The **Rough Guide** to

France

written and researched by

**David Abram, Ruth Blackmore, Colleen Brousil,
Brian Catlos, Hilary Heuler, Anette dal Jensen,
James McConnachie, Charlotte Melville,
Sophie Nellis, Kate Turner, Neville Walker,
Greg Ward, Richard Watkins and Lucy White**

ROUGH
GUIDES

www.roughguides.com

Contents

French wines
colour section
following p.360

Walking in France
colour section
following p.744

◀◀ Poppy field, Haute-Loire ◀ Château de Beynac, Dordogne

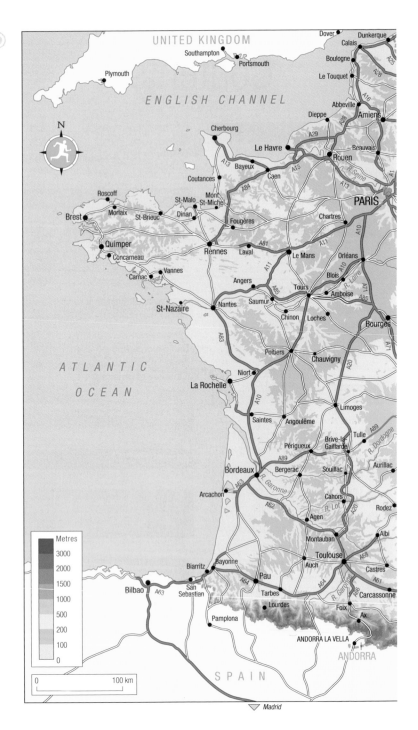

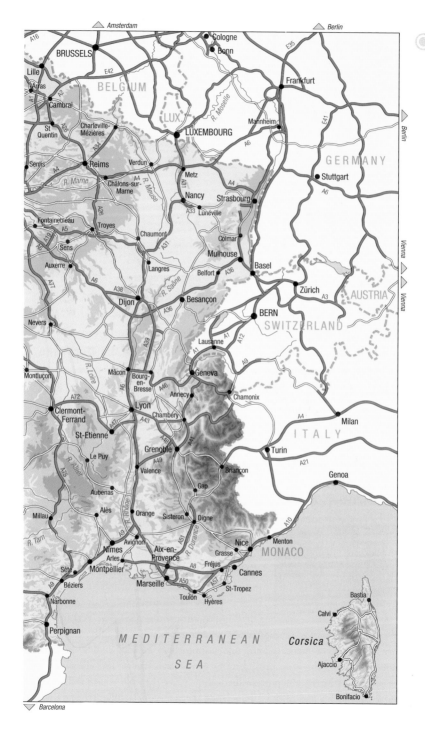

△ Amsterdam △ Berlin

Cologne
BRUSSELS Bonn
Lille
Arras Frankfurt
Cambrai BELGIUM
St LUX
Quentin LUXEMBOURG
Charleville-Mézières Mannheim
Senlis Reims Verdun
Châlons-sur-Marne Metz GERMANY
R. Marne Nancy Strasbourg Stuttgart
Fontainebleau Lunéville
Troyes Chaumont Colmar
Sens Mulhouse
Auxerre Langres Basel
Belfort Zürich
Dijon Besançon AUSTRIA
Nevers BERN
SWITZERLAND
Lausanne
Montluçon Mâcon Bourg-en-Bresse Geneva
Lyon Annecy Chamonix
Clermont-Ferrand Chambéry Milan
St-Etienne Grenoble Turin
Le Puy ITALY
Valence Briançon
Aubenas Gap Genoa
Millau Alès Orange Sisteron Digne
Nîmes Avignon Nice Menton
Arles Aix-en-Provence Grasse MONACO
Sète Montpellier Fréjus
Béziers Marseille Cannes
Narbonne Toulon St-Tropez
Perpignan Hyères

Bastia
Calvi

MEDITERRANEAN Corsica

SEA Ajaccio

Bonifacio

△ Berlin
△ Vienna
△ Vienna

▽ Barcelona

5

Introduction to

France

The sheer physical diversity of France would be hard to exhaust in a lifetime of visits. Landscapes range from the fretted coasts of Brittany and the limestone hills of Provence to the canyons of the Pyrenees and the half-moon bays of Corsica, and from the lushly wooded valleys of the Dordogne and the gentle meadows of the Loire valley to the glaciated peaks of the Alps. Each region looks and feels different, has its own style of architecture, its own characteristic food and often its own dialect. Though the French word *pays* is the term for a whole country, people frequently refer to their own region as *mon pays* – my country – and this strong sense of regional identity has persisted despite centuries of centralizing governments, from Louis XIV to de Gaulle.

Industrialization came relatively late to France, and for all the millions of French people that live in cities, the idea persists that theirs is a rural country. The importance of the land reverberates throughout French culture, manifesting itself in areas as diverse as regional pride in local cuisine and the state's fierce defence of Europe's agricultural subsidies. Perhaps the most striking feature of the French countryside is the sense of space. There are huge tracts of woodland and undeveloped land without a house in sight, and, away from the main urban centres, hundreds of towns and villages have changed only slowly and organically over the years, their old houses and streets intact, as much a part of the natural landscape as the rivers, hills and fields.

Despite this image of pastoral tranquillity, France's history is notable for its extraordinary vigour. For more than a thousand years the country has been in the vanguard of European development, and the accumulation of wealth and experience is evident everywhere in the astonishing variety of **things to see**, from the Dordogne's prehistoric cave-paintings and the Roman monuments of the south, to the Gothic cathedrals of the north, the châteaux of the Loire, and the cutting-edge architecture of the *grands projets* in Paris. This legacy of

Horseriding in Normandy

history and culture – **le patrimoine** – is so widely dispersed across the land that even the briefest of stays will leave the visitor with a powerful sense of France's past.

The importance of these traditions is felt deeply by the French state, which fights to preserve and develop its national **culture** perhaps harder than any other country in the world, and private companies, which also strive to maintain French traditions in arenas as diverse as *haute couture*, pottery and, of course, food. The fruits of these efforts are evident in the subsidized **arts**, notably the film industry, and in the lavishly endowed and innovative **museums and galleries**. From colonial history to fishing techniques, aeroplane design to textiles, and migrant shepherds to manicure, these collections can be found across the nation, but, inevitably, first place must go to the fabulous displays of fine art in Paris, a city which has nurtured more than its share of the finest creative artists of the last century and a half, both French – Monet and Matisse for example – and foreign, such as Picasso and Van Gogh.

There are all kinds of pegs on which to hang a holiday in France: a city, a region, a river, a mountain range, gastronomy, cathedrals, châteaux. All that open space means there's endless scope for outdoor activities – from walking, canoeing and cycling to skiing and sailing – but if you need more urban stimuli – clubs, shops, fashion, movies, music – then the great cities provide them in abundance.

Where to go

Travelling around France is easy. Restaurants and hotels proliferate, many of them relatively inexpensive when compared with other developed Western European countries. Train services are admirably efficient, as is the road network – especially the (toll-paying) autoroutes – and cyclists are much admired and encouraged. **Information** is highly organized and available from tourist offices across the country, as well as from specialist organizations for walkers, cyclists, campers and so on.

As for specific destinations, **Paris**, of course, is the outstanding cultural centre, with its impressive buildings and atmospheric backstreets, its art, nightlife and ethnic diversity, though the great **provincial cities** – Lyon, Bordeaux, Toulouse, Marseille – all now vie with the capital and each other for prestige in the arts, ascendancy in sport and innovation in attracting visitors.

For most people, however, it's the unique characters of the **regions** – and not least their cuisines – that will define a trip. Few holiday-makers stay long in the largely flat, industrial **north**, but there are some fine cathedrals and energetic cities to leaven the mix. The picture is similar in **Alsace-Lorraine** where Germanic influences are strong, notably in the food. On the northern Atlantic coast, **Normandy** has a rich heritage of cathedrals, castles, battlefields and beaches – and, with its cream-based sauces, an equally rich cuisine. To the west, **Brittany** is more renowned for its Celtic links, beautiful coastline, prehistoric sites and seafood, while the **Loire** valley, extending inland towards Paris, is famed for soft, fertile countryside and a marvellous parade of châteaux.

▲ Typical Alsace house

9

Further east, the green valleys of **Burgundy** shelter a wealth of Romanesque churches, and the wines and food are among the finest in France. More Romanesque churches follow the pilgrim routes through rural **Poitou-Charentes** and down the Atlantic coast to **Bordeaux**, where the wines rival those of Burgundy. Inland from Bordeaux, visitors flock to the gorges, prehistoric sites and picturesque fortified villages of the **Dordogne** and neighbouring

Limousin, drawn too by the truffles and duck and goose dishes of Périgord cuisine. To the south, the great mountain chain of the **Pyrenees** rears up along the Spanish border, running from the Basque country on the Atlantic to the Catalan lands of **Roussillon** on the Mediterranean; there's fine walking and skiing to be had, as well as beaches at either end. Further along the Mediterranean coast, **Languedoc** offers dramatic landscapes, medieval towns and Cathar castles, as well as more beaches, while the **Massif Central**, in the centre of the country, is undeveloped and little visited, but beautiful nonetheless, with its rivers, forests and the wild volcanic uplands of the **Auvergne**. The **Alps**, of course, are prime skiing territory, but a network of signposted paths makes walking a great way to explore too; to the north, the wooded mountains of the **Jura** provide further scope for outdoor pursuits. Stretching down from the Alps to the Mediterranean is **Provence**, which, as generations of travellers have discovered, seems to have everything: Roman ruins, picturesque villages, vineyards and lavender fields – and legions of visitors. Its cuisine is similarly diverse, encompassing fruit, olives, herbs, seafood, lamb and an unusual emphasis on vegetables. Along the Provençal coast, the beaches, towns and chic resorts of the **Côte d'Azur** form a giant smile extending from the down-at-heel but vibrant city of **Marseille** to the super-rich Riviera hotspots of Nice and Monaco. For truly fabulous beaches, however, head for the rugged island of **Corsica**, birthplace of Napoleon and home to an Italian-leaning culture and cuisine and some fascinating Neolithic sculptures.

The French

According to the clichés, the French are stylish, romantic and passionate. They also have a reputation for rudeness – and yet they are courteous with each other to the point of formality. It's common for someone entering a shop to wish customers and shopkeeper alike a general "good morning", and foreigners on business quickly learn the importance of shaking hands, asking the right questions and maintaining respectful eye contact. At the same time, if they want something, many French people can be direct in ways that are disconcerting for Anglo-Saxons. To foreigners stumbling over the language, never mind the cultural gap, this can seem like rudeness; it isn't. It's fairer to say that the French are proud. Opinions tend to be held and argued strongly – it's not for nothing that so many revolutions have shaken the political landscape. Culture, too, is a source of great pride, and artists, writers and thinkers are held in high esteem even beyond elite circles. And French people everywhere are proud of their locality. Whether it's for a village shopfront, a civic floral display or another landmark building for the French state, no effort is too great.

When to go

The single most important factor in deciding when to visit France is tourism itself. As most French people take their holidays in their own country, it's as well to consider avoiding the main **French holiday periods** – mid-July to the end of August. At this time almost the entire country closes down, except for the tourist industry itself. You can easily walk a kilometre and more in Paris, for example, in search of an open boulangerie, and the city sometimes seems deserted by all except fellow tourists. Prices in the resorts rise to take full advantage and often you can't find a room for love nor money, and on the Côte d'Azur not even a space in the campsites. The seaside is the most crowded, but the mountains and popular regions like the Dordogne are not far behind. Easter, too, is a bad time for Paris: half of Europe's schoolchildren seem to descend on the city. For the same reasons, ski buffs should keep in mind the February school ski break. And no one who values life, limb and sanity should ever be caught on the roads during the last weekend of July or August, and least of all on the weekend of August 15.

Generally speaking, **climate** needn't be a major consideration in planning when to go. If you're a skier, of course, you wouldn't choose the mountains between May and November; and if you want a beach holiday, you wouldn't head for the seaside out of summer – except for the Mediterranean coast, which is at its most attractive in spring. **Northern France**, like nearby Britain, is wet and unpredictable. **Paris** has a marginally better climate than New York, rarely reaching the extremes of heat and cold of that city, but only **south of the Loire** does the weather become significantly warmer. **West coast** weather, even in the south, is tempered by the proximity of the Atlantic, subject to violent storms and close thundery days even in summer. The **centre** and **east**, as you leave the coasts behind, have a more continental climate, with colder

▲ Produce at a market in Aix-en-Provence

winters and hotter summers. The most reliable weather is along and behind the **Mediterranean** coastline and on **Corsica**, where winter is short and summer long and hot.

Average daily temperatures and rainfall

For a recorded weather forecast you can phone the main forecasting line on ☎08.92.68.08.08, or check online at ⓦwww.meteofrance.com.

	Jan	Feb	Mar	Apr	May	Jun	Jul	Aug	Sep	Oct	Nov	Dec
Paris												
Max/min (°C)	6/2	7/2	11/4	14/6	18/9	21/12	24/14	23/14	20/12	16/9	10/5	7/2
Max/min (°F)	43/35	45/35	51/39	57/42	64/49	70/54	74/58	74/57	68/53	60/47	49/40	44/36
Rainfall mm	54	46	52	45	62	57	54	51	57	59	59	55
St-Malo												
Max/min (°C)	8/3	9/3	11/4	13/6	17/9	20/11	22/13	22/13	20/12	16/10	12/6	9/4
Max/min (°F)	47/38	48/38	52/40	56/43	62/48	67/53	71/56	71/56	68/54	61/49	53/43	48/40
Rainfall mm	82	68	63	50	57	48	41	48	62	75	95	89
Lyon												
Max/min (°C)	6/0	8/1	12/3	15/6	19/9	23/13	27/15	26/14	23/12	17/8	10/4	6/1
Max/min (°F)	42/32	47/34	53/37	60/42	67/49	74/55	80/59	78/58	73/53	62/46	50/38	43/33
Rainfall mm	58	58	66	69	89	78	61	77	78	79	73	64
Toulouse												
Max/min (°C)	9/2	11/3	14/4	16/7	20/10	24/13	28/15	27/15	24/13	19/10	13/5	10/3
Max/min (°F)	49/35	52/37	56/39	61/44	68/49	75/55	82/60	80/59	76/55	67/49	56/41	49/37
Rainfall mm	59	59	57	67	77	71	44	57	67	58	63	69
Nice												
Max/min (°C)	11/3	11/4	13/6	15/8	19/12	22/15	26/18	26/18	23/16	19/12	14/7	12/5
Max/min (°F)	51/38	52/39	55/42	60/47	66/53	72/59	78/64	78/64	73/60	67/54	58/45	53/40
Rainfall mm	77	79	74	66	61	46	22	43	65	104	101	78

30

things not to miss

It's not possible to see everything that France has to offer in one trip — and we don't suggest you try. What follows is a selective taste of the country's highlights: natural wonders and outstanding sights, plus the best activities and experiences. They're arranged in five colour-coded categories, so you can browse through to find the very best things to see and do. All highlights have a page reference to take you straight into the Guide, where you can find out more.

01 Châteaux of the Loire Page **393** • The River Loire is lined with gracious châteaux, of which Azay-le-Rideau is surely the most staggeringly impressive, both for its size and the double-spiral staircase designed by Leonardo da Vinci.

02 **The Issenheim altarpiece** Page **245** • The village of Colmar might be excessively twee, but it's still worth a visit for Grünewald's amazing altarpiece, one of the most extraordinary works of art in the country.

04 **Les Gorges du Verdon** Page **889** • The mighty gorges are Europe's answer to the Grand Canyon, and offer stunning views, a range of hikes, and colours and scents that are uniquely, gorgeously Provençal.

03 **Champagne tasting at Épernay** Page **216** • Dom Pérignon might be the most famous, but there are plenty of other bubblies to try in the atmospheric cellars of Épernay's *maisons*.

05 Corsican beaches Page **984** • Some of the best of France's many beautiful beaches are found on Corsica, including the plage de Saleccia, with its soft white shell sand and turquoise water.

06 Bordeaux Page **524** • Stylish and lively Bordeaux was the principal English stronghold in France for three hundred years, and is still known for the refined red wines – claret – which the English popularized.

07 Jardin du Luxembourg
Page **114** • Paris's most beautiful park, in the heart of the laid-back Left Bank, is the ideal spot for relaxing.

08 Amiens cathedral
Page **203** • The largest Gothic building in all France, this lofty cathedral has a clever evening light show that gives a vivid idea of how the west front would have looked when it was coloured.

09 The Louvre
Page **94** • The palace of the Louvre cuts a grand Classical swathe through the centre of Paris and houses what is nothing less than the gold standard of France's artistic tradition.

10 Carnac
Page **364** • Archeologically, Brittany is one of the richest regions in the world and the alignments at Carnac rival Stonehenge.

12 Bastille Day Pages **49** & **107** • July 14 sees national celebrations commemorating the beginning of the French Revolution, with fireworks and parties across the whole country.

11 St-Ouen Page **130** • It's easy to lose track of an entire weekend morning browsing the acres of fine antiques, covetable curios and general bric-a-brac at St-Ouen, the mother of Paris's flea markets.

13 Tour de France Page **51** • Cycling is an ideal way to explore France's scenic back roads, and there are some great long-distance cycle routes, too, such as the one that follows the Loire river.

14 **Mont St-Michel** Page **304** • Second only to the Eiffel Tower as France's best-loved landmark, the *merveille* of Mont St-Michel is a splendid union of nature and architecture.

15 **Dining out in a Lyon bouchon** Page **826** • Famed for its gastronomy and home to super chefs such as Paul Bocuse, Lyon offers no end of wonderful eating places, not least the old-fashioned *bouchons*, traditional colourful bistros, where you can sample *quenelles* (pike sausages), *andouillettes* (chunky sausages made from chitterlings) and other local specialities.

16 **Bastide towns** Page **565** • Monpazier is one of the best preserved of the fortified towns – *bastides* – built in the Dordogne region during the turbulent medieval period when there was almost constant conflict between the French and English.

17 **Canal du Midi** Page **695** • A calm, watery avenue, stretching from beyond Toulouse to the Mediterranean. Cycling, walking or drifting along its tree-shaded course is the most atmospheric way of savouring France's southwest.

18 **Aix-en-Provence** Page **880** • Marseille may be the biggest city in Provence, but aristocratic Aix is the region's capital, and it's a wonderful place to shop, eat and linger under the plane trees with a *pastis*.

19 **Annecy** Page **784** • One of the prettiest towns in the Alps, Annecy has a picture-postcard quality which even the crowds can't mar.

20 **Les Calanques** Page **916** • The limestone cliffs on the stretch of coast between Marseille and Cassis offer excellent hiking, and you can scramble down to isolated coves that are perfect for swimming.

21 **War memorials** Page **297** • World Wars I and II left permanent scars on the French countryside – and on its psyche. The dead are remembered in solemn, sometimes overwhelming cemeteries, such as the one at Colleville-sur-Mer in Normandy.

22 **Cathar castles**
Page **651** • These gaunt fortresses are grim but fascinating relics of the brutal crusade launched by the Catholic church and northern French nobility against the heretic Cathars.

23 **Bayeux Tapestry** Page **293** • This 70-metre-long tapestry is an astonishingly detailed depiction of the 1066 Norman invasion of England, and one of the finest artistic works of the early medieval era.

24 **Prehistoric cave art**
Page **574** • Prehistoric art can be seen in several places around France, but perhaps the most impressive paintings are those at Lascaux in the Dordogne.

25 **The GR20** Page **990** & *Walking in France* colour section • Arguably France's most dramatic – and most demanding – long-distance footpath climbs through and over Corsica's precipitous mountains for some 170km.

26 **Fontenay Abbey** Page **455** • One of the most complete monastic complexes anywhere, this Burgundian monastery has a serene setting in a stream-filled valley.

27 **Gorges de l'Ardèche** Page **751** • The fantastic gorges begin at the Pont d'Arc and cut their way through limestone cliffs before emptying into the Rhône valley.

28 **Carcassonne** Page **693** • So atmospheric is this medieval fortress town that it manages to resist even relentless commercialization and summer's throng of visitors.

29 **Medieval Provençal villages** Page **877** • Provence's hilltop villages attract visitors by the score. Though Gordes is one of the most famous, there are others less well known but equally beautiful.

30 **Winter sports in the Alps** Page **769** • The French Alps are home to some of the world's most prestigious ski resorts, offering a wide range of winter sports.

Basics

Basics

Getting there

The quickest way to reach France from most parts of the United Kingdom and Ireland is by air. From southern England, however, the Eurostar provides a viable alternative, making the journey from London to Paris in as little as two and a quarter hours. The Channel Tunnel is the most flexible option if you want to take your car to France, though cross-Channel ferries are usually cheaper. It's also worth bearing in mind that if you live west of London, the ferry services to Roscoff, St-Malo, Cherbourg, Caen and Le Havre can save a lot of driving time. From the US and Canada a number of airlines fly direct to Paris, from where you can pick up onward connections. You can also fly direct to Paris from South Africa, while the best fares from Australia and New Zealand are generally via Asia.

Whether you are travelling by air, sea or rail, prices increasingly depend on how far in advance you book, but will also depend on the **season**. Fares are at their highest from around early June to the end of August, when the weather is best, drop during the "shoulder" seasons – roughly September to October and April to May – and are at their cheapest during the low season, November to March (excluding Christmas and New Year when prices are hiked up and seats are at a premium). Note also that flying at weekends can be more expensive; price ranges quoted below assume midweek travel, and include all taxes and surcharges.

Flights from the UK and Ireland

Since the rise of the **budget airlines**, flights between the UK, Ireland and France are plentiful and often cheap, even from regional airports. The main budget airlines are bmibaby, easyJet, flybe and Ryanair, which between them cover nearly thirty airports across France, including Bergerac, Carcassonne, Chambéry, La Rochelle, Montpellier, Nantes, Pau, Toulon and Tours, as well as more established hubs such as Paris, Lyon and Nice. Routes change frwequently and some destinations are not served all year round, so keep an eye on the airlines' websites. It's also worth double-checking exactly where the airport is in relation to your destination; Ryanair claims to fly to Paris, for example, but in reality flies to Beauvais, a ninety-minute coach drive from

the city centre. **Tickets** work on a quota system, and it's wise to book as early as possible for the really cheap seats, which can cost as little as £10–25/€8–32 each way, including taxes. Surcharges for checked-in baggage, priority boarding or paying by credit card can all bump up the price however, so the price you actually pay will probably be higher than these figures.

It's worth checking out the **traditional carriers**, such as Air France, British Airways and Aer Lingus, which have streamlined their schedules and lowered prices in response to the budget airline challenge. Low-season return fares to Paris start at around £106 from London, £100 from Edinburgh and €90 from Dublin; to Nice you'll pay upwards of £130 from London and €110 from Dublin.

Air France flies direct to Paris Charles-de-Gaulle (CDG) several times daily from London Heathrow, Dublin and regional airports such as Birmingham, Manchester and Southampton and from London City to Paris Orly (ORY); flights to most other French destinations involve a change at Paris or Amsterdam. **British Airways** has several flights a day to Paris CDG from London Heathrow and at least one direct from Birmingham and Manchester. BA also operates flights from London to Bordeaux, Lyon, Marseille, Nice and Toulouse. In Ireland, **Aer Lingus** offers nonstop flights from Dublin and Cork to Paris CDG; from Dublin to Bordeaux, Lyon, Marseille, Nice, Rennes and Toulouse; and from Cork to La Rochelle and Nice.

Flights from the US and Canada

Most major airlines operate scheduled flights to Paris from the US and Canada. Air France has the most frequent service, with good onward regional connections and competitive fares that sometimes undercut US carriers; it also operates a code share with Delta. One possible disadvantage, if your destination is not Paris, is that while Air France transatlantic flights often terminate at Charles-de-Gaulle, domestic connections frequently depart from Orly, entailing an inconvenient transfer between the two airports. Other airlines offering **nonstop** services to Paris from a variety of US cities include: American Airlines from New York, Boston, Chicago, Dallas and Miami; Continental from Newark and Houston; Delta from Atlanta and Cincinnati; United from Chicago, Philadelphia and Washington DC and US Airways from Charlotte and Philadelphia. Air Canada offers nonstop services to Paris from Montréal and Toronto, while Air Transat offers good-value scheduled and **charter flights** to Paris from a number of bases and to other destinations from Montréal, Québec or Toronto. Another option is to fly with a European carrier – such as British Airways, Iberia or Lufthansa – to its European hub and then continue on to Paris or a regional French airport.

Thanks to intense competition, trans-atlantic **fares** to France are still pretty reasonable. An off-season midweek return fare to Paris can be as low as US$580 before taxes from New York, US$850 from Los Angeles and US$586 from Houston. From Canada, prices to Paris start at around CAN$970 from Montréal or Toronto.

Flights from Australia, New Zealand and South Africa

Most travellers from **Australia and New Zealand** choose to fly to France via London, although the majority of airlines can add a Paris leg (or a flight to any other major French city) to an Australia/New Zealand–Europe ticket. Flights via Asia or the Gulf States, with a transfer or overnight stop at the airline's home port, are generally the cheapest option; those routed through the US tend to be slightly pricier. Return **fares** start at around AUS$2200 from Sydney, AUS$2100 from Perth, AUS$2100 from Melbourne and NZ$2400 from Auckland.

From **South Africa**, Johannesburg is the best place to start, with Air France flying direct to Paris from around R6800 return; from Cape Town, they fly via Johannesburg or Amsterdam and are more expensive, starting at around R8,000. BA, flying via London, costs upwards of R8,000 from Johannesburg and R9,000 from Cape Town.

By train

Eurostar operates high-speed passenger trains daily from St Pancras International to France through the **Channel Tunnel**; many but not all services stop at either Ebbsfleet or Ashford in Kent (15min and 30min from London, respectively). There are 1–2 services an hour from around 5.30am to 8pm for Paris Gare du Nord; fast trains take 2 hour 15 minutes; while a handful stop at Calais (1hr) or Lille (1hr 20min), where you can connect with TGV trains heading south to Bordeaux, Lyon and Marseille. In addition, Eurostar runs direct trains from London to Disneyland Paris (daily; 2hr 40min), to Avignon (mid-July to early Sept; Sat; 6hr), and a special weekly ski service to Moutiers, Aime-la-Plagne and Bourg-St-Maurice in the French Alps (mid-Dec to mid-April; around 6hr 30min).

Standard **fares** from London to Paris start at £69 (£65 to Lille, £99 to Avignon) for a non-refundable, non-exchangeable return; availability is limited so it's best to book as early as possible. Another option is the non-refundable "semi-flexible" ticket (from £250/236/299 respectively), where you can change the dates for a fee. Otherwise, you're looking at £309/270/349 for a fully refundable ticket with no restrictions. Return fares to Disneyland Paris start at £69 for adults (£44 for children aged 4–11). Under-4s travel for free provided they travel on the lap of a fare-paying passenger.

Tickets can be bought online or by phone from Eurostar, as well as through travel agents and websites like lastminute.com. InterRail and Eurail **passes** (see opposite) entitle you to discounts on Eurostar trains. For information about taking your bike on Eurostar, see opposite. For rail contacts, see p.32.

By car via the Channel Tunnel

The simplest way to take your car to France from the UK is on one of the drive-on drive-off shuttle trains operated by **Eurotunnel**. The service runs continuously between Folkestone and Coquelles, near Calais, with up to four departures per hour (one every 2hr from midnight–6am) and takes 35 minutes. It is possible to turn up and buy your ticket at the check-in booths, though you'll pay a premium and at busy times booking is strongly recommended; if you have a booking, you must arrive at least thirty minutes before departure. Note that Eurotunnel is not allowed to transport cars fitted with LPG or CNG tanks.

Standard **fares** start at £53 one-way if you book far enough ahead and/or travel offpeak, rising to £157. Fully refundable and changeable FlexiPlus fares cost £149 each way for a short stay (up to 5 days) and £199 for longer periods. There's room for only six **bicycles** on any departure, so book ahead in high season – a standard return costs £32 for a bike plus rider.

Rail passes

There is a variety of rail passes useful for travel within France, some of which need to be bought in your home country (for details of railcards that you can buy in France, see p.34). **Rail Europe** (see p.32) the umbrella company for all national and international rail purchases, is the most useful source of information on availability and cost.

InterRail Pass

InterRail Passes are only available to European residents, or those who have lived in a European country for at least six months, and you will be asked to provide proof of residency (and long-stay visa if applicable) before being allowed to buy one.

They come in first or second class senior (over 60), first or second class over-26 or second class under-26 versions, and cover thirty European countries. Children from 4–12 years pay half; those under 4 travel free, though they may not get a seat.

There are two types of passes: global and one-country. The global pass covers all thirty countries with various options: five days travel in a ten-day period (under-26 £135/over-26 £209); ten days travel within a 22-day period (£199/305); 22 days continuous travel (£259/399); and one month (£339/509) continuous travel. Similarly, the one-country pass allows you to opt for various periods, ranging from three days in one month (£105/165) to eight days in one month (£165/255). In each case, first-class passes are also available.

Inter-Rail Passes do not include travel within your country of residence, though pass holders are eligible for discounts on rail fares to and from the border of the relevant zone as well as reductions on Eurostar.

Eurail Pass

Eurail Passes are not available to European residents but once ordered can be delivered to a European address. Again, there are various options; the most useful are likely to be the **regional passes**, covering France with Germany, Italy, Spain or Switzerland. The France-Italy pass offers four days of unlimited train travel within two months for €174 for under-26, €227 for an adult travelling second class, or up to ten days within two months for €296 under-26/€385 adult. The Saverpass offers the same benefits for two to five people travelling together.

By ferry

Though slower than travelling by plane or via the Channel Tunnel, the ferries plying

---

Travelling with pets from the UK

If you wish to take your dog (or cat) to France, the **Pet Travel Scheme (PETS)** enables you to avoid putting it in quarantine when re-entering the UK as long as certain conditions are met. Current regulations are available on the Department for Environment, Food and Rural Affairs (DEFRA) website ⓦ www.defra.gov.uk /wildlife-pets/pets/travel/index.htm or through the PETS Helpline (☏ 0870 241 1710).

Travel your way, in your car.

Taking your car with P&O Ferries is a great way to experience the very best that France has to offer.

You'll arrive in the north of France, with beautiful scenery within easy driving distance. Calais is also a great starting point for exploring everywhere from big cities to tiny picturesque villages, all in your own time. With P&O Ferries, you have the freedom to go when you want to make the very most of your break.

It's quick too. Drive onto one of our magnificent ferries in Dover and in less than 90 minutes (just enough time to enjoy our restaurants, bars, shops and many other facilities), you'll be in Calais and on your way. You can take as much or bring back as much as you want too. Because after all, there are no baggage restrictions.

Check out our best prices online and book now.

POferries.com
08716 64 64 64

Calls cost 10p per minute plus network extras. Calls from mobiles will be higher.

P&O Ferries

dover calais • **hull** zeebrugge / rotterdam • **cairnryan / troon** larne • **liverpool** dublin

between Dover and Calais offer the cheapest means of travelling to France **from the UK** and are particularly convenient if you live in southeast England. If you're coming from the north of England or Scotland, you could consider the overnight crossing from Hull (13hr) to Zeebrugge (Belgium) operated by P&O Ferries. **From Ireland**, putting the car on the ferry from Cork (14hr) or Rosslare (17hr 30min) to Roscoff in Brittany, or from Rosslare to Cherbourg (18hr 30min) in Normandy cuts out the drive across Britain to the Channel.

Ferry **prices** are seasonal and, for motorists, depend on the type of vehicle. In general, the further you book ahead, the cheaper the fare and it's well worth playing around with dates and times to find the best deals: midweek sailings are usually cheapest. At the time of writing, one-way fares for a car and up to five passengers are available for as little as £13 with Norfolkline (DFDS Seaways) on the Dover–Dunkerque route off season, while one-way fares on the Dover–Calais crossing start at around £25. One-way fares from Ireland kick off at around €99 for a car and two adults.

Some ferry companies (but not Norfolkline (DFDS Seaways)) also offer fares for **foot passengers**, typically £20–30 return on cross-Channel routes; accompanying **bicycles** can usually be carried free.

By bus

Eurolines runs regular services from London Victoria to nearly forty French cities (fewer in winter), including seven a day to Paris, crossing the Channel by ferry or Eurotunnel. Prices are lower than for the same journey by train, with adult return "Promo" fares (must be booked at least seven days in advance) starting at around £40 to Paris and £38 to Lille. If you're travelling frequently, a Eurolines Discount Card (three months £23/six months £43) will give you 25 percent off fares. Subject to certain restrictions – you're only allowed one return journey to any one city – a Eurolines pass offers Europe-wide travel between 43 cities for fifteen or thirty days. Prices range from £159 for a fifteen-day youth pass in low season to £389 for a peak-season thirty-day adult pass.

Airlines, agents and operators

There are a vast number of travel agents and tour operators offering holidays in France, with options varying from luxury, château-based breaks to adventure trips involving skiing and hiking. The following pages list the most useful contacts.

Airlines

Aer Arann ⓦ www.aerarann.com.
Aer Lingus ⓦ www.aerlingus.com.
Air Canada ⓦ www.aircanada.com.
Air France ⓦ www.airfrance.com.
Air Transat ⓦ www.airtransat.com.
American Airlines ⓦ www.aa.com.
bmi ⓦ www.flybmi.com.
bmibaby ⓦ www.bmibaby.com.
British Airways ⓦ www.ba.com.
Cathay Pacific ⓦ www.cathaypacific.com.
Continental Airlines ⓦ www.continental.com.
Delta ⓦ www.delta.com.
easyJet ⓦ www.easyjet.com.
Emirates ⓦ www.emirates.com.
flybe ⓦ www.flybe.com.
Jet2 ⓦ www.jet2.com.
KLM ⓦ www.klm.com.
Lufthansa ⓦ www.lufthansa.com.
Qantas ⓦ www.qantas.com.
Ryanair ⓦ www.ryanair.com.
Singapore Airlines ⓦ www.singaporeair.com.
South African Airways ⓦ www.flysaa.com.
United Airlines ⓦ www.united.com.
US Airways ⓦ www.usair.com.

Agents and operators

Allez France ⓦ www.allezfrance.com. UK tour operator offering accommodation only as well as short breaks and other holiday packages throughout France.
Austin-Lehman Adventures US ☎ 1-800-575-1540, ⓦ www.austinlehman.com. Good range of bike and walking tours all over France for family groups or solo travellers.
Belle France UK ☎ 01580/214 010, ⓦ www.bellefrance.co.uk. Walking, cycling and boating holidays throughout France.
Bonnes Vacances Direct UK ☎ 0844 804 2000, ⓦ www.bvdirect.co.uk. Agent for property owners in France for self-catering and B&B accommodation.
Canvas Holidays UK ☎ 0845 268 0827, ⓦ www.canvas.co.uk. Tailor-made caravan and camping holidays.
Chez Nous UK ☎ 0845 268 1102, ⓦ www.cheznous.com. Thousands of self-catering and B&B properties online, including ski rentals.

Corsican Places UK ☎ 0845 330 2059, ⓦ www
.corsica.co.uk. Corsica specialists.
Cycling for Softies UK ☎ 0161/248 8282,
ⓦ www.cycling-for-softies.co.uk. Easy-going cycle
holiday operator to rural France.
Discover France US ☎ 1-800-960-2221, ⓦ www
.discoverfrance.com. Self-guided cycling and walking
holidays throughout France.
Eurocamp UK ☎ 0844 406 0402, ⓦ www
.eurocamp.co.uk. Camping holidays with kids'
activities and single-parent deals.
Fields Fairway France ☎ +33 (0)3.21.33.65.64,
ⓦ www.fieldsfairway.co.uk. British-run, France-
based company offering all-inclusive golfing holidays.
France Afloat UK ☎ 0870 011 0538, ⓦ www
.franceafloat.com. Canal and river cruises across
France.
French Affair UK ☎ 020/7381 8519, ⓦ www
.frenchaffair.com. Wide range of self-catering
accommodation in southern France and Corsica.
French Travel Connection Australia ☎ 02/9966
1177, ⓦ www.frenchtravel.com.au. Offers large
range of holidays to France.
Headwater UK ☎ 01606/720 199, Republic of
Ireland ☎ 01/295 8901, US ☎ 1-800-567-6286,
Australia ☎ 1300/363 055, New Zealand ☎ 09/524
5118; ⓦ www.headwater.com. UK-based operator
offering walking, cycling, and canoeing tours
throughout France, and cross-country skiing.
Holiday France ⓦ www.holidayfrance.org.uk.
Website that allows you to search for French tour
operators by holiday type and location.
Inntravel UK ☎ 01653/617 001, ⓦ www.inntravel
.co.uk. Broad range of activity holidays, including
riding, skiing, walking and cycling, as well as
property rental.
Keycamp Holidays UK ☎ 0844 406 0200,
Republic of Ireland ☎ 021/425 2399; ⓦ www
.keycamp.com. Caravan and camping holidays,
including transport to France.
Le Boat US ☎ 1-866-570-3202, ⓦ www.leboat
.com. Self-drive canal holidays all over France.
Locaboat UK ☎ 01756/706517, Republic of
Ireland ☎ 071/964 5923, US ☎ 401-849-1112;
ⓦ www.locaboat.com. French company specializing
in holidays on pénichettes (scaled-down replicas of
commercial barges).
North South Travel UK ☎ 01245/608 291,
ⓦ www.northsouthtravel.co.uk. Friendly, competitive

travel agency, offering discounted fares worldwide.
Profits are used to support projects in the developing
world, especially the promotion of sustainable tourism.

Rail, Channel Tunnel and bus contacts

Eurolines UK ☎ 0871 781 8181, ⓦ www
.eurolines.co.uk
European Rail UK ☎ 020/7619 1083, ⓦ www
.europeanrail.com.
Eurostar UK ☎ 08432 186 186, ⓦ www.eurostar
.com.
Eurotunnel UK ☎ 08448 79 73 79, ⓦ www
.eurotunnel.com.
International Rail UK ☎ 0871 231 0790, ⓦ www
.international-rail.com.
Rail Europe (SNCF French Railways) UK ☎ 0844
848 4064, US ☎ 1-800-622-8600, Canada
☎ 1-800-361-7245; ⓦ www.raileurope.com.
Rail Plus Australia ☎ 1300 555 003, New
Zealand ☎ 09/377 5415; ⓦ www.railplus.com.au.
Trainseurope UK ☎ 0871 700 7722, ⓦ www
.trainseurope.co.uk.
World Travel South Africa ☎ 011/628 2319,
ⓦ www.world-travel.co.za.

Ferry contacts

Brittany Ferries UK ☎ 0871 244 0744,
ⓦ www.brittanyferries.co.uk; Republic of Ireland
☎ 021/4277 801, ⓦ www.brittanyferries.ie.
Condor Ferries UK ☎ 0845 609 1024, ⓦ www
.condorferries.co.uk.
EuroDrive UK ☎ 0844 371 8021, ⓦ www
.eurodrive.co.uk.
Ferryoffers ⓦ www.ferryoffers.co.uk. Ferry,
Eurotunnel and Eurostar tickets.
Ferry Savers UK ☎ 0844 371 8021, ⓦ www
.ferrysavers.com.
Irish Ferries Republic of Ireland ☎ 0818/300 400,
ⓦ www.irishferries.com.
LD Lines UK ☎ 0844 576 8836, ⓦ www.ldlines
.com.
Norfolkline (DFDS Seaways) UK ☎ 0871 574
7235 (Dover-Calais), ☎ 0871 574 7300
(Rosyth-Zeebrugge); ⓦ www.norfolkline.com.
P&O Ferries UK ☎ 08716 64 21 21, ⓦ www
.poferries.com.
Sea France UK ☎ 0871 423 7119, ⓦ www
.seafrance.com.

Getting around

With the most extensive train network in Western Europe, France is a great country in which to travel by rail. The national rail company, SNCF (Société Nationale des Chemins de Fer), runs fast, efficient trains between the main towns. Buses cover rural areas, but services can be sporadic, with awkward departure times. If you want to get off the beaten track the best option is to have your own transport. Approximate journey times and frequencies of the main train, bus, plane and ferry services can be found in the "Travel details" at the end of each chapter.

By train

SNCF (☎36 35, €0.34/min; ⓦwww .voyages-sncf.com) operates one of the most efficient, comfortable and user-friendly railway systems in the world. Staff are generally courteous and helpful, and its trains – for the most part, fast, clean and reliable – continue, in spite of the closure of some rural lines, to serve most of the country.

Trains

Pride and joy of the French rail system is the high-speed **TGV** (*train à grande vitesse*), capable of speeds of up to 300kph, and its offspring Eurostar. The continually expanding TGV network has its main hub at Paris, from where main lines head north to Lille, east to Strasbourg and two head south: one to Marseille and the Mediterranean, the other west to Bordeaux and the Spanish frontier. Spur lines service Brittany and Normandy, the Alps, Pyrenees and Jura.

Latest-generation **iDTGV** (ⓦwww.idtgv .com) trains compete with low-cost airlines with keen fares and facilities to watch DVDs and play computer games. Currently available on routes to 29 destinations from Paris including Bordeaux, Mulhouse, Marseille, Nice, Perpignan, Toulouse, Strasbourg and Hendaye, tickets are sold online and can only be changed for an additional fee. **Corail** trains provide intercity services on routes not yet upgraded to TGV. Though not as fast, they have good facilities, particularly the refurbished Téoz trains linking Paris to Clermont-Ferrand, Limoges and Toulouse and Bordeaux to Marseille and Nice. **Lunéa** are comfortable sleeper trains. Local services are covered by **TER** regional express trains.

Aside from the regular lines there are a number of special **tourist trains**, usually not part of the SNCF system or covered by normal rail passes, though some offer a discount to rail pass holders. One of the most popular is the spectacular Petit Train Jaune, which winds its way up through the Pyrenees (see p.663).

Tickets and fares

Tickets can be bought online (see opposite) or at train stations (*gare SNCF*). If you have language problems or there are long queues at the counter, use one of the touch-screen vending machines with instructions in English, which are available at most stations. All tickets – but not passes or computerized tickets printed out at home – must be validated in the orange machines located beside the entrance to the platforms, and it's an offence not to follow the instruction *Compostez votre billet* ("validate your ticket").

Regional **timetables** and leaflets covering particular lines are available free at stations. The word *Autocar* (often abbreviated to *car*) on the timetable signifies that the service is covered by an SNCF bus, on which rail tickets and passes are valid.

Fares are cheaper if you travel off-peak (*période bleue* or blue period) rather than during peak hours (*période blanche* or white period); peak period generally means

Monday mornings and Friday and Sunday evenings. One-way "Loisir" fares from Paris to Toulouse by TGV start at around €55, and from Paris to Nice €62 in second class. **Seat reservations** are obligatory on TGV, Téoz and Lunéa trains.

Discounts and rail passes

On certain mainline routes a limited number of **discount tickets**, known as *tarifs Prem's* (one-way fares from €12 for shorter trips on TGVs), can be bought up to ninety days in advance; these are non-refundable and cannot be changed. Internet-only TGV fares (from €19 one-way) are available on iDTGVs. These discount fares carry certain restrictions, so check when you book.

SNCF also offers a range of **travel cards**, which are valid for one year, and can be purchased online, by phone, through accredited travel agents and from main *gares SNCF*. Anyone aged 26 to 59 years, for example, is eligible for the *Carte Escapades* (€85). This guarantees a minimum reduction for journeys of at least 200km of 25 percent on standard peak fares, rising to 40 percent off-peak; you need to either travel at weekends or stay away for a Saturday or Sunday night. Similar deals are available for 12- to 25-year olds (*Carte 12–25*; €49), over-60s (*Carte Senior*; €56) and families with children under the age of 12 (*Carte Enfant +*; €70).

Non-Europeans also have the option of picking up the **France Rail Pass** before arriving in France. For information on this and other passes available outside the country, see "Getting there" (p.29).

By bus

The most convenient **bus services** are those operated by SNCF, which run between train stations and serve areas not accessible by rail. In addition to SNCF buses, private, municipal and departmental buses can be useful for local and some cross-country journeys, though if you want to see much outside the main towns be prepared for early starts and careful planning – the timetable is often constructed to suit market and school hours. As a rule, buses are cheaper and slower than trains.

Larger towns usually have a *gare routière* (bus station), often next to the *gare SNCF*. However, the private bus companies don't always work together and you'll frequently find them leaving from an array of different points (the local tourist office should be able to help locate the stop you need).

By ferry

Most of France's coastal islands, which are concentrated around Brittany and the Côte d'Azur, can only be reached by **ferry**. Local companies run services, with timetables and prices varying according to season. Some routes have a reduced schedule or cease to operate completely in winter months, while in high season booking ahead is recommended on all but the most frequent services. Information on these local companies is listed in the Brittany and Normandy and Côte d'Azur chapters in the Guide. For details of ferry services from the mainland to Corsica, see p.974.

By air

Arriving by air from outside Europe, you may be able to get a good deal on add-on **domestic flights**. Air France operates the most routes within the country, although competition is hotting up, with the likes of easyJet running internal discount flights from Paris or Lyon to Biarritz, Brest, Corsica, Nice and Toulouse.

By car

Driving in France can be a real pleasure, with a magnificent network of autoroutes providing sweeping views of the countryside. If you're in a hurry, it's worth paying motorway tolls to avoid the slow, often congested toll-free *routes nationales* (marked, for example, RN116 or N116 on signs and maps), many of which have been reclassified as *routes départementales* in recent years. Many of the more minor *routes départementales* (marked with a D) are uncongested and make for a more scenic drive.

There are times when it's wiser not to drive at all: in big cities; around major seaside resorts in high season; and at peak holiday migrations such as the beginning and end of

Save money on your Paris Sightseeing

Entry to your choice of over 60 top attractions including: The Louvre, Notre Dame Cathedral, Seine River Cruise, Open Top Bus Tour and many more

FREE guidebook in 3 languages

Plus **many exclusive offers** in shops and restaurants

Save 10% by visiting
www.parispass.com
quoting offer code **roughguide**

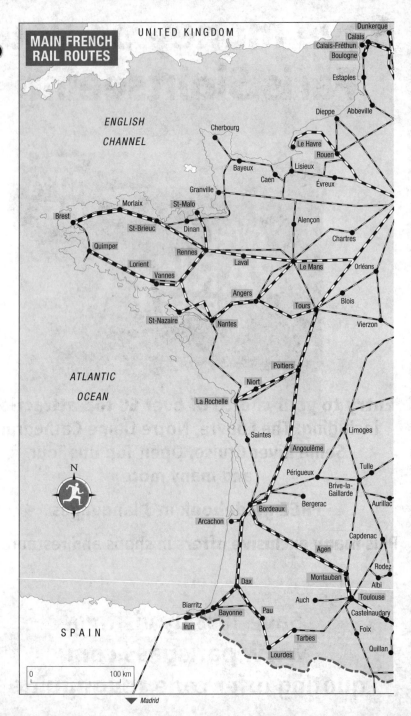

MAIN FRENCH
RAIL ROUTES

UNITED KINGDOM

Dunkerque
Calais
Calais-Fréthun
Boulogne

Estaples

ENGLISH
CHANNEL

Cherbourg

Dieppe   Abbeville

Le Havre
Bayeux   Rouen
Caen   Lisieux
Évreux

Granville

Morlaix   St-Malo
Brest
St-Brieuc   Dinan
Quimper   Rennes   Laval
Lorient
Vannes

Alençon
Chartres

Le Mans
Orléans

Angers
Tours   Blois
St-Nazaire   Nantes
Vierzon

ATLANTIC
OCEAN

Poitiers
Niort
La Rochelle

Saintes

Limoges
Angoulême

Périgueux   Tulle
Brive-la-
Gaillarde
Bergerac   Aurillac
Bordeaux
Arcachon
Capdenac

Agen
Rodez

Dax   Montauban   Albi
Auch   Toulouse
Biarritz   Castelnaudary
Bayonne   Pau
Irún   Foix
Tarbes
SPAIN   Quillan
Lourdes

N

0   100 km

Madrid

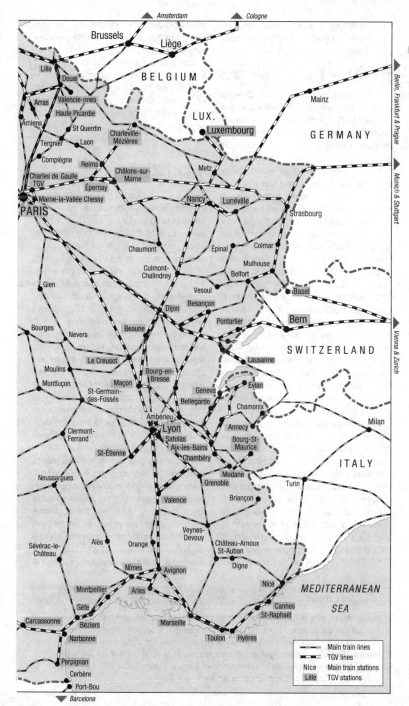

▲ Amsterdam ▲ Cologne

Brussels
Liège

BELGIUM

Lille
Douai
Arras
Valencie-nnes
Haute Picardie
Amiens
St Quentin
Tergnier
Laon
Compiègne
Reims
Charleville-Mézières

LUX.

Luxembourg

Mainz

GERMANY

Charles de Gaulle TGV
Châlons-sur-Marne
Metz
Épernay
Nancy
Lunéville
Marne-la-Vallée Chessy

PARIS

Chaumont
Épinal
Colmar
Strasbourg

Culmont-Chalindrey
Mulhouse
Belfort

Gien
Vesoul
Basel

Dijon
Besançon

Bourges
Nevers
Beaune
Pontarlier
Bern

Le Creusot
Lausanne
SWITZERLAND

Moulins
Bourg-en-Bresse

Montluçon
Mâcon
St-Germain-des-Fossés
Geneva
Évian
Bellegarde
Chamonix

Clermont-Ferrand
Ambérieu
Lyon
Satolas
Aix-les-Bains
Annecy
Bourg-St-Maurice
Milan

St-Étienne
Chambéry
ITALY

Neussargues
Modane
Grenoble
Turin

Valence
Briançon

Veynes-Devouy

Sévérac-le-Château
Alès
Orange
Château-Arnoux St-Auban

Nîmes
Digne

Montpellier
Avignon

Arles
Nice

Carcassonne
Sète
Cannes
St-Raphaël

Béziers
Marseille
MEDITERRANEAN

Narbonne
Toulon
Hyères
SEA

Perpignan

Cerbère

Port-Bou

▼ Barcelona

Legend:
— Main train lines
▪▪▪ TGV lines
Nice Main train stations
Lille TGV stations

the month-long August holiday, and the notoriously congested weekends nearest July 14 and August 15.

Practicalities

US, Canadian, Australian, New Zealand, South African and all EU **driving licences** are valid in France, though an International Driver's Licence makes life easier. The minimum driving age is 18 and you must hold a full licence. Drivers are required to carry their licence with them when driving, and you should also have the insurance papers with you in the car. If the vehicle is rented, its registration document (*carte grise*) must also be carried.

All the major car manufacturers have garages and service stations in France, which can help if you run into mechanical difficulties. You'll find them listed in the Yellow Pages of the phone book under "*Garages d'automobiles*"; for breakdowns, look under "*Dépannages*". If you have an accident or suffer theft, contact the local police – and keep a copy of their report in order to file an insurance claim. Within Europe, most car **insurance policies** cover taking your car to France; check with your insurer. However, you're advised to take out extra cover for motoring assistance in case your car breaks down.

Note that **petrol stations** in rural areas tend to be few and far between, and those that do exist usually open only during normal shop hours – don't count on being able to buy petrol at night or on Sunday. An increasing number of stations are equipped with automated 24-hour pumps, but many of these only accept French bank cards. Most sell unleaded (*sans plomb*), and diesel (*gazole* or *gasoil*); some also sell LPG and an increasing number are selling SP95-E10, a form of unleaded which includes 10 percent ethanol. Not all cars can run on this, so check with the manufacturer before using it.

Most autoroutes have **tolls**: rates vary, but to give you an idea, travelling by motorway from Calais to Montpellier costs roughly €62; pay in cash or by credit card (get in a lane marked CB at the toll-gates). You can work out routes and costs of both petrol and tolls online at the useful ⓦwww .viamichelin.com.

Rules of the road

Since the French **drive on the right**, drivers of right-hand-drive cars must adjust their **headlights** to dip to the right. This is most easily done by sticking on glare deflectors, which can be bought at most motor accessory shops, at the Channel ferry ports or the Eurostar terminal and on the ferries. It's more complicated if your car is fitted with High-Intensity Discharge (HID) or halogen-type lights; check with your dealer about how to adjust these well in advance.

All non-French vehicles must display their **national identification letters** (GB, etc) either on the number plate or by means of a sticker, and all vehicles must carry a **red warning triangle** and a **reflective safety jacket**. You are also strongly advised to carry a spare set of bulbs, a fire extinguisher and a first-aid kit. **Seat belts** are compulsory and children under 10 years are not allowed to sit in the front of the car.

The law of *priorité à droite* – **giving way** to traffic coming from your right, even when it is coming from a minor road – has largely been phased out. However, it still applies on some roads in built-up areas and the occasional roundabout, so be vigilant at junctions. A sign showing a yellow diamond on a white background indicates that you have right of way, while the same sign with a diagonal

Road information

Up-to-the-minute information regarding traffic jams and road works throughout France can be obtained from the Bison Futé free-dial recorded information service (☏08.00.10.02.00; French only) or their website ⓦwww.bison-fute.equipement .gouv.fr. For information regarding autoroutes, you can also consult the bilingual website ⓦwww.autoroutes.fr. In the south of France, Radio Trafic 107.7GM provides 24-hour music and updates on traffic conditions.

Buy-back leasing schemes

If you are not resident in an EU country and will be touring France for between 17 days (21 in the case of Peugeot and Renault) and six months, it's worth investigating the special **buy-back leasing schemes** operated by Peugeot ("Peugeot Open Europe"), Citroën ("Citroën DriveEurope" and Renault ("Renault Eurodrive"). Under these deals, you purchase a new car tax-free and the manufacturer guarantees to buy it back from you for an agreed price at the end of the period. In general, the difference between the purchase and repurchase price works out considerably less per day than the equivalent cost of car hire. Further details are available from Peugeot, Citroën and Renault dealers and online at ⓦwww.peugeot-openeurope.com, ⓦwww.citroendriveeurope.com and ⓦwww.eurodrive.renault.com.

black slash across it warns you that vehicles emerging from the right have priority. *Cédez le passage* means "Give way".

If you have an **accident** while driving, you must fill in and sign a *constat d'accident* (declaration form) or, if another car is also involved, a *constat aimable* (jointly agreed declaration); in the case of a hire car, these forms should be provided with the car's insurance documents.

Unless otherwise indicated **speed limits** are: 130kph (80mph) on *autoroutes*; 110kph (68mph) on dual carriageways; 90kph (55mph) on other roads; and 50kph (31mph) in towns. In wet weather, and for drivers with less than two years' experience, these limits are 110kph (68mph), 100kph (62mph) and 80kph (50mph), respectively, while the town limit remains constant. Fixed and mobile radars are now widely used. The **alcohol limit** is 0.05 percent (0.5 grams per litre of blood), and random breath tests and saliva tests for drugs are common. There are stiff **penalties** for driving violations, ranging from on-the-spot **fines** for minor infringements to the immediate confiscation of your licence if you're caught exceeding the speed limit by more than 40kph or prison for the most serious offences. Note that radar detectors are illegal in France.

Car rental

To rent a car in France you must be over 21 and have driven for at least two years. Car rental costs upwards of €70 a day and €240 for a week; reserve online well in advance to get the best price. You'll find the big-name international firms – Avis, Hertz and so on –

represented at airports and in most major towns and cities; some alternatives to these are listed below. Local firms can be cheaper but they won't have the agency network for one-way rentals and you should check the small print. Unless you specify otherwise, you'll get a car with manual (stick shift) transmission.

Car-rental agencies

Avis ⓦwww.avis.com.
Argus Car Hire ⓦwww.arguscarhire.com.
Auto Europe ⓦwww.autoeurope.com.
Europcar ⓦwww.europcar.com.
Europe by Car ⓦwww.europebycar.com.
Hertz ⓦwww.hertz.com.
Holiday Autos ⓦwww.holidayautos.com.

By scooter and motorbike

Scooters are ideal for pottering around locally. They're easy to rent – places offering bicycles often also rent out scooters. Expect to pay in the region of €30 and up a day for a 50cc machine. You don't need a licence, just a passport or some other form of ID.

For anything over 125cc you'll need to have held a full **motorbike** licence for at least two years. Rental prices are around €70 a day for a 125cc bike and expect to leave a hefty deposit by cash or credit card – over €1000 is the norm – which you may lose in the event of damage or theft. Crash helmets are compulsory on all bikes, and the headlight must be switched on at all times. It is recommended to carry a first-aid kit and a set of spare bulbs.

Canal and river trips

With over 7000km of navigable rivers and canals, **boating** is one of the most relaxed ways of exploring France. Expect to pay between around €700 and €2500 per week, depending on the season and level of comfort, for a four- to six-person boat. Details of firms offering canal and river holidays can be found on p.31, or contact the Fédération des Industries Nautiques (☎01.44.37.04.00, ⓦwww .france-nautic.com). If you want to bring your own boat, Voies Navigables de France (VNF) (ⓦwww.vnf.fr) has information in English on maximum dimensions, documentation, regulations and so forth.The **principal areas** for boating are Brittany, Burgundy, Picardy-Flanders, Alsace and Champagne. The eighteenth-century Canal de Bourgogne and 300-year-old Canal du Midi in particular are fascinating examples of early canal engineering, the latter being a UNESCO World Heritage Site.

By bicycle

Bicycles (*vélos*) have high status in France, where cyclists are given respect both on the roads and as customers at restaurants and hotels. In addition, local authorities are actively promoting cycling, not only with urban cycle lanes, but also with comprehensive networks in rural areas (often on disused railways). Most towns have well-stocked repair shops, but if you're using a foreign-made bike with non-standard wheels, it's a good idea to carry spare tyres.

You can take your bike free of charge without reservation on many TER and Intercité trains; look out for trains marked on the timetable with a bicycle symbol. Folding bikes travel free on TGV, Téoz and Lunéa trains if they're packed into a bag no more than 90cmx120cm; for non-folding bikes

you'll have to pay a €10 fee. Another option is to have your bicycle delivered with your luggage to your destination; prices start at €28. Eurostar has similar arrangements. **Ferries** usually carry bikes free (they count as your "vehicle" when you book), as do some **airlines** such as British Airways, while others now charge – check when making your booking.

Bikes – usually mountain bikes (*vélos tout-terrain* or VTT) or hybrid bikes (*vélos tout-chemin* or VTC) – are often available to **rent** from campsites and hostels, as well as from specialist cycle shops and some tourist offices for around €15 per day. Many cities, including Lyon, Marseille, Nice and Paris, now have public self-service bike hire schemes with hire points scattered widely throughout the city.

Accommodation

At most times of the year, you can turn up in any French town and find a room or a place in a campsite. Booking a couple of nights in advance can be reassuring, however, as it saves you the effort of trudging round and ensures that you know what you'll be paying; many hoteliers, campsite managers and hostel managers speak at least a little English. In most places, you'll be able to get a simple double for €35–40, though expect to pay at least €50 for a reasonable level of comfort. Paris and the Côte d'Azur are more expensive, however, with equivalent rates of roughly €60 and €100. We've detailed a selection of hotels throughout the Guide, and given a price range for each (see box below); as a general rule the areas around train stations have the highest density of cheap hotels.

Problems may arise between mid-July and the end of August, when the French take their own vacations en masse. During this period, hotel and hostel accommodation can be hard to come by, particularly in the coastal resorts, and you may find yourself falling back on local tourist offices for help.

All **tourist offices** can provide lists of hotels, hostels, campsites and bed-and-breakfast possibilities, and some offer a booking service, though they can't guarantee rooms at a particular price. With campsites, you can be more relaxed about finding an empty pitch, though it may be more difficult with a caravan or camper van or if you're looking for a place on the Côte d'Azur.

Hotels

French hotels are graded in six bands, from zero for the simplest through one, two, three and four to five stars for the most exclusive. The price more or less corresponds to the number of stars, though the system is a little haphazard, having more to do with ratios of bathrooms per guest and so forth than genuine quality; some unclassified and single-star hotels can be very good. An alternative system, HotelCert (Ⓦ www.hotelcert .org), focuses instead on cleanliness and the quality of the service in general. Single rooms – if the hotel has any – are only marginally cheaper than doubles, so sharing slashes costs, especially since many hotels willingly

---

Accommodation price categories

All the hotels and guesthouses listed in this book have been price coded according to the scale below. The prices quoted are for the cheapest available double room in high season, although remember that many of the cheap places will also have more expensive rooms with more facilities. For accommodation in the ❶ bracket, expect simple rooms, occasionally with communal (*dans le palier*) showers (*douches*) and toilets (WC or *toilettes*). ❷ will probably guarantee you a separate bathroom (*salle de bain*), while ❸ should get you a TV, phone and better furnishings. At around ❹, the rooms will be more spacious and attractively decorated, if not state of the art; anything from ❺ upwards tends towards luxury, with all the mod cons you would expect, except in the larger cities, where luxury rooms tend to start at around ❻. Rooms from ❼ upwards will be increasingly plush and by the time they get to a ❾, sumptuous rooms will often be accompanied by a sauna, gym, swimming pool and many other services.

❶ €40 and under	❹ €66–80	❼ €121–150
❷ €41–50	❺ €81–100	❽ €151–200
❸ €51–65	❻ €101–120	❾ €201 and over

provide rooms with extra beds for three or more people.

Big cities tend to have a good variety of cheap establishments; in small towns and rural areas, you may not be so lucky, particularly as the cheaper, family-run hotels find it increasingly hard to survive. Swanky resorts, particularly those on the Côte d'Azur, have very high **prices** in July and August, but even these are still cheaper than Paris, which is far more expensive than the rest of the country. If you're staying for more than three nights in a hotel it's often possible to negotiate a lower price, particularly out of season.

Breakfast, which is never included in the quoted price, will add anything between €6 and €30 per person to a bill – though there is no obligation to take it.

Note that many **family-run hotels** close for two or three weeks a year in low season. In smaller towns and villages they may also close for one or two nights a week, usually Sunday or Monday. Details are given where relevant in the Guide, but dates change from year to year; the best precaution is to phone ahead to be sure.

A very useful option, especially if you're driving and are looking for somewhere late at night, are the **chain hotels** located at motorway exits and on the outskirts of major towns. They may be soulless, but you can usually count on a decent and reliable standard. Among the cheapest (from around €30 for a three-person room with communal toilets and showers) is the one-star Formule 1 chain (℡08.92.68.89.00, ⓦwww.hotel formule1.com). Other budget chains include B&B (℡02.98.33.75.29, ⓦwww.hotel-bb .com), the slightly more comfortable Première Classe (℡08.92.68.81.23, ⓦwww.premiere classe.fr) and Etap Hôtel (℡08.92.68.89.00, ⓦwww.etaphotel.com). Slightly more upmarket are Ibis (℡08.92.68.66.86, ⓦwww .ibishotel.com) and Campanile (ⓦwww .campanile.fr), where en-suite rooms with satellite TV and often broadband internet access cost from around €50–60.

There are a number of well-respected **hotel federations** in France. The biggest and most useful of these is Logis de France (℡01.45.84.83.84, ⓦwww.logis-de-france .fr), an association of over three thousand hotels nationwide. They produce a free annual guide, available in French tourist offices, from Logis de France itself and from member hotels. Two other, more upmarket federations worth mentioning are Châteaux & Hôtels de France (℡01.58.00.22.00,

www.chateauxhotels.com) and the Relais du Silence (☎01.44.49.90.00, Ⓦwww .silencehotel.com), both of which offer high-class accommodation in beautiful older properties, often in rural locations.

Bed and breakfast and self-catering

In country areas, in addition to standard hotels, you will come across **chambres d'hôtes** – bed-and-breakfast accommodation in someone's house, château or farm. Though the quality varies widely, on the whole standards are pretty high, and the best can offer more character and greater value for money than an equivalently priced hotel. If you're lucky, the owners may also provide traditional home cooking and a great insight into French life. Prices generally range between €40 and €80 for two people including breakfast; payment is almost always expected in cash. Some offer meals on request (*tables d'hôtes*), usually evenings only.

If you're planning to stay a week or more in any one place it's worth considering renting self-catering accommodation. This will generally consist of self-contained country cottages known as **gîtes**. Many *gîtes* are in converted barns or farm outbuildings, though some can be quite grand. "Gîtes Panda" are *gîtes* located in a national park or other protected area and are run on environmentally friendly lines.

You can get lists of both *gîtes* and *chambres d'hôtes* from the government-funded agency Gîtes de France (☎01.49.70.75.75, Ⓦwww .gites-de-france.com), or search on their website for accommodation by location or theme (for example, *gîtes* near fishing or riding opportunities). In addition, every year the organization publishes a number of national guides, such as *Nouveaux Gîtes Ruraux* (listing new addresses); these guides are available to buy online or from departmental offices of Gîtes de France, as well as from bookstores and tourist offices. Tourist offices will also have lists of places in their area which are not affiliated to Gîtes de France.

Hostels and student accommodation

At €13–24 per night for a **dormitory bed**, usually with breakfast thrown in, youth

hostels – *auberges de jeunesse* – are invaluable for single travellers of any age on a budget. Some now offer rooms, occasionally en suite, but they don't necessarily work out cheaper than hotels – particularly if you've had to pay a taxi fare to reach them. However, many allow you to cut costs by eating in the hostels' cheap canteens, while in a few you can prepare your own meals in the communal kitchens. In the Guide we give the cost of a dormitory bed.

In addition to those belonging to the two French hostelling associations listed below, there are now also several independent hostels, particularly in Paris. At these, dorm beds cost €20–30, with breakfast sometimes extra.

In July and August, there's sometimes the possibility of staying in **student accommodation** at prices similar to hostels. Contact CROUS (☎01.40.51.36.00, Ⓦwww.crous -paris.fr) for further information.

Youth hostel associations

Slightly confusingly, there are two rival **French hostelling associations** – the

Fédération Unie des Auberges de Jeunesse (℡01.44.89.87.27, ⓦwww.fuaj.org) and the much smaller Ligue Française (℡01.44.16.78.78, ⓦwww.auberges-de -jeunesse.com). In either case, you normally have to show a current Hostelling International (HI) **membership card**. It's usually cheaper and easier to join before you leave home, provided your national youth hostel association is a full member of HI. Alternatively, you can purchase an HI card in certain French hostels for €16 (€11 for those under 26), or (at Ligue hostels) a "one night card" for €1.50 per night.

Gîtes d'étape and refuges

In the countryside, another hostel-style option exists in the form of **gîtes d'étape**. Aimed primarily at hikers and long-distance bikers, *gîtes d'étape* are often run by the local village or municipality and are less formal than hostels, providing bunk beds and primitive kitchen and washing facilities from around €12 per person. They are marked on the large-scale IGN walkers' maps and listed in the individual Topo guides (see "Walking and climbing" p.53). In addition, mountain areas are well supplied with **refuge huts**, mostly run by the Fédération Française des Clubs Alpins et de Montagne (FFCAM; ℡01.53.72.87.00, ⓦwww.ffcam.fr). These huts, generally only open in summer, offer dorm accommodation and meals, and are the only available shelter once you are above the villages. Costs are €14–25 for the night, or half of this if you're a member of a climbing organization affiliated to FFCAM, plus around €18–20 for breakfast and dinner, which is good value when you consider that in some cases supplies have to be brought up by mule or helicopter.

More information can be found either online or in the guides *Gîtes d'Étape et de Séjours* (€10), published by Gîtes de France (see p.43).

Camping

Practically every village and town in France has at least one **campsite** to cater for the thousands of people who spend their holiday under canvas. Most sites open from around Easter to September or October. Most are graded – from one to four stars –

by the local authority. One-star sites are basic, with toilets and showers (not necessarily with hot water) but little else, and standards of cleanliness are not always brilliant. Facilities improve with more stars: at the top end of the scale, four-star sites are far more spacious, have hot-water showers and electrical hook-ups; most will also have a swimming pool (sometimes heated), washing machines, a shop and sports facilities, and will provide refreshments or meals in high season. A further designation, **Camping Qualité** (ⓦwww.campingqualite .com), indicates campsites with particularly high standards of hygiene, service and privacy, while the **Clef Verte** (ⓦwww .laclefverte.org) label is awarded to sites run along environmentally friendly lines. For those who really like to get away from it all, camping **à la ferme** – on somebody's farm – is a good, simple option. Lists of sites are available at local tourist offices or from Gîtes de France (see p.43).

The Fédération Française de Camping et de Caravaning (℡01.42.72.84.08, ⓦwww .ffcc.fr) publishes an annual **guide** (€12) covering over ten thousand campsites, details of which can also be found online on the excellent Camping France website (ⓦwww.campingfrance.com). If you'd rather have everything organized for you, a number of companies specialize in camping holidays; see p.32 for details.

Most campsites charge per emplacement and per person, usually including a car, with extra charges for electricity. As a rough guide, two people with a tent and car should expect to pay from €12 per day at a one-star site in low season, rising to as much as €50 at a four-star in high season. In peak season it's wise to book ahead, and note that many of the big sites now have caravans and even chalet bungalows for rent.

Lastly, a word of caution: always ask permission before **camping rough** (*camping sauvage*) on anyone's land. If the dogs don't get you, the guns might – farmers have been known to shoot first, and ask later. Camping on public land is not officially permitted and is often strongly discouraged, particularly in the south where in summer the risk of forest fires is high.

Food and drink

France is famous for producing some of the most sublime food in the world, whether it's the rarefied delicacies of haute cuisine or the robust, no-nonsense fare served up at country inns. Nevertheless, French cuisine has taken a bit of a knocking in recent years. The wonderful ingredients are still there, as every town and village market testifies, but those little family restaurants serving classic dishes that celebrate the region's produce – and where the bill is less than €20 – are increasingly hard to find. Don't be afraid to ask locals for their recommendations; this will usually elicit strong views and sound advice.

In the complex world of **haute cuisine**, where the top chefs are national celebrities, a battle has long been raging between traditionalists, determined to preserve the purity of French cuisine, and those who experiment with different flavours from around the world. At this level, French food is still brilliant – in both camps – but can be astronomically expensive: at a three-star Michelin restaurant, even the set lunch *menu* is likely to cost €80, though you might get away with less than half that at a – still very impressive – one-star restaurant.

France is also a great place for **foreign cuisine**, in particular North African, Caribbean (known as *Antillais*) and Asiatic.

Breakfast and lunch

A croissant or *pain au chocolat* (a chocolate-filled, light pastry) in a café or bar, with tea, hot chocolate or coffee, is generally the most economical way to eat breakfast, costing from €4. If there are no croissants left, it's perfectly acceptable to go and buy your own at the nearest baker or patisserie. The standard hotel breakfast comprises bread and/or pastries, jam and a jug of coffee or tea, and orange juice if you're lucky, from around €6. More expensive places might offer a breakfast buffet or even hot dishes cooked to order.

The main meal of the day is traditionally eaten at **lunchtime**, usually between noon and 2pm. Midday, and sometimes in the evening, you'll find places offering a *plat du jour* (daily special) for €8–12, or *formules* (or simply *menus*), limited *menus* typically offering a main dish and either a starter or a

dessert for a set price. **Crêpes**, or pancakes with fillings, served at ubiquitous crêperies, are popular lunchtime food. The savoury buckwheat variety (*galettes*) provide the main course; sweet, white-flour crêpes are dessert. **Pizzerias**, usually *au feu du bois* (baked in wood-fired ovens), are also very common. They are somewhat better value than crêperies, but quality and quantity vary greatly.

For **picnics**, the local outdoor market or supermarket will provide you with almost everything you need, from tomatoes and avocados to cheese and pâté. Cooked meat, prepared snacks, ready-made dishes and assorted salads can be bought at charcuteries (delicatessens), which you'll find even in most small villages, and at supermarket cold-food counters. You purchase by weight, or you can ask for *une tranche* (a slice), *une barquette* (a carton) or *une part* (a portion) as appropriate.

Snacks

Outside tourist areas the opportunities for snacking on the run are not always as plentiful or obvious in France as in Britain or North America; the local boulangerie is often the best bet. Popular snacks include *Croques-monsieur* or *croques-madame* (variations on the toasted cheese-and-ham sandwich) – on sale at cafés, brasseries and many street stands – along with *frites* (fries), crêpes, *galettes*, *gauffres* (waffles), *glaces* (ice creams) and all kinds of fresh-filled baguettes (which usually cost between €3 and €5 to take away). For variety, in bigger towns you can find Tunisian snacks like *brik à l'œuf* (a fried pastry with an egg inside), *merguez* (spicy North African sausage) and Middle Eastern falafel (deep-fried chickpea balls served in flat bread with salad). Wine bars are good for regional sausages and cheese, usually served with brown bread (*pain de campagne*).

Regional dishes

French cooking is as varied as its landscape, and differs vastly from region to region. In **Provence**, in close proximity to Italy, local dishes make heavy use of olive oils, garlic and tomatoes, as well as Mediterranean vegetables such as aubergines (eggplant) and peppers. In keeping with its close distance to the sea, the region's most famous dish is *bouillabaisse*, a delicious fish stew from Marseille. To the southwest, in **Languedoc** and **Pays Basque**, hearty *cassoulet* stews and heavier meals are in order, with certain similarities to Spanish cuisine. **Alsace**, in the northeast, shows Germanic influences in dishes such as *choucroute* (sauerkraut), and a hearty array of sausages. **Burgundy**, famous for its wines, is the home of what many people consider classic French dishes such as *coq au vin* and *boeuf bourguignon*. In the northwest, **Normandy** and **Brittany** are about the best places you could head for

seafood, as well as for sweet and savoury crêpes and *galettes*. Finally, if you're in the **Dordogne**, be sure to sample its famous foie gras or pricey truffles (*truffes*).

For more on which regional dishes to try, see the boxes at the start of each chapter in the Guide.

Vegetarian food

On the whole, **vegetarians** can expect a somewhat lean time in France. Most cities now have at least one specifically vegetarian restaurant, but elsewhere your best bet may be a crêperie, pizzeria or North African restaurant. Otherwise you may have to fall back on an omelette, salad or crudités (raw vegetables) in an ordinary restaurant. Sometimes restaurants are willing to replace a meat dish on the fixed-price *menu* (*menu fixe*); at other times you'll have to pick your way through the *carte*. Remember the phrase *Je suis végétarien(ne); est-ce qu'il y a quelques plats sans viande?* ("I'm a vegetarian; are there any non-meat dishes?"). **Vegans**, however, should probably stick to self-catering.

Drinking

In France, drinking is done at a leisurely pace whether it's a prelude to food (*apéritif*) or a sequel (*digestif*), and **café-bars** are the standard places to do it. By law the full price

Cheese

Charles de Gaulle famously commented "How can you govern a country that has 246 kinds of cheese?" For serious **cheese**-lovers, France is the ultimate paradise. Other countries may produce individual cheeses which are as good as, or even better than, the best of the French, but no country offers a range that comes anywhere near them in terms of sheer inventiveness. In fact, there are officially over 350 types of French cheese, and the way they are made are jealously guarded secrets. Many cheese-makers have successfully protected their products by gaining the right to label their produce **AOC** (*appellation d'origine contrôlée*), covered by laws similar to those for wines, which – among other things – controls the amount of cheese that a particular area can produce. As a result, the subtle differences between French local cheeses have not been overwhelmed by the industrialized uniformity that has plagued other countries.

The best, or most traditional, restaurants offer a well-stocked *plateau de fromages* (cheeseboard), served at room temperature with bread, but not butter. Apart from the ubiquitous Brie, Camembert and numerous varieties of goat's cheese (*chèvre*), there will usually be one or two local cheeses on offer – these are the ones to go for. If you want to buy cheese, local markets are always the best bet, while in larger towns you'll generally find a *fromagerie*, a shop with dozens of varieties to choose from. We've indicated the best regional cheeses throughout the Guide.

list, including service charges, must be clearly displayed. You normally pay when you leave, and it's perfectly acceptable to sit for hours over just one cup of coffee, though in this case a small tip will be appreciated.

Wine

For an introduction to French **wines** (*vins*), see the *French wines* colour section.

Choosing wine is an extremely complex business and it's hard not to feel intimidated by the seemingly innate expertise of all French people. Many *appellations* are mentioned in the text, but trusting your own taste is the best way to go. The more interest you show, the more helpful advice you're likely to receive. The only thing the French cannot tolerate is people ordering Coke or the like to accompany a gourmet meal.

The best way of **buying wine** is directly from the producers (*vignerons*) at their vineyards or at Maisons or Syndicats du Vin (representing a group of wine-producers), or Coopératifs Vinicoles (producers' co-ops). At all these places you can usually sample the wines first. It's best to make clear at the start how much you want to buy (particularly if it's only one or two bottles) and you'll not be popular if you drink several glasses and then fail to make a purchase. The most economical option is to buy *en vrac*, which you can do at some wine shops (*caves*), filling an easily obtainable plastic five- or ten-litre container (usually sold on the premises) straight from the barrel. Supermarkets often have good bargains, too.

The basic wine terms are: *brut*, very dry; *sec*, dry; *demi-sec*, sweet; *doux*, very sweet; *mousseux*, sparkling; *méthode champenoise*, mature and sparkling.

Beer and spirits

Familiar light Belgian and German brands, plus French brands from Alsace, account for most of the **beer** you'll find. Draught beer (*à la pression*) – very often Kronenbourg – is the cheapest drink you can have next to coffee and wine; *une pression* or *un demi* (0.33 litre) will cost around €3. For a wider choice of draught and bottled beer you need to go to the special beer-drinking establishments such as the English- and Irish-style pubs

found in larger towns and cities. A small bottle at one of these places can set you back double what you'd pay in an ordinary café-bar. Buying bottled or canned beer in supermarkets is, of course, much cheaper.

Spirits, such as cognac and armagnac, and liqueurs are consumed at any time of day, though in far smaller quantities these days thanks to the clampdown on drink-driving. *Pastis* – the generic name of aniseed drinks such as Pernod and Ricard – is served diluted with water and ice (*glace* or *glaçons*). It's very refreshing and not expensive. Among less familiar names, try Poire William (pear brandy) or Marc (a spirit distilled from grape pulp). Measures are generous, but they don't come cheap: the same applies for imported spirits like whisky (*Scotch*). Two drinks designed to stimulate the appetite – *un apéritif* – are *pineau* (cognac and grape juice) and kir (white wine with a dash of Cassis – blackcurrant liqueur – or with champagne instead of wine for a Kir Royal). Cognac, armagnac and Chartreuse are among the many aids to digestion – *un digestif* – to relax over after a meal. Cocktails are served at most late-night bars, discos and clubs, as well as upmarket hotel bars and at every seaside promenade café; they usually cost at least €5.

Soft drinks, tea and coffee

You can buy cartons of unsweetened **fruit juice** in supermarkets, although in cafés the bottled (sweetened) nectars such as apricot (*jus d'abricot*) and blackcurrant (*cassis*) still hold sway. Fresh orange (*jus d'orange*) or lemon juice (*citron pressé*) is much more refreshing – for the latter, the juice is served in the bottom of a long ice-filled glass, with a jug of water and a sugar bowl to sweeten it to your taste. Other soft drinks to try are syrups (*sirops*) – mint or grenadine, for example, mixed with water. The standard fizzy drinks of lemonade (*limonade*), Coke (*coca*) and so forth are all available, and there's no shortage of bottled mineral **water** (*eau minérale*) or spring water (*eau de source*) – whether sparkling (*gazeuse*) or still (*plate*) – either, from the big brand names to the most obscure spa product. But there's not much wrong with the tap water (*l'eau de robinet*), which will always be brought free to your table if you ask for it. The only time you shouldn't drink the tap water is if the tap is labelled *eau non potable*.

Coffee is invariably espresso – small, black and very strong. *Un café* or *un express* is the regular; *un crème* is with milk; *un grand café* or *un grand crème* are large versions. *Un déca* is decaffeinated, now widely available. Ordinary **tea** (*thé*) – Lipton's nine times out of ten – is normally served black (*nature*) or with a slice of lemon (*limon*);

to have milk with it, ask for *un peu de lait frais* (some fresh milk). *Chocolat chaud* – **hot chocolate** – unlike tea, lives up to the high standards of French food and drink and is very common in cafés and bars. After meals, herb teas (*infusions* or *tisanes*), offered by most restaurants, can be soothing. The more common ones are *verveine* (verbena), *tilleul* (lime blossom), *menthe* (mint) and *camomille* (camomile).

The media

French newspapers and magazines are available from newsagents (*maisons de la presse*) or any of the ubiquitous street-side kiosks, while TV, satellite and otherwise, is easy to track down in most forms of accommodation. A limited range of British and US newspapers and magazines is widely available in cities and occasionally in even quite small towns.

Newspapers and magazines

Of the **French daily papers**, *Le Monde* (🌐www.lemonde.fr) is the most intellectual; it's widely respected, and somewhat austere, though it does now carry such frivolities as colour photos. Conservative, and at times controversial, *Le Figaro* (🌐www.lefigaro.fr) is the most highly regarded of the more right-wing papers. *Libération* (🌐www.liberation .com), founded by Jean-Paul Sartre in the 1960s, is moderately left-wing, pro-European, independent and more colloquial, while rigorous left-wing criticism of the government comes from *L'Humanité* (🌐www.humanite .presse.fr), the Communist Party paper, though it is struggling to survive. The top-selling **tabloid**, predictably more readable and a good source of news, is *Aujourd'hui* (🌐www.aujourdhui-en-france.fr, published in Paris as *Le Parisien*), while *L'Équipe* (🌐www .lequipe.fr) is dedicated to sports coverage. The widest circulations are enjoyed by the **regional dailies**, of which the most important is the Rennes-based *Ouest-France* (🌐www .ouest-france.fr). For visitors, these are mainly of interest for their listings.

Weekly **magazines** of the *Newsweek/Time* model include the wide-ranging and left-leaning *Le Nouvel Observateur* (🌐www .nouvelobs.com), its right-wing counterpoint *L'Express* (🌐www.lexpress.fr) and the centrist with bite, *Marianne* (🌐www.marianne-en -ligne.fr). The best investigative journalism is found in the weekly satirical paper *Le Canard Enchaîné* (🌐www.lecanardenchaine.fr), while *Charlie Hebdo* (🌐www.charliebedo.fr) is roughly equivalent to the UK's *Private Eye*. There's also *Paris Match* (🌐www.parismatch .com), for gossip about stars and royalty, and, of course, the French versions of *Vogue*, *Elle* and *Marie-Claire*, and the relentlessly urban *Biba*, for women's fashion and lifestyle.

English-language newspapers which are printed locally, such as the *International Herald Tribune*, are available on the day of publication. Others usually arrive the following day, and the prices are all heavily marked up.

Television and radio

French **terrestrial TV** has six channels: three public (France 2, France 3 and Arte/France 5); one subscription (Canal Plus – with some unencrypted programmes); and two commercial (TF1 and M6). Of these, TF1 (ⓦwww.tf1.fr) and France 2 (ⓦwww.france2.fr) are the most popular channels, showing a broad mix of programmes.

In addition there are any number of **cable and satellite channels**, including CNN, BBC World, Euronews, Eurosport, Planète (which specializes in documentaries) and Canal Jimmy (*Friends* and the like in French). The main French-run music channel is MCM.

Radio France (ⓦwww.radio-france.fr) operates eight stations. These include France Culture for arts, France Info for news and France Musique for classical music. Other major stations include Europe 1 (ⓦwww.europe1.fr) for news, debate and sport. Radio France International (RFI, ⓦwww.rfi.fr) broadcasts in French and various foreign languages, including English, on 89 FM and the internet.

Festivals

It's hard to beat the experience of arriving in a small French village, expecting no more than a bed for the night, to discover the streets decked out with flags and streamers, a band playing in the square and the entire population out celebrating the feast of their patron saint. As well as nationwide celebrations such as the Fête de la Musique (around June 21; ⓦwww.fetedelamusique.culture.fr), Bastille Day (July 14) and the Assumption of the Virgin Mary (Aug 15), there are any number of festivals – both traditional and of more recent origin – held in towns and villages throughout France. For more information see ⓦwww.culture.fr and www.viafrance.com.

Festival calendar

January and February

Nantes La Folle Journée (late Jan to early Feb; ⓦwww.follejournee.fr).

February to April

Menton Fête du Citron (two weeks following Mardi Gras, forty days before Easter; ⓦwww.feteducitron.com); parades, concerts and fireworks.
Nice Carnival (Feb–March; ⓦwww.nicecarnaval.com).

May

Cannes Festival de Cannes (ⓦwww.festival-cannes.com); international film festival.

Les Saintes-Maries-de-la-Mer Fête de Ste Sarah (May 24–25); Romany festival.
Nîmes La Féria de Nîmes (Pentecost, seven weeks after Easter); bullfights.

June

Annecy Festival International du Film d'Animation (early June; ⓦwww.annecy.org); animated films.
Bordeaux Fête le Vin (late June in even-numbered years; ⓦwww.bordeaux-fete-le-vin.com).
Châlons-en-Campagne Festival Furies (early June; ⓦwww.festival-furies.com); street theatre.
Lyon Les Nuits de Fourvière (June and July; ⓦwww.nuitsdefourviere.fr); performance arts.
Montpellier Montpellier Danse (mid-June to early July; ⓦwww.montpellierdanse.com).
Paris La Marche des Fiertés Lesbienne, Gai, Bi & Trans (late June; ⓦwww.inter-lgbt.org).
Paris Festival Django Reinhardt (late June; ⓦwww.festivaldjangoreinhardt.com); jazz.
Paris Festival de St-Denis (May–June; ⓦwww.festival-saint-denis.com); classical and world music festival.
Strasbourg Festival de Musique de Strasbourg (ⓦwww.festival-strasbourg.com); classical music.
Uzès Uzès Danse (ⓦwww.uzesdanse.fr); contemporary dance.
Vienne Jazz à Vienne (late June to early July; ⓦwww.jazzavienne.com).

July

Aix-en-Provence Festival International d'Art Lyrique (ⓦwww.festival-aix.com); classical music and opera.

Alès Cratère/Surfaces (early July; www.lecratere.fr); street theatre.

Arles Les Suds à Arles (mid-July; www.suds-arles.com); world music.

Avignon Festival d'Avignon (www.festival-avignon.com); contemporary dance and theatre.

Beaune Festival International d'Opéra Baroque (www.festivalbeaune.com).

Belfort Eurockéennes (early July; festival.eurockeennes.fr); rock and indie music.

Carhaix Festival des Vieilles Charrues (mid-July; www.vieillescharrues.asso.fr); contemporary music festival.

Chalon-sur-Saône Chalon dans la Rue (third week July; www.chalondanslarue.com); street theatre.

Colmar Festival International de Colmar (early July; www.festival-colmar.com); classical music.

Gannat (near Vichy) Les Cultures du Monde (late July; www.gannat.com).

Grenoble Rencontres du Jeune Théâtre Européen (early July; www.crearc.fr); contemporary theatre.

Juan-les-Pins Jazz à Juan (mid-July; www.jazzajuan.fr).

La Rochelle Festival International du Film (early July; www.festival-larochelle.org). Francofolies (mid-July; www.francofolies.fr); contemporary French music.

La Roque d'Anthéron Festival International de Piano (mid-July to mid-Aug; www.festival-piano.com).

Nice Jazz Festival (late July; www.nicejazzfestival.fr).

Orange Chorégies d'Orange (mid-July to early Aug; www.choregies.asso.fr); opera.

Prades Festival Pablo Casals (late July to mid-Aug; www.prades-festival-casals.com); chamber music.

Reims Flâneries Musicales d'Été (www.flaneriesreims.com); open-air concerts.

Rennes Les Tombées de la Nuit (early July; www.lestombeesdelanuit.com); concerts, cinema and performance arts.

Saintes Festival de Saintes (mid-July; www.abbayeauxdames.org); classical music.

Vaison-la-Romaine Vaison Danse (mid- to late July; www.vaison-festival.com); contemporary dance.

August

Aurillac Festival International de Théâtre de Rue (www.aurillac.net); street theatre.

Lorient Festival Interceltique (early Aug; www.festival-interceltique.com); Celtic folk festival.

Menton Festival de Musique (www.musique-menton.fr); chamber music.

Mulhouse Festival du Jazz (mid- to late Aug; www.jazz-mulhouse.org).

Paris Rock en Seine (late Aug; www.rockenseine.com).

Périgueux Mimos (early Aug; www.mimos.fr); international mime festival.

Quimper Semaines Musicales (www.semaines-musicales-quimper.org); baroque, classical and contemporary music.

St-Malo La Route du Rock (mid-Aug; www.laroutedurock.com).

September

Limoges Les Francophonies en Limousin (late Sept to early Oct; www.lesfrancophonies.com); contemporary theatre.

Lyon Biennale de la Danse (next in 2012; www.biennaledeladanse.com).

Paris Biennial des Antiquaires (next in 2012; www.bdafrance.eu) antiques fair; Jazz à la Villette (early Sept; www.jazzalavillette.com); Festival d'Automne (mid-Sept to mid-Dec; www.festival-automne.com); theatre, concerts, dance, films and exhibitions.

Perpignan Visa pour l'Image (early to mid-Sept; www.visapourlimage.com); international photojournalism.

Puy-en-Velay Fête Renaissance du Roi de l'Oiseau (mid-Sept; www.roideloiseau.com); historical pageants, fireworks and recreations.

Strasbourg Musica (late Sept to early Oct; www.festival-musica.org); contemporary music.

October

Bastia Les Musicales (www.musicales-de-bastia.com); chanson and world music.

Nancy Jazz Pulsations (www.nancyjazzpulsations.com).

Paris Foire International d'Art Contemporain (late Oct; www.fiac.com).

November and December

Rennes Rencontres Transmusicales (early Dec; www.lestrans.com); contemporary music.

Strasbourg Jazz d'Or (Nov; www.jazzdor.com).

Sports and outdoor activities

France has much to offer sports fans, whether spectator or participant. It's not difficult to get tickets for football and rugby matches, while the biggest event of all, the Tour de France, is free. And if you prefer to participate, there's a host of activities and adventure sports available.

Spectator sports

More than any cultural jamboree, it's **sporting events** that excite the French – particularly cycling, football, rugby and tennis. In the south, bullfighting and the Basque game of pelota are also popular. At the local, everyday level, the rather less gripping but ubiquitous game of *boules* is the sport of choice.

Cycling

The sport the French are truly mad about is **cycling**. The world's premier cycling race is the **Tour de France**, held over three weeks in July and covering around 3500 kilometres. The course changes each year, but always includes some truly arduous mountain stages and time trials, and ends on the Champs-Élysées. An aggregate of each rider's times is made daily, the overall leader wearing the coveted yellow jersey (*maillot jaune*). Huge crowds turn out to cheer on the cyclists and the French president himself presents the jersey to the overall winner. The last French cyclist to win the Tour, however, was Bernard Hinault in 1985.

Other classic long-distance bike races include the **Paris–Roubaix**, instigated in 1896 and held in April, which is reputed to be the most exacting one-day race in the world; the **Paris–Brussels** (Sept), held since 1893; and the rugged seven-day **Paris–Nice** event (March). Details for all the above can be found at ⓦ www.letour.fr.

Football

Football (soccer) is France's number-one team sport. After its legendary win at the 1998 World Cup, the national team's chequered recent history reached its nadir at the 2010 World Cup in South Africa, when the players refused to train after Nicolas Anelka was expelled from the squad for verbally abusing coach Raymond Domenech; a disastrous World Cup performance subsequently ended with defeat 2-1 by the host nation and an ignominious exit from the competition in the first round.

The **domestic game** has been on the up in recent years, and average attendances have improved. The leading club sides include AS Monaco, Olympique Lyonnais and Olympique de Marseille. For the latest information visit the website of the *Ligue de Football Professionel* at ⓦ www.lfp.fr.

Tickets to see domestic clubs are available either from specific club websites,

Sporting calendar

January Monte Carlo Car Rally (ⓦ www.acm.mc).

February–March Six Nations rugby tournament (Paris; ⓦ www.rbs6nations.com).

April Paris Marathon (ⓦ www.parismarathon.com); Le Mans 24-hour motorcycle rally (ⓦ www.lemans.org).

May Roland Garros International Tennis Championship (Paris; ⓦ www.rolandgarros.com); Monaco Formula 1 Grand Prix (ⓦ www.acm.mc).

June Le Mans 24-hour car rally (ⓦ www.lemans.org).

July Tour de France (ⓦ www.letour.fr).

October Grand Prix de l'Arc de Triomphe (Paris; ⓦ www.prixarcdetriomphe.com).

or in the towns where they are playing; ask at local tourist offices. To watch the national team, you can get tickets online at ⓦwww .fff.fr (Fédération Française de Football), or try ⓦwww.francebillet.com. Prices tend to start at around €10–15.

Rugby

Although most popular in the southwest, **rugby** enjoys a passionate following throughout France. French rugby's greatest moment to date came in the 1999 World Cup, when they trounced the favourites New Zealand in the semi-finals, though then lost to an Australian side that never had to rouse itself out of second gear. They also made it to the semi-finals in 2003 and 2007, losing to England on both occasions.

More international fare is provided by the **Six Nations** tournament – the other five nations being England, Wales, Scotland, Ireland and Italy. France has been the most consistent team in recent years, clinching Grand Slams in 2002 and 2004, and again in 2010.

Domestic clubs to watch for include Toulouse (winner of the French Championship in 2008), Paris's Stade Français, Perpignan and Brive (all past winners or runners up in the Europe-wide Heineken Cup), Agen, and the Basque teams of Bayonne and Biarritz, which still retain their reputation as keepers of the game's soul.

Tickets for local games can be bought through the clubs themselves, with prices starting around €10. For bigger domestic and international games, they are available online at ⓦwww.francebillet.com. Information can be found on the Fédération Française de Rugby's website (ⓦwww.ffr.fr).

Pelota

In the Basque country (and also in the nearby Landes), the main draw for crowds is **pelota**, a lethally (sometimes literally) fast variety of team handball or raquetball played in a walled court with a ball of solid wood. The most popular form today is played with bare hands in a two-walled court called a *fronton*. In other varieties wooden bats are used or wicker slings strapped to the players' arms. Ask at local tourist offices for details of where to see the game played.

Bullfighting

In and around the Camargue, the number-one sport is **bullfighting**. Different from the Spanish version, the *course camarguaise* involves variations on the theme of removing cockades from the base of the bull's horns, and it's generally the fighters, rather than the bulls, who get hurt. Further west, particularly in the Landes *département*, you'll come across the similar *courses landaises*, where men perform acrobatics with the by no means docile local cows.

Spanish bullfights, known as *corridas*, do take place – and draw capacity crowds – in southern France. The major events of the year are the Féria de Nîmes (see p.673) at Pentecost (Whitsun) and the Easter *féria* at Arles (p.869). See the local press or ask at tourist offices for details of where to pick up tickets.

Boules

In every town or village square, particularly in the south, you'll see beret-clad men playing *boules* or its variant, *pétanque* (in which contestants must keep both feet on the ground when throwing). Although more women are taking up *boules*, at competition level it remains very male-dominated: there are café or village teams and endless championships.

Outdoor activities

France provides a fantastically wide range of outdoor activities. Most have a national federation (listed in the text where relevant), which can provide information on local clubs.

Walking and climbing

France is covered by a network of some 60,000km of long-distance footpaths, known as *sentiers de grande randonnée* or **GRs**. They're signposted and equipped with campsites, refuges and hostels (*gîtes d'étape*) along the way. Some are real marathons, like the GR5 from the coast of Holland to Nice, the trans-Pyrenean GR10, the Grande Traversée des Alpes (the GTA) and the magnificent GR20 in Corsica (see box, p.990). There are also thousands of shorter *sentiers de promenade et de randonnée*, the **PRs**, as well as nature walks and many other local footpaths.

Each GR and many PRs are described in the **Topo-guide series** (available outside France in good travel bookshops), which give a detailed account of each route, including maps, campsites, refuges, sources of provisions, and so on. In France, the guides are available from bookshops and some tourist offices, or direct from the principal French walkers' association, the Fédération Française de la Randonnée Pédestre (☏01.44.89.93.90, ⊛www .ffrandonnee.fr). In addition, many tourist offices have guides to local footpaths.

Mountain climbing is possible all year round, although bear in mind that some higher routes will be snowbound until quite late in the year, and require special equipment such as crampons and ice axes; these shouldn't be attempted without experience or at least a local guide. See p.44 for information about staying in mountain refuges.

You'll need plenty of water, decent footwear, waterproofs and a map, compass and possibly GPS system.

In mountain areas associations of professional **mountain guides**, often located in the tourist office, organize walking expeditions for all levels of experience. In these and more low-land areas, particularly the limestone cliffs of the south and west, you'll also find possibilities for **rock climbing** (*escalade*). For more information you could contact the Fédération Française de la Montagne et de l'Escalade (☏01.40.18.75.50, ⊛www.ffme.fr).

Details of tour operators specializing in walking holidays are listed on p.31.

Cycling

There are around 50,000km of marked cycle paths (*pistes cyclables*) in France. Many towns and cities have established cycle lanes, while in the countryside there are an increasing number of specially designated **long-distance cycle routes** (*véloroutes* and *voies vertes*). Burgundy is particularly well served, with an 800km circuit, while the Loire à Vélo cycle route will eventually run almost the complete length of the Loire valley. The Fédération Française de Cyclisme (☏01.49.35.69.00, ⊛www.ffc.fr) produces a guide to mountain-biking sites and tourist offices can provide details of local cycle ways; the Fédération Française de Cyclotourisme (☏01.56.20.88.88, ⊛www.ffct.org) provides links to local cycling clubs, and lists local trips. IGN produces a number of departmental "Cycloguides", with maps at 1:25,000, specially aimed at cyclists. Otherwise, their France-wide 1:100,000 maps are the best option (see p.59).

For information on the practicalities of cycling in France, see "Getting around", p.40. Details of tour operators specializing in cycling holidays are on p.32.

Skiing and snowboarding

Millions of visitors come to France to go **skiing** and **snowboarding**, whether it's downhill, cross-country or ski-mountaineering. These can be arranged in France or before you leave (most travel agents sell all-in packages). Though it's possible to ski from early November through to the end of April at high altitudes, peak season is February and March.

The best skiing and boarding is generally in the **Alps**. The higher the resort the longer the season, and the fewer the anxieties you'll have about there being enough snow. For a brief rundown of all the main Alpine skiing areas, see the box on p.769. The foothills of the Alps in **Provence** offer skiing on a smaller scale; snow may be not as reliable. The **Pyrenees** are a friendlier range of mountains, less developed (though that can be a drawback if you want to get in as many different runs as possible per day) and warmer, which means a shorter season and – again – less reliable snow.

Cross-country skiing (*ski de fond*) is being promoted hard, especially in the smaller ranges of the Jura and Massif Central. It's easier on the joints, but don't be fooled into thinking it's any less athletic. For the really experienced and fit, though, it's a good way of getting about, using snowbound GR routes to discover villages still relatively uncommercialized. Several independent operators organize **ski-mountaineering courses** in the French mountains (see p.31).

Lift **passes** start at around €25 a day, but can reach €50 in the pricier spots; six-day passes cost from €150 to around €250. **Equipment** hire is available at most resorts, and comes in at around €20 per day for skis and boots, while a week's hire will set you back anything from €80–120, but can climb to €200 for the most high-tech or stylish gear.

The Fédération Française de Ski (☏04.50.51.40.34, ⊛www.ffs.fr) provides links to local clubs, while ⊛www.skifrance.fr is a good overall source of **information**, with links to all the country's ski resorts.

Adventure sports

Hang-gliding and **paragliding** are popular in the Hautes-Alpes of Provence, the Pyrenees and Corsica. Prices start at around €70 for a tandem trip; contact local tourist offices for more information.

Caving is practised in the limestone caverns of southwest France and in the gorges and ravines of the Pyrenees, the Alps and the Massif Central. You'll need to make an arrangement through a local club; they usually organize beginner courses as well as half- or full-day outings. For more information, contact the Fédération Française de Spéléologie (☏04.72.56.09.63, ⊛www.ffspeleo.fr).

As for all adventure sports, it is important to make sure that your **insurance** covers you for these rather more risky activities. See p.58 for details.

Horseriding

Horseriding is an excellent way to explore the French countryside. The most famous and romantic region for riding is the flat and windswept Camargue at the Rhône Delta, but practically every town has an equestrian centre (centre équestre) where you can ride with a guide or unaccompanied. **Mule-** and **donkey-trekking** are also popular, particularly along the trails of the Pyrenees and Alps. An hour on horseback costs from around €20; a day's horse- or donkey-trekking will cost €50 or more.

Lists of **riding centres** and events are available from the Comité National de Tourisme Équestre (☏02.54.94.46.80, ⊛www.tourisme-equestre.fr), or from local tourist offices.

Watersports and activities

France's extensive coastline has been well developed for recreational activities, especially in the south. In the towns and resorts of the Mediterranean coast, you'll find every conceivable sort of beachside activity, including boating, sea-fishing and diving, and if you don't mind high prices and crowds, the blue waters and sandy coves are unbeatable. The wind-battered western Mediterranean is where **windsurfers** head to enjoy the calm saltwater inlets (étangs) that typify the area. The Atlantic coast is good for **sailing**, particularly around Brittany, while the best **surfing** (Fédération Française de Surf; ⊛www.surfingfrance.com) is in Biarritz; further north, Anglet, Hossegor and Lacanau regularly host international competitions. Corsica is the most popular destination for **diving** and snorkelling; contact the Fédération Française d'Études et de Sports Sous-Marins (☏04.91.33.99.31, ⊛www.ffessm.fr) for more information.

Most towns have a **swimming pool** (piscine), though outdoor pools tend to open only in the height of summer. You may be requested to wear a bathing cap and men to wear trunks (not shorts), so come prepared. You can also swim at many river beaches (usually signposted) and in the real and artificial lakes that pepper France. Many lakes have leisure centres (bases de plein air or centres de loisirs) at which you can rent pedaloes, windsurfers and dinghies, as well as larger boats and, on the bigger reservoirs, jet-skis.

Canoeing (Fédération Française de Canoë-Kayak; ⊛www.ffck.org) is very popular in France, and in summer practically every navigable stretch of river has outfits renting out boats and organizing excursions. The rivers of the southwest (the Dordogne, Vézère, Lot and Tarn) in particular offer tremendous variety.

For information on **canal-boating**, see the box on p.40 in "Getting around".

Tourist offices will be able to put you in touch with local companies to help you arrange activities, or contact the national federations listed in the text. For tour operators organizing holidays around these activities, see p.31.

Shopping

France in general is a paradise for shoppers. Even outside Paris, most main towns have a range of excellent department stores, such as Printemps and Galeries Lafayette, as well as a host of independent shops which make superb targets for window-shopping (known as *lèche-vitrines*, or literally "window-licking" in French).

Food is a particular joy to shop for; well-stocked supermarkets are easy to find, while on the outskirts of most towns of any size you'll come across at least one *hypermarché*, enormous supermarkets selling everything from food to clothes and garden furniture. The most well-known chains include Auchan, Carrefour, Leclerc and Casino. Every French town worth its salt holds at least one **market** (*marché*) a week. These tend to be vibrant, mostly morning affairs when local producers gather to sell speciality goods such as honey, cheese and alcohol, alongside excellent-quality vegetable, meat and fish stalls. Boulangeries are the best places to buy bread, while patisseries offer a broader range of pastries, cakes and sometimes also sandwiches and other snacks.

Regional specialities are mostly of the edible kind. If you're travelling in Brittany, be sure to pick up some of the local cider (*cidre*), while Normandy is famous for its calvados,

and the south for its *pastis*. Provence is well known for its superb olive oil (*huile d'olive*) and pricey truffles (*truffes*), as is the Dordogne. No matter where you go, each region will produce at least one local cheese, and wine of course also varies from region to region. Cognac (p.519) and the Champagne region (pp.211–224) are also obvious destinations if you're looking to stock up.

Other items to look out for include **lace** (*dentelle*) in the north, **pottery** in Brittany and **ceramics** in Limoges. The northeast, especially Lorraine, is renowned for its **crystal** production, while Provence, particularly the town of Grasse (pp.1000–1067), is *the* place in France to buy **perfume**.

Non-EU residents are able to claim back **VAT** (*TVA*) on purchases that come to over €175. To do this, make sure the shop you're buying from fills out the correct paperwork, and present this to customs before you check in at the airport for your return flight.

Travel essentials

Costs

Recent surveys have suggested France is one of the more expensive European countries to visit, but how much a visit will cost depends on where in the country you go and when. Much of France is little or no more expensive than its Eurozone neighbours, with reasonably priced accommodation and restaurant food. But in prime tourist spots hotel prices can go up by a

third during July and August, and places like Paris and the Côte d'Azur are always more expensive than other regions. If you're visiting a chic tourist hotspot like St Tropez, be prepared for a wallet-bashing.

For a reasonably comfortable existence – staying in hotels, eating lunch and dinner in restaurants, plus moving around, café stops and museum visits – you need to allow a **budget** of around €100 (£83/$128) a day per person, assuming two people sharing a mid-range room. By counting the pennies – staying at youth hostels or camping and being strong-willed about extra cups of coffee and doses of culture – you could probably manage on €60 (£50/$77) a day.

Admission charges to museums and monuments can also eat into your budget, though many state-owned museums have one day of the week when they're free or half-price. Reductions are often available for those under 18 (for which you'll need your passport as proof of age) and for students under 26, while many are free for children under 12, and almost always for kids under 4. Several towns and regions offer multi-entry tickets covering a number of sights (detailed in the Guide).

Discount cards

Once obtained, various official and quasi-official youth/student ID cards soon pay for themselves in savings. Full-time students are eligible for the **International Student ID Card** (ISIC, @www.isiccard.com, or www.isic.org in the US and Canada), which entitles you to special air, rail and bus fares and discounts at museums and for certain services.

You have to be 26 or younger to qualify for the **International Youth Travel Card (IYTC)**, while teachers are eligible for the **International Teacher Card (ITIC)**. See @www.isic.org for further details. A **university photo ID** might open some doors, but is not always as easily recognizable as the above cards.

Some cities issue their own discount cards, offering free or reduced price entry to museums or on public transport. These are mentioned in the relevant sections of the book.

Emergency numbers

Police ☏17
Medical emergencies/ambulance ☏15
Fire brigade/paramedics ☏18
Emergency calls from a mobile phone ☏112
Rape crisis (Viols Femmes Informations) ☏08.00.05.95.95
All emergency numbers are toll-free.

Crime and personal safety

Theft and assault

While violent crime involving tourists is rare in France, **petty theft** is endemic in all the big cities, on beaches and at major tourist sights. In Paris, be especially wary of pickpockets at train stations and on the métro and RER lines; RER line B, serving Charles de Gaulle airport and Gare du Nord, has recently been the scene of several serious assaults. There is a growing incidence of violent attacks against tourists by groups of young people in Paris, usually late at night and close to major tourist attractions. Cars with foreign numberplates face a high risk of break-ins; vehicles are rarely stolen, but luggage makes a tempting target. Thefts from cars stuck in traffic are also common, particularly in the south. Card skimming and ATM fraud are rising, particularly at automated service stations and in tourist areas.

To **report a theft**, go to the local gendarmerie or Commissariat de Police (addresses are given in the Guide for major cities). Remember to take your passport, and vehicle documents if relevant. The duty officer will usually find someone who speaks English if they don't themselves.

Drugs

Drug use is just as prevalent in France as anywhere else in Europe – and just as risky. The authorities make no distinction between soft and hard drugs. People caught smuggling or possessing drugs, even just a few grams of marijuana, are liable to find themselves in jail. Should you be arrested on any charge, you have the right to contact your consulate (addresses given in the Guide), though don't expect much sympathy.

Racism

Though the self-proclaimed home of "liberté, égalité, fraternité", France has an unfortunate reputation for **racism and anti-Semitism**. The majority of racist incidents are focused against the Arab community, although black and Asian visitors may also encounter an unwelcome degree of curiosity or suspicion from shopkeepers, hoteliers and the like. It is not unknown for hotels to claim they are fully booked when they're not, for example, and the police are far more likely to stop Arab and black people and demand to see their ID. In the worst cases, you might be unlucky enough to experience outright hostility. If you suffer a **racial assault**, contact the police, your consulate or one of the local anti-racism organizations (though they may not have English-speakers); SOS Racism (⊕www.sos-racisme.org) and Mouvement contre le Racisme et pour l'Amitié entre les Peuples (MRAP; ⊕www.mrap.asso.fr) have offices in most regions of France. Alternatively, you could contact the **English-speaking helpline** SOS Help (⊕01.46.21.46.46, daily 3–11pm; ⊕www.soshelpline.org). The service is staffed by trained volunteers who not only provide a confidential listening service, but also offer practical information for foreigners facing problems in France.

Electricity

Voltage is generally 220V, using **plugs** with two round pins. If you need an adapter, it's best to buy one before leaving home, though you can find them in big department stores in France.

Entry requirements

Citizens of **EU countries** can enter France freely, while those from many **non-EU countries**, including Australia, Canada, New Zealand and the United States, among others, do not need a visa for a stay of **up to ninety days**. South African citizens require a short-stay visa for up to ninety days, which should be applied for in advance, and costs €60.

All non-EU citizens who wish to remain **longer than ninety days** must apply for a long-stay visa, for which you'll have to show proof of – among other things – a regular income or sufficient funds to support yourself and medical insurance. Be aware, however, that the situation can change and it's advisable to check with your nearest French embassy or consulate before departure. For further information about visa regulations consult the Ministry of Foreign Affairs website: ⊕www.diplomatie.gouv.fr.

French embassies and consulates

Australia Canberra ⊕02/6216 0100, ⊕www.ambafrance-au.org.
Britain London ⊕020/7073 1000; Edinburgh ⊕0131/225 3377; ⊕www.ambafrance-uk.org.
Canada Montréal ⊕514/878 4385, ⊕www.consulfrance-montreal.org; Toronto ⊕416/847 1900, ⊕www.consulfrance-toronto.org.
Ireland Dublin ⊕01/277 5000, ⊕www.ambafrance-ie.org.
New Zealand Wellington ⊕04/384 2555, ⊕www.ambafrance-nz.org.
South Africa Johannesburg ⊕011/77 85 600, ⊕www.consulfrance-jhb.org.
US Washington ⊕202/944 6000, ⊕www.ambafrance-us.org.

Gay and lesbian France

In general, France is as liberal as other western European countries. The age of consent is 16, and same-sex couples have been able to form civil partnerships, called PACs, since 1999.

Gay male communities thrive, especially in Paris and southern towns such as Montpellier and Nice. Nevertheless, gay men tend to keep a low profile outside communities and specific gay venues, parades, and the prime gay areas of Paris and the coastal resorts. Lesbian life is rather less upfront, although Toulouse has a particularly lively lesbian community. The biggest annual event is the Gay Pride march in Paris (⊕www.gaypride.fr), which takes place every June.

In **Corsica**, attitudes remain much more conservative than on the mainland. At the same time, the island has long been a popular destination for discreet gay couples and no one is likely to raise much more than an eyebrow.

Addresses of local gay and/or lesbian establishments are listed in the Guide. Also useful is the French tourist board website FranceGuide (⊕www.franceguide.com), and the *France Gay et Lesbian* guide published by Petit Futé (⊕www.petitfute.com).

Useful contacts

Spartacus Published by Bruno Gmünder Verlag, the English-language *Spartacus International Gay Guide* has an extensive section on France and contains some information for lesbians.

Têtu ⓦwww.tetu.com. France's best-selling gay/lesbian magazine with events listings and contact addresses; you can buy it in bookshops or through their website, which is also an excellent source of information.

Health

Visitors to France have little to worry about as far as health is concerned. No vaccinations are required, there are no nasty diseases and tap water is safe to drink. The worst that's likely to happen to you is a case of sunburn or an upset stomach from eating too much rich food. If you do need treatment, however, you should be in good hands: the French healthcare system is rated one of the best in the world.

Under the French health system, all services, including doctors' consultations, prescribed medicines, hospital stays and ambulance call-outs, incur a charge which you have to pay upfront. **EU citizens** are entitled to a refund (usually 70 percent) of medical and dental expenses, providing the doctor is government-registered (*un médecin conventionné*) and provided you have a European Health Insurance Card (EHIC; *Carte Européenne d'Assurance Maladie*). Note that everyone in the family, including children, must have their own EHIC card, which is free. In the UK, you can apply for them online (ⓦwww.ehic.org.uk), by phone (☎0845/606 2030) or by post – forms are available at post offices. Even with the EHIC card, however, you might want to take out some additional insurance to cover the shortfall. All **non-EU visitors** should ensure they have adequate medical insurance cover. For minor complaints go to

a **pharmacie**, signalled by an illuminated green cross. You'll find at least one in every small town and even in some villages. They keep normal shop hours (roughly 9am–noon & 3–6pm), though some stay open late and in larger towns at least one (known as the *pharmacie de garde*) is open 24 hours according to a rota; details are displayed in all pharmacy windows, or the local police will have information.

For anything more serious you can get the name of a **doctor** from a pharmacy, local police station, tourist office or your hotel. Alternatively, look under "Médecins" in the Yellow Pages of the phone directory. The consultation fee is in the region of €21 to €25; note that some practitioners charge an additional fee on top of the official rate. You'll be given a *Feuille de Soins* (Statement of Treatment) for later insurance claims. Any prescriptions will be fulfilled by the pharmacy and must be paid for; little price stickers (*vignettes*) from each medicine will be stuck on the *Feuille de Soins*.

In serious **emergencies** you will always be admitted to the nearest general hospital (*centre hospitalier*). Phone numbers and addresses of hospitals in all the main cities are given in the Guide.

Insurance

Even though EU citizens are entitled to health-care privileges in France, they would do well to take out an **insurance policy** before travelling in order to cover against theft, loss, illness or injury. Before paying for a new policy, however, it's worth checking whether you are already covered: some all-risks home insurance policies may cover

---

Rough Guides travel insurance

Rough Guides has teamed up with WorldNomads.com to offer great **travel insurance** deals. Policies are available to residents of over 150 countries, with cover for a wide range of **adventure sports**, 24hr emergency assistance, high levels of medical and evacuation cover and a stream of **travel safety information**. Roughguides.com users can take advantage of their policies online 24/7, from anywhere in the world – even if you're already travelling. And since plans often change when you're on the road, you can extend your policy and even claim online. Roughguides.com users who buy travel insurance with WorldNomads.com can also leave a positive footprint and donate to a community development project. For more information go to ⓦ**www.roughguides.com/shop**.

your possessions when overseas, and many private medical schemes include cover when abroad.

After investigating these possibilities above, you might want to contact a **specialist travel insurance** company. A typical travel insurance policy usually provides cover for the loss of baggage, tickets and – up to a certain limit – cash or cheques, as well as cancellation or curtailment of your journey. Most exclude so-called **dangerous sports** unless an extra premium is paid.

Rough Guides has teamed up with World Nomads to offer you **travel insurance** that can be tailored to suit the length of your stay. There are also annual **multi-trip** policies for those who travel regularly. You can get a quote on our website (⊛www .roughguides.com/website/shop).

Laundry

Self-service **laundries** are common in French towns – just ask in your hotel or the tourist office, or look in the phone book under "*Laveries automatiques*" or "*Laveries en libre-service*". Most **hotels** forbid doing laundry in your room, though you should get away with just one or two items.

Mail

French **post offices**, known as La Poste and identified by bright yellow-and-blue signs, are generally open from around 9am to 6pm Monday to Friday, and 9am to noon on Saturday. However, these hours aren't set in stone: smaller branches and those in rural areas are likely to close for lunch (generally noon to 2pm) and finish at 5pm, while big city centre branches may be open longer.

You can **receive letters** using the poste restante system available at the central post office in every town. They should be addressed (preferably with the surname first and in capitals) "Poste Restante, Poste Centrale, Town x, post code". You'll need your passport to collect your mail and there'll be a charge of €0.58 per item. Items are kept for 15 days.

For **sending mail**, standard letters (20g or less) and postcards in France and beyond cost €0.58; to other European Union countries a charge of €0.05 per 10g is added to the basic fee for heavier letters and of €0.11 per 10g to all other countries. You can also buy stamps from *tabacs* and newsagents. To post your letter on the street, look for the bright yellow postboxes.

For **further information** on postal rates, among other things, log on to the post office website ⊛www.laposte.fr.

Maps

In addition to the maps in this guide and the various free town plans and regional maps you'll be offered along the way, the one extra map you might want is a good, up-to-date **road map** of France. The best are those produced by Michelin (1:200,000; ⊛www.viamichelin.fr) and the Institut Géographique National (IGN; 1:250,000; ⊛www.ign.fr), either as individual sheets or in one large spiral-bound *atlas routier*.

Rough Guides also produces a national map of France, a city map of Paris, and regional maps of Brittany, Corsica and the Pyrenees.

Money

France's **currency** is the euro, which is divided into 100 cents (often still referred to as *centimes*). There are seven notes – in denominations of 5, 10, 20, 50, 100, 200 and 500 euros – and eight different coins – 1, 2, 5, 10, 20 and 50 cents, and 1 and 2 euros. At the time of writing, the **exchange rate** for the euro was around €1.21 to the pound sterling (or £0.82 to €1) and €0.77 to the dollar (or $1.28 to €1). See ⊛www .xe.com for current rates.

You can change cash at most **banks** and main **post offices**, and travellers' cheques at post offices and some BNP Paribas branches. Rates and commission vary, so it's worth shopping around. There are **money-exchange counters** (*bureaux de change*) at French airports, major train stations and usually one or two in city centres as well, though they don't always offer the best exchange rates.

By far the easiest way to access money in France is to use your credit or debit card to withdraw cash from an **ATM** (known as a *distributeur* or *point argent*); most machines give instructions in several European languages. Note that there is often a transaction fee, so it's more efficient to take out a sizeable sum each time rather than making lots of small withdrawals.

Credit and debit cards are also widely accepted, although some smaller establishments don't accept cards, or only for sums above a certain threshold. Visa – called Carte Bleue in France – is widely recognized, followed by MasterCard (also known as EuroCard). American Express ranks a bit lower.

Opening hours and public holidays

Basic **hours of business** are Monday to Saturday 9am to noon and 2 to 6pm. In big cities, **shops** and other businesses stay open throughout the day, as do most **tourist offices** and museums in July and August. In rural areas and throughout southern France places tend to close for at least a couple of hours at lunchtime. Small food shops may not reopen till halfway through the afternoon, closing around 7.30 or 8pm, just before the evening meal. The standard **closing day** is Sunday, even in larger towns and cities, though some food shops and newsagents are open in the morning. Some shops and businesses, particularly in rural areas, also close on Mondays.

Banking hours are typically Monday to Friday 8.30am to 12.30pm and 1.30/2 to 5 or 6pm. Some branches, especially those

---

Public holidays

January 1 New Year's Day

March/April (variable) Easter Monday

Ascension Day (forty days after Easter)

Whit Monday (seventh Monday after Easter)

May 1 Labour Day

May 8 Victory in Europe (VE) Day 1945

July 14 Bastille Day

August 15 Assumption of the Virgin Mary

November 1 All Saints' Day

November 11 Armistice Day

December 25 Christmas Day

---

in rural areas, close on Monday, while those in big cities may remain open at midday and may also open on Saturday morning. All are closed on Sunday and public holidays.

Museums tend to open from 9 or 10am to noon and from 2 or 3pm to 5 or 6pm, though in the big cities some stay open all day and opening hours tend to be longer in summer. Museum closing days are usually Monday or Tuesday, sometimes both. **Churches** are generally open from around 8am to dusk, but may close at lunchtime and are reserved for worshippers during services (times of which will be posted on the door).

France celebrates eleven **public holidays** (*jours fériés*), when most shops and businesses (though not necessarily restaurants), and some museums, are closed.

Phones

Payphones (*cabines*) are increasingly rare due to the proliferation of mobile phones. You can make and receive calls – look for the number in the top right-hand corner of the information panel. The vast majority of public phones require a prepaid phonecard (*télécarte*) available from Orange outlets, tabacs and newsagents; they come in units of 50 and 120 units (€7.50 and €15 respectively). Alternatively, a more flexible option is one of the many prepaid phone cards which operate with a unique code (*cartes téléphoniques*) on sale at Orange outlets, post offices, tabacs, newsagents and many supermarkets, which can be used from both private and public phones. The post office, for example, sells e.Ticket prepaid cards for domestic and European calls (€5 and €10) and for international calls (€7.50 and €15); the €15 card buys up to 858 minutes to the US and Canada. Orange also provides a wide range of "Ticket Téléphone" cards. You can also use credit cards in many call boxes. Coin-operated phones have almost completely disappeared except in cafés and bars.

Calling within France

For calls within France – local or long distance – simply dial all ten digits of the number. Numbers beginning ☎08.00 and ☎08.05 are free-dial numbers; those beginning ☎08.1 and ☎08.6 are charged as a local call; anything else beginning ☎08 is premium-rated. Note that some of these ☎08 numbers cannot be accessed from abroad. Numbers starting ☎06 and 07 are mobile numbers and are therefore more expensive to call.

Mobile phones

If you want to use your **mobile/cell phone**, contact your phone provider to check whether it will work in France and what the call charges are – they tend to be pretty exorbitant, and remember you're likely to be charged extra for receiving calls. French mobile phones operate on the European GSM standard, so US cellphones won't work in France unless you have a tri-band phone. If you are going to be in France for any length of time and will be making and receiving a lot of local calls, it may be worth buying a **French SIM card** and prepaid recharge cards (*mobicartes*) from any of the big mobile providers (Orange, SFR and Bouygues Telecom), all of which have high-street outlets. They cost around €30, including a certain amount of credit, and you need to give an address in France – that of your hotel or a friend will usually suffice – and provide a copy of your ID card to register.

Smoking

Smoking is banned in all public places, including public transport, museums, cafés, restaurants and nightclubs.

Time

France is in the Central European Time Zone (GMT+1). This means it is one hour ahead of the UK, six hours ahead of Eastern Standard Time and nine hours ahead of Pacific Standard Time. Between March and October France is the same time as South Africa, eight hours behind eastern Australia and ten hours behind New Zealand; from October to March it is one hour behind South Africa, 10 hours behind southeastern Australia and 12 hours behind New Zealand. Daylight Saving Time (GMT+2) in France

lasts from the last Sunday in March to the last Sunday in October.

Tipping

At restaurants you only need to leave an additional cash **tip** if you feel you have received service out of the ordinary, since restaurant prices always include a service charge. It's customary to tip porters, tour guides, taxi drivers and hairdressers a couple of euros.

Tourist information

The **French Government Tourist Office** (Maison de la France; ⊛www.franceguide.com) generally refers you to their website for information, though they still produce a free magazine, *Traveller in France*, and dispense the Logis de France book (see "Accommodation" p.42). For more detailed information, such as hotels, campsites, activities and festivals in a specific location, it's best to contact the relevant regional or departmental tourist offices; contact details can be found online at ⊛www.fncrt.com and ⊛www.fncdt.net respectively.

In France itself you'll find a tourist office – usually an **Office du Tourisme** (OT) but sometimes a **Syndicat d'Initiative** (SI, run by local businesses) – in practically every town and many villages. Addresses, contact details and opening hours are detailed in the Guide, or try ⊛www.tourisme.fr. All local tourist offices provide specific information on the area, including hotel and restaurant listings, leisure activities, car and bike rental, bus times, laundries and countless other things; many can also book accommodation for you. If asked, most offices will provide a town plan (for which you may be charged a nominal fee), and will have maps and local walking guides on sale. In mountain regions they display daily meteorological information and often share premises with the local hiking and climbing organizations. In the big cities you can usually pick up free *What's On* guides.

Tourist offices and government sites

Australia and New Zealand ⊛au.franceguide.com.
Canada ⊛ca-en.franceguide.com.

Ireland ⓦ ie.franceguide.com.
South Africa ⓦ za.franceguide.com.
UK ⓦ uk.franceguide.com.
US ⓦ us.franceguide.com.

Travellers with disabilities

The French authorities have been making a concerted effort to improve facilities for **disabled travellers**. Though haphazard parking habits and stepped village streets remain serious obstacles for anyone with mobility problems, ramps or other forms of access are gradually being added to hotels, museums and other public buildings. All but the oldest hotels are required to adapt at least one room to be wheelchair accessible and a growing number of *chambres d'hôtes* are doing likewise. Accessible hotels, sights and other facilities are gradually being inspected and, if they fulfil certain criteria, issued a "Tourisme & Handicap" certificate and logo – recognized establishments now number more than 3700.

For **getting to France**, Eurotunnel (see p.22) offers the simplest option for travellers from the UK, since you can remain in your car. Alternatively, Eurostar trains have two wheelchair spaces per train at £60 return (a companion can also travel for the same fare); it's wise to reserve well in advance, when you might also like to enquire about the special assistance that Eurostar offers. If you're flying, it's worth noting that, while airlines are required to offer access to travellers with mobility problems, the level of service provided by some low-cost airlines may be fairly basic. All cross-Channel ferries have lifts for getting to and from the car deck, but moving between the different passenger decks may be more difficult.

Within France, most train stations now make provision for travellers with reduced mobility. SNCF produces a free booklet outlining its services, which is available from main stations or to download from SNCF's dedicated website for travellers with disabilities: ⓦ www.accessibilite.sncf.com, where you can also find information on accessible stations. Reductions on fares for travellers with disabilities and their companions are calculated on the degree of disability as indicated by the holder's carte d'invalidité.

Drivers of **taxis** are legally obliged to help passengers in and out of the vehicle and to carry guide dogs. Specially adapted taxi services are available in some towns: contact the local tourist office for further information or one of the organizations listed opposite. All the big **car hire** agencies can provide automatic cars if you reserve sufficiently far in advance, while Hertz offers cars with hand controls on request in Paris, Marseille and Nice – again, make sure you give them plenty of notice.

As for finding suitable **accommodation**, guides produced by Logis de France (see p.42) and Gîtes de France (see p.43) indicate places with specially adapted rooms, though it's essential to double-check when booking that the facilities meet your needs.

Up-to-date **information** about accessibility, special programmes and discounts is best obtained before you leave home from the organizations listed below. French readers might want to get hold of the *Handi-tourisme* guide, published by Petit Futé (ⓦ www.petitfute.com), available online or from major bookstores.

Useful contacts

Access in Paris ⓦ www.accessinparis.org. Comprehensive information on accessible Paris in book form or as downloadable pdfs (donation requested).

Association des Paralysés de France (APF) ⓦ www.apf.asso.fr. National association which can answer general enquiries and put you in touch with their departmental offices.

Door to Door ⓦ www.dptac.gov.uk/door-to-door /index.htm. General online travel information from the UK's Disabled Persons Transport Advisory Committee.

Fédération Française Handisport France ⓦ www.handisport.org. Among other things, this federation provides information on sports and leisure facilities for people with disabilities.

Irish Wheelchair Association Ireland ⓦ www .iwa.ie. Useful information about travelling abroad with a wheelchair, and good links.

Mobile en Ville France ⓦ www.mobile-en-ville .asso.fr. Information on getting around, mainly in Paris but also other cities and towns (French only).

Mobility International USA US ⓦ www.miusa .org. Provides information and referral services and international exchange programmes.

Tourism for All UK ⓦ www.toursimforall.org.uk. Masses of useful information.

Travelling with children

France is a relatively easy country in which to travel with children. They're generally welcome everywhere and young children and babies in particular will be fussed over. There are masses of family-oriented theme parks and no end of leisure activities geared towards kids, while most public parks contain children's play areas.

Local **tourist offices** will have details of specific activities for children, which might include anything from farm visits, nature walks or treasure hunts to paintball and forest ropeways for older children. In summer most seaside resorts organize clubs for children on the beach, while bigger campsites put on extensive programmes of activities and entertainments. Children under 4 years travel free on public transport, while those between 4 and 11 pay half-fare. Museums and the like are generally free to under-12s and half-price or even free up to the age of 18.

Hotels charge by the room, with a small supplement for an additional bed or cot, and family-run places will usually babysit or offer a listening service while you eat or go out. Some youth hostels also now offer family rooms. Nearly all **restaurants** offer children's *menus*. Disposable **nappies/diapers** (*couches à jeter*) are available at most pharmacies and supermarkets, alongside a vast range of **baby foods**, though many have added sugar and salt. **Milk powders** also tend to be sweet, so bring your own if this is likely to be a concern. Note that **breastfeeding** in public tends to be frowned on.

Further information

Family Travel ⓦ www.family-travel.co.uk. Slightly outdated but useful for basic information on where to go, health and what to pack.
The Rough Guide to Travel with Babies and Young Children Comprehensive guide to hassle-free family travel.

Women travellers

Despite a relatively strong feminist movement, France can still feel like a very male-dominated country, with many men still holding rather strong chauvinist ideas.

While change is in the air, with female politicians starting to take a higher profile and giving the male ruling class a run for their money, for the moment many women still suffer the double burden of being housewife and earner.

French men tend to be on the predatory side, but are usually easily brushed off if you don't want the attention. It's not unusual, however, to be chatted up regularly, or have men (more often boys) call at you from cars in the street, and make comments as they pass you. The best way to deal with this is simply to avoid making eye contact and fail to react, and they'll soon get the message.

Work and study in France

EU citizens are able to work in France on the same basis as a French citizen. This means that you don't have to apply for a residence or work permit except in very rare cases – contact your nearest French consulate for further information (see "Entry requirements", p.57). The criteria for working in France if you're not an EU citizen are strict: your would-be employer needs authorisation to hire you and you'll need to qualify for one of several specific work permits. On arrival in France you'll have to present an endorsed employment contract and obtain a medical certificate from the ANAEM (*Agence Nationale de l'Acceuil des Étrangers et des Migrations*); again, contact your nearest French consulate to check what rules apply in your particular situation.

When **looking for a job**, a good starting point is to read one of the books on working abroad published by Vacation Work (ⓦ www.vacationwork.co.uk). You might also want to search the online recruitment resource Monster (ⓦ www.monster.fr) and Job Etudiant (ⓦ www.jobetudiant.net) which focuses on jobs for students. In France, try the youth information agency CIDJ (ⓦ www .cidj.com), or CIJ (Centre d'Information Jeunesse) offices in main cities, which have information about temporary jobs and about working in France.

A degree and a TEFL (Teaching English as a Foreign Language) or similar qualification are normally required for **English-language** teaching posts. The annual *EL Gazette Guide to English Language Teaching Around the World* (🅦 www.elgazette.com) provides lists of schools and other practical information. Other useful resources are *Teaching English Abroad* published by Vacation Work and the TEFL website (🅦 www.tefl.com), with its database of English-teaching vacancies.

Foreign **students** pay the same as French nationals to enrol for a course, and you'll be eligible for subsidized accommodation. French universities are relatively informal, but there are strict entry requirements, including an exam in French for undergraduate courses. For full details and prospectuses, contact the Cultural Service of any French embassy or consulate (see p.57).

Embassies and consulates can also provide details of **language courses** at French universities and colleges, which are often combined with lectures on French "civilization" and usually very costly. Alternatively, you can sign up to one of the hundreds of language-learning courses offered by private

organizations – contact the tourist board for details.

Further contacts

AFS Interncultural Programs 🅦 www.afs.org. Opportunities for high-school students to study in France for a term or full academic year, living with host families.

American Institute for Foreign Study US 🅦 www.aifs.com. Language study and cultural immersion for the summer or school year.

Council on International Educational Exchange (CIEE) US 🅦 www.ciee.org. A non-profit organization with summer, semester and academic-year programmes in France.

Erasmus UK 🅦 www.britishcouncil.org/erasmus. EU-run student exchange programme enabling students at participating EU universities to study in another European member country.

Experiment in International Living US 🅦 www .usexperiment.org. Summer programmes for high-school students.

World Wide Opportunities on Organic Farms (WWOOF) 🅦 www.wwoof.fr. Volunteer to work on an organic farm in return for board and lodging.

Guide

Guide

1

Paris and around

UNITED KINGDOM

ENGLISH CHANNEL

BELGIUM

GERMANY

LUX

4 **1** **2**

3

5

6 **7**

SWITZERLAND

ATLANTIC
OCEAN

8

13

ITALY

9 **12** **14**

N

15

11 **16**

10

17

0   250 km

SPAIN

MEDITERRANEAN
SEA

CHAPTER 1 # Highlights

✳ **Sainte-Chapelle** The stunning stained-glass windows of the Sainte-Chapelle rank among the finest achievements of French High Gothic. See p.88

✳ **Musée Jacquemart-André** One-time sumptuous residence of a wealthy Second-Empire couple, who built up a choice collection of Italian, Dutch and French masters. See p.91

✳ **The Louvre** One of the world's greatest museums, containing a vast display of French and Italian paintings and notable Ancient Egyptian, Roman and Greek collections. See p.94

✳ **Marais** Arguably the city's most lively and attractive district, characterized by narrow streets, fine Renaissance mansions and trendy bars. See p.102

✳ **Jardin du Luxembourg** The haunt of old men playing *boules*, children riding donkeys, students reading textbooks and couples kissing, these gardens capture Paris at its most warm-hearted. See p.114

✳ **Palais de Tokyo** This cool 1930s structure houses two of Paris's most exciting art spaces. See p.118

✳ **Musée Rodin** Rodin's intense sculptures are displayed to powerful effect in his eighteenth-century town house. See p.123

✳ **Puces de St-Ouen** Even if it's less of a flea market now, and more of a mega-emporium for arty bric-a-brac and antiques, the St-Ouen market is a wonderful place for relaxed weekend browsing. See p.130

▲ The Louvre at night

1

Paris and around

L ong considered the paragon of style, **PARIS** is perhaps the most glamorous city in Europe. It is at once deeply traditional – a village-like metropolis whose inhabitants continue to be notorious for their hauteur – and famously cosmopolitan. The city's reputation as a magnet for writers, artists and dissidents lives on, and it remains at the forefront of Western intellectual, artistic and literary life.

The most tangible and immediate pleasures of Paris are found in its street life and along the banks and bridges of the River Seine. Cafés, bars and restaurants line every street and boulevard, and the city's compactness makes it possible to experience the individual feel of the different *quartiers*. You can move easily, even on foot, from the calm, almost small-town atmosphere of **Montmartre** and parts of the **Quartier Latin** to the busy commercial centres of the **Bourse** and **Opéra-Garnier** or the aristocratic mansions of the **Marais**. The city's lack of open space is redeemed by unexpected havens like the **Mosque**, **Arènes de Lutèce** and the **place des Vosges**, and courtyards of grand houses like the **Hôtel de Sully**. The gravelled paths and formal beauty of the **Tuileries** create the backdrop for the ultimate Parisian Sunday promenade, while the islands and quaysides of the Left and Right Banks of the **River Seine** and the Quartier Latin's two splendid parks, the **Luxembourg** and the **Jardin des Plantes**, make for a wonderful wander.

Paris's architectural spirit resides in the elegant streets and boulevards begun in the nineteenth century under Baron Haussmann. The mansion blocks that line them are at once grand and perfectly human in scale, a triumph in city planning proved by the fact that so many remain residential to this day. Rising above these harmonious buildings are the more arrogant monuments that define the French capital. For centuries, an imposing Classical style prevailed with great set pieces such as the **Louvre**, **Panthéon** and **Arc de Triomphe**, but the last hundred years or so has seen the architectural mould repeatedly broken in a succession of ambitious structures, the industrial chic of the **Eiffel Tower** and **Pompidou Centre** contrasting with the almost spiritual glasswork of the Louvre **Pyramide** and **Institut du Monde Arabe**. Paris is remarkable, too, for its **museums** – there are over 150 of them, ranging from giants of the art world such as the Louvre, **Musée d'Orsay** and Pompidou Centre to lesser-known gems like the Picasso, Rodin and Jewish museums – and the diversity of **entertainment**, from cinema to jazz music, on offer.

Some history

Paris's **history** has conspired to create a sense of being apart from, and even superior to, the rest of the country. To this day, everything beyond the capital is known quite ordinarily as *province* – the provinces. Appropriately, the city's first

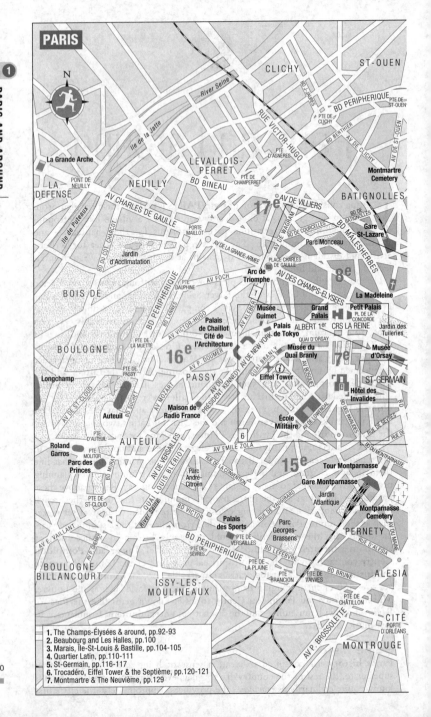

PARIS

N

River Seine

CLICHY

ST-OUEN

BD PERIPHERIQUE
PTE DE ST-OUEN

PTE DE CLICHY

BD DE CLICHY

BD BERTHIER

Montmartre
Cemetery

La Grande Arche

PONT DE NEUILLY

LEVALLOIS-PERRET

BD BINEAU

PTE D'ASNERES

RUE VICTOR-HUGO

AV DE CLICHY

PTE DE CHAMPERRET

AV DE VILLIERS

17e

BATIGNOLLES

BD DE BATIGNOLLES

LA DEFENSE

Île de la Jatte

NEUILLY

AV CHARLES DE GAULLE

Île de Puteaux

BD DU COL CHARCOT

PORTE MAILLOT

BD DE COURCELLES

Gare
St-Lazare

Jardin
d'Acclimatation

AV DE LA GRANDE-ARMEE

AV DE WAGRAM

Parc Monceau

BD MALESHERBES

BOIS DE

PTE DAUPHINE

PLACE CHARLES DE GAULLE

Arc de Triomphe

8e

La Madeleine

AV FOCH

1

AV DES CHAMPS-ELYSEES

PTE DAUPHINE

AV VICTOR-HUGO

AV KLEBER

Musée
Guimet

Grand
Palais

Petit Palais

PL DE LA CONCORDE

BOULOGNE

Palais
de Chaillot
Cité de
l'Architecture

Palais
de Tokyo

ALBERT 1er

Jardin des
Tuileries

PTE DE LA MUETTE

16e

AV P. DOUMER

QUAI D'ORSAY

CRS LA REINE

Musée
d'Orsay

Longchamp

PTE DE PASSY

PASSY

AV DU PRESIDENT KENNEDY

Musée du
Quai Branly

7e

ST-GERMAIN

BD LANNES

AV MOZART

Maison de
Radio France

Eiffel Tower

AV DE SUFFREN

Hôtel des
Invalides

RUE DE SEVRES

RUE DE

Auteuil

AV DE ST-CLOUD

BD SUCHET

École
Militaire

BD DES INVALIDES

AV DE LOWENDAL

Roland
Garros

PTE D'AUTEUIL

PTE MOLITOR

AUTEUIL

AV DE VERSAILLES

AV EMILE ZOLA

15e

Tour Montparnasse

BD DU MONTPARNASSE

Parc des
Princes

BD MURAT

RUE DE LA CONVENTION

Gare Montparnasse

PTE DE ST-CLOUD

QUAI LOUIS BLERIOT

Parc
André-Citroën

RUE DE VAUGIRARD

Jardin
Atlantique

Montparnasse
Cemetery

AV DU MAINE

River Seine

BD VICTOR

Palais
des Sports

Parc
Georges-Brassens

PERNETY

PTE DE VERSAILLES

BD PERIPHERIQUE

BD LEFEBVRE

RUE D'ALESIA

BOULOGNE
BILLANCOURT

ISSY-LES-MOULINEAUX

PTE DE SEVRES

PTE DE LA PLAINE

PTE BRANCION

PTE DE VANVES

PTE DE BRUNE

ALESIA

PTE DE CHÂTILLON

CITÉ
PORTE
D'ORLÉANS

AV E. VAILLANT

AV P. GRENIER

AV P. BROSSOLETTE

MONTROUGE

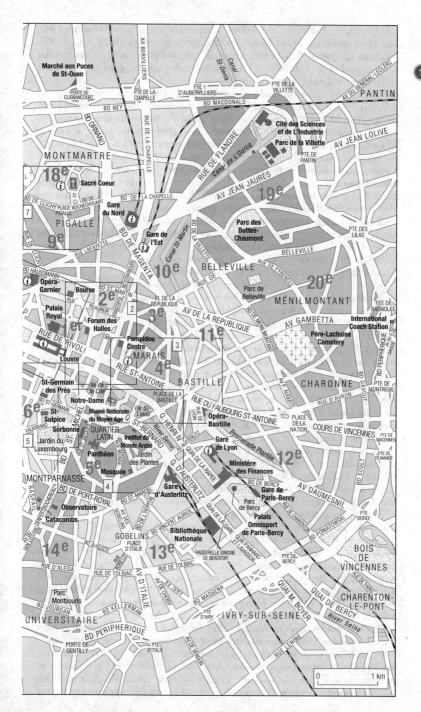

inhabitants, the **Parisii**, a Celtic tribe that arrived in around the third century BC, had their settlement on an island: Lutetia, probably today's Île de la Cité. The **Romans** conquered the city two centuries later, and preferred the more familiar hilly ground of the Left Bank. Their city, also called Lutetia, grew up around the hill where the Panthéon stands today.

This hill, now known as the Montagne Ste-Geneviève, gets its name from Paris's first patron saint, who, as legend has it, saved the town from the marauding army of Attila in 451 through her exemplary holiness. Fifty years later **Geneviève** converted another invader to Christianity: Clovis the Frank, the leader of a group of Germanic tribes, went on to make the city the capital of his kingdom. His newly founded Merovingian dynasty promptly fell apart under his son Childéric II.

Power only returned to Paris under **Hugues Capet**, the Count of Paris. He was elected king of France in 987, although at the time his territory amounted to little more than the Île de France, the region immediately surrounding Paris. From this shaky start French monarchs gradually extended their control over their feudal rivals, centralizing administrative, legal, financial and political power as they did so, until anyone seeking influence, publicity or credibility, in whatever field, had to be in Paris – which is still the case today. The city's cultural influence grew alongside its **university**, which was formally established in 1215 and swiftly became the great European centre for scholastic learning.

The wars and plagues of the fourteenth and fifteenth centuries left Paris half in ruins and more than half abandoned, but with royal encouragement, the city steadily recovered. During the **Wars of Religion** the capital remained staunchly Catholic, but Parisians' loyalty to the throne was tested during the mid-seventeenth-century rebellions known as the Frondes, in which the young Louis XIV was forced to flee the city. Perhaps this traumatic experience lay behind the king's decision, in 1670, to move the court to his vast new palace at **Versailles**. Paris suffered in the court's absence, even as grand Baroque buildings were thrown up in the capital.

Parisians, both as deputies to the Assembly and mobs of *sans-culottes*, were at the forefront of the **Revolution**, but many of the new citizens welcomed the return to order under Napoleon I. The emperor adorned the city with many of its signature monuments, Neoclassical almost-follies designed to amplify his majesty: the Arc de Triomphe, Arc du Carrousel and the Madeleine. He also instituted the Grandes Écoles, super-universities for the nation's elite administrators, engineers and teachers. At the fall of the Empire, in 1814, Paris was saved from destruction by the arch-diplomat Talleyrand, who delivered the city to the Russians with hardly a shot fired. Nationalists grumbled that the occupation continued well into the Restoration regime, as the city once again became the playground of the rich of Europe, the ultimate tourist destination.

The greatest shocks to the fabric of the city came under Napoléon III. He finally completed the Louvre, rebuilding much of the facade in the process, but it was his Prefect of the Seine, **Baron Haussmann**, who truly transformed the city, smashing through the slums to create wide boulevards that could be easily controlled by rifle-toting troops – not that it succeeded in preventing the **1871 Commune**, the most determined insurrection since 1789. It was down these large boulevards, lined with grey bourgeois residences, that **Nazi troops** paraded in June 1940, followed by the Allies, led by General Leclerc, in August 1944.

Although riotous street protests are still a feature of modern Parisian life – most famously in **May 1968**, when students burst onto the streets of the Quartier Latin – the traditional barricade-builders have long since been booted into the depressing satellite towns, known as *la banlieue*, alongside the under-served populations of immigrants and their descendants. Integrating these communities, riven with poverty, unemployment and discontent, is one of the greatest challenges facing the city today – perhaps one that can be met by the ambitious **Grand Paris** plan, launched by the government in 2009. Ten leading architects were invited to submit proposals, which included covering up railway lines with huge green spaces and building new waterways and high-speed rail links between the city and suburbs. Whether any of these grand plans will ever come to fruition remains to be seen, but what is certain is that Paris can no longer afford to ignore its burgeoning suburbs.

Bold initiatives have certainly been the hallmark of the city's Socialist mayor, **Bertrand Delanoë**, who has held the post since 2001. Two of his most popular innovations have been the introduction of Paris Plage, which sees a stretch of the Seine's *quais* converted into a beach every summer, and Velib', inexpensive bikes for rent dotted all round the city. The latter has proved enormously successful and is soon to be followed up with Autolib', a similar scheme in which over two thousand cars will be available to rent at various locations in the city. These initiatives, together with the huge expansion of cycle and bus lanes and the building of tramways on the city outskirts, are having some success in easing traffic congestion and are all part of Delanoë's vision of a greener, happier city.

Arrival

Many British travellers to Paris arrive by Eurostar at the central **Gare du Nord train station**, while more far-flung visitors are likely to land at one of Paris's two main airports: Charles de Gaulle and Orly. Trains from other parts of France or continental Europe arrive at one of the six central mainline stations. Almost all the **buses** coming into Paris – whether international or domestic – arrive at the main *gare routière* at 28 av du Général-de-Gaulle, Bagnolet, at the eastern edge of the city; métro Gallieni (line 3) links it to the centre. If you're **driving** in yourself, don't try to go straight across the city to your destination. Use the ring road – the *boulevard périphérique* – to get around to the nearest *porte*: it's much quicker, except at rush hour, and far easier to navigate, albeit pretty terrifying. For more on car parks in Paris, see Ⓦ www.parkingsdeparis.com.

By air

The two main Paris airports that deal with international flights are **Roissy-Charles de Gaulle** and **Orly**, both well connected to the centre. Detailed information in English can be found online at Ⓦ www.adp.fr. The more distant **Beauvais** airport is used by some budget airlines, including Ryanair.

Roissy-Charles de Gaulle Airport

Roissy-Charles de Gaulle Airport (24hr information in English Ⓣ 01.70.36.39.50), usually referred to as Charles de Gaulle and abbreviated to CDG or Paris CDG, is 23km northeast of the city. The airport has two main **terminals**, CDG 1 and CDG 2. A third terminal, CDG 3 (sometimes called CDG-T3), handles various low-cost airlines, including easyJet. Make sure you know which terminal your flight is departing from when it's time to leave Paris, so you take the correct bus or get off at the right train station. A TGV station links the airport (CDG 2) with Bordeaux, Brussels, Lille, Lyon, Nantes, Marseille and Rennes, among other places.

The least expensive and probably quickest way into the centre of Paris is to take the suburban train line **RER B3**, sometimes called Roissy-Rail, which runs every ten to fifteen minutes from 5am until midnight; the journey time is thirty minutes and tickets cost €8.40 one way (no return tickets). To get to the RER station from CDG 1 you have to take a free shuttle bus (*navette*) to the RER station, but from CDG 2 and CDG-T3 it's simpler to take the pedestrian walkway, though the station is also served by a shuttle bus. The RER train stops at stations including Gare du Nord, Châtelet–Les Halles and St-Michel, at all of which you can transfer to the ordinary métro system – your ticket is valid through to any métro station in central Paris.

Various bus companies provide services from the airport direct to various city-centre locations, but they're slightly more expensive than Roissy-Rail, and may take longer. A more useful alternative is the Paris Blue door-to-door minibus service, which costs from €30 for two people, with no extra charge for luggage. Bookings must be made at least 24 hours in advance on T01.30.11.13.00 or, for the best rates, online at W www.paris-blue-airport-shuttle.fr.

Taxis into central Paris from CDG cost around €50 on the meter, plus a small luggage supplement (€1 per item), and should take between fifty minutes and one hour. Note that if your flight gets in after midnight your only means of transport is a taxi or the minibus.

Orly Airport

Orly Airport (information in English daily 6am–11.30pm; T01.70.36.39.50), 14km south of Paris, has **two terminals**, Orly Sud and Orly Ouest, linked by shuttle bus but easily walkable; Ouest (West) is used for domestic flights while Sud (South) handles international flights.

The easiest way into the centre is via Orlyval, a fast **train shuttle** link to the suburban RER station Antony, where you can pick up RER line B trains to the central RER/métro stations Denfert-Rochereau, St-Michel and Châtelet-Les Halles; Orlyval runs every four to seven minutes from 6.10am to 11pm (€9.30 one way; 35min to Châtelet). A useful alternative is the **Orlybus**: a shuttle bus takes you direct to RER line B station Denfert-Rochereau, on the Left Bank, with good onward métro connections; Orlybus runs every fifteen to twenty minutes from roughly 6am to 11.20pm (€6.10 one way; total journey around 30min). **Taxis** take about 35 minutes to reach the centre of Paris and cost around €35.

Beauvais Airport

Ryanair passengers arrive at Beauvais Airport (T08.92.68.20.66, W www .aeroportbeauvais.com), some 65km northwest of Paris. **Coaches** (€13 one way) shuttle between the airport and Porte Maillot, at the northwestern edge of Paris, where you can pick up métro line 1 to the centre. Coaches take about an hour, and leave between fifteen and thirty minutes after the flight has arrived and about three hours before the flight departs on the way back.

By train

Paris has six mainline train stations. **Eurostar** (T08.92.35.35.39, W www .eurostar.com) terminates at the busy **Gare du Nord**, rue Dunkerque, in the northeast of the city. Coming off the train, turn left for the métro, the RER and the tourist office, and right for taxis (expect to pay around €10 to central Paris). Just short of the taxi exit, head down the escalators for left luggage (*consignes*) and the various car rental desks. Two bureaux de change (neither offers a good deal) allow you to change money at the station, or you can use your card in one of the ATM cash machines. The Gare du Nord is also the arrival point for trains from Calais and other north European countries.

Nearby, the **Gare de l'Est** (place du 11-Novembre-1918, 10e) serves eastern France and central and eastern Europe. The **Gare St-Lazare** (place du Havre, 8e), serving the Normandy coast and Dieppe, is the most central, close to the Madeleine and the Opéra-Garnier. Still on the Right Bank but towards the southeast corner is the **Gare de Lyon** (place Louis-Armand, 12e), for trains to Italy and Switzerland and TGV lines to southeast France. South of the river, **Gare Montparnasse** (boulevard de Vaugirard, 15e) is the terminus for Chartres, Brittany, the Atlantic coast and TGV lines to Tours and southwest France. **Gare d'Austerlitz** (boulevard de l'Hôpital, 13^e) serves the Loire Valley and the Dordogne. The **motorail station**, Gare de Paris-Bercy, is down the tracks from the Gare de Lyon on boulevard de Bercy, 12^e.

Orientation

Finding your way around Paris is remarkably easy, as the centre is fairly small for a major capital city, and very **walkable**. The city proper is divided into twenty arrondissements, or districts. These are marked on the map on pp.70–71 and are included as an integral part of addresses throughout the chapter. Arrondissements are abbreviated as 1er (premier = first), 2e (deuxième = second), 3e, 4e and so on; the numbering is confusing until you work out that it spirals out from the centre.

The **Seine** flows in a downturned arc from east to west, cutting the city in two. In the middle of the Seine lie two islands, while north of the river is the busy, commercial **Right Bank**, or *rive droite*. Most of the city's sights are found here, within the historic central arrondissements (1er to 4^e). South of the river is the relatively laid-back **Left Bank**, or *rive gauche* (5^e to 7^e). The outer arrondissements (8^e to 20^e) were mostly incorporated into the city in the nineteenth century. Generally speaking, those to the east accommodated the working classes while those to the west were, and still are, the addresses for the aristocracy and new rich. For a brief rundown of Paris's different quarters, see the introduction to the city on p.69.

Paris proper is encircled by the *boulevard périphérique* ring road. The sprawling conurbation beyond is known as the **banlieue**, or suburbs. There are few sights for the tourist here, and only one of significant interest: St-Denis, with its historic cathedral.

Information

At Paris's tourist offices (ⓦ www.parisinfo.com) you can pick up **maps** and information, book accommodation and buy travel passes and the Paris Museum Pass (see box below). The most usefully located branches are at 25 rue Pyramides, 1er

Reductions and the Museum Pass

The permanent collections at all municipal museums are free all year round, while all national museums (including the Louvre, Musée d'Orsay and Pompidou Centre) – see ⓦ www.rmn.fr for a full list – are free on the first Sunday of the month and to under-18s. Elsewhere, the cut-off age for free admission varies between 18, 12 and 4. Reduced admission is usually available for 18 to 26-year-olds and for those over 60 or 65; you'll need to carry your passport or ID card around with you as proof of age. Some discounts are available for students with an ISIC Card (International Student Identity Card; ⓦ www.isiccard.com). If you're planning to visit a great many museums in a short time it might be worth buying the **Paris Museum Pass** (€32 two-day, €48 four-day, €64 six-day; ⓦ www.parismuseumpass.fr). Available from the tourist office and participating museums, it's valid for 35 or so of the most important museums and monuments including the Louvre (but not special exhibitions) inside Paris, and allows you to bypass ticket queues (though not the security checkpoints).

(June–Oct daily 9am–7pm; Nov–May Mon–Sat 10am–7pm, Sun 11am–7pm; M° Pyramides), and in the Carrousel du Louvre, accessed from 99 rue de Rivoli, 1ᵉʳ (daily 10am–6pm; M° Palais Royal-Musée du Louvre). The latter also has information on the region around Paris, the Île de France. Montmartre has its own little office at 72 bd Rochechouart (daily 10am–6pm; M° Anvers) and there are booths at the Gare du Nord (daily 8am–6pm), Gare de l'Est (Mon–Sat 8am–7pm) and Gare de Lyon (Mon–Sat 8am–6pm).

Of Paris's inexpensive weekly **listings magazines**, sold at newsagents and kiosks, *Pariscope* has the edge, with a comprehensive section on films. On Wednesdays, *Le Monde* and *Le Figaro* also bring out free listings supplements, while for more detail, the **Webzines** *Paris Voice* (Ⓦ www.parisvoice.com) and *GoGo Paris* (Ⓦ www.gogoparis.com) cover the latest events and trends. For a comprehensive A–Z map, your best bet is one of the pocket-sized "*L'indispensable*" series booklets, sold throughout the city.

City transport

While walking is undoubtedly the best way to discover Paris, the city's integrated **public transport system** of bus, métro and trains – the RATP (Régie Autonome des Transports Parisiens) – is cheap, fast and meticulously signposted. Free métro and bus **maps** of varying sizes and detail are available at most stations, bus terminals and tourist offices: the largest and most useful is the *Grand Plan de Paris numéro 2*, which overlays the métro, RER and bus routes on a map of the city so you can see exactly how transport lines and streets match up. If you just want a handy pocket-sized métro/bus map ask for the *Petit Plan de Paris* or the smaller *Paris Plan de Poche*. You can also **download maps**, including a wallet-sized version of the métro map and a very useful searchable interactive online version of *Grand Plan de Paris numéro 2* at Ⓦ www.ratp.fr.

The métro and RER

The métro, combined with the RER (Réseau Express Régional) suburban express lines, is the simplest way of getting around. The métro runs from 5.20am to 1.20am, RER trains from 4.45am to 1.30am. Stations (abbreviated: M° Concorde, RER Luxembourg, etc) are evenly spaced and you'll rarely find yourself more than 500m from one in the centre, though the interchanges can involve a lot of legwork, including many stairs. In addition to the free maps available (see above), every station has a big plan of the network outside the entrance and several inside, as well as a map of the local area. The lines are colour-coded and designated by numbers for the métro and by letters for the RER, although they are signposted within the system with the names of the terminus stations: for example, travelling from Montparnasse to Châtelet, you follow the sign "Direction Porte-de-Clignancourt"; from Gare d'Austerlitz to Grenelle on line 10 you follow "Direction Boulogne–Pont-de-St-Cloud". The numerous interchanges (*correspondances*) make it possible to travel all over the city in a more or less straight line. For RER journeys beyond the city, make sure the station you want is illuminated on the platform display board.

Buses

The city's buses are not difficult to use, and of course you do see much more from a bus than on the métro. Every bus stop displays the name of the stop, the numbers of the buses that stop there, a map showing all the stops on the route, and the times of the first and last buses. You can buy a single ticket (€1.70 from the driver), or use a

Tickets and passes

For a short stay in the city, **carnets** of ten tickets can be bought from any station or *tabac* (€11.40, as opposed to €1.60 for an individual ticket). The city's integrated transport system, the RATP (@www.ratp.fr), is divided into **five zones**, and the métro system itself more or less fits into zones 1 and 2. The same tickets are valid for the buses (including the night bus), métro and, within the city limits and immediate suburbs (zones 1 and 2), the RER express rail lines, which also extend far out into the Île de France. Only one ticket is ever needed on the métro system, and within zones 1 and 2 for any RER or bus journey, but you can't switch between buses or between bus and métro/RER on the same ticket. For RER journeys beyond zones 1 and 2 you must buy an RER ticket. In order to get to La Défense on the RER rather than on the métro, for example, you need to buy a RER ticket, as La Défense is in zone 3. Children under 4 travel free and from ages 4 to 10 at half-price. Don't buy from the touts who hang round the main stations – you may pay well over the odds, quite often for a used ticket – and be sure to keep your ticket until the end of the journey as you'll be fined on the spot if you can't produce one.

If you're doing a fair number of journeys in one day, it might be worth getting a **Mobilis day pass** (€6.10 for zones 1 & 2), which offers unlimited access to the métro, buses and, depending on which zones you choose, the RER. Other possibilities are the **Paris Visite** passes (@www.ratp.info/touristes/), one-, two-, three- and five-day visitors' passes at €9, €14.70, €20 and €28.90 for Paris and close suburbs, or €18.90, €28.90, €40.50 and €49.40 to include the airports, Versailles and Disneyland Paris (make sure you buy this one when you arrive at Roissy-Charles de Gaulle or Orly to get maximum value). A half-price child's version is also available. You can buy them from métro and RER stations, tourist offices and online from @www.helloparis.co.uk. Paris Visite passes can begin on any day and entitle you to unlimited travel (in the zones you have chosen) on bus, métro, RER, SNCF and the Montmartre funicular; they also allow you discounts at certain monuments and museums.

For those who arrive early in the week and are staying more than three days, it's more economical to buy a **Navigo weekly pass** (*le passe Navigo découverte*). It costs €18.35 for zones 1 and 2 and is valid for an unlimited number of journeys from Monday morning to Sunday evening. You can only buy a ticket for the current week until Wednesday; from Thursday you can buy a ticket to begin the following Monday. A monthly pass costs €60.40 for zones 1 and 2. The Navigo swipe card itself costs €5, and you'll also need a passport photo.

---

pre-purchased carnet ticket or pass (see box above); remember to validate your ticket by inserting it into one of the machines on board. Press the red button to request a stop and an *arrêt demandé* sign will then light up. Most buses are easily accessible for wheelchairs and prams. Generally speaking, buses run from 5.30am to 8.30pm with some services continuing to 1.30am. Around half the lines don't operate on Sundays and holidays – the *Grand Plan de Paris* (see opposite) lists those that do. You can download a **map** of the most useful tourist routes from @www.ratp.fr.

From mid-April to mid-September, a special orange-and-white **Balabus service** (not to be confused with Batobus, see p.80) passes all the major tourist sights between the Grande Arche de la Défense and Gare de Lyon. These buses run on Sundays and holidays every fifteen to twenty minutes from noon to 9pm. Bus stops are marked "Balabus", and you'll need one to three bus tickets, depending on the length of your journey: check the information at the bus stop or ask the driver. The Paris Visite and Mobilis passes are all valid too.

Night buses (Noctilien; @www.noctilien.fr) ply 45 routes at least every hour from 12.30am to 5.30am between place du Châtelet, west of the Hôtel de Ville, and the suburbs. Details of the routes are available online.

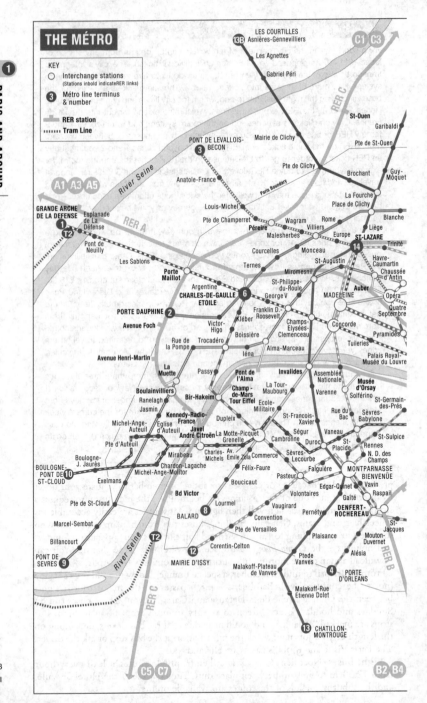

THE MÉTRO

KEY

○ Interchange stations
(Stations inbold indicateRER links)

③ Métro line terminus
& number

▬ RER station

······ Tram Line

LES COURTILLES
13B Asnières-Gennevilliers

Les Agnettes

Gabriel Péri

C1 C3

RER C

St-Ouen

Garibaldi

PONT DE LEVALLOIS-
③ BECON

Mairie de Clichy

Pte de St-Ouen

Pte de Clichy

Brochant

Guy-
Môquet

Anatole-France

Paris Boundary

La Fourche
Place de Clichy

A1 A3 A5

RER A

Louis-Michel

Pte de Champerret

Wagram
Rome
Villiers

Blanche

GRANDE ARCHE
DE LA DEFENSE
①

Esplanade
de La
Défense

T2

Péreire

Malesherbes

Europe

Liège

ST-LAZARE

Pont de
Neuilly

Courcelles

Monceau

St-Augustin

14

Trinité

Les Sablons

Porte
Maillot

Ternes

Miromesnil

Havre-
Caumartin
Chaussée
d'Antin

Argentine
CHARLES-DE-GAULLE
ETOILE

St-Philippe-
du-Roule

George V

Auber

Opéra

6

MADELEINE

PORTE DAUPHINE
②

Franklin D.-
Roosevelt

Quatre
Septembre

Victor-
Hugo

Kléber

Champs-
Elysées-
Clemenceau

Concorde

Pyramides

Avenue Foch

Rue de
la Pompe

Trocadéro

Boissière

Iéna

Alma-Marceau

Tuileries

Palais Royal-
Musée du Louvre

Avenue Henri-Martin

La
Muette

Passy

Pont de
l'Alma

Invalides

Assemblée
Nationale

Musée
d'Orsay

Boulainvilliers

Ranelagh

Bir-Hakeim

Champ -
de-Mars
Tour Eiffel

La Tour-
Maubourg

Varenne

Solférino

St-Germain-
des-Prés

Jasmin

Kennedy-Radio-
France

Ecole-
Militaire

Rue du
Bac

Sèvres-
Babylone

Michel-Ange-
Auteuil

Eglise
d'Auteuil

Dupleix

St-Francois-
Xavier

Vaneau

St-Sulpice

Javel
André Citroën

La Motte-Picquet
Grenelle

Ségur

Duroc

St-
Placide

Rennes

Pte d'Auteuil

Mirabeau

Charles-
Michels

Av.
Emile Zola

Commerce

Cambronne

Sèvres-
Lecourbe

N. D. des
Champs

Boulogne-
J. Jaurès

Chardon-Lagache

Félix-Faure

Falguière

MONTPARNASSE
BIENVENÜE

BOULOGNE-
PONT DE
ST-CLOUD
⑩

Michel-Ange-Molitor

Boucicaut

Pasteur

Vavin

Exelmans

Bd Victor

Edgar-Quinet

Raspail

Pte de St-Cloud

⑧ Lourmel

Vaugirard

Gaîté

DENFERT-
ROCHEREAU

Marcel-Sembat

BALARD

Volontaires

Pernéty

Billancourt

Convention

St-
Jacques

⑫

Corentin-Celton

Pte de Versailles

Plaisance

Mouton-
Duvernet

PONT DE
SEVRES ⑨

T2

MAIRIE D'ISSY

Ptede
Vanves

Alésia

RER B

River Seine

Malakoff-Plateau
de Vanves

④

PORTE
D'ORLEANS

RER C

Malakoff-Rue
Etienne Dolet

⑬ CHATILLON-
MONTROUGE

C5 C7

B2 B4

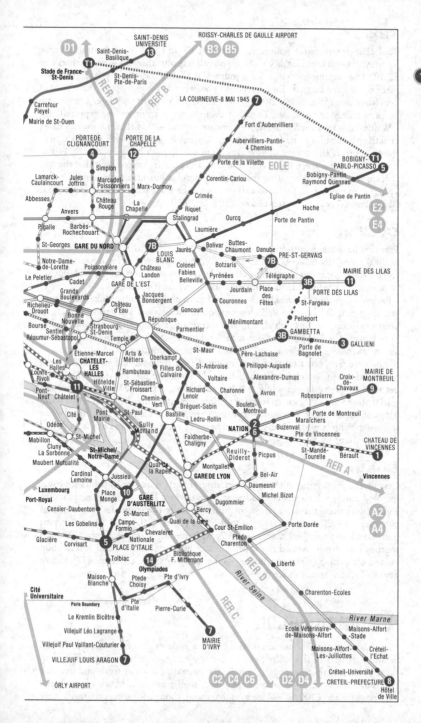

Taxis

Taxi charges are fairly reasonable: between €7 and €12 for a central daytime journey, though considerably more if you call one out; there's a pick-up charge of €2.10. The minimum charge for a journey is €6.10, and you'll pay €1 for each piece of luggage carried. Taxi drivers do not have to take more than three passengers (they don't like people sitting in the front); if a fourth passenger is accepted, an extra charge of €2.95 will be added. A tip of ten percent will be expected.

Waiting at a **taxi rank** (*arrêt taxi* – there are around 470 of them) is usually more effective than hailing one from the street. Currently, the large white light signals the taxi is free; the orange light means it's in use, though by the end of 2011 this is set to change: a green light will mean that the taxi is free, a red light that the taxi is occupied. Taxis can be rather thin on the ground at lunchtime and any time after 7pm, when you might prefer to **call** one out – the three main firms, Alpha, Taxis Bleues and G7, can all be reached on ☏01.45.30.30.30.

Cycling

Parisians have taken enthusiastically to **Vélib'**, the self-service bike scheme set up in 2007. More than 24,000 sleek, modern – and heavy – bicycles are stationed at some 17,500 locations around the city and close suburbs; you simply pick one up at one rack, or *borne*, ride to your destination, and drop it off again.

Passes – one-day €1, weekly €5 – are sold from meters at bigger bike stations, or any shop that displays the Vélib' logo, or online at ⓦ www.velib.paris.fr; plug in your credit card details (which will also secure a €150 deposit, not cashed unless you damage the bike). Once your card is paid up, you simply press it against the automatic readers to release a bike. The first thirty minutes on top of the cost of the pass are free, but after that costs mount; €1 for the next half-hour, €3 for the next, and €4 for every further half-hour. Helmets are not provided. There are between twelve and twenty bike stands at each *borne*, which are around 300m apart – so if the *borne* you come to is full, or empty, you shouldn't have too far to walk. Maps of the network are displayed at the *bornes*, and available to print in advance from the Vélib' website. Sadly, the incidence of theft and vandalism is high and there is talk of higher charges in order to offset this.

Boats

One of the most enjoyable ways to get around Paris is on the **Batobus** (ⓦ www.batobus.com), which operates all year round, apart from January, stopping at eight points along the Seine, from the Eiffel Tower to the Jardin des Plantes. Boats run every 15–30 minutes (Feb to mid-March, Nov & Dec 10.30am–4.30pm; mid-March to June, Sept & Oct 10am–7pm; June–Aug 10am–9.30pm). The total journey time from one end to the other is around thirty minutes and you can hop on and off as many times as you like – a day-pass costs €13, two days €17 and five days €20 (there are no single tickets).

Accommodation

Paris has some two thousand hotels offering a wide range of comfort, price and location. Hotels in the budget and mid-range category are **less expensive** than those in many other European capitals. By contrast, the city's four- and five-star hotels are among Europe's most expensive. Smaller two-star hotels often charge between €60 and €100 (❸–❺) for a double room, though for something with a bit

Boat trips

Most tourists are keen, rightly, to take a **boat trip** on the Seine. The faithful old Bateaux-Mouches is the best-known operator. Leaving from the Embarcadère du Pont de l'Alma on the Right Bank in the 8ᵉ (reservations and information ☎01.42.25.96.10, Ⓦwww.bateaux-mouches.fr; Mᵒ Alma-Marceau), the rides last 1 hour 10 minutes, cost €10 (€5 for children and over-65s) and take you past the major Seine-side sights, such as Notre-Dame and the Louvre. From April to September boats leave every 45 minutes from 10.15am to 6.30pm, then every twenty minutes from 7 to 11pm; winter departures are less frequent. The night-time cruises use lights to illuminate the streetscapes that are so bright they almost blind passers-by – much more fun on board than off – and at all times a narration in several languages blares out. The outrageously priced lunch and dinner trips, for which "correct" dress is mandatory, are probably best avoided. Bateaux-Mouches has many competitors, all much of a muchness and detailed in *Pariscope* under "Croisières" in the "Promenades et Loisirs" section.

Another option, which takes you past less-visited sights, is to take a **canal boat trip** run by Canauxrama (☎01.42.39.15.00, Ⓦwww.canauxrama.com) on the Canal St-Martin in the east of the city. Departing daily from May to September at 9.45am and 2.30pm from the Port de l'Arsenal (opposite 50 bd de la Bastille; Mᵒ Bastille, exit Opera), and at 9.45am and 2.45pm from the Bassin de la Villette (Mᵒ Jaurès), the ride lasts 2 hours 30 minutes and costs €16 (children €8.50); reservations are advisable on weekends. Trips run less frequently from October to April – it's best to email or phone for information and reservations during this period. **Paris Canal** (Ⓦwww .pariscanal.com) also runs canal trips (reservations online) between the Musée d'Orsay (quai Anatole-France by the Pont Solférino, 7ᵉ; Mᵒ Solférino) and the Parc de la Villette ("La Folie des Visites du Parc", on the canal by the bridge between the Grande Salle and the Cité des Sciences, 19ᵉ; Mᵒ Porte de Pantin), which last nearly three hours. Boats depart from the Musée d'Orsay at 9.30am and at 2.25pm. Parc de la Villette departures are at 10am and 2.30pm. Trips take place daily from mid-March to mid-November and cost €18, 12–25s and over-60s €15, 2–11s €11.

of style you'll probably have to pay upwards of €100 (⑥), and €120 or more (⑦) in swankier areas. Bargains exist in the 10ᵉ, especially around place de la République, and you can also get good deals in quieter areas further out, in the 13ᵉ and 14ᵉ, south of Montparnasse.

If you want to secure a really good room it's worth **booking** a couple of months or more in advance, as even the nicer hotels often leave their pokiest rooms at the back for last-minute reservations, and the best places will sell out well in advance in all but the coldest months. If you find yourself stuck on arrival, the main **tourist office** (see p.75 for addresses) will find you a room in a hotel or hostel free of charge. The tourist office also offers a free **online** reservation service (Ⓦwww .paris-info.com), with discounts on some hotels.

Our hotel recommendations are divided by area (see map, pp.70–71). Hostels and student accommodation are listed separately on pp.86–87.

The Champs-Élysées and around

See map, pp.92–93.

Le 123 123 rue du Faubourg Saint-Honorè, 8ᵉ ☎01.53.89.01.23, Ⓦwww.astotel.com; Mᵒ Saint-Philippe-du-Roule. A giant puffball light greets you in the lobby of this stylish hotel, 5min walk from the Champs-Élysées. Rooms are a good size with high ceilings, laminate floors and bathtubs. Each one has at least one antique – a chaise longue, nest of tables or desk – to take the edge off the minimalism. Public rates start at €299, but frequent special offers bring this down to around €150. ⑤

De L'Élysée Faubourg Saint-Honoré 12 rue des Saussaies, 8ᵉ ☎01.42.65.29.25, Ⓦwww.france -hotel-guide.com/h75008efsh.htm; Mᵒ Champs-Élysées-Clemenceau. This comfy three-star, a mere chandelier swing from the Élysée Palace, has sixty rooms decorated in traditional style, with *toile de Jouy* wallpaper, solid mahogany furniture and jacquard bedspreads. **8**

Lancaster 7 rue de Berri, 8ᵉ ℡01.40.76.40.76, ⓦwww.hotel-lancaster.fr; Mº George-V. Once the pied-à-terre for the likes of Garbo, Dietrich and Sir Alec Guinness, this elegantly restored nineteenth-century town house is still a favourite hide-out today for those fleeing the paparazzi. The rooms retain original features and are chock-full of Louis XVI and rococo antiques, but with a touch of contemporary chic. To top it all off, there's a Michelin-starred restaurant and zen-style interior garden. It's worth checking their site for special offers, otherwise doubles usually start at €520. **9**

De Sers 41 av Pierre 1ᵉʳ de Serbie, 8ᵉ ℡01.53.23.75.75, ⓦwww.hoteldesers.com; Mº George-V. A seriously chic boutique hotel, just off the Champs-Élysées, offering rooms in minimalist style, with rosewood furnishings and decor in white, grey, deep reds and pinks; facilities include CD/DVD player and huge TV. The two suites on the top floor have fabulous panoramic terraces. Doubles from €450. **9**

The Louvre and Tuileries
See map, pp.92–93.

Brighton 218 rue de Rivoli, 1ᵉʳ ℡01.47.03.61.61, ⓦwww.paris-hotel-brighton.com; Mº Tuileries. An elegant hotel dating back to the late nineteenth century and possessing a certain period charm. The "classic" rooms, with internal views and striped blue-and-white walls, are fine but nothing special; the "superior" rooms are much better, particularly those on the upper floors, with magnificent views of the Tuileries gardens and nice touches such as two basins in the bathrooms. "Classic" €200–240, "superior" €250–300. **9**

Relais St-Honoré 308 rue St-Honoré, 1ᵉʳ ℡01.42.96.06.06, ⓦrelaissainthonore.com; Mº Tuileries. A snug little hotel set in a stylishly renovated seventeenth-century town house. The pretty wood-beamed rooms are decorated in warm colours and rich fabrics. Doubles from €208. **9**

Thérèse 5–7 rue Thérèse, 1ᵉʳ ℡01.42.96.10.01, ⓦwww.hoteltherese.com; Mº Palais Royal-Musée du Louvre. A very attractive boutique hotel, on a quiet street within easy walking distance of the Louvre, offering more expensive "traditional" rooms, which are pared-down and stylish, with dark wood fittings, and "classic" rooms, which are small but good value. Book well in advance as it's very popular, especially during the fashion shows. **8**

Grands Boulevards and around
See map, pp.92–93.

Chopin 46 passage Jouffroy, entrance on bd Montmartre, near rue du Faubourg-Montmartre, 9ᵉ ℡01.47.70.58.10, ⓦwww.bretonnerie.com /chopin; Mº Grands-Boulevards. A lovely period building hidden away at the end of an elegant 1850s *passage* (shopping arcade), with quiet and pleasantly furnished rooms, though the cheaper ones are on the small side and a little dark. **5**

Mansart 5 rue des Capucines, 1ᵉʳ ℡01.42.61.50.28, ⓦwww.paris-hotel-mansart.com; Mº Opéra/Madeleine. This gracious hotel is situated on the corner of place Vendôme, just a stone's throw from the *Ritz*, but with rooms at a fraction of the price, and while they're not quite in the luxury bracket they're attractively decorated in Louis XIV style, with plenty of antique furniture, old prints and quality fabrics, and most are fairly spacious by Parisian standards. **7**

Vivienne 40 rue Vivienne, 2ᵉ ℡01.42.33.13.26, ©paris@hotel-vivienne.com; Mº Grands-Boulevards. A 10min walk from the Louvre, this is a friendly, family-run place, with good-sized, cheery rooms and modern bathrooms – a pretty good deal considering the location. **5**

Beaubourg and Les Halles
See map, p.100.

Relais du Louvre 19 rue des Prêtres St-Germain l'Auxerrois, 1ᵉʳ ℡01.40.41.96.42, ⓦwww.relaisdulouvre.com; Mº PalaisvRoyal-Musée du Louvre. A small, discreet hotel set on a quiet back street opposite the church of St-Germain l'Auxerrois. The decor is traditional but not stuffy, with rich, quality fabrics, old prints, Turkish rugs and solid furniture. All rooms have cable TV and wi-fi access; the cheaper ones are rather small. **8**

De Roubaix 6 rue Greneta, 3ᵉ ℡01.42.72.89.91, ⓦwww.hotel-de-roubaix.com; Mº Réaumur-Sébastopol or Mº Arts-et-Métiers. An old-fashioned two-star hotel run by a pleasant elderly couple, who don't speak much English. The 53 rooms are small and done out with floral wallpaper and rickety furniture, but they're pretty good value when you consider the location, just 5min walk from the Pompidou Centre. A basic breakfast consisting of a hunk of crusty bread and a hot drink is included in the price. **4**

Tiquetonne 6 rue Tiquetonne, 2ᵉ ℡01.42.36.94.58; Mº Etienne-Marcel. Located on a pedestrianized street a block away from Montorgueil street market and around the corner from the rue Saint Denis red light district, this excellent-value budget hotel dates back to the 1920s and looks as though it's probably changed little since. The simple rooms are well maintained, many quite spacious, though walls are thin. Non-en-suite rooms are equipped with a sink and bidet. There are no TVs and breakfast is served in your room. ❷

The Marais, islands and Bastille

See map, pp.104–105.

Beaumarchais 3 rue Oberkampf, 11ᵉ ☎01.43.38.16.16, ⓦwww.hotelbeaumarchais.com; Mᵒ Filles-du-Calvaire/Oberkampf. A funky, gay-friendly hotel, though the garish fifties-inspired decor may be a bit much for some: rooms have pink, yellow or orange walls, red bedspreads, swirly carpets and crazy paving-style tiles in the bathrooms. All 31 rooms are en suite with a/c and cable TV. There's a little patio for breakfast on fine days.❻

Caron de Beaumarchais 12 rue Vieille-du-Temple, 4ᵉ ☎01.42.72.34.12, ⓦwww.carondebeaumarchais .com; Mᵒ Hôtel-de-Ville. A pretty boutique hotel, named after the eighteenth-century French playwright Beaumarchais, who lived just up the road. Everything – down to the original engravings and Louis XVI-style furniture, not to mention the piano-forte in the foyer – evokes the refined tastes of high-society pre-Revolutionary Paris. Rooms overlooking the courtyard are small but cosy, while those on the street are more spacious, some with a balcony. ❼

Grand Hôtel du Loiret 8 rue des Mauvais Garçons, 4ᵉ ☎01.48.87.77.00, ⓦwww.hotel-du-loiret.fr; Mᵒ Hôtel-de-Ville. A budget hotel, grand in name only. The rooms are essentially uneventful and very small, but acceptable for the price; cheaper ones have washbasin only, all have TV and telephone. ❸

De Lutèce 65 rue St-Louis-en-l'Île, 4ᵉ ☎01.43.26.23.52, ⓦwww.paris-hotel-lutece.com; Mᵒ Pont Marie. Twenty-three tiny but appealing rooms, decorated in contemporary style and equipped with sparkling-white bathrooms, are eked out of this old wood-beamed town house situated on the most desirable island in France. ❻

De Nevers 53 rue de Malte, 11ᵉ ☎01.47.00.56.18, ⓦwww.hoteldenevers.com; Mᵒ République/Oberkampf. A hospitable budget hotel with very simple but cheerfully decorated rooms – the best are the en-suite doubles at the front; courtyard-facing rooms are dark and poky. ❸

Pavillon de la Reine 28 place des Vosges, 3ᵉ ☎01.40.29.19.19, ⓦwww.pavillon-de-la-reine .com; Mᵒ Bastille. A perfect honeymoon hideaway in a beautiful ivy-covered mansion secreted away off the adorable Place des Vosges. It preserves an intimate ambience, with friendly, personable staff. The rooms mostly have a distinctively 1990s "hip

hotel" feel, and could probably use another makeover. Doubles €300–500. ❾

Du Petit Moulin 29–31 rue du Poitou, 3ᵉ ☎01.42.74.10.10, ⓦwww.paris-hotel-petitmoulin .com; Mᵒ Saint-Sébastien-Froissart/Filles du Calvaire. An ultra-stylish boutique hotel, set in an old bakery and designed top to bottom by Christian Lacroix. Each room bears the designer's hallmark flamboyancy and is a fusion of different styles, from elegant Baroque to Sixties kitsch. ❽

De la Porte Dorée 273 av Daumesnil, 12ᵉ ☎01.43.07.56.97, ⓦwww.hoteldelaportedoree .com; Mᵒ Porte Dorée. A good-value hotel, a considerable step above the two-star norm: all rooms have private shower or bath, cable TV, comfy beds and pleasant decor. Traditional features such as ceiling mouldings, fireplaces and the elegant main staircase have been retained and many of the furnishings are antique. Bastille is seven minutes away by métro or a pleasant twenty-minute walk along the Promenade Plantée. ❸

🏃 **St-Louis Marais** 1 rue Charles-V, 4ᵉ ☎01.48.87.87.04, ⓦwww.saintlouismarais .com; Mᵒ Sully-Morland. Formerly part of the seventeenth-century Célestins Convent, this cosy place retains its period feel, with stone walls, exposed beams and tiled floors. Rooms are done out with terracotta-coloured fabrics and old maps of Paris, and have wi-fi access. A major plus is its location on a very quiet road, just a short walk from all the Marais action further north, and the Left Bank is easily reached over the Pont de Sully. The cheaper rooms are very small. ❸

Sévigné 2 rue Malher, 4ᵉ ☎01.42.72.76.17, ⓦwww.le-sevigne.com; Mᵒ St-Paul. A pleasant family-run budget hotel set in a narrow town house, with small, simple rooms in shades of pale yellow and red, and modern tiled bathrooms. Double glazing helps muffle the traffic noise from nearby rue de Rivoli. Good value for the area. ❺

Quartier Latin

See map, pp.110–111.

Hôtel du Commerce 14 rue de la Montagne-Ste-Geneviève, 5ᵉ ☎01.43.54.89.69, ⓦwww .commerce-paris-hotel.com; Mᵒ Maubert-Mutualité. Business-like but very central budget hotel with a range of rooms from washbasin-only cheapies (❷) up to modern en suites and family rooms. Communal kitchen and free internet access. ❺

🏃 **Hôtel Degrés de Notre Dame** 10 rue des Grands Degrés, 5ᵉ ☎01.55.42.88.88, ⓦwww.lesdegreshotel.com; Mᵒ St-Michel/Maubert-Mutualité. This charming, superbly idiosyncratic hotel has just ten rooms, so book in advance. The building is ancient and the rooms all very different, with prices corresponding to size. Unique, personal touches are everywhere: hand-painted murals, antique mirrors and curious nooks. Perhaps the loveliest room of all is under the roof, with its own stairs. Breakfast included. ❼

Hôtel Esmeralda 4 rue St-Julien-le-Pauvre, 5ᵉ ☎01.43.54.19.20, ✉hotel.esmeralda@orange.fr; M° St-Michel/Maubert-Mutualité. Dozing in an ancient house on square Viviani, this rickety old hotel offers a deeply old-fashioned, faded feel, with resolutely unmodernized en-suite rooms done up in worn red velvet or faded florals. ❺, or ❻ with superb views of Notre-Dame.

Familia Hôtel 11 rue des Ecoles, 5ᵉ ☎01.43.54.55.27, ⓦwww.familiahotel.com; M° Cardinal-Lemoine/Maubert-Mutualité/Jussieu. Big, friendly, family-run hotel on a busy road. Rooms are small but attractive, with beams and *toile de Jouy* wallpaper; some have views of Notre-Dame, others have balconies. Breakfast included. ❹

🏃 **Hôtel des Grandes Ecoles** 75 rue du Cardinal-Lemoine, 5ᵉ ☎01.43.26.79.23, ⓦwww.hotel-grandes-ecoles.com; M° Cardinal-Lemoine. Follow the cobbled alleyway to a large, peaceful garden and this tranquil hotel, with its pretty, old-fashioned rooms. Reservations are taken three months in advance, on the 15th of the month; don't be even a day late. ❼

Hôtel Marignan 13 rue du Sommerard, 5ᵉ ☎01.43.54.63.81, ⓦwww.hotel-marignan.com; M° Maubert-Mutualité. Great-value place, totally sympathetic to the needs of rucksack-toting foreigners, with free wi-fi, laundry, ironing and kitchen facilities, a library of guidebooks – and rooms for up to five people. The cheapest share bathrooms with one other room. No credit cards. ❸

Hôtel Port-Royal 8 bd Port-Royal, 5ᵉ ☎1.43.31.70.06, ⓦwww.hotelportroyal.fr; M° Gobelins. A friendly, good-value one-star that has been in the same family since the 1930s. Doubles, though small, are attractive and very clean; those with shared bath are considerably cheaper (€52.50, showers €2.50). It's in a quiet, residential area at the rue Mouffetard end of the boulevard, near the métro and the Quartier Latin. No credit cards. ❹

🏃 **Hôtel Résidence Henri IV** 50 rue des Bernardins, 5ᵉ ☎01.44.41.31.81, ⓦwww .residencehenri4.com; M° Maubert-Mutualité. Set back from busy rue des Ecoles on a cul-de-sac, this hotel is discreet and elegant, with classically styled rooms. Some have period features such as fireplaces, and all have miniature kitchenettes. ❼

Select Hôtel 51 place de la Sorbonne, 5ᵉ ☎01.46.34.14.80, ⓦwww.selecthotel.fr;

M° Cluny-Sorbonne. Situated right on the *place*, this hotel has had the full designer makeover, with exposed stone walls, leather and recessed wood trim much in evidence. ❽

St-Germain

See map, pp.116–117.

🏃 **Hôtel de l'Abbaye** 10 rue Cassette, 6ᵉ ☎01.45.44.38.11, ⓦwww.hotelabbayeparis .com; M° St-Sulpice. An atmosphere of hushed, luxurious calm presides over this four-star hotel. The rooms have loads of floral fabric and brass fittings, and there's a fair-sized courtyard garden and conservatory out back. Doubles from €240. ❾

Hôtel du Globe 15 rue des Quatre-Vents, 6ᵉ ☎01.43.26.35.50, ⓦwww.hotel-du-globe.fr; M° Odéon. Welcoming hotel in a tall, narrow, seventeenth-century building decked out with four-posters, stone walls, roof beams and the like. Rooms can be small, but aren't expensive for the location. ❼

L'Hôtel 13 rue des Beaux-Arts, 6ᵉ ☎01.44.41.99.00, ⓦwww.l-hotel.com; M° Mabillon/St-Germain-des-Prés. Extravagant designer hotel, with twenty sumptuous rooms accessed by a wonderful spiral staircase, and with a tiny pool in the basement. Oscar Wilde died here, "fighting a duel" with his wallpaper. Prices start in the high €200s. ❾

🏃 **Hôtel Michelet-Odéon** 6 place de l'Odéon, 6ᵉ ☎01.53.10.05.60, ⓦwww.hotelmichelet odeon.com; M° Odéon. A serious bargain for a hotel so close to the Jardin du Luxembourg. Rooms are unusually attractive (especially those facing onto the *place*) and larger than most at this price. ❻

Hôtel de Nesle 7 rue de Nesle, 6ᵉ ☎01.43.54.62.41, ⓦwww.hoteldenesleparis.com; M° St-Michel. Eccentric and sometimes chaotic hotel whose rooms are decorated with cartoon historical murals that you'll either love or hate. Rooms are tiny, but inexpensive for the central location. ❹

Relais Christine 3 rue Christine, 6ᵉ ☎01.40.51.60.80, ⓦwww.relais-christine.com; M° Odéon. Elegant, romantic four-star in a sixteenth-century former convent set around a deliciously hidden courtyard. It's well worth paying the 20 percent premium for one of the *supérieure* rooms. Doubles from €290. ❾

Relais Saint-Sulpice 3 rue Garancière, 6ᵉ ☎01.46.33.99.00, ⓦwww.relais-saint-sulpice.com; M° St-Sulpice/St-Germain-des-Prés. Set in an aristocratic townhouse immediately behind St-Sulpice's apse, this is a discreet and classy small hotel with well-furnished rooms painted in cheerful Provençal colours. The sauna is a nice touch. ❼

Hôtel de l'Université 22 rue de l'Université, 7e ⓣ01.42.61.09.39, ⓦwww.hotel universite.com; M° Rue du Bac. Cosy, quiet boutique three-star with antique details, including beamed ceilings and fireplaces in the larger, slightly pricier rooms. ⓻

Trocadéro, Eiffel Tower and the Septième

See map, pp.120–121.

🏃 **Hôtel du Champ-de-Mars** 7 rue du Champ-de-Mars, 7e ⓣ01.45.51.52.30, ⓦwww.hotelduchampdemars.com; M° École-Militaire. Cosy, colourful, excellent-value rooms in a well-run hotel. The location is great, too, in a nice neighbourhood just off the lively rue Cler market. ⓹

🏃 **Hôtel du Palais Bourbon** 49 rue de Bourgogne, 7e ⓣ01.44.11.30.70, ⓦwww .hotel-palais-bourbon.com; M° Varenne. This substantial, handsome old building on a quiet street in the hushed, posh district near the Musée Rodin offers spacious, prettily furnished rooms, with parquet floors and plenty of period detail. Homely family rooms (€235) and singles (€110) are also available. Breakfast is included in the price. ⓼

Montmartre and Northern Paris

See map, p.129.

Hôtel Amour 8 rue Navarin, 9e ⓣ01.48.78.31.80, ⓦwww.hotelamourparis.fr; M° Pigalle. Designer hotel for an achingly cool clientele, with old parquet, new paintwork and a deliberately boho Pigalle porn theme. Every room is decorated differently – one is all black with disco balls above the bed – but none has phone or TV, and all have iPod speakers. There's also a spacious dining area and a vodka bar. ⓻

🏃 **Hôtel des Arts** 5 rue Tholozé, 18e ⓣ01.46.06.30.52, ⓦwww.arts-hotel-paris .com; M° Blanche/Abbesses. Homely but efficient, with the family dog lolling by the reception desk and courteous staff. Rooms are a little small and bland, but cosy and the location on a romantic cobbled Montmartre street is fantastic. ⓹

🏃 **Hôtel Bonséjour** Montmartre 11 rue Burq, 18e ⓣ01.42.54.22.53, ⓦwww.hotel -bonsejour-montmartre.com; M° Abbesses. Rooms are basic and old-fashioned (with shower, but WC down the hall), but the location and price are superb. Ask for the corner rooms 23, 33, 43 or 53, which have balconies. ⓷

🏃 **Hôtel Eldorado** 18 rue des Dames, 17e ⓣ01.45.22.35.21, ⓦwww.eldoradohotel.fr; M° Place-de-Clichy. Idiosyncratic hotel in the bohemian Batignolles village. Rooms with some vintage fittings are brightened up with vivid colour

schemes and furnishings, and there's a secluded annexe at the back of the courtyard garden. Good onsite *bistro*. ⓸

Hôtel Ermitage 24 rue Lamarck, 18e ⓣ01.42.64.79.22, ⓦwww.ermitagesacrecoeur.fr; M° Anvers. Hushed, family-run hotel set on the lofty heights behind Sacré-Coeur. Rooms are old-fashioned and chintzy; those at the back have views across northern Paris. Complimentary breakfast served in rooms. Approach via the funicular to avoid a steep climb. No credit cards. ⓹

🏃 **Hôtel Langlois** 63 rue St-Lazare, 9e ⓣ01.48.74.78.24, ⓦwww.hotel-langlois .com; M° Trinité. Despite having all the facilities of a two-star, this genteel hotel in an untouristy quarter has barely changed in the last century, with antique furnishings and some spacious, handsome rooms. ⓻

🏃 **Hôtel Particulier** Montmartre 23 av Junot, 18e ⓣ01.53.41.81.40, ⓦwww.hotel -particulier-montmartre.com; M° Abbesses/ Lamarck-Caulaincourt. An exceptional hotel for a treat – or perhaps a honeymoon retreat, given its secluded location in a garden off a private passage set back from one of Paris's most exclusive streets. Set in an elegant Neoclassical mansion, this discreet boutique hotel has just five rooms, all *très* designer and all €400 and up. ⓽

Style Hôtel 8 rue Ganneron, 18e ⓣ01.45.22.37.59; M° Place-de-Clichy. An unpromising exterior in Batignolles hides a good budget place, with wooden floors, marble fireplaces and a secluded courtyard. Great value, especially the rooms with shared bathrooms (⓶). Otherwise ⓷

Eastern Paris

🏃 **Mama Shelter** 109 rue de Bagnolet, 20e ⓣ01.43.48.48.48, ⓦwww.mamashelter .com; M° Alexandre-Dumas. Currently one of the most talked-about hotels in Paris, *Mama Shelter*, owned by Club Med founders the Trigano family, justifies the hype. Philippe Starck-designed, with a hip, industrial-chic theme, it's also extremely good value. The sharp en suites come with an arty graffiti motif on the carpets and ceilings, swanky bathrooms, iMacs and decorative superhero masks. An excellent bar-restaurant, sun terrace and top-notch service complete the package. ⓺

Southern Paris

Hôtel de la Loire 39bis rue du Moulin-Vert, 14e ⓣ01.45.40.66.88, ⓦwww.hoteldelaloire-paris .com; M° Pernety/Alésia. On a pedestrianized street lies this delightful family hotel. En-suite doubles, with spotless, if tiny, bathrooms, are a bargain. There are cheaper options (with shared WC) in the slightly darker rooms in the annexe, which runs the length of the peaceful garden. Each room is different, and all have charming personal touches. Free wi-fi. ❹

Hôtel Mistral 24 rue Cels, 14ᵉ ☏ 01.43.20.25.43, ⓦ www.hotel-mistral-paris.com; Mᵒ Pernety/Alésia. Welcoming, cosy and pleasantly refurbished hotel on a very quiet street, with a little courtyard garden and a shared dining room/kitchen. Some rooms come with showers and shared WC facilities only (€70). ❺

Solar Hôtel 22 rue Boulard, 14ᵉ ☏ 01.43.21.08.20, ⓦ www.solarhotel.fr; Mᵒ Denfert-Rochereau. Set on an old-fashioned Montparnasse street, this budget hotel has paintings by local artists on the walls, cultural events in the back garden and strives to be ecological, with low-energy fittings, organic breakfasts and free bike rental. Don't be put off by the exterior: rooms are basic, but comfortable and bright, with a/c, TV and free wi-fi. Guests have use of a kitchen and living room. ❸

Hostels and student accommodation

Hostels won't necessarily be cheaper than sharing a room in a budget hotel, but they offer a more communal and often livelier atmosphere. Most take advance bookings, including the hostel groups: FUAJ (ⓦ www.fuaj.fr), which is part of Hostelling International, and MIJE (ⓦ www.mije.com), which runs three excellent hostels in historic buildings in the Marais. (There is a third big hostel group, UCRIF, but it caters largely to groups, so we haven't listed their hostels here; full details can be found online at ⓦ www.ucrif.asso.fr.) Independent hostels tend to be noisier places, often with bars attached. There is no effective age limit at any of these places.

The utterly budget option, of course, is camping. Only one site is reasonably close to central Paris, *Camping du Bois de Boulogne* (ⓦ www.campingparis.fr). It's by the Seine and gets booked out in summer; there's a free shuttle bus to the Porte-Maillot métro station. *Camping de la Colline*, in Torcy, on the RER line A4 (ⓦ www.camping-de-la-colline.com) is better for Disneyland, with shuttle buses to the park. Both campsites offer inexpensive bungalow accommodation.

Hostels

D'Artagnan 80 rue Vitruve, 20ᵉ ☏ 01.40.32.34.56, ⓦ www.fuaj.org; Mᵒ Porte-de-Bagnolet. This colourful, modern HI hostel is the largest in France with 440 beds and facilities including a small cinema, restaurant and bar, internet access and a swimming pool nearby. Guests have to vacate the rooms between 11am and 3pm for cleaning. It's very popular, so get here early or book online or by phone on the central reservations number: ☏ 01.44.89.87.27. Doubles and rooms for three to five are a few euros more per head than the dorm price. Dorm beds from €23.50.

BVJ Louvre 20 rue Jean-Jacques Rousseau, 1ᵉʳ ☏ 01.53.00.90.90, ⓦ www.bvjhotel.com; Mᵒ Louvre/Châtelet-Les-Halles. With 200 beds, the *BVJ Louvre* attracts an international studenty crowd, though dorms (sleeping eight) have a slightly institutional feel. Single rooms are available. Restaurant open daily except Sun. Dorm beds €29, twins €62.

BVJ Paris Quartier Latin 44 rue des Bernardins, 5ᵉ ☏ 01.43.29.34.80, ⓦ www.bvjhotel.com; Mᵒ Maubert-Mutualité. Spick and span hostel in a good location. Single rooms (€45) and dorm beds are good value; for double rooms (€66) you can do better elsewhere. Dorm beds €29.

Le Fauconnier 11 rue du Fauconnier, 4ᵉ ☏ 01.42.74.23.45, ⓦ www.mije.com; Mᵒ St-Paul/Pont Marie. MIJE hostel in a superbly renovated seventeenth-century building. Dorms sleep three to eight, and there are some single (€49) and double rooms too (€72), with en-suite showers. Dorm beds €30.

Le Fourcy 6 rue de Fourcy, 4ᵉ ☏ 01.42.74.23.45; Mᵒ St Paul. Another excellent MIJE hostel (same prices and deal as *Le Fauconnier*, see above). Housed in a beautiful mansion, this place has a small garden and an inexpensive restaurant. Doubles and triples also available.

Jules Ferry 8 bd Jules-Ferry, 11ᵉ ☏ 01.43.57.55.60, ⓦ www.fuaj.fr; Mᵒ République. Fairly central HI hostel, in a lively area at the foot of the Belleville hill. Difficult to get a place, but they can help find a bed elsewhere. Two to four people in each room. Dorm beds from €23.

Maubuisson 12 rue des Barres, 4ᵉ ☏ 01.42.74.23.45; Mᵒ Pont Marie/Hôtel de Ville. A MIJE hostel in a magnificent medieval building on a quiet street. Shared use of the restaurant at *Le Fourcy* (see above). Dorms only, sleeping four. Dorm beds €30.

Oops 50 av des Gobelins, 5ᵉ ℡ 01.47.07.47.00, ⓦ www.oops-paris.com; Mᵒ Gobelins. This "design hostel" is brightly decorated with funky patterns. All dorms are en suite, there's free wi-fi, a/c and a basic breakfast, and it's open 24 hours. Private doubles from €60. Unexceptional location, but it's just a couple of métro stops south of the Quartier Latin. Dorm beds €23–30.

Plug-inn Boutique Hostel 7 rue Aristide Bruant, 18ᵉ ℡ 01.42.58.42.58, ⓦ www.plug-inn.fr; Mᵒ Blanche/Abbesses. This friendly pocket hostel has a cool designer decor, in parts, and offers free wi-fi and breakfast (and no curfew), but the best thing is the location on the slopes of Montmartre. Dorm beds from €25, double rooms from €60.

St Christopher's Paris 68–74 quai de la Seine, 19ᵉ ℡ 01.40.34.34.40, ⓦ www.st-christophers.co .uk/paris-hostels; Mᵒ Crimée/Laumière. Massive new hostel overlooking the waters of the Bassin de la Villette – a long way from the centre. Rooms sleep six to eight and are pleasant in a functional, cabin-like way, but there's a great bar, inexpensive restaurant, and free internet access. As well as dorms there are also twins and doubles available (€42–80). Dorm beds €25–30.

Le Village Hostel 20 rue d'Orsel, 18ᵉ ℡ 01.42.64.22.02, ⓦ www.villagehostel.fr; Mᵒ Anvers. Attractive independent hostel in a handsome building, with good facilities and a view of Sacré-Coeur from the terrace. Doubles €35–45 and triples €32–38 per person, including breakfast. Small discounts in winter. Dorm beds €28.

Woodstock Hostel 48 rue Rodier, 9ᵉ ℡ 01.48.78.87.76, ⓦ www.woodstock.fr; Mᵒ Anvers/St-Georges. A reliable hostel with its own bar, set in a great location on a pretty street near Montmartre. Twin rooms also available €22–25 per person, breakfast included. Dorm beds €19–22.

Young and Happy Hostel 80 rue Mouffetard, 5ᵉ ℡ 01.47.07.47.07, ⓦ www.youngandhappy.fr; Mᵒ Monge/Censier-Daubenton. Noisy, basic and studenty independent hostel in a lively, touristy location. Dorms beds from €20.

The City

Rather than slavishly following the boundaries of the official twenty arrondissements (see map, pp.70–71), this book divides Paris into several quarters, each with their own distinct identities. The account begins with the **Île de la Cité**, the ancient heart of Paris and home of the cathedral of **Notre-Dame**. Heading north onto the **Right Bank**, we take in the Arc de Triomphe and follow the Voie Triomphale through the glamorous **Champs-Élysées** area to the Louvre palace. Immediately north is the expensive **Opéra district**, home of the shopping arcades of the *passages*, ritzy Place Vendôme and the tranquil gardens of the Palais Royal. East, the bustle and tacky shops of **Les Halles** and **Beaubourg** give way to the aristocratic and fashionable **Marais** and still-trendier **Bastille** quarters. Detouring via the Île St-Louis, Paris's second island, we cross the Seine onto the (southern) **Left Bank**, moving west from the studenty **Quartier Latin** through elegant and international **St-Germain** and into the aristocratic, museum-rich area around the **Eiffel Tower**, taking in the **Trocadéro** quarter, immediately across the river. We then explore outlying areas of the city, visiting first **Montparnasse** and southern Paris, then heading out west to the wealthy **Beaux Quartiers**, the green space of the Bois de Boulogne and the outlying business district of La Défense. Lastly, we move up to **Montmartre** and the northern arrondissements before finishing in the grittier eastern end of the city, which incorporates the vast Père-Lachaise cemetery.

Île de la Cité

The **Île de la Cité** is where Paris began. The earliest settlements were built here, followed by the small Gallic town of Lutetia, overrun by Julius Caesar's troops in 52 BC. A natural defensive site commanding a major east–west river trade route, it was an obvious candidate for a bright future. In 508 it became the stronghold of the Merovingian kings, then of the counts of Paris, who in 987 became kings of France.

The Frankish kings built themselves a splendid palace at the western tip of the island, of which the **Sainte-Chapelle** and **Conciergerie** survive today. At the other end of the island, they erected the great cathedral of **Notre-Dame**. By the early thirteenth century this tiny island had become the bustling heart of the capital, accommodating twelve parishes, not to mention numerous chapels and convents. It's hard to imagine this today: virtually the whole medieval city was erased by heavy-handed nineteenth-century demolition and much of it replaced by four vast edifices largely given over to housing the law. The warren of narrow streets around the cathedral was swept away and replaced with a huge, rather soulless square, but it does at least afford uncluttered views of the cathedral.

Pont-Neuf and the quais, Sainte-Chapelle and the Conciergerie

One of the most popular approaches to the island is via the graceful, twelve-arched **Pont-Neuf**, which despite its name is Paris's oldest surviving bridge, built in 1607 by Henri IV. It takes its name ("new") from the fact that it was the first in the city to be built of stone. Henri is commemorated with an equestrian statue halfway across, and also lends his nickname to the **square du Vert-Galant**, enclosed within the triangular stern of the island and reached via steps leading down behind the statue. "Vert-Galant", meaning a "green" or "lusty gentleman", is a reference to Henri's legendary amorous exploits, and he would no doubt have approved of this tranquil, tree-lined garden, a popular haunt of lovers.

Back on Pont-Neuf, opposite the square du Vert-Galant, red-bricked seventeenth-century houses flank the entrance to **place Dauphine**, one of the city's most appealing squares. Traffic noise recedes in favour of the gentle tap of *boules* being played in the shade of the chestnuts. At the further end looms the huge facade of the **Palais de Justice**, which swallowed up the palace that was home to the French kings until Étienne Marcel's bloody revolt in 1358 frightened them off to the greater security of the Louvre.

A survivor of the old palace complex is the magnificent **Sainte-Chapelle** (daily: March–Oct 9.30am–6pm; Nov–Feb 9am–5pm; €8, combined admission to the Conciergerie €11; M° Cité), accessed from the boulevard du Palais. It was built by Louis IX between 1242 and 1248 to house a collection of holy relics, including Christ's crown of thorns and a fragment of the True Cross, bought at extortionate rates from the bankrupt empire of Byzantium. Though much restored, the chapel remains one of the finest achievements of French High Gothic. Its most radical feature is its seeming fragility – created by reducing the structural masonry to a minimum to make way for a huge expanse of exquisite stained glass. The impression inside is of being enclosed within the wings of a myriad brilliant butterflies.

Further along boulevard du Palais is the entrance to the **Conciergerie** (same hours as Sainte-Chapelle; €7, combined ticket with Ste-Chapelle €11; M° Cité), Paris's oldest prison, where Marie-Antoinette and, in their turn, the leading figures of the Revolution were incarcerated before execution. Inside are several splendidly vaulted late-Gothic halls, vestiges of the old Capetian kings' palace. The most impressive is the Salle des Gens d'armes, originally the canteen and recreation room of the royal household staff. A number of rooms and prisoners' cells, including Marie-Antoinette's, have been reconstructed to show what they might have been like at the time of the Revolution.

Heading east from here, along the north side of the island, you come to **place Lépine**, named after the police boss who gave Paris's cops their white truncheons and whistles. The old police headquarters, better known as the Quai des Orfèvres to readers of Georges Simenon's Maigret novels, stands on one side of the square, while the other side is enlivened by an exuberant **flower market**, held daily and augmented by a chirruping bird market on Sundays.

Cathédrale de Notre-Dame

One of the masterpieces of the Gothic age, the **Cathédrale de Notre-Dame** (daily 8am–6.45pm; free; Mᵒ St-Michel/Cité) rears up from the Île de la Cité's southeast corner like a ship moored by huge flying buttresses. It was among the first of the great Gothic cathedrals built in northern France and one of the most ambitious, its nave reaching an unprecedented 33m.

Built on the site of the old Merovingian cathedral of Saint-Étienne, Notre-Dame was begun in 1160 under the auspices of Bishop de Sully and completed around 1345. In the seventeenth and eighteenth centuries it fell into decline, suffering its worst depredations during the French Revolution when the frieze of Old Testament kings on the facade was damaged by enthusiasts who mistook them for the kings of France. It was only in the 1820s that the cathedral was at last given a much-needed restoration, a task entrusted to the great architect-restorer, Viollet-le-Duc, who carried out a thorough – some would say too thorough – renovation, including remaking most of the statuary on the facade (the originals can be seen in the Musée National du Moyen Âge, see p.109) – and adding the steeple and baleful-looking gargoyles, which you can see close up if you brave the ascent of the **towers** (daily: April–June & Sept 10am–6.30pm; July & Aug Mon–Fri 10am–6.30pm, Sat & Sun 10am–11pm; Oct–March daily 10am–5.30pm; €8). Queues for the towers often start before they open, so it pays to get here early or to come in the evening, when it's often quieter. The same goes for visiting the cathedral itself.

The cathedral's **facade** is one of its most impressive exterior features; the Romanesque influence is still visible, not least in its solid H-shape, but the overriding impression is one of lightness and grace, created in part by the delicate filigree work of the central rose window and gallery above. Of the facade's magnificent **carvings**, the oldest, dating from the twelfth century, are those in the right portal, depicting the Virgin Enthroned, elegantly executed and displaying all the majesty of a royal procession.

The interior

Inside Notre-Dame, the immediately striking feature is the dramatic contrast between the darkness of the nave and the light falling on the first great clustered pillars of the choir. It's the end walls of the transepts that admit all this light: they are nearly two-thirds glass, including two magnificent rose windows coloured in imperial purple. These, the vaulting and the soaring columns are all definite Gothic elements, though there remains a strong sense of Romanesque in the stout round pillars of the nave. Free guided tours (1hr–1hr 30min) take place in English on Wednesdays and Thursdays at 2pm and on Saturdays at 2.30pm; the gathering point is the welcome desk near the entrance. There are free organ concerts every Sunday, usually at 4.30pm, plus four Masses on Sunday morning and one at 6.30pm.

The kilomètre zéro and crypte archéologique

On the pavement by the west door of the cathedral is a spot known as **kilomètre zéro**, the symbolic heart of France, from which all main road distances in the country are calculated. At the far end of the *place* is the entrance to the atmospheric **crypte archéologique** (Tues–Sun 10am–6pm; €4), a large excavated area under the square revealing the remains of the original cathedral, as well as remnants of the streets and houses that once clustered around Notre-Dame: most are medieval, but some date as far back as Gallo-Roman times and include parts of a Roman hypocaust (heating system).

Le Mémorial de la Déportation

At the eastern tip of the island is the symbolic tomb of the 200,000 French who died in Nazi concentration camps during World War II – Resistance fighters, Jews and forced labourers among them. The stark and moving **Mémorial de la Déportation** (daily 10am–noon & 2–5pm; free) is scarcely visible above ground; stairs hardly shoulder-wide descend into a space like a prison yard and then into the crypt, off which is a long, narrow, stifling corridor, its wall covered in thousands of points of light representing the dead. Floor and ceiling are black, and it ends in a raw hole, with a single naked bulb hanging in the middle. Above the exit are the words "Pardonne, n'oublie pas" ("Forgive, do not forget").

The Champs-Élysées and around

Synonymous with Parisian glitz and glamour, the **Champs-Élysées** cuts through one of the city's most exclusive districts, studded with luxury hotels and top fashion boutiques. The avenue forms part of a grand, nine-kilometre axis that extends from the Louvre, at the heart of the city, to the Grande Arche de la Défense, in the west. Often referred to as the Voie Triomphale, or Triumphal Way, it offers impressive vistas all along its length and incorporates some of the city's most famous landmarks – the **Tuileries** gardens, **place de la Concorde**, the **Champs-Élysées** avenue and the **Arc de Triomphe**. The whole ensemble is so regular and geometrical it looks as though it was laid out by a single town planner rather than by successive kings, emperors and presidents, all keen to add their stamp and promote French power and prestige.

The Arc de Triomphe

The best view of the Voie Triomphale is from the top of the **Arc de Triomphe** (daily: April–Sept 10am–11pm; Oct–March 10am–10.30pm; €9; M° Charles-de-Gaulle-Étoile), towering above the traffic in the middle of **place Charles-de-Gaulle**, better known as l'Étoile ("star") on account of the twelve avenues radiating out from it. Access is via underground stairs from the north corner of the Champs-Élysées. The arch was started by Napoleon as a homage to the armies of France and himself, but it wasn't actually finished until 1836 by Louis-Philippe, who dedicated it to the French army in general. The names of 660 generals and numerous French battles are engraved on the inside of the arch, and reliefs adorn the exterior: the best is François Rude's extraordinarily dramatic *Marseillaise*, in which an Amazon-type figure personifying the Revolution charges forward with a sword, her face contorted in a fierce rallying cry. A quiet reminder of the less glorious side of war is the **tomb of the unknown soldier** placed beneath the arch and marked by an eternal flame that is stoked up every evening at 6.30pm by war veterans. If you're up for climbing the 280 steps to the top you'll be amply rewarded by the panoramic views; the best time to come is towards dusk on a sunny day, when the marble of the Grande Arche de la Défense sparkles in the setting sun and the Louvre is bathed in warm light.

The Champs-Élysées

The celebrated **avenue des Champs-Élysées**, a popular rallying point at times of national crisis and the scene of big military parades on Bastille Day, sweeps down from the Arc de Triomphe towards the place de la Concorde. Seen from a distance it's an impressive sight, but close up can be a little disappointing, with its constant stream of traffic, fast-food outlets and chain stores. Over the last decade or so, however, it's been steadily regaining something of its former cachet as a chic address: top fashion stores have moved in, once dowdy shops such as the Publicis ad agency and the Renault car showroom have undergone stylish makeovers and acquired cool bar-restaurants, while new, fashionable cafés and restaurants in the streets around have injected fresh buzz and glamour. Just off the avenue, **rue Francois 1er** and **avenue Montaigne**, part of the *"triangle d'or"* (golden triangle), are home to the most exclusive names in fashion: Dior, Prada, Chanel and many others.

The Champs-Élysées began life as a leafy promenade, an extension of the Tuileries gardens. It was transformed into a fashionable thoroughfare during the Second Empire when members of the *haute bourgeoisie* built themselves splendid mansions along its length and high society would come to stroll and frequent the cafés and theatres. Most of the mansions subsequently gave way to office blocks and the *beau monde* moved elsewhere, but remnants of the avenue's glitzy heyday live on at the *Lido* cabaret, *Fouquet's* café-restaurant, the perfumier Guerlain's shop and the former *Claridges* hotel, now a swanky shopping arcade.

North of the Champs-Élysées

Just north of the Champs-Élysées are a number of *hôtels particuliers* housing select museums, the best of which is the **Musée Jacquemart-André**, with its magnificent art collection. North of here is the small and formal **Parc Monceau**, surrounded by grand residences. **Rue de Lévis** (a few blocks up rue Berger from M° Monceau) has one of the city's most strident, colourful and appetizing markets every day of the week except Monday.

Musée Jacquemart-André

The **Musée Jacquemart-André** at 158 bd Haussmann, 8e (daily 10am–6pm; €10; Ⓦ www.musee-jacquemart-andre.com; M° Miromesnil/St-Philippe-du-Roule), is a splendid mansion laden with the outstanding works of art which its owners, banker Édouard André and his wife Nélie Jacquemart, collected on their extensive trips abroad. Free, informative audioguides (available in English) take you through sumptuous *salons*, mainly decorated in Louis XV and Louis XVI style, among them a room open to the floor above and surrounded by a carved wooden balcony from which musicians would have entertained guests at the glittering soirees that the Jacquemart-Andrés were renowned for. The pride of the couple's collection was their early Italian Renaissance paintings, on the upper floor. At the top of the stairs is a huge, animated fresco by Tiepolo depicting the French king Henri III being received by Frederigo Contarini in Venice. Other highlights are Uccello's *St George and the Dragon*, a haunting *Virgin and Child* by Mantegna, and another by Botticelli. An excellent way to finish off a visit is a reviving halt at the museum's **salon de thé**, with its lavish interior and ceiling frescoes by Tiepolo.

South of the Rond-Point des Champs-Élysées

The lower stretch of the Champs-Élysées, between the Rond-Point des Champs-Élysées and place de la Concorde, is bordered by chestnut trees and flowerbeds and is the most pleasant part of the avenue for a stroll. The gigantic Neoclassical building topped with a glass cupola that rises above the greenery to the south is the **Grand Palais** (Ⓦ www.grandpalais.fr), created with its neighbour, the Petit Palais, for the 1900 Exposition Universelle. The cupola forms the centrepiece of the *nef* (nave), a huge, impressive exhibition space, used for large-scale installations, fashion shows and trade fairs. In the Grand Palais' north wing is the **Galeries nationales** (Mon & Wed–Sun 10am–8pm, till 10pm on Wed; €11), the city's prime venue for blockbuster art exhibitions.

The **Petit Palais** (Tues–Sun 10am–6pm; free; Ⓦ www.petitpalais.paris.fr), facing the Grand Palais on avenue Winston-Churchill, is hardly "petit" but certainly palatial, boasting beautiful spiral wrought-iron staircases, stained-glass windows, ceiling frescoes and a grand gallery on the lines of Versailles' Hall of Mirrors. At first sight it looks like it's mopped up the leftovers after the other city's

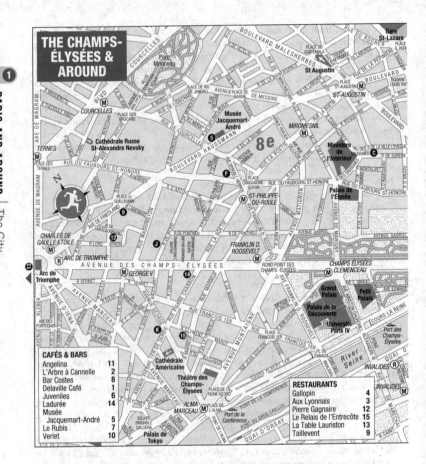

THE CHAMPS-ÉLYSÉES & AROUND

CAFÉS & BARS	
Angelina	11
L'Arbre à Cannelle	2
Bar Costes	8
Delaville Café	1
Juveniles	6
Ladurée	14
Musée Jacquemart-André	5
Le Rubis	7
Verlet	10

RESTAURANTS	
Gallopin	4
Aux Lyonnais	3
Pierre Gagnaire	12
Le Relais de l'Entrecôte	15
La Table Lauriston	13
Taillevent	9

galleries have taken their pick, but there are some real gems here, such as Monet's *Sunset at Lavacourt* and Courbet's provocative *Young Ladies on the Bank of the Seine*.

On the other side of the avenue, to the north of place Clemenceau, combat police guard the high walls round the presidential **Palais de l'Élysée** and the line of ministries and embassies ending with the US in prime position on the corner of place de la Concorde. On Thursdays and at weekends you can see more national branding in the **postage-stamp market** at the corner of avenues Gabriel and Marigny.

Place de la Concorde and the Tuileries

At the lower end of the Champs is the vast **place de la Concorde**, where crazed traffic makes crossing over to the middle a death-defying task. As it happens, some 1300 people did die here between 1793 and 1795, beneath the Revolutionary guillotine – Louis XVI, Marie-Antoinette, Danton and Robespierre among them. The centrepiece of the square is a stunning gold-tipped **obelisk** from the temple of Luxor, offered as a favour-currying gesture by the viceroy of Egypt in 1829. From here there are sweeping vistas in all directions; the Champs-Élysées looks particularly impressive, and you can admire the alignment of the Assemblée

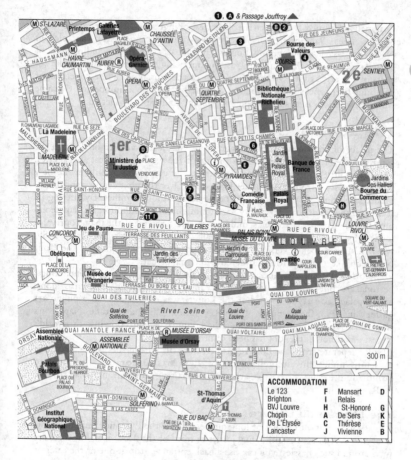

On the map:

● , Ⓐ & Passage Jouffroy ▲

Ⓜ ST-LAZARE — Printemps — Galeries Lafayette
PLACE DIAGHILEV
CHAUSSÉE D'ANTIN
BOULEVARD DES ITALIENS
RUE DES JEUNEURS
RUE DE CLÉRY
Ⓑ❷
❸
RUE VIVIENNE
Bourse des Valeurs
❹
HAUSSMANN
Opéra Garnier
Ⓜ AUBER Ⓡ
BOURSE
RUE REAUMUR
RUE DE LA BOURSE
PL. DE LA BOURSE
2e
SENTIER Ⓜ
LEOPOLD BELLAN
Ⓜ
Opéra Ⓜ
BOULEVARD DES CAPUCINES
PL. DE L'OPÉRA
RUE DU QUATRE SEPTEMBRE
RUE DES FILLES ST-THOMAS
Bibliothèque Nationale Richelieu
RUE DU LOUVRE
ABACKSALMONT
RUE MARCHANT
La Madeleine
MADELEINE Ⓜ
RUE DE SEZE
RUE DES CAPUCINES
RUE DANIELLE CASANOVA
RUE DES PETITS CHAMPS
PLACE DES VICTOIRES
RUE ETIENNE MARCEL
1er
Ministère de la Justice
PLACE VENDOME
❻
Jardin du Palais Royal
Banque de France
COQUILLIÈRE
Jardins des Halles
Bourse du Commerce
RUE ROYALE
RUE SAINT-HONORÉ
PYRAMIDES Ⓜ
❼ ❺
Comédie Française
Palais Royal
Ⓗ
R. ST-HONORÉ
RUE ST-HONORÉ
LOUVRE
❽
❿
RUE DU MONT THABOR
PLACE A. MALRAUX
PLACE DU PALAIS ROYAL
RIVOLI
Ⓜ
CONCORDE Ⓜ
Jeu de Paume
RUE DE RIVOLI
TUILERIES
PALAIS ROYAL Ⓜ MUSÉE DU LOUVRE
RUE DE RIVOLI Ⓜ
PL. DU LOUVRE
Obélisque
TERRASSE DES FEUILLANTS
Jardin des Tuileries
Jardin du Carrousel
PLACE DU CARROUSEL
Pyramide COUR NAPOLEON
COUR CARRÉE
R. PRÊTRES ST-GERMAIN L'AUXERROIS
PLACE DE LA CONCORDE
Musée de l'Orangerie
TERRASSE DU BORD DE L'EAU
JARDIN DE L'INFANTE
SQUARE DU VERT-GALANT
QUAI DES TUILERIES
QUAI DU LOUVRE
Quai de Solférino
River Seine
Quai du Louvre
Quai Malaquais
PLACE DE L'INSTITUT
QUAI DE CONTI
Assemblée Nationale
QUAI ANATOLE FRANCE
Ⓡ MUSÉE D'ORSAY
QUAI VOLTAIRE
QUAI MALAQUAIS
ORSAY
ASSEMBLÉE NATIONALE Ⓜ
Musée d'Orsay
RUE DE LILLE
RUE DE LILLE
0   300 m
Palais Bourbon
BOULEVARD ST-GERMAIN
RUE DE L'UNIVERSITÉ
RUE DE L'UNIVERSITÉ
RUE DE VERNEUIL
Institut Géographique National
RUE SAINT-DOMINIQUE
St-Thomas d'Aquin
RUE DU BAC
PGE DE ST-THOMAS D'AQUIN
SOLFERINO Ⓜ
Ⓜ

ACCOMMODATION			
Le 123	F	Mansart	D
Brighton	I	Relais	
BVJ Louvre	H	St-Honoré	G
Chopin	A	De Sers	
De L'Élysée	C	Thérèse	K
Lancaster	J	Vivienne	B

Nationale in the south with the church of the Madeleine – sporting an identical Neoclassical facade – to the north.

The symmetry continues beyond place de la Concorde in the formal layout of the **Jardin des Tuileries**, the formal French garden *par excellence*. It dates back to the 1570s, when Catherine de Médicis had the site cleared of the medieval warren of tilemakers (*tuileries*) to make way for a palace and grounds. One hundred years later, Louis XIV commissioned renowned landscape artist Le Nôtre to redesign them and the results are largely what you see today: straight avenues, formal flowerbeds and splendid vistas. Shady tree-lined paths flank the grand central alley, and ornamental ponds frame both ends. The much-sought-after chairs strewn around the ponds are a good spot from which to admire the landscaped surroundings and contemplate the superb statues executed by the likes of Coustou and Coysevox, many of them now replaced by copies, the originals transferred to the Louvre.

The two buildings flanking the garden at the Concorde end are the **Jeu de Paume** (Tues noon–9pm, Wed–Fri noon–7pm, Sat & Sun 10am–7pm; €7; Ⓦ www.jeudepaume.org; M° Concorde), by rue de Rivoli, once a royal tennis court and now a venue for major photographic exhibitions, and the **Orangerie**.

Originally designed to protect the Tuileries' orange trees, the Orangerie (daily except Tues 9am–6pm; €7.50; Ⓦ www.musee-orangerie.fr), an elegant Neoclassical-style building, now houses a private art collection including eight of Monet's giant water-lily paintings, vast, mesmerizing canvases executed in the last years of the artist's life. On the lower floor of the museum is a fine collection of paintings by Monet's contemporaries. Highlights include a number of Cézanne still lifes, sensuous nudes by Renoir and vibrant landscapes by Derain.

The Louvre

The palace of the **Louvre** cuts a magnificent Classical swathe right through the centre of the city – a fitting setting for one of the world's grandest art galleries. Originally little more than a feudal fortress, the castle was rebuilt in the new Renaissance style from 1546, under François I. Over the next century and a half, France's rulers steadily aggrandized their palace without significantly altering its style, and the result is an amazingly harmonious building. Admittedly, Napoleon's pink marble Arc du Carrousel, standing at the western end of the main courtyard, looks a bit out of place, but the only really radical makeover dates from 1989, when I.M. Pei's controversial **Pyramide** erupted from the centre of the Cour Napoléon like a visitor from another architectural planet.

The origins of the art gallery, the **Musée du Louvre**, lie in the French kings' personal art collections. The royal academy mounted exhibitions, known as salons, in the palace as early as 1725, but the Louvre was only opened as a public **art gallery** in 1793, in the midst of the Revolution. Within a decade, Napoleon's wagonloads of war booty transformed the Louvre's art collection into the world's largest – and not all the loot has been returned.

Quite separate from the Louvre proper, but still within the palace, are three museums under the umbrella name of **Les Arts Décoratifs**, dedicated to fashion and textiles, decorative arts, and advertising; the entrance is at 107 rue de Rivoli.

The Musée du Louvre

It's easy to be put off by tales of long queues outside the Pyramide, miles of foot-wearying corridors or multilingual jostles in front of the *Mona Lisa*, but there are ways around such hassles: you can use a back entrance, stop at one of the cafés or make for a less well-known section. Ultimately, the draw of the mighty collections of the **Musée du Louvre** is irresistible.

Orientation

From the Hall Napoléon under the **Pyramide**, stairs lead into each of the three wings: Denon (south), Richelieu (north) and Sully (east, around the giant quadrangle of the Cour Carré). Few visitors will be able to resist the allure of the *Mona Lisa*, in the **Denon** wing, housed along with the rest of the Louvre's Italian paintings and sculptures and its large-scale French nineteenth-century canvases. A relatively peaceful alternative would be to focus on the grand chronologies of French painting and sculpture, in the **Richelieu** wing. For a complete change of scene, descend to the **Medieval Louvre** section on the lower ground floor of Sully where you'll find the dramatic stump of Philippe-Auguste's keep and vestiges of Charles V's medieval palace walls.

A **floor plan**, available free from the information booth in the Hall Napoléon, will help you find your way around. It's wise not to attempt to see too much – even if you spent the entire day here you'd only see a fraction of the collection. The museum's size does at least make it easy to get away from the crowds – beyond the Denon wing you can mostly explore in peace. You can always step outside for a break, but three moderately expensive **cafés** are enticing and open all day. *Café Richelieu* (first floor, Richelieu), elegant and relatively quiet, has a summer-only terrace, with views of the Pyramide. *Café Denon* (lower ground floor, Denon) is cosily romantic, while *Café Mollien* (first floor, Denon) has a summer terrace and some inexpensive snacks. The various cafés and restaurants under the Pyramide are mostly noisy and overpriced.

Antiquities

Oriental Antiquities covers the sculptures, stone-carved writings, pottery and other relics of the ancient Middle and Near East, including the Mesopotamian, Sumerian, Babylonian, Assyrian and Phoenician civilizations, plus the art of ancient Persia. The highlight of this section is the boldly sculpted stonework, much of it in relief. Watch out for the statues and busts depicting the young Sumerian prince Gudea, and the black, two-metre-high Code of Hammurabi, a hugely important find from the Mesopotamian civilization, dating from around 1800 BC. The utterly refined **Arts of Islam** collection is next door.

Egyptian Antiquities contains jewellery, domestic objects, sandals, sarcophagi and dozens of examples of the delicate naturalism of Egyptian decorative technique, such as the wall tiles depicting a piebald calf galloping through fields of papyrus, and a duck taking off from a marsh. Among the major exhibits are the Great Sphinx, carved from a single block of pink granite, the polychrome Seated Scribe statue, the striking, life-size wooden statue of Chancellor Nakhti, a bust of Amenophis IV and a low-relief sculpture of Sethi I and the goddess Hathor.

The collection of **Greek and Roman Antiquities**, mostly statues, is one of the finest in the world. The biggest crowd-pullers in the museum, after the *Mona Lisa*, are here: the *Winged Victory of Samothrace*, at the top of Denon's great staircase, and the *Venus de Milo*. Venus is surrounded by hordes of antecedent Aphrodites, from the graceful marble head known as the "Kaufmann Head" and the delightful *Venus of Arles* to the strange *Dame d'Auxerre*. In the Roman section a sterner style takes over, but there are some very attractive mosaics from Asia Minor and vivid frescoes from Pompeii and Herculaneum.

Sculpture

The **French Sculpture** section is arranged on the lowest two levels of the Richelieu wing, with the more monumental pieces housed in two grand, glass-roofed court-yards: the four triumphal *Marly Horses* grace the Cour Marly, while Cour Puget has Puget's dynamic *Milon de Crotone* as its centrepiece. The surrounding rooms trace the development of sculpture in France from painful Romanesque Crucifixions to the lofty public works of David d'Angers. The startlingly realistic Gothic pieces – notably the Burgundian *Tomb of Philippe Pot*, complete with hooded mourners – and the experimental Mannerist works are particularly rewarding, but towards the end of the course you may find yourself crying out for an end to all those gracefully perfect nudes and grandiose busts. You'll have to leave the Louvre for Rodin, but an alternative antidote lies in the intense **Italian and northern European** sections, on the lower two floors of Denon, where you'll find such bold masterpieces as two of Michelangelo's writhing *Slaves*, Duccio's virtuoso *Virgin and Child Surrounded by Angels*, and some severely Gothic Virgins from Flanders and Germany.

Objets d'Art

The vast **Objets d'Art** section, on the first floor of the Richelieu wing, presents the finest tapestries, ceramics, jewellery and furniture commissioned by France's wealthiest and most influential patrons. Walking through the entire 81-room chronology affords a powerful sense of the evolution of aesthetic taste at its most refined and opulent. The exception is the **Middle Ages** section, which is of a decidedly pious nature, while the apotheosis of the whole experience comes towards the end, as the circuit passes through the breathtakingly plush **apartments** of Napoléon III's Minister of State.

Painting

The largest section by far is **Painting**. A good place to start a tour of **French painting** is in the Sully wing with the master of French Classicism, Poussin, whose profound, mythological themes influenced artists such as Lorrain, Le Brun and Rigaud. After this grandly Classical suite of rooms, the more intimate paintings of Watteau come as a relief, followed by Chardin's intense still lifes and the inspired Rococo sketches by Fragonard known as the *Figures of Fantasy*. From the southern wing of Sully to the end of this section, the chilly wind of Neoclassicism blows through the paintings of Gros, Gérard, Prud'hon, David and Ingres, contrasting with the more sentimental style that begins with Greuze and continues into the Romanticism of Géricault and Delacroix. The final set of rooms takes in Millet, Corot and the Barbizon school of painting, prefiguring the Impressionists.

The nineteenth century is most dramatically represented in the second area of the Louvre devoted to painting, on the first floor of the Denon wing. A pair of giant rooms is dedicated to Nationalism and Romanticism, respectively, featuring some of France's best-known works including such gigantic, epic canvases as David's *Coronation of Napoleon in Notre-Dame*, Géricault's *The Raft of the Medusa*, and Delacroix's *Liberty Leading the People*, the icon of nineteenth-century revolution.

Denon also houses the frankly staggering **Italian collection**. The high-ceilinged Salon Carré – which has been used to exhibit paintings since the first "salon" of the Royal Academy in 1725 – displays the so-called Primitives, with works by Uccello, Giotto, Cimabue and Fra Angelico. To the west of the Salon, the famous Grande Galerie stretches into the distance, parading all the great names of the Italian Renaissance – Mantegna, Filippo Lippi, Leonardo da Vinci, Raphael, Correggio, Titian. The playfully troubled Mannerists kick in about halfway along, but the second half of the Galerie dwindles in quality and representativeness as it moves towards the eighteenth century. Leonardo's *Mona Lisa*, along with Paolo Veronese's huge

Marriage at Cana, hangs in the Salle des États, a room halfway along the Galerie. If you want to catch *La Joconde* – as she's known to the French – without a swarm of admirers, go first or last thing in the day. At the far end of Denon, the relatively small but worthwhile **Spanish** collection has some notable Goya portraits.

The western end of Richelieu's second floor is given over to a more selective collection of **German**, **Flemish** and **Dutch** paintings, with a brilliant set of works by Rubens and no less than twelve Rembrandts, including some powerful self-portraits. Interspersed throughout the painting section are rooms dedicated to the Louvre's impressive collection of **prints and drawings**, exhibited in rotation.

Les Arts Décoratifs

The westernmost wing of the Louvre palace houses a separate museum, **Les Arts Décoratifs** ("applied arts"; entrance at 107 rue de Rivoli; Tues, Wed & Fri–Sun 11am–6pm, Thurs 11am–9pm; €9; ⓦwww.lesartsdecoratifs.fr). The core of the collection is the **Musée des Arts Décoratifs**, whose eclectic collection of art objects and superbly crafted furnishing certainly fits the "design" theme. The works in the "historical" rooms (from the medieval period through to Art Nouveau) may seem humble in comparison with those in the Louvre's Objets d'Art section, but these furnishings were made to be used, and feel more accessible as a result. There are curious and beautiful chairs, dressers and tables, religious paintings, Venetian glass and some wonderful tapestries. A number of "period rooms" have been reconstituted top-to-toe in the style of different eras; there's even an entire 1903 bedroom by Hector Guimard, the Art Nouveau designer behind Paris's métro stations. The topmost floors show off designer furnishings from the 1940s through to the present day, with some great examples from the prince of French design, Philippe Starck. Separate galleries focus on jewellery and toys.

The **Musée de la Mode et du Textile** holds high-quality exhibitions demonstrating the most brilliant and cutting edge of Paris fashions from all eras. Recent exhibitions have included couture handbags, a history of fashion curated by Christian Lacroix, and a retrospective of the Parisian designer, Sonia Rykiel. Immediately above, the **Musée de la Publicité** shows off its collection of advertising posters through cleverly themed, temporary exhibitions. Designed by the French über-architect Jean Nouvel, the space mixes exposed brickwork and steel panelling with crumbling Louvre finery.

The Opéra district

Between the Louvre and **boulevards Haussmann**, **Montmartre**, **Poissonnière** and **Bonne-Nouvelle** to the north lies the city's main **commercial and financial district**. Right at its heart stand the solid institutions of the Banque de France and the Bourse, while just to the north, beyond the glittering **Opéra-Garnier**, are the large department stores **Galeries Lafayette** and **Printemps**. More well-heeled shopping is concentrated on the rue **St-Honoré** in the west and the streets around aristocratic place Vendôme, lined with top couturiers, jewellers and art dealers. Scattered around the whole area are the delightful, secretive **passages** – nineteenth-century arcades that hark back to shopping from a different era.

The passages

Among the most attractive of the *passages* is the **Galerie Vivienne**, between rue Vivienne and rue des Petits-Champs, its decor of Grecian and marine motifs providing a suitably flamboyant backdrop for its smart shops, such as a branch of Jean-Paul Gaultier. But the most stylish examples are the three-storey **passage du Grand-Cerf**, between rue St-Denis and rue Dussoubs, and **Galerie Véro-Dodat**, between rue Croix-des-Petits-Champs and rue Jean-Jacques-Rousseau, named after the two pork butchers who set it up in 1824. This last is the most homogeneous and aristocratic *passage*, with painted ceilings and faux marble columns. North of rue St-Marc, the several arcades making up the **passage des Panoramas** are more workaday, although they do retain a great deal of character: there's an old brasserie with carved wood panelling (now a tea shop, *L'Arbre à Cannelle*, see p.138) and a printshop with its original 1867 fittings, as well as bric-a-brac shops, and stamp and secondhand postcard dealers. **Passage Jouffroy**, across boulevard Montmartre, harbours a number of quirky shops, including one selling antique walking sticks and another stocking exquisite dolls' house furniture.

The Madeleine and the Opéra-Garnier

Set back from the boulevard des Capucines and crowning the avenue de l'Opéra is the dazzling **Opéra-Garnier**, which was constructed from 1860 to 1875 as part of Napoléon III's new vision of Paris. The building's architect, Charles Garnier, whose golden bust by Carpeaux can be seen on the rue Auber side of his edifice, pulled out all the stops to provide a suitably grand space in which Second Empire high society could parade and be seen. The facade is a fabulous extravaganza of white, pink and green marble, colonnades, rearing horses, winged angels and niches holding gleaming gold busts of composers. You can look round the equally sumptuous **interior** (daily 10am–4.30pm; €9), including the plush auditorium – rehearsals permitting – the colourful ceiling of which is the work of Chagall, depicting scenes from well-known operas and ballets. The visit includes the **Bibliothèque-Musée de l'Opéra**, dedicated to the artists connected with the Opéra throughout its history, and containing model sets, dreadful nineteenth-century paintings and rather better temporary exhibitions on operatic themes.

West of the Opéra, occupying nearly the whole of the place de la Madeleine, the imperious-looking **Église de la Madeleine** is the parish church of the cream of Parisian high society. Modelled on a Greek classical temple, it's surrounded by 52 Corinthian columns and fronted by a huge pediment depicting the Last Judgement. Originally intended as a monument to Napoleon's army, it narrowly escaped being turned into a railway station before finally being consecrated to Mary Magdalene in 1845. Inside, a wonderfully theatrical sculpture, *Mary Magdalene Ascending to Heaven,* draws your eye to the high altar.

If the Madeleine caters to spiritual needs, the rest of the square is given over to nourishment of quite a different kind, for this is where Paris's top gourmet food stores Fauchon and Hédiard are located. On the east side of the Madeleine church is one of the city's oldest **flower markets** dating back to 1832, open every day except Monday while, nearby, some rather fine Art Nouveau public toilets are definitely worth inspecting.

Place Vendôme

A short walk east of the Madeleine along ancient rue St-Honoré, a preserve of top fashion designers and art galleries, lies **place Vendôme**, one of the city's most impressive set pieces. Built by Versailles' architect Hardouin-Mansart, it's a pleasingly symmetrical, eight-sided *place*, enclosed by a harmonious ensemble of elegant mansions, graced with Corinthian pilasters, *mascarons* and steeply pitched roofs. Once the grand residences of tax collectors and financiers, they now house such luxury establishments as the *Ritz* hotel, Cartier, Bulgari and other top-flight jewellers, lending the square a decidedly exclusive air. No. 12, now occupied by Chaumet jewellers, is where Chopin died in 1849.

Somewhat out of proportion with the rest of the square, the centrepiece is a towering triumphal **column**, surmounted by a statue of Napoleon dressed as Caesar, raised in 1806 to celebrate the Battle of Austerlitz – bronze reliefs of scenes of the battle, cast from 1200 recycled Austro-Russian cannons, spiral their way up the column.

The Palais Royal and Bibliothèque Nationale

At the eastern end of rue St-Honoré stands the handsome, colonnaded **Palais Royal**, built for Cardinal Richelieu in 1624, though much modified and renovated since. The current building houses various governmental bodies and the **Comédie Française**, a long-standing venue for the classics of French theatre. To its rear lie gardens lined with stately three-storey houses built over arcades housing quirky antique and designer shops. It's an attractive and peaceful oasis, with avenues of limes, fountains and flowerbeds. You'd hardly guess that this was a site of gambling dens, brothels and funfair attractions until the Grands Boulevards took up the baton in the 1830s. Folly, some might say, has returned in the form of Daniel Buren's art installation, which consists of black and white striped pillars, rather like sticks of Brighton rock, all of varying heights, dotted about the palace's main courtyard.

The gardens are a handy short cut from the rue de Rivoli to the **Bibliothèque Nationale** (Ⓦ www.bnf.fr) on the north side; you can enter free of charge and peer into the atmospheric reading rooms, though some look rather bereft, as many books have now been transferred to the new François Mitterrand site on the Left Bank. Visiting the library's temporary exhibitions (closed Mon) will give you access to the beautiful **Galerie Mazarine**, with its panelled ceilings painted by Romanelli (1617–62). It's also worth calling into the **Cabinet des Monnaies, Médailles et Antiques** (Mon–Fri 1–5.45pm, Sat 1–4.45pm, Sun noon–6pm; free), a permanent display of coins and ancient treasures, such as Charlemagne's ivory chess set, built up by successive kings from Philippe-Auguste onwards.

Les Halles and around

Les Halles was the city's main food market for over eight hundred years. It was moved out to the suburbs in 1969, despite widespread opposition, and replaced by a large underground shopping and leisure complex, known as the Forum des Halles, and an RER/métro interchange. Unsightly, run down, even unsavoury in parts, the complex is now widely acknowledged as an architectural disaster – so much so that steps are under way to give it a major facelift. The French architect David Mangin, who won the competition to redevelop the site, plans to suspend a **vast glass roof** over the forum, allowing light to flood in, while also redesigning the gardens and creating a wide promenade on the model of Barcelona's Ramblas. Work is due to be completed by 2014.

The **Forum des Halles** centre stretches underground from the Bourse du Commerce rotunda to rue Pierre-Lescot and is spread over four levels. The overground section comprises aquarium-like arcades of shops, arranged around a sunken patio, and landscaped gardens. The shops are mostly devoted to high-street fashion and there's also a large FNAC bookshop and the Forum des Créateurs, an outlet for young fashion designers. It's not all commerce, however: there's scope for various diversions including swimming, billiards and movie-going.

Although little now remains of the former working-class quarter, you can still catch a flavour of the old Les Halles atmosphere in some of the surrounding bars and bistros and on the lively market street of **rue Montorgueil** to the north, where traditional grocers, horse butchers and fishmongers continue to ply their trade.

At the foot of rue Montorgueil stands another survivor from the past, the beautiful, gracefully buttressed church of **St-Eustache**. Built between 1532 and 1637, it's a glorious fusion of Gothic and Renaissance styles, with soaring vaults, Corinthian pilasters and arcades. It was the scene of Molière's baptism, and Rameau and Marivaux are buried here.

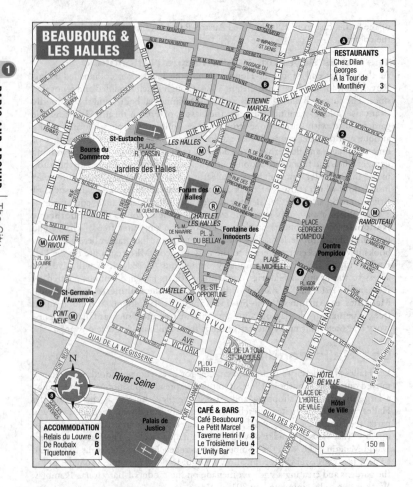

Centre Georges Pompidou

The **Centre Georges Pompidou** (aka Beaubourg; Ⓦ www.centrepompidou.fr; Mº Rambuteau/Hôtel-de-Ville), housing the Musée National d'Art Moderne, is one of the twentieth century's most radical buildings and its opening in 1977 gave rise to some violent reactions. Since then, however, it has won over critics and public alike, and has become one of the city's most recognizable landmarks. Architects Renzo Piano and Richard Rogers freed up maximum gallery space inside by placing all infrastructure outside: utility pipes and escalator tubes, all brightly colour-coded according to their function, climb around the exterior in crazy snakes-and-ladders fashion. The transparent escalator on the front of the building, giving access to the modern art museum, affords superb views over the city. Aside from the museum there are two cinemas, performance spaces and a library.

Tickets for the museum cost €10 and include entry to temporary exhibitions. Under-18s, plus EU residents aged 18-25, get in free – pick up a pass at the ticket office. Admission to the museum and exhibitions is free for everyone on the first Sunday of the month.

Musée National d'Art Moderne

The superb **Musée National d'Art Moderne** (daily except Tues 11am–9pm; see above for admission) presides over the fourth and fifth floors of the Centre Pompidou, with the fifth floor covering 1905 to 1960 and the fourth 1960 to the present day. Thanks to an astute acquisitions policy and some generous gifts, the collection is a near-complete visual essay on the history of twentieth-century art and is so large that only a fraction of the fifty thousand works are on display at any one time. Since the opening of the museum's sister site in Metz (see p.257) in 2010 many more of the museum's holdings have been brought out of storage and put on display.

In the section covering the years **1905 to 1960** Fauvism, Cubism, Dada, abstract art, Surrealism and abstract expressionism are all well represented. There's a particularly rich collection of Matisses, ranging from early Fauvist works to his late masterpieces – a stand-out is his *Tristesse du Roi*, a moving meditation on old age and memory. Other highlights include a number of Picasso's and Braque's early Cubist paintings and a substantial collection of Kandinskys, including his pioneering abstract works *Avec l'arc noir* and *Composition à la tache rouge*. A whole room is usually devoted to the characteristically colourful paintings of Robert and Sonia Delaunay, contrasting with the darker mood of more unsettling works on display by Surrealists Magritte, Dalí and Ernst.

In the post-1960s section the works of Yves Klein are perhaps the most arresting, especially his luminous blue "body prints", made by covering female models in paint and using them as human paintbrushes. Established **contemporary artists** you're likely to come across include Claes Oldenburg, Christian Boltanski and Daniel Buren. Christian Boltanski is known for his large *mise-en-scène* installations, often containing veiled allusions to the Holocaust. Daniel Buren's works are easy to spot: they all bear his trademark stripes, exactly 8.7cm in width. Some space is dedicated to **video art**, with changing installations by artists such as Jean-Luc Vilmout, Dominique Gonzalez-Foerster and Pierre Huyghe.

Atelier Brancusi

On the northern edge of the Pompidou Centre, down some steps off the sloping piazza, in a small separate building, is the **Atelier Brancusi** (free; daily except Tues 2–6pm), the reconstructed home and studio of Constantin Brancusi. The sculptor bequeathed the contents of his workshop to the state on condition that the rooms be arranged exactly as he left them, and they provide a fascinating insight into how he lived and worked. Studios one and two are crowded with Brancusi's trademark abstract bird and column shapes in highly polished brass and marble, while studios three and four comprise the artist's private quarters.

Quartier Beaubourg and the Hôtel de Ville

The *quartier* around the Centre Pompidou, known as **Beaubourg**, is home to more contemporary art. Jean Tinguely and Niki de St Phalle created the colourful moving sculptures and fountains in the pool in front of Église St-Merri on **place Igor Stravinsky**. This squirting waterworks pays homage to Stravinsky – each fountain corresponds to one of his compositions (*The Firebird*, *The Rite of Spring* and so on) – and shows scant respect for passers-by. On the west side of the square is the entrance to **IRCAM**, a research centre for contemporary music founded by the composer Pierre Boulez and an occasional venue for concerts. To the north are numerous commercial art galleries, occupying the attractive old *hôtels particuliers* on pedestrianized **rue Quincampoix**.

Heading back towards the river along rue Renard will bring you to the **Hôtel de Ville**, the seat of the city's government. It's a mansion of gargantuan proportions in florid neo-Renaissance style, modelled pretty much on the previous building burned down in the Commune in 1871. In front of the Hôtel de Ville, the huge square – a notorious guillotine site in the French Revolution – becomes the location of a popular ice-skating rink from December to March.

The Marais, the Île St-Louis and Bastille

The **Marais** is one of the most seductive districts of Paris. Having largely escaped the heavy-handed attentions of Baron Haussmann, and unspoiled by modern development, the *quartier* is full of handsome Renaissance *hôtels particuliers* (mansions), narrow lanes and inviting cafés and restaurants.

There's a significant Jewish community here, established in the twelfth century and centred on **rue des Rosiers**, and with its long-lasting reputation for tolerance of minorities, the area has become popular with gay Parisians. Prime streets for wandering are **rue des Francs-Bourgeois**, lined with fashion and interior design boutiques, **rue Vieille-du-Temple** and **rue des Archives**, their trendy cafés and bars abuzz at all times of day and night, and **rue Charlot and rue de Poitou** with their art galleries and chic fashion outlets. The Marais' animated streets and atmospheric old buildings would be reason enough to visit, but the *quartier* also boasts a high concentration of excellent museums, not least among them the **Musée Picasso**, the **Carnavalet** history museum and the **Musée d'Art et d'Histoire du Judaïsme**, all set in fine mansions.

Rue des Francs-Bourgeois

Rue des Francs-Bourgeois begins with the eighteenth-century magnificence of the **Palais Soubise**, which houses the Archives Nationales de France and the **Musée de l'Histoire de France**. The palace's fabulous rococo interiors are the setting for changing exhibitions (Mon & Wed–Fri 10am–12.30pm & 2–5.30pm, Sat & Sun 2–5.30pm; €3) drawn from the archives. The adjacent Hôtel de Rohan is also occasionally used for exhibitions from the archives and has more sumptuous interiors, notably the charming Chinese-inspired Cabinet des Singes, whose walls are painted with monkeys acting out various aristocratic scenes.

Musée Carnavalet

Further down rue des Francs-Bourgeois and just off it at 23 rue de Sévigné stands the **Musée Carnavalet** (Tues–Sun 10am–6pm; free; M° St-Paul), which presents the history of Paris from its origins up to the Belle Époque through an extraordinary collection of paintings, sculptures, decorative arts and archeological finds. The museum's setting in two beautiful Renaissance mansions, Hôtel Carnavalet and Hôtel Le Peletier, surrounded by attractive gardens, makes a visit worthwhile in itself. There are 140 rooms in all, with hardly a dull one among them. The **collection** begins with nineteenth- and early twentieth-century shop and inn signs (beautiful objects in themselves) and fascinating models of Paris through the ages. Other highlights on the ground floor include the renovated orangery, which houses a significant collection of Neolithic finds such as wooden pirogues unearthed during the 1990s redevelopment of the Bercy riverside area.

On the **first floor** is a succession of richly decorated Louis XV and Louis XVI salons and boudoirs rescued from buildings destroyed to make way for Haussmann's boulevards, and remounted here more or less intact. Rooms 128 to 148 are largely devoted to the *belle époque*, evoked through vivid paintings of the period and some wonderful Art Nouveau interiors, among which is the sumptuous peacock-green interior designed by Alphonse Mucha for Fouquet's jewellery shop in the rue Royale. José-Maria Sert's Art Deco ballroom, with its extravagant gold-leaf decor and grand-scale paintings, including one of the Queen of Sheba with a train of elephants, is also well preserved. Nearby is a section on literary life at the beginning of the twentieth century, including a reconstruction of Proust's cork-lined bedroom. The **second floor** has rooms full of mementos of the **French Revolution**: models of the Bastille, the original *Declaration of the Rights of Man and the Citizen*, tricolours and liberty caps, sculpted allegories of Reason, crockery with Revolutionary slogans, models of the guillotine and execution orders to make you shed a tear for royalists as well as revolutionaries.

Musée Picasso

To the north of the rue des Francs-Bourgeois, at 5 rue de Thorigny, is the **Musée Picasso** (daily except Tues: April–Sept 9.30am–6pm; Oct–March 9.30am–5.30pm; €6.50; free first Sun of the month; ⓦwww.musee-picasso.fr; Mº Filles du Calvaire/St-Paul), closed until 2012 for a major renovation and the addition of an extension. Set in the magnificent seventeenth-century Hôtel Salé, this is the largest collection of Picassos anywhere, representing almost all the major periods of the artist's life from 1905 onwards. Many of the works were owned by Picasso and on his death in 1973 were seized by the state in lieu of taxes owed. The result is an unedited body of work, which, although not including the most recognizable of Picasso's masterpieces, does provide a sense of the artist's development and an insight into the person behind the myth. In addition, the collection includes paintings Picasso bought or was given by contemporaries such as Matisse and Cézanne, his African masks and sculptures and photographs of him in his studio taken by Brassaï.

The **exhibition** covers the artist's blue period; his experiments with Cubism and Surrealism; larger-scale works on themes of war and peace; and numerous paintings of the Minotaur and bullfighting, reflecting his later preoccupations with love and death. Perhaps some of the most striking works on display are Picasso's more personal ones – those of his children, wives and lovers – such as *Olga Pensive* (1923), in which his first wife is shown lost in thought, the deep blue of her dress reflecting her mood.

The museum also holds a substantial number of Picasso's **engravings**, **ceramics** and **sculpture**, showcasing the remarkable ease with which the artist moved from one medium to another. Some of the most arresting sculptures are those he created from recycled household objects, such as the endearing *La Chèvre* (Goat), whose stomach is made from a basket, and *Tête de Taureau*, an ingenious pairing of a bicycle seat and handlebars.

The Jewish quarter

One block south of the rue des Francs-Bourgeois, the area around narrow **rue des Rosiers** has traditionally been the **Jewish quarter** of the city, though recent incursions by trendy fashion boutiques are threatening to change the character of the quarter. Some Jewish shops survive, however, such as the odd kosher food shop, a Hebrew bookstore and falafel takeaways, testimony to the influence of the North African *Sephardim*, who replenished Paris's Jewish population, depleted when its *Ashkenazim* were rounded up by the Nazis and the French police and transported to the concentration camps.

That fate befell some of the inhabitants who once lived in the Hôtel de St-Aignan, at 71 rue de Temple, just northeast of the Centre Pompidou, now fittingly home to the **Musée d'Art et d'Histoire du Judaisme** (Mon–Fri 11am–6pm, Sun 10am–6pm; €6.80; ⓦwww.mahj.org; Mº Rambuteau), tracing the culture, history and artistic endeavours of the Jewish people from the Middle Ages to the present day. The focus is on the history of Jews in France, but there are also many artefacts from the rest of Europe and North Africa. Some of the most notable exhibits are a Gothic-style Hanukkah lamp, one of the very few French Jewish artefacts to survive from the period before the expulsion of the Jews

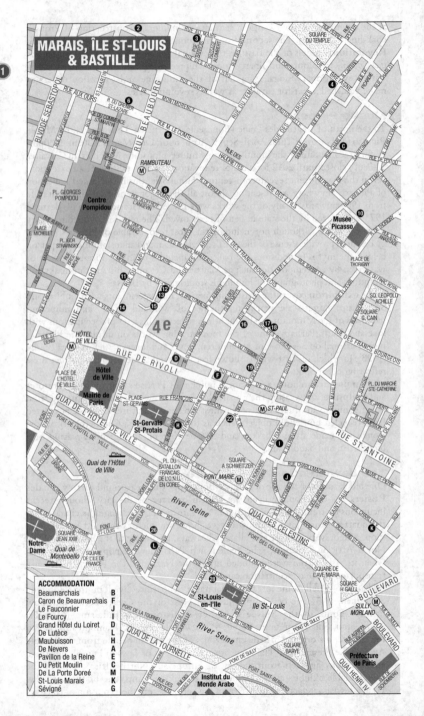

MARAIS, ÎLE ST-LOUIS & BASTILLE

ACCOMMODATION

Beaumarchais	B
Caron de Beaumarchais	F
Le Fauconnier	J
Le Fourcy	I
Grand Hôtel du Loiret	D
De Lutèce	L
Maubuisson	H
De Nevers	A
Pavillon de la Reine	E
Du Petit Moulin	C
De La Porte Dorée	M
St-Louis Marais	K
Sévigné	G

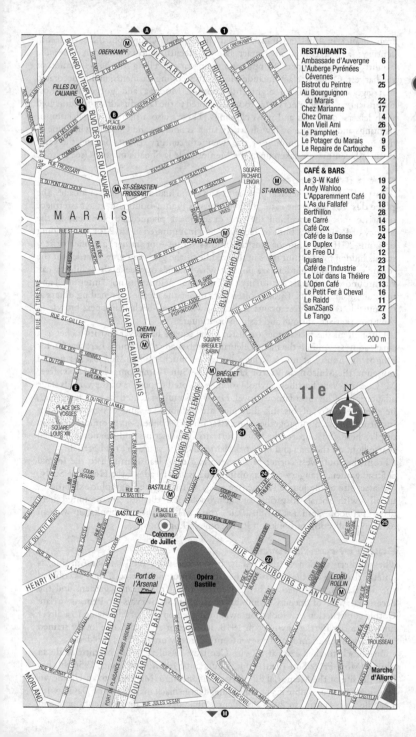

RESTAURANTS

Ambassade d'Auvergne	6
L'Auberge Pyrénées Cévennes	1
Bistrot du Peintre	25
Au Bourguignon du Marais	22
Chez Marianne	17
Chez Omar	4
Mon Vieil Ami	26
Le Pamphlet	7
Le Potager du Marais	9
Le Repaire de Cartouche	5

CAFÉ & BARS

Le 3-W Kafé	19
Andy Wahloo	2
L'Apparement Café	10
L'As du Fallafel	18
Berthillon	28
Le Carré	14
Café Cox	15
Café de la Danse	24
Le Duplex	8
Le Free DJ	12
Iguana	23
Café de l'Industrie	21
Le Loir dans la Théière	20
L'Open Café	13
Le Petit Fer à Cheval	16
Le Raidd	11
SanZSanS	27
Le Tango	3

0 _____ 200 m

11e

from France in 1394; an Italian gilded circumcision chair from the seventeenth century; and a completely intact late nineteenth-century Austrian *sukkah*, a brightly painted wooden hut built as a temporary dwelling for the celebration of the harvest. Other artefacts include Moroccan wedding garments, highly decorated marriage contracts from eighteenth-century Modena and gorgeous, almost whimsical, spice containers. One room is devoted to the **Dreyfus affair**, documented with letters, postcards and press clippings. There's also a significant collection of paintings and sculpture by Jewish artists, such as Soutine and Chagall, who came to live in Paris at the beginning of the twentieth century. Events beyond the early twentieth century are taken up at the Mémorial de la Shoah's museum (see below).

Place des Vosges

A vast square of symmetrical pink brick and stone mansions built over arcades, the **place des Vosges**, at the eastern end of rue des Francs-Bourgeois, is a masterpiece of aristocratic elegance and the first example of planned development in the history of Paris. It was built by Henri IV and inaugurated in 1612 for the wedding of Louis XIII and Anne of Austria; Louis's statue – or, rather, a replica of it – stands hidden by chestnut trees in the middle of the grass and gravel gardens at the square's centre. The gardens are popular with families on weekends – children can run around on the grass (unusually for Paris the "pelouse" is not "interdite") and mess about in sandpits. Buskers often play under the arcades, serenading diners at the outside tables of restaurants and cafés, while well-heeled shoppers browse in the upmarket art, antique and fashion boutiques.

Through all the vicissitudes of history, the square has never lost its cachet as a smart address. Among the many celebrities who made their homes here was Victor Hugo: his house, at no. 6, where he wrote much of *Les Misérables*, is now a museum, the **Maison de Victor Hugo** (Tues–Sun 10am–6pm; closed hols; free; M° Chemin-Vert/Bastille); a whole room is devoted to posters of the various stage adaptations of his most famous novel. Hugo was multi-talented: as well as writing, he drew – many of his ink drawings are exhibited – and designed his own furniture; he even put together the extraordinary Chinese-style dining room on display here. That apart, the usual portraits, manuscripts and memorabilia shed sparse light on the man and his work, particularly if you don't read French.

From the southwest corner of the square, a door leads through to the formal château garden, orangery and exquisite Renaissance facade of the **Hôtel de Sully**, the sister site to the Jeu de Paume (see p.93). Changing photographic exhibitions, usually with social, historical or anthropological themes, are mounted here (Tues–Fri noon–7pm, Sat & Sun 10am–7pm; €7), and there's a bookshop with an extensive collection of books on Paris, some in English.

South of rue de Rivoli

The southern section of the Marais, below rues de Rivoli and St-Antoine, is quieter than the northern part and has some atmospheric streets, such as cobbled rue des Barres, perfumed with the scent of roses from nearby gardens and the occasional waft of incense from the church of **St-Gervais-St-Protais**, a late Gothic construction that looks somewhat battered on the outside owing to a direct hit from a Big Bertha howitzer in 1918. Its interior contains some lovely stained glass, carved misericords and a seventeenth-century organ – Paris's oldest.

One block further east, at 17 rue Geoffroy-l'Asnier, is the **Mémorial de la Shoah** (Mon–Fri & Sun 10am–6pm, Thurs until 10pm; free). Since 1956 this has been the site of the Mémorial du Martyr Juif Inconnu (Memorial to an Unknown Jewish Martyr), a sombre crypt containing a large black marble star of David, with a candle at its centre. In 2005 President Chirac opened a new museum here and unveiled a Wall of Names: four giant slabs of marble engraved with the names of the 76,000 French Jews sent to death camps from 1942 to 1944.

The museum gives an absorbing and moving account of the history of Jews in France, especially Paris, during the German occupation. There are last letters from deportees to their families, videotaped testimony from survivors, numerous ID cards and photos. The museum ends with the Mémorial des Enfants, a collection of photos, almost unbearable to look at, of 2500 French children, each with the date of their birth and the date of their deportation.

A little further east, between rues Fourcy and François-Miron, the handsome Hôtel Hénault de Cantoube, with its two-storey crypt, is home to the **Maison Européenne de la Photographie** (Wed–Sun 11am–8pm; €6.50, free Wed after 5pm; ⓦwww.mep-fr.org; Mº St-Paul/Pont-Marie) and hosts excellent exhibitions of contemporary photography; the entrance is at 5/7 rue du Fourcy.

The Île St-Louis

Often considered the most romantic part of Paris, the peaceful **Île St-Louis** is prime strolling territory. Unlike its larger neighbour, the Île de la Cité, the Île St-Louis has no heavyweight sights, just austerely handsome seventeenth-century houses on single-lane streets, tree-lined *quais*, a school, church, restaurants, cafés, interesting little shops, and the best sorbets in the world at *Berthillon*, 31 rue St-Louis-en-l'Île (see p.137). The island is particularly atmospheric in the evening, and an arm-in-arm wander along the *quais* is a must in any lover's itinerary.

Bastille

The landmark column topped with the gilded "Spirit of Liberty" on **place de la Bastille** was erected not to commemorate the surrender in 1789 of the prison – whose only visible remains have been transported to square Henri-Galli at the end of boulevard Henri-IV – but the July Revolution of 1830 that replaced the autocratic Charles X with the "Citizen King" Louis-Philippe. When Louis-Philippe fled in the more significant 1848 Revolution, his throne was burnt beside the column and a new inscription added. However, it is the events of July 14, 1789, symbol of the end of feudalism in Europe, that France celebrates every year on Bastille Day.

The Bicentennial in 1989 was marked by the inauguration of the **Opéra-Bastille**, President Mitterrand's pet project. Filling almost the entire block between rues de Lyon, Charenton and Moreau, it has shifted the focus of place de la Bastille, so that the column is no longer the pivotal point; in fact, it's easy to miss it altogether when dazzled by the night-time glare of lights emanating from this "hippopotamus in a bathtub", as one critic dubbed the Opéra.

The building's construction destroyed no small amount of low-rent housing, but, as with most speculative developments, the pace of change is uneven, and cobblers and ironmongers still survive alongside cocktail haunts and sushi bars, making the **quartier de la Bastille** a simultaneously gritty and stylish quarter. **Place** and **rue d'Aligre**, east of square Trousseau, still have their raucous daily market and, on **rue de Lappe**, *Balajo* is one remnant of a very Parisian tradition: the *bals musettes*, or music halls of 1930s *gai Paris*, frequented between the wars by Piaf, Jean Gabin and Rita Hayworth. It was founded by one Jo de France, who introduced glitter and spectacle into what were then seedy gangster dives, and brought Parisians from the other side of the city to the rue de Lappe lowlife. Now the street is crammed with bars drawing a largely tourist crowd. Bars and cafés have also sprung up in the surrounding streets, especially on **rue de Charonne**, also home to fashion boutiques and wacky interior designers, while alternative, hippy outfits cluster on **rues Keller** and **de la Roquette**.

Just south of here you can find quiet havens in the courtyards of **rue du Faubourg-St-Antoine**. Since the fifteenth century, this has been the principal artisan and working-class *quartier* of Paris, the cradle of revolutions and mother of street-fighters. From its beginnings the principal trade associated with it has been **furniture-making**, and the maze of interconnecting yards and *passages* are still full of the workshops of the related trades: marquetry, stainers, polishers and inlayers.

Quartier Latin

South of the river, the **Rive Gauche** (Left Bank) has long maintained an "alternative" identity, opposed to the formal ambience of the Right Bank. Generally understood to describe the 5e and 6e arrondissements, the Left Bank was at the heart of *les évènements*, the revolutionary political "events" of May 1968. Since that infamous summer, however, rampant gentrification has transformed the artists' garrets and beatnik cafés into designer pads and top-end restaurants, and the legend is only really kept alive by the student population of the **Quartier Latin** – so-called for the learned Latin of the medieval scholars who first settled here, or possibly for the abundant Roman ruins. The pivotal point of this "Latin quarter" is **place St-Michel**, where the tree-lined **boulevard St-Michel** begins. It's a busy commercial thoroughfare these days, but the universities on all sides still give an intellectual air to the place, and the cafés and shops are still jammed with young people.

Around St-Séverin

The touristy scrum is at its most intense around **rue de la Huchette**, just east of the place St-Michel. Hemmed in by cheap bars and Greek restaurants the tiny Théâtre de la Huchette (see p.153) is the last bastion of the area's postwar beatnik heyday, still showing Ionesco's absurdist plays more than fifty years on. Connecting rue de la Huchette to the riverside is **rue du Chat-qui-Pêche**, a narrow slice of medieval Paris as it was before Haussmann got to work.

At the end of rue de la Huchette, **rue St-Jacques** follows the line of the main street of Roman Paris, and was the road up which millions of medieval pilgrims trudged at the start of their long march to Santiago (Saint Jacques, in French) de Compostela in Spain. One block south of rue de la Huchette, just west of rue St-Jacques, is the mainly fifteenth-century church of **St-Séverin**, whose entrance is on rue des Prêtres St-Séverin (Mon–Sat 11am–7.30pm, Sun 9am–8.30pm; M° St-Michel/Cluny–La Sorbonne). It's one of the city's more intense churches, its flamboyant (distinguished by *flamboyant*, or flame-like, carving) choir resting on a virtuoso spiralling central pillar and its windows filled with edgy stained glass by the modern French painter Jean Bazaine. East of rue St-Jacques, and back towards the river, **square Viviani** provides a perfect view of Notre-Dame and a pleasant patch of green. The mutilated church behind is **St-Julien-le-Pauvre** (daily 9.30am–1pm & 3–6.30pm; M° St-Michel/Maubert-Mutualité). The same age as Notre-Dame, it used to be the venue for university assemblies until rumbustious students tore it apart in 1524. Across rue Lagrange from the square, rue de la Bûcherie is the home of the celebrated English-language bookshop **Shakespeare and Co** (see p.154), which acts as an informal hostel for wannabe Hemingways who sleep on lumpy divans on the top floor. The original shop with the Shakespeare name – owned by Sylvia Beach, the first publisher of Joyce's *Ulysses* – was on rue de l'Odéon, but even the replacement has become a classic.

The riverbank and Institut du Monde Arabe

A short walk from square Viviani on the riverbank, you'll find old books, postcards and prints on sale from the **bouquinistes**, whose green boxes line the parapets of the **riverside quais**. It's a pleasant walk upstream to **Pont de Sully**, which leads across to the Île St-Louis and offers a dramatic view of Notre-Dame.

Opposite Pont de Sully, you can't miss the bold glass and aluminium mass of the **Institut du Monde Arabe** (Tues–Sun 10am–6pm; Ⓦ www.imarabe.org; M° Jussieu/Cardinal-Lemoine), a cultural centre built to further understanding of the Arab world. Designed by Paris's favourite architect, Jean Nouvel, its broad southern facade, which mimics a *moucharabiyah*, or traditional Arab latticework, is made up of thousands of tiny, photo-sensitive metallic shutters. Inside, a **museum** (€6) traces the evolution of art in the Islamic world but you're better off coming for one of the temporary exhibitions (around €12) or concerts of Arab music. There's also a library and specialist bookshop, and the rooftop **café-restaurant** is a fantastic place to enjoy a mint tea and the view towards the apse of Notre-Dame.

The Musée National du Moyen Age and the Sorbonne

The area around the slopes of the **Montagne Ste-Geneviève**, the hill on which the Panthéon stands, is good for a stroll. The best approach is from **place Maubert** (which has a market on Tues, Thurs & Sat mornings) or from the St-Michel/ St-Germain crossroads, where the walls of the third-century **Roman baths** are visible in the garden of the **Hôtel de Cluny**, a sixteenth-century mansion built by the abbots of the powerful Cluny monastery as their Paris pied-à-terre. It now houses the richly rewarding **Musée National du Moyen Age**, 6 place Paul-Painlevé, off rue des Écoles (daily except Tues 9.15am–5.45pm; €8.50; Ⓦ www.musee-moyenage.fr; M° Cluny-La Sorbonne), a treasure house of medieval sculpture, stained glass, books and *objets d'art*. The real beauties here, however, are the **tapestries**, and supreme among them is *La Dame à la Licorne* ("The Lady with the Unicorn"), a fifteenth-century masterpiece depicting the five senses along with an ambiguous and distinctly erotic image that may represent the virtue in controlling them. You can also see the vaults of the former Roman cold room, or *frigidarium*, which now shelter the beautifully carved Gallo-Roman *Pillar of St-Landry*. The museum puts on high-quality **concerts** of medieval music, including hour-long drop-by recitals (€6) on Monday lunchtimes (12.30pm) and Sunday afternoons (4pm).

The forbidding-looking buildings on the other side of rue des Écoles are the elite educational institutions of the **Sorbonne**, **Collège de France** and the prestigious **Lycée Louis-le-Grand**, which numbers Molière, Robespierre, Sartre and Victor Hugo among its pupils. The hub of the quarter is **place de la Sorbonne**, overlooked by the dramatic Counter-Reformation facade of the Sorbonne's chapel, built in the 1640s by the great Cardinal Richelieu, whose tomb it houses. With its lime trees, fountains and cafés, the square is a lovely place to sit.

The Panthéon, St-Étienne-du-Mont and around

The Montagne Ste-Geneviève is topped by the grandly domed and porticoed **Panthéon** (daily: April–Sept 10am–6.30pm; Oct–March 10am–6pm; €8; Ⓦ pantheon.monuments-nationaux.fr; RER Luxembourg/M° Cardinal-Lemoine), Louis XV's grateful response to Ste-Geneviève, patron saint of Paris, for curing him of illness. The Revolution transformed it into a mausoleum, and the remains of giants of French culture such as Voltaire, Rousseau, Hugo and Zola are entombed in the vast, barrel-vaulted crypt below, along with Marie Curie (the only woman), and Alexandre Dumas, of musketeers fame, who was only "panthéonized" in 2002. The interior is overwhelmingly monumental, bombastically Classical in design – and has a working model of **Foucault's Pendulum** swinging from the dome. The French physicist Léon Foucault devised the experiment to demonstrate vividly the rotation of the earth: while the pendulum appeared to rotate over a 24-hour period, it was in fact the earth beneath it turning. Huge crowds turned up here in 1851 to watch the ground move beneath their feet, and you can do the same today. In summer, guided tours (April–Sept

QUARTIER LATIN

Palais de Justice

Hôtel Dieu

Ile de la Cité

Crypte Archéologique

RUE D'ARCOLE

QUAI AUX FLEURS

RUE DE LA CITÉ

RUE DES URSINS

RUE CHANOINESSE

PONT ST-MICHEL

QUAI DU MARCHE NEUF

PLACE DU PARVIS NOTRE-DAME

PONT AU DOUBLE

QUAI DE LA CORSE

QUAI ST-MICHEL

PLACE ST-MICHEL

RUE DE LA HUCHETTE

PLACE DU PETIT PONT

Notre-Dame

SQUARE JEAN XXIII

RUE DU CLOITRE NOTRE-DAME

6e

RUE DE SAVOIE

R. DES GRANDS AUGUSTINS

RUE ST-ANDRÉ DES ARTS

RUE SUGER

COUR DU COMMERCE ST-ANDRE

RUE DANTON

RUE SERPENTE

BOULEVARD ST-GERMAIN

ST-MICHEL NOTRE-DAME

St-Séverin

RUE DE LA PARCHEMINERIE

St-Julien-le-Pauvre

QUAI DE MONTEBELLO

PONT DE MONTEBELLO

Quai de Montebello

SQUARE DE L'ILE DE FRANCE

QUAI

CLUNY LA SORBONNE

RUE DE L'ECOLE DE MEDECINE

Musée National du Moyen Age

RUE RACINE

SQUARE ET PLACE P. PAINLEVE

RUE DU SOMMERARD

RUE DE LATRAN

MAUBERT MUTUALITE

PLACE MAUBERT

RUE MONGE

RUE DE BIEVRE

RUE DE PONTOISE

RUE DE POISSY

BLVD

RUE DOMAT

RUE DANTE

RUE LAGRANGE

RUE GALANDE

RUE DE LA BÛCHERIE

BOULEVARD ST-MICHEL

RUE DE VAUGIRARD

RUE DE MEDICIS

Fontaine Médicis

PLACE EDMOND ROSTAND

La Sorbonne

Chapelle de la Sorbonne

RUE SAINT-JACQUES

RUE CUJAS

RUE SOUFFLOT

RUE CHAMPOLLION

RUE DE LA SORBONNE

SQ. F. A. MARIETTE

PLACE M. BERTHELOT

CIMETIERE SAINT BENOIT

RUE DE LA MONTAGNE STE

RUE DES CARMES

RUE DE L'ECOLE POLYTECHNIQUE

RUE VALETTE

RUE LAPLACE

RUE DES ECOLES

SQUARE P. LANGEVIN

RUE DES ÉCOLES

RUE ST-VICTOR

RUE DE LA BUCHERIE

RUE D'ARRAS

Jardin de Navarre

CARDINAL LEMOINE

RUE DU CARDINAL LEMOINE

RUE MONGE

Panthéon

St-Etienne-du-Mont

PLACE DU PANTHEON

PLACE STE GENEVIEVE

RUE CLOVIS

RUE DESCARTES

5e

RUE ROLLIN

RUE MONGE

St-Jacques-du-Haut-Pas

LUXEMBOURG

BOULEVARD ST-MICHEL

RUE GAY-LUSSAC

RUE ST-JACQUES

RUE MALEBRANCHE

RUE ROYER-COLLARD

RUE DE L'ESTRAPADE

PLACE DE L'ESTRAPADE

RUE PIERRE ET MARIE CURIE

PLACE DE LA CONTRESCARPE

RUE THOUIN

R. BLAINVILLE

RUE LHOMOND

RUE DE L'ARBALETE

RUE ST-MÉDARD

SQ. ORTOLAN

PLACE ORTOLAN

RUE ORTOLAN

PLACE MONGE

MONGE

Ecole Nat. Sup. de Chimie

Ecole Nat. Sup. des Arts Decoratifs

Institut Curie

RUE DES URSULINES

RUE L. THUILLIER

RUE ERASME

RUE DU POT DE FER

RUE RATAUD

RUE AMYOT

PLACE L. HERR

PLACE P. LAMPUE

Ecole Normale Supérieure

RUE DES FEUILLANTINES

RUE P. BROSSOLETTE

RUE J. CALVIN

R. DE L'EPEE DE BOIS

RUE MIRBEL

GRACIEUSE

PASTEUR

CENSIER DAUBENTON

RUE HENRI-BARBUSSE

RUE PIERRE NICOLE

RUE ST-JACQUES

PL. DU VAL-DE-GRACE

PLACE A. LAVERAN

Val-de-Grâce

PGE DES POSTES

RUE VAUQUELIN

RUE CLAUDE BERNARD

RUE DE L'ABBÉ-DE-L'EPEE

RUE DAUBENTON

RUE MOUFFETARD

St-Médard

0   150 m

110

K (400m)

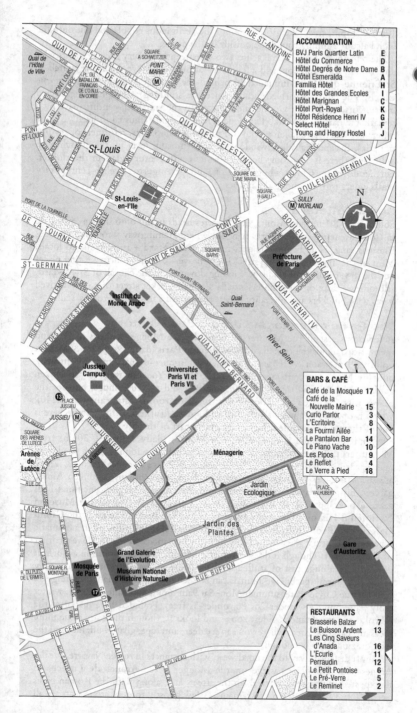

ACCOMMODATION

BVJ Paris Quartier Latin	E
Hôtel du Commerce	D
Hôtel Degrés de Notre Dame	B
Hôtel Esmeralda	A
Familia Hôtel	I
Hôtel des Grandes Ecoles	C
Hôtel Marignan	K
Hôtel Port-Royal	G
Hôtel Résidence Henri IV	F
Select Hôtel	J
Young and Happy Hostel	

BARS & CAFÉ

Café de la Mosquée	17
Café de la Nouvelle Mairie	15
Curio Parlor	3
L'Ecritoire	8
La Fourmi Ailée	1
Le Pantalon Bar	14
Le Piano Vache	10
Les Pipos	9
Le Reflet	4
Le Verre à Pied	18

RESTAURANTS

Brasserie Balzar	7
Le Buisson Ardent	13
Les Cinq Saveurs d'Anada	16
L'Ecurie	11
Perraudin	12
Le Petit Pontoise	6
Le Pré-Verre	5
Le Reminet	2

10am–5.15pm; free) take groups up into the vertiginous cupola and out onto the high balcony running round the outside of the dome.

The remains of Pascal and Racine, two seventeenth-century literary giants who didn't make the Panthéon, and a few relics of Ste-Geneviève, lie in the church of **St-Étienne-du-Mont**, immediately behind the Panthéon on the corner of rue Clovis. The church's garbled facade conceals a stunning and highly unexpected interior, its flamboyant Gothic choir linked to the sixteenth-century nave by a remarkable narrow catwalk. This rood screen is highly unusual in itself, as most others in France have fallen victim to Protestant iconoclasts, reformers or revolutionaries. Exceptionally tall windows at the triforium level fill the church with light, and there is also some beautiful seventeenth-century glass in the cloister. Further down rue Clovis, a huge piece of Philippe-Auguste's twelfth-century **city walls** emerges from among the houses.

Rue Mouffetard

South of St-Étienne-du-Mont, rue Descartes heads uphill onto the tiny **place de la Contrescarpe** – once an arty hangout where Hemingway wrote and Georges Brassens sang. Here begins the ancient **rue Mouffetard** – rue Mouff' to locals. Most of the upper half of the street is given over to rather touristy eating places but the lower half, a cobbled lane winding downhill to the church of **St-Médard**, still offers a taste of the quintessentially Parisian market street that once thrived here, with butchers and speciality cheese shops, and a few greengrocers' stalls.

The Paris mosque and Jardin des Plantes

A few steps east of rue Mouffetard, beyond place Monge, with its market and métro stop, stands the crenellated **Mosquée de Paris** (daily except Fri & Muslim holidays 9am–noon & 2–6pm; €3; ⓦwww.mosquee-de-paris.org; Mᵒ Jussieu), built by Moroccan craftsmen in the early 1920s. You can walk in the sunken garden and patios with their polychrome tiles and carved ceilings, but not the prayer room. There's also a lovely courtyard **tearoom/restaurant** (see p.140), which is open to all, and an atmospheric **hamam** (Turkish bath); bathing here is one of the most enjoyable things to do in this part of the city.

Behind the mosque is the **Jardin des Plantes** (daily 7.30am–7.30pm; free; Mᵒ Austerlitz/Jussieu/Censier-Daubenton), which was founded as a medicinal herb garden in 1626 and gradually evolved into Paris's botanical gardens. There are shady avenues of trees, lawns to sprawl on, rose gardens, a sunken Alpine garden, historic glasshouses, museums and even a zoo. Magnificent floral beds make a fine approach to the collection of buildings that forms the **Muséum National d'Histoire Naturelle** (ⓦwww.mnhn.fr). Best of the lot is the **Grand Galerie de l'Évolution** (daily except Tues 10am–6pm; €9), housed in a dramatic nineteenth-century glass-domed building (the entrance is at the southwest corner of the gardens). Though it doesn't actually tell the story of evolution as such, it does feature a huge cast of stuffed animals, some of them striding dramatically across the central space. Live animals can be seen in the rather mangy **menagerie** near the rue Cuvier gate (summer Mon–Sat 9am–6pm, Sun 9am–6.30pm; winter daily 9am–5pm; €8, under-26s €6, under-3s free). Founded here just after the Revolution, it is France's oldest zoo – and looks it, though there are some more pleasant, park-like areas where you can see deer, antelope, goats, buffaloes and the like, grazing happily enough.

A short distance away to the northwest, with entrances in rue de Navarre, rue des Arènes and through a passage on rue Monge, is the **Arènes de Lutèce**, an unexpected backwater hidden from the street and, along with the Roman baths (see p.109), Paris's only Roman remains. A few ghostly rows of stone seats are all that's left of an amphitheatre that once seated ten thousand; old men playing *boules* in the sand provide the only show.

St-Germain

The northern half of the 6ᵉ arrondissement, centred on **place St-Germain-des-Prés**, is one of the most attractive, lively and wealthy square kilometres in the city – and one of the best places to shop for upmarket clothes. The most dramatic approach is to cross the river from the Louvre by the footbridge, the **Pont des Arts**, from where there's a classic upstream view of the Île de la Cité, with barges moored at the quai de Conti, the Tour St-Jacques and Hôtel de Ville breaking the skyline of the Right Bank. The dome and pediment at the end of the bridge belong to the **Institut de France**, seat of the Académie Française, an august body of writers and scholars whose mission is to safeguard the purity of the French language. This is the most grandiose part of the Left Bank riverfront: to the left is the **Hôtel des Monnaies**, redesigned as the Mint in the late eighteenth century; to the right is the **Beaux-Arts**, the School of Fine Art, whose students throng the *quais* on sunny days, sketchpads on knees. More students can be found relaxing in the **Jardin du Luxembourg**, bordering the Quartier Latin towards the southern end of the *sixième*, which is one of the largest, loveliest and best-loved green spaces in the city.

The riverside

The riverside chunk of the 6ᵉ arrondissement is cut lengthwise by rue St-André-des-Arts and rue Jacob. It's an area full of bookshops, commercial art galleries, antique shops, cafés and restaurants, and if you poke your nose into the courtyards and side streets, you'll find foliage, fountains and peaceful enclaves removed from the bustle of the city. The houses are four to six storeys high, seventeenth- and eighteenth-century, some noble, some bulging and skew, all painted in infinite gradations of grey, pearl and off-white. Broadly speaking, the further west you go the posher the houses get.

Historical associations are legion: Picasso painted *Guernica* in rue des Grands-Augustins; Molière started his career in rue Mazarine; Robespierre et al split ideological hairs at the *Café Procope* in rue de l'Ancienne-Comédie. In rue Visconti, Racine died, Delacroix painted and Balzac's printing business went bust. In the parallel rue des Beaux-Arts, Oscar Wilde died, Corot and Ampère (father of amps) lived and the poet Gérard de Nerval went walking with a lobster on a lead.

If you're looking to eat, you'll find numerous places on **place** and **rue St-André-des-Arts** and along **rue de Buci**, up towards boulevard St-Germain. Rue de Buci preserves a strong flavour of its origins as a market street, with food shops, delis and some excellent cafés and brasseries. Before you get to rue de Buci, there is an intriguing little passage on the left, **Cour du Commerce St-André**, where Marat had a printing press and Dr Guillotin perfected his notorious machine by lopping off sheep's heads.

A delightful corner for a quiet picnic is around rue de l'Abbaye and rue de Furstenberg. Halfway down rue de Furstenburg at no. 6, opposite a tiny square and backing onto a secret garden, Delacroix's old studio is now the **Musée Delacroix** (daily except Tues 9.30am–5pm; €5; Mᵒ Mabillon/St-Germain-des-Prés), with a small collection of the artist's personal belongings as well as minor exhibitions of his work. This is also the beginning of some very upmarket shopping territory, in rue Jacob, rue de Seine and rue Bonaparte in particular.

St-Germain-des-Prés to St-Sulpice

Place St-Germain-des-Prés, the hub of the *quartier*, is only a stone's throw away from the Musée Delacroix, with the famous *Deux Magots* café (see p.141) on the corner of the square, *Flore* (see p.141) adjacent and *Lipp* (see p.141) across the boulevard St-Germain. All three are renowned for the number of philosophical and literary backsides that have shined – and continue to shine – their banquettes, along with plenty of celebrity-hunters. Picasso's bust of a woman, dedicated to the poet Apollinaire, recalls the district's creative heyday. The tower opposite the *Deux Magots* belongs to the **church of St-Germain-des-Prés**, all that remains of an enormous Benedictine monastery. Inside, the transformation from Romanesque to early Gothic is just about visible under the heavy green and gold nineteenth-century paintwork. The last chapel on the south side contains the tomb of the philosopher René Descartes.

South of boulevard St-Germain, the streets around St-Sulpice are calm and classy. **Rue Mabillon** is pretty, with a row of old houses set back below the level of the modern street. On the left are the shops of the **Halles St-Germain**, on the site of a nineteenth-century market. Rue St-Sulpice leads through to the front of the enormous, early eighteenth-century church of **St-Sulpice** (daily 7am–7.30pm; M° St-Sulpice), an austerely Classical building with Doric and Ionic colonnades and Corinthian pilasters in the towers. On the south tower centuries-old uncut masonry blocks protrude from the top, still awaiting the sculptor's chisel. Three Delacroix murals can be seen in the first chapel on the right, but most visitors these days come to see the **gnomon**, a kind of solar clock whose origins and purpose were so compellingly garbled by *The Da Vinci Code*.

All is expensive elegance around **place St-Sulpice**, but if you're heading east towards boulevard St-Michel, the glitzy shops quickly fade into the worthy bookshops and inexpensive restaurants around the École de Médecine.

Jardin du Luxembourg

The Jardin du Luxembourg (daily dawn to dusk) offers formal lawns, gravel paths and resplendent floral parterres, all dotted with sculptures, citrus and olive trees in giant pots (taken inside in winter) and elegant sage-green chairs. Sprawling on the lawns is strictly forbidden, except on the southernmost strip, which gets fantastically crowded on sunny days. The shady **Fontaine de Médicis**, in the northeast corner, is a pleasant place to sit, and there's a delightful **café** roughly 100m northeast of the central pond. The western side of the park is the more active area, with tennis courts and a **puppet theatre** that has been in the same family for the best part of a century, and still puts on enthralling shows (Wed, Sat, Sun and daily during school holidays at 3pm; €4.50). The quieter, wooded southeast corner ends in a miniature orchard of elaborately espaliered pear trees.

The gardens belong to the **Palais du Luxembourg**, which fronts onto **rue de Vaugirard**, Paris's longest street. It was constructed for Marie de Médicis, Henri IV's widow, to remind her of the Palazzo Pitti and Giardino di Boboli of her native Florence. Today, it's the seat of the French Senate. The **Musée du Luxembourg**, at no. 19 rue de Vaugirard, hosts some of the city's largest and most exciting temporary art exhibitions (Mon, Fri & Sat 10.30am–10pm, Tues–Thurs 10.30am–7pm, Sun 9.30am–7pm; around €10–15; Ⓦwww .museeduluxembourg.fr).

Musée d'Orsay

The **Musée d'Orsay** (Tues–Sun 9.30am–6pm, Thurs till 9.45pm; €8, free on first Sun of the month and to under-18s; €12 with the Musée Rodin, see p.123; Ⓦwww.musee-orsay.fr; M° Solférino/RER Musée-d'Orsay) hides its electrifying collection of **Impressionist** works behind the stony facade of a former railway station. Actually, it's not just Impressionism: the museum showcases French painting and sculpture between 1848 and 1914, thus bridging the gap between the

"Classical" Louvre and the "modern" art of the Centre Pompidou. You could spend half a day meandering through in chronological order, but the layout makes it easy to confine your visit to a specific section.

The two **cafés** are fine – if pricey – places to take stock: the tearoom on the upper level has a summer terrace and wonderful views of Montmartre through the giant railway clock, while the café-restaurant on the middle level is resplendently gilded in stunning period style.

The ground level

The **ground floor**, under the great glass arch, is devoted to pre-1870 work, with a double row of sculptures running down the central aisle like railway tracks, and paintings in the odd little bunkers on either side. You'll find works by Ingres, Delacroix and the serious-minded painters and sculptors acceptable to the mid-nineteenth century salons (rooms 1–3), as well as the relatively unusual works of Puvis de Chavannes, Gustave Moreau and the younger Degas (rooms 11–13). The influential **Barbizon school** and the **Realists** (rooms 4–7) are showcased alongside works by Daumier, Corot and Millet – all of which prepares the ground for Manet's scandalous *Déjeuner sur l'herbe* and his provocative *Olympia* (both 1863), the paintings held to have announced the arrival of **Impressionism**. Gentler essays in Realist and early Impressionist landscapes hang next door (rooms 19–23), with works by Pissarro, Sisley and Monet – don't miss his well-loved *Coquelicots* (*Poppies*).

The upper level

To continue chronologically you have to go straight to the **upper level**, done up like a suite of attic studios. After the shock of the Realist portraits by Eugène Carrière and Henri Fantin-Latour in room 29 – not everybody at this time was painting light and colour – you arrive in deep **Impressionist** territory. From this point on, you'll have to fight off a persistent sense of familiarity or recognition – Manet's waterlilies, Degas' *Au Café du L'Absinthe*, Renoir's *Bal du Moulin de la Galette*, Monet's *Femme à l'Ombrelle* – in order to appreciate Impressionism's vibrant, experimental vigour. There's a host of small-scale landscapes and outdoor scenes by Renoir, Sisley, Pissarro and Monet, paintings which owed much of their brilliance to the novel practice of setting up easels in the open to capture the light. Degas' ballet-dancers demonstrate his principal interest in movement and line as opposed to the more common Impressionist concern with light, while his domestic scenes of ordinary working life are touchingly humane. Berthe Morisot, the first woman to join the early Impressionists, is represented by her famous *Le Berceau* (1872), among others. More heavyweight masterpieces can be found in rooms 34 and 39, devoted to **Monet** and **Renoir** in their middle and late periods – the development of Monet's obsession with light is shown with five of his extraordinary Rouen Cathedral series, each painted in different light conditions. Room 35 explodes with the fervid colours and disturbing rhythms of **Van Gogh**, while **Cézanne** attempts to restore his own particular kind of order in room 36.

Passing the **café** you arrive at a dimly lit, melancholy chamber (40) devoted to **pastels** by Redon, Mondrian and others; close by hang **Toulouse-Lautrec**'s deliciously smoky caricatures, including *Dance Mauresque,* a work that depicts the celebrated cancan dancer La Goulue entertaining a washed-up and obese Oscar Wilde. The next and final suite of rooms on this level is given over to the various offspring of Impressionism, and has an edgier, more modern feel, with a much greater emphasis on psychology. It begins with Rousseau's dreamlike *La Charmeuse de Serpents* (1907) and continues past **Gauguin**'s ambivalent Tahitian paintings to **Pointillist** works by Seurat (the famous *Cirque, 1891*), Signac and others.

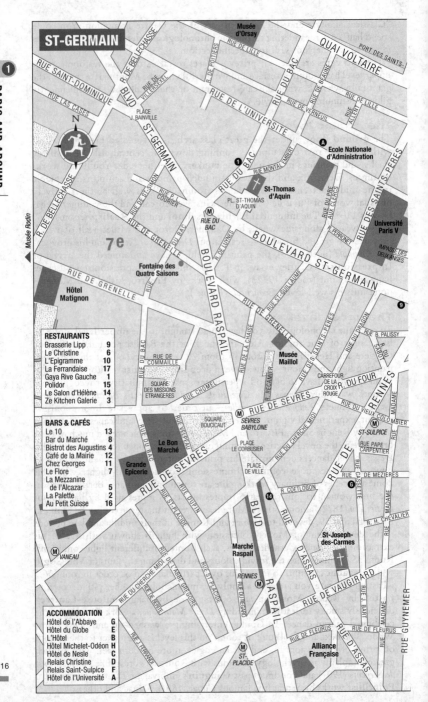

ST-GERMAIN

Musée d'Orsay

QUAI VOLTAIRE
PORT DES SAINTS-

RUE DE LILLE
RUE DE POITIERS
R. DE BELLECHASSE
RUE DE BEAUNE
RUE DU BAC
RUE DE VERNEUIL
RUE DE LILLE
RUE ALLENT

RUE SAINT-DOMINIQUE
BLVD
RUE DE VILLERSEXEL
RUE DE L'UNIVERSITÉ

RUE LAS CASES
PLACE J. BAINVILLE
ST-GERMAIN

Ecole Nationale d'Administration

RUE DU PRE AUX CLERCS
RUE DES SAINTS-PÈRES

St-Thomas d'Aquin

RUE MONTALEMBERT
RUE DU BAC

N

RUE DE BELLECHASSE
RUE DE ST-SIMON
RUE P. COURIER

PL. ST-THOMAS D'AQUIN

Université Paris V

IMPASSE DES DEUX-ANGES

▲ Musée Rodin

M
RUE DU BAC

R. PERRONET

RUE DE GRENELLE
7e
RUE DE LUYNES

BOULEVARD ST-GERMAIN

RUE DE GRENELLE

Fontaine des Quatre Saisons

RUE DE ST-GUILLAUME
RUE DE GRENELLE

RUE DU DRAGON
RUE B. PALISSY
RUE DU SABOT

Hôtel Matignon

BOULEVARD RASPAIL

RUE DE LA CHAISE

RUE DES SAINTS-PÈRES

RESTAURANTS
Brasserie Lipp   9
Le Christine   6
L'Epigramme   10
La Ferrandaise   17
Gaya Rive Gauche   1
Polidor   15
Le Salon d'Hélène   14
Ze Kitchen Galerie   3

RUE DU BAC
RUE DE COMMAILLE

Musée Maillol

RUE RECAMIER

CARREFOUR DE LA CROIX ROUGE
R. DU FOUR

RENNES

SQUARE DES MISSIONS ETRANGERES
RUE CHOMEL

RUE DU VIEUX COLOMBIER
RUE MADAME

BARS & CAFÉS
Le 10   13
Bar du Marché   8
Bistrot des Augustins   4
Café de la Mairie   12
Chez Georges   11
Le Flore   7
La Mezzanine
  de l'Alcazar   5
La Palette   2
Au Petit Suisse   16

M
RUE DE SEVRES

SQUARE BOUCICAUT

SÈVRES BABYLONE

PLACE LE CORBUSIER

RUE DU CHERCHE MIDI

M
ST-SULPICE

RUE PAPE CARPENTIER

RUE DE MEZIERES

Le Bon Marché

PLACE DE VILLE

R. COETLOGON

RUE CASSETTE

G

Grande Epicerie

RUE DE SEVRES

RUE DUPIN

BLVD

14

RUE D'ASSAS

St-Joseph-des-Carmes

R. H. CHEVALIER

M
VANEAU

RUE ST-PLACIDE

Marché Raspail

RUE DU CHERCHE MIDI

RUE DE L'ABBÉ GREGOIRE

RUE ST-PLACIDE

RENNES

RUE DU REGARD

M
RENNES

RASPAIL

RUE DE VAUGIRARD

RUE J. BART

RUE MADAME

RUE GUYNEMER

ACCOMMODATION
Hôtel de l'Abbaye   G
Hôtel du Globe   E
L'Hôtel   B
Hôtel Michelet-Odéon   H
Hôtel de Nesle   C
Relais Christine   D
Relais Saint-Sulpice   F
Hôtel de l'Université   A

RUE J FERRANDI
RUE DE BERTEL

M
ST-PLACIDE

RUE DE FLEURUS
RUE DE FLEURUS

Alliance Française

RUE D'ASSAS

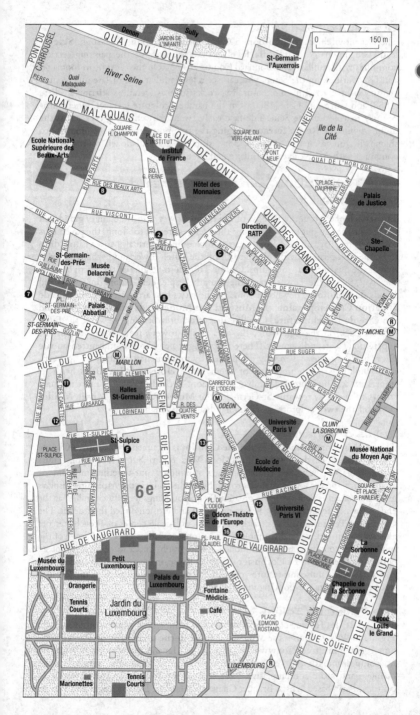

The middle level

The Kaganovitch collection (room 50) – Bonnard, Gauguin, Van Gogh, Sisley – leads you down to the **middle level**, where the flow of the painting section continues with Vuillard and Bonnard (rooms 70–72). On the far side, in rooms 55 and 58, overlooking the Seine, you can see a less familiar side of late nineteenth-century painting, with epic, naturalist works such as Detaille's stirring *Le Rêve* (1888) and Cormon's *Caïn* (1880). On the parallel sculpture terraces, nineteenth-century marbles on the Seine side face early twentieth-century pieces across the divide, while the **Rodin terrace** bridging the two puts almost everything else to shame. If you've energy to spare, don't skip the last half-dozen rooms, which contain superb Art Nouveau furniture and *objets*.

The Trocadéro, Eiffel Tower and the Septième

The stretch of Paris in the shadow of the **Eiffel Tower** is so sweepingly grand that it can take the fun out of exploration: the avenues are just too long, the pavements somehow too hard and the buildings too forbiddingly formal. Most visitors drop in by métro (or sail in by Batobus), to climb the Eiffel Tower and perhaps call in at one of the quarter's fine museums. On the Trocadéro heights of the north bank of the river, facing the Tower, stand the brutally resplendent **Palais de Tokyo** and **Palais de Chaillot**. They house some of the city's best art museums: the **Site de Création Contemporaine**, the **Musée d'Art Moderne de la Ville de Paris** and the **Cité de l'Architecture**. Chaillot also offers breathtaking views of the Eiffel Tower. Back on the Left Bank, the area at the tower's feet, to the east, is the **septième** (7ᵉ) arrondissement. There is a villagey neighbourhood centred on **rue Cler**, but the *septième* is mostly dominated by monumental military and government buildings. Most imposing of them is the **Hôtel des Invalides**, with its impressive war museum and tomb of Napoleon. Tucked away in the more intimate streets to the east, towards St-Germain, the **Musée Rodin** and **Musée Maillol** show off the two sculptors' works in handsome private houses.

Palais de Chaillot

The northern wing of the ugly **Palais de Chaillot** is occupied by the superb **Cité de l'Architecture et du Patrimoine** (Mon, Wed & Fri–Sun 11am–7pm, Thurs 11am–9pm; €8; Ⓦwww.citechaillot.fr), a stunningly put-together museum of architecture. On the loftily vaulted ground floor, the **Galerie des Moulages** displays giant plastercasts taken from the greatest French buildings (chiefly churches) at the end of the nineteenth century, before pollution and erosion dulled their detail. The Galerie des Peintures Murales, with its radiant, full-scale copies of French frescoes and wall-paintings, is equally impressive. The top floor offers a sleek rundown of the modern and contemporary, with models, photographs and a reconstruction of an entire apartment from **Le Corbusier**'s Cité Radieuse, in Marseille. You could spend half a day at the museum; restore yourself afterwards on the terrace of the ground-floor **café**, with its eye-popping views of the Eiffel Tower.

The Palais de Tokyo

The **Palais de Tokyo**, contemporary with Chaillot, and nearby on avenue du Président-Wilson, houses the **Musée d'Art Moderne de la Ville de Paris** (Tues–Sun 10am–6pm; free; Ⓦwww.mam.paris.fr; Mº Iéna/Alma-Marceau). While it's no competition for the Pompidou Centre, the cool Modernist setting is more fitting – and more contemplative – for a collection focused on early twentieth-century, Paris-based artists. Braque, Chagall, Delaunay, Derain, Léger and Picasso are well represented, and many works were expressly chosen for their Parisian themes. The enormous centrepieces are the two versions of Matisse's glorious mural, *La Danse,* and Dufy's gigantic *La Fée Électricité*, a mural commissioned by the electricity board to illustrate the story of electricity from Aristotle to the then-modern power station. Temporary exhibitions fill the ground-floor space.

The western wing of the palace is occupied by the **Site de Création Contemporaine** (Tues–Sun noon–midnight; €6; ⓦ www.palaisdetokyo.com), a cutting-edge gallery whose semi-derelict interior focuses exclusively on contemporary and avant-garde art. A constantly changing flow of exhibitions and events – anything from a concept show by Turner Prize-winning Jeremy Deller to a temporary "occupation" by squatter-artists – keeps the atmosphere lively, with a genuinely exciting countercultural buzz.

Musée de la Mode de la Ville and Musée Guimet

Behind the Palais de Tokyo, at 10 av Pierre 1er de Serbie, the stately, Italianate Palais Galliera is home to the **Musée de la Mode de la Ville de Paris** (closed until autumn 2011; Mᵒ Iéna/Alma-Marceau), which rotates its magnificent collection of clothes and accessories from the eighteenth century to the present day in a few themed exhibitions a year.

A short walk away, on place d'Iéna, the remarkable **Musée National des Arts Asiatiques-Guimet** (daily except Tues 10am–6pm; €7.50; ⓦ www.museeguimet .fr; Mᵒ Iéna) boasts a stunning display of Asian and especially Buddhist art. Four floors groan under the weight of statues of Buddhas and gods, while a roofed-in courtyard provides an airy space in which to show off the museum's world-renowned collection of **Khmer sculpture**.

The Eiffel Tower

It's hard to believe that the **Eiffel Tower**, the quintessential symbol both of Paris and of the brilliance of industrial engineering, was designed to be a temporary structure for a fair. Late nineteenth-century Europe had a decadent taste for such giant-scale, colonialist-capitalist extravaganzas, but the 1889 Exposition was particularly ambitious, and when completed the tower, at 300m, was the tallest building in the world. Reactions were violent. Outraged critics protested "in the name of menaced French art and history" against this "useless and monstrous" tower. "Is Paris", they asked, "going to be associated with the grotesque, mercantile imaginings of a constructor of machines?"

Curiously, Paris's most famous landmark was only saved from demolition by the sudden need for "wireless telegraphy" aerials in the first decade of the twentieth century. The tower's role in telecommunications – its only function apart from tourism – has become increasingly important, and the original crown is now masked by an efflorescence of antennae. After dark, the tower is particularly spectacular, an urban lighthouse illuminated by a double searchlight and, for the first ten minutes of every hour, by thousands of effervescent lights that fizz across its gridlines.

Though you may have to wait a while for the lifts, it's arguable that you simply haven't seen Paris until you've seen it from the top (daily: mid-June to Sept 9am–12.45am; Sept to mid-June 9.30am–11.45pm; last entry 45min before closing time. Top level €13.10; second level €8.10, or €4.50 by stairs [access closes 6pm Sept to mid-June]; ⓦ www.tour-eiffel.fr). While the views are almost better from the second level, especially on hazier days, there's something irresistible about going all the way to the top, and looking down over the surreally microscopic city below.

Stretching back from the legs of the Eiffel Tower, the long rectangular gardens of the **Champs de Mars** lead to the eighteenth-century buildings of the **École Militaire**, originally founded in 1751 by Louis XV for the training of aristocratic

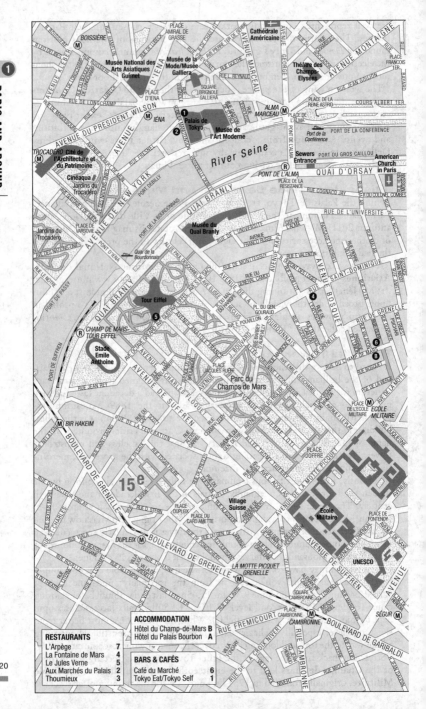

RESTAURANTS
L'Arpège   7
La Fontaine de Mars   4
Le Jules Verne   5
Aux Marchés du Palais   2
Thoumieux   3

ACCOMMODATION
Hôtel du Champ-de-Mars   B
Hôtel du Palais Bourbon A

BARS & CAFÉS
Café du Marché   6
Tokyo Eat/Tokyo Self   1

TROCADÉRO, EIFFEL TOWER AND THE SEPTIÈME

IMPASSE D'ANTIN
CHAMPS ELYSÉES (M) CLEMENCEAU
AVENUE DES CHAMPS-ELYSÉES
RUE JEAN GOUJON
AVENUE FRANKLIN D. ROOSEVELT
Grand Palais
Palais de la Découverte
Université Paris IV
Petit Palais
RUE FRANÇOIS TER
PLACE DU CANADA
RUE DE PONTHIEU
AVENUE DES CHAMPS-ELYSÉES
RUE DE RIVOLI
CONCORDE (M)
Obélisque
Jeu de Paume
TERRASSE DES FEUILLANTS
PLACE DE LA CONCORDE
AVE WINSTON CHURCHILL
AVE EDWARD TUCK
COURS LA REINE
PONT DES INVALIDES
PORT DES
CHAMPS ELYSÉES
Port des Champs-Elysées
PONT ALEXANDRE III
Musée de l'Orangerie
TERRASSE DU BORD DE L'EAU
Jardin des Tuileries
PLACE DE FINLANDE
QUAI D'ORSAY
INVALIDES (R)
INVALIDES (M)
QUAI ANATOLE FRANCE
Quai de Solférino
PORT DE SOLFERINO
QUAI DES TUILERIES
Ministère des Affaires Étrangères
Palais Bourbon Assemblée Nationale
ASSEMBLÉE NATIONALE (M)
Musée de la Légion d'Honneur
PLACE H. DE MONTHERLANT
MUSÉE D'ORSAY (R)
RUE DE L'UNIVERSITÉ
Esplanade des Invalides
PL. DU PALAIS BOURBON
PL. DU PRÉSIDENT E. HERRIOT
RUE DE L'UNIVERSITÉ
Musée d'Orsay
I N V A L I D E S
RUE SAINT-DOMINIQUE
BOULEVARD DE LA TOUR MAUBOURG
RUE FABERT
AVENUE DE LA MOTTE-PICQUET
AVENUE DE TOURVILLE
RUE DE CONSTANTINE
Institut Géographique National
RUE SAINT-DOMINIQUE
SOLFÉRINO (M)
Ste-Clotilde
PLACE DES INVALIDES
SQUARE SANTIAGO DU CHILI
SQUARE D'AJACCIO
LA TOUR MAUBOURG (M)
Musée de l'Armée
Hôtel des Invalides
Musée des Plans-Reliefs
Musée de l'Ordre de la Libération
St-Louis-des-Invalides
Église des Soldats
Église du Dôme
Jardin de l'Intendant
VARENNE (M)
Musée Rodin
RUE DE GRENELLE
RUE DE BELLECHASSE
RUE DE VARENNE
PLACE J. BAINVILLE
7e
Fontaine des Quatre Saisons
BOULEVARD RASPAIL
St-Thomas d'Aquin
RUE DU BAC
RUE DE GRENELLE
Hôtel Matignon
AVENUE DE TOURVILLE
PLACE VAUBAN
Esplanade du Souvenir Français
RUE DE CHANALEILLES
RUE VANEAU
RUE DE BABYLONE
SQUARE DES MISSIONS ÉTRANGÈRES
SÈVRES BABYLONE (M)
AVENUE DE LOWENDAL
AVENUE DUQUESNE
RUE D'ESTRÉES
PLACE EL SALVADOR
PLACE ANDRÉ TARDIEU
ST-FRANÇOIS XAVIER (M)
RUE OUDINOT
RUE MASSERAN
Jardin de Babylone
Grande Épicerie
RUE DE SÈVRES
PLACE LE CORBUSIER
PLACE DE VILLE
AVENUE DE SÉGUR
VILLA DE SAXE
PLACE DU PRÉSIDENT MITHOUARD
BOULEVARD DES INVALIDES
Hôpital Laënnec
SQUARE BOUCICAUT
AVENUE DE BRETEUIL
AVENUE DE SAXE
PLACE DE BRETEUIL
AVENUE DUROC
AVENUE LECOURBE
RUE DE SÈVRES
VANEAU (M)
PLACE L. P. FARGUE
RUE DU CHERCHE MIDI
RENNES (M)
ST-PLACIDE (M)
DUROC (M)
Hôpital Necker Enfants Malades
SÈVRES LECOURBE (M)
BLEVD DU MONTPARNASSE
RUE DE VAUGIRARD

N

0   200 m

121

army officers, and attended by Napoleon, among other fledgling leaders. The surrounding *quartier* may be expensive and sought after as an address, but it's mostly uninspiring to visit.

Musée du Quai Branly

A short distance upstream of the Eiffel Tower, on quai Branly, stands the intriguing **Musée du Quai Branly** (Tues, Wed & Sun 11am–7pm, Thurs–Sat 11am–9pm; €8.50; ⓦ www.quaibranly.fr; Mᵒ Iéna/RER Pont de l'Alma), which gathers together hundreds of thousands of non-European objects bought or purloined by France over the centuries. The museum was the pet project of President Chirac, whose passion for what he would no doubt call *arts primitifs* ("*primitive art*") helped secure funding. Designed by the French state's favourite architect, Jean Nouvel, the building unfurls in a sleek curve through the middle of a splendid **garden** – which, with its "green wall" and exotic plantings is worth a visit on its own account. Inside, areas devoted to Asia, Africa, the Americas and the Pacific ("Oceania") snake through semi-dark rooms lined by curving "mud" walls in brown leather. The 3500 **folk artefacts** on display at any one time are as fascinating as they are beautiful, but there's an uneasy sense that they are being presented in terms of their exotic "otherness" as much as for their artistic quality.

The riverside

Just beyond the museum, opposite the Pont d'Alma on the northeast side of the busy junction of place de la Résistance, is the entrance to the **sewers**, or *les égouts* (Sat–Wed: May–Sept 11am–5pm; Oct–April 11am–4pm; €4.30). Once you're underground it's dark, damp and noisy from the gushing water; the main exhibition, which runs along a gantry walk poised above a main sewer, renders the history of the city's water supply and waste management surprisingly fascinating. Children, however, may be disappointed to find that it's not all that smelly.

A little further upstream still, the **American Church** on quai d'Orsay, together with the American College nearby at 31 av Bosquet, is a focal point in the well-organized life of Paris's large American community. Immediately to the south lies a villagey wedge of early nineteenth-century streets. This tiny neighbourhood, between rue St-Dominique and rue de Grenelle, is full of appealingly bijou shops, hotels and restaurants, with the lively market street of **rue Cler** at the centre of it all.

Les Invalides

The noble **Esplanade des Invalides** strikes due south from the resplendent **Pont Alexandre III** towards the proud dome of the **Hôtel des Invalides**, which was built as a home for soldiers on the orders of Louis XIV. The building still belongs to the army today, but now houses a vast museum of war and weapons. Even if that doesn't appeal, it's worth coming to visit the complex's two magnificent churches, one of which now contains the mortal remains of Napoleon.

The most interesting section of the vast **Musée de l'Armée** (April–Sept Mon Mon–Wed & Fri–Sun 10am–6pm, Thurs 10am–9pm; Oct–March daily 10am–5pm; Oct–June closed first Mon of the month; €8 ticket also valid for Napoleon's tomb; ⓦ www.invalides.org; Mᵒ La Tour-Maubourg/Varenne), covers the two World Wars, explaining the battles, the resistance and the slow, final liberation using memorabilia and stirring contemporary news reels, most of which have an English-language option. The simplest artefacts – a rag doll found on a battlefield, plaster casts of mutilated faces, an overcoat caked in mud from the trenches – tell a stirring human story. The **Historial Charles de Gaulle** section, in the basement, pays high-tech audiovisual tribute to the Resistance leader and, later, President. The collection of medieval and Renaissance armour in the west wing of the royal courtyard is distinctly fabulous, while the super-scale three-dimensional maps of French ports and fortified cities in the **Musée des Plans–Reliefs**, under the roof of the east wing, are well worth a visit. The remainder of the museum, dedicated to the history of the French army from Louis XIV up to the 1870s, uniforms and weaponry, is perhaps more for enthusiasts.

The Invalides churches and Napoleon's tomb

The two Invalides churches have separate entrances. The lofty **Église des Soldats** (free; entrance from main courtyard of Les Invalides) is the spiritual home of the French army. The walls are hung with almost one hundred enemy standards captured on the battlefield, the rump of a collection of some three thousand that once adorned Notre-Dame. The proud simplicity of this "Soldiers' Church" stands in stark contrast to the lavish **Église du Dôme** (same hours and ticket as Musée de l'Armée above, except July & Aug open till 7pm; entrance from south side of Les Invalides), which lies on the other side of a dividing glass wall – a design innovation that allowed worshippers to share the same high altar without the risk of coming into social contact. The domed "Royal church" is a supreme example of the architectural pomposity of Louis XIV's day, with grandiose frescoes and an abundance of Corinthian columns and pilasters. **Napoleon**, or rather his ashes, lies in a hole in the floor in a cold, smooth sarcophagus of red porphyry, installed there on December 14, 1840. Freshly returned from St Helena, his remains were carried through the streets from the newly completed Arc de Triomphe to the Invalides. As many as half a million people came out to watch the emperor's last journey, and Victor Hugo commented that "it felt as if the whole of Paris had been poured to one side of the city, like liquid in a vase which has been tilted".

Musée Rodin

Immediately east of Les Invalides stands what is arguably Paris's loveliest museum: the **Musée Rodin** (Tues–Sun: April–Sept 9.30am–5.45pm, garden closes 6.45pm; Oct–March 9.30am–4.45pm, garden closes 5pm; house and gardens €6, €12 with the Musée d'Orsay, see p.114, garden only €1; Ⓦwww.musee-rodin.fr; Mº Varenne). It occupies a beautiful eighteenth-century mansion on the corner of rue de Varenne, a house the sculptor leased from the state in return for the gift of all his work at his death. Today, major projects like *The Burghers of Calais*, *The Thinker*, *The Gate of Hell* and *Ugolini* are exhibited in the extensive and peaceful gardens – the latter forming the centrepiece of the ornamental pond. Indoors, the mould-breaking, stormy vigour of the sculptures sits beautifully with the time-worn elegance of the wooden panelling. Well-loved works like the touchingly erotic *The Kiss* and *The Hand of God* get most of the attention, but you can explore quieter rooms full of tortured clay figures that still bear the imprint of the artist's hands. Don't miss the room dedicated to Camille Claudel, Rodin's ill-starred pupil, muse and lover.

Musée Maillol and around

The rest of rue de Varenne and the parallel rue de Grenelle is full of aristocratic mansions, including the Hôtel Matignon, the prime minister's residence. At 61 rue de Grenelle, a handsome eighteenth-century house has been turned into the Musée Maillol (Mon, Wed, Thurs, Sat & Sun 10.30am–7pm, Fri 10.30am–9.30pm; €11; Ⓦwww.museemaillol.com; Mº Rue du Bac), stuffed with Aristide Maillol's endlessly buxom sculpted female nudes, copies of which can be seen to better effect in the Louvre's Jardin du Carrousel. His paintings follow a similar theme, and there are also minor works by contemporaries like Picasso, Degas, Cézanne, Gauguin and Suzanne Valadon, as well as some excellent exhibitions.

From here, **rue du Bac** leads south to rue de Sèvres, cutting across **rue de Babylone**, another of the *quartier*'s livelier streets. Don't miss **La Pagode** at no. 57bis (Mº St-François-Xavier). Built in 1895 for the wife of a director of Paris's elegant Le Bon Marché department store, this Orientalist folly was turned into an arts cinema in the 1930s – in 1959 it premiered Jean Cocteau's *Le Testament d'Orphée*, and it remains one of Paris's classic art-house venues.

Montparnasse and southern Paris

The entertainment nexus of **Montparnasse** divides the well-heeled opinion-formers and powerbrokers of St-Germain and the 7ᵉ from the relatively anonymous populations to the south. The three arrondissements to the south have suffered from large-scale housing developments, most notably along the riverfronts to both east and west, but villagey areas such as **rue du Commerce** in the 15ᵉ, **Pernety** in the 14ᵉ and the **Buttes-aux-Cailles** in the 13ᵉ are well worth a foray. On the fringes of the city proper, hard up against the *périphérique* ring road, are three fantastic **parks**: André Citroën, Georges Brassens and Montsouris.

Like other Left Bank *quartiers*, Montparnasse trades on its association with the wild characters of the interwar artistic and literary boom. Many were *habitués* of the cafés *Select, Coupole, Dôme, Rotonde* and *Closerie des Lilas*. The cafés are all still going strong on **boulevard du Montparnasse**, while the glitterati have mostly ended up in the nearby **Montparnasse cemetery**. The quarter's artistic traditions are maintained in a couple of second-tier, but fascinating, art museums, while elsewhere you can ascend the **Tour Montparnasse**, Paris's first and ugliest skyscraper, and descend into the bone-lined **catacombs**.

Around Montparnasse station

Most of the life of the quarter is concentrated between the junction with boulevard Raspail, where Rodin's *Balzac* broods over the traffic, and at the station end of boulevard du Montparnasse, where the colossal **Tour Montparnasse** has become one of the city's principal and most despised landmarks. Although central Paris is more distant, the view from the top is better than the one from the Eiffel Tower in that it includes the Eiffel Tower – and excludes the Tour Montparnasse. It also costs less to ascend (daily: May–Sept 9.30am–11.30pm; Oct–April 9.30am–10.30pm; €11; ⓦwww.tourmontparnasse56.com). Alternatively, you could sit down for an expensive drink in the 56th-storey café-gallery, from where you get a tremendous view westwards. Sunset is the best time to visit.

One block northwest of the tower, on rue Antoine-Bourdelle, a garden of sculptures invites you into the fascinating **Musée Bourdelle** (Tues–Sun 10am–6pm; €7; Mº Montparnasse-Bienvenüe/Falguière), which has been built around the sculptor's atmospheric, musty and slightly ghostly old studio. As Rodin's pupil and Giacometti's teacher, Bourdelle's bronze and stone works moved sculpture on from a naturalistic style – as in the wonderful series of Beethoven busts – towards a more geometric, Modernist approach, seen in his better-known, monumental sculptures, some of which are dotted around the garden.

Montparnasse station was once the great arrival and departure point for travellers heading across the Atlantic, a connection commemorated in the unexpected **Jardin Atlantique**, suspended above the train tracks behind the station. Hemmed in by cliff-like high-rise apartment blocks, the park is a wonderful example of French design, with fields of Atlantic-coast grasses, wave-like undulations in the lawns (to cover the irregularly placed concrete struts below) – and well-hidden ventilation holes that reveal sudden glimpses of TGV roofs and rail sleepers below.

Montparnasse cemetery and the Fondation Henri Cartier-Bresson

Just south of boulevard Edgar-Quinet (which has a good food market) is the main entrance to the **Montparnasse cemetery** (mid-March to Nov 5 Mon–Fri 8am–6pm, Sat 8.30am–6pm, Sun 9am–6pm; Nov 6 to mid-March closes 5.30pm; free; M° Raspail/Gaîté/Edgar Quinet). Second in size and celebrity to Père Lachaise, its ranks of miniature temples pay homage to illustrious names from Baudelaire to Beckett and Gainsbourg to Saint-Saëns; pick up a free map at the entrance gate to track down your favourites. The simple joint grave of Jean-Paul Sartre and Simone de Beauvoir lies immediately right of the main entrance; a couple of poignant monuments are marked by artist Niki de Saint Phalle's distinctive mosaic sculptures. In the southwest corner is an old windmill, remains of one of the seventeenth-century taverns frequented by the carousing students who caused the district to be named after Mount Parnassus, the legendary home of the muses of poetry and song, and of Bacchus's drunken revels.

Cutting across avenue du Maine to the west, you come to the tiny Impasse Lebouis, where the slender steel-and-glass front of the **Fondation Henri Cartier-Bresson** (Tues, Thurs, Fri & Sun 1–6.30pm, Wed 1–8.30pm, Sat 11am–6.45pm; closed Aug; €6; ⓦ www.henricartierbresson.org; M° Gaîté) is hidden away. The foundation houses the archive of the grand old photographer of Paris. Exhibitions of work by HCB himself, and his contemporaries, alternate with exhibitions promoting younger photographers.

The catacombs, the Fondation Cartier and the Observatoire

For a surreal, somewhat chilling experience, head down into the **catacombs** (Tues–Sun 10am–4pm; €8; M° Denfert-Rochereau) in nearby **place Denfert-Rochereau**, formerly place d'Enfer (Hell Square). Abandoned quarries stacked with millions of bones, which were cleared from overstocked charnel houses and cemeteries between 1785 and 1871, the catacombs are said to hold the remains of around six million Parisians. Lining the gloomy passageways, long thigh bones are stacked end-on, forming a wall to keep in the smaller bones and shards, which can just be seen in dusty, higgledy-piggledy heaps behind. These high femoral walls are further inset with gaping, hollow-eyed skulls and plaques carrying macabre quotations. It's undeniably a fascinating place, but note that there are a good couple of kilometres to walk – it's 500m through dark, damp, narrow passageways before you even get to the ossuary – and it can quickly become claustrophobic in the extreme.

Rue Schoelcher and boulevard Raspail, on the east side of Montparnasse cemetery, have some interesting examples of twentieth-century architecture, from Art Nouveau to the modern glass-and-steel façade of the **Fondation Cartier pour l'Art Contemporain** at 261 bd Raspail (Tues 11am–10pm, Wed–Sun 11am–8pm; €7.50; ⓦ www.fondation.cartier.fr; M° Raspail). Built in 1994 by Jean Nouvel, this presents contemporary installations, videos and multimedia in high-quality temporary exhibitions. About 500m to the east, on avenue de l'Observatoire, the classical **Observatoire de Paris** sat on France's zero meridian line from the 1660s, when it was constructed, until 1884. After that date, they reluctantly agreed that 0° longitude should pass through a small village in Normandy that happens to be due south of Greenwich. You can see one of the bronze markers of the "Arago line" set into the cobbles of the observatory's courtyard.

The 14e below Montparnasse

The jokey quasi-Classical Ricardo Bofill apartment complex around place de Catalogne gives way to a walkway along the old rue Vercingétorix and to the cosy district of **Pernety**, which was long an artists' haunt. Wandering around Cité Bauer, rue des Thermopyles and rue Didot reveals adorable houses, secluded courtyards and quiet mews, and on the corner of rue du Moulin Vert and rue Hippolyte-Maindron you'll find Giacometti's old ramshackle studio and home. There are more artistic associations south of rue d'Alésia near the junction with avenue Réné-Coty: Dalí, Lurçat, Miller and Durrell lived in the tiny cobbled street of Villa Seurat off rue de la Tombe-Issoire; Lenin and his wife lodged across the street at 4 rue Marie-Rose; Le Corbusier built the studio at 53 avenue Reille, close to the secretive and verdant square du Montsouris which links with rue Nansouty; and Georges Braque's home was in the cul-de-sac now named after him off this street.

The nearby **Parc Montsouris** (RER Cité-Universitaire) is a pleasant place to stroll, with its unlikely contours, winding paths and waterfall above the lake – even the RER tracks cutting right through it fail to dent its charm.

The 15ᵉ arrondissement

Though it's the largest and most populous of them all, the **15ᵉ arrondissement** falls off the agenda for most visitors as it lacks a single important building or monument. It does have a pleasant villagey heart, however, in the **rue du Commerce**, a lively, old-fashioned high street full of small shops and shuttered houses, with one fine old restaurant, the *Café du Commerce* (see p.145). And it offers an appealing offbeat riverside stroll, on the narrow midstream island, the **Allée des Cygnes**, which you can reach in a short stroll south of the Eiffel Tower, via the Pont de Bir-Hakeim. The chief landmarks of the 15ᵉ, however, are its parks. In the southwest corner lies the hyper-designed **Parc André Citroën** (Mᵒ Balard), so named because the site used to be the Citroën motor works. Its best features are the glasshouses full of exotic-smelling shrubs, the dancing fountains – which bolder park-goers run through on hot days – and the tethered **balloon** (fine days only: 9am to roughly one hour before dusk; Mon–Fri €10, Sat & Sun €12), which offers spectacular views. The **Parc Georges Brassens**, in the southeast corner (Mᵒ Convention/Porte-de-Vanves), is a delight, with a garden of scented herbs and shrubs (best in late spring), puppets and rocks and merry-go-rounds for kids, a mountain stream with pine and birch trees, beehives and a tiny terraced vineyard. On the west side of the park, in a secluded garden in passage Dantzig, off rue Dantzig, stands an unusual polygonal studio space known as **La Ruche**. Home to Fernand Léger, Modigliani, Chagall, Soutine and many other artists at the start of the last century, it's still used as studios. In the sheds of the old horse market between the park and rue Brancion, a **book market** is held every Saturday and Sunday morning.

The 13ᵉ arrondissement

The 13ᵉ is one of the most disparate areas of the city. Place d'Italie, with the ornate *mairie* and vast Gaumont cinema, is the hub, with each of the major roads radiating out into very different *quartiers*. North of the mega-roundabout of **Place d'Italie**, the genteel neighbourhood around the ancient **Gobelins** tapestry works has more in common with the adjacent Quartier Latin. Between boulevard Auguste-Blanqui and rue Bobillot, meanwhile, is the lively hilltop quarter of the **Butte-aux-Cailles**. If you're looking for unpretentious, youthful and vaguely lefty restaurants and nightlife, it's well worth the short métro ride out from the centre. The easiest route is to walk up rue Bobillot from place d'Italie.

Over to the east, in the middle of a cluster of high-rise social housing, is the **Chinese quarter** of Paris. Avenues de Choisy and d'Ivry are full of Vietnamese, Chinese, Thai, Cambodian and Laotian restaurants and food shops, as is **Les Olympiades**, a weird semi-derelict pedestrian area seemingly suspended between giant tower blocks.

Following rue Tolbiac or boulevard Vincent-Auriol to the river, you reach the new district of **Paris Rive Gauche**, whose star attraction is the impressive **Bibliothèque Nationale de France** (Mon 2–7pm, Tues–Sat 9am–7pm, Sun 1–7pm; €3.30 for a reading room pass; Ⓦwww.bnf.fr). Accessible from its northern and southern corners (M° Quai-de-la-Gare or Bibliothèque-François-Mitterrand), it has four enormous towers – intended to look like open books – framing a sunken pine copse. Jaw-dropping as it is, architect Dominique Perrault's design attracted widespread derision after shutters had to be added to the towers to protect the books and manuscripts from sunlight. It's worth wandering around inside, to see the pair of wonderful globes that belonged to Louis XIV and occasional small-scale exhibitions; the garden level is reserved for accredited researchers only. From the Bibliothèque Nationale down to the *boulevard périphérique*, almost every stick of street furniture and square metre of tarmac is shiny and new. The still-underpopulated cafés and apartment blocks, and the **Passerelle Simone de Beauvoir**, a €21-million footbridge that crosses the Seine in a hyper-modern double-ribbon structure, give the area a futuristic frontier-town feel. Between the bridge and the pont de Bercy, several tethered **barges** have made the area a nightlife attraction in its own right (see p.147); among them, the floating swimming pool **Piscine Josephine Baker**, on its own barge, is wonderful. Immediately south of rue Tolbiac, the giant, decaying warehouse of **Les Frigos** was once used for cold-storage of meat and fish destined for Les Halles, but was taken over immediately after the market's closure by artists and musicians. It has been run as an anarchic studio space ever since, with a bar-restaurant on site and open-door exhibitions once or twice a year.

Newest of all, the former warehouses on the bleak Quai d'Austerlitz are currently being transformed into **Docks en Seine**, whose centrepiece is the **Cité de la Mode et du Design**, a combined fashion institute and retail opportunity. Its intrusive design of twisting, lime green tubes, by Dominique Jacob and Brendan MacFarlane, is supposed to recall the sinuous shape of the river. Inside, the **Institut Français de la Mode** (Ⓦwww.ifm-paris.com) is expected to host frequent exhibitions, and a café-restaurant complex, with a riverside terrace, is underway.

The Beaux Quartiers and Bois de Boulogne

Commonly referred to as the **Beaux Quartiers**, Paris's well-manicured western arrondissements, the 16ᵉ and 17ᵉ, are mainly residential with few specific sights, the chief exception being the **Musée Marmottan**, with its dazzling collection of late Monets. Bordering the area to the west is the **Bois de Boulogne**, with its trees, lakes, cycling trails and the beautiful floral displays of the Parc de Bagatelle. Further west bristle the gleaming skyscrapers of the purpose-built commercial district of **La Défense**, dominated by the enormous Grande Arche.

The Musée Marmottan

The **Musée Marmottan** (daily except Mon 11am–6pm, Tues until 9pm; €9; Ⓦwww.marmottan.com; M° Muette), at 2 rue Louis-Boilly, showcases Impressionist works, the highlight of which is a dazzling collection of canvases from Monet's last years at Giverny, including several *Nymphéas* (Water Lilies). The collection also features some of his contemporaries – Manet, Renoir and Berthe Morisot.

Bois de Boulogne

The **Bois de Boulogne** (M° Porte Maillot) is an area of extensive parkland running down the west side of the 16ᵉ. The "bois" of the name is somewhat deceptive, though it does contain some remnants of the once great Forêt de Rouvray. Once the playground of the wealthy, it also established a reputation as the site of the sex trade and its associated crime. The same is true today and you should avoid it at night. By day, however, the park is an extremely pleasant spot for a stroll. One of the main attractions is the **Parc de Bagatelle** (bus #244 from M° Porte Maillot, or bus #43 from M° Pont de Neuilly), which features beautiful displays of tulips, hyacinths and daffodils in the first half of April, irises in May, water lilies and roses at the end of June. The highlight for children is the **Jardin d'Acclimatation** (daily: April–Sept 10am–7pm, Oct–March 10am–6pm; €2.70; rides €2.50; ⓦwww .jardindacclimatation.fr; M° Les Sablons/Porte Maillot), a cross between a funfair, zoo and amusement park. Temptations range from bumper cars, go-karts and pony and camel rides to sea lions, birds, bears and monkeys. The best way to get to the park is via the *petit train* (€5.40 return, including entrance fee) which leaves every fifteen minutes from behind the *L'Orée du Bois* restaurant near Porte Maillot métro station. The Jardin d'Acclimatation is also the location for a new contemporary arts space, the **Fondation Louis Vuitton pour la Création**, designed by Frank Gehry and due for completion at the end of 2012.

La Défense

An impressive complex of gleaming skyscrapers, **La Défense** (M°/RER Grande-Arche-de-la-Défense) is Paris's prestige business district and a monument to late twentieth-century capitalism. Its most popular attraction is the huge **Grande Arche**, an astounding 112-metre hollow cube clad in white marble, standing 6km out from the Arc de Triomphe at the far end of the Voie Triomphale. It's no longer possible to take a lift up to the rooftop, but it's no great loss, as the views from the base of the arch are impressive enough – from here you can see as far as the Louvre on a clear day.

Montmartre and northern Paris

Perched on Paris's highest hill, towards the northern edge of the city, **Montmartre** was famously the home and playground of artists such as Renoir, Degas, Picasso and Toulouse-Lautrec. The crown of the Butte Montmartre, around place du Tertre, is a scrum, overrun with tourists these days, but the steep streets around **Abbesses** métro preserve an attractively festive, village-like atmosphere – and seem to become more gentrified and more fashionable every year. Even **Pigalle**, the brassy sprawl at the southern foot of the Butte, is turning trendy, with fashionable shops and boutique hotels springing up around rue des Martyrs. The **Goutte d'Or**, to the east, remains vibrantly multi-ethnic. Out at the northern city limits, the mammoth **St-Ouen market** hawks everything from extravagant antiques to the cheapest flea-market hand-me-downs.

Place des Abbesses and up to the Butte

In spite of being one of the city's chief tourist attractions, the **Butte Montmartre** manages to retain the quiet, almost secretive, air of its rural origins. The most popular access route is via the rue de Steinkerque and the steps below the Sacré-Coeur (the funicular railway from place Suzanne-Valadon is covered by normal métro tickets). For a quieter approach, wind your way up via place des Abbesses or rue Lepic.

Place des Abbesses, featuring one of the few complete surviving Guimard métro entrances, is the hub of a lively neighborhood. To the east, at the Chapelle des Auxiliatrices in rue Yvonne-Le-Tac, Ignatius Loyola founded the Jesuit movement in 1534. It's also supposed to be the place where St-Denis, the first bishop of Paris, was beheaded by the Romans around 250 AD (see p.159). Today, the streets are full of clothes shops, buzzing wine bars and laid-back restaurants.

One quiet and attractive way to get from place des Abbesses to the top of the Butte is to climb up rue de la Vieuville and the rue Drevet stairs to the minuscule **place du Calvaire**, with a lovely view back over the city; you could also head up rue Tholozé, turning right below the **Moulin de la Galette** – the last survivor of Montmartre's forty-odd windmills, immortalized by Renoir – into rue des Norvins. Artistic associations abound hereabouts: Zola, Berlioz, Turgenev, Seurat, Degas and Van Gogh lived in the area. Picasso, Braque and Gris invented Cubism in an old piano factory in place Émile-Goudeau, known as the **Bateau-Lavoir**; it still serves as artists' studios, though the original building burnt down years ago. Toulouse-Lautrec's inspiration, the **Moulin Rouge**, survives too, albeit as a shadow of its former self, on the corner of boulevard de Clichy and place Blanche.

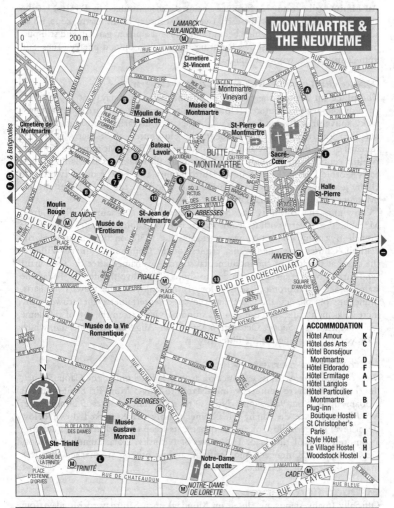

MONTMARTRE &
THE NEUVIÈME

0 — 200 m

ACCOMMODATION

Hôtel Amour	K
Hôtel des Arts	C
Hôtel Bonséjour Montmartre	D
Hôtel Eldorado	F
Hôtel Ermitage	A
Hôtel Langlois	L
Hôtel Particulier Montmartre	B
Plug-inn Boutique Hostel	E
St Christopher's Paris	
Style Hôtel	I
Le Village Hostel	H
Woodstock Hostel	J

BARS & CAFÉS				RESTAURANTS			
Café des Deux Moulins	8	Au Rendez-Vous des Amis	5	Café Burq	4	Le Relais Gascon	12
Chez Camille	6	Le Relais de la Butte	3	Au Grain de Folie	11	Wepler	9
La Fourmi	13	Le Sancerre	10	Le Mono	7		
L'Été en Pente Douce	1			Á la Pomponnette	2		

The intriguing little **Musée de Montmartre**, in a quiet spot at 12 rue Cortot (June–Sept Tues–Sun 11am–6pm; July & Aug Tues–Thurs 11am–6pm, Fri–Sun 11am–7pm; €8; Ⓦ www.museedemontmartre.fr; M° Lamarck-Caulaincourt), recaptures something of the feel of those bohemian days with old posters, paintings and photos and recreations of period rooms. The house, rented at various times by Renoir, Dufy, Suzanne Valadon and her alcoholic son Utrillo, also offers views over the neat terraces of the tiny **Montmartre vineyard** – which produces some 1500 bottles a year – on the north side of the Butte. You can walk round to the vineyard, where the steep rue de Saules falls away past the famous cabaret club **Au Lapin Agile** at no. 22. Famously painted and patronized by Picasso, Utrillo and other leading lights of the early twentieth-century Montmartre scene, it's an adorable little building, hidden behind shutters and a pretty garden, and still puts on old-fashioned cabaret shows featuring French chanson and poetry (Tues–Sun 9pm–2am; €24; Ⓦ www.au-lapin-agile.com).

Place du Tertre and the Sacré-Coeur

The **place du Tertre**, the core of old Montmartre, is today best avoided. It's been sucked dry of all interest, clotted with tour groups, overpriced restaurants, tacky souvenir stalls and jaded artists knocking out garish paintings. Between place du Tertre and the Sacré-Coeur, the old church of St-Pierre is all that remains of the Benedictine abbey that occupied the Butte Montmartre from the twelfth century on. Though much altered, it still retains its Romanesque and early Gothic feel. In it are four ancient columns, two by the door, two in the choir, leftovers from a Roman shrine that stood on the hill – *mons mercurii* (Mercury's Hill), the Romans called it.

Crowning the Butte is the **Sacré-Coeur** (daily 6.45am–10.30pm; free; M° Abbesses/Anvers) with its iconic ice-cream-scoop dome. Construction of this French–Byzantine confection was started in the 1870s on the initiative of the Catholic Church to atone for the "crimes" of the Commune. **Square Willette**, the space at the foot of the monumental staircase, is named after the local artist who turned out on inauguration day to shout "Long live the devil!" Today the staircase acts as impromptu seating for visitors enjoying the views over Paris, munching on picnics and watching the street entertainers; the crowds only increase as night falls. You can also get stunning **views** from the top of the dome (daily: April, May, Sept & Oct 9am–6.45pm; Jun–Aug 9.30am–8pm; €5), which takes you almost as high as the Eiffel Tower.

Montmartre cemetery

West of the Butte, with its entrance on avenue Rachel under rue Caulaincourt, lies the **Montmartre cemetery** (mid-March to Nov 5 Mon–Fri 8am–6pm, Sat 8.30am–6pm, Sun 9am–6pm; Nov 6 to mid-March closes 5.30pm; free; M° Blanche/Place de Clichy). It's a melancholy place, tucked down below street level in the hollow of an old quarry, its steep tomb-dotted hills creating a sombre ravine of the dead. The graves of Nijinsky, Zola, Stendhal, Berlioz, Degas, Feydeau, Offenbach and Truffaut, among others, are marked on a free map available at the entrance.

St-Ouen flea market

Officially (many stands are closed on Monday) open Saturday to Monday from 9am to 6.30pm – unofficially, from 5am – **the puces de St-Ouen** (M° Porte de Clignancourt) claims to be the largest flea market in the world. Nowadays it's predominantly a proper – and expensive – antiques market (mainly furniture, but including old café-bar counters, telephones, traffic lights, jukeboxes and the like), with many quirky treasures to be found. Of the twelve or so individual markets, you could concentrate on Marché **Dauphine**, good for movie posters, chanson and jazz records, comics and books, and Marché **Vernaison** for curios and bric-a-brac. Under the flyover of the *périphérique*, along rue J.H. Fabre, vendors hawk counterfeit clothing, sunglasses and pirated DVDs, while cup-and-ball scam merchants try their luck on hapless victims.

Pigalle

From place Clichy in the west to Barbès-Rochechouart in the east, the hill of Montmartre is underlined by the sleazy **boulevards de Clichy and Rochechouart**. In the middle, between place Blanche and place **Pigalle**, sex shows, sex shops, girly bars and streetwalkers (both male and female) vie for custom. In this appropriate setting you'll find the surprisingly classy **Musée de l'Erotisme**, 72 bd Clichy (daily 10am–2am; €8; ⓦ www.musee-erotisme.com; Mº Blanche), which bristles with sacred, ethnographic and ribald erotic art and sculpture from around the world. There's also a fascinating history of Parisian brothels, and regular, high-quality themed exhibitions. Only a few steps south of the Pigalle maelstrom, the atmosphere shifts as you enter the more genteel and increasingly trendy 9ᵉ arrondissement. Rue des Martyrs, long known for its neighbourhood food shops, is fast acquiring a hot reputation for boutique clothes shops too.

Goutte d'Or

Along the north side of the grotty boulevard de la Chapelle, between boulevard Barbès and the Gare du Nord rail lines, stretches the *quartier* of the **Goutte d'Or** ("Drop of Gold"), a name that derives from the medieval vineyard that occupied this site. After World War I, when large numbers of North Africans were first imported to replenish the ranks of Frenchmen dying in the trenches, the area gradually became an immigrant ghetto. Today, while the *quartier* remains poor, it is a vibrant place, home to a host of mini-communities, predominantly West African and Congolese, but with pockets of South Asian, Haitian, Turkish and other ethnicities as well. Countless shops sell ethnic music and fabrics, but the main sight for visitors is on rue Dejean, a few steps east of métro Château Rouge, where the **Marché Dejean** (closed Sun afternoon and Mon) heaves with African groceries and thrums with shoppers. Another, more general market takes place in the mornings twice weekly (Wed & Sat) underneath the métro viaduct on the **boulevard de la Chapelle**.

Canal St-Martin and La Villette

The **Bassin de la Villette** and the **canals** at the northeastern gate of the city were for generations the centre of a densely populated working-class district, whose main source of employment were the La Villette abattoirs and meat market. These have long gone, replaced by the huge complex of La Villette, a postmodern park of science and technology.

The Villette complex stands at the junction of the **Ourcq** and **St-Denis canals**. The first was built by Napoleon to bring fresh water into the city; the second is an extension of the Canal St-Martin built as a short cut to the great western loop of the Seine around Paris. The canals have undergone extensive renovation, and derelict sections of the *quais* have been made more appealing to cyclists, rollerbladers and pedestrians. A major new arts centre, **Le 104**, is also helping to regenerate the area.

Canal St-Martin and place de Stalingrad

The **Canal St-Martin** runs underground at Bastille to surface again in boulevard Jules-Ferry by rue du Faubourg-du-Temple. The canal still has a slightly industrial feel, especially along its upper stretch. The lower part is more attractive, with plane trees, cobbled *quais* and elegant, high-arched footbridges, as well as lively bars and stylish boutiques frequented by artsy, media folk. The area is particularly lively on Sunday afternoons, when the *quais* are closed to traffic, and pedestrians, cyclists and rollerbladers take over the streets; on sunny days a young crowd hangs out along the canal's edge, nursing beers or softly strumming guitars.

The canal disappears underground again further north at **place de Stalingrad**. To one side of the square stands the beautifully restored Palladian-style Rotonde de la Villette, one of Ledoux's tollhouses in Louis XVI's tax wall, where taxes were levied on all goods coming into the city – a major bone of contention in the lead-up to the 1789 Revolution. The *rotonde* is currently being converted into a cultural space and restaurant and is due to open at the end of 2010.

Beyond the square is the renovated **Bassin de la Villette** dock, once France's premier port. It's been recobbled and the dockside buildings have been converted into brasseries and a multiplex cinema (the MK2), which has screens on both banks, linked by a boat shuttle. In August, as part of the Paris Plage scheme (see p.157), there are canoes, pedaloes for children and other boating activities. At rue de Crimée a unique hydraulic bridge marks the end of the dock and the beginning of the Canal de l'Ourcq. If you keep to the south bank on quai de la Marne, you can cross directly into the Parc de la Villette.

The Parc de la Villette

The **Parc de la Villette** music, art and science complex (daily 6am–1am; free; Ⓦwww.villette.com), between avenues Corentin-Cariou and Jean-Jaurès, has so many disparate and disconnected elements that it's hard to know where to start. To help you get your bearings, it's worth picking up a map at the **information centre** at the entrance by Mº Porte de Pantin, to the south.

The main attraction is the enormous **Cité des Sciences et de l'Industrie** (Tues–Sat 10am–6pm, Sun 10am–7pm; €8 or €11 with the planetarium; Ⓦwww .cite-sciences.fr; Mº Porte de la Villette). This high-tech museum devoted to science and all its applications is built into the concrete hulk of the abandoned abattoirs on the north side of the Canal de l'Ourcq. Four times the size of the Pompidou Centre, it's a colossal glass-walled building, surrounded by a moat. Inside are crow's-nests, cantilevered platforms, bridges and suspended walkways, the different levels linked by lifts and escalators around a huge central space open to the full forty-metre height of the roof. The permanent exhibition, called Explora, covers subjects such as sound, robotics, energy, light, ecology, maths, medicine, space and language. As the name suggests, the emphasis is on exploring, encouraged through interactive computers, videos, holograms, animated models and games.

When all the interrogation and stimulation becomes too much, you can relax in cafés within Explora, before joining the queue for the **planetarium**. Back on the ground floor there's the **Louis Lumière Cinema**, which shows 3-D films (included in Cité des Sciences et de l'Industrie ticket), and the Cité des Enfants for children. The **Cité des Enfants**, which has areas for 2- to 7-year-olds and 5- to 12-year-olds, is hugely engaging. The kids can touch, smell and feel things, play about with water, construct buildings on a miniature construction site, manipulate robots and race their own shadows. Sessions run for ninety minutes (Tues–Fri 9.45am, 11.30am, 1.30 & 3.15pm; Sat & Sun 10.30am, 12.30, 2.30 & 4.30pm; €6; children must be accompanied by at least one adult; book in advance during busy holiday periods via the website or on ☏08.92.69.70.72).

Children are also likely to enjoy the Imax films shown at the **Géode cinema** (hourly shows Mon 10.30am–6.30pm, Tues–Sun 10.30am–8.30pm; €10.50), located in front of the Cité complex, and those at the **Cinaxe**, between the Cité and the Canal St-Denis (screenings every 15min Tues–Sun 11am–1pm & 2–5pm;

€4.80), which combines 70mm film shot at thirty frames a second with seats that move, enabling viewers to experience the sensation of speeding and flying. Beside the Géode is a real 1957 French **submarine**, the **Argonaute** (Tues–Sat 10am–5.30pm, Sun 10am–6.30pm; €3). South of the canal are landscaped **themed gardens** of "mirrors", "mists", "winds and dunes" and "islands", and over to the east is the **Zénith** inflatable rock music venue. To the south, the largest of the old **market halls** is now a vast and brilliant exhibition space, the **Grande Salle**.

South of the Grande Salle stands the **Cité de la Musique** (Ⓦ www.cite-musique.fr), in two fine contemporary buildings to either side of the Porte-de-Pantin entrance. To the west is the national music academy, while to the east are a concert hall, the chic *Café de la Musique* and the excellent **Musée de la Musique** (Tues–Sat noon–6pm, Sun 10am–6pm; €8), presenting the history of music from the end of the Renaissance to the present day, both visually – through a collection of 4500 instruments – and aurally, with headsets and interactive displays.

Le 104

Three blocks west of the Bassin de la Villette, a former funeral parlour, built in the 1870s, has been converted into an impressive multimedia arts space, **Le 104** (Ⓦ www.104.fr), covering some 39,000 square metres. Thirty-odd established and new artists have set up studios here; one of the stipulations is that they regularly open their studios to the public, with the aim of stimulating debate and the exchange of ideas. Each week has an artistic theme, and there are regular dance and music performances, lectures, exhibitions and other events, some suitable for children; see the website for details. Also on site are a restaurant, café and bookshop.

Belleville, Ménilmontant and Père-Lachaise

Traditionally working class, with a history of radical and revolutionary activity, the gritty **eastern districts** of Paris, particularly the old villages of **Belleville** and **Ménilmontant**, are nowadays some of the most diverse and vibrant parts of the city, home to sizeable ethnic populations, as well as students and artists, attracted by the low rents. The main visitor attraction in the area is the **Père-Lachaise cemetery**, final resting place of many well-known artists and writers. Visiting the modern **Parc de Belleville** will reveal the area's other main asset – wonderful views of the city below. Another park well worth seeing is the fairytale-like **Parc des Buttes-Chaumont**.

Parc des Buttes-Chaumont

At the northern end of the Belleville heights, a short walk from La Villette, is the **parc des Buttes-Chaumont** (M° Buttes-Chaumont/Botzaris), constructed by Haussmann in the 1860s to camouflage what until then had been a desolate warren of disused quarries and miserable shacks. Out of this rather unlikely setting a wonderfully romantic park was created – there's a grotto with a cascade and artificial stalactites, and a picturesque lake from which a huge rock rises up topped with a delicate Corinthian temple.

Belleville and Ménilmontant

The route from Buttes-Chaumont to Père-Lachaise will take you through the one-time villages of **Belleville** and **Ménilmontant**. Absorbed into Paris in the 1860s and subsequently built up with high-rise blocks to house migrants from rural districts and the ex-colonies, this area might not be exactly "belle", but it's certainly vibrant and happening. The main street, rue de Belleville, abounds with Vietnamese, Thai and Chinese shops and restaurants, and numerous artists live and work in the area, attracted by the availability of affordable and large spaces; the best time to view their work is during the **Journées portes ouvertes ateliers d'artistes de Belleville** in mid-May (for exact dates see Ⓦ www.ateliers-artistes-belleville.org).

You get fantastic views down onto the city centre from the higher reaches of Belleville and Ménilmontant: the best place to watch the sun set is the **Parc de Belleville** (Mᵒ Couronnes/Pyrénées), which descends in a series of terraces and waterfalls from rue Piat. And from **rue de Ménilmontant**, by rues de l'Ermitage and Boyer, you can look straight down to the Pompidou Centre. On rue de Ménilmontant and its extension **rue Oberkampf** trendsetting bars and cafés jostle for space alongside the ethnic bakeries, cheap goods stores and grocers.

Père-Lachaise cemetery

Père-Lachaise cemetery (Mon–Fri 8am–5.30pm, Sat 8.30am–5.30pm, Sun 9am–5.30pm; Mᵒ Gambetta/Père-Lachaise/Alexandre-Dumas/Philippe-Auguste), final resting place of numerous notables, is an atmospheric, eerily beautiful haven, with little cobbled footpaths, terraced slopes and magnificent old trees which spread their branches over the tombs as though shading them from the outside world. The cemetery was opened in 1804, after an urgent stop had been put to further burials in the overflowing city cemeteries and churchyards. The civil authorities had Molière, La Fontaine, Abelard and Héloïse reburied here, and to be interred in Père-Lachaise quickly acquired cachet. A free **map** of the cemetery is available at all the entrances or you can buy a more detailed one for around €2 at nearby newsagents and florists.

Among the most visited graves is that of **Chopin** (Division 11), often attended by Poles bearing red-and-white wreaths and flowers. Fans also flock to the ex-Doors lead singer **Jim Morrison** (Division 6), who died in Paris at the age of 27.

Femme fatale Colette's tomb, close to the main entrance in Division 4, is very plain, though always covered in flowers. The same holds true for those of Sarah Bernhardt (Division 44) and Edith Piaf (Division 97). Marcel Proust lies in his family's black-marble, conventional tomb (Division 85).

Cutting a rather romantic figure, French president Félix Faure (Division 4), who died in the arms of his mistress in the Elysée palace in 1899, lies draped in a French flag, his head to one side. Corot (division 24) and Balzac (division 48) both have superb busts, while Géricault reclines on cushions of stone (division 12), paint palette in hand. One of the most impressive of the individual tombs is Oscar Wilde's (Division 89), topped with a sculpture by Jacob Epstein of a mysterious Pharaonic winged messenger (sadly vandalized of its once prominent member, last seen being used as a paperweight by the director of the cemetery). Nearby, in division 96, is the grave of **Modigliani** and his lover Jeanne Herbuterne, who killed herself in crazed grief a few days after the artist died in agony from meningitis.

In Division 97 are the memorials to the victims of the Nazi concentration camps and executed Resistance fighters. The sculptures are relentless in their images of inhumanity, of people forced to collaborate in their own degradation and death. Marking one of the bloodiest episodes in French history is the Mur des Fédérés (Division 76), the wall where the last troops of the Paris Commune were lined up and shot in the final days of the battle in 1871. The man who ordered their execution, Adolphe Thiers, lies in the centre of the cemetery in division 55.

Bercy, the Promenade Plantée and Bois de Vincennes

The riverside **Bercy** *quartier*, which extends southeast from the Gare de Lyon, was where the capital's wine supplies used to be unloaded from river barges. Much of the area has been turned into a welcome green space, the extensive **Parc de Bercy**

(M° Bercy), cleverly incorporating elements of the old warehouse district such as disused railway tracks and cobbled lanes.

The impressive building resembling a pack of falling cards that overlooks the east side of the park, at 51 rue de Bercy, was designed by Bilbao's Guggenheim architect Frank Gehry and houses the **Cinémathèque** (Ⓦ www.cinematheque.fr; M° Bercy), the repository for a huge archive of films dating back to the earliest days of cinema. Regular retrospectives of French and foreign films are screened in the four cinemas and it also has an engaging museum (Mon, Wed–Sat noon–7pm, Sun 10am–8pm; €5), with lots of early cinematic equipment and silent-film clips, as well as the dress that Vivien Leigh wore in *Gone with the Wind*.

Continuing eastwards through the Parc de Bercy, you come to **Bercy Village** (M° Cour Saint-Émilion), the main thoroughfare of which is the Cour Saint-Émilion, a pedestrianized street lined with former wine warehouses converted into cafés, restaurants and shops. The ochre-coloured stone and the homogeneity of the buildings make for an attractive ensemble and it's an agreeable spot for a wander.

Even better for a stroll, especially if you feel like escaping from the bustle of the city for a bit, is the **Promenade Plantée** (M° Bastille/Ledru-Rollin), a stretch of disused railway line, much of it along a viaduct, that has been converted into an elevated walkway and planted with a profusion of trees and flowers. The walkway starts near the beginning of avenue Daumesnil, just south of the Bastille opera house, and is reached via a flight of stone steps – or lifts – with a number of similar access points all the way along. It takes you to the Parc de Reuilly, then descends to ground level and continues nearly as far as the *périphérique*, from where you can follow signs to the Bois de Vincennes. The whole walk is around 4.5km long, but if you don't feel like doing the entire thing you could just walk the first part – along the viaduct – which also happens to be the most attractive stretch, running past venerable old mansion blocks and giving a bird's-eye view of the area below and of small architectural details not seen from street level. What's more, the arches of the viaduct itself have been ingeniously converted into spaces for artisans' *ateliers* and craftshops, collectively known as the **Viaduc des Arts**. There are 51 of them, including furniture restorers, interior designers, cabinet-makers and fashion and jewellery boutiques.

The Bois de Vincennes

The **Bois de Vincennes** is a favourite family Sunday retreat and the largest green space that the city has to offer, aside from the Bois de Boulogne in the west. It's rather crisscrossed with roads, but there are some very pleasant corners, including the picturesque Lac Daumesnil, where you can hire boats, and the **Parc Floral** (daily: summer 9.30am–8pm; winter 9.30am–dusk; €1; Ⓦ www.parcfloraldeparis.com; M° Château de Vincennes then bus #112 or a 15min walk), perhaps Paris's best gardens, with an adventure playground attached. Flowers are always in bloom in the Jardin des Quatres Saisons; you can picnic amid pines and rhododendrons, then wander through concentrations of camellias, cacti, ferns, irises and bonsai trees. Just north of Lac Daumesnil is the city's largest **zoo**, currently closed for major renovation and due to reopen in 2013.

On the northern edge of the *bois* lies the **Château de Vincennes** (daily: May–Aug 10am–6pm; Sept–April 10am–5pm; donjon €8, Ste-Chapelle €8, combined ticket €12; M° Château de Vincennes), the country's only surviving medieval royal residence, built by Charles V, subsequently turned into a state prison, then porcelain factory, weapons dump and military training school. Enclosed by a high defensive wall and still preserving the feel of a military barracks, it presents a rather austere aspect on first sight, but it's worth visiting for its Gothic **Chapelle Royale**, decorated with superb Renaissance stained-glass windows; and the restored fourteenth-century **donjon** (keep), where you can see some fine vaulted ceilings, Charles V's bedchamber and graffiti left by prisoners, whose number included one Marquis de Sade.

Eating and drinking

Eating and drinking are among the chief delights of Paris. An incredible number of restaurants remain defiantly traditional, offering the classic *cuisine bourgeoise* based on well-sauced meat dishes, or regional French cuisines, notably from the southwest. You can find a tremendous variety of foods, from Senegalese to Vietnamese, however, and contemporary French gastronomy is increasingly willing to embrace spices and exotic ingredients. There is a huge diversity of ambiences to choose from: luxurious, hushed **restaurants** decked with crystal and white linen; noisy, elbow-to-elbow bench-and-trestle-table joints; intimate neighbourhood **bistros** with specials on the blackboard; grand seafood **brasseries** with splendid, historic interiors; and artfully distressed **cafés** serving dishes of the day.

Eating out is expensive nowadays, with evening meals rarely less than €30. Lunchtime set *menus* (known as *menus* or *formules*) can still cost as little as €12–16, however. The big boulevard cafés and brasseries, especially those in more touristy areas, can be significantly more expensive than those a little further removed. Students with an ISIC card can eat very inexpensively at university cafeterias – for full details see ⓦ www.crous-paris.fr.

It's worth budgeting for at least one meal in one of Paris's spectacular Michelin-starred **gourmet restaurants**. You'll need to dress smartly; most prefer men to wear a jacket and perhaps a tie. Prices are often significantly lower at weekday lunchtimes; otherwise count on €100–150 as a minimum, and there's no limit on the amount you can pay for wine. Spin-off bistros of celebrity chefs like Alain Ducasse, Pierre Gagnaire and Guy Savoy are something of a fashion at the moment, and well worth considering.

Drinking venues range from the many **cafés** that move seamlessly from coffees to cocktails as evening approaches, to the tiny, dedicated **wine bars** offering little-known vintages from every region of France. There are cavernous **beer cellars**, designer **bars** with DJ *soirées* at weekends and the ubiquitous Irish/British/Canadian **pubs**. You can take coffee and cakes in a chintzy **salon de thé**, in a bookshop or gallery, or even in the courtyard of a mosque. Many bars have happy hours, but prices can double after 10pm, and any clearly trendy, glitzy or stylish place is bound to be expensive.

The different **eating** and **drinking establishments** are listed here by area. They are divided into restaurants, including brasseries and bistros, and bars and cafés, a term used to incorporate anywhere you might go for a drink or a lighter meal – cafés, ice-cream parlours and *salons de thé*. Restaurant **opening times** are typically noon–2/2.30pm and 7.30–10.30/11pm; exceptions to this are noted in the text. Where possible, we have marked restaurants listed on the maps. It's best to **book ahead** for evening meals, especially from Thursday to Saturday; for most places it's usually enough to book on the day, though for the top gourmet restaurants you'll need to book at least two or three weeks in advance. Note that a surprising number of places don't accept credit cards.

The Islands

See maps, p.100 and pp.104–105.

Berthillon 31 rue St-Louis-en-l'Île, 4e; Mo Pont Marie. You may well have to queue for one of *Berthillon*'s exquisite ice creams or sorbets – arguably the best in Paris. Wed–Sun 10am–8pm.

🏃 **Mon Vieil Ami** 69 rue St-Louis-en-l'Île, 4e ☎01.40.46.01.35; Mo Pont Marie. Charming little bistro, with appealing contemporary decor of chocolate browns and frosted-glass panels. The excellent cuisine is bold and zesty, using seasonal ingredients, and the wine list includes some choice vintages. Three courses cost around €40. Closed Mon & Tues, and three weeks in Jan & Aug.

Taverne Henri IV 13 place du Pont Neuf, Île de la Cité, 1er; Mo Pont Neuf. An old-style wine bar that's probably changed little since Yves Montand used to come here with Simone Signoret. It's especially lively at lunchtime when lawyers from the nearby Palais de Justice drop in for generous platters of meats and cheeses and toasted sandwiches. Mon–Fri 11.30am–9.30pm, Sat noon–5pm; closed Sun & Aug.

The Champs-Élysées and around

See map, pp.92–93.

Bars and cafés

Ladurée 75 av des Champs-Élysées, 8e; Mo George V. This Champs-Élysées branch of the *Ladurée* tearooms, with its luxurious gold and green decor, is perfect for a shopping break. Try the delicious macaroons or the thick hot chocolate. Daily 7.30am–11.30pm.

Musée Jacquemart-André 158 bd Haussmann, 8e ☎01.45.62.11.59; Mo St-Philippe-du-Roule/Miromesnil. Part of the Musée Jacquemart-André but with independent access, this is the most sumptuously appointed *salon de thé* in the city. Admire the ceiling frescoes by Tiepolo while savouring fine pastries or salads. Daily 11.45am–5.30pm.

Restaurants

Pierre Gagnaire *Hôtel Balzac*, 6 rue Balzac, 8e ☎01.58.36.12.50; Mo George V. Regularly rated as one of the top ten restaurants in the world by *Restaurant* magazine, *Pierre Gagnaire* is a gastronomic adventure. The lunch *menu* costs €105, dinner around €270. Mon–Fri noon–1.30pm & 7.30–9.30pm, Sun 7.30–9.30pm.

Le Relais de l'Entrecôte 15 rue Marbeuf, 8e; Mo Franklin-D.-Roosevelt. No reservations are taken at this bustling diner, so you may have to queue for the single main course on the *menu*:

steak and *frites*. This is no ordinary steak though – the secret is in the delicious, buttery sauce. Around €30 for three courses. Daily; closed Aug.

La Table Lauriston 129 rue Lauriston, 16e ☎01.47.27.00.07; Mo Trocadéro. A slightly older, well-off crowd from the neighbourhood usually dines at this traditional bistro run by chef-to-the-stars Serge Rabey. Game terrine with chanterelle mushrooms and *poularde fondante au vin jaune* (chicken croquettes with Arbois wine) are indicative of the upscale dishes here, and be sure to taste their famed Baba au Rhum. You'll easily spend €50 per person, but the *cuisine bourgeoise* is excellent. Closed Sat lunch & all day Sun.

Taillevent 15 rue Lamennais, 8e ☎01.44.95.15.01; Mo Charles-de-Gaulle. One of Paris's finest gourmet restaurants. The Provençal-influenced cuisine and wine list are exceptional, the decor classy and refined. There's a set *menu* for €80 at lunch only, otherwise reckon on an average of €150 a head, excluding wine, and book well in advance. Closed Sat, Sun & Aug.

The Louvre, Tuileries and Palais Royal

See map, pp.92–93.

Angelina 226 rue de Rivoli, 1er; Mo Tuileries. This elegant old *salon de thé*, with its murals, gilded stuccowork and comfy leather armchairs, does the best hot chocolate in town – a generous jugful with whipped cream on the side is enough for two. Mon–Fri 8am–7pm, Sat & Sun 9.15am–7pm; closed Tues in July & Aug.

Bar Costes *Hotel Costes*, 239 rue St-Honoré, 8e; Mo Concorde/Tuileries. A favourite haunt of fashionistas and celebs, this is a romantic place for an aperitif or late-night drinks amid decadent nineteenth-century decor of red velvet, swags and columns, set around an Italianate courtyard. Cocktails around €17. Daily until 2am.

Juveniles 47 rue de Richelieu, 2e; Mo Palais-Royal. A very popular tiny wine bar run by a Scot. Wine costs from €15 a bottle and there are usually around ten varieties available by the glass (from €4); *plats du jour* cost around €16, cheese platters and tapas-style dishes are also available. Tues–Sat 11am–11pm, Sun noon–2pm, Mon 7.30–11pm.

🏃 **Verlet** 56 rue St-Honoré, 1er; Mo Palais Royal-Musée du Louvre. A heady aroma of coffee greets you as you enter this charming old-world coffee merchant's and café done out with wood furnishings and green-leather benches. You can dither over 25 varieties of coffee, and there's a selection of teas and light snacks, too. Mon–Sat 9am–7pm.

The Grands Boulevards and around

See map, pp.92–93.

Bars and cafés

L'Arbre à Cannelle 57 passage des Panoramas, 2e; Mo Grands Boulevards. Tucked away in an attractive *passage*, this *salon de thé* with exquisite wood panelling, frescoes and painted ceilings makes an excellent spot to treat yourself to salads and quiches, and desserts such as pear and chocolate tart. Mon–Sat 11.30am–6pm.

Delaville Café 34 bd de la Bonne-Nouvelle, 10e; Mo Bonne-Nouvelle. This ex-bordello, with grand staircase, gilded mosaics and marble columns, draws in crowds of hipsters, who sling back a mojito or two before moving on to one of the area's clubs. Daily 11am–2am.

Le Rubis 10 rue du Marché St-Honoré, 1er; Mo Pyramides. This very small and very crowded wine bar is one of the oldest in Paris, known for its excellent wines – mostly from the Beaujolais and Loire regions – and home-made *rillettes* (a kind of pork pâté). Mon–Fri 7.30am–9pm, Sat 9am–3pm; closed mid-Aug.

Restaurants

Gallopin 40 rue Notre-Dame des Victoires, 2e ☏01.42.36.45.38; Mo Bourse. An utterly endearing old brasserie, with all its original brass and mahogany fittings and a beautiful painted glass roof in the back room. The classic French dishes, especially the *foie gras maison*, are well above par, and *menus* start at €24.50. Daily noon–midnight.

Aux Lyonnais 32 rue St-Marc, 2e ☏01.42.96.65.04; Mo Bourse/Richelieu-Drouot. This revamped old bistro, with lovely *belle époque* tiles and mirrored walls, serves up delicious Lyonnais fare – try the *quenelles* (light and delicate fish dumplings) followed by the heavenly Cointreau soufflé for dessert. Three-course set *menu* €34. Closed Sat lunch, Sun & Mon.

Beaubourg and Les Halles

See map, p.100.

Bars and cafés

Café Beaubourg 43 rue St-Merri, 4e; Mo Rambuteau/Hôtel-de-Ville. Seats under the expansive awnings of this stylish café command frontline views of the Pompidou piazza and are great for people-watching. It's also good for a relaxing Sunday brunch. Daily 8am–1am.

Le Petit Marcel 63 rue Rambuteau, 4e; Mo Rambuteau. Speckled tabletops, mirrors and Art Nouveau tiles, a cracked and faded ceiling and about eight square metres of drinking space. There's a small dining area, too, where you can get reasonably cheap and filling bistro food such as *frites* and omelette or steak tartare. Mon–Sat till 2am.

Restaurants

Chez Dilan 13 rue Mandar, 2e ☏01.42.21.14.88; Mo Les Halles/Sentier. An excellent-value Kurdish restaurant, strewn with kilims and playing taped Kurdish music. Starters include melt-in-your mouth *babaqunuc* (stuffed aubergines) and mains *beyti* (spiced minced beef wrapped in pastry, with yoghurt, tomato sauce and bulgar wheat). Mains cost from €12. Closed Sun.

Georges Centre Georges Pompidou, 4e ☏01.44.78.47.99; Mo Rambuteau/Hôtel-de-Ville. On the top floor of the Pompidou Centre, this trendy minimalist restaurant with outdoor terrace commands stunning views over Paris and makes a stylish place for lunch or dinner. The international cuisine is pretty good, if overpriced. Main courses from €30. Daily except Tues noon–midnight.

À la Tour de Montlhéry (Chez Denise) 5 rue des Prouvaires, 1er ☏01.42.36.21.82; Mo Louvre-Rivoli/Châtelet. A quintessential old-style Parisian bistro, going back to the Les Halles market days. Diners sit elbow to elbow at long tables in a narrow dining room and tuck into substantial meaty dishes, such as *andouillette* (tripe sausage), offal and steak, accompanied by perfectly cooked *frites*. Mains cost €20–25. Mon–Fri noon–3pm & 7.30pm–5am. Closed mid-July to mid-Aug.

The Marais

See map, pp.104–105.

Bars and cafés

Andy Wahloo 69 rue des Gravilliers, 3e ☏01.42.71.20.38; Mo Arts-et-Métiers. A very popular bar decked out in original Pop Art-inspired Arabic decor. Tasty mezze appetizers are available until midnight and the bar serves a few original cocktails, including the Wahloo Special (rum, lime, ginger, banana and cinnamon). DJs play a wide range of dance music. Tues–Sat noon–2am.

L'Apparemment Café 18 rue des Coutures St-Gervais, 3e; Mo St-Sébastien Froissart. A chic and cosy café resembling a series of comfortable sitting rooms, with quiet corners and deep sofas. The salads, which you compose yourself by ticking off your chosen ingredients and handing your order to the waiter, are recommended, as is the popular Sunday brunch (€21). Mon–Fri noon–2am, Sat 4pm–2am, Sun 12.30pm–midnight.

L'As du Fallafel 34 rue des Rosiers, 4ᵉ ☎01.48.87.63.60; Mᵒ St-Paul. The best falafel shop in the Jewish quarter. Falafels to take away cost only €4, or you can pay a bit more and sit in the little dining room. Daily noon–midnight; closed Fri eve & Sat.

Le Loir dans la Théière 3 rue des Rosiers, 4ᵉ; Mᵒ Saint-Paul. A laid-back and very popular *salon de thé* where you can sink into comfy sofas and feast on enormous portions of home-made cakes and vegetarian quiches. Come early for the popular Sunday brunch. Mon–Fri 11am–7pm, Sat & Sun 10am–7pm.

Le Petit Fer à Cheval 30 rue Vieille-du-Temple, 4ᵉ; Mᵒ St-Paul. A very attractive small drinking spot with original *fin-de-siècle* decor, including a marble-topped bar in the shape of a horseshoe (*fer à cheval*). You can snack on sandwiches or something more substantial in the little back room furnished with old wooden métro seats. Mon–Fri 9am–2am, Sat & Sun 11am–2am; food noon–midnight.

Restaurants

Ambassade d'Auvergne 22 rue du Grenier St-Lazare, 3ᵉ ☎01.42.72.31.22; Mᵒ Rambuteau. Suited, mustachioed waiters serve scrumptious Auvergnat cuisine that would have made Vercingétorix proud. There's a set *menu* for €38, but you may well be tempted by some of the house specialities, like the roast guinea fowl with garlic. Open daily; closed last two weeks in Aug.

Au Bourguignon du Marais 52 rue François Miron, 4ᵉ ☎01.48.87.15.40; Mᵒ St-Paul. A warm, relaxed restaurant, with attractive contemporary decor and tables outside in summer, serving excellent Burgundian cuisine with carefully selected wines to match. Mains cost around €20. Mon–Fri noon–3pm & 8–11pm; closed three weeks in Aug.

Chez Marianne 2 rue des Hospitalières St-Gervais, 4ᵉ ☎01.42.72.18.86; Mᵒ St-Paul. A Marais institution, this homely place with cheery red awnings specializes in Middle Eastern and Jewish delicacies. A platter of mezze for two (from €26) might include tabbouleh, aubergine purée, chopped liver and hummus, and there's a good selection of wines. Daily noon–midnight.

Chez Omar 47 rue de Bretagne, 3ᵉ; Mᵒ Arts-et-Métiers. No reservations are taken at this popular North African couscous restaurant, so it's best to arrive early, though it's no hardship to wait at the bar for a table, taking in the handsome old brasserie decor and the buzzy atmosphere. Portions are copious and reasonably priced, and the couscous light and fluffy. No credit cards. Daily except Sun lunch noon–2.30pm & 7–11.30pm.

Le Pamphlet 38 rue Debelleyme, 3ᵉ ☎01.42.72.39.24; Mᵒ Filles du Calvaire. This is one of the Marais' best restaurants, where the cuisine is *haute*, but the prices aren't. There's an excellent-value seven-course tasting menu for €70 or you could just go for the two-course menu at €30, which might include duck croquettes, smoked *magret de canard* and tomato with cumin for starters, and pork fillet, chorizo and prunes with lentil salad for mains. Though billed as a bistro, it's more like a comfy restaurant, with upholstered chairs, tasteful decor and well spaced tables. Mon 8–10.30pm, Tues–Fri noon–2pm & 8–10.30pm, Sat 8–10.30pm. Closed two weeks mid-Aug.

Le Potager du Marais 22 rue Rambuteau, 4ᵉ ☎01.42.74.24.66; Mᵒ Rambuteau. Come early or book in advance for a place at this tiny vegetarian restaurant, which has only 25 covers at a long communal table. The ingredients are all organic and there's plenty for vegans and those with gluten allergies, too. Dishes include goat's cheese with honey, "crusty" quinoa burger, and ravioli with basil. Set *menu* €25. Mon–Fri noon–3pm & 6–10.30pm, Sat & Sun noon–10.30pm.

Bastille

See map, pp.104–105.

Bars and cafés

Iguana 15 rue de la Roquette, corner of rue Daval, 11ᵉ; Mᵒ Bastille. A place to be seen in, with a decor of trellises, colonial fans and a brushed bronze bar. By day, the clientele studies recherché art reviews over excellent coffee, while things hot up at night with a youngish, high-spirited crowd. DJ on Thurs. Cocktails around €10. Daily 9am–5am.

Café de l'Industrie 16 rue St-Sabin, 11ᵉ; Mᵒ Bastille. One of the best Bastille cafés (actually two cafés, across the road from each other), packed out at lunch and every evening. There are rugs on the floor around solid old wooden tables, mounted rhinoceros heads, old black-and-white photos on the walls and a young, unpretentious crowd enjoying the comfortable absence of minimalism. Simple *plats du jour* such as sausage and mash and pasta dishes cost around €9. The waitresses are charming, though service can be slow. Daily 10am–2am.

SanZSanS 49 rue du Faubourg St-Antoine, 11ᵉ; Mᵒ Bastille. Gothic getup of red velvet, oil paintings and chandeliers, popular with a young crowd, especially on Fri & Sat evenings, when DJs play funk, Brazilian beats and house. Drinks are reasonably priced. Daily 9am–5am.

Restaurants

L'Auberge Pyrénées Cévennes 106 rue de la Folie Méricourt, 11e ⓣ 01.43.57.33.78; Mº République. Make sure you come hungry to this homely little place serving hearty portions of country cuisine. The garlicky *moules marinière* and the wonderful cassoulet, served in its own copper pot, are fantastic. Around €30 a head. Closed Sat lunch and all day Sun.

Bistrot du Peintre 116 av Ledru-Rollin, 11e ⓣ 01.47.00.34.39; Mº Faidherbe-Chaligny. A traditional neighbourhood bistro, where small tables are jammed together beneath faded Art Nouveau frescoes and wood panelling. The emphasis is on traditional cuisine, with dishes such as beef tartare and *confit de canard* for around €15. Mon–Sat 7am–2am, Sun 10am–1am.

Le Repaire de Cartouche 8 bd des Filles du Calvaire, 11e ⓣ 01.47.00.25.86; Mº Filles du Calvaire. Supposedly the house where eighteenth-century brigand Cartouche once hid away, this cosy, rustic-style restaurant is a popular bolthole with locals, who come for the excellent classic French cuisine and the exceptional wine list of over 400 vintages. Around €50 a head for three courses and wine. Closed Mon & Sun.

Quartier Latin
See map, pp.110–111.

Bars and cafés

Café de la Mosquée 39 rue Geoffroy-St-Hilaire, 5e; Mº Monge. Drink mint tea and eat sweet cakes in the Algerian-styled courtyard haven of the Paris mosque. Consider the hammam-massage-meal option. Daily 9am–midnight.

🏃 **Café de la Nouvelle Mairie** 19 rue des Fossés St-Jacques, 5e; Mº Cluny-La Sorbonne/RER Luxembourg. Sleek café-wine bar with a university clientele (note it's shut at weekends). Serves satisfying mains like linguine or lamb steaks, as well as *assiettes* of cheese or charcuterie (all around €10). On warm days there are outside tables on the picturesque square. Mon, Wed & Fri 9am–8pm, Tues & Thurs 9am–midnight.

Curio Parlor 16 rue des Bernardins, 5e; Mº Maubert-Mutualité. This secretive – spot the entrance if you can – pocket cocktail bar is much patronised by Paris's gilded youth. DJs play in the designer-dressed basement. Tues–Thurs & Sun 6pm–2am, Fri & Sat 6pm–4am.

L'Ecritoire 3 place de la Sorbonne, 5e; Mº Cluny-La Sorbonne/RER Luxembourg. This classic university café has outside tables right beside the Sorbonne. Daily 7am–midnight

🏃 **La Fourmi Ailée** 8 rue du Fouarre, 5e; Mº Maubert-Mutualité. Simple, filling food is

served in this relaxed *salon de thé*. A high, mural-painted ceiling and background jazz contribute to the atmosphere. Around €12 for a *plat*. Daily noon–11pm.

Le Pantalon Bar 7 rue Royer-Collard, 5e; RER Luxembourg. This archetypal student dive sports weathered mirrors and graffiti-covered walls, and serves very cheap drinks. Daily 5.30pm–2am.

Le Piano Vache 8 rue Laplace, 5e; Mº Cardinal-Lemoine. Venerable, grungy bar crammed with students drinking at little tables. Mon–Fri noon–2am, Sat & Sun 9pm–2am.

Les Pipos 2 rue de l'École Polytechnique, 5e; Mº Maubert-Mutualité/Cardinal-Lemoine. This antique bar has a decor that's heavy on old wood, and a local clientele. Serves wines from €5 a glass along with simple plates of Auvergnat charcuterie, cheese and the like (€10–15). Mon–Sat 8.30am–1am; closed 2 weeks in Aug.

Le Reflet 6 rue Champollion, 5e; Mº Cluny-La Sorbonne. This cinema café has a pleasingly scruffy black decor, and its rickety tables packed with artsy film-goers. Perfect for a pre-film drink, perhaps accompanied by a steak or quiche from the blackboard specials. Daily 10am–2am.

Le Verre à Pied 118bis rue Mouffetard, 5e; Mº Monge. Deeply old-fashioned market bar where traders take their morning *vin rouge*, or sit down to eat a *plat du jour* for €11. Some have been doing it so long they've got little plaques on their tables. Tues–Sat 9am–8.30pm, Sun 9am–3.30pm.

Restaurants

Brasserie Balzar 49 rue des Écoles, 5e ⓣ 01.43.54.13.67; Mº Maubert-Mutualité. This classic, high-ceilinged brasserie with its attentive, suited waiters feels almost intimidatingly Parisian – though if you're unlucky, or eat early, the tourist clientele can spoil the Left Bank mood. À la carte is around €40. Daily 8am–11.30pm.

🏃 **Le Buisson Ardent** 25 rue Jussieu, 5e ⓣ 01.43.54.93.02; Mº Jussieu. Generous helpings of first-class cooking with vivacious touches: think *velouté* of watermelon followed by a perfectly cooked sea bream. The dining room is high-ceilinged, panelled and muralled and the atmosphere convivial. Lunch *menu* €15, dinner €29. Mon–Fri noon–2pm & 7.30–10pm; Sat 5.30–10pm; closed two weeks in Aug.

Les Cinq Saveurs d'Anada 72 rue du Cardinal-Lemoine, 5e ⓣ 01.43.29.58.54; Mº Cardinal-Lemoine. Airy and informal restaurant serving delicious organic vegetarian food. Salads (€8) are good, as are more robust dishes such as tofu soufflé with ginger (around €14–18). Tues–Sun noon–2.30pm & 7.30–10.30pm.

L'Ecurie 58 rue de la Montagne Ste-Geneviève, corner of rue Laplace, 5ᵉ ☎ 01.46.33.68.49; Mᵒ Maubert-Mutualité/Cardinal-Lemoine. Shoehorned into a former stables, this family-run restaurant is bustling and lovable. Outside tables provide a few extra seats. Serves mostly meat dishes grilled with *frites* for less than €20. Mon–Sat noon–3pm & 7pm–midnight, Sun 7pm–midnight.

Perraudin 157 rue St-Jacques, 5ᵉ ☎ 01.46.33.15.75; RER Luxembourg. Mon–Fri noon–2pm & 7.30–10.15pm; closed last 2 weeks in Aug. One of the classic *bistros* of the Left Bank, featuring enjoyable homely cooking. The place is brightly lit, packed and thick with Parisian chatter. Lunch *menu* at €18, evening *menu* at €28.

Le Petit Pontoise 9 rue de Pontoise, 5ᵉ ☎ 01.43.29.25.20; Mᵒ Maubert-Mutualité. This relaxed, young *bistro* is as authentically Parisian as you can get this close to the river: lace café-curtains, little wooden tables, a bar in one corner and blackboard specials like haricot bean salad with prawns, or duck breast. Puddings are outstanding. Around €35 a head.

🏃 **Le Pré-Verre** 8 rue Thénard 5ᵉ ☎ 01.43.54.59.47; Mᵒ Maubert-Mutualité. This sleek *bistro à vins* has a great wine list, and interesting modern French food with a fine judiciously oriental touches – you might find swordfish on blue poppy seeds and artichoke, or chicken with avocado and ginger. *Menus* at €28.50, or just €13.50 at lunch. Tues–Sat noon–2pm & 7.30–10.30pm; closed 3 weeks in Aug.

Le Reminet 3 rue des Grands Degrés, 5ᵉ ☎ 01.44.07.04.24; Mᵒ Maubert-Mutualité. This artful, chandelier-hung little *bistro*-restaurant graces high-quality traditional French ingredients with imaginative sauces. Gastronomic *menu* at around €50, with a bargain lunch *menu* at €14. Mon & Thurs–Sun noon–3pm & 7.30–11pm; closed 2 weeks in Aug.

St-Germain

See map, pp.116–117.

Bars and cafés

Le 10 10 rue de l'Odéon, 6ᵉ; Mᵒ Odéon. Classic Art Deco-era posters line the walls of this small, dark, studenty bar. The atmospherically vaulted cellar bar gets noisy in the small hours. Daily 6pm–2am.

Bar du Marché 75 rue de Seine, 6ᵉ; Mᵒ Mabillon. A thrumming, fashionable café where the *serveurs* are cutely kitted out in flat caps and aprons, and the rue de Buci market bustles on the doorstep. Lively by night or day. Daily 7am–2am.

🏃 **Bistrot des Augustins** 39 quai des Grands Augustins, 6ᵉ; Mᵒ St-Michel. That a wine bar this friendly and traditional should be found on

the riverbank between the Pont Neuf and Place St-Michel is quite incredible. Serves good charcuterie, salads and hot *gratins*, all for around €10. Daily 10am–midnight.

🏃 **Café de la Mairie** 8 place St-Sulpice, 6ᵉ; Mᵒ St-Sulpice. A peaceful, pleasant café on the sunny north side of this gorgeous square, right opposite the church of St-Sulpice. Perfect for basking at an outdoor table, admiring the neighbourhood's beautiful people. Mon–Sat 7am–2am.

Chez Georges 11 rue des Canettes, 6ᵉ; Mᵒ Mabillon. This dilapidated wine bar is one of the few authentic addresses in an area dominated by big, noisy theme pubs (you'll find plenty in the vicinity if you're in the market). The young, studenty crowd gets good-naturedly rowdy later on in the cellar bar. Tues–Sat noon–2am; closed Aug.

🏃 **Le Flore** 172 bd St-Germain, 6ᵉ; Mᵒ St-Germain-des-Prés. The great rival and immediate neighbour of the equally famous (and rather similar) *Les Deux Magots*. There's a unique hierarchy: tourists on the *terrasse*, beautiful people inside, intellectuals upstairs. Sartre, de Beauvoir, Camus and Marcel Carné used to hang out here. Try the hot chocolate. Daily 7am–1.30am.

La Mezzanine de l'Alcazar 62 rue Mazarine, 6ᵉ; Mᵒ Odéon. Daily 7pm–2am. Cool, expensive cocktail bar set on a mezzanine level overlooking Conran's *Alcazar* restaurant. Most nights start off relaxed and finish with dancing, with hardcore types moving on to the *WAGG* club below. DJs Wed–Sat.

La Palette 43 rue de Seine, 6ᵉ; Mᵒ Odéon. This once-famous Beaux-Arts student hangout is now frequented by art dealers, though it still attracts a trendy young crowd in the evenings. There's a roomy *terrasse* outside, and some good daily specials on the *menu*. Mon–Sat 9am–2am.

Au Petit Suisse 16 rue de Vaugirard, 6ᵉ; RER Luxembourg/Mᵒ Cluny-La Sorbonne. The perfect retreat from the Jardin du Luxembourg, with everything you'd need from a café, including a lovely outdoor terrace. Mon–Sat 7am–midnight, Sun 7am–11.30pm.

Restaurants

🏃 **Brasserie Lipp** 151 bd St-Germain, 6ᵉ ☎ 01.45.48.53.91; Mᵒ St-Germain-des-Prés. One of the most celebrated of all the classic Paris brasseries, with a wonderful 1900s wood-and-glass interior. There are decent *plats du jour*, including the famous *choucroute* (sauerkraut), for under €20, but exploring à la carte gets expensive. Daily noon–12.45am

Le Christine 1 rue Christine, 6ᵉ ☎ 01.40.51.71.64; Mᵒ St-Germain-des-Prés. Mixes old-fashioned and innovative, satisfyingly: old wooden beams and stone walls are set off by contemporary paintings, and duck leg and *filet de boeuf* jostle with dishes like poached eggs with violet artichokes. *Menus* €35 and up. Mon–Fri noon–2.30pm & 6.30pm–midnight, Sat & Sun 6.30pm–midnight.

L'Epigramme 9 rue de l'Eperon, 6ᵉ
☎01.44.41.00.09; Mᵒ Odéon. This tiny, simple restaurant offers quality French cooking, stripped bare of pretensions. Prices around €30, plus wine. Tues–Sun noon–2.30pm & 7.30–11.30pm.

La Ferrandaise 8 rue de Vaugirard, 6ᵉ
☎01.43.26.36.36; Mᵒ St-Germain-des-Prés. relaxed, airy restaurant near the Jardin du Luxembourg offering rich dishes such as crab ravioli, oven-steamed pike-perch or the richest shoulder of lamb. Evening *menu* €32. Mon–Thurs noon–2pm & 7.30–10.30pm, Fri noon–2pm & 7.30–11pm. Sat 7.30pm–midnight.

Gaya Rive Gauche 44 rue du Bac, 6ᵉ
☎01.45.44.73.73; Mᵒ Rue du Bac. This hyper-designed, upscale mini-restaurant is the fishy satellite of celebrity chef Pierre Gagnaire's empire. Imagine *pressé* of skate with a bloody mary sauce, or grilled swordfish on a bed of caramel, soya and Asian mushrooms. Around €90 a head with wine. Mon–Sat noon–2.30pm & 7.30–11pm.

Polidor 41 rue Monsieur le Prince, 6ᵉ
☎01.43.26.95.34; Mᵒ Odéon. Open since 1845, this Left Bank classic is still bright and bustling with aproned waitresses and noisy regulars dining until late. Serves solid French classics like *confit de canard* or guinea fowl with *lardons,* from around €13. Mon–Sat noon–2.30pm & 7pm–12.30am, Sun noon–2.30pm & 7pm–12.30am.

Le Salon d'Hélène 4 rue d'Assas, 6ᵉ
☎01.42.22.00.11; Mᵒ St-Sulpice/Sèvres-Babylone. Celebrated chef Hélène Darroze's gastronomic, Michelin-starred *Restaurant d'Hélène* (lunch *menus* from €52, evenings from €125) has a more relaxed ground-floor "salon", where you can find similarly imaginative, southern-European tinged dishes, in tapas portions. Don't let the lack of windows put you off: this is interesting cooking at low prices for the quality – from €28 up to €105 for the tasting *menu* with wine. Tues–Sat 12.30–2.15pm & 7.30–10.15pm; closed Aug.

Ze Kitchen Galerie 4 rue des Grands-Augustins, 6ᵉ ☎01.44.32.00.32; Mᵒ St-Michel. Halfway between restaurant and trendy art gallery in atmosphere, the food mixes Asian influences with contemporary Mediterranean cuisine – try gnocchetti with squid and *nori,* or pork croquettes with Thai herbs. At dinner, expect to pay upwards of €60, without wine. Mon–Fri noon–2.30pm & 7–11pm, Sat 7–11pm.

Trocadéro, Eiffel Tower and the Septième

See map, pp.120–121.

Bars and cafés

Café du Marché 38 rue Cler, 7ᵉ; Mᵒ La Tour-Maubourg. Big, busy café-brasserie in the middle of the rue Cler market, serving reasonably priced meals and chunky salads. There's outdoor seating, and a covered *terrasse* in winter. Mon–Sat 7am–midnight.

Tokyo Eat/Tokyo Self Palais de Tokyo, 16ᵉ
☎01.47.20.00.29; Mᵒ Iéna/Alma-Marceau. The restaurant inside the Site de Création Contemporaine is a self-consciously cool place to eat, with its futuristic, colourful decor, arty clientele and Mediterranean fusion menu. The more dressed-down *Tokyo Self* café is a reliable bet for a drink and a snack. Tues–Sun noon–1am, bar till 2am.

Restaurants

L'Arpège 84 rue de Varenne, 7ᵉ ☎01.45.05.09.06; Mᵒ Varenne. Mon–Fri noon–2.30pm & 8–11pm. Alain Passard is one of France's great chefs – and he really pushes boundaries here by giving vegetables the spotlight. Dishes such as grilled turnips with chestnuts or duck with black sesame and orange brandy are astounding. The lunch *menu* costs €130, and you'll pay €200–300 à la carte.

La Fontaine de Mars 129 rue Saint-Dominique, 7ᵉ ☎01.47.05.46.44; Mᵒ La Tour-Maubourg. Heavy, pink-checked tablecloths, leather banquettes, tiled floor, attentive service: this quintessentially French restaurant serves reliable, meaty southwestern French cuisine, and has lovely outside tables – no wonder President Obama ate here. Starters at €11–15, *plat du jour* €20. Daily noon–2.30pm & 7.30–11pm.

Le Jules Verne Pilier Sud, Eiffel Tower, 7ᵉ
☎01.45.55.61.44; Mᵒ Bir-Hakeim. Dining halfway up the Eiffel Tower is enough of a draw in itself, but since Alain Ducasse's team took over in 2007, the gastronomic food is worthy of the setting. Best at dinner (€200), but cheaper for a weekday lunch (a mere €85). Reserve months in advance, and don't expect a window table. Daily noon–2pm & 7–10pm.

Aux Marchés du Palais 5 rue de la Manutention, 16ᵉ ☎01.47.23.52.80; Mᵒ Iéna. Simple, traditionally styled *bistro*, with sunny tables on the pavement opposite the side wall of the Palais de Tokyo. You can eat heartily around €35, and there's nothing half as satisfying anywhere nearby. Mon–Fri noon–2pm & 7.30–10.30pm, Sat 7.30–10.30pm.

Thoumieux 79 rue St-Dominique, 7ᵉ
☎01.47.05.49.75; Mᵒ La Tour-Maubourg. The fashionable Costes-Pièges team has given this classic address a gastronomic makeover, while mostly leaving the be-mirrored and banquette-heavy

Art Deco interior blessedly intact. Big-hearted brasserie classics with a twist – imagine pork belly with Asian spices. Around €50 à la carte. Daily noon–2.30pm & 7–11pm.

Montmartre and le Neuvième

See map, p.129.

Bars and cafés

Café des Deux Moulins 15 rue Lepic, 18ᵉ ℡01.42.54.90.50; Mᵒ Blanche. Having seen its early-2000s heyday of fans on the trawl of *Amélie* lore (she waited tables here in the film), this diner-style café is back to what it always was: a down-to-earth neighbourhood hangout, preserved in a bright, charming 1950s interior. Sunday brunch is popular. Mon–Sat 7am–2am, Sun 9am–2am.

Chez Camille 8 rue Ravignan, 18ᵉ; Mᵒ Abbesses. This delightful little bar on the slopes of the Butte has a stylish interior of old mirrors, ceiling fans and mismatched seating, and a fashionable young clientele. Tues–Sat 9am–2am, Sun 9am–8pm.

La Fourmi 74 rue des Martyrs, 18ᵉ; Mᵒ Pigalle/Abbesses. The glamorous decor, long bar and high-ceilinged spaciousness draw the discerning *bourgeois-bohemians* of Abbesses and the 10ᵉ for cocktails, wine and chatter, to the tune of lounge music. Mon–Thurs 8am–2am, Fri & Sat 8am–4am, Sun 10am–2am.

L'Été en Pente Douce 23 rue Muller, 18ᵉ (corner of rue Paul-Albert) ℡01.42.64.02.67. Mᵒ Château-Rouge. The big salads and *plats* (around €14) are unspectacular, but the big outdoor terrace alongside the steps leading up to Sacré-Cœur is delightful on a sunny day. Daily noon–midnight.

Au Rendez-Vous des Amis 23 rue Gabrielle, 18ᵉ; Mᵒ Abbesses. Halfway up the Butte, this small, ramshackle, smoky and community-spirited hangout is a magnet for Montmartre locals, especially the young, artsy and alternative-leaning. Daily 8.30am–2am.

Le Relais de la Butte 12 rue Ravignan, 18ᵉ; Mᵒ Abbesses. Come for the outdoor café tables on the expansive terrace, with its amazing views over Paris. The food is unexceptional – salads and *plats* for around €15. Daily 8.30am–midnight.

Le Sancerre 35 rue des Abbesses, 18ᵉ; Mᵒ Abbesses. A much-loved and always thrumming hangout under the southern slope of Montmartre, with a row of outside tables perfect for watching the world go by. The food can be disappointing. Daily 7am–2am.

Restaurants

Café Burq 6 rue Burq, 18ᵉ ℡01.42.52.81.27; Mᵒ Abbesses.

Ultra-relaxed bar-restaurant offering (from 8pm to midnight) zesty-flavoured dishes such as an asparagus *velouté*, veal with lime cream sauce, or honey-roast Camembert. You'll jostle elbows with a trendy clientele, whose noisy conversation competes with the DJ soundtrack. Mon–Sat 7pm–2am.

Au Grain de Folie 24 rue de La Vieuville, 18ᵉ ℡01.42.58.15.57; Mᵒ Abbesses. A tiny, simple and colourfully dilapidated vegetarian place where all the food is inexpensive and organic and there's always a vegan option. Tues–Sat 12.30–2.30pm & 7.30–10.30pm, Sun 12.30–10.30pm.

Le Mono 40 rue Véron, 18ᵉ ℡01.46.06.99.20; Mᵒ Abbesses. Welcoming, family-run Togolese restaurant. Mains (around €12) are mostly grilled fish or meat served with sour, hot sauces, with rice or cassava on the side. Enjoyable atmosphere, with soukous on the stereo, Afro-print tablecloths and Togolese carvings on the walls. Thurs–Tues 7.30–11pm.

Á la Pomponnette 42 rue Lepic, 18ᵉ ℡01.46.06.08.36; Mᵒ Blanche/Abbesses. A genuine old Montmartre *bistro*, with posters, drawings and a zinc-top bar. The traditional French food is just as it should be, with an evening *menu* at €34. Tues–Thurs noon–2.30pm & 7–11pm, Fri & Sat noon–2.30pm & 7pm–midnight.

Le Relais Gascon 6 rue des Abbesses, 18ᵉ ℡01.42.58.58.22; Mᵒ Abbesses. Serving hearty, filling meals all day, this two-storey restaurant provides a welcome blast of straightforward Gascon heartiness in this touristy part of town. The enormous warm salads cost €11.50, and there are equally tasty *plats* for around €12. Daily 10am–2am.

Northern Paris

Bars, cafés and restaurants

Chez Casimir 6 rue de Belzunce, 10ᵉ ℡01.48.78.28.80; Mᵒ Gare du Nord. It's astonishing to find a restaurant this good so close to the Gare du Nord. Serves inexpensive (€22 at lunch, or €29 in the evening) but well-cooked dishes in basic, unrenovated *bistrot* surroundings. The Sunday "brunch" (€25) is more scallops and cod casserole than eggs and ham. Mon 7.30–10.30pm, Tues–Fri noon–2pm & 7.30–10.30pm.

Julien 16 rue du Faubourg St-Denis, 10ᵉ ℡01.47.70.12.06; Mᵒ Strasbourg-St-Denis. Utterly handsome brasserie, all globe lamps, hat stands, white linen, brass and polished wood, with frescoes of flowery Art Deco maidens. Even the poor service and crammed-in clientele can't spoil it. Serves satisfying if unsophisticated fish and seafood dishes, with *menus* from €30 and up. Daily noon–3pm & 7pm–1am.

Paris for vegetarians

The chances of finding vegetarian main dishes on the menus of traditional French restaurants are not good, though these days some of the newer, more innovative establishments will often have one or two on offer. It's also possible to put together a meal from vegetarian starters, omelettes and salads. Your other option is to go for a Middle Eastern or Indian restaurant or head for one of the city's handful of proper **vegetarian restaurants** – they do tend to be based on a healthy diet principle rather than *haute cuisine*, but at least you get a choice. Try **Les Cinq Saveurs d'Anada** (see p.140) and **Le Potager du Marais** (see p.139).

Olympic Café 20 rue Léon, 10ᵉ ⊛ www.rueleon
.net; Mᵒ Château Rouge. In the heart of the poor and peeling Goutte d'Or, this boho café-restaurant pumps out life and energy like a lighthouse. The basement venue features six gigs a week, from African rock to klezmer, Bulgarian folk and French *chanson*. Tues–Sun 11am–2am.

Wepler 14 place de Clichy, 18ᵉ
⊕ 01.45.22.53.24; Mᵒ Place-de-Clichy. Now over a hundred years old, and still a beacon of conviviality amid the hustle of place de Clichy. Its clientele has moved upmarket since it was depicted in Truffaut's *Les 400 Coups*, but as palatial brasseries go, *Wepler* has remained unashamedly *populaire*. Serves honest brasserie fare and classic seafood platters (€40–45 à la carte). Daily noon–1am, café from 8am.

Eastern Paris

Bars and cafés

Le Baron Rouge 1 rue Théophile-Roussel, corner of place d'Aligre market, 12ᵉ; Mᵒ Ledru-Rollin. This traditional *bar à vins* is perfect for a light lunch or aperitif after shopping at the place d'Aligre market. If it's crowded inside (as it often is), join the locals standing around the wine barrels on the pavement lunching on *saucisson* or mussels washed down with a glass of Muscadet. Tues–Sat 10am–2pm & 5–9.30pm, Sun 10am–2pm.

Café Charbon 109 rue Oberkampf, 11ᵉ;
Mᵒ St-Maur/Parmentier. The place that pioneered the rise of the Oberkampf bar scene is still going strong and continues to draw in a fashionable mixed crowd. Part of the allure is the attractively restored *fin-de-siècle* decor. Thurs–Sat 9am–4am, Sun–Wed 9am–2am.

Le Cannibale 93 rue Jean-Pierre Timbaud, 11ᵉ; Mᵒ Couronnes. A cool retro café-bar, where nattily dressed locals sit at their laptops or chill out at the bar against a soundtrack of electro lounge. Classic dishes such as *blanquette de veau* are served in the dining area, and there's live music (chanson, jazz funk, Cuban) most Sundays at 6pm. Daily 8am–2am.

Aux Folies 8 rue de Belleville, 20ᵉ; Mᵒ Belleville. *Aux Folies* offers a real slice of Belleville life: its outside terrace and 1930s long brass bar, with mirrored tiles and red neon lights, are packed day and night with a cosmopolitan and artsy crowd sipping inexpensive cocktails and beer. Daily 6.30am–1am.

Pause Café 41 rue de Charonne, corner of rue Keller, 11ᵉ; Mᵒ Ledru-Rollin. Or maybe "Pose Café" – given its popularity with the *quartier's* young and fashionable who bag the pavement tables at lunch and aperitif time. *Plats du jour* around €12. Mon–Sat 8am–2am, Sun 8.45am–8pm.

Restaurants

Bistrot Paul Bert 18 rue Paul Bert, 11ᵉ
⊕ 01.43.72.24.01; Mᵒ Faidherbe-Chaligny. A quintessential Parisian bistro, patronized by a mix of locals and visitors drawn by the cosy, friendly ambience and high-quality simple fare such as *poulet rôti* as well as more sophisticated dishes such as guinea fowl and morel mushrooms. Reckon on around €35 a head for dinner, and the wine list is reasonably priced, with an excellent selection of familiar and rarer vintages. Closed Mon & Sun and three weeks in Aug.

Flo 7 cour des Petites-Écuries, 10ᵉ
⊕ 01.47.70.13.59; Mᵒ Château d'Eau. Tucked away down a secret side alley, this is a dark, handsome and extremely atmospheric old-time brasserie. Sound but not scintillating fish and seafood are the specialities, along with snooty wait-staff. From around €30. Daily noon–3pm & 7pm–1.30am.

Julien 16 rue du Faubourg St-Denis, 10ᵉ
⊕ 01.47.70.12.06; Mᵒ Strasbourg-St-Denis. So splendid is the decor – globe lamps, brass, murals, white linen and polished wood, with frescoes of flowery Art Deco maidens – that not even the patchy service and crammed-in clientele can't spoil it. Waiters in ankle-length aprons bring satisfying if unsophisticated fish and seafood dishes, along with brasserie classics like salt pork with lentils. Expect to pay €30–50 a head. Daily noon–3pm & 6.30pm–1am.

Lao Siam 49 rue de Belleville, 19e
℡ 01.40.40.09.68; M° Belleville. The surroundings
are nothing special, but the excellent Thai and
Laotian food, popular with locals, makes up for it.
From around €20 a head. Mon–Fri noon–3pm &
6–11.30pm, Sat & Sun noon–12.30am.
Pooja 91 passage Brady, 10e ℡ 01.48.24.00.83;
M° Strasbourg-St-Denis/Château d'Eau. Not quite
London, let alone Mumbai, but friendly and located
in a glazed passage that is lined with Indian
restaurants, all offering good if rather similar fare.
Costs around €20 in the evening. Daily noon–3pm
& 7–11pm.

🏃 **Le Train Bleu** Gare de Lyon, 12e
℡ 01.43.43.09.06; M° Gare de Lyon. The
sumptuous decor of what must be the world's
most luxurious station buffet is straight out of a
bygone golden era – everything drips with gilt, and
chandeliers hang from high ceilings frescoed with
scenes from the Paris–Lyon–Marseilles train route.
The traditional French cuisine has a hard time
living up to all this, but is still pretty good, if a tad
overpriced. The set *menu* costs €52, including half
a bottle of wine; for à la carte reckon on around
€70. Daily 11.30am–3pm & 7–11pm.
Waly Fay 6 rue Godefroy-Cavaignac, 11e
℡ 01.40.24.17.79; M° Charonne. A moderately
priced West African restaurant with a cosy, stylish
atmosphere, the dim lighting, rattan and old, faded
photographs creating an intimate, faintly colonial
ambience. Smart young Parisians come here to
dine on perfumed, richly spiced stews and other
West African delicacies. Mon–Sat noon–2pm &
7.30–11pm, Sun 11am–5pm; closed last two
weeks of Aug.

Southern Paris

Bars and cafés

🏃 **L'Entrepôt** 7–9 rue Francis de Pressensé,
14e; M° Pernety. A spacious, relaxed café –
part of an arty cinema – with lovely seats in its green
courtyard. Serves a great Sunday brunch (€25), has
plats du jour for around €15–25, and holds
occasional evening concerts. Mon–Sat noon–2am.
La Folie en Tête 33 rue Butte-aux-Cailles, 13e;
M° Place-d'Italie/Corvisart. Surveying the Butte
aux-Cailles from its prime corner spot, this vibrant,
friendly and distinctly lefty café-bar is a classic.
The walls are littered with bric-a-brac and musical
instruments and there's usually something cool
playing on the system – laid-back underground
beats, perhaps, or a young singer-songwriter's
latest album. Mon–Sat 6pm–2am.
Le Merle Moqueur 11 rue Butte-aux-Cailles,
13e; M° Place d'Italie/Corvisart. This bohemian
Butte-aux-Cailles bar once saw the Paris debut of

Manu Chao. It maintains an alternative edge,
though most days serves up 1980s French rock
CDs and home-made flavoured rums to young
Parisians. If you don't fancy the playlist when you
arrive, you can always try the very similar
Le Diapason, two doors along. Daily 5pm–2am.
Le Select 99 bd du Montparnasse, 6e; M° Vavin. If
you want to visit one of the great Montparnasse
cafés, as frequented by Picasso, Matisse, Henry
Miller and F. Scott Fitzgerald, make it this one. It
has changed least; only the brasserie-style food is
disappointing. Daily 7am–2am, Fri & Sat till 4am.
Café Tournesol 9 rue de la Gâité, 14e; M° Edgar
Quinet. This corner café-bar attracts bohemian
twenty-somethings for its distressed chic, outside
tables and cool playlists. Fashionable yet
welcoming – a rare combination. Daily 7am–2am.
Le Rosebud 11bis rue Delambre, 14e; M° Vavin.
A hushed, faintly exclusive Art Nouveau bar just off
the bd Montparnasse, serving wonderful Martinis
from €12. Daily 7pm–2am.

Restaurants

🏃 **L'Avant Goût** 37 rue Bobillot, 13e
℡ 01.45.81.14.06; M° Place d'Italie. Small
neighbourhood restaurant with bright red leather
banquettes and a reputation for exciting modern
French cuisine. Superb value *menus*, lunch €14,
dinner €31. Tues–Sat 12.30–2pm & 7.45–10.45pm

🏃 **Le Bambou** 70 rue Baudricourt, 13e
℡ 01.45.70.91.75; M° Tolbiac. Tiny Asian-
quarter restaurant crammed with local punters
tucking into giant, inexpensive pho soups and
Vietnamese specialities. Last orders at 10.30pm,
but you can stay till midnight. Tues–Sun
11.45am–3.30pm & 6.45–10.30pm.
Chez Gladines 30 rue des Cinq Diamants, 13e
℡ 01.45.80.70.10; M° Corvisart. This tiny, Basque-
run corner bistro is always warm, welcoming and
packed with young people. Serves rich Basque and
southwest dishes such as *magret de canard*. Giant
salads cost under €10, and you'll pay less than €20
for a (very) full meal. Mon & Tues noon–3pm &
7pm–midnight; Wed–Sun noon–3pm & 7pm–1am.

🏃 **Le Café du Commerce** 51 rue du
Commerce, 15e ℡ 01.45.75.03.27;
M° Emile Zola. Once a 1920s workers' canteen,
this is still a buzzing place to eat, with tables set
on three storeys of galleries. Honest, high-quality
meat is the speciality, but there's always a fish and
vegetarian dish too. Expect to pay €15–20 for a
plat, though the lunch *menu* is a bargain €15. Daily
noon–3pm & 7pm–midnight.
La Coupole 102 bd du Montparnasse, 14e
℡ 01.43.20.14.20; M° Vavin. The largest and most
enduring arty-chic Parisian brasserie, *La Coupole*

still buzzes with conversation and clatter under its high, chandeliered roof. The menu runs from oysters to Welsh rarebit, with plenty of fishy and meaty classics in between. Evening *menu* at €30.50. Daily 8am–1am.

L'Os à Moelle 3 rue Vasco de Gama, 15ᵉ ☎ 01.45.57.27.27; Mᵒ Lourmel. The highlight of this relaxed *bistro* is the €35 four-course *menu*, which brings you everything from

Jerusalem artichoke and black truffle soup to fine steaks, via scallops and giant snails. You can also dine across the road at the no-frills *La Cave de l'Os à Moelle* (☎ 01.45.57.28.88/28), where you sit at communal tables, helping yourself to a steaming pot of stew or the like (*menu* €22.50). Reserve well in advance at either. Tues–Sun noon–3pm & 7pm–midnight; closed 3 weeks in Aug.

Music and nightlife

Paris's fame as the quintessential home of decadent, hedonistic **nightlife** has endured for centuries. That reputation is sustained today by a vibrant **bar and club scene** and a world-class **live music** programme. World music and jazz are particularly strong, but you'll find everything from house and electro-lounge to home-grown rock and chanson.

Information and tickets

The listings magazine *Pariscope* is the traditional first port of call. For more detail, try *Nova* magazine (ⓦ www.novaplanet.com), also available from newsstands, or specialist websites such as ⓦ www.radiofg.com and www.triselectif.net. To find the latest club nights seek out flyers – or word-of-mouth tips – in one of the city's trendier bars. The easiest places to get **tickets** for concerts, whether rock, jazz, chanson or classical, are at one of Paris's many FNAC stores – the main branch is in the Forum des Halles, 1–5 rue Pierre-Lescot, 1ᵉʳ (Mon–Sat 10am–8pm; ☎ 08.25.02.00.20, ⓦ www.fnac.com; Mᵒ Châtelet-Les Halles).

Live music venues

Most of the **venues** listed here are primarily concert venues, though some double up as clubs on certain nights, or after-hours. The majority host bands on just a couple of nights a week. Admission **prices** vary depending on who's playing. Note too that some clubs host gigs earlier on in the evening, and jazz venues (see p.148) often branch out into world music and folk.

Le Bataclan 50 bd Voltaire, 11ᵉ ☎ 01.43.14.00.30, ⓦ www.myspace.com/bataclanparis; Mᵒ Oberkampf. Classic pagoda-styled, ex-theatre venue (seats 1200) with one of the best and most eclectic line-ups covering anything from international and local dance and rock acts – Francis Cabrel, Chemical Brothers, Khaled, Hole – to *chanson*, opera, comedy and techno nights.
Café de la Danse 5 passage Louis-Philippe, 11ᵉ ☎ 01.47.00.57.59, ⓦ www.cafedeladanse.com; Mᵒ Bastille. Rock, pop, world, folk and jazz music played in an intimate and attractive space. Open nights of concerts only.
La Cigale 120 bd de Rochechouart, 18ᵉ ☎ 01.49.25.81.75, ⓦ www.lacigale.fr; Mᵒ Pigalle. Since 1987 and a Philippe Starck renovation this historic, 1400-seat Pigalle theatre has become a

leading venue for French rock, world music and indie acts. You might see anything from Rock dinosaur Marc Lavoine to Electro superstars Beat Torrent, or from actress/chanteuse Charlotte Gainsbourg to Ivory Coast reggae star Tiken Jah Fakoly.
Le Divan du Monde 75 rue des Martyrs, 18ᵉ ☎ 01.40.05.06.99, ⓦ www.divandumonde.com; Mᵒ Anvers. A youthful venue in a café whose regulars once included Toulouse-Lautrec. One of the city's most diverse and exciting programmes, ranging from techno to Congolese rumba, with dancing till dawn on weekend nights.
Elysée Montmartre 72 bd de Rochechouart, 18ᵉ ☎ 01.55.07.06.00, ⓦ www.elyseemontmartre.com; Mᵒ Anvers. A cavernous historic Montmartre nightspot that pulls in a young, excitable crowd

with its rock, soul, R&B and hip-hop acts – the Pharcyde, the Hives, Public Enemy. Also hosts up-tempo Latin and club nights.
Maroquinerie 23 rue Boyer, 20ᵉ ℡01.40.33.35.05, ⊛www.lamaroquinerie.fr; Mᵒ Gambetta. The smallish concert venue is the downstairs part of a trendy arts centre. The line-up is rock, folk and jazz, with a particularly good selection of French musicians.

Point Ephemère 200 quai de Valmy, 10ᵉ ℡01.40.34.02.48, ⊛www.pointephemere.org; Mᵒ Jaurès. Run by an arts collective in a disused warehouse, this superbly dilapidated venue lives up to its reputation as a nexus for alternative and underground performers of all kinds. There are gigs most nights, covering anything from electro to Afro-jazz via folk-rock, as well as dance studios, rehearsal spaces and the like.

Clubs

Where deep house and techno once ruled, you can now find hip-hop, electro-lounge and even rock nights. The **clubs** listed here support good programmes and attract interesting crowds, but it really depends who is running the individual *soirée*. It's worth also checking the listings for **live music** venues (see opposite), which often hold DJ-led sessions after hours, as well as **gay and lesbian** clubs (see p.150).

Most clubs **open** between 11pm and midnight, but venues rarely warm up before 1 or 2am. Trendier places may turn away the scruffier or less fashionably dressed, though booking online in advance and being very obviously a tourist can prevent problems. **Entry prices** vary from one night to another, and may be free or reduced before midnight, but almost always include one "free" drink (*consommation*). Given the difficulty of finding a **taxi after hours** (see p.80), many Parisian clubbers keep going until the métro starts up at around 5.30am, or take advantage of Vélib bikes (see p.80).

Bâteau Concorde Atlantique Port de Solférino, 23 quai Anatole France, 7ᵉ ℡01.40.56.02.82; Mᵒ Assemblée Nationale/RER Musée d'Orsay. Summer-only club (roughly late June to mid-Sept), which takes over this two-level boat for hedonistic parties in the hot months. The boat doesn't actually go anywhere, but a drink on the deck is a fine way to chill out before heading back down to the dancefloor. Soirées vary, but it's mostly house or techno. Entry around €15. Daily 11pm–5am.

Batofar Opposite 11 quai François Mauriac, 13ᵉ ℡01.56.29.10.33, ⊛www.batofar.org; Mᵒ Etienne Marcel. This old lighthouse boat moored at the foot of the Bibliothèque Nationale is a small but classic address. The programme is electro, house, techno, hip-hop, whatever – with the odd experimental funk night or the like thrown in. Entry €8–12. Tues–Thurs 8pm–2am, Fri 11pm–dawn, Sat 11pm–noon.

Le Cab Place du Palais-Royal, 1ᵉʳ ℡01.58.62.56.25; Mᵒ Palais-Royal-Musée du Louvre. This is a smallish, upmarket venue – on weekend nights you'll need to look good to get in. Designer retro-meets-futuristic lounge decor, with a similar music policy. Entry €20. Mon–Sat 11.30pm–5am.

Mix Club 24 rue de l'Arrivée, 15ᵉ ℡01.56.80.37.37; Mᵒ Montparnasse-Bienvenüe. Massive sound system, massive dancefloor, massive DJs: big night out. Mon–Sat 11pm–6am, Sun 5pm–1am. Entry €12–20.

Le Nouveau Casino 109 rue Oberkampf, 11ᵉ ℡01.43.57.57.40, ⊛www.nouveaucasino.net; Mᵒ Parmentier. Right behind *Café Charbon* (see p.144), this adventurous concert venue makes way for a relaxed, dancey crowd later on, with music ranging from electro-pop or house to rock and world music. From free up to around €15. Tues & Wed 9pm–2am, Thurs–Sat midnight–5am.

Rex Club 5 bd Poissonnière, 2ᵉ ℡01.42.36.10.96; Mᵒ Bonne-Nouvelle. The clubbers' club: spacious but not intimidatingly so, and serious about its music, which is strictly electronic, notably techno. Attracts big-name DJs. Entry €10–15. Wed–Sat 11.30pm–5am.

Showcase Pont Alexandre III, 8ᵉ ℡01.45.61.25.43, ⊛www.showcase.fr; Mᵒ Champs-Élysées-Clemenceau/Les Invalides. This big club underneath the Alexandre III bridge is spacious and atmospheric, with its stone arches. Committed to showcasing (geddit) good electronic music. Entry €10–15.

Social Club 142 rue Montmartre, 2ᵉ ℡01.40.28.05.55, ⊛www.parissocialclub.com; Mᵒ Bourse. *Les physios* (the bouncers) won't turn you away at this small, unpretentious, music-loving club. The mad futuristic interior, with skeletal grid and strip lights tells the story: this is electro-land. Entry costs vary. Open daily till 6am.

WAGG 62 rue Mazarine, 6ᵉ ℡01.55.42.22.00; Mᵒ Odéon. Adjoining Terence Conran's flashy

Alcazar restaurant and bar, the *WAGG* offers glossy good times, with Seventies-themed "Carwash" nights on Fri, Eighties and Nineties grooves on Sat, and Latino/salsa on Sun. Entry €12, Sun and Fri & Sat before midnight free. Fri & Sat midnight–6am, Sun 5pm to midnight.

Jazz venues

Le Baiser Salé 58 rue des Lombards, 1er Ⓣ01.42.33.37.71, Ⓦwww.lebaisersale.com; M° Châtelet. Small, crowded upstairs room with live music every night from 10pm – usually jazz, rhythm & blues, fusion, reggae or Brazilian. The downstairs bar is great for just chilling out. Admission €12–20. Mon–Sat 5.30pm–6am.

Caveau de la Huchette 5 rue de la Huchette, 5e Ⓣ01.43.26.65.05, Ⓦwww.caveaudelahuchette.fr; M° St-Michel. One of the city's oldest jazz clubs dating back to the mid-1940s. Both Lionel Hampton and Sidney Bechet played here. Live jazz, usually trad and big band, to dance to on a floor surrounded by tiers of benches. Admission Sun–Thurs €12, Fri & Sat €14; drinks around €8. Daily 9.30pm–2am or later.

New Morning 7–9 rue des Petites-Écuries, 10e Ⓣ01.45.23.51.41, Ⓦwww.newmorning.com; M° Château-d'Eau. This cavernous, somewhat spartan venue, an ex-printing press, is the place to hear the big international names on the circuit. It's often standing room only unless you get here early. Admission €15–21. Usually Mon–Sat 8pm–1.30am (concerts start around 9pm).

Le Sunside/Le Sunset 60 rue des Lombards, 1er Ⓣ01.40.26.46.60, Ⓦwww.sunset-sunside.com; M° Châtelet-Les Halles. Two clubs in one: *Le Sunside* on the ground floor features mostly traditional jazz, whereas the downstairs *Sunset* is a venue for electric and fusion jazz. The *Sunside* concert usually starts at 9 or 9.30pm and the *Sunset* at 10pm, so you can sample a bit of both. Admission €20–25. Daily 9pm–2.30am.

Chanson venues

Casino de Paris 16 rue de Clichy, 9e Ⓣ01.49.95.99.99, Ⓦwww.casinodeparis.fr; M° Trinité. This decaying, once-plush former casino in one of the seediest streets in Paris is a venue for all sorts of performances – including chansons, poetry combined with flamenco guitar and cabaret. Check the listings magazines under "*Variétés*" and "*Chansons*". Most performances start at 8.30pm. Tickets from €25.

Au Limonaire 18 Cité Bergère, 9e Ⓣ01.45.23.33.33, Ⓦlimonaire.free.fr; M° Grands Boulevards. Tiny backstreet venue, perfect for Parisian chanson nights showcasing young singers and zany music/poetry/performance acts. Dinner beforehand – traditional, inexpensive and fairly good – guarantees a seat for the show at 10pm (Tues–Sat) – otherwise you'll be crammed up against the bar, if you can get in at all.

Les Trois Baudets 64 bd de Clichy, 18e Ⓣ01.42.62.33.33, Ⓦwww.lestroisbaudets.com; M° Blanche/Pigalle. Refitted in 2009, this chanson venue has already found a proud place on the Pigalle nightlife scene. It specializes in developing young, upcoming French musicians, so concerts are something of a lucky dip, but tickets are inexpensive at around €10–15. The venue is pleasingly intimate (250 seats), and there are often after events with DJs at the lively bar/restaurant. Tues–Sat 6.30pm–1.30am.

Classical music

Paris is a stimulating environment for **classical music**, both established and contemporary. The former is well represented in performances within churches – sometimes free or very cheap – and in an enormous choice of commercially promoted concerts held every day of the week.

Concert venues

Some of the city's most dynamic and eclectic programming is found at the **Cité de la Musique** at La Villette (Ⓦwww.cite-musique.fr; M° Porte-de-Pantin). Ancient music, contemporary works, jazz, chanson and music from all over the world can be heard at the complex's two major concert venues: the **Conservatoire** (the national music academy) at 209 av Jean-Jaurès, 19e (Ⓣ01.40.40.46.46); and the **Salle des Concerts** at 221 av Jean-Jaurès, 19e (Ⓣ01.44.84.44.84). Soon these will be eclipsed however by a new state-of-the-art 2400-seater auditorium that's being built on the same site and is due to be completed in 2012.

The city's other top **concert halls** are the Salle Pleyel, 252 rue du Faubourg St-Honoré, 8e (Ⓣ08.25.00.02.52, Ⓦwww.pleyel.com; M° Concorde); the Salle

Gaveau, 45 rue de La Boétie, 8ᵉ (℡01.49.53.05.07, Ⓦwww.sallegaveau.com; Mᵒ Miromesnil); Théâtre des Champs-Élysées, 15 av Montaigne, 8ᵉ (℡01.49.52.50.50, Ⓦwww.theatrechampselysees.fr; Mᵒ Alma-Marceau); and the Théâtre Musical de Paris (Ⓦwww.chatelet-theatre.com; Mᵒ Châtelet). **Tickets** are best bought at the box offices, though for big names you may find overnight queues, and a large number of seats are always booked by subscribers. The price range is very reasonable.

Churches and **museums** are also good places to hear classical music. Regular concerts can be caught at the Église St-Séverin, 1 rue des Prêtres St-Séverin, 5ᵉ (℡01.48.24.16.97; Mᵒ St-Michel); the Église St-Julien le Pauvre, 23 quai de Montebello, 5ᵉ (℡01.42.26.00.00; Mᵒ St-Michel); and the Sainte-Chapelle, 4 bd du Palais, 1ᵉʳ (℡01.42.77.65.65; Mᵒ Cité).

The Musée du Louvre, the Musée d'Orsay and Musée Carnavalet host chamber music recitals in their auditoriums, while the Musée National du Moyen-Âge regularly holds recitals of medieval music. Radio France lunchtime concerts are held every Thursday (12.30pm Sept–June) in the Petit Palais' auditorium – turn up half an hour or so in advance to claim a free ticket.

Opera

The city's main opera house is the **Opéra-Bastille**, Mitterrand's most extravagant legacy to the city, opened in 1989. Opinions differ over the acoustics, but the orchestra is first-rate and nearly every performance is a sell-out. Its current director, Nicolas Joel, concentrates on the mainstream repertoire, with A-list performers. Tickets (€5–172) can be bought online (Ⓦwww.opera-de-paris.fr). You can also book by phone (Mon–Fri 9am–6pm, Saturday 9am–1pm; ℡08.92.89.90.90 or 331.72.29.35.35 from abroad), or at the ticket office (Mon–Sat 11am–6.30pm). Unfilled seats are sold at a discount to students fifteen minutes before the curtain goes up, and 62 standing tickets at €5 are available for Opéra-Bastille performances one and a half hours before the curtain goes up.

The Opéra-Bastille enjoys a friendly rivalry with the **Théâtre du Châtelet**, 1 place du Châtelet, 1ᵉʳ (℡01.40.28.28.40; Mᵒ Châtelet), which also puts on large-scale productions. Operas are still staged at the old **Opéra-Garnier**, place de l'Opéra, 9ᵉ (℡08.92.89.90.90, Ⓦwww.operadeparis.fr; Mᵒ Opéra), though these days it hosts mostly ballets; the procedure for getting tickets for the latter is the same as for the Opéra-Bastille above. Operetta, as well as more daring modern operas, are performed at the **Opéra-Comique**, Salle Favart, 5 rue Favart, 2ᵉ (℡01.42.44.45.46, Ⓦwww.opera-comique.com; Mᵒ Richelieu-Drouot).

Festivals

Festivals are plentiful in all the diverse fields that come under the far too general term of "classical". The **Festival d'Art Sacré** consists mainly of concerts and recitals of early sacred music (end of Nov to mid-Dec; Ⓦwww.festivaldartsacre .new.fr); concerts feature in the general arts **Festival d'Automne** (mid-Sept to end Dec; Ⓦwww.festival-automne.com); and a **Festival Chopin** is held in the lovely setting of the Bois de Boulogne's Orangerie (mid-June to mid-July; Ⓦwww.frederic-chopin.com).

For details of these and more, the current year's **festival schedule** is available from tourist offices or their website (Ⓦwww.parisinfo.com).

Gay and lesbian Paris

Paris is one of Europe's great centres for **gay men**, with the scene's focal point in the **Marais**, around rue Sainte-Croix de la Bretonnerie. **Lesbians** have fewer dedicated addresses, but the community is becoming more energetic and visible. The high spots of the calendar are the annual **Marche des Fiertés LGBT**, or gay pride march, which normally takes place on the last Saturday in June, and the **Bastille Day Ball** – open to all – held on the quai de Tournelle, 5e (M° Pont Marie) on July 13.

Information and contacts

The gay and lesbian community is well catered for by the media, the best source of information being *Têtu* (W www.tetu.com), France's main gay monthly magazine – the name means "headstrong". Alternatively, have a look at "Two Weeks", W www.2xparis.fr, the city's premier free gay paper for nightlife listings, small ads, services, etc; the print edition comes out every Thursday.

Centre Gai et Lesbien de Paris 63 rue Beaubourg, 3e ☎01.43.57.21.47, W cglparis.org; M° Bastille/Ledru-Rollin/Voltaire. The first port of call for information and advice – legal, social, psychological and medical. Also has a good library and puts on small exhibitions. Mon 6–8pm, Tues–Thurs 3–8pm, Fri & Sat 12.30–8pm, Sun 4–7pm.

Les Mots à la Bouche 6 rue Ste-Croix de la Bretonnerie, 4e ☎01.42.78.88.30, W www .motsbouche.com; M° Hôtel-de-Ville. The main gay and lesbian bookshop, with exhibition space and meeting rooms; a selection of literature in English, too. Lots of free listings maps and club flyers to pick up, and one of the helpful assistants usually speaks English. Mon–Sat 11am–11pm, Sun 1–9pm.

Bars and clubs

Parisians like to complain about the nightlife scene in Paris relative to rival cities, but in truth there's a fair range of gay and lesbian **bars**, especially in the "pink triangle" of the Marais. A few classic **club** addresses are given here, but many, if not most, mainstream clubs run gay *soirées,* so check also the listings on pp.147–148. The best option with clubs, of course, is to keep an eye on flyers or ask around in bars. Club **opening hours** are largely irrelevant: they're all pretty empty before at least 1am and keep going till at least dawn. Club **entry prices** are generally around €10–20 (usually including a *conso,* or "free" drink), depending on venue size and the popularity of the individual *soirée.*

Mainly women – bars

3W-Kafé 8 rue des Ecouffes, 4e ☎01.48.87.39.26; M° Hôtel-de-Ville. Swish lipstick-lesbian lounge-café, full of sophisticated professionals earlier on, but warming up considerably at weekends, when the cellar bar gets moving. Daily 5.30pm–2am.

La Champmeslé 4 rue Chabanais, 2e ☎01.42.96.85.20; M° Pyramides. Long-established, community-oriented lesbian address in a handsome old building. Popular among thirty-somethings, though packs everyone in for the live music or cabaret nights from Thursday to Saturday. Daily 4pm–4am.

Le Troisième Lieu 62 rue Quincampoix, 4e ☎01.48.04.85.64; M° Rambuteau. Buzzy, upbeat and welcoming new disco-diner offering all things: (inexpensive) cocktail bar, restaurant and dancing at weekends. Daily 6pm–2am.

L'Unity Bar 176 rue St-Martin, 3e; M° Rambuteau. Predominantly butch bar where life is centred on the beer tap and the pool table. Daily 4pm–2am.

Mainly men – bars

Le Carré 18 rue du Temple, 4e ☎01.44.59.38.57; M° Hôtel-de-Ville. Stylish, designer café with good food, comfortable chairs, cool lighting and an excellent *terrasse* on the street, with occasional video projects or fashion shows on the side. Mon–Thurs & Sun 11am–2am, Fri & Sat 11am–4am.

Café Cox 15 rue des Archives, 3e ☎01.42.72.08.00; M° Hôtel-de-Ville. Muscular types up for a seriously good time pack out this loud, riotous neon-coloured bar. Friendly – if your face fits – with DJs at weekends. Mon–Thurs 12.30pm–2am, Fri–Sun 1.30pm–2am.

Le Duplex 25 rue Michel-le-Comte, 3ᵉ ☎01.42.72.80.86; Mᵒ Rambuteau. Arty little bar that's popular with intellectual or media types for its relatively relaxed and chatty atmosphere. Mon–Thurs & Sun 8pm–2am, Fri & Sat 8pm–4am.

Le Free DJ 35 rue Ste-Croix de la Bretonnerie, 4ᵉ ☎01.42.78.26.20; Mᵒ Hôtel-de-Ville. This stylish, fairly recent addition to the scene draws the young and *très looké* – beautiful types – and offers house and disco-funk in the basement club. Mon–Wed & Sun 6pm–3am, Fri & Sat 6pm–4am.

L'Open Café 17 rue des Archives, 3ᵉ ☎01.48.87.80.25; Mᵒ Arts-et-Métiers. The first gay café-bar to have tables out on the pavement, and they're still there, with overhead heaters in winter. Expensive and now touristy, but still good fun. Mon–Thurs & Sun 11am–2am, Fri & Sat 11am–4am.

Le Raidd 23 rue du Temple, 4ᵉ; Mᵒ Hôtel-de-Ville. One of the city's biggest, glossiest (and most expensive) bars, famous for its beautiful staff, topless waiters and go-go boys' shower shows every hour. Daily 5pm–2am.

Clubs

CUD 12 rue des Haudriettes, 3ᵉ; Mᵒ Rambuteau. The "Classic Up and Down" is just that: bar upstairs, miniature club below. Low-key: no queues, door policies or overpriced drinks. More for bears than boys, though it's pretty mixed.

Queen 102 av des Champs-Élysées, 8ᵉ ⓦwww.queen.fr; Mᵒ George V. The legendary gay club of the 1980s has bounced back from its inevitable fall, though it's still a bit packed out with eager provincials – except on the kitsch, gay-leaning Sunday nights.

Le Rive Gauche 1 rue du Sabot, 6ᵉ ⓦwww.lerivegauche.com; Mᵒ St-Germain-des-Prés. Currently very fashionable among gorgeous young gamines, this pocket club is a historic 1970s address preserving some of its gold mirror-mosaic decor.

Le Tango 13 rue au Maire, 3ᵉ ☎01.42.72.17.78; Mᵒ Arts-et-Métiers. Unpretentious and inexpensive gay and lesbian club with a traditional Sunday-afternoon *bal* from 7pm, featuring proper slow dances as well as tangos and disco classics. Turns into a full-on club later on, and on Fri and Sat nights.

Film, theatre and dance

Cinema-goers have a choice of around three hundred films showing in Paris in any one week. The city's plethora of little arts cinemas screen unrivalled programmes of classic and contemporary films, and you can find mainstream movies at almost any time of the day or night. The city also has a vibrant **theatre** scene. Several superstar directors are based here, including Peter Brook and Ariane Mnouchkine. **Dance** enjoys a high profile, enhanced by the opening of the Centre National de la Danse, Europe's largest dance academy, in 2004.

The main **festivals** include the **Festival de Films des Femmes** (March; ☎01.49.80.38.98, ⓦwww.filmsdefemmes.com) at the Maison des Arts in Créteil, just southeast of Paris (Mᵒ Créteil-Préfecture); the **Festival Exit** (March; ⓦwww.maccreteil.com), which features international contemporary dance, performance and theatre, at the same venue; **Paris Quartier d'Été** (mid-July to mid-Aug; ⓦwww.quartierdete.com), with music, theatre and cinema events around the city; the **Festival d'Automne** (Sept–Dec; ⓦwww.festival-automne.com), with traditional and experimental theatrical, musical, dance and multi-media productions from all over the world; and the **Festival du Cinéma en Plein Air** (July to mid-Aug; ⓦwww.cinema.arbo.com) at Parc de la Villette, showing free films in the park.

Information and tickets

You can easily find **film listings** online at sites including ⓦwww.allocine.fr, but the handiest guide is still the inexpensive weekly magazine, *Pariscope*. Watch out for its small *Reprises* section, which lists British or American classics, often one-off afternoon screenings. You can almost always find a current foreign film somewhere in the original language – *version originale* or *v.o.* in the listings. Dubbed films are listed as *v.f.* Average cinema ticket prices are around €8, but there are many reduced-rate periods, especially for students; you rarely need to book in advance.

Stage productions are detailed in *Pariscope* and *L'Officiel des Spectacles* with brief résumés or reviews. Ticket prices are often around €15–30, though you may pay less in smaller venues, and more for many commercial and major state productions (most closed Sun & Mon). Half-price previews are advertised in *Pariscope* and *L'Officiel des Spectacles*, and there are weekday student discounts. Tickets can be bought directly from the theatres, from FNAC shops and the Virgin Megastore (52–60 av des Champs-Élysées, 8ᵉ; Mᵒ Franklin D. Roosevelt (Mon–Sat 10am–midnight, Sun noon–midnight), or at the **ticket kiosks** on place de la Madeleine, 8ᵉ, opposite no. 15, and on the *parvis* of the Gare du Montparnasse, 15ᵉ (Tues–Sat 12.30–7.45pm, Sun 12.30–3.45pm). They sell half-price same-day tickets and charge a small commission, but be prepared to queue.

Film

Paris is littered with fine cinemas, from the megaplexes on the boulevards to the pocket venues in the Quartier Latin. Among the more interesting arts venues are L'entrepôt, 7–9 rue Francis de Pressensé, 14ᵉ (@www.lentrepot.fr); Montmartre's le Studio 28, 10 rue de Tholozé, 18ᵉ (@www.cinemastudio28.com); and the cluster of venues around rue Champollion and rue des Ecoles, 5ᵉ – check out in particular the mini-chains operated by the Reflet Médicis (@www.lesecransdeparis.fr) and the Action chain (@www.actioncinemas.com). For big-screen movies, there's a fine pair of art deco venues on the boulevard Poissonnière, 2ᵉ: Le Grand Rex (@www.legrandrex.com) and Max Linder Panorama (@maxlinder.cine.allocine.fr).

But for the seriously committed film-freak, the best venue in Paris is the Gehry-designed **Cinémathèque Française**, 51 rue de Bercy (Mᵒ Bercy; ℡01.71.19.33.33, @www.cinemathequefrancaise.com; see p.135). You get a choice of around two dozen films and shorts every week, and tickets are only €6.50. At the **Forum des Images**, 2 Grande Galerie, Porte St-Eustache, Forum des Halles (℡01.44.76.63.00, @www.forumdesimages.net), several films (or projected videos) are screened daily, with tickets at just €5. Many cultural institutions and embassies also offer regular screenings.

Theatre

Looking at the scores of métro posters advertising theatre in Paris, you might think bourgeois farces form the backbone of French theatre. To an extent, that's true, though the classics – Molière, Corneille and Racine – are also staple fare, and well worth a try if your French is up to it. You can easily get by with quite basic French, however, at one of the frequent performances of plays by the great postwar generation of Francophone dramatists, including Genet, Camus, Sartre, Ionesco, Cocteau and Beckett. For monolingual visitors, the most rewarding theatre in Paris is likely to be the genre-busting, avant-garde, highly styled and radical kind best represented by **Ariane Mnouchkine** and her Théâtre du Soleil, based at the Cartoucherie in Vincennes, and **Peter Brook**, the British director of the Bouffes du Nord theatre, though Brook is due to retire in 2011.

Bouffes du Nord 37bis bd de la Chapelle, 10ᵉ ℡01.46.07.34.50, @www.bouffesdunord.com; Mᵒ La Chapelle. Peter Brook resurrected the derelict Bouffes du Nord in 1974 and has been based here ever since.

Cartoucherie Rte du Champ-de-Manoeuvre, 12ᵉ; Mᵒ Château-de-Vincennes. Home to several interesting theatre companies including workers' co-op Théâtre du Soleil, set up by Ariane Mnouchkine (℡01.43.74.24.08, @www .theatre-du-soleil.fr).

Comédie Française 2 rue de Richelieu, 1ᵉʳ ℡01.44.58.15.15, @www.comedie-francaise.fr; Mᵒ Palais-Royal. This venerable national theatre stages mainly Racine, Molière and other classics, but also twentieth-century greats such as Anouilh and Genet.

Odéon Théâtre de l'Europe 1 place Paul Claudel, 6ᵉ ☎01.44.41.36.36, ⓦwww.theatre-odeon.fr; Mᵒ Odéon. Contemporary plays and foreign-language productions in the theatre that became an open parliament during May 1968.

Théâtre de la Huchette 23 rue de la Huchette, 5ᵉ ☎01.43.26.38.99; Mᵒ Saint-Michel. Almost sixty

years on, this intimate little theatre, seating ninety, is still showing Ionesco's *La Cantatrice Chauve* (*The Bald Prima Donna*; 7pm) and *La Leçon* (8pm), two classics of the Theatre of the Absurd.

Théâtre National de Chaillot Palais de Chaillot, place du Trocadéro, 16ᵉ ☎01.53.65.30.00, ⓦwww.theatre-chaillot.fr; Mᵒ Trocadéro. Puts on an exciting programme and often hosts foreign productions; Deborah Warner and Robert Lepage are regular visitors.

Dance

The status of dance in the capital received a major boost with the inauguration in 2004 of the **Centre National de la Danse**, committed to promoting every possible dance form from classical to contemporary, and including ethnic traditions. While Paris itself has few home-grown companies (government subsidies go to regional companies expressly to decentralize the arts) it makes up for this by regularly hosting all the best contemporary practitioners. Names to look out for are Régine Chopinot's troupe from La Rochelle, Maguy Marin's from Rillieux-la-Pape and Angelin Preljocaj's from Aix-en-Provence. Plenty of space and critical attention are also given to tango, folk and visiting traditional dance troupes from all over the world. As for ballet, the principal stage is at the Palais Garnier, home to the Ballet de l'Opéra National de Paris, directed by Brigitte Lefèvre. It still bears the influence of **Rudolf Nureyev**, its charismatic, if controversial, director from 1983 to 1989, and frequently revives his productions, such as *Swan Lake* and *La Bayadère*. Many of the venues listed above under "Theatre" also host dance productions.

Centre National de la Danse 1 rue Victor Hugo, Pantin ☎01.41.83.27.27, ⓦwww.cnd.fr; Mᵒ Hoche/RER Pantin. The capital's major dance centre occupies an impressively large building, ingeniously converted from a disused 1970s monolith into an airy high-tech space. Though several of its eleven studios are used for performances, the main emphasis of the centre is to promote dance through training, workshops and exhibitions.

Opéra-Garnier Place de l'Opéra, 9ᵉ ☎08.36.69.78.68, ⓦwww.opera-de-paris.fr;

Mᵒ Opéra. Main home of the Ballet de l'Opéra National de Paris.

Théâtre des Abbesses 31 rue des Abbesses, 18ᵉ; Mᵒ Abbesses. The Théâtre de la Ville's sister company, with a slightly more risk-taking programme – including Indian and other international dance.

Théâtre de la Ville 2 place du Châtelet, 4ᵉ ☎01.42.74.22.77, ⓦwww.theatredelaville-paris .com; Mᵒ Châtelet. Specializes in avant-garde dance by top European choreographers, such as Anne Teresa de Keersmaeker.

Shopping

The Parisian love of style and fierce attachment to small local traders have kept alive a wonderful variety of speciality shops. The nineteenth-century **arcades**, or *passages*, in the **2ᵉ and 9ᵉ arrondissements**, are particularly rich in intriguing boutiques, while the square kilometre around **place St-Germain-des-Prés** is hard to beat for anything from books to shoes, and from antiques to artworks. Other atmospheric and rewarding places for browsing include the aristocratic **Marais**, the trendy **Bastille quartier**, the quirky **Abbesses** quarter of **Montmartre**, and the broadly bohemian **Oberkampf** and **Canal Saint-Martin** areas of northeastern Paris. For **haute couture** the traditional bastions are avenue Montaigne, rue François 1ᵉʳ and the upper end of **rue du Faubourg St-Honoré** in the 8ᵉ. The traditional shopping heart of the city, **Les Halles**, is very commercial, and mostly downmarket.

Books

The most atmospheric places for **book** shopping are the Seine *quais*, with their rows of mostly secondhand bookstalls perched against the river parapet. The **quartier Latin** is the home of most of the city's best independent bookshops.

Artcurial 9 av Matignon, 8ᵉ; Mᵒ Franklin D. Roosevelt. The best art bookshop in Paris, set in an elegant town house. Sells French and foreign editions, and there's also a gallery and stylish café. Mon–Sat 10.30am–7pm; closed two weeks in Aug.

FNAC 74 av des Champs-Élysées, 8ᵉ; Mᵒ George V; Forum des Halles, niveau 2, Porte Pierre-Lescot, 1ᵉʳ; Mᵒ/RER Châtelet-Les Halles; 136 rue de Rennes, 6ᵉ; Mᵒ Montparnasse; ⓦwww.fnac.com. Not the most congenial of bookshops, but it's the biggest and covers everything. Mon–Sat 10am–7.30pm; the Champs-Élysées branch is open till midnight daily.

Gibert Jeune 5 place St-Michel and around; 5ᵉ ⓦwww.gibertjeune.fr; Mᵒ St-Michel. A Latin Quarter institution for student/academic books, with nine, slightly chaotic, stores on and around Place St-Michel. There's a secondhand selection at 2 pl St-Michel, and foreign-language titles at 10 pl St-Michel. Mon–Sat 9.30am–7.30pm.

Shakespeare & Co 37 rue de la Bûcherie, 5ᵉ ⓦwww.shakespeareandcompany.com; Mᵒ Maubert-Mutualité. Cosy, welcoming literary haunt (see p.108), staffed by earnest young wannabe Hemingways, selling the best selection of English-language books in town and running regular readings and events. Mon–Fri 10am–11pm, Sat & Sun 11am–11pm.

Village Voice 6 rue Princesse, 6ᵉ ⓦwww.villagevoicebookshop.com; Mᵒ Mabillon. A welcoming neighbourhood bookstore in St-Germain, with a good selection of contemporary titles and British and American classics. Frequent readings and author signings. Mon 2–7.30pm, Tues–Sat 10am–7.30pm, Sun noon–6pm.

Clothes

If you're looking for a one-stop hit of Paris fashion, the **department stores** (see box below) are probably the place to go. For more picturesque browsing, make for the streets **around St-Sulpice métro**, on the Left Bank: you'll find rich pickings if you wander down rues du Vieux Colombier, de Rennes, Madame and du Cherche-Midi – the last is particularly good for shoes. The home of couture and designer labels is the wealthy, manicured "golden triangle" off the **Champs-Élysées**, especially avenue François 1ᵉʳ, avenue Montaigne and rue du Faubourg St-Honoré. Younger designers have colonized the lower reaches of the latter street, between rue Cambon and rue des Pyramides.

On the eastern side of the city, around the **Marais**, **Canal St Martin** and **Bastille**, the clothes, like the residents, are younger, cooler and more relaxed. Chic boutiques cluster on rue Charlot, rue du Poitou and rue Saintonge in the Haut Marais, and

Department stores

Le Bon Marché 38 rue de Sèvres, 7ᵉ, ⓦwww.lebonmarche.fr; Mᵒ Sèvres-Babylone. The world's oldest department store, founded in 1852, is a beautiful building and a classy place to shop, with a legendary food hall. Mon–Wed, & Sat 10am–8pm, Thurs & Fri 10am–9pm.

Galeries Lafayette 40 bd Haussmann, 9ᵉ, ⓦwww.galerieslafayette.com; Mᵒ Havre-Caumartin. Three floors are given over to high fashion for women, while an adjoining three-storey store is devoted to men's clothing. Then there's a huge *parfumerie* and a host of big names in mens and women's accessories – all under a superb 1900 dome. Lafayette Maison, the huge, impressive home store, is just up the road at 35 bd Haussmann. Mon–Sat 9.30am–7.30pm, Thurs till 9pm.

Printemps 64 bd Haussmann, 9ᵉ, ⓦwww.printemps.com; Mᵒ Havre-Caumartin. Recently revamped and taken a notch upmarket, Printemps has an excellent fashion collection for men and women and a *parfumerie* even bigger than that of rival Galeries Lafayette. Mon–Sat 9.35am–7pm, Thurs till 10pm.

young, trendy designers and hippie outfits congregate on Bastille streets rue de Charonne and rue Keller. There's also a good concentration of one-off designer boutiques around the foot of **Montmartre** – try rue des Martyrs, and the streets around rue des **Trois-Frères**. For more streetwise clothing, the area surrounding the Forum des Halles is a good place to browse; Rue Etienne Marcel and (pedestrianized) **rue Tiquetonne** are good for clothes with a young, urban edge.

agnès b 6 rue du Jour, 1er (M° Châtelet-Les Halles), 6 & 10 rue du Vieux Colombier, 6e (M° St-Sulpice). The queen of classic understatement, for men and women of all persuasions. Relatively affordable for designer gear.

Anne Willi 13 rue Keller, 11e; M° Ledru-Rollin/Voltaire. Original pieces of clothing in gorgeous fabrics that respect classic French sartorial design. Prices from around €60 upwards. Mon 2–8pm, Tues–Sat 11.30am–8pm.

APC 38 rue Madame, 6e (M° St-Sulpice); 112 rue Vieille du Temple, 3e (M° St-Sébastien Froissart). Effortlessly classic but youthful fashion – like a Parisian take on Gap, and all the better for it. Mon–Sat 11am–7.30pm.

Comptoir des Cotonniers 30 rue de Buci 6e; M° Mabillon; 10 rue du Jour, 1er (M° Les Halles); 33 rue des Francs-Bourgeois 4e (M° St-Paul). Utterly reliable chain (there are some thirty shops in Paris) stocking comfortable, well-cut women's basics that make well-judged concessions to contemporary fashions without being modish. Trousers, shirts and dresses for around €100. Opening hours generally Mon–Sat 10am–7pm.

Isabel Marant 16 rue de Charonne, 11e; M° Bastille. Marant excels in feminine and flattering clothes in quality fabrics such as silk and cashmere. Prices from around €90 upwards. Mon–Sat 10.30am–7.30pm.

Jacques Le Corre 193 rue Saint-Honoré, 1er; M° Tuileries. Creative, original hats, footwear and handbags. The stylish, unisex hats here come in interesting colours and shapes; Jacques is famed for his classic cotton *cloche*, perfecting the vagrant-chic look. Mon–Sat 11am–7pm.

Le Mouton à Cinq Pattes 138 bd St-Germain, 6e; M° Odéon/Mabillon. You might just find a Gaultier among the racks of last-season bargains – though often the labels are cut out so you'll have to trust your judgement. Mon–Sat 10am–7pm. There's a branch at 18 rue St-Placide, 6e, and one just for women's clothes at 8 rue St-Placide, 6e (both Mon–Sat 10am–7pm; M° Sèvres-Babylone).

No Good Store 52 rue des Martyrs, 9e; M° Pigalle. The most celebrated of this street's trendy boutiques, stocking younger designers with a boho or urban edge. Caters for men and women, with prices generally in the €100–200 range. See also Roxan at 34 rue des Martyrs and Annabel at no.36. Mon noon–7pm, Tues–Sat 11am–8pm.

Paul & Joe 62–66 rue des Saints-Pères, 7e; M° Sèvres-Babylone. Quintessential Parisian chic: classic but quirky, feminine (and that goes for the men's clothes too) but with an edge. Mon–Sat 10.30am–7.30pm. Branch at 46 rue Etienne Marcel, 2e (M° Sentier).

Sonia/Sonia Rykiel 61 rue des Saints-Pères, 6e; M° Sèvres-Babylone. Sonia Rykiel has been a St-Germain institution since opening a store on bd St-Germain in 1968; "Sonia" is a younger, less expensive offshoot. Mon–Sat 10.30am–7pm.

Spree 16 rue de la Vieuville, 18e; M° Abbesses. Funky, feminine clothing store/gallery led by designers such as Vanessa Bruno, Isabel Marant and Christian Wijnants. Also vintage pieces, accessories, furniture and beauty products. Clothing mostly falls in the €100–250 range Mon–Sat 10am–7pm.

Vanessa Bruno 25 rue St-Sulpice, 6e; M° Odéon. Effortlessly beautiful women's fashions with a hint of floaty, hippy chic. Mon–Sat 10.30am–7.30pm. Branch at 100 rue Vieille du Temple, 4er (M° St-Sébastien/Froissart).

Zadig & Voltaire 1 & 3 rue du Vieux Colombier, 6e; M° St-Sulpice. The women's clothes at this moderately expensive Parisian chain are pretty and feminine: not a million miles from agnès *b*, but with a more wayward flair. Branches all over Paris, generally open Mon–Sat 10.30am–7pm.

Food and drink

Barthélémy 51 rue de Grenelle, 7e ☏01.45.48.56.75; M° Bac. Purveyors of carefully ripened and meticulously stored seasonal cheeses to the rich and powerful. Delivery available. Tues–Sat 8.30am–1pm & 4–7.15pm; closed Aug.

Les Caves Augé 116 bd Haussmann, 8e; M° St-Augustin. This old-fasioned, wood-panelled shop is the oldest *cave* in Paris and sells not only fine wines, but also a wide selection of port, armagnac, cognac and champagne. Mon 1–7.30pm, Tues–Sat 9am–7.30pm.

Debauve and Gallais 30 rue des Sts-Pères, 7ᵉ; Mº St-Germain-des-Prés/Sèvres-Babylone. A beautiful, ancient shop specializing in ambrosial chocolates. Mon–Sat 9.30am–7pm.

Fauchon 26 place de la Madeleine, 8ᵉ; Mº Madeleine. A dazzling range of exquisite groceries and wine; just the place for presents of tea, jam, truffles, chocolates, exotic vinegars and mustards etc. There's a *traiteur* which stays open until 9pm and a swish restaurant. Mon–Sat 9am–7pm.

Hédiard 21 place de la Madeleine, 8ᵉ; Mº Madeleine. The aristocrat's grocer since 1850; there are several other branches throughout the city. Mon–Sat 9am–10pm.

Mariage Frères 30 rue du Bourg Tibourg, 4ᵉ; Mº Hôtel-de-Ville. Hundreds of teas, neatly packed in tins, line the floor-to-ceiling shelves of this 100-year-old emporium. There's a *salon de thé* in the back with exquisite pastries (daily noon–7pm). Daily 10.30am–7.30pm.

Poilâne 8 rue du Cherche-Midi, 6ᵉ ⓦww.poilane .fr; Mº Sèvres-Babylone. You can order the famous, traditionally made sourdough pain Poilâne online, or visit the delicious-smelling store for loaves and baked goods. Mon–Sat 7.15am–8.15pm. Branch at 49 bd de Grenelle, 15ᵉ (Mº Dupleix), open Tues–Sun.

Food markets

Many of Paris's most historic market streets, such as those on rue Mouffetard (5ᵉ) and rue des Martyrs (9ᵉ) are lined with food shops, now, not stalls, but this is still one of the world's great cities for outdoor shopping. A few of the more classic or unusual markets are recommended here; for a full list, arranged by arrondissement, see the town hall site, ⓦwww.paris.fr, under "Marchés Parisiens". Unless stated otherwise, markets open between 7 and 8am and tail off sometime between 1 and 2.30pm.

Belleville Bd de Belleville, 20ᵉ; Mº Belleville/Ménilmontant. Mediterranean and African foods. Tues & Fri.

Dejean Place du Château-Rouge, 18ᵉ; Mº Château Rouge. African foods. Tues–Sun.

Enfants-Rouges 39 rue de Bretagne, 3ᵉ; Mº Filles-du-Calvaire. Tues–Sat 8am–1pm & 4–7pm, Sun 8am–2pm.

Maubert Place Maubert, 5ᵉ; Mº Maubert-Mutualité. Tues, Thurs & Sat.

Monge Place Monge, 5ᵉ. Mº Monge. Wed, Fri & Sat.

Montorgueil Rue Montorgueil & rue Montmartre, 1ᵉʳ; Mº Châtelet-Les Halles/Sentier. Tues–Sat 8am–1pm & 4–7pm, Sun 9am–1pm.

Place d'Aligre 12ᵉ; Mº Ledru-Rollin. Tues–Sun until 12.30pm.

Raspail Bd Raspail, between rue du Cherche-Midi & rue de Rennes, 6ᵉ; Mº Rennes. Tues & Fri, plus celebrated organic market on Sun (9am–3pm).

Richard Lenoir Bd Richard Lenoir, 11ᵉ; Mº Bastille/Richard Lenoir. Thurs & Sun.

Ternes Rue Lemercier, 17ᵉ; Mº Ternes. Specializes in flowers. Tues–Sun 8am–7.30pm.

Flea markets

Paris's **flea markets**, or *marchés aux puces*, are increasingly oriented towards genuine antiques rather than junk, but you can still find some quirky bargains, and the festive atmosphere is unbeatable. Arrive early.

Place d'Aligre 12ᵉ; Mº Ledru-Rollin. A small flea market and the only one located in the city proper, peddling secondhand clothes and bric-a-brac – anything from old gramophone players to odd bits of crockery. Tues–Sun 7.30am–12.30pm.

Porte de Montreuil 20ᵉ; Mº Porte-de-Montreuil. The most junkyard-like of them all, and the best for secondhand clothes – it's cheapest on Monday when leftovers from the weekend are sold off. Also good for old furniture and household goods. Sat, Sun & Mon 7am–7.30pm.

Porte de Vanves Av Georges Lafenestre/av Marc Sangnier, 14ᵉ; Mº Porte de Vanves. The best for bric-a-brac and Parisian knick-knacks. Sat & Sun 7am–1pm (Marc Sangnier), all day (Georges Lafenestre).

St-Ouen/Porte de Clignancourt 18ᵉ; Mº Porte de Clignancourt. The biggest and most touristy flea market, with nearly a thousand stalls selling new and used clothes, shoes, records, books and junk of all sorts, along with expensive antiques. Mon, Sat & Sun 7.30am–6pm.

Listings

Banks and exchange Cash machines (ATMs) are located at all airports and mainline train stations, and at most of the banks in town. Beware of money-exchange bureaux and automatic exchange machines, however, which may advertise the selling rather than buying rate and add on hefty commission fees.

Embassies/Consulates Australia, 4 rue Jean-Rey, 15^e ☎01.40.59.33.00, ⓦwww.france.embassy.gov.au, M^o Bir-Hakeim; Canada, 35 av Montaigne, 8e ☎01.44.43.29.00, ⓦwww.amb-canada.fr, M^o Franklin D. Roosevelt; Germany, 13–15 av Franklin D. Roosevelt, 8e ☎01.53.83.45.00, ⓦwww.paris.diplo.de, M^o Franklin D. Roosevelt; Ireland, 4 rue Rude, 16e ☎01.44.17.67.00, ⓦwww.embassyofirelandparis.com, M^o Charles-de-Gaulle-Étoile; New Zealand, 7ter, rue Léonardo-de-Vinci, 16e ☎01.45.01.43.43, ⓦwww.nzembassy.com/france, M^o Victor-Hugo; South Africa, 59 Quai d'Orsay, 7e ☎01.53.59.23.23, ⓦwww.afriquesud.net, M^o Invalides; UK, 35 rue du Faubourg St-Honoré, 8e ☎01.44.51.31.00, ⓦhttp://ukinfrance.fco.gov.uk, M^o Concorde; US, 2 av Gabriel, 8e ☎01.43.12.22.22, ⓦfrance.usembassy.gov, M^o Concorde.

Festivals There are free concerts and street performers all over Paris for the Fête de la Musique, which coincides with the summer solstice (June 21; ⓦwww.fetedelamusique.culture.fr). Gay Pride follows swiftly afterwards, on the last Sat of June. July 14 (Bastille Day) is celebrated with official pomp in parades of tanks down the Champs-Élysées, firework displays, concerts and *bals pompiers* in the fire stations (head for rue Blanche and rue du Vieux Colombier). The Tour de France finishes along the Champs-Élysées on the third or fourth Sun of July. For a month afterwards, the *quais* are transformed into a sandy beach along the Seine as part of the wildly popular Paris Plages scheme. In early Oct, the Nuit Blanche ("sleepless night") persuades Parisians to stay up all night for an energetic programme of arts events and parties all over the city. For further details on these and many others, see "*Sorties & événements*" on the tourist board website ⓦwww.parisinfo.com.

Health The private association SOS Médecins ☎08.20.33.24.24 offers 24hr medical help.

Hospitals In emergencies, call an ambulance on ☎15. If you require longer-term out-patient care, perhaps, or if you prefer not to avail yourself of France's superb healthcare system, then consider one of the English-speaking private, not-for-profit hospitals. These include the Hertford British Hospital, 3 rue Barbès, Levallois-Perret (☎01.46.39.22.22, ⓦwww.british-hospital.org; M^o Anatole France) and the American Hospital, 63 bd Victor-Hugo, Neuilly-sur-Seine (☎01.46.41.25.25, ⓦwww.american-hospital.org; M^o Porte Maillot then bus #82 to terminus).

Left luggage Lockers are available at all train stations.

Lost property Your first port of call should be the Commissariat de Police for the arrondissement where you think the loss took place; the next step is the central police Bureau des Objets Trouvés, 36 rue des Morillons, 15e (☎08.21.00.25.25; M^o Convention; Mon–Thurs 8.30am–5pm, Fri 8.30am–4.30pm). For property lost on métro/RER and bus services, try the station where you might have lost it first, then call ☎08.92.68.77.14. If you lose your passport, report it to a police station and then your embassy.

Pharmacies 24hr service at: Dhéry, 84 av des Champs-Élysées, 8e ☎01.45.62.02.41 (M^o George V); 6 place Clichy, 9e ☎01.48.74.65.18. All pharmacies, if closed, post the address of one nearby that stays open late (*pharmacie de garde*).

Police ☎17 (☎112 from a mobile) for emergencies. To report a theft, go to the Commissariat de Police of the arrondissement in which the theft took place.

Post office Main office at 52 rue du Louvre 1er; M^o Châtelet-Les Halles. Open daily 24hr for letters, poste restante, faxes, telegrams and phone calls. Other offices are usually open Mon–Fri 8am–7pm, Sat 8am–noon.

Travellers with disabilities Paris's narrow pavements are notoriously difficult for people with limited mobility or wheelchair-users, and the métro is hopeless. Buses, however, are now equipped with platforms and wheelchair spaces, and museums are finally equipping themselves with disabled facilities. A new edition of the extremely handy publication *Access in Paris* (ⓦwww.accessinparis.org) came out in 2008 and the text can be downloaded from the website.

Around Paris

The region around the capital – the **Île de France** – and the borders of the neighbouring provinces are studded with large-scale **châteaux**. Many were royal or noble hunting retreats, while some – like gargantuan **Versailles** – were for more serious state show. **Vaux-le-Vicomte** has perhaps the most harmonious architecture, **Chantilly** the finest art collection and **Fontainebleau** the most gorgeous interiors. Two of the world's loveliest cathedrals also lie within easy reach of Paris: at **St-Denis**, on the edge of Paris, the Gothic style was born; at **Chartres**, it reached its exquisite pinnacle. St-Denis also offers a fascinating collection of royal tombs, while Chartres rises from a delightful medieval town. The most popular attraction by far, however, is **Disneyland Paris**, out beyond the satellite town of **Marne-la-Vallée**. All of the places detailed in this chapter are easily accessible from Paris by public transport.

St-Denis

For most of the twentieth century, **ST-DENIS**, 10km north of the centre of Paris (M° Basilique de St-Denis), was one of the most heavily industrialized communities in France, and a bastion of the Communist party. Since then, factories have closed, unemployment is rife and immigration has radically altered the ethnic mix. The centre of St-Denis retains traces of small-town origins, but the area abutting its cathedral has been transformed into a fortress-like housing and shopping complex, with a vibrant, cheap **market** at its core.

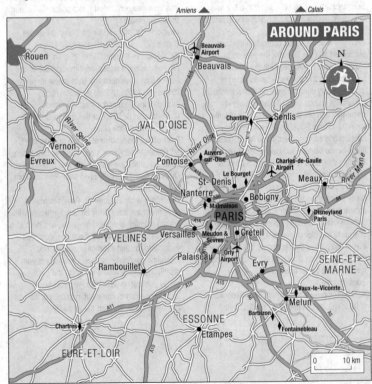

The town's chief claim to fame, though, is its magnificent cathedral, which stands 300m south of the Basilique de Saint-Denis métro stop. Begun in the first half of the twelfth century, the **Basilique St-Denis** (April–Sept Mon–Sat 10am–6.15pm, Sun noon–6.15pm; Oct–March Mon–Sat 10am–5pm, Sun noon–5.15pm; €7) is generally regarded as the birthplace of the Gothic style in European architecture. With its two towers (the northern one collapsed in 1837), three large sculpted portals and high rose window, the west front set the pattern of Gothic facades to come, but it's in the choir that you best see the emergence of the new style: the use of the pointed arch, the ribbed vault and the long shafts of half-column rising from pillar to roof. It's beautifully lit, thanks to the transept windows – so big that they occupy their entire end walls – and the clerestory, which is almost entirely made of glass – another first.

Legend holds that the first church here was founded by a mid-third-century Parisian bishop, later known as St-Denis. The story goes that after he was beheaded for his beliefs at Montmartre (Mount of the Martyr), he picked up his head and walked to St-Denis, thereby establishing the abbey. The site's **royal history** began with the coronation of Pepin the Short in 754, but it wasn't until the reign of Hugues Capet, in 996, that it became the customary burial place of the kings of France. Since then, all but three of France's kings have been interred here, and their fine tombs and effigies are distributed about the **necropolis** (closed during services) in the transepts and ambulatory.

Immediately on the left of the entrance, in the south transept, is one of the most bizarre sights: the bare feet of **François 1er** and his wife Claude de France peeking out of their enormous Renaissance memorial. Beside the steps to the ambulatory lies **Charles V**, the first king to have his funeral effigy carved from life, on the day of his coronation in 1364. Alongside him is his wife Jeanne de Bourbon, who clutches the sack of her own entrails to her chest – a reminder that royalty was traditionally eviscerated at death, the flesh boiled away from the bones and buried separately. Up the steps and round to the right, a florid Louis XVI and busty **Marie-Antoinette** – often graced by bouquets of flowers – kneel in prayer. The pious scene was sculpted in 1830, long after their execution.

Chantilly

CHANTILLY, a small town 40km north of Paris, is famous for its horses. Scores of thoroughbreds can be seen thundering along the forest rides of a morning, and two of the season's classiest flat races, the Jockey Club and the Prix de Diane, are held here. **Trains** run almost every hour from Paris's Gare du Nord to Chantilly Gouvieux station (30min). Free shuttle buses to the château meet some but not all trains – in any case it's a pleasant two-kilometre stroll through the forest; turn right outside the station, then left at the major roundabout on the signposted **footpath**.

The château and the Musée Vivant du Cheval

The Chantilly estate used to belong to two of the most powerful clans in France: first the Montmorencys, then, through marriage, to the Condés. The present **Château** (daily except Tues: château April–Oct 10am–6pm, Nov–March 10.30am–5pm; park April–Oct 10am–8pm, Nov–March 10.30am–6pm; château and park €12, park only €6; ℗ www.chateaudechantilly.com) was built in the late nineteenth century on the ruins of the Grand Château, for the Grand Condé, who helped Louis XIV smash Spanish power in the mid-seventeenth century. It's a beautiful structure, graceful and romantic, surrounded by water and looking out over a formal arrangement of pools and pathways designed by Le Nôtre, Louis XIV's gardener. A major restoration, funded by local resident the Aga Khan, is now in progress, so expect certain areas of the château and park to be closed for works – and, as time goes on, anticipate new rooms to open for the first time.

The entrance is across a moat, past two realistic bronzes of hunting hounds. The bulk of what you'll see in the château is from the enormous collection of **paintings and drawings** owned by the Institut de France. Stipulated to remain as organized by Henri d'Orléans (the donor of the château), the arrangement is haphazard but immensely satisfying. Some highlights can be found in the Rotunda of the picture gallery – Piero di Cosimo's *Simonetta Vespucci* and Raphael's *La Vierge de Lorette* – and in the so-called Sanctuary, with Raphael's *Three Graces* displayed alongside Filippo Lippi's *Esther et Assuerius* and forty miniatures from a fifteenth-century Book of Hours attributed to the great French Renaissance artist Jean Fouquet. Pass through the Galerie de Psyche, with its series of sepia stained glass illustrating Apuleius' *Golden Ass*, to the room known as the Tribune, where Italian art, including Botticelli's *Autumn*, takes up two walls, and Ingres and Delacroix have a wall each.

The sixteenth-century wing known as the Petit Château includes the well-stocked **library**, where a facsimile of the museum's single greatest treasure is on display, *Les Très Riches Heures du Duc de Berry*, the most celebrated of all the Books of Hours. The remaining half-dozen rooms on the tour of the **Grands Appartements** mostly show off superb furnishings, with exquisite *boiseries* panelling the walls of the Monkey Gallery, wittily painted with allegorical stories in a pseudo-Chinese style. A grand parade of canvases in the long gallery depicts the many battles won by the Grand Condé.

Five minutes' walk back towards town along the château drive stands a palatial stable block, **Les Grandes Ecuries**. It is now a "living museum" of horses and horsemanship, the **Musée Vivant du Cheval** (April–Oct daily except Tues 10am–6pm; Nov Mon & Wed–Fri 1–5pm, Sat & Sun 10.30am–5.30pm; Dec–March Mon & Wed–Fri 1–5pm, Sat & Sun 1–6pm; €9, €17 combined ticket with château and park; Ⓦ www.museevivantducheval.fr). The building was erected at the beginning of the eighteenth century by the incumbent Condé prince, who believed he would be reincarnated as a horse and wished to provide accommodation for 240 of his future relatives. Breeds from around the world are stalled in the vast main hall, with a central ring for meticulous equestrian **demonstrations** (held most days at 2.30pm, and often at 11am too, but check in advance online). The **Potager des Princes**, or "kitchen garden of the princes" (mid-March to Oct daily except Tues 2–7pm; €7.50; Ⓦ www.potagerdesprinces.com), a few hundred metres down from the stables, is a huge horticultural haven of herbs, salad plants and artistically planted vegetables, as designed for the Grand Condé by the ubiquitous Le Nôtre.

Disneyland Paris

There are no two ways about it: children will love **Disneyland Paris** (Ⓦ www .disneylandparis.co.uk) – and most adults too, for all the rampant commercialism. If you're not staying in one of the resort hotels, in Disney Village, it's easy to visit in a day-trip from the capital, 25km away. There are two main areas: **Disneyland Park**, which has most of the really big rides, and **Walt Disney Studios Park**, which offers more technological rides based on animation – though there are plenty of thrill rides too.

Arrival, information and accommodation

To reach Disneyland from Paris, take RER line A from Châtelet-Les Halles, Gare de Lyon or Nation to Marne-la-Vallée/Chessy station, which is opposite the main park gates. The journey takes around 40 minutes and costs €8.50 one way. If you're coming straight **from the airport**, there are shuttle buses from Charles de Gaulle and Orly, taking 45 minutes from each (every 20min–1hr from 8.30am; check Ⓦ www.vea.fr/uk for timetables and pickup points; there are also shuttles from Beauvais, but they take half a day); shuttle tickets cost €18 one-way, or €13 for children aged 3 to 12. Marne-la-Vallée/Chessy also has its own TGV train station, linked to Lille and Lyon, as well as London (via special Eurostar trains). By car, the park is a 32-kilometre drive east of Paris along the A4: take the "Porte de Bercy" exit off the *périphérique*, then follow "direction Metz/Nancy", leaving at exit 14. From Calais follow the A26, changing to the A1, the A104 and finally the A4.

Most people buy their Disney **admission passes** online, but you can also get them, along with the relevant train tickets, at all Paris's RER line A and B stations, tourist offices and major metro stations. A "1-day/1-Park" ticket costs €53 for an adult or €45 for a child (aged 3–11); the ticket allows entry to either the Disneyland Park or Walt Disney Studios Park, not both. One-day tickets, allowing access to both parks cost €67/57; multi-day tickets are also available. The website details various seasonal offers. **Opening hours** vary, and should be checked when you buy your ticket, but are usually 9/10am–6/8pm, or until 11pm in high summer.

Disney's six themed, heavily designed **hotels** are a mixed bag, and only worth staying in as part of a multi-day package booked through an agent, or through Disneyland. To really economize, you could camp at the nearby *Camping du Parc de la Colline*, route de Lagny, 77200 Torcy (Ⓦ www.camping-de-la-colline.com), which is open all year and provides minibus service to the parks.

Disneyland Park

Disneyland Park has a variety of good thrill rides, though the majority of attractions remain relatively sedate. The Magic Kingdom is divided into four "lands" radiating out from **Main Street USA**. **Fantasyland** appeals to the tinies, with "It's a Small World", Sleeping Beauty's Castle, Peter Pan's Flight and Dumbo the Flying Elephant among its attractions. **Adventureland** has the most outlandish sets and two of the best rides – Pirates of the Caribbean and Indiana Jones and the Temple of Peril. **Frontierland**, loosely set in the Wild West, features the hair-raising roller coaster Big Thunder Mountain, modelled on a runaway mine train, and the gothic Phantom Manor. In **Discoveryland** there's a high-tech 3-D experience called "Honey, I Shrunk The Audience", an interactive Buzz Lightyear laser battle, and the terrifyingly fast Space Mountain roller coasters. The grand **parade** of floats representing all your favourite characters sallies down Main Street USA at about 7pm every day, with smaller events, special shows and fireworks displays occurring regularly.

Walt Disney Studios Park

Though it has its share of big rides – among them the Rock 'n' Roller Coaster Starring Aerosmith, a corkscrew-looping, metal-playing white-knuckler, and the Twilight Zone Tower of Terror, with its gut-churning elevator drop – the **Walt Disney Studios Park** largely focuses on what Disney was and is still renowned for – animation. You can try your hand at drawing, be part of the audience in a mocked-up film or TV set, and enjoy special effects and stunt shows. The virtual-reality Armageddon ride is genuinely thrilling – your space-station is bombarded by meteors – the tram tour through the collapsing Catastrophe Canyon is good fun, and smaller children will be bowled over by their live interactions with that alarmingly crazed blue alien, Stitch.

Vaux-le-Vicomte

Of all the great mansions within reach of a day's outing from Paris, the classical **Château of Vaux-le-Vicomte** (April–June & Sept to mid-Nov Mon, Tues &

Thurs–Sun 10am–6pm, July & Aug daily 10am–6pm; €14; ⓦ www.vaux-le
-vicomte.com), 46km southeast of Paris, is the most architecturally harmonious
and aesthetically pleasing – and the most human in scale.

To get there, take a train from Gare de Lyon to Melun (25min), from where a
sparse shuttle-bus service (April–Oct Sat & Sun; €7 return) covers the final 7km to
the château. Otherwise, a taxi from the rank at the station costs €17 one-way.

The château

Louis XIV's finance minister, Nicholas Fouquet, had the **château** built between
1656 and 1661 at colossal expense, using the top designers of the day – architect
Le Vau, painter Le Brun and landscape gardener Le Nôtre. The result was magnificence and precision in perfect proportion, and a bill that could only be paid by
someone who occasionally confused the state's accounts with his own. In September
1661, weeks after his sumptuous and showy housewarming party, he was arrested
– by d'Artagnan of **Musketeer** fame – charged with embezzlement, of which he
was certainly guilty, and clapped into jail for life. Thereupon, the design trio was
carted off to build the king's own piece of one-upmanship, the palace of Versailles.

Seen from the entrance, the château is an austere grey pile surrounded by an
artificial moat. It's only when you go through to the south side – where clipped
box and yew, fountains and statuary stand in formal gardens – that you can look
back and appreciate the very harmonious and very French combination of steep,
tall roof and central dome with classical pediment and pilasters.

Inside, the main artistic interest lies in the work of Le Brun. He was responsible
for the two fine **tapestries** in the entrance, made in the local workshops set up by
Fouquet specifically to adorn his house, and **painted ceilings** including the Salon
des Muses, *Sleep* in the Cabinet des Jeux and the so-called King's Bedroom, whose
decor is the first example of the style that became known as "Louis Quatorze".

Other points of interest are the **kitchens**, which have not been altered since
construction, and a room displaying letters in the hand of Fouquet, Louis XIV and
other notables. One, dated November 1794 (mid-Revolution), addresses the
incumbent Duc de Choiseul-Praslin as *tu*. "Citizen," it says, "you've got a week to
hand over one hundred thousand pounds ...", and signs off with "Cheers and
brotherhood".

The **Musée des Equipages** in the stables comprises a collection of horse-drawn
vehicles, complete with model horses. On Saturday evenings in summer
(May–Sept Sat 8pm–midnight; €17) the state rooms and gardens are illuminated
with two thousand candles, as they probably were on the occasion of Fouquet's
fateful party; the classical music, sadly, is no longer live. The **fountains** can be seen
in action on the second and last Saturdays of each month (3–6pm).

Fontainebleau

From the Gare de Lyon it's a forty-minute train journey to **FONTAINEBLEAU**,
famous for its ramblingly magnificent **Château** (daily except Tues: April–Sept
9.30am–6pm; Oct–March 9.30am–5pm; €8; ⓦ www.musee-chateau-fontainebleau
.fr). The connecting buses #A and #B from Fontainebleau-Avon station take you to
the château gates in fifteen minutes.

The château owes its existence to the surrounding forest, which made it the perfect
base for royal hunting expeditions. A lodge was built here as early as the twelfth
century, but it only began its transformation into a luxurious palace during the 1500s
on the initiative of François I, who imported a colony of Italian artists – most notably
Rosso il Fiorentino and Niccolò dell'Abate – to carry out the decoration. Their work
is best seen in the celebrated **Galerie François I** – a sumptuously decorated long
gallery which had a seminal influence on the development of French aristocratic art

and design – and the dazzlingly frescoed **Salle de Bal**. A few years later, Henri IV commissioned the resplendent decoration of the **chapelle de la Trinité**.

The palace continued to enjoy royal favour well into the nineteenth century; Napoleon spent huge amounts of money on it, as did Louis-Philippe. The sober elegance of Napoleon's **Petits Appartements** – the private rooms of the emperor, his wife, and their intimate entourage – makes a dramatic contrast to the fabulous Italianate interiors. Along with the **Musée Napoléon**, which displays a wide variety of personal and official souvenirs, they can only be visited as part of a **guided tour** (€12.50 including château admission). The **Musée Chinois** (included in château admission but only sporadically open), displays the Empress Eugénie's private collection of Chinese and Thai *objets d'art* in their original Second Empire setting.

The **gardens** are equally splendid, but if you want to escape to the relative wilds, the surrounding **forest** of Fontainebleau is full of walking and cycling trails, all marked on the Michelin map *Environs de Paris*.

Versailles

Twenty kilometres southwest of Paris, the royal town of **VERSAILLES** is renowned for Louis XIV's extraordinary **Château de Versailles** (Tues–Sun: April–Sept 9am–6.30pm; Oct–March 9am–5.30pm; ⓦ www.chateauversailles .fr). With 700 rooms, 67 staircases and 352 fireplaces alone, Versailles is, without doubt, the apotheosis of French regal indulgence. While it's possible to see the whole complex in one day, it's undeniably tiring. The best plan to avoid the worst of the crowds is to head in the morning through the glorious **gardens** (free), with their perfectly symmetrical lawns, grand vistas, statuary, fountains and pools, to **Marie Antoinette's estate**, leaving the main palace to the tour buses. You can then work your way backwards, leaving the palace, and in particular the Hall of Mirrors, till as late as possible.

Distances are considerable, so at some point you may want to make use of the **petit train** that shuttles between the terrace in front of the château and the Trianons. You could also rent a **buggy** (you'll need a driving licence) or a **bike** to get around. There are a number of cafés and restaurants dotted around the gardens, should you need to refuel.

The palace

Driven by envy of his finance minister's château at Vaux-le-Vicomte (see p.161), the young Louis XIV recruited the same design team – architect Le Vau, painter Le Brun and gardener Le Nôtre – to create a **palace** a hundred times bigger. Construction began in 1664 and lasted virtually until Louis XIV's death in 1715. Second only to God, and the head of an immensely powerful state, Louis was an institution rather than a private individual. His risings and sittings, comings and goings, were minutely regulated and rigidly encased in ceremony, attendance at which was an honour much sought after by courtiers. Versailles was the headquarters of every arm of the state, and the entire court of around 3500 nobles lived in the palace (in a state of squalor, according to contemporary accounts).

Following the king's death, the château was abandoned for a few years before being reoccupied by Louis XV in 1722. It remained a residence of the royal family until the Revolution of 1789, when the furniture was sold and the pictures dispatched to the Louvre. Thereafter Versailles fell into ruin until Louis-Philippe established his giant museum of French Glory here – it still exists, though most is mothballed. In 1871, during the Paris Commune, the château became the seat of the nationalist government, and the French parliament continued to meet in Louis XV's opera building until 1879.

Versailles practicalities

To **get to Versailles**, take the RER line C5 from Champ de Mars/Tour Eiffel or another Left Bank station to Versailles-Rive Gauche; the palace is an eight-minute walk away. The **Passeport Versailles** (April–Oct Tues–Fri €18, Sat & Sun €25; Nov–March €18; under 26s resident in the EU and under-18s free) is a one-day pass that gives you access to all the main sights, including the Trianons and the Grandes Eaux Musicales, and includes audioguides. Tickets for the **château alone** cost €15, including audioguide, while admission to **Marie-Antoinette's estate**, including both Trianon palaces, is €10. All tickets, including the Passeport, can be bought and printed out from ⊛ www.chateauversailles.fr. You can also buy the Passeport at the château itself up until 3pm on the day, though this of course means queuing. Excellent, English-language **guided tours** (€14.50) take you to wings that you wouldn't otherwise get to see; they can be booked in the morning at the information point – turn up early to make sure of a place.

Without a guide you can visit the **State Apartments**, used for the king's official business. A procession of gilded drawing rooms leads to the dazzling **Galerie des Glaces** (Hall of Mirrors), where the Treaty of Versailles was signed after World War I. More fabulously rich rooms, this time belonging to the **queen's apartments**, line the northern wing, beginning with the queen's bedchamber, which has been restored exactly as it was in its last refit, of 1787, with hardly a surface unadorned with gold leaf.

The Trianons and Domaine de Marie-Antoinette

Hidden away in the northern reaches of the gardens is the **Domaine de Marie-Antoinette** (Tues–Sun: April–Oct noon–6.30pm; Nov–March noon–5pm), the young queen's country retreat, where she found relief from the stifling etiquette of the court. Here she commissioned some dozen or so buildings, sparing no expense and imposing her own style and tastes throughout (and gaining herself a reputation for extravagance that did her no favours).

The centrepiece is the elegant Neoclassical **Petit Trianon** palace, built by Gabriel in the 1760s for Louis XV's mistress, Mme de Pompadour, and given to Marie-Antoinette by her husband Louis XVI as a wedding gift. The interior boasts an intriguing *cabinet des glaces montantes*, a pale-blue salon fitted with sliding mirrors that could be moved to conceal the windows, creating a more intimate space. West of the palace, in the formal **Jardin français**, is the **Petit Théâtre** where Marie-Antoinette would regularly perform, often as a maid or shepherdess, before the king and members of her inner circle.

On the other side of the palace lies the bucolic **Jardin anglais**, impossibly picturesque with its little winding stream, grassy banks and grotto, and the enchanting, if bizarre, **Hameau de la Reine**, a play village and farm where the queen indulged her fashionable Rousseau-inspired fantasy of returning to the "natural" life.

The Italianate **Grand Trianon** palace, designed by Hardouin-Mansart in 1687 as a country retreat for Louis XIV, was refurbished in Empire style by Napoleon, who stayed here intermittently between 1805 and 1813.

Chartres

About 80km southwest of Paris, **CHARTRES** is a modest but charming market town whose existence is almost entirely overshadowed by its extraordinary Gothic **cathedral** (daily 8.30am–7.30pm; free). Built between 1194 and 1260, it was one of the quickest ever constructed and, as a result, preserves a uniquely harmonious design. The cathedral's official name, Notre-Dame (Our Lady), and its staggering size and architectural richness are owed to its holiest relic, the **Sancta Camisia** – supposed to have been the robe Mary wore when she gave birth to Jesus – which was discovered here, miraculously unharmed, three days after an earlier Roman-esque structure burnt down in 1194. In the heyday of the pilgrimage to Santiago de Compostela hordes of medieval pilgrims would stop here on their way to Spain – note the sloping floor, which allowed it to be washed down more easily. The Sancta Camisia still exists, though it has been rolled up and put into storage.

The geometry of the building is unique in being almost unaltered since its consecration, and virtually all of the magnificent **stained glass** is original thirteenth-century work. But the paint and gilt that once brought the portal sculptures to life has vanished, while the walls have lost the whitewash that reflected the vivid colours of the stained glass. Worse still, the high altar has been brought down into the body of the church, among the hoi polloi, and chairs usually cover the thirteenth-century **labyrinth** on the floor of the nave. The cathedral's **stonework**, however, is still captivating, particularly the **choir screen**, which curves around the ambulatory. Like the south tower and spire that abuts it, the mid-twelfth-century **Royal Portal** actually survives from the earlier Romanesque church. You have to pay extra to visit the crypt and treasury, though these are relatively unimpressive. Crowds permitting, it's worth climbing the **north tower** (May–Aug 9.30am–noon & 2–5.40pm, Sun 2–5.30pm; Sept–April Mon–Sat 9.30–noon & 2–4.30pm, Sun 2–4.30pm; free) for its bird's-eye view of the sculptures and structure of the cathedral.

The **Musée des Beaux Arts** (May–Oct Mon & Wed–Sat 10am–noon & 2–6pm, Sun 2–6pm; Nov–April Mon & Wed–Sat 10am–noon & 2–5pm, Sun 2–5pm; €3.10), in the former episcopal palace just north of the cathedral, has some beautiful tapestries, work by the French Fauvist Vlaminck, and the Spanish Baroque painter Zurbarán's *Sainte Lucie*. Behind the museum, rue Chantault leads

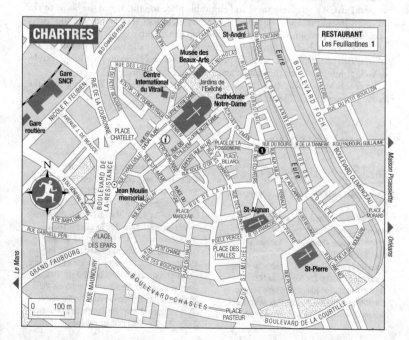

past old town houses to the River Eure and Pont du Massacre. You can follow the river upstream, passing ancient wash houses. A left turn at the end of rue de la Tannerie, then third right, will bring you to the **Maison Picassiette**, at 22 rue du Repos (April Mon & Wed–Sat 10am–noon & 2–5pm, Sun 2–5pm; May–Sept Mon & Wed–Sat 10am–noon & 2–6pm, Sun 2–6pm; Oct Sat 10am–noon & 2–6pm, Sun 2–6pm; €5.10), a work of naïve genius created out of broken pottery mosaics by local road-mender, cemetery-caretaker and eccentric, Raymond Isidore. Back at the end of rue de la Tannerie, the bridge over the river brings you back to the medieval town. A food **market** takes place on place Billard and rue des Changes, and there's a flower market on place du Cygne (Tues, Thurs & Sat).

Practicalities

Trains run from Paris's Gare Montparnasse at least hourly on weekdays (1hr). The *gare SNCF* is five minutes' walk from the cathedral, and from the old town, where you'll find the **tourist office** in the medieval Maison du Saumon, on Place de la Poissonnerie (April–Sept Mon–Sat 9am–7pm, Sun 9.30am–5.30pm; Oct–March Mon–Sat 9am–6pm, Sun 9.30am–5.30pm; ℡02.37.18.26.26), which is right by the cathedral. For a **snack**, there are lots of places on rue Cloître-Notre-Dame. For a **restaurant** meal, try *Les Feuillantines*, 4 rue Bourg, just down the road from the tourist office (℡02.37.30.22.21); it's welcoming, has some outside tables, and the traditional food on the €24 *menu* is good enough to satisfy even locals.

Malmaison

The **Château of Malmaison** (April–Sept Mon & Wed–Fri 10am–noon & 1.30–5pm, Sat & Sun 10am–noon & 1.30–5.30pm; Oct–March Mon & Wed–Fri 10am–noon & 1.30–4.30pm, Sat & Sun 10am–noon & 1.30–5pm; €5; ⓦwww.chateau-malmaison.fr), set in the beautiful grounds of the **Bois-Préau**, about 15km west of central Paris, is a relatively small and enjoyable place to visit. It was the home of the Empress Josephine, and – during the 1800–04 Consulate – of Napoleon, too. After their divorce, Josephine stayed on, building up her superb rose garden and occasionally receiving visits from the emperor until her death in 1814. Visitors can see the official apartments, which perfectly preserve the austerely elegant First Empire style, as well as Josephine's clothes, china and personal possessions.

To **reach** Malmaison, take the metro line 1 (or RER A) to La Défense, then the fairly frequent bus #258 to Malmaison-Château.

Travel details

Trains

Gare de'Austerlitz to: Tours (18 daily; 1hr–2hr 30min).

Gare de l'Est to: Metz (14 daily; 1hr 25min–2hr 45min); Nancy (12 daily; 1hr 30–2hr 20min); Reims (12 daily; 45min–2hr); Strasbourg (17 daily; 2hr 20min–3hr).

Gare de Lyon to: Avignon (21 daily; 2hr 40min); Besançon (15 daily; 2hr 30min–3hr 50min); Dijon (18 daily; 1hr 40min); Grenoble (hourly; 2hr 50min–4hr); Lyon (hourly; 2hr); Marseille (hourly; 3–4hr); Nice (15 daily; 5hr 40min).

Gare Montparnasse to: Bayonne (6 daily; 4hr 45min–6hr 30min); Bordeaux (at least hourly; 3hr–3hr 30min); Brest (8 daily; 4hr 20min–5hr 20min); Nantes (11 daily; 2hr); Pau (7 daily; 5hr 15min–7hr 20min); Poitiers (14 daily; 1hr 40min); Rennes (at least hourly; 2hr); Toulouse (10 daily; 5hr–6hr 30min); Tours (hourly; 1hr–1hr 30min).

Gare du Nord to: Amiens (at least hourly; 1hr 45min); Arras (roughly every 2hr; 50min); Boulogne (at least hourly; 2hr 10min); Lille (hourly; 1hr).

Gare St-Lazare to: Caen (hourly; 1hr 50min–2hr 30min); Cherbourg (roughly every 2hr; 3hr–3hr 30min); Dieppe (2 daily; 2hr 15min); Le Havre (every 2–3hr; 2hr–2hr 30min); Rouen (hourly; 1hr 15min).

2

The north

CHAPTER 2   # Highlights

* **Marquenterre Bird Sanctuary**
  From geese and godwits to
  storks and spoonbills, a huge
  variety of birds make their home
  amid briny meres and tamarisk-
  fringed dunes. See p.186

* **Lillois cuisine** Eat anything
  from the ubiquitous *moules-
  frites*, washed down with
  micro-brewed beer, to fried
  escargots with onions roasted
  in lavender oil in the historic
  centre of Lille, the cultural
  capital of northern France.
  See p.192

* **World War I monuments in
  the Somme** Moving memorials
  by Lutyens and others to the
  victims of the trenches.
  See p.200

* **Son et lumière at Amiens
  Cathedral** The biggest Gothic
  building in France, brought to
  life by sound and light shows
  on summer evenings.
  See p.203

* **The Ardennes** The
  spectacular scenery and
  forested hills of the rugged
  Meuse river valley make for
  wonderful hiking, cycling and
  boat trips. See p.211

* **Champagne tasting at
  Épernay or Reims** Taste
  vintage bubbly in the
  atmospheric cellars of
  world-famous sparkling
  wine emporia. See p.217
  & p.218

▲ The River Meuse

2

The north

When conjuring up exotic holiday locations, you're unlikely to light upon the **north** of France. Even among the French, the most enthusiastic tourists of their own country, it has few adherents. Largely flat Artois and Flanders include some of the most heavily industrialized parts of the country, still feeling the effects of post-industrial depression, while across the giant fields of sparsely populated Picardy and Champagne a few drops of rain are all that is required for total gloom to descend. Coming from Britain it's likely, however, that you'll arrive and leave France via this region, possibly through the busy ferry port of **Calais**, and there are several good reasons to stop off in the area. **Dunkerque** offers a bustling, university atmosphere and poignant war memorials, and just inland, the delightful village of **Cassel** is a rare example of a Flemish hill settlement. **St-Omer** and **Montreuil-sur-Mer** are also strong contenders in terms of charm and interest.

Northern France has been on the path of various invaders into the country, from northern mainland Europe as well as from Britain, and the events that have taken place in Flanders, Artois and Picardy have shaped French and world history. The bloodiest battles were those of World War I, above all the **Battle of the Somme**, which took place north of Amiens, and **Vimy Ridge**, near Arras, where the trenches have been preserved in perpetuity; a visit to any of these is highly recommended to understand the sacrifice and futility of war.

On a more cheerful note, **Picardy** boasts some of France's finest cathedrals, including those at **Amiens**, **Beauvais** and **Laon**. Further south, the vineyards and cellars of the world-famous **Champagne** region are the main draw, for which the best bases are **Épernay** and **Reims**; the latter is home to another fine cathedral. Other attractions include the bird sanctuary of **Marquenterre**; the wooded wilderness of the **Ardennes**; industrial archeology in the coalfields around **Douai**, where Zola's *Germinal* was set; the great medieval castle of **Coucy-le-Château**; and the battle sites of the Middle Ages, **Agincourt** and **Crécy**, familiar names in the long history of Anglo–French rivalry.

In city centres from **Lille** to **Troyes**, you'll find your fill of food, culture and entertainment in the company of locals similarly intent on having a good time.

The Channel ports and the coast

The millions of British day-trippers who come to the northern tip of France every year are mostly after a sniff of something foreign: a meal, a shopping bag full of produce or a few crates of cheap wine. Until the end of the twentieth century the chief function of the northern Channel ports – **Calais**, **Boulogne-sur-Mer** and

THE NORTH

Liège

River Meuse

Antwerp

A13

A2

A3

A4

A4

A15

BELGIUM

BRUSSELS

A1

A10

A8

A4

N63

N4

A89

THE ARDENNES

Sedan

D31

Givet

Monthermé

River Meuse

Charleville-Mézières

Revin

D960

Charleroi

Mons

D966

N51

Rethel

Maubeuge

N2

N2

River Oise

St-Quentin

A26

Laon

N2

Le Cateau-Cambrésis

N43

Coucy-le-Château Auffrique

N31

Valenciennes

A2

Cambrai

N44

Noyon

Compiègne

Roubaix

A23

Lewarde

Doual

A2

A26

A17

Ostend

FLANDERS

Lille

Lens

Vimy

Bapaume

Peronne

A1

A28

A25

Hazebrouck

Béthune

Arras

D937

N25

Somme Battlefields

D929

Albert

D934

A29

Dunkerque

A16

Cassel

St-Omer

A26

ARTOIS

PICARDY

Amiens

N1

Beauvais

Calais

A16

Calais-Fréthun

Eperlecques

N42

La Coupole

D928

Azincourt

N39

Hesdin

River Somme

A16

Abbeville

D901

A28

A29

A26

Sangatte

Escalles

Wissant

D940

Boulogne-sur-Mer

Côte d'Opale

Étaples

Le Touquet

Berck-Plage

N1

Montreuil-sur-Mer

Crécy

Rue

Marquenterre Bird Sanctuary

Le Crotoy

St-Valéry

Rouen

A29

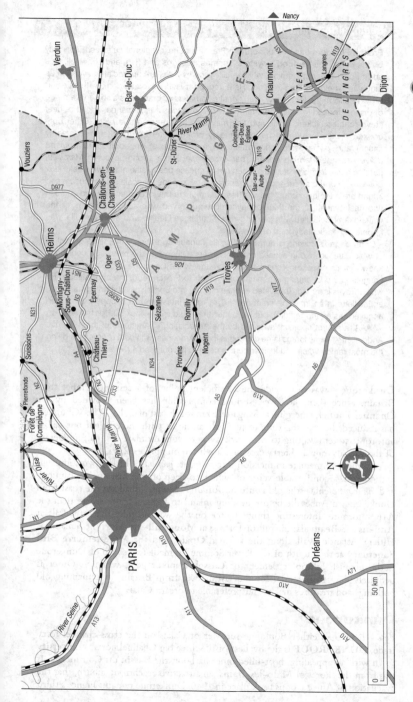

Nancy

Verdun

Bar-le-Duc

Langres

Chaumont

PLATEAU

DE LANGRES

Dijon

A31

N19

River Marne

St-Dizier

Colombey-
les-Deux-
Églises

A4

Châlons-en-
Champagne

N19

Bar-sur-
Aube

A5

Vouziers

D977

C H A M P A G N E

A26

Reims

Oger

D951

D9

Troyes

N77

Montigny-
Sous-Châtillon

A3

N51

Épernay

D3

Sézanne

Romilly

N61

A5

Soissons

N31

A4

Château-
Thierry

N34

Provins

Nogent

A19

A6

Pierrefonds

N2

D3

D33

A5

Forêt de
Compiègne

River Oise

River Marne

A6

N1

A13

River Seine

PARIS

A10

A71

Orléans

A11

A10

A10

N

50 km

0

Regional food and drink

French Flanders has one of northern France's richest regional cuisines. Especially on the coast, the **seafood** – oysters, shrimps, scallops and **fish**, and above all, sole and turbot – are outstanding, while in Lille *moules-frites* are appreciated every bit as much as in neighbouring Belgium. Here, too, **beer** is the favourite drink, with pale and brown Pelforth the local brew. Traditional *estaminets* or brasseries also serve a range of dishes cooked in beer, most famously *carbonnades à la flamande*, a kind of beef stew; rabbit, chicken, game and fish may also be prepared *à la bière*. Other pot–cooked dishes include *hochepot* (a meaty broth), *waterzooi* (chicken in a creamy sauce) and *potjevlesch* (white meats in a rich sauce). In addition to *boulette d'Avesnes*, the **Flemish cheese** *par excellence* is the strong-flavoured *Maroilles*, used to make *flamiche*, a kind of open tart of cheese pastry also made with leeks (*aux poireaux*). For the sweet-toothed, *crêpes à la cassonade* (pancakes with muscovado sugar) are often on menus, but **waffles** (*gaufres*) are the local speciality and come in two basic varieties: the thick honeycomb type served with sugar or cream, or the wafer-like biscuit filled with jam or syrup. Charles de Gaulle, who was from Lille, was apparently particularly fond of the latter.

Champagne's cuisine is dominated by its famous **sparkling wine**, large quantities of which are sloshed in sauces or over sorbets. Otherwise, the province's cooking is known for its **cheeses** – sharp-tasting, creamy white Chaource and orange-skinned Langres – and Champagne's main contribution to French food, the **andouillette**, for which Troyes is famed. Translated euphemistically into English as "chitterling sausage", andouillette is an intestine crammed full of more intestines, all chopped up. It's an acquired taste (and texture), but it's better than it sounds – look out for the notation AAAAA, a seal of approval awarded by the Association of Amateurs of the Authentic Andouillette. Game looms large on menus in the Ardennes, with *pâté d'Ardennes* being the most famous dish and juniper berries used to flavour food *à l'ardennaise*.

Dunkerque – was to provide cheap, efficient points of access into France from Britain. Since then, however, serious competition has been provided by the **Channel Tunnel**, emerging at Sangatte, 5km southwest of Calais. The "Chunnel" has reduced the crossing time to just half an hour, with the efficient but pricey autoroute system waiting to whisk you away to your ultimate destination. Details of the various train and ferry crossings are listed on pp.28–32.

For a more immediate immersion into *la France profonde* – little towns, idiosyncratic farms, a comfortable verge on which to sleep off the first cheese, baguette and *vin rouge* picnic – the old **route nationale N1**, which shadows the coast from Dunkerque to Abbeville before heading inland to Paris, is more sedate than the A16 autoroute. Interesting things to see on the way include: the cathedrals at **Amiens** and **Beauvais**; the hilltop fortress at **Montreuil-sur-Mer**; the remains of Hitler's Atlantic Wall along the **Côte d'Opale**; and the **Marquenterre Bird Sanctuary** at the mouth of the River Somme. Immediately south of Dunkerque is the Flemish hilltop settlement of **Cassel**, a minor gem, while **St-Omer** is definitely day-trip material for the visitor over from Britain; its remaining old buildings and treasures make it far preferable to dreary Calais.

Dunkerque

Less reliant than either Boulogne-sur-Mer or Calais on the cross-channel ferry trade, **DUNKERQUE** is the liveliest of the three big Channel ports, a university town with an appealing, boat-filled inner harbour, the **Bassin du Commerce**. It was from the shores of **Malo-les-Bains**, an attractive beachfront suburb, that the evacuation of Allied troops took place in 1940. Dunkerque remains France's third largest port and a massive industrial centre, its oil refineries and steelworks producing a quarter of the total French output. Devastated during World War II, it is not exactly beautiful; although its postwar rebuild was more ambitious and stylish than those of Calais or Boulogne-sur-Mer, these days the 1950s architecture could do with a good scrub.

Arrival, information and accommodation

From Dunkerque's **gare SNCF** – where **buses** also stop – it's a short walk to rue de l'Amiral Ronarc'h and the **tourist office** (Mon–Fri 9.30am–12.30pm & 1.30–6.30pm, Sat 9.30am–6.30pm, Sun & public hols 10am–noon & 2–4pm; ℡03.28.66.79.21, ⓦwww.ot-dunkerque.fr), which is housed in a fifteenth-century belfry. If you're looking to rent a **car**, there's a branch of Avis at the station (℡03.28.66.67.95). For internet access head for Point Micro, tucked into a car park at impasse Pierre et Marie Curie (Mon–Sat 12.30–8pm). **Accommodation** is split between business-oriented town-centre offerings and more individual options in Malo-les-Bains. There's also a **campsite**, *La Licorne*, close to the beach at 1005 bd de l'Europe in Malo (℡03.28.69.26.68; closed Dec–March).

Hotels and hostel

Au Bon Coin 49 av Kléber, Malo-les-Bains ℡03.28.69.12.63, ⓦwww.restaurantauboncoin .com. More a "restaurant with rooms" than a hotel, but comfortable, characterful and convenient for the beach. ❸
Borel 6 rue L'Hermite ℡03.28.66.51.80, ⓦwww .hotelborel.fr. A comfortable but slightly anonymous three-star option, right on the Bassin du Commerce. ❺
Hirondelle 46/48 av Faidherbe, Malo-les-Bains ℡03.28.63.17.65, ⓦwww.hotelhirondelle.com.

Bright modern Logis de France hotel with a good restaurant and comfortable en-suite rooms, including three adapted for people with limited mobility. ❹
Select 25/27 place de la Gare ℡03.28.66.64.47. Reasonably priced two-star hotel with just nine rooms, right opposite the train station. ❷
Youth Hostel Place Paul Asseman ℡03.28.63.36.34, ⓦwww.fuaj.org. Basic HI hostel a 20min walk east of the centre and close to the beach; dorm beds from €17, including breakfast. Bus #3, stop at "Malo Plage".

The Town

Central Dunkerque is largely the brick-built product of postwar reconstruction, much of it fairly utilitarian but with occasional stylistic flourishes on prominent corner sites, where some buildings affect a sculptural, almost Art Deco look. Among the few buildings of any significance that survived World War II (or were at least rebuilt afterwards) are the tall medieval brick **belfry**, the town's chief landmark (guided tours: April–Sept Mon–Sat every 45min 10am–5.45pm; July & Aug also Sun & public hols 10am, 11am, 2pm & 3pm; Oct–March Sat every 45min 2–5pm; €2.90); the impressive, bullet-ridden fifteenth-century **church of St-Éloi** opposite, to which the belfry belonged; and, a few blocks north of the church on place Charles-Valentin, the early twentieth-century **Hôtel de Ville**, a giant Flemish fancy to rival that of Calais.

Dunkerque also has a few worthwhile museums. The **Mémorial du Souvenir** (April–Sept daily 10am–noon & 2–5pm; €3.50; ⓦwww.dynamo-dunkerque .com), north of the centre at 32 Courtines du Bastion, is the place to go if you want to find out more about the 1940 evacuations; it has an important collection of photographs as well as maps, uniforms and military equipment relating to the period. In the park just to the south of the Mémorial du Souvenir, the **LAAC (Lieu d'Art et Action Contemporaine)**, or Modern Art Museum (April–Oct daily 10am–12.15pm & 2–6.30pm, Thurs until 8.30pm; Nov–March Tues–Sun 10am–12.15pm & 2–5.30pm; €4.50), specializes in the period from 1950 to 1980 and features works by Andy Warhol, Pierre Soulages and César. More interesting,

Dunkerque's 1940 evacuation

The evacuation of 350,000 Allied troops from the beaches of **Dunkerque** from May 27 to June 4, 1940, has become legendary, conveniently concealing the fact that the Allies, through their own incompetence, almost lost their entire armed forces in the first weeks of the war.

The German army had taken just ten days to reach the English Channel and could easily have cut off the Allied armies. Hitler, unable to believe the ease with which he had overcome a numerically superior enemy, ordered his generals to halt their advance, giving Allied forces trapped in the Pas-de-Calais time to organize **Operation Dynamo**, the largest wartime evacuation ever undertaken. Initially it was hoped that around 10,000 men would be saved, but thanks to low-lying cloud and the help of more than 1,750 vessels – including pleasure cruisers, fishing boats and river ferries – 140,000 French and more than 200,000 British soldiers were successfully shipped back to England. The heroism of the boatmen and the relief at saving so many British soldiers were the cause of national celebration.

In France, however, the ratio of British to French evacuees caused bitter resentment, since Churchill had promised that the two sides would go *bras dessus, bras dessous* ("arm in arm"). Meanwhile, the British media played up the "remarkable discipline" of the troops as they waited to embark, the "victory" of the RAF over the Luftwaffe and the "disintegration" of the French army all around. In fact, there was widespread indiscipline in the early stages as men fought for places on board; the battle for the skies was evenly matched; and the French fought long and hard to cover the whole operation, some 150,000 of them remaining behind to become prisoners of war. In addition, the Allies lost seven destroyers and 177 fighter planes and were forced to abandon more than 60,000 vehicles. After 1940, Dunkerque remained occupied by Germans until the bitter end of the war. It was the last French town to be liberated in 1945.

especially for children, is the **Musée Portuaire** (daily except Tues: July & Aug 10am–6pm; Sept–June 10am–12.45pm & 1.30–6pm; €4), housed in a restored brick warehouse at 9 quai de la Citadelle on the Bassin du Commerce, which illustrates the history of Dunkerque from its beginnings as a fishing hamlet, using ship models and panoramas as well as period film footage. It also mounts engrossing temporary exhibitions on related themes, such as the ocean liners that were once built at Dunkerque.

The **Bassin du Commerce** itself is a lively and attractive stretch of water, housing not just fishing boats and yachts but a miscellany of preserved historic ships, including the three-masted sailing ship **Duchesse Anne**, built in Germany in 1901. It and several other vessels can be visited as part of the **Musée à Flot** (daily July & Aug; guided tours 2.30pm, 3.30pm, 4.30pm; Sept–June guided tours Wed & Sun at 3.30pm; €7.50, or €10 joint ticket with Musée Portuaire) – the "floating" half of the city's maritime museum.

Malo-les-Bains
MALO-LES-BAINS is a pleasant nineteenth-century seaside suburb on the east side of Dunkerque (buses #3 & #2), from whose vast sandy beach the Allied troops embarked in 1940. Digue des Alliés is the urban end of an extensive beachfront promenade lined with cafés and restaurants, though things are rather nicer further east along Digue de Mer, away from Dunkerque's industrial inferno. Much of the promenade's attractive architecture somehow survived wartime destruction; there's more *fin-de-siècle* charm a few blocks inland, along avenue Faidherbe and its continuation avenue Kléber, around leafy place Turenne with its dainty old-fashioned bandstand.

Eating and drinking

Dunkerque's best options for **eating and drinking** are close to the water: there's a decent line-up of restaurants and bars along quai de la Citadelle on the Bassin du Commerce, with plenty more in Malo-les-Bains.

L'Auberge de Jules 9 rue de la Poudrière ☎03.28.63.68.80. Funky modern restaurant just off the Bassin du Commerce, Michelin-listed and with plenty of fish on offer; *plats* from €14. Closed Sun.

Au Bon Coin 49 av Kléber, Malo-les-Bains ☎03.28.69.12.63. Oysters, lobster and a selection of *plateaux de fruits de mer* (€35 to €116) grace the menu of this plush Malo restaurant. Closed Sun eve & Mon.

Le Désirade 6 quai de la Citadelle ☎03.28.61.53.85. Classy harbourside restaurant, serving plenty of meat-based dishes. *Menus* from €20. Closed Sun & Wed.

Hirondelle 46/48 av Faidherbe, Malo-les-Bains ☎03.28.63.17.65. There's a strong seafood emphasis here, with everything from marinated herring to a variety of salmon dishes; *menus* at €19.50 and €27. Closed Sun eve & Mon lunch.

La Marie-Jane 13 quai de la Citadelle. Lively portside bar with nautical decor and regular live music.

La Moule Rit 175 Digue de Mer, Malo-les-Bains ☎03.28.29.06.07. More than fifty *moules* dishes at €13.50 per portion, plus sea views through the huge windows, welcome visitors to this beachfront place. Closed Mon.

Cassel

Barely 30km southeast of Dunkerque and just off the A25 autoroute to Lille, is the tiny hilltop town of **CASSEL**. Hills are rare in Flanders, and consequently Cassel was much fought over from Roman times onwards. During World War I, Marshal Foch spent some of the "most distressing hours" of his life here, and it was supposedly to the top of Cassel's hill that the "Grand Old Duke of York" marched his ten thousand men in 1793, though, as implied in the nursery rhyme, he failed to take the town.

As its name suggests, Cassel was originally a Flemish-speaking community – until use of the language was suppressed by the authorities – and it still boasts a very Flemish **Grand'Place**, lined with some magnificent mansions, from which narrow cobbled streets fan out to the ramparts. From the public gardens in the upper town, you have an unrivalled view over Flanders, with Belgium just 10km away. Here you'll find the eighteenth-century **Kasteel Meulen**, the last of Cassel's 29 wooden windmills (April–Sept daily 10am–12.30pm & 2–6pm; Oct–March Sat, Sun & school hols 10am–12.30pm & 2–6pm; €2.80), still occasionally pounding out flour and linseed oil as a demonstration of how it once worked.

Practicalities

There's no bus into town from Cassel's **gare SNCF** (a regular train service on the Dunkerque–Lille line); those without their own transport have to walk the 3km. The town's **tourist office** is on the Grand'Place (June–Aug Mon–Sat 8.45am–noon & 1.30–6pm, Sun 2–6.30pm; April, May, Sept & Oct Mon–Sat 8.30am–noon & 1.30–5.45pm, Sun 2–5.45pm; Nov–March Mon–Fri 8.30am–noon & 1.30–5.30pm, Sat 9am–noon; ☎03.28.40.52.55, ⓦwww.cassel-horizons.com); it houses a small but enjoyable exhibition, **Cassel Horizons**, on the history of the town (same hours as tourist office; €2.80). An upmarket **accommodation** option is the very smart *Châtellerie de Schoebeque* at 32 rue Foch (☎03.28.42.42.67, ⓦwww.schoebeque.com; ❽).

On the southern side of the Grand'Place many of the **cafés and restaurants** have fabulous views over the surrounding countryside. *La Taverne Flamande* at no. 34 (closed Tues eve & Wed; from €12) specializes in Flemish cuisine, while *Le Sauvage*, no. 38 (☎03.28.42.40.88), offers classic French fare (*menus* from €20). Up near the windmill at 8 rue St-Nicolas, cosy little *T'Kasteel Hof* (☎03.28.40.59.29; mains from €10) oozes local ambience and has a variety of beers to go with the simple Flemish cuisine, which includes a delicious *carbonnade*; book ahead on weekends. It also has a small shop selling traditional local produce. Cassel's big annual event is its Easter Monday **Carnival**, when giant effigies are paraded through the town's streets.

Calais and around

CALAIS is less than 40km from Dover – the Channel's shortest crossing – and is by far the busiest French passenger port. The port, petrochemical industries and out-of-town shopping dominate the place, and there's little else here. In World War II, the British destroyed Calais to prevent it being used as a base for a German invasion, but the French still refer to it as "the most English town in France", an influence that began after the battle of Crécy in 1346, when Edward III seized it for use as a beachhead in the Hundred Years' War. It remained in English hands for over two hundred years until 1558, when its loss famously caused Mary Tudor to say: "When I am dead and opened, you shall find Calais lying in my heart." The association has continued over the centuries, and today Calais welcomes over nine million British travellers and day-trippers per year.

Arrival, information and accommodation

There's a daytime **bus** (€1 one way) from the **ferry terminal** to place d'Armes and the central Calais-Ville **gare SNCF**, from where **buses** depart for Dunkerque, Boulogne-sur-Mer and the out-of-town shopping centres. To get to the outlying Calais-Fréthun **gare TGV** for Eurostar trains to London and Paris, take the *navette*,

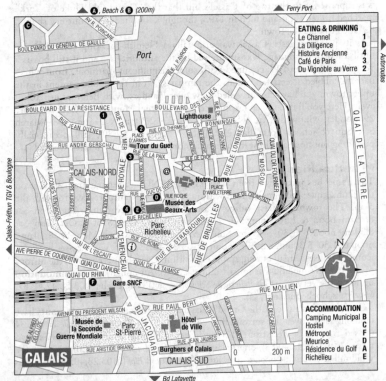

EATING & DRINKING
Le Channel	1
La Diligence	D
Histoire Ancienne	4
Café de Paris	3
Du Vignoble au Verre	2

ACCOMMODATION
Camping Municipal	B
Hostel	C
Métropol	F
Meurice	D
Résidence du Golf	A
Richelieu	E

usually a shuttle bus, occasionally a TER train. It's free on presentation of a SNCF ticket (otherwise €2). If you're driving and keen to avoid Calais, take a left out of the ferry terminal – the *autoroute* bypass begins almost immediately, leading to the A26 and the N1. To **rent a car**, try Avis (℡03.21.34.66.50) in place d'Armes and at the car ferry terminal, or Budget (℡03.55.33.14.34) at the ferry terminal; a cheaper option, also at the ferry terminal, is National/Citer (℡03.21.34.58.45). For details of ferry crossings, see p.31. Via the **tunnel**, road connections to Calais and the autoroutes are well signposted and straightforward.

If you decide to stay in Calais, there is plenty of **accommodation** available, though it's wise to book ahead in the high season. The **tourist office** at 12 bd Clémenceau, the continuation of rue Royale (mid-Sept to March Mon–Sat 10am–6pm; April to mid-June daily 10am–7pm; mid-June to mid-Sept daily 9am–7pm; ℡03.21.96.62.40, Ⓦ www.calais-cotedopale.com), has a free accommodation booking service as well as a list of *gîtes* and hotels in the region. For internet access, head to the cybercafé at rue Seigneur de Gourdon, across from Notre-Dame.

Hotels

Métropol 45 quai du Rhin ℡03.21.97.54.00, Ⓦ www.metropolhotel.com. Situated beside the canal close to the train station, this is a comfortable but nondescript hotel with small rooms, satellite TV and a bar. ➍

Meurice 5 rue Edmond-Roche ℡03.21.34.57.03, Ⓦ www.hotel-meurice.fr. Comfortable three-star with a grand entrance, luxurious jacuzzi baths and antique furniture in a quiet street behind the Musée des Beaux-Arts. ➎

Résidence du Golf 745 Digue G. Berthe ℡03.21.96.88.99, Ⓦ www.hoteldugolf-calais.com. Neat, bright motel-style rooms which, although lacking in character, have the advantages of kitchenettes and views of the water. Some can accommodate up to 4 people. ➌

Richelieu 17 rue Richelieu ℡03.21.34.61.60, Ⓦ www.hotelrichelieu-calais.com. Overlooking the park of the same name, this hotel has light and airy rooms – try to get one of the attractively refurbished ones if you can. ➌

Hostel and campsite

Camping Municipal 26 av Raymond-Poincaré ℡03.21.97.89.79. A large, exposed site at the harbour end of Calais' beach; closed Nov to mid-April.

Hostel Av du Maréchal-de-Lattre-de-Tassigny ℡03.21.34.70.20, Ⓦ www.auberge-jeunesse -calais.com. Modern, well-appointed hostel just one block from the beach. Dorm beds from €19 in two- or three-bed rooms; single rooms €25; breakfast included.

The Town

Most of Calais' modest sights are in **Calais-Nord**, the Old Town rebuilt after the war, with drab place d'Armes and more appealing rue Royale as its focus. The **Tour du Guet**, on place d'Armes, is the only medieval building on the square to have survived wartime bombardment. From here, rue de la Paix leads to the **church of Notre-Dame**, where Charles de Gaulle married local girl Yvonne Vendroux in 1921. There is an unusual lacemaking exhibition, plus a small but interesting collection of sixteenth- to twentieth-century art, including paintings by Picasso and Dubuffet, and a Rodin sculpture, in the **Musée des Beaux-Arts et de la Dentelle** on rue Richelieu (Tues–Sat 10am–noon & 2–5pm, Sun 2–5pm; closes 6pm June–Sept; €4). Walk north up rue Royale and cross the bridge to reach the city's **beach**, where the waters are chilly but swimmable, and from which on a fine day a white strip of English shore is visible; get a panoramic view from the top of the 59m **lighthouse** at place Henri-Barbusse (daily 2–5.30pm, also 10am–noon on weekends; closes 6.30pm June–Sept; €4.50).

Just over the canal bridge in **Calais-Sud**, the town's landmark, the **Hôtel de Ville**, raises its belfry over 60m into the sky; this Flemish extravaganza was finished in 1926, and miraculously survived World War II. Nearby, Rodin's famous bronze, the *Burghers of Calais*, records for ever the self-sacrifice of local dignitaries, who offered their lives to assuage the blood lust of the victor at Crécy,

Shopping in Calais

For truly epic cross-border shopping it's best to head out of town, either to the **hypermarkets**, malls and outlet centres, or to one of the many **wine and beer** stores. The best hypermarket is **Auchan** on avenue Roger Salengro west of town (Mon–Sat 8.30am–9.30pm, open till 10pm Fri & Sat; bus #1), closely followed by **Carrefour/Mi-Voix**, on the east side of town, on avenue Georges-Guynemer (Mon–Sat 8.30am–9pm; bus #2 or #4). **Cité Europe**, a vast shopping mall on boulevard du Kent by the Channel Tunnel terminal (bus #1), offers another Carrefour (Mon–Sat 8.30am–9pm, open till 10pm Fri & Sat) plus high-street clothing and food shops (Mon–Thurs 10am–8pm, Fri 10am–9pm, Sat 10am–8pm). You could also visit the nearby **Marques Avenue** outlet centre on boulevard du Parc (Mon–Sat 10am–7pm; bus #1), where the discounted brands include Adidas, Nike and Puma. For cheap wine, head for the British-run **Wine & Beer World** on the eastern side of town at rue de Judée, Zone Marcel Doret (daily 8am–8pm; bus #7), with another branch close to the Channel Tunnel terminal in the La Francaise *zone industrielle* (daily 9am–7pm; bus #1); alternatively, head for the more Francophile **Franglais Vins** at junction 44 of the A16 (Mon–Sat 9am–7pm, Sun 9.30am–6pm).

In downtown Calais, **La Maison du Fromage et des Vins** (daily except Tues, Mon am and Sun pm; 8.30am–12.30pm & 3–7.30pm) just off place d'Armes is worth a visit for a good selection of cheese and wine. In Calais-Sud, the **Les 4 Boulevards** complex (Mon–Sat 9am–7pm) on boulevard Jacquard is the town centre's response to the big malls, though more colourful are the markets around place d'Armes (Wed & Sat am) and place Crèvecoeur (Thurs & Sat am).

Edward III – only to be spared at the last minute by the intervention of Queen Philippa, Edward's wife. For a record of Calais' wartime travails, visit the fascinating **Musée de la Seconde Guerre Mondiale** (Feb–April & Oct–Nov daily except Tues 11am–5pm; May–Sept daily 10am–6pm; €6; ⓦmuseeguerrecalais .free.fr). It is set in a former German *Blockhaus* (bunker) in the Parc St-Pierre.

Eating and drinking

Calais is full of **restaurants** catering to its transient visitors, but there are enough decent ones to make eating one of the best uses of your time here. Place d'Armes and rue Royale are where the concentration is thickest. **Drinking** establishments ranging from Gaelic theme pubs to trendier offerings are concentrated on rue Royale and its continuation, rue de la Mer. *La Mauvaise Herbe* on rue Royale is about the hippest of Calais-Nord's watering holes, while *Le Bekeur* is a **gay bar** just east of place d'Armes at 40 rue de Thermes.

Le Channel 3 bd de la Résistance Ⓣ03.21.34.42.30. Generous *menus* (€19–52) and stylish decor. Beautifully prepared but safely unadventurous food, with a wide range of delicious desserts, and views over the yacht basin. Closed Sun eve, Tues & 2 weeks in summer; booking recommended.
La Diligence 7 rue Edmond-Roche ⓉM03.21.34.57.03. The well-regarded restaurant of the *Meurice* hotel is snug and atmospheric, with wood-panelled walls, beamed ceilings and *menus* at €25–50.
Histoire Ancienne 20 rue Royale ⓉM03.21.34.11.20. Michelin-listed brasserie with a charming, vaguely

Art Deco interior; the mainly French menu includes a separate list for vegetarians. *Menus* from €12.50 for lunch and early dinner; otherwise from €18.50. Closed Sun & Mon eve.
Café de Paris 72 rue Royale ⓉM03.21.34.76.84. This lively Calais-Nord brasserie is popular with locals and tourists alike for its inexpensive dishes; *plats du jour* from €9, *menu* at €17.50.
Du Vignoble au Verre 43 place d'Armes ⓉM03.21.34.83.29. The cosy interior matches the traditional French cooking – including pâté made on the premises – and there's an emphasis on wine, including a reasonable selection by the glass. *Menus* from €18.50.

St-Omer

Away from the ports, the first stop for many is **ST-OMER**, an attractive old Flemish town of yellow-brick houses 43km southeast of Calais. The Hôtel de Ville on place Foch and the chapel of the former Jesuit college on rue du Lycée are genuine flights of architectural fancy, but for the most part the style is simple but handsome, though some parts of the town are rather run-down. The Gothic **Basilique Notre-Dame** (daily 9.45am–12.30pm & 2.30–4.30pm) contains some fine statues, and the fascinating **Musée de l'Hôtel Sandelin** at 14 rue Carnot (Wed–Sun 10am–noon & 2–6pm; €4.50) is worth a stop as well. The centrepiece of this eighteenth-century mansion is the suite of panelled rooms on the ground floor, and the museum displays focus on eleventh- to fifteenth-century Flemish art, fine arts (including a Breughel) and ceramics. One highlight is a glorious piece of medieval goldsmithing known as the *Pied de Croix de St-Bertin*.

The pleasant **public gardens** to the west of town are also worth a visit, as are the nearby **marais**, a network of Flemish waterways cut between plots of land on reclaimed marshes along the river. Boat trips, or *bateaux-promenade*, run by Isnor Location (☏03.21.39.15.15, ⓦwww.isnor.fr), leave from the church in nearby Clairmarais. For further information and details of kayak and canoe rental, contact the tourist office (see below).

Practicalities

To get to the centre of town from the exuberant 1903 **gare SNCF**, cross over the canal and walk down rue François Ringot, which leads through place du Vainquai and rue Faidherbe into rue Carnot. The **tourist office** is in the western end of town near the park at 4 rue du Lion d'Or (Easter–Sept Mon–Sat 9am–6pm, Sun 10am–1pm; Oct–Easter Mon–Sat 9am–12.30pm & 2–6pm; ☏03.21.98.08.51, ⓦwww.tourisme-saintomer.com).

For **accommodation**, try the pretty *Hôtel St-Louis* at 25 rue d'Arras (☏03.21.38.35.21, ⓦwww.hotel-saintlouis.com; ❹; *Le Flaubert* restaurant from €15.50) or the *Bretagne*, 2 place du Vainquai, near the train station (☏03.21.38.25.78, ⓦwww.hotellebretagne.com; ❹; *Le Vainquai* restaurant from €14.50). The closest **campsite** is *Le Clair Marais* on rue du Romelaëre near the Forêt de Clairmarais, 4.5km east of St-Omer (☏03.21.38.34.80, ⓦwww.camping-clairmarais.com; closed mid-Dec to end Jan), but there's no transport between it and the town. For **places to eat** other than the hotels, try the establishments around place Foch: *Les Trois Caves*, at no. 18 has the best reputation, specializing in local and Flemish dishes (☏03.21.39.72.52; closed Mon & Wed; *menu* €18).

The Blockhaus at Éperlecques

In the Forêt d'Éperlecques, 12km north of St-Omer off the D300, you can visit the largest ever **Blockhaus**, or concrete bunker, built in 1943–44 by the Germans – or rather by six thousand of their half-starved prisoners of war (daily: March 11am–5pm; April & Oct 10am–noon & 2.45–6pm; May–Sept 10am–7pm; Nov 2.45–5pm; €9). It was designed to launch V2 rockets against London, but the RAF and French Resistance bombed it so heavily – killing many Allied prisoners at the same time – that it was never ready for use. As well as the Blockhaus, you will see remnants of weapons that were used to attack (or were meant to attack) London, including a 45m ramp for launching V1 rockets.

The Blockhaus is hard to reach without your own transport: it's a 4km walk from the station at Watten, on the eastern edge of the forest, to which there are several trains daily from Calais.

La Coupole

Of all the converted World War II bunker museums, **La Coupole** (daily: July & Aug 10am–7pm; Sept–June 9am–6pm; closed for 2 weeks over Christmas and New Year; €9; ⓦ www.lacoupole-france.com), 5km southwest of St-Omer, is the most stimulating. As you walk around the site of an intended V2 rocket launch pad, you can listen on multilingual infrared headphones to a discussion of the occupation of northern France by the Nazis, the use of prisoners as slave labour, and the technology and ethics of the first liquid-fuelled rocket – advanced by Hitler and later developed for the space race by the Soviets, the French and the Americans. Visits last two and a half hours. Getting there by car is easy: it's just off the D928 (A26 junctions 3 & 4), but there are only a few buses running from St-Omer train station (ring La Coupole or St-Omer tourist office for times).

The Côte d'Opale

The **Côte d'Opale** is the stretch of Channel coast between Calais and the mouth of the River Somme, characterized by huge, windswept beaches more attractive than anything to be found in the port cities. Along the northern stretch, as far as Boulogne, the beaches are fringed by white chalk cliffs, as on the English side of the Channel. Here, between the prominent headlands of **Cap Blanc-Nez** and **Cap Gris-Nez**, the D940 coast road winds high above the sea, allowing you to appreciate the "opal" in the name – the sea and sky merging in an opalescent, oyster-grey continuum. The southern part of the coast is flatter, and the beach, uninterrupted for 40km, is backed by pine-anchored dunes and brackish tarns, punctuated by German pillboxes toppled on their noses by the shifting sands. An organization called Eden 62 (ⓣ 03.21.32.13.74, ⓦ www.eden62.fr) offers **guided walks** all year round.

Cap Blanc-Nez to Cap Gris-Nez

Six kilometres west of Calais by the sedate seaside village of Sangatte, the Channel Tunnel comes ashore, though the actual terminal is 5km inland outside the village of Fréthun. From Sangatte, the D940 winds up onto the grassy windswept heights of **Cap Blanc-Nez**, topped by an obelisk commemorating the Dover Patrol, who kept the Channel free from U-boats during World War I. From here, 130m above sea level, you can spot the Channel craft plying the water to the north, while to the south you look down on Wissant and its enormous beach from which Julius Caesar sailed for Britain in 55 BC. Before arriving in Wissant, you pass through the beachside village of **Escalles**, where you can stay at the smart, appropriately named *Escale* (ⓣ 03.21.85.25.00, ⓦ www.hotel -lescale.com; ❶; restaurant from €16.50).

WISSANT itself is a small, attractive place, popular with windsurfers and weekending Britons. The **tourist office** (Mon–Fri 9.30am–noon & 2–6pm, Sat 9.30am–noon; ⓣ 08.20.20.76.00, ⓦ www.terredes2caps.fr) is on place de la Mairie. **Hotels** here include the picturesque old *Hôtel de la Plage*, 1 place Édouard-Houssin (ⓣ 03.21.35.91.87, ⓦ www.hotelplage-wissant.com; ❷; good restaurant from €16), with rooms arranged around a wide courtyard, and the two-star *Bellevue*, rue Paul Crampel (ⓣ 03.21.35.91.07, ⓦ www.wissant-hotel-bellevue .com; ❸). Wissant also has a **campsite**, *La Source* (ⓣ 03.21.35.92.46; closed mid-Nov to mid-March).

The GR du Littoral footpath passes through Wissant and continues up to **Cap Gris-Nez**, just 28km from the English coast. To get to the cape by road, take the turn-off north 1km outside **AUDINGHEN**, from which it's another three kilometres. The remainder of the drive along the D940 towards Boulogne-sur-Mer is lined with beautiful and undeveloped dunes with frequent turn-offs for **walking paths** to the shore, each of which is tempting on a fine day.

Boulogne-sur-Mer

BOULOGNE-SUR-MER is the smallest of the three main channel ports, and although the **ville basse** is pretty unprepossessing, rising above the lower town is a diminutive medieval quarter, the **ville haute**, contained within the old town walls and dominated by a grand, domed basilica.

Arrival, information and accommodation

The centre is a ten-minute walk across the river from the **ferry terminal** into town; there is no bus. The centre is a ten-minute walk from the **gare SNCF** (Boulogne-Ville), down boulevard Voltaire then right along boulevard Diderot. The **tourist office** (July & Aug Mon–Sat 9am–7pm, Sun 10.30am–1pm & 2.30–5pm; Sept–June Mon–Sat 9.30am–12.30pm & 2–6pm, Sun 10am–1pm; Nov–Jan closed Sun; ☎03.21.10.88.10, ⓦwww.tourisme-boulognesurmer .com), at Pont Marguet, can advise on rooms, which get booked up in advance in summer. There's plenty of inexpensive **accommodation** in Boulogne, plus a couple of upmarket places around the centre.

Hotels

Enclos de L'Evêché 6 rue de Pressy ☎03.91.90.05.90, ⓦwww.enclosde leveche.com. Classy *chambres d'hôtes* with five individually designed rooms, in a fine townhouse in the heart of the medieval quarter. ❹

Faidherbe 12 rue Faidherbe ☎03.21.31.60.93, ⓦwww.hotelfaidherbe.fr. Great-value two-star near the water and shops, with elegant rooms and friendly proprietors. ❸

Hamiot 1 rue Faidherbe, corner of bd Gambetta ☎03.21.31.44.20, ⓦwww.hotelhamiot.com. Harbourside hotel over a popular bistro. Renovated rooms have bath and double-glazing; some have balconies. ❺

Hostel Place Rouget-de-Lisle ☎03.21.99.15.30, ⓦwww.fuaj.org. HI hostel opposite the *gare SNCF* in the middle of a housing estate. Friendly modern hostel with rooms for 3–4 people at €19.25 per person, breakfast included. En-suite doubles €21.25.

La Matelote 80 bd Ste-Beuve ☎03.21.30.33.33, ⓦwww.la-matelote.com. Very smart rooms on the seafront, opposite Nausicaá and above a famed restaurant; all have minibar, a/c, cable TV and tasteful decor. ❻

The Town

Boulogne's number one attraction – and one of the most visited in northern France – is the Centre National de la Mer, or **Nausicaá**, on boulevard Ste-Beuve (daily: July & Aug 9.30am–7.30pm; Sept–June 9.30am–6.30pm; closed for 3 weeks in Jan; €17.40; ⓦwww.nausicaa.fr), though in May and June the place is crawling

---

Shopping in Boulogne

For the serious **hypermarkets**, catch bus #20 for the Leclerc or bus #8 for the huge Auchan complex, 8km along the N42 towards St-Omer – certainly the most convenient place for large-scale food and wine shopping. More fastidious foodies should stay in town and head for the **Grande Rue** and streets leading off it, but be aware that most are closed all day Monday. For charcuterie, locals' favourite Bourgeois is at 1 Grande Rue, and check out the fabulous fish displays at Aux Pêcheurs d'Étaples, at no. 31; you can also sample the seafood at the brasserie tucked behind. A shop definitely not to be missed is Philippe Olivier's famous *fromagerie*, just around the corner at 43 rue Thiers, which has a selection of over two hundred cheeses in various states of maturation. To go with it you'll find a great choice of wines at Les Vins de France, 11 rue Nationale, but to buy in bulk try Le Chais at 49 rue des Deux-Ponts, in the Bréquerecque district by the gare SNCF. On Wednesday and Saturday mornings place Dalton hosts a **market**, or for basic groceries head for the Centre Commercial Liane on the corner of boulevards Diderot and Daunou.

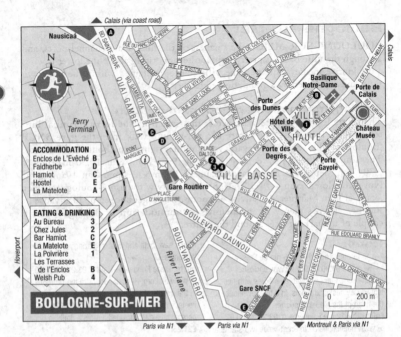

ACCOMMODATION
Enclos de L'Evêché	B
Faidherbe	D
Hamiot	C
Hostel	E
La Matelote	A

EATING & DRINKING
Au Bureau	3
Chez Jules	2
Bar Hamiot	
La Matelote	C
La Poivrière	1
Les Terrasses de l'Enclos	B
Welsh Pub	4

BOULOGNE-SUR-MER

with French and British school groups, and you may find it best to stay away. With ultraviolet lighting and New Age music creating a suitably weird ambience, you wander from tank to tank while hammerhead sharks circle overhead, a shoal of tuna lurks in a diamond-shaped aquarium, and giant conger eels conceal themselves in rusty pipes. Compared with the creatures themselves, some of the educational stuff (all in French and English – one in five visitors is British) is rather dull. Environmental issues are touched on in some of the display materials and, as you'd expect in France, there's an emphasis on the sea as a source of food – visit the chic bistro, where you can sample appropriately fresh fish and wine.

The quiet cobbled streets of the **ville haute**, southeast of Nausicaá and uphill along Grande Rue, make a pleasant respite from the more workaday **ville basse**. The most impressive sight here is the **medieval walls** themselves, which are decked out with rose beds, gravel paths and benches, and provide impressive views of the city below; it takes about 45 minutes to walk around them. Within the walls, the domed **Basilique Notre-Dame** (April–Aug 9am–noon & 2–6pm; Sept–March 10am–noon & 2–5pm) is an odd building – raised in the nineteenth century by the town's vicar without any architectural knowledge or advice – yet it seems to work. In the vast **crypt** (Tues–Sun 2–5pm; €2) you can see frescoed remains of the Romanesque building and relics of a Roman temple to Diana. In the main part of the church sits a bizarre white statue of the Virgin and Child on a boat-chariot, drawn here on its own wheels from Lourdes over the course of six years during a pilgrimage in the 1940s.

Nearby, the **Château Musée** (Mon & Wed–Sat 10am–12.30pm & 2–5.30pm, Sun 10am–12.30pm & 2.30–6pm; €4.50) contains Egyptian funerary objects, an unusual set of Eskimo masks and a sizeable collection of Greek pots. A short walk down the main tourist street, **rue de Lille**, will bring you to the **Hôtel de Ville**, whose twelfth-century belfry is the most ancient monument in the Old Town; it's only accessible via guided tour arranged with the tourist office.

Three kilometres north of Boulogne on the N1 stands the **Colonne de la Grande Armée** where, in 1803, Napoleon is said to have changed his mind about invading Britain and turned his troops east towards Austria. The column was originally topped by a bronze figure of Napoleon symbolically clad in Roman garb – though his head, equally symbolically, was shot off by the British navy during World War II; a replacement statue now tops the column.

For a pleasant excursion on a fine day, take bus #1 10 minutes north to Wimereux, a charming seaside village with a broad promenade and a network of walking paths leading up into the wind-swept headlands. The quickest route south of Boulogne is the A16 Boulogne–Abbeville autoroute, which continues all the way to Paris.

Eating and drinking

As a fishing port, Boulogne is a good spot to **eat** fish and seafood, with plenty of possibilities around place Dalton and a scattering in the *ville haute* (mostly on rue de Lille). If you're just after a **drink**, there is a handful of bars in the *ville haute* and a rather livelier selection in place Dalton, with *Au Bureau* and the smart *Welsh Pub* being the most popular.

Chez Jules 8–10 place Dalton ☎03.21.31.54.12. On the square of the *ville basse* and a great place to watch the Wednesday and Saturday markets. Typical brasserie fare with *menus* from €16.

Bar Hamiot 1 rue Faidherbe ☎03.21.31.44.20. Under the hotel of the same name, this brasserie remains popular with locals and tourists alike, offering everything from €7 omelettes and €15 fish dishes to €25–32 *menus*.

La Matelote 80 bd Ste-Beuve ☎03.21.30.17.97. The best restaurant near the water, featuring a *menu dégustation* at €70. If you'd rather not spend that much, you could go for the €29 *menu* or à la carte fish from €30. Much care is taken over the food, but service can be rather snooty.

La Poivrière 15 rue de Lille ☎03.21.80.18.18. Set in a parade of rather mediocre eateries in the prettiest part of the *ville haute*, offering traditional French cuisine starting with a very reasonable €19.50 *menu*. Closed Wed.

Les Terrasses de l'Enclos 6 rue de Pressy ☎03.91.90.05.90. This is the smartest restaurant in the *ville haute*, focusing on freshness, with excellent meat and fish. *Menus* €17–46. Closed Sun eve & Mon.

Le Touquet and around

Situated among dunes and wind–flattened tamarisks and pines, leafy **LE TOUQUET** (officially called Le Touquet–Paris–Plage) is not so different to some of the snootier places on the English south coast. This is no real surprise, given its interwar popularity with the British smart set: Noel Coward spent weekends here, while the author P.G. Wodehouse lived in the town from 1934 to 1940. He was captured here by the rapidly advancing Germans, then interned, later making his notorious wartime broadcasts from Berlin. Though the town's seafront has been colonized by modern apartments, magnificent villas still hide behind the trees a few blocks inland. One treat worth indulging in – especially if you've got kids – is Le Touquet's **Aqualud** swimming complex right on the beach (July & Aug daily 10am–7pm; Sept–June mostly 10.15am–7.45pm but days of opening vary; closed mid-Nov to mid-Feb; July & Aug €18.50, otherwise €16.50), which boasts three giant water slides and a series of indoor and outdoor themed pools.

Practicalities

To get to Le Touquet, either take the train from Boulogne to Étaples, from where a local bus covers the last four kilometres, or take the slow bus (Mon–Sat only; timetable from local tourist offices) directly from Boulogne; it heads down the coast through Le Touquet to Berck-sur-Mer. Le Touquet's **tourist office** is in the Palais de l'Europe on place de l'Hermitage (April–Sept Mon–Sat 9am–7pm, Sun

10am–7pm; Oct–March Mon–Sat 9am–6pm, Sun 10am–6pm; ℡03.21.06.72.00, Ⓦwww.letouquet.com), which also houses the casino.

If you're looking for somewhere reasonable to **stay**, try the hostel *Riva Bella* just 30m from the sandy beach at 12 rue Léon-Garet (℡03.21.05.08.22, Ⓦwww .rivabella-touquet.com; ❷), or the two-star *Armide*, 56 rue Léon-Garet (℡03.21.05.21.76, Ⓦwww.hotelarmide.com; ❸). If you fancy splashing out there's plenty of choice, including the very English-looking *Le Manoir* on avenue du Golf (℡03.21.06.28.28, Ⓦwww.opengolfclub.com; ❼) and *Le Westminster*, avenue du Verger (℡03.21.05.48.48, Ⓦwww.westminster.fr; ❽). There's also a **caravan site**, the *Stoneham* (℡03.21.05.16.55, Ⓔcaravaning.stoneham@letouquet .com; closed mid-Nov to mid-Feb), on avenue François-Godin, 1km from the centre and the beach. Places to **eat** can be expensive in Le Touquet. For an affordable treat, visit *Le Café des Arts*, 80 rue de Paris, which specializes in fish dishes (℡03.21.05.21.55; closed Tues & Wed; *menus* from €18), or *Les Sports*, 22 rue St-Jean (℡03.21.05.05.22), which has been serving classic brasserie fare since 1911 (*menus* from €17). For more upscale cuisine try the *Auberge de la Dune aux Loups* on the avenue of the same name (℡03.21.05.42.54; *menus* from €25), where you can eat on the terrace in a quiet residential area.

Étaples

On the other side of the River Canche is the much more workaday **ÉTAPLES**, a fishing port whose charm lies in its relaxed air. Between April and September **boat trips** departing from the port can be booked via the **tourist office** (April–Sept daily 10am–1pm & 2–6.30pm; Oct–March Mon–Sat 10am–noon & 2–6pm, Sun 2–6pm; ℡03.21.09.56.94, Ⓦwww.etaples-tourisme.com) at La Corderie, a former fish filleting plant on boulevard Bigot–Descelers. You can choose between a 45-minute sea jaunt (€6.40) and a more rigorous twelve-hour fishing stint with experienced fishermen (€45). If you've still not had your fill of fish afterwards, you can visit the Centre de Découverte de la Pêche en Mer (**Sea Fishing Discovery Centre**: April–Sept daily 10am–1pm & 2–6.30pm; Oct–March Tues–Sun 10am–12.30pm & 2–6pm; €6) in the same building as the tourist office. The village also boasts a good seafood **restaurant**, *Aux Pêcheurs d'Étaples* (℡03.21.94.06.90; from €16), situated upstairs from the bustling and well-stocked **fish market** on quai de la Canche.

Apart from **Étaples**, the seaside towns in this area are only interesting in that they provide access to the beaches, which really are worth getting to. Their eerie beauty is best experienced by walking the coastal GR path (or any one of the several marked trails that the local tourist offices promote). For drivers, the D119 between Boulogne and just north of Dannes is a little closer to the water with turn-offs directly into the dunes.

Montreuil-sur-Mer

Once a port, **MONTREUIL-SUR-MER** is now stranded 13km inland, owing to the silting up of the River Canche. Perched on a hilltop above the river and surrounded by ancient walls, it's an appealing place. Quite compact, it's easily walkable, with its hilltop ramparts offering fine views. Laurence Sterne spent a night here on his *Sentimental Journey*, and it was the scene of much of the action in Victor Hugo's *Les Misérables*, perhaps best evoked by the steep cobbled street of Cavée St-Firmin, first left after the Porte de Boulogne, a short climb from the *gare SNCF*.

Two heavily damaged Gothic churches grace the main square: the **church of St-Saulve** and a tiny wood-panelled **chapelle** tucked into the side of the red-brick hospital. To the south there are numerous cobbled lanes to wander down, all lined with little artisan houses. In the northwestern corner of the walls lies Vauban's

Citadelle (daily except Tues: mid-April to mid-Oct 10am–noon & 2–6pm; Feb to mid-April & mid-Oct to Nov 10am–noon & 2–5pm; Dec 2–5pm; €4) – ruined and overgrown, with subterranean gun emplacements and a fourteenth-century tower that records the coats of arms of the French noblemen killed at Agincourt. A path following the top of the walls provides views out across the Canche estuary.

In mid-August, Montreuil puts on a surprisingly lively mini arts **festival** of opera, theatre and dance, Les Malins Plaisirs.

Practicalities

The **tourist office** is by the citadelle at 21 rue Carnot (April–June, Sept & Oct Mon–Sat 10am–12.30pm & 2–6pm, Sun 10am–12.30pm; July & Aug Mon–Sat 10am–6pm, Sun 10am–12.30pm & 3–5pm; Nov–March Mon–Sat 10am–12.30pm & 2–5pm; ☏03.21.06.04.27, ⓦwww.tourisme-montreuillois.com). To **stay** in style, try the classy, expensive *Château de Montreuil* (☏03.21.81.53.04, ⓦwww .chateaudemontreuil.com; ⓪), overlooking the citadelle, which also has a top-class restaurant (closed Mon outside high season; *menus* €75). For good food and accommodation at more manageable prices, try *Le Darnétal*, in place Darnétal (☏03.21.06.04.87; ❸; closed Mon & Tues; restaurant from €21). However, the most atmospheric hotel in town is the *Hôtel de France* on rue Petit Cocquempot, a renovated sixteenth-century inn with rooms looking out onto a pretty courtyard of weathered brick (☏03.21.06.05.36, ⓦwww.hoteldefrance1.com; closed Jan; ❺). There's also a basic **youth hostel** (☏03.21.06.10.83; closed Nov–Feb; reception 10am–6pm except Tues; dorm beds €11.40) in one of the citadelle's outbuildings, and a **campsite**, *La Fontaine des Clercs* (☏03.21.06.07.28; open all year), below the walls, by the Canche on rue de'Église.

The Crécy and Agincourt battlefields

Agincourt and Crécy, two of the bloodiest Anglo–French battles of the Middle Ages, took place near the attractive little town of **HESDIN** (familiar to Simenon fans from the TV series *Inspector Maigret*). Getting to either is difficult without your own transport; by car, it takes around an hour from Boulogne.

Twenty kilometres southwest of Hesdin, at the **Battle of Crécy**, Edward III inflicted the first of his many defeats of the French in 1346. This was the first appearance on the continent of the new English weapon, the six-foot longbow, and the first use in European history of gunpowder. There's not a lot to see today: just the **Moulin Édouard III** (now a watchtower), 1km northeast of **Crécy-en-Ponthieu** on the D111 to Wadicourt, site of the windmill from which Edward watched the hurly-burly of battle. Further south, on the D56 to Fontaine, the battered **croix de Bohème** marks the place where King John of Bohemia died fighting for the French, having insisted on leading his men into battle despite his blindness.

Ten thousand men died in the heaviest defeat ever of France's feudal knighthood at the **Battle of Agincourt** on October 25, 1415. Forced by muddy conditions to fight on foot in heavy armour, the French, though more than three times as numerous, were easy prey for the lighter, mobile English archers. The rout took place near present-day **AZINCOURT**, about 12km northeast of Hesdin off the D928, where a colourful, well-organized museum, the **Centre Historique Médiéval d'Azincourt** (April–June & Sept–Oct daily 10am–6pm; July–Aug daily 9.30am–6.30pm; Nov–March daily except Tues 10am–5pm; €7.50; ⓦwww .azincourt-medieval.fr), uses video and interactive facilities to bring the story to life. The museum can give you a map indicating the position of the English and French lines, and southeast of the village, by the crossroads of the D104 and the road to Maisoncelle, there's an informative orientation point at the foot of a stone obelisk.

The Marquenterre Bird Sanctuary

Even if you know nothing about birds, the **Parc Ornithologique du Marquen-terre** (daily: Feb, March & Oct to mid-Nov 10am–6pm; April–Sept 10am–7.30pm; mid-Nov to Jan 10am–5pm; €9.90), 30km south of Étaples off the D940 between the Canche and Somme estuaries, will still be a revelation. The landscape is beautiful and strange: all dunes, tamarisks and pine forest, full of salty meres and ponds thick with water plants.

Binoculars can be hired (€4); otherwise, rely on the guides posted at some of the observation huts, who set up portable telescopes and will tell you about the nesting birds. There's a choice of itineraries – two longer, more interesting walks (2–3hr) and a shorter one (roughly 1hr 30min); you can expect to see dozens of species – ducks, geese, oyster-catchers, terns, egrets, redshanks, greenshanks, spoonbills, herons, storks, godwits – some of them residents, most taking a breather from their epic migratory flights. In April and May they head north, returning from the end of August to October, while in early summer the young chicks can be spotted.

Keen natural historians might also want to drop into the **Maison de la Baie de Somme et de l'Oiseau** on the other side of the bay, between St-Valéry-sur-Somme and Cayeux-sur-Mer (daily: July & Aug 9.30am–7pm; April–June & Sept to mid-Oct 9.30am–6pm; mid-Oct to March 10am–5pm; €6.90; ☎03.22.26.93.93), which has displays relating to birds and seals of the Somme bay and organizes seal excursions.

The Somme estuary

After Marquenterre, the D940 meanders through yet more silted-up fishing hamlets, whose crouching cottages are reminders of their former poverty. Some, like **LE CROTOY**, have enough sea still to attract the yachties, and have enjoyed a boom in second homes. Le Crotoy's south-facing beach has attracted numerous writers and painters over the years: Jules Verne wrote *Twenty Thousand Leagues under the Sea* here.

Across the bay lies **ST-VALÉRY-SUR-SOMME**, accessible from April to Oct by **steam train** (see website for timetables; €7.60–10.80; ⓦwww.chemin -fer-baie-somme.asso.fr) from Le Crotoy and Noyelles, and by four buses a day from Abbeville. This is where William, Duke of Normandy, set sail to conquer England in 1066. With its intact medieval citadelle and brightly painted quays, St-Valéry is the jewel of the coast. The only notable sight is the **Écomusée Picarvie** at 5 quai du Romerel (April–Sept Wed–Sun 10am–12.30pm & 1.30–6pm; €5.90), with its interesting collection of tools and artefacts relating to vanished trades and ways of life. Otherwise, there are plenty of **activities**, including boat trips from €9 (☎03.22.60.74.68), cycling (guided cycle rides from €15; ☎03.22.29.07.51) and guided walks (☎03.22.26.92.30). Digging for shellfish is also popular, but you have to be extremely careful about the tide. When it's high it reaches up to the quays, but withdraws 14km at low tide, creating a dangerous current; equally, it returns very suddenly, cutting off the unwary.

The town's **tourist office** (daily 9.30am–12.30pm & 2–6pm, closed Mon Sept–May; ☎03.22.60.93.50) is situated on the quayside. There are two attractive **hotel-restaurants**: the three-star *Hôtel du Port et des Bains* (☎03.22.60.80.09, ⓦwww.hotelhpb.fr; ❹; restaurant *menu* from €16), right on the quayside by the tourist office; and the two-star *Les Pilotes* (☎03.22.60.80.39, ⓦwww.lespilotes .com; ❹), which fronts both rue de la Ferté and the quayside and serves mussels in over thirty different ways (*menus* from €16).

Abbeville

ABBEVILLE lies about halfway from Calais to Paris and makes a convenient stop-off on the N1. Until hit by a German air raid in 1940, it was a very beautiful town. Remnants of its small-scale charm can still be found in the pretty, winding streets north and east of the tourist office, especially along rue des Teinturiers. But the town's crowning glory is the splendid late Gothic **church of St-Vulfran**, marooned now amid regimented postwar shopping streets. Restoration work on the church, which was badly scarred during the war, only finished in 1993; the nave retains a real feeling of dusty antiquity but the restorers' touches are obvious in the choir. The original builders' ambitions exceeded their reach; funds ran out, and the grandiose nave and modest choir seem to belong to different churches.

The **tourist office** is at 1 place de l'Amiral-Courbet (mid-April to Sept Mon–Sat 9.30am–7pm, Sun 10am–1pm; Oct to mid-April Mon–Sat 9.30am–12.30pm & 1.30–5.30pm, Sun 10am–1pm; ℡ 03.22.24.27.92, Ⓦ www.ot-abbeville.fr). In terms of **accommodation**, Abbeville has few establishments with individual charm. The most comfortable and central of the chains is the *Mercure Hôtel de France*, in place du Pilori in the town centre (℡ 03.22.24.00.42, Ⓦ www.mercure .com; ❺; *menus* from €17), while a cheap local option is the neat but basic *Le Liberty*, 5 rue Ste-Catherine (℡ 03.22.24.21.71; ❶). For a **meal**, try *L'Escale en Picardie* at 15 rue des Teinturiers (℡ 03.22.24.21.51; *menus* from €25), which specializes in fresh fish with crisp white wines.

The Flemish cities and world war battlefields

From the Middle Ages until the late twentieth century, great Flemish cities like **Lille**, **Roubaix**, **Douai** and **Cambrai** flourished, mainly thanks to their textile industries. The other dominating – now virtually extinct – presence in this part of northern France was the **coalfields** and related industries, which, at their peak in the nineteenth century, formed a continuous stretch from Béthune in the west to Valenciennes in the east. At **Lewarde** you can visit one of the pits, while in the region's big industrial cities you can see what the masters built with their profits: noble townhouses, magnificent city halls, ornate churches and some of the country's finest art collections. Lille is a major trans-European communications hub with a thriving centre of interest to locals and tourists alike.

On a more sombre note, Picardy, Artois and Flanders are littered with the monuments, battlefields and cemeteries of the two world wars, nowhere as intensely as the region northeast of Amiens, between **Albert** and the appealing market town of **Arras**. It was here, among the fields and villages of the Somme, that the main battle lines of World War I were drawn. They can be visited most spectacularly at **Vimy Ridge**, just off the A26 north of Arras, where the trenches have been left *in situ*. Lesser sites, often more poignant, dot the countryside around Albert along the **Circuit du Souvenir**.

Lille and around

LILLE (Rijsel in Flemish), northern France's largest city, surprises many visitors with its impressive architecture, the winding streets of its tastefully restored old quarter (Vieux Lille), its plethora of excellent restaurants and bustling nightlife. It boasts a large university, a modern métro system and a very serious attitude to culture, with some great museums. At the same time, the city spreads far into the countryside in every direction, a jumble of suburbs and factories, and for the French it remains the very symbol of the country's heavy industry and working-class politics. Lille is facing up to many of the tough issues of contemporary France: poverty and racial conflict, a crime rate similar to that of Paris and Marseille, and a certain regionalism – Lillois sprinkle their speech with a French–Flemish patois ("Ch'ti") and to some extent assert a Flemish identity.

Arrival, information and accommodation

The central Grand'Place is just a few minutes' walk from **Gare Lille-Flandres** (originally Paris's Gare du Nord, brought here brick by brick in 1865), served by regional trains plus a regular service to Paris. TGV and Eurostar services from London, Brussels and further afield stop at the modern **Lille-Europe** station, a few minutes' walk from the centre, or one stop on the métro. If you arrive by air at **Lesquin airport**, a shuttle-bus service (hourly on the hour; ☏08.91.67.32.10; €5 one way) whisks you to Euralille, just by Gare Lille-Flandres, in twenty minutes. Despite being the fifth-largest city in France, Lille's centre is small enough to walk round and, unless you choose to visit the modern art museum at Villeneuve-d'Ascq or La Piscine in Roubaix, you won't even need to use the city's efficient **métro** system (tickets €1.30 per trip; day pass €3.60).

The **tourist office** in place Rihour (Mon–Sat 9.30am–6.30pm, Sun & public hols 10am–noon & 2–5pm; ☏08.91.56.20.04, ⓦwww.lilletourism.com), ten minutes' walk from the station along rue Faidherbe through place du Théâtre and the Grand'Place, runs four-hour tours of the surrounding world war battlefields every Saturday (€38 per person). It also offers help with booking hotels, and sells a **City Pass** (one day €20, two days €30 and three days €45), which offers free entry to various sites and attractions and free use of public transport.

Accommodation in Lille is plentiful and tends to be of a good standard, though good budget options are scarce.

Hotels

Brueghel 3–5 parvis St-Maurice ☏03.20.06.06.69, ⓦwww.hotel-brueghel.com. Very attractive and typically Flemish two-star hotel with antique-furnished rooms and charming, understated service. ❹

Carlton 3 rue de Paris ☏03.20.13.33.13, ⓦwww.carltonlille.com. Smart four-star rooms decorated in Louis XV and Louis XVI style with marble bathrooms. Noted for its magnificent reception halls. ❾

Flandre Angleterre 13 place de la Gare ☏03.20.06.04.12, ⓦwww.hotel-flandre-angleterre.fr. Much the classiest of the hotels near the train station: impressively large en-suite rooms with TV & free wireless internet. ❹

Le Grand 51 rue Faidherbe ☏03.20.06.31.57, ⓦwww.legrandhotel.com. Comfortable two-star; rooms are en-suite and soundproofed, with satellite TV & wi-fi. ❹

De la Paix 46bis rue de Paris ☏03.20.54.63.93, ⓦwww.hotel-la-paix.com. The nicest, and most expensive, two-star in town, with a great location, a gleaming wooden staircase, and rooms decorated with classy modern art posters. All rooms come with shower, toilet and TV. ❺

De la Treille 7–9 place Louise-de-Bettignies ☏03.20.55.45.46, ⓦwww.hoteldelatreille.com. Bright, cheerful Vieux Lille hotel, with marble bathrooms and pastel-walled bedrooms. ❻

Hostel and campsite

Camping de l'Image 140 rue Brune ☏03.20.35.69.42, ⓦwww.campingimage.com. Situated in Houplines northwest of Lille, this campsite has the advantage of being open all year round. Take the métro to St-Philibert, then bus #75 to rue Brune.

Hostel 12 rue Malpart, off rue de Paris ☏03.20.57.08.94, ⓦwww.fuaj.org. HI hostel in a fairly central position. Kitchen facilities and internet access available. Dorm beds €19 including breakfast. Closed Jan.

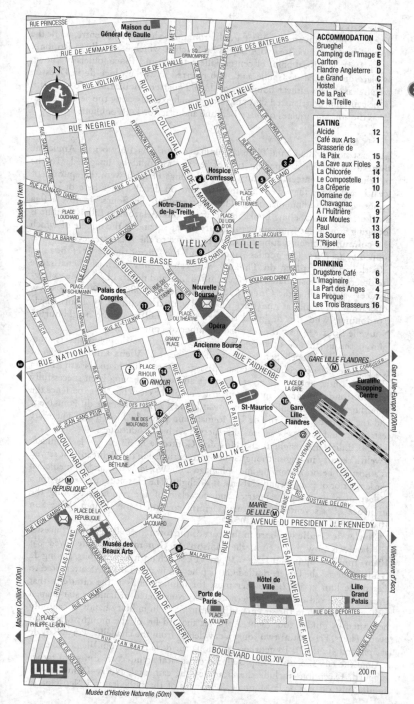

ACCOMMODATION

Brueghel	G
Camping de l'Image	E
Carlton	B
Flandre Angleterre	D
Le Grand	C
Hostel	H
De la Paix	F
De la Treille	A

EATING

Alcide	12
Café aux Arts	1
Brasserie de la Paix	15
La Cave aux Fioles	3
La Chicorée	14
Le Compostelle	11
La Crêperie	10
Domaine de Chavagnac	2
A l'Huîtrière	9
Aux Moules	17
Paul	13
La Source	18
T'Rijsel	5

DRINKING

Drugstore Café	6
L'Imaginaire	8
La Part des Anges	4
La Pirogue	7
Les Trois Brasseurs	16

Maison du Général de Gaulle

Hospice Comtesse

Notre-Dame-de-la-Treille

VIEUX LILLE

Palais des Congrès

Nouvelle Bourse

Opéra

Ancienne Bourse

GRAND' PLACE

RIHOUR

St-Maurice

Euralille Shopping Centre

Gare Lille-Flandres

GARE LILLE FLANDRES

PLACE DE LA GARE

RÉPUBLIQUE

MAIRIE DE LILLE

Musée des Beaux Arts

Porte de Paris

Hôtel de Ville

Lille Grand Palais

▲ Citadelle (1km)

▲ Gare Lille-Europe (200m)

▲ Villeneuve d'Ascq

◄ Maison Coilliot (100m)

Musée d'Histoire Naturelle (50m) ▼

0   200 m

LILLE

The City

The city's museums are all a bit of a walk from the pedestrianized centre, while the hottest museum associated with Lille is **La Piscine**, which is actually in **Roubaix** (see p.193). The focal point of central Lille is the **Grand'Place** (officially known as place du Général-de-Gaulle and often referred to as the **place de la Déesse**), which marks the southern boundary of the old quarter, **Vieux Lille**. To the south is the central pedestrianized shopping area, which extends along rue de Béthune as far as the adjacent squares of place Béthune and place de la République.

Vieux Lille

The east side of the Grand'Place is dominated by the lavishly ornate **Ancienne Bourse**, as perfect a representative of its age as could be imagined. To the merchants of seventeenth-century Lille, all things Flemish were the epitome of wealth and taste; they were not men to stint on detail, either here or on the imposing surrounding mansions. The courtyard of the Bourse is now a **flea market**, with stalls selling books in the afternoons. A favourite Lillois pastime is lounging around the fountain at the centre of the square, in the middle of which is a **column** commemorating the city's resistance to the Austrian siege of 1792, topped by *La Déesse* (the goddess), modelled on the wife of the mayor at the time.

In the adjacent **place du Théâtre**, you can see how Flemish Renaissance architecture was assimilated and Frenchified in grand flights of Baroque extravagance – above all at the **Opéra** (closed July–Sept; ☎08.20.48.90.00, ⓦwww.opera-lille.fr), built at the start of the twentieth century by Louis-Marie Cordonnier, who also designed the extravagant **belfry** of the neighbouring Nouvelle Bourse – now the regional chamber of commerce.

From the north side of these two squares, the smart shopping streets, rues Esquermoise and Lepelletier, lead towards the heart of **Vieux Lille**, a warren of red-brick terraces on cobbled lanes and passages. Once a dilapidated North African ghetto, it's now an area of great character and charm, having been successfully reclaimed and reintegrated into the mainstream of the city's life. To experience the atmosphere of Vieux Lille, head up towards rue d'Angleterre, rue du Pont-Neuf and the Porte de Gand, rue de la Monnaie and place du Lion d'Or. There are restaurants and bars everywhere, interspersed with chic boutiques.

Vieux Lille's main sight is the **Hospice Comtesse** at 32 rue de la Monnaie. Twelfth century in origin, though much reconstructed in the eighteenth, it served as a hospital before becoming an orphanage after World War I, and its medicinal garden, a riot of poppies and verbena, is a delight. The Hospice is the setting for a collection of paintings, tapestries and porcelain of the region, recreating the ambience of a seventeenth-century Flemish convent (Mon 2–6pm, Wed–Sun 10am–12.30pm & 2–6pm; €3.50).

Charles de Gaulle was born in this part of the town in 1890, at 9 rue Princesse. His house is now a museum, the **Maison du Général de Gaulle** (Wed–Sat 10am–1pm & 2–6pm, Sun 1.30–6.30pm; €6), which normally exhibits, among de Gaulle's effects, the bullet–riddled Citroën he was in when the OAS attempted to assassinate him in 1962. Another must for military buffs is the **citadelle** that overlooks the old quarter to the northwest, constructed in familiar star-shaped fashion by Vauban in the seventeenth century. Still in military hands, it can only be visited by guided tour (Sept–April 1st and 3rd Fri of the month; May–Aug every Thurs, Fri & Sun; two tours a day depart from the citadelle's Porte Royale at 3pm and 4pm; €7). To get there, go along rue de la Barre from Vieux Lille.

Amid the city's secular pomp, Lille's ecclesiastical architecture can seem rather subdued. Exceptions include the facade of the cathedral, **Notre-Dame-de-la-Treille**, just off rue de la Monnaie. The body of the cathedral is a Neo-Gothic construction begun in 1854, but the new facade, completed in 1999, is a translucent marble skin supported by steel wires, best appreciated from inside, or at night when lit up from within. More traditional, but also impressive, is the **church of St-Maurice**, close to the station on rue de Paris, whose white stone front hides a classic Flemish Hallekerke, its five aisles characteristic of the style.

South of the Grand'Place

Just south of the Grand'Place is **place Rihour**, a largely modern square flanked by brasseries and the remains of an old palace that now houses the tourist office, hidden behind a war memorial of gigantic proportions. Close by, the busiest shopping street, rue de Béthune, leads into place de Béthune, home to some excellent cafés, and beyond to the **Musée des Beaux-Arts** on place de la République (Mon 2–6pm; Wed–Sun 10am–6pm; €5). The late 1990s redesign is almost too sleek and spacious, but the museum does contain some important works. Flemish painters form the core of the collection, from "primitives" like Dirck Bouts, through the northern Renaissance to Ruisdael, de Hooch and the seventeenth-century greats, including several painted by Rubens for the Capuchin convent in Lille. French works include paintings by Delacroix, Courbet and Monet. The museum's temporary exhibitions cost extra, but can be worthwhile.

A few hundred metres south of the museum, near the green avenue Jean-Baptiste Lebas, is the **Musée d'Histoire Naturelle**, 19 rue de Bruxelles (Mon & Wed–Fri 9am–noon & 2–5pm, Sun 10am–5pm; €2.70). It's a small museum, a manageable size for children, with a lovely collection of dinosaur bones, fossils, and an impressive array of stuffed birds, including a dodo.

West of the Musée des Beaux-Arts, on rue de Fleurus, lies **Maison Coilliot**, one of the few houses built by Hector Guimard, who made his name designing the Art Nouveau entrances to the Paris métro – it's worth taking a look at the facade. Built at the height of the Art Nouveau movement, it's as striking today as it was to the conservative burghers of Lille (there are no other such buildings in the city), but it also displays the somewhat muddled eclecticism of the style, coming over as half brick-faced mansion, half timber-framed cottage. East of the museum, near the triumphal arch of Porte de Paris, is the city's odd but serviceable **Hôtel de Ville**, executed in a Flemish-modernist style not unlike German *Jugendstil*, with an extremely tall belfry.

Euralille

Thanks to Eurostar and the international extension of the TGV network, Lille has become the transport hub of northern Europe, a position it is trying to exploit to turn itself into an international business centre: hence **Euralille**, the burgeoning complex of shops and offices behind the old *gare SNCF*. Some of the structures are by big-name architects like Rem Koolhaas and Jean Nouvel, but some of the glitter is already coming off this "new" Lille: the TGV station is bustling and audacious, but the shopping mall opposite is dull, the brutal concrete expanse between the two stations is popular only with drunks and vagrants, and the weed-infested kerbs and dirty fountains point to a lack of adequate maintenance.

Villeneuve d'Ascq: the Musée d'Art Moderne

The suburb of Villeneuve d'Ascq is a mark of Lille's cultural ambition. Acres of parkland, an old windmill or two, and a whole series of mini-lakes form the setting for the **Musée d'Art Moderne** (Tues–Sun 10am–6pm; €7; park open Mon 2–7pm, Tues–Sun 9am–7pm), newly reopened after four years of renovation. It houses an unusually good, if small, collection in its uninviting red-brick buildings. The ground floor is generally given over to exhibitions of varying quality by contemporary French artists, while the permanent collection, on the first floor, contains canvases by Picasso, Braque, Modigliani and Rouault. The museum also holds a substantial collection of art brut ("raw art"), which includes graffiti and pieces by primitive artists working outside the fine art tradition.

Eating, drinking and entertainment

A Flemish flavour and a taste for mussels characterize the city's traditional cuisine, with the main central concentration of cafés, **brasseries** and **restaurants** around **place Rihour** and along rue de Béthune. Vieux Lille has gained a reputation for gastronomic excellence, and for something more innovative or atmospheric it's here, particularly on the eastern side towards and along **rue de Gand**, where you'll find the thickest concentration of worthwhile places. The **student quarter** along rues Solférino and Masséna is good for ethnic eating – the former mostly Chinese or Japanese, the latter dominated by cheap kebab shops. Foodies should make a pilgrimage to Philippe Olivier's *fromagerie* with its three hundred cheeses at 3 rue du Curé-St-Étienne.

The **cafés** around the Grand'Place and place Rihour are always buzzing with life. Up near the cathedral in Vieux Lille, rue Royale, rue de la Barre, rue Basse and place Louise-de-Bettignies have trendier spots, with a few stretched out along rue de la Monnaie too. West of the centre, Celtic-style pubs dominate in studenty rue Masséna, attracting a young crowd. For **gay bars**, of which there are several, try *Vice Versa* on rue de la Barre or *Le Privilège* just opposite. Art and music events are always worth checking up on – there's a particularly lively **jazz** scene. Pick up a copy of the free weekly listings magazine, *Sortir*, from the tourist office, or look in the local paper, *La Voix du Nord*.

Restaurants and cafés

Alcide 5 rue Débris St-Étienne ☎03.20.12.06.95. A Lillois institution, this upmarket brasserie is tucked down a narrow alleyway near the Grand'Place. Reliable, hearty fare (*flamiche*, fish, *crêpes à la cassonade*) and home-made ice creams served in a wood-panelled dining room. *Menus* from €19. Closed Sun eve.

Café aux Arts 1 place du Concert. Good old-fashioned café with wicker chairs on its terrace, in an unbeatable vantage point over the market.

Brasserie de la Paix 25 place Rihour ☎03.20.54.70.41. Sumptuous brasserie specializing in mussels and seafood. *Menus* from €18. Closed Sun.

La Cave aux Fioles 39 rue de Gand ☎03.20.55.18.43. The jazz-themed decor and chill-out music here create a mellow ambience. Food ranges from classic French dishes and Flemish specials to more adventurous fare. *Menus* from €35 or *plats* from €18. Closed Sat lunch, Sun & Mon.

La Chicorée 15 place Rihour ☎03.20.54.00.23. Open until dawn for late-nighters, this bustling brasserie serves simple, hearty fare for around €10, plus some good-value lunch specials.

Le Compostelle 4 rue St-Étienne ☎03.28.38.08.30. In a much-renovated Knights Templar Renaissance palace, this airy restaurant

with indoor trees offers refined versions of traditional French specialities, including vegetarian options. *Menus* from €29.

La Crêperie 4 rue Débris St-Étienne ☎03.20.42.12.16. Stylish modern crêperie with a good choice of sweet and savoury pancakes plus *tartines* and salads; *plats* around €10. There's another branch on rue de Gand.

Domaine de Chavagnac 43 rue de Gand ☎03.20.06.53.51. Unpretentious, old-fashioned French cuisine specializing in foie gras, cassoulet and other *produits du terroir* from the owner's farm (the *produits* can also be purchased). Mains from €9.50. Closed lunch Sun–Wed.

🏃 **A l'Huîtrière** 3 rue des Chats-Bossus ☎03.20.55.43.41. A wonderful shop (worth a visit just to look at the mosaics and stained glass) with an expensive, chandelier-hung restaurant at the back – acclaimed as Lille's best – specializing in fish and oysters at €40-plus a dish; there's an impressive €118 menu. Closed Sun eve.

Aux Moules 34 rue de Béthune ☎03.20.57.12.46. The best place to eat mussels; they've been serving them here in the Art Deco-style interior since 1930. Nothing costs much over €12 and it's all excellent value. Daily noon–11pm.

Paul Place du Théâtre, corner of rue Faidherbe. *Paul* is an institution in Lille; although it has now become an international chain, it all started here with the boulangerie, patisserie and *salon de thé* all under one roof.

La Source 13 rue du Plat ℡03.20.57.53.07. Vegetarian restaurant and health food store, best at lunchtime. From €9.

T'Rijsel 25 rue de Gand ℡03.20.15.01.59. Traditional Flemish *estaminet*, serving the whole gamut of regional dishes and over 40 beers. *Plats* from €8. Closed Sun & Mon.

Bars and clubs

Drugstore Café 21 rue Royale. Trendy Vieux Lille bar on three levels, with 1970s-style decor and an eclectic music policy playing everything from oldies and jazz to electro.

L'Imaginaire Place Louise-de-Bettignies, next door to the *Hôtel Treille*. Arty young bar with paintings adorning the walls. Mon–Sat 11pm–3am.

La Part des Anges 50 rue de la Monnaie. Trendy wine bar with an enviable cellar, serving simple meals and oysters to accompany the wine.

La Pirogue 16 rue Jean-Jacques Rousseau. Antilles-themed bar with reasonably priced cocktails, especially popular with local students.

Les Trois Brasseurs 22 place de la Gare. Dark, smoke-stained dining stalls surround copper cauldrons in this brasserie that brews its own beer. Food is also served but the beer is the main attraction.

THE NORTH | The Flemish cities and world war battlefields

Listings

Banks Several major banks have branches on rue Nationale; they're mostly open on Sat until lunchtime.

Books Le Furet du Nord, 15 place Général-de-Gaulle, is a huge bookshop on eight floors with a wide selection of books in English.

Car rental Mostly from the two train stations: Avis, Gare Flandres ℡03.20.06.35.55, Gare Europe ℡03.20.51.12.31; Europcar, Gare Flandres ℡03.20.06.10.04, Gare Europe ℡03.20.06.01.46; Hertz, Gare Flandres ℡03.28.36.28.70, Gare Europe ℡03.28.36.25.90.

Cinema Lille's two main cinemas, Le Majestic and UGC, are along the rue de Béthune; UGC at no. 40 shows blockbusters with usually at least one film in English, Le Majestic at nos. 54–56 is artier and sometimes runs festivals.

Festivals The major festival of the year, the Grande Braderie, takes place over the first weekend of September, when a big street parade and vast flea market fill the streets of the Old Town by day, and the evenings see a *moules-frites* frenzy in all the restaurants.

Health SOS Médecins ℡03.20.29.91.91.

Internet Allo Monde at 9 rue de Molinel ℡03.20.39.40.99.

Laundry There are several outlets of Lavotec, most central at 137 rue Solférino, open daily 7am–9pm. There's another, unnamed laundry close to the youth hostel on the corner of rue Ovigneur and rue Monnoyer (daily 7am–8pm).

Markets The loud and colourful Wazemmes flea market, selling food and clothes, spills around place de la Nouvelle Aventure, to the west of central Lille. Main day Sun but also open Tues and Thurs (7am–2pm). A smaller food market takes place in Vieux Lille on place du Concert (Wed, Fri & Sun 7am–2pm).

Police Commissariat Central, 5 bd du Maréchal Vaillant ℡03.20.62.47.47.

Post office 8 place de la République (℡03.28.36.10.20; Mon–Fri 8am–7pm, Sat 8.30am–12.30pm) and 13–15 rue Nationale (℡03.28.38.18.40; Mon 10am–6.30pm, Tues–Fri 9am–6.30pm, Sat 10am–1pm & 2–4pm).

Taxi Gare ℡03.20.06.64.00; Taxi Union ℡03.20.06.06.06.

Roubaix

Just 15km northeast of Lille, right up against the Belgian border, **ROUBAIX** is a once-great Flemish textile city that fell into decline and is striving to rejuvenate itself. The city centre is not especially attractive: even the modest outlet shopping mall on its southern fringe is somehow dispiriting. Nevertheless, Roubaix is worth a quick visit to **La Piscine**, or the **Musée d'Art et d'Industrie** (Tues–Thurs 11am–6pm, Fri 11am–8pm, Sat & Sun 1–6pm; temporary and permanent collection €7; permanent collection only €4.50), halfway between the *gare SNCF* and the Grand'Place at 23 rue de l'Espérance. This fascinating museum opened its doors in 2001 in the improbable setting of one of France's most beautiful swimming pools, originally built in the early 1930s. Architect Jean-Paul Philippon's contemporary

193

conversion retains various aspects of the baths – part of the pool, the shower-cubicles, the changing rooms and the bathhouses – and uses each part of the complex to display a splendid collection of mostly nineteenth- and early twentieth-century sculpture and painting, plus *haute couture* clothing, textiles and photographs of the pool in its heyday.

A short way southeast of central Roubaix, at 25 rue de la Prudence, is the **Manufacture des Flandres**, a working tapestry factory, where you'll find the **Musée du Jacquard** (Tues–Sun 2–6pm; €6). One-hour guided tours take you round an interesting collection of looms and other machinery, plus tapestries from the Middle Ages to the present day, and finish in a boutique selling the factory's wares. The quickest way to Roubaix is by **métro** from Lille, which stops at Roubaix Gare/Jean-Baptiste-Lebas, Grand'Place and Eurotéléport, the last of which, just east of Grand'Place, is also the terminus of the tram from Lille's Eurostar station.

Douai

Right in the heart of mining country, 40km south of Lille, **DOUAI** is an unpre-tentious, surprisingly attractive town, despite being badly damaged in both world wars. Its handsome streets of eighteenth-century houses are cut through by the River Scarpe and a canal. Once a haven for English Catholics fleeing Protestant oppression in Tudor England, Douai later became the seat of Flemish local govern-ment under Louis XIV, an aristocratic past evoked in the novels of Balzac.

Most of what's worth seeing in Douai is west of the central **place d'Armes**, from which rue de la Mairie leads to the splendid fifteenth-century Gothic **Hôtel de Ville** (guided tours through the tourist office: July & Aug daily 10am, 11am & hourly 2–6pm; Sept–June Mon 3pm, 4pm & 5pm, Tues–Sun 11am, 3pm, 4pm & 5pm; €3.80). It's topped by a belfry of fairytale fabulousness, popularized by Victor Hugo and renowned for its carillon of 62 bells – the largest single collection in Europe. There are concerts every Saturday at 10.45am.

One block north of the town hall, on **rue Bellegambe**, is an outrageous Art Nouveau facade fronting a very ordinary children's store. At the end of the street, rising above the Old Town, is the **church of St-Pierre**, its Baroque nave bracketed by a stone west tower, begun in 1513 but not finished until 1690, and by a dumpy round tower and dome at the opposite end. The church contains – among other treasures – a spectacular carved Baroque organ case. With the exception of the 1970s extension to the old Flemish Parliament, the riverfront west of the town hall is pleasant to wander along; across the river to the west are quiet streets of handsome two-storey houses. Here, at 130 rue des Chartreux, the **Ancienne Chartreuse** has been converted into a wonderful **museum** (daily except Tues: 10am–noon & 2–6pm; €4; free first Sun of the month), with a fine collection of paintings by Flemish, Dutch and French masters, including Van Dyck, Jordaens, Rubens and Douai's own Jean Bellegambe. The adjacent chapel displays an array of sculptures including a poignant *Enfant prodige* by Rodin.

Practicalities

The **gare SNCF** is a five-minute walk from the centre – from the station head straight along avenue Georges Clémenceau, cross place Carnot and turn left down rue Saint-Jacques, the main shopping street, to reach place d'Armes. The **tourist office** (April–Sept Mon–Sat 10am–1pm & 2–6.30pm, Sun 3–6pm; Oct–March Mon–Sat 10am–12.30pm & 2–6.30pm; ℡03.27.88.26.79, ⓦwww.ville-douai.fr) is at no. 70.

For **accommodation**, there's the classy *La Terrasse* at 36 terrasse St-Pierre (℡03.27.88.70.04, ⓦwww.laterrasse.fr; ❸), to one side of the church of St-Pierre; alternatively, try the *Ibis* (℡03.27.87.27.27, ⓦwww.ibishotel.com; ❹) on pretty place St-Amé, housed in a historic mansion. **Eating** in Douai tends towards the cheap and informal – kebabs, crêpes, pizza – but the restaurant at *La Terrasse* is an exception, with a superb €27 *menu* including wine. Also worth trying is *Au Turbotin* (☎03.27.87.04.16, *menus* from €24), west of the river at 9 rue de la Massue. For **drinking**, head for the atmospheric *Taverne les Grès* on place St-Amé, where you can catch occasional live bands.

Lewarde

A visit to the colliery at **LEWARDE**, 7km east of Douai, is a must for admirers of Zola's *Germinal*. It offers visitors a fascinating insight into the gruelling conditions of a nineteenth-century coal mine, much like the one that Zola described. Surrounded by flat, featureless beet fields, Lewarde's dour brick dwellings line streets named after Pablo Neruda, Jean-Jacques Rousseau, Georges Brassens and other luminaries of the Left. This is the traditional heart of France's coal-mining country, though you'll look in vain for winding towers or slag heaps hereabouts, demolition and landscaping having removed almost all visible traces.

From Douai's place de Gaulle, catch tram A to Bougival, where you can either take bus #1 one more stop or walk twenty minutes down the D132 towards Erchin to get to the colliery. The **Centre Historique Minier** (guided tours: March–Oct daily 9am–5.30pm; Nov–Feb Mon–Sat 1–5pm, Sun 10am–5pm; 1hr 30min; €11.50) is on the left in the old Fosse Delloye. Visitors can tour the exhibition and surface installations with an English-language audioguide, but the tours of the mine itself are led by retired miners, many of whom are not French, but Polish, Italian or North African. These pits were deep and hot, with steeply inclined narrow seams that forced the miners to work on slopes of 55 degrees and more, just as Étienne and the Maheu family do in Zola's story. They also had a poor safety record; the worst disaster occurred at Courrières in 1906, when 1,100 men were killed. Incredibly, although the owners made little effort to search for survivors, thirteen men emerged after twenty days without food, water or light. The first person they met thought that they were ghosts and fainted in fright. More incredible still, a fourteenth man surfaced alone four days later.

Cambrai

Despite the tank battle of November 1917 (see box, p.196), and the fact that the heavily defended Hindenburg Line ran through the town centre for most of World War I, **CAMBRAI** has kept enough of its character to make a fleeting visit worthwhile, though it is less attractive than either Douai, 27km to the north, or Arras to the northwest.

The huge, cobbled main square, **place Aristide-Briand**, is dominated by the Neoclassical Hôtel de Ville. The imposing building still hints at the town's former wealth, which was based on textiles and agriculture. Cambrai's chief ecclesiastical treasure is the **Church of St-Géry**, off rue St-Aubert west of the main square, worth a visit for a celebrated *Mise au Tombeau* by Rubens. The appealingly presented **Musée de Cambrai** (Wed–Sun 10am–noon & 2–6pm; €3.10; free entry first weekend of the month) at 15 rue de l'Épée, a short way south of the town square, is also worthwhile. Paintings by Velázquez, Utrillo and Ingres feature prominently alongside works by various Flemish old masters, plus great twentieth-century artists like Zadkine and Van Dongen. Don't turn down the audio-guided tour and be sure to check out the archeological display in the basement, where you can see some fascinating exhibits including elegant statues rescued from Cambrai's cathedral, destroyed after the Revolution.

Cambrai 1917

At dawn on November 20, 1917, the first full-scale **tank battle** in history began at Cambrai, when over four hundred British tanks poured over the Hindenburg Line. In just 24 hours, the Royal Tank Corps and British Third Army made the biggest advance by either side since the trenches were dug in 1914. A fortnight later, however, casualties had reached 50,000, and the armies were back where they'd started.

Although the tanks were ahead of their time, they still relied on cavalry and plodding infantry as back-up. The tanks were primitive, operated by a crew of eight who endured almost intolerable conditions – with no ventilation, the temperature inside could reach 48°C. The steering alone required three men, each on separate gearboxes, communicating by hand signals through the mechanical din. Maximum speed (6kph) dropped to barely 1kph over rough terrain, and refuelling was necessary every 55km. Of the 179 tanks lost at Cambrai, few were destroyed by the enemy; most broke down and were abandoned by their crews.

Cambrai's **tourist office** is housed in the Maison Espagnole on the corner of avenue de la Victoire at 48 rue de Noyon (Mon–Sat 9.30am–12.30pm & 2–6pm, Sun 2.30–5.30pm; ℡03.27.78.36.15, Ⓦwww.tourisme-cambrai.fr). Central **accommodation** includes *Le Mouton Blanc*, 33 rue d'Alsace-Lorraine (℡03.27.81.30.16, Ⓦwww.mouton-blanc.com; ❸), convenient, moderately priced and close to the station, with a posh **restaurant** inside (from €23.50; closed Sun eve & Mon, plus last week of July & 1st week Aug), and the very pleasant *Hôtel de France* nearby at 37 rue de Lille (℡03.27.81.38.80, Ⓦhoteldefrance-cambrai.fr; ❸), which also has a good restaurant. The nearest **campsite** is *Les Colombes* at Aubencheul-au-Bac (April–Oct; ℡03.27.89.25.90), 10km away off the N43 to Douai.

Le Cateau–Cambrésis

Twenty-two kilometres east of Cambrai along an old Roman road, the small town of **LE CATEAU-CAMBRÉSIS** is the birthplace of Henri Matisse (1869–1954). As a gift to his home town, the artist bequeathed it a collection of his works, some of which are displayed in the **Musée Matisse** (daily except Tues 10am–6pm; €4.50, free first Sun of month), housed in Palais Fénelon in the centre of town. Although it contains no major masterpieces, this is the third-largest Matisse collection in France, and the paintings here are no less attractive and interesting than the better-known ones exhibited elsewhere. The collection includes several studies for the chapel in Vence, plus a whole series of his characteristically simple pen-and-ink sketches. Also worth a look is the work of local Cubist Auguste Herbin, particularly his psychedelic upright piano. For somewhere to **stay** and **eat** there's the simple but comfortable *Hostellerie du Marché* at 45 rue Landrecies (℡03.27.84.09.32, Ⓦwww.hostelleriedumarche.com; ❸; menus €18.50).

The Somme battlefields and around

Some of the fiercest and most futile battles of World War I took place around **Arras** and **Albert**. Arras, easily accessible from Paris and Lille by TGV, is the best base for exploring the battlefields. Nearby, at **Vimy Ridge**, is where Canadians fell by the thousands, while at the site of the Notre-Dame de Lorette church, the French suffered the same fate; the battlefields and cemeteries of the Somme lie to the south, around **Albert** and **Péronne**.

Arras

ARRAS is one of the most architecturally striking towns in northern France, the cobblestoned squares of its old centre surrounded by ornate baroque townhouses that hark back to its Flemish past. It was renowned for its tapestries in the Middle Ages, giving its name to the hangings behind which Shakespeare's Polonius was killed by Hamlet. The town later fell under Spanish control, and many of its citizens today claim that Spanish blood runs in their veins. Only in 1640 was Arras returned to French control, with the help of Cyrano de Bergerac. During World War I, the British dug tunnels under the town to try to surprise the Germans to the northeast, while the Germans bombarded the town. Only one of the famous medieval Arras tapestries survived the centuries of wartime destruction; it's now on display in a cathedral in Belgium.

Arrival, information and accommodation

From the **gare SNCF** it's a ten-minute walk up rue Gambetta then traffic-free rue Ronville and its extension, to place des Héros and the **tourist office**, located in the Hôtel de Ville (April to mid-Sept Mon–Sat 9am–6.30pm, Sun 10am–1pm & 2.30–6.30pm; mid-Sept to March Mon 10am–noon & 2–6pm, Tues–Sat 9am–noon & 2–6pm, Sun 10am–12.30pm & 2.30–6.30pm; ℡03.21.51.26.95, Ⓦwww.ot-arras.fr); they have details of transport and tours of local battlefields (see "Vimy Ridge", p.198). To reach the Vimy memorial and the cemeteries around Neuville–St-Vlaast, you can rent a car from Hertz, boulevard Carnot (℡03.21.23.11.14).

There are two good **hotels** on the central squares: the *Diamant*, 5 place des Héros (℡03.21.71.23.23, Ⓦwww.arras-hotel-diamant.com; ❹), a comfortable, reliable two-star; and *Ostel Les Trois Luppars*, 49 Grand'Place (℡03.21.60.02.03, Ⓦwww.ostel-les-3luppars.com; ❹), a friendly place with modern facilities in a charming old building. For a more luxurious night, go to the *Univers*, a beautiful former monastery around a courtyard at 3 place de la Croix-Rouge, near the Abbaye St-Vaast (℡03.21.71.34.01, Ⓦwww.hotel-univers-arras.com; ❼; restaurant *menu* €29). Facing the train station there are more hotels in nearly every price range.

The Town

Reconstruction after the war was meticulous, and the townhouses lining the grand arcaded Flemish- and Dutch-style squares in the centre – **Grand'Place** and the smaller **Place des Héros** – preserve their historic character. Both were once lively market squares, but unfortunately they've since been covered over with parking spaces, making them less pleasant places to linger. Still, the architecture is impressive; on every side are restored seventeenth- and eighteenth-century mansions and, on place des Héros, the railing around the grandly ornate **Hôtel de Ville** displays an interesting photographic history of the town's wartime destruction and subsequent reconstruction.

Also inside the town hall is the entrance to the **belfry** viewing platform, 150m high – a lift takes you up most of the way, though there are still 43 steps to climb (€2.70) – and **les souterrains** (or *les boves*) – cold, dark passageways and spacious vaults beneath the city centre, tunnelled since the Middle Ages and extended by the British during World War I (frequent bilingual guided tours – ask for times in the tourist office; €5). Once down, you're escorted on a forty-minute tour and given an interesting survey of local history. The rooms – many of which have fine, tiled floors and lovely pillars and stairways – were used as a British barracks and hospital. Pictures from this period are on display, as is a bilingual newspaper published for the soldiers. Arras boasts a further subterranean attraction in the newly opened **Carrière Wellington**, just off the Bapaume road southeast of the centre at rue Delétoile (daily 10am–12.30pm & 1.30–6pm; €6.50). It's a network of medieval chalk quarries adapted by New Zealand mining engineers to create secret underground quarters for the 24,000 allied troops awaiting the start of the Battle of Arras, a diversionary attack in preparation for the Chemin des Dames assaults. The troops emerged to mount their surprise attack on 9 April 1917; the visit is accompanied but there are also individual audioguides, and there's a film on the battle at the end of the tour.

Next to its enormous cathedral is Arras's other main above-ground sight, the **Benedictine Abbaye St-Vaast**, a grey-stone classical building – still pockmarked by wartime shrapnel – erected in the eighteenth century by Cardinal Rohen. The abbey now houses the **Musée des Beaux–Arts**, with its entrance at 22 rue Paul-Doumer (daily except Tues 9.30am–noon & 2–5.30pm; €4), which contains a motley collection of paintings, including a couple of Jordaens and Brueghels, plus fragments of sculpture and local porcelain. Figuring among the highlights are a pair of delicately sculpted thirteenth-century angels, the *Anges de Saudemont,* and a room on the first floor filled with vivid seventeenth-century paintings by Philippe de Champaigne and his contemporaries, including his own *Présentation de la Vierge au Temple.*

Thirty minutes away by foot on the mournful southwestern edge of town, along boulevard Général-de-Gaulle from the Vauban barracks, is a **war cemetery** and memorial by the British architect Sir Edwin Lutyens. It's a movingly elegiac, classical colonnade of pristine brick and stone, commemorating 35,928 missing soldiers, their names inscribed on the walls. Around the back of the barracks, alongside an overgrown moat, is the stark **Mémorial des Fusillés**; its plaques commemorate two hundred Resistance fighters shot by firing squad during World War II – many of them of Polish descent, nearly all of them miners, and most of them Communists.

On a lighter note, on the last Sunday of August the town transforms itself into an open-air bistro for **La Fête de l'Andouillette**, with parades, colourful costumes and tasting of the sausage itself.

Eating

Restaurants worth trying include *La Rapière,* 44 Grand'Place (☎03.21.55.09.92), with excellent regional food and *menus* from €12.50; and, for a splurge, the gourmet *La Faisanderie,* across the square at no. 45 (☎03.21.48.20.76; from €30). Nearer the station at 26 bd de Strasbourg is an attractive, old-fashioned brasserie, *La Coupole,* where you'll find locals and tourists eating oysters and other fresh seafood, as well as traditional brasserie dishes (☎03.21.71.88.44; closed Sun & Mon; *menus* €25).

There's a good *fromagerie, L'Alpage,* just off the Grand'Place on rue de la Taillerie. Saturday is the best day for food and wine, when the squares are taken over by a morning **market**.

Vimy Ridge

Eight kilometres north of Arras on the D49, **Vimy Ridge**, or Hill 145, was the scene of some of the fiercest trench warfare of World War I: almost two full years of battle, culminating in its capture by the Canadian Corps in April 1917. It's a vast site, given in perpetuity to the Canadian people out of respect for their sacrifices, and the churned land has been preserved, in part, as it was during the conflict. You really need your own transport to get here as the Arras–Lens bus will get you no closer than the N17, which is still a long walk from the ridge (for details contact the tourist office in Arras). It is well worth the journey – of all the battlefields, this is the best place to gain an impression of the lay of the land, and to imagine how it may have felt to be part of a World War I battle.

There's a **visitor centre** (daily: April–Oct 10am–6pm; Nov–March 9am–5pm; free; ℡03.21.50.68.68) supervised by friendly, bilingual Canadian students, who run free guided **tours** (daily except Mon; call to pre-book, as tours are heavily over-subscribed). Tours are available of the "subway", the Canadian term for the series of interlinking underground tunnels used as secret passageways and to hoard ammunition and equipment, and of the cemeteries and battlefields. The visitor centre's exhibition illustrates the well-planned Canadian attack and its importance for the Canadians: this was the first time they were recognized as fighting separately from the British, thus adding to their growing sense of nationhood.

Near the information centre, long veins of neat, sanitized **trenches** wind through the earth, still heavily pitted by shell bursts beneath the planted pines. Under the ground lie countless rounds of unexploded ammunition – visitors are warned not to stray from the paths.

On the brow of the ridge to the north, overlooking the slag-heap-dotted plain of Artois, a great white **monument** reaches for the heavens, inscribed with the names of 11,285 Canadians and Newfoundlanders whose bodies were never found. It must have been an unenviable task to design a fitting memorial to such slaughter, but this one, aided by its setting, succeeds dramatically. Back from the ridge lies a memorial to the **Moroccan Division** who also fought at Vimy, and in the woods behind, on the headstones of another exquisitely maintained **cemetery**, you can read the names of half the counties of rural England.

La Targette and Notre-Dame de Lorette

At the crossroads (D937/D49) of **LA TARGETTE**, 8km north of Arras, the **Musée de la Targette** (irregular hours: officially 9am–8pm daily; €4; ℡03.21.59.17.76) contains an interesting collection of World War I and II artefacts. It's the private collection of one David Bardiaux, inspired by his grandfather, a veteran of Verdun. Its appeal lies in the precision with which the mannequins of British, French, Canadian and German soldiers are dressed and equipped, down to their sweet and tobacco tins and such rarities as a 1915 British cap with earflaps – very comfortable for the troops but withdrawn because the top brass thought it made their men look like yokels. All the pieces exhibited have been under fire; some have stitched-up tears of old wounds.

North and south of La Targette along the D937 are several **cemeteries**. There's a small British one, a huge French one, and south of the crossroads an equally vast and moving German one, containing the remains of 44,833 Germans, four to a cross or singly under a Star of David. To the north, a Polish memorial and a Czech cemetery face each other across the D937 between La Targette and Souchez.

On a bleak hill a few kilometres further north in the village of Ablain-St-Nazaire (and 5km north of La Targette) is the church of **Notre-Dame de Lorette**, scene of a costly French offensive in May 1915. The original church was blasted to bits during the war – its ruins can be seen in the village below the cemetery; afterwards a Neo-Byzantine church was built, grey and dour outside but rich and bejewelled within. It stands at the centre of a vast graveyard with over 20,000 crosses laid out in pairs, back to back, each separated by a cluster of roses. There are 20,000 more buried in the ossuary, and there's a small **Musée Vivant 1914–1918** (daily 9am–8pm; €5) behind the church, displaying photographs, uniforms and other paraphernalia.

Albert and around

The church at **ALBERT**, 40km south of Arras and 30km northeast of Amiens, was one of the minor landmarks of World War I. Its tall tower was hit by German bombing early on in the campaign, leaving the statue of the Madonna on top leaning

The Battle of the Somme

On July 1, 1916, the British and French launched the **Battle of the Somme** to relieve pressure on the French army defending Verdun. The front ran roughly northwest–southeast, 6km east of Albert across the valley of the Ancre and over the almost treeless high ground north of the Somme. The windy terrain had no intrinsic value, nor was there any long-term strategic objective; the region around Albert was the battle site simply because it was where the two Allied armies met.

There were 57,000 British casualties on the first day alone, approximately 20,000 of them dead, making it the costliest defeat the British army has ever suffered. **Sir Douglas Haig** is the usual scapegoat, yet he was only following the military thinking of the day, which is where the real problem lay. As historian A.J.P. Taylor put it, "Defence was mechanized: attack was not." Machine guns were efficient, barbed wire effective, and, most important of all, the rail lines could move defensive reserves far faster than the attacking army could march. The often ineffective heavy bombardment that presaged an advance only made matters worse, warning the enemy of an offensive and churning the trenches into a giant muddy quagmire.

Despite the bloody disaster of the first day, the battle wore on until bad weather in November made further attacks impossible. The cost of this futile struggle was roughly 415,000 British, 195,000 French and 600,000 German casualties.

---

at a precarious angle. The British, entrenched over three years in the region, came to know it as the "Leaning Virgin". Superstition had it that when she fell the war would end, a myth inspiring frequent pot shots from disgruntled troops. Before visiting the battle sites and war cemeteries along the Circuit du Souvenir, you might want to stop in at the **Musée "Somme 1916"** (daily: Feb–May & Oct to mid–Dec 9am–noon & 2–6pm; June–Sept 9am–6pm; €5; ⓦ www.musee-somme-1916.eu), an underground museum containing re-enactments of fifteen different scenes from life in the Somme trenches in 1916. The mannequins look slightly too jolly and eager but it does go some way to bringing the props to life. The final section recreates the actual battle, complete with flashing lights and the sound of exploding shells.

As you arrive (trains from Amiens or Arras), the town's "new" church tower, capped by an equally improbably posed statue, is the first thing that catches your eye. The **tourist office** is close by at 9 rue Gambetta (April–Oct Mon–Fri 9am–12.30pm & 1.30–6.30pm, Sat 9am–noon & 2–6.30pm, Sun 10am–12.30pm; Nov–March Mon–Sat 9am–12.30pm & 1.30–5pm; ☏03.22.75.16.42). Of the town's **hotels**, the best choice is *La Paix*, a friendly establishment with eight cosy rooms and a decent restaurant, at 43 rue Victor-Hugo (☏03.22.75.01.64; ❹; restaurant closed Sat & Sun eve; *menus* from €16.50).

The Circuit du Souvenir

Was it for this the clay grew tall?
O what made fatuous sunbeams toil
To break earth's sleep at all?

Wilfred Owen, Futility

The **Circuit du Souvenir** conducts you from graveyard to mine crater, trench to memorial. There's little to show the scale of the destruction that happened here less than a century ago. Nor do you get much sense of battle tactics. But you will find that, no matter what the level of your interest in the Great War, you have embarked on a sort of pilgrimage, as each successive step evokes a more harrowing slice of history.

The **cemeteries** are deeply moving – beautifully ordered, with the grass perfectly mown and flowers at the foot of every gravestone. There are tens of thousands of them, all identical, with a man's name, if it's known (nearly half the British dead have never been found), his rank and regiment and, often, a personal message chosen by the bereaved family. In the lanes between Albert and Bapaume you'll see cemeteries everywhere: at the angle of copses, halfway across a field, in the middle of a wood.

The Circuit du Souvenir heads east from Albert to the giant mine crater of **Lochnagar** at La Boisselle before swinging north to **BEAUMONT-HAMEL**, where, pipes playing, the 51st Highland Division walked abreast to their deaths. On the hill where most of them died, a series of trenches, now grassed over and eroding, is preserved. You'll get a good sense of what happened here at the visitor centre at the **Newfoundland Memorial** (daily: Nov–March 9am–5pm; April–Oct 10am–6pm), a few minutes' walk south; of eight hundred Newfoundlanders who took part in the push, just 86 returned. Across the river, near the village of **THIEPVAL**, the five thousand Ulstermen who died in the Battle of the Somme are commemorated by the **Ulster Memorial**, a replica of Helen's Tower at Clandeboyne near Belfast (café and exhibition open May–Sept Tues–Sun 10am–6pm; March–April & Oct–Nov Tues–Sun 10am–5pm; closed Dec–Feb). Probably the most famous of Edwin Lutyens' many memorials is also at Thiepval: the colossal **Memorial to the Missing**, inscribed with the names of the 73,367 British troops whose bodies were never recovered at the Somme, is visible for miles around. Here, too, there's an informative **visitor centre** (daily 10am–6pm), with a poignant photo wall of some of the missing, an exhibition on the Somme Offensive and short films in English on related themes.

Delville Wood, known as "**Devil's Wood**", lies some 10km to the east at **LONGUEVAL**. Here, where thousands of **South Africans** lost their lives, a memorial to the dead from both world wars has been erected, as well as a **museum** (daily except Mon: April–Oct 10am–5.45pm; Nov & March 10am–3.45pm). It describes not just the battle in France but also the longest march of the war, thousands of kilometres away, when South African troops walked 800km to drive the Germans out of East Africa (now Tanzania). The display is brought up to date with a short section documenting the armed struggle against apartheid.

The most informative of the museums is at **PÉRONNE**, on the River Somme some 25km east of Albert – the **Historial de la Grande Guerre** (mid-Jan to mid-Dec 10am–6pm; €7.50). Newsreel and film footage, commemorative plates, Otto Dix drawings, artificial limbs and displays of hardware all provide a broad, modern view of the catastrophe, including the political and cultural tensions that led to war.

There's a **TGV** station about 15km from Péronne – the **Gare Haute Picardie** – which is thirty minutes from the Eurostar stop at Lille-Europe; for a taxi to or from the station, call Confort Taxi (℡03.22.84.40.00) or Taxi Nico (℡03.22.84.59.22). The **tourist office** is at place André Audinot, opposite the museum (July & Aug Mon–Sat 9am–noon & 2–6.30pm, Sun 10am–noon & 2–5pm; April–June & Sept Mon–Sat 10am–noon & 2–6.30pm; Oct–March Mon–Sat 10am–noon & 2–5pm;

Getting around on the Circuit du Souvenir

It would be difficult to see all four hundred Commonwealth cemeteries in the area, though visiting one or two small ones can be rewarding. The easiest way to explore the circuit is by car, though the distances are short enough that it is also possible by bicycle. Both Albert to the west and Péronne to the southeast (see above) make good starting points, their tourist offices and museums offering free **maps** of the circuit. The route is marked (somewhat intermittently) by arrows and poppy symbols, with Commonwealth graves also indicated in English.

☎03.22.84.42.38, ⓦwww.ville-peronne.fr). **Accommodation** includes the pricey *Saint Claude*, on the main square at 42 place Louis Daudré (☎03.22.79.49.49, ⓦwww.hotel-saintclaude.com; ❺; restaurant from €15), or the more reasonable *Campanile* (☎03.22.84.22.22, ⓦwww.campanile.fr; ❷), just out of town on the N17 to Roye and Paris.

Near **VILLERS-BRETONNEUX**, 18km from Albert near the River Somme, stands another fine Lutyens creation. As at Vimy, the landscaping of the **Australian Memorial** is dramatic – for the full effect, climb up to the viewing platform of the stark white central tower. The monument was one of the last to be inaugurated, in July 1938, when the prospects for peace were again looking bleak, and it was damaged during fighting not long afterwards – bullet holes are still visible. There's a small **Franco–Australian Museum** (Mon–Sat: March–Oct 9.30am–5.30pm; Nov–Feb 9.30am–4.30pm; €4) on the first floor of the school in the village, just south of the memorial.

Picardy

To the southeast of the Somme, away from the coast and the main Paris through-routes, the often rainwashed and dull province of Picardy becomes considerably more inviting. **Amiens** is a friendly city whose life revolves around its canals, while both the Amiens and Beauvais cathedrals are highlights of the region. In the *départements* of **Aisne** and **Oise**, where Picardy merges with neighbouring Champagne, there are some real attractions amid the lush wooded hills. **Laon**, **Soissons** and **Noyon** all have handsome Gothic cathedrals, while at **Compiègne**, Napoleon Bonaparte and Napoléon III enjoyed the luxury of a magnificent château. The most rewarding overnight stop is off the beaten track in the tiny fortified town of **Coucy-le-Château-Auffrique**, perched on a hill between Soissons and Laon. **Transport** is good, too, with a network of bus connections from Amiens and good train links with Paris.

Amiens

AMIENS was badly scarred during both world wars, but sensitively restored. The cathedral is the main reason to visit, but **St-Leu**, the renovated medieval artisans' quarter north of the cathedral with its network of canals, has considerable charm, while a few minutes' walk from the train station the *hortillonnages* (see p.204) transport you into a peaceful rural landscape. A sizeable student presence ensures there's enough life in the evening to make an overnight stay worthwhile.

Arrival, information and accommodation

The main **gare SNCF** (Amiens-Nord) is on the place Alphonse Fiquet; the **gare routière** is concealed beneath the Amiens 2 shopping complex just next door. Much of central Amiens is traffic-free – the rest of it is full of cars circling endlessly in search of non-existent parking spaces. The **tourist office** is next to the cathedral on place Notre-Dame (April–Sept Mon–Sat 9.30am–6.30pm, Sun 10am–noon & 2–5pm; Oct–March Mon–Sat 9.30am–6pm, Sun 10am–noon & 2–5pm; ☎03.22.71.60.50, ⓦwww.amiens-tourisme.com). If you intend to spend much time in Amiens it's worth considering the **Pass Amiens**, which for €8 entitles the holder to a string of reductions on everything from museum entry to city transport, bicycle hire and restaurants.

Amiens has many two-star **hotels**, all with similar prices and fairly nondescript, though they tend to fill up fast.

Central et Anzac 17 rue Alexandre-Fatton
℡03.22.91.34.08, ⓦwww.hotelcentraletanzac
.com. Fewer creature comforts than its neighbour
Spatial, but perfectly decent and in a good, central
location. ❷

Hôtel de Normandie 1bis rue Lamartine
℡03.22.91.74.99, ⓦwww.hotelnormandie-80
.com. Comfortable two-star hotel in a little side
street close to the *gare SNCF*. ❶

Le Prieuré 17 rue Porion ℡03.22.71.16.71,
ⓦwww.hotel-prieure-amiens.com. Quiet little hotel

close to the cathedral, slightly more upmarket than
the *Victor Hugo*. ❸

Spatial 15 rue Alexandre-Fatton ℡03.22.91.53.23,
ⓦwww.hotelspatial.com. The slightly more
comfortable of two neighbouring hotels in a side
street opposite the *gare SNCF*, with rooms
equipped with flat-screen TVs. ❷

Victor Hugo 2 rue de l'Oratoire ℡03.22.91.57.91,
ⓦwww.hotel-a-amiens.com. Good-value renovated
hotel near the cathedral with the feel of a country
bed-and-breakfast. ❷

The City

The **Cathédrale Notre-Dame** (daily: April–Sept 8.30am–6.30pm; Oct–March
8.30am–5.30pm) dominates the city by sheer size – it's the biggest Gothic building
in France – but its appeal lies mainly in its unusual uniformity of style. Begun in
1220 under architect Robert de Luzarches, it was effectively finished by 1269, thus
escaping the influence of succeeding architectural fads. A laser scrub, used on the
west front, has revealed traces of the original polychrome exterior, in stark
contrast to its sombre, grey modern appearance. An evening **sound and light
show** (daily mid-June to mid-Sept, starts at dusk; free) gives a vivid idea of how

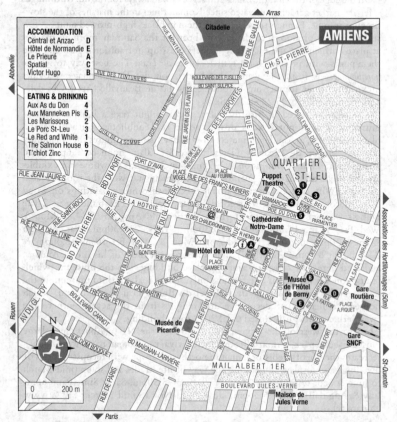

the west front would have looked when coloured, with an explanation of the various statues on the facade first in French and then in English. The interior, on the other hand, is a light, calm and unaffected space. Ruskin thought the apse "not only the best, but the very first thing done perfectly in its manner by northern Christendom". The later embellishments, like the sixteenth-century choir stalls, are works of breathtaking virtuosity, as are the sculpted panels depicting the life of St Firmin, Amiens' first bishop, on the right side of the choir screen. The choir itself can be visited at 3.30pm daily but is otherwise locked. Those with strong legs can mount the cathedral's front **towers** (daily except Tues and Sun am: April–June & Sept 2.30–5.15pm, weekends 2.30–4pm; July & August 11am guided tour, 2.30–5.15pm; Oct–March 3.45pm guided tour; €7). One of the most atmospheric ways of seeing the cathedral is to attend a Sunday morning Mass (9am and 10.30am) and listen to the sublime Gregorian chants.

Just north of the cathedral is the **quartier St-Leu**, a Flemish-looking network of canals and cottages that was once the centre of Amiens' textile industry. The city still produces much of the country's velvet, but the factories moved out to the suburbs long ago, leaving St-Leu to rot away in peace – until, that is, the property developers moved in. The slums have been tastefully transformed into neat brick cottages on cobbled streets, and the waterfront has been colonized by restaurants and bars.

On the edge of the city, the canals still serve as waterways for the **hortillonnages** – fertile market gardens cultivated since Roman times in the marshes of the slow-flowing Somme. Farmers travel between them in black, high-prowed punts. A few still take their produce into the city by boat for the Saturday morning **market** at place Parmentier, and each June farmers dress up in traditional garb and load their punts with produce for a festive *marché sur l'eau*. The best way to see the *hortillonnages* is from the water: the Association des Hortillonnages provides inexpensive **boat tours** from its office at 54 bd de Beauvillé (April–Oct daily 1.30–5pm; €5.70; ☎03.22.92.12.18).

If you're interested in Picardy culture, you might take a look at Amiens' museums. Five minutes' walk down rue de la République, south of central place Gambetta, an opulent nineteenth-century mansion houses the splendidly laid out **Musée de Picardie** (Tues, Fri & Sat 10am–noon & 2–6pm; Wed 10am–6pm; Thurs 10am–noon & 2–9pm; Sun 2–7pm; €5), whose star exhibits are the Puvis de Chavannes paintings on the main stairwell, the room created by Sol LeWitt, and a collection of rare sixteenth-century paintings on wood donated to the cathedral by a local literary society. The building at 2 rue Dubois was once the **house of Jules Verne** (mid-April to mid-Oct Mon & Wed–Fri 10am–12.30pm & 2–6.30pm, Tues 2–6.30pm, Sat & Sun 11am–6.30pm; mid-Oct to mid-April Mon & Wed–Fri 10am–12.30pm & 2–6pm, Sat & Sun 2–6pm; €7). The author spent most of his life in Amiens, and died here. It's a historic and attractive building, but the museum, which focuses on Verne's life, is one for fans only. There is also a third museum in the seventeenth-century **Musée de l'Hôtel de Berny** near the cathedral, which houses a collection of decorative arts ranging from the seventeenth to the twentieth century; it is closed until 2012 for rebuilding.

Just to the west of the city, at Tirancourt off the N1 to Abbeville, a large museum-cum-park, **Samara** (from Samarobriva, the Roman name for Amiens), recreates the life of prehistoric man in northern Europe with reconstructions of dwellings and displays illustrating the way of life, trades and so on (mid-March to June & Sept to mid-Nov Mon–Fri 9.30am–5.30pm, Sat & Sun 10am–6pm; July & Aug daily 10am–6.30pm; closed mid-Nov to mid-March; €9; ⓦ www .samara.fr).

Eating, drinking and entertainment

By far the most attractive area to eat is around **St-Leu**, where many of the **restaurants** have outdoor seating overlooking a canal and the cathedral, especially on rue Bélu.

Bars and pubs abound in the area – try the lively *Aux Manneken Pis* on place du Don for a good selection of Belgian beers. There is also a trendy late-night gay bar, *Le Red and White*, at 9 rue de la Dodane.

In late March and early April Amiens bursts into life for its annual international **jazz festival**; on the third weekend in June, the local costumes come out for the **Fête d'Amiens**, which is the best time of year to visit the *hortillonnages*. Traditional Picardy **marionette** (*cabotans*) performances take place at the Théâtre de Marionnettes Chés Cabotans d'Amiens, 31 rue Edouard-David (℡ 03.22.22.30.90, 🖳 www.ches-cabotans-damiens.com; tickets €10). To purchase or take a look at handmade marionettes, visit the workshop of Jean-Pierre Facquier at 67 rue du Don.

Restaurants

Aux As du Don 1 place du Don. On a pretty, cobbled square below the cathedral, with a *menu du jour* for €16 and a heated terrace.

Les Marissons 69 rue Marissons ℡ 03.22.92.96.66. By the canal at the Pont de la Dodane, this is Amiens' best gourmet restaurant. Lunch *menu* €18.50, evening *menu* €28; closed Wed & Sat lunch & all day Sun.

Le Porc St-Leu 45/47 rue Bélu ℡ 03.22.80.00.73. More traditional than its trendy neighbours, serving *cochon de lait* (suckling pig) and *menus* from €29.

The Salmon House 14/16 rue Cormont ℡ 03.22.91.27.83. Right by the south door of the cathedral, this restaurant offers salmon in every conceivable form, plus a few meat dishes. *Menus* from €13; closed Sun.

T'chiot Zinc 18 rue de Noyon. Handsome, diminutive place serving traditional country fare, with *menus* at €16 & €22.

Beauvais

As you head south from Amiens towards Paris, the countryside becomes broad and flat; **BEAUVAIS**, 60km from Amiens, seems to fit into this landscape. Rebuilt in tasteful but dull fashion after World War II, it's not a town that repays aimless wandering, but it is redeemed by its audacious, eccentric Gothic cathedral, the **Cathédrale St-Pierre** (daily: June–Sept 9am–6.15pm; May & Oct 9am–12.15pm & 2–6.15pm; Nov–April 9am–12.15pm & 2–5.30pm), which rises above the town. It's a building that, perhaps more than any other in northern France, demonstrates the religious materialism of the Middle Ages – its main intention was to be taller and larger than its rivals. The choir, completed in 1272, was once 5m higher than that of Amiens, though only briefly, as it collapsed in 1284. Its replacement, only completed three centuries later, was raised by the sale of indulgences. This, too, fell within a few years and, the authorities having overreached themselves financially, the church remained as it is today: unfinished, mutilated and really rather odd. At over 155m high, the interior vaults are undeniably impressive, giving the impression that the cathedral is of a larger scale than at Amiens; at the same time, the network of props and brackets that reinforce the structure internally attests to its fragility. The building's real beauty lies in its glass, its sculpted doorways and the remnants of the so-called Basse-Oeuvre, a ninth-century Carolingian church incorporated into (and dwarfed by) the Gothic structure. It also contains a couple of remarkable **clocks**: a 12m-high astronomical clock built in 1865, on which figures mimic scenes from the Last Judgement on the hour; and a medieval clock that's been working for seven hundred years. Ongoing restoration work means much of the exterior is likely to be shrouded in scaffolding for some time to come.

Alongside the cathedral, the **Galerie Nationale de la Tapisserie** (April–Sept Tues–Sun 10.30am–5.30pm; Oct–March Tues–Sun 10am–12.30pm & 2–5pm; free), a museum of tapestry, manufacture of which Beauvais was once renowned, houses a collection ranging from the fifteenth century to the present day. There's also a **Musée Départemental de l'Oise** (daily except Tues: July–Sept 10am–6pm; Oct–June 10am–noon & 2–6pm; free), devoted to painting, local history and archeology, in the sharp, black-towered building west of the cathedral.

Practicalities

Beauvais is just over an hour by train from Paris, and the **gare SNCF** is a short walk from the centre of town – take avenue de la République, then turn right up rue de Malherbe. The Paris-Beauvais **airport** – served by Ryanair from the UK and Ireland – is just outside the town (shuttle bus €4; 8 daily; 17min to cathedral). The **tourist office** (Mon–Sat 9.30am–12.30pm & 1.30–6pm; April–Oct also Sun 10am–5pm; ☏03.44.15.30.30, ⓦwww.beauvaistourisme.fr) is just across from the Galerie Nationale de Tapisserie, at 1 rue Beauregard.

If you want to **stay** the night, plump for the modest *Hôtel du Palais*, within sight of the cathedral at 9 rue St-Nicolas (☏03.44.45.12.58, ⓦwww.hoteldupalais beauvais.com; ❷), or try the *Cygne*, 24 rue Carnot (☏03.44.48.68.40, ⓦwww .hotelducygne-beauvais.com; ❷). There's a **campsite** (☏03.44.02.00.22; July & Aug only) just out of town on the Paris road. Beauvais' best **food** is served just south of the town centre at *La Maison Haute*, 128 rue de Paris (☏03.44.02.61.60), which has *menus* from €32 and offers cookery classes. Less expensive is the charming *L'Auberge de la Meule*, 8 rue du 27 juin (closed Sun, Mon & Thurs eve), situated in one of Beauvais' few surviving streets of half-timbered houses and specializing in salads and fondues (from €12.50).

Laon

Looking out over the plains of Champagne and Picardy from the spine of a high narrow ridge, still protected by its gated medieval walls, **LAON** (pronounced "Lon") is one of the highlights of the region. Dominating the town are the five great towers of one of the earliest and finest Gothic cathedrals in the country. Of all the cathedral towns in the Aisne, Laon is the one to head for.

Arrival, information and accommodation

Arriving by train or road, you'll find yourself in the dreary lower town, or **ville basse**. To get to the upper town – **ville haute** – without your own transport, you can make the stiff climb up the steps at the end of avenue Carnot, or take the **Poma 2000** (Mon–Sat 7am–8pm every 5min; same-day return ticket €1.10), a cable railway; you board next to the train station and alight by the town hall (Terminus "Hôtel de Ville") on place Général-Leclerc; from here, a left turn down rue Sérurier brings you nose to nose with the cathedral. The **tourist office** (April–Sept daily 9.30am–1pm & 2–6.30pm; Oct–March Mon–Sat 9.30am–12.30pm & 2–5.30pm, Sun 2–5.30pm; ☏03.23.20.28.62, ⓦwww.tourisme-paysdelaon.com) is right by the western end of the cathedral, housed in the Gothic Hôtel-Dieu, built in 1209; ask for information about local *gîtes* and guesthouses. If you need **accommodation** in the *ville basse*, try *Hôtel Welcome* (☏03.23.23.06.11, ⓔhotel-welcome.laon@orange.fr; ❶), at 12 av Carnot, a few minutes' walk from the *gare SNCF*. In the *ville haute*, try the charming, *Les Chevaliers*, at 3–5 rue Sérurier, near the Poma stop (☏03.23.27.17.50, ⓔhotel chevaliers@aol.com; ❷), or the three-star *Hôtel de la Bannière de France*, 11 rue Franklin-Roosevelt (☏03.23.23.21.44, ⓦwww.hoteldelabannieredefrance.com; ❹; restaurant from €22). *La Chênaie* (☏03.23.20.25.56; May–Sept), Laon's **campsite**, is on allée de la Chênaie, on the northwest side of town.

The Town

Laon really only has one attraction, its magnificent **Cathédrale Notre-Dame** (daily 9am–7pm; guided tours at 2.30pm or 4pm; different tours available – enquire at tourist office). Built in the second half of the twelfth century, the cathedral was a trendsetter in its day. Elements of its design – the gabled porches, the imposing towers and the gallery of arcades above the west front – were repeated at Chartres, Reims and Notre-Dame in Paris. When wrapped in thick mist, the towers seem otherworldly. The creatures craning from the uppermost ledges, looking like reckless mountain goats borrowed from a medieval bestiary, are reputed to have been carved in memory of the valiant horned steers who lugged the cathedral's masonry up from the plains below. Inside, the effects are no less dramatic – the high white nave is lit by the dense ruby, sapphire and emerald tones of the stained glass, which at close range reveals the appealing scratchy, smoky quality of medieval glass.

Crowded in the cathedral's lee is a quiet, rather sad jumble of grey stone streets; for all its beauty, Laon is no chic weekenders' haunt and even the lunchtime bustle along rue Châtelaine can't disguise the number of vacant commercial premises. South of the cathedral on rue Ermant is the crumbly little twelfth-century octagonal **Chapelle des Templiers** – the Knights Templar – set in a secluded garden. Next door is the **Musée de l'Art et de l'Archéologie**, 32 rue Georges-Ermant (June–Sept Tues–Sun 11am–6pm; Oct–May Tues–Sun 2–6pm; €3.60), which contains a rather stuffy collection of classical antiquities, albeit with some fine Grecian ceramics among them, and a jumble of furniture and paintings including an acclaimed seventeenth-century work, *Le Concert*, by local lad Mathieu Le Nain. The rest of the *ville haute*, which rambles along the ridge to the west of the cathedral, is enjoyable to wander around, with sweeping views north from the **ramparts**.

Eating, drinking and entertainment

Eating and drinking in Laon is inexpensive and unpretentious. *Crêperie L'Agora*, on place du Marché opposite the cathedral, is a cheap Breton place (open till 11pm; closed Mon eve & Wed; *menu* €8.90); at *Le Chant des Voyelles*, midway along rue Châtelaine, you can tuck into omelettes for less than €7 or more substantial *plats du jour* for around €9. Even fancy **restaurants** in Laon tend to be good value: Michelin-listed *La Petite Auberge,* at 45 bd Pierre-Brossolette in the *ville basse* near the station, falls into this category, serving a five-course *menu gourmand* using the freshest ingredients for a remarkable €37 (☎03.23.23.02.38, booking recommended; closed Sat lunch, Sun and Mon eve). They also own the adjacent bistro, which offers simpler fare.

There's usually something going on at the **Maison des Arts de Laon** (MAL), based in a theatre on place Aubry to the north of the cathedral, including a concentration of events during Les Médiévales de Laon in May and big-name classical concerts during the Festival de Laon in October, either in the cathedral or MAL venues (details from the tourist office).

Soissons

Half an hour by train, or 30km down the N2, **SOISSONS** can lay claim to a long and highly strategic history. Before the Romans arrived it was already a town, and in 486 AD the last Roman ruler, Syagrius, suffered a decisive defeat here at the hands of Clovis the Frank, making Soissons one of the first real centres of the Frankish kingdom. Napoleon, too, considered it a crucial military base, a judgement borne out in the twentieth century by extensive war damage.

The town boasts the fine, if shell-pocked and battered, **Cathédrale St Gervais-St Protais** (daily 9.30am–noon & 2–4.30pm) at the west end of the oversized main square, place Fernand Marquigny. It's thirteenth century for the most part, with majestic glass and vaulting. More impressive still is the ruined **Abbaye de St-Jean-des-Vignes**, to the south of place Marquigny down rue St-Martin and then right down avenue Thiers. The gaping west front of the tremendous Gothic abbey rises sheer and grand, impervious to the empty space behind it – you get a superb view of it from the peaceful abbey precincts, but the ruin itself is in crumbly condition and fenced off. The rest of the complex, save for remnants of a **cloister** and **refectory** (free to visit), was dismantled in 1804.

Practicalities

Soissons is relatively compact, but to get to the main square from the **gare SNCF** (good services to Laon and Paris) it's a twenty-minute walk along avenue du Général-de-Gaulle, which becomes rue St-Martin. The **gare routière** is closer to the centre by the river on avenue de l'Aisne; buses leave for Compiègne early in the morning, at lunchtime and at the end of the afternoon during school term times, but otherwise less frequently. The **tourist office** is on place Fernand Marquigny near the cathedral (May–Sept Mon–Sat 10am–6pm, Sun 11am–4pm; Oct–April Mon–Sat 9am–5pm, Sun 10am–1pm; ℡03.23.53.17.37, Ⓦwww .tourisme-soissons.fr).

The town is more of a place to stop en route than to **stay**, and the hotels are mostly dull and overpriced. But if you're keen to explore the nearby forest or are simply stuck, try the two-star hotel *Terminus* above a bar by the station at 56 av du Général-de-Gaulle (℡03.23.53.33.59; ❷), or the **campsite** (℡03.23.74.52.69), north of the centre on avenue du Mail. An excellent place for *galettes* is *La Galetière* (from €5; closed Sun & Mon) at 1 rue du Beffroi by the cathedral. There's also a good Tunisian **restaurant**, the *Sidi Bou*, at 4 rue de la Bannière down towards the river, and a pretty **salon de thé**, *L'Arthé*, on the same street.

Coucy-le-Château-Auffrique

About 30km west of Laon and 15km north of Soissons, in hilly countryside on the far side of the forest of St-Gobain, lie the straggling ruins of one of the greatest castles of the Middle Ages, **Coucy-le-Château** (daily: May to early Sept 10am–1pm & 2–6.30pm; early Sept to April 10am–1pm & 2–5.30pm; €5). The castle's walls still stand, encircling the attractive village of **COUCY-LE-CHÂTEAU-AUFFRIQUE**. In the past this was a seat of great power and the influence of its lords, the Sires de Coucy, rivalled and often even exceeded that of the king – "King I am not, neither Prince, Duke nor Count. I am the Sire of Coucy" was Enguerrand III's proud boast. The retreating Germans capped the destruction of World War I battles by blowing up the castle's keep as they left in 1917, but enough remains, crowning a wooded spur, to be extremely evocative.

Enter the village through one of three original gates, squeezed between powerful, round flanking towers – there's a footpath around the outside which is open even when the castle is not. A small museum, the **Tour de Coucy Musée Panorama** (no fixed hours, ask at tourist office; free), at the **Porte de Soissons** on the south side of the walled part of town, has a display of photographs showing how the castle looked pre-1917, which can be compared with today's postwar reconstruction from the vantage point of the roof.

Practicalities

It's hard to get to Coucy-le-Château without a car, though there are around five buses a day from Soissons. The **tourist office** is in the central square (Mon–Fri 9am–6pm, Sat & Sun 2–6pm; ℡03.23.52.44.55), just north of the Porte de Soissons. There are lots of medieval spectacles offered in this magical town, so it's worth checking events (such as Coucy à la Merveille; ⓦ www.coucyalamerveille .com) in advance of your visit so you can book tickets.

Staying the night here, especially if you have children, is something special: try the *Hôtel Belle Vue* within the walls, although the bedrooms have seen better days (ⓣ 03.23.52.69.70, ⓦ www.hotel-bellevue-coucy.com; closed Fri & Sat in Dec; ❷). Its restaurant specializes in Picardy cuisine (*menus* from €21), and serves special "medieval" meals (€18) on certain summer nights when medieval re-enactments are held across town. There is also a *chambre d'hôte* in a pretty old house just down the road from the hotel, at 3 rue Traversière (ⓣ 03.23.52.76.64; ❷).

Compiègne

Thirty-eight kilometres west of Soissons lies **COMPIÈGNE**, whose reputation as a tourist centre rests on the presence of a vast royal palace, built at the edge of the Forêt de Compiègne in order that generations of French kings could play at "being peasants", in Louis XIV's words. It's an attractive town, a good base for seeing the sites associated with the two world wars and for walks in the surrounding forest.

Arrival, information and accommodation

The **gares routière** and **SNCF** are adjacent to each other, just a few minutes' walk from the centre of town: cross the wide River Oise and go up rue Solférino to place de l'Hôtel-de-Ville. The **tourist office** (April–Sept Mon–Sat 9.15am–12.15pm & 1.45–6.15pm; Oct–March Mon 1.45–5.15pm, Tues–Sat 9.15am–12.15pm & 1.45–5.15pm; open Sun Easter–Oct 10am–12.15pm & 2.15–5pm; ⓣ 03.44.40.01.00, ⓦ www.compiegne-tourisme.fr) takes up part of the ornate Hôtel de Ville. It offers a free hotel booking service, and can provide a town map detailing an exhaustive visitors' route, including the forest paths (see p.210).

As for **accommodation**, the friendly, family-run *Hôtel du Puy du Roy* has tidy rooms and a pretty garden, though it's about a ten-minute walk west of the centre at 131 rue de Paris (ⓣ 03.44.23.36.44; ❶). Similarly priced and more central, the *Hôtel de Flandre*, at 16 quai de la République (ⓣ 03.44.83.24.40, ⓦ www.hoteldeflandre .com; ❶), has some good-value, simple doubles with hall showers alongside its more expensive, plusher offerings. It's near the train station and overlooks the river.

The Town

Compiègne itself is a handsome and lively place of pale stone houses, white shutters and dark slate roofs, though the entire town plays foil to its star attraction, the opulent **Château de Compiègne**, with extensive gardens that make excellent picnicking territory. The eighteenth-century château, two blocks east of the Hôtel de Ville along rue des Minimes, inspires a certain fascination despite its pompous excess. The interior is particularly impressive (daily except Tues 10am–6pm, last admission 5.15pm; €5.50–€7.50, more during temporary exhibitions). Napoleon commissioned a renovation of the former royal palace in 1807, and the work was completed in time for the emperor to welcome his second wife, Marie-Louise of Austria – a relative of Marie-Antoinette – here in 1810. The ostentatious post-revolutionary apartments stand in marked contrast to the more sober Neoclassicism of the few surviving late royal interiors, a monument to the unseemly haste with which Napoleon I moved in, scarcely a dozen years after the Revolution. The self-guided tour includes the temporary exhibitions of the Musée du Second Empire, but if you also want to see the **Musée de la Voiture** (same ticket) you have to join a one-hour guided tour. It contains a wonderful array of antique bicycles, tricycles and aristocratic carriages, as well as the world's first steam coach. The **Théâtre Impérial**, first planned by Napoléon III, was finally completed in 1991 at a cost of some thirty million francs. Originally designed with just two seats for Napoleon and his wife, it now seats nine hundred and is used for concerts.

You can visit the palace gardens separately (daily: March to mid-April & mid-Sept to Oct 8am–6pm; mid-April to mid-Sept 8am–7pm; Nov–Feb 8am–5pm; free). Much of the original French-style garden was replanted on Napoleon's orders after 1811. The result is monumental; the great avenue that extends 4.5km into the Forêt de Compiègne (see below) was inspired by the Austrian imperial summer residence at Schönbrunn on the outskirts of Vienna.

The centre of town is more handsome than picturesque, though several half-timbered buildings remain on rue Napoléon and rue des Lombards, south of the main place de l'Hôtel-de-Ville. The **Hôtel de Ville** itself – Louis XII Gothic – features ebullient nineteenth-century statuary including the image of Joan of Arc, who was captured in this town before being handed to the English. By the side of the town hall is the **Musée de la Figurine Historique** (Tues–Sat 9am–noon & 2–6pm, Sun 2–6pm; closes 5pm in winter; €3), which reputedly holds the world's largest collection of toy soldiers in mock-up battles; the huge diorama of the Battle of Waterloo is the most impressive.

Southwest of the town centre at 2bis av des Martyrs de la Liberté, the sombre **Mémorial de l'Internement et de la Déportation** (daily except Tues 10am–6pm; €3) occupies the former barracks of Royallieu, transformed into a prisoner of war camp by the German army in 1940 and later used as a transit camp for political prisoners, Jews and others. It was from here in March 1942 that the first deportation from France to Auschwitz took place.

Eating and drinking

Compiègne lacks a wide variety of good places to **eat**. Notable establishments include the homey, family-run *Le Cordelier*, 1 rue des Cordeliers (T 03.44.40.23.38; open Mon–Sat lunch, Thurs–Sat dinner; from €12), and *Le Bistrot de Flandre* on the ground floor of the hotel of the same name, which offers a *menu* of local specialities for €20. One of Compiègne's best restaurants is the *Bistrot des Arts* at 35 cours Guynemer, serving traditional bistro food with a twist, accompanied by excellent wines, for around €25 a head (T 03.44.20.10.10). The bustling *Le Saint Clair*, 6 rue des Lombards (T 03.44.40.58.18; from €12), guarantees a good meal, a big selection of Belgian beers and a warm welcome for students and gay travellers. There is an **internet** café, *L'Évasion*, at 7 rue Jean Legendre.

The Forêt de Compiègne and the Clairière de l'Armistice

Very ancient, and cut through by a succession of hills, streams and valleys, the **Forêt de Compiègne**, with the GR12 running through it, is ideal for walkers and cyclists. East of Compiègne, some 6km into the forest and not far from the banks of the Aisne, is the green, sandy clearing known as the **Clairière de l'Armistice**. Here, in what was a rail siding for rail-mounted artillery, World War I was brought to an end on November 11, 1918. A plaque commemorates the deed: "Here the criminal pride of the German empire was brought low, vanquished by the free peoples whom it had sought to enslave." To avenge this humiliation, Hitler had the French sign their capitulation on June 22, 1940, on the same spot, in the same rail carriage. The original car was taken to Berlin and destroyed by fire in the last days of the war. Its replacement, housed in a small **museum** (daily except Tues: April to mid-Oct 9am–12.30pm & 2–6pm; mid-Oct to March 9am–noon & 2–5.30pm; last admission 30min before closing; €4), is similar, and the objects inside are the originals.

Thirteen kilometres southeast of Compiègne at **PIERREFONDS** there's a classic medieval **château** (May–Aug daily 9.30am–6pm; Sept–April Tues–Sun 10am–1pm & 2–5.30pm; €7). It was built in the twelfth century, dismantled in the seventeenth and restored by order of Napoléon III in the nineteenth to create a fantastic fairytale affair of turrets, towers and moat. Other sights include **Vieux-Moulin** and **St-Jean-aux-Bois,** picturesque villages right in the heart of the forest, the latter retaining part of its twelfth-century fortifications.

Noyon

Further up the Oise and a possible day-trip from Compiègne, **NOYON** is another of Picardy's cathedral towns. Its quiet provinciality belies a long, illustrious history, first as a Roman prefecture, then as seat of a bishopric from 531. Here, in 768, Charlemagne was crowned king of Neustria, largest of the Frankish kingdoms; in 987, Hugues Capet was crowned king of France; and Jean Calvin was born here in 1509.

Rowing along the Oise on his *Inland Journey* of 1876, Robert Louis Stevenson stopped briefly at Noyon, which he described as "a stack of brown roofs at the best, where I believe people live very respectably in a quiet way". It's still like that, though the **cathedral**, to which Stevenson warmed, is impressive enough. Spacious and a little stark, it successfully blends Romanesque and Gothic, and is flanked by the ruins of thirteenth-century cloisters and a strange, exquisitely shaped Renaissance library. On the south side of the cathedral, the old episcopal palace houses the **Musée du Noyonnais** (Tues–Sun 10am–noon & 2–6pm; Nov–March closes 5pm; €3), a small, well-presented collection of local archeological finds and cathedral treasure. Close by, signs direct you to the **Musée Calvin** (same hours and ticket), ostensibly on the site of the reformer's birthplace. The respectable citizens of Noyon were never among their local boy's adherents and tore down the original building long before its tourist potential was appreciated.

The **tourist office** is in the Hôtel de Ville on place Bertrand Labarre (Mon 2–6.15pm, Tues–Sat 9am–noon & 2–6.15pm, Sun 10am–noon; closed Sun Nov–March; ☎03.44.44.21.88, ⓦwww.noyon-tourisme.com). The best **accommodation** option is *Le St-Éloi*, at 81 bd Carnot (☎03.44.44.01.49, ⓦwww.hotelsainteloi.fr; ❹; restaurant *menus* from €34), just off the round-about between the train station and cathedral.

Champagne and the Ardennes

The bubbly stuff is the reason most people visit **Champagne**. The cultivation of vines here was already well established in Roman times, when Reims was the capital of the Roman province of Belgae (Belgium), and by the seventeenth century still wines from the region had gained a considerable reputation. Contrary to popular myth, however, it was not Dom Pérignon, cellar master of the Abbaye de Hautvillers near Épernay, who "invented" champagne. He was probably responsible for the innovation of mixing grapes from different vineyards, but the wine's well-known tendency to re-ferment within the bottle was not controllable until eighteenth-century glass-moulding techniques produced vessels strong enough to contain the natural effervescence.

Much of the area is taken up with cultivating wheat and cabbages, but the region's capital, the cathedral city of **Reims**, is worth a visit, and has a reasonably full cultural calendar. Some of the most extravagant champagne houses are here, the *caves* beneath them notable for their vaulted ceilings and kilometres of bottles.

Épernay, a smaller town set in the scenic heart of the region, is dominated by an avenue of champagne *maisons*, where visitors can float from one to another like so many bubbles. The region's other major attraction is **Troyes**, some way to the southwest, a town of cobbled streets, half-timbered houses and cut-price shopping. Further south still, the small, far-flung towns of **Chaumont** and **Langres** also merit a stop, if only for an hour or two. Meanwhile the breathtakingly wild landscape of the **Ardennes**, in the far north on the Belgian border, offers nature-lovers a tempting array of hiking, cycling and boating opportunities.

Reims

Laid flat by the shells of World War I, **REIMS** (pronounced like a nasal "Rance", and traditionally spelled Rheims in English) was rebuilt afterwards with tact and touches of Art Nouveau and Art Deco, but consequently lacks any great sense of antiquity. It makes up for this with a walkable centre, beneath which lies its real treasure – kilometre upon kilometre of bottles of fermenting champagne. Its status as champagne capital of the world aside, Reims possesses one of the most impressive Gothic cathedrals in France – formerly the coronation church of dynasties of French monarchs going back to Clovis, first king of the Franks, and later painted obsessively by Monet. These attractions, plus a handful of interesting museums and a big city buzz unusual in this part of France, make it worth a day or two's stopover.

Arrival, information and accommodation

The cathedral is less than ten minutes' walk from the **gare SNCF** and **gare routière**. The **tourist office**, 2 rue Guillaume-de-Machault (May–Sept Mon–Sat 9am–7pm, Sun 10am–6pm; Oct–March Mon–Sat 9am–6pm, Sun 10am–1pm; April Mon–Sat 9am–6pm, Sun 10am–6pm; ℡08.92.70.13.51, Ⓦwww.reims -tourisme.com), is next to the cathedral in a picturesque ruin; for €5 you can hire an English audioguide to the city from them, though note that if you want to do the circuit more than once you'll have to pay again. They also sell the Reims City Card (€15), which includes entry to various museums, an audioguide to the cathedral and a tour of a champagne cellar. **Internet access** is available at *Clique et Croque*, 19 rue Chanzy (Mon–Sat 10am–9pm, Sun 2–8pm).

Rooms are fairly easy to come by in Reims, but since the city is an easy day-trip from Paris it may not be necessary to stay at all.

Hotels and hostel

De la Cathédrale 20 rue Libergier ℡03.26.47.28.46, Ⓦwww.hotel-cathedrale-reims .fr. Old-fashioned but comfortable two-star near the cathedral. ❸

Centre International de Séjour 1 chaussée Bocquaine, Parc Léo Lagrange ℡03.26.40.52.60, Ⓦwww.cis-reims.com. HI hostel with 3- to 5-bed dorms plus doubles & singles (dorm beds €19.80, doubles €40, breakfast included). Bus H from theatre to "Charles de Gaulle", or a 15min walk from the station on the other side of the A4 autoroute.

Château Les Crayères 64 bd Henry-Vasnier ℡03.26.24.90.00, Ⓦwww.lescrayeres.com. This refined hotel in a restored eighteenth-century château has a beautiful garden, luxurious rooms and impeccable service, as well as one of the region's most sophisticated restaurants (see p.216). ❾

Crystal 86 place Drouet-d'Erlon ℡03.26.88.44.44, Ⓦwww.hotel-crystal.fr. Small rooms, charming service and a pretty courtyard garden which blocks out much of the noise from the local nightlife. ❶

Gambetta 9–13 rue Gambetta ℡03.26.47.22.00, Ⓦwww.hotel-gambetta-reims.fr. Neat, well-designed, modern rooms, all with shower and toilet, above a pleasant café across the street from the *conservatoire* of music and dance. ❸

Grand Hôtel Continental 93 place Drouet-d'Erlon ℡03.26.40.39.35, Ⓦwww.grandhotelcontinental .com. Very central hotel, with rather grand public areas and quiet rooms, all with bathroom and TV. ❹

Univers 41 bd Foch ℡03.26.88.68.08, Ⓦwww .hotel-univers-reims.com. Handsomely located on the tree-lined Hautes Promenades, this smart Art Deco-style establishment, with double-glazing, is the best mid-range hotel in the city. ❺

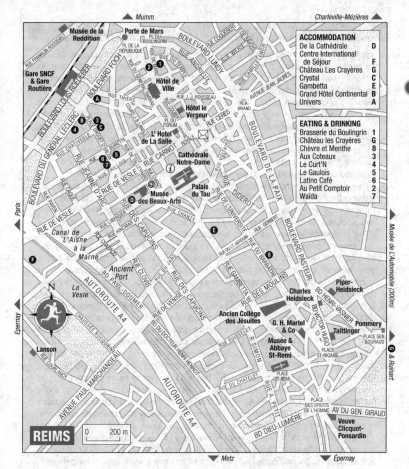

ACCOMMODATION

De la Cathédrale	D
Centre International de Séjour	F
Château Les Crayères	G
Crystal	C
Gambetta	E
Grand Hôtel Continental	B
Univers	A

EATING & DRINKING

Brasserie du Boulingrin	1
Château les Crayères	G
Chèvre et Menthe	8
Aux Coteaux	3
Le Curt'N	4
Le Gaulois	5
Latino Café	6
Au Petit Comptoir	2
Waïda	7

REIMS   0   200 m

The City

The old centre of Reims stretches from the **cathedral** north to place de la République's triumphal Roman arch, the **Porte de Mars**, punctuated by the grand squares of place Royale, place du Forum and place de l'Hôtel-de-Ville. To the west, place Drouet d'Erlon is the focus of the city's nightlife and an almost-complete example of the city's 1920s reconstruction. To the south, about fifteen minutes' walk from the cathedral, is the other historical focus of the town, the **Abbaye St-Remi**, with the Jesuits' College nearby. To the east of here are most of the **champagne maisons** and, further east still, a museum of cars.

The cathedral and around

The glorious Gothic thirteenth-century **Cathédrale Notre-Dame** (daily 7.30am– 7.30pm) features prominently in French history: in 1429 Joan of Arc managed to get the Dauphin crowned here as Charles VII – an act of immense significance when France was more or less wiped off the map by the English and their allies. In all, 26 French kings were crowned here.

The chief draw inside the cathedral is the kaleidoscopic patterns in the stained glass, with fantastic Marc **Chagall** designs in the east chapel and champagne

Champagne: the facts

Nowhere else in the world are you allowed to make a drink called **champagne**, though many people do, calling it "champan", "shampanskoye" and all manner of variants. You can blend grape juice harvested from chalk–soil vineyards, double-ferment it, store the result for years at the requisite constant temperature and high humidity in sweating underground *caves*, turn and tilt the bottles little by little to clear the sediment, add some vintage liqueur, and finally produce a bubbling golden (or pink) liquid; but according to international law you may refer to it only as "*méthode champenoise*". The jealously guarded monopoly helps keep the region's sparkling wines in the luxury class, although the locals will tell you the difference comes from the squid fossils in the chalk, the lay of the land and its climate, the evolution of the grapes, the regulated pruning methods and the legally enforced quantity of juice pressed.

Three authorized **grape varieties** are used: chardonnay, the only white grape, growing best on the Côte des Blancs and contributing a light and elegant element; pinot noir, grown mainly on the Montagne de Reims slopes, giving body and long life; and pinot meunier, cultivated primarily in the Marne valley, adding flowery aromas.

The **vineyards** are owned either by *maisons*, who produce the *grande marque* champagne, or by small cultivators called *vignerons*, who sell the grapes to the *maisons*. The *vignerons* also make their own champagne and will happily offer you a glass and sell you a bottle at two-thirds the price of a *grande marque* (ask at any tourist office in the Champagne region for a list of addresses). The difference between the two comes down to capital. The *maisons* can afford to blend grapes from up to sixty different vineyards and to tie up their investment while their champagne matures for several years longer than the legal minimum (one year for non-vintage, three years vintage). So the wine they produce is undoubtedly superior – and not a lot cheaper here than in a good discount off-licence/liquor store in Britain or the US.

If you could visit the head offices of Cartier or Dior, the atmosphere would probably be similar to that of the champagne *maisons*, whose palaces are divided between Épernay and Reims. Visits to the handful that organize regular **tours** are not free, and most require appointments, but don't be put off – their staff all speak English and a generous *dégustation* is generally thrown in. Their audiovisuals and (cold) cellar tours are on the whole very informative, and do more than merely plug brand names. Local tourist offices can provide full lists of addresses and times of visits.

If you want to work on the **harvest**, contact any of the smaller *maisons* direct, the Agence Nationale pour l'Emploi, 30 rue de Sézanne, Épernay (☎03.26.51.01.33), or one of the champagne houses' offices in Rheims – see ⓦwww.anpe.fr for details.

---

processes glorified in the south transept. But the greatest appeal is outside: an inexplicable joke runs around the restored but still badly mutilated statuary on the west front – the giggling angels who seem to be responsible for disseminating the prank are a delight. Not all the figures on the cathedral's west front are originals – some have been removed to spare them further erosion and are now at the former bishop's palace, the Palais du Tau. The **towers** of the cathedral are open to the public (by guided tour only; mid-March to April & Sept–Oct Sat at 10 & 11am, Sat & Sun at 2, 3 & 4pm; May–Sept Tues–Sun 10am, 11.30am, 2pm, 5pm; €7, or combined ticket with the Palais du Tau €9.50); as well as a walk round the transepts and chevet, you get to see inside the framework of the cathedral roof; tickets available from the Palais du Tau.

At the **Palais du Tau** (daily: early May to early Sept 9.30am–6.30pm; early Sept to early May 9.30am–12.30pm & 2–5.30pm; €4.50, or combined ticket with the towers €9.50; ⓦpalais-tau.monuments-nationaux.fr), next door to the cathedral, you can appreciate the expressiveness of the statuary from close up – a view that would never have been possible in their intended monumental positions on the cathedral. Apart from the grinning angels, there is also a superb Eve, shiftily clutching the monster of sin, while embroidered tapestries of the Song of Songs line the walls. The palace also preserves the paraphernalia of Charles X's coronation in 1824, right down to the Dauphin's hat box.

West of the cathedral on rue Chanzy, the **Musée des Beaux-Arts** (daily except Tues & public hols 10am–noon & 2–6pm; €3) is the city's principal art museum, which, though ill-suited to its ancient building, effectively covers French art from the Renaissance to the present. Few of the works are among the artists' best but the collection includes one of David's replicas of his famous Marat death scene, a set of 27 Corots, two great Gauguin still lifes, and some beautifully observed sixteenth-century portraits by the German artists Lucas Cranach the Elder and Younger.

Just north of the cathedral, the **Musée-Hôtel Le Vergeur**, 36 place du Forum (Tues–Sun 2–6pm; €4), is a stuffed treasure house of all kinds of beautiful objects, including two sets of Dürer engravings – an *Apocalypse* and *Passion of Christ* – but you have to go through a long guided tour to see them. Opposite the museum there's access to sections of the partly submerged arcades of the **crypto-portique Gallo–Romain** (June to mid-Oct Tues–Sun 2–6pm; free), which date back to 200 AD. Reims's other Roman monument, the quadruple-arched **Porte de Mars**, on place de la République, belongs to the same era.

West of the Porte, behind the station in rue Franklin-Roosevelt, is the **Musée de la Reddition** ("Museum of the Surrender"; daily except Tues & public hols 10am–noon & 2–6pm; €3), based around an old schoolroom that served as Eisenhower's HQ from February 1945. In the early hours of May 7, 1945, General Jodl agreed to the unconditional surrender of the German army here, thus ending World War II in Europe. The room has been left exactly as it was (minus the ashtrays and carpet), with the Allies' battle maps on the walls.

The Abbaye St-Remi, Jesuits' College and surrounding museums

Most of the early French kings were buried in Reims's oldest building, the eleventh-century **Basilique St-Remi**, fifteen minutes' walk from the cathedral on rue Simon (daily 8am–dusk, closed during services; music & light show July–Sept Sat 9.30pm; free), part of a former Benedictine abbey named after the 22-year-old bishop who baptized Clovis and three thousand of his warriors. An immensely spacious building, it preserves its Romanesque transept walls and ambulatory chapels, some of them with modern stained glass that works beautifully. Albert Nicart, the bellringer of St-Remi, was the inspiration for Victor Hugo's fictional Quasimodo in *The Hunchback of Notre Dame;* Hugo met Nicart and the gypsy girl Esméralda in 1825 while visiting Reims to attend Charles X's coronation. The spectacular abbey buildings alongside the church house the **Musée St-Remi** (Mon–Fri 2–6.30pm, Sat & Sun 2–7pm; €3), the city's rather dry archaeological and historical museum that includes the reconstructed façade of a thirteenth-century house destroyed by World War I German shelling. The museum's twelfth- to thirteenth-century chapterhouse has been listed as a UNESCO World Heritage Site.

The **Ancien Collège des Jésuites** (closed for renovation: temporary exhibitions open daily 2–6pm; €3), a short walk north on rue du Grand-Cerf, was founded in Reims in 1606, and the building completed in 1678. Extensive renovation work, likely to continue until 2012, means it is currently only possible to visit the temporary exhibitions of modern art, just inside the main entrance.

If you have even a passing interest in old cars you should not miss the **Musée de l'Automobile**, 84 av Georges-Clemenceau (daily except Tues: April–Oct 10am–noon & 2–6pm; Nov–March 10am–noon & 2–5pm; also open Tues July & Aug; €7), fifteen minutes' walk southeast of the cathedral. The collection contains many prototypes and rarities; highlights include a string of sleek, powerful Delahaye coupés designed by Philippe Charbonneaux in the 1940s and 1950s, and a stunning Panhard et Levassor Dynamic 130 Coupé from 1936 – pure Art Deco on wheels.

Eating and drinking

Place Drouet-d'Erlon, a wide pedestrianized boulevard lined with **bars** and **restaurants**, is where you'll find most of the city's nightlife, which is geared more to pavement café lounging than high-octane partying. There's also a big Saturday **market** in place du Boulingrin (6am–1pm).

Brasserie du Boulingrin 48 rue de Mars ☎03.26.40.96.22. Charming, good-value brasserie, dating back to 1925, famed for its seafood platters and *fondant au chocolat*. Weekday *menus* at €18 and €23, including wine. Closed Sun.

Château les Crayères 64 bd Henry-Vasnier ☎03.26.24.90.00. Reputed to be one of France's finest gastronomic restaurants – with prices and style to match. Closed Mon & Tues lunch; à la carte around €200.

Chèvre et Menthe 63 rue du Barbâtre ☎03.26.05.17.03. A homey, inexpensive establishment recommended for vegetarians, with a range of gourmet salads from €5.50. Daily à la carte dishes (some of which contain meat) plus the eponymous goat's cheese and fresh mint quiche. Closed Sun & Mon.

Aux Coteaux 86–88 place Drouet-d'Erlon ☎03.26.47.08.79. Dependable cheapie on Reims's main café strip, with a wide range of pizzas and salads from under €9. Closed Sun & Mon.

Au Petit Comptoir 17 rue de Mars ☎03.26.40.58.58. Close to the Marché du Boulingrin, with traditional and inventive dishes from €15 and a *menu* at €31, served in modern surroundings. Closed Sun & Mon.

Waïda 3–5 place Drouet-d'Erlon. Beautiful *patissier-glacier* and *salon de thé*, with pastries and ice cream made on the premises, plus one of the best original Art Deco interiors in Reims. Closed Mon.

Nightlife and entertainment

For **drinking** into the early hours there are plenty of large terrace cafés on place Drouet-d'Erlon; try *Le Gaulois*, at nos. 2–4, which serves excellent cocktails. One of Drouet-d'Erlon's livelier spots is *Latino Café* at no. 33, open until 3am, with hispanic food and music, plus occasional live entertainment. If you want to **dance**, try *Le Curt'N* at 7 bd Général-Leclerc (daily from 11pm; admission €12 with drink Fri & Sat).

From mid-June to early August, over a hundred classical concerts – many of them free – take place as part of **Les Flâneries Musicales d'Été**; pick up a leaflet at the tourist office.

Épernay

There's no question that **ÉPERNAY**, 26km south of Reims, is a single-industry town. But it's beautifully situated below rolling, vine-covered hills, and the industry in question – champagne production – is a compelling reason for a visit. The town contains some of the most famous champagne *maisons* as well as several smaller houses, and makes a sensible base for exploring the surrounding villages and vineyards.

Arrival, information and accommodation

Épernay's **gare SNCF** and **gare routière** are next to each other, a five-minute walk north of the central place de la République, which is reached via rue Jean-Moët. The **tourist office** is at 7 av de Champagne (mid-April to mid–Oct Mon–Sat 9.30am–12.30pm & 1.30–7pm, Sun 11am–4pm; mid-Oct to mid-April Mon–Sat 9.30am–12.30pm & 1.30–5.30pm; ☎03.26.53.33.00, ⓦwww.ot-epernay.fr) and has information about a huge selection of tours ranging from minibuses to hot-air balloons. If you feel like touring the vineyards by **mountain bike** (**VTT**), either independently or in an organized group, contact Bulleo, in Parc Roger Menu (☎03.26.53.35.60; from €10 per half day).

Champagne-tasting in Reims

Tours of the Reims champagne houses and *caves* generally need to be pre-booked. Those in the southern part of town near the Abbaye St-Remi tend to have the most impressive cellars – some have been carved in cathedral-esque formations from the Gallo–Roman quarries used to build the city, long before champagne was invented.

Non-appointment houses

Taittinger 9 place St-Niçaise ⓣ03.26.85.45.35, ⓦwww.taittinger.com. Starts with a film show before a guided stroll through the ancient cellars, some of which have doodles and carvings added by more recent workers; there are also statues of St Vincent and St Jean, patron saints respectively of *vignerons* and cellar hands. Mid-March to mid-Nov daily 9.30am–1pm & 2–5.30pm (last tour at 4.30); mid-Nov to mid-March Mon–Fri same hours; closed Sat & Sun; tour 1hr; €10.

Mumm 34 rue du Champ-de-Mars ⓣ03.26.49.59.69, ⓦwww.mumm.com. Known for its red-slashed Cordon Rouge label, Mumm's un-French-sounding name is the legacy of its founders, German wine-makers from the Rhine Valley who established the business in 1827. The guided tour includes a short film, and ends with a generous glass of either Cordon Rouge, the sweeter Cordon Vert, or the Extra Dry. March–Oct daily 9–11am & 2–5pm; Nov–Feb by appointment only on weekdays, Sat 9–11am & 2–5pm; €10.

Appointment-only houses

Most houses nowadays prefer that you call or email in advance, but in summer it may be worth showing up on the off-chance. This is not a comprehensive list of all the *maisons* in the city, but includes the most visitor-friendly.

Lanson 66 rue de Courlancy ⓣ03.26.78.50.50, ⓦwww.lanson.fr. Worth the trip across the river because the in-depth tours here actually bring you into the factory, and demonstrate the mechanized process of champagne-making. Most days you'll see the machines degorging the bottles, as well as labelling and filling them in preparation for the second fermentation. By appointment Mon–Fri only; closed Aug; €10.

G.H.Martel & Co 17 rue des Créneaux, near the Basilique St-Remi ⓣ03.26.82.70.67, ⓦwww.champagnemartel.com. At €9, this is a good-value tour, with a *dégustation* of three champagnes as well as a film show and guided visit. Open daily year round (10am–7pm, last tour at 5.45pm).

Pommery 5 place du Général-Gouraud ⓣ03.26.61.62.55, ⓦwww.pommery.fr. The creator of the cute one-eighth size "Pop" bottles has excavated Roman quarries for its cellars – it claims to have been the first *maison* to do so. Daily: April to mid-Nov 9.30am–7pm; mid-Nov to March 10am–6pm; from €12.

Ruinart 4 rue des Crayères ⓣ03.26.77.51.51, ⓦwww.ruinart.com. The fanciest of the champagne houses, in a swanky mansion. Reserved and upmarket, the tours are nonetheless informative. €20.

Veuve Clicquot-Ponsardin 1 place des Droits-de-l'Homme ⓣ03.26.89.53.90, ⓦwww.veuve-cliquot.com. In 1805 the widowed Mme Clicquot not only took over her husband's business – *veuve* means "widow" in French – but also later bequeathed it to her business manager rather than to her children. The *maison* is one of the least pompous, and its *caves* some of the most spectacular, sited in ancient Gallo–Roman quarries. 10am–6pm (last tour at 4.15pm): April–Oct Tues–Sat; Nov–March Tues–Fri; €13.

The best of the cheap **hotels** in Épernay is the friendly, one-star *St-Pierre*, 1 rue Jeanne-d'Arc (ⓣ03.26.54.40.80, ⓦwww.villasaintpierre.fr; ❶), in a quiet street away from the centre. More comfort is to be had at the excellent *Les Berceaux*, at

13 rue des Berceaux (T 03.26.55.28.84, W www.lesberceaux.com; ⑤), which also has one of the best restaurants in town (see opposite), or the elegant *Clos Raymi*, 3 rue Joseph-de-Venoge (T 03.26.51.00.58, W www.closraymi-hotel.com; ⑦), in a beautiful red-brick house once belonging to the Chandon family. For even more luxury out of town, head for the *Royal Champagne*, 5km north on the N2051 to Champillon (T 03.26.52.87.11, W www.royalchampagne.com; ⑨). The local **campsite** is 2km to the north on route de Cumières in the Parc des Sports, on the south bank of the Marne (T 03.26.55.32.14; closed Oct–April).

The Town

Since you're only here for the alcohol, you may as well make a beeline for the appropriately named **avenue de Champagne**, running east from place de la République. Dubbed "the most drinkable street in the world" by Winston Churchill, it's worth strolling for its imposing eighteenth- and nineteenth-century champagne *maisons*; it may, in effect, be no more than an exalted industrial zone – as a short detour down one of the side streets will prove – but it's pretty showy for all that. You can tour some of the *maisons*, and many others welcome visitors to taste and buy. The Épernay tourist office's *guide touristique* has details.

The largest, and probably the most famous *maison*, though neither the most beautiful nor necessarily the most interesting to tour, is **Moët et Chandon**, 18 av de Champagne (9.30–11.30am & 2–4.30pm; mid-Nov to March closed Sat & Sun; from €14.50 including *dégustation* of the Brut Impérial; W www.moet .com), one of the keystones of the LVMH (Louis Vuitton, Moët and Hennessy) empire which owns Mercier, Veuve Clicquot, Dior perfumes and a variety of other concerns. The house is also the creator of the iconic **Dom Pérignon** label. The tour is rather generic, beginning with a mawkish video, followed by a walk through the cellars adorned with mementos of Napoleon (a good friend of the original M. Moët), and concluding with a tasting of their truly excellent champagne.

Further up the street, **Mercier**, at 70 av de Champagne, runs a fairly rewarding tour around its cellars in an electric train (mid-March to mid-Nov 9.30–11.30am & 2–4.30pm; closed Tues & Wed out of season; €8.50, including *dégustation*; W www.champagnemercier.fr). Nowadays Mercier is known as the lower-end champagne of French supermarkets, showing that M. Mercier was successful in his goal: he founded the house, aged 20, in 1858 with a plan to make champagne more accessible to the French people. In 1889 he carted a giant barrel that held 200,000 bottles' worth to the Paris Exhibition – only to be upstaged by the Eiffel Tower. The barrel is on display in the lobby.

Castellane, by the station at 57 rue de Verdun (April–Dec daily 10am–noon & 2–6pm; €8 including *dégustation*; W www.castellane.com), provides Épernay with its chief landmark: a pastel edifice resembling a kind of Neoclassical water tower. Along with the cellars, the visit shows off the working assembly lines that fill the champagne bottles, and the huge vats that hold the grape juice prior to fermentation. After the tour you can wander the little museum and climb the tower for a great view of the surrounding vineyards.

Épernay has a few other *grandes maisons* that can be visited by appointment, but perhaps more worthwhile are the many smaller houses. Since these have fewer employees it's best to call or email well in advance. Try **Leclerc-Briant** at 67 rue Chaude-Ruelle, west of the town centre (Mon–Fri 9am–noon & 1.30–5pm, or by appointment on weekends; T 03.26.54.45.33, W www.leclercbriant.com); for €8 they give a tour of their presshouse, museum and cellars, as well as a tasting of three vintages and a souvenir champagne glass.

Eating and drinking

Restaurants in Épernay are not necessarily cheap. One good-value option is *Les Berceaux*, 13 rue des Berceaux (℡03.26.55.28.84; closed Mon & Tues; *menus* from €26), while *La Table Kobus*, 3 rue Dr-Rousseau, is good for traditional French fare (℡03.26.51.53.53; *menus* from €28). Call in advance to squeeze into *La Cave à Champagne* at 16 rue Gambetta (℡03.26.55.50.70; closed Tues & Wed; from €17). For a major blowout, the *Royal Champagne*, north of town (see opposite), serves *menus* at €65 and €90.

Around Épernay

The villages in the appealing **vineyards** of the Montagne de Reims, Côte des Blancs and Vallée de la Marne surrounding Épernay host a range of curiosities, including the world's largest champagne bottle and cork in **Mardeuil** and a traditional *vigneron*'s house and early twentieth-century school room at **Oeuilly**. Many of the villages have a sleepy, old-stone charm: **Vertus**, 16km south of Épernay, is particularly pretty, and so too is **Hautvillers**, 6km north of town, where you can see the abbey of Dom Pérignon fame (though it is closed to the public).

The best reason for venturing out into the countryside is simply to view the vines and taste less well-known but often delicious champagnes. One such house is Charlier & Fils, set in an attractive *maison* surrounded by flowers at 4 rue des Pervenches, **MONTIGNY-SOUS-CHÂTILLON**, 15km west of Épernay (℡03.26.58.35.18, ⓦwww.champagne-charlier.com).

For somewhere to **stay** that offers real luxury in an atmosphere of faded elegance, base yourself in **Etoges** at *Château d'Etoges*, 4 rue Richebourg (℡03.26.59.30.08, ⓦwww.etoges.com; ❾). This small château offers 28 characterful bedrooms, and a top-notch restaurant.

Troyes

It is easy to find charm in the leaning medieval half-timbered houses and churches of **TROYES**, the ancient capital of the Champagne region. The town also offers top-quality museums and shopping outlets, and is a good place to try the regional speciality, *andouillette* (see box, p.172).

Arrival, information and accommodation

The **gare SNCF** and **gare routière** are side by side off boulevard Carnot. Not all buses use the main station, though, and if you're heading for the outlet stores or the countryside it's best to check first with the **tourist office** (ⓦwww.tourisme-troyes.com). There are two branches: the station branch is at 16 bd Carnot (Mon–Sat 9am–12.30pm & 2–6.30pm; also open Sun Nov–March 10am–1pm; ℡03.25.82.62.70); and the town-centre branch is on rue Mignard facing the Église St-Jean (April–June & mid-Sept to Oct Mon–Sat 10am–1pm & 2–6pm, Sun 10am–noon and 2–6pm; July to mid-Sept daily 10am–7pm; Nov–March closed; ℡03.25.73.36.88). They sell a good-value **museum pass** (€15) that includes entry to all Troyes' museums, two champagne *dégustations*, a chocolate tasting, thirty minutes of internet use and discount vouchers for the factory outlets. If you want to **rent a car** try Hertz at 28 rue Voltaire, near the station (℡03.25.71.35.50).

Accommodation is plentiful, most of it in the Old Town – the tourist office has information about places to stay in the wine villages around Troyes.

Hotels

Hôtel Arlequin 50 rue de Turenne ℡03.25.83.12.70, ⓦwww.hotelarlequin.com. Pleasant, sunny rooms in a characterful antique building, tucked in among the rambling alleyways of the Old Town. ❷

Les Comtes de Champagne 54 rue de la Monnaie ☎03.25.73.11.70, ⓦwww.comtesde champagne.com. Central and charming two-star in a twelfth-century house with slanted floors. Friendly proprietors and covered parking. ❷

La Maison de Rhodes 18 rue Linard-Gonthier ☎03.25.43.11.11, ⓦwww .maisonderhodes.com. A fine Renaissance house with Templar links, near the cathedral, which has been transformed into a four-star boutique hotel with contemporary interior decor and an abundance of medieval wooden beams. The internal courtyard is a tranquil place for a quality evening meal. ❽

Le Relais St-Jean 51 rue Paillot-de-Montabert ☎03.25.73.89.90, ⓦwww.relais-st-jean.com. Posh hotel in a half-timbered building right in the centre, though the modern interior comes as a surprise. ❺

Le Royal 22 bd Carnot ☎03.25.73.19.99, ⓦwww .royal-hotel-troyes.com. Decent, pleasantly restored hotel behind a stern facade near the station; spacious bathrooms and a copious breakfast. ❺

Hostel and campsite
Camping municipal 7 rue Roger-Salengro, Pont Ste-Marie ☎03.25.81.02.64, ⓦwww .troyescamping.net. 5km out on the N60 to Châlons, on the left, with good facilities including washing machines and children's play area. Minimum two-night reservation, closed mid-Oct to March.

HI hostel Chemin Ste-Scholastique, Rosières ☎03.25.82.00.65, ⓦwww.fuaj.org. Decent hostel located in a former fourteenth-century priory, 5.5km out of town on the Dijon road; take bus #8 direction "Rosières", stop "Liberté". Open year-round. Dorm beds €15.20, including breakfast.

The Town
The centre of Troyes between the station and cathedral is scattered with marvellous **churches**, four of which are open to the public. The first you come to is the sumptuous, high-naved **St-Pantaléon** (Mon–Sat 10am–12.30pm & 2–5pm, Sun 2–5pm) on rue de Vaulisant, which is filled with sixteenth-century sculpture, having been used to rescue statuary from the ravages of the Revolution. A short walk to the north is Troyes' oldest church, twelfth-century **Ste-Madeleine**, on the road of the same name (same hours as St-Pantaléon) and remodelled in the sixteenth century, when the delicate stonework rood screen – used to keep the priest separate from the congregation – was added. A short way to the southeast, between rues Émile-Zola and Champeaux, is **St-Jean-au-Marché**, the church where Henry V of England married Catherine of France after being recognized as heir to the French throne in the 1420 Treaty of Troyes. Between it and the cathedral is the elegant Gothic **Basilique St-Urbain**, on place Vernier (same hours as St-Pantaléon), its exterior dramatizing the Day of Judgement.

Across the Canal de la Haute Seine lies the city's most outstanding museum, the **Musée d'Art Moderne** (Tues–Sun 10am–1pm & 2–6pm; €5, or part of museum pass), housed in the old bishops' palace next to the cathedral on place St-Pierre. The museum displays the private collection built up by industrialist Pierre Lévy (1907–2002) and his wife Denise. Lévy developed a strong friendship with the Fauvist André Derain, and it's Derain's work (including the famous paintings of Hyde Park and Big Ben) that forms the collection's core. For the rest, there are works by Degas, Courbet, Gauguin and Max Ernst, but it's in no sense a greatest hits of modern art and therein lies its charm: entire rooms are devoted to a particular theme or to the works of lesser-known artists. Another room is given over to a beautiful collection of African carvings.

The ancient **quartier de la Cité**, across the canal from the centre, is home to many of the city's oldest buildings. They all huddle around the **Cathédrale St-Pierre-et-St-Paul** (July to mid-Sept daily 10.15am–1pm & 2–6.45pm; mid-Sept to June Tues–Sat 8.30am–noon & 1–5pm, Sun 2.15–4.45pm), whose pale Gothic nave is mottled with reflections from the wonderful stained glass. On the other side of the cathedral from the Musée d'Art Moderne, at 1 rue Chrétien-de-Troyes, the once glorious **Abbaye St-Loup** houses the **Musée Saint-Loup** (Tues–Sun 9am–noon & 1–5pm; €4, or part of museum pass), seemingly endless galleries of mostly French

Clothes shopping in Troyes

Troyes made its name in the clothing trade, and today the industry still accounts for more than half of the town's employment. **Factory outlets** are one of the chief attractions here: designer-label clothes can be picked up at two-thirds or less of the normal shop price. The best array is at the giant **Marques Avenue**, avenue de la Maille, St-Julien-les-Villas, a couple of kilometres south of the city on the N71 to Dijon or on bus #2 (Mon–Fri 10am–7pm, Sat 9.30am–7pm; ⓦwww.marquesavenue.com); there's also a special "shed" for household goods at 230 faubourg Croncels, including luxury glass and chinaware. At Pont–Ste-Marie, a short way to the northeast of Troyes between the D677 to Reims and the D960 to Nancy, are **Marques City** (Mon–Fri 10am–7pm, Sat 9.30am–7pm; ⓦwww.marquescity.fr) and **McArthur Glen** (same hours as Marques City; ⓦwww.mcarthurglen.fr). Buses for the outlets depart from the bus stops by Marché les Halles (ask at the tourist offices for details).

paintings, including a couple by Watteau and an impressive collection of medieval sculpture. Down rue de la Cité (entrance on quai des Comtes de Champagne) is the **apothicairerie**, a richly decorated sixteenth-century pharmacy (Tues–Sun 9am–noon & 1–5pm; €2, or part of museum pass) occupying a corner of the majestic eighteenth-century **Hôtel-Dieu-le-Comte**; rows of painted wooden "silènes" boxes dating from the eighteenth century adorn its shelves, each illustrating the medicines once found inside.

Despite being raked by numerous fires since the Middle Ages, Troyes' Old Town has retained many timber-framed buildings. The most famous fire, in 1524, led to a massive rebuilding scheme that resulted in Troyes' wealth of Renaissance palaces. An outstanding example, just east of the church of St-Pantaléon, is the sixteenth-century Hôtel de Mauroy, 7 rue de la Trinité, once an orphanage, then a textile factory, but now the **Maison de l'Outil et de la Pensée Ouvrière** (March–Sept daily 10am–6pm; Oct–Feb Wed–Mon 10am–6pm; €6.50, or part of museum pass). Troyes' most original museum, it exhibits traditional tools of a myriad of trades, ranging from chair-caning to glove-making. Its beautifully lit displays provide a window into the world of the workers, while video monitors throughout the museum demonstrate how the tools were used. Be sure to pick up the English-language guide at the entrance.

Hosiery ("bonneterie") and woollens have been Troyes' most important industry since the late Middle Ages. Some of the old machines and products used for creating garments can be seen in the sixteenth-century palace, the **Hôtel de Vauluisant**, at 4 rue de Vauluisant, part of which houses the rather dry **Musée de la Bonneterie** (Tues–Sun 9am–noon & 1–5pm; €3, or part of museum pass); it houses an array of looms, sewing machines and the like, as well as historic photographs and a collection of socks and stockings from the nineteenth and twentieth centuries. The palace also houses the more compelling **Musée Historique de Troyes et de la Champagne Méridionale** (same hours and ticket – English language leaflet available at entrance), which contains some gorgeous sixteenth-century sculptures of the Troyes school as well as some fine winged triptychs.

Eating, drinking and entertainment

Self-caterers should head for the Marché les Halles, a daily covered **market** on the corner of rue Général-de-Gaulle and place St-Rémy, close to the Hôtel de Ville. Central Troyes is sprinkled with **places to eat**, but quality is uneven and there's a preponderance of crêperies. Most of the places worth tracking down cluster in the narrow streets around St-Jean. *Le Tricasse* is a perennially popular **bar** at 2 rue Charbonnet, on the corner with narrow rue Paillot-de-Montabert – which is also where you'll find the tiny and consistently packed-out *Bar des Bougnats des Pouilles*. Back on rue Charbonnet, *Cotton Club* at no. 8 has a busy programme of DJ nights and live music, including jazz.

From late June to late July, the city organizes free **Ville en Musique** concerts in picturesque locations in the historic centre; the programme ranges from classical and jazz to rock and hip-hop – pick up a schedule at the tourist office.

Bistroquet Place Langevin ℡03.25.73.65.65. A classic place to try the regional speciality of *andouillette* (see box, p.172), along with delicious home-style cooking; *menus* from €22.20; closed Sun eve.

Le Champo 12 rue Champeaux ℡03.25.43.90.27. A good place to come for *fondues* and *raclettes* (around €15), served up in a lovely old Rennaissance building.

Aux Crieurs de Vins 4 place Jean-Jaurès ℡03.25.40.01.01. Delightfully uncomplicated wine bar with *andouillettes* on the menu and a jumble of different furniture; *plats du jour* from €11.

La Mignardise 1 ruelle des Chats ℡03.25.73.15.30. Troyes' best restaurant, set in a sixteenth-century building with a quiet courtyard, serving a traditional French *menu* from €29. Closed Sun eve and Mon.

Le Valentino 35 rue Paillot de Montabert (entrance cours de la Rencontre) ℡03.25.73.14.14. Chic, intimate place serving gastronomic delights at reasonable prices. Reservations essential; closed Sun & Mon; *menus* €25 for lunch, from €33 for dinner.

The Plateau de Langres

The Seine, Marne, Aube and several other lesser rivers rise in the **Plateau de Langres** between Troyes and Dijon, with main routes between the two towns skirting this area. To the east, the N19 (which the train follows) takes in **Chaumont** and **Langres**, two towns that could briefly slow your progress if you're in no hurry, and the home village of Charles de Gaulle, **Colombey-les-Deux-Églises**.

Chaumont

Situated on a steep ridge between the Marne and Suize valleys, **CHAUMONT** (Chaumont-en-Bassigny to give its full name), lies 93km southeast of Troyes. It is best approached by train, which enables you to cross the town's stupendous mid-nineteenth-century viaduct, which took an average of 2500 labourers working night and day two years to construct. It's also possible to walk across the viaduct, which gives you fine views of the Suize valley.

The town's most interesting historic building is the **Basilique St-Jean-Baptiste**. Though built with the same dour, grey stone of most Champagne churches, it has a wonderful Renaissance addition to the Gothic transept of balconies and turreted stairway, and a superb church organ. The decoration includes an *Arbre de Jessé* of the early sixteenth-century Troyes school, in which all the characters are sitting in the tree, dressed in the style of the day.

You shouldn't leave without taking a look at **Les Silos**, 7–9 av Foch, near the *gare SNCF* (Tues, Thurs & Fri 2–7pm, Wed & Sat 10am–6pm; free), a 1930s agricultural co-op transformed into a graphic arts centre and *médiathèque*. As well as hosting temporary exhibitions, it's the main venue for Chaumont's international **poster festival** (Festival de l'Affiche), held every year from mid-May to mid-June. As for the rest of the Old Town, there's not much to do except admire the twelfth-century castle keep of the Comtes de Champagne, the delightfully named Tour d'Arse at the foot of the Vieille Ville – all that remains of the thirteenth-century town gate – and the strange, bulging stair towers of the houses.

The **tourist office** is opposite the *gare SNCF* on place du Général-Charles-de-Gaulle (Mon–Sat 9.30am–12.30pm & 2.30–6pm; ℡03.25.03.80.80, ⓦwww.tourisme-chaumont-champagne.com), which is also where you'll find *Le Terminus Reine* (℡03.25.03.66.66, ⓦwww.relais-sud-champagne.com; ❹), an old-fashioned hotel with great charm; its restaurant is the best place to eat.

Colombey-les-Deux-Églises

Twenty-seven kilometres northwest of Chaumont, on the N19 to Troyes, is **COLOMBEY-LES-DEUX-ÉGLISES**, the village where Gaullist leaders come to pay their respects at the grave of **General Charles de Gaulle**. The former president's family home, **La Boisserie**, opens its ground floor to the public (April–Sept daily 10am–6.30pm; Oct–March daily except Tues 10am–5.30pm; €4), but more impressive are the pink-granite **Cross of Lorraine**, symbol of the French Resistance movement, standing over 40m high on a hill just west of the village, and the spanking (and pricey) new **Mémorial Charles de Gaulle** (May–Sept daily 9.30am–7pm; Oct–April daily except Tues 10am–5.30pm; €12.50; ⓦwww.memorial-charlesdegaulle.fr), an exhaustive chronicle of the man's life and times in an ultra-sleek museum beneath the cross.

The best place to **stay** here is the splendid *Hostellerie La Montagne-Restaurant Natali*, rue de Pisseloup (☎03.25.01.51.69, ⓦwww.hostellerielamontagne .com; ❼; *menus* from €28), where the rooms are individually designed and truly top-notch. Run by a father and son team, it's really a restaurant with rooms – chef Jean-Baptiste Natali worked previously at a Michelin-starred restaurant in Cannes. A more modest option, with a simple country dining room and smartly renovated rooms, is *La Grange du Relais* (☎03.25.02.03.89, ⓦwww.lagrangedurelais.fr; ❸; *menus* from €18) on the RN19 at the bottom of the town.

Langres

LANGRES, 35km south of Chaumont and just as spectacularly situated above the Marne, retains its near-complete encirclement of gateways, towers and ramparts. If you're just here for an hour or so, the best thing to do is to walk this circuit, with its great views east to the hills of Alsace and southwest across the Plateau de Langres. Don't miss the **St-Ferjeux tower** with its beautiful metal sculpture, *Air and Dreams*. Wandering inside the walls is also rewarding – Renaissance houses and narrow streets give the feel of a place time has left behind, swathed in the mists of southern Champagne. Langres was home to the eighteenth-century Enlightenment philosopher **Diderot** for the first sixteen years of his life, and people like to make the point that, if he were to return to Langres today, he'd have no trouble finding his way around.

The **Hôtel du Breuil de St-Germain**, at 2 rue Chambrûlard, is one of the best of the town's sixteenth-century mansions, though it can only be viewed from outside. The **Musée d'Art et Histoire** on place du Centenaire, near the cathedral (daily except Tues: April–Oct 10am–noon & 2–6pm; until 5pm Nov–March; €4) devotes a section to Diderot, with his encyclopedias and various other first editions of his works, plus a portrait by Van Loos. The highlight of the museum is the superbly restored Romanesque **chapel of St-Didier** in the old wing, housing a fourteenth-century painted ivory *Annunciation*. Sixteenth-century tiles from Rouen are on display in one of the nave chapels of the **Cathédrale St-Mammès**, where you'll also find an amusing sixteenth-century relief of the Raising of Lazarus, in which the apostles watch, totally blasé, while other characters look like kids at a good horror movie.

Practicalities

The **tourist office** is just inside the town's main gate, the Porte des Moulins, on place Bel'Air (April–Sept daily 9am–noon & 1.30–6.30pm; Oct–March Mon–Sat 9am–noon & 1.30–6pm, Sat 9.30am–noon & 1.30–6pm; ☎03.25.87.67.67, ⓦwww.tourisme-langres.com), on the other side of town from the **gare SNCF** (connections to Reims and Dijon); staff can give you a useful map of the main sights in town, and also have information on the four lakes in the surrounding region.

For **accommodation**, there's a **hostel** close by the Porte des Moulins on place des États-Unis (℡03.25.87.09.69; book ahead for Sat & Sun as the reception closes at weekends; dorm beds from €15, breakfast and bedding extra), and the reasonable *Auberge Jeanne d'Arc*, 26 rue Gambetta (℡03.25.86.87.88; ❷), in the centre of town. More comfortable rooms can be found at the characterful *Cheval Blanc*, in a converted church at 4 rue de l'Estres (℡03.25.87.07.00, ⓦwww.hotel-langres .com; ❹), or in the less elegant seventeenth-century *Grand Hôtel de l'Europe*, 23–25 rue Diderot (℡03.25.87.10.88, ⓦwww.relais-sud-champagne.com; ❹). For good but expensive **food**, try *Restaurant Diderot* at the *Cheval Blanc* (closed Sun eve; *menus* from €32). Better value is to be had at the *Lion d'Or* (℡03.25.87.03.30), a restaurant and hotel just outside the town on the route de Vesoul with views of the surrounding lakes. Langres has its own highly flavourful, strong-smelling – and excellent – cheese, which you can buy at the Friday **market** on place Bel'Air.

The Ardennes

To the northeast of Reims, the scenery of the **Ardennes** region along the Meuse valley knocks spots off any landscape in Champagne. Most of the hills lie over the border in Belgium, but there's enough of interest on the French side to make it well worth exploring.

In war after war, the people of the Ardennes have been engaged in protracted last-ditch battles down the valley of the Meuse, which, once lost, gave invading armies a clear path to Paris. The rugged, hilly terrain and deep forests (frightening even to Julius Caesar's legionnaires) gave an advantage to World War II Resistance fighters, but during peacetime life here has never been easy. The land is unsuitable for crops, and the slate and ironworks, the main source of employment during the nineteenth century, closed in the 1980s. The only major investment in the region has been a nuclear power station, to which locals responded by etching "Nuke the Élysée!" high on a half-cut cliff of slate just downstream.

This said, tourism, the main growth industry, is developing apace – there are walking and boating possibilities, plus good train connections – though the isolated atmosphere of this region still lingers.

Charleville-Mézières

CHARLEVILLE-MÉZIÈRES – an agglomeration of former stand-alone towns Charleville and Mézières – provides a good base for exploring the northern part of the region, which spreads across the meandering Meuse before the valley closes in and the forests take over.

The splendid seventeenth-century **place Ducale**, in the centre of town, was the result of the local duke's envy of the contemporary place des Vosges in Paris, which it somewhat resembles. Despite the posh setting, the shops in the arcades remain very down-to-earth and the cafés charge reasonable prices to sit outside. From 31 place Ducale you can reach the complex of old and new buildings that house the **Musée de l'Ardenne** (Tues–Sun 10am–noon & 2–6pm; €4, combined ticket with Musée Arthur Rimbaud), a typically eclectic local museum which includes archeological finds from a local Merovingian cemetery, fascinating historic models of Charleville and Mézières in the seventeenth century, and paintings on nineteenth-century industrial and political themes by Paul Gondrexon.

The most famous person to emerge from the town was Arthur Rimbaud (1854–91), who ran away from Charleville four times before he was 17, so desperate was he to escape its provincialism. He is honoured in the **Musée Arthur Rimbaud**, housed in a very grand stone windmill – a contemporary of the place Ducale – on quai Arthur Rimbaud, two blocks north of the main square (same hours and ticket as Musée de l'Ardenne). It contains paintings and sketches of him and his contemporaries, including his lover Verlaine, as well as facsimiles of his writings and related documents. A few steps down the quayside is the spot where he composed his most famous poem, *Le Bateau Ivre*. After penning poetry in Paris, journeying to the Far East and trading in Ethiopia and Yemen, Rimbaud died in a Marseille hospital. His body was brought back to his home town – probably the last place he would have wanted to be buried – and true Rimbaud fanatics can visit his **tomb** in the cemetery west of the place Ducale at the end of avenue Charles Boutet.

Charleville is a major international puppetry centre (its school is justly famous), and every three years it hosts one of the largest puppet festivals in the world, the **Festival Mondial des Théâtres de Marionnettes** (W www.festival -marionnette.com). Up to 150 professional troupes – some from as far away as Mali and Burma – put on something like fifty shows a day on the streets and in every available space in town. Tickets are cheap, and there are shows for adults as well as the usual stuff aimed at kids. If you miss the festival you can still catch one of the puppet performances year-round at the **Institut de la Marionnette** on place Winston Churchill (T 03.24.33.72.50; tickets around €12). If you're passing by here during the day, you can see one of the automated episodes of the *Four Sons of Aymon* enacted on the facade's clock every hour, or all twelve scenes on Saturday at 9.15pm.

Practicalities

From the **gare SNCF**, place Ducale is a ten-minute walk; the **gare routière** is a couple of blocks west of the square, by the Marché Couvert. The **regional tourist office** for the Ardennes is at 22 place Ducale (Mon–Sat: May–Sept 10am–12.30pm & 1.30–7pm; Oct–April closes 6pm; T 03.24.56.06.08), with Charleville-Mézières' **tourist office** at no. 4 (Mon–Fri 9am–noon & 1–6pm, Sat & Sun 9am–noon & 1–5pm; July & Aug closes 7pm; T 03.24.55.69.90, W www .charleville-tourisme.com).

For **accommodation**, three places worth trying are: the *Dormeur du Val*, a four-star boutique hotel with colourful, stylish rooms at 32 rue de la Gravière (T 03.24.42.04.30, W www.dormeur.fr; 6); the *Hôtel de Paris*, 24 av Georges Corneau, which offers free internet access (T 03.24.33.34.38, W www.hotelde paris08.fr; 3); and *Le Relais du Square*, 3 place de la Gare (T 03.24.33.38.76, W www.hotel-charleville-mezieres.com; 2), a two-star hotel in a tree-filled square near the station. The town's **campsite**, *Camping du Mont Olympe* (T 03.24.33.23.60, E camping-charlevillemezieres@orange.fr; open April–Sept), is north of place Ducale, over the river and left along rue des Paquis. There are plenty of places to **eat and drink**. For something a bit special, *La Côte à l'Os*, at 11 cours Aristide-Briand (T 03.24.59.20.16), specializes in *fruits de mer* and local cuisine; daily *menus* start at €13.50. At 33 rue du Moulin, the Michelin-listed *La Clef des Champs* (T 03.24.56.17.50) offers *menus* from €23.

North of Charleville-Mézières

Writing about the stretch of the Meuse that winds through the Ardennes, George Sand said: "its high wooded cliffs, strangely solid and compact, are like some inexorable destiny that encloses, pushes and twists the river without permitting it a single whim or any escape". What all the tourist literature emphasizes, however, are the legends of medieval struggles between Good and Evil whose characters have given names to some of the curious rocks and crests. The grandest of these, where the schist formations have taken the most peculiar turns, is the **Roc de la Tour**, also known as the "Devil's Castle", up a path off the D31, 3.5km out of **Monthermé**.

The journey through this frontier country should ideally be done on foot or skis, by bicycle, or **by boat**. The alternatives for the last are good old *bateau-mouche*-type cruises or live-in pleasure boats – not wildly expensive if you can split the cost four or six ways. For cyclists, the Trans-Ardennes Green Track provides over 80km of off-road bike trails following the Meuse Valley; the regional tourist office at Charleville-Mézières (see p.224) can provide free route maps, as well as information on hiking, canoeing or riding. For **public transport** from Charleville-Mézières, trains follow the Meuse towards Belgium, while local buses run as far as **Nouzonville**.

The **GR12** is a good walking route, circling the **Lac des Vieilles Forges**, 17km northwest of Charleville-Mézières, then meeting the Meuse at Bogny and crossing over to Hautes-Rivières in the even more sinuous **Semoy Valley**. There are plenty of other tracks, too, though beware of *chasse* (hunting) signs – French hunters tend to hack through the undergrowth with their safety catches off and are notoriously trigger-happy. They're mostly after the local wild boar, who are nowhere near as dangerous as their pursuers, and would seem to be more intelligent, too, rooting about near the crosses of the Resistance memorial near **Revin**, while hunters stalk the forest. A good place to stay, overlooking the river at Revin, is the *Hôtel François-1ᵉʳ*, 46 quai Camille-Desmoulins (℡03.24.40.15.88; ❶).

Travel details

Trains

Amiens to: Albert (frequent; 20min); Arras (frequent; 40–50min); Compiègne (frequent; 1hr 30min); Laon (8 daily; 1hr 40min); Lille (frequent; 1hr 25min); Paris (every 30min–1hr; 1hr 30min); Reims (7 daily; 3hr).

Arras to: Albert (approx. every 1–2hr; 25min); Boulogne (6 daily; 1hr 50min); Calais (frequent; 2hr); Douai (frequent; 15–20min); Étaples-Le Touquet (9 daily; 1hr 30min); Lille (approx. every 1–2hr; 45min); Paris (frequent; 50min).

Beauvais to: Paris (every 45min–1hr; 1hr 10min).

Boulogne–Ville to: Abbeville (11 daily; 1hr); Amiens (frequent; 1hr 20min); Arras (4 daily; 2hr); Calais-Ville (approx. hourly; 30min); Étaples-Le Touquet (frequent; 20–30min); Lille (approx. every 30 min; 2hr); Montreuil–sur-Mer (frequent; 40min); Paris (10 daily; 2hr 40min).

Calais-Fréthun to: Lille (frequent; 30min); Paris (5 daily; 1hr 30min).

Calais-Ville to: Abbeville (10 daily; 2hr); Boulogne-Ville (approx. hourly; 30min); Dunkerque (frequent; 1hr 20min); Étaples-Le Touquet (approx. every hour; 1hr); Lille (approx. every hour; 1hr 30min); Paris (7 daily; 1hr 40min).

Compiègne to: Paris (frequent; 50min).

Dunkerque to: Calais-Ville (frequent; 1hr 20min); Cassel (approx. hourly; 25min).

Laon to: Paris (approx. every hour; 1hr 45min); Soissons (approx. every 1–2hr; 30min).

Lille to: Arras (approx. every 1–2hr; 40min); Boulogne (approx. hourly; 1hr 30min); Brussels (TGV 7 daily; 40min); Charleville-Mézières (3 daily; 2hr); Dunkerque (approx. hourly; 1hr); Lyon (TGV frequent; 3hr); Marseille (TGV 6 daily; 4hr 30min); Paris (TGV frequent; 1hr).

Reims to: Charleville-Mézières (almost hourly; 50min); Épernay (frequent; 35min); Laon (7 daily; 45min); Paris (frequent; 45min).

Troyes to: Chaumont (approx. every 1–2hr; 50min); Langres (9 daily; 1hr 15min); Paris (frequent; 1hr 30min).

Buses

Abbeville to: St Valéry-sur-Somme (4 daily; 30min).

Amiens to: Abbeville (2 daily; 1hr 25min); Albert (4 daily; 45min–1hr 8min); Beauvais (14 daily; 1hr 20min); Péronne (2 daily; 1hr 40min).

Boulogne to: Calais (4 daily; 40min); Dunkerque (4 daily; 1hr 20min); Le Touquet (5 daily; 1hr 20min).

Calais to: Boulogne (5 daily; 40min); Dunkerque (12 daily; 1hr 45min).

Dunkerque to: Boulogne (5 daily; 1hr 30min); Calais (11 daily; 45min).

Reims to: Laon (1 daily; 1hr 30min); Troyes (5 daily; 2hr 10min).

Soissons to: Compiègne (9 daily; 1hr 15min); Coucy (5 daily; 25min).

3

Alsace and Lorraine

CHAPTER 3 # Highlights

✳ **Strasbourg cathedral**
Climb the lofty spire of this
magnificent Gothic cathedral
for stunning views as far as
the Black Forest. See p.234

✳ **The Route des Vins**
Surrounded by a sea of vines,
Alsace's picturesque wine
villages are overlooked by
a wealth of ruined castles,
perched on pine-clad fringes
of the Vosges. See p.239

✳ **The Issenheim Altarpiece,
Colmar** Luridly expressive,
this Renaissance masterpiece
alone makes quaint Colmar
worth a visit. See p.245

✳ **Bugattis at Mulhouse's Cité
de l'Automobile** A unique
collection of vintage motors in
the city where the French car
industry was set in motion.
See p.249

✳ **Place Stanislas, Nancy**
Along with some outstanding
Art Nouveau architecture,
elegant Nancy is home to
one of the most grandiose
eighteenth-century squares in
all France. See p.252

✳ **Centre Pompidou-Metz**
Explore the brand-new branch
of the famous Parisian Centre
Pompidou. See p.257

▲ Place Stanislas, Nancy

Alsace and Lorraine

D isputed for centuries by French kings and the princes of the Holy Roman Empire, and subsequently embroiled in a bloody tug-of-war between France and Germany, France's easternmost provinces, Alsace and Lorraine, share a tumultuous history. It's no surprise then that almost everything, from the architecture to the cuisine and the language, is an enticing mixture of French and German – so much so that you might begin to wonder which country you're actually in.

Cute Hansel-and-Gretel-type houses – higgedly-piggledy creations with oriel windows, carved timberwork, toy-town gables and geranium-filled window boxes – are a common feature in **Alsace**, especially along the winding **Route des Vins**, which traces the eastern margin of the forests of the Vosges mountains. This road also represents the region's chief tourist *raison d'etre* – wine – best accompanied with a regional cuisine that's more Germanic than French: think hefty portions of pork, cabbage and pungent cheese. Ruined medieval castles are scattered about, while outstanding churches and museums are concentrated in the handsome regional capital of **Strasbourg** and smaller, quainter **Colmar**. A noticeably wealthy province, Alsace has historically churned out cars and textiles, not to mention half the beer in France.

Alsace's less prosperous rival, **Lorraine**, shares borders with Luxembourg, Germany and Belgium, and is part farmland, part rust belt. Although less scenic than Alsace, the elegant former capital, **Nancy**, home to a major school of Art Nouveau, is well worth a visit, as is leafy **Metz**, with its sparkling new contemporary art gallery. The bloody World War I battlefields around **Verdun** also attract a large number of visitors. Gastronomically less renowned than other French provinces, Lorraine has nonetheless bequeathed to the world one of its favourite savoury pies – the *quiche lorraine*.

Alsace

Although it can sometimes seem unfeasibly quaint, there's no denying that **Alsace** is charming, thanks to its old stone towns and villages set along the fertile Rhine valley and amid the thickly wooded hills of the Vosges. **Strasbourg**, the capital of Alsace, is undoubtedly one of the most attractive cities in France. South of the city, the famous wine road – the **Route des Vins** – is surrounded on all sides by

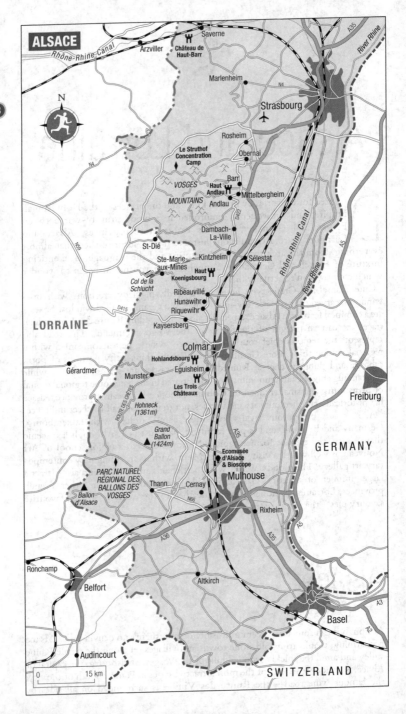

ALSACE

N

Rhône–Rhine Canal
Arzviller
Saverne
Château de Haut-Barr
Marlenheim
N4
Strasbourg
River Rhine
A35

Rosheim
Obernai
Le Struthof Concentration Camp
VOSGES MOUNTAINS
Barr
Haut Andlau
Mittelbergheim
Andlau
Dambach-La-Ville
St-Dié
Kintzheim
Sélestat
Ste-Marie-aux-Mines
Haut Koenigsbourg
Col de la Schlucht
Ribeauvillé
Hunawihr
Riquewihr
Kaysersberg
Rhône–Rhine Canal
River Rhine
A5

LORRAINE

Colmar
Hohlandsbourg
Eguisheim
Les Trois Châteaux
Gérardmer
Munster
ROUTE DES CRÊTES
Hohneck (1361m)
Grand Ballon (1424m)
Freiburg
GERMANY

PARC NATUREL RÉGIONAL DES BALLONS DES VOSGES
Ballon d'Alsace
Thann
Cernay
N66
Ecomusée d'Alsace & Bioscope
Mulhouse
Rixheim
A36
A35
A5

Ronchamp
Belfort
Altkirch
Basel
A3
A2

Audincourt

SWITZERLAND

0   15 km

Alsatian food

The cuisine of Alsace is quite distinct from that of other regions of France. The classic dish is *choucroute*, the aromatic pickled cabbage known in German as **sauerkraut**. The extra ingredient here is the inclusion of juniper berries in the pickling stage and the addition of goose grease or lard. Traditionally it's served with large helpings of smoked pork, ham and sausages, but some restaurants offer a succulent variant replacing the meat with fish (*choucroute aux poissons*), usually salmon and monkfish. The qualification *à l'alsacienne* after the name of a dish means "with *choucroute*". **Baeckoffe**, a three-meat hotpot, comprising layers of potato, pork, mutton and beef marinated in wine and baked for several hours, is a speciality. **Onions**, too, crop up frequently on *menus*, either in the guise of a tart (*tarte à l'oignon*), made with a béchamel sauce, or as *flammeküche* (*tarte flambée*), a mixture of onion, cream and pieces of chopped smoked pork breast, baked on a thin, pizza-like base.

Alsatians are fond of their **pastries**. In almost every patisserie, you'll find a mouth-watering array of fruit tarts made with rhubarb (topped with meringue), wild blueberries, red cherries or yellow *mirabelle* plums. Cake-lovers should try *kugelhopf*, a dome-shaped cake with a hollow in the middle made with raisins and almonds.

For the classic Alsatian eating experience, you should go to a **winstub**, loosely translated as a "wine bar", a cosy establishment with bare beams, wood wall panels and benches and a convivial atmosphere. The food revolves around Alsatian classics, such as *choucroute*, all accompanied by local wines (or, in a *bierstub*, beer).

---

countless picturesque medieval hamlets, all with half-timbered houses and cobbled streets. Pretty **Colmar** is well worth a visit, particularly for Grünewald's beautiful Issenheim altarpiece, one of the most striking pieces of religious art in France. By contrast, less-visited (and far less twee) **Mulhouse**, although thoroughly industrial, boasts eclectic museums devoted to subjects as varied as cars, trains and wallpaper.

Every town has its own **tourist office** (Ⓦ www.tourisme-alsace.com), which is often housed in the *mairie* or Hôtel de Ville; almost all provide free maps. A comprehensive TER **train** network links Strasbourg with all major towns and many of the wine villages along the Route des Vins. Buses fill in a few of the gaps.

Strasbourg

STRASBOURG is a hybrid city: part medieval village, characterized by lovely half-timbered houses, soaring Gothic cathedral and narrow winding streets, and part modern European powerhouse, with sleek, glassy buildings inhabited by important European Union bodies. Boasting the largest university in France, the city is a lively, metropolitan place that deserves at least three or four days' visit.

The city owes both its Germanic name – "the City of the Roads" – and its wealth to its strategic position on the west bank of the Rhine. Self-styled *Le Carrefour de l'Europe* ("Europe's Crossroads"), it is geographically closer to Frankfurt, Zurich and even Milan than to Paris, although the TGV renders the French capital within two and a half hours' reach. Strasbourg's medieval commercial pre-eminence was damaged by its involvement in the religious struggles of the sixteenth and seventeenth centuries, but recovered with its absorption into France in 1681. Along with the rest of Alsace, the city was annexed by Germany from 1871 to the end of World War I and again from 1940 to 1944. Today, old animosities have been submerged in the **European Union**, with Strasbourg the seat of the Council of Europe, the European Court of Human Rights and the European Parliament.

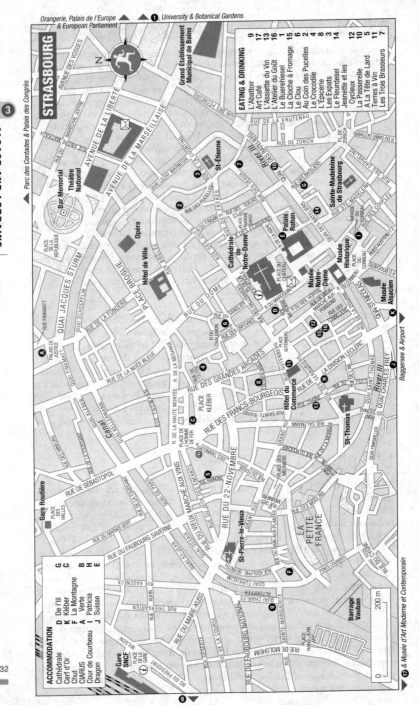

STRASBOURG

Orangerie, Palais de l'Europe & European Parliament

University & Botanical Gardens

Parc des Contades & Palais des Congrès

Grand Etablissement Municipal de Bains

EATING & DRINKING

L'Abattoir	9
Art Café	17
L'Assiette du Vin	13
L'Atelier du Goût	16
Le Buerehiesel	1
La Cloche à Fromage	15
Le Clou	6
Au Coin des Pucelles	2
Le Crocodile	4
L'Epicerie	8
Les Expats	3
Le Fleurdesel	14
Jeanette et les Cycleux	12
La Passerelle	10
A La Tête de Lard	5
Terres à Vin	11
Les Trois Brasseurs	7

ACCOMMODATION

Cathédrale	D	De l'Ill	G
Cerf d'Or	K	Kléber	C
Chut	F	La Montagne	B
CIARUS	A	Verte	H
Cour de Courbeau	I	Patricia	E
Dragon	J	Suisse	

Avenue des Vosges

Avenue de la Liberté

Avenue de la Marseillaise

Bat Memorial
Théâtre National

Opéra

Hôtel de Ville

Place Broglie

St-Étienne

Cathédrale de Notre-Dame

Palais Rohan

Musée Notre-Dame

Musée Historique

Musée Alsacien

Sainte-Madeleine de Strasbourg

Rue de Zurich

Place de Zürich

Rue de la Krutenau

Rue de Sébastopol

Gare Routière

Place des Halles

Rue des Grandes Arcades

Rue des Francs-Bourgeois

Place Kléber

Hôtel du Commerce

St-Thomas

River Ill

Rue de la Division Leclerc

Rue du 22-Novembre

St-Pierre-le-Vieux

Marché aux Vins

LA PETITE FRANCE

Barrage Vauban

Gare SNCF

Baggersee & Airport

& Musée d'Art Moderne et Contemporain

0   200 m

Arrival and information

The **gare SNCF** lies on the west side of the city centre, fifteen-minutes' walk from the cathedral. The **airport shuttle bus** (*navette*), departing Entzheim international airport every twenty minutes (5.20am–11.20pm), drops off at Baggersee, south of the centre, from where you can catch the tram into central Strasbourg (€3.60 combined ticket from the airport).

The main **tourist office** is at 17 place de la Cathédrale (daily 9am–7pm; ☏03.88.52.28.28, ⓦwww.otstrasbourg.fr), which can provide you with a map (€1 for one with museums and sights marked on it; free otherwise). There's another branch in the underground shopping complex just in front of the train station (Mon–Sat 9am–7pm; Sun 9am–12.30pm & 1.45–7pm). Depending on your itinerary, it may be worth investing in a **Strasbourg Pass** (€12.40), which entitles you to one free museum entry, one half-price museum entry, a boat tour, a half-day of bike hire, and the cathedral tower and clock; it's valid for three days.

With much of the city centre geared for pedestrian use, there are several car parks available (ⓦwww.parcus.com). While the compact centre can easily be explored on foot, the city boasts an efficient public transport system, which includes five tram lines (€1.50 single; ⓦwww.cts-strasbourg.fr). Strasbourg is a very **bicycle**-friendly city, and its 300km of cycle lanes make bike hire a tempting option (see p.238).

Accommodation

When looking for a place to **stay**, bear in mind that once a month (except Aug, but twice in Oct) the European Parliament is in session for the best part of a week, bringing hundreds of MEPs and their entourages into town. To find out in advance when the parliament is sitting, contact the main tourist office.

Hotels

Cathédrale 12–13 place de la Cathédrale ☏03.88.22.12.12, ⓦwww.hotel-cathedrale .fr. Bang next to the cathedral, the location of this charming hotel can't be beaten. If you can, fork out for the pricier rooms, which boast wonderful cathedral views. **❹–❼**

Cerf d'Or 6 place de l'Hôpital ☏03.88.36.20.05, ⓦwww.cerf-dor.com. Attractive, family-run place in a sixteenth-century building, with a small swimming pool/sauna and its own restaurant (lunch *menu* €25). Closed mid-Dec to mid-Jan and three weeks of July. **❸–❻**

🏃 **Chut** 4 rue du Bain-aux-Plantes ☏03.88.32.05.06, ⓦwww.hote-strasbourg .fr. Living up to its name – which translates as "shh" – this rambling and beautifully designed hotel is an oasis of calm in a touristy area of La Petite France. Each of its eight fresh and sophisticated rooms comes with elegant antique furniture, wooden floorboards and walk-in showers. Restaurant (*plats* from €19.50) closed Sun & Mon. Parking €10. **❺**

🏃 **Cour de Courbeau** 6–8 rue des Couples ☏03.90.00.26.26, ⓦwww.cour-corbeau .com. Housed in an exquisite sixteenth-century building with an intricate wooden courtyard and 300-year-old cobbles in the dining room, *Cours de Courbeau* lays claim to being the oldest hotel in

Europe. The pale, white-washed rooms, some with views of the cathedral, are luxurious and spacious and the service is suitably attentive. **❼**

Dragon 2 rue de l'Écarlate ☏03.88.35.79.80, ⓦwww.dragon.fr. Painted in a pleasing shade of burnt orange, this seventeenth-century house situated near the river has a little cobbled courtyard and comfortable rooms in soothing shades of grey. **❹**

De l'Ill 8 rue des Bateliers ☏03.88.36.20.01, ⓦwww.hotel-ill.com. Clean, simple rooms over several stories of an old townhouse, on a quiet street just 50m from the river; the only drawback is the absence of a lift. Closed end of Dec to mid-Jan. **❸**

Kléber 29 place Kléber ☏03.88.32.09.53, ⓦwww .hotel-kleber.com. Thirty quirky, bijou rooms named after enticing flavours, fruits and puddings; take your pick from almond, rose, damson, pavlova, honey and cappuccino, among others. **❹**

Patricia 1a rue du Puits ☏03.88.32.14.60, ⓦwww.hotelpatricia.fr. In a great location in the backstreets of the Old Town, this basic hotel has a range of decent rooms up an old wooden staircase lined with oriental rugs. Reception has limited opening hours. **❷**

Suisse 2–4 rue de la Râpe ☏03.88.35.22.11, ⓦwww.hotel-suisse.com. Friendly hotel in a labyrinthine old house just a stone's throw from the cathedral. It's a superb location, although the rooms (with the exception of the family rooms) are rather cramped. **4**

Hostel and campsite

CIARUS 7 rue Finkmatt ☎03.88.15.27.88, ⓦwww.ciarus.com. Very central hostel; it's just behind the Palais de Justice, a 15min walk around the river from the train station. 8-bed dorms

€26.50 including breakfast, single rooms **2**, twin rooms **1**

La Montagne Verte 2 rue Robert-Forrer ☎03.88.30.25.46, ⓦwww.camping-montagne -verte-strasbourg.com. Well-equipped campsite; take bus #2 from train station, direction "Campus d'Illkirch", to "Nid des Cigognes", or tram B or C from place Homme de Fer to "Montagne Verte", then bus #2, #13 or #15 to "Nid des Cigognes".

The City

It isn't difficult to find your way around Strasbourg on foot, as the flat city centre is concentrated on a small island encircled by the **River Ill** and an old canal. The magnificent filigree spire of the pink-sandstone **cathedral** is visible throughout the city. Immediately south of the cathedral are the best of the museums, while to the northwest, **place Kléber** is the heart of the commercial district. The more attractive **place Gutenberg** to the south is nominally the city's main square. About a ten-minute walk west, on the tip of the island, is picturesque **La Petite France**, where timber-framed houses and canals hark back to the city's medieval trades of tanning and dyeing. Across the canal to the east of the centre is the late nineteenth-century **German quarter**, the **University** and the city's **European institutions**.

The cathedral and place Gutenberg

The **Cathédrale de Notre-Dame** (daily 7–11.30am & 12.40–7pm; closed during services; free) soars out of the close huddle of medieval houses at its feet with a single spire of such delicacy that it seems the work of confectioners rather than masons. It's worth slogging up the 332 steps to the spire's **viewing platform** (daily: April–Sept 9am–7.15pm; Oct–March 10am–5.15pm; June & July until 9.45pm on Fri and Sat; €4.70) for the superb view of the Old Town, and, in the distance, the Vosges to the west and the Black Forest to the east.

The **interior**, too, is magnificent, the high nave a model of proportion enhanced by a glorious sequence of stained-glass windows. The finest are in the south aisle next to the door, depicting the life of Christ and the Creation, but the modern glass in the apse designed in 1956 by Max Ingrand to commemorate the city's first European institutions is also beautiful. On the left of the nave, the cathedral's organ perches precariously above one of the arches, while further down on the same side is the late fifteenth-century pulpit, a masterpiece of intricacy in stone by the aptly named Hans Hammer.

In the south transept are the cathedral's two most popular sights. The **Pilier des Anges** is a slender triple-tiered central column, decorated with some of the most

---

The Alsatian language

Travelling through the province, you'll hear locals converse in **Elsässisch** – a High German dialect known to philologists as Alemannic. There are two versions – High and Low Alemannic. Given the province's turbulent history, it's in many ways a miracle that the dialect has survived: Elsässisch was suppressed during the French Revolution only for French to be ousted by German after the Prussian victory in 1870, and again under the Nazi occupation. Nowadays, most daily transactions are conducted in French. Yet Elsässisch remains a living language and is still spoken by young and old throughout Alsace. A renaissance of regional identity has meant that it's beginning to reappear on signs, too.

graceful and expressive statuary of the thirteenth century. The huge and enormously complicated **astrological clock** (tickets can be bought from the postcard stand 9am–11.30am, then at the cash desk at the south door 11.35am–noon; €2) was built by Schwilgué of Strasbourg in 1842. It is a favourite with the tour-group operators, whose customers roll up in droves at midday to witness the clock's crowning daily performance, striking the hour of noon, which it does with unerring accuracy at 12.30pm – that being 12 o'clock "Strasbourg time".

Narrow rue Mercière, busy with cathedral-gazers, funnels west to **place Gutenberg**, with its steep-pitched roofs and brightly painted facades. It was named after the printer and pioneer of moveable type, Johannes Gutenberg, who lived in the city in the early fifteenth century and whose statue occupies the middle of the square.

The museum quarter

Next to the cathedral, place du Château is enclosed to the south by the imposing **Palais Rohan**, designed for the immensely powerful Rohan family, who, for several generations, cornered the market in cardinals' hats. It now contains three museums (Mon & Wed–Fri noon–6pm, Sat & Sun 10am–6pm; closed public hols; €4 each): the **Musée des Arts Décoratifs**; the **Musée des Beaux-Arts**; and the rather specialist **Musée Archéologique**. Of the three museums, the Arts Décoratifs stands out; its collections include some fine eighteenth-century faïence tiles crafted in the city by Paul Hannong and some impressive trompe-l'oeil crockery. The palace itself fell victim to the vicissitudes of the Revolution, following which the original furnishings were sold off. Although refurnished in period style, its vast, ostentatious rooms are not especially interesting.

Next door, the excellent **Musée de l'Oeuvre Notre-Dame** (Tues–Fri noon–6pm, Sat & Sun 10am–6pm; closed Mon & public hols; €5) houses the original sculptures from the cathedral exterior, damaged in the Revolution and replaced today by copies. Other treasures here include mesmeric stained-glass windows and impressive still lifes by the sixteenth-century Strasbourg painter Sebastian Stoskopff.

Past the picturesque place du Marché-aux-Cochons-de-Lait is the **Musée Historique** (Sept–June Tues–Fri noon–6pm, Sat & Sun 10am–6pm; July & Aug daily except Mon 10am–6pm; closed public hols; €5). Interactive exhibits, and an over-enthusiastic but worthwhile audio guide, steer you through Strasbourg's political and social history, as a prosperous free city of the Holy Roman Empire, through the theological controversies of the Reformation to French annexation by Louis XIV and the revolutionary fervour of 1789. The prize exhibit is an enormous 3D relief map of the city, commissioned in the 1720s to show the state of the city's fortifications. The narrative ends rather abruptly in the 1830s; exhibits on the nineteenth and twentieth centuries are currently being amassed and are due to be unveiled in 2012. Across the river, in a rickety and typically Alsatian house on quai St-Nicolas, the delightful **Musée Alsacien** (Mon & Wed–Fri noon–6pm, Sat & Sun 10am–6pm; closed public hols; €4) celebrates all things Alsatian: reconstructed rooms – a kitchen, nursery, bedroom, even a *winstub* and a farmyard – are packed with local artefacts, which come together to paint a vivid picture of Alsatian life in the eighteenth and nineteenth centuries.

Musée d'Art Moderne et Contemporain

Housed in a purpose-built, glass-fronted building overlooking the river and Vauban's dam (see p.236), the light and airy **Musée d'Art Moderne et Contemporain** (Tues, Wed & Fri noon–7pm, Thurs noon–9pm, Sat & Sun 10am–6pm; €5) hosts temporary exhibitions, alongside its well-presented permanent collections, which include a sprinkling of minor works by some of the most celebrated twentieth-century French artists. Most interesting is the ground floor, which confronts the themes of modern European art from the late nineteenth century through to the 1950s. Starting with a small group of Impressionist paintings, by the likes of Pissarro and Renoir, the collection features Kandinsky's studies for the ceramic *salon de musique*, a couple of Picassos, plus a good section on Surrealism, with plenty of folkloric, mystical paintings by Brauner. There's a room devoted to the voluptuous, smooth curves sculpted by Strasbourg's own Jean Arp, who was influenced by Dada and Surrealism before turning to sculpture. The collections are not extensive – but there are some interesting works by lesser known artists. Upstairs, the emphasis switches to more conceptual "contemporary art", primarily Arte Povera, before finishing up with stripey creations by Daniel Buren and temporary installations. The museum also has a great café upstairs (see opposite).

La Petite France and the rest of the old city

The attractive Pont St-Martin marks the beginning of the district known as **La Petite France**, where the city's millers, tanners and fishermen used to live. At the far end of a series of canals are the so-called **Ponts Couverts** (they are in fact no longer covered), built as part of the fourteenth-century city fortifications. Just beyond is the **barrage Vauban**, a dam built by Vauban (daily 9am–7.30pm; free) to protect the city from waterborne assault. The whole area is picture-postcard pretty, with winding streets – most notably rue du Bain-aux-Plantes – bordered by sixteenth- and seventeenth-century houses adorned with flowers and elaborately carved woodwork.

The area east of the cathedral, where rue des Frères leads to place St-Étienne, is good for a stroll, too. **Place du Marché-Gayot**, tucked away off rue des Frères behind the cathedral, is a lively cobbled square lined with café-bars and is one of the city's top nightspots. From the north side of the cathedral, rue du Dôme leads to the eighteenth-century **place Broglie**, with the Hôtel de Ville, the bijou **Opéra** and some imposing eighteenth-century mansions.

The German quarter (Neustadt) and the European institutions

Across the canal from the cathedral, **place de la République** is surrounded by vast German Neo-Gothic edifices erected during the Prussian occupation, one example being the main **post office** on avenue de la Marseillaise. At the other end of avenue de la Liberté, across the confluence of the Ill and Aar, is the city's **university**, where Goethe studied. From in front of the university, alleé de la Robertsau, flanked by handsome *fin-de-siècle* bourgeois residences, leads to the headquarters of three major European institutions: the bunker-like **Palais de l'Europe**, the 1970s-built home of the 44-member Council of Europe; the glass and steel curvilinear **European Parliament building**, opened in 1999; and the glass entrance and silver towers of Richard Rogers's **European Court of Human Rights**, completed in 1995. Individuals can arrange to visit the European Parliament during plenary sessions (free; ⓦwww.europarl.europa.eu); the European Court of Human Rights has public court hearings (free; ⓦwww.echr.coe.int). Booking is also required to visit the Council of Europe (free; ⓦwww.coe.int). Opposite the Palais de l'Europe, the **Orangerie**, Strasbourg's best bit of greenery, hosts a variety of exhibitions and free concerts. There's also a small zoo with monkeys and exotic birds.

Eating and drinking

Traffic-free place du Marché-Gayot ("PMG") near the cathedral is one of the best spots for **café-bars**, most of which stay open until 1.30am. In summer, when the sun comes out, the floating cafés and deckchairs along the **quai des Pêcheurs** make great hangouts. There's a good selection of less touristy **restaurants**, ranging from upmarket *winstubs* to simple neighbourhood eateries, along the quai des Pêcheurs and on surrounding streets, such as rue de Zürich and rue de la Krutenau.

Restaurants

L'Assiette du Vin 5 rue de la Chaîne ☎03.88.32.00.92. Questionable decor in the window – a medley of plastic goldfish and some musical instruments – but there's nothing confused about the tasty food in this bright, cheery restaurant. Tuck into sea bream with a lemon crust and braised fennel (€22) and for pudding a "pina colada" – coconut mousse with fresh pineapple and rum granita (€6.50). Closed Sun.

L'Atelier du Goût 17 rue des Tonneliers ☎03.88.21.01.01. A mix of modern and old – lime green banquettes and slick lighting along with wood panelled walls and dried flowers – this restaurant places heavy emphasis on serving fresh, locally sourced food. Starters could include smoked octopus with spring peas (€14) and fried foie gras with a poppy-seed crust, glazed vegetables and a citrus sauce (€26.50). Kitchen closes at 1.30pm at lunch time and 9.30pm in the evening. Closed Sat & Sun.

Le Buerehiesel 4 parc de l'Orangerie ☎03.88.45.56.65. Run by Eric Westermann, son of the much-lauded, Michelin-starred chef Antoine Westermann, *Buerehiesel* is housed in a delightful, rustic farmhouse in the Parc de l'Orangerie. It's pricey – *menus* start at €65, and à la carte mains hover around the €30 mark. Closed Sun & Mon.

La Cloche à Fromage 27 rue des Tonneliers ☎03.88.23.13.19. Don't come here if you don't like cheese: everything on the *menu* centres around it, from the delicious oven-baked goats' cheese profiteroles (€18.30) to the *raclettes* (from €25.50) and fondues (from €22.90). They also have an excellent cheese shop across the road at number 32 (Mon–Fri 10am–12.15pm & 2.30–7pm, Sat 8am–6pm).

Le Clou 3 rue du Chaudron ☎03.88.32.11.67. Reliable, ever-popular *winstub* tucked away close to the cathedral, serving hearty meals such as *bratwurst* and sautéed potatoes (€13). Closed Wed lunch & Sun.

Au Coin des Pucelles 12 rue des Pucelles ☎03.88.35.35.14. Atmospheric little *winstub* in a cosy, panelled old house, serving mounds of *choucroute* and other tasty old Alsatian dishes until 1am, alongside a good selection of local wines. Lighter meals such as omelettes are also on offer (€9.60). Closed Sun & Mon.

Le Crocodile 10 rue de l'Outre ☎03.88.32.13.02. Named after the stuffed beast in the entrance, this elegant restaurant has earned a Michelin star for its excellent cuisine: exquisite *plats* could include milk-fed lamb with asparagus and a chickpea puree (€43) or meaty sturgeon in Moroccan spices (€45).

Le Fleurdesel 22 quai des Bateliers ☎03.88.36.01.54. Stylish restaurant in an old house beside the river. The cuisine has a Mediterranean slant, incorporating lots of tasty tomatoes, peppers and mozzarella. *Plats* €18.

A La Tête de Lard 3 rue de Hannong ☎03.88.32.13.56. Relaxed, low-key restaurant with rustic decor that serves good-value *plats* such as a tasty Munster cheese and onion tart flavoured with cumin (€12.10) and *choucroute* (€17.40).

Cafés and bars

L'Abattoir 1 quai Charles Altorffer. With its funky lamps, painted black walls and wooden benches, *L'Abattoir* is a very relaxed café-bar. Delicious snacks are on offer – for a sugary pick-me-up, try the strawberry crumble (€3.50) or the waffles (from €3.50) – all day, as well as shisha pipes. There's a lounging area with strange circular beds as well as two outside areas for a drink in the sunshine.

Art Café 1 rue Hans-Jean Arp ☎03.88.22.18.88. You don't have to get a ticket to the museum to come up to its superb café-restaurant serving everything from teas and coffees to light snacks; *tartes* from €9.50. There's a large terrace that looks out over the whole of Strasbourg, perfect for brunch (Sun only; €12). Tues–Sat 11am–2pm, Sun until 6pm. Closed Mon.

L'Épicerie 6 rue du Vieux-Seigle ☎03.88.32.52.41. This fun café-bar is a reconstructed grocers, with jolly tablecloths, ramshackle wooden furniture, and vintage advertisements. It's always packed out with people enjoying very reasonably priced *tartines* (open sandwiches), served daily until midnight. *Tartine* with prunes and *fourme d'ambert* cheese €5.20. Daily 11.30am–1.30am.

Les Expats 3 rue de la Courtine. Appealing little bar draped with plastic stars and butterflies and plastered with eclectic posters. Snacks – tapas, *tartes flambées* and pizza – served. Sun–Wed 11.30am–10.30pm, Thurs–Sat 11.30am–1.30am.

Jeanette et les Cycleux 30 rue des Tonneliers. A cycling theme dominates at this trendy little bar, which serves a variety of coffees, cocktails, milkshakes and wines. Substantial snacks on offer include salads (€9.50; served noon–2pm) and delicious *planchettes* of cold meat and cheese (from €4.50).

La Passerelle 38 quai des Bateliers. Chic late-night bar with velvet sofas and soft purple lighting. Popular with a smart set that come to sip cocktails and shimmy to the music – which can be anything from electro to salsa and rock. Tues & Wed 8pm–1.30am, Thurs–Sat 8pm–4am. Closed Sun & Mon.

Terres à Vin 1 rue du Miroir ☏ 03.88.51.37.20. Excellent boutique wine shop/bar stocking over 2500 different wines from high-quality producers around France, with an emphasis on bio-dynamic wines and *vins naturelles*. There are a variety of snacks to accompany your tipple (glass from €2.50). Daily 10.30am–10pm.

Les Trois Brasseurs 22 rue des Veaux. Buzzing *bierstub*, which brews its own beers. There's a piano bar in the cellar Thurs–Sat from 9.30pm. Open daily till 1am.

Entertainment

Strasbourg usually has lots going on, particularly when it comes to music. Pick up the free monthly magazine *Spectacles à Strasbourg et alentours* (ⓦ www.spectacles -publications.com) for entertainment info and **listings**. **Free concerts** are held regularly in the Parc des Contades and Parc de l'Orangerie (see p.236).

There are theatre, dance and musical **festivals** throughout the summer; with a particular focus on classical music in mid-June, jazz in July, and "contemporary classical" music at the Musica festival (ⓦ www.festivalmusica.org) from mid-September to early October. If you happen to be in town from July to the first week of August don't miss the impressive illumination of the cathedral facade, accompanied by music (10.30pm–1am). At the **Marché de Noël** (late Nov to Dec 24), an increasingly commercial event dating back over 400 years, central Strasbourg is taken over by wooden stalls selling mulled wine, crafts of varying quality and spicy Christmas cookies known as *bredele*.

Listings

Bike rental Vélocation, 10 rue des Bouchers (☏ 03.88.24.05.61, ⓦ www.velocation.net) for €8 per day/€5 half-day.

Boat trips Batorama (☏ 03.88.84.13.13, ⓦ www .batorama.fr) runs cruises on the Ill, which depart from in front of the Palais Rohan (daily: April–Oct every 30min 9.30am–9pm; rest of year at least four sailings). The itinerary includes La Petite France, the Vauban dam, the European Parliament and the Palais de l'Europe. The trip lasts 1hr 10min and costs €8.40 (discounts for students and children).

Buses Eurolines has an office at place d'Austerlitz (☏ 03.90.22.14.60); its international coaches depart from the southern outskirts of the city (tram stop "Couffignal"). Buses to destinations in Alsace leave from the place des Halles.

Car rental Europcar, airport ☏ 08.25.00.41.01, 16 place de la Gare ☏ 08.25.85.74.79; Avis, airport ☏ 08.20.61.17.00, place de la Gare ☏ 08.20.61.16.98; Hertz, 10 bd de Metz by the *gare SNCF* ☏ 03.88.32.57.62.

Cinemas Le Star, 27 rue du Jeu-des-Enfants and Le Star St Exupéry, 18 rue du 22-novembre; L'Odyssée (ⓦ www.cinemaodyssee.com), 3 rue des Francs-Bourgeois, a sumptuous restored cinema with red velvet seats, showing a combination of classic and contemporary films, many in *v.o.*

Health Clinique de la Toussaint, 11 rue de la Toussaint ☏ 03.88.21.75.75.

Internet *Cyber Café L'Utopie*, 21 rue du Fossé des Tanneurs.

Markets Place Broglie hosts a large market of produce and bric-a-brac every Wed & Fri (7am–6pm); there are fruit, vegetable and local produce markets every Tues and Sat am on bd de la Marne and in the place du Vieux-Marché aux Poissons on Sat. The flea market is on Wed and Sat on rue du Vieil-Hôpital (near the cathedral).

Police 32 rue 22-novembre ☏ 03.88.84.13.05.

Post offices 5 av de la Marseillaise and place de la Cathédrale.

Taxis Taxis 13 ☏ 03.88.36.13.13.

The Route des Vins

Flanked to the west by the rising forests of the southern Vosges, which stretch all the way down to Belfort, Alsace's picturesque **Route des Vins** ("Wine Route") follows the foot of the mountains along the western edge of the wide and flat Rhine valley. Beginning in Marlenheim, west of Strasbourg, the *route* snakes its way over 180km to Thann, near Mulhouse, through exquisitely preserved medieval towns and villages characterized by quaint half-timbered houses, narrow cobbled streets and neighbouring ancient ruined castles – testimony to the province's turbulent past. The *route* is blanketed with neat terraces of vines, which produce the region's famous white wines (see box below). Tasting opportunities are plentiful, particularly during the region's countless wine festivals that mainly coincide with the October harvest. To get away from the heavily touristed villages, you can duck into the vines themselves by following various *sentiers vinicoles* (vineyard paths); ask at the local tourist offices for information.

Obernai

Picturesque little **OBERNAI**, on the D422 (or the Strasbourg–Molsheim–Sélestat train line), is the first place most people head for when travelling south from Strasbourg. Miraculously unscathed by the last two world wars, Obernai has retained almost its entire **rampart system**, including no fewer than fifteen towers, along with street after street of carefully maintained medieval houses. Not surprisingly, it gets more than its fair share of visitors.

The **tourist office** is on place du Beffroi (April–June, Sept & Oct daily 9am–noon & 2–6pm; July & Aug daily 9.30am–12.30pm & 2–7pm; Nov–March Mon–Sat 9am–noon & 2–5pm; ℡03.88.95.64.13). **Hotels** include *Le Gouverneur* at 13 rue de Sélestat (℡03.88.95.63.72, ⓦwww.hotellegouverneur.com; ❹), a peaceful sixteenth-century building housing 32 comfortable rooms; showers only, no baths. Slap bang in the centre of town, at 23 place de la Mairie, is *La Diligence*

The wines of Alsace

Despite the long, tall bottles and Germanic names, Alsatian wines are unmistakably French in their ability to complement the region's traditional cuisine. This is white wine country – if you do spot a local red, it will be light-bodied, fresh and often served chilled. Winemakers take advantage of the long, dry autumns to pick extremely ripe grapes producing wines with a little more sweetness than elsewhere in France, but good wines will have a refreshing natural acidity, too. Each of the three main grape varieties listed below can be made with a sweetness level ranging from off-dry right through to *"Sélection des Grains Nobles"* for the most highly-prized dessert wines (*vendanges tardives* being the label for the slightly less sweet late-harvested wines). *Grand Cru* labelled wines come from the best vineyard sites.

Riesling the ultimate thirst-quencher, limey, often peachy, excellent with fish dishes (most obviously trout).

Gewurztraminer Alsace's most aromatic grape, with roses, lychees, honey, spices and all manner of exotic flavours. Try with pungent Munster cheese or rich paté.

Pinot Gris rich, fruity, smoky and more understated than Gewurztraminer. A versatile food wine; try with white meat in creamy sauces and milder cheeses.

Other wines you're likely to come across include the grapey **Muscat**, straightforward **Sylvaner**, and delicate **Pinot Blanc/Auxerrois**, which also forms the base of the region's excellent sparkling **Crémant d'Alsace**. **Pinot Noir** is used for light, fruity reds and rosés.

(☎03.88.95.55.69, ⓦwww.hotel-diligence.com; ❸), with neat rooms above a pleasant *salon de thé*. A smarter option is *Hôtel à la Cour d'Alsace* (☎03.88.95.07.00, ⓦwww.cour-alsace.com; ❼), tucked away next to the rampart walls at 3 rue de Gail; it has a pool, garden terrace, two restaurants and a fancy junior suite (❾). For **food**, you have your fill of some very touristy *winstubs* in the town centre; a particularly popular spot is *La Dime*, 5 rue des Pèlerins (☎03.88.95.54.02; closed Wed; *menus* from €12.60).

Barr

For some reason **BARR**, 6km south of Obernai, is overlooked by mass tourism. Every bit as charming as Obernai, it's easy to while away a couple of hours wandering its twisting cobbled streets, at their busiest during the lively mid-July **wine festival**, when you can taste over two hundred local wines in the town hall. The town makes a good base from which to strike out on the walks and bicycle paths that begin behind the Hôtel de Ville, or there are shorter trails around the local *Grand Cru* vineyards.

To break up the wine and the walking, you might like to drop into **La Folie Marco** (June & Oct Sat & Sun 10am–noon & 2–6pm; July–Sept daily except Tues 10am–noon & 2–6pm; €5) at 30 rue du Docteur-Sultzer, an eighteenth-century house on the outskirts of town along the road from Obernai, which has interesting displays of period furniture.

A good place to stay is *Hôtel Le Manoir* (☎03.88.08.03.40, ⓦwww.hotel-manoir .com; ❻), 11 rue St-Marc. Its light and spacious rooms, furnished with elegant drapes and antiques, are housed in a nineteenth-century winemaker's villa. *Les Hortensias* (☎03.88.58.56.00, ⓦwww.hortensias-hotel.com; ❺) on the other side of town at 19 rue du Docteur Sultzer has a swimming pool, fresh rooms and a cool, contemporary feel, while down-to-earth *Hôtel/Restaurant Maison Rouge* (☎03.88.08.90.40, ⓦwww.maison-rouge-barr.com; ❸) at 1 av du Docteur Marcel Krieg, has comfortable accommodation above a *bierstub* boasting over sixty different types of beer and a restaurant serving excellent *tartes flambées* for €6.90 (closed Wed). If you're under canvas, try the municipal **campsite**, *Les Reflets du Mont Ste-Odile,* 4km north of town at 137 rue de la Vallée (☎03.88.08.02.38, ⓦwww.les-reflets.com; Easter–Nov).

For **food**, there's the *Maison Rouge*, or the *Winstub Le Manoir*, 6 rue Saint Marc, a cosy place serving traditional Alsatian dishes as well as *tartes flambées* to take away (from €9). Anyone with a sweet tooth will find it hard to resist *J Oster*, a superb patisserie and *salon de thé* at 31 rue du Collège, stuffed with glistening strawberry tarts and plump *kugelhopf*.

Mittelbergheim and Andlau

A delightful stop on the Route des Vins, a couple of kilometres south of Barr, is **Mittelbergheim**, a peaches-and-cream cluster of houses lining narrow, undulating streets. The focus of the little village is wine; virtually every other house is a wine cellar offering *dégustations*. If you're to make the most of the *vin* round here, stay over at ⚘ *Hotel Gilg* (☎03.88.08.91.37, ⓦwww.hotel-gilg.com; ❸), an atmospheric old inn with a vertiginous stone staircase spiralling up to fifteen simple rooms with en-suite bathrooms. The restaurant serves good food, such as *choucroute* for €17, as well as more sophisticated dishes like lamb fillet with thyme-infused ratatouille (€25).

Another worthwhile hotel in this area lies in the small village of **ANDLAU** around two kilometres south of Mittelbergheim; the quirky *Zinck* (☎03.88.08.27.30, ⓦwww.zinckhotel.com; ❷) occupies a former *moulin* (windmill) and each room has a different theme, from the 1930s browns and beiges in "Jazzy" to the more traditional "Vigneronne" and the colourful "Zen" suites.

Alsace under the Nazi occupation

After the conclusion of the **Armistice** on June 22, 1940, the Bas-Rhin, Haut Rhin and Moselle *départements* were annexed to the German Reich. Over the next four years, Alsace experienced a sustained programme of **Nazification**: the use of French was prohibited; town, street and personal names were translated into German; children were indoctrinated by the Hitler Youth; and thousands of "undesirables", Jews and "francophiles", were expelled from the region. Most unpalatable to the local population, from August 1942 Hitler imposed **conscription** of all eligible Alsatian men of "German race"; the vast majority of these 130,000 young men – the "*Malgré Nous*" (against our will), as they were known – were sent to fight Stalin's forces on the inhospitable Eastern Front, where more than 40,000 of them perished.

Le Struthof concentration camp

One significant reminder of this painful past lies deep in the forests and hills of the Vosges, over 20km west of Barr – **Le Struthof-Natzwiller concentration camp** (daily: mid-March to mid-April 9am–5pm; mid-April to mid-Oct 9am–6.30pm; mid-Oct to Dec 9am–6.30pm; €6; ⓦwww.struthof.fr). It was the only concentration camp to be built on French soil and, set up shortly after Hitler's occupation of Alsace-Lorraine, it is thought that over 10,000 people died here. The site is almost perversely beautiful, its stepped terraces cut into the hillside giving fantastic views across the Bruche valley. The barbed wire and watchtowers are as they were, though only two of the prisoners' barracks remain, one of which is now a museum. An arson attack on the museum by neo-Nazis in 1976 only served to underline the need for such displays; captions are in French only, but the pictures suffice to tell the story. At the foot of the camp is the crematorium with its ovens still intact, while a couple of kilometres down the road to the west, towards Schirmeck, the Germans built a gas chamber. To the east are the two main granite quarries worked by the internees.

Andlau itself, cradled in a verdant valley, is a charming place, and has a venerable abbey that dates back to 880.

Sélestat

Less touristy than the pretty little villages that surround it, **SÉLESTAT**, midway between Strasbourg and Colmar, is a good base for exploring the most popular section of the Route des Vins.

For a brief period in the late fifteenth and early sixteenth centuries, Sélestat was the intellectual centre of Alsace; its Latin School attracted a group of humanists led by Beatus Rhenanus, whose personal library was one of the most impressive collections of its time. Rhenanus's library is now on display in the **Bibliothèque Humaniste**, housed in the town's former corn exchange (Mon & Wed–Fri 9am–noon & 2–6pm; July & Aug also Sat 9am–noon & 2–5pm, Sun 2–5pm; €4). Alongside Rhenanus's humanist texts, the library holds rare books and manuscripts dating back to the seventh century, including the 1507 *Cosmographiae Introductio*, the first document ever to use the word "America". Sélestat's second museum, the **Maison du Pain** at 8 rue Sel (Tues–Sat 9am–12.30pm & 2–6pm, Sun 9am–12.30pm & 2.30–6pm; €4.60), deals with bread, and the making of it, and while the museum itself isn't particularly remarkable, the enticing bakery on the ground floor makes the best croissants and *pains au chocolat* in town.

It's worth dropping into the town's two churches, the romanesque **Ste-Foy**, much restored since its construction by the monks of Conques and, close by, the attractive Gothic **St-Georges**, which sports spectacularly multicoloured roof tiles and some very beautiful stained glass.

Sélestat's **gare SNCF** is west of the town centre down avenue de la Liberté. The **tourist office** is on boulevard du Général-Leclerc (Sept–June Mon–Fri 9am–noon & 2–5.45pm, Sat 9am–noon & 2–5pm; July & Aug Mon–Fri 9.30am–12.30pm & 1.30–6.30pm, Sat 9am–12.30pm & 2–5pm, Sun and public hols 10.30am–3pm; ☏03.88.58.87.20, ⓦwww.selestat-tourisme.com). If you fancy splashing out on a place to **stay**, try the upmarket *Abbaye de Pommeraie* (☏03.88.92.07.84, ⓦwww.pommeraie.fr; ❽), which has elegant rooms, a refined restaurant and absolutely impeccable service. Another good choice is the friendly *Auberge des Alliés*, 39 rue des Chevaliers (☏03.88.92.09.34, ⓦwww .auberge-des-allies.fr; ❸). There's also a **campsite**, *Les Cigognes* (☏03.88.92.03.98; April–Sept), just south of the centre behind the ramparts. *L'Acoustic* (☏03.88.92.29.40; Mon–Thurs 9am–4pm, Fri & Sat 12.30–10pm) is a dinky organic **café-bar** just by the church of Ste-Foy, which serves tasty snacks and main meals – *plats* around €7, *menus* from €11; on Saturday evenings there are amateur performances ranging from jazz and classical concerts to comedy and drama (*menu* €22 for three courses, plus €5 for the show).

Bergheim

From Mittelbergheim you'll drive 30km through a few medieval villages of varying attractiveness to reach the peaceful walled town of **BERGHEIM**. Stop by for a wander and perhaps a bite to eat with the locals at the diminutive *La Mosaique*; the *plat du jour* is extremely good value (usually around €8), and their house speciality, *matafan* – thick crêpes covered with a bechamel sauce and filled with onions, bacon and cheese – is particularly delicious. Pop over the square to 10 place Walter to fill your bags full of wonderful jams at ⚜*Eglantine de Bergheim* (ⓦwww.bergheim-confitures.com), whose house speciality, and namesake, is a sticky, sweet rosehip jam (*confiture d'eglantine*). A good place to stay the night is the cheerful *La Cour Bailli* at 57 Grand'Rue (☏03.89.73.73.46, ⓦwww.cour-bailli .com; ❹), with studios and rooms housed in a charming lavender-coloured building – there's also a rather incongruous, but welcome, spa. Further up the monetary scale is *Auberge de l'Ill* (☏03.89.71.89.00, ⓦwww.auberge-de-l-ill.com; closed Mon & Tues all day, Feb–March eve only), an expensive hotel-restaurant in the little village of **Illhaeusern**, seven kilometres southeast of Bergheim. Rooms are stylish and pricey (❾, rooms from €290), but it's the three Michelin-starred restaurant that's the star of the show: behind a traditional, half-timbered façade, the restaurant's decor is a modern medley of camouflage carpet, crystal chandeliers and cream-coloured furniture, while the food and wines are pretty spectacular. Expect a fair dent in your bank account, with *plats* starting at €43 and rising to €65 – *menus* are €121 at lunch and €158 at dinner.

Hunawihr

Around 8km southwest of Bergheim lies the beguiling hamlet of **HUNAWIHR**, with its fourteenth-century walled church standing proud amid the green vines. Hunawihr is at the forefront of the Alsatian ecological movement aimed at protecting the stork – the *cigogne* – of the region, and there's a **reserve** for them along with otters (*loutres*) to the east of the village, the **Centre de Réintroduction des Cigognes et des Loutres** (daily: April 10am–12.30pm & 2–5.30pm, Sat & Sun 10am–5.30pm; May & Sept 10am–12.30pm & 2–6pm; June 10am–6pm; July 10am–6.30pm; Aug 10am–7pm and late opening the first three Thurs; call to check show times; €8.50; ☏03.89.73.72.62, ⓦwww.cigogne-loutre.com). Next door you can admire some rather beautiful butterflies in the Jardins des Papillons (April–Sept 10am–6pm; Oct 10am–5pm; €7.50; ⓦwww.jardinsdespapillons.fr).

Riquewihr

An exceptionally well-preserved medieval town a couple of kilometres south of Hunawihr, **RIQUEWIHR** has its fair share of visitors but is still a lovely place to stay a night or two, if only to take advantage of the renowned **restaurant**, *Table du Gourmet* (T03.89.86.54.54, Wwww.jlbrendel.com) run by illustrious chef, Jean-Luc Brendel. *Menus* (from €39) are a sensation for the taste buds; expect adventurous delights such as frog-leg doughnuts and chicken with prawns in a lemon and coconut sauce. Brendel also manages a few beautiful **hotel suites** nearby at 48 rue du Général de Gaulle, sumptuous, elegant rooms with exposed stone walls, wooden beams and enormous four-poster beds (contact details as above; ❸). Next door, at 52 rue du Général de Gaulle, is a cheaper place to stay – the family-run *Le Dolder* (T03.89.47.92.56, Wwww.dolder.fr; ❸) sits above a lively *winstub* that serves traditional food. To distract you from the tempting *dégustations* at wine cellars that dot Riquewihr's cobbled streets, there's a small museum investigating the development of communications – the **Musée de la Communication en Alsace** (daily: April–Oct & Dec 10am–5.30pm; €4.50).

Kaysersburg

Considered one of the most beautiful villages on the Route des Vins, **KAYSERSBURG** suffers from a deluge of summertime visitors, thanks to its pretty Hansel and Gretel houses clustered in chocolate-box fashion around the River Weiss and its

---

Four fabulous Alsace fortresses

Alsace is dotted with medieval fortresses, heirlooms from a quarrelsome past. Here's a rundown of the very best castles in the region:

Bernstein Explore the marvellous ruins of this castle perched 562m up on a hill overlooking the pretty village of Dambach-la-Ville (which has a train station, 1km east of town); it's a 45-minute walk from the village past the chapel of St-Sébastien. Free access.

Haut Koenigsbourg A massive pile of honey-coloured sandstone that sits astride a 757m bluff, this castle dates from the twelfth century. It was heavily restored in the twentieth century under the tenacious management of Kaiser Wilhelm II and is today the fourth most visited monument in France – try to come mid-week or out of season to avoid the crowds. While it's easy to criticise some of the detail of the restoration, it's still a stunning spot with fantastic views on a clear day. Daily: March & Oct 9.45am–4.30pm; April, May & Sept 9.30am–5pm; June, July & Aug 9.30am–6pm; Nov–Feb 9.45am–noon & 1–4.30pm; €7.50; Wwww.haut-koenigsbourg.net.

Château Hohlandsbourg Six kilometres outside Eguisheim, this enormous castle surrounded by massive walls is the largest in the region. It was extensively damaged during the Thirty Years' War but there's still plenty to see, including beautiful gardens. The castle is also a venue for cultural activities, music concerts and children's workshops – check the website for events. July & Aug daily 10am–7pm; April, June & Sept Mon–Sat 2–6pm; May Sat & Sun 11am–6pm; Oct Sat 2–6pm, Sun 11am–6pm; €4.20; Wwww.chateau-hohlandsbourg.com.

Kintzheim Small but wonderful ruined castle built around a cylindrical refuge-tower and located just south of Haut Koenigsbourg (see above). Today Kintzheim is an aviary for birds of prey – the Volerie des Aigles – and puts on magnificent displays of aerial prowess by resident eagles and vultures. March–May & Sept–Nov Mon–Fri demonstrations twice daily, three demonstrations on Sat & Sun; June–Aug three or four demonstrations daily – consult website for demonstration times; €9; Wwww .voleriedesaigles.com.

fortified bridge. Along with a wonderful sixteenth-century altarpiece in its Gothic church, the town's main claim to fame is as the birthplace of Nobel Peace Prize-winner Albert Schweitzer, who founded a leprosy hospital at Lambaréné in French Equatorial Africa. He is honoured with the **Centre Culturel Albert Schweitzer**, 126 rue du Général de Gaulle (April–Nov daily 9am–noon & 2–6pm; €2). The top hotel hereabouts is *Le Chambard* on the same street at nos. 9–13 (T03.89.47.10.17, W lechambard.fr; ❼), with modern rooms decked out in a sleek black and white colour scheme. They also have an inviting pool and spa, a refined restaurant and a more wallet-friendly *winstub*. Best of all is their affiliated restaurant, *Flamme et Co*, at no. 4. In a glitzy space that would seem more appropriate for a nightclub, they've taken the traditional *tarte flambée* and flung it into the twenty-first century: fillet of beef with béarnaise sauce (€14.70), snail and parsley (€14.90) and lemon meringue pie (€8.80) are just some of the mad-cap varieties here.

Colmar

The old centre of **COLMAR**, a fifty-minute train ride south of Strasbourg and lying east of the main Route des Vins villages, is *echt* Alsatian, with picturesque crooked half-timbered and painted houses. As the proud home of Mathias Grünewald's magnificent Issenheim altarpiece, the town is a magnet for tourists all year round.

Arrival and information

From the **gare SNCF** it's a ten-minute walk down avenue de la République to the **tourist office** on place d'Unterlinden (Mon–Sat 9am–noon & 2–6pm; T03.89.20.68.92, W www.ot-colmar.fr). You can get up close to the charming half-timbered houses in La Petite Venise by taking a peaceful **boat trip** with either La Krutenau (Mon–Sat 10am–6.30pm, April–Oct also Sun 10am–5pm; €6; T03.89.41.18.80, E lakrut.resto.jpw@orange.fr) from 1 rue de la Poissonnerie, or with Sweet Narcisse (April–Sept daily 10am–noon & 1.30–7pm; €6; T03.89.41.01.94, W www.sweetnarcisse.com) which has a thirty-minute commentary, from 10 rue de la Herse; English is spoken. **Bicycles** can be rented from Vélo & Oxygen, 6 bd du Champ de Mars (Tues–Sat 8.30am–noon & 2–6pm; €11 per day). **Internet** is available at *Cyber Didim* (Mon–Sat 10am–10pm, Sun 2–10pm; €2.50 per hour), 9 rue du Rempart, above a doner kebab shop.

Accommodation

Accommodation is not overpriced, and there's a wide range of places to stay, including an excellent boutique hotel and a friendly B&B.

Hotels

Chez Leslie 31 rue de Mulhouse
T03.89.79.98.99, W www.chezleslie.com. Great B&B situated in a residential area of Colmar, with easy access to the train station. The hostess, Leslie, couldn't be friendlier and the rooms are bright and spacious, with large, marshallow-soft beds. A generous breakfast buffet is included. Leslie also rents out an apartment for up to four people in Petite Venise (€400 per week). ❹

Le Colombier 7 rue de Turenne
T03.89.23.96.00, W www.hotel-le-colombier.fr. Colmar's only boutique hotel in the heart of the Petite Venise quarter. Modern rooms

are swathed in cool lavender tones and back onto a calm internal courtyard. Large family suites available, too. ❺–❽

St-Martin 38 Grand'Rue T03.89.24.11.51, W www.hotel-saint-martin.com. A riot of flowery wallpaper, flounces and painted headboards, but the hotel couldn't be more central. ❺

Les Têtes 19 rue des Têtes
T03.89.24.43.43, W www.maisondestetes.com. Well-appointed seventeenth-century house with a wonderful facade covered in grimacing faces. The rooms are clad in wood panelling and there's a refined restaurant downstairs (*plats* around €20). ❻

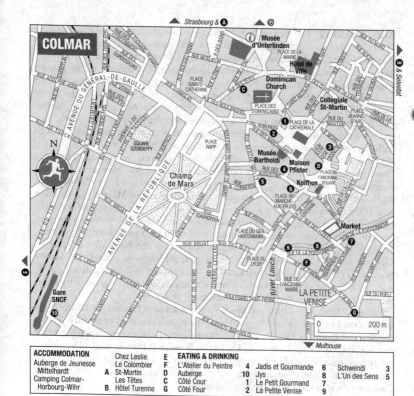

ACCOMMODATION			EATING & DRINKING				
Auberge de Jeunesse Mittelhardt		**A**	Chez Leslie	**E**	L'Atelier du Peintre	**4**	Jadis et Gourmande	**6**	Schwendi	**3**
Camping Colmar-Horbourg-Wihr		**B**	Le Colombier	**F**	Auberge	**10**	Jys	**8**	L'Un des Sens	**5**
			St-Martin	**D**	Côté Cour	**1**	Le Petit Gourmand	**7**		
			Les Têtes	**C**	Côté Four	**2**	La Petite Venise	**9**		
			Hôtel Turenne	**G**						

Hôtel Turenne 10 rte de Bâle ☏03.89.21.58.58, Ⓦwww.turenne.com. Functional, multi-coloured rooms in a jolly little hotel a few metres from Petite Venise. Free wi-fi. ③

Hostel and campsite

Auberge de Jeunesse Mittelhardt 2 rue Pasteur ☏03.89.80.57.39, Ⓔauberge.jeunesse@ville-colmar.com. The town's only youth hostel is perfectly adequate but gets extremely busy in summer. It's 1km from town; take bus #4, #5 or #15 to Pont Rouge. Closed Jan. Dorms (up to 9 beds) €9.30. Breakfast extra.

Camping Colmar-Horbourg-Wihr Rte de Neuf-Brisach ☏03.89.41.15.94, Ⓦwww.campingdelill.com. Inexpensive campsite 2km from Colmar. Take bus #1 from the station, direction "Wihr", stop "Plage de l'Ill". Closed Jan & Feb.

The Town

Colmar's foremost attraction, the **Musée d'Unterlinden** at 1 rue d'Unterlinden, is housed in a former Dominican convent with a peaceful cloistered garden (May–Oct daily 9am–6pm; Nov–April daily except Tues 9am–noon & 2–5pm; closed public hols; €7; Ⓦwww.musee-unterlinden.com). The museum's *pièce de résistance* is the **Issenheim altarpiece**, thought to have been made between 1512 and 1516 for the monastic order of St Anthony at Issenheim, whose members dedicated themselves to caring for those afflicted by ergotism and other nasty skin diseases. The extraordinary painted panels are the work of Mathias Grünewald (1480–1528). The luridly expressive centre panel depicts the Crucifixion: a tortured Christ of exaggerated dimensions turns his outsize hands upwards, fingers splayed in pain, flanked by his pale, fainting mother and saints John and

Mary Magdalene. The face of St Sebastian, on the right wing, is believed to have been modelled on Grünewald's own likeness. The reverse panels depict the annunciation, Christ's resurrection, the nativity and a vivid, flamboyant orchestra of angels, all splendidly bathed in transcendental light. On another set of painted panels, you'll find a truly disturbing representation of the temptation of St Anthony, who is engulfed by a grotesque pack of demons; note the figure afflicted with the alarming symptoms of ergotism. Altarpieces by Martin Schongauer, in the same room as the *Issenheim*, are also worth a quick look, as is the museum's collection of modern paintings, also on the ground floor, which includes some Impressionist works and a couple of Picassos.

A short walk away, the austere **Dominican church** on rue des Serruriers (April–Dec daily 10am–1pm & 3–6pm; €1.50) has some fine glass and a beautiful altarpiece known as *The Virgin in a Bower of Roses*, painted in 1473 by Schongauer. At the other end of the street you reach the **Collégiale St-Martin** (daily except Sun am, 8am–6pm; free) on a busy café-lined square. It's known locally as "the cathedral"; peek in to see its stonework and stained glass. The sixteenth-century **Maison Pfister**, with external painted panels, is on the south side of the church. Frédéric Auguste Bartholdi, the sculptor responsible for New York's Statue of Liberty, was born at 30 rue des Marchands, which now houses the **Musée Bartholdi** (March–Dec daily except Tues 10am–noon & 2–6pm; closed public hols; €4.50). It contains Bartholdi's personal effects and the original designs for the statue, along with sundry Colmarabilia.

Rue des Marchands continues south to the Ancienne Douane or **Koïfhus**, its gaily painted roof tiles loudly proclaiming the town's medieval prosperity. This is the heart of Colmar's Old Town, a short step away from the picturesque quarter down the Grand'Rue known as **La Petite Venise** (Little Venice). The dolly-mixture colours of the old fishing cottages on quai de la Poissonnerie contrast with the much taller, black-and-white, half-timbered tanners' houses on **rue des Tanneurs**, which leads off from the Koïfhus.

Eating and drinking

There's no shortage of places to eat and drink in Colmar but restaurants are often overpriced. A tempting alternative is to gather together a sumptuous picnic from the town's patisseries and charcuteries – La Fromagerie St-Nicolas at 18 rue St-Nicolas is a great place for some delicious local cheeses. If you're after some **wine-tasting**, try La Sommelière (Ⓦlasommeliere.kiubi-web.com), at 19 place de la Cathédrale, which stocks over six hundred different wines, with prices ranging from €5 to over €3000.

L'Atelier du Peintre 1 rue Schongauer ☏03.89.29.51.57. Interesting dishes with influences from the Mediterranean and Scotland (the chef worked in the latter for three years), served up in an attractive restaurant, all lime green and distressed wood. *Plats* could include swordfish fillet with rhubarb confit (€27) and for pudding a crunchy chocolate caramel strudel with peanut ice cream (€9). Lunchtime *menu* from €18. Closed Sun & Mon.

Auberge 7 place de la Gare ☏03.89.23.59.59. Roomy Alsatian brasserie with a relaxed vibe, situated in the *Grand Hôtel Bristol* opposite the train station. *Menus* start at €13.50.

Côté Four, Côté Cour Two restaurants in one – the "Four" (11–13 rue des Serruriers) is the popular sit-in bakery selling baguettes, *bretzels* and

tempting cakes, while behind is the "Cour" (place de la Cathédrale ☏03.89.21.19.18), a large brasserie set round a courtyard – dishes here might include a sticky lemon glazed duck or a creamy vanilla crème brûlée. Both closed Sun & Mon.

Jadis et Gourmande 8 place du Marché-aux-Fruits. Quaint *salon de thé* serving daytime *plats* and a great line in delicious cakes and puddings – the *chocolat gourmand* (hot chocolate with chocolate mousse and a mini chocolate brownie) is great, and intense (€5).

Jys 17 rue de la Poissonnerie ☏03.89.21.53.60. Sitting by the canal with a lovely outdoor terrace, this is one of the top gastronomic restaurants in Colmar. Inside, the decor is cool and contemporary, and the food simply sublime. For pudding, tuck into their fresh strawberry millefeuille with a sweet bergamot cream. Two courses €30, three courses €36. Closed Sun & Mon.

Le Petit Gourmand 9 quai de la Poissonnerie ⊤03.89.41.09.32. Traditional Alsatian cuisine with a degree of finesse and a delightful little terrace overlooking the canal, for which it's advisable to book. *Menu* €26; *baeckoffe* €16.50. Closed Sun eve & Mon.

La Petite Venise 4 rue de la Poissonnerie ⊤03.89.41.72.59. It's like eating dinner in an old Alsatian house here – pots and pans, wooden benches and even an old oven adorn the interior. Alsatian classics as well as other mains like gratin

of cod and prawns with coconut milk (€20). Closed Tues lunch, Thurs & Sun lunch.

Schwendi 23 Grand'Rue ⊤03.89.23.66.26. Exposed wooden beams, tightly packed tables and vintage posters on the wall give this place a warm, convivial feel. The *menu* is varied and good value; salads (from €8), onion soup (€4) and the house speciality, a hearty and deliciously salty potato rösti (€11).

L'Un des Sens 18 rue Berthe-Molly. Excellent *cave à vins*, where you can taste a wide range of wines and nibble on plates of cold meat and cheese (€5–16). Buy the wines you liked at the front from the boutique.

Munster

Some 19km west of Colmar, and accessible by train, the peaceful town of **MUNSTER** owes its existence and its name to a band of Irish monks who founded a successful monastery (monasterium = Munster) here in the seventh century. Today its name is associated with a rich, creamy and exceedingly smelly **cheese**, the crowning glory of many an Alsatian meal. Overlooked by Le Petit Ballon (1272m) and Le Hohneck (1363m), among the highest peaks of the Vosges, the town itself is not as picturesque as the wine villages further east but nevertheless makes a pleasant day-trip from Colmar.

From the train station walk up rue de la Gare and turn right down rue Sébastopol to reach the centre. The **tourist office**, 1 rue du Couvent (Jan–March & Nov–Dec Mon–Fri 10am–noon & 2–5pm, Sat 10am–noon & 2–4pm; April–June & Sept–Oct Mon–Fri 9.30am–noon & 2–6pm, Sat 10am–noon & 2–4pm; July & Aug Mon–Sat 9.30am–12.30pm & 1.30–6.30pm, Sun 10am–12.30pm; ⊤03.89.77.31.80, ⓦwww.la-vallee-de-munster.com), can provide information about hiking in the Munster valley and the *parc régional*, as can the Maison du Parc, 1 cour de l'Abbaye (July–Sept daily except Mon 10am–noon & 2–6pm; Oct–June Mon–Fri 2–6pm; closed public hols; ⊤03.89.77.70.34, ⓦwww.parc-ballons-vosges.fr).

There are plenty of enticing *fromageries* and charcuteries along the main street selling the famous Munster cheese, or you could try the cheerful little *L'Agneau d'Or* (⊤03.89.77.34.08; closed Mon & Tues) at 2 rue St-Grégoire, where you can sample the cheese three ways – traditional, *aux raisins* and grilled. *Plats* are around €20, and *menus* start at €35.

The Route des Crêtes

Above Munster, the main road west to the little town of Gérardmer crosses the mountains by the principal pass, the Col de la Schlucht, where it intersects the "**Route des Crêtes**" (Crest Road), built for strategic purposes during World War I to facilitate the movement of munitions and supplies. It's a spectacular road traversing thick forest and open pasture, and in winter it becomes one long cross-country ski route. Starting in Cernay, 15km west of Mulhouse, it follows the main ridge of the Vosges, including the highest peak of the range, the **Grand Ballon** (1424m), north as far as Ste-Marie-aux-Mines, 20km west of Sélestat. From Munster it's also accessible by a twisting minor road through Hohrodberg, which takes you past beautiful glacial lakes and the eerie World War I battlefield of Linge, where the French and German trenches, once separated by just a few metres, are still clearly visible.

Écomusée d'Alsace and Bioscope

Around 25km south of Colmar, just outside the small village of **Ungersheim**, lie a couple of very worthwhile attractions, particularly if you have children in tow: the fantastic open-air Écomusée d'Alsace, and the nearby science museum, Bioscope. You'll need to have your own wheels to access these, as public transport is non-existent.

Opened in 2007, the **Écomusée d'Alsace** (daily 10am–6pm; July & Aug 10am–7pm; €13 with Bioscope; ⊤03.89.74.44.74, Ⓦ www.ecomusee-alsace .fr) is a successful reconstruction of a typical early twentieth-century Alsatian village – the seventy or so half-timbered huts were dismantled from elsewhere in the region and rebuilt in fields here, using Alsatian building methods. Visitors can wander at will around the farmyard and stables – complete with farm animals – pottery, school, bakery, ironmongers and buzzing apiary. There's even a barber, where brave visitors can treat themselves to a shave and haircut *à l'alsatian*. Enthusiastic staff dressed in traditional Alsatian garb – white aprons, ribboned headdresses and the like – are on site to help explain the ins and outs of the history. Throughout the year, usually on Sundays, there are festivals and various workshops, ranging from pottery to stonemasonry. The only negative is that information signs are all in French or German, but don't let this put you off – there's still plenty to feast your eyes on, and you could easily spend a couple of hours here.

A kilometre west of the Écomusée, the **Bioscope** (€13 with Écomusée; ⊤03.89.62.43.00, Ⓦ www.lebioscope.com) is a lively cross between an adventure park and a science museum, which endeavours to explore the relationship between man and the environment via a series of fun, interactive quizzes, acrobatic displays and theatre. Shows are put on virtually every hour, so you could easily spend a day here with your increasingly environmentally aware offspring.

Mulhouse

A large, sprawling, industrial city 35km south of Colmar, **MULHOUSE** was Swiss until 1798 when, at the peak of its prosperity (founded on printed textiles), it voted to become part of France. Today it bills itself as a "museum town", with at least four that might grab your interest. The city itself isn't very attractive; better to make Colmar or the surrounding villages your base and visit for the day. Mulhouse also happens to be the birthplace of Alfred Dreyfus, the unfortunate Jewish army officer erroneously convicted of espionage in 1894, provoking a national furore (see p.1032).

Arrival and information

The main square, place de la Réunion, is five minutes' walk north of the **gare SNCF**. The main **tourist office** is on the ground floor of the Hôtel de Ville (July, Aug & Dec daily 10am–7pm; Jan–June & Sept–Nov Mon–Sat 10am–6pm, Sun and public hols 10am–noon & 2–6pm; ⊤03.89.66.93.13, Ⓦ www.tourisme -mulhouse.com). There's also a tram; Ⓦ www.solea.info has routes and timetables.

The museums

Close to the *gare SNCF* is the **Musée de l'Impression sur Étoffes**, 14 rue Jean-Jacques-Henner (daily except Mon 10am–noon & 2–6pm; Ⓦ www.musee -impression.com; €7 or €11 for a combined ticket with the missable **Musée du**

Papier-Peint – wallpaper museum – in the village of Rixheim, 6km east; bus #18 direction "Chemin–Vert", stop "Temple"; same hours, but closed Tues Oct–May). Mostly displayed in temporary exhibitions, the museum's vast collection of sumptuous fabrics includes the eighteenth-century Indian and Persian imports that revolutionized the European ready-to-wear market and made Mulhouse a prosperous manufacturing centre. It's worth trying to coincide with one of the daily demonstrations of fabric printing (consult the website). The **Hôtel de Ville** on central place de la Réunion contains a beautifully presented history of the city in the **Musée Historique** (daily except Tues: July & Aug 10am–noon & 2–6.30pm; Sept–June 10am–noon & 2–6pm; free).

Some way to the west of the centre, in the direction of the A36 autoroute, is the **Cité du Train – Musée Français du Chemin de Fer**, 2 rue Alfred-de-Glehn (daily: April–Oct 10am–6pm; Nov–Dec & Feb–March 10am–5pm; Jan closed weekdays pm; €10, combined ticket with Cité de l'Automobile, €17.50; take bus #20 from *gare SNCF* to stop "Anvers"; ⓦwww.citedutrain.com). Slick and inter-active, the museum has impressive railway rolling stock on display, including Napoléon III's aide-de-camp's drawing room and a luxuriously appointed 1926 dining car from the *Golden Arrow*.

A couple of kilometres north of the city centre the **Cité de l'Automobile, Musée National-Collection Schlumpf**, 192 av de Colmar (daily: April–Oct 10am–6pm; Nov–Dec 10am–5pm; Jan closed weekdays am; €10.50, combined ticket with Cité du Train, €17.50; take tram #1 from *gare SNCF* to stop "Musée Auto"; ⓦwww.collection-schlumpf.com), houses an overwhelming collection of over six hundred cars, originally belonging to local brothers Hans and Fritz Schlumpf, who made their fortunes running a nearby spinning mill. Lined up in endless rows, the impeccably preserved vehicles range from the industry's earliest attempts, like the extraordinary wooden-wheeled Jacquot steam "car" of 1878 and the very first attempt at an environmentally friendly, solar-powered car made in 1942 to the 1968 Porsche racers. The highlight is the locally made Bugatti models: dozens of alluringly displayed, glorious racing cars, coupés and limousines, the pride of them being the two Bugatti Royales, out of only seven that were constructed – one of them Ettore Bugatti's own, with bodywork designed by his son. Car enthusiasts will want to spend hours here – those who are less keen can hole up in the spacious **café**.

Lorraine

Lorraine derives its name from the Latin, *Lotharii regnum*, "the kingdom of Lothar", one of the three grandsons of Charlemagne, among whom his empire was divided in 843 AD. Much of the province is a rolling plateau of dull farmland; that said, **Nancy**, the smart former capital, is definitely worth a visit, if only to marvel at its harmoniously proportioned Neoclassical square. North of Nancy, the pleasant present-day capital of **Metz** is justly famed for its magnificent cathedral and new Pompidou-Metz museum.

West of Metz, several sites connected with the province's bloody history make an interesting detour. During World War II, when de Gaulle and the Free French

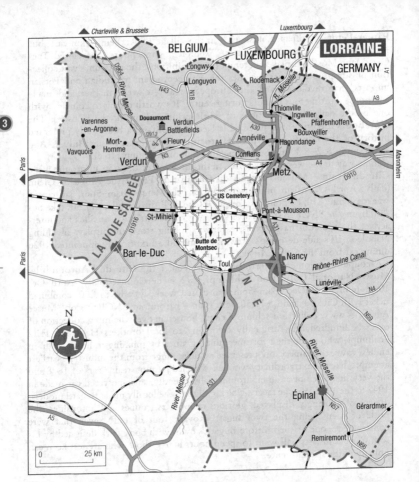

chose Lorraine's double-barred cross as their emblem, they were making a powerful point. For over a thousand years Lorraine had been the principal route of invasion from across the Rhine. Long the cause of disputes between France and the dukes of Burgundy, the duchy of Lorraine was only fully subsumed into France in 1766. It was on the heights above Metz that Napoléon III's troops suffered their humiliating defeat at the hands of the Prussians in 1870, precipitating the annexation of Alsace and the Moselle. During the twentieth century, Lorraine became once again the site of horrific fighting; of all the battles, **Verdun** remains etched in national memory as one of the most costly and protracted conflicts of the First World War. If you intend to visit the poignant **battlefields** surrounding Verdun, you need your own transport. The SNCF network will take you to and between Nancy, Metz and Verdun – but little further.

Nancy

The city of **NANCY**, on the River Meurthe, is justly famed for the magnificent place Stanislas, cited as a paragon of eighteenth-century Neoclassical urban planning and today the finest in France. The city is also home to some impressive examples of Art Nouveau furniture and glassware hailing from the days of the **École de Nancy**, founded at the end of the nineteenth century by glassmaster and furniture maker, Émile Gallé. For its spectacularly grand centre, Nancy has the last of the independent dukes of Lorraine to thank, the dethroned king of Poland and father-in-law of Louis XV, Stanislas Leszczynski. During the twenty-odd years of his office in the mid-eighteenth century, he ordered some of the most successful construction of the period in all France.

Arrival and information

The part of Nancy you're likely to want to see extends no more than a ten- or fifteen-minute walk either side of **rue Stanislas**, the main axis connecting the **gare SNCF** and **place Stanislas**. The **tourist office**, on the south side of place Stanislas in the Hôtel de Ville (April–Oct Mon–Sat 9am–7pm, Sun & public hols 10am–5pm; Nov–March Mon–Sat 9am–6pm, Sun 10am–1pm; ☏ 03.83.35.22.41, ⓦ www.ot-nancy.fr), is well stocked with information about both the city and the region. **Internet** access is available at Cybercafé at 11 rue des Quatre-Églises (Mon 11am–9pm, Tues–Fri 9am–9pm & Sat 11am–9pm; €4.60 per hour). Nancy's main **public transport** hub is place de la République, just around the corner from the train station; the STAN information centre there (Mon–Sat 7am–7.30pm; ⓦ www.reseau-stan.com) has timetables and tickets for local bus and tram routes.

Accommodation

The place to stay in Nancy is the *Grand Hôtel de la Reine* on place Stanislas, but if your budget doesn't quite stretch to that there are a few more wallet-friendly options dotted about town.

Hotels

Grand Hôtel de la Reine 2 place Stanislas ☏ 03.83.35.03.01, ⓦ www.hoteldelareine .com. The grandest hotel in Nancy, situated on the elegant main square. You pay for the location – upwards of €260 for a room. Their restaurant serving à la carte meals and *menus* from €16 is open for lunch only. **❼**

De Guise Rue de Guise, just off Grande-Rue ☏ 03.83.32.24.68, ⓦ www.hoteldeguise .com. An eighteenth-century seigneurial residence, atmospherically furnished with antiques and tucked away on a quiet side street off the lively, restaurant-lined Grande-Rue. **❹**

Jean-Jaurès 14 bd Jean-Jaurès ☏ 03.83.27.74.14, ⓦ www.hotel-jeanjaures.fr. Small, friendly hotel a 5min walk south of the station in a homely, four-storey house; a solid budget option. **❸**

Portes d'Or 21 rue Stanislas ☏ 03.83.35.42.34, ⓦ www.hotel-lesportesdor.com. Located just a few steps from place Stanislas, this is an absolute bargain. Each room is adorned in a different, rather lurid colour – take your pick from lavender, pink, orange and green. **❷**

Des Prélats 56 place du Monseigneur-Ruch ☏ 03.83.30.20.20, ⓦ www.hoteldesprelats .com. Attractive rooms in an airy seventeenth-century house. Eat breakfast in the conservatory. **❻**

Hostel and campsite

Camping de Brabois ☏ 03.83.27.18.28, ⓦ www .camping-brabois.com. Set in a large park near the hostel. To get there take bus #126 direction "Villers Clairlieu", stop "Camping". April to mid-Oct.

Château de Rémicourt 149 rue de Vandoeuvre ☏ 03.83.27.73.67, ⓔ aubergeremicourt@mairie -nancy.fr. Spacious and pretty hostel, set in a sixteenth-century castle, but a fair trek from the centre in the suburb of Villers-lès-Nancy. To get there, take tram #1 from the station to "Le Reclus", then it's a 10min walk; bus #134 or #135 to terminus "Lycée Stanislas", or bus #126 in the direction of "Villers Clairlieu", stop "St-Fiacre". €14.40 including breakfast in 3- or 4-bed dorm; 2-bed private rooms **❶**

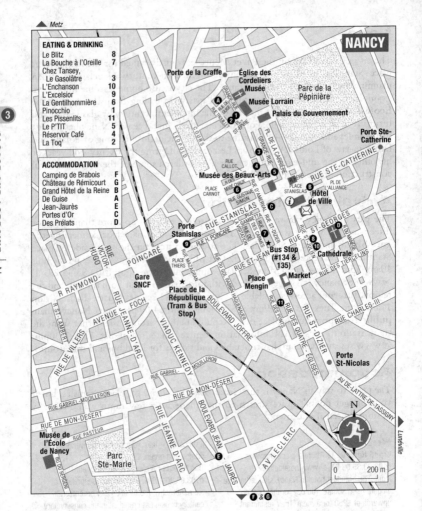

EATING & DRINKING

Le Blitz	8
La Bouche à l'Oreille	7
Chez Tansey, Le Gasolâtre	3
L'Enchanson	10
L'Excelsior	9
La Gentilhommière	6
Pinocchio	1
Les Pissenlits	11
Le P'TIT	5
Réservoir Café	4
La Toq'	2

ACCOMMODATION

Camping de Brabois	F
Château de Rémicourt	G
Grand Hôtel de la Reine	B
De Guise	A
Jean-Jaurès	E
Portes d'Or	C
Des Prélats	D

NANCY

The Town

From the *gare SNCF*, walk through Neoclassical **Porte Stanislas**, straight down rue Stanislas to reach **place Stanislas**. Both this gate and porte St-Catherine opposite are meticulously aligned with place Stanislas's solitary statue – that of the portly **Stanislas Leszczynski**, who commissioned architect Emmanuel Héré to design the square in the 1750s. On the south side of the square stands the imposing **Hôtel de Ville**, its roof topped by a balustrade ornamented with florid urns and winged cupids. Along its walls, lozenge-shaped lanterns dangle from the beaks of gilded cockerels; similar motifs adorn the other buildings bordering the square – look out for the fake, two-dimensional replacements. The square's entrances are enclosed by magnificent wrought-iron gates; the particularly impressive railings on the northern corners frame fountains dominated by statues of Neptune and Amphitrite.

In the corner where rue Stanislas joins the square, the **Musée des Beaux-Arts** (daily except Tues 10am–6pm; €6; ☎03.83.85.30.72) presents some excellent nineteenth- and twentieth-century French art, including a number of beautiful paintings by Émile Friant and Nancy's own Victor Prouvé on the ground floor. The rest of the collection upstairs, encompassing Italian, German, northern European and more French painting, is less interesting. Time is better spent in the basement, where works from Nancy's glass company, Daum, are beautifully lit in black rooms. The layout of the basement follows the shape of fortifications constructed from the fifteenth century through to Vauban's seventeenth-century alterations, discovered during the museum's 1990s renovation. For a glimpse of Daum's contemporary creations you can visit their shop on place Stanislas.

On its north side, place Stanislas opens into the long, tree-lined **place de la Carrière**. Its far end is enclosed by the classical colonnades of the **Palais du Gouvernement**, former residence of the governor of Lorraine. Behind it, housed in the fifteenth-century Palais Ducal is the **Musée Lorrain**, 64 Grande-Rue (daily except Mon 10am–12.30pm & 2–6pm, closed public hols; €4 or €5.50 combined ticket with Musée des Cordeliers). It displays many local treasures – pottery, sculptures, Renaissance painting – along with a worthwhile little annexe showing off a collection of Gallo-Roman skeletons found in the Lorraine region. Back in the main building there's also a room full of superb etchings by the Nancy-born seventeenth-century artist, Jacques Callot, whose concern with social issues, evident in series such as *The Miseries of War*, presaged much nineteenth and twentieth-century art. Next door, in the Église des Cordeliers et Chapelle Ducale, the **Musée des Cordeliers** (same hours as Musée Lorrain; €3.50, €5.50 combined ticket with Musée Lorrain) illustrates the history of rural life in the region. You can access the church and adjacent octagonal chapel, which contain a few tombs belonging to various dukes of Lorraine. On the other side of the Palais du Gouvernement, you can collapse with exhaustion on the green grass of the attractive **Parc de la Pépinière**, which also contains a free zoo with resident macaque monkeys, ponies and a few sheep.

A half-hour walk or a ten-minute bus ride (bus #123; stop "Nancy-Thermal") southwest of the train station, the **Musée de l'École de Nancy**, 36 rue du Sergent-Blandan (Wed–Sun 10.30am–6pm; €6), is housed in a 1909 villa built for the Corbin family, founders of the Magasins Réunis chain of department stores. Even if you're not into Art Nouveau, this collection is exciting. Although not all of it belonged to the Corbins, the museum is arranged as if it were a private house. The furniture is outstanding – all swirling curvilinear forms – and the standards of workmanship are superlative. In particular, there's some extraordinary glassware by Émile Gallé, whose expressive naturalistic motifs and experimental glass-making techniques,

Stanislas Leszczynski

Stanislas Leszczynski, born in the Polish–Ukrainian city of Lemberg (now Lviv) in 1677, lasted just five years as the king of Poland before being forced into exile by Tsar Peter the Great. For the next twenty-odd years he lived on a French pension in northern Alsace, but after fifteen years Stanislas's luck changed when he managed, against all odds, to get his daughter, Marie, betrothed to the 15-year-old king of France, **Louis XV**. Marie was not so fortunate: married by proxy in Strasbourg Cathedral, having never set eyes on the groom, she gave birth to ten children, only to be rejected by Louis, who preferred the company of his mistresses, Madame de Pompadour and Madame du Barry. Bolstered by his daughter's marriage, Stanislas had another spell on the Polish throne from 1733 to 1736, but gave it up in favour of the comfortable dukedom of Barr and Lorraine. He lived out his final years in aristocratic style in the capital, Nancy, which he transformed into one of France's most beautiful towns.

particularly in colouring and etching, brought him international recognition from the 1880s. Some of Gallé's marquetry and furniture is also on display – look out for the stunning *Aube et Crépuscle* (Dawn and Dusk) bed, with its beautifully curvaceous headboard and exotic moths, inlaid with mother of pearl. The **garden**, planted with irises, magnolias, saxifrages and all kinds of plants that inspired the School of Nancy's creations, is also worth exploring.

Eating, drinking and entertainment

There's a cluster of **restaurants** along and around the Grande-Rue, rue des Maréchaux and the rue des Ponts, although some of those on the rue des Maréchaux cater primarily to tourists and are overpriced. Cheaper establishments are based around the covered market on rue St-Dizier and on rue des Quatre-Églises. For a drink, the **cafés** on place Stanislas make great people-watching points. At night, head up the Grande-Rue towards place St-Epvre, with its various lively bars. The tourist office stocks the free listings magazine *Spectacles à Nancy*, while Ⓦ www .nancybynight.com has information on nightlife and entertainment.

Restaurants

La Bouche à l'Oreille 42 rue des Carmes ℡03.83.35.17.17. Hearty Alsatian food using lots of cheese is served in this adorable restaurant covered ceiling to floor in knick-knacks – think old clocks, earthenware pots, faded pictures, wonky lamps and so on. *Tartiflette*, omelettes and crêpes are on the large and varied *menu* (all from €9). Another slightly less festooned branch is at 17 rue Stanislas (℡03.83.37.22.87). Both closed Mon lunch, Sat lunch & Sun.

Chez Tansey, Le Gastrolâtre 23 Grande-Rue ℡03.83.35.51.94. Wonderful little restaurant run by jovial chef, Patrick Tansey. *Plats* are tasty and unusual – try the melt-in-the-mouth scallops served on a rhubarb compote (€28). The high-quality food is reflected in the *menu* price – from €43.50. Booking recommended. Closed Sun, Mon & Tues lunch.

L'Excelsior 50 rue Henri-Poincaré, opposite the train station ℡03.83.35.24.57. A lively *fin-de-siècle* Art Nouveau brasserie; now part of the *Flo* brasserie chain, but managing to retain its good classic food (mains from €15).

La Gentilhommière 29 rue des Maréchaux ℡03.83.32.26.44. One of the trendier establishments on this street of restaurants, with a busy terrace and generous portions, particularly of fish. *Menus* at €22 and €36. Closed Sun & Sat lunch.

Les Pissenlits 25bis rue des Ponts. Real old-fashioned bistro cuisine in a less touristy spot; lunch *menu* €8.40. A sommelier is on hand to help

choose the wine to accompany your meal. Closed Sun & Mon.

La Toq' 1 rue Monseigneur Trouillet, just off place St-Epvre ℡03.83.30.17.20. One of the finest gourmet restaurants in Nancy, serving inventive, seasonal cuisine. The cheapest set *menu*, the "*Retour du marché*", is a very reasonable €20 (2 courses; Tues & Fri lunch only); otherwise, *menus* from €27 and rising to €55. Closed Sun eve, Mon & Wed lunch.

Cafés and bars

Le Blitz 76 rue St-Julien. Relaxed little bar, which comes alive at the weekend with danceable music; plastic seats outside and a youthful clientele. Happy hour 7–9pm. Open until 2am. Closed Sun.

L'Enchanson 9 rue de la Primatiale. Local watering hole that's endearingly shabby and weathered, and popular with Nancy's artier students. They serve over 200 wines – ask the knowledgeable barman for advice about which to pick. Closed Sun & Mon. Closes at 9.30pm.

Pinocchio 9 place St-Epvre. Features attractive wooden interior furnishings and has a busy summer terrace, facing the church of St-Epvre; good for drinks at all hours. Closed Sun.

Le P'TIT 8 Grande-Rue. Tiny, down-to-earth bar, regularly packed with a crowd that spills out onto the street. Open until 2am.

Réservoir Café 13 rue Callot. Leather armchairs and chilled out music add to the cosiness of this fashionable café-bar known for its stiff cocktails. Closed Mon.

Metz

METZ (pronounced "Mess"), the capital of Lorraine, lies on the east bank of the River Moselle, close to the Autoroute de l'Est linking Paris and Strasbourg, and the main Strasbourg–Brussels train line. Today the city has another connection to the capital in the much-awaited and much-lauded satellite branch of the Centre Pompidou. Along with its rather splendid cathedral, a strong dining scene (inspired by the Renaissance writer, Rabelais, who lived here for two years), large and beautiful flower-lined public spaces and riverside setting, the honey-coloured city of Metz is currently something of an undiscovered gem.

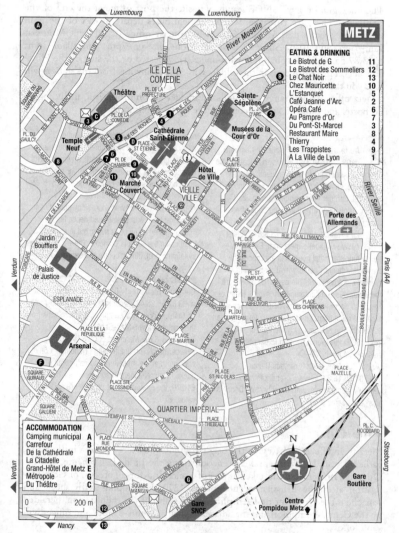

EATING & DRINKING
Le Bistrot de G 11
Le Bistrot des Sommeliers 12
Le Chat Noir 13
Chez Mauricette 10
L'Estanquet 5
Café Jeanne d'Arc 2
Opéra Café 6
Au Pampre d'Or 7
Du Pont-St-Marcel 3
Restaurant Maire 8
Thierry 4
Les Trappistes 9
A La Ville de Lyon 1

ACCOMMODATION
Camping municipal A
Carrefour B
De la Cathédrale D
La Citadelle F
Grand-Hôtel de Metz E
Métropole G
Du Théâtre C

The city's origins go back at least to Roman times, when, as now, it stood astride major trade routes. On the death of Charlemagne it became the capital of Lothar's portion of his empire. By the Middle Ages it had sufficient wealth and strength to proclaim itself an independent republic, which it remained until its absorption into France in 1552. Caught between warring influences, Metz has endured more than its share of historical hand-changing; reluctantly ceded to Germany in 1870, it recovered its liberty at the end of World War I, only to be re-annexed by Hitler until the Liberation.

Arrival, information and accommodation

The huge granite **gare SNCF** stands opposite the **post office** at the end of rue Gambetta. The **gare routière**, where regional buses depart, is east of the train station on avenue de l'Amphithéâtre. The **tourist office** (April–Sept Mon–Sat 9am–7pm, Sun 10am–5pm; Oct–March Mon–Sat 9am–7pm, Sun 10am–3pm; ℡03.87.55.53.76, Ⓦtourisme.mairie-metz.fr) is located by the side of the Hôtel de Ville on place d'Armes in the Old Town. Almost any bus from the station will take you there.

Metz offers a good range of hotels and budget **accommodation**, including an HI hostel and campsite, plus a couple more ritzy establishments.

Hotels

De la Cathédrale 25 place de Chambre ℡03.87.75.00.02, Ⓦwww.hotelcathedrale -metz.fr. Lovely hotel in a seventeenth-century townhouse, wonderfully located opposite the cathedral. Parquet floors, original beams and elegant furnishings give this place bags of character. ➎

La Citadelle 5 av Ney ℡03.87.17.17.17, Ⓦwww.citadelle-metz.com. Extremely stylish four-star hotel housed in an impeccably converted fifteenth-century military building overlooking a peaceful little park. The rooms are chic, spacious and contemporary, with a touch of Japanese decor about them. There's also an excellent restaurant, Le Magasin aux Vivres (closed Sat lunch, Sun & Mon; lunch menus from €43; from €65 in the evening), offering beautifully presented cuisine. ➑–➒

Grand-Hôtel de Metz 3 rue des Clercs ℡03.87.36.16.33, Ⓦwww.grandhotelmetz.com. Centrally located hotel with friendly staff. Decor is fussy but bearable. ➍

Métropole 5 place du Général de Gaulle ℡03.87.66.26.22, Ⓦwww.hotelmetropole-metz .com. A great option near the station with cheerful rooms (some for smokers). Look out for the resident chirping budgies in their cage by the staircase. ➌

Du Théâtre 3 rue du Pont-St-Marcel ℡03.87.31.10.10, Ⓦwww.port-saint-marcel.com. Upmarket hotel with pastel-hued decor, less charming than some of its rivals, but in a pretty location on the Île de la Comédie. There's an outdoor swimming pool, fitness centre and sauna. ➏

Hostel and campsite

Camping municipal Allée de Metz-Plage ℡03.87.68.26.48, Ⓔcampingmetz@mairie-metz .fr. Quiet, very central campsite, a 10min walk from the centre of town. May–Sept.

Carrefour 6 rue Marchant ℡03.87.75.07.26, Ⓔascarrefour@orange.fr. Large HI hostel, a 5min walk north of the museums and cathedral; it's packed with teenagers in summer. Four-bed dorms €16.70; the en-suite private rooms are excellent value. ➊

The City

Metz is, in effect, two towns: the original French quarters of the **Vieille Ville**, gathered round the cathedral and encompassing the Île de la Comédie, and the **Quartier Impérial**, undertaken as part of a once-and-for-all process of Germanification after the Prussian occupation in 1870. Developing with speed and panache is the **Quartier de l'Amphithéâtre**, south of the train station, heralded by the Centre Pompidou and the adjacent sports stadium – shops and offices will soon follow.

Centre Pompidou-Metz

The **Centre Pompidou-Metz** (Mon & Wed 11am–6pm; Thurs & Fri 11am–8pm; Sat 10am–8pm; Sun 10am–6pm; €7, free for under 26-year-olds; ⓦwww .centrepompidou-metz.fr), the first decentralized branch of the Georges Pompidou Centre in Paris, opened with much pomp and ceremony in Metz's *Quartier de l'Amphithéâtre* in May 2010. Designed by architects Shigeru Ban and Jean de Gastines, it's a curious, bright white building resembling a swimming stingray and, with its huge glass windows and wooden scaffolding, is extremely light and inviting. The same spirit reigns here as in Paris: showing off a varying percentage of the Parisian stock, the aim of the museum is to bring modern art to the masses, and judging by the queues awaiting the excellent first exhibition, "What is a masterpiece?", it's working. Expect to spend around two hours here; there's a café, as well as workshops for children (ask at reception for details).

To get here, turn right out of the station and head under the bridge. The museum is a few hundred yards in front of you – you can't really miss it.

Quartier Impérial

The **Quartier Impérial** makes up the southern section of the city, an elegant and stately collection of rose and yellow sandstone buildings, unmistakably Teutonic in style: the **gare SNCF** sets the tone, a vast and splendid granite structure of 1870 in Rhenish Romanesque, a bizarre cross between a Scottish laird's hunting lodge and a dungeon. Its gigantic dimensions reflect the Germans' long-term intention to use it as the hub of their military transport system. It's matched in style by the **post office** opposite and by some imposing bourgeois apartment buildings on the surrounding streets. The whole quarter was meant to serve as a model of superior town planning, in contrast to the squalid Latin hugger-mugger of the old French neighbourhoods further north.

To the northwest of the *gare SNCF*, the place de la République is a major parking area, bounded on the east side by shops and cafés, with army barracks to the south and the formal gardens of the **Esplanade**, overlooking the Moselle, to the west. To the right, as you look down the esplanade from the square, is the handsome **Palais de Justice**. To the left, a gravel drive leads past the old arsenal, now converted into a prestigious concert hall, **L'Arsenal**.

Vieille Ville

From the north side of place de la République, **rue des Clercs** cuts through the attractive, bustling and largely pedestrianized heart of the Vieille Ville. Past the **place St-Jacques**, with its numerous outdoor cafés, you come to the eighteenth-century **place d'Armes**, where the lofty Gothic **Cathédrale Saint-Étienne** towers above the colonnaded classical facade of the Hôtel de Ville. Its nave is the third tallest in France – after Beauvais and Amiens cathedrals – but its best feature is without doubt the stained glass (*vitraux*), both medieval and modern, including windows dating from the thirteenth century. Pride of place, however, goes to **Chagall**'s 1963 masterpiece in the western wall of the north transept, representing the Garden of Eden, while his slightly earlier works in the ambulatory vividly depict Old Testament scenes – Moses and David, Abraham's Sacrifice and Jacob's Dream.

From the cathedral, a short walk up rue du Chanoine Collin brings you to the city's main museum complex, the **Musées de la Cour d'Or**, 2 rue du Haut-Poirier (Mon & Wed–Fri 9am–5pm, Sat & Sun 10am–5pm; €4.60, free first Sun of month; ⓦmusees.metzmetropole.fr), a very large and rather confusingly laid-out treasure house of Gallo-Roman sculpture, which contains the remains of the city's Roman baths, excavated during the museum's extension in the 1930s. Space is also given over to objects dating from the year 1000, including paintings from the fifteenth century as well as artefacts illustrating the city's ancient Jewish community.

Some ten-minutes' walk to the east of the cathedral along En-Fournirue is the popular drinking spot **place St-Louis**, with its Gothic arcades. On the way, wander up the Italianate streets climbing the hill of Sainte-Croix to your left, the legacy of the Lombard bankers who came to run the city's finances in the thirteenth century. It's also worth continuing east down the rue des Allemands to have a look at the Porte des Allemands – a massive, fortified double gate that once barred the eastern entrances to the medieval city.

For the city's most compelling townscape, go down to the riverbank and cross over to the tiny **Île de la Comédie**, dominated by its classical eighteenth-century square and theatre (the oldest in France) and a rather striking Protestant church erected under the German occupation.

Eating, drinking and entertainment

Metz celebrates Lorraine specialities with enthusiasm – you'll find *choucroute*, quiche and plum tarts everywhere, as well as many a *menu rabelais*, involving such earthy delights as pigs' trotters, foie gras and snails. Place de Chambre, beside the cathedral, place St-Jacques and place St-Louis all have their fair share of restaurants and bars. For a picnic or snack, head to the covered market (Tues–Sat 8am–6pm). On Saturday mornings, nearby place Jean Paul II is taken over by the weekly fruit and vegetable market.

If you're after **live music** or **dance**, have a look at the programme at L'Arsenal (℡03.87.39.92.00, Ⓦwww.arsenal-metz.fr). Les Trinitaires at 10–12 rue des Trinitaires (℡03.87.20.03.03, Ⓦwww.lestrinitaires.com) is the place to go for jazz, rock, folk and *chanson* on Thursday, Friday and Saturday nights (from 8.30pm; tickets from €6).

Restaurants

Le Bistrot de G 9 rue du Faisan ℡03.87.37.06.44. Atmospheric Parisian-style bistro serving anything from *tartines au jambon* (€9.50) to an expensive *menu* at €51 involving an intense chocolate fondue. Closed Sun & Mon.

Le Bistrot des Sommeliers 10 rue Pasteur ℡03.87.63.40.20. Affordable *plats du jour* (€9) at this down-to-earth bistro, popular with the locals. *Menu* at €15. Closed Sat eve & Sun.

Le Chat Noir 30 rue Pasteur ℡03.87.56.99.19. Oozing modernity with its sleek black decor and leopard-print chairs, this place does a great line in seafood and has *menus* at €30 and €50. The foie gras with figs, grapefruit and toasted brioche is delicious (€20). Closed Sun eve & Mon eve.

Au Pampre d'Or 31 place de Chambre ℡03.87.74.12.46. Starched tablecloths, smart decor and attentive service at this excellent restaurant with *menus* at €25 and €39. Closed Sun eve.

Du Pont-St-Marcel 1 rue du Pont St-Marcel ℡03.87.30.12.29. On the twee side, admittedly, but this seventeenth-century establishment, where the staff don regional costume, is renowned for its excellent local specialities and fine Moselle wines. *Menus* from €18. Closed Sun eve & Mon.

Restaurant Maire 1 rue du Pont des Morts ℡03.87.32.43.12. The decor here may be fussy but this is one of Metz's top gastro restaurants, with a lovely location overlooking the inky waters of the River Moselle. *Menus* start at €31.

Thierry 5 rue des Piques ℡03.87.74.01.23. Delicious and adventurous fusion cuisine – you could happen upon North African influences one day, Carribbean the next. The pineapple, apple and banana crumble is unusual but very moreish. *Menus* from €23.50. Closed Sun & Wed.

À La Ville de Lyon 7 rue des Piques ℡03.87.36.07.01. This atmospheric restaurant in a vaulted building is tucked away beneath the shadow of the cathedral and, as the name suggests, specialises in recipes from Lyon, so expect hearty meat dishes such as pigeon confit with celeriac mousse. *Menus* are expensive, from €62. Closed Sun eve & Mon.

Cafés and bars

Chez Mauricette Marché couvert, place de la Cathédrale. Serves vast sandwiches, made with the finest local cheese and charcuterie on crusty rustic bread; eat in or take away from €2.

L'Estanquet 27 rue des Roches. Friendly riverside bar open daily with live music at weekends and lots of outside seating in summer, serving snacks from €7.

Café Jeanne d'Arc Place Jeanne-d'Arc. Medieval beams and frescoes inside, and an attractive terrace centred around a trickling fountain. An ideal spot to catch one of the free jazz concerts which

take place in the square every Thursday evening in summer. Closed Sun.

Opéra Café 39 place de Chambre. One of the most popular drinking spots on this lively square – it stays open till late (Mon–Thurs 10–2am; Fri & Sat 10–3am; Sun 5pm–midnight).

Les Trappistes 20 place de Chambre. Charming bar with outside seating in a prime people-watching spot. Closed Sun.

Verdun and the battlefields

VERDUN lies in a bend of the River Meuse, some 70km west of Metz. Of no great interest in itself, what makes this sleepy provincial town remarkable is its association with the ghastly battle that took place on the bleak uplands to the north between 1916 and 1918. In 1916, aiming to break the stalemate of trench warfare, the German General Erich von Falkenhayn chose Verdun as the target for an offensive that ranked among the most devastating ever launched in the annals of war. His troops advanced to within 5km of Verdun, but never captured the town. Gradually the French clawed back the lost ground, but final victory came only in the last months of the war with the aid of US troops. The price was high: hundreds of thousands of men died on both sides. To this day, memorials in every village, hamlet and town of France are inscribed with the names of men slaughtered at Verdun.

Arrival, information and accommodation

With a skeletal timetable from both Metz and Paris, Verdun's **gare SNCF**, on avenue Garibaldi, is poorly served. The official **tourist office** (Jan, Feb & Dec Mon–Sat 10am–12.30pm & 2–5pm, Sun & public hols 10am–12.30pm; March–June & Sept–Nov Mon–Sat 9.30am–12.30pm & 1.30–6pm, Sun & public hols 10am–noon & 2.30–5pm; July & Aug Mon–Sat 9am–7pm, Sun & public hols 10am–noon & 2–6pm; ☎03.29.84.55.55, Ⓦwww.tourisme-verdun.fr) lies just across the River Meuse from the Porte Chaussée and is well stocked with free information on the battlefields. Opposite, the Maison du Tourisme (☎03.29.86.14.18, Ⓦwww.verdun-tourisme.com) runs a variety of guided minibus **tours** (May–Sept; booking advised; €29–55 depending on the tour) around some of the battlefields, memorials and forts. The Maison also sells a **Pass Musées** (€18.50 or €13.50, valid for all of the below except the Citadelle), which allows discounted entry to the Citadelle, Fort de Vaux, Fort de Douaumont, Ossuaire de Douaumont and the Mémorial de Verdun.

A lack of decent, good-value **accommodation** in Verdun means it's best to visit just for the day, as there's much more to choose from in Metz or Nancy. However, if you're determined to stay, head for the simple family-run *Hôtel Montaulbain*, 4 rue de la Vieille-Prison (☎03.29.86.00.47; ➋) or alternatively try the *Auberge de Jeunesse* (☎03.29.86.28.28, Ⓔverdun@fuaj.org; closed Jan), between the cathedral and Centre Mondial (4, 5, 6 or 12-bed dorms €17.20, including breakfast).

The Town

Perhaps surprisingly, given the pounding it received during the course of two world wars, Verdun's centre is not entirely unattractive. Memorials to the town's unfortunate history aside, however, there's not a vast amount to see or do. Near the railway station, the **Rodin memorial**, a disturbing statue of winged Victory, stands beside a handsome eighteenth-century gateway at the northern end of rue St-Paul where it joins avenue Garibaldi. Nearby, a simple engraving lists all the years between 450 and 1916 that Verdun has been involved in conflict. The fourteenth-century **Porte Chaussée** guards the river-crossing in the middle of town. Beyond it, further along rue Mazel, a flight of steps climbs up to the **Monument de la Victoire**, where a helmeted warrior leans on his sword in commemoration of the 1916 battle, while in the crypt below a roll is kept of all the soldiers, French and American, who took part.

The rue de la Belle Vierge leads round to the **Cathedral of Notre-Dame**, whose outward characteristics are Gothic; its earlier Romanesque origins were only uncovered by shell damage in 1916. The elegant **bishop's palace** behind it has been converted into the **Centre Mondial de la Paix et des Droits de l'Homme** (Tues–Sun 9.30am–noon & 2–6pm; July & Aug 9.30am–7pm; €5), hosting exhibitions on themes such as peacekeeping and human rights.

Rue de Ru, the continuation of rue Mazel, takes you to the underground galleries of the **Citadelle** (daily: Feb 10am–noon & 2–5pm; March, Oct & Nov 9.30am–5.30am; April–June & Sept 9am–6pm; July & Aug 9am–7pm; Dec 10am–12.30pm & 2–5pm; €6), used as shelter for thousands of soldiers during the battle. The Unknown Soldier, whose remains now lie under the Arc de Triomphe in Paris, was chosen from among the dead who lie here.

Eating

You shouldn't have trouble finding somewhere to **eat**: there are plenty of cafés along the river. A good bet is *Le Clapier* (T03.29.86.20.14; closed Sun & Mon) at 34 rue des Gros-Degrés, a quaint little restaurant serving traditional *plats* such as brie tart from €9 and *menus* from €11.90.

The battlefields

The **Battle of Verdun** opened on the morning of February 21, 1916, with a German artillery barrage that lasted ten hours and expended two million shells. The battle concentrated on the forts of Vaux and Douaumont, which the French had built after the 1870 Franco–Prussian War. By the time the main battle ended ten months later, nine villages had been pounded into oblivion; not a single trace of them is detectable in aerial photos taken at the time.

The most visited part of the battlefield extends along the hills north of Verdun, but the fighting also spread to the west of the Meuse, to the hills of Mort-Homme and Hill 304, to Vauquois and the Argonne, and south along the Meuse to St-Mihiel, where the Germans held an important salient until dislodged by US forces in 1918. Unless you take an organised tour, the only viable way to explore the area is with your own transport. The main sights are reached via two minor roads that snake through the battlefields, forming a crossroads northeast of Verdun: the D913 and D112.

The monument to André Maginot and the Fort de Souville

The D913 branches left from the main N3 to Metz, 5km east of Verdun; the D112 leaves the same N3 opposite the Cimetière du Faubourg-Pavé on the eastern outskirts of Verdun and is soon enclosed by gloomy conifer plantations.

If you take the D112, on the right you pass a **monument to André Maginot**, later French Minister of War, who was wounded in the battle. Shortly afterwards, a sign points out a forest ride to the **Fort de Souville**, the furthest point of the

German advance in 1916. The site is not on the main tourist beat, and is a very moving, if rather frightening, twenty-minute walk over ground absolutely shattered by artillery fire, with pools of black water standing in the now grassy shell-holes. The fort itself lies half-hidden among the scrub, the armoured gun turrets still louring in their pits. A little way beyond the fort, where the D112 intersects the D913, a **stone lion** marks the spot at which the German advance was checked. To the left the D913 continues to Fleury, 1km from the crossroads, and on to Douaumont, before curling back round to the D964.

Fleury and the Fort de Vaux

The full horror of the battle is graphically documented at **FLEURY**, in the **Memorial de Verdun** (daily: Feb & March 9am–noon & 2–6pm; April to mid-Nov 9am–6pm; mid-Nov to mid-Dec 9am–noon & 2–6pm; €7; ⓦwww .memorial-de-verdun.fr), where, alongside contemporary newsreels and photos, a section of the shell-torn terrain that was once the village of Fleury has been reconstructed as the battle left it.

Another major monument is the **Fort de Vaux**, 4km east of Fleury (daily: Feb, March, Oct & Nov 10am–5pm; April 10am–5.30pm; May–Aug 10am–6.30pm; Sept 10am–5.30pm; Dec 10am–4.30pm; €3). After six days' hand-to-hand combat in the gas-filled tunnels, the French garrison was left with no alternative but to surrender. On the exterior wall, a plaque commemorates the last messenger pigeon sent to the command post in Verdun asking, in vain, for reinforcements. Having delivered its message, the pigeon expired, poisoned by the gas-filled air above the battlefield. It was posthumously awarded the Légion d'Honneur.

Douaumont

The principal memorial to the carnage stands in the middle of the battlefield a short distance along the D913 beyond Fleury. The **Ossuaire de Douaumont** (daily: Feb 2pm–5pm; March & Oct 9am–noon & 2–5.30pm; April 9am–6pm; May–Aug 9am–6.30pm; Sept 9am–noon & 2–6pm; Nov 9am–noon & 2–5pm; Dec 2–5pm; €3.50) is a vast and surreal structure, with a central tower shaped like a projectile aimed at the heavens. Its vaults contain the bones of thousands upon thousands of unidentified soldiers, some of them visible through windows set in the base of the building. When the battle ended in 1918, the ground was covered in fragments of corpses; 120,000 French bodies were identified, perhaps a third of the total killed. Across the road, a **cemetery** contains the graves of 15,000 men, including Muslims of the French colonial regiments while a nearby wall, beneath, an eerily tree-less ridge top, commemorates the Jewish dead.

St-Mihiel and the Voie Sacrée

As early as 1914, the Germans captured the town of **St-Mihiel** on the River Meuse to the south, which gave them control of the main supply route into Verdun. The only route left open to the French was the N35 (now downgraded to the D1916, winding north from Bar-le-Duc over the open hills and wheat fields. In memory of all those who kept the supplies going, the road is called **La Voie Sacrée** (The Sacred Way) and marked with milestones capped with the helmet of the *poilu* (the slang term for infantryman). In St-Mihiel itself, the **Église St-Michel** contains the **Sépulcre** or *Entombment of Christ*, by local sculptor **Ligier Richier** – a set of thirteen stone figures, carved in the mid-sixteenth century and regarded as one of the masterpieces of the French Renaissance. Just beyond the town to the east, on the Butte de Montsec, is a **memorial** to the Americans who died here in 1918 and a US **cemetery** at Thiancourt on the main road.

The **Fort de Douaumont** (daily: Feb & March 10am–5pm; April 10am–6pm; May–Aug 10am–6.30pm; Sept 10am–6pm; Oct 10am–5.30pm; Nov & Dec 10am–5pm; €3) is 900m down the road from the cemetery. Completed in 1912, it was the strongest of the 38 forts built to defend Verdun. Inexplicably, however, the armament of these forts was greatly reduced in 1915, and when the Germans attacked in 1916, twenty men were enough to overrun the garrison. The fort is on three levels and its claustrophobic, dungeon-like galleries are hung with stalactites. The Germans held the fort for eight months while under continuous siege, housing three thousand men in these cramped, unventilated quarters, infested with fleas and lice and plagued by rats that attacked the sleeping and the dead indiscriminately.

Travel details

Trains

Barr to: Obernai (hourly; 14 min); Sélestat (10 daily; 25min); Strasbourg (14 daily; 40min).
Colmar to: Mulhouse (every 30min; 20min); Munster (every 30min; 25min); Sélestat (every 30min; 11min); Strasbourg (every 30min; 35–45min).
Dambach-la-Ville to: Obernai (10 daily; 20min); Sélestat (10 daily; 10min); Strasbourg (10 daily; 1hr).
Metz to: Luxembourg (every 30min; 55min); Nancy (hourly; 40min–1hr); Paris-Est (TGV 7 daily; 1hr 25min); Strasbourg (every 1–2hr; 1hr 30–50min; Verdun (2 daily; 1hr 15min).
Mulhouse to: Basel (every 30min; 20min); Belfort (every 1–2hr; 35min); Sélestat (every 30min–hourly; 30min); Strasbourg (every 30–40min; 50min).
Nancy to: Metz (every 30min; 35min–1hr); Paris-Est (TGV 6 daily; 1hr 30min); Strasbourg (hourly; 1hr 20min).
Obernai to: Rosheim (hourly; 7min); Sélestat (10 daily; 30min); Strasbourg (every 30min; 30min).
Sélestat to: Barr (10 daily; 30min); Obernai (10 daily; 25min); Rosheim (10 daily; 45min); Strasbourg (every 40min; 20min).

Strasbourg to: Barr (14 daily; 45min); Basel (hourly; 1hr 15min); Colmar (frequent; 30–50min); Dambach-la-Ville (10 daily; 1hr); Ingwiller (hourly; 30min); Lille (TGV 3 daily; 3hr 40min); Lyon (5 daily; 5hr 30min); Metz (every 1–2hr; 1hr 30–50min); Mulhouse (every 30–40min; 50min); Nancy (every 1–2hr; 1hr 20min); Nantes (TGV 1 daily; 5hr 15min); Obernai (frequent; 40min); Paris-Est (TGV hourly; 2hr 20min); Sélestat (10 daily; 20min).
Verdun to: Metz (2 daily; 1hr 20min).

Buses

Colmar to: Bergheim (5 daily; 40min); Freiburg, Germany (11 daily; 1hr 20min); Illhaeusern (7 daily; 25min); Mulhouse (4 daily; 1hr 20min); Munster (hourly; 30min); Ribeauvillé (7 daily; 30min); Riquewihr (every 1–2hr; 30min).
Dambach-la-Ville to: Sélestat (4 daily; 25min).
Metz to: Verdun (4 daily Mon–Fri; 1hr 30min).
Mulhouse to: Freiburg (2 daily; 1hr 30min).
Sélestat to: Dambach-la-Ville (4 daily; 25min); Ribeauvillé (5 daily; 30min).
Strasbourg to: Obernai (every 30min; 50min).

Normandy

CHAPTER 4 # Highlights

* **Rouen** This fine old medieval city would still seem familiar to Joan of Arc, whose life came to a tragic end in its main square. **See p.275**

* **Château Gaillard** Richard the Lionheart's sturdy fortress commands superb views of the River Seine. **See p.283**

* **Giverny** Claude Monet's house and garden remain just as he left them. **See p.283**

* **The Bayeux Tapestry** One of the world's most extraordinary historical documents, embroidering the saga of William the Conqueror in every colourful detail. **See p.293**

* **The war cemeteries** Memories of D-Day abound in Normandy, but nowhere more so than in the American cemetery at Colleville-sur-Mer. **See p.297**

* **Mont St-Michel** Second only to the Eiffel Tower as France's best-loved landmark, the *merveille* of Mont St-Michel is a magnificent spectacle. **See p.304**

* **The Pays d'Auge** With luscious meadows and half-timbered farmhouses, the Pays d'Auge is a picture-perfect home for Camembert and other legendary cheeses. **See p.308**

▲ Cathédrale de Notre-Dame, Rouen

Normandy

Though firmly incorporated into the French mainstream, the seaboard province of **Normandy** has a history of prosperous independence as one of the crucial powers of medieval Europe. Colonized by Scandinavian Vikings (or Norsemen) from the ninth century onwards, it colonized in turn during the eleventh and twelfth centuries, with military expeditions conquering not only England but as far afield as Sicily and areas of the Near East. Later, as part of France, it was instrumental in the settlement of Canada.

Normandy has always had large ports: **Rouen**, on the Seine, is the nearest navigable point to Paris, while **Dieppe**, **Le Havre** and **Cherbourg** have important transatlantic trade. Inland, it is overwhelmingly agricultural – a fertile belt of tranquil pastureland, where the chief interest for most visitors will be the groaning restaurant tables of regions such as the **Pays d'Auge**. Significant portions of the coast are overdeveloped, whether because of industry, as with the huge sprawl of Le Havre, or tourism – during the nineteenth century, the last French emperor created a "Norman Riviera" around **Trouville** and **Deauville**, and an air of pretension still hangs about their elegant promenades. However, more ancient harbours such as **Honfleur** and **Barfleur** remain irresistible, and numerous seaside villages lack both crowds and affectations. The banks of the Seine, too, hold several delightful little communities.

Normandy also boasts extraordinary Romanesque and Gothic architectural treasures, although only the much-restored capital, Rouen, retains a complete medieval centre. Elsewhere, the attractions are more often single buildings than entire towns. Most famous of all is the spectacular *merveille* on the island of **Mont St-Michel**, but there are also the monasteries at **Jumièges** and **Caen**, the cathedrals of **Bayeux** and **Coutances**, and Richard the Lionheart's castle above the Seine at **Les Andelys**. In addition, **Bayeux** has its vivid and astonishing tapestry, while more recent creations include Monet's garden at **Giverny**. Furthermore,

Transport in Normandy

The main towns and cities of Normandy are well served by **rail links**, though many routes in Haute Normandie require passengers to change at Rouen, and services are much less frequent at weekends. **Bus services** vary by *département*: by far the best served is Calvados, where Bus Verts (ⓦ www.busverts.fr), for example, link Caen to the D-Day beaches, and Honfleur to Le Havre. To explore the countryside, you'll need a **car**; bus services to rural areas such as villages in the Pays d'Auge are at best infrequent, more likely non-existent. A car also makes it much easier to explore the coast, although tours from Bayeux and Caen make a good alternative for the D-Day beaches.

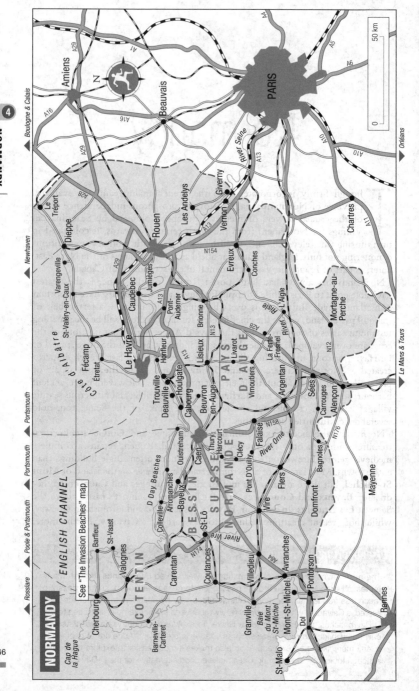

NORMANDY

ENGLISH CHANNEL

50 km

N

PARIS

Amiens

Beauvais

Rouen

Le Havre

Caen

Cherbourg

Rennes

Chartres

Évreux

Alençon

See "The Invasion Beaches" map

Côte d'Albâtre

COTENTIN

BESSIN

SUISSE NORMANDE

PAYS D'AUGE

◀ Rosslare   ◀ Poole & Portsmouth   ◀ Portsmouth   ◀ Portsmouth   ◀ Newhaven   ◀ Boulogne & Calais

▶ Le Mans & Tours

▶ Orléans

Normandy's vernacular architecture makes it well worth exploring inland – rural back roads are lined with splendid centuries-old half-timbered manor houses. It's remarkable how much has survived – or, less surprisingly, been restored – since the Allied landings in 1944 and the subsequent **Battle of Normandy**, which has its own legacy in a series of war museums, memorials and cemeteries.

To the French, at least, the essence of Normandy is its produce. The land of Camembert and Calvados, cider and seafood, and butter- and cream-based cuisine has a proud disdain for most things *nouvelle*. Economically, however, the richness of the dairy pastures has been Normandy's downfall in recent years. EU milk quotas have liquidated many small farms, and stringent regulations have forced many small-scale traditional cheese factories to close. Parts of inland Normandy are now among the most depressed in the whole country, and in the forested areas to the south, where life has never been easy, things have not improved.

Seine Maritime

The *département* of Seine Maritime comprises three distinct sections: Normandy's dramatic **northern coastline**, home not only to major ports like Dieppe and Le Havre but also to such delightful resorts as **Étretat**; the meandering course of the **River Seine**, where unchanged villages stand both up- and downstream of the provincial capital of Rouen; and the flat, chalky **Caux plateau**, which makes for pleasant cycling country but holds little of note to detain visitors.

Dieppe in particular offers a much more appealing introduction to France than its counterparts further north in Picardy, and with the impressive white cliffs of the aptly named **Côte d'Albâtre** (Alabaster Coast) stretching to either side it makes a good base for a long stay. The most direct route to Rouen from here is simply to head due south, but it's well worth tracing the shore all the way west to **Le Havre**, and then following the Seine inland.

Driving along the D982 on the northern bank of the Seine, you'll often find your course paralleled by mighty container ships out on the water. Potential stops en route include the medieval abbey of **Jumièges**, but **Rouen** itself is the prime destination, its association with the execution of Joan of Arc the most compelling episode in its fascinating history. Further upstream, Monet's wonderful house and garden at **Giverny** and the English frontier stronghold of Château Gaillard at **Les Andelys** also justify taking a slow route into Paris.

Dieppe

Squeezed between high cliff headlands, **DIEPPE** is an enjoyably small-scale port that used to be more of a resort. During the nineteenth century, Parisians came here by train to take the sea air, promenading along the front while the English indulged in the peculiar pastime of swimming.

Though ferry services have diminished in recent years, Dieppe remains a nice little place, and you won't regret spending an afternoon or evening here. With kids in tow, the aquariums of the **Cité de la Mer** and the strip of pebble beach are the

The food of Normandy

The **food of Normandy** owes its most distinctive characteristic – its gut-bursting, heart-pounding richness – to the lush orchards and dairy herds of its agricultural heartland, especially the area southeast of Caen known as the Pays d'Auge. Menus abound in **meat** such as veal (*veau*) cooked in *vallée d'Auge* style, which consists largely of the profligate addition of **cream** and **butter**. Many dishes also feature orchard fruit, either in its natural state or in successively more alcoholic forms – either as apple or pear cider, or perhaps further distilled to produce brandies.

Normans relish blood and guts. In addition to gamier meat and fowl such as rabbit and duck (a speciality in Rouen, where the birds are strangled to ensure that all their blood gets into the sauce), they enjoy such intestinal preparations as *andouilles*, the sausages known in English as chitterlings, and *tripes*, stewed for hours *à la mode de Caen*. A full blowout at a country restaurant will also traditionally entail one or two pauses between courses for the *trou normand*: a glass of the apple brandy Calvados to let you catch your breath before struggling on with the feast.

Normandy's long coastline ensures that it is also a wonderful region for **seafood**. Many of the larger ports and resorts have long waterfront lines of restaurants competing for attention, each with its "*copieuse*" *assiette de fruits de mer*. **Honfleur** is probably the most enjoyable, but **Dieppe**, **Étretat** and **Cherbourg** also offer endless eating opportunities. The menus tend to be much the same as those on offer in Brittany, if perhaps slightly more expensive.

The most famous products of Normandy's meadow-munching cows are, of course, their **cheeses**. Cheese-making in the Pays d'Auge started in the monasteries during the Dark Ages. By the eleventh century the local products were already well defined; in 1236, the *Roman de la Rose* referred to Angelot cheese, identified with a small coin depicting a young angel killing a dragon. The principal modern varieties began to emerge in the seventeenth century – **Pont l'Evêque**, which is square with a washed crust, soft but not runny, and **Livarot**, which is round, thick and firm, and has a stronger flavour. Although Marie Herel is generally credited with having invented **Camembert** in the 1790s, a smaller and stodgier version of that cheese had already existed for some time. A priest fleeing the Revolution stayed in Madame Herel's farmhouse at Camembert, and suggested modifications in her cheese-making in line with the techniques used to manufacture Brie de Meaux – a slower process, gentler on the curd and with more thorough drainage. The rich full cheese thus created was an instant success in the market at Vimoutiers, and the development of the railways (and the invention of the chipboard cheesebox in 1880) helped to give it a worldwide popularity.

obvious attractions; otherwise, you could settle for admiring the cliffs and the castle as you stroll the seafront lawns.

Arrival and information

The only **ferry** services between Dieppe's **gare maritime**, east of the centre, and Newhaven in England, are the four-hour crossings operated by Transmanche Ferries, using conventional vessels (2 daily; ☎08.00.65.01.00, ⓦwww.transmancheferries.com). Trains to Rouen and Paris leave from Dieppe's **gare SNCF**, 500m south of the tourist office, on boulevard Clemenceau; buses set off along the coast from the **gare routière** alongside.

Dieppe's **tourist office** (May, June & Sept Mon–Sat 9am–1pm & 2–6pm, Sun 10am–1pm & 2–5pm; July & Aug Mon–Sat 9am–7pm, Sun 10am–1pm & 2–5pm; Oct–April Mon–Sat 9am–noon & 2–6pm; ☎02.32.14.40.60, ⓦwww.dieppetourisme.com) is on the pont Ango, which separates the ferry harbour from the pleasure port. **Bicycles** can be rented cheaply from Vélo Service, just across the bridge (☏06.24.56.06.27). **Internet access** is available at the main **post office**, 2 bd Maréchal-Joffre (Mon–Fri 8am–6pm, Sat 8am–12.30pm; ☏02.35.04.70.14).

Accommodation

Dieppe has plenty of **hotels**, with the more expensive ones concentrated along the seafront, which is among the quietest areas of town.

Les Arcades de la Bourse 1–3 arcades de la Bourse ☏02.35.84.14.12, ⓦlesarcades.fr. Long-established central hotel under the arcades facing the port; you couldn't ask for a better location. Cheaper rooms face the street. Restaurant with full, good-value *menus* from €18. ❸

Camping Vitamin Chemin des Vertus ☏02.35.82.11.11, ⓦwww.camping-vitamin.com. Three-star site, well south of town in an unremarkable setting in St-Aubin-sur-Scie. It's really only convenient for motorists, even if it is served by bus #2. April to mid-Oct.

Grand Duquesne 15 place St-Jacques ☏02.32.14.61.10, ⓦaugrandduquesne.free.fr.

This small, central hotel offers 12 slightly old-fashioned plain rooms at bargain rates, and good food in the downstairs restaurant. ❷

Manoir d'Archelles Rte de Neufchâtel, Arques-La-Bataille ☏02.32.83.40.51, ⓦwww.manoir-darchelles.fr. Simple rooms, including some large family rooms, in an eccentric old château set in gorgeous gardens, 6km southeast of central Dieppe; restaurant next door. ❹

La Plage 20 bd de Verdun ☏02.35.84.18.28, ⓦwww.plagehotel.fr.st. Seafront hotel with something to suit all budgets, from the upmarket sea-view ones to smaller but perfectly pleasant courtyard-facing doubles. No restaurant. ❸–❺

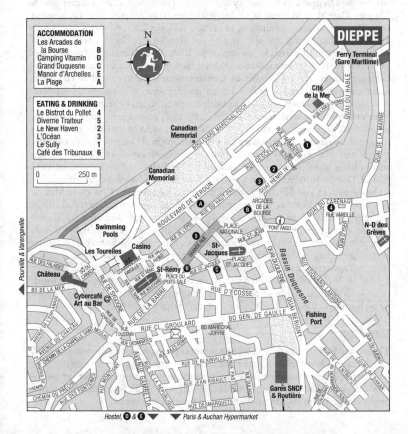

ACCOMMODATION
Les Arcades de la Bourse	B
Camping Vitamin	D
Grand Duquesne	C
Manoir d'Archelles	E
La Plage	A

EATING & DRINKING
Le Bistrot du Pollet	4
Diverne Traiteur	5
Le New Haven	2
L'Océan	3
Le Sully	1
Café des Tribunaux	6

DIEPPE

The Town

Modern Dieppe is laid out along the three axes dictated by its eighteenth-century town planners. The **boulevard de Verdun** runs for over a kilometre along the seafront, from the fifteenth-century castle in the west to the port entrance, and passes the Casino, along with the grandest and oldest hotels. A large area near the Casino is taken up by "Les Bains", a massive complex of indoor and outdoor **swimming pools**, along with a sauna, Turkish bath and fitness facilities (hours vary enormously; pool access €5.90; ☎ 02.32.82.80.90, ⓦ vert-marine.com /les-bains-dieppe-76. A short way inland, parallel to the seafront, is the **rue de la Barre** and its pedestrianized continuation, the Grande Rue. Along the harbour's edge, an extension of the Grande Rue, **quai Henri IV**, has a colourful backdrop of cafés, brasseries and restaurants.

The **place du Puits-Salé**, at the centre of the Old Town, is dominated by the huge, restored **Café des Tribunaux**, built as an inn towards the end of the seventeenth century. Two hundred years later, it was favoured by painters and writers such as Renoir, Monet, Sickert, Whistler and Pissarro. For English visitors, its most evocative association is with the exiled and unhappy Oscar Wilde, who drank here regularly. It's now a cavernous café, popular with college students and open until after midnight.

The medieval **castle**, overlooking the seafront from the west, is home of the **Musée de Dieppe** and temporary exhibitions (June–Sept daily 10am–noon & 2–6pm; Oct–May Mon & Wed–Sat 10am–noon & 2–5pm, Sun 10am–noon & 2–6pm; €3.60). Its permanent collection includes carved ivories – virtuoso pieces of sawing, filing and chipping of the plundered riches of Africa, shipped back to the town by early Dieppe explorers. It also holds paintings of local scenes by artists such as Pissarro, Renoir, Dufy, Sickert and Boudin, and works by Georges Braque, the co-founder of **Cubism**, who went to school in Le Havre, spent summers in Dieppe and is buried not far west at Varengeville-sur-Mer. A separate, much newer wing of the castle stages temporary exhibitions.

An exit from the western side of the castle leads onto a path up to the **cliffs**, where there are impressive views of Dieppe and beyond. On the other side, a flight of steps heads down to the **square du Canada**, originally named in commemoration of the role played by Dieppe sailors in the colonization of Canada. Now a small plaque is dedicated to the Canadian soldiers who died in the suicidal 1942 raid on Dieppe, justified later as a trial run for the 1944 Normandy landings.

On the eastern end of town just back from the harbour, the **Cité de la Mer**, at 37 rue de l'Asile-Thomas, is a museum and scientific research centre for all things sea-related (daily 10am–noon & 2–6pm; €6; ⓦ estrancitedelamer.free.fr). Unless you are a maritime history or marine biology enthusiast, little is likely to hold your attention for long: the small museum races through the history of seagoing vessels, including a Viking *drakkar* reconstructed using methods depicted in the Bayeux Tapestry, and an exhibition details Dieppe's relationship with the sea, with a pungent display of dried, salted fish. Visits culminate with the large **aquariums**, filled with the marine life of the Channel: flatfish with bulbous eyes and twisted faces, retiring octopuses, battling lobsters, and hermaphrodite scallops.

Eating

The most promising area to look for **restaurants** in Dieppe is along the quai Henri IV, which makes a lovely place to stroll and compare *menus* of a summer's evening. The beach itself, by contrast, offers no formal restaurants, just a couple of open-air bistro-type cafés and a handful of crêpe stands. The café-lined Place St-Jacques, dominated by the Gothic Église St-Jacques, is an ideal spot for a relaxed drink.

Dieppe's main shopping streets are rue de la Barre and the Grande Rue; Saturday sees an all-day open-air **market** in the place Nationale and along Grande Rue.

Le Bistrot du Pollet 23 rue de la Tête du Boeuf ☎02.35.84.68.57. Little local restaurant just east of Pont Ango, especially cosy on a winter's evening, selling fresh seafood at low prices. Closed Sun, Mon, second fortnight in April and second fortnight in Aug.

Diverne Traiteur 138 Grande Rue ☎02.35.84.13.87. Chic patisserie and tearoom serving up delicious cakes.

Le New Haven 53 quai Henri IV ☎02.35.84.89.72. Reliable seafood specialist, towards the quieter end

of the quayside, with good *menus* from €18. Closed Tues eve, plus Mon & Wed in winter.

L'Océan 23 quai Henri IV ☎02.32.90.97.80. Big, sprawling quayside bistro, ideal for a large group; its long menu offers every imaginable permutation of meat, fish and shellfish, with set *menus* from €11 to €32.

Le Sully 97 quai Henri IV ☎02.35.84.23.13. This smart indoor restaurant offers some of the finest seafood along the quayside, on bargain *menus* from just €12 up to €34, or on lavish platters.

The Côte d'Albâtre

The shoreline of the Côte d'Albâtre is eroding at such a ferocious rate that the small resorts tucked among the cliffs at the ends of its successive valleys may not last more than another century or so. For the moment, however, they are quietly prospering, with casinos, sports centres and yacht marinas ensuring a modest but steady summer trade. From Dieppe, the obvious direction to head is west, where both **Fécamp** and **Étretat** make attractive bases.

Varengeville

If the museum in Dieppe (see opposite) awakened your interest in **Georges Braque**, you may be interested in visiting his grave in the clifftop church further up the coast at **VARENGEVILLE**, 8km west of Dieppe. Braque's marble **tomb** is topped by a sadly decaying mosaic of a white dove in flight. More impressive is his vivid blue *Tree of Jesse* stained-glass window inside the church, through which the sun rises in summer.

Back along the road towards Dieppe from the church, the house at the **Bois des Moutiers** was built by architect **Edwin Lutyens** from 1898 onwards. Its magnificent **gardens**, designed by owner Guillaume Mallet with Gertrude Jekyll, are at their most spectacular in the second half of May (tickets on sale mid-March to mid-Nov daily 10am–noon & 2–6pm; house open those hours, gardens open April–Oct 10am–8pm; €8 May & June, otherwise €7).

Nearby, 300m south of the D75, the **Manoir d'Ango** was the "summer palace" of sixteenth-century Dieppe's leading shipbuilder (mid-April to Sept daily 10am–12.30pm & 2–6pm; Oct Sat & Sun 10am–12.30pm & 2–6pm; €5; ⓦwww .manoirdango.fr). Jean Ango's former home consists of a rectangular ensemble of fine brick buildings arranged around a central courtyard. The intricate patterning of red bricks, shaped flint slabs, stone blocks and supporting timbers is at its finest in the remarkable central **dovecote**.

Varengeville's one **accommodation** option is absolutely irresistible – the lovely ⚐ *Hôtel de la Terrasse*, a *logis* set amid the pines on the route de Vastérival (☎02.35.85.12.54, ⓦwww.hotel-restaurant-la-terrasse.com; closed mid-Oct to mid-March; ❸). Reached via a right turn off the main highway as you head west of town, it's perched high above the cliffs, with great sea views. Fish *menus* in its panoramic dining room start at €22, and you can follow footpaths down through narrow cracks in the cliffs to reach the rocky beach below.

Fécamp

FÉCAMP, just over halfway from Dieppe to Le Havre, is a serious fishing port with a pleasant seafront promenade. Its most distinctive tourist attraction is the **Benedictine Distillery**, at 110 rue Alexandre-le-Grand, a back street parallel to the port (daily: early Feb to March & mid-Oct to Dec 10.30–11.45am & 2–5pm; April to mid-July & Sept to mid-Oct 10am–noon & 2–5.30pm; mid-July to Aug 10am–6pm; €7; ⓦbenedictine.fr). Ninety-minute guided **tours**, which start by trekking through a museum of local antiquities and oddments, culminate in the old distillery, where boxes of herbs are flung with gusto into copper vats and alembics, though commercial production has long since moved to an out-of-town site. Finally, you're offered a *dégustation* of the liqueur in their bar across the road – either neat, in a cocktail, or on crêpes. If your aesthetic sensibilities need soothing after this, head for the soaring medieval nave and Renaissance carved screens of the **church of the Trinité**, up in the town centre, or the **Musée des Terres-Neuvas et de la Pêche**, on the seafront at 27 bd Albert 1ᵉʳ (July & Aug daily 10am–7pm; Sept–June daily except Tues 10am–noon & 2–5.30pm; €3). Adorned with miniature model boats and amateur paintings, it focuses on the long tradition whereby the fishermen of Fécamp decamp en masse each year to catch cod in the cold, foggy waters off Newfoundland. Sailing vessels continued to make the trek from the sixteenth century right up until 1931; today vast refrigerated container ships have taken their place.

Practicalities

Fécamp's **tourist office** is on the seafront on quai Sadi-Carnot (Sept–March Mon–Fri 9am–6pm, Sat 9.30am–12.30pm & 2–6pm; April–June Mon–Fri 9am–6pm, Sat & Sun 10am–6.30pm; July & Aug daily 9am–6.30pm; ⓣ02.35.28.51.01, ⓦwww.fecamptourisme.com). Most of the **hotels** are set on side streets away from the sea, but there are a couple of good options near the waterfront. Only the higher rooms at the rather genteel *Hôtel de la Plage*, 87 rue de la Plage (ⓣ02.35.29.76.51, ⓦhoteldelaplage-fecamp.com; ➋), have sea views, but all are comfortable and the location is quiet. The good-value *De la Mer*, on the seafront at 89 bd Albert 1ᵉʳ (ⓣ02.35.28.24.64, ⓦwww.hotel-dela-mer.com; ➋), is nicer inside than it looks from the outside. A lovely **campsite** with beautiful views of the coast, *Camping de Reneville* (ⓣ02.35.28.20.97, ⓦcampingdereneville .com; closed mid-Nov to mid-March), stands a short walk out of town on the western cliffs.

Well-priced fish **restaurants** include *La Marée*, 77 quai Bérigny (ⓣ02.35.29.39.15; closed Sun eve & Mon), attached to a fish shop and offering just one set *menu* at €30, and the friendly little *Marine*, 23 quai de la Vicomté (ⓣ02.35.28.15.94), where an excellent *choucroute de la mer* costs €18.

Étretat

Delightful little **ÉTRETAT** is very different to Fécamp. Here the alabaster cliffs are at their most spectacular – their arches, tunnels and the solitary "needle" out to sea adorn countless tourist brochures – and the town itself has grown up simply as a pleasure resort. There isn't even a port of any kind: the seafront consists of a sweeping unbroken curve of concrete above a shingle beach.

Thanks partly to its superb setting, and the lovely architectural ensemble that surrounds its central **place Foch**, Étretat is a very pretty little place. The old wooden market *halles* still dominate the main square, the ground floor now converted into souvenir shops, but the beams of the balcony and roof are bare and ancient.

As soon as you step onto the beach you're confronted by the stunning **cliffs** to either side. To the south, on the **Falaise d'Aval**, a straightforward walk – made unnerving by the scary drops nearby – leads up the crumbling side of the cliff, with lush lawns and pastures to the inland side, and German fortifications on the shore side extending to the point where the turf abruptly stops. From the windswept top you can see further rock formations and sometimes even glimpse Le Havre, but the views back to the town sheltered in the valley, and the **Falaise d'Amont**, on its northern side, are what stick in the memory. The cliff itself presents an idyllic rural scene, with a gentle footpath winding up the green hillside to the little chapel of Notre-Dame.

Practicalities

The biggest drawback to visiting Étretat is that it gets so crowded; drivers can find it impossible to park in summer. The **tourist office** is beside the main through road, on place Maurice Guillard (mid-March to mid-June & mid-Sept to mid-Nov Mon–Sat 10am–noon & 2–6pm; mid-June to mid-Sept daily 10am–7pm; mid-Nov to mid-March Fri & Sat 10am–noon & 2–6pm; ☎02.35.27.05.21, ⓦetretat.net). Coastal **buses** stop just outside.

The main hub for **hotels** is the area around place Foch; *L'Escale*, on the *place* itself (☎02.35.27.03.69; ❸), has simple but pleasant rooms, and a low-key restaurant downstairs specializing in *moules-frites* and crêpes. Just off the square, *La Résidence*, 4 bd René-Coty (☎02.35.27.02.87, ⓦwww.hotels-etretat.com; ❶–❼), is a dramatic half-timbered old mansion where guest rooms vary enormously; the cheapest option lacks en-suite facilities, while others are positively luxurious. Campers will find the municipal **campsite** spreading beside the D39, 1km out of town (☎02.35.27.07.67; closed mid-Oct to mid-April).

The top local **restaurant** is the *Galion*, adjoining *La Résidence* at 4 bd René-Coty (☎02.35.29.48.74; closed Tues & Wed in low season); its €22 *menu* makes a definitive introduction to Norman cuisine.

Le Havre

While **LE HAVRE** – Normandy's largest town, at the mouth of the Seine – may hardly be picturesque or tranquil, neither is it the soulless urban sprawl some travellers suggest. Its port, the second largest in France after Marseille, does take up half the Seine estuary, but the town itself at the core, home to a population of almost 200,000, is a place of pilgrimage for devotees of contemporary architecture.

The city was originally built in 1517 to replace the ancient ports of Harfleur and Honfleur, then silting up. Under the simple name of Le Havre – "The Harbour" – it became the principal trading post of France's northern coast. In the years before 1939, it was the European home of the great luxury liners such as the *Normandie*, *Île de France* and *France*.

Le Havre suffered the heaviest damage of any European port during World War II. Following its near-total destruction, it was rebuilt by a single architect, **Auguste Perret**, between 1946 and 1964, an enterprise circumscribed by constraints of time and money. The sheer sense of space can be exhilarating: the showpiece monuments have a winning self-confidence, and the few surviving relics of the old city have been sensitively integrated into the whole. While the endless mundane residential blocks can be dispiriting, even those visitors who fail to agree with Perret's famous dictum that "concrete is beautiful" may enjoy a stroll around his city.

EATING & DRINKING

Le Grignot	3
Le Lyonnais	4
Le Nuage Dans La Tasse	2
La Petite Auberge	1

0   500 m

ACCOMMODATION

Best Western Art Hôtel	B
Celtic	C
Richelieu	D
Vent d'Ouest	A

Arrival, information and accommodation

Le Havre's **gare SNCF** and adjoining **gare routière** are ten minutes' walk from the town centre down the boulevard de Strasbourg, not far from the **ferry port**, which welcomes daily sailings from Portsmouth operated by LD Lines (℡ 08.25.30.43.04, Ⓦ ldlines.co.uk). The town's large **tourist office** is on the main seafront drag, at 186 bd Clemenceau (July & Aug Mon–Sat 9am–7pm, Sun 10am–12.30pm & 2.30–6pm; May, June, Sept & Oct Mon–Sat 9am–6.45pm, Sun 10am–12.30pm & 2.30–5.45pm; Nov–April Mon–Fri 9am–6.30pm, Sat 9am–12.30pm & 2–6.30pm, Sun 10am–1pm; ℡ 02.32.74.04.04, Ⓦ www.lehavretourisme.com). The **post office** at 62 rue Jules-Siegfried (Mon–Fri 8am–7pm, Sat 8am–noon) offers **internet** access.

Le Havre holds two main concentrations of **hotels**: one group faces the *gare SNCF*, while most of the rest lie within walking distance of the ferry terminal.

Best Western Art Hôtel 147 rue Louis Brindeau ℡ 02.35.22.69.44, Ⓦ www.art-hotel.fr. Very smart, comfortable hotel on the north side of the Espace Oscar Niemeyer, facing the Volcano cultural centre. All rooms have flat-screen TVs and wi-fi. ❺

Celtic 106 rue Voltaire ℡ 02.35.42.39.77, Ⓦ hotelceltic.com. Facing the *Art Hôtel*, this place tells it like it is, with three distinct room categories: "budget" (with showers but sharing toilets); "comfort"; and "pleasure". ❶–❸

Richelieu 135 rue de Paris ℡ 02.35.42.38.71, Ⓔ hotel.lerichelieu@orange.fr. For a mid-priced hotel in a very central location with bright, comfortable rooms, this hotel is hard to beat. ❸

🏃 **Vent d'Ouest** 4 rue de Caligny ℡ 02.35.42.50.69, Ⓦ www.ventdouest.fr. Le Havre's smartest hotel is a stylishly designed boutique affair, with comfortable, well-equipped rooms decorated with a nautical or mountain theme. Apartments sleeping 4 are also available. ❻

The Town

One reason visitors often dismiss Le Havre out of hand is that it's easy to get to and from the city without ever seeing its downtown area. For those who do make the effort, the Perret-designed central **Hôtel de Ville** is a logical first port of call, a long, low, flat-roofed building topped by a seventeen-storey concrete tower. Surrounded by pergola walkways, flowerbeds and cascading fountains, the square in which it sits is an attractive, lively place, while the Hôtel de Ville itself hosts imaginative exhibitions.

Perret's other major creation, southwest of the town hall, is the **church of St-Joseph**, built on a cross of which all four arms are equally short. From the outside it's a mass of speckled concrete, the main doors thrown open to hint at dark interior spaces within. When you get inside it all makes sense: the altar is right in the centre, with the hundred-metre bell tower rising directly above. Very simple patterns of stained glass, extending right the way up the tower, create a bright interplay of coloured light, focusing on the altar.

Le Havre's boldest specimen of modern architecture is a post-Perret creation – the cultural centre known as the **Volcano** (or less reverentially as the "yoghurt pot"), dominating the Espace Oscar Niemeyer. Niemeyer, a Brazilian architect, is best known for overseeing the construction of Brasilia, and was still hard at work – at the age of 102 – at the time of writing. He designed this slightly asymmetrical gleaming white cone in the 1970s.

Overlooking the harbour entrance, the **Musée Malraux** (Mon & Wed–Fri 11am–6pm, Sat & Sun 11am–7pm; €5) ranks among the best-designed art galleries in France, making full use of natural light to display an enjoyable assortment of nineteenth- and twentieth-century French paintings. Its principal highlights are over two hundred canvases by Eugène Boudin, including greyish landscapes produced all along the Normandy coastline with views of Trouville, Honfleur and Étretat, as well as an entire wall of miniature cows, and a lovely set of works by Raoul Dufy (1877–1953), which make Le Havre seem positively radiant, whatever the weather outside.

Eating and drinking

Le Havre's restaurants are concentrated in the same areas as its hotels. There are plenty of **bars**, **cafés** and **brasseries** around the *gare SNCF*, and all sorts of restaurants, from traditional French to Japanese, in the back streets of the waterside St-François district.

Le Grignot 53 rue Racine ☎02.35.43.62.07. Traditional brasserie, with brisk, efficient service and good food at very reasonable prices.
Le Lyonnais 7–9 rue de Bretagne ☎02.35.22.07.31. Small, cosy restaurant with chequered tablecloths and a welcoming atmosphere. The house speciality is baked fish, though dishes from Lyon, such as *andouillettes*, are also available on *menus* that start at €12.50 for lunch, and €16 for dinner. Closed Sun & Mon eve.

Le Nuage Dans La Tasse 93 av Foch ☎02.35.21.64.94. Huge salads and simple, good-value bistro meals near the town hall. Closed Sun, & lunch Mon–Wed.
La Petite Auberge 32 rue de Ste-Adresse ☎02.35.46.27.32. High-class traditional French cooking, aimed more at local businesspeople than at tourists, and offering few surprises but no disappointments. Closed Sun eve, Wed lunch & Mon.

Rouen and around

ROUEN, the capital of Upper Normandy, is one of France's most ancient cities. Standing on the site of Rotomagus, built by the Romans at the lowest point where they could bridge the Seine, it was laid out by the Viking Rollo, the first duke of Normandy, in 911. Captured by the English in 1419, after a long siege, it became the stage in 1431 for the trial and execution of Joan of Arc, before returning to French control in 1449.

Bombing during World War II, specifically during the fierce onslaught that preceded the D-Day landings, destroyed all Rouen's bridges, the area between the cathedral and the *quais*, and much of the left bank's industrial quarter. The city has since been almost entirely rebuilt, turning its inner core of streets, a few hundred metres north of the river, into the closest approximation to a medieval city that modern imaginations could conceive. Rouen today can be very seductive, its lively and bustling centre well equipped with impressive churches and museums. Sadly, however, the immediate riverside area has never been adequately restored.

While Rouen proper is home to a population of 110,000, its metropolitan area holds five times that number, and it remains the fourth largest port in the country. The city spreads deep into the loop of the Seine, with its docks and industrial infrastructure stretching endlessly away to the south, and it is increasingly expanding up into the hills to the north as well.

Arrival and information

Rouen is a difficult and unpleasant city to **drive** into. All traffic is funnelled into the hideous multi-lane highways that line either bank of the river, while many of the central streets, north of the river, have been pedestrianized. It's best to park as soon as you can – there are plenty of central underground car parks, especially near the cathedral and the place du Vieux-Marché – and explore the city on foot.

The main **gare SNCF**, Gare Rive Droite, stands at the north end of rue Jeanne-d'Arc. It's connected to the centre by a **métro** system, which follows the line of the rue Jeanne-d'Arc, making two stops before it resurfaces to cross the river by bridge. Individual journeys cost €1.40; a book of ten tickets is €11.40, or you can buy an all-day pass for €4.10. All **buses** from the *gare SNCF* except #2A run down rue Jeanne-d'Arc to the centre, which takes five minutes. From the fifth stop, the "Théâtre des Arts" by the river, the **gare routière** is one block west in rue des Charrettes, tucked away behind the riverfront buildings.

Rouen's **tourist office** stands opposite the cathedral at 25 place de la Cathédrale (May–Sept Mon–Sat 9am–7pm, Sun 9.30am–12.30pm & 2–6pm; Oct–April Mon–Sat 9.30am–12.30pm & 1–6pm; ℡02.32.08.32.40, ⓦwww.rouentourisme .com). They provide audio-guides for self-guided city **walking tours** for €5, while a motorized **"petit train"** makes a forty-minute tour from the tourist office in summer (April–Oct daily 10am, 11am, noon, 2pm, 3pm, 4pm & 5pm; €6.50, ages 3–11 €4.50). The city-sponsored Cy'clic network enables credit-card holders to unlock a simple **bike** from "stations" scattered along the streets, and leave it at any other station; journeys of less than thirty minutes are free. Details on ⓦcyclic .rouen.fr. The **post office** is at 45 rue Jeanne-d'Arc, in the centre of town (Mon–Fri 8am–7pm, Sat 8.30am–12.30pm). For **internet** access, head to Cyber-Net, 47 place du Vieux-Marché (Mon–Sat 10am–7pm).

Accommodation

With more than three thousand **hotel** rooms in town, there should be no difficulty finding accommodation in Rouen, even at the busiest times. Few of the city's hotels have restaurants, chiefly because there's such a wide choice of places to eat.

Hotels

Andersen 4 rue Pouchet ℡02.35.71.88.51, ⓦhotelandersen.com. Very friendly place with plenty of character, a short walk west of the Gare Rive Droite, and set back beyond a small gravel yard. The exterior is run-down, and the bathrooms are a little basic, but the bedrooms are large, light and colourful. ❸

Arts et Seine 6 rue St-Étienne-des-Tonneliers ℡02.35.88.11.44, ⓦartsetseine.com. Inexpensive, renovated hotel, a block north of the river not far from the cathedral, with friendly owners and

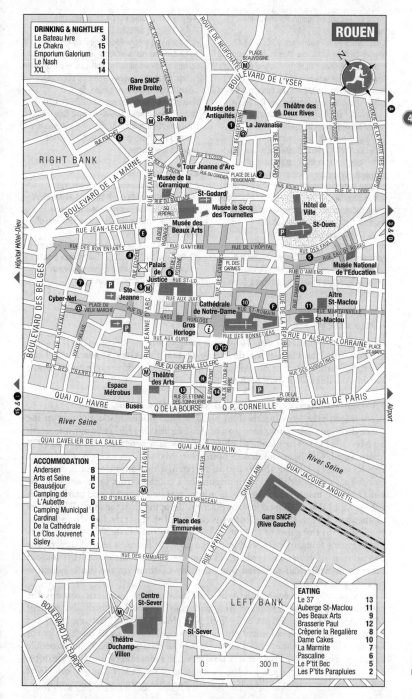

ROUEN

NORMANDY

4

DRINKING & NIGHTLIFE
Le Bateau Ivre	3
Le Chakra	15
Emporium Galorium	1
Le Nash	4
XXL	14

Gare SNCF (Rive Droite)

St-Romain

Musée des Antiquités

Théâtre des Deux Rives

La Javanaise

RIGHT BANK

BOULEVARD DE L'YSER

PLACE BEAUVOISINE

ROUTE DE NEUFCHATEL

RUE DU CHAMP DES OISEAUX

BOULEVARD DE LA MARNE

RUE POUCHET

Tour Jeanne d'Arc

Musée de la Céramique

St-Godard

Musée le Secq des Tournelles

Hôtel de Ville

St-Ouen

RUE JEAN-LECANUET

Musée des Beaux Arts

RUE DES BON ENFANTS

RUE GANTERIE

RUE DE L'HÔPITAL

RUE DES FAULX

RUE EAU DE ROBEC

Musée National de l'Education

BOULEVARD DES BELGES

Cyber-Net

Ste-Jeanne

Palais de Justice

PLACE DU VIEUX MARCHÉ

RUE DU GROS HORLOGE

Cathédrale de Notre-Dame

Gros Horloge

Aître St-Maclou

St-Maclou

RUE MARTAINVILLE

RUE D'ALSACE-LORRAINE

PLACE ST-MARC

VIEUX PALAIS

RUE DES CHARRETTES

Espace Métrobus

Théâtre des Arts

Buses

QUAI DU HAVRE

Q DE LA BOURSE

Q P. CORNEILLE

QUAI DE PARIS

PL DE LA RÉPUBLIQUE

River Seine

QUAI CAVELIER DE LA SALLE

QUAI JEAN MOULIN

River Seine

QUAI JACQUES ANQUETIL

ACCOMMODATION
Andersen	B
Arts et Seine	H
Beauséjour	C
Camping de L'Aubette	D
Camping Municipal	I
Cardinal	G
De la Cathédrale	F
Le Clos Jouvenet	A
Sisley	E

AV. DE BRETAGNE

BD D'ORLEANS

COURS CLEMENCEAU

Gare SNCF (Rive Gauche)

Place des Emmurées

RUE DES EMMURÉES

Centre St-Sever

LEFT BANK

Théâtre Duchamp-Villon

St-Sever

BOULEVARD DE L'EUROPE

EATING
Le 37	13
Auberge St-Maclou	11
Des Beaux Arts	9
Brasserie Paul	12
Crêperie la Regalière	8
Dame Cakes	10
La Marmite	7
Pascaline	6
Le P'tit Bec	5
Les P'tits Parapluies	2

0   300 m

Hôpital Hôtel-Dieu

clean, well-equipped rooms of varying levels of comfort. ❹

Beauséjour 9 rue Pouchet ☎02.35.71.93.47, ⓦhotel-beausejour76.com. Good-value, revamped hotel near the station (turn right as you come out). Beyond the orange facade and nice garden courtyard, the rooms are nothing fancy, but they're crisply decorated with large-screen TVs and wi-fi; one cheaper single room lacks its own shower. Closed second half of July. ❸

Cardinal 1 place de la Cathédrale ☎02.35.70.24.42, ⓦcardinal-hotel.fr. Very good-value hotel in a stunning location facing the cathedral. Rooms are spacious and clean, with good en-suite facilities, flat-screen TVs and wi-fi access. Two family rooms available. All have views of the cathedral (the higher ones from balconies). Ample buffet breakfasts for €8. ❹

De la Cathédrale 12 rue St-Romain ☎02.35.71.57.95, ⓦwww.hotel-de-la-cathedrale.fr. Attractive hotel, in a pedestrian lane beside the cathedral, with a pleasant olde-worlde theme, nice breakfast room and flower-filled courtyard. Discounts at public car park nearby. Buffet breakfasts €8.50. ❹

Le Clos Jouvenet 42 rue Hyacinthe Langlois ☎02.35.89.80.66, ⓦleclosjouvenet.com. Four beautifully decorated, comfortable rooms in an immaculate nineteenth-century house ten minutes' walk east of the train station. Breakfast is served in the conservatory, overlooking the enclosed garden. ❺

Sisley 51 rue Jean-Lecanuet ☎02.35.71.10.07, ⓔhotelsisley@gmail.com. Very central little budget hotel, where each of the bright, newly renovated rooms is decorated in keeping with a different Impressionist painter. ❷

Campsites

Camping de l'Aubette 23 Vert Buisson in St-Léger du Bourg-Denis ☎02.35.08.47.69. Basic site in a more rural, but much less accessible setting than the *Camping Municipal*, 4km east of town on bus route #8.

Camping Municipal Rue Jules-Ferry in Déville-lès-Rouen ☎02.35.74.07.59. Surprisingly small site, 4km northwest of town, geared towards caravans rather than tents; bus #2.

The City

North of the Seine at any rate, Rouen is a real pleasure to explore. As well as some great sights – the **Cathédrale de Notre-Dame**, the **Aître St-Maclou**, all the delightful twisting streets of timbered houses – there's history aplenty too, most notably the links with **Joan of Arc**.

Place du Vieux-Marché to the cathedral

Alongside a huge cross (nearly 20m high), a small plaque marks the spot in the **place du Vieux-Marché** where Joan of Arc (see box opposite) was burnt to death on May 30, 1431. The memorial **church** to the saint here was dedicated in 1979 (daily: April–Oct 10am–noon & 2–6pm; Nov–March 10am–noon & 2–5.30pm). A wacky, spiky-looking thing, said to represent either an upturned boat or the flames that consumed Joan, it's indisputably a triumph, part of an ensemble of buildings that manages to incorporate in similar style a covered food market (daily except Mon) that's designed less for practical shopping than for show. The theme of the church's fish-shaped windows is continued in the scaly tiles that adorn its roof, which is elongated to form a walkway across the square. The outline of its predecessor's foundations is visible on the adjacent lawns, which also mark the precise spot of Joan's martyrdom. The square itself is surrounded by fine old brown-and-white half-timbered houses, many of those on the south side now serving as restaurants.

From place du Vieux-Marché, rue du Gros-Horloge leads east towards the cathedral. Just across rue Jeanne d'Arc stands the **Gros Horloge** itself (daily except Mon: April–Oct 10am–1pm & 2–7pm; Nov–March 2–6pm; last admission 1hr before closing; €6). A colourful one-handed clock, it used to be on the adjacent Gothic belfry until it was moved down by popular demand in 1529, so that people could see it better. The lower storey now serves as a museum of the clock's history, and visitors can climb up rather too many steps to see its intricate workings, and enjoy marvellous views of the old city, with its startling array of towers and spires.

Despite the addition of all sorts of different towers, spires and vertical extensions, the **Cathédrale de Notre-Dame** (mid-March to Oct Mon 2–7pm, Tues–Sat 7.30am–7pm, Sun 8am–6pm; Nov to mid-March Mon 2–6pm, Tues–Sat 7.30am–noon & 2–6pm, Sun 8am–6pm) remains at heart the Gothic masterpiece that was built in the twelfth and thirteenth centuries. The west facade of the cathedral, intricately sculpted like the rest of the exterior, was Monet's subject for over thirty studies of changing light, which now hang in the Musée d'Orsay in Paris. Monet might not recognize it now, however – in the last few years, it's been scrubbed a gleaming white, free from the centuries of accreted dirt he so carefully recorded.

On summer nights, colours inspired by Monet's cathedral paintings are projected onto the church's façade in a thirty-minute light show known as **La Cathédrale de Monet aux Pixels** (daily: July 11pm, August 10.30pm; free), transforming it quite magnificently into a series of giant Monet-esque canvases. Inside the cathedral, the **ambulatory** and **crypt** – closed on Sundays and during services – hold the assorted tombs of various recumbent royalty, such as Duke Rollo, who died "enfeebled by toil" in 933 AD, and the actual heart of Richard the Lionheart.

Joan of Arc

When the 17-year-old peasant girl known to history as **Joan of Arc** (Jeanne d'Arc in French) arrived at the French court early in 1429, the Hundred Years' War had already dragged on for over ninety years. Most of northern France was in the grip of an Anglo–Burgundian alliance, but Joan, who had been hearing voices since 1425, was certain she could save the country, and came to present her case to the as-yet-uncrowned Dauphin. Partly through recognizing him despite a simple disguise he wore to fool her at their first meeting, she convinced him of her divine guidance. After a remarkable three-week examination by a tribunal of the French *parlement*, she went on to secure command of the armies of France. In a whirlwind **campaign**, which culminated in the raising of the siege of Orléans on May 8, 1429, she broke the English hold on the Loire Valley. She then escorted the Dauphin deep into enemy territory so that, in accordance with ancient tradition, he could be crowned King Charles VII of France in the cathedral at Reims, on July 17.

Within a year of her greatest triumph, Joan was **captured** by the Burgundian army at Compiègne in May 1430, and held to ransom. Chivalry dictated that any offer of payment from the vacillating Charles must be accepted, but in the absence of such an offer Joan was handed over to the English for 10,000 ducats. On Christmas Day, 1430, she was imprisoned in the château of Philippe-Auguste at Rouen.

Charged with heresy, on account of her "false and diabolical" visions and refusal to give up wearing men's clothing, Joan was put on trial for her life on February 21, 1431. For three months, a changing panel of 131 assessors – only eight of them English-born – heard the evidence against her. Condemned, inevitably, to death, Joan recanted on the scaffold in St-Ouen cemetery on May 24, and her sentence was commuted to life imprisonment. The presiding judge, Bishop Pierre Cauchon of Beauvais, reassured disappointed English representatives that "we will get her yet". The next Sunday, Joan was tricked into breaking her vow and putting on male clothing, and taken to the archbishop's chapel in rue St-Romain to be condemned to death for the second time. On May 30, 1431, she was burned at the stake in the place du Vieux-Marché; her ashes, together with her unburned heart, were thrown into the Seine.

Joan passed into legend, until the discovery and publication of the full transcript of her trial in the 1840s. The forbearance and devout humility she displayed throughout her ordeal added to her status as France's greatest religious heroine. She was canonized as recently as 1920, and soon afterwards became the country's patron saint.

St-Ouen and around

The **church of St-Ouen**, next to the Hôtel de Ville (which itself occupies buildings that were once part of the abbey), is larger than the cathedral and has far less decoration, so from the outside there's nothing to diminish the instant impact of its vast Gothic proportions and the purity of its lines. Inside, it holds some stunning fourteenth-century stained glass, though much was destroyed during the Revolution (April–Oct Mon & Fri–Sun 10am–noon & 2–6pm; Nov–March Mon & Fri–Sun 10am–noon & 2–5.30pm). The world that produced it – and, nearer the end of the era, the lightness and grace of the **church of St-Maclou** not far to the south – was one of mass death from the plague: thus the **Aître St-Maclou** immediately to the east, a cemetery for the victims, was an integral part of the St-Maclou complex (daily: mid-March to Oct 8am–8pm; Nov to mid-March 8am–7pm; free). It's now the tranquil garden courtyard of the Fine Arts school, but if you examine the one open lower storey of the surrounding buildings you'll discover the original deathly decorations and a mummified cat.

The museums

Rouen's imposing **Musée des Beaux-Arts** commands the square Verdrel from just east of the central rue Jeanne-d'Arc (daily except Tues 10am–6pm; €5, combined ticket including Musée de la Céramique and Musée Le Secq des Tournelles €8). The grand edifice is home to an absorbing permanent collection, as well as regular temporary exhibitions, for which there may be an extra charge. Unexpected highlights include dazzling Russian icons from the sixteenth century onwards, and an entertaining eighteenth-century crib from Naples. Many of the biggest names among the painters – Caravaggio (the centrepiece *Flagellation of Christ*), Velázquez, Rubens – tend to be represented by a single minor work, but there are several Modiglianis and a number of Monets, including *Rouen Cathedral* (1894), the *Vue Générale de Rouen* and *Brume sur la Seine* (1894). The central sculpture court, roofed over but very light, holds a small tearoom.

Rouen's history as a centre for *faïencerie*, or earthenware pottery, is recorded in the **Musée de la Céramique**, raised above the north side of the square Verdrel nearby (daily except Tues 10am–6pm; €5). A series of beautiful rooms, some of which incorporate sixteenth-century wood panelling rescued from a demolished nunnery of St-Amand, display specimens from the 1600s onwards. Assorted tiles and plates reflect the eighteenth-century craze for *chinoiserie*.

Behind the Beaux-Arts, housed in the old, barely altered church of St-Laurent on rue Jacques-Villon, the **Musée Le Secq des Tournelles** (daily except Tues 10am–1pm & 2–6pm; €3) consists of a gloriously eccentric and uncategorizable collection of wrought-iron objects of all dates and descriptions, among them nutcrackers and door knockers, a huge double bed from sixteenth-century Italy, spiral staircases that lead nowhere and hideous implements of torture.

A short walk north at the top of rue Beauvoisine, the **Musée des Antiquités** (Mon & Wed–Sat 10am–12.15pm & 1.30–5.30pm, Sun 2–6pm; €3) provides a dry but comprehensive run-through of ancient artefacts found in or near Rouen. Starting with an impressive pointed helmet from the Bronze Age and an assortment of early iron tools, it continues with some remarkably complete and beautifully presented Roman mosaics from villas in the vicinity. Then comes a long gallery filled with woodcarvings rescued from long-lost Rouen houses – including a lovely bas-relief of sheep that served as the sign for a medieval draper's shop – and also some fine fifteenth-century tapestries.

The Tour Jeanne d'Arc

The **Tour Jeanne d'Arc** (daily except Tues: Mon–Sat 10am–noon & 2–6pm, Sun 2–6.30pm; €1.50), a short way southeast of the *gare SNCF*, is all that remains of the castle of Philippe-Auguste, built in 1205 and scene of the imprisonment and trial of Joan of Arc. It served as the castle's keep and entrance-way, and was itself fully surrounded by a moat. It was not, however, Joan's actual prison – that was the Tour de la Pucelle, demolished in 1809 – while the trial took place first of all in the castle's St-Romain chapel, and then later in its great central hall, both of which were destroyed in 1590. The tall, sharp-pointed tower was bought by public subscription in 1860, and restored to its present state. After seeing a small collection of Joan-related memorabilia, you can climb a steep spiral staircase to the very top, but you can't see out over the city, let alone step outside into the open air.

Eating, drinking and nightlife

Rouen's bars and restaurants are largely concentrated around the streets which radiate out from the place du Vieux-Marché, with rue Martainville offering some excellent, often less touristy alternatives.

Restaurants

Le 37 37 rue St-Étienne-des-Tonneliers ⓣ02.35.70.56.65. Classy modern bistro, just up from the river and belonging to top Rouennais chef Gilles Tournadre. Good-value contemporary cuisine in stylishly minimal surroundings; €19 lunch *menu*, dinner is twice that. Closed Sun & Mon.

Auberge St-Maclou 224–226 rue Martainville ⓣ02.35.71.06.67. Half-timbered building in shadow of St-Maclou church, with outdoor tables on a busy pedestrian street, and an old-style ambience. Well-priced traditional French *menus* – lunch is €12 or €15, dinner €21 or €26. Closed Sun eve (except March–June), Mon, three weeks in Aug & two weeks in Feb.

Des Beaux Arts 34 rue Damiette ⓣ02.35.70.17.15. Very good-value Algerian cuisine, on a pretty, pedestrianized street north of St-Maclou church: couscous from €8 or tajine from €12.50, with all kinds of sausages and assorted meats.

Brasserie Paul 1 place de la Cathédrale ⓣ02.35.71.86.07. Rouen's definitive bistro, an attractive *belle époque* place facing the cathedral. Daily lunch specials, with a €15 *formule* or Simone de Beauvoir's favourite goat's cheese and smoked duck salad for €12.50.

Crêperie la Regalière 12 rue Massacre ⓣ02.35.15.33.33. This quaint, inexpensive but good-quality crêperie, with some outdoor seating just off the place du Vieux-Marché, is one of central Rouen's best bargains, with *menus* at €9.50 and €13. Open daily until 11pm.

Dame Cakes 70 rue St-Romain ⓣ02.35.07.49.31. Elegant tearoom, with a little garden, on a quiet street next to the cathedral, tempting the tastebuds with delicious desserts, savoury tarts and salads.

La Marmite 3 rue de Florence ⓣ02.35.71.75.55, ⓦlamarmiterouen.com. Romantic little place just north of the place du Vieux-Marché, offering beautiful, elegantly presented gourmet dishes on well-priced *menus* from €19 to €55. Closed Sun eve, Mon & Tues lunch.

Pascaline 5 rue de la Poterne ⓣ02.35.89.67.44. Classic bistro, located to the north of the Palais de Justice, near the flower market, with a green wooden enclosure attached to the front of a half-timbered house. Set *menus* from €13 to €28.50, and live jazz some Thursdays.

Le P'tit Bec 182 rue Eau-de-Robec ⓣ02.35.07.63.33. Friendly brasserie that's a popular lunch spot. Simple *menus* at €13 and €15.50 include a fish or meat main course, plus vegetarian options. There's seating indoors as well as out on the pedestrianized street, in view of several fine half-timbered mansions. Closed Sun, plus Mon & Thurs eve June–Aug, Sun–Thurs eve Sept–May.

Les P'tits Parapluies 46 rue Bourg-l'Abbé, place de la Rougemare ⓣ02.35.88.55.26, ⓦlesptits-parapluies.com. Elegant, secluded half-timbered restaurant not far north of the Hôtel de Ville, on the edge of an attractive little square. Counting your calories (or your pennies) is not really an option; set *menus* start at €30 and include such delights as foie gras and oysters. €5 extra gets two glasses of wine per person. Closed Sat lunch, Sun eve & Mon.

Bars and Clubs

Le Bateau Ivre 17 rue des Sapins ⓣ02.35.70.09.05, ⓦbateauivre.rouen.free.fr. Low-key but atmospheric hangout a long way northeast of the centre. Mostly rock-oriented programme of music and performance, with some open-mic nights. Tues & Wed 10pm–2am, Thurs–Sat 10pm–4am. Closed Sun, Mon & all Aug.

Le Chakra 4 bd Ferdinand-de-Lesseps ☏ 02.32.10.12.02, ⊛ lechakra.fr. Busy, sweaty club, beside the Seine a couple of kilometres west of the centre, where big-name DJs play "100% Electro" to a young crowd. Fri 11pm–4am, Sat 5–9pm & 11pm–4am, Sun 5–9pm.

Emporium Galorium 151 rue Beauvoisine ☏ 02.35.71.76.95, ⊛ emporium-galorium.com. Busy, half-timbered student-dominated bar, a short walk north of the centre, hosting small-scale gigs and theatrical productions. Tues & Wed 8pm–2am, Thurs–Sat 6pm–4am. Closed 2 weeks in Aug.

Le Nash 97 rue Écuyère ☏ 02.35.98.25.24. Relaxed bar popular with locals. The interior has a lounge-like feel with its mood lighting and zebra stripes, while the outdoor terrace is much more akin to a classic French café, and serves light snacks. Music from ambient to Latin. Mon–Fri 11.30am–2pm & 6pm–2am, Sat 6pm–2am.

XXL 25–27 rue de la Savonnerie ☏ 02.35.88.84.00, ⊛ xxl-rouen.com. Gay (very largely male) bar near the river, just south of the cathedral, with theme nights and a small basement dance floor. Tues & Wed 9pm–2am, Thurs–Sat 9pm–4am, Sun 10pm–2am.

Entertainment

As you would expect in a conurbation of half a million, there's always plenty going on in Rouen, from classical concerts in churches to alternative events. Several **theatres** work largely to winter seasons. The most highbrow venue, the **Théâtre des Arts**, 7 rue du Dr-Rambert (☏ 08.10.81.11.16, ⊛ www.operaderouen.com), puts on opera, ballet and concerts. The **Théâtre des Deux Rives** (☏ 02.35.70.22.82, ⊛ cdr2rives.com), opposite the Antiquités museum at the top end of rue Louis Ricard, is a more adventurous repertory company. Major **concerts** often take place in **Hangar 23** in the St-Sever complex (☏ 02.32.18.28.10, ⊛ hangar23.fr), accessible by métro (stop "St-Sever").

Around Rouen

As well as idyllic pastoral scenery, the banks of the Seine in either direction of Rouen hold some unmissable historical and cultural attractions. Until relatively recently, Rouen itself marked the lowest spot on the river to be crossed by a bridge. These days, however, several bridges lie further **downstream**. The magnificent **Pont de Brotonne**, the closest to Rouen, sets off from the north bank 34km west of the city, near sleepy Caudebec, while the immense **Tancarville** suspension bridge is another 26km west of that, and the colossal **Pont de Normandie** spans the rivermouth itself, enabling motorists to zip between Le Havre and Honfleur. If you're driving this lovely riverside route, be sure to stop off at the intriguing ruins of the **Jumièges** abbey.

Upstream from Rouen, on the other hand, high cliffs on the north bank of the Seine imitate the coast, looking down on waves of green and scattered river islands. By the time you reach the splendid medieval castle at **Les Andelys**, 25km southeast of Rouen, you're within 100km of Paris, while another 30km brings you to one of Normandy's most visited tourist attractions, the village of **Giverny**.

Abbaye de Jumièges

The true highlight of the Seine valley nestles in an especially delightful loop of the river, just 23km west of Rouen. The majestic **abbey** of **JUMIÈGES** (mid-April to mid-Sept daily 9.30am–6.30pm; mid-Sept to mid-April daily 9.30am–1pm & 2.30–5.30pm; €5, ages 18–25 €3.50, under-18s free), is said to have been founded by St Philibert in 654 AD. A haunting ruin, the abbey was burned by marauding Vikings in 841, rebuilt a century later, then destroyed again – as a deliberate act – during the Revolution. Its main surviving outline, as far as it can still be discerned, dates from the eleventh century – William the Conqueror himself attended its reconsecration in 1067. The twin towers, 52m high, are still standing, as is one arch of the roofless nave, while a one-sided yew tree stands in the centre of what were once the cloisters.

The *Auberge des Ruines*, across from the abbey at 17 place de la Mairie (℡02.35.37.24.05; closed Sun eve, Tues eve, Wed and second fortnight of Aug), is a truly superb restaurant, with outdoor seating on a shaded terrace. Its dinner *menus* start at €35.

Les Andelys

The most dramatic sight anywhere along the Seine has to be Richard the Lionheart's **Château Gaillard**, perched high above **LES ANDELYS**. Constructed in a position of impregnable power, it looked down over all movement on the river at the frontier of the English king's domains. Built in less than a year (1196–97), the castle might have survived intact had Henri IV not ordered its destruction in 1603. As it is, the stout flint walls of its keep, roughly 4m thick, remain reasonably sound, and the outline of most of the rest is still clear, arranged over assorted green and chalky knolls (daily except Tues 10am–1pm & 2–6pm; guided tours mid-March to mid-Nov at 11am, 3pm & 4.30pm; entry €3.50, tour €5.20). On foot, you can make the steep climb up via a path that leads off rue Richard-Coeur-de-Lion in Petit Andely. The only route for motorists is extraordinarily convoluted, following a long-winded one-way system that starts opposite the church in Grand Andely.

The **tourist office** for Les Andelys is in Petit Andely, at 24 rue Philippe-Auguste (Mon–Sat 10am–noon & 2–6pm, Sun 10am–noon & 2–5pm; ℡02.32.54.41.93, Ⓦ ville-andelys.fr). The nicest **hotel** is the riverfront 🍴 *Chaîne d'Or*, opposite the thirteenth-century St-Sauveur church at 27 rue Grande (℡02.32.54.00.31, Ⓦ hotel-lachainedor.com; ❺; restaurant closed Mon lunch in Aug, Sun eve & Mon Sept–July), though the wonderful food in its **restaurant** is expensive. The neighbouring *Normandie*, at 1 rue Grande (℡02.32.54.10.52, Ⓦ hotelnormandie -andelys.com; ❸; restaurant closed Wed eve & Thurs, whole place closed Dec), is significantly cheaper and it too has a good restaurant. There's also a lovely riverside **campsite**, far below the château, the *L'Île des Trois Rois* (℡02.32.54.23.79, Ⓦ camping-troisrois.com; closed mid-Nov to mid-March).

Giverny

The house where **Claude Monet** lived from 1883 until his death in 1926 remains much as he left it – complete with water-lily pond – at **GIVERNY**, 20km south of Les Andelys near the north bank of the Seine (April–Oct daily 9.30am–6pm; last entry 5.30pm; €6; ℡02.32.51.28.21, Ⓦ www.fondation-monet.com). As none of Monet's original paintings is on display – most are in the Orangerie and Musée d'Orsay in Paris – although the **gardens** that he laid out are still lovingly tended in all their glory, art lovers who make the pilgrimage here tend to be outnumbered by garden enthusiasts.

Visits start in the huge **studio**, built in 1915, where Monet painted the last and largest of his many depictions of waterlilies (*nymphéas*). It now serves as a well-stocked book and gift shop. The **house** itself is a long two-storey structure, painted pastel pink with green shutters. Almost all the main rooms are crammed floor-to-ceiling with Monet's collection of Japanese prints. Most of the original furnishings are gone, but you get a real sense of how the dining room used to be, with all its walls and fittings painted a glorious bright yellow; Monet designed his own yellow crockery to harmonize with the surroundings.

The flower-filled **gardens** stretch down towards the river, though these days the footpath that drops to the **waterlily pond** is forced to burrow beneath the main road. Once there, paths around the pond, as well as arching Japanese footbridges, offer differing views of the waterlilies, cherished by gardeners in rowing boats. May and June, when the rhododendrons flower and the wisteria is in bloom, are the best times to visit. Whenever you come, however, you'll have to contend with camera-happy crowds jostling to capture their own impressions of the waterlilies.

A few minutes' walk up Giverny's village street, the **Musée des Impressionismes**, while unattractive from the outside, holds a spacious and well-lit gallery (April–Oct Tues–Sun 10am–6pm; €5.50, free first Sun of each month; ⓦwww.maag.org). It originally opened in 1992 to celebrate the work of Monet's many American followers, but its brief now covers his contemporaries of all nationalities.

Giverny's one **hotel**, the *Musardière*, stands not far beyond Monet's house at 123 rue Claude-Monet (ⓣ02.32.21.03.18, ⓦlamusardiere.fr; closed Nov–March; ❺); dinner *menus* in its restaurant start at €26. The nearest inexpensive accommodation is the *Hôtel d'Évreux*, 11 place d'Évreux (ⓣ02.32.21.16.12; ⓦwww.hoteldevreux .fr; ❷), across the river in the heart of the town of **VERNON**, where the cheapest rooms share bathrooms. Connecting buses from outside Vernon's **gare SNCF** run to a car park close to the gardens in Giverny (€4 return) and are timed to coincide with trains between Paris and Rouen.

Basse Normandie

As you head west along the coast of Basse Normandie from Le Havre, you come to a succession of somewhat exclusive resorts: **Trouville** and **Deauville** are the busiest centres here, while **Honfleur** is a delightful medieval port. Continuing west brings you to the beaches where the Allied armies landed in 1944, and then to the wilder, and in places deserted, shore around the **Cotentin Peninsula**.

Honfleur and the Norman Riviera

HONFLEUR, the best preserved of the old ports of Normandy and the most easterly on the Calvados coast, is a near-perfect seaside town that lacks only a beach. It used to have one, but with the accumulation of silt from the Seine the sea has steadily withdrawn, leaving the eighteenth-century waterfront houses of **boulevard Charles-V** stranded and a little surreal. The ancient port, however, still functions – the channel to the beautiful Vieux Bassin is kept open by regular dredging – and though only pleasure craft now use the moorings in the harbour basin, fishing boats tie up alongside the pier nearby.

While picturesque enough to attract hundreds of visitors daily, Honfleur remains recognizable as the fishing village that so appealed to nineteenth-century artists. Its compact size, quaint waterside setting and abundance of restaurants make it an ideal destination for a weekend break.

Arrival and information

Honfleur's **gare routière**, ten minutes' walk east of the Vieux Bassin, is served by frequent **buses** from Caen and Le Havre (Bus Verts; ⓣ08.10.21.42.14, ⓦwww .busverts.fr). However, the nearest **train station** is 20km south at Pont-l'Évêque, connected to Honfleur by the Lisieux bus #50 (20min ride).

The **tourist office**, on quai Le Paulmier, between the Vieux Bassin and the *gare routière* (Easter–June & Sept Mon–Sat 9.30am–12.30pm & 2–6.30pm, Sun 10am–12.30pm & 2–5pm; July & Aug Mon–Sat 9.30am–7pm, Sun 10am–5pm; Oct–Easter Mon–Sat 10am–12.30pm & 2–6pm; ☎02.31.89.23.30, ⊛ot-honfleur .fr), arranges **guided tours** in summer, and offers cheap **internet access**. Also in summer, several **cruises** sail upriver each day from either side of the Avant Port, for a closer look at the Pont de Normandie (40min trip; €6; ☎02.31.89.07.77).

Accommodation

It's hard to find a reasonably priced room in Honfleur in summer; budget travellers are better off simply visiting for the day. No hotels overlook the harbour itself, while motorists will find it hard to park anywhere near most central hotels. A two-star **campsite**, *Du Phare* (☎02.31.89.10.26, ⊛www.campings-plage.fr; closed Oct–March), is at the west end of boulevard Charles V on place Jean-de-Vienne.

Les Cascades 17 place Thiers ☎02.31.89.05.83, ⊛lescascades.com. Seventeen-room hotel-restaurant opening onto both place Thiers and the cobbled rue de la Ville behind. Slightly noisy rooms upstairs, and a good-value restaurant with outdoor seating; *menus* €16–35. Closed Mon & Tues in low season, plus mid-Nov to early Feb. ❸

La Cour Sainte-Catherine 74 rue du Puits ☎02.31.89.42.40, ⊛giaglis.com. Beautiful B&B tucked down a quiet street beyond Ste-Catherine church. Comfortable, well-decorated rooms around a plant-filled courtyard, with breakfast served in the old cider press. ❹

L'Ex Voto 8 place Albert-Sorel ☎02.31.89.19.69. Two clean, well-priced rooms above a friendly family-run bar, a short walk inland along the main

road from the Vieux Bassin. Both rooms have a bidet, but share a shower and toilet. Rates include breakfast. Closed Wed Sept–June, plus all Nov & Dec. ❸

Des Loges 18 rue Brûlée ☎02.31.89.38.26, ⊛www.hoteldesloges.com. Smart, brightly refurbished hotel, spread through three houses on a cobbled street 100m from Ste-Catherine church. It's run by helpful staff and offers good but expensive accommodation. Closed Jan. ❻

Monet Charrière du Puits ☎02.31.89.00.90, ⊛hotel-monet-honfleur .com. Spruce, modern en-suite rooms, in a welcoming ivy-covered house in a very quiet spot ten minutes' walk uphill from the centre. Courtyard parking available. ❹

The Town

Visitors to Honfleur inevitably gravitate towards the old centre, around the **Vieux Bassin**, where slate-fronted houses, each one or two storeys higher than seems possible, harmonize despite their tottering and ill-matched forms. They create a splendid backdrop for the **Lieutenance** at the harbour entrance, the former dwelling of the King's Lieutenant, which has been the gateway to the inner town since at least 1608, when Samuel Champlain sailed from Honfleur to found Québec.

Squeezed into the church of **St-Étienne** on the eastern side of the *bassin*, the **Musée de la Marine** combines a collection of model ships with several rooms of antique Norman furnishings (mid-Feb to March & Oct to mid-Nov Tues–Fri 2.30–5.30pm, Sat & Sun 10am–noon; April–Sept daily except Mon 10am–noon & 2–6.30pm; closed mid-Nov to mid-Feb; €3.50, €4.70 with Musée de Vieux Honfleur, €9.40 with Boudin & Satie museums as well). Alongside, on tiny rue de la Prison, a nice little ensemble that once held Honfleur's prison now serves as the **Musée du Vieux Honfleur** (same hours and entrance fee), filling ten rooms with a fascinating assortment of everyday artefacts from old Honfleur.

The town's artistic past – and its present concentration of galleries and painters – owes most to Eugène Boudin, forerunner of Impressionism, who was born here. He worked in the town, trained the 18-year-old Monet and was joined for various periods by Pissarro, Renoir and Cézanne. Boudin was among the founders of what's now the **Musée Eugène Boudin** (mid-March to Sept daily except Tues

10am–noon & 2–6pm; Oct to mid-March Mon & Wed–Fri 2.30–5.30pm, Sat & Sun 10am–noon & 2.30–5.30pm; €6.50), west of the port on place Érik-Satie, and he left 53 works to it after his death in 1898. His pastel seascapes and sunsets hold an especial resonance in this setting, where panoramic windows offer superb views of the Seine estuary.

Honfleur's most remarkable building has to be the church of **Ste-Catherine** (daily: summer 9am–6pm; winter 9am–5.30pm), which like its distinctive detached **belfry** (one of Monet's favourite subjects in his younger days) is built almost entirely of wood. The church itself has the added peculiarity of being divided into twin naves, with one balcony running around both. The belfry holds random ethnographic oddities, and visitors are not permitted above ground level (same hours as Eugène Boudin museum; €2 on its own, or free entry with museum ticket).

The red-timbered former home of composer **Érik Satie**, down the hill from the Musée Boudin at 67 bd Charles-V, is open to visitors as **Les Maisons Satie** (daily except Tues: May–Sept 10am–7pm; mid-Feb to April & Oct–Dec 11am–6pm; last entry 1hr before closing; €5.50). From the outside it looks unchanged since the composer was born there in 1866. Step inside, however, and you'll find yourself in Normandy's most unusual and eccentric museum. It's worth finding out a little about Satie before visiting, as the unconventional exhibits provide few facts. Instead, as befits a close associate of the Surrealists, Satie is commemorated by all sorts of weird and wonderful interactive surprises. It would be a shame to give too many of them away here; suffice it to say that you're immediately confronted by a giant pear, bouncing into the air on huge wings to the strains of his best-known piano series, *Gymnopédies*.

Eating

With its abundance of visitors, Honfleur supports an astonishing number of **restaurants**, many specializing in seafood. Few face onto the harbour itself; most of the narrow buildings around its edge are home to crêperies, cafés and ice-cream parlours.

Le Bréard 7 rue du Puits ☏02.31.89.53.49, ⓦ www.restaurant-lebreard.com. Highly creative, contemporary take on classic French cuisine, just off the church square. Lunch €20 (Thurs–Sat only), dinner *menus* €28–49. Closed 3 weeks in Dec, closed for lunch Mon–Wed.

La Fleur de Sel 17 rue Haute ☏02.31.89.01.92. Elegant, formal option, with indoor seating only, offering gourmet *menus* at €28, €38 and €58 that are equally strong on meat and fish. Closed Tues & Wed, plus all Jan.

La Lieutenance 12 place Ste-Catherine ☏02.31.89.07.52. Not by the Lieutenance, despite the name, but facing both church and belfry on the cobbled square, with plenty of outdoor seating. Gourmet dining with a heavy emphasis on oysters;

menus start at €15 for two courses, €19 for three. Closed Sun eve in winter.

Au P'tit Mareyeur 4 rue Haute ☏02.31.98.84.23. No distance from the centre, but all the seating is indoors and there are no views. Very good fish dishes, plus plenty of creamy *pays d'Auge* sauces and superb desserts. Lunch *menus* from €25, dinner from €30. Closed Mon, Tues & Jan.

Au Vieux Honfleur 13 quai St-Étienne ☏02.31.89.15.31. The best restaurant on the harbour, with spacious alfresco dining – in shade at lunchtime – on its pedestrianized eastern side. Simple *menus*, but the seafood is very good, as befits the price of €31 ("des Peintres") or €49 ("des Poètes").

Trouville and Deauville

Heading west along the corniche from Honfleur, green fields and fruit trees lull the land's edge, and cliffs rise from sandy beaches all the way to Trouville, 15km away. The resorts aren't cheap but if you want to stop along the coast this is a good place to do it. The next stretch is what you might call the Riviera of Normandy, where Trouville plays "Nice" to Deauville's "Cannes".

TROUVILLE is perhaps more of a real town, with a constant population and industries other than tourism. But it's still a resort, with a tangle of pedestrian streets just back from the beach that are alive with restaurants and hotels, and a busy boardwalk running along a sandy beach. On Wednesday mornings, a lively market selling everything from fluorescent underpants to local produce runs along the quayside. Although Trouville has been a chic destination ever since Napoléon III started bringing his court here every summer in the 1860s, its glamour has faded somewhat, while that of **DEAUVILLE** next door has only grown. One of Napoléon's dukes, looking across the river that now separates the two towns, saw, instead of marshlands, money – and lots of it, in the form of a racetrack. His vision materialized, and villas appeared between the racetrack and the sea. Now Deauville is slightly larger than its neighbour, and significantly smarter, its sleek streets lined with designer boutiques and chic cafés. In summer, life revolves around the beach and the *planches*, 650m of boardwalk, beyond which rows of primary-coloured parasols obscure the view of the sea.

Deauville's **American Film Festival** (Ⓦwww.festival-deauville.com), held in the first week of September, is the antithesis of Cannes, with public admission to a wide selection of previews.

Practicalities

Trouville and Deauville share their **gare SNCF** and **gare routière**, located in between the two just south of the marina. Each day, ten of the hourly buses from Caen continue along the coast to Honfleur. In summer only, CityJet (Ⓦcityjet .com) **flies** from London's City Airport direct to Deauville.

Deauville's **tourist office** is on place de la Mairie (mid-June to mid-Sept Mon–Sat 9am–7pm, Sun 10am–6pm; mid-Sept to mid-June Mon–Sat 10am–6pm, Sun 10am–1pm & 2–5pm; Ⓣ02.31.14.40.00, Ⓦdeauville.org). Trouville's equivalent is at 32 quai Fernand Moureaux (April–June, Sept & Oct Mon–Sat 9.30am–noon & 2–6.30pm, Sun 10am–1pm; July & Aug Mon–Sat 9.30am–7pm, Sun 10am–4pm; Nov–March Mon–Sat 9.30am–noon & 1.30–6.30pm, Sun 10am–1pm; Ⓣ02.31.14.60.70, Ⓦwww.trouvillesurmer.org).

As you might imagine, **hotels** tend to be luxurious, overpriced or both. If you fancy staying right on the seafront, it's hard to beat the *Flaubert*, rue Gustave-Flaubert (Ⓣ02.31.88.37.23, Ⓦwww.flaubert.fr; ❺), a grand, faux-timbered mansion with spacious, comfortable rooms at the start of Trouville's boardwalk. Cheaper options include the *Hôtel des Sports*, behind Deauville's fish market at 27 rue Gambetta (Ⓣ02.31.88.22.67; closed Feb & Nov, plus Sun in winter; ❸), and Trouville's closest equivalent, *Le Trouville*, 50m from the beach at 1 rue Thiers (Ⓣ02.31.98.45.48, Ⓦwww.hotelletrouville.com; closed Jan; ❹). Deauville, meanwhile, has a **campsite**, *La Vallée de Deauville*, 3km from the centre on route de Beaumont-en-Auge in St-Arnoult (Ⓣ02.31.88.58.17, Ⓦwww.camping-deauville.com; open April–Oct).

A good **place to eat** in Deauville is *Chez Miocque* at 81 rue Eugène-Colas (Ⓣ02.31.88.09.52; closed Tues in winter, plus all Jan), a top-quality Parisian-style bistro where a three-course meal costs around €40. Trouville also has its fair share of good fish restaurants, including *La Petite Auberge*, 7 rue Carnot (Ⓣ02.31.88.11.07; closed Tues all year, plus Wed except in Aug).

Houlgate

A hundred years ago, **HOULGATE**, 15km west of Deauville, was every bit as glamorous and sophisticated a destination as its immediate neighbours. What makes it different today is that it has barely changed since then. Its long straight beach remains lined with a stately procession of nineteenth-century villas, while the town's handful of commercial enterprises are confined to the narrow parallel street, the **rue des Bains**, fifty metres inland. As a result, Houlgate is the most relaxed of the local resorts, ideal if you're looking for a peaceful family break where the only stress is deciding whether to paddle or play mini-golf.

The **tourist office** is well back from the sea on boulevard des Belges (Easter–June & Sept Mon–Sat 10am–1pm & 2–6pm, Sun 10.30am–1pm & 2–4pm; July & Aug daily 10am–1pm & 2–6.30pm; Nov–Easter Mon–Sat 10am–1pm & 2–6pm; ℡02.31.24.34.79, ⓦwww.ville-houlgate.fr). The *Hostellerie Normande*, just off the rue des Bains at 11 rue Émile Deschanel (℡02.31.24.85.50, ⓦhotel-houlgate .com; ❹), is a pretty but rather impersonal little **hotel** covered with ivy and creeping flowers, with a €16.50 lunch *menu*. Above the Vaches Noires ("Black Cows") cliffs on the corniche road east of town, ⚲ *La Ferme Auberge des Aulnettes* (℡02.31.28.00.28; ❸) is a lovely half-timbered country house in pleasant gardens, where the cheapest rooms have showers but share a WC. A pleasant restaurant with outdoor seating serves *menus* from €18.

Caen and around

CAEN, capital and largest city of Basse Normandie, is not a place that many tourists go out of their way to visit: it was completely devastated during the fighting of 1944. Its central feature is a ring of ramparts that no longer have a castle to protect, and a busy road network fills the wide spaces where prewar houses stood. However, the former home to William the Conqueror remains impressive in parts, adorned with the scattered spires and buttresses of two abbeys and eight old churches, plus some pretty pedestrianized shopping streets and a restaurant-lined marina. It also makes a convenient and pleasant base for exploring the D-Day beaches.

Arrival and information

Caen's **gare SNCF** stands a kilometre south of the centre across the river Orne, with the **gare routière** alongside. Local **buses** and **trams** are run by TWISTO (℡02.31.15.55.55, ⓦtwisto.fr), which has ticket and information centres at 15 rue de Geôle (just north of the tourist office), and on boulevard Maréchal-Leclerc. Single journeys cost €1.20, and a 24-hour pass €3.55. The main tram route connects the southern and northern suburbs, running through the heart of the city from the *gare SNCF* up avenue du 6-juin to the university and beyond.

The local **tourist office** is on place St-Pierre across from the church of St-Pierre (March Mon–Sat 9.30am–1pm & 2–6.30pm; April–June & Sept Mon–Sat 9.30am–1pm & 2–6.30pm, Sun 10am–1pm; July & Aug Mon–Sat 9am–7pm, Sun 10am–1pm & 2–5pm; Oct–Feb Mon–Sat 9.30am–1pm & 2–6pm; ℡02.31.27.14.14, ⓦwww.tourisme.caen.fr). You can go **online** at Espace Micro, on place Courtonne at 1 rue Basse, or at the main **post office** on place Gambetta (Mon–Fri 8am–7pm, Sat 8.30am–12.30pm).

Accommodation

Caen has a great number of **hotels**, though, as ever in the rebuilt bomb-damaged cities of Normandy, few could be called attractive. They're not particularly concentrated in any one area, but you'll find clusters just west of the castle and tourist office, as well as around the pleasure port, and a handful facing the *gare SNCF*.

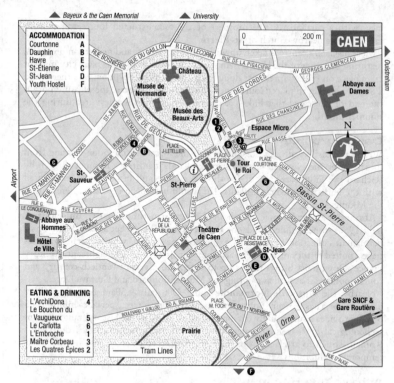

ACCOMMODATION
Courtonne   A
Dauphin   B
Havre   E
St-Étienne   C
St-Jean   D
Youth Hostel   F

EATING & DRINKING
L'ArchiDona   4
Le Bouchon du
   Vaugueux   5
Le Carlotta   6
L'Embroche   1
Maître Corbeau   3
Les Quatres Épices   2

Tram Lines

Courtonne 5 rue des Prairies St-Gilles
☎02.31.93.47.83, ⌨hotelcourtonne.com.
Welcoming, modernized hotel overlooking the
place Courtonne and the pleasure port, though the
building is so narrow it's easy to miss. All rooms
have bath or shower, phone and TV. **③**
Dauphin 29 rue Gémare ☎02.31.86.22.26,
⌨le-dauphin-normandie.com. Upmarket Best
Western hotel behind the tourist office. The
public areas are impressive, while the rooms
are comfortable but relatively compact, at least
at the lower end of the price scale. Sauna and
fitness facilities are available, plus a grand
restaurant; dinner €17.50 weekdays, €34 or €56
weekends. **⑤**
Havre 11 rue du Havre ☎02.31.86.19.80,
⌨hotelduhavre.com. Modern, cosy,
welcoming and very good-value budget hotel, a

block south of St-Jean church, close to the trams
and with free parking. **②**
St-Étienne 2 rue de l'Académie ☎02.31.86.35.82,
⌨hotel-saint-etienne.com. Friendly budget hotel
housed in a venerable stone house in the characterful St-Martin district, not far from the Abbaye
aux Hommes. The cheapest rooms share
bathrooms; en-suite ones cost little more. **①**
St-Jean 20 rue des Martyrs ☎02.31.86.23.35.
Simple but well-equipped rooms – all have shower
or bath – facing St-Jean church. Free parking. **②**
Youth Hostel Foyer Robert-Remé, 68bis rue
Eustache Restout, Grâce-de-Dieu
☎02.31.52.19.96, ⌨www.fuaj.org/Caen. Lively
and welcoming hostel, situated in a sleepy area
500m southwest of the *gare SNCF*. Beds in both
four-bed dorms or two-bed private rooms cost €14
per person. Reception 5–9pm. Open June–Sept.

The City

A virtue was made of the postwar necessity of clearing away the rubble of Caen's
medieval houses, which formerly pressed up against its ancient **château ramparts**.
The resulting open green space has left those walls fully visible for the first time in
centuries. In turn, walking the circuit of the ramparts gives a good overview of the

city, with a particularly fine prospect of the reconstructed fourteenth-century facade of the nearby church of **St-Pierre**.

Most of Caen's centre is taken up with shopping streets and pedestrian precincts, featuring branches of the big Parisian stores and local rivals. The main city **market** takes place on Friday, spreading along both sides of Fosse St-Julien, and there's also a Sunday market in place Courtonne. The **Bassin St-Pierre**, the pleasure port at the end of the canal that links Caen to the sea, is the liveliest area during the summer months.

Castle grounds

Within the castle walls, it's possible to visit the former **Exchequer** – dating from shortly after the Norman Conquest of England, it hosted a banquet thrown by Richard the Lionheart en route to the Crusades – and inspect a garden planted with the herbs and medicinal plants that would have been cultivated here during the Middle Ages.

Also inside the castle precinct, though in new structures, are two **museums**. A light 1960s stone building holds the **Beaux-Arts** (daily except Tues 9.30am–6pm; permanent collection free, special exhibitions €5 or €7), where upstairs galleries trace a potted history of European art from Renaissance Italy to eighteenth-century France. Downstairs brings things up to date with diverse twentieth-century and contemporary art as well as paintings by Monet, Bonnard and Gustave Doré.

Nearby, the **Musée de Normandie** (June–Oct daily 9.30am–6pm; Nov–May daily except Tues 9.30am–6pm; permanent collection free, special exhibitions €5 or €7) provides a surprisingly cursory overview of Norman history, ranging from archeological finds from the megalithic period and glass jewellery from Gallo-Roman Rouen to artefacts from the Industrial Revolution. It also hosts regular temporary exhibitions.

Abbaye aux Hommes

The magnificent **Abbaye aux Hommes**, at the west end of rue St-Pierre, was founded by William the Conqueror and designed to hold his tomb within the huge, austere Romanesque church of St-Étienne (Mon–Sat 8.30am–12.30pm & 1.30–7pm, Sun 8.30am–12.30pm & 2.30–7pm; free; 1hr 15min guided tours leave adjacent Hôtel de Ville daily 9.30am, 11am, 2.30pm & 4pm; tours in English mid-July to Aug only, times vary; €2.50, free on Sun). However, his burial here, in 1087, was hopelessly undignified. The funeral procession first caught fire and was then held to ransom, as various factions squabbled over his rotting corpse for any spoils they could grab. During the Revolution the tomb was again ransacked, and now holds a solitary thigh-bone rescued from the river. Still, the building itself is a spectacular Romanesque monument. Adjoining the church are the abbey buildings, designed during the eighteenth century and now housing the Hôtel de Ville.

William's queen, Mathilda, lies across town in the **Abbaye aux Dames** at the end of rue des Chanoines. She had commissioned the building of the abbey church, La Trinité, well before the Conquest. It's starkly impressive, with a gloomy pillared crypt, superb stained glass behind the altar, and odd sculptural details like the fish curled up in the holy-water stoup (daily 2–5.30pm; guided tours 2.30pm & 4pm; free).

The Caen Memorial

Just north of Caen, at the end of avenue Marshal-Montgomery, the **Caen Memorial** (late Jan to mid-Feb and mid-Nov to Dec daily except Mon 9.30am–6pm; mid-Feb to mid-Nov daily 9am–7pm; closed 3 weeks in Jan; last entry 1hr 15min before closing time; May–Sept €18.50, Oct–April €18; ⓦwww.memorial-caen.fr) stands on a plateau named after General Eisenhower on a clifftop beneath which the Germans had their HQ in June and July 1944. It's served by bus #2 from the "Tour le Roi" stop in the centre of town.

The museum is a typically French, high-tech novel-architecture conception, with excellent displays divided into several distinct sections. Having started out as a "museum for peace", its brief has expanded to cover history since the Great War; allow two hours at the very least for a visit. It begins with the rise of fascism in Germany, follows with resistance and collaboration in France, then charts all the major battles of World War II, with a special emphasis on D-Day and its aftermath. Further areas examine the Cold War, and Berlin in particular. Most of the captions, though not always the written exhibits themselves, are translated into English. The memorial also hosts regular temporary exhibitions, and has a good-value self-service restaurant.

Eating

Caen's town centre offers two major areas for **eating**: with cosmopolitan restaurants in the pedestrianized **quartier Vaugueux** and more traditional French restaurants on the streets off **rue de Geôle**, near the western ramparts.

L'ArchiDona 8 rue des Croisiers ☏ 02.31.85.30.30, ⊛ www.archidona.fr. This classy and atmospheric restaurant belies its stately setting by serving delightfully fresh Mediterranean-influenced cuisine, ranging from simple entrée-plus-dessert meals at €14 up to the €33 "seduction" and €46 "emotion" *menus*. Closed Sun, Mon & three weeks in Aug.

Le Bouchon du Vaugueux 12 rue du Graindorge ☏ 02.31.44.26.26. Intimate little brasserie in the Vaugueux quarter, offering well-prepared French classics on just two *menus*, at €18 and €26. Closed Mon & Sun, plus first three weeks of Aug.

Le Carlotta 16 quai Vendeuvre ☏ 02.31.86.68.99, ⊛ www.lecarlotta.fr. Smart, busy, fashionable Paris-style brasserie beside the pleasure port, which serves good Norman cooking both à la carte and on *menus* at €23 (not Sat), €27 and €36. Closed Sun.

L'Embroche 17 rue de la Porte au Berger ☏ 02.31.93.71.31. Cosy little place, where the open kitchen whips up simple regional specialities in full view of appreciative diners, with lunch from €17.50 and dinner from €25. Closed Sat lunch, Sun & Mon lunch.

Maître Corbeau 8 rue Buquet ☏ 02.31.93.93.00. Large, eccentric restaurant with an entirely cheese-related menu featuring fondue, *raclette* and *tartiflette* to name but a few. The kitsch decor ties in with the theme too. A typical fondue costs around €14, while non-fondue *menus* start from €19. Closed Sat lunch, Sun, Mon lunch & three weeks in Aug.

Les Quatres Épices 25 rue de la Porte au Berger ☏ 02.31.93.40.41. Lively West African restaurant, just off rue du Vaugueux. Everything is à la carte – prawns with sweet potato for €19.50, grilled fish with ginger and spices for €16.50, plus plantains and meat galore – and African music plays nonstop.

Bayeux

BAYEUX, with its perfectly preserved medieval ensemble, magnificent **cathedral** and world-famous **tapestry**, stands just 23km west of Caen. It's a smaller and much more intimate town, and, despite the large crowds of summer tourists, a far more enjoyable place to visit. A mere 10km from the coast, Bayeux was the first French city liberated in 1944, the day after D-Day. Occupied so quickly that it escaped serious damage, it briefly became capital of Free France.

Arrival and information

Bayeux's **gare SNCF** is fifteen minutes' walk southeast of the town centre, just outside the ring road, while **buses** stop both there and on the other side of town, on the north side of place St-Patrice.

The **tourist office** stands in the very centre of town, on the arched pont St-Jean (Jan–March & Nov–Dec Mon–Sat 9.30am–12.30pm & 2–5.30pm; April–May &

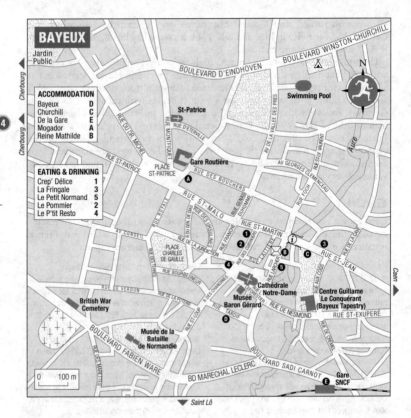

Sept–Oct daily 9.30am–12.30pm & 2–6pm; June–Aug Mon–Sat 9am–7pm, Sun 9am–1pm & 2–6pm; ☎02.31.51.28.28, ⓦbessin-normandie.fr). **Internet** access is available at the **post office**, just around the corner at 14 rue Larcher (Mon–Fri 8.15am–6.30pm, Sat 8.15am–noon; ☎02.31.51.24.90).

Accommodation

Bayeux is well equipped with **accommodation**, though its hotels tend to be more expensive than elsewhere in Normandy. There's a large three-star **campsite** on boulevard d'Eindhoven (☎02.31.92.08.43, ⓦwww.mairie-bayeux.fr; May–Sept), on the northern ring road (RN13) near the river.

Bayeux 9 rue Tardif ☎02.31.92.70.08, ⓦlebayeux.com. Good-value central hotel, across from the Baron Gérard museum, with several large family rooms ideal for sharers. No restaurant. ❸

Churchill 14–16 rue St-Jean ☎02.31.21.31.80, ⓦhotel-churchill.fr. Perfectly situated in the heart of town, with its own free parking, this beautifully furnished 32-room hotel has no restaurant, but offers personal and friendly service. Closed Dec–Feb. ❻

De la Gare 26 place de la Gare ☎02.31.92.10.70, ⒺHotel-delagare.bayeux@orange.fr. Set beside the station, a 15min walk from the cathedral, this is a basic but perfectly adequate hotel, with a simple brasserie. Tours of D-Day beaches arranged through Normandy Tours (see p.295), who are based here. ❶

Mogador 20 rue Chartier ☎02.31.92.24.58, Ⓔhotel.mogador@orange.fr. Friendly little hotel facing Bayeux's main square; the rooms are simple but very presentable, with the quieter ones overlooking the inner courtyard. ❸

Reine Mathilde 23 rue Larcher ⓣ02.31.92.08.13, ⓦhotel-reinemathilde.com. Simple but well-equipped en-suite rooms backing onto the canal, between the tapestry and the cathedral. There's a nice open-air brasserie/crêperie downstairs. Closed Dec–Feb. ❸

The Town

The extraordinary **Bayeux Tapestry**, also known to the French as the *Tapisserie de la Reine Mathilde*, is housed in a grand eighteenth-century seminary on rue de Nesmond, remodelled as the **Centre Guillaume le Conquérant** (daily: mid-March to April & Sept to early Nov 9am–6.30pm; May–Aug 9am–7pm; early Nov to mid-March 9.30am–12.30pm & 2–6pm; last admission 45min before closing; €7.80; ⓦtapisserie-bayeux.fr).

Created over nine centuries ago, this 70m strip of linen recounts the story of the Norman Conquest of England. The brilliance of its coloured wools has barely faded, and the tale is enlivened throughout with scenes of medieval life, popular fables and mythical beasts; its draughtsmanship, and the sheer vigour and detail, are stunning. The work is thought to have been carried out by nuns in England, commissioned by Bishop Oddo, William's half-brother, for the inauguration of Bayeux Cathedral in 1077.

Visits are highly atmospheric, if somewhat exhausting. Unexpectedly, the first thing you see is the tapestry itself, with an interesting audio-guided commentary explaining the events depicted so vividly on the canvas. It looks – and reads – much like a modern comic strip. Harold is every inch the villain, with his dastardly little moustache and shifty eyes. He looks extremely self-satisfied as he breaks his oath to accept William as king of England and seizes the throne for himself, but his come-uppance swiftly follows, as William, the noble hero, crosses the Channel and defeats the English armies at Hastings. Only afterwards comes an exhibition detailing the theories that surround the tapestry's creation, and explaining more about its turbulent history, followed by a film (shown in English at least once an hour in summer) that gives more of the historical background.

The **Cathédrale Notre-Dame** (daily: Jan–March 9am–5pm; April–June & Oct–Dec 9am–6pm; July–Sept 9am–7pm; free), the first home of the tapestry, is just a short walk from its latest resting place. The original Romanesque plan of the building is still intact, although only the crypt and towers date from the original work of 1077. The crypt is a beauty, its columns graced with frescoes of angels playing trumpets and bagpipes, looking exhausted by their performance for eternity. Alongside the cathedral, the **Musée Baron Gérard** displays a large collection of beautifully decorated porcelain and intricate lacework, donated to the archbishops of Bayeux (daily: July & Aug 10am–12.30pm & 2–7pm; Sept–June 10am–12.30pm & 2–6pm; €3.50, free with tapestry ticket).

Set behind massive guns on the southwest side of town, Bayeux's **Musée Mémorial de la Bataille de Normandie** (daily: May–Sept 9.30am–6.30pm; Oct–April 10am–12.30pm & 2–6pm; €6.50) provides a readily accessible, visceral and highly visual, overview of the Battle of Normandy. Rather than endless military hardware, it's filled with colour photos, maps and display panels that trace the development of the campaign, with good sections on German counter-attacks and the role of the press. The understated and touching **British War Cemetery** stands immediately across the road (see box, p.297).

Eating

Several of Bayeux's hotels hold good **restaurants** or brasseries. Otherwise, most restaurants are in the rue St-Jean leading east from the river, or near the main door of the cathedral.

4

Crep' Délice 16 rue des Cuisiniers
☎02.31.51.71.16. Cheap but chic crêperie serving
an imaginative range of savoury *galettes* followed
by sweet crêpes.
La Fringale 43 rue St-Jean ☎02.31.21.34.40. The
nicest of the pavement restaurants along rue
St-Jean, offering lunch *menus* from €16, and also
generous salads and snacks, plus formal fish
dinners. Closed Wed, plus mid-Dec to mid-Feb.
Le Petit Normand 35 rue Larcher
☎02.31.22.88.66. Below the cathedral, offering
good traditional cooking, with seafood specialities
and local cider. Lunch *menus* from €13, dinner

from €19. Closed Tues & Wed, plus mid-Dec
to Jan.
Le Pommier 38–40 rue des Cuisiniers
☎02.31.21.52.10. Traditional restaurant near the
cathedral, with a tiny terrace. Meat- and dairy-rich
Norman cuisine on *menus* from €15 (lunch only) up
to €30, including a vegetarian option. Closed
mid-Dec to mid-Jan.
Le P'tit Resto 2 rue Bienvenue ☎02.31.51.85.40.
Tiny old place opposite the cathedral, where the
"creative cuisine" extends to veal chop fried in
wasabi, and rolled monkfish with tandoori stuffing.
Menus from €16 at lunch, €20 at dinner. Closed Sun.

The D-Day beaches

At dawn on **D-Day**, June 6, 1944, Allied troops landed at points along the
Normandy coast from the mouth of the Orne to the eastern Cotentin Peninsula.
For the most part, the shore consists of innocuous beaches backed by gentle dunes,
and yet this foothold in Europe was won at the cost of 100,000 lives. That the
invasion happened here, and not nearer to Germany, was partly due to the failure
of the Canadian raid on Dieppe in 1942, which demonstrated the even more
appalling casualties that would have resulted from an assault on a cliff-dominated
coastline. The ensuing **Battle of Normandy** killed thousands of civilians and
reduced nearly six hundred towns and villages to rubble, but within a week of its
eventual conclusion, Paris was liberated.

The various beaches are still often referred to by their wartime code names. The
British and Commonwealth forces landed on **Sword**, **Juno** and **Gold** beaches
between Ouistreham and Arromanches; the Americans, further west on **Omaha**
and **Utah** beaches. Substantial traces of the fighting are rare, the most remarkable
being the remains of the astounding **Mulberry Harbour** at **Arromanches**, 10km
northeast of Bayeux. Further west, at **Pointe du Hoc** on Omaha Beach, the cliff
heights are deeply pitted with German bunkers and shell holes, while the church
at **Ste-Mère-Église**, from whose steeple the US paratrooper dangled during
heavy fighting throughout *The Longest Day*, still stands, and now has a model
parachute permanently fastened to the roof. Just about every coastal town has its
war museum. These tend as a rule to shy away from the unbearable reality of war
in favour of *Boy's Own*-style heroics, but the wealth of incidental human detail can
nonetheless be overpowering.

Bus Verts (☎08.10.21.42.14, ⓦwww.busverts.fr) run all along this coast. From
Bayeux, bus #75 goes to Arromanches, Courseulles and Ouistreham, and bus #70
to the Pointe du Hoc, the US cemetery at Colleville-sur-Mer and Port-en-Bessin.
From Caen, bus #30 runs inland to Bayeux, express bus #1 to Ouistreham, and
express bus #3 to Courseulles.

Normandie Pass

If you plan to visit several D-Day-related sights, it's worth paying €1 extra on your first
admission to a participating attraction to buy a **Normandie Pass** (ⓦwww.normandie
pass.com). The card offers discounts varying from €0.30 to €4.50 on entry to 26
museums and sights on the D-Day circuit, including the Caen Memorial, the Musée du
Débarquement at Arromanches and the Pegasus Memorial. It can also be used at
certain other Basse Normandie attractions, such as Cherbourg's Cité de la Mer.

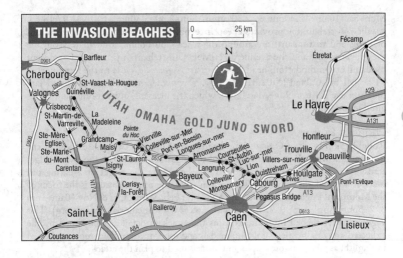

THE INVASION BEACHES

The Caen Memorial (see p.290) organizes expensive but informative bilingual **guided tours** of the beaches in small groups of around eight people, combining four or five hours on the road with a visit to the Memorial, either at your own pace (€75) or with a guide (€109.50; includes lunch). Other operators offering D-Day **tours**, at typical prices of around €50 for half a day and €80 for a full day, include Normandy Sightseeing Tours (☎02.31.51.70.52, ⓦd-daybeaches .com), Victory Tours (☎02.31.51.98.14, ⓦvictorytours.com), Battlebus (☎02.31.22.28.82, ⓦwww.battlebus.fr) and Normandy Tours (☎02.31.92.10.70, ⓦwww.normandy-landing-tour.com).

Ouistreham and around

Although **OUISTREHAM-RIVA BELLA**, on the coast 15km north of Caen, has been connected by ferry with Portsmouth, England since 1986, it remains at heart a small seaside village. From the port itself at its eastern end, it's easy to drive straight out of town on the fast dual carriageway towards Caen. Head west instead, immediately outside the terminal, and you'll soon come to the handful of charming old streets at the heart of the old town. The sea itself lies a couple of hundred metres north of here, along the semi-pedestrianized **avenue de la Mer**, home to several inexpensive snack bars and restaurants. Strictly speaking, the waterfront, backing a long straight beach, is a separate community known as **Riva Bella**. Its large central **casino**, on place Alfred-Thomas, has been remodelled as a 1930s passenger liner, housing an expensive restaurant and cocktail bar, while gloriously old-fashioned bathing huts face onto the sands.

Nearby, the **Musée du Mur de l'Atlantique** (daily: Feb, March & Oct–Dec 10am–6pm; April–Sept 9am–7pm; €7; ⓦwww.musee-grand-bunker.com) is housed in a lofty bunker – hence its alternative name, the Grand Bunker. Now heavily restored, the bunker was headquarters to several German batteries that defended the mouth of the River Orne, and fell to Allied forces on June 9, 1944. Inside, displays re-create the living quarters, with newspapers, cutlery and cigarette packets adding a welcome human touch to the moderately interesting explanations of the generators, gas filters and radio room.

The **tourist office**, alongside the casino on the beach (April–June & Sept daily 10am–12.30pm & 2–6.30pm; July & Aug daily 10am–1pm & 2–7pm; Oct–March

Mon–Sat 10am–12.30pm & 2.30–6pm, Sun 2.30–5.30pm; ℡02.31.97.18.63, Ⓦville-ouistreham.fr), provides cheap **internet access**. The main concentrations of **cafés** and **restaurants** are around the place Courbonne, immediately outside the *gare maritime*, and the avenue de la Mer, Ouistreham's main drag. For decent food and accommodation, head for the smart *Normandie*, close to the ferry port at 71 av Michel-Cabieu (℡02.31.97.19.57, Ⓦwww.lenormandie.com; closed Jan, plus Sun eve & Mon Nov–March; ❹), which has pleasant, quiet rooms, and serves good *menus* from €21.

Pegasus Bridge

Roughly 5km south of Ouistreham, the main road towards Caen passes close by the site now known as **Pegasus Bridge**. On the night before D-Day, the twin bridges across the Caen canal and the River Orne here were the target of a daring but successful Allied glider assault. Replaced in 1994, the original bridge is the focus of the **Mémorial Pegasus** immediately east (daily: Feb, March, Oct & Nov 10am–1pm & 2–5pm; April–Sept 9.30am–6.30pm; €6; Ⓦwww.memorial-pegasus.org). This vaguely glider-shaped museum explains the attack in detail, accompanied by the expected array of helmets, goggles, medals and other memorabilia, most captioned in English, as well as photographs and models used to plan the attack.

Arromanches

While basically a little seaside village, **ARROMANCHES**, cradled between high cliffs 31km west of Ouistreham, has the strongest identity of all the resorts along this shoreline. This was the location of the artificial **Mulberry Harbour**, "Port Winston", that facilitated the landings of two and a half million men and half a million vehicles. Two of these prefab concrete constructions were built in segments in Britain, then towed across the Channel at 6kph as the invasion began. The seafront **Musée du Débarquement**, in Arromanches' main square (daily: Feb, Nov & Dec 10am–12.30pm & 1.30–5pm; March & Oct 9.30am–12.30pm & 1.30–5.30pm; April 9am–12.30pm & 1.30–6pm; May–Aug 9am–7pm; Sept 9am–6pm; closed Jan; €6.50; Ⓦmusee-arromanches.fr), recounts the whole story. A huge picture window enables visitors to look straight out to the bulky remains of the harbour (the other one, further west on Omaha Beach, was destroyed by a storm within a few weeks). Several other war memorials are scattered throughout Arromanches, including a crucifix and a statue of the Virgin Mary, high up on the cliffs above the invasion site.

Nonetheless, Arromanches somehow manages to be quite a cheerful place to stay, with a lively pedestrian street of **bars** and **brasseries**, and a long expanse of sand where you can rent windsurf boards. Its **tourist office** is just back from the sea at 2 rue Maréchal-Joffre (daily: July & Aug 9am–6pm; Sept–June 10am–noon & 2–5pm; ℡02.31.22.36.45, Ⓦwww.arromanches.com).

The spacious three-star municipal **campsite** is 200m back from the seafront (℡02.31.22.36.78; closed Nov to late March). *La Marine*, at 2 quai Canada (℡02.31.22.34.19, Ⓦhotel-de-la-marine.fr; ❹), is a slightly expensive **hotel**, with well-appointed rooms – many of which enjoy superb sea views – and an excellent restaurant serving fish *menus* from €22; there's also a cheaper brasserie, the *Winston*, alongside. Across the square, the *Arromanches*, 2 rue du Colonel René Michel (℡02.31.22.36.26, Ⓦhoteldarromanches.fr; closed Jan, plus Tues & Wed in low season; ❹), is less well situated but just as comfortable, and its *Pappagall* restaurant has reasonable *menus*.

Colleville-sur-Mer and Utah Beach

The clifftop village of **COLLEVILLE-SUR-MER**, above Omaha Beach 21km along, marks the start of the long approach road to the larger of the two

The war cemeteries

The World War II cemeteries that dot the Normandy countryside are filled with foreigners; most of the French dead are buried in the churchyards of their home towns. After the war, some felt the soldiers should remain in the makeshift graves dug where they fell. Instead, commissions gathered the remains into cemeteries devoted to the separate warring nations. In total, over 140,000 young men were disinterred; more than half of the 31,744 US casualties were repatriated.

The 27 **British and Commonwealth cemeteries** are magnificently maintained, and open in every sense. They tend not to be screened off with hedges or walls, or to consist of expanses of manicured lawn, but are instead intimate, punctuated with flowers. The family of each soldier suggested an inscription for his tomb, making each grave very personal, yet part of a common attempt to bring meaning to the carnage. Some epitaphs are questioning – "One day we will understand"; some are accepting – "Our lad at rest"; some matter-of-fact, simply giving the home address. Interspersed among them all is the chilling refrain of the anonymous: "A soldier... known unto God". Thus the cemetery outside Ryes, northeast of Bayeux, where so many graves bear the date of D-Day, and so many victims are under 20, remains immediate and accessible. Even the monumental sculpture is subdued, a very British sort of fumbling for the decent thing to say. The understatement of the memorial at Bayeux, with its contrived Latin epigram commemorating the return as liberators of "those whom William conquered", conveys deep humility and sadness.

What the **German cemeteries** might have been like had the Nazis won doesn't bear contemplation. As it is, they are sombre places, inconspicuous to minimize the bitterness they still arouse. At Orglandes, 10km south of Valognes, ten thousand lie buried, three to each of the plain headstones in the long flat lawn. There are no noble slogans and the plain entrance is without a dedicatory monument. At the superb site of Mont d'Huisnes, 6km east of Mont St-Michel, ten thousand more are filed away in the cold concrete tiers of a circular mausoleum. There is no attempt to defend the indefensible, and yet one feels an overpowering sorrow – that there is nothing to be said in such a place bitterly underlines the sheer waste.

The largest **American cemetery** is at Colleville-sur-Mer near the Pointe du Hoc. Neat rows of crosses cover the clifftop lawns, with no individual epitaphs, just gold lettering for a few exceptional warriors. At one end, a muscular giant dominates a huge array of battlefield plans and diagrams covered with surging arrows and pincer movements. Barack Obama is the latest of many US presidents to have paid his respects here; another president's son, General Theodore Roosevelt Jr, is among those buried.

American war cemeteries, a sombre place, described above. The vast **Normandy American Cemetery and Memorial** also holds a high-tech visitor centre (daily 9am–6pm; free; Ⓦabmc.gov), which explains the events of 1944 and the American role in them. Touching multimedia displays focus on the personal angle, highlighting the stories of both casualties and survivors.

The westernmost of the Invasion Beaches, **Utah Beach** stretches up the eastern shore of the Cotentin Peninsula, running 30km north towards St-Vaast (see p.301). From 6.30am onwards on D-Day, 23,000 men and 1700 vehicles landed here. A minor coast road, the D421, traces the edge of the dunes and enables visitors to follow the course of the fighting, though in truth there's precious little to see these days. Ships deliberately sunk to create artificial breakwaters are still visible at low tide, while markers along the seafront commemorate individual fallen heroes.

Two museums now tell the story. In the comprehensive **Musée du Débarquement d'Utah-Beach** in **STE-MARIE-DU-MONT** (daily: Feb, March & Nov

10am–5.30pm; April, May & Oct 10am–6pm; June–Sept 9.30am–7pm; last admission 45min before closing; closed Dec & Jan; €6; ⓦutah-beach.com), huge sea-view windows lend immediacy to the copious models, maps, films and diagrams. The **Mémorial de la Liberté** in **QUINÉVILLE** (late March to mid-Nov daily 10am–7pm; €6; ⓦwww.memorial-quineville.com) focuses on everyday life for the people of Normandy under Nazi occupation.

The Cotentin Peninsula

Hard against the frontier with Brittany, and cut off from the rest of Normandy by difficult marshy terrain, the **Cotentin Peninsula** has traditionally been seen as something of a backwater, far removed from the French mainstream. It nonetheless makes a rewarding goal for travellers, and one that by sea at least is very easily accessible. Ferries from both England and Ireland dock at the peninsula's major port, **Cherbourg**, a city turned resolutely seaward. Nearby are a plethora of attractive little villages, such as **Barfleur** and **St-Vaast**, nestled amid the hills to the east, and the handsome landscapes of heather-clad cliffs and stone-wall-divided patchwork fields to be found in La Hague to the west.

For many visitors the Cotentin's long western flank, with its flat beaches, serves primarily as a prelude to **Mont St-Michel**, with hill towns such as **Coutances** and **Avranches** cherishing architectural and historical relics associated with the abbey. Halfway down, however, the walled port of **Granville**, a popular destination with French holiday-makers, is a sort of small-scale mirror-image of Brittany's St-Malo.

Cherbourg

Though its heyday as a transatlantic passenger port is now long past, the sizeable town of **CHERBOURG** is still an appealing place to arrive in France. Despite its busy network of pedestrian streets lined with attractive stone facades, the labyrinth of alleyways known as *boëls*, some lively bars, and an impressive **maritime museum** in a converted Art Deco ferry terminal, many visitors head straight out and on, lured in part by the delightful villages that lie within a few kilometres to either side. Napoleon inaugurated the transformation of what had been a rather poor, but perfectly situated, natural harbour into a major port, by means of massive artificial breakwaters. An equestrian statue commemorates his boast that in Cherbourg he would "recreate the wonders of Egypt". As yet, however, there are no pyramids nearer than the Louvre in Paris.

Arrival and information

Cross-Channel ferries sail into Cherbourg's **gare maritime**, not far east of the town centre. Regular €1.20 shuttle buses connect the terminal with the **tourist office** at 2 quai Alexandre III (June Mon–Sat 9am–12.30pm & 2–6.30pm; July & Aug Mon–Sat 9am–6.30pm, Sun 10am–12.30pm; Sept–May Mon–Fri 9am–noon & 2–6pm, Sat 9am–12.30pm & 2–6pm; ⓣ02.33.93.52.02, ⓦot-cherbourg -cotentin.fr), and the **gare SNCF** further south. Tourisme Verney (ⓣ02.33.44.32.22) run buses from the **gare routière** opposite.

Accommodation

By usual Norman standards, **room rates** in Cherbourg are very reasonable and there's no reason for ferry passengers to avoid spending a night here, though traffic and the lack of parking space can be problematic.

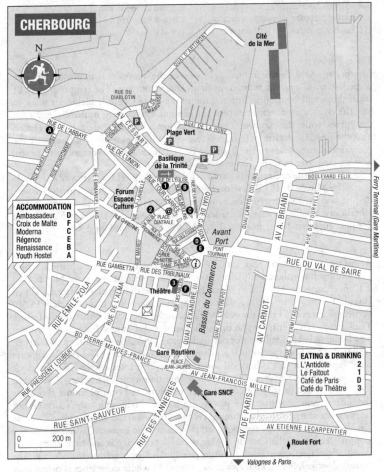

CHERBOURG

N

ACCOMMODATION

Ambassadeur	D
Croix de Malte	F
Moderna	C
Régence	E
Renaissance	B
Youth Hostel	A

EATING & DRINKING

L'Antidote	2
Le Faitout	1
Café de Paris	D
Café du Théâtre	3

0   200 m

Ferry Terminal (Gare Maritime)

Valognes & Paris

Ambassadeur 22 quai de Caligny
☏02.33.43.10.00, ⓦambassadeurhotel.com.
Inexpensive, good-value central hotel, on the
quayside with four storeys of en-suite rooms
(there's a lift). ②
Croix de Malte 5 rue des Halles
☏02.33.43.19.16, ⓦhotelcroixmalte.com. Simple
hotel on three upstairs floors, one block back from
the harbour near the theatre. The clean, renovated
rooms all have TVs and at least a shower. The
cheapest rates are for the perfectly acceptable
windowless rooms in the attic. ②
Moderna 28 rue de la Marine ☏02.33.43.05.30,
ⓦmoderna-hotel.com. Friendly small hotel with
reasonable, very well-priced en-suite rooms,
slightly back from the harbour. ②

Régence 42–44 quai de Caligny ☏02.33.43.05.16,
ⓦlaregence.com. Slightly more upmarket than
Cherbourg's other offerings, this Logis de France
has small, neat rooms overlooking the harbour. The
dining room downstairs starts with a reasonable
€20 *menu*, and ranges up to €35; it's not the best
restaurant along the *quai*, but there's something to
be said for eating where you sleep. ④
Renaissance 4 rue de l'Église ☏02.33.43.23.90,
ⓦhotel-renaissance-cherbourg.com. Nicely refurbished rooms, all with either shower or bath and
some with sea views, in a friendly hotel facing the
port in the most appealing quarter of town. The
"Église" of the address is the attractive Trinité. ③
Youth Hostel 55 rue de l'Abbaye
☏02.33.78.15.15, ⓦfuaj.org/Cherbourg-Octeville.

Well-equipped red-brick hostel, fifteen minutes' walk west of the centre, offering dorm beds for €18, including breakfast. Two bedrooms are designed for visitors with limited mobility. Check-in 9am–1pm & 6–11pm, closed mid-Dec to mid-Jan.

The Town

Cherbourg's **Old Town**, immediately west of the quayside, is an intriguing maze of pedestrian alleys that abounds in shops and restaurants. The tempting array of small shops and boutiques clustered round the place Centrale includes a place to buy the city's most famous product, the genuine **Cherbourg umbrella**, at 30 rue des Portes, while the excellent Thursday **market** is held on and off rue des Halles, near the majestic theatre with its *belle époque* facade. A pleasant stroll north of the commercial zone leads to the Basilique de la Trinité and the former town beach, now grassed over to form the "Plage Vert".

Southeast of the centre, you can climb up to **Roule Fort** for a view of the whole port. The **Musée de la Libération** here commemorates the period in 1944 when, despite the massive destruction wrought by the Nazis before they surrendered, Cherbourg briefly became the busiest port in the world (May–Sept Mon & Sun 2–6pm, Tues–Sat 10am–noon & 2–6pm; Oct–April Wed–Sun 2–6pm; €3).

La Cité de la Mer

Across from the pleasure port, **La Cité de la Mer** combines a large aquarium with a visitable nuclear submarine (daily: May, June & Sept 9.30am–6pm; July & Aug 9.30am–7pm; Oct–Dec & Feb–April 10am–6pm, with irregular variations; closed Jan; last entry 1hr before closing; April–Sept €18, Oct–March €15.50; ⓦcitedelamer.com). From the outside, the complex appears to centre on the former Transatlantic ferry terminal that simply houses its ticket offices. Instead, displays in a new building behind tell the story of underwater exploration in history and fiction, while fish tanks hold species such as jellyfish, seahorses and large squid, and walkways offer views into a vast cylindrical aquarium at ever greater depths. In a dry dock alongside, the *Redoutable* was France's first ballistic-missile submarine. Visitors can scramble through its labyrinth of tube-like walkways and control rooms, though as the nuclear generator that once powered it has been removed, there's a cavernous empty space at its heart. The cramped crew quarters will feel very familiar if you've just shared a cabin on an overnight ferry crossing. The separate "Walking into the Depths" section of the Cité de la Mer is aimed primarily at children. Entry is by timed admission; once inside, visitors are divided into teams to undertake the "mission" of helping an underwater explorer. The whole experience is pretty long at around 45 minutes, but the final "surprise" is undeniably amusing.

Eating

Restaurants in Cherbourg divide readily into the glass-fronted seafood places along the quai de Caligny, each with its "copious" *assiette de fruits de mer*, and the more varied, less expensive little places tucked away in the pedestrianized streets and alleyways of the Old Town. This is also where you'll find some animated **bars**, especially along rue de l'Union.

L'Antidote 41 rue au Blé ⓣ02.33.78.01.28. Central and very friendly restaurant/wine bar, tucked away in the tangled lanes but offering some outdoor seating, serving *menus* starting just under €20. Closed Sun.

Le Faitout 25 rue Tour-Carrée ⓣ02.33.04.25.04. Stylish, faux-rustic fishing-themed restaurant that offers traditional

French cuisine, including mussels prepared with celery, apples and the like for around €13, and has good *menus* at €19 and €33. It's so popular in summer that you may have to reserve. Dinner daily, lunch Tues–Sat.

Café de Paris 40 quai de Caligny ⓣ02.33.43.12.36. As well as fish-heavy *menus* from €21.50–36.50, you can work your way up through the ranks of *assiettes de fruits de mer*, from the €18.50 *Matelot* to the *Corsaire* at €55 for two. Closed Sun, plus Mon lunch.

Café du Théâtre 8 place de Gaulle ☎02.33.43.01.49. Attractive set-up adjoining the theatre, with a café behind plate-glass windows on the ground floor and a full-scale brasserie upstairs. It's a place used by the community as a whole rather than being a typical tourist restaurant. The varied *menus*, from €14, offer more than just seafood. Closed Sun.

Around the Cotentin

Once you get away from Cherbourg, the largely rural Cotentin Peninsula is geographically an area of transition. Little ports such as **Barfleur** on the indented northern headland presage the rocky Breton coast, while inland the meadows resemble the farmlands of the Bocage and the Bessin. **La Hague** is an underexplored gem, offering activities from sailing and diving to riding and rambling. In any case, the temptation to race south towards Mont St-Michel is likely to be thwarted by slow traffic on the peninsula's narrow roads, even if the Cherbourg–St-Lô route is now mostly four-lane, so you might as well stop off in the towns and resorts that line its western shore, such as **Granville** and **Avranches**.

Barfleur

The pleasant little harbour village of **BARFLEUR**, 25km east of Cherbourg, was the biggest port in Normandy seven centuries ago. Its population having dwindled along with its fortunes, it's now a surprisingly low-key place, where the sweeping crescent of the picturesque grey-granite quayside sees little tourist activity.

The nicer of its two **hotels**, ⚜ *Le Conquérant*, is set in a gorgeous, rambling old townhouse a short way from the sea at 16–18 rue St-Thomas-à-Becket (☎02.33.54.00.82, ⓦhotel-leconquerant.com; closed mid-Nov to mid-March; ❹). Accommodation at *Le Moderne*, south of the main road at 1 place de Gaulle (☎02.33.23.12.44, ⓦhotel-restaurant-moderne-barfleur.com; closed Tues eve & Wed mid-Sept to mid-July, plus all Jan to mid-Feb; ❸), is not quite as appealing, but the **restaurant** is quite superb, with the €34 *menu* including the house speciality, oysters, stuffed or raw. A basic but appealing **campsite** stands a couple of kilometres north in Le Crabec: *La Ferme du Bord du Mer* (☎02.33.54.01.77) is exactly what its name suggests, a farm beside the sea, alongside a scruffy flat beach.

Although no hotels, and barely any bars or other businesses face the harbour itself, the waterfront quai Henri-Chardon does hold a couple of good **restaurants**, the charming *Comptoir de la Presqu'île* at no. 30 (☎02.33.20.37.51), and the *Café de France* at no. 12 (☎02.33.54.00.38), both of which serve delicious fish.

St-Vaast

Pretty **ST-VAAST-LA-HOUGUE**, 11km south of Barfleur, is more of a resort than Barfleur, with lots of tiny Channel-crossing yachts moored in the bay where Edward III landed on his way to Crécy, and a string of fortifications from Vauban's time. The *Hôtel de France et des Fuchsias*, just back from the sea at 18 rue du Maréchal-Foch (☎02.33.54.42.26, ⓦwww.france-fuchsias.com; closed Jan–Feb, plus Mon in winter; ❸–❼), has splendid gardens and an excellent restaurant, and makes an ideal stopover for ferry passengers.

West from Cherbourg: the Cape de la Hague

The stretch of coast immediately west of Cherbourg is similar to that to the east, with the windswept **Cap de la Hague** at its westernmost tip being the main goal for most visitors. Two ancient villages, **Omonville-la-Petite** and **Omonville-la-Rogue**, 20km out of Cherbourg, make lovely places to stroll around, and all the way along you'll find wild and isolated countryside where you can lean against the wind, watch waves smashing against rocks or sunbathe in a spring profusion of wild flowers. The one drawback of the area is that the discharges of "low-level" radioactive wastes from the **nuclear reprocessing plant** near the Cap de la Hague, which is closed to visitors, may discourage you from swimming.

The main road, the D901, continues a couple of kilometres beyond the plant to **GOURY**, where the fields finally roll down to a craggy pebble coastline. Facing the octagonal lifeboat station in this splendidly windswept spot, the *Auberge de Goury* (℡02.33.52.77.01; closed Mon) serves wonderful seafood.

From the cape of **La Hague** itself, the northern tip of the peninsula, bracken-covered hills and narrow valleys run south to the cliffs of the **Nez de Jobourg**, claimed in wild local optimism to be the highest in Europe. South of that, a great curve of sand – some of it military training ground – takes the land's edge to **Flamanville** and another nuclear installation. Halfway along, in the picturesque village of **VAUVILLE**, the tropical-looking garden at the **Château de Vauville** is famed for its huge palm grove (April–Sept daily 2–6pm; Oct Wed & Fri–Sun 2–6pm; €6; ⓦwww.jardin-vauville.fr).

Barneville and Carteret

The next two sweeps of beach down to Carteret, backed by sand dunes like miniature mountain ranges, are among the best **beaches** in Normandy if you have transport and want solitude. **CARTERET** itself, sheltered by a rocky headland, is the nearest harbour to the English-speaking island of **Jersey**, just 25km away across seas made treacherous by the fast Alderney current.

Carteret's old port area is not especially attractive, but does have several seafront **hotels**, including the elegant, tastefully restored *Hôtel des Ormes*, quai Barbey d'Aurévilly (℡02.33.52.23.50, ⓦhoteldesormes.fr; closed Jan; ➐), which has a good restaurant. Visitors who prefer to be beside a beach should head instead for Carteret's twin community of **BARNEVILLE**, directly across the mouth of the bay. Here, an endless exposed stretch of clean, firm sand is backed by a long row of weather-beaten villas and the odd hotel, including the *Hôtel des Isles*, at 9 bd Maritime (℡02.33.04.90.76, ⓦhoteldesisles.com; closed Feb; ➐), which has a heated outdoor swimming pool and a superb **restaurant**.

Two **campsites** are located in the dunes north of town: the two-star *Le Ranch* at **Le Rozel** (℡02.33.10.07.10, ⓦcamping-leranch.com; closed Oct–March), and the three-star *Les Mielles* at **Surtainville** (℡02.33.04.31.04, ⓦwww.surtainville.com).

Coutances

The old hill town of **COUTANCES**, 65km south of Cherbourg, confined by its site to just one main street, is crested by the landmark **Cathédrale de Notre-Dame**. Essentially Gothic, it remains very Norman in its unconventional blending of architectural traditions, and the octagonal lantern crowning the nave is nothing short of divinely inspired. The *son et lumière* on Sunday evenings and throughout the summer is a true complement to the light stone building. Also illuminated on summer nights (and left open) are the formal fountained **public gardens**.

Coutances's **gare SNCF**, 1.5km southeast of the centre at the bottom of the steep hill, doubles as the stop for through **buses**. The **tourist office** is housed behind the Hôtel de Ville in place Georges-Léclerc (July & Aug Mon–Fri 9.30am–6pm, Sat 10am–12.30pm & 2–6pm, Sun 10am–1pm; Sept–June Mon–Fri 9.30am–12.30pm & 2–6pm, Sat 10am–12.30pm & 2–5pm; ℡02.33.19.08.10, ⓦtourisme-coutances .fr). Central Coutances is very short of **hotels**. In the cathedral square, the *Taverne du Parvis* (℡02.33.45.13.55; ➌; restaurant closed Sun) has unexciting but adequate rooms, above a reasonable brasserie. A more comfortable alternative is the large *Cositel* (℡02.33.19.15.00, ⓦwww.hotelcositel.com; ➍), halfway up the hill west of town towards Agon. It stands next to an excellent year-round municipal **campsite**, *Les Vignettes* (℡ 02.33.45.43.13).

Granville

The striking fortified coastal town of **GRANVILLE**, 25km southwest of Coutances, is the Norman equivalent of Brittany's St-Malo, with a similar history of piracy and an imposing, severely elegant citadel – the **haute ville** – guarding the approaches to the bay of Mont St-Michel across from Cancale. Here, however, the fortress was originally built by the English, early in the fifteenth century, as the springboard for an attack on Mont St-Michel that never came to fruition.

Granville today is a deservedly popular tourist destination. Thanks in part to the long beach that stretches away north of town, which disappears almost completely at high tide, it's the busiest resort in the area. Traffic in the maze-like new town, down below the headland, can be nightmarish, but the beaches are excellent, with facilities for watersports of all kind.

The great difference between Granville and St-Malo is that Granville's walled, fortified **citadel** stands separate from the modern town, an intriguing enclave that remains resolutely uncommercialized. Sheltered behind a rocky outcrop that juts out into the Channel, it's reached by steep stairs from alongside the beach and casino, or circuitous climbing roads from the port. Once up there, you'll find three or four long narrow parallel streets of grey-granite eighteenth-century houses – some forbidding and aloof, some adorned with brightly painted shutters – that lead to the church of Notre-Dame.

In pride of place at the inland end of the *haute ville*, the **Musée d'Art Moderne Richard Anacréon** (April–Sept daily except Mon 11am–6pm; Oct–March Wed–Sun 2–6pm; €2.70) houses art accumulated by a Parisian bookseller from 1940 onwards. Filled with sketches and autographs from the likes of Jean Cocteau and André Derain, it's not all that compelling, but the gallery itself is impressive, and hosts interesting temporary exhibitions.

Practicalities

The **tourist office** is below the citadel at 4 cours Jonville (July & Aug Mon–Sat 9am–1pm & 2–7pm, Sun 10am–1pm & 3–6pm; May, June & Sept Mon–Sat 9am–12.30pm & 2–6pm, Sun 10am–1pm & 3–6pm; Oct–April Mon–Sat 9am–noon & 2–6pm; ℡ 02.33.91.30.03, ⓦ granville-tourisme.fr). Trains between Paris and Cherbourg arrive well to the east at the **gare SNCF** on avenue du Maréchal-Leclerc, which also serves as the **gare routière**. **Ferries** connect Granville with the Îles Chausey, an hour or so offshore, and the Channel Islands.

With so many visitors in summer, it's well worth booking **accommodation** in advance. Most is concentrated in the new town that sprawls below the citadel, either beneath the walls on the seaward side, or near the station. The only option in the citadel itself is the *Logis du Roc*, 13 rue St-Michel (℡ 02.33.50.75.71, ⓦ lelogisduroc .com; ❸), a nicely furnished B&B with three en-suite rooms; otherwise, the *Michelet*, just below at 5 rue Jules-Michelet (℡ 02.33.50.06.55, ⓦ www.hotel-michelet -granville.com; ❶), offers reasonably well-equipped but rather characterless rooms, the cheapest of which lack en-suite facilities. The modern, oceanfront *Centre Régional de Nautisme* (℡ 02.33.91.22.62, ⓦ crng.fr; closed Sat & Sun Nov–Feb; dorm beds €16, private rooms ❷), a kilometre south of the station in the town centre, serves as Granville's **hostel**, with dorms and private rooms.

Where Granville really does excel is in its waterfront **restaurants**, below the citadel walls, though the port here is commercial rather than a delightful harbour. The best are the ⚜ *Restaurant du Port*, 19 rue du Port (℡ 02.33.50.00.55; closed Sun eve, plus Mon in low season), with its mouthwatering assortment of very fishy *menus*, and the *De la Mer*, at no. 74 (℡02.33.50.01.85; closed Mon, plus Tues in low season). Up in the Old Town, *L'Échauguette*, 24 rue St-Jean (℡02.33.50.51.87), serves good crêpes and simple meals cooked over an open fire.

Avranches

Perched high above the bay on an abrupt granite outcrop, **AVRANCHES** is the nearest large town to Mont St-Michel, and has always had close connections with the abbey. The Mont's original church was founded by a bishop of Avranches, spurred on by the Archangel Michael, who became so impatient with the lack of progress that he prodded a hole in the bishop's skull. Robert of Torigny, a subsequent abbot of St-Michel, played host in the town on several occasions to Henry II of England, the most memorable being when Henry was obliged, barefoot and bareheaded, to do public penance for the murder of Thomas Becket, on May 22, 1172.

A more vivid evocation of the area's medieval splendours comes from the illuminated manuscripts, mostly created on the Mont, on display in a state-of-the-art new museum in the place d'Estouteville, the **Scriptorial d'Avranches** (Feb–April & Oct–Dec Tues–Fri 10am–12.30pm & 2–5pm, Sat & Sun 10am–12.30pm & 2–6pm; May–June & Sept daily except Mon 10am–6pm; July & Aug daily 10am–7pm; closed Jan; €7; ⊕scriptorial.fr). Additional exhibits trace the history of Avranches, and bring the story up to date by covering modern book-production techniques.

Avranches's **gare SNCF** is a long way below the town centre; the walk up discourages most rail travellers from stopping here at all. The **tourist office** is at no. 2 in the central place Général-de-Gaulle (July & Aug Mon–Sat 9.30am–12.30pm & 2–7pm, Sun 9.30am–12.30pm & 2–6pm; Sept–June Mon–Fri 9.30am–12.30pm & 2–6pm, Sat 10am–12.30pm & 2.30–5pm; ℡02.33.58.00.22, ⊕www.ot-avranches.com). In summer, one **bus** per day runs to Mont St-Michel from right outside.

The nicest **hotel** is the gloriously old-fashioned ⚜ *Croix d'Or*, near the Patton monument at 83 rue de la Constitution (℡02.33.58.04.88, ⊕hoteldelacroixdor .fr; closed Jan, plus Sun eve in winter; ❹), which boasts beautiful hydrangea-filled gardens and the best **restaurant** in town.

Mont St-Michel

The island at the very frontier of Normandy and Brittany, which for over a millennium has housed the stupendous abbey of **MONT ST-MICHEL**, was once known as "the Mount in Peril from the Sea". Many a pilgrim in medieval times drowned while trying to cross the bay to this 80m-high rocky outcrop. The Archangel Michael was its vigorous protector, with a marked propensity to leap from rock to rock in titanic struggles against Paganism and Evil. The abbey dates back to the eighth century, when the archangel appeared to Aubert, bishop of Avranches, who duly founded a monastery on the island. Since the eleventh century – when work on the sturdy church at the peak commenced – new buildings have been grafted to produce a fortified hotchpotch of Romanesque and Gothic buildings clambering to the pinnacle of the graceful church, forming probably the most recognizable silhouette in France after the Eiffel Tower.

Although the abbey was a fortress town, home to a large community, even at its twelfth-century peak it never housed more than sixty monks. When the Revolution came the monastery was converted into a prison, but in 1966, exactly a thousand years after Duke Richard the First originally brought the order to the Mont, the Benedictines were invited to return. They departed again in 2001, after finding that the present-day island does not exactly lend itself to a life of quiet contemplation. In their place, a dozen nuns and monks from the Monastic Fraternity of Jerusalem now maintain a presence.

For many years, the Mont has not, strictly speaking, been an island, as the causeway (*digue*) that leads to it is never submerged. However, a dam has now been constructed at the mouth of the river Couesnon, in order to stop the build-up of silt, and the causeway will shortly be replaced by a bridge, with shuttle buses to spare visitors the 2km walk from the mainland. Currently scheduled for completion in 2014, this should not only make tourist numbers easier to control but also enable the sea to wash away much of the accumulated silt.

The abbey

The **abbey**, an architectural ensemble incorporating the high-spired, archangel-topped church and the magnificent Gothic buildings known since 1228 as the **Merveille** ("The Marvel") – which in turn includes the entire north face, with the cloister, Knights' Hall, Refectory, Guest Hall and cellars – is visible from all around the bay, but becomes, if anything, more awe-inspiring the closer you get.

The Mont's rock comes to a sharp point just below what is now the transept of the **church**, a building where the transition from Romanesque to Gothic is only too evident in the vaulting of the nave. In order to lay out the church's ground plan in the traditional shape of the cross, supporting crypts had to be built up from the surrounding hillside, and the Chausey granite has always had to be sculpted to match the exact contours of the hill. Space was always limited, and yet the building has grown through the centuries, with an architectural ingenuity that constantly surprises – witness the shock of emerging into the light of the cloisters from the sombre Great Hall.

Not surprisingly, the building of the **monastery** was no smooth progression: the original church, choir, nave and tower all had to be replaced after collapsing. The style of decoration has varied, too, along with the architecture. That you now walk through halls of plain grey stone is a reflection of modern taste. In the Middle Ages, the walls of public areas such as the refectory would have been festooned with tapestries and frescoes, while the original coloured tiles of the cloisters have long since been stripped away to reveal bare walls.

The rest of the island

The base of Mont St-Michel rests on a primeval slime of sand and mud. Just above that, you pass through the heavily fortified **Porte du Roi** onto the narrow **Grande Rue**, climbing steadily around the base of the rock and lined with medieval gabled houses and a jumble of postcard and souvenir shops.

The rather dry **Musée Maritime** offers an insight into the island's ties with the sea, while the Archangel Michael manages in just fifteen minutes to lead visitors on a voyage through space and time in the **Archéoscope**, with the full majestic panoply of multimedia mumbo jumbo. Further along the Grande Rue and up the steps towards the abbey church, next door to the eleventh-century **church of St-Pierre**, the absurd **Musée Grévin** contains such edifying specimens as a wax model of a woman drowning in a sea of mud (all open Feb to mid-Nov daily 9am–6pm; €18 for all, or €9 each one).

Large crowds gather each day at the **North Tower** to watch the tide sweep in across the bay. Seagulls wheel away in alarm, and those foolish enough to be wandering too late on the sands have to sprint to safety.

Practicalities

Mont St-Michel has its own **tourist office**, in the lowest gateway (April–June & Sept Mon–Sat 9am–12.30pm & 2–6.30pm, Sun 9am–noon & 2–6pm; July & Aug daily 9am–7pm; Oct–March Mon–Sat 9am–noon & 2–6pm, Sun 10am–noon & 2–5pm; ☏02.33.60.14.30, ⓦwww.ot-montsaintmichel.com). Regular **buses** connect it with the SNCF stations at Pontorson (see below), Rennes and St-Malo.

The island holds a surprising number of **hotels**, albeit not enough to cope with the sheer number of visitors. Most are predictably expensive, and all charge extra for a view of the sea. The cheapest option is the *Du Guesclin* (☏02.33.60.14.10; ⓦhotelduguesclin.com; closed Nov–March; ❹), a Logis de France where all the rooms have been reasonably spruced up, and five have sea views; the nicest is the *Croix Blanche* (☏02.33.60.14.04, ⓦhotel-la-croix-blanche.com; closed mid-Nov to mid-Feb; ❻); and the *Mouton Blanc* (☏02.33.60.14.08, ⓦlemoutonblanc.com; ❺) falls somewhere in between.

Sadly, however, the **restaurants** on Mont St-Michel, both independent and in the hotels, are consistently worse than almost anywhere in France. It's impossible to make any confident recommendations, other than that ideally you should aim to eat elsewhere – for example, Cancale, which has a fabulous selection of restaurants. In addition, the main approach road, the D976, is lined shortly before the causeway by around a dozen large and virtually indistinguishable hotels and motels, each with its own brasserie or restaurant. Typical among these are the *De la Digue* (☏02.33.60.14.02, ⓦladigue.eu; ❻), and the *Formule Verte* (☏02.33.60.14.13, ⓦle-mont-saint-michel.com; ❸). The three-star, 350-pitch *Camping du Mont St-Michel* (☏02.33.60.22.10, ⓦcamping-montsaintmichel.com; closed mid-Nov to early Feb) is nearby.

Many visitors to Mont St-Michel choose instead to stay at **PONTORSON**, 6km inland, which has the nearest **gare SNCF**, connected by a bus service. The **hotels** here are not especially interesting, but the *Montgomery* is housed in a fine old ivy-covered mansion at 13 rue du Couesnon (☏02.33.60.00.09, ⓦhotel-montgomery.com; closed last two weeks in Nov; ❹), and has fairly appealing rooms and a good restaurant, as does the *Bretagne*, just along the main road at 59 rue du Couesnon (☏02.33.60.10.55; closed Feb; ❷).

Inland Normandy

Seeking out specific highlights is not really the point when you're exploring **inland Normandy**. The pleasure of a visit lies not so much in show-stopping sights, or individual towns, as in the feel of the landscape – the lush meadows, orchards and forests of the Norman countryside. On top of that, of course, there's the **food**, a major attraction in these rich dairy regions. To the French, the **Pays d'Auge**, **Calvados** and the **Suisse Normande** are synonymous with cheeses, cream, apple and pear brandies, and ciders.

This is also a place to be active. The **Suisse Normande** is canoeing and rock-climbing country, and there are countless good walks in the stretch along the southern border of the province designated as the **Parc Naturel Régional de Normandie-Maine**. Of the towns, **Conches** is the most charming, **Falaise** has William the Conqueror as a constant fall-back attraction, and **Lisieux** has its religious significance.

South of the Seine

Heading south from the Seine you can follow the River Risle from the estuary just east of Honfleur, or the Eure and its tributaries from upstream of Rouen. Between the two stretches the long featureless **Neubourg Plain**. The lowest major crossing point over the Risle is at **Pont-Audemer**, where medieval houses lean out at alarming angles over the crisscrossing roads, rivers and canals. From here, perfect cycling roads lined with timbered farmhouses follow the river south.

Le Bec-Hellouin

The size and tranquil setting of the **Abbaye de Bec-Hellouin**, upstream from Pont-Audemer just before Brionne, lend a monastic feel to the whole Risle valley. Bells echo across the water and white-robed monks go soberly about their business. From the eleventh century onwards, the abbey was an important intellectual centre; the philosopher Anselm was abbot here before becoming Archbishop of Canterbury in 1093. Thanks to the Revolution, most of the monastery buildings are recent – the monks only returned in 1948 – but some have survived amid the appealing clusters of stone ruins, including the fifteenth-century **bell tower of St-Nicholas** and the cloister. Visitors are welcome to wander through the grounds for no charge (daily 8am–9pm); to get a better sense of what you're seeing, join a **guided tour** (Mon & Wed–Sat 10.30am, 3pm & 4pm, plus extra tour at 5pm June–Sept only; Sun & hols noon, 3pm & 4pm; €5; Ⓦ abbayedubec.com).

The tiny and rather twee adjacent village of **BEC-HELLOUIN** holds a pretty, half-timbered **hotel-restaurant**, the *Auberge de l'Abbaye* (Ⓣ 02.32.44.86.02, Ⓦ hotelbechellouin.com; closed Tues, plus all Dec & Jan, & Wed Oct–March; ❾). At the local **riding stables**, the Centre Equestre du Bec-Hellouin, horses can be booked by the hour or the day (Ⓣ 02.32.44.86.31).

Conches-en-Ouche

Forty kilometres south of Bec-Hellouin across the wild and open woodland of the **Forêt de Conches**, standing above the River Rouloir on an abrupt and narrow spur, the classic old Norman town of **CONCHES-EN-OUCHE** can have changed little since the nineteenth century. At the highest point, in the middle of a row of medieval houses, is the **church of Ste-Foy**, its windows a stunning sequence of Renaissance stained glass. Behind are the gardens of the **Hôtel de Ville**, where a robust stone boar gazes proudly over a spectacular view. Next to that, you can scramble up the slippery steps of the ruined twelfth-century **castle**.

The town's **tourist office**, close to the castle in place Aristide-Briand (Tues–Sat 10am–12.30pm & 2–6pm, plus Sun 10am–noon in July & Aug only; ☎02.32.30.76.42, ⓦconches-en-ouche.fr), hires out mountain bikes. The best **accommodation** option is *Le Cygne*, a Logis de France at 2 rue Paul-Guilbaud at the north end of town (☎02.32.30.20.60, ⓦlecygne.fr; closed Sun eve & Mon; ❷), which has a good restaurant where *menus* start at €18. On Thursday the whole town is taken up by a **market**.

Lisieux and the Pays d'Auge

The rolling hills and green twisting valleys of the **Pays d'Auge** stretch south of **Lisieux** and are scattered with magnificent manor houses. The pastures here are the lushest in the province, their produce the world-famous cheeses of Camembert, Livarot and Pont L'Evêque. They are intermingled with orchards yielding the best of Norman ciders, both apple and pear (*poiré*), as well as Calvados apple brandy.

For really good, solid Norman cooking visit one of this area's *fermes auberges*, working farms which welcome paying visitors to share their meals. Local tourist offices can provide copious lists of these and of local producers from whom you can buy your cheese and booze.

Lisieux

LISIEUX, the main town of the Pays d'Auge, hosts a large street **market** on Wednesday and Saturday which is a great opportunity to get acquainted with its cheeses and ciders. Most visitors, however, arrive as pilgrims. **Ste Thérèse**, the most popular French spiritual figure of the last hundred years, was born here in 1873 and lived just 24 years. Passivity, self-effacement and a self-denial that verged on masochism were her trademarks, and she is honoured by the gaudy and gigantic **Basilique de Ste-Thérèse**, completed in 1954 on a slope southwest of the centre. The huge modern mosaics that decorate the nave are undeniably impressive, but the overall impression is of a quasi-medieval hagiography. The faithful can ride on a white, flag-bedecked fairground train around the holiest sites, which include the infinitely restrained and sober **Cathédrale St-Pierre**.

Lisieux's **tourist office**, 11 rue d'Alençon, is the best place to gather information on the rural areas further inland (mid-June to Sept Mon–Sat 8.30am–6.30pm, Sun 10am–12.30pm & 2–5pm; Oct to mid-June Mon–Sat 8.30am–noon & 1.30–6pm; ☎02.31.48.18.10, ⓦlisieux-tourisme.com). The town is full of good-value **hotels**, such as the *Terrasse*, near the basilica at 25 av Ste-Thérèse (☎02.31.62.17.65, ⓦlaterrassehotel.com; closed mid-Jan to mid-Feb, plus Mon in winter; ❸), and the smart, central *Azur Hôtel*, just north of the Église St-Jacques at 15 rue au Char (☎02.31.62.09.14, ⓦazur-hotel.com; closed mid-Dec to mid-Jan; ❹).

Crèvecoeur-en-Auge

While it's always fun to stumble across dilapidated old half-timbered farms in the Pays d'Auge, here and there it's possible to visit prime specimens that have been beautifully restored and preserved. An especially fine assortment has been gathered just west of **CRÈVECOEUR-EN-AUGE**, 17km west of Lisieux on the N14, in the grounds of a small twelfth-century **château** (April–June & Sept daily 11am–6pm; July & Aug daily 11am–7pm; Oct Sun 2–6pm; guided tours July & Aug Sun 2.30–4.30pm; €6; Ⓦchateau-de-crevecoeur.com). Around the pristine lawns of a recreated village green, circled by a shallow moat, this photogenic group of golden adobe structures includes a manor house, a barn and a tall thin dovecote that date from the fifteenth century. The little twelfth-century chapel that adjoins the château holds a fascinating exhibition on the music and instruments of the Middle Ages, although almost all the explanatory captions are in French.

Beuvron-en-Auge

By far the prettiest of the Pays d'Auge villages is **BEUVRON-EN-AUGE**, 7km north of the N13 halfway between Lisieux and Caen. It consists of an oval central *place*, ringed by a glorious ensemble of multicoloured half-timbered houses, including the yellow-and-brown sixteenth-century Vieux Manoir. The very centre of the square is taken up by the top-notch *Pavé d'Auge* **restaurant** (℡02.31.79.26.71, Ⓦpavedauge.com; closed Mon, plus Tues Sept–June), where regularly changing *menus* start at €36; it also offers four rooms in the separate *Pavé d'Hôtes* (❺).

Orbec and Livarot

The town of **ORBEC**, 19km southeast of Lisieux, epitomizes the simple pleasures of the Pays d'Auge. Along the rue Grande, you'll see several houses in which the gaps between the timbers are filled with intricate patterns of coloured tiles and bricks. Debussy composed *Jardin sous la Pluie* in one of these, and the oldest and prettiest of the lot – a tanner's house dating back to 1568, known as the **Vieux Manoir** – holds a museum of local history. On the whole, though, it's more fun just to walk down behind the church to the river, its watermill and paddocks.

The centre of the cheese country is venerable **LIVAROT**, where the **Fromagerie Graindorge**, on the route de Vimoutiers (Mon–Fri 9.30am–noon & 1.30–5pm, Sat 9.30am–noon; free; Ⓦwww.graindorge.fr), gives you a closer look at how the town's eponymous cheese is made. For superb views of the valley, climb up to the thirteenth-century church of **St-Michel de Livet**, just above town. Livarot holds one, simple **hotel** – the *De La France* in the place de la Gare (℡02.31.31.59.35; ❶) – and a tiny one-star municipal **campsite** (℡02.31.32.01.18; closed Sept–April).

Vimoutiers and Camembert

The pretty little town of **VIMOUTIERS**, due south of Livarot, is home to the **Musée du Camembert**, at 10 av Général-de-Gaulle (April–Oct only, Mon & Thurs–Sun 2–5.30pm; €3), a rather homespun affair which explains the production process of the famous cheese, with tastings at the end.

A statue in the town's main square honours Marie Harel, who, at the nearby village of Camembert, developed the original cheese early in the nineteenth century, promoting it with a skilful campaign that included sending free samples to Napoleon. Marie is confronted across the main street by what might be called the statue of the Unknown Cow.

Vimoutiers hosts a **market** on Monday afternoons. The **tourist office**, 21 place de Mackau (June–Sept Mon 2–6pm, Tues–Sat 9.30am–12.30pm & 2–6pm, Sun 10am–12.30pm & 2–6pm; Oct–May Mon 2–5.30pm, Tues–Sat 10am–12.30pm & 2–5.30pm; ℡02.33.67.49.42, Ⓦvimoutiers.fr), can advise on myriad cheese-related attractions. *La Couronne*, 9 rue du 8 mai (℡02.33.67.21.49, Ⓦhotelrestaurant lacouronne.fr; ❷), the better of the two central **hotels**, has a reasonable restaurant.

A short way south of Vimoutiers, en route to Camembert, the beautifully sited lake known as the **Escale du Vitou** offers everything you need for windsurfing, swimming and horseriding, as well as its own comfortable, rural **hotel**, *L'Escale du Vitou* (℡ 02.33.39.12.04, Ⓦ domainedelescaleduvitou.com; ❸). There's also a clean and very cheap **campsite** nearby on boulevard Docteur-Dentu, the two-star *La Campière* (℡ 02.33.39.18.86, Ⓦ vimoutiers.fr; closed Oct–April).

CAMEMBERT itself, 3km southeast of Vimoutiers, is tiny, hilly and very rural, home to far more cows than humans. On one side of its little central square, the largest Camembert producers, **La Ferme Président**, run their own, surprisingly amateurish, museum (April–Oct Mon 2–6pm, Tues–Sat 9am–noon & 2–6pm, Sun 10am–noon & 2.30–6pm; €3; Ⓦ www.fermepresident.com), which whirls through the history of the cheese and the methods, both traditional and modern, used to make it. Afterwards comes a cheese tasting at **La Maison du Camembert** on the other side of the square, which also serves as an information centre and café (March, April, Sept & Oct Wed–Sun 10am–6pm; May–Aug daily 10am–6pm; free).

The **Fromagerie Durand**, below Camembert on the road towards Trun (Ferme de la Hérronière; Mon–Sat 9.30am–12.30pm & 3–6pm; free), offers an alternative experience: a visit to the last farm in the region which produces Camembert made the traditional way, using unpasteurized milk. An interesting film explains – you've guessed it – the cheese production process, while four windows allow visitors to glimpse the cheese at various stages in its life, and you're also likely to catch a glimpse of the artisan at work. The end product and other local produce are on sale in the shop.

Falaise

William the Conqueror, or William the Bastard as he is more commonly known here, was born in **FALAISE**, 40km southwest of Lisieux. His mother, Arlette, a laundrywoman, was spotted by his father, Duke Robert of Normandy, at the washing place below the château. She was a shrewd woman, scorning secrecy in her eventual assignation by riding publicly through the main entrance to meet him. During her pregnancy, she is said to have dreamed of bearing a mighty tree that cast its shade over Normandy and England.

Falaise's **castle** keep, firmly planted on the massive rocks of the cliff (*falaise*) that gave the town its name, and towering over the **Fontaine d'Arlette** down by the river, is one of the most evocative historic sights imaginable. Nonetheless, it was so heavily damaged during the war that it took over fifty years to reopen for regular visits (Feb–June & Sept–Dec daily 10am–6pm; July & Aug daily 10am–7pm; closed Jan; English-language tours in July & Aug daily 11.30am & 3.30pm, otherwise Sat & Sun 11.30am; €7.50; Ⓦ chateau-guillaume -leconquerant.fr). Huge resources have been lavished on restoring the central **donjon**, reminiscent of the Tower of London with its cream-coloured Caen stone. Steel slabs, concrete blocks, glass floors and tent-like canvas awnings have been slapped down atop the bare ruins, and metal staircases squeezed into the wall cavities. The raw structure of the keep, down to its very foundations, lies exposed to view, while the newly created rooms are used for changing exhibitions that focus on the castle's fascinating past.

The whole of Falaise was devastated in the struggle to close the "Falaise Gap" in August 1944 – the climax of the **Battle of Normandy**, as the Allied armies sought to encircle the Germans and cut off their retreat. By the time the Canadians entered the town on August 17, they could no longer tell where the roads had been and had to bulldoze a new 4m strip straight through the middle. The full bloody story is told in horrific detail at the **Musée Août 44**, beyond the château in a former cheese factory, on the chemin des Rochers (April to mid-Nov daily 10am–noon & 2–6pm; €6; Ⓦ normandie-museeaout44.com).

Practicalities

Falaise's modern, well-stocked **tourist office** is on the boulevard de la Libération (May to mid-June Mon–Sat 9.30am–12.30pm & 1.30–6.30pm; mid-June to mid-Sept same hours plus Sun 10am–12.30pm & 2–4pm; mid-Sept to April Mon–Sat 9.30am–12.30pm & 1.30–5.30pm; ℡02.31.90.17.26, Ⓦfalaise-tourisme.com).

Now that central Falaise is bypassed by the motorway, it's a quiet place to spend the night. The best-value **hotel** is the *Poste*, near the tourist office at 38 rue Georges-Clemenceau (℡02.31.90.13.14, Ⓔhotel.delaposte@orange.fr; ❸; hotel closed Jan, restaurant closed Fri eve, Sun eve & Mon), which serves good food on *menus* from €16. The three-star municipal **campsite**, *Camping du Château* (℡02.31.90.16.55; closed Oct–April), is in a great location, next to Arlette's fountain and the local swimming pool.

The Suisse Normande

The area known as the **Suisse Normande** starts roughly 25km south of Caen, along the gorge of the River Orne, between Thury-Harcourt and Putanges. While the name is a little far-fetched – there are certainly no mountains – it is quite distinctive, with cliffs, crags and wooded hills at every turn. There are plenty of opportunities for outdoor pursuits: you can race along the Orne in canoes and kayaks, cruise more sedately on pedalos, or dangle on ropes from the sheer rock faces high above. For mere walkers the Orne can be frustrating: footpaths along the river are few and far between, and often entirely overgrown.

The Suisse Normande is usually approached from Caen or Falaise and contrasts dramatically with the prairie-like expanse of wheat fields en route. Cycling or driving, the most attractive access is via the D235 from Caen (signed to Falaise then right through Ifs). Bus Verts #34 will take you to **Thury-Harcourt** or **Clécy** on the way from Caen to Flers.

Thury-Harcourt and Clécy

At **THURY-HARCOURT**, the **tourist office** on place St-Sauveur (May, June & Sept Tues–Sat 10am–12.30pm & 2.30–6.30pm, Sun 10am–12.30pm; July & Aug same hours plus Mon 10am–12.30pm; Oct–April Mon 2.30–5pm, Tues–Fri 10am–12.30pm & 2.30–5pm, Sat 10am–12.30pm; ℡02.31.79.70.45, Ⓦwww.ot-suisse-normande.com) can suggest walks, rides and *gîtes d'étape* throughout the Suisse Normande. Thury-Harcourt is home to a **hotel**, the *Relais de la Poste* (℡02.31.79.72.12, Ⓦhotel-relaisdelaposte.com; closed March, in summer, all Fri and Sat lunch in winter; ❹), and also an attractive four-star **campsite**, the *Vallée du Traspy* (℡02.31.79.61.80; closed Oct–March), beside the river on the rue du Pont-Benoit.

CLÉCY, 10km to the south, is a slightly better bet for finding a room, although visitors outnumber residents in peak season. The **hotel** facing the church in the village centre, *Au Site Normand*, 1 rue des Châtelets (℡02.31.69.71.05, Ⓦhotel-clecy.com; closed mid-Dec to mid-Feb; ❷), has pleasant, comfortable rooms in a modern annexe, and an old-fashioned and good-value dining room in the main timber-framed building itself. The river is a kilometre away, down the hill. En route, in the Parc des Loisirs, is a **Musée du Chemin de Fer Miniature** (March–Easter, Oct & Nov Sun 2–5.30pm; Easter–June daily except Mon 10am–noon & 2–6pm; July & Aug daily 10am–6pm; second half of Sept daily except Mon 2–6pm; €6.80; Ⓦchemin-fer-miniature-clecy.com), featuring a gigantic model railway certain to appeal to children.

The western riverbank is lined with restaurants, takeaways and snack bars as far as the two-star municipal **campsite** (T02.31.69.70.36, Wwww.ocampings.com /campingclecy; closed Nov–March).

Pont d'Ouilly

If you're planning to walk, or cycle, a good central base is **PONT D'OUILLY**, at the point where the main road from Vire to Falaise crosses the river. It's just a village, with a few basic shops, an old covered market hall and a promenade (with bar) slightly upstream alongside the weir. Continuing upstream, a pleasant walk leads for 3.5km to the pretty little village of Le Mesnil Villement.

As well as a **campsite** overlooking the river (T02.31.69.46.12; closed Oct–Easter), Pont d'Ouilly offers an attractive **hotel**, the *Du Commerce* (T02.31.69.80.16, Wrelaisducommerce.fr; closed Sun eve & Mon; ❹), with bland but comfortable rooms and a reasonable restaurant. About a kilometre north, the *Auberge St-Christophe*, covered with ivy and geraniums, offers seven en-suite rooms in a beautiful setting on the right bank of the Orne (T02.31.69.81.23; closed Sun eve, Mon & three weeks in Feb–March; ❸).

A short distance south of Pont d'Ouilly, the **Roche d'Oëtre** is a high rock with a tremendous view into the deep and totally wooded gorge of the Rouvre, a tributary of the Orne. The river widens soon afterwards into the **Lac de Rabodanges**, formed by the many-arched Rabodanges Dam.

Southern Normandy

As an alternative to the more northerly routes across Normandy, motorists heading west from Paris towards Brittany may prefer to cut directly across, following the N12 through **Alençon** and then heading northwest on the N176. Much of the terrain along Normandy's southern border is taken up by the dense woodlands of the **Forêt d'Écouves** and the **Forêt des Andaines**, so there's plenty of good walking, while the hill towns of **Carrouges** and **Domfront** make great stopovers.

Alençon

ALENÇON, a medium-sized and lively town, is known for its traditional – and now pretty much defunct – lacemaking industry. The **Musée des Beaux-Arts et de la Dentelle** (daily 10am–noon & 2–6pm; closed Mon Sept–June; €3.20) is housed in a former Jesuit school and has all the best trappings of a modern museum. The highly informative history of lacemaking upstairs, can, however, be tedious for anyone not already riveted by the subject. It also contains an unexpected collection of gruesome Cambodian artefacts like spears and lances, tiger skulls and elephants' feet, gathered in the nineteenth century. The paintings in the adjoining Beaux-Arts section are nondescript, except for a few works by Courbet and Géricault. Wandering around the town will take you to St Thérèse's birthplace on rue St-Blaise, just in front of the **gare routière**.

The **Forêt d'Écouves**, which starts 10km north of Alençon, is a dense mixture of spruce, pine, oak and beech, unfortunately a favoured spot of the military – and, in autumn, deer hunters, too. You can usually ramble along the cool paths, happening upon wild mushrooms and even the odd wild boar.

Practicalities

The **tourist office** is housed in the fifteenth-century Maison d'Ozé on place La Magdelaine (July & Aug Mon–Sat 9.30am–7pm, Sun 10am–12.30pm & 2.30–5pm;

Sept–June Mon–Sat 9.30am–12.30pm & 1.30–6pm; ☎02.33.80.66.33, ⓦpaysda lencontourisme.com). The **gare routière** and **gare SNCF** are both to the northeast, in an area that holds Alençon's prime concentration of **hotels**. The cheapest, the *Hôtel de Paris*, is above a bar facing the *gare SNCF* at 26 rue Denis-Papin (☎02.33.29.01.64; ❶); even its en-suite rooms cost under €40. *Le Chapeau Rouge*, just across the river west of the centre at 3 bd Duchamp (☎02.33.26.20.23; ❷; restaurant closed Sat lunch & Sun), has large comfortable rooms and offers decent meals in its adjoining restaurant.

Good **restaurants**, cafés and shops are scattered through the central pedestrianized streets. For a well-priced meal, drop into *Le Hangar*, near the lace museum at 12 place Avoine (☎02.33.82.04.27; closed Sat & Sun), where the daily *menu* costs around €15. High spots on the thriving **bar** scene include *La Cave Aux Boeufs*, spreading across the pedestrian rue de la Cave Aux Boeufs (☎02.33.82.99.45), which also serves a simple brasserie *menu*.

Le Perche

Famous for the percheron horses who derive their name from this rural region, **Le Perche** is a pleasant spot for a few days' relaxation, or as a base to explore the countryside of southern Normandy. An obvious place to stay is the region's capital, the pretty town of **MORTAGNE-AU-PERCHE**, 38km east of Alençon. The tourist office (mid-May to Sept Tues–Sat 9.30am–12.30pm & 2.30–6pm; Oct to mid-May Tues–Sat 10am–12.30pm & 3–6pm; ☎02.33.85.11.18, ⓦot-mortagne auperche.fr) is situated in the former Halle aux Grains in the café-lined central square, the place Général de Gaulle. The town's historical centre includes the sixteenth-century Église Notre-Dame, and an impressive Hôtel de Ville set in some lovely formal gardens, which have an excellent view of the countryside beyond.

The nicest **hotel** in town has to be the ⚜ *Hôtel du Tribunal*, on the sleepy little tree-lined place du Palais (☎02.33.25.04.77, ⓦhotel-tribunal.fr; ❸), which holds a good **restaurant**. For something a bit different, try the modern, comfortable B&B rooms on offer at the ⚜ *Ferme du Gros Chêne*, just outside Mortagne on the D8 towards Logny-au-Perche (☎02.33.25.02.72, ⓦfermedugroschene.com; ❸). This working farm has five guest rooms in a converted barn, and offers self-catering facilities plus the option of a three-course dinner for €20.

Le Perche is also home to a beautiful, château-studded natural park. For information on walks, attractions and events, drop in at its visitor centre, the **Maison du Parc**, housed in the impressive Manoir de Courboyer in Nocé (daily: April–June & Sept–Oct 10.30am–6pm, July & Aug 10.30am–7pm, Nov–March 10.30am–5.30pm; ☎02.33.85.36.36, ⓦwww.parc-naturel-perche.fr), which can itself be visited during these hours (€2/€3 including a guided tour). Occasional equestrian displays feature the percheron horses that graze nearby.

Carrouges

An alternative base to Alençon, at the western end of the Forêt d'Écouves, is the hill town of **CARROUGES**, with its impressive moat-encircled **château** set in spacious grounds at the foot of the hill (daily: April to mid-June & Sept 10am–noon & 2–6pm; mid-June to Aug 9.30am–noon & 2–6.30pm; Oct–March 10am–noon & 2–5pm; €7; ⓦcarrouges.monuments-nationaux.fr). Its two highlights are a superb restored brick staircase, and a room in which hang portraits of fourteen successive generations of the Le Veneur family, an extraordinary illustration of the processes of heredity. Local craftsmen sell their work in the **Maison de Métiers**, the former castle chapel.

On the narrow rue Ste-Marguerite that runs through the heart of Carrouges – a noisier location than it might look – the *Hôtel du Nord* (☎02.33.27.20.14; closed mid-Dec to mid-Jan, plus Fri eve & Sun eve Sept–June; ❷) offers reasonably large en-suite **rooms** at low rates, and delicious local cuisine on *menus* that start at €18.

Bagnoles-de-l'Orne

West of Carrouges, the quaint spa town of **BAGNOLES-DE-L'ORNE** is quite unlike anywhere else in this part of the world, attracting the moneyed sick and convalescent from all over France to its thermal baths, along with mainly elderly visitors wanting to indulge themselves in the various spas. The layout is formal and spacious, centering on a lake surrounded by well-tended gardens. With so many visitors to keep entertained, there are also innumerable cultural events of a restrained and stressless nature, such as tea dances and stage shows. Anyone wishing for slightly more active pursuits has the choice of mini golf or a pedalo trip around the lake. Whether you'd actually want to spend time in Bagnoles depends on your disposable income as well as your health. Furthermore, the town as a whole operates to a season that lasts roughly from early April to the end of October; arrive in winter, and you may find everything shut.

The **tourist office** on place du Marché (April–Oct Mon–Sat 9.30am–12.30pm & 2–6pm, Sun 10am–12.30pm & 2.30–6.30pm; Nov–March Mon–Sat 9.30am–12.30pm & 2–6pm; ☏02.33.37.85.66, ⓦbagnolesdelorne.com) will give details on accommodation in Bagnoles and its less exclusive sister town of **TESSE-MADELEINE**.

The numerous hotels are, on the whole, expensive and sedate places, and the three-star **campsite**, *De la Vée* (☏02.33.37.87.45; open mid-March to Oct), south of town, is rather forlorn. The nicest **hotel**, *Ô Gayot*, by the tourist office at 2 av de la Ferté-Macé (☏02.33.38.44.01, ⓦogayot.com; ❷–❺), offers a contemporary take on the spa experience with its minimalist rooms, and has a pleasant **restaurant** with outdoor seating. More traditional alternatives include the neighbouring *Bagnoles Hôtel*, 6 place de la République (☏02.33.37.86.79, ⓦbagnoles-hotel.com; closed Nov–March; ❸), which has its own bistro.

Domfront

The road through the forest from Bagnoles, the D335 and then the D908, climbs above the lush woodlands and progressively narrows before entering the pretty hilltop town of **DOMFRONT**.

A public park, near the long-abandoned former train station, leads up to some redoubtable castle ruins perched on an isolated rock. Eleanor of Aquitaine was born in this **castle** in October 1162, and Thomas Becket came to stay for Christmas 1166, saying Mass in the **Notre-Dame-sur-l'Eau** church down by the river, which has sadly been ruined by vandals. The views from the flower-filled gardens that surround the mangled keep are spectacular, including an impressive panorama of the ascent you've made to get up. A slender footbridge connects the castle with the narrow little village itself, which boasts an abundance of half-timbered houses.

The **tourist office** is beside the castle at 12 place de la Roirie (Tues–Sat 10am–12.30pm & 2–6pm; ☏02.33.38.53.97, ⓦdomfront.com). On two summer afternoons a week (July & Aug Tues & Thurs 4.30pm), they run **guided tours** of old Domfront. A couple of pleasant Logis de France **hotels** stand side by side below the Old Town, where they're somewhat exposed to traffic noise. The *Relais St-Michel*, 5 rue du Mont St-Michel (☏02.33.38.64.99, ⓦhotellerelaisstmichel .com; ❶–❸), offers rooms with and without en-suite facilities, plus *menus* from €19, while the *France*, 7 rue du Mont St-Michel (☏02.33.38.51.44, ⓦhotelde france-fr.com; ❷), has a nice bar and garden as well as a restaurant.

The Bocage

The region that centres on **St-Lô**, just south of the Cotentin, is known as the **Bocage**; the word describes a type of cultivated countryside common in western France, where fields are cut by tight hedgerows rooted into walls of earth well over a metre high. An effective form of smallhold farming in pre-industrial days, it also proved to be a perfect system of anti-tank barricades. When the Allied troops tried to advance through the region in 1944, it was almost impenetrable – certainly bearing no resemblance to the East Anglian plains where they had trained. The war here was hand-to-hand slaughter, and the destruction of villages was often wholesale.

St-Lô

The city of **ST-LÔ**, 60km southeast of Cherbourg and 36km southwest of Bayeux, is still known as the "Capital of the Ruins". Memorial sites are everywhere and what is new speaks as tellingly of the destruction as the ruins that have been preserved. In the main square, the gate of the old prison commemorates Resistance members executed by the Nazis, people deported east to the concentration camps and soldiers killed in action. When the bombardment of St-Lô was at its fiercest, the Germans refused to take measures to protect the prisoners; this gate was all that survived.

The newness of so much in St-Lô reveals the scale of fighting. It took sixty years for the canalized channel of the Vire, running between the *gare SNCF* and the castle rock, to be relandscaped. Now known as **Port-St-Lô**, it's an attractive area to walk around, and pedalos are available for rent. But the most visible – and brilliant – reconstruction is the **Cathédrale de Notre-Dame**. The main body of this, with its strange southward-veering nave, has been conventionally repaired and rebuilt. Between the shattered west front and base of the collapsed north tower, however, a startling sheer wall of icy green stone makes no attempt to mask the destruction. By way of contrast, a lighthouse-like 1950s folly spirals to nowhere on the main square. Should you feel the urge, you can climb its staircase and make your way into the new and even more pointless labyrinth of glass at its feet for a €1.50 admission fee.

St-Lô's **tourist office** stands alongside the folly on the main square (July & Aug Mon–Fri 9.30am–6.30pm, Sat 10am–1pm; Sept–June Mon 2–6pm, Tues–Fri 10am–12.30pm & 2–6pm, Sat 10am–1pm; ☏02.33.77.60.35, ⓦwww.mairie -saint-lo.fr). The largest **hotel**, the *Mercure Saint-Lô*, stands just across the river beside the **gare SNCF**, ranged atop a ridge at 1 av Briovère (☏02.33.05.10.84; ❺); it's home to the *Tocqueville* **restaurant** (dinner only; closed Sun) which serves *menus* from €17. If you'd rather be up in town, *La Crémaillère*, at 8 rue de la Chancellerie (☏02.33.57.14.68; closed Fri eve & Sat in low season; ❷), also has a good restaurant, where all the *menus*, which start at €10 for lunch and €14.50 for dinner, include a buffet of hors d'oeuvres.

The Vire Valley

Once St-Lô was taken in the Battle of Normandy, the armies speedily moved southwest towards their next confrontation. The **Vire Valley**, trailing south from St-Lô, saw little action – and its towns and villages seem to have been rarely touched by any historic or cultural mainstream. The motivation in coming to this landscape of rolling hills and occasional gorges is essentially to consume the region's cider, Calvados apple brandy (much of it bootleg), fruit pastries and sausages made from pigs' intestines.

La Chapelle-sur-Vire

The best section of the valley is south of St-Lô through the Roches de Ham to Tessy-sur-Vire. The **Roches de Ham** are a pair of sheer rocky promontories high above the river. Though these are promoted as "viewing tables", the pleasure lies as much in the walk up, through lanes lined with blackberries, hazelnuts and rich orchards. Downstream from the Roches at **LA CHAPELLE-SUR-VIRE**, the church that towers majestically above the river has been an object of pilgrimage since the twelfth century. In a traditional cottage nearby, the ♨ *Auberge de la Chapelle* (☎ 02.33.56.32.83; ❷) is a good **restaurant** that also offers a few cheap **rooms** (rates include breakfast). *Menus* at €22 and €28 feature plenty of fresh river fish.

Travel details

Trains

Alençon to: Caen (8 daily; 1hr 10min); Le Mans (11 daily; 40min).

Caen to: Cherbourg (10 daily; 1hr 15min), via Bayeux (20min); Lisieux (21 daily; 30min); Le Mans (5 daily; 2hr), via Alençon (1hr 15min); Paris-St-Lazare (11 daily; 2hr 10min); Rennes (4 daily; 3hr), via St-Lô (50min), Coutances (1hr 15min) and Pontorson (2hr); Rouen (6 daily; 2hr).

Cherbourg to: Paris (8 daily; 3hr), via Valognes (15min) and Caen (1hr 15min).

Dieppe to: Paris-St-Lazare (19 daily; 2hr 10min), via Rouen (16 daily; 50min).

Granville to: Coutances (7 daily; 30min).

Le Havre to: Paris (11 daily; 2hr 30min); Rouen (15 daily; 50min).

Rouen to: Paris-St-Lazare (25 daily; 1hr 20min); Vernon (12 daily; 30min).

St-Lô to: Caen (12 daily; 50min), via Bayeux (25min); Rennes (4 daily; 2hr 10min), via Coutances (20min) and Pontorson (1hr 15min).

Trouville-Deauville to: Lisieux (5 daily in winter, much more frequently in summer; 20min); Paris (5 daily in winter, much more frequently in summer; 2hr).

Buses

Alençon to: Bagnoles (3 daily; 1hr); Mortagne (2–3 daily; 1hr); Vimoutiers (1–3 daily; 1hr 30min).

Bayeux to: Arromanches (4 daily; 30min); Ouistreham (3 daily; 1hr 15min).

Caen to: Arromanches (1 daily; 1hr 10min); Bayeux (3 daily; 50min); Clécy (4 daily; 50min); Falaise (7 daily; 1hr); Honfleur (13 daily; 2hr), via Cabourg (50min), Houlgate (1hr) and Deauville (1hr 51min), of which 5 continue to Le Havre (2hr 30min); Le Havre (3 daily express services; 1hr 20min), via Honfleur (1hr); Ouistreham (20 daily; 30min); Thury-Harcourt (5 daily; 40min).

Cherbourg to: St-Lô (3 daily; 1hr 30min); St-Vaast (3 daily; 1hr 10min) via Barfleur (1hr).

Dieppe to: Fécamp (4 daily; 2hr 20min).

Le Havre to: Étretat (12 daily; 45min); Fécamp (11 daily; 1hr 20min); Honfleur (7 daily; 30min).

Mont St-Michel to: Rennes (5 daily; 1hr 20min); St-Malo (4 daily; 1hr 30min).

Rouen to: Le Havre (hourly; 2hr 45min), via Jumièges (30min); Lisieux (2 daily; 2hr 30min).

St-Lô to: Bayeux (8 daily; 30min); Coutances (5 daily; 1hr).

Brittany

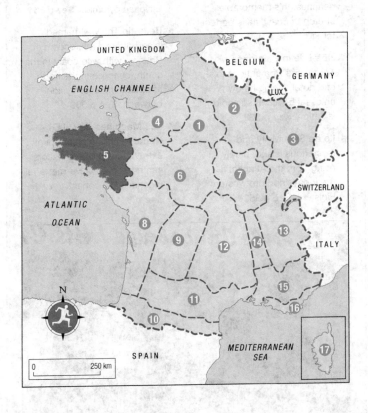

CHAPTER 5 # Highlights

* **Cancale** The stalls and restaurants in Cancale's little harbour will have oyster-lovers in raptures. See p.331

* **The Côte de Granit Rose** With its bizarre pink rock formations and gem-like beaches, this memorable stretch of coastline is perfect for kids. See p.338

* **Hôtel de la Baie des Trépassés** Romantic land's-end hotel, facing its own colossal beach in splendid isolation. See p.352

* **Île de Sein** Misty and mysterious island, barely rising from the Atlantic; a great day-trip from western Finistère. See p.352

* **The Inter-Celtic Festival** Celebrate the music and culture of the Celtic nations at Brittany's best-loved summer festival. See p.363

* **Carnac** France's most extraordinary megalithic monuments, predating even the Egyptian pyramids. See p.364

* **Belle-Île** The well-named island offers a microcosm of Brittany, with wild coast in the south, beaches in the north, and beautiful countryside between. See p.369

* **Les Machines de L'Île, Nantes** Thrilling steam-punk extravaganza, where visitors can ride on a twelve-metre-tall mechanical elephant. See p.381

▲ Cancale oysters

5

Brittany

No one area – and certainly no one town – in **Brittany** encapsulates the character of the province; that lies in its people and in its geographical unity. For generations Bretons risked their lives fishing and trading on the violent seas and struggled with the arid soil of the interior. This toughness and resilience is tinged with **Celtic** culture: mystical, musical, sometimes morbid and defeatist, sometimes vital and inspired.

Although archeologically Brittany is among the richest regions in the world – the alignments at **Carnac** rival Stonehenge – it first appeared in recorded history as the quasi-mythical "Little Britain" of Arthurian legend. In the days when travel by sea was safer and easier than by land, it was intimately connected with "Great Britain" across the water. Settlements such as St-Malo, St-Pol and Quimper were founded by Welsh and Irish missionary "saints" whose names won't be found in any official breviary. Brittany remained **independent** until the sixteenth century, its last ruler, Duchess Anne, only managing to protect the province's autonomy through marriage to two consecutive French monarchs. After her death, in 1532, François I took her daughter and lands, and sealed the **union with France** with an act supposedly enshrining certain privileges. The successive violations of this treaty by Paris, and subsequent revolts, form the core of Breton history since the Middle Ages.

Many Bretons continue to regard France as a separate country. Few, however, actively support Breton nationalism (which it's a criminal offence to advocate) much beyond putting Breizh (Breton for "Brittany") stickers on their cars. But there have been many successes in reviving the Breton language, and the economic resurgence of the last three decades, helped partly by summer tourism, has largely been due to local initiatives, like Brittany Ferries re-establishing an old trading link, carrying produce and passengers across to Britain and Ireland. At the same time a Celtic artistic identity has consciously been revived, and local festivals – above all August's **Inter-Celtic Festival** at Lorient – celebrate traditional Breton music, poetry and dance, with fellow Celts treated as comrades.

For most visitors, the Breton **coast** is the dominant feature. Apart from the Côte d'Azur, this is the most popular resort area in France, for both French and foreign tourists. Its attractions are obvious: warm white-sand beaches, towering cliffs, rock formations and offshore islands and islets, and everywhere the stone dolmens and menhirs of a prehistoric past. The most frequented areas are the **Côte d'Émeraude** around **St-Malo**; the **Côte de Granit Rose** in the north; the **Crozon peninsula** in far western **Finistère**; the family resorts such as **Bénodet** just to the south; and the **Morbihan coast** below **Vannes**. Hotels and campsites here are plentiful, if pushed to their limits from mid-June to the end of August. Be aware, though, that many coastal resorts close down completely out of season.

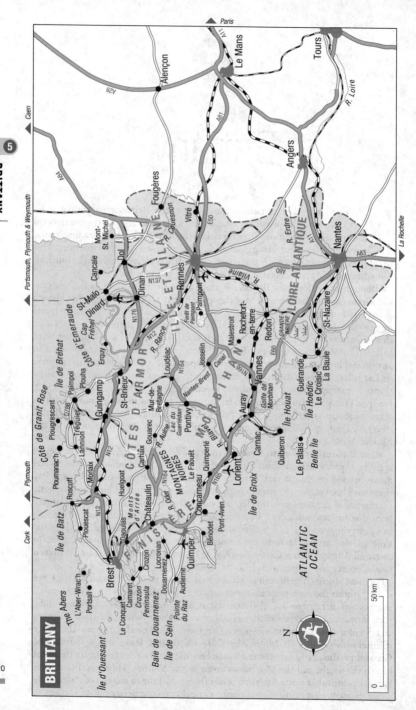

BRITTANY

Paris

Caen

Portsmouth, Plymouth & Weymouth

Plymouth

Cork

La Rochelle

Le Mans

Tours

Alençon

Angers

Nantes

St-Nazaire

La Baule

Le Croisic

Île du Hoëdic

La Palais

Belle Île

Quiberon

Île de Houat

Guérande

GRANDE BRIÈRE

LOIRE-ATLANTIQUE

Redon

Rochefort-en-terre

Malestroit

Vannes

Golfe du Morbihan

Auray

Carnac

Lorient

Île de Groix

Concarneau

Pont-Aven

Bénodet

Quimper

Audierne

Pointe du Raz

Île de Sein

Baie de Douarnenez

Quimperlé

Le Faouët

MONTAGNES NOIRES

Gourarec

Mur-de-Bretagne

Pontivy

Josselin

Paimpont

Forêt de Paimpont

Rennes

Dol

Mont-St. Michel

Cancale

St-Malo

Dinard

Cap Fréhel

Côte d'Émeraude

Erquy

Dinan

Paimpol

Île de Bréhat

Plouha

St-Brieuc

Loudéac

Guingamp

Tréguier

Lannion

Plougrescant

Ploumanac'h

Côte de Granit Rose

Roscoff

Île de Batz

Plouescat

Portsall

L'Aber-Wrac'h

The Abers

Brest

Le Conquet

Camaret

Crozon Peninsula

Crozon

Locronan

Douarnenez

Châteaulin

Daoulas

Huelgoat

Monts d'Arrée

Morlaix

Ploumarac'h

Carhaix

FINISTÈRE

CÔTES D'ARMOR

ILLE-ET-VILAINE

MORBIHAN

Fougères

Vitré

Laval

Lac du Guerlédan

ATLANTIC OCEAN

Île d'Ouessant

R. Loire

R. Erdre

R. Vilaine

R. Rance

R. Aulne

R. Blavet

Nantes-Brest Canal

Canal

A11

A81

A28

A84

A83

A80

E50

E60

N12

N137

N176

N164

N24

N165

N166

D786

D764

Bénodet

N

50 km

0

Brittany's proudest addition to the great cuisines of the world has to be the **crêpe** and its savoury equivalent the **galette**; crêperies throughout the region attempt to pass them off as satisfying meals, serving them with every imaginable filling. However, gourmet types are more likely to be enticed by the magnificent array of **seafood** on offer. Restaurants in resorts such as St-Malo and Quiberon jostle to attract fish connoisseurs, while some smaller towns – like Cancale, widely regarded as the best place in France for oysters (*huîtres*), and Erquy, with its scallops (*coquilles St-Jacques*) – depend wholly on one specific mollusc for their livelihood.

Although they can't claim to be uniquely Breton, two appetizers feature on every self-respecting menu. These are **moules marinière**, giant bowls of succulent orange mussels steamed in a combination of white wine, shallots and parsley (and perhaps enriched with cream or *crème fraîche* to become *moules à la crème*), and **soupe de poissons** (fish soup), traditionally served with a pot of the garlicky mayonnaise known as *rouille* (coloured with pulverized sweet red pepper), a mound of grated *gruyère*, and a bowl of croutons. Jars of fresh *soupe de poissons* are always on sale in seaside *poissonneries*, and make an ideal way to take a taste of France home with you. Paying a bit more in a restaurant – typically on *menus* costing €25 or more – brings you into the realm of the **assiette de fruits de mer**, a mountainous heap of langoustines, crabs, oysters, mussels, clams, whelks and cockles, most raw and all delicious.

Main courses tend to be plainer than in Normandy, with fresh local fish being prepared with relatively simple sauces. Skate served with capers, or salmon baked with a mustard or cheese sauce, are typical dishes, while even the **cotriade**, a stew containing sole, turbot or bass, as well as shellfish, is distinctly less rich than its Mediterranean equivalent, the *bouillabaisse*. Brittany is also better than much of France in maintaining its respect for fresh **vegetables**, thanks to the extensive local production of peas, cauliflowers, artichokes and the like. Only with the **desserts** can things get a little heavy; **far Breton**, considered a great delicacy, is a baked concoction of sponge and custard dotted with chopped plums, while *îles flottantes* are soft meringue icebergs adrift in a sea of *crème anglaise*, a light egg custard.

Strictly speaking, no **wine** is produced in Brittany. However, along the lower Loire valley, the *département* of Loire-Atlantique, centred on Nantes, is still generally regarded as "belonging" to Brittany – and is treated as such in this chapter. Vineyards here are responsible for the dry white Muscadet – normally used in *moules marinière* – and the even drier Gros-Plant.

Whenever you come, don't leave Brittany without visiting one of its scores of **islands** – such as the **Île de Bréhat**, the **Île de Sein**, or **Belle-Île** – or taking in cities like **Quimper** or **Morlaix**, testimony to the riches of the medieval duchy. Allow time, too, to leave the coast and explore the interior, even if the price you pay for the solitude is sketchy transport and a shortage of accommodation.

If you're looking for traditional Breton fun, and you can't make the Lorient festival (or the smaller Quinzaine Celtique at Nantes in June/July), look out for gatherings organized by **Celtic folklore groups** – Circles or Bagadou. You may also be interested by the **pardons**, pilgrimage festivals commemorating local saints. However, despite guidebooks (and tourist offices) that promote these as exciting spectacles, they're not phoney affairs kept alive for tourists, but deeply serious and rather gloomy religious occasions.

Brittany is well served by **public transport**. Separate TGV **train** lines from Paris – one ending at Brest, the other at Quimper – serve the major cities along the north and south coasts respectively, and high-speed trains also connect Lille with both Rennes or Nantes. All are complemented by local buses and trains. **Driving** too is straightforward, and none of Brittany's autoroutes charges tolls.

A Breton glossary

Although estimates of the number of **Breton-speakers** range from 400,000 to 800,000, you're unlikely to encounter it spoken as a first, day-to-day language. Learning Breton is not really a viable prospect for visitors without a grounding in Welsh, Gaelic or some other Celtic language. However, as you travel through the province, it's interesting to note the roots of Breton place names, many of which have a simple meaning in the language. Below are some of the most common:

aber	estuary	*lann*	heath
argoat	land	*lech*	flat stone
armor	sea	*mario*	dead
avel	wind	*men*	stone
bihan	little	*menez*	(rounded) mountain
bran	hill	*menhir*	long stone
braz	big	*meur*	big
coat	forest	*nevez*	new
cromlech	stone circle	*parc*	field
dol	table	*penn*	end, head
dolmen	stone table	*plou*	parish
du	black	*pors*	port, farmyard
enez	island	*roc'h*	ridge
goaz	stream	*ster*	river
gwenn	white	*stivel*	fountain, spring
hir	long	*traez henn*	beach
ker	village or house	*trou*	valley
kozh	old	*ty*	house
lan	holy place	*wrach*	witch

Eastern Brittany and the north coast

All roads in Brittany curl eventually inland to **Rennes**, the capital. East of Rennes, the fortified citadels of **Fougères** and **Vitré** protected the eastern approaches to medieval Brittany, which vigorously defended its independence against incursors. Along the north coast, west of Normandy's Mont St-Michel, stand some of Brittany's finest old towns. A spectacular introduction to the province greets ferry passengers from Portsmouth: the **River Rance**, guarded by magnificently preserved **St-Malo** on its estuary, and beautiful medieval **Dinan** 20km upstream. Further west stretches a varied coastline that culminates in the seductive **Île de Bréhat**, and the colourful chaos of the **Côte de Granit Rose**.

Rennes and around

For a city that has been the capital and power centre of Brittany since the 1532 union with France, **Rennes** is – outwardly at least – uncharacteristic of the province, with its Neoclassical layout and pompous major buildings. What potential it had to be a picturesque tourist spot was destroyed in 1720, when a drunken carpenter managed to set light to virtually the whole city. Only the area known as **Les Lices**, at the junction of the canalized Ille and the River Vilaine, was undamaged.

The subsequent remodelling of the rest of the city left it, north of the river at any rate, as a muddle of grand eighteenth-century public squares interspersed with intimate little alleys of half-timbered houses. It's a lively enough place though, with over forty thousand university **students**, to stimulate its cultural life, and a couple of major annual **festivals**, the Tombées de la Nuit and the Transmusicales, to lure in outsiders.

Arrival and information

For drivers, it's best to park as soon as you reach the city centre; the most convenient **car parks** are beneath the place des Lices, and between the *quais* Duguay-Trouin and Lamennais.

Rennes' **gare SNCF** (☏08.36.35.35.35), on the Paris–Brest TGV line, is south of the Vilaine, twenty minutes' walk from the tourist office and a little more from the medieval quarter. A fast, efficient **métro** system connects the *gare SNCF*, the place de la République beside the canal in the heart of town, and the place

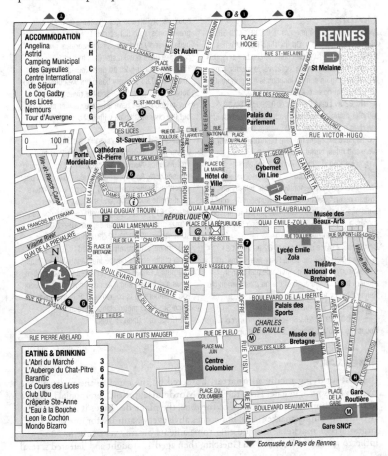

ACCOMMODATION
Angelina — E
Astrid — H
Camping Municipal des Gayeulles — C
Centre International de Séjour — A
Le Coq Gadby — B
Des Lices — D
Nemours — F
Tour d'Auvergne — G

EATING & DRINKING
L'Abri du Marché — 3
L'Auberge du Chat-Pitre — 6
Barantic — 4
Le Cours des Lices — 5
Club Ubu — 8
Crêperie Ste-Anne — 2
L'Eau à la Bouche — 9
Leon le Cochon — 7
Mondo Bizarro — 1

RENNES

Ecomusée du Pays de Rennes

Ste-Anne. Like the extensive local **bus** network, which radiates out from place de la République, it's run by STAR (one journey €1.20, all-day pass €3.50; ⓦstar.fr).

The long-distance **gare routière** stands alongside the *gare SNCF* on boulevard Solférino. Rennes is a busy junction, with direct services to St-Malo (Illenoo: ⓣ02.99.82.26.26, ⓦillenoo.fr), and Mont-St-Michel (Keolis Emeraude: ⓣ02.99.19.70.80, ⓦwww.keolis-emeraude.com).

The **tourist office** stands in a disused medieval church, the Chapelle St-Yves, just north of the river at 11 rue St-Yves (July & Aug Mon–Sat 9am–7pm, Sun 11am–1pm & 2–6pm; Sept–June Mon 1–6pm, Tues–Sat 10am–6pm, Sun 11am–1pm & 2–6pm; ⓣ02.99.67.11.11, ⓦwww.tourisme-rennes.com). **Internet access** is available at the France Telecom shop, next to the post office on place de la République (Mon–Sat 9am–7pm).

Accommodation

Hotels are scattered near the river and in old Rennes, the best area for restaurants and nightlife. There's a wider choice of options further out, made practical by the excellent public transport system.

Hotels

Angelina 1 quai Lammenais ⓣ02.99.79.29.66, ⓦangelina-hotel.com. On the third floor of what initially seems a rundown commercial building, this budget hotel offers large, great-value rooms; the one snag with its central location is the potential for late-night noise outside. ❸

Astrid 32 av Louis Barthou ⓣ02.99.30.82.38, ⓦhotel-astrid-rennes.eu. Peaceful hotel, south of the river near the *gare SNCF*, where the large rooms have excellent modern bathrooms. Lower weekend rates, buffet breakfasts €8. ❸

🏃 **Le Coq Gadby** 156 rue d'Antrain ⓣ02.99.38.05.55, ⓦlecoq-gadby.com. Family-run for four generations, this self-styled "urban resort", set in superb seventeenth-century buildings, offers eleven luxurious period-furnished rooms, an open-fire lounge, on-site spa and Michelin-starred restaurant. ❽

Des Lices 7 place des Lices ⓣ02.99.79.14.81, ⓦwww.hotel-des-lices.com. Forty-five rooms, all with balcony, in a very comfortable and friendly modern hotel on the edge of the prettiest part of old Rennes, handy for the place des Lices car park. ❹

🏃 **Nemours** 5 rue de Nemours ⓣ02.99.78.26.26, ⓦhotelnemours.com. Recast as a boutique hotel, this central option has spotless, stylish and well-lit rooms in white and green tones, with flat-screen TVs and comfortable beds. Friendly and professional service, and you can take good breakfasts (€10) in bed. ❹

Tour d'Auvergne 20 bd de la Tour-d'Auvergne ⓣ02.99.30.84.16. Very basic but welcoming option between the *gare SNCF* and the river. Some low-priced rooms have en-suite shower facilities, but the cheapest come with just a sink. ❶

Hostel and campsite

Camping Municipal des Gayeulles Rue du Prof-Maurice-Audin ⓣ02.99.36.91.22, ⓦcamping-rennes.com. An appealingly verdant site, 1km east of central Rennes on bus #3, in a park that offers good shade and a pool and sporting facilities nearby. €13 for two people with car. Open all year.

Centre International de Séjour 10–12 Canal St-Martin ⓣ02.99.33.22.33, ⓦfuaj.org/rennes. Welcoming, attractively positioned HI hostel, 3km north of the centre beside the Canal d'Ille et Rance. Charging €19 per person per night for a dorm bed, it has a cafeteria and a laundry; hostelling association membership is compulsory. Bus #18 from the place Ste-Anne métro station, direction "St-Gregoire". Open all year.

The City

Rennes' surviving **medieval quarter**, bordered by the canal to the west and the river to the south, radiates from the **Porte Mordelaise**, the old ceremonial entrance to the city. Immediately northeast of the *porte*, the **place des Lices** is dominated by two usually empty market halls, but comes alive every Saturday for one of France's largest **street markets**. In a jousting tournaments on this very spot in 1337, the hitherto unknown Bertrand du Guesclin, then aged 17, fought and defeated several older opponents. That set him on his career as a soldier, during which he was to save Rennes when it was under siege by the English. However, after the Bretons were defeated at Auray in 1364, he fought for the French, and twice invaded Brittany.

The one central building to escape the 1720 fire was the **Palais du Parlement** on rue Hoche downtown. Ironically, however, the Palais was all but ruined by a mysterious conflagration in 1994, sparked by a flare during a demonstration by Breton fishermen. Since then, the entire structure has been rebuilt and restored, and is once more topped by an impressive array of gleaming gilded statues. Inside, its lobby stages temporary exhibitions.

If you head south from the Palais, you'll soon reach the **River Vilaine**, which flows through the centre of Rennes, narrowly confined into a steep-sided channel. The south bank is every bit as busy as the north, and is home to the **Musée des Beaux-Arts**, 20 quai Émile-Zola (Tues 10am–6pm, Wed–Sun 10am–noon & 2–6pm; €5.72; ⓦmbar.org). Unfortunately many of its finest artworks – which include drawings by Leonardo da Vinci, Botticelli, Fra Lippo Lippi and Dürer – are not usually on public display. Instead you'll find indifferent Impressionist views of Normandy by the likes of Boudin and Sisley, interspersed with the occasional treasure such as Veronese's depiction of a flying *Perseus Rescuing Andromeda*. Picasso makes a cameo appearance, with a nude from 1923, a simple *Baigneuse à Dinard* from 1928, and a very late and surprisingly Cubist canvas from 1970.

The showpiece **Musée de Bretagne**, housed in the modern Champs Libres, five hundred metres south on the cours des Alliés, provides a high-tech overview of Breton history and culture (Tues noon–9pm, Wed–Fri noon–7pm, Sat & Sun 2–7pm; €4, or €7 for museum and Éspace des Sciences; ⓦwww.musee-bretagne .fr). It starts with a hearth used by humans in a Finistère sea cave half a million years ago that ranks among the oldest signs of fire in the world. From here on, a quick, entertaining skate through regional history covers the dolmens and menhirs of the megalith builders, some magnificent jadeite axes and Bronze Age swords, and the arrival of first the Celts, next the Romans, and later still the spread of Christianity from the fifth century onwards. Labels are in English as well as French and Breton. Under the same roof, and sharing the same hours and entrance fees, the **Éspace des Sciences** is a peculiar sort of scaly volcano that contains two floors of rather dry scientific displays, this time with no English captions.

Eating and drinking

Most of Rennes' more interesting **bars** and **restaurants** are in the streets just south of the **place Ste-Anne**, with the bar-lined **rue St-Michel** and rue Penhoët, each with a fine assemblage of ancient wooden buildings, as the epicentre. Ethnic alternatives are concentrated along **rue St-Malo** just to the north, and also on **rue St-Georges** near the place du Palais. Rue Vasselot is the nearest equivalent south of the river.

Restaurants

L'Abri du Marché 9 place des Lices ☎02.99.79.73.87. Nothing but the Breton staples of *moules* (€10) and *galettes* (€3–9) are served at this local favourite, where the pleasant dining room is smothered in old Breton trinkets.

L'Auberge du Chat-Pitre 18 rue du Chapitre ☎02.99.30.36.36. Enjoyable recreation of medieval dining, seated at long communal tables in a very pretty red half-timbered mansion close by the cathedral, and interrupted by the odd jester.

Hearty stews and roasts predominate; there's a €24 *menu*, or starters cost around €7, main courses €13–19. Cheaper salads and tarts at lunchtime, with no entertainment. Closed Sun.

Le Cours des Lices 18 place des Lices ☎02.99.30.25.25, ⓦlecourdeslices.fr. Top-notch French restaurant, perfectly positioned to take advantage of the fresh produce in the adjoining market. Dinner *menus* from €19 (weekdays only), €27 and €39. Closed Sun & Mon.

Crêperie Ste-Anne 5 place Ste-Anne ⓣ 02.99.79.22.72, ⓦ creperiesainteanne.com. Appealing crêperie nicely situated on the place Ste-Anne opposite the church, with plenty of outdoor seating and a good selection of *galettes* for €5–8. Closed Sun.

L'Eau à la Bouche 12 rue de l'Arsenal ⓣ 02.23.40.27.95, ⓦ restaurant-leaualabouche.fr. Exquisite little restaurant that servies a modern take on classic French cuisine on ever-changing dinner *menus* that range €16–34, and lays on a special brunch on Sat & Sun.

Leon le Cochon 1 rue Maréchal-Joffre ⓣ 02.99.79.37.54, ⓦ leonlecochon.com. Tasteful, contemporary but classically French restaurant; the simple €12.50 lunch *menu* includes wine, while

dinner *menus* start at €26. Closed Sun in July & Aug.

Bars and clubs

Barantic 4 rue St-Michel ⓣ 02.99.79.29.24. One of the city's favourite bars, putting on occasional live music for a mixed crowd of Breton nationalists and boisterous students; if it's too full, half a dozen similar alternatives lie within spitting distance.

Mondo Bizarro 264 av Général-Patton ⓣ 02.99.87.22.00, ⓦ mondobizarro.free.fr. Rock, metal and especially punk club, 1km northeast of the centre on bus line #15, and kept busy most nights with local bands and international punk stalwarts, plus a leavening of tribute bands, ska, reggae and jazz.

Festivals and Entertainment

Rennes is at its best in the first ten days of July, when the **Festival des Tombées de la Nuit** takes over the whole city to celebrate Breton culture with music, theatre, film, mime and poetry (ⓦ lestombeesdelanuit.com). A pocket version of same festival is also held in the week between Christmas and New Year. In the first week of December, the **Transmusicales** rock festival attracts big-name acts from all over the world, though still with a Breton emphasis (ⓦ lestrans.com). The **Théâtre National de Bretagne**, 1 rue St-Helier (ⓣ 02.99.31.12.31, ⓦ www.t-n-b.fr), puts on varied events throughout the year, except in July and August. All year round, in a different auditorium on the same premises, *Club Ubu* (ⓣ 02.99.31.12.10, ⓦ ubu-rennes.com) is the venue for large-scale rock concerts.

Vitré

VITRÉ, just north of the Le Mans–Rennes motorway, 30km east of Rennes, rivals Dinan as the best-preserved medieval town in Brittany. While its walls are not quite complete, the thickets of medieval stone cottages that lie outside them have hardly changed. The towers of the **castle**, which dominates the western end of the ramparts, have pointed slate-grey roofs in best fairytale fashion, looking like freshly sharpened pencils, but sadly the municipal offices and **museum** of shells, birds, bugs and local history inside are not exactly thrilling (May–Sept daily except Tues 10am–12.45pm & 2–6pm; Oct–April Mon & Wed–Sat 10am–12.15pm & 2–5.30pm, Sun 2–5.30pm; €4).

Vitré's principal **market** is held on Mondays in the square in front of **Notre-Dame church**. The old city is full of twisting streets of half-timbered houses, a good proportion of which are bars – **rue Beaudrairie** in particular has a fine selection.

The local **gare SNCF** is on the southern edge of the centre, where the ramparts disappear and the town blends into its newer sectors. Left of the station, on place Général de Gaulle, you'll find the **tourist office** (July & Aug Mon–Sat 9.30am–12.30pm & 2–6.30pm, Sun 10am–12.30pm & 3–6pm; Sept–June Mon 2.30–6pm, Tues–Fri 9.30am–12.30pm & 2.30–6pm, Sat 10am–12.30pm & 3–5pm; ⓣ 02.99.75.04.46, ⓦ ot-vitre.fr), which runs an intricate schedule of guided tours in summer.

Most of the **hotels** are nearby. The good-value *Petit Billot*, 5bis place du Général-Leclerc (ⓣ 02.99.75.02.10, ⓦ petit-billot.com; ❷), has the excellent *Potager* restaurant downstairs, while higher rooms in the *Hôtel du Château*, 5 rue Rallon (ⓣ 02.99.74.58.59, ⓦ premiumorange.com/hotel-du-chateau; ❷; closed

Sun in low season), just below the castle, have views of the ramparts. Of the **restaurants**, *La Soupe aux Choux*, 32 rue Notre-Dame (T02.99.75.10.86; closed Sat lunch, plus Sun in low season), prepares simple but classic French food, with the occasional eccentricity like kangaroo cooked in cider (€14) thrown in.

St-Malo and around

Walled with the same grey granite stone as Mont St-Michel, the elegant, ancient, and beautifully positioned city of **ST-MALO** was originally a fortified island at the mouth of the Rance, controlling not only the estuary but the open sea beyond. Now inseparably attached to the mainland, it's the most visited place in Brittany, thanks partly to its superb **old citadelle** and partly to its ferry service to England. The busy, lively streets that lie within the walls – the area known as *Intra-muros* – are packed with restaurants, bars and shops. Yes, the summer crowds can be oppressive, but even then a stroll atop the ramparts should restore your equilibrium, and vast, clean beaches beyond the walls are a huge bonus if you're travelling with kids in tow.

Arrival and information

St-Malo is always busy with **boats**. From the **Terminal Ferry du Naye**, Brittany Ferries (T02.99.40.64.41, Wbrittany-ferries.com) sails to Portsmouth, while Condor Ferries (T02.99.40.78.10, Wcondorferries.co.uk) connects with Weymouth. Portsmouth and Poole (via Jersey or Guernsey) during spring and summer; for details, see p.29. Between April and early November, regular passenger **ferries to Dinard** operate from the **quai Dinan**, just outside the southernmost point of the ramparts (€4.30 single, €6.70 return; bikes €2.50 single, €4 return; T08.25.13.80.35, Wcompagniecorsaire.com); the trip across the estuary takes an all-too-short ten minutes.

St-Malo's **gare SNCF** is 2km out from the citadelle, convenient neither for the old town nor the ferry. Almost all local and long-distance **buses** stop there as well as on the esplanade St-Vincent, just outside the walls. Illenoo (T02.99.82.26.26, Willenoo.fr) runs services to Dinard, Rennes and, in summer, Mont-St-Michel; Kéolis Emeraude (T02.99.19.70.80, Wwww.keolis-emeraude.com) runs express services to Mont-St-Michel; and Tibus (T08.10.22.22.22, Wwww.tibus.fr) serves Dinard and Dinard.

The helpful local **tourist office** is alongside the *gare routière* (April–June & Sept Mon–Sat 9am–1pm & 2–6.30pm, Sun 10am–12.30pm & 2.30–6pm; July & Aug Mon–Sat 9am–7.30pm, Sun 10am–6pm; Oct–March Mon–Sat 9am–1pm & 2–6pm; T08.25.13.52.00, Wwww.saint-malo-tourisme.com). You can get **internet access** here, or in Cyber' Com, west of the *gare SNCF* at 29bis bd des Talards (T02.99.56.05.83, Wwww.cybermalo.com).

Bicycles can be rented from Les Velos Bleus, 19 rue Alphonse-Thébault (T02.99.40.31.63, Wwww.velos-bleus.fr; closed Nov–March), or Espace Nicole, 11 rue R-Schuman, Paramé (T02.99.56.11.06, Wcyclesnicole.com).

Accommodation

St-Malo boasts over a hundred **hotels**, including the seaside boarding houses just off the beach, along with several **campsites** and a **hostel**. In high season it needs every one of them, so make reservations well in advance. Some *intra-muros* hotels take advantage of summer demand by insisting you eat in their own restaurants. Cheaper rates can be found by the *gare SNCF*, or in suburban Paramé.

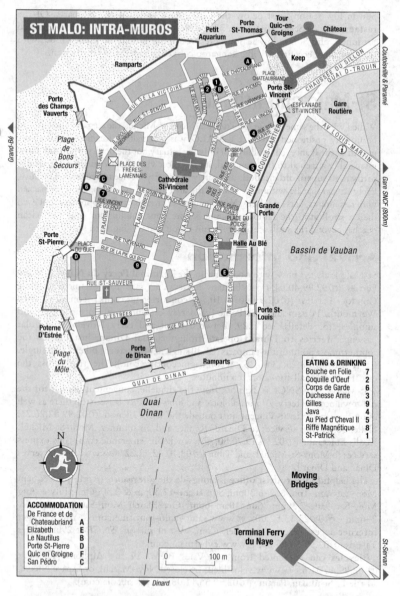

ST MALO: INTRA-MUROS

EATING & DRINKING

Bouche en Folie	7
Coquille d'Oeuf	2
Corps de Garde	6
Duchesse Anne	3
Gilles	9
Java	4
Au Pied d'Cheval II	5
Riffe Magnétique	8
St-Patrick	1

ACCOMMODATION

De France et de Chateaubriand	A
Elizabeth	E
Le Nautilus	B
Porte St-Pierre	D
Quic en Groigne	F
San Pédro	C

N

0   100 m

▼ Dinard

Hotels in the citadelle

De France et de Chateaubriand Place Chateaubriand ☏02.99.56.66.52, ⊛www.hotel-fr-chateaubriand.com. Elegant rooms (though standards vary; look first) at surprisingly reasonable prices in the imposing birthplace of the writer Chateaubriand, approached via a courtyard from the main square. Higher rooms have sea views; breakfast is €11 and parking €15. ⑤

Elizabeth 2 rue des Cordiers ☏02.99.56.24.98, ⊛st-malo-hotel-elizabeth.com. Seventeenth-century mansion, just back from the walls and grandly furnished to a Far Eastern theme. Ten spacious guest rooms with rather small bathrooms, plus cheaper but modern and comfortable rooms in "the Skippers", an annexe 100m away. Breakfast €11. ❼, Skippers ❹

🏃 **Le Nautilus** 9 rue de la Corne de Cerf
    ☎02.99.40.42.27, ⓦlenautilus.com. Colourfully refitted hotel (with a lift), not far in from the Porte St-Vincent, with small, bright, good-value rooms, all with shower and WC. Friendly staff ensure it's hugely popular with younger travellers. Bar but no restaurant. Closed mid-Nov to early Feb. ❸

Porte St-Pierre 2 place du Guet ☎02.99.40.91.27, ⓦhotel-portestpierre.com. Comfortable Logis de France, peeping over the walls of the citadelle, near the small Porte St-Pierre and very handy for the beach. Predominantly fish-based dinner *menus*, in the separate restaurant across the alley (closed Tues, plus Thurs lunch & Sun eve), run from €29 upwards. Closed mid-Nov to Feb. ❹

Quic en Groigne 8 rue d'Estrées
☎02.99.20.22.20, ⓦquic-en-groigne.com. Friendly little hotel at the far end of the citadelle, with attractive en-suite rooms. ❹

🏃 **San Pédro** 1 rue Ste-Anne
    ☎02.99.40.88.57, ⓦsanpedro-hotel.com. Twelve compact but tastefully and stylishly refurbished rooms in a nice quiet setting, just inside the walls in the north of the citadelle. Great breakfasts and friendly advice. Higher rooms (reached via a minuscule lift) enjoy sea views, and cost around €10 extra. Closed mid-Nov to Feb. ❸

Hotels outside the walls

Le Beaufort 25 chaussée du Sillon, Coutoisville ☎02.99.40.99.99, ⓦwww.hotel-beaufort.com. Grand sea-view hotel, half an hour's walk along the beach from the citadelle. Beautifully restored rooms – some with lovely balconies – and a fine restaurant. ❼

De l'Europe 44 bd de la République
☎02.99.56.13.42, ⓦhoteldeleurope-saintmalo.com.

Year-round cheap but clean rooms (the cheapest don't have en-suite facilities) in a genuinely friendly (if noisy) hotel near the *gare* SNCF, with a cosy café. Some rooms accommodate up to six people; for groups of four or more, it works out cheaper than the hostel. ❶

🏃 **La Rance** 15 quai Sébastopol, St-Servan
    ☎02.99.81.78.63, ⓦlarancehotel.com. Small, tasteful and airy option in sight of the Tour Solidor, that boasts eleven spacious rooms and a much more tranquil atmosphere than St-Malo itself. ❹

Hostel and campsites

Centre Patrick Varangot 37 av du Père-Umbricht, Paramé ☎02.99.40.29.80, ⓦcentrevarangot.com. One of France's busiest hostels, near the beach 2km northeast of the *gare* SNCF, and usually dominated by lively young travellers. Dorm beds at €17.50 in a room with just a washbasin, €19.80 with en-suite facilities; private rooms €15 extra; hostelling association membership required. Rates include breakfast, and there's also a cut-price cafeteria, kitchen facilities and tennis courts. No curfew, open all year.

🏃 **Cité d'Alet** Allée Gaston Buy, St-Servan
    ☎02.99.81.60.91, ⓦwww.ville-saint-malo
.fr/tourisme/les-campings. The nicest local campsite is also by far the nearest to the citadelle, a municipally run gem in a dramatic location on the headland southwest of St-Malo, overlooking the city from within the wartime German fortified stronghold. Bus #1 from *gare SNCF* or Porte St-Vincent. €13.40 for two. Closed Oct to early May.

Les Îlôts Av de la Guimorais, Rothéneuf
☎02.99.56.98.72, ⓦwww.ville-saint-malo.fr
/tourisme/les-campings. Green little municipal site, five minutes' walk inland from either of two crescent beaches, roughly 5km east of the citadelle. €13.40 for two. Closed Sept–June.

The Town

The **citadelle** of St-Malo was long joined to the mainland only by a causeway; then the construction of the harbour basin concealed the original line of the coast forever. Although its streets of restored seventeenth- and eighteenth-century houses get terribly crowded in summer, away from the more popular thoroughfares random exploration is fun, and you can always escape to the **ramparts** – first erected in the fourteenth century – to enjoy wonderful all-round views.

Ancient as they look, the **buildings** within the walls are almost entirely reconstructed; following the bombardment that forced the German surrender in 1944, eighty percent of the city was lovingly and precisely rebuilt, stone by stone. One notable survivor of this, and the fire in 1661, is the **Maison International des Poètes et Écrivains** at 5 rue Pélicot (Tues–Sat 2–6pm; ⓦwww.mipe.asso.fr), which holds exhibitions and literary events and stocks a library of world poetry.

Besides the prominent **Grande Porte**, the main gate of the citadelle is the **Porte St-Vincent**. To the right is the **castle**, inside which the **Musée de la Ville** (April–Sept daily 10am–12.30pm & 2–6pm; Oct–March Tues–Sun 10am–noon & 2–6pm; €5.60) commemorates the "prodigious prosperity" enjoyed by St-Malo during its days of piracy, colonialism and slave trading. Climbing the 169 steps of the keep, you pass a fascinating mixture of maps, diagrams and exhibits – chilling handbills from the Nazi occupation, accounts of the "infernal machine" used by the English to blow up the port in 1693, and savage four-pronged *chausse-trapes* (a kind of early version of barbed wire), thrown by pirates onto the decks of ships being boarded to immobilize their crews. At the top a gull's-eye prospect takes in the whole citadelle.

The beach

At several points, you can pass through the ramparts to reach the open shore, where a huge **beach** stretches away east beyond the rather featureless resort-suburb of **Paramé**. When the tide is low, it's safe to walk out to the small island of **Grand-Bé** – the walk is so popular that sometimes you even need to queue to get onto the short causeway. Solemn warnings are posted of the dangers of attempting to return from the island when the tide has risen too far – if you're caught there, there you have to stay. The one "sight" is the tomb of the nineteenth-century writer-politician **Chateaubriand** (1768–1848).

Beyond the citadelle

The **St-Servan** district, within walking distance along the corniche south of the citadelle, was the city's original settlement, converted to Christianity by St Malou (or Maclou) in the sixth century; only later, in the twelfth century, did the townspeople move to the impregnable island now called St-Malo. St-Servan is dominated by the distinctive **Tour Solidor**, which consists of three linked towers built in 1382, and looks in cross-section just like the ace of clubs. It now holds a **museum** of Cape Horn clipper ships, open for ninety-minute guided visits (April–Sept daily 10am–12.30pm & 2–6pm; Oct–March Tues–Sun 10am–noon & 2–6pm; €5.60). Most of the great European explorers of the Pacific are covered, from Magellan onwards, but naturally the emphasis is on French heroes like Bougainville. Tours culminate with a superb view from the topmost ramparts.

Follow the main road due south from St-Servan, ignoring signs for the Barrage de la Rance – or take bus #5 from the *gare SNCF* – and high above town you'll come to the **Grand Aquarium** (daily: April–June & Sept 10am–7pm; first two weeks in July & second two weeks in Aug 9.30am–8pm; mid-July to mid-Aug 9.30am–10pm; Oct–March 10am–6pm as a rule, but wide variations and some closures; last admission one hour before closing; €15.50, under-15s €9.50; ⓦ www.aquarium-st-malo.com). This postmodern structure can be a bit bewildering at first, but once you get the hang of it it's an entertaining place, where you can either learn interesting facts about slimy monsters of the deep or simply pull faces back at them. Its eight distinct fish tanks, which hold fish from all over the world, include one shaped like a Polo mint, where dizzy visitors stand in the hole in the middle as myriad fish whirl around them.

Eating and drinking

Intra-muros St-Malo boasts even more **restaurants and bars** than hotels, but prices are probably higher than anywhere else in Brittany, especially on the open café terraces – apart from the *Duchesse Anne*, avoid all those around rue Jacques-Cartier and Porte St-Vincent. Bear in mind that most crêperies also serve *moules* and similar snacks.

Markets are held in the Halle au Blé within the walls of St-Malo on Tuesdays and Fridays, in St-Servan on Mondays and Fridays, and in Paramé on Wednesdays and Saturdays. The fish market is on Saturdays in the place de la Poissonerie, also within the walls.

Restaurants

Bouche en Folie 14 rue du Boyer
☎06.72.49.08.89, ⓦboucheenfolie.eresto.net. This tiny little place offers classic French dishes, with a good lunch *menu* for €12, and excellent dinner *menus* for €22 and €28. Some outdoor seating. Closed Mon & Tues.

Coquille d'Oeuf 20 rue de la Corne de Cerf
☎02.99.40.92.62. Stylish, open-kitchen restaurant, priding itself on serving "slow food"; at busy times, it can be too slow for comfort. But the food is seriously good; €22 lets you choose from the simple daily *menu*, with fish or meat for each course. Lunch Sun only, dinner nightly except Mon.

Corps de Garde 3 montée Notre Dame
☎02.99.40.91.46. The only restaurant that's right up on St-Malo's ramparts is just an ordinary crêperie, serving standard €2.40–9 crêpes. However, the views from its large open-air terrace (covered when necessary) are sensational, looking out over the beach to dozens of little islets. Closed mid-Nov to mid-Feb.

Duchesse Anne 5–7 place Guy-la-Chambre
☎02.99.40.85.33. St-Malo's best known upmarket restaurant, beside Porte St-Vincent, works hard to keep up its reputation – and its prices. The only set *menu* is a €78 lobster option; you might manage to get a lunch for under €25, but dinner will cost well over twice that. Whole baked fish is the speciality.

Closed Wed & Mon lunch, Sun eve in low season, plus all Dec & Jan.

Gilles 2 rue de la Pie-qui-Boit ☎02.99.40.97.25. Bright, modern, good-value restaurant, just off the central pedestrian axis. The €17 lunch *menu* is fine; for dinner, €24.70 brings you oysters or smoked salmon, and a fabulous fish hotpot. Closed Wed & Thurs, plus late Nov to mid-Dec.

Au Pied d'Cheval II 6 rue Jacques Cartier
☎02.99.40.98.18, ⓦau-pied-de-cheval.com. This offshoot of the casual little waterfront gem in nearby Cancale – see below – is more of a place to linger, but serves exactly the same well-priced *menu*, heavy on oysters and mussels for under €10, with a delicious *assiette de fruits de mer* for two at €45.

Bars

Java 3 rue Ste-Barbe ☎02.99.56.41.90, ⓦwww .lajavacafe.com. An entertaining and unique cider bar, with swings at the bar, old dolls on the wall, and an elevator door into the toilet.

Riffe Magnétique 20 rue de la Herse
☎02.99.40.85.70, ⓦleriffmagnetique.com. Lively, friendly bar, with a fine choice of wines plus regular café-concerts, and DJs at the weekend. Closed Sun & Mon.

St-Patrick 24 rue Ste-Barbe ☎02.99.56.66.90. Cosy Irish pub, tucked away not far from the château.

The Pointe du Grouin and Cancale

Along the coast east of St-Malo, the perilous and windy heights of the **Pointe du Grouin** offer spectacular views of the pinnacle of Mont St-Michel and the bird sanctuary of the **Îles des Landes** to the east. Just south of the *pointe*, and less than 15km from St-Malo across the peninsula, **CANCALE** is France's most renowned spot for **oysters**. In the old church of St-Méen at the top of the hill, the town's obsession is documented with meticulous precision by the small **Musée des Arts et Traditions Populaires** (May Fri–Sun 2.30–6.30pm; June & Sept Mon & Fri–Sun 2.30–6.30pm; July & Aug Mon 2.30–6.30pm, Tues–Sun 10am–noon & 2.30–6.30pm; €3.50; ⓦmuseedecancale.fr). Cancale oysters were found in the camps of Julius Caesar, taken daily to Versailles for Louis XIV and even accompanied Napoleon on the march to Moscow.

From the rue des Parcs next to the jetty, you can see at low tide the *parcs* where the oysters are grown. The rocks of the cliff behind are streaked and shiny like mother-of-pearl; underfoot the beach is littered with countless generations of empty shells. The port area is pretty and very smart, with a long line of upmarket glass-fronted hotels and restaurants.

Cancale's **hotels** mostly insist that you eat in if you want to stay; among the best value are ⚓ *La Houle*, 18 quai Gambetta (☎02.99.89.62.38; ❶–❸), where the cheapest rooms lack en-suite facilities, but paying a little more gets you an excellent bathroom, and more still a sea-view balcony, and the *Phare*, 6 quai

Thomas (℡02.99.89.60.24, Ⓦlephare-cancale.com; ❸), which offers good rooms above a top-notch restaurant. Budget travellers can also head for the **hostel**, near the beach 2km north of town at Port Picain (℡02.99.89.62.62, Ⓦfuaj.org /cancale-baie-de-saint-michel; closed Dec & Jan), where a dorm bed costs €19 with breakfast, and you can also camp.

🏃 *Au Pied de Cheval*, 10 quai Gambetta (℡02.99.89.76.95), is a ramshackle, gloriously atmospheric little place to sample a few oysters, with great baskets of them spread across its wooden quayside tables. A dozen raw oysters on a bed of seaweed can cost just €5.

Dinan

The wonderful citadel of **DINAN** has preserved almost intact its 3km encirclement of protective masonry, along with street upon colourful street of late medieval houses. However, despite its slightly unreal perfection, it's seldom overrun with tourists. There are no essential museums, the most memorable architecture is vernacular rather than monumental, and time is most easily spent wandering from crêperie to café and down to the pretty port.

Arrival and information

Both the Art Deco **gare SNCF** and the **gare routière** (℡08.10.22.22.22, Ⓦwww .tibus.fr) are in the rather gloomy modern quarter, on place du 11-Novembre, ten minutes' walk west of the walls. The **tourist office**, which also offers **internet access**, is just off the place Du Guesclin at 9 rue du Château (July & Aug Mon–Sat 9am–7pm, Sun 10am–12.30pm & 2.30–6pm; Sept–June Mon–Sat 9am–12.30pm & 2–6pm; ℡02.96.87.69.76, Ⓦwww.dinan-tourisme.com).

Between May and October, **boats** sail along the Rance between Dinan's port and Dinard and St-Malo (Compagnie Corsaire: ℡08.25.13.81.20, Ⓦcompagnie corsaire.com). The trip takes 2 hours 45 minutes, with the exact schedule varying according to the tides (adults €23.50, under-13s €14). It's only possible to do a day return by boat (adults €29.50, under-13s €17.70) if you start from St-Malo or Dinard; starting from Dinan, you have to come back by bus or train.

Accommodation

Many of Dinan's **hotels** lie within the walled town or down by the port. Both locations are convenient if you're on foot, but motorists should note that parking can be difficult in summer. Most hotels are in the mid-range category, with only a couple of genuine budget options.

Hotels and B&Bs

Le d'Avaugour 1 place du Champ ℡02.96.39.07.49, Ⓦavaugourhotel.com. Smart, elegant hotel, entered from the main square but backing onto the ramparts, with very tasteful renovated rooms and lovely gardens. Closed Nov–Feb.

🏃 Logis du Jerzual 25–27 rue du Petit Fort ℡02.96.85.46.54, Ⓦlogis-du-jerzual.com. Friendly B&B, with a lovely garden terrace, halfway up the exquisite little lane that leads from the port. The five rooms have wonderful character, with

four-poster beds, modern bathrooms and romantic views over the rooftops. ❹
De la Porte St-Malo 35 rue St-Malo ℡02.96.39.19.76, Ⓦhotelportemalo.com. Simple but very comfortable rooms in a welcoming and tasteful small hotel just outside the walls, beyond the Porte St-Malo, away from the bustle of the centre. ❸
Théâtre 2 rue Ste-Claire ℡02.96.39.06.91. Nine basic rooms above a friendly bar, right by the Théâtre des Jacobins; the cheapest come only with a sink, but even those with en-suite bathrooms still

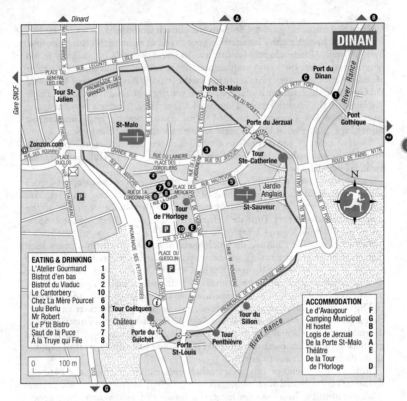

DINAN

▲ Dinard   ▲ Ⓐ   ▲ Ⓑ

5

BRITTANY | Dinan

EATING & DRINKING

L'Atelier Gourmand	1
Bistrot d'en bas	5
Bistrot du Viaduc	2
Le Cantorbery	10
Chez La Mère Pourcel	6
Lulu Berlu	9
Mr Robert	4
Le P'tit Bistro	3
Saut de la Puce	7
À la Truye qui File	8

0   100 m

ACCOMMODATION

Le d'Avaugour	F
Camping Municipal	G
HI hostel	B
Logis de Jerzual	C
De la Porte St-Malo	A
Théâtre	E
De la Tour de l'Horloge	D

cost under €30, which is amazing for such a central location. ❶

De la Tour de l'Horloge 5 rue de la Chaux ☎02.96.39.96.92, ⓦwww.hotel-dinan.com. So long as you don't mind climbing forty-plus stairs to reach them, the rooms in this nice and very central little hotel are spacious, clean and good value; the bells on the namesake clock tower start ringing at 7am. ❹

Hostel and campsite

Camping Municipal 103 rue Châteaubriand ☎02.96.39.11.96. In a quiet spot just outside the western ramparts, with just fifty pitches. Closed late Sept to late May.

HI hostel Moulin de Méen, Vallée de la Fontaine-des-Eaux ☎02.96.39.10.83, ⓦfuaj .org/dinan. Attractive, rural former watermill, beside the river in green fields below the town centre. No bus access: to walk there, follow the quay downstream from the port on the town side. Dorm bed €13.20, double room same price per person, breakfast €3; in addition, camping is permitted in the grounds. Closed Oct–Feb.

The Town

Like St-Malo, Dinan is ideally seen when arriving by boat up the Rance. By the time the ferries get to the lovely **port du Dinan**, down below the thirteenth-century ramparts, the river has narrowed sufficiently to be spanned by a small but majestic old stone bridge. High above it towers a former railway viaduct. The steep, cobbled **lane that** twists up from the quayside makes a wonderful climb, passing ancient flower-festooned edifices of wood and stone, as well as several crêperies and even a half-timbered poodle parlour, before it enters the city through the **Porte du Jerzual**.

333

Above that imposing gateway, **St-Sauveur church** sends the skyline even higher. It's a real hotchpotch, with a Romanesque porch and an eighteenth-century steeple. Even its nine Gothic chapels feature five different patterns of vaulting in no symmetrical order; the most complex pair, in the centre, would make any spider proud. By contrast, a very plain cenotaph on the left contains the heart of **Bertrand Du Guesclin**, the fourteenth-century Breton warrior who fought and won a single combat with the English knight Thomas of Canterbury, in what's now the large, central **place Du Guesclin**, in 1364. That square hosts a large **market on Thursdays**, and serves as Dinan's main car park for the rest of the week.

The true heart of town consists of two much smaller squares, the **place des Merciers** and the **place des Cordeliers**, which hold a wonderful assortment of medieval wood-framed houses.

Unfortunately, you can only walk along one small stretch of the **ramparts**, from behind St-Sauveur church to just short of Tour Sillon overlooking the river. You can, however, get a good general overview from the wooden balcony of the central, fifteenth-century **Tour de l'Horloge** (daily: April, May & Sept 2–6pm; June–Aug 10am–6.30pm; €2.95).

Now known as the **Château de Duchesse Anne**, the fourteenth-century keep that once protected the town's southern approach offers access to two separate towers (daily: June–Sept 10am–6.30pm; Oct–Dec & Feb–May 1.30–5.30pm; €4.50). The keep itself, or *donjon*, consists of four storeys, each of which holds an unexpected hotchpotch of items, including two big old looms and assorted Greek and Etruscan perfume jars; at ground level, well below the walls, there's a slender, closed drawbridge. Nearby, the ancient **Tour Coëtquen** is all but empty, though if you descend the spiral staircase to its waterlogged bottom floor, you'll find a group of stone fifteenth-century notables resembling some medieval time capsule, about to depetrify at any moment.

On the last weekend of July, every other (even-numbered) year, the **Fête des Remparts** is celebrated with medieval-style jousting, banquets, fairs and processions, culminating in an immense fireworks display (Ⓦ fete-remparts-dinan.com).

Eating and drinking

All sorts of specialist **restaurants**, including several ethnic alternatives, are tucked away in the old streets of Dinan. Take an evening stroll through the town and down to the port, and you'll pass at least twenty places. For **bars**, explore the series of tiny parallel alleyways between place des Merciers and rue du Marchix. Along rue de la Cordonnerie, the busiest of the lot, the various hangouts define themselves by their taste in music: *À la Truye qui File* at no. 14 is a contemporary folky Breton dive, while *Lulu Berlu*, next door at no. 12 (closed Sun & Mon), and *Saut de la Puce* opposite, are considerably more raucous.

L'Atelier Gourmand 4 rue de Quai
Ⓣ 02.96.85.14.18. This delightful riverside spot, beside the bridge with indoor and outdoor seating, serves a well-priced *menu* of *tartines* (€9), *moules* (€10–12), and assorted main courses (€12–15). Closed Sun eve & all Mon in low season.

Bistrot d'en bas 20 rue Haute Voie
Ⓣ 02.96.85.44.00. This lively little pub and wine bar hosts popular jazz and folk performances, and serves salads and *tartines* too. Closed Sun evening & Mon.

Bistrot du Viaduc 22 rue du Lion d'Or
Ⓣ 02.96.85.95.00, Ⓦ www.bistrot-du-viaduc.fr.

Traditional French cuisine and good wine served just across the viaduct from town, with superb views over the port and valley. Lunch *menu* €19.50, dinner from €32. Closed Sat lunch, Sun eve & Mon.
Le Cantorbery 6 rue Ste-Claire Ⓣ 02.96.39.02.52.
High-class food served in an old stone house with rafters, a spiral staircase and a real wood fire. Lunch from €13, while traditional dinner *menus* start with a good €25 option that includes fish soup and veal kidneys. Closed Sun eve & Wed in low season.
Chez La Mère Pourcel 3 place des Merciers
Ⓣ 02.96.39.03.80, Ⓦ chezlamerepourcel.com.
Beautiful half-timbered fifteenth-century house in the

central square. Good à la carte options are served all day, while the dinner *menus*, ranging at €23–35, are gourmet class. Closed Sun eve & Mon in low season.
Mr Robert 11 place des Cordeliers ☎02.96.85.20.37, ⓦwww.mrrobertrestaurant.fr. Named for its Irish chef-owner, this excellent central option offers a handful of tables on the square itself but plenty of room indoors. Classic

French cuisine with subtle Asian-influenced flavourings, on dinner *menus* from €21.50. Closed Sun eve & Mon.
Le P'tit Bistro 4 rue de l'École ☎02.96.39.76.77. Friendly, central bistro/pub, serving inexpensive *tartines* (€8) and fruit tarts at wooden tables on its pavement deck, and hosting local music evenings on Fridays.

The north coast from Dinard to Lannion

The coast that stretches from the resort of **Dinard** to Finistère at the far western end of Brittany is divided into two distinct regions, either side of the bay of **St-Brieuc**. Between Dinard and St-Brieuc are the exposed green headlands of the **Côte d'Émeraude**, while beyond St-Brieuc, along the **Côte de Goëlo**, the shore becomes more extravagantly indented, with a succession of secluded little bays and an increasing proliferation of huge pink-granite boulders, seen at their best on the **Côte de Granit Rose** near Tréguier.

Dinard

Originally a fishing village, now a smart little resort blessed with several lovely beaches, **DINARD** sprawls around the western approaches to the Rance estuary, just across the water from St-Malo but a good twenty minutes' drive away. With its casino, spacious shaded villas and social calendar of regattas and ballet, it might not feel out of place on the Côte d'Azur.

Although Dinard is a hilly town, undulating over a succession of pretty little coastal inlets, it attracts great numbers of older visitors; as a result, prices tend to be high, and pleasures sedate.

Central Dinard faces north to the open sea, across the curving bay that holds the attractive **plage de l'Écluse**. Hemmed in by venerable Victorian villas rather than hotels or shops, the beach itself has a low-key atmosphere, despite the casino and summer crowds. An unexpected statue of **Alfred Hitchcock** dominates its main access point. Standing on a giant egg, with a ferocious-looking bird perched on each shoulder, he was placed here to commemorate the town's annual festival of English-language films. Enjoyable **coastal footpaths** lead off in either direction from the principal beach, enlivened by notice boards holding reproductions of paintings produced at points along the way. Surprisingly Pablo Picasso's *Deux Femmes courants sur la Plage* and *Baigneuses sur la Plage*, both of which look quintessentially Mediterranean with their blue skies and golden sands, were in fact painted here in Dinard during his annual summer visits throughout the 1920s.

Practicalities

Dinard's small **airport**, 4km southeast of the town centre, off the D168 near **Pleurtuit**, is served by Ryanair flights from London Stansted. The connecting Illenoo bus #990 (€4) runs via Dinard's tourist office to St-Malo. Many visitors simply come for the day on the Companie Corsaire **boats** from St-Malo (see p.332). The **tourist office** is in the heart of town at 2 bd Féart (July & Aug Mon–Sat 9.30am–1pm & 2–7pm, Sun 10am–12.15pm & 2–6.30pm; Sept–June Mon–Sat 9.30am–12.30pm & 2–6.30pm, Sun 10am–12.15pm & 2.15–6pm; ☎02.99.46.94.12, ⓦot-dinard.com).

On the whole, Dinard is an expensive place to stay, but it does at least have a wide selection of **hotels** (many are listed on ⓦdinard-hotel-plus.com). Good mid-range options include the *Printania*, 5 av Georges-V (℡02.99.46.13.07, Ⓦwww.printaniahotel.com; ❹; closed mid-Nov to mid-March), on a quiet street as it drops down to the port, where a great terrace restaurant looks out towards St-Malo. ☆ *Didier Méril*, 1 place du Général-de-Gaulle (℡02.99.46.95.74, Ⓦrestaurant-didier-meril.com; ❺), is another wonderful restaurant that also offers luxurious designer bedrooms. The best local **campsite** is the municipal *Port Blanc*, with shady pitches right by the plage du Port-Blanc for under €20, on rue du Sergent-Boulanger (℡02.99.46.10.74, Ⓦcamping-port-blanc.com; closed Oct–March).

The Côte d'Émeraude

The splendidly attractive **Côte d'Émeraude**, west of Dinard, is one of Brittany's most traditional family resort areas, with old-fashioned holiday towns, and safe sandy beaches. It also offers wonderful camping, at its best around the heather-backed beaches near **Cap Fréhel**, a high, warm expanse of heath and cliffs where views can extend as far as Jersey and the Île de Bréhat.

Fort la Latte

The fourteenth-century **Fort la Latte**, at the tip of a lesser headland 2km southeast of Cap Fréhel, is a gorgeous little gem. Visitors enter across two drawbridges; outbuildings scattered within include a cannonball factory, and there's also a medieval herb garden, but the highlight is the keep, which contains historical exhibits. Precarious walkways climb to its very summit, for superb coastal views (early July to late Aug daily 10.30am–7pm; April to early July, and late Aug to Sept daily 10.30am–12.30pm & 2–6.30pm; Oct–March Sat, Sun & hols 1.30–5.30pm; €5; Ⓦcastlelalatte.com).

Erquy

In the delightful little family resort of **ERQUY**, 20km west of Cap Fréhel, a perfect crescent beach nestles into a vast natural bay. At low tide, the sea disappears way beyond the harbour entrance, leaving gentle ripples of sand. You can walk right across its mouth, from the grassy wooded headland on the left side to the picturesque little lighthouse on the right.

Erquy's **tourist office** is at 3 rue du 19 Mars (April–June Mon–Sat 9.30am–12.30pm & 2–6pm, Sun 10am–12.30pm; July & Aug Mon–Sat 9.30am–1pm & 2–7pm, Sun 10am–1pm & 4–6pm; first fortnight of Sept Mon–Sat 9.30am–12.30pm & 2–6pm; mid-Sept to March Mon–Sat 9.30am–12.30pm & 2–5pm; ℡02.96.72.30.12, Ⓦerquy-tourisme.com).

The ☆ *Hôtel Beauséjour*, poised above the southern end of the beach at 21 rue de la Corniche (℡02.96.72.30.39, Ⓦbeausejour-erquy.com; ❸; closed Sun eve, plus Mon & Thurs eve in low season), is Erquy at its most quirky, adorned with dungaree-wearing teddies, but the rooms are nice, and its panoramic **restaurant** is excellent. There's also tasteful **B&B** accommodation in a grand nineteenth-century villa nearby, ☆ *La Villa Nazado*, 2 rue des Patriotes (℡02.96.63.67.14, Ⓦvillanazado.com; ❸). **Campsites**, on the promontory north of town, include the three-star, seafront *St-Pabu* (℡02.96.72.24.65, Ⓦwww.saintpabu.com; closed mid-Nov to March).

The Côte de Goëlo

Moving northwest towards Paimpol along the **Côte de Goëlo**, the shoreline becomes wilder and harsher and the seaside towns tend to be crammed into narrow rocky inlets or set well back in river estuaries.

Paimpol and around

At the top of the Côte de Goëlo, **PAIMPOL** is an attractive town with a tangle of cobbled alleyways and fine grey-granite houses, though stripped of some character from its transition from working fishing port to pleasure harbour. It was once the centre of a cod and whaling fleet, which sailed to Iceland each February. From then until September the town would be empty of its young men. Thanks to naval shipyards and the like, the open sea is not visible from Paimpol; a maze of waterways leads to its two separate **harbours**. Both are usually filled with the high masts of yachts, but are still also used by the fishing vessels that keep a fish market and a plethora of *poissonneries* busy.

A couple of kilometres short of town, in a superbly romantic setting, the D786 passes the substantial ruins of the **Abbaye de Beauport** (daily: mid-June to mid-Sept 10am–7pm, with regular 1hr 30min guided tours; mid-Sept to mid-June 10am–noon & 2–5pm; €5.50; W abbaye-beauport.com), established in 1202 by Count Alain de Goëlo. Its stone walls are covered with wild flowers and ivy, the central cloisters are engulfed by a huge tree, and birds fly everywhere. The Norman Gothic chapterhouse is the most noteworthy building to survive, and its roofless halls hold relics from all periods of its history. In summer, the abbey reopens for late-night visits, with imaginative lighting effects (July & Aug, Wed & Sun 10pm–1am; €6), and also hosts weekly Breton music concerts (mid-July to mid-Aug Thurs 9pm; €13).

Paimpol's **tourist office** is 100m from the pleasure port on place de la République (July & Aug Mon–Sat 9.30am–7.30pm, Sun 10am–12.30pm & 4.30–6.30pm; Sept–June Mon–Fri 9.30am–12.30pm & 2–6.pm, Sat 9.30am–12.30pm & 2–6.30pm; T 02.96.20.83.16, W paimpol-goelo.com). The **gare SNCF** and **gare routière** are nearby, side by side on avenue du Général-de-Gaulle.

Hotels include the grand old ♣ *K'Loys*, overlooking the small-boat harbour from 21 quai Morand (T 02.96.20.50.13, W k-loys.com; ❸–❻), whose comfortable rooms vary in price according to size and view; the kitsch but very hospitable *Berthelot*, 1 rue du Port (T 02.96.20.88.66; ❶) offers a dozen simple rooms at exceptionally low prices. As for **restaurants**, *La Cotriade*, on the far side of the harbour on the quai Armand-Dayot (T 02.96.20.81.08, W la-cotriade.com; closed all day Mon, Fri evening & Sat lunch), is the best bet for authentic fish dishes, with *menus* from €25.

The Île de Bréhat

Two kilometres offshore at Pointe de l'Arcouest, 6km northwest of Paimpol, the **ÎLE DE BRÉHAT** – really, two islands joined by a tiny bridge – appears to span great latitudes. On its north side are windswept meadows of hemlock and yarrow, sloping down to chaotic erosions of rock; on the south, you're in the midst of palm trees, mimosa and eucalyptus. All around is a multitude of little islets – some accessible at low tide, others *propriété privée*, most just pink-orange rocks. All in all, it's among the most beautiful places in Brittany, renowned as a sanctuary not only for rare species of wild flowers – especially blue acanthus – but also for birds of all kinds.

Boats to Bréhat (see p.338) arrive at the small harbour of **PORT-CLOS**, though depending on the tide passengers may have to walk several hundred metres before setting foot on terra firma. **Cars** are banned, so many visitors rent **bikes** at the port, for €15 per day. However, it's easy enough to explore on foot; walking from one end to the other takes less than an hour.

Each batch of new arrivals heads first to Bréhat's village, **LE BOURG**, 500m up from the port. As well as a handful of hotels, restaurants and bars, it also holds a limited array of shops, and hosts a small **market** most days. In high season, the attractive central square tends to be packed fit to burst, with exasperated holiday-home owners pushing their little shopping carts through the throngs of day-trippers.

Continue a short distance north of Le Bourg, however, and you'll soon cross over the slender **Pont ar Prat** bridge to the northern island, where the crowds thin out, and countless little coves offer opportunities to sprawl on the tough grass or clamber across the rugged boulders. At the northernmost tip, the Paon lighthouse stands erect over the rock-scattered waters – girls of the island used to throw rocks into the wash, believing that if it landed in the water without hitting a rock they would marry their love, but if it hit a rock, it would be a cold bed for another year. Though the coastal footpath around this northern half offers the most attractive walking on the island, the best **beaches** line the southern shores, with the **Grève du Guerzido** at its southeastern corner being the pick of the crop.

Practicalities

Bréhat is connected regularly by **ferry** from the Pointe de l'Arcouest, 6km northwest of Paimpol, and served by summer buses from its *gare SNCF*. Broadly speaking, sailings, with Les Vedettes de Bréhat (T 02.96.55.79.50, W vedettesde brehat.com), are half-hourly in July and August, hourly between April and June and in September, and every 1 hour 30 minutres otherwise, with the first boat out to Bréhat at 8.15am in summer, and the last boat back at 7.45pm. The return trip costs €9 (bikes, €15 extra, are only allowed outside peak crossing times). The same company also offers crossings in summer from Erquy and St-Quay-Portrieux, and boat tours of the island (€13).

Bréhat's **tourist office** is in Le Bourg's main square (July & Aug Mon–Sat 10am–1pm & 2–5pm, Sun 10am–1pm; March–June & Sept Mon, Tues & Thurs–Sat 10am–12.30pm & 1.30–4.30pm; Oct–Feb Mon & Thurs–Sat 10am–12.30pm & 1.30–4.30pm; T 02.96.20.04.15, W brehat-infos.fr). All the island's **hotels** tend to be booked throughout the summer, and to insist on *demi-pension*. The *Bellevue* is right by the *embarcadère* in Port-Clos (T 02.96.20.00.05, W hotel-bellevue-brehat .fr; ⑥; closed mid-Nov to mid-Feb), while Le Bourg holds the *Vieille Auberge* (T 02.96.20.00.24, W www.brehat-vieilleauberge.eu; ⑦; closed Nov–Easter), and the smaller *Aux Pêcheurs* (T 02.96.20.00.14; ④; closed Jan). There's also a wonderful municipal **campsite** in the woods high above the sea west of the port (T 02.96.20.02.36; closed mid-Sept to mid-June); when it's closed, you can pitch your tent almost anywhere.

The Côte de Granit Rose

The entire northernmost stretch of the Breton coast, from Bréhat to Ploumanac'h, has loosely come to be known as the **Côte de Granit Rose**. There are indeed great

La petite maison de Plougrescant

Perhaps the best-known photographic image of Brittany is of a small seafront cottage somehow squeezed between two mighty pink-granite boulders. Surprisingly few visitors, however, see the house in real life. It stands 10km north of Tréguier, and just 2km out from the village of **Plougrescant**. The precise spot tends to be marked on regional maps as either **Le Gouffre** or Le Gouffre du Castel-Meuru. Although you can't visit the cottage itself – which actually faces inland, across a small sheltered bay, with its back to the open sea, the shoreline nearby offers superb short walks – and a summer-only café sells snacks. The owners of the cottage recently won a large financial settlement against advertisers who used its image without permission, so you may not see it quite so often in future.

granite boulders scattered in the sea around the island of Bréhat, and at the various headlands to the west, but the most memorable stretch of coast lies north of **Tréguier**, where the pink-granite rocks are eroded into fantastic shapes.

Tréguier

The D786 turns west from Paimpol, passing over a green *ria* on the bridge outside Lézardrieux before arriving at **TRÉGUIER**, one of Brittany's very few hill-towns. Its central feature is the **Cathédrale de St-Tugdual**, which contains the tomb of St Yves, a native of the town who died in 1303 and – for his incorruptibility – became the patron saint of lawyers. Attempts to bribe him continue to this day; his tomb is surrounded by marble plaques and an inferno of candles invoking his aid.

Out of town to the south, near Trédarzec, the **Jardins de Kerdalo** (July & Aug Mon–Sat 2–6pm; April–June & Sept Mon & Sat 2–6pm; €8), originally planted by Russian Peter Wolkonsky, rank among the finest in France. Rare and exotic breeds ramble through the grounds, making a joyful change from the exacting straight-line gardening of so many châteaux.

Tréguier's **tourist office** is at 67 rue Ernest-Renan, down by the commercial port (mid-June to mid-Sept Mon–Sat 9am–7pm, Sun 10am–1pm & 2–6pm; mid-Sept to mid-June Tues–Sat 10am–1pm & 2–6pm; ℗02.96.92.22.33, ⓦpaysdetreguier .com). Of **hotels** down here, the fancy *Aigue-Marine* has a swimming pool and jacuzzi (℗02.96.92.97.00, ⓦwww.aiguemarine.fr; ⑤), while the much more basic *d'Estuaire* (℗06.15.08.77.03; ①), has great views from its reasonably-priced upstairs dining room. The upper town holds a fine array of places to **eat**. The *Poissonnerie Moulinet*, above a fish shop just below the cathedral at 2 rue Ernest-Renan (℗02.96.92.30.27), is a sort of tasting room where you can buy superb seafood platters at low prices, perhaps to take away and eat in the square.

Château de la Roche-Jagu

About 10km inland from Tréguier, the fifteenth-century **Château de la Roche-Jagu** (daily: Feb–Easter & Nov 2–5pm; Easter–June & mid-Sept to Oct 10am–noon & 2–6pm; July to mid-Sept 10am–1pm & 2–7pm; park access free, château €4, or more during special exhibitions; ⓦcotesdarmor.fr/larochejagu) stands on a heavily wooded slope above the meanders of the Trieux river. A really gorgeous building, it hosts lavish **annual exhibitions**, usually on some sort of Celtic theme. Outside, the modern landscaped park is traced through by several **hiking trails**.

Ploumanac'h

A great walk along the **Sentier des Douaniers** pathway winds round the clifftops from plage Trestraou at the missable town of Perros-Guirec to the tiny resort of **PLOUMANAC'H**, past an astonishing succession of deformed and water-sculpted rocks. Birds wheel overhead towards the offshore bird sanctuary of **Sept-Îles**, and battered boats shelter in the narrow inlets or bob uncontrollably out on the waves. There are patches and brief causeways of grass, clumps of purple heather and yellow gorse. The small golden yellow beach here is a surreal treat, in an alcove of soft shaped and smooth pink granite formations protected by numerous other outcrops in the bay, one of which barely separates a glorious private house from the waves.

Ploumanac'h offers several **hotels**, including the *Hôtel du Parc*, just back from the sea at 175 place St-Guirec (℗02.96.91.40.80, ⓦwww-hotelduparc.com; ③), which serves good seafood *menus* as well as lavish buffet breakfasts, and the much more lavish beachfront *Castel Beau Site* (℗02.96.91.40.87, ⓦcastelbeausite.com; ⑧), which has its own delicious, expensive restaurant. The nicest place to **camp** is the four-star *Ranolien* (℡02.96.91.65.65, ⓦwww.leranolien.fr; closed late Sept to March; €15–40 depending on the season), in a superb position near a little beach halfway along the Sentier des Douaniers, but directly accessible on the other side by road, and boasting a great array of swimming pools, waterslides, a spa and a cinema.

The Bay of Lannion

Despite being set significantly back from the sea on the estuary of the River Léguer, **Lannion** gives its name to the next bay west along the Breton coast – and it's the bay rather than the town that is most likely to impress visitors. One enormous beach stretches from **St-Michel-en-Grève**, which is little more than a bend in the road, as far as **Locquirec**; at low tide you can walk hundreds of metres out on the sands.

Lannion

Set amid plummeting hills and stairways, **LANNION** is a historic city with streets of medieval housing and a couple of interesting old churches, which as a centre for high-tech telecommunications is one of modern Brittany's real success stories. Hence its rather self-satisfied nickname, *ville heureuse* or "happy town". In addition to admiring the half-timbered houses around the **place du Général-Leclerc** and along **rue des Chapeliers**, it's well worth climbing from the town up the 142 granite steps that lead to the twelfth-century Templar **Église de Brélévenez**. The views from its terrace are stupendous.

Lannion's **tourist office** is at 2 quai d'Aiguillon (July & Aug Mon–Sat 9am–7pm, Sun 10am–1pm; Sept–June Mon–Sat 9.30am–12.30pm & 2–6pm; ℡02.96.46.41.00, ⓦwww.ot-lannion.fr). The only central **hotel** – the *Ibis*, opposite the station at 30 av du Général-de-Gaulle (℡02.96.37.03.67, ⓦwww .ibishotel.com; ❹) – has modern rooms, but no restaurant, but there's also a **hostel** nearby, *Les Korrigans* at 6 rue du 73ᵉ Territorial (℡02.96.37.91.28, ⓦfuaj.org/lannion-les-korrigans; dorm beds €18 including breakfast), which has a restaurant and bar.

The Cairn du Barnenez

In a glorious position at the mouth of the Morlaix estuary, 13km north of Morlaix itself, the prehistoric stone **Cairn du Barnenez** surveys the waters from the summit of a hill (May–Aug daily 10am–6.30pm; Sept–April Tues–Sun 10am–12.30pm & 2–5.30pm; €5; ⓦbarnenez.monuments-nationaux.fr). As on the island of Gavrinis in the Morbihan, its ancient masonry has been laid bare by excavations, and provides a stunning sense of the architectural prowess of the megalith builders. Dated by radiocarbon testing to 4500 BC, this is one of the oldest large monuments in the world.

The two distinct stepped pyramids rise in successive tiers, built of large flat stones chinked with pebbles; the second was added onto the side of the first, and the two are encircled by a series of terraces and ramps. The whole thing measures roughly 70m long by 15–25m wide and 6m high. Both pyramids were long buried under the same eighty-metre-long earthen mound. While the actual cairns are completely exposed to view, most of the passages and chambers that lie within them are sealed off. The two minor corridors that are open simply cut through the edifice from one side to the other but visitors are not permitted to pass through. Local tradition has it that one tunnel runs right through this "home of the fairies", and continues out deep under the sea.

Finistère

It's hard to resist the appeal of the **Finistère coast**, with its ocean-fronting cliffs and headlands. Summer crowds may detract from the best parts of the **Crozon peninsula** and the **Pointe de Raz**, but elsewhere you can enjoy near-solitude. Explore the semi-wilderness of the **northern stretches** beyond Brest and the little fishing village of **Le Conquet**, or take a ferry trip to the misty islands of **Ouessant** and **Sein**. From the top of **Ménez-Hom** visitors can admire the anarchic limits of western France, while the cities of **Morlaix** and **Quimper** display modern Breton life as well as ancient splendours, and the **parish closes** south of Morlaix reveal much about the beliefs of the past.

Léon

Memories of the days when Brittany was "Petite Bretagne", as opposed to "Grande Bretagne" across the water, linger in the names of Finistère's two main areas, **Léon** (once Lyonesse), the northern peninsula, and its southern neighbour Cornouaille (Cornwall). Both feature prominently in Arthurian legend. In the north of Léon, the ragged **coastline** is the prime attraction, indented with a succession of estuaries or **abers**, each of which shelters its own tiny harbour. Heading west from either the thriving historic town of **Morlaix** or the appealing little Channel port of **Roscoff**, there are possible stopping places all the way to **Le Conquet**. From Le Conquet, you can reach the island of **Ouessant** across a treacherous stretch of ocean. Inland, by contrast, the ornate medieval village churches known as **parish closes** hold some of Brittany's finest religious architecture.

Morlaix

MORLAIX, one of the great old Breton ports, thrived on trade with England during the "Golden Period" of the late Middle Ages. Built up the slopes of a steep valley with sober stone houses, the town was originally protected by an eleventh-century castle and a circuit of walls. Little is left of either, but the old centre remains in part medieval with its cobbled streets and half-timbered houses. The present grandeur comes from the pink-granite **viaduct** carrying trains from Paris to Brest towering above the town centre.

The **Jacobin convent** that fronts place des Jacobins, which once housed the five-year-old Mary Queen of Scots on her way to the French court, now houses the **Musée de Morlaix**, which hosts two temporary exhibitions per year (March & June Mon & Wed–Sat 10am–noon & 2–5pm; April, May & Sept Mon & Wed–Sat 10am–noon & 2–6pm, Sun 2–6pm; July & Aug daily 10am–12.30pm & 2–6.30pm; Oct Mon & Wed–Sat 10am–noon & 2–5pm, Sun 2–6pm; €4; Ⓦ www.musee.ville .morlaix.fr). The same ticket entitles you to a guided tour of the fabulously restored, sixteenth-century **Maison à Pondalez**, at 9 Grand'Rue (same hours), a fabulously restored house that takes its name from the Breton word for the sculpted wooden internal gallery that dominates the ground floor.

Practicalities

Morlaix's **tourist office** is all but beneath the viaduct, in place des Otages (July & Aug Mon–Sat 9am–12.30pm & 1.30–7pm, Sun 10.30am–12.30pm; Sept–June

Mon–Sat 9am–12.30pm & 2–6pm; ℡02.98.62.14.94, ⒲tourisme.morlaix.fr). All **buses** conveniently depart from place Cornic, right under the viaduct, but the **gare SNCF** is on rue Armand-Rousseau, high above the town at the western end of the viaduct.

On the whole, Morlaix's **hotels** are uninspiring, though the eccentric old *De l'Europe*, above a simple but good brasserie at 1 rue d'Aiguillon (℡02.98.62.11.99, ⒲hotel-europe-com.fr; ❺), holds plain but modern rooms. Cheaper alternatives include the *Hôtel de la Gare*, close to the *gare SNCF* at 25 place St-Martin (℡02.98.88.03.29, ⒲hotelgare29.com; ❷).

The best hunting ground for **restaurants** is between St-Mélaine church and place des Jacobins, where choices include *La Marée Bleue*, 3 rampe St-Mélaine (℡02.98.63.24.21; closed Oct, plus Sun evening & Mon), a well-respected seafood place.

The enclos paroissiaux

Morlaix makes an excellent base for visiting the countryside towards Brest, where **enclos paroissiaux** (walled churchyards incorporating cemetery, calvary and ossuary), celebrate the distinctive character of Breton Catholicism – closer to the Celtic past than to Rome – in elaborately sculpted scenes. Stone calvaries are covered in detailed depictions of the Crucifixion above a crowd of saints, Gospel stories and legends; in richer parishes, a high stone arch leads into the churchyard, adjoining an equally majestic ossuary, where bones would be taken when the tiny cemeteries filled up. Most of the parish closes date from Brittany's wealthiest period, the two centuries either side of the union with France in 1532.

The most famous *enclos* lie in three neighbouring parishes, on a clearly signposted route off the N12 between Morlaix and Landivisiau. At **ST-THÉGONNEC**, the church **pulpit**, carved by two brothers in 1683, is the acknowledged masterpiece, albeit so swamped with detail – symbolic saints, sibyls and arcane figures – that it is almost too intricate to take in. At the pretty flower-filled village of **GUIMILIAU**, 6km southwest, the **calvary** is an incredible ensemble of over two hundred granite figures, depicting scenes from the life of Christ and rendered all the more dramatic by being covered with what has been called "secular lichen". A uniquely Breton illustration, just above the Last Supper, depicts the unfortunate Katell Gollet – Katherine the Damned, a figure from local myth who stole consecrated wafers to give to her lover, who naturally turned out to be the Devil – being torn to shreds by demons. At **LAMPAUL-GUIMILIAU**, the painted wooden baptistry, the dragons on the beams and the suitably wicked faces of the robbers on the calvary are the key components.

In St-Thégonnec the ⚐ *Auberge de St-Thégonnec*, 6 place de la Mairie (℡02.98.79.61.18, ⒲aubergesaintthegonnec.com; ❺; closed Sun Sept–March, plus mid-Dec to mid-Jan), is a surprisingly smart **hotel** for such a small village, and has a superb **restaurant**.

Roscoff

The opening of the deep-water port at **ROSCOFF** in 1973 was part of a general attempt to revitalize the Breton economy. Its cross-Channel **ferry services** aim not just to bring tourists, but also to revive the traditional trading links between the Celtic nations of Brittany, Ireland and southwest England. In fact, Roscoff had already long been a significant port. Mary Queen of Scots landed here in 1548 on her way to Paris to be engaged to François, the son of Henri II of France, as did Bonnie Prince Charlie, the Young Pretender, in 1746, after his defeat at Culloden.

Arrival and information

Boats from Plymouth, Cork and Rosslare dock not in Roscoff's original natural harbour, but at the Port de Bloscon, a couple of kilometres east (and just out of sight) of the town. In summer, direct **buses** to Morlaix and Quimper leave from the ferry terminal (daily 8.05am; Penn-ar-Bed; T08.10.81.00.29, Wviaoo29.fr). From the **gare SNCF**, a few hundred metres south of the town centre, a restricted rail service (often replaced by buses) runs to Morlaix, with connections beyond. Most **local buses** also go from here, including a direct service to Brest (T02.98.83.45.80, Wbihan.fr).

The helpful **tourist office** is on the quayside in town, at 46 rue Gambetta (July & Aug Mon–Sat 9am–12.30pm & 1.30–7pm, Sun 10am–12.30pm & 2–7pm; Sept–June Mon–Sat 9.15am–noon & 2–6pm; T02.98.61.12.13, Wwww.roscoff -tourisme.com).

Accommodation

For a small town, Roscoff is well equipped with **hotels**, which are accustomed to late-night arrivals from the ferries. However, most are relatively expensive and close for some or all of the winter. There's also a **hostel** on the Île de Batz (see p.344), and a two-star **campsite**, the beachfront *Aux Quatre Saisons*, 2km west in Perharidy, just off the route de Santec (T02.98.69.70.86, Wcamping-aux4saisons .com; €12; closed early Oct to March).

Des Arcades 15 rue de l'Amiral-Réveillère T02.98.69.70.45, Wwww.hotel-les-arcades-roscoff .com. Sixteenth-century building with superb views from some of its modernized rooms and from the restaurant, which has economical *menus* at €11, with a good €26.90 option. En-suite facilities cost around €12 extra. Closed mid-Nov to mid-Feb. ❷

Du Centre 5 rue Gambetta T02.98.61.24.25, Wchezjanie.com. Family hotel above the café-bar *Chez Janie*, entered via the main street but looking out on the port. Modern, tastefully furnished rooms; sea views cost €25 extra. Closed mid-Nov to mid-Feb. ❹

Les Chardons Bleus 4 rue de l'Amiral-Réveillère T02.98.69.72.03, Wwww .roscoffhotel.com. Very friendly hotel in the heart of the old town, with a good restaurant (closed Thurs & Sun eve Sept–June) where dinner *menus* start at €20. Closed three weeks in Feb. ❸

Le Temps de Vivre 19 place Lacaze-Duthiers T02.98.19.33.19, Wwww .letempsdevivre.net. Ultra-stylish contemporary hotel, in an old mansion near the Notre-Dame church; luxuriously spacious rooms with designer bathrooms, and wonderful sea views. Off-season rates are at least €60 lower. ❽

The Town

Roscoff itself is still just a small resort where almost all activity is confined to **rue Gambetta** and to the old port. The sixteenth-century church, **Notre-Dame-de-Croas-Batz**, at the far end of rue Gambetta, is embellished with an ornate Renaissance belfry, complete with sculpted ships and a protruding stone cannon. Some way beyond is Roscoff's best **beach**, at Laber, surrounded by expensive hotels and apartments.

The old **harbour** is livelier, mixing an economy based on fishing with relatively low-key pleasure trips to the Île de Batz. The **Criée de Roscoff** (fish auction) on port de Bloscon (April–June & Sept–Oct Wed 3pm; July & Aug Mon–Thurs 11am, 3pm, 5pm; €4) opens up the fisherman's life from catch to sale, with exhibitions, films, games and knot-tying to hoover up the kids' attention.

In 1828, Henri Ollivier took **onions** to England from Roscoff, thereby founding a trade that flourished until the 1930s. The story of the "Johnnies" – that classic French image of men in black berets with strings of onions hanging over the handlebars of their bicycles – is told at **La Maison des Johnnies et de l'Oignon Rosé de Roscoff**, 48 rue Brizeux, near the *gare SNCF* (mid-June to mid-Sept Mon–Fri 11am, 3pm & 5pm; mid-Feb to mid-June & mid-Sept to Dec Mon, Tues, Thurs, Fri & Sun 3pm; €4).

Eating

The obvious places to **eat** in Roscoff are the dining rooms of the hotels themselves – *Le Temps de Vivre* is especially recommended – but the town does hold a few specialist **restaurants** as well, plus appealing crêperies around the old harbour. If you're arriving on an evening ferry out of season, it can be difficult to find a restaurant still serving any later than 9.15pm.

Crêperie de la Poste 12 rue Gambetta ☎02.98.69.72.81, ⓦcreperiedelaposte.fr. Cosy old stone house, just back from the port in the heart of town, offering inexpensive à la carte meals of sweet and savoury pancakes; more exotic seafood crêpes cost up to €9. They also serve fish soup, mussels and other simple meals. Daily 11.30am until late; closed mid-Nov to mid-Jan, plus Wed Sept–June, Tues July & Aug.

L'Écume des Jours Quai d'Auxerre ☎02.98.61.22.83, ⓦwww.ecume-roscoff.fr. Romantic restaurant in a grand old house facing the port, offering good-value set lunches for €15 on weekdays, plus dinner *menus* from €29, featuring such delights as braised oysters or scallops with local pink onions. Closed mid-Dec to Jan & Tues, plus Wed lunch in summer, all Wed in low season.

The Île de Batz

The long, narrow, and very lovely **ÎLE DE BATZ** (pronounced "Ba") mirrors Roscoff across the water, separated from it by a sea channel that's barely 200m wide at low tide but perhaps five times that when the tide is high. Appearances from the mainland are deceptive: the island's old town fills much of its southern shoreline, but those areas not visible from Roscoff are much wilder and more windswept. With no cars permitted, and some great expanses of sandy beach, it makes a wonderfully quiet retreat for families in particular.

Ferries from Roscoff arrive at the quayside of the old town. A nice small beach lines the edge of the harbour, but it turns into a morass of seaweed at low tide. All arriving passengers make the obvious 500m walk towards the town. Turning left when you get to the **church** will bring you to the hostel (see below), and the 44-metre **lighthouse** on the island's peak, all of 23m above sea level (second half of June & first half of Sept Thurs–Tues 2–5pm; July & Aug daily 1–5.30pm; €2). Turning right, on the other hand, leads you towards the best beach, the white-sand **Grève Blanche** at its eastern end. Nearby, the **Jardin Exotique Georges-Delaselle** (April–June, Sept & Oct daily except Tues 2–6pm; July & Aug daily 1–6.30pm; €4.60) is a 75-year-old garden that takes advantage of the temperate Batz microclimate to sustain its palm trees and other out-of-context flora.

Practicalities

Three separate **ferry** companies make the ten-minute crossing from Roscoff to Batz (10min; €7.50 return; bikes €7), with frequent services between 8am and 8pm daily. Compagnie Maritime Armein (☎02.98.61.77.75), CFTM (☎02.98.61.78.87, ⓦvedettes-ile-de-batz.com), and Armor Excursions (☎02.98.61.79.66, ⓦvedettes .armor.ile.de.batz.fr) sell tickets at the landward end of Roscoff's long pier; in summer only, tickets are valid on any ferry. At low tide, the boats sail from the far end of the pier, a good five minutes' walk further on.

The island's nicest **hotel**, the *Grand Hôtel Morvan* at the centre of the harbour (☎02.98.61.78.06; ❷; closed Dec to mid-March), serves good meals on its large seafront terraces. There's a **hostel** in a beautiful beachfront setting at the evocatively named Creach ar Bolloc'h (☎02.98.61.77.69, ⓦaj-iledebatz.org; closed Nov–March; €15.50). The best **B&B** is *Ti Va Zadou* (☎02.98.61.76.91; ❸), with comfortable rooms, a good view and big breakfasts. As for **eating** and **drinking**, a quirky little **crêperie-restaurant**, *Les Couleurs du Temps* (☎02.98.61.75.75, closed Oct–Easter), near the ferries, sells sweet and savoury pancakes for €5–7, and prepares the Breton speciality *kig ha farz*, seafood stew topped by a crêpe. ※ *Le Bigorneau Langoureux* (℡02.98.61.74.50) is a very pleasant spot to be languorous over a bottle from the good selection of Basque wines.

The abers

The coast west of Roscoff is among the most dramatic in Brittany, a jagged succession of **abers** – deep, narrow estuaries – that hold a succession of small, isolated resorts. It's a little on the bracing side, especially if you're making use of the numerous **campsites**, but that just has to be counted as part of the appeal. In summer, at least, the temperatures are mild enough, and things get progressively more sheltered as you move around towards Le Conquet and Brest.

Around the abers

The first real resort west of Roscoff, **PLOUESCAT**, is not quite on the sea itself, but there are **campsites** nearby on each of three adjacent beaches, the nicest being *La Baie du Kernic* (℡02.98.69.86.60, ⓦ www.village-center.com/bretagne; closed mid-Sept to early April). Of the **hotels**, the best value is the little *Roc'h-Ar-Mor*, 18 rue Ar Mor (℡02.98.69.63.01, ⓔ roch.ar.mor@orange.fr; ②; closed Nov–Feb); though it's right on the beach at Porsmeur, none of its rooms actually give sea views. Roscoff to Brest **buses** stop at Plouescat before turning inland.

Pretty little **BRIGNOGAN-PLAGES**, on the next *aber*, has a small natural harbour, once the lair of wreckers, with beaches and weather-beaten rocks to either side, as well as its own menhir. The two high-season **campsites** are the central municipal site at Kéravezan, the *Côte des Legendes* (℡02.98.83.41.65, ⓦ www.campingcotedeslegendes.com; closed Nov–Easter), and the *Du Phare*, east of town (℡02.98.83.45.06, ⓦ camping-du-phare.com; closed Oct–March). There are also schools of sailing and riding.

The *aber* between Plouguerneau and **L'ABER-WRAC'H** has a stepping-stone crossing just upstream from the bridge at Lannilis, built in Gallo-Roman times, where long cut stones still cross the three channels of water. L'Aber-Wrac'h itself, perched over the western side of the vast mouth of the Baie des Anges, is a small and attractive resort within reach of several sandy beaches. At the start of the bay, commanding this stunning view, the irresistible ※ *Hôtel la Baie des Anges*, 350 rte des Anges (℡02.98.04.90.04, ⓦ baie-des-anges.com; ⑥; closed Feb), makes a peaceful and exceptionally comfortable place to stay. It has no dining room, but there's a classy bar with a small waterfront terrace, reserved for guests only. The best local **restaurant**, *Le Brennig* (℡02.98.04.81.12, ⓦ restaurant.brennig.free.fr; closed Tues & Nov–Feb), is back at the other end of the coastal road through town.

Le Conquet

LE CONQUET, at the far western tip of Brittany 24km beyond Brest, is a wonderful place, scarcely developed, with a long beach of clean white sand, protected from the winds by the narrow spit of the Kermorvan peninsula. It's very much a working fishing village, with grey-stone houses leading down to the stone jetties of a cramped harbour. It occasionally floods, causing great amusement to locals who watch the waves wash over cars left there by tourists taking the ferry out to Ouessant. A good walk 5km south brings you to the lighthouse at **Pointe St-Mathieu**, with its much-photographed view out to the islands from its site among the ruins of a Benedictine abbey.

Right by the jetty, the *Relais du Vieux Port*, 1 quai Drellac'h (℡02.98.89.15.91, ⓦ www.lerelaisduvieuxport.com; ③; closed Jan), offers a handful of inexpensive but attractive rooms, and has a crêperie that also serves fine seafood. There's also a well-equipped, two-star **campsite** over on the Kermorvan peninsula, *Les Blancs Sablon* (℡02.98.89.06.90, Ⓦlescledelles.com; closed Oct–March).

The Île d'Ouessant

The **Île d'Ouessant** ("Ushant" to the English) lies 30km northwest of Le Conquet, and its lighthouse at **Creac'h** (said to be the strongest in the world) is regarded as the entrance to the English Channel. The island is the last in a chain of smaller islands and half-submerged granite rocks. Most are uninhabited, or like Beniguet the preserve only of rabbits, though the **Île de Molène**, midway, has a village.

You arrive on **Ouessant** at the modern **harbour** in the ominous-sounding Baie du Stiff. There's a scattering of houses here, but the only town is 4km distant at **LAMPAUL**, and that's where everyone heads, either by the bus that meets each arriving ferry (€3.50 return to Lampaul, €12 for a full island tour), by bike, or in a long walking procession that straggles along the one road. **Bicycle** rental (€10–15 per day; operators wait at the port) is the most convenient option, as the island is too big to explore on foot.

There's not a lot to Lampaul. The best beaches are sprawled around its bay, while the cemetery's **war memorial** lists all the ships in which townsfolk were lost, alongside graves of unknown sailors washed ashore and a chapel of wax "*proëlla* crosses" symbolizing the many islanders who never returned.

At **NIOU**, 1km northwest, the **Maisons du Niou** – one's a museum of island history, the other a reconstruction of a traditional island house – jointly form the **Éco-Musée d'Ouessant** (April–Jun & Sept daily 11am–6pm in school hols, 11am–5pm otherwise; July & Aug daily 10.30am–6pm; Oct–March daily except Mon 1.30–5.30pm; €3.50, or €7 with Musée des Phares et Balises).

Another kilometre west, past **Niou**, the **Créac'h lighthouse** boasts a 500-million-candlepower beam capable of being seen from England's Lizard Point. You can't visit the lighthouse tower itself, but the complex at its base holds the **Musée des Phares et Balises** (same hours; €4.50), a large museum about lighthouses and buoys. None of the information is in English, however, and photography is not permitted.

The Créac'h lighthouse makes a good starting point from which to set out along the barren and exposed rocks of the north coast. Particularly in September and other times of migration, it's a remarkable spot for birdwatching, frequented by puffins, storm petrels and cormorants.

Getting to Ouessant

Penn Ar Bed (℡02.98.80.80.80, Ⓦpennarbed.fr) sail to Ouessant all year, with one to six daily departures from Le Conquet, and one to three daily from **Brest**. The timetables are extremely intricate, but broadly speaking the first sailing from Le Conquet is at 8am early July to late Aug, at 9am in the spring and autumn, and at 9.45am in winter. Corresponding times from Brest are half an hour earlier. Between early July and early September, they also depart from **Camaret** to Ouessant at 8.15am daily except Sundays, with some additional 11am sailings, while between early April and early July, and from early September until late September they sail from Camaret at 8.15am on Thursdays only. In every instance, whether you leave from Brest, Le Conquet, or Camaret, the round-trip **fare** is the same (June–Sept €30.20, Oct–May Mon–Fri €18, Sat & Sun €21).

In addition, you can **fly** to Ouessant in just fifteen minutes from Brest's Guipavas airport with Finist'Air (Mon–Sat 8.30am & 4.45pm, Sun 9am & 4.45pm; one way €65, return, not on same day, €93 ℡02.98.84.64.87, Ⓦwww.finistair.fr).

Practicalities

General information is available from Lampaul's central **tourist office** (mid-July to Aug Mon–Sat 9am–1pm & 1.30–7pm, Sun 9.30am–1pm; Sept to mid-July Mon–Sat 10am–noon & 2–5pm, Sun 10am–noon; ℡02.98.48.85.83, ⓦwww .ot-ouessant.fr). The town has a small **hostel**, *La Croix Rouge*, north towards Niou (℡02.98.48.84.53, ⓦauberge-ouessant.com; closed Dec & Jan), where a dorm bed plus breakfast costs €17.50. The best **hotel** is the colourful and comfortable *Ti Jan Ar C'hafé* (℡02.98.48.82.64, ⓦrocharmor.pagesperso-orange .fr; ❹; closed mid-Nov to mid-March), with a fine terrace, too. There's also a small **campsite**, the *Penn ar Bed*, just outside town (℡02.98.48.84.65; closed Oct–March) whose €10 pitches are protected from the wind by the surrounding relics of a military installation. *Hôtel Fromveur*, by the church in Lampaul (℡02.98.48.81.30; ❸), serves good traditional island cooking; expect to pay around €20 for lunch.

Brest

Set in a magnificent natural harbour, known as the Rade de Brest, the city of **BREST** is doubly sheltered from ocean storms by the bulk of Léon to the north and by the Crozon peninsula to the south. Today home to France's Atlantic Fleet, Brest has been a naval town since the Middle Ages. During World War II, it was continually bombed to prevent the Germans from using it as a submarine base a and when liberated on September 18, 1944, after a six-week siege, it was devastated beyond recognition. The architecture of the postwar town is raw and bleak and though there have been attempts to green the city, it has proved too windswept to respond. While it's reasonably lively, most visitors tend to pass through, using the town's rail and ferry links.

Arrival and information

Brest's **gare SNCF** and **gare routière** stand shoulder-to-shoulder in place du 19ème RI at the bottom of avenue Clemenceau. The **airport**, at Guipavas 9km northeast, is served by flights from London Luton on Ryanair, and from Birmingham and Southampton on British European, and also offers local connections to Ouessant (see opposite).

As well as the sailings to Ouessant, detailed opposite, in summer boats make the 25-minute crossing from Brest's Port de Commerce to Le Fret (see p.349) on the Crozon peninsula (April–June & Sept 3 sailings daily except Mon; July & Aug 3 sailings daily; €17 return; ℡02.98.41.46.23, ⓦazenor.fr). The same company also sails from both the port and Océanopolis to Camaret (July & Aug 3 sailings daily except Sat; €17 return), and offers excursions around the Rade de Brest (1hr 30min; usually around €15.50).

The helpful **tourist office**, on avenue Clemenceau facing place de la Liberté, runs an excellent website (July & Aug Mon–Sat 9.30am–7pm, Sun 10am–noon; Sept–June Mon–Sat 9.30am–6pm; ℡02.98.44.24.96, ⓦbrest-metropole -tourisme.fr).

Accommodation

Used more by business travellers than tourists, the vast majority of Brest's **hotels** remain open throughout the year, and many offer discounted **weekend** rates. Only a few, however, maintain their own restaurants.

Abalys 7 av Clemenceau ⊕02.98.44.21.86, ⓦabalys.com. Small but good-value accommodation (especially with weekend reductions) in a spruce little hotel above a bar near the stations. Not all rooms have en-suite facilities, and even in those that do the bathrooms can be tiny. ❷

Citôtel de la Gare 4 bd Gambetta ⊕02.98.44.47.01, ⓦhotelgare.com. Convenient, good-value option very near the stations. The cheapest rooms have a shower but no WC, while for a bit extra you can get a magnificent view of the Rade de Brest from the upper storeys. ❸

Continental Place de la Tour d'Auvergne ⊕02.98.80.50.40, ⓦoceaniahotels.com. Despite the dull concrete facade, this grand luxury hotel has some fine Art Deco features, and is very popular with business travellers. Spotlessly clean rooms; several on the fourth floor have large balconies. Good weekend rates. ❻

Pasteur 29 rue Louis-Pasteur ⊕02.98.46.08.73, ⓦhotel.pasteur.free.fr. Clean, good-value budget hotel, offering plain if potentially noisy en-suite rooms above a bar, a couple of blocks south of the St-Louis church. ❶

The Town

The one major site in Brest's city centre is its fifteenth-century **château**, perched on a headland where the Penfeld river meets the bay, and offering a tremendous panorama of both the busy port and the roadstead. Not quite as much of the castle survives as its impressive facade might suggest, though new buildings in the grounds still house the French naval headquarters. Three still-standing medieval towers, however, hold Brest's portion of the **Musée National de la Marine** (daily: Feb, March & Oct–Dec 1.30–6.30pm; April–Sept 10am–6.30pm; closed Jan; €5.50; ⓦwww.musee-marine.fr). Collections include ornate carved figureheads and models, as well as a German "pocket submarine" based here during World War II, and visitors can also stroll the parapets to enjoy the views.

Across the river, the fourteenth-century **Tour Tanguy**, with its conical slate roof, serves as a history museum of Brest before 1939 (June–Sept daily 10am–noon & 2–7pm; Oct–May Wed & Thurs 2–5pm, Sat & Sun 2–6pm; free).

A futuristic complex of **aquariums** and related attractions, **Océanopolis** sprawls a couple of kilometres east of the city centre (mid-Jan to March & Oct–Dec Tues–Fri 10am–5pm, Sat & Sun 10am–6pm; April–June & Sept daily 10am–6pm; July & Aug daily 9am–7pm; bus #3; adults €16.50, under-18s €11.50; ⓦwww .oceanopolis.com). Its original white dome, now known as the **Temperate Pavilion**, focuses on the Breton littoral and Finistère's fishing industry, holding all kinds of fish, seals, molluscs, seaweed and sea anemones. To that has been added a **Tropical Pavilion**, with a tankful of ferocious-looking sharks plus a myriad of rainbow-hued smaller fish that populate a highly convincing coral reef; a **Polar Pavilion**, complete with polar bears and penguins; and a **Biodiversity Pavilion**. Everything's very high-tech, and perhaps a little too earnest for some visitors' tastes, but it's possible to spend a whole entertaining day here.

Eating

As well as several low-priced places near the stations, Brest offers a wide assortment of **restaurants**. Rue Jean-Jaurès, climbing east from the place de la Liberté, has plenty of bistros and bars, while place Guérin to the north is the centre of the student-dominated quartier St-Martin.

La Fleur de Sel 15bis rue de Lyon ⊕02.98.44.38.65, ⓦwww.lafleurdesel.com. Brest's finest restaurant serves largely traditional cuisine in highly sophisticated and flavourful combinations. Lunch *menu* €21, dinner €27–40. Closed Sat lunch, Sun, & first three weeks in Aug.

La Maison de l'Océan 2 quai de la Douane ⊕02.98.80.44.84, ⓦmaisondelocean .over-blog.com. Blue-hued fish restaurant down by the port, with a terrace facing across to the island ferries. Open daily for lunch and dinner, and serving wonderful seafood on *menus* from €16.50 to €38.

Pensée Sauvage 13 rue d'Aboville
☎ 02.98.46.36.65. Popular and informal neighbourhood budget restaurant in the St-Martin district, which offers a bargain €9 lunch special and inexpensive meat or fish dinners from €14. Closed Sat lunch, plus all Sun & Mon.

The Crozon peninsula

The **Crozon peninsula**, a craggy outcrop of land shaped like a long-robed giant, arms outstretched, is the central feature of Finistère's jagged coastline. Much the easiest way for cyclists and travellers relying on public transport to reach the peninsula from Brest is via the **ferries** to Le Fret (see p.347).

As you approach the Crozon peninsula, it's well worth making a slight detour to climb the hill of **Ménez-Hom** ("at the giant's feet") for a fabulous preview of the alternating land and water across the southern side of the peninsula out to the ocean.

Crozon and Morgat

The main town on the peninsula proper, **CROZON**, has a nice little stone-built core that serves as the commercial hub for the surrounding communities, and plays host to a large-scale **market** on alternate Wednesdays. As it's also, unfortunately, a traffic hub, its one-way traffic system distributing tourists among the various resorts, and in any case it's set back from the sea, it's more of a place to pass through than to linger. It does hold the **tourist office** for the whole peninsula, however, just west of the centre in the *gare routière* (July & Aug Mon–Sat 9.15am–1pm & 2–7pm, Sun 10am–1pm; Sept–June Mon–Sat 9.15am–noon & 2–5.30pm; ☎ 02.98.27.07.92, ⓦ crozon.com).

MORGAT, just down the hill, makes a more enticing base. It has a long crescent beach that ends in a pine slope, and a well-sheltered harbour full of pleasure boats on the short haul from England and Ireland. The main attractions are **boat trips** around the various headlands, such as the **Cap de la Chèvre** (which is a good

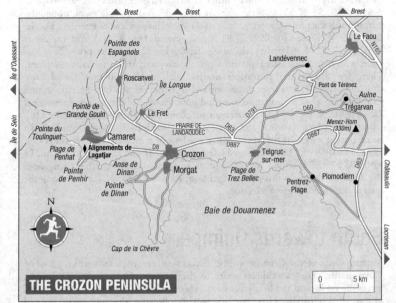

THE CROZON PENINSULA

0   5 km

clifftop walk if you'd rather make your own way). The most popular is the 45-minute tour of the **Grottes** with Vedettes Rosmeur (daily April to late Sept; ☏02.98.27.10.71, ⊛grottes-morgat.com; €11). From these multicoloured caves in the cliffs, accessible only by sea but with steep "chimneys" up to the clifftops, saints are said to have emerged in bygone days to rescue the shipwrecked.

The pick of the **accommodation** in Morgat is *Kermaria* (☏02.98.26.20.02, ⊛www.kermaria.com; ❺), a luxury guest house with high ceilings and leather armchairs, and gardens leading onto the beach. Of the hotels, *Julia*, 400m from the beach at 43 rue de Tréflez (☏02.98.27.05.89, ⊛hoteljulia.fr; ❸; obligatory half-board in summer; closed Jan & Feb), is the best bet. For **campers** the best option is the three-star site at *Plage de Goulien* (☏02.98.26.23.16, ⊛camping-crozon -laplagedegoulien.com; closed mid-Sept to May; well under €15). The best place to **eat** is the central *Saveurs et Marée*, 52 bd de la Plage (☏02.98.26.23.18), which serves great seafood, and has the bonus of outdoor seating.

Camaret

One of the loveliest seaside towns in all Brittany, the sheltered port of **CAMARET**, nestles at the western tip of the peninsula. Its most prominent building is the pink-orange **château de Vauban**, standing at the end of the long jetty that runs parallel to the main town waterfront. Walled, moated, and accessible via a little gatehouse reached by means of a drawbridge, it was built in 1689 to guard the approaches to Brest; these days it guards no more than a motley assortment of decaying half-submerged fishing boats, abandoned to rot beside the jetty. There are two beaches nearby – a small one to the north and another, larger and more attractive, in the low-lying (and rather marshy) Anse de Dinan. There are also some good wreck dives and submerged islands for scuba-diving enthusiasts – head to *Léo-Lagrange*, 2 rue du Stade (⊛club-leo-camaret.net). In summer, **ferries** run from Camaret to the islands of Ouessant (see p.350) and Sein (see p.352).

Camaret has its own little **tourist office** at 15 quai Kléber (Mon–Sat 9am–noon & 2–6pm; ☏02.98.27.93.60, ⊛camaret-sur-mer.com). A short walk away, around the port towards the protective jetty, the quai du Styvel holds a row of excellent **hotels**. Both the ⚓ *Vauban* (☏02.98.27.91.36; ❷; closed Dec & Jan) and *Du Styvel* (☏02.98.27.92.74, ✉hotelstyvel@orange.fr; ❷; closed Jan) are exceptionally hospitable, with rooms that look right out across the bay; only the *Styvel* has a restaurant. There are also several **campsites** nearby, such as the four-star *Grand Large* (☏02.98.27.91.41, ⊛www.campinglegrandlarge.com; closed Oct–March; around €25) boasting a water slide in its pool and great views, and the two-star municipal *Lannic* (☏02.98.27.91.31, ⊛camaret-sur-mer.com; closed Nov–March; under €10).

Back along the quayside in the centre of town, the quai Toudouze, you'll find a succession of excellent **fish restaurants**, the best of which are *Les Frères de la Côte* at no. 11 (☏02.98.27.95.42; closed late Sept to April), and the *Côté Mer* at no. 12 (☏02.98.27.93.79; closed Wed & Thurs in low season). *Rhum*, rather than *cidre* is the drink of choice in this part of Finistère; *Rhumerie La Goël*, further along the quai at no. 36, has a good selection.

South towards Quimper

Moving south of the Crozon peninsula, you soon enter the ancient kingdom of **Cornouaille**. The most direct route to the region's principal city, **Quimper**, leaves the sea behind and heads due south, passing close to the unchanged medieval village of **Locronan**. However, it's worth following the supremely isolated coastline instead around the Baie de Douarnenez to the **Pointe du Raz**, the western tip of Finistère. With a few exceptions – most notably its "land's end" capes – this stretch of coast has kept out of the tourist mainstream, and nowhere does that hold more true than on the remarkable, remote **Île de Sein**.

Locronan

LOCRONAN, a short way from the sea on the minor road that leads down from the Crozon peninsula, is a rare example of architectural unity. From 1469 through to the seventeenth century, rich medieval houses built up in the centre as the town thrived on woven "lin" (linen), supplying sails to the French, English and Spanish navies. It was first rivalled by Vitré and Rennes, before suffering the "agony and ruin" so graphically described in its small **museum** (Feb–June & Sept Mon–Fri 10am–noon & 2–6pm; July & Aug Mon–Sat 10am–1pm & 2–6pm, Sun 2–6pm; €2). Film directors love this sense of time warp, even if Roman Polanski, filming *Tess*, deemed it necessary to change all the porches, put new windows on the Renaissance houses, and bury the main square in mud to make it all look a bit more English.

Today Locronan prospers on tourism, but this commercialization shouldn't put you off making at least a passing visit, as the town itself is genuinely remarkable, centred around the focal **Église St-Ronan**. Be sure to take the time to walk down the hill of the **rue Moal**, to the lovely little stone chapel of Notre-Dame de Bonne Nouvelle.

The **tourist office** is next to the museum (same hours; ☎02.98.91.70.14, Ⓦlocronan.org). The one **hotel**, *du Prieuré*, at 11 rue du Prieuré on the main approach street (☎02.98.91.70.89, Ⓦhotel-le-prieure.com; ❹; closed mid-Nov to mid-March) is not particularly attractive, but offers well-equipped rooms and a good restaurant.

Douarnenez

Though it's still home to the largest fish canneries in Europe, the sheltered, historic port of **DOUARNENEZ** has been transformed over the last two decades into a superb living museum. Since 1993, **Port-Rhû**, on the west side of town, has been designated as the **Port-Musée**, with its entire waterfront taken up with fishing and other vessels gathered from throughout northern Europe, five of which you can roam through. Its centrepiece, the **Musée du Bateau** (Boat Museum) in place de l'Enfer (April–June & Sept to early Nov daily except Mon 10am–12.30pm & 2–6pm; July & Aug daily 10am–7pm; €7.50; Ⓦwww.port-musee.org), houses slightly smaller vessels, such as Gallic coracles and a Portugese *moliceiro*, and displays exhaustive explanations on boat construction techniques and a strong emphasis on fishing.

Of the three separate harbour areas still in operation, by far the most appealing is the rough-and-ready **port du Rosmeur**, on the east side, which is nominally the fishing port used by the smaller local craft. Its quayside, still far from commercialized, holds a reasonable number of relaxed waterside cafés and restaurants.

Douarnenez's **tourist office** is a short walk up from the Port-Musée at 1 rue du Dr-Mével (April–June Mon–Sat 10am–12.30pm & 2–6pm, Sun 10.45am–12.45pm; July & Aug Mon–Sat 10am–7pm, Sun 10am–1pm & 4–6.30pm; Sept Mon–Sat 10am–12.30pm & 2–6pm; Oct–March Mon–Sat 10am–12.30pm & 2–5.30pm; ☎02.98.92.13.35, Ⓦdouarnenez-tourisme.com). Good-value **hotels** nearby include *Le Bretagne*, 23 rue Duguay-Trouin (☎02.98.92.30.44, Ⓦle-bretagne .fr; ❸) and the more upmarket *De France*, 4 rue Jean Jaurès (☎02.98.92.00.02, Ⓦlafrance-dz.com; ❹; closed Mon, Sat lunch & Sun eve), both of which boast restaurants (the latter with *menus* starting at €25). Close by on the bay, at Tréboul/ Les Sables Blancs, there's a two-star **campsite**, *Croas Men* (☎02.98.74.00.18, Ⓦcroas-men.com; €11; closed Oct–Easter). In addition to the hotel **restaurants**,

Les Bigorneaux Amoureux, 2 bd Richepin (☎02.98.92.35.55; closed Mon), is a good seafood place with a terrace overlooking the plage des Dames.

The Pointe du Raz and the Baie des Trépassés

Thirty kilometres west of Douarnenez, the **Pointe du Raz** – the Land's End of both Finistère and France – is designated a "Grand Site National", and makes a magnificent spectacle. Buffeted by wind and waves and peppered with deep gurgling fissures, it's quite a wild experience to walk to the end and back. Don't expect to have the place to yourself; with three million visitors every year, they've had to build a huge car park 1km short of the actual headland (€5 cars, €3 motorcycles), alongside an information complex (April–June & Sept daily 10.30am–6pm; July & Aug daily 9.30am–7pm; ☎02.98.70.67.18, Ⓦwww .pointeduraz.com). To get to the *pointe*, take the free *navette*, then walk the most direct route, along an undulating, arrow-straight track or take a longer stroll along the footpath that skirts the top of the cliffs.

The **Baie des Trépassés** (Bay of the Dead), along the coast to the north, gets its grim name from the shipwrecked bodies that used to be washed up here. However, it's actually a very attractive spot; green meadows, too exposed to support trees, end abruptly on the low cliffs to either side; there's a huge expanse of flat sand (in fact little else at low tide); and out in the crashing waves surfers and windsurfers get thrashed to within an inch of their lives. Beyond them, you can usually make out the white-painted houses along the harbour on the Île de Sein, while the various uninhabited rocks in between hold a veritable forest of lighthouses.

In total, less than half a dozen scattered buildings intrude upon the emptiness, including the two parts of a **hotel**, both with tremendous views. The pink ⚜ *Hôtel de la Baie des Trépassés* (☎02.98.70.61.34, Ⓦwww.baiedestrepasses.com; ❹; closed mid-Nov to mid-Feb) is a truly romantic hideaway, sitting alone on the grass just behind its wide, fine-sand beach. The rooms are simply decorated and comfortable – there is one cheaper room (❶) without en-suite facilities, and the restaurant serves *menus* of wonderfully fresh seafood from €18.50.

The Île de Sein

Of all the Breton islands, the tiny **Île de Sein**, just 8km off the end of the Pointe du Raz, has to be the most extraordinary. It's hard to believe anyone could truly survive here; nowhere does it rise more than six metres above the surrounding ocean, and for much of its 2.5km length it's barely broader than the breakwater wall of bricks that serves as its central spine. In fact, the island has been inhabited since prehistoric times, and it was reputed to have been the very last refuge of the druids in Brittany. It also became famous during World War II, when its entire male population answered General de Gaulle's call to join him in exile in England. Today, over three hundred islanders continue to make their living from the sea, gathering rainwater and seaweed, and fishing for scallops, lobster and crayfish.

Never mind cars, not even bicycles are permitted here. Depending on the tide, boats pull in at one or other of the two adjoining harbours that constitute Sein's one tight-knit village, in front of which a little beach appears at low tide. There is a **museum** of local history here (June & Sept daily 10am–noon & 2–4pm; July & Aug daily 10am–noon & 2–6pm; €2.50), packed with black-and-white photos and press clippings, and displaying a long list of shipwrecks from 1476 onwards. The basic activity for visitors, however, is to take a bracing walk, preferably to the far end of the island, from where you can see the **Phare Ar-men** lighthouse, peeking out of the waves 12km further west into the Atlantic.

Practicalities

The principal departure point for **boats** to Sein is Ste-Evette beach, just outside **Audierne**; the crossing takes around an hour. Services are operated by Penn Ar Bed (daily: early July to late Aug 3–5 sailings daily, with first at 8.45am; late Aug to early July 1–2 daily, with first at 9.30am; ☎02.98.70.70.70, ⊛pennarbed.fr). On Sundays from late June to early September, Penn Ar Bed also runs trips to Sein from **Brest** (departs 9am; 1hr 30min) via **Camaret** (9.30am; 1hr). The round-trip **fare** on every route is the same (June–Sept €30.20, Oct–May Mon–Fri €15.20, Sat & Sun €16.80).

Sein is hardly bursting with facilities, but it does have two **hotels**. The nicest, the *d'Armen* (⚑☎02.98.70.90.77, ⊛hotel-armen.net; ❸), is the very last building as you walk west out of town, which makes it the last restaurant in Europe. All its simple but lovely rooms face the sea, and the excellent €20 dinner *menu* features mussels in cider, skate, and delicious home-baked bread. Back in town, above a bar in the middle of the port, the *Trois Dauphins*, 16 quai des Paimpolais (☎02.98.70.92.09, ⊛hoteliledesein.com; ❷), offers cosy and attractive rooms, not all en suite or with sea views.

Quimper

Pretty, historic, laid-back **QUIMPER** ranks high among the most attractive cities in Brittany. Still "the charming little place" known to Flaubert, it takes at most half an hour to cross it on foot. Though relaxed, it's active enough to have the bars and atmosphere to make it worth going out café-crawling. The word "kemper" denotes the junction of the two rivers, the Steir and the Odet, around which lie the cobbled streets (now mainly pedestrianized) of the medieval quarter, dominated by the cathedral towering nearby. With no great pressure to rush around monuments or museums, the most enjoyable option may be to take a boat and drift down the Odet "the prettiest river in France" to the open sea at Bénodet. Overlooking all is tree-covered Mont Frugy; climb to its 87m peak for good views over the city.

Capital of the ancient diocese, kingdom and later duchy of Cornouaille, Quimper is the oldest Breton city. According to the only source – legend – its first bishop, St Corentin, came with the first Bretons across the English Channel to Brittany, the place they named Little Britain, at some point between the fourth and seventh centuries.

Arrival and information

The **gare SNCF** and **gare routière** stand side by side on avenue de la Gare, 1km east of the centre on bus route #6. All city buses pass the tourist office, on either side of the river, depending on which direction you're heading. To reach the coast on public transport, the **bus** is your only option (CAT: (☎02.98.90.68.40, ⊛cat29.fr).

The **tourist office**, which organizes guided tours in season, is on the south bank of the Odet at 7 rue de la Déesse, place de la Résistance (April & May Mon–Sat 9.30am–12.30pm & 1.30–6.30pm; June & Sept Mon–Sat 9.30am–12.30pm & 1.30–6.30pm, Sun 10am–12.45pm; July & Aug Mon–Sat 9am–7pm, Sun 10am–12.45pm & 3–5.45pm; Oct–March Mon–Sat 9am–12.30pm & 1.30–6pm; ☎02.98.53.04.05, ⊛www.quimper-tourisme.com). For internet access, call in at Wok Café, 53 bd de Kerguélen (☎02.98.64.40.07, ⊛wokcafe.fr).

Between June and September you can **cruise** from Quimper down the Odet to Bénodet, which takes about 1 hour 15 minutes each way, on Vedettes de l'Odet (☎02.98.57.00.58, ⊛vedettes-odet.com; €25 return). Between one and four boats

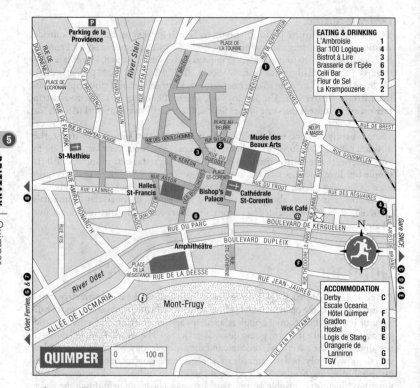

EATING & DRINKING
L'Ambroisie   1
Bar 100 Logique   4
Bistrot à Lire   3
Brasserie de l'Epée 6
Ceili Bar   5
Fleur de Sel   7
La Krampouzerie   2

ACCOMMODATION
Derby   C
Escale Oceania
  Hôtel Quimper   F
Gradlon   A
Hostel   B
Logis de Stang   E
Orangerie de
  Lanniron   G
TGV   D

QUIMPER   0   100 m

sail every day (except Sun in July & Aug), with schedules and precise departure points varying with the tide and season; the tourist office sells tickets.

Accommodation

The old streets in the centre of Quimper hold remarkably few **hotels**, though several can be found near the station. Rooms can be especially difficult to find in late July or early August; reserve ahead.

Hotels

Derby 13 av de la Gare ☎02.98.52.06.91, ⓦwww.hotel-le-derby.fr. Inexpensive, surprisingly quiet option above a corner bar facing the station. ②

Escale Oceania Hôtel Quimper 6 rue Théodore Le Hars ☎02.98.53.37.37, ⓦoceaniahotels.com. Comfortable central hotel, next to a parking garage, that offers slightly characterless, but reliably clean and quiet rooms, helpful service and €9 buffet breakfasts. ⑤

Gradlon 30 rue de Brest ☎02.98.95.04.39, ⓦwww.hotel-gradlon.fr. Central but quiet, this exceptionally friendly hotel is an ideal base, and has a pleasant garden. Tastefully decorated rooms, plus a good bar, with an open fire in winter. ⑥

Logis du Stang Allée du Stang-Youen ☎02.98.52.00.55, ⓦlogis-du-stang.com. Delightful B&B, east of the centre in a nineteenth-century house, with five well-furnished en-suite rooms and a hortensia-filled garden. ⑤

TGV 4 rue de Concarneau ☎02.98.90.54.00, ⓦhoteltgv.com. Plain but clean rooms with shower and TV at bargain rates, opposite the station. Avoid the first floor, which gets a bit noisy. ①

Hostel and Camping

Hostel 6 av des Oiseaux, Bois de Seminaire ☎02.98.64.97.97, ⓦfuaj.org/quimper. Unremarkable but clean hostel, 2km west of the centre on bus #1. Kitchen, rental bikes, and a quiet garden. The €12.70 price for a dorm bed includes sheets, but breakfast is €3 extra. Closed Oct–March.

Orangerie de Lanniron Route de Bénodet ☎ 98.90.62.02, ⓦ www.lanniron.com. Four-star campsite, 4km south in the grounds of a château, with swimming pool and tennis court, and also chalets and stone cottages for rent. Closed mid-Sept to mid-May.

The Town

Quimper's focal point, the enormous **Cathédrale St-Corentin**, is said to be the most complete Gothic cathedral in Brittany, though its neo-Gothic spires date from 1856. When the nave was being added to the old chancel in the fifteenth century, the extension would either have hit existing buildings or the swampy edge of the then-unchannelled river. So the nave was placed at a slight angle – a peculiarity which, once noticed, makes it hard to concentrate on the other Gothic splendours within. The exterior, however, gives no hint of the deviation, with King Gradlon mounted in perfect symmetry between the spires.

Alongside the cathedral, the quirky-looking Bishop's Palace holds the beautifully laid-out **Musée Départemental Breton** (June–Sept daily 9am–6pm; Oct–May Tues–Sat 9am–noon & 2–5pm, Sun 2–5pm; €4; ⓦ museedepartementalbreton.fr). Collections start with Bronze Age spear- and axe-heads and prehistoric golden jewellery, move rapidly through Roman and medieval statues, and culminate with a remarkable assortment of Breton oddments and objets d'art.

The **Musée des Beaux Arts**, immediately north of the cathedral, is even more compelling (April–June, Sept & Oct daily except Tues 10am–noon & 2–6pm; July & Aug daily 10am–7pm; Nov–March Mon & Wed–Sat 10am–noon & 2–6pm, Sun 2–6pm; €4.50; ⓦ musee-beauxarts.quimper.fr). Impressively refurbished, with new floors and suspended walkways, it focuses on an amazing assemblage of drawings by Max Jacob – who was born in Quimper – and his contemporaries. Look out also for the museum's Gauguin, a goose he painted on the door of Marie Henry's inn in Pont-Aven itself.

Ancient half-timbered buildings, in the heart of **old Quimper**, west of place St-Corentin, hold the city's liveliest shops and cafés, including the Breton Keltia-Musique record shop at 1 place au Beurre (ⓦ keltiamusique.com), and the Celtic shop, Ar Bed Keltiek, 2 rue du Roi-Gradlon (ⓦ arbedkeltiek.com). The **Halles St-Francis** marketplace, on rue Astor, is a delight, not just for the food, but for the view past the upturned boat rafters through the roof to the cathedral's twin spires. It's open from Monday to Saturday, with an extra-large market spreading into the surrounding streets on Saturdays.

As you walk through Quimper, it is impossible to ignore the local ceramic tradition of **faïence**, or tin-glazed earthenware. The major atelier **H-B Henriot**, which continues to produce hand-painted pottery in the allées de Locmaria not far west of the tourist office, has a gift shop and also offers tours (July & Aug Mon–Sat 9.15–11.15am & 1.30–4.15pm; Sept–June Mon–Fri 10.15–11.15am & 2–4.15pm; ☎ 02.98.90.09.36, ⓦ hb-henriot.com; €5).

Eating and drinking

Although the pedestrian streets west of the cathedral are unexpectedly short on places to eat, there are quite a few **restaurants** further east on the north side of the river, en route towards the *gare SNCF*. For crêperies, the place au Beurre, a short walk northwest of the cathedral, is a good bet.

Restaurants

L'Ambroisie 49 rue Élie-Fréron ☎ 02.98.95.00.02, ⓦ ambroisie-quimper.com. Upmarket French restaurant a short climb north from the cathedral, featuring fine seafood (including tuna) and meat dishes on *menus* from €23. Closed Mon, plus Sun eve in winter.

Bistrot à Lire 18 rue des Boucheries ☎ 02.98.95.30.86. This café specializes in two things: desserts and detective thrillers. The fruit crumbles are an excellent choice for the former; you can pick the latter off the bookshelves and read while you eat. Lunchtime *plats du jour* for €88. Closed Sun & Mon.

Brasserie de l'Epée 14 rue du Parc ℡ 02.98.95.28.97, Ⓦ quimper-lepee.com. Lovely Art Nouveau brasserie, facing the river near the cathedral. Good-value dinner *menus* at €25 or €35, or *moules frites* for €13, and it stays open late – you can still get a meal at 11pm, rare indeed for Brittany. Closed Sun & Mon.

Fleur de Sel 1 quai Neuf ℡ 02.98.55.04.71, Ⓦ fleur-de-sel-quimper.com. Gourmet French cooking not far west of the centre on the north, with largely fish *menus* (dinner €27 or €38). Closed lunch on both Sat & Sun.

La Krampouzerie 9 rue du Sallé ℡ 02.98.95.13.08. Great crêperies, with outdoor seating on the place au Beurre. Most crêpes, such as the one with Roscoff onions and seaweed, cost around €4, though a wholewheat *galette* with smoked salmon and cream cheese is €6. Closed Sun, plus Mon in winter.

Bars

Bar 100 Logique 9 rue des Réguaires ℡ 02.98.95.44.69, Ⓦ le100logiquequimper.skyrock. com. Classy little bar that makes the most of being Quimper's only gay and lesbian hangout. Closed Mon.

Ceili Bar 4 rue Aristide Briand ℡ 02.98.95.17.61. This lively and convivial bar is the place to go for all things Breton: beer and opinionated conversation, plus live traditional Celtic bands and occasionally jazz. Open until 1am.

Entertainment

Quimper's **Festival de Cornouaille** started in 1923, and is still going from strength to strength. This great jamboree of Breton music, costumes, theatre and dance is held in the week before the fourth Sunday in July, attracting guest performers from the other Celtic countries and a scattering of other, sometimes highly unusual, ethnic-cultural ensembles. The whole thing culminates in an incredible Sunday parade through the town. The official programme does not appear until July, but you can get provisional details in advance from the tourist office or at Ⓦ www .festival-cornouaille.com. Accommodation is at a premium during the festival.

Not so widely known are the **Semaines Musicales**, which follow in the first three weeks of August (Ⓦ www.semaines-musicales-quimper.org), and bring the rather stuffy nineteenth-century theatre on boulevard Dupleix alive. The music is predominantly classical, favouring French composers.

South from Quimper

More tourists flock to Finistère's southern coast than to any other part of the region, with the busiest segment of all in summer centring on the family-friendly resort of **Bénodet**. The beaches between here and **La Forêt-Fouesnant** to the east rank among the finest in Brittany. A little further along the coast, the walled, sea-circled old town of **Concarneau** makes a perfect day-trip destination, though a prettier place to spend a night or two would be the flowery village of **Pont-Aven**, immortalized by Paul Gauguin, slightly further east.

Bénodet and around

Once out of its city channel, the Odet spreads out to lake proportions then turns narrow corners between gorges until it reaches **BÉNODET** at the mouth of the river. This partially redeveloped family resort has a long, sheltered beach on the ocean side that's packed in summer but good fun for children. A good **hotel** near the port and beach is *Les Bains de Mer*, 11 rue de Kerguélen (℡ 02.98.57.03.41, Ⓦ lesbainsdemer .com; ❹; closed Jan), which has comfortable rooms and a heated outdoor pool.

Bénodet also has several large **campsites**, including comfortable and well-equipped four-stars such as the enormous *Camping du Letty*, southeast alongside the plage du Letty, on rue du Canvez (℡02.98.57.04.69, ⓦcampingduletty.com; €17; closed early Sept to mid-June); and the *Camping du Port de Plaisance* near the pleasure port (℡02.98.57.02.38, ⓦcampingbenodet.fr; €39; closed late Sept to March), which has its own covered water park.

East of Bénodet, the coast is rocky and repeatedly cut by deep valleys. After 12km, clustered along the waterfront at the foot of a hill so steep that caravans are banned from even approaching, **LA FORÊT-FOUESNANT** is known for its beaches and cider. Attractive **hotels** include *l'Espérance*, place de l'Église (℡02.98.56.96.58, ⓦwww.hotel-esperance.org; ❷), and *du Port*, 4 corniche de la Cale (℡02.98.56.97.33, ⓦwww.hotelduport.fr; ❸; closed Dec–March; restaurant closed Mon, plus Sun eve & all Tues in low season). Sample award-winning organic cider at *Cidre Séhédic* (℡02.98.56.85.18, ⓦwww.cidre-sehedic.fr) on the road to Bénodet.

Concarneau

The first sizeable town you come to east of Bénodet is **CONCARNEAU**, where the third most important fishing port in France does a reasonable job of passing itself off as a holiday resort. Its greatest asset is its small and very well-fortified old city, located just a few metres offshore on an irregular rocky island.

Arrival and information

There's no rail service to Concarneau, but SNCF **buses** connect the town with Quimper, from the quai d'Aiguillon next to the **tourist office** (May, June & first fortnight of Sept Mon–Sat 9am–12.30pm & 1.45–6.30pm, Sun 10am–1pm; July & Aug daily 9am–7pm; mid-Sept to April Mon–Sat 9am–noon & 2–6pm; ℡02.98.97.01.44, ⓦwww.tourismeconcarneau.fr).

Accommodation

Concarneau's accommodation options are concentrated in the mainland backstreets. There are also some lovely **campsites** close to the Sables-Blancs beach; the spacious *Prés Verts* (℡02.98.97.09.74, ⓦpresverts.com; closed Oct–April) spreads through verdant fields at Kernous Plage at the far end.

De France et d'Europe 9 av de la Gare
℡02.98.97.00.64, ⓦhotel-france-europe.com.
Bright, modernized and very central hotel near the main bus stop, which has a small gym. Closed Sat in winter. ❸
Des Halles Place de l'Hôtel de Ville
℡02.98.97.11.41, ⓦhoteldeshalles.com. Spruce pastel-orange hotel near the fish market, across from the entrance to the Ville Close, offering well-equipped rooms at reasonable rates. ❸
Hostel Place de la Croix ℡02.98.97.03.47, ⓦajconcarneau.com. Budget travellers will like this very central hostel, which enjoys magnificent ocean views just around the south tip of the headland from the town centre, and has a windsurfing shop nearby. Dorm beds €15.30 including breakfast.
Ker Moor Plage les Sables-Blancs ℡02.98.97.02.96, ⓦhotel-kermor.com. Classic, beautifully restored seafront hotel, nautically themed throughout, on the beach 2km west of town. All the rooms have sea views, but you can pay extra for a balcony. ❻

The Town

Concarneau's walled core, the **ville close**, is a real delight, even if it does get too crowded for comfort in high summer. Like those of the citadelle at Le Palais on Belle-Île, its ramparts were completed by Vauban in the seventeenth century. The island itself, however, had been inhabited for at least a thousand years before that.

Concarneau boasts that it is a *ville fleurie*, and the flowers are most in evidence inside the walls, where climbing roses and clematis swarm all over the various gift shops, restaurants and crêperies. Walk the central pedestrianized street to the far

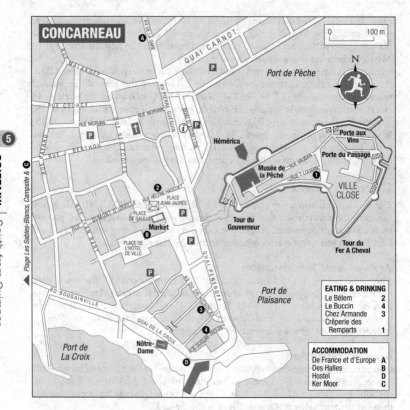

CONCARNEAU

0   100 m

Port de Pèche

Port de Plaisance

Port de La Croix

Nôtre-Dame

VILLE CLOSE

Porte aux Vins
Porte du Passage
Musée de la Pêche
Hémérica
Tour du Gouverneur
Tour du Fer A Cheval

Market
PLACE JEAN-JAURÈS
PLACE DE GAULLE
PLACE DE L'HÔTEL DE VILLE

EATING & DRINKING
Le Bélem	2
Le Buccin	4
Chez Armande	3
Crêperie des Remparts	1

ACCOMMODATION
De France et d'Europe	A
Des Halles	B
Hostel	D
Ker Moor	C

end, and you can pass through a gateway to the shoreline to watch the fishing boats go by. The best views of all come from the promenade on top of the **ramparts**; you can't stroll all the way round to make a complete circuit of the walls, but here and there you can climb up for short stretches.

By exploring the history of fishing all over the world, the **Musée de la Pêche**, immediately inside the *ville close* (daily: July & Aug 9.30am–8pm; April–June & Sept 10am–6pm; Oct–March 10am–noon & 2–6pm but closed Sun morning in Oct only; €6; Ⓦmusee-peche.fr), provides an insight into the traditional life Concarneau shared with so many other Breton ports. Oddities on show include a three-thousand-year-old anchor from Crete, the swords of swordfish and the saws of sawfish, and a genuine trawler, moored on the other side of the city walls behind the museum.

Eating and drinking

Eating options in the *ville close* are generally overpriced; you can get far better value around the market just over the road.

Le Bélem 2 rue Hélène Hascoët ☏02.98.97.02.78, Ⓦlebelem.voila.net. Pretty little indoor restaurant, next to the market on the mainland, serving mussels for €10 and good seafood *menus* from €20. Closed Wed, plus Thurs eve & Sun eve in low season.

Le Buccin 1 rue Duguay-Trouin ☏02.98.50.54.22, Ⓦrestaurantlebuccin.fr. Traditional little place near the southern tip of the headland, with lunchtime *formules* from €8.40 and dinner *menus* at €25 and €34. Closed Wed, plus Tues morning in low season.

Chez Armande 15 av du Dr-Nicholas ☎02.98.97.00.76. Excellent seafood not far south of the market on the mainland, on *menus* starting from €12.65 at lunch, €18.50 in the evening. Closed Wed, & Tues in winter.

Crêperie des Remparts 31 rue Théophile Luarn ☎02.98.50.65.66. Good inexpensive crêpes, slightly off the beaten track behind the main street in the walled city, served either indoors or on a nice terrace. There's also a good €12 lunch *menu*. Closed Wed in low season, & Nov–Easter.

Pont-Aven

PONT-AVEN, 14km east of Concarneau and just inland from the tip of the Aven estuary, is a small port packed with art galleries – and tourists. This was where **Paul Gauguin** came to paint in the 1880s before he left for Tahiti, and inspired the **Pont-Aven School** of fellow artists, including Émile Bernard. Despite this, the town has no permanent collection of his work: the **Musée des Beaux Arts** (daily: Feb, March, Nov & Dec 10am–12.30pm & 2–6pm; April–June, Sept & Oct 10am–12.30pm & 2–6.30pm; July & Aug 10am–7pm; €4.50) in the *mairie* holds changing exhibitions of the school and other artists active during the same period.

Gauguin aside, Pont-Aven is pleasant in its own right. Just upstream of the little granite bridge at the heart of town, the **promenade Xavier-Grall** crisscrosses the tiny river itself on landscaped walkways, offering glimpses of the backs of venerable mansions, dripping with ivy, and a little "chaos" of rocks in the stream itself. A longer walk – allow an hour – leads into the romantically named **Bois d'Amour**, wooded gardens which have long provided inspiration to painters, poets and musicians.

Practicalities

Pont-Aven's **tourist office** is at 5 place de l'Hôtel de Ville (April–June & Sept Mon–Sat 10am–12.30pm & 2–6pm, Sun 3–6pm; July & Aug Mon–Sat 9.30am–7pm, Sun 10am–1pm & 3–6.30pm; Oct–March Mon–Sat 10am–12.30pm & 2–6pm; ☎02.98.06.04.70, ⑩pontaven.com). Much the best of the three relatively expensive **hotels** is the central *Ajoncs d'Or*, 1 place de l'Hôtel de Ville (☎02.98.06.02.06, ⑩ajoncsdor-pontaven.com; ❸; closed Jan, plus Mon & Sun eve in low season), where gourmet *menus* start at €25. There's also a lovely B&B, *Castel Braz*, 12 rue du Bois d'Amour (☎02.98.06.07.81, ⑩castelbraz.com; ❸), where each of the six rooms is decorated to a different theme. The nicest local **campsite** is the four-star *Domaine de Kerlann* (☎02.98.06.01.77, ⑩siblu.fr /domainedekerlann; closed late Sept to early April), set in a large wooded park with a swimming pool, tennis courts and mini-golf.

The Nantes–Brest canal

Completed in 1836, the **Nantes–Brest canal** is a meandering chain of waterways that connects Finistère to the Loire. Interweaving rivers with stretches of canal, it was built at Napoleon's instigation to bypass the belligerent English fleets off the coast. As a focus for exploring **inland Brittany**, whether by barge, bike, foot, or all three, the canal is ideal. Not every stretch is accessible, but detours can be made away from it, such as into the wild and desolate **Monts d'Arrée** to the north of the canal in Finistère.

The canal passes through riverside towns, such as **Josselin**, that long predate its construction; the old port of **Redon**, a patchwork of water, where the canal crosses the River Vilaine; and a sequence of scenic splendours, including long, narrow **Lac de Guerlédan**, created by the construction of the **Barrage de Guerlédan**, near Mur-de-Bretagne.

Châteaulin and Carhaix

CHÂTEAULIN, the first real town on the canal route, is a quiet place ideal for fishing and walking. Within a couple of minutes' walk upstream from the statue to **Jean Moulin** – the Resistance leader who was sous-préfet here from 1930 to 1933 – and the town centre, you'll find yourself on towpaths full of rabbits and squirrels. Hotel *Le Chrismas*, 33 Grande-Rue (☎02.98.86.01.24, ✉le-chrismas @orange.fr; ❸), serves excellent food.

There's little reason to visit **CARHAIX**, a further 25km east, other than for the third weekend of July, when it hosts France's biggest **rock festival**, the massive four-day **Vieilles Charrues** (ⓦvieillescharrues.asso.fr); recent headliners have included Bruce Springsteen. The most interesting building in town, the granite Renaissance **Maison du Sénéchal** on rue Brizeux, houses the **tourist office** (July & Aug Mon–Sat 9am–12.30pm & 1.30–7pm, Sun 10am–1pm; June & Sept Mon–Sat 9am–noon & 2–6pm; Oct–May Mon 2–6pm, Wed–Sat 10am–noon & 2–5.30pm; ☎02.98.93.04.42).

Huelgoat and its forest

HUELGOAT, next to its own small **lake** halfway between Morlaix and Carhaix on the minor road D769, makes a pleasant overnight stop. Spreading north and east from the village is the **Forêt de Huelgoat**, a landscape of trees, giant boulders and waterfalls tangled together in primeval chaos. Various paths lead into the depths of the woods, allowing for long walks amid spectacularly wild scenery.

The *Hôtel du Lac*, beside the lake at 9 rue du Général-de-Gaulle (☎02.98.99.71.14, ⓦhoteldulac-huelgoat.com; ❸; closed Mon Sept–June, plus mid-Jan to mid-Feb), offers well-refurbished rooms and hearty food. Also beside the lake, on the road towards Brest, there's the two-star *Camping du Lac* (☎02.98.99.78.80; closed Sept–June).

Le lac de Guerlédan

For the 15km between Gouarec and Mur-de-Bretagne, the N164 skirts the edge of **Quénécan Forest**, within which is the artificial **Lac de Guerlédan** created by the dam of the same name completed in 1928. It's a beautiful stretch of river, peaceful enough despite the summer influx of campers and caravans.

Just off the N164, at the western end of the lake, at the tiny village of **BON REPOS**, the ravishing 🍴 *Les Jardins de l'Abbaye* (☎02.96.24.95.77, ⓦabbaye .jardin.free.fr; ❷; closed Tues eve & Wed in low season) is an irresistible (and inexpensive) **hotel-restaurant**, nestling beside the water at the end of an impressive avenue of ancient trees. It's housed in the cosy slate outbuildings of a twelfth-century Cistercian abbey, which plays host to *son-et-lumière* spectacles on the first two weekends in August (☎02.96.24.85.28, ⓦpays-conomor.com; €19).

From just west of **CAUREL**, 7km east of St-Gelven, the brief loop of the D111 leads to tiny sandy beaches – a bit too tiny in season. At the spot known justifiably as **Beau Rivage**, the *Hôtel Beau Rivage* (☎02.96.28.52.15; ❸; closed Mon & Tues), commands magnificent views of the lake and serves great food, with dinner *menus* from €20 and even crêpes for breakfast.

French wines

French wines, drunk at just about every meal and social occasion, are unrivalled in the world for their range, sophistication, diversity and status. With the exception of the northwest of the country and the mountains, wine is produced almost everywhere. Champagne, Burgundy and Bordeaux are the most famous wine-producing regions, closely followed by the Loire and Rhône valleys and the up-and-coming Languedoc region.

Harvesting grapes ▲

Champagne cork ▼

Arbois Chardonnay ▼

Within each region there's enormous diversity, with differences generated by the type of grape grown (there are over sixty varieties), the individual skill of the *vigneron* (producer) and something the French refer to as *terroir*, an almost untranslatable term meaning the combination of soil, lie of the land and climate. Even a slight variation in soil or climate between one vineyard and its neighbour can result in very different-tasting wines, and it is this sheer variety and unpredictability that makes tasting French wines such a delight.

The most obvious guide to the quality of a wine is its classification. All French wine is classed into one of four categories: at the lowest level is the humble *vin de table*, suitable for everyday drinking. Next comes *vin de pays*, mostly designating decent quaffable fare, but also including some very good wines that fall outside the strict AOC rules. AOC (*appellation d'origine contrôlée*), the highest category, accounts for around forty percent of all French wine and is intended as a guarantee of origin and quality, though, through various flaws in the system, not all AOC wines merit their status. Within the AOC category a number of exceptional wines also qualify for the superior labels of Premier Cru or Grand Cru.

Wine regions

▶▶ Burgundy's luscious reds and crisp white wines can be truly sublime. The best wines come from the Côte de Nuits, producing Burgundy's headiest reds, made from the richly fruity Pinot Noir grape, and the Côte de Beaune, which yields the region's great white burgundy, made from the buttery Chardonnay grape. To the south, the Côte Chalonnaise and the

Mâconnais also produce good-quality whites, while further south still the Beaujolais is famous for its light, fruity reds. Out on its own, further north, is the Chablis region, known for its wonderfully fresh, flinty whites.

▶▶ The Bordeaux wine-producing region, three times the size of Burgundy, produces a huge quantity of very fine, medium-bodied reds, delicious sweet whites, notably Sauternes, and dry whites of varying quality. The best-known area is the Médoc, known for its long-lived, rich reds, including such legendary names as Margaux and Lafite, made from a blend of wines, chiefly the blackcurranty Cabernet Sauvignon. Graves produces the best of the area's dry white wines, while St-Emilion, where the Merlot grape thrives, yields warmer, fruitier wines.

▶▶ Champagne's status as the luxury celebration drink goes back to a time when it was used to anoint French kings, and at its best is an extraordinarily complex and rich sparkling wine. This far north – Champagne is just an hour from Paris – where good weather cannot be relied on year in year out, the only way to achieve consistent quality is by blending the produce of different vineyards and vintages. The leading Champagne houses, known as *maisons*, such as Bollinger and Moët et Chandon, blend up to sixty different wines and allow them to age for some years before selling. Needless to say, they produce the best and most expensive champagnes; those of smaller growers are more variable in quality.

▶▶ Nowhere else in France produces such a variety of wines: dry and sweet, white, red and rosé, still and sparkling. With some exceptions, however, the Loire's wines tend to be rather overlooked, probably because their hallmark is subtlety and

▲ Taittinger champagne cellar

▼ Merlot grapevines, Bordeaux

▼ Sancerre wines

Châteauneuf-du-Pape winery ▲

Le Baron Rouge, Paris ▲

Oysters and wine, Île-de-Ré ▼

elegance rather than intensity and punch. Sauvignon Blanc is the dominant white grape variety, as manifested in the dry, fragrant Sancerre and the smoky Pouilly-Fumé, arguably the region's finest whites. Steely Muscadet, made from the hardy Melon de Bourgogne grape, is not to everyone's taste, but the best (try Sèvre-et-Maine) make a great accompaniment to seafood. The region's top reds include the light, aromatic Chinon and Bourgueil.

▶▶ The Rhône is best known for its warm, flavoursome reds such as the blackberry-scented Hermitages, the peppery Gigondas and most famously of all the rich, spicy Châteauneuf-du-Pape. The Languedoc has the largest area of vineyards in the world, too many of them unfortunately producing rather mediocre wine, though recently some great-quality wines have been emerging, such as the heady, full-bodied reds from Faugères and Collioure.

Accompaniments...

Pairing food with wine is an art taken very seriously in France. The basic principle is to match subtle flavours, such as white fish, with lighter-bodied wines, and more flavoursome foods with heavier-bodied wines. Here are some suggestions:

Sea fish lighter wines, such as Chablis and dry white Bordeaux.

Trout and other river fish stronger-flavoured wines, such as white Burgundy, Sancerre, Riesling and dry rosé.

Mussels and oysters Muscadet or Chablis. Oysters also go down nicely with Champagne. Crab, lobster and scallops: white Burgundy, Riesling or Sancerre.

Beef red Burgundy

Lamb red Bordeaux

Game peppery Rhône or Cahors reds

MÛR-DE-BRETAGNE, set back from the eastern end of the lake, is a lively town with a wide and colourful pedestrianized zone around its church. The **tourist office** here, at 1 place de l'Église (July–Aug Mon–Sat 10am–12.30pm & 2–6.30pm, Sun 10.30am–12.30pm; Sept–June Mon–Fri 10am–noon & 2–5pm; ☏02.96.28.51.41, ⓦwww.guerledan.fr) organizes bike rides, horseriding, canoeing and jet-skiing.

Josselin

The three Rapunzel towers of the **château** at **JOSSELIN**, embedded in a vast sheet of stone above the water, are the most impressive sight along the Nantes–Brest canal. However, they turn out on close inspection to be no more than a facade. The building behind was built in the last century, the bulk of the original castle having been demolished by Richelieu in 1629 in punishment for Henri de Rohan's leadership of the Huguenots. It's still owned by the Rohan family, which used to own a third of Brittany.

Although tours of the castle's oppressively formal apartments are not very compelling, the duchess's collection of ancient **dolls**, housed in the **Musée des Poupées** behind, is something special (early April to mid-July daily 2–6pm; mid-July to Aug daily 11am–6pm; Sept daily 2–5.30pm; Oct Sat, Sun & hols 2–5.30pm; tours €7, museum €7, combined ticket €12; ⓦchateaujosselin.com).

The town itself is full of medieval splendours, from the gargoyles of the **basilica**, Notre-Dame-du-Roncier, to the castle **ramparts**, and the half-timbered houses in between.

Its **tourist office** is in a superb old house on the place de la Congrégation, by the castle entrance (April–June & Sept Mon–Sat 10am–noon & 2–6pm; Sun 2–6pm; July & Aug daily 10am–6.30pm; Oct–March Mon–Fri 10am–noon & 2–6pm; ☏02.97.22.36.43, ⓦwww.josselin.com). The lovely ⚞ *Hôtel du Chateau*, facing the castle from across the river at 1 rue du Général-de-Gaulle (☏02.97.22.20.11, ⓦwww.hotel-chateau.com; ❸; closed Feb), makes a perfect place to **stay**. Rooms with château views are slightly more expensive, but worth it – the whole place looks fabulous lit up at night – while the food, with dinner *menus* from €17.20, is first-rate. The nearest good **campsite** is the three-star *Bas de la Lande* (☏02.97.22.22.20, ⓦwww.guegon.fr; €8.30; closed Nov–March), half an hour's walk west from the castle, south of the river in Guégon, where simple rental chalets are also available.

Redon

Situated at the junction not only of the rivers Oust and Vilaine and the canal, but also of the train lines to Rennes, Vannes and Nantes, and of six major roads, **REDON** is not easy to avoid. And you shouldn't try to, either. A wonderful mess of water and locks, it's a town with history, charm and life.

Until World War I, Redon was the seaport for Rennes. Its industrial docks – or what remains of them – are therefore on the Vilaine, while the canal, even in the very centre of town, is almost totally rural, its towpaths shaded avenues. Shipowners' houses from the seventeenth and eighteenth centuries can be seen along quai Jean-Bart by the *bassin* and quai Duguay-Truin next to the river. A rusted wrought-iron workbridge, equipped with a gantry, still crosses the river, but the main users of the port now are cruise ships heading down the Vilaine to La Roche-Bernard.

Redon was once also a religious centre, its first abbey founded in 832 by St Conwoion. The most prominent church today is **St-Sauveur**. Its unique four-storeyed Romanesque belfry is squat, almost obscured by later roofs and the high choir, and best seen from the adjacent cloisters; the Gothic tower was entirely separated from the main building by a fire. In the crypt, you'll find the tomb of the judge who tried the legendary Bluebeard – Joan of Arc's friend, Gilles de Rais.

Redon's helpful **tourist office** is in the place de la République, north across the railway tracks from the town centre (July & Aug Mon–Sat 9am–7pm, Sun 10am–1pm & 4–6pm; Sept–June Mon & Wed–Fri 9.30am–noon & 2–6pm, Tues 2–6pm, Sat 10am–12.30pm & 3–5pm; ☏02.99.71.06.04, ⓦtourisme-pays-redon .com). The **gare SNCF** is five minutes' walk west. Most of the **hotels** are concentrated in town and near the *gare SNCF* rather than in the port area. The off-white, good-value *France* looks down on the canal from 30 rue Duguesclin (☏02.99.71.06.11, ⓦlefrance.chez-alice.fr; ❷); not all its rooms are en-suite. Nearer the station, the upmarket *Chandouineau*, 1 rue Thiers (☏02.99.71.02.04, ⓦhotel-restaurant-chandouineau.com; ❹; closed Sat & Sun eve), has just seven bedrooms, and a gourmet **restaurant**.

The southern coast

Brittany's **southern coast** is best known for mainland Europe's most famous prehistoric site, the megalithic alignments of **Carnac**, complemented by ancient relics around the beautiful, island-studded **Golfe de Morbihan**. The beaches are not as spectacular as in Finistère, but there are more safe places to swim and the water is warmer. Of the cities, **Lorient** has Brittany's most compelling **festival** and **Vannes** a lively medieval centre, while you can also escape to the islands of **Belle-Île**, **Hoëdic** and **Houat**.

Lorient and around

Brittany's fourth largest city, **LORIENT**, lies on an immense natural harbour, sheltered by the Île de Groix. A functional, rather depressing port today, it was once a key base for French colonialism, and was founded in the mid-seventeenth century by the Compagnie des Indes, an equivalent of the Dutch and English East India Companies. Apart from the name, little else remains to suggest the plundered wealth that once arrived here.

During the last war, Lorient was a major target for the Allies; by the time the Germans surrendered, in May 1945, the city was almost completely destroyed. The only substantial traces to survive were the **U-boat pens**, a couple of kilometres south of the centre in the port district of **Kéroman**. Subsequently expanded to hold French nuclear submarines, they're now open for **guided tours** in summer (July & Aug daily 10am–7pm; otherwise daily 10am–6pm in school hols, or Tues–Sun 10am–12.30pm & 2–6pm; ☏02.97.84.78.06, ⓦwww.la-flore.fr; €7.50, or €12.60 with submarine visit).

The adjoining **Cité de la Voile Éric Tabarly**, at the mouth of the Ter river, is a large, modern, interactive museum of **sailing** (Feb–June & Sept–Dec daily except Mon 10am–6pm, open Mon in school hols; July & Aug daily 10am–7pm; closed Jan; last admission 1hr 30min before closing; €11.50; ⓦcitevoile-tabarly.com).

M Tabarly himself was a champion yachtsman and Breton hero who drowned in 1998. Several of his yachts – all of which were called *Pen Duick*, which roughly means "little black head" – are moored alongside, and can be visited.

If you have time it's worth catching a ferry across to **Port-Louis** from the Embarcadère des Rades (Mon–Sat 6.45am–8pm, Sun 10am–7pm; €1.20; ℗02.97.21.28.29). In the citadel here, the **Musée de la Compagnie des Indes** traces the history of French imperialism in Asia, with displays covering both the trading voyages and the goods they brought home (Feb–April & Sept to mid-Dec, daily except Tues 1.30–6pm; May–Aug daily 10am–6.30pm; closed mid-Dec to Jan; €6; ⓦmusee.lorient.fr).

Practicalities

Lorient's **tourist office**, beside the pleasure port on the quai de Rohan (early April to early July and late Aug to late Sept, Mon–Fri 10am–noon & 2–6pm, Sat 10am–noon & 2–5pm; early July to late Aug Mon–Sat 9.30am–1pm & 2–7pm, Sun 10am–1pm, except during the festival, when it's daily 9am–8pm; late Sept to early April Mon–Fri 10am–noon & 2–5pm, Sat 10am–1pm; ℗02.97.84.78.00, ⓦwww.lorient-tourisme.fr), can provide full details on local boat trips and organizes some excursions itself. Lorient holds a surprisingly large number of **hotels**, though demand is of course high during the Inter-Celtic Festival. The central *Victor Hugo*, 36 rue Lazare-Carnot (℗02.97.21.16.24, ⓦwww.hotel victorhugo-lorient.com; ❷), has good-value sound-proofed rooms and a pleasant restaurant, while the basic but acceptable *Pecheurs*, 7 rue Jean Lagarde (℗02.97.21.19.24, ⓦwww.hotel-lespecheurs.com; ❶), is even cheaper. There's also a **hostel**, next to the River Ter at 41 rue Victor-Schoelcher (℗02.97.37.11.65, ⓦfuaj.org/lorient) 3km out on bus line C1 from the *gare SNCF*, where dorm beds cost €14.20, and they have space for **camping** in summer.

A good central **restaurant** is *Café Leffe* (℗02.97.21.21.30; closed Jan), in the same building as the tourist office, facing the port, which is particularly strong on seafood. Celts are famed for their **pubs**, and there's a fine selection in Lorient: you can get good, hearty meat and fish dishes at *Tavarn ar Boue Morvan* on place Polig-Monjarret (℗02.97.21.61.57), as well as home-made cider and live traditional music; *Galway Inn* on 18 rue Belgique (℗02.97.64.50.77) is the Irish–Celtic alternative, with Guinness and rock instead.

The Inter-Celtic Festival

The main reason visitors come to Lorient is for the **Inter-Celtic Festival**, held for ten days from the first Friday to the second Sunday in August. The largest Celtic event anywhere, it welcomes representatives from all the Celtic nations of Europe – Brittany, Ireland, Scotland, Wales, Cornwall, the Isle of Man, Asturias and Galicia. In a celebration of cultural solidarity, well over half a million people come to more than a hundred different shows, five languages mingle, and Scotch and Guinness flow with French and Spanish wines and ciders. There's a certain competitive element, with championships in various categories, but mutual enthusiasm and conviviality is paramount. Various activities – embracing music, dance and literature – take place all over the city, with mass celebrations around both the central place Jules-Ferry and the fishing harbour, and the biggest concerts at the local football stadium, the Parc du Moustoir.

For full schedules, which are not usually finalized until June, see ⓦfestival -interceltique.com. Tickets for the largest events should be reserved well in advance.

Carnac and around

CARNAC is the most important prehistoric site in Europe – in fact this spot is thought to have been continuously inhabited longer than anywhere else in the world. Its **alignments** of two thousand or so menhirs stretch over 4km, with great burial tumuli dotted amid them. In use since at least 5700 BC, the site long predates Knossos, the Pyramids, Stonehenge and the great Egyptian temples of the same name at Karnak. As a holiday centre, Carnac has a special charm, especially in late spring and early autumn when it is less crowded – and cheaper.

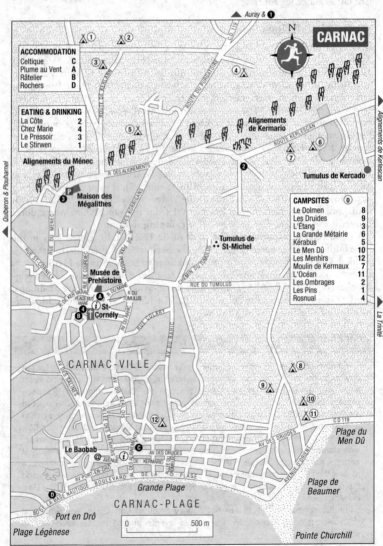

Auray & ①

CARNAC

N

ACCOMMODATION
Celtique   C
Plume au Vent   A
Râtelier   B
Rochers   D

EATING & DRINKING
La Côte   2
Chez Marie   4
Le Pressoir   3
Le Stirwen   1

Alignements du Ménec

Alignements de Kermario

ROUTE KERLESCAN

Tumulus de Kercado

Alignements de Kerlescan

R. DES ALIGNEMENTS

Maison des Mégalithes

RUE DU MÉNEC

RUE DES KORRIGANS

RUE ST-CORNÉLY

RUE DE KER VARKER

R. DE LA COURDIEC

Tumulus de St-Michel

CHEMIN DU TUMULUS

RUE DU TUMULUS

RUE DU TUMULUS

CAMPSITES   ⓞ
Le Dolmen   8
Les Druides   9
L'Étang   3
La Grande Métairie   6
Kérabus   5
Le Men Dû   10
Les Menhirs   12
Moulin de Kermaux   7
L'Océan   11
Les Ombrages   2
Les Pins   1
Rosnual   4

Musée de Préhistoire

PLACE DU MANÉ

St-Cornély

AV. DU KERLOIS

R DU MANÉ

AV. DES SALINES

CARNAC-VILLE

ALLÉE DES MENHIRS

Le Baobab

AV. DES DRUIDES

AV DES DRUIDES

Plage du Men Dû

AVENUE D'ORIENT

AVENUE

AL. DES ALIGNEMENTS

AV. DE KERMARIO

ALLÉE DES ORMES

AV. PORT-EN-DRO

BOULEVARD DE LA PLAGE

BD DE LA BASE NAUTIQUE

Grande Plage

CARNAC-PLAGE

Plage de Beaumer

Port en Drô

Plage Légénèse

Pointe Churchill

0   500 m

C.D 119

La Trinité

Quiberon & Plouharnel

Arrival and information

In July and August, when the Tire-Bouchon **rail** link runs between Auray and Quiberon, trains call at Plouharnel, 4km northwest of Carnac. The main **tourist office**, where **buses** from Auray, Quiberon and Vannes stop, is slightly back from the main beach at 74 av des Druides (July & Aug daily 9am–7pm, Sun 3–7pm; Sept–June Mon–Sat 9.30am–12.30pm & 2–6pm; ℡02.97.52.13.52, Ⓦot-carnac .fr). **Bicycles** can be rented from Le Randonneur, 20 av des Druides, Carnac-Plage (℡02.97.52.02.55), or local campsites like the *Grande Métairie* (see below), which also arranges horseback tours. There's a **market** in Carnac-Ville on Wednesday and Sunday mornings.

Accommodation

Hotel prices in Carnac are among the most expensive in all Brittany, and at a premium in July and August. As befits such a family-oriented place, Carnac features as many as twenty **campsites**. Among the best are the three-star *Dolmen* (℡02.97.52.12.35, Ⓦcampingledolmen.com; closed Oct–March; up to €27), an easy walk from the sea just north of Carnac-Plage, or the more expensive four-star *Grande Métairie* (℡02.97.52.24.01, Ⓦlagrandemetairie.com; closed early Sept to late March; up to €43), near the Kercado tumulus.

Celtique 82 av des Druides, Carnac-Plage ℡02.97.52.14.15, Ⓦhotel-celtique.com. Luxurious option, by the beach and affiliated to Best Western, with an indoor pool, spa and billiard room. ❼

🏃 **Plume au Vent** 4 venelle Notre-Dame, Carnac-Ville ℡06.16.98.34.79, Ⓦplume -au-vent.com. Central, welcoming and brilliantly decorated B&B, drawing tastefully on the nautical theme (for once), with pastel colours and some great found artefacts. ❺

Râtelier 4 chemin de Douët, Carnac-Ville ℡02.97.52.05.04, Ⓦle-ratelier.com. Old, ivy-clad stone hotel with comfortable rooms characterized by rustic colours and open wooden beams; some have showers but not toilets. Top-quality food on *menus* from €22.50. Restaurant closed Tues & Wed Oct–Easter, hotel closed mid-Nov to mid-Dec & all Jan. ❹

Rochers 6 bd de la Base Nautique, Carnac-Plage ℡02.97.52.10.09, Ⓦwww.les-rochers.com. This well-kept, family-friendly hotel is the best beach-front value, especially if you want a sea-view balcony. Closed Nov–Easter. ❻

The town and beaches

Divided between the original **Carnac-Ville** and the seaside resort of **Carnac-Plage**, Carnac swarms with holiday-makers in July and August. For most, the alignments are, if anything, only a sideshow. The town and seafront remain well wooded, and the tree-lined avenues and gardens are a delight, the climate being mild enough for evergreen oak and Mediterranean mimosa to grow alongside native stone pine and cypress.

The rather dry **Musée de Préhistoire**, at 10 place de la Chapelle (April–June & Sept Wed–Mon 10am–12.30pm & 2–6pm; July & Aug daily 10am–6pm; Oct–March Wed–Mon 10am–12.30pm & 2–5pm; €5; Ⓦwww.museedecarnac.com), traces the history of the area from earliest times, starting with 450,000-year-old chipping tools and leading by way of the Neanderthals to the megalith builders and beyond (descriptions are in French only). As well as authentic physical relics, it holds reproductions and casts of the carvings at Locmariaquer, a scale model of the Alignements de Menec, and diagrams of how the stones may have been moved into place.

The town's five **beaches** extend for nearly 3km in total. The two most attractive, usually counted as one of the five, are **plages Men Dû** and **Beaumer**, which lie to the east towards La Trinité beyond Pointe Churchill. They're especially popular these days with **kite surfers**.

The megaliths of Carnac

The **megaliths** of Carnac make up three distinct major alignments, running roughly in the same northeast–southwest direction, but each with a slightly separate orientation. These are the **Alignements de Menec**, "the place of stones" or "place of remembrance", with 1169 stones in eleven rows; the **Alignements de Kermario**, "the place of the dead", with 1029 stones in ten rows; and the **Alignements de Kerlescan**, "the place of burning", with 555 stones in thirteen lines. All three are sited parallel to the sea alongside the **Route des Alignements**, 1km or so to the north of Carnac-Ville.

Visitors are only allowed to walk freely around the best-preserved sites between October and March (daily 10am–5pm). Access between April and September is on guided tours only (€4.50), some of which are in English. A tour is worthwhile as without any background, you can feel as though you're simply staring at rocks in a field. To pick up the tour schedule, see some interesting displays, examine a model of the entire site, and buy books and maps, call in at the official visitor centre, the **Maison des Mégalithes**, across the road from the Alignements de Menec (daily: May & June 9am–7pm, July & Aug 9am–8pm, Sept–April 10am–5pm; ☏02.97.52.29.81, ⊛carnac.monuments-nationaux.fr).

Eating and drinking

Besides some good hotel **restaurants**, Carnac has a range of eating options – the better ones found away from the beach – and a busy nightlife fuelled by the large seasonal-worker population.

La Côte 3 impasse Parc-er-Forn ☏02.97.52.02.80, ⊛restaurant-la-cote.com. An old stone building, but with inventive, modern gourmet cuisine, which you can try at lunch for just €25, or from €35 in the evening. Closed all Mon and Tues eve, plus Sun eve Sept–June.

The megaliths of Brittany

Along with Newgrange in Ireland, Stonehenge in England and the Ring of Brodgar in the Orkneys, the tumuli, alignments and single standing stones of Brittany are of pre-eminent importance among the **Megalithic sites** of Europe. Dated at 5700 BC, the tumulus of Kercado at Carnac is the earliest known stone construction in Europe. Little is known of their creators; the few skeletons found in graves here indicate a short, dark, hairy race with a life expectancy of no more than the mid-30s. What is certain is that their civilization was long-lasting; the earliest and the latest constructions at Carnac are over five thousand years apart.

Each megalithic centre had its own distinct styles and traditions. Brittany has relatively few stone circles, or **cromlechs**, and a greater proportion of free-standing stones, **menhirs**; fewer burial chambers, known as **dolmens**, and more evidence of ritual fires; and different styles of carving. Carnac's alignments are unique in their sheer complexity.

As for their actual **purpose**, the most fashionable theory sees them as part of a vast astronomical observatory centred on the fallen Grand Menhir of Locmariaquer. However, controversy rages as to whether the Grand Menhir ever stood at all, or, even if it did, whether it fell or was broken up before the surrounding sites came into being. Moreover, sceptics say, these measurements ignore the fact that the sea level in southern Brittany 6600 years ago was 10m lower than it is today. Alternative theories interpret the menhirs as a series of territorial or memorial markers. This annual or occasional setting-up of a new stone is easier to envisage than the vast effort required to erect them all at once – in which case the fact that they were arranged in lines, mounds and circles might have been of peripheral importance.

Chez Marie 3 place de l'Église ☎ 02.97.52.07.93. A old favourite in Carnac-Ville, this busy stone-clad, crêperie serves good €12 *menus*, including a full *galette*. Closed Nov to early Feb.
Le Pressoir By the Ménec alignments ☎ 02.97.52.01.86. Good crêperie that prides itself on natural ingredients and serves more-ish local cider. Closed Sept–Easter.
Le Stirwen ☎ 02.97.52.80.80. Nightclub institution in the woods just north of town, which draws heavily on the crowd of seasonal workers. Open weekends in season, until 4am.

Locmariaquer

LOCMARIAQUER stands right at the narrow mouth of the Gulf of Morbihan. On the ocean side, there's a long sandy beach, on the Gulf side, a small tidal port. Like Carnac, however, the main reason to visit Locmariaquer is for its fine crop of **megaliths**.

Its principal site (daily: May & June 10am–6pm, July & Aug 10am–7pm; Sept–April 10am–12.30pm & 2–5.15pm; €5, under-18s free; ⓦ locmariaquer .monuments-nationaux.fr) was thought until 1991 to hold two monuments – the broken fragments of the **Grand Menhir Brisé**, which having originally stood twenty metres tall is the largest ever discovered, and a massive dolmen, the **Table des Marchands**. Then archeologists realized that the car park had inadvertently been created atop a third, even larger relic. Now known as **Er Grah**, it consists of a series of partially reconstructed stone terraces, the purpose of which remains unknown.

Locmariaquer holds a couple of reasonable small **hotels**, both with good restaurants: *L'Escale*, on the waterfront at 2 place Dariorigum (☎ 02.97.57.32.51, ⓦ escale-hotel.com; ❸; closed Oct–March), and the more basic *Lautram,* set slightly back on place de l'Église (☎ 02.97.57.31.32, ⓦ hotel-golfe-morbihan .com; ❷; closed Oct–March). **Campsites** in Locmariaquer include the excellent *Ferme Fleurie* (☎ 02.97.57.34.06, ⓦ campinglafermefleurie.com; €15; closed Dec & Jan), 1km towards Kerinis, and the *Lann Brick* (☎ 02.97.57.32.79, ⓦ www .camping-lannbrick.com; €18.50; closed Nov to mid-March), 1.5km further on, nearer the beach.

The Presqu'île de Quiberon

The **Presqu'île de Quiberon**, south of Carnac, is as close to being an island as any peninsula could conceivably be; the long causeway of sand that links it to the mainland narrows to as little as 50m in places. In summer, it's packed with tourists, here not so much for the towns, which, other than lively **Quiberon**, are generally featureless, but to use them as a base for trips out to **Belle-Île** or around the peninsula's contrasting coastline. The ocean-facing shore, known as the **Côte Sauvage**, is wild and highly unswimmable, where the stormy seas look like snowy mountain tops. The sheltered eastern side has safe and calm sandy beaches, and plenty of campsites.

Quiberon

Despite recent construction on the peninsula, **QUIBERON**, at the peninsula's southern tip, is still the only real town. Its most active area, **Port-Maria**, is home to the **gare maritime** for the islands of Belle-Île, Houat and Hoëdic, and also has a sardine-fishing harbour of former glory.

Arrival and information

In July and August, the special Tire-Bouchon ("corkscrew") **train** links Quiberon's *gare SNCF*, a short way above the town proper, with Auray. Bus #1 (TIM; ☎02.97.24.26.20) runs right to the *gare maritime* from Vannes, via Auray and Carnac.

The **tourist office**, 14 rue de Verdun (July & Aug daily 9am–1pm & 2–7pm; Sept–June Mon–Sat 9am–12.30pm & 2–5.30pm; ☎08.25.13.56.00, ⊛quiberon .com), has a 24-hour computer terminal outside showing which hotels are full, hour by hour. **Bicycles** can be rented from Cycl'omar, 47 place Hoche (☎02.97.50.26.00, ⊛cyclomar.com).

Accommodation

For most of the year, it's hard to get a **room** in Quiberon. In July and August, the whole peninsula is packed, while in winter it's so quiet that virtually all its facilities close down. The nicest area to stay is along the seafront in Port-Maria, where several good hotel-restaurants face the Belle-Île ferry terminal.

Au Bon Accueil 6 quai de Houat ☎02.97.50.07.92. Seafront hotel that's Port-Maria's best option for budget travellers. The rooms are basic but inexpensive, and there's a good restaurant downstairs. Closed mid-Nov to mid-Feb. ❷

De la Mer 8 quai de Houat ☎02.97.50.09.05, ⊛hotel-de-la-mer.fr. Blue-trimmed hotel at the western end of Port-Maria's seafront strip, offering adequate comfort and sea views from some rooms, but rather poor en-suite bathrooms. Heated swimming pool, and another good restaurant. Closed mid-Nov to March, & Thurs. ❹

Filets Bleus 45 rue du Roc'h-Priol ☎02.97.50.15.54, ⊛fuaj.org/quiberon. Well-situated but basic hostel, where some rooms don't have windows. Better to camp under the pine trees in the back. €11.20, camping €6 or €8 if you use the tents they provide. Closed Sept–March.

Neptune 4 quai de Houat ☎02.97.50.09.62, ⊛hotel-neptune-quiberon.com. Great-value hotel, where all rooms have either sea or garden views – some with private balconies – and there's a very good restaurant (see below) with a terrace overlooking the water. Closed Jan to mid-Feb, plus Mon in low season. ❹

The Town

At Quiberon's centre is a busy little park and miniature golf course, but few of the streets further back hold anything of great interest. The exception is the little hill that leads down to the port from the **gare SNCF**, where browsing around is rewarded with some surprisingly good clothes and antique shops. Stretching away to the east of the harbour is a long curve of fine sandy **beach**, lined for several hundred yards with bars, cafés and restaurants.

Eating and drinking

A line of seafood **restaurants** compete to attract ferry passengers at Port-Maria. As for **cafés**, those by the long bathing beach are the most enjoyable.

Chaumine 36 place de Manémeur ☎02.97.50.17.67. Manémeur is technically a separate village, though it's not too far to walk around the headland west of the port. Set close to the menhir in the main square, this lovely little fish restaurant serves *menus* from €19, with a €28 option featuring salmon braised in champagne. Closed Mon, plus Sun eve in low season; closed altogether early Nov to March.

De la Criée 11 quai de l'Océan ☎02.97.30.53.09. Superb local fish

restaurant, serving whatever may be fresh from the morning's catch; choose from the baskets arrayed along the front. For €21, you can get either the one set *menu*, which may include ling and sea bass, for example, or a great seafood couscous. Closed Jan & Sun eve & Mon in low season.

Neptune 4 quai de Houat ☎02.97.50.09.62. Hotel dining room that serves exceptionally good seafood *menus* at €19 and €23. The portions are small, but the food is exquisite. Closed Jan & Mon in low season.

Belle-Île

Considerably larger than the other Breton islands, gorgeous **BELLE-ÎLE**, 15km or 45 minutes by ferry south of Quiberon, feels significantly less isolated than the rest, what with its bus tours and traffic. However, its towns – **Le Palais**, **Sauzon** and **Bangor** – are consistently lovely, and it offers wonderful opportunities for walking and cycling. At different times in its turbulent history the island belonged to the monks of Redon, the English – who in 1761 swapped it for Menorca – and Lorient's Companie des Indes.

Docking at the port and main town of **LE PALAIS**, the abrupt star-shaped fortifications of the **citadelle** are the first thing you see. Built along stylish and ordered lines by the great fortress-builder, Vauban, it is startling in size – filled with doorways leading to mysterious cellars and underground passages and deserted cells. Much of it has recently been converted into an expensive hotel, but it still houses a **museum**, documenting the island's history in fiction as much as in fact (daily: April–June, Sept & Oct 9.30am–6pm; July & Aug 9am–7pm; Nov–March 9.30am–5pm; €6.50; ⓦcitadellevauban.com).

The island is far too large to stroll round, but a coastal footpath runs on bare soil for the length of the exposed **Côte Sauvage** with its sparse heather-covered cliffs facing out into the sea. To appreciate this and the rich and fertile landward side, some form of transport is advisable – **rental bikes** are widely available in Le Palais.

Near the west end you'll find the **Grotte de l'Apothicairerie**, so called because it was once full of cormorants' nests, arranged like the jars on a pharmacist's shelves. Inland, on the D25 back towards Le Palais, you pass the two **menhirs**, Jean and Jeanne, said to be lovers petrified as punishment for wanting to meet before

Getting to Belle-Île, Houat and Hoëdic

All year, **Compagnie-Océane** (☏08.20.05.61.56, or 02.97.35.02.00, ⓦwww .compagnie-oceane.fr) sends at least six **ferries** daily – and up to fifteen in high summer – from **Port-Maria** on the Quiberon peninsula to **Le Palais** on Belle-Île. The first departure is around 8am, and the crossing normally takes 45 minutes, though the high-speed vessel *Locmaria 56* makes up to five crossings daily between mid-April and August in just 20 minutes. The return fare is €28.15. Small cars can be taken on the slower crossings only, for €134.30 return, while bikes cost €16.70 return. Reserve in advance during peak periods. Between early July and the end of August, the same company also sends the *Locmaria 56* on one daily trip to **Sauzon** from **Port-Maria**, for the same fare. Compagnie-Océane also runs between one and six daily ferries to **Houat** and **Hoëdic** all year, to widely varying schedules (40min to Houat, another 25min to Hoëdic; €29.65 return).

From early April until September, **Compagnie des Îles** (☏08.25.13.41.40, ⓦcompagniedesiles.com) also connects Port-Maria with both **Le Palais** and **Sauzon** on Belle-Île, operating two services daily except Monday for most of the season, and three daily between mid-July and late August (€27 return). The same company also sails direct to Le Palais from La Turballe (☏08.25.13.41.80), between Piriac and Guérande on the coast not far north of La Baule. The crossing takes 1 hour 45 minutes (sporadic sailings May to mid-July & late Aug to end Sept; early July to late Aug daily; €39 return, under-15s €24.50). Between early July and late Aug, they also run day-trips from **Le Croisic** (☏08.25.13.41.70; same fares).

From April until mid-October, **Navix** (☏08.25.13.21.00, ⓦnavix.fr; €30–44) operates day-trips to Belle-Île from **Vannes**, **Locmariaquer**, and Port-Navalo. In July & Aug they run afternoon excursions to **Houat** from **La Trinité**, to a very irregular schedule (€28.50).

their marriage. Another larger menhir used to lie near these two; it was broken up to help construct the road that separates them.

If you're staying any length of time, Belle-Île's second town, **SAUZON**, a beautiful little village arrayed along one side of a long estuary, or inland town of **Bangor** present less touristy places to base yourself.

Practicalities

Belle-Île's **tourist office** is next to the **gare maritime** in Le Palais (July & Aug Mon–Sat 8.45am–7pm, Sun 8.45am–1pm; Sept–June Mon–Sat 9am–12.30pm & 2–6pm; ℡02.97.31.81.93, ⓦwww.belle-ile.com). Several waterfront outlets, including Didier Banet (℡02.97.31.84.74, ⓦwww.location2roues.com), rent **bikes** at around €12 per day, while Locatourisle (℡02.97.31.83.56, ⓦlocatourisle .com), rents **cars**, from around €65 per day. Belle-Île also has its own **bus** system (℡02.97.31.32.32, ⓦtaol-mor.com), offering around eight daily connections in summer to each of Sauzon, Bangor and Locmaria.

Accommodation in Le Palais includes the simple *Frégate*, above a nice little bar on the quayside (℡02.97.31.54.16; ❸; closed mid-Nov to March), and the comfortable *Atlantique* (℡02.97.31.80.11, ⓦhotel-atlantique.com; ❸), which has an excellent sea-view **restaurant**. There are also three **campsites**, including the three-star *Camping de l'Océan* (℡02.97.31.83.86, ⓦcamping-ocean-belle-ile.com; €19; closed Oct–March), and an often fully booked **hostel** (℡02.97.31.81.33, ⓦfuaj.org/belle-ile-en-mer; €13.20; closed Oct), a short way out of town along the clifftops from the citadelle at Haute-Boulogne.

Sauzon has one good hotel in a magnificent setting, the 🍴 *Du Phare* (℡02.97.31.60.36, ⓦhotelduphare.blogspot.com; ❸; closed Nov–March), which serves delicious fish dinners with *menus* from €17.50, and two two-star **campsites**, including *Pen Prad* (℡02.97.31.64.82, ⓦwww.sauzon.fr; €8.70; closed Oct–March). Across the island on the wilder south shore, outside Bangor, the orange-pink *Grand Large* (℡02.97.31.80.92, ⓦhotelgrandlarge.com; ❺; closed Nov to late March), charges premium rates for its finest sea views.

Houat and Hoëdic

You can't take your car to Belle-Île's two smaller sisters, **Houat** and **Hoëdic**. Known as the *"îles de silence"*, both islands have a feeling of being left behind by the passing centuries. However, the younger fishermen of Houat have revived the island's fortunes by establishing a successful fishing cooperative, and it also holds excellent **beaches** – as ever on the sheltered (eastern) side – that fill up with campers in the summer (even though camping is not strictly legal). The more traditional and less developed Hoëdic on the other hand has a large municipal **campsite**, overlooking the port (℡02.97.52.48.88; closed Sept–June; €7). There are a couple of small **hotels** on Houat – *L'Ezenn* (℡02.97.30.69.73; ❸; closed Feb) and the pricier *Hôtel-Restaurant des Îles* (℡02.97.30.68.02, ⓦhouat.chez.com; ❹; closed Nov–Jan) – and one on Hoëdic, *Les Cardinaux* (℡02.97.52.37.27, ⓔhotel-les -cardinaux@orange.fr; ❹; closed Feb, plus Sun pm & Mon in winter).

The Golfe de Morbihan and Vannes

The sheltered **Golfe du Morbihan** – *mor bihan* means "little sea" in Breton – is one of the loveliest stretches of Brittany's coast. While its only large town, medieval **Vannes**, is well worth visiting, its endlessly indented shoreline is the major attraction, with superb vistas at every turn, and countless secluded **beaches**.

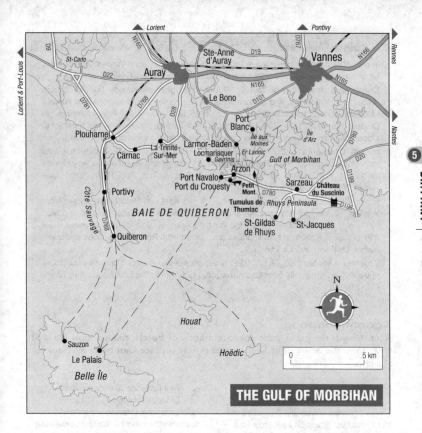

THE GULF OF MORBIHAN

By popular tradition the gulf used to hold an **island** for every day of the year, but rising seas have left fewer than one per week. A **boat tour** around them, or at least a trip out to **Gavrinis** near the mouth of the gulf, is a compelling experience, with megalithic ruins and stone circles dotted around the beguiling maze of channels and solitary menhirs looking down from small hillocks.

Vannes

At the head of the Golfe de Morbihan, **VANNES**, southern Brittany's major tourist town, is such a large and thriving community that the size of the small walled town at its core, **Vieux Vannes**, may well come as a surprise. Its focal point, the old gateway of the **Porte St-Vincent**, commands a busy little square at the northern end of a canalized port leading to the gulf itself. Inside the ramparts, the winding car-free streets – crammed around the cathedral, and enclosed by gardens and a tiny stream – are great strolling territory.

Arrival and information

Vannes' **gare SNCF** and **gare routière** (☎02.97.01.22.01, ⓦlactm.com) face each other 25 minutes' walk north of the centre. **Parking** can be a problem, but there's plenty of space on Quai Tabarly on the port's west side, near the **tourist office** (July & Aug Mon–Sat 9am–7pm, Sun 10am–6pm; Sept–June Mon–Sat 9.30am–noon & 2–6pm; ☎08.25.13.56.10, ⓦtourisme-vannes.com).

Gulf tours

In season, dozens of boats leave for **gulf tours** each day from Vannes, Port Navalo, La Trinité, Locmariaquer, Auray, Le Bono and Larmor-Baden. Options include:

Compagnie des Îles ☎08.25.13.41.00, ⓦcompagniedesiles.com. Daily gulf tours (€15–29) from **Vannes**, and a more limited programme of cruises from **Port Navalo** (☎08.25.13.41.20), **Locmariaquer** (☎08.25.13.41.30), and **Port-Haliguen** in Quiberon (☎08.25.13.41.40). The price of each cruise depends on the number of stops you make, with possibilities of getting off at Île aux Moines and Île d'Arz.

Izenah Croisières ☎02.97.57.23.24 or 02.97.26.31.45, ⓦwww.izenah-croisieres .com. Gulf tours from **Port Blanc** at **Baden** in summer, and a year-round ferry service to the Île aux Moines (daily every 30min: July & Aug 7am–10pm, Sept–June 7am–7.30pm; €4.10 return).

Navix ☎08.25.13.21.00, ⓦnavix.fr. Between mid-April and September, cruises from **Vannes** include half-day (€22.50) and full-day (€29) trips around the gulf, and also lunch and dinner cruises, where the cost depends on your choice of *menu* (total €50–56). Similar tours at similar prices also depart from **Port Navalo**, **Locmariaquer**, **Auray**, **Le Bono** and **La Trinité**.

Vedettes Angelus ☎02.97.57.30.29, ⓦvedettes-angelus.com. Up to five gulf tours of varying le ngths daily from **Locmariaquer** (mid-April to Sept; first departure 10am; €13–25).

Accommodation

Vannes holds the gulf's greatest concentration of **hotels**, though most are well away from the centre. The liveliest area to stay is **place Gambetta** overlooking the port.

Hotels

Le Bretagne 36 rue du Méné ☎02.97.47.20.21, ⓦhotel-lebretagne-vannes.com. Reasonable and friendly hotel just outside the walls, around the corner from the Porte-Prison, with nicely refitted en-suite rooms. ❸

Escale Océania av Jean-Monnet ☎02.97.47.59.60, ⓦoceaniahotels.com. Dependable upscale hotel a short walk northwest of the walled town, offering 65 large, soundproofed, en-suite and air-conditioned rooms, plus an adequate restaurant that's closed at weekends, when hotel rates are cheaper. ❺

Marina 4 place Gambetta ☎02.97.47.00.10, ⓦhotellemarina.fr. Fifteen pleasantly refurbished but plain rooms – double-glazed to keep the noise out – above a busy bar right by the port with sea views and morning sun. En-suite facilities cost €5 extra. ❷

Villa Catherine 89 av du Président Édouard-Herriot ☎02.97.42.48.59, ⓦvilla-catherine.fr. Charming four-room B&B, in a late nineteenth-century townhouse, restored using ecologically sustainable materials, and serving an entirely organic breakfast. ❺

Hostel and campsite

Camping Conleau Av du Maréchal-Juin ☎02.97.63.13.88, ⓔcamping@mairie-vannes.fr. Very pleasant three-star municipal campsite, the closest to central Vannes, is set right beside the gulf at the far end of avenue du Maréchal-Juin, 2km southwest of the centre. €18 for two with car. Closed Oct–March.

Centre International de Séjour Rte de Moustérian, Séné ☎02.97.66.94.25, ⓦlesasterides.com. Budget hostel, with dorm beds at €13.50, 4km southeast of the town centre on bus route #4 from place de la République. Closed July & Aug.

The Town

Modern Vannes centres on **place de la République**; the focus was shifted outside the medieval city during the nineteenth-century craze for urbanization. The grandest of the public buildings here, guarded by a pair of sleek bronze lions, is the **Hôtel de Ville** at the top of rue Thiers. By day, however, the streets of the old

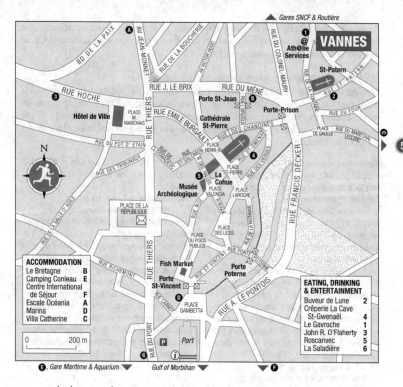

▲ Gares SNCF & Routière

VANNES

ACCOMMODATION
Le Bretagne   **B**
Camping Conleau   **E**
Centre International
de Séjour   **F**
Escale Océania   **A**
Marina   **D**
Villa Catherine   **C**

EATING, DRINKING
& ENTERTAINMENT
Buveur de Lune   **2**
Crêperie La Cave
St-Gwenaël   **4**
Le Gavroche   **1**
John R. O'Flaherty   **3**
Roscanvec   **5**
La Saladière   **6**

0   200 m

E, Gare Maritime & Aquarium ▼   Gulf of Morbihan ▼   ▼ **F**

BRITTANY | The Golfe de Morbihan and Vannes

---

city, with their overhanging, witch-hatted houses and busy commercial life, are the chief source of pleasure.

La Cohue, an impressive building on place St-Pierre, was where the Breton *États* assembled in 1532 to ratify the Act of Union with France. It currently houses the **Musée des Beaux Arts** (daily: June–Sept 10am–6pm; Oct–May 1.30–6pm; €6 with history museum), of interest primarily for its temporary exhibitions. Opposite, the **Cathédrale St-Pierre** is a rather forbidding place, with a stern main altar almost imprisoned by four solemn grey pillars. Light, purple through new stained glass, spears in to illuminate the desiccated finger of the Blessed Pierre Rogue, who was guillotined on the main square in 1796.

A sombre fifteenth-century mansion at 2 rue Noé holds Vannes' summer-only **Musée d'Histoire et Archéologie** (mid-May to mid-June daily 1.30–6pm, mid-June to Sept daily 10am–6pm; €6 with Beaux Arts museum). Its collection of prehistoric artefacts is said to be one of the world's finest, but they're tediously arrayed in formal patterns in glass cases, and the Middle Ages exhibit on the upper floors is more entertaining.

Vannes' major tourist attraction, its modern **aquarium**, 500m south of place Gambetta in the **Parc du Golfe**, claims to hold Europe's finest collection of tropical fish (daily: April–June & Sept 10am–noon & 2–6pm; July & Aug 9am–7.30pm; Oct–March 2–6pm, except school hols 10am–noon & 2–6pm; adults €10.80, under-12s €7.50; ⓦaquarium-du-golfe.com). Certainly it holds some pretty extraordinary specimens, including a type of fish from Venezuela with four sexes and four eyes; cave fish from Mexico that have no eyes at all; and *arowana* from Guyana, which jump two metres out of the water to catch birds.

373

Alongside, the separate **Jardin aux Papillons**, or Butterfly Garden, consists of a huge glass dome containing hundreds of free-flying butterflies (same hours; €9, or €16 for combined ticket with aquarium).

Eating, drinking and entertainment

Dining out in old Vannes can be expensive, whether you eat in the intimate little restaurants along the rue des Halles, or down by the port. Other, cheaper restaurants abound in the St-Patern quarter, outside the walls in the northeast. At the end of July, the open-air concerts of the **Vannes Jazz Festival** take place in the Théâtre de Verdure.

Buveur de Lune 8 rue Saint-Patern ⊕02.97.54.32.32. A relaxed and good-natured spot for a drink with the night sky across the ceiling and fairly priced drinks. Closed Mon & Tues.
Crêperie La Cave St-Gwenaël 23 rue St-Gwenaël ⊕02.97.47.47.94. Atmospheric, good-value crêperie in the cellar of a lovely old house, alongside the cathedral. Closed Sun, plus Mon Sept–June, & all Jan.
Le Gavroche 17 rue de la Fontaine Pasteur ⊕02.97.54.03.54, ⊛www.restaurant -legavroche.com. A godsend for meat-lovers in a region dominated by seafood. Here the steaks are cooked to perfection and original starters such as pig's trotters – along with the complimentary glass of home-made rum – will put hairs on your chest. *Menus* start from €15.50. Closed Sun.
John R. O'Flaherty 22 rue Hoche ⊕02.97.42.40.11. A real Irish pub with the right ales on tap, various bits of junk on the walls and traditional Irish folk live on Friday nights. Closed Sun.
Roscanvec 17 rue des Halles ⊕02.97.47.15.96, ⊛roscanvec.com. Superb formal restaurant, in a lovely half-timbered house, with some outdoor seating. Lunch at €25 is a bargain, while even the cheapest dinner *menu*, at €30, features unusual dishes such as *carbonara d'huîtres*. Given the standard, you might even be tempted by the €60 *Dégustation menu*. Closed Sun in summer, Sun eve & all Mon Sept–June.
La Saladière 36 rue du Port ⊕02.97.42.52.10, ⊛lasaladiere-vannes.com. Large, tasty, fresh-made salads for €11–15, in an inexpensive restaurant just west of the port, which also serves full lunch *menus* from €10 and dinner from €16. Closed Sun in low season.

Gavrinis

The reason to visit the island of **Gavrinis**, which can only be reached on guided boat tours from Larmor-Baden, the closest spot on the mainland immediately north, is its **megalithic site**. The most impressive and remarkable in Brittany, it stands comparison with Newgrange in Ireland and – in shape as well as size and age – with the earliest pyramids of Egypt.

The megalithic structure is essentially a **tumulus**, an earth mound covering a stone cairn and "passage grave". However, half of the mound has been peeled back and the side of the cairn that faces the water was reconstructed to make a facade resembling a step-pyramid. Inside, every stone of both passage and chamber is covered in carvings, with a restricted "alphabet" of fingerprint whorls, axe-heads and other conventional signs, including the spirals familiar in Ireland but seen only here in Brittany.

Gavrinis can be reached between March and November only. Tides permitting, **ferries** leave Larmor-Baden at half-hourly intervals, and the cost includes a 45-minute guided tour of the cairn (April, June & Sept daily 9.30am–12.30pm & 1.30–6.30pm; May Mon–Fri 1.30–6.30pm, Sat & Sun 9.30am–12.30pm & 1.30–6.30pm; July & Aug daily 9.30am–12.30pm & 1.30–7pm; March, Oct & Nov daily except Wed 1.30–5pm; €12; ⊕02.97.57.19.38, ⊛gavrinis.info). The last boats of the morning and afternoon leave Larmor-Baden an hour and a half before the closing time.

South to the Loire

When you cross the **Vilaine** on the way south, you're not only leaving the Morbihan *département* but also technically leaving Brittany itself. Roads veer firmly east and west, avoiding the marshes of the **Grande-Brière**. For centuries these 20,000 acres of peat bog have been deemed to be the common property of all who lived in them. The scattered population, the *Brièrons*, still make their living by fishing for eels in the streams, gathering reeds and – on the nine days permitted each year – cutting peat. Tourism has arrived relatively recently, and is resented. The touted attraction is renting a punt to get yourself lost for a few hours with your pole tangled in the rushes.

Guérande

No visitor to the region should miss the gorgeous walled town of **GUÉRANDE**, inland on the southwestern edge of the Grande-Brière marshes. Guérande derived its fortune from controlling the saltpans that form a chequerboard across the surrounding inlets. This "white country" is composed of bizarre-looking *oeillets*, each 70 to 80 square metres, in which sea-water has been collected and evaporated since Roman times, leaving piles of white salt.

A tiny little place, Guérande is still entirely enclosed by its stout fifteenth-century **ramparts**. A spacious promenade leads right the way around the outside, passing four fortified gateways; for half its length, the broad old moat remains filled with water. Within the walls, pedestrians throng the narrow cobbled streets during high season; the main souvenir on sale is locally produced salt, but abundant shops sell trinkets from all over the world, and there are lots of restaurants and crêperies. So long as the crowds aren't too oppressive, it makes a great day out, with the old houses bright with window-boxes. On Wednesdays and Saturdays, a market is in full swing in the centre, next to the **church of St-Aubin**.

Guérande's **tourist office** is just outside the Porte St-Michel at 1 place du Marché aux Bois (June & Sept Mon–Sat 9.30am–6pm; July & Aug Mon–Sat 9.30am–7pm; Oct–May Mon–Sat 9.30am–12.30pm & 1.30–6pm; ☏08.20.15.00.44, ⓦot-guerande.fr). Tucked out of sight behind the market, the pretty ⚜ *Roc-Maria*, 1 rue des Halles (☏02.40.24.90.51, ⓦhotelcreperierocmaria.com; ❹; closed Mon in low season), offers cosy **rooms** above a crêperie in a fifteenth-century town house. Also in the old town, by the Porte Vannetaise, the hugely attractive ⚜ *La Guérandière* (☏02.40.62.17.15, ⓦguerande.fr; ❹) is a beautifully restored and decorated manor-house **B&B**, where breakfast is served in a pleasant garden.

Piriac-sur-mer

Still readily recognizable as an old fishing village, but lively all through summer with holidaying families, **PIRIAC-SUR-MER**, 13km west from Guérande is a ravishing old-fashioned seaside resort that knocks the socks of its giant neighbour La Baule. Although the adjacent headland offers fine sandy **beaches** within a couple of minutes' walk from the centre, the village itself turns its back on the Atlantic, preferring to face the protective jetty that curls back into the little bay to shield its small fishing fleet and summer array of yachts.

The red-striped ⚜ *De la Plage*, at no. 2 on the quiet seafront place du Lehn (☏02.40.23.50.05, ⓦhoteldelaplage-piriac.com; ❷), is the most perfect French seaside **hotel** imaginable. The cheapest rooms lack en-suite facilities, but all are cheery and comfortable, and almost all have views of the sea.

La Baule

The upscale resort of **LA BAULE** may boast a wonderful crescent of sandy beach, but it feels utterly unlike the rest of Brittany. With its endless Riviera-style oceanfront boulevard, lined with palm-tree-fronted hotels and residences, it firmly imagines itself in the south of France. It can be fun if you feel like a break from the more subdued Breton attractions – and the beach is undeniably impressive. It's not a place to imagine you're going to enjoy strolling around in search of hidden charms, however; the backstreets have an oddly rural feel, but hold nothing of any interest.

La Baule's **gare SNCF**, served by TGVs from Paris, is on place Rhin-et-Danube, away from the seafront. The **tourist office** is nearby at 8 place de la Victoire, close to the *gare routière* (July & Aug daily 9.30am–7.30pm; Sept–June Mon & Wed–Sat 9.15am–12.30pm & 2–6pm, Tues 10.15am–12.30pm & 2–6pm, Sun 10am–1pm; ℡02.40.24.34.44, 🌐labaule.fr).

Few of the **hotels** are cheap, particularly in high season, and in low season more than half are closed. Relatively lower-priced options near the station include the comfortable *Marini*, 22 av Clemenceau (℡02.40.60.23.29; ④), while the *Mascotte*, 26 av Marie-Louise (℡02.40.60.26.55, 🌐la-mascotte.fr; ⑤), is a quieter and classier option less than 100m back from the beach.

Le Croisic

The small port of **LE CROISIC**, sheltering from the ocean around the corner of the headland, but stretching right across the peninsula, makes an attractive alternative to La Baule. These days it's basically a pleasure port, but fishing boats do still sail from its harbour, near the very slender mouth of the bay, and there's a modern **fish market** near the long Tréhic jetty, where you can watch the day's catch being auctioned.

Le Croisic holds a couple of excellent **hotels**: *Castel Moor*, 500m beyond the centre on the sheltered side of the headland (℡02.40.23.24.18, 🌐castel-moor .com; ④; closed Jan), where there's a good restaurant, and *Les Nids*, set slightly back from the ocean side at 15 rue Pasteur (℡02.40.23.00.63, 🌐hotellesnids .com; ④; closed Nov–March), which has a small indoor swimming pool.

Close by, all around the rocky sea coast known as the **Grande Côte**, are a range of **campsites**, including the *Océan* (℡02.40.23.07.69, 🌐camping-ocean.com; closed Oct–March; upto €42).

For equally good beaches, you could alternatively go east from La Baule to **PORNICHET** (though its overpriced, aseptic marina is worth avoiding) or to tiny **ST-MARC**, where in 1953 Jacques Tati filmed *Monsieur Hulot's Holiday*.

Nantes

Over the last decade, the rejuvenated, go-ahead city of **NANTES** has transformed itself into a likeable metropolis that deserves to figure on any tourist itinerary. At the heart of this ambitious regeneration project stands a must-see attraction, the **Machines de l'Île** – home of the Grand Éléphant – but the city as a whole is also scrubbed, gleaming, and suffused with a remarkable energy.

As the capital of an independent Brittany, Nantes was a considerable medieval centre. Great wealth came later, however, when it prospered from colonial expeditions, and was by the end of the eighteenth century the principal port of France. An estimated 500,000 Africans were carried into **slavery** in the Americas in vessels based here, and even after abolition in 1817 the trade continued illegally. Subsequently the

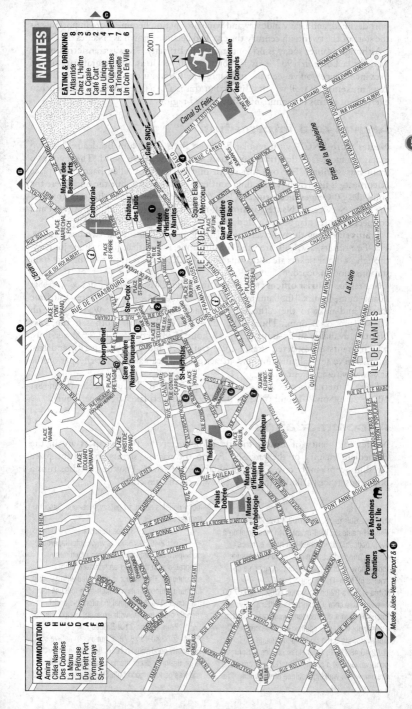

EATING & DRINKING

L'Atlantide	8
Chez L Huître	3
La Cigale	5
Café Cult'	2
Lieu Unique	4
Les Oubliettes	1
La Trinquette	7
Un Coin En Ville	6

0   200 m

N

ACCOMMODATION

Amiral	G
Citéa Nantes	H
Des Colonies	E
La Manu	C
La Pérouse	D
Du Petit Port	A
Pommeraye	F
St-Yves	B

port declined, and heavy industry and wine production became more important. At the start of the twentieth century the city had become known as "Nantes the Grey".

Although Nantes today is no longer even in Brittany – it was transferred to the Pays de la Loire in 1962 – its inhabitants still see it as an integral part of the province. Once you've seen the machines, the **Château des Ducs** and the **Beaux Arts museum** are well worth visiting, but this is also a place to enjoy a little urban excitement in this predominantly slow-paced region.

Arrival and information

Nantes' **gare SNCF**, with regular TGVs to Paris, Lyon and Bordeaux, has two exits; for most facilities (tramway, buses, hotels) use Accès Nord. There are two main **bus** stations. The one just south of the centre on allée Baco, near place Ricordeau, is used by buses heading south and southwest, while the one where the cours des 50 Otages meets rue de l'Hôtel de Ville serves routes that stay north of the river. Services to Nantes' **airport** (Ⓦnantes.aeroport.fr), 12km southwest and connected by regular buses, include daily flights from London City Airport.

Trams run along the old riverfront, past the *gare SNCF* and the two bus stations. Flat-fare tickets, at €1.80, are valid for one hour, rather than just a single journey, though 24-hour tickets are also available for €4.20. Tickets must be bought at tram stations, not on board.

Nantes has **tourist offices** at 3 cours Olivier-de-Clisson (Mon, Tues & Wed–Sat 10am–6pm, Thurs 10.30am–6pm; ℡08.92.46.40.44, Ⓦwww.nantes-tourisme .com), and next to the cathedral at 2 place St-Pierre (Tues, Wed & Fri–Sun 10am–1pm & 2–6pm, Thurs 10.30am–1pm & 2–6pm). Both sell the **Pass Nantes**, available in 24-hour (€18), 48-hour (€28) and 72-hour (€36) versions, which grants unrestricted use of local transport and some car parks, and free admission to several museums and attractions; you can also buy it cheaper online at Ⓦwww.resanantes.com.

There's internet access at **Cyberpl@net**, 18 rue de l'Arche Sèche (Mon–Sat 10am–2am, Sun 2–10pm; ℡02.51.82.47.97, Ⓦcyberplanet.fr; €3 per hour).

Accommodation

Nantes has plenty of **hotels** to suit all budgets; the two hotspots are in the immediate vicinity of the *gare SNCF*, and the narrow streets around the place Greslin. Surprisingly few are in the older part of town. The tourist office runs a booking service (℡08.92.46.40.44, Ⓦwww.resanantes.com).

Hotels

Amiral 26bis rue Scribe ℡02.40.69.20.21, Ⓦhotel-nantes.fr. Well-maintained little hotel on a lively pedestrianized street just north of place Graslin, and perfect for nightlife. All the en-suite rooms have double-glazing, but some noise still creeps in. Mon–Fri ❺, Sat & Sun ❸

Citéa Nantes 82 bd St-Aignan ℡02.28.20.07.00, Ⓦwww.citea.com. Comfortable suites at a great price, albeit in a dull residential neighbourhood, a ten-minute tram ride southwest of the centre. ❹

Des Colonies 5 rue du Chapeau Rouge ℡02.40.48.79.76, Ⓦhoteldescolonies.fr. Spruce, good-value hotel a couple of blocks up from place Graslin, within walking distance of everything. The lobby doubles as an art gallery. Weekend discount. No restaurant. ❹

La Pérouse 3 allée Duquesne ℡02.40.89.75.00, Ⓦwww.hotel-laperouse .fr. Superb contemporary building ingeniously integrated with the older architecture that surrounds it. The interior is decorated with 1930s furniture, stucco and high-tech touches like flat-screen TVs. An original, comfortable and friendly place to stay, with excellent breakfasts. ❺

Pommeraye 2 rue Boileau ℡02.40.48.78.79, Ⓦhotel-pommeraye.com. Extremely good-value modern boutique hotel with large, designer-decor rooms, beautiful bathrooms and free parking; good buffet breakfast for €9.40. ❹

St-Yves 154 rue du Général Buat ℡ 02.40.74.48.42, @ hotel-saintyves.fr. Very attractive, great-value little ten-room hotel, ten minutes' walk north of the railway station, with friendly staff, a nice garden and big breakfasts for €6.50. ❷

Hostel and campsite
La Manu 2 place de la Manufacture ℡ 02.40.29.29.20, @ fuaj.org/nantes. Nantes' hostel, which has a cafeteria, is housed in a postmodern former tobacco factory a few hundred metres east of the gare SNCF, five minutes from the centre on tramway #1. Beds in 4- or 6-bed dorms for €18.20 including breakfast. Reception daily 8am–noon & 4–10.30pm, closed mid-Dec to early Jan.
Du Petit Port 21 bd du Petit-Port ℡ 02.40.74.47.94, @ www.nge-nantes.fr/camping. Well-managed, four-star campsite, with a pool, in a pleasant tree-shaded setting north of the city centre on tram route #2 (stop "Morrhonnière"). Open all year.

The City

Huge redevelopment schemes are currently attempting to shift the focus of Nantes back towards the **Loire**, the original source of its riches. As recently as the 1930s, the river crossed the city in seven separate channels, but German labour as part of reparations for World War I filled in five of them. For the moment, however, the main distinction still lies between the older **medieval city**, concentrated around the cathedral, with the château prominent in its southeast corner, and the elegant **nineteenth-century town** to the west.

The old town

Though no longer on the waterfront, the **Château des Ducs** still preserves the form in which it was built by two of the last rulers of independent Brittany, François II, and his daughter Duchess Anne, born here in 1477. The list of famous people who have been guests or prisoners, defenders or belligerents, of the castle includes Gilles de Rais (Bluebeard), publicly executed in 1440; Machiavelli, in 1498; John Knox as a galley-slave in 1547–49; and Bonnie Prince Charlie preparing for Culloden in 1745. In addition, the **Edict of Nantes** was signed here in 1598 by Henri IV, ending the Wars of Religion by granting a degree of toleration to the Protestants. It had far more crucial consequences when it was revoked, by Louis XIV, in 1685.

The stout **ramparts** of the château remain pretty much intact, and most of the encircling moat is filled with water, surrounded by well-tended lawns that make a popular spot for lunchtime picnics. Visitors can pass through the walls, and also stroll atop them for fine views over the city, for no charge (July & Aug daily 9am–8pm; Sept–June daily 10am–7pm).

The rather incongruous potpourri of buildings within includes a major exhibition space used for year-long displays on differing subjects; the pleasant Oubliettes café/restaurant (see p.381); and the high-tech **Musée d'Histoire de Nantes** (July & Aug daily 9.30am–7pm; Sept–June daily except Mon 10am–6pm; €5, €9 combined with temporary exhibitions; @ www.chateau-nantes.fr). The latter covers local history in exhaustive detail. Highlights include a fascinating scale model of the city in the thirteenth century, and a determined attempt to come to terms with Nantes' slave-trading past, displaying pitiful trinkets used to buy slaves in Africa.

In 1800 the Spaniards Tower, the castle's arsenal, exploded, shattering the stained glass of the fifteenth-century **Cathédrale de St-Pierre-et-St-Paul** over 200m away. This was just one of many disasters that have befallen the unlucky church. It was used as a barn during the Revolution, bombed during World War II, and damaged by fire in 1972. Restored and finally reopened, its soaring height and lightness are emphasized by its clean white stone. It contains the tomb of François II and his wife Margaret – with symbols of Power, Strength and Justice for him and Fidelity, Prudence and Temperance for her.

Nantes' **Musée des Beaux-Arts**, east of the cathedral on rue Clemenceau, has a respectable collection and good temporary exhibitions (Mon, Wed & Fri–Sun 10am–6pm, Thurs 10am–8pm; €3.50, €2 after 4.30pm). Not all its Renaissance and contemporary works are on display at any one time, but try to catch *David Triumphant* by Delaunay, Chagall's *Le Cheval Rouge* and Monet's *Nymphéas*.

The nineteenth-century town

The financier Graslin took charge of the development of the western part of the city in the 1780s, when Nantes was at its richest. **Place Royale**, with its distinctive fountain, was laid out at the end of the eighteenth century, and has been rebuilt since it was bombed in 1943; the 1780s also produced the nearby **place Graslin**, named after its creator, with the elaborately styled **Grand Théâtre**, whose Corinthian portico contrasts with the 1895 Art Nouveau of the not-to-be-missed *La Cigale* brasserie (see opposite) on the corner.

Rue Voltaire runs west of the place Graslin, leading to the **Musée d'Histoire Naturelle** at no. 12 (daily except Tues 10am–6pm, Ⓦ www.museum.nantes.fr; €3.50). This holds an eccentric assortment of oddities, including rhinoceros toenails, a coelecanth, an aepyornis egg and an Egyptian mummy. There's even a complete tanned human skin, taken in 1793 from the body of a soldier whose dying wish was to be made into a drum.

Les Machines de l'Île

Inaugurated in 2007, and centring on the fabulous **Grand Éléphant**, the **Machines de l'Île** is a truly world-class attraction. Part *hommage* to the sci-fi creations of Jules Verne and the blueprints of Leonardo da Vinci, part street-theatre extravaganza, this is the lynchpin of Nantes' urban regeneration. The "machines" in question are the astonishing contraptions created by designer/engineer François Delarozière and artist Pierre Orefice; the "island" is the Île de Nantes, a 3km-long, whale-shaped island in the Loire, ten minutes' walk southwest of the tourist office, that was once the centre of the city's shipbuilding industry.

While the machines are kept and constructed in vast hangars (which you can pay to enter), you can see the **elephant** for free as it emerges for regular walks along the huge esplanade outside. Twelve metres high and eight metres wide, it's phenomenally realistic, down to the articulation of its joints as it "walks", and its trunk as it flexes and sprays water. Paying for a ride (see box opposite) allows you to wander through its hollow belly and climb the spiral stairs within to reach the balconies and vantage points around its canopied howdah.

Inside the main hangar, the **Workshop** can be viewed from an overhead walkway, while the **Gallery** displays a changing assortment of completed machines. At the time of writing, these were the various components of the multi-tiered Marine Worlds carousel, due to be fully assembled and operational in 2012. Those visitors who volunteer quickly enough – mostly but not necessarily children – get to ride such oddball devices as the Giant Crab, the Bus of the Abyss, and the Reverse-Propelling Squid.

Eating and drinking

Restaurants fill the winding lanes of the old city, so it shouldn't take long to find somewhere once you start wandering the central pedestrian streets. Nantes is large enough to have all sorts of ethnic alternatives as well, with North African, Italian, Chinese, Vietnamese and Indian places concentrated especially along the rue de la Juiverie. Bars can be found around place du Commerce and place du Bouffay.

Machines de l'Île times and tickets

Opening hours for the Machines de l'Île vary enormously throughout the year; check Ⓦ www.lesmachines-nantes.fr or ☏ 08.10.12.12.25 for up-to-date information.

Early Jan to mid-Feb: closed

Second half of Feb: Daily except Mon 2–7pm

March to mid-April: Wed–Fri 2–6pm, Sat & Sun 2–7pm

Mid-April to early May & late May to June: Tues–Fri 10am–6pm, Sat & Sun 10am–7pm

Middle fortnight of May: Mon–Fri 10am–6pm, Sat & Sun 10am–7pm

July & Aug: daily 10am–8pm

Sept to early Nov: Tues–Fri 10 am–6 pm, Sat & Sun 10am–7pm

Early Nov to late Dec: Wed–Fri 2–6pm, Sat & Sun 2–7pm

Late Dec to early Jan: Daily except Mon 2–7pm

Tickets for an elephant ride *or* the gallery cost €7 for adults and €5.50 for under-18s. Either ticket gives access to the Workshop. Elephant rides cannot be reserved in advance; tickets are sold for same-day rides only, with a limit of 49 passengers per ride. Provided those times fall within that day's opening hours, rides are scheduled for 10.30am, 11.15am, noon, 12.45pm, 3.30pm, 4.15pm, 5pm & 5.45pm. Only the Gallery is free with the Pass Nantes (see p.378), and holders still have to queue. The ticket office shuts an hour before the site closes.

Restaurants

L'Atlantide Centre des Salorges, 16 quai Ernest-Renaud ☏ 02.40.73.23.23, Ⓦ restaurant-atlantide .net. Designer restaurant, with big river views from the fourth floor of a modern block, serving the contemporary French cuisine of chef Jean-Yves Gueho. Fish is the speciality, but expect quirky twists like the bananas braised in beer. *Menus* €30–95. Closed Sat lunch & all Sun, plus late July to late Aug.

Chez L'Huître 5 rue des Petites-Écuries ☏ 02.51.82.02.02. Much as the name suggests, this lovely little restaurant, with outdoor seating on a pedestrian street, specializes in oysters of all sizes and provenance. The *apérihuître* consists of six oysters and a glass of Muscadet for €6; there's also a €17.50 set *menu*. Open until late nightly, closed Sun lunch.

La Cigale 4 place Graslin ☏ 02.51.84.94.94, Ⓦ www.lacigale.com. Fabulous Belle Epoque brasserie, offering fine meals in opulent surroundings, with seating either at tiled terrace tables or in a more formal indoor dining room. Fish is a speciality, with lunch options like a €17 *tartare de thon* or salmon platter. Assorted set *menus* are served until midnight. Daily 7.30am–12.30am.

Les Oubliettes 4 place Marc Elder ☏ 02.51.82.67.04, Ⓦ lesoubliettes.fr. Despite the address, this little daytime-only restaurant is splendidly and very spaciously set in the château

courtyard, far from the traffic, with indoors and open-air seating. Breakfast, tea and good-value lunches, with large *plats* and specials for around €10.

Un Coin En Ville 2 place Bourse ☏ 02.40.20.05.97, Ⓦ uncoinenville.com. This hip, cellar-like restaurant serves classic French cuisine with a fusion edge. Lunchtime *plats* for under €10, or set lunch with carpaccio for €13; the full dinner *menu* is €27, and they serve until at least 11pm. Closed Sat lunch, & all Sun & Mon.

Cafés and bars

Café Cult' 2 rue des Carmes ☏ 02.40.47.18.49, Ⓦ cafe-cult.com. Friendly, good-value café housed in a beautiful old half-timbered house. They serve two-course lunches for just €12, dinner for €20, and cheap drinks later on, when it becomes a lively bar. Until 2am, closed Sun.

Lieu Unique Quai Ferdinand Favre ☏ 02.51.82.15.00, Ⓦ www.lelieuunique.com. As unique as its name proclaims, this former LU biscuit factory now plays host to concerts, theatre, dance, art exhibitions, a bookshop, a fair brasserie and a great bar, open until late.

La Trinquette 3 quai de la Fosse ☏ 02.51.72.39.05. This youthful central bar, with friendly English-speaking owners, serves *tartines* and *croques monsieur* to go with its fine *aperitifs*, and gets especially lively on market day, Sat, when DJs play. Mon–Fri 8.30am–10pm, Sat 7.30am–8pm.

Travel details

Trains

Brest to: Le Mans (2 daily; 3hr 50min); Morlaix (16 daily; 30min); Paris-Montparnasse (7 TGVs daily; 4hr 20min); Quimper (7 daily; 1hr 15min); Rennes (8 daily; 2hr 15min).

Guingamp to: Paimpol (2–5 daily; 45min).

Nantes to: Bordeaux (2 daily; 4hr 20min); Le Croisic (10 daily; 1hr 10min); Paris-Montparnasse (6 TGVs daily; 2hr 10min).

Quimper to: Lorient (6 daily; 40min); Nantes (5 daily; 2hr 30min); Paris-Montparnasse (7 TGVs daily; 4hr 20min); Redon (6 daily; 1hr 45min); Vannes (12 daily; 1hr 15min).

Rennes to: Brest (5 TGVs daily; 2hr 15min, plus 6 daily slower services, 2hr 40min); Caen (4 daily; 3hr) and Pontorson (1hr); Lille (2 daily; 3hr 45min); Morlaix (10 daily; 1hr 45min); Nantes (10 daily; 45min); Paris-Montparnasse (10 TGVs daily; 2hr 10min); Quimper (9 daily; 2hr 15min); Vannes (6 daily; 1hr); Vitré (5 daily; 20min).

Roscoff to: Morlaix (4 daily; 35min).

St-Malo to: Rennes (14 daily; 50min; connections for Paris on TGV).

Buses

Brest to: Brignogan (8 daily; 1hr); Camaret (1–3 daily; 1hr 10min); Le Conquet (8 daily; 45min); Quimper (5 daily; 1hr 15min); Roscoff (5 daily; 1hr 45min).

Quimper to: Bénodet (8 daily; 40min); Camaret (3 daily; 1hr 20min); Concarneau (7 daily; 30min); Crozon (3 daily; 1hr 10min); Douarnenez (10 daily; 40min); Locronan (3 daily; 20min); Pointe du Raz (5 daily; 1hr 30 min); Roscoff (1 daily; 2hr 30min).

Rennes to: Dinan (6 daily; 1hr 20min); Dinard (5 daily; 1hr 40min); Fougères (10 daily; 1hr); Mont St-Michel (5 daily; 1hr 20min).

Roscoff to: Morlaix (5 daily; 1hr).

St-Malo to: Cancale (6 daily; 45min); Dinan (6 daily; 45min); Dinard (10 daily; 30min); Fougères (3 daily; 2hr 15min); Mont St-Michel (4 daily; 1hr 30min); Pontorson (4 daily; 1hr 15min); Rennes (3 daily; 1hr 30min).

Vannes to: Carnac (7 daily; 1hr 20min); Quiberon (7 daily; 2hr).

Ferries

For details of ferries to Dinard from St-Malo, see p.327; to Bréhat, see p.338; to Batz, see p.344; to Ouessant, see p.346; from Brest to the Crozon peninsula, see p.347; to Sein, see p.353; to Belle-Île, see p.369; and for tours of the Gulf of Morbihan see p.372.

6

The Loire

UNITED KINGDOM

BELGIUM

GERMANY

LUX.

ENGLISH CHANNEL

ATLANTIC
OCEAN

SWITZERLAND

ITALY

N

0   250 km

SPAIN

MEDITERRANEAN
SEA

CHAPTER 6 # Highlights

✴ **Châteaux à vélo** 300km
of bike paths that ramble
through forests, fields and
pretty stone villages, an idyllic
way to visit the stunning
châteaux around Blois.
See p.385

✴ **Stained glass at Bourges
cathedral** Some of France's
finest stained-glass windows
are preserved in Bourges'
extravagant Gothic cathedral.
See p.402

✴ **Château de Blois** A brilliantly
conceived building with an
epic history – a must-see for
all visitors. See p.411

✴ **Amboise** Beautiful,
archetypal Loire Valley town,
and a brilliant base for an
exploration of the outlying
regions. See p.423

✴ **The gardens at Villandry**
These superb gardens
are home to allegorical
Renaissance hedge-work.
See p.424

✴ **The Tapestry of the
Apocalypse** Dramatically
displayed in Angers' half-
ruined château, this is an
astonishingly well-preserved
piece of medieval doom-
mongering. See p.435

▲ Tending the gardens at Villandry

6

The Loire

The Loire has a justifiable reputation as one of the greatest, grandest and most striking rivers anywhere in Europe. In its most characteristic stretch, from the hills of Sancerre to the city of Angers, it flows past an extraordinary parade of castles, palaces and fine mansions; unsurprisingly, when it came to choosing which should be awarded the title of World Heritage Site, UNESCO simply bestowed the label on the entire valley. Although the most striking feature is the beautiful views, there are simpler pleasures, such as the outstanding food and drink and the noticeably gentler pace of life.

The region's heartland, **Touraine**, long known as "the garden of France", has some of the best wines, the tastiest goat's cheese, and the most regal history in France, including one of the finest châteaux in **Chenonceau**. Touraine also takes in three of the Loire's pleasantest tributaries: the **Cher**, **Indre** and **Vienne**. If you have just a week to spare for the region, then these are the parts to concentrate on. The attractive towns of **Blois** and **Amboise**, each with their own exceptional châteaux, make good bases for visiting the area upstream of Tours. Numerous grand châteaux dot the wooded country immediately south and east of Blois, including **Chambord**, the grandest of them all, while the wild and watery region of the **Sologne** stretches away further to the southeast. Downstream of Tours, around handsome **Saumur**, quirky troglodyte dwellings have been carved out of the rock faces.

Along with its many châteaux, the region has a few unexpected sights, most compelling of which are the gardens at **Villandry**, outside Tours, and the abbey

The Loire by bike

Thanks to the **Loire à Vélo** scheme (ⓦwww.loire-a-velo.fr), the Loire valley is now one of the most charming places in the world to have a cycling holiday or take a day out on a hired bike. A mix of dedicated cycle paths and meticulously signposted routes along minor roads now runs all the way along the Loire from Orléans to beyond Angers – a distance of more than 300km. The region around Blois offers an additional 300km network, **Châteaux à vélo** (ⓦwww.chateauxavelo.com; see p.412). These routes thread inland among the forests, linking the area's many châteaux.

Tourist offices provide detailed maps and other information, and you can download most details, including maps, online. French villages are accustomed to cyclists, and all larger towns have at least one hire agency. Bikes can also be hired at hotels, campsites, tourist offices, train stations and even restaurants along the way. Many have signed up to the **Détours de Loire scheme** (ⓣ02.47.61.22.23, ⓦwww .locationdevelos.com), which allows you to pick up a bike in one place and drop it off in another, paying inexpensive drop-off costs per zone crossed – on top of the bike rental charge.

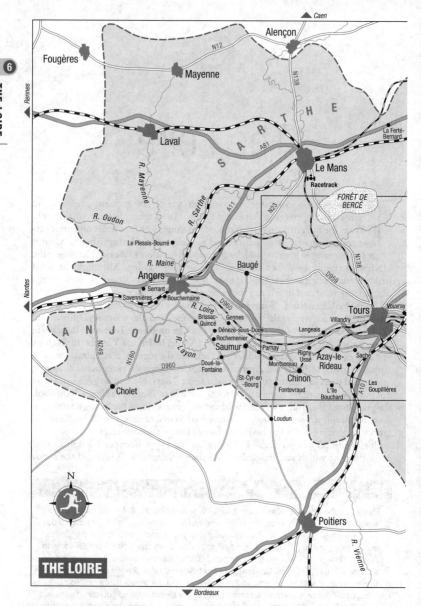

at **Fontevraud**. The major towns of Angers, Tours, Le Mans and Orléans seem disappointing in comparison, though each has its charms, from Tours' astonishing cathedral to the apocalyptic tapestry sequence at Angers.

The Loire itself is often called the last wild river in France, mostly because unpredictable currents and shallow water brought an end to commercial river traffic as soon as the railways arrived, and the many quays remain largely forgotten, except by the occasional tour boat. Such an untamed river also makes for dramatic floods,

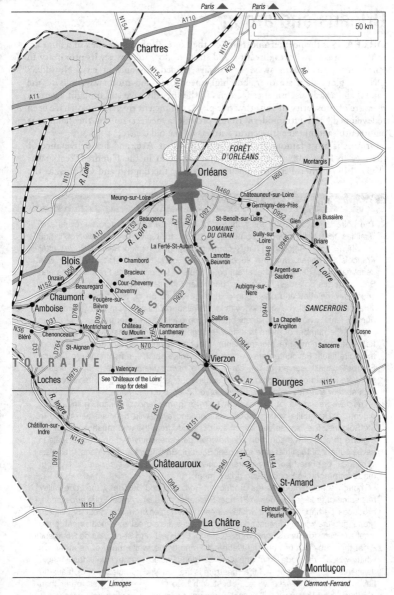

but for most of the year it meanders gently past its shifting sandbanks, shaded by reeds and willows, and punctuated by long, sandy islands beloved by birds.

Though most sites are accessible by public transport, buses and trains can be rather limiting. It's a good idea to hire some means of transport, at least for occasional forays away from the crowds. Hiring a bike is perhaps the most enjoyable option of all: this is wonderful and easy **cycling** country, especially on the dedicated cycle routes that make up the new Loire à Vélo network (see box, p.385).

Orléans and around

ORLÉANS is the northernmost city on the Loire, sitting at the apex of a huge arc in the river as it switches direction and starts to flow southwest. Its proximity to Paris, just over 100km away, has always shaped this ancient city. Nowadays Orléans' glory days are over, but high-speed train and motorway links to the capital and a rash of cosmetics factories in the suburbs have still brought a certain measure of prosperity. It's an attractive place; the ancient riverside quays have been redeveloped, and ultramodern trams provide a perfect foil to the handsome eighteenth- and nineteenth-century streets of the old centre.

Orléans is most famous for its heroine, **Joan of Arc**, and her deliverance of the city in May 1429. This was the turning point in the Hundred Years' War (1337–1453), when Paris had been captured by the English and Orléans, as the

Food and drink of the Loire

The Loire is renowned for the softness of its climate and the richness of its soil, qualities that help produce some of the best **fruit** and **vegetables** you'll find anywhere. From Anjou's orchards come greengages, named *Reine Claudes* after François I's queen, and the succulent Anjou pear. Market stalls overflow with seasonal fruits, particularly local apricots. Tours is famous for its French beans and Saumur for its potatoes. Asparagus, particularly the fleshy white variety, appears in soufflés, omelettes and other egg dishes as well as on its own, accompanied by vinaigrette made (if you're lucky) with local walnut oil. Finally, from Berry, comes the humble lentil, whose green variety often accompanies salmon or trout.

Given the number of rivers that flow through the region, it's hardly surprising that **fish** features on most restaurant menus, though this doesn't guarantee that it's from the Loire itself. Favourites are *filet de sandre* (pike-perch – a fish native to Central Europe), usually served in the classic Loire *beurre blanc* sauce; stuffed bream; *matelote* (a kind of stew) of local eels softened in red wine; salmon (often flavoured with sorrel); and little smelt-like fishes served deep-fried (*la friture*).

The favoured meat of the eastern Loire is **game**, and pheasant, guinea fowl, pigeon, duck, quails, young rabbit, venison and even wild boar are all hunted in the Sologne. They are served in rich sauces made from the wild **mushrooms** of the region's forests or the common *champignon de Paris*, cultivated on a huge scale in caves cut out of the limestone rock near Saumur. Both Tours and Le Mans specialize in *rillettes*, or potted **pork**; in Touraine charcuteries you'll also find *pâté au biquion*, made from pork, veal and young goat's meat.

Though not as famous as the produce of Bordeaux and Burgundy, the Loire valley has some of the finest **wines** in France. Sancerre, the easternmost Loire *appellation*, produces perhaps the finest white wines in the region from the great Sauvignon grape, and the whites of Muscadet around Nantes are a great accompaniment to the local shellfish. Touraine's finest reds – Chinon, Bourgueil and St-Nicolas de Bourgueil – get their ruby colour from the Cabernet Franc grape, while many of its attractive white wines are made from the Chenin Blanc including the highly fashionable Jasnières. At the other end of the spectrum is the honeyed complexity of Côteaux du Layon's so-called dessert wines – best with blue cheese or foie gras rather than pudding – and Vouvray's still, sweet and semi-sweet whites, which only release the best of the Chenin Blanc grape after decades in the bottle.

Touraine makes something of a cult of its **goat's cheese**, and a local *chèvre fermier* (farm-produced goat's cheese) can be a revelation. Four named goats' cheeses are found on most boards: Ste-Maure is a long cylinder with a piece of straw running through the middle; Pouligny-St-Pierre and Valençay are pyramid-shaped; and Selles-sur-Cher is flat and round.

key city in central France, was under siege. Joan, a 17-year-old peasant girl in men's clothing, had talked her way into meeting Charles, the heir to the French throne, and persuaded him to reconquer his kingdom. Her legend has probably coloured her actual achievements, but she was undeniably an important symbolic figure. Less than three years later she was captured in battle, tried as a heretic, and burnt at the stake. Today, the Maid of Orléans is an omnipresent feature, whether in museums, hotels or in the stained glass of the vast Neo-Gothic cathedral. One of the best times to visit is on May 8 (**Joan of Arc Day**) or the evening before, when the city is filled with parades, fireworks and a medieval fair.

Upstream from Orléans, the rambling Forêt d'Orléans spreads north. Along the river are plenty of lesser-known attractions, most notably the **abbey at St-Benoît**, the **château at Sully-sur-Loire**, the small town of **Gien**, the **aqueduct at Briare** and the hilltop town of **Sancerre**, where the famous dry white wines are produced.

Arrival and information

The **gare SNCF** leads straight into the modern shopping centre on place d'Arc, which fronts onto a huge swathe of busy roads; the Old Town centre lies on the far side. The **gare routière**, on rue Marcel-Proust, is just north of place d'Arc. The main **tourist office**, 2 place de l'Étape (Mon–Sat: March 10am–1pm & 2–5.30pm; April 10am–1pm & 2–6pm; May & Sept 9.30am–1pm & 2–6pm; June 9.30am–1pm & 2–6.30pm; July & Aug 9am–7pm, also Sun 10am–1pm & 2–5pm; Oct–Feb 10am–1pm & 2–5pm; ☎02.38.24.01.69, ⓦwww.tourisme -orleans.com), is in the old centre, opposite the cathedral.

Accommodation

Accommodation in Orléans is nothing spectacular, and you might want to consider staying in nearby Beaugency or Sully-sur-Loire instead. If you do stop off here, these are some of the best options.

D'Arc 37 rue de la République ☎02.38.53.10.94, ⓦwww.hoteldarc.fr. This long-established Art Nouveau hotel has touches of grandeur, though it's now a Best Western and starting to look a bit generic. The most attractive rooms have small balconies with window boxes looking down onto the pedestrianized street below. ⑥

Hôtel Archange 1 bd de Verdun ☎02.38.54.42.42, ⓦwww.hotelarchange.com. An unassuming exterior hides a number of quirky, individually designed rooms decorated with everything from pink satin to portraits of Jimi Hendrix. Definitely the most original option in town. ②

Auberge de Jeunesse d'Orléans-La Source Stade Omnisports, 7 av Beaumarchais ☎02.38.53.60.06, ⓔauberge.crjs45@orange.fr. Clean, decent hostel, with modern facilities, but far from the centre underneath a stand of Orléans' stadium: take tram A from the train station to "Université l'indien" (30min), then walk 500m east down av du Président-Kennedy. Closed at weekends; reception open Mon–Fri 8am–7pm. Dorm beds €13, €21 for singles.

Le Brin de Zinc 62 rue Ste-Catherine ☎02.38.53.38.77, ⓦwww.brindezinc.fr. Half a dozen sparsely furnished but decent, cheap rooms in an old building above a popular and very central restaurant. The marble chimneys add a welcome note of class. ②

Camping Gaston Marchand Chemin de la Roche, St-Jean-de-la-Ruelle ☎02.38.88.39.39. The municipal campsite, and the closest to Orléans, 3km out on the Blois road beside the Loire; bus #26, stop "Petite Espère". Showers and a shop on site. Closed Sept–June.

Des Cèdres 17 rue Maréchal-Foch ☎02.38.62.22.92, ⓦwww.hoteldescedres.com. The best hotel in town; comfortable and clean with some touches of personality, including a leafy courtyard out back. ④

Charles Sanglier 8 rue Charles-Sanglier ☎02.38.53.38.50. Very central, so tends to get booked up. The modern building is unprepossessing, and the rooms are small and a little shabby, but it's a friendly place, and comfortable enough. ②

Marguerite 14 place du Vieux-Marché ☎02.38.53.74.32, ⓦwww.hotel-orleans.fr. Central, friendly and well run. Large, immaculate rooms painted in cheery modern colours – the few unrenovated rooms are cheaper. ④

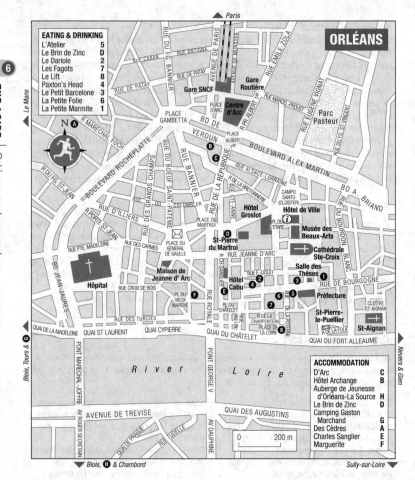

◀ Le Mans

◀ Blois, Tours & G

◀ Blois, H & Chambord

Paris ▲

Nevers & Gien ▶

Sully-sur-Loire ▶

EATING & DRINKING
L'Atelier 5
Le Brin de Zinc D
Le Dariole 2
Les Fagots 7
Le Lift 8
Paxton's Head 4
Le Petit Barcelone 3
La Petite Folie 6
La Petite Marmite 1

ACCOMMODATION
D'Arc C
Hôtel Archange B
Auberge de Jeunesse
 d'Orléans-La Source H
Le Brin de Zinc D
Camping Gaston
 Marchand G
Des Cèdres A
Charles Sanglier E
Marguerite F

The City

In pride of place in the large, central **place du Martroi**, a mostly pedestrianized square at the end of rue de la République, rises an unflattering mid-nineteenth-century likeness of St Joan on horseback. Just beyond place du Martroi, the grand nineteenth-century stretch of rue Jeanne-d'Arc marches arrow-straight up to the doors of the **Cathédrale Sainte-Croix** (daily 9.15am–5pm), where Joan celebrated her victory over the English – although the uniformly Gothic structure actually dates from well after her death. Huguenot iconoclasts destroyed the transepts in 1568, and in 1601 Henri IV inaugurated a rebuilding programme that lasted until the nineteenth century. The lofty towers of the west front, which culminate in a delicate stone palisade, were only completed at the time of the Revolution. Inside, skeletal columns of stone extend in a single vertical sweep from the cathedral floor to the vault. Joan's canonization in 1920 is marked by a garish monumental altar next to the north transept, supported by two jagged golden leopards that represent the English. In the nave, the late nineteenth-century stained-glass windows tell the story of her life, starting from the north transept. In a series of cartoon-like images, *L'Anglois Perfide*, or perfidious Albion, gets a rough ride, while the role of the Burgundians in her capture and the French clergy in her trial is rather brushed over. Across place d'Étape from the cathedral, outside the red-brick Renaissance **Hôtel Groslot**, the old Hôtel de Ville, Joan appears again, in pensive mood, her skirt now shredded by World War II bullets.

The interesting **Musée des Beaux-Arts** (Tues–Sun 10am–6pm; €3), opposite the Hôtel Groslot, is probably the cultural highpoint of the city. The highlights of the main French collection on the first floor include Claude Deruet's *Four Elements*, the Le Nain brothers' dream-like and compelling *Bacchus Discovering Ariane on Naxos*, and an exquisite collection of eighteenth-century pastel portraits. The suite of rooms on the mezzanine level leads from nineteenth-century Neoclassicism through Romanticism and on to a large chamber devoted to the early Realists, dominated by Antigna's taut, melodramatic *The Fire*. Foreign art, mainly Flemish and Italian sixteenth- and seventeenth-century works, is on the second floor – look out for Correggio's renowned *Holy Family* (1522) and Velázquez's *St Thomas*. Twentieth-century art lurks in the basement, where the big names include Picasso and Gauguin; a small inner chamber has a number of African-influenced sculptures by Henri Gaudier-Brzeska (1891–1915), who was born just outside Orléans at St-Jean-de-Braye. English information sheets are supplied in each room.

If you follow rue Jeanne-d'Arc west from the cathedral and turn left down rue Charles-Sanglier, you'll find the ornate **Hôtel Cabu** (May, June & Sept Tues–Sat 1.30–5.45pm, Sun 2–6pm; July & Aug Tues–Sat 9.30am–12.15pm & 1.30–5.45pm, Sun 2–6pm; Oct–April Wed 1.30–5.45pm, Sun 2–6pm; same ticket as Musée des Beaux-Arts), whose three tiers faithfully follow the three main classical orders in strict Renaissance style. Inside, a small historical and archeological museum houses the extraordinary **Trésor de Neuvy-en-Sullias**, a collection of bronze animals and figurines found near Orléans in 1861. The cache was probably buried in the second half of the third century AD, either to protect it from Germanic invaders or to stop it being melted down for coinage at a time of rampant inflation, and possibly represents the last flourishing of Celtic religion at the end of the Gallo-Roman period. The floors above house various medieval oddities and Joan-related pieces, as well as exhibits on the history of Orléans. The entrance is on square Abbé-Desnoyers.

If you haven't had enough of Jeanne d'Arc by this stage, head to place du Général-de-Gaulle, where you'll find the semi-timbered **Maison de Jeanne d'Arc** (Tues–Sun: May–Oct 10am–12.30pm & 1.30–6.30pm; Nov–April 1.30–6pm; €2), a 1960s reconstruction of the house where Joan stayed, an entertaining enough diversion for an hour. Despite the consistency in artists' renderings of the saint, it seems the pageboy haircut and demure little face are part of the myth – there is no contemporary portrait of her, save for a clerk's doodle in the margin of her trial proceedings, kept in the National Archives in Paris.

The riverfront and around

The scattered vestiges of the old city are to the east, down towards the river. **Rue de Bourgogne** was the Gallo-Roman main street, and is now lined with lively bars and restaurants. The **Salles des Thèses** is all that remains of the medieval university of Orléans where the hardline Reformation theologian Calvin studied Roman law.

To the south, the attractive narrow streets of the old industrial area lead to the river. Once semi-derelict, this neighbourhood is now the focus of a campaign to make the riverfront once more the focus of the city. On the **place de la Loire**, which slopes down to the river from a nine-screen cinema complex, the flagstones are inset with a pattern that's supposed to suggest waves. At least two of the quarter's churches are on the list of precious monuments: the remains of **St-Aignan** and its well-preserved eleventh-century crypt; and the Romanesque **St-Pierre-le-Puellier**, a former university church now used for concerts and exhibitions. St-Aignan was destroyed during the English siege and rebuilt by the Dauphin, then grew to become one of the greatest churches in France under Louis XII. More sieges of the city during the Wars of Religion took their toll, leaving just the choir and transepts standing. Tours of the **crypt**, which was built in the early eleventh century to house the relics of St-Aignan, are occasionally conducted by the tourist office.

Eating and drinking

Rue de Bourgogne is the main street for **restaurants** and **nightlife**. You can choose from among French, Spanish, North African, Middle Eastern, Indian and Asian cuisines, all of which can be sampled at very reasonable prices. You can buy your own provisions in the covered **market halls** on place du Châtelet, near the river.

Restaurants

Le Brin de Zinc 62 rue Ste-Catherine. Bustling bistro just off place du Martroi in the hotel of the same name. The outside tables are usually packed with a noisy crowd tucking into huge seafood platters (€17–39).

Le Dariole 25 rue Étienne-Dolet ☎ 02.38.77.26.67. Tearoom-cum-restaurant in a picture-postcard half-timbered building that serves good quality food at inexpensive prices (*menus* from €17.50). Open Mon–Fri lunch, Tues & Fri dinner.

Les Fagots 32 rue du Poirier ☎ 02.38.62.22.79. Wonderfully convivial place that looks as if it has been crammed into someone's grandmother's kitchen. Traditional mains and grilled meats feature on the €12 and €15 *menus*. Closed Sun & Mon.

Le Lift Place de la Loire ☎ 02.38.53.63.48. Run by a renowned chef, Philippe Bardau, this modern restaurant features finely prepared cuisine and a terrace with views of the Loire; the "brunch" specials (€18 including wine) are particularly good value. Evening *menus* from €48.

La Petite Folie 223 rue de Bourgogne ☎ 02.38.53.39.87. Youthful, designer bar-restaurant serving fresh, light and exciting food – you might

have asparagus flan, chicken with *sauce Canadienne*, then strawberry soup with wine – all for around €22 for the set *menu*. Closed Sun & Mon.

La Petite Marmite 178 rue de Bourgogne ☎ 02.38.54.23.83. The most highly regarded restaurant on this busy street combines a stylish but homey atmosphere with excellent regional cuisine. The €22 *menu du terroir* features local produce, such as rabbit and mushrooms from the Sologne. Closed Tues.

Bars and nightlife

L'Atelier 203 rue de Bourgogne. Arty, studenty place, with regular concerts and exhibitions. Possibly slightly too insular if you don't speak the language as well as the bohemian regulars, but quite fun if you do.

Paxton's Head 264–266 rue de Bourgogne. If you're homesick for an archetypal English pub, this will just about fit the bill. Not the cheapest place in town, though. Daily 3pm–3am.

Le Petit Barcelone 218 rue de Bourgogne. Friendly, informal student bar with cheapish drinks (around €3–4 for a beer or glass of wine) and meals served from April to December.

Listings

Bike hire The only central option is CAD, 95 rue Faubourg-Bannier ☎ 02.38.81.23.00. Otherwise, try Kit Loisirs, 1720 rue Marcel-Belot (☎ 02.38.66.29.40, ⓦ www.kitloisirs.com), out in the suburb of Olivet.

Car rental Avis, Gare SNCF ☎ 02.38.62.27.04; Rent-a-Car, 3 rue Sansonnières ☎ 02.38.62.22.44; Europcar, 17 av de Paris ☎ 02.38.63.88.00.

Festivals Fête de Jeanne d'Arc is a series of period-costume parades held on April 29, May 1 and May 7–8, with the big set-pieces occurring in front of the cathedral on the night of the 7th and the morning of the 8th of May. The Festival de Jazz d'Orléans is held right through June, culminating in concerts held in the Campo Santo (ⓦ www.orleans jazz.fr). Every Sept in odd years, the Loire Festival takes place, with five days of concerts and shows beside the Châtelet quay.

Health Centre Hospitalier, 1 rue Porte-Madeleine ☎02.38.51.44.44; emergencies ☎15.

Internet Leader Best Phone, 196 rue de Bourgogne (10am–9pm).

Police Courtyard of Hôtel Groslot, place de l'Étape ☎02.38.79.29.44; emergencies ☎17.

Château de Meung

Little streams known as *les mauves* flow between the houses in the village of **MEUNG-SUR-LOIRE**, 14km southwest of Orléans on the Blois rail line. During the summer months they leave slimy green high-water marks, but the sound of water is always pleasant, and Meung is an agreeable place to spend an afternoon, having accumulated a number of literary associations over the centuries.

In the late thirteenth century, Jean de Meun, or de Meung, added eighteen thousand lines to the already four thousand line-long *Roman de la Rose*, a poetic hymn to sexuality written half a century earlier (by Guillaume de Lorris, from the town of the same name in the nearby Forêt d'Orléans). Inspired by the philosophical spirit of the times, de Meun transformed the poem into a finely

Must-see châteaux

First things first; though it is tempting to try and pack in as many châteaux as you can in a short period of time, this is counter-productive and frustrating. It's far better to aim to visit three or four of the best in the area in which you're staying, possibly with a one-day trip to one of the most spectacular set-piece châteaux in the region.

Of the most famous, **Azay-le-Rideau** (see p.425) and **Chenonceau** (see p.403) both belong exclusively to the Renaissance period, and their respective settings in the middle of a moat and a river are very beautiful, rivalled only by the wonderful Renaissance gardens of **Villandry** (see p.424). Azay-le-Rideau, in particular, is a marvellous encapsulation of a long-gone period of grandeur and power, in a beautifully serene setting conveniently hidden from public view. **Blois** (see p.411), with its four wings representing four distinct eras, is extremely impressive, as is the monstrously huge **Chambord** (see p.414), the triumph of François I's Renaissance. The latter is something of an acquired taste, not least because it's always busy. The key feature here is the dual-spiral staircase; legend has it this was designed by Leonardo da Vinci. At **Valençay** (see p.406), the interior of the Renaissance château is Napoleonic, while **Cheverny** (see p.413) is the prime example of seventeenth-century magnificence.

For an urban château, **Amboise** (see p.423), which rears above the Loire like a cliff, is one of the most compelling and striking, even if the interior decoration leaves something to be desired. For an evocation of medieval times, the citadel of **Loches** (see p.407) is hard to beat.

Other châteaux are more compelling for their contents than for their architecture: **Beauregard** (see p.414) is most famous for its portrait gallery and **La Bussière** (see p.397) for its obsessive nineteenth-century decoration, entirely dedicated to freshwater fishing. **La Ferté-St-Aubin** is a living aristocratic home, and at **Angers** (see p.435) the stark, largely ruined medieval castle houses the Tapestry of the Apocalypse, the greatest work of art in the Loire valley, and worth a visit in itself.

Entry prices are undeniably steep, particularly for the châteaux that have remained in private hands – and there are a surprising number of French aristocrats still living in their family homes. This means that picking and choosing the best really will help you. There is no consistency in concessions offered, and children rarely go free. If you're over 65, under 25, a student or still at school, check for any reductions and make sure you've got proof of age or a student card with you.

argued disquisition on the nature of love, and inspired generations of European writers. Most recently, the town featured in the works of Georges Simenon – his fictional hero, Maigret, takes his holidays here.

Looming at the western edge of the old town centre is the **Château de Meung** (March–Oct daily 10am–7pm; Nov–Feb Sat & Sun 2–6pm; €8), which remained in the hands of the bishops of Orléans from its construction in the twelfth century right up to the Revolution, though since then it has passed through seven or eight private owners. The exterior of the château on the side facing the old drawbridge looks grimly defensive with its thirteenth-century pepper-pot towers, while the park side presents a much warmer facade, its eighteenth-century windows framed by salmon-pink stucco. You can explore the older part on your own, even poking around under the roof, but bear in mind that most of this pleasantly shambolic section of the building was remodelled in the nineteenth century, and little sense of its history remains. More impressive is the eighteenth-century wing, where the bishops entertained their guests in relative comfort. Below here are the **cellars** where criminals condemned by the Episcopal courts were imprisoned. The most famous of the detainees was the poet François Villon, who was kept under lock and key between May and October 1461.

Beaugency

Six kilometres southwest of Meung along the Loire, **BEAUGENCY** is a pretty little town, which, in contrast to its innocuous appearance today, played its part in the conniving games of early medieval politics. In 1152 the marriage of Louis VII of France and Eleanor of Aquitaine was annulled by the Council of Beaugency in the church of Notre-Dame, allowing Eleanor to marry Henry Plantagenet, the future Henry II of England. Her huge land holdings in southwest France thus passed to the English crown – which already controlled Normandy, Maine, Anjou and Touraine – and the struggles between the French and English kings over their claims to these territories, and to the French throne itself, lasted for centuries.

Liberated by the indefatigable Joan of Arc on her way to Orléans in 1429, Beaugency was a constant battleground during the Hundred Years' War due to its strategic significance as the only bridge crossing point of the Loire between Orléans and Blois. Remarkably, the 26-arch **bridge** still stands. The once heavily fortified medieval heart of the town clusters tightly around a handful of central squares. **Place St-Firmin**, with its statue of Joan, is overlooked by the only remaining tower of a church destroyed during the Revolution, while **place Dunois** is bordered by the massive eleventh-century **Tour de César**, formerly part of the rather plain, fifteenth-century **Château Dunois**, which is closed to visitors for major structural works. The square is completed by the severe Romanesque **abbey church of Notre-Dame**, the venue for the council's fateful matrimonial decision in 1152. Shady place du Docteur-Hyvernaud, two blocks north of place Dunois, is dominated by the elaborate sixteenth-century facade of the **Hôtel de Ville**. Inside, the main council chamber is graced by eight fine **embroidered wall hangings** from the era of Louis XIII, but you'll have to ask at the tourist office (on the same square) to be allowed inside to have a look. One set illustrates the four continents as perceived in the seventeenth century, with the rest dramatizing pagan rites such as gathering mistletoe and sacrificing animals.

Practicalities

There's a small **tourist office** (May–Sept Mon–Sat 9.30am–12.30pm & 2.30–6.30pm, Sun 10am–noon; Oct–April Mon–Sat 9.30am–noon & 2.30–6pm; ☎02.38.44.54.42, ⊛www.beaugency.fr) on place Docteur-Hyvernaud. Two charming **hotels** make the most of Beaugency's atmosphere of genteel charm: the

☆ *Hôtel de l'Abbaye*, 2 quai de l'Abbaye (☎02.38.45.10.10, ⓦwww.hotel-abbaye -beaugency.com; ❻), is set in a beautiful seventeenth-century abbey with painted ceilings and beds on raised platforms, offering traditional luxury at a reasonable price; while the small, delightful *Hôtel de la Sologne*, 6 place St-Firmin (closed Dec 20 to Jan 15; ☎02.38.44.50.27, ⓦwww.hoteldelasologne.com; ❸), has some rooms with views of the Tour de César. The family-run *Relais de Templiers*, 68 rue du Pont (☎02.38.44.53.78, ⓦwww.hotelrelaistempliers.com; ❸), is also relatively inexpensive; a good option if the other two are full. There's also a decent **HI Youth Hostel** 2km to the north at 152 rue de Châteaudun, but there's no bus into town (☎02.38.44.61.31, ⓦwww.fuaj.org; closed Dec; dorm beds €13.20).

Le Relais du Château, 8 rue du Pont (☎02.38.44.55.10; closed Wed), is a decent, traditional **restaurant** with *menus* from €15; alternatively, *Le P'tit Bateau*, at no. 54 (☎02.38.44.56.38; closed Mon), has a pleasant terrace, ideal for summer dining, and slightly more elevated gastronomic ambitions, with *menus* from €20 upwards. Midway between the two, *La Crep'zeria*, at no. 32, serves decent pizzas and crêpes on its sunny terrace.

Château de la Ferté-St-Aubin and around

The **Château de la Ferté-St-Aubin** lies 20km south of Orléans (daily: mid-Feb to March & Oct to mid-Nov 2–6pm; April–Sept 10am–7pm; €8.50; ⓦwww .chateau-ferte-st-aubin.com), at the north end of the village of **LA FERTÉ-ST-AUBIN**. The late sixteenth- and early seventeenth-century building presents an enticing combination of salmon-coloured brick, creamy limestone and dark slate roofs, while the interior is a real nineteenth-century home – and you are invited to treat it as such, which makes a real change from the stuffier attitudes of most grand homes. You can wander freely into almost every room, playing billiards or the piano, picking up the old telephone, sitting on the worn armchairs or washing your hands in a porcelain sink; only the rather fancier grand salon is cordoned off. Roughly every hour there are demonstrations down in the kitchens of how to make Madeleine cakes – the sweet spongy biscuit that so inspired Proust. At the rear of the château, also enclosed by the moat, there's a play fort with sponge balls supplied for storming it, little cabins with dummies acting out fairy tales, and a toy farm.

The **gare SNCF** is roughly 200m southwest of the village square; there are regular services from Orléans, as well as south to Vierzon and Bourges. For **eating**, an inexpensive option is the *Auberge Solognote* (closed Tues eve & Wed), behind the covered market on place Halle, La Ferté's main square.

Germigny-des-Prés and St-Benoît-sur-Loire

Heading east of Orléans on the D960, you pass through **Châteauneuf-sur-Loire** – whose château has very pleasant gardens of rhododendrons and magnolias and a small museum of traditional Loire shipping – en route to **GERMIGNY-DES-PRÉS**, 30km from the city. It's a pleasant afternoon's bike ride. The small, plain **church** (daily: April–Oct 8.30am–7.30pm; Nov–March 8.30am–6pm; €2 coin needed for lighting) incorporates at its east end one of the few surviving buildings from the Carolingian Renaissance, a tiny, perfectly formed church in the shape of a Greek cross. The oratory's sheer antiquity is spoiled by too-perfect restoration work, but the unique gold and silver mosaic on the dome of the eastern chapel preserves all its rare beauty.

Five kilometres further upstream, along the D60, **ST-BENOÎT-SUR-LOIRE** offers the striking edifice of the Romanesque **Abbaye de Fleury** (daily 6.30am–10pm; ⓦwww.abbaye-fleury.com), which is populated by a small community of some forty Benedictine monks who still observe the original Rule – poverty, chastity and obedience – and whose Gregorian chants can be heard at the daily midday mass (11am on Sun).

Built in warm, cream-coloured stone between 1020 and 1218, the church dates from the abbey's greatest epoch. The oldest part, the porch tower, illustrates St John's vision of the New Jerusalem in Revelation – foursquare, with open gates on each side. The fantastically sculpted capitals of the heavy pillars are alive with acanthus leaves, birds and exotic animals. Three of them depict scenes from the Apocalypse, while another shows Mary's flight into Egypt. Inside, the choir is split into two levels: above, a marble mosaic of Roman origin covers the chancel floor; in the ancient crypt below lie the relics of St-Benoît.

Sully-sur-Loire and around

SULLY-SUR-LOIRE lies on the south bank of the Loire, 7km east of St-Benoît and accessible by bus from Orléans. The grand **château** here (April–June & Sept Tues–Sun 10am–6pm; July & Aug daily 10am–6pm; Oct–Dec & Feb–March Tues–Sun 10am–noon & 2–5pm; €6) is pure fantasy, despite savage wartime bombing that destroyed the nearby bridge. From the outside, rising massively out of its gigantic moat, it has all the picture-book requirements of pointed towers, machicolations and drawbridge. Sully's **international Music Festival** (Ⓦwww .festival-sully.com) runs right through June, featuring classical concerts held in a huge marquee in the château grounds.

The **village** of Sully itself is uninteresting, but the quiet riverbank roads are worth exploring by bike, or you can venture north into the Forêt d'Orléans on the far bank.

Practicalities

The **gare SNCF**, on the Bourges–Étampes line, is 500m from the centre of the village. The **tourist office** can be found on central place de Gaulle (May–Sept Mon–Sat 9.45am–12.15pm & 2.30–6.30pm, Sun 10.30am–1pm; Oct–April Mon 10am–noon, Tues, Wed, Fri & Sat 10am–noon & 2–6pm, Thurs 2–6pm; Ⓣ02.38.36.23.70, Ⓦwww.sully-sur-loire.fr). Bikes can be hired from Passion Deux Roues, 10 rue des Épinettes (Ⓣ02.38.35.13.13).

The town's two best **hotels** both lie in the centre. The top choice is the beautifully renovated ⚘ *Hôtel la Closeraie* at 14 rue Porte-Berry (Ⓣ02.38.05.10.90, Ⓦwww.hotel-la-closeraie.fr; ❸), which features hardwood floors, bathtubs and fireplaces, while the rambling *Hôtel de la Tour*, above a bar at 21 rue Porte-de-Sologne (Ⓣ02.38.36.21.72; ❸), has simple rooms freshly done up in a modern style. The town's campsite, *Camping Hortus* (Ⓣ02.38.36.35.94, Ⓦwww.camping -hortus.com), is on the opposite side of the Loire. For **eating** out, *Côtes et Jardin*, 8 rue du Grand-Sully (closed Sun, Tues eve & Wed; Ⓣ02.38.36.35.89), on the château side of the village, is the best bet, with an exceptionally good-value lunchtime *menu* for €15, including wine.

Gien and around

The pretty town of **GIEN** has been restored to its late fifteenth-century quaintness after extensive wartime bombing, and the sixteenth-century stone **bridge** spanning the river gives excellent views as you approach from the south. The fifteenth-century **château** in the town centre – where the young Louis XIV and his mother, Anne of Austria, hid during the revolts against taxation known as the *Frondes* (see p.1028) – has been turned over to the **Musée international de la Chasse et de la Nature** (Feb, March & Oct–Dec Mon & Wed–Sun 10am–noon & 2–5pm; April–June & Sept Mon & Wed–Sun 10am–6pm; July & Aug daily

10am–6pm; closed Jan; €5). Perhaps unsurprisingly, the emphasis lies more on *la chasse* – hunting horns, tapestries, exquisite watercolours of horseback hunts, guns and falconers' gear – than *la nature*. One of the significant consequences of the French Revolution for rural people was the right to hunt, a right still jealously guarded today. The château itself is modest, but unusual in its brick construction, a pattern of dark red interrupted by geometric inlays of grey; the interior is similarly striking, with its warm combination of brick and timber.

Gien has also long been known in France for its fine china. If you're a fan it's worth paying a visit to the **Musée de la Faïencerie**, immediately adjacent to the factory shop (Jan & Feb Mon–Sat 2–6pm, Sun 9am–noon & 2–6pm; March–June & Sept–Dec Mon–Sat 9am–noon & 2–6pm, Sun 10am–noon & 2–6pm; July & Aug Mon–Sat 9am–6pm, Sun 10am–noon & 2–6pm; €3.50; ⓦwww.gien.com), which displays the more extravagant ceramic knick-knacks produced over the last 180-odd years, ranging from exquisitely worked vases to some monstrously pretentious *objets d'art*.

Practicalities

Gien's **tourist office** is on place Jean-Jaurès, between the château and the river (Oct–April Mon–Sat 9.30am–noon & 2–5.30pm; May, June & Sept Mon–Sat 9.30am–12.30pm & 2–6pm; July & Aug Mon–Sat 9.30am–6.30pm, Sun 10am–12.30pm; ⓣ02.38.67.25.28, ⓦwww.gien.fr). **Bus** #3, which runs between Briare and Orléans, stops at place Leclerc, at the north end of the bridge. For **accommodation**, *La Poularde*, 13 quai de Nice (ⓣ02.38.67.36.05, ⓔcontacte@lapoularde.fr; ❸), on the way out of town on the road to Briare, has some lovely rooms looking out onto the river, and an excellent restaurant (*menus* €29–50). Adjacent is the **campsite** (ⓣ02.38.67.12.50, ⓦwww.camping-gien .com; closed mid-Nov to Feb), which has a swimming pool and offers a number of outdoor activities, including bike hire and canoe trips. For an alternative to the **restaurant** at *La Poularde*, make for the small strip of decent places on quai Lenoir, by the bridge; the pick of the bunch is the *Restaurant de la Loire*, at no. 18 (ⓣ02.38.67.00.75; closed Mon), a refined place serving a wide variety of fish dishes for around €30.

La Bussière

Twelve kilometres northeast of Gien is another château dedicated to country pursuits – this time fishing. The so-called **Château des Pêcheurs** at **LA BUSSIÈRE** (April–June & Sept to mid-Nov Mon & Wed–Sun 10am–noon & 2–6pm; July & Aug daily 10am–6pm; €7.50; ⓦwww.chateau-labussiere.com) is moored like a ship on its enormous fishpond, connected to a formal arrangement of gardens and huge outbuildings on the mainland. Initially a fortress, the château was turned into a luxurious residence at the end of the sixteenth century, but only the gateway and one pepper-pot tower are recognizably medieval. Guided tours are available, but you're free to wander around, soaking up the genteel atmosphere evoked by the handsome, largely nineteenth-century furnishings and the eccentrically huge collection of freshwater fishing memorabilia bequeathed by Count Henri de Chasseval, whose widow lives in an apartment in one of the outbuildings.

Briare

The small town of **BRIARE**, 10km southeast of Gien on the Orléans–Nevers road and the Paris–Nevers rail line, is notable for its *belle époque* iron aqueduct, the **Pont Canal**. It links the Canal de Briare to the north with the Canal Lateral à la Loire, making it the longest bridge-canal in Europe. The design of the Pont Canal came from the workshops of Gustav Eiffel (of Tower fame), but parts of the canal scheme date back to the early seventeenth century. Poised high above the Loire, you can walk along the aqueduct's extraordinary 625m span, with its wrought-iron crested lamps and railings.

On the opposite side of town from the canal, at the northern end, the tiny **Maison des Deux Marines** (daily: March–May & Oct to mid-Nov 2–6pm; June–Sept 10am–12.30pm & 2–6.30pm; €5) is dedicated to the rival boatmen who plied the Loire and the Canal Lateral; its basement houses a modest aquarium of Loire species. Just across the street, the **Musée de la Mosaïque et des Emaux** (daily: June–Sept 10am–6.30pm; Oct–Dec & Feb–May 2–6pm; €5) has a small collection of reproduction and contemporary mosaics made using locally manufactured tiles – Briare's wares adorn sites as prestigious and varied as the mosque at Medina and Paris's RER stations.

The **tourist office**, 1 place Charles-de-Gaulle (April to mid-Aug daily 10am–noon & 2–6pm; mid-Aug to Sept Mon–Sat 10am–noon & 2–6pm, Sun 10am–noon; Oct–March Mon–Sat 10am–noon & 2–6pm; ℡02.38.31.24.51, Ⓦwww.briare-le -canal.com), can provide details of canal boats and canoe rental as well as maps of footpaths, towpaths and the locks (the one at Châtillon-sur-Loire, 4km upstream, is particularly charming). For **accommodation**, the modern *Auberge du Pont Canal* at 19 rue du Pont-Canal (℡02.38.31.24.24; ❷) is right next to the bridge.

Sancerre and around

Huddled at the top of a steep, round hill with vineyards below, **SANCERRE** could almost be in Tuscany. The village trades heavily on its famous wines – there are endless *caves* offering tastings – rather than any particular sights or attractions, but it's certainly picturesque and the rolling hills of the Sancerrois, to the northwest, make an attractive venue for walks and cycle rides. First port of call for wine enthusiasts should be the **Maison des Sancerre**, 3 rue du Méridien (April, May, Oct & Nov 10am–6pm; June–Sept 10am–7pm; €5; Ⓦwww.maison-des -sancerre.com), which has an elaborate permanent exhibition on winemaking in Sancerre, and a garden of aromatic plants which represent the sixty key flavours found in Sancerre wines. The building itself is a fine fourteenth-century townhouse, with a great view over the rolling vine-clad hills around.

Wine outlets in the village itself tend to belong to the most famous names, with prices to match, but the tourist office can supply a list. Well suited to the wines is the local *crottin de Chavignol*, a goat's cheese named after the neighbouring village in which it's made; signs in Chavignol direct you to **fromageries** open to visitors.

The vineyards of Sancerre

If you're going to be staying in Sancerre, your first priority is probably going to be the wine, and so it makes sense during your visit to have an idea of which are the best **vineyards** in the area. There are numerous quirks of wine production here that may come as something of a surprise; for instance, wines here aren't allowed to carry an individual vineyard's name, instead being sold under the name of the producer or, very occasionally, the *cuvée*, which means that seeking out good local vineyards is best done with the help of a guide.

The Daumy family, based in Crézancy-en-Sancerre (℡02.48.79.05.75), has been making excellent **organic wines** for three generations, including the wonderful but much less commonly made red Sancerre. For a more unusual buy than the well-known white Sancerre, it's well worth exploring the neighbouring areas of **Menetou-Salon** and **Pouilly-Fumé**. The informative Aronde Sancerroise, at 4 rue de la Tour, just off the central Nouvelle Place (℡02.48.78.05.72), offers excellent, free tastings as well as tours of local vineyards by minibus.

Practicalities

The town is difficult to access by public transport, save for an infrequent bus service to and from Bourges. Private transport, such as a car or chartered bus, is more convenient, especially where visiting the vineyards is concerned. The **tourist office**, on Nouvelle Place (daily: July–Sept 10am–6.30pm; Oct–March 10am–12.30pm & 2–5pm; April–June 10am–12.30pm & 2–6pm; ☎02.48.54.08.21, ⓦwww.sancerre .fr), is an invaluable source of local information, especially when it comes to wine.

The choice of **hotels** in Sancerre is surprisingly poor, but two charming *chambres d'hôtes* more than make up for it: *Le Logis du Grillon*, 3 rue du Chantre (☎02.48.78.09.45; ➎); and *La Belle Époque*, rue St-André (☎02.48.78.00.04; ➌). The best hotel in the area is by the river in St-Satur: the antique-furnished, extremely comfortable and picturesque ⚑ *Hôtel de la Loire*, 2 quai de la Loire (☎02.48.78.22.22, ⓦwww.hotel-de-la-loire.com; ➍). The welcoming youth hostel, *Auberge de St-Thibault*, 37 rue Jacques Combes (☎02.48.78.04.10), a block away from the river, has the best-value rooms in the area (dorm beds €25). There's an excellent **campsite** (☎02.48.72.10.88; closed Oct–April) a little further along the quay, beyond the kayak shop.

There are two fine **restaurants** in Sancerre: *La Pomme d'Or*, 1 rue de la Panneterie (☎02.48.54.13.30; closed Tues & Wed eve), and the more formal *La Tour*, 31 place de la Halle (☎02.48.54.00.81), both with *menus* (around €25) to suit all pockets. *Auberge Joseph Mellot*, Nouvelle Place (☎02.48.54.20.53; closed Sun, Tues eve & Wed), serves good, simple meals designed to complement its own top-notch wines.

Bourges

BOURGES, the chief town of the rather distant region of Berry, is some way from the Loire valley proper but linked to it historically. The presence of one of the finest Gothic cathedrals in France, rising gloriously out of the unpretentious and handsome medieval quarter, provides enough reason for making a detour, but the city also offers an impressive mansion belonging to the Dauphin's financial adviser, Jacques Coeur.

Bourges's **festival** programme is excellent. Les Printemps de Bourges (ⓦwww .printemps-bourges.com) features hundreds of contemporary music acts from rock to rap, and lasts for one week during the French Easter holidays. Atmospheric ambient lighting transforms the streets of the Old Town every evening in July and August (and from Thurs–Sat in May, June & Sept).

Arrival, information and accommodation

The **gare routière** is west of the city beyond boulevard Juranville on rue du Prado. The **gare SNCF** lies 1km north of the centre; it's a straightforward walk along avenues Henri Lauder and Jean-Jaurès to place Planchat, from where rue du Commerce connects with the main street, **rue Moyenne**. The **tourist office** is just off the top end of rue Moyenne, at 21 rue Victor-Hugo (April–Sept Mon–Sat 9am–7pm, Sun 10am–6pm; Oct–March Mon–Sat 9am–6pm, Sun 2–5pm; ☎02.48.23.02.60, ⓦwww.bourges-tourisme.com), facing the south facade of the cathedral. The old medieval quarter falls away to the east, below the cathedral.

Accommodation in Bourges mostly fails to make the best of the charming old city, with the exception of one superb *chambre d'hôte*.

D'Angleterre Place des Quatre-Piliers ☎02.48.24.68.51, ⓦwww.bestwestern -angleterre-bourges.com. This is the old, traditional town-centre hotel, with an excellent location right next to the Palais de Jacques-Coeur. It has a degree of old-fashioned charm, along with modern facilities. The less expensive rooms are very small for the price. **⑥**

Les Bonnets Rouges 3 rue de la Thaumassière ☎02.48.65.79.92, ⓦbonnets-rouges.bourges.net. Five beautifully furnished chambres d'hôtes in a striking seventeenth-century house with views of the cathedral from the attic rooms. **④**

De Bourbon Bd de la République ☎02.48.70.70.00, ⓦhoteldebourbon.fr. Between the town centre and the railway station; a luxurious hotel converted from a seventeenth-century abbey, though inside it's standard luxury-hotel-chain fare. **⑥**

Camping Robinson 26 bd de l'Industrie ☎02.48.20.16.85. Decent-sized three-star site located south of the HI hostel. Bus #1 from place

Cujas, stop "Piscine Robinson", or a 10min walk from the *gare routière*. Closed mid-Nov to mid-March.

Le Cèdre Bleu 14 rue Voltaire ☎02.48.25.07.37, ⓦwww.lecedrebleu.fr. An intimate *chambre d'hôte* with attractively decorated rooms. The nineteenth-century house overlooks a lovely courtyard garden that once belonged to a convent. **③**

HI Hostel 22 rue Henri-Sellier ☎02.48.24.58.09, ⓦwww.fuaj.org. Friendly hostel located a short way southwest of the centre, with a garden on the River Auron. Bus #1 from the station towards "Golf", stop "Condé"; or a 10min walk from the cathedral or *gare routière*. Reception hours mid-Jan to mid-Dec daily 8–10am & 6–10pm. Dorm beds €14.40.

The City

Bourges's museums may be modest, but they are housed in some beautiful medieval buildings. Rue Bourbonnoux, parallel to rue Moyenne to the east of the cathedral, is worth a wander for the early Renaissance **Hôtel Lallemant**, richly decorated in an Italianate style. It houses the **Musée des Arts Décoratifs** (Jan–March 10am–noon & 2–5pm; April–June & Sept–Dec 10am–noon & 2–6pm; July & Aug 10am–12.30pm & 1.30–6pm; closed Mon & Sun am; free), a diverting enough museum of paintings, tapestries, furniture and *objets d'art*, including works by the Berrichon artist Jean Boucher (1575–1633). Halfway along the street, you can take a narrow passage up to the remains of the Gallo-Roman town **ramparts**, lined with old houses and trees. On rue Edouard Branly, you'll find the fifteenth-century **Hôtel des Échevins**, home to the **Musée Estève** (same hours as Musée des Arts Décoratifs; closed Tues & Sun am; free), dedicated to the highly coloured, mostly abstract paintings and tapestries by the locally born artist, Maurice Estève, who died in 2001.

The continuation of rue Édouard Branly, **rue Jacques-Coeur**, was the site of the head office, stock exchange, dealing rooms, bank safes and home of Charles VII's finance minister, Jacques Coeur (1400–56). A medieval shipping magnate, moneylender and arms dealer, Coeur dominates Bourges as Joan of Arc does Orléans – Charles VII doesn't get a look-in. The **Palais de Jacques-Coeur** (daily: May & June 9.30–noon & 2–6.15pm; July & Aug 9.30am–12.30pm & 2–6.30pm; Sept–April 9.30–noon & 2–5.15pm; €7; guided tours every 30min–1hr, depending on the season) is one of the most remarkable examples of fifteenth-century domestic architecture in France. The visit starts with the fake windows on the entrance front from which two realistically sculpted half-figures look down. There are hardly any furnishings, but the house's stonework recalls the man who had it built, including a pair of bas-reliefs on the courtyard tower that may represent Jacques and his wife, and numerous hearts and scallop shells inside that playfully allude to his name.

Steps lead down beside the palace to rue des Arènes, where the sixteenth-century **Hôtel Cujas** houses the **Musée du Berry** (same hours as Musée des Arts Décoratifs; closed Tues & Sun am; free), which has an interesting collection of local artefacts, most notably ten of the forty *pleurants* that survived the breaking up of Jean de Berry's tomb; Rodin considered these weeping statues so beautiful that he paid six thousand francs for one shortly before his death. Etruscan bronzes and Roman funerary monuments bear witness to Bourges's

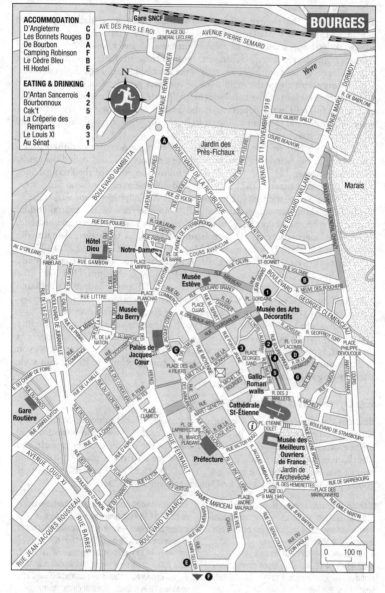

BOURGES

ACCOMMODATION
D'Angleterre   C
Les Bonnets Rouges   D
De Bourbon   A
Camping Robinson   F
Le Cèdre Bleu   B
HI Hostel   E

EATING & DRINKING
D'Antan Sancerrois   4
Bourbonnoux   2
Cak't   5
La Crêperie des
  Remparts   6
Le Louis XI   3
Au Sénat   1

ancient history, while an exhibition on the theme of traditional rural life occupies the first floor.

Next to the cathedral in place Étienne Dolet, the **Musée des Meilleurs Ouvriers de France** (same hours as Musée des Arts Décoratifs; free) displays show-off pieces by French artisans. The theme changes each year, and recent features have included glassblowing, lingerie and pastry-making.

The cathedral

The exterior of the twelfth-century **Cathédrale St-Étienne** (daily: April–Sept 8.30am–7.15pm; Oct–March 8.15am–5.45pm) is characterized by the delicate, almost skeletal appearance of its flying buttresses. A much-vaunted example of Gothic architecture, it's modelled on Notre-Dame in Paris but incorporates improvements on the latter's design, such as the astonishing height of the inner aisles.

The **tympanum** above the main door of the west portal could engross you for hours with its tableau of the Last Judgement. Thirteenth-century imagination has been given full rein in the depiction of the devils, complete with snakes' tails and winged bottoms and faces appearing from below the waist, symbolic of the soul in the service of sinful appetites.

The interior's best feature is the twelfth- to thirteenth-century **stained glass**. The most glorious windows, with astonishing deep colours, are around the choir, all created between 1215 and 1225. You can follow the stories of the Prodigal Son, the Rich Man and Lazarus, the life of Mary, Joseph in Egypt, the Good Samaritan, Christ's Crucifixion, the Last Judgement and the Apocalypse – binoculars come in handy for picking out the exquisite detail. On either side of the central absidal chapel, polychrome figures kneel in prayer; these are **Jean de Berry** and his wife. The painted decoration of the **astronomical clock** in the nave celebrates the wedding of Charles VII, who married Marie d'Anjou here on April 22, 1422.

On the northwest side of the nave aisle is the door to the **Tour de Beurre** (daily except Sun am: April & Sept 9.45–11.45am & 2–5.30pm; May & June 9.30–11.30am & 2–5.30pm; July & Aug 9.30am–12.30pm & 2–6pm; Oct–March 9.30–11.30am & 2–4.45pm; €7, or €9 with the crypt and Palais de Jacques-Coeur), which you can climb unsupervised for fantastic views over the old city. You can also join a guided tour of the **crypt** (same hours and ticket; tours roughly every hour), where you can see the alabaster statue of a puggish Jean de Berry, a small bear, symbol of strength, lying asleep at his feet. The same ticket allows you to climb unsupervised to the top of the north **tower**, rebuilt in flamboyant style after the original collapsed in 1506.

Eating and drinking

Bourges's main centre for **eating** is along rue Bourbonnoux, which runs between place Gordaine and the cathedral. Those with a sweet tooth should head for the excellent **patisserie** *Aux Trois Flûtes*, on the corner of rues Joyeuse and Bourbonnoux. On warm nights, a great spot for a **drink** is place Cujas, at the foot of rue Porte Jaune; the bar *Le Cujas* has plenty of outside seating. Another good option is the cocktail bar *Le Damier*, at 5 rue Émile Deschamps.

D'Antan Sancerrois 50 rue Bourbonnoux ☎02.48.65.96.26. Excellent local dishes, specializing in fish and game (à la carte mains all €28); closed Sun & Mon.

Bourbonnoux 44 rue Bourbonnoux ☎02.48.24.14.76. A friendly place offering some ambitious regional *menus* (€19–32). Closed Sat lunch, Fri & Sun eve.

Cak't Promenade des Remparts ☎02.48.24.94.60. Tucked under the old ramparts just off rue Bourbonnoux, this deliciously refined tearoom serves home-made quiches and tarts at lunchtime and for afternoon tea. Closed Mon.

La Crêperie des Remparts 59 rue Bourbonnoux ☎02.48.24.55.44. A better-than-usual range of crêpes and salads – those made with the local goat's cheese are especially good. Closed Sun & Mon.

Le Louis XI 11 rue Porte Jaune ☎02.48.70.92.14. Just 200m down from the cathedral, *Le Louis XI* serves impeccable steaks and chargrilled meats for around €15 in a small, informal dining room. Closed Sun.

Au Sénat 8 rue de la Poissonnerie ☎02.48.24.02.56. Just off attractive, medieval place Gordaine, this smart Bourges institution cooks excellent traditional dishes, and has tables out on the street (*menus* €17–25). Closed Wed & Thurs.

The Cher and upper Indre

Of all the Loire's many tributaries, the slow-moving **Cher** and **Indre** are closest to the heart of the region, watering a host of châteaux as they flow northwest from this little-visited region to the south. Twenty kilometres southeast of Tours, spanning the Cher, the **Château de Chenonceau** is perhaps the quintessential Loire château for its architecture, site, contents and atmosphere. Further upstream, **Montrichard** and **St-Aignan** make quieter diversions from the endless stream of castle tours. To the south is the **Château de Valençay**, with its exquisite Empire interiors. A short drive west of here, on the River Indre itself, **Loches** possesses the most magnificent medieval citadel in the region.

Château de Chenonceau

Unlike the Loire, the gentle River Cher flows so slowly and passively between the exquisite arches of the **Château de Chenonceau** (daily: April & May 9am–7pm; June & Sept 9am–7.30pm; July & Aug 9am–8pm; Oct 9am–6.30pm; Nov–Jan 9.30am–5pm; Feb & March 9.30am–6pm; €10.50; Ⓦ www.chenonceau.com) that you're almost always assured of a perfect reflection. The château is not visible from the road so you have to pay before even getting a peek at the residence. While the tree-lined path to the front door is dramatic, head through the **gardens** for a more intimate approach. They were laid out under Diane de Poitiers, mistress of Henri II.

During summer the place teems with people and it can become uncomfortably crowded, so aim to visit first thing in the morning if possible. Visits are unguided – a relief, for there's an endless array of arresting tapestries, paintings, ceilings, floors and furniture on show. It's worth seeking out the numerous portraits of the château's female owners. On the ground floor, the **François I room** features two contrasting images of the goddess Diana; one is a portrait of Diane de Poitiers by Primaticcio, and the other represents a relatively aristocratic Gabrielle d'Estrées. The room also features works by or attributed to Veronese, Tintoretto, Correggio, Murillo and Rubens, among others. The tiled floors throughout, many original, are particularly lovely. There are some unique decorative details as well, such as the seventeenth-century window frame in the **César de Vendôme room**, supported by two carved caryatids, and the moving ceiling in the bedroom of Louise de Lorraine, which mourns her murdered husband Henri III in black paint picked out with painted tears and the couple's intertwined initials. The vaulted **kitchens**, poised above the water in the foundations, are also well worth a look.

The section of the château that spans the Cher is relatively empty. The seemingly incongruous chequerboard flooring of the elegant long **gallery** is in fact true to the Renaissance design, though potted plants have replaced the classical statues that Louis XIV carried off to Versailles. Catherine de Médicis used to hold wild parties here, all naked nymphs and Italian fireworks. She intended the door on the far side to continue into another building on the south bank, but the project was never begun, and these days the gallery leads to quiet, wooded gardens. During the war, the Cher briefly formed the boundary between occupied and "free" France, and the current proprietors, who rode out Nazi occupation, claim the château's gallery was much used as an escape route. In July and August, as part of the "Nocturne à Chenonceau", the gardens and château are lit up between 9.30pm and 11pm, and classical music is played through speakers. You can take **boats** out onto the Cher in the summer months.

Practicalities

The tiny village of **Chenonceaux** – spelt with an "x" on the end – has been almost entirely taken over by a handful of rather swish **hotels**. All of them are on rue du

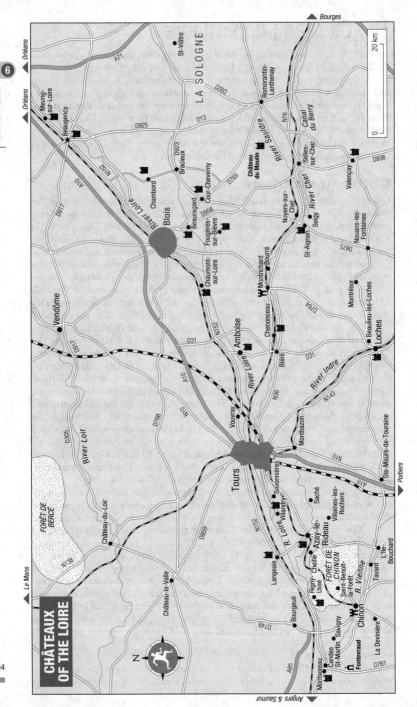

CHÂTEAUX OF THE LOIRE

Docteur-Bretonneau, within easy reach of the **gare SNCF** and the château. The *Hostel du Roy* at no. 9 (☎02.47.23.90.17, ✆www.hostelduroy.com; ❸) is comfortable and relatively inexpensive; *La Roseraie*, at no. 7 (☎02.47.23.90.09; ❹), is very welcoming, with good food, extensive grounds and a swimming pool; and at no. 6, the luxurious *Auberge du Bon Laboureur* (☎02.47.23.90.02, ✆www.bonlaboureur .com; ❼) is spread around five former village houses. For **camping**, the municipal site (closed Oct–May; ☎02.47.23.62.80) is between the railway line and the river.

Montrichard and Bourré

In many ways just a laid-back market town, **MONTRICHARD** also happens to have a full complement of medieval and Renaissance buildings, plus a hilltop **fortress**, of which just the keep remains after Henri IV broke down the rest of the defences at the end of the sixteenth century. Between mid-July and mid-August costumed medieval spectacles (daily at 4pm for €8, and at 10pm for €15) in the former château grounds entertain mainly younger audiences. At any time, you can climb up the hill for the view of the Cher – though the keep itself is out of bounds. Montrichard's Romanesque **church** was where the disabled 12-year-old princess, Jeanne de Valois, who would never be able to have children, married her cousin the Duc d'Orléans. When he became King Louis XII, after the unlikely death of Charles VIII at Amboise, politics dictated that he marry Charles VIII's widow, Anne of Brittany. Poor Jeanne was divorced and sent off to govern Bourges, where she founded a new religious order and eventually took the veil herself, before dying in 1505. In summer, you can rent pedalos and **kayaks** (July & Aug; ☎02.54.71.49.48) at the pleasant artificial **beach** on the opposite bank of the Cher. Some hardy locals swim from here, but be sure to seek advice before entering the water.

Three kilometres to the east of Montrichard, the hills around **BOURRÉ** are riddled with enormous, cave-like quarries, dug deep to get at the famous château-building stone that gets whiter as it weathers. Some of the caves are now used to cultivate mushrooms – big business in the Loire – a peculiar process that you can witness at the **Caves Champignonnières**, 40 route des Roches (mid-March to mid-Nov guided visits daily at 10am, 11am, 2pm, 3pm, 4pm & 5pm; also at noon & 6pm July & Aug; €6.50; ✆www.le-champignon.com). A second tour takes you to a "subterranean city" (€6.50, or €10.50 for both tours) sculpted in recent years as a tourist attraction, and there's an excellent shop including rare varieties of mushrooms, mushroom soup, dried mushrooms, and so on. You can also visit a fascinating troglodyte dwelling at **La Magnanerie**, 4 chemin de la Croix-Bardin (guided visits only: April–Aug daily except Tues at 11am, 3pm, 4pm & 5pm; Sept daily except Tues & Wed at 3pm, 4pm & 5pm; Oct Fri–Sun at 4pm; €7). The owner demonstrates how his family and their ancestors lived a troglodyte life here, quarrying the soft stone using huge saws, and producing silk in a chamber riddled with pigeonhole-like niches and stocked with living silkworms.

Practicalities

Montrichard's **tourist office** is in the Maison Ave Maria (April & May Mon–Sat 10am–noon & 2–6pm, Sun 10am–1pm; June & Sept 10am–6pm; July & Aug 10am–7pm; Oct–March Mon–Sat 10am–noon & 2–5pm; ☎02.54.32.05.10, ✆www.officetourisme-montrichard.com), an ancient house with saints and beasts sculpted down its beams, on rue du Pont. The only really enticing **hotel** is *La Tête Noire*, 24 rue de Tours (☎02.54.32.05.55, ✆www.latetenoire.com; ❸), with its terrace on the river, though the atmospheric *Manoir de la Salle du Roc*, 69 route de Vierzon (☎02.54.32.73.54, ✆manoirdelasalleduroc.monsite.orange .fr; ❹), offers grand *chambres d'hôtes* set in an ancient manor house above the main road leading west from Bourré. There's also a **campsite**, *L'Étourneau* (closed mid-Sept to March; ⓣ02.54.32.06.08), right in town, on the banks of the Cher. Decent meals can be had at *Les Tuffeaux*, a straightforward brasserie on Montrichard's main square, place Barthélémy-Gilbert.

St-Aignan

ST-AIGNAN, 15km southeast of Montrichard, is a small town comprising a cluster of houses below a huge Romanesque collegiate church and sixteenth-century private château. The lofty **Collégiale de St-Aignan** (daily 9am–7pm, Sun closed during services at 11am & 5.30pm) features some fine capitals carved in the twelfth century, though many more are nineteenth-century recreations. The crypt is renowned for its remarkably preserved, brightly coloured twelfth- and thirteenth-century frescoes, some of which show the beginnings of naturalistic Gothic tendencies. A flight of 144 steps climbs from the *collégiale* to the grand gravelled terrace of the **château**, enclosed on one side by the L-shape of the Renaissance *logis*, and on the other by the remnants of the eleventh-century fortress. Private ownership means it's closed to visitors, but you're free to stroll around – the far corner of the terrace leads through to a great **view** of the river, which you can reach via a flight of steep steps. Ask at the tourist office for details of **boat trips** on the Cher, or you can hire windsurfers, canoes and sail boats at the lake a couple of kilometres upstream in **Seigy**. The Maison du Vin, on place Wilson (July & Aug daily 10am–noon & 3–6pm; Sept–June Tues & Thurs 9am–noon), is open for tastings and sales of Côteaux du Cher wines.

One of the region's biggest tourist attractions is the excellent **Zoo Parc Beauval** (daily: 9am–dusk; €21, children aged 3–10 €15; ⓦ www.zoobeauval.com), 2km to the south of town on the D675. The space given to the animals is ample, and it's part of a Europe-wide programme for breeding threatened species in captivity. Sumptuous flowerbeds give way to little streams and lakes where islands provide natural enclosures for some of the monkeys.

Practicalities

The **tourist office**, 60 rue Constant-Ragot (mid-July to mid-Aug Mon–Sat 9am–7pm; rest of the year Mon–Sat 9.30am–12.30pm & 2–6pm; also open Sun mid-June to mid-Aug 10am–12.30pm & 3–6pm; ⓣ02.54.71.77.23, ⓦ www .tourisme-valdecher-staignan.com), is just off the car-park-like place Président-Wilson, in the upper part of town. The only two **hotels** are both alongside the river, on either side of the bridge: *Hôtel du Moulin*, 7 rue Novilliers (ⓣ02.54.75.15.54; ❶), is fairly basic but friendly, while *Le Grand Hôtel St-Aignan*, 7 quai Jean-Jacques Delorme (ⓣ02.54.75.18.04, ⓦ www.grand-hotel-saint -aignan.com; ❷), is a hushed, well-furnished affair, with a good restaurant (*menus* €13–36). St-Aignan has an excellent **campsite** on the bank of the river near Seigy, the *Camping des Cochards* (ⓣ02.54.75.15.59, ⓦ www.lescochards.com; closed mid-Oct to March). For an alternative to the hotel **restaurants**, the *Mange-Grenouille*, 10 rue Paul Boncour (ⓣ02.54.71.74.91; closed Tues eve & Wed; *menus* €25-30), has delightful sixteenth-century decor and outside seating in its courtyard. The welcoming *L'Amarena*, place de la Paix (ⓣ02.54.75.47.98; closed Sun & Mon afternoons), serves inexpensive Italian food on an attractive square, with pizza from €5.20.

Château de Valençay

There is nothing medieval about the fittings and furnishings of the **Château de Valençay**, 20km southeast of St-Aignan on the main Blois–Châteauroux road (daily: mid-March to April 10.30am–6pm; May & Sept 10am–6pm; June

Cave Dwellers of the Loire

One of the peculiarities of the Loire Valley is the unusual number of **troglodyte dwellings** quarried out of the soft tufa rock of the cliffs, the same material used to build the châteaux. Some have been inhabited for centuries. It is estimated that in the twelfth century, half the local population lived in caves, and today the stretch between Saumur and Angers boasts more troglodytes than anywhere else in France. These days most of the caves have been modernised – don't be surprised to see satellite dishes sprouting from the rock. Many are still being lived in, but others are used as bars or wine cellars. A number of tours of troglodyte sites are available, including one in Bourré (page p.405). If you fancy sleeping in a cave, head to *Troglododo*, a comfortable *maison d'hôte* in Azay-le-Rideau (see p.426).

9.30am–6.30pm; July & Aug 9.30am–7pm; Oct to mid-Nov 10.30am–5.30pm; €11; Ⓦ www.chateau-valencay.fr), for all its huge pepper-pot towers and turreted, decorated keep. This refined castle was originally built to show off the wealth of a sixteenth-century financier, but the lasting impression of a visit today is the imperial legacy of its greatest owner, the **Prince de Talleyrand**.

One of the great political operators and survivors, Talleyrand owes most of his fame to his post as Napoleon's foreign minister. A bishop before the Revolution, with a reputation for having the most desirable mistresses, he proposed the nationalization of church property, renounced his bishopric, escaped to America during the Terror, backed Napoleon and continued to serve the state under the restored Bourbons. One of his tasks for the emperor was keeping Ferdinand VII of Spain entertained for six years here after the king had been forced to abdicate in favour of Napoleon's brother Joseph. The Treaty of Valençay, signed in the château in 1813, put an end to Ferdinand's forced guest status, giving him back his throne. The interior is consequently largely First Empire: elaborately embroidered chairs, Chinese vases, ornate inlays to all the tables, faux-Egyptian details, finicky clocks and chandeliers. A single discordant note is struck by the leg-brace and shoe displayed in a glass cabinet along with Talleyrand's uniforms – the statesman's deformed foot was concealed in every painting of the man, including the one displayed in the portrait gallery that runs the length of the graceful Neoclassical wing.

The château **park** (same hours) keeps a collection of unhappy-looking camels, zebras, llamas and goats, and there's a small, imaginative maze. In the village, about 100m from the château gates, a **car museum** (daily: June 10am–12.30pm & 2–6.30pm; July & Aug 10am–12.30pm & 1.30–7pm; April, May, Sept & Oct 10.30am–12.30pm & 2–6pm; €5.50) houses an excellent collection of sixty-odd mostly prewar cars.

Loches

LOCHES, 42km southeast of Tours, is the obvious place to head for in the Indre valley. Its walled **citadel** is by far the most impressive of the Loire valley fortresses, with its unbreached ramparts and the Renaissance houses below still partly enclosed by the outer wall of the medieval town. Tours is only an hour away by bus, but Loches makes for a quiet, relatively untouristy base for exploring the Cher valley, or the lesser-known country to the south, up the Indre.

The **Old Town** is dominated by the Tour St-Antoine belfry, close to the handsome place du Marché that links rue St-Antoine with Grande Rue. Two fifteenth-century gates to the Old Town still stand: the **Porte des Cordeliers**, by the river at the end of Grande Rue, and the **Porte Picois** to the west, at the end of rue St-Antoine. Rue du Château, lined with Renaissance buildings, leads to the twelfth-century towers of **Porte Royale**, the main entrance to the citadel.

Arrival, information and accommodation

From Tours, trains and buses alike arrive at the **gare SNCF** on the east side of the Indre, just up from place de la Marne, where the **tourist office** is housed in a little wooden chalet (March & April Mon–Sat 9.30am–12.30pm & 2–6pm; May & June Mon–Sat 9am–12.30pm & 1.30–6pm, Sun 10am–12.30pm & 2.30–5pm; July & Aug Mon–Sat 9am–7pm, Sun 9.45am–12.30pm & 2.15–6pm; Sept Mon–Sat 9.30am–12.30pm & 1.30–6.30pm, Sun 9.45am–12.30pm & 2.15–6pm; Oct–Feb Mon–Sat 10am–12.30pm & 2.30–6pm; ℡02.47.91.82.82, ⓦwww .loches-tourainecotesud.com).

The best **accommodation** option is the old-fashioned and characterful *Hôtel de France*, 6 rue Picois (℡02.47.59.00.32, ⓦwww.hoteldefranceloches.com; ❸), which has a good restaurant. The *Hôtel George Sand*, 37 rue Quintefol (℡02.47.59.39.74, ⓦwww.hotelrestaurant-georgesand.com; ❹), just below the eastern ramparts, has its best rooms at the back, looking onto the river; the restaurant also has a lovely terrace overlooking the Indre. Less expensive rooms can be found at the charmingly tumbledown *Hôtel de Beaulieu*, 3 rue Foulques-Nerra (℡02.47.91.60.80, ⓦwww.hotel-restaurant.hoteldebeaulieu.fr; ❷), right next to the abbey in Beaulieu-les-Loches, 1km across the river. The municipal **campsite** *La Citadelle* (℡02.47.59.05.91; closed mid-Oct to mid-March) is between two branches of the Indre by the swimming pool and stadium.

The citadel

Behind the Porte Royale, the **Musée Lansyer** (June–Sept daily except Tues 10am–noon & 2–6pm; April, May & Oct Wed–Fri 2–5pm, Sat & Sun 10am–noon & 2–5pm; €3) occupies the house of local nineteenth-century landscape painter Emmanuel Lansyer, done up in period style. Straight ahead is the Romanesque church, the **Collégiale de St-Ours**, with its distinctively odd roofline – the nave bays are capped by two octagonal stone pyramids, sandwiched between more conventional spires. The porch has some entertainingly grotesque twelfth-century monster carvings, and the stoup, or basin for holy water, is a Gallo-Roman altar. But the church's highlight is the shining white **tomb of Agnès Sorel**, the mistress of the Dauphin Charles VII, a beautiful recumbent figure tenderly watched over by angels. The alabaster is rather more pristine than it should be, as it had to be restored after anticlerical revolutionary soldiers mistook her for a saint – an easy error to make.

The northern end of the citadel is taken up by the **Logis Royal**, or Royal Lodgings, of Charles VII and his three successors (daily: Jan–March & Oct–Dec 9.30am–5pm; April–Sept 9am–7pm; €7 including the *donjon*). It has two distinct halves; the older section was built in the late fourteenth century as a kind of pleasure palace for the Dauphin Charles and Agnès Sorel. A copy of Charles's portrait by Fouquet can be seen in the antechamber to the Grande Salle, where in June 1429 the Dauphin met Joan of Arc, who came here victorious from Orléans to give the defeatist Dauphin another pep talk about coronations.

From the Logis Royal, cobbled streets lined with handsome townhouses wind through to the far end of the elevated citadel, where the **donjon** (same hours and ticket as Logis Royal) stands in grim ruin. You can climb up to the top of the massive keep, but the main interest lies in the dungeons and lesser towers. The Tour Ronde was built under Louis XI and served as a prison for his adviser, Cardinal Balue, who was kept locked up in a wooden cage in one of the upper rooms. Perhaps he was kept in the extraordinary graffiti chamber on the second floor, which is decorated with an enigmatic series of deeply carved, soldier-like figures that may date from the thirteenth century. From the courtyard, steps lead down into the bowels of the Martelet, which was home to a more famous prisoner: Ludovico "il Moro" Sforza, duke of Milan, patron of Leonardo da Vinci and captive of Louis XII. In the four years he was imprisoned here, from 1500, he found time to decorate his cave-like cell with ruddy wall paintings, still faintly visible. The dungeons peter out into quarried-out galleries which produced the stone for the keep.

Eating and drinking

For an alternative to the hotel **restaurants**, *L'Entracte*, 4 rue du Château (T02.47.94.05.70; closed Sun; *menus* from €18), does hearty and generous bistro food, and has a lovely courtyard out back. The recreations of medieval recipes at *Le Vicariat*, next to the château on place Charles-VII (T02.47.59.08.79; closed Mon & Sun eve, Tues lunch; "medieval *menu*" €35), can be fun, and there is a great outside terrace. The best option of all is to stock up at the superb **market**, held on Wednesday and Saturday mornings in the winding streets just above the château gate.

Blois and around

The château at **BLOIS**, the handsome former seat of the dukes of Orléans, is magnificent; it's the main reason for visiting the town. The château's great facade rises above the modern town like an Italianate cliff, with the dramatic esplanade and courtyard behind and the rooms within steeped in (sometimes bloody) history. There are several stretches of woodland within striking distance including the **Forêt de Blois** to the west of the town on the north bank of the Loire, and the **Parc de Chambord** and **Forêt de Boulogne**, further upstream. To the south and east, the forested, watery, game-rich area known as the **Sologne** lies between the Loire and Cher, stretching beyond Orléans almost as far as Gien.

Arrival and information

Blois is easy to get around: avenue Jean-Laigret is the main street leading east from the **gare SNCF** to place Victor-Hugo and the château, and past it to the town centre. The **gare routière** is directly in front of the *gare SNCF*, with **buses** leaving up to three times a day for Cheverny and Chambord. The **tourist office**, 23 place du Château (daily: Jan–March 10am–5pm; April, May & Sept 9am–6pm; June–Aug 9am–7pm; T02.54.90.41.41, Wwww.loiredeschateaux.com), organizes hotel rooms for a small fee and has information on day coach tours of Chambord and Cheverny. It also sells combined tickets to various local châteaux for between €20.50 and €30.50. Regional information is available online at Wwww.chambordcountry.com. **Bikes** can be hired from Détours de Loire, 3 rue de la Garenne (April–Oct; T02.54.56.07.73), and Traîneurs de Loire, 12bis rue St-Lubin (April to mid-Nov; T02.54.79.36.71, Wwww.traineursdeloire.com).

Accommodation

The hotels in Blois are acceptable, if not terribly exciting. But with so many châteaux in the area, you will probably find yourself spending at least one night here.

Anne de Bretagne 31 av Jean-Laigret T02.54.78.05.38, Wannedebretagne.free.fr. Charming, vine-covered hotel set a little way back from the station, more peaceful than many others in its category. ❸

Du Bellay 12 rue des Minimes ☏02.54.78.23.62, Ⓦhoteldubellay.free.fr. Comfortable budget option with twelve well-worn but clean little rooms, much cheered up by pictures of local sights and the odd wooden beam. Good location at the top of the hill, above the town centre. ❶

Camping Rives de Loire Vineuil ☏08.00.30.04.10. On the south bank of the river, 4km from the town centre. Bus #3C (stop "Mairie Vineuil") only runs twice a day during the summer, but the campsite offers bike hire. Closed Oct–May.

Côté Loire 2 place de la Grève ☏02.54.78.07.86, Ⓦwww.coteloire.com. Charming boutique hotel, tucked away in a quiet corner by the river. Rooms have antique furnishings and brand-new bathrooms, and those at the front have views of the river. ❸

Hôtel de France et de Guise 3 rue Gallois ☏02.54.78.00.53. Dating from the 19th century, this sprawling old hotel provides a pleasant mix of old-world charm and modern amenities. Rooms on the lower floors can be noisy, but the owners are friendly and the location is hard to beat. ❸

HI Hostel 18 rue de l'Hôtel-Pasquier ☏02.54.78.27.21, Ⓦwww.fuaj.org. Five kilometres downstream from Blois, between the Forêt de Blois and the river. Bus #4 runs twice an hour, but stops at around 7.30pm. Reception open 6.45–10am & 6–10pm; closed mid-Nov to Feb. Dorm beds €11.

Le Monarque 61 rue Porte Chartraine ☏02.54.78.02.35, Ⓦannedebretagne.free.fr. Professional and energetically managed hotel with rooms cheerfully renovated in a modern style. Conveniently located at the top end of town. ❸

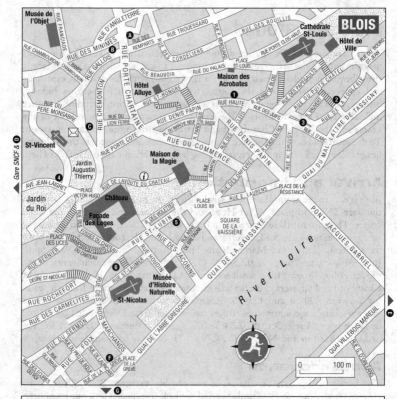

ACCOMMODATION				EATING & DRINKING			
Anne de Bretagne	D	Hôtel de France et		Les Banquettes Rouges	6	Le St-James	2
Du Bellay	B	de Guise	C	Le Castelet	5	Velvet Jazz Lounge	1
Camping Rives de Loire	E	HI Hostel	G	Hendrix Bar	3		
Côté Loire	F	Le Monarque	A	L'Orangerie du Château	4		

The château

The **Château de Blois** (daily: April–June & Sept 9am–6.30pm; July & Aug 9am–7pm; Oct 9am–6pm; Nov–March 9am–12.30pm & 1.30–5.30pm; €9.50; ⓦwww.chateaudeblois.fr) was home to six kings, and countless more aristocratic and noble visitors. The impression given is one of grandiloquent splendour, mixed with awe-inspiring spectacle, especially the way in which the predominantly Renaissance north wing is dominated by a superb spiral staircase. The grandly Classical west wing was built in the 1630s by François Mansart for Gaston d'Orléans, the brother of Louis XIII. Turning to the south side, you go back in time 140-odd years to Louis XII's St-Calais chapel, which contrasts with the more exuberant brickwork of his flamboyant Gothic east wing.

The signposts point you straight ahead and up Mansart's breathtaking staircase, which leads you round to the less interesting **François I wing**; the garish decor here dates from Félix Duban's mid-nineteenth-century efforts to turn an empty barn of a château into a showcase for sixteenth-century decorative motifs. One of the largest rooms is given over to paintings of the notorious murder of the Duke of Guise and his brother, the Cardinal of Lorraine, by Henri III. As leaders of the radical Catholic League, the Guises were responsible for the summary execution of Huguenots at Amboise. The king had summoned the States-General to a meeting in the Grande Salle, only to find that an overwhelming majority supported the Duke, along with the stringing-up of Protestants, and aristocratic over royal power. Henri had the Duke summoned to his bedroom in the palace, where he was ambushed and hacked to death, and the cardinal was murdered in prison the next day. Their deaths were avenged a year later when a monk assassinated the king himself.

The château was also home to Henri III's mother and manipulator, Catherine de Médicis, who died here a few days after the murders in 1589. The most famous of her suite of rooms is the study, where, according to Alexandre Dumas' novel, *La Reine Margot*, she kept poison hidden in secret caches in the skirting boards and behind some of the 237 narrow carved wooden panels; they now contain small Renaissance *objets d'art*. In the nineteenth century, revolutionaries were tried in the Grande Salle for conspiring to assassinate Napoléon III, a year before the Paris Commune of 1870. You can return to the courtyard via the vast space of the Salle des États, where the arches, pillars and fireplaces are another riot of nineteenth-century colour.

If you're still not flagging, you can head back across the courtyard to the ground floor of the François I wing, where an **archaeological museum** displays original stonework from the staircase and dormer windows, as well as carved details rescued from other châteaux.

French-speakers may want to take the two-hour guided **visite insolite** (April–Sept every Sun at 10.30am; also Tues & Thurs in July & Aug; €10), which explores parts of the château you won't normally see, such as the roof and cellars. You can usually just turn up at the gate for the **son et lumière** (April–Sept daily; €7, or €13 including château entry; in English on Wed), which takes place at dusk on summer evenings. It's one of the best in the region, rising above the usual mix of melodrama, light and musical effects by making the most of the château's fascinating history and lovely courtyard setting, and thrillingly recreates the murder of the Duc de Guise.

The rest of the town

Just below the château on rue St-Laumer, the **church of St Nicholas** (daily 9am–6.30pm) once belonged to an abbey, and the choir is a handsome example of the humble Benedictine treatment of the Romanesque style. The **Maison de la Magie** faces the château on the far side of the esplanade (April–Aug daily 10am–12.30pm & 2–6.30pm; Sept Mon–Fri 2–6.30pm, Sat & Sun 10am–12.30pm & 2–6.30pm; €8 or €14 with château entry; ⓦwww.maisondelamagie.fr); it sounds interesting but is actually rather boring. Slightly more instructive is the **Musée d'Histoire Naturelle**, 6 rue des Jacobins (daily except Mon 2–6pm; €2.80), with some good dioramas showing the different environments of the region, and the birds and animals that live in them.

At the north end of town, the superb **Musée de l'Objet**, 6 rue Franciade (April–June & Sept–Nov Fri–Sun 1.30–6.30pm; July & Aug Wed–Sun 1.30–6.30pm; €4), celebrates modern sculptures created from found objects rather than traditional materials. A forest of hammers hanging from the staircase ceiling gradually morphs into handbags, and the two long, spacious galleries are filled with similarly witty or alarming artworks, including some by major figures in modern art such as Man Ray and Salvador Dalí.

In the east of town, the Gothic **cathédrale St-Louis** (daily 9am–6.30pm) leans against a weighty bell tower whose lowest storey dates from the twelfth century. The interior is unexceptional, but an interesting feature is the modern **stained-glass windows**, completed in 2003 by the Dutch artist Jan Dibbets. Leading off place St-Louis, rue du Palais connects with rue St-Honoré, where, at no. 8, you'll find the elaborate **Hôtel Alluye**; the private house of the royal treasurer Florimond Robertet, it is one of the few surviving relics of Blois' golden years under Louis XII.

Eating and drinking

Most of Blois' traditional **restaurants** can be found on or around rue St-Lubin, between the château and the river. *Le Castelet*, 40 rue St-Lubin (ⓣ02.54.74.66.09; closed Wed & Sun; meals from €18), specializes in homely Loire cuisine, using regional produce. The house wines by the carafe are excellent; avoid the throat-stripping cognac. A little further along the same stretch, *Les Banquettes Rouges*, 16 rue des Trois Marchands (ⓣ02.54.78.74.92; closed Sun & Mon), serves modern French, Mediterranean-influenced food, with evening *menus* from €26. The best gastronomic experience in town is *L'Orangerie du Château*, 1 av Jean-Laigret (ⓣ02.54.78.05.36; *menus* €33–77; closed Wed & Sun eve), with acclaimed Michelin-starred cuisine, although the atmosphere can be a bit snooty.

The small square at the end of rue Vauvert, on the east side of town, has a number of crêperies and pizzerias with tables set out under the trees; the *Hendrix Bar* is a fun place to grab a drink. Immediately below, rue de la Foulerie is the best place for ethnic food – Portuguese, Moroccan and Indian – and for late-night **bars** as well. The cocktail bar *Le St-James*, 50 rue de la Foulerie, is a good bet, as is the *Velvet Jazz Lounge*, nearby at 15bis rue Haute.

Around Blois

A good reason to use Blois as a base is its proximity to several **châteaux**. By car you could call at all of them in a couple of days, but they also make ideal cycling or walking targets if you arm yourself with a map and strike out along minor roads and woodland paths. It's particularly pleasant to be able to visit them by bicycle, as local **public transport** in the area is very poor, with even the main routes served by only a couple of commuter buses a day. Note, however, that the local bus company TLC (ⓣ02.54.58.55.55, ⓦwww.tlcinfo.net) runs **coach trips** to Chambord and Cheverny, with two morning and one lunchtime departure from Blois' *gare SNCF* (April–Aug; €6 one-way); tickets can be bought at the tourist office. You can also charter a taxi from Taxi Radio Blois (☎02.54.78.07.65), but expect to pay at least €29 one-way, more if the driver waits for you at the château.

Château de Chaumont

Catherine de Médicis forced Diane de Poitiers to hand over Chenonceau in return for the **Château de Chaumont** (daily: April–June & Sept 10am–6.30pm; July & Aug 10am–7pm; Oct 10am–6pm; Nov–March 10am–4.15pm; €8; grounds open daily 9.30am–dusk; free), 20km downstream from Blois. Diane got a bad deal, but this is still one of the lovelier châteaux.

The original fortress was destroyed by Louis XI in the mid-fifteenth century in revenge for the part its owner, Pierre d'Amboise, played in the "League of Public Weal", an alliance of powerful nobles against the ever-increasing power of the monarch. But Pierre found his way back into the king's favour, and with his son, Charles I, built much of the quintessentially medieval castle that stands today. Proto-Renaissance design is more obvious in the courtyard, which today forms three sides of a square, the fourth side having been demolished in 1739 to improve the spectacular views over the river. Inside, the heavy nineteenth-century decor of the ground-floor rooms dates from the ownership of the Broglie family, but a few rooms on the first floor have been remodelled in Renaissance style. The large council chamber is particularly fine, with seventeenth-century majolica tiles on the floor and its walls adorned with wonderfully busy sixteenth-century tapestries showing the gods of each of the seven planets known at the time.

The Broglie family also transformed the landscaped **park** into the fashionable English style and built the remarkable *belle époque* **stables**, with their porcelain troughs and elegant electric lamps for the benefit of the horses at a time before the château itself was wired – let alone the rest of the country. A corner of the château grounds now plays host to an annual **Festival des Jardins** (May to mid-Oct daily 9.45am to dusk; €9.50, or €13 with château entry), which shows off the extravagant efforts of contemporary garden designers.

On weekends in summer, you can secure the best view of the château from the deck of a traditional Loire boat. Contact the Association Millière Raboton (☎06.88.76.57.14, ⊛www.milliere-raboton.net), whose hour and a half-long **boat trips** (€12–15) leave from the quay immediately below the château. The regular dawn excursions are best for wildlife spotting, and you can organize longer trips – even camping out overnight on an island sandbank.

Château de Cheverny

Fifteen kilometres southeast of Blois, the **Château de Cheverny** (daily: April–June & Sept 9.15am–6.15pm; July & Aug 9.15am–6.45pm; Oct 9.45am–5.30pm; Nov–March 9.45am–5pm; €7.50; ⊛www.chateau-cheverny .fr) is the quintessential seventeenth-century château. Built between 1604 and 1634, and little changed since, it presents an immaculate picture of symmetry, harmony and the aristocratic good life. This continuity may well be because descendants of the first owners still own, live in and go hunting from Cheverny today. Its stone, from Bourré on the River Cher, lightens with age, and the château gleams in its acres of rolling parkland. The interior decoration has only been added to, never destroyed, and the extravagant display of paintings, furniture, tapestries and armour against the gilded, sculpted and carved walls and ceilings is extremely impressive. The most precious objects are hard to pick out from the sumptuous whole, but some highlights are the painted wall panels in the dining room telling stories from *Don Quixote*; the vibrant, unfaded colours of the Gobelin tapestry in the arms room; and the three rare family portraits by François I's court painter, François Clouet, in the gallery.

You can explore the elegant **grounds** on foot, or take a sedate tour by golf buggy and boat (April to mid-Nov; €12.20 including château entry). The **kennels** near the main entrance are certainly worth a look: a hundred lithe hounds mill and loll about while they wait for the next stag, and feeding time (5pm) is something to be seen. Cheverny's hunt culls around thirty deer a year, a figure set by the National Forestry Office.

You can **stay** in the rustic *Hôtel des Trois Marchands* (☎02.54.79.96.44, ⓦwww .hoteldes3marchands.com; ❷), in **COUR-CHEVERNY**, 1km north. The hotel's restaurant is rather smart, or there's the inexpensive bar and grill next door.

Château de Beauregard

A pleasant cycle ride from Blois, the little-visited **Château de Beauregard** (April, May & Sept daily 9.30am–12.30pm & 2–6.30pm; June–Aug daily 9.30am–6.30pm; Oct & Nov daily 9.30am–12.30pm & 2–5pm; Dec & Jan daily except Wed 9.30am–noon & 2–5pm; Feb & March daily except Wed 9.30am–12.30pm & 2–5pm; €8; ⓦwww.beauregard-loire.com), 7km south of Blois on the D956 to Contres, lies in the Forêt de Russy. It was – like Chambord – one of François I's hunting lodges, but its transformation in the sixteenth century was one of beautification rather than aggrandizement. It was added to in the seventeenth century and the result is sober and serene, very much at ease in its manicured geometric park.

The highlight of the château is a richly decorated, long **portrait gallery**, whose floor of Delft tiling depicts an army on the march. The walls are entirely panelled with 327 portraits of kings, queens and great nobles, including European celebrities such as Francis Drake, Anne Boleyn and Charles V of Spain. All of France's kings are represented, from Philippe VI (1328–50), who precipitated the Hundred Years' War, to Louis XIII (1610–43), who occupied the throne when the gallery was created. Kings, nobles and executed wives alike are given equal billing – except for Louis XIII, whose portrait is exactly nine times the size of any other. It's worth strolling down through the grounds to the sunken **Jardin des Portraits**, a Renaissance-influenced creation by contemporary landscaper Gilles Clément, who was responsible for Paris's futuristic Parc André Citroën (see p.126). It could be better tended, but the garden's formal arrangement – by colour of flower and foliage – is fascinating.

Château de Chambord

The **Château de Chambord** (daily: April to mid-July & mid-Aug to Sept 9am–6.15pm; mid-July to mid-Aug 9am–7.30pm; Oct–March 9am–5.15pm; April–Sept €9.50, Oct–March €8.50; ☎02.54.50.40.00, ⓦwww.chambord.org), François I's little "hunting lodge", is the largest and most popular of the Loire châteaux and one of the most extravagant commissions of its age. If you are going to visit – and it's one of the region's absolute highlights – try to arrive early, and avoid weekends, when the crush of visitors can be both unpleasant and overwhelming. Its patron's principal object – to outshine the Holy Roman Emperor Charles V – would, he claimed, leave him renowned as "one of the greatest builders in the universe"; posterity has judged it well.

Before you even get close, the gargantuan scale of the place is awe-inspiring: there are more than 440 rooms and 85 staircases, and a petrified forest of 365 chimneys runs wild on the roof. In architectural terms, the mixture of styles is as outrageous as the size. The Italian architect Domenico da Cortona was chosen to design the château in 1519 in an effort to establish prestigious Italian Renaissance art forms in France, though the labour was supplied by French masons. The château's plan (attributed, fancifully, to da Vinci) is pure Renaissance: rational, symmetrical and totally designed to express a single idea – the central power of its owner. Four hallways run crossways through the central keep, at the heart of which the Great Staircase rises up in two unconnected spirals before opening out into the great lantern tower, which draws together the confusion on the roof like a great crown.

The cold, draughty size of the château made it unpopular as an actual residence – François I himself stayed here for just 42 days in total – and Chambord's role in history is slight. A number of rooms on the first floor were fitted out by Louis XIV and his son, the Comte de Chambord, and as reconstructed today they feel like separate apartments within the unmanageable whole. You can explore them freely, along with the adjacent eighteenth-century apartments, where the château was made habitable by lowering ceilings, building small fireplaces within the larger ones, and cladding the walls with the fashionable wooden panelling known as *boiseries*. The second floor houses a rambling **Museum of Hunting** where, among the endless guns and paintings that glorify hunting, are two superb seventeenth-century tapestry cycles: one depicts Diana, goddess of the hunt; another, based on cartoons by Lebrun, tells the story of Meleager, the heroic huntsman from Ovid's *Metamorphoses*.

The **Parc de Chambord** around the château is an enormous walled game reserve – the largest in Europe. Wild boar roam freely, though red deer are the beasts you're most likely to spot. You can explore on foot, or by bike or boat – both rentable from the jetty where the Cosson passes alongside the main facade of the château.

Practicalities

The **events and festivals** calendar is a busy one, with evening lighting displays, guided nature walks, cycle rides and jeep tours in the forest, costumed tours for children and a twice-daily dressage display, among other attractions. A free leaflet available at the château gives details.

Accommodation in the village of **Chambord** itself can be found opposite the château (and beside the cafeterias and postcard stalls) at the *Hôtel du Grand St-Michel* (☎02.54.20.31.31, ⓦwww.saintmichel-chambord.com; ⑤), although what it gains in ease of location it loses in charm and value for money. In **BRACIEUX**, a small village just beyond the southern wall of the Parc de Chambord, 8km from the château, the *Hôtel de la Bonnheure*, 9 rue René Masson (☎02.54.46.41.57, ⓦwww.hoteldelabonnheur.com; ❸), has various rooms and apartments set around floral gardens. Bracieux also has an excellent but pricey **restaurant**, *Le Relais de Bracieux* (☎02.54.46.41.22; €38–150; closed Tues, Wed & Jan), and a large **campsite** (☎02.54.46.41.84, ⓦwww.campingdeschateaux.com; closed Dec–March) with a summer-only pool.

The Sologne

Stretching southeast of Blois, **the Sologne** is one of those traditionally rural regions of France that help keep alive the national self-image. Depending on the weather and the season, it can be one of the most dismal areas in central France: damp, flat, featureless and foggy. But at other times its forests, lakes, ponds and marshes have a quiet magic – in summer, for example, when the heather is in bloom and the ponds are full of water lilies, or in early autumn when you can collect mushrooms. Wild boar and deer roam here, not to mention the ducks, geese, quails and pheasants, who far outnumber the small human population. It was this remote, mystical landscape that provided the setting for Alain Fournier's novel *Le Grand Meaulnes*; Fournier himself spent his childhood in La Chapelle d'Angillon, 34km north of Bourges, and the story's famous "fête étrange" certainly took place in the Sologne. It's worth passing through by bike on a fine day, but there's little to see otherwise.

Two *grandes randonnées* lead through the Sologne, both variants of the main GR3 along the Loire. The northern **GR3C** runs through Chambord and east mostly along forest roads to Thoury and La Ferté-St-Cyr, where it rejoins the southern branch, the **GR31**, which takes a more attractive route through Bracieux and along footpaths through the southern part of the Forêt de Chambord. There are numerous other well-signposted paths, and tourist offices in most of Sologne's towns and villages can provide maps and details of bike rental or horseriding, as well as accommodation details. If you're exploring the Sologne during the hunting season (Oct 1 to March 1), don't stray from the marked paths: there are depressingly frequent stories of people being accidentally shot.

Tours and around

Straddling a spit of land between the rivers Loire and Cher, the ancient cathedral city of **TOURS** is the chief town of the Loire valley. It has the usual feel of a mid-sized provincial city, with uneasy shifts between the strikingly grand and depressingly modern. It has its charms, however, with some good bars and cafés and some fine restaurants. It has a prettified and animated **old quarter**, some unusual **museums** – of wine, crafts, stained glass and an above-average Beaux-Arts museum – and a great many fine buildings, not least **St-Gatien cathedral**. It's also the main transport link to the great châteaux of **Villandry**, **Langeais**, **Azay-le-Rideau** and **Amboise**.

Arrival and information

The **gare routière** and **gare SNCF** are situated a short way southeast of the cathedral district, facing the futuristic Centre de Congrès Vinci, which was hugely expensive and has proved to be something of a local white elephant. Most TGVs stop at **St-Pierre-des-Corps** station, in an industrial estate outside the city, but frequent trains (or sometimes buses) provide a link to the main station. The excellent **tourist office** is on the corner of rue Bernard-Palissy and busy boulevard Heurteloup (April–Sept Mon–Sat 8.30am–7pm, Sun 10am–12.30pm & 2.30–5pm; Oct–March Mon–Sat 9am–12.30pm & 1.30–6pm, Sun 10am–1pm; ℡02.47.70.37.37, ⓦwww.ligeris.com), just across the square from the train and bus stations; it offers information on **château tours**.

Château tours

It's possible to get to most of the more-visited châteaux by public transport, but if you're short of time it's worth considering a minibus trip. The main drawback is that you're usually limited to fairly brief visits. A number of companies run **excursions** from Tours, and on most schedules you'll find the following châteaux: Amboise, Azay-le-Rideau, Blois, Chambord, Chenonceau, Cheverny, Clos-Lucé (in Amboise), Fougères-sur-Bièvre, Langeais, Ussé and Villandry. **Ticket** prices are steep: usually around €20 for a morning trip, taking in a couple of châteaux, and €40–50 for a full-day tour. These prices do not usually include entrance fees or lunch. Ask at tourist offices or contact the following Touraine-based **agencies** directly: Acco Dispo (℡06.82.00.64.51, ⓦwww.accodispo-tours.com); Saint-Éloi Excursions (℡06.70.82.78.75, ⓦwww.chateauxexcursions.com); Alienor Excursions (℡06.10.85.35.39, ⓦwww.alienortours.com); and Quart de Tours (℡06.30.65.52.01, ⓦwww.quartdetours.com). There's little to choose between them, and most pick up from the tourist office in Tours or from your hotel.

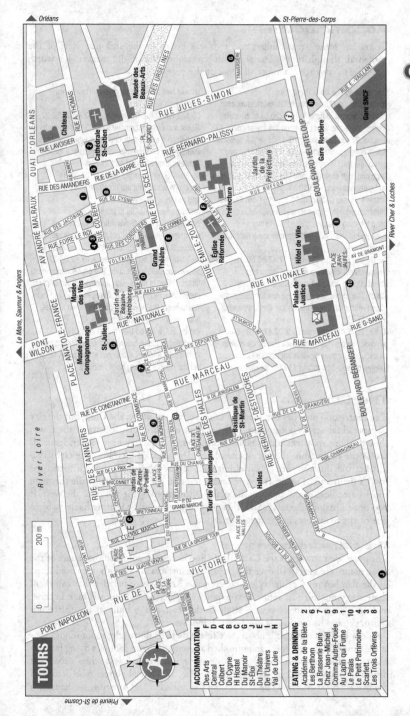

▲ Orléans

▲ St-Pierre-des-Corps

6

THE LOIRE

◄ Le Mans, Saumur & Angers

River Cher & Loches ▶

Prieuré de St-Cosme ◄

TOURS

N

0   200 m

ACCOMMODATION

Des Arts	F
Central	C
Colbert	A
Du Cygne	B
HI Hostel	G
Du Manoir	J
St-Éloi	C
Du Théâtre	E
De l'Univers	I
Val de Loire	H

EATING & DRINKING

Académie de la Bière	2
Les Berthom	6
La Brasserie Buré	7
Chez Jean-Michel	5
Comme Autre-Fouée	9
Au Lapin qui Fume	1
Le Palais	10
Le Petit Patrimoine	4
Scarlett	3
Les Trois Orfèvres	8

417

Accommodation

Tours has some great budget and two-star hotels in the area just west of the cathedral, though there's less choice at the higher end of the market. It's worth booking in advance at almost all times of the year.

Des Arts 40 rue de la Préfecture ☎02.47.05.05.00, ⓦwww.hoteldesartstours.com. Warmly decorated hotel with a choice of en-suite rooms; there are larger ones on the lower floors. ❸

Central 21 rue Berthelot ☎02.47.05.46.44, ⓦwww.tours-online.com/central-hotel. It's overpriced and part of the Best Western chain, but the rooms are large and high-ceilinged, and there's a small garden and garage parking for €10 a night. ❹

Colbert 78 rue Colbert ☎02.47.66.61.56, ⓦwww.hotelcolbert.net. Pleasant, well-furnished hotel in a good location near the cathedral. Rooms overlooking the small back garden are a little more expensive. ❷

Du Cygne 6 rue du Cygne ☎02.47.66.66.41, ⓦwww.hotel-cygne-tours.com. Pleasantly old-fashioned and well-run hotel on a quiet street. The rooms are dated but comfortable and preserve the flavour of the house. Garage parking available. ❸

HI Hostel 5 rue Bretonneau ☎02.47.37.81.58, ⓦwww.fuaj.org. Large, modern youth hostel with an excellent central location near place Plumereau. Singles or twin-bed rooms €19.50. Inexpensive

bicycle hire available for guests. Reception 8am–noon & 5–11pm.

Du Manoir 2 rue Traversière ☎02.47.05.37.37, ⓦsite.voila.fr/hotel.manoir.tours. Set in an over-modernized nineteenth-century townhouse, but friendly and comfortable with a peaceful location between the cathedral and train station. ❸

St-Éloi 79 bd Béranger ☎02.47.37.67.34. Excellent-value intimate hotel, carefully decorated and run by a friendly family. ❶

Du Théâtre 57 rue de la Scellerie ☎02.47.05.31.29, ⓦwww.hotel-du-theatre37.com. Charming, friendly hotel set in a tastefully restored medieval townhouse in the cathedral quarter. ❸

De l'Univers 5 bd Heurteloup ☎02.47.05.37.12, ⓦwww.oceaniahotels.com. The grandest and most historic hotel in town, with an enviable list of past guests including Churchill, Georges Sand and Pete Townshend; it's now considerably down at heel, and caters mainly to tour groups. ❽

Val de Loire 33 bd Heurteloup ☎02.47.05.37.86. Charming, antique-laden townhouse hotel close to the station, and a real bargain at the price. Noisy, but the double glazing does help. ❷

The City

The centre of Tours lies between the Loire and its tributary, the Cher, but the city has spread far across both banks. Neither river is a particular feature of the town, though there are parks on islands in both, and an attractive new footbridge leads across the Loire from the site of the old castle on quai d'Orléans. The city's two distinct old quarter part lie on either side of **rue Nationale**, which forms the town's main axis. The quieter part centres around the **cathedral**, while the main tourist area lies around picturesque **place Plumereau**, some 600m to the west. It was once a major pilgrimage site; these days, the pilgrimage is more likely to be to one of the many bars in the neighbourhood.

The cathedral quarter

The great west towers of the **Cathédrale St-Gatien**, standing on the square of the same name, are visible all over the city. Their surfaces crawl with decorated stone in the flamboyant Gothic style, and even the Renaissance belfries that cap them share the same spirit of refined exuberance. Inside, the style moves back in time, ending with a relatively severe High Gothic east end – built in the thirteenth century – and its glorious stained-glass windows.

A door in the north aisle leads to the **Cloître de la Psalette** (closed for renovations at the time of writing). It has an unfinished air, with the great foot of a flying buttress planted in the southeast corner and a missing south arcade – lost when a road was driven through in 1802 by the same progressive, anticlerical prefect who destroyed the basilica of St-Martin. The area behind the cathedral and museum, to the east, is good for a short stroll. There's a fine view of the spidery buttresses supporting the cathedral's painfully thin-walled apse from **place Grégoire de Tours**. Overlooking the square is the oldest wing of the **archbishop's palace**, whose end wall is a mongrel of Romanesque and eighteenth-century work, with an early sixteenth-century projecting balcony once used by clerics to address their flock.

Just south of the cathedral, the **Musée des Beaux-Arts** (daily except Tues 9am–12.45pm & 2–6pm; €4) is housed in the former archbishop's palace. Other than Mantegna's intense, unmissable *Agony in the Garden* (1457–59) in the basement, there are few celebrity works in the large collection. Even Rembrandt's much-advertised *Flight into Egypt* is a small oil study rather than a finished work. But the stately, loosely chronological progression of palatial seventeenth- and eighteenth-century rooms, each furnished and decorated to match the era of the paintings it displays, is extremely attractive. Local gems include Boulanger's portrait of Balzac, and the engravings *The Five Senses* by the locally born Abraham Bosse, which have been interpreted as full-size canvases in the handsome Louis XIII room.

On the other side of the cathedral, between rue Albert-Thomas and the river, just two towers remain of the ancient royal **château** of Tours. You can get inside when an exhibition is on but there's nothing much left of the interior.

The old quarter

To the west, the pulse of the city quickens as you approach **place Plumereau** – or place Plum' as it's known locally. The square's tightly clustered, ancient houses have been carefully restored as the city's showpiece, transforming what was once a slum into the epicentre of social life. On sunny days, the square is packed almost end-to-end with café tables, and students and families drink and dine out until late in the evening.

If you're looking for peace, slip down **rue Briçonnet** into a miniature maze of quiet, ancient streets. Opposite an oddly Venetian-looking, fourteenth-century house, at no. 41 rue Briçonnet, a passageway leads past a palm tree and an ancient outdoor staircase to the quiet and insulated **Jardin de St-Pierre-le-Puellier**, laid out around the dug-out ruins of a conventual church.

To the south lay the pilgrim city once known as **Martinopolis** after St Martin, the fourth-century bishop of Tours who went on to become a key figure in the spread of Christianity through France. He is usually remembered for giving half his cloak to a beggar, an image repeated in stained-glass windows all over the region. The Romanesque **basilica** stretched along rue des Halles from rue des Trois-Pavés-Ronds almost to place de Châteauneuf: the outline is traced out in the street, but only the north tower, the Tour de Charlemagne, and the western clock tower survived the iconoclastic Huguenot riots of 1562. The new **Basilique de St-Martin**, on rue Descartes, is a late nineteenth-century neo-Byzantine affair built to honour the relics of St Martin, rediscovered in 1860. They are now housed in the crypt, watched over by hundreds of votive prayers carved into the walls. A short distance away, down rue des Halles, lies the huge, modern **Halles**, or covered market – an excellent place to browse for a picnic in the morning.

Around rue Nationale

At the head of **rue Nationale**, Tours' main street, statues of Descartes and Rabelais – both Touraine-born – overlook the scruffy walkways running along the bank of the Loire. A short walk back from the river brings you to the Benedictine **church of St Julien**, whose old monastic buildings are home to two fairly missable museums. The **Musée des Vins**, 16 rue Nationale (Fri–Sun 9am–noon & 2–6pm; €3.30), is a bit of a let-down, as all the exhibits are in French and there is no opportunity to taste wines. Behind the museum, a Gallo-Roman winepress from Cheillé sits in the former cloisters of the church. The **Musée de Compagnonnage**, at 8 rue Nationale (mid-June to mid-Sept daily 9am–12.30pm & 2–6pm; mid-Sept to mid-June daily except Tues 9am–noon & 2–6pm; €5), is housed in the eleventh-century guesthouse and sixteenth-century monks' dormitory. It honours the peculiarly French cult of the artisan, displaying the "masterpieces" that craftsmen had to create in order to join their guilds (*compagnonnage*) as master craftsmen. The skills are unquestionable but many of these showpieces are rather mundane, displaying arts as diverse as cake-making, carpentry, clog-making and cooperage.

At the southern end of rue Nationale, the huge, traffic-ridden place Jean-Jaurès is the site of the grandiose Hôtel de Ville and Palais de Justice. To the west of place Jean-Jaurès, a giant **flower market** takes over boulevard Béranger on Wednesdays and Saturdays, lasting from 8am into the early evening.

St-Cosme

In May, when the roses are in full bloom, the **Prieuré de St-Cosme**, 3km west of the centre (mid-March to April & Sept to mid-Oct daily 10am–6pm; May–Aug daily 10am–7pm; mid-Oct to mid-March daily except Tues 10am–12.30pm & 2–5pm; €4.50), is one of the most appealing sights in the area even if it is hemmed in by suburbs and barred off from the nearby Loire by a trunk road. Once an island priory, now a semi-ruin, it was here that Pierre de Ronsard, France's greatest Renaissance poet, lived as prior from 1565 until his death in 1585. Vestiges of many monastic buildings survive but the most affecting sight is the lovingly tended garden of roses, which has some two thousand rose bushes, and 250 varieties – including the tightly rounded pink rose called "Pierre de Ronsard". To get here by public transport, take **bus** #3 from immediately outside the Palais de Justice, on place Jean-Jaurès, towards La Riche-Petit Plessis, getting off at the La Pléiade stop.

Eating

The streets around place Plumereau, especially rue du Grand-Marché, are overrun with **cafés**, **bars** and **bistros**; if you don't mind paying a little extra for the bustling atmosphere and an outside table, this is the area to head for. Don't expect too many culinary fireworks though. On the cathedral side of rue Nationale, rue Colbert is lined with much less touristy bars and ethnic eateries, as well as a few good restaurants serving regional cuisine. For a quiet tea break in the afternoon, make for *Scarlett*, a relaxed tearoom at 70 rue Colbert.

La Brasserie Buré 1 place de la Résistance ⓣ02.47.05.67.74. This bustling brasserie has become something of a local institution, serving both seafood and grilled meats on its crowded terrace. Mains around €20.

Chez Jean-Michel 123 rue Colbert ⓣ02.47.20.80.20. Intimate wine bar and restaurant that manages to be elegant and relaxed at the same time. Serves good regional dishes to go along with the excellent local wines. *Menus* from €25. Closed Sat & Sun.

Comme Autre-Fouée 11 rue de la Monnaie ⓣ02.47.05.94.78. The food served here is a revival of the archaic *fouace* (or *fouée*) breads immortalized by Rabelais, served hot and heavily garnished with local titbits. An excellent option for a unique meal, with a good-value lunch *menu* for €10. Closed Sun & Mon.

Au Lapin qui Fume 90 rue Colbert ⓣ02.47.66.95.49. Tiny, relaxed but elegant restaurant serving a good menu that's half Loire and half south of France. Lots of tasty *lapin* (rabbit) – it comes as a terrine, as a *fricassée* with rosemary, or *confit* – but it's not obligatory. Evening *menus* around the €24 mark.

Le Petit Patrimoine 58 rue Colbert ⓣ02.47.66.05.81. Romantic little place serving rich, lovingly prepared Loire dishes and good Loire wines, including the famous red Sancerre. *Menus* €18–28.

Drinking and nightlife

Packed with tables and chairs, place Plumereau is *the* place to start the evening with an open-air aperitif and to finish it with a restorative coffee. There's a slightly depressing absence of bars and pubs with really individual character in the area, but there are plenty of less commercial places to be found in the surrounding streets, with some good **café-bars** on rue du Commerce – try *Les Berthom*, which has lots of outside tables. In the cathedral quarter, the bars on rue Colbert are overpriced and unfriendly to non-locals, with the exception of the *Académie de la Bière* just up from the cathedral at 43 rue Lavoisier; it's a lively, student-friendly place, with an excellent range of beers. If you're around during the university term, it might be worth a visit to *Le Palais* on 15 place Jean-Jaurès on a Monday night, where you can speak in a variety of different languages to the students during an event called Café des Langues.

Even in summer, when local students are away, the **nightclubs** just off place Plumereau fill up with backpackers, locals and language students – try *Les Trois Orfèvres*, 6 rue des Orfèvres, though things don't usually get going until past midnight. For details of **classical music** concerts, stop by the tourist office to pick up *Détours et des Nuits*, a free monthly magazine of exhibitions, concerts and events in Touraine.

Listings

Airport Aéroport Tours Val de Loire ☎02.47.49.37.00, ⓦwww.tours-aeroport.fr. A shuttle bus runs to the airport from the centre of town (€5).

Bike hire Détours de Loire, 35 rue Charles Gille ☎02.47.61.22.23, ⓦwww.locationdevelos.com. Runs the Détours de Loire scheme (see p.385), which allows you to drop off the bike at various locations along the river, for a small extra charge. The *Hôtel Moderne* at 1 rue Laloux also rents bikes to the public (☎02.47.05.32.81).

Car hire Avis, gare de Tours ☎02.47.20.53.27; Europcar, 194 av Maginot ☎02.47.85.85.85; Hertz, 57 rue Marcel-Tribut ☎02.47.75.50.00. All offer pick-up and drop-off at Tours airport, at St-Pierre-des-Corps TGV station or near the *gare SNCF* in Tours.

Health Ambulance ☎15; different hospital departments are spread around the city – call ☎02.47.47.47.47 to check where to head.

Internet Central options include: Alliance Micro, 7 rue de la Monnaie (Mon–Sat 9.30am–6pm); Cyber Gate, 11 rue Merville (Mon–Sat 10am–midnight, Sun 3–9pm); and Top Communication, 129 rue Colbert (Mon–Sat 9am–10pm, Sun 2–10pm).

Police Commissariat Général, 70–72 rue Marceau ☎02.47.33.80.69.

Amboise

Twenty kilometres upstream of Tours, **AMBOISE** is one of the highlights of the Loire region, with a beguiling mix of beauty, excellent food and drink and a genuine sense of history. The **château** dominates the town, but there are many other attractions, most famously Leonardo da Vinci's residence of **Clos-Lucé**, with its exhibition of the great man's inventions. Amboise draws a busy tourist trade that may detract from the quieter pleasures of strolling around town, but makes it a good destination for children. In July and August, **son et lumière** shows are held around 10pm at the château (Wed & Sat; adults €13, children 6–12 €7; ⓦwww.renaissance-amboise.com), with Leonardo images projected on the walls and costumed actors prancing about to loud Renaissance-style music.

Arrival, information and accommodation

The **gare SNCF** is on the north bank of the river, at the end of rue Jules-Ferry, about 1km from the château. There are frequent connections to Tours and Blois. Information on Amboise and its environs, including the vineyards of the Touraine-Amboise *appellation*, is available at the **tourist office** on quai du Général-de-Gaulle,

Staying in a château

One of the great privileges of visiting the Loire is that there are a variety of châteaux that accommodate visitors. The standards range enormously: at the top end of the market, you are guaranteed deluxe accommodation, with room service, all mod cons, excellent food and all the amenities you would expect from a top-class hotel; at the other end, you are effectively staying in a bed and breakfast in someone's house, which can be pot luck. The following are the pick of the hotels in the Tours area:

Château D'Artigny Near Montbazon (take D17 from there) ℡02.47.34.30.30, ⓦwww .grandesetapes.fr/en/Chateau-hotel-artigny. Stunning, beautifully restored château originally owned by the perfumier François Coty, and decorated in a Neoclassical style. The rooms are all large, lavishly appointed and very comfortable, and the excellent restaurant has sweeping views across the Loire valley. ❽

Domaine de Beauvois Near Luynes ℡02.47.55.50.11, ⓦwww.grandesetapes.fr/en /Chateau-hotel-beauvois. Much of the appeal of this beautiful sixteenth-century mansion comes from its peaceful seclusion, with long country walks and beautiful bike rides the order of the day. There are some lovely, quirky touches in the rooms, too, which have beamed ceilings and painted frescoes, and the restaurant offers excellent food. ❽

Domaine de la Tortinière Near Montbazon ℡02.47.34.35.00, ⓦwww.tortiniere.com. Delightful family-run hotel, with friendly bilingual owners. Rooms range from the modestly comfortable to the spectacularly luxurious (such as the suites in the turrets, complete with circular bedrooms) and very good food is served in the dining room, overlooking an open-air swimming pool. ❼

on the riverfront (June & Sept Mon–Sat 9.30am–6.30pm, Sun 10am–1pm & 2–5pm; July & Aug Mon–Sat 9am–8pm, Sun 10am–6pm; Oct–May Mon–Sat 10am–1pm & 2–6pm; ℡02.47.57.09.28, ⓦwww.amboise-valdeloire.com).

Bikes can be hired from Cycles Richard, 2 rue Nazelles, near the station (℡02.47.57.01.79), or Locacycle, on rue Jean-Jacques-Rousseau (℡02.47.57.00.28). **Canoes** are available from the Club de Canoë-Kayak, at the Base de l'Île d'Or (℡02.47.23.26.52, ⓦwww.loire-aventure.com), which also runs guided trips.

Hotels in Amboise vary enormously in price, but tend to be of a good standard.

Belle-Vue 12 quai Charles-Guinot ℡02.47.57.02.26, ⓔbellevuehotel.amboise @orange.fr. Long-established Logis de France three-star just below the château, with comfortable, old-fashioned bedrooms. Some rooms at the front overlook the Loire – and the main road. Closed mid-Nov to mid-March. ❹

Le Blason 11 place Richelieu ℡02.47.23.22.41, ⓦwww.leblason.fr. Very smartly kept but homey hotel in a quiet location. The furnishings are modern, but all rooms have pretty, exposed beams. Triples and quads available. Free internet access. ❸

Café des Arts Place Michel-Debré ℡02.47.57.25.04. Simple but friendly backpacker-oriented place – think pine bunkbeds and hard-wearing carpet – above a popular local café. ❶

Camping de l'Île d'Or Île d'Or ℡02.47.57.23.37, ⓦwww.camping-amboise.com. Pleasant, leafy campsite, with access to the pool. Closed Oct–March.

Centre Charles Péguy Île d'Or ℡02.47.30.60.90, ⓦwww.mjcamboise.fr. Ordinary but clean and relatively comfortable hostel in a pleasant location on the midstream island, halfway across the town bridge; fills up fast, so it's best to reserve in advance. Prices vary, but beds cost around €14 a night, plus €3 for sheets. Reception Mon–Fri 2–8pm, Sat & Sun 6–8pm.

Le Choiseul 36 quai Charles-Guinot ℡02.47.30.45.45, ⓦwww.le-choiseul.com. Widely acknowledged to be the best hotel in Amboise, this luxurious place has grandly appointed and very comfortable rooms, an excellent restaurant and all the other touches you'd expect. ❼

Le Vieux Manoir 13 rue Rabelais ℡02.47.30.41.27, ⓦwww.le-vieux-manoir .com. Run by an utterly charming American couple, this lovingly restored manor house is the best bed and breakfast in the region, some might say the country. Lots of lovely touches abound, from the glass of Loire wine waiting on your arrival to the sweet self-contained cottage. ❼

Château d'Amboise

Rising above the river are the remains of the **château** (daily: April–June 9am–6.30pm; July & Aug 9am–7pm; Sept & Oct 9am–6pm; first 2 weeks Nov & March 9am–5.30pm; mid-Nov to Jan 9am–12.30pm & 2–4.45pm; Feb 9am–12.30pm & 1.30–5pm; €9.70; ⓦwww.chateau-amboise.com), once five times its present size, but much reduced by wars and lack of finance; it still represents a highly impressive accomplishment. It was in the late fifteenth century, following his marriage to Anne of Brittany at Langeais, that Charles VIII decided to turn the old castle of his childhood days into an extravagant palace, adding the flamboyant Gothic wing that overlooks the river and the **chapelle de St-Hubert**, perched incongruously atop a buttress of the defensive walls. But not long after the work was completed, he managed to hit his head, fatally, on a door frame. He left the kingdom to his cousin, Louis XII, who spent most of his time at Blois but built a new wing at Amboise (at right angles to the main body) to house his nearest male relative, the young François d'Angoulême, thereby keeping him within easy reach. When the young heir acceded to the throne as François I he didn't forget his childhood home. He embellished it with classical stonework (visible on the east facade of the Louis XII wing), invited Leonardo da Vinci to work in Amboise under his protection, and eventually died in the château's collegiate church.

Henri II continued to add to the château, but it was during the reign of his sickly son, François II, that it became notorious. The Tumult of Amboise was one of the first skirmishes in the Wars of Religion. Persecuted by the young king's powerful advisers, the Guise brothers, Huguenot conspirators set out for Amboise in 1560 to "rescue" their king and establish a more tolerant monarchy under their tutelage. But they were ambushed by royal troops in the woods outside the town, rounded up and summarily tried in the Salle des Conseils. Some were drowned in the Loire below the château, some were beheaded in the grounds, and others were hung from the château's balconies.

After such a history, the interior of the château is comparatively restrained, though the various rooms still retain some sense of their historical grandeur. The last French king, Louis-Philippe, also stayed in the château, hence the abrupt switch from the solid Gothic furnishings of the ground floor to the 1830s post-First Empire style of the first-floor apartments. The **Tour des Minimes**, the original fifteenth-century entrance, is architecturally the most exciting part of the castle. With its massive internal ramp, it was designed to allow the maximum number of fully armoured men on horseback to get in and out as quickly as possible. These days it leads down to the pleasant gardens, which in turn lead to the exit.

Clos-Lucé

Following his campaigns in Lombardy, François I decided that the best way to bring back the ideas of the Italian Renaissance was to import one of the finest exponents of the new arts. In 1516, **Leonardo da Vinci** ventured across the Alps in response to the royal invitation, carrying with him the *Mona Lisa* among other paintings. For three years before his death in 1519, he made his home at the **Clos-Lucé**, at the end of rue Victor-Hugo (daily: Jan 10am–6pm; Feb–June, Sept & Oct 9am–7pm; July & Aug 9am–8pm; Nov & Dec 9am–6pm; March to mid-Nov €12.50, mid-Nov to Feb €9.50). Leonardo seems to have enjoyed a semi-retirement at Amboise, devoting himself to inventions of varying brilliance and impracticability, and enjoying conversations with his royal patron, but it seems that no work of any great stature was produced here. The house – an attractive brick mansion with Italianate details added by Charles VIII – is now a museum to Leonardo. The gardens are over-designed, but it's nevertheless interesting to browse through the forty models of his mechanical inventions.

Beyond the town centre

If you take the main road south out of Amboise and turn right just before the junction with the D31, you'll come to an eighteenth-century **pagoda**, once part of the enormous but now demolished château of Chanteloup. You can climb to the top for an expansive view and explore the grounds of the surrounding park (April daily 10am–6pm; May & Sept daily 10am–6.30pm; June daily 10am–7pm; July & Aug daily 9.30am–7.30pm; Oct & Nov Sat & Sun 10am–noon & 2–5pm; €8). Turn left on the D31 itself to reach the park **Mini-Châteaux** (daily: April & May 10.30am–7pm; June & July 10am–7pm; Aug 10am–8pm; Sept to mid-Nov 10.30am–6pm; €13.50, children 4–14 years €9.50), which houses more than forty surprisingly good scale models of the chief Loire châteaux.

At Lussault, 5km west towards Tours, the mammoth **Aquarium du Val de Loire** (daily: April & May 10.30am–7pm; June & July 10am–7pm; Aug 10am–8pm; Sept–March 10.30am–6pm; closed last 2 weeks Jan & last 2 weeks Nov; adults €13.50, children 4–14 years €9.50; ⓦwww.aquariumduvaldeloire .com) boasts ten thousand fish, along with turtles, alligators and a tunnel through a large shark tank.

Eating and drinking

The best restaurant in town is Pascal Bouvier's celebrated dining room at the hotel ⚘ *Le Choiseul* (ⓣ02.47.30.45.45; *menus* €45–€80); the food is expensive but excellent, and the views over the Loire are stunning. *L'Épicerie*, 46 place Michel-Debré (ⓣ02.47.57.08.94; *menus* €22–34; closed Mon & Tues except July & Aug), is overlooked by the chapelle St-Hubert and serves good country cuisine with a good-value set lunch at €10, and *L'Alliance*, 14 rue Joyeuse (ⓣ02.47.30.52.13; *menus* €29–50; closed Tues & Wed), is a good option mainly serving fish; in summer, both need to be booked in advance. *Brasserie de l'Hôtel de Ville*, 1 rue François-I (ⓣ02.47.57.26.30; *menus* €16–29), a bustling place next to the Hôtel de Ville, has good lunchtime *menus* and pleasant outdoor seating out back. If you fancy a late drink, head over to the Île d'Or, where you'll find the cocktail **bar** *Le Shaker* (6pm–3am; closed Mon), whose outside terrace has great views across to the château. The *Caveau des Vignerons d'Amboise* at the base of the château offers a wide variety of local wines to taste.

Château de Villandry

Even if gardens aren't normally your thing, those at the **Château de Villandry** are unmissable (daily: March 9am–5.30pm; April–June, Sept & Oct 9am–6pm; July & Aug 9am–6.30pm; first 2 weeks Nov & Feb 9am–5pm; last 2 weeks Dec 9.30am–4.30pm; closed mid-Nov to mid-Dec & Jan; €9 château and gardens, €6 gardens only; ⓦwww.chateauvillandry.com). Thirteen kilometres west of Tours along the Cher, this recreated Renaissance garden is as much symbolic as ornamental or practical. At the topmost level is a large, formal water garden in the elevated Classical spirit. Next down, beside the château itself, is the ornamental garden, which features geometrical arrangements of box hedges symbolizing different kinds of love: tender, passionate, fickle and tragic. But the highlight, spread out at the lowest level across 12,500 square metres, is the potager, or Renaissance kitchen garden. Carrots, cabbages and aubergines are arranged into intricate patterns, while rose bowers and miniature box hedges form a kind of frame. Even in winter, there is almost always something to see, as the entire area is replanted twice a year. At the far end of the garden, overlooked by the squat tower of the village church, beautiful vine-shaded paths run past the medieval herb garden and the maze.

The elegant **château** was erected in the 1530s by one of François I's royal financiers, Jean le Breton, though the keep – from which there's a fine view of the gardens – dates back to a twelfth-century feudal castle. It's worth a quick visit, but pales in comparison to its gardens. Le Breton's Renaissance structure is arranged around three sides of a *cour d'honneur*, the fourth wing having been demolished in the eighteenth century. To get here, a number of **minibus companies** make the trip from Tours, a service that usually includes a stop in Azay-le-Rideau (see below); they leave from the tourist office and cost around €20 return. In July and August, there are also two local buses a day from Tours' *gare routière*.

There are some top-class options for **eating** out in and around Villandry. In the centre of the tiny village, just down from the château, the wine bar, deli and restaurant 🍴 *L'Épicerie Gourmande* (☎02.47.43.57.49) matches Loire wines with delicious delicatessen specialities, served all day; there's a good crêpe *menu* for €12. For something hearty, head 1km down the D121 towards Druye, where you'll find a farmhouse restaurant, the *Étape Gourmande* at the Domaine de la Giraudière (☎02.47.50.08.60; closed mid-Nov to mid-March; *menus* €17–33); its courtyard throngs with families enjoying honest home-cooked fare, with the farm's own goat's cheese featuring prominently. Right beside the Loire in Berthenay, a tiny village across the Cher from Villandry – you have to make a 7km round trip via Savonnières – 🍴 *Au Bout du Monde* (☎02.47.43.51.50; evening *menus* €17–32; closed Sun eve & Tues) serves fresh, light, imaginative cuisine in a lovely garden setting.

Château de Langeais

Twenty-three kilometres west of Tours, the small riverside town of **LANGEAIS** huddles in the shadow of its forbidding **château** (daily: Feb & March 9.30am–5.30pm; April–June & Sept to mid-Nov 9.30am–6.30pm; July & Aug 9am–7pm; mid-Nov to Jan 10am–5pm; €8.20; ⓦwww.chateau-de-langeais.com), which was built to stop any incursions up the Loire by the Bretons. This threat ended with the marriage of Charles VIII and Duchess Anne of Brittany in 1491, which was celebrated in the castle, and a diptych of the couple portrays them looking less than joyous at their union – Anne had little choice in giving up her independence. The event is also recreated in waxworks in the chapel.

The main appeal here is in the way that the interior has resisted modernization to give a genuine sense of what life would have been like in the fifteenth century. There are fascinating tapestries, some rare paintings, cots and beds and a number of *chaires*, or seigneurial chairs. In the huge marriage chamber, the gilded and bejewelled wedding coffer of Charles and Anne is carved with a miniature scene of the Annunciation and figures of the apostles, the wise and foolish virgins depicted on the lid.

Langeais has a pleasant **hotel**, the *Errard-Hosten*, 2 rue Gambetta (☎02.47.96.82.12, ⓦwww.errard.com; ❹), with a good restaurant (*menus* from €29). The *Anne de Bretagne*, 27 rue Anne de Bretagne (☎02.47.96.08.52, ⓦwww.chambresdhotes-langeais.fr; ❸), offers some exceptional *chambres d'hôtes* in a restored early nineteenth-century home. Sixteen kilometres north along the D57, just outside the village of Hommes, the *Vieux Château d'Hommes* (☎02.47.24.95.13, ⓦwww.le-vieux-chateau-de-hommes.com; ❻) offers well-furnished rooms in a fifteenth-century outhouse of the main château, and can prepare meals for guests on request.

Azay-le-Rideau and around

Even without its striking **château** (daily: April–June & Sept 9.30am–6pm; July & Aug 9.30am–7pm; Oct–March 10am–12.30pm & 2–5.30pm; €8), the quiet village of **AZAY-LE-RIDEAU** would bask in its serene setting, complete with an old mill by the bridge and curious, doll-like Carolingian statues embedded in the facade of the church of St Symphorien. Perhaps unsurprisingly, it has become a magnet for tourists, and much of its charm is being gradually eroded by the sheer number of visitors it attracts. On its little island in the Indre, the château is one of the loveliest in the Loire: perfect turreted early Renaissance, pure in style right down to the blood-red paint of its window frames. Visiting the interior, furnished in mostly period style, doesn't add much to the experience although the grand staircase is worth seeing, and it's fun to look out through the mullioned windows across the moat and park and imagine yourself the *seigneur*. In summer, the château's grounds are the setting for a restrained and rather lovely **son et lumière** (July & Aug daily 9pm; €10, or €14 with daytime château entry).

Practicalities

Azay's **tourist office** sits just off the village's main square, place de la République (May, June & Sept Mon–Sat 9am–1pm & 2–6pm, Sun 10am–1pm & 2–5pm; July & Aug Mon–Sat 9am–7pm, Sun 10am–6pm; Oct–April Mon–Sat 9am–1pm & 2–6pm; ☏02.47.45.44.40, ⓦwww.ot-paysazaylerideau.fr). The **bus stop** is next to the tourist office on the main road, but the **gare SNCF** is awkwardly situated a fifteen-minute walk west of the centre, along avenue Adélaïde-Riché – trains from Tours call at Azay-le-Rideau on their way to Chinon roughly every two hours (some services are replaced by *SNCF* buses). You can hire **bikes** from Cycles Leprovost, 13 rue Carnot (☏02.47.45.40.94), and in summer **canoes** can be hired from beside the bridge on the road out towards Chinon (June–Aug daily 1–7pm; ☏02.47.45.39.45).

Azay-le-Rideau has some of the best **accommodation** in the area, with two very pleasant hotels on or just off the main square. The *Hôtel de Biencourt*, 7 rue Balzac (closed mid-Nov to mid-March; ☏02.47.45.20.75, ⓦwww.hotel biencourt.com; ❸), is attractive and friendly, while *Le Grand Monarque*, 3 place de la République (☏02.47.45.40.08, ⓦwww.legrandmonarque.com; ❸), is indeed rather grand, and has a wide range of rooms. But the best options are all *chambres d'hôtes*: the *Manoir de la Rémonière* (☏02.47.45.24.88, ⓦwww.manoir delaremoniere.com; ❼), 1km from Azay on the opposite side of the Indre, on the road to Saché, was once the château's fifteenth-century hunting lodge and the two rooms offered by M. et Mme Sarrazin at ⚷ *Troglododo*, 9 chemin des Caves Mecquelines (☏02.47.45.31.25, ⓦwww.troglododo.fr; ❸), are both in troglodyte chambers hollowed out of the rock. Every hotel gets booked up a fair way in advance; don't even think about turning up in summer without a reservation. Upstream from the château is a large **campsite**, the *Camping du Sabot* (closed Nov–March; ☏02.47.45.42.72), signposted off the D84 to Saché.

For **restaurants**, *La Ridelloise*, 24 rue Nationale (☏02.47.45.46.53; *menus* €13–27), has a family atmosphere and inexpensive but decent cooking. In summer, *L'Aigle d'Or*, 10 av Adélaïde-Riché (☏02.47.45.24.58; closed Wed & Sun eve), serves elegant cuisine in its delightful garden, with *menus* from €26 to €44. The more commercial *Les Grottes*, 23 rue de Pineau (☏02.47.45.21.04; mains from €12), offers the novel sensation of dining in a cave, but the food doesn't match up to the experience.

Château d'Ussé

Fourteen kilometres west of Azay-le-Rideau, as the Indre approaches its confluence with the Loire, is the **Château d'Ussé** in **RIGNY-USSÉ** (daily: mid-Feb to March 10am–6pm; April–Aug 10am–7pm; Sept to mid-Nov 10am–6pm; €13; ⓦwww.chateaudusse.fr). With its shimmering white towers and terraced gardens, this is the ultimate fairy-tale château – so much so that it's supposed to have inspired Charles Perrault's classic retelling of the Sleeping Beauty myth. Whether you find it an unmissable spectacle or a faintly embarrassing testament to kitsch depends entirely on personal taste. The exterior resembles nothing so much as a Disney fantasy; you half expect to see Beauty and the Beast emerge. Inside, things are more restrained, apart from the tacky tableaux telling the story of Sleeping Beauty, but the **gardens**, designed by Le Nôtre, are pleasant to wander in. The loveliest feature of all is the Renaissance **chapel** in the grounds, shaded by ancient cedars.

The tiny village of **Rigny-Ussé** has a welcoming, family-run **hotel-restaurant**, *Le Clos d'Ussé* (℡02.47.95.55.47; ❶), with eight simple rooms. Behind the château, in a tranquil, wooded fold of the valley, the *Domaine de la Juranvillerie*, 15 rue des Fougères (℡02.47.95.57.85, ⊛www.lajuranvillerie.com; ❹), is a charming little group of cottages, two housing simple, attractive *chambres d'hôtes*. The friendly owners are enthusiastic naturalists and can advise on walks in the Forêt de Chinon.

Chinon and around

CHINON lies on the north bank of the Vienne, 12km from its confluence with the Loire, and is surrounded by some of the best vineyards in the Loire valley. While the cobbled medieval streets give a marvellous sense of history, it's a quiet town, and the actual sights won't keep you occupied for any more than a day or two.

Arrival, information and accommodation

The **gare SNCF** lies to the east of the town, from where rue du Dr-P.-Labussière and rue du 11-novembre lead to place Jeanne-d'Arc, where Joan is sculptured in mid-battle charge. Keep heading west and you'll soon reach the old quarter. The **tourist office** is on place d'Hofheim, on the central rue Jean-Jacques-Rousseau (May–Sept daily 10am–7pm; Oct–April Mon–Sat 10am–12.30pm & 2.30–6pm; ℡02.47.93.17.85, ⊛www.chinon-valdeloire.com), and can provide addresses of local vineyards where you can taste Chinon's famous red wine. Just beside the campsite, Chinon Loisirs Activités Nature (℡06.23.82.96.33, ⊛www.loisirs -nature.fr) hires out **canoes** and kayaks, and runs half-day and full-day guided trips in summer.

Most of the hotels in Chinon are decent and inexpensive, but if you're after something more extravagant it's worth visiting one of the nearby châteaux.

Agnès Sorel 4 quai Pasteur ℡02.47.93.04.37, ⊛www.agnes-sorel.com. The location down by the main road, at the western edge of the Old Town, lacks atmosphere and is awkward for the train station, but it's very clean and welcoming inside. ❷

Camping de l'Île Auger ℡02.47.93.08.35. Overlooks the Old Town and château from the south bank of the Vienne; turn right from the bridge along quai Danton. Closed mid-Oct to April.

Diderot 7 rue Diderot ℡02.47.93.18.87, ⊛www .hoteldiderot.com. Solidly bourgeois hotel offering an old-fashioned welcome in a venerable townhouse. Has some grand old rooms with antique furnishings in the main building, and some brighter modern ones in the annexe. ❸

De France 47–49 place du Général-de-Gaulle ℡02.47.93.33.91, ⊛www.bestwestern.fr. Historic hotel overlooking the leafy main square. Rooms are attractive and cosy, with big comfy beds, beams and exposed stone walls. ❸

Hostellerie Gargantua 73 rue Haute St-Maurice ℡02.47.93.04.71, ⊛www.hotel-gargantua.com. Housed in a fifteenth-century building – formerly the royal courts – the rooms here are fairly austere, but the original stonework makes up for it. There is also a pretty terrace restaurant out front. ❸

Le Plantagenêt 12 place Jeanne-d'Arc ℡02.47.93.36.92, ⊛www.hotel-plantagenet .com. Decent, welcoming two-star hotel on the large market square on the eastern edge of town. Rooms in the main nineteenth-century house are pleasantly decorated; those in the garden annexe are characterless but have a/c. Family rooms available. ❹

La Treille 4 place Jeanne-d'Arc ℡02.47.93.07.71. Tiny, spartan and full of character, with four basic rooms shoe-horned into an ancient building. ❶

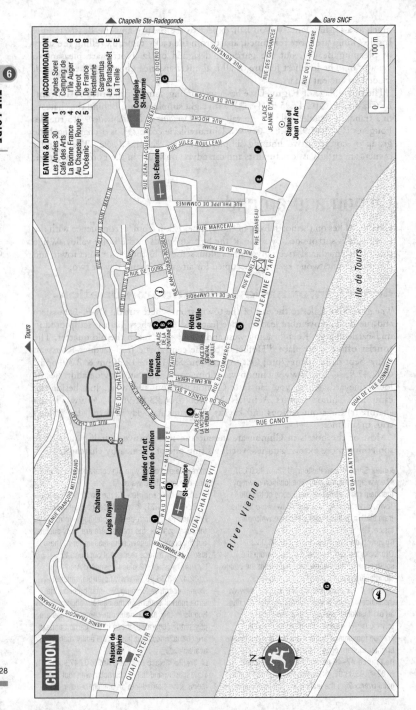

CHINON

Maison de la Rivière

Château
Logis Royal

Musée d'Art et
d'Histoire de Chinon

St-Maurice

Hôtel de Ville

Caves
Peinctes

Colégiale
St-Mexme

St-Étienne

Statue of
Joan of Arc

PLACE
JEANNE D'ARC

River Vienne

Ile de Tours

▲ Tours

▲ Chapelle Ste-Radegonde   ▲ Gare SNCF

EATING & DRINKING
Les Années 30   1
Café des Arts   3
La Bonne France   4
Au Chapeau Rouge   2
L'Océanic   5

ACCOMMODATION
Agnès Sorel   A
Camping de
l'Île Auger   G
Diderot   C
De France   B
Hostellerie
Gargantua   D
Le Plantagenêt   F
La Treille   E

0   100 m

RUE DU CHÂTEAU
RUE JEANNE D'ARC
RUE HAUTE SAINT-MAURICE
RUE PARMENTIER
QUAI CHARLES VII
QUAI PASTEUR
AVENUE FRANÇOIS MITTERRAND
QUAI DE L'ÎLE SONNANTE
QUAI DANTON
RUE CANOT
PLACE DE
LA VICTOIRE
DE VERDUN
RUE ÉMILE HÉBERT
RUE DU GRENIER À SEL
RUE DU COMMERCE
PLACE DU
GÉNÉRAL
DE GAULLE
RUE VOLTAIRE
PLACE
DE LA
FONTAINE
RUE DE TOURS
RUE DU PUITS DE BANCY
RUE DU COTEAU SAINT-MARTIN
RUE DE LA LAMPROIE
RUE RABELAIS
QUAI JEANNE D'ARC
RUE DU JEU DE PAUME
RUE MIRABEAU
RUE PHILIPPE DE COMMINES
RUE MARCEAU
RUE JEAN-JACQUES ROUSSEAU
RUE JULES ROULLEAU
RUE HOCHE
RUE DE BUFFON
RUE DIDEROT
RUE RONSARD
RUE DES COURANCES
RUE DU 11-NOVEMBRE

The Town

A fortress existed at Chinon from the Stone Age until the time of Louis XIV, the age of its most recent ruins. Henry Plantagenet added a new castle to the first medieval fortress on the site, built by his ancestor Foulques Nerra, and died here, crying vengeance on his son Richard, who had treacherously allied himself with the French king Philippe-Auguste. After a year's siege in 1204–5, Philippe-Auguste finally took the castle, ending the Plantagenet rule over Touraine and Anjou.

Over two hundred years later, Chinon was one of the few places where the Dauphin Charles, later Charles VII, could safely stay while Henry V of England held Paris and the title to the French throne. When Joan of Arc arrived here in 1429, she was able to talk her way into meeting him. The story depicted in a tapestry on display on the site is that as Joan entered the great hall, the Dauphin remained hidden anonymously among the assembled nobles, as a test, but that Joan picked him out straight away. Joan herself claimed that an angel had appeared before the court, bearing a crown. She begged him to allow her to rally his army against the English. To the horror of the courtiers, Charles said yes.

The **château** (daily: April–Sept 9am–7pm; Oct–March 9.30am–5pm; €3) has been covered with scaffolding for years, and is slowly reopening to the public after extensive restoration. You can visit the scene of Joan's encounter, the **Logis Royal**, and the castle's towers offer good panoramic views of the town.

Below, the medieval streets with their half-timbered and sculpted townhouses are pleasant enough to wander through, or you could duck into one of the town's low-key museums. The **Musée d'Art et d'Histoire de Chinon**, 44 rue Haute St-Maurice (June–Sept daily 2–6pm; Oct–May Mon–Fri 2–6pm; €2), has some diverting oddments of sculpture, pottery and paintings related to the town's history, as well as a fascinating recreation of a room in a sixteenth-century inn, complete with half-eaten food. Though it's better with a good meal, if you want to try a glass of Chinon you could visit the **Caves Peinctes**, off rue Voltaire, a deep cellar carved out of the rock where a local winegrowers' guild runs **tastings** (July & Aug daily except Mon 11am, 3pm, 4.30pm & 6pm; €3). "Peincte" was supposedly the name of a wine cellar owned by the father of Rabelais, who was born at the manor farm of **La Devinière**, 6km southwest of town, where there's a good but rather dry museum. An antiques and flea market takes place every third Sunday of the month, while regular **market day** is Thursday.

Eating and drinking

Chinon has a number of good **eating** options. The main square, place du Général-de-Gaulle, is enticingly filled with outdoor tables, and there are cosy restaurants to be found down the side streets as well.

Les Années 30 78 rue Haute St-Maurice ℡02.47.93.37.18. Cosy and old-fashioned, but with some adventurous dishes on the *menus* (€27 and €43).

Café des Arts 4 rue Jean-Jacques-Rousseau ℡02.47.93.09.84. Offers reliable and reasonably priced brasserie fare at around €15.

La Bonne France 4 place de la Victoire de Verdun ℡02.47.98.01.34. A good, homey restaurant hidden away on an intimate square a short walk west of place du Général-de-Gaulle; closed Thurs lunch & Wed.

Au Chapeau Rouge 49 place du Général-de-Gaulle ℡02.47.98.08.08. Top-quality regional cuisine on the main square, with *menus* from €20.

L'Océanic 13 rue Rabelais ℡02.47.93.44.55. The place to go if you're in the mood for some local fish, with an impressive cheese selection as well; closed Mon.

Forêt de Chinon

Northeast of Chinon, the elevated terrain of the *landes* is covered by the ancient **Forêt de Chinon**, which makes for great cycling and walking territory. If you want to **stay** in the area, there's a good *chambres d'hôtes* near Rigny-Ussé (see p.427). Just outside Saint-Benoît-la-Forêt, the village in the heart of the forest, is a woodland adventure park, **Saint-Benoît Aventure** (May & June Sat & Sun 2–7pm; July & Aug daily 10.30am–7.30pm; Sept & April 2–6.30pm; adults €22, children €8–20; ☏06.89.07.18.96, ⓦwww.saintbenoitaventure.com). It offers a chance to let the kids off the leash – or rather attach them to it – in the form of an alarming aerial ropeway assault course which threads its way through the trees. There's also a mountain bike circuit and a nature walk.

Tavant

Sixteen kilometres southeast of Chinon, the village of **TAVANT** hides the great **St-Nicolas church** (April–Sept Wed–Sun 10am–12.30pm & 2.15–6pm; March, Oct & Nov Mon–Fri, same hours; crypt €3). The appeal lies in the twelfth-century Romanesque **wall paintings** in its **crypt**, which rank among the finest in Europe. It's not clear why this crypt was so richly painted, as it hasn't been identified with any major relic cult or tomb. It's thought that the entire structure, inside and out, would once have been painted in bright colours, but today just fragments survive in the upper church, as well as a giant figure of Christ in Majesty on the half-dome of the apse. If the chapel isn't open when you arrive, ask for the guardian at the nearby *mairie*.

Saumur and around

SAUMUR is a civilized town notable for two things in particular: the excellent sparkling wine (some would say as good as Champagne) and the wealth of aristocratic military associations, based on its status as home to the French Cavalry Academy and its successor, the Armoured Corps Academy. The stretch of the Loire from Chinon to Angers, which passes through Saumur, is particularly lovely, with the bizarre added draw of **troglodyte dwellings** carved out of the cliffs. The land on the south bank, under grapes and sunflowers, gradually rises away from the river, with long-inactive windmills still standing. Across the water cows graze in wooded pastures.

Arrival, information and accommodation

Saumur spreads along both banks of the Loire and over the Île d'Offard in the middle of the river. Arriving at the **gare SNCF**, you'll find yourself on the north bank: turn right onto avenue David-d'Angers and either take bus #30 to the centre or cross the bridge to the island on foot. From the island the old **Pont Cessart** leads across to the main part of the town on the south bank, where you'll find the **gare routière**, a couple of blocks west of the bridge on place St-Nicolas, and the **tourist office**, next to the bridge on place de la Bilange (mid-May to mid-Oct Mon–Sat 9.15am–7pm, Sun 10.30am–5.30pm; mid-Oct to mid-May Mon–Sat 9.15am–12.30pm & 2–6pm, Sun 10am–noon; ℡02.41.40.20.60, ⓦwww .ot-saumur.fr). The **old quarter**, around St-Pierre and the castle, lies immediately behind the Hôtel de Ville, on the riverbank just east of the bridge.

Accommodation in Saumur is of an acceptable standard, with several decent budget offerings and one outstanding hotel.

Anne d'Anjou 32 quai Mayaud ℡02.41.67.30.30, ⓦwww.hotel-anneanjou.com. Comfortable hotel, with a wide range of attractively decorated, if uniform, rooms in a grand eighteenth-century listed building. ❻

Camping de l'Île d'Offard Rue de Verden, Île d'Offard ℡02.41.40.30.00, ⓦwww.cvtloisirs.com. Big, well-run site right next door to the hostel.

Château de Verrières 53 rue Alsace ℡02.41.38.05.15, ⓦwww.chateau -verrieres.com. One of the finest buildings in the town is given over to this exceptional bed and breakfast, with friendly and dynamic owners dedicated to making your stay a special one. The rooms are ornate and lavish, the atmosphere luxurious. No restaurant, but meals are prepared for groups by special request. ❽

Cristal 10–12 place de la République ℡02.41.51.09.54, ⓦwww.cristal-hotel.fr. One of the nicer hotels in town, with a great situation on the riverfront, and friendly proprietors. Rooms on the side street can be noisy, but those with river or château views are usually fine. Some inexpensive attic rooms are also available. ❶

Hostel Rue de Verden, Île d'Offard ℡02.41.40.30.00, ⓦwww.hebergement-international-saumur.fr. Large hostel at the east end of the island with laundry facilities, swimming-pool access and views of the château. Dorm beds €17, singles €25. Reception 9am–noon & 2.30–7pm. Closed Nov–Feb.

St-Pierre 8 rue Haute-St-Pierre ℡02.41.50.33.00, ⓦwww.saintpierresaumur.com. Charming boutique hotel, slightly in need of updating. Its main appeal lies in the convenient and picturesque location; the rooms remain fairly ordinary. ❹

Le Volney 1 rue Volney ℡02.41.51.25.41, ⓦwww.levolney.com. This simple, budget hotel on the south side of town is a bit tired round the edges, but has friendly management and some inexpensive but cosy little rooms under the roof. ❶

The Town

Set high above town, Saumur's impressive **château** (interior closed for restoration works; exterior daily except Mon: April–June 10am–1pm & 2–5.30pm; July & Aug 10am–6pm; Sept & Oct 10am–1pm & 2–5.30pm; €3) may seem oddly familiar, but then its famous depiction in *Les Très Riches Heures du Duc de Berry*, the most celebrated of all the medieval illuminated prayer books, is reproduced all over the region. It was largely built in the latter half of the fourteenth century by Louis I, Duc d'Anjou, who wanted to compete with his brothers Jean de Berry and Charles V. The threat of marauding bands of English soldiers made the masons work flat out – they weren't even allowed to stop for feast days. Part of the château has been closed since April 2001, when a huge chunk of the star-shaped outer fortifications collapsed down the hill towards the river. In the aftermath, the alarmed authorities decided to embark on a major renovation programme. But several collections are still on display, including china-like *faïences* from the Musée des Arts Décoratifs and an impressive equestrian exhibit taken from the château's Musée du Cheval.

Down by the public gardens south of the château, Saumur's oldest church, **Notre-Dame de Nantilly** (daily 9am–6pm, closes 5pm in winter), houses a large tapestry collection in its Romanesque nave. The original Gothic **church of St-Pierre**, in the centre of the Old Town, is closed for renovation works through 2010. But once it reopens it's worth taking a look at the Counter-Reformation façade, built as part of the church's efforts to overawe its persistently Protestant population – Louise de Bourbon, abbess of Fontevraud, called the town a "second Geneva", horrified at the thought that Saumur might become a similarly radical Calvinist power base.

For relief from military and ecclesiastical history, try a glass of the famous Saumur *méthode champenoise* wines at the **Maison du Vin** on quai Lucien-Gautier (April–Sept Mon 2–7pm, Tues–Sat 9.30am–1pm & 2–7pm, Sun 9.30am–1pm; Oct–March Tues–Sat 10am–1pm & 2–6.30pm; ⓦwww.interloire.com), which can also provide addresses of wine-growers and *caves* to visit. Alternatively, make for the Caves des Vignerons at St-Cyr-en-Bourg (daily 9.30am–12.30pm & 2–6pm; €2.50; ⓣ02.41.53.06.18), a short train hop south of Saumur and near St-Cyr station, where there are kilometres of cellars.

Beyond the town centre

Saumur's cavalry traditions are displayed in all their glory at the **École Nationale d'Équitation**, in St-Hilaire-St-Florent, a suburb to the east of the centre (take bus #31 from the south end of rue Franklin-Roosevelt to the "Alouette" stop, then continue down the route de Marson, turning right at the signpost; it's a walk of a little over 1km). The Riding School (Mon pm to Sat am: mid-Feb to March tours at 9.30am, 11am, 2pm & 4pm; April to mid-Oct tours every 30min 9.30–11.30am & 2–4pm; €7) provides guided tours during which you can watch training sessions (mornings are best) and view the stables. Displays of dressage and anachronistic battle manoeuvres by the crackshot Cadre Noir, the former cavalry trainers, are regular events (programme details from the tourist office or online at ⓦwww .cadrenoir.fr). The history of the tank – traditionally considered as cavalry not infantry – is covered in the separate **Musée des Blindés**, at 1043 rue Fricotelle, to the southeast of the centre (daily: May, June & Sept daily 10am–6pm; July & Aug daily 9.30am–6.30pm; Oct–April Mon–Fri 10am–5pm, Sat & Sun 11am–6pm; €7; ⓦwww.museedesblindes.fr).

The main activity in the suburb of St-Hilaire-St-Florent, especially along the main stretch of the riverside road, along rue Ackerman and rue Leopold-Palustre, is the manufacture of **sparkling wine**. You can visit the impressive rock-carved cellars of Ackerman-Laurance, Bouvet-Ladubay, Langlois-Château, Gratien & Meyer, Louis de Grenelle and Veuve Amiot. Choosing between them is a matter of personal taste, and possibly a question of opening hours, though most are open all day every day throughout the warmer months (generally 10am–6pm, though most close for a couple of hours at lunchtime out of season). Buy a couple of bottles to take away, and you'll probably be impressed by both the taste and the price difference between this inexpensive wine and champagne.

Eating and drinking

There are several reasonably inexpensive places around place St-Pierre, many of which offer a chance to enjoy a glass of sparkling Saumur brut at an outside table.

Auberge Reine de Sicile 71 rue Waldeck-Rousseau, Île d'Offard ⓣ02.41.67.30.48. Over the bridge on the Île d'Offard, with an atmospherically ancient dining room. Stick to the excellent local fish, and you're unlikely to be disappointed. *Menus* at €19–35; closed Mon & Sun eve.

Les Forges de St-Pierre 1 place St-Pierre ⓣ02.41.38.21.79. Specializing in grilled meats, this is one of the busy, touristy but relatively good-value restaurants on the atmospheric old square. Steaks around €11–16; closed Sun & Mon.
Le Grand Bleu 6 rue du Marché ⓣ02.41.67.41.83. Specializes in sea fish – Brittany is, after all, not so

far away. Pleasant situation on a miniature square, with outside seating in summer. *Menus* €15–27; closed Wed & Tues eve.

Les Ménestrels *Hôtel Anne d'Anjou*, 32 quai Mayaud ☎ 02.41.67.71.10. Saumur's best place for serious, formal gastronomy, though the stone walls and exposed beams add a note of rustic relaxation. *Menus* €32–68.

Le Pot de Lapin 35 rue Rabelais ☎ 02.41.67.12.86. Relaxed, contemporary bistro-restaurant on the way out towards Notre-Dame des Ardilliers. There's a sleek bar area, a pleasant summer terrace and a focus on fresh game and *tapas*. Mains around €12; closed Tues lunch, Sun eve & Mon.

The Abbaye de Fontevraud

At the heart of the stunning Romanesque complex of the **Abbaye de Fontevraud** (daily: April–June, Sept & Oct 9.30am–6.30pm; July & Aug 9.30am–7.30pm; Nov–March 10am–5.30pm; €8.40; ☎ 02.41.51.73.52, ⓦ www.abbaye -fontevraud.com), 13km southeast of Saumur, are the tombs of the Plantagenet royal family, eerily lifelike works of funereal art that powerfully evoke the historical bonds between England and France. A religious community was established in around 1100 as both a nunnery and a monastery with an abbess in charge – an unconventional move, even if the post was filled solely by queens and princesses. The remaining buildings date from the twelfth century and are immense, built as they were to house and separate not only the nuns and monks but also the sick, lepers and repentant prostitutes. There were originally five separate institutions, of which three still stand in graceful Romanesque solidity. Used as a prison from the Revolution until 1963, it was an inspiration for the writer Jean Genet, whose book *Miracle of the Rose* was partly based on the recollections of a prisoner incarcerated here.

The **abbey church** is an impressive space, not least for the four tombstone effigies: Henry II, his wife Eleanor of Aquitaine, who died here, their son Richard the Lionheart and daughter-in-law Isabelle of Angoulême, King John's queen. Carved as they were at the time of their deaths, the figures are eerily lifelike. The strange domed roof, the great cream-coloured columns of the choir and the graceful capitals of the nave add to the atmosphere. Elsewhere in the complex you can explore the magnificent **cloisters**, the **chapterhouse**, decorated with sixteenth-century murals, and the vast **refectory**. All the cooking for the religious community, which would have numbered several hundred, was done in the – now perfectly restored – Romanesque **kitchen**, an octagonal building as extraordinary from the outside (with its 21 spiky chimneys) as it is from within.

The abbey is now the **Centre Culturel de l'Ouest** (CCO), the cultural centre for western France, and one of Europe's most important centres of medieval archaeology; it is used for a great many activities, from concerts to lectures, art exhibitions and theatre. Programme details are available at the abbey or from the Saumur tourist office. **Bus** #1 runs from Saumur to Fontevraud, but it's not a frequent service and certain times have to be booked in advance; check with the tourist office for details.

Angers and around

ANGERS, capital of the ancient county of Anjou and dominated by its monolithic château, seems a less welcoming and friendly destination than many others around it. The main reason to visit is to see its two stunning **tapestry** series, the fourteenth-century *Apocalypse* and the twentieth-century *Le Chant du Monde*.

Arrival, information and accommodation

The **gare SNCF** is just south of the centre, while the **gare routière** is down by the river, just past the Pont de Verdun on place Molière. The main **tourist office** is on place Kennedy (May–Sept Mon 10am–7pm, Tues–Sat 9am–7pm, Sun 10am–6pm; Oct–April Mon 2–6pm, Tues–Sat 10am–6pm, Sun 10am–1pm; ℡02.41.23.50.00, Ⓦwww.angersloiretourisme.com), facing the château; it sells a **city pass** (€12 for 24hr, €19 for 48hr), which allows access to the tapestries as well as the city's museums and galleries.

There's a wide range of **accommodation** on offer and finding a room shouldn't present too many problems, though it's still wise to book ahead in summer.

D'Anjou 1 bd du Maréchal Foch ℡02.41.21.12.11, Ⓦwww.hoteldanjou.fr. An adequate Best Western option, with all the usual comforts of the chain. ⑥
Auberge de Jeunesse Darwin 3 rue Darwin ℡02.41.22.61.20, Ⓦwww.foyerdarwin.com. Attractive youth hostel by a lake, 5km west of town, with kitchen facilities available; take bus #1 or #8 to "Lakanal". Dorm beds €11.10, singles €14.30.
Camping Lac de Maine 49 av du Lac de Maine ℡02.41.73.05.03, Ⓦwww.lacdemaine.fr. Agreeably situated next to a lake, complete with

extensive sports facilities. 20min southwest of the town on bus #6 (bus #11 from 7.30pm–midnight, bus #26 on Sun) either from the train station or bd Général-de-Gaulle. Closed Oct–March.
Centre 12 rue St-Laud ℡02.41.87.45.07. Reasonably comfortable hotel above a lively bar. Double-glazing keeps out the worst of the street noise. ②
Des Lices 25 rue des Lices ℡02.41.87.44.10. A real bargain in a balustraded townhouse on a distinctly posh central street. Closed Aug 1–15. ②

EATING & DRINKING
Boléro	6
La Cantina	7
Les Caves du Ralliement	4
Bar du Centre	B
La Descente de la Marine	8
Le Grandgousier	3
Le Mid'Star	1
Le Petit Comptoir	5
La Soufflerie	2
Villa Toussaint	9

ACCOMMODATION
D'Anjou	D
Auberge de Jeunesse Darwin	F
Camping Lac de Maine	G
Centre	B
Des Lices	E
Du Mail	A
St-Julien	C

Du Mail 8 rue des Ursules ☎02.41.25.05.25, ⓦwww.hotel-du-mail.com. The best hotel in the town by miles, with comfortable, inexpensive rooms, a friendly welcome, a beautiful location and a good breakfast. Parking available. ❸

St-Julien 9 place du Ralliement ☎02.41.88.41.62, ⓦwww.hotelsaintjulien.com. Large hotel right in the centre of the city, offering a good spread of modernized rooms. Some of the pretty little ones under the roof have views over town. ❸

The City

The **château** dominates Angers, and it's not hard to see why. It's an impressive, sturdy fortress by the river, its moat now filled with striking formal flower arrangements and softened by trees. From here, it's just a fifteen-minute stroll east to the **cathedral** and its entourage of several smaller churches and museums. Across the pont de Verdun from the château is the suburb of **La Doutre**, where the **Hôpital St-Jean** houses the modern response to the castle's *Apocalypse* tapestry, *Le Chant du Monde*. Further out in the suburbs is a rash of interesting museums, easily reached by bus, exalting everything from early aeroplanes to Cointreau and communication methods.

The château and Apocalypse tapestry

The **Château d'Angers** (daily: May–Aug 9.30am–6.30pm; Sept–April 10am–5.30pm; €6) is a formidable early medieval fortress. The sense of impregnability is accentuated by its dark stone, the purple-brown schist characteristic of western Anjou. The château's mighty kilometre-long curtain wall is reinforced by seventeen circular towers, their brooding stone offset by decorative bands of pale tufa. Inside are a few miscellaneous remains of the counts' royal lodgings and chapels, but the chief focus is the astonishing **Tapestry of the Apocalypse**. Woven between 1373 and 1382 for Louis I of Anjou, it was originally 140m long, of which 100m now survives. From the start, it was treated as a masterpiece, and only brought out to decorate the cathedral of Angers on major festival days. The sheer grandeur of the conception is overwhelming but the tapestry's reputation rests as much on its superb detail and stunning colours, preserved today by the very low light levels in the long viewing hall. If you plan to follow the apocalypse story right through, the English-language audio guide (€4.50) comes in handy, but a Bible would be even better. In brief: the Day of Judgement is signalled by the breaking of the seven seals – note the four horsemen – and the seven angels blowing their trumpets. As the battle of Armageddon rages, Satan appears first as a seven-headed red dragon, then as the seven-headed lion-like Beast. The holy forces break the seven vials of plagues, whereupon the Whore of Babylon appears mounted on the Beast. She is challenged by the Word of God, seen riding a galloping horse, who chases the hordes of Satan into the lake of fire, allowing the establishment of the heavenly Jerusalem. It's spellbinding, operatic stuff, and will appeal whatever your religious views.

If you need a drink after all that, head straight out of the castle and into the **Maison du Vin Anjou Saumur**, 5bis place Kennedy (April–Sept Mon 2–7pm, Tues–Sat 9.30am–1pm & 2–7pm, Sun 10.30am–1pm; Oct–March Tues–Fri 10.30am–12.30pm & 3–6pm, Sat 10.30am–12.30pm & 2.30–6.30pm), where the helpful staff will offer you wine to taste before you buy, and can provide lists of wine-growers to visit.

The cathedral and around

The most dramatic approach to the **Cathédrale St-Maurice** is via the quayside, from where a long flight of steps leads straight up to the mid-twelfth-century portal, which shows another version of the apocalypse. Built in the 1150s and 1160s, the cathedral exemplifies the Plantagenet style – in fact, it's probably the earliest example in France of this influential architectural development. The interior is somewhat prosaic, but the fifteenth-century windows are impressive.

Arguably the greatest stoneworks in Angers are the creations of the famous local sculptor David d'Angers (1788–1856), whose Calvary adorns the cathedral. His great civic commissions can be seen all over France, but these large-scale marbles and bronzes are almost all copies of the smaller plaster-of-Paris works created by the artist himself. These plaster originals are exhibited in the **Galerie David d'Angers**, 37bis rue Toussaint (June–Sept daily 10am–6.30pm; Oct–May Tues–Sun 10am–noon & 2–6pm; €4), set impressively in the glazed-over nave of a ruined thirteenth-century church, the **Église Toussaint**.

The **Musée des Beaux-Arts**, 10 rue du Musée (June–Sept daily 10am–6.30pm; Oct–May Tues–Sun 10am–noon & 2–6pm; €4), is housed in the **Logis Barrault**, a proudly decorated mansion built by a wealthy late fifteenth-century mayor. Eighteenth- and nineteenth-century paintings dominate the collection, with works by Watteau, Chardin and Fragonard, as well as Ingres' operatic *Paolo et Francesca* – the same subject depicted by Rodin in *The Kiss* – and a small collection devoted to Boucher's *Génie des Arts*.

La Doutre

The district facing the château across the Maine is known as **La Doutre** (literally, "the other side"), and still has a few mansions and houses dating from the medieval period, despite redevelopment over the years.

In the north of the area, a short way from the Pont de la Haute-Chaine, the **Hôpital St-Jean** at 4 bd Arago was built by Henry Plantagenet in 1174 as a hospital for the poor, a function it continued to serve for nearly 700 years. Today it houses the **Musée Jean Lurçat et de la Tapisserie Contemporaine** (June–Sept daily 10am–6.30pm; Oct–May Tues–Sun 10am–noon & 2–6pm; €4), which contains the city's great twentieth-century tapestry, **Le Chant du Monde**. The tapestry sequence was designed by Jean Lurçat in 1957 in response to the Apocalypse tapestry, though he died nine years before its completion. It hangs in a vast vaulted space, the original ward for the sick, or Salle des Malades. The first four tapestries deal with *La Grande Menace*, the threat of nuclear war: first the bomb itself; then *Hiroshima Man*, flayed and burnt with the broken symbols of belief dropping from him; then the collective massacre of the *Great Charnel House*; and the last dying rose falling with the post-Holocaust ash through black space – the *End of Everything*. From then on, the tapestries celebrate the joys of life: *Man in Glory in Peace*; *Water and Fire*; *Champagne* – "that blissful ejaculation", according to Lurçat; *Conquest of Space*; *Poetry*; and *Sacred Ornaments*. Subject matter and treatment are intense, and the setting helps: it's a huge echoey space, with rows of columns supporting soaring Angevin vaulting. The artist's own commentary is available in English. The Romanesque cloisters at the back, with their graceful double columns, are also worth a peek.

There are more modern tapestries in the building adjoining the Salle des Malades, where the collection includes several of Lurçat's paintings, ceramics and tapestries, along with the highly tactile but more muted abstract tapestries of Thomas Gleb and Josep Grau Garriga. With four local *ateliers*, Angers is a leading centre for contemporary tapestry. The neighbouring **Atelier de Tapisserie d'Angers Création**, 3 bd Daviers (☎02.41.88.31.92), can put you in touch with local artists and let you know where to find private exhibitions, though they are only open by appointment.

South of the Hôpital St-Jean, on La Doutre's central square, place de la Laiterie, the church of the ancient **Abbaye de Ronceray** is used to mount art exhibitions, worth visiting just to see the Romanesque galleries of the old abbey and admire their beautiful murals. When there's no exhibition, you can only visit as part of the tourist office's weekly tour of La Doutre. Inside the adjacent twelfth-century **Église de la Trinité**, an exquisite Renaissance wooden spiral staircase fails to mask a great piece of medieval bodging used to fit the wall of the church around a part of the abbey that juts into it.

Eating

The streets around place du Ralliement and place Romain have a wide variety of **cafés** and **restaurants**, many of them very inexpensive.

La Cantina 9 rue de l'Oisellerie ℡02.41.87.36.34. Relaxed café-bistro serving southwestern dishes such as *magret de canard* (duck steak). Good value for lunch, with straightforward fish and meat *plats* and salads for around €16. Closed Mon.

Les Caves du Ralliement 9 place du Ralliement ℡02.41.88.47.77. Busy brasserie underneath the posh and well-regarded *Provence Caffé*. Good for inexpensive *moules-* or *steak-frites* at lunchtime, and oysters or eels with a glass of wine in the evening at one of the outside tables on the square. *Menus* from €19. Closed Mon eve.

Le Grandgousier 7 rue St-Laud ℡02.41.87.81.47. Serves meats grilled over a wood fire, complemented by so-so local wines,

which are included in the price of the €16 and €24 *menus*. Closed Sun.

Le Petit Comptoir 40 rue David d'Angers ℡02.41.88.81.57. Impressive restaurant specializing in local dishes with both a traditional and modernist focus; the €19 lunch menu is excellent value. Closed Sun & Mon.

La Soufflerie 8 place du Pilori ℡02.41.87.45.32. Popular café specializing in soufflés, both large and savoury (at around €12) and small and sweet (around €10). Closed Sun, Mon & 4 weeks in July/Aug.

Villa Toussaint 43 rue Toussaint ℡02.41.88.15.64. Currently the hippest place in town, specializing in sushi and seafood for around €28. The leafy terrace is a lovely spot in summer. Closed Sun.

Drinking and nightlife

Late-opening **bars** congregate around rue St-Laud: *Bar du Centre*, below *Hôtel Centre*, is full of students, and there's a cluster of popular Irish-type places at the bottom end of the road around place Romain. Over in La Doutre, *La Descente de la Marine*, at 28 quai des Carmes, is an old-time bar with a strong nautical flavour, attracting lots of students and young people who come down for an early evening *apéro* on the quay. Among Angers' numerous **clubs**, *Boléro*, 38 rue St-Laud, is popular and central, with an unpretentious, sometimes cheesy music policy. *Le Mid'Star*, 25 quai Félix-Faure, is the biggest and best-known clubbing venue, with a more serious playlist.

Listings

Bike hire The tourist office rents out bikes.
Boat hire Numerous companies hire out canoes and run guided kayak trips on the five rivers in the vicinity of Angers. Try: Canoe Kayak Club d'Angers, 75 av du Lac de Maine (on the Maine and Lac de Maine) ℡02.41.72.07.04, ⊛ckca.fr; Club Nautique d'Écouflant, rue de l'Île St-Aubin, Écouflant (Sarthe, Mayenne, Loire, Maine) ℡02.41.34.56.38, ⊛www.kayakecouflant.com; and Club de Canoe Kayak les Ponts de Cé, 30 rue Maximin-Gélineau, Les Ponts de Cé (on the Loire) ℡02.41.44.65.15, ⊛www.canoe-kayak -lespontsdece.fr. The tourist office has details of more sedate trips on sightseeing boats.
Car hire Avis, *Gare SNCF* ℡02.41.88.20.24; Europcar, *Gare SNCF* ℡02.41.87.87.10; Hertz, *Gare SNCF* ℡02.41.88.15.16.
Festivals At the end of May, the Tour de Scènes festival brings rock and world music acts to the

city centre for four days of concerts. The Festival Angers l'Été features jazz and world music gigs in the atmospheric Cloître Toussaint, the cloisters behind the Galerie David d'Angers, on Tues & Thurs evenings throughout July and Aug; book through the tourist office. In early Sept, the festival Les Accroche Coeurs brings in a host of theatrical companies, musicians and street performers for three days of surreal entertainment.
Health Ambulance ℡15; Centre Hospitalier, 4 rue Larrey (℡02.41.35.36.37); for late-night pharmacies, phone ℡3915.
Internet Go online at 42 rue de Mail and 25 rue de la Roë, just east of place de la République.
Market There's a flower market on place Leclerc and an organic produce market on rue Saint-Laud, both on Sat.
Police Commissariat, 15 rue Dupetit-Thouars ℡02.41.43.98.38.

Around Angers

Angers can be a good base, as long as you have your own transport. You can easily reach the château of **Le Plessis-Bourré** near Ecuillé (impossible to get to by public transport), 17km to the north. Or, for a more accessible glimpse of a real monster of a mansion, head for the **Château de Serrant**, just outside St-Georges-sur-Loire, on the infrequent #7 bus from Angers – the tourist office has timetables.

Château du Plessis-Bourré

Five years' work at the end of the fifteenth century produced the fortress of **Le Plessis-Bourré** (mid-Feb to end March, Oct & Nov daily except Wed 2–6pm; April–June & Sept Mon, Tues & Fri–Sun 10am–noon & 2–6pm, Thurs 2–6pm; July & Aug daily 10am–6pm; closed Dec–Feb; €9; ⓦwww.plessis-bourre.com), between the Sarthe and Mayenne rivers. Despite the vast, full moat, spanned by an arched bridge with a still-functioning drawbridge, it was built as a luxurious residence rather than a defensive castle. The treasurer of France at the time, Jean Bourré, received important visitors here, among them Louis XI and Charles VIII.

Given the powerful medieval exterior, the first three rooms on the ground floor come as a surprise; they are beautifully decorated and furnished in the Louis XVI, XV and Régence styles, respectively, though things revert to type in the Gothic Salle du Parlement. The highlight of the tour comes in the Salle des Gardes, just above, where the original, deeply coffered ceiling stems from Bourré's fashionable interest in alchemy. Every inch is painted with allegorical scenes: sixteen panels depict alchemical symbols such as the phoenix, the pregnant siren and the donkey singing Mass, while eight cartoon-like paintings come with morals attached – look out for "Chicheface", the hungry wolf that only eats faithful women, whose victim is supposed to be Jean Bourré's wife.

Château de Serrant

At the **Château de Serrant**, 15km west of Angers beside the N23 near **ST-GEORGES-SUR-LOIRE**, the combination of dark-brown schist and creamy tufa gives a rather pleasant cake-like effect to the exterior (guided tours only, departing on the hour; mid-March to June & Sept daily except Tues 9.45am–noon & 2–5.15pm; July & Aug daily 9.45am–5.15pm; Oct to mid-Nov Wed–Sun 9.45am–noon & 2–5.15pm; €9.50; ⓦwww.chateau-serrant.net). But with its heavy slate bell-shaped cupolas pressing down on massive towers, the exterior is grandiose rather than graceful. The building was begun in the sixteenth century and added to up until the eighteenth century. In 1755 it belonged to an Irishman, Francis Walsh, to whom Louis XV had given the title Count of Serrant as a reward for Walsh's help against the old enemy, the English. The Walsh family married into the ancient La Trémoille clan, whose descendants – via a Belgian offshoot – still own the château. The massive rooms of the interior are packed with all the trappings of old wealth. Much of the decor dates from the late nineteenth and early twentieth centuries, but it's tastefully – and expensively – done, and you are also shown the Renaissance staircase, the sombre private chapel designed by Mansart, a bedroom prepared for Napoleon (who only stopped here for a couple of hours), and the attractive vaulted kitchens.

Le Mans and around

LE MANS, the historic capital of the Maine region, is synonymous with its famous 24-hour car race in June. During the rest of the year, it's a much quieter place; what it lacks in obvious beauty it makes up for in historical background, being the

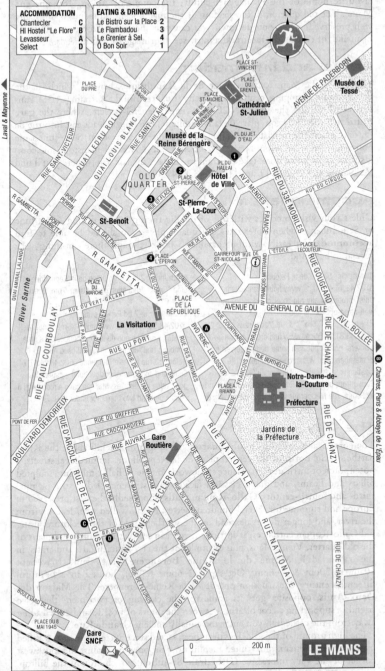

N

Laval & Mayenne ◄

ACCOMMODATION
Chantecler	C
HI Hostel "Le Flore"	B
Levasseur	A
Select	D

EATING & DRINKING
Le Bistro sur la Place	2
Le Flambadou	3
Le Grenier à Sel	4
Ô Bon Soir	1

PLACE ST-VINCENT

AVENUE DE PADERBORN

Musée de Tessé

PLACE DU PRE

PLACE ST-MICHEL

PLACE DU GRENIER

PONT YSSOIR

QUAI LOUIS BLANC

QUAI DU DU ROLLIN

RUE SAINT-HILAIRE

RUE DE LA REINE BÉRENGÈRE

Cathédrale St-Julien

PL DU JET D'EAU

RUE DU 33E MOBILES

RUE DU CIRQUE

Musée de la Reine Bérengère

GRANDE RUE

OLD QUARTER

PLACE ST-PIERRE

RUE ST-FLACEAU

PL DU HALLAI

Hôtel de Ville

AV P. MENDES - FRANCE

RUE SAINT-VICTOR

St-Pierre-La-Cour

R GAMBETTA

PONT PERRIN

PONT GAMBETTA

St-Benoît

RUE DE LA GALÈRE

RUE DE L'ANCIEN EVÊCHÉ

RUE DE LA BARILLÈRE

CARREFOUR ST-NICOLAS

RUE DE L'ÉTOILE

PLACE L. LECOUTEUX

RUE GOUGEARD

QUAI AMIRAL LALANDE

River Sarthe

R GAMBETTA

PLACE L'ÉPERON

RUE ST-MARTIN

RUE BOLTON

AVENUE FRANÇOIS MITTERRAND

(i)

PLACE DU MARCHÉ

RUE DU CORNET

RUE BONHOMMET

AVENUE DU GENERAL DE GAULLE

AVL. BOLLÉE

RUE DU VERT-GALANT

PLACE DE LA RÉPUBLIQUE

RUE DE CHANZY

La Visitation

RUE PASTEUR

RUE BARBIER

RUE DU PORT

BVD RENÉ- LEVASSEUR

RUE COURTHARDY

RUE BERTHELOT

Notre-Dame-de-la-Couture

Préfecture

B. Chartres, Paris & Abbaye de l'Épau ►

BOULEVARD DEMORIEUX

RUE PAUL COURBOULAY

RUE DES MINIMES

RUE DE CONSTANTINE

RUE DU TERTOT

AVENUE FRANÇOIS MITTERRAND

PLACE BRIAND

Jardins de la Préfecture

RUE DE CHANZY

PONT DE FER

RUE D'ARCOLE

RUE DU GREFFIER

RUE CROCHARDIÈRE

RUE AUVRAY

Gare Routière

RUE DE RICHEBOURG

RUE NATIONALE

RUE DE LA PELOUSE

RUE D'IÉNA

RUE DE MARENGO

RUE DE WAGRAM

RUE DU CHANOINE LELIÈVRE

C

RUE FOISY

R.P. MERSENNE

D

AVENUE GÉNÉRAL-LECLERC

RUE DE WAGRAM

RUE DU BOURG BELÉ

RUE NATIONALE

RUE DE CHANZY

BOULEVARD DE LA GARE

RUE DE FLEURUS

PLACE DU 8 MAI 1945

Gare SNCF

BD E. ZOLA

0	200 m

LE MANS

Tours & Racing Circuits ▼

favourite home of the Plantagenet family, the counts of Anjou, Touraine and Maine. The old quarter, in the shadow of the magnificent cathedral, is unusually well preserved, while outside town you can visit the serene Cistercian abbey of Épau and, of course, the racetrack, a must-see pilgrimage for petrolheads.

Arrival and information

The hub of Le Mans today is **place de la République**, beneath which, in the underground shopping centre, is the city **bus terminal**. A tram (€1.35) runs between here and the **gare SNCF** via avenue Général-Leclerc, where the **gare routière** is located. From place de la République, rue Bolton leads east into rue de l'Étoile, where the **tourist office** (July & Aug Mon–Sat 9am–6pm; Sept–June same hours but closed Sat noon–2pm; ℡02.43.28.17.22, ⓦwww.lemanstourisme.com) is situated. To hire a **bike**, take the tram to "Espal", the last stop, where you'll find Vel'Nature at 43 rue de l'Estérel (℡02.43.47.47.49).

Accommodation

Unless your visit coincides with one of the big **racing events** during April, June or September – when hotel rates can quadruple – you should be able to find **accommodation** easily without having to book, though there's nothing very special to be found.

Chantecler 50 rue de la Pelouse ℡02.43.14.40.00, ⓦwww.hotelchantecler.fr. Quiet, professionally run hotel, offering dull but well-fitted-out rooms and parking. ⑤

HI Hostel "Le Flore" 23 rue Maupertuis ℡02.43.81.27.55, ⓦwww.fuaj.org. Mainly a workers' hostel, but with some beds reserved for HI members, and with a cheap canteen. The location is fairly central: take av du Général-de-Gaulle from place de la République, continue along av Bollée; rue Maupertuis is the third on the left; or

catch the #12 bus from place de la République to stop "Flore". Reception open 10am–7pm. Dorm beds €15.

Levasseur 5–7 bd René-Levasseur ℡02.43.39.61.61, ⓦwww.hotel-le-mans.net. Well located just off place de la République, but a little rambling and functional in feel. Closed Aug. ③

Select 13 rue du Père-Mersenne ℡02.43.24.17.74. Clean and comfortable budget hotel – especially good value for families, who can have a room with a double bed and two bunks for under €60. ②

The City

The complicated web of the **old quarter** lies atop a minor hill above the River Sarthe, to the north of the central place de la République. Its medieval streets, a hotchpotch of intricate Renaissance stonework, medieval half-timbering, sculpted pillars and beams, and grand classical facades, are still encircled by the original third- and fourth-century **Gallo-Roman walls**, supposedly the best preserved in Europe and running for several hundred metres. Steep, walled steps lead up from the river, and longer flights descend on the southern side of the enclosure, using old Gallo-Roman entrances. If intrigued, you can see pictures, maps and plans of the old quarter, Vieux Mans, plus examples of the city's ancient arts and crafts, in the rather dull **Musée de la Reine Bérengère** (Tues–Sun: May–Sept 10am–12.30pm & 2–6pm; Oct–April 2–6pm; €2.80), housed in a beautiful fifteenth-century construction on rue de la Reine-Bérengère. The **Maison des Deux-Amis**, opposite, gets its name for the carving of two men (the "two friends") supporting a coat of arms between the doors of nos. 18 and 20. Heading away from the cathedral, you enter the equally ancient **Grande Rue**.

The high ground of the Old Town has been sacred since ancient times, as testified by a strangely human, pink-tinted menhir now propped up against the southwest corner of the very impressive **Cathédrale St-Julien**, which crowns the hilltop.

The nave of the cathedral was only just completed when Geoffroi Plantagenet, the count of Maine and Anjou, married Matilda, daughter of Henry I of England, in 1129, thus founding the English dynastic line. Inside, for all the power and measured beauty of this Romanesque structure, it's impossible not to be drawn towards the vertiginous High Gothic choir, filled with coloured light filtering through the stained-glass windows. At the easternmost end of the choir, the vault of the chapelle de la Vierge is painted with angels singing, dancing and playing medieval musical instruments.

In the 1850s a road was tunnelled under the old quarter – a slum at the time – helping to preserve its self-contained unity. On the north side of the quarter, the road tunnel comes out by an impressive **monument to Wilbur Wright** – who tested an early flying machine in Le Mans – which points you into place du Hallai. From here, you can walk northeast alongside the park to the **Musée de Tessé**, on avenue de Paderborn (Tues–Sun 10am–12.30pm & 2–6pm; €4), where the highlight is an exquisite enamel portrait of Henry II's father, Geoffroi Le Bel, which was originally part of his tomb in the cathedral. Otherwise it's a mixed bag of paintings, furnishings and sculptures, while in the basement there's a full-scale reconstruction of the ancient Egyptian tomb of Queen Nefertari.

On summer nights in July and August, the cathedral and various other buildings in the Old Town are illuminated in Le Mans' **son et lumière** show, called *La Nuit des Chimères*. The daily displays are free and last two hours, starting at dusk. The highlight is a parade of mythical monsters projected along the length of the Gallo-Roman walls.

Le Mans racing

The first big race at Le Mans was in 1906, and two years later aviator **Wilbur Wright** took off here, remaining in the air for a record-breaking one hour, 31 minutes and 30 seconds. The first 24-hour car race was run as early as 1923, on the present 13.6km Sarthe circuit, with average speeds of 92kph (57mph) – these days, the drivers average around 210kph (130mph). The Sarthe circuit, on which the now world-renowned **24 Heures du Mans** car race takes place every year in mid-June, stretches south from the outskirts of the city, along ordinary roads. During the race weekend, you'll need a ticket to get anywhere near the circuit. These can be bought direct from the organizers at ⓦ www.lemans.org, or via the tourist office; they cost €65 for the whole event, €27 for trial days (Wed & Thurs), and €42 for race day, which is always on a Sunday. You'll need a separate ticket (€62–105) to get access to the grandstands, and be sure to book well in advance. Many enthusiasts' clubs and ticket agencies offer tour packages including accommodation – otherwise impossible to find at race times – and the crucial parking passes; try ⓦ www.clubarnage.com, or look through the adverts in a motorsports magazine. True petrolheads can book themselves a place at one of the circuit-side campsites.

At other times of year, you can watch practice sessions, and there's the bikers' **24 Heures Moto** in early April and the **Le Mans Classic** in September. Outside race days, the simplest way to get a taste of the action is just to take the main road south of the city towards Tours, a stretch of ordinary highway which follows the famous **Mulsanne straight** for 5.7km – a distance that saw race cars reach speeds of up to 375kph, until two chicanes were introduced in 1989. Alternatively, visit the **Musée de l'Automobile** (mid-April to Sept daily 10am–6pm; Oct to mid-April Wed–Fri 11am–5pm; €8), on the edge of the Bugatti circuit – the dedicated track section of the main Sarthe circuit, where the race starts and finishes. It parades some 150 vehicles, ranging from the humble 2CV to classic Lotus and Porsche race cars.

Eating and drinking

In the centre of town, the **cafés** and **brasseries** on place de la République stay open till late, while nearby place de l'Éperon holds the best restaurant in town, ⚜ *Le Grenier à Sel* (☏02.43.23.26.30; *menus* from €20; closed Sun & Mon), particularly good for local game dishes. The most atmospheric restaurants, however, are located in the old quarter. For a special occasion, make for the rustically styled *Le Flambadou*, 14bis rue St-Flaceau (☏02.43.24.88.38; closed Sat lunch, Sun & Mon lunch), which offers meaty *menus* from Périgord and the Landes from €25. Nearby on place St-Pierre, *Le Bistro sur la Place* (☏02.43.14.25.74; closed Sun & Mon) has pleasant outside seating facing the Hôtel de Ville and serves moderately priced classic French cuisine, while the wine bar *Ô Bon Soir* at 12 place du Hallai (☏02.43.77.13.95; open eve only) offers an impressive list of local wines and a tempting cheese selection to accompany them. There's a daily **market** in the covered halls on place du Marché, plus a bric-a-brac market on Wednesday, Friday (when there's also food) and Sunday mornings on place du Jet-d'Eau, below the cathedral in the new town.

The Abbaye de L'Épau

If car racing holds no romance, there's another outing from Le Mans of a much quieter nature, to the Cistercian **Abbaye de l'Épau** (May–Oct daily 9am–noon & 2–6pm; Nov, Dec, March & April Wed–Sun 10am–noon & 2–5pm; €3; ☏02.43.84.22.29, ⊛www.sarthe.com), 4km out of town off the Chartres–Paris road – take the tram to "Épau". The abbey was founded in 1229 by Queen Berengaria, consort of Richard the Lionheart, and it stands in a rural setting on the outskirts of the Bois de Changé more or less unaltered since its fifteenth-century restoration after a fire. The visit includes the dormitory, with the remains of a fourteenth-century fresco, the abbey church and the scriptorium, or writing room. The church contains the recumbent figure of Queen Berengaria over her tomb.

Travel details

Trains

Angers to: Le Mans (frequent; 40min–1hr 20min); Nantes (frequent; 45min); Paris (frequent; 1hr 40min); Saumur (frequent; 20–30min); Tours (frequent; 1hr–1hr 30min).
Bourges to: Nevers (frequent; 50min); Orléans (frequent; 1hr 15min); Tours (frequent; 1hr 40min).
Le Mans to: Angers (frequent; 40min–1hr 20min); Nantes (frequent, 55min–1hr 45min); Paris (frequent; 1hr); Rennes (frequent; 2hr); Saumur (2 daily; 1hr 50min); Tours (frequent; 1hr).
Orléans to: Beaugency (frequent; 20min); Blois (frequent; 40min); La Ferté-St-Aubin (frequent; 15–25min); Meung-sur-Loire (frequent; 15min); Paris (at least hourly; 1hr); Tours (frequent; 1hr–1hr 30min).
Tours to: Amboise (frequent; 20min); Azay-le-Rideau (8 daily; 30min); Blois (frequent; 40min); Chenonceaux (8 daily; 30min); Chinon (8 daily; 45min); Langeais (10 daily; 20min); Le Mans (8 daily; 1hr); Montrichard (11 daily; 40min); Orléans

(frequent; 1hr 30min); Paris (hourly; 2hr 30min, TGVs via St-Pierre-des-Corps 1hr); Saumur (frequent; 45min).

Buses

Angers to: St-Georges-sur-Loire (3 daily; 45min).
Blois to: Chambord (3 daily; 45min); Cour-Cheverny (7 daily; 20min); St-Aignan (2–3 daily; 1hr 10min).
Bourges to: Sancerre (1–2 daily; 1hr 15min).
Orléans to: Beaugency (10 daily; 1hr); Chartres (9 daily; 1hr 10min–1hr 45min); Germigny-des-Prés (3 daily; 1hr); Gien (8 daily; 1hr 50min); Meung-sur-Loire (10 daily; 35min); St-Benoît-sur-Loire (3 daily; 1hr); Sully-sur-Loire (8 daily; 1hr 20min).
Saumur to: Fontevraud (4–6 daily; 35min).
Tours to: Amboise (8 daily; 50min); Azay-le-Rideau (3 daily; 50min); Chinon (3 daily; 1hr 10min); Loches (12 daily; 50min); Richelieu (3 daily; 1hr 50min); Villandry (July & Aug only; 2 daily; 30min).

Burgundy

CHAPTER 7   # Highlights

✳ **À la bourguignonne**
Voluptuaries, prepare
to indulge – Burgundy's
ambrosial sauces are based
on its full-flavoured red wines.
See box, p.445

✳ **Noyers-sur-Serein** Buried
in beautiful countryside east
of Auxerre, this stunningly
unspoilt medieval town has
the added bonuses of an
impressive museum and an
excellent place to sleep and
dine. See p.452

✳ **Fontenay Abbey** Stunningly
simple, serene and austere
Fontenay perfectly evokes
the stark atmosphere of a
Cistercian community.
See p.455

✳ **Dijon** This affluent and
cosmopolitan city has a
charming historic centre
and is a great place for both
eating and drinking.
See p.468

✳ **The Côte d'Or** Home to
Burgundy's most renowned
vineyards, the towns and
villages that line the road from
Dijon to Beaune are full of
possibilities for wine tasting.
See p.474

✳ **Beaune's Hôtel-Dieu** Topped
by a myriad of glazed,
multicoloured tiles, the
medieval hospice at Beaune
also houses Rogier van der
Weyden's *Last Judgement*.
See p.477

▲ Beaune's Hôtel-Dieu

Burgundy

L ocated in the heart of the country, **Burgundy** is one of France's most prosperous regions. Its peaceful way of life, celebrated wine, delectable food and numerous outdoor activities all combine to make this region the ideal place to discover and appreciate *la vie française*. For centuries Burgundy's powerful dukes remained independent of the French crown, and during the Hundred Years War they even sided with the English, selling them the captured Joan of Arc. By the fifteenth century their power extended over all of Franche-Comté, Alsace and Lorraine, Belgium, Holland, Picardy and Flanders, and their state was the best organized and richest in Europe. It finally fell to the French kings when Duke Charles le Téméraire (the Bold) was killed besieging Nancy in 1477.

There's evidence everywhere of this former wealth and power, both secular and religious: the dukes' capital of **Dijon**, the great abbeys of **Vézelay** and **Fontenay**, the ruins of the monastery of **Cluny** (whose abbots' influence was second only to the pope's), and the châteaux of **Tanlay** and **Ancy**.

The food of Burgundy

The richness of Burgundy's **cuisine** is largely due to two factors: the region's heavy red wines and its possession of one of the world's finest breeds of beef cattle, the Charollais. **Wines** are often used in the preparation of sauces, earning a dish the title *à la bourguignonne*. Essentially, this means that the dish is cooked in a red wine sauce to which baby onions, mushrooms and *lardons* (pieces of bacon) are added. The classic Burgundy dishes cooked in this manner are *bœuf bourguignon* and *coq au vin*. Another term which frequently appears on menus is *meurette*, also a red wine sauce but made without mushrooms and flambéed with a touch of *marc* brandy. It's used with eggs, fish and poultry as well as red meat.

Snails (*escargots*) are hard to avoid in Burgundy, and the local style of cooking involves stewing them for several hours in the white wine of Chablis with shallots, carrots and onions, then stuffing them with garlic and parsley butter and finishing them off in the oven. **Other specialities** include the parsley-flavoured ham (*jambon persillé*); calf's head (*tête de veau*, or *sansiot*); a *pauchouse* of river fish (that is, poached in white wine with onions, butter, garlic and *lardons*); and a *poussin* (tender chicken) from Bresse.

Like other regions of France, Burgundy produces a variety of **cheeses**. The best known are the creamy white Chaource, the soft St-Florentin from the Yonne valley, the orange-skinned Époisses and the delicious goat's cheeses from the Morvan. And then there is *gougère*, a savoury pastry made with cheese, best eaten warm with a glass of Chablis.

During the Middle Ages, Burgundy became, along with Poitou and Provence, one of the great church-building areas in France. Practically every village has its Romanesque church, especially in the country around Cluny and Paray-le-Monial, and where the Catholic Church built, so had the Romans before, with their legacy visible in the substantial Roman remains at **Autun**. And the history goes back further: **Bibracte**, on the vast, windswept hill of Mont-Beuvray, was an

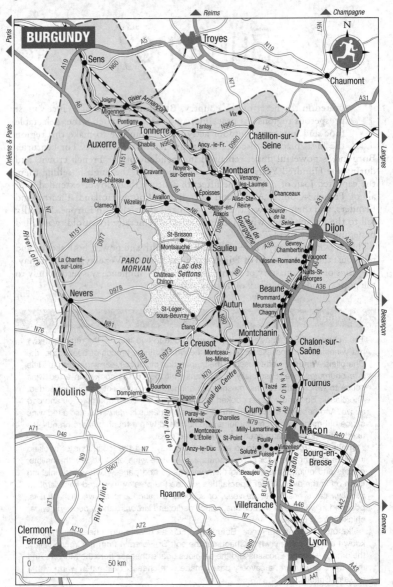

important Gallic capital, and **Alésia** was the scene of Julius Caesar's epic victory over the Gauls in 52 BC.

Wine is, of course, the region's most obvious attraction, and devotees head straight for the great vineyards, whose produce has played the key role in the local economy since Louis XIV's doctor prescribed wine as a palliative for the royal dyspepsia. If you lack the funds to indulge your taste for expensive drink, go in September or October when the *vignerons* are recruiting harvesters.

Between bouts of gastronomic indulgence, you can engage in some moderate activity: for walkers there's a wide range of hikes, from the gentle to the relatively demanding, in the Parc Régional du Morvan and the Côte d'Or. The region's many canals can be explored by rented barge, while their towpaths often form part of a rapidly expanding network of cycle paths (Ⓦ www.la-bourgogne-a-velo.com).

Burgundy has a pretty good **public transport** network, with *départmental* buses filling in most of the gaps left by the SNCF, albeit with somewhat skeletal timetables (see Ⓦ www.mobigo-bourgogne.com for more information on bus networks in each *départment*).

The road to Dijon

The old road to Dijon, the **Nationale 6**, runs from Paris down to the Côte d'Azur, and was the route taken by the National Guardsmen of Marseille when they marched on Paris singing the *Marseillaise* in 1792. It enters the province of Burgundy just south of Fontainebleau, near where the River Yonne joins the Seine, and follows the Yonne valley through the historic towns of **Sens**, **Joigny** and **Auxerre**. Scattered in a broad corridor to the east and west of the road, in the valleys of the Yonne's tributaries – the Armançon, Serein, Cure and Cousin rivers – is a fascinating collection of abbeys, châteaux, towns, villages and other sites as ancient as the history of France. It makes for a far more interesting, albeit slower route, than speeding around the bland curves of its modern replacement, the **Autoroute du Soleil** (A6), use of which requires toll payment.

Sens

The northernmost town in Burgundy, **SENS** is a quiet, relaxed place on the banks of the River Yonne. Its name commemorates the Senones, the Gallic tribe who all but captured Rome in 390 BC; they were only thwarted by the Capitoline geese cackling and waking the garrison. Sens' heyday as a major ecclesiastical centre was in the twelfth and thirteenth centuries, but it lost its pre-eminence in the ensuing centuries.

The town's ancient centre is dominated by the **Cathédrale St-Étienne**. Begun around 1130, it was the first of the great French Gothic cathedrals, and having been built without flying buttresses – these were added later for stability – its profile is relatively wide and squat. The architect who completed it, William of Sens, went on to rebuild the choir of Canterbury Cathedral in England – the other spiritual home of Thomas Becket, who had spent several years in exile around Sens. The story of Thomas's murder is told in the twelfth-century windows in the north aisle of the choir.

Next door is the thirteenth-century **Palais Synodal**. Originally designed to accommodate the ecclesiastical courts, it now houses part of the **Musée de Sens** (June–Sept daily except Tues 10am–noon & 2–6pm; Oct–May Wed, Sat & Sun 10am–noon & 2–6pm, Mon, Thurs & Fri 2–6pm; €4.20), the highlight of which is an extensive **art collection** donated in 2002 by the Marrey brothers (wealthy

Parisians with a soft spot for Sens), including a tremendous statue by Rodin and a lively crowd scene by Brueghel the younger. The museum ticket gives access to the cathedral's **treasury**, containing a number of rich tapestries and vestments – among them those of the evidently rather corpulent Thomas Becket. In summer there are guided tours of the cathedral (2.30pm), treasury (3.30pm) and museum (4.30pm), lasting 1 hour each (July & Aug daily; €5/€8 per tour or €12 for all three).

Practicalities

The **tourist office** is in place Jean-Jaurès (July & Aug Mon–Sat 9.30am–1pm & 2–6.30pm; Sept–June Mon–Sat 9.30am–12.30pm & 2–6pm; May–Oct Sun 10.30am–1pm & 2–4.30pm; ☎03.86.65.19.49, ⓦwww.office-de-tourisme -sens.com). *Hôtel Brennus* (☎03.86.64.04.40, ⓦwww.hotel-brennus.fr; ❷) at 21 rue de Trois Croissants, has charming rooms, some of which offer views of the cathedral, while *Hôtel de Paris et de la Poste* (☎03.86.65.17.43, ⓦwww.hotel -paris-poste.com; ❹), at 97 rue de la République, opposite the elaborate facade of the town hall, is grander still and has a respected but expensive restaurant (from €30). The local **campsite**, *Entre-deux-Vannes*, is at 191 av de Sénigallia (☎03.86.65.64.71, Ⓔespacesverts@mairie-sens.fr; mid-May to mid-Sept), a 20min walk south of town.

The café terraces on place de la République are a great spot for a **drink** or light meal. For more substantial **dining**, try the friendly, bustling crêperie *Au P'tit Creux* (☎03.86.64.99.29; closed Tues eve & Wed) on the doorstep of the cathedral at 3 rue de Brennus. For excellent seafood, try *Le Soleil Levant*, 51 rue Emile-Zola (☎03.86.65.71.82; closed Wed, Sun eve & Aug; *menus* €16–38), near the train station.

Joigny and around

As you travel from Sens towards Auxerre, the next place of any size on the Yonne is the modest town of **JOIGNY**. The first fort was created here at the end of the tenth century, but much of the original settlement was destroyed by a fire in 1530. The town is not worth a prolonged visit, but makes a pleasant rest stop, particularly on market days (Wed & Sat). Buildings worthy of attention are the classical **Château des Gondi**, built by Cardinal Gondi in the sixteenth century, and the remains of the twelfth-century **ramparts** on Chemin de la Guimbard. A few half-timbered houses that somehow escaped the 1530 fire are on **rue Montant-au-Palais**, the street leading up to the church of St-Jean, including the best known, **Maison du Pilori**, which combines Gothic and Renaissance styles, with some carvings strangely reminiscent of crocodile heads.

From the **gare SNCF** it's a long, straight walk up avenues de Gaulle and Gambetta to the bridge over the river to the old town. By the bridge, you'll find the **tourist office** (July–Sept Mon 2–5pm, Tues–Fri 9am–12.30pm & 2–7pm, Sat 9am–1pm & 2–6pm, Sun 10am–1pm; Oct–June Mon 2–5pm, Tues–Sat 9am–noon & 2–5/6pm; ☎03.86.62.11.05, ⓦwww.tourisme-joigny.fr) and the market halls. The nicest place to stay and eat is 5km west of town along the D182 in Thèmes. *Le Petit Claridge* (☎03.86.63.10.92, ⓦwww.lepetitclaridge .com; ❷) has rooms full of charm and a restaurant offering a very good-value *menu* at €16 (closed Sun eve to Tues).

An interesting side trip from Joigny, located about 45 minutes away by car, is the village of **ST-SAUVEUR-EN-PUISAYE** and the birthplace, in 1873, of the French writer Colette. The **Musée Colette** is in the château (April–Oct daily except Tues 10am–6pm; Nov–March Sat & Sun 2–6pm, closed mid-Nov to mid-Dec; €5) and includes a reconstruction of her apartment in Paris, as well as personal items and original manuscripts.

Auxerre

A further 15km up the Yonne from Joigny is **AUXERRE**, a pretty old town of narrow lanes and lovely open squares. It looks its best from Pont Paul-Bert and the riverside **quais**, where houseboats and barges moor, its churches soaring dramatically and harmoniously above the surrounding rooftops.

Arrival, information and accommodation

The **gare SNCF**, on rue Paul-Doumer, is across the river from the town: follow signs for the *centre ville*, crossing Pont Paul-Bert. The **tourist office** (mid-June to mid-Sept Mon–Sat 9am–1pm & 2–7pm, Sun 9.30am–1pm & 3–6.30pm; mid-Sept to mid-June Mon–Sat 9.30am–12.30pm & 2–6pm, Sun 10am–1pm; ☎03.86.52.06.19, ⊛www.ot-auxerre.fr), sits by the river at 2 quai de la République with an annexe on place de l'Hôtel de Ville. It also rents out **bikes** (€18 per day) and small **electric boats** on the river (€20 per hour), and sells a **pass** (€2) giving reductions to most of the sights in Auxerre. To enjoy some local colour, and local produce, try the **market** in place de l'Arquebuse (Tues & Fri morning). There's **internet** at Speed Informatique 89, 32 rue du Pont (Mon–Sat 2–9pm; €5 per hour), while **car hire** firms line the roads near the station: Avis (☎03.86.46.83.47) is closest at 3 rue Paul Doumer (closed Sun).

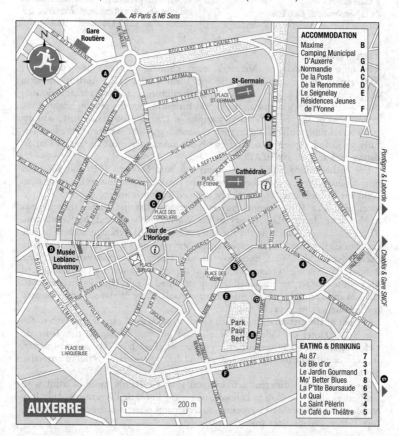

▲ A6 Paris & N6 Sens

ACCOMMODATION

Maxime	B
Camping Municipal D'Auxerre	G
Normandie	A
De la Poste	C
De la Renommée	D
Le Seignelay	E
Résidences Jeunes de l'Yonne	F

EATING & DRINKING

Au 87	7
Le Ble d'or	3
Le Jardin Gourmand	1
Mo' Better Blues	8
La P'tite Beursaude	6
Le Quai	2
Le Saint Pèlerin	4
Le Café du Théâtre	5

AUXERRE

0   200 m

Hotels

Maxime 2 quai de la Marine ℡03.86.52.14.19, ⓦwww.lemaxime.com. Rooms here are stylishly monotone and luxurious (all have a/c, wi-fi and modern furnishings). Ask for one with river views, as they are not necessarily more expensive – it's the size that matters. ❺

Normandie 41 bd Vauban ℡03.86.52.57.80, ⓦwww.hotelnormandie.fr. Just outside the old town centre, this fairly swanky, creeper-covered chain hotel occupies a former nineteenth-century country house, though the rooms boast all modern trimmings. Other facilities include a sauna, a gym and a billiards room. ❹

De la Poste 9 rue d'Orbandelle ℡03.86.52.12.02, ⓦwww.hoteldelaposte.biz. Don't be put off by the bizarre coconut-matting-clad walls of the corridors – they lead to charmingly decorated, airy, modern rooms. A great central location and a high-quality restaurant to boot (three courses €28; closed Sun & Mon lunch). ❸

De la Renommée 27 rue d'Eglény ℡03.86.51.31.45. A reliable, family-run budget option, though it's a good half-hour uphill walk from the train station. Restaurant from €14.50. Closed Sun & Aug. ❶

Le Seignelay 2 rue du Pont ℡03.86.52.03.48, ⓦwww.leseignelay.com. A popular mid-range choice with friendly staff and a restaurant (closed Sat lunch & Mon) in the courtyard, where you can have a good *menu bourguignon* for €22. Closed Feb. ❸

Hostel and campsite

Camping Municipal D'Auxerre 8 rte de Vaux ℡03.86.52.11.15, ⒺCamping.mairie@auxerre.com. Next to the riverside football ground, a pleasant site on the south side of town. Mid-April to Sept.

Résidences Jeunes de l'Yonne 16 bd Vaulabelle ℡03.86.52.45.38, ⓦwww.residences-jeunes -yonne.fr. Hard to find (it's behind a block of flats just to the right of the Citroen garage), this hostel offers spartan, single rooms reminiscent of a student residence, each with an en-suite shower and toilet. Friendly staff and a canteen offering four courses for just €8.25. €16 including breakfast.

The Town

The most interesting of Auxerre's many churches is the abbey church of **St Germain** (daily except Tues: May–Sept 10am–6.30pm; Oct–April 10am–noon & 2pm–5pm; €4.80). The monks' former dormitories, around a classical cloister, now house a historical and archeological **museum**, but the real highlight is the **crypt**. One of the few surviving examples of Carolingian architecture, with its plain barrel vaults still resting on their thousand-year-old oak beams, the wonderfully vivid and expressive ochre frescoes are among the most ancient in France, dating back to around 850 AD.

The **cathedral** itself (7.30am–5/6pm) was built between 1215 and 1560 but remains unfinished; the southernmost of the two west front towers has never been completed. Look out for the richly detailed sculpture of the porches and the glorious colours of the original thirteenth-century glass that still fills the windows of the choir, despite the savagery of the Wars of Religion and the Revolution. There has been a church on the site since about 400 AD, though nothing visible survives earlier than the eleventh-century **crypt** (mid-March to mid-Nov daily except Sun 10am–5pm; mid-Nov to mid-March Mon–Sat 9am–6pm, Sun 2–6pm; €3). Among its frescoes is a unique depiction of a warrior Christ mounted on a white charger, accompanied by four mounted angels. Upstairs, manuscripts, chalices and a number of interesting ivory ornaments are displayed in the **treasury** (same hours as the crypt; €1.90).

In front of the cathedral, rue Fourier leads to place des Cordeliers and off to the left is the Hôtel de Ville and the old city gateway known as the **Tour de l'Horloge**, with its fifteenth-century coloured clock face. The whole quarter, from place Surugue through rue Joubert and down to the river, is full of attractive old houses.

For an altogether different activity, and almost certainly more of a hit with youngsters, drive the 5km to Laborde, where the **Forêt de l'Aventure** (daily July & Aug; €20; ⓦwww.foret-aventure-auxerre.com) offers a course of high wires, rope ladders and zip lines around the treetops.

Eating, drinking and entertainment

Auxerre boasts a number of good **restaurants**, some revelling in, others diverging from, the much-loved Burgundian staples. Place de l'Hôtel de Ville is a good spot to go for an aperitif, especially in summer, as there are several bars and cafés with sunny terraces. If you're here in July or August, be sure to pick up a programme for the "Garçon la Note" series of **free concerts**, held on different café terraces every evening from Monday to Saturday.

Au 87 87 rue du Pont. A pleasant café-bar that serves an impressive array of teas, as well as coffee, organic beer, and wine. Closed Sun eve & Mon.

Le Blé d'or 5 rue d'Orbandelle ℡03.86.48.16.84. A popular little crêperie, offering filling, tasty food at fair prices. Salads, *galettes* and crêpes all €7–8. Closed Sun & Mon.

Le Jardin Gourmand 56 bd Vauban ℡03.86.51.53.52. Polished glass, crisp linen and immaculate decor; this is truly fine dining. Although the *menu* changes regularly, you are guaranteed gastronomic dishes made from locally sourced ingredients. The *menu du marché* is €70 and you get the full works, including wine, for €100. It only seats 15 so it's best to reserve in advance. Closed Mon & Tues.

Mo' Better Blues 36–38 rue du Puits des Dames ℡03.86.51.36.64. This jazz bar regularly has live music and there are concerts every weekend. There's a lively atmosphere and entry is usually free. Wed–Sat 9pm onwards.

La P'tite Beursaude 55 rue Joubert ℡03.86.51.10.21. With exposed beams and waitresses wearing traditional Morvan dress, this popular restaurant has a rustic feel to it. Specialising in regional cuisine, it has *menus* from €17.50 (lunch) and €25 (dinner). Reservations advised. Closed Tues & Wed.

Le Quai Place St-Nicholas ℡03.86.51.66.67. Grab a seat on the outdoor terrace of this popular brasserie, which overlooks a pretty square. Reasonably priced *plats* and pizzas (€10–12) have a light, modern feel, with more salad and less rich Burgundy sauce.

Le Saint-Pèlerin 56 rue St-Pèlerin ℡03.86.52.77.05. The centrepiece of this quiet, relaxed dining room is the wood fire on which the restaurant's speciality *grillades* are prepared. Good choice of meats and fish, with a *menu* for €18.50. Closed Sun & Mon.

Le Café du Théâtre 46 rue Joubert. A few doors up from the striking Art-Deco theatre, this friendly café is ideal if you fancy a quiet drink. It also does light meals. Closed Sun & Mon.

Around Auxerre

On or close to the D965, in the open, rolling country east of Auxerre and particularly along the valley of the aptly named **Serein River**, lie several towns deserving of a visit, for reasons ranging from architecture to wine to sheer secluded beauty. Rapides de Bourgogne (Ⓦwww.rapidesdebourgogne.com) runs buses from Auxerre to Pontigny (line 2) and Chablis (line 4), and from Avallon to Noyers-sur-Serein (line 5), but you usually need to reserve the day before you want to travel (℡08.00.30.33.09) and it's not always possible to do a round trip on the same day.

Pontigny

PONTIGNY lies 18km northeast of Auxerre, and its beautifully preserved twelfth-century **abbey church** (daily: June–Sept 9am–7pm; Oct–Nov 9.30am–6pm; Dec–Feb 10am–5pm; March–April 10am–6pm; free), stands on the edge of the village. There's no tower, no stained glass and no statuary to distract from its austere, harmonious lines, though the effect is marred by the seventeenth-century choir that occupies much of the nave.

Three Englishmen played a major role in the abbey's early history, all of them archbishops of Canterbury: Thomas Becket took refuge from Henry II in the abbey in 1164, Stephen Langton similarly hid here during an argument over his eligibility for the primacy from 1207 to 1213, and Edmund Rich retired here in 1240 after unsuccessfully trying to stand up to Henry III.

If you're looking for a **restaurant**, in the neighbouring village of Montigny-la-Resle is the classic *Le Soleil d'Or* (℡03.86.41.81.21, Ⓦwww.lesoleil-dor.com), which specializes in regional cuisine and has *menus* from €12 (lunch) and €28 (dinner). To **stay** the night, though, head to **Ligny-le-Chatel**, 4km east of Pontigny, which has a comfortable hotel, the *Relais St-Vincent* (T 03.86.47.53.38, W www.relais-saint-vincent.fr; ❷–❸) at 14 Grande-Rue, and a **campsite** by the Serein off the D8 Auxerre road (T 03.86.47.56.99; May–Sept).

Chablis

Sixteen kilometres to the south of Pontigny on the winding D965, the pretty red-roofed village of **CHABLIS** is home to the region's famous dry white wines. Lying in the valley of the River Serein, the town is surrounded by rows of vines, interspersed with yellow splashes of fields full of sunflowers. While wandering around the village take a look at the side door of the **church of St-Martin**, decorated with ancient horseshoes and other bits of rustic ironwork left as *ex votos* by visiting pilgrims. Legend has it that Joan of Arc was one of them.

The **tourist office** is just over the Serein bridge at 1 rue du Maréchal de Lattre de Tassigny (daily 10am–12.30pm & 1.30–6pm; Nov–March closed Sun; T 03.86.42.80.80, W www.chablis.net), and can provide lots of information about local vineyards and wine-tasting. Hotels in Chablis tend to be quite pricey but if you want to **stay** the night, a great choice is the nearby *Hôtel du Vieux Moulin* (T 03.86.42.47.30, W www.larochehotel.fr; closed Jan; ❼) at 18 rue des Moulins, a luxurious mix of traditional and contemporary architecture, with stylish rooms. Cheaper rooms are available above a bar at the *Hôtel de la Poste*, 24 rue Auxerroise (T 03.86.42.11.94, W www.hotel-poste-chablis.com; ❸), though some have the toilet in the room, offering no privacy. An attractive **campsite**, the *Camping de Chablis* (T 03.86.42.44.39, W www.chablis.net/camping; June–Sept), lies beside the river just outside the village.

For **food**, *Hôtel du Vieux Moulin*'s restaurant, *Laroche* (contact details as above; closed both Fri & Sat lunchtime, Sun & Mon), has *menus* from €22 and staff will happily advise you on a choice of wine from their extensive list. *Le Bistrot des Grand Crus* (T 03.86.42.19.41), 8 rue Jules-Rathier, has a very affordable *plat*-plus-wine deal at €9.50 and a *menu* full of local touches, offering, for example, guinea fowl or Charollais beef in rich Chablis sauces.

Caves abound in Chablis, where you can taste and purchase a good bottle of **wine** from €10 upwards. The best choice is the ☆ *La Cave du Connaisseur* (daily 10am–6pm; T 03.86.42.87.15, W www.chablis.net/caveduconnaisseur), on rue des Moulins, which is located in a thirteenth-century wine-cellar and offers an excellent selection of the area's wine, as well as wine from other parts of Burgundy. Friendly staff, all of whom speak English, offer customers free tastings and can organise group visits.

Noyers-sur-Serein

Twenty-three kilometres to the southeast of Chablis, you come to the beautiful little town of **NOYERS-SUR-SEREIN**. Half-timbered and arcaded houses, ornamented with rustic carvings – particularly those on place de la Petite-Étape-aux-Vins and round place de l'Hôtel-de-Ville – are corralled inside a loop of the river and the town walls, and pleasant hours can be passed wandering the path between the river and the irregular walls, with their robust towers. The Serein here is as pretty as in Chablis, but Noyers, being remarkably free of commercialism, has more charm.

Considering that it is based in such a small town, the **Musée de Noyers** (July & Aug daily except Tues 10am–6.30pm; June & Sept daily except Tues 11am–12.30pm & 2–6pm; Oct–May Sat & Sun 2.30–6.30pm; closed Jan; €4) certainly punches above its weight. It comprises one of the best collections in the country of the Naive painters, who had no formal training and were often workers lacking academic education (one, Augustine Lesage, worked as a miner for sixty years before he started painting). Some star exhibits include Gérard Lattier's morbid comic-strip-style work, the excellent collages of Louis Quilici and dreamy early twentieth-century paintings of Jacques Lagrange. If you fancy some exercise, you might want to attempt the hike up to the hill behind the town, at the top of which are a ruined twelfth-century **castle** and a beautiful panorama over the town. To find the path up, follow the signs for the *Vieux Château*.

Tourist information can be obtained from the friendly **Syndicat d'Initiative** on place de l'Hôtel-de-Ville (daily 10am–1pm & 2–6pm; mid-Sept to May closed Sun; ℡03.86.82.66.06, ⓦwww.noyers-et-tourisme.com). The best place to **stay** and **eat** is the ivy-covered seventeenth-century ⚑ *La Vieille Tour* (closed Sept–March; ℡03.86.82.87.69; ❸) in place du Grenier-à-Sel. Owned by a Dutch art historian, the five beautifully furnished and charmingly rustic *chambres d'hôtes* are rife with personality and enjoy views across the gardens to the river. Visitors also have access to cooking facilities and a common room. The restaurant (℡03.86.82.87.36; closed Thurs), just down the road, offers wonderful meals featuring all the regional classics plus a vegetarian option; set *menus* start at €14.50 and are accompanied by an equally good-value wine list. Reservations are essential.

The valley of the Yonne

If you're travelling south from Auxerre and want a break from the main roads, head along the D163, a twisting minor road which follows the course of the **River Yonne** through a score of peaceful rural villages. Several have places to both stay and eat, making for a much more restful overnight stop than the towns. **VAUX** and **ESCOLIVES-STE-CAMILLE**, the first villages you come to, both have attractive Romanesque churches, whilst **VINCELOTTES** and **IRANCY**, on the opposite bank of the river, are flower-decked and picturesque. A nice **place to stay** hereabouts is the hotel-restaurant *Le Castel* (℡03.86.81.43.06, ⓦwww.lecastelmailly.com; ❸) on place de l'Église in **MAILLY-LE-CHÂTEAU**, a further 10km along the river, which has *menus* from €15. The main part of the village is on high ground above the river, but there's also a lovely riverside quarter, with ancient houses huddling under cliffs.

The Canal de Bourgogne

From Migennes – near Joigny, on the N6 – the River Armançon and the **Canal de Bourgogne** branch off to the north of the River Yonne. Along or close to the canal are several places of interest: the Renaissance châteaux of **Ancy-le-Franc** and **Tanlay**, **Abbaye de Fontenay**, and the site of Julius Caesar's victory over the Gauls at **Alésia**. Just east of the Canal, perched above the River Armançon, is the picturesque town of **Semur-en-Auxois**. Further east the canal encompasses the upper reaches of the River Seine: at **Châtillon-sur-Seine** is the famous Celtic Treasure of Vix.

Cycling along the Canal de Bourgogne

There are signposted **cycle routes**, partly but not wholly, on the traffic-free canal towpath. The paths run all the way from Migennes to Dijon (212km) and make for a pleasant and flattish ride. Maps and info, including suggestions for places to stay and eat along the route, are available at ⓦwww.le-tour-de-bourgogne-a-velo.com.

Tonnerre

On the Paris–Sens–Dijon TGV train route, **TONNERRE** is a useful, though unexciting, base for exploring this corner of the region. Clearly not as prosperous as its neighbour Chablis, it nonetheless has a few sights worth a look.

The best of these is the huge medieval hospice (entrance through the tourist office; €4.50), which hosts a wonderfully realistic sculpture of the Entombment of Christ in the Burgundian style. Around the corner you can see the elaborate facade of the **Hôtel d'Uzès**, birthplace of Tonnerre's quirkiest claim to fame, a gentleman with the fittingly excessive moniker Charles-Geneviève-Louis-Auguste-André-Timothé Déon de Beaumont (b.1728). He tickled his contemporaries' prurience by going about his important diplomatic missions for King Louis XV dressed in women's clothes. Bookmakers took bets on his real sex and the results of the autopsy after his death were eagerly awaited by the gossip columnists of the day.

Another unlikely attraction sits at the foot of the steep hill crowned by the Église Saint-Pierre. The **Fosse Dionne** is a fascinating blue-green pool encircled by an eighteenth-century *lavoir* (wash house). A number of legends are attached to the spring (the name derives from Divona, Celtic goddess of water), including suggestions that it was a gateway to hell or the lair of a ferocious serpent slain by a local saint. Divers have penetrated 360m along a narrow underwater passageway, with no end in sight, but further exploration is now banned as three people have died in attempts.

The super-friendly **tourist office** is on place Marguerite-de-Bourgogne (daily 9.30am–noon & 1.30–5.30pm; Nov–March closed Sun; ℡03.86.55.14.48, Ⓦwww.tonnerre.fr). Here you can hire **bikes** (€18 per day) and pick up an interesting town history-trail leaflet. Directly opposite, at 65 rue de l'Hôpital, is the least expensive **accommodation** in town, the *Hôtel du Centre* (℡03.86.55.10.56, Ⓔhotelducentre.tonnerre@orange.fr; ❶), a relaxed, provincial hotel with a reasonable little restaurant (*menus* from €10.50). Directly overlooking the spring, the *Ferme de la Fosse Dionne*, 11 rue de la Fosse Dionne (℡03.86.54.82.62, Ⓦwww.fermefossedionne.fr; closed mid-Nov to mid-Dec; breakfast included ❸), is a tiny, sensitively restored former farm, with lovely rooms in bright colours and a beamed, covered balcony overlooking a small courtyard. The friendly owners also offer a *table d'hôte* for €20 in the evening. The local **campsite**, *La Cascade* (℡03.86.55.15.44; April to mid-Nov), is between the River Armançon and the Canal de Bourgogne.

The châteaux of Ancy-le-Franc and Tanlay

Close to Tonnerre are two of the finest, though least-known and least-visited, châteaux in France: **Ancy-le-Franc** and **Tanlay**. The former has the edge for architectural purity, the latter for romantic appeal. Unfortunately, there's **no public transport** to either château so you'll need a car.

The **Château d'Ancy-le-Franc** (guided tours only, April to mid-Nov Tues–Sun at 10.30am, 11.30am, 2pm, 3pm & 4pm; plus April–Sept 5pm; €9) is 25km from Tonnerre and was built in the mid-sixteenth century for the brother-in-law of the notorious Diane de Poitiers, mistress of Henri II. More Italian than French, with its textbook classical countenance, it is the work of the Italian Sebastiano Serlio, one of the most important architectural theorists of the Renaissance, who was brought to France in 1540 by François I to work on his palace at Fontainebleau. The exterior is rather austere and forbidding, but the inner courtyard is a refined embodiment of the principles of classical architecture. Some of the apartments are sumptuous, decorated by the Italian artists Primaticcio and Niccolò dell'Abbate, who also worked at Fontainebleau. Concerts are occasionally held in the courtyard, the price of which includes a tour of the château; Ⓦwww.chateau-ancy.com has the programme.

The **Château de Tanlay** (April–Oct guided tours daily except Tues: 10am, 11.30am & hourly 2.15–5.15pm; ⓦwww.chateaudetanlay.fr; €9) is a pleasant 8km walk or cycle along the canal from Tonnerre. This 1559 construction, very French in feel and full of ambience, is only slightly later in date than its near-neighbour, but those extra few years were enough for the purer Italian influences visible in Ancy to have become Frenchified. Encircling the château are water-filled moats and standing guard over the entrance to the first grassy courtyard is the grand lodge, from where you enter the château across a stone drawbridge.

Châtillon-sur-Seine

About 30km east of Tonnerre is **CHÂTILLON-SUR-SEINE**, and for those interested in pre-Roman France, there is one compelling reason for going there: the so-called **Treasure of Vix**. Discovered in 1953, the treasure consists of the finds from the sixth-century BC tomb of a Celtic princess buried in a four-wheeled chariot at **Vix**, 6km northwest of Châtillon. The most interesting piece of treasure is the famous Vase of Vix. Weighing 208kg and measuring 1.64m in height, it is the largest bronze vase of Greek origin known from antiquity. Around its rim is a superbly modelled high-relief frieze, with Gorgons' heads for handles. The vase is displayed in the **Musée du Pays Châtillonnais** (daily 9am–noon & 2–4pm; July & Aug 10am–7pm; €6; ℡03.80.91.51.76, ⓦwww.musee-vix.fr); which also boasts an impressive collection of objects from Celtic, Gallo-Roman and Medieval periods found in the Châtillonnais region.

Archeology aside, Châtillon makes for a picturesque stop. Here the Seine embarks on a gloriously complex series of tangents and S-bends, many spanned by picture-postcard, flower-decked bridges. On the rocky bluff overlooking the steep-pitched roofs of the old quarter are the ruins of a **castle** and the beautifully spare, early Romanesque **church of St Vorles**. At its foot in a luxuriantly verdant spot, a **spring** swells out of the rock forming an enchanting pool before tumbling off to join the infant Seine.

The **tourist office** is on place Marmont (July & Aug Mon–Sat 9am–7pm, Sun 10am–1pm; Sept–June Mon–Sat 9am–noon & 2–6pm; ℡03.80.91.13.19, ⓦwww.pays-chatillonnais.fr). Hotels include *Sylvia* (℡03.80.91.02.44, ⓦwww .sylvia-hotel.com; ❷), north of the centre at 9 av de la Gare, with charming rooms and great breakfasts, which include home-made jam and *brioche*; and, in the middle of town at 2 rue Charles-Ronot the *Hôtel de la Côte d'Or* (℡03.80.91.13.29; closed Jan & Feb; ❸), a wonderfully atmospheric old post-house, complete with hunting trophies on the walls. It also has a very good **restaurant** with *menus* at €19, €29 and €40. Otherwise *O Chapo Ron* (℡03.80.91.32.41; closed Mon & Tues), at 21 rue de la Liberation, is a great refreshment stop, with a large terrace and a blazing cooking fire. Grilled dishes start at €9 and *galettes* are around €7. Or kick back with a pint of Belgian draught and scoff down a baguette (€4) along the banks of the river at *Pub le Splendide*, on quai de la Seine by the bridge.

Montbard and Abbaye de Fontenay

One base worth knowing about if you're counting on **public transport** in the area is the rather unexciting hillside town of **MONTBARD**, which is on the main railway line between Dijon and Paris and where buses leave for both Châtillon and Semur. The *Hôtel de la Gare* (℡03.80.92.07.21, ⓦwww.hotel-de-la-gare-montbard .com; ❸), just opposite the station, has reasonably priced rooms. The restaurant has *menus* (€14–29) and also serves salads and sandwiches if you fancy a quick bite.

Six kilometres away, along the GR213 footpath, the privately owned **Abbaye de Fontenay** (daily: April–Oct 10am–6pm, guided visits every hour except 1pm,

Nov–March 10am–noon & 2–5pm; ⓦwww.abbayedefontenay.com; €9.20) is probably the biggest draw in the area. Founded in 1118, it's the only Burgundian monastery to survive intact, despite conversion to a paper mill in the early nineteenth century. It was restored in the early 1900s to its original form and is one of the world's most complete monastic complexes, including caretaker's lodge, guesthouse and chapel, dormitory, hospital, prison, bakery, kennels and abbot's house, as well as a church, cloister, chapterhouse and even a forge.

On top of all this, the abbey's physical setting, at the head of a quiet stream-filled valley enclosed by woods of pine, fir, sycamore and beech, is superb. There's a bucolic calm about the place, particularly in the graceful cloister, and in these surroundings the spartan simplicity of Cistercian life seems utterly attractive. Hardly a scrap of decoration softens the church and there's no direct lighting in the nave, just an other-worldly glow from the square-ended apse. The effect is beautiful but daunting, the perfect structural embodiment of St Bernard's ascetic principles.

Alésia

A few kilometres south of Montbard is the site of the 52 BC **Battle of Alésia**, where the Gauls, united under the leadership of Vercingétorix, made their last stand against the military might of Rome. Julius Caesar himself commanded the Roman army, which surrounded the final Gallic stronghold and starved the Gauls out, bloodily defeating all attempts at escape. Vercingétorix surrendered to save his people, was imprisoned in Rome for six years until Caesar's formal triumph, and then strangled. The battle was a fundamental turning point in the fortunes of the region. Thereafter, Gaul remained under Roman rule for four hundred years.

The **site** of Alésia (daily: Feb–March 10am–5pm; April–June 9am–6pm; July–Aug 9am–7pm; Sept 9am–6pm; Oct to mid-Nov 10am–5pm; closed mid-Nov to Jan; €3), treeless and exposed, is on Mont Auxois, above the village of **ALISE-STE-REINE**. You can recreate the scenes of the battle in your mind's eye as well as visit the excavations of the town, including the theatre and a Gallo-Roman house.

On the hilltop opposite, and visible for miles around, is a great bronze **statue of Vercingétorix**. Erected by Napoléon III, whose influence popularized the rediscovery of France's pre-Roman roots, the statue represents Vercingétorix as a romantic Celt – half virginal Christ, half long-haired 1970s matinee idol. On the plinth is inscribed a quotation from Vercingétorix's address to the Gauls as imagined by Julius Caesar: "United and forming a single nation inspired by a single ideal, Gaul can defy the world." Napoléon signs his dedication, "Emperor of the French", inspired by a vain desire to gain legitimacy by linking his own name to that of a "legendary" Celt.

The whole site looks set to be revolutionized over the coming years by the construction of a brand new, hi-tech **MuséoParc**, comprising two new buildings 2km apart: an Interpretation Centre and an Archaeological Museum. The centre is due to open in summer 2011, and the museum in several years' time (ⓦwww.alesia.com).

Practicalities

Trains from Dijon or Montbard will get you as far as the station of "Les Laumes – Alésia", but from here it's a 3km ascent to the real centre of interest. The most attractive stopover is in Alise-Ste-Reine at the *Hôtel-Restaurant Alésia* (☎03.80.96.19.67; ➊), 16 rue du Miroir, a welcoming, family-run hotel with a simple restaurant; all rooms have shared bathroom facilities. A little further up the street at no. 9, the elegant *L'Auberge du Cheval Blanc* (☎03.80.96.01.55; closed Mon) serves excellent regional cuisine, with wonderful *menus* from €15 – specialities include snails, and *foie gras de canard*.

The Château de Bussy-Rabutin

Eight kilometres east of Alésia, on the D954, stands the handsome **Château de Bussy-Rabutin** (daily except Mon 9.15am–noon & 2–5/6pm; €7). It was built for Roger de Rabutin, a member of the Academy in the reign of Louis XIV and a notorious womanizer. The scurrilous tales of life at the royal court told in his book *Histoires Amoureuses des Gaules* earned him a spell in the Bastille, followed by years of exile in this château. There are some interesting portraits of great characters of the age, including its famous female beauties, each underlined by an acerbic little comment such as: "The most beautiful woman of her day, less renowned for her beauty than the uses she put it to".

The source of the Seine

You'll need your own car to get to the **source of the Seine**, which lies some 15km east of Alésia. No more than a trickle here, it rises in a tight little vale of beech woods. The spring is now covered by an artificial grotto complete with a languid nymph, Sequana, spirit of the Seine. In Celtic times it was a place of worship, as is clear from the numerous votive offerings discovered here, including a neat bronze of Sequana standing in a bird-shaped boat, now in the Dijon archeological museum.

Semur-en-Auxois

Extraordinarily beautiful, the small fortress town of **SEMUR-EN-AUXOIS** sits on a rocky bluff – a place of cobbled lanes, medieval gateways and ancient gardens tumbling down to the River Armançon. Thirteen kilometres west of Alésia, all roads here lead to place Notre-Dame, a handsome square dominated by the large thirteenth-century **church of Notre-Dame** (another Viollet-le-Duc restoration) characterized by its huge entrance porch and the narrowness of its nave. Inside, the windows of the second chapel on the left commemorate the dead of World War I – Semur was the general headquarters of the American 78th division, and the battlefields were not far away.

Down the street in front of the church you come to the four sturdy towers of Semur's once-powerful **castle**, all that remains after the body of the fortress was dismantled in 1602 because of its utility to enemies of the French crown. You can explore the winding streets around the castle – there's scarcely a lane in town without some building of note – and continue down to the delightful stretch of river between the Pont Pinard and the Pont Joly, from where there are beautiful views of the town.

Cheese connoisseurs might like to take a twelve-kilometre hop **further** west on the Avallon road to **ÉPOISSES**, not just for its village and château (gardens open all year round; €2; castle open July & Aug daily except Tues 10am–noon & 3–6pm; @www.chateaudepoisses.com; €7), but for its distinctive, soft orange-skinned cheese of the same name, washed in *marc de Bourgogne*.

Practicalities

Semur's **tourist office** is on the small place Gaveau (Mon–Sat 9am–noon & 2–6pm; July & Aug Sun 10am–1.30pm; ☎03.80.97.05.96, @www.ville-semur-en-auxois .fr), at the junction of rues de l'Ancienne-Comédie, de la Liberté and Buffon.

The least expensive **hotel** is *Le Commerce* at 19 rue de la Liberté (☎03.80.96.64.40, @hotelducommerce21@orange.fr; ❷), which has clean but rather basic rooms. Downstairs is a bar-restaurant with **internet** access (€4 per hour). Inside the medieval city proper is the more traditional *Hôtel des Cymaises* (☎03.80.97.21.44, @www.hotelcymaises.com; ❸–❹), in a grand old mansion with a walled courtyard at 7 rue du Renaudot. The local **campsite** is at Lac-de-Pont (☏03.80.97.01.26; April–Sept), 7km south of town.

Semur has a number of nice places to **eat**. The stylish café and art gallery *Spiral-inthe* (☏03.80.89.45.18; open 8am–late; closed Sun) on 4 place Gaveau serves light meals all day, including quiche, *tartines* and a *plat du jour* for €13. Alternatively, the bustling old-fashioned bistro *Le Saint-Vernier* (☏03.80.97.32.96) at 13 rue Févret, has a filling lunch *menu* for €12, alongside its speciality *tartiflettes* (from €12). For something really special, it is well worth wandering down to the river and the Pont des Minimes, where the *Maison-Dieu Les Minimes* (☏03.80.97.26.86; *menus* from €11.50; closed Sun & Mon) is a great find: excellent food, a warm atmosphere and extremely good-value – look out for their delicious recommended wines. In the heart of the old town, the **patisserie-chocolaterie**, at 14 rue Buffon (closed Mon) sells the local speciality *semurettes*, addictive little nuggets of chocolate made without butter. For savoury treats, head to ✹ *L'Epicerie chez Serge* on rue de la Liberté (open daily), where you'll find a wonderful selection of locally produced gourmet food products, wine, champagne, fresh fruit & vegetables, and the owner's charming collection of Dinky toys.

The Morvan

The **Morvan** region lies in the middle of Burgundy between the valleys of the Loire and the Saône, stretching roughly from **Clamecy**, **Vézelay** and **Avallon** in the north to **Autun** and **Le Creusot** in the south. It's a land of wooded hills and, with poor soil and pastures only good for a few cattle, villages and farms are few and far between. In the old days, supplying firewood and charcoal to Paris was the main business and large tracts of hillside are now covered in coniferous plantations. But as a result of the decline in industry, parts of this region are some of the poorest in the country, with few resources to trade on and little inspiration for outside investment.

The creation of a **parc naturel régional** in 1970 did something to promote the area as a place for outdoor activities, but it was the election of François Mitterrand, local politician and former mayor of **Château-Chinon**, as president of the Republic that rescued the Morvan from oblivion. In addition to lending it some of the glamour of his office, he took concrete steps to beef up the local economy. Plentiful local information can be found **online** at Ⓦwww.morvan.com.

West of the Morvan, the landscape softens as it descends towards the River Loire and the fine medieval town of **Nevers**, on Burgundy's western border.

Avallon

Approaching **AVALLON** along the N6 from the north, you might not, mistakenly, give the place a second look. The southern aspect is altogether more promising, clustered high on a ridge above the wooded valley of the River Cousin, looking out over the hilly, sparsely populated country of the Morvan regional park. Once a staging post on the Romans' *Via Agrippa* from Lyon to Boulogne, it's a small and ancient town of stone facades and sleepy cobbled streets.

Arrival, information and accommodation

The **tourist office** is at 6 rue Bocquillot (June–Sept daily 9am–7pm; Oct–May Mon–Sat 9.30am–12.30pm & 2–6pm; ☏03.86.34.14.19, Ⓦwww.avallonnais -tourisme.com), between the clock tower and the church, and offers **internet access** (€4 per hour) and **bike hire** (€18 per day).

Hotels

Les Capucins 6 av Doumer ☏03.86.34.06.52, ⓦwww.avallonlescapucins.com. This delightful mid-range hotel is close to the train station and has pleasant rooms all boasting a/c, en-suite bathrooms and wi-fi. ❸

Hostellerie de la Poste 13 place Vauban ☏03.86.34.16.16, ⓦwww.hostelleriedelaposte .com. A former coaching inn with sumptuous, exquisitely furnished rooms set around a cobbled courtyard lined with wooden balconies. Napoleon stayed here on his way back from Elba. It also has a restaurant (from €25; closed Sun & Mon), which serves a five-course *menu gastronomique* for €48. Closed Jan & Feb. ❼

Le Moulin des Ruats 4km outside Avallon, on the scenic riverside road to Vézelay (D427) ☏03.86.34.97.00, ⓦwww.moulindesruats.com.

This eighteenth-century former flour mill offers calm and elegant rooms, some of which have a view of the river. The restaurant (from €29.50; open Tues–Sun eve plus Sun lunch) specializes in regional cuisine. Closed mid-Nov to mid-Feb. ❺

Le Pub Vauban 3 rue Mathé ☏03.86.34.02.20, ⓔpubvauban@orange.fr. Four simple but clean rooms situated above a bar – ask for one with a view of the street, as the price is the same. Breakfast (€6) includes the owner's delicious home-made jam. ❶

Campsite

Camping Municipal de Sous-Roche Rue Sous-Roche, 2km south of town ☏03.86.34.10.39, ⓔcampingsousroche@ville-avallon.fr. Attractive riverside site, not far from hiking and mountain biking trails. April–Oct.

The Town

Bisecting the town north to south, the narrow **Grande-Rue-Aristide-Briand** leads to the arch of the fifteenth-century **Tour de l'Horloge** – the spire of which dominates the town – to the pilgrim **church of St-Lazare**, on whose battered Romanesque facade you can still decipher the graceful carvings of the zodiac signs. Almost opposite, in a fifteenth-century house, is the tourist office, with the **Musée Avallonnais** (July–Sept daily except Tues 2–6pm; Oct–June Sat & Sun 2–6pm; free) behind it. The archeological section includes a second-century mosaic from a Gallo-Roman villa, while the highlight of the fine arts department is Alfred Boucher's sculpture of a very life-like Jason pinching the Golden Fleece. There's also the rather quaint **Musée du Costume** at 6 rue Belgrand (April–Nov daily 10.30am–12.30pm & 1.30–5.30pm; €4), just off Grande-Rue, with a collection of regional dress.

Continuing from St-Lazare, down what's now called rue Bocquillot, brings you to the lime-shaded **Promenade de la Petite Porte**, with precipitous views across the plunging valley of the Cousin. From here, you can walk the perimeter of the outside walls. From the **Parc des Chaumes**, on the east side of town, there's a great view back to the old quarter, snug within its walls, with garden terraces descending on the slope beneath.

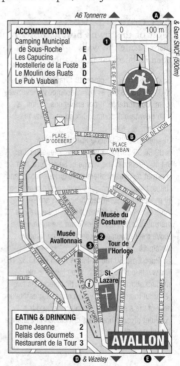

Eating and drinking

For **food** in town, the *Relais des Gourmets* (daily; Nov–March closed Sun eve & Mon; ☏03.86.34.18.90), 45–47 rue de

Paris, has a large choice of *menus* – for under €20 you get the regional classics, snails and beef, while €36 involves more upmarket cuisine, including lobster. On Grande Rue, in the heart of the old town, the friendly *Restaurant de la Tour* (daily; Nov–March closed Sun & Mon) does pizzas and *plats* for €8–10, while the refined tea room *Dame Jeanne* (closed Thurs) has a wonderful selection of teas and does light, predominantly vegetarian, lunches for around €8 in a flowery courtyard.

Vézelay

The coach buses winding their way like ants up the steep incline to **VÉZELAY** should not deter you from visiting this attractive hilltop hamlet, surrounded by ramparts and with some of the most picturesque, winding streets and crumbly buildings in Burgundy.

Arrival and information

In summer, you can get here by **bus** from Clamecy or Avallon; during the rest of the year there is only one Rapides de Bourgogne bus that runs to and from Vézelay from Avallon on a Saturday, and you have to reserve it the night before (℡08.00.30.33.09). Alternatively, you can go to Semizelles-Vézelay, north of Vézelay, by train and then get a **taxi** (a reliable company is Annette Devry, ℡03.86.32.36.63; the journey takes around 15min). Vézelay's friendly **tourist office** (daily 10am–1pm & 2–6pm; Oct–May closed Sun & Thurs; ℡03.86.33.23.69, Ⓦwww.vezelaytourisme.com), on rue St-Pierre provides various services, including taking reservations for **hot-air balloon** flights over the town and surrounding countryside (from €185 per person; Ⓦwww.france -montgolfiere.com).

Accommodation

Most of the town's **hotels** cluster round the bustling place du Champ-de-Foire, just outside the walls at the foot of town. At weekends and in high season you'll need to book far in advance.

Le Compostelle 1 place du Champ de Foire ℡03.86.33.28.63, Ⓦwww.lecompostellevezelay .com. Comfortable, if not enormous rooms, all with private bathrooms. Closed mid-Nov to mid-Feb. ❷–❸

L'Espérance 25 Grande Rue, Saint-Père ℡03.86.33.39.10, Ⓦwww.marc.meneau.com. Below Vézelay, in the village of Saint-Père, this gourmet restaurant offers 34 luxurious rooms and suites. Filled with antique furniture, but providing all modern conveniences, the rooms are set in three locations, *Le Moulin* (the mill), *Le pré des marguerites* (the daisy field) and the main house above the restaurant. Closed mid-Jan to early March. ❽

Au Porc Épic 80 rue St-Pierre ℡03.86.33.32.16, Ⓦwww.le-porc-epic.com. In a charming old building above an art gallery, this place has two beautiful rooms, one of which offers a breathtaking view of the surrounding countryside, and the excellent organic breakfast is included in the price. Closed Dec–Feb. ❻

De la Poste et du Lion d'Or Place du Champ de Foire ℡03.86.33.21.23, Ⓦwww.laposte-liondor .com. A grand and luxurious choice whose plush rooms have imposing old wooden furniture and great views of either the old town or the sweeping valley behind. Restaurant *menus* from €25. Closed Jan & Feb. ❺

Hostels

Youth Hostel Rte de l'Étang ℡03.86.33.24.18. About 1km outside of Vézelay, this friendly hostel offers lovely views of the surrounding countryside. Best to ring in advance as it is often closed in the afternoon. Beds €10 (bed linen not provided) and camping space available. Closed Nov–March.

Centre Sainte-Madeline Rue Saint-Pierre ℡03.86.33.22.14. Right at the top of the hill, near the Basilica, this lovely former convent offers dormitory accommodation to tourists and pilgrims alike. Rooms are simple but clean and prices range from €12 to €25, depending on the number of people in a dormitory. Bed linen can be rented for €4.

The Town

Pilgrims journey to Vézelay to venerate the relics of Mary Magdalene, housed in one of the seminal buildings of the Romanesque period, the **Basilica Ste-Marie Madeleine** (daily sunrise–sunset). The church's west front begins with the colossal narthex, added to the nave around 1150 to accommodate the swelling numbers of pilgrims. Inside, your eye is drawn to the sculptures of the central doorway, on whose tympanum a Pentecostal Christ is shown swathed in exquisitely figured drapery. From Christ's outstretched hands, the message of the Gospel shoots out to the apostles in the form of beams of fire, while the frieze below depicts the converted and the pagans – among those featured are giants, pygmies (one mounting his horse with a ladder), a man with breasts and huge ears, and dog-headed heathens. The arcades and arches are edged with fretted mouldings, and the supporting pillars are crowned with finely cut capitals, depicting scenes from the Bible, classical mythology, allegories and morality stories.

The abbey declined in subsequent centuries, due to rumours that Mary Magdalene's bones were false relics, then pillaging by Protestants in the sixteenth-century Wars of Religion, and finally the dismantling of much of the complex during the Revolution. Today, a significant Franciscan community has been re-established, and pilgrims stream here en route to Santiago de Compostela in Spain.

As well as pilgrims, Vézelay is a popular destination for art-lovers, and there are a number of small galleries and antique shops on rue St-Pierre. The **Musée Zervos** (July & Aug daily, March–Nov daily except Tues; €3), which displays a number of interesting modernist works, including several Picassos and a Calder mobile, is definitely worth a visit.

Eating and drinking

Auberge de la Coquille 81 rue St-Pierre ℡03.86.33.35.57. Close to the basilica, this restaurant has a lovely courtyard and serves a range of reasonably priced dishes, from crêpes (around €8) to delicious Burgundian specialities (*menus* from €11.80). Closed Thurs eve & Nov–March.

Le Bougainville 28 rue St-Pierre ℡03.86.33.27.57. Good regional cuisine served in a genteel dining room, *menus* from €22. The house terrine, made with *Époisses* cheese, ham and artichoke, is delicious. Closed Tues, Wed & mid-Nov to mid-Feb.

L'Espérance 25 Grande Rue, Saint-Père ℡03.86.33.39.10. Below Vézelay, in the village of Saint-Père, is one of Burgundy's most famous restaurants. Celebrated chef Marc Meneau's gourmet restaurant takes a traditional dish and adds modern touches – such as roasted lobster with polenta and to follow, peaches poached in pink champagne. Lunch *menus* from €57, dinner from €150. Closed Mon lunch, Tues, Wed lunch, and mid-Jan to early March.

Le Saint Etienne 39 rue St-Pierre ℡03.86.33.27.34. Owned by Gilles Lafontaine, former chef of the well-known *George V* in Paris, this gourmet restaurant specialises in traditional French cuisine. *Menus* start at €25 and Madame Fontaine is happy to advise clients about the food, explain how dishes are made, and even disclose a few of the chef's secrets. Reservations necessary. Closed Wed & Thurs, Jan & Feb.

Clamecy

CLAMECY, 23km to the west of Vézelay on the banks of the River Yonne, has less to offer than its rustic neighbours, but is worth a day-trip. It was the centre of the Morvan's logging trade from the sixteenth century to the completion of the Canal du Nivernais in 1834. Individual woodcutting gangs working in the hills floated their logs down the river as far as Clamecy, where they were made up into great rafts for shipment on to Paris. You can see one of these rafts in the timber-floating exhibition in the **Romain Rolland Art and History Museum** on Avenue de la République (daily except Tues & Sun morning 10am–noon & 2–6pm; Oct–May closed Mon; closed Jan; €3), which has a collection of works ranging from Gallo-Roman objects to twentieth-century abstract art. The modernist posters designed by renowned poster artist Charles Loupot and the collection of paintings donated by President Mitterand are definitely worth a look.

Winding your way up the narrow streets that lead to the well-preserved historic centre of the town, you'll pass a number of fifteenth- to eighteenth-century buildings, particularly on rue de la Monnaie, rue de la Tour and rue Bourgeoise. At the top of the hill is the church of St Martin, a veritable gem of flamboyant Gothic architecture, parts of which date back to the twelfth century. The **tourist office** is further up the hill from St Martin's on rue Grand Marché (daily except Sun & Mon 9.30am–12.30pm, 2–5/6pm, July & Aug Mon 2–6pm & Sun 10am–1pm; ℡03.86.27.02.51, ⓦwww.vaux-yonne.com). Should you be in need of some light refreshments, the tearoom *Portal Emmanuel* (closed Mon) on rue de la Monnaie serves delicious cakes and pastries.

Saulieu

An old market town with a reputation for its gastronomy, **SAULIEU** suffered something of a decline as a result of the depopulation of the Morvan. Every year the town waits hungrily for its Charollais **festival** on the third weekend of August – a super-gourmet festival featuring mountains of meat and other local produce. Saulieu is also a good springboard for the cycling, hiking and riding possibilities of the Parc du Morvan (see below), and the tourist office rents out bikes for €18 per day. The main sight of the old town is the twelfth-century **Basilique St-Andoche** (closed Sun morning & Mon), noted for its lovely capitals (probably carved by a disciple of Gislebertus, the master sculptor of Autun), but little else. Next door, the **Musée François-Pompon** (Mon 10.30am–noon, Wed–Sun 10am–12.30pm & 2–5/6pm; closed Jan & Feb; €4) is surprisingly interesting, with good local folklore displays and a large collection of works by the local nineteenth-century animal sculptor, François Pompon.

From the **train station**, walking up avenue de la Gare brings you to a wide market place (market Sat morning), around which you'll find the **tourist office** (Jan–March Mon–Sat 10am–1pm & 2–5pm; April–Dec Mon–Sat 9am–1pm & 2–5/6pm; June, July & Aug also Sun; ℡03.80.64.00.21, ⓦwww.saulieu.fr) and some six or seven hotel-restaurants. Among the best options is *La Borne Imperiale*, 14–16 rue d'Argentine (℡03.80.64.19.76, ⓦwww.borne-imperiale.com; ❸; closed Mon eve & Tues). Run by a charming couple, it has rooms facing a peaceful garden and a great restaurant with an attractive terrace and classic Burgundian *menus* from €23.50. Should your trust fund mature while in Saulieu, head for *Le Relais Bernard Loiseau* (℡03.80.90.53.53, ⓦwww.bernard-loiseau.com; ❻), practically next door. This hotel-restaurant-spa was created by the famed chef Bernard Loiseau (and made even more famous after his suicide in 2003 following a long bout with depression). It is an elegant, beyond-luxurious place of rich woods, stone arches and plush furnishings that exude wealth. Unfortunately it'll also drain yours; the cheapest rooms are €255, while the restaurant starts at €66 for lunch and €145 for dinner. Alternatively, there is a **campsite** (℡03.80.64.16.19, ⓔcamping.saulieu@orange.fr; April–Sept), 1km out along the Paris road, which also rents out mini chalets.

The Parc du Morvan

Carpeted with forest and etched by cascading streams, the **Parc Régional du Morvan** was only officially created in 1970, when 170,000 hectares of hilly countryside were set aside in an attempt to protect the local cultural and physical environment with a series of nature trails, animal reserves, museums and local craft shops. The Maison du Parc, its official **information centre** (daily Mon–Fri

Exploring the Parc du Morvan

Outdoor activities

There is a plethora of **cycle** routes in the Parc du Morvan, and tourist offices sell a pack of large-scale maps for around €10. **Bikes** are available from most campsites in the area (see below): for a complete list ask at any tourist office, or check online for VTT (mountain bikes) at Ⓦwww.morvan.com. For **walkers**, the most challenging trip is the three- to four-day hike along the GR13 footpath, crossing the park from Vézelay to Mont Beuvray and taking in the major lakes, which are among the park's most developed attractions. There are also numerous less strenuous possibilities including the 4km walk from Saulieu to Lac Chamboux. **Riding** is a fairly popular way of seeing the park, and numerous *gîtes d'étape* offer pony-trekking facilities – again, tourist offices can advise.

Accommodation and provisions

Every other village in the park seems to have its own **campsite** (most of which are open from April or May–Sept), and the larger ones often have a couple of simple **hotels** as well. There are several campsites and small, beach-resortish hotels round the large, wooded **Lac des Settons**, in the heart of the park, which has watersports facilities, café-restaurants and small beach areas. The plain, modern village of **Montsauche**, 4km to the northwest of the lake, is a good bet for provisions, including camping gas, and has a municipal campsite; **Moux**, a similar distance to the southeast, can provide the same facilities, and also has a couple of decent hotels.

9.30am–12.30pm & 2–5.30pm, Sat 10am–12.30pm & 2–5pm, Sun 10am–1pm; July & Aug Sun 10am–1pm, 2–5pm; ☎03.86.78.79.57, Ⓦwww.parcdumorvan .org), is located 13km from Saulieu in beautiful grounds about a kilometre outside **St-Brisson** on the D6. Although there's no public transport to get you there, if you're walking or cycling it's a good place to head for, as they have information on all the routes and facilities in the park. There's also a small **museum** (July & Aug daily 10am–1pm & 2–5/6pm, April to mid-Nov daily except Tues & Sat morning; €4), devoted to the region's World War II Resistance movement, which was particularly active in this hard-to-patrol forested backwater.

Château-Chinon

Although it nestles in beautiful countryside dotted with evergreens, lakes and limestone deposits, **CHÂTEAU-CHINON** – the most substantial community in the park – is a rather ugly village. President Mitterrand was mayor here from 1959 to 1981 and, thanks largely to him, the village now boasts a major hosiery factory and military printing works, both of which have provided much needed employment to an isolated and often forgotten region. Buscéphale runs buses from Autun to Château-Chinon but the schedules won't allow you to come for a day-trip (see Ⓦwww.buscephale.fr for more information).

In the **Musée du Septennat** (July & Aug daily 10am–1pm & 2–7pm; March–June & Sept–Dec daily except Tues 10am–noon & 2–6pm; €4), at 6 rue du Château, you can see the extraordinary gifts Mitterrand received as head of state: carpets from the Middle East, ivory from Togo, Japanese puppets, and the bizarre table decorated with butterfly wings. Another of the town's attractions is the **Musée du Costume**, 4 rue du Château (same times and price), featuring a collection of over five thousand articles, allowing you to trace developments in French provincial fashion from the eighteenth century to the present.

Mitterrand's preferred **hotel** was *Le Vieux Morvan* (☎03.86.85.05.01, Ⓦwww .auvieuxmorvan.com; ❸), at 8 place Gudin, with a restaurant (from €15) which has a panoramic view of the surrounding countryside. Cheaper is the cosy and comfortable *Lion d'Or* (☎03.86.85.13.56; **②**; restaurant from €11) at 10 rue des Fossés; be sure to ask for one of the rooms with views of the surrounding hillside. There's also a **campsite** here, *Le Perthuy d'Oiseau* (☎03.86.85.08.17; May–Sept).

Autun

With its Gothic spire rising against the backdrop of the Morvan hills, **AUTUN** is scarcely bigger than the circumference of its medieval **walls**, which follow the line of earlier Roman fortifications. The emperor Augustus founded the town in about 10 BC as part of a massive and, ultimately, highly successful campaign to pacify the brooding Celts of defeated Vercingétorix. The splendour of Augustodunum, as it was called, was designed to eclipse the memory of **Bibracte** (see p.446), the neighbouring capital of the powerful tribe of the Aedui, and it did indeed become one of the leading cities of Roman Gaul. Today, Autun is a sleepy but picturesque provincial town, and an excellent base for exploring the surrounding countryside, particularly the Parc du Morvan.

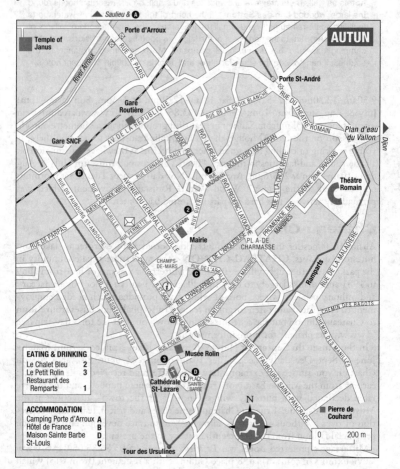

AUTUN

EATING & DRINKING
Le Chalet Bleu — 2
Le Petit Rolin — 3
Restaurant des Remparts — 1

ACCOMMODATION
Camping Porte d'Arroux — A
Hôtel de France — B
Maison Sainte Barbe — D
St-Louis — C

Arrival, information and accommodation

The **gare SNCF** and **gare routière** are just a short walk from the central square of the Champs-de-Mars, where you'll find the main **tourist office** at 13 rue Général-Demetz (July & Aug Mon–Sat 9am–7pm, Sun 10am–1pm & 3–6pm; May, June & Sept Mon–Sat 9am–1pm & 2–6/7pm; Oct–April Mon 2–6pm, Tues–Sat 9.30am–12.30pm & 2–6pm; ℡03.85.86.80.38, @www.autun-tourisme.com).
Internet access is available at the stylish *Elge*, which also serves tea and coffee, at 6 Grande-rue Chauchien (€4 per hour; closed Sat & Sun).

Hotels

Hôtel de France 18 av de la République ℡03.85.52.14.00, @hotel-restaurant.hotel-de-france-autun.fr. Family-run hotel opposite the station that provides basic but clean rooms. The cheaper ones have shared facilities. Closed Aug & Feb. ❶–❷

Maison Sainte-Barbe 7 place Sainte-Barbe ℡03.85.86.24.77, @www.maisonsaintebarbe.com. Run by a charming couple, this former rectory has four spacious and beautifully furnished *chambres d'hôtes*, and a lovely garden with a view of the neighbouring chapel. ❸

St-Louis 6 rue de l'Arbalète ℡03.85.52.01.01, @www.hotelsaintlouis.net. The now slightly faded but once magnificent *St-Louis* is situated just behind the cathedral. Napoleon and Josephine stayed here on several occasions and for €250 you can sleep in the emperor's suite itself, still containing much of its original furniture. There are cheaper rates on the internet. Closed mid-Nov to mid-Feb. ❺

Campsite

Camping Porte d'Arroux Rue du Traité d'Anvers ℡03.85.52.10.82, @www.camping-autun.com. The campsite is located just across the river on the road to Saulieu. Bike hire available. Open April–Oct.

The Town

This city's Roman past remains very tangible. Two of its four Roman gates survive: **Porte St-André**, spanning rue de la Croix Blanche in the northeast, and **Porte d'Arroux** in the northwest. In a field just across the River Arroux stands a lofty section of wall known as the **Temple of Janus**, which was probably part of the sanctuary of a Gallic deity. On the east side of the town, on avenue du 2ème-Dragons, you can see the remains of what was the largest **Roman theatre** in Gaul, with a capacity of fifteen thousand – in itself a measure of Autun's importance at that time. An artificial lake below the football pitch, the **Plan d'eau du Vallon**, provides the usual watersports. The most enigmatic of the Gallo-Roman remains in the region is the **Pierre de Couhard**, off Faubourg St-Pancrace to the southeast of the town. It's a 27-metre-tall stone pyramid situated on the site of one of the city's necropolises, thought to date from the first century, and most probably either a tomb or a cenotaph.

The Cathédrale St-Lazare and the Musée Rolin

Autun's great twelfth-century **Cathédrale St-Lazare** was built nearly a thousand years after the Romans had gone, and its greatest claim to artistic fame lies in its sculptures, the work of Gislebertus, generally accepted as one of the most outstanding Romanesque sculptors.

The tympanum of the **Last Judgement** above the west door bears his signature – *Gislebertus hoc fecit* ("Gislebertus made this") – beneath the feet of Christ. To his left are the Virgin Mary, the saints and the apostles, with the saved rejoicing below them; to the right the Archangel Michael disputes souls with Satan, who tries to cheat by leaning on the scales, while the damned despair beneath. During the eighteenth century the local clergy decided the tympanum was an inferior work and plastered over it, saving it from almost certain destruction during the Revolution. The head of Christ, however, was hacked off, and only rediscovered – hiding in the collection of the Musée Rolin – in 1948.

The interior of the cathedral, whose pilasters and arcading were modelled on the Roman architecture of the city's gates, was also decorated by Gislebertus, who carved most of the capitals himself. Conveniently for anyone wanting a close look, some of the finest are now exhibited in the old chapter library, up the stairs on the right of the choir, among them a beautiful *Flight into Egypt* and *Adoration of the Magi*.

Just outside the cathedral on rue des Bancs, the **Musée Rolin** (daily except Tues 10am–noon & 2–5/6pm; €5) occupies a Renaissance *hôtel* built by Nicolas Rolin, chancellor of Philippe le Bon. In addition to interesting Gallo-Roman pieces, the star attractions are Gislebertus's representation of Eve as an unashamedly sensual nude, and the Maître de Moulins' brilliantly coloured *Nativity*.

Eating and drinking

For traditional French **cuisine** your best options lie behind the Hôtel de Ville: *Le Chalet Bleu*, 3 rue Jeannin (℡03.85.86.27.30; *menus* €16.50–58; closed both Sun & Mon eve & Tues) is innovative and distinctly stylish, while at 17 rue Mazagran the *Restaurant des Remparts* (℡03.85.52.54.02; *menu du jour* €13.50, dinner from €21; closed Tues & Wed eve) is a convivial place with great-value *menus* featuring regional specialities. You'll find lighter meals and more picturesque outdoor seating around the cathedral on place St-Louis, with a pair of pizzerias and *Le Petit Rolin* (℡03.85.86.15.55; closed Mon & Tues), serving *grillades* (€12) and crêpes (€8) in a cosy downstairs dining room.

Le Creusot

LE CREUSOT (not to be confused with Le Creuset, the northern French town of cast-iron cookware fame) means one thing to French ears: the **Schneider iron and steelworks**, maker of the first French locomotive in 1838, the first steamship in 1839, the 75mm field gun – mainstay of World War I artillery – and the ironwork of the Pont Alexandre-III and the Gare d'Austerlitz in Paris.

The town's main attraction is the **Château de la Verrerie** on place Schneider. Built as a glassworks in 1787, the château was sold to the Schneider family in 1838 and transformed into their private residence. Paternalistic but despotic employers, the Schneiders provided housing, schools and health care for their workers, but expected "gratitude and obedience" in return. The last Schneider died in 1960 and the château now houses the interesting **Musée de l'Homme et de l'Industrie** (July & Aug daily 10am–noon & 1–6pm, Sat & Sun 2.30–6.30pm; Sept–June daily except Tues 10am–noon & 2–6pm, Sat & Sun 2–6pm; €6), a museum dedicated to the iron and steel industry, accompanied by paintings of various Schneiders. The peculiar cone-shaped constructions in the courtyard of the château were glass furnaces; one of them was transformed into a tiny Neoclassical theatre where the Schneiders' wealthy and influential guests were entertained, and can be visited on regular tours.

A more recent development in town is the huge **Parc Touristique des Combes** (July & Aug daily 11am–7pm; April–June, Sept & Oct Sat & Sun 2–7pm; ⓦwww.parcdescombes.com), which boasts a narrow-gauge steam train (€6.70), a karting track, and a 435-metre-long dry luge piste (€2.80).

Practicalities

The **tourist office**, in the gatehouse of the Château de la Verrerie (May to mid-Sept Mon–Fri 9.30am–12.30pm & 2–6pm, Sat & Sun 2–6pm; mid-Sept to April Mon–Fri 10am–noon & 2–5.30pm, Sat 2–6pm; ℡03.85.55.02.46, ⓦwww .le-creusot.fr), sells tickets to the Musée de l'Homme et de l'Industrie. The local train station is a short walk away down rue Leclerc, but the grander **TGV station** is 6km away in Montchanin. There are a couple of buses to the station per day (see

ⓦ www.monrezo.org for more information); alternatively a taxi (☏ 03.85.80.97.18) will cost about €22. Presentable but unexciting **rooms** are on offer at *Le Bourgogne* on place Schneider (☏ 03.85.80.32.02; ➌), which has a decent brasserie downstairs.

Nevers

Some sixty kilometres west of the Parc du Morvan, **NEVERS** is a pretty provincial city on the confluence of the rivers Loire and Nièvre, known for its *nougatine* sweets and fine porcelain, hand-painted with a deep blue colour known as *bleu de Nevers*. **Faïence**, as it's also called, has been a hallmark of Nevers since the seventeenth century and you can still see artisans at work in the shops on rue du 14 Juillet.

Arrival, information and accommodation

Avenue de Gaulle leads from the train and bus stations straight to place Carnot and the **tourist office** (June–Sept Mon–Sat 9.30am–1pm & 2–6.30pm, Sun 10am–1pm & 3–6pm; Oct–May Mon–Sat 10am–12.30pm & 2–6pm; ☏ 03.86.68.46.00, ⓦ www.nevers-tourisme.com). On the near bank of the Loire, next to the railway bridge, is an excellent base for outdoor activities: Le Bureau des Guides de Loire et Allier rents out **bikes** (€15 per day) and organizes canoe trips from a few hours to several days (April–Sept; ☏ 03.86.57.69.76, ⓦ www.l-o-i-r-e.com).

Hotels

Hôtel Beauséjour 5bis rue Saint-Gildard ☏ 03.86.61.20.84, ⓦ www.hotel-beausejour -nevers.com. Close to the station and opposite the convent of St-Gildard, this hotel offers very reasonably priced rooms and friendly service. Some of the cheaper ones have shared facilities. ➊

Hotel de La Chasseigne 5 rue Fonmorigny ☏ 03.86.36.61.69. Just behind the church of St-Étienne, the charming owners of this sixteenth-century *hôtel* (private residence) run two beautifully decorated *chambres d'hôtes*, both of which look out onto a delightful garden. ➍

Hôtel de Cleves 8 rue St Didier ☏ 03.86.61.15.87, ⓦ www.hoteldecleves.fr. A quiet and comfortable hotel in the centre of the town, run by friendly and energetic owners. The rooms are pleasant – some were recently redecorated – and all of them have wi-fi. ➌

Campsite

Camping de Nevers Rue de la Jonction ☏ 06.84.98.69.79, ⓦ www.campingnevers.com. The municipal campsite, located beside the river, across the Pont de Loire, offers a splendid view of the Palais Ducal and Cathédrale de St-Cyr. Mid-April to mid-Oct.

The Town

Place Carnot is the hub of the centre, and it's here that you'll find the fifteenth-century **Palais Ducal**, former home of the dukes of Nevers, with octagonal turrets and a central tower adorned with elegantly carved hunting scenes. That aside, Nevers' main attractions are its religious monuments. The stunning **Cathédrale de St-Cyr**, with its wonderful display of jutting gargoyles, reveals French architectural styles from the tenth to the sixteenth centuries; it even manages to have two opposite apses, one Gothic, the other Romanesque. On the far side of the commercial pedestrian precinct around rue Mitterand is the even more interesting and aesthetically satisfying late eleventh-century **church of St-Étienne**. Behind its plain exterior lies one of the prototype pilgrim churches, with galleries above the aisles, ambulatory and three radiating chapels around the apse.

Of spiritual rather than architectural appeal is the **convent of St-Gildard**, where Bernadette of Lourdes ended her days. A steady flow of pilgrims comes to visit her tiny, embalmed body, displayed in a glass-fronted **shrine** (daily 7.30am–noon & 2–6pm) in the convent chapel. Next door, a small but very engaging museum displays some of her belongings and correspondence (€2.30).

Eating and drinking

There are some great places to eat in Nevers, with the best **restaurants and bars** in the area around St-Étienne.

L'Assiette 7bis rue Ferdinand-Gambon ⑦03.86.36.24.99. Trendy restaurant offering themed *assiettes* (plates) for around €15. Whatever the theme, the starter and the main course are served together on the same plate. Open for lunch Mon–Sat, dinner Fri & Sat.

La Cour St-Étienne 33 rue St-Étienne ⑦03.86.36.74.57. Attractive restaurant with an elegant half-timbered dining room, which serves high-quality, traditional food, with *menus* starting at €18.50. Closed Sun eve, Mon & Tues eve.

Le Goémon 9 rue du 14 Juillet ⑦03.86.59.54.99. The decor of this bustling crêperie is rather uninspiring but the crêpes (around €6) are delicious and the staff are friendly. Closed Sun & Mon.

🏃 **Jean-Michel Couron** 21 rue St-Étienne ⑦03.86.61.19.28. Located in a former chapel, Jean-Michel Couran's restaurant gives traditional dishes a modern edge, offering gourmet French cuisine at reasonable prices. *Menus* start at €21.50 during the week and €34 at weekends. Closed Sun eve, Mon & Tues lunch.

Dijon

In Celtic times, **DIJON** held a strategic position on the tin merchants' route from Britain to the Adriatic. It became the capital of the dukes of Burgundy around 1000 AD, and in the fourteenth and fifteenth centuries, under the auspices of dukes Philippe le Hardi (the Bold – as a boy, he had fought the English at Poitiers), Jean sans Peur (the Fearless), Philippe le Bon (the Good – he sold Joan of Arc to the English), and Charles le Téméraire (also the Bold), Dijon flourished. The dukes used their tremendous wealth and power – especially their control of Flanders, the dominant manufacturing region of the age – to make Dijon one of the greatest centres of art, learning and science in Europe. It lost its capital status on incorporation into the kingdom of France in 1477, but has remained one of the country's pre-eminent provincial cities. Today, it's an affluent university town: elegant, modern and dynamic, especially when the students are around.

Arrival and information

Dijon is not an enormous city and the area you'll want to see is confined to the eminently walkable centre. The **gare SNCF**, with the **gare routière** next door, is a five-minute walk away from place Darcy and the city centre – just head down avenue Maréchal Foch.

The main **tourist office** is in the heart of the city at 11 rue des Forges (April–Sept Mon–Sat 9.30am–6.30pm, Sun 10am–6pm; Oct–March Mon–Sat 9.30am–1pm & 2–6pm, Sun 10am–4pm; ⑦08.92.70.05.58, ⓦwww.visitdijon.com) and organizes lots of guided tours, including minibus tours of local vineyards. It also sells the **Dijon Pass** (from €18), which offers significant reductions on museum entry fees and a number of free guided tours. There's a second office at 15 Cour de la Gare (same hours), which is handier if coming from the station. A tramway is currently being constructed in the city, due to be finished in 2013.

Accommodation

Dijon has plenty of reasonably priced **hotels** in the centre of town, but it's worth booking at least a week in advance if you plan to stay in the busy summer months.

Hotels

Le Chambellan 92 rue Vannerie ☎03.80.67.12.67, ⓦwww.hotel-chambellan.com. This hotel has relaxing rooms and sparkling bathrooms, clustered around a pretty seventeenth-century courtyard. The cheapest rooms have shared facilities. ❶–❸

Le Jacquemart 32 rue Verrerie ☎03.80.60.09.60, ⓦwww.hotel-lejacquemart.fr. Run by the same charming management as *Le Chambellan* (see above), the high-ceilinged rooms of this elegant hotel are comfortable and quiet. ❶–❸

Du Palais 23 rue du Palais ☎03.80.67.16.26, ⓦwww.hoteldupalais-dijon.com. Relatively grand rooms with tall windows in a pleasant eighteenth-century townhouse. The garret-style ones have good views over the city's rooftops. Slightly faded, though, compared to the other options in this price range. ❷

Philippe le Bon 18 rue Sainte-Anne ☎03.80.30.73.52, ⓦwww.hotelphilippelebon.com. An elegant old building set in an agreeable garden opposite the Musée de la Vie Bourguignonne. The most expensive rooms are lovely; full of character and beautifully restored, the others are plush but a little bland in comparison. ❺

Quality Hotel du Nord Place Darcy ☎03.80.50.80.50, ⓦwww.hotel-nord.fr. Housed in a lovely old building and run by the same family for four generations, this is one of Dijon's more upscale places with modern but slightly anonymous bedrooms. Central with a decent restaurant downstairs. ❺

Hôtel du Sauvage 64 rue Monge ☎03.80.41.31.21, ⓦwww.hotellesauvage.com. This delightful former coaching inn has elegant rooms overlooking a vine-draped courtyard, and, despite being in the liveliest quarter of town, it's quiet. ❸

Hotel Sofitel La Cloche 14 place Darcy ☎03.80.30.12.32, ⓦwww.hotel-lacloche.com. A grand nineteenth-century building located between the station and the centre of the town, this hotel has uber-luxurious rooms and a gourmet restaurant downstairs. Rooms start at €210. ❾

Hostel and campsite

Camping du Lac Kir 3 bd Chanoine Kir ☎03.80.43.54.72, ⓦwww.camping-dijon.com. Popular site with a wealth of activities. It's about 1km out of town near Lake Kir: follow the signs for Paris, or take bus #3 from the train station, direction "Fontaine d'Ouche". Open April–Oct.

Centre de Rencontres Internationales 1 bd Champollion ☎03.80.72.95.20, ⓦwww.cri-dijon.com. An HI hostel in a modern complex 2km from the centre, with well-kept dorm rooms, a self-service canteen and sports facilities next door. Often teeming with adolescent school groups. Take bus #4 to stop "Épirey CRI" from rue des Godrans. Buses run until midnight.

The City

The **rue de la Liberté** forms the spine of the town, running east from the wide, attractive **place Darcy** and the eighteenth-century triumphal arch of **Porte Guillaume** – once a city gate – past the **palace** of the dukes of Burgundy on the semicircular **place de la Libération**. From this elegant, classical square, rue Rameau continues directly east to place du Théâtre, from where rue Vaillant leads on to the **church of St-Michel**, which is lined with smart shops, mammoth department stores and elegant old houses. Most places of interest are within ten-minutes' walk to the north or south of this main axis.

The Palais des Ducs

The geographical focus of a visit to Dijon is inevitably the seat of its former rulers, the **Palais des Ducs**, which stands at the hub of the city. Facing the main courtyard is the serene **place de la Libération**, built by Jules Hardouin-Mansart, one of the architects of Versailles, towards the end of the seventeenth century. It's now something of a suntrap on a good day, and the decision to close it to traffic has stimulated a boom in café trade. The fourteenth-century **Tour de Bar** dominates the courtyard in front of the east wing, and now houses the Musée des Beaux-Arts, while the loftier, fifteenth-century **Tour Philippe-le-Bon** can be visited only on guided tours (April–Nov, 11 tours daily; Dec–March tours at 1.30pm, 2.30pm & 3.30pm on Wed; six tours Sat & Sun; €2.30). The view from the top is particularly worthwhile for the views of the glazed Burgundian tiles of the Hôtel de Vogüé and the cathedral, and on a clear day the Alps loom on the horizon.

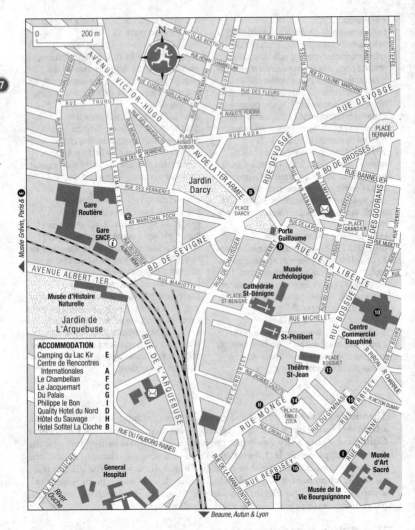

Beaune, Autun & Lyon

The **Musée des Beaux Arts** (daily except Tues, May–Oct 9.30am–6pm; Nov–April 10am–5pm; free) has an interesting collection of works from the Middle Ages to the twentieth century; among the highlights are the Flemish paintings, particularly the *Nativity* by the so-called Master of Flémalle, a shadowy figure who ranks with van Eyck as one of the first artists to break from the chilly stranglehold of International Gothic, Burgundy's homespun phase of Gothic art.

Visiting the museum also provides the opportunity to see the surviving portions of the original ducal palace, including the vast **kitchen** and the magnificent **Salle des Gardes**. Displayed here are the lavish, almost decadent, **tombs** of Philippe le Hardi and Jean sans Peur and his wife, Marguerite de Bavière, with their startling, painted effigies of the dead, surrounded by gold-plated angels.

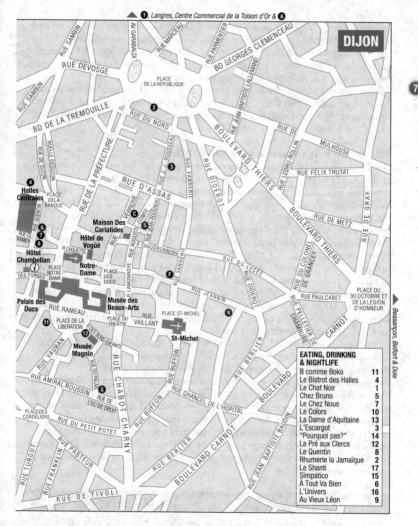

Langres, Centre Commercial de la Toison d'Or & ❶ ❷ ❸ ❹ ❺ ❻ ❼ ❽ ❾ ❿

DIJON

Beaançon, Belfort & Dole

EATING, DRINKING & NIGHTLIFE

B comme Boko	11
Le Bistrot des Halles	4
Le Chat Noir	1
Chez Bruno	5
Le Chez Nous	7
Le Colors	10
La Dame d'Aquitaine	13
L'Escargot	3
"Pourquoi pas?"	14
Le Pré aux Clercs	12
Le Quentin	8
Rhumerie la Jamaïque	2
Le Shanti	17
Simpatico	15
À Tout Va Bien	6
L'Univers	16
Au Vieux Léon	9

The Quartier Notre-Dame

Architecturally more interesting than the palace, and much more suggestive of the city's former glories, are the lavish townhouses of the rich burghers. These abound in the streets behind the duke's palace: rue Verrerie, rue Vannerie, rue des Forges, rue Chaudronnière, rue Chouette. Some are half-timbered, with storeys projecting over the street, others are in more formal and imposing Renaissance stone. Particularly fine are the Renaissance **Hôtel de Vogüé**, 8 rue de la Chouette, the **Hôtel Chambellan** at no. 34 rue des Forges, and the **Maison des Cariatides** at no. 28 rue Chaudronnière.

Also in this quarter, in the angle between rue de la Chouette and rue de la Préfecture, is the **church of Notre-Dame**, built in the early thirteenth century in the Burgundian Gothic style. In the south transept there is a ninth-century wooden "black" Virgin. Known as "Our Lady of Good Hope", she is credited with twice miraculously saving the city from fighting, most recently when German troops left peacefully in 1944. Outside, in the north wall of the church on rue de la Chouette, is a small, sculpted owl – *chouette*. Locals believe that touching it as you walk past will bring you good luck.

From here rue Musette leads west, passing just south of the **market square** and the covered *halles*. The whole area is full of sumptuous displays of food and attractive cafés and restaurants, and is thronged with people on market days (Tues, Thurs, Fri & Sat).

South of the place de la Libération

On the south side of the place Darcy–church of St-Michel axis, and especially in the *quartier* behind place de la Libération, there's a concentration of magnificent *hôtels* from the seventeenth and eighteenth centuries. These were built, for the most part, by men who had bought themselves offices and privileges with the Parliament of Burgundy, which had been established by Louis XI in 1477 as a means of winning the compliance of this newly acquired frontier province. One of them, 4 rue des Bons Enfants, houses the **Musée Magnin** (Tues–Sun 10am–noon & 2–6pm; €3.50). Installed in this seventeenth-century *hôtel particulier* – complete with its original furnishings – is an assembly of French and Italian paintings that was bequeathed to the State by two collectors in 1938. Other noteworthy houses are nearby in rue Vauban, some showing the marks of sculptor Hugues Sambin's influence in their decorative details (lions' heads, garlands of fruit, tendrils of ivy and his famous *chou bourguignon*, or "Burgundy cabbage"), notably, numbers 3, 12 and 21.

Continuing south from Musée Magnin, to rue Ste-Anne, a beautiful seventeenth-century former Cistercian convent is home to two museums. The **Musée de la Vie Bourguignonne** (daily except Tues May–Sept 9am–12.30pm & 1.30–6pm; Oct–April 9am–noon & 2–6pm; free) explores nineteenth-century Burgundian life, and features costumes, furniture and a number of fun reconstructions of rooms and shops. Practically next door at no. 15, the **Musée d'Art Sacré** (same hours; free) contains an important collection of church treasures, including a seventeenth-century statue of St Paul, the first in the world to be restored using an extraordinary technique that involves injecting the stone with resin and then solidifying the resulting compound using gamma rays. Formerly crumbling to dust, the statue is now completely firm.

Tickle your tastebuds

Dijon is home to a good few gastronomic specialities, from spicy condiments to sticky, sweet pastries. Here's a run-down of what tasty treats you can expect:

Mustard Impossible to forget that Dijon is the high temple of mustard – the shop of leading producer, Maille, is at 30 rue de la Liberté (closed Sun), selling a range from mild to cauterizing.

Pain d'épices A gingerbread made with honey and spices and eaten with butter or jam. Visit the headquarters of renowned *pain d'épices* producer, Mulot et Petitjean at 13 place Bossuet (closed Sun & Mon morn).

Chocolate Another Dijon speciality – try *Le Fabrice Gillotte* at 21 rue du Bourg.

Wine As capital of the Burgundy region, Dijon presides over some great wine-making country: head to Au Vieux Millésime, 82 rue Monge (closed Sun & Mon), where Ludovic Flexas offers helpful advice on wines from the region and further afield; prices start at around €5. See box, p.475 for more.

Eating

There are a large number of excellent **restaurants** throughout the city, particularly around rue Monge, while pretty place Émile Zola is packed with the open-air tables of reasonably priced pizzerias.

B comme Boko 14 place de la Libération ☎03.80.43.27.05. Classic French dishes are given a modern twist, and served in elegant glass pots at this trendy café-bar-restaurant. Friendly staff and a large, sunny terrace that's ideal for admiring the grandeur of the Palais des Ducs. *Menus* from €13. 9am–midnight.

Le Bistrot des Halles 10 rue Bannelier ☎03.80.49.94.15. Located alongside the market, this popular bistro has a charming outdoor terrace and serves good, traditional Burgundy cuisine (*jambon persillé, escargots, boeuf bourguignon*). Lunch *menu* €17, à la carte around €30. Closed Sun & Mon.

La Dame d'Aquitaine 23 place Bossuet ☎03.80.30.45.65. While the *menus* (€28–43) are composed of the usual regional suspects, the setting of this restaurant is highly unusual: a handful of tables set spaciously beneath the stone vaults of a twelfth-century crypt, with classical music playing in the background. Closed Sun & Mon lunch.

L'Escargot 43 rue J.J. Rousseau ☎03.80.73.33.85. Attractive restaurant with surprisingly low prices, making it a great place to try the local classics. The *oeufs en meurette* are particularly delicious. 3 courses from €22. Closed Sun.

"Pourquoi pas?" 13 rue Monge ☎03.80.50.11.77. A simple but sophisticated restaurant that serves classic French cuisine, with a specials *menu* that changes daily. Try the *montgolfière escargots*, a wonderful combination of snails and puff-pastry that's made to look like a hot-air balloon. Lunch from €13.30, dinner from €22, à la carte around €30. Closed Sun & Mon.

Le Pré aux Clercs 13 place de la Libération ☎03.80.38.05.05, ⊛www.le-pre-aux-clercs.com. The *crème de la crème* of Dijon restaurants; under the direction of chef Jean-Pierre Billoux this restaurant serves gourmet cuisine in an elegant dining room. Lunch *menu* €35, dinner €50 and €95. Closed Sun eve & Mon.

Simpatico 30 rue Berbisey ☎03.80.30.53.53. Excellent Italian restaurant which serves modern Italian dishes accompanied by an, almost defiantly, Italian wine list. Stylish decor and live jazz on Friday evenings. Lunch from €12, dinner from €25. Closed Sun & Mon.

À Tout Va Bien 12 rue Quentin ☎03.80.49.15.36. A friendly, brightly decorated restaurant with a lively ambiance, particularly on market days. Specialising in traditional cuisine (*tête de veau, hachis parmentier*), there's a *menu du jour* for €12.50. Daily 5am–5pm, closed Sun.

Drinking and nightlife

Dijon is an important university city as well as one of France's main conference centres, so **nightspots** at both ends of the range are worth exploring. Rue Berbisey is a good place to start a night out. The English/Irish theme pubs are predictably popular, but there are plenty of alternatives. For **information** on bands and DJs, pick up a free *Mag de la Nuit* (⊛www.magdelanuit.fr) at the tourist office or various establishments around the city.

Le Chat Noir 20 av Garibaldi. Just off place de la République, this is Dijon's most serious clubbing venue. €12 entry includes a drink. Usually Thurs–Sat, but ⊛www.lechatnoir.fr has the up-to-date programme.

Chez Bruno 80 rue J.J. Rousseau. A charming wine bar-*cave* with a wine list of around 800 wines and an amiable proprietor after whom the bar is named. To complement his wines, Bruno also serves a variety of delicious cheese and charcuterie plates for under €10 each. Open till 11pm.

Le Chez Nous Impasse Quentin. Tucked down a tiny alleyway just off rue Quentin, this is an authentic community bar with a proudly alternative ethos. Expect mismatched old tables, exhibitions and impromptu performances. Also does cheap bar snacks and fine wines by the glass. Open till 1am.

Le Colors Centre Commercial Dauphine. A popular student club, with the added advantage that it's dead central. Themed nights are organized regularly during term time, and entry is between €3 and €10. ⊛www.lecolors.net has full details of the programme.

Le Quentin 6 rue Quentin. Cool café-bar with a terrace that looks onto the market. Ideal for

people-watching on market days or an *apero* on a sunny evening. Open till 2am Fri & Sat.
Rhumerie la Jamaïque 14 place de la République. With its pricey cocktails and rock-opera decor, this place is popular with a trendy late-20s/early-30s crowd. They have live bands most evenings at 11pm, and a dancefloor and DJ at weekends. Open Tues–Sat till 4am.
Le Shanti 69 rue Berbisey. Great little hookah joint, decked out with divans in transcendental South Asian decor, serving delicious teas,

non-alcoholic cocktails, *lassis* and flavoured *sheesha* (€9 for a tobacco pipe). Mon–Sat till 2am.
L'Univers 47 rue Berbisey. Trendy and dark, this pub-bar is popular with students and puts on regular blues, jazz and rock concerts. The French singer Yves Jamait began his career here and has written several songs about it. Open till 2am.
Au Vieux Léon 52 rue Jeannin. Decorated like an old-fashioned French café on acid, this bar has a lively, friendly atmosphere and is a favourite amongst the student crowd. Mon–Sat till 2am.

Listings

Bike hire Available at the central tourist office for €18 per day.
Car hire Numerous outlets at the station, like Hertz (☎03.80.53.14.00) or Europcar (☎03.80.45.90.60).
Cinemas L'Eldorado, 21 rue Alfred-de-Musset (☎08.92.68.01.74, Ⓦwww.cinema-eldorado.fr), is a small arts cinema showing all films in original language with a concentration of foreign films. Devosge, 6 rue Devosge (☎08.92.68.73.33, Ⓦwww.cinealpes.fr), shows most films in the original, and tries to deviate from the obvious blockbusters.
Festivals The city has a good summer music season, offering classical concerts throughout June as part of its Été Musical programme. L'Estivade, which takes place between June and September,

puts on endless music, dance and street theatre performances. The Fête de la Vigne, in late August and early September is a traditional costume and folklore jamboree; while the Foire gastronomique, during the first two weeks of November, celebrates all things edible.
Health Pharmacy at the junction of rue Berbisey and rue Charrue (Mon–Sat 8.45am–7pm).
Internet Cybersp@ce21 (46 rue Monge; Mon–Sat 11am–midnight, Sun 2pm–midnight; €4 per hour) is a good option in the centre of the old town.
Police 2 place Suquet ☎03.80.44.55.00.
Swimming pool Oxygène-Parc Aquatique, Centre Commercial de la Toison d'Or (Wed, Sat & Sun; ☎03.80.74.16.16; adults €10, children €8; bus #2 or #7). Has a wave machine, jacuzzi and water slides.

The Côte d'Or

South of Dijon, the attractive countryside of the **Côte d'Or** is characterized by the steep scarp of the *côte*, wooded along the top and cut by sheer little valleys called *combes*, where local rock climbers hone their skills (footpaths **GR7** and **GR76** run the whole length of the wine country as far south as Lyon). Spring is a good time to visit this region; you can avoid the crowds and the landscape is a dramatic symphony of browns – trees, earth and vines – punctuated by millions of bone-coloured vine stakes, standing like crosses in a vast war cemetery.

The place names that line the N74 – Gevrey-Chambertin, Vougeot, Vosne-Romanée, Nuits-St-Georges, Pommard, Volnay, Meursault, Beaune – are music to the ears of wine buffs. These prosperous towns are full of *caves*, where you can get good advice on different vintages, but be prepared to pay for your tasting if you don't go on to make a significant purchase. You can taste and buy direct from the source at most of the **vineyards** by just turning up and asking (tourist offices can provide you with a map), though few have regular opening hours.

You may find it cheaper and easier to use Dijon as a base for getting around the Côte d'Or, as there are good connections by train and Transco buses (see Ⓦwww.mobigo-bourgogne.com for timetables), which serve all the villages down the N74.

Château du Clos-de-Vougeot

If you're interested in French wine culture, it's worth visiting the **Château du Clos-de-Vougeot**, 20km south of Dijon between Gevrey-Chambertin and Nuits-St-Georges, to see the wine-making process (daily: April–Sept 9am–6.30pm; Oct–March 9–11.30am & 2–5.30pm; €3.90). Particularly impressive are the mammoth thirteenth-century winepresses installed by the Cistercian monks who owned these vineyards for nearly seven hundred years. The land now belongs to over eighty different owners, each growing and marketing their own wine. Just down the road from the château is the nineteenth-century Château de la Tour (daily except Tues 10am–6pm; Ⓦ www.chateaudelatour.com), which sells the very expensive Clos-Vougeot wines, as well as other Cote d'Or wines, and offers tasting sessions for €5.

Château de Meursault and Le Cassisium

The **Château de Meursault** in Meursault (daily 9.30am–12/12.30pm & 2/2.30–6pm; Ⓦ www.chateau-meursault.com) is one of the few *caves* that has regular opening hours. It has extensive and beautiful grounds and is the most prestigious producer of white wine. The visit costs €15, though, before you've bought a single bottle. Fans of *cassis* (blackcurrant liqueur) should drop by **Le Cassisium** on the outskirts on Nuits-Saint-Georges (April–Nov daily

The wines of Burgundy

Burgundy farmers have been growing grapes since Roman times, and Burgundy's **wines** are some of the most renowned in the world. In recent years, though, Burgundy's vineyards, and those in other regions of France, have suffered due to competition from the southern hemisphere. However, because of stringent legal restrictions banning watering and other interference, French wines, more than others, remain a faithful reflection of the *terroir* where they are produced, and Burgundy experts remain confident that the climate and soil of their region will fight off any temporary economic challenges.

Burgundy's best wines come from a narrow strip of hillside called the **Côte d'Or** that runs southwest from Dijon to Santenay, and is divided into two regions, Côte de Nuits (the better reds) and Côte de Beaune (the better whites). High-quality wine is certainly produced further south as well though, in the **Mâconnais** and on the **Côtes Chalonnaises**, while **Beaujolais** is famous (some might say notorious) for its cheap, fruity *nouveau,* which is drunk very young. Reds from the region are made almost exclusively from the Pinot Noir grape, while whites are largely from Chardonnay. Of the latter, particularly renowned are the light, dry vintages of **Chablis**, which are divided into *Grands Crus* (the most prestigious, and therefore dearest), *Premiers Crus* (the next level down) and the still very drinkable *Petit Chablis*. Fans of bubbly should look out for the often highly regarded **sparkling** whites, which crop up across the region and won't set you back half as much as a bottle of Champagne.

The single most important factor determining the "character" of wines is the **soil**. In both the Côte d'Or and Chablis, its character varies over very short distances, making for an enormous variety of taste. Chalky soil makes a wine *virile* or *corsé*, in other words "heady" – *il y a de la mâche*, they say, "something to bite on" – while clay makes it *féminin*, more *agréable*.

For an **apéritif** in Burgundy, you should try *kir*, named after the man who was both mayor and MP for Dijon for many years after World War II – two parts dry white wine, traditionally *aligoté*, and one part *cassis*. To round the evening off there are many **liqueurs** to choose from, but Burgundy is particularly famous for its *marcs*, of which the best are matured for years in oak casks.

10am–1pm & 2–7pm; Dec–March Tues–Sat 10.30am–1pm & 2–5.30pm; Ⓦwww.cassissium.com; €7.50), where you can enjoy a guided tour of the *cassis* factory and learn about the history of the blackcurrant.

Beaune

BEAUNE, the principal town of the Côte d'Or, manages to maintain its attractively ancient air, despite a near constant stream of tourists and rampant commercialism. Narrow cobbled streets and sunny squares dotted with cafés make it a lovely, albeit expensive, spot to sample the region's wine. If you're keen to indulge in a **wine-tasting** session, head to the *Marché aux Vins* on rue Nicholas Rolin (daily: mid-June to Aug 9.30am–5.30pm; Sept to mid-June 9.30–11.30am & 2–5.30pm; €10; ☏03.80.25.08.20), where you can wander freely through the atmospheric Église des Cordeliers and its *caves*, sampling fifteen wines along the way. To **buy wine** in Beaune, pay the Cellier de la Vieille Grange a visit at 27 bd Georges Clemenceau (Tues–Sat 9am–noon & 2–7pm, Sun–Wed by appointment; ☏03.80.22.40.06); prices start at €5, you can buy in bulk, and the tasting is free of charge, even if you're not purchasing.

Arrival and information

Beaune's **gare SNCF** is five minutes' walk away from the old walls to the east of the centre on avenue du 8 Septembre, and buses also stop here. The **tourist office**,

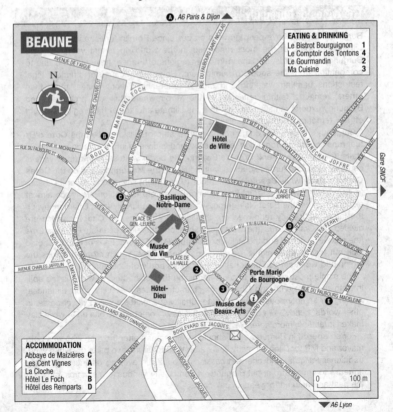

6 bd Perpreuil (April–Oct Mon–Sat 9am–6.30/7pm, Sun 9–6pm; Nov–March Mon–Sat 9am–noon & 1–6pm, Sun 10am–12.30pm & 1.30–5pm; ☏03.80.26.21.30, ⓦwww.beaune-tourisme.fr), offers **internet access** (€5 per hour) and organizes a number of tours and visits in the area. You can rent **bikes** from Bourgogne Randonnées at avenue du 8 Septembre (☏03.80.22.06.53; €4 per hour, €17 per day).

Accommodation

If you're going to **stay** within the town walls of Beaune, be prepared to book in advance and pay over €50. Outside of the walls tends to be a little cheaper.

Hotels

Abbaye de Maizières 19 rue Maizières ☏03.80.24.74.64, ⓦwww.beaune-abbaye -maizieres.com. Located in a twelfth-century abbey, this hotel has beautifully decorated rooms with exposed stone walls, wall hangings and medieval-style tapestries. Beware the steep stairs. ❻

La Cloche 40 rue du Faubourg Madeleine ☏03.80.24.66.33, ⓦwww.hotel-lacloche-beaune .com. Near to the station, this recently refurbished hotel offers brightly decorated, modern rooms which complement the elegant old building. ❸

Hôtel Le Foch 24 bd du Maréchal Foch ☏03.80.24.05.65, ⓦwww.hotelbeaune-lefoch.fr. A good choice if you're on a budget, this hotel

offers simple but pleasant rooms above a café/bar just outside the city walls. ❷

Hôtel des Remparts 48 rue Thiers ☏03.80.24.94, ⓦwww.hotel-remparts -beaune.com. Run by a delightful former headmistress, this is a wonderful hotel, sensitively restored and full of old beams and ancient stone. You can still see the ramparts that give it its name from the windows of some of the more expensive rooms. ❺

Campsite

Les Cent Vignes 10 rue Auguste Dubois ☏03.80.22.03.91. This pretty campsite is about 1km north of town, off rue du Faubourg St-Nicolas (the N74 to Dijon), before the bridge over the *autoroute*. Booking is advisable. March–Oct.

The Town

Beaune's town centre is a tightly clustered, rampart-enclosed *vieille ville*, and its chief attraction is the fifteenth-century hospital, the **Hôtel-Dieu** (daily April to mid-Nov 9am–6.30pm; mid-Nov to March 9–11.30am & 2–5.30pm; €6.50), on the corner of place de la Halle. The cobbled courtyard is surrounded by a wooden gallery overhung by a massive roof patterned with diamonds of gaudy tiles – green, burnt sienna, black and yellow – and similarly multicoloured steep-pitched dormers and turrets. Inside is a vast paved hall with a glorious arched timber roof, the Grande Salle des Malades, with the original enclosed wooden beds. Passing through two smaller, furnished wards, one with some stunning seventeenth-century frescos, then the kitchen and the pharmacy, you reach a dark chamber housing the splendid fifteenth-century altarpiece of the *Last Judgement* by Rogier van der Weyden.

The former residence of the dukes of Burgundy on rue d'Enfer now houses the **Musée du Vin** (April–Nov daily 9.30am–6pm; Dec–March daily except Tues 9.30am–5pm; €5.50), with giant winepresses, a collection of traditional tools of the trade and a relief map of the vineyards that helps to make sense of it all. If you feel like visiting all three museums in one day, a **combined ticket** into the Musée du Vin, the Hôtel-Dieu and the town's **Musée des Beaux Arts** costs €11.

Eating and drinking

Eating out in Beaune is an expensive business and the wine list is often more important than the menu when it comes to choosing where to eat; many **restaurants** pride themselves on how many wines they offer. If you're on a budget, most of the brasseries on place Carnot have a *plat du jour* for under €12.

Le Bistrot Bourguignon 8 rue Monge ☎03.80.22.23.24. This relaxed and friendly bistro and wine-bar specialises in regional cuisine (main courses around €15) and prides itself on having been the first wine bar in Beaune to serve wine by the glass. Look out for the pet goldfish and the jazz on Saturday nights. Closed Sun & Mon.
Le Comptoir des Tontons 22 rue du Faubourg Madeleine ☎03.80.24.19.64. Just outside the town walls, this down-to-earth restaurant serves a lot of organic products, including organic wine. *Menus* start at €27. Closed Sun & Mon.

Ma Cuisine Passage Ste-Hélène ☎03.80.22.30.22. Simple yet stylish, this restaurant serves traditional French cuisine, with a *menu* at €24, and has a wine list of no less than 900 wines. Closed Wed, Sat & Sun.
Le Gourmandin 8 place Carnot ☎03.80.24.07.88. One of the more upmarket restaurants on place Carnot, this sophisticated restaurant has an excellent *menu bourguignon* for €37 and a lunch *menu* for €18.

The Saône valley

The **Saône valley** is prosperous and modern, nourished by tourism, industry (especially metal-working in Chalon and Mâcon), and the wine trade. But turn your back on the river and head west and you immediately enter a different Burgundy, full of hilly pastures and woodland. Utterly rural, every village clusters under the tower of a Romanesque church, spawned by the influence of Cluny in the 1000s and 1100s. It is only when you reach the Loire and encounter the main traffic routes that you re-enter the modern world.

It's beautiful country for **cycling**, though there are few places that actually rent bikes. There are, however, plenty of buses (see ⓦwww.buscephale.fr for more information) and train connections.

Chalon-sur-Saône

CHALON is a sizeable port and bustling town on a broad meander of the Saône. It's old riverside quarter has an easy charm, and it makes a good base for exploring the more expensive areas of the Côte d'Or. You may be tempted to visit for the pre-Lent carnival (Feb or March), which features a parade of giant masks and a confetti battle, or for the national festival of street artists and theatre in July (ⓦwww.chalondanslarue.com).

Arrival, information and accommodation
The **gares SNCF** and **routière** are a fifteen-minute walk from the centre, if you go up avenue Jaurès and boulevard de la République you'll come to the town centre. Then bear right towards the attractive riverfront and its **tourist office**, 4 place du Port Villiers (July & Aug Mon–Sat 9am–12.30pm & 2–7pm, Sun 10am–noon & 3–7pm; Sept–June Mon–Sat 9am–12.30pm & 2–6/6.30pm; May–June & Sept Sun 3–6pm; ☎03.85.48.37.97, ⓦwww.chalon-sur-saone.net).

Hotels
Des Jacobines 10 rue des Jacobines ☎03.85.48.12.24, ⓦwww.hotel-lesjacobines.com. On a quiet street near the centre, this is the cheapest hotel in town with comfortable but rather garishly decorated rooms. Check-in closed from 1–5pm. ❶
St-Jean 24 quai Gambetta ☎03.85.48.45.65, ⓦwww.hotelsaintjean.fr. Right on the riverbank, this hotel offers classical-style rooms, some of

which are rather old-fashioned in their decor. Ask for a room with a view of the Saône. ❸
A La Villa Boucicaut 33bis av Boucicaut ☎03.85.48.37.97, ⓦwww.la-villa-boucicaut.fr. Undoubtedly the nicest place to stay in Chalon, this peaceful hotel is a few minutes' walk from the station. Run by a charming couple, who designed each of the beautifully furnished and decorated rooms themselves. ❺

Hostel and campsite

Camping du Pont de Bourgogne Rue Julien
Leneveu, St-Marcel ℡03.85.48.26.86, ⍉www
.camping-chalon.com. Cross one of Chalon's bridges
and head east – the campsite is 1km out of town on
the south bank of the Saône in St-Marcel. April–Sept.

Residences Chalon Jeunes 18 av Pierre Nugues
℡03.85.46.44.90, ⍉www.etudiant-chalon.com.
A twenty-minute walk east of the town, this hostel
offers basic but clean rooms for €15.50 a night,
and a cafeteria-style restaurant.

The Town

The highlight of the **old town**, set just back from the river, is the stunning **place
St-Vincent**, where you can sit outside a café and admire the twin towers of the
cathedral, surrounded by medieval timber-framed houses. Also here is the unusual
Musée Niépce, 28 quai des Messageries (daily except Tues: July & Aug
10am–6pm; Sept–June 9.30–11.45am & 2–5.45pm; free). Nicéphore Niépce,
who was born in Chalon, is credited with inventing photography in 1816 –
though he named it "heliography". The museum possesses a fascinating range of
cameras, from the first machine ever to the Apollo moon mission's equipment, plus
an interesting selection of photographs.

You should also make a beeline for the ⚜ **Maison des Vins** on Promenade
Ste-Marie (Mon–Sat 9am–7pm), where you can taste and buy a carefully selected
range of Côte Chalonnaise wines at low prices – starting at €5.

Eating and drinking

Rue de Strasbourg, across Pont St-Laurent on the so-called *île aux restos*, is lined
with excellent **places to eat**, including Italian, Indian and French. At no. 31 is
the bright-red *Le Bistrot* (℡03.85.93.22.01; closed Sat & Sun), chic to an almost
Parisian degree, offering serious quality for around €30. *Chez Jules* at no. 11
(℡03.85.48.08.34; *menus* €19; closed Sat lunch & Sun) is a good choice for
traditional favourites. Back on the mainland is a rare treat for vegetarians: ⚜ *La
Pierre Vive,* 33 rue de Lyon (℡03.85.93.26.50; closed eve and weekends), where
there is a buffet menu of delicious home-made vegetable dishes for just €12.80.
A handful of **bars** can be found on rue de Strasbourg and also on place
St-Vincent. There are food **markets** in place de l'Hôtel de Ville (Fri) and place
St-Vincent (Wed & Sat).

Tournus

Graced by ancient, golden buildings, **TOURNUS** is a beautiful little town on the
banks of the Saône, 28km south of Chalon. Its main attraction is the old abbey
church of St-Philibert, one of the earliest and most influential Romanesque
buildings in Burgundy.

Arrival, information and accommodation

The **gare SNCF** is on avenue Gambetta and a ten-minute walk from the **tourist
office** at 2 place de l'Abbaye (July & Aug daily 9.30am–7pm; Sept–June
Mon–Sat 9.30am–12.30pm & 2–5pm; Nov–Feb closed Mon; ℡03.85.27.00.20,
⍉www.tournugeois.fr). Here staff will reserve accommodation for you
(€2.50) and let you use the **internet** (€1 for 15min). For **accommodation**, just
next door to the tourist office at 5 place de l'Abbaye, is the turreted mansion
Hôtel Restaurant Greuze (℡03.85.51.77.77, ⍉www.hotelgreuze.com; ➑),
which offers plush rooms with all the standard luxuries. The most expensive
rooms offer a stunning view of the abbey. A much cheaper alternative, on the
other side of the river, is the *Hôtel Restaurant Rive de Saône* (℡03.85.51.20.65,
Ⓔ contact@hotel-restaurant-rivedesaone.com; ➊–➋), which has cheerful,
modern rooms and a splendidly tranquil riverside location. **Campers** should

head for the municipal site on the riverbank (℡03.85.51.16.58, ⓦwww
.camping-tournus.com; April–Sept), a fifteen-minute walk north out of town,
up rue René-Cassin.

The Town

Construction of the **church of St-Philibert** began around 900 AD but the present
building dates back to the first half of the eleventh century. The facade, with its
powerful towers and simple decoration of Lombard arcading, is somewhat reminiscent of a fortress. A narrow staircase leads up to a **high chapel** whose main arch is
inset with two extraordinary sculptures. It is possible that they represent the abbot
responsible for the rebuilding (on the right, holding a hammer and giving a blessing)
and the sculptor himself (on the left, full-face), who may even be the "Gerlamus" of
the inscription – in which case this is one of the earliest self-portraits of the medieval
period. In 2002, restoration work revealed one further treasure: some twelfth-
century, but very Roman-looking, **mosaics**, which can be seen in the ambulatory.

To the south of town is the **Hôtel Dieu** (April–Oct daily except Tues 10am–1pm
& 2–6pm; €4), a seventeenth-century charity hospital. You can still see the rows
of solid, oak beds, in which patients, fleas and lice cohabited until 1982, but the
real highlight is the elaborate dispensary, complete with a host of faïence pots and
hand-blown glass jars. The building also houses the **Musée Greuze**, which pays
homage to one of Tournus' best-known citizens, the Enlightenment painter Jean-
Baptiste Greuze.

Eating and drinking

The best **restaurant** in Tournus is the restaurant in the *Hôtel Restaurant Greuze* (see
p.479; ℡03.85.51.09.11; closed Wed & both Tues & Thurs lunch; *menus* €35–80),
run by the highly regarded chef Yohann Chapuis. A cheaper alternative is the
restaurant at *Hôtel Restaurant Rive de Saône* (see p.479; from €16; closed Wed lunch)
which serves standard dishes but offers a fine view of the town, while *Le Bourgogne*
on rue du Docteur Privey (℡03.85.51.12.23; *menus* €15–25; closed Tues & Wed)
is popular with the locals and serves good quality, traditional French dishes.

Mâcon

MÂCON is a lively, prosperous town on the banks of the River Saône, 58km
south of Chalon and 68km north of Lyon, with excellent transport connections
between the two. It has no great sights, despite being a centre for the wine trade,
but it does have a surprisingly relaxed, seaside atmosphere, thanks to its long café-
lined **riverbank** and free outdoor concerts in late June, July and August.

Arrival, information and accommodation

The **gare SNCF** (adjacent to the **gare routière**) lies on rue Bigonnet at the southern
end of rue Victor-Hugo, but TGV trains leave from Mâcon-Loché station 6km out
of town – there are half a dozen buses to the station daily, or it's a short taxi ride.
The **tourist office**, 1 place St-Pierre (Nov–April Tues–Sat 10am–noon & 2–6pm;
May–June & Sept–Oct Mon–Sat 9.30am–12.30pm & 2–6.30pm; July & Aug daily
9am–12.30pm & 2–7pm; ℡03.85.21.07.07, ⓦwww.macon-tourism.com), is well
stocked with info on the area.

Hotels

Hôtel de Bourgogne 6 rue Victor Hugo
℡03.85.21.10.23, ⓦwww.hoteldebourgogne.com.
Located near to the train station, this hotel offers
luxurious but rather standard rooms. The restaurant

serves regional specialities, with *menus* starting
at €19. ❹
Hôtel d'Europe et d'Angleterre 29 quai Jean-
Jaurès ℡03.85.38.27.94, ⓦwww.hotel
-europeangleterre-macon.com. With a touch of only

slightly-faded grandeur, this hotel has finely furnished, high-ceilinged rooms, some of which have a view of the river. ❸

Hôtel de Promenade 266 quai Lamartine ☎ 03.85.38.10.98. With few budget options to choose from, this hotel offers cheap but basic rooms. ❶

Campsite

Camping Municipal 1 rue des Grandes-Varennes ☎ 03.85.38.16.22, ⓔ camping@ville-macon.fr. The local campsite is about 3km north of town on the N6. Mid-March to Oct.

The Town

Lamartine, the nineteenth-century French Romantic poet (see box, p.482), was born in Mâcon in 1790 and his name is much in evidence. He is remembered in the handsome eighteenth-century mansion, the Hôtel Senecé, 41 rue Sigorgne, which houses the **Musée Lamartine** (Tues–Sat 10am–noon & 2–6pm, Sun 2–6pm; €2.50), part of which is dedicated to documents and other memorabilia relating to his personal, political and poetic lives. Nearby, in a seventeenth-century convent, is the **Musée des Ursulines** (same hours and price as Musée Lamartine; combined ticket €3.40), which features Gallo-Roman artefacts, an exhibition dedicated to the history of Mâcon, and a collection of sixteenth- to twentieth-century paintings. On the corner of place des Herbes where a summertime fruit and veg market is held, stands an elaborately carved wooden house built around 1500 and known as the **Maison du Bois Doré**, with a wonderful bar/café downstairs that serves cocktails until 1am.

On the far side of the St-Laurent bridge over the Saône you'll find the embarcation point for a more restful couple of hours: **cruises**, to be reserved at the tourist office (April–Oct: Tues, Thurs & Sat 3pm, 5.30pm & 7pm; €12), allow you to see the waterfront from a new perspective.

The most enjoyable way to bone up on the Mâcon, Chalonnais and Beaujolais **wines** is to head off on one of the much-signposted wine roads (Ⓦwww .bourgogne-tourisme.com), which extend north into the Mâconnais, and south into the Beaujolais, sampling as you go. If you're without transport, however, you could make do with the **Maison Mâconnaise des Vins**, 484 avenue Lattre-de-Tassigny (daily 9am–7pm; ☎ 03.85.22.91.11), on the riverbank fifteen minutes' walk north of the centre. It has a selection of reasonably priced wines from around the region, starting at €6. The staff will offer free tastings, as long as you look likely to purchase.

Eating and drinking

Bars and restaurants are plentiful down by the river.

Le Carline 226 quai Lamartine ☎ 03.85.37.10.98. Offering classic French cuisine, including frogs' legs and *poulet de Bresse*, this restaurant has a laid-back atmosphere and reasonable prices. Lunch €11.20, dinner from €17.50. Closed Sun.

Dolce Vita 23 place Émile Violet ☎ 03.85.39.13.11. A good budget option: you can eat good pizza and pasta dishes here for around €10. And there's a nice little outdoor seating area during the summer. Closed Sun & Mon.

St Laurent 1 quai Bouchacourt ☎ 03.85.39.29.19. Classy fish restaurant next to the river that offers wonderful views of the city. *Menus* from around €18 (lunch) and €28 (dinner). Closed last two weeks of November.

Restaurant Pierre 7 rue Dufour ☎ 03.85.38.14.23. This elegant restaurant in the centre of the town offers gourmet French cuisine, with *menus* ranging from €21 (lunch during the week) to €73. Closed Sun eve, Mon & Tues lunch.

The Mâconnais, Beaujolais and Charollais

West of the valley of the Saône lies a tract of hilly country that is best known for its produce: the white wines of the **Mâconnais** are justly renowned, while the fashion for drinking the young red wine of **Beaujolais** has spread far beyond France. Further west still, the handsome white cattle that luxuriate in the green fields of the **Charollais** are an obvious sign that this is serious beef country.

In the past, however, the region was famed for its religion, and many large and powerful abbeys were established in the eleventh and twelfth centuries under the influence of the great monastery at Cluny. Few monks remain, and little is left of the abbey at **Cluny**, but Romanesque churches are almost as thick on the ground as cattle, and few are more impressive than the great basilica at **Paray-le-Monial**.

The Mâconnais

The **Mâconnais** wine-producing country lies to the west of the Saône, a 20km wide strip stretching from Tournus to Mâcon. The region's best white wines come from the southern part of this strip, around the pretty villages of **POUILLY**, **VINZELLES** and **FUISSÉ**. Should you yearn for rustic rest, the *Hôtel La Vigne Blanche* in Fuissé (T 03.85.35.60.50; W www.vigne-blanche.com; 3) will provide just the setting you're looking for, with simple rooms, good regional cooking (*menus* from €25) and, of course, the chance to sample some of the local wines.

Directly above these villages rises the distinctive and precipitous 500-metre rock of **Solutré**, which served as an ambush site for hunters in prehistoric times – around 20,000 BC. The bones of 100,000 horses have been found in the soil beneath the rock, along with mammoth, bison and reindeer carcasses. The history and results of the excavations are displayed in a museum at the foot of the rock, the **Musée Départemental de Préhistoire** (daily: April–Sept 10am–6pm; Oct–March 10am–noon & 2–5pm; closed Dec; €3.50). A steep path climbs to the top of the rock, where, on a clear day, you get a superb view as far as Mont Blanc and the Matterhorn. Looking down on the huddled roofs of **SOLUTRÉ-POUILLY** the slopes beneath you are covered with the vines of the Chardonnay grape, which makes the exquisite greenish Pouilly-Fuissé wine.

Aside from the sheer pleasure of wandering about in such reposeful landscapes, there are some specific places to make for. One is the sleepy hamlet of **ST-POINT**, where the poet Lamartine (see box above) spent much of his life in the little medieval **Château de St-Point**, now a museum dedicated to him (guided visits 11am, 3pm, 4pm, 5pm, 6pm; April–June, Sept & Oct weekends only; daily July

& Aug; €7; ☎03.85.50.50.30, ⓦwww.chateaulamartine.com). Next door is the Romanesque church where he's buried.

Cluny

Scattered among the houses of the attractive modern-day town, the **abbey of CLUNY** is this region's major tourist destination. The monastery was founded in 910 in response to the corruption of the existing church, and it took only a couple of vigorous early abbots to transform the power of Cluny into a veritable empire. Second only to that of the pope, the abbot's power in the Christian world made even monarchs tremble. However, Cluny's spiritual influence gradually declined and the abbey became a royal gift in the twelfth century. Centuries later, in the wake of the Revolution, Hugues de Semur's vast and influential eleventh-century **church**, which had been the largest building in Christendom until the construction of St Peter's in Rome, was dismantled.

Arrival and information

There is no train station in Cluny but there are regular buses from both Mâcon and Chalon-sur-Saône. Buses stop on Rue Portre-de-Paris, just five minutes' walk from the town centre. The **tourist office** is beside the Tours des Fromages at 6 rue Mercière (May–Sept daily 9.30am–7pm; Oct–April Mon–Sat 10am–12.30pm & 2.30–5/6.45pm; ☎03.85.59.05.34, ⓦwww.cluny-tourisme.com). **Bikes** can be hired from Ludisport (☎03.85.22.10.62, ⓦwww.ludisport.com) next to the abandoned train station.

Hotels

Hôtel de Bourgogne Place de l'Abbaye ☎03.85.59.00.58, ⓦwww.hotel-cluny.com. Right in the centre of Cluny, this hotel has luxurious rooms, including one with disabled access, which look onto either the abbey or the pretty breakfast garden. Closed Dec & Jan. ❺–❼

Le Clos de l'Abbaye 6 place du Marché ☎03.85.59.22.06, ⓦwww.bnb-gite-leclos.com. A great mid-range choice, run by a friendly couple. There are four stylishly decorated *chambres d'hôtes*, three of which have a view of the abbey. ❸

Hôtel du Commerce 8 place du Commerce ☎03.85.59.03.09, ⓦwww.hotelducommerce -cluny.com. This hotel offers simple but clean rooms, good for those on a budget. Some of the cheaper rooms have shared facilities. ❶

Le Potin Gourmand 4 place du Champ de Foire ☎03.85.59.02.06, ⓦwww.potingourmand.com. A lovely, rambling old building set around an inner courtyard and garden. The rooms are charming and all individually decorated – look out for the *Jungle Book* wallpaper in one of the family rooms. Closed Jan. ❸

Hostel and campsite

Camping St-Vital Rue Griottons ☎03.85.59.08.34, ⒺCamping.st.vital@orange.fr. Sits across the Pont de la Levée in the direction of Tournus. May–Sept.

Cluny Séjour 22 rue Porte-de-Paris ☎03.85.59.08.83, ⓦwww.cluny-sejour.blogspot .com. Located in a large old building near to the town bus stop, this friendly hostel offers dormitory accommodation from €16. Closed mid-Dec to mid-Jan.

The abbey and town

What you see of the former **abbey** today (daily May–Aug 9.30am–6.30pm; Sept–April 9.30am–noon & 1.30–5pm; €7 combined ticket with museum) is an octagonal belfry and the huge south transept. Standing amid these fragments of a once huge construction gives a tangible and poignant insight into the Revolution's enormous powers of transformation. Access to the belfry is through the Grand École des Ingénieurs, one of France's elite higher-education institutions, and you can often see the students in their grey lab coats. At the back of the abbey is one of France's national stud farms, **Haras de Cluny** (April–June daily 2pm & 4pm; July–Sept daily 2pm, 3.30pm & 5pm; Oct & Nov Wed & Sun 2pm; Feb–March Wed, Fri & Sun 2pm; €6; ☎06.22.94.52.69), which you can visit but only on a guided tour. The **Musée d'Art et d'Archéologie** (same hours and ticket as abbey), in the fifteenth-century palace of the last freely elected abbot, helps to flesh out the ruins with an interesting 3D film, and from the top of the **Tour des Fromages** (entrance through the tourist office; €2) you can try to picture it in the landscape below. If you want to indulge in a glass of Burgundy wine or enjoy a wine-tasting session, head to ⅄ *Le Cellier de l'Abbaye* at 13 Rue Municipale (daily 10am–7pm, Sun 10am–12.30pm; ℡03.85.59.04.00), a wonderful medieval building that once belonged to the abbey. As well as wine, there's a great selection of gourmet food products, spirits, and wine accessories.

Eating and drinking

Auberge du Cheval Blanc 1 rue Porte de Macon ℡03.85.59.01.13. This restaurant serves good regional cuisine and has been run by the same family for three generations. *Menus* from €17.50. Closed Fri eve & Sat.

Hôtel de Bourgogne Place de l'Abbaye ℡03.85.59.00.58. This top-notch restaurant works gastronomic wonders with local produce, offering *menus* from €25. Closed Tues & Wed.

Café du Centre 4 rue Municipale ℡03.85.59.10.65. Right in the centre of town, with a charming terrace, this lively old-fashioned bistro offers simple but tasty *plats* from €8. Closed Sun eve & Mon.

Le Potin Gourmand 4 place du Champ de Foire ℡03.85.59.02.06. A beautiful rustic restaurant, set around a courtyard. Combining local products with more exotic flavours, the enticing *menus* begin at €22. Closed Mon lunch.

The Beaujolais

As you continue south towards Burgundy's border with the Rhône Valley (see Chapter 14), the Mâconnais becomes the **Beaujolais**, a larger area of terraced hills producing lighter, fruity red wines, which it is now fashionable to drink very early. The Beaujolais grape is the Gamay, which, unlike in other wine regions, thrives here on the granite soil. Of the four *appellations* of Beaujolais, the best are the *crus*, which come from the Burgundy part of the region between St-Amour and Brouilly. If you have transport, you can follow the *cru* trail south from Mâcon by turning right at Crêches-sur-Saône up the D31 to St-Amour, and then south along the D68. The well-marked **route de Beaujolais** winds down through the wine villages into the Rhône Valley. **Villefranche**, not far from Lyon, is a good base for the route (see p.830).

Paray-le-Monial

Fifty kilometres west of Cluny, across countryside that becomes ever gentler and flatter as you approach the broad valley of the Loire, is **PARAY-LE-MONIAL**, whose major attraction is its **Basilique du Sacré-Coeur** (daily 9am–8pm). Not only is it an exquisite building in its own right, with a marvellously satisfying arrangement of apses and chapels stacking up in sturdy symmetry to a fine octagonal belfry, it's the best place to get an idea of what the abbey of Cluny looked like, as it was built shortly afterwards in devoted imitation of the mother church. Aside from just browsing down the main street – rue de la République/ rue des Deux-Ponts/rue Victor-Hugo – one secular building definitely worth a look is the highly ornamented **Maison Jayet** on place Guignault, which was built in the 1520s.

Practicalities

The **tourist office** is right outside the Basilique (July & Aug daily 9am–7pm, Sun 10am–7pm; Sept–June Mon–Sat 9am–noon & 1.30–6pm; April–June & Sept–Oct Mon–Sat 9am–noon & 1.30–6pm, Sun 10am–12.30pm & 2.30–5.30pm;

T 03.85.81.10.92, W www.paraylemonial.fr) and has some leaflets written in English about the history of the Basilica and other monuments in the town. It also rents out **bikes** (€9 per day) as well as offering **internet** access (€1 for 15min).

For **accommodation**, an excellent bet is the pleasantly old-fashioned *Grand Hôtel de la Basilique*, 18 rue de la Visitation (T 03.85.81.11.13, W www.hotelbasilique .com; closed Nov–March; ❶–❷) which has a fine restaurant with *menus* from €15. Rather swankier, but still not overpriced, the *Hostellerie des Trois Pigeons* at 2 rue Daugard (T 03.85.81.03.77, W www.h-3-p.com; closed Dec–Feb; ❸), boasts plusher rooms and a classy restaurant with *menus* from €18.50. The *Mambré* **campsite** is at 19 rue Gué-Léger (T 03.85.88.89.20, W www.campingdemambre .com; May–Sept). For **food**, as well as the hotel-restaurants above, rue Victor Hugo and place Guignault provide options for light meals.

The Charollais

The **Charollais** takes its name from the pretty little water-enclosed market town of **CHAROLLES**, with its 32 bridges, on the main N79 road. In turn, it gives its name to one of the world's most illustrious breeds of cattle: the white, curly-haired, stocky Charollais, bred for its lean meat. Throughout this region, scattered across the rich farmland, are dozens of small villages, all with Romanesque churches, the offspring of Cluny's vigorous youth.

ANZY-LE-DUC, about 15km south of Paray off the main D982 to Roanne, boasts an exquisite complex of buildings: a perfect Romanesque church with jackdaw chatter echoing off the octagonal belfry, side by side with the remains of the old priory incorporated into a sort of fortified farm looking out over the Arconce valley, all built in a rich, warm stone. **MONTCEAUX-L'ÉTOILE**, a little nearer to Paray, has its special charm too: a quiet, worn church with beautiful sculptures adorning the porch, also standing above the Arconce valley, and, a little way down the village street, a curious tower-like house where a Marquis of Vichy is said to have practised alchemy with the notorious Italian wizard, Cagliostro.

Travel details

Trains

Autun to: Avallon (2–4 daily; 1hr 50min); Chalon-sur-Saône (1–6 daily; 1hr 10min–1hr 50min); Le Creusot-Ville (2–6 daily; 45min); Saulieu (2–5 daily; 50min).

Auxerre to: Avallon (3–7 daily; 1hr 10min); Clamecy (3–7 daily; 1hr–1hr 20min); Dijon (5–10 daily; 2hr); Joigny (14–20 daily; 35–50min); Paris (frequent daily; 1hr 30min–2hr 30min); Sens (14–20 daily; 1hr).

Avallon to: Autun (1–2 daily; 1hr 50min–2hr 30min); Auxerre (4–9 daily; 1hr 10min); Saulieu (1–2 daily; 50min–1hr).

Beaune to: Dijon (frequent; 25min); Lyon (frequent; 1hr 40min).

Dijon to: Auxerre (5–7 daily; 1hr 50min–2hr 20min); Beaune (frequent; 25min); Chalon-sur-Saône (frequent; 40min); Laroche-Migennes (10–14 daily; 1hr 30min); Les Laumes-Alésia (frequent; 30–50min); Lyon (9–13 daily; 2hr 10min); Mâcon (frequent; 1hr–1hr 20min); Nevers (6–9 daily; 2hr 10min–2hr 30min); Paris (frequent; 1hr 40min–3hr 15min); Tonnerre (10–14 daily; 1hr–1hr 30min); Tournus (frequent; 1hr).

Laroche-Migennes to: Auxerre (frequent; 20min).

Mâcon to: Dijon (frequent; 1hr–1hr 20min); Geneva (4–8 daily; 1hr 40min–3hr 30min); Lyon (frequent; 1hr).

Montbard to: Dijon (7–11 daily; 50min); Laroche-Migennes (9–13 daily; 1hr).

Montchanin to: Le Creusot (6–10 daily; 10min); Paray-le-Monial (8–10 daily; 50min).

Nevers to: Clermont-Ferrand (6–9 daily; 1hr 30min–2hr); Le Creusot-Ville (5–9 daily; 1hr 30min); Dijon (5–9 daily; 2hr 30min); Paris (frequent; 2–3hr).

Paray-le-Monial to: Dijon (2–4 daily; 1hr 50min); Lyon (3–5 daily; 1hr 50min–2hr 30min).

Sens to: Auxerre (10–15 daily; 40min–1hr); Dijon (8–15 daily; 2hr–2hr 50min); Joigny (frequent; 30min); Paris (frequent; 1hr–1hr 30min); Tonnerre (4–6 daily; 1hr).

Tournus to: Chalon-sur-Saône (frequent; 20min); Mâcon (frequent; 20min).

Buses

Autun to: Chalon-sur-Saône (3 daily; 1hr–1hr 15min); Château-Chinon (Mon–Fri 1 daily; 1hr); Le Creusot Gare TGV (2–5 daily; 45min); St-Léger-sous-Beuvray (1 weekly; 30min).

Auxerre to: Chablis (2–3 daily, reservations required; 35min); Pontigny (2–4 weekly, reservations required; 30min); Tonnerre (2–3 daily, reservations required; 1hr).

Avallon to: Dijon (1–3 daily; 2hr–2hr 30min); Semur-en-Auxois (2–3 daily; 1hr); Vézelay (summer only 1–3 daily; 30min).

Chablis to: Auxerre (2–3 daily, reservations required; 35min); Tonnerre (2–3 daily, reservations required; 30min).

Chalon-sur-Saône to: Autun (1–5 daily; 1hr–1hr 15min); Le Creusot (2–10 daily; 1hr); Le Creusot Gare TGV (2–10 daily; 45min); Mâcon (3 daily; 2hr); Tournus (1 daily; 30min).

Châtillon-sur-Seine to: Dijon (1–3 daily; 1hr 30min–2hr).

Cluny to: Chalon-sur-Saône (3–5 daily; 1hr 15min); Charolles (1–2 daily; 45min); Mâcon (6 daily; 50min); Paray-le-Monial (1–2 daily; 1hr); Taizé (5–7 daily; 10min).

Dijon to: Avallon (2–3 daily; 1–2hr); Beaune (2–6 daily; 1hr 20min); Châtillon-sur-Seine (2–3 daily; 1hr 30min–2hr 15min); Saulieu (1–2 daily; 1hr 30min).

Mâcon to: Charolles (1–2 daily; 1hr 10min); Cluny (5–7 daily; 45min); Paray-le-Monial (1–2 daily; 1hr 30min); Tournus (1 daily; 50min)

Semur-en-Auxois to: Montbard (2–4 daily; 20min–1hr); Saulieu (2–4 daily; 30min).

Poitou-Charentes and the Atlantic coast

CHAPTER 8 # Highlights

* **Romanesque churches**
The facade of Notre-Dame
in Poitiers is one of the
most absorbingly intricate,
but other humbler churches
throughout the region are just
as beautiful. **See p.492**

* **Marais Poitevin** The "green
Venice", an intricate network
of land and water that's
perfect to explore by bike.
See p.498

* **La Rochelle** This charming
and unspoilt port town is the
jewel of the west coast, with a
well-preserved historic centre
and some exquisite seafood
restaurants. **See p.501**

* **Île de Ré** Visitors come from
far and wide to relax on this
peaceful little island, famous
for its pretty villages and
delicious seafood.
See p.507

* **Angoulême** Wholly
underrated, this enchanting
old-school town hosts an
animated nightlife and some
fine restaurants, and is an
essential pilgrimage for
any fan of comics.
See p.520

* **Bordeaux** Lively, stylish city
surrounded by some of the
world's best vineyards.
See p.524

▲ La Rochelle

Poitou-Charentes and the Atlantic coast

Newsstands selling *Sud-Ouest* remind you where you are: this is not the Mediterranean, certainly, but in summer the quality of the light, the warm air, the fields of sunflowers and the shuttered siesta-silence of the farmhouses give you the first exciting promises of the south. While it has great charm in places, particularly out of season on the islands of **Noirmoutier**, **Ré** and **Oléron**, it's a family, camper-caravanner seaside, largely popular for land and water-based outdoor pursuits. The principal port in the north, **La Rochelle**, is one of the prettiest and most distinctive towns in France, its strong fortifications just one of many remaining vestiges of the region's important history. Sandy **beaches** are beautiful everywhere, particularly down on the dune-backed **Côte d'Argent**, south of Bordeaux, although the Atlantic rollers can be outright dangerous.

Inland, the valley of the slow and green **River Charente** epitomizes blue-overalled, Gauloise-smoking, peasant France. The towpath is accessible for long stretches, on foot or mountain bike, and there are boat trips from **Saintes** and **Cognac**. The **Marais Poitevin**, too, with its myriad poplar groves and meandering canals, is both an unusual landscape and easy-going walking or cycling country.

But perhaps the most memorable aspect of the countryside – and indeed of towns like **Poitiers** and **Angoulême** – is the presence of exquisite Romanesque churches. This region formed a significant stretch of the medieval pilgrim routes across France and from Britain and northern Europe to the shrine of St Jacques (St James, or Santiago as the Spanish know him) at Compostela in northwest Spain, and was well endowed by its followers. The finest of the churches, among the best in all of France, are in the countryside around Saintes and Poitiers.

Lastly, of course, remember that this is a region of seafood – fresh and cheap in every market for miles inland – and, around the modern, charismatic urban centre that is **Bordeaux**, some of the world's top **vineyards**.

Public transport users will find all the main urban centres covered here well connected by trains, with most of the smaller towns and villages also

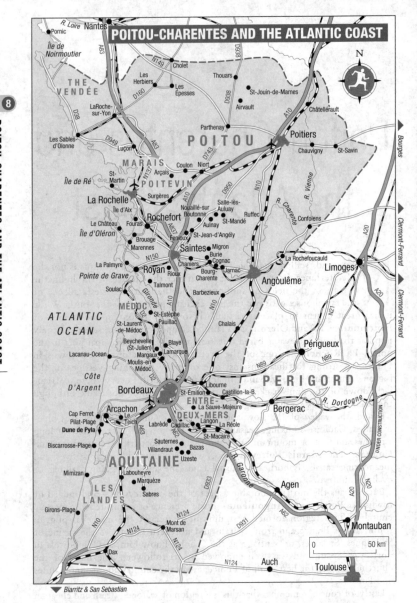

POITOU-CHARENTES AND THE ATLANTIC COAST

N

Biarritz & San Sebastian

accessible by regular, if infrequent, bus services. Off the main routes, though, particularly in the Bordeaux wine region and on the islands, having your own transport can be a major advantage – although cycling is often an attractive alternative.

Poitou

Most of the old province of **Poitou** comprises a huge expanse of rolling wheat fields and sunflower and maize plantations crowned by wind turbines and great arcs of white water shot from giant sprinklers over the fields in summertime. Heartland of the domains of Eleanor, Duchess of Aquitaine, whose marriage to King Henry II in 1152 brought the whole of southwest France under English control for three hundred years, it is also the northern limit of the *langue d'oc*-speaking part of the country, whose Occitan dialect survives among the older generations even today.

Poitiers

Sitting on a hilltop overlooking two rivers, **POITIERS** is a charming country town that comes from a long and sometimes influential history – as the seat of the dukes of Aquitaine, for instance – discernible in the winding lines of the streets and the breadth of architectural fashions represented in its buildings. Its pedestrian precincts and wonderful central gardens make for comfortable sightseeing, while the large student population ensures a lively atmosphere in the restaurants and pavement cafés.

Arrival and information

It's a short taxi ride (around €10) into the centre from Poitiers-Biard **airport**, located to the west of town, while the **gare SNCF** is on boulevard du Grand Cerf, part of the ring-road system that encircles the base of the hill on which Poitiers is built. The *gare routière* is on the ground floor of the conference centre just next door. The **tourist office** (mid-June to mid-Sept Mon–Sat 10am–7pm, Sun 10am–6pm; Sept to mid-June Mon–Sat 10am–6pm; ℡05.49.41.21.24, ⓦwww.ot-poitiers.fr) is a fifteen-minute walk away, up the hill at 45 place Charles-de-Gaulle, and can supply **walkers** and cyclists with various guides to the regional opportunities: the GR364 sets out from here, reaching the Vendée coast via Parthenay.

Accommodation

Hotels along boulevard du Grand Cerf by the train station don't come recommended, bar one; for more agreeable surroundings it's only a short uphill walk to the town centre.

Hotels and hostel

Au Chapon Fin ll rue Lebascles ℡05.49.88.02.97, ⓦwww.hotel-chaponfin.com. A bargain, popular with backpackers, in a most central location off place du Maréchal Leclerc. ❶–❸
Continental 2 bd Solférino ℡05.49.37.93.93, ⓦwww.continental-poitiers.com. Comfortable and secure two-star opposite the station, whose sound-proofed rooms are fully equipped. It's worth paying an extra couple of euros for a quiet room at the back. ❸
Le Grand 28 rue Carnot ℡05.49.60.90.60, ⓦwww.grandhotelpoitiers.fr. This hotel boasts a great location, comfortable and spotless rooms, with Art Deco-style furnishings, off-street parking and a swanky bar complete with sun terrace. The large rooms all have TV and mini-bar; most are a/c. ❹
HI Hostel 1 allée Roger-Tagault ℡05.49.30.09.70, ⓔpoitiers@fuaj.org. Good, modern hostel with a field reserved for camping. Take bus #7 from the *station* to "Bellejouanne", 3km away. Well signposted, it's to the right off the N10 Angoulême road.
Du Plat d'Étain 7 rue du Plat d'Étain ℡05.49.41.04.80, ⓦwww.poitiers-leplatdetain .com. A pleasant, well-run hotel in a central, quiet street just off the main shopping precinct. ❸

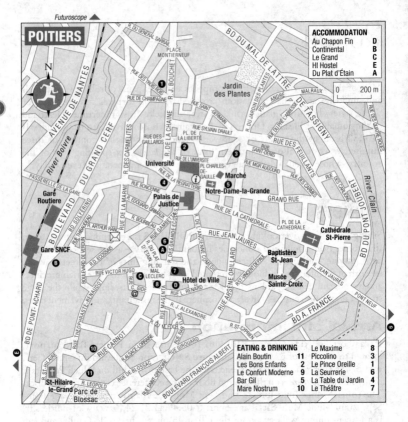

The Town

The two centres of communal life in Poitiers are the tree-lined **place du Maréchal Leclerc**, with its popular cafés and lively outdoor culture, and **place Charles de Gaulle** to the north, where a big and bustling food and clothes **market** takes place (Mon–Sat 7am–1pm). Between the two is a warren of prosperous streets – as far along as the half-timbered medieval houses of **rue de la Chaine**. Rue Gambetta cuts north past the old **Palais de Justice** (Mon–Fri 9am–6pm; free), whose nineteenth-century facade hides a much older core, including the magnificent thirteenth-century Gothic grand hall.

The church of Notre-Dame-la-Grande

The Palais de Justice looks down on one of the greatest and most idiosyncratic churches in France, **Notre-Dame-la-Grande**, begun in the twelfth-century reign of Eleanor and renovated most recently in the mid-1990s – the lower parts of the facade had suffered considerable erosion due to salt from the market stalls of fishmongers seeping up into the stone over centuries.

The most exceptional thing about the church is the west front, which is wonderfully transformed in a display of coloured lights at 10.30pm every evening in summer. You can't call the facade beautiful, at least not in a conventional sense, squat and loaded as it is with detail to a degree that the modern eye could regard as fussy. And yet it's this detail which is enthralling, ranging from the domestic to the disturbingly anarchic. Such elaborate sculpted facades – and domes like pine cones on turret and belfry – are the hallmarks of the Poitou brand of Romanesque. The interior, which is crudely overlaid with nineteenth-century frescoes, is not nearly as interesting.

The cathedral and around

At the eastern edge of the old town stands the enormous **Cathédrale St-Pierre**, on whose broad, pale facade pigeons roost and plants take root. Some of the stained glass dates from the twelfth century, notably the Crucifixion in the central window of the apse, in which the features of Henry II and Eleanor are supposedly discernible. The choir stalls, too, are full of characteristic medieval detail, but it's the grand and deafening eighteenth-century organ, the Orgue Clicquot, which is the cathedral's most striking feature, often put to good use in summer concerts.

Opposite – literally in the middle of rue Jean-Jaurès – you come upon the chunky, mid-fourth-century **Baptistère St-Jean** (April–June & Sept daily except Tues 10.30am–12.30pm & 3.30–6pm; July & Aug same times, daily; Oct–March daily except Tues 2.30–4.30pm €1.50), reputedly the oldest Christian building in France and, until the seventeenth century, the only place in town you could have a proper baptism. The "font" was the octagonal pool sunk into the floor. Water pipes uncovered in the bottom show the water could not have been more than 30–40cm deep, which casts doubt on the popular belief that early Christian baptism was by total immersion. Next to the baptistery is the town museum, the **Musée Sainte-Croix**, 3bis rue Jean-Jaurès (June–Sept Tues–Fri 10am–noon & 1.15–6pm, Sat & Sun 10am–noon, 2–8pm; Oct–May Tues–Fri 10am–noon & 1.15–5pm, Sat & Sun 2–6pm; €4, free on Tues and 1st Sun of the month; Ⓦ www.musees-poitiers.org), featuring an interesting Gallo-Roman section with some handsome glass, pottery and sculpture, notably a white marble Minerva of the first century. Taking the **riverside path** – on the right across Pont Neuf – upstream to Pont St-Cyprien makes for a relaxing walk. On the far bank, you'll see a characteristic feature of every French provincial town: neat, well-manured *potagers* – vegetable gardens – coming down to the water's edge with a little mud quay at the end and a moored punt.

Eating, drinking and entertainment

Along with traditional, fine dining places, Poitiers has a good range of ethnic options. The most formal gastronomic establishments are on rue Carnot, but there's often a friendlier atmosphere, if less grandeur, in the smaller restaurants around place de la Liberté, where the town's student population also assures the liveliest **nightlife**. If you're keen to make your money last, you can ask about student/youth offers at the Centre Information Jeunesse (CIJ), 64 rue Gambetta (Ⓣ05.49.60.68.68).

Restaurants and cafés

Alain Boutin 65 rue Carnot Ⓣ05.49.88.25.53.
A good bet for regional dishes like *cailles au Pineau* (quails cooked in a brandy liqueur), with a small, carefully chosen selection; *menus* from €25. Closed Sun.

Bar Gil 2 Place Charles de Gaulle Ⓣ05.49.41.11.56. Great place for tight budgets; this café-bar serves enormous and very tasty sandwiches (€4) all day. Bar open till 2am.

Les Bons Enfants 11bis rue Cloche Perse Ⓣ05.49.41.49.82. Scrumptious home cooking served at this tiny restaurant; try the house speciality of *escargots* melted in a parsley-buttered baked potato. Reservations essential. Closed Sun & Mon.

Mare Nostrum 74 rue Carnot Ⓣ05.49.41.58.80.
A boisterous welcome and delicious Mediterranean specialities including moussaka and *kawage*, a baked ratatouille-style dish with aubergine and *haricots verts*. *Menus* from €15.

Le Maxime 4 rue St-Nicolas ℡ 05.49.41.09.55. *Gastronomique* cuisine at its finest: delicious dishes served in an elegant setting. Lunch here is popular with the well-to-do business crowd. Evening *menus* upwards of €25. Closed Sat & Sun.

Piccolino 37 rue Augouard ℡ 05.49.01.84.53. Friendly Italian serving pizzas from a wood fire in a large, open dining room. Popular with families. Closed Sun.

La Serrureri 28 rue des Grandes Ecoles. Bright and bustling, this popular bistro, open late, serves up delicious smoothies and steaming bowls of pasta from €8.

La Table du Jardin 42 rue du Moulin à Vent ℡ 05.49.41.68.46. Traditional and creative cooking with fresh ingredients, served in a relaxed atmosphere with outside seating on a pretty square. The *menu du marché* is good value at €20. Closed Sun & Mon.

Clubs and venues

Le Confort Moderne 185 rue du Faubourg du Pont-Neuf Ⓦ www.confort-moderne.fr. Ultra-modern club and exhibition space that holds an electic range of nights, from experimental jazz to electronica.

Le Pince Oreille 11 rue des 3 Rois Ⓦ www .lepince.oreille.com. A trendy live music joint that hosts artists from all over the world.

Le Théâtre Place du Maréchal Leclerc Ⓦ www .tap-poitiers.com. Shows films from across the ages in their original language with French subtitles.

Listings

Bike rental Cyclamen (℡ 05.49.88.13.25) 60 bd Pont-Achard. Closed Sun & Mon.
Car rental National/Citer (℡ 05.49.58.51.58), 48 bd du Grand Cerf; Hertz (℡ 05.49.58.24.24) 105 bd Grand Cerf.
Internet Cybercorner, 18 rue Charles Gide (daily 10am–late; €2 per hour).

Police 38 rue de la Marne (℡ 05.49.58.51.58).
Post Office 38 rue Monseigneur Augouard.
Taxis Radio Taxi (℡ 05.49.88.12.34); Taxis Independants (℡ 05.49.01.10.01).

Around Poitiers

The area immediately surrounding Poitiers is dominated by the post-modern cinema theme park **Futuroscope**, to the north (see box opposite). Families are also catered for by a number of *parcs animaliers*, reserves for various exotic species which distinguish themselves from zoos by an absence of cages. The best is the **Vallée des Singes** ("Valley of the Apes"), thirty minutes' drive to the south near Romagne (daily March–Nov 10am–6pm; €14; Ⓦ www.la-vallee-des-singes.fr), where monkeys of all sizes roam in relative freedom. Information and cut-price tickets for this and similar attractions (snakes, birds of prey and crocodiles are all within reach) are available at the Maison du Tourisme, the tourist office for the Vienne region, at 35 place Charles de Gaulle in Poitiers (℡ 05.49.37.48.48, Ⓦ www.tourisme-vienne.com). More traditional attractions can be found at **Chauvigny** and **St-Savin**, which boast medieval centres and two fine Romanesque churches.

Chauvigny and St-Savin

East of Poitiers, the towns of **CHAUVIGNY** and **ST-SAVIN** are both accessible by bus, though you'll need an early start if you want to see both in one day.

Chauvigny is a busy market town on the banks of the Vienne which boasts five **medieval castles** whose imposing ruins stand atop a precipitous rock spur. Its pride and joy, however, are the sculpted capitals in the Romanesque **church of St-Pierre**. If you take rue du Château, which winds up the spur from the central place de la Poste, you'll pass the ruins of the Château Baronnial, which belonged to the bishops of Poitiers and now hosts displays by birds of prey, then the

Futuroscope

This giant, cutting-edge film theme park is Poitiers' best-known attraction, and sits 8km north of the city. The collection of increasingly ambitious virtual-reality rides draws visitors into the action on screen – you can be flung around on a robot's arm one minute and catapulted through the solar system in vertigo-inducing nightmare the next. New attractions appear each year; recent additions include spectacular evening shows to supplement the virtual-reality films that are the park's *raison d'être*.

Practicalities

An early start to beat the queues is recommended. The Paris Montparnasse–Poitiers TGV stops at Futuroscope; there are also regular buses (line #9; €2.60 return, family ticket €4.80 one way) from Poitiers' Hôtel de Ville or *gare SNCF*. The park is open all year apart from January, from 10am until shortly after sunset, when the laser show has finished. **Tickets** are valid for one or two days (adult one-day pass €35, child aged 5–16 €26; adult two-day pass €66, child €47) and to avoid queues at the park it's best to purchase tickets in advance from the Maison du Tourisme in Poitiers (see opposite). **Food** is predictably expensive inside, and bringing a picnic lunch can cut costs substantially. There are various deals available that include admission, plus a wide selection of accommodation on site, the cheapest of which costs €66 per adult in a four-bed room (ⓦwww.futuroscope.com).

The futuristic **cinema pavilions** housing the 26 attractions are well spread out across several acres of greenery; to see everything, including a break for lunch and a ride on the oversized floating bicycles on the park's lakes, takes about ten exhausting hours. To orientate yourself, head first for **La Gyrotour** where a lift takes you to the top of the high rotating tower and you can get the full effect of your new futuristic setting.

All the films are in French, with English commentaries on headphones often available but, as it's the visual impact that's most important anyway, it's generally better to do without. Apart from the films and robots, there's a **laser show**, "La Forêt des Rêves", a phenomenal display of music, colour and effects focused on the park's dancing fountains (shows start daily just after sunset).

Current top 5 attractions

Arthur, the 4D Adventure A hair-raising ride in 4D astride a giant ladybird in search of lost Arthur – not for the faint hearted.

Moi, Van Gogh (Brush with Genius) For the more discerning visitor, an in-depth look at the artist's work and inspirations.

La Citadelle de la Vertige A topsy-turvy tour of a virtual universe from the unusual perspective of walking on the ceiling.

Danse avec les Robots Strapped to the arm of a giant robot, fly around the room to a waltz or rock-and-roll rhythm of your choice.

Imax Solido An enormous screen, measuring 540 square metres, in conjunction with 3D-vision glasses brings you face to face with dinosaurs or stunning sea creatures – depending on which film is showing.

---

better-preserved Château d'Harcourt, before coming to the attractive and unusual east end of St-Pierre.

The choir capitals inside the church of St-Pierre are a visual treat. Each one is different, evoking a terrifying, nightmarish world. Graphically illustrated monsters – bearded, winged, scaly, human-headed with manes of flame – grab hapless mortals – naked, upside-down and puny – ripping their bowels out and crunching their heads. The only escape offered is in the serene events of the Nativity. On the second capital on the south side of the choir, for instance, the Angel Gabriel announces Christ's birth to the shepherds while just around the corner the Archangel Michael weighs souls in hand-held scales and a devil tries to grab one for his dinner.

Coinciding your visit with the Saturday or Thursday **market** gives an extra dimension to a day-trip here. Held between the church of Notre-Dame and the river, it offers a mouthwatering selection of food – oysters, prawns, crayfish, cheeses galore and pâtés in aspic. The cafés are fun, too, bursting with noisy wine-flushed farmers.

St-Savin is scarcely more than a hamlet in comparison, but it is worth a visit for its **abbey church** alone, now listed as a UNESCO monument of universal importance. Built in the eleventh century, possibly on the site of a church founded by Charlemagne, it rises strong and severe above the gazebos, vegetable gardens and lichened tile roofs of the houses at its feet. Inside, the entire vault is covered with paintings and, though colours are few, they're full of light and grace, depicting scenes from the stories of Genesis and Exodus. Some are instantly recognizable: Noah's three-decked ark, or Pharaoh's horses rearing at the engulfing waves of the Red Sea. Attached to the abbey is a fascinating multimedia **museum** (in French; Feb–June & Sept–Dec daily except Sun morn 10am–noon & 2–5pm; July & Aug daily 10am–7pm; €6; ⓦ www.abbaye-saint -savin.com) of Romanesque art history with a number of innovative exhibits about medieval monastic life and architecture.

Parthenay and around

Directly west of Poitiers, and served by regular SNCF buses, the attractive small town of **PARTHENAY** was once an important stop on the pilgrim routes to Compostela and is now the site of a major cattle market every Wednesday. Its medieval heart is worth a quick stopover if you're heading north to Brittany or west to the sea.

Buses arrive into the abandoned train station. From here, avenue de Gaulle leads straight to the central place du Drapeau, from which you can cut through a largely pedestrianized shopping district to the Gothic **Porte de l'Horloge**, the fortified gateway to the old citadelle on a steep-sided neck of land above a loop of the River Thouet.

Through the gateway, on rue de la Citadelle, the Romanesque **church of Sainte-Croix** faces the *mairie* across a small garden. The views over the western ramparts and the **gully of St-Jacques**, with its scramble of medieval houses and vegetable plots, are glorious. Further along rue de la Citadelle is a handsome but badly damaged Romanesque door, all that remains of the castle chapel of **Notre-Dame-de-la-Couldre**. Of the castle itself, practically nothing is left, but from the tip of the spur where it once stood you can look down on the twin-towered **gateway** and the **Pont St-Jacques**, a thirteenth-century bridge through which the nightly flocks of pilgrims poured into the town for shelter and security. To reach it, turn left under the Tour de l'Horloge and down the medieval lane known as **Vaux St-Jacques**. The lane is highly evocative of that period, with crooked half-timbered dwellings crowding up to the bridge.

Practicalities

The **tourist office** (May–Sept Mon–Fri 9am–12.30pm & 2–6pm, Sat 2.30–6.30pm; Oct–April Mon 2–6pm, Tues–Fri 9.30am–12.30pm & 2–6pm, Sat 9.30am–12.30pm; ☏05.49.64.24.24, ⓦ www.cc-parthenay.fr) is at 8 rue de la Vaux Saint-Jacques, right next to the old bridge. Nearby, at no. 10 place du

Vauvert, is the town's most attractive **accommodation**, the extremely welcoming ⚘ *chambres d'hôtes* run by the Giboury family (☎05.49.64.12.33; ❶). The rooms are full of character, set in an old house in the heart of the medieval quarter. If convenience is a higher priority than romance, try the smart two-star *Hôtel du Nord* right opposite the station (☎05.49.94.29.11, ⓦwww.hotelnordparthenay .com; ❸; restaurant from €14). **Campers** will find a four-star site at *Le Bois Vert* (☎05.49.64.78.43; April–Oct), part of the huge Base de Loisirs riverbank recreation area, about 3km west of Parthenay on the D949.

Parthenay also has several very good restaurants including *Le Fin Gourmet*, 28 rue Ganne (☎05.49.64.04.53; closed Sun eve, Mon & Wed lunch) which combines high-quality cuisine with a jovial atmosphere; *menus* start at €26. *La Citadelle* 9 place Georges Picard (☎05.49.64.12.25) is slightly cheaper but equally noteworthy, with rich and delicious local dishes starting at €11. Good-value brasseries with outside seating can be found on place du Drapeau, of which *L'Esplanade* has a tasty lunch *menu* for €10.

Churches around Partenay

There are three beautiful **Romanesque churches** within easy reach of Parthenay. One – with a sculpted facade depicting a mounted knight hawking – is a twenty-minute walk away on the Niort road, at **Parthenay-le-Vieux**. The others are at **Airvault**, 20km northeast of Parthenay and accessible by the Parthenay–Thouars SNCF bus route, and **St-Jouin-de-Marnes**, 9km northeast of Airvault (no public transport). A trip to St-Jouin can easily be combined with a visit to the sixteenth-century **Château d'Oiron**, 8.5km to the northwest. Alternatively, you could go on north to **Thouars**, 21km from Airvault or 16km from St-Jouin, to see the abbey church of St-Laon.

Niort

NIORT, 50km southwest of Poitiers, and connected to it by regular trains, makes a useful stopover if your goal is the Marais Poitevin (see p.498). The town, built on two small hills, has enough of interest to fill a pleasant morning's stroll, and it's the last place before the marshes to get a really wide choice of provisions. The most interesting part of the town is the mainly pedestrian area around **rue Victor-Hugo** and **rue St-Jean**, full of stone-fronted or half-timbered medieval houses. The old **town hall** on rue St Jean is a triangular building of the early sixteenth century with lantern, belfry and ornamental machicolations, perhaps capable of repelling drunken revellers but no match for catapult or sledgehammer. Along the tree-lined river **Sèvre Niortaise** lie the ruins of a glove factory, the last vestige of Niort's once thriving leather industry. At the time of the Revolution, it kept more than thirty cavalry regiments in breeches. Today Niort's bourgeois reputation is thanks to its new key industry: insurance. Accordingly, restaurants are usually packed at lunchtime, and well-heeled shoppers throng the pedestrianized streets, giving it an animated, affluent feel. Just downstream is the **market hall** and, beyond, vast and unmistakable on a slight rise, the keep of a **castle** begun by Henry II of England.

Practicalities

Coming from the *gare SNCF* on rue Mazagran, take rue de la Gare as far as rue du 14 Juillet, then turn right into place de la Brèche where you will find the excellent **tourist office** (daily 10am–6pm; ☎05.49.24.18.79, ⓦwww.niortourisme.com). They have helpful maps of the town and plenty of information about walking itineraries around the Marais, also selling large-scale maps of cycle routes (€1).

A number of **car rental** agencies line rue de la Gare by the station, including Avis at no. 89 (☎05.49.24.36.98).

There are plenty of **hotels** in Niort; by far the best value is the *Hôtel Saint-Jean*, 21 av St-Jean d'Angély (☎05.49.79.20.76, Ⓦwww.niort-hotel-saint-jean .com; ❷), a little budget hotel with welcoming, helpful owners, not far from the medieval quarter. Closer to the station is the impeccably smart *Ambassadeur*, 82 rue de la Gare (☎05.49.24.00.38, Ⓦwww.ambassadeur-hotel.com; ❸), while real luxury can be found at the sumptuous boutique hotel *La Chamoiserie*, 10 rue de l'Esplinade (☎05.49.78.07.07, Ⓦwww.hotelparticulierniort.com; ❺). **Restaurants** are congregated around place de la Brèche, however *L'Address,* at 247 av de la Rochelle (☎05.49.79.41.06; closed Sun & Mon; *menus* from €24), is worth the fifteen-minute walk from the centre for its distinctive local *menus*. For lunches, *Sucrée Salée*, 2 rue du Temple, specializes in tarts and crumbles *à l'anglaise; menus* from €10.50.

The Marais Poitevin

Calm and lush, the **Marais Poitevin** is a strange landscape of fens and meadows, shielded by poplar trees and crisscrossed by an elaborate network of canals, dykes and sluggish rivers. It's known as "La Venise Verte" – Green Venice – and indeed, farmers here use flat-bottomed punts to travel through the marshes to access their fields. The area is growing increasingly popular with summer visitors, attracted by the peace and tranquillity and absorbing scenery. Whether walking or cycling, it's best to stick to the marked paths, as shortcuts invariably end in fields surrounded by water.

Access to the eastern edge of the marsh is easiest at the whitewashed village of **COULON**, on the River Sèvre, just 11km from Niort. The #20 bus from place Brèche in Niort sets you down outside the post office on rue Gabriel Auchier. From here it's a ten-minute walk south to the place de l'Eglise, where bikes can be rented from La Libellule (☎05.49.35.83.42; €18 per day). A further five-minute stroll takes you onto Quai Louis Tardy from which La Pigouille (☎05.49.35.80.99; €19 per person with guide) rents punts, with or without a guide. The **tourist office** is on place de la Coutume and houses a free museum that explores the history of the area (Mon–Sat 10am–1pm & 2–7pm, ☎05.49.35.99.29, Ⓦwww .marais-poitevin.fr).

The best **hotel** in the village is the family-run 𝔸 *Central*, 4 rue d'Autremont (☎05.49.35.90.20, Ⓦwww.hotel-lecentral-coulon.com; ❸), which has tasteful rooms and an excellent, traditional restaurant for which it's wise to reserve (*menus* €19–40; closed Sun & Mon). If you're **camping**, try *Camping Venise Verte* (☎05.49.35.90.36, Ⓦwww.camping-laveniseverte.com; April–Oct), which is attractively situated in a meadow 2km downstream (a 25min walk). The tourist office can provide details of other campsites and *chambres d'hôtes* further into the marshes. Of the latter, *Le Paradis*, in Le Vanneau (€55; ☎05.49.35.33.95, Ⓦwww .gite-le-paradis.com; ❸), is a particularly good deal.

Ten kilometres west of Coulon you arrive at the village of **ARÇAIS**, with a simple nineteenth-century church and a substantial port, testimony to the earlier role of the canals as a serious means of agricultural transportation. Nowadays, it is another spot from which to hire canoes or punts. Beyond Arçais, there's practically no traffic, just meadows and cows. At the seaward end of the marsh – the area south of **LUÇON** – the landscape changes, becoming all straight lines and fields of sunflowers. The villages cap low mounds that were once islands.

The Vendée

The northwest of the Poitou region falls within the rural *département* of the **Vendée**, whose main attraction is the 80km of golden coast that stretches between the seaside town of **Les Sables-d'Olonne** and the northernmost tip of the scenic **Île de Noirmoutier**. Inland, the main focus is the marvellous summertime *spectacle* at **Les Épesses**.

Les Sables-d'Olonne

Although the town fringes are rather overdeveloped, the centre of **LES SABLES-D'OLONNE** retains some gaudy charm and is a popular destination for its vast curve of pristine beach. In summer, the wide seafront boulevard is cheerful and predictable, lined with pricey restaurants and hotels, and myriad brightly coloured shops selling sweets and inflatable dinghies. There is plenty to see and do here; the surf is perfect for beginners and, at the western end of the drag, the **tourist office** (July & Aug daily 9am–7pm; Sept–June Mon–Sat 9am–12.30pm & 1.30–6pm, Sun 10.30am–noon & 3.30–5.30pm; ☏02.51.96.85.85) has information on the full range of **activities** in the area, from museum visits to parachute jumps. The **Musée de l'Abbaye Sainte-Croix** on rue de Verdun houses a respectable modern-art section (mid-June to Sept Tues–Sun 10am–noon & 2.30–6.30pm; Oct to mid-June Tues–Sun 2.30–5.30pm; €5), and a stroll up from the seafront to the Île Penotte quarter, where the houses are famously decorated with *coquillages* – colourful seashell mosaics – is a must. **Hotels** fill up well in advance in July and August. The comfortable *Hôtel Antoine*, 60 rue Napoléon (☏02.51.95.08.36, ⓦwww .antoinehotel.com; March–Oct; ❸), offers bright, spacious rooms while the welcoming but basic *Relais des Voyageurs*, 84 av Alcide Gabaret, between the station and the beach, is the cheapest in town (☏02.51.95.15.96; ❶–❷). Alternatively, the *Atlantic Hotel* (☏02.51.95.08.37.71, ⓦwww.atlantichotel .fr; ❼) has the final word on ocean views and polished walnut interiors. The four-star **campsite** *Les Roses* (☏02.51.95.10.42, ⓦwww.chadotel.com; April–Oct) on rue des Roses, is 500m from the beach and town centre.

   Good-quality fish **restaurants** line the port on quai Guiné and opposite on quai des Boucaniers, reached via the shuttle ferry which crosses the port channel (daily 6am–midnight; €0.93).

The Île de Noirmoutier

The twenty-kilometre-long **Île de Noirmoutier**, 60km north of Les Sables-d'Olonne on the D38, was a seventh-century monastic settlement; today it bows to pilgrims of a different type, serving as a relatively plush tourist resort. Although tourism is the island's main economy, it doesn't dominate everything. Salt marshes here are still worked, spring vegetables sown and fishes fished. The island can be reached in two hours by bus from La Roche-sur-Yon or Nantes, and is connected to the shore by both bridge and the *Passage du Gois*, a channel across which you can drive your car at low tide. Once you've arrived, cycling is the ideal way to explore: there are paths around almost the entire perimeter, and it's perfectly flat.

Noirmoutier-en-l'Île

The island town **NOIRMOUTIER-EN-L'ÎLE** is a low-key place that comes alive with visitors in summer. It has a twelfth-century **castle**, a **church** with a Romanesque crypt, an **aquarium**, an excellent **market** (Tues, Fri & Sun) in place de la République and most of the island's **nightlife** in the form of port-front bars and cafés. The helpful **tourist office** (Sept–June Mon–Sat 9.30am–12.30pm & 2–6pm; July & Aug daily 9am–7pm; ℗02.51.39.12.42, ⓌWww.ile-noirmoutier .com) on rue du Général Passaga can brief you on all the island's activities, from fishing to kite and windsurfing, as well as lists of the island's campsites and basic maps of cycle routes. Of the dozens of **bike** rental outlets, Vel-hop, 55 av Joseph Pineau (℗02.51.39.01.34, Ⓦwww.cyclhop.fr; €11 per day) will deliver to your hotel. **Hotels** need to be booked in advance in summer. The cheapest in town is also a very agreeable one: *Bamboo*, 37 av Joseph Pineau (℗02.51.39.08.97; ❸), has brand-new rooms decorated in light colours of sea and sand. Closer to the beach is the modern *Bois de la Chaize*, 23 av de la Victoire (℗02.51.39.04.62, Ⓦwww .hotel-noirmoutier.com; ❹), while there are more elegant and luxurious surroundings on offer at the *Général d'Elbée* (℗02.51.39.10.29, Ⓦwww.general delbee.com; mid-May to Oct; ❼) in an atmospheric eighteenth-century building right opposite the castle.

Escape the overpriced pizzerias and crêperies of the pedestrianized centre for the finer **restaurants** beneath the curtain wall and sparkling white keep of the château, like the long-standing *Le Grand Four*, 1 rue de la Cure (℗02.51.39.61.97), with *menus* from €23.

The rest of the island

One beautiful **beach**, the Plage des Dames, is a ten-minute cycle ride east of Noirmoutier town, but the curving sands of the western and southern coasts are the least populated in the summer. The northern side dips in and out of little bays interspersed with rocky promontories. *Le Goéland*, 15 route du Gois (℗02.51.39.68.66, Ⓦhotel.legoeland.voila.net; ❺), in the southern village of Barbâtre is a stone's throw from the beach. Inland, the saltwater dykes are the only reminder you that you're out to sea, while the village centres are built around pretty whitewashed and ochre-tiled houses, typical of La Vendée and southern Brittany. Spring weather is often stormy and the summer heat entices the mosquitoes, so come prepared.

Les Épesses

Some 80km inland from Les Sables (on the N160 if you're driving), at the ruined castle-cum-medieval theme park **Château du Puy du Fou** in the village of **LES ÉPESSES**, a remarkable lakeside extravaganza takes place during the summer months (June–Sept Fri & Sat 10.30pm; 1hr 40min; booking essential; ℗02.51.64.11.11, Ⓦwww.puydufou.com; €24). It's an astonishing affair: the enactment of the life of a local peasant from the Middle Ages to World War II, complete with fireworks, lasers, dances on the lake and Comédie Française voice-overs. The story, available in English through a headset (€7) is interesting but incidental – the massive spectacle itself is the real attraction.

To get to Les Épesses by public **transport**, you'll need to venture to **Cholet** (connected by train from Nantes) and take a bus south from there; Puy du Fou itself is 2.5km from Les Épesses on the D27 to Chambretaud. The tourist office in Cholet (℗02.41.49.80.00, Ⓦwww.ot-cholet.fr) can provide information about transport. There is one reasonably priced **hotel** in Les Épesses, *La Crémaillère*, 2 rue de la Libération (℗&℗02.51.57.30.01; ❷), and further accommodation options 10km west in **Les Herbiers**.

La Rochelle and around

The coast around **La Rochelle** – especially the **islands** – is great for young families, with miles of safe sandy beaches and shallow water. Be aware, however, that in August, unless you're camping or book in advance, accommodation is a near-insuperable problem. Out of season you can't rely on sunny weather, but that shouldn't deter you since the quiet misty seascapes and working fishing ports have their own melancholy romance. La Rochelle and **Royan** are the largest urban centres but **Rochefort**, cheaper than the former and more attractive than the latter, makes an excellent base. All three are connected by regular trains, while elsewhere you'll have to take pot luck with the rather quirky bus routes.

La Rochelle

LA ROCHELLE is the most attractive and unspoilt seaside town in France. Thanks to the foresight of 1970s mayor Michel Crépeau, its historic seventeenth- to eighteenth-century centre and waterfront were plucked from the clutches of the developers and its streets freed of traffic. An outrage at the time, the policy has since been adopted across the country – even surpassing Crépeau's successful yellow bicycle plan, since imitated in Paris and London.

La Rochelle has a long history, as you would expect of such a sheltered Atlantic port. Eleanor of Aquitaine gave it a charter in 1199, which released it from its feudal obligations, and it expanded rapidly through the salt and wine trade and by skilfully exploiting the Anglo–French quarrels. The Wars of Religion, however, were particularly destructive for La Rochelle. It turned Protestant and, because of its strategic importance, drew the remorseless enmity of Cardinal Richelieu, who besieged the city in 1627. To the dismay of the townspeople, who reasoned that no one could effectively blockade seasoned mariners like themselves, he succeeded in sealing the harbour approaches with a dyke. The English dispatched the Duke of Buckingham to their aid, but he was caught napping on the Île de Ré and badly defeated. By the end of 1628 Richelieu had starved the city into submission. Out of the pre-siege population of 28,000, only 5000 survived. The walls were demolished and the city's privileges revoked. La Rochelle later became the principal port for trade with the French colonies in the Caribbean Antilles and Canada. Indeed, many of the settlers, especially in Canada, came from this part of France.

Arrival, information and transport

Ryanair serves La Rochelle daily from Stansted. Bus #7 runs every twenty minutes between the **airport** and town centre (Mon–Sat 7am–7.20pm; €1.20; 10min). From the grandiose **gare SNCF** on boulevard Joffre, take avenue de Gaulle opposite to reach the town centre; on the left as you reach the waterfront you'll see the efficient **tourist office**, on quai Georges Simenon (April & May Mon–Sat 9am–6pm, Sun 10.30am–5.30pm; June & Sept Mon–Sat 9am–7pm, Sun 10.30am–12.30pm; July & Aug Mon–Sat 9am–8pm, Sun 10.30am–6pm; Oct–March Mon–Sat 9am–6pm, Sun 10am–1pm; ☎05.46.41.14.68, ⓦwww .larochelle-tourisme.com), which has excellent maps and sells the **Pass' Rochelais** (2 days €5.60; 1 week €8.40), covering you for all city transport and discount entry into attractions. The office also leads **walking tours** of the old town (July

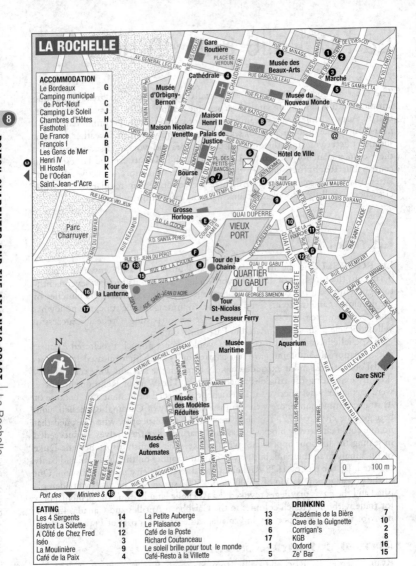

LA ROCHELLE

ACCOMMODATION

Le Bordeaux	G
Camping municipal de Port-Neuf	C
Camping Le Soleil	J
Chambres d'Hôtes	H
Fasthotel	L
De France	A
François I	B
Les Gens de Mer	I
Henri IV	D
HI Hostel	K
De l'Océan	E
Saint-Jean-d'Acre	F

EATING				
Les 4 Sergents	14	La Petite Auberge	13	
Bistrot La Solette	11	Le Plaisance	18	
A Côté de Chez Fred	12	Café de la Poste	6	
Iséo	3	Richard Coutanceau	17	
La Moulinière	9	Le soleil brille pour tout le monde	1	
Café de la Paix	4	Café-Resto à la Villette	5	

DRINKING	
Académie de la Bière	7
Cave de la Guignette	10
Corrigan's	2
KGB	8
Oxford	16
Ze' Bar	15

& Aug Mon–Sat 10.30am; €7), and rather more amusing two-hour evening tours of the city, led by a local donning medieval garb (mid-June to mid-Sept Thurs 8.30pm; €11). Most things you'll want to see are in the area behind the water-front; in effect, between the harbour and the place de Verdun, where the **gare routière** is situated. **Internet** is available at Continuum, rue Amelot (daily 10.30am–7.30pm; €2 per hour).

There are two municipal **bike parks**, heir to Michel Crépeau's original pick-up-and-leave scheme: one in place de Verdun (all year), the other on quai Valin near the tourist office (May–Sept only). You get two hours of free bike time after handing over ID; after this it's €1 per hour. **Car rental** is available from all major companies outside the station, like Rent-A-Car, 29 av de Gaulle (☎05.46.27.27.27).

La Rochelle is the area's hub for **maritime transport**, with services to the Île de Ré, Île d'Oléron, Île d'Aix and to **Fort Boyard**, a fortress-turned-prison-turned-gameshow-set, stranded in the middle of the ocean. Companies with departures from the port here include Navipromer (☎05.46.34.40.20, ⊛www.navipromer .com) and Interîles (☎08.25.13.55.00, ⊛www.inter-iles.com); times and prices vary seasonally, and weather and tides may affect crossings.

Accommodation

Accommodation in La Rochelle is in short supply and particularly pricey in summer, when booking is essential even for campers. There's no such thing as a budget hotel here, though an outstanding youth hostel goes some way to making amends. As an alternative to hotels, you might try the **self-catering apartments** that abound, particularly around Les Minimes – the tourist office has lists.

Hotels

Le Bordeaux 43 rue St-Nicolas ☎05.46.41.31.22, ⊛www.hotel-bordeaux-fr.com. Modern and comfortable hotel, whose fully-equipped rooms all look onto the lively, pedestrianized area below. Conveniently located between station and port. ❹

🏃 **Chambres d'hôtes** 4 rue Sur les Murs ☎06.14.54.39.45, ✉bconchin@hotmail .com. Situated almost underneath the Tour de la Chaine, this wonderful B&B could not be more thoughtfully run. Friendly owner Bruno Conchin is the former chef to British nobility, so a delicious breakfast is a definite. It's pricey, but fair for the location and views of the port. ❺

Fasthotel 20 rue Alfred Kastler, Les Minimes ☎05.46.45.46.00, ⊛www.fasthotel.com. Excellent-value hotel made up of modern bungalows. It's well out of the action, though – a 15min walk from the port des Minimes. Larger rooms are available for families. ❸

De France 43 rue du Minage ☎05.46.28.06.00, ⊛www.hotel-larochelle.com. A hidden pocket of grandeur right in the town centre. The calm, luxurious rooms here surround an ivy-covered courtyard. Rooms and suites are expensive for what they are (❼), but the very similar "studios" are a good deal (❹).

François I 15 rue Bazoges ☎05.46.41.28.46, ⊛www.hotelfrancois1er.fr. A touch expensive, but well situated in a historic building within a secluded walled courtyard. It's been modernized since François himself used to stop off here, with wireless internet and other mod cons now standard. ❺

Les Gens de Mer 20 av du Général-de-Gaulle ☎05.46.41.26.24, ⊛www.lesgensdemer.fr. Business-like hotel, but relatively good-value. Rooms are fully kitted-out, and it's in a handy spot for the station. ❸

Henri IV 31 rue des Gentilshommes ☎05.46.41.25.79, ⊛www.henri-iv.fr. This popular hotel has sparkling rooms right in the town centre in a sixteenth-century building on place de la Caille, a short stroll from the harbourfront. ❺

De l'Océan 36 cours des Dames ☎05.46.41.31.97, ⊛www.hotel-ocean-larochelle .com. Comfortable two-star hotel in an enviable location, with a/c rooms – many with views of the port. ❹

Saint-Jean-d'Acre 4 place de la Chaine ☎05.46.41.73.33, ⊛www.hotel-la-rochelle.com. This modern, luxurious chain hotel offers good-sized rooms with probably the city's best views of the towers and harbour from the more expensive ones. ❺–❼

Hostel and campsites

Camping municipal de Port-Neuf On the northwest side of town ☎05.46.43.81.20. This rather shabby but well-shaded campsite is about 40min walk from the town centre. Take bus #20 from place de Verdun, direction "Port-Neuf". Open all year.

Camping Le Soleil Av Michel Crépeau ☎05.46.44.42.53. In a great location near the hostel and close to the beaches, this site is often crowded with raucous young holiday-makers. Take bus #10 from place de Verdun to Les Minimes. Open late June to late Sept.

🏃 **HI Hostel** Av des Minimes ☎05.46.44.43.11, ⊛www.fuaj-aj -larochelle.com. A big modern hostel with a veranda overlooking the marina at Port des Minimes. It has all facilities, including a bar and cafeteria serving decent grub for €5 in the evening. Dorm-beds €17, single rooms €28. Bus #10 or walk from the train station, following the signs to the left.

The Town

The **Vieux Port** is very much the focus of the town, with pleasure boats moored in serried ranks in front of the two impressive towers guarding the entrance to the port. Leading north from the **Porte de la Grosse Horloge**, the **rue du Palais** runs towards the cathedral and several of the museums on rue Thiers. You can stroll very pleasantly for an hour or more along the seafront in either direction from the harbour, down to the **Port des Minimes**, a huge modern marina development 2km south of the centre, or west along an attractive promenade and through a beautiful strip of parkland towards the **Port Neuf**.

The Vieux Port

Dominating the inner harbour, the heavy Gothic gateway of the **Porte de la Grosse Horloge** straddles the entrance to the old town to the north and out towards the tree-lined pedestrianized cours des Dames to the south, where sailors' wives used to anxiously await the return of their husbands from the high seas. There is a view here of all three of the famous **towers**, which can be visited with a combined ticket (daily: April–Sept 10am–6.30pm; Oct–March 10am–1pm & 2.15–5.30pm; €6 for one tower, €8 for all three). Architecturally speaking, the **Tour St-Nicolas** is the most interesting, boasting two spiral staircases which intertwine but never meet. Opposite, the **Tour de la Chaine**, from which a colossal chain used to be slung across to close the harbour at night, now houses a gently informative exhibition on seventeenth-century emigration from La Rochelle to French Canada. You can then climb along the old city walls to the third tower, known as the **Tour de la Lanterne** or Tour des Quatre Sergents, named after four sergeants imprisoned and executed for defying the Restoration monarchy in 1822. All three towers have fine views back to the port, and the entry ticket also includes a trip on the nifty **electric ferry**, the *passeur*, which crosses all day from one side of the water to the other (€0.75).

The rue du Palais and around

The real charm of La Rochelle lies in the environs of the city's main shopping street **rue du Palais**, that leads up under the Grosse Horloge to place de Verdun. Lining the street are eighteenth-century houses, some grey-stone, some half-timbered, with distinctive Rochelais-style slates overlapped like fish scales, while the shop-fronts are set back beneath the ground-floor arcades. Among the finest are the **Hôtel de la Bourse** – actually the Chamber of Commerce – and the **Palais de Justice** with its colonnaded facade, both on the left-hand side. A few metres further on, in **rue des Augustins**, there is another grandiose affair built for a wealthy Rochelais in 1555, the so-called **Maison Henri II**, complete with loggia, gallery and slated turrets, where the regional tourist board has its offices. Place de Verdun itself is rather characterless, home to an uninspiring, humpbacked, eighteenth-century **cathedral** on the corner and the bike rental park (see p.502).

To the west of rue du Palais, especially in **rue de l'Escale**, paved with granite setts brought back from Canada as ballast in the Rochelais cargo vessels, you get the discreet residences of the eighteenth-century shipowners and chandlers, veiling their wealth with high walls and classical restraint. Look for the rather less modest abode of a seventeenth-century doctor, Nicolas Venette, on the corner of **rue Fromentin**, who adorned his house-front with the statues of famous medical men – Hippocrates, Galen and others. East of rue du Palais, and starting out from place des Petits-Bancs, rue du Temple takes you up alongside the **Hôtel de Ville** (guided tours daily 3pm & 4pm; €4), protected by a decorative but seriously fortified wall. Begun in the reign of Henri IV, it's a beautiful specimen of

Frenchified Italian taste, adorned with niches and statues and coffered ceilings in a stone the colour of ripe barley. Just up rue des Merciers, the other main shopping area, is the **market square**, where a busy food market takes place every morning as locals watch on from the encircling cafes.

Various **museums** are concealed in the townhouses around rue du Palais. The **Musée des Beaux-Arts** in rue Gargoulleau (Mon & Wed–Fri 1.30–5pm; Sat & Sun 2.30–6.30pm; €5) has a modest collection, including the exotic works of Eugène Fromentin, one of the town's most beloved sons, whose statue you can admire beneath the Grosse Horloge. More out of the ordinary is the **Musée du Nouveau Monde** (Mon & Wed–Fri 10am–12.30pm & 1.30–5pm, Sat & Sun 2.30–6pm; €4), whose entrance is in rue Fleuriau. It occupies the former residence of the Fleuriau family, rich shipowners and traders who, like many of their fellow Rochelais, made fortunes out of the slave trade and Caribbean sugar, spices and coffee. There's a fine collection of prints, paintings and photos of the old West Indian plantations; seventeenth- and eighteenth-century maps of America; and an interesting display of aquatint illustrations for Marmontel's novel *Les Incas*.

The quartier du Gabut and south to the Port des Minimes

On the east side of the old harbour behind the Tour St-Nicolas is the **quartier du Gabut**, the one-time fishermen's quarter of wooden cabins and sheds, now converted into bars, shops and eating places. Right on the quayside is the spectacular **aquarium** (daily: April–June & Sept 9am–8pm; July & Aug 9am–11pm; Oct–March 10am–8pm; adults €13, children €10; Ⓦwww.aquarium-larochelle.com), whose pride and joy are its twenty species of shark. Opposite the aquarium is the **Musée Maritime** (April–Sept 10am–6pm; €8; Ⓦwww.museemaritimelarochelle.fr), consisting of two ships: an old weather station and a trawler whose working days are over.

A further ten-minute walk brings you to the **Musée des Automates** (daily: July & Aug 9.30am–7pm; Sept–June 10am–noon & 2–6pm; adults €7.50, children €5, or joint ticket with Musée des Modèles Réduits, adults €11, children €6.50; Ⓦwww.museedesautomates.com) on rue de la Désirée, a fascinating collection of three hundred automated puppets, drawing you into an irresistible fantasy world. Further down the same street is the **Musée des Modèles Réduits** (same hours and ticket prices as the Automates). Scale models of every variety and era are on show, starting with cars and including models of a submerged shipwreck and La Rochelle train station.

The **Port des Minimes** itself houses thousands of yachts and also has a beautiful beach, where the young and gorgeous flock out to parade at weekends and on summer evenings. You can get here on bus #10 from place de Verdun, or more entertainingly on the **"bus de mer"**, a small boat which runs from the old port (April–June & Sept hourly 10am–7pm except 1pm; July & Aug half-hourly 9am–11.30pm; Oct–March Sat & Sun hourly 10am–6pm except 1pm; €1.30 one way).

Eating

Provided you resist the lure of the touristy establishments along the cours des Dames, eating very well is easy. The best place to start is the attractive rue St-Jean-du-Pérot, where the highest-quality traditional **restaurants** are located, as well as a couple of ethnic eateries. A handful of charismatic, authentic little places further inland around the market square are also worth seeking out. *Ernest Le Glacier*, 15 rue du Port, and *Olivier Glacier*, 21 rue St-Jean-du-Pérot, both serve excellent **ice cream** well into the evening.

Les 4 Sergents 49 rue St-Jean-du-Pérot
℡05.46.41.35.80. Despite its smart appearance,
the food here is not quite *haute cuisine*, but it's
tasty nonetheless; the restaurant has its own wine
cave two doors down. *Menus* from €18. Closed
Mon.

Bistrot La Solette 11 place de la Fourche. In a
charming cobbled square off bustling Rue Saint-
Nicholas, this appealing little café dishes up
oysters and sorbets (not necessarily at the same
time) plus a lunch and early dinner *menu* for €16.
Open daily until 8pm.

A Côté de Chez Fred 30–32 rue St-Nicolas
℡05.46.41.65.76. A welcoming restaurant with
oak tables and watercolours of seaside scenes.
A blackboard *carte* changes daily to reveal what
the morning's catch brought in. The excellent
menu de la mer costs €27. Booking advisable.
Closed Sun.

Iséo Place du Marché, northern side. Run by three
chefs – one Japanese, one Thai and one French –
this hugely popular fusion restaurant is proof that
too many cooks do not spoil the sushi. On the
contrary, they make it superb. Price varies
according to each piece of sushi; around €13 for 8
pieces of sushi.

La Moulinière 24 rue St-Sauveur
℡05.46.41.18.16. This is the place to come for
mussels, which are served in a dozen different
ways (from €8). It's in a pleasant spot, too, right
opposite the church of St-Sauveur. Closed Sun, and
Mon eve out of season.

Café de la Paix Place de Verdun. A superbly
decadent *belle-époque* café that is the highlight of
an otherwise dull square. All mirrors, gilt and plush;
La Rochelle's ladies of means come here to sip
lemon tea and nibble daintily at sticky cakes. The

plats du jour are also in the finest French brasserie
tradition.

La Petite Auberge 25 rue St-Jean-du-Pérot
℡05.46.41.28.43. An extremely comfortable, high-
quality seafood restaurant with a wine list
stretching to Spain. *Menu* at €29 (Mon–Sat).

Le Plaisance 77 av des Minimes ℡05.46.44.41.51.
One of a row of good-value fish restaurants near the
beach in Les Minimes. *Menus* for just €13, enjoyed
on a covered terrace from which you can watch the
sun go down behind the marina.

Café de la Poste Place de l'Hôtel de Ville. A chic
spot to admire the ornate town hall over a late
breakfast or a drink in the afternoon. Brasserie
staples all on offer, like the classic *steak-frites* for
around €12.

Richard Coutanceau Plage de la
Concurrence ℡05.46.41.48.19.
Unquestionably a great place to splash out.
Located on the seafront just to the west of the
old harbour, with a perfect view out over the
beach and sea, this Michelin starred restaurant is
a veritable palace of gastronomic excellence.
Menus €52–95. Closed Sun.

Le soleil brille pour tout le monde
13 rue des Cloutiers ℡05.46.41.11.42.
Cheerful and colourful home cooking in friendly
surroundings. The vegetarian *tartes* (€8) are
outstanding and, like everything else here, are
made from fresh ingredients from the market down
the road. Seafood and meat feature on the *plats du
jour*. Very popular, so book or get here early. Closed
Sun & Mon.

Café-Resto à la Villette 4 rue de la Forme,
behind the market. Tiny, traditional place popular
with locals; good *plats du jour* from €8.90. Lunch
only, Mon–Sat.

Nightlife and entertainment

Nightlife is in rich abundance in La Rochelle, from excellent arthouse cinemas
to moody bars and cheesy nightclubs. While nightlife along rue St-Nicolas
stays busy all year round, the lively, late-night student bars on the quai de
Gabut, behind the tourist office, can quieten during the holidays. The monthly
magazine *Sortir* has listings for mainstream and classical music events, as well
as for theatre and film. In mid-July La Rochelle hosts the major **festival** of
French-language music, Les Francofolies (ⓦwww.francofolies.fr), which
features musicians from overseas as well as France and attracts the best part of
100,000 fans to the city.

Two arthouse cinemas include La Coursive at 4 rue St-Jean-du-Pérot (ⓦwww
.la-coursive.com) and Dragon Cinema at 8 Cours des Dames, which shows films in
the original language with subtitles.

Bars and clubs

Académie de la Bière 10 cour du Temple, off rue des Templiers. An agreeable, low-key bar full of *blondes, brunes* and *blanches* that make it a must for beer aficionados.

Cave de la Guignette 8 rue St-Nicolas. This old-school watering hole could be described as either dingy or atmospheric depending on your taste, but serves unquestionably good wine.

Corrigan's 20 rue des Cloutiers. Proof that Irish pubs don't have to be ghastly and inauthentic. Affable owner Barry appeals to a mainly local clientele and puts on regular live music nights, including Irish folk on Sundays.

KGB 14 cour du Temple, off rue des Templiers. This fun little nightclub (less intimidating than it sounds) has a good-times music policy and a late licence (5am).

Oxford Plage de la Concurrence. Bigger than the KGB and with a techno/house line-up more often than not, plus regular "girls get in free" nights.

Zé Bar 13bis rue de la Chaine. Organic wines and cool lounge jazz are on the menu until late at this ultramodern brasserie.

The Île de Ré

There a few sights easier on the eye than the low-lying landscape of the **ÎLE DE RÉ**: sandy beaches fringe the assortment of whitewashed villages, marshy oyster beds and golden wheat fields as birds of prey soar in an expansive sky. Out of season the island has a slow, misty charm, and life in its little ports revolves exclusively around the cultivation of oysters and mussels. In season, however, upwards of 400,000 visitors pass through, keen to explore the network of cycle paths and sample the delicious, but expensive, local cuisine.

Arrival and information

A regular bus service runs from place de Verdun in La Rochelle to the **Île de Ré**, or you could drive over the **toll bridge** (€16.50 summer, €9 winter) which begins at the commercial port of **La Pallice**. Alternatively, the cruise companies in La Rochelle (see p.503) do boat trips to St-Martin (1hr; €17).

Buses and ferries deposit visitors at the island's tiny capital **ST-MARTIN-DE-RÉ**. Each village has its own **tourist office**, but the branch on the *îlot* in the middle of the harbour (Mon–Sat 10am–1pm & 2–6pm; Sun 10am–1pm; ℡05.46.09.20.06, ⓦwww.saint-martin-de-re.fr), is the biggest and most comprehensive with useful maps of the island's numerous **cycle routes**. **Bikes** can be rented from operators across the island such as Cyclosurf (℡05.46.09.08.28, ⓦwww.cyclo-surf.com) and Cycland (℡05.46.09.08.66, ⓦwww.cycland.fr) for around €12 per day.

Accommodation

Hotels are plentiful and pricey in all the island's villages, and packed in July and August. There are even more **campsites** on the island than there are hotels, and it shouldn't be difficult finding a place, except perhaps in desirable locations near the southern beaches at the height of the summer. Check ⓦwww.campings-ile-de-re.com for more information.

Hotels

Le Français 1 cours Félix-Faure, La Flotte ℡05.46.09.60.06, ⓦwww.hotellefrancais.com. Bright and welcoming, the hotel has beautiful views over the harbour and lighthouse. Closed mid-Nov to March. ❸

Le Galion Allée de la Guyane ℡05.46.09.03.19, ⓦwww.hotel-legalion.com. Tucked away along the harbour wall, with many rooms facing the sea, this hotel offers the best value in St-Martin. ❺

L'Océan 172 rue St-Martin in Le-Bois-Plage ℡05.46.09.23.07, ⓦwww.re-hotel-ocean.com.

Cosy spa hotel with an excellent restaurant, and a beautiful pool. Rooms are decorated by local artisans, *menus* €24. Closed Jan. ❹

Le Sénéchal 6 rue Gambetta, opposite the church in Ars-en-Ré ☏ 05.46.29.40.42, ⓦ www.hotel-le -senechal.com. Tasteful rooms decked out in exposed brickwork and wooden furnishings. A pretty garden makes the perfect spot for breakfast. Closed Jan. ❺

Hotel de Toiras 1 quai Job Foran, in St-Martin; ☏ 05.46.35.40.32, ⓦ www.hotel-de -toiras.com. Dominating the eastern entrance to the harbour, this hotel is a real splurge in unbridled Napoleonic decadence, with most rooms overlooking a glorious courtyard garden. ❾

Campsites

Camp du Soleil Ars-en-Ré ☏ 05.46.29.40.62, ⓦ www.campdusoleil.com. A charming three-star campsite with grassy pitches. Mid-March to mid-Nov.

L'Île Blanche La Flotte ☏ 05.46.09.52.43, ⓦ www.ileblanche.com. Situated 1.5km from the sea, this site has an outdoor heated pool and restaurant. April–Sept.

L'Océan 50 rte d'Ars in La Couarde ☏ 05.46.29.87.70, ⓦ www.campingocean.com. Four-star campsite boasting the best swimming complex of them all. April–Sept.

The island

The island's atmospheric little capital, **ST-MARTIN**, is the main hub of activity. Like many of the architecturally identical villages (all the buildings on Ré must abide by height restrictions and incorporate the typical local features of white-washed walls, curly orange tiles and green-painted shutters) the centre of St-Martin encircles a pretty stone harbour, from where trawlers and flat-bottomed oyster boats, piled high with cage-like devices used for "growing" oysters, slip out every morning on the muddy tide. To the east of the harbour you can walk along the almost perfectly preserved **fortifications** – redesigned by Vauban in the late seventeenth century – to the citadelle, long used as a prison. From 1860 until 1938, it served as departure point for the *bagnards* – prisoners sentenced to hard labour in the penal colonies of French Guiana and New Caledonia.

Packing a **picnic** and cycling off to the sandy beaches to the south or the rocky bays to the north is perhaps the best and most economical way to spend a day on the island, although a range of pursuits from windsurfing to horseriding can also be organised through the tourist offices. Drop by the migratory bird reserve, the **Maison du Fier et Reserve Naturelle** in the village of **LES-PORTES-EN-RÉ** (daily except Saturday morn: April–Aug 10am–12.30pm & 2.30–6pm; Sept to mid-Nov 2.30–6pm; €4; ⓦ www.lilleau.niges.reserves-naturelles.org). The **Écomusée du Marais Salant** (daily: mid-Feb to mid-April & mid-Sept to early Nov 2.30–5.30pm; mid-April to mid-June 2.30–6pm; mid-June to mid-Sept 10am–12.30pm & 2–7pm; €4.80; ⓦ www.marais-salant.com), near the village of **LOIX**, offers a glimpse into one of the island's more traditional industries, salt-harvesting. A little further into the island, through an intricate maze of salt and oyster beds, you come to the pretty village of **ARS-EN-RÉ**, easily recognizable by its distinctive black and white steeple belonging to a rather beautiful church, the lower parts of which date from the twelfth century.

Eating and drinking

Each village has a food market and *épicerie* for picnic-goers; **restaurants** can be eye-wateringly expensive but the seafood is fresh and in abundance.

Bar Basque 18 quai Sénac, La Flotte. For a change from local cuisine, you'll find excellent Basque dishes here for as little as €5 in a relaxed, informal atmosphere. Dishes are best accompanied by a glass of their sangria.

🏃 **Le Belem** 29 quai de la Poithevinière ☏ 05.46.09.56.56. The least pretentious

and best value of the restaurants overlooking the harbour in St-Martin, with an excellent three-course *menu* for €19.50 and far superior service to its neighbour, *The Skipper*.

🏃 **Cabanajam** 500m west of St-Martin along the cycle path ☏ 05.46.66.45.89. The best of the oyster-producer-cum-rudimentary-restaurants on the island. The freshest of the day's harvest can be bought to eat at home or gorged on at a picnic bench on site with a glass of chilled white wine. May–Oct.

K'Ré d'Ars 9 quai de la Criée ℡05.46.29.94.94. Another seafood specialist with *menus* from €19

and lovely terrace overlooking the harbour. Mid-Feb to Jan.

La Salicorne 16 rue de l'Olivette, La Couarde ℡05.46.29.82.37. An airy terraced restaurant with a high standard of cuisine starting at €25.

Rochefort and around

ROCHEFORT dates from the seventeenth century, when it was created by Colbert, Louis XIV's navy minister, to protect the coast from English raids and to keep an eye on troublesome La Rochelle. It remained an important naval base until modern times with its shipyards, sail-makers, munitions factories and hospital. Built on a grid plan with regular ranks of identical houses, the town is a monument to the tidiness of the military mind, and is charming with it. **Place Colbert** is exactly as the seventeenth century left it, complete with lime trees, and cobblestones brought from Canada as ships' ballast. The banks of the **Charente** are beautiful here, too, dominated by the eighteenth-century royal ropeworks, while the extraordinary house of explorer and novelist Pierre Loti is worth the trip in its own right.

Arrival and information

The **gare SNCF** is located at the northern end of avenue du Président-Wilson, about a fifteen-minute walk from the centre of town. The town has two **tourist offices**; the main one is on avenue Sadi-Carnot (Mon–Sat: July & Aug 9.30am–7pm; Sept–June 9.30am–12.30pm & 2–6pm; ℡05.46.99.08.60, ⓦwww.pays-rochefortais .com) two blocks north of the **gare routière**, where, in July and August, you can also hire **bikes** for just €1 per hour. A smaller office is also open on Sundays by the Musée de la Marine (Sun 10am–1pm & 2–5pm). **Internet** access is available at Cybernet Copy 17, 38 rue du Dr-Peltier (Mon–Sat 9am–noon & 2–6pm; €4 per hour).

Accommodation

Rochefort's **hotels** are good value, and the town is a more relaxed, as well as more economical, place to stay than neighbouring La Rochelle.

Hotels

La Corderie Royale Rue Audebert ℡05.46.99.35.35, ⓦwww.corderieroyale.com. The smartest hotel in Rochefort, with luxurious rooms and its own swimming pool. It's situated in the lovely grounds of the ropeworks (see p.510) – the top-end rooms have views of this. Closed Feb. ⑥–⑧

Roca Fortis 14 rue de la République ℡05.46.99.26.32, ⓦwww.hotel-rocafortis.com. Exceptionally good value, this central hotel offers bright, comfortable rooms, many of them overlooking a flowery inner courtyard. ❷

Le Welcome Place Françoise-Dorléac ℡05.46.99.00.90, ⓦwww.le-welcome-rochefort.fr. A very budget hotel opposite the station, but it is safe and rooms are more than acceptable; you pay

a touch more for a private bathroom. There's also a garden and a reasonable brasserie. ❶

Hostel and campsite

HI Hostel 20 rue de la République ℡05.46.99.74.62, ⓔrochefort@fuaj.org. A basic hostel with clean rooms, communal kitchen and a pleasant garden area; no breakfast though. Dorm beds cost €16.30. Call beforehand if you know you'll be arriving on a Sunday, as the reception will be closed.

Municipal campsite ℡05.46.82.67.70. A long haul if you've arrived at the *gare SNCF*: take avenue du Président-Wilson and keep going straight, until you reach the bottom of rue Toufaire, where you turn right, then left – about half an hour all the way. March–Nov.

The Town

If you have a taste for the wild and opulent, an essential visit is to the house of the novelist Julien Viaud (1850–1923), alias Pierre Loti. Forty years a naval officer, he wrote numerous bestselling romances with exotic settings and characters. The **Maison Pierre Loti** (guided tours: daily except Tues 10–11.30am & 2–5pm; reservations essential; €9.50; ☎05.46.99.16.88), at 141 rue Pierre Loti, is part of a row of modestly proportioned grey-stone houses, outwardly a model of petit-bourgeois conformity and respectability, inside an outrageous and fantastical series of rooms decorated to exotic themes, from medieval Gothic to an Arabian room complete with minaret. You can see how the house suited Loti's private life: he threw extravagant fancy dress parties and, rather more scandalously, fathered more children with his Basque mistress, kept in a separate part of the house, than with his more sober French wife.

Loti is in further evidence, along with the town's other explorer sons the Lesson brothers, at the nearby **Musée d'Art et d'Histoire** (Tues–Sun 10.30am–12.30pm & 2–6pm; free), 63 rue de Gaulle, which has various objects brought back from far-flung places and some nautically themed works of art.

A **combined ticket** available at both the museums and the tourist office costing €18 will get you into the three main museums below; the first and grandest is the **Corderie Royale** or royal ropeworks (July & Aug 9am–8pm; Sept–June 10am–noon & 2–5pm; single ticket €8; ⓦwww.corderie-royale.com), off rue Toufaire. It's a rare and splendid example of seventeenth-century industrial architecture, substantially restored after damage in World War II; from 1660 until the Revolution, it furnished the entire French navy with rope. From here, you can stroll along an enchanting path through gardens by the river and examine the rest of the admirably restored **Arsenal**. After a few minutes, you come to Rochefort's latest pride and joy: a shipyard, meticulously rebuilding the **Hermione** (daily: April–Sept 9am–7pm; Oct–March 10am–12.30pm & 2–6pm; single ticket €8), the frigate aboard which La Fayette set sail from here in 1780 to assist the American bid for independence from the British. From here it is a further five-minute walk to the **Musée National de la Marine**, a modest but attractive collection of sculptures and models of the Arsenal (May–Sept 10am–6pm; Oct–April 1.30–6.30pm; single ticket €5.50).

Eating and drinking

Strolling through Rochefort, you should have no trouble finding somewhere to **eat**, though few establishments are culinary standouts. One lovely spot is the terrace of *Le Galion* (☎05.46.87.03.77) on rue Toufaire opposite the entrance to the Arsenal, where there are fish dishes and a few classics; *menus* from €14.50. More formal is *Les Quatres Saisons*, 76 rue Grimaux (☎05.46.83.95.12; closed Sun & Mon), with *menus* from €23.

Fouras

FOURAS, some 30km south of La Rochelle and accessible by the regular bus G from Rochefort, is the main embarkation point for the tiny Île d'Aix (see opposite), where Napoleon spent his last days in Europe. The ferry dock, **Pointe de la Fumée**, is at the tip of the 3km long peninsula which is bordered by oyster beds. The finger of land is hemmed by sea-dashed fortresses, originally intended to protect the Charente, and particularly La Rochelle, against Norman attack, and later employed against the Dutch in the seventeenth century and the English in the eighteenth. The seventeenth-century **Fort Vauban** (daily except Monday morning

10am–noon & 3–6.30pm) now houses a small local history museum (€3.20), and its esplanade offers a magnificent panorama of neighbouring forts and islands, including the lesser visited **Île Madame**, which is accessible at low tide from Port des Barques, via the Passe aux Boeufs causeway. A rather desolate-looking place, especially at low tide, the island also has a grim history as the site of the internment, and in most cases death, of scores of priests from the region, victims of the anti-clerical terror unleashed in the 1790s.

Fouras's **tourist office**, which also serves the Île d'Aix, is situated on avenue du Bois Vert on the peninsula (Mon–Sat 9am–12.30pm & 2–6pm, Sun 10am–12.30pm & 2.30–6pm; ℡05.46.84.60.69, Ⓦwww.fouras.net). The town has a couple of reasonably priced **hotels**: the *Roseraie*, at 2 rue Eric Tabarly on the peninsula (℡05.46.84.64.89, Ⓦwww.hotel-fouras.com; ❸), has bright rooms and friendly owners, while a few paces from the beach and the fort the rather quirky *Commerce du Courreau*, 20 rue Bruncher (℡05.46.84.22.62, Ⓦwww.hotel-restaurant-commerce-fouras.fr; ❸), has the bonus of a good restaurant (*menus* €16.50).

Île d'Aix

Less frequented than the bigger islands in the area, the car-free, crescent-shaped **Île d'Aix** (pronounced "eel-dex") is small enough – just 2km long – to be walked around in about three hours. It's a well-defended little place, with forts and ramparts; over the course of history the whole island, particularly **Fort Liédot**, has served as a prison, notably during the Crimean and First World Wars. There's a **museum** (daily except Tues: 9.30am–12.30pm & 2–6pm; €5 with Musée Africain; Ⓦwww.musees-nationaux-napoleoniens.org) in the house constructed to Napoleon's orders. He lived in it for a week in 1815 while he was planning his escape to America, only to find himself en route to St Helena and exile, via Portsmouth. Extensive displays fill ten rooms with the emperor's works of art, clothing, portraits and arms. The white dromedary from atop which Napoleon conducted his Egyptian campaign was stuffed and is now lodged nearby in the **Musée Africain** (same hours and ticket as Musée Napoléon), with its collection devoted to African wildlife.

Access to the island is by frequent ferry (half-hourly in summer, five daily in winter, according to tide schedule – check Ⓦwww.service-maritime-iledaix.com) from Pointe de la Fumée (℡05.46.84.26.77), or with Interîles from La Rochelle (May–Sept 2–4 daily). Recently renovated to a very high standard, the island's only hotel, the *Napoléon* (℡05.46.84.00.77, Ⓦwww.hotel-ile-aix.com; ❺) boasts a modern fusion restaurant, *Chez Josephine* (*menus* from €19.50). Another accommodation option is the three-star *Fort de la Rade* campsite (℡05.46.84.28.28; May–Sept).

Brouage and Marennes

Eighteen kilometres southwest of Rochefort, **BROUAGE** is another seventeenth-century military base, this time created by Richelieu after the siege of La Rochelle. A useful tourist office at the northern gate has plenty of interesting facts on the town's history, and a small art gallery.

The way into Brouage is through the **Porte Royale** in the north wall of the mid-seventeenth-century fortifications, which remain totally intact. Locked within its 400 square metres, the town now seems abandoned and somnolent; even the sea has retreated, and all that's left of the harbour are the partly fresh-water pools, or *claires*, where oysters are fattened in the last stage of their rearing (see box, p.512).

Within the walls, the streets are laid out on a grid pattern, lined with low two-storey houses. On the second street to the right is a **memorial** to Samuel de Champlain, the local boy who founded the French colony of Québec in 1608. In the same century, Brouage witnessed the last painful pangs of a royal romance: here, Cardinal Mazarin, successor to Richelieu, locked up his niece, Marie Mancini, to keep her from her youthful sweetheart, Louis XIV. The politics of the time made the Infanta of Spain a more suitable consort for the King of France than his daughter – in his own judgement. Louis gave in, while Marie pined and sighed on the walls of Brouage. Returning from his marriage in St-Jean-de-Luz, Louis dodged his escort and stole away to see her. Finding her gone, he slept in her room and paced the walls in her footsteps.

Half a dozen kilometres south of Brouages, you come to the village of **MARENNES**. This is the centre of oyster production for an area that supplies over sixty percent of France's requirements. There are various opportunities to visit the oyster beds and learn about the business, either on foot or by boat; enquire at the **tourist office** on place Chasseloup-Laubat (April–June & Sept Mon–Fri 9.30am–noon & 2–5pm, Sat 9.30am–noon & 2–4pm; July & Aug Mon–Sat 9.30am–6.30pm; Oct–March Tues–Sat 10am–noon & 2–4pm; ℡05.46.85.04.36). For **accommodation** in Marennes, try the inexpensive *Hôtel du Commerce* at 9 rue de la République (℡05.46.85.00.09; ❶), with a good restaurant (*menus* from €15). Another option for food is *La Verte Ostréa* at the end of the pier at La Cayenne, where oysters and shellfish form the basis of every *menu* (from €13).

The Île d'Oléron

The **Île d'Oléron** is France's largest island after Corsica and a favourite of day-trippers and families in the summer months. Joined to the mainland by a bridge just north of Marennes, it's reachable in an hour on **bus** #6 from Rochefort and in July and August, minibuses also connect the main towns on the island; see ⓦwww.lesmouettes-transport.com for timetables.

Outside the tourist season, the island is a peaceful retreat, comprising a rich network of little villages, pine-studded forests and gleaming muddy tributaries lined with fishing boats that creep all the way up to the beautiful sandy beaches. In July and August, however, the island is taken over by holidaymakers and their campervans, and much of that tranquillity is lost.

Oysters

Marennes' speciality is fattening the **oysters** known as *creuses*. It's a lucrative but precarious business, extremely vulnerable to storm damage, changes of temperature or salinity in the water, the ravages of starfish and umpteen other improbable natural disasters. That said, the industry proved its resilience following the attack of Hurricane Xynthia in March 2010; the vast majority of business has resumed after a one-month fishing ban.

Oysters begin life as minuscule larvae, which are "born" about three times a year. When a birth happens, the oystermen are alerted by a special radio service, and they all rush out to place their "collectors" – usually arrangements of roofing tiles – for the larvae to cling to. There the immature oysters remain for eight or nine months, after which they are scraped off and moved to *parcs* in the tidal waters of the sea: sometimes covered, sometimes uncovered. Their last move is to *claires* – shallow rectangular pools where they are kept permanently covered by water less salty than normal sea water. Here they fatten up and acquire the greenish colour the market expects. With "improved" modern oysters, the whole cycle takes about two years, as opposed to four or five with the old varieties.

There are a few places that still retain some charm, however, not least of which is the main town in the south of the island, **LE CHÂTEAU**, named after the **citadelle** that still stands, along with some seventeenth-century **fortifications**. The town thrives on its traditional oyster farming and boat building, and there's a lively **market** in place de la République every morning. The chief town in the north – and most picturesque of the island's settlements – is **ST-PIERRE**, whose market square has an unusual thirteenth-century monument, **La Lanterne des Morts**. The best beach, meanwhile, is at **LA BRÉE LES BAINS**, in the northeast. Activities abound, from cycling to **surfing**, and a great **aqua park** opens between June and September in the village of Dolus d'Oléron in the centre of the island. A pleasant place to spend an afternoon is at the bird park of **Le Marais aux Oiseaux** (daily: April–June & Sept 10am–1pm & 2–6pm; July & Aug 10am–7pm; €4.50; Ⓦwww.centre -sauvegarde-oleron.com). Off the D126 between St-Pierre and Dolus, right in the middle of the island, this is a breeding centre with many examples of rare or endangered species.

Practicalities

The main **tourist office** is on place de la République in Le Château (daily: Mon–Sat 9.30am–12.30pm & 2.30–7pm, plus July & Aug Sun 10am–12.30pm; Ⓣ05.46.47.60.51, Ⓦwww.oleron.org). **Bikes** can be rented from Vélos 17 (Ⓣ05.46.47.14.05, Ⓦwww.velos17loisirs.com), which has outlets in all the towns on the island.

In St-Pierre, the best **accommodation** is the friendly hotel *Le Square*, place des Anciens Combattants (Ⓣ05.46.47.00.35, Ⓦwww.le-square-hotel.fr; ❹), where you should ask for a room at the back next to the pretty pool. In St-Trojan-les-Bains there's good value at *L'Albatros*, 11 bd du Dr-Pineau (Ⓣ05.46.76.00.08, Ⓦwww.albatros-hotel-oleron.com; closed Oct–Feb; ❸). A nicely situated, small hotel on the harbour in the pretty fishing village of **LA COTINIÈRE**, 🍴 *L'Écailler* (Ⓣ05.46.47.10.31, Ⓦwww.ecailler-oleron .com; closed Dec & Jan; ❺) is also an outstanding place to **eat**, with super-fresh seafood *menus* for under €20. Otherwise, the greatest choice of restaurants is in St-Pierre's pedestrian streets.

There are **campsites** all over the island: at La Brée, where the best beaches are, there's *Pertuis d'Antioche* (Ⓣ05.46.47.92.00, Ⓦwww.camping-antiochedoleron .com; April–Sept), 150m from the beach off the D273. Further down the east coast, *Signol* at Boyardville (Ⓣ05.46.47.01.22, Ⓦwww.signol.com; April–Sept) is pleasantly sited near pine forests. For stays of a week or longer, the tourist offices have lists of **holiday apartments** for rent.

Royan and around

Before World War II, **ROYAN**, at the mouth of the Gironde, was a fashionable resort for the bourgeoisie. It's still popular, but the prestige of its heyday lies very palpably in the past. The modern town has lost its elegance to the dreary rationalism of 1950s town planning: broad boulevards, car parks, shopping centres and planned greenery have shorn the town of its glamour and left the seafront crowded and uninspiring. The occasion for this planners' romp was provided by Allied bombing, an attempt to dislodge a large contingent of German troops who had withdrawn into the area after the D-Day landings. The **beaches** remain one good reason to come here, though. Particularly out towards the northern suburb of

Pontaillac, they are enticingly beautiful expanses of fine pale, and meticulously manicured, sand.

Arrival and information

The **gare routière** and **gare SNCF** are located on cours de l'Europe. The **tourist office** (mid-June to Aug Mon–Sun 9am–7.30pm; Sept to mid-June Mon–Sat 9am–12.30pm & 2–6pm; ℡ 05.46.05.04.71, ⊛ www.royan-tourisme .com) and **PTT** lie on the Rond-Point-de-la-Poste at the east end of the seafront. You can hire **bikes** for €12 per day from Cycles Horseau at 107 cours de l'Europe (℡ 05.46.39.96.43) and **cars** from most major firms also near the station.

Accommodation

Accommodation in Royan is expensive and in short supply in season, when your best bet is to visit for the day from Saintes or Rochefort.

Hotels

Les Bleuets 21 façade de Foncillon ℡ 05.46.38.51.79, ⊛ www.hotel-les-bleuets.com. A nautically themed hotel right on the seafront. All rooms have shower and TV, while for a little more money you can get a small balcony with a sea view. ❹

Le Crystal 1 bd Aristide-Briand ℡ 05.46.05.00.64, ℻ 05.46.05.32.41. Bargain basement prices and rudimentary rooms – showers are on the landing and cost €3. ❶

Miramar 173 av de Pontaillac ℡ 05.46.39.03.64, ⊛ www.miramar-pontaillac.com. Right opposite the beach, this well-run hotel has large, comfortable and sparkling rooms, while downstairs are an attractive bar and a breakfast terrace looking out over the sea. ❺

De la Plage 26 Front de Mer ℡ 05.46.05.10.27, ℻ 05.46.38.37.79. Decent value, located on the weary-looking main promenade. Rooms are ordinary but comfortable; those at the front are slightly noisier but have balconies. ❸

Campsites

Clairefontaine Allée des Peupliers towards Pontaillac ℡ 05.46.39.08.11, ⊛ www.camping-clairefontaine .com. A fairly pricey site. May to mid-Oct.

La Triloterie Off av d'Aquitaine – the road to Bordeaux ℡ 05.46.05.26.91, ⊛ www.camping royan.com. Municipal campsite.

The Town

A sight worth seeing in Royan is the 1950s **church of Notre-Dame**, designed by Gillet and Hébrard, in a tatty square behind the main waterfront. Though the concrete has weathered badly, the overall effect is dramatic and surprising. Tall V-sectioned columns rise dramatically to culminate in a 65-metre bell tower, like the prow of a giant vessel. The interior is even more striking: using uncompromisingly modern materials and designs, the architects have succeeded in out-Gothicking Gothic.

The most attractive area in Royan is around **boulevard Garnier**, which leads southeast from Rond-Point-de-la-Poste along the beach, and once housed Parisian high society in purpose-built, *belle-époque* holiday villas. Some of these have survived, including **Le Rêve**, 58 bd Garnier, where Émile Zola lived and wrote; **Kosiki**, 100 av du Parc (running parallel to boulevard Garnier), a nineteenth-century folly of Japanese inspiration; and **Tanagra**, 34 av du Parc, whose facade is covered in sculptures and balconies.

Various **cruises** are organized from Royan in season, including one to the **Cordouan lighthouse**, erected by Edward III's son, the Black Prince, and commanding the mouth of the Gironde River. There's a frequent thirty-minute **ferry** crossing (one way: pedestrians €3.10, bikes €1.60, motorbikes €10, cars €21.90) to the headland on the other side of the Gironde, the **Pointe de Grave**, from where a **bicycle trail** and the **GR8** head down the coast through the pines and dunes to the bay of Arcachon.

Eating and drinking

The seafront itself is lined with brasseries, all serving fresh fish dishes at reasonable prices, so you won't go far wrong. That said, the better **restaurants** are at least a few paces off the touristy thoroughfare. The bars along the front are certainly the best place for an evening **drink**, though, and some occasionally have live music.

Les Filets Bleus 14 rue Notre-Dame ℡05.46.05.74.00. Near the cathedral, this place serves up French specialities from seafood to foie gras; the decor has a muted maritime feel. A treat for all budgets, with *menus* from €15 to €40. Closed Sat lunch & Mon.
Le Relais de la Mairie 1 rue du Chay ℡05.46.39.03.15. A bit of a walk from town off avenue de Pontaillac, this restaurant is a bit of a local secret, offering lavish seafood dishes, like hake with shrimps, on *menus* from €15. Closed Sun, Mon & Thurs eve.
La Siesta Rue Gambetta ℡05.48.38.36.53. Delicious seafood and lovely view make this one of the best restaurants in town, a couple of minutes' walk from the Front de Mer: two-course lunch *menus* start at €13.

La Palmyre and Talmont

If you have children to entertain, head to the **zoo park** in **LA PALMYRE** (daily: April–Sept 9am–7pm; Oct–March 9am–6pm; €14; ⓦ www.zoo-palmyre.fr), 10km northwest of Royan up the D25 coast road; an exciting range of exotic species belies the slightly tacky advertising. **Buses** run there all day from Royan's *gare routière* and the place Charles-de-Gaulle.

An ideal bicycle or picnic excursion just over an hour's ride from Royan is to **TALMONT**, 16km up the Gironde on the GR360 – apart from a few ups and downs through the woods outside Royan, it's all level terrain. The low-crouching village clusters about the twelfth-century **church of Ste-Radegonde**, standing at the edge of a cliff above the Gironde. With gabled transepts, a squat tower and an apse simply but elegantly decorated with blind arcading – all in weathered tawny stone and pocked like a sponge – it stands magnificently against the forlorn browny-grey seascapes typical of the Gironde. The inside is as unpretentiously beautiful as the exterior.

The Charente

It's hard to believe that the tranquil, fertile valley of the **River Charente** was once a busy industrial waterway, bringing armaments from **Angoulême** to the naval shipyards at Rochefort. Today peaceful, ochre-coloured farms crown the valley slopes, with green rows of vineyards sweeping up to the walls, and the graceful turrets of minor châteaux – properties of wealthy cognac-producers – poke up from out of the woods. The towns and villages may look old-fashioned, but the prosperous shops and classy new villas are proof that where the grape grows, money and modernity are not far behind.

Pineau des Charentes

Roadside signs throughout the Charente advertise **Pineau des Charentes**, a sweet liqueur that's a blending of grape juice stopped in its fermentation by adding cognac from the same vineyard. It's best drunk chilled as an aperitif; the locals also like it with oysters and love cooking with it. Favourite dishes include *moules au Pineau* (mussels cooked with tomatoes, *Pineau*, garlic and parsley) and *lapin à la saintongeaise* (rabbit casseroled with *Pineau rosé*, shallots, garlic, tomatoes, thyme and bay leaves).

The **valley** itself is easy to travel as the main road and train lines to Limoges run this way. North and south, Poitiers, Périgueux (for the Dordogne) and Bordeaux are also easily reached by train. Otherwise, for cross-country journeys, you're heavily reliant on your own transport.

Saintes and around

SAINTES was formerly much more important than its present size suggests. Today a busy market town, it was once capital of the old province of Saintonge and a major Roman administrative and cultural centre. It still retains some impressive remains from that period, as well as two beautiful Romanesque pilgrim churches and an attractive town centre. A highly regarded classical music festival takes place in mid-July, when concerts are held in the atmospheric Abbaye aux Dames (Ⓦwww.abbayeauxdames.org; tickets from €10).

Arrival and information

Saintes' **gare SNCF** is on avenue de la Marne at the east end of the main road, avenue Gambetta. The **tourist office** is on place Bassompierre by the Arc de Germanicus (July–Aug 9am–7pm daily; Sept–June Mon–Sat 9.30am–12.30pm & 2–5.30pm; ℡05.46.74.23.82, Ⓦwww.saintes-tourisme.fr). The office organizes **boat trips** on the Charente during the summer (from €5) and offers maps with self-guided walking tours marked out as well as regular guided tours to many of the sites described below.

Accommodation

Saintes' **hotels** are inexpensive, and a couple are in really prime position to make the most of the old town.

Hotels

De France 56 rue Frédéric Mestreau
℡05.46.93.01.16, Ⓦwww.hotel-restaurant-17.fr. The best of the options near the train station, with comfortable rooms. Quieter ones at the back look out over a pretty garden. ❹
Des Messageries Rue des Messageries
℡05.46.93.64.99, Ⓦwww.hotel-des-messageries .com. In a seventeenth-century building, set back on a quiet courtyard in the middle of the pedestrianised old town: most rooms are a/c and all have TV and minibar. ❹

Saveurs de l'Abbaye 1 place St-Pallais
℡05.46.94.17.91, Ⓦwww.saveurs-abbaye .com. Right opposite the Abbaye aux Dames, this is a stylish and welcoming hotel with parquet floors and very attractive rooms – particularly those on the top floor. Downstairs is a super restaurant (closed Sun & Mon) with excellent-value *menus* from €15. ❸

Hostel and campsite

HI Hostel 2 place Geoffroy Martel
℡05.46.92.14.92, Ⓔsaintes@fuaj.org. In a superb position in behind the Abbaye aux Dames, the

facilities here are modern and breakfast is included. Dorm beds are €16.30. Reception open 8am–noon & 5–10pm.

Municipal campsite Quai de l'Yser ☎05.46.93.08.00, ⊛www.camping-saintes-17 .com. By the river. Mid-April to mid-Oct.

The Town

The abbey church, the **Abbaye aux Dames** (daily: April–Sept 10am–12.30pm & 2–7pm; Oct–March 2–6pm; entry €2, guided tour €3.50), is as quirky as Notre-Dame in Poitiers (see p.492). A sculpted doorway conceals the plain, domed interior. Its rarest feature is the eleventh-century tower, by turns square, octagonal and lantern-shaped, flanked with pinnacles and capped with the Poitou pine cone.

Nearby on the riverbank is the imposing **Arc de Germanicus**, which originally stood on the bridge until 1843 when it was demolished to make way for the modern crossing and rebuilt here. The arch was dedicated to the emperor Tiberius, his son Drusus and nephew Germanicus in 19 AD. In a stone building next door is the **Musée Archéologique** (April–Sept Tues–Sat 10am–12.30pm & 1.30–6pm, Sun 1.30–6pm; Oct–March Tues–Sun 2–5pm; €1.70), with a great many more Roman bits and pieces strewn about, mostly rescued from the fifth-century city walls into which they had been incorporated.

A footbridge crosses from the Musée Archéologique to the covered market on the west bank of the river and place du Marché, which sits at the foot of the rather uninspiring **Cathédrale de St-Pierre**. The cathedral began life as a Romanesque church but was significantly altered in the aftermath of damage inflicted during the Wars of Religion, when Saintes was a Huguenot stronghold. North of the cathedral, an early seventeenth-century mansion on rue Victor-Hugo houses the **Musée Présidial** (same hours and price as Musée Archéologique), containing a collection of local pottery and some decent fifteenth- to eighteenth-century paintings. Just down the road is the **Musée de l'Echevinage** (same hours and price as Musée Archéologique), with nineteenth- and twentieth-century paintings, mainly by local artists of the Saintongeaise and Bordelaise schools. A ticket costing €4.20 will get you into both galleries, the Musée Archéologique and the **Musée Dupuy-Mestreau** (same hours and price as Musée Archéologique) down on the riverbank, which houses a vast personal collection of objects ranging from model ships to headdresses.

Saintes' Roman heritage is best seen at **Les Arènes** (June–Sept daily 10am–8pm; Oct–May Mon–Sat 10am–5pm, Sun 1.30–5pm; €2). The remains of the Roman amphitheatre are perhaps all the more extraordinary for their location. This

monumental vestige from an ancient past, now a little grassy in parts, sits embedded in a valley almost completely surrounded by bland suburbia; a forgotten, sleeping relic dating from 40 AD, the oldest surviving example in France. To find it take the small footpath beginning by 54 cours Reverseaux.

On the way back from the amphitheatre drop into the eleventh-century **church of St-Eutrope**. The upper church, which lost its nave in 1803, has some brilliant capital carving in the old choir. But it's the crypt – entered from the street – which is most atmospheric and primitive: here massive pillars carved with stylized vegetation support the vaulting in semi-darkness, and there's a huge old font and the third-century tomb of Saintes' first bishop, Eutropius himself.

Eating and drinking

Saintes is a quiet town, but boasts a couple of lovely **restaurants** and a few cheerful watering holes; most of them can be found along the quai de la Republique opposite the Arc de Germanicus.

La Crêperie Victor Hugo 20 rue Victor-Hugo. Popular for its wide selection and outdoor seating.
Moulin de la Baine 10km upstream in Chaniers ☎05.46.91.12.92. Beautifully situated restaurant with delicious local dishes such as stuffed quail on a bed of grapes caramelised in *Pineau des Charentes*. *Menus* from €19.50. March–Oct.
Opéra Latin Rue des Messageries, opposite the post office. This quirky lounge bar hosts live salsa performances at weekends after which you're invited to share the floor.

Le Point Central On the corner of Cours National and rue Alsace-Lorraine. A relaxed, social hub that serves drinks until midnight if there is enough demand.
La Table de Marion 10 place Blair ☎05.46.74.16.38. The finest restaurant in Saintes, with a daily *menu* from the market for €27, though you have to pay a bit more to experience the distinguished chef at his best. Closed Tues eve & Wed.

Around Saintes

If you have a car, you could explore several of the marvellous Romanesque churches within easy reach of Saintes. In **FENIOUX**, 29km to the north towards St-Jean-d'Angély, there's superb St-Eutrope with its mighty spire, while the church at **RIOUX**, 12km to the south, is well worth visiting for its detailed facade. There's also the fine **Château of Roche-Courbon**, 18km northwest off the Rochefort road – once described by Pierre Loti (see p.510) as the Sleeping Beauty's castle – with some stylish interiors and gardens.

One place worth any amount of trouble to get to is the twelfth-century pilgrim **church of St-Pierre** at **AULNAY**, 37km northeast of Saintes, and sadly not served by public transport. On the building's main facade, two blind arches flank the central portal. The tympanum of the right depicts Christ in Majesty; the left, St Peter, crucified upside down with two lithe soldiers balancing on the arms of his cross to get a better swing at the nails in his feet. Inside, there is more extraordinary carving: capitals depicting Delilah cutting Samson's hair and human-eared elephants bearing the Latin inscription *Hic sunt elephantes* – "Here are elephants" – presumably for the edification of ignorant locals.

You might also like to visit **Nuaillé-sur-Boutonne**, 9km west of Aulnay, which boasts another remarkable church; and, even nearer just down the D129 east of Aulnay, you can walk to **Salles-lès-Aulnay** (20min), or **St-Mandé** (1hr), which has humbler churches of the same period.

Cognac and around

Anyone who does not already know what **COGNAC** is about will quickly nose its quintessential air as they stroll about the medieval lanes of the town's riverside quarter. For here is the greatest concentration of *chais* (warehouses), where the high-quality brandy is matured, its fumes blackening the walls with tiny fungi. Cognac *is* cognac, from the tractor driver and pruning-knife wielder to the manufacturer of corks, bottles and cartons. Untouched by recession (eighty percent of production is exported), it is likely to thrive as long as the world has sorrows to drown – a sunny, prosperous, self-satisfied little place.

Arrival and information

From the industrial **gare SNCF**, to get to the central place François-I, go down rue Mousnier, right on rue Bayard, past the PTT and up rue du 14-Juillet. The square is dominated by an equestrian statue of the king rising from a bed of begonias; in fine weather the cafés here teem with locals. The **tourist office** is at 16 rue du 14-Juillet (May, June & Sept Mon–Sat 9.30am–5.30pm; July & Aug Mon–Sat 9am–7pm, Sun 10am–4pm; Oct–April Mon–Sat 10am–5pm; ☏ 05.45.82.10.71, Ⓦ www.tourism-cognac.com), where you can ask about visiting the various *chais*, as well as get information on river trips. **Internet access** is available at Je Console, 24 allée de la Corderie (€3.50 per hour).

Accommodation

Hotels

Chambres d'Hôtes 29 rue Grande ☏ 06.07.01.71.57, Ⓦ www.bedandbreakfastin cognac.com. Wonderfully comfortable B&B in the heart of the old town with sixteenth-century cellars and a garden for breakfast. ❹

Le Cheval Blanc 6 place Bayard ☏ 05.45.82.09.55, Ⓦ www.hotel-chevalblanc.fr. Not a huge amount of character, but good-value rooms, fully equipped with flat-screen TVs, a/c and wi-fi, mostly surrounding a quiet patio. ❸

Hôtel Heritage 25 rue d'Angoulême ☏ 05.45.82.01.26, Ⓦ www.hheritage.com. Vibrantly themed rooms may come as a surprise in this grand, well-situated hotel, but they are spotless and comfortable. The restaurant is extremely popular, with *menus* starting at €16.50. ❹

L'Oliveraie 6 place de la Gare ☏ 05.45.82.04.15, Ⓦ www.oliveraie-cognac.com. Opposite the station, quiet rooms in a villa-style outbuilding are spacious for the price and have a/c. ❸

Les Pigeons Blancs 110 rue Jules Brisson ☏ 05.45.82.16.36, Ⓦ www.pigeons-blancs.com. A 20min walk from the town centre, set in lovely open grounds on top of a hill. Rooms are luxurious and there is a high-quality restaurant (*menus* around €30). ❺

Campsite

Camping de Cognac Bd de Châtenay ☏ 05.45.32.13.32, Ⓦ www.campingdecognac.com. Four-star campsite on the willow-lined banks of the river. May–Oct.

The Town

Cognac has a number of medieval stone and half-timbered buildings in the narrow streets of the old town, of which rue Saulnier and rue de l'Île-d'Or make atmospheric backdrops for a stroll, while picturesque **Grande-Rue** winds through the heart of the old quarter to the *chais*, down by the river. The attractive Hôtel de Ville is set in pleasant gardens just to the east.

All the major cognac houses offer tours, but the **Otard** *chais* (guided tours; April–Oct daily 11am–5pm; Nov–Dec Mon–Fri; €8.50; Ⓦ www.otard.com) has an added historical attraction. François I was born here in 1494, while the castle made a miserable prison for British prisoners after the Seven Years War in 1754;

the prisoners' graffiti can still be seen on the walls of the great hall. The hour-long tour (at least once a day in English) recounts some history of the château, before explaining the general principles (though no closely guarded secrets) of cognac production. A tasting at the end allows you to test your nose and compare different vintages.

Eating

For **eating** out, try the chic restaurant *La Belle Epoque* (℡ 05.45.82.01.26) at 25 rue d'Angoulême, at the striking *Hôtel Heritage* (see p.519). *Menus* proposing the finest regional recipes and produce start at €18. Another possibility is *Le Patio* (℡ 05.45.32.40.50), 42 av Victor-Hugo, with a range of steak and duck dishes and a *menu* for €20.

Around Cognac

The area around Cognac is gentle enough for some restful walks, taking in some pretty little Charentais villages. The tourist office sells large-scale maps of the best possibilities for €3.50. Particularly pleasant is the towpath or *chemin de halage* that follows the south bank of the Charente upstream to Pont de la Trâche, then on along a track to the idyllic village of **BOURG-CHARENTE** (about 8km in all), known far and wide for its excellent riverside **restaurant** called ⚑ *La Ribaudière* (℡ 05.45.81.30.54; closed Sun eve, Mon & Tues lunch; *menus* from €42). From here, you can amble to the village's interesting castle and Romanesque church. Alternatively, follow the GR4 the other way to the hamlet of **RICHEMONT**, 5km northwest of Cognac, where you can swim in the pools of the tiny River Antenne below an ancient church on a steep bluff lost in the woods.

It's an 18km drive northwest of Cognac to the fascinating **Écomusée du Cognac** (June–Sept daily 10am–12.30pm & 2.30–6.30pm; rest of year by reservation; €5; ℡ 05.46.94.91.16), which illustrates the history of the distillation process and includes a tasting of cognacs and liqueurs; follow the D731 to St-Jean-d'Angély for 13km as far as Burie, then turn right onto the D131, 4km from Migron.

A particularly beautiful excursion is upstream to **Jarnac**, where you can take boat trips on the Charente from €7.50, arranged by the tourist office (May–Sept; ℡ 05.45.82.09.35, ⓦ www.jarnac-tourisme.com). The town proudly boasts its connection with the late President Mitterrand, who was both born and buried here. The **Musée François-Mitterrand**, 10 quai de l'Orangerie (July & Aug daily 10am–12.30pm & 2.30–6.30pm; Jan–June, Sept & Oct Wed–Sun 2–6pm; €5; ℡ 05.45.81.38.8), houses a permanent exhibition on the public works carried out during Mitterrand's two terms of office.

Angoulême and around

The pretty cathedral city of **ANGOULÊME** was once dominated by paper mills that employed thousands and bolstered the city's prosperity. Today only a couple of small, specialized mills still function but tourism has revived the economy and the town now has a lively, prosperous air.

In the past, the former capital of the Angoumois province was a much-coveted city politically, being heavily fought over during the fourteenth-century Anglo–French squabbles and again in the sixteenth century during the Wars of Religion, when it was a Protestant stronghold. After the revocation of the Edict of Nantes, a good proportion of its citizens – among them many of its skilled papermakers – emigrated to Holland, never to return.

Arrival and information

Angoulême is easily accessible by **train** from Cognac, Limoges and Poitiers. From the **gare SNCF**, avenue Gambetta leads uphill to the town centre through place Pérot, a fifteen-minute walk. Buses leave from either the train station or place Bouillaud, at the top of the hill, while the **tourist office**, 7 rue du Chat (July & Aug Mon–Sat 9.30am–6.30pm, Sun 10am–1pm; Sept–June Mon–Sat 9.30am–12.30pm & 1.30–6pm, Sun 9.30am–12.30pm & 1.30–5.30pm; ☎05.45.95.16.84, ⓦwww.angouleme-tourisme.com), is on place des Halles, opposite the large covered market (daily 7am–1pm). **Internet** access is available at 72 av Gambetta (Mon–Sat 10.30am–6.30pm, €2 per hour).

Accommodation

The tourist office can help with **accommodation**; but if you go it alone you'll find a clutch of cheap hotels around the station and some more attractive options nearer the town centre. Prices rise opportunistically during the Festival de la Bande Dessinée (see p.523), during which it is essential to book in advance.

Hotels

Chambres d'Hôtes 69 rue Saint-Ausone ☎06.66.10.95.76, ⓔcecile.bezada @laposte.net. A delightfully bohemian B&B run by Cécile Bezada, situated on a quiet street a steep ten-minute walk out of town. Guests can eat breakfast in the garden watched over by the enormous family rabbit. ❶

Le Crab 27 rue Kléber ☎05.45.93.02.93, ⓔlecrab.angouleme@orange.fr. In a quiet backstreet, clearly signed from the station, the spotless rooms here are secure and good value, as are the simple daily *menus* at the restaurant downstairs (€12; closed weekends). ❸

Du Palais 4 place Francis Louvel ☎05.45.92.54.11, ⓦwww.hotel -angouleme.fr. A charming hotel in an elegantly preserved former convent. A recent revamp has preserved the building's authenticity, with exposed beams and ancient stone a feature in most rooms. Those on higher floors have balconies that look out onto the central square. ❹

La Palma 4 rampe d'Aguesseau ☎05.45.95.22.89, ⓦwww.restaurant-hotel-palma .com. Friendly and attentive hotel with nine a/c rooms and free wi-fi. ❹

Campsite

Camping du Plan d'Eau Impasse des Rouyères, St-Yrieix ☎05.45.92.14.64, ⓦcamping-du-plan -deau.cabanova.fr. This sparkling three-star site can be reached by #3 bus to St-Yrieix from the *gare routière*.

The Town

Overlooking a bend in the Charente and contained within stone ramparts atop a steep-sided plateau, the **old town** is an attractive natural fortress. On the southern edge stands the **cathedral**, whose west front – like Notre-Dame at Poitiers – is a fascinating display board for some expressive twelfth-century sculpture, culminating in a Risen Christ with angels about his head. The lively frieze beneath the tympanum commemorates the recapture of Spanish Zaragoza from the Moors, showing a bishop transfixing a Moorish giant with his lance and Roland killing the Moorish king.

Wander round the old town and you'll happen across frescoes of a different kind; brightly coloured cartoons and murals painted on various town walls allude to the city's position as world-leader of the *bandes dessinées,* or comic books. The tourist office has a leaflet detailing the location of every wall mural. Every year in

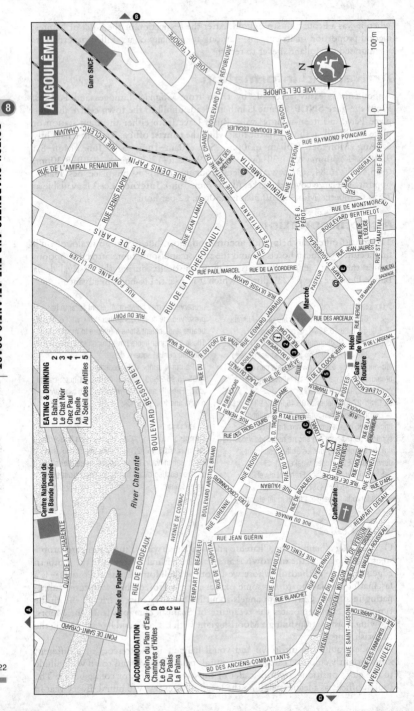

POITOU-CHARENTES AND THE ATLANTIC COAST

8

ANGOULÊME

Gare SNCF

Centre National de la Bande Desinée

Musée du Papier

River Charente

EATING & DRINKING
Le Bahia	2
Le Chat Noir	3
Chez Paul	4
La Ruelle	1
Au Soleil des Antilles	5

ACCOMMODATION
Camping du Plan d'Eau	A
Chambres d'Hôtes	D
Le Crab	B
Du Palais	C
La Palma	E

N

0   100 m

QUAI DE LA CHARENTE
PONT DE SAINT-CYBARD
RUE DE BORDEAUX
BOULEVARD BESSON BEY
RUE DU PORT
RUE DE L'AMIRAL RENAUDIN
RUE LECLERC-CHAUVIN
RUE DENIS PAPIN
RUE DE PARIS
RUE FONTAINE DU LIZIER
RUE DE LA ROCHEFOUCAULT
RUE JEAN LAMAUD
RUE PAUL MARCEL
RUE DE LA CORDERIE
RUE ULYSSE GAYON
AVENUE GAMBETTA
RUE FONTAINE DE CHANDE
RUE DES METONS
BOULEVARD DE LA RÉPUBLIQUE
VOIE DE L'EUROPE
VOIE DE L'EUROPE
RUE ST-ROCH
RUE ÉDOUARD ESCALIER
RUE RAYMOND POINCARÉ
RUE DE L'ÉPERON
RUE DE PÉRIGUEUX
RUE JEAN FOUGERAT
RUE DE MONTMOREAU
BOULEVARD BERTHELOT
PLACE G. PÉROT
RUE DE L'ÉGLISE
RUE ST-MARTIAL
RUE JEAN JAURÈS
RUE DU SAUVAGE
RAMPE D'AGUESSEAU
Marché
RUE PASTEUR
RUE DES ARCEAUX
RUE HERGÉ
RUE DE VILLE
R DE L'ARSENAL
Hôtel de Ville
R DE L'ARSENAL
RUE LÉONARD JARRAUD
BOULEVARD PASTEUR
RUE DU CHAT
RUE DU CHEVAL BLANC
RUE DE GENÈVE
R DE LA CLOCHE VERTE
Gare Routière
RUE DES POSTES
AV. G. CLEMENCEAU
RUE D'ARDOLE
RUE DE LA GENDARMERIE
RUE DES ARTISANS
PLACE DU PALET
R DU FORT DE VAUX
FORT DE VAUX
RUE HENRI IV
R. E. ÉTIENNE
RUE DES ACACIAS
R. T. TRAVIEUX
RUE DES TROIS FOURS
R. D. TROIS NOTRE DAME
R TAILLETER
PL. F. LOUVEL
RUE FROIDE
RUE TURENNE
RUE DU SOLEIL
RUE DES CORDONNIERS
RUE VAUBAN
RUE DU MINAGE
RUE DE BEAULIEU
RUE TISON D'ARGENCE
RUE DE L'ÉVÊCHÉ
RUE MOLIÈRE
RUE CORNEILLE
RUE D'ARC
RUE DESAIX
BOULEVARD ARISTIDE BRIAND
AVENUE DE COGNAC
REMPART DE BEAULIEU
RUE DE L'HÔPITAL
RUE JEAN GUÉRIN
RUE FENELON
RUE DE BEAULIEU
RUE D'ÉPERON
Cathédrale
REMPART DU MIDI
RUE DE L'ÉGLISE DROIT
AV. DE VERDUN
AVENUE DU PRÉSIDENT WILSON
REMPART DESAIX
RUE WALDECK-ROUSSEAU
RUE BLANCHET
BD DES ANCIENS COMBATTANTS
RUE SAINT-AUSONE
RUE ÉMILE JARRETON
RUE DES TANNERIES
AVENUE JULES

the last weekend of January the city hosts the extremely popular **Festival de la Bande Dessinée**, when thousands come to see the latest developments in what is most certainly regarded as a serious art form. It is also permanently represented by the **Cité Internationale de la Bande Dessinée** (€6 for the museum, library and reading room; free for library only; Ⓦ www.cnbdi.fr), which owns a vast collection of original drawings that includes Astérix, Peanuts and Tintin, and traces the 150-year development of the comic strip. The new building in a former riverside warehouse includes a vast library, much of it in English, where you're welcome to relax on cushions and have a read.Close by is the **Musée du Papier**, a tribute to the declining industry, which was closed for major refurbishment at the time of writing.

Eating and drinking

Angoulême has some great **restaurants**, which line the narrow streets that wind from place des Halles to place Louvel. The place des Halles is the ideal spot for a glass of chilled *Pineau des Charentes* and some people-watching.

Le Bahia 13 place des Halles ℡ 05.45.95.94.55. A South American-themed brasserie opposite the market. Sangria and bottled Mexican beers are on offer, as is a more conventional French *plat du jour* for €8.90. There are salsa nights every Thurs out of season, and live music in summer. Closed Sun.

Le Chat Noir 24 rue de Genève ℡ 05.45.95.26.27. A beloved meeting place for locals every day of the week, *Le Chat Noir* is popular for its great-value salads and omelettes at lunchtime, and for its *bruschetta* (€7) and relaxed atmosphere in the evenings. Closed Sun.

Chez Paul 8 place Francis Louvel ℡ 05.45.90.04.61. A high-class restaurant serving bistro-style dishes with a modern twist (*menus* from €26), with a large terrace and garden. Inside there is a rather trendy bar, open until midnight.

La Ruelle 6 rue 3 Notre-Dame ℡ 05.45.95.15.19. A really fine restaurant, with impeccable service and some of the best food in the region, combining local staples with exotic delicacies. So you might have, for example, foie gras with a beetroot, mango and chilli chutney followed by lobster in lemon butter. *Menus* from €38. Closed Sun & Mon.

Au Soleil des Antilles 19 rue des 3 Notre-Dame ℡ 05.45.94.70.15. For something a bit different, try the tropical house cocktails and delicious creole *menus* (from €13) at this laid-back restaurant. On Fri & Sat the chef leaves the kitchen after dinner to offer some musical accompaniment. Closed Sun & Mon.

Around Angoulême

LA ROCHEFOUCAULD, 22km east of Angoulême, is the site of a huge Renaissance **château** on the banks of the River Tardoire, which still belongs to the family that gave its name to the town a thousand years ago. The stately pile (Easter–Nov daily except Tues 10am–7pm; €8) stages a massive son et lumière with a brigade-sized cast in August. A lovely place to **stay** here is *La Vieille Auberge* at 1 rue de Vitrac (℡ 05.45.62.02.72, Ⓦ www.hotel-restaurant-lavieilleauberge .com; ❷–❸).

Further east, the country becomes hillier and more wooded, with buttercup pastures grazed by liver-coloured Limousin cattle. One place to aim for is the beautiful, if now rather touristy little town of **CONFOLENS**, about 40km northeast of La Rochefoucauld. Its ancient houses are stacked up a hillside above a broad brown sweep of the river Vienne, here crossed by a long narrow medieval bridge. Having come this far, it's worth continuing the extra 6km to the minuscule village of **St-Germain-de-Confolens**, huddled by the riverside beneath the romantic towers of its ruined castle.

Aquitaine

In Roman times, **Bordeaux** was capital of the province of Aquitania Secunda. With the marriage of Eleanor of Aquitaine and King Henry II of England in 1152, it quickly became the principal English foothold for their three-hundred-year Aquitanian adventure, and it was largely due to their taste for its red wines – imported back to England and termed "claret" – that the region owed its first great economic boom. The second boom, which financed the building of the gracious eighteenth-century centre of Bordeaux, came with the expansion of colonial trade.

The surrounding countryside is more notable for its **wines** and **vineyards** than its scenery, though the hills of **Entre-Deux-Mers** and the pretty town of **St-Émilion** are worth visiting in their own right. Quite different are the vast pine-covered expanse of **Les Landes** and the glistening, wild Atlantic beaches of the **Côte d'Argent** to the south – you need your own transport to explore it fully.

Bordeaux

The city of **BORDEAUX** cuts a fine figure, its sparkling quaysides over the River Garonne a showcase of grand classical architecture and modern resourcefulness, with former warehouses gradually transformed into chic designer outlets and restaurants. Behind this impressive facade, a thriving multicultural population of over half a million eat, sleep, work and play. The Romans set up a lively trading centre here and today the city still functions as the regional transport hub for Aquitaine, the proud pioneer of a space-age tram network – a modern, electric aspect that juxtaposes nicely with its classical architecture. First-rate museums, gastronomic excellence and a fantastic nightlife make Bordeaux an absorbing town, well worth a few days of anybody's time.

Arrival and information

Bordeaux-Mérignac **airport** is 12km west of the city and is connected by shuttle buses (every 45min; €7) to the main tourist office. Arriving by **train**, you'll find yourself at the gare St-Jean, right at the heart of a somewhat insalubrious area nearly 3km south of the city centre; bus #16 and tramline C run into the centre. There's no central **gare routière**, but the hub of bus transport is the south side of the esplanade des Quinconces, on allées de Munich, where you'll also find the information centre (℡05.57.57.88.88, ⊛www.infotbc.com) for all local transport. Troublesome exceptions are buses to Blaye, which leave from "Buttinière" (take tram line A), and buses to Margaux and Pauillac, which leave from "place Ravezies" (tram line C).

Tram services operate on the three lines frequently from 5am to midnight, and extend several kilometres into Bordeaux's suburbs. You can purchase either single tickets (€1.40) or carnets of ten (€10.30), available from the machines at tram stops or at *tabacs* all over the city. Though the city is certainly walkable, some sights are a fair distance away from each other, and if you're going to be here for a few days, it pays to buy an **unlimited-use pass**, available for between one and seven days.

For drivers, there are numerous underground **car parks** in the town centre, though it's cheaper to use the ones next to the tram stations on the east bank of the Garonne: buy a round-trip park-and-ride ticket (€2.60), and hop on a tram into the centre.

Bordeaux's main **tourist office**, near the Grand Théâtre on 12 cours du 30-Juillet (May–Oct Mon–Sat 9am–7pm, Sun 9.30am–6.30pm; Nov–April Mon–Sat 9am–6.30pm, Sun 9.45am–6.30pm; ☎05.56.00.66.00, 🖥www.bordeaux -tourisme.com), can book accommodation free of charge, and it has useful information on the city and surrounding vineyards, to which it also arranges tours (see box, p.533).

Accommodation

The city has a wealth of **hotels** ranging from cheerful basic to plush luxury – far better to venture into the centre than pick from the selection by the station on rue Charles Domercq and cours de la Marne, rife with grotty one- and two-star hotels. Rooms are not difficult to come by, with the notable exception of the week of the Vinexpo trade fair (in odd-numbered years) and Fête du Vin (in even-numbered years) in June, when Bordeaux is packed to the gunnels.

🏃 **L'Avant-Scène** 36 rue Borie
☎05.57.29.25.39, 🖥www.lavantscene.fr.
Well located in the Chartrons district, this fabulous boutique hotel has nine exquisitely decorated rooms, effortlessly mixing the original features of the seventeenth-century building with sharp, contemporary design. The charming gay management welcomes one and all. ⑥

🏃 **Ecolodge des Chartrons** 23 rue Raze
☎06.98.39.50.15, 🖥www.ecolodgedes chartrons.com. On a quiet road in the northerly Chartrons district, these five *chambres d'hôtes* have been renovated to be as environmentally sustainable as possible – from using sheep's wool as insulation to heating water with solar panels. The rooms are also very attractive, combining antique furniture and original beams, stone and hearths with brand-new bathrooms and wi-fi. ⑥

La Maison du Lierre 57 rue Huguerie
☎05.56.51.92.71, 🖥www.maisondulierre.com.
An attractive, quiet and friendly hotel with twelve rooms, all with parquet floors. Those at the front have balconies, while those at the back are more peaceful. Closed Feb. ④

Notre-Dame 36 rue Notre-Dame
☎05.56.52.88.24, 🖥www.hotelnotredame33.fr.
A great spot in the Chartrons district. Quiet, modest and impeccably clean, all rooms have a/c and are decorated with posters of Bordeaux. Also an option for families; they will put two rooms together (⑤) and offer free breakfast to children. ③

Regina 34 rue Charles Domercq
☎05.56.91.66.07, 🖥www.hotelreginabordeaux .com. This old hotel just opposite the station offers excellent value. All rooms are in good

condition, though you pay slightly more for en-suite facilities or a television. Very backpacker-friendly, with left-luggage and kitchen facilities thrown in. ②

Seeko'o 54 quai de Bacalan ☎05.56.48.00.14,
🖥www.seekoo-hotel.com. The Inuit word for iceberg is "Seeko'o", and that's just what the rooms in this sumptuous four-star boutique hotel are – gigantic, splendid, and extremely cool. The city views from the cocktail bar are marvellous, as is the hammam spa. ⑧

Studio 26 rue Huguerie ☎05.56.48.00.14,
📧studio@hotel-bordeaux.com. Easily the best deal in town, offering simple single rooms with shower and TV for a paltry €19, so very popular with backpackers. There's not much sound-proofing though, so your night's sleep is slightly pot luck. ①

De la Tour Intendance 14–16 rue de la Vieille-Tour ☎05.56.44.56.56, 🖥www.hotel-tour -intendance.com. This sweet yellow and blue hotel has smart, homely rooms and lift access, is a stone's throw from the action on place Gambetta but nicely secluded in a small back-street. ⑥

Une Chambre en Ville 35 rue Bouffard
☎05.56.81.34.53, 🖥www.bandb-bx.com. This stylish *chambres d'hôtes* in the old city is a comfortable option. The five rooms are full of character, unusually spacious and all en suite. Delicious fresh orange juice for breakfast, too. ⑤

Hostel and campsite

Camping de Bordeaux Lac Bd du Parc des Expositions ☎05.57.87.70.60, 🖥www.camping -bordeauxlac.com. A lovely campsite located north

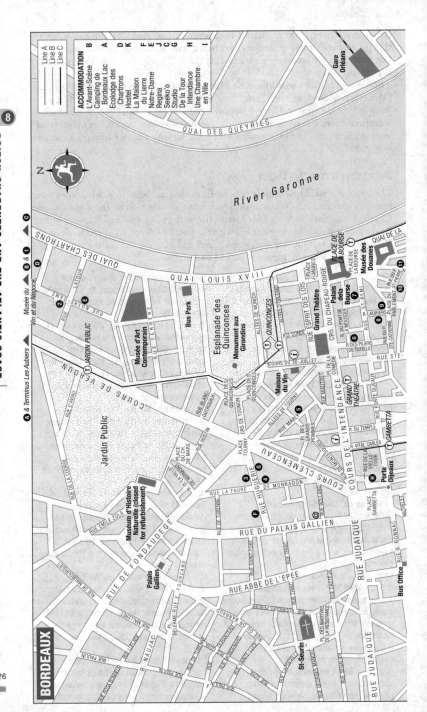

BORDEAUX

N

River Garonne

QUAI DES QUEYRIES

Gare Orléans

A & Terminus Les Aubiers

Musée du Vin et du Négoce

QUAI DES CHARTRONS

QUAI LOUIS XVIII

PLACE DE LA BOURSE

QUAI DE LA

QUAI DES DOUANES

Musée des Douanes

Line A
Line B
Line C

ACCOMMODATION
L'Avant-Scène   B
Camping de
  Bordeaux Lac   A
Écolodge des
  Chartrons   D
Hostel   K
La Maison
  du Lierre   F
Notre-Dame   E
Regina   J
Seeko'o   C
Studio   G
De la Tour
  Intendance   H
Une Chambre
  en Ville   I

RUE NOTRE-DAME
RUE FERRÈRE
RUE LATOUR

JARDIN PUBLIC

Musée d'Art
Contemporain

Bus Park

Esplanade des
Quinconces

Monument aux
Girondins

ALLÉES D'ORLÉANS

ALLÉES DE MUNICH

COURS DE VERDUN

Jardin Public

Muséum d'Histoire
Naturelle (closed
for refurbishment)

RUE D'AVIAU

RUE DE LA COURSE

RUE ÉMILE ZOLA

Palais
Gallien

RUE DE FONDAUDÈGE

RUE DE MAUBOURGUET

RUE DE LA VILLE
PLACE DU
DR L'HONNEUR
PLACE DU DOCTEUR
DE MARS

RUE HUSTIN

PLACE
TOURNY

Maison
du Vin

ALLÉES DE TOURNY

RUE BLANC
(AUTROUBE)

PLACE DES
QUINCONCES

CRS DE TOUNON

RUE MABLY

PLACE DES
GRANDS
HOMMES

RUE MONTESQUIEU

COURS DE L'INTENDANCE

GRAND THÉÂTRE

COURS DU 30-JUILLET

Grand Théâtre

Palais
de la
Bourse

PLACE
J-JAURÈS

RUE ESPRIT DES LOIS

RD CONDÉ

RUE DU CHAPEAU-ROUGE

RUE DU PONT DE
LA MOUSQUE

CRS. DU CHAPEAU-ROUGE

RUE DE LA
COMÉDIE

RUE ST-RÉMI

PLACE DU
PARLEMENT

RUE DES PILIERS
DE TUTELLE

RUE LAURIERS

RUE DU P

RUE STE-CATHERINE

RUE DE

RUE STE-

COURS CLEMENCEAU

RUE HUGUERIE

RUE LA FAURE

RUE TIBERNE

DE MONBADON

RUE SAINT-FORT

RUE THIAC

RUE DU PALAIS GALLIEN

RUE ABBÉ DE L'ÉPÉE

RUE E. FOURCAND

RUE F. DELERME

RUE DR BARRAUD

RUE RODRIGUES PEREIRE

RUE DES MARTYRS
DE LA RÉSISTANCE

St-Seurin

RUE JUDAÏQUE

RUE JUDAÏQUE

RUE G. BONNAC

RUE BONNAC

Bus Office

RUE CASTÉJA

RUE MALLERET

RUE DU TEMPLE

RUE VITAL CARLES

RUE PORTE DIJEAUX

Porte
Dijeaux

PLACE
GAMBETTA

GAMBETTA

MICHELET

RUE DE LA VIEILLE
TOUR

RUE ROLLAND

RUE DE GRASSI

RUE SÉGALIER

RUE LAPEVERIE

RUE SAINTE-LUCE

RUE TURENNE

RUE DE L'ORME

RUE SAINT-SERNIN

RUE PAULIN

RUE NAUJAC

RUE LIBÉRÉ

RUE MALLERET

RUE DES
FRÈRES BONIE

RUE GOYA

RUE PADOU

RUE ROSA BONHEUR

RUE GEORGES MANDEL

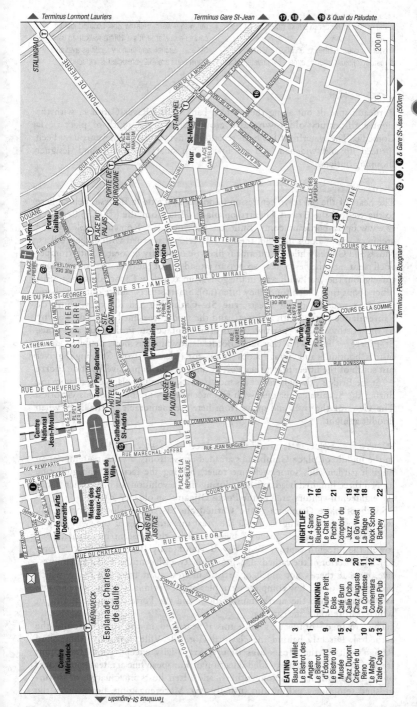

of the centre by Bordeaux's lake (tramline C to Les Aubiers).

Hostel 22 cours Barbey ⓣ05.56.91.59.51, ⓔresa@bxaj.au. A slightly expensive private hostel, but with a warm, relaxed vibe. Located just off cours de la Marne, it's a 10min walk from gare St-Jean. Kitchen and laundry facilities available. Dorm beds are €22; breakfast is included.

The City

Bordeaux spreads out along the western bank of the River Garonne, with the eighteenth-century **old town** based around and to the south of place de la Comédie. The waterfront has been recently reinvigorated; boulevards have been spruced up and widened, and are lined with smart restaurants and designer shopping outlets.

Vieux Bordeaux

The heart of the old town centres on imposing **place de la Bourse**. Behind here to the west, is the **Grand Théâtre** on **place de la Comédie** (ⓣ05.56.00.85.95, ⓦwww.opera-bordeaux.com). Built on the site of a Roman temple by the architect Victor Louis in 1780, the lofty exterior is adorned with endless pillars, Muses and Graces while the interior is likewise opulently decorated with trompe-l'oeil paintings; the best way to see it is to attend one of the operas or ballets staged throughout the year, with seats in the gods from as little as €8, or ask at the tourist office about the guided tours they offer (€6). Smart streets radiate out from here: the city's main shopping streets, **rue Ste-Catherine** and the ritzy **cours de l'Intendance** to the south and west, and the sandy, tree-lined **allées de Tourny** to the northwest. The narrow streets around **place du Parlement** and **place St-Pierre** – lined with charming Bordelais townhouses now doubling up as bistros, boutiques and vintage shops – make for a pleasant stroll. Crossing the river just south of the fifteenth-century Porte Cailhau is the impressive **Pont de Pierre** – "Stone Bridge", though in fact it's mostly brick – built at Napoleon's command during the Spanish campaigns, with seventeen arches in honour of his victories. The views of the river and quays from here are memorable, particularly when floodlit at night.

Place Gambetta, the cathedral and around

In the middle of **place Gambetta**'s arcaded house fronts, a valiant attempt at an English garden adds some welcome relief, belying the fact that the guillotine lopped three hundred heads off here during the Revolution. In one corner stands the eighteenth-century arch of the **Porte Dijeaux**, an old city gate.

South of place Gambetta is the **Cathédrale St-André** (closed Mon morn), whose most eye-catching feature is the great upward sweep of the twin steeples over the north transept, an effect heightened by the adjacent but separate bell tower, the fifteenth-century **Tour Pey-Berland** (daily 10am–1.15pm & 2–6pm; €5). The interior of the cathedral, begun in the twelfth century, is vast and impressive, even if there's not much of artistic interest apart from the choir, which provides one of the few complete examples of the florid late Gothic style known as Rayonnant, and the north transept door and the Porte Royale to the right, which feature some fine carving.

The cream of Bordeaux's museums is scattered in the streets around the cathedral. Directly behind the classical Hôtel de Ville, formerly Archbishop Rohan's palace, the **Musée des Beaux-Arts** (daily except Tues 11am–6pm; free) has a small but star-studded selection of European fine art, featuring works by Titian and Rubens among others, and often hosts imaginative or distinguished temporary exhibitions (usually €5). More engaging, however, is the

Musée des Arts Décoratifs (daily except Tues 2–6pm; free), two blocks north on rue Bouffard and housed in a handsome eighteenth-century house; the exhibits are fine paintings, porcelain and furniture. The museum's *salon de thé* is well worth a visit.

Continuing to circle clockwise round the cathedral, you'll pass the **Centre National Jean-Moulin** (Tues–Sun 2–6pm; free), an interesting museum dedicated to the local Resistance, featuring a history of the occupation of Bordeaux and a harrowing permanent exhibit of Holocaust-inspired paintings by French artist J.J. Morran. South of here is the **Musée d'Aquitaine**, on cours Pasteur (Tues–Sun 11am–6pm; free), one of the city's best museums, tracing its development since Roman times through a variety of objects and art. If archeological bric-a-brac is not your bag you might want to move swiftly through the ground floor, but the upstairs is more varied, including a section on the wine trade and some documentary films with old footage of prewar Aquitaine life.

North of the centre

North of the Grand Théâtre, cours du 30-Juillet leads into the bare, gravelly expanse of the **esplanade des Quinconces**, crowned at the western end by the **Monument aux Girondins**, a glorious *fin-de-siècle* ensemble of statues and fountains built in honour of the influential local deputies to the 1789 Revolutionary Assembly, later purged by Robespierre as moderates and counter-revolutionaries. During World War II, in a fit of anti-French spite, the occupying Germans made plans to melt the monument down, only to be foiled by the local Resistance, who got there first and, under cover of darkness, dismantled it piece by piece and hid it in a barn in the Médoc for the duration of the war.

To the northwest is the beautiful formal park, the **Jardin Public**, containing the city's botanical gardens as well as a small **natural history museum** (closed for refurbishment until 2012). Behind it, to the west and north, lies a quiet, provincial quarter of two-storey stone houses among which, on rue du Dr Albert Barraud, sit the remains of the **Palais Gallien**, in fact a third-century arena that's all that remains of Burdigala, Aquitaine's Roman capital. Nearby, on place Delerme, the unusual round **market hall** makes a focus for a stroll through the quarter.

To the east of the gardens, closer to the river, the **Musée d'Art Contemporain** on rue Ferrère (Tues & Thurs–Sun 11am–6pm, Wed 11am–8pm; €5) occupies a converted nineteenth-century warehouse. The vast, arcaded hall is magnificent in its own right and provides an ideal setting for the mostly post-1960 sculpture and installation-based work by artists such as Richard Long and Sol LeWitt. The main space is usually filled by temporary exhibitions. There's a superb collection of glossy art books in the library and an elegant café-restaurant on the roof (lunch only). Following the curve of the river north from here, you soon reach the down-at-heel but historic former wine trade district of **Chartrons**. A little off the beaten track, the area has developed a distinct bohemian edge, with antiques shops, artists' ateliers and some excellent restaurants. The quayside is taken over with a delectable, sprawling farmers' market every Sunday. The worthwhile **Musée du Vin et du Négoce** (daily 10am–6pm; €7) is a ten-minute walk from here on rue Borie where the history of the wine trade, with an inevitable focus on Bordeaux, is engagingly presented.

Eating and drinking

Bordeaux is packed with **restaurants**, many of them top-notch, and due to its proximity to the Atlantic coast, fresh seafood features prominently on many a Bordelais menu. A large number of fast-food joints are dotted about the city, but there are also some more upmarket options, particularly around place du Parlement and towards Chartrons. For **picnic fodder**, head to the **market** in the place des Grands-Hommes, while on rue de Montesquieu (just off place des Grands-Hommes), Jean d'Alos runs the city's best *fromagerie*, with dozens of farm-produced cheeses. The student population ensures a collection of young, lively **bars**, especially around place de la Victoire, while the city has a strong **gay scene**. Several venues offer live music and the weekend generally seems to begin on Thursdays.

Cafés and restaurants

Baud et Millet 19 rue Huguerie ☏05.56.79.05.77. The ultimate cheese-and-wine feast consumed around a few tables at the back of a wine shop where you choose your own bottle from the shelves. Portions are generous and the food rich, so one dish goes a long way. You can have a platter of cheese and cold meat with wine for €12.50, while *raclette* is another option. Closed Sun.

Le Bistrot des Anges 19 rue Rode, Marché des Halles ☏05.56.79.14.57. This is one of many lovely bistros that set up tables in the market square in the evenings. Cheerful and animated, it is a great place to spend a balmy evening. Favourite dishes include a goat cheese and duck salad (€12) and some of the finest chocolate-based desserts known to man, such as a baked chocolate fondant pudding with home-made vanilla ice cream.

Le Bistrot d'Édouard 16 place du Parlement ☏05.56.81.48.87. In a great position on a lovely square, with outdoor seating in summer, this is a perfect spot to enjoy a three-course *menu* for €13.50.

Le Bistro du Musée 37 place Pey-Berland ☏05.56.54.99.69. Under the spires of the cathedral, this formal restaurant has first-rate service and serves beautifully presented traditional cuisine such as duck breast, *pommes dauphinoises* and an orange reduction; *menus* from €23.50.

Chez Dupont 45 rue de Notre-Dame ☏05.56.81.49.59. Bustling, old-fashioned restaurant in the Chartrons district, with wooden floors, old posters and waiters sporting colourful waistcoats. Prices are very reasonable, with a *plat du jour*, fresh from the market, for €8.50.

Crêperie du Reno 34 rue du Parlement St-Pierre. A colourful restaurant whose kitchen is in one corner of the dining room. It also has seats outside on a pleasant pedestrian street. *Galettes* are €8 or you could go for the lunchtime *menu* for €9.

Le Mably 12 rue Mably ☏05.56.44.30.10. Informal, friendly and popular restaurant with a warm, homely atmosphere. The food is of excellent quality and very traditional, most dishes featuring either duck or rabbit. *Menus* from €22. Closed Sun, Mon & three weeks in August.

Table Cayo 19 rue du Cerf Volant ☏05.56.44.16.36. Warm and elegant restaurant not far from Porte Cailhau, delighting guests with a blend of traditional Basque and French cuisine, creatively presented, such as veal in a delicately spiced sauce on a stack of seasonal vegetables. *Menus* from €23.

Bars

L'Autre Petit Bois Place du Parlement. Along with its sister *Le Petit Bois* on rue du Chai des Farines, this hip bar has a loyal fan base thanks in no small part to the efficient bar staff. Quaint and chintzy with a great wine list and selection of sharing platters, this is the best spot for an early evening aperitif.

Café Brun 45 rue Rémi. A classic bar popular with students for its warm welcome and reasonably priced beer. What it lacks in cleanliness it makes up for with atmosphere and a late licence. If you ask nicely, you can bring food in as they don't have a kitchen.

Calle Ocho 24 rue des Piliers-de-Tutelle. Bordeaux's best-known salsa bar has an unrivalled party atmosphere and is packed out most nights till 2am. They serve real Cuban rum and *mojitos*, and the self-inebriating bar staff frequently showers the crowds with water sprayed from the bar tap.

Chez Auguste Place de la Victoire. Friendly bar with plenty of outside seating on the sunny side of the square, loved by a young crowd for the cocktail list as long as your arm.

La Comtesse 25 rue du Parlement. Beautiful young things fill up this trendy music bar nearly every night of the week, sipping on pricey drinks and chatting under moody lighting, while the jukebox keeps the beat.

Connemara 18 cours d'Albret. As typical an Irish pub as ever you'll find, the Guinness is cold and the football always pulls a good crowd. Happy hour is 6–8pm daily, and they host weekly free live music and open mic nights.

Strong Pub 43 rue Lafaurie de Monbadon. A great watering hole for the gay community, set out like an English pub with stools at the bar and good range of beers, and a few bear (the animal) posters. Lively themed parties take place once a month.

Nightlife and entertainment

Since Bordeaux's **clubs** are constantly changing it's best to ask around for the latest hotspots, but the majority of clubs are spread out along southerly quai de Paludate, where things don't really get going until one in the morning and continue till closing time at four. The best **publication** on music is *Clubs & Concerts*, a monthly low-down revealing what's on in the major venues. The tourist office also issues *Bordeaux Magazine*, a free monthly in French with coverage of more highbrow cultural events around town. To buy **tickets** for city and regional events, contact the venue direct or head for the Box Office (℡05.56.48.26.26, ⊕www.box-office.fr) in the nineteenth-century Galerie Bordelaise arcade, wedged between rue Ste-Catherine and rue des Piliers-de-Tutelle. Virgin Megastore (℡05.56.56.05.55) on place Gambetta also has a ticket outlet, as does the FNAC on rue Ste-Catherine (℡05.56.00.21.30).

Clubs and venues

Le 4 Sans 40 rue d'Armagnac ⊕www.le4sans .com. Showcases alternative music (mainly electro and techno) and often hosts international DJs. Open weekends until 4am.

Blueberry 61 rue Sauvageau ℡05.56.94.16.87. A great place for live jazz, notable for its discerning crowd and fruity cocktail menu. Open until 2am daily except Sunday.

Le Chat Qui Peche 50 cours de la Marne ℡05.56.31.11.39. Favourite with students for the great-value drinks and jazz on offer.

Comptoir du Jazz 57 quai du Paludate ⊕www .leportdelalune.com. Charges next to nothing for

the privilege of watching live jazz and blues into the wee small hours.

Le Go West 3 rue Duffour-Dubergier ⊕www .legowest.com. Uber-modern gay club aimed mostly at boys but welcomes lesbians and gay-friendly straights. Open until 2am.

La Plage 40 quai du Paludate ℡05.56.43.08.46. Fun, cheesy disco in a tropical-beach setting, open daily until 4am.

Rock School Barbey 18 cours Barbey ⊕www .rockschool-barbey.com. Those prone to falling for the frontman can head to Bordeaux's home of rock music, the *Rock School Barbey*, which hosts recognized international bands quite regularly.

Listings

Bike rental Liberty Cycles (℡05.56.92.77.18; closed Sat afternoon & Sun) at 104 cours de l'Yser rents out bikes from €9 per day. Another option is Station Vélo Services, just down the road at 48 cours de l'Yser. Both shops also do repairs.

Books and newspapers Presse Gambetta, on place Gambetta, sells all the main English-language papers in addition to some regional guides and maps, while Bordeaux's largest bookstore, Mollat, 15 rue Vital Carles, has a better selection. They also stock a few English-language titles, though there's more choice at helpful Bradley's Bookshop, 8 cours d'Albret.

Car rental Numerous rental firms are located in and around the train station, including Europcar ℡05.56.33.87.40; Hertz ℡05.57.59.05.95; and National/Citer ℡05.56.92.19.62. They all have outlets at the airport as well.

Cinema Original-language (*version originale* or *v.o.*) films at the wonderful art-house cinema

Utopia, 5 place Camille-Jullian (℡05.56.52.00.03, ⊕www.cinemas-utopia.org), in a converted church. For more standard fare, there's the vast, seventeen-screen Megarama (℡08.92.69.33.17, ⊕www.megarama.fr) across the Pont de Pierre in the old Gare d'Orléans. The free weekly *Bordeaux Plus* has details of other cinemas and full programmes.

Consulates UK, 353 bd du Président-Wilson ℡05.57.22.21.10; USA, 10 place de la Bourse ℡05.56.48.63.80.

Health Centre Hospitalier Pellegrin-Tripode, place Amélie Raba-Léon (℡05.56.79.56.79), to the west of central Bordeaux.

Internet Iphone, 24 rue du Palais Gallien (daily 10am–midnight), or La Cyb, 23 cours Pasteur (daily), though the latter has the disadvantage of crowds of enthusiastic internet gamers.

Police Commissariat Central, 23 rue François-de-Sourdis (℡05.57.85.77.77 or ℡17 in emergencies).

The Bordeaux wine region

Touring the **vineyards** and sampling a few local wines is one of the great pleasures of the Bordeaux region. The wine-producing districts lie in a great semicircle around the city, starting with the **Médoc** in the north, then skirting east through **St-Émilion**, before finishing south of the city among the vineyards of the **Sauternes**. In between, the less prestigious districts are also worth investigating, notably those of **Blaye**, to the north of Bordeaux, and **Entre-Deux-Mers**, to the east.

There's more to the region than its wine, however. Many of the Médoc's eighteenth-century châteaux are striking buildings in their own right, while the town of Blaye is dominated by a vast fortress, and there's a far older, more ruined castle at Villandraut on the edge of the Sauternes. St-Émilion is the prettiest of the wine towns, and has the unexpected bonus of a cavernous underground church. For scenic views, however, you can't beat the green, gentle hills of Entre-Deux-Mers and its ruined abbey, **La Sauve-Majeure**.

The main towns are well served by **public transport**, but to fully explore the region and its châteaux you need your own wheels. There are train lines from Bordeaux running north through the Médoc to Margaux and Pauillac, and south along the Garonne valley to St-Macaire and La Réole. St-Émilion, meanwhile, lies on the Bordeaux–Sarlat line, but the station is a couple of kilometres out of town. In addition, there's a very comprehensive regional bus network for which you can pick up timetables from the office on allées de Munich in Bordeaux. Buses are operated by several different companies, the largest being Citram Aquitaine (☎05.56.43.68.43). **Cycling** is another option, as many of the towns are interconnected by well-marked, clean, tarmac cycle-paths that wend their way through the woods.

The Médoc

The landscape of **the Médoc**, a slice of land northwest of Bordeaux wedged between the forests bordering the Atlantic coast and the Gironde estuary, is itself rather monotonous: its gravel plains, occupying the west bank of the brown, island-spotted estuary, rarely swell into anything resembling a hill. Paradoxically, however, this poor soil is ideal for viticulture – vines root more deeply if they don't find the sustenance they need in the topsoil and, firmly rooted, they are less subject to drought and flooding. The D2 wine road, heading off the N15 from Bordeaux, passes through Margaux, St-Julien, Pauillac and St-Estèphe and, while the scenery might not be stunning, the many famous – albeit mostly inaccessible – châteaux are. **Accommodation** is not plentiful in the Médoc, so an alternative is to visit the area on a day-trip from Bordeaux.

Château Margaux

Easily the prettiest of the Bordeaux châteaux, Château Margaux (by appointment only Mon–Fri; closed Aug and during harvest; ☎05.57.88.83.83, ⓦwww .chateau-margaux.com; free) is an eighteenth-century villa set in extensive, sculpture-dotted gardens close to the west bank of the Gironde, some 20km north of Bordeaux. Its wine, a classified Premier Grand Cru and world-famous in the 1940s and 1950s, went through a rough patch in the two succeeding decades but improved in the 1980s after the estate was bought by a Greek family. The château does not offer tastings or sell directly, but you can visit the grounds if you book a couple of weeks in advance.

In the small village of **MARGAUX** itself, there's a friendly **Maison du Vin** (June–Sept Mon–Sat 10am–1pm & 2–6pm, Sun 11am–1pm & 2–5pm; Oct–May

With Burgundy and Champagne, the **wines of Bordeaux** form the "Holy Trinity" of French viticulture. Despite producing as many whites as reds, it is the latter – known as claret to the British – that have graced the tables of the discerning for centuries. The countryside that produces them encircles the city, enjoying near-perfect climatic conditions and soils ranging from limestone to sand and pebbles. It's the largest quality wine district in the world, turning out around 500 million bottles a year – over half the country's quality wine output and ten percent, by value, of the world's wine trade. While the niche market of the big names is largely immune to economic factors, smaller châteaux have been feeling the squeeze of competition from the new world in recent years and have been forced to be more inventive. One result is a growing fashion for "green" or organic wines.

The Gironde estuary, fed by the Garonne and the Dordogne, determines the lie of the land. The **Médoc** lies northwest of Bordeaux between the Atlantic coast and the River Gironde, with its vines deeply rooted in poor, gravelly soil, producing good, full-bodied red wines; the region's **eight appellations** are Médoc, Haut Médoc, St-Estèphe, Pauillac, St-Julien, Moulis en Médoc, Listrac-Médoc and Margaux. Southwest of Bordeaux are the vast vineyards of **Graves**, producing the best of the region's dry white wines, along with some punchy reds, from some of the most prestigious communes in France – Pessac, Talence, Martillac and Villenave d'Ornon among them. They spread down to Langon and envelop the areas of **Sauternes** and **Barsac**, whose extremely sweet white dessert wines are considered among the world's best.

On the east side of the Gironde estuary and the Dordogne, the **Côtes de Blaye** feature some good-quality white table wines, mostly dry, and a smaller quantity of reds. The **Côtes de Bourg** specialize in solid whites and reds, spreading down to the renowned **St-Émilion** area. Here, there are a dozen producers who have earned the accolade of **Premiers Grands Crus Classés**, and their output is a full, rich red wine that doesn't have to be kept as long as the Médoc ones. Lesser-known neighbouring areas include the vineyards of **Pomerol**, **Lalande** and **Côtes de Francs**, all producing reds similar to St-Émilion but at more affordable prices.

Between the Garonne and the Dordogne is **Entre-Deux-Mers**, an area which yields large quantities of inexpensive, drinkable table whites, mainly from the Sauvignon grape. Stretching along the north bank of the Garonne, the vineyards of the **Côtes de Bordeaux** feature fruity reds and a smaller number of dry and sweet whites.

The **classification** of Bordeaux wines is an extremely complex affair. Apart from the usual *appellation d'origine contrôlée* (AOC) labelling – guaranteeing origin but not quality – the wines of the Médoc châteaux are graded into five crus, or growths. These were established as long ago as 1855, based on the prices the wines had fetched over the last few hundred years. Four were voted the best or **Premier Grand Cru Classé**: Margaux, Lafite, Latour and Haut-Brion. With the exception of Château Mouton-Rothschild, which moved up a class in 1973 to become the fifth *Premier Grand Cru Classé*, there have been no official changes, so divisions between the *crus* should not be taken too seriously.

If you're interested in **buying wines**, head for the châteaux themselves, where you'll get the best price and the opportunity to sample and receive expert advice before purchasing. To **visit the châteaux**, ask at the Maison du Vin in each wine-producing village. In Bordeaux, the best place to sample wines is La Vinothèque. (Mon–Sat 10am–7.30pm), next to the tourist office. The tourist office offers **guided tours**, covering all the main wine areas (from €28 per person). Generally interesting and informative, the guide translates the wine-maker's commentary into English and answers any questions. Tastings are generous, and expert tuition on how to go about it is part of the deal.

Mon–Sat 10am–1pm & 2–6pm; ℡05.57.88.70.82) that can help find accommodation and advise on visits to the *appellation*'s châteaux. At the other end of the village, the enterprising and inviting cellar La Cave d'Ulysse (daily 9am–7pm, closed Sun in winter; ⓦwww.caveulysse.com) provides free tastings from a variety of Margaux châteaux, giving you a chance to try and buy (and ship, if you need) some very good wines. Prices range from a €5 run-of-the-mill Médoc to €2400 for a delicate, rare 1990 Petrus. Margaux has a very comfortable **hotel**, *Le Pavillon de Margaux* (℡05.57.88.77.54, ⓦwww.pavillondemargaux.com; ❺). They also serve a selection of tasty charcuterie and cheese platters to accompany your glass, or bottle, of wine from the bar. Otherwise, try the *chambre d'hôte Le Domaine les Sapins* (℡05.56.58.18.26; ❷) in Moulis, 10km to the west.

Fort Médoc

The seventeenth-century Fort Médoc sits off the D2 road between Margaux and St-Julien by the banks of the estuary. It was designed by the prolific military architect Vauban to defend the Gironde estuary against the British. The remains of the fort are scant but scrambleable, and in summer its Toytown aspect has a leafy charm, marred only by the view of a nuclear power station across the river to the north of Blaye. A little further south, **LAMARQUE** is a very pretty village, full of flowers and centred around a church with a distinctive, minaret-like tower. A couple of kilometres from the village is the port, from which you can take a ferry (4–9 daily; one-way passengers €3.10, cycles €1.60, cars €13) across the muddy Gironde to Blaye (see opposite). It's also a pleasant place to stop for refreshments, with a couple of café-restaurants with outside seating, including *L'Escale* (*menus* from €12; closed Tues & eve off season).

Pauillac and around

PAUILLAC is the largest town in the Médoc region and central to the most important vineyards of Bordeaux: no fewer than three of the top five *grands crus* come from around here.

The huge **Maison du Tourisme et du Vin** along the waterfront (July & Aug Mon–Sat 9.30am–7pm, Sun 10am–1pm & 2–6pm; Sept–June Mon–Sat 9.30am–12.30pm & 2–6.30pm, Sun 10.30am–12.30pm & 3–6pm; ℡05.56.59.03.08, ⓦwww.pauillac-medoc.com) can provide you with a list of *gîtes* and, for a modest fee, make appointments for you to visit the surrounding châteaux. To explore the area by **bike**, head to Sport Nature, 6 rue Joffre (℡05.57.75.22.60), which has decent rates for full-or half-day rental, though it's best to reserve in advance. Pauillac itself is not a great **place to stay**, but should you wish to, try the *Hôtel de France et d'Angleterre*, opposite the little harbour (℡05.56.59.01.20, ⓦwww.hoteldefrance-angleterre.com; closed Christmas & New Year; ❸), with a good restaurant (closed Sun off-season), or the welcoming riverfront **campsite** further south on route de la Rivière (℡05.56.59.10.03; April–Sept). Campsites are rare in the Médoc: the only other alternative is the three-star *Camping Le Paradis* at **ST-LAURENT-DE-MÉDOC** (℡05.56.59.42.15, ⓦwww.leparadismedoc.com; March–Oct).

The most famous of the **Médoc châteaux** – Château Lafite-Rothschild (9km northwest of Pauillac; ℡05.56.73.18.18), Château Latour (3km south of Pauillac; ℡05.56.73.19.80) and Château Mouton-Rothschild (8km northwest of Pauillac; ℡05.56.73.21.29) – can be visited by appointment only, either direct (all have English-speaking staff) or through the Maison du Vin. Their vineyards occupy larger single tracts of land than elsewhere in the Médoc, and consequently neighbouring wines can differ markedly: a good vintage Lafite is perfumed and refined, whereas a Mouton-Rothschild is strong and dark and should be kept for at least ten years. **Château Mouton-Rothschild** and its wine **museum** (which can only be visited as part of the tour; €6 or €25 with a tasting) is the most absorbing of the big houses: as well as the viticultural stuff, you also get to see the Rothschilds' amazing collection of art treasures, all loosely connected with wine.

St-Estèphe

North of Pauillac, the wine commune of **ST-ESTÈPHE** is Médoc's largest *appellation*, consisting predominantly of *crus bourgeois* properties and growers belonging to the local *cave coopérative*, **Marquis de St-Estèphe**, on the D2 towards Pauillac (tastings July & Aug daily 10am–noon & 2–6pm; Sept–June by appointment; ☏05.56.73.35.30). One of the *appellation*'s five *crus classés* is the distinctive **Château Cos d'Estournel**, with its over-the-top nineteenth-century French version of a pagoda; the *chais* (warehouses) can be visited by appointment (Mon–Fri; ☏05.56.73.15.50; English spoken, reserve a week ahead). The village of St-Estèphe itself is a sleepy affair dominated by its landmark, the eighteenth-century **church of St-Étienne**, with its highly decorative interior. The small, homespun **Maison du Vin** (June & Sept Mon–Fri 10am–5pm, Sat 1.30–5.30pm; July & Aug Mon–Sat 10am–7pm; Oct–May Mon–Fri 10am–12.30pm & 1.30–5pm; ☏05.56.59.30.59, ⊛www.vins-saint-estephe.com) is hidden in the church square.

Château Pomys (☏05.56.59.73.44; ⊛www.chateaupomys.com; ❺), just south of the village, is an elegant place to **stay**. There are also several good *chambres d'hôtes* in the area – ask at the tourist office for a list.

Blaye

The green slopes north of the Garonne, the **Côtes de Bourg** and **Côtes de Blaye**, were home to wine production long before the Médoc was planted. The wine is a rather heavier, plummier red, and cheaper than anything found on the opposite side of the river. The **Maison du Vin des Premières Côtes de Blaye** on cours Vauban (Mon–Sat 8.30am–12.30pm & 2–6.30pm), the main street of the pretty little town of **BLAYE**, serves a representative selection of the local produce, with some ridiculously inexpensive wines – you can get a good bottle for around €5.

Blaye has long played a strategic role defending Bordeaux, and was fortified by Vauban in the seventeenth century. The cobblestone **citadelle** deserves a wander: people still live here, and it's a strange combination of peaceful village and tourist attraction. A beautiful spot, it has some appealing bar-restaurants and glorious views over the Gironde estuary. Blaye is also the last resting place of the heroic paladin **Roland**, whose body was brought here in 778 after the battle of Roncevaux. However, his mausoleum is now no more than a heap of rocks.

The **tourist office**, at 33 allées Marines (daily 9.30am–12.30pm & 2–5.30pm; closed Sun Oct–March; ☏05.57.42.12.09, ⊛www.tourisme-blaye.com), can reserve rooms and give out details on wine tasting. If you fancy **staying** here, try the outstanding ⚜ *Auberge du Porche*, 5 rue Ernest Régnier (☏05.57.42.22.69, ⊛www.auberge-du-porche.com; ❸), which has finely decorated rooms in an old building on the riverfront. It also has a high-quality but unpretentious restaurant with seasonal *menus* for €22.50 and an excellent local wine list. Alternatively, there's the more expensive *Hôtel La Citadelle* (☏05.57.42.17.10, ⊛www.hotella citadelle.com; ❺, half-board required July & Aug; restaurant from €25) within the old fort, with views over the Garonne and a swimming pool. Finally, there's a small municipal **campsite** spectacularly situated within the citadelle (☏05.57.42.00.20; May–Sept).

St-Émilion

ST-ÉMILION, 35km east of Bordeaux, and a short train trip, is an essential visit. The old grey houses of this fortified medieval town straggle down the steep south-hanging slope of a low hill, with the green froth of the summer's vines crawling over its walls. Many of the growers still keep up the old tradition of planting roses at the ends of the rows, which in pre-pesticide days served as an early-warning system against infection, the idea being that the commonest bug, *oïdium*, went for the roses first, giving three days' notice of its intentions.

Arrival, information and accommodation

The super-efficient **tourist office** on place des Créneaux by the belfry (daily: June–Sept 9.30am–7/8pm; Oct–May 9.30am–12.30pm & 1.30–6/6.30pm; ℡05.57.55.28.28, Ⓦwww.saint-emilion-tourisme.com) organizes guided tours around the town (daily every hour 10am–5pm; €7; one a day in English) as well as bilingual (French and English) vineyard tours in season (June–Sept; €10). They also have **bikes** for rent (€15 per day or €150 per month).

If you're short of funds or without your own transport, St-Émilion is best seen as a day-trip from Bordeaux, as there's a chronic shortage of budget **accommodation** within the town. If you have money to spend, however, try ⚑*Palais Cardinal* (℡05.57.24.72.39, Ⓦwww.palais-cardinal.com; ❻) on place du 11 Novembre 1918, a warm, family-run establishment with a pleasant summer restaurant and a pool in rose-filled gardens. The tourist office can furnish you with an extensive list of *chambres d'hôtes* in the area, many of which are very reasonably priced (from €40). Within the town itself, the two-star *Auberge de la Commanderie* on rue des Cordeliers (℡05.57.24.70.19, Ⓦwww.aubergedelacommanderie.com; closed late-Dec to mid-Feb; ❹) is the cheapest option, although its starkly modernist decor won't be to everybody's taste. Two kilometres northwest on the road to Montagne, there's a fantastic three-star campsite, *La Barbanne* (℡05.57.24.75.80, Ⓦwww.camping-saint-emilion.com; April–Sept).

The Town

The only way to see St Émilion's historical highlights is via a **guided tour** (see above). The tour begins in the **grotte de l'Ermitage**, where St Émilion supposedly lived a hermit's life in the eighth century, with a stone ledge serving as his bed and a carved seat as his chair – infertile women reputedly still come to sit here in the hope of getting pregnant. The tour continues above, in the half-ruined thirteenth-century **Trinity Chapel**, which was built in honour of St Émilion and converted into a cooperage during the Revolution; some strikingly well-preserved frescoes are still visible, including a kneeling figure who is thought to be the saint himself. On the other side of the yard, a passage tunnels beneath the **belfry** to the **catacombs**, where three chambers dug out of the soft limestone were used as ossuary and cemetery from the eighth to the eleventh centuries.

Below is the church itself: simple and huge, the entire structure – barrel-vaulting, great square piers and all – has been hacked out of the rock. The impact has been somewhat diminished, however, by the installation of massive metal supports after cracks were discovered in the unusually tall and heavy bell tower above in 1990. The whole interior was painted once, but only faint traces survived the Revolution, when a gunpowder factory was installed here. These days, every June, the wine council – *La Jurade* – assembles in the church in distinctive red robes to evaluate the previous season's wine and decide whether each *viticulteur*'s produce deserves the *appellation contrôlée* rating.

Behind the tourist office, the town comes to an abrupt end with a grand view of the **moat** and old **walls**. To the right is the twelfth-century **collegiate church**, with a handsome but badly mutilated doorway and a lovely fourteenth-century **cloister**, accessed via the tourist office (same hours; free).

You should take advantage of the produce of this well-respected wine region, ideally by visiting one of the local vineyards for a tasting: Château Fonplégade (☎05.57.74.43.11) is friendly and convenient from the train station, if a bit expensive, while Château Canon (☎05.57.55.23.45; by appointment only), just west of the town, has impressive buildings and respected wines. The **Maison du Vin**, opposite the tourist office in St-Émilion (daily 10am–12.30pm & 2–6pm; ⓦwww.vins-saint-emilion.com), has a small, free interactive museum and can advise further on which vineyards to visit as well as itself selling wine from the region at reasonable prices.

Eating and drinking

You should try the town's foodie speciality while you're here: **macaroons** were devised here by the Ursuline sisters in 1620, and the one authentic place to buy them is at the Fabrique de Macarons, 9 rue Guadet, where the tiny melt-in-the-mouth biscuits are baked to the original recipe. An excellent place for a **meal** is the relaxed contemporary bistro *L'Envers du Décor* (closed Sun Nov–April) on rue du Clocher, with a creative *menu* for €29 and local wine by the glass. Alternatively, try the homely-looking *Les Giron Dines* at 5 rue des Girondins, which has a fine *menu* for €19.50 and a lovely terrace.

Entre-Deux-Mers

The landscape of **Entre-Deux-Mers** (literally "between two seas") – so called because it's sandwiched between the tidal waters of the Dordogne and Garonne – is the prettiest of the Bordeaux wine regions, with its gentle hills and scattered medieval villages. Its wines, including the *Premières Côtes de Bordeaux*, are mainly dry whites produced by over forty *caves coopératives*, and are regarded as good but inferior to the Médocs or super-dry Graves to the south. It's a region which can be explored, at least in part, by public transport.

La Sauve-Majeure

One place you shouldn't miss is the ruined **Abbey** (June–Sept daily 10am–6pm; Oct–May Tues–Sun 10.30am–1pm & 2.30–5.30pm; €6.50) at **LA SAUVE-MAJEURE**, some 25km east of Bordeaux, an important stop for pilgrims en route to Santiago de Compostela in Spain. It was once all forest here, the abbey's name being a corruption of the Latin *silva major* (big wood). Founded in 1079, the treasures of what remains are the twelfth-century Romanesque apse and apsidal chapels and the outstanding sculpted capitals in the chancel. The finest are the ones illustrating stories from the Old and New Testaments (Daniel in the lions' den and so on), while others show fabulous beasts and decorative motifs. There is a small **museum** at the entrance, with some keystones from the fallen roofs. But what makes the visit so worthwhile is not just the capitals, but the remote, undisturbed nature of the site.

St-Macaire and La Réole

If you're heading south through Entre-Deux-Mers, Langon is the first town of any size you come to. But **ST-MACAIRE**, across the Garonne, is far better for a rest or food stop. The village still has its original **gates** and **battlements** and a beautiful medieval church, the **Église-Prieuré**, with significant, freshly restored wall paintings (the switch to illuminate them is on the left side of the nave by the door to the Sacristie). The **tourist office**, 8 rue Canton (June–Sept daily 10am–1pm & 3–7pm; April & May Tues–Sun same hours; March & Oct Tues–Fri

2–6pm, Sat & Sun 10am–noon & 2–6pm; Nov–Feb same hours, also closed Tues; ℡05.56.63.32.14), also sells delicious local produce, principally honey and wine. Staff can help arrange visits to the *chais*, and in season (July & Aug daily) they organize tastings hosted by various local winemakers. Good-value **accommodation** in the form of studio apartments is offered by *Les Tilleuls* (℡05.56.62.28.38, Ⓦwww.tilleul-medieval.com; ❷), based just outside the medieval city. More elegant, though, is *Les Feuilles d'Acanthe* (℡05.56.62.33.75, Ⓦwww.feuilles -dacanthe.fr; closed mid-Dec to mid-Jan; ❺), opposite the tourist office, whose stone-walled, wooden-beamed rooms offer some fine views out over the rooftops. As well as a jacuzzi and south-facing terrace, the hotel also has one of the town's best **restaurants**, which serves traditional meaty dishes with *menus* from €21.

LA RÉOLE, on the north bank 18km further east, boasts a wealth of medieval architecture among its narrow, hilly streets – pick up a map from the tourist office on place Richard-Coeur-de-Lion. France's oldest **town hall**, constructed for Richard the Lionheart in the twelfth century, and the well-preserved simple **Abbaye des Bénédictins** – with a fantastic view over the River Garonne and the surrounding countryside – reward a stroll through the town, although little remains of the fortified **castle**.

Sauternes and around

The **Sauternes** region, which extends southeast from Bordeaux for 40km along the left bank of the Garonne, is an ancient wine-making area, originally planted during the Roman occupation. The distinctive golden wine of the area is certainly sweet, but also round, full-bodied and spicy, with a long aftertaste. It's not necessarily a dessert wine, either: try it with some Roquefort cheese. Gravelly terraces with a limestone subsoil help create the delicious taste, but mostly it's due to a peculiar microclimate of morning autumn mists and afternoons of sun and heat which causes *Botrytis cinerea* fungus, or "noble rot", to flourish on the grapes, letting the sugar concentrate and introducing some intense flavours. When they're picked, they're not a pretty sight: carefully selected by hand, only the most shrivelled, rotting bunches are taken. The wines of Sauternes are some of the most highly sought-after in the world, with bottles of **Château d'Yquem**, in particular, fetching thousands of euros. Sadly that particular château does not offer tastings, but you can wander around its attractive buildings and grounds, two minutes' drive north of Sauternes.

SAUTERNES itself is a sleepy little village surrounded by vines and dominated by the **Maison du Sauternes** (Mon–Fri 9am–7pm, Sat & Sun 10am–7pm; ℡05.56.76.69.83, Ⓦwww.maisondusauternes.com) at one end of the village, with a pretty church at the other. The *maison* is a room full of treasures, the golden bottles with white and gold labels being quite beautiful objects in themselves. A non-profit organization, it offers tastings, expert advice and unbeatable prices.

For a luxurious place to **stay**, try the sumptuous *Relais du Château d'Arche*, on the D125 just outside Sauternes heading north (℡05.56.76.67.67, Ⓦwww .chateaudarche-sauternes.com; ❼). **Food-wise**, there's the *Auberge Les Vignes*, by the church (℡05.56.76.60.06; closed Sun & Mon eve and Feb), a typical country restaurant with regional specialities like *grillades aux Sauternes* (meats grilled over vine clippings), a great wine list and a lunch *menu* at €13.

Ten kilometres south of Sauternes, the ruinous curtain walls and corner towers of a colossal moated **château** (July & Aug daily 10am–7pm; Sept–June 2–6pm; €3.50) still dominate **VILLANDRAUT**. The castle was built by Pope Clement V, a native of the area who caused a schism by moving the papacy to Avignon in the fourteenth century. You can visit his tomb in the even smaller village of **UZESTE** en route to **BAZAS**, 15km east, which has a laid-back, southern air. Bazas' most attractive feature is the wide, arcaded place de la Cathédrale, overlooked by the grey, lichen-covered **Cathédrale St-Jean-Baptiste**, which displays a harmonious blend of Romanesque, Gothic and classical styles in its west front. On the southern outskirts of the town is a luxurious place to **stay**: the *Domaine de Fompeyre* (T05.56.25.98.00, W www.monalisahotels.com; ⓖ) has tempting rooms set in extensive grounds with a pool. For more modestly priced lodgings, ask at Bazas' tourist office (T05.56.25.25.84, W www.ville-bazas.fr) for the list of *chambres d'hôtes* in the area, whose rates begin at around €45. Don't miss Bazas' excellent **restaurant**, *Les Remparts* (T05.56.25.25.52; closed Sun eve & Mon) on place de la Cathédrale, which has a good view from its terrace and sophisticated, gastronomic cuisine on set *menus* for €25 or €50.

The Côte d'Argent

The **Côte d'Argent** is the long stretch of coast from the mouth of the Gironde estuary to Biarritz, which – at over 200km – is the longest, straightest and sandiest in Europe. The endless beaches are backed by high sand dunes, while behind lies the largest forest in western Europe, **Les Landes**. No motorable road follows the coast for most of the way; instead a cycle path, built at the end of World War II, winds through more than 75km of pine-forested dunes from the upmarket holiday village of Cap Ferret to the resort of Soulac in the north. The lack of conventional tourist sights means that outside July and August the coast gets comparatively few visitors, and away from the main resorts it's still possible to find deserted stretches of coastline.

Arcachon and around

On summer weekends, the Bordelais escape en masse to **ARCACHON**, the oldest resort on the Côte d'Argent and a forty-minute train ride across flat, sandy forest from Bordeaux. The beaches of white sand are magnificent but can be crowded, and its central jetties are busy with boats going off on an array of cruises.

Four little districts quaintly named after the seasons make up the core of the town. The seafront promenades and commercial streets of the **ville d'été** (summer town) are a little tacky these days, especially in summer, but the **ville d'hiver** (winter town) on the hillside south of the beach still retains its former elegance, with wide shady streets full of fanciful, if slightly faded, Second Empire mansions. To reach it, follow the boulevard de la Plage west of Jetée Thiers until you reach the lively pedestrianized rue du Maréchal-de-Lattre-de-Tassigny; at the end of this mouthful of a street, a rather curious public lift carries you up to the flower-filled, wooded **Parc Mauresque** that separates the *ville d'hiver* from the *ville d'été* below. From the park, there are fine views over the seafront. The residential **ville d'automne** (autumn town) stretches east along the boulevard de la Plage, a gentle 15min walk from the *ville d'été*. It's far enough away from the main drag to boast quieter stretches of beach.

At **LE TEICH**, about 14km east of Arcachon, one of the most important expanses of wetlands remaining in France has been converted into a bird sanctuary, the **Parc Ornithologique du Teich** (daily 10am–6pm; €7.20; W www.parc-ornithologique -du-teich.com), one of only two in the country. There's no **accommodation** in Le Teich beyond **campsites**, but it's an easy day-trip by train from Arcachon.

Practicalities

A well-stocked **tourist office**, on esplanade Georges-Pompidou (April–June & Sept Mon–Sat 9am–6.30pm, Sun 10am–1pm & 2–5pm; July & Aug daily 9am–7pm; Oct–March Mon–Fri 9am–6pm, Sat 9am–5pm; T05.57.52.97.97,

Ⓦwww.arcachon.com) is a short, straight walk back from place Thiers. In summer, boats leave the jetties of Thiers and Eyrac on various **cruises**, including the Île aux Oiseaux (1hr 45min; €14), and an exploration of the Arcachon basin with a look at the Dune du Pyla (2hr 45min; €21). There's also a regular boat service from here to Cap Ferret on the opposite peninsula (30min; €11.50 return). Discounted tickets can be purchased for all excursions at the tourist office.

Be prepared to pay resort prices for **hotels** in summer. No one can match the decadent *Arc Hôtel sur Mer* (Ⓣ05.56.83.06.85, Ⓦwww.arc-hotel-sur-mer.com; ❼) at 89 bd de la Plage for its views of the basin, while uphill in the tranquil *ville d'hiver* is *Marinette* (Ⓣ05.56.83.06.67, Ⓦwww.hotel-marinette.com; ❸), 800m from the beach at 15 allée José-Maria de Heredia, with shady rooms in a villa-style building. **Camping** is another option, with plenty of sites around the Arcachon basin, though only the excellent three-star *Le Camping Club*, allée de la Galaxie (Ⓣ05.56.83.24.15), is actually within the town. **Restaurants** can be expensive and disappointingly bland in the centre of town; head away from the pedestrian areas for the best food. The charming *Salon de thé bio* on place Fleming in the *ville d'hiver* serves one or two delicious simple dishes, such as home-made goat's cheese tortilla (€8) and numerous tea varieties, while a 500m walk along boulevard de la Plage towards the *ville d'automne* brings you to a cluster of decent spots, in particular *Calypso*, with Caribbean-style decor and a delicious *bouillabaisse* for €18. There are also some serious gastronomic heavyweights on boulevard du Général-Leclerc, such as *Chez Yvette*, which serves immense seafood platters for €34.

Cap Ferret

Apart from the occasional surf shack or beach restaurant, the only settlements of any size along the coast are **Lacanau–Océan** – with its great beaches and golf courses – and **Cap Ferret**, which can be reached by boat from Arcachon (see p.539). Once considered to be the poor man's Arcachon, the tiny peninsula town of Cap Ferret has been elevated to the summertime playground of the wealthy Paris and Bordeaux bourgeoisie in recent years. **Hotels** here are pricey and exclusive for the most part, but a good bet is *Hôtel des Pins* at 23 rue des Fauvettes (Ⓣ05.56.60.60.11, Ⓦwww.hoteldespins.eu; closed mid-Nov to Jan; ❾), with beautiful gardens and veranda. If funds are low, go for the youth hostel at 87 av de Bordeaux (Ⓣ05.56.60.64.62; open July & Aug only). Some 10km to the north there's a campsite at Grand Crohot, Bremontier (Ⓣ05.56.60.03.99; June to mid-Sept). There are several very smart **restaurants** in Cap Ferret, like chic *Le Chacouette* at 52 bd de la Plage, far enough from the hub of tourist traps along the Allée de la Jetée and serving fine *menus* from €30.

The Dune du Pyla

At over 100m, the **Dune du Pyla** is the highest sand dune in Europe – a mountain of wind-carved sand, about 12km south of Arcachon. Bus #1 leaves from the *gare SNCF* in Arcachon every hour in July and August – two to five a day at other times. If you're driving, it costs €4 to use the obligatory car park. There's the inevitable group of stands selling ice cream, *galettes* and junk, but from the top you get a superb view over the bay of Arcachon and the forest of the Landes stretching away to the south. It's a great sandy slide down to the sea (the sides are as steep as an Olympic ski-jump) and a long haul back up but well worth the effort. A wonderful **hotel** is a short distance from here at **Pyla-sur-Mer**, the ⚶ *Côte du Sud* (Ⓣ05.56.83.25.00, Ⓦwww.cote-du-sud.com; ❻), which has charming themed rooms all facing the sea and a breezy terrace restaurant.

Les Landes

Travelling south from Bordeaux by road or rail, you pass for what seems like hours through an unremittingly flat, sandy pine forest known as **Les Landes**. Containing nearly 10,000 square kilometres of trees and designated a *parc naturel régional* since 1970, it is, in the main, a region for outdoor pursuits rather than cultural enrichment.

Mont-de-Marsan

The administrative centre of Les Landes, **MONT-DE-MARSAN**, 100km south of Bordeaux and served by regular trains, makes a good base for exploring the inland part of the region. The **tourist office** on place du Général-Leclerc (Mon–Sat: July & Aug 9am–6pm; Sept–June 9am—5pm; ☎05.58.05.87.37, ⓦwww.tourisme-montdemarsan.com) can provide you with large-scale maps of local walking and cycling routes (€1.50 each). Another outdoor activity on offer is canoeing on one of the three rivers whose confluence is at Mont-de-Marsan: Canoë Loisir (☎05.58.45.62.21, ⒺCanoe-loisir@orange.fr) is based at Latrillette, just off the N134 to the west of town, and offers half-day trips for €15 per person.

The town itself boasts various medieval remnants, most notably a **twelfth-century keep** which now contains a collection of work by two local sculptors (daily except Tues 10am–noon & 2–6pm; free). The **Parc Jean Rameau**, on the north bank of the river Douze, is the most attractive section of the town; immaculately kept lawns and blooming flowerbeds, interwoven with shady paths, make a great spot to spend a hot afternoon watching the locals play *boules*. If you're lucky enough to be in the area at the right time in summer, you should definitely make the effort to see the **festival** for which Mont-de-Marsan is best known. Les Fêtes Madeleine (mid-July; ⓦwww.fetesmadeleine.fr) consist of a week of parades, sports and carnival atmosphere, when the town's Basque identity is most tangible, with flamenco dancing and bullfighting playing a major role.

Apart from festival period, **accommodation** shouldn't be hard to come by. You could have a reasonably priced luxury stay at *Le Renaissance*, 1km from the centre at 225 av de Villeneuve (☎05.58.51.51.51, ⓦwww.le-renaissance.com; ⑤) with its own outdoor swimming pool and restaurant serving a gastronomic *menu* for €51. Various cheaper and more central options are also available, another good bet being *Le Richelieu*, 3 rue Wlérick (☎05.58.06.10.20, Ⓔle.richelieu@orange.fr; ③), which has comfortable, fully equipped rooms in the heart of the town. For **eating**, good-value brasseries line rue Gambetta, while the *Créperie la Floralie* on rue Wlérick serves a slice of Brittany for €8.50 at lunchtime.

Travel details

Trains

Angoulême to: Bordeaux (20 daily; 1hr–1hr 30min); Limoges (7 daily; 1hr 30min–2hr); Poitiers (23 daily; 40min–1hr 10min); Royan (4 daily; 2hr).
Bordeaux to: Angoulême (13 daily; 1hr–1hr 30min); Arcachon (frequently; 50–55min); Bayonne (7–10 daily; 1hr 40min–2hr 10min); Bergerac (6–10 daily; 1hr 15min–1hr 30min); Biarritz (6–12 daily; 2hr–2hr 45min); Brive (2–4 daily; 2hr 15min); Dax (15 daily; 1hr 10min–1hr 40min);

Hendaye (3–5 daily; 2hr 30min); Irun (3 daily; 2hr 30min); La Rochelle (4–6 daily; 2hr – 2hr 20min); Lourdes (1–3 daily; 2hr 20min–3hr); Marseille (9 daily; 6–7hr); Mont-de-Marsan (7 daily; 1hr 30min); Nice (6 daily; 9–10hr); Paris-Montparnasse (14–18 daily; 3hr–3hr 30min); Périgueux (10–12 daily; 1hr–1hr 25min); Pointe de Grave (frequently to Lesparre; 1hr 45min; then bus 713 to Pointe de Grave 55min, frequently); Poitiers (7–10 daily; 1hr 45min); Saintes (5–10 daily; 1hr 30min); Sarlat (6 daily; 2hr 30min–3hr);

St-Émilion (3–7 daily; 40min); St-Jean-de-Luz
(8–12 daily; 2hr–2hr 40min); Toulouse
(10–17 daily; 2hr–2hr 40min).

La Rochelle to: Bordeaux (7 daily; 2hr 20min); La
Roche-sur-Yon (5 daily; 1hr); Nantes (5 daily; 1hr
50min); Paris-Montparnasse (15–20 daily; 3hr
10min–3hr 30min); Rochefort (frequently; 20min);
Saintes (9 daily; 50min–1hr).

La Roche-sur-Yon to: Les Sables-d'Olonne
(14 daily; 30min).

Les Sables-d'Olonne to: Nantes (10–14 daily;
1hr 30min–1hr 45min).

Poitiers to: Angoulême (17 daily; 45min–1hr 15min);
Bordeaux (3–15 daily; 1hr 45min–2hr 30min);
Châtellerault (12 daily; 20min); La Rochelle (15 daily;
1hr 20min–1hr 45min); Limoges (6–9 daily; 2hr);
Niort (6–14 daily; 45min); Paris-Montparnasse
(frequently; 1hr 45min); Surgères (10–14 daily; 1hr).

Royan to: Saintes (5–7 daily; 30min).

Saintes to: Angoulême (9 daily; 1hr 20min);
Cognac (9 daily; 20min); Rochefort (6 daily; 30min).

Buses

Bordeaux to: Blaye (4–10 daily; 1hr 45min); Cap
Ferret (4–10 daily; 1hr 30min); Lacanau (5 daily;

1hr 25min); La Sauve-Majeure (1–4 daily; 50min);
Margaux (4–10 daily; 45min–1hr); Pauillac
(2–8 daily; 45min–1hr 10min).

La Rochelle to: St-Martin-de-Ré
(6–16 daily; 1hr).

La Roche-sur-Yon to: Cholet (4–6 daily; 1hr
15min); Nantes (3 daily; 1hr 30min); Noirmoutier-
en-l'Île (2–4 daily; 1hr 30min–2hr).

Les Sables-d'Olonne to: Luçon (2–4 daily; 2hr);
La Roche-sur-Yon (8 daily; 45min–1hr).

Parthenay to: Airvault (several daily; 25min);
Niort (8 daily; 50min); Thouars (at least
10 daily; 1hr).

Poitiers to: Châteauroux (2–3 daily; 2hr);
Chauvigny (3–5 daily; 45min); Le Blanc (3–5 daily;
1hr 25min); Limoges (6–8 daily; 2hr 30min);
Parthenay (6–10 daily; 1hr 30min); Ruffec
(7–9 daily; 2hr 30min); St-Savin (3–5 daily;
1hr 30min).

Rochefort to: Château-d'Oléron (8 daily;
50min–1hr 10min); La Fumée-Île-d'Aix (5–8 daily;
40min); Marennes (8 daily; 40min).

Saintes to: Rochefort (4 daily; 1hr 20min);
St-Pierre-d'Oléron (5 daily; 1hr 50min–2hr 20min).

The Limousin, Dordogne and Lot

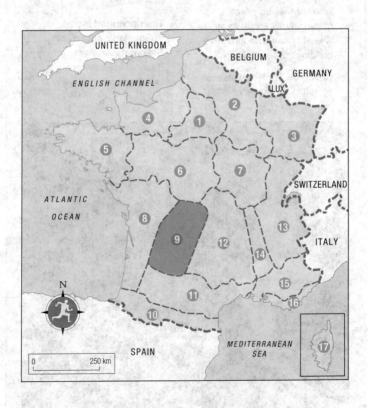

CHAPTER 9   Highlights

* **Cuisine** The Dordogne is the place to sample French country cooking at its best. See p.558

* **Monpazier** An almost perfectly preserved *bastide* (fortified town). See p.566

* **Sarlat** Wander the narrow lanes of this archetypal medieval town, with its *vieille ville* of honey-coloured stone buildings. See p.568

* **Grotte de Font-de-Gaume** Stunning examples of

prehistoric cave art, including the spectacular frieze of five bison. See p.572

* **Châteaux of Beynac and Castelnaud** Two of the region's most majestic castles eye each other across the Dordogne valley. See p.576

* **The carving of Isaiah in Souillac's church of Ste-Marie** An extraordinary masterpiece of Romanesque art. See p.579

▲ *Saucissons* on market stall

The Limousin, Dordogne and Lot

The region covered in this chapter forms a rough oval bordered to the east by the uplands of the Massif Central and to the west by the Atlantic plains. It's the area which was most in dispute between the English and the French during the Hundred Years' War, and has been most in demand among English visitors and second-home buyers in more recent times. Although it doesn't coincide exactly with either the modern French administrative boundaries or the old provinces of Périgord and Quercy, which constitute the core of the region, the land has a physical and geographical homogeneity thanks to its great rivers: the **Dordogne**, the **Lot** and the **Aveyron**, all of which drain westwards from the Massif Central into the mighty **Garonne**, which forms the southern limit covered by this chapter.

The wartime Resistance was very active in these out-of-the-way regions, and the roadsides are dotted with memorials to those killed in ambushes or shot in reprisals. There is also one monstrous monument to wartime atrocity: the ruined village of **Oradour-sur-Glane**, still as the Nazis left it after massacring the population and setting fire to the houses.

From **Limoges** in the province of Limousin in the north to the Garonne valley in the south, the country is gently hilly, full of lush hidden valleys and miles of woodland, mainly oak. The northerly **Limousin** is slightly greener and wetter, the south more open and arid. But you can travel a long way without seeing a radical shift, except in the uplands of the **Plateau de Millevaches**, where the rivers plunge into gorges and the woods are beech, chestnut and conifer plantations. The other characteristic landscape is the *causses*, the dry scrubby limestone plateaux like the **Causse de Gramat** between the Lot and Dordogne and the **Causse de Limogne** between the Lot and Aveyron. Where the rivers have cut their way through the limestone, the valleys are walled with overhanging cliffs, riddled with fissures, underground streams and caves. And in these caves – especially in the valley of the Vézère around **Les Eyzies** – is some of the most awe-inspiring **prehistoric art** to be found anywhere in the world.

The other great artistic legacy of the area is the Romanesque sculpture, most notably adorning the churches at **Souillac** and **Beaulieu-sur-Dordogne**, but all modelled on the supreme example of the cloister of St-Pierre in **Moissac**. And the dearth of luxurious châteaux is compensated for by the numerous splendid

fortresses of purely military design, such as **Bonaguil**, **Najac**, **Biron**, **Beynac** and **Castelnaud**.

There are no great cities in the area: its charm lies in the landscapes and the dozens of harmonious small towns and villages. Some, like **Sarlat** and **Rocamadour**, are so well known that they are overrun with tourists. Others, like **Figeac**, **Villefranche-de-Rouergue**, **Gourdon**, **Montauban**, **Monflanquin** and the

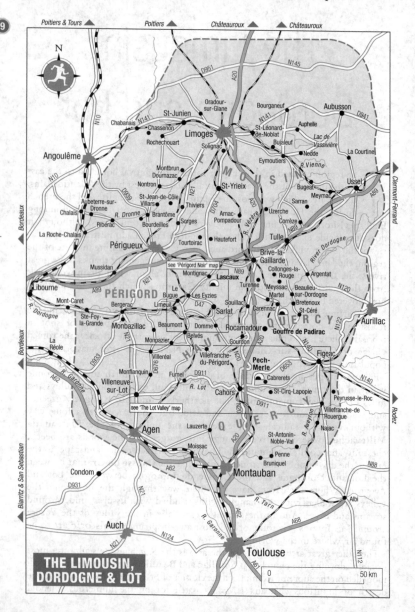

THE LIMOUSIN,
DORDOGNE & LOT

0   50 km

many *bastides* (fortified towns) that pepper the area between the Lot and Dordogne, boast no single notable sight but are perfect organic ensembles.

For **getting around**, all the region's main towns are linked by rail and/or bus services, while a fair number of smaller places have sporadic public transport links. To really make the most of the area, though, particularly the Plateau de Mille-vaches, you'll need your own wheels.

The Limousin

The **Limousin** – the country around **Limoges** – is hilly, wooded, wet and not particularly fertile: ideal pasture for the famous Limousin breed of cattle. This is herdsman's country, from where the widespread use of the shepherd's cape known as a *limousine* gave its name to the big, wraparound covered twentieth-century car.

The modern Limousin region stretches south to the Dordogne valley to include **Brive, Uzerche and Turenne**. But while these places, together with Limoges itself, are not without interest, the star of the show is the countryside – especially in the east on the **Plateau de Millevaches,** between **Eymoutiers** and **Meymac**. Walkers, cyclists and other outdoor sports enthusiasts are well catered for and there are plenty of small hotels, *gîtes* and campsites to accommodate the wanderer.

Limoges

LIMOGES is a pleasant city, if not one that calls for a long stay. Its main draw is the craft industries that made the city a household name: enamel in the Middle Ages and, since the eighteenth century, china, including some of the finest ever produced. If these appeal, then the city's unique museum collections – and its Gothic cathedral – will reward a visit. But it has to be said that the porcelain industry today seems a spent tradition, hard hit by recession and changing tastes among the wealthy. The local *kaolin* (china clay) mines that gave Limoges china its special quality are exhausted, and the workshops survive mainly on the tourist trade, though some are now successfully diversifying into high-tech ceramics.

Arrival, information and accommodation

Limoges's magnificent Art Deco **gare des Bénédictins** and neighbouring **gare routière** (☏ 05.55.45.10.72) lie slightly northeast of the centre on avenue de-Gaulle, where you'll find **car rental** at ADA at no. 27 (☏ 05.55.79.61.12). The **tourist office** is on place Wilson (May to mid-June & mid-Sept to end Sept Mon–Sat 9am–7pm; mid-June to mid-Sept Mon–Sat 9am–7pm, Sun 10am–5.30pm; Oct–April Mon–Sat 9.30am–6pm; ☏ 05.55.34.46.87, ⓦ www.limoges-tourisme.com).

Hotels

Jeanne d'Arc 17 av de-Gaulle ☏ 05.55.77.67.77, ⓦ www.hoteljeannedarc-limoges.fr. The elegant entrance, tastefully decorated rooms and grand breakfast hall make this a more appealing option than the *Mercure* (see below). Rooms with showers are on the small side – better to upgrade to one with a bath, and overlooking the interior courtyard. ❹

Mercure Place de la République ☏ 05.55.34.65.30, ⓦ www.mercure.com. The only

9

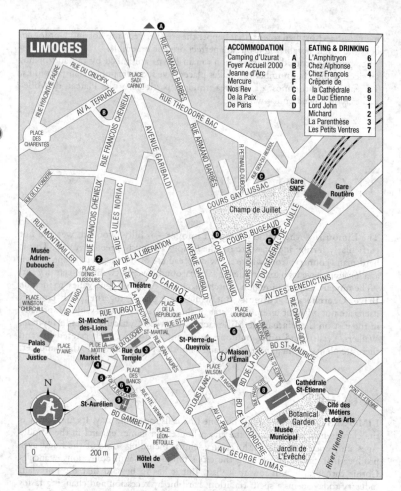

ACCOMMODATION	
Camping d'Uzurat	A
Foyer Accueil 2000	B
Jeanne d'Arc	E
Mercure	F
Nos Rev	C
De la Paix	G
De Paris	D

EATING & DRINKING	
L'Amphitryon	6
Chez Alphonse	5
Chez François	4
Crêperie de la Cathédrale	8
Le Duc Étienne	9
Lord John	1
Michard	2
La Parenthèse	3
Les Petits Ventres	7

hotel in the old quarter, this is a surprisingly unattractive, concrete affair, though the rooms are a decent size and boast three-star facilities, including room service and wi-fi. More expensive rooms have balconies looking over the square. ❺

Nos Rev 16 rue du Général-du-Bessol ☎05.55.77.41.43, ⓦwww.hotelnos-rev.com. The contemporary decor makes this tiny hotel stand out as a mid-range option. It's set back off a quietish street near the station. ❸

De la Paix 25 place Jourdan ☎05.55.34.36.00, ⓕ05.55.32.37.06. A wonderful old hotel, doubling as a museum of gramophones, which decorate the breakfast room in all shapes and sizes. Bedrooms are large and nicely furnished for the price. The cheapest have no en-suite bathrooms. ❷–❸

De Paris 5 cours Vergniaud ☎05.55.77.56.96, ⓦwww.hoteldeparis-limoges.com. You'll need to book ahead for this well-located budget hotel, where good-sized rooms – the cheapest with washbasin only – make up for the rather worn furnishings. ❷

Hostel and campsite

Camping d'Uzurat 40 av d'Uzurat ☎05.55.38.49.43, ⓦwww.campinglimoges.fr. About 5km out of town in Limoges's northern suburbs; take bus #20 from the *gare SNCF*. March–Oct.

Foyer Accueil 2000 20 rue Encombe-Vineuse ☎05.55.77.63.97, ⓔfjt.accueil-2000@orange.fr. A hike out on the north side of town, but you still need to book well ahead. €18 per night includes breakfast, and there is also a communal kitchen.

The City

The **Cathédrale St-Étienne**, a landmark for miles around, was begun in 1273 and modelled on the cathedral of Amiens, though only the choir, completed in the early thirteenth century, is pure Gothic. The rest of the building was added piecemeal over the centuries, the western part of the nave not until 1876. The most striking external feature is the sixteenth-century facade of the north transept, built in full flamboyant style with elongated arches, clusters of pinnacles and delicate tracery in window and gallery. At the west end of the nave, the tower, erected on a Romanesque base that had to be massively reinforced to bear the weight, has octagonal upper storeys, in common with most churches in the region. It once stood as a separate campanile and probably looked the better for it. Inside, the effects are much more pleasing. The sense of soaring height is accentuated by all the upward-reaching lines of the pillars, the net of vaulting ribs, the curling, flame-like lines, and, as you look down the nave, by the narrower and more pointed arches of the choir.

The best of the city's museums – with its showpiece collections of enamelware dating back to the twelfth century – is the **Musée des Beaux-Arts de Limoges** in the old bishop's palace next to the cathedral. At the time of writing, the museum was closed for long-term renovation though due to reopen at the end of 2010 with twice the amount of exhibition space, charting the progression from the simple Byzantine-influenced *champlevé* (copper filled with enamel), to seventeenth- and eighteenth-century work using a far greater range of colours and indulging in elaborate, virtuoso portraiture. Meanwhile, contemporary enamel work is on display at the nearby **Maison d'Émail** at 18 bd de la Cité (Wed–Sat 2–7pm; free; Ⓦwww.enamel-house.com), which also runs introductory half-day classes (€41) if you'd like to try your hand.

Behind the cathedral, the well-laid-out **botanical garden** (daily sunrise to sunset; free) is an inviting prospect, descending gracefully towards the River Vienne. In the garden's northern corner an old refectory now houses the excellent **Cité des Métiers et des Arts** (Easter–May Wed, Sat & Sun 2–6pm; June, Sept & Oct daily 2–6pm; July & Aug daily 10.30am–1pm & 2.30–7pm; €5; Ⓦwww .cma-limoges.com) displaying pieces – mostly carpentry – by France's top crafts-guild members.

The best area for a relaxed stroll is the partly renovated **old quarter** of the town, over to the west, where you'll find rue de la Boucherie, for a thousand years the domain of the butchers' guild. The dark, cluttered **chapel of St-Aurélien** belongs to them, while one of their former shophouses makes an interesting little museum, the **Maison de la Boucherie**, at no. 36 (July–Sept daily 10am–1pm & 2.30–7pm; free). At the top of the street, the **market hall** is in place de la Motte and, to the right, partly hidden by adjoining houses, the fourteenth- and fifteenth-century **church of St-Michel-des-Lions**, named after the two badly weathered Celtic lions guarding the south door and topped by one of the best towers and spires in the region. The inside is dark and atmospheric, with two beautiful, densely coloured fifteenth-century windows either side of the choir.

Further east, the concrete stretch of place de la République conceals the fourth-century **crypt** of the long-vanished **Abbey of St-Martial** (July–Sept daily 9.30am–noon & 2.30–7pm; free), containing the saint's massive sarcophagus, discovered during building work in the 1960s. Nearby is the **church of St-Pierre-du-Queyroix** under another typically Limousin belfry. The interior, partly twelfth century, has the same slightly pink granite glow as the cathedral. There's more fine stained glass here, including an eye-catching window at the end of the south aisle depicting the Dormition of the Virgin, signed by the great enamel artist Jean Pénicault in 1510.

Limoges's renowned **porcelain** is best displayed in the **Musée Adrien-Dubouché** (daily except Tues 10am–12.25pm & 2–5.40pm; €4.50; @www .musee-adriendubouche.fr), west of the old quarter on place Winston-Churchill. The well-presented collection is more interesting than you might expect, including samples of the local product and china displays from around the world, as well as various pieces from celebrity services ordered for the likes of Abraham Lincoln, Queen Elizabeth and sundry French royals.

Eating and drinking

Limoges has an abundance of good and not too expensive **places to eat**. For **drinks** at any time of the day, one option is the not very attractive place de la République; a slightly nicer choice is lively place Denis-Dussoubs, a short walk further west, where you'll find fine beers on tap at the *Michard* micro-brewery (closed Sun). *Le Duc Etienne*, at 19 rue de la Boucherie, is a relaxed, wood-timbered bar in the old quarter, while over on the other side of town the *Lord John* is a welcoming, British-style pub with concerts some weekends.

Restaurants

L'Amphitryon 26 rue de la Boucherie
℡05.55.33.36.39. There's no better place for a real treat of subtle and sophisticated cuisine, well deserving its Michelin star. You'll be offered a good choice of seafood as well as beef, veal and other local fare. The lunchtime *formule* is €23, while the evening *menus* are €44 and €72. Closed Sun, Mon, two weeks in Aug/Sept & one week in Jan, March & May.

Chez Alphonse 5 place de la Motte
℡05.55.34.34.14. Welcoming and popular bistro, complete with red-check cloths and bustling waiters, which specializes in local dishes such as pig's trotters and sweetbreads, plus a broader range of daily specials. Around €30 a head for three courses. Closed Sun.

Chez François Place de la Motte. For a good-value lunch and a lively atmosphere, head straight to the central market hall to join the locals round communal tables. Colourful pictures of market life adorn the walls, and you'll pay around €15 a head. If it's full, try the *Bistrot d'Olivier* next door. Closed eves, Sun & Aug.

Crêperie de la Cathédrale 3 rue Haute-Cité. One of a cluster of brasseries with outside seating on this attractive pedestrianized street by the cathedral. It's good value at lunchtime, with a *plat du jour*, dessert and drink for €11.

La Parenthèse Cour du Temple. Tucked away in an attractive courtyard off rue du Temple, this is a great place for a light lunch or tea break. They offer various *formules* including a drink and one of their scrumptious desserts from €14, as well as good, fresh salads and a *plat du jour*. Closed eves & Sun.

Les Petits Ventres 20 rue de la Boucherie
℡05.55.34.22.90. This elegant restaurant in a timbered, seventeenth-century building will delight lovers of brain, brawn, tongue and other unmentionable cuts – though they also do plenty of more everyday dishes and even a vegetarian platter. You'll pay €11 for the *plat du jour*, while three-course *menus* start at €24.50. Closed Sun & Mon.

Festivals

In late September, there's an interesting and important gathering of writers, dramatists and musicians from other French-speaking countries at the **Festival International des Francophonies** (@www.lesfrancophonies.com). For one week in mid-August brass instruments take pride of place in the **Cuivres en Fête** music festival (@www.cuivres-en-fete.com), while gourmets of a certain persuasion should make sure their visit coincides with the third Friday in October for the **Frairie des Petits Ventres food fair**, when the entire population turns out to gorge on everything from pig's trotters to sheep's testicles in the rue de la Boucherie. Otherwise, there's **Urbaka**, a festival of street theatre held at the end of June (@www.urbaka.com), and the **Danse Emoi** contemporary dance festival every two years in January, the next being in 2012.

Around Limoges

There's a clutch of villages within a day's reach of Limoges. A route linking places of interest on the south bank of the Vienne, such as the **château** of **Rochechouart** is detailed in the *Route Richard-Coeur-de-Lion* leaflet (available at local tourist offices), so called because of its associations with the English king. The route also takes you close to **Solignac**'s abbey church and the **Château de Châlucet**, now reduced to atmospheric ruins. North of the Vienne, the charred walls of **Oradour-sur-Glane** stand testimony to a World War II massacre, while east of Limoges, beyond the attractive market town of **St-Léonard-de-Noblat**, the master weavers of **Aubusson** have been producing tapestries for more than six hundred years, and carpets since 1743.

Visiting all these places really requires a car, but some are accessible by a combination of public transport, walking and patient hitching.

Oradour-sur-Glane

Twenty-five kilometres northwest of Limoges, the village of **ORADOUR-SUR-GLANE** stands just as the soldiers of the SS left it on June 10, 1944, after killing 642 of the inhabitants in reprisal for attacks by French *maquisards*. The entire village has been preserved both as a shrine and a chilling reminder of human brutality.

Before entering the village, the **Centre de la Mémoire**, immediately southeast of Oradour on the Limoges road (daily: Feb & Nov to 15 Dec 9am–5pm; March to 15 May & 16 Sept to Oct 9am–6pm; 16 May to 15 Sept 9am–7pm; closed 16 Dec–Jan; entry to village free, exhibition €7.70; ⓦwww.oradour.org), sets the historical context and attempts to explain how – and why – such acts of brutality took place.

From here an underground passage leads into the village itself, where a sign admonishes *Souviens-toi* ("Remember"), and the main street leads past roofless houses gutted by fire. Telephone poles, iron bedsteads and gutters are fixed in tormented attitudes where the fire's heat left them; prewar cars rust in the garages; cooking pots hang over empty grates; last year's grapes hang wizened on a vine whose trellis has long rotted away.

To the north of the village a dolmen-like slab on a shallow plinth covers a crypt containing relics of the dead, and the awful list of names, while to the southeast, by the stream, stands the church where the women and children – five hundred of them – were burnt to death.

There are **buses** from Limoges to Oradour, or alternatively you can take the train to **ST-JUNIEN** and pick up a bus there.

Rochechouart

ROCHECHOUART, a beautiful little walled town roughly 45km west of Limoges, has two claims to fame. Two hundred million years ago it was the site of one of the largest **meteorites** ever to hit earth, a monster 1.5km in diameter and weighing some 6 billion tonnes. The traces of this cosmic calamity still attract the curiosity of astronomers, though the only evidence that a layman might notice is the unusual-looking breccia stone many of the region's older buildings are made of: the squashed, shattered, heat-transformed and reconstituted result of the collision. A small museum in town, the **Espace Météorite**, 16 rue Jean Parvy (late June to mid-Sept & school hols Mon–Fri 10am–12.30pm & 1.30–6pm, Sat & Sun 2–6pm; rest of year Mon–Fri 2–6pm, though phone to be sure; €4; ⓉT05.55.03.02.70, ⓦwww.espacemeteorite.com), uncovers the history of the meteorite with interactive displays, models and videos.

One building using the stone from the impact is Rochechouart's other source of pride: the handsome **château** that stands at the town's edge. It started life as a rough fortress before 1000 AD, was "modernized" in the thirteenth century (the sawn-off keep and entrance survive from this period) and embellished with Renaissance additions in the fifteenth. Until it was acquired as the *mairie* in 1832, it had belonged to the de Rochechouart family for 800 years. Today it houses not only the town hall, but also the very well-regarded **Musée Départemental d'Art Contemporain** (daily except Tues: March–Sept 10am–12.30pm & 1.30–6pm; Oct to mid-Dec 10am–12.30pm & 2–5pm; closed mid-Dec to Feb; €4.60; Ⓦwww.musee-rochechouart.com), with an important collection of works by the Dadaist Raoul Haussmann, who died in Limoges in 1971. In another room decorated with its original sixteenth-century frescoes of the Labours of Hercules, the British artist Richard Long has created a special installation of white stones, while in the garden Giuseppe Penone's metal sculpture grapples with a tree.

The Rochechouart **tourist office** is at 6 rue Victor-Hugo (July & Aug Mon–Sat 10am–12.30pm & 2.30–6pm; Sept–June Mon–Sat 10am–noon & 2–5pm; Ⓣ05.55.03.72.73, Ⓦwww.rochechouart.com). Should you wish to **stay**, there are two well-priced **hotels** on place Octave-Marquet: the *Hôtel de France* (Ⓣ05.55.03.77.40, Ⓦwww.hoteldefrance-rochechouart.fr; ❷), with the better restaurant (closed Sun eve; *menus* €13–33.50), and the slightly smarter *Météorite* (Ⓣ05.55.02.86.80; ❸; *menus* from €13).

Solignac and Châlucet

A dozen kilometres south of Limoges in the lovely wooded valley of the Briance, the church of **SOLIGNAC** and the Château de Châlucet make the most attractive outings from the city. There are **buses** and **trains** to Solignac-Le Vigen station, 1km away on the Limoges–Brive line, and occasional buses to Solignac itself, but beware that no combination allows you to see Solignac and get back in one day. There is, however, a comfortable **hotel** opposite the church, *Le St-Éloi* (Ⓣ05.55.00.44.52, Ⓦwww.lesainteloi.fr; closed three weeks in Jan, one in June & one in Sept; ❹; restaurant around €30, closed Sat lunch, Sun eve & Mon).

Approaching from Le Vigen you see Solignac's Romanesque **abbey church** ahead of you, simple and sturdy, with the tiled roofs of its octagonal apse and neat little brood of radiating chapels. The twelfth-century facade has little sculpture, as the granite is too hard to permit intricate carving. Inside it's beautiful, with a flight of steps leading down into the nave with a dramatic view of the length of the church. There are no aisles, just a single space roofed with three big domes – an absolutely plain Latin cross in design.

The **Château de Châlucet** is a good 5km up the valley of the Briance in the other direction. At the highest point of the climb there is a dramatic view across the valley to the romantic, ruined keep of the castle, rising above the woods. Built in the twelfth century, the château was in English hands during the Hundred Years' War and, in the lawless aftermath, became the lair of a notorious local brigand, Perrot le Béarnais. It was dismantled in 1593 for harbouring Protestants and has been much restored recently. You can borrow an explanatory guide from the visitors' centre (daily: mid-March to mid-June & mid-Sept to mid-Nov 9.30am–12.30pm & 1.30–6pm; mid-June to mid-Sept 11am–6.30pm) on the path up to the ruins.

St-Léonard-de-Noblat

ST-LÉONARD-DE-NOBLAT, twenty minutes by train from Limoges or thirty minutes by bus, is an appealing little market town of narrow streets and medieval houses with jutting eaves and corbelled turrets. There's a very lovely eleventh- and twelfth-century church, with a six-storey tower, high dome and barrel-vaulted interior. A couple of kilometres northwest, demonstrations of papermaking and printing are on offer at a fifteenth-century paper mill, the **Moulin du Got** (guided visits: May, June & Sept Wed, Sat & Sun 2.30pm & 4pm; July & Aug Tues–Fri 10.30am, 2.15–5.15pm, Sat–Mon 2.15–5.15pm; school hols Tues–Sat 2.30pm & 4pm; rest of year Wed & Sat 2.30pm & 4pm; closed Jan; €6.50; ⓦwww.moulindugot.com). In the town centre, the **HistoRail museum**, 18 rue de Beaufort (July & Aug only, Mon–Fri 10am–noon & 2–6pm; €4.50; ⓦwww.historail.com), is good fun, with some excellent working model railways.

The **tourist office** on place du Champs-de-Mars (April–June & Sept Mon–Sat 10am–12.15pm & 2.15–5.30pm; July & Aug Mon–Sat 10am–6.30pm, Sun 10am–12.30pm; Oct–March Mon–Sat 10am–12.15pm & 2.15–5pm; ⓣ05.55.56.25.06, ⓦwww.otsi-noblat.fr) offers ideas for local walks and will point you to *chambres d'hôte* possibilities round about. A good **place to stay** or **eat** is the *Relais St-Jacques* on the boulevard encircling the Old Town (ⓣ05.55.56.00.25, ⓦlogis-de-france-hotel.lerelaissaintjacques.com; ❸; restaurant from €19; closed Sun eve & Mon lunch Oct–May), and you can also **eat** well just round the corner at the welcoming *Le Gay-Lussac*, 18 rue Victor-Hugo, which offers great-value *menus* featuring local and seasonal produce (weekday lunches from €11.50, weekends & eve from €19). There's a spruce **campsite**, the *Camping de Beaufort* (ⓣ05.55.56.02.79, ⓦwww.campingdebeaufort.fr; May–Sept), a couple of kilometres out of town on the D39.

Aubusson

AUBUSSON is 90km east of Limoges and served by regular buses and trains. A neat grey-stone town in the bottom of a ravine formed by the River Creuse, it's known for its reputation as a centre for weaving **tapestries**, second only to the Gobelins works in Paris. The **Musée Départemental de la Tapisserie**, in avenue des Lissiers (July & Aug Mon & Wed–Sun 10am–6pm, Tues 2–6pm; Sept–June daily except Tues 9.30am–noon & 2–6pm; €5), traces the history of Aubusson tapestries over six centuries, up to the modern-day works of Jean Lurçat (see p.583). The **Maison du Tapissier** next to the tourist office (same hours as tourist office; €6) is also worth a quick look for its overview of weaving techniques and local history displayed in the sixteenth-century home of a master weaver.

For information about further exhibitions and workshop visits ask at the **tourist office** in rue Vieille (March–June, Sept & Oct Mon–Sat 9.30am–12.30pm & 2–6pm; July & Aug daily 9.30am–6pm; Nov–Feb Mon–Sat 10am–12.30pm & 3–5pm; ⓣ05.55.66.32.12, ⓦwww.ot-aubusson.fr). As for **hotels**, a reliable budget place is the *Chapitre*, on the main Grande-Rue above a bar at no. 53 (ⓣ05.55.66.18.54, ⓦwww.hotellechapitre.com; ❶). For something smarter, try *Le France* at 6 rue des Déportés (ⓣ05.55.66.10.22, ⓦwww.aubussonlefrance.com; ❸), with elegant rooms and a decent formal **restaurant** (*menus* from €20) plus a cheaper brasserie open for lunch only (closed Sun). The town's *La Croix Blanche* **campsite** (ⓣ05.55.66.18.00, ⓔcamping23@orange.fr; April–Sept) is by the river on the Felletin road.

The Plateau de Millevaches

Millevaches, the plateau of a thousand springs, is undulating upland country rising to 800–900m in altitude, on the northern edge of the Massif Central, with a wild and sparsely populated landscape and villages few and far between. Those that do exist appear small, grey and sturdy, inured to the buffeting of upland weather. It's a magnificent country of conifer plantations and natural woodland – of beech, birch and chestnut – interspersed with reed-fringed tarns, man-made lakes and pasture grazed by sheep and cows, much of it now designated a **natural regional park** (Ⓦwww.pnr-millevaches.fr). It's an area to walk or cycle in, or at least savour at a gentle pace, stopping in the attractive, country inns scattered across the plateau.

The small towns, like **Eymoutiers** and **Meymac**, have a primitive architectural beauty and an old-world charm largely untouched by modern development. Not that the modern world has passed the area by. Near Eymoutiers, the **Lac de Vassivière** offers all sorts of sports activities and a beautiful setting for a contemporary art museum.

Getting around by car is easiest, but there is access by public transport. Both Eymoutiers and Meymac lie on a cross-country rail line connecting Limoges and Ussel, while Meymac and Égletons are on the main line between Brive and Clermont-Ferrand.

Eymoutiers and around

EYMOUTIERS, 45km southeast of Limoges, is an upland town of tall, narrow stone houses crowding round a much-altered Romanesque **church**. Not interesting enough for a prolonged stay, it nonetheless makes an agreeable stopover, especially for campers, as it has a simple but magnificently sited municipal **campsite**, the *St-Pierre Château* (Ⓣ05.55.69.27.81; June–Sept), on a hill 2km southeast of town off the Bugeat road. If you prefer a **hotel**, you'll find simple rooms and hearty food at *Le Ranch des Lacs* (Ⓣ05.55.69.15.66, Ⓦwww.le-ranch -des-lacs.com; closed Dec 24 to Jan 26; ❶; *menus* €15–40) about 7km northwest of Eymoutiers, signposted off the Bujaleuf road.

Eymoutiers is also the jumping-off point for the **Lac de Vassivière**. This man-made lake, with 45km of indented shoreline, provides some lovely spots for walking and cycling – and no fewer than six **campsites**. In summer, the lake is also a popular destination for watersports enthusiasts, with opportunities for sailing, windsurfing and water skiing, among other activities. An island, accessed by a causeway, provides a wonderful home for the **Centre International d'Art et du Paysage** (June–Oct daily 11am–7pm; Nov–June Tues–Sun 11am–1pm & 2–6pm; exhibition hall €3; Ⓣ05.55.69.27.27, Ⓦwww.ciapiledevassiviere.com), a contemporary art centre where many of the pieces lie scattered among the trees. There's also a hall hosting temporary exhibitions and a **café** where you can get light meals while admiring the views (May–Sept daily). The main **information** centre for the lake is the Maison de Vassivière (July & Aug daily 9am–1pm & 2–6pm; Sept–June Mon–Fri 9am–1pm & 2–5pm; Ⓣ05.55.69.76.70, Ⓦwww.lelacdevassiviere.com), at **AUPHELLE**, on the western shore.

Ten kilometres southeast of Eymoutiers, the small village of **NEDDE** nestles beside the Vienne river. The reason for coming here, particularly if you've got children in tow, is the **Cité des Insectes** (April–June & Sept–Oct Wed, Sat & Sun 10.30am–7pm; July & Aug daily 10.30am–7pm; closed Nov–March; €7; Ⓦwww .lacitedesinsectes.com), a couple of kilometres to the south. Exhibits trace the history of entomology and delve into their secret lives, ending with living examples of weird and wonderful insects from around the world. Nedde also boasts a welcoming little **hotel** and **restaurant**, *Le Verrou* (Ⓣ05.55.69.98.04, Ⓦwww.leverrou.com; closed mid-Nov to March; ❷–❸), where the more expensive rooms have been tastefully restored. Alternatively, head 15km further southeast to **TARNAC**, another mountain village, where the *Hôtel des Voyageurs* (Ⓣ05.55.95.53.12, Ⓦwww.hotel -voyageurs-correze.com; closed mid-Dec to mid-Jan, last week in Feb and last week in June; ❷) is a simple but appealingly old-fashioned, country **hotel** with a good traditional **restaurant** to match (closed Sun eve & Mon; *menus* €18–32).

Meymac and around

Pepper-pot turrets and steep slate roofs adorn the ancient grey houses of **MEYMAC**, 50km southeast of Eymoutiers, on the southern fringes of the plateau. The village is packed tightly around its Romanesque church and the Benedictine **abbey**, whose foundation a thousand years ago brought the town into being. Part of the abbey now houses the innovative **Centre National d'Art Contemporain** (daily except Mon: July & Aug 10am–1pm & 2–7pm; Sept–June 2–6pm; closed Jan; €5; ⓦ www.centre-art-contemporain-meymac.com), featuring changing exhibitions of young, local artists as well as big-name retrospectives. It's also worth popping into the adjacent **Musée de la Fondation Marius Vazeilles** (May–June & Sept–Oct Tues, Wed & Fri–Sun 2.30–6pm; July & Aug daily 10am–noon & 2.30–7pm; closed Nov–April; €3) to learn about the history and traditions of the plateau.

Grande-Rue, the main street, ends in steps that climb past the round **bell tower**, the town's landmark, to a pretty square in front of the town hall. Here you'll also find the **tourist office** (Mon–Fri 10am–noon & 2–5.30pm; ☎05.55.95.18.43, ⓦ www.ot-meymac.visite.org), which has plenty of information on hiking, among other things.

There's a reasonable two-star **hotel** on the main road, the *Limousin*, 76 av Limousine (☎05.55.46.12.11, ⓦ www.logishotels.com; closed Sat from Sept to June & Sun eve all year; ❷; restaurant from €9). Alternatively, book ahead for one of the four rooms in a sixteenth-century tower at *Chez Françoise*, up the hill from the tourist office (☎05.55.95.10.63; ❷). They also run a well-respected **restaurant** serving local specialities, with a vast wine list (closed Sun eve & Mon; *menus* €15–35). Finally, there's a municipal **campsite**, *La Garenne* (☎05.55.95.22.80, ⓔmairie@meymac.fr; mid-May to mid-Sept), close at hand on the Sornac road.

Brive-la-Gaillarde and around

BRIVE-LA-GAILLARDE is a major rail junction and the nearest thing to an industrial centre for miles around. Nevertheless, it has an attractive old centre and makes an agreeable base for exploring the Corrèze *département* and its beautiful villages, as well as the upper reaches of the Vézère and Dordogne rivers.

Though it has no commanding sights, Brive does have a few distractions. At its centre is the much-restored **church of St-Martin**, originally Romanesque in style, though only the transept, apse and a few comically carved capitals survive from that era. St Martin himself, a Spanish aristocrat, arrived in pagan Brive in 407 AD on the feast of Saturnus, smashed various idols and was promptly stoned to death by the outraged onlookers.

Numerous streets fan out from the central square, place du Général-de-Gaulle, with a number of turreted and towered houses, some dating back to the thirteenth century. The most impressive is the sixteenth-century **Hôtel de Labenche** on boulevard Jules-Ferry, now housing the town's archeological finds as well as a collection of seventeenth-century tapestries in the **Musée Labenche** (daily except Tues: April–Oct 10am–6.30pm; Nov–March 1–6pm; €4.70; ⓦ www.musee-labenche.com). There's also the **Centre National d'Études Edmond Michelet** at 4 rue Champanatier (Mon–Sat 10am–noon & 2–6pm; free), based in the former house of this minister of de Gaulle, and one of the town's leading *résistants*, with exhibitions portraying the occupation and Resistance through photographs, posters and objects of the time.

From the **gare SNCF**, it's a five-minute walk north along avenue Jean-Jaurès to the boulevard ringing the Old Town. The **tourist office** is outside the ring road to the north on place 14-juillet (April–June & Sept Mon–Sat 9am–12.30pm & 1.30–6.30pm; July & Aug Mon–Sat 9am–7pm, Sun 3–7pm; Oct–March Mon–Sat 9am–noon & 2–6pm; ☎05.55.24.08.80, ⊛www.brive-tourisme.com), where you'll also find the modern market hall and the **gare routière**. The best place to go for **internet** access is the Centre Culturel at 31 av Jean-Jaurès (Mon, Tues & Thurs–Sat 9am–noon & 2–7pm, Wed 9am–noon).

There's a decent **HI hostel** a 25-minute walk across town at 56 av du Maréchal Bugeaud (☎05.55.24.34.00, ⊛www.fuaj.org/Brive-la-Gaillarde; dorm beds €13.20) while the best of the cheap **hotels** is *L'Andréa*, near the station at 39 av Jean-Jaurès (☎05.55.74.11.84, ℗05.55.17.25.73; ❷), with pleasant rooms, a small garden terrace and a bar. *Le Collonges*, on the ring road at 3 place Winston-Churchill (☎05.55.74.09.58, ⊛www.hotel-le-collonges.com; ❸), is a welcoming, family-run place, nothing fancy but the rooms are perfectly acceptable. From there it's a big jump up to *La Truffe Noir*, 22 bd Anatole-France (☎05.55.92.45.00, ⊛www.la-truffe-noire.com; ❻), Brive's grandest hotel, with a gourmet restaurant (from around €40 a head). Despite the impressive lobby, the rooms are disappointingly ordinary, though they're well equipped and air-conditioned.

For **places to eat**, try *Les Viviers St-Martin*, at 4 rue Traversière (closed two weeks each in March & late Sept; evening *menus* from €26), tucked down an alley near St-Martin, which serves brasserie-style food, including plenty of fish dishes. Though it doesn't look much from the outside, *Le Boulevard*, at 8 bd Jules-Ferry (☎05.55.23.07.13; closed Sun eve & Mon; *menus* from €15), hides a cosy dining room where locals come for dishes such as duck breast with local mustard. For something smarter, *La Crémaillère*, at 53 av de Paris (closed Sun; *menus* from €24), has a well-deserved reputation for its classic regional cuisine.

Turenne and Collonges-la-Rouge

TURENNE, just 16km south of Brive, was capital of the viscountcy of Turenne, whose most illustrious seigneur was Henri de la Tour d'Auvergne – the "Grand Turenne", born 1611, whom Napoleon rated the finest tactician of modern times. Mellow stone houses crowd in the lee of the sharp bluff on whose summit sprout two towers, all that remains of the castle. One, known as **La Tour de César**, can be visited (April–June, Sept & Oct daily 10am–noon & 2–6pm; July & Aug daily 10am–7pm; Nov–March Sun 2–5pm; €4; ⊛www.chateau-turenne.com) and is worth climbing for vertiginous views to the mountains of Cantal.

With its red-sandstone houses, pepper-pot towers and pink-candled chestnut trees, **COLLONGES-LA-ROUGE**, 7km east of Turenne, is the epitome of rustic charm – make sure you get here early in the day to avoid the crowds. Though small-scale, there's a certain grandeur about the place, befitting the status of the resident Turenne administrators. On the main square a twelfth-century **church** testifies to the imbecility of shedding blood over religious differences: here, side by side, Protestant and Catholic conducted their services simultaneously. Outside, the covered **market hall** still retains its old-fashioned baker's oven.

If you want to **stay**, it's best to head east 2km to **MEYSSAC**, a town built in the same red sandstone, though less grandly, to the very pleasant *Relais du Quercy* (☎05.55.25.40.31, ⊛www.relaisduquercy.com.fr; closed one week each in March & Nov; ❸; restaurant *menus* €12–36). On the way you'll pass a three-star **campsite**, *Moulin de la Valanne* (☎05.55.25.41.59, ⊛www.meyssac .fr; May–Sept).

The Dordogne

To the French, the **Dordogne** is a river. To the British, it is a much looser term, covering a vast area roughly equivalent to what the French call Périgord. This starts south of Limoges and includes the Vézère and Dordogne valleys. The Dordogne is also a *département*, with fixed boundaries that pay no heed to either definition. The central part of the *département*, around Périgueux and the River Isle, is known as **Périgord Blanc**, after the light, white colour of its rock outcrops; the southeastern half around Sarlat as **Périgord Noir**, said to be darker in aspect because of the preponderance of oak woods. To confuse matters further, the tourist authorities have added another two colours to the Périgord patchwork: **Périgord Vert**, the far north of the *département*, so called because of the green of its woods and pastureland; and **Périgord Pourpre** in the southwest, purple because it includes the wine-growing area around Bergerac.

This southern region is also known for its **bastides** – fortified towns – built during the turbulent medieval period when there was almost constant conflict between the French and English. In the reaches of the **upper Dordogne**, the colour scheme breaks down, but the villages and scenery in this less travelled backwater still rival anything the rest of the region has to offer.

Périgord Vert and Périgord Blanc

The close green valleys of **Périgord Vert** are very rural, with plenty of space and few people, large tracts of wood and uncultivated land. Less well known than the Périgord Noir, its largely granite landscape bears a closer resemblance to the neighbouring Limousin than to the rest of the Périgord. It's partly for this reason that in 1998 the most northerly tip, together with the southwestern part of the Haute-Vienne, was designated as the **Parc Naturel Régional Périgord-Limousin** in an attempt to promote "green" tourism in this economically fragile and depopulated area.

Périgueux, in the centre of **Périgord Blanc**, is interesting for its domed cathedral and its Roman remains, whose existence is a reminder of how long these parts have been civilized. But it's in the countryside that the region's finest monuments lie. One of the loveliest stretches is the **valley of the Dronne**, from **Aubeterre** on the Charente border through **Brantôme** to the marvellous Renaissance château of **Puyguilhem** and the picture-postcard village of **St-Jean-de-Côle**, and on to the Limousin border, where the scenery becomes higher and less intimate. Truffle-lovers might like to take a look at **Sorges**, where there's a nature trail through truffle country and a museum to explain it all.

Périgueux

PÉRIGUEUX, capital of the *département* of the Dordogne and a central base for exploring the countryside of Périgord Blanc, is a small, busy market town with an attractive medieval and Renaissance core of stone-flagged squares and narrow alleys harbouring richly ornamented merchants' houses.

Arrival, information and accommodation

Périgueux's **gare SNCF** lies to the west of town at the end of rue des Mobiles-de-Coulmiers, the continuation of rue du Président-Wilson. Regional **buses** run by

The two great stars of Périgord cuisine are **foie gras** and **truffles** (*truffes*). Foie gras is best eaten either chilled in succulent, buttery slabs, or lightly fried and served with a fruit compote to provide contrasting sweetness and acidity. Truffle is often dished up in omelettes and the rich *périgourdin* sauces which accompany many local meat dishes, but to appreciate the delicate earthy flavour to the full, you really need to eat truffle on its own, with just a salad and some coarse, country bread.

The other mainstay of Périgord cuisine is the grey Toulouse **goose**, whose fat is used in the cooking of everything, including the flavourful potato dish, *pommes sarladaises*. The goose fattens well: *gavé* or crammed with corn, it goes from six to ten kilos in weight in three weeks, with its liver alone weighing nearly a kilo. Though some may find the process off-putting, small local producers are very careful not to harm their birds, if for no other reason than that stress ruins the liver. Geese are also raised for their meat alone, which is cooked and preserved in its own thick yellow grease as *confits d'oie*, which you can either eat on its own or use in the preparation of other dishes, like *cassoulet*. **Duck** is used in the same way, both for foie gras and *confits*. *Magret de canard*, or duck-breast fillet, is one of the favourite ways of eating duck and appears on practically every restaurant menu.

Another goose delicacy is *cou d'oie farci* – goose neck stuffed with sausage meat, duck liver and truffles, while a popular favourite salad throughout the region is made with warm *gésiers* or goose gizzards. Try not to be put off by fare such as this, or your palate will miss out on some delicious experiences – like *tripoux*, sheep's stomach stuffed with tripe, trotters, pork and garlic, which is really an Auvergnat dish but is quite often served in neighbouring areas like the Rouergue. Other less challenging specialities include stuffed *cèpes*, or wild mushrooms; *ballottines*, fillets of poultry stuffed, rolled and poached; the little flat discs of goat's cheese known as *cabécou* or *rocamadour*; and for dessert there's *pastis*, a light apple tart topped with crinkled, wafer-thin pastry laced with armagnac.

The **wines** should not be scorned, either. There are the fine, dark, almost peppery reds from Cahors, and both reds and whites from the vineyards of Bergerac, of which the sweet, white Monbazillac is the most famous. Pécharmant is the fanciest of the reds, but there are some very drinkable Côtes de Bergerac, much like the neighbouring Bordeaux and far cheaper. The same goes for the wines of Duras, Marmande and Buzet. If you're thinking of taking a stock of wine home, you could do much worse than make some enquiries in Bergerac itself, Ste-Foy, or any of the villages in the vineyard areas.

CFTA Périgord (℡05.53.08.43.13, ⊛www.cftaco.fr) stop at both the *gare SNCF* and on place Francheville, a wide, open square with underground parking. On the east side of this square, next to Tour Mataguerre, the last surviving bit of the town's medieval defences, you'll find the **tourist office** (June–Sept Mon–Sat 9am–7pm, Sun 10am–1pm & 2–6pm; Oct–May Mon–Sat 9am–12.30pm & 2–6pm; ℡05.53.53.10.63, ⊛www.tourisme-perigueux.fr), which organizes various guided visits on foot and by bike in summer. For **internet** access go to Ouratech on place du Général-Leclerc (Mon–Fri 10am–7pm, Sat 2–7pm).

Hotels

Des Barris 2 rue Pierre-Magne ℡05.53.53.04.05, ⊛www.hoteldesbarris.com. With views across the river to the cathedral from some rooms, this small, city-centre hotel offers good-value simple rooms. Double-glazing cuts out the road noise, and there's a decent restaurant downstairs with a riverside terrace (*menus* €23–42). ❸

Bristol 37 rue Antoine-Gadaud ℡05.53.08.75.90, ⊛www.bristolfrance.com. A good find, in a quiet area 2min from the town centre. Rooms are large, and all have a/c and wireless internet. There is also free parking for guests. ❹

Mercure 7 place Francheville ℡05.53.06.65.00, ⊛www.mercure.com. This new three-star on the main square offers spacious rooms decked out in

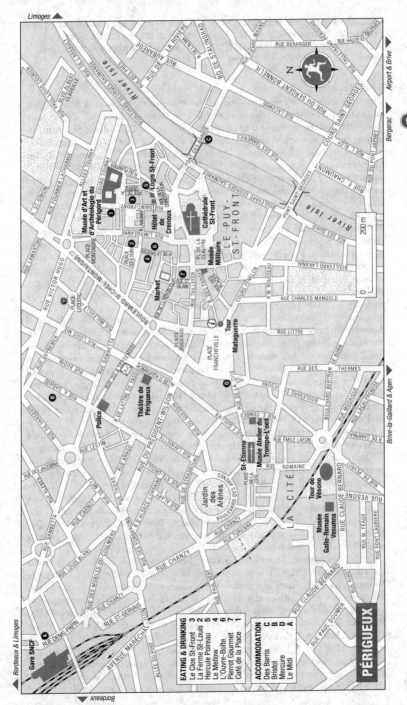

Limoges

Airport & Brive

Bergerac

RUE BERANGER
RUE HAUTE-ST-GEORGES
RUE PIERRE MAGNE
RUE DU SERGENT BONNELIE
RUE SAINT GEORGES
RUE LACOMBE
COURS SAINT GEORGES
BD. DE STALINGRAD
RUE DE LA RIVIERE
RUE DE L'AUBARÉDE
RUE DES TANNERIES
RUE DU PONT JAPHET
RUE E. CHAUMONT
RUE DU PONT JAPHET
RUE L. BLOY

RUE DE LA MAIN
RUE DES PRÈS
BOULEVARD GEORGES SAIGNE
RUE DE L'ARSAULT
BLVD ALBERT CLAVELLE
BLVD LOUIS COURIER
R. ST-SIMON
RUE FOURNIER LACHARME

River Isle
N
Brive

Limoges

RUE DES BARRIS
C

Musée d'Art et d'Archéologie du Périgord
Logis St-Front
5
3
Hôtel de Crenoux
Cathédrale St-Front
Musée Militaire
LE PUY ST-FRONT
PL DE LA CLAÎTRE
COURS TOURNY
ALLÉES TOURNY
PL. DE LA CITÉ
RUE SAINT-FRONT
RUE LIMOGEANNE
PLACE ST-LOUIS
2
6
4
PLACE MONTAIGNE
BOULEVARD MICHEL MONTAIGNE
R DE LA SAGESSE
Market
7
RUE TAILLEFER
RUE ST SILAIN
RUE SALINIÈRE
RUE AUBERGERIE
R. DE L'ÉGLISE
COURS FÉNELON
RUE DES FARGES
RUE CHARLES MANGOLD
R W. ROUSSEAU
BOULEVARD LAKANAL

River Isle
PONT SAINT GEORGES
RUE DES QUAIS
BOULEVARD GEORGES SAUMANDE

200 m
0

RUE LAMARTINE
RUE VICTOR HUGO
RUE MALVILLE
PLACE LECLERC
PLACE BUGEAUD
PLACE FRANCHEVILLE
Tour Mataguerre
i
RUE LITTRE
RUE DE BORN
0
RUE DE LA CITÉ
RUE VÉSONE
RUE DES THERMES
BOULEVARD BERTRAN DE BORN
RUE MODAGUE
RUE LACAL PRENÈDE
R DE CAMPNIAC

RUE LOUIS MIE
RUE BODIN
RUE A. GADAUD
RUE BOYMEYER
ALLÉE D'AQUITAINE
RUE DE LATTRE DE TASSIGNY
Théâtre de Périgueux
Police
RUE DE LA BRETONNIE
RUE DU GUESDE
RUE DU PRÉSIDENT-WILSON
RUE ARAGO
RUE LAFAYETTE
RUE STE-URSULE
RUE ALFA
RUE DE STRASBOURG
PLACE DE LA CITÉ
St-Étienne
Musée Atelier du Trompe-l'oeil
RUE DE COMBES
RUE E BOUILLER
RUE ÉMILE LAFON
RUE ROMAINE
La Cité
Tour de Vésone
Musée Gallo-Romain Vesunna
RUE CLAUDE BERNARD
RUE VÉSONE
RUE M. FEIX
RUE FONT LAURIÈRE

8

RUE DE VARSOVIE
RUE DES JACOBINS
RUE GAMBETTA
RUE DU LIEZ
RUE THIERS
RUE DES FORGERONS
RUE CARNOT
RUE DES MOBILES-DU-COULMIERS
RUE LOUIS BLANC
RUE DE LA BOÉTIE
RUE LESTIN
RUE D'ALSACE-LORRAINE
BOULEVARD DES ARÈNES
Jardin des Arènes
PLACE DE LA CITÉ
RUE TURENNE
RUE CHANZY
RUE ST-GERVAIS
RUE CHANZY
RUE PAUL MAZY
RUE GAMBETTA
RUE CHANZY
AVENUE MARÉCHAL JUIN
ALLÉE DU PORT
RUE DENIS-PAPIN
Gare SNCF
A
RUE PAUL DOUMER
RUE BIBOU
RUE PR. FÉVOLA

Bordeaux & Limoges
Bordeaux
Brive-la-Gaillard & Agen

9781848367234
559

PÉRIGUEUX

EATING & DRINKING

Le Clos St-Front	3
La Ferme St-Louis	2
Hercule Poireau	5
Le Mellow	6
L'Ouvre-Boîte	4
Pierrot Gourmet	7
Café de la Place	1

ACCOMMODATION

Des Barris	C
Bristol	B
Mercure	D
Le Midi	A

earth tones. Facilities include secure parking, flat-screen satellite TVs and internet access. ⑥
Le Midi 18 rue Denis-Papin ☎05.53.53.41.06, ⓦwww.hotel-du-midi.fr. A decent budget hotel

opposite the station, with a restaurant serving set *menus* from €14.50 to €28. The collection of toy cars on display downstairs is worth a visit in its own right. ❷

The Town

The main hub of the modern town is the tree-shaded **boulevard Montaigne**, which marks the western edge of the *vieille ville*. At its southern end, a short walk along rue Taillefer brings you to the domed and coned **Cathédrale St-Front**, its square, pineapple-capped belfry surging far above the roofs of the surrounding medieval houses. It's no beauty, having suffered from the attentions of the nineteenth-century restorer Abadie, best known for the white elephant of Paris's Sacré-Coeur. The result is an excess of ill-proportioned, nipple-like projections: "a supreme example of how not to restore", Freda White tartly observed in her classic travelogue, *Three Rivers of France*. It's a pity, since when it was rebuilt in 1173 following a fire, it was one of the most distinctive Byzantine churches in France, modelled on St Mark's in Venice and the Holy Apostles in Constantinople. Nevertheless, the Byzantine influence is still evident in the interior in the Greek-cross plan – unusual in France – and in the massive clean curves of the domes and their supporting arches. The big Baroque altarpiece, carved in walnut wood in the gloomy east bay, is worth a look, too, depicting the Assumption of the Virgin, with a humorous little detail in the illustrative scenes from her life of a puppy tugging the infant Jesus' sheets from his bed with its teeth.

In front of the cathedral, there's a fresh produce market on Wednesday and Saturday mornings in **place de la Clautre**, at the heart of the renovated streets of the medieval town, the most attractive of which is the narrow **rue Limogeanne**, lined with Renaissance mansions, now turned into boutiques and delicatessens, intermingled with fast-food outlets. The surrounding streets are also scattered with fine Renaissance houses; particularly handsome are the **Logis St-Front**, 7 rue de la Constitution, and the more sedate **Hôtel de Crenoux** at no. 3. Another striking building is at 17 rue de l'Éguillerie, on the corner of the attractive **place St-Louis**, where a turreted watchtower leans out over the street.

At the northern end of rue Limogeanne, on tree-lined cours Tourny, the **Musée d'Art et d'Archéologie du Périgord** (April–Sept Mon & Wed–Fri 10.30am–5.30pm, Sat & Sun 1–6pm; Oct–March Mon & Wed–Fri 10am–5pm, Sat & Sun 1–6pm; €4.50) is best known for its extensive and important prehistoric collection and some beautiful Gallo-Roman mosaics. Exhibits include copies of a 70,000-year-old skeleton, the oldest yet found in France, and a beautiful engraving of a bison's head. More lively but of less general interest is the **Musée Militaire**, near the cathedral at 32 rue des Farges (Jan–March Wed & Sat 2–6pm; April–Dec Mon–Sat 2–6pm; €4), which contains some unusual exhibits, particularly relating to the French colonial wars in Vietnam.

Roman Périgueux, known as **La Cité**, lies to the west of the town centre towards the *gare SNCF*. The most prominent vestige is the high, brick **Tour de Vésone**, the last remains of a temple to the city's guardian goddess, standing in a public garden just south of the train tracks. Beside the tower, the foundations of an exceptionally well-preserved Roman villa form the basis of the **Musée Gallo-Romain Vesunna** (April–June & Sept Tues–Fri 9.30am–5.30pm, Sat & Sun 10am–12.30pm & 2.30–6pm; July & Aug daily 10am–7pm; Oct–March Tues–Fri 9.30am–12.30pm & 1.30–5pm, Sat & Sun 10am–12.30pm & 2.30–6pm; €6; ⓦwww.vesunna.fr). This was no humble abode: the villa, complete with under-floor heating, thermal baths and colonnaded walkways around the central garden with its cooling pond and fountains, boasted at least sixty rooms. Visitors can see the remains of first-century murals of river and marine life, the colours still amazingly vibrant, and here and there, graffiti of hunting scenes, gladiatorial combat and even an ostrich – no doubt the work of some bored Roman urchin.

Eating and drinking

The best area to look for **places to eat** is the *vieille ville*, particularly around place St-Louis, place St-Silain and in the streets behind the tourist office. As for **cafés**, *Café de la Place*, on place du Marché-du-Bois, is a relaxed, traditional place with a shady terrace and good-value brasserie food. For the best of Périgueux's limited **nightlife**, head for rue de la Sagesse, where you'll find *Le Mellow* (Tues–Sat) and *L'Ouvre-Boîte* (Wed–Sun), both lively bars with music and cocktails.

Restaurants

Le Clos St-Front 5 rue de la Vertu
☏ 05.53.46.78.58. High-quality *menus* served in a leafy, walled courtyard or elegant dining rooms. You can eat for under €30, but for the €62 set *menu* you get the best of the best, with wine included. Sept–June closed Sun eve & Mon.

La Ferme St-Louis Place St-Louis
☏ 05.53.53.82.77. The most appealing of the many restaurants on the square, it has a small terrace and a homely, stone-walled interior. Food-wise, you can't get much more local than the duck breast in a truffle-based sauce. You'll pay €24 for two courses at lunchtime and €27 in the evening. Closed Sun & Mon.

Hercule Poireau 2 rue de la Nation
☏ 05.53.08.90.76. An atmospheric, stone-vaulted restaurant serving seriously gourmet food at very reasonable prices. Their speciality is *rossini de canard* (duck with foie gras in a truffle sauce). Three courses from €29. Closed Wed.

Pierrot Gourmet 6 rue de l'Hôtel-de-Ville. This gourmet deli has a few tables during the daytime (10am–5pm), where you can choose from a range of fresh, top-quality dishes such as mushroom pâté and pears poached in red wine for around €12. Closed Sun & Mon.

Brantôme and the valley of the Dronne

Although **Brantôme** itself is very much on the tourist trail, the country to both the west and east of the town along the **River Dronne** remains largely undisturbed. It's tranquil and very beautiful, and best savoured at a gentle pace, perhaps by bike or even by canoeing along the river.

Brantôme

BRANTÔME, 27km north of Périgueux on the Angoulême road, sits on an island in the River Dronne, whose still, water-lilied surface mirrors the limes and weeping willows of the riverside gardens. On the north bank of the river are the church and convent buildings of the former **Benedictine abbey** that has been Brantôme's focus ever since it was founded, possibly by Charlemagne. The other big name associated with the abbey is that of its most notorious abbot, Pierre de Bourdeilles, the sixteenth-century author of scurrilous tales of life at the royal court. Brantôme's best architectural feature, however, is the Limousin-style Romanesque **belfry**, built into the cliff face behind the church and only accessible on a guided tour arranged by the tourist office (daily except Tues 15 June to 15 Sept; €6). There are also pleasant views to be had wandering the nearby **gardens** and the balustraded riverbanks, while in summer you can take a leisurely **boat trip** on the river (Easter to mid-Oct; €7).

Five days a week (Mon, Wed & Fri–Sun), **buses** connect Brantôme with Périgueux and the TGV in Angoulême. The **tourist office** (May, June & Sept daily except Tues 10am–noon & 2–6pm; July & Aug daily 10am–6pm; Oct–April daily except Tues 10am–noon & 2–5pm; ☏ 05.53.05.80.52, ⓦ www.ville-brantome.fr) is next to the abbey church. From April to September you can rent **canoes** from Brantôme Canoë (☏ 05.53.05.77.24, ⓦ www.brantome-canoe.com), on the east side of town on the road to Thiviers, while **bikes** are available at Spadzone, 2 av des Martyrs (℡05.53.08.02.65, Ⓦwww.spadzone.com), north on the Angoulême road.

One of the nicest **places to stay** is ☆ *Maison Fleurie*, an English-owned *chambres d'hôte* at 54 rue Gambetta (℡05.53.35.17.04, Ⓦwww.maison-fleurie.net; ❸), with elegant rooms and a quiet courtyard garden and pool. On the other side of the road, overlooking the river, is *Hôtel Restaurant Charbonnel* (℡05.53.05.70.15, Ⓦwww.lesfrerescharbonnel.com; closed Feb & mid-Nov to mid-Dec; ❸), offering comfortable, pretty rooms and a gourmet restaurant (three-course *menus* €29.50–66; closed Sun eve & Mon Oct–June). Cheaper **accommodation** is to be found at *Hôtel Coligny*, 8 place de Gaulle (℡05.53.05.71.42; closed mid-Dec to March; ❸; *menu périgourdin* for €19.50), its eight rooms decorated in simple, contemporary style. Other good **eating** options include *Les Jardins de Brantôme*, with an attractive garden, a short walk north of town at 33 rue Pierre-de-Mareuil (closed Wed & Thurs; *menus* €21–36), and *Au Fil de l'Eau*, on quai Bertin, which specializes in fish dishes (closed mid-Oct to Easter; *menus* from €29), and has outside seating on a picturesque riverside terrace. Campers should head for the *Le Peyrelevade* **campsite** just east of Brantôme on the D78 Thiviers road (℡08.25.00.20.30, Ⓦwww.camping-dordogne.net; mid-May to mid-Sept).

Bourdeilles

BOURDEILLES, 16km down the Dronne from Brantôme by a beautiful back road, is a sleepy backwater. The ancient village clusters round its **château** (Feb, March, Nov & Dec Mon, Wed, Thurs & Sun 10am–12.30pm & 2–5.30pm; April–June, Sept & Oct daily except Tues 10am–12.30pm & 2–6pm; July & Aug daily 10am–7pm; €6; Ⓦwww.semitour.com) set on a rocky spur above the river. The château consists of two buildings: one a thirteenth-century fortress, the other an elegant Renaissance residence begun by the lady of the house as a piece of unsuccessful favour-currying with Catherine de Médici – unsuccessful because Catherine never came to stay and the château remained unfinished. Climb the octagonal keep for a good view over the town's clustered roofs and along the valley of the Dronne.

The château is now home to an exceptional collection of **furniture** and **religious statuary** bequeathed to the state by its former owners. Among the more notable pieces are some splendid Spanish dowry chests and a sixteenth-century Rhenish Entombment with life-sized statues, embodying the very image of the serious, self-satisfied medieval burgher. The *salon doré*, the room in which de Médici was supposed to sleep, has also been preserved.

Lesser mortals wanting to **stay** the night could try the appealing *Hostellerie Le Donjon* (℡05.53.04.82.81, Ⓦwww.hostellerie-ledonjon.fr; closed mid-Nov to Easter; ❸; *menus* €23 & €29), on the main street, with seven nice, simple rooms around a charming courtyard, or the more upmarket *Hostellerie Les Griffons* (℡05.53.45.45.35, Ⓦwww.griffons.fr; closed Nov–Easter; ❻) in a sixteenth-century house beside the old bridge, with a restaurant serving top-notch regional cuisine (*menus* from €33.50; open daily for dinner, but only Sun for lunch).

Aubeterre-sur-Dronne

Rather touristy, but very beautiful with its ancient galleried and turreted houses, **AUBETERRE-SUR-DRONNE** hangs on a steep hillside above the river some 30km downstream of Ribérac. Its principal curiosity is the cavernous **Église Monolithe** (daily 9.30am–noon & 2–6pm; €4.50), carved out of the soft rock of the cliff face in the twelfth century, with its rock-hewn tombs going back to the sixth. A (blocked-off) tunnel connects with the **château** on the bluff overhead. There's also the extremely beautiful church of **St-Jacques**, with an eleventh-century facade sculpted and decorated in the richly carved Poitiers style on the street leading uphill from the square.

The **tourist office** is beside the main car park (June & Sept Mon & Sat 2–6pm, Tues–Fri 10am–noon & 2–6pm; July & Aug Mon 2–7pm, Tues–Sun 10am–12.30pm & 2–7pm; Oct–May Mon–Fri 2–6pm; ☎05.45.98.57.18, ⓦaubeterresurdronne .com). You'll find comfortable **accommodation** and a fine restaurant just below the village at the *Hostellerie du Périgord*, beside the bridge (☎05.45.98.50.46, ⓦwww.hostellerie-perigord.com; ❸; *menus* €15.50–43.50; closed Sun eve & Mon). There's also a **campsite** (☎05.45.98.60.17; May–Sept) across the other side of the river. An early-morning **bus** runs to Angoulême (Mon–Fri, also Sat in July & Aug), while Chalais, which is on the Angoulême train line, is only 12km away.

South of Aubeterre the country gradually changes. Farmland gives way to an extensive forest of oak and sweet chestnut, bracken and broom, interspersed with sour, marshy pasture. Sparsely populated, it is ideal cycling and picnicking country.

St-Jean-de-Côle and around

Twenty kilometres northeast of Brantôme, **ST-JEAN-DE-CÔLE** ranks as one of the loveliest villages in the Dordogne. Its ancient houses huddle together in typical medieval fashion around a wide sandy square dominated by the charmingly ill-proportioned eleventh-century **church of St-Jean-Baptiste** and the rugged-looking **Château de la Marthonie** (not generally open to the public). The château, which dates from the twelfth century, has acquired various additions in a pleasingly organic fashion.

The **tourist office** (mid-June to mid-Sept daily 10am–12.30pm & 2–6.30pm; mid-Sept to mid-June Thurs–Sun 10am–1pm & 2–6pm; ☎05.53.62.14.15, ⓦwww.ville-saint-jean-de-cole.fr) is also on the square, as is the attractive **restaurant** *La Perla*, serving salads and light lunches (daily July & Aug, otherwise closed Mon & Oct–March). However, for good traditional fare like truffle omelette, you can't beat the wisteria-covered *St-Jean* (☎05.53.52.23.20; closed Sun eve & Mon; *menus* from €15) on the main road through the village.

Around 10km west of St-Jean, just outside the village of **VILLARS**, the **Château de Puyguilhem** (May–Aug daily 10am–12.30pm & 2–6.30pm; Sept–April Wed–Sun 10am–12.30pm & 2–5.30pm; €5; ⓦpuyguilhem.monuments-nationaux .fr) sits on the edge of a valley backed by oak woods. It was erected at the beginning of the sixteenth century on the site of an earlier military fortress. With its octagonal tower, broad spiral staircase, steep roofs, magnificent fireplaces and false dormer windows, it's a perfect example of French Renaissance architecture. From the gallery at the top of the stairs you get a close-up of the roof and window decoration, as well as a view down the valley, which once was filled by an ornamental lake.

A short distance north of Villars, the **Grotte de Villars** (daily: April–June & Sept 10am–noon & 2–7pm; July & Aug 10am–7.30pm; Oct 2–6.30pm; closed Nov–March; €7.50; ⓦwww.grotte-villars.com) boasts a few prehistoric paintings – notably of horses and a still unexplained scene of a man and a bison. The main reason for coming here, is to see the impressive array of stalactites and stalagmites.

Château de Hautefort

Forty kilometres east of Périgueux (take the D5 along the River Auvézère for the most attractive route), the **Château de Hautefort** (March & Nov 1–11 Sat & Sun 2–6pm; April & May daily 10am–12.30pm & 2–6.30pm; June–Sept daily 9.30am–7pm; Oct daily 2–6pm; closed Nov 12 to Feb; €8.50; ⓦwww.chateau -hautefort.com) enjoys a majestic position at the end of a wooded spur above its feudal village. A magnificent example of good living on a grand scale, the castle has an elegance that is out of step with the usual rough stone fortresses of Périgord. The approach is across a wide esplanade flanked by formal gardens, over a drawbridge, and into a stylish Renaissance courtyard, open to the south. In 1968 a fire gutted the castle, but it has since been meticulously restored using traditional techniques; it's all unmistakably new, but the quality of the craftsmanship is superb.

Hautefort has a very pleasant **hotel**, the *Auberge du Parc* (☎05.53.50.88.98, Ⓦ www.aubergeduparc-hautefort.fr; closed mid-Dec to Feb; ❷; restaurant *menus* €17.50–40; closed Sun eve & Wed), just beneath the castle walls.

Périgord Pourpre

The area known as the **Périgord Pourpre** takes its name from the wine-growing region concentrated in the southwest corner of the Dordogne *département*, most famous for the sweet white wines produced around **Monbazillac**. The only town of any size is **Bergerac**, which makes a good base for exploring the vineyards and the uplands to the south. These are peppered with *bastides*, medieval fortified towns (see box opposite), such as the beautifully preserved **Monpazier**, and here also you'll find the **Château de Biron**, which dominates the countryside for miles around.

Bergerac

BERGERAC, "capital" of Périgord Pourpre, lies on the riverbank in the wide plain of the Dordogne. Once a flourishing port for the wine trade, it is still the main market centre for the surrounding maize, vine and tobacco farms. Devastated in the Wars of Religion, when most of its Protestant population fled overseas, Bergerac is now essentially a modern town with some interesting and attractive reminders of the past.

Arrival and information

The **gare SNCF** is at the end of cours Alsace-Lorraine, ten minutes' walk north from the Old Town, while the **airport** (☎05.53.22.25.25) lies 5km southeast of Bergerac (roughly €15 by taxi). The main **tourist office** is at 97 rue Neuve-d'Argenson, two minutes' walk northeast of the Old Town (July & Aug Mon–Sat 9.30am–7.30pm, Sun 10.30am–1pm, 2.30–7pm; Sept–June Mon–Sat 9.30am–1pm & 2–7pm; ☎05.53.57.03.11, Ⓦ www.bergerac-tourisme.com), and a second office opens in summer behind the Maison des Vins in the Cloître des Récollets (July & Aug daily 10.30am–1pm & 2.30–7pm). You can rent motorbikes, scooters and **bicycles** from Apolo Cycles (☎06.20.64.59.25, Ⓦ www.apolo-cycles.com), which has an outlet by the port in summer (June–Sept) and will otherwise deliver to your hotel. A vast **market** takes place on Wednesday and Saturday mornings in the covered *halles* in the Old Town centre and around Notre-Dame church. If you're here in July, don't miss the magnificent La Table de Cyrano **food festival** in the week of July 14.

Accommodation

There's a decent range of **accommodation** to choose from. The best budget option is *Le Moderne*, opposite the station (☎05.53.57.19.62, Ⓕ05.53.61.80.50; ❶), a welcoming, well-kept place with a brasserie (closed Sun eve; *menus* from €20). For something more comfortable, try one of the two three-star hotels on place Gambetta between the station and the Old Town, both with open-air swimming pools: the *France* (☎05.53.57.11.61, Ⓦ www.hoteldefrance-bergerac.com; ❸), with small, simple rooms, some with balconies and air conditioning, or the *Bordeaux* (☎05.53.57.12.83, Ⓦ www.hotel-bordeaux-bergerac.com; ❹), with bright, comfortably furnished rooms; in both cases rooms at the back are quieter than those on the square. There's also a municipal **campsite**, *La Pelouse* (☎05.53.57.06.67, ⒺⒸcamping@ville-bergerac.fr; mid-Feb to Oct), on the south bank of the river.

The Town

The compact **vieille ville** is a beguiling area to wander through, with numerous late-medieval houses and one or two beautiful squares. In rue de l'Ancien-Pont, the splendid seventeenth-century Maison Peyrarède houses an informative **Musée du Tabac** (March 15 to Nov 15 Tues–Fri 10am–noon & 2–6pm, Sat 10am–noon & 2–5pm, Sun 2.30–6.30pm; Nov 16 to March 14 Tues–Fri 10am–noon & 2–6pm, Sat 10am–noon; €3.50), detailing the history of the plant, with collections of pipes and tools of the trade.

Bergerac has a couple of other museums, the best of which is the small **Musée du Vin et de la Batellerie** in rue des Conférences in the heart of the Old Town (Tues–Fri 10am–noon & 2–5.30pm, Sat 10am–noon; mid-March to mid-Nov also Sun 2.30–6.30pm; €2.50), focusing on viticulture, barrel-making and the town's once bustling river trade. Nearby, on the picturesque place de la Myrpe and further up the hill on place Pélissière, are two statues in honour of **Cyrano de Bergerac**, the town's most famous association. The big-nosed hero of Edmond

Bastides

From the Occitan word *bastida*, meaning a group of buildings, **bastides** were the new towns of the thirteenth and fourteenth centuries. Although they are found all over southwest France, from the Dordogne to the foothills of the Pyrenees, there is a particularly high concentration in the area between the Dordogne and Lot rivers, which at that time formed the disputed "frontier" region between English-held Aquitaine and Capetian France.

That said, the earliest *bastides* were founded largely for economic and political reasons. They were a means of bringing new land into production – in an era of rapid population growth and technological innovation – and thus extending the power of the local lord. But as tensions between the French and English forces intensified in the late thirteenth century, so the motive became increasingly military. The *bastides* provided a handy way of securing the land along the frontier, and it was generally at this point that they were fortified.

As an incentive, anyone who was prepared to build, inhabit and defend the *bastide* was granted various benefits in a founding charter. All new residents were allocated a building plot, garden and cultivable land. The charter might also offer asylum to certain types of criminal or grant exemption from military service, and would allow the election of consuls charged with day-to-day administration – a measure of self-government remarkable in feudal times. Taxes and judicial affairs, meanwhile, remained the preserve of the representative of the king or local lord under whose ultimate authority the *bastide* lay.

The other defining feature of a *bastide* is its layout. They are nearly always square or rectangular in shape and are divided by streets at right angles to each other, producing a chequerboard pattern. The focal point is the market square, often missing its covered *halle* nowadays, but generally still surrounded by arcades, while the church is relegated to one side.

The busiest *bastide* founders were Alphonse de Poitiers, on behalf of the French crown, after he became Count of Toulouse in 1249, and King Edward I of England (1272–1307), who wished to consolidate his hold on the northern borders of his Duchy of Aquitaine. The former chalked up a total of 57 *bastides*, including **Villeneuve-sur-Lot** (1251) and **Monflanquin** (1252), while Edward was responsible for **Beaumont** (1272) and **Monpazier** (1284), among others. While many *bastides* retain only vestiges of their original aspect, both Monpazier and Monflanquin have survived almost entirely intact.

Rostand's play, though fictional, was inspired by the seventeenth-century philosopher of the same name, who, sadly, had nothing to do with the town.

Wine-lovers should make a beeline for the **Maison des Vins**, down by the river on quai Salvette (Feb–June & Sept–Dec Tues–Sat 10.30am–12.30pm & 2–6pm; July & Aug daily 10am–7pm; closed Jan; ⓦwww.vins-bergerac.fr), which offers free tastings and beginners' courses in July and August (Ⓣ05.53.63.57.55; €5). It also sells a selection of local wines and provides information about visiting the surrounding vineyards.

Eating

For **eating**, *Côté Noix*, on place Pélissière (closed Sun & Mon), makes a great pit-stop with its mouth-watering array of home-made cakes and light lunches, while *La Blanche Hermine*, beside the covered market (closed Sun & Mon), is a cheerful crêperie dishing up an imaginative range of buckwheat crêpes as well as copious salads – all at very reasonable prices. Nearby, *La Table du Marché*, 21 place de la Bardonnie (*menu* €22; closed Wed & Thurs eve and Sun), offers innovative takes on classic dishes, such as cucumber gazpacho or prawn and mango *ceviche*.

Monpazier and around

MONPAZIER, founded in 1284 by King Edward I of England (who was also Duke of Aquitaine), is one of the most complete of the surviving *bastides*. Picturesque and placid though it is today, the village has a hard and bitter history, being twice – in 1594 and 1637 – the centre of peasant rebellions provoked by the misery following the Wars of Religion. Both uprisings were brutally suppressed: the 1637 peasants' leader was broken on the wheel in the square. Sully, the Protestant general, describes a rare moment of light relief in the terrible wars, when the men of the Catholic *bastide* of Villefranche-du-Périgord planned to capture Monpazier on the same night as the men of Monpazier planned to capture Villefranche. By chance, both sides took different routes, met no resistance, looted to their hearts' content and returned home congratulating themselves on their luck and skill, only to find in the morning that things were rather different. The peace terms required that everything was returned to its proper place.

Monpazier follows the typical *bastide* layout, with a grid of streets built around a gem of a central square. Deep, shady arcades pass under all the houses, which are separated from each other by a small gap to reduce fire risk; at the corners the buttresses are cut away to allow the passage of laden pack animals. There's also an ancient *lavoir* where women used to wash clothes, and a much altered church.

The **tourist office** is on the central square (July & Aug daily 10am–12.30pm & 2–7pm; Sept–June Tues–Sun 10am–12.30pm & 2–6pm; ⓉP05.53.22.68.59, ⓦwww.pays-des-bastides.com), where you'll also find reasonable **accommodation** and a good traditional **restaurant** at the *Hôtel de France*, 21 rue St-Jacques (ⓉP05.53.22.60.06, ⓦwww.hoteldefrancemonpazier.fr; closed Nov–Easter; ❷; *menus* from €17, closed Tues eve & Wed, open daily July & Aug). A more luxurious option is the *Hôtel Edward 1ᵉʳ* (ⓉP05.53.22.44.00, ⓦwww.hoteledward1er.com; closed mid-Nov to mid-March; ❺) at 5 rue St-Pierre, a few minutes' walk from the main square, with its own swimming pool and a restaurant with *menus* from €29.50 (reservations required; closed Wed eve & mid-Nov to mid-March). The best of the local **campsites** is the luxurious *Moulin de David*, roughly 3km south on the road to Villeréal (ⓉP05.53.22.65.25, ⓦwww.moulin-de-david.com; April to mid-Sept).

The Château de Biron

Eight kilometres south of Monpazier, the vast **Château de Biron** (Feb, March, Nov & Dec Tues–Thurs & Sun 10am–12.30pm & 2–5.30pm; April–June daily

10am–6pm; July & Aug daily 10am–7pm; Sept & Oct Tues–Sun 10am–12.30pm & 2–6pm; €6.50; Ⓦwww.semitour.com) was begun in the eleventh century and added to piecemeal afterwards. You can take a guided tour (in French only), but it's better to borrow the English-language translation and wander at will around the rooms and the grassy courtyard, where there is a restored Renaissance chapel and guardhouse with tremendous views over the roofs of the feudal village below.

A single street runs through the village of **BIRON**, past a covered **market** on timber supports iron-hard with age, and out under an arched gateway, where well-manured vegetable plots interspersed with iris, lily and Iceland poppies lie under the tumbledown walls. At the bottom of the hill, another group of houses stands on a small square with a well in front of the village **church**, its Romanesque origins hidden by motley alterations.

Périgord Noir

Périgord Noir encompasses the central part of the valley of the Dordogne, and the valley of the Vézère. This is the distinctive Dordogne country: deep-cut valleys between limestone cliffs, with fields of maize in the alluvial bottoms and dense oak woods on the heights, interspersed with patches of not very fertile

farmland. Plantations of walnut trees (cultivated for their oil), flocks of low-slung grey geese (their livers enlarged for foie gras) and prehistoric-looking stone huts called *bories* are all hallmarks of Périgord Noir.

The well-preserved medieval architecture of **Sarlat**, the wealth of **prehistory** and the staggering cave paintings of the **Vézère valley**, and the stunning beauty of the château-studded **Dordogne** have all contributed to making this one of the most heavily touristed inland areas of France, with all the concomitant problems of crowds, high prices and tack. If possible, it's worth coming out of season, but if you can't, seek accommodation away from the main centres, and always drive along the back roads – the smaller the better – even when there is a more direct route available.

Sarlat and around

SARLAT-LA-CANÉDA, "capital" of Périgord Noir, lies in a hollow between hills 10km or so back from the Dordogne river. You hardly notice the modern town, as it's mainly fifteenth- and sixteenth-century houses of the *vieille ville* in mellow, honey-coloured stone that draw the attention.

Arrival and information

The **gare SNCF** is just over 1km south of the Old Town, where on rue Tourny you'll find the **tourist office** (April & Sept–Nov Mon–Sat 9am–noon & 2–6pm, Sun 10am–1pm; May & June Mon–Sat 9am–6pm, Sun 10am–1pm & 2–5pm; July & Aug Mon–Sat 9am–7pm, Sun 10am–noon & 2–6pm; Dec–March Mon–Sat 9am–noon & 2–5pm; ☎05.53.31.45.45, ⓦwww.sarlat-tourisme.com). You can rent **bicycles** from Bike Bus (☎06.08.94.42.01, ⓦwww.multitravel.co.uk), through their outlet at Cycles Sarladais, avenue Aristide-Briand, while there is **internet** access at the *Salon de Thés*, opposite the *Mairie* on place de la Liberté (closed Mon, also Jan & Feb) – it's free if you eat there or €2.50 an hour otherwise.

Accommodation

One of the nicest and most reasonable **places to stay** in Sarlat is *La Couleuvrine* at 1 place de la Bouquerie, occupying a tower in the former ramparts on the northeast side of the Old Town (☎05.53.59.27.80, ⓦwww.la-couleuvrine .com; ❸); most of the rooms are quite small, though cosily furnished with solid dark furniture and pretty fabrics, and its fine, bustling restaurant takes up most of the ground floor (*menus* from €15). The *Hôtel des Récollets*, 4 rue Jean-Jacques Rousseau (☎05.53.31.36.00, ⓦwww.hotel-recollets-sarlat.com; ❸), is another good-value place, set in an old cloister around a little courtyard, with modern, rather functional small rooms, while the modern three-star *Hôtel de Selves*, 93 av de Selves (☎05.53.31.50.00, ⓦwww.selves-sarlat.com; closed mid-Jan to mid-Feb; ❺), boasts a pool and small garden. Ideal for families, groups or people wanting a longer stay is *La Villa des Consuls*, 3 rue Jean-Jacques Rousseau (☎05.53.31.90.05, ⓦwww.villaconsuls.fr; ❺), which, besides standard double rooms, also offers eight attractive, spacious apartments with their own kitchens and terraces. The nearest **campsite**, *Les Périères*, on Sarlat's northern outskirts (☎05.53.59.05.84, ⓦwww.lesperieres.com; March to mid-Nov), is very well equipped if pricey; a cheaper alternative is *Les Terrasses du Périgord*, about 2.5km north of Sarlat near Proissans village (☎05.53.59.02.25, ⓦwww.terrasses-du -perigord.com; April–Sept).

The Town

The **vieille ville** is an excellent example of medieval organic urban growth. It was also the first town to benefit from culture minister André Malraux's law of 1962

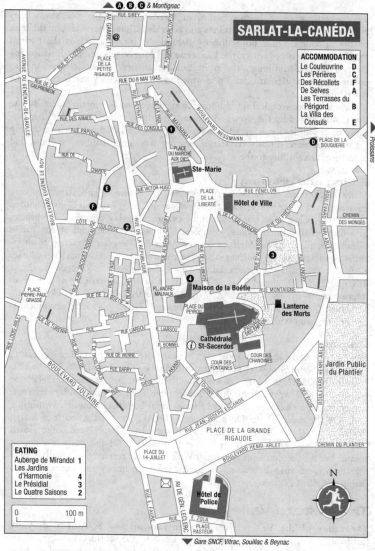

Within the map:

SARLAT-LA-CANÉDA

▲ Ⓐ, Ⓑ, Ⓒ & Montignac

RUE SIREY

AV. GAMBETTA

RUE ST-CYPRIEN

AVENUE DU GÉNÉRAL-DE-GAULLE

AVENUE DU GÉNÉRAL-DE-GAULLE

T. FOURNIER-SARLOVÈZE

@

PLACE DE LA PETITE RIGAUDIE

RUE DE LA CALPRENÈDE

RUE 8 MAI 1945

RUE DES ARMES

RUE PETRAT

RUE MAGNANAT

BOULEVARD NESSMANN

RUE PAPUCIE

RUE DES CONSULS ❶

PLACE DU MARCHÉ AUX OIES

RUE DE LA CHARITÉ

BOULEVARD EUGÈNE LE ROY

Ⓔ

RUE VICTOR-HUGO

Ste-Marie

PLACE DE LA LIBERTÉ

RUE FÉNELON

PLACE DE LA BOUQUERIE

Ⓓ

Poissans ▶

BOULEVARD HENRI-ARLET

CHEMIN DES MONGES

Ⓕ

CÔTE DE TOULOUSE

❷

RUE DE LA RÉPUBLIQUE

RUE ALBÉRIC-CAUSIET

RUE DE LA RÉPUBLIQUE

Hôtel de Ville

R. DE LA SALAMANDRE

RUE DU PRÉSIDAL

RUE D'ALBUSSE

❸

RUE LANDRY

PLACE PIERRE-PAUL GRASSÉ

RUE JEAN-JACQUES-ROUSSEAU

RUE DE LA BOÉTIE

RUE DE TAGE

R. BLANCHET

ROUSSET

PL. ANDRÉ-MALRAUX

❹ **Maison de la Boétie**

RUE DE LA BRÈCHE

RUE MONTAIGNE

RUE DE TURENNE

R. LIARSOU

RUE LIARSOU

PLACE DU PEYROU

Lanterne des Morts

PASSAGE DES ENFERS

RUE LOUIS-ARLET

RUE DE VIENNE

R. BONNEL

ⓘ **Cathédrale St-Sacerdos**

COUR DES CHANOINES

BOULEVARD HENRI-ARLET

Jardin Public du Plantier

RUE DU SIÈGE

RUE DES TROIS CONTES

RUE BARRY

RUE LAKANAL

COUR DES FONTAINES

RUE DES ÉCUS

BOULEVARD VOLTAIRE

RUE DU SIÈGE

RUE TOURNY

RUE JEAN-JOSEPH-ESCANDE

PLACE DE LA GRANDE RIGAUDIE

CHEMIN DU PLANTIER

PLACE DU 14-JUILLET

BOULEVARD HENRI-ARLET

AV. DU GÉN. LECLERC

N

Hôtel de Police

RUE E. FAURE

E. ZOLA

PLACE PASTEUR

▼ Gare SNCF, Vitrac, Souillac & Beynac

ACCOMMODATION

Le Couleuvrine	D
Les Périères	C
Des Récollets	F
De Selves	A
Les Terrasses du Périgord	B
La Villa des Consuls	E

EATING

Auberge de Mirandol	1
Les Jardins d'Harmonie	4
Le Présidial	3
Le Quatre Saisons	2

0   100 m

---

which created the concept of a *secteur sauvegardé* (protected area), and boasts no fewer than 65 protected buildings and monuments. The old centre is violated only by the straight swath of the rue de la République which cuts through its middle. The west side remains relatively quiet, whereas the east side is where most people wander. Approaching from the south, rue Lakanal leads to the large and unexciting **Cathédrale St-Sacerdos**, mostly dating from its seventeenth-century renovation. Opposite stands the town's finest house, the **Maison de La Boétie** (not open to the public) where the poet and humanist Étienne de La Boétie was born in 1530, with its gabled tiers of windows and characteristic steep roof stacked with heavy limestone tiles (*lauzes*).

For a better sense of the medieval town, wander through the cool, shady lanes and courtyards – **cour des Fontaines** and **cour des Chanoines** – around the back of the cathedral. On a slope directly behind the cathedral stands the curious twelfth-century coned tower, the **Lanterne des Morts**, whose exact function has escaped historians, though the most popular theory is that it was built to commemorate St Bernard, who performed various miracles when he visited the town in 1147.

There are more wonderful old houses in the streets to the north, especially **rue des Consuls**, and up the slopes to the east. Eventually, though, Sarlat's labyrinthine lanes will lead you back to the central **place de la Liberté**, where the big Saturday **market** spreads its stands bearing foie gras, truffles, walnuts and mushrooms, according to the season.

Eating and drinking

Many **restaurants** in Sarlat open only for the summer and standards vary enormously. Two safe choices are the *Auberge de Mirandol*, 7 rue des Consuls (closed Dec to mid-Feb & Mon out of season), serving reasonably priced local delicacies in a fourteenth-century house, complete with its own *cave*, and ℀ *Les Jardins d'Harmonie*, place André-Malraux (closed Mon & Tues), an attractive teashop-cum-restaurant serving gourmet salads and main dishes at lunchtime (two courses €20). For something a bit special, try *Le Quatre Saisons*, 2 côte de Toulouse (℡05.53.29.48.59; closed Tues & Wed out of season; *menus* €20–49), with an interior courtyard, or *Le Présidial*, 6 rue Landry (℡05.53.28.92.47; closed Sun, Mon lunch, Thurs lunch & Nov–March; *menus* €19–39), in a lovely seventeenth-century mansion with a walled garden.

Carsac

Not far from Sarlat there are some very pleasant alternatives to staying – or eating – in Sarlat. Some 5km to the east, just outside the village of **CARSAC**, *La Villa Romaine* (℡05.53.28.52.07, Ⓦwww.lavillaromaine.com; closed mid-Feb to mid-March & 2 weeks in Nov; ❼; *menus* from €29, eve only) offers extreme pampering in a cluster of attractive former farm buildings around a swimming pool. On the banks of the Dordogne at **VITRAC**, about 7km south of Sarlat, ℀ *Hôtel La Treille* (℡05.53.28.33.19, Ⓦwww.latreille-perigord.com; closed mid-Nov to mid-Dec, also Mon & Tues Oct–March; ❸) also has a few decent rooms, but it's the excellent restaurant with its sunny terrace that's really worth coming for, offering dishes such as roast duck with honey and juniper berries (*menus* €16.50–45).

The Vézère valley

The **valley of the Vézère** river between **Limeuil** and **St-Amand-de-Coly** justifiably styles itself as the **prehistory** capital of the world. The high, rocky outcrops which overlook acres of thick forest are riddled with caves which have provided shelter for humans for tens of thousands of years. It was here that the first skeletons of **Cro-Magnon people** – the first Homo sapiens, tall and muscular with a large skull – were unearthed in 1868 by labourers building the Périgueux–Agen train line. Since then, an incomparable wealth of archeological and artistic evidence of late Stone Age people has been revealed, most famously in the breathtakingly sophisticated **cave paintings** of **Lascaux** and **Font de Gaume**.

Away from the throngs of visitors at the caves, there is much to appreciate in the peace and quiet of the Vézère valley. It's best enjoyed from a **canoe**, where you'll often find yourself alone in a bend of the river, rather than part of a vast armada, as tends to be the case on the Dordogne.

Limeuil

Built into the steep slope at the confluence of the Dordogne and Vézère rivers, the beautiful village of **LIMEUIL** is a picturesque place to while away a couple of hours. From the riverbank – an ideal picnic spot, with a pebbly beach for those who fancy a dip – the narrow, cobbled rue du Port leads steeply uphill, winding in between medieval houses and through the old gateways. At the top, the best views out over the village and surrounding countryside have been monopolized by the **Parc Panoramique** (April–June & Sept–Nov Sun–Fri 10am–12.30pm & 2.30–6pm; July & Aug daily 10am–8pm; €6), a wilderness of trees, shrubs and crumbling stone walls. For an even more classic view of the Dordogne valley, however, head west on the D31 towards Trémolat to find a vantage point looking down on one of two huge meanders in the river.

Canoes can be rented for trips on either river at the "port" (℡05.53.63.38.73, Ⓦ www.canoes-rivieres-loisirs.com), where there are also a couple of **eating** options: the bar-brasserie *À l'Ancre de Salut* (closed Nov–March & eve except in July & Aug; *menus* from €15.50), and the slightly more formal *Le Chai* (closed Wed & mid-Nov to early Feb; *menus* from €21.50), serving pizzas plus local cuisine and a vast range of ice creams and sorbets.

Les Eyzies-de-Tayac

The main base for visiting many of the prehistoric painted caves is **LES EYZIES-DE-TAYAC**, a one-street village lined with gift shops and foie gras outlets. While you're here, it's worth visiting the excellent **Musée National de Préhistoire** (June & Sept daily except Tues 9.30am–6pm; July & Aug daily 9.30am–6.30pm; Oct–May daily except Tues 9.30am–12.30pm & 2–5.30pm; €5; Ⓦ www.musee-prehistoire-eyzies.fr), which contains many important prehistoric artefacts found in the various caves in the region. Look out for the oil lamp from Lascaux and the exhibits from La Madeleine, to the north of Les Eyzies, including a superb bas-relief of a bison licking its flank.

The **tourist office** (April to mid-June Mon–Sat 9am–noon & 2–6pm, Sun 10am–noon & 2–5pm; mid-June to mid-Sept Mon–Sat 9am–7pm, Sun 10am–noon & 2–6pm; mid-Sept to March Mon–Fri 9am–noon & 2–6pm, Sat 10am–noon & 2–5pm; ℡05.53.06.97.05, Ⓦ www.tourisme-terredecromagnon.com), on the main street, offers **bike** rental, **internet** access and information on local *chambres d'hôtes* and *gîtes d'étape*, among other things. For **canoe** rental, try AVCK (℡05.53.06.92.92, Ⓦ www.vezere-canoe.com), which offers trips between Thonac and Le Bugue.

Hotels are pricey and may require half-board in high season, while most are closed in winter. A good-value option is *La Rivière*, in a quiet spot about 1km away on the Périgueux road, with a handful of bright, well-kept rooms (℡05.53.06.97.14, Ⓦ www.lariviereleseyzies.com; closed Nov–March; ❷) and a restaurant serving simple meals. There is also a **campsite** here (April–Oct), under the same management. In a lovely spot by a millrace just east of the centre nestles ivy-covered *Le Moulin de la Beune* (℡05.53.06.94.33, Ⓦ www.moulindelabeune.com; closed Nov–March; ❸), with simple, spacious rooms and an excellent restaurant (closed for lunch Tues, Wed & Sat; *menus* €18–48). North of the centre, near the tiny railway station, is the elegant ⚹ *Les Glycines* (℡05.53.06.97.07, Ⓦ www.les-glycines-dordogne.com; closed Nov–March; ❺; three-course *menus* from €39), offering very pretty, romantic rooms with drapes and frills, some overlooking the extensive, beautiful grounds and swimming pool; the hotel's *potager* provides much of the produce used in the fine restaurant. Another nice place to stay is *Hôtel du Château* (℡05.53.07.23.50, Ⓦ www.hotelcampagne24.fr; closed mid-Oct to Easter; ❸) in **CAMPAGNE**, a pretty village 6km downstream; here you'll find big, bright rooms and regional *menus* from €20.

When it comes to **eating**, you're best off dining in one of the hotel restaurants mentioned above. Alternatively, there's a clutch of cheap and cheerful bar-brasseries around the tourist office, or you could take a picnic down to the river.

Around Les Eyzies

There are more **prehistoric caves** around Les Eyzies than you could possibly hope to visit in one day. Besides, the compulsory guided tours are tiring, so it's best to select just a couple of the ones listed below.

Most of these caves were not used as permanent homes, and there are various theories as to the purpose of such inaccessible spots. Most agree that they were sanctuaries and, if not actually places of worship, at least had religious significance. One suggestion is that making images of animals that were commonly hunted – like reindeer and bison – or feared – like bears and mammoths – was a kind of sympathetic magic intended to help men either catch or evade these animals. Another is that they were part of a fertility cult: sexual images of women with pendulous breasts and protuberant behinds are common. Others argue that these cave paintings served educational purposes, making parallels with Australian aborigines who used similar images to teach their young vital survival information as well as the history and mythological origins of their people. But much remains unexplained – the abstract signs that appear in so many caves, for example, and the arrows which clearly cannot be arrows, since Stone Age arrowheads looked different from these representations.

Grotte de Font-de-Gaume

Since its discovery in 1901, dozens of polychrome paintings have been found in the **Grotte de Font-de-Gaume** (daily except Sat: mid-May to mid-Sept 9.30am–5.30pm; mid-Sept to mid-May 9.30am–12.30pm & 2–5.30pm; €7; ⊤05.53.06.86.00, ⓔ fontdegaume@monuments-nationaux.fr), 1.5km along the D47 to Sarlat. Be aware that only 180 people are allowed to visit the cave each day and tickets sell out fast. You are advised to book (by phone or email) at least a month ahead in high season and well in advance at other times. You have to pay at the same time (€1.50 reservation fee; credit cards accepted) and tickets cannot be cancelled, though you can change the date and time if necessary. If you want to chance it, it's still worth enquiring on site first thing in the morning, as some tickets may be held back to be sold on the day.

The **cave** was first settled by Stone Age people during the last Ice Age – about 25,000 BC – when the Dordogne was the domain of roaming bison, reindeer and mammoths. The entrance is no more than a fissure concealed by rocks and trees above a small lush valley, leading to a narrow twisting passage. The first painting you see is a frieze of bison, reddish-brown in colour, massive, full of movement and very far from the primitive representations you might expect. Further on comes the most miraculous image of all, a **frieze** of five bison discovered in 1966 during cleaning operations. The colour, remarkably sharp and vivid, is preserved by a protective layer of calcite. Shading under the belly and down the thighs is used to give three-dimensionality with a sophistication that seems utterly modern. Another panel consists of superimposed drawings, a fairly common phenomenon in cave painting, sometimes the result of work by successive generations, but here an obviously deliberate technique. A reindeer in the foreground shares legs with a large bison behind to indicate perspective.

Stocks of **artists' materials** have also been found: kilos of prepared pigments; palettes – stones stained with ground-up earth pigments; and wooden painting sticks. Painting was clearly a specialized, perhaps professional, business, reproduced in dozens of caves located in the central Pyrenees and northern Spain.

Grotte des Combarelles

The **Grotte des Combarelles** (same hours as Font-de-Gaume; maximum six people per tour; €7), 2km along the D47 towards Sarlat, was discovered in 1910. The innermost part of the cave is covered with **engravings** from the Magdalenian period (about 12,000 years ago). Drawn over a period of two thousand years, many are superimposed one upon another, and include horses, reindeer, mammoths and stylized human figures – among the finest are the heads of a horse and a lioness. As with Font-de-Gaume, pre-booking is essential, especially in peak season (same phone and email); collect tickets from Font-de-Gaume.

Abri du Cap Blanc and the Château de Commarque

Not a cave but a natural rock shelter, the **Abri du Cap Blanc** (same hours as Font-de-Gaume, but phone to check in the off-season; €7; ℡05.53.06.86.00) lies on a steep wooded hillside about 7km east of Les Eyzies. The shelter contains a **sculpted frieze** of horses and bison dating from the Middle Magdalenian period, about 14,000 years ago. Of only ten surviving prehistoric sculptures in France, this is undoubtedly the best. The design is deliberate, with the sculptures polished and set off against a pockmarked background. But what makes this place extraordinary is not just the large scale, but the high relief of some of the sculptures. This was only possible in places where light reached in, which in turn brought the danger of destruction by exposure to the air. Cro-Magnon people actually lived in this shelter, and a female skeleton some two thousand years younger than the frieze was found here.

For a non-cave detour, continue a little further up the heavily wooded Beune valley to visit the romantic ruins of the **Château de Commarque** (daily: April 10am–6pm; May, June & Sept 10am–7pm; July & Aug 10am–8pm; €6.40; ⓦwww.commarque.com). Dating from the twelfth century, it was originally a **castrum**, a fortified village made up of six separate fortresses, each belonging to a different noble family. The ruins have now been made structurally sound and it's possible to climb the 30m-high tower for views over the surrounding countryside. You can reach the château by a footpath starting below Cap Blanc. Cars have to approach from the south, following signs from the D47 Sarlat road.

Grotte du Grand Roc

As well as prehistoric cave paintings, you can see some truly spectacular **stalactites** and **stalagmites** in the area around Les Eyzies. Some of the best examples are off the D47 towards Périgueux, 2km north of Les Eyzies, in the **Grotte du Grand Roc** (daily: Easter–June, Sept–Nov & Christmas hols 10am–6pm; July & Aug 9.30am–7pm; €7.50), whose entrance is high up in the cliffs that line much of the Vézère valley. There's a great view from the mouth of the cave and, inside, along some eighty metres of tunnel, a fantastic array of rock formations.

La Roque St-Christophe

The enormous prehistoric dwelling site, **La Roque St-Christophe** (daily: Feb, March & Oct 10am–6pm; April–June & Sept 10am–6.30pm; July & Aug 10am–8pm; Nov–Jan 2–5pm; €7; ⓦwww.roque-st-christophe.com), 9km northeast of Les Eyzies along the D706 to Montignac, is made up of about a hundred **rock shelters** on five levels, hollowed out of the limestone cliffs. The whole complex is nearly a kilometre long and about eighty metres above ground level, where the River Vézère once flowed. The earliest traces of occupation go back over 50,000 years. There are frequent guided visits in summer, or you could just take an English-language leaflet and wander at your own pace.

Montignac

Some 26km up the Vézère valley, **MONTIGNAC** is the main base for visiting the Lascaux cave. It's a more attractive place than Les Eyzies, with several wooden-balconied houses leaning appealingly over the river, a good **market** (Wed & Sat) and a lively annual **arts festival** (third week of July), featuring international folk groups. The **tourist office** is on place Bertran-de-Born (Feb–June, Sept & Oct Mon–Sat 9am–noon & 2–6pm; July & Aug daily 9am–7pm; Nov–Jan Mon–Sat 10am–noon & 2–5pm; ℡05.53.51.82.60, Ⓦwww.tourisme-montignac.com) and offers **internet** access. You can rent **canoes** from Kanoak (or ℡06.75.48.60.47, Ⓦc.farcache.free.fr) below the old bridge.

Hotels, as everywhere around here, get booked up quickly in summer. The cheapest rooms on offer – but still nice and cheerful – are at *Le P'tit Monde*, just out of the centre on the road to Sarlat (℡05.53.51.32.76, Ⓦwww.hotellepetitmonde .com), and it also has a reasonably priced restaurant. The nearby *Hôtel de la Grotte*, rue du 4-septembre (℡05.53.51.80.48, Ⓦwww.hoteldelagrotte.fr; ❸), is another good, reasonably priced option, with a restaurant and small but pleasant garden beside a stream; ask for rooms off the main road. A step up in price is the three-star *Relais du Soleil d'Or*, also on the main rue du 4-septembre (℡05.53.51.80.22, Ⓦwww.le-soleil-dor.com; closed two weeks in Feb; ❹), with a gourmet restaurant (Nov–March closed Sun eve & Mon; *menus* from €26.50) and its own pool set in a lovely garden, though the rooms are rather ordinary and a little old-fashioned. More character is to be found in the pretty, period rooms of the ivy- and wisteria-clad *Hostellerie de la Roseraie*, also with a pool and flower-filled garden, across the river in quiet place d'Armes (℡05.53.50.53.92, Ⓦwww.laroseraie-hotel.com; closed Nov–March; ❺; restaurant *menus* €25–50). Finally, there's a well-tended three-star **campsite**, *Le Moulin du Bleufond* (℡05.53.51.83.95, Ⓦwww.bleufond.com; April to mid-Oct), on the riverbank 500m downstream.

Grotte de Lascaux and Lascaux II

The **Grotte de Lascaux** was discovered in 1940 by four boys who were looking for their dog and stumbled across a deep cavern decorated with marvellously preserved **paintings** of animals. Executed by Cro-Magnon people 17,000 years ago, the paintings are among the finest examples of prehistoric art in existence. There are five or six identifiable styles, and subjects include bison, mammoths and horses, plus the biggest known prehistoric drawing, of a 5.5m bull with astonishingly expressive head and face. In 1948, the cave was opened to the public, and over the course of the next fifteen years more than a million tourists came to Lascaux. Sadly, because of deterioration caused by the heat and breath of visitors, the cave had to be closed in 1963; now you have to be content with the replica known as **Lascaux II**, 2km south of Montignac on the D704 (Feb, March, Nov & Dec Tues–Sun 10am–12.30pm & 2–5.30pm; April–June & Sept daily 9am–6.30pm; July & Aug daily 9am–7pm; Oct daily 10am–12.30pm & 2–6pm; closed Jan; €12.50; Ⓦwww.semitour.com). There are two thousand tickets on sale each day but these go fast in peak season; you can buy them in person a day or so in advance, while telephone bookings are accepted only in July and August (℡05.53.51.95.03). Note also that in winter (Oct–Easter) tickets are normally on sale at the site, while in summer (Easter–Sept) they are only available from an office (daily: July & Aug 9am–7pm; Sept & Easter to June 9am–6pm) beside Montignac tourist office – the system and opening times are somewhat fickle, however, so it's safest to check in Montignac before heading up to the cave.

Opened in 1983, Lascaux II was the result of eleven years' painstaking work by twenty artists and sculptors, using the same methods and materials as the original cave painters. While the visit can't offer the excitement of a real cave, the reconstruction rarely disappoints the thousands who trek here every year. The guided tour lasts forty minutes (commentary in French or English). For an enhanced appreciation of the cave itself, especially if you have children, it's worth visiting the combined animal park and museum, called the "Espace Cro-Magnon", at **Le Thot first** (Feb, March, Nov & Dec Tues–Sun 10am–12.30pm & 2–5.30pm; April–June & Sept daily 10am–6pm; July & Aug daily 10am–7pm; Oct daily 10am–12.30pm & 2–6pm; closed Jan; €6.50; Ⓦwww.semitour.com), 5km down the Vézère near **THONAC**. The video showing the construction of Lascaux II is particularly interesting, and there are Disneyesque mock-ups of prehistoric scenes and live examples of some of the animals featured in the paintings: European bison, long-horned cattle and Przewalski's horses, rare and beautiful animals from Mongolia believed to resemble the prehistoric wild horse – notice the erect mane.

St-Amand-de-Coly

Nine kilometres east of Montignac, the village of **ST-AMAND-DE-COLY** boasts a superbly beautiful fortified Romanesque church, a magical venue for concerts in the summer. Despite its bristling military architecture, the twelfth-century church manages to combine great delicacy and spirituality, with its purity of line and simple decoration most evocative in the low sun of late afternoon or early evening. Its defences left nothing to chance: the walls are four metres thick, a ditch runs all the way round, and a passage once skirted the eaves, with numerous positions for archers to rain down arrows and blind stairways to mislead attackers. Near the church, the unpretentious *Hôtel Gardette* (Ⓣ05.53.51.68.50, Ⓦwww .hotel-gardette.com; closed Oct–March; ❷; restaurant *menus* from €19) makes it possible to stay overnight in this tiny, idyllic place.

The middle Dordogne valley

The most familiar images of the River Dordogne are those from around **Beynac** and **La Roque-Gageac**, where the scenery is at its most spectacular, with clifftop châteaux facing each other across the valley. The most imposing of these date from the Hundred Years' War, when the river marked the frontier between French-held land to the north and English territory to the south. Further upstream, the hilltop *bastide* village of **Domme** offers stunning views, but is as crowded as Sarlat in summer.

Just south of the river, the **Abbaye de Cadouin** lies tucked out of harm's way in a fold of the landscape, hiding a lovely Gothic cloister. The train line from Bergerac to Sarlat runs along the river for this stretch, offering some wonderful views but unfortunately not stopping anywhere very useful; to appreciate the villages covered here, you need your own transport or, better still, a canoe.

The Abbaye de Cadouin

Before setting off up the Dordogne, it's worth taking a detour about 6km south of **LE BUISSON** to the twelfth-century Cistercian **Abbaye de Cadouin**. For eight hundred years until 1935 it drew flocks of pilgrims to wonder at a piece of cloth first mentioned by Simon de Montfort in 1214 and thought to be part of Christ's shroud. In 1935 the two bands of embroidery at either end were shown to contain an Arabic text from around the eleventh century. Since then the main attraction has been the finely sculpted but badly damaged capitals of the flamboyant Gothic **cloister** (Feb, March, Nov & Dec Mon, Wed, Thurs & Sun 10am–12.30pm & 2–5.30pm; April–June, Sept & Oct daily except Tues 10am–12.30pm & 2–6pm; July & Aug daily 10am–7pm; closed Jan; €5.50; Ⓦwww.semitour.com). Beside it stands a Romanesque **church** with a stark, bold front and wooden belfry roofed with chestnut shingles (chestnut trees abound around here – their timber was used in furniture-making and their nuts ground for flour during frequent famines).

Inside the church, the nave is slightly out of alignment; this is thought to be deliberate and perhaps a vestige of pagan attachments, as the three windows are aligned so that at the winter and summer solstices the sun shines through all three in a single shaft.

You can **stay** across the road at the *Restaurant de l'Abbaye* (℡05.53.63.40.93, Ⓔdelpech@orange.fr; ❷; restaurant closed Sun eve & Mon), which has five simple en-suite rooms and serves hearty, reasonably priced meals, all starting with a complimentary helping of the delicious house *soupe tourane* (garlic soup). You can also stay in the monks' dormitories themselves, now an excellent HI **youth hostel** (℡05.53.73.28.78, Ⓦwww.fuaj.org/cadouin; closed mid-Dec to Jan; dorm beds €18.40), and there's a small **campsite** in the village, *Les Jardins de l'Abbaye* (℡05.53.61.89.30, Ⓦwww.dordogne-perigord.com/jardins-abbaye; April–Oct).

The châteaux of Les Milandes and Castelnaud

The first of the string of châteaux that line the Dordogne east of Le Buisson is **Les Milandes** (daily: April & Oct Mon–Fri 10am–6.15pm, Sat 1.30–6.15pm, Sun 10am–6.15pm; May, June & Sept 10am–6.15pm; July & Aug 9.30am–7.30pm; €8.50; Ⓦwww.milandes.com), perched high on the south bank. Built in 1489, it was the property of the de Caumont family until the Revolution, but its most famous owner was the Folies Bergères star, Josephine Baker (see box opposite), who lived here from 1936 to 1968. The stories surrounding the place are more intriguing than the château itself, which contains a motley collection of Ms Baker's effects. The garden, meanwhile, hosts daily displays by birds of prey.

Further along on the same side of the river, the **Château de Fayrac** was an English forward position in the Hundred Years' War, built to watch over Beynac, on the opposite bank, where the French were holed up. All slated pepper-pot towers, it's unfortunately closed to the public, but you can visit the partially ruined **Château de Castelnaud** (daily: Feb, March & Oct 10am–6pm; April–June & Sept 10am–7pm; July & Aug 9am–8pm; Nov–Jan 2–5pm; €7.80, or €13.40 for a joint ticket with Marqueyssac; Ⓦwww.castelnaud.com), a little to the south of Fayrac and the true rival to Beynac in terms of impregnability – although it was successfully captured by the bellicose Simon de Montfort as early as 1214. The English held it for much of the Hundred Years' War, and it wasn't until the Revolution that it was finally abandoned. Fairly heavily restored in recent years, it now houses a highly informative **museum of medieval warfare**. Its core is an extensive collection of original weaponry, including all sorts of bizarre contraptions, and a fine assortment of armour.

Beynac-et-Cazenac

Clearly visible on an impregnable cliff on the north bank of the river, the eye-catching village and castle of **BEYNAC-ET-CAZENAC** was built in the days when the river was the only route open to traders and invaders. By road, it's 3km to the **château** (daily 10am–6pm; €7) but a steep lane leads up through the village and takes only 15 minutes by foot. It's protected on the landward side by a double wall; elsewhere the sheer drop of almost two hundred metres does the job. The flat terrace at the base of the keep, which was added by the English, conceals the remains of the houses where the beleaguered villagers lived. Richard the Lionheart held the place for a time, until a gangrenous wound received while besieging the castle of Châlus, north of Périgueux, ended his term of blood-letting.

Originally, to facilitate defence, the rooms inside the keep were only connected by a narrow spiral staircase. The division of domestic space into dining rooms and so forth only came about when the advent of artillery made these old châteaux-forts militarily obsolete. From the roof there's a stupendous – and vertiginous – view

Josephine Baker and the Rainbow Tribe

Born on June 3, 1906, in the black ghetto of East St Louis, Illinois, **Josephine Baker** was one of the most remarkable women of the twentieth century. Her mother washed clothes for a living, her father was a drummer who soon deserted his family, yet by the late 1920s Josephine was the most celebrated cabaret star in France, primarily due to her role in the legendary Folies Bergères show in Paris. On her first night, de Gaulle, Hemingway, Piaf and Stravinsky were among the audience, and her notoriety was further enhanced by her long line of illustrious husbands and lovers, which included the Crown Prince of Sweden and the crime novelist Georges Simenon. She also kept a pet cheetah called Mildred, with whom she used to walk around Paris. During the war, Baker was active in the Resistance, for which she won the Croix de Guerre, and later became involved in the civil rights movement in North America, where she insisted on playing to non-segregated audiences, a stance which got her arrested in Canada and tailed by the FBI in the US.

By far her most bizarre project was the château of **Les Milandes**, which she rented from 1936 and then bought in 1947, after she married the French orchestra leader Jo Bouillon. Having converted the place into two hotels with a mini-golf course, tennis court and an autobiographical wax museum, she opened the château to the general public as a model multicultural community, popularly dubbed the "*village du monde*". In the course of the 1950s, she adopted babies (mostly orphans) of different ethnic and religious backgrounds from around the world, and by the end of the decade had twelve children at Les Milandes, including a black Catholic Colombian and a Buddhist Korean, along with her mother, brother and sister from East St Louis.

Over 300,000 people a year visited the château in the 1950s, but the conservative local population was never very happy about Les Milandes and what Josephine dubbed her "Rainbow Tribe". In the 1960s, Baker's financial problems, divorce and two heart attacks spelled the end for the project and, despite a sit-in protest by Baker herself (by then in her 60s), the château was sold off in 1968. Josephine died of a stroke in 1975 and was given a state funeral at La Madeleine in Paris, mourned by thousands of her adopted countryfolk.

upriver to the **Château de Marqueyssac**, whose beautiful seventeenth- and nineteenth-century **gardens** extend along the ridge (same hours as Castelnaud; €7.20, or €13.40 for a joint ticket with Castelnaud).

For a different perspective of these châteaux, it's worth taking a **river cruise** with Gabarres de Beynac (April–Oct daily 10am–12.30pm & 2–6pm; €7.50; Ⓦwww.gabarre-beynac.com) on a replica *gabarre*, the traditional wooden river-craft. This is also classic **canoeing** country, with rental available from Canoë Copeyre (Ⓣ05.53.28.95.01, Ⓦwww.canoe-copeyre.com), among numerous outlets along this stretch of river.

The best of Beynac's **hotels** is the *Hôtel du Château* (Ⓣ05.53.29.19.20, Ⓦwww .hotelduchateau-dordogne.com; closed Dec to mid-Jan; ❸), with fresh, bright rooms, a small swimming pool and a good restaurant (*menus* from €21.50) with a terrace overlooking the river; though it's on the busy main road, rooms are double-glazed and some have air-conditioning. A little further east there's also a **campsite**, *Le Capeyrou* (Ⓣ05.53.29.54.95, Ⓦwww.campinglecapeyrou.com; April–Sept).

La Roque-Gageac

The village of **LA ROQUE-GAGEAC** is almost too perfect, its ochre-coloured houses sheltering under dramatically overhanging cliffs. It inevitably pulls in the tourist buses, and since the main road separates the village from the river, the noise and fumes of the traffic can become oppressive. The best way to escape is to slip away through the lanes and alleyways that wind up through the terraced houses. Alternatively, hop on a *gabarre* for a leisurely **river trip** (daily: April–Sept 10am–6pm; Oct 2–5pm; €8.50; Ⓦwww.gabarres.com), or rent a **canoe** (Ⓣ05.53.28.17.07, Ⓦwww.canoevacances.com) and paddle over to the opposite bank, where you can picnic and enjoy a great view of the village, at its best in the burnt-orange glow of the evening sun.

Most people just come here for the afternoon, so there's usually space if you want to **stay** the night, most pleasantly at *La Belle Étoile* (Ⓣ05.53.29.51.44, Ⓦwww.belleetoile.fr; closed Nov–March; ❸), whose restaurant serves good traditional cuisine (closed Mon & lunch Wed; *menus* from €26), and whose more expensive rooms have lovely views out over the river. Of the many **campsites** in the vicinity, *Le Beau Rivage* (Ⓣ08.25.00.20.30, Ⓦwww.village-center.com; April–Sept), on the D703 towards Sarlat, is a good three-star choice with lots of activities on offer.

Domme

High on a cliff on the river's south bank, **DOMME** is an exceptionally well-preserved *bastide*. Its attractions, in addition to its position, include three original thirteenth-century **gateways** and a section of the old **walls**. From the northern edge of the village, marked by a drop so precipitous that fortifications were deemed unnecessary, you look out over a wide sweep of river country. Beneath the village is a warren of **caves** (daily: Feb to mid-Nov & Christmas hols; contact the tourist office for times & tickets; €8) in which the townspeople took refuge in times of danger. Unfortunately, the rock formations can't compare with the area's other caves; the only good point is the exit onto the cliff face with a panoramic lift up to the top. The entrance to the complex is under the market hall, opposite the **tourist office** (Feb–June & Sept to mid-Nov daily 10am–noon & 2–6pm; July & Aug daily 10am–7pm; mid-Nov to Dec Mon–Fri 10am–12.30pm & 1.30–4.30pm; closed Jan; Ⓣ05.53.31.71.00, Ⓦwww.ot-domme.com).

The smartest **hotel** in town is *L'Esplanade*, right on the cliff edge (Ⓣ05.53.28.31.41, Ⓦwww.esplanade-perigord.com; closed Nov–March; ❺), with a fine restaurant (closed Mon & lunchtime Wed; *menus* from €45); some of the rooms have wonderful views over the river. A cheaper alternative is *Le Nouvel Hôtel*, at the top of the Grand'Rue (Ⓣ05.53.28.36.81, Ⓦwww.domme-nouvel-hotel.com; closed mid-Nov to Easter; ❷), which has several simple, reasonably priced rooms above an inexpensive restaurant. The closest **campsite** is the one-star municipal site (Ⓣ05.53.28.31.91, Ⓔmairie.cenac@orange.fr; mid-June to mid-Sept) down by the river at **Cénac**.

Canoeing on the Dordogne and Vézère

Canoeing is hugely popular in the Dordogne, especially in summer, when the Vézère and Dordogne rivers are shallow and slow-flowing – ideal for beginners. There are rental outlets at just about every twist in both rivers. Although it's possible to rent one-person kayaks or two-person canoes by the hour, it's best to take at least a half-day or longer (some outfits offer up to a week's rental), and simply cruise downstream. The company you book through will either take you to your departure point or send a minibus to pick you up from your final destination. **Prices** vary according to what's on offer; expect to pay around €20–25 per person per day. Most places function daily in July and August, on demand in May, June and September, depending on the weather, and are closed the rest of the year. All companies must provide life-jackets (*gilets*) and teach you basic safety procedures, most importantly how to capsize and get out safely. You must be able to swim.

The upper Dordogne

East of Sarlat and Domme, you leave the crowds of Périgord Noir behind, but the Dordogne valley retains all of its beauty and interest. **Martel** and **Carennac** are wonderfully preserved medieval villages, and there are exceptional examples of Romanesque sculpture in the churches at **Souillac** and **Beaulieu**. Travel is difficult without a car, but Souillac is reachable by train and has bus routes to Sarlat and Martel. Cyclists can follow the "*voie verte*", a 23km-long cycle route from Sarlat to Souillac along a decommissioned train track.

Souillac

The first place of any size east of Sarlat is **SOUILLAC**, at the confluence of the Borrèze and Dordogne rivers and on a major road junction. Virginia Woolf stayed here in 1937, and was pleased to meet "no tourists ... England seems like a chocolate box bursting with trippers afterward". There are still few tourists, since Souillac's only real point of interest is the twelfth-century **church of Ste-Marie**, west of the main road. Roofed with massive domes like the cathedrals of Périgueux and Cahors, its spacious interior creates just the atmosphere for cool reflection on a summer's day. On the inside of the west door are some of the most wonderful Romanesque sculptures, including a seething mass of beasts devouring each other. The greatest piece of craftsmanship, though, is a **bas-relief of Isaiah**, fluid and supple, thought to be by one of the artists who worked at Moissac. Next to the church, the **Musée de l'Automate** (April–June, Sept & Oct Tues–Sun 10am–noon & 3–6pm; July & Aug daily 10am–7pm; Nov–March Wed–Sun 2.30–5.30pm; €6) contains an impressive collection of nineteenth- and twentieth-century mechanical dolls and animals, which dance, sing and perform magical tricks; look out for the irresistible laughing man.

The **tourist office** (July & Aug Mon–Sat 9.30am–12.30pm & 2–7pm, Sun 10am–noon & 3–6pm; Sept–June Mon–Sat 10am–noon & 2–6pm; ☎05.65.37.81.56, ⓦwww.tourisme-souillac.com) is on the main boulevard Louis-Jean-Malvy. For **accommodation**, head to the old quarter, where you'll find beautifully renovated rooms in the sixteenth-century *Pavillon St-Martin*, on place St-Martin in the shadow of the old belfry (☎05.65.32.63.45, ⓦhotel -saint-martin-souillac.com; ❷–❸). If they're full, try *La Vieille Auberge*, 1 rue de la Recège (☎05.65.32.79.43, ⓦwww.la-vieille-auberge.com; closed mid-Nov to March; ❹), which has a pool and is best known for its excellent **restaurant** (closed Sun eve & Mon; *menus* €20–68). For simpler meals, head to *Le Beffroi* on place St-Martin (closed Sun eve & Mon; *menus* from €15), with its lovely, wisteria-shaded terrace. There's also a large riverside **campsite**, *Les Ondines* (☎05.65.37.86.44, ⓦwww.camping-lesondines.com; May–Sept). You can rent **bicycles and canoes** from Copeyre Canoë (☎05.65.32.72.61, ⓦwww.copeyre .com), next to the campsite.

Martel

About 15km east of Souillac and set back even further from the river, **MARTEL** is a minor medieval masterpiece, built in a pale, almost white stone, offset by warm reddish-brown roofs. A Turenne-administered town (see p.556), its heyday came during the thirteenth and fourteenth centuries, when the viscounts established a court of appeal here.

The main square, **place des Consuls**, is mostly taken up by the eighteenth-century **market hall** (market Sat & Wed am), but on every side there are reminders of the town's illustrious past, most notably in the superb Gothic **Hôtel de la**

Raymondie. Begun in 1280, it served as the Turenne law courts, though it doubled as the town's refuge, hence the distinctive corner turrets. Facing the *hôtel* is the **Tour des Pénitents**, one of the many medieval towers which gave the town its epithet, *la ville aux sept tours* ("the town with seven towers"). The Young King Henry, son of Henry II, died in the striking **Maison Fabri**, in the southeast corner of the square. One block south, rue Droite leads east to the town's main **church**, St-Maur, built in a fiercely defensive, mostly Gothic style, with a finely carved Romanesque tympanum depicting the Last Judgement above the west door.

The nicest place to **stay** is the ivy-covered ⚜ *Relais Ste-Anne* (☎05.65.36.40.56, ⓦwww.relais-sainte-anne.com; open March–Nov; ⑤), a former girls' boarding school, surrounded by attractive gardens with a small heated pool and a fine restaurant (*menus* from €23); the rooms are very tastefully furnished in contemporary style, some with their own terrace. Cheaper accommodation is available in eight simple rooms at the *Auberge des 7 Tours* (☎05.65.37.30.16, ⓦwww.auberge7tours .com; ❷; restaurant *menus* from €19.80, closed out of season on Sun eve & Mon). There's also a basic municipal **campsite**, *La Callopie* (☎05.65.37.30.03, Ⓔmairie demartel@orange.fr; May–Sept), on the northern edge of town, and the more attractive riverside *Camping les Falaises* (☎05.65.37.37.78, ⓦwww.camping -lesfalaises.com; mid-June to mid-Sept), 5km away in the village of **GLUGES**, where you can also rent **canoes and bikes** from Port-Loisirs down by the water (☎05.65.32.27.59, ⓦwww.portloisirs.com).

Railway enthusiasts might be interested in the **steam and diesel tourist trains** (April–Sept; ☎05.65.37.35.81, ⓦwww.trainduhautquercy.info), which run on a restored line between Martel and St-Denis and afford wonderful views as they climb the steep cliffs overlooking the river valley. The return trip (€9.50) lasts about an hour.

Carennac and Castelnau-Bretenoux

CARENNAC is without doubt one of the most beautiful villages along this part of the Dordogne River. Elevated just above the south bank of the river, 13km or so east of Martel, it's best known for its typical Quercy architecture, its Romanesque priory, where the French writer Fénelon spent the best years of his life, and for its greengages.

Carennac's feature, as so often in these parts, is the Romanesque tympanum – in the Moissac style – above the west door of its church, the **Église St-Pierre**. Christ sits in majesty with the Book of Judgement in his left hand, with the apostles and adoring angels below him. Next to the church, don't miss the old **cloisters and chapterhouse** (April–June, Sept & Oct Mon–Sat 10am–noon & 2–6pm; July & Aug daily 10am–1pm & 2–7pm; Nov–March Mon–Fri 10am–noon & 2–5pm; €2.50), which contain an exceptionally expressive life-size *Entombment of Christ*.

Perhaps the nicest **place to stay** in Carennac is the welcoming *chambres d'hôtes*, ⚜ *La Farga* (☎05.65.33.18.97, ⓦlafarga.wordpress.com; ❸), on the main street, with five appealingly simple, tastefully decorated rooms and an apartment, some overlooking the garden with its heated pool and children's play area; meals using local organic ingredients are available for around €20 in the communal dining room. Nearby, the village's only **hotel**, the *Hostellerie Fénelon* (☎05.65.10.96.46, ⓦwww.hotel-fenelon.com; closed mid-Nov to mid-March; ❸), offers simple, old-fashioned but perfectly adequate rooms, the nicer ones overlooking the river. It also has a pool and a good **restaurant** specializing in traditional regional cuisine (*menus* from €23.50, out of season closed Fri & for lunch on Mon & Sat). There's a **campsite**, *L'Eau Vive*, 1km further east along the river (☎05.65.10.97.39, ⓦwww.dordogne-soleil.com; May to mid-Oct).

Another 10km further upstream, the sturdy towers and machicolated red-brown walls of the eleventh-century **Château de Castelnau-Bretenoux** (April–June & Sept daily 10am–12.30pm & 2–5.30pm; July & Aug daily 10am–7pm; Oct–March daily except Tues 10am–12.30pm & 2–5.30pm; €7; ⓦwww.monuments -nationaux.fr) dominate a sharp knoll above the Dordogne. Most of it has now been restored and refurnished.

Beaulieu-sur-Dordogne

In a picturesque spot on the banks of the Dordogne, 8km upriver from Castelnau-Bretenoux, **BEAULIEU-SUR-DORDOGNE** boasts another of the great masterpieces of Romanesque sculpture on the porch of the **church of St-Pierre**. This doorway is unusually deep-set, with a tympanum presided over by an oriental-looking Christ with one arm extended to welcome the chosen. All around him is a complicated pattern of angels and apostles, executed in character-istic "dancing" style, similar to that at Carennac. The dead raise the lids of their coffins hopefully, while underneath a frieze depicts monsters crunching heads. Take the opportunity also to wander north along rue de la Chapelle past some handsome sculpted facades and down to the river.

One of the most appealing **hotels** is 🍴 *Le Relais de Vellinus*, 17 place du Champ-de-Mars (☎05.55.91.11.04, ⓦwww.vellinus.com; closed Christmas & New Year hols; ❹), imaginatively decorated in warm, contemporary colours. You'll find the same attention to detail in its **restaurant**, which serves good-value *menus* from €22 in the evening. Another pleasant option, also with a decent restaurant, is the riverside *Les Charmilles* (☎05.55.91.29.29, ⓦwww.auberge-charmilles.com; ❸; *menus* from €19; Oct–April closed Wed), harbouring eight pretty rooms. The welcoming HI **hostel** is at the far end of rue de la Chapelle in a magnificent half-timbered and turreted building, with surprisingly modern rooms inside (☎05.55.91.13.82, Ⓔbeaulieu@fuaj.org; closed Nov–March; dorm beds €13.50). There are river-bathing and canoeing possibilities and a good riverside **campsite**, *Camping des Îles*, close by (☎05.55.91.02.65, ⓦwww.campingdesiles.fr; mid-April to mid-Oct).

The Lot

The core of this section is formed by the old provinces of **Haut Quercy** and **Quercy**: the land between the Dordogne and the Lot rivers and between the Lot and the Garonne, Aveyron and Tarn. While it largely corresponds to the modern-day Lot *département*, we have extended it slightly eastwards to include the gorges of the River **Aveyron** and Villefranche-de-Rouergue on the edge of the province of Rouergue.

The area is hotter, drier, less well known and, with few exceptions, less crowded than the Dordogne, though no less interesting. The cave paintings at **Pech-Merle** are on a par with those at Les Eyzies. **Najac**, **Penne** and **Peyrusse** have ruined castles to rival those of the Dordogne. Towns such as **Figeac** and **Villefranche-de-Rouergue** are without equal, as are villages such as **St-Antonin–Noble-Val**, and stretches of country such as that below **Gourdon**, around **Les Arques** where Ossip Zadkine had his studio, and the **Célé valley**.

Again, without transport, many places are out of reach. Some consolation, however, is the existence of the Brive–Toulouse train line that makes Figeac, Villefranche-de-Rouergue and Najac accessible, while **Moissac** and **Montauban** are on the Bordeaux–Toulouse line.

Rocamadour and around

Halfway up a cliff in the deep and abrupt canyon of the Alzou stream, the spectacular setting of **ROCAMADOUR** is hard to beat. Since medieval times the town has been inundated by pilgrims drawn by the supposed miraculous ability of Rocamadour's Black Madonna. Nowadays, pilgrims are outnumbered by more secular-minded visitors, who fill the lanes lined with shops peddling incongruous souvenirs, but who come here mainly to wonder at the sheer audacity of the town's location, built almost vertically into its rocky backdrop.

Legend has it that the history of Rocamadour began with the arrival of **Zacchaeus**, a tax-collector in Jericho at the time of Christ. According to one legend he was advised by the Virgin Mary to come to France, where he lived out his years as a hermit. When in 1166 a perfectly preserved body was found in a grave high up on the rock, it was declared to be Zacchaeus, or **St Amadour**. The place soon became a major pilgrimage site and a staging post on the road to Santiago de Compostela in Spain. St Bernard, numerous kings of England and France and thousands of others crawled up the chapel steps on their knees to pay their respects and seek cures for their illnesses. Young King Henry, son of Henry II of England, was the first to plunder the shrine, but he was easily outclassed by the Huguenots, who tried in vain to burn the saint's corpse and finally resigned themselves simply to hacking it to bits. A reconstruction was produced in the nineteenth century, in an attempt to revive the flagging pilgrimage.

Arrival and information

Getting to Rocamadour without your own transport is awkward unless you're prepared to walk or take a taxi the 4km from the Rocamadour-Padirac **gare SNCF** on the Brive–Capdenac line. If you arrive by car, you'll have to park in L'Hospitalet, on the hilltop above Rocamadour (which has the best view of the town), or else in the car park several hundred metres below. There are two **tourist offices**: the main one in l'Hospitalet (☎05.65.33.22.00, ⓦwww.rocamadour .com), and a second next to the Hôtel de Ville, on rue de la Couronnerie. Inconveniently, the distribution of hours between the two offices changes significantly most years, though you're assured that at least one will be open on any given day.

Accommodation and eating

Rocamadour's **hotels** close for the winter months, and you need to book early in summer. There's good value at the *Lion d'Or*, on rue de la Couronnerie (☎05.65.33.62.04, ⓦwww.liondor-rocamadour.com; closed mid-Nov to Easter; ❷), plus a decent restaurant with inexpensive *menus*, and at *Le Terminus des Pèlerins*, at the bottom of the Via Sancta, with fine views of the valley (☎05.65.33.62.14, ⓦwww.terminus-des-pelerins.com; closed Nov to mid-March; ❷–❸; restaurant from around €20). For a night of luxury, try the *Beau Site*, also on rue de la Couronnerie (☎05.65.33.63.08, ⓦwww.bestwestern .com; closed mid-Nov to early Feb; ❺), which has an excellent restaurant, the *Jehan de Valon* (lunch *menus* from €21), plus a cheaper bistro. Up in L'Hospitalet, the *Belvédère* (☎05.65.33.63.25, ⓦwww.hotel-le-belvedere.fr; closed Jan to mid-March; ❸–❹) enjoys prime views from its more expensive rooms and from its more formal – and recommended – restaurant (*menus* from €18). **Campers** should head for the nearby three-star site, *Les Cigales* (☎05.65.33.64.44, ⓦwww.camping-cigales.com; Easter–Sept). Apart from the hotels, a reliable **place to eat** is the homely *Chez Anne-Marie*, on rue de la Couronnerie (☎05.65.33.65.81), which offers good-value *menus* from €17. Or try *Les Jardins de la Louve*, at the far end of rue de la Couronnerie, with tables in the garden in fine weather (closed mid-Nov to Easter; *menus* from €17).

The Town

Rocamadour is easy enough to find your way around. There's just one street, rue de la Couronnerie, strung out between two medieval gateways. Above it, the steep hillside supports no fewer than seven churches. There's a lift dug into the rock face (€3 return), but it's far better to climb the 223 steps of the Via Sancta, up which the devout drag themselves on their knees to the little **Chapelle Notre-Dame** where the miracle-working twelfth-century Black Madonna resides. The tiny, crudely carved walnut statue glows in the mysterious half-light, but the rest of the chapel is unremarkable. From the rock above the entrance door hangs a rusty sword, supposedly Roland's legendary blade, Durandal.

Just east of here you can either hop in another lift (€4 return) or take a winding, shady path, La Calvarie, past the Stations of the Cross, to the little hamlet of **L'Hospitalet**, where you can walk around the ancient **ramparts** (daily 8am–9pm; €2) and enjoy vertiginous views across the valley. There are two different **wildlife centres** worth visiting in L'Hospitalet: the **Rocher des Aigles** (April–June & Sept Tues–Sun 2–5pm; July & Aug daily 1–7pm; closed Oct–March; €9; ⓦwww.rocherdesaigles.com), a breeding centre for birds of prey – don't miss the demonstrations of the birds in flight; and the **Forêt des Singes**, off the D673 (April–June & first two weeks Sept daily 10am–noon & 1–5.30pm; July & Aug daily 9.30am–6.30pm; mid-Sept to Oct Mon–Fri 1–5pm, Sat & Sun 10am–noon & 1–5pm; €8.50; ⓦwww.la-foret-des-singes.com), where more than one hundred Barbary apes roam the plateau in relative freedom.

Gouffre de Padirac

The **Gouffre de Padirac** (daily guided tours: April–June 9.30am–5pm; July 9.30am–6pm; Aug 8.30am–6.30pm; Sept to mid-Nov 10am–5pm; €9.20; ⓦwww.gouffre-de-padirac.com) is about 20km east of Rocamadour on the other side of the main Brive–Figeac road. An enormous limestone sinkhole, about 100m deep and over 100m wide, it gives access to an underground river system containing some spectacular rock formations and magical lakes, but is very, very popular. There is no system for reservations, so in summer you're advised to arrive before 10am. Visits are partly on foot, partly by boat, and the guided tours last an hour and a half. In wet weather you'll need a waterproof jacket.

St-Céré

East of Padirac and about 9km from **Bretenoux**, you come to the medieval town of **ST-CÉRÉ**, full of ancient houses crowding around place du Mercadial, and dominated by the brooding ruins of the **Château de St-Laurent-les-Tours**, whose two powerful keeps were once part of a fortress belonging to the Turenne. During World War II, the artist Jean Lurçat operated a secret Resistance radio post here; after the war he turned it into a studio, and it's now a **museum** of his work, with mainly huge tapestries but also sketches, paintings and pottery (daily: two weeks at Easter & mid-July to Sept 9.30am–noon & 2.30–6.30pm; €2.50). At over 200m altitude, the site is spectacular, with stunning views all around.

St-Céré has two pleasant and reasonable **places to stay**: the *Hôtel Victor-Hugo*, avenue Victor-Hugo, by the river (℡05.65.38.16.15, ⓦwww.hotel-victor-hugo .fr; closed two weeks in Feb & three in Oct/Nov; ❸; restaurant *menus* from €17.50, closed Sun eve and Mon), and the modern, more upmarket *Hôtel de France*, on avenue François-de-Maynard (℡05.65.38.02.16, ⓦwww.lefrance-hotel.com; closed late-Dec to Jan; ❸; restaurant *menus* from €25, eve only Mon–Sat, dinner and lunch on Sun), with a pool. Otherwise, there's *Le Soulhol* riverside **campsite** (℡05.65.38.12.37, ⓦwww.campinglesoulhol.com; May–Sept) near the *Victor-Hugo*.

Bikes can be rented from Cycles St-Chamant, 45 rue Faidherbe (℡05.65.38.03.23) – one of the best trips you could do is to cycle to the extremely pretty little village of **AUTOIRE**, in a tight side valley about 10km to the west of St-Céré. Much hillier but glorious country lies to the east along the road to Aurillac via Sousceyrac and Laroquebrou.

Gourdon and around

GOURDON lies between Sarlat and Cahors, conveniently served by the Brive–Toulouse train line, and makes a quiet, agreeable base for visiting some of the major places in this part of the Dordogne and Lot. It's 17km south of the River Dordogne and pretty much at the eastern limit of the luxuriant woods and valleys of Périgord, which give way quite suddenly, at the line of the N20, to the arid limestone landscape of the **Causse de Gramat**.

In the Middle Ages, Gourdon was an important place, deriving wealth and influence from the presence of four monasteries. It was besieged and captured in 1189 by Richard the Lionheart, who promptly murdered its feudal lords. Legend has it that the archer who fired the fatal shot at Richard during the siege of Châlus was the last surviving member of this family. But more than anything it was the devastation of the Wars of Religion that dispatched the place into centuries of oblivion.

Gourdon is a striking town, its medieval centre of yellow-stone houses attached like a swarm of bees to a prominent hilltop, neatly ringed by modern boulevards containing all the commerce. The main street through the Old Town, with a fortified **gateway** at one end, is rue du Majou. It's lined all the way up with splendid stone houses, some, like the **Maison d'Anglars** at no. 17, dating back to the thirteenth century. At the top you emerge into a lovely, intimate square in front of the massive but not particularly interesting fourteenth-century **church of St-Pierre**. From the square, steps climb to the top of the hill, where the castle once stood and from where there is a superb view stretching for miles.

A couple of kilometres along the Sarlat road, in the direction of Cougnac from Gourdon, are some interesting caves, the **Grottes de Cougnac**, discovered in 1949 (April–June & Sept daily 10–11.30am & 2.30–5pm; July & Aug daily 10am–6pm; Oct Mon–Sat 2–4pm; closed Nov–March; €7; ⓦwww.grottesdecougnac.com). Inside are beautiful rock formations as well as some fine prehistoric paintings rather similar to those at Pech-Merle (see p.594) and, intriguingly, sharing some of the same unexplained symbols.

Practicalities

Gourdon's **train station** lies roughly 1km northeast of the centre; from the station, walk south on avenue de la Gare, then turn right onto avenue Gambetta to reach the boulevard encircling the Old Town. Turn left here to find rue du Majou and the **tourist office** at no. 24 (March–June, Sept & Oct Mon–Sat 10am–noon & 2–6pm; July & Aug Mon–Sat 10am–7pm, Sun 10am–noon; Nov–Feb Mon–Sat 10am–noon & 2–5pm; ☎05.65.27.52.50, ⊛www.tourisme-gourdon.com). **Bikes** can be rented from Nature Évasion, 73 av Cavignac (☎05.65.37.65.12), out on the west side of town.

For an overnight **stay**, the *Hôtel de la Promenade*, on the northwest side of the ring road at 48 bd Galiot-de-Genouillac (☎05.65.41.41.44, ⊛www.lapromenade gourdon.fr; ❷; restaurant closed Sat lunch & Sun), is a cheerful place with well-priced rooms and an inexpensive pub-style restaurant. On the opposite side of town, tucked down a quiet cul-de-sac, is the agreeable *Hostellerie de la Bouriane*, place du Foirail (☎05.65.41.16.37, ⊛www.hotellabouriane.fr; closed Feb to mid-March & one week in Oct; ❹), with a fine, traditional restaurant (eves only, closed Mon; *menus* from €26). There's a well-equipped **campsite**, *Domaine Le Quercy* (☎05.65.41.06.19, ⊛www.domainequercy.com; Easter–Sept), 1.5km north on the D704 Périgueux road.

In addition to the hotels above, you'll find cafés and **restaurants** scattered around the ring road.

Les Arques

Twenty-five kilometres southwest of Gourdon on the Fumel road, you come to a pretty but unremarkable *bastide* called **Cazals**. A left turn here takes you along the bottom of the valley of the Masse and up its left flank to the exquisite hamlet of **LES ARQUES**. This is quiet, remote, small-scale farming country, emptied of people by the slaughter of the two World Wars and by migration to the towns in search of jobs.

Les Arques' main claim to fame is the Russian Cubist/Expressionist sculptor Ossip Zadkine, who bought an old house by the church here in 1934. Some of his sculptures are on display outside the church and in its lovely interior, and there's also a **museum** with a number of his works (Tues–Sun: April–Oct 10am–1pm & 3–7pm; Nov–March 2–6pm; closed Jan; €3).

The other reason to come here is the old village school, now transformed into a wonderful **restaurant**, ⚞ *La Récréation* (☎05.65.22.88.08; closed Wed & Thurs, also Nov–Feb; reservations highly recommended), where you are served a copious and delicious meal beneath the chestnut trees of the school yard or in one of the converted classrooms for €22 at lunch in July and August, or otherwise for €34. On a summer night, with the swifts flying overhead, it's idyllic.

On the other side of the valley, and well signposted, the tiny Romanesque **chapel of St-André-des-Arques** has some very lovely fifteenth-century frescoes discovered by Zadkine. The chapel is locked, but you can borrow the key from the museum in Les Arques (see p.585); you'll be asked for your passport, driving licence or other form of identification.

Cahors and around

CAHORS, on the River Lot, was the capital of the old province of Quercy. In its time, it has been a Gallic settlement; a Roman town; a briefly held Moorish posses-sion; a town under English rule; a bastion of Catholicism in the Wars of Religion, sacked in consequence by Henri IV; a university town for 400 years; and birthplace of the politician Léon Gambetta (1838–82), after whom so many French streets and squares are named. Modern Cahors is a sunny southern backwater, with two inter-esting sights in its **cathedral** and the remarkable **Pont Valentré**.

While you're in the Cahors area, don't miss out on the local **wine**, heady and black but dry to the taste and not at all plummy like the Gironde wines from Blaye and Bourg, which use the same Malbec grape.

Arrival, information and accommodation

The **gare SNCF** is at the end of avenue Jean-Jaurès off rue du Président-Wilson. For further information on the area, make for the **tourist office** (Mon–Sat 9am–12.30pm & 1.30–6pm; July & Aug also Sun 10am–1pm; ℡05.65.53.20.65, ✆www.tourisme-cahors.com) on place François-Mitterrand in the town centre. You can get **internet** access at Cyber Caviole, 118 rue du Président-Wilson (Mon–Fri 8am–12.30pm & 1.30–5pm). A leisurely way to enjoy some of the Lot's scenery is on one of the **cruises** run by Croisières Fénelon (℡05.65.30.16.55, ✆www.bateau-cahors.com). They offer day-trips from €54 in July and August, for example to St-Cirq-Lapopie, where the boat moors to allow you time to explore the village.

Cahors boasts several attractive, mid-range hotel options. There's less choice for those on a tight budget, beyond a riverside **campsite**, *Camping Rivière de Cabessut* (℡05.65.30.06.30, ✆www.cabessut.com; April–Sept), across the Pont de Cabessut.

Hotels

La Chartreuse St-Georges ℡05.65.35.17.37, ✆www.hotel-la-chartreuse.com. In a nice quiet spot on the south bank, over the river from the town centre, this modern, concrete hotel has a small pool and a decent, inexpensive restaurant. Ask for a room overlooking the river. ❹

Château La Roussille Chemin du Moulin, Labéraudie ℡05.65.22.84.74, ✆www .chateauroussille.com. A welcoming *chambres d'hôtes*, five minutes' drive from Cahors centre; take the D8 in the direction of Moulin de Labéraudie. It has two rooms and two suites, all with their own individual character, plus a lounge and billiard room. It is set in a large garden with a swimming pool. Open end March to mid-Nov. ❹

Jean XXII 2 rue Edmond-Albe ℡05.65.35.07.66, ✆www.hotel-jeanxxii.com. Situated in the fourteenth-century buildings of the Palais Duèze, at the north end of bd Gambetta, this small, friendly hotel offers modern, fairly functional rooms, done out with paisley prints, with free wi-fi internet access and the option of a/c. ❸

Terminus 5 av Charles-de-Freycinet ℡05.65.53.32.00, ✆www.balandre.com. Cahors' most characterful hotel, in an elegant nineteenth-century house just up from the station, with a fine restaurant (closed Sun; dinner *menus* €36–75). The rooms don't quite match up to the public areas, but boast all the modern three-star comforts such as double-glazing and a/c. ❹

The Town

Small and easily walkable, Cahors sits on a peninsula formed by a tight loop in the River Lot. It's best known for its dramatic fourteenth-century **Pont Valentré**, one of the finest surviving medieval bridges. Its three powerful towers, originally closed by portcullises and gates, made it effectively an independent fortress, guarding the river crossing on the west side of town.

Dominating the centre is the **cathedral**, which, consecrated in 1119, is the oldest and simplest in plan of the Périgord-style churches. The exterior is not exciting: a heavy square tower dominates the plain west front, whose best feature is the north portal, where a Christ in Majesty dominates the tympanum, surrounded by angels and apostles, while cherubim fly out of the clouds to relieve him of his halo. Side panels show scenes from the life of St Stephen. The outer ring over the portal shows a line of naked figures being stabbed and hacked with axes.

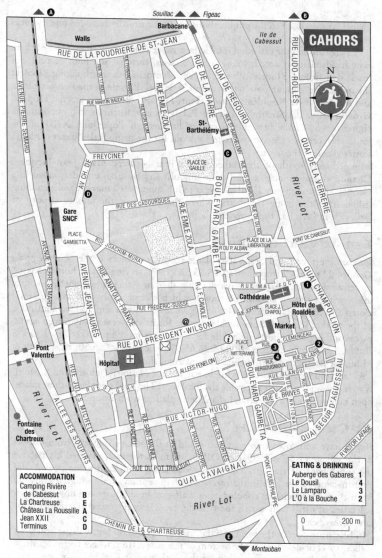

CAHORS

N

Souillac ▲ ▲ Figeac

Barbacane

Walls

RUE DE LA POUDRIERE DE ST-JEAN

Ile de
Cabessut

RUE DE LA BARRE

QUAI DE REGOURD

RUE LUDO-ROLLES

QUAI DE LA VERRERIE

River Lot

RUE MARTIN BAUDEL

RUE EMILE-ZOLA

St-
Barthélémy

FREYCINET

AV. CH. DE

PLACE DE
GAULLE

BOULEVARD GAMBETTA

PONT DE CABESSUT

Gare
SNCF

RUE DES CADOURQUES

RUE EMILE-ZOLA

PLACE DE LA
LIBERATION

PLACE
GAMBETTA

RUE JOACHIM-MURAT

R DU P. ALBAN

AVENUE PIERRE SEMARD

AVENUE PIERRE SEMARD

AVENUE JEAN-JAURES

RUE ANATOLE-FRANCE

RUE MAL. FOCH

Cathédrale

QUAI CHAMPOLLION

RUE FREDERIC-SUISSE

R. J. F. CAVIOLE

RUE JOFFRE

PLACE J.
CHAPOU

Hôtel de
Roaldès

@

RUE DU PRÉSIDENT-WILSON

Market

RUE G. CLEMENCEAU

Pont
Valentré

i

PLACE
F.
MITTERAND

RUE DE LASTIE

Hôpital

ALLEES FENELON

RUE
BERGOUGNIOUX

RUE BLANQUI

River Lot

RUE S. GERY

ALLEE DES SOUPIRS

RUE JULES MICHELET

BOULEVARD GAMBETTA

RUE E. BRIVES

QUAI SEGUR D'AGUESSEAU

R. VICTOR LAFAGE

Fontaine
des
Chartreux

RUE VICTOR-HUGO

RUE SAINT-MAXINE

RUE HAUTESSERRE

RUE DES HORTES

RUE DU POT TRINQUAT

RUE FONDDIEU

QUAI CAVAIGNAC

PONT LOUIS PHILIPPE

CHEMIN DE LA CHARTREUSE

River Lot

Montauban

EATING & DRINKING
Auberge des Gabares	1
Le Dousil	4
Le Lamparo	3
L'O à la Bouche	2

ACCOMMODATION
Camping Rivière de Cabessut	B
La Chartreuse	E
Château La Roussille	A
Jean XXII	C
Terminus	D

0   200 m

Inside, the cathedral is much like Périgueux's St-Front, with a nave lacking aisles and transepts, roofed with two big domes; in the first are fourteenth-century frescoes of the stoning of St Stephen, while over the west door are faded but beautiful Creation scenes from the same era. To the right of the choir a door opens into a delicate **cloister** in the flamboyant style, still retaining some intricate, though damaged, carving. On the northwest corner pillar the Virgin is portrayed as a graceful girl with broad brow and ringlets to her waist. In the cloister's northeast corner St Gaubert's chapel holds the Holy Coif, a cloth said to have covered Christ's head in the tomb, which according to legend was brought back from the Holy Land in the twelfth century by Bishop Géraud de Cardaillac. The chapel is now closed to the public, though it is occasionally included on city tours – ask at the tourist office.

The area around the cathedral is filled by a warren of narrow lanes, most of them now handsomely restored. Many of the houses, turreted and built of thin, flat brick, date from the fourteenth and fifteenth centuries. It's worth taking a look at the impressive, though now rather crumbly, **Hôtel d'Issale** in rue Bergougnioux and the **Hôtel de Roaldès** in place Henri-IV; also of interest are the **Hôpital Grossia** in rue des Soubirous and the **Palais Duèze**, further north opposite the church of St-Barthélémy, built for the brothers of Pope John XXII in the fourteenth century. As you wander, look out for the many little "secret gardens" scattered round the town.

Immediately south of the cathedral, the lime-bordered **place Jean-Jacques-Chapou** commemorates a local trade unionist and Resistance leader, killed in a German ambush on July 17, 1944. Next to it is the covered **market** and a building still bearing the name Gambetta, where the family of the famous deputy of Belleville in Paris had their grocery shop.

Eating and drinking

One of the nicest and best-value places to eat in Cahors is the ⚔ *Auberge des Gabares*, 24 place Champollion (☎05.65.53.91.47), serving hearty home cooking on its wisteria-covered terrace overlooking the Lot – there's just one five-course *menu*, with a certain amount of choice, which changes daily (€15, Sat eve €21; closed Sun & Mon). *Le Lamparo* (☎05.65.35.25.93; closed Sun), on the south side of the market square, is a perennial favourite for its very reasonably priced *menus*, pizzas and generous portions, while for something more upmarket, try *L'O à la Bouche*, 124 rue St-Urcisse (☎05.65.35.65.69; *menus* from €26.50; closed Sun & Mon), for its nicely presented and imaginative dishes.

As for drinking, *Le Dousil*, a **wine bar** at 124 rue Nationale (closed Sun & Mon), is a great venue in which to sample the local reds. The food's not bad either: salads, open sandwiches and cheese and charcuterie platters from around €13.

St-Cirq-Lapopie

If you have your own transport you could easily make a side trip from Cahors to the village of **ST-CIRQ-LAPOPIE**, 30km to the east, perched high above the south bank of the Lot. The village was saved from ruin when poet André Breton came to live here in the early twentieth century, and though it's now an irresistible draw, with its cobbled lanes, half-timbered houses and flower-strewn balconies, it's still well worth the trouble, especially if you're visiting early or late in the day.

Public transport in the form of a bus, run by Les Bus du Lot, will get you from Cahors to Tour-de-Faure, at the bottom of the valley, from where there's no alternative but to leg it up the steep hill for the final 2km. St-Cirq has only one hotel, the pretty *Auberge du Sombral*, on the central square (☎05.65.31.26.08, ⓦlesombral .com; closed mid-Nov to March; ❹; restaurant *menus* from €15, open for dinner on Fri & Sat and for lunch daily, except Thurs out of season), with plain but perfectly adequate rooms. There's also a very comfortable *gîte d'étape* in the centre (☎05.65.31.21.51, ⓔmaisondelafourdonne46@orange.fr; closed Mon & mid-Nov to March), and a well-run **campsite**, *Camping de la Plage* (☎05.65.30.29.51, ⓦwww.campingplage.com; open all year), down by the river, with various activities on offer, including swimming, canoeing and horseriding.

When it comes to **restaurants**, you can eat very well at *L'Oustal* (☎05.65.31.20.17; closed Mon & Nov–March; *menus* from €13 at lunch, €17.50

eve), tucked into a corner of rue de la Pélissaria just south of the church. At the top of the village, with views from its terrace over jumbled roofs, *Lou Bolat* serves a varied menu of salads, pizzas and regional dishes (closed mid-Nov to Feb, also Mon eve & Tues lunch; lunch *menu* €12, eve €19).

For **canoeing**, from hourly rental to week-long expeditions on the Lot and Célé rivers, contact Kalapca Loisirs (☎05.65.30.29.51, ⓦwww.kalapca.com), which has a base below St-Cirq.

Downstream from Cahors

West of Cahors the vine-cloaked banks of the Lot are dotted with ancient villages. The first of these, **Luzech** and the dramatic **Puy-l'Évêque**, are served by SNCF buses that thread along the valley from Cahors via Fumel to Monsempron-Libos, on the Agen–Périgueux train line. You'll need your own transport, however, to reach the splendid **Château de Bonaguil**, in the hills northwest of Puy-l'Évêque, worth the effort for its elaborate fortifications and spectacular position. From here the Lot valley starts to get ugly and industrial, though **Villeneuve-sur-Lot** provides a pleasant enough base for exploring the villages around. Prettiest are **Pujols**, to the south, which also boasts a number of excellent restaurants, and **Penne-d'Agenais**, overlooking the Lot to the east. **Monflanquin**, a *bastide* to the north of Villeneuve, is also well worth a visit for its hilltop location and almost perfect arcaded central square.

Luzech, Puy-l'Évêque and the Château de Bonaguil

Twenty kilometres downriver from Cahors you come to **LUZECH**, with scant Gaulish and Roman remains of the town of L'Impernal, and the **Chapelle de Notre-Dame-de-l'Île**, dedicated to the medieval boatmen who transported Cahors wines to Bordeaux. The town stands in a huge river loop, overlooked by a thirteenth-century keep, with some picturesque alleys and dwellings in the quarter opposite place du Canal.

Several bends in the river later – 22km by road – **PUY-L'ÉVÊQUE** is probably the prettiest village in the entire valley, with many grand houses built in honey-coloured stone and overlooked by both a **church** and the **castle** of the bishops of Cahors. The best view is from the bridge across the Lot. For an overnight **stay**, the classy *Bellevue* (☎05.65.36.06.60, ⓦwww.hotelbellevue-puyleveque.com; closed two weeks in Nov and four weeks in Jan/Feb; ④), perched on the cliff edge, has stylish rooms and a good restaurant (closed Sun & Mon; *menus* from €35, or €13.50 in the brasserie). For something cheaper, at the bottom of the town, the *Henry* has excellent-value, air-conditioned rooms (☎05.65.21.32.24, ⓦwww.hotel-henry .com; closed two weeks in Jan; ①), a garden and a good traditional restaurant (closed Sun eve; *menus* from €17), and there's a well-tended riverside **campsite**, *Camping Les Vignes* (☎05.65.30.81.72, ⓦwww.camping-lesvignes.fr; April–Sept), 3km to the south.

With your own transport, follow the Lot as far as Duravel and then cut across country via the picturesque hamlet of St-Martin-le-Redon to reach the **Château de Bonaguil** (March–May & Oct daily 10.30am–12.30pm & 2–5.30pm; June & Sept daily 10am–12.30pm & 2–6pm; July & Aug daily 10am–7pm; Nov Sun 10.30am–12.30pm & 2–5pm; Christmas hols daily 2–5pm; €7; ⓦwww.bonaguil .org) some 15km later, spectacularly perched on a wooded spur. Dating largely from the fifteenth and sixteenth centuries, with a double ring of walls, five huge towers and a narrow boat-shaped keep designed to resist artillery, Bonaguil was the last of a dying breed, completed just when military architects were abandoning such elaborate fortifications.

Villeneuve-sur-Lot and around

VILLENEUVE-SUR-LOT, 75km west and downstream from Cahors, is a pleasant, workaday sort of town which makes a useful base. While there are no very interesting sights, the handful of attractive timbered houses in the Old Town and the arcaded central square go some way to compensate. If you're reliant on public transport, note that SNCF runs regular bus services to Agen, on the Bordeaux–Toulouse line.

The town's most striking landmark is the red-brick tower of the **church of St-Catherine**, completed as late as 1937 in typically dramatic neo-Byzantine style. A couple of towers alone survive from the fortifications of this originally *bastide* town, and to the south the main avenue, rue des Cieutats, crosses thirteenth-century **Pont des Cieutat**, resembling the Pont Valentré in Cahors but devoid of its towers.

The helpful **tourist office**, 3 place de la Libération (July & Aug Mon–Sat 9.30am–12.30pm & 2.30–7pm, Sun 9.30am–1pm; Sept–June Mon–Sat 9am–noon & 2–6pm; ℡05.53.36.17.30, Ⓦwww.grandvilleneuvois.fr), lies just outside the town's northern gate. The best place to look for **accommodation** is around the former train station, now the **gare routière**, five minutes' walk south of the centre, where the welcoming *La Résidence* hotel, 17 av Lazare-Carnot (℡05.53.40.17.03, Ⓦwww.hotellaresidence47.com; ❶–❷), offers excellent value for money. Closer to the centre, *Les Platanes*, 40 bd de la Marine (℡05.53.40.11.40, Ⓦwww.hoteldes platanes.com; ❷), offers unfussy but spacious and well-kept rooms and a popular brasserie restaurant. For **campers**, there's the *Camping du Rooy*, signed off the Agen road 1.5km south of the centre (℡05.53.70.24.18; mid-April to Sept).

When it comes to **eating**, *La Crêperie de la Tour*, at 5 rue Arnaud d'Aubasse, does good crêpes, *galettes* and salads (closed Mon & Sun; *menus* from €7.50). *Chez Câline*

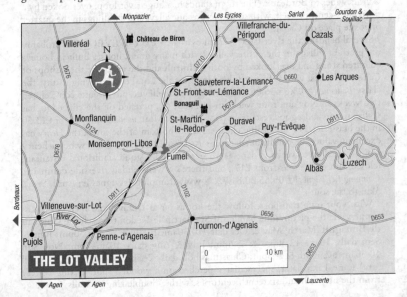

(☎05.53.70.42.08), near the old bridge at 2 rue Notre-Dame, is a pretty little restaurant serving fresh, inventive dishes in a tiny brick-vaulted room with a small terrace overlooking the Lot (closed Sun and Tues & Wed eve; *menus* from €12), while for a more upmarket ambience and good-value regional cooking make for *L'Entracte* (☎05.53.49.25.50) at 30 bd de la Marine (closed Wed; *menus* from €13.90), with a terrace under the plane trees. Alternatively, head south to Pujols.

Pujols

Three kilometres south of Villeneuve, the tiny hilltop village of **PUJOLS** makes a popular excursion, partly to see the faded Romanesque frescoes in the **church of Ste-Foy** and partly for the views over the surrounding country. But the main reason locals come here is for the quality of its **restaurants**. Top of the list is the excellent ⚜ *La Toque Blanche* (☎05.53.49.00.30, ⓦ www.la-toque-blanche.com; closed Sun eve to Tues lunch; *menus* from €39), just south of Pujols with views back to the village. The panorama is even better, however, from their less formal outlet, *Lou Calel*, overlooking the Lot valley in Pujols itself, where you can sample beautifully cooked, traditional but light *menus* (☎05.53.70.46.14; closed Tues eve to Thurs lunch; from around €20).

Monflanquin

Some 30km north of Villeneuve-sur-Lot, pretty **MONFLANQUIN**, founded by Alphonse de Poitiers in 1256, is another perfectly preserved *bastide*, less touristy than Monpazier and even more impressively positioned on the top of a hill that rises sharply from the surrounding country. It conforms to the regular pattern of right-angled streets leading from a central square to the four town gates. The square – **place des Arcades** – with its distinctly Gothic houses, derives a special charm from being tree-shaded on a slope. On the square's north side you'll find the informative **Musée des Bastides** (May, June, Sept & Oct Mon–Sat 10am–noon & 2–6pm, Sun 3–5pm; July & Aug daily 10am–7pm; Nov–April Mon–Sat 10am–noon & 2–5pm; €4), detailing the life and history of *bastides*.

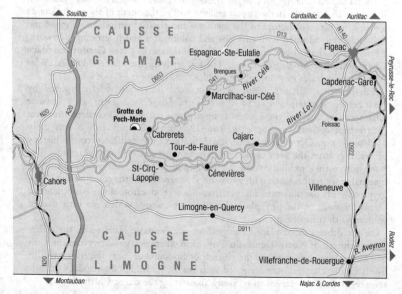

The museum is above the **tourist office** (same hours as the Musée des Bastides; ℡05.53.36.40.19, ⓦwww.cc-monflanquinois.fr), which can furnish you with lists of *chambres d'hôtes*. The nicest hotel in the area is the *Moulin de Boulède* (℡05.53.36.16.49, ⓦwww.lemoulindeboulede.com; ❸), just west of Monflanquin on the D124 to Cancon, which has a handful of pleasant rooms and a first-rate restaurant specializing in fish (closed Wed; evening *menus* from €26). **Campers** are well served by the four-star *Camping des Bastides* (℡05.53.40.83.09, ⓦwww.campingdesbastides.com; mid-April to Sept), 10km east of Monflanquin, near the village of Salles. The place des Arcades makes a fine setting for a number of **cafés** and **restaurants**; the best are British-owned *La Bastide* (closed Mon), which serves crêpes and salads from around €8, and the reasonably priced *Bistrot du Prince Noir* (April, May & Oct–Dec closed Tues & Wed; open daily June–Sept; closed Jan–March), both a wine bar and restaurant, offering traditional dishes and more unusual specialities such as vegetable tempura with spicy Thai sauce.

Figeac and around

FIGEAC lies on the River Célé, 71km east of Cahors. It's a beautiful town with an unspoilt medieval centre not too encumbered by tourism. Like many other provincial towns hereabouts, it owes its beginnings to the foundation of an abbey in the early days of Christianity in France, one which quickly became wealthy because of its position on the pilgrim routes to both Rocamadour and Compostela. In the Middle Ages it became a centre of tanning, which partly accounts for why many houses' top floors have *solelhos*, or open-sided wooden galleries used for drying skins and other produce. Again, it was the Wars of Religion that pushed it into eclipse, for Figeac sided with the nearby Protestant stronghold of Montauban and suffered the same punishing reprisals by the victorious royalists in 1662.

In the Old Town centre, the **Hôtel de la Monnaie** surveys place Vival. It's a splendid building dating back to the thirteenth century, when the city's mint was located in this district. In the streets radiating off to the north of the square there's a delightful range of houses of the medieval and classical periods, both stone and half-timbered, adorned with carvings and colonnettes and interesting ironwork. At the end of these streets are the two adjacent squares of **place Carnot** and **place Champollion**, both of great charm. The former is the site of the old *halles*, under whose awning cafés now spread their tables.

Jean-François Champollion, who cracked Egyptian hieroglyphics by deciphering the triple text of the Rosetta Stone, was born at 4 impasse Champollion, just off the square. It now forms part of an excellent **museum** (April–June & Sept Tues–Sun 10.30am–12.30pm & 2–6pm; July & Aug daily 10.30am–6pm; Oct–March Tues–Sun 2–5.30pm; €4) dedicated to the history of writing, from the very earliest cuneiform signs some 50,000 years ago. The most interesting exhibits relate to Champollion's life and work, including original manuscripts tracing his and others' progress towards cracking the hieroglyphs. Beside the museum, a larger-than-life reproduction of the Rosetta Stone forms the floor of the tiny **place des Écritures**, above which is a little garden planted with tufts of papyrus.

On the other side of place Champollion, rue Boutaric leads up to the cedar-shaded **church of Notre-Dame-du-Puy**, from where you get views over the roofs of Figeac. More interesting is the **church of St-Sauveur**, near the river, with its lovely Gothic chapterhouse decorated with heavily gilded but dramatically realistic seventeenth-century carved wood panels illustrating the life of Christ.

Practicalities

The **gare SNCF** is a few minutes' walk to the south of the Old Town, across the river at the end of rue de la Gare and avenue des Poilus. SNCF **buses** leave from the train station, and others from the **gare routière** on avenue Maréchal-Joffre, a few minutes' walk west of place Vival, which is where you'll find the **tourist office** in the Hôtel de la Monnaie (May, June & Sept Mon–Sat 10am–12.30pm & 2.30–6pm, Sun 10am–1pm; July & Aug daily 10am–7pm; Oct–April Mon–Sat 10am–12.30pm & 2.30–6pm; ℡05.65.34.06.25, ⓦwww.tourisme-figeac.com).

One of the nicest places to **stay** in Figeac is *Le Soleilho*, 8 rue Prat (℡05.65.34.64.41, ⓦwww.location-gites-lot.com; ❹), a stylish *chambres d'hôtes* with four rooms in a fourteenth-century mansion near the St-Sauveur church. Among the hotels, the riverside *Des Bains*, 1 rue du Griffoul (℡05.65.34.10.89, ⓦwww.hoteldesbains.fr; mid-Nov to Feb closed Fri–Sun, also closed Christmas & New Year; ❷), a former swimming baths, has nineteen well-kept rooms, some a little spartan, the nicest with balconies overlooking the river. The nearby *Pont d'Or*, 2 av Jean-Jaurès (℡05.65.50.95.00, ⓦwww.hotelpontdor.com; ❻), is a smartish chain hotel with sauna, gym, rooftop pool and reasonably priced restaurant. Or treat yourself to a night of pure luxury at the *Château du Viguier du Roy*, rue Émile-Zola (℡05.65.50.05.05, ⓦwww.chateau-viguier-figeac.com; closed mid-Oct to mid-April; ❾), a fourteenth-century château with huge rooms, a cloister garden, small (unheated) pool and a gourmet restaurant (closed Mon & Sat lunch; *menus* from €28.50).

There's also a well-equipped riverside **campsite**, *Les Rives du Célé* (℡05.61.64.88.54, ⓦwww.lesrivesducele.com; April–Sept), just east of town, where you can rent **bikes** and **canoes** in summer; at other times contact the Office Intercommunal des Sports at 2 av de Gaulle (℡05.65.34.52.54).

Figeac boasts some excellent **restaurants**. One of the nicest is the elegant *La Cuisine du Marché*, 15 rue Clermont (℡05.65.50.18.55; closed all day Sun & Mon lunch), just north of St-Sauveur church, offering well-prepared seasonal dishes on *menus* ranging from €26 to €38 (with lunch at €17). Off place Champollion, *Les Anges Gourmands*, 4 rue Séguier (open for lunch Tues–Sat & dinner Fri & Sat), is a funky little place dishing up tasty salads, open sandwiches and a couple of more substantial options, with ices or home-made cakes to follow; try one of their "medieval aperitifs". The *Pizzeria del Portel*, 9 rue Ortabadial (closed Sun lunch & Mon), is a convivial place serving an extensive menu of pizzas, salad platters, *moules* and the like, with the benefit of outside seating; most dishes are under €12.

Peyrusse-le-Roc

About 20km southeast of Figeac, following a series of beautiful lanes across the *causse*, you happen upon one of the most remarkable old villages in this corner of France, **PEYRUSSE-LE-ROC**. The "modern" village sits astride a ridge above a narrow wooded valley: a tiny huddle of long-eaved, half-timbered houses gathered round a seventeenth-century church. On the slopes below, hidden in the steep woods, lie the remains of a medieval stronghold, abandoned around 1700, that once stood guard over the silver-rich country round about. Cobbled paths connect the ruins of a Gothic church, a synagogue and a hospital, while a vertiginous ladder gives access to the twin towers of the old fort. The site is gradually being excavated and some of the buildings restored, but it still remains a moving and atmospheric place.

The valley of the Célé

For the last stretch of its course from Figeac to Conduché, where it joins the Lot, the **River Célé** flows through a luxuriant canyon-like valley cut into the limestone uplands of the Causse de Gramat. A twisting minor road follows the river: a silent backwater of a place, hot in summer, frequented mainly by canoeists. The **GR651** follows the same route, sometimes close to the river, sometimes on the edge of the *causse* on the north bank.

Espagnac-Ste-Eulalie and Marcilhac-sur-Célé

Downstream from Figeac, two villages in particular are worth a stop. The first is **ESPAGNAC-STE-EULALIE**, about 18km west of Figeac. It's a tiny and beautiful hamlet on the south bank of the river, reached across an old stone bridge, under the limestone outcrops of the *causse*. An eye-catching octagonal lantern crowns the belfry of the **church** (guided visits: daily 10.30am, 4.30pm & 6pm by appointment, call Mme Bonzani on ℡05.65.40.06.17; €2), and under a weathered tower next door, an ancient gateway houses a *gîte d'étape* (℡05.65.11.42.66; closed mid-Nov to March). There's an attractive and good-value *chambres d'hôtes*, *Les Anons du Célé*, 2.5km north of Espagnac on the D41 (℡05.65.50.26.57, ⓦlesanonsducele.free .fr; ❷; dinner €18), and two quiet riverside **campsites** in the next hamlet, **Brengues**: *Le Moulin Vieux* (℡05.65.40.00.41, ⓦwww.brengues.com; April– Sept), and the smaller municipal site (℡05.65.40.06.82, same website; June–Sept).

The second village of real interest is **MARCILHAC-SUR-CÉLÉ**, 9km downstream of Brengues, whose partially ruined **abbey** (July to mid-Sept 2–4.30pm by appointment – call ℡05.65.40.65.52; €3), with its gaping walls and broken columns, conjures a strongly romantic atmosphere. Very early and rather primitive ninth-century Carolingian sculpture decorates the lintel, and there are some handsome Romanesque capitals in the chapterhouse. In the damp interior are frescoes from around 1500 and old coats of arms of the local nobility, testimony to Marcilhac's once mighty power, when even Rocamadour was under its sway. During World War II, it was the scene of one of the *maquis'* first theatrical gestures of turning the tables on the occupier: on November 11, 1943 – Armistice Day – Jean-Jacques Chapou's group (see p.588) briefly occupied the village and laid a wreath at the war memorial.

There's a well-tended **campsite**, *Pré de Monsieur*, just north of the village (℡05.65.40.77.88, ⓦwww.camping-marcilhac.com; April to mid-Oct), with a decent little **restaurant** serving snacks, salads and main meals.

Grotte de Pech-Merle

Discovered in 1922, the **Grotte de Pech-Merle** (Easter to Oct daily 9.30am–noon & 1.30–5pm; €8; ℡05.65.31.27.05, ⓦwww.pechmerle.com) is less accessible than the caves at Les Eyzies but still attracts sufficient visitors to warrant restricting numbers to seven hundred per day; it's advisable to book ahead in July and August either by phone (three or four days ahead) or online (at least a week ahead). The cave is well hidden on the scrubby hillsides above Cabrerets, which lies 15km from Marcilhac and 4km from Conduché. The cave itself is far more beautiful than those at Padirac or Les Eyzies, with galleries full of the most spectacular stalactites and stalagmites – structures tiered like wedding cakes, hanging like curtains, or shaped like discs or pearls.

The first **drawings** you come to are in the "Chapelle des Mammouths", executed on a white calcite panel that looks as if it's been specially prepared for the purpose. There are horses, bison – charging head down with tiny rumps and arched tails – and tusked, whiskery mammoths. Next comes a vast chamber where the glorious horse panel is visible on a lower level; it's remarkable how the artist used the relief of the rock to do the work, producing an utterly convincing mammoth in just two black lines. The ceiling is covered with finger marks, preserved in the soft clay. You pass the skeleton of a cave hyena that has been lying there for 20,000 years –

wild animals used these caves for shelter and sometimes, unable to find their way out, starved to death. And finally, the most spine-tingling experience at Pech-Merle: the footprints of an adolescent preserved in a muddy pool.

The admission charge includes an excellent film and **museum**, where prehistory is illustrated by colourful and intelligible charts, a selection of objects (rather than the usual ten thousand flints), skulls and beautiful slides displayed in wall panels.

There's a **campsite**, *Le Cantal* (☏ 05.65.31.26.61, ℱ 05.65.31.20.47; April–Oct), close by at **CABRERETS**, a tiny place which also boasts a pair of two-star **hotels**: the spick-and-span *Auberge de la Sagne*, 1km outside the village on the road to Pech-Merle (☏ 05.65.31.26.62, ⓦ www.hotel-auberge-cabrerets.com; closed mid-Sept to mid-May; ❸), which has a pool and a good restaurant (eves only; *menu* €16); and the welcoming riverside *Les Grottes* (☏ 05.65.31.27.02, ⓦ www.hoteldesgrottes .com; closed Nov–Easter; ❷), also with a decent traditional restaurant (*menus* from €15) and a small pool. There's also pretty and well-equipped *chambres d'hôtes* accommodation at *Un Jardin dans la Falaise* (☏ 05.65.30.85.35, ⓦ www .unjardindanslafalaise.com; closed mid-Nov to mid-Jan; ❸), perched above the village with wonderful views; meals available on request (around €20).

For **canoes** and **bikes**, contact the Bureau des Sports Nature (☏ 05.65.24.21.01, ℮ bureau.sports.nature@orange.fr; April–Oct), a few kilometres further south at **Conduché**, where the Célé joins the Lot. It also organizes various other activities, including rock-climbing, caving and canyoning.

The valley of the Aveyron

Thirty-odd kilometres south of Figeac, **Villefranche-de-Rouergue** lies on a bend in the River Aveyron, clustered around its perfectly preserved, arcaded market square. From here the Aveyron flows south through increasingly deep, thickly wooded valleys, past the hilltop village of **Najac**, and then turns abruptly west as it enters the **Gorges de l'Aveyron**. The most impressive stretch of this gorge begins just east of **St-Antonin-de-Noble-Val**, an ancient village caught between soaring limestone cliffs, and continues downstream to the villages of **Penne** and **Bruniquel**, perched beside their crumbling castles. Bruniquel marks the end of the gorges, as you suddenly break out into flat alluvial plains where the Aveyron joins the great rivers of the Tarn and Garonne.

Villefranche-de-Rouergue

No medieval junketing, barely a craft shop in sight, **VILLEFRANCHE-DE-ROUERGUE** must be as close as you can get to what a French provincial town used to be like. It's a small town, lying on a bend in the Aveyron, 35km due south of Figeac and 61km east of Cahors across the **Causse de Limogne**. Built as a *bastide* by Alphonse de Poitiers in 1252 as part of the royal policy of extending control over the recalcitrant lands of the south, the town became rich on copper from the surrounding mines and its privilege of minting coins. From the fifteenth to the eighteenth centuries, its wealthy men built the magnificent houses that grace the cobbled streets to this day.

Rue du Sergent-Boriès and rue de la République, the main commercial street, are both very attractive, but they are no preparation for **place Notre-Dame**, the loveliest *bastide* square in the region. It's built on a slope and you enter at the corners underneath the buildings. All the houses are arcaded at ground-floor level, providing for a **market** (Thurs am) where local merchants and farmers spread out their weekly produce – the quintessential Villefranche experience. The houses are unusually tall and some are very elaborately decorated, notably the so-called **Maison du Président Raynal** on the lower side at the top of rue de la République.

The square's east side is dominated by the **church of Notre–Dame** with its colossal porch and bell tower, nearly 60m high. The interior has some fine late fifteenth-century stained glass, carved choir stalls and misericords.

On the boulevard that forms the northern limit of the Old Town, the seventeenth-century **Chapelle des Pénitents–Noirs** (April–June & Oct Tues–Sat 2–6pm; July & Aug daily 10am–noon & 2–6pm; Sept Tues–Sat 2–6pm; closed Nov–March; €4) boasts a splendidly Baroque painted ceiling and an enormous gilded retable. Another ecclesiastical building worth the slight detour is the **Chartreuse St–Sauveur** (same hours; €5), about 1km out of town on the Gaillac road. It was completed in the space of ten years from 1450, giving it a singular architectural harmony, and has a very beautiful cloister and choir stalls by the same master as Notre-Dame in Villefranche, which, by contrast, took nearly three hundred years to complete.

Practicalities

The **gare SNCF** lies a couple of minutes' walk south across the Aveyron from the Old Town. For information about buses, contact the **tourist office** just north of the river on promenade du Guiraudet (May–June & Sept Mon–Fri 9am–noon & 2–7pm, Sat 9am–noon & 2–6pm; July & Aug also open Sun 10am–12.30pm; Oct–April Mon–Fri 9am–noon & 2–6pm, Sat 9am–noon; ℡05.65.45.13.18, Ⓦwww.villefranche.com), beside the bridge. They also lay on guided tours of the town in summer, and can provide you with an audioguide out of season.

The nicest place to **stay** is *Le Claux de la Bastide*, 8 rue Ste-Émile-de-Rodat (℡06.70.74.61.57, Ⓦwww.leclauxdelabastide.fr; ❹), a lovely *chambres d'hôtes* in an elegant townhouse one block north of the tourist office. If you'd prefer a hotel, the *Aveyron*, near the station at 4 rue Lapeyrade (℡05.65.45.17.88, Ⓔhotel-restaurant.aveyron@orange.fr; closed Christmas & New Year hols and weekends out of season; ❷), offers simple rooms and a decent, inexpensive restaurant (closed eve & weekends). The other option is to head 3km north on the Figeac road to where *Le Relais de Farrou* (℡05.65.45.18.11, Ⓦwww.relaisdefarrou.com; ❹) offers much more luxurious surroundings and a fine restaurant (closed Sat lunch, Sun eve & Mon; *menus* from €22), albeit in a rather unpromising location. Back in Villefranche, there's an excellent *Foyer de Jeunes Travailleurs* **HI hostel** (℡05.65.45.09.68, Ⓦwww.fjtvillefranche.fr; dorm beds €15), next to the *gare SNCF*. There's also a *gîte d'étape* by the river at La Gasse (℡05.65.45.10.80; closed Nov to mid-April), 3km out of town on the D269 back road to La Bastide-L'Évêque, at the start of GR62b, plus a three-star **campsite**, the *Camping du Rouergue* (℡05.65.45.16.24, Ⓦwww.campingdurouergue.com; mid-April to Sept), 1.5km to the south on the D47 to Monteils.

For **eating**, in addition to the two hotel restaurants mentioned, the terrace of *Le Dali's*, on the cathedral square, has an unbeatable location, while the food is perfectly acceptable (closed Nov, also eve Mon–Fri & lunch Sat & Sun except July & Aug; *menus* from €16.50). You'll eat very well at the *Assiette Gourmande*, one block north of the cathedral on place André-Lescure (closed Tues & Sun eve & Wed; *menus* €15–35), which specializes in local cuisine, and at the aptly named *L'Épicurien* (℡05.65.45.01.12; closed Sun eve, Mon & Tues; from around €30 for dinner), a gourmet establishment near the station on avenue Raymond-St-Gilles.

Najac

NAJAC occupies an extraordinary site on a conical hill isolated in a wide bend in the deep valley of the Aveyron, 25km south of Villefranche-de-Rouergue and on the Aurillac–Toulouse train line. Its magnificent castle, which graces many a travel poster, sits right on the peak of the hill, while the half-timbered and stone-tiled village houses tail out in a single street along the narrow back of the spur that joins the hill to the valley side.

The **château** (daily: April, May, Sept & Oct 10.30am–1pm & 3–5.30pm; June to mid-July 10.30am–1pm & 3–6.30pm; mid-July to Aug 10.30am–7pm; closed Nov–March; €4.50) is a model of medieval defensive architecture and was endlessly fought over because of its impregnable position in a region once rich in silver and copper mines. In one of the chambers of the keep are sculpted portraits of St Louis, king of France, his brother Alphonse de Poitiers and Jeanne, the daughter of the count of Toulouse, whose marriage to Alphonse was arranged in 1229 to end the Cathar wars by bringing the domains of Count Raymond and his allies under royal control. It was Alphonse who "modernized" the castle and made the place we see today – a model in one of the turrets shows his fortifications as they were in the castle's prime in 1253. The main reason to visit, however, is the magnificent all-round view from the top of the keep, a full 200m above the river.

At the foot of the castle, in the centre of what was the medieval village, stands the sturdy **church of St-Jean** (April–Sept daily 10am–noon & 2–6pm; Oct Sun 10am–noon & 2–6pm; free), which the villagers of Najac were forced by the Inquisition to build at their own expense in 1258 as a punishment for their conversion to Catharism. In addition to a collection of reliquaries and an extraordinary iron cage for holding candles, the church has one architectural oddity: its windows are solid panels of stone from which the lights have been cut out in trefoil form. Below the church, a surviving stretch of **Roman road** leads downhill to where a thirteenth-century bridge spans the Aveyron.

Heading the other way, a narrow street overlooked by ancient houses leads from the castle to what is now the village centre, **place du Faubourg**, a sort of elongated square bordered by houses raised on pillars, like the central square of a *bastide*.

Here you'll find the **tourist office** (April–Sept Mon–Sat 9.30am–12.30pm & 2.30–6pm, Sun 10am–1pm; Oct–March Mon–Fri 9.30am–noon & 2.30–5.30pm, Sat 9.30am–noon; ☏05.65.29.72.05, ⊛www.tourisme-najac.com) and a very comfortable **hotel**, *L'Oustal del Barry* (☏05.65.29.74.32, ⊛www.oustaldelbarry.com; closed Nov–March; ❸), which has simple but warmly decorated rooms with solid wood furnishings; the best room has a balcony with wonderful panoramic views of the château and countryside. Its restaurant is renowned for its subtle and inventive cuisine (closed Mon & Tues lunch except July & Aug; *menus* €18.50–50). Another attractive option is the *Belle Rive* (☏05.65.29.73.90, ⊛www.lebellerive.com; closed Nov–March; ❸), in a nice, peaceful spot down by the river, with a pool and a restaurant serving good-value regional cooking (*menus* €20–36). Nearby is a four-star **campsite**, *Le Païsserou* (☏05.65.29.73.96, or 05.65.47.45.72 off season, ⊛www.lescledelles.com; May–Sept), with a *gîte d'étape* (same contact details; open all year). You can also rent **canoes** and **bikes** down here (☏05.65.29.73.94, ⊛www.aagac.com).

St-Antonin-Noble-Val

One of the finest and most substantial towns in the valley is **ST-ANTONIN-NOBLE-VAL**, 30km southwest of Najac. It sits on the bank of the Aveyron beneath the beetling cliffs of the Roc d'Anglars, and has endured all the vicissitudes of the old towns of the southwest: it went Cathar, then Protestant, and each time was walloped by the alien power of the kings from the north. It recovered its prosperity, manufacturing cloth and leather goods, and was endowed by its wealthy merchants with a heritage of medieval houses in all the streets leading out from the lovely **place de la Halle**. Here stands the town's finest building, the **Maison des Consuls**, whose origins go back to 1120. It now houses the town museum, **Musée du Vieux St-Antonin** (July & Aug daily except Tues 10am–1pm & 3–6pm; €2.50), with an uninspiring collection of objects illustrating the former life of the place.

The **tourist office** is in the "new" town hall next to the church (March & Oct Mon 2–5.30pm, Tues–Sun 10am–12.30pm & 2–5.30pm; April–June & Sept daily 9.30am–12.30pm & 2–6pm; July & Aug daily 9am–1pm & 2–7pm; Nov–Feb Mon & Sat 2–5pm, Tues–Fri 10am–12.30pm & 2–5pm; ℡05.63.30.63.47, Ⓦwww.saint-antonin-noble-val.com), and can supply information about canoeing on the Aveyron, nearby walks and **chambres d'hôtes**. Arguably the best *chambres d'hôtes* is the smart and welcoming *La Résidence* (℡05.63.67.37.56, Ⓦwww .laresidence-france.com; ❹) at 37 rue Droite; its rooms are large and airy, one with its own roof terrace, and meals are available for €25 a head. The closest of several **campsites** is the quiet and well-kept *Camping Le Ponget*, 500m north of the centre (℡05.63.28.21.13, Ⓔcamping.leponget@orange.fr; May–Sept). One of the nicest **restaurants** is the *Auberge Côté Pont*, 6 bd des Thermes (℡05.63.30.63.75; closed Mon & Tues lunch & Sun eve; *menu* at €18), with an inventive and constantly changing menu. You'll also eat well across the river at *Le Festin de Babette* (closed Wed), which offers good-value *menus* (€18–35) and lovely views of the village.

Penne and Bruniquel

Twenty kilometres downstream of St-Antonin you come to the beautiful ridge-top village of **PENNE**, once a Cathar stronghold, with its ruined castle impossibly perched on an airy crag. Everything is old and leaning and bulging, but holding together nonetheless, with a harmony that would be impossible to create purposely.

BRUNIQUEL, a few kilometres further on, is another hilltop village clustered round its **castle** (daily: March–June, Sept & Oct 10am–6pm; July & Aug 10am–7pm; 1–11 Nov 10am–5pm; €2.50, or €3.50 including guided visit; Ⓦwww.bruniquel.org). You can also visit a handsome house in the village, the aristocratic **Maison des Comtes de Payrol** (April–Sept daily 10am–6pm; €3). If you want to **stay**, Marc de Badouin runs a good *chambres d'hôte* to the right of the church (℡05.63.67.26.16, Ⓦwww.chambres-bruniquel.fr; ❸; meals around €20); he's a keen mountain-biker and can advise on local trails and footpaths. There's also a small two-star **campsite**, *Le Payssel* (℡05.63.67.25.95, Ⓔgugu2@orange.fr; July–Sept), about 2km south on the D964 to Albi.

Montauban and around

MONTAUBAN today is a prosperous, provincial city, capital of the largely agricultural *département* of Tarn-et-Garonne. It lies on the banks of the River Tarn, 53km from Toulouse, close to its junction with the Aveyron and their joint confluence with the Garonne. It is also, conveniently, on the main road and railway between Toulouse and Bordeaux.

The city's **history** goes back to 1144, when the count of Toulouse decided to found a *bastide* here as a bulwark against English and French royal power. In fact, it's generally regarded as the first *bastide*, and that plan is still clearly evident in the old city centre.

Montauban has enjoyed periods of great prosperity, as one can guess from the proliferation of fine townhouses. The first followed the suppression of the Cathar heresy and the final submission of the counts of Toulouse in 1229, and was greatly enhanced by the building of the Pont-Vieux in 1335, making it the best crossing-point on the Tarn for miles around. The Hundred Years' War did its share of damage, as did Montauban's opting for the Protestant cause in the Wars of Religion, but by the time of the Revolution it had become once more one of the richest cities in the southwest, particularly successful in the manufacture of cloth.

Arrival, information and accommodation

At Montauban's centre lies the perfect **place Nationale**, with the cathedral five minutes' walk to the south on the unattractive **place Roosevelt**. From here, rue de l'Hôtel-de-Ville leads directly to the Pont-Vieux and across the river to avenue de Mayenne, at the end of which is the **gare SNCF**. There's no central *gare routière*, so you'll need to ask for bus information at the **tourist office**, on the northern corner of boulevard Midi-Pyrénées (July & Aug Mon–Sat 9.30am–6.30pm, Sun 10am–noon; Sept–June Mon–Sat 9.30am–12.30pm & 2–6.30pm; ℡05.63.63.60.60, Ⓦwww.montauban-tourisme.com). **Internet** access is available at Arobaze, 112 faubourg Lacapelle (Tues–Thurs 10am–9pm, Fri & Sat 10am–11pm), on the southwest side of town.

Among a limited choice of **hotels**, the best deal is the attractive *Du Commerce*, 9 place Roosevelt (℡05.63.66.31.32, Ⓦwww.hotel-commerce-montauban .com; ❸), near the cathedral. The *Mercure*, opposite at 12 rue Notre-Dame (℡05.63.63.17.23, Ⓦwww.mercure.com; ❻), offers larger rooms and three-star services, as well as a reasonably priced restaurant, but less character. Otherwise, your best option is the *Hôtel d'Orsay*, 32 rue Salengro, opposite the train station (℡05.63.66.06.66, Ⓦwww.hotel-restaurant-orsay; closed Sun; ❸), which has dated but comfortable rooms and an excellent restaurant (*menus* €21.70–65; closed Sun, plus Mon & Sat lunch).

The Town

Montauban couldn't be easier to navigate. The greatest delight is simply to wander the streets of the compact city centre, with their lovely pink-brick houses. The finest point of all is **place Nationale**, the *bastide*'s central square, rebuilt after a fire in the seventeenth century and surrounded on all sides by exquisite double-vaulted arcades with the octagonal belfry of St-Jacques showing above the western rooftops.

The adjacent **place du Coq** on rue de la République is also pretty, and if you follow the street down it brings you out by the **church of St-Jacques** (first built in the thirteenth century on the pilgrim route to Compostela) and the end of the **Pont-Vieux** with a wide view of the river. At the near end of the bridge, the former bishop's residence is a massive half-palace, half-fortress, begun by the Black Prince, the son of King Edward III of England, in 1363 but never finished because the English lost control of the town. It's now home to the **Musée Ingres** (April–June, Sept & Oct Tues–Sun 10am–noon & 2–6pm; July & Aug daily 10am–6pm; Nov–March Tues–Sat 10am–noon & 2–6pm, Sun 2–6pm; €4.50), based on a collection of drawings and paintings that artist Jean-Auguste-Dominique Ingres, a native of Montauban, left to the city on his death. It's a collection the city is very proud of, though his supremely realistic, luminous portraits won't be to everyone's taste. The museum also contains a substantial collection of sculptures by another native, Émile-Antoine Bourdelle.

The **Cathédrale Notre-Dame**, ten minutes' walk up rue de l'Hôtel-de-Ville, is a cold fish: an austere and unsympathetic building erected just before 1700 as part of the triumphalist campaign to reassert the glories of the Catholic faith after the cruel defeat and repression of the Protestants. Apart from being a rare example of a French cathedral built in the classical style, its most interesting features are the statues of the four evangelists which triumphantly adorn the facade. Those on show now are recent copies, but the weather-beaten originals can be seen just inside.

Eating

The simplest way of finding a place to **eat** is to browse the cafés, bars and brasseries around **place Nationale**. For a light lunch along the lines of home-made quiche and salad or afternoon tea and cakes, head for *Crumble Tea*, in a courtyard at 25 rue de la République (℡05.63.20.39.43; closed Sun & eve) – it's a good idea to reserve. *Le Contre Filet*, just off place Nationale at 4 rue Princesse (closed Wed & Sun), serves tasty and inexpensive platters of local produce and excellent *faux filet*. For fine gourmet cuisine, head for *Le Ventadour*, magnificently sited in an old house on the west bank near the Pont-Vieux at 23 quai Villebourbon (℡05.63.63.34.58; closed Sat lunch, Sun & Mon; evening *menus* €30 & €40).

Moissac

There's nothing very memorable about the modern town of **MOISSAC**, 30km northwest of Montauban, largely because of the terrible damage done by the flood of March 1930, when the Tarn, swollen by a sudden thaw in the Massif Central, burst its banks, destroying 617 houses and killing 120 people.

Luckily, the one thing that makes Moissac a household name in the history of art survived: the cloister and porch of the **abbey church of St-Pierre**, a supreme masterpiece of Romanesque sculpture. Indeed, the fact that it has survived numerous wars, including siege and sack by Simon de Montfort senior in 1212 during the crusade against the Cathars, is something of a miracle. During the Revolution it was used as a gunpowder factory and billet for soldiers, which damaged many of the sculptures. In the 1830s it only escaped demolition to make way for the Bordeaux–Toulouse train line by a whisker.

Legend has it that Clovis the Frank first founded a monastery here, though it seems more probable that its origins belong in the seventh century, which saw the foundation of so many monasteries throughout Aquitaine. The first Romanesque church on the site was consecrated in 1063 and enlarged in the following century. The famous south **porch**, with its magnificent tympanum and curious wavy door jambs and pillars, dates from this second phase of building, and its influence can be seen in the decoration of porches on countless churches across the south of France. It depicts Christ in Majesty, right hand raised in benediction, the Book of Life in his hand, surrounded by the evangelists and the elders of the Apocalypse as described by St John in the Book of Revelation. There's more fine carving in the capitals inside the porch, and the interior of the church, which was remodelled in the fifteenth century, is interesting too, especially for some of the wood and stone statuary it contains.

The adjoining **cloister** (same hours as tourist office – see opposite; €5) is entered through the tourist office, and is most peaceful first thing in the morning. The cloister surrounds a garden shaded by a majestic cedar, and its pantile roof is supported by 76 alternating single and double marble columns. Each column supports a single inverted wedge-shaped block of stone, on which are carved with extraordinary delicacy all manner of animals and plant motifs, as well as scenes from Bible stories and the lives of the saints. An inscription on the middle pillar on the west side explains that the cloister was made in the time of Abbot Ansquitil in the year of Our Lord 1100.

Practicalities

The **tourist office** (April–June, Sept & Oct Mon–Fri 9am–12.30pm & 2–6pm, Sat & Sun 10am–12.30pm & 2–6pm; July & Aug daily 9am–7pm; Nov–March Mon–Fri 10am–noon & 2–5pm, Sat & Sun 2–5pm; ℡ 05.63.04.01.85, ⓦ www .moissac.fr) is next to the cloister, with the **gare SNCF** further west along avenue Pierre-Chabrié. There's a weekend **market** in place des Récollets at the end of rue de la République, which leads away from the abbey, a marvel of colour and temptation.

The *Moulin de Moissac* (℡ 05.63.32.88.88, ⓦ www.lemoulindemoissac.com; ❺; restaurant *menus* from €28, closed Sat lunch & Sun), occupying a former mill on the river is the town's top **hotel**; the building is large and not particularly attractive, but the interior has been beautifully refurbished. Alternatively, *Le Chapon Fin*, on place des Récollets (℡ 05.63.04.04.22, ⓦ www.lechaponfin-moissac .com; ❸), has simple but clean and comfortable rooms. For **campers**, there's a shady site across the river on the *Île du Bidounet* (℡ 05.63.32.52.52, ⓦ www .camping-moissac.fr; April–Sept), and for walkers a *gîte d'étape* at 5 sente du Calvaire (℡ 05.63.04.62.21, Ⓔ accueil.cafmoissac@orange.fr) on the hill above town. The nicest **place to eat** is the magnolia-shaded *Auberge du Cloître* (℡ 05.63.04.37.50; closed Mon, & Wed & Sun eve; evening *menus* from €21), beside the tourist office. Or, in summer, head to the river bank just up from the *Moulin de Moissac*, where the *Kiosque de l'Uvarium* has a large terrace and serves a varied menu of grills, salads, pasta and the like; you'll eat well for around €20 a head (closed Mon & Oct–April).

Travel details

Trains

Bergerac to: Bordeaux (7–10 daily; 1hr 10min–1hr 30min); Le Buisson (3–7 daily; 30–40min); St-Émilion (4–7 daily; 55min); Sarlat (3–7 daily; 1hr 15min–1hr 30min).

Brive to: Bordeaux (3–10 daily; 2hr 15min–4hr); Cahors (4–6 daily; 1hr 5min); Gourdon (2–5 daily; 40min); Limoges (1–2 hourly; 1hr–1hr 20min); Meymac (4–6 daily; 1hr 30min); Montauban (3–6 daily; 1hr 50min); Paris-Austerlitz (6–8 daily; 4hr–4hr 30min); Périgueux (4–5 daily; 50min–1hr); Pompadour (3–7 daily; 40min); Souillac (2–5 daily; 25min); Toulouse (4–8 daily; 2hr–2hr 30min); Uzerche (4–8 daily; 25–30min).

Cahors to: Brive (6–8 daily; 1hr–1hr 10min); Montauban (6–9 daily; 40min); Toulouse (9–11 daily; 1hr 20min).

Figeac to: Rodez (3 daily; 1hr 30min); Toulouse (4–6 daily; 2hr 30min); Villefranche-de-Rouergue (4–6 daily; 50min).

Limoges to: Angoulême (3–6 daily; 2hr); Aubusson (1 daily except Sat; 1hr 45min); Bordeaux (3–5 daily; 2hr 30min); Brive (1–2 hourly; 1hr–1hr 50min); Eymoutiers (4–9 daily; 45min); Meymac (3–5 daily; 1hr 40min–2hr 15min); Paris-Austerlitz (1–2 hourly; 3hr–3hr 30min); Périgueux (7–15 daily; 1hr–1hr 20min); Poitiers (3–6 daily; 2hr); Pompadour (1–2 daily; 1hr 10min); St-Junien (2–6 daily; 40min); St-Léonard (6–10 daily; 20min); Solignac-Le Vigen (1–3 daily; 10min).

Montauban to: Bordeaux (hourly; 1hr 30min–2hr 15min); Moissac (5–7 daily; 15–20min); Toulouse (1–2 hourly; 25–35min).

Périgueux to: Bordeaux (6–12 daily; 1hr 15min–1hr 45min); Brive (3–6 daily; 45min–1hr); Le Buisson (2–6 daily; 50min); Les Eyzies (2–6 daily; 35min); Limoges (6–12 daily; 1hr–1hr 30min); Monsempron-Libos (2–5 daily; 1hr 30min).

Sarlat to: Bergerac (5–8 daily; 1hr 10min–1hr 30min); Bordeaux (4–6 daily; 2hr 40min); Le Buisson (5–8 daily; 40min).

Buses

Bergerac to: Périgueux (Mon–Fri 3–5 daily; 1hr).
Brive to: Arnac-Pompadour (Mon–Sat 1 daily; 1hr 45min); Beaulieu-sur-Dordogne (school term Mon–Sat 1–3 daily; July & Aug Mon, Tues & Thurs–Sat 1–2 daily; rest of year Tues, Thurs & Sat 1–2 daily; 1hr 20min); Collonges-la-Rouge (Mon–Sat 1–3 daily; 30min); Figeac (3–6 daily; 1hr 55min); Meyssac (Mon–Sat 1–3 daily; 35min); Montignac (school term Mon–Fri 1 daily; 1hr 15min); Rocamadour-Padirac (3–6 daily; 45min); Turenne (school term Mon–Sat 1 daily; 20min); Uzerche (Mon–Sat 2 daily; 1hr).
Cahors to: Figeac (3–7 daily; 1hr 30min–2hr); Fumel (4–6 daily; 1hr 10min); Luzech (4–9 daily; 25min); Monsempron-Libos (4–6 daily; 1hr 15min);

Puy-l'Évêque (4–9 daily; 45min); Tour-de-Faure (3–6 daily; 35min).
Figeac to: Brive (6 daily; 1hr 50min).
Limoges to: Aubusson (1–4 daily; 1hr 40min); Oradour-sur-Glane (Mon–Sat 2–3 daily; 30–40min); Rochechouart (Mon–Sat 3–4 daily; 1hr–1hr 30min); St-Junien (Mon–Sat 3–4 daily; 1hr); St-Léonard (2–4 daily; 35min); Solignac (Mon–Sat 1 daily; 30min); Le Vigen (Mon–Sat 2–4 daily; 30min).
Périgueux to: Angoulême (Mon, Wed, Fri, Sat & Sun 1–2 daily; 1hr 40min); Bergerac (Mon–Fri 3–5 daily; 1hr–1hr 30min); Brantôme (Mon, Wed, Fri, Sat & Sun 1–2 daily; 35min); Ribérac (Mon–Fri 3–4 daily; 1hr).
Souillac to: Martel (Mon–Sat 2–4 daily; 20min); Sarlat (2–4 daily; 50min).

The Pyrenees

CHAPTER 10 # Highlights

* **Surfing the Côte Basque**
Catch a wave at Biarritz
or Anglet, Europe's top
destination for both boogie-
boarders and classic surfers.
See p.611 & p.614

* **Cauterets** Several lake-
spangled valleys above this
agreeable spa offer superb
trekking, whether modest
day-loops or more ambitious
multi-day traverses. See p.636

* **The Cirque de Gavarnie** A
vast alpine amphitheatre with
wind-blown cascades and
traces of glacier. See p.637

* **Niaux cave** The upper Ariège
valley hosts a cluster of
prehistoric caves painted by
Cro-Magnon humans over

10,000 years ago; Niaux
contains the best preserved
and most vivid of these
images. See p.644

* **Cathar castles** The imposing
castles of the upper Aude
and Corbières region testify
to southwestern Languedoc's
era of independence.
See p.651

* **Musée d'Art Moderne, Céret**
An astonishing collection
of paintings from the prime
movers of the early twentieth-
century avant garde.
See p.659

* **Petit Train Jaune** Rumble
up the dramatic Têt valley of
Roussillon in an open-car,
narrow-gauge train. See p.663

▲ Cathar castle

The Pyrenees

B asque-speaking, wet and green in the west; craggy, snowy, Gascon-influenced in the middle; dry, Mediterranean and Catalan-speaking in the east – the **Pyrenees** are physically beautiful, culturally varied and less developed than the Alps. The whole range is marvellous walkers' country, especially the central region around the **Parc National des Pyrénées**, with its 3000-metre-high peaks, streams, forests and wildlife. If you're a committed **hiker**, it's possible to traverse these mountains, usually from the Atlantic to the Mediterranean, along the **GR10** or the higher, more difficult **Haute Randonnée Pyrénéenne** (HRP). There are numerous spa resorts as well – **Cauterets**, **Luz-St-Sauveur, Barèges, Ax-les-Thermes** – with shorter hikes nearby to suit all abilities, as well as skiing opportunities in winter.

As for the more conventional tourist attractions, the **Côte Basque** – peppered with fun-loving towns like **Bayonne** and **Biarritz** – is lovely, sandy but very popular, suffering from seaside sprawl and a surfeit of caravan-colonized

Hiking in the Pyrenees

There are plenty of walkers' **guidebooks** to the area in both French and English (see p.1072), plus two series of widely available **maps**. The most detailed of the latter are the French IGN 1:25,000 "TOP 25" series (ⓦ www.ign.fr); #1547OT, #1647ET, #1647OT, #1748ET and #1748OT cover the Parc National des Pyrénées, while #1848OT covers the Luchon area. Less demanding walkers can make do with Rando Éditions' *Cartes de Randonnées*, which covers the range at 1:50,000 in eleven sheets numbered from west to east (#9 is out of print).

The **walking season** usually lasts from mid-June until late September; earlier in the year, few staffed refuges function, and you'll often find snow on parts of the GR10 (even more so the HRP) until early July. These are big mountains and should be treated with respect: tackling any of the main walks means **proper preparation**. Before setting out, check weather forecasts – posted at the local tourist office – and be properly equipped and provisioned. Above all, don't take chances: mountain conditions change very quickly: sunny, warm weather in the valley doesn't mean it will be the same higher up, three hours later. If you are not experienced, it's best not to embark on anything other than a well-frequented path unless you're accompanied by someone who is.

One kilometre in twelve minutes (5kph) is a rather brisk average **walking pace** for level ground; if you're going uphill, allow an hour for every 350m in elevation gained. Much terrain is so steep, and trail surface so uneven, that going downhill isn't any faster. Be mindful of the punishment your knees will take: bring or buy telescopic walking poles or a traditional walking stick.

campsites. The foothill towns are on the whole rather dull, although **Pau** merits at least a day, while monstrously kitsch **Lourdes** has to be seen whether you're a devout pilgrim or not. **Roussillon** in the east, focused on busy **Perpignan**, has beaches every bit as popular as those of the Côte Basque, nestled into the compact coves of its rocky coast, while its interior consists of craggy terrain split by spectacular canyons, sprouting a crop of fine Romanesque abbeys and churches – **St-Michel-de-Cuixà**, **St-Martin-de-Canigou** and **Serrabona** being the most dramatic – and a landscape bathed in Mediterranean light. Finally, the sun-drenched foothills just to the northwest harbour the famous **Cathar castles**, legacies of the once-independent and ever-rebellious inhabitants of southwestern Languedoc.

The Pays Basque

The three **Basque provinces** – Labourd (Lapurdi), Basse Navarre (Behe Nafarroa) and Soule (Zuberoa) – share with their Spanish neighbours a common language – Euskera – and a strong sense of identity. The language is widely spoken, and Basques refer to their country as Euskal-herri (or, across the border in Spain, Euskadi). You'll see bilingual French/Euskera toponym signage and posters throughout the region (sometimes only in Euskera), so in this section we have given the Euskera for all

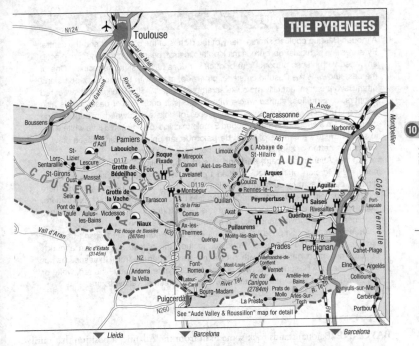

locations in brackets after the French. Unlike some of their Spanish counterparts, few French Basques favour an independent state or secession from France, though a Basque *département* has been mooted. For decades the French authorities turned a blind eye to the Spanish Basque terrorist organization ETA, which used the region as a safe haven and organizational base. Since the millennium, however, as France has extradited suspected terrorists to Spain, incidents of violence and vandalism associated with nationalists have increased, notably around Bayonne and Pau. Such events, however, are so exceptional as to not concern visitors.

Apart from the language and the traditional broad beret, the most obvious manifestations of Basque national identity are the ubiquitous *trinquets* (enclosed) or *frontons* (open) concrete courts in which the national game of **pelota** is played. Pairs of players wallop a hard leather-covered ball, either with their bare hands or a long basket-work extension of the hand called a *chistera* (in the variation known as *cesta punta*), against a high wall blocking one end of the court. It's extraordinarily dangerous – the ball travels at speeds of up to 200kph – and knockouts or worse are not uncommon. Trials of strength (*force Basque*), rather like Scottish Highland games, are also popular, including tugs-of-war, lifting heavy weights, turning massive carts and sawing or axing giant tree trunks.

The Côte Basque

Barely 30km long from the Spanish frontier to the mouth of the Adour, the **Basque coast** is easily accessible by air, bus and train, and reasonably priced accommodation is not difficult to find – except from mid-July through August, when space should be reserved at least six weeks in advance.

Basque country cuisine

Although Basque cooking shares many of the dishes of the southwest and the central Pyrenees – in particular **garbure**, a thick potato, carrot, bean, cabbage and turnip soup enlivened with pieces of pork, ham or duck – it does have distinctive recipes. One of the best known is the Basque omelette, **pipérade**, made with tomatoes, peppers and often Bayonne ham, actually more like scrambled eggs. Another delicacy is sweet red peppers, or **piquillos**, stuffed whole with *morue* (salt cod). *Poulet basquaise* is also common, especially as takeaway food: pieces of chicken browned in pork fat and casseroled in a sauce of tomato, ground Espelette chillis, onions and a little white wine. In season there's a chance of **salmi de palombe**, an onion-and-wine-based stew of wild doves netted or shot as they migrate north over the Pyrenees.

With the Atlantic adjacent, **seafood** is also a speciality. The Basques inevitably have their version of fish soup, called *ttoro*. Another great delicacy is elvers or *pibales*, netted as they come up the Atlantic rivers. Squid are common, served here as *txiperons*, either in their own ink, stuffed and baked or stewed with onion, tomato, peppers and garlic. All the locally caught fish – tuna (*thon*), sea bass (*bor*), sardines (*sardines*) and anchovies (*anchois*) – are regular favourites, too.

Cheeses mainly comprise the delicious ewe's-milk *tommes* and *gasna* from the high pastures of the Pyrenees. Puddings include the *gâteau basque*, an almond-custard pie often garnished with preserved black cherries from Itxassou. As for alcohol, the only Basque AOC wine is the very drinkable Irouléguy – as red, white or rosé – while the local digestif liqueur is the potent green or yellow Izzara.

Bayonne

BAYONNE (Baïona) stands back some 5km from the Atlantic, a position that until recently protected it from any real touristic exploitation. The city is effectively the economic and political capital of the Pays Basque and to the lay person, at least, its Basque flavour predominates, with tall half-timbered dwellings and woodwork painted in the traditional green and red. Here, too, Basques fleeing from Franco's Spain came without hesitation to seek refuge among their own. For many years the Petit Bayonne quarter on the Nive's right bank was a hotbed of violent Basque nationalism, until the French government clamped down on such dangerous tendencies.

Sitting astride the confluence of the River Ardour and the much smaller Nive, Bayonne is a small-scale, easily manageable city, at the hub of all major road and rail routes from the north and east. Although there are no great sights, it's a pleasure to walk the narrow streets of the old town, still wrapped in the fortifications of **Sébastien le Preste de Vauban**, Louis XIV's military engineer. The cathedral is on the west bank in **Grand Bayonne**, the museums east of the river in **Petit Bayonne**.

Arrival and information

From the **airport**, city buses #6 or C take you into town. The **gare SNCF** and **gare routière** for destinations in Béarn, Basse Navarre and Soule are next door to each other, just off place de la République on the north bank of the Adour, across the wide Pont St-Esprit from the city centre. In addition, **bus stops** in place des Basques on the Adour's south bank serve Biarritz and Anglet (though most of these lines stop at the *gare SNCF* too), as well as destinations in the Nive valley. There is a free shuttle service available daily except Sunday into the city centre (Ⓦwww.bus-stab.com). The **tourist office** is also in place des Basques (July & Aug Mon–Sat 9am–7pm, Sun 10am–1pm; Sept–June Mon–Fri 9am–6.30pm, Sat 10am–6pm; Ⓣ08.20.42.64.64, Ⓦwww.bayonne-tourisme.com). All **car hire** outfits – for example Ada (Ⓣ05.59.50.37.10, Ⓔada.bayonne@orange.fr) at 10bis quai de Lesseps – are in the St-Esprit quarter, within sight of the *gare SNCF*.

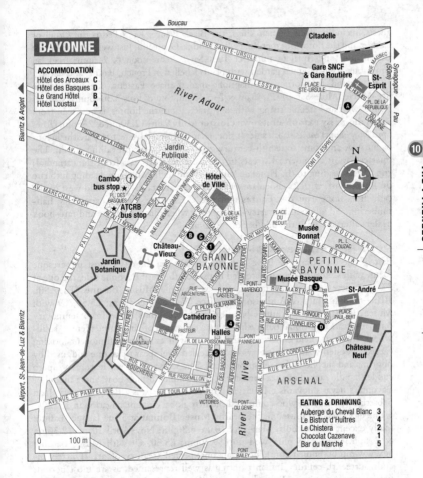

BAYONNE

ACCOMMODATION
Hôtel des Arceaux	C
Hôtel des Basques	D
Le Grand Hôtel	B
Hôtel Loustau	A

EATING & DRINKING
Auberge du Cheval Blanc	3
Le Bistrot d'Huîtres	4
Le Chistera	2
Chocolat Cazenave	1
Bar du Marché	5

Accommodation

Hôtel des Arceaux 26 rue du Port-Neuf ☏05.59.59.15.53, Ⓦwww.hotel-arceaux.com. Comfortable hotel with pastel-hued rooms furnished with a few antique pieces of furniture. ③

Hôtel des Basques 4 rue des Lisses ☏05.59.59.08.02. Most agreeable budget hotel in town. ①

Le Grand Hôtel 21 rue Thiers ☏05.59.59.62.00, Ⓦwww.bw-legrandhotel.com. Part of the Best

Western chain and set in a nineteenth-century town house. There are some slightly more expensive suites (⑥). ⑤

Hôtel Loustau Place de la République ☏05.59.55.08.08, Ⓦwww.hotel-loustau.com. Overlooks the river beside Pont St-Esprit, and has a well-regarded restaurant. ⑤

Grand Bayonne

In Grand Bayonne, just up avenue du 11 novembre from the tourist office, stands the town's fourteenth-century **castle** (closed to the public except for an exclusive, by-appointment-only restaurant 3 nights weekly; booking info posted). The oldest part, the Château-Vieux, is a genuine example of no-nonsense late-medieval fortification; a plaque on the east wall lists some of the more famous willing or unwilling

609

guests, including four French kings, the Black Prince, King Pedro the Cruel of Castile, and the notorious mercenary Bertrand de Guescelin. Just west lies the **Jardin Botanique** (mid-April to mid-Oct Tues–Sat 9.30am–noon & 2–6pm; free), an enormous, well-designed garden with plants labelled in French, Basque and Latin.

Just around the corner on magnolia-shaded place Pasteur, the **Cathédrale Ste-Marie** (Mon–Sat 10–11.45am & 3–5.45pm, Sun & hols 3.30–6pm), with its twin towers and steeple rising with airy grace above the houses, is best seen from across the grassy expanse of its own **cloister** (daily 9am–12.30pm & 2–5pm, closes 6pm May–Sept) on its south side. Inside, its most impressive features are the height of the nave and some sixteenth-century glass, set off by the prevailing gloom. The smartest, most commercial streets in town extend northeast from the cathedral: **rue Thiers** leading to the Hôtel de Ville, and **rue de la Monnaie**, leading into **rue du Port-Neuf**, with its chocolate *confiseries* and restaurants. South and west of the cathedral, along **rue des Faures** and **rue d'Espagne**, there's exemplary half-timbering and a bohemian, artsy-craftsy feel, where antique shops and rare-book dealers alternate with the odd bar or restaurant.

Petit Bayonne and St-Esprit

East of the cathedral, the Nive's riverside **quays** are the city's most picturesque focus, with sixteenth-century arcaded houses on the Petit Bayonne side, the one at 37 quai des Corsaires containing the worthwhile **Musée Basque** (Tues–Sun 10am–6.30pm, July & Aug also Mon; free Wed 6.30–9.30pm; €5.50, €9 with Musée Bonnat; Ⓦwww.musee-basque.com). Its exhibits (aside from temporary ones) illustrate traditional Basque life using a collection of farm implements – solid-wheeled oxcarts, field rollers and the like, as well as *makhilak* (innocent-looking carved, wooden walking sticks with a concealed steel spear tip at one end, used by pilgrims and shepherds for self-protection). The seafaring gallery features a superb rudder handle carved as a sea-monster, a wood-hulled fishing boat, and a model of Bayonne's naval shipyards c.1805; Columbus's skipper was a Basque, as was Juan Sebastián de Elakano, who completed the first global circumnavigation in 1522.

The city's second museum, the nearby **Musée Bonnat** at 5 rue Jacques Laffitte (daily except Tues & hols: May–Oct 10am–6.30pm; Nov–April 10am–12.30pm & 2–6pm; July–Aug plus Wed until 9.30pm; €5.50, €9 with Musée Basque; Ⓦwww.musee-bonnat.com), holds an unexpected treasury of art. Thirteenth- and fourteenth-century Italian painting is well represented, as are most periods before Impressionism. Highlights include Goya's *Self-Portrait* and *Portrait of Don Francisco de Borja*, Rubens' powerful *Apollo and Daphne* and *The Triumph of Venus*, plus works by Murrillo, El Greco and Ingres. A whole gallery is devoted to high-society portraits by Léon Bonnat (1833–1922), whose personal collection formed the original core of the museum. There are also frequent, worthwhile temporary exhibits in the annexe at 9 rue Frédéric-Bastiat.

Apart from the view back across the river, there's relatively little on the northern bank of the Adour. A deliberately inconspicuous, early nineteenth-century **synagogue** at 33 rue Maubec is a legacy of Bayonne's Jewish community, which settled here on arrival from Portugal during the sixteenth century. St-Esprit in effect became their ghetto after an expulsion order in 1602, when Grand Bayonne was consecrated to the Virgin and off-limits to unbelievers. The **church of St-Esprit**, opposite the station, is all that remains of a hostel that once served Chemin de St-Jacques pilgrims – it's worth a peek inside for a fine fifteenth-century wood sculpture of the *Flight into Egypt*. Just above the train station looms Vauban's massive **citadelle**; built in 1680 to defend the town against Spanish attack, it actually saw little action until the Napoleonic wars, when its garrison resisted a four-month 1813 siege by Wellington before falling the next year.

Eating, drinking and entertainment

The most popular areas for **eating** and **drinking** are along the right-bank of the Nive between Pont Marengo and Pont Pannecau, or along quai Jauréguiberry between Pont Pannecau and Pont du Genie on the Grand Bayonne side – though restaurants here tend to be more notable for their number than their quality. The backstreets either side of the river can be rewarding, especially in Petit Bayonne or the area south and west of the *halles*.

Bayonne's biggest annual **festival** is the Fêtes de Bayonne, which usually starts on the last Wednesday in July and consists of five days and nights of continuous boozing and entertainment. There are *corridas* (bullfights) the last two days, plus a few more in the run-up to August 15. A well-established, three-day **jazz festival**, La Ruée au Jazz (Ⓦ www.larueeaujazz.com), takes place in mid-July.

Auberge du Cheval Blanc 68 rue Bourg-Neuf, Petit Bayonne Ⓣ 05.59.59.01.33. Formerly Michelin-starred, this seafood restaurant is still considered the best in town. Weekday lunch *menu* is offered, but assume €90 expenditure; booking essential. Closed part July, all Sun eve, Sat noon & Mon except Aug.
Le Bistrot d'Huîtres Southeast corner of the *halle* Ⓣ 05.59.46.10.10. One of three such oyster bars based in the market, with a good-value €19 *formule*.
Le Chistera 42 rue du Port-Neuf, Grand Bayonne. Doyenne of a row of three similar restaurants under the arcades here, offering gazpacho, fish soup, plenty of hake dishes, a few meat platters and good home-made desserts; best order à la carte (allow €27) and/or off the daily specials board rather than the dull *menu*. Closed Mon, part May, plus Tues & Wed eves except July & Aug.

Chocolat Cazenave 19 rue du Port-Neuf, Grand Bayonne Ⓣ 05.59.59.25.93. The local chocolate tradition is duly honoured with a handful of *chocolateries* on, or just off this street. This, the most famous one, serving hot whipped chocolate and cold cocoa-based desserts at tables under the arcade or in its Art Nouveau interior. Closed Sun.

Bar du Marché 39 rue des Basques, Grand Bayonne. Despite the name, this begins serving food and drink – including good beer on tap – at 5am to market sellers and continues with good-value *plats du jour* at lunchtime. The decor is accented by posters for Basque-country beverages, and the San Fermín bull-running at Pamplona. Closed eves & all Sun.

Biarritz

A few minutes by rail or road from Bayonne, **BIARRITZ** (Miarritze) was, until the 1950s, the Monte Carlo of the Atlantic coast, transformed by Napoléon III during the mid-nineteenth century into a playground for monarchs, aristos and glitterati. With the 1960s rise of the Côte d'Azur, however, the place went into seemingly terminal decline, despite having been discovered by the first surfers in 1957. But from about 1994, Biarritz was rediscovered by Parisian yuppies, a new generation of the international surfing fraternity and a slightly alternative family clientele, who together have put the place back on the map.

Arrival and information

The **gare SNCF** lies 3km southeast of the centre at the end of avenue Foch/avenue Kennedy in the *quartier* known as La Négresse (STAB bus #2 or B from or to square d'Ixelles). There is a free shuttle service available Mon–Sat in the city centre (Ⓦ www .bus-stab.com). The **tourist office**, also selling tickets for local events and spectacles, is on square d'Ixelles (daily: July & Aug 8am–8pm; Sept–June Mon–Sat 10am–6pm, Sun 10am–5pm; Ⓣ 05.59.22.37.00, Ⓦ www.biarritz.fr). Alternatives to the STAB bus are basically fairly pricey hired **mountain bikes** or **scooters** (best rates from Cycle Océan at Carrefour d'Hélianthe Ⓣ 05.59.24.94.47, Ⓦ www.cycleocean.com).

Accommodation

Accommodation is booked out weeks in advance during July and August, especially the more affordable choices.

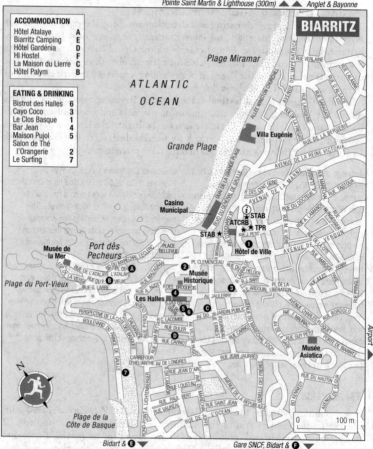

THE PYRENEES | The Côte Basque

10

Pointe Saint Martin & Lighthouse (300m) ▲ ▲ Anglet & Bayonne

BIARRITZ

ACCOMMODATION

Hôtel Atalaye	A
Biarritz Camping	E
Hôtel Gardénia	D
HI Hostel	F
La Maison du Lierre	C
Hôtel Palym	B

EATING & DRINKING

Bistrot des Halles	6
Cayo Coco	3
Le Clos Basque	1
Bar Jean	4
Maison Pujol	5
Salon de Thé l'Orangerie	2
Le Surfing	7

ATLANTIC OCEAN

Plage Miramar

Grande Plage

Villa Eugénie

Casino Municipal

Musée de la Mer

Port dês Pecheurs

Plage du Port-Vieux

Plage de la Côte de Basque

Les Halles

Musée Historique

Hôtel de Ville

Musée Asiatica

Airport

0   100 m

Bidart & **E** ▼   Gare SNCF, Bidart & **F** ▼

Hotels

Hôtel Atalaye 6 rue des Goélands ☎05.59.24.06.76, ⓦwww.hotelatalaye.com. The best rooms here have balconies facing a quiet square and, obliquely, the sea. En-suite bathrooms throughout. **③–④**

Hôtel Gardénia 19 av Carnot ☎05.59.24.10.46, ⓦwww.hotel-gardenia.com. Very popular place, though not all rooms are en suite. Wi-fi available. **③**

La Maison du Lierre 3 av du Jardin Public ☎05.59.24.06.00, ⓦwww.maisondulierre.com. Offers good-sized, wood-floored rooms in a comfortable, restored mansion. **⑤**

Hôtel Palym 7 rue du Port-Vieux ☎05.59.24.16.56, ⓦwww.le-palmarium.com.

With a variety of old-fashioned rooms and a ground-floor bar-restaurant, this a solid budget option, though owing to nearby bars isn't great for those after an early night. **②–③**

Hostel and campsite

Biarritz Camping 28 rte d'Harcet, the inland continuation of avenue de la Plage ☎05.59.23.00.12, ⓦwww.biarritz-camping.fr. Behind plage de la Milady south of town. Early May to mid-Sept.

Hostel 2km southwest of the centre on the shore of Lac Mouriscot ☎05.59.41.76.07, ⓦaubergejeune.biarritz@orange.fr. Just walkable from the *gare SNCF*; otherwise take bus #2 or B from the centre, stop "*Bois de Boulogne*".

The Town

The focus of Biarritz is the **Casino Municipal**, just behind the Grande Plage, now restored to its 1930s grandeur. Inland, the town forms a surprisingly amorphous, workaday sprawl, with the sole cultural attractions being the **Musée Asiatica**, 1 rue Guy Petit (school holidays Mon–Fri 10.30am–6.30pm, Sat & Sun 2–7pm, otherwise daily 2–6.30pm, Sat & Sun to 7pm; €7), exhibiting the collection of Indian and Tibetan art specialist Michel Postel, and the **Musée Historique de Biarritz** in the former Anglican church (Tues–Sat 10am–12.30pm & 2–6.30pm; €4), tracing the town's fortunes from its beginnings as a medieval whaling station to its Belle Époque heyday.

Between this and the plage du Port-Vieux are the only streets and squares conducive to relaxed strolling. The **halles**, divided into a seafood wing and a produce, cheese and ham division, is friendly and photogenic, the streets around it lined with places to eat and drink. To the west, **place de l'Atalaye**, high above the port and named for a nearby whalers' lookout tower, is fringed by elegant mansions; just below, characterful if touristy **rue du Port-Vieux** leads down to its namesake beach.

The **ocean**, however, is undeniably beautiful – if not especially clean, with beaches occasionally closed during spells of extreme contamination (see @www .surfrider.eu) – and also treacherous, thus heavily lifeguard-patrolled (June–Sept). White breakers crash on sandy strands, where beautiful people bronze their limbs cheek by jowl with families and surf bums, against a backdrop of ocean-liner hotels, ornate churches, Gothic follies and modern apartment blocks. The **beaches** – served by local bus operator STAB's La Navette des Plages ten times daily during July and August – extend northwards from plage de la Milady through plage Marbella, Côte des Basques (with several surfing schools), plage du Port-Vieux, Grande Plage and plage Miramar to the Pointe St-Martin with its lighthouse. Most of the action takes place between the plage du Port-Vieux and the plage Miramar, overlooked by the huge **Hôtel du Palais** (formerly the Villa Eugénie), built by Napoléon III in the mid-nineteenth century for his wife, whom he met and courted in Biarritz.

Just beside the **plage du Port-Vieux**, the most sheltered and intimate of the beaches, a rocky promontory sticks out into the sea, ending in the **Rocher de la Vierge**, an offshore rock topped by a white statue of the Virgin, and linked to the mainland by an Eiffel-built iron catwalk. Around it are scattered other rocky islets where the swell heaves and combs. On the bluff above the Virgin stands the **Musée de la Mer** (daily: June & Sept 9.30am–7pm; July & Aug 9.30am–midnight; Oct–May 9.30am–12.30pm & 2–6pm; closed Jan 7–21 & Mon Nov–March; €8; @www.museedelamer.com), which contains interesting displays on the fishing industry and the region's birds, and an aquarium of North Atlantic fish as well as the obligatory seal tank with twice-daily feedings.

Just below is the picturesque **Port des Pêcheurs**, most easily approached by a pedestrian lane. The fishermen are long gone, replaced by pleasure boats, two **scuba outfitters** (the more established being BAB ☎06.09.26.22.65, @www .babsub.fr) and pricey seafood restaurants. To the northeast lies the **Grande Plage**, an immaculate sweep of sand once dubbed the "Plage des Fous" after the 1850s practice of taking lunatics to bathe here as a primitive form of thalassotherapy.

Eating, drinking and nightlife

Away from the touristy snack bars on rue du Port-Vieux, it's possible to eat well for an affordable price, especially near the *halles*.

Bistrot des Halles 1 rue du Centre
℡05.59.24.21.22. Cosy place (groups should book) doing generously portioned, tasty fish or meat-under-sauce dishes. *Menu* at lunch only, allow €29–35 à la carte. Closed Sun eve except school holidays.

Cayo Coco 5 rue Jaulerry. A Cuban theme bar (Thurs–Sat eves) offering free salsa dance lessons.

Le Clos Basque 12 rue Louis Barthou
℡05.59.24.24.96. A popular favourite bistro – booking is mandatory even in spring/autumn – with meaty, hearty fare. *Menus* at €24–26 give a wide choice. Closed Mon & low-season Sun eve.

 Bar Jean 5 rue Halles. Semi-subterranean Spanish-theme outfit with tapas or seafood meals for about €25; also has tables on the pavement.

Maison Pujol 1 rue du Centre. Basically a deli (specialising in foie gras) that also does very reasonable tapas, bigger platters of ham or seafood and wine in any measure at impromptu seating around barrel-tables out front.

Salon de Thé l'Orangerie 1 rue Gambetta. Start your day off well at this little salon serving forty varieties of tea and a reasonably copious breakfast. Closed Wed.

Le Surfing Plage de Côte des Basques
℡05.59.24.78.72. A seaview shrine to the sport, this place is festooned with antique boards and serves decent seafood grills and *frites*.

Anglet

Immediately north and east of Biarritz, resolutely residential **ANGLET** (Angelu) sprawls up the coast from the Pointe St-Martin to the mouth of the Adour at La Barre. Tourism revolves around a half-dozen contiguous, superb beaches, broader and wilder than any at Biarritz. The most frequented are **Chambre d'Amour**, so named for two lovers trapped in their trysting place by the tide, and adjacent **Sables d'Or** and **Marinella**, both much favoured by the surfers and with schools operating in season. On the downside, parking in season (even scooters) is hopeless and a sharp drop-off means bathers hug the shore.

The summertime Navette des Plages calls here, too, or you can walk from Biarritz in about thirty minutes, along avenue de l'Impératrice, avenue MacCroskey, then second left down to the seaside boulevard des Plages. Anglet has a **HI hostel** at 19 route des Vignes (℡05.59.58.70.00; mid-Feb to mid-Nov; stop "Les Corsaires" on Navette des Plages or STAB bus #4 or C).

St-Jean-de-Luz

With its fine sandy bay – the most protected of the Basque beaches – and magnificent old quarter speckled with half-timbered mansions, **ST-JEAN-DE-LUZ** (Donibane Lohitzun) remains the most attractive resort on the Basque coast, despite being fairly overrun by families in peak season. As the only natural harbour between Arcachon and Spain, it has long been a major port, with whaling and cod-fishing the traditional occupations of its fleets. Even now, St-Jean remains one of France's busiest fisheries, and the principal one for landing anchovy and tuna.

Arrival, information and accommodation

St-Jean's **gare SNCF** is on the southern edge of the town centre, 500m from the beach, while **buses** arrive at the *halte routière* diagonally opposite. The **tourist office** (April–June & Sept Mon–Sat 9am–12.30pm & 2–7pm, Sun 10am–1pm; July & Aug Mon–Sat 9am–7.30pm, Sun 10am–1pm & 3–7pm; Oct–March Mon–Sat 9am–12.30pm & 1.30–6.30pm, Sun 10am–1pm; ℡05.59.26.03.16, Ⓦwww.saint-jean-de-luz.com) stands opposite the fish market on the corner of boulevard Victor Hugo and rue Bernard Jauréguiberry. There are numerous **campsites**, seaward of the N10 between St-Jean and Guéthary.

Hotels

Les Goëlands 4–6 av d'Etcheverry ☎05.59.26.10.05, ⓦwww.hotel -lesgoelands.com. Consists of two *belle-époque* villas, with parking and a restaurant (Easter–Oct). ❻
Lafayette 18–20 rue de la République ☎05.59.26.17.74, ⓦwww.hotelpaysbasque.com.
On a pedestrianised street, the best rooms here have balconies. ❸–❹
Hôtel Ohartzia 28 rue Garat ☎05.59.26.00.06, ⓦwww.hotel-ohartzia.com. Located just inland from the beach, with rear rooms overlooking the garden where breakfast is served. ❹–❺

The Town

The wealth and vigour of St-Jean's seafaring and mercantile past is evident in surviving seventeenth- and eighteenth-century town houses. One of the finest, adjacent to the Hôtel de Ville on plane-tree-studded place Louis XIV, is the turreted **Maison Louis XIV** (guided visits only: June & Sept to mid-Oct 11am, 3pm, 4pm, 5pm; July & Aug Mon–Sat 10.30am–12.30pm & 2.30–6.30pm; by appointment only otherwise; €5), built for the Lohobiague family in 1635, but renamed after the young King Louis stayed here for a month in 1660 during the preparations for his marriage to Maria Teresa, Infanta of Castile. She lodged in the equally impressive pink Italianate villa known as the **Maison de l'Infante** (mid-June to mid-Oct 11am–12.30pm & 2.30–6.30pm; €3), overlooking the harbour on the quay.

The couple's sumptuous wedding took place in the **church of St-Jean–Baptiste** on pedestrianized **rue Gambetta**, the main shopping-and-tourism street today. The door through which they left the church – right of the existing entrance – has been sealed up ever since. Even without this curiosity, the church deserves a look inside: the largest French Basque church, its barn-like nave roofed in wood and lined on three sides with tiers of dark oak galleries accessed by wrought-iron stairways. These are a distinctive feature of Basque churches, reserved for the men, while the women sat at ground level. Equally Basque is the elaborate gilded retable of tiered angels, saints and prophets behind the altar. Hanging from the ceiling is an *ex voto* model of the Empress Eugénie's paddle steamer, the *Eagle*, which narrowly escaped being wrecked outside St-Jean in 1867.

Ciboure, the harbour and Urrugne

On the far side of the harbour and Nivelle river mouth, **CIBOURE** (Ziburu), seems a continuation of St-Jean but is in fact a separate community, terminating in the little fortress of **Socoa** (**Sokoa**), today home to a watersports club and small beach (shuttle boat 9am–7pm from St-Jean beach, €2). Ciboure's streets are prettier and emptier than its neighbour's, especially waterfront **quai Maurice Ravel** (the composer was born at no. 12) and the parallel **rue Pocolette** just inland, an exquisite terrace of wide-fronted, half-timbered, balconied town houses gaily painted in typical Basque colours. The octagonal tower protruding above the houses belongs to the sixteenth-century **church of St-Vincent**, where you'll find more characteristic Basque galleries, a Baroque altarpiece and yet another *ex voto* model ship; the entrance is via a paved courtyard with gravestones embedded in it.

Also worth considering is a visit to the **Château d'Urtubie** (guided tours April–Oct 10.30am–12.30pm & 2–6.30pm, July–Aug no lunchbreak; €6; ⓦwww.chateaudurtubie.net) at **URRUGNE** (Urruña), just outside Ciboure, 3km southwest of St-Jean-de-Luz, which has belonged to the same family since its construction as a fortified château in 1341. It was enlarged and gentrified during the sixteenth and eighteenth centuries, and provided hospitality for the French King Louis XI, as well as for Maréchal Soult and later Wellington during the Napoleonic Wars. If you fancy following in their footsteps, note that it's also a very upmarket **hotel** (☎05.59.54.31.15; ❻–❽); otherwise just visit and take tea in the *salon* afterwards for €4 extra.

Eating and drinking

Leading off place Louis XIV – with its cafés, sidewalk artists and free summertime **evening concerts** in the bandstand – rue de la République has several **restaurants**, including cheap-and-cheerful *La Ruelle* (closed Mon, also Tues in low season) at no. 19, with two seafood *menus* (€18–23), though service is "relaxed" and drinks stiffly priced. The next street east, rue Tourasse, also offers possibilities, including *La Vieille Auberge* at no. 22 (closed Wed, & Tues lunch), with *menus* from €14.

Hendaye and Château d'Abbadia

HENDAYE (Hendaïa), 15km southwest of St-Jean-de-Luz, is the last French town before the Spanish frontier. The main local sight is the **Château d'Abbadia** (ⓦwww.academie-sciences.fr/Abbadia.htm), home of nineteenth-century Dublin-born explorer Antoine d'Abbadie, on the headland closing off Hendaye-Plage on the east, just off the route de la Corniche (Feb–May & Oct to mid-Dec Tues–Sat guided visits only 2–5pm; June–Sept Mon–Fri guided visits 10–11.30am & 2–5pm, without guide 12.30–2pm; Sat & Sun visit without guide 2–6pm; €5.50 unguided, €6.60 guided Musicale visits (July & Aug Wed at 7pm; €10) and English tours by reservation (ⓣ05.59.20.04.51). After expeditions in Ethiopia and Egypt, d'Abbadie had the Neo-Gothic château built between 1860 and 1870; the architect was Eugène Viollet-le-Duc, and the result a bizarre Franco-Hibernian folly with every surface painted, carved or fabric-covered, filled with objects collected by d'Abbadie on his travels. Visits take in the chapel, a ground-floor bedroom in red with Arabic calligraphy, upstairs rooms with Ethiopian inscriptions and a round reception room, blue-motifed like d'Abbadie's own quarters.

Practicalities

Hendaye's **tourist office** is at 67B boulevard de la Mer in Hendaye-Plage (April–June & Sept–Oct Mon–Sat 9am–12.30pm & 2–6pm; July & Aug Mon–Sat 9am–7.30pm, Sun 10.30am–1pm; Nov–March Mon–Sat 9am–12.30pm & 2–5pm; ⓣ05.59.20.00.34, ⓦwww.hendaye.com). Ten local **campsites** are all east of Hendaye-Plage, just off the Route de la Corniche; one of the more tent-friendly, and closest to the beach, is *Alturan* (ⓣ05.59.20.04.55; June–Sept), on rue de la Côte. The best **hotels** are both on boulevard de la Mer: *Hôtel Uhainak* at no. 3 (ⓣ05.59.20.33.63, ⓦwww.hotel-uhainak.com; Feb–Nov; ❹); and mock-Moorish *Hôtel Valencia* at no. 29 (ⓣ05.59.20.01.62, ⓦwww.hotelvalencia.fr; most of year; ❹), with wi-fi and free parking (a selling point as beachside street-parking is charged for all day). **Restaurants** are overwhelmingly fishy if not too numerous; cheap – because prosaically set by a car park – and popular is *La Petite Marée* at 2 av des Mimosas, one block inland. For a sea view, head west to the yacht and fishing port, where *La Cabane du Pêcheur* (closed Sun eve & Mon) does full seafood meals (weekday *menus* €25). Just around the corner at 4 rue des Orangers, ⭐ *Le Parc à Huîtres* (closed Tues) is a superb oyster-bar-cum-takeaway-deli with seating outdoors and in; make a meal of it with salad, oysters or other tapas, desserts and oyster-compatible wines *en vrac* or by the bottle.

Labourd and Basse Navarre

Without your own transport, the simplest forays into the soft, seductive landscapes of the Basque hinterland – **Labourd** (Lapurdi) and **Basse Navarre** (Behe Nafarroa) – are along the St-Jean-de-Luz–Sare bus route past **La Rhune**, **Ascain** and **Sare**, or the Bayonne–St-Jean-Pied-de-Port train line through the **Vallée de la Nive**. Both give a representative sample of the area.

La Rhune and Ascain

The 905-metre cone of **La Rhune** (Larrun), straddling the frontier with Spain, is the westernmost skyward thrust of the Pyrenees before they decline into the Atlantic. As *the* landmark of Labourd, in spite of its unsightly multipurpose antennae, and duly equipped with a rack-and-pinion rail service, it's a predictably popular vantage point, offering fine vistas way up the Basque coast and east along the Pyrenees. Two or three **buses** a day (July–Aug Mon–Sat; Sept–June Mon–Fri), run by Le Basque Bondissant, ply the route from St-Jean-de-Luz, stopping also at Ascain, Col de St-Ignace and Sare.

ASCAIN (Azkaine), where Pierre Loti wrote his romantic novel *Ramuntcho*, is like so many Labourdan villages – postcard-perfect to the point of tweeness with its galleried church, *fronton* and polychrome, half-timbered houses. Loti's house on place du Fronton is now the central **hotel-restaurant** *De la Rhune* (T05.59.54.00.04, @hoteldelarhune@orange.fr; ④) with a garden at the back, one of several accommodation options in the village.

You could walk up La Rhune from here in about two and a half hours, or take the **rack-and-pinion tourist train** from **Col de St-Ignace** (mid-March to Oct; every 35min 9am–5pm peak season, much less otherwise; current fares/schedules at Wwww.rhune.com). The ascent takes 35 minutes, but you should allow up to two hours for the round trip. Be warned: it's very popular in summer, with long queues and two snack bars near the base station taking full advantage of a captive clientele.

Sare and Ainhoa

With or without the bus, it's worth continuing to **SARE** (Sara), a perfectly proportioned Basque knoll-top village ringed by satellite hamlets. Several scattered **hotels** make for a more attractive overnight than Ascain; most central – and poshest – choice is the three-star *Arraya* on the village square (T05.59.54.20.46, Wwww.arraya.com; April–Oct; ⑤), a former hospice on the Santiago pilgrimage route. More affordable are the *Baratxartea*, 1km northeast in Ihalar hamlet (T05.59.54.20.48, Wwww.hotel-baratxartea.com; mid-March to mid-Nov; ③), or the *Pikassaria* in Lehenbizkai 1.5km south of the square (T05.59.54.21.51, Wwww.hotel-pikassaria.com; ③), with a good restaurant (dinner only except Sun; *menus* from €16). The only independent **restaurant** is popular *Lastiry* opposite the *Arraya*, offering *nouvelle Basquaise* cuisine under the arcade (*menus* from €23). The more consistently open of two **campsites** is *La Petite Rhune* (T05.59.54.23.97; May–Sept), near *Hôtel Pikassaria*.

Instead of going back to St-Jean-de-Luz from Sare, an easy three- to four-hour stint on the GR10 brings you to **AINHOA**, another gem of a village. It consists of little more than a single street lined with substantial, mainly seventeenth-century houses, whose lintel plaques offer mini-genealogies as well as foundation dates. Take a look at the bulky towered **church** with its gilded Baroque altarpiece of prophets and apostles in niches, framed by Corinthian columns. Indoor **accommodation** is only for well-heeled trekkers (or drivers); best value among three pricey hotels is *Hôtel Oppoca* (T05.59.29.90.72, Wwww.oppoca.com; mostly closed mid-Nov to April; ⑤) with a **restaurant** (closed Mon; *menus* from €26). Otherwise it's *Camping Harazpy* near the village centre (T05.59.29.89.38; mid-June to mid-Sept).

Vallée de la Nive

The **River Nive** valley is the only public transport corridor southeast into the Basque hinterland, with several daily trains making the riverside journey from Bayonne to St-Jean-Pied-de-Port. The luminous green landscape on the approach to the mountains is scattered with peaceful villages untouched by speculative development.

Cambo-les-Bains

The first major stop is **CAMBO–LES–BAINS** (Kanbo), an old spa resort whose favourable microclimate made it ideal for the treatment of tuberculosis in the nineteenth century; it's an attractive place, green and open, but suffers from the usual genteel stuffiness of spas. The "new" town, with its ornate houses and hotels, radiates out from the baths over the heights above the River Nive, while the old quarter of Bas Cambo lies beside the river and *gare SNCF*.

The main local sight is the **Villa Arnaga**, 1.5km northwest of town on the Bayonne road (guided or "free" visits: March 2.30–6pm; April–June & Sept to mid-Oct 10am–12.30pm & 2.30–7pm; July–Aug 10am–7pm; mid-Oct to early Nov 2.30–6pm; €6), built for Edmond Rostand, author of *Cyrano de Bergerac*, who came here to cure his pleurisy in 1903. This larger-than-life Basque house, painted in deep-red trim, overlooks an almost surreal formal garden with discs and rectangles of water and segments of grass punctuated by blobs, cubes and cones of topiary box, with a distant view of green hills. Inside, it's very kitsch, with a minstrels' gallery, fake pilasters, allegorical frescoes, numerous portraits and various memorabilia.

The **tourist office** is at the start of the road down to Bas Cambo (mid-July to Aug Mon–Sat 9am–6.30pm, Sun 9am–12.30pm; Sept to mid-July Mon–Sat 9am–12.30pm & 2–5.30pm; ☎05.59.29.70.25, ⓦwww.cambolesbains.com). For an overnight **stay**, try *Auberge de Tante Ursule* in Bas Cambo by the *pelota* court (☎05.59.29.78.23, ⓦwww.auberge-tante-ursule.com; ➋), with old-fashioned rooms upstairs from the excellent **restaurant** (*menus* from €16). The nearest year-round **campsite** is *Ur-Hégia* on route des Sept Chênes (☎05.59.29.72.03), also in Bas Cambo.

Espelette, Itxassou and Laxia

Buses cover the 5km southwest from Cambo to **ESPELETTE** (Ezpeleta), a somewhat busy village of wide-eaved houses, with a **church** notable for its heavy square tower, painted ceiling (climb the triple gallery for a closer look) and keyhole-shaped, inscribed-slab gravestones (the oldest are by the church, under the lime trees). The village's principal source of renown is its dark red **chilli peppers** – much used in Basque cuisine, hung to dry in summer on many housefronts – and its **pottok** markets. *Pottoks* are the indigenous Basque pony, once used in British coal mines but now reared mainly for meat and riding. The annual sales happen on the last Tuesday and Wednesday in January; the pepper jamboree takes place on the last Sunday in October. There's a very good **hotel-restaurant** in Espelette, *Euzkadi*, on the main street at the northeast edge of the village (☎05.59.93.91.88; ➌; restaurant closed Mon, & Tues low season), with calmer rear rooms facing a pool and three *menus* (from €23) featuring hearty Basque country cooking.

About the same distance south from Cambo-les-Bains, next stop up the train line (though only one train a day stops here), is the delightful village of **ITXASSOU** (Itsasu), quieter than most of the others in the area, and surrounded by green wooded hills. The main point of interest is the little seventeenth-century **church of St-Fructueux**, about 1km out on the minor D349 road towards Pas de Roland and Laxia hamlet, its vast cemetery harbouring a significant collection of both modern and ancient keyhole-shaped gravestones; inside, its three-tiered wooden galleries and sumptuous retable are worth a quick look. Itxassou is a great base for a gentle recharge of the batteries, with about a half-dozen **hotel-restaurants** scattered locally. Best-value and quietest are – next to

St-Fructueux – the ⚘ *Hôtel du Chêne* (℡05.59.29.75.01, 🖷05.59.29.27.39; closed mid-Dec to Feb; ❸), with bright, wood-floored rooms and a well-kept restaurant (closed Mon, also Tues low season) offering *menus* featuring *pipérade*, salad, game and dessert, and – at bucolic **LAXIA** – the *Hôtel Ondoria* (℡05.59.29.75.39, 🖳www.ondoria.fr; closed mid-Dec to Jan & Mon; ❷), where meals are taken at a wisteria-festooned terrace overlooking the river.

Bidarray

The GR10 from Ainhoa, the train line (station Pont-Noblia) and a perilously narrow road beyond Laxia all converge at **BIDARRAY** (Bidarrai), which at first glance seems restricted to a few houses clustered around its medieval bridge over the Nive, the **Pont d'Enfer**. Further investigation, however, reveals the upper village, scattered appealingly on a ridge with superb views. On the way into the village on the GR10 is a *gîte d'étape* spread over two buildings, the *Auñamendi* (℡05.59.37.71.34), while the central place de l'Église is flanked by the *Hôtel Barberaenea* (℡05.59.37.74.86, closed mid-Nov to mid-Dec; ❶–❸), with a decent **restaurant**. A short walk east, equidistant from upper and riverside quarters, lies the tent-only *Camping Errekaldia* (℡05.59.37.72.36).

St-Étienne-de-Baïgorry

Like many other Basque villages, **ST-ÉTIENNE-DE-BAÏGORRY** (Baigorri) is divided into distinct quarters, more like separate hamlets than a unified settlement. A prosperous, sleek place, its business is still predominantly agriculture rather than tourism, with the Pays Basque's only vineyards scattered around, producing the Irouléguy (Irulegi) wine named after the village 5km east; the vintner's on the D15 road offers *dégustation* and sales. The "sights" here comprise a seventeenth-century, barrel-vaulted **church** with a fine organ over the southwest door in addition to the usual galleries and altarpiece, plus a picturesque medieval bridge posing against a backdrop of the romantic Château de Etchaux and distant hills.

The **tourist office** is opposite the church (Mon–Fri 9am–noon & 2.30–6pm; ℡05.59.37.47.28 🖳www.saintjeanpieddeport-paysbasque-tourisme.com). **Accommodation** includes the municipal **campsite** *Irouléguy* (℡05.59.37.43.96; March to mid-Dec), opposite the swimming pool on the St-Jean road, plus *Hôtel-Restaurant Juantorena* on the through road in Bourg quarter (℡05.59.37.40.78; ❷), with a pleasant terrace and parking in the back. If you have transport, head for tranquil, stream-side *Hôtel Manechenea*, 5km north in the hamlet of **Urdos** (Urdoze) (℡05.59.37.41.68, 📧hotel-manechenea@orange.fr; ❸; closed Nov–March), with a good restaurant (*menus* from €19).

St-Jean-Pied-de-Port

The old capital of Basse Navarre, **ST-JEAN-PIED-DE-PORT** (Donibane Garazi) lies in a circle of hills at the foot of the Bentarte pass into Spain. It owes its name to its position "at the foot of the *port*" – the pass leading into Spain. Only part of France since the 1659 Treaty of the Pyrenees, it was an important halt on the **pilgrimage to Santiago de Compostela** in the Middle Ages. The routes from Paris, Vézelay and Le Puy converged just northeast of here at Ostabat, before struggling over the ridge to the Spanish monastery of Roncesvalles (Roncevaux in French).

The old town consists of a single cobbled street, **rue de la Citadelle**, which runs downhill from the fifteenth-century **Porte St-Jacques** – the gate by which pilgrims entered the town, St Jacques being French for Santiago – to the **Porte Notre-Dame**, commanding the bridge over the Nive, with a constantly photographed view of balconied houses overlooking the stream.

The GR65 south from St-Jean

The final French leg of the **GR65** pilgrim route starts from St-Jean and follows the line of the old Roman road across to Roncesvalles in Spanish Navarra, a walk of 27km (allow 7–8hr). Follow the star-ray yellow-on-blue signs south from the Porte d'Espagne, soon adopting the one-lane D428 with which you will stay for more than half the route; the typical yellow waymarks of the Chemin de St-Jacques guide you, as do newer red-and-white ones. Though the climb on tarmac is initially dull, there are attractive farmhouses to look at, with immensely broad roofs – one side short, the other long to cover stalls and tools – plus views out across the valleys east and west. After about ninety minutes you'll reach the tiny hamlet of **Honto**, which for late starters in particular offers excellent *chambres d'hôtes* (as well as cheaper dorm beds) and hearty evening meals at *Ferme Ithurburia* (☏05.59.37.11.17; ❷; year round). Beyond Honto, the grade sharpens, but there's only one brief path short-cut from the D428 before you arrive, an hour further along, at the well-sited *Refuge-Auberge Orisson* (☏06.81.49.79.56, ⓦwww.refuge-orisson.com; 18 bunks; March–Oct), your last chance for meals and shelter before Roncesvalles. After passing a pennant-festooned altar, you'll finally leave the D428 for a proper trail at Pic Urdanarré (1240m), some four hours along and just before the frontier and spring at Col de Bentarte (c.1340m), where sheep and vultures are everywhere.

Information and accommodation

The **tourist office** is at 14 place du Général-de-Gaulle (July & Aug Mon–Sat 9am–7pm, Sun 9.30am–1pm & 2.30–5pm; Sept–June Mon–Sat 9am–noon & 2–6pm; ☏05.59.37.03.57, ⓦwww.terre-basque.com), while a handful of newsagents and bookstores sell guides and IGN maps. The **gare SNCF** lies a ten-minute walk away at the end of avenue Renaud, north of the centre.

Chambres d'hôtes, as well as cheaper dormitory lodgings for pilgrims and hikers, are numerous: try along rue de la Citadelle.

Hotels and gîtes d'étape

Central Place du Général-de-Gaulle ☏05.59.37.00.22. Has a restaurant with *menus* from €19.50, some river-view rooms and parking. Closed Dec–Feb, Tues low season. ❺

L'Esprit du Chemin 40 rue de la Citadelle ☏05.59.37.24.68, ⓦwww.espritduchemin .org. Inexpensive place with 14 bunks run by Dutch volunteers, offering moral support to pilgrims and walkers. Dorm bed €8. Open April–Sept.

Etchegoin 9 rte d'Uhart, on the Bayonne road ☏05.59.37.12.08. Helpful and basic *gîte d'étape* with 12 bunks. Dorm bed €10.

Ramuntcho 1 rue de France ☏05.59.37.03.91. Just inside the city walls, with some balconied rooms. There's parking near by and a popular restaurant (*menu* from €16.50). Closed late-Nov to mid-Jan; Tues–Wed low season. ❹

Les Remparts 16 place Floquet ☏05.59.37.13.79, ⓦwww.touradour.com/hotel-remparts.htm. The best budget choice among the hotels, this relatively quiet place is located just before you cross the Nive coming into town on the Bayonne road. Closed Nov to mid-Feb. ❸

Campsite

Plaza Berri ☏05.59.37.11.19. Municipal campsite on the south bank of the Nive, off avenue du Fronton. Easter to early Nov.

Eating and drinking

Restaurants are mostly slapdash bistros and "café-snacks" aimed squarely at the day-tripper trade. Two exceptions are popular *Paxkal Oillarburu* at 8 rue de l'Église just inside the Porte de Navarre (closed Tues low season, book on ☏05.59.37.06.44 in summer), and *Hurrup Eta Klik* at 3bis rue de la Citadelle (☏05.59.37.09.18; closed Wed), just inside the Porte Notre-Dame and serving country cooking and generous measures of cider.

Estérençuby and Béhérobie

From St-Jean, the D301 follows the deepening valley of the Nive to the southeast, past small farms and bucolic villages, while the GR10 stays well northeast of the river, first on paved lanes and then on track or trail along Handiamendi ridge. Both routes converge at **ESTÉRENÇUBY** (Ezterenzubi), 8km from St-Jean and an attractive spot. *Auberge Carricaburu* by the *fronton* is the most appealing **restaurant** (*menus* €18–22) and has a lively village bar. *Hôtel Andreinia-Larramendy* is over the bridge (℡05.59.37.09.70, ⓦwww.hotel-andreinia.com; closed mid-Nov to Dec, Wed low season; ❷); they also run a 19-bunk *gîte d'étape* (March–Nov).

Beyond Estérençuby the valley-floor D428 road continues alongside the Nive, now no more than a mountain stream, tumbling down between steep green slopes, covered in hay and bracken. Some 4km from Estérençuby the road reaches tiny **BÉHÉROBIE** (Beherobia) before climbing up to the border by the Col de Bentarte and looping back to St-Jean – an excellent bike-ride or drive. At Béhérobie the ⅍ *Hôtel des Sources de la Nive* (℡05.59.37.10.57, ⓦwww.hotel-sourcesdelanive.com; ❷–❺ half-board; closed Jan to mid-Feb and Tues low season, booked out in Oct by pigeon-shooters), beside the stream, is ideal for a quiet stay despite the rooms being decidedly 1970s, with a restaurant where frog's legs, *cèpes*, trout, roebuck and pigeon feature on copious *menus*.

Just before the bridge at Béhérobie, a lane leads to the left, signposted to "**Sources de la Nive**". With a car, you can drive 400m to the asphalt's end, then continue on foot along the dirt track going left, not the one going over the bridge. After fifteen minutes, you'll reach the springs, where water percolates a thousand metres down through the karstic slopes to well up as surging rapids. Hidden in dense beech woods, it's a magic spot in any weather, with a faint mist often rising from the surface of the young stream.

Haute Soule

East of the Nive valley, you enter largely uninhabited country, the old Basque county known as the **Haute Soule**, threaded only by the GR10 and a couple of minor roads. The border between Basse Navarre and Soule skims the western edge of the **Forêt d'Iraty**, one of Europe's largest surviving beech woods, a popular summer retreat and winter cross-country skiing area. There are no shops or proper hotels until you reach **Larrau**, the only real village hereabouts, though the scattered hamlet of **Ste-Engrâce** in the east of the district has accommodation, as do **Licq** and **Tardets-Sorholus**, foothill settlements some way down the valley.

Haute Soule is a land of open skies, where griffon vultures turn on the thermals high above countless flocks of sheep (their occasional corpses providing sustenance), with three vast gorges to explore. It's not a great distance between the Nive valley and Béarn, but the slowness of the roads (there's no public transport), the GR10 – it's two days' hiking from Estérençuby to Larrau – and the grandeur of the scenery seems to magnify it.

The Forêt d'Iraty

To drive to the **Forêt d'Iraty** (Irati), follow the D301 east out of the Nive valley from the junction on the D428, where the forest is signposted. The road is steep, narrow and full of tight hairpins and ambling livestock – it's best avoided at night or in misty conditions – but as you climb up the steep spurs and around the heads of labyrinthine gullies, ever more spectacular views open out over the valley of the Nive, St-Jean and the hills beyond. Solar-powered sheep ranches abound, with cheese on sale. Beech copses fill the gullies, shadowing the lighter grass whose green is so intense it seems almost theatrical – an effect produced by a backdrop of purplish rock outcrops.

Once past the north flank of **Occabé** (Okabe; 1456m), you're in Haute Soule, and from here the road loops down to meet the D18 on the **plateau d'Iraty**, with its small lake and *Le Cayolar* snack bar. A minor road that soon turns into a jeep track leads south towards Ochagavia (in Spain) passing *Chalet Pedro* (1km along), a basic hikers' *gîte* with eight beds which is open in July and August, but also offering comfier apartments sleeping eight (℡05.59.28.55.98, Ⓦwww.chaletpedro.com; mid-June to Aug) as well as the best **restaurant** in the area (*menus* €23–29, featuring trout, *cèpes*, Iberian ham). The GR10 emerges here from its descent of flat-topped Occabé (75min up from here), with its Iron Age **stone circle** up top. Continuing east from the plateau, the D18 road enters the densest part of the forest, climbing past another small lake and a **campsite** half-hidden in the magnificent beeches, to nine wooden chalets and a *gîte d'étape* at the **Col de Bagargi-Iraty** (1327m). An **information** office here (open all year; ℡05.59.28.51.29) takes bookings for the chalets and the *gîte*; across the car park is a small shop and reasonably priced **restaurant**. From here you descend slightly to the nearby **Col d'Orgambidexka**, which is one of the prime viewing fields for the autumn bird migrations. As you emerge into the open beyond Orgambidexka, the ground drops sharply away on the left into the **Vallée de Larrau**, 600m lower.

Larrau

The first thing you notice coming into **LARRAU** (Larraiñe) from the west is how different the architecture is from the villages in Labourd and Basse Navarre. In contrast to the usual painted, half-timbered facades and tiled roofs, the houses here are grey and stuccoed, with Béarnais-style, steep-pitched slate roofs to shed heavy snow. Despite its size, it's nonetheless very quiet – almost dead out of season. There are two friendly **hotels**: the simple, old-fashioned *Hôtel Despouey* (℡05.59.28.60.82; ❷; closed mid-Nov to Easter), and the fancier ⚑ *Hôtel-Restaurant Etchémaïté* (℡05.59.28.61.45, Ⓦwww.hotel-etchemaite.fr; closed Sun eve & Mon and various months – contact the hotel for details; ❷–❸), with an excellent restaurant serving eels, *cèpes*, pigeon and decadent desserts (closed early Jan to mid-Feb; *menus* €18–42).

There's one **campsite** in Larrau, the *Ixtila* (℡05.59.28.63.09; April to mid-Nov), and the *Auberge Logibar*, a *gîte d'étape* (℡05.59.28.61.14) with a bar-restaurant (closed Dec–Feb) 3km away at **LOGIBAR**, close to the mouth of the **Gorges d'Holzarte**. This is one of several locally, cutting deep into northern slopes of the ridge that forms the frontier with Spain. A short track leads from Logibar across a lively, chilly stream to a car park, from where a steep, usually very busy path – a variant of the GR10 – climbs through beech woods in about 45 minutes to the junction of the Holzarte gorge with the **Gorges d'Olhadubi**. Slung across the mouth of the latter is a spectacular Himalayan-style **suspension bridge**, the *passerelle*, which bounces and swings alarmingly as you walk out over the 180-metre drop.

The Gorges de Kakuetta and Gorges d'Ehujarré

Fifteen kilometres east of Larrau, well beyond the turning for Licq and Tardets, you reach the **Gorges de Kakuetta** (mid-March to mid-Nov 8am–nightfall; €4.50), having veered off the D26 and onto the D113. About 4km along the latter, minuscule **CASERNES** hamlet offers a shop opposite the *mairie*, and the attractive riverside **campsite** *Ibarra* (℡05.59.28.73.59; Easter–Oct).

Kakuetta gorge is truly dramatic and, outside peak season, not crowded at all; allow about two hours to visit. It pays to be well shod – the metal catwalk and narrow path, by turns, are slippery in places and provided with safety cables where needed. The walls of the gorge rise up to 300m high and are scarcely more than 5m apart in spots, so little sunlight penetrates except at midday from May to July. The air hangs heavy with mist produced by dozens of seeps and tiny waterfalls, nurturing tenacious ferns, moss and other vegetation that thrives in the hothouse atmosphere. Within an hour, the path brings you to a small cave beyond which only technical climbers need apply; just before it a twenty-metre waterfall (which you can walk behind) gushes out of a hole in the rock.

There's another, scarcely visited gorge, the **Gorges d'Ehujarré**, a short distance east at Senta, the easternmost of the three hamlets that comprise Ste-Engrâce (see below). It's a straightforward walk up along the east flank – this route has been used for centuries for moving sheep up to the pastures of Pic Lakhoura – and then down along the gorge floor, a five-hour round trip.

Ste-Engrâce

Le bout du monde – "the end of the earth" – is what they used to call tiny **STE-ENGRÂCE** (Ⓦ www.sainte-engrace.com) hidden in its cul-de-sac valley beneath the Spanish frontier at the easternmost extremity of the Basque country. And, although a road now runs through it to Béarn and La-Pierre-St-Martin, the place remains beautifully remote and peaceful. Life is not so idyllic for the locals – there's no work and the young don't stay – but for an outsider it has great charm.

Ste-Engrâce's hallmark is the eleventh-century Romanesque **church** in the hamlet of **SENTA**, which features in most coffee-table books about the Pyrenees. Focus of a popular **festival** the last two Sundays in July, it stands with heavily buttressed walls, belfry and assymetrical roof, a sharply defined and angular assertion of humanity against the often mist-shrouded bulwarks of the mountains behind. Inside, it has some excellent carved column capitals depicting among other things the Adoration of the Magi, lions devouring Christians, and King Solomon copulating with the Queen of Sheba. There's a 30-bunk **gîte d'étape** opposite the church, the *Auberge Elichalt* (Ⓣ 05.59.28.61.63), with a few *chambres d'hôtes* (❸), a garden to camp in and a café-bar serving light meals.

The Central Pyrenees

The **Central Pyrenees**, immediately east of the Pays Basque, hosts the range's highest mountain peaks, the most spectacular section by the border being protected within the **Parc National des Pyrénées**. Getting here by public transport is straightforward, at least as far as the foothill towns, served by frequent trains on the Bayonne–Toulouse line. But travelling uphill, and around once there, can be very slow. Buses – and most other traffic – keep mainly to the north–south valleys, making it difficult to switch from one valley system to the next without having to emerge from the mountains each time.

Highlights – apart from the lakes, torrents, forests and 3000-metre peaks around **Cauterets** – are the cirques of **Lescun**, **Gavarnie** and **Troumouse**, each with its distinctive character. And for less *sportif* interests, there's many a flower-starred

10

624

PARC NATIONAL DES PYRÉNÉES

Sentier de Grande Randonnée (GR10)
High Level Route (HRP)
Mountain Refuge Hut

0   10 km

Campan
Oule
La Mongie
Pic du Midi de Bigorre (2877m)
Col du Tournalet (2115m)
Lac d'Orédon Orédon
Barèges
P. Néouvielle (3091m)
Turon (3035m)
Lac de Cap-de-Long
RÉSERVE NATURELLE DE NÉOUVIELLE
Cirque de Troumouse
Pic de la Munia (3133m)
HRP
Argelès-Gazost
Pierrefitte-Nestalas
Gèdre
Héas
Espuguettes
Maillet
Grd. Astazou (3071m)
Marboré (3248m)
Mte. Perdido (3335m)
Lourdes
Cauterets
Luz-St-Sauveur
Gavarnie
St-Savin
GR10 LOW VARIANT
Moun Né (2324m)
VALLÉE DU LUTOUR
Grange de Holle
Cirque
Brèche de Roland
N21
D920
Estom
Baysellance
Sarradets
PARQUE NACIONAL DE ORDESA
Arrens-Marsous
VALLÉE D'ESTAING
Ilhéou
Pont d'Espagne
Lac de Gaube
Oulettes de Gaube
GR10 HIGH VARIANT
Port de Gavarnie
SPAIN
Lac d'Estaing
Wallon
Vignemale (3298m)
Col de Soulor (1475m)
D918
Larribet
Arrémoulit
HRP NORTH VARIANT
HRP NORM VARIANT
Col d'Aubisque (1709m)
Gourette
Lac d'Artouste
Respumoso
HRP SOUTH VARIANT
Pau
Aste-Béon
Béost
Laruns
Eaux-Bonnes
Eaux-chaudes
VALLÉE D'OSSAU
Téléphérique
Lac de Fabrèges
Pic de la Sagette (2031m)
Sallent de Gállego
N260
Huesca
Pombie
Pic Du Midi d'Ossau (2884m)
Col du Pourtalet
Gabas
D934
D'Ayous
Lacs d'Ayous
Col du Somport (1632m)
Candanchu
Canfranc
N330
Jaca
Chem. de la Mâture
Urdos
Fort du Portalet
Borce
GR10
Etsaut
Cette-Eygun
VALLÉE D'ASPE
L'Estanguet
N134
Sarrance
Bedous
Lourdios-Ichère
Osse-en-Aspe
Cirque de Lescun
Lescun
HRP
Arlet
La-Pierre-St-Martin

N

The **Parc National des Pyrénées** was created in 1967 to protect at least part of the high Pyrenees from modern touristic development – ski resorts, paved roads, mountain-top restaurants, car parks and other inappropriate amenities. It extends for more than 100km along the Spanish border from Pic de Laraille (2147m), south of Lescun, in the west, to beyond Pic de la Munia (3133m), almost to the Aragnouet–Bielsa tunnel. Varying in altitude between 1070m and 3298m at the Pic de Vignemale, south of Cauterets, the park includes the spectacular Gavarnie and Troumouse cirques, as well as 220 lakes, more than a dozen valleys and about 400km of marked walking routes.

By the **banning of hunting** and all dogs and vehicles (except local herders), the park has also provided sanctuary for many rare, endangered species of birds and mammals. These include chamois, marmots, ermines, genets, griffon vultures, golden eagles, eagle owls and capercaillies, to say nothing of the rich and varied flora. The most celebrated animal – extinct as of 2004 – is the Pyrenean **brown bear**, whose pre-1940 numbers ran to as many as two hundred; the dozen current specimens are descended from introduced Slovenian brown bears. Although largely herbivorous, bears will take livestock opportunistically, and most mountain shepherds are their remorseless enemies. To appease them, local authorities pay prompt and generous compensation for any losses, but the restocking programme remains highly controversial, with pro- and anti-bear graffiti prominent on the road approaches to the park, and troublesome animals being shot illegally by aggrieved farmers or herders on a regular basis.

The **GR10** runs through the entire park on its 700-kilometre journey from coast to coast, starting at Banyuls-sur-Mer on the Mediterranean and ending at Hendaye-Plage on the Atlantic; the tougher **Haute Randonnée Pyrénéenne** (HRP) also finishes its course in Hendaye-Plage and runs roughly parallel to the GR10, but takes in more rugged, alpine terrain. While the Pyrenees have a modest maximum altitude by world-mountain standards, their climate can be as extreme as in ranges twice their height.

There are **Maisons du Parc** (park information centres) in Etsaut, Cauterets, Luz-St-Sauveur, Gavarnie, Laruns and Arrens-Marsous, giving information about the park's wildlife and vegetation and the best walks. There are over a dozen wardened refuges in *parc* territory and plenty of hotels, campsites and *gîtes* just outside it, listed in the text or highlighted on the map opposite. Backcountry camping (*camping sauvage*) is forbidden in many areas, except for emergency bivouacs above 2000m elevation which must be disassembled by 9am. For an update on weather conditions in the *département* of Hautes-Pyrénées, telephone ☎08.92.68.02.65, or 3250, option 4.

mountain meadow accessible by car, especially near **Barèges** and **Luchon**, in which to picnic. The only real urban centres are **Pau**, a probable entry point to the area, dull **Tarbes** and the tacky pilgrimage target of **Lourdes**. Great man-made monuments – except for the fortified churches at **Luz-St-Sauveur**, **St-Savin** and **St-Bertrand-de-Comminges** – are equally scarce, though there are wonderful Romanesque carvings on smaller churches at **Oloron-Ste-Marie**, **St-Aventin** and **Valcabrère**.

Pau and around

From humble beginnings as a crossing on the Gave de Pau (*gave* is "mountain river" in Gascon dialect), **PAU** became the capital of the ancient viscountcy of Béarn in 1464, and of the French part of the kingdom of Navarre in 1512. In 1567 its sovereign, Henri d'Albret, married the sister of French King François I, Marguerite d'Angoulême, who transformed the town into a centre of the arts and nonconformist thinking.

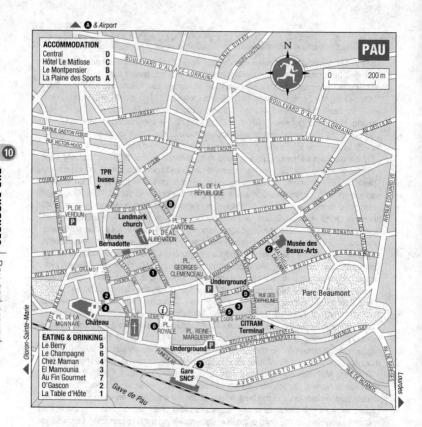

The least-expected thing about Pau is its **English connection**: seduced by its climate and persuaded (mistakenly) of its curative powers by Scottish doctor Alexander Taylor, the English flocked to Pau throughout the nineteenth century, bringing along their cultural idiosyncracies – fox-hunting, horse-racing, polo, croquet, cricket, golf (the first eighteen-hole course in continental Europe in 1860, and the first to admit women), tea salons and parks. When the railway arrived here in 1866, the French came, too: writers like Victor Hugo, Stendhal and Lamartine, as well as socialites. The first French rugby club opened here in 1902, after which the sport spread throughout the southwest. During the 1950s, natural gas was discovered at nearby Lacq, bringing new jobs and subsidiary industries, as well as massive sulphur-dioxide-based pollution, now reduced by filtration – and the imminent depletion of the gas field. In addition, there's a well-respected university, founded in 1972, whose 15,000 students give the town a youthful buzz.

Arrival and information

Pau's busy **airport** (☎05.59.33.33.00, ⓦwww.pau.aeroport.fr) is served by year-round no-frills arrivals from the UK and Holland. A bus runs from the airport to the *gare SNCF* hourly from 7.40am–7.40pm, while another runs from the *gare SNCF* to the airport hourly from 6.30am–7.50pm. The fare is €1. The **gare SNCF**, for both trains and SNCF buses, is on the southern edge of the city centre by the riverside. TPR buses leave from a terminal at 4 rue Lapouble, near place de Verdun, while CITRAM buses leave from a stop at the west end of the Parc Beaumont. Services run south down the Vallée d'Ossau and to Oloron-Ste-Marie, with onward connections from there to the Vallée d'Aspe. **Parking** (and driving) is predictably nightmarish; there are a few free spaces at the far west end of boulevard des Pyrénées and many more on place de Verdun, otherwise shell out for kerbside meters or use the giant underground car park at place Georges Clemenceau.

A **free funicular** carries you up from the train station to the boulevard des Pyrénées, opposite place Royale. At the far end of the *place* is the **tourist office** (July & Aug Mon–Fri 9am–6.30pm, Sat 9am–6pm, Sun 9am–1pm & 2–6pm; Sept–June Mon–Sat 9am–6pm, Sun 9.30am–1pm; ℡05.59.27.27.08, ⓦwww.pau-pyrenees.com). Librairie des Pyrénées at 14 rue St-Louis stocks books and maps on the mountains.

Accommodation

Hotel and campsite

Central 15 rue Léon Daran ℡05.59.27.72.75, ⓦwww.hotelcentralpau.com. Excellent-value hotel with tasteful room decor and wi-fi. ❸

Hôtel le Matisse 17 rue Mathieu Lalanne ℡05.59.27.73.80. A friendly and relatively quiet budget hotel opposite the Musée des Beaux-Arts. All rooms have showers, some have toilets. ❶

Le Montpensier 36 rue Montpensier ℡05.59.27.42.72, ⓦwww.hotel-montpensier-pau.com. Stylish three-star hotel housed in an eighteenth-century building with private parking. ❹

La Plaine des Sports Bd du Cami-Salié ℡05.59.02.30.49. Municipal campsite off avenue Sallenave towards the autoroute, on the northern edge of town; open June to mid-Sept.

The Town

Pau has no must-see sights or museums, so you can enjoy its relaxed elegance without any sense of guilt. The parts to wander in are the streets behind the **boulevard des Pyrénées**, especially the western end, which stretches along the escarpment above the Gave de Pau, from the castle to the Palais Beaumont, now a convention centre, in the English-style **Parc Beaumont**. On a (rare) clear day, the view from the boulevard encompasses a broad sweep of the highest Pyrenean peaks, with the distinctive Pic du Midi d'Ossau slap in front of you.

In the narrow streets between the castle and ravine-bed chemin du Hédas are numerous cafés, restaurants, bars and boutiques, with the main Saturday **market** in the *halles* just northeast on place de la République. The **château** (exterior gardens free, unenclosed) is very much a landmark building, though not much remains of its original fabric beyond the southeasterly brick keep built by Gaston Fébus in 1370. The handsome Renaissance windows and other details on the inner courtyard were added by Henri d'Albret. Louis-Philippe renovated it in the nineteenth century after two hundred years of dereliction, and Napoléon III and Eugénie titivated it further with stellar vaulting, chandeliers and coffered ceilings. The **Musée National** inside is visitable by a French-only, one-hour guided tour (daily: mid-June to mid-Sept 9.30am–12.15pm & 1.30–5.45pm; mid-Sept to mid-June 9.30–11.45am & 2–5pm; €5 except €3.50 Sun, free first Sun of month), but this is the only way to see the vivid eighteenth-century tapestries with their wonderfully observed scenes of rural life, or Henri IV memorabilia like the giant turtle shell that purportedly served as his cradle.

A short distance northeast of the château, the mildly interesting **Musée Bernadotte**, 6 rue Tran (Tues–Sun 10am–noon & 2–5pm; €3), is the birthplace of the man who, having served as one of Napoleon's commanders, went on to become Charles XIV of Sweden. As well as fine pieces of traditional Béarnais furniture, the house contains some valuable works of art collected over his lifetime. Pau's other museum, the **Musée des Beaux-Arts** in rue Mathieu Lalanne (daily except Tues 10am–noon & 2–6pm; €3), has an eclectic collection of little-known works from European schools spanning the fourteenth to twentieth centuries; the only really world-class items are Rubens' *The Last Judgement* and Degas' *The Cotton Exchange*, a slice of finely observed *belle-époque* New Orleans life.

Eating and drinking

Pau's better **restaurants** are concentrated in the pedestrianized lanes around the château, on place Royal or in rue du Hédas, though there are a few choices elsewhere. **Bars** cluster immediately west of place Reine Marguerite, about halfway along boulevard des Pyrénées.

Le Berry Rue Gachet, near corner rue Louis Barthou ☎05.59.27.42.95. Less than brilliant siting, by the "rabbit hole" of the subterranean car park, but compensated for by excellent brasserie grub (*magret de canard*, Châteaubriand steaks). Expect a wait for interior tables; service until 11pm; budget €20–28 à la carte.

Le Champagne 5 place Royale ☎05.59.27.72.12. Popular, upscale brasserie with *carte* and *menus* from €14.50 up – even the cheapest nets you a solid lamb-based main course, salad and dessert. There's been an establishment here since 1843, and the current interior with swirling fans and original art (larger parties can book the back room) vies for allure with tables on the *place* in fine weather. Service is consistently leisurely, however.

Chez Maman 6 rue du Château. Simple crêperie/*cidrerie* right opposite the castle; a good option for vegetarians, with big salads – €20 will about cover two courses and a bit of cider. Tues–Sun 11am–midnight.

El Mamounia 7 rue des Orphelines ☎05.59.27.12.44. Competent Moroccan restaurant; lunch *menus* from €12, otherwise allow up to around €30. Closed Mon lunch & Sun.

Au Fin Gourmet 24 av Gaston Lacoste, opposite the *gare SNCF* ☎05.59.27.47.71. Trim, modern place with a few game-oriented lunch *menus* (pigeon, rabbit) from €19, but best allow €40-plus à la carte. Closed Sun eve–Tues lunch, plus 2 weeks in mid-summer.

O'Gascon 13 rue du Château ☎05.59.27.64.74. The most popular and reasonable of the four non-pizzerias on this little place; their €29 *menu tradition* – big salad, stuffed quail, free dessert choice – is excellent. Dinner only except Sun lunch. Closed Tues.

La Table d'Hôte 1 rue du Hédas ☎05.59.27.56.06. Elegant bare-brick restaurant in a former warehouse, one of the first to colonize this trendy area. There's a heavy emphasis on duck, pork, foie gras and fish like *rouget or lotte*. Menus €18–31; service can be laid-back. Closed Sun & Mon.

Around Pau

One worthwhile excursion from Pau, particularly for families, is to the **Grottes de Bétharram** (guided visits only late-March to Oct daily 9am–noon & 1.30–5.30pm; Feb to late-March groups only Mon–Fri 2.30–4pm; €12.50; ⓦwww.grottes-de-betharram.com) at St-Pé-de-Bigorre, just off the D937 between Pau and Lourdes, 14km from the latter. Part of the eighty-minute tour around its spectacular stalactites and stalagmites takes place in a barge on an underground lake; the remaining kilometre is by miniature railway.

In the opposite direction from Pau lies tourist-board-dubbed **Béarn des Gaves**, so called because several *gaves* – de Pau, d' Oloron, the Saleys and the Saison – slant across the landscape before mingling with each other or, ultimately, the Adour. The four major destinations here have strategic riverside locations, and three were traditional halts on the **Chemin de St-Jacques**, though the main variant of the modern GR65 traces a course across the southeast of the territory.

Orthez

Thirty kilometres northwest of Pau, **ORTHEZ** was the original capital of Béarn, its wealth due largely to a beautiful, still-surviving thirteenth-century **Pont-Vieux**, which controlled the most important commercial route across the Gave de Pau for English and Flemish textiles, Aragonese wool, olive oil and wine, as well as the Chemin de St-Jacques (there's still a pilgrims' hostel at 14 rue de l'Horloge; March–Nov). The town also serves as a gateway to Haute Soule in the Pays Basque: SNCF **buses** run from Puyôo, 12km west, to Salies-de-Béarn, Sauveterre-de-Béarn and Mauléon.

The **tourist office** (July–Aug Mon–Sat 9.30am–12.30pm & 2–6.30pm, Sun 9.30am–12.30pm; Sept–June Mon–Sat 9am–noon & 2–6pm; T05.59.69.37.50) occupies the sixteenth-century Maison Jeanne d'Albret on rue du Bourg-Vieux, which also hosts a **Musée de Protestantisme en Béarn** on the second floor (Mon–Sat 10am–noon & 2.30–6.30pm; €4.50). Other fine old houses are dotted around the town centre, especially along **rue Moncade**, the uphill continuation of rue du Bourg-Vieux, leading to five-sided, thirteenth-century **Tour Moncade** (June–Aug daily 10am–12.30pm & 3–7pm; Sept daily & May/Oct weekends 10am–12.30pm & 2.30–6.30pm; €3), all that remains of Orthez's castle, though the town retains some of its medieval walls. **Staying** overnight, your best option is historic *Hôtel Restaurant Au Temps de la Reine Jeanne*, opposite the tourist office at 42–44 rue du Bourg-Vieux (T05.59.67.00.76; ❹), with a traditional **restaurant** (*menus* from €14.50 lunch/€30 dinner), sauna and in-house jazz events (March–May).

Salies-de-Béarn

Fifteen kilometres west from Orthez (TPR bus from Pau), **SALIES-DE-BÉARN** is a typical Béarnais village of winding lanes and flower-decked houses with brightly painted woodwork. The River Saleys, hardly more than a stream here, runs through the middle of it, separating the old village from the nineteenth-century quarter that sprang up to exploit the powerful saline spring for which it has long been famous. You can try the curative waters at the wonderful **thermal baths** (Wwww.thermes-de-salies.com), in place du Jardin Public, starting from €8 for a one-hour plunge in the outdoor, 32°C pool (daily May–Sept). The **tourist office** is 150m around the corner on rue des Bains (mid-June to mid-Sept Mon–Sat 9.30am–12.30pm & 3–7pm, Sun 9.30am–12.30pm; mid-Sept to mid-June Mon–Sat 9.30am–noon & 2–6pm; T05.59.38.00.33, Wbearn-gaves.blogspot.com).

Accommodation includes the economical *Au Petit Béarn* (T05.59.38.17.42; ❶; restaurant closed Fri eve & Sat lunch Oct–June) on rue Bellecave, off the road to Sauveterre. A plusher but good-value option is the *Helios* (T05.59.38.37.59, Wwww.golfsalies.com; ❸–❹), on the northeastern outskirts of town, by the twelve-hole course. The closest local **campsite** is *Mosqueros*, 1km from the *thermes* (T05.59.38.12.94; mid-March to Oct).

Sauveterre-de-Béarn

Heading south from Salies-de-Béarn, the D933 winds over hilly farming country to **SAUVETERRE-DE-BÉARN**, another pretty country town beautifully set on a bluff high above the Gave d'Oloron, just before it mingles with the Saison. From the terrace by the thirteenth-century **church of St-André** – over-restored but still retaining a fine west-portal relief of Christ in Glory – you look down over the river and the remains of fortified, half-ruined **Pont de la Légende**, while at the west end of the compact *cité médiévale* stand the ruins of a Gaston Fébus **château**. A pedestrian-only lane leads down to the bridge and river, full of bathers (and **canoers/rafters**, see Ⓦwww.aboste.com) on hot days despite its murky greenness; many come from the adjacent, tent-friendly *Camping du Gave* (Ⓣ05.59.38.53.30, Ⓦwww.campingdugave.fr; mid-April to mid-Oct). Alluring indoor **accommodation** comprises *Auberge du Saumon* (Ⓣ05.59.38.53.20; closed mid-Jan to mid-Feb & Sat low season; ❷), an old coaching inn across the river on the road south out of town, and less remote *La Maison de Navarre* in quartier St-Marc (Ⓣ05.59.38.55.28, Ⓦwww.lamaisondenavarre.com; closed Nov, restaurant closed Sun & Wed eve; ❸), a converted mansion set in a garden.

Navarrenx and L'Hôpital-S-Blaise

From Sauveterre-de-Béarn, the D936 bears southeast along the flat valley bottom to **NAVARRENX**, 20km away on the Pau–Mauléon bus route, a sleepy, old-fashioned market town built as a *bastide* in 1316 and still surrounded by its medieval **walls**. Having crossed the medieval **bridge** over the Gave d'Oloron – claimed here as the salmon-fishing capital of France – you enter from the west by the fortified **Porte St-Antoine**. The friendly *Hôtel du Commerce* just inside on place des Casernes makes an agreeable place to **stay** (Ⓣ05.59.66.50.16, Ⓦwww .hotel-commerce.fr; ❸; closed Jan). Its restaurant opposite is excellent, the basis of good half-board prices and a decent buffet breakfast. The only alternative is courtyarded *Le Relais du Jacquet* (Ⓣ06.75.72.89.33; ❷), a *chambres d'hôtes* at 42 rue Saint-Germain, the main street. There's also a riverside **campsite**, the *Beau Rivage*, in allée des Marronniers southwest of the ramparts (Ⓣ05.59.66.10.00, mid-March to mid-Oct).

Just off the Navarrenx-Oloron highway on the road to Mauléon, **L'HÔPITAL-ST-BLAISE** (Ospitalepea) is named for its cross-in-square, twelfth-century central **church** (daily: 10am–7pm; 8min audioguide with synchronized lighting for "donation"; Ⓦwww.hopital-saint-blaise.fr), all that remains of a vanished pilgrims' hospice. A Romanesque–Gothic–Islamic melange, it juxtaposes Basque features like a carved-wood gallery over the west door with Moorish-tracery windows and arches, plus stellar vaulting inside the octagonal dome. The surrounding valley-bottom hamlet offers two **hotel-restaurants**, *L'Auberge du Lausset* opposite the church (Ⓣ05.59.66.53.03; ❷) being more reliably open.

Lourdes

LOURDES, 37km southeast of Pau, has just one function. Over seven million Catholic pilgrims arrive here yearly, and the town is totally dedicated to looking after and exploiting them. Lourdes was hardly more than a village before 1858, when Bernadette Soubirous, 14-year-old daughter of a poor local miller, had the first of eighteen visions of the Virgin Mary in the Grotte de Massabielle by the Gave de Pau. Since then, Lourdes has become the most visited attraction in this part of France, with many pilgrims hoping for a miraculous cure for conventionally intractable ailments.

Myriad shops are devoted to the sale of unbelievable religious kitsch: Bernadette and/or the Virgin in every shape and size, adorning barometers, thermometers, plastic tree trunks, empty bottles that you can fill with holy water, bellows, candles and illuminated plastic grottoes. Clustered around the miraculous grotto are the churches of the Domaine de la Grotte, an annexe to the town proper that sprang up in the century following Bernadette's visions. The first to be built was an underground crypt in 1866, followed by the flamboyant double **Basilique du Rosaire et de l'Immaculée Conception** (1871–83), and then in 1958 by the massive subterranean **Basilique St-Pie-X**, which can apparently fit 20,000 people at a time. The **Grotte de Massabielle** itself is the focus of pilgrimage – a moisture-blackened overhang by the riverside with a marble statue on high of the Virgin, where pilgrims queue to circumambulate, stroking the grotto wall with their left hand. To one side are taps for filling souvenir containers with the holy spring water; to the other are the *brûloirs* or rows of braziers where enormous votive candles burn, prolonging the prayers of suppliants.

Lourdes' only secular attraction is its **château**, poised on a rocky bluff east of the Gave de Pau, guarding the approaches to the valleys and passes of the central Pyrenees. Inside, it houses the surprisingly excellent **Musée Pyrénéen** (daily: April–Sept 9am–noon & 1.30–6.30pm, no lunchbreak mid-July to Aug; Oct–March daily 9am–noon & 2–6pm, 5pm on Fri; last entry 50min before closing; €5; Ⓦwww.lourdes-visite.com). Its collections include Pyrenean fauna, all sorts of fascinating pastoral and farming gear, and an interesting section on the history of Pyrenean mountaineering.

Practicalities

Tarbes-Ossun-Lourdes **airport** is served by no-frills flights from Britain. The Maligne Gave #2 bus stops at the airport and connects to Tarbes, Lourdes, Argelès-Gazost, Luz-Saint-Sauveur and Barèges (Ⓦwww.transports-maligne.fr); single tickets are €2. Lourdes' **gare SNCF** is on the northeast edge of the town centre, at the end of avenue de la Gare; the **gare routière** is in central place Capdevielle, and the **tourist office** is in place Peyramale (Easter–June & Sept to mid-Oct Mon–Sat 9am–7pm, Sun 11am–6pm; July & Aug Mon–Sat 9am–7pm, Sun 10am–6pm; mid-Oct to Easter Mon–Sat 9am–noon & 2–6pm; ℡05.62.42.77.40, Ⓦwww.lourdes-infotourisme.com).

Lourdes has more **hotels** than any city in France outside Paris. A modestly priced option. One modestly priced hotel is the *LogisHotel de Nevers* (℡05.62.94.90.88; Ⓦwww.hoteldenevers-lourdes.com; open early to mid-Feb & March to mid-Nov; ❸) located in a former convent at 13 av Maransin, within easy walking distance of the pilgrimage site. Near the castle, with its **restaurant** open for hearty meals, including full breakfasts, is English-run *chambres d'hôtes*, *D'Angel*, at 3 chaussée du Bourg (℡05.62.94.09.96).

Tarbes

Twenty minutes away by train to the north of Lourdes, **TARBES** is a fairly dull town dominated by its history as a military stronghold (a paratroop regiment is still based here), but useful for launching into the mountains to the south. Tarbes' only real highlight is the stud farm dating from Napoleonic times, **Les Haras**, entered from chemin de Mauhourat (1hr guided visits only depart July–Aug & school holidays Mon–Fri at 2, 3 & 4pm; rest of year by appointment only; ℡05.62.56.30.80; €8), best known for the *cheval Tarbais*, bred from English, Basque and Arabian stock as a cavalry horse. Highlight of the horse-year is the late July/early August Equestria Festival (Ⓦwww.festivalequestria.com).

The **gare SNCF** is on avenue Maréchal Joffre, about 500m north of the centre, and the **gare routière** on the other side of town on place au Bois, off rue Larrey. The **tourist office** is near the central place de Verdun, at 3 cours

Gambetta (Mon–Sat 9am–noon & 2–6pm; ☎05.62.51.30.31, ⊛www
.tarbes.com). One modestly priced **hotel** near the station is friendly *Hôtel de
l'Avenue,* 80 av Bertrand Barère (☎05.62.93.06.36, ⊛www.hotel-avenue
-tarbes.fr; ❶), though most people will probably only stop long enough for
a **meal**. A bit out of the way, but worth the trek east of the oasis-like **Jardin
Massey**, is ⚘ *Chez Patrick* at 6 rue Adolphe d'Eichtal (☎05.62.36.36.82), a
cheery workaday institution that fills by 12.30pm with a five-course *menu*
(€11 includes wine and coffee). In the centre, rue Abbé-Torné and cross-
streets host many restaurants and bistros, in particular *L'Epicerie* at 1 rue de
la Victoire (☎05.62.34.20.98), specializing in fish and *magret aux cèpes*
(closed Sat lunch & Sun).

The Vallée d'Aspe

The **Vallée d'Aspe** presents the central Pyrenees at their most undeveloped,
primarily because inappropriate topography and unreliable snow conditions have
precluded ski-resort construction.

Oloron-Ste-Marie

The Vallée d'Aspe begins at the grey town of **OLORON-STE-MARIE**, 45km
west of Lourdes and only 33km southwest of Pau, where the *gaves* of the Aspe and
Ossau meet to form the Gave d'Oloron. It's served by train from Pau as well as by
CITRAM buses, with SNCF buses rolling up the valley to Urdos, a few of these
continuing as far as Canfranc in Spain. Oloron was long famous as the manufacturing centre for the famous woollen pancake-shaped *beret basque*, once the
standard headgear for all French men but now seldom seen; the single surviving
factory has had to branch out into more fashionable hats.

There is little here to detain the visitor other than the Romanesque **Cathédrale
Ste-Marie** across the Gave d'Aspe, with its beautiful west portal in Pyrenean
marble. In the upper arch, the elders of the Apocalypse play violins and rebecs,
while in the second arch scenes from medieval life – a cooper, slaying wild boar,
fishing for salmon – are represented. The gallant knight on horseback over the
outer column on the right is Gaston IV, Count of Béarn, who commissioned the
portal on his return from the first Crusade at the beginning of the twelfth century
– hence the inclusion of Saracens in chains among the sculptures. Inside, well away
from the main area of worship, stands a stoup reserved for use by the Cagots, a
stark reminder of centuries-long persecution and segregation of this mysterious
Pyrenean tribe, now thought to have been of Visigothic origin. Across the river in
Oloron, hilltop **Sainte-Croix** is one of the oldest Romanesque structures in
Béarn, its unusual interior vaulting created by thirteenth-century Spanish stone-
masons in imitation of the Great Mosque in Córdoba.

Oloron's **tourist office** lies west of the Aspe in the Villa Bourdeu (July–Aug
Mon–Sat 9am–7pm, Sun 10am–1pm; Sept–June Mon–Sat 9am–12.30pm &
2–6pm; ☎05.59.39.98.00, ⊛www.tourisme-oloron.com). **Accommodation**
includes *Hôtel de la Paix* at 24 av Sadi-Carnot opposite the train station
(☎05.59.39.02.63; ❸), quiet despite the location and with easy parking. The
closest **campsite** is *Camping du Stade*, on the D919 Arette road (☎05.59.39.11.26;
April–Sept). **Restaurants** are not especially numerous; try cheap and cheerful
La Cour des Miracles (closed Tues eve & Sun) at 13 place de la Cathédrale, opposite
the Romanesque portal, or *Samia*, a late-serving Moroccan restaurant on place
Amédée Gabe.

Lescun and its cirque

Six steep kilometres southwest of the N134 and valley floor at L'Estanguet, the ancient stone-and-stucco houses of **LESCUN** huddle on the northeast slopes of a huge and magnificent green **cirque**. The floor of the cirque and the lower slopes, dimpled with vales and hollows, have been gently shaped by generations of farming, while to the west it's overlooked by the great grey molars of **Le Billare**, Trois Rois and Ansabère, beyond which rises the storm-lashed bulk of the **Pic d'Anie** (2504m). Over 1km below the village by the stream draining the cirque, grassy *Camping Le Lauzart* (℡05.59.34.51.77; May–Sept) has a matchless position with unimpeded views of the peaks. Lescun itself has a lovely old antique-furnished **chambres d'hôtes**, the *Pic d'Anie* (℡05.59.34.71.54, ℻05.59.34.53.22; ❷–❸; April–Sept), with a restaurant (guests only) and co-managed *gîte d'étape* opposite.

Cette-Eygun to the border

A couple of kilometres beyond the turn-off for Lescun, **CETTE-EYGUN** offers, in its upper Cette quarter, the excellent, welcoming 🍴 *Au Château d'Arance* (℡05.59.34.75.50, ⓦwww.hotel-auchateaudarance.com; ❸), a converted and modernised twelfth-century manor; meals (*menus* €12–19) and leisurely breakfasts (7.30–11am) are served on a terrace with unbeatable views, while co-managed *Chambres d'Hôtes Pouquette* (ⓦchambre-hotes-aspe-bearn-pouquette.com; ❷) occupy a nearby house, next to the swimming pool.

Some 3.5km southeast at **ETSAUT**, the **Maison du Parc** (July–Aug only daily 10am–12.30pm & 2–6pm; ℡05.59.34.88.30) inhabits the old *gare SNCF*. There's a **gîte d'étape** beyond the church, *Auberge La Garbure* (℡05.59.34.88.98, ⓦwww.garbure.net), and a **hotel** on the square, *Des Pyrénées* (℡05.59.34.88.62; ❶; closed mid-Dec to mid-Jan) with a restaurant, though you may prefer the wi-fi-equipped *Bar Tabac Le Randonneur* across the *place*, which does *plats du jour* in the bar or full meals in the attractive diner upstairs.

BORCE, a more appealing medieval village 1km away on the west flank of the valley, is home to more **gîtes**: *La Communal* (℡05.59.34.86.40; 18 places) in the centre, above the bar-*épicerie*, plus the historic *Hospitalet de Borce* (no phone; 6 places) on the north outskirts, next to the original pilgrims' church, which is now an annexe of the Ecomusée in Sarrance.

Further upstream at one of the narrowest, rockiest, steepest points of the Aspe squats the menacing **Fort du Portalet** (privately owned), which served as a prison for 1930s Socialist premier Léon Blum under Pétain's Vichy government, and then for Pétain himself after the liberation of France. Just before the fort, the GR10 threads east along the **Chemin de la Mâture**, an eighteenth-century mule path hacked out of the sides of a dizzying ravine, facilitating the transport of tree trunks felled for use as ships' masts. The really spectacular part – which, however, has minimal exposure and attracts lots of young families – ends after about 45min from the upper parking area (1hr from the lower car park at Pont de Cebers south of Etsaut); the GR10 continues to the Lacs d'Ayous refuge opposite the Pic du Midi d'Ossau in five-plus hours, but by careful study of *Carte de Randonnée* no. 3, "Béarn", it's easy to form a three-hour loop hike returning you to the Pont de Cebers parking area on local trails.

Less than 2km south of the fort, **URDOS** is the last village on the French side of the frontier, and has one of the best **hotel–restaurants** in the valley: 🍴 *Hôtel des Voyageurs* (℡05.59.34.88.05, ⓦwww.hotel-voyageurs-aspe.com; ❶–❷), which serves wonderful, four-course *menus* (from €12). From here, you (and the odd bus) can continue through the free tunnel under the **Col de Somport** and on to Canfranc in Spain, the terminus for trains from Jaca, though in fine weather the far more scenic road over the pass is not that strenuous a drive.

Vallée d'Ossau

The **Vallée d'Ossau** is notable mainly for its distinctive **Pic du Midi**, around which are some beautiful lakes set in rugged country; the usual base for visiting is tiny **Gabas** hamlet. The main valley market town of **Laruns** is pleasant enough, and the route east via the spa of **Eaux-Bonnes** and the ski resort of **Gourette** has its appeal. CITRAM provides a service most of the year to Eaux-Bonnes and Gourette.

Aste-Béon and Laruns

Between Pau and Laruns, few places compel a stop. One is **ASTE-BÉON**, home to **La Falaise aux Vautours** (daily: April 2–5pm; May, Sept & school hols in Oct, Dec & Feb 2pm–5.30pm; June 2–6pm; July & Aug 10.30am–12.30pm and 2–6.30pm; €7; visit duration 1hr 30min; Ⓦwww.falaise-aux-vautours.com), a vulture-watching installation where over a hundred breeding pairs and their chicks are observable nesting naturally.

Otherwise unremarkable **LARUNS**, on the valley bottom just before steep wooded heights rise towards the border, comes alive for its Aug 15 **festival**, with revellers in traditional dress and live music. The **tourist office** on the main place de la Mairie (summer Mon–Sat 9am–12.30pm & 2–6.30pm, Sun 9am–1pm & 2–6pm; Ⓣ05.59.05.31.41) stands back-to-back with a **Maison du Parc** (mid-June to mid-Sept daily 10am–1pm & 2–6.30pm; Ⓣ05.59.05.41.59). **Accommodation** includes cheerful *Hôtel de France*, at the eastern end of town opposite the disused *gare SNCF* (Ⓣ05.59.05.33.71; ❷); more or less opposite stands pilgrim-friendly *Chalet-Refuge L'Embaradère* (Ⓣ05.59.05.41.88; 28 places; cheap meals; closed Mon–Tues low season). Two **restaurants** are on rue du Bourguet off the square: *L'Arrégalet* at no. 37 (closed lunch Mon & Tues; *menus* from €15), strong on local recipes, and *Auberge Bellevue* at no. 55 (closed Mon eve & all Tues low season), with varied *menus* from €13. Just across the river in **BÉOST**, *Auberge Chez Trey* (Ⓣ05.59.05.15.89; Ⓦwww.trey.fr) is an excellent traditional grill.

Eaux-Chaudes and Gabas

The road to Gabas, 13km south, winds steeply into the upper reaches of the Gave d'Ossau valley, through **EAUX-CHAUDES** spa, whose few bright spots include the excellent 🍴 *Auberge La Caverne* (Ⓣ05.59.05.36.40, Ⓦwww.aubergelacaverne.com; closed Oct–Nov), run by a hard-working couple who offer both dorms (€13 dorm bed; breakfast €6) and en-suite doubles (❶) in an atmospheric old building, as well as *table d'hôte* meals (from €15). Another is the restored nineteenth-century **spa** itself (May–Oct 3.30–6.30pm; from €6) by the river.

Primarily a base for climbers and walkers, there's little to **GABAS** beyond a minuscule chapel and limited **accommodation** – which fills quickly in summer. The preferable of two hotels, at Gabas' north entrance, *Chez Vignau* (Ⓣ05.59.05.34.06, Ⓦwww.hotelvignau.fr; ❷) has basic rooms, some with toilets down the hall, plus a decent restaurant. There's also the CAF *Chalet-Refuge* (Ⓣ05.59.05.33.14; 46 places; June–Sept & winter weekends except mid-Oct to mid-Nov) 700m above Gabas, with unusually good food.

The **Pic du Midi d'Ossau**, with its craggy, mitten-shaped summit (2884m), is a classic Pyrenean landmark, visible for kilometres around. From Gabas, it's a steep 4.5-kilometre climb on the D231 road (1 daily morning bus) to the artificial **Lac de Bious-Artigues**, so named because it flooded the *artigue* or "mountain pasture" that formerly existed here. Drivers will be directed by *parc national* wardens to one of two car parks, the higher one just above the dam. There are no

facilities of note here, so come prepared. For more information see Ⓦwww
.picdumidi.com.

Lac d'Artouste and Le Petit Train

Some 6.5km out of Gabas, the Pourtalet road passes the dammed **Lac de
Fabrèges**, with an access drive around the east shore leading to a huge ski-chalet
complex, among which is concealed the *billeterie* for a *télécabine*. This attains the
base of **Pic de la Sagette** (2031m) to connect with **Le Petit Train**, a miniature rail
line running 10km southeast through the mountains to **Lac d'Artouste**. Built in
the 1920s to service a hydroelectric project which raised this lake's level 25m, it
was later converted for tourist purposes. Weather permitting, the train starts
operating in late May and continues until late September (low season 8.30am–
2.30pm, July–Aug 8am–4.30pm; reserve on Ⓣ05.59.05.36.99 or Ⓦwww.train
-artouste.com). It's a beautiful trip, lasting about four hours, including the
télécabine; you've time to walk down to the lake and back (and to *Refuge Arrémoulit*;
Ⓣ05.59.05.31.79; 40 places) if you set a brisk pace. **Prices** are a stiff €21 return,
€16 one-way (useful for trekkers). In **winter** the same lift gives access to the small
downhill **ski centre** northeast of the Col de la Sagette.

Gourette and Eaux-Bonnes

The only way of reaching the Gave de Pau by road without going back towards
Pau is along the minor D918 east over the Col d'Aubisque, via Eaux-Bonnes and
Gourette, 12km east of Laruns and the favourite **ski centre** of folk from Pau. The
base development is ugly but the skiing, on 28 north-facing runs from a top point
of 2400m, is more than respectable. You can of course stay here, but the spa village
of **EAUX-BONNES**, 8km below Gourette, is more elegant and pleasant. Here
the old-fashioned *Hôtel de la Poste* on the central park-square (Ⓣ05.59.50.33.06,
Ⓦwww.hotel-dela-poste.com; closed late spring & mid-Oct to Christmas; ❷) is
excellent value, especially at half-board rates with a *table d'hôte* dinner. About the
only independent restaurant is *La Farandole*, specializing in crêpes and fondue.

The **Col d'Aubisque** itself (1709m), a grassy saddle with a souvenir stall/café on
top, usually sees the Tour de France come through, making the pass irresistible to
any French cyclist worth his salt. Once over the next, lower Col du Soulor
(1475m), the route descends, 18km in all, to attractive **ARRENS-MARSOUS**, at
the head of the Val d'Azun. Despite being another gateway to the PNP, with
information (including local walking guidebooks) from the Maison du Val
d'Azun (Ⓣ05.62.97.49.49, Ⓦwww.valdazun.com; Mon–Sat 9am–noon &
3–6/7pm), **accommodation** is limited to *Gîte Camélat*, in a fine, rambling house
from 1887 just off the central *place* (Ⓣ05.62.97.40.94, Ⓦwww.gite-camelat.com;
50 places; all year) with both doubles (❷) and dorm space.

The Gave de Pau

From its namesake city, the **Gave de Pau** forges southeast towards the mountains,
bending sharply south at Lourdes and soon fraying into several tributaries: the **Gave
d'Azun**, the **Gave de Cauterets**, the **Gave de Gavarnie** and the **Gave de Bastan**,
dropping from the Col du Tourmalet. All four valleys, and their villages, are served
by SNCF buses from Lourdes or Argelès-Gazost. **Cauterets**, 30km due south of
Lourdes, and **Gavarnie** 37km southeast of Argelès, are busy, established resorts on
the edge of the PNP, but the countryside they adjoin is so spectacular that you

forgive their deficiencies. If you want a smaller, more manageable base, then either **Barèges**, up a side valley from the spa resort of **Luz-St-Sauveur**, or Luz itself, are better bets. But pick your season – or even the time of day – right, and you can enjoy the most popular sites in relative solitude. At Gavarnie few people stay the night, so it's quiet early or late, and the **Cirque de Troumouse**, which is just as impressive (though much harder to get to without a car), has far fewer visitors.

Cauterets

CAUTERETS is a pleasant if unexciting little town that owes its fame and rather elegant Neoclassical architecture (especially on boulevard Latapie-Flurin) to its spa, and more recently to its role as one of the main Pyrenean ski and mountaineering centres.

The town is small and easy to get around; most of it is still squeezed between the steep wooded heights that close the mouth of the Gave de Cauterets valley. Next door to the **gare routière** on the north edge of the centre, where SNCF coaches stop, the **Maison du Parc** (daily 9.30am–noon & 3.30–7pm; ☏05.62.92.52.56) has a small display of flora and fauna. In the centre, five minutes' walk distant, you'll find the **tourist office** in place Maréchal Foch (Mon–Sat: July & Aug 9am–12.30pm & 2–7pm; Sept–June 9am–noon & 2–6pm; ☏05.62.92.50.50, Ⓦwww.cauterets.com).

Several well-equipped **campsites** line the road north of town, the closest being *La Prairie* (☏05.62.92.07.04; June–Sept). Inexpensive **hotels** include *Le Grum* at 4 rue Victor-Hugo, off rue de la Raillère (☏05.62.92.53.01; closed late Oct to early Dec; ❷), with a mix of rooms en suite and not; and *Le Pas de l'Ours*, 21 rue de la Raillère (☏05.62.92.58.07, Ⓦwww.lepasdelours.com; ❹), which also runs a *gîte*. For a more upmarket stay, try the atmospheric *Lion d'Or* at 12 rue Richelieu (☏05.62.92.52.87, Ⓦwww.liondor.eu; closed mid-Oct to Christmas & 3 weeks after Easter; ❺), or the elegant *Astérides-Sacca* at 11 bd Latapie-Flurin (☏05.62.92.50.02; Ⓦwww.asterides-sacca.com; closed mid-Oct to mid-Dec; ❻). As many hotels require half-board in peak season, independent **restaurants** are thin on the ground.

There are a number of excellent excursions and **hikes** from Cauterets – ask at the tourist office for details.

Luz-St-Sauveur

The only road approach to the Gavarnie and Troumouse zones is through **LUZ-ST-SAUVEUR**, astride the GR10 and SNCF bus route from Lourdes. Like Cauterets, this was a nineteenth-century spa, patronized by Napoléon III and Eugénie, and elegant Neoclassical facades in the left-bank St-Saveur quarter date from them. The principal sight, at the top of Luz's medieval, right-bank quarter, is **St-André church** (daily May 15 to Sept 30 3–6pm; €2). Built in the late twelfth century, it was fortified in the fourteenth by the Knights of St John with a crenellated outer wall and two stout towers. The north entrance sports a handsome portal surmounted by a Christ in Majesty carved in fine-grained local stone.

The **tourist office** (all year minimum hours Mon–Sat 9am–7.30pm, Sun 9am–12.30pm & 4.30–7.30pm; ☏05.62.92.30.30, Ⓦwww.luz.org), edges the central place du Huit-Mai. One worthwhile central **hotel** is *Les Templiers* (☏05.62.92.81.52, Ⓦwww.hotellestempliers.com; closed April or May; ❷–❸), opposite the church with half-board offered and pricier rooms with view. Best value for three-star comfort is in adjoining Esquièze-Sère village at ⚜ *Le Montaigu* (☏05.62.92.81.71, Ⓔhotel.montaigu@orange.fr; ❺, half-board ❼), with large balconied rooms. The better of two **campsites**, also with a *gîte* on site, is smallish *Les Cascades* (☎05.62.92.94.14; Dec–Sept), uphill from the church, with a pool. **Restaurants** aren't numerous; two reliable ones are *La Tasca* on place St-Clement, great for Spanish tapas and seafood, and ✹ *Chez Christine* (daily summer & school hols, closed Nov & Sun–Wed low season) near the post office, specializing in pizzas, own-made pasta and desserts, plus locally sourced lamb and trout.

Gavarnie and its cirque

A further 8km up the ravine from Gèdre, **GAVARNIE** is connected with Luz-St-Sauveur by two daily **bus services** (July–Aug only; otherwise just 3 weekly, or a taxi from Luz). You can walk it on the higher variant of the GR10 from Cauterets in two days. If you drive in, a **parking** fee (July to mid-Sept 8am–5pm; €4) is charged; otherwise there is ample free parking around the shops and hotels. Once poor and depopulated, Gavarnie found the attractions of mass tourism – much of it excursions from Lourdes – too seductive to resist, and it's now populated with souvenir shops and snack bars. As with other overly popular sites, visit in shoulder season and/or before 9am or after 5pm, to avoid the bus-borne hordes.

However, the **cirque** itself – Victor Hugo called it "Nature's Colosseum" – is magnificent, a natural amphitheatre scoured out by glaciers. Over 1500m high, it consists of three sheer bands of rock streaked by seepage and waterfalls, separated by sloping ledges covered with snow and glacier remnants. On the east, it's dominated by jagged **Astazou** and **Marboré** peaks, both over 3000m. In the middle, a cornice sweeps round to the **Brèche de Roland**, a curious vertical slash, 100m deep and about 60m wide, said to have been hewn from the ridge by Roland's sword, Durandal. In winter, there's good beginner-to-intermediate **skiing** at the nearby 24-run resort of **Gavarnie-Gèdre**, with great views of the cirque from the top point of 2400m.

Practicalities

La Bergerie (☎05.62.92.48.41, ⓦwww.camping-gavarnie-labergerie.com; mid-May to Oct), on the east bank of the *gave* on the cirque side of the village, must be one of the most stunningly located Pyrenean **campsites**, with views compensating for basic facilities. Otherwise, **dorm-type** accommodation is available at high-standard *Gîte Auberge Le Gypaëte* (☎05.62.92.40.61; 45 places; most of year), below the main car park. Fair-value **hotel** options include en-suite *Le Taillon* (☎05.62.92.48.20, ⓦwww.hotelletaillon.com; closed end-Oct to end-Dec; ❹), with a competent restaurant, and smallish *Hôtel Compostelle* by the church (☎05.62.92.49.43, ⓦwww.compostellehotel.com; closed Oct–Christmas, part Jan; ❸), with most rooms facing the cirque. You can park next to, or near, both but the village is closed to traffic in high season 10am–6pm. Most idyllically set, by the *gave*, are two *chambres d'hôtes* at *La Chaumière* (☎05.62.92.48.08, ⓦlachaumiere.gavarnie.free.fr; closed Oct–Christmas; ❶).

The best **restaurant** is duck and trout specialist ✹ *Les Cascades*, next to the **Maison du Parc** (Mon–Sat 9am–noon & 1.30–6.30pm, Sun 10am–noon & 3–6pm; ☎05.62.92.42.48) on the north side of the village, with the top tables overlooking the cirque (reserve on ☎05.62.92.40.17), a good wine list and *menus* (from €18). Other **information** sources include the tourist office by the car parks (daily summer 9am–noon & 2–6pm; ☎05.62.92.49.10, ⓦwww.gavarnie.com), and the CRS mountain rescue unit opposite *La Bergerie*, for accurate snow and weather reports.

The cirque and around

It's an easy walk from Gavarnie into the cirque along the *gave* draining it, using either the main east-bank track or the longer, steeper west-bank trail. Luckily, the scale of the place is sufficient to dwarf humans, but for a bit of serenity it's still best to use the west-bank path, or go up early or late. The broad track ends after 45 minutes at the *Hôtel du Cirque et de la Cascade*, once a famous meeting place for mountaineers and now a popular snack bar in summer. To get to the foot of the cirque walls, you face a steeper, final half-hour on a dwindling, increasingly slippery path which ends in a spray-bath at the base of the **Grande Cascade**, fed by Lago Helado on the Spanish side, and at 423m the highest waterfall in Europe. This plummets and fans out in three stages down the rock faces – a fine sight in sunny weather, with rainbows in the wind-teased plumes.

The Cirque de Troumouse

Much bigger than Gavarnie and, in bad weather, rather intimidating, the **Cirque de Troumouse** lies up a wild valley whose only habitations are the handful of farmsteads and pilgrimage chapel with its ancient polychrome statuette of the Virgin and Child which make up the scattered hamlet of **HÉAS** – among the loneliest outposts in France before the road in was constructed. The only **rooms** are at *Auberge de la Munia* (℡05.62.92.48.39, Ⓦwww.aubergedelamunia.com; closed mid-Oct to mid-Dec; half-board only ❹), by the chapel, though you've more choice in **meals** (eg, *Le Refuge* 400m along, *menu* €18.50), near which you can **camp**. By *Le Refuge* there's a **tollgate** (9am–6pm; €4 per car), after which the road climbs in tight hairpins 4km to the *Auberge du Maillet* (℡05.62.92.48.97; Ⓦwww.aubergedumaillet.free.fr; mid-May to Oct; 33 dorm places, also doubles

---

Skiing and hiking around Barèges

With its links to the adjacent, equal-sized *domaine* of **La Mongie** over 10km east on the far side of the Col du Tourmalet, Barèges offers access to the largest **skiing** area in the French Pyrenees, including downhill pistes totalling 125km (1850–2400m) and 31km of cross-country trails through the Lienz plateau forest (1350–1700m). Beginners' runs finishing in Barèges village are much too low (1250m) to retain snow, so all skiers usually have to start from the Tournaboup or Tourmalet zones. High-speed, state-of-the-art chair lifts are the rule at Barèges, and runs have been regraded to make the resort more competitive, but La Mongie over the hill, despite its hideous purpose-built development, offers even higher, longer pistes. For more information consult Ⓦwww.tourmalet.fr.

Hiking

The **GR10** passes through Barèges on its way southeast into the lake-filled **Néouvielle Massif**, part of France's oldest (1935) natural reserve, and a great hiking area. The best trailhead for **day-hikes**, with limited parking, lies 3km east at **Ponte de la Gaubie** (1538m), from where the classic seven-hour day-loop takes in the Vallée des Aygues Cluses plus the lakes and peak of Madamète, followed by a descent via Lac Nère and Lac Dets Coubous back to Gaubie. For those **traversing** with full packs, a seven-hour walking day from Barèges via either the Col de Madamète or the Horquette d'Aubert brings you into the Néouvielle reserve for an overnight at either the mammoth, modernized *Chalet du Lac d'Orédon* (℡05.62.23.05.72.60, Ⓦwww.refuge-pyrenees -oredon.com; mid-June to mid-Sept; doubles ❷ & dorms), or the *Chalet-Hôtel de l'Oule* (℡05.62.98.48.62; 28 places; open early June to mid-Sept & ski season). Lakeside *Refuge de Bastan* (℡05.62.98.48.80; 24 places; June–Sept), over the Horquette Nère from Aygues Cluses, is also a tempting target.

half-board only ❹), beside a small tarn at 1837m. Beyond, the road climbs again, even more steeply over 3km, beneath snow-streaked crags, to a car park at 2103m. Nearby, a prominent statue of the Vierge d'Héas crowns a grassy knoll amid enough moorland pasture for thousands of animals, enclosed by the vast cirque. Beneath its eastern walls are scattered a half-dozen blue glacial lakelets, the **Lacs des Aires**. A *parc national* path arrives here, starting from just before the Héas toll-booth (2hr 30min uphill).

Vallée de Bastan

Luz-St-Sauveur marks the start of climb east along the D918 through the **Vallée de Bastan**, culminating after 18km in the **Col du Tourmalet** (2115m), one of the major torments of the Tour de France and the fulcrum of a giant **skiing** *domaine*. North of the pass rises the landmark **Pic du Midi de Bigorre** (2877m), with its wonderful observatory reachable by funicular (June–Sept daily 9am–4.30pm; sporadic, complicated schedule otherwise; €34 adult, €84 family, includes admission to museum; Ⓦwww.picdumidi.com) from La Mongie.

Barèges

The only major village in the Bastan is **BARÈGES**, served by SNCF bus (change at Pierrefite-Nestalas). It's primarily a skiing, mountaineering and paragliding centre, and the most congenial, low-key resort around the Gave de Pau.

The central **tourist office** (July & Aug Mon–Sat 9am–12.30pm & 2–6.30pm, Sun 10am–noon & 4–6pm; Sept–June shorter afternoon hours; Ⓣ05.62.92.16.00, Ⓦwww.bareges.com) can supply accommodation lists and ski-lift plans. The through road (rue Ramond) is lined with a half-dozen **hotels**, all with a fairly similar summer opening season (May–Oct) and price (typically ❸); best value among these is charming *Hôtel La Montagne Fleurie* (Ⓣ05.62.92.68.50, Ⓦwww .hotel-bareges.fr) at no. 21. Equally distinctive are two high-quality, English-run *chambres d'hôtes*: 🏠 *Les Sorbiers* on the main street (Ⓣ05.62.92.86.68, Ⓦwww .lessorbiers.co.uk; ❸), offering vegetarian meals on request, and 🏠 *Mountain Bug* (Ⓣ05.62.92.16.39, Ⓦwww.mountainbug.com; ❼) behind the butcher's, a superbly restored eighteenth-century farmhouse with modern bathrooms and tasteful wood-floored common areas; proprietors Robert and Emma are certified guides offering local walking holidays. The cosier of two **gîtes d'étape** is welcoming, Anglo–French-run *L'Oasis*, right behind the spa (Ⓣ05.62.92.69.47, Ⓦwww.gite-oasis.com; 40 places; closed April & Oct), offering evening meals and reasonable half-board rates.

The Comminges

Stretching from **Luchon** almost to Toulouse, the **Comminges** is an ancient feudal county encompassing the upper Garonne River valley. It also hosts one of the finest buildings in the Pyrenees, magnificent **St-Bertrand-de-Comminges** cathedral, built over three distinct periods. The mountainous southern part is the most visited; access is via the unprepossessing little town of Montréjeau, from where there are daily bus and train services to Luchon.

Valcabrère

VALCABRÈRE, some 10km south of Montréjeau on the main Bayonne–Toulouse rail line, can be reached by SNCF bus (direction "Luchon") to the hamlet of Labroquère, by the Garonne, and then a short stroll across the river. It's a sleepy village of rough stone barns and open lofts for drying hay, with an exquisite Romanesque church, **St-Just** (daily: July–Sept 9am–noon & 2–7pm; Oct–Dec & March–June Sat & Sun 10 am–noon and 2–6 pm; €2), whose square tower rises above a cypress-studded cemetery. The north portal is girded by four elegant full-length sculptures and overtopped by a relief of Christ in Glory borne heavenward by angels. Both interior and exterior are full of recycled masonry from the Roman **Lugdunum Convenarum**, whose remains are visible at the crossroads just beyond the village. Founded by Pompey in 72 BC, this had 60,000 inhabitants in its prime, making it one of the most important towns in Roman Aquitaine.

St-Bertrand-de-Comminges

Around 2km southwest of Valcabrère is **ST-BERTRAND-DE-COMMINGES**, whose grey fortress-like **cathedral** (March, April & Oct Mon–Sat 10am–noon & 2–6pm, Sun 2–6pm; May–Sept Mon–Sat 9am–7pm, Sun 2–6.30pm; Nov–Feb Mon–Sat 10am–noon & 2–5pm, Sun 2–5pm; admission to cloister and choir €4) commands the plain from the knoll ahead, the austere white-veined facade and heavily buttressed nave totally subduing the clutch of fifteenth- and sixteenth-century houses huddled at its feet. To the right of the west door a Romanesque twelfth-century cloister with carved capitals looks out across a lush valley to the foothills, haunt of Resistance fighters during World War II. In the aisleless interior, the church's great attraction is the central choir, built by Toulousain craftsmen and installed 1523–35. The interior features a wealth of detail including 66 elaborately carved stalls, each one the work of a different craftsman; they are a feast of virtuosity, mingling piety, irony and satire – though sadly roped off-limits and difficult to see in detail even from a metre away.

Practicalities

Traffic into the old quarter is sporadically controlled, and **parking** (except for a few spaces near the cathedral) is restricted to two car parks at the south and southwest outskirts. During July and August the cathedral and St-Just in Valcabrère, both with marvellous acoustics, host the musical **Festival du Comminges** (Ⓦwww.festival-du-comminges.com). The **tourist office** is installed in the nineteenth-century Olivétain chapel and monastery on the cathedral square (daily 10.30am–12.30pm & 3–7pm; ℡05.61.88.32.00 or 05.61.95.44.44), doubling as an adjunct festival box office.

Staying overnight is an attractive proposition, at least outside peak season. Opposite the cathedral, friendly *Hôtel du Comminges* (℡05.61.88.31.43, Ⓕ05.61.94.98.22; April–Sept; ❷–❸) makes a fine, slightly old-fashioned option. **Restaurant** choices include *Vieille Auberge* in the lower town and friendly 🍴*Chez Simon* near the cathedral, the latter featuring duck, game, paté and regional dishes on a €16 *menu* or à la carte (allow €24); there's a lovely terrace or beam-ceilinged interior with fireplace.

The Grottes de Gargas

About 6km from St-Bertrand in the direction of St-Laurent, the **Grottes de Gargas** (half-hourly guided tours daily: July & Aug 10am–noon & 2–7pm; rest of year by prior arrangement, but reservations usually necessary ℡05.62.39.72.39, Ⓦgrottesdegargas.free.fr; €7) are renowned for their 231 prehistoric painted hand-prints. Outlined in black, red, yellow or white, they mostly seem deformed – perhaps the result of leprosy, frostbite or ritual mutilation, though no one really knows why. There are representations of large animals as well.

Luchon

There's none of the usual spa-town fustiness about **LUCHON** (formerly Bagnères de Luchon), long one of the focuses of Pyrenean exploration. The main **allées d'Étigny**, lined with cafés and brasseries, has a metropolitan elegance and bustle. There is not, however, much to see, apart from the **Musée du Pays de Luchon** (daily 9am–noon & 2–6pm; €1.60) next to the tourist office, containing an extraordinarily eclectic collection of engravings and travel posters, ancient climbing or skiing gear, and strange rural impedimenta, and the nineteenth-century **baths** (ⓦ www.thermes-luchon.fr) at the end of allées d'Étigny behind the **Parc des Quinconces** and its duck-lake. Luchon is best reckoned a comfortable base for exploring the surrounding mountains in summer, and for **skiing** at the nearby centres of Superbagnères and Peyragudes in winter. Because of the

---

Hiking and skiing around Luchon

There are several classic hikes south and southwest of Luchon, though there's no public transport to most of the various trailheads. The exception, 14km southwest of Luchon, is **Granges d'Astau** jump-off point for the **Lac d'Oô** , served by two daily shuttle buses (July to early Sept). Here, you'll find the *Auberge d'Astau* (ⓣ 05.61.79.35.63; May–Oct; 16 places in dorms, also doubles ❷), with a restaurant, though many hikers prefer *Le Mailh d'Astau* next door for **meals** . From the car park here a busy section of the GR10 climbs an hour to the dammed lake, where the pricey *Refuge-Auberge du Lac d'Oô* (1504m; ⓣ 05.61.79.12.29, ⓦ www .refuge-lac-oo.com; 25 places; May–Oct) perches beyond the west end of the dam. The onward path leads to the *Refuge d'Espingo* exactly an hour above Oô, just below the Col d'Espingo. This hut (1967m; ⓣ 05.61.79.20.01; 70 places; June to mid-Oct) overlooks beautiful, undammed **Lac d'Espingo**, and the frontier ridge; most day-trippers stop here, as the grade stiffens considerably beyond. You can also get here by taking the *télécabine* from Luchon up to Superbagnères (June & Sept weekends 1.30–6pm; July & Aug, daily 9am–12.45pm & 2–6pm; €7.90 return, €5.90 one way), then continuing west on the GR10 to the *Refuge d'Espingo* (4hr 30min total).

Another possible walking route from Luchon involves following the Pique valley south 11km, partly on the D125, to the **Hospice de France** (1385m), originally founded by the Knights of St John and now open as a refuge (ⓣ 05.67.79.32.47, ⓦ www.hospicedefrance.com; May–Nov; ❷), from where a signposted path climbs a steep, narrow valley to the **Boums du Port** (just under 2hr with daypack), four small, scenic lakes; beside the middle one sits the small but welcoming *Refuge de Vénasque* (ⓣ 05.61.79.26.46; mid-June to mid-Sept). Next you tackle the short, sharp path-climb to the notch on the frontier ridge known as the **Port de Vénasque** (3hr from *Hospice de France*), with superb views of the **Maladeta massif** and the **Pico d'Aneto**, highest summit of the Pyrenees (3404m). Return the same way, or fashion a classic loop taking in the frontier ridge to the east, then a descent of the Vallée de la Frèche back to the *Hospice*.

Skiing

Luchon has two downhill **ski resorts** within striking distance, of which **Peyragudes** (ⓦ www.peyragudes.com), 15km west of Luchon overlooking each approach to Peyresourde, is much better. Its 43 runs, mostly of intermediate calibre and broad by Pyrenean standards, start from 2400m, with superb views of the frontier ridge and a decent lift system. Lower-altitude **Superbagnères** (ⓦ www.luchon.com), right above the town and accessible by a 15-kilometre road or the *télécabine* (included in ski pass), has 28 mostly beginnner-to-intermediate pistes lamentably exposed to morning sun and thus often mushy.

peculiar local topography, the valley here is also one of the major Pyrenean centres for **paragliding** and **light aviation**.

Practicalities

The **gare SNCF**, also the **gare routière**, is in avenue de Toulouse across the River One in the northern part of the town. The **tourist office** is at 18 allée d'Étigny (daily: July–Aug & peak ski season 9am–7pm, rest of year same but closed for lunch; ☏05.61.79.21.21, ⓦwww.luchon.com), which stocks leaflets detailing lodging and currently-operating activity outfitters.

You're best off avoiding obvious **accommodation** on allées d'Étigny for better value in quieter side streets. Possibilities there include *Hôtel des Deux Nations* to the west at 5 rue Victor-Hugo (☏05.61.79.01.71, ⓦwww.hotel-des2nations .com; ❸), a popular choice with a busy downstairs restaurant; east of the main street, *Hôtel la Petite Auberge*, 15 rue Lamartine (☏05.61.79.02.88; ❷), in a *belle-époque* mansion, with ample parking and a *table d'hôte* restaurant; and south, just over the municipal boundary in St-Mamet at 4 av de Gascogne, friendly, chalet-style ❧ *Hôtel La Rencluse* (☏05.61.79.02.81; ⓦwww.hotel-larencluse.com; ❸), with attic rooms, decent buffet breakfast and ample parking. There's no *gîte*, but the least cramped of eight **campsites** in the vicinity is *Camping La Lanette* (☏05.61.79.00.38; mid-Dec to Oct), 1.5km down rue Lamartine) towards Montauban-de-Luchon.

As with lodging, the best **restaurant** prospects are some distance away from the allée d'Etigny. *Hôtel La Rencluse*'s diner is excellent, serving until 10pm or so, with *table d'hôte* dinners at €14.50, plus palatable own-label wine. With transport and more funds, try *L'Auberge de Castel-Vielh*, 3km south on the D125 (☏05.61.79.36.79; April–Oct Wed–Sun; Nov–March weekends only; *menus* from €28), in a converted country house, purveying game and regional dishes, including snails, offal and trout; or – 7km west in **BILLIÈRE** village – ❧ *La Ferme d'Espiau* (☏05.61.79.69.69, ⓦwww.restaurant-luchon.com; ❸ *menus* from €17; closed Mon, also Tues–Wed low season; also *chambre d'hôte* at ❷), which excels at local meat or game and foie gras served amid antique rustic decor.

The Eastern Pyrenees

The dominant climatic influence of the **Eastern Pyrenees**, excluding the misty Couserans region, is the Mediterranean; the climate is warmer, the days sunnier, the landscape more arid than elsewhere in the Pyrenees. Dry-weather plants like cistus, broom and thyme make their appearance, and the foothills are planted with vines. The proximity of Spain is evident, with much of the territory definitively incorporated into France in 1659 previously belonging to historical Catalonia. As with the rest of the Pyrenees, the countryside is spectacular, and densely networked with hiking trails. Historical sights, with the exception of the painted caves of the **Ariège** and the Cathar castles and medieval towns of the **upper Aude**, are concentrated towards the coast in French Catalonia, comprising **Roussillon** and the Cerdagne (Rosilló and Cerdanya in Catalan).

The Ariège valley

Whether you're coming from the western Pyrenees or heading south from the major transport hub of Toulouse, the **Ariège valley** marks the start of the transition to the Mediterranean zone. The river, extending from high peaks along the Andorran border around the spa of **Ax-les-Thermes** down to agricultural plains north of **Foix**, forms the main axis of the eponymous *département*. In between lie a wealth of **caves**, most notably near **Tarascon** and **Mas d'Azil**. Transport is no problem as long as you stick to the valley.

Foix

France's smallest *départemental* capital, **FOIX,** lies 82km south of Toulouse on the Toulouse–Barcelona train line. It's an agreeable country town of narrow alleys and sixteenth- to seventeenth-century half-timbered houses, with an attractive old quarter squeezed between the rivers Ariège and Arget. Dominating all around are the three distinctive hilltop towers of the **Château des Comtes de Foix**, which contains a dull handful of themed exhibits (May, June & Sept daily 9.45am–noon & 2–6pm; July & Aug daily 9.30am–6.30pm; Oct–April Wed–Sun 10.30am–noon & 2–5.30pm; €4) – though the views merit the climb.

The **gares SNCF and routière** are together on avenue de la Gare, off the N20 on the right (east) bank of the Ariège. The **tourist office** is on rue Théophile Delcasse (July & Aug Mon–Sat 9am–7pm, Sun 9am–noon & 2–6pm; Sept–June Mon–Sat 9am–noon & 2–6pm; ☎05.61.65.12.12, ⓦwww.ot-foix.fr).

Most **accommodation** is in the old town, on the left bank of the Ariège, though little of it is inspiring. The quietest and most comfortable option is three-star *Hôtel Lons*, on 6 place Duthil, near the Pont-Vieux (☎05.61.65.52.44, ⓦwww.hotel-lons-foix.com; ❸; closed late Dec to early Jan), with a respected restaurant. The *Eychenne* at 11 rue Noël Peyrevidal (☎05.61.65.00.04, ⓦwww.hotel-eychenne .com; ❸) has a busy ground-floor café, but no restaurant. Opposite at no. 16, *Auberge Léo Lagrange* (☎05.61.65.09.04, ⓦwww.leolagrange-foix.com) is more an activity centre (rafting, etc) than hostel, but offers 74 bunks in doubles or quads, plus economical weekday lunches in its downstairs *foyer*.

A prime area for **eating** is rue de la Faurie and lanes leading off it, the old blacksmiths' bazaar at the heart of the old town. At no. 17, *Le Jeu de l'Oie* does classic French country-bistro cuisine – *cassoulet*, duck dishes, *terrines*, offal, good desserts, Leffe draught beer – at low prices (*menus* from under €10), which guarantees a lunch-time crush, though service doesn't suffer unduly. Also popular is *Les Quatre Saisons* at no. 11 (☎05.61.02.71.58; *menus* from €14; closed Sun–Thurs eve low season), whose speciality is *pierrade* – hot ceramic plates at your table to grill fish and meat.

Mas d'Azil

Twenty-five kilometres west of Foix, the **Mas d'Azil** was one of the first prehistoric caves to yield evidence of human habitation, but its most impressive feature is a magnificent 500-metre-long natural tunnel, scoured by the River Arize, which now carries the D119 road from here towards Pamiers.

A few animal bones and other artefacts found during excavation remain on view in glass cases in the caves, but the best pieces are now on display in the attractive, sleepy village of **LE MAS-D'AZIL**, 1km to the north, in the **Musée de la Préhistoire** (March Sun 5.15–6.15pm; April–May daily except Mon 3–6pm; June daily except Monday 2–6pm; July & Aug daily 11am–1pm & 2–7pm; Sept daily except Monday 2–6pm; Oct–Nov Sun 3–6pm; €4.60). Among other engraved tools and weapons,

Grotte de Niaux 4 km south of Tarascon. A huge cave complex under an enormous rock overhang 2km north of the hamlet of Niaux. There are 4km of galleries in all, with paintings of the Magdalenian period (c.11,000 BC) scattered throughout, although tours see just a fraction of the complex. No colour is used to render the subjects – horses, ibex, stags and bison – just a dark outline and shading to give body to the drawings, executed with a "crayon" made of bison fat and manganese oxide. 45min guided tours: July–Sept daily 9am–5.45pm, English tours at 9am & 1pm; April–June & Oct 10.30am–5pm; Nov–Jan & March, tours at 11am, 2.30pm & 4.15pm; €9.40; max group size 20, advance reservations mandatory on ℡05.61.05.10.10.

Grotte de la Vache Alliat, right across the valley from Niaux. A relatively rare example of an inhabited cave where you can observe hearths, embossed bones, tools and other remnants *in situ*. 90min guided tours: April–June, Sept & school holidays 2.30 & 4pm; July & Aug daily 10am–5.30pm; otherwise by arrangement; ℡05.61.05.95.06, ⓦwww.grotte-de-la-vache.org; €9.

Grotte de Bédeilhac Above Bédeilhac village. Take the D618 from Tarascon west towards Saurat; after 5km, the cave entrance yawns in the Soudour ridge. Inside are examples of every known technique of Paleolithic art; while not as immediately powerful as at Niaux, its diversity – including modelled stalagmites and mud reliefs of beasts – compensates. Same tour length and schedule as de la Vache, plus every Sun at 3pm; ⓦwww.grotte-de-bedeilhac.org; €8.

Parc de La Préhistoire Just west of Tarascon-sur-Ariège on the Route de Banat. This museum presents a circuit of discovery that shows the life and art of people from the Magdalenian period who lived in this area 14,000 years ago. Outdoor exhibits here feature engaging workshop demonstrations on archeology, prehistoric hunting, firemaking and art techniques; as well as a recreation of a Magdalenian encampment. July–Aug daily 10am–8pm, last ticket at 5.30pm; April–May & Sept weekdays 10am–6pm & weekends 10am–7pm; end-Sept to selected dates in Nov daily 10am–6pm; closed Mon in May; €9.70.

the museum's most outstanding exhibit is the beautiful carved antler known as *le faon aux oiseaux* (fawn with birds), perhaps used as a spear-thrower. There's just one **hotel** here on the central *place*, Gardel (℡05.61.69.90.05; ❷; closed mid-Nov to mid-March), as well as a municipal **campsite** (℡05.61.69.71.37; mid-June to mid-Sept) 1.5km away. The best of three spots to **eat** is *Le Jardin de Cadettou* (closed Sat lunchtime, Sun eve, Mon, mid-Dec to April), with excellent regional *menus* (€16–26); they also have *chambres d'hôtes* (℡05.61.69.95.23; ❸).

Tarascon-sur-Ariège

TARASCON-SUR-ARIÈGE lies 17km south of Foix, where the N20 crosses the Ariège (a bypass diverts the worst of the traffic). Once a centre for the now-defunct iron-mining industry, it's a hot, unexciting little town enclosed by high wooded ridges. However, Tarascon is convenient for the nearby prehistoric caves, and more pleasant than first impressions suggest. From the east bank of the Ariège with its riverside cafés, narrow **rue de Barri** leads to St-Michel church in the old quarter, presiding over a partly arcaded square. Two items of the mostly razed medieval walls survive: the **Tour St-Michel** and the **Porte-d'Espagne**.

The combined **gare SNCF/halte routière** is a few minutes' walk north from the centre, on the west bank. The **tourist office** is also just west of the bridge in the Éspace François Mitterrand (Mon–Sat 9am–1pm & 2–6pm, also Sun 9.30am–1pm peak summer/ski season; ℡05.61.05.94.94, ⓦwww.paysdetarascon.com).

Accommodation options include quiet *Hôtel Confort* on riverside quai Armand Sylvestre (☎05.61.05.61.90; closed Jan; ❶), with some rooms facing a courtyard; for rooms facing the river, try *Hostellerie de la Poste* (☎05.61.05.60.41, ⓦwww .hostellerieposte.com; all year; ❷), on the main street. This also has the town's best **restaurant** (closed Mon noon and Tues), with summer seating facing a lawn-garden and four *menus* (including one vegetarian) at €13–38. The **campsite**, *Pré Lombard* (☎05.61.05.61.94; ⓦwww.prelombard.com), is on the left bank of the river, ten minutes' walk upstream from the bridge.

Ax-les-Thermes

Twenty-six kilometres east of Tarascon, still on the banks of the Ariège, the spa town of **AX-LES-THERMES** is completely hemmed in by shaggy mountains; Ax is the last sizeable place before the Andorran and Spanish frontiers. The town is small and agreeable enough, but there's little to see once you've wandered rue de l'École and rue de la Boucarie with their few medieval buildings in the quarter west of the N20, which forms the main through road, avenue Delcassé. Above place du Breilh, the **church of St-Vincent** retains a Romanesque tower; on the *place* itself you can dangle your feet for free in the **Bassin des Ladres**, a pool of sulphurous water – one of forty local *sources* as hot as 77°C – which is all that remains of the hospital founded in 1260 by St Louis for soldiers wounded in the Crusades.

The **gare SNCF** is off avenue Delcassé on the northwest side of town. The **tourist office** (July & Aug daily 9am–1pm & 2–7pm; Sept–June 9am–noon & 2–6pm; ☎05.61.64.60.60, ⓦwww.vallees-ax.com) is halfway through town on the north side of the main road. There's a **campsite**, *Le Malazéou* (☎05.61.64.09.14; closed Nov), on the riverbank 500m downstream from the *gare SNCF*. For indoor **accommodation**, a good budget choice at part-pedestrianized 6 place Roussel is *Hôtel Le P'tit Montagnard* (☎05.61.64.22.01, ⓦwww.leptitmontagnard.fr; ❶–❷). Alternatively there's *Hôtel Restaurant Le Grillon* on rue St-Udaut, 300m southeast of place du Breilh (☎05.61.64.31.64, ⓦwww.hotel-le-grillon.com; closed Easter to late May; ❷). But much the best deal in town is ⚡ *Hôtel Restaurant Le Chalet* at 4 av Turrel, opposite the *thermes* (☎05.61.64.24.31, ⓦwww.le-chalet.fr; ❸), managed by a friendly, energetic young couple. All the airy rooms over two wings are unique, but share parquet floors and plasma TV, and most have balconies overlooking the river. **Restaurants** here include *Le P'tit Montagnard* (*menus* from €17), *Le Grillon* (weekday *menu*, otherwise à la carte), or at the riverside diner of *Le Chalet* (*menus* from €18; closed Sun eve & Mon). For **snacks** and **drinks**, try *Crêperie L'Oiseau Bleu* behind *Le P'tit Montagnard*.

The Pays de Sault

The **Pays de Sault** – a magnificent upland bounded by the rivers Ariège and Aude, and the D117 road from Foix to Quillan – marks the start of "Cathar country" (for more, see p.651). The region's main town, **Lavelanet**, is a nondescript place on the banks of the River Touyre, 28km from Foix and 35km from Quillan, offering little beyond bus connections – including north to **Mirepoix** – covered on p.647, though not strictly in the *pays*.

Roquefixade

ROQUEFIXADE sits roughly 19km east of Foix on the D117 (or a bit less on the minor D9a); the ruinous (free, unclosed) eleventh-century castle towers above

The fall of Montségur

Between 1204 and 1232, Montségur's castle was reconstructed by Guilhabert de Castres as a strongpoint for the **Cathars** (see p.651). By 1232 it – and the village at the base of the *pog* or rock pinnacle – had become the effective seat of the beleaguered Cathar Church, under the protection of a garrison commanded by Pierre-Roger de Mirepoix, with a population of some five hundred, clergy as well as ordinary believers fleeing Inquisition persecution.

Provoked by de Mirepoix's raid on Avignonet in May 1242, in which the eleven chief Inquisitors were hacked to pieces, the forces of the Catholic Church and the king of France laid siege to the castle in May 1243. By March 1244, Pierre-Roger, despairing of relief, agreed to terms. At the end of a fortnight's truce, the 225 Cathar civilians who still refused to recant their beliefs were burnt on a communal pyre on March 16.

Four men who had escaped Montségur unseen on the night of March 15 recovered the Cathar "treasure", hidden in a cave for safekeeping since late 1243, and vanished. Two of them later reappeared in Lombardy, where these funds were used to support the refugee Cathar community there for another 150 years. More recent New-Agey speculations, especially in German writings, identify this "treasure" as the Holy Grail, and the Cathars themselves as the Knights of the Round Table.

the village. Nearby accommodation is a thirteenth-century *bastide* with a quality *gîte d'étape* (℡05.61.03.01.36; Ⓦwww.gite-etape-roquefixade.com; all year; 15 places), which does meals.

Montségur

From Lavelanet, there's no public transport south towards Montségur, so whether you approach via Montferrier (12km) or via Bélesta and Fougax-et-Barrineuf (21km in all) is a matter of taste. The village of **MONTSÉGUR** straggles in long terraces at the foot of its castle-rock, a modified version of a *bastide* (the original settlement was up by the castle). Depopulated now except as a second-home venue, the place comes to life only with the influx of tourists, most of them day-trippers.

A footpath from the top of the village shortens the way up to the saddle of the hill and the **Prats des Cramats**, the field where the Cathar martyrs were burnt. From here it's a steep, slick-when-wet, twenty-minute climb to the **Château de Montségur** (daily: Feb 10am–4pm; March 10am–5pm; April & Sept–Oct 9.30am–6pm; May–Aug 9am–7.30pm; Nov 10am–5.30pm; Dec 10am–4pm; €4), of which all that remain are the stout, now truncated curtain walls and keep. The space within is terribly cramped, and one can easily imagine the sufferings of the besieged. The walls are off-limits (a prohibition universally defied for postcard views over kilometres of forested hills and snowy peaks), though you can climb to the west keep.

There's a seasonal **tourist office** in the village (July–Sept daily 10am–1pm & 2–6pm; ℡05.61.03.03.03, Ⓦwww.montsegur.fr). Several **accommodation** options fill quickly in (and even out of) season; the least expensive hotel is the old-fashioned *Couquet* (℡05.61.01.10.28; ❷), a rambling *pension* fronted by pollarded lime trees. An even cosier option is ⚘ *Maison d'Hôte L'Oustal* at the north end of the village (℡05.61.02.80.70, Ⓦwww.montsegur.org/html /oustal/; ❷), with superb, four-course dinners (€18). If Montségur is full and you've transport, consider another excellent *chambres d'hôtes* 8km downhill in **FOUGAX-ET-BARRINEUF**, opposite the post office: English/Canadian-run ⚘ *Tindleys* (℡05.61.01.34.87, Ⓦtindleys.com; ❸), with three rooms, a copious breakfast and dinner on request. The region lacks stand-alone **restaurants**; one of the few to aim for is *Le Rendez Vouz* at the north edge of **MONTFERRIER** (℡05.61.05.20.92; *menus* from €13 at lunch, €20 at dinner; closed Sun, Mon, Sat lunch).

The Gorges de la Frau

From either Montségur or Fougax-et-Barrineuf, you can take an impressive half-day walk through the **Gorges de la Frau**, emerging at Comus hamlet in the heart of the Pays de Sault. The route from Montségur initially follows the "Sentier Cathare" until linking up with the **GR107** (ex-GR7B) at Pelail in the valley of the Hers river, which has carved out the gorge. Starting from Fougax, just follow the minor D5 south along the Hers until, beyond Pelail, tarmac dwindles to a rough, steep track as you enter the *gorges* proper, where thousand-metre-high cliffs admit sunlight only at midday. The canyon bottom is densely wooded, though it is in fact a major pastoral-migratory route; each mid-October hundreds of cattle which have summered on the Sault plateau are driven down en masse. The defile ends some 3.5km before Comus, where the track broadens and the grade slackens. **COMUS** itself has a good *gîte d'étape* in the former school (℡04.68.20.33.69, ⓦwww.gites-comus.com; 38 places, some doubles ❶); here you're just 2.5km shy of the D613 road between Ax-les-Thermes and Quillan, with a daily bus to the latter.

Mirepoix

Heading north from Lavelanet towards Carcassonne, it's definitely worth stopping in at **MIREPOIX**, a late thirteenth-century *bastide* built around one of the finest surviving arcaded market squares – **Les Couverts** – in the country. The square is bordered by houses dating from the thirteenth to the fifteenth centuries, and a harmonizing modern *halle* on one side, but its highlight is the medieval **Maison des Consuls** (council house), whose rafter-ends are carved with dozens of unique portrayals of animals and monsters, and caricatures of medieval social groups and professions, as well as ethnic groups from across the world. Just south of Les Couverts, the early Gothic cathedral of **St-Maurice** is claimed to have the largest undivided nave in France, supported only by airy rib vaulting.

There's a **tourist office** in the main square (Mon–Sat 9am–noon & 2–6pm; ℡05.61.68.83.76, ⓦwww.tourisme-mirepoix.com). The best-value **accommodation** and **eating** – you often have to reserve a table – is at modest 🍴*Hôtel-Restaurant Le Commerce*, 20 cours du Docteur-Chabaud by the cathedral (℡05.61.68.10.29, ⓦlecommerce/chez.com; ❷), where three generous à la carte courses (including foie gras, *cassoulet, confit de canard* and fish) plus house wine won't much top €26 – *menus* are varied but not much cheaper. More comfort is on offer at no. 6 of the arcaded square, at *Maison des Consuls* (℡05.61.68.81.81, ⓦwww.maisondesconsuls.com; all year; ❺), its plushly furnished units just above the carved rafters. There's a municipal **campsite** on the Limoux road (℡05.61.01.55.44; June–Sept).

Those with transport have another **accommodation** option 13km southeast in the medieval village of **CAMON**, easiest reached off the D625 Lavelanet-Mirepoix road. Here the twelfth- to fourteenth-century **fortified Benedictine abbey** at the summit of things has been transformed by English owners into *chambres d'hôtes* with a difference, 🍴*L'Abbaye-Château de Camon* (℡05.61.60.31.23, ⓦwww.chateaudecamon.com; closed early Jan to mid-March; ❼). There's a large pool, a part of the original cloister, eighteenth-century canvases in the lounge, a frescoed chapel, plus all the echoing galleries and spiral staircases you could want; the gourmet **restaurant** does dinner for all comers (€38 *table d'hôte*).

Vallée de l'Aude

South of Carcassonne, the D118 and the (mostly disused) rail line both forge steadily up the twisting **Vallée de l'Aude** between scrubby hills and vineyards, past **L'Abbaye de St-Hilaire** and its carved sarcophagus, river-straddling **Limoux** and sleepy **Alet-les-Bains**, before reaching **Quillan** where the topography changes. The route squeezes through awesome gorges either side of **Axat** before emerging near the river's headwaters on the Capcir plateau, east of the Carlit massif. It's a magnificent drive or slightly hair-raising cycle-ride up to isolated **Quérigut**, then easier going on to **Formiguères**.

Limoux

Some 24km south of Carcassonne, **LIMOUX** is served regularly by **SNCF buses**; those arriving by car will find free **parking** on the riverbanks by the picturesque old bridge. Life revolves around pretty **place de la République** in the heart of the old town, with its Friday market, brasseries and cafés, and the nineteenth-century **promenade du Tivoli**, in effect a bypass road on the west. Previously known for its wool and leather-tanning trades, Limoux's recent claim to fame is the excellent regional sparkling wine, Blanquette de Limoux, cheaper than champagne, and easiest found at the Aimery-Sieur d'Arques Co-operative in avenue du Mauzac (daily 9am–noon & 2.30–7pm).

Blanquette was supposedly invented 11km northeast by minor road in 1531 at the **Abbaye de St-Hilaire**, which dominates the centre of the eponymous village. The Gothic cloister (always open) doubles as the village square, but the main attraction is the so-called **sarcophagus** in the south chapel of the thirteenth-century cathedral (daily: Nov–March 10am–noon & 2–5pm; April–June & Sept–Oct, same hours, closes 6pm; July–Aug 10am–7pm; €4). This is one of the masterpieces of the mysterious **Maître de Cabestany**, an itinerant sculptor whose work – found across the eastern Pyrenees on both sides of the border – is distinguished by the elongated fingers, pleated clothing and cat-like, almond-eyed faces of the human figures. Here the arrest of evangelizing **St Sernin** (Saturnin), patron of Toulouse, his martyrdom through dragging by a bull, and burial by female disciples is portrayed on three intricately carved side panels of what's actually a twelfth-century marble reliquary too small to contain a corpse.

Limoux's **tourist office** is at promenade du Tivoli 32 (July–Aug daily 9am–7pm; Sept–June Mon–Fri 9am–noon & 2–6pm, Sat–Sun 10am–noon & 2–5pm; ℡04.68.31.11.82; Ⓦwww.limoux.fr). The better-value of two **hotel** choices is *Des Arcades*, north of St-Martin church at 96 rue St-Martin (℡04.68.31.02.57; closed latter half of Dec & Wed; ❷). The best **restaurant** is *Maison de la Blanquette*, at 46bis promenade du Tivoli (closed Tues; *menus* from €17.50; ℡04.68.31.01.63).

Alet-les-Bains

South of Limoux, the next place to halt is the thermal resort of **ALET-LES-BAINS**; the spa on the outskirts is incidental to the lovely half-timbered houses and arcaded *place* inside the fortifications. There's also a ruined Romanesque abbey, next to the tourist office which has the keys (daily: 10am–noon & 2.30–6pm), and an excellent **hotel** partly occupying the old bishop's palace, the *Hostellerie de l'Évêché* (℡04.68.69.90.25, Ⓦwww.hotel-eveche.com; April–Oct; ❸), by the abbey. Their elegant **restaurant** (the only one here) has *menus* from €26.

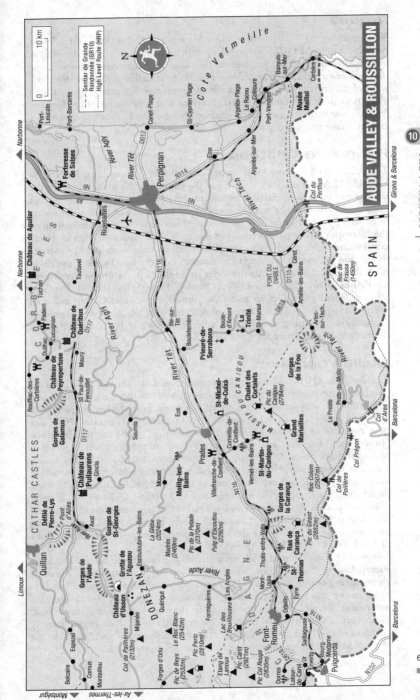

AUDE VALLEY & ROUSSILLON

0 ———— 10 km

Sentier de Grande
Randonnée (GR10)
High Level Route (HRP)

N

Côte Vermeille

Narbonne

Port-
Leucate
Port-Barcarès

Port-
Barcarès

Forteresse
de Salses

River Agly

River Têt

Canet-Plage

St-Cyprien Plage

Argelès-Plage
Le Racou
Collioure
Port-Vendres

Banyuls-
sur-Mer

Cerbère

Musée
Maillol

10

Château de Aguilar

Tuchan

Padern

Cucugnan

Château de
Quéribus

River Agly

Ille-sur-Têt

Perpignan

N114

6N

6N

Rivesaltes

A9

N116

Elne

Argelès-sur-Mer

River Tech

Col du
Perthus

Girona & Barcelona

SPAIN

Duilhac

Rouffiac-
des-Corbières

Château de
Peyrepertuse

Maury

St-Paul-de-
Fenouillet

Tautavel

D117

D115

Céret

PONT DU
DIABLE

Roc de
Frausa
(1450m)

D618

Amélie-les-Bains

Boule-
d'Amont

St-Marsal

La
Trinité

Prieuré-de-
Serrabona

Boulternère

Gorges de
Galamus

Château de
Puilaurens

Gincla

D117

Eus

Soumia

Mosset

St-Michel-
de-Cuixà

Cornellà-de-
Conflent

Chalet des
Cortalets

Pic du
Canigou
(2784m)

MASSIF DU CANIGOU

Gorges
de la Fou

Arles-
sur-Tech

River Tech

Barcelona

CATHAR CASTLES

Défilé de
Pierre-Lys

Quillan

Gorges de
St-Georges

Pont
d'Aliès

Axat

Gorges de
l'Aude

Grotte de
l'Aguzou

Château
d'Usson

Escouloubre-les-Bains

La Glèbe
(2024m)

Madrès
(2469m)

Pic de la Pelade
(2370m)

Puig d'Escoutou
(2292m)

Prades

Molitg-les-
Bains

Villefranche-de-
Conflent

Vernet-les-Bains

St-Martin-
du-Canigou

Grand
Maraïlles

Roc Colom
(2507m)

La Preste

Prats-de-Mollo

Col de
Poillières

Col Pregon

Col
d'Ares

Barcelona

DONEZAN

Querigut

Forges d'Orlu

Le Roc Blanc
(2542m)

Pic de Beys
(2532m)

Mijanès

River Aude

Gorges de
la Carança

Thuès-entre-Valls

Ras de
Carança

Pic du Géant
(2882m)

St-
Thomas

Col de
Pailhères
(2132m)

Belcaire

Espezel

Comus

Montaillou

Ax-les-Thermes

Montségur

Limoux

Narbonne

Narbonne

Pic Peric
(2810m)

Formiguères

Les Angles

Lac des
Bouillouses

Mont-
Louis

Eyne

Font-
Romeu

Saillagouse

N116

N116

N152

CERDAGNE

Pic Carlit
(2921m)

Pic Col Rouge
(2835m)

Étang de
Lanoux

Dorres

Angoustrine

Bourg-
Madame

Puigcerdà

Latour-
de-Carol

Enveitg

649

Arques

With transport, it's worth taking a detour left south of Alet at Couiza for 10km to twelfth-century **ARQUES** castle (ⓦ www.chateau-arques.fr; closed Jan–Feb & mid-Nov to end-Dec; €5), just west of the village of Arques (one restaurant, one *chambre d'hôte*), perhaps the most domesticated of the Cathar castles (see opposite). Most of the curtain wall, except for the southwest tower, is gone, but the place's glory is its thirteenth-century central **donjon**, with four round corner *bartizans* (turrets), one containing the spiral staircase giving access to four upper storeys – and fine views to a wooded ridge.

Rennes-le-Château

The D52 climbs 4.5km southeast out of Couiza towards mountaintop **RENNES-LE-CHÂTEAU**. The views alone repay the effort, but the main reason for the jaunt is the mysterious **parish church** run by Abbé Bérenguer Saunière from 1885 until 1910, when he was defrocked by the bishop of Carcassonne for failing to explain how he financed his comfortable lifestyle and lavish redecoration of the fifteenth-century church (free admission). This is supposedly full of veiled symbols and codes, which – say some (others will see only lavish kitsch) – indicate that he had discovered Solomon's lost treasure, brought here by the Visigoths in the fifth century. This and other theories are explored in the **Musée Presbytère de l'Abbé** (daily: July to mid-Sept 10am–7.15pm; May–June & late Sept 10am–6.15pm: early Oct to mid-Oct 10am–5.45pm; mid-Oct to end Oct 10am–5.15pm; Nov–April 10am–1pm & 2–5.15pm; €4.25; ⓦ www.rennes-le-chateau.fr) comprising Saunière's Villa Béthania – where he lived openly with his mistress Marie Denardaud – and its gardens.

Quillan and Axat

Pleasant little **QUILLAN**, 28km upstream from Limoux, is a useful staging post en route south into the mountains or east to the Cathar castles (see opposite). The only monument is the ruined castle, burnt by the Huguenots in 1575 and partly dismantled in the eighteenth century. The **gare SNCF** and **gare routière** sit together on the main bypass road, while the **tourist office** (June–Sept Mon–Sat 9am–noon & 2–7pm, Sun 9am–noon; Oct–May Mon–Fri 9am–noon & 2–6pm, Sat 9am–1pm; ☎ 04.68.20.07.78) stands opposite in the former Art Deco public baths. **Accommodation** options on the same (noisy) boulevard are the *Canal* at no. 36 (☎ 04.68.20.08.62, ⓦ www .hotel-canal.com; ❷) and the *Cartier* at no. 31 (☎ 04.68.20.05.14, ⓦ www .hotelcartier.com; ❷–❸; closed mid-Jan to Feb). A good **restaurant** is *Pizzeria des Platanes* at 2 av Pasteur, towards the river by the cinema, with seating outdoors under the namesake trees. The *Sapinette* **campsite** is at 21 rue René Delpech (☎ 04.68.20.13.52; April–Oct).

Beyond Quillan, the road heads southeast 11km, through the narrow **Défilé de Pierre-Lys**, to **Pont d'Aliès**, where there's another campsite and a clutch of **river-rafting** outfitters, the Aude being a major venue for watersports. Just 1km south of the *pont* is **AXAT**, covering both banks of the river; you can **eat** (not Sun pm) at *Auberge La Petite Ourse*, no. 88 on the main highway, and **stay** at basic *Hôtel Axat* at no. 101 (☎ 04.68.20.93.76; ❷). Otherwise, Axat is the westerly terminus of the Train du Pays Cathare et du Fenouillèdes (see p.652), and the last town of any size before entering the rocky canyons to the south.

The Aude gorges, the Donezan and the Capcir

On its first 20km south of Axat, the D618 threads hazardously through two consecutive canyon systems: the **Gorges de St-Georges** and the **Gorges de l'Aude**. Beyond the second set of narrows is a magnificent cave, the **Grotte de l'Aguzou**. It's expensive to visit (reservation only; contact guide Philippe Moreno ℡04.68.20.45.38, Ⓦwww.grotte-aguzou.com; €60 full day, bring your own picnic), but – accoutred like a pro – as near to real speleology as you can get without being a caver. The closest indoor **accommodation** is 8km up the Aude at **ESCOULOUBRE-LES-BAINS**, where *Chambre d'Hôte Maison Roquelaure* (℡04.68.20.47.29, Ⓦwww.maison-roquelaure.com; ❶), in the old thermal establishment, makes evening meals for hikers and cyclists, and still has a spring-fed spa pool on the ground floor.

Upstream, the road divides just above abandoned Usson-les-Bains (the easterly fork goes to Escouloubre-les-Bains). On a shaggy bluff between the arms of the fork, dwarfed in turn by crags either side, stands forlornly ruined **Château d'Usson** (Feb & Easter hols, Sept 2–6pm; July–Aug daily 10am–1pm & 3–7pm; €4), allegedly the hiding place of the "Cathar treasure" after the siege of Montségur. This is the gateway to the **Donezan** region, beautifully forested but the most neglected and depopulated corner of the Ariège.

From Mijanès a road heads 8km up-valley to **QUÉRIGUT**, last settlement before the border with Roussillon and end of the infrequent summer bus line. The high, chilly village is guarded by the ruined **Château de Donezan**, last refuge of Cathars who held out for eleven years after the fall of Montségur. There's a single, central, skier/cyclist-friendly **hotel-restaurant**, *Auberge du Donezan* (℡04.68.20.42.40, Ⓦwww.auberge-du-donezan.com; ❷).

The Cathar castles

Romantic and ruined, the medieval fortresses which pepper the hills between Quillan and Perpignan have become known as the **Cathar castles**, though many were built either before or after the Cathar era. Roussillon, Languedoc and the eastern Ariège were this twelfth-century sect's power-base; their name derives from the Greek word for "pure", *katharon*, as they abhorred the materialism and worldly power of the established Church, were initially pacifist and denied the validity of feudal vows or allegiances. While the Cathars probably never accounted for more than ten percent of the population, they included many members of the nobility and mercantile classes, which alarmed the powers that were.

Once disputational persuasion by the ecclesiastical hierarchy proved fruitless, Pope Innocent III anathemized the Cathars as heretics in 1208 and persuaded the French king to mount the first of many "Albigensian" crusades, so called after Albi, a Cathar stronghold. Predatory northern nobles, led for a decade by the notoriously cruel Simon de Montfort, descended on the area with their forces, besieging and sacking towns, massacring Cathar and Catholic civilians alike, laying waste or seizing the lands of local counts. The effect of this brutality was to unite both the Cathars and their Catholic neighbours in southern solidarity against the barbarous north. Though military defeat became inevitable with the capitulation of Toulouse in 1229 and the fall of Montségur in 1244, it took the informers and torturers of the Holy Inquisition another 180 years to root out Catharism completely.

Visiting the castles

The best of the castles stud the arid, herb-scented hills of the **Corbières** which separate Roussillon from Languedoc. **Walking** is the most direct way to experience them; the **GR36**, crossing from Carcassonne to St-Paul-de-Fenouillet, and the **Sentier Cathare**, traversing east to west from Port-la-Nouvelle to Foix, together pass most of the sites. The Sentier Cathare is described in *Le Sentier Cathare* Topo-guide (Rando Éditions).

Without transport or walking boots, the best way to tackle the castles is from the south, as the most spectacular ones are close to the Quillan–Perpignan road. This route is served by bus, but a better option is the narrow-gauge **Train du Pays Cathare et du Fenouillèdes** (ⓣ04.68.59.96.18, ⓦwww.tpcf.fr), which runs from Rivesaltes or Espira de l'Agly, just north of Perpignan, to Axat, stopping at the main towns along the way. The service (sometimes only St-Paul-de-Fenouillet to Axat) runs Sun–Wed in May, June, Sept & Oct, daily July & Aug (adult fare €11–18 depending on direction and distance).

If you're planning on visiting several of the Cathar-related and other medieval sites in the Aude (including many in Chapter 11), consider purchasing the **Passeport des Sites du Pays Cathare**, available for €3 at any of the nineteen participating monuments in the *département*. The card (valid per calendar year) gives €1 off adult admission, and free child tickets, for the ramparts of Carcassonne, Lastours, Saissac, Caunes-Minervois, St-Hilaire, Lagrasse, Fontfroide, Puilaurens, Usson, Peyrepertuse, Quéribus, Aguilar, Arques and other sites. For more information see ⓦwww.payscathare.org.

Accommodation

A popular base for visiting Quéribus (and Peyrepertuse) is **Cucugnan**, in the valley roughly halfway between the two. There's ample **accommodation** in *chambres d'hôtes* and hotels, the latter including central *Auberge du Vigneron* at 2 rue Achille Mir (ⓣ04.68.45.03.00, ⓦwww.auberge-vigneron.com; ❸; restaurant *menus* from €22, closed Mon, also mid-Nov to mid-March) and the *Auberge de Cucugnan* (ⓣ04.68.45.40.84, ⓦwww.auberge-de-cucugnan.com; closed Jan–March; ❸), with smallish rooms but a pleasant rear courtyard, and a decent restaurant (closed Thurs; *menus* from €18).

A second possible base is **Rouffiac-des-Corbières**, around 9km north of Cucugnan, where there's a **hotel**, the *Auberge de Peyrepertuse* (ⓣ04.68.45.40.40; closed mid-Dec to Jan, plus Wed; ❷), with well-appointed en-suite rooms and a restaurant (*menus* from €17).

Puilaurens

The westernmost Cathar castle, **Puilaurens**, can be reached by road from Quillan or rail from Axat, from the Lapradelle station of the seasonal train (see above). Lapradelle, 6km east of Axat, is in turn 2km north of the turnings for dramatically sited **Château de Puilaurens** (daily: Feb, April & Oct to mid-Nov 10am–5pm; March (weekends) 10am–5pm; May 10am–6pm; June & Sept 10am–7pm; July & Aug 9am–8pm; closed mid-Nov to Jan; €4). You can either drive up a 1500-metre side road starting 500m south of Puilaurens hamlet, or there's a shorter and fairly gentle path up from the hamlet through forest alive with cuckoos. The castle perches atop a hill at 700m, its fine crenellated walls sprouting organically from the rock outcrops. It sheltered many Cathars up to 1256, when Chabert de Barbera, the region's *de facto* ruler, was captured and forced to hand over this citadel and Quéribus further east to secure his release. The castle remained strategically important –

being close to the Spanish border – until 1659, when France annexed Roussillon and the frontier was pushed south. Highlights of a visit are the **west donjon** and **southeast postern gate**, where you're allowed briefly on the curtain wall for views, and the **Tour de la Dame Blanche**, with a rib-vaulted ceiling.

Quéribus

The **Château de Quéribus** (daily: Feb 10am–5.30pm; March 10am–6pm; Nov–Dec 10am–5pm; April–June & Sept 9.30am–7pm; July–Aug daily 9am–8pm; Oct 10am–6.30pm; closed most Jan; €5), 30km further east towards Perpignan, overlooks the vine-ringed village of Cucugnan (see opposite) from the ridge that marked the French–Spanish border until 1659. The history of Quéribus is similar to that of Puilaurens, holding out until 1255 or 1256; not reduced by siege, its role as a Cathar sanctuary ended with the capture of the luckless Chabert, though the garrison escaped to Spain. Spectacularly situated above the Grau de Maury pass 6km north of the Quillan–Perpignan road, the castle balances on a storm-battered rock pinnacle above sheer cliffs – access is forbidden in bad weather. Because of the cramped topography, the space within the walls is stepped in terraces, linked by a single stairway and dominated by the polygonal keep. High point, in all senses, is the so-called **Salle du Pilier**, whose vaulted ceiling is supported by a graceful pillar sprouting a canopy of intersecting ribs. A spiral staircase leads to the roof terrace and fantastic views (best outside summer) in every direction, including Canigou, the Mediterranean and northwest to the next Cathar castle, Peyrepertuse.

Peyrepertuse

If you only have time for one of the Cathar castles, make it the **Château de Peyrepertuse** (daily: Feb, Nov & Dec 10am–5pm; April–June & Sept 9am–7.30pm; July–Aug 9am–8.30pm; March & Oct daily 10am–6.30pm; last entry 20min before close; closed last 3 weeks in Jan; €5), not only for the unbeatable site and stunning views, but also because it's unusually well preserved. The castle was obtained by treaty with the Kingdom of Aragón in 1258, and most of the existing fortifications were built afterwards, staying in use until 1789. The 3.5-km access road starts in Duilhac village or, alternatively, you can walk up from Rouffiac-des-Corbières village (see opposite) to the north via the GR36 – a tough, hot climb of over an hour. Either way the effort is rewarded, for Peyrepertuse is among the most awe-inspiring castles anywhere, draped the length of a jagged rock-spine with sheer drops at most points. Access is banned during fierce summer thunderstorms, when (as at Quéribus) the ridge makes an ideal lightning target.

Tickets are sold by the southerly car park, but you then walk fifteen minutes through thickets of box to the entrance on the north side. The bulkiest fortifications enclose the lower, eastern end of the ridge, with a **keep** and **barbican** controlling the main gate. Things get increasingly airier as you progress west along the ridge past and through various cisterns, chapels and bastions, culminating in a **stairway** of over a hundred steps carved into the living rock, which leads to a keep, tower and the **chapel of San Jordi** at the summit.

Aguilar

Just east of Tuchan, overlooking the Côtes de Roussillon-Villages wine *domaine*, is the isolated, thirteenth-century **Château d'Aguilar** (daily: March, Oct & Nov 10am–1pm & 2–5pm; April–June & Sept 10am–1pm & 2–6pm; July & Aug 10am–7pm; closed Dec–Feb; €5). Perched at the end of a steep, one-lane drive, its hexagonal curtain wall shelters a keep with the chatelain's lodge on the top floor.

Roussillon

The area comprising the eastern fringe of the Pyrenees and the lowlands down to the Mediterranean is known as **Roussillon**, or **French Catalonia**. Catalan power first emerged in the tenth century under the independent counts of Barcelona, who then became kings of Aragón as well in 1163. The Catalan zenith was reached during the thirteenth and fourteenth centuries, when the Franco–Catalan frontier traced the Corbières hills north of Perpignan. But Jaume I of Aragón and Valencia made the mistake of dividing his kingdom between his two sons at his death in 1276, thus ensuring continuous see-saw battles and annexations that ended only with the Treaty of the Pyrenees, negotiated by Louis XIV and the Spanish king in 1659.

Although there's no real separatist impetus among French Catalans today, their sense of identity remains strong: the language is very much alive (not least in bilingual place-signage), and their red-and-yellow flag is ubiquitous. The **Pic du Canigou**, which completely dominates Roussillon despite its modest (2784m) elevation, shines as a powerful beacon of Catalan nationalism, attracting hordes of Catalans from across the border to celebrate St John's Eve (June 23–24). At its feet the little town of **Prades**, place of exile from Franco's Spain of cellist Pablo (Pau) Casals, served as a focus of Catalan resistance until 1975.

Most of the region's attractions are easily reached by public transport from Roussillon's capital, **Perpignan**. The coast and foothills between it and the Spanish frontier are beautiful, especially at **Collioure**, though predictably crowded and in most places overdeveloped. You'll find the finest spots in the **Tech** and **Têt valleys** which slice southwest towards the high peaks, among them the Romanesque monasteries of **Serrabona**, **St-Michel-de-Cuixà** and **St-Martin-du-Canigou**, the world-class modern art museum at **Céret** and **Mont Canigou** itself, lapped by foothill orchards of peaches and cherries.

Perpignan

This far south, climate and geography alone would ensure a palpable Spanish influence. Moreover, a good part of **PERPIGNAN**'s population is of Spanish origin – refugees from the Civil War and their descendants. The southern influence is further augmented by a substantial contingent of North Africans, including both Arabs and white French settlers repatriated after Algerian independence in 1962. Bearing in mind the town's relatively grubby appearance, few will want to stay here for more than a day or two; with your own transport, you may prefer to base yourself somewhere in the surrounding area.

Arrival, information and accommodation

From the **airport** at Rivesaltes, 6km north (no-frills flights from UK), there are up to six daily shuttle buses into town (€5), which call at the **gare routière** just off avenue du Général-Leclerc, near the Pont Arago; a taxi will cost about three times as much. The **gare SNCF** is on avenue du Général-de-Gaulle in the west of town. Both stations are a fifteen-minute walk from the **municipal tourist office** in the Palais des Congrès at the end of boulevard Wilson (mid-June to mid-Sept

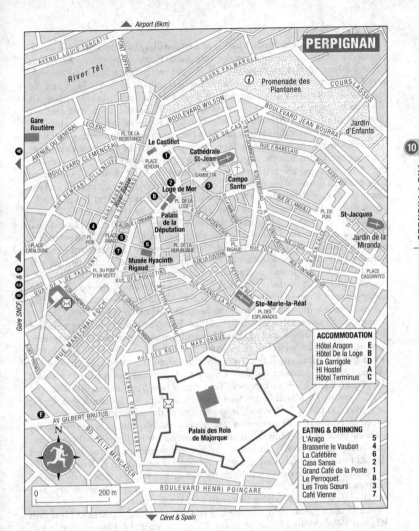

PERPIGNAN

Airport (6km)

River Têt

Gare Routière

Gare SNCF

i Promenade des Plantanes

Jardin d'Enfants

Le Castillet

Cathédrale St-Jean

Campo Santo

Loge de Mer

Palais de la Députation

Musée Hyacinth Rigaud

St-Jacques

Jardin de la Miranda

PLACE CASSANYES

Ste-Marie-la-Réal

PLACE CATALOGNE

Palais des Rois de Majorque

N

0   200 m

Céret & Spain

ACCOMMODATION

Hôtel Aragon	E
Hôtel De la Loge	B
La Garrigole	D
HI Hostel	A
Hôtel Terminus	C

EATING & DRINKING

L'Arago	5
Brasserie le Vauban	4
La Cafétière	6
Casa Sansa	2
Grand Café de la Poste	1
Le Perroquet	8
Les Trois Sœurs	3
Café Vienne	7

Mon–Sat 9am–7pm, Sun 10am–4pm; rest of year Mon–Sat 9am–6pm, Sun 9am–noon; ℡04.68.66.30.30, Ⓦwww.perpignantourisme.com).

Hotels

Hôtel d'Aragon 17 av Gilbert Brutus ℡04.68.54.04.46, Ⓦwww.aragon-hotel.com. A bit out of the way, but handy for the Palais des Rois de Majorque, *Aragon* is a two-star with non-fusty rooms, wi-fi signal and parking nearby. ❸

Hôtel de la Loge 1 Fabriques d'en Nabot ℡04.68.34.41.02, Ⓦwww.hoteldelaloge.fr. Situated in the centre of town, this is a well-renovated medieval mansion with a central courtyard, on a quiet alley. ❸

Hôtel Terminus 2 av du Général-de-Gaulle ℡04.68.34.32.54, Ⓦwww.au-terminus.com. Decent hotel right opposite the station. ❷

Hostel and campsite

La Garrigole Rue Maurice Lévy ℡04.68.54.66.10. 1.8 km from the hostel (see below).

HI hostel ℡04.68.34.63.32. Welcoming, if somewhat traffic-noisy hostel behind the Parc de la Pépinière by Pont Arago (entrance from av de Grande-Bretagne). Closed mid-Nov to Feb.

The City

The best place to begin explorations is at **Le Castillet**, built as a gateway in the fourteenth century and now home to the **Casa Païral** (Wed–Mon: May–Sept 10am–6.30pm; Oct–April 11am–5.30pm; €4), an interesting museum of Roussillon's Catalan rural culture and the anti-French rebellions of 1661–74, when the tower held captured Catalan insurgents. A short distance down rue Louis Blanc lies **place de la Loge**, focus of the pedestrianized heart of the old town, with a voluptuous Venus statue by Aristide Maillol (see p.659) in the centre. Dominating the cafés and brasseries of the narrow square is Perpignan's most interesting building, the 1397-vintage Gothic **Loge de Mer**. Designed to hold the city's stock exchange and maritime court, it features gargoyles, lancet windows and lacy balustrades up top. Adjacent stand the sixteenth-century **Hôtel de Ville**, with its magnificent wrought-iron gates and another Maillol (*La Méditerranée*) in the courtyard, and the fifteenth-century **Palais de la Députation**, once the parliament of Roussillon.

From place de la Loge, rue St-Jean leads northeast to the fourteenth-century **Cathédrale St-Jean** on place Gambetta (daily 7.30am–6.30pm; free), its external walls built of alternating bands of river stones and brick. The dimly lit interior is most interesting for its elaborate Catalan altarpieces and for the fourteenth-century, Rhenish polychrome Crucifixion known as the *Dévôt Christ*; it's in the fifth side chapel along the north wall, probably brought from the Low Countries by a travelling merchant. Out of the side door, a few steps on the left is the entrance to the **Campo Santo**, a vast enclosure that's one of France's oldest cemeteries, now used for summer concerts (otherwise closed May–Sept; Oct–April Tues–Sun 11am–5pm).

South of the cathedral, rue de la Révolution-Française and rue de l'Anguille lead into the teeming, dilapidated **Maghrebian and Romany quarters**, where women congregate on the secluded inner lanes but are seldom seen on the busier thoroughfares. Here you'll find North African shops and cafés, especially on rue Llucia, and a daily market on place Cassanyes. Uphill and north from this stands the elegant church of **St-Jacques** (Tues–Sun 11am–5pm) dating from around 1200, abutting **La Miranda gardens** (daily: June–Sept 8–11.45am & 2–5.45pm; Oct–May 8–11am & 3.30–6pm), atop a section of the old city walls.

A twenty-minute walk southwest through place des Esplanades brings you to the main entrance of the **Palais des Rois de Majorque** (daily: June–Sept 10am–6pm; Oct–May 9am–5pm; €4), crowning the hill that dominates the southern part of the old town. Although Vauban's walls surround it now, and it suffered generally from ongoing military use until 1946, the two-storey palace and its partly arcaded courtyard date originally from the late thirteenth century. There are frequent worthwhile temporary exhibits in the former king's apartments.

Finally, at 16 rue de l'Ange near place Arago, you'll find the **Musée Hyacinth Rigaud** (Wed–Mon: May–Sept noon–6.30pm; Oct–April 11am–5.30pm; €4). The collection is largely devoted to Catalan painters, most notably Minorcan-born **Pierre Daura** (1896–1976), a Republican and godson of Pablo Casals long exiled in the US, his sympathies evident in two symbolic canvases of the post-civil-war Republican refugee camps at nearby Argelès. One room has a few Maillol sketches and statues, and three portraits by Picasso.

Eating, drinking and entertainment

For a place of Perpignan's size, **restaurants** are quite thin on the ground. Festivals, on the other hand, are more plentiful, including the July Estivales, the late-September Trobades (which celebrates the medieval heritage of the region), and the October-long Jazzèbre festival. But Perpignan's best-known spectacle is **La Procession de la Sanch**, the Good Friday procession of red-hooded penitents that goes from the church of St-Jacques to the cathedral between 3pm and 5pm.

L'Arago 1 Place Arago ☎04.68.51.81.96.
Brasserie cuisine with a pleasant alfresco setting.
Mains from €15.
Brasserie le Vauban 29 quai Vauban
☎04.68.51.05.10. Art Deco place situated just
across the river serving elegant, Parisian-style food.
La Cafétière Opposite the Hyacinth Rigaud
museum. Tiny café serving the best cup of coffee
in the city (both flavoured and premium grade).
Casa Sansa 3 rue Fabriques-Couvertes
☎04.68.34.21.84. Smart surroundings, traditional
Catalan cuisine, bullfight posters and old photos.
There's a seafood annexe adjacent.

Grand Café de la Poste Place de Verdun
☎04.68.51.25.65. Great for people-watching,
especially on summer evenings when the Catalan
sardana dance might be spontaneously performed
here. Live music Tuesday and Saturday.
Le Perroquet 1 av de Gaulle ☎04.68.34.34.36.
A good selection of reasonably priced Catalan
dishes. Closed Wed Sept–April.
Les Trois Sœurs 2 rue Fontfroide. The most
reliable central bar, with novelty acts and theme
evenings (Wed–Sun).
Café Vienne 3 place Arago ☎04.68.34.80.00.
Delicious seafood dishes from €11.

Around Perpignan

CANET-PLAGE, 12km east of Perpignan, is the nearest place for a Mediterranean dip, although there's nothing to recommend it except that the beach is wide and sandy and the sea is wet; take a CTP bus #1 from place Catalogne. Perhaps more interesting, 15km north and served by regular trains, is the late-fifteenth-century Forteresse de Salses (daily: June–Sept 9.30am–7pm; Oct–May 10am–12.15pm & 2–5pm; €7; ⓦwww.salses.monuments-nationaux.fr). This was one of the first forts to be designed with a ground-hugging profile to protect it from artillery fire.

Another place, with not much to see but interesting anthropologically, is vine-girt TAUTAVEL, 25km northwest off the St-Paul-de-Fenouillet road. In 1971 the remains of the oldest known European human being – dated to around 450,000 BC – were discovered in the nearby Caune d'Arago cave, and a reconstruction of the skull and other cave finds are displayed in the village's Musée de la Préhistoire (daily: April–June & Sept 10am–12.30pm & 2–6pm; July–Aug 10am–7pm; Oct–March 10am–12.30pm & 2–5pm; €8; ⓦwww.tautavel.com).

Fourteen kilometres southeast of Perpignan lies ELNE. This small town once had the honour of seeing Hannibal camp below its walls en route to Rome, and used to be the capital of Roussillon. Today, it's worth a stop for its fortified, partially Romanesque cathedral of Ste-Eulalie and extremely beautiful cloister (daily May–Sept 10am–7pm; Oct–April daily except Mon 10am–12.30pm & 2–5.30pm; ⓦwww.ot-elne.fr/anglais/patrimoine.html; €5). The four colonnades of the cloister demonstrate a gradual transition from Romanesque to Gothic styles, clockwise from the south bay (twelfth century) to the east bay (fourteenth), intricately carved with biblical and secular scenes, plus mythical creaures. It's the best possible introduction to Roussillon Romanesque, especially if you're planning to visit Serrabona and St-Michel-de-Cuixà further west. Around the cathedral are the strollable lanes of the old town, and a certain amount of accommodation, including *Hôtel Restaurant Cara-Sol* at 10 bd Illibéris (☎04.68.22.10.42, ⓦwww.hotelcarasol.com; ❺); their restaurant has seating with an unbeatable view on the ramparts outside.

The Côte Vermeille

The Côte Vermeille, where the Pyrenees meet the sea, is the last patch of French shoreline before Spain, its seaside villages once so remote that the Fauvist painters of the early 1900s hid out here. Mass tourism has ended any sense of exclusivity or unspoiltness, but in low season at least they remain attractive, and well served by public transport.

Argèles-Plage

Argèles-Plage is the first resort beyond Elne. It's a fun, neon-licked resort town packed cheek by jowl with typical tourist diversions, including windsurfing, miniature golf and sea kayaking. The **tourist office** (daily 8.30am–8pm; off-season Mon–Sat 9am–noon & 2–6pm, Sun 9am–noon; ℡04.68.81.15.85, Ⓦen.argeles-sur-mer.com) is located on place de l'Europe across from the police station. Accommodation is many and varied. If you're keen to **stay**, try *L'Auberge du Roua* located on the edge of town beyond the RN 114 on Chemin du Roua (℡04.68.95.85.85, Ⓦwww.aubergeduroua.com; ❼), which offers stylish rooms in a seventeenth-century Catalan mansion. The grounds and pool feature a sundrenched terrace with peaceful views of stately palms, lush vineyards and the rolling mountains of Les Alberes. **Camping** includes *La Sardane* (℡01.68.95.82.18, Ⓦwww.campinglasardane.com), a family friendly beachside resort on avenue du Grau 200 metre from the beach.

Collioure

Eleven kilometres southeast of Elne, **COLLIOURE** is achingly picturesque. Palm trees line the curving main beach of **Port d'Avall**, while slopes of vines and olives rise to ridges crowned with ruined forts and watchtowers. Its setting and monuments inspired Henri Matisse and André Derain to embark in 1905 on their explosive Fauvist colour experiments. Collioure is dominated by its twelfth-century **Château Royal** (daily: June–Sept 10am–5.15pm; Oct–May 9am–4.15pm; €4), founded by the Templars and subject to later alterations by the kings of Mallorca and Aragón, and again after the Treaty of the Pyrenees gave Collioure to France. The mediocre permanent "collection" inside scarcely merits the entrance fee; attend instead a concert in the courtyard. Collioure's other landmark is the distinctive round belfry of the seventeenth-century **church of Notre-Dame-des-Anges** (daily 9am–noon & 2–6pm), formerly the harbour lighthouse. Behind it two small **beaches** are divided by a causeway leading to the **chapel of St-Vincent**, built on a former islet, while west from here a concrete path follows the rocky shore to the bay of **Le Racou**.

Just north of the château lies the **old harbour**, still home to a bare handful of brightly painted lateen-rigged fishing boats – now more likely used as pleasure craft – all that remains of Collioure's traditional fleet. Beyond this, the stone houses and sloping lanes of the old **Mouré** quarter are the main focus of interest. The **tourist office** is here on place du 18 Juin (July & Aug Mon–Sat 9am–8pm & Sun 10am–6pm; Sept–June Tues–Sat 9am–noon & 2–6.30pm; ℡04.68.82.15.47, Ⓦwww.collioure.com).

The most central place to **stay** is atmospheric *Hostellerie des Templiers* (℡04.68.98.31.10, Ⓦwww.hotel-templiers.com; closed for five weeks from end-Jan; ❸–❺) at 12 av Camille Pelletan, crammed with artwork and housing overflow in various annexes. With a car (central **parking** is nightmarish) and/or desire for a sea view, opt instead for *Hôtel Triton*, Port d'Avall beach (℡04.68.98.39.39, Ⓦwww.hotel-triton-collioure.com; ❹) or remoter *Hôtel Caranques* (℡04.68.82.06.68, Ⓦwww.les-caranques.com; ❹) at the east side of the bay on route de Port-Vendres, very friendly and with direct access to a lido from the terraced gardens. The best **campsite** is seaside, caravan-free *La Girelle* (℡04.68.81.25.56; April–Sept), at plage d'Ouille, west of town on the coastal path to Le Racou. Rue Camille Pelletan and its side lanes have some cafés and **restaurants**, but you'll fork out well over the odds for listless grub. Get, at least, what you pay for at *Amphytrion* on Port d'Avall, crowded even off-season for the sake of good-sized, seafood-based *menus* (€18–21).

Banyuls-sur-Mer

South towards **BANYULS-SUR-MER**, 10km from Collioure, both the main highway and minor D914 wind through attractive vineyards, with the Albères hills rising steeply on the right. The town itself, facing a broad sweep of pebble beach, is pleasant (and is where the GR10 meets the Mediterranean) but lacks the overt charm of Collioure. There are, however, several local attractions. One is the seafront **aquarium** of the Laboratoire Arago (daily: July–Aug 9am–1pm & 2–8.30pm; Sept–June 9am–noon & 2–6.30pm; €4.80) run by the Sorbonne's marine biology department, whose tanks contain a comprehensive collection of the region's submarine life; this is protected in a nearby *réserve marine*, France's best, which can be explored with local **scuba outfitters**. Also worth a look are the works of sculptor **Aristide Maillol** (1861–1944), who was born near Banyuls; they are best seen at the **Musée Maillol** (daily: May–Sept 10am–noon & 4–7pm; Oct–April 10am–noon & 2–5pm; €3.50), 4km outside the town in the Vallée de Roume, where he is buried under his statue *La Pensée*. Make sure you sample the dark, full-bodied Banyuls dessert **wine**, an *appellation* which applies only to the vineyards of the Côte Vermeille.

The **tourist office** stands diagonally opposite the *mairie* on the seafront (July & Aug daily 9.30am–12.30pm & 2.30–7pm; Sept–June Mon–Sat 9am–noon & 2–6pm; ℡04.68.88.31.58, Ⓦwww.banyuls-sur-mer.com). The only budget **hotel** is *Canal*, 9 rue Dugommier a block inland (℡04.68.88.00.75; ❷–❸), basic but adequate and with wi-fi signal throughout, while with a bit more to spend try *Les Elmes* at the eponymous sandy cove 1.5km north (℡04.58.88.03.12, Ⓦwww .hotel-des-elmes.com; ❺), with quieter rear-facing rooms, or *Al-Fanal* (℡04.68.88.00.81; ❹) overlooking the yacht port, with parking. This also has its own seafood **restaurant**, but the best value in town – on an otherwise touristy street – is provided by seafood and shellfish specialists ⅄ *Les Canadells* opposite the *mairie*, with big portions and good own-label wine. Also worth considering is the tapas-bar *La Casa Miguel* at 3 rue St-Pierre; inside are original Maillol lithographs and photos of old Banyuls.

Vallée du Tech

The D115 winds its way through the beautiful Vallée du Tech all the way up to the Spanish border, just past the medieval walled town of **Prats-de-Mollo**. The first tempting stop is **Céret**, capital of the Vallespir region, served like the rest of the valley by regular buses from Perpignan.

Céret

Céret is a delightful place, with a wonderfully shady old town overhung by huge plane trees; central streets are narrow and winding, opening onto small squares like the **Plaça de Nou Reigs** ("Nine Spouts" in Catalan), named after its central fountain; on avenue d'Espagne, two remnants of the medieval walls, the **Porte de France** and **Porte d'Espagne**, are visible. Céret is also known for its cherries from surrounding orchards (June festival), plus July *corridas* (bullfights) and Pamplona-style running of bulls. Other annual events include the Easter Sunday procession of the Resurrected Christ, and an international *sardana* jamboree in July.

Céret's main sight, however, is the remarkable **Musée d'Art Moderne** (mid-June to mid-Sept daily 10am–7pm; mid-Feb to mid-Sept daily 10am–6pm; Oct to mid-Sept same hours; closed Tues; ℡04.68.87.27.76, Ⓦwww.musee-ceret.com; €8), at 8 bd Maréchal Joffre. Between about 1910 and 1935, Céret's charms – coupled with the residence here of the Catalan artist and sculptor Manolo – drew a number of avant-garde artists to the town, including Matisse and Picasso, who personally dedicated a number of pictures to the museum. The holdings are too extensive to mount everything at once, but works on show should include some Chagall, Miró, Pignon, Picasso and Dufy, among others.

The **tourist office** is at 1 av Clemenceau (July & Aug Mon–Sat 9.30am–12.30pm & 2–7pm; Sept–May Mon–Fri 9am–noon & 2–5pm, Sat 9.30am–12.30pm; ℡04.68.87.00.53, Ⓦwww.ceret.fr). Best of the **accommodation** is friendly ⚘ *Hôtel Vidal* at 4 place Soutine (℡04.68.87.00.85, Ⓦwww.hotelceret.com; closed Nov; ❷), a tastefully converted episcopal palace. They have a good restaurant, *El Bisbe* (closed Tues & Wed low season), with gourmet *menus* at €31. Alternative **eating** options include *Pizzeria Quattrocento* (closed Tues) on Plaça de Nou Reigs; and *Côte Jardin* at 12 rue St-Ferréol down from the museum, with a €16 lunch *menu*.

Arles-sur-Tech and Gorges de la Fou

West of Céret, past the single span of its fourteenth-century **Pont du Diable**, the view opens towards the towering eminence of the Canigou massif. Once past congested Amélie-les-Bains (8km), it's 4km further to **ARLES-SUR-TECH**, a more interesting proposition. The Carolingian origins of its Romanesque **Abbaye de Ste-Marie** (July–Aug 9am–7pm; Sept–June Mon–Sat 9am–noon & 2–5pm; also Sun April–Oct 2–5pm; €3.50) are thought to account for the back-to-front alignment of altar at the west end and entrance at the east. Entry is via the pleasant thirteenth-century cloister. The unique and compelling feature of the massive church interior is a band of still-vividly coloured twelfth-century **frescoes** high up in the apse of the eastern antichapel dedicated to St-Michel, appropriately featuring the archangel.

Outside the east facade – surmounted by an impressive Romanesque relief of Christ and the Tetramorphs – stands a very ancient (fourth- or fifth-century) sarcophagus, known as the **Sainte-Tombe**, which has the mysterious habit of slowly filling with very pure water. Every July 30, when Arles celebrates its *fête* dedicated to SS Abdon and Sennen (two Roman martyrs whose bones used to lodge inside), the water is siphoned out and distributed after Mass to worshipful pilgrims. The town's other festivals include the probably prehistoric **Fête de l'Ours**, devised to exorcize human fear of awakening bears, traditionally held in late February when hibernation ended; there's also a torchlit **Procession de la Sanch** at Easter. Arles is an important stage on the **GR10**, which from here heads northwest towards the Canigou massif or southeast towards Las Illas.

The **tourist office** (Mon–Sat 9am–noon & 2–6pm, Sun 2–6pm; ℡04.68.39.11.99, Ⓦwww.ville-arles-sur-tech.fr) also serves as the abbey ticket office. **Accommodation** is limited to the *Hôtel les Glycines* on rue du Jeu-de-Paume (℡04.68.39.10.09; Feb–Nov; ❷), with a terrace restaurant (from €18), and *Chambre d'Hôte La Corrent Sana* (℡04.68.83.92.09, Ⓦla-corrent-sana .com; ❷), on the edge of town. There's also a **campsite**, *Riuferrer* (℡04.68.39.11.06), on the west side of town.

Just west of Arles, on the road to Prats-de-Mollo, is the entrance to the **Gorges de la Fou** (Ⓦwww.les-gorges-de-la-fou.com), 2km long, very narrow and up to 250m deep (April–Nov daily 10am–6pm weather permitting, closes at 5pm Oct–Nov; €7). It's spectacular, but inevitably a tourist trap, with snack stalls and a metal catwalk all along the bottom.

Prats-de-Mollo

Beyond the Gorges de la Fou, the D115 climbs steadily, between valley sides thick with walnut, oak and sweet chestnut, 19km to **PRATS-DE-MOLLO**, the end of the bus line. Prats is the last French town before the **Spanish frontier**, 13km beyond at Col d'Ares, but it has none of the usual malaise of border towns and is the most attractive place in the valley since Céret. Hub of the newer quarter is **El Firal**, the huge square used for markets since 1308; the walled and gated **ville haute** just south makes for a wonderful wander, with steep cobbled streets and a weathered church with marvellous ironwork on the door. The old town's walls were rebuilt in the seventeenth century after the suppression of a local revolt against onerous taxation imposed by Louis XIV on his new, post-Treaty Pyrenees holdings. Vauban's **Fort Lagarde** (April–June & Sept–Oct Tues–Sun 2–6pm; July & Aug daily 11am–1pm; guided visits only, apply to tourist office; €2.50), on the heights above the town, also dates from this period, built to intimidate the local population as much as to keep the Spanish out.

The **tourist office** is on El Fioral (July–Aug daily 9am–12.30pm & 2–6.30pm; Sept–June Mon–Fri 9am–noon & 2–6pm, Sat 9am–noon; ℡04.68.39.70.83; ⓦwww.pratsdemollolapreste.com). There's ample good-quality **accommodation**, which makes Prats a good base or transit stopover; in the walled quarter, go for *Hostellerie Le Relais* at 3 place Josep de la Trinxeria (℡04.68.39.71.30, ⓦwww.hostellerie-le-relais.com; ❷), with cheerful pastel-hued rooms and a south-facing garden restaurant. Just outside, overlooking El Firal, is *Hôtel Le Bellevue* (℡04.68.39.72.48, ⓦwww.uk.hotel-le-bellevue.fr/; closed Dec to mid-Feb; ❸), with private parking and a restaurant (*menu* from €21).

Les Aspres

The only direct route between the **valleys of the Tech and the Têt**, best covered with a small car or cycle, is the D618 from Amélie-les-Bains to Bouleternère. It's 44 slow kilometres of mountain road, twisting through hillside meadows and magnificent woods, past isolated *masies* (Catalan farmsteads), many now tenanted by foreigners or French *soixante-huitard* idealists drawn to **Les Aspres**, as this region is known. The only amenities en route, 20km along, are in tiny **ST-MARSAL** with its broad vistas, at *Hôtel Auberge de Saint-Marsal* (℡04.68.39.42.68; ❶), a converted *mas*. Some 5km further, the Romanesque **Chapelle de la Trinité** stands by the road, opposite the *mairie* of Prunet-Belpuig. Inside (usually open) is a fine, serene *majestat*, the particularly Catalan wood-carved Crucifixions of the eleventh or twelfth centuries; most of the Spanish examples were destroyed in 1936.

From here the D618 descends into the Boulès valley, through the pretty hamlet of **Boule d'Amont**, before reaching the steep D84 side road climbing 4km to the remarkable, bluff-top **Prieuré de Serrabona** (formerly Serrabonne; daily except major holidays 10am–6pm; €3). One of the finest examples – arguably *the* finest – of Roussillon Romanesque, the interior of the church (consecrated 1151) is starkly plain, making the beautifully carved column-capitals of its rib-vaulted tribune even more striking: lions, centaurs, griffins and human figures with Asiatic faces and hairstyles – motifs brought back from the Crusades – executed in pink marble from Villefranche-de-Conflent, by students of the Maître d'Cabestany if not himself.

The Têt valley

The upper **Têt valley**, known as the **Pays de Conflent**, is utterly dominated by the **Pic du Canigou**. The valley bottoms are lush with fields and orchards, but the vast and uncompromising mountain presides over all. Continuing upstream, the valley narrows and steepens until you emerge onto the Cerdagne plateau.

Prades and Molitg-les-Bains

Chief valley town is **Prades**, easily accessible by train and bus on the Perpignan–Villefranche–Latour-de-Carol route, and the obvious starting point for all excursions in the Canigou region. Although there are no great sights beyond the **church of**

St-Pierre in central place de la République, the town enjoys a status disproportionate to its size. This is largely thanks to Catalan cellist Pablo (Pau) Casals, who settled here as an exile and fierce opponent of the Franco regime in Spain. In 1950 he instituted the internationally renowned **chamber music festival** (ⓦwww.prades-festival-casals.com), held annually from late July to mid-August, the usual venue being the abbey of St-Michel-de-Cuixà (see below). Prades (or Prada) also hosts a Catalan university in mid-August and has the first Catalan-language primary school in France.

The **tourist office** is at 4 rue des Marchands (July & Aug Mon–Sat 9am–12.30pm & 2–7pm, Sun 9am–noon; Sept–June Mon–Fri 9am–noon & 2–6pm; ⓣ04.68.05.41.02, ⓦwww.prades-tourisme.fr). The best **accommodation** is *Castell Rose* (ⓣ04.68.96.07.57, ⓦwww.castellrose-prades.com; ❺–❻), lovely *chambres d'hôtes* just west of town on chemin de la Llitera, in a converted manor house set in extensive grounds with a pool and tennis court. If that's beyond your budget, and you've transport, make for welcoming *Hôtel St Joseph*, 7km west across the river in gorge-set **MOLITG-LES-BAINS** (ⓣ04.68.05.02.11, ⓦwww.hotel-saint-joseph.com; rooms ❶, studios ❷), though **eating**'s much better next door at *Royal*, where the €16 tasting *menu* includes wine and coffee. Back in Prades, the best **restaurant** is *La Meridienne* at 20 rue des Marchands (book in season on ⓣ04.68.05.98.31), with *menus* from €16.

St-Michel-de-Cuixà

Three kilometres south of Prades stands one of the loveliest abbeys in France, originally eleventh-century **St-Michel-de-Cuixà** (May–Sept Mon–Sat 9.30–11.50am & 2–6pm, Sun 2–6pm; Oct–April Mon–Sat 9.30–11.50am & 2–5pm, Sun 2–5pm; €4). Although mutilated after the Revolution it is still beautiful, with its crenellated tower silhouetted against the wooded – sometimes snowy – slopes of Canigou. You enter via the labyrinthine, vaulted crypt, with a round central chamber, before proceeding to the church with its strange Visigothic-style "keyhole" arches. But the glory of the place is the **cloister** and its twelfth-century column capitals. Although most of the north and east bays were taken to the Cloisters Museum in New York early in the last century, the remaining west and south series – filled in with capitals from the vanished tribune in the church – rival Serrabona and Elne for virtuosity, sharing Serrabona's rose marble, and possibly artist (the Maître de Cabestany, or a disciple). They feature highly stylized figures strongly reminiscent of Sumerian, Assyrian or Persian relief art: often monsters, either alone or being grappled by human keepers displaying an array of Asiatic beards, exotic headgear and corpulent anatomies.

Vernet-les-Bains and St-Martin-du-Canigou

An innocuous little hillside spa, **VERNET-LES-BAINS**, 12km along the minor, foothill-skimming D27 from the abbey, has a **tourist office** in place de la Mairie (Mon–Fri 9am–noon & 2–6pm, Sat 9am–noon, Sun 10am–12.30pm; ⓣ04.68.05.55.35, ⓦwww.vernet-les-bains.fr). Two of the best **hotels** are *Les Sources* (ⓣ04.68.05.52.84, ⓦwww.thermes-vernet.com; ❷) and the *Princess* on rue des Lavandières (ⓣ04.68.05.56.22, ⓦwww.hotel-princess.com; ❸). There are two **campsites** outside Vernet and a *gîte d'étape* (ⓣ04.68.05.51.30) next to the municipal pool.

A half-hour walk (no car access) above the hamlet of Casteil, itself 2.5km south of Vernet, lies the stunning abbey of **St-Martin-du-Canigou** (ⓦstmartinducanigou.org), founded in 1001. Resurrected from ruins between 1902 and 1982, and now occupied by a working religious community, the monastery at over 1000m altitude occupies a narrow promontory of rock surrounded by chestnut and oak woods, while above it rise the precipitous slopes of Canigou. Below, the ground drops sheerly into the ravine of the Cady stream rushing down from the Col de Jou. The place is visitable in French-narrated tours (year-round Mon–Sat 10am, 11am, 2pm, 3pm, 4pm; also June–Sept noon & 5pm; Sun/hols 10am & 12.30pm; closed Jan & Mon Oct–May; €5). What you see is a beautiful little garden and cloister overlooking the ravine, a low-ceiling, atmospheric chapel beneath the church, and the main church itself.

From the monastery, a **path** leads up to a rocky viewpoint from which most photographs of the place are taken. This trail continues to meet the GR10 at the Col de Segalès, and from there to the *Refuge Grand Mariailles* (1718m; ☎04.68.04.49.86; 55 bunks; late May to early Oct) on Canigou's west flank. For a **day-loop** walk back to Casteil, another path drops down into the Cady ravine just at the start of the monastery buildings.

Villefranche-de-Conflent

A medieval garrison town listed in July 2008 as a UNESCO World Heritage Site as part of the fortifications of Vauban (Ⓦwww.sites-vauban.org), **VILLEFRANCHE-DE-CONFLENT**, 6km up the Têt from Prades and a similar distance below Vernet-les-Bains, is today a tourist trap of the first order. Founded in 1092 by the counts of Cerdagne to block incursions from rivals in Roussillon, then remodelled by Vauban in the seventeenth century after annexation by France, its streets and fortifications have remained untouched by subsequent events, aside from becoming one giant, uninterrupted *tchatchka* stall. Worth a look is **St-Jacques church**, with a primitively carved thirteenth-century baptismal font just inside the door; you can also walk the **walls** (daily: Feb–May & Oct–Dec 10.30am–12.30pm & 2–5/6pm; June–Sept 10am–8pm; closed Jan; €4.50). If you do, you'll see why in 1681 Vauban constructed the **Château-Fort Libéria** on the heights above town to protect it from "aerial" bombardment. Getting up there (daily: June & Sept 9am–7pm; July–Aug 9am–8pm; Oct–May 10am–5/6pm; Ⓦwww.fort-liberia .com; €6) involves taking the free minibus or jeep leaving from near the town's main gate; you can return to Villefranche by descending a subterranean stairway of a thousand steps, emerging at the end of rue St-Pierre.

The **tourist office** (Feb–Dec daily 10am–12.30pm & 2–5.30pm; ☎04.68.96.22.96, Ⓦwww.villefranchedeconflent.fr) is in place d'Église. The best-value local **restaurant**, in the old town at 31 rue St-Jean, is *La Casa de la Nine* (most of year Wed–Sat pm & Sun lunch; *menus* from €28).

The upper Têt

The next sizeable village upstream from Villefranche, 10km along, is sleepy **OLETTE**, perched in tiers on the north flank of the Têt with an excellent, English-run **chambre d'hôte**, 🍴 *La Fontaine* (☎04.68.97.03.67, Ⓦwww.atasteofcatalonia .co.uk; closed Jan; ❸), with very tasteful rooms and good dinners (around €20).

Some 7km southwest of Olette on the south side of the valley, the wild, wooded **Gorges de la Carança** cut south through the mountains towards Spain. A clear

Petit Train Jaune

The narrow-gauge **Petit Train Jaune** runs from Villefranche-de-Conflent to Latour-de-Carol on the Spanish frontier. It climbs along the Têt at a cyclist's pace, soaking up marvellous views, especially in summer when some of the carriages are open-air (☎04.68.96.56.62, Ⓦwww.trainstouristiques-ter.com). The summertime frequency of the trains makes it practical to hop off and on, allowing you to explore the areas around smaller, isolated stations, many of them *haltes facultatifs* (ask to be set down).

path follows the canyon to the GR10 at the basic *Refuge Ras de Carança* (3–4hr; 1831m; ☏04.68.04.13.18; ⓦrefuge.caranca.free.fr; 30 places; June to mid-Sept). **THUÈS-ENTRE-VALLS** is the closest village to the *gorges* and its **car park** (€2), with a *halte facultatif* on the Petit Train Jaune (see box, p.663), and an unsigned **gîte** 🏠 *Mas de Bordes* (☏04.68.97.05.00; most of year; doubles ❷, s/c family quads ❸), up the single lane from the train line. This also offers dorms, a camping meadow and an on-site **hot spring** (free, 40°C) a 25-minute tough but scenic walk distant.

At **Fontpédrouse**, 4km beyond Thuès, a minor side road veers south across the river and up a grassy spur above the River Aigues towards the village of Prats-Balaguer. Bearing right instead at a fork leads, 3km from Fontpédrouse station, to the organized **Bains de St-Thomas** (daily 10am–7.40pm, last admission 8.40pm July/Aug; closed mid-Nov to early Dec; €5.50; ⓦwww.bains-saint-thomas.fr), with open pools at a pleasant 37–38°C.

The Cerdagne

Another 10km up the N116 from Fontpédrouse, or three stops on the train, brings you onto the wide, grassy **Cerdagne** plateau, whose once-powerful counts controlled lands from Barcelona to Roussillon. It's a region that's never been sure whether it is Spanish or French. After the French annexation of Roussillon, it was partitioned, with Spain retaining – as it still does – the enclave of Llívi. The Petit Train Jaune snakes laboriously across the entire plateau, though stations aren't always convenient for the settlements they nominally serve.

The Têt ultimately has its source in the Carlit massif, which looms above dammed **Lac des Bouillouses**, 13km northwest of Mont-Louis by the D60 and very busy in summer. Car access along this road is limited to a *navette* during peak season, or you can hike in along the GR10 from Mont-Louis in under four hours. On arrival you'll find a choice of **accommodation**; best, east of the dam, is *Auberge du Carlit* (☏04.68.04.22.23, ⓦaubergeducarlit.free.fr), with rooms (❺ half-board) and a 32-bunk *gîte* in a separate building.

The Petit Train Jaune continues past Mont-Louis, though the drama of the ride is diminished compared with the lower Têt valley. A good intermediate spot to alight is **SAILLAGOUSE**, where cheerful *Hôtel Planes-Planotel* (☏04.68.04.72.08, ⓦwww.planotel.fr; closed Nov–May) offers **rooms** in the 1895-built *vieille maison* (❸) or a nearby modern annexe (❹), and excellent-value **meals**. Ur-les-Escaldes is the closest (5km) station to more hot springs in **DORRES**, the **Bains Romans** (daily 8.30/8.45am–7.40/8.15pm; ☏04.68.04.66.87; €3.90), with open-air granite pools (39–40°C) at their best in ski season. End of the line is **LATOUR-DE-CAROL** with its fine old quarter 1km northwest of Enveitg station; on the main road the 🏠 *Auberge Catalane* (☏04.68.04.80.66, ⓦwww.auberge-catalane.fr; ❸; closed Sun night & Mon) has been going since 1929, with soundproofed rooms and a restaurant where *menus* (from €18) encompass fish, foie gras, *gésiers* and *boudin noir*.

Travel details

Trains

Bayonne to: Biarritz (14 daily; 10min); Bordeaux (6–12 daily; 1hr 40min–2hr 10min); Cambo-les-Bains (4–5 daily; 25min); Hendaye (14 daily;

35min); Lourdes (5–8 daily; 1hr 45min–2hr); Orthez (5–6 daily; 45min–1hr); Pau (7–8 daily; 1hr 15min); St-Gaudens (7–8 daily; 2hr 45min); St-Jean-de-Luz (16–20 daily; 25min); St-Jean-Pied-de-Port (4–5 daily; 1hr); Tarbes (7–8 daily;

2hr); Toulouse (7–12 daily; 3hr–5hr 30min).
Foix to: Ax-les-Thermes (11–13 daily, some on SNCF bus; 55min); Barcelona (3–4 daily; 5hr–5hr 30min); Latour-de-Carol (7 daily, some on SNCF bus; 1hr 45min–2hr); Tarascon-sur-Ariège (11–13 daily; 15–20min); Toulouse (11–13 daily; 1hr 20min–1hr 45min).
Luchon to: Montréjeau (5–6 daily; usually SNCF coach; 45–55min).
Pau to: Bordeaux (5–7 daily; 1hr 15min–2hr); Oloron-Ste-Marie (6–9 daily; 35min); Orthez (5–6 daily; 20min).
Perpignan to: Argelès-sur-Mer (8–12 daily; 20min); Banyuls-sur-Mer (8–12 daily; 30min); Cerbère (8–12 daily; 40min); Collioure (8–12 daily; 25min); Elne (8–12 daily; 10min); Narbonne (10–13 daily; 35–50min); Prades (5–8 daily; 45min); Salses (7–9 daily; 15min); Toulouse (10–12 daily; 2hr 30min–3hr); Villefranche-de-Conflent (5–8 daily; 55min).
Quillan to: Carcassonne (4–5 daily, SNCF coach except in summer; 55min–1hr 15min); Limoux (6–7 daily, SNCF coach; 30–40min).
Tarbes to: Bordeaux (6–9 daily; 3hr 15min); Dax (6–9 daily; 1hr 50min); Lourdes (11–14 daily; 15min); Orthez (3–5 daily; 1hr 10min).
Villefranche-de-Conflent to: Latour-de-Carol (3–6 daily; 2hr 45min); Mont–Louis (4–7 daily; 1hr 35min).

Buses

Bayonne to: Ainhoa (2–3 daily; 30min); Biarritz (local transport; 15–20min); Cambo-les-Bains (several daily; 30–40min); Orthez (3 daily; 50min); Pau (2–3 daily; 1hr 10min); San Sebastian (2 daily Mon–Sat; 1hr 45min); St-Jean-de-Luz (5–7 daily; 40min).
Biarritz to: Hendaye (5–7 daily; 35min); Orthez (2–3 daily; 1hr 45min); Pau (2–3 daily; 2hr 30min); St-Jean-de-Luz (11–16 daily; 25min); Salies-de-Béarn (2 daily; 1hr 20min).

Foix to: Lavelanet (2–3 daily; 30min); Mirepoix (2–3 daily; 45min); Quillan (1 daily Mon–Sat; 1hr 30min).
Lourdes to: Bagnères-de-Bigorre (2–3 daily; 45min); Barèges, usually changing at Pierrefitte-Nestalas (6–7 daily on SNCF coach or SALT bus; 1hr 10min); Cauterets, changing at Pierrefitte-Nestalas (4–7 daily; 50min); Gavarnie, changing at Luz-St-Sauveur (July–Aug 2 daily, otherwise 3 weekly; 1hr 15min); Luz-St-Sauveur (5–7 daily; 45min); Pau (4–8 daily; 1hr 15min).
Oloron-Ste-Marie to: Bedous (4–6 daily on SNCF coach; 30min); Urdos (4–6 daily; 50min); 3–4 continue to Canfranc, Spain.
Pau to: Agen (1–2 daily; 3hr); Bayonne (3–4 daily on TPR; 2hr 15min); Biarritz (2–3 daily on TPR; 2hr 30min); Eaux-Bonnes (3–4 daily on CITRAM; 1hr 15min); Gourette (2 daily on CITRAM; 1hr 30min); Laruns (5–8 daily via Buzy; 1hr 10min); Oloron-Ste-Marie (2–3 daily on CITRAM; 45min); Orthez (2–3 daily; 45min); Salies-de-Béarn (3 daily; 1hr 10min).
Perpignan to: Arles-sur-Tech (6 daily; 1hr 15min); Axat (2 daily, 1hr 40min); Banyuls-sur-Mer (3 daily; 1hr 10min); Céret (14 daily; 55min); Collioure (3 daily; 45min); Latour-de-Carol (2–3 daily; 3hr); Mont-Louis (3–4 daily; 2hr 15min); Prades (7 daily; 1hr); Prats-de-Mollo (6 daily; 1hr 40min); Villefranche-le-Conflent (7 daily; 1hr 15min).
Prades to: Molitg-les-Bains (4–5 daily; 10min).
Quillan to: Carcassonne (2 daily; 1hr 20min); Perpignan (1 daily; 1hr 30min); Quérigut (3 weekly in summer; 1hr 30min).
St-Girons to: Foix (4 daily; 1hr); Toulouse (2–3 daily; 2hr).
St-Jean-de-Luz to: Cambo-les-Bains (2–4 daily; 45min); Espelette (2 daily; 35min); Hendaye (9–17 daily; 20min); Sare (2–3 daily; 30min).
Tarbes to: Auch (2–6 daily; 1hr 40min); Bagnères-de-Bigorre (4–6 daily by SNCF coach; 40min); Lourdes (hourly; 30min); Luz-St-Sauveur (5–7 daily on SALT bus; 1hr); Pau (6 daily; 1hr).

Languedoc

CHAPTER 11 # Highlights

* **Bulls** Whether in the ring or on your plate as a succulent *boeuf à la gardienne*, the *taureaux* of the plains of Languedoc are famous. See p.673

* **Pont du Gard** This graceful aqueduct is an emblem of southern France and a tribute to Roman determination. See p.676

* **St-Guilhem-le-Désert** The ancient Carolingian monastery and the tiny hamlet at its feet present a quintessential Occitan panorama. See p.682

* **Water-jousting** A Setois tradition, in which teams of rowers charge at each other in gondolas. See p.685

* **Carcassonne** The Middle Ages come alive in this walled fortress town. See p.693

* **The Canal du Midi** Cycling, walking or drifting along this tree-shaded canal is the most atmospheric way of savouring France's southwest. See p.695

* **Les Abattoirs** This former slaughterhouse in Toulouse contains an important collection of modern and contemporary art. See p.703

* **Toulouse-Lautrec museum, Albi** The most comprehensive collection of Toulouse-Lautrec's work is in the former Bishop's Palace of his home town. See p.707

▲ Diving at the Pont du Gard

Languedoc

anguedoc is more an idea than a geographical entity. The modern *région* covers only a fraction of the lands where Occitan or the *langue d'oc* – the language of *oc*, the southern Gallo-Latin word for *oui* – once dominated. These stretched south from Bordeaux and Lyon into Spain and northwest Italy. The heartland today is the Bas Languedoc – the coastal plain and dry, stony vine-growing hills between Carcassonne and Nîmes. It's here that the **Occitan** movement has its power base, demanding recognition of its linguistic and cultural distinctiveness. A good part of its character derives from resentment of political domination by remote and alien Paris, aggravated by the area's traditional poverty. In recent times this has been focused on Parisian determination to drag the province into the modern world, with massive tourist development on the coast and the drastic transformation of the cheap wine industry. It is also mixed up in a vague collective folk memory with the brutal repression of the Protestant Huguenots around 1700, the thirteenth-century massacres of the Cathars and the subsequent obliteration of the brilliant *langue d'oc* troubadour tradition. The resulting antipathy towards central authority has made an essentially rural and conservative population vote traditionally for the Left – at least until the elections of 2002, which saw wide support for Le Pen's resurgent Front National. Although a sense of Occitan identity remains strong in the region, it has very little currency as a spoken or literary language, despite the popularity of university-level language courses and the foundation of Occitan-speaking elementary schools.

Nîmes has extensive Roman remains, and there are great swathes of **beach** where – away from the major resorts – you can still find a kilometre or two to yourself. **Montpellier**'s university ensures it has an exciting cultural vibe which outstrips the city's modest size. **Toulouse**, the cultural capital of medieval and modern Languedoc, lies outside the administrative *région* but is included in this chapter and is a high point among numerous other attractions. There are great stretches of dramatic landscape and river gorges, from the **Cévennes** foothills in the east to the **Montagne Noire** and **Corbières** hills in the west. There's ecclesiastical architecture in **Albi** and **St-Guilhem-le-Désert**, and medieval towns at **Cordes** and **Carcassonne**, the latter providing access to the romantic Cathar castles to the south.

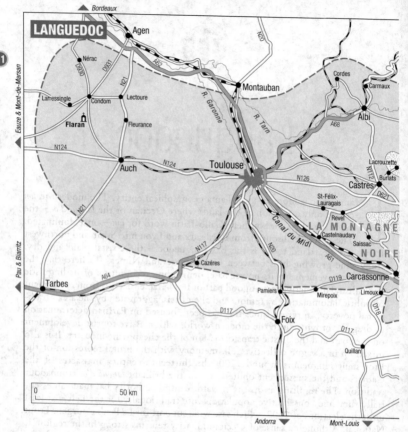

Bordeaux ▼

Andorra ▼   Mont-Louis ▼

Eastern Languedoc

Heading south from Paris via Lyon and the Rhône valley, you can go one of two
ways: east to Provence and the Côte d'Azur – which is what most people do – or
west to **Nîmes**, **Montpellier** and the comparatively untouched Languedoc
coast. Nîmes itself, while not officially in the administrative *région*, makes a good
introduction to the area, a hectic modern town impressive for its Roman past
and some scattered attractions, such as the **Pont du Gard** nearby. **Montpellier**
is also worth a day or two, not so much for historical attractions as for a heady
vibrancy and easy access to the ancient villages, churches and fine scenery of the
upper **Hérault valley**.

This is the heartland of Languedoc, a region that has resolutely resisted the
power of Northern France since the Middle Ages. This resistance came in the form
of medieval Catharism, early-modern Protestantism, its support of the revolutions
of 1789 and 1848, the nineteenth-century revival of Occitan culture, wartime
resistance against the Nazis, and finally a democratic populism which has found its

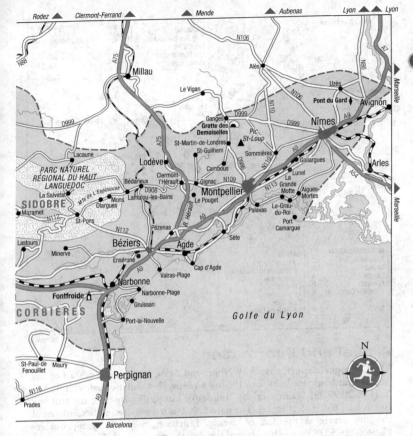

voice both in the extreme left and the extreme right. Such resistance often provoked reprisals on the part of Paris and the north, that together with this region's enduring rural character has helped establish a distinct Languedocian identity expressed as opposition to the status quo.

Nîmes and around

On the border between Provence and Languedoc, the name of **NÎMES** is inescapably linked to two things – denim and Rome. The latter's influence resulted in some of the most extensive Roman remains in Europe, while the former (*de Nîmes*), was first manufactured in the city's textile mills, and exported to the southern USA in the nineteenth century to clothe slaves. The city is worth a visit, in part for the ruins but also to experience its new-found energy and direction, having enlisted the services of a galaxy of architects and designers – including Norman Foster, Jean Nouvel and Philippe Starck – in a bid to wrest southern supremacy from neighbouring Montpellier.

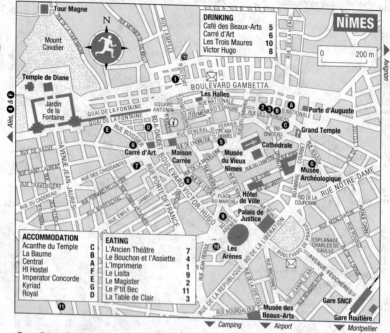

DRINKING

Café des Beaux-Arts	5
Carré d'Art	6
Les Trois Maures	10
Victor Hugo	8

NÎMES

0 — 200 m

ACCOMMODATION

Acanthe du Temple	C
La Baume	B
Central	A
HI Hostel	F
Imperator Concorde	E
Kyriad	G
Royal	D

EATING

L'Ancien Théâtre	7
Le Bouchon et l'Assiette	4
L'Imprimerie	1
Le Lisita	9
Le Magister	2
Le P'tit Bec	11
La Table de Clair	3

Arrival and information

The Camargue **airport**, shared by Nîmes and Arles, lies 20km southeast of the city. A shuttle service links it to the town centre (2–4 daily, timed with flights; ☎04.66.29.27.29; "Gambetta" or "Imperator" stop; €5). By taxi, the trip will cost at least €30 (€35 at night). The **gare SNCF** is ten minutes' walk southeast of the city centre at the end of avenue Feuchères, with the **gare routière** (☎04.66.29.52.00) just behind (access through the train station). The main **tourist office** is at 6 rue Auguste, by the Maison Carrée (Mon–Fri 8.30am–7/8pm, Sat 9am–6.30/7pm & Sun 10am–5/6pm; ☎04.66.58.38.00, ⓦwww.ot-nimes.fr).

Accommodation

There are several decent **hotels** in Nîmes, located in two main zones: a cluster north of the train station and in the old city. An attractive **HI hostel** with tent space can be found on chemin de la Cigale, 2km northwest of the centre (☎04.66.68.03.20, ⓦwww.hinimes.com; July & Aug membership required; Sept–June no curfew; dorm beds €13.35, rooms ➋); take bus #2 direction "Alès/ Villeverte" from the *gare SNCF* to stop "Stade" – the last bus goes at 8pm. The municipal **campsite** (☎04.66.62.05.82, ⓦwww.camping-nimes.com; year-round) is on route de Générac, 5km south of the city centre, beyond the modern Stade Costières and the autoroute.

Acanthe du Temple 1 rue Charles Babout ☎04.66.67.54.61, ⓦwww.hotel-temple .com. A clean and economical hotel, with friendly staff, good amenities and 24hr access. This is one of the Old Town's best bargains. Closed Jan. ➌

La Baume 21 rue Nationale ☎04.66.76.28.42, ⓦwww.new-hotel.com. Located in a tastefully decorated former mansion with an in-house bar and friendly and professional service: slightly pricey, but worth it. Junior suites available. ➑

Central 2 place du Château ℡04.66.67.27.75, ⓦwww.hotel-central.org. Just behind the temple and the Porte d'Auguste, with English-speaking management, this small but cosy hotel features simple but comfortable rooms and also has secure parking. ❷

Imperator Concorde Quai de la Fontaine ℡04.66.21.90.30, ⓦwww.hotel-imperator.com. The city's finest choice, and a favourite of Hemingway's, located by the Jardin de la Fontaine. The luxuriously appointed rooms have a/c and satellite TV, the service is excellent and there is private parking. Prices quadruple during *ferias*. ❾

Kyriad 10 rue Roussy ℡04.66.76.16.20, ⓦwww .hotel-kyriad-nimes.com. One of Nîmes' newer

hotels, the *Kyriad* is a solid two-star option with an impressive range of amenities, including a/c, Canal Plus, wi-fi and a generous breakfast buffet. Its location just outside the Old Town makes street parking a convenient possibility. ❺

Royal 3 bd Alphonse-Daudet ℡04.66.58.28.27, ⓦwww.royalhotel -nimes.com. The *Royal* has a cool Spanish-style decor which draws in passing *toreros*. The rooms are individually decorated with a distinctly Iberian flavour, and the place exudes a certain cool chic. Amenities include HDTV and wi-fi. It's also home to the *Bodeguita* tapas bar. ❹

The City

Most of what you'll want to see is contained within the boulevards de la Libération, Amiral-Courbet, Gambetta and Victor-Hugo, and there's much pleasure to be had from wandering the narrow lanes that they enclose, discovering unexpected squares with fountains and cafés. If you're planning on making the rounds of museums and monuments, opt for the Billet Nîmes Romaine and Forfait Musée (from the tourist office; €9.80 for the Roman ruins, €9 for the museums).

Les Arènes

The focal point of the city is a first-century Roman arena, known as **Les Arènes** (daily: March–May & Sept–Oct 9am–6/6.30pm; June–Aug 9am–7/8pm; Nov–Feb 9.30am–5pm; €4.50), at the junction of boulevards de la Libération and Victor-Hugo. One of the best-preserved Roman arenas in the world, its arcaded two-storey facade conceals massive interior vaulting, riddled with corridors and supporting raked tiers of seats with a capacity of more than twenty thousand spectators, whose staple fare was the blood and guts of gladiatorial combat. When Rome's sway was broken by the barbarian invasions, the arena became a fortress and eventually a slum, home to an incredible two thousand people when it was

The bullfight

Nîmes' great passion is **bullfighting**, and its *ferias* are acknowledged and well attended by both aficionados and fighters at the highest level. The wildest and most famous is the Feria de Pentecôte, which lasts five days over the Whitsun weekend. A couple of a million people crowd into the town (hotel rooms need to be booked a year in advance), and seemingly every city native opens a bodega at the bottom of the garden for dispensing booze. There are *corridas*, which end with the killing of the bull, *courses* where *cocards* are snatched from the bull's head, and semi-amateur *courses libres* when a small posse of bulls is run through the streets and the daring try to snatch the *cocards* from their heads. In 1996, Nîmes witnessed the acclamation of the first-ever woman matador, Cristina Sanchez, though she took early retirement in 1999, blaming the profession's machismo. Recently events have been marked by small but vocal protests and in 2006 several organizers of the local *tauromachie* world were injured by letter bombs. Two other *ferias* take place: one at carnival time in February, when the inflatable roof of the Arènes is pulled over for protection from the weather; the other in the third week of September at grape-harvest time, the Feria des Vendanges. The **tourist office** can supply full details and advise about accommodation if you want to visit at *feria* time.

cleared in the early 1800s. Today it has recovered something of its former role, with passionate summer crowds still turning out for some blood-letting – Nîmes has the premier bullfighting scene outside Spain.

The Hôtel de Ville and museums

Just to the north of the Roman arena lies the warren of narrow streets that makes up Nîmes' compact Old Town. Among the mostly seventeenth- and eighteenth-century mansions you'll find the **Hôtel de Ville**, set between rue Dorée and rue des Greffes, the interior of which has been redesigned by the architect Jean-Michel Wilmotte to combine high-tech design with classical stone. Look out for the stuffed crocodiles suspended from chains above the stairwells – a gift from wealthy and contented eighteenth-century burghers. At the eastern end of rue des Greffes is the combined **Musée Archéologique** and **Muséum d'Histoire Naturelle** (Tues–Sun 10am–6pm; free); housed in a seventeenth-century Jesuit chapel at no. 13, they are full of Roman bits and bobs, assorted curios, and stuffed animals.

The Cathédrale Notre-Dame-et-St-Castor and Porte d'Auguste

When banned from public office, the Protestants put their energy into making money. The results of their efforts can be seen in the seventeenth- and eighteenth-century *hôtels* they built in the streets around the cathedral – rues de l'Aspic, Chapitre, Dorée and Grand'Rue, among others. At the end of Grand'Rue, the former bishop's palace is now the **Musée du Vieux Nîmes** (Tues–Sun 10am–6pm; free), with displays of Renaissance furnishings and decor and documents to do with local history. Opposite, the **Cathédrale Notre-Dame-et-St-Castor** sports a handsome sculpted frieze on the west front, illustrating the story of Adam and Eve, and a pediment inspired by the Maison Carrée. It's practically the only existing medieval building in town, as most were destroyed in the turmoil that followed the Michelade, the St Michael's Day massacre of Catholic clergy and notables by Protestants in 1567. Despite brutal repression in the wake of the Camisard insurrection of 1702, Nîmes was, and remains, a dogged Protestant stronghold. Apart from that, the cathedral is of little interest, having been seriously mutilated in the Wars of Religion and significantly altered in the nineteenth century. The author Alphonse Daudet was born in its shadow, as was Jean Nicot – a doctor, no less – who introduced tobacco into France from Portugal in 1560 and gave his name to the world's most widely consumed drug.

North of the cathedral stands Nîmes' surviving Roman gate, **Porte d'Auguste** at the end of rue Nationale, the former Roman main street. Already a prosperous city on the Via Domitia, the main Roman road from Italy to Spain, Nîmes did especially well under Augustus. He gave the city its walls, remnants of which surface here and there, and its gates, as the inscription on the Porte records. He is also responsible for the chained crocodile, which figures on Nîmes' coat of arms. The device was copied from an Augustan coin struck to commemorate his defeat of Antony and Cleopatra after he settled veterans of that campaign on the surrounding land.

The Maison Carrée and the Carré d'Art

Meandering west from the cathedral are the narrow lanes of the medieval city, at the heart of which is the delightful **place aux Herbes**, with two or three cafés and bars and a fine twelfth-century house on the corner of rue de la Madeleine. Heading west along **rue de l'Horloge** will take you to the city's other famous landmark, the **Maison Carrée** (daily: March & Oct 10am–6pm; April, May & Sept 10am–6.30pm; June–Aug 10am–7/8pm; Nov–Feb 10am–1pm & 2–4.30pm;

€4.50), a neat, jewel-like temple celebrated for its integrity and harmonic proportions. Built in 5 AD, it's dedicated to the adopted sons of Emperor Augustus – all part of the business of inflating the imperial personality cult. No surprise, then, that Napoleon, with his love of flummery, took it as the model for the Madeleine church in Paris. The temple stands in its own small square opposite rue Auguste, where the Roman forum used to be, with pieces of Roman masonry scattered around. On the west side of place de la Maison Carrée, there's a gleaming example of the architectural boldness characteristic of the city, the **Carré d'Art**, by British architect Norman Foster. In spite of its size, this box of glass, aluminium and concrete sits modestly among the ancient roofs of Nîmes, its slender portico echoing that of the Roman temple opposite. Light pours in through the walls and roof, giving it a grace and weightlessness that makes it not in the least incongruous. Housed within the Carré d'Art is the excellent **Musée d'Art Contemporain** (Tues–Sun 10am–6pm; €5), containing an impressive collection of French and Western European art from the last four decades. There's a roof-terrace café at the top, overlooking the Maison Carrée.

Beyond the Old Town

Perhaps the most refreshing thing you can do in Nîmes is head east of the centre to the **Jardin de la Fontaine**, France's first public garden, created in 1750. Behind the formal entrance, where fountains, nymphs and formal trees enclose the **Temple de Diane**, steps climb the steep wooded slope, adorned with grottoes and nooks and artful streams, to the **Tour Magne** (daily: March & Oct 9.30am–1pm & 2–6pm; April, May & Sept 9.30am–6.30pm; June–Aug 9am–7/8pm; Nov–Feb 9.30am–1pm & 2–4.30pm; €2.70). The 32m tower, left over from Augustus's city walls, gives terrific views over the surrounding country – as far, it is claimed, as the Pic du Canigou on the edge of the Pyrenees. At the foot of the slope flows the gloriously green and shady **Canal de la Fontaine**, built to supplement the rather unsteady supply of water from the *fontaine*, the Nemausus spring, whose presence in a dry, limestone landscape gave Nîmes its existence.

The city's remaining sights lie south of the Arènes. The **Musée des Beaux-Arts**, in rue de la Cité-Foulc (Tues–Sun 10am–6pm; €5), prides itself on a huge Gallo-Roman mosaic showing the Marriage of Admetus, but is otherwise pretty ordinary. Further afield, out on the southern edge of town, you'll find examples of the revolutionary civic architecture for which Nîmes was once famed. Jean Nouvel's pseudo-Mississippi-steamboat housing project, named **Nemausus** after the deity of the local spring that gave Nîmes its name, squats off the Arles road behind the *gare SNCF*, and the magnificent sports stadium, the **Stades des Costières**, by Vittorio Gregotti, looms close to the autoroute along the continuation of avenue Jean-Jaurès.

Eating and drinking

The best places to hang out for **coffee and drinks** are the numerous little squares scattered through the Old Town: place de la Maison-Carrée, place du Marché and place aux Herbes (breakfast here early at the *Café des Beaux-Arts* to watch the sun creep up behind the cathedral tower). *Les Trois Maures*, in boulevard des Arènes, is a classic Nîmes café. For a quiet evening, head to the *Carré d'Art* piano bar on rue Gaston-Bossier, near the canal and the post-modern place d'Assas, while the *Victor Hugo*, a music-bar at 36 bd Victor-Hugo attracts a younger, livelier crowd.

For **eating**, boulevard de la Libération and boulevard Amiral-Courbet harbour a stock of reasonably priced brasseries and pizzerias, and the squares are full of possibilities.

Restaurants

L'Ancien Théâtre 4 rue Racine ☎04.66.21.30.75. Just a 5min stroll west from the Maison Carrée, with solid Gard cuisine, and home-made breads and pastries. *Menus* from €18. Closed Sat lunch, Sun, Mon & early Aug.

Le Bouchon et l'Assiette 5bis rue de Sauve ☎04.66.62.02.93. Come here for elaborate *gastronomique* variations on traditional *tarnaise* themes. Very reasonably priced, with *menus* from €17 to €45. Closed Tues & Wed, part Jan & most of Aug.

L'Imprimerie 3 rue Balore ☎04.66.29.57.16. A favourite of local artists, this former printing shop features an ever-changing *carte* drawing on influences as far off as North Africa. Mon–Fri, with tapas till 10pm on Fri.

Le Lisita 2b bd des Arènes ☎04.66.67.29.15. Hands-down, the city's best *gastronomique*, run by two former staff of Michel Roux's famous London restaurant Le Gavroche. *Menus* start from as little as €35.

Le Magister 5 rue Nationale ☎04.66.76.11.00. Daring experimentation is the order of the day at this good *gastronomique* restaurant. The €30 *menu* is a solid option, and includes wine; otherwise à la carte is pricey. Closed Sat lunch & Sun, part of Feb, July & Aug.

Le P'tit Bec 87bis rue de la République ☎04.66.38.05.83. The best mid-range place for typical Gardoise cuisine. The dining room is pleasant and airy and the service is friendly. Closed Sun eve & Mon.

La Table de Clair Place des Esclafidous ☎04.66.67.55.61. This funky and unprepossessing restaurant features eclectic cuisine; everything is good. The house speciality is local beef, grilled and smothered in Cassis mustard sauce. *Menus* at €19 & €32. Closed Mon, Wed lunch & Sun eve.

The Pont du Gard

Some twenty kilometres northeast from Nîmes, the **Pont du Gard** is the greatest surviving stretch of a 50km-long Roman aqueduct built in the middle of the first century AD to supply fresh water to the city. With just a 17m difference in altitude between start and finish, the aqueduct was quite an achievement, running as it does over hill and dale, through a tunnel, along the top of a wall, into trenches and over rivers; the Pont du Gard carries it over the River Gardon. Today the bridge is a UNESCO World Heritage Site and something of a tourist trap, but is nonetheless a supreme piece of engineering and a brilliant combination of function and aesthetics; it made the impressionable Rousseau wish he'd been born Roman.

Three tiers of **arches** span the river, with the covered water conduit on the top, rendered with a special plaster waterproofed with a paint apparently based on fig juice. A visit here used to be a must for French journeymen masons on their traditional tour of the country, and many of them have left their names and home towns carved on the stonework. Markings made by the original builders are still visible on individual stones in the arches, such as "FR S III – frons sinistra", front side left no. 3. The Pont du Gard has recently undergone a massive restoration programme and now features an extensive multimedia complex, the **Site Pont du Gard**, which includes a state-of-the-art **musuem** (daily 9.30am–5/7pm; €7; ⓦ www.pontdugard.fr), botanical **gardens** and a range of regular children's activities. With the swimmable waters of the Gardon and ample picnic possibilities available, you could easily spend a day here.

Uzès

Seventeen kilometres further on, near the start of the aqueduct and served by daily buses from Nîmes, **UZÈS** is a lovely old town perched on a hill above the River Alzon. Half a dozen medieval towers – the most fetching is the windowed Pisa-like **Tour Fenestrelle**, tacked onto the much later cathedral – rise above its tiled roofs and narrow lanes of Renaissance and Neoclassical houses. The latter were the residences of the seventeenth- and eighteenth-century local bourgeoisie, who had grown rich, like their fellow Protestants in

Nîmes, on textiles. From the mansion of Le Portalet, with its view out over the valley, walk past the Renaissance church of **St-Étienne** and into the medieval place aux Herbes, where there's a Saturday morning market, and up the arcaded rue de la République. The Gide family used to live off the square, the young André spending summer vacations with his granny here. To the right of rue de la République is the **castle of Le Duché** (1hr 30min guided tours: daily: July & Aug 10am–12.30pm & 2–6.30pm; Sept–June 10am–noon & 2–6pm; €15), still inhabited by the same family a thousand years on, and dominated by its original keep, the **Tour Bermonde** (tower only €10). Today, there are guided tours around the castle and exhibits of local history and vintage cars. Opposite, the courtyard of the eighteenth-century **Hôtel de Ville** holds summer concerts.

For details of these and other summer events, including more bull-running, consult the **tourist office** in place Albert-1er on boulevard Gambetta (June–Sept Mon–Fri 9am–6/7pm, Sat & Sun 10am–1pm & 2–5pm; Oct–May Mon–Fri 9am–12.30pm & 2–6pm, Sat 10am–1pm; ☎04.66.22.68.88, ⓦwww.uzes-tourisme.com). The **gare routière** (☎04.66.22.00.58) is further west on avenue de la Libération. Should you need **accommodation**, head for the friendly *Hostellerie Provençale* in two old row houses at 1 rue Grand Bourgade, south of the church of St-Étienne (☎04.66.22.11.06, ⓦwww.hostellerieprovencale.com; ⑥), or the attractively renovated ⚞ *La Taverne* (☎04.66.22.13.10, Ⓔlataverne.uzes @orange.fr; ④), a small and welcoming hotel with good amenities (including wi-fi) set behind the tourist office at 4 rue Xavier-Sigalon, and with a good *terroir* restaurant up the road at no. 7 (€20). The town's *de luxe* option is the *Général d'Entraigues*, 8 rue de la Calade (☎04.66.22.32.68, ⓦwww.hoteldentraigues .com; ⑥), in a converted fifteenth-century mansion opposite the cathedral. Alternatively, there's a municipal **campsite** off avenue Maxime Pascal (☎04.66.22.38.55; mid-June to mid-Sept) on the Bagnols-sur-Cèze road running northeast of town.

Montpellier and around

A thousand years of trade and intellectual activity have made **MONTPELLIER** a teeming, energetic city. Benjamin of Tudela, the tireless twelfth-century Jewish traveller, reported its streets crowded with traders from every corner of Egypt, Greece, Gaul, Spain, Genoa and Pisa. After the king of Mallorca sold it to France in 1349 it became an important university town in the 1500s, counting the radical satirist François Rabelais among its alumni. Periodic setbacks, including almost total destruction for its Protestantism in 1622, and depression in the wine trade in the early years of the twentieth century, have done little to dent its progress. Today it vies with Toulouse for the title of the most dynamic city in the south. The reputation of its university especially, founded in the thirteenth century and most famous for its medical school, is a long-standing one: more than sixty thousand students still set the intellectual and cultural tone of the city, the average age of whose residents is said to be just 25. In many senses the best time to visit is during the academic year (Oct–June), when the city teems with students looking for stimulation of every kind.

Montpellier is renowned for its **cultural life**, and hosts a number of annual **festivals**, notably Montpellier Danse (late June to mid-July), and for music, Le Festival de Radio-France et de Montpellier (second half of July). The tourist office provides information about programmes and booking.

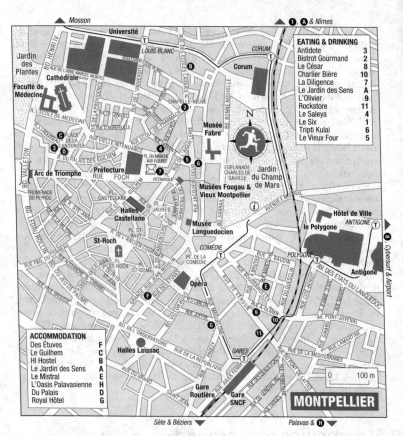

Map labels (Montpellier):

EATING & DRINKING
Antidote	3
Bistrot Gourmand	2
Le César	8
Charlier Bière	10
La Diligence	7
Le Jardin des Sens	A
L'Olivier	9
Rockstore	11
Le Saleya	4
Le Six	1
Tripti Kulai	6
Le Vieux Four	5

ACCOMMODATION
Des Étuves	F
Le Guilhem	C
HI Hostel	B
Le Jardin des Sens	A
Le Mistral	E
L'Oasis Palavasienne	H
Du Palais	D
Royal Hôtel	G

MONTPELLIER

Arrival and information

The **gare SNCF** (no left luggage) and **gare routière** are next to each other at the opposite end of rue Maguelone from the central place de la Comédie. The **airport**, Montpellier-Méditerranée (montpellier.aeroport.fr), is 8km to the southeast beside the Étang de Mauguio; from here a **navette** (timed for flights; 15min; €5.50) runs to the stop on rue de Crète (by the Léon Blum tramstop); it will cost you €14–30 by **taxi** depending on the time of day and traffic conditions. Much of the city centre is pedestrianized, but you can street park outside the centre and there are many well-signed municipal garages.

The **tourist office** (Mon–Fri 9.30am–7.30pm, Sat 9.30am–6pm, Sun 9.30am–1pm & 2.30–6pm; ☎04.67.60.60.60, ⓦwww.ot-montpellier.fr), which has money exchange facilities, lies at the east end of place de la Comédie, opposite the Polygone shopping centre. They also sell the one-, two- and three-day City Card, which includes public transport, free admission to many sites and other discounts. TAM **city buses** run between the stations and outer districts as far as Palavas (€1.30; day ticket for €3.20). The green transport policies of Montpellier have also resulted in the construction of a **tramway**, sweeping across town from northwest to southeast, as well as over 120km of **bike paths** running throughout the city and to the sea.

For the best route out into the country of the Bas Languedoc from Montpellier take the N109 to **Lodève** (regular bus service). This takes you into an out-of-the-way corner of Languedoc, best for its relatively untouristed villages, as well as excellent hiking and rafting opportunities.

Accommodation

Most hotel **accommodation** is conveniently concentrated in the streets between the train station and place de la Comédie, or in the nearby centre of the Old Town. There's a well-equipped **hostel** in a renovated old building in impasse Petite Corraterie, off rue des Écoles Laïques (☎04.67.60.32.22, ⓦwww.fuaj.org/Montpellier; bus #6 "Ursulines"; closed part Dec; dorm beds €16.70 including breakfast), plus several **campsites** around Montpellier, particularly in nearby Palavas (bus #28); the most central and expensive is *L'Oasis Palavasienne* (☎04.67.15.11.61, ⓦwww.oasis-palavasienne.com; April to mid-Oct), just south of town on the D21 (to Palavas; bus #28), which also has a waterpark.

Des Étuves 24 rue des Étuves ☎04.67.60.78.19, ⓦwww.hoteldesetuves.fr. Simple, spotless rooms in the south of the old city, all with en-suite bathrooms, free wi-fi and TV. ❷

Le Guilhem 18 rue Jean-Jacques Rousseau ☎04.67.52.90.90, ⓦwww.leguilhem.com. Beautifully restored sixteenth-century townhouse, with cheerful rooms mostly overlooking quiet gardens, and a sunny breakfast terrace. Free wi-fi. A good alternative to the *Du Palais*, if full. ❻

🏃 **Le Jardin des Sens** 11 av St-Lazare ☎04.67.79.63.38, ⓦwww.jardindessens .com. The best of the upper-bracket hotels, and the epitome of restrained and tasteful luxury, the four-star *Le Jardin* boasts a swimming pool, elegant rooms and one of the region's most acclaimed restaurants. ❾

Le Mistral 25 rue Boussairolles ☎04.67.58.45.25, ⓦwww.hotel-le-mistral.com. Comfortable and clean, an excellent economy-range option, offering satellite TV, free wi-fi and garage parking (€5 extra). ❸

Du Palais 3 rue du Palais ☎04.67.60.47.38, ⓦwww.hoteldupalais-montpellier.fr. Tastefully renovated eighteenth-century mansion on the west side of the Old Town, blending modern and antique touches. Cosy rooms, most en suite. An excellent mid-range option. Free wi-fi. ❹

Royal Hôtel 8 rue Maguelone ☎04.67.92.13.36, ⓦwww.royalhotelmontpellier.com. Good amenities (including Canal Plus) in this three-star hotel between the Comédie and the *gare*, with an old-world ambience. ❺

The City

Montpellier's city centre – the **Old Town** – is small, compact and architecturally homogeneous, full of charm and life, except in July and August when the students are on holiday and everyone else is at the beach. The place is almost entirely pedestrianized, so you can walk the narrow streets without looking anxiously over your shoulder.

Place de la Comédie and the Old Town

At the hub of the city's life, joining the old part to its newer additions, is **place de la Comédie**, or "L'Oeuf" ("the egg") to the initiated. This colossal oblong square, paved with cream-coloured marble, has a fountain at its centre and cafés either side. One end is closed by the **Opéra**, an ornate nineteenth-century theatre; the other opens onto the **Esplanade**, a beautiful tree-lined promenade that snakes its way to the **Corum concert hall**, dug into the hillside and topped off in pink granite, with splendid views from the roof. South of the Corum, the city's most trumpeted museum, the **Musée Fabre** (Tues, Thurs, Fri & Sun 10am–6pm, Wed 1–9pm & Sat 11am–6pm; €6), has reopened after a major renovation. Its huge collection features seventeenth- to nineteenth-century European painting, including works by Delacroix, Zurbaran, Raphael, Jan van Steen and Veronese, as well as ceramics and contemporary art.

From the north side of L'Oeuf, **rue de la Loge** and **rue Foch**, opened in the 1880s in Montpellier's own Haussmann-izing spree, slice through the heart of the old city. Either side of them, a maze of narrow lanes slopes away to the encircling modern boulevards. Few buildings survive from before the 1622 siege, but the city's busy bourgeoisie quickly made up for the loss, proclaiming their financial power through austere seventeenth- and eighteenth-century mansions. Known as "Lou Clapas" (rubble), the area is rapidly being restored and gentrified. It's a pleasure to wander through and come upon secretive little squares like the places St-Roch, St-Ravy and de la Canourgue.

First left off rue de la Loge is **Grande-Rue Jean-Moulin**, where Moulin, hero of the Resistance, lived at no. 21. To the left, at no. 32, the present-day chamber of commerce is located in one of the finest eighteenth-century *hôtels*, the Hôtel St-Côme, originally built as a demonstration operating theatre for medical students. On the opposite corner, rue de l'Argenterie forks up to **place Jean-Jaurès**. This square is a nodal point in the city's student life: early on fine evenings you get the impression that half the population is sitting here and in the adjacent place du Marché-aux-Fleurs. Through the Gothic doorway of no. 10 is the so-called palace of the kings of Aragon, named after the city's thirteenth-century rulers. Also on the square, the **Musée de l'Histoire de Montpellier** (Tues–Sat 10.30am–12.30pm & 1.30–6pm; €1.50), housed in an ancient crypt, offers reconstructions of the city's past. Close by is the **Halles Castellane**, a graceful, iron-framed market hall.

A short walk from place Jean-Jaurès, the lively little rue des Trésoriers-de-France has one of the best seventeenth-century houses in the city, the **Hôtel Lunaret**, at no. 5, while round the block on rue Jacques-Coeur you'll find the **Musée Languedocien** (Mon–Sat 2/2.30pm–5.30/6pm; €6), which houses a mixed collection of Greek, Egyptian and other antiquities.

Jardin des Plantes and around

On the hill at the end of rue Foch, from which the royal artillery bombarded the Protestants in 1622, the formal gardens of the **Promenade du Peyrou** look out across the city and away to the Pic St-Loup, which dominates the hinterland behind Montpellier, with the distant smudge of the Cévennes beyond. At the farther side a swagged and pillared water-tower marks the end of an eighteenth-century aqueduct modelled on the Pont du Gard. Beneath the grand sweep of its double-tiered arches is a daily fruit and veg market and a huge Saturday **flea market**. At the city end of the promenade, the vainglorious **Arc de Triomphe** shows Louis XIV as Hercules, stomping on the Austrian eagle and English lion, forcefully reminding the locals of his victory over their Protestant "heresy".

Lower down the hill, on boulevard Henri-IV, the lovely but slightly run-down **Jardin des Plantes** (July & Aug noon–8pm; Sept–June 2–5pm; free), with avenues of exotic trees, is France's oldest botanical garden, founded in 1593. Across the road is the long-suffering **cathedral**, with its massive porch, sporting a patchwork of styles from the fourteenth to the nineteenth centuries. Inside is a memorial to the bishop of Montpellier, who sided with the half-million destitute vine-growers who came to demonstrate against their plight in 1907 and were fired on by government troops. Above the cathedral, in the university's prestigious medical school on rue de l'École-de-Médecine, the **Musée Atger** (Mon, Wed & Fri 1.30–5.45pm; free) has a distinguished academic collection of French and Italian drawings.

Antigone

South of place de la Comédie stretches the controversial quarter of **Antigone**, a chain of post-modern squares and open spaces designed to provide a mix of fair-rent housing and offices, aligned along a monumental axis from the place du Nombre-d'Or, through place du Millénaire, to the glassed-in arch of the Hôtel de la Région. It's more interesting in scale and design than most attempts at urban renewal, but it has failed to attract the crowds away from the place de la Comédie and is often deserted. The enclosed spaces in particular work well, with their theatrical references to classical architecture, like oversized cornices and columns supporting only sky. The more open spaces are, however, disturbing, with something dystopian and inhuman about their scale and blandness.

Eating, drinking and entertainment

Montpellier's year-round vitality supports a variety of **restaurants** and **bars** to suit all budgets and tastes. **Cafés** line every square while some of the more expensive restaurants use the city's ancient interiors to stunning effect. And Montpellier's youthful population ensures an energetic bar and **nightclub** scene right through to the early hours.

There's always plenty of **drinking** activity in the place de la Comédie, place du Marché-aux-Fleurs and place Jean-Jaurès. Two places that stand out are *Charlier Bière*, a grungy beer bar at 22 rue Olivier, and *Antidote*, a snappy cocktail joint on place de la Canourgue, which attracts the arty set. The old perennial for late-night dancing and live gigs is the *Rockstore*, near the station at 20 rue de Verdun (Ⓦwww .rockstore.fr).

In addition to its clubs, bars and live music, Montpellier has a very lively **theatre scene**, as well as a tradition of engaging *café-littéraires* on a variety of themes; *Le César* at 17 place du Nombre-d'Or (℡04.67.20.27.02) hosts two such gatherings, the *café des femmes* and the *café des arts* – check for days and times. For what's on at the various venues, look for posters around town or check the free weekly listings magazines, *Le Sortir* and *Olé*. The best central food **markets** are Halles Castellane, on rue de la Loge, and Laissac, place Laissac (daily 7.30am–1pm).

Restaurants and cafés

Bistrot Gourmand 7 place de la Chapelle Neuve ℡04.67.66.08.09. Excellent-value Languedocian cuisine (both inland and coastal varieties) with a wonderful shaded terrace. The *pâtés de canard* are particularly notable, and the wine list is excellent. *Menus* €12 at lunch and €18 at dinner. Closed off season Sun & Wed.

La Diligence 2 place Pétrarque ℡04.67.66.12.21. Atmospheric vaulted medieval setting for innovative dishes infused with Asian influence. *Menus* are €36–60 (€20 at lunch), and a good-value dip into the finest French cuisine. Closed Sat lunch, Sun & Mon.

Le Jardin des Sens 11 av St-Lazare ℡04.67.79.63.38. One of the top restaurants in Languedoc and universally acclaimed as Montpellier's best. Excellent *terroir*-based creations of the famed Pourcel brothers, served in elegant surroundings. *Menus* €50–190. Closed Sun, Mon & Wed lunch.

L'Olivier 12 rue Aristide-Olivier ℡04.67.92.86.28. Pretty little restaurant north of the station offering excellent-value and imaginative cuisine, such as salmon with oyster tartare, and leg of rabbit stuffed with wild mushrooms. *Menus* €32–47. Closed Sun, Mon and Aug.

Le Saleya Place du Marché aux Fleurs ℡04.67.60.53.92. In fine weather, join the locals at the outdoor tables to feast on a daily selection of market-fresh fish and regional fare for €12. A long-standing Montpellier institution. Closed Sun in rainy weather.

Le Six 55bis rue de la Cavalerie ℡04.99.58.18.91. Elegant but modern restaurant featuring a range of dishes, from fresh shellfish to specialities of Aveyron. Open for dinner till 11.30pm with *menus* from €15 to €25.50 and a lunch special for €10. Closed Sat & Sun lunch.

Tripti Kulai 20 rue Jacques-Coeur. Quirky, friendly vegetarian/vegan restaurant. Dishes with oriental flair, including a good choice of salads, from €9. The lassis and home-made chai are superb. Closed Sun.

Le Vieux Four 59 rue de l'Aiguillerie ℡04.67.60.55.95. Carnivores will love this cosy, candlelit place specializing in *grillades au feu de bois* – meats roasted on an open spit. The *andouillette* (offal sausage) is excellent. *Menus* €14–25. Eves only; closed Sun in summer.

Listings

Bike rental Montpellier's municipal *Vélomagg* (Ⓦ www.tam-way.com) stations around town rent bikes for 4 hours (€1) and by the day (€2).
Books English books at Book in Bar, 8 rue du Bras de Fer, and Book Shop, 4 rue de l'Université.
Health Ⓣ 04.67.22.81.67 or 15; Centre Hospitalier de Montpellier, 555 rte de Ganges (Ⓣ 04.67.33.93.02) – take bus #16 from the *gare* to "Route de Ganges" or the tram to "Hôpital Lapeyronie".
Internet There are lots of cybercafés around town, including Cybersurf, 22 place du Millénaire in

Antigone (Mon–Fri 8am–9pm, Sat & Sun 10am–6pm).
Post office The main office is on place Rondelet, 34000 Montpellier (Mon–Fri 9am–7pm, Sat 9am–noon).
Shopping The most convenient place is the Polygone mall, which contains FNAC and Galeries Lafayette stores.
Swimming The nearest beaches for a dip are at Palavas (tram direction "Odysseum" to Port Marianne, then bus #28), but the best are slightly to the west of the town.

St-Guilhem-le-Désert and the caves

The small town of **Gignac** lies amid vineyards 30km west of Montpellier. It is here that the highway (and buses) turn off for the glorious abbey and village of **ST-GUILHEM-LE-DÉSERT**, which lies in a side ravine, 6km further north up the Hérault beyond the famed medieval Pont du Diable. A ruined castle spikes the ridge above, and the ancient tiled houses of the village ramble down the banks of the rushing Verdus, which is everywhere channelled into carefully tended gardens. The grand focus is the tenth- to twelfth-century **abbey church** (daily 8am–12.10pm & 2.30–6.20pm; free), founded at the beginning of the ninth century by St Guilhem, comrade-in-arms of Charlemagne. The church is a beautiful and atmospheric building, though architecturally impoverished by the dismantling and sale of its cloister – now in New York – in the nineteenth century. It stands on place de la Liberté, surrounded by honey-coloured houses and arcades with traces of Romanesque and Renaissance domestic styles in some of the windows. The interior of the church is plain and somewhat severe compared to the warm colours of the exterior, best seen from rue Cor-de-Nostra-Dama/Font-du-Portal, where you get the classic view of the perfect apse.

Along the way from Gignas, cave enthusiasts will enjoy the **Grotte de Clamouse** (Feb–Nov daily 10.30am–5/7pm; €8.50). This extensive and beautiful stalactite cave is entered along a subterranean river and opens up into three expansive grottoes. North of St-Guilhem, through dramatic river gorges almost as far as Ganges, you reach the **Grotte des Demoiselles** (tours: March & Oct daily 10 & 11am & 2–4.30pm; April–June & Sept daily 10am–5.30pm; July & Aug daily 10am–6pm; Nov–Feb Mon–Fri 2–4pm, Sat & Sun 10 & 11am & 2–4pm; €8.90), the most spectacular of the region's many caves: a set of vast cathedral-like caverns hung with stalactites descending with millennial slowness to meet the limpid waters of eerily still pools. Located deep inside the mountain, it's reached by funicular (hourly departures).

In season the village of St-Guilhem is on every tour operator's route, making early mornings and late afternoons better for visiting. The best **hotel** is *Le Guilhaume d'Orange* (Ⓣ 04.67.57.24.53, Ⓦ www.guilhaumedorange.com; ❹), while budget travellers should head to the English-speaking *Gîte de la Tour* (Ⓣ 04.67.57.34.00; ❶). The nearest **campsite** is *Le Moulin de Siau* (Ⓣ 04.67.57.51.08, Ⓦ www.camping-moulin-de-siau.com; June to early Sept), near Aniane on the road back down to Gignac.

Lodève

Another 24km west of Gignac, at the point where the swift A75 autoroute brings heavy traffic down from Clermont-Ferrand sits **LODÈVE**, a town at the confluence of the Lergues and Soulondre rivers. In addition to being a pleasant, old-fashioned place to pause on your way up to Le Caylar or La Couvertoirade, it also has an art museum that puts on world-class temporary exhibitions. The **cathedral** – a stop on the pilgrim route to Santiago de Compostela – is also worth a look, as is the unusual World War I **Monument aux Morts**, in the adjacent park, by local sculptor Paul Dardé. This spooky *mise en scène* of civilians mourning a soldier fallen on the field is a departure from the usual stiff commemorations of the "Morts pour la France". More of his work is displayed at the town **museum** in the Hôtel Fleury (Tues–Sun 9.30am–noon & 2–6pm; €3.50) and the **Halle Dardé** (daily 9am–7pm; free) in the place du Marché.

The **tourist office** is at 7 place de la République (Mon–Fri 9.30am–noon & 2.30–6pm, Sat 9.30am–noon; ☏04.67.88.86.44, ⓦwww.lodeve.com), next door to the **gare routière**, where you can catch buses to Montpellier, Béziers, Millau, Rodez and St-Affrique. The best place to **stay** in town is the *Hôtel du Nord* (☏04.67.44.10.08, ⓦwww.hotellodeve.com; ❸) at 18 bd de la Liberté, or the family-run *Hôtel de la Paix* (☏04.67.44.07.46, ⓦwww.hotel-dela-paix.com; closed Jan & Feb; ❸) on 11 bd Montalangue. There's a big **market** on Saturdays, and local farmers bring in their produce three times a week in summer.

The Languedoc coast

On the face of it, the **Languedoc coast** isn't particularly enticing, lined with bleak beaches and treeless strands, often irritatingly windswept and cut off from the sea by marshy *étangs* (lagoons). The area does, however, have long hours of sunshine, 200km of only sporadically populated sand and relatively unpolluted water. Resorts – mostly geared towards families who settle in for a few weeks at a time – have sprung up, sometimes engulfing once quiet fishing towns, but there's still enough unexploited territory to make this coast a good getaway from the crowds, and many of the old towns have managed to sustain their character and traditions despite the summer onslaught.

La Grande-Motte, Le Grau-du-Roi and Aigues-Mortes

The oldest of the new resorts, on the fringes of the Camargue, **LA GRANDE-MOTTE** is a 1960s vintage beach-side Antigone – a "futuristic" planned community which has aged as gracefully as the bean bag and eight-track tape. In summer, its seaside and streets are crowded with semi-naked bodies; in winter, it's a depressing, wind-battered place with few permanent residents. If you plan on **staying**, you could try *Camping le Garden* (☏04.67.56.50.09, ⓦwww.legarden.fr; March–Oct), which offers excellent facilities a couple of minutes' walk from the beach. The most appealing among the town's dozen or so near-identical **hotels** is the *Azur Bord de Mer* (☏04.67.56.56.00, ⓦwww.hotelazur.net; ❹), set dramatically on the extremity of the town's quay.

A little way east are Port-Camargue, with a sprawling, modern marina, and **LE GRAU-DU-ROI**, which manages to retain something of its character as a working fishing port. Tourist traffic still has to give way every afternoon at 4.30pm when the swing bridge opens and lets in the trawlers to unload the day's catch onto the quayside, from where it's whisked off to auction – *la criée* – now conducted largely by electronic means rather than shouting. For a reasonable place to **stay**, try the *Bellevue et d'Angleterre*, quai Colbert (℡04.66.51.40.75, Ⓦwww .hotelbellevueetdangleterre.com; closed Jan; ❹).

Eight kilometres inland lies the appealingly named town of **AIGUES-MORTES** ("dead waters"), built as a fortress port by Louis IX in the thirteenth century for his departure on the Seventh Crusade. Its massive walls and towers remain virtually intact. Outside the ramparts, amid drab modern development, flat salt pans lend a certain otherworldly appeal, but inside all is geared to the tourist. If you visit, consider a climb up the **Tour de Constance** on the northwest corner of the town walls (daily: May–Aug 10am–7pm; Sept–April 10am–5pm; €7), where Camisard women were imprisoned (Marie Durand was incarcerated here for 38 years), and a walk along the wall, where you can gaze out over the weird mist-shrouded flats of the Camargue.

Sète

Some 28km southwest of Montpellier, twenty minutes away by train, **SÈTE** has been an important port for three hundred years. The upper part of the town straddles the slopes of the Mont St-Clair, which overlooks the vast Bassin de Thau, a breeding ground for mussels and oysters, while the lower part is intersected by waterways lined with tall terraces and seafood restaurants. It has a lively workaday bustle in addition to its tourist activity, at its height during the summer *joutes nautiques* (see box opposite).

Arrival, information and accommodation

The **gare routière** is awkwardly placed on quai de la République, and the **gare SNCF** is further out still on quai Maréchal-Joffre – though it is on the main bus route, which circles Mont St-Clair (last bus about 7pm). **Ferries** for Morocco (1–2 weekly) and Mallorca (1–3 weekly) depart from the *gare maritime* at 4 quai d'Alger (℡04.67.46.68.00). The **tourist office**, at 60 Grand'Rue Mario-Roustan (April–Oct daily 9.30am–6/7.30pm; Nov–March Mon–Fri 9.30am–6pm, Sat & Sun 9.30am–12.30pm & 2–5.30pm; ℡04.67.74.71.71, Ⓦwww.ot-sete.fr), has a good array of English-language information.

For **accommodation**, a great option is the *belle époque* splendour of the *Grand Hôtel*, 17 quai de Lattre-de-Tassigny (℡04.67.74.71.77, Ⓦwww.legrandhotelsete .com; ❼), which also has apartments, and ⚹ *L'Orque Bleu* at 10 quai Aspirant-Herber (℡04.67.74.72.13, Ⓦwww.hotel-orquebleu-sete.com; ❺), which offers an equally charming alternative at a lower price. The **HI hostel** (℡04.67.53.46.68, Ⓦwww.fuaj.org/Sete; mid-Jan to Nov; dorm beds €20) is high up in the town on rue du Général-Revest. Campers should ask the tourist office for details of the numerous campsites in the area.

The Town

A short climb up from the harbour is the **cimetière marin**, the sailors' cemetery, where poet Paul Valéry is buried. Adjacent to the cemetery, the small **Musée Paul Valéry**, in rue Denoyer (10am–noon & 2–6pm: July & Aug daily; Sept–June Wed–Sun; €4), opposite the cemetery, and the **Éspace Brassens** (June– Sept daily 10am–noon & 2–7pm; Oct–May Tues–Sun 10am–noon & 2–6pm; €5), dedicated to the locally born singer-songwriter George Brassens, will be of scarce interest to non-fans. More interesting is the **Musée International des Arts Modestes** (10am–noon & 2–6pm: July & Aug daily; Sept–June Tues–Sun; €6), at 23 quai Maréchal de Lattre-de-Tassigny, containing a collection of art made from cast-off goods. For €11.50 you can get the "Pass Musée" for all three museums.

Joutes nautiques

Water-jousting is a venerable coastal tradition which pits boat-borne jousting teams against each other in an effort to unseat their opponents. Two sleek boats, each manned by eight oarsmen and bearing a lance-carrying jouster, charge at each other on a near head-on course. As the boats approach, the jousters attempt to strike their adversary from his mount. There are about a dozen *sociétés des joutes* in Sète itself, and you can see them in action all through the summer.

Eating and drinking

There's a barrage of **restaurants** along quai du Général-Duran, from the Pont de la Savonnerie right down to the fish market at the mouth of the pleasure port, all offering seafood in the €15–35 bracket. Local favourite ℳ *La Palangrotte* (℡04.67.74.80.35; closed Sun eve, plus Mon & Wed off season), at 1 rampe Paul-Valéry, is famous for its mussels and *bouillabaisse* (€23–36; reservations recommended) and solid wine list. Another good choice is *La Galinette*, 26 place des Mouettes (dinner only in summer; otherwise closed Sun & Thurs eve, Fri & Sat lunch; ℡04.67.51.16.77), on the north side of town.

Agde and around

Midway between Sète and Béziers, at the western end of the Bassin de Thau, **AGDE** is the most interesting of the coastal towns. Originally Phoenician, and maintained by the Romans, it thrived for centuries on trade with the Levant. Outrun as a seaport by Sète, it later degenerated into a sleepy fishing harbour.

Today, it's a major tourist centre with a good deal of charm, notably in the narrow back lanes between rue de l'Amour and the riverside, where fishing boats tie up. There are few sights apart from the impressively fortified **cathedral**, though the **waterfront** is attractive, and by the bridge you can watch the Canal du Midi slip modestly into the River Hérault on the very last leg of its journey from Toulouse to the Bassin de Thau and Sète.

The **tourist office** (daily 9am–noon & 2–6pm; ℡04.67.94.29.68, ⓦwww .capdagde.com) for the Old Town of Agde (the *cité*) and nearby Cap d'Agde and Grau d'Agde is unmissable, set on the roundabout at the entrance to Cap, travelling from the *cité*. The pick of the town's **hotels** is ℳ *La Galiote* (℡04.67.94.45.58, ⓦwww.lagaliote.fr; ❺), located in the old bishop's palace on place Jean-Jaurès, with excellent service and restrained elegance, while *La Voile d'Or*, in place du Globe, Cap d'Agde (℡04.67.01.04.11, ⓦwww.lavoiledor.com; April–Nov; ❻), is a modern resort-style alternative with lots of amenities including two pools. Aside from the numerous places to **eat** around La Promenade, a good bet is the quayside *La Table de Stéphane* (℡04.67.26.45.22) at 2 rue du Moulin à Huile, where you can enjoy elaborate creations such as jellied oysters in squid's ink (*menus* from €26; closed Mon, Sat lunch & Sun eve). One of the area's best restaurants is at *Le Jardin de Beaumont* (℡04.67.21.19.23; closed Sept–June Thurs–Sat eve & Sun noon), set in a wine *domaine* 3km north of town, where you can dine on tapas and excellent wines indoors or out (about €30).

An hourly **bus service** operates between the town and the sea at **Cap d'Agde** (see p.686); you can pick it up at the *gare SNCF* at the end of avenue Victor-Hugo, at the bridge and on La Promenade. Should you want to explore the Canal du Midi, **boat trips** are organized by Bateaux du Soleil, 6 rue Chassefières (℡04.67.94.08.79, ⓦwww.penichesdefrance.com).

Cap d'Agde

CAP D'AGDE lies to the south of Mont St-Loup, 7km from Agde. The largest (and by far the most successful) of the newer resorts, it sprawls out from the volcanic mound of St-Loup in an excess of pseudo-traditional buildings that offer every type of facility and entertainment – all of which are expensive. It is perhaps best known for its colossal **quartier naturiste** (ⓦ www.village naturiste-agde.com), one of the largest in France, with the best of the beaches, space for twenty thousand visitors, and its own restaurants, banks, post offices and shops. Access is possible if you're not actually staying here (€10 per car, €5 on foot; both until 8pm only).

If you have time to fill, head for the **Musée de l'Éphèbe** (daily 10am–noon & 2–6pm; €8.50), which displays antiquities discovered locally, many of them from the sea. Alternatively, the **Fort de Brescou** (mid-June to early-Sept; €3), which dates back to 1680, lies on a rocky, seagull-infested island just offshore; it can be reached by ferries from the centre port at Cap d'Agde (Sarl Croisières: July & Aug Thurs–Mon 10.30am, 2.30 & 6.30pm; €6) and le Grau d'Agde (Île de Brescou: July & Aug daily 2.30 & 4.30pm; €7).

Southern Languedoc

Southern Languedoc presents an exciting and varied landscape, its coastal flats stretching south from the mouth of the Aude towards Perpignan, interrupted by occasional low, rocky hills. Just inland sits **Béziers**, its imposing cathedral set high above the languid River Orb, girded in the north by the amazingly preserved Renaissance town of **Pézenas** and in the south by the pre-Roman settlement of the **Ensérune**. It's also a gateway to the spectacular uplands of the **Monts de l'Espinouse** and the **Parc Naturel Régional du Haut Languedoc**, a haven for ramblers. Just south of Béziers, the ancient Roman capital of **Narbonne** guards the mouth of the Aude. Following the course of this river, which is shadowed by the historic **Canal du Midi**, you arrive at the quintessential medieval citadel, the famous fortress-town of **Carcassonne**. Once a shelter for renegade **Cathar** heretics, this is also a fine departure point for the Cathar castles (see p.651) – a string of romantic ruins.

Béziers and around

Though no longer the rich city of its nineteenth-century heyday, **BÉZIERS** has risen out of its recent dreariness with admirable panache. The town is the capital of the Languedoc **wine** country and a focus for the **Occitan** movement, as well as being the birthplace of Resistance hero **Jean Moulin**. Today local resistance takes the form of the CRIV, a radical clandestine group championing the area's besieged vintners, which occasionally employs modest but violent acts of terrorism. The town is also home to two great Languedocian adopted traditions: English **rugby** and the Spanish **corrida**, both of which are followed with a passion. The best time to visit is during the mid-August **feria**, a raucous four-day party that can be enjoyed even if bullfighting isn't to your taste.

Arrival, information and accommodation

From the **gare SNCF** on boulevard Verdun, the best way into town is through the landscaped gardens of the Plateau des Poètes opposite the station entrance and up the allées Paul-Riquet. The **gare routière** is in place de Gaulle, at the northern end of the *allées*, while the **tourist office** is in the new Palais des Congrès at 29 av Saint-Saëns (June & Sept daily 9am–12.30pm & 1.30–6pm; July & Aug Mon–Sat 9am–6.30pm, Sun 10am–1pm & 3–6pm; Oct–May daily 9am–noon & 2–5/6pm; ☏04.67.76.47.00, ⓦwww.beziers-tourisme.fr). Béziers has one of the star **rugby** clubs in France, A.S.B.H., based at the Stade de la Méditerranée in the eastern suburbs (☏04.67.11.03.76, ⓦwww.asbh.net). If you fancy pottering along the Canal du Midi, you can rent **bikes** at La Maison du Canal (☏04.67.62.18.18) beside the Pont-Neuf, south of the *gare SNCF*.

For a central place to **stay**, try the *Hôtel des Poètes*, 80 allées Paul-Riquet (☏04.67.76.38.66, ⓦwww.hoteldespoetes.net; ❸), at the southern end overlooking the garden. The town's deluxe option, *Hôtel Impérator* (☏04.67.49.02.25, ⓦwww.hotel-imperator.fr; ❺), at 28 allées Paul-Riquet, is a notch above the rest but won't break the bank. There's no **campsite** in Béziers, but you can head to *Les Berges du Canal* (☏04.67.39.36.09, ⓦwww.lesbergesdu canal.com; mid-April to mid-Sept) in Villeneuve-lès-Béziers, about 4km southeast of the town centre, or 6km east to Clairac (☏04.67.76.78.97; April–Sept).

The City

The finest view of the Old Town is from the west, as you come in from Carcassonne: crossing the willow-lined River Orb by the Pont-Neuf, you can look upstream at the sturdy arches of the **Pont-Vieux**, above which rises a steep-banked hill crowned by the **Cathédrale St-Nazaire** which, with its crenellated towers, resembles a castle more than a church. The best approach to the cathedral is up the medieval lanes at the end of Pont-Vieux, rue Canterelles and passage Canterellettes. Its architecture is mainly Gothic, the original building having burned down in 1209 during the sacking of Béziers, when Armand Amaury's crusaders massacred some seven thousand people at the church of the Madeleine for refusing to hand over about twenty Cathars. "Kill them all", the pious abbot is said to have ordered, "God will recognize his own!"

From the top of the cathedral **tower**, there's a superb view out across the vine-dominated surrounding landscape. Keep an eye on small kiddies, however, lest they slip through the potentially perilous gaps in the wall. Next door, you can wander through the ancient **cloister** (free) and out into the shady **bishop's garden** overlooking the river. The nearby **place de la Révolution** is home to the **Musée des Beaux-Arts** (Tues–Sun: July & Aug 10am–6pm; Sept–June 9/10am–noon & 2–5/6pm; €2.70) which, apart from an interesting collection of Greek Cycladic vases, won't keep you long. Nearby, **Hôtel Fayet**, at 9 rue du Capus (same hours and ticket), has been pressed into service as an annexe to the museum, though it's as much of interest for its period interiors as its collection of nineteenth- and early twentieth-century art and works by local sculptor Jean-Antoine Injalbert.

The city's other museum, the **Musée du Biterrois** (same hours; €2.70), holds an important collection ranging from locally produced pottery to funerary monuments and artefacts dredged from ancient shipwrecks, but the highlight is the "treasure of Béziers" – a rich cache of silver platters found in a nearby field.

⑪

Eating

A string of **restaurants** with terraces are lined along the west side of allées Paul-Riquet, serving the usual *steak-frites*-type *menus* for about €14. Better fare can be found in the old quarter; rue Viennet has a good choice of places. The best overall establishment is probably ⚘ *Le Cep d'Or*, at no. 7, a bistro with a charming old-fashioned air, serving mostly seafood (closed Sun eve & Mon out of season; *menus* €15–23), while *L'Ambassade* (⊕04.67.76.06.24; closed Sun & Mon), at 22 bd de Verdun is another top choice, its cuisine a local favourite.

Pézenas

PÉZENAS lies 18km east of Béziers on the old N9. Market centre of the coastal plain, it looks across to rice fields and shallow lagoons, hazy in the heat and dotted with pink flamingos. The town was catapulted to glory when it became the seat of the parliament of Languedoc and the residence of its governors in 1465, and reached its zenith in the late seventeenth century when the prince Armand de Bourbon made it a "second Versailles". The legacy of this illustrious past can be seen in the town's exquisite array of fourteenth- to seventeenth-century mansions.

The town also plays up its association with **Molière**, who visited several times with his troupe in the mid-seventeenth century, when he enjoyed the patronage of Prince Armand, and put on plays at the **Hôtel d'Alfonce** on rue Conti. Although Molière features in the eclectic **Musée Vulliod St-Germain** (June–Sept Tues–Sun 10am–noon & 3–7pm, plus Wed & Fri 9–11pm in July & Aug; Feb–May & Oct to mid-Nov Tues–Sun 10am–noon & 2–5.30pm; €2.50), housed in a sixteenth-century palace just off the square, it's the grand salon, with its Aubusson tapestries and collection of seventeenth- and eighteenth-century furniture, that steals the show. The tourist office, at the main entrance to the Old Town, distributes a guide to all the town's eminent houses, taking in the former **Jewish ghetto** on rue des Litanies and rue Juiverie, but you can just as easily follow the explanatory plaques posted all over the centre, starting at the east end of rue François-Outrin where it leaves the town's main square, place du 14-juillet.

Practicalities

The **tourist office** (July & Aug Mon, Tues, Thurs & Sat 9am–7pm, Wed & Fri 9am–10pm, Sun 10am–7pm; Sept–June Mon–Sat 9am–noon & 2–6pm, Sun 10am–noon & 2–5pm; ⊕04.67.98.36.40, ⊛www.ot-pezenas-valdherault.com) is in place des États du Languedoc. The **gare routière** is on the opposite side of the square on the riverbank, with buses to Montpellier, Béziers and Agde, while an enormous **market** takes place each Saturday on cours Jean-Jaurès, a five-minute walk away.

There are two **hotels** in old Pézenas: *Le Saint Germain*, at 6 av Paul Vidal (⊕04.67.09.75.75, ⊛www.hotel-saintgermain.com; ❸), and the splendid *Molière*, 18 place du 14-juillet (⊕04.67.98.14.00, ⊛www.hotel-le-moliere.com; ❹). There are plenty of **restaurants** to choose from, most with *menus* for under €20. *Les Palmiers,* 50 rue de Mercière (⊕04.67.09.42.56; mid-April to mid-Sept), is a beautiful and welcoming establishment serving inventive Mediterranean-style cuisine from about €28, while the excellent *Après le Déluge*, 5 rue Maréchal de Plantavit (⊕04.67.98.10.77; closed Mon eve), is in a fourteenth-century building with several separate dining rooms (*terroir menus* €14–45). The wine lists at both places are superb. Those with a sweet tooth should sample two local delicacies: flavoured sugar-drops called *berlingots*, and *petits pâtés* – bobbin-shaped pastries related to mince pies, reputedly introduced by the Indian cook of Clive of India, who stayed in Pézenas in 1770.

Narbonne and around

On the Toulouse–Nice main train line, 25km west of Béziers, is **NARBONNE**, once the capital of Rome's first colony in Gaul, Gallia Narbonensis, and a thriving port in classical times and the Middle Ages. Plague, war with the English and the silting up of its harbour finished it off in the fourteenth century. Today, it's a pleasant provincial city with a small but well-kept Old Town, dominated by the great truncated choir of its cathedral and bisected by a grassy esplanade on the banks of the Canal de la Robine.

Arrival, information and accommodation

The **gare routière** and the **gare SNCF** are next door to each other on avenue Carnot on the northwest side of town. The **tourist office** is on place Salengro, next to the cathedral (April to mid-Sept daily 9am–7pm; mid-Sept to March Mon–Sat 10am–12.30pm & 1.20–6pm, Sun 9am–1pm; ☎04.68.65.15.60, Ⓦwww.narbonne-tourisme.fr).

The best budget **accommodation** is the modern and friendly *MJC Centre International de Séjour*, in place Salengro (☎04.68.32.01.00, Ⓦwww.cis-narbonne .com; ❶). Two of the more reasonable hotels are *Will's Hotel*, 23 av Pierre-Sémard (☎04.68.90.44.50, Ⓦwww.willshotel-narbonne.com; ❸), a homely backpackers' favourite near the station, and the spruce *Hôtel de France*, 6 rue Rossini (☎04.68.32.09.75, Ⓦwww.hotelnarbonne.com; ❷), beside the attractive market hall. But best is ☘ *Grand Hôtel du Languedoc*, 22 bd Gambetta (☎04.68.65.14.74, Ⓦwww.hoteldulanguedoc.com; ❹), set in a dignified nineteenth-century house. The nearest **campsite** is *Les Mimosas* (☎04.68.32.01.00, Ⓦwww.cis-narbonne .com), located 6km south of town on the Étang de Bages (no public transport).

The Town

One of the few Roman remnants in Narbonne is the **Horreum**, at the north end of rue Rouget-de-l'Isle (April–Sept daily 9.30am–12.15pm & 2–6pm; Oct–March Tues–Sun 10am–noon & 2–5pm; €3.70 or €5.20 for a pass to the town's four museums), an unusual underground grain store divided into a series of small chambers leading off a rectangular passageway. At the opposite end of the same street, close to the attractive tree-lined banks of the **Canal de la Robine**, is Narbonne's other principal attraction, the enormous Gothic **Cathédrale St-Just-et-St-Pasteur**. With the Palais des Archevêques and its 40m-high keep, it forms a massive pile of masonry that completely dominates the restored lanes of the Old Town. In spite of its size, it's actually only the choir of a much more ambitious church, whose construction was halted to avoid wrecking the city walls. The immensely tall interior has some beautiful fourteenth-century stained glass in the chapels on the northeast side of the apse and imposing Aubusson tapestries – one of the most valuable of these is kept in the **Salle du Trésor** (July–Sept Mon–Sat 11am–6pm & Sun 2–6pm; Oct–June 2–5/6pm; €2.20), along with a small collection of ecclesiastical treasures.

The adjacent **place de l'Hôtel-de-Ville** is dominated by the great towers of St-Martial, the Madeleine and Bishop Aycelin's keep. From here the passage de l'Ancre leads through to the **Palais des Archevêques** (Archbishops' Palace), housing a fairly ordinary **museum of art** and a good **archeology museum** (both same hours and price as the Horreum), whose interesting Roman remains include a massive 3.5m wood and lead ship's rudder, and a huge mosaic. Across into the southern part of the town, the small early Christian crypt of the church of **St-Paul**, off rue de l'Hôtel-Dieu (Mon–Sat 9am–noon & 2–6pm, Sun 9am–noon;

free), is worth a quick look, as is the deconsecrated church of **Notre-Dame-de-Lamourguié**, which now houses a collection of Roman sculptures and epigraphy (same hours and cost as the Horreum).

Eating

As for **food**, you'll find a string of alfresco snack bars and brasseries along the terraces bordering the Canal de la Robine in the town centre, while *L'Estagnol* (℡04.68.65.09.27; closed Sun & Mon eve; *menus* €12–28), across the canal on Cours Mirabeau, attracts the crowds with its simple, good-value fare. *L'Alsace*, at 2 av Pierre-Sémard (℡04.68.65.10.24; closed Sun eve & Wed) is Narbonne's best restaurant hands down, featuring mammoth servings of excellent *terroir* and northeastern French dishes, plus local seafood dishes (from €14) – baked sea wolf is the house speciality.

Fontfroide

For a side trip from Narbonne – only 15km southwest, but nigh impossible without transport of your own – the lovely **abbey of FONTFROIDE** enjoys a beautiful location, tucked into a fold in the dry cypress-clad hillsides. The extant buildings go back to the twelfth century, with some elegant seventeenth-century additions in the entrance and courtyards, and were in use from their foundation until 1900, first by Benedictines, then Cistercians. It was one of the Cistercian monks, Pierre de Castelnau, whose murder as papal legate set off the Albigensian Crusade against the Cathars in 1208.

Visits to the restored abbey are only possible on a **guided tour** (daily: April–June & Sept 10am–12.15pm & 1.45–5.30pm; July & Aug 10am–6pm; Oct 10am–12.15pm & 1.45–4.45pm; Nov–March 10am–noon & 2–4pm; €9). Star features include the cloister, with its marble pillars and giant wisteria creepers, the church itself, some fine ironwork and a rose garden. The stained glass in the windows of the lay brothers' dormitory consists of fragments from churches in north and eastern France damaged in World War I.

Parc Naturel Régional du Haut Languedoc

Embracing Mont Caroux in the east and the Montagne Noire in the west, the **Parc Naturel Régional du Haut Languedoc** is the southernmost extension of the Massif Central. The west, above Castres and Mazamet, is Atlantic in feel and climate, with deciduous forests and lush valleys, while the east is dry, craggy and calcareous. Except in high summer you can have it almost to yourself. Buses serve the **Orb valley** and cross the centre of the park to **La Salvetat** and **Lacaune**, but you really need transport of your own to make the most of it.

Bédarieux and the Orb valley

Some 34km north of Béziers, the pleasant if unremarkable town of **BÉDARIEUX** lies on the edge of the park. Served by buses from both Béziers and Montpellier, and by train from Béziers, it makes a good base for entering the park, especially as the bus service continues along the Orb and Jaur valleys to St-Pons beneath the southern slopes of the Monts de l'Espinouse.

The best part of town is to the east of the river, where the tall, crumbly old houses are redolent of a rural France long since vanished in more prosperous areas. You'll find the **tourist office** on place aux Herbes (Mon–Fri 9am–noon & 2–6pm, Sat 9am–noon; ℡04.67.95.08.79, Ⓦwww.bedarieux.fr). The town's only **hotel**, *Hôtel de l'Orb* (℡04.67.23.35.90, Ⓦwww.hotel-orb.com; ❸), is on route de St-Pins, near the station, and there's a municipal **campsite** on boulevard Jean-Moulin (℡04.67.23.30.19, Ⓔgites.bedarieux@orange.fr; mid–June to Aug). There's an excellent **restaurant**, *La Forge* (℡04.67.95.13.13; Tues–Sun), at 22 av Abbé Tarroux, with a cosy, vaulted dining-room and *terroir menus* from €16.

Continuing west, the D908 (on the Bédarieux bus route) moves through spectacular scenery, with the peaks of the Monts de l'Espinouse rising up to 1000m on your right. The spa town of **LAMALOU-LES-BAINS**, 8km on, is notably livelier than neighbouring settlements, boasting the attraction of **recuperative springs** where the likes of André Gide and crowned heads of Spain and Morocco soothed their aches and pains. At the west end of the town by the main road, the **cemetery** is an untypically grand necropolis crowned with ornate mausoleums, while the ancient **church** on the north side of town contains carvings left by Mozarab (Christian) refugees from Islamic Spain.

Olargues and St-Pons-de-Thomières

About 15km after Lamalou, you reach the medieval village of **OLARGUES**, scrambling up the south bank of the Jaur above its thirteenth-century single-span bridge. The steep twisting streets, presumably almost unchanged since the bridge was built, lead up to a thousand-year-old belfry crowning the top of the hill. With the river and gardens below, the ancient and earth-brown farms on the infant slopes of Mont Caroux beyond, and swifts swirling round the tower in summer, you get a powerful sense of age and history. There's a tiny **tourist office** on rue de la Place near the church (July & Aug Tues–Sat 10am–12.30pm & 4–7pm, Sun 9.30am–noon; Sept–June Tues–Sat 9.30am–12.30pm & 3–6pm; ℡04.67.97.71.26, Ⓦwww.olargues.org), as well as an old train station now served only by SNCF **buses**. There is a deluxe country **hotel**, the *Domaine de Rieumégé* (℡04.67.97.73.99, Ⓦwww.domainederieumege.fr; March–Dec; ❻), just outside the town on the St-Pons road, but a better deal is the homely 🍴 *Les Quatr' Farceurs* in rue de la Comporte (℡04.67.97.81.33, Ⓦwww.olargues.co.uk; ❸), which also serves huge meals with free-flowing wine for €20. Olargues has a seasonal municipal **campsite** (℡04.67.97.71.50; July to mid-Sept) and **bikes** can be rented from Oxygène (℡04.67.97.87.00).

ST-PONS-DE-THOMIÈRES, 18km further west, is a little larger and noisier: it's on the Béziers–Castres and Béziers–La Salvetat bus routes, as well as the Bédarieux–Mazamet route. This is the "capital" of the park, with the **Maison du Parc** housed in the local **tourist office** (July & Aug Mon–Sat 9.30am–12.30pm & 2.30–7.30pm, Sun 9.30am–1pm; Sept–June Tues–Fri 10am–noon & 2–6pm, Sat 9am–noon & 2–5pm; ℡04.67.97.06.65, Ⓦwww.saint-pons-tourisme.com) on place du Forail. Sights include the **cathedral** – a strange mix of Romanesque and classical – and a small and reasonably interesting **Musée de Préhistoire Régionale** (April to mid-June & mid-Sept to end Sept Thurs–Sun 3–6pm; mid-June to mid-Sept Tues–Sun 10am–noon and 3–6pm; rest of year closed to public; €3.50), across the river from the tourist office.

If you need to **stay**, try the basic *Le Somail* (℡04.67.97.00.12; ❶). The municipal **campsite** (℡04.67.97.34.85) is on the main road east to Bédarieux. Deluxe accommodation can be found at the 🍴 *Bergeries de Ponderach* 1km east of town (℡04.67.97.02.57, Ⓦbergeries-ponderach.com; ❼), a luxurious seventeenth-century country estate with a fine **restaurant**.

The park's uplands

The uplands of the park are wild and little travelled, dominated by the towering peak of **Mont Caroux** and stretching west along the ridge of the **Monts de l'Espinouse**. This is prime hiking territory, where thick forest of stunted oak alternates with broad mountain meadows, opening up to impressive vistas. Civilization appears again to the west in the upper Agout valley, where **Fraïsse** and **La Salvetat** have become thriving bases for outdoor recreation, and to the north, at the medieval spa town of **Lacaune**. There's no transport crossing the uplands, but the D180 takes you from Le Poujol-sur-Orb, 2km west of Lamalou-les-Bains, to Mont Caroux and L'Espinouse.

Into the Agout valley

The D180 is the most spectacular way to climb into the park. Soon after leaving the main highway, you'll pass the **Forêt des Écrivains–Combattants**, named after the French writers who died in World War I. Just above the hamlet of Rosis, the road levels out in a small mountain valley, whose slopes are brilliant yellow with broom in June. Continuing north, the D180 climbs another 12km above deep ravines, offering spectacular views to the summit of **L'Espinouse**. The Col de l'Ourtigas is a good place to stretch your legs and take in the grandeur. Here the landscape changes from Mediterranean cragginess to marshy moor-like meadow and big conifer plantations, and the road begins to descend west into the valley of the River Agout. It runs through tiny Salvergues, with plain workers' cottages and a striking fortress-church; Cambon, where the natural woods begin; and postcard-pretty **FRAÏSSE-SUR-AGOUT** – where you can **stay** at the homely *Auberge de l'Espinouse* (T04.67.95.40.46, W aubergespinouse.net; ❸), which also has a good *gastronomique* **restaurant** (May–Nov; *menu* €18).

Next, you'll reach **LA SALVETAT-SUR-AGOUT**, another attractive mountain town built on a hill above the river, with car-wide streets and houses clad in huge slate tiles, situated between the artificial lakes of La Raviège and Laouzas. It's usually half asleep except at holiday time, when it becomes a busy outdoor activities centre. There are four campsites within walking distance; the nearest is *La Blaquière* on allée St-Étienne de Cavall just north of the centre (T04.67.97.61.29, W www.campingblaquiere.com; June–Aug). Inexpensive rooms and generous portions of home-cooked local food (for guests only) can be found at *La Plage* (T04.67.97.69.87, W www.pageloisirs.com/hotel-la-plage; ❸), a small, lakeside hotel 1km from the town centre. There's a **tourist office** in place des Archers at the top of the hill (Mon–Fri 9am–noon & 2–6pm, Sat & Sun 10am–noon & 2–5pm; Sept–June closed Sun; T04.67.97.64.44, W www.lasalvetatot.com).

Lacaune

Twenty kilometres further north, **LACAUNE** makes another agreeable stop if you're heading for Castres. Surrounded by rounded wooded heights, it's very much a mountain town. It was one of the centres of Protestant Camisard resistance at the end of the seventeenth century, when its inaccessibility was ideal for clandestine worship.

The air is fresh, and the town, though somewhat grey in appearance because of the slates and greyish stucco common throughout the region, is cheerful enough. **Buses** stop at place de la République, where a small **tourist office** (mid-June to mid-Sept Mon–Fri 9am–noon & 2–6.30pm, Sat & Sun 10am–noon & 2–6.30pm; mid-Sept to mid-June Mon 2–5pm, Tues–Fri 9am–noon & 2–5pm, Sat 10am–noon & 2–5pm; T05.63.37.04.98, W www.lacaune.com) rents out **bikes**. To **stay** the night, the small family-run hotel *Calas*, tucked away in the place de la Vierge (T05.63.37.03.28, W pageloisirs.com/calas; closed mid-Dec to mid-Jan; ❷), is home to a highly praised

bistro (closed Fri & Sat eve Oct–Easter; *menus* €11–45). House specialities include pigeon and pigs' feet with truffles. The local municipal campsite is on the Murat road (℡05.63.37.03.59, Ⓦwww.pageloisirs.com/le-clot; year-round).

From here to Castres the most agreeable route is along the wooded **Gijou valley**, following the now defunct train track, past minuscule Gijounet and **LACAZE**, where a nearly derelict **château** strikes a picturesque pose in a bend of the river.

Carcassonne and around

Right on the main Toulouse–Montpellier train link, **Carcassonne** couldn't be easier to reach. For anyone travelling through this region it is a must – one of the most dramatic, if also most-visited, towns in the whole of Languedoc. Carcassonne owes its division into two separate "towns" to the wars against the Cathars. Following Simon de Montfort's capture of the town in 1209, its people tried in 1240 to restore their traditional ruling family, the Trencavels. In reprisal, King Louis IX expelled them from the **Cité**, only permitting their return on condition they built on the low ground by the River Aude – what would become the **ville basse**.

Arrival and information

Arriving by **train**, you'll find yourself in the *ville basse* on the north bank of the Canal du Midi at the northern limits of the town. To reach the **centre** from the train station, cross the canal bridge by an oval lock, pass the Jardin Chénier and

CARCASSONNE: VILLE BASSE

ACCOMMODATION
La Bastide — B
La Cité Campsite — C
Montségur — D
Du Soleil Terminus — A

EATING
L'Écurie — 2
Roberto Rodríguez — 1

follow rue Clemenceau, which will take you through the central **place Carnot** and out to the exterior boulevard on the southern side of town (a 15min walk). The **gare routière** (in fact a series of bus stops with no actual building) is on boulevard de Varsovie on the northwest side of town, south of the canal, while the **airport** (ⓦ www.carcassonne.aeroport.fr) lies just west of the city. A *navette* service (€5; hourly, 15min trip) leaves from outside the terminal and stops at the *gare SNCF*, square Gambetta and the Cité; a taxi to the centre will cost €8–15. If you are planning on visiting other medieval sites in the vicinity of Carcassonne (including the Cathar castles), you might purchase the **Intersite Pass**, which gives you a discounted admission price to many castles and monuments (see p.654 for details).

The **tourist office** is at 28 rue de Verdun (Mon–Sat 9am–6pm & Sun 9am–noon; ⓣ 04.68.10.24.30, ⓦ www.carcassonne-tourisme.com), west of square Gambetta, where the main road from Montpellier enters the town across the Pont-Neuf and the River Aude. There's also an annexe (daily: June & Sept 9am–6pm; July & Aug 9am–7pm; Oct–May 9am–5pm) just inside the main gate to the medieval Cité, Porte Narbonnaise.

Accommodation

There is plenty of **accommodation** on offer in both the *ville basse* and the Cité, although the latter, while more atmospheric, tends to be much more expensive. In any case, you should book well ahead, particularly in high season. There's a **campsite**, *La Cité*, on route St-Hilaire (ⓣ 04.68.25.11.17, ⓦ www.camping -carcassonne.info; mid-March to mid-Oct), with good shady sites, a shop and some bungalows. Tucked off amid parkland to the south of town, it can be reached by local bus (line 8) or by foot (about 20min) from the Cité.

La Bastide 81 rue de la Liberté ⓣ 04.68.71.96.89, ⓦ www.hotel-bastide.fr. A good economy option and surprisingly well-equipped. ❸

🏃 **De La Cité** Place Auguste-Pierre Pont ⓣ 04.68.71.98.71, ⓦ www.hoteldelacite .com. Carcassonne's luxury option, with prices to match, featuring rooms and suites in the opulent surroundings of a medieval manor house, with a heated swimming pool and stunning views from the battlemented walls. ❾

Le Donjon 2 rue Comte-Roger ⓣ 04.68.11.23.00, ⓦ www.hotel-donjon.fr. A shade less luxurious than the *Cité* and correspondingly less expensive. It offers four-star amenities in a medieval building near the castle. ❼

Espace Cité 132 rue Trivalle ⓣ 04.68.25.24.24, ⓦ www.hotelespacecite.fr. Located just outside the main gate of the Cité this represents the best value for money – excellent location, mod cons and efficient service at reasonable prices. ❹

HI Hostel Rue Trencavel ⓣ 04.68.25.23.16, ⓦ www.fuaj.org/Carcassonne. This modern, clean hostel offers the cheapest accommodation in town (€16 for dorm beds) and is located in the heart of the Cité. Tends to book up far in advance.

Montségur 27 allée d'Iéna ⓣ 04.68.25.31.41, ⓦ www.hotelmontsegur.com. A comfortable, nineteenth-century townhouse, with ample-sized rooms, but quite far from the Cité. ❻

Du Soleil Terminus 2 av du Maréchal-Joffre ⓣ 04.68.25.25.00, ⓦ soleilvacances.com. Pride of place goes to the *Terminus*, a station-side hotel of decaying steam-age luxury, with a splendid *fin-de-siècle* façade. ❹

The Cité

The attractions of the well-preserved and lively *ville basse* notwithstanding, what everybody comes for is the **Cité**, the double-walled and turreted fortress that crowns the hill above the River Aude. From a distance it's the epitome of the fairytale medieval town. Viollet-le-Duc rescued it from ruin in 1844, and his "too-perfect" restoration has been furiously debated ever since. It is, as you would expect, a real tourist trap. Yet, in spite of the chintzy cafés, crafty shops and the crowds, you'd have to be a very stiff-necked purist not to be moved at all.

Canal du Midi

The **Canal du Midi** runs for 240km from the River Garonne at Toulouse via Carcassonne to the Mediterranean at Agde. It was the brainchild of **Pierre-Paul Riquet**, a minor noble and tax collector, who succeeded in convincing Louis XIV (and more importantly, his first minister, Colbert) of the merits of linking the Atlantic and the Mediterranean via the Garonne.

The work, begun in 1667, took fourteen years to complete, using tens of thousands of workers. The crux of the problem from the engineering point of view was how to feed the canal with water when its high point at Naurouze, west of Carcassonne, was 190m above sea level and 58m above the Garonne at Toulouse. Riquet responded by building a system of reservoirs in the Montagne Noire, channelling run-off from the heights down to Naurouze. He spent the whole of his fortune on the canal and, sadly, died just six months before its inauguration in 1681.

The canal was a success and sparked a wave of prosperity along its course, with traffic increasing steadily until 1857, when the Sète–Bordeaux railway was opened, reducing trade on the canal to all but nothing. Today, the canal remains a marvel of engineering and beauty, incorporating no fewer than 99 locks (*écluses*) and 130 bridges, almost all of which date back to the first era of construction. A double file of trees lines most of its length, giving it a distinctive "Midi" look and impeding loss of water through evaporation, while the greenery is enhanced in spring by the bloom of yellow irises and wild gladioli. With all of this and the occasional glimpses afforded of a world beyond – a distant smudge of hills and the towers of Carcassonne – the canal is a pleasure to travel. You can follow it by road, and many sections have foot or bicycle paths, but the best way to see it is, of course, by boat.

Outfits in all the major ports rent houseboats and barges, and there are many cruise options to choose from as well. For **boat rental and cruises**, contact Crown Blue Line (℡04.68.94.52.72, www.crownblueline.com) or Locaboat (℡03.86.91.72.72, www.locaboat.com), both of which have a number of branches in Languedoc and the Midi. Canal **information** can be found at the port offices of Voies Navigables de France, at 2 Port St-Étienne in Toulouse (℡05.61.36.24.24, www.vnf.fr), who also have English-speaking offices at the major canal ports. For a green option, try the solar-power 14-berth barges (accessible for passengers with mobility issues) available from Naviratous starting at €700 per week (℡04.68.46.37.98, www.naviratous2.com).

To reach the Cité from the *ville basse*, take bus #2 from outside the station, or a *navette* from square Gambetta. Alternatively, you can walk it in under thirty minutes, crossing the Pont-Vieux and climbing rue Barbacane, past the church of St-Gimer to the sturdy bastion of the **Porte d'Aude**. This is effectively the back entrance – the main gate is **Porte Narbonnaise**, on the east side.

There is no charge for admission to the streets or the grassy *lices* – "lists" – between the walls, though cars are banned from 10am to 6pm. However, to see the inner fortress of the **Château Comtal** and walk the walls, you'll have to join a **guided tour** (daily: April–Sept 10am–6.30pm; Oct–March 10am–5pm; €8). These – including several per day in English (June–Sept) – assume some knowledge of French history, and point out the various phases in the construction of the fortifications, from Roman and Visigothic to Romanesque and the post-Cathar adaptations of the French kings.

In addition to wandering the narrow streets, don't miss the beautiful **church of St-Nazaire** (Mon–Fri 8.45am–12.45pm & 1.45–5/6pm, Sat & Sun 8.45–10.30am & 2–5/6pm; free), towards the southern corner of the Cité at the end of rue St-Louis. It's a serene combination of nave with carved capitals in the Romanesque style and a Gothic choir and transepts, along with some of the loveliest stained glass in Languedoc. In the south transept is a tombstone believed to belong to

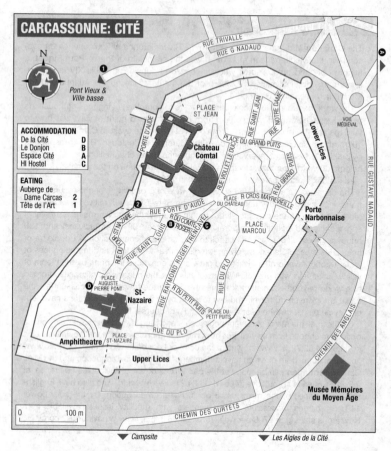

CARCASSONNE: CITÉ

Pont Vieux &
Ville basse

RUE TRIVALLE
RUE G NADAUD

PLACE
ST JEAN

PORTE D'AUDE

RUE SAINT JEAN
RUE NOTRE DAME
PLACE DU GRAND PUITS

Château
Comtal

VOIE
MEDIÉVAL

RUE VOLLET LE DUC

Lower Lices

RUE DU GRAND PUITS

ACCOMMODATION
De la Cité   D
Le Donjon   B
Espace Cité   A
HI Hostel   C

EATING
Auberge de
  Dame Carcas   2
Tête de l'Art   1

RUE PORTE D'AUDE

R CROS MAYREVIEILLE
PLACE
DU CHÂTEAU

R DU COMTE DEL

Roger

PLACE
MARCOU

RUE GUSTAVE NADAUD

Porte
Narbonnaise

RUE DU PLO

PLACE
AUGUSTE
PIERRE PONT

RUE SAINT LOUIS

RUE RAYMOND ROGER TRENCAVEL

R DU PETIT PUITS

St-
Nazaire

PLACE DU
PETIT PUITS

Amphitheatre

PLACE
ST-NAZAIRE

RUE DU PLO

Upper Lices

CHEMIN DES ANGLAIS

Musée Mémoires
du Moyen Âge

0   100 m

CHEMIN DES OURTETS

▼ Campsite   ▼ Les Aigles de la Cité

Simon de Montfort. You can also climb the **tower** (same hours; €1.50), for spectacular views over the Cité.

Eating, drinking and entertainment

With over fifty **restaurants** within its walls, the Cité is a good place to look for somewhere to eat, though it tends to be expensive. First choice is the *Auberge de Dame Carcas*, 3 place du Château (☎04.68.71.23.23; closed Sun eve, Mon lunch & Feb; *menus* €15–26), a traditional bistro offering cassoulet and other regional dishes. Otherwise try *Tête de l'Art* (☎04.68.71.23.11), at 37bis rue Trivalle, which has an arty atmosphere and excellent *terroir* fare from €16 to €34 with a filling vegetarian option at €13.

There's a greater variety of affordable places in the *ville basse*, which are easy enough to stumble upon. For something more sophisticated, try ⚜ *L'Écurie* (☎04.68.72.04.04) at 43 bd Barbès, offering local cuisine with adventurous touches, such as roast lamb with thyme and garlic (closed Sun eve & Wed; *menus* €15–30), or the highly inventive cuisine of *Restaurant Roberto Rodriguez* (☎04.68.47.37.80; closed Wed eve & Sun; *menus* €40–70) at 39 rue Coste Reboulh. For picnic provisions, head for the market on place Carnot (Tues, Thurs & Sat am).

A major summertime event worth catching is the **Festival de Carcassonne** from late June through mid-August, featuring world-class dance, theatre and music, the highpoint of which is the mammoth fireworks display on Bastille Day (July 14).

Castelnaudary

Thirty-six kilometres west of Carcassonne, on the main road from Toulouse, **CASTELNAUDARY** is one of those innumerable French country towns that boasts no particular sights but is nonetheless a pleasure to spend a couple of hours in, having coffee or shopping in the market. Today it serves as an important commercial centre for the rolling Lauragais farming country hereabouts, as it once was for the traffic on the Canal du Midi. In fact, the most flattering view of the town is still that from the canal's **Grand Bassin**, which makes it look remarkably like a Greek island town, with its ancient houses climbing the hillside from the water's edge.

In town you'll find some fine old **mansions**, a restored **windmill** and an eighteenth-century **semaphore** tower. However, Castelnaudary's chief claim to fame is as the world capital of **cassoulet**, which, according to tradition, must be made in an earthenware pot from Issel (a *cassolo*) with beans grown in Pamiers or Lavelanet, and cooked in a baker's oven fired with rushes from the Montagne Noire. *La Belle Époque* (T04.68.23.39.72; closed Tues eve & Wed), at 55 rue du Général-Dejean, serves a great one (basic *menu* €12).

The **tourist office** is in Castelnaudary's central Halle aux Grains (June & Sept Mon–Sat 9am–12.30pm & 2.30–6pm; July & Aug daily 9am–1pm & 2–7pm; Oct–May Mon–Fri 9am–12.30pm & 2.30–6pm, Sat 9am–12.30pm; T04.68.23.05.73, Wwww.castelnaudary-tourisme.com). The best **hotels** are the friendly canalside *Hôtel du Canal* (T04.68.94.05.05, Wwww.hotelducanal.com;), at 2 av Arnaut-Vidal – a comfortable place with all mod cons (family rooms available), and *Hôtel du Centre et du Lauragais* (T04.68.23.25.95, Wwww.hotel-centre-lauragais.com; closed Jan to mid-Feb;), a converted nineteenth-century house, at 31 cours de la République.

The Montagne Noire and Revel

There are two good routes from Carcassonne north into the **Montagne Noire**, which forms the western extremity of the Parc Naturel Régional du Haut Languedoc: Carcassonne–Revel and Carcassonne–Mazamet by the valley of the Orbiel. Neither is served by public transport, but both offer superlative scenery. **The Revel route** follows the N113 out of Carcassonne, then the D629 through Montolieu (17km) and Saissac. **MONTOLIEU**, semi-fortified and built on the edge of a ravine, has set itself the target of becoming France's secondhand book capital (a conscious imitation of Wales's Hay-on-Wye), with shops overflowing with dog-eared and antiquarian tomes. Drop in to the Librairie Booth, by the bridge over the ravine, for English titles.

SAISSAC, 8km further on, is much more an upland village. Conifers and beech wood, interspersed with patches of rough pasture, surround it, and gardens are terraced down its steep slopes. Remains of towers and fortifications poke out among the ancient houses, and on a spur below the village stand the romantic ruins of its castle and the church of St-Michel. If you wish to **stay** in the area, head north of town to *Domaine du Lampy-Neuf* (T04.68.24.46.07, Wwww.domaine lampy-neuf.com), a lakeside estate which offers deluxe *chambres d'hôtes* () and *gîte* dorms (€15) as well as meals (€20).

Some 14km west of Saissac on the D103 (or just a few kilometres southwest of the *Bout du Monde* campsite), the ancient village of **ST-PAPOUL**, with its walls and Benedictine **abbey**, makes for a gentle side trip. The abbey is best known for the sculpted corbels on the exterior of the nave, executed by the "Master of

Cabestany". These can be viewed free at any time, although the interior of the church and its pretty fourteenth-century cloister (April–June & Sept–Oct daily 10–11.30am & 2–5.30pm; July & Aug daily 10am–6.30pm; Nov–March Sat, Sun & hols 10–11.30am & 2–6.30pm; €3.50) are also worth a peek.

Back on the "main" D629, the road winds down through the forest, past the Bassin de St-Férréol, constructed by Riquet to supply water to the Canal du Midi, and on to **REVEL**. Revel is a *bastide* dating from 1342, featuring an attractive arcaded central square with a superb wooden-pillared medieval *halle* in the middle. Now a prosperous market town (Saturday is market day), it makes an agreeably provincial stopover. The *Auberge du Midi* at 34 bd Gambetta (℡05.61.83.50.50, Ⓦwww.hotelrestaurantdu midi.com; closed late Nov to early Dec; ❹) is set in a refined old nineteenth-century mansion, and also has the town's best **restaurant** (*menus* €19–45).

Lastours and the valley of the Orbiel

The alternative route from Carcassonne into the Montagne Noire takes you through the region known as the **Cabardès**. Cut by the deep ravines of the Orbiel and its tributary streams, it's covered with Mediterranean scrub lower down and forests of chestnut and pine higher up. The area is extremely poor and depopulated, with rough stone villages and hamlets crouching in the valleys. Until relatively recently, its people lived off beans and chestnut flour and the meat from their pigs, and worked in the region's copper, iron, lead, silver and gold mines. Nothing now remains save for the gold mine at Salsigne, a huge and unsightly open pit atop a bleak windswept plateau.

The most memorable site in the **Orbiel valley** is the **Châteaux de Lastours** (Feb, March, Nov & Dec Sat, Sun & hols 10am–5pm; April–June & Sept daily 10am–6pm; July & Aug daily 9am–8pm; Oct daily 10am–5pm; €5), the most northerly of the Cathar castles, 16km north of Carcassonne. There are, in fact, four castles here – their ruined keeps jutting superbly from a sharp ridge of scrub and cypress that plunges to rivers on both sides. The two oldest, Cabaret (mid-eleventh century) and Surdespine (1153), fell into de Montfort's hands in 1211, after their lords had given shelter to the Cathars. The other two, Tour Régine and Quertinheux, were added after 1240, when the site became royal property, and a garrison was maintained here as late as the Revolution. Today, despite their ruined state, they look as impregnable and beautiful as ever. A path winds up from the roadside, bright in early summer with iris, cistus, broom and numerous others.

Toulouse and western Languedoc

With its sunny, cosmopolitan charms, **Toulouse** is a very accessible kick-off point for any destination in the southwest of France. Of the immediately surrounding places, **Albi**, with its highly original cathedral and comprehensive collection of Toulouse-Lautrec paintings, is the number-one priority. Once you've made it that far, it's worth the extra hop to the well-preserved medieval town of **Cordes**. West of Toulouse the land opens up into the broad plains of the **Gers**, a sleepy and rather dull expanse of wheat fields and rolling hills. Those in search of a solitary, little-visited France will enjoy its uncrowded monuments, especially lovers of rich terrines and Armagnac.

Toulouse

TOULOUSE, with its beautiful historic centre, is one of the most vibrant provincial cities in France. This is a transformation that has come about since World War II, under the guidance of the French state, which has poured in money to make Toulouse the think-tank of high-tech industry and a sort of premier trans-national Euroville. Long an **aviation** centre – St-Exupéry and Mermoz flew out from here on their pioneering airmail flights over Africa and the Atlantic in the 1920s – Toulouse is now home to Aérospatiale, the driving force behind Concorde, Airbus and the Ariane space rocket. Moreover, the city's 110,000 students make it second only to Paris as a **university** centre. But it's not to the burgeoning suburbs of factories, labs, shopping and housing complexes that all these people go for their entertainment, but to the old **Ville Rose** – pink not only in its brickwork, but also in its left-leaning politics.

This is not the first flush of pre-eminence for Toulouse. From the tenth to the thirteenth centuries the counts of Toulouse controlled much of southern France. They maintained a resplendent court, renowned especially for its troubadours, the poets of courtly love, whose work influenced Petrarch, Dante and Chaucer and thus the whole course of European poetry. The arrival of the hungry northern French nobles of the Albigensian Crusade put an end to that; in 1271 Toulouse became crown property.

Arrival and information

The **gare SNCF** (better known to locals as **gare Matabiau**) and **gare routière** (℡05.61.61.67.67) stand side by side in boulevard Pierre-Sémard on the bank of the tree-lined Canal du Midi. This is where you might find yourself if you arrive by air as well – the **airport shuttle** (every 20min; €4) puts you down at the bus station (with stops in allées Jean-Jaurès and at place Jeanne-d'Arc). It's also the best spot to aim for if you're in a car: leave the **boulevard périphérique** at exit 15.

To reach the city centre from the train station takes just five minutes by **métro** to Capitole (€1.40, covering one hour's transport by métro and Tisseo-Connex city buses within the city centre), or twenty minutes on foot. Turn left out of the station, cross the canal and head straight down allées Jean-Jaurès, through place Wilson and on into place du Capitole, the city's main square. Just before it lie the shady and much-frequented gardens of the square Charles-de-Gaulle, where the main **tourist office** (June–Sept Mon–Sat 9am–7pm, Sun 10am–5.15pm; Oct–May Mon–Fri 9am–6pm, Sat 9am–12.30pm & 2–6pm, Sun 10am–12.30pm & 2–5pm; ℡05.61.11.02.22, Ⓦ www.toulouse-tourisme.com) is housed in a sixteenth-century tower that has been restored to look like a castle keep; the Capitole métro stop is right outside. To save on admissions, the "Toulouse en liberté" card (€10) offers discounts at a range of hotels, museums, cultural events and shops. For getting around the city, you can use the **municipal bike** system, VéloToulouse (see p.706).

Accommodation

The best place to **stay** is in the city centre, where there are a number of excellent-value hotels, as well as many more upmarket establishments. The area around the

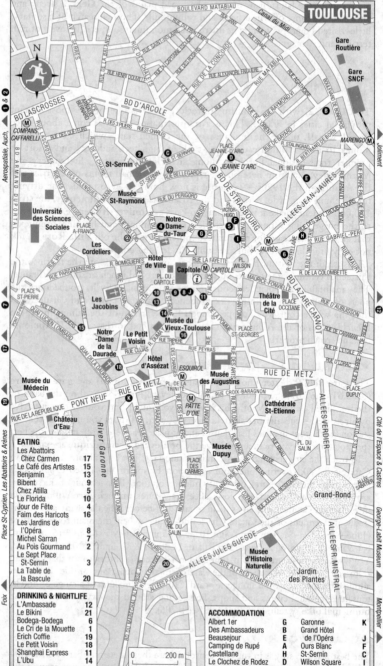

TOULOUSE

N20 & **A**

Albi

Gare Routière

Gare SNCF

MARENGO **M**

Joliment

Aerospatiale, Auch,

Place St-Cyprien, Les Abattoirs & Arènes

Foix

Cité de l'Espace & Castres

George-Labit Museum

Montpellier

Grand-Rond

Jardin des Plantes

EATING

Les Abattoirs	
Chez Carmen	17
Le Café des Artistes	15
Benjamin	13
Bibent	9
Chez Atilla	5
Le Florida	10
Jour de Fête	4
Faim des Haricots	16
Les Jardins de l'Opéra	8
Michel Sarran	7
Au Pois Gourmand	2
Le Sept Place St-Sernin	3
La Table de la Bascule	20

DRINKING & NIGHTLIFE

L'Ambassade	12
Le Bikini	21
Bodega-Bodega	6
Le Cri de la Mouette	1
Erich Coffie	19
Le Petit Voisin	18
Shanghai Express	11
L'Ubu	14

ACCOMMODATION

Albert 1er	G	Garonne	K
Des Ambassadeurs	B	Grand Hôtel	
Beausejour	E	de l'Opéra	J
Camping de Rupé	A	Ours Blanc	F
Castellane	H	St-Sernin	C
Le Clochez de Rodez	D	Wilson Square	I

train station, though charmless and still retaining some of its red-light seediness, has a few acceptable options. There's no hostel, and the closest **campsite** is *Camping de Rupé*, chemin du Pont du Rupé (℡05.61.70.07.35, Ⓔcampinglerupe31@orange.fr; bus #59, stop "Rupé").

Albert 1er 8 rue Rivals ℡05.61.21.17.91, Ⓦwww.hotel-albert1.com. This small, comfortable and good-value establishment is set in a quiet side street just off the Capitole and close to the central market in place Victor-Hugo. Check for special weekend deals. ❹

Des Ambassadeurs 68 rue de Bayard ℡05.61.62.65.84, Ⓦwww.hotel-des-ambassadeurs .com. Very friendly little hotel just down from the station. All rooms have TV, en-suite bath and phone – a surprisingly good deal given the price. ❸

Beausejour 4 rue Caffarelli ℡05.61.62.77.59, Ⓔhotelbeausejour@cegetel.net. Basic, but dirt cheap, and with a great copper-balconied facade and soundproofed rooms. Best of the hotels in the slightly dodgy but engagingly gritty neighbourhood around place de Belfort. ❷

Castellane 17 rue Castellane ℡05.61.62.18.82, Ⓦwww.castellanehotel.com. A cheerful hotel with a wide selection of room sizes and types – most are bright and quiet. One of the few wheelchair-accessible hotels in this price range. ❺

🏃 **Le Clochez de Rodez** 14 place Jeanne-d'Arc ℡05.61.62.42.92, Ⓦwww.hotel -clochez-toulouse.com. Comfortable and central, with secure parking and all mod cons. Despite its size, it exudes a very personal hospitality. ❺

Garonne 22 descente de la Halle-aux-Poissons ℡05.34.31.94.80, Ⓦwww.hotelsgaronne.com.

A chic little hotel with fourteen rooms of under-stated luxury looking out over the river and the Old Town. Check the website for excellent-value weekend and off-season specials. The most romantic of the city's hotels. ❾

Grand Hôtel de l'Opéra 1 place du Capitole ℡05.61.21.82.66, Ⓦwww.grand-hotel-opera.com. The grande dame of Toulouse's hotels presides over the place du Capitole in the guise of a seventeenth-century convent. The rich decor, peppered with antiques and artwork, underlines the atmosphere of sophistication, and there's a fitness centre for working off that second helping of foie gras. ❾

Ours Blanc 25 place de Victor-Hugo ℡05.61.21.62.40, Ⓦwww.hotel-ours-blanc.com. Right by the covered market and steps from the Capitole, this welcoming hotel is one of the city's better bargains. Solid amenities including TV, a/c, wi-fi and phone, as well as private bath. ❺

St-Sernin 2 rue St-Bernard ℡05.61.21.73.08, Ⓦwww.hotelstsernin.com. Well-renovated old hotel in one of the best districts of the Old Town, around the basilica – close to all the action, but far enough away to provide peace in the evening. ❺

Wilson Square 12 rue d'Austerlitz ℡05.61.21.67.57, Ⓦwww.hotel-wilson.com. Clean and well-kept place at the top end of rue Austerlitz, with TV, a/c and a lift. Also has a great patisserie at street level. ❹

The City

The part of the city you'll want to see forms a rough hexagon clamped round a bend in the wide, brown River Garonne and contained within a ring of nineteenth-century boulevards, including Strasbourg, Carnot and Jules Guesde. The Canal du Midi, which here joins the Garonne on its way from the Mediterranean to the Atlantic, forms a further ring around this core. Old Toulouse is effectively quartered by two nineteenth-century streets: the long shopping street, **rue d'Alsace-Lorraine/rue du Languedoc**, which runs north–south; and **rue de Metz**, which runs east–west onto the Pont-Neuf and across the Garonne. It's all very compact and easily walkable, and the city's métro is of little use for getting to sites of interest.

In addition to the general pleasure of wandering the streets, there are three very good museums and some real architectural treasures in the churches of **St-Sernin** and **Les Jacobins** and in the magnificent Renaissance townhouses – *hôtels particuliers* – of the merchants who grew rich on the woad-dye trade. This formed the basis of the city's economy from the mid-fifteenth until the mid-sixteenth century, when the arrival of indigo from the Indian colonies wiped it out.

Place du Capitole is the centre of gravity for the city's social life. Its smart cafés throng with people at lunchtime and in the early evening, when the dying sun flushes the pink facade of the big town hall opposite. This is the scene of a mammoth Wednesday **market** for food, clothes and junk, and a smaller organic food market on Tuesday and Saturday mornings. From place du Capitole, a labyrinth of narrow medieval streets radiates out to the town's other squares, such as place Wilson, the more intimate place St-Georges, the delightful triangular place de la Trinité and place St-Étienne, in front of the cathedral.

For green space, you have to head for the sunny banks of the Garonne or the lovely formal gardens of the **Grand-Rond** and **Jardin des Plantes** in the southeast corner of the centre. A less obvious but attractive alternative is the towpath of the Canal du Midi; the best place to join it is a short walk southeast of the Jardin des Plantes, by the neo-Moorish pavilion of the Georges-Labit Museum, which houses a good collection of Egyptian and Oriental art.

The Capitole and the hôtels particuliers

Occupying the whole of the eastern side of the eponymous square, the **Capitole** has been the seat of Toulouse's city government since the twelfth century. In medieval times it housed the *capitouls*, who made up the oligarchic and independent city council from which its name derives. Today, these medieval origins are disguised by an elaborate pink and white classical facade (1750) of columns and pilasters, from which the flags of Languedoc, the Republic and the European Union are proudly flown. If there are no official functions taking place, you can peek inside (Mon–Fri 9am–5pm, Sat 9am–1pm; free) the Salle des Illustres and a couple of other rooms covered in flowery, late nineteenth-century murals and some more subdued Impressionist works by Henri Martin.

Many of the old *capitouls* built their **hôtels** in the dense web of now mainly pedestrianized streets around here. The material they used was almost exclusively the flat Toulousain brick, whose rosy colour gives the city its nickname of *Ville Rose*. It is an attractive material, lending a small-scale, detailed finish to otherwise plain facades, and setting off admirably any wood- or stonework. Although many of the *hôtels* survive, they are rarely open to the public, so you have to do a lot of nonchalant sauntering into courtyards to get a look at them. The best known, open to visitors thanks to its very handsome Bemberg collection of paintings, is the **Hôtel d'Assézat**, at the river end of rue de Metz (Tues–Sun 10am–12.30pm & 1–6pm, Thurs until 9pm; €4.60). Started in 1555 under the direction of Nicolas Bachelier, Toulouse's most renowned Renaissance architect, and never finished, it is a sumptuous palace of brick and stone, sporting columns of the three classical orders of Doric, Ionic and Corinthian, plus a lofty staircase tower surmounted by an octagonal lantern. The paintings within include works by Cranach the Elder, Tintoretto and Canaletto as well as moderns like Pissarro, Monet, Gauguin, Vlaminck, Dufy and a roomful of Bonnards. From April to October there's also a *salon de thé* in the entrance gallery.

Other fine houses exist just to the south: on rue Pharaon, in place des Carmes, on rue du Languedoc and on rue de la Dalbade, where the Hôtel Clary (also known as de Pierre) at no. 25 is unusual for being built of stone.

The Musée des Augustins, the cathedral and the riverside

Right at the junction of rue de Metz and rue d'Alsace-Lorraine stands the **Musée des Augustins** (Wed 10am–9pm, Thurs–Tues 10am–6pm; €3). Outwardly unattractive, the nineteenth-century building incorporates two surviving cloisters of an Augustinian priory (one now restored as a monastery garden) and contains outstanding collections of Romanesque and medieval sculpture, much of it saved from the now-vanished churches of Toulouse's golden age. Many of the pieces form a fascinating, highly naturalistic display of contemporary manners and fashions: merchants with forked beards touching one another's arms in a gesture of familiarity, and the Virgin represented as a pretty, bored young mother looking away from the Child who strains to escape her hold.

To the south of the museum, just past the Chambre de Commerce, **rue Croix-Baragnon**, full of smart shops and galleries, opens at its eastern end onto the equally attractive **place St-Étienne**, which boasts the city's oldest fountain, the Griffoul (1546). Behind it stands the lopsided **cathedral of St-Étienne**, whose construction was spread over so many centuries that it makes no architectural sense at all. But there's ample compensation in the quiet and elegant streets of the quarter immediately to the south, and in the **Musée Paul-Dupuy**, a few minutes' walk away along rue Tolosane and rue Mage at 13 rue de la Pléau (daily: June–Sept 10am–6pm; Oct–May 10am–5pm; €3), which has a beautifully displayed and surprisingly interesting collection of clocks, watches, clothes, pottery and furniture from the Middle Ages to the present day, as well as a good display of religious art.

If you follow the rue de Metz westward from the Musée des Augustins, you come to the **Pont-Neuf** – begun in 1544, despite its name – where you can cross over to the **St-Cyprien quarter** on the left bank of the Garonne. At the end of the bridge on the left, an old water tower, erected in 1822 to supply clean water to the city's drinking fountains, now houses the **Galerie Municipale du Château d'Eau** (Tues–Sun 1–7pm; €2.50), a small but influential photography exhibition space and information centre, with frequently changing exhibitions. Next door in the old hospital buildings there's a small **medical museum** (Thurs & Fri 1–5pm; 1st Sun of the month 10am–6pm; free), housing a selection of surgical instruments and pharmaceutical equipment.

But the star of the left bank is undoubtedly Toulouse's contemporary art gallery, **Les Abattoirs**, at 76 allées Charles-de-Fitte (Tues–Sun 11am–7pm; €6; ⓦwww .lesabattoirs.org). This splendid venue is not only one of France's best contemporary art museums, but an inspiring example of urban regeneration, constructed in a vast brick abattoir complex dating from 1828. The space itself is massive, with huge chambers perfectly suited to display even the largest canvases. The collection comprises over two thousand works (painting, sculpture, mixed- and multimedia) by artists from 44 countries; the most striking piece is undoubtedly Picasso's massive 14m by 20m theatre backdrop, *La dépouille du Minotaure en costume d'Arlequin*, painted in 1936 for Romain Rolland's *Le 14 juillet*, which towers over the lower gallery.

The churches of Les Jacobins and St-Sernin

A short distance west of place du Capitole, on rue Lakanal, you can't miss the **church of the Jacobins**. Constructed in 1230 by the Order of Preachers (Dominicans), which St Dominic had founded here in 1216 to preach against Cathar heretics, the church is a huge fortress-like rectangle of unadorned brick, buttressed – like Albi cathedral – by plain brick piles, quite unlike what you'd normally associate with Gothic architecture. The interior is a single space divided by a central row of ultra-slim pillars from whose minimal capitals spring an elegant splay of vaulting ribs – 22 from the last in line – like palm fronds. Beneath the altar lie the bones of the philosopher St Thomas Aquinas. On the north side, you step out into the calming hush of a **cloister** with a formal array of box trees and cypress in the middle, and its adjacent art **exhibition hall** (daily 9am–7pm; €3). Nearby, at the corner of rue Gambetta and rue Lakanal, poke your nose into the stone-galleried courtyard of the **Hôtel de Bernuy**, one of the city's most elaborate Renaissance houses.

From the north side of place du Capitole, **rue du Taur** leads past the belfry wall of **Notre-Dame-du-Taur**, whose diamond-pointed arches and decorative motifs are the acme of Toulousain bricklaying skills, to place St-Sernin. Here you're confronted with the largest Romanesque church in France, the **basilica of St-Sernin**, begun in 1080 to accommodate the passing hordes of Santiago pilgrims, and one of the loveliest examples of its genre. Its most striking external features are the octagonal brick belfry with rounded and pointed arches, diamond lozenges, colonnettes and mouldings picked out in stone, and the apse with nine radiating chapels. Entering from the south, you pass under the Porte Miégeville, whose twelfth-century carvings launched the influential Toulouse school of sculpture. Inside, the great high nave rests on brick piers, flanked by double aisles of diminishing height, surmounted by a gallery running right around the building. The fee for the **ambulatory** (daily 10am–6pm; €2) is worth it for the exceptional eleventh-century marble reliefs on the end wall of the choir and for the extraordinary wealth of reliquaries in the spacious **crypt**.

Right outside St-Sernin is the city's archeological museum, **Musée St-Raymond** (daily 10am–6/7pm; €3), housed in what remains of the block built for poor students of the medieval university and containing a large collection of objects ranging from prehistoric to Roman, as well as an excavated necropolis in the basement. On Sunday mornings the whole of place St-Sernin turns into a marvellous, teeming **flea market**.

The suburbs

To see something of the modern face of Toulouse, it's necessary to venture out into the suburbs, where you can visit a high-tech amusement park and a specialized but surprisingly interesting aircraft assembly plant. The first of these is the **Cité de l'Espace** (Feb–Aug daily 9am–5/7pm; €22, under-5s free), beside exit 17 of the A612 *périphérique* on the road to Castres, or take bus #19 from place Marengo (school hols only). The theme is space and space exploration, including satellite communications, space probes and, best of all, the opportunity to walk inside a mock-up of the Mir space station – fascinating, but chilling. Many of the exhibits are interactive, and though it's a bit on the pricey side, you could easily spend a half-day here, especially with children in tow.

At **Aérospatiale's** Usine Clément Ader, Airbus passenger jets are assembled, painted and tested in a vast hangar before taking their maiden flights from next-door Blagnac airport. The plant can be visited on a highly informative guided tour (normally in French; €14; ☏ 05.34.39.42.00, ⓦ www.taxiway.fr), but you need to apply in advance (a few days for EU citizens, two weeks for others). After a brief bus tour and a short film, you climb high above the eerily quiet assembly bays where just one hundred people, ably assisted by scores of computerized robots, churn out the latest Airbus, the A380, a two-storey superliner which dwarfs even the Jumbo.

Eating, drinking and nightlife

Regular daytime **café-lounging** can be pursued around the popular arty hangout of place Arnaud-Bernard, while place du Capitole is the early evening meeting place. Place St-Georges remains popular, though its clientele is no longer convincingly bohemian, and place Wilson also has its enthusiasts.

For lunch, a great informal option is the row of five or six small restaurants jammed in line on the mezzanine floor above the gorgeous **food market** in place Victor-Hugo, off boulevard de Strasbourg. They only function at midday, are all closed on Monday, and cost as little as €12 for market-fresh *menus*. Both food and atmosphere are perfect.

Cafés

Le Café des Artistes Place de la Daurade. Lively young café overlooking the Garonne. A perfect spot to watch the sun set on warm summer evenings, as floodlights pick out the brick buildings along the *quais*.

Bibent 5 place du Capitole. On the south side of the square, this is Toulouse's most distinguished café, with exuberant plasterwork, marble tables and cascading chandeliers.

Le Florida 12 place du Capitole. Relaxed café with a retro air. One of the most pleasant places to hang out on the central square.

Jour de Fête 43 rue du Taur. Trendy tearoom and brasserie with a small street-side patio. Friendly service and a young university-set crowd.

Restaurants

Les Abbatoirs Chez Carmen 97 allée Charles-de-Fitte ℡05.61.42.04.95. Family-run for two generations, this is one of the last of the traditional slaughterhouse-side meat emporia, with a reputation for top-of-the-line intestinal delicacies, as well as calves' brains and pigs' feet. *Menus* from €18. Closed Sun, Mon & Aug.

Benjamin 7 rue des Gestes ℡05.61.22.92.66. A long-standing institution for economical *terroir* food; service is pleasant and professional, although the atmosphere is somewhat anonymous. There's a wide selection of duck-based lunch and dinner *menus* from €11–€19. Open daily.

Chez Atilla Market, place Victor-Hugo. The best of the market restaurants, this no-nonsense lunchtime establishment is also one of Toulouse's best options for seafood – their Spanish *zarzuela* stew is a fish-lover's dream. *Menus* from €12. Closed Mon & part Aug.

Faim des Haricots 3 rue du Puits Vert ℡05.61.22.49.25. Toulouse's best vegetarian option, with generous *formules* starting at €11. Mon–Sat lunch & Thurs–Sat dinner; closed first half Aug.

Les Jardins de l'Opéra 1 place du Capitole ℡05.61.21.05.56. The *Grand Hôtel*'s restaurant is Toulouse's best and most luxurious. If you fancy a splurge you will pay for it – a basic *menu* starts at €29 at lunch and dinner is around €100 – but the food is outstanding. Closed Sun, Mon & part Aug.

🏃 **Michel Sarran** 21 bd Armand-Duportal ℡05.61.12.32.32. Justifiably renowned *gastronomique* restaurant, a 15min walk from the place du Capitole (follow rue des Lois and rue des Salenques to the end, and turn left). Imaginative dishes with a strong Mediterranean streak are served with style and warmth. *Menus* from €44 at lunch and €95 at dinner. Closed Wed lunch, Sat, Sun & part Aug.

Au Pois Gourmand 3 rue Émile-Heybrard ℡05.34.36.42.00. Great location in a riverside nineteenth-century house with a beautiful patio. The quality French cuisine does not come cheap here (*menus* €22–64), but is of a predictably high standard, and the *carte* presents a pleasant departure from purely regional dishes. Bus #66 or #14 from métro St-Cyprien-République. Closed Sat & Mon lunch & Sun.

🏃 **Le Sept Place St-Sernin** 7 place St-Sernin ℡05.62.30.05.30. A small house behind the basilica conceals a lively and cheerful restaurant serving inventive and original cuisine with a constantly changing *carte*, followed by dazzling desserts. *Menus* from €23. Closed Sat lunch & Sun.

La Table de la Bascule 14 av Maurice-Hauriou ℡05.61.52.09.51. A Toulouse institution. Its chromey interior is pure Art Deco and the food well prepared and presented. The menu includes regional dishes like cassoulet, *foie de canard* and oysters from the Bay of Arcachon. Expect to spend €25 or more. Closed Sat lunch & Sun.

Bars and clubs

L'Ambassade 22 bd de la Gare. Downbeat club where funk and soul rule. Live jazz on Sun nights. Mon–Fri 7pm–2am, Sat & Sun 7pm–5am.

Le Bikini 55 chemin des Étroits, rte de Lacroix-Falgarde ⓦwww.lebikini.com. On the city's southern outskirts, this is the hangout of Toulouse rockers, and a prime venue for live gigs. Open Thurs–Sun.

Bodega-Bodega 1 rue Gabriel-Péri. The old *Telegraph* newspaper building makes a superb venue for this bar-restaurant, with its hugely popular disco after 10pm. Daily 7pm–2am, till 4am on Sat.

Le Cri de la Mouette Place Héraklès ⓦwww.lecridelamouette.com. Popular disco featuring reggae, rock, funk and soul. Cover from €5. Daily 11pm–5am.

Erich Coffie 9 rue Joseph-Vié ℡05.61.42.04.27. Just west of the river in the *quartier* St-Cyprien, this is one of the city's liveliest and most enjoyable music bars (food available), with an eclectic music policy. Live bands most evenings. Tues–Sat from 10pm.

Le Petit Voisin 37 rue Peyrolières. A neighbourhood place, just like the name says, laid-back during the day, and with DJs at night. Mon–Fri 7.30am–2am, Sat 8am–4am. Closed part Aug.

Shanghai Express 12 rue de la Pomme. One of the city's most established gay and lesbian clubs, which attracts a mixed crowd including transvestites and transsexuals. Wed–Sun 11pm–late (on Sat right through to Sun 1pm).

L'Ubu 16 rue St-Rome ℡05.61.23.26.75. Long-standing pillar of the city's dance scene, which remains as popular as ever. Mon–Sat 11pm till dawn.

Film, theatre and live music

Drinking and dancing aside, there's plenty to do at night in Toulouse. Several **cinemas** regularly show *v.o.* films, including: ABC, 13 rue St-Bernard (℡05.61.29.81.00, ⓦwww.abc-toulouse.net); Cinémathèque, 68 rue du Taur (℡05.62.30.30.10, ⓦwww.lacinemathequedetoulouse.com); Le Cratère, 95 Grande-Rue St-Michel (℡05.61.52.50.53); and Utopia, 24 rue Montardy (℡05.61.23.66.20, ⓦwww.cinemas-utopia.org). There's also a vibrant **theatre** culture here. The tourist office can give you a full list of venues, which range from the official Théâtre de la Cité, 1 rue Pierre-Baudis (℡05.34.45.05.05, ⓦwww .tnt-cite.com), to the workshop Nouveau Théâtre Jules-Julien, 6 av des Écoles-Jules-Juliens (Mon–Fri 9am–noon & 2–5pm; ℡05.61.25.79.92). The larger venues, such as Odyssud, 4 av du Parc Blagnac (℡05.61.71.75.15; bus #66), feature both theatre and **opera**, while the Orchestre National du Capitole has its base in the Halle aux Grains on place Dupuy (℡05.61.99.78.00, ⓦwww.onct .mairie-toulouse.fr). The city's biggest **concert venue** (9000 seats), specializing in rock, is Zénith, at 11 av Raymond Badiou (℡05.62.74.49.49; métro Arènes), while Cave-Poésie at 71 rue du Taur (℡05.61.23.62.00) is home to literary workshops and gatherings of a decidedly bohemian spirit.

Listings

Airport Aéroport Toulouse-Blagnac ℡05.61.42.44.00 and 05.24.61.80.00, ⓦwww.toulouse.aeroport.fr; buses from 5am–8.20pm every 20min, returning 7.35–12.15am; €4; tickets can be bought from driver.

Bike rental Municipal bikes (subscribe for €1 per day, €5 per week, at ⓦwww.velo.toulouse.fr) are available for free up to 30min at a time from over 200 automated stations. You are charged extra (approx. €2 per hour) if you exceed half an hour.

Books The best general bookshops are Castéla, on place du Capitole, and FNAC, at 16 allées Franklin Roosevelt. There are book markets on Thursday mornings in place Arnaud-Bernard, and all day Saturday in place St-Étienne.

Consulates Canada, 10 rue Jules de Resseguier ℡05.61.52.19.06, ⓔconsulat.canada-st _pierreetmiquelon@amb-canada.fr; USA, 25 allées Jean-Jaurès ℡05.34.41.36.50, ⓦfrance .usembassy.gov; the closest British Consulate is in Bordeaux at 353 bd Wilson (℡05.57.22.21.10; ⓦukinfrance.fco.gov.uk); there is an Honorary Consulate in Toulouse (℡05.61.30.37.91).

Gay and lesbian For information, contact the gay and lesbian students' group Jules et Julies, Comité des Étudiants, Université du Mirail, 5 allée Machado, 310589, or Gais et Lesbiennes en Marche (℡06.11.87.38.81, ⓔgelem@altern.org).

Health For medical emergencies contact SAMU (℡115). The network of university hospitals has facilities all over the city. For non-emergencies check their website for the appropriate centre (ⓦwww.chu-toulouse.fr).

Internet Cyber Media-Net, 19 rue des Lois (Mon–Fri 9am–11.30pm, Sat 10am–midnight), or @fterbug, 12 place St-Sernin (Mon–Fri noon–2am, Sat noon–5am, Sun 2.30–10.30pm).

Pharmacy The Pharmacie de Nuit, 70–76 allées Jean-Jaurès (entry on rue Arnaud-Vidal) is open 8pm–8am.

Police 23 bd de l'Embouchure ℡05.61.12.77.77.

Taxi Capitole ℡05.34.25.02.50; Taxi Radio Toulousain ℡05.61.42.38.38. For taxis to the airport call ℡05.61.30.02.54.

Albi and around

ALBI, 77km and an hour's train ride northeast of Toulouse, is a small industrial town with two unique sights: a museum containing the most comprehensive collection of Toulouse-Lautrec's work (Albi was his birthplace); and one of the most remarkable Gothic cathedrals you'll ever see. Its other claim to fame comes from its association with Catharism; though not itself an important centre, it gave its name – Albigensian – to both the heresy and the crusade to suppress it.

The town hosts three good **festivals** over the course of the year: jazz in May, theatre at the end of June and beginning of July, and classical music at the end of July and beginning of August. During July and August there are also free organ recitals in the cathedral (Wed 5pm & Sun 4pm). The tourist office can supply information and programmes.

Arrival, information and accommodation

From the **gare SNCF** on place Stalingrad it's a ten-minute walk into town along avenues Maréchal-Joffre and de-Gaulle; you'll see the **gare routière** on your right in place Jean-Jaurès as you reach the limits of the Old Town. The **tourist office** is in one corner of the Palais de la Berbie (July & Aug Mon–Sat 9am–7pm, Sun 10am–12.30pm & 2.30–6.30pm; Sept–June Mon–Sat 9am–12.30pm & 2–6/6.30pm, Sun 10am–12.30pm & 2.30–5pm; T05.63.49.48.80, Wwww.albi -tourisme.fr); ask for a copy of their English-language leaflet describing three walking tours round Albi. Also recommended is the "Albi Pass" (€6.50) which gives free or discounted admission to the town's sights.

There are two attractive **hotels** near the station on avenue Maréchal-Joffre, which have now merged: *La Régence*, at no. 27, and the *George V*, at no. 29 (T05.63.54.24.16, Wwww.hotelgeorgev.com; ❸). On the opposite side of the town, on the north bank of the river, you'll find the luxurious *Mercure Albi Bastides* (T05.63.47.66.66, Wlemoulin-albi.fr; ❹) at 41 rue Porta. In the heart of old Albi near the cathedral, the *Hôtel St-Clair*, 8 rue St-Clair (T05.63.54.25.66, Wwww .hotel-albi-saintclair.com; ❸), is a good bargain, but ✕ *Le Vieil Alby*, 25 rue Toulouse-Lautrec (T05.63.54.14.69, Wlevieilalby.com; ❹) is a real find – cheap and comfortable, with a friendly owner and excellent home-cooked food available. Otherwise, there's a caravan park and **campsite** (T05.63.60.37.06; Easter–Oct) in the Parc de Caussels, about 2km east on the D999 Millau road.

The Town

The **Cathédrale Ste-Cécile** (daily: June–Sept 9am–6.30pm; Oct–May 9am– noon & 2.30–6.30pm; free; entry to choir €3, to treasury €3), begun about 1280, is visible from miles around, dwarfing the town like some vast bulk carrier run aground, the belfry its massive superstructure. The comparison sounds unflat- tering, and this is not a conventionally beautiful building; it's all about size and boldness of conception. The sheer plainness of the exterior is impressive on this scale, and it's not without interest: arcading, buttressing, the contrast of stone against brick – every differentiation of detail becomes significant. Entrance is through the south portal, by contrast the most extravagant piece of flamboyant- Gothic sixteenth-century frippery. The interior, a hall-like nave of colossal proportions, is dominated by a huge mural of the Last Judgement, believed to be the work of Flemish artists in the late fifteenth century. Above, the vault is covered in richly colourful paintings of sixteenth-century Italian workmanship, while a rood screen, delicate as lace, shuts off the choir: Adam makes a show of covering himself, Eve strikes a flaunting model's pose beside the central doorway, and the rest of the screen is adorned with countless statues.

Next to the cathedral, a powerful red-brick castle, the thirteenth-century **Palais de la Berbie**, houses the **Musée Toulouse-Lautrec** (April–June & Sept daily 9/10am–noon & 2–6pm; July & Aug daily 9am–6pm; Oct–March Wed–Mon 10am–noon & 2–5/6pm; €5.50). It contains paintings, drawings, lithographs and posters from the earliest work to the very last – an absolute must for anyone inter- ested in *belle époque* seediness and, given the predominant Impressionism of the time, the rather offbeat painting style of its subject. But perhaps the most impressive

ALBI

▲ Castelnau & Lescure

N

RUE ST-MARIE
RUE DE LA MADELEINE
RUE DE CANTEPAU
RUE RINALDI
RUE PORTA
RUE DU PORT
RUE PORTA
RK PERROTY
RUE RINALDI
RUE PORTA
RUE DU TENDAT

A
1

PONT DU 22 AOÛT 1944

RUE ÉDOUARD BRANLY

River Tarn

2

RUE PONT-VIEUX

R. BASSE DES MOULINS
RUE DE LA RIVIERE
R. EMILE GRAND

Gabares
Pier

SENTIER DES BERGES DU TARN

3 QUAI CHOISEUL

RUE DE LA VIGNE
RUE DE LA GDE CÔTE
RUE ST AFRIC
RUE DE LA RUDDE

LICES GEORGES POMPIDOU

RUE DE LA RÉPUBLIQUE

Palais
de la Berbie

RUE DE LA SOUQUE
R ST ÉTIENNE

Covered
Market

R.BONNE CAMBE R.D'ELBENE
R.STE RHONE
RUE DE
CLAIRE

Musée
Toulouse-
Lautrec

DE LA TEMPORALITÉ
R.D FARGUES
PLACE DU
MARCHÉ
R.D FOISSANTS
RUE ST CLAIRE
RUE CANDEIL

i

R DE LA MAITRISE

RUE
SAINT
JULIEN

RUE AUGUSTIN MALROUX

PLACE DE LA TRÉBAILLE

PLACE
SAINTE
CÉCILE

RUE MARIES

Cathédrale Ste-Cécile

St-Salvy

PLACE DU
CLOITRE

RUE STE-MARIE
IMP STE-MARIE

R DE LA CROIX VERTE

R CAMINADE
RUE DE LA PIALE
R.D PEYRES
R DE LA CROIX BLANCHE
RUE STE CÉCILE
R DE L'OULMET
R.D PUITS DE LA GRACE
IMP TIMBAL
IMP TIMBAL
RUE TIMBAL
RUE D'EMPEYRALOTS

R SERE DE RIVIERE

BD GÉNÉRAL SIBILLE

R DU C BRIOT
R P BERENGUIER
R DU PLANCAT
R ST SAUNA
R ROQUELAURE
RUE DES PÉNITENTS
Hôtel
du Ville

PLACE
DU
VIGAN

LICES JEAN MOULIN

B
4
C

RUE T. LAUTREC
R DES NOBLES
RUE DE VERDUSSE
RUE DE L'HÔTEL DE VILLE
5 RUE DE L'ORT EN SALVY
R DU BOURGUET

R ST ANTOINE

BD DU GÉNÉRAL SIBILLE
BD DU GÉNÉRAL SIBILLE

PLACE DU
PALAIS

R.LOCTEUR DEVISON
RUE DU SEL
R.DES MUETES
RUE LA VIOLETTE
RUE DE LA PORTE NEUVE
R DU MINE
RUE DU DOCTEUR CAMBOULIVES

PLACE
LAPEROUSE

RUE DE LA BERCHERE
CHEMIN DE MERVILLE

Jardin National

RUE HIPPOLYTE SAVARY

Gare
Routière

BD ÉDOUARD ANDRIEU

AV CHARLES DE GAULLE
R.D CORBELIERS
RUE DE GENÈVE
AV GAMBETTA

0   200 m

▼ **D, E** & Gare SNCF (250m)

Castres & Toulouse ▼

thing about this museum is the building itself, its parapets, gardens and walkways giving stunning views over the river and its bridges.

Opposite the east end of the cathedral, rue Mariés leads into the shopping streets of the Old Town, most of which has been impeccably renovated and restored. The little square and covered passages by the church of St-Salvy are worth a look as you go by. Eventually you come to the broad Lices Georges Pompidou, the main thoroughfare of modern Albi, which leads down to the river and the road to Cordes. Less touristy, this is the best place to look for somewhere to eat and drink.

Eating

Albi's cuisine is predominantly *terroir* – local cooking notable only for *lou tastou*, the local version of tapas. One of the best *terroir* **restaurants** is *La Viguière d'Alby* at 7 rue Toulouse-Lautrec, long an Albigeois *terroir* institution, now with a *gastronomique* twist (℡05.63.54.76.44; closed Wed eve & Thurs off season; from €15 at lunch to €60 eve). *Le Robinson*, at 142 rue Édouard Branly (℡05.63.46.15.69; closed Tues & Wed off season & Nov–March; from €17), is set apart by its park-like surroundings, while *L'Esprit du Vin*, 11 quai Choiseul (℡05.63.54.60.44; closed Sun, Mon & mid-Feb to May; from €30), has imaginative cuisine. *Tournesol*, off place du Vigan (℡05.63.38.38.14; Tues–Sat lunch only & Fri dinner), is Albi's vegetarian option (from about €20).

Cordes

One of the region's "don't miss" sights is **CORDES**, perched on a conical hill 24km northwest of Albi, from which it's a brief trip by train (as far as Cordes-Vindrac, 5km away, with bike rental from the station) or bus (daily except Sun). Founded in 1222 by Raymond VII, Count of Toulouse, Cordes was a **Cathar** stronghold, and the ground beneath the town is riddled with tunnels for storage and refuge in time of trouble. As one of the southwest's oldest and best-preserved *bastides*, complete with thirteenth- and fourteenth-century houses climbing steep cobbled lanes, Cordes is inevitably a major tourist attraction: medieval banners flutter in the streets and artisans practise their crafts. The **Musée Charles-Portal** (July & Aug daily 2–6pm; Sept–June Sat & Sun 2–5/6pm; €2.50) depicts the history of the town. Also of interest is the **Musée d'Art Moderne et Contemporain** (daily: Feb, March, Nov & Dec 2–5pm; April, May & Oct 11.30am–12.30pm & 2–6.30pm; June–Sept 11am–12.30pm & 2–7pm; €4), which features works by the figurative painter Yves Brayer, who lived in Cordes from 1940. The best **hotel** in town is the splendid ☀ *Grand Écuyer* (℡05.63.53.79.50, ⓦwww.legrandecuyer.com; closed mid-Oct to Easter; ❽) – from its gargoyle-studded facade to the ponderous stone of the interior, this former palace of Count Raymond VII of Toulouse is an evocative combination of medieval atmosphere and modern amenities. Just down the street, the *Vieux Cordes* (℡05.63.53.79.20, ⓦwww.vieuxcordes.com; closed Jan; ❹) is housed in a medieval building.

Castres

In spite of its industrial activities, **CASTRES**, 40km south of Albi and 55km east of Toulouse, has kept a lot of its charm, in the streets on the right bank of the Agout and, in particular, the riverside quarter where the old tanners' and weavers' houses overhang the water. The centre is a bustling, businesslike sort of place, with

Jean Jaurès

Jean Jaurès, the nineteenth-century labour activist, politician and martyr, was born in Castres in 1859. He showed exceptional promise as a student and won a scholarship to complete his studies in Paris. After graduating, rather than stay in the capital he returned to his home *département* of Tarn and taught philosophy in Albi, while lecturing at the University of Toulouse. But the miserable living and working conditions of his working-class neighbours drew him out of the academy. At the young age of 26 Jaurès was elected a legislative representative. Under his guidance the glass-workers at Albi founded the collectively run VOA bottle factory, which still operates today. In 1893, as socialist deputy for Carmaux, he supported the miners' struggle, and his renown as a social reformer began to spread.

However, Jaurès's desire for reform was not limited to local causes, and in 1898 he joined other liberals, including Zola, in defence of the Jewish army captain, **Alfred Dreyfus**, convicted on unfounded charges of espionage, and helped to obtain his eventual pardon. The patriotically charged issue temporarily cost Jaurès his popularity, but he was soon back, founding the Communist daily **L'Humanité** in 1904 (still one of France's major newspapers; ⓦwww.humanite.fr) and helping found the socialist SFIO party. With the dawn of World War I, Jaurès's internationalism was manifested in an outspoken and unpopular pacifist stand which led to his **assassination** in Paris by a nationalist extremist called Villain in July 1914. He was hailed as a martyr, and became the hero of the Tarn – a local politician who fought for this marginalized region, and who wasn't afraid to take on the political establishment of Paris in order to defend a higher justice.

There could be no better epitaph than his own last article in *L'Humanité*, in which he wrote: "The most important thing is that we should continue to act and to keep our minds perpetually fresh and alive... That is the real safeguard, the guarantee of our future."

a big morning **market** on Saturdays on place Jean-Jaurès. By the rather unremarkable old cathedral, the former bishop's palace holds the Hôtel de Ville and Castres' **Musée Goya** (July & Aug daily noon–6pm; Sept–June Tues–Sun 9am–noon & 2–5/6pm; €2.30), home to the biggest collection of Spanish paintings in France outside the Louvre. Goya is represented by some lighter political paintings and a large collection of engravings, and there are also works by other famous Iberian artists, like Murillo and Velázquez.

Castres' other specialist museum is the **Musée Jean-Jaurès** (same hours as Goya museum; €1.50), dedicated to its famous native son (see box above). It's located in place Pélisson, and getting to it takes you through the streets of the Old Town, past the splendid seventeenth-century **Hôtel Nayrac**, on rue Frédéric-Thomas. The museum was opened in 1988 by President Mitterrand – appropriately enough, because Mitterrand's Socialist Party is the direct descendant of Jaurès's SFIO, founded in 1905, which split at the Congress of Tours in 1920 when the "Bolshevik" element left to form the French Communist Party. The slightly hagiographic museum nonetheless pays well-deserved tribute to one of France's boldest and best political writers, thinkers and activists of modern times.

Practicalities

Arriving from Toulouse by train, you'll find the **gare SNCF** a kilometre southwest of the town centre on avenue Albert-1ᵉʳ. The **gare routière** is on place Soult, with bus services to Mazamet and Lacaune. The **tourist office** stands beside the Pont Vieux at 3 rue Milhau-Ducommun (July & Aug daily 9.30am–12.30pm &

1.30–6.30pm; Sept–June Mon–Sat 9.30am–12.30pm & 2–6pm; ☏05.63.62.63.62, ⓦwww.ville-castres.fr).

Castres has two marvellous seventeenth-century mansions converted into luxurious but affordable **hotels**: the marginally more luxurious 𝄡 *Renaissance* is at 17 rue Victor-Hugo (☏05.63.59.30.42, ⓦwww.hotel-renaissance.fr; ❺); and the *Rivière*, 10 quai Tourcaudière (☏05.63.59.04.53, ⓦpagesperso-orange.fr /hotelriviere; ❸), has helpful staff and pleasant views over the Agout. The municipal **campsite** (☏05.63.59.33.51, ⓦwww.campingdegourjade.net; closed Oct–March) is in a riverside park 2km northeast of town on the road to Roque-courbe, which you can also reach by river-taxi (round-trip €5).

As for **restaurants**, *La Mandragore*, 1 rue Malpas (☏05.63.59.51.27; closed Sun & Mon lunch), is praised both for its *gastronomique* cuisine and selection of wines (*menus* €13–36), while *Le Médiéval* at 44 rue Milhau-Ducommun (☏05.63.51.13.78; closed Sun & Mon), has great atmosphere and a riverside location (*menus* from €18).

The Gers

West of Toulouse, the *département* of **Gers** lies at the heart of the historic region of Gascony. In the long struggle for supremacy between the English and the French in the Middle Ages it had the misfortune to form the frontier zone between the English base at Bordeaux and the French at Toulouse. The attractive if unspectacular rolling agricultural land is dotted with ancient, honey-stoned farms. Settlement is sparse and – with the exception of **Auch**, the capital – major monuments are largely lacking, which keeps it well off the beaten tourist trails.

The region's traditional sources of renown are its stout-hearted mercenary warriors – of whom Alexandre Dumas' d'Artagnan and Edmond Rostand's Cyrano de Bergerac are the supreme literary exemplars – its rich cuisine and its **Armagnac**. The food and brandy still flourish: Gers is the biggest producer of **foie gras** in the country.

Auch

The sleepy provincial capital of the Gers, **AUCH** is most easily accessible by rail from Toulouse, 78km to the east. The Old Town, which is the only part worth exploring, stands on a bluff overlooking the tree-lined River Gers, with the cathedral towering dramatically over the town.

It is this building – the **Cathédrale Ste-Marie** – which makes a trip to Auch worthwhile. Although not finished until the latter part of the seventeenth century, it is built in broadly late-Gothic style, with a classical facade. Of particular interest are the choir stalls (daily: mid-July to Aug 8.30am–6.30pm; Sept–June 8.30/9am–noon & 2–5/6pm; closed during services; €2) and the stained glass; both were begun in the early 1500s, though the windows are of clearly Renaissance inspira-tion, while the choir remains Gothic. The stalls are thought to have been carved by the same craftsmen who executed those at St-Bertrand-de-Comminges, and show the same extraordinary virtuosity and detail. The eighteen windows, unusual in being a complete set, parallel the scenes and personages depicted in the stalls. They are the work of a Gascon painter, Arnaud de Moles, and are equally rich in detail.

Immediately south of the cathedral, in the tree-filled place Salinis, is the 40m-high **Tour d'Armagnac**, which served as an ecclesiastical court and prison in the fourteenth century. Descending from here to the river is a

Armagnac

Armagnac is a dry, golden brandy distilled in the district extending into the Landes and Lot and Garonne *départements*, divided into three distinct areas: Haut-Armagnac (around Auch), Ténarèze (Condom) and Bas-Armagnac (Éauze), in ascending order of output and quality. Growers of the grape like to compare brandy with whisky, equating malts with the individualistic, earthy Armagnac distilled by small producers, and blended whiskies with the more consistent, standardized output of the large-scale houses. Armagnac grapes are grown on sandy soils and, importantly, the wine is distilled only once, giving the spirit a lower alcohol content but more flavour. Aged in local black oak, Armagnac matures quickly, so young Armagnacs are relatively smoother than corresponding Cognacs.

Distilled originally for medicinal reasons, Armagnac has many claims made for its efficacy. Perhaps the most optimistic are those of the priest of Éauze de St-Mont, who held that the eau de vie cured **gout** and hepatitis. More reasonably, he also wrote that it "stimulates the spirit if taken in moderation, recalls the past, gives many joys, above all else, conserves youth. If one retains it in the mouth, it unties the tongue and gives courage to the timid."

Many of the producers welcome visitors and offer tastings, whether you go to one of the bigger *chais* of Condom or Éauze, or follow a faded sign at the bottom of a farm track. For more **information**, contact the Bureau National Interprofessionnel de l'Armagnac, place de la Liberté, 32800 Éauze (☎05.62.08.11.00, ⓦwww.cognacnet .com/armagnac).

monumental stairway of 234 steps, with a statue of d'Artagnan gracing one of the terraces. From place de la République, in front of the cathedral's main west door, rue d'Espagne connects with rue de la Convention and what is left of the narrow medieval stairways known as the **pousterles**, which give access to the lower town. On the north side of place de la République, the tourist office inhabits a splendid, half-timbered fifteenth-century house on the corner with rue Dessoles, a pedestrianized street boasting an array of fine buildings. Just down the steps to the east of rue Dessoles, on place Louis-Blanc, the former convent, now the **Musée des Jacobins** (Feb, March, Nov & Dec Mon–Fri 2–5pm, Sat & Sun 10am–noon & 2–5pm; April–Oct daily 10am–noon & 2–6pm; €4), houses one of the best collections of pre-Columbian and later South American art in France, left to the town by an adventurous son, M. Pujos, who had lived in Chile in the last years of the nineteenth century. Also of interest is its small collection of traditional Gascon furniture, religious artefacts and Gallo-Roman remains.

Practicalities

The **tourist office** (May to mid-July & mid-Aug to Sept Mon–Sat 9.15/ 10am–noon & 2–6pm, Sun 10am–12.15pm; mid-July to mid-Aug Mon–Sat 9.30am–6.30pm, Sun 10am–12.15pm & 3–6pm; Oct–April Mon–Sat 9.15/10am–noon & 2–6pm; Oct Sun only 10am–12.15pm; ☎05.62.05.22.89, ⓦwww.auch-tourisme.com) stands at the corner of place de la République and rue Dessoles. West of here, place de la Libération leads to the allées d'Étigny, with the **gare routière** off to the right.

In terms of **accommodation**, the only choice in the centre is the relatively luxurious *Hôtel de France* at 2 place de la Libération (☎05.62.61.71.71, ⓦwww .hoteldefrance-auch.com; ⑨), right by the *mairie* and only a few minutes' walk west of the cathedral. The best hotel is 2km northwest of the town centre: the *Château les Charmettes* (☎05.62.62.10.10, ⓦwww.chateaulescharmettes.com; ⑧).

An economical alternative is the *Hôtel de Paris*, 38 av de la Marne (☏ 05.62.63.26.22, ⓔ hotelparis.auch@orange.fr; closed Nov; ❷). To get here from the **gare SNCF**, turn right on avenue de la Gare, follow it to the end, then turn left. Otherwise, the municipal **campsite** (☏ 05.62.05.00.22; mid-April to mid-Oct) is beside the river on the south side of town.

Avenue d'Alsace, in the lower town, is the best place to look for inexpensive places to **eat**. Alternatively, up by the cathedral, place de la République and place de la Libération boast a fair selection of cafés and brasseries; try *Café Daroles* by the fountain (*menus* from €19, or €10 at lunch). For something traditional, *La Table d'Oste*, off rue Dessoles at 7 rue Lamartine, offers good Gascon fare from €16–24 (closed Sat–Mon, depending on season). The well-regarded restaurant of the *Hôtel de France* has *menus* from €18, although à la carte will set you back considerably more.

Travel details

Trains

Béziers to: Agde (18 daily; 45min); Arles (10–14 daily; 2hr 10min); Avignon (4–10 daily; 2hr); Bédarieux (4–8 daily; 40min); Carcassonne (22 daily; 45min–1hr 45min); Clermont-Ferrand (3 daily; 6–7hr); Marseille (8 daily; 3hr 10min); Millau (4–6 daily; 2hr); Montpellier (26 daily; 45min); Narbonne (18 daily; 14min); Nîmes (20 daily; 1hr 15min); Paris (30 daily; 4hr 30min–12hr); Perpignan (18 daily; 40min–1hr); Sète (23 daily; 25min).

Carcassonne to: Arles (4–8 daily; 2hr 40min–3hr 30min); Béziers (22 daily; 45min–1hr 45min); Bordeaux (18–22 daily; 3hr 20min–4hr 30min); Limoux (16 daily; 25min); Marseille (12–18 daily; 3hr 20min–5hr 30min); Montpellier (18 daily; 1hr 30min–4hr); Narbonne (22 daily; 35min); Nîmes (26 daily; 2hr 5min–3hr 10min); Quillan (6 daily; 1hr 15min); Toulouse (22 daily; 45min–1hr).

Montpellier to: Arles (10–14 daily; 1hr 20min); Avignon (22 daily; 1hr 15min–2hr); Béziers (18 daily; 40min); Carcassonne (22 daily; 1hr 15min); Lyon (18 daily; 1hr 40min–3hr 30min); Marseille (18–22 daily; 2hr 20min); Mende (18 daily; 3hr 40min–4hr 30min); Narbonne (26 daily; 45min–1hr 15min); Paris (16 daily; 3hr 15min–6hr); Perpignan (12 daily; 2hr 15min); Sète (22 daily; 15–20min); Toulouse (18 daily; 2hr 15min–2hr 55min).

Narbonne to: Arles (18–22 daily; 2hr); Avignon (4–8 daily; 2hr 10min); Béziers (18 daily; 14min); Bordeaux (18–22 daily; 3hr 45min–6hr); Carcassonne (22 daily; 35min); Cerbère (12–16 daily; 1hr–1hr 30min); Marseille (20 daily; 2hr 40min–3hr 30min); Montpellier (26 daily; 45min–1hr 15min); Nîmes (20 daily; 1hr 45min);

Perpignan (24 daily; 36–45min); Sète (23 daily; 45min); Toulouse (18 daily; 1hr 30min).

Nîmes to: Arles (22 daily; 30–40min); Avignon (14–18 daily; 30min); Béziers (36 daily; 1hr 15min); Carcassonne (26 daily; 2hr 5min–3hr 10min); Clermont-Ferrand (12–16 daily; 5–6hr); Marseille (20 daily; 40min–1hr 15min); Montpellier (26 daily; 30min); Narbonne (20 daily; 1hr 45min); Paris (23 daily; 3hr–9hr 30min); Perpignan (12 daily; 2hr 45min); Sète (22 daily; 48min).

Toulouse to: Albi (17 daily; 1hr); Auch (18–20 daily; 1hr 15min–2hr 30min); Ax-les-Thermes (6 daily; 1hr 55min); Bayonne (18–22 daily; 2hr 25min–3hr 45min); Bordeaux (18–22 daily; 2hr 30min); Castres (11 daily; 1hr 5min); Foix (13 daily; 47min–1hr 15min); La-Tour-de-Carol (6 daily; 2hr 30min); Lourdes (8–16 daily; 1hr 40min); Lyon (14–18 daily; 4–6hr); Marseille (22 daily; 3hr 30min–6hr); Mazamet (11 daily; 1hr 30min–1hr 55min); Paris (13 daily; 5hr 20min–6hr 45min); Pau (6–10 daily; 2hr–2hr 30min); Tarascon-sur-Ariège (13 daily; 1hr 20min); Tarbes (6–13 daily; 1hr 45min).

Buses

Albi to: Cordes-sur-Ciel (2 daily; 35min).

Auch to: Bordeaux (1 daily; 3hr 40min); Condom (1–2 daily; 40min); Lectoure (4–8 daily; 40min); Montauban (generally up to 3 daily, check before leaving; 2hr); Tarbes (3–4 daily; 2hr); Toulouse (1–4 daily; 1hr 30min).

Bédarieux to: Olargues (1–2 daily; 40min); St-Pons-de-Thomières (3 daily; 1hr 20min).

Béziers to: Agde (2 daily & 4–6 in summer; 25min); Bédarieux (generally up to 2 daily, check before leaving; 1hr); Castres (2 daily; 2hr 50min);

La Salvetat (generally up to 2 daily, check before leaving; 2hr 10min); Mazamet (2 daily; 2hr); Pézenas (4–11 daily; 32min); St-Pons-de-Thomières (4 daily; 1hr 20min).
Carcassonne to: Castelnaudary (3–5 daily; 45min); Quillan (2 daily; 1hr 20min).
Montpellier to: Aigues-Mortes (2–4 daily; 1hr); Bédarieux (3–4 daily; 1hr 35min); Gignac (for St-Guilhem: 6–8 daily; 40min); La Grande-Motte (8–12 daily; 1hr 5min; hourly in summer); Grau-du-Roi (4–8 daily; 1hr 10min); Le Vigan (3–5 daily; 1hr 40min); Lodève (4 daily; 1hr 15min); Millau (2–8 daily; 2hr 20min); Palavas (local service); Rodez (1–3 daily; 3hr 55min); St-Pons-de-

Thomières (1–3 daily; 2hr 55min).
Narbonne to: Gruissan (3–6 daily; 45min); Narbonne-Plage (2–8 daily; 45min).
Nîmes to: Aigues-Mortes (17 daily; 55min); Ganges (2–3 daily; 1hr 30min); La Grande-Motte (2–9 daily; 1hr 30min); Le Grau-du-Roi (12–18 daily; 1hr 15min); Le Vigan (3–5 daily; 1hr 50min); Pont du Gard (8 daily; 45min); Sommières (8 daily; 45min); Uzès (8–12 daily; 30min–1hr).
Sète to: Montpellier (3–15 daily; 1hr 5min).
Toulouse to: Albi (12–16 weekly; 2hr 40min); Carcassonne (1 daily; 2hr 20min); Castres (8–12 weekly; 1hr 40min–2hr); St-Girons (3 daily; 2hr 30min).

The Massif Central

CHAPTER 12 # Highlights

✳ **Cheese** The pasture lands of France's central region produce some of its best cheeses: Roquefort, Laguiole and St-Nectaire. See p.719

✳ **Puy de Dôme** Four hundred metres above Clermont-Ferrand, this long-extinct volcano offers staggering vistas of the Massif Central. See p.724

✳ **Conques** Modern pilgrims trek to this monastery town, once an important way-station on the medieval Chemin de St-Jacques, for the church's Romanesque facade and treasury of early medieval reliquaries. See p.739

✳ **Canoeing** The river gorges of the Tarn, Lot and Ardèche provide near limitless opportunities for kayaking and canoeing. See p.744 & p.751

✳ **Cirque de Navacelles** Cutting 150m down into the limestone *causse*, the River Vis doubles back on itself, leaving a tiny island that was capped centuries ago by a farming hamlet. See p.745

✳ **Gorges de l'Ardèche** From the natural bridge at Pont d'Arc, the rushing Ardèche has carved out a dramatic descent through wooded and cave-riddled cliffs. See p.751

▲ Canoeing on the Ardèche River

The Massif Central

One of the loveliest spots on earth…a country without roads, without guides, without any facilities for locomotion, where every discovery must be conquered at the price of danger or fatigue…a soil cut up with deep ravines, crossed in every way by lofty walls of lava, and furrowed by numerous torrents.

The Marquis de Villemer.

Thus one of George Sand's characters described the Haute-Loire, the central *département* of the **Massif Central**, and it's a description that could still be applied to some of the region. Thickly forested and sliced by numerous rivers and lakes, these once volcanic uplands are geologically the oldest part of France and culturally one of the most firmly rooted in the past. Industry and tourism have made few inroads here, and the people remain rural and somewhat taciturn, with an enduring sense of regional identity.

The Massif Central takes up a huge portion of the centre of France, but only a handful of towns have gained a foothold in its rugged terrain: **Le Puy**, spiked with theatrical pinnacles of lava, is the most compelling, with its steep streets and majestic cathedral; the spa town of **Vichy** has an antiquated elegance and charm; even heavily industrial **Clermont-Ferrand**, the capital, has a certain cachet in the black volcanic stone of its historic centre and its stunning physical setting beneath the **Puy de Dôme**, a 1464m-high volcanic plug. There is pleasure, too, in the unpretentious provinciality of **Aurillac** and in the untouched medieval architecture of smaller places like **Murat**, **Besse**, **Salers**, **Orcival**, **Sauveterre-de-Rouergue** and **La Couvertoirade**, and in the hugely influential abbey of **Conques**. But, above all, this is a country where the sights are landscapes rather than towns, churches and museums.

The heart of the region is the **Auvergne**, a wild and unexpected scene of extinct volcanoes (*puys*), stretching from the grassy domes and craters of the **Monts-Dômes** to the eroded skylines of the **Monts-Dore**, and the deeply ravined **Cantal mountains** to the forest of darkly wooded pinnacles surrounding Le Puy. It's one of the poorest regions in France and has long remained outside the main national lines of communication: much of it is above 1000m in height and snowbound in winter. However, the new Clermont–Montpellier *autoroute* now provides a convenient means of travel from the capital to the gorges of the Tarn and Ardèche.

Many of France's greatest rivers rise in the Massif Central: the **Dordogne** in the Monts-Dore, the **Loire** on the slopes of the Gerbier de Jonc in the east, and in the Cévennes the **Lot** and the **Tarn**. It is these last two rivers which create the distinctive character of the southern parts of the Massif Central, dividing and defining the special landscapes of the *causses*, or limestone plateaux, with their stupendous gorges. This is territory tailor-made for walkers and lovers of the **outdoors**, and everywhere you go tourist offices will supply ideas and routes for walks and bike rides.

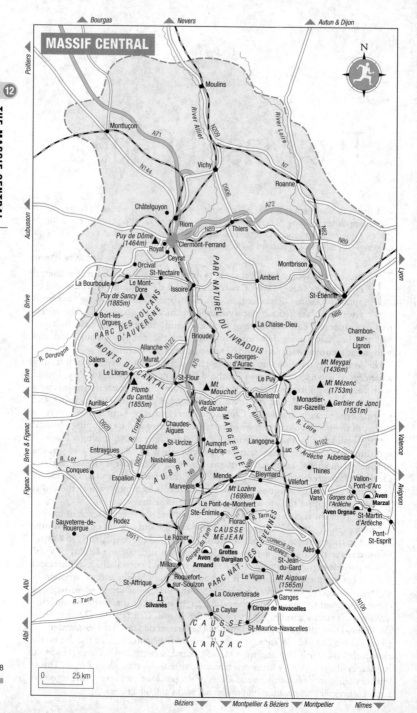

MASSIF CENTRAL

N

Bourgas   Nevers   Autun & Dijon

Poitiers

Aubusson

Brive

Brive

Brive & Figeac

Figeac

Brive & Figeac

Albi

Albi

Albi

Moulins

Montluçon   A71

N144

Vichy   N7

Châtelguyon   Roanne   A72

Riom   N89   Thiers   N82   N89

Puy de Dôme   Clermont-Ferrand   Montbrison
(1464m)
Royat   Ceyrat   St-Étienne   Lyon
Orcival   Ambert   N88
La Bourboule   Le Mont-   St-Nectaire
Dore   Issoire
Puy de Sancy   PARC NATUREL DU LIVRADOIS
(1885m)
Bort-les-   La Chaise-Dieu   Chambon-
Orgues   sur-
PARC DES VOLCANS   Lignon
D'AUVERGNE   Brioude
Allanche   N122   St-Georges-   Mt Meygal
Salers   d'Aurac   (1436m)
Murat   A75   Le Puy   Mt Mézenc
Le Lioran   St-Flour   Mt   (1753m)
Mouchet   Monistrol   Monastier-   Gerbier de Jonc
MONTS DU CANTAL   sur-Gazeille   (1551m)
Plomb   Viaduc
du Cantal   de Garabit
(1855m)   R. Loire
Aurillac   Chaudes-   Langogne   N102
Aiguès   Aumont-   Aubenas
Laguiole   St-Urcize   Aubrac   Luc
Entraygues   Nasbinals   Le   Thines
R. Lot   Bleymard   Valence
Conques   Espalion   Mende   Villefort   Vallon-
AUBRAC   Mt Lozère   Les   Pont-d'Arc
(1699m)   Vans
Marvejols   Gorges de   Avignon
Sauveterre-de-   Le Pont-de-Montvert   l'Ardèche   Aven
Rouergue   Rodez   Ste-Énimie   Aven Orgnac   Marzal
Florac   St-Martin-
CAUSSE   R. Tarn   d'Ardèche
Le Rozier   MEJEAN   Pont-
St-Esprit
Gorges du Tarn   Grottes
Millau   Aven   de Dargilan   St-Jean-   Alès
Armand   du-Gard
St-Affrique   Roquefort-   PARC NAT. DES CÉVENNES   N106
R. Tarn   sur-Soulzon   Mt Aigoual
Le Vigan   (1565m)
Silvanès   La Couvertoirade   Ganges
Le Caylar   Cirque de Navacelles
CAUSSE   St-Maurice-Navacelles
DU
LARZAC

River Allier   N209   River Loire

R. Dordogne

PARC NATUREL DU LIVRADOIS

MARGERIDE

CORNICHE DES CÉVENNES

R. Truyère   D921   R. Allier   N88   R. Ardèche

D920   N9   R. Tarn   D986

D911

0   25 km

Béziers ▼   Montpellier & Béziers ▼   Montpellier ▼   Nîmes ▼

The food of the Massif Central

Don't expect anything very refined from the cuisine of the Auvergne and Massif Central: it's solid peasant fare as befits a traditionally poor and rugged region. The best-known dish is **potée auvergnate**, basically a kind of cabbage soup, easy to make and very nourishing. The ingredients – potatoes, pork or bacon, cabbage, beans, turnips – though added at different intervals, are all boiled up together. Another popular cabbage dish is **chou farci**, cabbage stuffed with pork and beef and cooked with bacon.

Two potato dishes are very common – **la truffade** and **l'aligot**. For *truffade*, the potatoes are sliced and fried in lard, then fresh Cantal cheese is added; for an *aligot*, the potatoes are puréed and mixed with cheese. Less palatable for the squeamish is **tripoux**, usually a stuffing of either sheep's feet or calf's innards, cooked in a casing of stomach lining. **Fricandeau**, a kind of pork pâté, is also wrapped in sheep's stomach.

By way of dessert, **clafoutis** is a popular fruit tart in which the fruit is baked with a batter of flour and egg simply poured over it. The classic fruit ingredient is black cherries, though pears, blackcurrants or apples can also be used.

The Auvergne and the Ardèche in the east produce some wines, though these are not of any great renown. **Cheese**, however, is a different story. In addition to the five great cow's milk cheeses – St-Nectaire (see p.729), Laguiole, Cantal, Fourme d'Ambert and Bleu d'Auvergne – this region also produces the prince of all cheeses, **Roquefort**, made from sheep's milk at the edge of the Causse du Larzac (see p.745).

The Parc des Volcans d'Auvergne

The **Parc Naturel Régional des Volcans d'Auvergne** encompasses the whole of the western edge of the Massif Central, from **Vichy** in the north to **Aurillac** in the south. It consists of three groups of extinct volcanoes – the **Monts-Dômes**, the **Monts-Dore** and the **Monts du Cantal** – linked by the high plateaux of Artense and the Cézallier. It's big, wide-open country, sparsely populated and with largely treeless pasture grazed by the cows whose milk produces Cantal and St-Nectaire cheese.

The park organization, whose headquarters are at the **Maison du Parc**, Château de Montlosier, 20km southwest of Clermont-Ferrand just off the Mont-Dore road (Feb–April & Nov–Dec Fri–Mon 9am–12.30pm & 1.30–5/6pm; May, June, Sept & Oct Mon–Sat 9am–12.30pm & 1–6pm; July & Aug daily 8am–12.30pm & 1.30–7pm; ☎04.73.65.64.00, ⓦwww.parc-volcans-auvergne.com), oversees various subsidiary *maisons du parc*, each a kind of museum devoted to different themes or activities: fauna and flora, shepherd life, peat bogs and so on.

If only because of the practicalities of transport, you are likely to pass through **Clermont-Ferrand**, capital of the *département*. Given its rather dramatic historical associations – it was the site of Pope Urban II's speech which launched the First Crusade in 1095 – the city may disappoint, but nonetheless it merits an afternoon's rambling. Otherwise, the towns in the area are few and of secondary interest, although **Orcival**, **Murat** and **Salers** are unexpectedly attractive; **St-Nectaire** contains an exceptionally beautiful small church in the distinct Auvergne version of Romanesque; and **St-Flour** and **Aurillac** have an agreeable provincial insularity.

Clermont-Ferrand

CLERMONT-FERRAND lies at the northern tip of the Massif Central. Although its situation is magnificent, almost encircled by the wooded and grassy volcanoes of the **Monts-Dômes**, it has for over a century been a typical smokestack

Drinking and Driving

In Clermont-Ferrand industrialization meant, first and foremost, Michelin. The company originated in 1829, thanks to the inventions of **Charles Mackintosh**, the Scotsman of raincoat fame. His niece married Édouard Daubrée, a Clermont sugar manufacturer, and brought with her some ideas about making rubber goods that she had learnt from her uncle. In 1889, the company became **Michelin and Co**, just in time to catch the development of the automobile and the World War I aircraft industry. The family ruled the town and employed 30,000 of its citizens until the early 1980s, when the industry went into decline. In the years since, the workforce has been halved, causing rippling unemployment throughout Clermont's economy.

Bibendum, or Dennis Dunlop, the famous Michelin Man mascot, was launched in 1894, appearing on a poster quaffing what was to initial appearances a large glass of beer. But although his name came from a Latin epigram meaning "Time to drink!" Bibendum's glass was full of obstacles and road hazards, which the company's tyres were said to be able to "drink up" with ease.

industrial centre, the home base of Michelin tyres, which makes it a rather incongruous capital for the rustic and isolated province of the Auvergne.

Its roots, both as a spa and a communications and trading centre, go back to Roman times. It was just outside the town, on the plateau of Gergovia to the south, that the Gauls, under the leadership of **Vercingétorix**, won their only victory against Julius Caesar's invading Romans. In the Middle Ages, the rival towns of Clermont and Montferrand were ruled respectively by a bishop and the count of Auvergne. Louis XIII united them in 1630, but it was not until the rapid industrial expansion of the late nineteenth century that the two really became indistinguishable.

As in many other traditional industrial towns hit by recession and changing global patterns of trade, Clermont has had to struggle to reorientate itself, turning to service industries and the creation of a university of 34,000 students. Nonetheless, many people have moved elsewhere in search of work, reducing the population by nearly a tenth. The town has changed physically, too, as many of the old factories have been demolished. Despite all of this, the old centre has a surprisingly hip and youthful feel, with pavement bars packed out in the evenings, as the boutiques and galleries which have sprung up start to wind down for the day.

Arrival and information

The **gare SNCF** is on avenue de l'Union Soviétique, a ten-minute bus journey away from place de Jaude, at the western edge of the cathedral hill. The **gare routière** (T04.73.29.70.05) is on boulevard François-Mitterrand, with a city transport information kiosk called Boutique T2C at 24 bd Charles-de-Gaulle (T04.73.28.70.00, Wwww.t2c.fr). The city **airport** (T04.73.62.71.00, Wwww.clermont-aeroport.com) is at Aulnat, 7km east, operating mainly internal flights, but also flights to London in summer. A local bus (line 20; €1.40 one way) connects the airport with the train and bus stations.

The **tourist office** is opposite the cathedral in place de la Victoire (June–Sept daily 9/10am–7pm; Oct–May Mon–Fri 9am–6pm, Sat 10am–1pm & 2–6pm, Sun 9.30am–12.30pm & 2–6pm; T04.73.98.65.00, Wwww.ot-clermont-ferrand.fr). For information on the *département* of Puy de Dôme and the region of Auvergne, start with Wplanetepuydedome.com and Wwww.auvergne-tourisme.info), while for detailed hiking or mountain-biking information see Wwww.chamina.com. **Bikes** are available from the SNCF, at the main station and at a central office at 20 place Remoux (T04.73.14.12.36). For **internet** access, try *CyberStrike* at 31 av de la Grande-Bretagne (Mon–Sat 10am–2am, Sun noon–2am; T04.73.92.96.78).

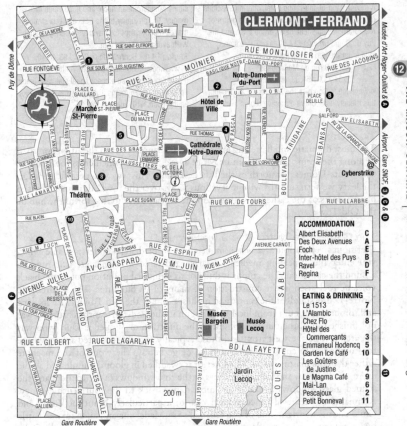

CLERMONT-FERRAND

ACCOMMODATION

Albert Elisabeth	C
Des Deux Avenues	A
Foch	E
Inter-hôtel des Puys	B
Ravel	D
Regina	F

EATING & DRINKING

Le 1513	7
L'Alambic	1
Chez Flo	8
Hôtel des Commerçants	3
Emmanuel Hodencq	5
Garden Ice Café	10
Les Goûters de Justine	4
Le Magma Café	9
Mai-Lan	6
Pescajoux	2
Petit Bonneval	11

Accommodation

Most of Clermont's **hotels** are concentrated just off the lively place de Jaude, close to the town's main shops, and around the rather characterless station area. There isn't a tremendous choice, but they are generally good value. Campers will find municipal **campsites** at Royat (*L'Indigo Royat*), 4km to the southwest (☎04.73.35.97.05, ⓦwww.camping-indigo.com; closed mid-Sept to early April; bus #41); Ceyrat (*Le Chanset*), 5km to the south (☎04.73.61.30.73, ⓦwww .campingdeceyrat63.com; bus #4C & #41, stop "Preguille"); and Cournon (*Le Pré des Laveuses*), 10km to the east, on the River Allier (☎04.73.84.81.30, ⓦwww.cournon-auvergne.fr; April–Oct; bus #3, stop "Plaine de jeux").

Albert Elisabeth 37 av Albert-Elisabeth ☎04.73.92.47.41, ⓦwww.hotel-albertelisabeth .com. Well-run family hotel, with pastel-coloured rooms; handy for the train station. Amenities include parking, wi-fi and a/c. ❸
Des Deux Avenues 4 av de la République ☎04.73.92.37.52, ⓦwww.hotel-2avenues.fr. This funky hotel near place Delille is the best option in town and offers clean airy rooms at budget rates;

about 5min walk from the station. Family rooms also available. ❷
Foch 22 rue Maréchal-Foch ☎04.73.93.48.40, ⓦwww.hotel-foch-clermont.com. Tucked away down a side street off place de Jaude, this is a good-value budget hotel, with bright, summery rooms. ❸
Inter-hôtel des Puys 16 place Delille ☎04.73.91.92.06, ⓦwww.hoteldespuys.com.

A modern, top-of-the-range hotel, offering spacious rooms, some with balconies. Its first-rate gourmet restaurant has splendid views of the town and the Puy de Dôme (*menus* €14.50–44). There's an indoor garage and rooms have wi-fi. ❺

🏃 **Ravel** 8 rue de Maringues ☎04.73.91.51.33, ℮hotelravel63 @wanadoo.fr. Opposite the old Marché St-Joseph, this friendly hotel offers attractive rooms, with sunny Mediterranean decor and good value for money. The proximity to the train and bus stations makes it convenient for travellers passing through. Wi-fi available. Closed Jan. ❸

Regina 14 rue Bonnabaud ☎04.73.93.48.40, Ⓦwww.hotel-foch-clermont.com. A little grubby outside, but inside an elegant spiral staircase leads up to fresh, clean rooms. Owned by the same folks as the *Foch*. Wi-fi and parking. ❸

The City

The most dramatic and flattering approach to Clermont is from the Aubusson road or along the scenic rail line from Le Mont-Dore, both of which cross the chain of the Monts-Dômes just north of the Puy de Dôme. This way you descend through the leafy western suburbs with marvellous views over the town, dominated by the black towers of the cathedral sitting atop the volcanic stump that forms the hub of the Old Town.

The Cathédrale Notre-Dame and around

Clermont's reputation as a *ville noire* becomes immediately understandable when you enter the appealing medieval quarter, clustered in a characteristic muddle around the cathedral. The colour is due not to industrial pollution but to the black volcanic rock used in the construction of many of its buildings. The **Cathédrale Notre-Dame** stands at the centre and highest point of the Old Town, with its dark and sombre walls built from local lava. Begun in the mid-thirteenth century, it was not finished until the nineteenth, under the direction of Viollet-le-Duc, who was the architect of the west front and those typically Gothic crocketed spires, whose too methodically cut stonework at close range betrays the work of the machine rather than the mason's hand. The interior is swaddled in gloom, illuminated all the more startlingly by the brilliant colours of the rose windows in the transept and the stained-glass windows in the choir, most dating back to the fourteenth century. Remnants of medieval frescoes survive, too: a particularly beautiful Virgin and Child adorns the right wall of the Chapelle Ste-Madeleine and an animated battle scene between the Crusaders and Muslims unfolds on the central wall of the Chapelle St-Georges. On a fine day it's worth climbing the **Tour de la Bayette** (Mon–Sat 9–11.15am & 2–5.15pm, Sun 3–5.30pm; €1.50) by the north transept door: you look back over the rue des Gras to the Puy de Dôme looming dramatically over the city, with white morning mist retreating down its sides.

Northeast of the cathedral, down the elegant old rue du Port, stands Clermont's other great church, the Romanesque **Basilique Notre-Dame-du-Port** – a century older than the cathedral and in almost total contrast both in style and substance, built from softer stone in pre-lava-working days and consequently corroding badly from exposure to Clermont's polluted air. For all that, it's a beautiful building in pure Auvergnat Romanesque style with an interior restored in 2008. Check out the Madonna and Child over the south door in the strangely stylized local form, both figures stiff and upright, the Child more like a dwarf than an infant. It was here in all probability that Pope Urban II preached the First Crusade in 1095 to a vast crowd who received his speech with shouts of *Dios lo volt* (Occitan for "God wills it"), which became the battle-cry of the crusaders.

For general shopping, drinking and eating, the streets between the cathedral and place de Jaude are best, with the main morning market taking place in the conspicuously modern **place St-Pierre** just off rue des Gras. **Place de Jaude** remains another monument to planners' deviation, in spite of the shops, the cafés well placed to take in the morning sun and an attempt to make it more attractive with trees and a fountain.

Outside the city centre

Away from these central streets, there are a few concrete sights to tempt the pedestrian. Among these are **rue Ballainvilliers**, whose eighteenth-century facades recall the sombre elegance of Edinburgh and lead to the **Musée Bargoin** (Tues–Sat 10am–noon & 1–5pm, Sun 2–7pm; €5, or €9 for all three museums), with its displays of archeological finds. These include an array of fascinating domestic bits: Roman shoes, baskets, bits of dried fruit, glass and pottery, as well as a remarkable burial find from nearby Martres-de-Veyre dating back to the second century AD. There is also a diverse collection of tapestries and textiles. Though not of great interest, the **Musée Lecoq**, directly behind the Musée Bargoin (Mon–Sat 10am–noon & 2–5/6pm, Sun 2–6pm; €5), is devoted mainly to natural history – and named after the gentleman who also founded the public garden full of beautiful trees and formal beds just across the street.

Clermont-Ferrand's most impressive museum, the **Musée d'Art Roger-Quilliot** (Tues–Fri 10am–6pm, Sat & Sun 10am–noon & 1–6pm; €5), is situated on place Louis-Deteix in **Montferrand**, some 2.5km northeast of the centre (bus #1, #9 or #16 from place de Jaude). Housed in a daringly renovated eighteenth-century Ursuline convent, this museum holds a broad collection of over two thousand works of art from the medieval to the contemporary. Notable pieces include a collection of carved capitals and a stunning enamelled reliquary of Thomas Becket. Montferrand is today little more than a suburb of larger Clermont, standing out on a limb to the north – if you journey out for the museum you should take time to stroll around. Built on the *bastide* plan, its principal streets, rue de la Rodade and rue Jules Guesde (the latter named after the founder of the French Communist Party, as Montferrand was home to many of the Michelin factory workers), are still lined with the fine townhouses of medieval merchants and magistrates.

Eating and drinking

For a daytime drink, *Garden Ice Café*, on the corner of place de Jaude, is one of the most popular places to hang out. More unusual is *Les Goûters de Justine,* a *salon de thé* tucked away in rue Pascal and furnished with antique chairs, old sofas and oriental carpets. At night one of the most fashionable places is *Le Magma Café* on place de la Victoire.

Restaurants

Le 1513 3 rue des Chaussetiers. Sited opposite the cathedral, this is the best of the cheaper places and very popular. The restaurant occupies a superb Renaissance mansion built in 1513. Lunchtime *menu* €10, otherwise from €14.

L'Alambic 6 rue Ste-Claire ℡04.73.36.17.45. A good-value *terroir* restaurant with a high-end feel, excellent food and service with mid-range prices. *Menus* from €26. Closed Mon, Wed lunch & Sun.

Chez Flo 18 rue du Cheval Blanc. A basic brasserie with excellent-value local cuisine. *Menus* from €12.80. Closed Sat eve.

Hôtel des Commerçants Opposite the station. Inexpensive and very friendly, with a terrace at the back (closed Sun; *menus* from €14).

Emmanuel Hodencq 6 place Marché St-Pierre ℡04.73.31.23.23. The city's finest restaurant has a pleasantly airy dining room and a *menu* ranging from lobster through truffle ravioli (expect to spend €70+). Closed Sun & Mon lunch.

Mai-Lan 41 bd Trudaine. Serves first-class Vietnamese cooking for around €18 (€10–14 at lunch). Closed Mon lunch & Sun.

Pescajoux 13 rue du Port. A good place for a quick snack, with a lunchtime crêpe *menu* starting from €10.50 (closed Sat lunch, Sun & Mon)

Petit Bonneval Av de la République, 5km southeast off the N9 Issoire road at Pérignat-lès-Sarliève ℡04.73.79.11.11, ⊛www.lepetitbonneval.com. A delicious stop for dinner; *menus* from €26. Closed Sun eve. Also has hotel rooms (⑥).

The Puy de Dôme

Visiting Clermont without going to the top of the **Puy de Dôme** (1464m) would be like visiting Athens without seeing the Acropolis. And if you choose your moment – early in the morning or late in the evening – you can easily avoid the worst of the crowds.

Clearly signposted from place de Jaude, it's about 15km from the city centre by the D941. The last 6.5km is a private road (March, April, Oct & Nov 8am–sunset; May–Sept 7am–sunset); there is also a shuttle bus (35min; 9am–7pm: May–June & Sept Sat & Sun; July & Aug daily; €5.50) serving the route when the road is closed to vehicles. If you're driving, make sure you pump your brakes on the descent; otherwise you may find yourself waiting a long time for your brakes to cool down before driving off. Alternatively, you can leave the car at the **Col de Ceyssat** and climb the Puy on foot in about an hour. The route is reserved for cyclists in summer (May–Sept Wed & Sun 7–9am).

The result of a volcanic explosion about 10,000 years ago, the Puy is a steep 400m from base to summit. Although the weather station buildings and enormous television mast are pretty ugly close up, the staggering views and sense of airy elevation more than compensate. Even if Mont Blanc itself is not always visible way to the east – it can be if conditions are favourable – you can see huge distances, all down the Massif Central to the Cantal mountains. Above all, you get a bird's-eye view of the other volcanic summits to the north and south, largely forested since the nineteenth century and including the perfect 100m-deep grassy crater of the **Puy de Pariou**.

Immediately below the summit are the scant remains of a substantial **Roman temple** (free entry) dedicated to the god Mercury, some of the finds from which are displayed in the Musée Bargoin in Clermont-Ferrand. Beside it is a memorial commemorating the exploits of Eugène Renaux, who landed a plane here in 1911 in response to the offer of a 100,000-franc prize by the Michelin brothers. Today's aviators are hang-gliders and paragliding enthusiasts, taking advantage of the updrafts and stunning scenery.

Riom

Just 15km north of Clermont-Ferrand, **RIOM** is a sedate and provincial town. One-time capital of the entire Auvergne, its Renaissance architecture, fashioned out of the local black volcanic stone, now secures the town's status as a highlight of the northern Massif. In 1942, just before the first trains of Jewish deportees were shipped to Nazi Germany, Léon Blum, Jewish prime minister and architect of the Socialist Popular Front government, was put on trial in Riom by Marshal Pétain, France's collaborationist ruler, in an attempt to blame the country's defeat in 1940 on the Left. Defending himself, Blum turned the trial into an indictment of collaboration and Nazism. Under pressure from Hitler, Pétain called it off, but nonetheless deported Blum to Germany, an experience which he survived, later giving evidence against Pétain after the war.

You may only want to spend a morning here, but Riom does provide a worthwhile stop for lunch if you're on the way up to Vichy. It's an aloof, old-world kind of place, still Auvergne's judicial capital, with a nineteenth-century **Palais de Justice** that stands on the site of a grand palace built when the dukes of Berry controlled this region in the fourteenth century. Only the Gothic **Ste-Chapelle** survives of the original palace, with fine stained-glass windows taking up almost the entirety of three of the walls (June & Sept Tues–Fri 3.30–5.30pm; July & Aug Tues–Fri 10am–noon & 2–5pm; €0.50).

The best way to admire the town's impressive ensemble of basalt-stone houses, with their red-tiled roofs, is to climb up to the viewing platform of the sixteenth-century clock tower, at 5 rue de l'Horloge, off the main street, rue du Commerce (July & Aug daily 10am–noon & 2–6pm, Wed till 9pm; Sept–June Tues–Sun 10am–noon & 2–5pm; €0.50). There's an interesting museum on the region's folk traditions at 10bis rue Delille, the **Musée Régional d'Auvergne** (Tues–Sun: April–June & Sept–Nov 10am–noon & 2–5.30pm; July & Aug daily 10am–6pm; €3, or €6 joint ticket with the Musée Mandet; free on Wed), with the **Musée Mandet**'s displays of Roman finds and bland paintings not far away at 4 rue de l'Hôtel-de-Ville (Tues–Sun: July & Aug 10am–6pm; Sept–June 10am–noon & 2–5.30pm; €3, free on Wed). At 44 rue du Commerce, the **church of Notre-Dame-du-Marthuret** (daily 9am–5/6pm) holds Riom's most valued treasures, two statues of the Virgin and Child – one a Black Madonna, the other, the so-called *Vierge à l'Oiseau*, a touchingly realistic piece of carving that portrays the young Christ with a bird fluttering in his hands. A copy stands in the entrance hall of the church (its original site), where you can see it with the advantage of daylight.

Practicalities

Riom's **tourist office** is at 27 place de la Fédération (July & Aug Mon–Sat 9.30am–12.30pm & 1–6.30pm, Sun 10am–12.30pm; Sept–June Mon–Sat 9.30am–12.30pm & 2–5.30pm, Mon & Thurs pm only; ☎04.73.38.59.45, ⓦwww.tourisme-riomlimagne.fr). For **internet** access go to Clic et tel at 19 rue Hyppolite Gomot (Mon–Sat 9am–9pm & Sun 2–9pm) or use the wi-fi at *Le Pacifique*. There's little **hotel** choice in town, but the best is *Le Pacifique* (☎04.73.38.15.65, ⓦwww.hotel-lepacifique-riom.com; ❹), a box-like, modern structure on the edge of town. *Le Magnolia*, at 11 av du Commandant Madeline, is one of Riom's finest **restaurants** for local cuisine (open Tues–Fri, Sat eve, Sun lunch; closed late July to early Aug; à la carte €16–43). Alternatively, follow the locals to *Ane Gris* at 13 rue Gomot (open Tues eve to Sat; closed part Aug), which has *menus terroir* from €12.50.

Vichy

VICHY is famous for two things: its World War II puppet government under Marshal Pétain, and its curative sulphurous springs, which attract thousands of ageing and ailing visitors, or *curistes*, every year. There's no mention of Pétain's government in town, but the fact that Vichy is one of France's foremost spa resorts colours everything you see here. The town is almost entirely devoted to catering for its largely elderly, genteel and rich population, which swells several-fold in summer; they come here to drink the water, wallow in it, inhale its steam or be sprayed with it. An attempt is now being made to rejuvenate the image of Vichy by appealing to a younger, more fitness-conscious generation.

Arrival, information and accommodation

Vichy's **gare SNCF** is about a ten-minute walk from the centre, on the eastern edge at the end of rue de Paris. The **gare routière** sits on the corner of rue Doumier and rue Jardet, by the central place Charles-de-Gaulle, and there's a public transport information line on ☎04.70.30.17.30. The building that used to house the wartime Vichy government at 19 rue du Parc is now home to the **tourist office** (April–June & Sept Mon–Sat 9am–12.30pm & 1.30–7pm, Sun 9.30am–12.30pm & 3–7pm; July & Aug Mon–Sat 9am–7pm, Sun 9.30am–12.30pm & 3–7pm; Oct–March Mon–Fri 9am–noon & 1.30–6pm, Sat 9am–noon & 2–6pm, Sun 2.30–5.30pm; ☎04.70.98.71.94, ⓦwww.vichy-tourisme.com). Internet access is available at Echap Internet Café, 12 rue Source de l'Hôpital (Tues–Sat noon–midnight, Sun 2pm–midnight).

There is an abundance of **hotels**, and finding a place to stay is not difficult. You'll find several around the station, but the most pleasant is the friendly, grand neo-Baroque *Midland*, 4 rue de l'Intendance, in a quiet street off rue de Paris (℡04.70.97.48.48, ⓦwww.hotel-midland.com; closed mid-Oct to mid-April; ❹; good restaurant with *menus* from €23). An excellent budget option is the clean and simple *Hôtel Cognac* (℡04.70.32.15.58, ⓦwww.hoteldecognac-vichy.com; ❷). There's a municipal **campsite**, *La Gravière*, at the Centre Omnisports (℡04.70.59.21.00; closed Oct to late May).

The Town

There's a real *fin-de-siècle* atmosphere about Vichy and a curious fascination in its continuing function. The town revolves around the **Parc des Sources**, a stately tree-shaded park that takes up most of the centre. At its north end stands the **Hall des Sources**, an enormous iron-framed greenhouse in which people sit and chat or read newspapers, while the various waters emerge from a large tiled stand in the middle, beside the just-visible remains of the Roman establishment. The *curistes* line up to get their prescribed cupful, and for a small fee you can join them. The Célestins is the only one of the springs that is bottled and widely drunk: if you're up for a taste experience, try the remaining five. They are progressively more sulphurous and foul, with the Source de l'Hôpital, which has its own circular building at the far end of the park, an almost unbelievably nasty creation. Each of the springs is prescribed for a different ailment and the tradition is that, apart from the Célestins, they must all be drunk on the spot to work – a dubious but effective way of drawing in the crowds.

Although all the springs technically belong to the nation and treatment is partially funded by the state, they are in fact run privately for profit by the Compagnie Fermière, first created in the mid-nineteenth century to prepare for a visit by the Emperor Napoléon III, whose interest in the waters brought Vichy to public notice. The Compagnie not only has a monopoly on selling the waters but also runs the casino and numerous hotels – it even owns the chairs conveniently dotted around the Parc des Sources.

Directly behind the Hall des Sources, on the leafy **Esplanade Napoléon III**, is the enormous, Byzantine-style **Grand Établissement Thermal**, the former thermal baths, decorated with Moorish arches, gold-and-blue domes and blue ceramic panels of voluptuous mermaids. All that remains inside of the original

Volvic to Laschamp walk

For a good day's walk and a thorough exploration of the *puys*, take the train from Clermont to Volvic-Gare. Follow the D90 road beside the train line for about 1km until you join up with the **GR441** path, where the road turns right under the track. Keep along your side of the train track for a few minutes longer and follow the GR441 round to the left, almost doubling back southwest along the line of the wooded Puys Nugères, Jumes and Coquille to the northern foot of the Puy de Chopine (2–3hr). Here you join up with the **GR4** and follow the combined GR4–441 across the Orcines–Pontgibaud road to the summit of the Puy de Dôme (about 2hr 30min from the road). From the Puy, descend to the Col de Ceyssat in half an hour (good chance of a lift back to Clermont), or continue to **Laschamp** (50min), where there is a **gîte d'étape** (total excursion time 7–8hr, 6hr for a very fit walker).

You should not set off without either the relevant section of the GR4 Topo-guide or, preferably, the IGN 1:25,000 map, the *Chaîne des Puys*, which also marks the GR441 from Volvic-Gare. If you don't feel up to a walk, you should investigate the beautiful train ride from Clermont to Le Mont-Dore, which follows the chain of the *puys*.

baths is the grand entrance hall, with its fountain and two beautiful murals, *La Bain* and *La Source*, painted by Osberd in 1903. The arcades leading off either side of the hall, once the site of gyms and treatment rooms, now house expensive boutiques.

After the waters, Vichy's curiosities are limited. There's a pleasant, wooded riverside in the **Parc de l'Allier**, also created for Napoléon III. And, not far from here, the Old Town boasts the strange **church of St-Blaise**, actually two churches in one, with a 1930s Baroque structure built onto the original Romanesque one – an effect that sounds hideous but is rather imaginative. Inside, another Auvergne Black Virgin, Notre-Dame-des-Malades, stands surrounded by plaques offered by the grateful healed who stacked their odds with both her and the sulphur.

Eating

For **eating**, apart from the hotel-restaurants listed above, the simplest solution is to head for the area around the junction of rue Clemenceau and rue de Paris, where there are several brasseries and cafés. To do so, however, would be to miss out on Vichy's surprising range of top-notch restaurants. Two of the best include the eclectic *Jacques Decoret* on 15 rue du Parc (℡04.70.97.65.06; closed Tues, Wed & Aug), which has *menus* drawing on flavours from places as jarringly diverse as Oaxaca and Marseille at €65–165, and the more affordable and less daring *La Table d'Antoine* at 8 rue Burnol (℡04.70.98.99.71; closed Sun lunch & Mon; from €22 at lunch).

The Monts-Dore

The **Monts-Dore** lie about 50km southwest of Clermont. Also volcanic in origin – the main period of activity was around five million years ago – they are much more rugged and more obviously mountainous than their gentler, younger neighbours, the Monts-Dômes. Their centre is the precipitous, plunging valley of the River Dordogne, which rises on the slopes of the **Puy de Sancy**, at 1885m the highest point in the Massif Central, just above the little town of **Le Mont-Dore**.

In spite of their relative ruggedness, there are few crags or rock faces and their upper slopes, albeit steep, are grassy and treeless for miles and miles. They are known as *montagnes à vaches* – mountains for cows – as they traditionally provided summer pastureland for herds of cows, raised above all for their milk and the production of **St-Nectaire** cheese. The herdsmen who milked them and made the cheese set up their primitive summer homes in the dozens of (now mainly ruined) stone huts, or *burons*, that dot the landscape.

Le Mont-Dore and the Puy de Sancy

Squeezed out along the narrow wooded valley of the infant Dordogne, grey-slated **LE MONT-DORE** is a long-established spa resort, with Roman remnants testifying to just how old it is. Its popularity goes back to the eighteenth century, when metalled roads replaced the old mule paths and made access possible, but reached its apogee with the opening of the rail line around 1900. It is an altogether wholesome and civilized sort of place.

The **Établissement Thermal** – the baths, which give the place its *raison d'être* – are in the middle of town and are certainly worth visiting (day-passes for the spa begin at €49). Early every morning, the *curistes* stream into its neo-Byzantine halls – an extravaganza of tiles, striped columns and ornate ironwork – hoping for a remedy in this self-proclaimed "world centre for treatment of asthma". For many Parisians, of all ages and walks of life, this is their annual mecca: whiling away days sniffing sulphur from bunsen burner tubes, and sitting in thick steam.

Walkers also frequent the town, the principal attraction being the **Puy de Sancy** (1885m), whose jagged skyline blocks the head of the Dordogne valley, 3km away (mid-May to Sept; 4 buses per day, 1 on Wed & Sun, from the tourist office;

€3.50). Accessible by *téléphérique* (May–Sept; €7.50 return) since the 1930s, it's one of the busiest tourist sites in the country. As a result, the path from the *téléphérique* station to the summit has had to be railed and paved with baulks of timber to prevent total erosion. Combined with the scars of access tracks for the ski installations, this has done little for its beauty.

Practicalities

Without a car, Le Mont-Dore is most easily accessible by train from Clermont. The **train** and **bus stations** are at the entrance to the town. A ten-minute walk down avenue Michelet takes you to the centre, where the **tourist office** sits in the park on avenue de la Libération (Mon–Sat 9am–noon & 2–6pm; Sun and hols 10am–noon & 2–4pm; ⓣ04.73.65.20.21, ⓦwww.sancy.com); the helpful staff will advise about walking and cycling possibilities (VTT rental), as well as day excursions to otherwise rather inaccessible places in the area. The web page also lists the schedule of the *navettes* which regularly serve the surrounding villages and connect them to Clermont-Ferrand. **Internet** access is available at Sancyber at 4 rue Georges-Lagaye (daily 10am–midnight).

Accommodation is not hard to come by, as the town is brimming with hotels. By the riverside, at 5 rue de la Saigne, the simple *Hôtel Helvétia* (ⓣ04.73.65.01.67, ⓔhotelhelvetia@orange.fr; open mid-April to mid-Nov; half- and full-*pensions* available; ❷) is very welcoming, while the stately nineteenth-century *Grand Hôtel*, nearby on rue Rigny (ⓣ04.73.65.02.64, ⓦwww.hotel-mont-dore.com; ❹), is excellent value. There's an efficient modern **hostel** on the Puy de Sancy road, with a stunning view of the mountains (ⓣ04.73.65.03.53, ⓔle-mont-dore@fuaj.org; closed mid-Nov to mid-Dec; dorm beds €17.20), and there's a municipal **campsite**, *Les Crouzets* (ⓣ04.73.65.21.60, ⓔcamping.crouzets@orange.fr; closed mid-Oct to mid-Dec), opposite the station.

As far as **eating** is concerned, there are large numbers of brasseries and cafés in the centre offering *plats* for €9–12. A particularly pleasant place is rustic *Le Bougnat*, 23 av Clemenceau, which serves various Auvergnat traditional dishes, as well as *raclette* and fondue (ⓣ04.73.65.28.19; *menus* from €20). A great place for a **drink** is the atmospheric 1940s-style *Café de Paris*, located on rue Jean-Moulin.

Orcival

Twenty-seven kilometres southwest of Clermont and about 20km north of Le Mont-Dore, lush pastures and green hills punctuated by the abrupt eruptions of the *puys* enclose the small village of **ORCIVAL**. A pretty, popular place, founded by the monks of La Chaise-Dieu in the twelfth century, it makes a suitable base for hiking in the region.

Orcival is dominated by the stunning Romanesque **church of Notre-Dame** (daily 8am–noon & 2–7pm), built of the same dark-grey volcanic stone as the cathedral in Clermont and topped with a spire and fanned with tiny chapels. Once a major parish, it counted no fewer than 24 priests in the mid-1200s, and the ironwork on the north door, with its curious forged human head motif, dates from that era. Inside, attention focuses on the choir, neatly and harmoniously contained by the semicircle of pillars defining the ambulatory. Mounted on a stone column in the centre is the celebrated **Virgin of Orcival**, a gilded and enamelled twelfth-century statue in typical Romance style; the object of a popular cult since the Middle Ages it is still carried through the streets on Ascension Day.

There's no public transport to Orcival itself; the nearest **bus station** is at Rochefort-Montagne, 6km away, served by buses from Clermont-Ferrand. There is, however, a helpful **tourist office** (June–Sept Mon–Sat 10am–noon & 2–6/7pm, plus Sun 10am–noon in July & Aug; rest of year holiday periods only Tues–Sat

Walking possibilities from Orcival include trips to **Lac de Servières** and **Lac de Guéry**. The first takes two and a half hours, the second some five hours. For Lac de Servières, follow the **GR141–30** south through the woods above the valley of the Sioule. The lake is a beauty; it's 1200m up, with gently sloping shores surrounded by pasture and conifers. You can either head southeast to the **gîte d'étape** at Pessade (☎04.73.79.31.07), or continue to the larger Lac de Guéry, lent a slightly eerie air by the black basalt boulders strewn across the surrounding meadows, where there's a romantically situated lakeside hotel, the *Lac de Guéry* (☎04.73.65.02.76, ⓌＷＷＷ .auberge-lac-guery.fr; closed mid-Oct to mid-Jan; ❹; restaurant from €20).

If you're driving to Le Mont-Dore, only 9km further on from here, just before the Lac de Guéry, the road takes you round the head of the **Fontsalade valley**, where two prominent rocks composed of banks of basalt organ-pipes rise spectacularly from the woods: the **Roche Tuilière** and the **Roche Sanadoire**. A footpath takes you on a two-hour walk round the valley, starting from the roadside belvedere overlooking Sanadoire. A little higher up, on the bare slopes of the **Puy de l'Aiguiller**, a roadside memorial commemorates some English airmen killed in an accident while making a parachute drop to the Maquis in March 1944.

2–5/6pm; ☎04.73.65.89.77, Ⓦwww.terresdomes-sancy.com), just below the church. Modest **accommodation** can be found at the *Hôtel des Touristes* (☎04.73.65.82.55, Ⓦwww.hoteldestouristes.fr; closed mid-Nov to mid-Feb; ❷; restaurant from €17) near the church. There's a lakeside **campsite**, *Camping de l'Étang de Fléchat* (☎04.73.65.82.96, Ⓦwww.campingdeflechat.com; closed Nov–May), 2km outside Orcival, but a better bet is the municipal site at St-Bonnet, 5km to the north of the village (☎04.73.65.83.32, Ⓦwww.camping-auvergne.info; closed Oct–April), on a hillside with wonderful views of the surrounding mountains.

St-Nectaire and around

ST-NECTAIRE lies some way to the southeast of Orcival, midway between Le Mont-Dore and Issoire. It comprises the old village of **St-Nectaire-le-Haut**, overlooked by a magnificent Romanesque **church** (daily April–Oct 9am–7pm & Nov–March 10am–5pm), and the tiny spa of **St-Nectaire-le-Bas**, whose main street is lined with grand but fading *belle époque* hotels. Like the church in Orcival and Notre-Dame-du-Port in Clermont, this is one of the most striking examples of the Auvergne's Romanesque architecture. The carved capitals around the apse retain the tantalizing hues of the paint which once covered the whole interior, while the church's treasures are guarded in the north transept and include a magnificent gilded bust of St Baudime (the third-century missionary of the Auvergne and parish-founder), a polychrome *Virgin in Majesty* and two enamelled plaques, all dating from the twelfth century. Among the town's other curiosities are a couple of caverns, and the **Maison du St-Nectaire** where you'll find an exhibition on the cheese-making process and a chance to visit a cheese-ripening cellar. The surrounding countryside is notable for its menhirs and other prehistoric megaliths; the tourist office has information on how to find them.

The **tourist office** (July & Aug Mon–Sat 9am–12.30pm & 1.30–7pm, Sun 9am–noon & 2–6pm; Sept–June Mon–Sat 9am–noon & 2–6pm; ☎04.73.88.50.86, Ⓦwww.ville-saint-nectaire.fr) is located in the "Grandes Thermes" complex on the main road and has information on six different circuit walks of various lengths that take from two to five hours to complete. For a **place to stay**, *Hôtel de la Paix*, situated at the base of the GR30 footpath below the church, offers comfortable

St-Nectaire cheese

St-Nectaire is an *appellation contrôlée*, to which only cheeses made from herds grazing in a limited area to the south of the Monts-Dore are entitled. It is made in two stages. First, a white creamy cheese or *tomme* is produced. This is matured for two to three months in a cellar at a constant temperature, resulting in the growth of a mould on the skin of the cheese which produces the characteristic smell, taste and whitish or yellowy-grey colour.

There are two kinds: St-Nectaire **fermier** and St-Nectaire **laitier**. The *fermier* is the strongest and tastiest and some of it is still made entirely on the farm. Increasingly, however, individual farmers make the *tomme*, then sell it on to wholesalers for the refining stage. The *laitier* is much more an "industrial" product, made from the milk of lots of different herds, sold onto a co-operative or cheese manufacturer for all its stages.

rooms and a reasonably priced restaurant (T04.73.88.49.07, Ehotelpaix63710 @aol.com; closed Nov–March; ❷; *menus* from €15). Greater comfort can be found at the *Mercure*, near the town centre, a converted spa renovated as a hotel (T04.73.88.57.00, Wwww.hotel-bains-romains.com; ❼), also with a fine restaurant (*menu* €25). The best-value campsite is the *Clé des Champs* (T04.73.88.52.33, Wwww.campingcledeschamps.com) located on the D996 on the right when heading in the direction of Champeix.

For shorter walks out of St-Nectaire, take the D150 past the church through the old village towards the **Puy de Mazeyres** (919m), and turn up a path to the right for the final climb to the summit (1hr), where you get a superb aerial view of the surrounding country. Alternatively, follow the D966 along the Couze de Chambon valley to **SAILLANT**, where the stream cascades down a high lava rock face in the middle of the village.

Murol

MUROL, 6km west of St-Nectaire by road (July & Aug twice-daily bus to Clermont) or 5.5km by footpath, is an attractive, sleepy little place best known for its striking medieval **château**, dramatically situated on top of a basalt cone commanding the approaches for kilometres around (April–Sept daily 10am–6pm; Oct–March Sat, Sun & hols 2–5pm; €5). In summer, a local organization re-enacts the medieval life of the castle in costume (€9 including castle admission).

Of the several small family-run **hotels** here, the *Hôtel de Paris*, on place de l'Hôtel-de-Ville (T04.73.88.60.09, Einfo@hoteldeparis-murol.com; May–Sept; ❷), is the best value. Of the **campsites**, the best deal is the *Ribeyre*, a short distance away at **JASSAT** (T04.73.88.64.29, Wlaribeyre.free.fr; closed mid-Sept to April).

Besse

Eleven kilometres due south of Murol, **BESSE** is one of the prettiest and oldest villages in the region. Its fascinating winding streets of noble lava-built houses – some fifteenth-century – sit atop the valley of the Couze de Pavin, with one of the original fortified town **gates** still in place at the upper end of the village.

Its wealth was due to its role as the principal market for the farms on the eastern slopes of the Monts-Dore, and its co-operative is still one of the main producers of St-Nectaire cheese (see box above). The annual **festivals** of the Montée and Dévalade, marking the ascent of the herds to the high pastures in July and their descent in autumn, are still celebrated by the procession of the Black Virgin of Vassivière from the **church of St-André** in Besse to the chapel of **La Vassivière**, west of **Lac Pavin**, and back again in autumn (July 2 & first Sun after Sept 21).

Lac Pavin lies 5km west of the village, on the way to the purpose-built downhill ski resort of **SUPER-BESSE** (both are connected to Besse by an hourly *navette*). It's a perfect volcanic lake, filling the now wooded crater. The **GR30** goes through, passing by the **Puy de Montchal**, whose summit (1407m) gives you a fine view over several other lakes and the rolling plateau south towards **ÉGLISE-NEUVE-D'ENTRAIGUES**, 13km by road, where the Parc des Volcans' **Maison du Fromage** gives a detailed account of the making of the different Auvergne cheeses (daily: mid-May to June & Sept 9am–12.30pm & 1.30–5pm; July & Aug 9am–12.30pm & 1.30–9pm; free).

Besse's **tourist office** is next to the church on place du Dr-Pipet (July & Aug Mon–Sat 9am–7pm, Sun 10am–noon & 2–6pm; Sept–June Mon–Sat 10am–noon & 2–6pm, Sun 10am–noon & 2–4/6pm; ☎04.73.79.52.84, Ⓦwww.sancy.com), and will provide information and advice about walking, mountain biking and skiing. For a place to **stay**, the atmospheric *Hostellerie du Beffroy*, 24 rue Abbé-Blot (☎04.73.79.50.08, Ⓦwww.lebeffroy.com; ❹), whose restaurant has an excellent *carte* (*menu* from €28), is worth a try. Good, simple **food** can be had next door at *Le Sancy*, which has a *plat du jour* for €9.

The Monts du Cantal

The **Cantal Massif** forms the most southerly extension of the Parc des Volcans. Still nearly 80km in diameter and once 3000m in height, it is one of the world's largest (albeit extinct) volcanoes, shaped like a wheel without a rim. The hub is formed by the three great conical peaks that survived the erosion of the original single cone: **Plomb du Cantal** (1855m), **Puy Mary** (1787m) and **Puy de Peyre-Arse** (1686m).

From this centre a series of deep-cut wooded valleys radiates out like spokes. The most notable are the **valley of Mandailles** and the **valleys of the Cère and Alagnon** in the southwest, where the road and rail line run, and in the north the **valleys of Falgoux and the Rhue**. Between the valleys, especially on the north side, are huge expanses of gently sloping grassland, including the **Plateau du Limon**. It's this grassland which has for centuries been the mainstay of life in the Cantal, as summer pasture for the cows whose milk makes the firm yellow Cantal cheese, pressed in the form of great crusty drums. But this traditional activity has long been in serious decline; as elsewhere, many of the herds are now beef cattle. And tourism is on the increase, in particular walking, horseriding and skiing.

You can trace the circumference of the Massif by car, following the sinuous and spectacular **Route des Crêtes**. But, be warned, if you hit a period of bad weather, you'll drive a long way seeing no more than white banks of mist illumined by your headlights. The main centres within the massif lie on the N122 between Murat and Aurillac: **LE LIORAN**, where the road and rail tunnels begin, and **SUPER-LIORAN**, the downhill and cross-country ski centre, with many hotels, including the rustic and comfortable *Rocher de Cerf* (☎04.71.49.50.14, Ⓦwww.lerocher ducerf.com; summer obligatory half-*pension*, for two ❽ otherwise ❹) and several *gîtes d'étape*, as well as a **tourist office** (April–Dec Mon–Sat 9.30am–12.30pm & 1.30–5/6pm, Sun 9.30am–12.30pm, except mid-July to mid-Aug daily 9am–6pm; Christmas–March daily 9am–6pm; ☎04.71.49.50.09, Ⓦwww.lelioran.com). At **THIEZAC**, 10km south, you can stay at *Hôtel Elancèze et la Belle Vallée* (☎04.71.47.00.22, Ⓦwww.elanceze.com; closed Nov–Dec 20; ❸; restaurant *menus* €16–32), or the municipal campsite, *La Bedisse* (☎04.71.47.00.41; closed mid-Sept to mid-May). Further south at **VIC-SUR-CÈRE** there's a riverside municipal **campsite** (☎04.71.47.54.18, Ⓦwww.camping-la-pommeraie.com; closed mid-Sept to April).

⑫

Aurillac

AURILLAC, the provincial capital of the Cantal, lies on the west side of the mountains, 98km east of Brive and 160km from Clermont-Ferrand. In spite of its good main-line train connections and the fact that its population has almost doubled in the last forty years to around 30,000, it remains one of the most out-of-the-way French provincial capitals. It was until recently a major manufacturer of umbrellas, though that seems doomed to eventual extinction, like its older traditional lace-making and tanning industries. It is now mainly an administrative and commercial centre, with important cattle markets in the suburb of Sistrières on Mondays.

The most interesting part of town is the kernel of old streets, now largely pedestrianized and full of good shops, just to the north of the central **place du Square**. **Rue Duclaux** leads through to the attractive **place de l'Hôtel-de-Ville**, where big markets are held (Wed & Sat) in the shadow of the handsome grey-stone **Hôtel de Ville**, built in restrained Republican-classical style in 1803. Beyond it, the continuation of **rue des Forgerons** leads to the beautiful little **place St-Géraud**, with a round twelfth-century fountain overlooked by a Romanesque house that was probably part of the original abbey guesthouse, and the externally rather unprepossessing **church of St-Géraud**, which nonetheless has a beautifully ribbed late Gothic ceiling.

At the back of the church, past a delightful small garden, **rue de la Fontaine** comes out on the riverbank by the Pont du Buis, with a shady walk back along cours d'Angoulême on the other side to the Pont-Rouge and **place Gerbert**, where there is an ancient *lavoir*, or washing place. On a steep bluff overlooking this end of town towers the eleventh-century keep of the Château St-Étienne, containing the town's only worthwhile museum, the **Muséum des Volcans** (late June to Sept Mon–Sat 10am–6.30pm & Sun 2–6.30pm; otherwise Tues–Sat 2–6pm; €4), with a good section on volcanoes and a splendid view over the mountains to the east.

Practicalities

The **gare SNCF** and **gare routière** are together on place Sémard, a ten-minute walk from the central place du Square along avenue de la République and rue de la Gare. The **tourist office** occupies a small kiosk on the downhill side of place du Square (Easter–June & Sept Mon–Sat 10am–noon & 1.30–6.30pm, Sun 10am–12.30pm; July & Aug daily 9am–7pm; Oct–April Mon–Sat 10am–noon & 1.30–6pm; ☎04.71.48.46.58, ⓦwww.iaurillac.com). There's **internet** access at the Absolut Games cybercafé, 1 place du Buis.

For a **place to stay** in the centre of town, try the smart and comfortable *Le Square*, 15 place du Square (☎04.71.48.24.72, ⓦwww.cantal-hotel.com; ❸), with a restaurant whose stuffed cabbage (from €15) has won several prizes. Rather more *de luxe* accommodation and attentive service can be found at the *Grand Hôtel de Bordeaux* at 2 av de la République (☎04.71.48.01.84, ⓦwww.hotel-de-bordeaux.fr; ❼), set in a nineteenth-century mansion.

There are a number of **restaurants** where you can sample Auvergnat specialities. The most popular is the atmospheric *Le Terroir du Cantal*, 5 rue du Buis (closed Sun lunch & Mon; from €17), with its rough-stone walls and wooden benches. Worth making the journey for is Aurillac's annual international **street theatre festival** (ⓦwww.aurillac.net), which lasts for one week in August, attracting performers from all over Europe and filling the town with rather more exotic characters than are normally to be seen in these provincial parts.

Salers

SALERS lies 42km north of Aurillac, at the foot of the northwest slopes of the Cantal and within sight of the Puy Violent. Scarcely altered in size or aspect since its sixteenth-century heyday, it remains an extraordinarily homogeneous example of the architecture of that time. If things appear rather grand for a place so small, it's because the town became the administrative centre for the highlands of the Auvergne in 1564 and home of its magistrates. Exploiting this past is really all it has left, but Salers still makes a very worthwhile visit.

If you arrive by the Puy Mary road, you'll enter town by the **church**, which is worth a look for the super-naturalistic statuary of the Entombment of Christ (1496), hidden in a side chapel near the entrance. In front of you, the cobbled **rue du Beffroi** leads uphill, under the massive clock tower, and into the central **place Tyssandier-d'Escous**. It is a glorious little square, surrounded by the fifteenth-century mansions of the provincial aristocracy with pepper-pot turrets, mullioned windows and carved lintels, among them the sturdy **Maison du Bailliage**, and, nearby, the **Maison des Templiers**, housing the small **Musée de Salers** (April–Sept daily 10.30am–noon & 2–7.30pm; closed Tues except July & Aug; €3). Though the museum itself is rather dull, with exhibitions on the Salers cattle breed, traditional costumes and the local cheese-making industry, it's worth having a look at the vaulted ceiling of the entrance passageway, with its carved lions and heads of saints, such as St John the Baptist, framed by wild flowing hair. Before you're done, be sure to make your way to the **Promenade de Barrouze** for the view out across the surrounding green hills and the Puy Violent.

The **tourist office** is in place Tyssandier-d'Escous (July & Aug 9.30am–7pm; Sept–June Tues–Sun 9.30am–noon & 2–5.30/6pm; ℡04.71.40.58.08, Ⓦwww.pays-de-salers.com). If you want to **stay**, try the *Hôtel des Remparts*, near the Promenade de Barrouze (℡04.71.40.70.33, Ⓦwww.salers-hotel-remparts.com; closed mid-Oct to mid-Dec; ❹), whose restaurant specializes in Auvergnat cuisine (from €14), or the more luxurious *Le Gerfaut* in route du Puy-Mary (℡04.71.40.75.75, Ⓦwww.salers-hotel-gerfaut.com; closed Nov–Easter; ❹). There's a municipal **campsite**, *Le Mouriol*, on the Puy Mary road (℡04.71.40.73.09, Ⓔmairie.salers@orange.fr; closed mid-Oct to April).

Murat

MURAT, on the eastern edge of the Cantal, is the closest town to the high peaks and a busy little place, its cafés and shops bustling uncharacteristically for the region. It is also the easiest to access, lying on the N122 road and main train line, about 12km northeast of Le Lioran. Rather than any particular sight, it's the ensemble of grey-stone houses that attracts, many dating from the fifteenth and sixteenth centuries. Crowded together on their medieval lanes, they make a magnificent sight, especially as you approach from the St-Flour road, with the backdrop of the steep basalt cliffs of the **Rocher Bonnevie**, once the site of the local castle and now surmounted by a huge white statue of the Virgin Mary. Facing the town, perched on the distinctive mound of the **Rocher Bredons**, on your left as you approach, there's the lovely Romanesque **Église de Bredons** (July & Aug daily 10am–noon & 2.30–6.30pm), containing some fine eighteenth-century altarpieces. One of the finest of the old houses is now open to the public as the **Maison de la Faune** (July & Aug Mon–Sat 10am–12.30pm & 2–7pm, Sun 10am–noon & 3–7pm; Sept–June Mon–Sat 10am–noon & 2–5pm, Sun 2–5pm; €4.30), full of stuffed animals and birds illustrating the wildlife of the Parc des Volcans.

The **monument** to deportees on place de l'Hôtel-de-Ville and the name of the **avenue des 12-et-24-juin-1944**, opposite the tourist office, both commemorate one of the blackest days in Murat's history. On June 12, 1944, a local Resistance group interrupted a German raid on the town and killed a senior SS officer. In reprisal, the Germans burnt several houses down on June 24 and arrested 120 people, eighty of whom died after deportation. Near the river, below the Rocher

Bredons, a stone with an inscription marks the spot where the villagers were assembled before being deported.

Practicalities

The **tourist office** is at 2 rue du faubourg Notre-Dame (July & Aug Mon–Sat 9am–12.30pm & 1.30–7pm, Sun 10am–12.30pm & 2.30–6.30pm; Sept–June Mon–Sat 9am–noon & 2–6pm, Sun 10am–noon; ⓣ04.71.20.09.47, ⓦwww .paysdemurat.fr/tourisme), and you can rent **mountain bikes** from La Godille, opposite, or from Bernard Escure, in place Gandilhon-Gens-d'Armes. The **gare SNCF** is on the main road, avenue du Dr-Mallet, where at no. 18 you'll find the comfortable **hotel** *Les Messageries* (ⓣ04.71.20.04.04, ⓦwww.hotel-les -messageries.com; ❸), which has larger rooms good for families, and a restaurant that serves good hearty meals (from €28–34), including home-made terrines and fruit tarts. The town's **campsite**, *Les Stalapos*, is southwest of the centre in rue du Stade (ⓣ04.71.20.01.83, ⓦwww.camping-murat.com; May–Sept).

St-Flour

Seat of a fourteenth-century bishopric, **ST-FLOUR** stands dramatically on a cliff-girt basalt promontory above the River Ander, 92km west of Le Puy and 92km south of Clermont-Ferrand. Prosperous in the Middle Ages because of its strategic position on the main road from northern France to Languedoc and the proximity of the grasslands of the Cantal whose herds provided the raw materials for its tanning and leather industries, it fell into somnolent decline in modern times, only partially reversed in the last thirty-odd years.

While the lower town that has grown up around the station is of little interest, the wedge of old streets that occupies the point of the promontory surrounding the cathedral has considerable charm. The best time to come is on a Saturday morning when the Old Town is filled with market stalls selling sausages, cheese and other local produce. If you're in a car, leave it in the car park in the chestnut-shaded square, **Les Promenades**. One end of the square is dominated by the **memorial** to Dr Mallet, his two sons and other hostages and assorted citizens executed in reprisals by the Germans during World War II.

The narrow streets of the Old Town lead off from here and converge on the **place d'Armes**, where the fourteenth-century **Cathédrale St-Pierre** stands, backing onto the edge of the cliff, with a terrace giving good views out over the countryside. From the outside, the plain grey volcanic rock of the cathedral makes for a rather severe and uninspiring appearance; it's an impression that is partly mitigated inside by the fine vaulting of the ceiling and a number of works of art, most notably a carved, black-painted walnut figure of Christ with a strikingly serene expression, dating from the thirteenth century.

Facing the cathedral on the place d'Armes are some attractive old buildings housing a couple of cafés under their arcades, while at the north and south extremities of the square stand the town's two museums. At the north end, the fine fourteenth-century building that was once the headquarters of the town's consuls contains the **Musée Alfred Douët**'s somewhat ragbag collections of furniture, tapestries and paintings (mid-April to mid-Oct daily 9am–noon & 2–6pm; mid-Oct to mid-April closed Sun; €3.50); the view from the cliffs behind the museum gives a sense of the impregnable position of the town. At the south end of the square, the current Hôtel de Ville, formerly the bishop's palace built in 1610, houses the more interesting **Musée de la Haute-Auvergne** (mid-April to mid-Oct daily 10am–noon & 2–6pm; mid-Oct to mid-April closed Sun; €3.50), whose collections include some beautifully carved Auvergnat furniture and exquisitely made traditional musical instruments, such as the *cabrette*, a kind of accordion peculiar to the Auvergne.

Practicalities

The **gare SNCF** is on avenue Charles-de-Gaulle in the lower town. A few trains from Clermont-Ferrand and Aurillac stop here, but most journeys involve changing at Neussargues onto a SNCF bus, which can drop you off on the Promenades in the Old Town, saving you the walk up. The **tourist office** is on the Promenades, opposite the memorial (May–June & Sept Mon–Sat 9am–12.30pm & 2–6.30pm, Sun 10am–12.30pm & 2.30–5.30pm; July & Aug Mon–Sat 9am–12.30pm & 1.30–7pm, Sun 10am–12.30pm & 2.30–5.30pm; Oct–April Mon–Sat 9am–noon & 2–6pm; ☎04.71.60.22.50, ⓦwww.saint-flour.com). **Internet** access can be found at Cg-Net on rue Marchande (daily 9.30am–9pm).

The best deal for **accommodation** in the atmospheric upper town is the magnificent, old-style *La Maison des Planchettes* at 7 rue des Planchettes (☎04.71.60.10.08, ⓦwww.maison-des-planchettes.com; ❷), which has half-*pensions* for as low as €35 and a *terroir* restaurant with *menus* from €12.90. The town's municipal **campsite**, *Les Orgues*, is off avenue des Orgues in the Old Town (☎04.71.60.44.01; June to mid-Sept). The best place for both local cuisine and *cuisine gastronomique* is *Le Nautilus* on 23 av Charles-de-Gaulle (☎04.71.60.11.36; closed Oct–May) with *menus* from €20. The *Viking* bar and brasserie has a good-value *carte* and stunning views of the valley.

The Margeride

South and east of St-Flour stretch the wild, rolling, sparsely populated wooded hills of the **Margeride**, one of the strongholds of the wartime Resistance groups. If you have your own transport, the D4 makes a slow but spectacular route east (92km) to Le Puy, crossing the forested heights of **Mont Mouchet**, at 1465m the highest point of the Margeride. A side turning, the D48 (signposted), takes you to the national Resistance **monument**. It is sited by the woodman's hut that served as HQ to the local Resistance commander in June 1944. Here, Resistance fighters battled to delay German reinforcements moving north to strengthen resistance to the D-day landings in Normandy. There's an **eco-museum** here (La Tour, Ruynes-en-Margeride; daily: July & Aug 10am–7pm; Sept–June 2–6pm; €4), sketching the progression of the Resistance movement in the area. The views back west from these heights to the Cantal are superb.

The southwest: Aubrac and Rouergue

In the southwest corner of the Massif Central, the landscapes start to change and the mean altitude begins to drop. The wild, desolate moorland of the **Aubrac** is cut and contained by the savage gorges of **the Lot and Truyère rivers**. To the south of them, the arid but more southern-feeling plateaux of the *causses* form a sort of intermediate step to the lower hills and coastal plains of Languedoc. And they in turn are cut by the dramatic trenches formed by the **gorges of the Tarn**, **Jonte** and **Dourbie**, along with the spectacular caves of the **Aven Armand** and **Dargilan**. These are places best avoided at the height of the holiday season, when they turn into overcrowded outdoor playgrounds for amateur canoeists, parties of schoolchildren, motorists and campers.

The bigger towns, like **Rodez** and **Millau** in the old province of the **Rouergue**, also have much more of a southern feel. Both are worth a visit, though their attractions need not keep you for more than half a day. Rodez has a fine cathedral and Millau is worth considering as a base for exploring the *causses* and river gorges of the Tarn and Jonte.

The two great architectural draws of the area are **Conques**, with its medieval village and magnificent abbey, which owes its existence to the Santiago pilgrim route (now the GR65), and the perfect little *bastide* town of **Sauveterre-de-Rouergue**.

The mountains of Aubrac

The **Aubrac** lies to the south of St-Flour, east of the valley of the River Truyère and north of the valley of the Lot. It's a region of bleak, windswept uplands with long views and huge skies, dotted with glacial lakes and granite villages hunkered down out of the weather. The highest points are between 1200m and 1400m, and there are more cows up here than people; you see them grazing the boggy, peaty pastures, divided by dry-stone walls and turf-brown streams. There are few trees, save for a scattering of willow and ash and the occasional stand of hardy beeches on the tops, and only the abandoned shepherds' huts testify to more populous times. It's an area that's invisible in bad weather, but which, in good conditions, has a bleak beauty, little disturbed by tourism or modernization.

Aumont-Aubrac and Aubrac

The waymarked **Tour d'Aubrac** footpath does a complete circuit of the area in around ten days, starting from the town of **AUMONT-AUBRAC**, where you'll find *Chez Camillou* at 10 rue Languedoc (☎04.66.42.80.22, ⓦwww.hotel -camillou.com; periodic closings mid-Nov to mid-Feb; ❹; restaurant from €25), the excellent-value *Relais de Peyre*, across the street at no. 9 (☎04.66.42.85.88, ⓦwww.lerelaisdepeyre.com; closed Jan; ❷; restaurant €16.50–30), and a municipal **campsite** (☎04.66.42.88.70, ⓔinfo@ot-aumont-aubrac.fr). The **tourist office** is on a small side street to the right of the town hall (Mon–Sat 9am–12.30pm & 2–4.30/7pm; ☎04.66.42.88.70, ⓦwww.ot-aumont-aubrac.fr). There is also a daily train connection on the Millau–St-Flour line.

The marathon **GR65** from Le Puy to Santiago de Compostela in Spain also crosses the area from northeast to southwest en route to Conques. In fact, the tiny village of **AUBRAC**, which gave its name to the region, owes its existence to this Santiago pilgrim route; around 1120, a way-station was opened here for the express purpose of providing shelter for the pilgrims on these inhospitable heights. Little remains of it today, beyond the windy **Tour des Anglais**, into which is incorporated the friendly *Hôtel de la Dômerie* (☎05.65.44.28.42, ⓦwww .hoteldomerie.com; closed mid-Nov to early Feb; ❹; restaurant €24–43).

St-Urcize

This is the wildest and most starkly beautiful part of the Aubrac. The close-huddled village of **ST-URCIZE**, 13km north of the town of Aubrac, hangs off the side of the valley of the River Lhère, with a lovely Romanesque church at its centre and a World War I **memorial**, with so many names on it you wouldn't have thought it possible such a small place could provide so much cannon fodder. The village is ghostly out of season, with most of the unspoiled granite houses owned by people who live elsewhere. Should you wish to **stay**, the place to head to is *Guy Prouhèze*, on 2 rte du Languedoc (☎04.66.42.80.07, ⓦwww.prouheze.com; closed Nov–March; ❹), an excellent-value hotel featuring a famed *gastronomique* restaurant (menu €60; closed Sun lunch & Mon) as well as a good *terroir* restaurant (€21), *Le Compostelle*.

Laguiole

Seventeen kilometres west of St-Urcize and 24km north of Espalion, **LAGUIOLE** passes for a substantial town in these parts. Derived from the Occitan word for "little church", it's a name that now stands for knives and cheese. The **knives**, which draw hordes of French to the town's many shops, are characterized by a long, pointed blade and bone handle that fits the palm; the genuine article should bear the effigy of a bee stamped on the clasp that holds the blade open. It's an industry that started here in the nineteenth century, then moved to industrial Thiers, outside Clermont-Ferrand, before returning to Laguiole in 1987. At this point, the Société Laguiole (the only outlet for the genuine article) opened a factory designed by Philippe Starck on the St-Urcize road, with a giant knife projecting from the roof of the windowless all-aluminium building. They have a shop on the main through-road, on the corner of the central marketplace (ⓦ www .forge-de-laguiole.com). Laguiole's **cheese-making** tradition dates back to the twelfth century; unpasteurized cow's milk is formed into massive cylindrical cheeses, and aged up to eighteen months. The hard, tangy result is a world apart from Roquefort; to sample or buy, the factory outlet on the north edge of town provides the best bargain.

The **tourist office** is in place du Mairie (July & Aug Mon–Sat 9.30am–1pm & 2–7pm, Sun 10am–noon & 2–5pm; Sept–June Mon–Sat 9.30am–12.30pm & 2–6pm; ⓣ 05.65.44.35.94, ⓦ www.laguiole-online.com). For first-class **accommodation**, *Michel Bras*, a highly rated **hotel** (ⓣ 05.65.51.18.20, ⓦ www.michel -bras.fr; ⓸) with one of the country's finest restaurants (*menus* €111–179), is located just outside of town on the route d'Aubrac. For something less extravagant there are several hotels on the main street. Try the *Aubrac* opposite the marketplace (ⓣ 05.65.44.32.13, ⓦ www.hotel-aubrac.fr; ⓷; restaurant from €11.50), or the *Grand Hôtel Auguy* (ⓣ 05.65.44.31.11, ⓦ www.hotel-auguy.fr; early April to mid-Nov; ⓸), 2 allée de l'Amicale, which has a good restaurant with a *menu terroir* at €29. For more economical accommodation try the tiny *Hôtel Noù 4* on rue Bardière, a cosy cross between a café-restaurant, boutique and hotel (ⓣ 05.65.51.68.30, ⓦ www.nou4.izihost.com; ⓷). There is a municipal **campsite** (ⓣ 05.65.44.39.72; closed mid-Sept to mid-May) on the St-Urcize road. Communications, however, are not good, and if you don't have a car your only chance of getting in or out of town is the daily bus to Rodez.

Rodez and the upper valley of the Lot

A particularly beautiful and out-of-the-way stretch of country lies on the southwestern periphery of the Massif Central, bordered roughly by the valley of the **River Lot** in the north and the **Viaur** in the south. The upland areas are open and wide, with views east to the mountains of the Cévennes and south to the Monts de Lacaune and the Monts de l'Espinouse. **RODEZ**, capital of the Rouergue, with a fine cathedral, is the only place of any size, accessible on the main train and bus routes.

Until the 1960s, Rodez and the Rouergue were synonymous with backcountry poverty and underdevelopment. Today, Rodez is an active and prosperous provincial town with a charming, renovated centre, even though the approach, through spreading commercial districts, is uninspiring. Built on high ground above the River Aveyron, the **Old Town**, dominated by the massive red-sandstone **Cathédrale Notre-Dame**, is visible for kilometres around. No matter which direction you approach from, you'll find yourself in the **place d'Armes**, where the cathedral's plain, fortress-like west front and the seventeenth-century bishop's palace sit side by side – both buildings were incorporated into the town's defences. The Gothic cathedral, its plain facade relieved only by an elaborately flowery rose window, was begun in 1277 and took three hundred years to complete. Towering over the square is the cathedral's 87m **belfry**, decorated with pinnacles, balustrades and statuary almost as fantastical as that of Strasbourg cathedral. The impressively spacious interior, architecturally as plain as the facade, is adorned with a magnificently extravagant seventeenth-century walnut organ loft and choir stalls that were crafted by André Sulpice in 1468.

Leaving by the splendid south porch, you find yourself in the tiny place Rozier in front of the fifteenth-century **Maison Cannoniale**, whose courtyard is guarded by jutting turrets. From the back of the cathedral to the north and the south, a network of well-restored medieval streets connects place de-Gaulle, place de la Préfecture and the attractive place du Bourg, with its fine sixteenth-century houses. At 14 place Raynaldy, the **Musée Fenaille** (Tues, Thurs & Fri 10am–noon/1pm & 1.30/2–6pm, Wed & Sat noon/1pm–6/7pm, Sun 2–6pm; plus Mon 10am–1pm & 1.30–6.30pm mid-June to Sept only; €3) holds an impressive collection of carved menhirs, going back over 5,000 years. In place Foch, just south of the cathedral, the Baroque chapel of the old **lycée** is worth a look for its amazing painted ceiling, while in place Raynaldy, the modern **Hôtel de Ville** and the **médiathèque** are interesting examples of attempts to graft modern styles onto old buildings.

Practicalities

The **tourist office** is situated on place Foch, just off boulevard Gambetta and the place d'Armes, near the cathedral (July & Aug Mon–Sat 9am–8.30pm & Sun 10am–noon; rest of year Mon–Sat 9am–12.30pm & 1.30–6pm; ☎05.65.75.76.77, Ⓦwww.ot-rodez.fr). The **gare routière** is on avenue Victor-Hugo (☎05.65.68.11.13), and the **gare SNCF** on boulevard Joffre, on the northern edge of town.

For reasonable hotel **accommodation**, try the *Hôtel du Clocher*, off the east end of the cathedral at 4 rue Séguy (☎05.65.68.10.16, Ⓦwww.hotel-clocher.com; ❹). Slightly more upmarket is *La Tour Maje*, on boulevard Gally behind the tourist office (☎05.65.68.34.68, Ⓦwww.hotel-tour-maje.fr; ❹), a modern building tacked onto a medieval tower. *Hôtel Le Broussy*, recognizable by its beautiful Art Deco facade on avenue Victor-Hugo next to the cathedral, provides stylish accommodation and a leisurely *terrasse* restaurant (☎05.65.68.18.71, Ⓦhotel.broussy.monsite.orange .fr; ❸; *menus* from €15). Rodez' municipal **campsite** (☎05.65.67.09.52; closed Oct–May) is on the riverbank in the quartier Layoule, about 1km from the centre.

As for **eating**, one of the best places to sample local cuisine is *La Taverne*, 23 rue de l'Embergue (closed Sun & Mon lunch; from about €12), with an attractive terrace at the back, while the place to go for gourmet food is the classy *Goûts et Couleurs*, 38 rue Bonald (closed Sun & Mon), where *menus* start at €30. *Le Bistroquet*, 17 rue du Bal, off place d'Olmet (closed Sun & Mon), does good salads and grills for around €15. For a **drink**, head for the *Café de la Paix* on place Jean-Jaurès, or *Au Bureau* in *La Tour Maje*. The most central **internet** access, Resolument Plus Net, is at 11 rue Béteille (☎05.65.75.66.87; Tues–Sat noon–10pm).

Sauveterre-de-Rouergue and the gorges of the Viaur

Forty kilometres southwest of Rodez, **SAUVETERRE-DE-ROUERGUE** makes the most rewarding side trip in this part of the Rouergue. It is a perfect, otherworldly *bastide*, founded in 1281, with a large, wide central square, part cobbled, part gravelled, and surrounded by stone and half-timbered houses built over arcaded ground floors. Narrow streets lead off to the outer road, lined with stone-built houses the colour of rusty iron. On summer evenings, *pétanque* players come out to roll their *boules* beneath chestnut and plane trees, while swallows and swifts swoop and dive overhead.

In summer, a **bus** runs once a weekday here in the late afternoon from Rodez. The **tourist office** is in the main square (June–Sept Mon–Sun 10am–1pm & 2.30–7pm, Fri until 9pm; ☎05.65.72.02.52, Ⓦwww.sauveterre-de-rouergue.eu). There are several agreeable **hotels**, including the cheap and charming 🍴 *Hôtel La Grappe d'Or*, on the outer road (☎05.65.72.00.62; April–Oct; ❷), whose restaurant offers an excellent *menu* at €12, with dishes like *gésiers chauds* and *tripoux*, and, for dessert, cheese, ice cream and *fouace* (a kind of sweet cake). More upmarket is

the *Sénéchal*, at the entrance to the village (℡05.65.71.29.00, Ⓦwww.hotel
-senechal.fr; closed Jan to mid-March; ❽), with an indoor pool and an excellent
restaurant (closed Mon plus Tues lunch; *menus* €27–120). There's also a **campsite**
just off the D997 (℡05.65.47.05.32).

Conques

CONQUES, 37km north of Rodez, is one of the great villages of southwest
France. It occupies a spectacular position on the flanks of the steep, densely wooded
gorge of the little **River Dourdou**, a tributary of the Lot. It was the abbey that
brought the village into existence. Its origins go back to a hermit called Dadon who
settled here around 800 AD and founded a community of Benedictine monks, one
of whom pilfered the relics of the martyred girl, Ste Foy, from the monastery at
Agen. Known for her ability to cure blindness and liberate captives, Ste Foy's
presence brought the pilgrims flocking to Conques in ever-increasing numbers,
earning the abbey a prime place on the pilgrimage route to Compostela.

Arrival, information and accommodation

Conques is not easy to get to. The only public transport to the village is a seasonal
bus that runs up the Tarn valley from Entraygues via Vieillevie and as far as
St-Geniez d'Olt. The shuttle makes one run in each direction (June & Sept Mon;
July & Aug Tues, Thurs & Sat; confirm departure times with the tourist office),
allowing you to visit Conques and return the same day. The **tourist office** is on
the square beside the church (internet access available; daily: April–Sept
9.30am–12.30pm & 2–6.30pm; Oct–March 10am–noon & 2–6pm;
℡05.65.72.85.00, Ⓦwww.conques.fr). Walkers can use sections of the **GR65** and
GR62, both of which pass through the village; the tourist office will provide
information about shorter local walks.

For somewhere central to **stay**, the *Auberge St-Jacques* (℡05.65.72.86.36, Ⓦwww
.aubergestjacques.fr; ❸), near the church, provides good-value, old-fashioned accommodation and also has a popular restaurant, with *menus* from €19. A good alternative
is the *Auberge du Pont Romain*, on the main road below the hill on which Conques
stands (℡05.65.69.84.07, Ⓔcaubel-francoise@orange.fr; closed Jan; ❷; *menus* from
€14) – it's a twenty-minute walk from here to the church. A little way upstream,
the attractive *Moulin de Cambelong* (℡05.65.72.84.77, Ⓦwww.moulindecambelong
.com; ❻) offers more comfort – some rooms have spacious wooden balconies with
great views of the river – and a first-rate restaurant, specializing in duck dishes
(lunchtime *menu* from €28 Mon–Fri, otherwise €55). There are several **campsites**
in Conques: try *Beau Rivage* (℡05.65.69.82.23, Ⓦwww.campingconques.com;
closed Oct–March), on the banks of the Dourdou, just below the village.

The Village

The **village** of Conques is very small, largely depopulated and mainly contained
within the medieval **walls**, parts of which still survive, along with three of its
gates. The houses date mainly from the late Middle Ages, and the whole ensemble
of cobbled lanes and stairways is a pleasure to stroll through. There are two main
streets, the old **rue Haute**, or "upper street", which was the route for the pilgrims
coming from Estaing and Le Puy and passing onto Figeac and Cahors through the
Porte de la Vinzelle; and the lane, now **rue Charlemagne**, which leads steeply
downhill through the **Porte de Barry** to the river and the ancient **Pont Romain**,
with the little **chapel of St-Roch** off to the left, from where you get a fine view
of the village and church. Better still: climb the road on the far side of the valley.
The rather grandiose-sounding **European Centre for Medieval Art and Civilization**, hidden in a bunker right at the top of the hill (daily 9am–noon & 2–6pm),

sometimes features exhibitions and displays in addition to a small permanent collection. Throughout August, the village hosts a prestigious **classical music festival**, most of the concerts taking place at the abbey church; contact the tourist office for more information.

The abbey church

At the village's centre, dominating the landscape, stands the renowned Romanesque **church of Ste-Foy**, whose giant pointed towers are echoed in those of the medieval houses clustered tightly around it. Begun in the eleventh century, its plain fortress-like facade rises on a small cobbled square beside the tourist office and pilgrims' fountain, the slightly shiny silver-grey schist prettily offset by the greenery and flowers of the terraced gardens.

In startling contrast to this plainness, the elaborately sculpted *Last Judgement* in the **tympanum** above the door admonishes all who see it to espouse virtue and eschew vice (ask at the tourist office for guided tours of the tympanum and the tribunes; 45min; €3.30). Christ sits in judgement in the centre, with the chosen on his right hand, among them Dadon the hermit and the emperor Charlemagne. Meanwhile, his left hand directs the damned to Hell, as usual so much more graphically and interestingly portrayed with all its gory tortures than the boring bliss of Paradise, depicted in the bottom left panel.

The **inside** of the church was designed to accommodate the large numbers of pilgrims and channel them down the aisles and round the ambulatory. From here they could contemplate Ste Foy's relics displayed in the choir, encircled by a lovely wrought-iron screen, still in place. There is some fine carving on the capitals, especially in the triforium arches, too high up to see from the nave: you need to climb to the organ loft, which gives you a superb perspective on the whole interior. This is also a good place to admire the windows, designed by the abstract artist Pierre Soulages, which consist of plain plates of glass that subtly change colour with the light outside.

The unrivalled asset of this church is the survival of its medieval treasure of extraordinarily rich, bejewelled **reliquaries**, including a gilded statue of Ste Foy, bits of which are as old as the fifth century, and one known as the *A of Charlemagne*, because it is thought to have been the first in a series given as presents by the emperor to monasteries he founded. Writing in 1010, a cleric named Bernard d'Angers gave an idea of the effect of these wonders on the medieval pilgrim: "The crowd of people prostrating themselves on the ground was so dense it was impossible to kneel down ... When they saw it for the first time [Ste Foy], all in gold and sparkling with precious stones and looking like a human face, the majority of the peasants thought that the statue was really looking at them and answering their prayers with her eyes." The treasure is kept in a room adjoining the now ruined cloister (daily: April–Sept 9.30am–12.30pm & 2–6.30pm; Oct–March 10am–noon & 2–6pm; €6.20); the second part of the Conques museum, displayed on three floors of a house on the cathedral square, consists of a miscellany of sixteenth-century and later tapestries, furnishings and assorted bits of medieval masonry.

By far the best way to experience the beauty of Conques is by visiting the church at around 9.30pm on a summer evening for the **Nocturne des Tribunes**. The church is opened to the public and is beautifully illuminated while an organist or pianist fills it with music (€5).

The upper valley

The most beautiful stretch of the **Lot Valley** is the 21.5km between the bridge of Coursavy, below **Grand-Vabre**, just north of Conques, and **Entraygues**: deep, narrow and wild, with the river running full and strong, as yet unaffected by the dams higher up, with scattered farms and houses high on the hillsides among long-abandoned terracing. The shady, tree-tunnelled road is level and not heavily used, making it ideal for cycling.

There is a good hotel 6.5km east in **VIEILLEVIE**, where canoe rental is also available: the *Hôtel de la Terrasse* (☎04.71.49.94.00, Ⓦwww.hotel-terrasse.com; April to mid-Nov; ❹; restaurant €22–37). A further possibility is the delightful *Auberge du Fel* (☎05.65.44.52.30, Ⓦwww.auberge-du-fel.com; closed mid-Nov to March; ❹; excellent restaurant with *menus* from €25), some 10km further on, high on the north slopes of the valley in the hamlet of **LE FEL**, which, by an unexpected quirk of climate, produces a little local wine. There is also a beautifully sited municipal **campsite** high on the hillside (☎05.65.44.51.86; closed Oct–May).

Entraygues and around

ENTRAYGUES, with its riverside streets and attractive grey houses, has an airy, open feel that belies its mountain sleepiness. It lies right in the angle of the junction of the Lot with the equally beautiful River Truyère. The brown towers of a thirteenth-century **château** overlook the meeting of the waters, and a magnificent four-arched **bridge** of the same date crosses the Truyère a little way upstream, alongside the ancient tanners' houses.

The **tourist office** is on place de la République (April–June & Sept Mon–Sat 10am–12.15pm & 2–6pm, Sun 10am–noon; July & Aug Mon–Sat 9.30am–12.30pm & 3–7pm, Sun 10am–12.30pm; Oct–March Mon 2–6pm, Tues–Fri 10am–12.15pm & 2–5/6pm; ☎05.65.44.56.10, Ⓦwww.tourisme-entraygues.com). It frequently remains open outside of its official hours and provides information about walking, mountain biking and canoeing in the area. The best overall **place to stay** is the *Lion d'Or*, on the corner of the main street and the bank of the Lot (☎05.65.44.50.01, Ⓦwww.hotel-lion-or.com; ❸), with a covered swimming pool and garden, assorted family-friendly amenities and attached restaurant (from €15). The best bargain is the *Hôtel Le Centre*, on the main street (☎05.65.44.51.19; ❶; *menus* €12–35). There's also a **campsite**, *Le Val-de-Saures* (☎05.65.44.56.92, Ⓦwww.camping-valdesaures .com; closed Oct–April), on the GR65 at **GOLINHAC**, about 7km south of Entraygues on the other side of the Lot. There is a **bus** to Aurillac (Tues–Fri 12.50pm from the post office) in the north and Rodez (Mon–Sat) to the south.

Also well worth a visit is the **Château de Calmont d'Olt** (daily: May, June & Sept 10am–noon & 2–6pm; July & Aug 10am–7pm; school hols 2–6pm; €8 in summer, otherwise €5.50; Ⓦwww.chateaucalmont.org), 10km south at **ESPALION**. It's a rough and atmospheric old fortress dating from the eleventh century, on the very peak of an abrupt bluff, 535m high and a stiff 1km climb above the town on the south bank – its views of the town and the country beyond are unbeatable. Particularly good for children is the regular programme of activities throughout the day (afternoon only out of season), including demonstrations of medieval siege engines and artillery.

Millau and around

MILLAU, now bypassed by the spectacular Millau viaduct, occupies a beautiful site in a bend of the River Tarn at its junction with the Dourbie. It's enclosed on all sides by impressive white cliffs, formed where the rivers have worn away the edges of the *causses*, especially on the north side, where the spectacular table-top hill of the **Puech d'Andan** stands sentinel over the town. From medieval until modern times, thanks to its proximity to the sheep pastures of the *causses*, the town was a major manufacturer of leather goods, especially gloves. Although outclassed by cheaper producers in the mass market and suffering serious unemployment as a result, Millau still leads in top-of-the-range goods.

In 2004, the town hit the headlines with the construction of the astonishing **Grand Viaduc de Millau**, a 2.5km bridge supported by seven enormous pillars that, at times, puncture through the cloud level (the tallest is 326m high, taller than the Eiffel tower). Designed by British architects Foster and Partners (of Sir Norman Foster fame), French engineer Michel Virlogeux (whose previous credits include the wonderful Pont de Normandie) and Eiffage, a construction firm that traces its heritage back to Gustave Eiffel, it is as much a work of art as it is a vital new link from Paris to the Languedoc coast.

Arrival, information and accommodation

From the **bus and train stations** it's about a ten-minute walk down rue Alfred-Merle to the main square, place du Mandarous. The **tourist office** is on place du Beffroi in the centre of the Old Town (July & Aug Mon–Sat 9am–7pm; Sept–June Mon–Sat 9am–12.30pm & 2–6.30pm, Sun 9.30am–4pm; ℡05.65.60.02.42, ⓦwww.ot-millau.fr). **Bikes and outdoor equipment** can be rented from Roc et Canyon, 55 av Jean-Jaurès.

The best-value **hotel** is *Des Causses*, set in an attractive building on the N9 at 56 av Jean-Jaurès (℡05.65.60.03.19, ⓦwww.hotel-des-causses.com; ❸). Even more atmospheric is the *Emma Calvé* at 28 rue Jean-Jaurès (℡05.65.60.13.49, ⓦwww.millau-hotel-emmacalve.com; ❸), once home of the popular nineteenth-century singer of that name and with decor and furnishings evocative of the old bourgeoisie. Though modern and characterless, *Hôtel de la Capelle* (℡05.65.60.14.72, ⓦwww.hotel-millau-capelle.com; ❸), overlooking the Puech d'Andan at 7 place de la Fraternité, is a good-value option, especially for groups of four. There are several **gîtes**, and over half a dozen **campsites**. The riverside *Les Érables* (℡05.65.59.15.13, ⓦwww.campingleserables.fr; closed Oct to late April) on avenue de Millau Plage is shady and not overly crowded. For **internet** access, Cyber-café at 5 rue Droite is the most central option (Mon–Sat 10am–8pm).

The Town

Millau is a very pleasant, lively provincial town whose clean and well-preserved old streets have a summery, southern charm. It owes its original prosperity to its position on the ford where the Roman road from Languedoc to the north crossed the Tarn, marked today by the truncated remains of a medieval **bridge** surmounted by a watermill jutting out into the river beside the modern bridge.

Whether you arrive from north or south, you'll find yourself sooner or later in **place du Mandarous**, the main square, where avenue de la République, the road to Rodez, begins. South of here, the **Old Town** is built a little way back from the river to avoid floods and contained within an almost circular ring of shady boulevards. The rue Droite cuts through the centre, linking the three squares: place Emma-Calvé, place des Halles and place Foch. The prettiest by far is **place Foch**, with its café, shaded by two big plane trees and bordered by houses supported on stone pillars; some are twelfth century. In one corner, the **church of Notre-Dame** is worth a look for its octagonal Toulouse-style belfry, originally Romanesque. In the other, there's the very interesting **Musée de Millau** (May–June & Sept daily 10am–noon & 2–6pm; July & Aug 10am–6pm; Oct–April closed Sun; €5.10), housed in a stately eighteenth-century mansion. Its collections revolve around the bizarre combination of archeology and gloves, and include the magnificent red pottery of the Graufesenque works (see opposite), as well as a complete 180-million-year-old plesiosaurus. Millau's other two squares have been the subject of some rather questionable attempts at reconciling old stones and Richard Rogers-inspired contemporary urban design. Off one of these, place Emma-Calvé, the **clock tower** (daily 10am–noon & 2–6pm; €3) is worth a climb for the great all-round view. Take a look also in the streets off the square – rue du Voultre, rue de la Peyrollerie and their tributaries – for a sense of the old working-class and bourgeois districts.

Clear evidence of the town's importance in Roman times is to be seen in the **Graufesenque pottery works** archeology museum, just upstream on the south bank (Tues–Sun: July & Aug 10am–12.30pm & 2.30–7pm; otherwise 10am–noon & 2–5/6pm; €4.10), whose renowned red terracotta ware (*terra sigillata*) was distributed throughout the Roman world.

Eating and drinking

For a quick **meal**, you'll find numerous brasseries and cafés on place du Mandarous. But for something more traditional, try the restaurant at the *Des Causses* hotel (Mon–Sat; from €30), featuring local variations on lamb sweetbreads and tripe as well as Lyonnaise dishes, or the less upmarket *La Braconne*, on place Foch (☎05.65.60.30.93; closed Sun eve & Mon; from €20), offering high-calorie fare such as stuffed goose and pork with juniper berries. Alternatively, head for boulevard de la Capelle on the northeast side of the Old Town, where two good establishments spread their tables under the trees: *La Mangeoire*, at no. 8 (☎05.65.60.13.16; closed Mon; *menus* €19–46), which serves grilled fish, meat and game dishes; and next door, *La Marmite*, featuring *menus* from €18, including dishes such as *aligot*. A popular place for a **drink** is *La Locomotive*, at 33 av Gambetta (till 2am), which has live music on summer evenings.

Roquefort-sur-Soulzon and the Abbey of Silvanès

Twenty-one kilometres south of Millau, the little village of **ROQUEFORT-SUR-SOULZON** has little to it apart from its cheese, and almost every building is devoted to the cheese-making process. What gives the cheese its special flavour is the fungus, *penicillium roqueforti*, that grows exclusively in the fissures in the rocks created by the collapse of the sides of the valley on which Roquefort now stands.

While the sheep's milk used in the making of the cheese comes from different flocks and dairies as far afield as the Pyrenees, the crucial fungus is grown here, on bread. Just 2g of powdered fungus are enough for four thousand litres of milk, which in turn makes 330 Roquefort cheeses; they are matured in Roquefort's many-layered cellars, first unwrapped for three weeks and then wrapped up again. It takes three to six months for the full flavour to develop.

Two of the cheese manufacturers run organized **visits**: **Société** (daily: April–June & Sept 9.30am–noon & 1–5pm; July & Aug 9am–6.30pm; Oct–March 10am–noon & 1–5pm; €3.50) and **Papillon** (April–June & Sept daily 9.30–11.30am & 1.30–5.30pm; July & Aug daily 9.30am–6.30pm; Oct–March Mon–Fri 9.30–11.30am & 1.30–4.30pm; free). Each visit consists of a short film, followed by a tour of the cellars and a tasting – not, in fact, very interesting, except to hardcore cheese fans.

Some 25km further south, deep in the isolation of the *causses*, squats the twelfth-century **Cistercian Abbey of Silvanès** (early-Jan to mid-Dec daily 9.15am–12.30pm & 2–6pm; €2), founded in 1137 and the first Cistercian house in the region. Having largely survived the depredations of war and revolution, the abbey serves today as a centre for sacred music and dance from the world over. Although you'll have to manage your own transport, it's worth visiting not only for the evocative setting, but also for the excellently preserved thirteenth-century church and the surviving monastic buildings, including a refectory and scriptorium dating back to the 1100s. There are a couple of **hotels** in the village by the abbey, but only 4km from the monastery is the magnificent and moderately priced sixteenth-century *Château de Gissac* (☎05.65.98.14.60, ⓦwww.chateau.gissac .com; ❺), which offers half- and full-*pensions*.

The Gorges du Tarn

Jam-packed with tourists in July and August, but absolutely spectacular nonetheless, the **Gorges du Tarn** cuts through the limestone plateaux of the Causse de Sauveterre and the Causse Méjean in a precipitous trench 400–500m deep and 1000–1500m wide. Its sides, cloaked with woods of feathery pine and spiked with pinnacles of eroded rock, are often sheer and always very steep, creating within them a microclimate in sharp distinction to the inhospitable plateaux above. The permanent population is tiny, though there's plenty of evidence of more populous times in abandoned houses and once-cultivated terraces. Because of the press of people and the subsequent overpricing of **accommodation**, the best bet, if you want to stay along the gorge, is to head up onto the Causse Méjean, where there are several small family-run hotels and *chambres d'hôtes*, among which is the attractively sited *Auberge de la Cascade* in St-Chély-du-Tarn (℡04.66.48.52.82, ⓦwww .aubergecascade.com; closed Nov–March; ❹; *menu* for €34).

The most attractive section of the gorge runs northeast for 53km from the pretty village of **LE ROZIER**, 21km northeast of Millau, to **ISPAGNAC**. If you want to stay in Le Rozier, good accommodation can be found at the *Grand Hôtel Voyageurs* (℡05.65.62.60.09, ⓦwww.grandhoteldesvoyageurs.fr; closed Nov–Easter; ❷; *menu* from €20), and there's also a municipal **campsite** (℡05.65.62.63.98, ⓦcamping-lerozier.com; closed Oct–April). A better bet, however, is *Le Vallon* (℡04.66.44.21.24, ⓦwww.hotel-vallon.com; ❷) in Ispagnac, a small hotel with an excellent *terroir* restaurant (from €16), offering family-size rooms and good-value half-*pensions*.

A narrow and very twisty road follows the right bank of the river from Le Rozier, but it's not the best way to see the scenery. For drivers, the best views are from the road to St-Rome-de-Dolan above Les Vignes, and from the roads out of La Malène and the attractive **STE-ÉNIMIE**, where you'll find a well-informed **tourist office** (July & Aug Mon–Sat 9am–1pm & 3–7pm, Sun 9am–12.30pm & 3–6pm; rest of year Mon–Sat 9am–noon & 2–4/6/7pm; ℡04.66.48.53.44, ⓦwww.gorgesdutarn.net). To **camp**, head for *Camping Couderc* (℡04.66.48.50.53, ⓦwww.campingcouderc.fr; mid-April to mid-Sept). Better than driving is to walk, or follow the river's course by boat or canoe. There are dozens of places to rent canoes (€18 per person for 2–3hr, plus pick-up), and maps for various walking routes can be downloaded from the Ste-Énimie tourist office website (look under "*téléchargements*").

Also worth seeing are two beautiful **caves** about 25km up the Jonte river from Le Rozier. **Aven Armand** (daily: late March to June & Sept to early Oct 10am–noon & 1.30–5pm; July & Aug 9.30am–6pm; €9.10), on the edge of the Causse Méjean, which is fitted with a funicular, claims the world's tallest stalagmite towering 30m above the cave floor. The **Grotte de Dargilan** (daily: April–June & Sept 10am–5.30pm; July & Aug 10am–6.30pm; Oct 10am–4.30pm; €8.50), on the south side of the river on the edge of the Causse Noir, known as the "pink cave" from the colour of its rock, is known as one of the country's most beautiful stalactite caverns. **HYELZAS**, near Aven Armand, has a *gîte*, *Du Four à Pain* (℡04.66.45.61.64, ⓦgitedufourapain.monsite-orange.fr; ❸), which also offers dorm beds for €10.

South of Millau

Heading south from Millau the autoroute skirts the barren and windswept Causse du Larzac. Two sights lie not far off the highway, but neither is served by public transport. **LA COUVERTOIRADE**, 5km off the main road (parking €3), is billed as a perfect "Templar" village, although its present remains postdate the dissolution of that Order in the late thirteenth century. It's still a striking site, completely enclosed by its towers and walls and almost untouched by renovation. Its forty

Walking in France

France is quite simply a walker's paradise. It has some 60,000km of long-distance footpaths, known as GRs (*sentiers de grande randonnée*), not to mention thousands of shorter routes (PRs, or *sentiers de promenade et de randonnée*), all well maintained and signposted. They take you through the best of France's beautiful and varied landscape, including the majestic Alps in the east, the volcanic plugs of the Massif Central and the lofty Pyrenees in the south.

Les Saisies, Mont Blanc ▲

Base camp at Cirque de Gavarnie ▼

Hut at the ascent of Mont Blanc ▼

The Alps

For sheer mountain grandeur the northern Alps are unbeatable. The area has over a hundred peaks topping 3000m – including the highest, Mont Blanc (4807m) – glaciers, soaring pinnacles, high Alpine meadows and rich flora and fauna. The two main areas for walking are the Chamonix valley, which offers plenty of impressive views of Mont Blanc, and the Parc National de la Vanoise, created to protect the wild ibex; you'll stand a good chance of seeing these wild goats on one of the spectacular high-level hikes through the park.

The southern Alps are generally more accessible to less experienced walkers; a good introduction to the area is the Parc Naturel Régional du Vercors, crisscrossed with around 2850km of waymarked paths. At its heart is the impressive Vercors plateau, edged with craggy limestone cliffs and riven with deep gorges. More Mediterranean in appearance is the Parc Naturel Régional du Queyras, with its meadows of violets, orchids and pinks.

The Pyrenees

Generally less formidable than the Alps, the Pyrenees are still serious mountains, with a number of peaks topping 3000m, and offer some of France's finest walking. The classic long-distance path is the GR10, which traverses the whole range from west to east and is about 800km long. There are plenty of shorter walks too, the best of which are to be found in the central Ariège region, characterized by steep lush-green valleys, meadows full of wild flowers and abundant wildlife, including vultures – lammergeiers and griffon vultures – and marmots.

The Auvergne and Cévennes

At the heart of France lies the sparsely populated **Auvergne** region of the Massif Central. It's wild and rugged terrain, formed by three volcanic mountain chains, the Monts-Dore, Monts du Cantal and the smaller Monts-Dômes. The biggest draw for walkers is the jagged Puy de Sancy (1885m), the source of the Dordogne River.

Just south of the Auvergne, the **Cévennes** region is a picturesque one of deep valleys clothed with chestnut trees, high limestone plateaux and soft rounded granite peaks. A number of long-distance paths wind their way through the area, the best known of which is the GR70, the route famously described by Robert Louis Stevenson in his book *Travels with a Donkey*.

Provence

This most beguiling region, with its lovely warm light and Mediterranean colours and scents, has numerous walking possibilities. You could hike through the dramatic and vast Gorges du Verdon, or ramble among the gentle hills and lavender fields of the Luberon. Towards the Italian border is the Parc National du Mercantour, an unspoilt Alpine wilderness, sheltering chamois, golden eagles and rare species of flowers.

Corsica

Corsica offers some of the most adventurous walking in France. Scores of footpaths give access to spectacular coastline, rocky gorges and mountainous peaks.

▲ Donkey, Cevennes

▼ Lac de Melo, Corsica

▼ Sunflower and lavender fields, Provence

Mont Blanc trails ▲

Aveyron, Conques ▼

Ten top walks in France

▶▶ Northern Alps: The classic Tour du Mont Blanc which crosses French, Italian and Swiss terrain and takes eight to ten days. See p.793.

▶▶ The Chemin de Saint-Jacques, the ancient pilgrimage route that starts in Le-Puy-en-Velay and ends at Santiago de Compostela in Spain (see p.752). To hike the whole thing would take weeks, but you could do just a section, such as the six-day stretch between Figeac and Moissac through the Lot valley.

▶▶ A two-day loop walk above Cauterets in the Pyrenees: Pont d'Espagne–Vallée du Gaube–Vallée de Lutour–Pont d'Espagne. See p.636.

▶▶ Corsica's nearly two-hundred-kilometre-long GR20, possibly Europe's most testing walk. It can take around twelve days if you're fit. Accommodation is in *refuges* – it's best to book these in advance in peak season. See p.990.

▶▶ The Côte de Granit Rose (see p.338). This attractive stretch of Brittany's coast is dotted with sculpted pink granite rocks. One of the best stretches is from Trégastel to Tréguier (a three-day hike) along the GR34.

▶▶ The ninety-minute walk up and down the rocky headlands from Cassis, on the Côte d'Azur, to the Calanque d'En Vau, with its beautifully secluded beach. See p.916.

▶▶ The circuit of the southern Alps' Parc National des Écrins (along the GR54), hard to beat for the grandeur of its scenery. See p.772.

▶▶ The Canyon du Verdon: the seven-hour walk from La Maline to the Point Sublime is by far the best way to explore the canyon. See p.889.

▶▶ The GR7 "Stevenson trail", which takes about a fortnight to walk, passing through the rugged Gévaudan highlands and the bare hilltops of Mont Lozère. See p.747.

remaining inhabitants live by tourism, and you have to pay to walk around the **ramparts** (daily: March–June & Sept to mid-Nov 10am–noon & 2–5/6pm; July & Aug 10am–7pm; €3, or €6 including a video presentation; English audio-guide available). Just outside the walls on the south side is a *lavogne*, a paved water-hole of a kind seen all over the *causse* for watering the flocks whose milk is used for Roquefort cheese. If you want to **stay**, there's the municipal *gîte d'étape* (☎05.65.58.17.75, ⓦwww.gite-chambre-d-hote-couvertoirade.com; ❸, dorm beds €15) in the far corner from the entrance, serving the GR71 and GR71C. A bus from Millau (Mon, Wed & Fri) serves the village during July and August.

A further 5km south, turn off at **Le Caylar** for the stunning road to **ST-MAURICE-NAVACELLES**, a small and sleepy hamlet with a fine World War I memorial by Paul Dardé at its centre. You'll want to keep going, however, to the **Cirque de Navacelles**, 10km north on the D25 past the beautiful ruined seventeenth-century sheep farm of La Prunarède. The cirque is a widening in the 150m-deep trench of the Vis *gorges*, formed by a now dry loop in the river that has left a neat pyramid of rock sticking up in the middle like a wheel hub. An ancient and scarcely inhabited hamlet survives in the bottom – a bizarre phenomenon in an extraordinary location, and you get literally a bird's-eye view of it from the edge of the cliff above. In the hamlet in the heart of the cirque you'll find the comfortable **hotel**, *Auberge de la Cascade* (☎04.67.81.50.95; April–Nov; ❸), which has a bar and restaurant.

The Cévennes and Ardèche

The **Cévennes** mountains and River **Ardèche** form the southeastern defences of the Massif Central, overlooking the Rhône valley to the east and the Mediterranean littoral to the south. The bare upland landscapes of the inner or western edges are those of the central Massif. The outer edges, Mont Aigoual and its radiating valleys and the tributary valleys of the Ardèche, are distinctly Mediterranean: deep, dry, close and clothed in forests of sweet chestnut, oak and pine.

Remote and inaccessible country until well into the twentieth century, the region has bred rugged and independent inhabitants. For centuries it was the most resolute stronghold of Protestantism in France, and it was in these valleys that the persecuted Protestants put up their fiercest resistance to the tyranny of Louis XIV and Louis XV. In World War II, it was heavily committed to the Resistance, while in the aftermath of 1968, it became the promised land of the hippies – *zippies*, as the locals called them; they moved into the countless abandoned farms and hamlets, whose native inhabitants had been driven away by hardship and poverty. The odd hippy has stuck it out, true to the last to the alternative life. In more recent times, it has been colonized by Dutch and Germans.

The author Robert Louis Stevenson crossed this terrain in 1878 with Modestine, a donkey he bought in Le Monastier-sur-Gazeille, near **Le Puy** and sold at journey's end in the former Protestant stronghold of **St-Jean-du-Gard**, a now-famous route described in *Travels with a Donkey* (see p.1068).

The Parc National des Cévennes

The **Parc National des Cévennes** was created in 1970 to protect and preserve the life, landscape, flora, fauna and architectural heritage of the Cévennes. North to south, it stretches from **Mende** on the Lot to **Le Vigan** and includes both **Mont Lozère** and **Mont Aigoual**. Access, to the periphery at least, is surprisingly easy, thanks to the Paris–Clermont–Alès–Nîmes train line and the Montpellier–Mende link.

The **main information office** for the park is at Florac (see opposite). It publishes numerous leaflets on the flora, fauna and traditions of the park, plus activities and routes for walkers, cyclists, canoeists and horseriders. It also provides a list of **gîtes d'étape** in the park and can provide information for those following Stevenson's route, including where to hire a donkey. In July and August, it's wise to book ahead for accommodation; otherwise you could find yourself sleeping outdoors.

Mende

Capital of the Lozère *département*, **MENDE** lies well down in the deep valley of the Lot at the northern tip of the Parc des Cévennes, and 40km north of Florac, with train and bus links to the Paris–Nîmes and Clermont–Millau lines. It's an attractive southern town, though much of its charm is lost in the newly commercialized streets of the city centre. What Mende lacks in authenticity it makes up for in practicality: it's a great place to purchase last-minute supplies before you head off to the mountains.

Standing against the haze of the mountain background, the town's main landmark, the **cathedral**, owes its construction to Pope Urban V, who was born locally and wished to give something back to his native soil. Although work began in 1369, progress was hampered by war and natural disasters and the building wasn't completed until the end of the nineteenth century. Inside is a handsome choir, and, suspended from the clerestory, eight great Aubusson tapestries, depicting the life of the Virgin. She's also present in one of the side chapels of the choir in the form of a statue made from olive wood, thought to have been brought back from the Middle East during the Crusades.

Aside from the cathedral, most pleasure resides in a quiet wander in the Old Town's minuscule squares and narrow medieval streets, with their houses bulging outwards, as though buckling under the weight of the upper storeys. In **rue Notre-Dame**, which separated the Christian from Jewish quarters in medieval times, the thirteenth-century house at no. 17 was once a synagogue. If you carry on down to the river, you'll see the medieval packhorse bridge, the **Pont Notre-Dame**, with its worn cobbles.

Practicalities

The **tourist office** is on place du Foirail located at the southern end of boulevard Henri-Bourrillon, the ring road that encircles the city centre (June & Sept Mon–Sat 9am–12.30pm & 2–6pm; July & Aug Mon–Sat 9am–12.30pm & 2–7pm, Sun 10am–noon & 2–4pm; Oct–May Mon–Fri 9am–12.30pm & 2–6/7pm, Sat 9am–noon; ☎04.66.94.00.23, ⓦwww.ot-mende.fr). The **gare SNCF** (☎04.66.49.00.39) lies across the river, north of the centre. **Buses** depart from either the station or place du Foirail.

For a place to **stay**, the best choice is the *Lion d'Or* at 12–14 bd Britexte (☎04.66.49.16.46, ⓔlion-dor48@orange.fr; ❸), set in a beautiful old building and featuring an excellent *terroir* restaurant (from €18). Another good choice is the pretty *Hôtel de France* on boulevard Lucien-Arnault, the northern part of the inner ring road (☎04.66.65.00.04, ⓦwww.hoteldefrance-mende.com; closed Dec & Jan; ❺; *menu* from €29). Slightly further out of town, on the river at 2 av du 11-novembre, the classy *Hôtel du Pont-Roupt* (☎04.66.65.01.43, ⓦwww.hotel-pont-roupt.com; ❺) offers such luxuries as an indoor pool, terrace and good restaurant; dishes include *truite au lard* and *salade au Roquefort* (*menus* €25–60). The best **restaurant** in town is *La Safranière* in Chabrits (☎04.66.49.31.54), which daringly blends *terroir* and *gastronomique* styles (*menus* from €20). Another good choice is *Le Mazel* (☎04.66.65.05.33; closed Mon eve & Tues; from €6), though the setting – in the only modern square in the Old Town – is a little disappointing.

Mont Lozère

Mont Lozère is a windswept and desolate barrier of granite and yellow grassland, rising to 1699m at the summit of **Finiels**, still grazed by herds of cows, but in nothing like the numbers of bygone years when half the cattle in Languedoc came up here for their summer feed. Snowbound in winter and wild and dangerous in bad weather, it has claimed many a victim among lost travellers. In some of the squat granite hamlets on the northern slopes, like Servies, Auriac and Les Sagnes, you can still hear the bells, known as *clochers de tourmente*, that tolled in the wind to give travellers some sense of direction when the cloud was low.

If you're travelling by car from Mende, the way to the summit is via the village of **LE BLEYMARD**, about 30km to the east on the bank of the infant River Lot, with accommodation in the form of the comfortably rustic *Hôtel La Remise* (℡04.66.48.65.80, ⓦwww.hotel-laremise.com; ❸; *terroir* restaurant from €17.50). From here, the D20 winds 7km up through the conifers to join up with the GR7, which has taken a more direct route from Le Bleymard. This is the route that Stevenson took, waymarked as the "Tracé Historique de Stevenson". Road and footpath run together as far as the **Col de Finiels**, where the GR7 strikes off on its own to the southeast. The source of the River Tarn is about 3km east of the col, the summit of Lozère 2km to the west. From the col, the road and Stevenson's route drop down in tandem, through the lonely hamlet of **FINIELS** to the pretty but touristy village of **LE PONT-DE-MONTVERT**.

At Le Pont, a seventeenth-century **bridge** crosses the Tarn by a stone tower that once served as a tollhouse. In this building in 1702, the Abbé du Chayla, a priest appointed by the Crown to reconvert the rebellious Protestants enraged by the revocation of the Edict of Nantes, set up a torture chamber to coerce the recalcitrant. Incensed by his brutality, a group of rebels under the leadership of one Esprit Séguier attacked and killed him on July 23. Reprisals were extreme; nearly twelve thousand were executed, thus precipitating the Camisards' guerrilla war against the state.

At the edge of the village, there's also an *écomusée* on the life and character of the region, the **Maison du Mont Lozère** (daily: April–May & Oct 3–6pm; June–Sept 10.30am–12.30pm & 2.30–6.30pm; Nov–March Sun only 3–6pm; €3.50). If you're tempted to **stay**, there's the small and atmospheric *Auberge des Cévennes* (℡04.66.45.80.01, ⓦauberge-des-cevennes.com; closed mid-Nov to March; ❺; restaurant from €16.50), overlooking the bridge.

Florac

Situated 39km south of Mende, **FLORAC** lies in the bottom of the trench-like valley of the Tarnon just short of its junction with the Tarn. Behind the village rises the steep wall that marks the edge of the Causse Méjean. When you get here, you will have already passed the frontier between the northern and Mediterranean landscapes; the dividing line seems to be the **Col de Montmirat** at the western end of Mont Lozère. Once you begin the descent, the scrub and steep gullies and the tiny abandoned hamlets, with their eyeless houses oriented towards the sun, speak clearly of the south.

The village, with some two thousand inhabitants, is strung out along the left bank of the Tarnon and the main street, **avenue Jean-Monestier**. There's little to see, though the close lanes of the village up towards the valley side have their charms, especially the plane-shaded **place du Souvenir**. It is worth visiting on a Thursday during summer for the **market**, when you'll find the tiny streets packed with merchants and local produce. A red-schist castle stands above the village, housing the **Centre d'Information du Parc National des Cévennes** (Easter–June & Sept daily 9.30am–12.30pm & 1.30–6pm; July & Aug daily 9am–6.30pm;

Oct–Easter Mon–Fri 9.30am–12.30pm & 1.30–6pm; ☎04.66.49.53.01, ⓦwww .cevennes-parcnational.fr). The **tourist office** is on avenue Jean-Monestier (Mon–Sat 9am–noon & 2–6pm; ☎04.66.45.01.14, ⓦwww.mescevennes.com); they provide details on the year-round "Festival of Nature" programme, with guided treks around the national park. **Mountain-bike rental** is available from Cévennes Evasion, in place Boyer (☎04.66.45.18.31).

The **accommodation** on offer is not fantastic. The best place is the *Grand Hôtel du Parc* on avenue Jean-Monestier (☎04.66.45.03.05, ⓦwww.grandhotelduparc.fr; closed Dec–March; ❸; restaurant €19–38), with pleasant gardens and a pool. *Les Gorges du Tarn* at 48 rue du Pêcher (☎04.66.45.00.63, ⓦwww.hotel-gorgesdutarn .com; ❸) is another comfortable option. The best-value **campsite** is the municipal one at Le Pont-du-Tarn out on the road towards Ispagnac (☎04.66.45.18.26, ⓦwww.causses-cevennes.com/erebuissonniere; April to mid-Sept).

Florac's Esplanade is a good place to look for somewhere to **eat**, otherwise the *Adonis* restaurant in the *Les Gorges* hotel serves high-quality local cuisine (April–Nov; closed Sun lunch; *menus* €16–28), while another good choice is the riverside *La Source du Pêcher* at 1 rue de Rémuret in the Old Town (☎04.66.45.03.01; *menus* €17–35; closed Nov–Easter).

Mont Aigoual

It's 24km by road up the beautiful valley of the Tarnon to the **Col de Perjuret**, where a right turn will take you on to the **Causse Méjean** and to the strange rock formations of **Nîmes-le-Vieux**, and a left turn along a rising ridge a further 15km to the 1565m summit of **Mont Aigoual** (GR6, GR7, GR66). From the latter, it is said that you can see a third of France, from the Alps to the Pyrenees, with the Mediterranean coast from Marseille to Sète at your feet. It's not a craggy summit, although the ground drops away pretty steeply into the valley of the River Hérault on the south side, but the view and the sense of exposure to the elements is dramatic enough. At the summit is an **observatory** which has been in use for over a century. A small but interesting **exhibition** (May–Sept daily 10am–6pm; free) shows modern weather-forecasting techniques alongside displays of old barometers and weather vanes.

The descent to Le Vigan by the valley of the Hérault is superb; a magnificent twisty road follows the deepening ravine through dense beech and chestnut woods, to come out at the bottom in rather Italianate scenery, with tall, close-built villages and vineyards beside the stream. The closest accommodation to the summit is the *Hôtel du Touring* (☎04.67.82.60.04, ⓦwww.hotel-restaurant -touring.com; closed April & Nov to mid-Dec; ❹; restaurant *menus* from €12) at **L'ESPÉROU**, a rather soulless mountain resort just below the summit. Better to go down to the charming village of **VALLERAUGUE**, with its brown-grey schist houses and leafy riverside setting. There are a number of hotels here, including the pleasantly sited *Les Bruyères* (☎04.67.82.20.06, ⓔhotelrestaurantles bruyeres@orange.fr; May to early-Oct; ❸; *menus* €16–35).

Le Vigan and the Huguenot strongholds

Only 64km from Montpellier and 29km from St-Guilhem-le-Désert, **LE VIGAN** makes a good starting point for exploring the southern part of the Cévennes. It's a leafy, cool and thoroughly agreeable place, at its liveliest during the **Fête d'Isis** at the beginning of August and the colossal fair that takes over the Parc des Châtaigniers on September 9 and 22.

The prettiest part of the town is around the central **place du Quai**, shaded by lime trees and bordered by cafés and brasseries. From here it's only a two-minute walk south, down rue Pierre-Gorlier, to reach the gracefully arched **Pont Vieux**.

Beside it stands the **Musée Cévenol** (April–Oct daily except Tues 10am–noon & 2–6pm; Nov–March Wed only 10am–noon & 2–6pm; €4.50), a well-presented look at traditional rural occupations in the area, including the woodcutter, butcher, shepherd and wolf-hunter. There's also a room devoted to the area's best-known twentieth-century writer, André Chamson, noted for his novels steeped in the traditions and countryside of the Cévennes. Interestingly, Coco Chanel also features in the museum: she had local family connections and it seems found inspiration for her designs in the *cévenol* silks.

The **tourist office** occupies a modern block in the centre of the place du Marché, at the opposite end of the place du Quai from the church (July & Aug Mon–Sat 8.45am–12.30pm & 2–6pm, Sun 9am–12.30pm; Sept–June Mon–Fri 9.30am–12.30pm & 2–6pm, Sat 9am–12.30pm & Easter–Oct also 3–6pm; ℡04.67.81.01.72, ⓦwww.cevennes-meridionales.com). For somewhere to **stay**, try the comfortable *Mas de la Prairie*, with many amenities including swimming pool, on avenue Sergent Triaire (℡04.67.81.80.80, ⓦwww.masdelaprairie.fr; ❷). The best alternative is a couple of kilometres out of town, south towards Montdardier on the D48: the handsome old *Auberge Cocagne* in the village of **AVÈZE** (℡04.67.81.02.70, ⓦwww.auberge-cocagne-cevennes.com; closed mid-Nov to mid-Feb; ❹; restaurant from €22). There is also a **campsite**, the well-shaded riverside *Val de l'Arre* (℡04.67.81.02.77, ⓦwww.valdelarre.com; closed Oct–March), 2km upriver from Le Vigan, on the opposite bank. One of the best places to eat in Le Vigan is *Le Jardin* (closed Mon), in place du Terral, just off the main square; *menus* start at €19 and feature French classics with a local twist, such as *filet mignon* with a chestnut sauce.

St-Jean-du-Gard and around

Thirty-two kilometres west of Alès, **ST-JEAN-DU-GARD** was the centre of Protestant resistance during the Camisard war in 1702–04. It straggles along the bank of the River Gardon, crossed by a graceful, arched eighteenth-century bridge, with a number of picturesque old houses still surviving in the main street, **Grande-Rue**. One of them contains the splendid **Musée des Vallées Cévenoles** (April–June & Sept–Oct daily 10am–12.30pm & 2–7pm; July & Aug 10am–7pm; Nov–March Tues–Sat 9am–noon & 2–6pm, Sun 2–6pm; €4.70), a museum of local life with displays of tools, trades, furniture, clothes, domestic articles and a fascinating collection of pieces related to the silk industry. The silk-spinning work was done by women in factories and lists of regulations and rules on display give some idea of the tough conditions in which they had to work.

The **tourist office** is just off the main street by the post office (July & Aug Mon & Wed–Fri 9am–1pm & 3–6pm, Tues & Sat 9am–7pm, Sun 10am–noon; Sept–June Mon–Fri 9am–12.30pm & 1.30–5pm, Sat 10am–12.30pm; ℡04.66.85.32.11, ⓦotsi.st.jeandugard.free.fr). They can advise you about operating times of the **steam train** between St-Jean and Anduze (April–Sept daily; Oct no service Mon & Fri; €13 return). There's a big **market** all along Grande-Rue on Tuesday mornings. The best bet for **accommodation** is *L'Oronge*, in a seventeenth-century building at 103 **Grande-Rue** (℡04.66.86.05.52, ⓦwww.hoteloronge.com; ❹; good restaurant from €14).

The Musée du Désert

Signposts at St-Jean direct you to the museum at **MAS SOUBEYRAN**, a minuscule hamlet of beautiful rough-stone houses in a gully above the village of Mialet, about 12km east. The **Musée du Désert** (daily: March–June & Sept–Nov 9.30am–noon & 2–6pm; July & Aug 9.30am–7pm; €5) is in the house that once belonged to Rolland, one of the Camisards' self-taught but most successful military leaders, and it remains much the same as it would have been in 1704, the year of his death. It catalogues the appalling sufferings and sheer dogged heroism of the Protestant Huguenots in defence of their freedom of conscience; and the "desert" they had to traverse between the Revocation of the Edict of Nantes in 1685 and the promulgation of the Edict of Tolerance in 1787, which restored their original rights (full emancipation came with the Declaration of the Rights of Man in the first heady months of the Revolution in 1789). During this period, they had no civil rights, unless they abjured their faith. They could not bury their dead, baptize their children or marry. Their ministers were forced into exile on pain of death. The recalcitrant were subjected to the infamous *dragonnades*, which involved the forcible billeting of troops on private homes at the expense of the occupants. As if this were not enough, the soldiers would beat their drums continuously for days and nights in people's bedrooms in order to deprive them of sleep. Protestants were also put to death or sent to the galleys for life and their houses were destroyed.

Not surprisingly, such brutality led to armed rebellion, inspired by the prophesying of the lay preachers who had replaced the banished priests, calling for a holy war. The rebels were hopelessly outnumbered and the revolt was ruthlessly put down in 1704. On display are documents, private letters and lists of those who died for their beliefs, including the names of five thousand who died as galley slaves (*galériens pour la foi*) and the women who were immured in the Tour de Constance prison in Aigues-Mortes. Also on show are the chains and rough uniform of a *galérien*.

Prafrance and the Mine Témoin

Twelve kilometres southeast of St-Jean in the direction of Anduze, **PRAFRANCE** is noteworthy for **La Bambouseraie** (March to mid-Nov daily 9.30am to closing time dependent on season and weather; €8), an extraordinary and appealing garden consisting exclusively of bamboos of all shapes and sizes; the project was started in 1855 by local entrepreneur Eugène Mazel. An easy way to get here is to take the steam train (see p.749) from St-Jean-du-Gard; it takes just ten minutes.

If you want to leave the area by main-line train, the place to head for is **ALÈS** on the Nîmes–Paris line. This was a major coal-mining centre, though 25,000 jobs have been lost and all but two open-cast pits closed in the last four decades. Today, it has a superb museum on the history and techniques of coal-mining, known as the **Mine Témoin**, in the underground workings of a disused mine on chemin de la Cité Ste-Marie in the Rochebelle district (French-only guided tours daily: March–June & Sept to mid-Nov 9.30am–12.30pm & 2–6pm; July & Aug 10am–7pm; €7; last visit 1hr 30min before closing).

Aubenas and the northern Cévennes

A small but prosperous, and surprisingly industrial, town of around twelve thousand, **AUBENAS** sits in the middle of the southern part of the Ardèche *département*, high up on a hill overlooking the middle valley of the River Ardèche. Located 91km southeast of Le Puy, the town, with a character and non-tourist-dependent economy of its own, makes a much better base than overly crowded places further downstream around Vallon-Pont-d'Arc.

The central knot of streets with their cobbles and bridges, occupying the highest point of town around **place de l'Hôtel-de-Ville**, have great charm, particularly towards place de la Grenette and place du 14-juillet. Place de l'Hôtel-de-Ville is dominated by the eleventh-century **château**, from which the local *seigneurs* ruled the area right up until the Revolution (90min guided tours: April–June & Sept Tues & Thurs–Sat 10.30am & 2pm; July & Aug daily 11am, 2pm & 5pm; Oct & Dec–March Tues, Thurs & Sat 2pm; closed hols; €3.50). Other sights include the heavily restored thirteenth-century **St-Laurent church**, which has the curious seventeenth-century hexagonal **Dôme Bênoit chapel** (July & Aug Mon–Fri 5pm; €3.50). There's a magnificent view of the Ardèche snaking up the valley from under an arch beside the castle, as there is from the end of boulevard Gambetta 200m downhill, where the **tourist office** is located on the main square (July & Aug Mon–Sat 9am–12.30pm & 2–7pm, Sun 9am–1pm; Sept–June Mon–Sat 9am–noon & 2–6pm; ℡04.75.89.02.03, Ⓦwww.aubenasvals.com). To use the **internet** go to Espace Informatique at 10 bd Saint-Didier (Mon noon–7pm, Tues–Sat 10am–7pm).

For somewhere to **stay**, the budget choice is the *Hôtel Le Provence* on boulevard de Vernon (℡04.75.35.28.43, Ⓦhotelleprovence.free.fr; ❶), which has clean simple rooms. At the top end of the scale the five-room *La Bastide du Soleil* (℡04.75.36.91.66, Ⓦwww.bastidesoleil.com; closed Dec & Jan; ❻) offers a splendid blend of antique charm and modern convenience (restaurant *menus* €19–30). There are many campsites to choose from in between Aubenas and Vallon. Cafés and brasseries line boulevard de Vernon on the south side of town; the best place for both food and atmosphere is *Le Fournil*, 34 rue du 4-septembre, set in a fifteenth-century house at the end of Béranger-de-la-Tour, in the heart of the Old Town (closed Sun & Mon; *menus* from €22), or you could try *Le Coyote*, 13 bd Jean-Mathon (℡04.75.35.01.28; closed Sun & Mon; *menus* at €21 & €30), whose specialities are fish and foie gras.

The Gorges de l'Ardèche

The **Gorges de l'Ardèche** begin at the **Pont d'Arc**, a very beautiful arch that the river has cut for itself through the limestone, just downstream from **VALLON**, itself 39km south of Aubenas. They continue for about 35km to **ST-MARTIN-D'ARDÈCHE** in the valley of the Rhône.

The fantastic gorges wind back and forth, much of the time dropping 300m straight down in the almost dead-flat scrubby Plateau des Gras. Unfortunately they are also an appalling tourist trap; the road following the rim, with spectacular viewpoints marked out at regular intervals, is jammed with traffic in summer. The river, down in the bottom, which is where you really want to be to appreciate the grandeur of the canyon, is likewise packed with canoes in high season. It is walkable, depending on the water level, but you would need to bivouac midway at either Gaud or Gournier. If you go in season, be prepared for heavy traffic, and book accommodation well ahead.

The plateau itself is riddled with caves. **Aven Marzal**, a stalactite cavern north of the gorge (daily 11.30am–5pm; €8.50, joint ticket with zoo €14.40), has a prehistoric **zoo**, which consists of reconstructions of dinosaurs and friends (Feb, March, Oct & Nov Sun & school hols 10.30am–6pm; April–Sept daily 11.30am–5pm; €8.50), but the frequency of visits to the cave depends on the number of visitors waiting – they are approximately every twenty minutes in July and August, falling to four per day in other months. Best of the area's caves is the **Aven Orgnac**, to the south of the gorge (90min tour daily: April, June & Sept 9.30am–5.30pm; July & Aug 9.30am–6pm; Oct to mid-Nov 9.30am–noon & 2–4.30pm; mid-Nov to March 10am–noon & 2–5pm; €10), one of France's most spectacular and colourful stalactite formations. In addition to the normal tours, you can also opt for the "*visites spéléologiques*" hardcore caving tours; they last three and eight hours respectively (reserve two weeks ahead; ℡04.75.38.65.10). There's also a very good prehistory **museum** (same hours as Aven Orgnac but closed mid-Nov to Jan; €5, joint ticket with Aven Orgnac €10).

Practicalities

Accommodation in the area can be a problem during the high season. By far the best option is *Le Manoir du Raveyron*, rue Henri-Barbusse (℡04.75.88.03.59, Ⓦchambre-confort-hotel-charme-logis-restaurant-gastronomique.manoir-du-raveyron.com; closed Oct to mid-March; ❸), with a good restaurant from €28, while another good option is the *Hôtel du Tourisme*, on rue du Miarou in Vallon (℡04.75.88.02.12, Ⓦwww.hotel-tourisme-pont-darc.com; closed Dec–Feb; ❹). The river is lined with **campsites**, the cheapest being the municipal one (℡04.75.88.04.73, Ⓦwww .municipalvallon.com; April–Sept). There's a **tourist office** on the south side of town (April & Oct Mon–Sat 9am–noon & 2–4/5pm; May, June & Sept Mon–Sat 9am–noon & 2–5/6pm, Sun 9.30am–12.30pm; July & Aug Mon–Sat 9am–1pm & 3–7pm, Sun 9.30am–12.30pm; Nov–March Mon–Fri 9am–noon & 2–5pm, Sat 9am–noon; ℡04.75.88.04.01, Ⓦwww.vallon-pont-darc.com).

Le Puy-en-Velay and the northeast

Right in the middle of the Massif Central, 78km from St-Étienne and 132km from Clermont, **LE PUY-EN-VELAY**, often shortened to Le Puy, is one of the most remarkable towns in the whole of France, with a landscape and architecture that are totally theatrical. Slung between the higher mountains to east and west, the countryside erupts in a chaos of volcanic acne: everywhere is a confusion of abrupt conical hills, scarred with dark outcrops of rock and topknotted with woods. Even in the centre of the town, these volcanic thrusts burst through.

In the past, Le Puy enjoyed influence and prosperity because of its ecclesiastical institutions, which were supported in part by the production of the town's famous green lentils. It was – and in a limited way, still is – a centre for pilgrims embarking

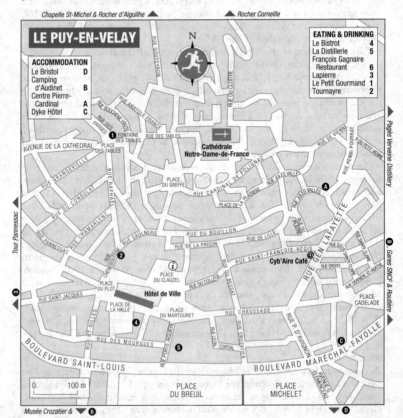

LE PUY-EN-VELAY

Chapelle St-Michel & Rocher d'Aiguilhe ▲ ▲ Rocher Corneille

ACCOMMODATION
Le Bristol   D
Camping
d'Audinet   B
Centre Pierre-
Cardinal   A
Dyke Hôtel   C

EATING & DRINKING
Le Bistrot   4
La Distillerie   5
François Gagnaire
Restaurant   6
Lapierre   3
Le Petit Gourmand   1
Tournayre   2

Cathédrale Notre-Dame-de-France

Cyb'Aire Café

Hôtel de Ville

0   100 m

PLACE DU BREUIL

PLACE MICHELET

Musée Crozatier & ▼ 6

on the 1600km trek to Santiago de Compostela. The specific starting point is place du Plot (also the scene of a lively Saturday market) and rue St-Jacques. History has it that Le Puy's Bishop Godescalk, in the tenth century, was the first pilgrim to make the journey. Recently, the town has fallen somewhat on hard times, and its traditional industries – tanning and lace – have essentially gone bust. Even today Le Puy is somewhat inaccessible for the capital of a *département*: the three main roads out all cross passes more than 1000m high, which causes problems in winter.

Arrival, information and accommodation

If you arrive at the **gare SNCF** or **gare routière** (℡04.71.09.25.60), facing each other in place du Maréchal-Leclerc, you'll find yourself around a ten-minute walk from the central place du Clauzel and the **tourist office** (Easter–June & Sept Mon–Sat 8.30am–noon & 1.30–6.15pm, Sun 9am–noon & 2–6pm; July & Aug daily 8.30am–7pm; Oct–Easter Mon–Sat 8.30am–noon & 1.30–6.15pm, Sun 10am–noon; ℡04.71.09.38.41, Ⓦwww.ot-lepuyenvelay.fr). There are quite a few places with **internet** access, the best option being Cyb'Aire at 17 rue du Général-Lafayette (Mon–Fri 9am–8pm; Sat 2–7pm).

Le Puy doesn't have a superabundance of **hotels**, so it's wise to book ahead in peak season. The budget options include the very well-equipped *Dyke Hôtel*, at no. 37 bd Maréchal-Fayolle (℡04.71.09.05.30, Ⓦwww.dykehotel.fr; ❷), which connects the station and place du Clauzel. The best bet, however, is ⚜ *Le Bristol*, 7 av Foch (℡04.71.09.13.38, Ⓦwww.hotelbristol-lepuy.com; ❹), set in one of the area's oldest buildings, a former pilgrims' hostel, with a restaurant offering an excellent regional set *menu* from €13.80. For those on a tight budget, there's a good **HI hostel**, the attractive *Centre Pierre-Cardinal* at 9 rue Jules-Vallès (℡04.71.05.52.40, Ⓔauberge.jeunesse@mairie-le-puy-en-velay.fr; closed weekends Oct–March; dorm beds €10.80), just off rue Lafayette, in the heart of the Old Town. **Campers** should head for the municipal *Camping d'Audinet* (℡04.71.09.10.18, Ⓦwww.brives-charensac.fr; April–Sept), near the River Loire in the northeast corner of town.

The Town

It would be hard to lose your bearings in Le Puy, for wherever you go there's no losing sight of the colossal, brick-red statue of the Virgin and Child that towers above the town on the **Rocher Corneille**, 755m above sea level and 130m above the lower town. The Virgin is cast from 213 guns captured at Sébastopol and painted red to match the tiled roofs below. You can climb up to the statue's base and, irreverent though it may seem, even up inside it (daily: Feb to mid-March & Oct to mid-Nov 10am–5pm; mid-March to April 9am–6pm; May–June & Sept 9am–7pm; July & Aug 9am–7.30pm; €3). From here you get stunning views of the city, the church of St-Michel atop its needle-pointed pinnacle a few hundred metres northwest, and the surrounding volcanic countryside.

In the maze of steep cobbled streets and steps that terrace the Rocher, lace-makers – a traditional, though now commercialized, industry – do a fine trade, with doilies and lace shawls hanging enticingly outside souvenir shops. The main focus here in the **Old Town** is the Byzantine-looking **Cathédrale Notre-Dame-de-France**, begun in the eleventh century and decorated with multi-coloured layers of stone and mosaic patterns and roofed with a line of six domes. It's best approached up the rue des Tables, where you get the full theatrical force of its five-storeyed west front towering above you. In the rather exotic eastern gloom of the interior, a black-faced Virgin in spreading lace and golden robes stands on the main altar, the copy of a revered original destroyed during the Revolution; the copy is still paraded through the town every August 15. Other lesser treasures are displayed at the back of the church in the sacristy, beyond which is the entrance to the exceptionally beautiful eleventh- and twelfth-century **cloister** (daily: late May to June & early Sept 9am–noon & 2–6.30pm, July & Aug 9am–6.30pm; late Sept to late May 9am–noon & 2–5pm; €5). The passageway to the cloisters takes you past the so-called **Fever Stone**, whose origins may have been as a prehistoric dolmen and which was reputed to have the power of curing fevers.

It's a ten-minute walk from the cathedral to the **Chapel of St-Michel** (signposts lead the way), perched atop the 82m needle-pointed lava pinnacle of the **Rocher d'Aiguilhe**. The little Romanesque church, built on Bishop Godescalk's return from his pilgrimage and consecrated in 962, is a beauty in its own right, and its improbable situation atop this striking pinnacle of rock is quite extraordinary – it's a long haul up 265 steps to the entrance (daily: Feb to mid-March 2–5pm; mid-March to April & Oct to mid-Nov 9.30am–noon & 2–5.30pm; May–Sept 9am–6.30pm; Christmas hols 2–5pm; €3).

Eating and drinking

For its size, Le Puy has an impressive array of fine yet economical **restaurants**, so there is little need to resort to the row of anonymous brasseries on the main street. The best of the eateries is the creative cuisine of the ☂ *François Gagnaire Restaurant* at 4 av Charbonnier (☎04.71.02.75.55, ⓦwww.francois-gagnaire-restaurant .com; closed Sun eve, Mon & Tues lunch; July & Aug closed Sun, Mon & Tues lunch; *menus* €25–145); try the *Saint-Jacques* with green lentils. Other good choices include *Tournayre*, set in a seventeenth-century building at 12 rue Chène-bouterie (☎04.71.09.58.94; closed Mon, Wed & Jan), specializing in regional fare (*menus* €23–67), and the *Lapierre* at 6 rue Capucins (☎04.71.09.08.44; closed Dec & Jan, Sun out of season & Sat), with *menus* from €20–29.

For a **drink** or light snack, the terrace of *Le Petit Gourmand*, at the bottom of rue des Tables, makes a pleasant stop in summer (closed Wed; *galettes* for €5, *menus* €10–19). Though lacking atmosphere, the large *La Distillerie* pub on place du Breuil has an impressive selection of regional speciality beers and liqueurs. *Le Bistrot* at 7 place de la Halle is a lively place for an evening drink.

La Chaise-Dieu

Located northwest of Le Puy, the little town of **LA CHAISE-DIEU** is renowned for the **abbey church of St-Robert** (Jan Sat 10am–noon & 2–5pm, Sun 2–5pm; otherwise daily except Sun am: Feb–June & mid-Aug to Dec 9/10am–noon & 2–5/6pm; July to mid-Aug 9am–7pm; €4), whose square towers dominate the town. Founded in 1044 and restored in the fourteenth century at the expense of Pope Clement VI, who had served as a monk here, the church was destroyed by the Huguenots in 1562, burnt down in 1692, and remained unfinished when the Revolution brought a wave of anticlericalism. It was only really finished in the twentieth century. Its interior contains the tomb of Clement VI, some magnificent Flemish tapestries of Old and New Testament scenes hanging in the choir, which also boasts some fine Gothic stalls, and a celebrated fresco of the **Danse Macabre**, depicting Death plucking at the coarse plump bodies of 23 living figures, representing the different classes of society. "It is yourself", says the fifteenth-century text below, as indeed it might easily have been in an age when plague and war were rife.

Nearby on the place de l'Echo, the **Salle de l'Echo** (Easter–Sept daily 10am–6pm, Oct–Easter Mon–Sat 10am–5pm; free) is another product of the risk of contagion – if not from plague, then from leprosy. In this room, once used for hearing confession from the sick and dying, two people can turn their backs on each other, stand in opposite corners and still have a perfectly audible conversation just by whispering.

A **classical music festival** takes place here in late August and early September, details of which are available from the **tourist office**, on place de la Mairie (Easter–June & Sept Tues–Sun 10am–noon & 2–6pm; July & Aug daily 9am–12.30pm & 1.30–7pm; Oct–Easter Tues–Sat 10am–noon & 2–6pm; ☎04.71.00.01.16, ⓦwww.la-chaise-dieu.info). The comfortable *De La Casadei* **hotel**, in place de l'Abbaye (☎04.71.00.00.58, ⓦwww.hotel-la-casadei.com; ❸; restaurant from €15–25), doubles as an art gallery. There's also a municipal **campsite**, *Les Parades*, on the Vichy side of the D906 (☎04.71.00.07.88; June–Sept).

Ambert

Twenty-five kilometres north of La Chaise-Dieu, the little town of **AMBERT** was, from the fourteenth to eighteenth centuries, the centre of papermaking in France. It especially supplied the printers of Lyon, a connection that brought the region into contact with new ideas, in particular the revolutionary teachings of the Reformed Church. Although those small-scale operations have long since been sidelined, there is still a **paper mill** in operation at Richard-de-Bas just east of the town, with its **Musée Historique du Papier** (daily: July & Aug 9am–7pm; Sept–June 9–11am & 2–5pm; €6.50) featuring exhibits and explanations from papyrus to handmade samples from medieval days. In the town itself, there's a small **museum** (early April–Oct, Tues–Sat 10am–12.30pm & 2.30–6.30pm; €5) devoted to the manufacture of the soft blue Fourme d'Ambert cheese, the region's speciality. An old diesel *train panoramique* runs between Ambert and **Sembadel** stopping at La Chaise-Dieu on the way (€14 return); a leisurely way to see the region. There is also a funky 1950s-era train named "Picasso" that will take you from Ambert to **La Chaise-Dieu** (€14.50 return, with time to visit), and an authentic steam train which goes to **Olliergues** (€15 return; see ⓦwww.agrivap .fr for details).

St-Étienne

ST-ÉTIENNE, 78km northeast of Le Puy, was until recently a particularly bland town. Almost entirely industrial, it was a major armaments manufacturer, enclosed for kilometres around by mineworkings, warehouses and factory chimneys. Like so many other industrial centres, it fell on hard times, and the demolition gangs have moved in to raze its archaic industrial past. Only in the last decades has an equilibrium been restored thanks to a concerted programme to revitalize the town.

The centre is now quite cheerful, buoyed by a collection of small new museums, the best of which is the **Musée d'Art Moderne** (Wed–Mon 2–6pm; €5) at La Terrasse (La Terrasse station is served by frequent trains from St-Étienne's central station, Châteaucreux; €1.20), in the north of the city. This justifies a detour for anyone with an interest in twentieth-century art. It's quite an unexpected treasure house of contemporary work, both pre- and post-World War II, with a good modern American section in which Andy Warhol and Frank Stella figure prominently, along with work by Rodin, Matisse, Léger and Ernst, and rooms filled entirely with French art, imaginatively laid out to exciting effect. The **Musée d'Art et d'Industrie**, 2 place Louis-Comte, is also good on St-Étienne's industrial background, including the development of the revolutionary Jacquard loom, and has an impressive exhibition of arms and armour (Wed–Mon 10am–6pm; €4.50).

St-Étienne's **tourist office** is on 16 av de la Libération (Mon–Sat 9.30am–12.30pm & 2–6.30pm; July & Aug also Sun 9.30am–12.30pm; ☎08.92.70.05.42, ⓦwww .tourisme-st-etienne.com), around ten minutes' walk from Châteaucreux train station along avenue Denfert-Rochereau. If you decide to stay, try the excellent-value *Hôtel de la Tour*, 1 rue Mercière (☎04.77.32.28.48, ⓦhoteldelatour.fr; ❷), the newly renovated and well-equipped *Le Cheval Noir*, 11 rue François-Gillet

(☎04.77.33.41.72, ⊛www.hotel-chevalnoir.com; ❺), or the funky *Hôtel Terminus du Forez*, 29–31 av Denfert-Rochereau (☎04.77.32.48.47, ⊛www.hotel -terminusforez.com; ❹). For a truly fine meal, **dine** at *La Bouche Pleine* at 2 place Chavanelle (☎04.77.33.92.47; closed Sat & Sun in Aug; *menus* from €20).

Travel details

Trains

Alès to: Nîmes (6–9 daily; 35min).
Aurillac to: Le Lioran (3–5 daily; 40min); Murat (3–5 daily; 50min); Toulouse (3–7 daily; 2hr 40min); Vic-sur-Cère (3–5 daily; 15min).
Clermont-Ferrand to: Aurillac (4–6 daily; 2hr 30min–5hr); Béziers (3 daily; 6–7hr); Brive (3 daily; 3hr 40min); La Bourboule (4 daily; 1hr 20min); Le Lioran (3–4 daily; 2–4hr); Le Mont-Dore (4 daily; 1hr 30min); Limoges (4 daily; 3hr 30min–4hr); Lyon (12–18 daily; 2hr 45min–3hr 30min); Marvejols (4 daily; 2hr 15min–3hr); Millau (1 daily; 4hr 15min); Murat (5–7 daily; 1hr 40min); Nîmes (12–16 daily; 5–6hr); Paris (5–10 daily; 2–5hr); Riom (12–14 daily; 10min); St-Étienne (2–3 daily; 2hr 10min); St-Flour (2 daily; 1hr 20min–2hr); Thiers (6 daily; 35min); Vic-sur-Cère (5–7 daily; 2hr 15min); Vichy (12–14 daily; 40min); Volvic (5 daily; 24min).
Le Puy to: St-Étienne (8 daily; 1hr 20min).
Mende to: La Bastide-Puylaurent (2–3 daily; 50min); Marvejols (3–5 daily; 40min); Montpellier (16–20 daily; 3hr–4hr 30min); Nîmes (16–20 daily; 2hr 30min–4hr); St-Flour (1–2 daily; 1hr 40min).
Millau to: Aumont-Aubrac (2–4 daily; 1hr 30min); Béziers (3 daily; 2hr); Marvejols (3–5 daily; 1hr 10min); Paris (2 daily direct; 8–9hr 30min).
Rodez to: Millau (5–7 daily; 1hr 10min–2hr 30min).
St-Étienne to: Clermont-Ferrand (3–6 daily; 2hr 40min); Lyon (3 daily; 45min); Paris (3 daily; 2hr 50min).
Vichy to: Clermont-Ferrand (12–14 daily; 40min); Nîmes (12–16 daily; 7–9hr); Paris (4 daily; 3hr 30min).

Buses

Ambert to: St-Étienne (1 daily; 2hr).
Aubenas to: Alès (2–3 daily; 2hr 10min); Entraygues (1–4 daily; 1hr); Les Vans (2–4 daily; 1hr 10min); Valence (5–7 daily; 2hr); Vallon-Pont-d'Arc (1–2 daily; 45min).
Aurillac to: Entraygues (1 daily; 1hr 30min); Murat (1 daily; 1hr 40min); St-Flour (1 daily; 2hr 10min);

Super-Lioran (1 daily; 1hr 20min); Vic-sur-Cère (1–3 daily; 40min).
Clermont-Ferrand to: Ambert (1–2 daily; 1hr 40min); Besse (July & Aug 2 daily; 1hr 35min); La Chaise-Dieu (1 Mon; 2hr); Le Puy (1 daily; 2hr 15min); Lyon (daily; 4hr); Murol (July & Aug 2 daily; 1hr 10min); Riom (2 daily; 40min); St-Flour (2 weekly; 2hr); St-Nectaire (July & Aug 2 daily; 1hr); Superbesse (July & Aug 2 daily; 1hr 45min); Thiers (several daily; 1hr); Vichy (4–5 daily; 1hr 40min).
Conques to: Entraygues (June–Sept several weekly; 35min); Espalion (June–Sept several weekly; 1hr 20min).
Le Puy to: Aubenas (2 weekly; 3hr 15min); La Chaise-Dieu (2 daily; 1hr); St-Étienne (4 daily; 2hr 10min).
Le Vigan to: Montpellier (1–3 daily; 2hr); Nîmes (3–5 daily; 1hr 50min).
Mende to: Le Puy (2 daily; 2hr); Marvejols (3 daily; 50min); St-Étienne (1 daily; 3hr).
Millau to: Aven Armand (July & Aug daily; 1hr 45min); Le Caylar (2–6 daily; 40min); Le Rozier (1–4 daily; 40min); Montpellier (3–8 daily; 2hr 20min); Rodez (4 daily; 1hr 30min); Roquefort (July & Aug 3 weekly; 30min); Ste-Énimie (July & Aug daily; 2hr 25min); Toulouse (2 daily; 4hr).
Riom to: Volvic (4–8 daily; 25min).
Rodez to: Albi (3 daily; 2hr); Conques (1 daily; 1hr); Entraygues (1–2 daily; 2hr); Espalion (3–4 daily; 45min); Laguiole (1 daily; 1hr 45min); Le Caylar (1–4 daily; 2hr 40min); Mende (1 daily; 3hr 30min); Millau (3–8 daily; 1hr 40min); Montpellier (1–4 daily; 3hr 55min); Sauveterre-de-Rouergue (5 weekly; 55min); Séverac-le-Château (several daily; 45min); Toulouse (2–4 daily; 3hr 30min); Villefranche-de-Rouergue (1–2 daily; 1hr 30min).
St-Flour to: Laguiole (several weekly; 3hr).
St-Martin-d'Ardèche to: Avignon (1 daily; 1hr 40min); Pont St-Esprit (2 daily; 15min); Vallon-Pont-d'Arc (2 daily; 1hr 10min).
Vichy to: Ambert (4 daily; 2hr 10min); La Chaise-Dieu (daily; 2hr 45min); Thiers (several daily; 40min).
Villefranche-de-Rouergue to: Conques (July & Aug Tues & Fri 1 daily; 2hr).

13

The Alps and
Franche-Comté

CHAPTER 13 # Highlights

* **Skiing and snowboarding** Test your skills from December to April in the world-class resorts of Chamonix, Méribel and Val d'Isère. See p.769

* **Briançon** Take in stunning views of Alpine peaks and valleys from the steep cobbled lanes of the fortified "Cité Vauban", and sample the "Vauban Menu". See p.771

* **Parc Naturel Régional du Queyras** Walk or drive through the empty mountain landscapes of the Queyras to St-Véran, one of the highest villages in Europe. See p.775

* **Annecy** Take a leisurely cruise on Annecy's beautiful lake and wander through the narrow lanes of its historic Old Town. See p.784

* **Aiguille du Midi** Brave one of the world's highest cable-car ascents for a spectacular view of Mont Blanc, the highest peak in Europe. See p.792

* **Lake Geneva** Enjoy the sedate pleasures of spa towns like Évian and Divonne on the French side of this huge and scenic lake, or hop on one of the frequent ferries to Switzerland. See p.796

* **Besançon** Explore the imposing Citadelle, the intriguing museums and the inviting cafés of the capital of Franche-Comté. See p.800

▲ Take a cable car at Aiguille du Midi

13

The Alps and Franche-Comté

The wild and rugged landscape of the Alps, formed by the collision of continental tectonic plates over tens of millions of years, and the eroding actions of multiple glaciers and fast-flowing rivers, contains some of Europe's most stunning mountain landscapes and picturesque rural settlements, while also providing plenty of enjoyable outdoor pursuits. Although you have to walk a long distance or, in winter, ski (see p.769) to see the more remote areas, there are also many awe-inspiring routes open to car-drivers and cyclists. Perhaps the most famous is the **Route des Grandes Alpes**, which crosses all the major mountain massifs from Thonon-les-Bains on Lake Geneva to Menton on the Mediterranean Sea.

The gentler region of Franche-Comté to the north sees far fewer visitors, but the mountains, forests and meadowland here are worth the trip, and nestled among them are some of the prettiest villages in France. One great way to explore this region is by walking on the **GR** (Grande Randonnée) footpaths, the network of long-distance trails that connect France with its European neighbours. Notable paths that pass through Franche-Comté include the GR5 from the Netherlands to the Mediterranean, and the GR9, which snakes its way through the Parc Régional du Haut-Jura.

The more remote areas of the Alps and Jura are **difficult to reach without a car**, but are best explored on foot or by bicycle. Nonetheless, there are frequent trains between the major towns and resorts, while during the skiing season of December to April and the summer months of July and August, more bus services become available. Drivers should remember that some high passes in the east of the region, including the Col du Galibier and the Col de l'Iseran, can remain closed well into June. This can force you to make long detours into Italy via expensive Alpine tunnels. As for accommodation, the **hotels** are often seasonal (closed in late spring and late autumn) and over-priced; it's always worth booking ahead to get the best deals. If you're on a budget, then campsites provide the cheapest and most numerous places to stay, although there are also hostels and *refuges* (huts) for those who don't want to carry camping equipment.

The **towns** in the Alps and Franche-Comté offer an excellent base to explore the surrounding countryside, but they also have many notable attractions of their own. **Grenoble**, the economic capital of the Alps, has a vibrant nightlife and lively cultural scene; **Annecy** is a town whose picture-postcard lakeside setting is sure to delight; **Besançon**, the capital of Franche-Comté, and **Briançon**, one of the

Colmar & Strasbourg

Mulhouse

Basel

BERN

SWITZERLAND

Lausanne

Sion

Martigny

Aosta

ITALY

Turin

Milan

N

THE ALPS &
FRANCHE-COMTÉ

0   25 km

Sisteron, Marseille & Cannes

There are seven national or regional parks in the area covered by this chapter: Vanoise, Chartreuse, Bauges, Écrins, Queyras, Vercors and Haut Jura. All of these contain gentle day-walks and more demanding treks – not least classic long-distance paths like the Tour du Mont Blanc – which require one or two weeks' walking. Most of these routes are clearly marked and dotted with *refuge* huts; the routes are also described in high detail by the Topo-guides guidebooks (see p.53). Nonetheless, even the most experienced walkers or skiers treat these mountains and their unpredictable weather conditions with due respect. Even low-level walks in the Alps during summer often require a good level of fitness and specialist equipment, such as crampons or ice axes. You should take due account of the weather conditions (which can vary considerably between the valleys and peaks), of the potentially debilitating effects of high altitude, and of the serious danger of avalanches.

The Alps was the first great centre for European rock climbers in the nineteenth century and still offers countless routes which can be enjoyed by both novices and world-class climbers. A more recent development has been the creation of Via Ferrata courses, in which wires and ladders are bolted onto the rock so that even inexperienced climbers (wearing harnesses and ropes) can make ascents which would otherwise be impossible for them. There are Via Ferrata courses being developed across the whole region, but at present two of the largest centres for this popular sport are at Serre Chevalier and in the Parc National des Écrins.

The **Bureau Info Montagne** office in Grenoble and the **Office de Haute Montagne** in Chamonix can provide information on the best guides and the most up-to-date information on all the **GR paths** and the best **Via Ferrata** courses, while local tourist offices often produce detailed maps of walks in their own areas.

highest towns in Europe, are still dominated by formidable fortresses that reflect the tumultuous past of this region on France's eastern frontier. The websites Ⓦwww.rhonealpes-tourisme.com and Ⓦwww.savoie-mont-blanc.com, plus the information on the Alps and Jura at Ⓦwww.franceguide.com provide excellent introductions to this picturesque corner of France.

The Alps

Europe's highest mountain range offers a plethora of exciting outdoor activities, ranging from extreme skiing to the most gentle of valley walks. Yet you'll also find plenty of charming villages and towns to explore, not least Grenoble, which is the region's easiest access point by car, train or plane.

Grenoble and around

Set serenely at the confluence of the Drac and Isère rivers, **GRENOBLE**, the self-styled "capital of the Alps", is watched over by the snow-capped peaks of the Belledonne, Vercors and Chartreuse massifs. It's a vibrant and cosmopolitan place, home to around 64,000 students and a lively cultural scene, while at its centre is a

Food and drink in the Alps and Franche-Comté

Indulging in an evening **feast** after a long day in the mountains is one of the greatest pleasures of travelling in the Alps and Franche-Comté, and it is a pleasure that can most often be attributed to the quality of the local ingredients – of the various cheeses, fish and herbs in particular – rather than to any great innovation in the cookery itself.

Most characteristic of Alpine cuisine is the liberal amounts of cheese made from the local cow, ewe and goat milk. The *fromageries* of Franche-Comté and the Northern Alps are full of cheeses like Reblochon, Tome des Bauges, Emmental, Chèvre, Comté and Beaufort. These are found not just in the famous fondue, but also *raclette* and *tartiflette* (both cheese-based dishes served with ham and potatoes). Other cheeses worth seeking out include the smooth blue-veined Bleu de Gex, produced exclusively in the Pays de Gex region, and creamy Saint Marcellin, from the Grenoble area.

Many restaurants feature **fish** (notably salmon and trout) from the Alpine lakes and use locally grown herbs, like thyme, basil and rosemary. These herbs are particularly in evidence in the Southern Alps around Briançon, where they are often used to flavour the *saucisson* (cured sausage), which you'll find in many a morning shopping market.

The region produces many light and fruity varieties of **wine**, of which the most popular is the dark red Mondeuse, with its faint taste of raspberries. By contrast, the expensive *vin jaune* from the Jura is a potent, golden wine, made from Sauvignon grapes with a fermentation process similar to that of sherry – it remains in the cask for 6–10 years before being bottled. *Vin jaune* is a favourite accompaniment for the local cheeses of Franche-Comté, and is used in speciality dishes such as *poulet au vin jaune* (chicken in a creamy sauce flavoured by the wine). It's also worth sampling some regional **liqueurs**. The most famous of these is undoubtedly **Chartreuse**, the drink produced by Carthusian monks since the sixteenth century, which contains 130 different herbs and is known as the "elixir of life", while Chambéry is famous for its high-quality **vermouth**, including the unique Chambéryzette, flavoured with strawberries.

quirky maze of streets, where modern and medieval buildings are packed close together.

Settled by the Celtic Allobroges tribe, who called their settlement Curaro, it was renamed Gratianopolis by the Romans in the fourth century and became the seat of a bishop. Grenoble was annexed by France in the fourteenth century, and it was here, far from Paris, that a local uprising in 1788 (known as the Journée des Tuiles) initiated the French Revolution. Grenoble is the final stop on the Route Napoléon; the French emperor arrived here on March 7, 1815, declaring "Before Grenoble, I was an adventurer. In Grenoble, I was a prince." The prosperity of the city was originally founded on glove-making, but in the nineteenth century its economy diversified to include industries as diverse as mining and hydroelectric power, while more recently it has forged a reputation as a centre for scientific research in the electronic and nuclear industries.

Grenoble's **Musée de Grenoble**, packed with paintings by notable nineteenth- and twentieth-century artists, is the region's outstanding art gallery, while the restaurants and cafés of the town provide relaxing spots in which to sit and admire the grandeur of this fantastic mountain setting. There are numerous events in Grenoble throughout the year and one definitely worth catching is **Cabaret Frappé** (Ⓦ www.cabaret-frappe.com), a nine-day celebration of contemporary jazz, soul, world and experimental music held at venues around town in late July.

Arrival and information

The Grenoble-Isère airport (℡04.76.65.48.48, ⓦwww.grenoble-airport.com) lies some 45km to the northwest of the city. It is served by several low-cost airlines; most of the flight connections are with Britain, although there are some less frequent services to Dublin, Rotterdam and Warsaw. There are buses every hour from the airport to the **gare routière** in Grenoble (45min; €12.50). In winter, there are also frequent buses between the airport and the ski resorts of Les Deux-Alpes and L'Alpe d'Huez (1hr 30min; €40).

The **gare SNCF** and the **gare routière** are next door to each other at the western end of avenue Félix-Viallet, just ten minutes' walk from the most interesting sections of the city, which are mainly on the left bank of the Isère. Not far from the central place Grenette, at 14 rue de la République, is the **tourist office** (May–Sept Mon–Sat 9am–6.30pm, Sun 10am–1pm & 2–5pm; Oct–April Mon–Sat 9am–6.30pm, Sun 10am–1pm; ℡04.76.42.41.41, ⓦwww.grenoble-tourisme.com), where you'll also find the local SNCF and public transport information offices. Walkers and climbers looking for suggestions and detailed information on *refuges* should check out the **Maison de la Montagne** (Mon–Fri 9.30am–12.30pm & 1–6pm, Sat 10am–1pm & 2–5pm; ℡04.76.44.67.03, ⓦwww.grenoble-montagne.com), at 3 rue Raoul-Blanchard, across the street from the rear of the tourist office.

Accommodation

Grenoble has plenty of **hotels** in all categories, but the city is busy from September to June with conferences and graduations, so it's worth booking ahead. The cheaper places tend to cluster around the train station area.

Hotels

Alizé 1 rue Amiral Courbet ℡04.76.43.12.91, ⓦwww.hotelalize.com. Small, basic, but clean rooms. It's the cheapest place in the centre and close to the train station. ❶

D'Angleterre 5 place Victor-Hugo ℡04.76.87.37.21, ⓦwww.hotel-angleterre -grenoble.com. A good central option with friendly staff, popular with business travellers. Jacuzzi baths and DVD players are nice extra touches, and there's free overnight parking. ❻

De L'Europe 22 place Grenette ℡04.76.46.16.94, ⓦwww.hoteleurope.fr. This good-value, central hotel is said to be the oldest in Grenoble, with a range of fairly simple but bright and modern rooms; the cheapest have shared bathrooms. ❷

Ibis 5 rue Miribel ℡04.76.47.48.49, ⓦwww .ibishotel.com. Standard mid-range facilities and simple but comfortable rooms are offered at this chain hotel, but there's also a good-value restaurant and substantial discounts (up to one-third of the room price) available at weekends. ❺

Institut 10 rue Barbillon ℡04.76.46.36.44, ⓦwww.institut-hotel.fr. This friendly two-star hotel provides rather small but artfully decorated rooms, internet connection and satellite TV. ❸

Mercure (Alpotel) 12 bd du Maréchal Joffre ℡04.76.87.88.41, ⓦwww.mercure.com. One of three Mercure hotels in Grenoble, this place has smart, comfortable rooms and a good restaurant. Closed Aug. ❺

Du Moucherotte 1 rue Auguste Gaché ℡04.76.54.61.40. This hotel is an inexpensive central option with clean, bright rooms with TVs. ❷

Park 10 place Paul-Mistral ℡04.76.85.81.23, ⓦwww.park-hotel-grenoble.fr. A luxury four-star

Grenoble passes

If you're in town for more than a day or two, it could be worth buying the full **Grenoble Pass** from the tourist office (€13.90). This gives you a guided tour of the Old Town, admission to the Musée de Grenoble, a return trip on the *téléphérique* and a ride on the *petit train*, a little locomotive which trundles around the city and is often a hit with kids. Cheaper passes, giving you a choice of either two (€9.90) or three (€11.90) of the above options are also available.

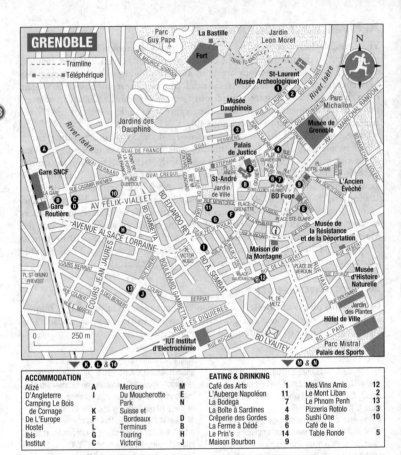

GRENOBLE

- - - - - Tramline
■ - ■ - ■ Téléphérique

0   250 m

ACCOMMODATION			
Alizé	A	Mercure	M
D'Angleterre	I	Du Moucherotte	E
Camping Le Bois		Park	N
de Cornage	K	Suisse et	
De L'Europe	F	Bordeaux	D
Hostel	L	Terminus	B
Ibis	G	Touring	H
Institut	C	Victoria	J

EATING & DRINKING			
Café des Arts	1	Mes Vins Amis	12
L'Auberge Napoléon	11	Le Mont Liban	2
La Bodega	7	Le Phnom Penh	13
La Boîte à Sardines		Pizzeria Rotolo	3
Crêperie des Gordes	8	Sushi One	10
La Ferme à Dédé	6	Café de la	
Le Prin's	14	Table Ronde	5
Maison Bourbon	9		

hotel with spacious and elegant rooms and suites, with onsite restaurant. Internet rates are significantly cheaper than the walk-in rates. Closed Aug. ⑧

Suisse et Bordeaux 6 place de la Gare ☎04.76.47.55.87, ⓦ www.hotel-sb-grenoble.com. Opposite the railway station, this grand nineteenth-century building houses small but cosy rooms with TVs and wi-fi access. ③

Terminus 10 place de la Gare ☎04.76.87.24.33, ⓦ www.terminus-hotel-grenoble.fr. This smart Best Western hotel has soundproof, air-conditioned rooms with satellite TVs near the *gare SNCF*. ⑤

Touring 26 av Alsace Lorraine ☎04.76.46.24.32, ⓦ www.france-touring-hotel.com. Overlooking one of the main tramlines into the city centre, this hotel offers a range of accommodation with showers or bathtubs, at reasonable rates. ③

Victoria 17 rue Thiers ☎04.76.46.06.36, ⓦ www .hotelvictoriagrenoble.com. This simple but clean and

comfortable two-star hotel offers free internet connection, satellite TV and private car park. Closed Aug. ③

Campsite and hostel

Camping Le Bois de Cornage Chemin du Camping, Vizille ☎06.83.18.17.87, ⓦ www.campingvizille.com. Situated 15km from the city centre, this three-star campsite has a swimming pool and restaurant on site. Take bus #3000 from the *gare routière* in Grenoble and get off at stop "Place du Chateau" in Vizille. Open May–September. €14.90 for a two-person tent, €350 per week for a chalet.

Hostel 10 av de Grésivaudan ☎04.76.09.33.52, ⓔ grenoble@fuaj.org. This ultramodern hostel provides simple meals, but also has good kitchen facilities and is near a supermarket. It's 5km south of the city centre in a large park in Echirolles; you can take bus #1 to the "Quinzaine" stop or tram A to "La Rampe". From €19 including breakfast.

The City

The best way to start your tour is to take the **téléphérique** (☎04.76.44.33.65, ⓦ www.bastille-grenoble.com; €6 return) or cable car from the riverside quai Stéphane-Jay to **Fort de la Bastille** on the steep slopes above the northern bank of the Isère. It's best to check the complicated operating times before arrival, but the cable car runs roughly every day at the following times: March–Sept 9.30am–midnight; Nov–Feb 11am–7.30pm. The ride is hair-raising, as you're whisked swiftly into the air in a transparent glass ball towards the Bastille 263m above. If you don't like the sound of the cable car, you can climb the steep footpath from the St-Laurent church on the northern bank of the Isère.

The well-preserved nineteenth-century fortifications on the hill were never tested in battle, and are interesting to explore. Part of the fort now houses the **Musée des Troupes de Montagne** (Tues–Sun 10am–6pm; free), dedicated to the history of the French mountain troops, featuring uniforms, dioramas and multimedia exhibitions. The site's main draw, though, is the view. At your feet, the Isère flows under old bridges which join the St-Laurent quarter (a home for Italian immigrants in the later 1800s) on the northern bank of the river to the nucleus of the medieval town. Even this far south, if you look northeast on a clear day you can see the distant white peaks of Mont Blanc further up the deep valley of the Isère. To the east, snowfields gleam in the high gullies of the Belledonne massif (2978m). To the southeast is the peak of Le Taillefer (2857m), while further to the south you can make out the mountain pass which the famous Route Napoléon crosses on its way northwards from the Mediterranean. This was the road towards Paris that Napoleon took after his escape from Elba in March 1815. Finally, to the west you can admire Moucherotte (1901m), the highest peak of the northern Vercors massif, and the mountain which most seems to dominate the city beneath.

The northern bank of the Isère

The **Église St-Laurent** on place St-Laurent is a former church, now displaying archaeological excavations showing evidence of pagan and Christian worship dating from the fourth century, as well as an eighth-century crypt and a medieval cloister. The museum here has been closed for some time but should reopen in 2011. Up a steep cobbled path opposite the St-Laurent footbridge, the **Musée Dauphinois**, 30 rue Maurice-Gignoux (daily except Tues: June–Sept 10am–7pm; Oct–May 10am–6pm; free), is located in a former convent, and is devoted to the history, arts and crafts of the Dauphiné province. In the basement, there's a Baroque chapel with grey and gold wall paintings depicting episodes from the New Testament and scenes from the life of St-François-de-Sales, the convent's founder. In the museum proper, there's plenty of information on the lives of the rugged and self-sufficient Dauphinois mountain people, but perhaps the most memorable exhibit details the evolution of skiing in the area over the last four thousand years, right through to the modern winter sports that came to Grenoble when it hosted the 1968 Winter Olympics.

The Old Town

The narrow streets of the Old Town on the southern bank of the Isère, particularly around places Grenette, Vaucanson, Verdun and Notre-Dame, make up the liveliest and most colourful quarter of the city. Near the bustling place Notre-Dame, on the riverbank at 5 place de Lavalette, is the **Musée de Grenoble** (daily except Tues 10am–6.30pm; €5; ⓦ www.museedegrenoble.fr), a modern complex that houses a large gallery of paintings ranging from the thirteenth century to the present day. There are works here by Chagall, Gauguin, Matisse, Picasso and Warhol, old masters by the likes of Rubens and Veronese, and a small collection of Egyptian antiquities.

On the eastern side of place Notre-Dame is the **Musee de l'Ancien Évêché** (Mon & Wed–Sat 9am–6pm, Tues 1.30–6pm, Sun 10am–7pm; free). Housed in the old bishop's palace, the museum offers a brisk tour through Grenoble's history from the Stone Age onwards. The remains of the Roman town walls and a fifth-century **baptistry** are on show in the basement, while upstairs you will find the oldest human skull found in the Alps, dating back 11,000 years, Iron Age jewellery and many Roman artefacts, including a colourful mosaic floor panel depicting a pair of parrots.

To the east of the *téléphérique* station on the southern bank of the Isère is the sixteenth-century **Palais de Justice** (open to the public), with place St-André and the **church of St-André** behind. Built in the thirteenth century, the church once served as the palace chapel of the princes of Dauphiné, though it has been heavily restored since.

A few blocks to the south at 14 rue Hébert is the **Musée de la Résistance et de la Déportation de l'Isère** (daily: July & Aug 10am–7pm, Tues 1.30–7pm; Sept–June 10am–6pm, Tues 1.30–6pm; free), which relates the history of the brutal Nazi occupation of the Dauphiné and the bravery of the members of the Resistance, with multimedia exhibitions and more poignant and personal wartime memorabilia.

Eating, drinking and nightlife

Eating in Grenoble is a pleasure and there are a wide variety of **restaurants** catering to all budgets and tastes; it's worth booking ahead at the restaurants listed below, especially in the evenings. Grenoble's large student population means that the **nightlife** is never dull. If you're looking for live music, try *Styx*, 6 place de Claveyson (Mon–Sat, 7pm–1am), a trendy bar with occasional DJs or, for brilliant live jazz, *La Soupe aux Choux*, 7 route du Lyon (Fri & Sat 8pm–1am). Further out, *Le Prin's*, 94 cours Jean-Jaurès (Thurs–Sun 11pm–5am), is a gay club playing retro and dance music for the over-25 crowd.

Restaurants

L'Auberge Napoléon 7 rue Montorge ☎04.76.87.53.64. A well-regarded, upmarket restaurant offering fine evening-only cuisine such as pigeon fillets (€35), scallops (€33) and guinea-fowl (€20). Closed Sun.

La Bodega 7 rue Brocherie ☎04.76.42.66.01. Convivial Spanish restaurant with an authentic feel, offering lots of tapas dishes (around €3) and traditional cusine including paella and steaks (*menus* €13–25). Closed Sun & Mon.

La Ferme à Dédé 1 place aux Herbes ☎04.76.54.00.33. Rustic regional fare is on the menu here, including *tête de veau* (€15.80) and hearty sausage casseroles, fondues and *tartiflette*. The *plat du jour* is good value at around €8.

Mes Vins Amis 11 rue de la Liberté ☎04.76.43.33.75. Small restaurant offering traditional and more exotic dishes, plus an excellent wine list. The *plats du jour* start at €9. Closed Sun, Mon & Tues eves & Aug.

Le Mont Liban 50 quai Xavier Jouvin ☎04.76.51.25.75. An inauspicious exterior masks the quality of this award-winning Lebanese restaurant, which provides three-course meals for €22. Closed Sun.

Le Phnom Penh 18 rue Thiers ☎04.76.46.07.62. Sample Chinese and Cambodian dishes here, including crayfish curry and pork satay, with *menus* starting at €12.80.

Pizzeria Rotolo 24 quai Perrière ☎04.76.47.40.01. One of a string of riverfront pizzerias, serving up a wide range of pizzas (€10–16) and pasta dishes.

Sushi One 28 av Félix Viallet ☎04.76.53.45.79. Modern Japanese place offering sushi *menus* from €12 and various sashimi and yakatori combinations. Takeaway is also available.

Cafés and bars

Café des Arts 36 rue St-Laurent ☎04.76.54.65.31. Situated on the northern bank of the river, *Café des Arts* has live music (including jazz, blues, folk and South American music) on Fri & Sat nights. Mon–Sat 8pm–midnight.

La Boîte à Sardines 1 place Claveyson. Rather cramped but popular little bar where you can get a small draught beer for €2.60 or try one of their inventive cocktails (€3.50–8). There are outside seats in summer. Closed Sun.

Crêperie des Gordes 3 place des Gordes. You can choose from a huge menu of sweet and savoury

crêpes and galettes here (€5.50–10), and they also serve ice cream and light salads (€11).
Maison Bourbon 3 place Notre-Dame. Popular patisserie selling freshly made sandwiches (around €3) as well as countless little cakes and bread. Mon–Sat 6am–8pm, Sun 6am–6.30pm.

Café de La Table Ronde 7 place St-André. France's second oldest café, founded in 1739, has always been a hotspot for writers, artists and tourists, and the mirrored interior is an atmospheric place to linger over a coffee. Closed Sun in winter.

Listings

Bike rental Metrovélo in the underpass of the *gare SNCF*, place de la Gare; €5 per day; ☎04.76.59.59.59, ⊛www.metrovelo.fr.
Bookshops BD Fugue, rue Jean-François Hache, is the place to go for French-language comic books, and it also has a Tintin-themed café. Librarie des Alpes, 1 rue Casimir Perier, has an excellent collection of coffee-table books on the Alps.
Car hire Several of the larger agencies have kiosks in or around the *gare SNCF* (closed on Sun): AVIS, *gare SNCF* ☎08.20.61.16.51; Europcar, *gare SNCF* ☎08.25.88.70.90; Hertz, *gare SNCF* ☎04.76.86.55.80; Rent-a-Car, 10 place de la Gare ☎04.76.86.27.60.

Internet Pl@net On-Line, 1 place Vaucanson (Mon–Sat 9am–midnight).
Health Centre Hospitalier Universitaire (CHU) ☎04.76.76.50.25; ambulance Alp'Azur (a private ambulance company) ☎04.76.21.11.11.
Pharmacy There are several large pharmacies in the centre which have long opening hours. Pharmacie Victor Hugo, 2 bd Agutte Sembat (open every day 8am–8pm) ☎04.76.46.04.15.
Police 36 bd Maréchal-Leclerc ☎04.76.60.40.40.
Taxi Grenoblois, 14 rue de la République ☎04.76.54.42.54. Provides a 24hr radio taxi service.

The Chartreuse massif

The Chartreuse massif, north of Grenoble, was designated in 1995 as the **Parc Naturel Régional de Chartreuse** (⊛www.parc-chartreuse.net), and is a place of spectacular landscapes, including sharp limestone peaks, mountain pastures and large areas of pine forest. The Grenoble **Maison de la Montagne** office (see p.790) publishes descriptions of the various hiking routes in the area.

The Grande Chartreuse Monastery and Voiron

The massif's main local landmark is the **Grande Chartreuse Monastery**, situated up the narrow Gorges du Guiers Mort, southeast of St-Laurent-du-Pont, and some 35km from Grenoble. Carthusian monks and nuns seek a life of contemplation following the example of their founder, the eleventh-century monk St Bruno, a life which involves long periods of solitude, silence, work and prayer. Members of the order live in cells and meet only for Mass and a weekly communal meal, eaten in silence. Since 1605, however, the Carthusians have also become famous as the producers of various **Chartreuses**. These powerfully alcoholic herbal elixirs range from the better-known green and yellow variants to a number of gentler fruit and nut liqueurs. The monastery is not open to the public, but near the village of **ST-PIERRE-DE-CHARTREUSE**, 5km back on the Grenoble road, you can visit the **Musée de la Grande Chartreuse**, formerly La Correrie monastery, which illustrates the life of the Carthusian Order (daily: April, Oct & early Nov 1.30–6pm; May–Sept 9.30am–6.30pm; €4; ⊛www.musee-grande-chartreuse.fr).

For those more interested in the liqueurs, a visit to **VOIRON**, 30km west of the park and on the train line from Grenoble to Lyon, is in order. The **Caves de la Chartreuse** on boulevard Edgar-Kofler (April to end Oct daily 9–11.30am & 2–6.30pm; Nov–March Mon–Fri 9–11.30am & 2–5.30pm; free; ⊛www .chartreuse.fr) are where the "elixir of life" is now bottled. The tour takes you through the world's largest liqueur cellars, and includes a film on the history of the monastery and the secret manuscript with the recipe of the original liqueur. The highlight of the tour, however, is a tasting of one of the beverages themselves. There's little else to see in Voiron, but if you're looking for a **hotel**, try the neat *La Chaumière*, rue de la Chaumière ℡04.76.05.16.24, ⓦwww.hotel-lachaumiere -voiron.com; ❸), which also has a restaurant (*menus* from €19).

Le Bourg-d'Oisans

Connecting Grenoble to Briançon, the **N91** twists through the precipitous valley of the Romanche and over the **Col du Lautaret** (2058m), which is kept open all year round and crossed at least a couple of times a day (and more often during the skiing season) by the Grenoble–Briançon bus. The first major settlement on the route, **LE BOURG-D'OISANS** (known as "Le Bourg"), 20km southeast of Grenoble, is of no great interest in itself, but it sits in a beautiful position in the valley and is a good base for summer sports. It's particularly popular with cyclists. You can pick up information on hiking routes from the **tourist office**, on quai Girard, by the river in the middle of town (July & Aug daily 9am–7pm; Sept–June Mon–Sat 9am–noon & 2–6pm; ℡04.76.80.03.25, ⓦwww.bourgdoisans.com), and the **Maison du Parc National des Écrins** on rue Gambetta (daily July & Aug 8am–noon & 3–7pm; Sept–June Mon–Fri 8am–noon & 2–5.30pm; ℡04.76.80.00.51). There are some good-value **hotels** here, among them *L'Oberland*, on avenue de la Gare (℡04.76.80.24.24, ⓦwww.hoteloberland.com; ❸), and the *Hôtel Le Terminus* on the same street (℡04.76.80.00.26, ⓦwww.leterminusoisans .com; ❸), which has just six rooms and a good restaurant, *Le Moulin des Truites Bleues* (grilled trout €20, salads €9). For **camping**, a good option is *La Cascade*, 1.5km outside town on the Route de l'Alpe d'Huez (℡04.76.80.02.42, ⓦwww .lacascadesarenne.com; open mid-Dec to Sept). There are several restaurants, including *La Crepizza*, place Jo Barruel (pizzas €7.50–10, *menus* from €16.80).

L'Alpe d'Huez and around

The ski resort of **L'ALPE D'HUEZ** is situated more than a vertical kilometre above the valley floor, and the 11km road, which crawls up the valley side, is often used as a stage in the Tour de France. As you ascend through the 21 hairpins, there's a fine view of the acutely crumpled strata of rock exposed by passing glaciers on the south side of the Romanche valley. During the winter, the extensive network of *télécabines* and *téléphériques* whisks skiers to the **Pic Blanc** (3330m), at the bottom of the Chaîne des Rousses ridge, from which two mammoth black runs (over two kilometres in length) descend. Yet while it is undoubtedly a skier's paradise in winter, the purpose-built resort itself has little character in July and August.

L'Alpe d'Huez's **tourist office** in the Maison de l'Alpe, place Paganon (May–June & Sept–Nov daily 9am–12.30pm & 2.30–6pm; Dec–April & July–Aug daily 9am–7pm; ℡04.76.11.44.44, ⓦwww.alpedhuez.com), provides detailed walking and mountain-biking maps; the Maison also houses the **ESF ski school** office (℡04.76.80.31.69, ⓦwww.esf-alpedhuez.com). Hotels here are generally expensive and unremarkable; one three-star hotel that provides excellent facilities and a central location near the pistes is *Le Dôme*, place du Cognet (℡04.76.80.32.11, ⓦwww.dome-alpedhuez.com; ❻). Another central option on route de la Poste is *Le Caribou* (℡04.76.80.15.31, ⓦwww.lecaribouhotel.com; ❻), a smaller, older place with simple rooms and a decent restaurant.

La Grave and the Col du Lautaret

Continuing on the N91 towards La Grave past the modern ski resort of **Les Deux-Alpes**, you'll pass two waterfalls issuing from the north side of the valley: early summer run-off enhances the 300m plume of the **Cascade de la Pisse** (the source

13

Skiing in the Alps

With their long and varied runs, extensive lift networks, and world-renowned après-ski, the French Alps offer some of the best skiing in Europe. Skiing first became a recreational sport in the early 1900s but the industry really began to boom in the Alps during the 1960s with the construction of dozens of high-altitude, purpose-built resorts that ensured good lasting snow cover. Some of the resorts have their detractors: the modern architects often created sprawling concrete settlements that had little in common with the traditional farming villages lower in the valleys, and in so doing they earned France a lasting reputation for "ski factories". Nonetheless, few can knock the efficiency of these resorts. They have an abundance of hotels, equipment outlets and ski schools, while at many you can simply clip your skis on at the hotel door and be skiing on some of the most challenging pistes on earth within minutes. If you are looking for more peaceful accommodation options, the villages at the foot of the valleys are now often linked to the major resorts by fast, modern lifts.

Unsurprisingly, given the size of the French Alps, you'll find opportunities for many different kinds of skiing. **Downhill skiing** is the most common form of the sport at all the resorts, but **cross-country or nordic skiing** has become increasingly popular on gentler slopes (particularly around Morzine and in the Parc Naturel Régional du Queyras), although the real magnet for cross-country skiers lies further to the north in Franche-Comté (see box, p.807). Back in the Alps, there are also several famous routes for **ski touring** (a form of cross-country skiing with uphill sections and across much longer distances), not least the **Haute Route** between Chamonix and Zermatt (Switzerland) and the **Grande Traversée des Alpes**, which leads south from Thonon-les-Bains on Lake Geneva through several national parks. There are also plenty of opportunities for **snowboarding**; many of the resorts now have snowparks expressly designed for snowboarders to refine their jumping technique.

The ski **season** runs from December to late April, with high season over Christmas and New Year, February half-term and (to a lesser extent) Easter; the weekends are also busy with crowds descending on resorts close to big urban centres and those with short airport transfers. During the summer more and more resorts are trying to attract **mountain bikers** and **hikers**; many ski lifts stay open during the summer, which makes many hiking and VTT (*vélo tout terrain*) biking trails more accessible.

of many a snigger by children from across Europe), while, 6km further on, the near-vertical fall of churning whitewater called the **Saut de la Pucelle** ("the virgin's leap") is a breathtaking sight.

LA GRAVE, 18km on from the Barrage du Lac du Chambon, lies at the foot of the Col du Lautaret, facing the majestic glaciers of the north side of **La Meije** (3984m). While it lies at the heart of a large and testing ski area, La Grave, with its small collection of stone buildings, could not be a more different environment than Les Deux-Alpes.

In addition to the skiing opportunities, it's also a good base for walkers and climbers; the **GR54** passes to the northwest of the village, and there are also two equipped Via Ferrata courses nearby (an easier one at Arsine and a tougher course at the Mines du Grand Clot). The **Bureau des Guides**, place du Téléphérique (T 04.76.79.90.21, W www.guidelagrave.com), provides guides for the different hiking paths in the area.

If you don't want to walk, then an easier way of appreciating the stunning vistas is provided by the *télécabine* (mid-June to early Sept & late Dec to early May; €22 return), which rises sharply from the centre of the village to the 3200m summit of **Le Rateau**, just west of La Meije. The 35-minute ride is very good value for money considering that the view of the barely accessible interior of the Écrins is normally seen only by the most intrepid mountaineers. The lift also provides access to acres of off-piste skiing, and the freezing conditions of the mountain's northerly face make it ideal for ice climbing. The **tourist office** is near the *télécabine* (℡04.76.79.90.05, Ⓦwww.lagrave-lameije.com).

For **accommodation**, a good-value central option is *Hôtel Castillan* (℡04.76.79.90.04, Ⓦcastillan.pagesperso-orange.fr; open Jan–Sept; ❹), where you'll find a swimming pool, bar and some good views out to La Meije.

From La Grave it's only 11km to the top of the **Col du Lautaret**, a pass which is generally kept clear for traffic during the winter months, despite its high altitude (2057m). Around the col is a huge expanse of meadow long known to botanists for its glorious variety of Alpine flowers, which are seen at their best in mid-July.

Serre Chevalier

Turning southeast at the Col du Lautaret, stay on the main N91 road, and 9km before reaching Briançon, you'll come to the skiing area of **SERRE CHEVALIER**, a name given to five traditional farming hamlets whose old wooden chalets have now been surrounded by small hotels and holiday homes.

This area is skiing central for the Southern Alps. In total, there's access to around 250km of ski runs with various degrees of difficulty, and you can generally guarantee good weather: the resort has an average of three hundred days of sunshine a year. The hamlets of Saint-Chaffrey and Chantemerle form Serre Chevalier 1350 (named for its altitude of 1350m); Villeneuve and La-Salle-les-Alpes make up Serre Chevalier 1400; and Le Monêtier-les-Bains is Serre Chevalier 1500. Each area is linked by a series of **ski lifts** and pistes which climb and descend the north-facing slopes of the valley, and there are ESF ski school offices in all three areas (Ⓦwww.esf-serrechevalier.com), as well as plenty of ski rental shops. Of all these settlements it is **Le Monêtier-les-Bains**, with its narrow streets weaving between old stone houses and rickety wooden balconies, which is most attractive. The village has been a thermal spa since Roman times, with two hot-water springs. The modern spa complex of *Les Grands Bains* (€20 3hr ticket; ℡04.92.40.00.00, Ⓦwww.lesgrandsbains.fr) is one of the largest in Europe, and features a plethora of pools, steam rooms and fitness centres.

The **tourist office** for the whole of Serre Chevalier is located in the centre of Villeneuve (℡04.92.24.98.98, Ⓦwww.serre-chevalier.com), while Le Monêtier-les-Bains in particular offers a good range of accommodation. *Auberge du Choucas* (℡04.92.24.42.73, Ⓦwww.aubergeduchoucas.com; closed May & Nov; ❾) is a beautiful old house with an excellent restaurant. A cheaper option close to the village at Pont de l'Alpe is the *Auberge Les Amis* (℡04.92.24.44.24, Ⓦwww .aubergelesamis.com; open mid-Dec to Oct; ❺ including breakfast).

The Hautes-Alpes

The **Hautes-Alpes** make up the area of high mountains to the southeast of Grenoble and south of the Massif de la Vanoise. To the east lies the Italian border and to the south, the Alpes de Provence. The region is sliced in two by the Durance valley with the **Parc National des Écrins** lying on the western side of the divide and the **Parc Naturel Régional du Queyras** on the eastern. At the head of the Durance valley, where the Guisane and Durance rivers converge, the ancient fortified city of **Briançon** makes an excellent base for exploring the surrounding region.

Briançon

Located 100km east of Grenoble along the N91, **Briançon** is the capital of the Écrins and one of Europe's highest towns at 1350m above sea level. An imposing citadel, it looms on the cusp of a rocky outcrop high above the Durance and Guisane valleys. Fortified originally by the Romans to guard the road from Milan to Vienne, the town is encircled by lofty ramparts and sheer walls constructed by the French architect and soldier, Sébastien Le Preste de Vauban in the seventeenth century (see box, p.772).

Arrival and information

The **gare SNCF** is along avenue de la République in the *ville basse*, 1.5km south of the old city. Local **buses** #1, #2 and #3 (from the shelter opposite the railway station) link the station and the Champ de Mars. Briançon's **tourist office** is at 1 place du Temple close to the porte Pignerol gateway (Mon–Sat 9am–noon & 2–6pm, Sun 10am–12.15pm & 2.30–5pm; ☏04.92.21.08.50, ⓦwww.briancon.com). For information about outdoor activities in the mountains, head for the **Bureau des Guides** in Parc Chancel (July & Aug 10am–noon & 3–7pm; Sept–June 5–7pm; ☏04.92.20.15.73, ⓦwww.guides-briancon.fr). The **Maison du Parc National des Écrins**, place du Médecin-Général-Blanchard (July & Aug daily 10am–noon & 1–7pm; Sept–June Mon–Fri 2–6pm; ☏04.92.21.42.15, ⓦwww.ecrins-parc national.fr), provides maps for those venturing into the nearby Écrins massif.

Accommodation

There's a good choice of **hotels** in town, although most are found in the relatively characterless *ville basse*. There are a few small hotels in or just outside the Old Town walls, which are more convenient for sightseeing.

Auberge de la Paix 3 rue Porte Méane ☏04.92.21.37.43, ⓦwww.auberge-de-la -paix.com. Set inside the Old Town walls, this is a small, friendly place with rather chic, spacious and colourful rooms, as well as two excellent restaurants. ❺

Camping des Cinq Vallées ☏04.92.21.06.27, ⓦwww.camping5vallees.com. Located at St-Blaise 2km to the south of the town, this is a three-star campsite with good facilities. Open June–Sept.

Hôtel de la Chaussée 4 rue Centrale ☏04.92.21.10.37, ⓦwww.hotel-de-la-chaussee .com. This is a good *ville basse* option, with neat rooms and a restaurant. ❹

Pension des Remparts 14 av Vauban ☏04.92.21.08.73, Ⓔannemarie.djaziri @orange.fr The cheapest option in town, just inside the Porte Pignerol, though facilities are pretty basic. ❶

Trois Chamois 9 place du Champ de Mars ☏04.92.21.02.29. Just outside the Old Town walls, this is a popular restaurant with five basic rooms upstairs. ❸

Vauban 13 av du Général de Gaulle ☏04.92.21.12.11, ⓦwww.hotel-vauban-briancon .com. This welcoming hotel in the *ville basse* features good-sized rooms, a gym and sauna. ❹

The Town

The steep, narrow streets of the **ville haute** (also known as the Cité Vauban), high above the urban spread of the modern town, are the main focus of interest. There are four **gates**: portes Dauphine and Pignerol lie to the north, porte d'Embrun to the southwest and porte de la Durance to the east. If you come by car the best option is to park at the **Champ de Mars** at the top of the hill and enter the town through the porte Pignerol. From here the narrow main street, Grande Rue – known as the *grande gargouille* because of the "gurgling" stream running down the middle – tips steeply downhill, bordered by mostly eighteenth-century houses. Almost halfway down and to the right is the sturdy **collegiate church**, designed under the supervision of Vauban, again with an eye to defence. Beyond it, there's a fantastic **view** from the walls, especially on a clear starry night, when the snows on the surrounding barrier of mountains give off a silvery glow. Continuing further down Grande Rue, and turning left, you'll find the blocky **Cordeliers church**, Briançon's sole surviving medieval building; it's only occasionally open to visitors, but there are some colourful, well-preserved fifteenth-century murals inside.

Vauban's **citadelle**, the highest point of the fortifications, is free to visit in July and August, and by guided tour during the rest of the year. These tours usually start at 3pm from the porte Pignerol and cost €5.50; there are English-language tours on Sundays (€6.50). The fortified keep, designed by Vauban, looks over the strategic intersection of five valleys and guards the start of the climb to the desolate and windswept **Col de Montgenèvre**, one of the oldest and most important passes into Italy.

Down in the *ville basse*, the **Télécabine du Prorel** shoots up from avenue René-Froger and links Briançon with the Serre Chevalier skiing resort area. It also provides a head start to mountain walkers (€11.10 return).

Eating and drinking

The *ville haute* is full of cafés and restaurants serving both local and Italian dishes. *Les Templiers*, near the tourist office at 20 rue du Temple (☎04.92.20.29.04), offers large fondues for €14–23 and pizzas from €9. For some exceptionally tasty traditional dishes, try ⚡ *Le Passé Simple* at the *Auberge de la Paix* (see p.771), which offers the "Vauban Menu" (€26), reviving dishes from the seventeenth-century (stuffed lettuce, lamb chops and *fromage blanc gâteau*) as well as plenty of local specialities like *tartiflette* and interesting dishes like snails in hazlenut sauce (€15). *Menus* are €19–38. Also worth a visit is *Le Rustique* at 35 rue du Pont d'Asfeld (☎04.92.21.00.10; closed Mon & Tues; *menus* from €25), which specialises in fresh trout, served in various ways, including with calvados (€19.40). They also offer a Vauban Menu, featuring nettle soup and salmon (€35). If you're after something lighter, the épicerie-cum-tearoom *Le Panier Alpin*, at 48 Grande Rue (☎04.92.20.54.65), serves an *assiette dégustation* for €11.90 consisting of a selection of local cheeses, cured meats and salad. It's also a nice place to rest up with a hot chocolate (€3) and the well-stocked shop sells a huge variety of local foodstuffs.

The Parc National des Écrins

The Écrins national park is worth a trip for the sheer variety of sports that it offers in a much less crowded setting than Mont Blanc. The best base for exploring the area is the village of **Vallouise**, southwest of Briançon on the D902. From Vallouise, there are several excellent shorter walks that take you into the heart of the Écrins or you can follow the GR54, which makes a circuit of the park and

---

Vauban and his fortresses

The citadelle in Briançon is just one example (albeit a spectacular one) of the many fortifications built on France's eastern borders by **Sébastien Le Preste de Vauban** (1633–1707), a Marshal and engineer in the army of Louis XIV. In all, Vauban built 33 fortresses and strengthened countless others in order to defend the new lands won by **Louis**, the so-called **"Sun King"**, during the wars of the seventeenth century. Vauban was highly innovative in the design of his fortresses, which were often built in the shape of a star so that the various defensive bastions could defend each other with covering fire. The other spectacular fortifications planned and constructed by him in the Alps and Franche-Comté are the citadelles at Besançon (see p.803) and Mont-Dauphin. Twelve of Vauban's fortresses, dotted around France, are now included on UNESCO's World Heritage List.

passes through the village. There's a tourist office in place de l'Église (daily except Sun & Mon 9am–noon & 2–6pm; ☎04.92.23.36.12, ⓦwww.paysdesecrins.com), and a Bureau des Guides hut in the main car park (☎04.92.23.32.29, ⓦwww .guides-ecrins.com). The Maison du Parc des Écrins provides hiking information (☎04.92.23.32.31).

Reaching Vallouise by **public transport** is difficult: there are several trains and SCAL buses that go between the *gare SNCF* in Briançon and Argentière, from where there are buses to Vallouise and the surrounding villages. It's best to contact the Vallouise tourist office for the latest transport information.

Vallouise has a handful of **gîtes and hotels**: the pick of the bunch is *Hôtel Les Vallois* (☎04.92.23.33.10, ⓦwww.lesvallois.com; open all year; ❹), where you can enjoy pleasant rooms and a garden with swimming pool. It also has a good restaurant serving local specialities and offers a good-value *plat du jour* for €9.90. *Menus* are €20–28. *Le Baoüti* (☎04.92.23.46.50, ⓦwww.gite-le-baouti.com; €14.50 per person per night) is a **gîte** with rooms for up to six people, a large common-room and self-catering facilities.

Briançon to the Queyras

The direct road from Briançon to Queyras (the D902) is a beautiful route that ascends steeply to the 2360m **Col d'Izoard** before descending into the **Casse Déserte**, a wild, desolate region with an abundance of scree running down from the peaks above. If the Col d'Izoard is closed (or if you don't fancy driving on the high, winding mountain roads), the Queyras can be reached from the north or the south on the N94.

From Briançon, the River Durance meanders through a wide valley, following the N94, until some 50km later it reaches **EMBRUN**, an attractive little town of narrow streets on a rocky bluff above the Durance and an excellent base if you want to spend a longer time exploring the Parc du Queyras. Embrun has been a fortress town for centuries. Emperor Hadrian made it the capital and main religious centre for this region, and from the third century to the Revolution it was the seat of an archbishopric. The chief sight is its twelfth-century **cathedral**, the largest in the French Alps, which has inspired numerous imitations throughout the region. The elaborate main porch, guarded by stone lions, and the fifteenth-century rose window, are especially impressive. The nearby **Tour Brune** was built in the thirteenth-century as a watchtower and today hosts regular exhibitions. **Guided tours**, in English, of the cathedral and its treasury (1hr 15min; €4.30) can be booked at the **tourist office**, located in the former chapel of the Cordeliers on place du Général Dosse (Mon–Sat 8.30am–noon & 2–6.30pm; ☎04.92.43.72.72, ⓦwww.tourisme-embrun.com), which is itself notable for the beautiful medieval frescoes which adorn the walls and ceilings. Helpful staff here can provide information on nearby walking routes, as well as on the wide range of other locally available outdoor activities including rafting, sailing and climbing, and watersports on nearby Lac de Serre-Ponçon.

A vehicle is useful for exploring the remoter areas of the Queyras, but there are also several **trains** and **buses** daily from Briançon to Embrun, as well as to Guillestre (see p.775) and Mont-Dauphin. For **accommodation**, the most agreeable option in Embrun is ⚑ *Le Pigeonnier* at 2 rue Victor Maurel (☎04.92.43.89.63, ⓦwww.pigeonnier.net; ❻), a lovely seventeenth-century house set in private gardens with just three very large, elegant rooms. On the central place de la Mairie, the recently renovated *Hôtel de la Mairie* (☎04.92.43.20.65, ⓦwww .hoteldelamairie.com; closed Oct & Nov; ❹) has a variety of bright rooms, some overlooking the square, and there's a good restaurant (mains from €15) that serves tasty local specialities. An alternative is *Le Boulevard* (☎04.92.43.25.70; *menus*

€16–20) on boulevard Pasteur, a popular brasserie offering light meals. There are also several **campsites**; at the southern end of town, *La Vieille Ferme* (T 04.92.43.04.08, W www.campingembrun.com; open May–Sept) has the most convenient location and the best facilities.

Some 10km south of Embrun, you'll come to **SAVINES-LE-LAC**, a town that was entirely relocated from what is now the bottom of the **Lac de Serre-Ponçon** to its current location. This wide expanse of water was created by the damming of the Durance, completed in 1961, and is still one of the largest man-made lakes in Europe. The town has a few reasonably priced hotels, including the peaceful *Les Sources* (T 04.92.44.20.52, W www.hotel-les-sources.com; ➋) on rue Barnafret, which has neat modern rooms as well as "mini-suites" with kitchenettes (€395 per week in July & Aug) and a shaded campsite. There's also a **hostel** overlooking the lake (T 04.92.44.20.16, E savines@fuaj.org; mid-June to Aug; dorm beds €16.70). Savines is on the bus route between Marseille and Briançon.

Gap

Continuing 10km west from Savines on the N94, you'll reach the departmental capital, **GAP**, a small, pleasant town on the Route Napoléon, whose origins reach back to Roman times. Gap prospered in the Middle Ages, partly thanks to its position on the pilgrim route to Santiago de Campostela, but suffered badly in the sixteenth-century Wars of Religion, and was burnt to the ground by the invading forces of the Duke of Savoy in 1692. Today the pedestrianised streets of the walled Old Town are lined with elegant, mainly eighteenth-century buildings.

Social life revolves around the café-filled place Jean-Marcellin, which is a good place to start a tour of the town. The house where Bonaparte spent a night in March 1815 is just off the square at 19 rue de France (look for the mural on the facade) while Gap's massive Romanesque-style **cathedral** is unmissable on place St-Arnoux. Completed in 1904, it incorporates elements from older churches, including marble altars and carved wooden angels. Outside the walled town on avenue du Maréchal Foch, the **Musée Départemental** (July to mid-Sept daily 10am–noon & 2–6pm; mid-Sept to June Wed–Fri & Mon 2–5pm, Sat & Sun 2–6pm; free) houses a diverting collection of local Iron Age and Roman archaeological finds, folk crafts and paintings.

A few kilometres north of the centre (and accessible via free shuttle buses in summer) are the lovely gardens of the **Domaine de Charance** (free), which, at around 1000m, offer fantastic views over the surrounding countryside and Gap's famous apple and pear orchards. The grand eighteenth-century château is closed to visitors, but the beautiful terraced gardens, featuring numerous apple trees and five hundred species of roses are worth the trip themselves. Behind the château is a wilder "English" garden, woodland and photogenic lake. Reasonably fit walkers can follow the trail from here to the **Pic de Charance** (1852m), which should take around three hours.

Practicalities

Gap's **tourist office**, at the western end of the Old Town at 2 cours Frédéric Mistral (Mon–Sat 9am–noon & 2–6pm; also open Sun 10am–1pm July–Aug; T 04.92.52.56.56, W www.gap-tourisme.fr), can provide information on nearby mountain-biking routes and the **airborne activities**, such as paragliding, parachuting and hot-air ballooning, for which the surrounding region is especially well known. The **gare SNCF** is just east of the centre on avenue des Alpes. If you want to stay, *La Cloche* (T 04.92.51.02.52; closed Oct & Nov; ➋), at 2 place Alsace-Lorraine has basic rooms above an Old Town café, while just outside the walls on boulevard Georges Pompidou, the more modern *Ibis* (T 04.92.53.57.57, www.accorhotel.com; ❹) offers the usual chain-hotel comforts. Those with their own transport can try 🎿 *Station Gap-Bayard* (℡04.92.50.16.83, Ⓦwww .gap-bayard.com; ❸ including half-board), 7km north of town on the N85, which offers simple but clean and bright rooms with great views over a stunning **golf course** (summer green fee €45). The complex is served by free shuttle buses from the city centre in summer; contact the tourist office for times.

There are plenty of places to **eat** in the Old Town; *Diversion* on place Jean Marcellin (℡04.92.52.08.20) offers pizzas (€8–11.20) and brasserie standards like *moules frites* (€12.90), with outdoor seating on the square, while *Le Lavandin* at 1 La Placette (℡04.92.51.15.46; closed Sun) is a good choice for light lunches such as salads and quiche (€8.50–11), as well as a wide range of tasty home-made pastries and desserts (around €4). For drinks, there are several **bars** on place Jean-Marcellin, or you can try *Le Fameux Café du Lycée* at 4 bd de la Libération (℡04.92.51.53.36), which is particularly well-known for its cocktails (€8–9).

Parc Naturel Régional du Queyras

Spreading southeast of Briançon to the Italian border, the **Parc Naturel Régional du Queyras** (Ⓦwww.queyras.com) is much more Mediterranean in appearance than the mountains to the north, with only shallow soils and low scrub covering the mountainsides. The open land along the park's rolling roads makes it particularly enjoyable to spend a few hours driving up to **St-Véran**, an Alpine village near the Italian border. There are some good walking opportunities: the **GR58** or **Tour du Queyras** path runs through St-Véran on its circuit of the park, and the **GR5** passes Ceillac and Arvieux on its way from Briançon towards Embrun.

Guillestre and Château-Ville-Vieille

The road into the Queyras park follows the River Guil from Mont-Dauphin. The first stop is **GUILLESTRE**, a pretty mountain village that only really comes to life in summer. Its houses, in typical Queyras style, have open granaries on the upper floors and its sixteenth-century church has an intriguing porch (reminiscent of the cathedral at Embrun) with squatting lions carved from limestone. If you want to **stay**, *Le Catinat Fleuri* (℡04.92.45.07.62, Ⓦwww.catinat-fleuri.com; ❸), just outside the village, has plain but cosy rooms in a complex which also includes a pool, gardens and campsite.

Continuing along the D947 from Guillestre, you'll come to the fortress of **Château-Queyras** (another of Vauban's constructions) which bars the way so completely that there's scarcely room for the road to squeeze around its base. Just beyond is **VILLE-VIEILLE**, a small village with a few old houses and a church still intact. A right turn here takes you towards St-Véran, but if you stay on the road parallel to the river Guil, you will pass through the villages of Aiguilles, Abriès and L'Échalp (all with *gîtes d'étape*), to the **Belvédère du Viso**, close to the Italian border and the **Monte Viso**, at 3841m the highest peak in the area.

St-Véran

Seven kilometres south of Château-Ville-Vieille lies **ST-VÉRAN**, which at 2042m is one of the highest villages in Europe. St-Véran's houses are part stone and part timber, and the seventeenth-century **Église de St-Véran** stands prettily on the higher of the two streets, with its white tower silhouetted against the bare crags on the other side of the valley. The **GR58** passes just south of the village; waymarked and easy to follow, the path eventually turns right down to the river, before continuing up the opposite bank through woods of pine and larch as far as the chapel of Notre-Dame-de-Clausis. There, above the line of trees, it crosses to the right bank of the stream and winds up grassy slopes to the **Col de Chamoussière**

(2884m), about three and a half hours from St-Véran. The ridge to the right of the col marks the frontier with Italy.

St-Véran's **tourist office** is halfway down the main high street (Mon–Sat 9am–12.30pm & 2–5.30pm; also open Sun in high season; ℡04.92.45.82.21, ⓦwww.saintveran.com). There's **internet access** available in the library (Mon, Wed & Fri 4.30–6.30pm) at the entrance to the village. In July and August, Petit Mathieu **buses** (℡04.92.46.71.56, ⓔcars.petitmathieu@orange.fr) link the village with the *gare SNCF* in Guillestre, although it's best to contact the tourist office for the most up-to-date times. One of the most tranquil places to stay is ⚜*Les Chalets du Villard* (℡04.92.45.82.88, ⓦwww.leschaletsduvillard.fr; mid-Dec to April & June to mid-Sept; ❸), which has spacious studio apartments with kitchen facilities and private terraces, as well as a spa and restaurant on site.

Chambéry and around

Nestling in a valley to the north of the Chartreuse Massif, the town of **CHAMBÉRY** commands the entrance to the mountain passes which lead towards Italy, and has thus held an important strategic position for the various armies and merchants who have crossed the Alps over the centuries. The town grew up around the château built by Count Thomas of Savoie in 1232, and became the Savoyard capital, enjoying a golden age in the fourteenth and fifteenth centuries. Although superseded as capital by Turin in 1562, it remained an important commercial and cultural centre, and the philosopher Rousseau spent some of his happiest years in the town during the 1730s. Only incorporated into France in 1860, modern Chambéry is a bustling provincial town with a wealth of grand Italianate architecture and a strong sense of its regional identity, discernible through the colourful red-and-white flags and the "Savoie Libre" bumper stickers which you'll see throughout the town. Around 13km north

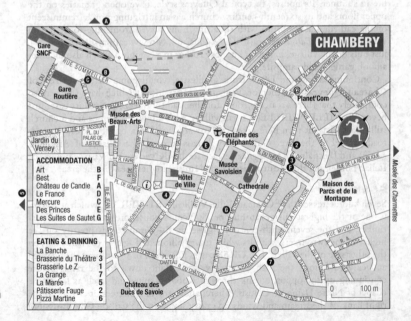

CHAMBÉRY

ACCOMMODATION
Art	B
Best	F
Château de Candie	A
Le France	D
Mercure	C
Des Princes	E
Les Suites de Sautet	G

EATING & DRINKING
La Banche	4
Brasserie du Théâtre	3
Brasserie Le Z	1
La Grange	7
La Marée	5
Pâtisserie Fauge	2
Pizza Martine	6

0   100 m

of Chambéry is the spa resort of **Aix-les-Bains**, with its famous thermal baths, as well as the **Lac du Bourget**, the largest natural lake in France and one of the best sites in the country for watersports.

Arrival, information and accommodation

The **gare SNCF** is on rue Sommeiller, 500m north of the Old Town, with the **gare routière** just outside on place de la Gare. The **tourist office** (July & Aug Mon–Sat 9am–6pm, Sun 10am–1pm; Sept–June Mon–Sat 9am–noon & 1.30–6pm; ☏04.79.33.42.47, ⓦwww.chambery-tourisme.com) is located near the Musée des Beaux-Arts at 5 place du Palais de Justice. There's **internet access** at the tourist office (same hours apply) or in the eastern part of the town centre at the internet shop Planet'Com, 9 faubourg Montmélian (☏04.79.71.96.50), as well as several other internet shops on the same street.

There's plenty of inexpensive **accommodation** scattered around the centre of Chambéry, but you can also enjoy some real luxury at fairly reasonable rates.

Art 154 rue Sommeiller ☏04.79.62.37.26, ⓦwww .arthotel-chambery.com. This place, close to the railway station, has simple but comfy rooms with satellite TV. Breakfast (€8) is served from 5.30am. **❸**

Best 9 rue Denfert-Rochereau ☏04.79.85.76.79, ⓦwww.besthotel.fr. The more expensive apartments here have balconies overlooking the place du Théâtre, but all the rooms are soundproofed and stylishly decorated. **❸**

Château de Candie Rue du Bois de Candie ☏04.79.96.63.00, ⓦwww.chateaudecandie.com. You'll find elegant, individually designed apartments and an excellent restaurant in this picturesque medieval château, standing a few km north of the town. **❽**

Le France 22 faubourg Reclus ☏04.79.33.51.18, ⓦwww.le-france-hotel.com. Located near the *gare SNCF*, this three-star place is a comfortable enough option, aimed more at business travellers. **❺**

Mercure 183 place de la Gare ☏04.79.62.10.11, ⓦwww.accorhotels.com. Conveniently situated opposite the train station, this large branch of the nationwide chain is a business-traveller favourite, with spacious rooms and friendly, professional service. **❺**

Des Princes 4 rue de Boigne ☏04.79.33.45.36, ⓦwww.hoteldesprinces.eu. There is a sense of colonial grandeur in the Indian-themed decor of this refined hotel, where the rooms are cosy and stylish. The €9 breakfast buffet is excellent value. **❺**

Les Suites de Sautet 6 rue Métropole ☏06.16.83.16.64, ⓦwww.hotel-chambery -sautet.fr. There are just two large and beautifully decorated rooms in this eighteenth-century townhouse set in a quiet courtyard, as well as a small lounge for guests. Breakfast, prepared by the friendly owners, is included, and you can borrow DVDs to watch on your flat-screen TV. **❻**

The Town

Halfway down the broad, leafy boulevard de la Colonne is Chambéry's most famous monument, the extravagant and somewhat off-scale **Fontaine des Éléphants**. The fountain was erected in homage to Général Comte de Boigne (1751–1830), a local boy who amassed a fortune working as a mercenary in India and subsequently used much of his vast wealth to fund major urban developments in his home town. **Musée Savoisien**, on nearby square de Lannoy-de-Bissy (Mon & Wed–Sun 10am–noon & 2–6pm; €3.10), chronicles the history of Savoie from the Bronze Age onwards. There's a diverse mix of exhibits: Iron Age pottery, Roman bronzes, paintings and the Cruet Mural, an important set of thirteenth-century wall-paintings depicting battle scenes and life at the royal court.

Next to the museum in place de la Métropole is the **cathedral**, which dates from the 1400s but has an interior decorated in elaborate nineteenth-century trompe-l'oeil. From here a passage leads to the fine old street of the **rue de la Croix-d'Or**, the hub of aristocratic Chambéry in the seventeenth century and now home to numerous restaurants. A few blocks to the south is the **rue de la République**, where there are several large public buildings, as well as the **Maison des Parcs et** de la Montagne (Tues–Sat 10am–noon and 2–7pm; free), which has a fun little museum with multimedia exhibits concerning the local mountains and lakes.

Heading west from the **rue de la Croix-d'Or**, you'll reach the long, rectangular, café-lined **place St-Léger** (home to Jean-Jacques Rousseau in 1735), which hosts a **flea market** on the second Saturday of every month. Further on, to your right, the smart **rue de Boigne**, with its elegant colonnades, is immediately reminiscent of Turin, while to your left, you will see the **Château des Ducs de Savoie**. A massive and imposing structure, the château was once the main home of the Dukes of Savoy, and is now occupied by the prefecture; the interior is only accessible by guided tours, which begin from the adjacent place du Château (May, June & Sept Tues–Sun 2.30pm; July & Aug daily 10.30am, 2.30, 3.30 and 4.30pm; Oct–April Tues–Sun 2.30pm; €2.50). The **Sainte-Chapelle**, in the internal courtyard, was once the repository of the Turin Shroud; it was damaged in a fire here in 1532 and was transferred to the Duke's new court in Turin in 1578. A short walk north from the castle exit along rue Jean-Pierre Veyrat brings you to the **Musée des Beaux-Arts** on place du Palais de Justice (closed for renovation until 2011), which is largely devoted to works by lesser-known Italian artists from the Renaissance; the pride of the collection is the fifteenth-century *Portrait of a Young Man,* attributed to Paolo Uccello. Chambéry's main food market, selling everything from regional cheeses to live poultry, sets up on this square on Saturday mornings.

Two kilometres south of town on the rustic chemin des Charmettes is Rousseau's other Chambéry address, **Les Charmettes**. This country cottage is now home to the **Musée des Charmettes** (April–Sept daily except Tues 10am–noon & 2–6pm; Oct–March daily except Tues 10am–noon & 2–4.30pm; free), a museum focused on Rousseau's writing and domestic life. The house is beautifully furnished in the style of the day, with eighteenth-century furniture, including the philosopher's writing desk on display, while the lovely formal gardens are laid out just as Rousseau would have remembered them. He only lived here a short while (1736–42) but claimed to have "savoured a century of life and a complete and pure happiness" in this isolated and tranquil location.

Eating and drinking

Tasty meals at decent prices are not hard to find in Chambéry. The town is an excellent place to indulge in some local Savoyard dishes, including fondues and fresh fish from the local lakes and rivers.

Restaurants

La Banche 10 place de l'Hôtel de Ville ☏04.79.85.36.10. Chambéry's oldest restaurant (recently refurbished) has been here in some form since the sixteenth century. It's a welcoming little place, offering a brief menu of typical brasserie dishes like *steak frites* and *moules* (mains from €15). Closed Sun & Mon.

Brasserie Le Z 12 av des Ducs de Savoie ☏04.79.85.96.87. This trendy spot offers an inexpensive and creative menu including lamb curry, tagines, salmon and smoked duck salad (*menus* from €15.50). Daily noon–2pm & 7–10pm.

La Grange 33 place Monge ☏04.79.85.60.31. This homely restaurant offers a variety of Savoyard specialities like fondue, *raclette* and *croziflette*. *Plats du jour* are €9, *menus* €22–27. Closed Sun.

La Marée 44 av Pierre Lanfrey ☏04.79.69.02.78. One of the best seafood restaurants in town, *La Marée* specialises in local fish, shellfish and *bouillabaisse* (€26–31). *Menus* €29–43. Closed Sun.

Pizza Martine 4 rue des Nonnes ☏04.79.85.51.91. Tiny place with a few indoor tables offering 32 different pizzas (€6–11) including some inventive local varieties like pizza *tartiflette*. Cheaper takeaway service available. Closed Mon.

Bars and cafés

Brasserie du Théâtre 14–16 rue Denfert-Rochereau. This traditional café/brasserie with outdoor seating, attached to the venerable theatre, is a popular place for locals to enjoy afternoon coffees and evening aperitifs. They also serve light meals like salads. *Plats du jour* from €9. Closed Sun.

Pâtisserie Fauge 20 rue d'Italie. There's a
wonderful array of artfully presented little cakes
here (€2–4) as well as savoury bites and
sandwiches. Tues–Sat 7.30am–12.30pm &
2–7.15pm, Sun 8am–12.30pm.

Aix-les-Bains and the Lac du Bourget

13km north of Chambéry is **AIX-LES-BAINS**, one of France's premier spa
resorts. The town's waters have been famous for their healing qualities since
Roman times but most of the elegant buildings here date from Aix's *belle époque*
heyday of the late 1800s, when members of European high society dropped by to
relax and take the waters; Queen Victoria was a frequent visitor. These days,
Aix-les-Bains is a sedate and genteel place, with thousands of French pensioners
descending on the town throughout the year for state-funded thermal treatments.
There are also some parks to amble through and plenty of cafés where you can sit
back with a *pastis* and watch the world go slowly by. It's also the best base for
enjoying the sights and outdoor activities at the nearby **Lac du Bourget**.

Arrival, information and accommodation

The **gare SNCF** in Aix-les-Bains is on the southern side of the town centre on
boulevard Président Wilson, and from here it's a brief stroll east up avenue
Charles-de-Gaulle to the central place Maurice Mollard. The **tourist office** (daily:
June–Aug 9am–6.30pm; Feb–May & Sept 9am–noon & 2–6pm; Oct–Jan 9am–
noon & 2–5.30pm, closed Sun; ☏04.79.88.68.00, ⓦwww.aixlesbains.com) is on
the north side of this square. It's only 2km from the town centre to the Grand Port
on the Lac du Bourget, but you can take bus #2 from the bus stop close to the
tourist office if you don't want to walk.

Aix-les-Bains has almost a hundred **hotels**, but they are busy year-round so
advance bookings are advisable. The historic, Art-Nouveau *Astoria*, 1 place des
Thermes (☏04.79.35.12.28, ⓦwww.hotelastoria.fr; ❻), is right in the centre and
has two restaurants and smart rooms with balconies or terraces. Next to the spa
complex at 2 rue Davat, the relaxing *Hôtel Thermal* (☏04.79.35.20.00, ⓦwww
.hotelthermal.fr; ❹) has a lovely garden, restaurant and lounges, including one
reserved for card games. The *Bristol*, 8 rue du Casino (☏04.79.35.08.14, ⓦwww
.bristolsavoie.com; ❹), is a marginally cheaper central option, with a range of
rooms on offer and a pleasant garden. One of the best-value options in town
though is the *Savoy*, 21 av Charles-de-Gaulle (☏04.79.35.13.33, ⓦwww.hotel
-savoy-aixlesbains.com; ❸). This hotel is in a recently renovated nineteenth-
century building and provides fresh and cosy rooms as well as cheaper ones with
shared facilities.

Closer to the lake itself, the Aix-les-Bains **hostel** is at Promenade du Sierroz
(☏04.79.88.32.88, ⓔaix-les-bains@fuaj.org; open Feb–Oct; dorm beds €18).
There are several **campsites** close by, including *Camping du Sierroz*, boulevard
Robert Barrier (☏04.79.61.21.43, ⓦwww.aixlesbains.com/campingsierroz).

The Town

The activities and sights of the town are focused around place Maurice Mollard,
where the most eye-catching landmark is **Arc de Campanus**, a Roman arch
erected in the first century BC as a funerary monument. The large Roman baths
that once stood near here are said to have incorporated over 24 kinds of marble; of
the surviving ruins in the square (some of which back on to the *mairie*), the
most intact is the Temple de Diane, a rectangular monument which now houses the
Musée Lapidaire (daily 10am–noon & 1.30–6pm; closed Tues pm; €5), where
there's a small collection of Gallo-Roman ceramics and statues.

A short walk north from here is the impressive spa centre, **Les Thermes Nationaux d'Aix-les-Bains** (daily 10am–7.45pm; €18 per day; ℡08.10.44.33.32, Ⓦwww.thermaix.com), one of the best places to experience the healing qualities of the local sulphurous water. Also north of the place Maurice-Mollard, at 10 bd des Côtes, is the **Musée Faure** (daily except Tues 10am–noon & 1.30–6pm; €4.60), an elegant villa with a small but impressive collection of nineteenth-century Impressionist art, including works by Cézanne, Pissarro and Sisley, as well as some lovely Degas pastels and sculptures by Rodin.

Lac du Bourget

Connected to the River Rhône by the Canal de Savières, the **Lac du Bourget** is France's biggest natural lake, at 18km long and 3.5km wide, and a place of great beauty, a protected wildlife reserve and home to the now scarce European beaver. "Nowhere could one find such perfect concord between water, mountains, earth and sky", enthused the nineteenth-century French writer Balzac, and it's clear what attracted him and so many other poets and artists to this place. The lake's "Côte Sauvage" rises precipitously above the sparkling blue water on its western bank, which is dominated at its southern end by the looming presence of the **Dent du Chat** (1390m). There are daily sightseeing **cruises** on the lake between April and October (1 1/2–2hr; €13.50–16), as well as more expensive lunch, dinner and evening cruises. Contact the Bateaux du Lac du Bourget office at the Grand Port in Aix-les-Bains (℡04.79.63.45.00, Ⓦwww.gwel.com).

There are also daily cruises (30min) to the picturesque **Abbaye d'Hautecombe** (audioguide tours in English and other languages; daily except Tues 10–11.15am & 2–5pm; €3) on the western side of the lake. The abbey is the final resting place of many members of the Savoie royals, including the last king and queen of Italy, Umberto II de Savoie and his wife Marie-José. The Abbaye lies close to the village of St-Pierre-de-Curtille, and is also accessible to cars via the D18 road.

Eating and drinking

There's a good choice of **restaurants** and **cafés** in town. Set in the Parc Thermal, ✻ *La Rotonde* (℡04.79.35.00.60) offers a tasty €24.50 set *menu*, as well as cheaper dishes like *moules frites* (€13). *Le Campanus* (℡04.79.35.04.96) at 11 place du Revard is a central brasserie with outdoor seating and a simpler menu including omelettes and salad (€8.90). Next to the lake at the Grand Port, you'll find the friendly *Skiff Pub* (℡04.79.63.41.00; closed Tues in winter), which serves fish from the lake, as well as seafood dishes like oysters and lobsters, and crêpes.

Watersports on the lake

Whatever your favourite watersport, the Lac du Bourget is likely to have a club and good facilities available. For **sailing**, you can visit the Club Nautique Voile d'Aix-les-Bains on boulevard Barrier at the Grand Port (℡04.79.34.10.74, Ⓦwww.cnva.com; 5 half-day sessions for €145). For **water-skiing**, contact the Ski Club Nautique, at the Plage Municipale to the east of the Petit Port (℡06.18.24.64.59, Ⓦwww.club-ski -nautique.com; €32 for a lesson). There's **kayaking and rowing** on offer at the Entente Nautique Aviron d'Aix-les-Bains, 22 av Daniel Rops (℡04.79.88.12.07, Ⓦaviron.ena.free.fr; €15 for a 2hr session).

The Isère valley and the Vanoise

The **Massif de la Vanoise**, a rugged set of mountains further to the east of Chambéry, rises to heights of over 3500m, and offers challenging routes for skiers, particularly along the steep slopes of the Isère valley. The glacier-capped southeast quadrant of the Vanoise forms the **Parc National de la Vanoise**, where hikers will find some of the most spectacular GR trails in France. The easiest road access to the Massif is from Chambéry or Grenoble, although driving the winding and precipitous old highways from Annecy or Chamonix is an adventure in itself.

The A43 from Chambéry cuts between the Massif des Bauges to the north and the Vanoise to the south, following the path of the lower **Isère River** as it flows down from Albertville. Following the river by road from here involves a 180km journey south, north and south again back to its source high in the mountains near the **Col de l'Iseran** (2770m), close to the Italian frontier. From Albertville, the N90 climbs southeast along the bends of the Isère River for 50km to Moûtiers, the turn-off for the massive **Les Trois Vallées** ski region. At Moûtiers, the river course swings northeast and following it will lead you to **Bourg-St-Maurice**, the town at the midpoint of the upper Isère valley. At Séez, a couple of kilometres further east, the road comes to an important junction: the N90 continues to climb steeply towards the **Col du Petit St-Bernard** (2188m), while the D902 heads south towards **Val d'Isère**.

Les Trois Vallées and Méribel

Just off the N90, south of the industrial town of Moûtiers, **Les Trois Vallées** (ⓦ www.les3vallees.com) is one of the world's largest linked skiing areas, with an ingenious lift network that makes skiing from village to village easy, and with endless off-piste possibilities. There are several component resorts: expensive and luxurious Courchevel (ⓦ www.courchevel.com); ugly and family-oriented Les Menuires (ⓦ www.lesmenuires.com), which has a number of cheap hotels; and lively Val Thorens (ⓦ www.valthorens.com), popular with younger crowds and the snowboarding set.

However, the main focus of interest of Les Trois Vallées is **MÉRIBEL**, a resort established in 1938 by the Scottish Colonel Peter Lindsay, and traditionally dominated by British tourists, which now offers a good range of cheap accommodation and après-ski activities. There are plenty of pubs and other British imports, but the small wooden chalets which climb the eastern side of the valley also manage to give the resort a traditional Savoyard feel. At the bottom of the valley is the large **Olympic Park** (Dec–April, July & Aug daily 2–7.45pm, until 9.30pm Tues & Thurs), which includes a swimming pool (€4.30) and ice rink (€4.60). Méribel's **tourist office** (daily 9am–noon & 3–7pm; ⓣ 04.79.08.60.01, ⓦ www.meribel.net) is at the top of the route de la Monte in the village centre. In summer, it's worth enquiring here about the **Méripass** card (valid for six days; €50) which gives you free access to both the Olympic Park and to the ski lifts in the area. The ESF ski school office (ⓣ 04.79.08.60.31) and the **Bureau des Guides** (ⓣ 04.79.00.30.38) are both located in the tourist office.

Accommodation tends to be pricey. *Hôtel La Croix Jean-Claude* (ⓣ 04.79.08.61.05, ⓦ www.croixjeanclaude.com; ⑤) is a smart, historic place in a central location. For sheer luxury, try the four-star *Hôtel Le Grand Coeur* on chemin du Grand Coeur (ⓣ 04.79.08.60.03, ⓦ www.legrandcoeur.com; ⑨), featuring stylish rooms with balconies or terraces, a spa and an excellent restaurant serving local specialities.

Bourg-St-Maurice and around

A pleasant if unremarkable town situated at the roaring confluence of the Isère and Chapieux rivers, **BOURG-ST-MAURICE** has some good shops – including a large Intersport (which rents out and sells ski gear) and a couple of supermarkets – which are useful for stocking up before heading to the resorts. The **tourist office** (Mon–Fri 9am–noon & 2–7pm, Sat 8.30am–7pm, Sun 9am–12.30pm & 3.30–7pm; ☎04.79.07.04.92) is across the main road from the building incorporating both the **gare SNCF** and the **gare routière**. In winter, there are regular bus services to Les Arcs and Val d'Isere, but in summer these are reduced to one or two a day.

There are a few reasonable **places to stay** in Bourg-St-Maurice. Located in a pretty, forested setting at 69 rte d'Hauteville, *L'Autantic* (☎04.79.07.01.70, Ⓦwww.autantic.fr; ❷–❻) is a modern chalet with a pool, sauna and variety of rooms, while *L'Angival* (☎04.79.07.27.97, Ⓦwww.angival.com; ❺) offers a choice of cosy rooms in the centre of town. The nearest **HI hostel**, *La Verdache* (☎04.79.41.01.93, Ⓔseez-les-arcs@fuaj.org; open late May to mid-Sept & mid-Dec to April; dorm beds €18.20), lies 4km away outside Séez among beautiful alpine woods, and has pleasant bedrooms but no kitchen facilities. A good **campsite** is *Camping Le Reclus* in Séez (☎04.79.41.01.05, Ⓦwww.campinglereclus.com). From Bourg-St-Maurice, you can take any bus towards Val d'Isere and ask to get off near the campsite or the hostel.

There are several major **ski resorts** in the mountains around Bourg-St-Maurice. On the northern slopes above the town, **Paradiski** (Ⓦwww.paradiski.com) is a ski area formed in 2003 when the resorts of La Plagne and Les Arcs were joined by a giant double-decker *téléphérique* that swings over the Ponthurin valley. **Les Arcs** (Ⓦwww.lesarcs.com), to the southeast of Bourg-St-Maurice and accessible from the town via a funicular railway, comprises four villages of varying altitude; while the resort has excellent snow and terrain for all levels, it also has a decidedly mellow après-ski scene and the villages lack atmosphere. **La Plagne** (Ⓦwww.la-plagne.com) is a huge ski station made up of ten resorts high above the Isère valley, with plenty of opportunities for both beginners and more advanced skiers. The most attractive (and exclusive) of these purpose-built resorts is **Belle Plagne**, where the emphasis is more on relaxation than lively nightlife; the **Centre Forme** (Mon–Fri 10am–12.30pm & 2–7.30pm, Sat 2–7.30pm; Ⓦwww.centre-forme-belle-plagne.com) at the heart of the resort offers heated pools, sauna, gym and all kinds of spa and beauty treatments.

Tignes

Beyond Bourg-St-Maurice and the road junction at Séez, the D902 follows the path of the Isère as it climbs towards Val d'Isère. After around 12km, the road brings you to the artificial **Lac de Chevril**, which sits below another popular and purpose-built ski resort: **TIGNES**. The resort is not attractive, and in summer has little to offer aside from a handful of lifts open for glacier skiing, yet in winter, the slopes nearby become irresistible for expert skiers. From Tignes, you can easily access 130km of pistes which pass over or around the 3656m **Grand Motte** to Val d'Isère (see opposite); these are collectively known as the **Espace Killy**, named after French downhill legend Jean-Claude Killy. The resort is usually filled with package-holidayers, but independent travellers can stay at the **HI hostel** *Les Clarines* (☎04.79.41.01.93, Ⓔtignes@fuaj.org; open late June to late July and late Sept to April; dorm beds €18.20). If you're looking for something a little more upmarket, the resort's **tourist office** (☎04.79.40.04.40, Ⓦwww.tignes.net) can help book accommodation (☎04.79.40.26.62, Ⓦwww.tignesreservation.net).

Val d'Isère

Once a tiny mountain village, **VAL D'ISÈRE** is now a sprawling mass of cafés, supermarkets, chalets and bars. Because of its distance from Bourg-St-Maurice and the larger towns to the west, the resort almost completely closes down in the off-season, with only one or two hotels remaining open in May. Nonetheless, Val d'Isère does make a convenient centre for walking in the summer, and you can ski year-round on the glacier.

The **skiing** around Val d'Isère is varied and demanding; many international experts never ski anywhere else. There are two beginner's slopes, one close to the resort centre and the other in nearby **Le Daille**. Of the three major skiing areas, **Le Fornet** provides the best slopes for novices, but it is also relatively undeveloped. The **Solaise** area provides easily accessible sheltered skiing between larch trees during bad weather, and has two free beginners' lifts near its swimming pool and ice-skating complex. **Le Rocher de Bellevard** is home to the Olympic downhill, and its east-facing slopes (site of the 1992 Olympics and the 2009 World Championships) are reserved for the most accomplished skiers.

Practicalities

The **tourist office** (daily 8.30am–7.30pm; ☏04.79.06.06.60, ⓦwww.valdisere .com) is next to the *mairie* in the centre of the resort. There is a **Bureau des Guides** (☏06.14.62.90.14, ⓦwww.guide-montagne-tarentaise.com) information desk in the Killy Sport Shop next to the tourist office; here you can find information and guides for the various climbs, Via Ferrata courses and hiking trails in the area, including those in the nearby **Parc National de la Vanoise** (see box below).

There are several **ski schools** in the town. The tried-and-trusted ESF (€48 for a group morning lesson; ☏04.79.06.02.34, ⓦwww.esfvaldisere.com) has an office in the centre at the Carrefour des Dolomites, while Misty Fly (€100 for private 2hr morning lesson, €205 for 5 group lessons; ☏04.79.41.95.71, ⓦwww.mistyfly valdisere.com) has fun-loving instructors, and also sells and rents ski and snowboard gear opposite the tourist office.

Val d'Isère is, unsurprisingly, a rather expensive place to stay. One central and comfortable **accommodation** option is the *Christiania* (☏04.79.06.08.25, ⓦwww .hotel-christiania.com; ⑨), which offers predictably swish rooms and a spa. One of the marginally more affordable hotels in town is the two-star *La Galise* (☏04.79.06.05.03, ⓦwww.lagalise.com; ⑧), where you'll find cosy wood-panelled rooms, a bar and billiard room. The cheapest spot in Val d'Isère, however, is the **campsite**: *Camping Les Richardes* (☏04.79.06.26.60, ⓦcampinglesrichardes.free.fr; open mid-June to mid-Sept) is 1km from the centre of the resort at Le Laisinant.

The Parc National de la Vanoise

The **Parc National de la Vanoise** (ⓦwww.vanoise.com) occupies the eastern end of the Vanoise Massif. It's extremely popular, with over 500km of marked paths, including the **GR5**, **GR55** and **GTA** (Grande Traversée des Alpes), and numerous *refuges* along the trails. For in-depth information on the various routes, head for the tourist offices in Val d'Isère, Bourg-St-Maurice and Méribel.

To cross the park, you can take the **GR55** from the Lac de Tignes and over the **Col de la Vanoise.** You can then connect with the **GR5**, which brings you out at the southern end of the park in the town of Modane. There are countless shorter but equally beautiful walks in the park. Settlements in the Arc Valley, like Bessans, are good bases to start exploring the park, but even the so-called ski resorts of Tignes, Val d'Isère and Méribel are good starting points.

As with the hotels, the resort's **restaurants** are mostly closed outside winter and prices tend to be on the high side. One reasonable option is the hotel restaurant at *Le Savoie* (℡04.79.00.01.15), which serves local fish dishes and grills (mains €16–28). There are also several popular bar-restaurants serving staples such as steak and chips. *Le Petit Danois* (℡04.79.06.27.97), for example, serves up hearty pub grub from around €18.

When it comes to **nightlife**, the most popular spot is just down from the Rond Point, where *Dick's Tea Bar* provides a mix of local bands and UK DJs until 4am (entry €10 after midnight). More central is *Le Graal*, where the resident DJ plays funky house music. During the winter, many of the bars close at 4am and open again just four hours later as the early-morning skiers hit the slopes. However, most bars shut down outside of the peak skiing season of November to April.

The Col de l'Iseran

From Val d'Isère, the **D902** veers south from the river and climbs towards the **Col de l'Iseran** (2770m), the highest pass with a paved road in the Alps. Despite the dangers of weather and the arduous climb, the pass has been used for centuries, mainly because it is by far the quickest route between the remote upper valleys of the Isère and Arc. From October to June, the pass is blocked by snow, but in summer, it's a must-see sight for tourists with cars, who have the option of moving on to the much less touristy villages of the **Arc Valley** that lie beyond the pass. If the weather is good and you are reasonably fit, you should consider walking from here along a steep path to the **Pointe des Lessières** (3041m), which offers beautiful views of the Vanoise Massif, as well as the fearsome Italian side of Mont Blanc.

Annecy

Lying 50km to the south of Lake Geneva, **ANNECY**, set on a sparkling turquoise lake, the Lac d'Annecy, is one of the most beautiful and popular resort towns of the French Alps. It enjoyed a brief moment of political and religious importance in the early sixteenth century, when Geneva embraced the Reformation and the Catholic bishop, François de Sales, decamped here with a train of ecclesiastics and a prosperous, cultivated elite.

These days, the delights of the town lie not just in its historical monuments, like the imposing château on the hill or the stronghold of the Palais de l'Île closer to the lake, but also in the stunning scenery, while its canals, watched over by Baroque and medieval churches and shuttered, flower-bedecked townhouses, lend the place a certain Venetian air.

Arrival, information and accommodation

The **gare SNCF** and **gare routière** complex is northwest of the town centre. The **tourist office** (Mon–Sat 9am–12.30pm & 1.45–6pm; June–Aug also Sun same hours; ℡04.50.45.00.33, ⓦwww.lac-annecy.com) is housed in the Centre Bonlieu, a modern civic centre on rue Jean-Jaurès, near the lake. For **internet access**, head for Planète Telecom at 2 rue Jean-Jaurès. There's **bike rental** from Roul' ma poule at 4 rue des Marquisats (℡04.50.27.86.83).

Annecy has no shortage of **hotels**, but these fill up quickly in July and August, so it's always good to reserve a bed well in advance.

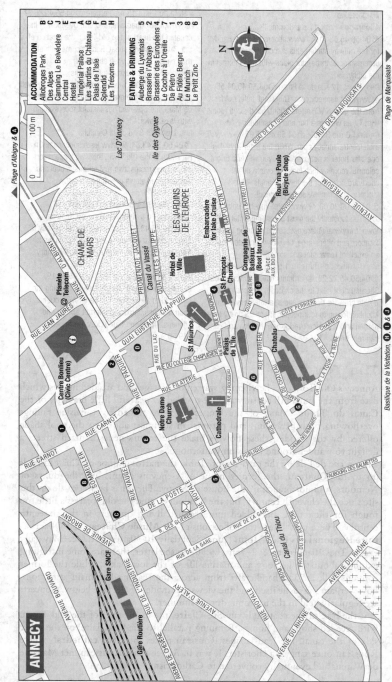

ANNECY

ACCOMMODATION

Allobroges Park	B
Des Alpes	C
Camping Le Belvédère	J
Central	E
Hostel	I
L'Impérial Palace	A
Les Jardins du Château	G
Palais de l'Isle	F
Splendid	D
Les Trésoms	H

EATING & DRINKING

Auberge du Lyonnais	5
Brasserie l'Abbaye	2
Brasserie des Européens	4
Le Cochon à l'Oreille	7
Da Pietro	1
Au Fidèle Berger	3
Le Munich	8
Le Petit Zinc	6

Plage d'Albigny & A

Lac D'Annecy

Ile des Cygnes

Basilique de la Visitation, H, I & J

Plage de Marquisats

Hotels

Allobroges Park 11 rue Sommeiller
☎04.50.45.03.11, Ⓦwww.allobroges.com. Handy for the railway station, this is a comfortable, if unremarkable, three-star place with free internet in the lobby. ❺

Des Alpes 12 rue de la Poste ☎04.50.45.04.56, Ⓦwww.hotelannecy.com. This small hotel not far from the *gare SNCF* offers bright, good-sized rooms with TV, as well as a bar and guest lounge. ❹

Central 6 rue Royale ☎04.50.45.05.37, Ⓦwww .hotelcentralannecy.com. While the exterior of this one-star hotel is not promising, you will find bright, colourful rooms which look out over a quiet courtyard or one of the town's canals. ❷

L'Impérial Palace Allée de l'Impérial
☎04.50.09.30.00, Ⓦwww.hotel-imperial-palace .com. Undoubtedly the most prestigious hotel in town, *L'Impérial Palace* occupies a stunning lakeside location, and offers large, tastefully decorated rooms, an excellent restaurant and spa. ❾

Les Jardins du Château 1 place du Château
☎04.50.45.72.28, Ⓔjardinduchateau@wanadoo.fr. Situated right next to the château, this *chambres d'hôte* provides doubles and apartments with small kitchens for up to four people. There's a pretty little garden and a terrace overlooking the city, and you can rent bikes. ❹

Palais de l'Isle 13 rue Perrière ☎04.50.45.86.87, Ⓦwww.hoteldupalaisdelisle.com. Overlooking the canal in the heart of the Old Town, the location of the *Palais* is hard to beat. Rooms come with all mod cons including wi-fi access. ❻

Splendid 4 quai Eustache Chappuis
☎04.50.45.20.00, Ⓦwww.hotel-annecy-lac.fr. Well placed opposite the grassy expanse of the Champ de Mars, the *Splendid* has tasteful rooms, some with lake views. ❻

Les Trésoms 3 bd de la Corniche
☎04.50.51.43.84, Ⓦwww.lestresoms.com. On a hill south of the Old Town, this swish spa resort offers large rooms, two restaurants, a pool and uninterrupted views over the lake below. ❽

Campsite and hostel

Camping Le Belvédère 8 rte du Semnoz
☎04.50.45.48.30, Ⓔcamping@ville-annecy.fr. The municipal campsite is just a 10min walk from the Old Town; there's a bar and laundry on site.

Hostel 4 rte du Semnoz ☎04.50.45.33.19, Ⓔannecy@fuaj.org. This hostel overlooking the lake is 2km away from the *gare SNCF*, but has good facilities, including internet access and kitchens. Open mid-Jan to Nov. Dorm beds €19.50.

The Town

Annecy's Old Town is a bewitching warren of passages and arcaded houses which date from the sixteenth century and are divided by peaceful little branches of the **Canal du Thiou**. Many of the houses here are ringed by canalside railings overflowing with geraniums and petunias in summer; added to the cool shade offered by the arcades, these flowers make the town's pedestrianized streets a delight to wander around on a sunny afternoon.

From rue de l'Île on the canal's south bank, the narrow rampe du Château leads up to the **Château**, the former home of Genevois counts and the dukes of Nemours, a junior branch of the house of Savoy. There has been a castle on this site since the eleventh century, but the Nemours found the old fortress a little too rough for their taste and added more refined living quarters in the sixteenth century. These now house the collections of the **Musée Château** and **Observatoire Régional des Lacs Alpins** (June–Sept daily 10.30am–6pm; Oct–May daily except Tues 10am–noon & 2–5pm; €4.90). In the latter, there are some intriguing exhibits about the geology and marine life of the local lakes, while the former contains folk art and handicrafts from across the region. The main attractions, however, are the castle itself and the views it provides of the lake below. Concerts are regularly held in the ballroom during summer.

At the base of the château is **rue Ste-Claire**, the main street of the Old Town, with arcaded shops and houses. Running parallel to rue Ste-Claire, on the other side of the canal, rue Jean-Jacques Rousseau passes the city's **cathedral**, where Rousseau once sang as a chorister. It was in Annecy that Rousseau met Madame de Warens and eventually converted to Catholicism.

Annecy's animation festival

The **International Animated Film Festiival** (⊕ www.annecy.org), which takes place in Annecy each June, should appeal to far more than just fans of old Disney movies. It's a renowned showcase for a wide range of international animated films, which increasingly displays the influence of Bollywood and Chinese film-makers. It's also great fun for kids, with many of the films using special effects and 3D glasses. A bus runs from the Centre Bonlieu to several venues around the town. Contact the tourist office for the latest details and programme.

Nearby, to the east, you'll find the photogenic **Palais de l'Île**, a small twelfth-century stronghold, beautifully constructed out of the local stone, which served in turn as a fortified residence, mint, court and prison; you can still read the graffiti left by French Resistance prisoners during World War II. It now houses the **Centre d'Interprétation de l'Architecture et du Patrimoine de l'Agglomération d'Annecy** (June–Sept daily 10.30am–6pm; Oct–May daily except Tues 10am–noon & 2–5pm; €3.60), a museum with several French-language audiovisual presentations on urban environments in the region. A combined ticket for the **Palais de l'Île** and the **Musée-Château** costs €6.40.

A few blocks to the north, the fifteenth-century **church of St-Maurice** conceals some wonderful fifteenth- and sixteenth-century frescoes. Across the lakeside road from here are the extensive lawns of the **Champ de Mars**; the quai Napoléon III skirts this area, and it is from here that boats leave on **cruises around the lake**.

From the Hôtel de Ville, a stroll south on rue des Marquisats leads along the lake to the free grassy **plage des Marquisats**. Alternatively, take avenue de Trésum up towards the **Basilica of the Visitation**, on avenue de la Visitation (daily 7am–noon & 2–7pm). Built in the 1920s, it houses the remains of both St François de Sales and St Jane de Chantal, held in Art Deco-style reliquaries in front of the altar. There's a tiny museum (daily 9am–noon & 2–5pm; free) displaying some of the saints' personal belongings, and panoramic views of the town below.

Eating and drinking

There are plenty of **bars and cafés** in Annecy from which you can admire the local architecture with a beverage in hand, but the **restaurants** tend to churn out rather unimaginative fare to feed the tourist crowds. You'll find a string of inexpensive places to eat overlooking the canal along quai Perrière and rue Ste-Claire.

Restaurants

Auberge du Lyonnais 9 rue de la République ⊕ 04.50.51.26.10. Excellent seafood is on the menu at this classy canalside restaurant, including oysters, clams and fresh fish from the lake. Lamb and beef dishes are also served. Mains €15–46.

Brasserie des Européens Place de l'Hôtel de Ville ⊕ 04.50.45.00.81. The seafood here is also wonderfully fresh (look out for the display of fish in the window) and there's an extensive wine list. Mains €17–24.

Le Cochon à l'Oreille Quai Perrière ⊕ 04.50.10.02.18. Decked out with countless porcelain pigs, this rustic restaurant offers plenty of pork dishes, sausages and traditional *tartiflettes*

and reasonably priced *menus* from €18. Closed Mon in winter.

Da Pietro 23 rue Sommeiller ⊕ 04.50.51.30.70. Situated north of most of the tourist restaurants, *Da Pietro* provides some excellent pizzas for €8–12, although the chef's specialities are his steaks (€18). Closed Sun.

Le Petit Zinc 11 rue Pont Morens ⊕ 04.50.51.12.93. This popular little bistro serves up tasty Savoyard favourites, including excellent fondues (€14–17). Daily noon–3pm & 7–11pm.

Bars and cafés

Brasserie l'Abbaye 4 rue du Pâquier. This lively brasserie favours Leffe beers, and has a large outdoor terrace where you can sit back with a 50cl glass for €4. The smart restaurant inside serves brasserie standards like *moules marinière* (€13.80) as well as pizzas from €8. Daily 8am–1am.

Au Fidèle Berger 2 rue Royale. This ever-busy *salon de thé* is a good spot to relax with a pot of Darjeeling or a coffee. They also sell a wide range of tempting chocolates, and light dishes such as salads for €12. Mon–Fri 9.15am–7pm, Sat 9am–7.30pm.

Le Munich 1 quai Perrière. *Le Munich* offers a huge menu of Belgian, German and international beers, with many on draught, but it's not cheap (from €6 for 50cl). Closed Mon.

Around Annecy

While the tourist crowds which flock to Annecy in the summer high season may only be bearable for a day or two, there are plenty of places around the lake to escape and run wild. As well as **boat tours**, **cycling** is an especially enjoyable means of appreciating the beauty of the Lac d'Annecy. Cycling the 40km road circuit of the lake is a very popular Sunday morning activity among sporty Annéciens; a traffic-free cycle route follows the west shore. The surrounding hills offer walking and mountain-biking excursions to suit all levels of ability and fitness. Experienced walkers should enjoy the relatively undemanding ascent of **La Tournette** (2351m) on the eastern side of the lake, while gentler walks and cycle routes are to be found in the forested **Semnoz mountains** on the lake's west side. Ten kilometres west of Annecy, the **Gorges du Fier** are among the most spectacular and beautiful natural gorges in France.

Around the lake

A **lake cruise** is the most peaceful way to travel between Annecy and the other settlements around the lake. Compagnie des Bateaux, 2 place aux Bois (☎04.50.51.08.40, ⓦwww.annecy-croisieres.com), runs several boats daily from the quai Napoléon III which stop off at various points around the lake; the price for a full circuit is €15.80. They also run 2- to 3-hour cruises which include lunch or dinner (as well as dancing in the evening) on the MS *Libellule*; prices start at €49.

Close to the village of **MENTHON-ST-BERNARD** on the eastern shore of the lake is the grand, turreted **Château de Menthon** (May, June & Sept Fri–Sun & hols 2–6pm; July & Aug daily noon–6pm; €7.50). The fortress has been inhabited since the twelfth century and was the birthplace of St Bernard, the patron saint of mountaineers. In the nineteenth century, however, it was extensively renovated in the romantic Gothic revival style and now possesses an impressive library containing some twelve thousand books. On weekends, costumed actors relate the château's history.

The village itself has a few places to stay. The most opulent **hotel** is the *Palace de Menthon*, 665 rte des Bains (☎04.50.64.83.00, ⓦwww.palacedementhon.com; ⑥), which offers smart rooms overlooking the lake and an excellent restaurant. There are more options a few kilometres down the road at the lovely lakeside village of **TALLOIRES**, whose eleventh-century Benedictine abbey has been converted into the luxurious *Hôtel de l'Abbaye de Talloires* on chemin des Moines (☎04.50.60.77.33, ⓦwww.abbaye-talloires.com; open Feb to mid-Nov; ⑥).

Hotels are cheaper on the western side of the lake. In **SEVRIER**, the *Auberge de Létraz* on route d'Albertville (☎04.50.52.40.36, ⓦwww.auberge-de-letraz .com; ⑥) has very neat modern rooms set in pleasant gardens.

Further south, the village of **DUINGT** occupies a peninsula which juts out into the narrowest point of the lake. There are two medieval **châteaux** here, one in ruins and the other partly rebuilt, which are unfortunately not open for visitors. Like Menthon-St-Bernard and Talloires, Duingt has a small beach, with the opportunity to rent pleasure craft. The waterfront *Auberge du Roselet* (☎04.50.68.67.19, ⓦwww .hotel-restaurant-leroselet.com; open Jan–Oct; ⑤) has cosy rooms and a lovely garden, while the four-star *Le Clos Marcel*, allée de la Plage (℡04.50.68.67.47, ⓦwww.closmarcel.fr; open June–Nov; ❼) offers a chic ambience with a spa, sauna and private beach. Both hotels have excellent restaurants.

South of Duingt at **BREDANNAZ**, the *Hôtel Port et Lac*, route d'Annecy (℡04.50.68.67.20, ⓦwww.hotel-port-et-lac74.com; open Feb–Oct; ❸) is one of the cheaper lakeside options, offering comfortable rooms, many with lake views, as well as a garden and restaurant.

The Gorges du Fier

West of Annecy, the River Fier has cut a narrow crevice through the limestone rock at the **Gorges du Fier** (daily: mid-March to mid-June & mid-Sept to mid-Oct 9.30am–6.15pm; mid-June to mid-Sept 9.30am–7.15pm; €5), which is signposted off the D14 at Lovagny. It's an awe-inspiring landscape of often bizarre geology, with eroded cliff faces, narrow rock fissures and curiously sculpted boulders, all formed by the rushing waters of the river below. Once you are inside the 300m-long gorge, you traverse a high-level walkway pinned to the gorge side. The crevice is so narrow that when it rains heavily the water can rise by around 25m in just a few hours. There's a shop, café and free car park on site.

Mont Blanc

Fifty kilometres to the east of Annecy on the Swiss and Italian borders looms **Mont Blanc** (4807m), Western Europe's highest peak. First climbed in 1786 by Jacques Balmat and Michel-Gabriel Paccard, two intrepid gentlemen from Chamonix, the mountain and its surrounding valleys are now the biggest tourist draw to the Alps.

The closest airport is in Geneva, but if you're coming from France then Annecy (see p.784) is the easiest city from which to approach the mountain, and, of the two road routes, the one east via Megève is the more picturesque. The two main approach roads to Mont Blanc come together at Le Fayet, a village just outside **St-Gervais-les-Bains**, where the **Tramway du Mont Blanc** begins its 75-minute haul to the **Nid d'Aigle** (2375m), a vantage point on the northwest slope (€31.50 return; ⓦwww.compagniedumontblanc.com). Experienced mountaineers can press on from here along the famous Goûter ridge to the summit of Mont Blanc itself.

It is the resort of **Chamonix-Mont-Blanc**, however, which is the primary French base for outdoor activities on or around Mont Blanc. "Cham" throngs with visitors throughout the year, but even the tourist hordes cannot diminish the grandeur of the Mont Blanc Massif, and if you're walking in the area, you can soon get away from the crowds.

Chamonix-Mont-Blanc

The bustling, cosmopolitan town of **CHAMONIX** (known officially as Chamonix-Mont-Blanc) may have long since had its village identity submerged in a sprawl of tourist development, flashy restaurants and boutiques, but the stunning backdrop of glaring snowfields, eerie blue glaciers and ridges of sharp peaks that surround Mont Blanc are ample compensation.

Arrival and information

The **gare SNCF** and **gare routière** are a short walk to the south of place du Triangle-de-l'Amitié, where you'll find the **tourist office** at no. 85 (daily: 9am–7pm; ℡04.50.53.00.24, ⓦwww.chamonix.com). The Chamonix multipass

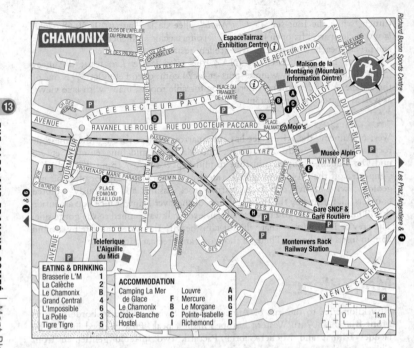

CHAMONIX

CLOS DE L'ATELIER
DU PEINTRE

CH. DES PAUSES

ROUTE DE LA ROUMNAZ

CH. DES CHARMILLES

VIA DES TRAZ

EspaceTairraz
(Exhibition Centre) ℹ

AV. DU SANTI

ALLÉE LOUIS
LACHENAL

ALLÉE RECTEUR PAYOT

Maison de la
Montagne (Mountain
Information Centre)

PLACE DU
TRIANGLE-
DE-L'AMITIÉ

ℹ

RUE VALLOT

AVENUE

CH. DES
VERALS

P

P

ALLÉE RECTEUR PAYOT

AVENUE RAVANEL LE ROUGE   RUE DU DOCTEUR PACCARD

B

A

C

D

2

PLACE
BALMAT

Mojo's

AV. DU MONT-BLANC

PASSAGE DE LA

RUE DU LYRET

Musée Alpin

R. WHYMPER

E

AVENUE CACHAT

RUE
D'ENTREVES

AVENUE DE COURMAYEUR

P

PROMENADE MARIE PARADIS

AV. DE L'AIGUILLE DU MIDI

CHEMIN DU SAPI

PLACE
EDMOND
DESAILLOUD

G

RUE DE LA TOURRETTE

RUE DES ALLOBROGES

RUE HELBRONNER

RUE DES FALÉS

H

Gare SNCF &
Gare Routière

AVENUE CACHAT

RUE DU LYRET

Teleferique
L'Aiguille
du Midi

P

CHEMIN DEVOUASSOUX

CH. DU
RUE DU LYRET

Montenvers Rack
Railway Station

P

N

0   1km

EATING & DRINKING
Brasserie L'M	1
La Calèche	2
Le Chamonix	B
Grand Central	4
L'Impossible	6
La Poêle	3
Tigre Tigre	5

ACCOMMODATION
Camping La Mer de Glace	F	Louvre	A
Le Chamonix	B	Mercure	H
Croix-Blanche	C	Le Morgane	G
Hostel	I	Pointe-Isabelle	E
		Richemond	D

(see p.792) and other mountain lift passes can also be purchased here, as well as at the foot of each cable-car ascent. The **websites** ⓦwww.chamonix.net and ⓦwww.chamex.com are also good sources of information on the town.

Near the tourist office at 190 place de l'Église, the **Maison de la Montagne** houses the **Compagnie des Guides** (daily 8.30am–noon and 3.30–7.30pm; ⓣ04.50.53.00.88, ⓦwww.chamonix-guides.com) which runs lessons in rock- and ice-climbing, as well as providing guides for those who don't want to ski off-piste or hike unaccompanied. The same building houses the **Office de Haute Montagne** (Mon–Sat 9am–noon & 3–6pm, also Sun in July & Aug; ⓣ04.50.53.22.08, ⓦwww.ohm-chamonix.com), which can give advice on *refuges* in addition to up-to-the-minute information on the weather in the mountains, and the details of countless local hiking routes. There's an **internet** café in the centre at *Mojo's*, place Balmat (daily 9am–8pm), as well as at *Grand Central* café further to the south in Chamonix Sud (see p.792).

There are plenty of **ski schools** in the town centre which provide lessons for skiers and snowboarders, as well as guides. The ESF office (ⓣ04.50.53.22.57, ⓦwww.esf-chamonix) is situated in the Maison de la Montagne; the guides here hold special lessons on the famous runs of the Vallée Blanche.

Accommodation

One of the biggest headaches in and around Chamonix is finding a bed. All hotels require booking in advance and tend to be expensive; however, there's also a good supply of *gîte* accommodation, as well as a clean and comfortable HI hostel a few kilometres to the west of the town centre. The tourist office also offers a **reservation service** (ⓣ04.50.53.23.33, ⓦreservation.chamonix.com), which can find you a room at even the busiest times. **High season** in Chamonix is February to

March and July and August, with the summer season being less expensive; many establishments close in May and October. If you're staying in a Chamonix hotel or at the hostel, then you should receive a free *Carte d'Hôte* on arrival; this guest card entitles you to free transport on the resort's public buses and on the SNCF train line between Servoz and Vallorcine.

Hotels

Le Chamonix 11 rue de l'Hôtel de Ville ☎04.50.53.11.07, ⓦwww.hotel-le-chamonix.com. This central hotel has wood-panelled rooms set above the lively hotel bar, and is within stumbling distance of the central restaurants and bars. ➎

Croix-Blanche 81 rue Vallot ☎04.50.53.00.11, ⓦwww.bestmontblanc.com. Dating from 1793, the *Croix-Blanche* is the oldest surviving hotel in Chamonix; its rooms combine an old-fashioned elegance with contemporary comfort. ➐

Louvre 95 impasse de l'Androsace ☎04.50.53.00.51, ⓦwww.hoteldulouvre.fr. The *Louvre* offers simple but clean rooms, free parking and a central location. Excellent value for money. ➌

Mercure 39 rue des Allobroges ☎04.50.53.07.56, ⓦwww.mercure.com. This large, modern outlet of the hotel chain is close to the *gare SNCF* and provides spacious rooms, all of which have balconies. ➐

Le Morgane 145 av de l'Aiguille du Midi ☎04.50.53.57.15, ⓦwww.morgane-hotel -chamonix.com. This stylish hotel has rooms designed in a minimalist (but very comfortable) fashion, and there's a pool, spa and bistro on site. ➐

Pointe-Isabelle 165 av Michel Croz ☎04.50.53.12.87. The *Pointe-Isabelle* has relatively inexpensive rooms with TVs and balconies close to the *gare SNCF*. Breakfast is €12 extra. ➏

Richemond 228 rue du Docteur Paccard ☎04.50.53.08.85, ⓦwww.richemond.fr. Set back from the busy rue Paccard, the *Richemond* has a pleasant garden, as well as spacious, airy rooms. ➏

Campsite and hostel

Camping La Mer de Glace 200 chemin de la Bagna, Les Praz ☎04.50.53.44.03, ⓦwww .chamonix-camping.com. A pleasant campsite with good facilities (including free internet access) 2km northeast of Chamonix. Open May–Sept.

Hostel 127 montée Jacques-Balmat, Les-Pèlerins-en-Haut ☎04.50.53.14.52, ⓔchamonix@fuaj.org. There's no communal kitchen, but this hostel has good facilities and provides cheap, filling meals in the evening. It's 2.5km out of the town centre; catch the #5 bus to the "Les Pèlerins – Auberge" stop. Open mid-May to Sept & Dec–April. Dorm beds €18.20.

The Town

The mountains provide the main sights and activities, but on days when the bad weather sets in, there are a few things to do in town. The **Musée Alpin**, off avenue Michel-Croz in the town centre (daily: mid-Dec to mid-June 3–7pm; mid-June to Oct 2–7pm; €5), is full of exhibits which detail the life of the valley since the first tourists began to arrive in the eighteenth century and displays on mountaineering equipment. The **Espace Tairraz** (same hours and ticket as the Musée Alpin) is an exhibition centre close to the tourist office in the Esplanade Saint-Michel; it hosts temporary photography exhibitions of the mountains, plus a permanent collection of crystals. The **Richard Bozon Sports Centre**, to the west of the town centre at 214 av de la Plage, has ice-skating, a pool, sauna and hammam, a climbing wall and tennis courts (hours vary; ☎04.50.53.23.70).

If you want to head into Italy from Chamonix, the most direct road is the N205, which takes you south out of Chamonix, then through the 11.6km **Mont Blanc Tunnel** (one way €33.20, return €41.40), and brings you out on the road to Aosta and Milan. There is often a waiting time of an hour or more on either side of the tunnel due to its narrowness.

Eating, drinking and nightlife

The choice of **bars**, **cafés and restaurants** reflects not only Chamonix's geographical location, with Swiss and Italian culinary influences, but also the tastes of the cosmopolitan mix of visitors. Japanese, fusion and hamburger places share the food scene with more traditional Savoyard restaurants, pizzerias and French haute cuisine. If you're after some **live music**, then either head for the pubs and clubs of rue des Moulins, or Chamonix Sud. The best **club** in town is *Le Garage* at 213 av de l'Aiguille-du-Midi (daily 1–4am), which regularly hosts top international DJs.

Restaurants

Brasserie L'M 87 rue Vallot ℡04.50.53.58.30. The multicoloured outdoor seating is the most striking feature of this central brasserie, but its tapas meals (€2–4 per dish) are also worth sampling; they include fish, cheese and sausages. Daily 11am–midnight.

La Calèche 18 rue du Docteur Paccard ℡04.50.55.94.68. Good central option serving traditonal Savoyard dishes like fondues and *raclette* (€23). Closed mid-Nov to early Dec.

L'Impossible 9 chemin du Cry ℡04.50.53.20.36. With a cosy farmhouse interior, some delicious dishes of grilled meats (€20–30), and an exceptional wine list (€12–40 for most bottles), *L'Impossible* is worth the 10min walk from the town centre. Closed Nov & Tues in May–June & Sept–Oct.

La Poêle 79 av de l'Aiguille-du-Midi ℡04.50.55.96.13. The speciality here is the omelettes. There's a range of options in terms of size, ingredients (including sausages, mushrooms and salmon) and price (€7–20). Daily noon–3pm & 6–11pm.

Tigre Tigre 239 av Michel Croz ℡04.50.55.33.42. British-style Indian meals like chicken tikka masala (€15) are on offer here, and there's also a stylish cocktail bar. Daily 4pm–2am.

Bars and cafés

Le Chamonix 11 rue de l'Hôtel de Ville. This hotel bar has several beers on tap (50cl for €5–7) and provides a nice spot to watch the world go by in the adjacent place de l'Église. Closed Sun.

Grand Central 62 promenade Marie Paradis, Chamonix Sud. This little café is a good place for light lunches with fresh fruit smoothies, healthy sandwiches and some tasty little cakes (€2–6). Daily 8am–7.30pm.

Excursions in the Chamonix Valley

Alongside the walking and skiing opportunities around Chamonix, there are several exhilarating excursions that can be made using the various ski lifts and mountain railways; it may be worth getting a **multipass** that covers all the lifts in the area (€49.50 for 24 hours, €55/70 for two/three consecutive days).

The cable-car and mountain railways

The most famous excursion is the very expensive, and often very crammed, **téléférique** (May to mid-June & Sept 8am–5pm; mid-June to Aug 7am–5pm, Oct 8.30am–4pm; Jan–April 8.30am–4.30pm; €41 return, advance reservations €2; call ℡08.92.68.00.67) to the **Aiguille du Midi** (3842m), one of the longest cable-car ascents in the world, rising 3000m above the valley floor in two extremely steep stages. Penny-pinching by buying a ticket only as far as the Plan du Midi is a waste of money: go all the way or not at all. If you do go up, make the effort to be on your way before 9am, as the summits tend to cloud over towards midday, and huge crowds may force you to wait for hours if you try later. Take warm clothes – even on a summer's day it'll be below zero at the top – and sunblock is also advisable to protect against the glare off the snow.

The Aiguille is an exposed granite pinnacle on which a restaurant and the *téléférique* dock are precariously balanced. The view is incredible. At your feet is the snowy plateau of the **Col du Midi**, with the glaciers of the Vallée Blanche and Géant sloping down the mountainside. From the Aiguille, the Three Monts climbing route takes mountaineers up the steep snowfield and exposed ridge to the summit of Mont Blanc with its final cap of ice. On the horizon lies rank upon rank of snow- and ice-capped monsters receding into the distance. Perhaps most impressive of all is the view from east to south, in which the Aiguille Verte, Triollet and the Jorasses, with the Matterhorn and Monte Rosa, form a cirque of needle-sharp peaks and sheer crags.

If you haven't tired of superb panoramic views, you can make for the **Monten-vers rack railway** (daily: May–June & Sept–Oct 8.30am–5pm; July & Aug 8am–6pm; Oct–April 10am–4pm; €18 return), a train service which has been running up from Chamonix to the Mer de Glace on the flanks of Mont Blanc since 1908. At the top you have the option of walking for twenty minutes or taking a short cable-car ride (an additional €6) down into an **ice cave** carved out of the Mer de Glace every summer.

Hiking and climbing

There are countless excellent **shorter walks** around Chamonix, including many on the northern side of the valley amid the lower but nonetheless impressive peaks of the **Aiguilles Rouges**. One easy, picturesque trail takes you from the village of Les Praz (just to the northeast of Chamonix itself) to **Lac Blanc**. Take the *téléférique* from Les Praz to Flégère and then the gondola to L'Index (a combined ticket is €21). The walk to the lake and back from L'Index takes around 2 hour 30 minutes and requires good walking boots.

   Climbing Mont Blanc should not be undertaken lightly. It is a semi-technical climb and fast-changing weather conditions mean that a guide is essential. There are several different routes, the most popular of which is the **Goûter** ridge route (three days); this ascends from the Nid d'Aigle at the top of the Tramway du Mont Blanc. The best season for climbing the mountain is mid-June to Sept, but even in this period the ascent should only be attempted by fit, acclimatized and well-prepared mountaineers.

Skiing

Despite its fame, Chamonix is not the most user-friendly of ski resorts and access to the slopes relies on shuttle buses, trains or a car. For advanced skiers, however, it's probably one of the best places in the Alps since it offers an impressive range of challenging runs and off-piste itineraries. It's not so much a single resort as a chain of unconnected ski areas set along both sides of the Chamonix valley and dominated by Mont Blanc. The **Brévent** and **Flégère** areas on the southern slopes both have a good variety of pistes and provide some fine views of the Mont Blanc massif across the valley, while **Argentière–Les Grands Montets** is a colder, north-facing area that is well suited to advanced skiers. The famous **Vallée Blanche** can be accessed by cable car from the Aiguille du Midi; skiing here involves a 20km descent which passes many crevasses and is not patrolled, so a guide is strongly recommended. Closer to Chamonix itself, the **Les Planards** and **Le Savoy** areas require artificial snow

The Tour du Mont Blanc

The classic way for walkers to admire Mont Blanc without putting themselves through the dangers of an ascent is to undertake the **Tour du Mont Blanc**, the trail which makes a 250km circuit of the mountain across French, Swiss and Italian terrain. The trail normally takes eight to twelve days, during which you can either camp or stay at the *refuges* (€20–25) en route. Many of the *refuges* provide food and other supplies, but it's worth checking the latest details with the **Office de Haute Montagne** in Chamonix, which can also provide maps of the route. Even in early July, many of the passes on the route can still be covered in snow, so walkers should carry crampons and heavy-duty waterproofs.

   Several tour companies in Chamonix can provide guides for the walk. The Compagnie des Guides (see p.790) is the oldest (it was established in 1821) and still the most recommended.

and snow cannons to stay open, but they are good spots for beginners to hone their technique.

Megève

It is the stunning views of Mont Blanc and a sense of old-world charm that make **MEGÈVE**, 15km to the west of Chamonix, one of the most beautiful French ski resorts. At the heart of the village is the traffic-free place de l'Église, a square surrounded by eighteenth-century buildings, centred on the fine medieval church of St John the Baptist. Combined with these carefully restored examples of older architecture, however, are the exclusive modern hotels, designer boutiques and ski-rental shops that lend Megève its rather chic ambiance.

While once Megève could guarantee snow during the winter, global warming has taken its toll; the resort's relatively low altitude now means that snow cannons are often required to provide adequate snow cover. There are, however, plenty of higher pistes nearby, quite gentle in comparison with those in Val d'Isère and Chamonix.

In summer, the Compagnie des Guides, in the Maison de la Montagne, 76 rue Ambroise Martin (Mon–Fri 9am–noon & 2.30–6pm; ☎04.50.21.55.11, ⓦwww .guides-megeve.com), provides guides for hikes in the area, as well as for rock climbing and mountain biking. There's also a sports centre, the Palais des Sports et des Congrès, on the north side of the town centre on the route du Palais des Sports. Here you'll find a climbing wall, swimming pool and ice rink (hours vary; ☎04.50.21.15.71).

Practicalities

The **tourist office** is at 70 rue Monseigneur Conseil (April to mid-June & Sept to mid-Dec Mon–Sat 9am–12.30pm & 2–6.30pm; rest of year 9am–7pm; ☎04.50.21.27.28, ⓦwww.megeve.com).

Upmarket **hotels** include the central and luxurious *Le Chalet St-Georges*, 159 rue Monseigneur Conseil (☎04.50.93.07.15, ⓦwww.hotel-chaletstgeorges.com; ⓽), which has a spa and gourmet restaurant. A cheaper but still central option is *La Chaumine*, 36 chemin des Bouleaux (☎04.50.21.37.05, ⓦwww.hotel -lachaumine-megeve.com; ⓺), while *Les Cimes*, 341 rue Charles Feige (☎04.50.21.11.13, ⓦwww.hotellescimes.info; ⓹), provides cosy rooms and a communal terrace just a few minutes' walk out of town. Some of the best-value accommodation is in **chambres d'hôtes**; *Les Oyats*, 745 chemin de Lady (☎04.50.21.11.56, ⓦwww.lesoyats.fr; ⓺), some 1.5km out of town, is an old farmhouse with lovely wood-panelled rooms. Situated 3km out of Megève at 57 route du Grand Bois is the local **campsite**, *Camp Bornand* (☎04.50.93.00.86, ⓦwww.camping-megeve.com; open May–Aug).

Megève has plenty of **restaurants**. In the centre, near the church, *Le Prieuré*, 116 place de l'Église (☎04.50.21.01.79), serves beautifully presented beef and lamb dishes (€32), while cheaper meals can be had at *Le Bistrot de Megève*, 76 rue Charles Feige (☎04.50.21.32.74), which serves salads (€8–12), omelettes (€14) and offers *menus* from €23. For light bites, *Le Comptoir du Père Sotieu*, 19 rue du Général Muffat, is a traditional patisserie offering a wide array of sandwiches (around €3.60) and lots of creamy cakes.

The Faucigny and the Cirque du Fer-à-Cheval

To the north of Chamonix is the **Faucigny**, a region of wide glacial valleys, gentle forested slopes and peaceful little villages that seem a world away from the party atmosphere of the resorts further south. **Samoëns**, lying 15km away from Chamonix, is one such village; despite its relatively low altitude, it has become popular with **skiers** thanks to a short transfer time from Geneva and its proximity

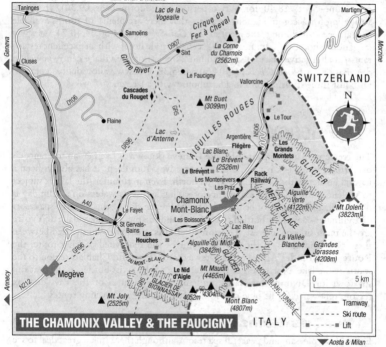

Map labels:

Évian & Morzine

Taninges

Lac de la Vogealle

Cirque du Fer à Cheval

Martigny

Samoëns

Sixt

La Corne du Chamois (2562m)

Geneva

Cluses

Giffre River

Le Faucigny

Vallorcine

SWITZERLAND

D106

Cascades du Rouget

Mt Buet (3099m)

AIGUILLES ROUGES

Le Tour

N506

Flaine

Lac d'Anterne

Argentière

Lac Blanc

Flégère

Les Grands Montets

GLACIER

Le Brévent (2526m)

Le Brévent

Les Montenevers

Rack Railway

MER DE GLACE

Aiguille Verte (4122m)

Mt Dolent (3823m)

A40

Le Fayet

Chamonix Mont-Blanc

Les Praz

Les Boissons

Lac Bleu

La Vallée Blanche

Grandes Jorasses (4208m)

St Gervais-Bains

Les Houches

Aiguille du Midi (3842m)

GLACIER

MONT BLANC TUNNEL

Annecy

N212

Megève

Le Nid d'Aigle

Mt Maudit (4465m)

4304m

4052m

Mt Joly (2525m)

Mont Blanc (4807m)

0   5 km

Tramway

Ski route

Lift

THE CHAMONIX VALLEY & THE FAUCIGNY

ITALY

Aosta & Milan

to the Grand Massif ski area (particularly the purpose-built resort of **Flaine**) via the Express du Grand Massif, a *télécabine* to the south of the village.

If you head east from Samoëns along the D907, you follow the valley as it narrows into the Gorges des Tines before opening out again at another delightful little village, **SIXT-FER-À-CHEVAL**. This pretty village lies on the confluence of two branches of the river Giffre: the Giffre-Haut, which comes down from Salvagny, and the Giffre-Bas, which flows all the way from the **Cirque du Fer-à-Cheval**. The cirque is a horseshoe-shaped ridge famed for the rugged beauty of its cliffs and waterfalls, and it is this which makes the journey away from Chamonix truly memorable.

The cirque begins about 6km from Sixt and you can reach it easily via the footpath on the left bank of the Giffre-Bas. It is a vast semicircle of limestone walls, up to 700m in height and 4–5km long, from which spring countless waterfalls, particularly in the summer months. The left-hand end of the cirque is dominated by a huge spike of rock known as La Corne du Chamois (The Goat's Horn). At its foot the valley of the Giffre bends sharply north to its source in the glaciers above the Fond de la Combe. The bowl of the cirque is thickly wooded except for a circular meadow in the middle where the road ends.

There's a **tourist office** and a park office in the place de la Gare of Sixt-Fer-à-Cheval (Mon–Fri 9am–noon & 2–6pm; ☏04.50.34.49.36, ⓦwww.sixteracheval .com), and the park office produces a useful and well-illustrated brochure of walks in the region. The village has a pleasant chalet-style **hotel**, *Le Petit Tetras* (☏04.50.34.42.51, ⓦwww.le-petit-tetras.fr; open late-Dec to March & June to mid-Sept; ⑤), with an outdoor pool and bar. The closest accommodation to the cirque itself is *Le Pelly* **campsite** (☏04.50.34.12.17, ⓔcamping.pelly@orange.fr;

open June–Sept; €8.40 for a two-person tent; dorm beds €9.30). If you're struggling for accommodation, be aware that there are plenty of rooms available in Samoëns, including the central *Le Gai Soleil* (T04.50.34.40.74, Wwww .augaisoleil-hotel-restaurant.com; ●), a chalet-style hotel with an excellent restaurant. An alternative place to stay, around 2km east of the village centre at Vallon d'en Bas, is *La Ferme d'en Bas* (T04.50.34.95.32, Wwww.vallonsdenbas.com; ●) with just three stylish rooms in a farmhouse with a jacuzzi.

Lake Geneva

The crescent-shaped expanse of **Lake Geneva** (known as Lac Léman in France) is over 70km long, 14km wide and an impressive 310m deep; it has always been a natural border with Switzerland to the north. Even in summer, the lake is subject to violent storms, yet the experience of sailing across its waters on a calm day is delightful, and should not be missed. On the French side of the lake, the spa resort of **Évian-les-Bains** (of bottled water fame) and the picturesque village of **Yvoire** are the main sites of interest. **Thonon-les-Bains**, a larger town situated between these two landmarks, is the starting point of the renowned touring route, the **Route des Grandes Alpes**, and a gateway to the beautiful Chablais region to the south of the lake. Northwest of the lake, close to the Swiss border, is the peaceful spa town of **Divonne-les-Bains**, and the green pastures of the Pays de Gex region, renowned for its blue cheese and scenic hiking and cycling routes.

Évian-Les-Bains

ÉVIAN is a pleasant and peaceful spa resort, although there isn't a great deal to see or do other than simply enjoy a stroll along the waterfront, or take leisurely trips on the lake. The waterfront is elegantly laid out with squares of immaculately mown grass, colourful flowerbeds and exotic trees; there is also mini-golf, water slides and other peaceful ways of amusing oneself if needed.

Évian is an excellent base for exploring other towns around the lake, thanks to the Compagnie General de Navigation (CGN) **ferries** (T00.41.84.81.18.48, Wwww.cgn.ch) which depart from the port here every day. These head towards several destinations, including Lausanne (19 daily; €24.20 return) and Geneva (2 daily; €50.70 return) in Switzerland, as well as Yvoire (3 daily; €33.10 return) and Thonon-les-Bains (4 daily; €19 return) on the French side.

Situated by the lake on the town's western outskirts and accessible only by a boat that leaves from the centre of Évian are the **Pré-Curieux** water gardens (3 boats daily: 10am, 1.45pm, 3.30pm in July & Aug; May, June and Sept boats run at the same times Wed–Sun only; €10 for boat trip and tour of gardens; Wwww .precurieux.com). These picturesque lakeside gardens are divided into various water-based ecosystems (including ponds, marshes and a waterfall), which each exhibit different forms of plant and animal life. Tickets for the gardens are available at the small kiosk in front of the casino and boats leave from the nearby quay.

If you fancy exploring the famous healing properties of the local water, then head for **Les Thermes Évian**, place de la Libération (T04.50.75.02.30, Wwww .lesthermesevian.com; one-day programmes start at €55), where you'll find a range of spa treatments such as "Zen-harmonic modelling massages" and activities including water aerobics.

The mineral water for which Évian is famous is now bottled at an industrial estate in Amphion, 3km along the lakeside (reserve at the tourist office for one of the 4 daily tours; €2; T04.50.26.80.29), but you can admire the **Source Cachat** on avenue des Sources, which gushes away behind the Évian company's Art Nouveau offices on rue Nationale.

Other points of interest include the grand **Palais Lumière** on quai Charles-Albert-Besson, built as a pump-room in 1902 and adorned with gorgeous stained-glass windows and Art Nouveau frescoes. Today it's a cultural centre, hosting regular exhibitions. The nearby **casino** (1912), with its "Neo-Byzantine" dome, is another example of *belle époque* exuberance.

Practicalities

The **tourist office** is on place d'Allinges (May, June & Sept Mon–Fri 9am–noon & 2–6.30pm, Sat 9am–noon & 2–6pm, Sun 10am–noon & 3–6pm; July & Aug Mon–Fri 9am–12.30pm & 2–7pm, Sat 9am–noon & 3–7pm, Sun 10am–noon & 3–6pm; Oct–April Mon–Fri 9am–noon & 2–6pm, closes 5pm on Sat, closed Sun; ☎04.50.75.04.26, ⓦwww.ville-evian.fr). The **gare SNCF** lies on the hill to the southwest of the town centre on avenue de la Gare; the **gare routière**, from which you can catch buses to Thonon-les-Bains and Yvoire, is next to the tourist office on quai Baron de Blonay.

Top-class **hotels** in town include the *Évian Royal Resort* (☎04.50.26.85.00, ⓦwww .evianroyalresort.com; ⓽), part of a luxury resort outside the town, with lavishly decorated rooms, a gourmet restaurant, spa and a beautiful golf course nearby. More affordable options are also available; occupying an eighteenth-century building in the centre of town, the *Hôtel de France* at 59 rue National (☎04.50.75.00.36, ⓦwww .hotel-france-evian.com; ⓸), has modern, stylish rooms and a pleasant breakfast garden. The *Terminus*, at 32 av de la Gare (☎04.50.75.15.07, ⓦwww.hotel-terminus -evian.com; ⓷), has basic rooms directly opposite the *gare SNCF*.

There are also some excellent **chambres d'hotes**, such as *Le Clos Gemme* (☎04.50.75.15.75, ⓦwww.gemme-plus.com; closed in Nov; ⓻), located on the heights above the resort and 10min from the town centre at 437 av du Flon. It provides a pool and spa, as well as an art gallery and meditation classes.

For **food** on a budget, one of the best local pizzerias is *La Pizza*, 4 place Charles de Gaulle (☎04.50.75.05.36; pizzas €8–12; closed Tues). *La R'mize* (☎04.50.74.61.44) at 58 rue National, offers a good range of Savoyard specialities as well as fresh lake fish, duck (€17) and steaks (€21). If you're looking for a more upmarket menu, it's worth making a trip to the restaurant at the *Hôtel les Cygnes* on 8 av de Grande-Rive (☎04.50.75.01.01; *menus* €16.50–55), which serves fresh fish, including perch, mackerel, swordfish and John Dory, as well as roast lamb and pork.

Yvoire

Situated some 25km to the west of Évian, **YVOIRE** is a pretty medieval village famous for its colourful flowers, which seem to abound on every street corner during

The Route des Grandes Alpes

Winding its way over mountain passes and secluded valleys all the way from Thonon-les-Bains to Menton on the Mediterranean coast is the most renowned tourist route of the French Alps, the 684km **Route des Grandes Alpes**. The route crosses six Alpine passes over 2000m, three of which – the Col de la Cayolle, the Col de l'Izoard and the Col de Vars – were only paved in 1934. The complete route opened in 1937 and has been a popular touring route for drivers, walkers and cyclists ever since. It can be covered in a couple of days by car, but only by rushing through the stunning mountain landscapes and intriguing settlements (including Morzine, Valloire, Briançon and Barcelonnette) that line the route.

the summer. The narrow cobbled lanes heave with day-trippers in July and August, but you can still find some peace and quiet even in those months. The main attraction is the **Labyrinthe-Jardin des Cinq Sens**, just off rue du Lac in the centre of the village (April–May & Sept to early Oct Tues–Sun 11am–6pm; June–Aug daily 10am–7pm; €10). These immaculate formal gardens are designed to stimulate each of the five senses: fruit bushes appeal to your tastebuds; the foliage in the Jardin des Textures encourages you to touch; geraniums provide vivid colours; lilies and honeysuckle produce attractive perfumes, while the central aviary is filled with birdsong. The **castle** and two stone gateways, both dating from the fourteenth century, are within easy walking distance of the gardens in the village centre. Guided visits of the medieval part of the village can be organized at the tourist office.

The **tourist office** is on place de la Mairie (Oct–March Mon–Fri 9.30am–12.30pm & 1.30–5pm; April–June Mon–Sat 9.30am–12.30pm & 1.30–5pm, Sun noon–4pm; July & Aug daily 9.30am–12.30pm & 1.30–6pm; ☎04.50.72.80.21, ⓦwww.yvoiretourism.com). Finding **accommodation** in the village can be difficult, especially in high season, but the tourist office can help. *Le Vieux Logis* on Grande Rue (☎04.50.72.80.24, ⓦwww.hotel-yvoire.org; open March–Dec; ❹) is a beautiful small hotel and restaurant in the heart of the medieval village. *Les Flots Bleus* (☎04.50.72.80.08, ⓦwww.flotsbleus-yvoire.com; open April–Oct; ❺) is located to the west of the main village in Port de Plaisance, and has chic, spacious rooms with lake-facing balconies or terraces.

Finding somewhere to **eat** is rather easier; both above-mentioned hotels have restaurants open to non-guests, and there are several more along the harbour. *Restaurant du Port* on rue du Port (☎04.50.72.80.17) offers *menus* from €25, featuring fresh perch from the lake.

Divonne-les-Bains

Passing Geneva and skirting the Swiss border northwards, you'll reach the alpine meadows and craggy peaks of the diverse Pays de Gex region, and the upmarket spa town of **DIVONNE-LES-BAINS**. Particularly handy if you're entering or leaving the region via Geneva airport, 15km away, Divonne is best known for its thermal spas. The **Thermes Paul Vidart** (March–Nov daily; treatments from €55; ☎04.50.20.05.70, ⓦwww.valvital.fr) on avenue des Thermes specialises in treating "nervous fatigue" and has jacuzzis, aquagym, hammam and numerous treatments on offer. The **Centre Nautique** (May–Sept daily 10am–8pm; €4; ☎04.50.20.03.81) on avenue des Alpes, has a heated Olympic swimming pool as well as paddling pools, slides and tennis courts and, nearby, a pleasant man-made lake, with a sandy beach (open June–Aug). There's also a renowned racecourse, the **Hippodrome de Divonne**, with meetings held in July and August. In addition, Divonne makes an excellent base for hiking, cycling or exploring the nearby **Parc Natural Régional du Haut-Jura** (ⓦwww.parc-haut-jura.fr).

The helpful **tourist office** is on rue des Bains (Mon–Sat 9am–noon & 2–6pm; ☎04.50.20.01.22, ⓦwww.divonnelesbains.fr). There are plenty of **hotels** here. Most luxurious is the ✣ *Domaine de Divonne* on avenue des Thermes (☎04.50.40.34.34, ⓦwww.domainedivonne.com; ❾), which offers large, elegantly furnished rooms, several restaurants, an English-style pub and a pool, as well as a casino, theatre, cinema and golf course. Cheaper options include *Le Beau Séjour*, 9 place Perdtemps (☎04.50.20.21.82, ⓦwww.hotel-beausejour-divonne .com; ❸), which has cosy, modern rooms and a restaurant. For an excellent **meal** of fine French cuisine, try the elegant *La Terrasse* at the *Domaine de Divonne* (closed Sun; *menus* €32–79). For something simpler, *Le Café de la Paix*, 93 Grande Rue (☎04.50.20.07.02; *menus* €13–21), is a popular brasserie serving traditional cheesy dishes like fondues and *tartiflette*.

Franche-Comté

The region of **Franche-Comté** (W www.franche-comte.org), which lies to the northwest of Lake Geneva, was once ruled by the Grand Dukes of Burgundy, and annexed by France in the late seventeenth century. The four *départements* of Franche-Comté – the Territoire-de-Belfort, the Haute-Saône, the Doubs and the

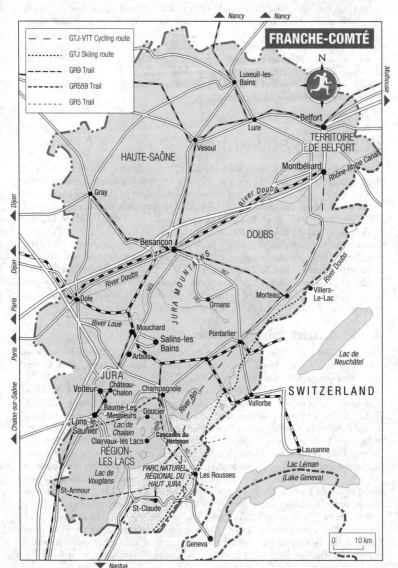

Legend:
- – – – GTJ-VTT Cycling route
- ·········· GTJ Skiing route
- – – – GR9 Trail
- – – – GR559 Trail
- – – – GR5 Trail

FRANCHE-COMTÉ

N

Nancy   Nancy

Mulhouse

Luxeuil-les-Bains

Belfort

Lure

TERRITOIRE DE BELFORT

Vesoul

HAUTE-SAÔNE

Montbéliard

Rhône-Rhine Canal

Gray

River Doubs

Besançon

DOUBS

Dijon

Dijon

Paris

Paris

River Doubs

JURA MOUNTAINS

N57

Morteau

Villers-Le-Lac

River Doubs

Dole

River Loue

Mouchard

Salins-les-Bains

Ornans

Pontarlier

Lac de Neuchâtel

Arbois

Chalon-sur-Saône

JURA

Voiteur

Château-Chalon

Champagnole

River Ain

SWITZERLAND

Baume-Les-Messieurs

Doucier

Vallorbe

Lons-le-Saunier

Lac de Chalain

Clairvaux-les Lacs

RÉGION-LES LACS

Cascades du Hérisson

Lausanne

St-Armour

Lac de Vouglans

PARC NATUREL RÉGIONAL DU HAUT JURA

Les Rousses

Lac Léman (Lake Geneva)

St-Claude

Geneva

0   10 km

Nantua

Jura are generally far more rural and less touristy than those in Rhone-Alpes. The region's capital, **Besançon**, is an attractive town built around imposing fortifications, developed by the French military engineer Vauban (see box, p.772) during the late 1600s.

Lying in the rich agricultural valley to the south of Besançon, the quiet town of **Lons-le-Saunier** provides a gateway to the Jura mountains to the east. Composed of gentle, forested slopes in the west, of more sheer crags in the east and of high-forested plateaux in between, these mountains have long been popular for cross-country sking, but the varied terrain also provides plenty of good trails for hikers. Readers should note that the official *département* of Jura in the south of Franche-Comté does not contain the whole of the mountain range commonly known as the Jura; these mountains also stretch northward into the Doubs *département* as well as into Switzerland. A particular highlight in these mountains is the **Région des Lacs**, which possesses beautiful lakes, pine forests and small farming communities as well as ski resorts. At the northern tip of the region, the historic town of **Belfort** is a rewarding destination in itself, and makes a handy base for exploring the area.

Besançon and around

The capital of Franche-Comté, **BESANÇON**, is an attractive town of handsome stone buildings that sits between the northern edge of the Jura mountains and a loop of the wide River Doubs. It is this natural defensive position that has defined the town's history. Besançon was briefly a Gallic fortress before Caesar smashed the Gauls' resistance in 58 BC. Strong outer walls were developed during the Middle Ages and the indefatigable military engineer Vauban added the still-extant Citadelle in the seventeenth century in order to guard the natural breach in the river, and a large French army presence remained in the area until well into the twentieth century. The Old Town, lying on the southern side of the Doubs, has a wealth of good museums and delightful cafés which make it a pleasure to explore. The modern town has sprawled to the north of the Doubs, and it is here that you will find the *gare SNCF* and the tourist office.

Arrival and information

The **gare SNCF** is at the end of avenue du Maréchal-Foch, a 10-minute walk to the north of the Old Town. There is an extensive **bus network**, with several major stops, including one at the *gare SNCF*. The Ginkobus office at no. 4 in the central place du 8 septembre (Mon–Sat 10am–7pm; ☎08.25.00.22.44, ⓦwww.ginkobus.com) offers information and timetables for buses departing to Ornans, Belfort or other towns in the area. The main **tourist office** is on the northern bank by the Pont de la République at place de la Première Armée Française (May–Sept Mon–Sat 10am–6pm; Oct–April closes 1pm; ☎03.81.80.92.55, ⓦwww.besancon-tourisme.com). There's a more central branch on place du 8 septembre (also open Sun 10am–1pm, same phone). **Internet access** is available at Cybercom (Mon–Thurs & Sat 10am–8pm, Fri 10am–noon & 3–8pm, Sun 2–8pm; €2 per hour) at 7b rue Battant. On the other side of the Pont de la République from the tourist office is the departure point for the **bateaux-mouches** or cruise boats (4 times daily July & Aug; €10.50), which follow the Doubs on its course around the outer limits of the town centre. The biggest **cultural event** of the year is the **Festival de Besançon**, a classical music festival which takes place in early September. The highlight is the international young conductors' competition.

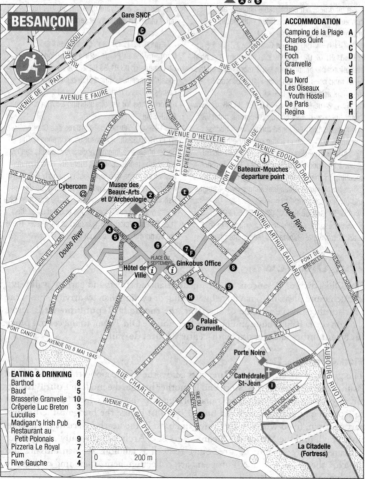

BESANÇON

N

Gare SNCF

Musee des
Beaux-Arts
et D'Archeologie

Cybercom

Bateaux-Mouches
departure point

Doubs River

Hôtel de
Ville

Ginkobus Office

PLACE DU
8 SEPTEMBRE

Palais
Granvelle

Porte Noire

Cathédrale
St-Jean

La Citadelle
(Fortress)

EATING & DRINKING
Barthod   8
Baud   5
Brasserie Granvelle   10
Crêperie Luc Breton   3
Lucullus   1
Madigan's Irish Pub   6
Restaurant au
 Petit Polonais   9
Pizzeria Le Royal   2
Pum   2
Rive Gauche   4

0   200 m

Accommodation

There's a good choice of mid-range **hotels** in the town centre, though cheaper options tend to be further out, in the "new town" or close to the train station.

Hotels

Charles Quint 3 rue du Chapitre ☎03.81.82.05.49, ⓦwww.hotel-charlesquint.com. This delightful hotel is set in an eighteenth-century building next to the Cathédrale St-Jean and close to the Citadelle, with large, comfortable rooms, a beautiful garden and a small swimming pool. Breakfast is €12. ⑤

Etap (Centre Gare) 5 av Foch ☎08.92.68.11.86, ⓦwww.etaphotel.com. Budget chain hotel offering

spacious, if rather simple, rooms with cable TV. It's also close to the *gare SNCF*. ②

Foch 7 av Foch ☎03.81.80.30.41, ⓦwww.hotel -foch-besancon.com. Another hotel close to the *gare SNCF*, *Foch* has cosy rooms (some with good views of the city) behind its rather drab concrete exterior. ③

Granvelle 13 rue du Général Lecourbe ☎03.81.81.33.92, ⓦwww.hotel-granvelle.fr. Set in a quieter corner of the Old Town, the rooms here are a bit dated, but comfortable enough, and, curiously, all windows are fitted with electric shutters rather than curtains. ❸

Ibis (Centre Ville) 21 rue Gambetta ☎03.81.81.02.02, ⓦwww.ibishotel.com. A central and affordable option, with large rooms and all the usual mod cons. Very popular with business travellers and regularly full. ❸

Du Nord 8 rue Moncey ☎03.81.81.34.56, ⓦwww.hotel-du-nord-besancon.com. A central hotel with comfortable, high-ceilinged rooms, wi-fi access and satellite TV, though it can be a little noisy. ❸

De Paris 33 rue des Granges ☎03.81.81.36.56, ⓦwww.besanconhoteldeparis.com. This former coaching inn has spacious, tastefully decorated rooms and good facilities including a gym, lounges and private car park. ❹

Regina 91 Grande-Rue ☎03.81.81.50.22, ⓦwww.besancon-regina.fr. Located right in the heart of town, the *Regina* still feels quite private,

set back in a courtyard off the road. The rooms are fairly plain but perfectly acceptable. ❸

Campsite and hostel

Camping de la Plage 12 rte du Belfort, Chalezeule ☎03.81.88.04.26, ⓦwww.laplage-besancon.com. Located 5km out of town, this campsite has a restaurant, pool and plenty of opportunities for various sporting activities. Open April–Sept.

Les Oiseaux Youth Hostel 48 rue des Cras ☎03.81.40.32.00, Ⓔfjtlesoiseaux@yahoo.fr. This hostel offers free internet access and guests can hire the nearby tennis court, but there are no communal kitchens and the free breakfast ends early (8am). It's a 15min walk from the *gare SNCF* along rue de Belfort, but difficult to find; head for the tourist office, where you can catch the #5 bus and get off at the "Les Oiseaux" stop, which is next to the hostel. There are no dorms; a double room costs €37.

The Old Town

The Old Town of Besançon, with its pedestrianized streets and narrow walkways, is much more pleasant to navigate by walking or cycling than by driving. From the tourist office on the far side of the river, the **rue de la République** leads across the pont de la République and into the heart of the Old Town, to the central **place du 8 septembre** and the sixteenth-century **Hôtel de Ville**.

The Grande-Rue

The principal street, **Grande-Rue**, cuts across the square along the line of an old Roman road. At its northwestern end is another bridge, the modern **Pont Battant**, a replacement for the original Roman bridge into the city, which (in a testament to Roman engineering) survived until 1953. Just before the bridge is the liveliest part of town, filled with inviting cafés and bars. In the nearby place de la Révolution, you'll find the **Musée des Beaux-Arts et d'Archéologie** (daily except Tues 9.30am–noon & 2–6pm; €5, free Sun). As well as fabulous Roman mosaics and bronzes there's also a fine European art collection here, including works by Rembrandt, Bronzino and Renoir.

Midway down Grande-Rue, it's clocks galore at the sixteenth-century **Palais Granvelle**, which houses the **Musée du Temps** (Wed–Sun: May–Sept 1–7pm; Oct–April 1–6pm; €5, free Sun), a museum packed with interactive exhibits on the important local clock-making industry, featuring timepieces from the seventeenth century onwards. There are also exhibitions on microtechnology and navigational instruments, and a Foucault's Pendulum. Continuing up the street, you pass place Victor-Hugo (he was born at no. 140) and arrive at the **Porte Noire**, a well-preserved Roman arch built in the second century AD in honour of Emperor Marcus Aurelius. The arch is currently undergoing long-term restoration. Beyond the arch is the eighteenth-century **Cathédrale St-Jean** (closed Tues); the principal interest here is the **Horloge Astronomique** (hourly guided visits in French; April–Sept daily except Tues 9.50–11.50am & 2.50–5.50pm; Oct–Dec & Feb–March daily except Tues & Wed same hours; €3), a remarkable astronomical clock built between 1858 and 1860 which contains some thirty thousand parts and indicates over a hundred terrestrial and celestial positions.

The Citadelle

The spectacular **citadelle** (daily: April–June & Sept–Oct 9am–6pm; July & Aug 9am–7pm; Nov–March 10am–5pm; Nov & Dec closed Tues; €8.20) is a steep fifteen-minute climb from the cathedral, and this higher ground offers a superb view of the Old Town. The citadelle itself is well-preserved and you can spend a fascinating hour or so exploring the walls, turrets and ditches that Vauban left as traps for any potential assailants. There are also several museums worth visiting, all of which have the same opening hours as the citadelle. The **Musée d'Histoire Naturelle** contains an aquarium, insectarium and zoo, while the **Musée Comtois** has collections of pottery, furniture and puppets. Best of all, however, is the **Musée de la Résistance et de la Déportation**, which details the activities of the wartime Resistance movement, both locally and throughout France. English audio commentary (€2.20) is available.

Eating, drinking and entertainment

While the Old Town doesn't have the wildest nightlife, you'll find plenty of popular **bars, cafés and restaurants** catering to all tastes and budgets.

Restaurants

Barthod 20–24 rue Bersot ☎03.81.82.27.14. With a classy wine shop at the entrance, the *Barthod* is a refined spot. There's an extensive wine list and some delicious steak and duck main courses to enjoy on the quiet inner terrace. *Menus* €20–58. Closed Sun & Mon.

Brasserie Granvelle Place Granvelle ☎03.81.81.05.60. Set in a shady little park with outdoor seating, the *Granvelle* is an agreeable spot to sit with a glass of wine or enjoy the simple *plats du jour* (€8.80) or pizzas (€11). Daily 8am–11pm.

Lucullus 46 rue Battant ☎03.81.81.57.45. Just over the Pont Battant in the "new town", *Lucullus* offers an interesting menu of local specialities such as chicken cooked in *Marc du Jura* wine (€16) and *cassolette d'escargots* (€10). *Menus* €16–35. Closed Tues eve & Wed & Sat lunchtime.

Restaurant au Petit Polonais 81 rue des Granges ☎03.81.81.23.67. Founded in 1870, this restaurant provides a small but tasty range of standard brasserie-type fare, such as hamburger and fries (€14) and quiche and salad (€8). Closed Sat eve & Sun.

Pizzeria Le Royal 33 rue des Granges ☎03.81.82.22.23. There's a large menu of pizzas (from €8) to choose from at this little place with outdoor seating, as well as pasta dishes from €7.50. Closed Sun.

Pum 1 rue Jean Petit ☎03.81.81.18.47. Great-value Thai restaurant with friendly service and tasty meat and vegetarian dishes. The vegetable green or red curry (€7.50 + €1 for choice of additional chicken, beef or pork) is particularly good. They also run a cookery school. Daily noon–2.30pm & 7–11.30pm.

Bars and cafés

Baud 4 Grande-Rue. This *chocolatier*-cum-café provides an irresistible array of chocolates to nibble on, as well as light meals like eggs Florentine (€9.80) and lots of teas and coffees. Closed Sun & Mon.

Crêperie Luc Breton 7 rue Luc Bretton. This stylish central crêperie provides a wide variety of *galettes* as well as plenty of sweet and savoury crêpes (€3.90–9.60). Closed Sun.

Madigan's Irish Pub 17 place du 8 septembre. A vast range of French and international beers is served at this lively pub (50cl around €5) – the knowledgeable waiters are able to reel off the brews of the moment.

Rive Gauche 2 quai Vauban. This sociable riverside café with outdoor seating is a popular place for locals to gather over an evening aperitif or a cold beer on a hot day. They also serve light meals like salads (€8–12). Closed Sun & Mon.

Ornans and the valley of the Loue

Lying around 10km to the southeast of Besançon, **ORNANS** looks like the typical picture-postcard Franche-Comté village. The town is best appreciated from its numerous footbridges, where you can watch the river Loue as it flows by the medieval balconied houses. The sixteenth-century **Église St-Laurent** was the subject of many paintings by Gustave Courbet, who was born here in 1819, and his old house is now the **Musée de la Maison Natale de Gustave Courbet**. The museum, housing a large collection of his paintings, sculptures and drawings, is currently under renovation and due to reopen in 2011.

Ornans is the main base for tourists looking to explore the beautiful **valley of the Loue**. The source of the river is a spring that lies a couple of kilometres above the village, and from this source you can continue on foot down the valley, a popular summer walking route past densely wooded limestone cliffs and pretty villages. Ornans' **tourist office** is at 7 rue Pierre-Vernier (April–June, Sept, Oct & school hols Mon–Sat 9.30am–noon & 2–6pm; July & Aug Mon–Sat 9am–12.30pm & 1.30-6pm, Sun 10am–noon & 2–4pm; Nov–March Mon–Fri 9.30am–noon & 2.30–5.30pm; ☎03.81.62.21.50, ⓦwww.valleedelaloue.com). There are a few good **hotels** in Ornans. The central three-star *Hôtel de France*, 51 rue Pierre-Vernier (☎03.81.62.24.44, ⓦwww.hoteldefrance-ornans.com; ❺), occupies the site of a sixteenth-century coaching inn, and provides stylish modern rooms and a pleasant garden. The *Hôtel-Restaurant La Table de Gustave*, at 11 rue Jacques-Gervais (☎03.81.62.16.79, ⓦwww.latabledegustave.com; ❸), is on the eastern side of the town centre; the rooms here are simpler, but still comfortable. There's a four-star **campsite**, *Le Chanet*, a couple of kilometres to the west of the town in a wooded park at 9 chemin le Chanet (☎03.81.62.23.44, ⓦwww.lechanet.com; open March–Oct), where you'll find a swimming pool, snack bar and shop.

If you're on the lookout for **places to eat**, note that both the hotels mentioned above have good restaurants serving traditional regional cuisine, with *menus* from €20. The *Pizzeria Le Chavot*, on 24 rue Pierre-Vernier (☎03.81.62.25.23), is a cheap and friendly restaurant with a terrace overlooking the river, serving home-made pizzas (€7–10).

Lons-le-Saunier and around

The origins of the sleepy little spa town and departmental capital of **LONS-LE-SAUNIER** date back to Roman times, although most of the town was destroyed by a fire in the early seventeenth century, and much of the old town you see today dates mainly from the 1700s. Lons was once a major, and very prosperous, centre for winemaking and salt production, and the legacy of this era can still be seen in the grand townhouses and public buildings. These days it's a rather quiet place, but there's a handful of sights worth spending a lazy afternoon looking over.

The central **place de la Liberté** is a good place to start your tour of the town. The **theatre clock** at the eastern end (silenced for repairs until 2012) chimes a familiar half-dozen notes from *La Marseillaise* to honour Lons' most famous citizen, Rouget de Lisle; he composed the anthem during his time as a campaigner in the French revolutionary army during the early 1790s. Running north from the square is the colonnaded thoroughfare of **rue du Commerce**, where you'll find some of Lons' oldest buildings. No. 24 on this street is the house where de Lisle was born; now the **Musée Rouget de Lisle** (July & Aug: Mon–Fri 10am–noon & 2–6pm, Sat & Sun 2–5pm; €1), it's mainly of interest for its fine eighteenth-century interior and furnishings.

At the northern end of rue du Commerce, in place Philibert de Chalon, stands the **Musée des Beaux Arts** (Tues–Fri 2–5pm, Sat & Sun 2–6pm; €2), which houses a collection of nineteenth-century sculptures, including those of the local artist Jean-Joseph Perraud. Spreadable cheese enthusiasts might be tempted to continue north to **La Maison de la Vache qui Rit** at 25 rue Richebourg

(April–June & Sept–Oct Tues–Fri 2–6pm, Sat & Sun 10am–6pm; July & Aug daily 10am–7pm; Dec & Feb–March Sat & Sun 10am–6pm; €7), a multimedia museum dedicated to the locally produced Laughing Cow cheese. Returning south along rue Richebourg to avenue Jean-Moulin, you'll come to a statue of de Lisle himself. It was created by Frédéric Bartholdi, the man who designed New York's Statue of Liberty.

A left turn here leads to the peaceful, tree-lined **Parc Édouard Guenon**, where you'll find the delightfully ornate *fin-de-siècle* **Thermes Ledonia**, or mineral baths. The baths are now run by **Thermes Valvital** (Mon & Wed 10am–8pm, Tues & Thurs 11.30am–8pm, Fri 10am–7pm, Sat 9am–6pm, Sun 9am–2pm; spa treatments from €15; ☏03.84.24.38.18, ⊛www.valvital.fr), and have a sauna, Turkish bath and jacuzzi.

Practicalities

Lons' **gare SNCF** is a ten-minute walk south of place de la Liberté; just head straight down avenue Aristide Briand (opposite the station entrance) to get into the centre. The **tourist office** (July & Aug Mon–Sat 9am–12.30pm & 1.30–6.30pm; Sept–June Mon–Fri 9am–noon & 2–6pm, Sat 10am–noon & 2–4pm; ☏03.84.24.65.01, ⊛www.lons-le-saunier.com) is in the same building as the theatre on place du 11 novembre. The **Comité Départemental du Tourisme du Jura**, 8 rue Louis-Rousseau (Mon–Fri 9am–noon and 2–5pm; ☏03.84.87.08.76, ⊛www.jura-tourism.com), can provide information about the Jura mountains.

There are two **hotels** on the busy road right opposite the *gare SNCF*; *Au Terminus*, 37 av Aristide-Briand, (☏03.84.24.41.83, ⊛www.hotel-terminus-lons .com; ❸), has bright, modern rooms with satellite TV, while the nearby *Gambetta*, 4 bd Gambetta (☏03.84.24.41.18, ⊛www.hotel-gambetta-lons.com; ❸), is a frendly, family-run place with a similar set-up. A more central choice is the *Hôtel du Parc*, 9 av Jean Moulin (☏03.84.86.10.20, ⊛www.hotel-parc.fr; ❾), where the light, simple rooms overlook the main square, and there's a popular restaurant downstairs.

For a delicious **meal**, call by *La Comédie*, 65 place de la Comédie (☏03.84.24.20.66; closed Sun & Mon; *menus* €18–28); dishes include roast rabbit, lamb and fish. For cheaper meals, including vegetarian options, try *L'Arc-en-ciel*, located opposite the Musée des Beaux Arts at 1 place Philibert de Chalon (☏03.84.86.06.64; closed Sun; *menus* €15), where you can tuck into salads or hamburger and chips (both €9). For truly indulgent pastries and chocolates, don't miss *Pelen*, 1 rue Saint-Désiré (☏03.84.24.31.39; *menus* €18–28), which in addition to the ground-floor chocolate shop (cakes around €3) has an upstairs tearoom with a short lunch *menu* including roast quail at €14.90 and salads from €11.60.

The Région des Lacs

If you drive east for 20km along the N78 road from Lons, you'll enter the **Région des Lacs**, an area of woods, pastures and lakes strung out along the valley of the River Ain. During the journey, the road begins its ascent to the peaks and gorges that define the border with Switzerland. With each bend in the climbing road, the views down to the tiny villages become all the more impressive. Some of the lakes charge parking fees during the day, but after 6pm, when the crowds and swimming supervisors have gone home, they are deserted and serenely peaceful – the perfect place for an evening picnic at sunset.

The region's main town is **CLAIRVAUX-LES-LACS**. It's near here that the River Ain flows into the northern tip of the serpentine **Lac de Vouglans**, which is dammed 25km downstream. The **Grand Lac**, just south of town, is the focus of summer resort activity, with a beach area and watersports facilities. It's calm and scenic, in spite of all the camping activity going on around it. The **Office du Tourisme du Pays des Lacs**, 36 Grande-Rue (Mon–Fri 9am–noon & 2–6pm, Sat 9am–noon; July & Aug Sat 9am–12.30pm & 2–6.30pm, also Sun 10am–noon; T 03.84.25.27.47, W www.juralacs.com), is the place to find information about the region and outdoor activities such as boat and bike rental and the 46 **hiking** routes in the area. There's a good-value **hotel** on the Grand Lac, *La Chaumière du Lac* (T 03.84.25.81.52, W www.juralacs.com/adherents/lachaumiere; open April– Sept; ❸), which provides simple rooms, plus a restaurant serving local fish and cheese (*menus* €15–35).

Lac de Chalain and the Cascades du Hérisson

Some 16km north of Clairvaux, near the village of **DOUCIER** and surrounded by hills, **Lac de Chalain** is a much more impressive setting. It's also a very popular spot for **camping**, hence the prices can be high. Of the **campsites** by the lake, *Le Grand Lac* (T 03.84.25.26.19, W www.odesiajura.com; open June to early Sept; up to €23 for a two-person tent, €85 for a four-person chalet), located on the lake at 52 rue du Langard, offers the best combination of good facilities (including a pool and snack bar) and value for money. Run by the same company, the nearby campsite *Le Fayolan* (same contact details; open May to mid-Sept) is pricier, but provides a sauna, three pools and disco, as well as more sporting activities and a restaurant.

One reason this area is so popular with campers is its proximity to the **Cascades du Hérisson**, the septet of waterfalls that has become one of the Jura's best-known natural spectacles. If you are **driving**, you can reach the main car park for the Cascades by passing through Val-Dessous, a village just to the southeast of Doucier, and then heading for the Parking de l'Éventail. A well-signposted path takes you from the car park to the highest of the falls, which descend a breath-taking 255m over just 7km. A gentle walk of around ten minutes from the car park leads to the prettiest of the falls, the **Éventail**. If you continue upstream, you'll arrive at the **Grand Saut** fall, where the water plummets down a sheer drop of some sixty metres. If you follow the pathway behind the waterfall, you can ascend a steep trail as it leads past several smaller springs as well as a drinks kiosk; from here another path leads south to the village of Bonlieu. Finally, the path ends at the uppermost fall, which is known as **Saut Girard**, close to the village of **ILAY**. In all, the walk should take around three hours for reasonably fit walkers. There's a choice of restaurants in Ilay, but only one **hotel**, the *Auberge du Hérisson*, 5 route des Lacs (T 03.84.25.58.18, W www.herisson.com; closed Nov–Jan; ❸; restaurant *menus* €15–40), where you can expect fairly simple but cosy rooms.

Les Rousses

A couple of kilometres before the frontier with Switzerland is the ski resort of **LES ROUSSES**; this is an outstanding area for cross-country skiing (see box opposite). Les Rousses is also very handy for hikers looking to explore the **Parc Naturel Régional du Haut-Jura** (W www.parc-haut-jura.fr), the regional park which runs south from Champagnole across the southern Jura mountains. There are several **GR** footpaths which can be accessed from Les Rousses. **GR9** passes through here as it moves along the crest of the ridge towards the Col de la Faucille; the **GR559**, a route which takes you on a tour of the lakes of Franche-Comté, begins here and ends in Lons-le-Saunier; even the much longer **GR5** passes within a few kilometres of the resort.

The **tourist office**, 495 rue Pasteur (T 03.84.60.04.31, W www.lesrousses.com), can provide information on the local skiing conditions. The ESF is also based in

13

Cross-country skiing and mountain biking in Franche-Comté

The high plateaux of the Jura mountains guarantee good snow cover in winter, but they also lack the steep gradients of the Alpine peaks further to the south; it is this high but level terrain which has made the Jura into France's most popular destination for **cross-country skiing**, or *ski de fond*. The goal of any superfit *fondeur* is the 175km **Grande Traversée du Jura** (GTJ), which crosses the high plateau from Villers-le-Lac to Giron, a town in the south of the Parc Naturel Régional du Haut-Jura.

The same gentle topography and established infrastructure that enable cross-country skiing have made this region an ideal high-summer venue for **mountain biking**, with hundreds of waymarked cross-country skiing pistes used out of season as trails for adventurous mountain bikers. The 360km **GTJ–VTT**, which starts near Montbéliard (just to the south of Belfort), has become the greatest long-distance biking challenge in the area. Many people cycle on the road; there aren't many cars, so if you can handle the hills, then go for it.

The headquarters of the departmental tourist board, the **Comité Départemental du Tourisme du Jura** in Lons-le-Saunier (℡03.84.87.08.76, ⓦwww.jura-tourism .com) can supply plenty of information, maps and literature (in English as well as French) on outdoor leisure opportunities of all kinds in the Jura.

---

the tourist office (℡03.84.60.01.61); their ski instructors organize lessons focusing specifically on cross-country skiing techniques.

There are plenty of **hotels** in Les Rousses: *La Ferme du Père François*, 214 rue Pasteur (℡03.84.60.34.62, ⓦwww.perefrancois.fr; ❺), offers smart rooms featuring lots of pine, and a very good restaurant in the centre; *Hôtel du Village*, just down the road at 344 rue Pasteur (℡03.84.34.12.75, ⓦwww.hotelvillage.fr; ❸), is a cheaper but perfectly comfortable option. To the east of the village and close to the ski slopes is *Le Chamois*, 230 montée le Noirmont (℡03.84.60.01.48, ⓦwww.lechamois.org; ❸), which has spacious rooms with all mod cons. At Le Bief-de-la-Chaille, 3.5km outside Les Rousses, is a **HI hostel** located in an old farmhouse by a stream (℡03.84.60.02.80, ⓔles-rousses@fuaj.org; open late Dec to March & mid-May to mid-Sept; dorm beds €18.50, with breakfast).

Many hotels in Les Rousses have restaurants and offer half- and full-board deals. For good local cuisine featuring local trout, ham and cheeses, try the restaurant at the *Hôtel Le Mont Saint-Jean*, 276 rte du Mont Saint-Jean (℡03.84.60.33.21, ⓦwww.lemontsaintjean.fr; closed first half of Dec; *menus* €23–39). There are also plenty of cafés and pizzerias in the town.

Château-Chalon and Poligny

10km to the north of Lons on the N83 road towards Besançon, the route known locally as the **Route des Vins du Jura**, you come to a turn-off on the D120 for **Voiteur**. This is an unremarkable provincial town, but just beyond it is one of the prettiest villages in Franche-Comté. **CHÂTEAU-CHALON** is a delight to wander around, with a beautiful church, the twelfth-century **Église Saint-Pierre**, and a medieval keep, which is all that remains of the grand Benedictine Abbey which once stood here. As well as holding a stunning position on top of a high rocky outcrop, the village is also noted for the unique variety of *vin jaune*, and there are several vineyards operating around the town. A good choice if you want to sample a range of local and regional wines is the vineyard of Jean Berthet-Bondet on the rue de la Tour (contact the vineyard to organize a tour; ℡03.84.44.60.48, ⓦwww.berthet-bondet.net), which offers tasting sessions. The **tourist office** in Voiteur, place de la Mairie (Sept–June Mon–Fri

⑬

9.30am–12.30pm, July & Aug Mon–Sat 9.30am–12.30pm & 2–6pm; ☎03.84.44.62.47, ⓦwww.hauteseille.com), can provide the latest details about the wine cellars and local accommodation options. *La Maison d'Eusébia* (☎03.84.44.92.10, ⓦwww.eusebia.fr; ❻), for example, provides comfortable rooms in the village, along with a superb restaurant serving creative local and seasonal food (*menus* €28.50–52).

Around 10km further along the N83 road, you reach the attractive little town of **POLIGNY**, at the southern end of the Culée de Vaux valley. The town is worth a stop for its medieval churches, as well as for the **Maison du Comté** (hourly guided tours; April–June & Sept–Oct Tues–Sun 2.30–4.30pm; July & Aug daily 10–11.30am & 2–5.30pm; €4; ☎03.84.37.78.40) on avenue de la Résistance. This old *fromagerie* is now the headquarters of the Comité Interprofessional du Gruyère du Comté, France's favourite cheese, and it includes an information centre with films, displays and tasting sessions.

A great **place to stay** locally is the *Hôtel de la Vallée Heureuse*, route de Genève (☎03.84.37.12.13, ⓦwww.hotelvalleeheureuse.com; ❺), located around 800m east of town in a lovely old converted mill with a pool, sauna and restaurant.

Arbois

Serious wine-lovers should head for **ARBOIS**, 10km to the north of Poligny. Wine emporia line the central place de la Liberté, all of which entreat you to sample the unusual local reds, whites and rosés in the shop windows. Of these local wines, the sweet *vin de paille* is the rarest; the name derives from its grapes, which are dried on beds of straw during the production process, thus giving the wine a strong aftertaste.

A few kilometres south of town on the D469 is the Château Pécauld, where you'll find the **Musée de la Vigne et du Vin** (March–June, Sept & Oct daily except Tues 10am–noon & 2–6pm; July & Aug daily 10am–noon & 2–6pm; Nov–Feb daily except Tues 2–6pm; €3.50; ☎03.84.66.40.45), which details the development and production of wine in the Jura. The château also has wine-tasting sessions, which must be booked in advance (☎03.84.66.40.53, ⓦwww.chateaupecauld.com).

The **tourist office** is at 17 rue de l'Hôtel de Ville (July & Aug Mon–Sat 9am–12.30pm & 2–6.30pm, Sun 10am–noon & 2–5pm; Sept–June Mon 3–6pm, Tues–Sat 9am–noon & 2–6pm; ☎03.84.66.55.50, ⓦwww.arbois.com); staff can provide details of vineyards in the area that offer tasting sessions of local wine.

If you're **staying** overnight, the three-star *Hôtel Jean-Paul Jeunet*, 9 rue de l'Hôtel de Ville (☎03.84.66.05.67; ⓦwww.jeanpauljeunet.com; ❼), offers the fanciest rooms, but if you'd prefer something cheaper, the *Hôtel Les Messageries*, 2 rue de Courcelles (☎03.84.66.15.45, ⓦwww.hoteldesmessageries.com; ❸), located in an old stone townhouse full of character, is a good choice. The **municipal campsite**, *Les Vignes*, on avenue du Général-Leclerc (☎03.84.25.26.19, ⓦwww.odesiajura.com; open May–Sept), is 1km east of the centre and has a grocery store, snack bar and swimming pool.

Of the **restaurants** in town, an excellent choice is *Les Caudalies*, 20 av Pasteur (☎03.84.73.06.54; closed Mon July & Aug, closed Mon & Tues Sept–June; *menus* €18–72), which serves delicious traditional cuisine in elegant surroundings. Another good option is *La Balance Mets et Vins*, 47 rue de Courcelles (☎03.84.37.45.00; closed Tues & Wed; *menus* €19.50–55), offering many classic regional specialities and an extensive list of local wines.

Belfort and around

Nestled in the gap between two mountain ranges – the Vosges to the north and the Jura to the south – lies **BELFORT**, a town assured of a place in French hearts for its history as an insurmountable stronghold on this obvious route for invaders. The town is remembered particularly for its long resistance to a siege during the 1870 Franco–Prussian War; it was this resistance that spared it the humiliating fate of being annexed into the German empire, a fate suffered by much of neighbouring Alsace-Lorraine. The commanding officer at the time was one Colonel Denfert-Rochereau (known popularly as the "Lion of Belfort"), who earned himself the honour of numerous street names throughout the country, as well as that of a Parisian square and métro station.

Arrival, information and accommodation

The **gare SNCF** and departure point for local **buses** is at the end of Faubourg-de-France, the main shopping street in the new town. The **tourist office** (Mon–Sat 9am–12.30pm & 2–6.30pm, mid-June to mid-Sept also Sun 10am–1pm; ☏03.84.55.90.90, ⓦwww.ot-belfort.fr) is at 2 rue Clemenceau. To reach the tourist office from the *gare SNCF*, walk for ten minutes down Faubourg-de-France as far as the river, then turn left and walk along quai Charles-Vallet until you reach rue Clemenceau. Free **internet access** is available at the tourist office.

There's an excellent choice of **hotels** in Belfort, but watch out for Eurockéennes (see p.810) and the other music festivals that take place here; these events make beds very difficult to find. Prices can vary, and many hotels offer much-reduced rates at weekends.

ATRIA Novotel Av de l'Espérance ☏03.84.58.85.00, ⓦwww.novotel.com. On the northern edge of the Old Town, this large three-star hotel in a stylish glass and steel building offers excellent facilities and there's a gym and restaurant on site. ❽

Boreal 2 rue du Comte de la Suze ☏03.84.22.32.32, ⓦwww.hotelboreal.com. This new-town hotel offers large, airy rooms in a quiet location, and is a popular stopover with business travellers. ❻

Camping International de l'Étang des Forges Rue du Général-Béthouart ☏03.84.22.54.92, ⓦwww.camping-belfort.com. The best local campsite, a few km north of the Old Town; here you'll find a grocery store, swimming pool, volleyball court and snack bar. Open April–Sept.

Grand Hôtel du Tonneau d'Or 1 rue Général Reiset ☏03.84.58.57.56, ⓦwww.tonneaudor.fr. Housed in an impressive building dating from 1902, the *Grand* provides spacious and pleasingly modern rooms. ❼

Kyriad 55 faubourg de Montbéliard ☏03.84.22.46.76, ⓦwww.hotel-kyriad-belfort.fr. Bright new chain hotel not far from the railway station, with weekend rates from €49. ❹

Saint-Christophe Place d'Armes ☏03.84.55.88.88, ⓦwww.hotelsaintchristophe.com. At the heart of the Old Town, the *Saint-Christophe* has neat, attractive rooms in a historic building with restaurant. ❹

Résidence Madrid 6 rue de Madrid ☏03.84.21.39.16, ⓦwww.fuaj.org/belfort. Belfort's hostel is located 1km west of the railway line, and is open year-round. Dorm beds €14.90.

The Town

Finding your way around Belfort is easy enough. The town is sliced in two by the River Savoureuse: the **new town** to the west is the commercial hub; lying beneath the impressive edifice of the red **Citadelle** on the eastern side is the quieter **Old Town**. This fortress was built by Vauban on the site of a medieval keep, of which only a single tower to the north of the castle remains. There are excellent views of Belfort's Old Town and of the surrounding countryside from up here. Vauban was also responsible for a new set of fortifications surrounding Belfort, and from the

Eurockéennes

First staged in 1989, today Eurockéennes is one of France's biggest and most diverse annual rock festivals, attracting top international artists as well as plenty of up-and-coming French acts. The three-day festival takes place over the first weekend in July in a lovely setting on the shores of the Lac du Malsaucy, 6km northeast of Belfort, and the vibe is suitably relaxed and friendly, despite crowds of 100,000 or more. Featured acts in 2010 included Mika, Massive Attack, Jay-Z, Charlotte Gainsbourg and The Hives. There's a free campsite nearby with 12,000 spaces for those who want the full rock festival experience. See ⓦ www.eurockeennes.fr for information.

castle you can see how these moulded the Old Town into a pentagonal shape. The street plan is still largely unchanged.

The Citadelle now houses the **Musée d'Histoire** (daily except Tues: April–May 10am–noon & 2–6pm; June–Sept 10am–6pm; Oct–March 10am–noon and 2–5pm; €2). The museum displays exhibits on the town's military history, as well as many Bronze and Iron Age artefacts.

Art lovers should head to the new **Musée des Beaux-Arts** (same times as Musée d'Histoire; €2), located in Tour 41 in the lower part of the fortifications on rue Pompidou, where paintings by the likes of Dürer and Doré and sculptures by Rodin and Carrière are on display. Also worth a visit is the **Donation Maurice Jardot** (same times; €2), on the northern edge of the new town at 8 rue de Mulhouse. It was founded at the behest of Maurice Jardot, an associate of Daniel-Henry Kahnweiler, one of the most noted art dealers of the twentieth century; when Jardot died in 1997, he left 150 works of art to the town, including some by Chagall, Braque and Picasso.

The most famous monument in town is an 11m-high red sandstone **lion** carved out of the rock face, which you pass on the way up to the castle. It was designed by Frédéric Bartholdi, of Statue of Liberty fame, as a monument to commemorate the 1870 siege, and was completed in 1880.

Belfort becomes a hotspot for **rock music** fans on the first weekend of July each year, when the **Eurockéennes** festival takes place at the nearby Malsaucy lake (see box above). Bargain hunters can visit the lively **flea market** (featuring over two hundred local artisans and antique-dealers) which takes place in the Old Town on the first Sunday of every month between March and December.

Eating and drinking

A good **dining** choice is the *Molière*, 6 rue de l'Etuve (ⓣ 03.84.21.86.38; closed Wed; mains from €19, *menus* €22–70), where you can enjoy some delicious, if pricey, local specialities. If your budget doesn't stretch that far, *Pizzeria La Marina*, opposite the station at 5 av Wilson (ⓣ 03.84.22.40.24; closed Sun), provides freshly made pizzas at reasonable prices (€9–12), while the central branch of the popular budget buffet chain *Flunch*, 18 Faubourg-de-France (ⓣ 03.84.21.54.55), offers the usual range of good-value dishes from around €6, with a free all-you-can-eat vegetable and salad bar.

Belfort has a good choice of **bars and cafés** dotted all around town. *Finnegans*, close to the river at 6 bd Carnot, is an ever-busy Irish pub, with lots of beers on tap (€3 for 25cl). *Café du Commerce*, 6 Faubourg-de-France, is the best place in town to sit down with a coffee (€2) and watch the world go by on the main pedestrian street. For a sweet treat, ⚘ *Jacques Belin Chocolatier* at 18 rue Metzger (closed Sun) offers a tempting array of handmade chocolates, including edible replicas of the nearby lion monument (€12).

Montbéliard

Just 16km south of Belfort, **MONTBÉLIARD**, which sits on the Rhône-Rhine Canal, was only incorporated into France in 1793, after centuries of rule by the German Dukes of Württemberg. Their palatial home, the **Château des Ducs de Wurtemberg** perched above rue du Château (daily except Tues 10am–noon & 2–6pm; €2), still dominates the town centre, and today houses a wide-ranging museum with exhibits on Gallo-Roman archaeology, natural history and art, as well as a room dedicated to the Montbéliard-born founder of palaeontology, Georges Cuvier.

Also worth a look is the **Musée d'Art et d'Histoire**, place Saint-Martin (daily except Tues 10am–noon & 2–6pm; €2), which houses displays of eighteenth- and nineteenth-century furniture, toys, textiles and silverware. Most interesting are the locally made music boxes and automata on the top floor. The attractive Parc de Prés-la-Rose, spread over an island between the River Allan and the canal, is a great place for kids, with play areas, outdoor scientific experiments and giant insect statues, and there are hands-on exhibits, including an earthquake simulator, at **Le Pavillon des Sciences** (April–June Mon, Tues, Thurs & Fri 9am–noon & 2–6pm, Wed 10am–noon & 2–6pm, Sat & Sun 2–6pm; July & Aug Mon–Fri 10am–7pm, Sat & Sun 2–7pm; rest of year opening times vary; ☎03.81.91.46.83; €4.50). Anyone interested in Montbéliard's car-making heritage should head north of the centre to the **Musée de l'Aventure Peugeot** at Carrefour de l'Europe in the Sochaux district (daily 10am–6pm; €7), where you can cast an appraising eye over a host of gleaming vintage motors dating from the early 1900s onwards.

Montbéliard's **gare SNCF** is off avenue des Alliés, on the northeastern edge of the town centre, not far from the **tourist office** at 1 rue Henri Mouhot (mid-June to mid-Sept Mon 1.30–7pm, Tues–Fri 9am–noon & 1.30–7pm, Sat 9am–noon & 1.30–6pm; mid-Sept to mid-June Mon 1.30–6pm, Tues–Sat 9am–noon & 1.30–6pm; ☎03.81.94.45.60, ⓦwww.ot-pays-de-montbeliard.fr).

Belfort is richer in **accommodation** options, but there are a couple of places to stay in town. The central *La Balance*, 40 rue de Belfort (☎03.81.96.77.41, ⓦwww.hotel-la-balance.com; ❹), has smart modern rooms in an historic building, while the *Hôtel de France*, 40 rte d'Audincourt (☎03.81.90.21.48, ⓦwww.hoteldefrance-montbeliard.com; ❹), has cosy rooms near the canal and the Parc de Prés-la-Rose. A good **restaurant** choice is *Malak*, 3 rue Saint-Martin (☎03.81.96.81.38; *menus* €15–30), where you can sample authentic Lebanese cuisine and wines, while *Ganesh*, 9 rue de l'Etuve (☎03.81.91.35.28; *menus* €13–20), serves tasty Indian curries, including vegetarian options. If you're just after a snack, *Le Doubs Bretzel*, 31 rue des Febvres (Mon–Sat 7.30am–7pm), sells a good range of sandwiches (€2.90–4) and cakes.

Travel details

Trains

Annecy to: Aix-les-Bains (frequent; 30min); Chambéry (frequent; 45min); Chamonix via St-Gervais (3 daily; 3hr); Grenoble (hourly; 2hr); Lyon (hourly; 2hr); Paris-Lyon (several daily; 4hr).

Annemasse, near Geneva to: Annecy (several daily; 1hr); Évian (frequent; 45min); Paris-Lyon via Bellegarde (4 daily; 4hr).

Belfort to: Besançon (every hour; 1hr 15min); Montbéliard (frequent; 15min); Mulhouse (8 daily; 30min); Paris-Est (5 daily; 4hr); Strasbourg (3 daily; 2hr).

13

Besançon to: Bourg-en-Bresse (4 daily; 1hr 30min); Dijon (several daily; 1hr); Paris-Lyon (5 daily; 2hr 30min).

Briançon to: Embrun (6 daily; 45min); Gap (6 daily; 1hr 25min); Grenoble (2 daily; 4hr); Marseille (4 daily; 5hr 30min).

Chambéry to: Aix-les-Bains (frequent; 15min); Annecy (frequent; 45min); Bourg-St-Maurice (several daily; 2hr); Geneva (3 daily; 1hr 30min); Grenoble (frequent; 45min); Lyon (frequent; 1hr 30min); Paris-Lyon (several daily; 3hr).

Évian to: Annecy via Annemasse (several daily; 2hr); Geneva via Annemasse (several daily; 1hr); Thonon-les-Bains (frequent; 10min).

Grenoble to: Annecy (hourly; 2hr); Briançon, changing at Gap (6 daily; 4hr 20min); Chambéry (hourly; 1hr); Lyon (frequent; 1hr 30min); Paris-Lyon (several daily; 3hr).

Lons-le-Saunier to: Annecy via Lyon (5 daily; 3hr 30min); Belfort via Besançon (several daily; 3hr); Besançon (frequent; 1hr); Geneva via Bourg-en-Bresse (3 daily; 2hr 30min); Paris-Lyon via Bourg-en-Bresse (4 daily; 3hr).

Buses

Annecy to: Geneva (2 daily; 1hr 15min); Lyon (5 daily; 2hr).

Besançon to: Ornans (3 daily; 40min).

Bourg-St-Maurice to: Aosta, Italy (1 daily in July & Aug; 2hr 30min); Les Arcs (5 on Sat only in July & Aug; 1hr); Tignes (2–3 daily; 1hr 15min); Val d'Isère (2–3 daily; 45min).

Briançon to: Col du Lautaret (3 daily; 50min); Gap (8 daily; 1hr 45min); La Grave (3 daily; 1hr 10min); Marseille (2 daily; 5–6hr); Le Monêtier-les-Bains (3 daily; 45min); St-Véran via Guillestre (1–2 daily; 1hr 40min); Vallouise via Argentière (1 daily; 2hr).

Chambéry to: Méribel, via Moutiers, depart from the airport (2 daily; 1hr).

Chamonix to: Geneva (2 daily; 2hr); other resorts in the Chamonix-Mont Blanc area: Argentière (12 daily; 20min); Les Houches (frequent; 20min).

Grenoble to: L'Alpe d'Huez (1–2 daily; 40min); Le Bourg-d'Oisans (7 daily; 1hr); Briançon (3 daily; 2hr 40min); Chambéry (13 daily; 2hr); Col du Lautaret (3 daily; 1hr 50min); La Grave (3 daily; 1hr 30min); Le Monêtier-les-Bains (3 daily; 2hr 10min); St-Pierre-de-Chartreuse (7 daily; 1hr 10min); Villard-de-Lans and other towns in the Vercors (6 daily; 1hr).

Thonon-les-Bains to: Évian (several daily; 25min); Yvoire (3–4 daily; 20min).

The Rhône valley

CHAPTER 14 # Highlights

✻ **Traboules** Follow in the footsteps of the plucky Resistance fighters, and explore Lyon's dark and winding *traboules*, hidden away behind hulking doorways. **See box, p.823**

✻ **Lyon's bouchons** Meat-lovers will be in heaven in the city famous for its earthy *bouchons* and award-winning chefs. **See p.826**

✻ **Pérouges** A short distance from Lyon, this is an impeccably preserved medieval hill-top village made up of sunkissed cobbled lanes and quaint houses. **See p.829**

✻ **Musée Internationale de la Chaussure** Fascinating historical museum in Romans-sur-Isère, displaying the world's wackiest designs in footwear – from early Egyptian sandals and tiny Chinese slippers to the latest Jimmy Choos. **See p.834**

✻ **Montélimar nougat** Without doubt, the best place to gorge on the moreish bonbon made of sweet honey and crunchy nuts. **See p.836**

▲ A traditional Lyon *bouchon*

The Rhône valley

T he **Rhône valley** stretches down from the compelling city of Lyon, the second biggest city in France, to just north of Orange, in Provence. The north–south route of ancient armies, medieval traders and modern rail and road, the valley has experienced some industrialization, but this has done little to affect the verdant, vine-dotted beauty of the countryside. The River Rhône is still a means of transport, but its waters now also cool the reactors of the Marcoule and Tricastin nuclear power stations between **Montélimar** and Avignon. Following the river is of limited appeal, with the exception of the scenic stretch of **vineyards** and fruit orchards between the Roman city of **Vienne** and the distinctly southern city of **Valence**. But the big magnet is, of course, the gastronomic paradise of **Lyon**, with its sophisticated bars and restaurants.

Lyon and around

Viewed from the Autoroute du Soleil, the first impression of **LYON** is of a major confluence of rivers and roads, around which only petrochemical industries thrive. In fact, from the sixteenth century right up until the postwar dominance of metalworks and chemicals, silk was the city's main industry, generating the wealth that left behind a multitude of Renaissance buildings. But what has stamped its character most on Lyon is the commerce and banking that grew up with its industrial expansion. Today, with its eco-friendly tram system and high-tech industrial parks that are home to international companies, Lyon is a modern city *par excellence*.

Most French people find themselves here for business rather than for recreation: it's a get-up-and-go place, with an almost Swiss sense of cleanliness, order and efficiency. But as a manageable slice of urban France, Lyon certainly has its charms. Foremost among these is **gastronomy**; there are more restaurants per Gothic and Renaissance square metre of the old town than anywhere else on earth, and the city could form a football team with its superstars of the international chef circuit. While the **textile museum** is the second famous reason for stopping here, Lyon's nightlife, cinema and theatre (including the famous Lyonnais puppets), its antique markets, music and other cultural festivities might tempt you to stay at least a few days. As if that weren't enough, Lyon's distinctive older quarters and its winding, secret *traboules* are an urban explorer's paradise.

Lyon is organized into nine arrondissements. A visit to the city will take you into the Presqu'île (1er and 2^e arrondissements), the area between the rivers Saône and Rhône, and you're likely to spend some time in Vieux Lyon (5^e) on the west bank of the Saône, as well as the east bank of the Rhône (3e), including the modern development known as La Part-Dieu.

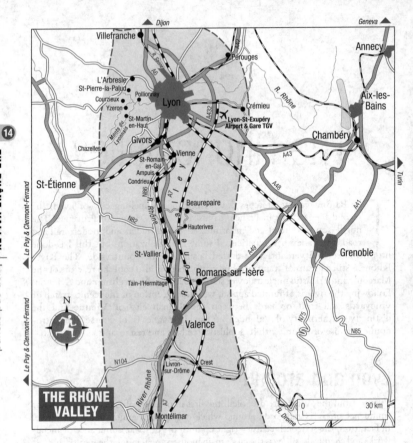

Arrival, information and city transport

The **Lyon-St-Exupéry international airport** (☎08.26.80.08.26, ⓦwww.lyon
.aeroport.fr) and its **TGV station** are off the Grenoble autoroute, 25km to the
southeast of the city, with a thirty-minute Rhône Express bus link to Part-Dieu
train station in the town centre (every 20min 6am–11.40pm; €8.60).

Central Lyon has two train stations: the **Gare de Perrache** on the Presqu'île is
used mainly for ordinary trains rather than TGVs, and has the bus station (**gare
routière**) alongside; and **Part-Dieu TGV station** is in the 3ᵉ arrondissement to
the east of the Presqu'île. Some TGV trains from Paris give the option of getting
off at either station; ask when buying your ticket. Central Lyon is linked to the
suburbs by an efficient **métro**, as well as trolleybuses and a slick **tram** system.

There's a **Bureau d'Information** in the Centre Perrache at the station (Mon–Fri
7.30am–6.30pm, Sat 9am–noon & 1.45–5pm; ⓦwww.tcl.fr), where you can pick
up a métro, tram, bus and funicular map; or it's just two stops on the métro to
place Bellecour, where the **central tourist office** stands on the southeast corner
(daily 9am–6pm; ☎04.72.77.69.69, ⓦwww.lyon-france.com). The tourist office
organizes and sells tickets for a number of **guided tours** that focus on different
aspects of the city; the silk tour, for example, explores the Croix-Rousse, where
many silk workers used to live, before visiting a silk-printing workshop; another

Lyon City Card and Discovery Weekend

The **Lyon City Card** (€19, €29 or €39 for one, two or three days) grants unlimited access to the metro, bus and tramway, nineteen museums (including the Roman ruins in St-Romain-en-Gal), guided city tours and several short boat trips. The card is available from the tourist office and the major TCL (public transit) offices.

The **Discovery Weekend** (from €150 per person) includes two nights in a two-, three- or four-star hotel, the City Card, and lunch at a local *bouchon*. The package is available online through the tourist office website.

tour delves into the complex web of Lyon's famous *traboules*. Tours last either 1 hour 30 minutes or 2 hours and cost €9–12, depending on duration and theme.

At métro stations or the city transport (TCL) offices, the cheapest way to buy **tickets** is in a carnet of ten (€12.80), or there's the *Ticket Liberté*, valid for one day (€4.70). Tickets on any form of transport (€1.60) are valid for one hour but limited to a single one-way journey with changes allowed. The métro runs 5am–12.15am, but some bus lines terminate as early as 8pm.

Accommodation

As a result of Lyon's commercial pre-eminence, hotel **rooms** can sometimes be hard to find, particularly on weekdays. If you're stuck, the tourist office offers a reservation service, though you'll have to stump up your deposit then and there.

If you're on a real budget, stop by the CROUS offices, 59 rue de la Madeleine, 7ᵉ (℡ 04.72.80.17.70, ⓦ www.crous-lyon.fr; Mᵒ Jean-Macé), or CRIJ offices, 10 quai Jean Moulin, 2ᵉ (℡ 04.72.77.00.66; Mᵒ Bellecour), which may be able to fix you up in student lodgings or residences closer to the centre during vacation time.

Hotels

Alexandra 49 rue Victor-Hugo, 2ᵉ ℡ 04.78.37.75.79, ⓦ www.hotel-alexandra-lyon.fr; Mᵒ Ampère Victor-Hugo. Comfortable well-run hotel overlooking place Ampère, a lively pedestrian zone. Parking available. ❹

Des Artistes 8 rue Gaspard-André, 2ᵉ ℡ 04.78.42.04.88, ⓦ www.hotel-des-artistes.fr; Mᵒ Bellecour. Smart hotel situated on the lovely Place des Célestins. Bathrooms are sparklingly clean, the beds are comfortable and there's an elegant dining room downstairs. ❼

Hotel d'Azur 64 rue Victor Hugo, 2ᵉ ℡ 04.78.42.51.26, ⓦ www.hotelazurlyon.com; Mᵒ Ampere Victor-Hugo. Double-glazed windows seal out the noise from the pedestrianized Victor-Hugo, while the cheerful yellow and blue decor of this pleasant hotel can't help but lift your mood. ❸

Hotelo 37 Cours de Verdun-Récamier, 2ᵉ ℡ 04.78.37.39.03, ⓦ www.hotelo-lyon.com; Mᵒ Perrache. Smart two-star hotel with well-appointed rooms decorated in neutral tones. ❺

Le Boulevardier 5 rue de la Fromagerie, 1ᵉʳ ℡ 04.78.28.48.22, ⓦ www.leboulevardier.fr; Mᵒ Cordeliers. Surprisingly peaceful despite its central location on a main pedestrian street and the popular jazz club downstairs. You can admire the stonework of the nearby church of St-Nizier from your window. Good value and friendly management. ❷

College 5 place St-Paul, 5ᵉ ℡ 04.72.10.05.05, ⓦ www.college-hotel.com; Mᵒ Vieux-Lyon. Imaginative decor with a "school" theme: there's a library, aged black and white prints of students in the lift and a reception featuring school gym equipment. Rooms are clean, white and coolly minimalist. ❼

Cour des Loges 2–8 rue du Boeuf, 5ᵉ ℡ 04.72.77.44.44, ⓦ www.courdesloges.com; Mᵒ Vieux-Lyon. Lyon's finest hotel, set in a seventeenth-century former Jesuit college, with a stunning dining area in the glazed atrium. Rooms from €240. ❾

Evasion Loft 21 cours Vitton, 6ᵉ ℡ 04.27.11.58.12, ⓦ www.evasion-loft .com; Mᵒ Masséna. Beautifully converted loft space offering chic bed and breakfast rooms and a relaxed atmosphere. ❺

Globe et Cécil 21 rue Gasparin, 2ᵉ ℡ 04.78.42.58.95, ⓦ www.globeetcecilhotel.com; Mᵒ Bellecour. Attractive, central and upmarket place with impeccable, attentive service. The comfortable rooms are all individually decorated. ❽

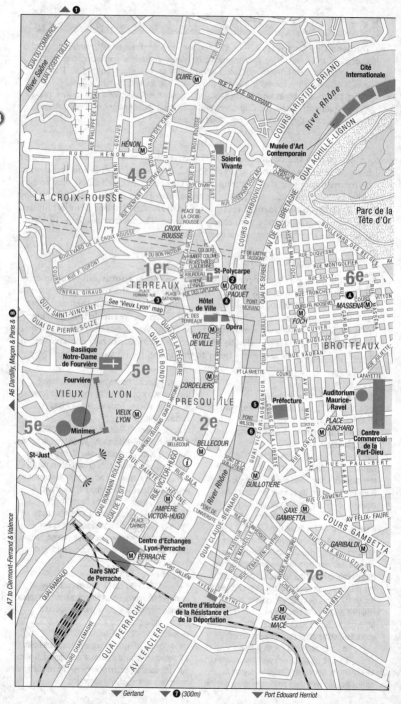

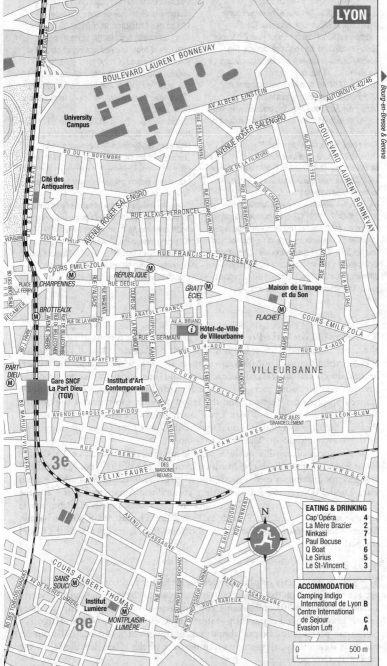

Bourg-en-Bresse & Geneva

BOULEVARD LAURENT BONNEVAY

AV ALBERT EINSTEIN

AUTOROUTE 42/46

University Campus

AVENUE ROGER SALENGRO

RUE DES ANTONINS

BD DU 11 NOVEMBRE

RUE DE LA FILATURE

BOULEVARD LAURENT BONNEVAY

RUE DU 8 MAI 1945

Cité des Antiquaires

AVENUE ROGER SALENGRO

RUE EDOUARD VAILLANT

RUE DE CHÂTEAU-GA

RUE DES BIENVENUS

RUE FLACHET

RUE GREUZE

RUE DU 8 MAI 1945

RUE ALEXIS-PERRONCEL

VERGUIN

COURS A.-PHILIP

RUE FRANCIS-DE-PRESSENSÉ

BD DES BELGES

PLACE
J. FERRY

COURS ÉMILE-ZOLA

CHARPENNES

RUE D'ALSACE

RUE MAGENTA

RÉPUBLIQUE

COURS DE LA RÉPUBLIQUE

GRATT ECIEL

Maison de L'Image et du Son

RECAMIER

BROTTEAUX

RUE DE LA VIABERT

RUE ANATOLE-FRANCE

RUE HIPPOLYTE KAHN

AV A. BRIAND

FLACHET

COURS ÉMILE ZOLA

BD J. FAVRE

AVENUE DE BELLECOMBE

RUE DE BELLECOMBE

RUE THIERS

GERMAIN

(i) **Hôtel-de-Ville de Villeurbanne**

RUE DU 4-AOÛT

RUE CAMILLE KOECHLIN

1ER MARS 1943

RUE DU 4-AOÛT

PART-DIEU

COURS LAFAYETTE

VILLEURBANNE

BD MARIUS VIVIER MERLE

Gare SNCF La Part Dieu (TGV)

Institut d'Art Contemporain

COURS CLÉMENT TOLSTOÏ

RUE DU

AVENUE GEROGES-POMPIDOU

AV MARC-SANGIER

PLACE JULES GRANDECLÉMENT

RUE LÉON-BLUM

RUE PAUL-BERT

PLACE DES MAISONS NEUVES

COURS JEAN-JAURÈS

3e

AV FÉLIX-FAURE

AVENUE PAUL-KRÜGER

AVENUE LACASSAGNE

RUE SAINT-ISIDORE

RUE BONNAND

N

BD DES TCHÉCOSLOVAQUES

COURS ALBERT-THOMAS

AV DE FRÈRES LUMIÈRE

SANS SOUCI

Institut Lumière

MONTPLAISIR-LUMIÈRE

RUE FEUILLAT

RUE DU PROFESSEUR ROCHAIX

RUE DU PROFESSEUR FLORENCE

RUE TRARIEUX

AVENUE LACASSAGNE

8e

EATING & DRINKING

Cap'Opéra	4
La Mère Brazier	2
Ninkasi	7
Paul Bocuse	1
Q Boat	6
Le Sirius	5
Le St-Vincent	3

ACCOMMODATION

Camping Indigo International de Lyon	B
Centre International de Sejour	C
Evasion Loft	A

0   500 m

Venissieux, **C**, ▼ St Exupéry Airport, TGV Station & Grenoble

Home Sweet Home 6 rue Cléberg, 5ᵉ
ⓣ04.72.32.15.66, ⓦwww.home-sweet-home
-lyon.com, Mᵒ Vieux-Lyon/Minimes. Three
chambres d'hôtes in a quiet spot near the Musée
Gallo-Romain and the Fourvière basilica. The
friendly owner provides a substantial breakfast. ❸
De la Marne 78 rue de la Charité, 2ᵉ
ⓣ04.78.37.07.46, ⓦwww.hoteldelamarne.fr;
Mᵒ Perrache. Conveniently located near the
Musée des Arts Décoratifs, this pleasant hotel has
comfortable, good-value rooms and is managed by
a friendly couple. ❸
Saint Paul 6 rue de la Lainerie, 5ᵉ
ⓣ04.78.28.13.29, ⓦwww.hotelstpaul.fr;
Mᵒ Vieux Lyon. Great location in the heart of Vieux
Lyon. Simple rooms built around a charming
fourteenth-century building. ❹
Hotel Simplon 11 rue Duhamel, 2ᵉ
ⓣ04.78.37.41.00, ⓦwww.hotel-du-simplon
-lyon.com; Mᵒ Perrache. This appealing hotel is run
by a friendly lady with a penchant for cherries; you'll
find her collection of cherry-adorned *objets* in the
dining room. Each room is cosily decorated in
different colours, although some of the bathrooms
are on the small side. Parking available. ❺

Hostels and campsite

Centre International de Séjour de Lyon
103 bd des États-Unis, 8ᵉ ⓣ04.37.90.42.42,
ⓦwww.cis-lyon.com. Large, modern hostel
with lots of beds, situated just out of earshot of
the main ring road. €19.50 for a dorm bed;
doubles and singles are also available. Take bus
#32 from Perrache or #36 from Part-Dieu, stop
"États-Unis-Beauvisage". Check-in from 2.30pm.
Open 24hr.
HI hostel (Vieux Lyon) 41–45 montée du Chemin
Neuf, 5ᵉ ⓣ04.78.15.05.50, ⓔlyon@fuaj.org;
Mᵒ Vieux-Lyon/Minimes. Modern hostel, set in a
steep part of the old town with great views over
Lyon. If you want to avoid the climb from Vieux
Lyon métro station get the funicular to Minimes.
Beds from €15.70.
Camping Indigo International de Lyon Dardilly
ⓣ04.78.35.64.55, ⓦwww.camping-indigo.com.
North along the A6 from Lyon or by bus #89 (stop
"Camping International") from the gare de Vaise.
Alternatively #3 from Hôtel de Ville. Pleasant though
expensive, with a tourist information bureau.
€18.40 for a tent and two people.

The City

The centre of Lyon is the **Presqu'île**, or "peninsula", the tongue of land between
the rivers Saône and Rhône, just north of their confluence. Most of it lies within
the 2ᵉ arrondissement, but it's known by its *quartiers*, which include **Bellecour**,
around the central square, and **Perrache**, around the station. At the top end of the
Presqu'île, as the Saône veers west, is the 1ᵉʳ arrondissement, known as **Terreaux**,
centred on place des Terreaux and the Hôtel de Ville. On the west bank of the
Saône is the old town, or **Vieux Lyon**, at the foot of Fourvière, on which the
Romans built their capital of Gaul, Lugdunum. Vieux Lyon forms the eastern end
of the 5ᵉ arrondissement. The 9ᵉ lies to its north.

To the north of the Presqu'île is the old silk-weavers' district of **La Croix-
Rousse**, the 4ᵉ arrondissement. **Modern Lyon** lies east of the Rhône, with the 7ᵉ
and 8ᵉ arrondissements to the south, the 3ᵉ arrondissement in the middle – with
Part-Dieu TGV station amid a bustling cultural and commercial area – and the
6ᵉ arrondissement, known as **Brotteaux**, to the north. North of Brotteaux is
Lyon's main open space, the **Parc de la Tête d'Or**. The district of **Villeurbanne**,
home to the university and the Théâtre National Populaire, lies east of the 6ᵉ and
the park.

The Presqu'île

The pink gravelly acres of **place Bellecour** were first laid out in 1617, and today
act as a focal point on the peninsula, with views up to the looming bulk of Notre-
Dame de Fourvière. Running south, **rue Auguste-Comte** is full of antique shops
selling heavily framed eighteenth-century art works, and **rue Victor-Hugo** is a
pedestrian precinct full of chic shops that continues north of place Bellecour on
rue de la République, all the way up to the back of the Hôtel de Ville below the
area of La Croix-Rousse.

South of place Bellecour

South of place Bellecour at 34 rue de la Charité is Lyon's best museum, the **Musée Historique des Tissus** (Tues–Sun 10am–5.30pm; €5.50), housed in the eighteenth-century former town palace of the Duke of Villeroy. It doesn't quite live up to its claim to cover the history of decorative cloth through the ages, but it does have brilliant collections from certain periods, notably third-century Greek-influenced and sixth-century Coptic tapestries, woven silk and painted linen from Egypt as well as silks from Baghdad and carpets from Iran, Turkey, India and China. The stuff produced in Lyon itself reflects the luxurious nature of the silk trade: seventeenth- to nineteenth-century hangings and chair covers, including hangings from Marie-Antoinette's bedroom at Versailles, from Empress Josephine's room at Fontainebleau and from the palaces of Catherine the Great of Russia. There are also some lovely twentieth-century pieces – including Sonia Delaunay's *Tissus Simultanés* – and couture creations from Worth to Mariano Fortuny, Paco Rabanne and Christian Lacroix. The **Musée des Arts Décoratifs** next door (same hours; entry included in Musée des Tissus ticket) displays faïence, porcelain, furniture and a couple of eighteenth-century rooms removed from old houses in the Presqu'Île, plus a collection of superb modern silverware by noted architects, including Richard Meier and Zaha Hadid.

To the south, the area around Perrache station is of little interest, but over the Rhône, across the adjacent pont Gallieni, at 14 av Berthelot, is the **Centre d'Histoire de la Résistance et de la Déportation** (Wed–Fri 9am–5.30pm, Sat & Sun 9.30am–6pm; €4; M° Perrache/Jean-Macé). In addition to a library of books, videos, memoirs and other documents recording experiences of resistance, occupation and deportation to the camps, there's an exhibition space housed over the very cellars and cells in which Klaus Barbie, the Gestapo boss of Lyon, tortured and murdered his victims. Barbie was brought back from Bolivia and tried in Lyon in 1987 for crimes against humanity; the principal "exhibit" is a moving and unsettling 45-minute video (five shows daily; French only) of the trial in which some of his victims recount their terrible ordeal.

North of place Bellecour

To the north of place Bellecour at the top of quai St-Antoine is the **quartier Mercière**, the old commercial centre of the town, with sixteenth- and seventeenth-century houses lining rue Mercière, and the **church of St-Nizier**, whose bells used to announce the nightly closing of the city's gates. In the silk-weavers' uprising of 1831 (see box, p.824), workers fleeing the soldiers took refuge in the church, only to be massacred. Today, traces of this working-class life are almost gone, edged out by bars, restaurants and designer shops, the latter along rue du Président Edouard-Herriot and the long pedestrian rue de la République in particular.

Further north is the monumental nineteenth-century **fountain** in front of the even more monumental **Hôtel de Ville** on place des Terreaux. It was designed by Bartholdi, of Statue of Liberty fame, although the rows of watery jets that sprout up unexpectedly across the rest of the square are a modern addition. Opposite is the vast the **Musée des Beaux-Arts** (Mon, Wed, Thurs, Sat & Sun 10.30am–6pm; Fri 10am–6pm; €7; audioguide included), housed in a former Benedictine abbey and whose collections are second in France only to those in the Louvre. The museum is organized roughly by genre, with nineteenth- and twentieth-century sculpture in the ex-chapel on the ground floor. The first floor houses a particularly interesting collection of Egyptian artefacts including coffins, amulets and stone tablets, in addition to a selection of medieval French, Dutch, German and Italian woodcarving and antiquities, coins and *objets d'art*. Upstairs, twentieth-century painting is represented by Picasso and Matisse, and there are also works by Braques, a brace of Bonnards and a gory Francis Bacon. The nineteenth century is covered by the Impressionists and their forerunners, Corot and Courbet; there are works by the Lyonnais artists Antoine Berjon and Fleury Richard, and from there you can work your way back through Rubens, Zurbarán, El Greco, Tintoretto and more. Keep an eye out for Rembrandt's earliest known work from 1625, *The Stoning of St Steven*.

Behind the Hôtel de Ville stands Lyon's **opera house** (tours every other Sat at 1pm; €9, book through the tourist office on place Bellecour). Radically redesigned in 1993 by the architect Jean Nouvel, its original Neoclassical elevations are now topped by a huge glass Swiss roll of a roof, and the interior is now entirely black with silver stairways climbing into the darkness.

La Croix-Rousse

La Croix-Rousse is the old silk-weavers' district and spreads up the steep slopes of the hill above the northern end of the Presqu'île. It's still a working-class area, but barely a couple of dozen people operate the modern high-speed computerized looms that are kept in business by the restoration and maintenance of France's palaces and châteaux. You can see an authentic silk worker's atelier at the **Soierie Vivante**, 21 rue Richan (Tues 2–6.30pm, Wed–Sat 9am–noon & 2–6.30pm; M° Croix-Rousse; €4). One of the original **traboules, Passage Thiaffait** on rue Réné-Leynaud, has been refurbished to provide premises for young couturiers.

Officially the *traboules* of La Croix-Rousse and Vieux-Lyon are public thoroughfares during daylight hours, but you may find some closed for security reasons, especially as the area is gradually being gentrified. The long climb up the part-pedestrianized **Montée de la Grande Côte**, however, still gives an idea of what the *quartier* was like in the sixteenth century, when the *traboules* were first built. Take a look at the pretty **place Sathonay** at the bottom, where a public garden and a lively local café are overlooked by Croix-Rousse Mairie.

The silk strike of 1831

Though the introduction of the Jacquard loom of 1804 made it possible for one person to produce 25cm of silk in a day instead of taking four people four days, **silk workers**, or *canuts* – whether masters and apprentices, or especially women and child workers – were badly paid whatever their output. Over the next three decades, the price paid for a length of silk fell by over fifty percent. Attempts to regulate the price were ignored by the dealers, even though hundreds of skilled workers were languishing in debtors' jails.

On November 21, 1831, the *canuts* called an all-out **strike**. As they processed down the Montée de la Grande Côte with their black flags and the slogan "Live working or die fighting", they were shot at and three people died. After a rapid retreat uphill they built barricades, assisted by half the National Guard, who refused to fire cannon at their "comrades of Croix-Rousse". For three days the battle raged on all four banks, the silk workers using sticks, stones and knives to defend themselves, and the bourgeoisie running scared, with only the area between the rivers, place des Terreaux and just north of St-Nizier still under their control. Unfortunately for the *canuts*, their employers were able to call on outside aid, and 30,000 extra troops arrived to quash the rebellion. Some 600 people were killed or wounded, and in the end the silk industrialists were free to pay whatever pitiful fee they chose, but the uprising was one of the first instances of organized labour taking to the streets during the most revolutionary fifty years of French history.

Vieux Lyon

Reached by one of the three *passerelles* (footbridges) crossing the Saône from Terreaux and the Presqu'île, **Vieux Lyon** is made up of the three villages of St-Jean, St-Georges and St-Paul at the base of the hill overlooking the Presqu'île.

South of place St-Paul, the cobbled streets of Vieux Lyon, pressed close together beneath the hill of **Fourvière**, form a backdrop of Renaissance and medieval facades, bright night-time illumination and a swelling chorus of well-dressed Lyonnais in search of supper or a midday splurge.

A short way south of the Hôtel Paterin on place du Petit-Collège, the **Musée Gadagne** (Wed–Sun 11am–6.30pm; €6 or €8 for both museums; ⓦ www .gadagne.musees.lyon.fr) encompasses the Musée d'Histoire de Lyon – which examines various decorative features in the city – and the rather more entertaining Musée de la Marionnette, a puppet museum showing off the eighteenth-century Lyonnais creations, Guignol and Madelon – the French equivalents of Punch and Judy.

The pedestrianized **rue St-Jean** ends at the twelfth- to fifteenth-century **Cathédrale St-Jean** (Mon–Fri 8am–noon & 2–7.30pm; Sat, Sun & holidays 8am–noon & 2–5pm). Though the west facade lacks most of its statuary as a result of various wars and revolutions, it's still impressive, and the thirteenth-century stained glass above the altar and in the rose windows of the transepts is in perfect condition. In the northern transept is a fourteenth-century astronomical clock, its mechanism cloaked by a beautiful Renaissance casing: it's capable of computing moveable feast days (such as Easter) until the year 2019, and most days on the strike of noon, 2pm, 3pm and 4pm the figures of the Annunciation go through an automated set piece, heralded by the lone bugler at the top of the clock.

Just beyond the cathedral, opposite avenue Adolphe-Max and pont Bonaparte, is the Vieux Lyon metro station and funicular stop, from where you can ascend to the town's Roman remains (direction "St-Just", stop "Minimes"). The antiquities consist of two ruined **theatres** dug into the hillside (entrance at 6 rue de l'Antiquaille; mid-April to mid-Sept 7am–9pm; mid-Sept to mid-April 7am–7pm; free) – the larger of which was built by Augustus and extended in the second century by Hadrian to seat ten thousand spectators – and an underground museum of Lyonnais life from prehistoric times to 7 AD, the **Musée Gallo-Romain**,

---

Top traboules

All around Lyon lurk *traboules*, alleyways and tunnelled passages originally built to provide shelter from the weather for the silk-weavers as they moved their delicate pieces of work from one part of the manufacturing process to another. The streets running down from boulevard de la Croix-Rousse, as well as many in Vieux Lyon, are intersected by these *traboules*. Usually hidden by plain doors, they are impossible to distinguish from normal entryways, proving an indispensable escape network for prewar gangsters, wartime Resistance fighters and, more recently, for anarchists, who used them in thwarting police efforts to capture them during the 2005 riots. Look out for subtle signs on the walls indicating the presence of a *traboule*.

Vieux Lyon Find the aptly named *longue traboule*, a dark winding passage connecting 27 rue du Boeuf with 54 rue St-Jean.

Vieux Lyon A *traboule* lies behind the door of 28 rue St-Jean, leading to the serene courtyard of a fifteenth-century palace.

La Croix-Rousse Go up rue René-Leynaud, passing St-Polycarpe on your right, then take rue Pouteau via a *passage*. Turn right into rue des Tables Claudiennes, and enter no. 55 emerging opposite 29 rue Imbert-Colomès. Climb the stairs into 14bis, cross three courtyards and climb the steps, where you finally arrive at place Colbert.

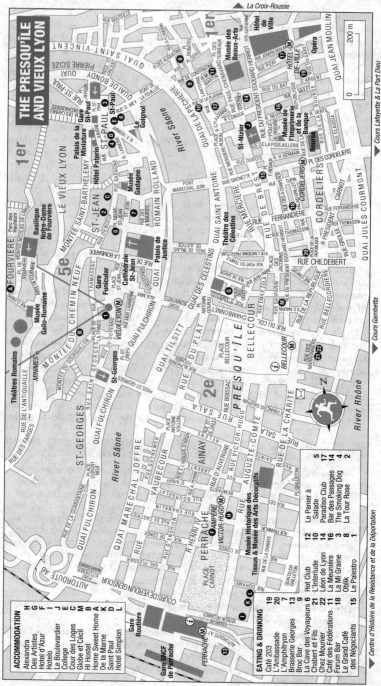

17 rue Cléberg (Tues–Sun 10am–6pm; €3.80). The fragments of a fine bronze engraving of a speech by the Lyon-born Emperor Claudius, as well as the sheer number and splendour of the mosaics here, serve to underline Roman Lyon's importance. Nowadays, the ancient theatres are the focal point for the **Nuits de Fourvière** music and film festival that takes place each summer (℡ 04.72.32.00.00, Ⓦ www.nuitsdefourviere.fr).

From the museum, it's just a moment's walk to the **Basilique Notre-Dame de Fourvière**, an incredibly ornate wedding cake of a church built, like the Sacré-Coeur in Paris, in the aftermath of the 1871 Commune to emphasize the defeat of the godless socialists. And like the Sacré-Coeur, its hilltop position has become a defining element in the city's skyline. At the time of writing, the cathedral was undergoing restoration, rendering its **Tour de l'Observatoire** inaccessible. Tours of the rooftop are an adequate and vertigo-worthy replacement, however (2.30pm & 4pm: April, May, Oct Wed & Sun; June–Sept daily; Nov 2.30pm & 3.30pm; 1hr 15min; €5). The Basilique is also accessible direct from the Vieux Lyon funicular station (alight at Fourvière): if you arrive by this route, it's worth walking down along the **montée St-Barthélémy** footpath, which winds back to Vieux Lyon through the hanging gardens below the church.

Modern Lyon

On the skyline from Fourvière, you can't miss the gleaming pencil-like skyscraper that belongs to Lyon's home-grown Crédit Lyonnais bank. This is the centrepiece of **Part-Dieu**, a business-culture-commerce hub which includes one of the biggest public libraries outside Paris, a mammoth concert hall and a busy shopping centre (M° Part-Dieu). The elegant tower aside, it's not the most aesthetically pleasing area. Penetrate the exterior of the main Halles market at 102 cours Lafayette, however, and you'll discover a gastronomic wonderland within, with superb seafood, poultry, cheese and charcuterie stalls (Tues–Sat 7am–noon & 3–5pm, Sun 7am–noon).

For a break from city buildings head north to the **Parc de la Tête d'Or** (M° Masséna, then walk up rue Masséna), where you'll find a boating lake, rose gardens, a botanical garden, a small zoo and lots of amusements for kids. It's overlooked by the bristling antennae of the international headquarters of Interpol, part of the **Cité Internationale**, which is made up of glass-heavy luxury apartments, slick restaurants, the **Palais des Congrès** conference centre and the enormous Amphitheatre. The complex is also home to the **Musée d'Art Contemporain**, at 81 quai Charles-de-Gaulle (Wed–Fri noon–7pm, Sat & Sun 10am–7pm; Ⓦ www.mac-lyon.com; €8; Line B to M° Saxe-Gambetta then bus #4, stop "Musée d'Art Contemporain"). The museum hosts excellent temporary exhibitions as well as the Lyon art biennial. Designed by Renzo Piano, it's a grand, white building with an imposing Neoclassical facade. The whole area looks smart, if a little artificial and immaculate behind its security barriers. To the east, dividing the park and the university, is boulevard de Stalingrad, where antique-fanciers can browse in the **Cité des Antiquaires** arcades at 117 boulevard de Stalingrad (Thurs–Sun 10am–5pm).

In Villeurbanne, not far to the east of Part-Dieu, is the **Institut d'Art Contemporain**, 11 rue du Dr-Dolard (Wed–Sun 1–7pm; ℡ 04.78.03.47.00, Ⓦ www.i-ac.eu; €4; bus #C3, stop "Institut d'Art Contemporain"), where thought-provoking and engaging exhibitions by contemporary artists question the function of art and architecture and their relation to society. It's also worth looking out for exhibitions at Villeurbanne's **Maison du Livre de l'Image et du Son**, to the east on avenue Émile-Zola (Mon 2–7pm, Tues–Fri 11am–7pm, Sat 10am–6pm; M° Flachet), which might feature anything from medieval illuminations to CD-ROMs.

Further south, on the edge of the 8ᵉ arrondissement, is the enlightening **Institut Lumière**, 25 rue du Premier-Film (Tues–Sun 11am–6.30pm; ⓦ www.institut -lumiere.org; €6; Mᵒ Monplaisir-Lumière), of real interest to film buffs. The building was the home of Antoine Lumière, father of Auguste and Louis, who made the first films, and the exhibits feature plenty of interactive displays, early magic lanterns and the cameras used by the brothers, as well as with touching family photographs. The Institut also shows several different films nightly; check their website for the schedule.

Right down in the south of the city, in the **Gerland quartier** (7ᵉ), is a developed area with a marina and a park on the Rhône's east bank, while across the bridge from the southern tip of the Presqu'île, just off place Docteurs Charles et Christophe Mérieux, squats the massive **Tony Garnier Hall** (Mᵒ Debourg), a former abbatoir, whose 17,000 cubic metres is completely free of roof-supporting columns. Its massive space lends itself freely to music concerts, conventions and sporting events; ask at the tourist office for what's on.

Eating and drinking

You'll find **restaurants** offering dishes from every region of France and overseas in Lyon. Vieux Lyon is the area with the greatest concentration of places to eat, though you'll find cheaper and less busy ones between place des Jacobins and place Sathonay at the top of the Presqu'île, with a particularly dense and atmospheric concentration in rue Mercière.

Restaurants

L'Amphitryon 33 rue St-Jean, 5ᵉ
ⓣ 04.78.37.23.68; Mᵒ Vieux-Lyon. Usually packed restaurant serving Lyonnais specialities; *menus* from €15. Service till midnight.

Brasserie Georges 30 cours de Verdun, 2ᵉ
ⓣ 04.72.56.54.54; Mᵒ Perrache. Bright, buzzing Art Deco brasserie founded in 1836. *Choucroutes* are the speciality; the local pork and pistachio sausages are also worth trying. *Menus* from €20.

Chabert et Fils 11 rue des Marronniers, 2ᵉ
ⓣ 04.78.37.01.94; Mᵒ Bellecour. *Bouchon* offering the ubiquitous *quenelle* and *andouillette* (offal sausage) specialities, along with other first-rate dishes. *Menus* from €17.50.

Chez Mounier 3 rue des Marronniers, 2ᵉ
ⓣ 04.78.37.79.26; Mᵒ Bellecour. Good-value *menus* from €12 at this unpretentious *bouchon*.

Serves imaginative options, such as tripe and cognac soufflé.

Café des Fédérations 8 rue du Major-Martin, 1ᵉʳ
ⓣ 04.78.28.26.00; Mᵒ Hôtel-de-Ville. Typical *bouchon* serving the earthiest of Lyonnais specialities (marinated tripe and black pudding). Cheerful green and white checked tables are complemented by rough wooden floorboards and jovial pictures on the walls. €25 dinner *menu*. Closed Sun.

Le Grand Café des Négociants 1 place Francisque Regaud, 1ᵉʳ ⓣ 04.78.42.50.05; Mᵒ Cordeliers. Despite a position on a busy road, this place attracts the punters for its sumptuous cuisine and sophisticated decor. Meat dishes go for up to €38 but pasta is cheaper at €14.

L'Interlude 8 rue de la Platière, 1ᵉʳ
ⓣ 04.78.28.35.96; Mᵒ Hôtel-de-Ville. Chic café-bar with a terrace near the Saône, serving tasty salads

The bouchon

The **bouchon**, the traditional Lyonnais eating establishment, is the best place to eat *quenelles*, sausages, tripe and the like. Its name derives either from *bouchon* (cork), or *bouchonner* (to rub down). One popular theory has it that wine bottles were lined up as the evening progressed, and at the end of the night the bill was determined by measuring from the first cork to the last. Another explanation, however, is that inns serving wine would attach small bundles of straw to their signs, indicating that horses could be cared for (*bouchonnés*) while the coachmen went inside to have a drink. Wandering around Vieux Lyon, you'll come across many *bouchons* – we've listed a few special ones above.

and a *plat du jour* for €8.50. Wine by the carafe is also good value.

Léon de Lyon 1 rue Pléney, 1ᵉʳ ☎04.72.10.11.12; Mº Hôtel-de-Ville. Delicious food, with original culinary creations as well as traditional Lyonnais recipes at this upmarket brasserie. Dishes from €19.50. Closed first three weeks in Aug.

La Mère Brazier 12 rue Royale, 1ᵉʳ ☎04.78.28.15.49; Mº Croix-Paquet. A beautiful setting complements the excellent food at this restaurant, still run by Mme Brazier, the grand-daughter of the couple who founded it in 1921. Closed Sat lunch, Sun, Tues & Aug.

La Meunière 11 rue Neuve, 1ᵉʳ ☎04.78.28.62.91; Mº Hôtel-de-Ville. Booking is essential at this excellent *bouchon*. Dishes include oxtail with tomatoes and shallots (€16). Closed Sun, Mon & mid-July to mid-Aug.

Paul Bocuse 40 rue de la Plage, Collonges-au-Mont-d'Or ☎04.72.42.90.90. Lyon's most famous restaurant, named after its celebrity chef-owner, is 9km north of the city, on the west bank of the Saône. Traditional French gastronomy is the bill of fare, with *menus* from €125 upwards.

Le Palestro 10 rue Mourguet, 5ᵉ ☎04.78.92.80.91; Mº Vieux-Lyon. Atmospheric Algerian restaurant with a friendly owner/chef and a changing nightly *menu* that can include dishes such as fish-filled pastry *briks*, *merguez* sausages and couscous. €30 for 3 courses, including an apéritif and mint tea.

Le Panier à Salade 1 place Neuve Saint-Jean 5ᵉ ☎04.78.37.22.85; Mº Vieux-Lyon. This popular restaurant on a pretty square offers a perfect compromise: meaty Lyonnais dishes for the carnivores, and interesting salads for the vegetarians. Salad and home-made dessert €15.

Le St-Vincent 6 place Fernand-Rey, 1ᵉʳ ☎04.72.07.70.43; Mº Hôtel-de-Ville. A dozen tables in a quiet, arty square shaded by mimosas. Very popular with locals. Lunch €12.50, eve *menu* €24. Closed Sun.

La Tour Rose 22 rue du Boeuf, 5ᵉ ☎04.78.92.69.10; Mº Vieux-Lyon. Gastronomic place with concoctions like terrine of *foie gras* with gingerbread and tomato chutney (€20). *Menus* from €30. Closed Sun eve.

Nightlife and entertainment

Lyon is almost as good a place for **nightlife** and **entertainment** as it is for eating, with a wide range of clubs, cinema, opera, jazz, classical music concerts and theatre. The best places to wander if you are looking for a **bar** are rue Mercière, the area around place des Terreaux and the Opéra (where most of Lyon's **lesbian and gay** scene is also found) and, most particularly, the streets of Vieux Lyon. Make a point of crossing the river by the *passerelles*; the whole district looks magnificent at night.

For **listings**, pick up a copy of the free weekly newspaper *Le Petit Bulletin* from tourist offices and outlets citywide. Alternatively buy a copy of the weekly *Lyon Poche*, available from newsagents (every Wed; €1), or look online at ⓦwww .lyonpoche.com.

Bars and clubs

Café 203 9 rue du Garet, 1ᵉʳ; Mº Hôtel-de-Ville. Lively bar that takes its name from the classic Peugeots parked out the front. Cheap *plats du jour* all day. Daily 7am–2am.

L'Ambassade 4 rue Stella, 2ᵉ; Mº Cordeliers. One of the best and hippest places to party in Lyon, this club features top DJs bashing out heavy house beats, hip-hop and some soul. Wed–Sat from 10.30pm.

Bar des Passages 8 rue du Plâtre, 1ᵉʳ; Mº Hôtel-de-Ville. Intimate wine bar adorned with candles and soft red lights. A glass of wine can be anything from €4 to €15 although in such luxurious surroundings you may be tempted to splash out on champagne. Closed Sun & Mon.

Broc Bar 20 rue Lanterne; Mº Hôtel-de-Ville. Trendy bar with a popular terrace; particularly lively during the Beaujolais *nouveau* festival.

Cap'Opéra 2 place Louis-Pradel, 1ᵉʳ; Mº Hôtel-de-Ville. Trendy, officially "mixed" (but really mostly gay) DJ bar close to the opera house. Mon–Sat 2pm–3am.

La Cave des Voyageurs 7 place Saint-Paul, 5ᵉ; Mº Vieux-Lyon. Small wine bar serving 450 varieties of wine that you can taste and take away. Serves plates of charcuterie to share. Closed Sun & Mon.

Forum Bar 15 rue des Quatre-Chapeaux, 2ᵉ; Mº Cordeliers. Convivial men's bar with bearish decor and clientele, down an alley just north of the places des Jacobins and de la République. Mon–Thurs 5pm–2am, Fri & Sat 5pm–3am.

Hot Club 26 rue Lanterne, 1er ☎04.78.39.54.74, ⓦwww.hotclubjazz.com; Mᵒ Hôtel-de-Ville. A variety of great jazz sessions and concerts in a vaulted cellar. Tues–Sat 9pm–1am; closed July & Aug.

La Mi Graine 11 place St-Paul, 5ᵉ; Mᵒ Vieux-Lyon. Welcoming small café on a sun-drenched square. Enjoy a drink and a sunbathe while listening to the café's relaxing jazz soundtrack. Mon–Sat 11.30am–3am, Sun 3–9pm.

Ninkasi 267 rue Marcel Mérieux, 7ᵉ; Mᵒ Gerland. Lyon's own microbrewery, with salads and burgers upstairs, bar, DJs and live music downstairs. Mon–Wed 10–1am, Thurs 10–2am, Fri 10–3am, Sat 10–4am & Sun 4pm–midnight.

Oblik 26 rue Hippolyte-Flandrin, 1er; Mᵒ Hôtel-de-Ville. Relaxed café/bar popular with gay men and lesbians. Tues–Sat 5pm–1am.

Paradiso Club 24 rue Pizay, 1ᵉʳ; Mᵒ Hôtel-de-Ville. Wild and funky place with transvestite or burlesque shows often entertaining the crowds. Daily 10pm–dawn.

Le Sirius Berges du Rhone Opposite 4 quai Augagneur; Mᵒ La Guillotière. Laid-back boat bar on the River Rhône with friendly staff, live music and late opening. Daily 2pm–3am.

The Smoking Dog 16 rue Lainerie, 5ᵉ; Mᵒ Vieux-Lyon. Very popular English-run pub with a large TV screen showing sports. Cosy decor, with book-filled shelves lining the walls. Daily 2pm–1am.

Theatre, music and film

Look out for **stage productions** by the Théâtre National Populaire (TNP), located at 24 rue Emile-Decorps (☎04.78.03.30.00; Mᵒ Laurent Bonnevay). Less radical stuff is shown at the city's gilded Théâtre des Célestins, in place des Célestins, 2ᵉ (☎04.72.77.40.00, ⓦwww.celestins-lyon.org; Mᵒ Bellecour). The **opera house**, one of the best in France, is on place de la Comédie, 1ᵉʳ (☎08.26.30.53.25, ⓦwww.opera-lyon.com; Mᵒ Hôtel-de-Ville), with cheap tickets sold just before performances begin. For avant-garde, classic and obscure **films**, usually in their original language, check the listings for the cinemas CNP Terreaux, Bellecour, Fourmi Lafayette, Opéra and Ambiance, as well as the Institut Lumière. Also, look out for the Lyon dance biennial, which brings in hundreds of artists and troupes from around the world (last three weeks of Sept in even-numbered years; ⓦwww.biennale-de-lyon.org).

Listings

Bike rental Holiday Bikes, 199 rue Vendôme, 3ᵉ ☎04.78.60.11.10, ⓦwww.holiday-bikes.com.

Boat trips Société Naviginter, 13bis quai Rambaud, 2ᵉ ☎04.78.42.96.81. Leaving from quai des Célestins, boats run up the Saône or down to the confluence with the Rhône at the Île Barbe (April & Sept–Oct Tues–Sun; May–Aug daily; €9). The same company offers lunch and dinner cruises from €44.

Car rental Europcar, 40 rue de la Villette, 3ᵉ ☎08.25.00.25.22; Hertz, 40 rue de la Villette, 3ᵉ ☎04.72.33.89.89; Avis, Gare Part-Dieu, 3ᵉ ☎04.72.33.37.19. All the above also have offices at the airport and at Perrache station.

Consulates Canada, 21 rue Bourgelat, 2ᵉ ☎04.72.77.64.07; UK, 24 rue Childebert, 2ᵉ ☎04.72.77.81.70; USA, 16 rue de la République, 2ᵉ ☎04.78.38.36.88.

Disabled travellers For information on facilities for the disabled contact Délégation Départementale APF, 73ter, rue Francis de Pressensé, Villeurbanne ☎04.72.43.01.01, ⓕ04.78.93.61.99.

Health Samu – emergency medical attention ☎15; Police ☎17; SOS Médecins ☎04.78.83.51.51.

Hospitals: Croix-Rousse ☎04.72.07.10.46; Hôpital Edouard-Herriot, place d'Arsonval, 3ᵉ (☎04.72.11.69.53). For house calls contact the medical referral centres (☎04.72.33.00.33).

Internet Planète Net Phone, 21 rue Romarin, 1ᵉʳ (Mon–Fri 10am–10pm, Sat till 9pm), has plenty of terminals; Raconte Moi de la Terre, 38 rue Thomassin, 2ᵉ (Mon–Sat noon–7.30pm) also serves snacks.

Lesbian and gay info ARIS (Accueil Rencontres Informations Services), 13 rue des Capucins (☎04.78.27.10.10), is a gay and lesbian centre organizing various activities and producing a useful scene guide. État d'Esprit, 19 rue Royale (☎04.78.27.76.53, ⓦwww.etatdesprit.free.fr), is a gay and lesbian bookstore that also holds cultural events. Online listings and activities are posted at the Forum Gai et Lesbien (ⓦwww.fgllyon.org). Lyon celebrates lesbian and gay pride in mid-June.

Police The main commissariat is at 47 rue de la Charité, 2ᵉ ☎04.78.42.26.56.

Post office PTT, place Antonin-Poncet, Lyon 69002.

Taxis ☎04.78.28.23.23 or 04.72.10.86.10.

Around Lyon

Within easy reach of the city, the **Monts du Lyonnais** to the south and west of Lyon may not reach spectacular heights, but they offer solitude among steep, forested hills and unassuming villages surrounded by cherry orchards, the region's main source of income. Tourism is low-key, but finding food and accommodation in the hostels of the mountain villages is rarely a problem for visitors to the area's parks and museums. **Bus** services from the main *gare routière* and the western *gare de Gorge de Loup* (M° Gorge-de-Loup; 9ᶜ) to the larger villages are reasonably frequent. The medieval town of **Pérouges** is particularly special, and deserves at least a half-day visit. It can be reached by train and bus from Gare de Part-Dieu (M° Part-Dieu). You might also like to visit the wine region of **Beaujolais**, 50km to the northeast of Lyon.

Pérouges

Twenty-nine kilometres northeast of Lyon, on the N84, **PÉROUGES** (Ⓦwww .perouges.org) is a lovely village of cobbled alleyways and ancient houses. By train from Lyon, you will arrive at the station in Meximieux where the tourist office on 1 rue de Genève (Ⓣ04.74.23.36.72, Ⓦwww.mairie-meximieux; Tues & Thurs 9.30am–noon & 3–6pm, Wed 9.30am–noon, Fri & Sat 2.30–6pm) will equip you with a choice of three walking routes to medieval Pérouges, perched high on a hill. Each route takes 30min and requires sturdy shoes; route 2 is perhaps the most scenic, skirting a fishing pond and traversing narrow stone bridges.

Pérouges' charm has not gone unnoticed by the French film industry – historical dramas such as *The Three Musketeers* were filmed within its fortifications – nor by some of the residents, who have fought long and hard for preservation orders on its most interesting buildings. The result is an immaculate work of conservation. Local traditional life is also thriving in the hands of a hundred or so workers who still weave locally grown hemp.

The simple and beautiful church of Marie-Madeleine, close to the medieval gate that serves as the entry-point to Pérouges, is worth an exploration. Built around 1440 it's built in a primarily early Gothic style with Romanesque features. The central square, the **place du Halle**, and Pérouges' main street, the **rue du Prince**, have some of the best-preserved French medieval remains. The **lime tree** on place du Halle is a symbol of liberty, planted in 1792. The place both to **stay** and eat in Pérouges, if you can afford it, is the *Hostellerie de Pérouges* (Ⓣ04.74.61.00.88, Ⓦwww.hostelleriedeperouges.com; Ⓞ), in a medieval town house fronting the square; its **restaurant** serves traditional mountain dishes of duck and carp, with *menus* from €35. Opposite, the *Ostellerie* runs a cheaper brasserie during summer, serving salads and omelettes for around €10. Those with a modest wallet should head for *Auberge du Coq*, rue des Rondes (Ⓣ04.74.61.05.47), where *menus* from €16.50 feature delights such as snail casserole and *coq au vin*. Pérouges' speciality is a delicious, sugary **galette**, washed down with cider; make for the *galette* shop also on rue des Rondes.

Beaujolais

Around 50km northeast of Lyon, the countryside becomes increasingly hilly as you approach the **Beaujolais** region, where the light, fruity red wines hail from. Fashionable to drink early, Beaujolais is made from the Gamay grape, which thrives on the area's granite soil. Of the four Beaujolais *appellations*, the best are the *crus*, which come from the northern part of the region between St-Amour and Brouilly. If you have your own transport, you can follow the *cru* trail that leads up the D68 to St-Amour, before wending your way along the D31. Beaujolais Villages produces the most highly regarded *nouveau*, which comes from the middle of the region, while plain Beaujolais and Beaujolais Supérieur are produced in the vineyards southwest of Villefranche-sur-Saône.

North of Lyon, **Villefranche** is an excellent base for an exploration of the Beaujolais region. Its tourist office at 96 rue de la Sous-Préfecture (Mon–Sat, May–Sept 9am–6pm; Oct–April 10am–5pm; ℡04.74.07.27.40, ⓦwww .villefranche-beaujolais.fr) has plenty of information about *caves* and wine tours. **Hotels** are clustered near the *gare SNCF*; one pleasant and reasonably priced option is *The Liberty's* at 81 rue d'Anse (℡04.74.68.36.13; ❷). Rue Nationale is the main axis of town, where you'll find most of the shops and the striking church of Notre-Dame, which boasts some fifteenth-century stained glass. This is also the area to head for lively cafés: *Le Saladier* (℡04.74.62.34.19), within a walled terrace at number 579, offers tasty *menus* from €16 and a good list of local wines.

Vienne and around

Heading south from Lyon on the A7, a twenty-kilometre stretch of oil refineries and factories, steel and chemical works may well tempt you to make a bee-line for the lavender fields of Provence further south. However, a short detour off the autoroute leads to **VIENNE**, which, along with **St-Romain-en-Gal**, just across the river, makes for an interesting stop on the Rhône.

With their riverside positions, Vienne and St-Romain prospered as Rome's major wine port and *entrepôt* on the Rhône, and many Roman monuments survive to attest to this past glory. Several important churches recall Vienne's medieval heyday as well: it was a bishop's seat from the fifth century and the home town of twelfth-century Pope Calixtus II. Today, the compact old quarter is crisscrossed with pedestrian precincts that make for enjoyable wandering, and there's a feeling that despite the distant rumble of the autoroute calling you to sunnier climes, the town has maintained its character and sense of purpose.

Arrival and information

The cours Brillier runs down from the **gare SNCF** to the river, with the **tourist office** (Mon–Sat 9am–noon & 1.30–6pm, Sun 10am–noon & 2–5pm; ℡04.74.53.80.30, ⓦwww.vienne-tourisme.com) at no. 3, near quai Jean-Jaurès, next to the pretty Jardin du 8 Mai 1945. Halfway up the cours, rue Boson leads up to the west front of the cathedral. For **internet** access, go to *World of Gamers Cybercafé*, 22 rue de la Table Ronde (Mon–Thurs 9.30am–6.45pm, Fri 9.30am–9.30pm, Sat 2–11pm), which also serves snacks and drinks.

Accommodation

Hotels and hostel

Grand Hotel de la Poste 47 cours Romestang ℡04.74.85.02.04, ⓦwww.hoteldelapostevienne .com. Comfortable rooms overlooking a pretty, tree-lined *cours*. ❹

Ibis ℡04.74.78.41.11, ⓦwww.ibishotel.com. Budget option near the *gare routière* in place Camille-Jouffray, just down from the tourist office. ❸

HI Hostel 11 quai Riondet ℡04.74.53.21.97, ℻04.74.31.98.93. Close to the centre of town on the other side of the gardens from the tourist office. €10 per person. Open for reservations Mon–Thurs 5–8pm, Fri 8am–noon.

La Reclusière 93 Montée Bon Accueil, 2km northwest of Vienne ℡04.74.85.04.78, ⓦwww.lareclusiere.com. Three beautiful, spacious *chambres d'hôtes* in a nineteenth-century mansion. The house, decorated with Art Deco treasures, is set in a walled garden with its own swimming pool. ❼

Vienne museum pass

The Musée Gallo-Romain de Saint-Roman-en-Gal, Théâtre Antique, Église and Cloître de St-André-le-Bas, Musée des Beaux-Arts et d'Archéologie, Musée de la Draperie and Musée Archéologique St-Pierre can be visited on a **single ticket** (€6), which can be picked up at any of the sites and is valid for 48 hours.

The Town

Roman monuments are scattered liberally around the streets of Vienne, including the magnificently restored **Temple d'Auguste et de Livie**, a perfect, scaled-down version of Nîmes' Maison Carrée, on place du Palais, and the remains of the **Jardin Archéologique de Cybèle**, off place de Miremont. The **Théâtre Antique**, off rue du Cirque at the base of Mont Pipet to the north (Tues–Sun 9.30am–5pm; €2.40, or €6 combined ticket with other museums), is a bit of a trek up a hill but it's definitely worth the effort for the view of the town and river from the very top seats. The theatre hosts many concerts throughout the summer, climaxing in **Jazz à Vienne,** a much-celebrated **international jazz festival** in the first two weeks of July (ⓦwww.jazzavienne.com). An **audioguide** (available in English, from the tourist office; €5) will give you more information on the city's glorious past at each of the main temples and ruins.

The **Musée Archéologique Eglise St-Pierre** (April–Oct Tues–Sun 9.30am–1pm & 2–6pm; Nov–March Tues–Fri 9.30am–12.30pm & 2–5pm, Sat & Sun 1.30–5pm; €2.40 or €6 combined ticket) stands on the site of one of France's first cathedrals. Since its origins in the fifth century, the building has suffered much reconstruction and abuse, including a stint as a factory in the nineteenth century, though the monumental portico of the former church is still striking. Today it has something of the atmosphere of an architectural salvage yard, housing substantial but broken chunks of Roman columns, capitals and cornices. Close by is one of Vienne's most prominent monuments, the **Cathédrale St-Maurice** (daily 8.30am–6pm; free), whose unwieldy facade, a combination of Romanesque and Gothic, appears as if its upper half has been dumped on top of a completely alien building. The interior, with its ninety-metre-long vaulted nave, is impressive though, spare and elegant, with some modern stained-glass windows and traces of fifteenth-century frescoes.

The **Église** and **Cloître de St-André-le-Bas** (same hours and ticket as St-Pierre) on place du Jeu de Paume, a few streets north of the cathedral, date from the ninth and twelfth centuries. The back tower of the church, on rue de la Table Ronde, is a remarkable monument, studded with tiny carved stone faces, while the cloister, entered through a space where temporary exhibits are held, is a beautiful little Romanesque affair, whose walls are decorated with local tombstones, some dating from the fifth century.

The **Musée des Beaux-Arts et d'Archéologie** on place de Miremont (€2.40 or €6 combined ticket, same hours as St-Pierre) is reminiscent of a dusty school hall, cluttered with a preponderance of eighteenth-century French pottery, assorted paintings and some Roman silverware. More enlightening is the small textile museum, the **Musée de la Draperie** (mid-April to mid-Sept Wed–Sun 2–6pm; €2.40 or €6 combined ticket), in the Espace St-Germain to the south of the centre off rue Vimaine, which, with the aid of videos, working looms and weavers, illustrates the complete process of cloth-making as it was practised in the city for over two hundred years.

Eating

Le Bec Fin 7 place St-Maurice ☏04.74.85.76.72. Classy and welcoming restaurant offering filling Lyonnais *menus* at €22 and €58. Closed Sun & Wed eve & Mon.

Le Cloître 2 rue des Cloîtres ☏04.74.31.93.57. Nice position, tucked in next to the Cathédrale Saint-Maurice. Serves traditional dishes such as foie gras (€21.90) and *crème brulée* (€8.50). Closed Sat & Sun lunch.

L'Entre Deux Next to the Musée Gallo-Romain ☏04.74.53.74.06. This riverside restaurant is a smart glass-fronted affair serving delicious Mediterranean dishes such as grilled sea bass on a bed of seasonal roasted vegetables. Lunch *menu* €18.

L'Estancot 4 rue de la Table Ronde ☏04.74.85.12.09. Cheery and inexpensive, this place does good seafood for under €20. Closed early to mid-Sept.

La Médina 71 rue de Bourgogne ☏04.74.53.51.35. Good-value Moroccan place serving huge portions of couscous and tagines. From €11.

St-Romain-en-Gal

Facing Vienne across the Rhône, several hectares of Roman ruins constitute the site of **ST-ROMAIN-EN-GAL**, also the name of the modern town surrounding it. The excavations just across the road bridge from Vienne attest to a significant community dating from the first century BC to the third AD, and give a vivid picture of the daily life and domestic architecture of Roman France. You enter through the excellent and child-friendly **Musée Gallo-Romain** (site & museum Tues–Sun 10am–6pm; €4 or €6 combined ticket, free Thurs), which displays frescoes, superb mosaics and other objects recovered from the site, along with explanatory models. The ruins themselves are clearly laid out, and be sure to check out the Romans' lavishly decorated marble public toilets. A detailed audioguide (included with entry) brings the exhibits inside and out to life.

Between Vienne and Valence

Between Vienne and Valence are some of the oldest, most celebrated **vineyards** in France: the renowned Côte Rotie, Hermitage and Crozes-Hermitage *appellations*. If you've got any spare luggage space, it's well worth stopping to pick up a bottle from the local co-op; even their *vin ordinaire* is superlative and unbelievably cheap, considering its quality. Just south of Ampuis on the west bank, 8km south of Vienne, is the tiny area producing one of the most exquisite and oldest French white wines, Condrieu, and close by one of the most exclusive – Château Grillet – an *appellation* covering just this single château (by appointment; ☏04.74.59.51.56).

Between **St-Vallier** and **Tain-l'Hermitage**, the Rhône becomes quite scenic, and after Tain you can see the Alps. In spring you're more likely to be conscious of orchards everywhere rather than vines. Cherries, pears, apples, peaches and apricots, as well as bilberries and strawberries, are cultivated in abundance and sold at roadside stalls.

Tain-l'Hermitage and Tournon-sur-Rhône

TAIN-L'HERMITAGE, accessible from both the N7 and the A7, is unpretentious and uneventful, but if you have a weakness for wine or chocolate, you'll love this place. There are cellars all over town where you can taste and buy wine but, for ease and expertise, head to the Cave de Tain-l'Hermitage at 22 route de Larnage (daily: 9am–12.30pm & 2–6.30pm; mid-May to mid-Sept & mid- to end Dec 9am–12.30pm & 1.30–7pm; ☏04.75.08.20.87, ⓦwww.cavedetain.com), walking distance from the *gare SNCF*, where they have all the wines of the distinguished

Hermitage and Crozes-Hermitage *appellations* you'll ever need. If your visit happens to fall on the last weekend in February you can try out wines from 78 vineyards in the Foire aux Vins des Côtes du Rhône Septentrionales, and on the third weekend of September, the different wine-producing villages celebrate their cellars in the **Fête des Vendanges**. But at any time of the year you can go bottle-hunting along the N86 for some 30km north of Tain along the right bank, following the *dégustation* signs and then crossing back over between Serrières and Chanas.

The famous Tain **chocolates** are made by Valrhona and can be sampled and purchased at the shop (Mon–Fri 9am–7pm, Sat 9am–6pm; ☎04.75.07.90.62) at 14 av du Président-Roosevelt (the RN7), past the junction with the RN95 as you're heading south.

It's worth crossing the oldest suspension bridge over the Rhône to wander around pretty **TOURNON-SUR-RHÔNE**, which boasts a riverside promenade and a hilltop château.

Practicalities

On the RN7 further north from the *chocolaterie*, the **tourist office** at place du 8-mai-1945 (Sept–May Mon–Sat 9am–noon & 2–6pm; June–Aug Mon–Sat 9am–5pm, Sun 9.30am–noon; ☎04.75.08.06.81, ⓦwww.tain-tourisme.com) can provide you with lists of vineyard addresses. For **accommodation**, try the riverside *Les 2 Côteaux* (☎04.75.08.33.01, ⓦwww.hotel-les-2-coteaux.com; ❸), a smart choice situated at 18 rue Joseph-Péala, next to the suspension bridge. If you have your own transport, an excellent option is *La Farella* (☎04.75.07.35.44, ⓦwww.lafarella.com; €63), a converted farm offering three self-catering *gîtes* and a *chambre d'hôte* in the countryside near Chanos-Curson, 3km from Tain on the Romans-sur-Isère road. For a bite to **eat**, try *Le Mangevins* (☎04.75.08.00.76; closed Sun & Mon) at 6 av du Docteur Paul-Durand, a cute little wine bar serving good-value international cuisine; salmon *tataki*, for example, is €8. *Brasserie La Table de Nath* (☎04.75.08.28.52; closed Tues eve & Wed) at 13 av Jean Jaurès is another reasonably priced option, serving simple but tasty local produce on a €15 three-course *menu*. The most upmarket choice, however, is *Le Quai* (☎04.75.07.05.90), opposite *Les 2 Côteaux*, at 17 rue Joseph-Péala. Delicious, inventive cuisine includes duck breast accompanied with a fig and raspberry vinegar tart and fried mushrooms (€17) and a *plat du jour* at €12.50.

Hauterives

HAUTERIVES, 25km northeast of Tain, is a small village with a remarkable creation – the manic, surreal **Palais Idéal** (daily: Jan & Dec 9.30am–12.30pm & 1.30–4.30pm; Feb, March, Oct & Nov 9.30am–12.30pm & 1.30–5.30pm; April–June & Sept 9am–12.30pm & 1.30–6.30pm; July & Aug 9am–12.30pm & 1.30–7pm; ⓦwww.facteurcheval.com; €5.50, joint ticket with Musée International de la Chaussure, €7.20) built by a local postman by the name of Ferdinand Cheval (1836–1912). The house is truly bizarre, a bubbling frenzy reminiscent of the *modernista* architecture of Spain, with features that recall Thai or Indian temples. The eccentric building took thirty years to carve, and Cheval designed an equally bizarre tombstone which can also be seen nearby. Various Surrealists have paid homage to the building and psychoanalysts have given it much thought, but it defies all classification. The *palais* is a tourist magnet, but the rest of the village is relatively unspoilt. If you want to **stay** here, you have the choice of the *Camping du Château* on the edge of town on the N538 (☎04.75.68.80.19, ⓕ04.75.68.90.94; April to mid-Oct) or the *chambres d'hôte* at the elegant *Villa Eugénie* (☎04.75.68.81.93, ⓦvillaeugenie.free.fr; ❹).

Romans-sur-Isère

Despite its bustle, **ROMANS-SUR-ISÈRE**, south of Hauterives and 15km east of the Rhône at Tain, isn't the most exciting of towns. The main attraction is a museum specializing in the town's principal and most-established industry: shoemaking. The vast **Musée International de la Chaussure** is in the former Convent of the Visitation at 2 rue Ste-Marthe (Jan–April & Oct–Dec Tues–Sat 10am–5pm; May, June & Sept Tues–Sat 10am–6pm; July & Aug Mon–Sat 10am–6pm; year-round Sun 2.30–6pm; ☎04.75.05.51.81; €5, or joint ticket with Palais Idéal, €7.20) and also includes a permanent exhibition on the Resistance. Your toes will curl in horror at the extent to which women have been immobilized by their footwear from ancient times to the present on every continent, while at the same time you can't help but admire the craziness of some of the creations. If inspired to replenish your own shoe stock, drop in to the Charles Jourdan factory shop at 1 bd Voltaire or the large shopping outlet, Marques Avenue, along avenue Gambetta.

The old town is pleasant enough, peppered with the inevitable shoe shops as well as establishments offering Romans' two other specialities – this time gastronomic: *pogne*, a ringed spongy bread flavoured with orange water, and *ravioles*, small cornflour-based ravioli with a cheese filling.

Practicalities

The **tourist office** is on place Jean-Jaurès (April–Oct Mon–Fri 9am–7pm, Sat 9am–6pm, Sun 9.30am–12.30pm; Nov–March Mon–Sat 9am–6pm, Sun 9.30am–12.30pm; ☎04.75.02.28.72, ⓦwww.ville-romans.com). **Hotels** include the lovely ⚘ *L'Orée du Parc* (☎04.75.70.26.12, ⓦwww.hotel-oreeparc.com; ❺) at 6 av Gambetta, a short walk from the main town. Housed in a 1920s mansion, the stylish rooms are immaculate and restful, and there's an inviting pool and terrace in the leafy back garden. A cheaper alternative is the decent *Cendrillon* on place Carnot by the station (☎04.75.02.83.77, ⓦwww.hotelcendrillon.com; ❸). The municipal **campsite**, *Les Chasses* (☎04.75.72.35.27; April–Oct), is 1km off the N92 northeast of the city, next to the aerodrome.

Agreeable places to **eat** include *Le Chevet de St-Barnard* (☎04.75.05.04.78; closed Sun eve, Tues eve, Wed & mid-July to Aug) on pretty little place aux Herbes, next to the cathedral; traditional *ravioles* here are €11.50. A good choice for a cheap meal is *Restaurant L'Impérial* (☎04.75.72.35.30) at 4 Place Jean Jaurès, which serves a huge selection of omelettes, crêpes and meat and fish dishes. Along with cafés and bars around place Charles de Gaulle, a popular place to have a **drink** is the daytime-only *Comptoir des Loges* on 76 rue Nicolas (☎04.75.45.40.92; closed Mon), which also does inexpensive meals.

Valence

At an indefinable point along the Rhône, there's an invisible sensual border, and by the time you reach **VALENCE**, you know you've crossed it. The quality of light is different and the temperature higher, bringing with it the scent of eucalyptus and pine, and the colours and contours suddenly seem worlds apart from the cold lands of Lyon and the north. Valence is the obvious place to celebrate your arrival in the **Midi** (as the French call the south), with plenty of excellent restaurants and convivial bars in the old town, although little in the way of sights.

Arrival and information

To the southeast of the old town are the **gare routière**, the **gare SNCF** and the **tourist office** on parvis de la Gare (June–Aug Mon–Sat 9.30am–6.30pm, Sun 10.30am–3.30pm; Sept–May Mon–Sat 9.30am–12.30pm & 1.30–6pm, Sun 10.30am–1.30pm; ☎08.92.70.70.99, ⓦwww.tourisme-valence.com). The **TGV** station is 10km northeast, along the autoroute to Romans. There are regular shuttles and trains (daily 6.30am–10.50pm; €2.20), which connect the *gare TGV* with the *gare SNCF*.

Accommodation

Hotel de France 16bd Général de Gaulle ☎04.75.43.00.87, ⓦwww.hotel-valence.com. Super-smart hotel with comfortable beds in a great position near Vieux Valence. ❺

De Lyon 23 av Pierre-Sémard ☎04.75.41.44.66, ⓦwww.hoteldelyon.com. A decent two-star located just opposite the station. Simply decorated with white walls and bright coloured bedspreads, but extras such as free wi-fi make it a good option. ❸

Les Négociants 27 av Pierre-Sémard ☎04.75.44.01.86, ⓦwww.hotel-lesnegociants valence.com. Close to the train station, this chic hotel features minimalist furniture and probably an orchid on your bedside table. ❷

Pic 285 av Victor-Hugo ☎04.75.44.15.32, ⓦwww .pic-valence.com. Fifteen incredibly luxurious rooms in an old coach house, along with a gastro-nomic restaurant and less expensive, but just as fantastic, brasserie (see p.836). Rooms range between €290 and €890. ❾

Clos Syrah Bd Pierre Tezier ☎04.75.55.52.52, ⓦwww.clos-syrah.com. Spacious rooms in a stylish modern building with park and pool, southeast of the city on the route de Montéléger. ❹

The Town

Valence is, for the most part, a spruce town basking in its new-found cleanliness and space: road work continues in an effort to give the town back to the pedes-trians as cars are forced out to suburban car parks. The result is a town made up of tidy boulevards, large public areas and fresh-looking facades as well as a very pleasant old quarter, Vieux Valence.

Vieux Valence

The focus of Vieux Valence, the **Cathédrale St-Apollinaire**, was consecrated in 1095 by Pope Urban II (who proclaimed the First Crusade), and largely recon-structed in the seventeenth century. More work was carried out later, including the horribly mismatched nineteenth-century tower, but the interior still preserves its original Romanesque grace – especially the columns around the ambulatory.

Between the cathedral and **Église de St-Jean** at the northern end of Grande-Rue, which has preserved its Romanesque tower and porch capitals, are some of the oldest and narrowest streets of Vieux Valence. They are known as **côtes**: côte St-Estève just northwest of the cathedral; côte St-Martin off rue du Petit-Paradis; and côte Sylvante off rue du Petit-Paradis' continuation, rue A.-Paré. Diverse characters who would have walked these steep and crooked streets include Rabelais, a student at the university founded here in 1452 and suppressed during the Revolution, and the teenage Napoleon Bonaparte, who began his military training as a cadet at the artillery school.

Though Valence lacks the cohesion of the medieval towns and villages further south, it does have several vestiges of the sixteenth-century city, most notably the Renaissance **Maison des Têtes** at 57 Grande-Rue. Be sure if you can to look at the ceiling in the passageway here (office hours only), where sculpted roses transform into the cherub-like heads after which the palace is named. Also worth a look is the **Maison Dupré-Latour**, on rue Pérollerie, which has a superbly sculptured porch and spiral staircase. On Sunday a **bric-a-brac market** fills the streets with stalls selling everything from underwear to oranges. Parc Jouvet, to the east of the town centre, offers a tranquil oasis to escape the town's bustle.

Eating and drinking

Café Bancel 7 bd Bancel ☎ 04.75.78.35.98. Black and chrome decor sets the tone for this slick, modern restaurant and bar, which serves imaginative dishes like chicken with caramelised ginger served with pea risotto (€16).

Chez Grand-Mère 3 place de la Pierre ☎ 04.75.62.09.98. Set on a lovely square dotted with restaurants, this cosy yet cool restaurant lets diners make up their own three-course *formule* from anything on the *menu* for just €19.80. Local dishes feature highly – the baked tomato and basil *ravioles* (€8.50) are delicious. Closed Sun & Mon.

Divinus 4 av André Lacroix ☎ 04.75.56.86.64. Fantastically inventive, good-value, cuisine – think lamb tagine with strawberries and almond milk (€16) – served on a pretty little terrace adorned with flowers and lanterns.

L'Épicerie 18 place Belat ☎ 04.75.42.74.46. Congenial restaurant overlooking a market place. Soft, restful decor and wonderful food – go for one of their excellent seafood platters – on *menus* from €25 to €68. Closed Sat lunch & Sun.

Le Marché 6 place des Clercs ☎ 04.75.42.17.78. Funky bar in the heart of the action surrounded by restaurants and overlooked by the cathedral. Six different beers (€3 per pint) on tap.

Le Milou 10 place de la Pierre ☎ 04.75.43.12.77. This joint dishes up Lyonnais classics for around €17 and is a great drinking spot, with an outdoor terrace.

Ly 2 rue Biffaut ☎ 04.75.25.70.32. Chic modern decor and a *menu* to match: main courses include oven-baked salmon fillets with tapenade cream and thyme (€14).

Pic 285 av Victor-Hugo ☎ 04.75.44.15.32. The city's top restaurant, but expect a wallet-bashing – there's a *menu* here for €320 (*plats* average €80). More affordable is *Le 7*, overseen by Anne Sophie Pic (the granddaughter of the restaurant's founder), which offers a *menu* with delights such as *filet mignon* with fondant potatoes and apple chutney. A lunchtime *plat du jour* is a reasonable €17. Closed Sun eve & Mon; *Le 7* open daily. For those who want to recreate the Pic family's gourmet creations, Anne-Sophie Pic runs cooking workshops at 243 av Victor-Hugo (☎ 04.75.44.14.14, ⊛ www .scook.fr; €49–240). Wine-tasting sessions are also on offer, and there's a delicatessen and kitchen regalia boutique.

Montélimar

If you didn't know it before, you'll soon realise what makes the pretty town of **MONTÉLIMAR**, 40km south of Valence, tick: nougat. Shops and signs everywhere proclaim the glory of the stuff, which has been made here for centuries. The *vieille ville* is made up of narrow lanes that radiate out from the main street, **rue Pierre-Julien**, which runs from the one remaining medieval **gateway** on the nineteenth-century ring of boulevards at place St-Martin, south past the **church of Sainte-Croix**, and on to place Marx-Dormoy.

Make sure you stop by the fascinating **Musée de la Miniature** (July & Aug daily 10am–6pm; Sept–June Wed–Sun 2–6pm; €3), at 19 rue Pierre Julien, opposite the post office. You have to look through a microscope to see many of these tiny exhibits, the most incredible of which are the minute necklaces and earrings, a caravan of twelve camels traipsing through the eye of a needle, and an amusing pair of mosquitoes playing mini-chess. Above the old town to the east is the impressive **Château des Adhémar** on rue du Château (daily 9.30am–noon & 2–6pm; closed Tues Nov–March; €3.50). Originally belonging to the family after whom the town ("Mount of the Adhémars") was named, the castle is mostly fourteenth-century, but also boasts a fine eleventh-century chapel and twelfth-century living-quarters.

If you're overwhelmed by the number of establishments offering nougat, visit the **Fabrique et Musée d'Arnaud Soubeyran** in the Zone Commerciale Sud

(Mon–Sat 9am–7pm, Sun 10am–noon & 2.30–5pm; free; bus line 1 from outside the train station towards Soleil Levant; stop "A. Pontaimery") where they'll show you how they concoct the sweet treat; there's also a fun museum outlining its history. The shop sells many flavours of nougat, including delicious orange and lavender.

To escape the heat of the streets and burn off all that nougat, head for **Base Nautique**, a 20-minute walk from the centre of town; there's swimming (supervised July & Aug), mini-golf and pétanque, among other activities, as well as a pleasant picnic area. In town, the extensive Jardin Public is an inviting spot for a stroll.

Practicalities

The **gare SNCF** is on the western corner of town. The modern **tourist office** is across the Jardin Public on the Montée Saint-Martin (Allées Provençales) and is well-stocked with information about the surrounding area (Mon–Sat 9am–12.15pm & 1.30–6pm; ☎04.75.01.00.20, Ⓦwww.montelimar-tourisme.com).

There are plenty of **hotels** around the boulevards, including the very pleasant *Sphinx* (☎04.75.01.86.64, Ⓦwww.sphinx-hotel.fr; ❸; closed mid-Dec to mid-Jan), in a seventeenth-century town house at 19 bd Marre-Desmarais, and the well-equipped *Hôtel la Crémaillère* (☎04.75.01.87.46, Ⓦwww.hotellacremaillere -montelimar.com; ❸), with its own pool, just outside the old town at 138 av Jean Jaurès. In the old town the *Pierre*, 7 place des Clercs (☎04.75.01.33.16; ❷), is – despite the unpromising exterior – comfortable and very peaceful, apart from the nearby bell of Sainte-Croix tolling the hours. The **campsite**, *La Graveline* (☎04.75.90.69.40, Ⓦwww.chateauneuf-du-rhone.fr), is on Chemin de la Graveline, 5km south of Montélimar.

The Allées Provençales are clustered with **bars** and **restaurants**, while the old town also features inviting restaurants such as *Méli-Mélo* (☎04.75.51.85.55) at 22 rue des Quatre Alliances, which serves organic dishes including chicken couscous with seasonal vegetables (€14). The modern St-Martin area near the tourist office is home to a couple of chic, inviting restaurants – *Le 45ème Bistro* on place des Oliviers offers *menus* from €13 and tempting modern à la carte dishes such as duck breast with lavender honey (€14).

Travel details

Trains

Lyon (La Part-Dieu or Perrache) to: Arles (4 daily; 2hr 40min); Avignon (15 daily; 2hr–2hr 40min); Avignon TGV (16 daily; 1hr 10min); Bourg-en-Bresse (9 daily; 1hr); Clermont-Ferrand (12 daily; 2hr 20min–2hr 50min); Dijon (1–2 hourly; 2hr); Grenoble (every 30min; 1hr 15min); Lille-Europe (8 daily; 3hr 10min); Marseille (frequent; 1hr 40min–3hr 45min); Montélimar (12 daily; 1hr 35min); Orange (11 daily; 2hr 5min); Paris (every 30min; 2hr); Paris CDG Airport (8 daily; 2hr 10min); Meximieux (for Pérouges) (6 daily; 30min); Valence (frequent; 1hr 10min); Valence TGV (11–18 daily; 35min); Vienne (frequent; 20–40min).

Lyon St-Exupéry TGV to: Paris (9 daily; 1hr 50min).

Valence to: Gap (5 daily; 2hr 20min–2hr 40min); Grenoble (frequent; 1hr–1hr 40min); Lyon (hourly; 1hr 10min); Montélimar (frequent: approx hourly at peak times; 30min); Tain-l'Hermitage (frequent; 12min).

Buses

Lyon to: Bourg-en-Bresse (27 daily; 1hr 10min–1hr 30min); Meximieux (for Pérouges 6 daily; 1hr); Vienne (20 daily; 1hr 10min).

15

Provence

CHAPTER 15   Highlights

* **Roman remains** Impressive arenas in Orange and Arles host summer festivals and concerts. See p.844 & p.865

* **Medieval hilltop villages** Les Baux and Gordes are the most famous, but many others are equally picturesque, and much less frequented. See p.848

* **Avignon** The former city of the popes has spectacular monuments and museums to go along with the annual Festival d'Avignon. See p.851

* **La Camargue** The marshland of the Rhône delta is home to white horses, flamingos and unearthly landscapes. See p.871

* **Aix** The most beautiful of Provence's major cities is a wonderful place for café idling, and has the most vibrant markets in the region. See p.880

* **Les Gorges du Verdon** The largest canyon in Europe, with stunning views and a full range of hikes. See p.889

* **Haute-Provence** The Parc National du Mercantour and the Vallée des Merveilles are Alpine gems off the beaten path. See p.896

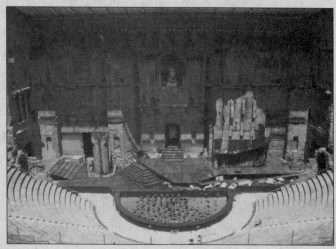

▲ The Roman Forum at Orange

Provence

O f all the areas of France, Provence is the most irresistible. Ranging from the snow-capped mountains of the southern Alps to the delta plains of the Camargue, it boasts Europe's greatest canyon, the Gorges du Verdon. Fortified towns guard its old borders; countless villages perch defensively on hilltops; and its great cities – Aix-en-Provence and Avignon – are full of cultural glories. The sensual inducements of Provence include sunshine, food and wine, and the heady perfumes of Mediterranean vegetation. Along with its coast – covered in Chapter 16 – the region has attracted the rich and famous, the artistic and reclusive, and countless arrivals who have found themselves unable to conceive of life elsewhere.

Despite the throngs of foreigners and French from other regions, **inland Provence** remains remarkably unscathed. The history of its earliest known natives, of the

Provençal food and drink

Provence boasts some of the most appetizing food in all France. It has many Mediterranean influences, such as the heavy use of **olives**: accompanying the traditional Provençal aperitif of *pastis*, they appear in sauces and salads, on tarts and pizzas, and mixed with capers in *tapenade* paste, spread on bread or biscuits. **Garlic** is another Provençal classic, used in *pistou*, a paste of olive oil, garlic and basil, and *aïoli*, the name for both a garlic mayonnaise and the dish in which it's served with salt cod.

Vegetables – tomatoes, capsicum, aubergines, courgettes and onions – are often made into **ratatouille**, while **courgette flowers** (*fleurs de courgettes farcies*), stuffed with pistou or tomato sauce, are an exquisite Provençal delicacy.

Sheep, taken up to the mountains in summer, provide the staple **meat**, of which the best is *agneau de Sisteron*, often roasted with Provençal herbs as *gigot d'agneau aux herbes*. But **fish** features most on traditional menus, with freshwater trout, salt cod, anchovies, sea bream, monkfish, sea bass and whiting all common, along with wonderful seafood such as clams, periwinkles, sea urchins and oysters.

Sweets include almond *calissons* from Aix and candied fruit from Apt, while the **fruit** – melons, white peaches, apricots, figs, cherries and Muscat grapes – is unbeatable. **Cheeses** are invariably made from goat's or ewe's milk. Two famous ones are Banon, wrapped in chestnut leaves and marinated in brandy, and the aromatic Picadon, from the foothills of the Alps.

The best **wines** come from around the Dentelles, notably Gigondas, and from Châteauneuf-du-Pape. To the east are the light, drinkable, but not particularly special wines of the Côtes du Ventoux and the Côtes du Lubéron *appellations*. With the exception of the Côteaux des Baux around Les Baux, and the Côtes de Provence in the Var *département*, the best wines of southern Provence come from along the coast.

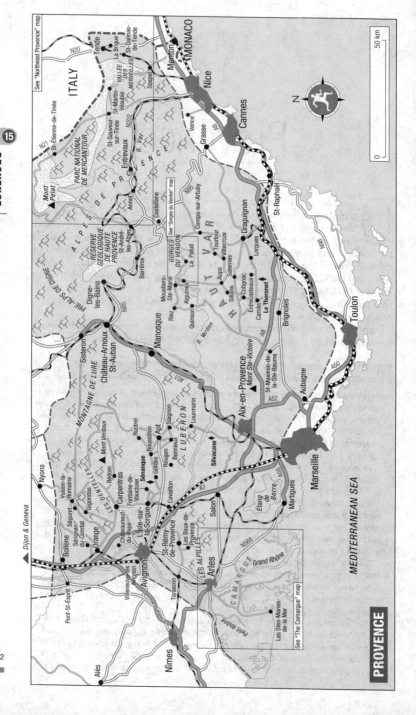

PROVENCE

Dijon & Geneva

See "Northeast Provence" map

ITALY

N20
Tende
La Brigue
St-Dalmas-de-Tende
Sospel
VALLÉE DES MERVEILLES
Menton
MONACO

N21
St-Étienne-de-Tinée
N202
St-Martin-Vésubie
St-Sauveur-sur-Tinée
Entrevaux
Nice

PARC NATIONAL DE MERCANTOUR
Mont Pelat
Annot
Vence
Grasse
Cannes
St-Raphaël

RÉSERVE GÉOLOGIQUE DE HAUTE PROVENCE
St-André-les-Alpes
Barrême
Castellane
Comps-sur-Artuby
See "Gorges du Verdon" map
Draguignan
N98

ALPES DE PROVENCE
Digne-les-Bains
N85
GORGES DU VERDON
Moustiers-Ste-Marie
La Palud
Tourtour
Villecroze
Lorgues
Salernes
Aups
H A U T   V A R

PRÉ-ALPES DE DIGNE
MONTAGNE DE LURE
Sisteron
Château-Arnoux
St-Auban
Manosque
Riez
Aiguines
Quinson
R. Verdon
Colignac
Entrecasteaux
Carcès
Le Thoronet
Brignoles

Nyons
Vaison-la-Romaine
Séguret
Séguret-du-Comtat
Gigondas
Mont Ventoux
Bédoin
LES DENTELLES
Carpentras
Fontaine-de-Vaucluse
Rustrel
Roussillon
Gordes
Bonnieux
Roupon
LUBÉRON
Salgnon
Apt
Lourmarin
A51
A52
Aix-en-Provence
Mont Ste-Victoire
St-Maximin-de-la-Ste-Baume
Aubagne
A50
A8
Toulon

Bollène
Pont-St-Esprit
Orange
Châteauneuf-du-Pape
Séguret
Sénanque
Cavaillon
L'Isle-sur-la-Sorgue
Silvacane
Salon
A7
Martigues
Étang de Berre
A55
Marseille

Villeneuve-les-Avignon
Avignon
St-Rémy-de-Provence
Les Baux-de-Provence
LES ALPILLES
Tarascon
Arles
N568
Grand Rhône

Nîmes
Alès
Petit Rhône
CAMARGUE
Les Stes-Maries-de-la-Mer
See "The Camargue" map

MEDITERRANEAN SEA

N

0   50 km

Greeks, then Romans, raiding Saracens, schismatic popes, and shifting allegiances to different counts and princes, remains everywhere apparent. Provence's complete integration into France dates only from the nineteenth century and, though the Provençal language is only spoken by a small minority, the accent is distinctive even to a foreign ear. In the east the rhythms of speech become clearly Italian.

Unless you're intending to stay for months, the main difficulty in visiting Provence is choosing where to go. In the west, along the **Rhône valley**, are the Roman cities of **Orange**, **Vaison-la-Romaine**, Carpentras and **Arles**, and the papal city of **Avignon**, with its fantastic summer festival. **Aix-en-Provence** is the mini-Paris of the region and was home to Cézanne, for whom the **Mont Ste-Victoire** was an enduring subject; Van Gogh's links are with **St-Rémy** and Arles. The **Gorges du Verdon**, **the Parc National du Mercantour** along the Italian border, **Mont Ventoux** northeast of Carpentras, and the flamingo-filled lagoons of the **Camargue** offer yet more stunning and widely disparate landscapes.

West Provence

The richest area of Provence, the Côte d'Azur apart, is the west. Most of the large-scale production of fruit, vegetables and wine is based here, in the low-lying plains beside the Rhône and the Durance rivers. The only heights are the rocky outbreaks of the Dentelles and the Alpilles, and the narrow east–west ridges of Mont Ventoux, the Luberon and Mont Ste-Victoire. The two dominant cities of inland Provence, Avignon and Aix, both boast rich histories and stage lively contemporary festivals of art; Arles, Orange and Vaison-la-Romaine hold impressive Roman remains. Around the Rhône delta, the Camargue is a unique self-contained enclave, as different from the rest of Provence as it is from anywhere else in France.

Orange

Thanks to its spectacular **Roman theatre**, the small town of **ORANGE**, west of the Rhône 20km north of Avignon, is famous out of all proportion to its size. It's also the former seat of the counts of Orange, whose best known scion was Prince William, who ascended the English throne with his consort Mary in the 1688 "Glorious Revolution" – his supporters in Ireland soon established the Protestant Orange Order.

Orange is at its best during the Chorégies **opera festival** in July. Otherwise, with its medieval street plan, fountained squares, houses with ancient porticoes, and Thursday market, it's an attractive enough place to stroll around, but there's no great reason to stay more than a day or two.

Arrival and information

Parking in the city centre is very limited; use the metered parking along cours Aristide Briand, or the underground car park east of the theatre. The *gare SNCF* is 1.5km east of the centre, at the end of avenue Frédéric Mistral.

The **tourist office** is at 5 cours Aristide Briand (April–June & Sept Mon–Sat 9am–6.30pm, Sun 10am–1pm & 2–6.30pm; July–Aug Mon–Sat 9am–7.30pm, Sun 10am–1pm & 2–7pm; Oct–March Mon–Sat 10am–1pm & 2–5pm; ℡04.90.34.70.88, ⓦwww.otorange.fr).

Accommodation

To get a real sense of the old town, pick a hotel in the centre. Accommodation only becomes hard to find during July's Chorégies festival.

L'Arène Place de Langes ℡04.90.11.40.40, ⓦwww.hotel-arene.fr. Very presentable hotel, with spacious rooms, on a quiet, pedestrianized (though not especially attractive) square. ❺
Glacier 46 cours Aristide Briand ℡04.90.34.02.01, ⓦwww.le-glacier.com. Comfortable, cosy Provençal-style rooms – think yellows and blues with pretty quilts and floral curtains. All en-suite and air-conditioned, but they vary widely in size and amenities. Closed Fri–Sun, Nov–Feb only. ❸–❼
L'Herbier 8 place aux Herbes ℡04.90.34.09.23, ⓦwww.lherbierdorange.com. Good budget option, in a seventeenth-century house overlooking a pretty square near the Théâtre Antique. Simple

clean rooms; the cheapest aren't en-suite, but there are some good-value family options. ❷
St-Florent 4 rue du Mazeau ℡04.90.34.18.53, ⓦwww.hotelsaintflorent.com. Very central, inexpensive hotel, with appealingly kitsch decor and a wide range of rooms; some have four-poster beds, not all are en-suite, and there are some extremely cheap singles. ❷–❺

Campsite

Le Jonquier Rue Alexis Carrel ℡04.90.34.49.48, ⓦwww.campinglejonquier.com. Popular campsite, 1.5km northwest of the centre, equipped with tennis courts, mini-golf and a pool. Closed mid-Sept to March.

The Town

Orange is small enough to cover easily on foot. Everything is dominated by the enormous wall of the **Théâtre Antique**, at the southern end of the medieval centre. Dating from 55 AD, and said to be the world's best-preserved Roman theatre, it's the only one with its stage wall still standing. It still hosts musical performances in summer, and is also open to visitors as an archeological site (daily: March & Oct 9.30am–5.30pm; April, May & Sept 9am–6pm; June–Aug 9am–7pm; Nov–Feb 9.30am–4.30pm; €8 including Musée d'Art et Histoire; Ⓦwww.theatre-antique.com).

Spreading a colossal 36m high by 103m wide, the Théâtre's outer face resembles a monstrous prison wall. Once inside, an excellent audioguide paints an evocative picture of its history and architecture. Its enormous **stage**, originally sheltered by a mighty awning, could accommodate vast numbers of performers, while the acoustics allowed ten thousand spectators to hear every word. Though missing most of its original decoration, the inner side of the wall above is extremely impressive. Below empty columned niches, a larger-than-life-size statue of Augustus, raising his arm in imperious fashion, looks down centre stage.

The best viewpoint over the entire theatre, on St-Eutrope hill, can be accessed without paying from both east and west. As you look down towards the stage, the ruins at your feet are those of the short-lived seventeenth-century castle of the princes of Orange. Louis XIV had it destroyed in 1673 and the principality of Orange was officially annexed to France forty years later.

Across from the Théâtre, the **Musée d'Art et Histoire** (daily: March & Oct 9.45am–12.30pm & 1.30–5.30pm; April, May & Sept 9.15am–6pm; June–Aug 9.15am–7pm; Nov–Feb 9.45am–12.30pm & 1.30–4.30pm; €4.60, or €8 with theatre) covers local history from the Romans onwards, and also hosts temporary exhibitions. Artefacts taken from the Théâtre complex include the largest known Roman land-survey maps, carved on marble and badly damaged when the museum itself collapsed in 1962, plus a couple of sphinxes and a mosaic floor.

Orange's old town is very small, hemmed in between the theatre and the River Meyne and shelters some pretty fountain-adorned squares and houses with ancient porticoes and courtyards. Don't miss the town's second major Roman monument, the **Arc de Triomphe**, situated to the north at the foot of Avenue de l'Arc de Triomphe. Built around 20 BC, its intricate frieze and relief celebrate imperial victories of the Roman Second Legion against the Gauls.

Eating and drinking

Sun-drenched **brasseries** and **bars** are situated in place de la République; those in place Clemenceau are slightly more touristy.

Le Bec Fin Rue Segond Weber ☎04.90.34.05.10. Large restaurant, with tables both indoors and sprawled along a narrow alley with slender views of the Théâtre Antique. Hearty salads and tasty pizzas for around €10, plus a really good €22 dinner *menu*, featuring gazpacho, whole roast monkfish and a delicious dessert.

Le Forum 3 rue du Mazeau ☎04.90.34.01.09. Small, intimate restaurant near the Théâtre. *Menus* (from €22) revolve around seasonal ingredients; in January, truffles feature heavily, while in May, it's asparagus. Often booked up, so reserve ahead. Closed Mon, plus Sat lunch.

Le Parvis 55 cours Pourtoules ☎04.90.34.82.00. The best Provençal food in Orange. Straight from the market, ingredients are whipped up into tempting, good-value dishes such as pikeperch with asparagus *millefeuille*. Lunch *menus* from €12, dinner from €24. Closed Sun & Mon, plus last 3 weeks in Nov & last 3 weeks in Jan.

La Roselière 4 rue du Renoyer ☎04.90.34.50.42. Lovely little restaurant by the Hôtel de Ville, where you can sample tasty veal and duck dishes on *menus* priced at €16–24. Closed Sun & Mon, plus all Aug.

Entertainment

Orange's main festival is the **Chorégies**, a programme of opera, oratorios and orchestral concerts that runs for three weeks from mid-July (Ⓦwww.choregies.asso.fr). The theatre is also used throughout the year for jazz, film, folk and rock concerts (full listings on Ⓦwww.theatre-antique.com).

Châteauneuf-du-Pape

Roughly halfway along the back road between Avignon and Orange, the large village of **CHÂTEAUNEUF-DU-PAPE** takes its name from the summer palace of the Avignon popes. However, neither the views down the Rhône valley from its ruined fourteenth-century **château** (freely accessible) nor its medieval streets give Châteauneuf its special appeal. It is, of course, the local **vineyards** that produce the magic, with the grapes warmed at night by large pebbles that cover the ground and soak up the sun's heat by day. Their rich ruby-red wine is one of the most renowned in France, though the lesser-known white, too, is exquisite.

As in so many Provençal villages, commercial activity in Châteauneuf is largely confined to the main road that loops around the base of its small central hill. Climb towards the castle from the busy little **place du Portail**, and you're soon in a delightful tangle of sleepy, verdant alleyways.

During the first full weekend of August, the **Fête de la Véraison** celebrates the ripening of the grapes, with free samples, as well as parades, dances, equestrian contests, and so forth. At other times, several places throughout the village offer free **tastings**, including the Musée du Vin on avenue Pierre-de-Luxembourg (daily: May to mid-Oct 9am–1pm & 2–7pm, mid-Oct to April 9am–noon & 2–6pm; free). No single outlet sells all the Châteauneuf-du-Pape wines; the best selection under one roof is at **La Maison des Vins**, 8 rue du Maréchal Foch (daily: mid-June to mid-Sept 10am–7pm; mid-Sept to mid-June 10.30am–noon & 2–6.30pm; Ⓦwww.vinadea.com).

Châteauneuf's **tourist office** is on place du Portail (June–Sept Mon–Sat 9am–6pm; Oct–May Mon, Tues & Thurs–Sat 9.30am–12.30pm & 2–6pm; ℡04.90.83.71.08, Ⓦwww.ccpro.fr/tourisme). Of the handful of pleasant small **hotel-restaurants** nearby, the lively *Mère Germaine*, on avenue Cdt-Lemaître (℡04.90.83.54.37, Ⓦwww.lameregermaine.com; ❸), has eight welcoming rooms and serves well-crafted Provençal cuisine on *menus* from €21. The charming *Sommellerie*, a renovated country house 3km north on route de Roquemaure (℡04.90.83.50.00, Ⓦwww.la-sommellerie.fr; closed Jan; ❺), has modern pastel-painted rooms, a pool, and a restaurant (closed Sat lunch & Mon lunch) producing superb dishes such as grilled lamb with garlic, rosemary and tapenade, on *menus* starting at €30 for lunch, €46 for dinner.

Vaison-la-Romaine and around

The charming old town of **VAISON-LA-ROMAINE**, 27km northeast of Orange, is divided into two very distinct halves, either side of the deep gorge cut by the River Ouvèze and connected by a single-arched Roman bridge. Throughout its history, the town centre has shifted from one side to the other, whenever its inhabitants needed the defensive position offered by the steep, forbidding hill south of the river. Now known as the Haute Ville, and topped by a ruined twelfth-century castle, this was the site of the original Celtic settlement. The Romans, however, built their homes on the flatter land north of the river, and that's where the modern town is now centred; the medieval lanes on the Haute Ville side attract throngs of day-trippers, but are largely residential.

Arrival and information

Vaison's **tourist office** (April–June & Sept to mid-Oct Mon–Sat 9am–noon & 2–5.45pm, Sun 9am–noon; July–Aug 9am–12.30pm & 2–6.45pm; mid-Oct to March Mon–Sat 9am–noon & 2–5.45pm; ℡04.90.36.02.11, ⓦwww.vaison-la -romaine.com) is on place du Chanoine-Sautel, between the two Roman sites. If there's no room to park on the central place Montfort, there should be spaces on quai Pasteur down by the river. The *gare routière* is on avenue des Choralies, east of the centre.

Accommodation

Vaison makes a lovely base for exploring the surrounding area, mostly because of its wonderful hotels. Make sure you book the following well in advance.

Le Beffroi Rue de l'Évêché ℡04.90.36.04.71, ⓦwww.le-beffroi.com. Beautiful, luxurious rooms in a sixteenth-century residence in the Haute Ville, with a pool, a great restaurant and unsurpassable views over the valley. Hotel closed Feb–March; restaurant closed Nov–March. ❺

Burrhus 1 place Montfort ℡04.90.36.00.11, ⓦwww.burrhus.com. Large, modern if somewhat characterless bedrooms in the heart of town, with tiled floors and very comfortable beds. It can be noisy at weekends, but the sunny breakfast balcony is a real plus. ❸

L'Évêché Rue de l'Évêché ℡04.90.36.13.46, ⓦwww.eveche-vaison.com. Lovely B&B in the Haute Ville, with comfortable modern rooms,

homely atmosphere, and a delightful little terrace at the back. ❺

La Fête en Provence Place du Vieux Marché ℡04.90.36.36.43, ⓦwww.hotellafete-provence .com. Gorgeous, comfortable rooms and apartments surrounding a pool and flower-decked patio in the Haute Ville. ❹

Campsite

Camping du Théâtre Romain Chemin du Brusquet, off av des Choralies, quartier des Arts ℡04.90.28.78.66, ⓦwww.camping-theatre.com. Small, four-star campsite 500m northeast of the centre, with good facilities. Reserve well ahead in summer. Closed early Nov to mid-March.

The Town

Vaison's two excavated Roman residential districts lie on either side of avenue Général-de-Gaulle. While you can peek through the railings for free, you'll get a much better sense of the style and luxury of the era if you pay for admission (€8 for both sites, plus cathedral cloisters), which includes an audio tour as well as the excellent museum.

The **Vestiges de Puymin** (daily: March & Oct 10am–12.30pm & 2–5.30pm; April & May 9.30am–6pm; June–Sept 9.30am–6.30pm; Nov–Feb 10am–noon & 2–5pm) stretch up a gentle hillside to the east. The ground plans of several mansions and houses are discernible in the foreground, while higher up the museum holds all sorts of detail and decoration unearthed from the ruins. Everyday artefacts include mirrors of silvered bronze, lead water pipes, weights and measures, taps shaped as griffins' feet and dolphin doorknobs, and there are also some impressive statues and stelae. A rather thrilling tunnel through the hillside leads to an ancient Roman theatre, which still seats seven thousand people during the July **dance festival** (ⓦwww.vaison-danses.com)

To the west, the **Vestiges de la Villasse** (daily except Tues morning: March & Oct 10am–12.30pm & 2–6pm; April & May 10am–noon & 2.30–6pm; June–Sept

10am–noon & 2.30–6.30pm; Nov–Feb 10am–noon & 2–5pm) are less substantial, but reveal a clearer picture of the layout of a comfortable, well-serviced town of the Roman ruling class. As well as a row of arcaded shops, there are more patrician houses, a basilica and the baths.

It says a great deal for Roman engineering that the **Pont Romain** survived relatively unscathed when the River Ouvèze burst its banks in 1992, killing thirty people and causing a great deal of material damage – unlike the modern road bridge to the west, which was completely destroyed. From its south side Rue du Pont Romain climbs upwards towards place du Poids and the fourteenth-century gateway to the medieval **Haute Ville**. More steep zigzags take you past the Gothic gate and overhanging portcullis of the belfry and into the heart of this sedately quiet, uncommercialized and rich *quartier*. There are pretty fountains and flowers in all the squares, and right at the top, from the twelfth- to sixteenth-century **castle**, you'll have a great view of Mont Ventoux. In summer, the Haute Ville livens up every Tuesday when Vaison's **market** spreads up here.

Eating and drinking

Vaison holds a large number of good **restaurants**, on both sides of the river. For a more local feel, stick to the modern town, particularly around place de Montfort and cours Taulignan, but the places in the Haute Ville cannot be beaten for their lovely views.

L'Auberge de Bartavelle 12 place Sus-Auze ☎04.90.36.02.6. Lively place in the modern town, with decent and affordable specialities from southwest France – rabbit ravioli, *confit de canard* and the like – on *menus* from €17 lunch, €24 dinner. Closed Mon, Fri lunch & Jan.
Le Brin d'Olivier 4 rue de Ventoux ☎04.90.28.74.79. Welcoming Provençal restaurant, serving lunch *menus* from €18 and dinner from €29

on a nice little terrace down the river. Closed Wed lunch & Sat lunch July–Sept, all Wed Oct–June.
La Lyriste 45 cours Taulignan ☎04.90.36.04.67. Of several restaurants spreading across the broad pavements of this quiet boulevard, just north of place Montfort, the *Lyriste* stands out for its changing, high-quality *menus*, based around themes like cheese, exotic fruits or scallops. The simple €18 *menu découverte* is great value.

Hill-top villages

All the **hill-top villages** around Vaison are worth visiting in their own right, and possess their own particular charm. South of Vaison, tiny, hill-top **LE CRESTET** is 3.5km down the Malaucène road, and off to the right. There's not a lot to do other than wander the steep and picturesque cobbled streets, earning a refreshment break at the restaurant at the top.

MONT VENTOUX, whose outline repeatedly appears upon the horizon from the Rhône and Durance valleys, rises some 20km east of Vaison. White with snow, black with storm-cloud shadow or reflecting myriad shades of blue, the barren pebbles of the uppermost 300m are like a weathervane for all of western Provence. Winds can accelerate to 250km per hour around the meteorological, TV and military masts and dishes on the summit, but if you can stand still for a moment the view in all directions is unbelievable. A road, the D974, climbs all the way to the top, though no buses go there. The road up the northern face from Malaucène is wider, straighter, and better surfaced than the southern ascent.

If you want to make the ascent on foot, the best path is from Les Colombets or Les Fébriers, two hamlets off the D974, east of **BEDOIN**, whose **tourist office** on the espace M.-L.-Gravier (mid–June to Aug Mon–Fri 9am–12.30pm & 2–6pm, Sat 9.30am–12.30pm & 2–6pm, Sun 9.30am–12.30pm; Sept to mid–June

Mon–Fri 9am–12.30pm & 2–6pm, Sat 9.30am–12.30pm; ℡04.90.65.63.95, Ⓦwww.bedoin.org) can give details of routes (including a once a week night-time ascent in July & Aug), plus addresses of campsites and *gîtes ruraux*.

Mont Ventoux is one of the great challenges revisited by the Tour de France. Within sight of the stony summit is a memorial to the British cyclist Tommy Simpson, who died here in 1967 from heart failure on one of the hottest days ever recorded in the race; according to race folklore his last words were "Put me back on the bloody bike."

The Dentelles

Running northeast to southwest between Vaison and Carpentras, the jagged hilly backdrop of the **DENTELLES DE MONTMIRAIL** is best appreciated from the contrasting landscape of level fields, orchards and vineyards lying to their south and west. The range is named after lace (*dentelles*) – the limestone protrusions were thought to resemble the contorted pins on a lace-making board – though the alternative connection with "teeth" (*dents*) is equally appropriate.

The area is best known for its wines. On the western and southern slopes lie the wine-producing villages of **Gigondas**, **Séguret**, **Beaumes-de-Venise**, **Sablet**, **Vacqueyras** and, across the River Ouvèze, **Rasteau**. Each one carries the distinction of having its own individual *appellation contrôlée* within the Côtes du Rhône or Côtes du Rhône Villages areas: in other words, their wines are exceptional.

Séguret

The star Dentelles village is **SÉGURET**, whose name means "safe place" in Provençal. Nine kilometres southwest of Vaison-la-Romaine, this alluring spot blends into the side of a rocky cliff, and is accompanied by a ruined castle soaring high above. With its steep cobbled streets, vine-covered houses and medieval structures, including an old stone laundry and a belfry with a one-handed clock, the village embodies many of Provence's charms. The **Fête des Vins et Festival Provençal Bravade** in the last two weeks of August involves processions for the Virgin Mary and the patron saint of wine-growers.

Perched near the top of the village, commanding fabulous views, there's a gorgeous hotel, 🍴 *La Table du Comtat* (℡04.90.46.91.49, Ⓦwww.table-comtat.fr; closed second half of Nov & mid-Feb to mid-March; ⑤). The rooms are comfortable and calming, and there's a small deck pool, but the real reason to come is to enjoy zestful Provençal food (closed Tues pm & Wed except in July & Aug), served on a delightful shaded terrace; there's a good-value lunch *menu* from €20 and dinner from €34, along with inexpensive organic wines.

Gigondas

Gigondas, 14km southwest of Seguret, is a worthwhile stop, its main draw being its exquisite **red wine**, which is strong with an aftertaste of spice and nuts. Sampling the varieties could not be easier; the **Syndicat des Vins** runs a *caveau des vignerons* (daily 10am–noon & 2–6pm) in place de la Mairie where you can taste and ask advice about the produce from forty different *domaines*.

Gigondas' **tourist office**, on place du Portail (April–June & Sept–Oct Mon–Sat 10am–12.30pm & 2.30–6pm; July & Aug Mon–Sat 10am–12.30pm & 2.30–6.30pm, Sun 10am–1pm; Nov–March Mon–Sat 10am–noon & 2–5pm; ℡04.90.65.85.46, Ⓦwww.gigondas-dm.fr), supplies lists of *domaines* or *caves* grouping several *vignerons* for the other villages.

At the entrance to the village, the *Gîte d'Etape des Dentelles* (℡ 04.90.65.80.85, Ⓦ gite-dentelles.com; closed Jan & Feb; ❶), offers cheap double rooms, and dorm beds (€13 per person). There's also a charming hotel, *Les Florets*, 2km towards the Dentelles (℡ 04.90.65.85.01, Ⓦ www.hotel-lesflorets.com; closed Jan & Feb; ❻), with an excellent **restaurant** (*menus* from €21; closed Wed). The best dining in the village centre is at *L'Oustalet*, on place du Portail in the village (℡ 04.90.65.85.30; Nov–April closed Mon), with a pleasant shaded terrace and dinner *menus* from €27.

Carpentras

With a population of around 30,000, **CARPENTRAS** is a substantial city for this part of the world. It's also a very old one, its known history commencing in 5 BC as the capital of a Celtic tribe. The Greeks who founded Marseille came to Carpentras to buy honey, wheat, goats and skins, and the Romans had a base here. For a brief period in the fourteenth century, it became the papal headquarters and gave protection to Jews expelled from France. Today, the town is in the throes of gradual refurbishment, so that immaculately restored squares and fountains alternate with gently decayed streets of seventeenth- and eighteenth-century houses, some forming arcades over the pavement.

The erotic fantasies of a seventeenth-century cardinal frescoed by Nicolas Mignard in the **Palais de Justice**, formerly the episcopal palace, were effaced by a later incumbent. The *palais* is attached to the dull **Cathédrale St-Siffrein**, behind which, almost hidden in the corner, stands a **Roman arch** inscribed with scenes of prisoners in chains. Fifteen hundred years after its erection, Jews – coerced, bribed or otherwise persuaded – entered the cathedral in chains to be unshackled as converted Christians. The door they passed through, the **Porte Juif**, is on the southern side and bears strange symbolism of rats encircling and devouring a globe. The **synagogue** (Mon–Thurs 10am–noon & 3–5pm, Fri 10am–noon & 3–4pm; closed Jewish holidays; free), near the Hôtel de Ville, is a seventeenth-century construction on fourteenth-century foundations, making it the oldest surviving place of Jewish worship in France.

Carpentras cheers up every Friday for the **market**, which from the end of November to early March specializes in truffles, and during **festival** time in the second half of July. The town is very proud of its sweet speciality of **berlingots** (you'll see them on signs, in shops, and at the end of your meal, as an accompaniment to your bill), small, striped *bonbons* made from fruit syrup – the mint flavour is the most famous, but the coffee one is absolutely delicious.

Practicalities

Carpentras' **tourist office** is on the south side of the old town, on place du 25 aout 1944 (July & Aug Mon–Sat 9am–1pm & 2–7pm, Sun 9.30am–1pm; Sept–June Mon–Sat 9.30am–12.30pm & 2–6pm; ℡ 04.90.63.00.78, Ⓦ www.carpentras -ventoux.com). **Buses** arrive nearby, either on avenue Victor-Hugo (from Marseille, Aix and Cavaillon) or at the *gare routière* on place Terradou (from Avignon, Vaison, and other points north and west). Central **accommodation** options include the kitsch but satisfactory *Malaga*, place Maurice Charretier (℡ 04.90.60.57.96; ❷). For something grander with greater character, try *Le Fiacre*, 153 rue Vigne (℡ 04.90.63.03.15, Ⓦ hotel-du-fiacre.com; ❹), an eighteenth-century town house; the owners are extremely friendly and can help plan walking and cycling tours. The local four-star **campsite**, *Lou Comtadou* (℡ 04.90.67.03.16; open Feb–Oct; Ⓦ campingloucomtadou.com), is 1km south on route St-Didier.

The Friday market and seasonality influence the **restaurant** menus. The cheery *La Petite Fontaine* (⊕04.90.60.77.83; closed Wed & Sun) is, as the name suggests, situated next to a little fountain on place du Colonel Mouret, and serves delicious, fresh food, with a *menu* at €25. *La Fraiseraie*, 125 bd Alfred Rogier (⊕04.90.67.06.39; closed Wed), draped in lush foliage, cooks up superb dishes like beef grilled in thyme (€15).

Avignon

AVIGNON, great city of the popes, has for centuries been one of the major artistic centres of France. With its spectacular monuments and museums, countless impressively decorated buildings, ancient churches, chapels and convents, it's a stunning medieval showcase, but also very much a lived-in city, capable of being unkempt and even intimidating away from the main tourist areas. Almost everything of interest to visitors lies within its impressive fortifications, an enclave that can be dauntingly crowded, and stiflingly hot, in summer. That of course is when Avignon is at its liveliest and most stimulating, especially during July's **Festival d'Avignon**.

The medieval walls that still enclose central Avignon were built in 1403 by the antipope Benedict XIII, the last of the nine **popes** based here during the fourteenth century. The first pope to come to Avignon, Clement V, was invited by the astute King Philippe le Bel ("the Good") in 1309, ostensibly to protect him from impending anarchy in Rome. In reality, Philippe saw a chance to extend his power by keeping the pope in Provence, during what came to be known as the Church's "Babylonian captivity". Clement's successor, **Jean XXII**, had previously been bishop of Avignon, so he reinstalled himself quite happily in the episcopal palace. The next Supreme Pontiff, **Benedict XII**, acceded in 1335; accepting the

The Festival of Avignon

Starting in the second week in July, the annual, three-week **Festival d'Avignon** focuses especially on theatre, while also featuring classical music, dance, lectures and exhibitions. The city's great buildings make a spectacular backdrop to the performances. Everywhere stays open late, and everything from accommodation to obscure fringe events gets booked up very quickly; getting around or doing anything normal becomes virtually impossible.

Founded in 1947 by actor-director **Jean Vilar**, the festival has included, over the years, theatrical interpretations as diverse as Euripides, Molière and Chekhov, performed by companies from across Europe. While big-name directors draw the largest crowds to the main venue, the Cour d'Honneur in the Palais des Papes, lesser-known troupes and directors also stage new works, and the festival spotlights a different culture each year.

The main **festival programme** is available from the second week in May from the Bureau du Festival d'Avignon, 20 rue du Portail Boquier (Ⓦwww.festival-avignon .com), or from the tourist office. Tickets go on sale on June 15 – via the festival's own website, the FNAC website (Ⓦfnac.com), FNAC shops all over France, or by phone (⊕04.90.14.14.14) – and remain available until three hours before each performance.

The fringe contingent known as the **Festival Off** (5 rue Ninon Vallin; ⊕04.90.85.13.08, Ⓦwww.avignonleoff.com) adds an additional element of craziness and magic, with a programme of innovative, obscure and bizarre performances taking place in more than a hundred venues as well as in the streets. A *Carte Public Adhérent* for €14 gives you thirty percent off all shows.

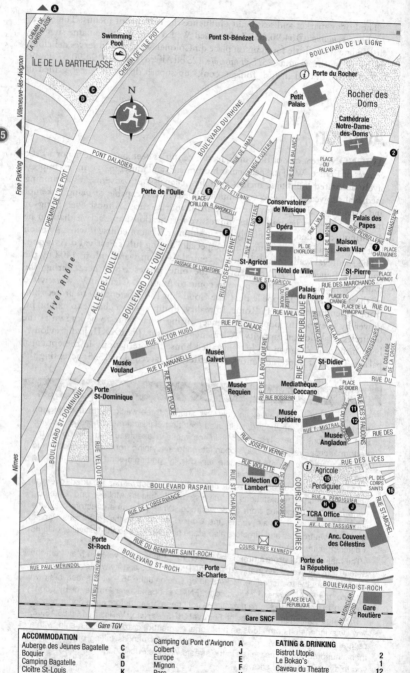

ÎLE DE LA BARTHELASSE

Swimming Pool

Pont St-Bénézet

BOULEVARD DE LA LIGNE

Porte du Rocher

CHEMIN DE L'ÎLE PIOT

N

Rocher des Doms

Petit Palais

Cathédrale Notre-Dame-des-Doms

PLACE DU PALAIS

BOULEVARD DU RHÔNE

PONT DALADIER

Porte de l'Oulle

Conservatoire de Musique

Palais des Papes

PLACE CRILLON R. BARONCELLI

Opéra

Maison Jean Vilar

PLACE CHÂTAIGNES

St-Agricol

PL. DE L'HORLOGE

Hôtel de Ville

St-Pierre

PLACE CARNOT

PASSAGE DE L'ORATOIRE

RUE ST-AGRICOL

Palais du Roure

PLACE DU CHANGE

PLACE DE LA PRINCIPALE

River Rhône

RUE VICTOR HUGO

RUE PTE. CALADE

RUE VIALA

Musée Vouland

RUE D'ANNANELLE

Musée Calvet

St-Didier

Porte St-Dominique

Musée Requien

Médiathèque Ceccano

PLACE ST-DIDIER

RUE BOISSERIN

Musée Lapidaire

RUE F. MISTRAL

RUE DES 3 FAUCONS

Musée Angladon

RUE DES

RUE JOSEPH VERNET

RUE VIOLETTE

RUE DES LICES

Agricole

Collection Lambert

Perdiguier

PL. DES CORPS SAINTS

BOULEVARD RASPAIL

RUE A. PERDIGUIER

RUE DE L'OBSERVANCE

TCRA Office

AV. L. DE TASSIGNY

Porte St-Roch

COURS JEAN-JAURÈS

Anc. Couvent des Célestins

RUE DU REMPART SAINT-ROCH

COURS PRES KENNEDY

BOULEVARD ST-ROCH

Porte St-Charles

Porte de la République

RUE PAUL-MÉRINDOL

AVENUE EISENHOWER

BOULEVARD ST-ROCH

PLACE DE LA RÉPUBLIQUE

Gare SNCF

AV. MONCLAR-NORD

Gare Routière

Gare TGV

ACCOMMODATION			
Auberge des Jeunes Bagatelle	C	Camping du Pont d'Avignon	A
Boquier	G	Colbert	J
Camping Bagatelle	D	Europe	E
Cloître St-Louis	K	Mignon	F
Le Clos du Rempart	B	Parc	H
		Splendid	I

EATING & DRINKING	
Bistrot Utopia	2
Le Bokao's	1
Caveau du Theatre	12
Chez Ginette & Marcel	16

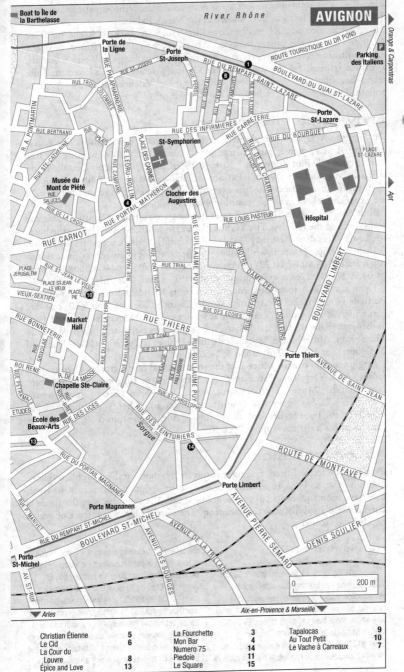

AVIGNON

Boat to Île de
la Barthelasse

River Rhône

Orange & Carpentras

Parking
des Italiens

ROUTE TOURISTIQUE DU DR PONS

Porte de
la Ligne

Porte
St-Joseph

RUE ST-JOSEPH

RUE PALAPHARNERIE

RUE TROIS
COLOMBES

RUE DU REMPART SAINT-LAZARE

BOULEVARD DU QUAI ST-LAZARE

RUE PERSIL

RUE SUREAU

RUE CREMADE

RUE TAMISIER

RUE TALOU

Porte
St-Lazare

PLACE
ST-LAZARE

15

PROVENCE

R. A. PONTMARTIN

RUE BERTRAND

RUE STE-CATHERINE

RUE 3
PALAIS

RUE DES INFIRMIERES

RUE CARRETERIE

RUE DE LA CHARRUE

RUE DU BOURGUET

Apt

RUE LEDRU-ROLLIN

RUE DES CARMES

PLACE
DES CARMES

St-Symphorien

RUE CAMPANE

Musée du
Mont de Piété

RUE
SALUCES

RUE DE LA CROIX

RUE PORTAIL MATHERON

Clocher des
Augustins

RUE LOUIS PASTEUR

Hôspital

RUE CARNOT

PLACE
JERUSALEM

RUE ST-JEAN LE VIEUX

PLACE ST-JEAN
LE VIEUX

VIEUX-SEXTIER

PLACE
PIE

RUE PAUL-SAIN

RUE PONT TROUCA

RUE TRIAL

RUE GUILLAUME PUY

RUE NOTRE DAME DES SEPT DOULEURS

RUE BUFFON

BOULEVARD LIMBERT

RUE BONNETERIE

Market
Hall

RUE THIERS

RUE COMU

RUE DU FOUR DE LA TERRE

RUE PHILONARDE

RUE DU BON PASTEUR

RUE DES ECOLES

Porte Thiers

AVENUE DE SAINT-JEAN

RUE
GRIVOLAS

ROI RENE

RUE PETRAMALE

Chapelle Ste-Claire

RUE
NOTRE-BIBE

RUE DE LA MASSE

RUE DE LA
PASSE

RUE GUILLAUME PUY

RUE ST-CHRISTOPHE

ETUDES

Ecole des
Beaux-Arts

RUE DES LICES

RUE DES TEINTURIERS

Sorgue

ROUTE DE MONTFAVET

RUE DU PORTAIL MAGNANEN

Porte Limbert

RUE P. MANIVET

Porte Magnanen

RUE DU REMPART ST-MICHEL

BOULEVARD ST-MICHEL

AVENUE DE LA TRILLADE

AVENUE PIERRE SEMARD

DENIS SOULIER

AVENUE DES SOURCES

Porte
St-Michel

AV. ST-RUF

0   200 m

Arles

Aix-en-Provence & Marseille

Christian Étienne	5	La Fourchette	3	Tapalocas	9
Le Cid	6	Mon Bar	4	Au Tout Petit	10
La Cour du		Numero 75	14	Le Vache à Carreaux	7
Louvre	8	Piedoie	11		
Épice and Love	13	Le Square	15		

impossibility of returning to Rome, he demolished the bishop's palace to replace it with an austere fortress, now known as the **Vieux Palais**.

Even when Gregory XI finally moved the Holy See back to Rome in 1378, Avignon's grip on the papacy persisted. After Gregory's death in Rome, dissident local cardinals elected their own pope in Avignon, provoking the Western Schism, a ruthless struggle for the control of the Church's wealth, which lasted until the pious Benedict fled Avignon for self-exile near Valencia in 1409. Avignon remained papal property right up to the Revolution.

Arrival and information

Driving into Avignon is a nightmare of junctions and one-way roads. The easiest **parking** is in two free, guarded car parks, connected with the centre by free shuttle buses: Île Piot (Mon–Fri 7.30am–8.30pm, Sat 1.30–8.30pm), on the Île de la Barthelasse, and the riverside Parking des Italiens (Mon–Sat 7.30am–8.30pm), northeast of town. Otherwise, the oversubscribed parking garages inside the walls are expensive; check whether your hotel offers parking.

Both Avignon's **gare SNCF** and the adjacent **gare routière** are just outside the walls south of the old city. The **TGV** station, 2km south, is linked by shuttle buses to cours Président-Kennedy (daily, 2–4 hourly; departures from station 6.18am–11.05pm, from town 5.44am–11.20pm; €3; ⓦwww.tcra.fr); a taxi into town (call ⓣ04.90.82.20.20) can cost €15 or more. Avignon-Caumont **airport** (ⓣ04.90.81.51.51, ⓦwww.avignon.aeroport.fr) is 8km southeast.

The main TCRA **local bus** stops are on cours Président-Kennedy and outside Porte de l'Oulle facing the river (tickets €1.20 each; book of ten €9.90; one-day pass €3.60; ⓦwww.tcra.fr). A free **boat** service crosses the river from east of Pont St-Bénézet to the Île de la Barthelasse, site of the city's campsites (July & Aug daily 11am–9pm; April–June & Sept daily 10am–12.30pm & 2–6.30pm; Oct–Dec Wed 2–5.30pm, Sat & Sun 10am–noon & 2–5.30pm).

Avignon's main **tourist office** is at the southern end of the city, at 41 cours Jean Jaurès (April–Oct Mon–Sat 9am–6pm, 9am–7pm in July, Sun 9.45am–5pm; Nov–March Mon–Fri 9am–6pm, Sat 9am–5pm, Sun 10am–noon; ⓣ04.32.74.32.74, ⓦwww.avignon-tourisme.com). There's another smaller branch by the Pont St-Bénézet (daily: July & Aug 10am–1pm & 2–7pm; April–June, Sept & Oct 10am–1pm & 2–6pm).

Accommodation

Even outside festival time, finding a **room** in Avignon can be a problem: cheap hotels fill fast, so book in advance. Villeneuve-lès-Avignon, just across the river, may have rooms when its larger neighbour is full. Between the two, the Île de la Barthelasse is an idyllic spot for **camping**. The tourist office keeps track of which hotels have vacancies.

Hotels and B&Bs

Boquier 6 rue du Portail Boquier
ⓣ04.90.82.34.43, ⓦwww.hotel-boquier
.com. Extremely welcoming little hotel near the tourist office, with funkily decorated, widely differing, and consistently inexpensive rooms, some very small, some sleeping three or four. ❸

Cloître St-Louis 20 rue du Portail Boquier
ⓣ04.90.27.55.55, ⓦwww.cloitre-saint-louis.com. Pleasant upscale hotel, with elegant modern decor in the seventeenth-century setting of a former Jesuit school. Some of the a/c rooms have attractive wood-beamed ceilings, and there's a rooftop pool. ❽

Le Clos du Rempart 35 rue Cremade
ⓣ04.90.86.39.14, ⓦwww.closdurempart
.com. Delightful B&B in a pretty nineteenth-century house behind the Palais des Papes, with two large, luxurious and very peaceful en-suite rooms; there's a wonderful wisteria-covered breakfast terrace and a hammock to doze in on sunny afternoons. ❼

Colbert 7 rue Agricol Perdiguier ☎04.90.86.20.20, ⓦwww.avignon-hotel-colbert.com. Warmly and imaginatively decorated rooms, mostly large, with helpful management and a pleasant courtyard. At the south end of town, handy for local trains and buses. Closed Nov–Feb. ❹

Europe 12 place Crillon ☎04.90.14.76.76, ⓦwww.heurope.com. A sixteenth-century town house, unpretentiously classy and set back in a shaded courtyard, with bright, modern, sound-proofed rooms, great home-made breakfasts and an excellent restaurant. ❾

Mignon 12 rue Joseph Vernet ☎04.90.82.17.30, ⓦwww.hotel-mignon.com. The decor may be a little too fussy, but this small hotel is great value for money considering its fantastic location on a chic street. Closed Jan. ❹

Parc 18 rue Agricol-Perdiguier ☎04.90.82.71.55, ⓦperso.modulonet.fr/hoduparc. Central budget option; very simple, clean rooms without TV, some overlooking a peaceful square. ❷

Splendid 17 rue Agricol-Perdiguier ☎04.90.86.14.46, ⓦwww.avignon-splendid-hotel .com. Very decent one-star in a great location just off the main drag; there's a steep narrow staircase to reach the upper floors. Fresh bathrooms and friendly management. Closed mid-Nov to mid-Dec. ❸

Hostel and campsites

Auberge des Jeunes Bagatelle Camping Bagatelle, Île de la Barthelasse ☎04.90.86.30.39, ⓦwww.campingbagatelle.com. Rather basic hostel facilities in the Bagatelle campsite. Beds in eight-person dorms for €18 per person, plus private rooms sleeping from two to four, with and without en-suite facilities; all rates include breakfast. ❶–❺

Camping Bagatelle Île de la Barthelasse ☎04.90.86.30.39, ⓦwww.campingbagatelle.com. Three-star campsite, with laundry facilities, a shop and café. It's the closest to the city centre, visible as you cross the Daladier bridge from Avignon; bus #20 from the post office to "Bagatelle" stop, or a 15-min walk from place de l'Horloge. Up to €23 for two people with a tent. Open all year.

Camping du Pont d'Avignon Île de la Barthelasse ☎04.90.80.63.50, ⓦwww.camping-avignon.com. Well shaded four-star site, with a lovely pool, on the island directly facing Pont St-Bénézet across the river, on bus route #20. Up to €24 for two people and a tent. Closed Nov to mid-March.

15

The City

Avignon's low walls still form a complete loop around the city. Despite their menacing crenellations, they were never a formidable defence, even when sections were girded by a now-vanished moat. Nevertheless with the gates and towers all restored, the old ramparts still give a sense of cohesion and unity to the old town, dramatically marking it off from the formless sprawl of the modern outskirts beyond.

The city's major monuments occupy a compact quarter inside the northern loop of the walls, just beyond its main square the **place de l'Horloge**, itself at the northern end of rue de la République, the old town's principal axis. Besides the colossal **Palais des Papes**, home to the medieval popes, other palaces are scattered around the centre, as well – of course – as several churches.

The Palais des Papes

The vast **Palais des Papes** soars above the east side of the cobbled place du Palais (daily: first half of March 9am–6.30pm; mid-March to June & mid-Sept to Oct 9am–7pm; July & first half of Sept 9am–8pm; Aug 9am–9pm; Nov–Feb 9.30am–5.45pm; last ticket 1hr before closing; €12.50, €15 with Pont St-Bénézet,

Avignon Passion passports

The tourist offices in Avignon and Villeneuve-lès-Avignon distribute free **Avignon Passion passports**. After paying the full admission price for the first museum you visit – for the best savings, make that a cheap one – you and your family receive discounts of 10–50 percent on the entrance fees of all subsequent museums in Avignon. The pass also gives discounts on tourist transport (such as riverboats and bus tours), and is valid for fifteen days after its first use.

€9.50/11 with Avignon Passion pass; Ⓦ www.palais-des-papes.com). With its massive stone vaults, battlements and sluices for pouring hot oil on attackers, the palace was built primarily as a fortress, though the two pointed towers that hover above its gate are incongruously graceful. Inside, however, so little remains of the original decoration and furnishings that it's easy to be deceived into thinking that all the popes and their retinues were as pious and austere as the last official occupant, Benedict XIII. The denuded interior leaves hardly a whiff of the corruption and decadence of fat, feuding cardinals and their mistresses, the thronging purveyors of jewels, velvet and furs, the musicians, chefs and painters competing for patronage, and the riotous banquets and corridor schemings. The first building on the audioguide tour (included in entrance fee) is the **Pope's Tower**, also known as the Tower of Angels; it's accessed via the vaulted **Treasury**, where the church's deeds and finances were handled. Four large holes concealed in the floor held the papal gold and jewels. The same cunning storage device was used in the **Chambre du Camérier** or Chamberlain's Quarters, off the Jesus Hall upstairs. In the adjoining **Papal Vestiary**, the Pope would dress before receiving sovereigns and ambassadors in the **Consistoire** of the Vieux Palais, on the other side of the Jesus Hall. On the floor above, the **kitchen** testifies to the scale of papal gluttony, with its square walls becoming an octagonal chimney piece for a vast central cooking fire. Major feasts were held in the **Grand Tinel**, or dining room, where only the pope was allowed to wield a knife. During the election of a new pope, the cardinals were locked into this room, adjourning to conspire and scheme in additional chambers to the south and west.

Once you've crossed from the Vieux Palais to the **Palais Neuf**, both Clement VI's bedroom and his study, the Chambre du Cerf, bear witness to this pope's secular concerns. The walls in the former are adorned with wonderful entwined oak- and vine-leaf motifs, the latter with superb hunting and fishing scenes. Providing almost the first dash of colour during the tour, these rooms can get unbearably crowded in high summer. As you continue, austerity resumes in the cathedral-like proportions of the **Grande Chapelle**, or Chapelle Clementine, and in the **Grande Audience**, its twin in terms of volume on the floor below.

The circuit also includes a walk along the roof terraces, which offer such tremendous views that it's worth heading up a little higher, to the rooftop café, even when the signs insist it's closed.

Around the Palais des Papes

Next to the Palais des Papes, the **Cathédrale Notre-Dame-des-Doms** might once have been a luminous Romanesque structure, but the interior has had a bad attack of Baroque, and the result is a stifling clutter. There's greater reward behind, in the peaceful **Rocher des Doms** park, which has fountains, ducks and views over the river to Villeneuve and beyond, along with a little café.

The absurdly misnamed **Petit Palais** (daily except Tues: June–Sept 10am–1pm & 2–6pm; Oct–May 9.30am–1pm & 2–5.30pm; €6), below the park's main entrance, is absolutely enormous. Its fabulous art collection focuses almost exclusively on thirteenth- to fifteenth-century painting and sculpture, most of it by masters from northern Italian cities. Pace yourself for a long haul – the peaceful courtyard café is a good place to break a visit – and watch out for such treasures as a supremely delicate *Virgin and Child* by the young Sandro Botticelli, and various works by the Sienese Simone Martini.

Behind the Petit Palais, and well signposted, is the half-span of Pont St-Bénézet, or the **Pont d'Avignon**, immortalized in the famous song *Sur le pont d'Avignon* ("… *l'on y danse, l'on y danse* …"). The song has existed in various forms for five centuries, but the modern words and tune come from nineteenth-century French operettas. It's generally agreed that the lyrics should really say "*Sous le pont*" (under the bridge), and referred to goings-on on the Île de Barthelasse, either of the general populace, who would dance on the island on feast days, or of the thief and trickster clientele of a tavern there, who danced with glee at the arrival of more potential victims.

The narrow bridge itself is open for visitors (same hours as Palais des Papes; €5, €15 combined ticket with Palais des Papes), while displays beneath its landward end explain the history of both bridge and song. After that, you're free to walk to the end and back, and dance upon it too, if you wish.

Around place de l'Horloge

Frenetically busy throughout the year, the café-lined **place de l'Horloge** holds the city's imposing **Hôtel de Ville** and **clock tower**, as well as the **Opéra**. Around the square, famous faces of past visitors to Avignon appear in windows painted on the buildings.

To the south, on rue Collège-du-Roure, the gateway and courtyard of the beautiful fifteenth-century **Palais du Roure** are well worth a look. A centre for Provençal culture, the palace often hosts temporary art exhibitions; for a rambling tour through the attics to see Provençal costumes, publications and presses, photographs of the Camargue in the 1900s and an old stagecoach, turn up at 3pm on Tuesday (€5).

Much as they did three hundred years ago, Avignon's most desirable addresses lie to the west of place de l'Horloge. The mellow stone facades along **rue Joseph Vernet** and **rue de la Petite-Fusterie** rise above the city's most luxurious shops.

The rest of the old city

The atmospheric and beautiful **quartier de la Banasterie**, immediately east of the Palais des Papes and north of place Pie, dates from the seventeenth and eighteenth centuries. Between Banasterie and **place des Carmes** lie a tangle of tiny streets where you're almost certain to get lost. Pedestrians have priority over cars on many streets, and there are plenty of tempting café or restaurant stops.

Avignon's main pedestrianized area, however, lies a little further south, stretching between the chainstore blandness of rue de la République and the modern **market hall** on place Pie (mornings Tues–Sun). **Rue des Marchands** and **rue du Vieux-Sextier** have their complement of chapels and late medieval mansions, while the Renaissance **church of St-Pierre** on place St-Pierre (Mon–Wed & Sun 10am–1pm; Thurs–Sat 10am–1pm & 2–6pm) holds superb doors sculpted in 1551. More Renaissance art is on show in the fourteenth-century **church of St-Didier** (daily 8am–6.30pm), chiefly *The Carrying of the Cross* by Francesco Laurana, commissioned by King René of Provence in 1478.

South of place Pie, the **Chapelle Ste-Clare** is where the poet Petrarch first saw and fell in love with Laura, during the Good Friday service in 1327. A little way east, the atmospheric **rue des Teinturiers** was a centre for calico printing during the eighteenth and nineteenth centuries. The cloth was washed in the Sorgue canal, which still runs alongside, though the four of its mighty watermills that survive no longer turn.

The museums

The excellent, airy **Musée Calvet** is housed in a lovely eighteenth-century palace at 65 rue Joseph Vernet (daily except Tues 10am–1pm & 2–6pm; €6, or €7 with Musée Lapidaire; Ⓦwww.musee-calvet.org). Highlights include a wonderful gallery of languorous nineteenth-century marble sculptures, including Bosio's *Young Indian*; the Puech collection of silverware and Italian and Dutch paintings;

and works by Soutine, Manet and Joseph Vernet, as well as Jacques-Louis David's subtle, moving *Death of Joseph Barra*. It also holds much more ancient artefacts, like enigmatic stelae from the fourth-century BC, carved with half-discernible faces.

Larger pieces from the Musée Calvet's archeological collection are displayed in the separate **Musée Lapidaire**, in a Baroque chapel at 27 rue de la République (daily except Tues 10am–1pm & 2–6pm; €2, or €7 with Musée Calvet; Ⓦwww .musee-calvet.org). Besides Egyptian statues and Etruscan urns, this abounds in Roman and Gallo-Roman sarcophagi, and early renditions of the mythical Tarasque (see p.869).

Nearby, the **Musée Angladon**, 5 rue Labourer (April–Nov Tues–Sun 1–6pm; Dec–March Wed–Sun 1–6pm; €6; Ⓦwww.angladon.com), displays what remains of the private collection of couturier Jacques Doucet. Apart from Antonio Forbera's extraordinary *Le Chevalet du Peintre*, a trompe-l'oeil painting from 1686 depicting the artist's easel, complete with sketches and palette as well as work in progress, the older works are largely outclassed by Doucet's contemporary collection. It includes Modigliani's *The Pink Blouse*, various Picassos, including a self-portrait from 1904, and Van Gogh's *The Railroad Cars*, his only Provençal painting on permanent display in the region.

Avignon's one contemporary art gallery, the thoughtfully curated and splendidly displayed **Collection Lambert** (July & Aug daily 11am–7pm; Sept–June Tues–Sun 11am–6pm; €5.50; Ⓦcollectionlambert.com), at 5 rue Violette just west of the tourist office, shows off works by the likes of Cy Twombly, Jasper Johns and Roni Horn. It also stages stimulating temporary exhibitions.

Eating and drinking

Avignon has an enormous number of **restaurants**, ranging from expensive gastronomic rendezvous to cheap snack places and takeaways. The large café-brasseries on the terraces of place de l'Horloge and rue de la République all serve quick, if not necessarily memorable, meals, while the old pedestrian lanes are packed with atmospheric possibilities.

Restaurants and cafés

Caveau du Théâtre 16 rue des Trois Faucons ☎04.90.82.60.91. Cheerful bistro, with pretty painted walls, jolly red tables and occasional live jazz, serving delicious dishes like market-fresh fish. Lunch *menu* €12, dinner *menus* €18 and €22. Closed Sat lunch, Sun, and 2nd half of Aug.

Chez Ginette & Marcel 27 place des Corps-Saints ☎04.90.85.58.70. The most attractive of several restaurants on this lively, youthful little square; if you sit outside, be sure to venture into the restaurant itself, a fun evocation of a 1950s' French grocery, filled with funky bric-a-brac. *Tartines* and salads are the speciality; you can get a substantial meal for well under €10.

Christian Étienne 10 rue de Mons ☎04.90.86.16.50. Avignon's best-known gourmet restaurant, in a twelfth-century mansion. Mouthwatering Provençal delights can include a whole menu devoted to tomatoes, or autumn vegetables – with meat and fish, naturally. Dinner *menus* range €65–125, but you can sample the delights for €31 at lunchtime. Closed Sun & Mon.

La Cour du Louvre 23 rue St-Agricol ☎04.90.27.12.66. Hidden peacefully away from the old-town bustle in a delightful interior courtyard at the end of a *cour*, with a romantic atmosphere and good Mediterranean cooking; *menus* from €32 for lunch, €29 for dinner. Closed Sun & Mon.

Épice and Love 20 rue des Lices ☎04.90.82.45.96. Dining in this friendly and hugely popular local restaurant feels like sharing hearty home cooking in someone's living room, stuffed with random gewgaws. Changing *menus* at €17 (three courses) or €15 (two), with staples like lasagne or tagine alongside subtler dishes like roasted squid or fish.

La Fourchette 17 rue Racine ☎04.90.85.20.93. Bright, busy yet refined restaurant serving up classic and sophisticated fish and meat dishes – try the tasty sardines marinated in coriander – on €33 and €42 dinner *menus*. Closed Sat, Sun & first three weeks in Aug.

Numero 75 75 rue Guillaume Puy ☎04.90.27.16.00. Housed in a beautiful mansion, with indoor and garden seating, this smart restaurant serves dinner *menus* from €32.50, but offers a €10 lunchtime *plat du jour*. Closed Sun, except in July.

Piedoie 26 rue des Trois Faucons ℡04.06.21.86.51.53. Romantic little restaurant specializing in fresh Provençal cuisine; the salads are recommended. Lunch sees a €18 market *menu*, while dinner *menus* start at €29. Closed Tues & Wed, plus two weeks in Feb & two weeks in Aug.

Le Square Square Agricol Perdiguier ℡04.06.21.86.71.94. There's nothing very exceptional about the food in this outdoor café/brasserie, sprawling in a spacious park behind the tourist office, but it makes a great spot for a summer-morning coffee, or a simple lunchtime salad or *plat* for under €10. Closed after sunset.

Au Tout Petit 4 rue d'Amphoux ℡04.90.82.38.86. Tiny, unpretentious place, tucked away down a side alley near Les Halles; the friendly owner prepares food that's imaginative, fresh and unbeatable. Two-course lunch for €11, dinner *menus* from €15. Closed Sun & Mon.

Bars and clubs

Bistrot Utopia 4 rue Escaliers Ste-Anne ℡06.37.57.52.31. In the shadow of the Palais des Papes, this café has changing exhibitions adorning the walls, live jazz some nights, and adjoins a good cinema. Daily noon–midnight.

Le Bokao's 9bis bd du Quai St-Lazare ℡04.90.82.47.95. Popular mainstream club, in a converted barn across from the river just outside the walls, playing an eclectic mix of music styles including house and techno at the weekends. Wed–Sat 10pm–5am.

Le Cid 11 place de l'Horloge ℡04.90.82.30.38. Trendy mixed gay/straight bar and terrace that opens up at 6.30am daily, and keeps going until 1am, long after everywhere else is closed.

Mon Bar 17 rue du Portail Matheron. Pleasantly old-fashioned café with a laid-back atmosphere. Daily 7am–10pm.

Tapalocas 15 rue Galante ℡04.90.82.56.84. Tapas and Spanish music, sometimes live, in a large, atmospheric bar. Daily noon–1am.

Le Vache à Carreaux 14 rue Peyrollerie ℡04.90.80.09.05. Intimate, homely wine bar that serves food and stays open until 1am.

Theatre, music and film

Though the city saves a lot of its energy for the festival, Avignon sees a fair amount of **nightlife** and **cultural events** all year round, particularly café-theatre. For more information, drop in at the tourist office. The **Opéra**, on place de l'Horloge (℡04.90.82.81.40, ⓦwww.operatheatredavignon.fr), stages a wide range of classical opera and ballet; Le Chêne Noir, 8bis rue Ste-Catherine (℡04.90.86.58.11, ⓦchenenoir.fr), is a theatre company worth seeing, with mime, musicals or Molière on offer; and plenty of **classical concerts** are performed in churches, usually for free. Cinéma Utopia, at La Manutention, 4 rue Escalier Ste-Anne (℡04.90.82.65.36, ⓦwww.cinemas-utopia.org), shows films in *version originale* (undubbed); the same complex houses the *AJMI Jazz Club* (℡04.90.86.08.61, ⓦwww.jazzalajmi.com), which hosts live jazz.

Listings

Bike rental Provence Bike, 52 bd St-Roch ℡04.90.27.92.61, ⓦwww.provence-bike.com; also scooters and motorbikes.

Boat trips Grands Bateaux de Provence, allée de l'Oulle ℡04.90.85.62.25, ⓦwww.mireio.net. Dinner cruises upstream towards Châteauneuf-du-Pape and downstream to Arles €48–65, meal included. Shorter cruises from €8.50. April–Sept.

Bookshops Shakespeare, 155 rue Carreterie ℡04.90.27.38.50, ⓦwww.shakespeare.bookshop .free.fr (closed Sun & Mon); FNAC, 19 rue de la République ⓦfnac.com (closed Sun).

Health Doctor/ambulance ℡15; hospital, Centre Hospitalier H.-Duffaut, 305 rue Raoul Follereau ℡04.32.75.33.33; night chemist, call police ℡04.90.85.13.13 for addresses.

Internet Chez W@M 41 rue du Vieux-Sextier; Webzone 3 rue St-Jean-le-Vieux/place Pie.

Police ℡17.

Post office Poste, cours Président-Kennedy, Avignon 84000.

Taxis Place Pie ℡04.90.82.20.20. Velocité (bicycle taxis €1 per km) ℡06.37.36.48.89.

Villeneuve-lès-Avignon

Pretty and prosperous, though little more than a village at its core, **VILLE-NEUVE-LÈS-AVIGNON** rises up a rocky escarpment above the west bank of the Rhône, looking down upon its older neighbour from behind far more convincing fortifications. Despite ongoing rivalry, Villeneuve has effectively been a suburb of Avignon for most of its history, with palatial residences constructed by the cardinals and a great monastery founded by Pope Innocent VI.

To this day, Villeneuve technically belongs to Languedoc not Provence, and might be better known were it further from Avignon, whose monuments it can almost match for colossal scale. It is, however, a very different – and really rather sleepy – kind of place, and as such retains a repose and a sense of timelessness that bustling Avignon inevitably lacks. In summer it provides venues for the Avignon Festival as well as alternative accommodation, and it's certainly worth a day's exploring, whatever time of year you visit.

Arrival and information

The half-hourly #11 bus takes ten minutes to reach Villeneuve from cours Président-Kennedy in Avignon, or just five minutes from Porte de l'Oulle. The unprepossessing place Charles-David where the bus stops is home to the **tourist office** (April–June, Sept & Oct Mon–Sat 9am–12.30pm & 2–6pm; July Mon–Fri 10am–7pm, Sat & Sun 10am–1pm & 2.30–7pm; Aug daily 9am–12.30pm & 2–6pm; Nov–March Mon–Sat 9.30am–12.30pm & 2–5pm; ℡04.90.25.61.33, Ⓦwww.villeneuvelezavignon.fr/tourisme), as well as **markets** on Thursday (food) and Saturday (bric-a-brac). The Avignon Passion pass detailed on p.855 is also valid in Villeneuve.

Accommodation

In terms of accommodation, Villeneuve is more a boutique destination than a mere alternative to Avignon, with a handful of charming, good-value hotels and B&Bs.

L'Atelier 5 rue de la Foire ℡04.90.25.01.84, Ⓦwww.hoteldelatelier .com. Very tasteful rooms in a charming sixteenth-century house with a central stone staircase bathed in light, plus huge open fireplaces and a delightful well-shaded courtyard garden with terraces. Closed Jan. ❹

Les Écuries des Chartreux 66 rue de la République ℡04.90.25.79.93, Ⓦecuries-des-chartreux .com. B&B in a light and airy rustic house with exposed stone walls and antique furniture. ❺

Jardin de la Livrée 4bis rue Camp de Bataille ℡04.90.26.05.05, Ⓦwww.la-livree.oxatis.com. Clean, comfortable B&B rooms in an old house in the centre of the village, with a swimming pool, and an appealing Mediterranean restaurant, closed Mon, that serves an €18 lunch *menu* and a €26 dinner *menu*. The one drawback is the noise of passing trains. ❺

Prieuré 7 place du Chapitre ℡04.90.15.90.15, Ⓦleprieure.com. If you fancy being surrounded by tapestries, finely carved doors, old oak ceilings and other baronial trappings, this old priory surrounded by a peaceful flower-filled garden is indisputably the first choice. The restaurant serves Provençal cuisine with a gourmet twist. Closed Nov–March. ❽

Hostel and campsite

Camping Municipal de la Laune Chemin St-Honoré ℡04.90.25.76.06, Ⓦcamping -villeneuvelezavignon.com. A three-star site off the D980, near the sports stadium and swimming pools. €15.50 for two people with a tent. Closed mid-Oct to March.

YMCA hostel 7bis chemin de la Justice ℡04.90.25.46.20, Ⓦwww.ymca-avignon.com. Beautifully situated overlooking the river by Pont du Royaume (the extension of Pont Daladier), with balconied rooms for one to four people (from €25 for dorm bed, or available as private rooms), with and without en-suite facilities, and an open-air swimming pool. ❶

The Town

Villeneuve today has a lazy small-town feel, its daily activity centred around the lovely little place Jean-Jaurès. Until 1770, however, the town was enclosed within the walls of the enormous **Fort St-André**, rising to the east. Then, the Rhône shifted its course south, and the fort lost its strategic importance. Now a hollow shell, it can be reached by climbing either the montée du Fort from place Jean-Jaurès, or the steeper, cobbled rue Pente Rapide, a cobbled street of tiny houses that leads off place Charles-David.

Once inside the fort's bulbous, double-towered gateway, you find yourself on the narrow former main street. Buying a ticket for the fort itself (daily: April to mid-May & last 2 weeks of Sept 10am–1pm & 2–5.30pm; mid-May to mid-Sept 10am–1pm & 2–6pm; Oct–March 10am–1pm & 2–5pm; €5) allows you to continue up the street, passing tumbledown ruins, and then walk along the parapets, where a cliff-face terrace offers tremendous views across the river. You can also pay separately to visit its former **abbey** (Tues–Sun: April–Sept 10am–12.30pm & 2–6pm; Oct–March 10am–12.30pm & 2–5pm; €4), which as well as more magnificent views holds gardens of olive trees, ruined chapels, lily ponds and dovecotes.

Below the fort, **La Chartreuse du Val du Bénédiction** (April–June daily 9.30am–6.30pm, July–Sept daily 9am–6.30pm; Oct–March Mon–Fri 9.30am–5pm, Sat & Sun 10am–5pm; €7), is one of France's largest Carthusian monasteries, founded by the sixth of the Avignon popes, Innocent VI. Its buildings are now totally unembellished, and except for the Giovanetti frescoes in the chapel beside the refectory, all its paintings and treasures have been dispersed. You're free to wander around unguided, through the three cloisters, the church, chapels, cells and communal spaces. Among the best venues for the Festival of Avignon, it also holds a great restaurant (see below).

Another festival venue, the fourteenth-century **Église Collégiale Notre-Dame** (daily: April–Sept 10am–12.30pm & 2–6.30pm; Oct–March 10am–noon & 2–5pm; free) and its cloister stand on place St-Marc close to the *mairie*. Notre-Dame's most important treasure is a rare fourteenth-century smiling Madonna and Child made from a single tusk of ivory. It's now housed in the **Musée Pierre-de-Luxembourg**, just to the north along rue de la République (Tues–Sun: Jan, March & Oct–Dec 10am–noon & 2–5pm; April–Sept 10am–12.30pm & 2–6.30pm; €3), along with many of the paintings from the Chartreuse, including the stunning *Coronation of the Virgin*, painted in 1453 by Enguerrand Quarton.

South of the centre, beside the main road from Avignon, the stout **Tour Philippe-le-Bel** (Tues–Sun: March, Oct & Nov 10am–noon & 2–5.30pm; April–Sept 10am–12.30pm & 2–6.30pm; €2.20) was built to guard the western end of Avignon's Pont St-Bénézet. The rather tricky climb to the top is rewarded with an overview of Villeneuve and Avignon.

Eating and drinking

Aubertin 1 rue de l'Hôpital ☏04.90.25.94.84. Set in the shade of the old arcades by the Collégiale Notre-Dame. Simple local dishes followed by fabulous desserts: try the chocolate and raspberry tart. €40 *menu*. Closed Sun & Mon.

La Banaste 28 rue de la République ☏04.90.25.64.20. Bountiful Provençal and Languedocien *terroir* meals. More pleasant indoors than on the cramped roadside terrace. *Menus* from €24 (two courses), €30 (three). Closed Thurs low season & last three weeks of Jan.

Les Jardins d'Été de la Chartreuse Cloître St-Jean, La Chartreuse ☏04.90.15.24.23. A truly memorable experience; between mid-June & Sept only, you can thread your way through the labyrinthine old monastery to find this open-air restaurant in a secluded courtyard. Some tables have lovely sunset views. Friendly service and *menus* of substantial Provençal cuisine; from €17 for lunch, €20 for dinner.

St-Rémy-de-Provence

The watery and intensely cultivated scenery of the Petite Crau plain south of Avignon changes abruptly with the eruption of the **Chaîne des Alpilles**, whose peaks look like the surf of a wave about to engulf the plain. The dreamy, little changed community of **ST-RÉMY-DE-PROVENCE**, where Van Gogh sought psychiatric help and painted some of his most lyrical works, nestles against the northern base of the Alpilles, 30km from either Arles or Avignon. St-Rémy is a beautiful spot, centring on a charmingly low-key old town – the Vieille Ville – that's barely five hundred metres across, and encircled by leafy boulevards. South of the old town, several exceptional sites and attractions lie within walking distance: Van Gogh's hospital of **St-Paul-de-Mausole**, a **Roman arch**, and the ruins of the ancient city of **Glanum**.

The best time to visit St-Rémy is during the **Fête de Transhumance** on Whit Monday (around mid- to late-May), when a two thousand-strong flock of sheep, accompanied by goats and donkeys, does a tour of the town before being packed off to the Alps for the summer.

Arrival and information

St-Rémy's **tourist office** is just south of the old town on place Jean-Jaurès (June–Sept Mon–Sat 9am–12.30pm & 2–6pm, Sun 10am–noon; Oct–May Mon–Sat 9am–noon & 2–6pm; ℡04.90.92.05.22, Ⓦsaintremy-de-provence.com). No trains serve St-Rémy; **buses** from Avignon, Aix and Arles drop passengers in place de la République, on the eastern edge of the old town. **Bikes** can be rented from Telecycles, who deliver anywhere in the area (℡04.90.92.83.15, Ⓦwww.telecycles-location.com).

Accommodation

Although no **accommodation** is available within the old town itself, St-Rémy has a fine selection of hotels, most within easy walking distance of the centre, and several campsites close by.

Cheval Blanc 6 av Fauconnet ℡04.90.92.09.28, Ⓦwww.hotelduchevalblanc.com. Inexpensive hotel, just outside the old town on its western edge. The cheapest rooms are not en-suite, but the four-person ones are especially good value. Closed Nov to mid-March. ❸

Sous les Figuiers 3 av Taillandier ℡04.32.60.15.40, Ⓦwww.hotel-charme-provence.com. Gorgeous place just north of the old town. Thirteen well appointed rooms, some with their own private garden terraces, plus swimming pool and an on-site artist's studio (art classes available). Closed mid-Jan to mid-March. ❺

Le Soleil 35 av Pasteur ℡04.90.92.00.63, Ⓦwww.hotelsoleil.com. Very welcoming hotel, set back from the main road a short walk south of the centre, with a pool and private parking. Nice, simple rooms but no restaurant. Closed early Nov to late March. ❸

Campsites

Le Mas de Nicolas Av Plaisance du Touch ℡04.90.92.27.05, Ⓦmasdenicolas.celeonet.fr. Four-star municipal site with its own pool, 800m from the centre on a turning off the route de Mollégès. Open mid-March to Oct.

Monplaisir Chemin Monplaisir ℡04.90.92.22.70, Ⓦwww.camping-monplaisir.fr. Family-run, five-acre, two-star campsite, 1km northwest of town along the rte de Maillane, with a pool and snack facilities. Open early March to Oct.

The Town

St-Rémy's compact **Vieille Ville** is an enchanting tangle of narrow lanes and alleyways, lined with stately residences and interspersed with peaceful squares.

While it only takes a few minutes to walk from one side to the other it's worth exploring every nook and cranny.

Be sure to call in on the **Musée des Alpilles**, halfway along the main axis, rue Carnot (daily except Mon, plus 1st Sun of month: July & Aug 10am–12.30pm & 2–7pm; March–June & Sept–Oct 10am–noon & 2–6pm; Nov–Feb 2–5pm; €3). Interesting sections on folklore, festivities and traditional crafts include an exhibit on cicadas, a symbol of Provence associated with author Frédéric Mistral. Another fine mansion, the eighteenth-century Hôtel d'Estrine at 8 rue Estrine, houses the **Centre d'Art Présence Van Gogh** (mid-March to April & Oct–Nov Tues–Sun 10.30am–12.30pm & 2–6pm; May–Sept Tues & Thurs–Sun 10am–12.30pm & 2–7pm, Wed 10am–7pm; €3.20), which hosts contemporary art exhibitions plus permanent displays on the painter, and has a well-stocked gift shop. Rue Hoche holds the house where astrologer Michel de Nostredame – **Nostradamus** – was born, but it's not open to visitors.

Between May 1889 and May 1890, **Vincent Van Gogh** was a voluntary psychiatric patient at the former monastery of **St-Paul-de-Mausole** (daily: April–Oct 9.30am–7pm; Oct–March 10.15am–5pm; €4), just east of the main road a little under 2km south of the old town. Amazingly enough, it's still a psychiatric hospital, and although tourists are kept well clear of the active area – be sure to follow the "Zone Touristique" signs – you get a real and profoundly moving sense of its ongoing work. Displays in the church and cloisters contrast Van Gogh's diagnosis and treatment with modern-day practices, and you can see a mock-up of his former room and walk in the glorious gardens, planted with lavender and poppies. Art therapy forms a major component of current treatment at the hospital, and patients' work is on sale in the on-site shop.

Across the main road from the monastery, an open patch of ground holds two Roman monuments, jointly known as **Les Antiques**. One is a triumphal arch celebrating the Roman conquest of Marseille, the other a well-preserved mausoleum thought to commemorate two grandsons of Augustus. Both display intricate patterning and a typically Roman sense of proportion.

Sharing the same car park (€2.50), the impressive ancient settlement of **GLANUM** (April–Aug daily 10am–6.30pm; Sept Tues–Sun 10am–6.30pm; Oct–March Tues–Sun 10am–5pm; €7; ⓦ glanum.monuments-nationaux.fr) was dug from the alluvial deposits at the foot of the Alpilles. This site originally held a Neolithic homestead, before the Gallo-Greeks built a city here between the second and first centuries BC. Then the Gallo-Romans constructed yet another town, which lasted until the third century AD.

A footpath drops from the site entrance to run through the centre of the ruins, with plenty of maps and captions along the way, but getting to grips with Glanum is far from easy. Not only were the later buildings moulded onto the earlier ones, but there was also a fashion at the time of Christ for building a deliberately archaic, Hellenistic style. Where the site narrows into a ravine at its southern end, a Greek edifice stands around the **spring** that made this location so desirable. Steps lead down to a pool, with a slab above for the libations of those too sick to descend. An inscription records that Agrippa restored it in 27 BC, and dedicated it to Valetudo, the Roman goddess of health. **Altars** to Hercules remain in evidence, however. The Gallo-Romans directed the water through canals to heat houses and, of course, to the **baths** that lie near the site entrance. There are superb sculptures on the Roman **Temples Geminées** (twin temples), as well as fragments of mosaics, fountains of both periods, and first-storey walls and columns.

Eating and drinking

You'll find plenty of **brasseries** and **restaurants** in and around old St-Rémy, the best of them on rue Carnot and on boulevards Mirabeau and Gambetta.

Bistrot Decouverte 19 bd Victor-Hugo ☏04.90.92.34.49. Straightforward, high-quality Provençal bistro, with a fabulous wine list, on the edge of the old town. There's a two-course *menu* for €16, and a full dinner *menu* at €30. Closed Sun pm & Mon, plus mid-Feb to mid-March.

La Gousse d'Ail 6 bd Marceau ☏04.90.92.16.87. Charming bistro on the western edge of the old town, with a €16 lunch *menu* and dinner for €27 or €34, its own vintage merry-go-round, and live jazz on Wednesday nights. Closed Thurs & Fri lunch.

La Maison Jaune 15 rue Carnot ☏04.90.92.56.14. Michelin-starred restaurant, with a garden terrace in the old town.

Tempting à la carte offerings such as polenta and pigeon roasted in Baux wines, and *menus* for €38, €58 (the lovely *Dégustation Provençale*), and €68. Closed Mon, plus Tues lunch, and also Sun eve in winter; closed Nov–Jan.

Taberna Romana Site of Glanum, av van-Gogh ☏04.90.92.65.97. Nice open-air lunch spot, overlooking the ruins of Glanum from a shady terrace. Its so-called "Roman food" is fun and a bit different, with a large mixed plate of, say, *samsa* (spicy olives), *cicerona* (chick peas) and goat's cheese for €17, or a *matza*, which closely resembles a chicken wrap, for €8. They also serve "Roman beer". Tues–Sun 10am–6.30pm, closed Nov–March.

Les Baux and the Val d'Enfer

At the top of the Alpilles ridge, 7km south of St-Rémy and 15km northeast of Arles, perches the unreal fortified village of **LES BAUX-DE-PROVENCE**. Unreal partly because the ruins of its eleventh-century castle merge almost imperceptibly into the plateau, and partly because this Ville Morte (Dead City) is accessible only via a turnstile from the living village below, which remains a too-perfect collection of sixteenth- and seventeenth-century churches, chapels and mansions.

After the medieval lords of Les Baux died out at the end of the fourteenth century, the town passed in due course to the kings of France who, in 1632, razed the feudal citadel to the ground. For the next two hundred years, both citadel and village were inhabited almost exclusively by bats and crows. The subsequent discovery of the mineral bauxite (named for Les Baux) in the neighbouring hills brought back some life, and tourism has more recently transformed the place. Today the population is around augmented by more than 1.5 million visitors each year. Even the former bauxite quarries, cut from the jagged rocks of the Val d'Enfer, are now tourist attractions, as home to the imaginative Cathédrale des Images. As the great majority of Les Baux's visitors are day-trippers, who tend to be thinning out by 5pm or so, it's well worth turning up later in the day.

The castle site

While Les Baux is undoubtedly a pretty village, the prime reason to come is to see its enormous and extraordinary **castle** (daily: March–June 9am–6.30pm; July & Aug 9am–8.30pm; Sept–Nov 9.30am–6pm; Dec–Feb 9.30am–5pm; €7.80; Ⓦwww.chateau-baux-provence.com), which though universally known as a château is in truth more of a large citadel. The only gate to the complex, at the far end of the main village street, leads first to open ground below the walls, scattered with replica siege engines and catapults, and then to footpaths over and through assorted buildings. These include the ruins of the feudal castle demolished on Richelieu's orders, the partially restored **Chapelle Castrale** and the **Tour Sarrasine**. The higher you climb, the more spectacular the views become.

The Val d'Enfer

It's said that Dante took his inspiration for the nine circles of the *Inferno* from a visit to the **Val d'Enfer** (Valley of Hell), immediately north of Les Baux. Jean Cocteau filmed parts of *Le Testament d'Orphée* in 1959 amid its contorted rocks and bauxite quarries. More recently, those same quarries have been turned into an audiovisual experience called the **Cathédrale des Images**, a few hundred metres north of the village along the D27 (daily: April–Sept 10am–6pm; Oct–March 10am–5pm; €7.50; ⓌWww.cathedrale-images.com). The effect is similar to entering an Egyptian temple carved from the rock, but here you're surrounded by images projected over the floor, ceilings and walls of the vast rectangular caverns, and by music that resonates strangely in the captured space. The precise content changes yearly, though it's often devoted to a particular artist or school of painting. Really, it makes little difference; the sensation is just mind-blowing, as you wander through the changing shapes and colours.

Practicalities

Les Baux village is pedestrianized. Parking costs €5 close to the gate, €3 a little lower down, and nothing at the Cathédrale des Images. The **tourist office** is at the beginning of Grande-Rue (daily: July & Aug 9am–7pm; Sept–June 9am–6pm; Ⓣ04.90.54.34.39, Ⓦwww.lesbauxdeprovence.com). Nothing in Les Baux comes cheap, least of all **accommodation**. The only moderately-priced hotel, the *Hostellerie de la Reine Jeanne* near the tourist office (Ⓣ04.90.54.32.06, Ⓦwww.la-reinejeanne .com; closed mid-Jan to mid-Feb; ❸), has very friendly staff, simple rooms with views of the citadel, and good *menus* starting at €25. There's also *Le Prince Noir*, an eccentric B&B in the uppermost house in the village, on rue de l'Orme (Ⓣ04.90.54.39.57, Ⓦwww.leprincenoir.com; ❺–❽; two-night minimum stay).

Arles

With its sun-kissed golden stone, small-town feel and splendid riverside setting, **ARLES** is one of the loveliest cities in southern France. It's also among the oldest; the extraordinarily well-preserved Roman amphitheatre at its heart, **Les Arènes**, is simply the most famous of several magnificent monuments. Originally a Celtic settlement, Arles became the Roman capital of Gaul, Britain and Spain, and served later as a base for the counts of Provence before unification with France.

For centuries, the port of Arles prospered thanks to the trade route up the Rhône. Decline set in with the arrival of the railways, however, and the town where **Van Gogh** spent a lonely and miserable – but highly prolific – period in the late nineteenth century was itself inward-looking and depressed.

Today's Arles is a gloriously laid-back place, its narrow lanes adorned with effortlessly artistic details. It's especially famous for its sense of style, most recently expressed via native designer Christian Lacroix. It springs to life for the **Saturday market**, thronged with farmers from the Camargue and La Crau, and during the busy bull-fighting season between Easter and All Saints. It also fills the year with a crowded calendar of festivals, of which the best known is the **Rencontres Internationales de la Photographie** (Ⓦwww.rencontres-arles.com), from July to mid-September.

Arrival and information

Arles' *gare SNCF* is a few blocks north of the Arènes. Most buses arrive at the unstaffed **gare routière** alongside, though all local services stop on boulevard

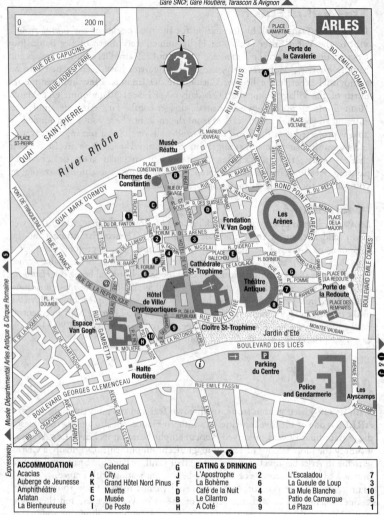

ARLES

0   200 m

N

PLACE
LAMARTINE

Porte de
la Cavalerie

BD. EMILE COMBES

RUE DES CAPUCINS

RUE ROBESPIERRE

SAINT-PIERRE

RUE MARIUS

RUE DE LA CAVALERIE

PLACE
VOLTAIRE

River Rhône

QUAI

PLACE
ST-PIERRE

QUAI MARX DORMOY

RUE A. FRANCE

PONT DE TRINQUETAILLE

Musée
Réattu

Thermes de
Constantin

PLACE
CONSTANTIN   R. DU GRAND PRIEURE

PL. MARIUS
JOUVEAU

RUE DU 4 SEPTEMBRE

R. BARBES

RUE AUGUSTIN TARDIEU

RUE PORTAGNEL

ROND POINT DES ARENES   R. DU REFUGE

R. RENAN

PLACE
DE LA
MAJOR

Les
Arènes

Fondation
V. Van Gogh

RUE DU DR. FANTON

R. DE LA LIBERTE

PL. DU
FORUM   R. DES ARENES

R. FAVORIN

R. HOTEL DE VILLE

R. NICOLAI

R. DIDEROT

PLACE
BALECHOU

PLACE
H. BORNIER

R. DE L'AMPHITHEATRE

PLACE
DE LA
REDOUTE

BOULEVARD EMILE COMBES

PLACE
DES
REMPARTS

Cathédrale
St-Trophime

PLACE
DE LA CALADE

R. PORTE DE LAURE

Théâtre
Antique

Hôtel
de Ville/
Cryptoportiques

RUE DU CLOITRE

PL. DE LA
REPUBLIQUE

RUE DE LA REPUBLIQUE

Cloître St-Trophime

Jardin d'Eté

MONTEE VAUBAN

R. VAUBAN

Espace
Van Gogh

RUE GAMBETTA

R. MOLIERE

BD DU PRE WILSON

R. DE LA ROTONDE

BOULEVARD DES LICES

P
Parking
du Centre

AVENUE DES ALYSCAMPS

Halte
Routière

i

Police
and Gendarmerie

Les
Alyscamps

BOULEVARD GEORGES CLEMENCEAU

AVE. SADI CARNOT

AVENUE DU M. LECLERC

RUE EMILE FASSIN

BD. EMILE ZOLA

Expressway ◄   Musée Départemental Arles Antique & Cirque Romaine ◄   Musée Départemental Arles Antique & Cirque Romaine ◄

K

ACCOMMODATION				EATING & DRINKING			
Acacias	A	Calendal	G	L'Apostrophe	2	L'Escaladou	7
Auberge de Jeunesse	K	City	J	La Bohème	6	La Gueule de Loup	3
Amphithéâtre	E	Grand Hôtel Nord Pinus	F	Café de la Nuit	4	La Mule Blanche	10
Arlatan	C	Muette	D	Le Cilantro	8	Patio de Camargue	5
La Bienheureuse	I	Musée	B	A Coté	9	Le Plaza	1
		De Poste	H				

Georges Clemenceau, just east of rue Gambetta. In summer, drivers are better off
parking on the periphery, such as in the Centre car park on boulevard des Lices,
rather than venturing into the central maze of narrow one-way streets. Bikes can
be rented from Europbike, 1 rue Philippe Lebon (℡06.85.55.44.71), or the hostel
(see opposite). The main **tourist office** is on boulevard des Lices (Easter–Sept
daily 9am–6.45pm; Oct–Easter Mon–Sat 9am–4.45pm, Sun 10am–1pm;
℡04.90.18.41.20, ⓦwww.arlestourisme.com); there's a summer annexe in the
gare SNCF (Easter–Sept Mon–Fri 9am–1.30pm & 2.30–5pm). For **internet
access**, go to Cyber-Saladelle, 17 rue de la République (Tues–Sat 10am–7pm,
℡04.90.93.13.56).

Accommodation

There's little shortage of **hotel** rooms at either end of the scale; it's nicer to stay in the historic centre, but cheap places are concentrated around Porte de la Cavalerie near the station.

Hotels

Acacias 2 rue de la Cavalerie ☎04.90.96.37.88, ⊛www.hotel-acacias.com. Modern, simple but cheerfully decorated – and sound-proofed – rooms in a friendly hotel, not far from the train station. Closed late Oct to March. ❹

Amphithéâtre 5–7 rue Diderot ☎04.90.96.10.30, ⊛hotelamphitheatre.fr. Very central hotel, where the spacious and beautifully decorated rooms feature warm colours, wrought ironwork, and large well-equipped bathrooms, Great-value four-person rooms. ❹

Arlatan 26 rue du Sauvage ☎04.90.93.56.66, ⊛www.hotel-arlatan.fr. Set in a beautiful antique-decorated fifteenth-century mansion, this hotel has plenty of character, and its own garage, but some rooms are rather small. Closed Jan. ❺

Calendal 5 rue Porte-de-Laure ☎04.90.96.11.89, ⊛www.lecalendal.com. Welcoming hotel, facing the Théâtre Antique and glowing at sunset, with bright a/c rooms overlooking a pleasant shaded garden. Closed Jan. ❻

Grand Hôtel Nord Pinus 14 place du Forum ☎04.90.93.44.44, ⊛www.nord-pinus.com. Chic, luxurious rooms in a grand mansion dominating a pretty, lively square in the heart of the old town. Much favoured by the *vedettes* of the bullring, it's decorated with assorted trophies and evocative photos. ❽

Muette 15 rue des Suisses ☎04.90.96.15.39, ⊛www.hotel-muette.com. Charming old stone hotel, close to Les Arènes, where the tasteful, tranquil rooms are decked out in beiges and creams. Nice buffet breakfast, and friendly management. Closed Jan & Feb. ❸

Musée 11 rue du Grand-Prieuré ☎04.90.93.88.88, ⊛www.hoteldumusee.com. Small, good-value, family-run place, in a quiet location opposite Musée Réattu, with a pretty, flower-filled terrace. Closed Jan & first fortnights of March & Dec. ❸

De Poste 2 rue Molière ☎04.90.52.05.76, ⊛www.hotelrelaisdeposte.fr. Simple but comfortable rooms in a fine old town house, on a surprisingly quiet place near the tourist office; its terrace restaurant opens for lunch only, Mon–Sat, with *menus* at €12 and €15. ❸

Hostel and campsites

Auberge de Jeunesse 20 av du Maréchal-Foch ☎04.90.96.18.25, ⊛www.fuaj.org/arles. Old-style hostel, 500m south of the centre (bus #3, stop "Clemenceau"), with rock-hard beds in large dorms (€16.70, including breakfast), and spartan facilities. Bike hire available. Reception 7–10am and 5–11pm (midnight in summer). Closed mid-Dec to mid-Feb.

La Bienheureuse On the N453 at Raphèle-lès-Arles ☎04.90.98.48.06, ⊛www.labienheureuse.com. Well-shaded three-star site that's the best of Arles' half-dozen campsites, 7km southeast on the Aix bus route, with a Provençal-styled restaurant. Open all year.

City 67 rte de Crau ☎04.90.93.08.86, ⊛www.camping-city.com. The closest campsite to town, 1.5km southeast on the Crau bus route, this two-star is not very attractive, but there's shade and a pool. Closed Oct–March.

The City

Although Arles is blessed with abundant monuments and museums, it's a delightful city simply to stroll around at random. The compact central core,

Discount Passes

Several passes grant free admission to differing combinations of Arles' Roman monuments, plus the cathedral cloisters, the Musée Départemental Arles Antique and the Musée Réattu. Sold at the tourist offices and the sites themselves, their precise details change each year, but the following passes were on sale at the time of writing (check ⊛www.arles-tourisme.com for current prices):

Liberté €9, valid for one month: any four Roman monuments, plus one museum.

Avantage €13.50, valid for one year, covers every site.

nestled against a ninety-degree curve in the river, is small enough to cross on foot in a few minutes, and holds all the major sights except the **Musée Départemental Arles Antique** to the southwest, and **Les Alyscamps** necropolis to the southeast. The main square, with the cathedral and town hall, is **place de la République**, while the hub of popular life is **place du Forum**.

Roman Arles

Roman Arles provided grain for most of the western empire and was one of the major ports for trade and shipbuilding. Under Constantine it became the capital of Gaul and reached its height as a world trading centre in the fifth century. Once the empire crumbled, however, Arles found itself isolated between the Rhône, the Alpilles and the marshlands of the Camargue – an isolation that allowed its Roman heritage to be preserved.

Arles' most dramatic monument, the amphitheatre known as **Les Arènes** (daily: March, April & Oct 9am–6pm; May–Sept 9am–7pm; Nov–Feb 10am–5pm; €6 with Théâtre Antique; Ⓦ www.arenes-arles.com), was the largest Roman building in all Gaul; its two tiers of sixty arches were originally topped by a third, and thirty thousand spectators would cram beneath its canvas roof to watch gladiator battles. During the Middle Ages, it became a fortress. Since two hundred medieval dwellings and three churches were cleared away in 1830, the Arènes has once more been used for entertainment. While it's impressive from the outside, it's only worth paying for admission when a performance is taking place, like a bullfight (see box opposite) or concert.

Just south of Les Arènes, but nowhere near as well preserved, the **Théâtre Antique** was quarried to build churches after the Roman Empire collapsed, and only one pair of columns is still standing. Once again, there's little to see on an ordinary day, but it's an atmospheric venue for performances and festivals year-round (daily: March, April & Oct 9am–noon & 2–6pm; May–Sept 9am–7pm; Nov–Feb 10am–noon & 2–5pm; €6 with Arènes; Ⓦ theatre-arles.com).

Arles' most unusual – and spookiest – Roman remains, the **Cryptoportiques** (daily: March, April & Oct 9am–noon & 2–6pm; May–Sept 9am–noon & 2–7pm; Nov–Feb 10am–noon & 2–5pm; €3.50) are reached via stairs that lead down from inside the Hôtel de Ville (see opposite). No one knows quite what these huge, dark and dank underground galleries were for; they may have been built simply to prop up one side of the town's level open forum, which stood above, and then used as a food store, or a barracks for public slaves. They're empty now, but make for an atmospheric subterranean stroll.

At the river end of rue Hôtel de Ville, the **Thermes de Constantin** (daily: March, April & Oct 9am–noon & 2–6pm; May–Sept 9am–noon & 2–7pm; Nov–Feb 1–5pm; €3), are the ruins of the biggest Roman baths in Provence. The most impressive feature is visible from outside on place Constantin: the elegant high wall of an apse that sheltered one of the baths, in alternating stripes of orange brick and grey masonry.

To get an overall sense of Roman Arles, be sure to visit the superb open-plan **Musée Départemental Arles Antique** (daily except Tues 10am–6pm; €6; Ⓦ www.arles-antique.cg13.fr). Excellent models show the changing layout of the city and the sheer size of its monuments, while thematic displays explore such topics as medicine, industry and agriculture, and the use of water power. Overhead walkways enable visitors to admire some fabulous mosaics.

Arles' Roman necropolis, **Les Alyscamps** (daily: March, April & Oct 9am–noon & 2–6pm; May–Sept 9am–7pm; Nov–Feb 10am–noon & 2–5pm; €3.50), is a few minutes' walk south of boulevard des Lices. Long after the Roman era ended, this was the most hallowed Christian burial ground in Europe; until the twelfth

The bullfight

Bullfighting, or more properly *tauromachie* (roughly, "the art of the bull"), comes in two styles in Arles and the Camargue. In the local **courses camarguaises**, held at *fêtes* from late spring to early autumn (the most prestigious of which is Arles' Cocarde d'Or in early July), *razeteurs* run at the bulls in an effort to pluck ribbons and cockades tied to the bulls' horns, cutting them free with special barbed gloves. The drama and grace is in the stylish way the men leap over the barrier away from the bull, and in the competition for prize money. In this gentler bullfight, people are rarely injured and the bulls are not killed.

More popular, however, are the brutal Spanish-style **corridas** (late April, early July & Sept at Arles), consisting of a strict ritual leading up to the all-but-inevitable death of the bull. After its entry into the ring, the bull is subjected to the *bandilleros* who stick decorated barbs in its back, the *picadors*, who lance it from horseback, and finally, the *torero*, who endeavours to lead the bull through as graceful a series of movements as possible before killing it with a single sword stroke to the heart. In one *corrida* six bulls are killed by three *toreros*, for whom injuries (sometimes fatal) are not uncommon.

Whether you approve or not, *tauromachie* has a long history here, and offers a rare opportunity to join in local life. It's also a great way to experience Arles' Roman arena in use. Assorted bullfighting events are staged at Les Arènes between Easter and October each year, including non-fatal *courses camarguaises* at 5.30pm each Wednesday from early July until late August; ticket prices typically range €9–35 (ⓦ www.arenes-arles.com).

century, mourners far upstream would launch sumptuous coffins to float down the Rhône, for collection at Arles. Only one of its many alleyways now survives, while the finest of its sarcophagi and statues have long since disappeared. Nonetheless, ancient tombs still line the shaded walk, as painted by Van Gogh, and the tranquil stroll ends at the wonderfully simple twelfth-century Romanesque church of **St-Honorat**.

The rest of the city

Superb twelfth-century Provençal stone carving around the doorway of the **Cathédrale St-Trophime** on the central **place de la République** depicts the Last Judgement, trumpeted by angels playing with the enthusiasm of jazz musicians. As the damned are led naked and chained down to hell, the blessed, all female and draped in long robes, process upwards. Work on the cathedral itself started in the ninth century. The high nave is now decorated with d'Aubusson tapestries, while there's more Romanesque and Gothic stone carving, including an image of Saint Martha leading away the tamed Tarasque (see p.858), in the beautiful **cloisters** (same hours as Les Arènes; €3.50), reached by a separate entrance to the right.

Also on place de la République, the palatial seventeenth-century **Hôtel de Ville** was inspired by the Palace of Versailles. A staircase inside leads down to the Roman **Cryptoportiques** (see opposite); the flattened vaulted roof of its entrance hall was expressly designed to minimize stress on the galleries below.

The must-see **Musée Réattu** (Tues–Sun: July–Sept 10am–7pm; Oct–June 10am–12.30pm & 2–6.30pm; €7; ⓦ www.museereattu.arles.fr) stands beside the river in a beautiful fifteenth-century priory. What's on display varies according to current temporary exhibitions, but it's always attractively laid out. The collection centres on 57 ink and crayon sketches, made between December 1970 and February 1971, donated by Pablo Picasso in appreciation of the many bullfights he'd seen in Arles. Among the split faces, clowns and hilarious Tarasque, there's a magnificently simple portrait of Picasso's mother, painted from life in 1923. Other twentieth-century pieces dotted about the landings, corridors and courtyard niches include *Odalisque*, Zadkine's polychromed sculpture of a woman playing a violin.

Van Gogh in Arles

At the back of the Musée Réattu, lanterns line the river wall where **Van Gogh** used to wander, wearing candles on his hat, watching the night-time light: *The Starry Night* is the Rhône at Arles. The café painted in *Café de Nuit* still stands in place du Forum, and the distinctive Pont Langlois drawbridge painted by the artist in March 1888 can be seen on the southern edge of the town (poorly signposted off the D35). Van Gogh had arrived by train in February 1888 to be greeted by snow and a bitter mistral wind. But he started painting straight away, and in this period produced such celebrated canvases as *The Sunflowers*, *Van Gogh's Chair*, *The Red Vines* and *The Sower*. Van Gogh found few kindred souls in Arles and finally managed to persuade Gauguin to join him in mid-autumn. Although the two were to influence each other substantially in the following weeks, their relationship quickly soured as the increasingly bad November weather forced them to spend more time together indoors. According to Gauguin, Van Gogh, feeling threatened by his friend's possible departure, finally succumbed to a fit of psychosis and attacked first Gauguin and then himself. He was packed off to the Hôtel-Dieu hospital on rue du Président-Wilson down from the Musée Arlaten, now the **Espace Van Gogh**, an academic and cultural centre with arty shops in its arcades and courtyard flower beds recreated according to Van Gogh's painting and descriptions of the hospital garden.

Arles has none of the artist's works but the **Fondation Vincent Van Gogh** (April–June daily 10am–6pm; July–Sept daily 10am–7pm; Oct–March Tues–Sun 11am–5pm; €7; Ⓦfondationvangogh-arles.org), facing the Arènes at 26 rond-point des Arènes, exhibits works by contemporary artists inspired by Van Gogh, including Roy Lichtenstein and David Hockney.

Eating and drinking

Arles holds a good range of **restaurants** – many excellent, many cheap, and a fair number both. Place du Forum is the centre of **café** life, with the *Café de la Nuit* attracting Van Gogh devotees, and a younger crowd at *l'Apostrophe*. Most of Arles, however, packs up for the night around 10.30pm.

La Bohème 6 rue Balze ⓉⒹ04.90.18.58.92. Very central Mediterranean restaurant, with vaulted ceilings. A good vegetarian *menu* costs €16, while the €21 *menu* includes a bream tartare.

Le Cilantro 31 rue Porte-de-Laure ⓉⒹ04.90.18.25.05. Serene, highly expensive restaurant serving beautifully executed, imaginative dishes. The meticulous young chef prepares excellent *plats*, such as pikeperch in a truffle crust, for around €30. Lunch *menus* from €25, dinner from €65. Closed Sat lunch & Sun, plus Mon lunch July & Aug, all Mon Sept–June.

A Coté 21 rue des Carmes ⓉⒹ04.90.47.61.13. The cheaper sister to the much more expensive, Michelin-starred *L'Atelier de Jean-Luc Rabanel*, at no. 7 on the same little alleyway, this is just as gastronomically satisfying, and has pleasant outdoor seating. Mouthwatering tapas include aubergine caviar (€6.50), full *plats*

are €12–24, and you can also get breakfast and fancy take-out sandwiches. Daily 9am–midnight.

L'Escaladou 23 rue Porte-de-Laure ⓉⒹ04.90.96.70.43. Behind its old-fashioned façade, above the Théâtre Antique, this local favourite holds three substantial dining rooms. It may be noisy, and the service perfunctory at times, but the honest local food is delicious. *Menus* from €18; magnificently garlicky fish specials include a sumptuous €26 Arlesian bouillabaisse. Closed Wed.

La Gueule de Loup 39 rue des Arènes ⓉⒹ04.90.96.96.69. Cosy stone-walled restaurant, squeezed into a venerable town house, and serving substantial traditional dishes such as bull *filet* with anchovy sauce. *Menus* from €12.50 lunch, €24 dinner; reservations recommended. Closed Sun & Mon lunch, plus Mon eve Nov–Easter.

La Mule Blanche 9 rue du Président-Wilson ⓉⒹ04.90.93.98.54. Laid-back brasserie/restaurant

with an enormous outdoor patio; the food is rich and fruity, with salads at €10, *plats* around €15, and a €25 dinner *menu* offering duck with honey. Occasional jazz. Closed Sun & first half of Jan.

Patio de Camargue 51bis Chemin Barriol ☏04.90.49.51.76, ⓦwww.chico.fr. Arles was the original base for the world-conquering *Gipsy Kings* group. Founder-member Chico now runs this riverfront restaurant-cum-music venue, roughly

1km southwest of the centre; check the website for upcoming events.

Le Plaza 28 rue du Dr-Fanton ☏04.90.96.33.15. Smart but very friendly place, also known as *La Paillote*, with a good €20 *menu* full of Provençal starters and main courses such as *papillote de taureau* (bull), and a €30 one of house specialities, with no choice. Reserve for outdoor seating. Closed Tues lunch & Wed eve.

The Camargue

Spreading across the Rhône delta and bounded by the Petit Rhône to the west, the Grand Rhône to the east, and the Mediterranean to the south, the drained, ditched and now protected land known as the **CAMARGUE** is utterly distinct from the rest of Provence. With land, lagoon and sea sharing the same horizontal plain, its shimmering horizons are infinite, its boundaries not apparent until you come upon them. The entire region is a Parc Naturel Régional, striving to find an equilibrium between tourism, agriculture, industry and hunting on the one hand, and the indigenous ecosystems on the other.

When the Romans arrived, the northern part of the Camargue was a forest; they felled the trees to build ships, then grew wheat. These days, the main crop is rice, but there's still some wheat, along with vines, fruit orchards and the ubiquitous rapeseed. To the east, along the final stretch of the Grand Rhône, the Camargue holds the biggest saltworks in the world.

The Camargue is divided into two separate sections by the Étang du Vaccarès at its heart, a lagoon that's out of bounds to visitors. The western side is much busier with tourists, who flock to the only sizeable town, **Stes-Maries-de-la-Mer**. Really just an overgrown village turned summer resort, it's a nice enough place, with a fascinating gypsy connection, but for a true sense of what makes the Camargue special, you're better off exploring its marshes and dunes, or following its waterfront nature trails.

There's no **ideal season** to visit. The Camargue's notorious **mosquitoes** can make the months from March to November unbearable; they're less prevalent

Tours and activities

- Around thirty Camargue farms offer **horseriding**, with typical rates ranging from €16 for an hour up to €85 per day. Recommended options include the Domaine Paul Ricard in Méjanes (☏04.90.97.10.62, ⓦwww.mejanes.camargue.fr); you can find full lists at ⓦwww.saintesmaries.com and ⓦwww.camargue.fr.

- **Bikes** can be rented in Stes-Maries from Le Vélociste, back from the sea on place Mireille (☏04.90.97.83.26, ⓦwww.levelociste.fr).

- **Canoes** and **kayaks** are available from Kayak Vert in Sylvéréal, beside the Petit-Rhône on the D38C 17km northwest of Stes-Maries (☏04.66.73.57.17, ⓦwww.kayakvert-camargue.fr).

- Ninety-minute river trips on the Petit Rhône, costing €10, are offered by the **paddle steamer** *Le Tiki III*, which sets off from the river mouth, 2.5km west of Stes-Maries (mid-March to early Nov, 1–5 trips daily; ☏04.90.97.81.68, ⓦtiki3.fr), and the *Camargue* (mid-March to mid-Oct, 1–5 trips daily; ☏04.90.97.84.72, ⓦwww.bateau-camargue.com), which leaves from the port in Stes-Maries.

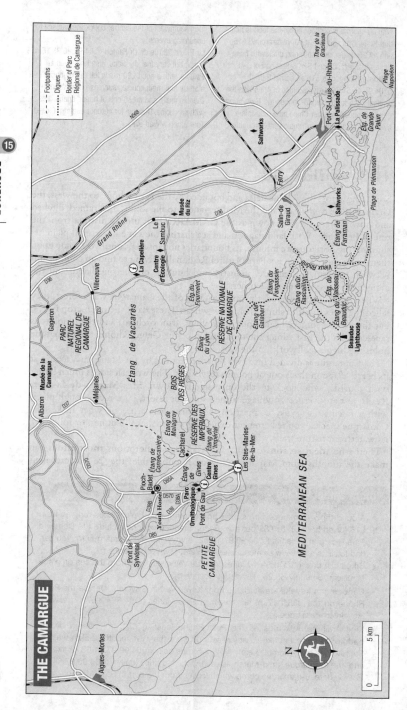

THE CAMARGUE

| Footpaths |
| Digues |
| Border of Parc Régional de Camargue |

They de la Gracieuse

Plage Napoléon

Port-St-Louis-du-Rhône

La Palissade

Saltworks

Etg. de Grande Palun

Ferry

Plage de Piémanson

Saltworks

Salin-de-Giraud

Musée du Riz

D36

Étang de Faraman

Étang du Tangassier

Vieux Rhône

Grand Rhône

Le Sambuc

La Capelière

Centre d'Écologie

Étg du Fournelet

RÉSERVE NATIONALE DE CAMARGUE

Villeneuve

D37

D36

Gageron

PARC NATUREL REGIONAL DE CAMARGUE

Étang de Vaccarès

Étang du Lyon

Étang de Galabert

Étang du Gr. Rascaillon

Étg. du Valsseau-Beauduc

Étang du

Beauduc Lighthouse

Albaron

Musée de la Camargue

Méjanes

BOIS DES RIEGES

RÉSERVE DES IMPÉRIAUX

Étang dit L'Impérial

D570

Étang de Malagroy

Cacharel

Les Stes-Maries-de-la-Mer

Pioch-Badet

Étang de Consecanière

Youth Hostel

D36

D570

D85A

Étang de Ginès

Parc Ornithologique

Pont de Gau

D85

Centre Ginès

D85

Pont de Sylvéréal

PETITE CAMARGUE

MEDITERRANEAN SEA

Aigues-Mortes

N

0   5 Km

beside the sea, but elsewhere you'll need serious chemical weaponry. Biting flies are also a problem, as are the strong autumn and winter winds, which make cycling hard despite the flat terrain. And finally, in summer the weather can be so hot and humid that the slightest movement is an effort.

The western Camargue

The main regional information centre is on the D570, 10km southwest of Arles, in the **Musée de la Camargue** (April–Sept daily 9am–12.30pm & 1–6pm; Oct–March daily except Tues 10am–12.30pm & 1–5pm; €4.50; ☎04.90.97.10.82, ⓦwww .parc-camargue.fr). Displays document the history, traditions and livelihoods of the Camarguais people, with particular emphasis on rice, wine and bulls.

Another 23km further on, at Pont de Gau, 4km north of Stes-Maries, hiking trails make birdwatching easy at the engrossing **Parc Ornithologique** (daily: April–Sept 9am–sunset; Oct–March 10am–sunset; €7; ⓦparcornithologique .com). Signs and information are plentiful, and some of the less easily spotted species are kept in aviaries.

The best **hiking trail** in the western Camargue follows a drover's path, the Draille de Cacharel, between Cacharel, 4km north of Stes-Maries, and the D37 just north of Méjanes.

Les Stes-Maries-de-la-Mer

The built-up seaside town of **LES STES-MARIES-DE-LA-MER**, 37km southwest of Arles, has more in common with France's other Mediterranean beach resorts than with the wild and empty land that surrounds it. Most famous for its annual gypsy festival on May 24–25, when Romanies celebrate Sarah, their patron saint, Stes-Maries is an attractive little place nonetheless. A line of beaches, sculpted into successive little crescents by stone breakwaters and busy with bathers and windsurfers throughout the summer, stretch away west from its central core of white-painted, orange-tiled houses, while the pleasure port to the east offers boat trips to the lagoons and fishing expeditions. With its *arènes* staging bullfights, cavalcades and other entertainment, and musicians playing in the street, a stay of a night or two can be good fun.

Arrival and information

The seafront tourist office is at 5 av Van-Gogh (daily: Jan, Feb, Nov & Dec 9am–5pm; March & Oct 9am–6pm; April–June & Sept 9am–7pm; July & Aug 9am–8pm; ☎04.90.97.82.55, ⓦwww.saintesmaries.com), with abundant car parking nearby. Buses from Arles arrive at the north end of place Mireille, 400m short of the sea.

Bulls, birds and beavers: Camarguais wildlife

The Camargue is a treasure trove of bird and animal species, both wild and domestic. Its most famous denizens are its bulls, and the white horses ridden by the region's *gardians* (herdsmen). Neither beast is truly wild, though both run in semi-liberty. Genuine wildlife ranges from wild boars, beavers and badgers; via tree frogs, water snakes and pond turtles; to marsh and sea birds, waterfowl and birds of prey. The best time for birdwatching is the mating season, from April to June. Of the region's fifty thousand or so flamingos, ten thousand remain in winter (Oct–March) when the rest migrate to north Africa. They're born grey, incidentally, then turn pink aged between four and seven.

Accommodation

At any time between April and October, and especially during the Romany festival, it's necessary to book **accommodation** well in advance. Don't worry too much if you can't find a room in Stes-Maries itself; appealing options are scattered through the marshlands nearby.

Hotels

Cacharel Rte de Cacharel ☎04.90.97.95.44, ⓦwww.hotel-cacharel.com. Luxurious rooms in an ancient farm, 4km north of Stes-Maries on the D85A, with open fires in winter, a pool in summer, and horseriding year-round, but no restaurant. **❼**

Le Dauphin Bleu/La Brise de Mer 31 av G-Leroy ☎04.90.97.80.21, ⓦwww.hotel-dauphin-bleu .camargue.fr. Good-value white-painted hotel-restaurant, on the seafront a few hundred metres from the centre at the east end of the beach road. The nicest of the rather austere rooms have balconies overlooking the sea. **❹**

🏇 **Mangio Fango** Rte d'Arles ☎04.90.97.80.56, ⓦwww.hotelmangio fango.com. Tranquil farmhouse, overlooking the marshes 600m north of central Stes-Maries, with a Mediterranean twist. Stylish, comfortable rooms, pricey restaurant, and a pool. Closed all Jan, open weekends only in Dec. **❻**

🏇 **Mediterranée** 4 av F-Mistral ☎04.90.97.82.09, ⓦwww.mediterranee hotel.com. Decked out in jolly flowers, this welcoming hotel has pretty Provençal rooms – sleeping up to four guests – and is in the heart of the town, seconds from the sea. **❷**

Hostel and campsites

Auberge de Jeunesse Pioch-Badet ☎04.90.97.51.72, ⓦwww.auberge-de-jeunesse .camargue.fr. Dorm beds in a former school, beside the D570 10km north of Stes-Maries cost €29.70, half-board; Bike rental, horse rides and other excursions available. Reservations essential.

Camping La Brise Rue Marcel Carrière ☎04.90.97.84.67, ⓦwww.camping-labrise.fr. Three-star site, near the sea on the east side of Stes-Maries, with a pool and laundry facilities. Tents, mobile homes or bungalows available for rent. Closed mid-Nov to mid-Dec.

Camping Le Clos du Rhône Rte d'Aigues-Mortes ☎04.90.97.85.99, ⓦwww.camping-leclos.fr. Busy four-star site at the mouth of the Petit Rhône, 800m west of central Stes-Maries along an easy seaside path, with a pool, laundry and shop. Closed early Nov to early April.

The Town

The spider's-web tangle of streets and alleyways at the heart of old Stes-Maries, filled with everything from supermarkets and delis to bucket-and-spade shops and art galleries, opens out into a sequence of spacious squares on all sides of its grey-gold Romanesque **church**. Fortified in the fourteenth century to shelter the entire population against pirate attacks, the church has beautifully pure lines and fabulous acoustics. Downstairs in the crypt, the tinselled and sequined statue of Sarah is surrounded by candles, abandoned crutches and calipers, and naïve ex-voto paintings dedicated in thanks for blessings and cures. Although you can't climb to the top of the tower, paying €2 allows you to scramble onto and over the church roof, for great views over the town (daily: July & Aug 10am–sunset; March–June & Sept to mid-Nov 10am–12.30pm & 2pm–sunset).

Eating and drinking

Of a summer evening, Stes-Maries gets very lively indeed, with the *terrasses* of its restaurants and bars sprawling out across the streets and squares, and flamenco guitarists and buskers everywhere. The town **market** takes place on place des Gitans every Monday and Friday.

La Bouvine Av F-Mistral ☎04.90.97.87.09. Large restaurant on Stes-Maries' main dining street, with outdoor seating and pretty much any French or Spanish dish you care to mention, from paella (€12) to *marmite de pêcheur* (€13.50), and a €15 set *menu*.

Brûleur de Loups Av Léon Gambetta ☎04.90.97.83.31. Smart, all-round Provençal restaurant with a terrace that's among the very few places in Stes-Maries where you get a sea view while you eat. *Menus* €18–40. Closed Tues pm, Wed, & mid-Nov to mid-Dec.

The eastern Camargue

To enjoy the finest scenery in the eastern half of the Camargue, follow the D36b along the eastern edge of the Étang de Vaccarès. An information centre at **La Capelière** (April–Sept daily 9am–1pm & 2–6pm, Oct–March daily except Tues 9am–1pm & 2–5pm; €3; T 04.90.97.00.97, W www.reserve-camargue.org), 23km out of Arles, holds rather faded displays on Camargue wildlife and how to see it. Outside, a short but excellent 1.5-km initiation trail circles a small lagoon, with superb bird-watching opportunities along the way from camouflaged hides equipped with telescopes. Another good hiking trail, which is also a prime observation point for **flamingos**, starts 5km west of the one town in these parts, industrial Salin-de-Giraud, and follows the dyke between the Étangs du Fangassier and Galabert.

From Avignon to the Luberon

Heading east from Avignon to the Luberon, worthwhile stops include pretty **Isle-sur-la-Sorgue**, and **Fontaine-de-Vaucluse**, at the source of the Sorgue. One of the most powerful natural springs in the world, it's a romantic spot, albeit deluged by tourists much of the time.

Isle-sur-la Sorgue

Isle-sur-la-Sorgue, 30km east of Avignon, straddles five branches of the River Sorgue, with little canals and waterways running through and around the centre. Its waters were once filled with otters and beavers, eels, trout and crayfish, and turned the power wheels of a **medieval cloth industry**. Tanneries, dyeing works, and subsequently silk and paper manufacturing, all ensured considerable prosperity for "the Island".

Nowadays, the huge blackened waterwheels turn for show only, and the mills and tanneries stand empty, plants growing through the crumbling brickwork. But in summer, fishing punts continue to crowd the streams and L'Isle is a cheerful place, particularly on Sundays, when people arrive for its well-known **antiques market**, which centres on the Village des Antiquaires on avenue de l'Égalité and spills out onto the boulevards.

L'Isle-sur-la-Sorgue's claim to be the Venice of Provence may stretch a point, but it's a pleasant waterside place to spend an afternoon. The central **place de l'Église** and **place de la Liberté** offer reminders of past prosperity, most obviously in the Baroque seventeenth-century **church** (closed Mon), the richest religious edifice for miles around. In addition, the little **Musée du Jouet et de la Poupée Ancienne** (daily 10.30am–6pm; €3.50; T 04.90.20.97.31) shows off a private collection of remarkably intact dolls dating from 1880 to 1920.

Practicalities

The **tourist office** (Mon–Sat 9am–12.30pm & 2.30–6pm; Sun 9am–12.30pm; T 04.90.38.04.78, W www.oti-delasorgue.fr) is next to the church. *La Prévôté*, 4 rue J.J. Rousseau (T 04.90.38.57.29, W www.la-prevote.fr; ➐) is a charming hotel with five rooms decked out in beautiful terracotta tiles and wooden beams, which also serves high-quality *menus* from €26 (restaurant closed Tues, plus Wed Sept–June). Cheaper alternatives include *La Gueulardière*, 1 cours René Char (T 04.90.38.10.52, W www.gueulardiere.com; restaurant closed Mon; ➍). For a true feast, head for the delightful *Vivier*, 800 cours Fernande Peyre (T 04.90.38.52.80, W levivier-restaurant.com; closed lunchtime Fri & Sat, Sun eve

& Mon), where *menus* start at €30 lunch, €45 dinner. The *Bistro de l'Industrie* on quai de la Charité (☎04.90.38.00.40) offers decent *plats du jour* for €10.

Fontaine-de-Vaucluse

The source of the Sorgue river is a mysterious tapering fissure, 7km east of Isle-sur-la-Sorgue at the foot of towering 230-metre cliffs. Among the most powerful natural springs in the world, and compellingly beautiful into the bargain, it's a hugely popular tourist attraction. All access is via the ancient riverside village of **FONTAINE-DE-VAUCLUSE**, downstream; from here a gentle 500m footpath, the chemin de la Fontaine, climbs through a narrowing gorge to the *fontaine* itself. Both the village and the full length of the path are heavily (albeit reasonably taste-fully) commercialized, but it's still a gorgeous spot, with the glorious green river cascading beneath thickly wooded slopes.

Seven centuries ago, the poet Petrarch spent sixteen unrequited years pining in this rustic backwater for his Laura. To learn a little more about the lovelorn rhymester, drop into the **Musée de Pétrarque**, just across the bridge south of the river (daily except Tues: April–May 10am–noon & 2–6pm; June–Sept 10am–12.30pm & 1.30–6pm; Oct 10am–noon & 2–5pm; €3.50).

The **tourist office** is beyond the village towards the spring, on chemin de la Fontaine (daily 10am–1pm & 2–6pm; ☎04.90.20.32.22, Ⓦwww.oti-delasorgue .fr). The most luxurious place to **stay** is *L'Hotel du Poète* (☎04.90.20.34.05, Ⓦwww.hoteldupoete.com; closed Dec–Feb; ❺), below the main D25 on the north bank of the river, just before the village, which has large, comfortable rooms and a pool. The *Sources* on the south bank (☎04.90.20.31.84, Ⓦwww .hoteldessources.com; closed mid-Nov to mid-Feb; ❸), offers nice old-fashioned rooms and a decent restaurant, while the pleasant **hostel**, 1km south towards Gordes (☎04.90.20.31.65, Ⓦwww.fuaj.org/fontaine-de-vaucluse; closed mid-Nov to Jan; €17.70 including breakfast), also offers camping in its grounds. *Les Prés* **campsite**, beside the river's south bank 500m downstream from the village, has a pool (☎04.90.20.32.38; closed Nov–Feb). Among the terraced **restaurants** and cafés that surround the central place de la Colonne is *Lou Fanau* (☎04.90.20.31.90; closed Wed), which has *menus* of regional food from €15.90.

The Luberon

Lying east of Avignon and north of Arles, **the Luberon** valley has long been a favoured escape for well-heeled Parisians, Dutch and British, but its beautiful wine-growing, lavender-carpeted countryside has also attracted a good number of artists. The Luberon's northern face is damper, more alpine in character than the Mediterranean-scented southern slopes, and gets extremely cold in winter. It's almost all wooded, except for the summer sheep pastures at the top, and there's just one main route across, the Combe de Lourmarin. Countless small **villages** cling stubbornly to the Luberon foothills – with their history, beauty and individuality, they make wonderful days out and even better places to stay.

With the aim of conserving the natural fauna and flora and limiting develop-ment, much of the area has been designated as the **Parc Naturel Régional du Luberon**. It's administered by the **Maison du Parc**, 60 place Jean-Jaurès in Apt (Mon–Fri 8.30am–noon & 1.30–6pm; April–Aug also Sat 8.30am–noon; ☎04.90.04.42.00, Ⓦwww.parcduluberon.fr). **Vélo Loisir en Luberon** (Ⓦwww .veloloisirluberon.com), a consortium of hotels, campsites and cycle hire and repair shops, promotes cycle tourism throughout the region.

Apt

The sole town base for exploring the Luberon is **APT**, a likeable and bustling little place that's gentrified rapidly during the last few years, and has one of the oldest cathedrals in Provence. It's especially worth visiting on a Saturday for the lively **market** when, as well as every imaginable Provençal edible, there are barrel organs, jazz musicians and stand-up comics on show.

Practicalities

Apt's **tourist office** is at 20 av Philippe-de-Girard, just to your left as you face the river from the main café-lined square (July & Aug Mon–Sat 9.30am–7pm, Sun 9.30am–12.30pm; June & Sept Mon–Sat 9.30am–12.30pm & 2.30–6.30pm, Sun 9.30am–12.30pm; Oct–May Mon–Sat 9.30am–12.30pm & 2.30–6.30pm; ☎04.90.74.03.18, ⓦwww.luberon-apt.fr). Arriving buses can drop you either in this square, place de la Bouquerie, or at the **gare routière** on avenue de la Libération at the eastern end of the town. No trains serve Apt. Bikes can be **hired** from Luberon Cycles at 86 quai du Général Leclerc (☎04.90.74.17.16).

The nicest place to **stay** is *Le Couvent*, 36 rue Louis Rousset (☎04.90.04.55.36, ⓦwww.loucouvent.com; ❺), a guesthouse in a former convent with five simple, spacious rooms. Cheaper central alternatives include the clean, basic but great-value *L'Aptois*, 289 cours Lauze-de-Perret (☎04.90.74.02.02, ⓦwww.aptois.fr; ❷). *Camping Les Cèdres* is within easy walking distance, across the bridge from place St-Pierre on avenue de Viton (☎04.90.74.14.61, ⓦwww.camping-les-cedres.fr; open mid-Feb to mid-Nov). Assuming you haven't stuffed yourself with chocolates and candied fruit, the local speciality, you can get a good **meal** at *Les Délices de Léa*, 87 rue de la République (☎04.90.74.32.77), which serves a €17 lunch *menu*.

The Luberon villages

In many ways, the **villages** that dot the Luberon valley epitomize the beauty of Provence: impossibly narrow cobbled streets, tumbledown houses strewn with flowers, and sun-baked *places*. As they possess few specific sights in themselves, most villages warrant just an hour or two of exploration. The best time to visit is on **market** day, when the whole village turns up to buy their baguettes, fruit and vegetables.

Ménerbes

Around 23km west of Apt, surrounded by sweeping countryside and perched on a hill, **MÉNERBES** boasts a fine collection of medieval and Renaissance-era houses and a dominant sixteenth-century citadelle. If you're feeling overwhelmed by the multitude of Luberon road signs directing you to various wine-tasting *caves* or *châteaux*, Ménerbes is the place to head for: the elegant **Maison de la Truffe et des Vins** (daily: April–Oct 10am–12.30pm & 2.30–6.30pm, Nov–March 3–6pm; ⓦwww.vin-truffe-luberon.com), on place de l'Horloge, houses wines from all three of Luberon's *appellations* and from over sixty vineyards, selling them for the same price as at the wholesalers. They arrange wine and truffle-tasting, and also act as the **tourist office** (same hours). **Market day** is Thursday.

Accommodation includes the luxurious *Mas du Magnolia* (☎04.90.72.48.00, ⓦwww.masmagnolia.com; ❼), just outside town on the D103, and the cheaper *Douze Oliviers* (☎04.90.72.23.80, ⓦwww.les-douze-oliviers.com; ❺), at the foot of town in Quartier Gaujas. To practise your newly acquired wine expertise, head for the popular **restaurant** *Le Gaboulet*, on avenue Marcellin Poncet (☎04.90.72.36.08; closed Wed), which serves good-quality, traditional Provençal dishes (*plats* €18); the smarter *Café Veranda* (☎04.90.72.33.33; closed Mon) next door offers much the same, at higher prices (lunch *menu* €16, dinner from €30).

Gordes and around

Not far from Ménerbes, on the north side of the D22, **Gordes** is an incredibly picturesque Provençal village much favoured by Parisian media personalities, film directors, artists and the like. A cluster of magnificent, honey-coloured buildings clinging to a sheer rockface, it's a spectacular sight. At the top of the village, a church and houses surround a mighty twelfth- to sixteenth-century **château**, housing the paintings of the contemporary Flemish artist Pol Mara (daily 10am–noon & 2–6pm; €4). **Market day** is Tuesday.

The **tourist office** is in the château (Mon–Sat 9am–noon & 2–6pm, Sun 10am–noon & 2–6pm; ☎04.90.72.02.75, ⊛www.gordes-village.com). Good-value hotels include the decent, seven-room *Provençal* (☎04.90.72.10.01, ⊛www.le-provencal.fr; ❹); the more luxurious *Bastide de Gordes* is built into the old ramparts in the old village (☎04.90.72.12.12, ⊛www.bastide-de-gordes .com; ❾); some of its rooms have vaulted ceilings, and the terrace boasts impressive views. Opposite the château, *l'Artégal* (☎04.90.72.02.54; closed Tues eve, plus Wed and Jan to mid-March), serves fabulous **food** on *menus* from €35.

Village des Bories

The **Village des Bories** (daily 9am–sunset; €6), 3.5km east off the D2 towards Cavaillon, comprises a collection of peculiar dry-stone dwellings. Although such buildings were first constructed in the Bronze Age, most of the constructions here – sheep-pens, wine vats, bread-ovens and the like – date from the eighteenth century and were inhabited until a hundred years ago. It's easiest to get here with your own car, although buses going to Cavaillon drop visitors off 1.7km from the village.

Abbaye de Sénanque

Four kilometres north of **Gordes**, set amid lavender fields in a deep cleft in the hills, stands the twelfth-century Cistercian **Abbaye de Sénanque** (visits by 1hr guided tour only, in French, to a very intricate schedule, ranging from 11 daily in summer down to 2 in winter, with the first tour at 9.50am in July & Aug, 10.30am Feb to mid-Nov, last usually at 4.30pm; closed Sun morning all year; reservations essential; ☎04.90.72.05.72, ⊛www.senanque.fr or enquire at abbey shop; €7). It's still in use as a monastery and you can visit the church, cloisters and all the main rooms of this substantial and austere building; a shop sells the monks' produce, including liqueur, honey and lavender essence.

Roussillon and around

The houses in the village of **ROUSSILLON**, 10km east of Gordes, radiate all the different shades of the seventeen ochre tints once quarried here. As colourful as an artist's palette itself, the town attracts a multitude of painters, potters and sculptors, whose works are on show and for sale throughout the town. To find out more about the ochre industry, head to the **Conservatoire des Ocres** (☎04.90.05.66.69; daily 9am–6pm; €6, includes optional guided tour; ⊛www .okhra.com), which demonstrates the various washing, draining, settling and drying procedures, and also hosts fascinating exhibitions. **Market day** is Thursday.

The **tourist office** (Mon–Sat 10am–noon & 1.30–5pm; ☎04.90.05.60.25, ⊛www.roussillon-provence.com) is on place de la Poste, just down from the swanky **hotel-restaurant** *Le Clos de la Glycine* (☎04.90.05.60.13, ⊛www .luberon-hotel.com; ❼), whose sumptuous rooms enjoy fabulous views over the valley. A cheaper, more charming option is *Les Rêves d'Ocres* on the route de

Gordes (℗04.90.05.60.50, Ⓦhotel-revesdocres.com; ❸). As for **food**, *Croq' La Vie*, upstairs in the imposing Maison Tachelle on place de la Mairie (℗04.90.71.55.72; open April–Sept only, closed Mon except in high summer), serves delicious simple *assiettes*, and has a lovely panoramic terrace, while *Le Pique-baure*, route de Gordes (℗04.90.05.79.65; closed Mon & Tues), offers *plats* for €12 and dinner *menus* from €24.

The Sentiers des Ocres and the Colorado Provençal

To further admire the lovely ochre hues of the Luberon – and to stretch your legs – head for the **Sentiers des Ocres**, a pretty natural park full of colourful and oddly shaped rocks and pinnacles. The entrance is next to Roussillon's cemetery, and you can follow the sandy, colour-coded walks (daily March to mid-Nov; €2.50).

The **Colorado Provençal** is a more dramatic valley, lying just outside the village of **Rustrel**, 9km northeast of Apt, and is signed off the D22 towards Gignac. You have to pay to park, either in the municipal car park (€2) or in a private car park (€6; map included) and then you're free to wander through the weird, fiery-red landscape.

Saignon

Four kilometres from Apt, tiny, immaculate **Saignon** is perhaps Luberon's most enchanting village, and remains somewhat undiscovered on the tourist circuit. For a breathtaking overview of the surrounding splendour, follow signs up to **Le Rocher**.

Saignon's best **hotel**, *Auberge du Presbytère*, stands on the dreamy, rose-covered place de la Fontaine (℗04.90.74.11.50, Ⓦwww.auberge-presbytere.com; closed mid-Jan to mid-Feb; ❹–❼); its sixteen lovely rooms are cosy and comfortable, and there's a rather pricey, but good, restaurant (full dinner *menu* €38; closed Wed). For something more rural and a bit less expensive, *La Bastide du Jas* (℗04.90.04.88.27, Ⓦwww.labastidedujas.com; ❹), at the bottom of the village among rambling gardens, has glorious, homely rooms and studios (two-bed studio €1200 per week), along with a swimming pool. Another **restaurant** worth trying is *La Cave Gourmande* (℗04.90.71.60.81; closed Mon; *menus* from €14), serving dishes such as Provençal lamb with olives, served on a snug terrace.

Bonnieux

It's very easy to get lost among the narrow, twisting lanes of **BONNIEUX**, built on several interlocking levels, 12km southwest of Apt. If all else fails, head to the top of the hill and dinky twelfth-century *église haute* where there are marvellous views across the valley. **Market day** is Friday.

The finest place to stay is the incredibly luxurious *Bastide du Capelongue* (℗04.90.75.89.78, Ⓦwww.capelongue.com; ❾), at the top of the village, which offers beautiful bedrooms, sitting rooms, terraces and pool. Its chef, Edouard Loubet, has received two Michelin stars and concocts fabulous dishes, such as duck breast with cauliflower mousse, at rather exorbitant prices. The more down-to-earth ⚘ *Mas del Sol*, 2.5km towards Goult (℗04.90.75.94.80, Ⓦwww.chambres-dhotes-bonnieux-luberon.com; ❻), is an immaculate B&B with a pool, run by a friendly young couple. They also prepare delicious dinners on request (€34).

The Abbaye de Silvacane

If you're heading for Aix-en-Provence from Apt, you'll pass close to another ancient Cistercian abbey contemporary with Sénanque, 29km south of Apt, just across the Durance. After a long history of abandonment and evictions, the **Abbaye de Silvacane** (June–Sept daily 10am–6pm; Oct–May daily except Tues 10am–1pm & 2–5pm; €6.50) is once again a monastic institution. Isolated from the surrounding villages on the bank of the Durance, its architecture has hardly changed over the last seven hundred years; you can visit the stark, pale-stoned splendour of the church, its cloisters and surrounding buildings.

Aix-en-Provence

AIX-EN-PROVENCE would be the dominant city of central Provence were it not for the great metropolis of Marseille, just 25km away. Historically, culturally and socially, the two cities are moons apart, and the tendency is to love one and hate the other. Aix is more immediately attractive, a stately and in parts pretty place that's traditionally seen as conservative, its riches based on landowning and the liberal professions. The proudest moment in its history was its fifteenth-century heyday as an independent fiefdom under the beloved King René of Anjou, while in the nineteenth century it was home to close friends Paul Cézanne and Émile Zola. Today, the youth of Aix dress immaculately; hundreds of foreign students, particularly Americans, come to study here; and there's a certain snobbishness, almost of Parisian proportions.

Arrival and information

Aix's **TGV** station, 10km southwest of town, is connected by regular minibuses (every 30min: daily 4am–11.30pm; €5) to the **gare routière** (℡08.91.02.40.25), on the south side of the old town on avenue de l'Europe. Local trains use the **gare SNCF** nearby, on rue Gustave Desplace. **Driving** into Aix can be confusing: the entire ring of boulevards encircling the old town is essentially one giant roundabout, circulating anticlockwise; hotels are signposted off in yellow. **Parking** in the old town is pretty nightmarish; the ring is probably the best bet for on-street parking, while some good underground car parks are dotted around the boulevards.

The busy **tourist office** is located on the *rond point* at the western end of cours Mirabeau at 2 place Général-de-Gaulle (June & Sept daily 8.30am–8pm; July & Aug 8.30am–9pm; Sept–May Mon–Sat 8.30am–7pm, Sun 10am–1pm & 2–6pm; ℡04.42.16.11.61, ⓦwww.aixenprovencetourism.com), between avenue des Belges and avenue Victor-Hugo.

Accommodation

For accommodation between mid-June and the end of July – festival time – it's essential to reserve a hotel room at least a couple of months in advance.

Arts 69 bd Carnot ℡04.42.38.11.77, ⓔhotelaix @yahoo.fr. Very cheap, rather bare and noisy rooms in the heart of town; no reservations, it's first-come, first-served. ❷

La Caravelle 29 bd Roi-René ℡04.42.21.53.05, ⓦwww.lacaravelle-hotel.com. Well kept, friendly hotel, by the ring roads southeast of the city. Not all rooms have a/c; the very cheapest share toilets, the more expensive ones overlook courtyard gardens. ❸

Cardinal 22–24 rue Cardinale ℡04.42.38.32.30, ⓦhotel-cardinal-aix.com. Clean, peaceful and welcoming establishment with 29 great-value, antique-furnished rooms. ❹

Globe 74 cours Sextius ℡04.42.26.03.58, ⓦwww.hotelduglobe.com. There's a slight chain-like feel to this large hotel, ten minutes' walk from the centre, but the rooms are adequate, and cater for families too. Modern breakfast room and roof-top terrace. Closed mid-Dec to mid-Jan. ❹

Le Manoir 8 rue d'Entrecasteaux ℡04.42.26.27.20, ⓦwww.hotelmanoir .com. Comfortable old hotel in a remarkably peaceful central location, in its own garden courtyard, with parking. Breakfast in the sixteenth-century cloister. ❹

Paul 10 av Pasteur ℡04.42.23.23.89, ⓔhotel .paul@wanadoo.fr. Basic but cheap and very central en-suite rooms; some have good views over the city, all get hot in summer. Pleasant garden. ❷

Pavillon de la Torse 69 cours Gambetta ☎04.42.27.90.15, ⓦwww.latorse.com. Grand five-room B&B, set in supremely tranquil grounds with an infinity pool, fifteen minutes' walk southeast of the centre. English-speaking hosts, free parking. ❼

Quatre-Dauphins 54 rue Roux-Alphéran ☎04.42.38.16.39, ⓦwww.lesquatredauphins.fr. Warm, old-world charm in the *quartier* Mazarin, with small but attractive rooms. ❹

St-Christophe 2 av Victor-Hugo ☎04.42.26.01.24, ⓦwww.hotel-saintchristophe.com. Comfortable 1920s-style place above a popular brasserie, close to the station and cours Mirabeau; some rooms have private terraces, the cheapest have showers not baths. ❺

Hostel and campsites

Airotel Camping Chantecler 41 av du Val St-André, rte de Nice ☎04.42.26.12.98, ⓦwww.campingchantecler.com. Set in a big park surrounding a Provençal country house, 3km southeast on bus #3. Open all year.

Camping Arc-en-Ciel 45 av Malacrida, Pont des Trois Sautets ☎04.42.26.14.28, ⓦwww.campingarcenciel.fr. Located 2km southeast of town on bus #3, near *Chantecler* above, this clean site has very good facilities, including a pool. No credit cards. Closed Oct–March.

Youth Hostel Jas de Bouffan 3 av Marcel-Pagnol ☎04.42.20.15.99, ⓦwww.auberge-jeunesse-aix.fr. Located 2km west of the centre, this hostel has small dorm rooms (€19), a restaurant, baggage deposit, tennis and volleyball courts, as well as parking. Take bus #4, direction "La Mayanelle", stop "V. Vasarély". Closed mid-Dec to mid-Jan.

The City

The **old city of Aix** is a great monument in its entirety, an enchanting ensemble that's far more compelling than any individual building or museum within it. With so many streets alive with people, so many tempting restaurants, cafés and shops, plus the best markets in Provence, it's easy to pass several days wandering around without the need for any itinerary or destination.

Vieil Aix

To explore the network of jumbled lanes and narrow roads that make up the heart of Aix, wander north from leafy **cours Mirabeau**, lined with plane trees, to anywhere within the ring of *cours* and boulevards. While the layout of **Vieil Aix** is not designed to assist your sense of direction, it hardly matters when there's a fountained square to rest in every few minutes, and a continuous architectural backdrop of treats from the sixteenth and seventeenth centuries. On Saturdays, and to a lesser extent on Tuesdays and Thursdays, when the centre is taken up with various **markets**, flowers and produce spill over in the cobbled alleyways.

On the central place des Prêcheurs is the **church of the Madeleine**, decorated with paintings by Rubens and Van Loo (who was born in Aix in 1684), and a three-panel medieval *Annunciation*. The **Hôtel de Ville** on place de l'Hôtel-de-Ville displays perfect classical proportions, while the massive foot of the goddess Cybele dangles over the architrave of the old corn exchange nearby, which now houses the post office.

A short way north, the **Cathédrale St-Sauveur** (daily: 7.30am–noon & 2–6pm) is a conglomerate of fifteenth- to sixteenth-century buildings. The finest of its many medieval art treasures is a dazzling triptych by Nicolas Froment, *Le Buisson Ardent*, which has become a Provençal icon. Commissioned by King René in 1475, the painting has recently been restored to a jewel-like intensity; the burning bush of the title is not the one seen by Moses, but an allegory of the virginity of Mary.

Just down from the cathedral, accessed via place des Martyrs-de-la-Résistance, the former bishop's palace, the **Ancien Archevêché**, houses the enjoyable **Musée des Tapisseries** (daily except Tues: mid-April to mid-Oct 10am–12.30pm & 1.15–6pm, mid-Oct to mid-April 1.30–5pm; €3.10). Highlights here include nine scenes from *Don Quixote*, woven in the 1730s.

AIX-EN-PROVENCE

▲ Sisteron
▲ Vauvenargues
▲ Pertuis, Manosque & Sisteron
▲ Atelier Cézanne
▲ Avignon & Puyricard
▼ & Avignon

VIEIL AIX

BOULEVARD F. & E. ZOLA

COURS ST-LOUIS

RUE SUFFREN

R. DE LA FONDERIE

RUE LACÉPÈDE

RUE PORTALIS

RUE CHASTEL

RUE MANUEL

RUE EMÉRIC-DAVID

Église de la Madeleine

RUE LISSE ST-LOUIS

PL DE LA MADELEINE

PLACE DES PRÊCHEURS

PLACE DE VERDUN

RUE MIGNET

RUE CONSTANTIN

RUE PEYRESC

RUE MONCLAR

Palais de Justice

RUE LOUBET

RUE DU PUITS NEUF

RUE BOEGODON

RUE MATHERON

RUE RIFLE-RAFLE

RUE CHAUDRONNIERS

BOULEVARD A. BRIAND

RUE P. & M. CURIE

VIEIL AIX

Ancien Archevêché

RUE GRIFFON

RUE CAMPRA

RUE GIBELIN

RUE PAUL-BERT

RUE LOUBON

RUE GRANET

Ancienne Halle Aux Grains

Musée d'Histoire Naturelle

AV. DE LA VIOLETTE

Cathédrale St-Sauveur

PLACE DES MARTYRS DE LA RÉSISTANCE

PLACE DE L'HÔTEL DE VILLE

PLACE RICHELME

RUE BELLEGARDE

RUE MASSILLON

RUE MAL-FOCH

AV. PAUL CÉZANNE

RUE J. DE LAROQUE

Musée Vieil Aix

RUE G. DE SAPORTA

Hôtel de Ville

RUE DE LA VERRERIE

RUE F. GAUT

AV. PASTEUR

RUE DES GUÉRIERS

RUE VENEL

RUE DU BON PASTEUR

PLACE DES CARDEURS

RUE CANCEL

RUE DES CORDELIERS

RUE DES MAGNANS

RUE MERINDOL

RUE LIEUTAUD

R. D'ENTRECASTEAUX

Thermes Sextius

RUE DE LA TREILLE

R. LISSE DES CORDELIERS

COURS SEXTIUS

VIEIL AIX

RUE VAN LOO

RUE CÉLONY

Pavillon de Vendôme

Jardin de Vendôme

EATING & DRINKING

Amphitryon	12
Bistrot des Philosophes	2
Carton Rouge	9
Crep Saultière	8
Deux Garçons	11
Hot Brass	1
Mediterranean Boys	5
Le Passage	14
Petit Verdot	7
Poivre d'Ane	3
La Rotonde	4
Le Scat	13
Ze Bistro	10
Zinc d'Hugo	6

ACCOMMODATION

Airotel Camping	E
Chartrecier	C
Arts	J
La Caravelle	G
Cardinal	F
Camping Arc-en-Ciel	B
Globe	D
Le Manoir	A
Paul	L
Pavillon de la Torse	I
Quatre-Dauphins	H
St-Christophe	K
Youth Hostel	

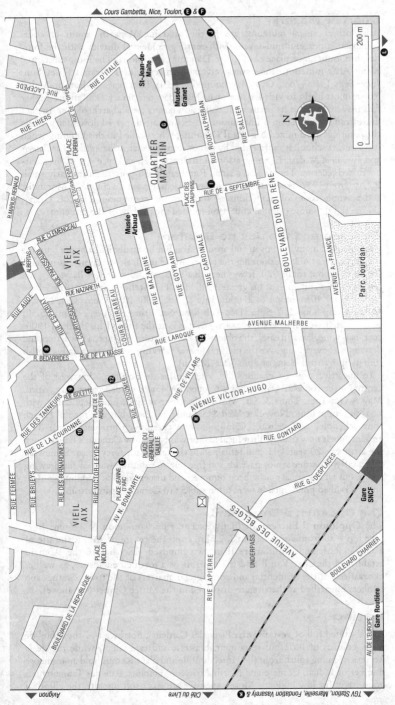

St-Jean-de-Malte

Musée Granet

❼

RUE D'ITALIE

RUE LACEPEDE

RUE DE L'OPERA

RUE THIERS

PLACE FORBIN

RUE TOURNEFORT

R. MARIUS-REINAUD

QUARTIER MAZARIN

RUE ROUX-ALPHERAN

RUE SALLIER

N

❶❺

PROVENCE

RUE CLEMENCEAU

RUE DU PARADIS

VIEIL AIX

ALBERTAS

❷

RUE NAZARETH

Musée Arbaud

RUE MAZARINE

RUE GOYRAND

RUE CARDINALE

PLACE DES 4 DAUPHINS

RUE DE 4 SEPTEMBRE

❶

BOULEVARD DU ROI RENE

AVENUE A.-FRANCE

Parc Jourdan

RUE AUDE

RUE ESPARIAT

R. COURTEISSADE

COURS MIRABEAU

R. BEDARRIDES

RUE DE LA MASSE

❽

RUE LAROQUE

❶❹

AVENUE MALHERBE

RUE DES TANNEURS

RUE ISOLETTE

❾

RUE P. DOUMER

PLACE DES AUGUSTINS

❶❷

RUE DE VILLARS

AVENUE VICTOR-HUGO

❶❶

RUE DE LA COURONNE

RUE DES BERNARDINES

❶❹

RUE VICTOR-LEYDET

❶❸

PLACE JEANNE D'ARC

AV. W. BONAPARTE

PLACE DU GENERAL DE GAULLE

ⓘ

❶❶

RUE GONTARD

RUE G.-DESPLACES

RUE FERMEE

RUE BRULEYS

VIEIL AIX

PLACE NIOLLON

PLACE DE LA REPUBLIQUE

RUE LAPIERRE

✉

UNDERPASS

AVENUE DES BELGES

Gare SNCF

BOULEVARD CHARRIER

Gare Routière

AV. DE L'EUROPE

❶ 200 m

0

Quartier Mazarin

Aix's other central museums are in the **quartier Mazarin**, south of cours Mirabeau, a peaceful mid-seventeenth-century residential district with the four-dolphin fountain of place des Quatre-Dauphins at its heart. The most substantial of all Aix's museums, the extensively modernized **Musée Granet** (Tues–Sun: June–Sept 11am–7pm, Oct–May noon–6pm; €4), faces place St-Jean-de-Malte. You're most likely to visit for one of its high-class temporary exhibitions (higher fees may apply), but its permanent collection covers art and archeology. Ancient finds from the Oppidum d'Entremont (see below) are displayed downstairs, while the paintings are a mixed bag. **Paul Cézanne**, who studied in this building when it was an art school, is represented by minor canvases such as *Bathsheba*, *The Bathers* and *Portrait of Madame Cézanne*, assorted student pieces, and even one of his paint-encrusted palettes. There's also a small Rembrandt self-portrait; a similarly small Picasso from 1937, *Femme au Ballon*; several Giacomettis and a couple of Morandis; and a whole room of depictions of ruins by the eponymous François Granet (1775–1849), whose original collection formed the nucleus of the museum.

Cezanne and the Jas de Bouffan

Cézanne used many studios in and around Aix, but he finally had a house built for the purpose in 1902, overlooking the city from the north at what is now 9 av Paul-Cézanne, on bus route #20. It was here that he painted the *Grandes Baigneuses,* the *Jardinier Vallier* and some of his greatest still lifes. The **Atelier Cézanne** (April–June & Sept daily 10am–noon & 2–6pm; July & Aug daily 10am–6pm; Oct, Nov & March 10am–noon & 2–5pm; Dec–Feb Mon–Sat 10am–noon & 2–5pm; €5.50; ⓦwww.atelier-cezanne.com) is exactly as it was at the time of his death in 1906: coat, hat, wineglass and easel, the objects he liked to paint, his pipe, a few letters and drawings … everything save the pictures he was working on. There's a daily English tour at 5pm (April–Sept) or 4pm (Oct–March).

To unearth more of Cezanne's life, visit the **Jas de Bouffan**, 4km west of the centre on the route de Galice, bus #6 (open for 45min guided tours only: April, May & Oct Tues, Thurs & Sat, with English tour at 2pm; June–Sept daily, with English tour at 2pm; Nov–Dec Wed & Sat only, no English tours; for full French tour schedule, see website; €5.50; ⓦwww.cezanne-en-provence.com). This elegant, albeit now shabby, Provençal manor was bought by Cezanne's father when the artist was 20 years old, and remained in the family for forty years. Somewhat reluctantly, Cezanne senior gave his son free rein to paint the walls of the drawing room, but all traces have now been removed and dispersed. The rambling gardens and duck-filled pond outside were often subject to Cezanne's paintbrush.

The Oppidum d'Entremont

The **Oppidum d'Entremont** (daily except Tues 9am–noon & 2–6pm; free; take bus #20 from cours Sextius), 2.5km from the centre of Aix, is the site of a Gallic settlement built more than two hundred years before the Romans established the city. You'll find the remains of a fortified enclosure, as well as excavations of the residential and commercial quarters of the town. Statues and trinkets unearthed at the site are displayed in the Musée Granet (see above).

Eating

Aix is stuffed full of **restaurants**. Place des Cardeurs, northwest of the Hôtel de Ville, consists of little but restaurant, brasserie and café tables, while rue de la Verrerie running south from the Hôtel de Ville and place Ramus hold an immense number of Indian, Chinese and North African restaurants. Rue des Tanneurs is a good street for low budgets. More expensive are Aix's soft biscuits, the elliptical candied-fruit and almond-flavoured *calissons*; the pretty Cure Gourmande shop at 16 place de l' Hôtel-de-Ville is a great place to sample a few. Local gourmet *chocolatier* Puyricard has a shop at 7 rue Rifle-Rafle.

Cafés and restaurants

Amphitryon 2 rue Paul Doumer ℡04.42.26.54.10. This excellent restaurant, serving eclectic cuisine on a flower-drenched terrace in a grotty side street of old Aix, won't break the bank. Lunch *menus* from €22, dinner from €30 before 8.30pm, or €40.50 for the day's market specialities. Closed Sun, Mon & second half Aug.

Bistrot des Philosophes 20 place des Cardeurs ℡04.42.21.64.35. The hippest and classiest of this busy square's many offerings, with tasty dishes like sardines and *ceviches* for €5.50, plenty of heartier *plats*, and seating both indoors and out.

Carton Rouge 7 rue Isolette ℡04.42.91.41.75. Cute little dinner-only bistro, serving traditional, home-made food (*plats* €22), accompanied by delectable wines. Closed Sun & Mon.

Crep Sautière 18 rue de Bédarrides ℡04.42.27.91.60. Delicious, fresh crêpes (from €5) to take away or enjoy squashed into the cosy, vaulted and often packed restaurant. Closed Sun & Mon.

Deux Garçons 53 cours Mirabeau ℡04.42.26.00.51. The erstwhile haunt of Camus is done up in faded 1900s style and still attracts a motley assortment of literati. A great place to sit, but the brasserie food is ordinary, and far from cheap. Service daily till midnight.

Le Passage 10 rue Villars ℡04.42.37.09.00. In this modern, airy three-storey complex, which has a pretty garden and incorporates a cooking school, the Mediterranean restaurant serves a wide range of traditional Provençal dishes. There's a €10 "Good Food" lunch *menu*, while dinner *menus* start at €30.

Petit Verdot 7 rue d' Entrecasteaux ℡04.42.27.30.12. Friendly restaurant where the tables are made from old wine boxes, and there's a strong emphasis on meat, with dishes like foie gras with coriander and nectarine chutney. Mains €15–24. Dinner Mon–Sat until midnight, lunch Sat only.

Poivre d'Âne 40 place des Cardeurs ℡04.42.21.32.66. Small restaurant on the fringes of the popular place des Cardeurs, with seating inside and out. Book ahead to enjoy good-value, wide ranging set *menus* of creative local cuisine, from €28 to €45. Dinner only, closed Wed in winter.

Ze Bistro 7 rue de la Couronne ℡04.42.39.81.88. Creative, relaxed old-town bistro, serving the freshest fish and local produce in simple surroundings, best sampled on good-value *dégustation menus*. Closed Sun & Mon, plus Sat lunch and first 3 weeks in Aug.

Zinc d'Hugo 22 rue Lieutaud ℡04.42.27.69.69. Snug wine bar with inventive cuisine. €19 gets you a delicious *assiette comptoire* of ham, cheeses and salad; there's a €24 set *menu*; and mains like tuna steak with raspberry balsamic vinegar cost €20–24. Closed Sun & Mon.

Drinking and nightlife

Nightlife in Aix divides readily between well-heeled visitors and the city's large student population. Local youth tends to congregate around the fountains and cafés near cours Mirabeau until midnight; the cool brasserie *La Rotonde*, at 2 place Jeanne d'Arc, is a rendezvous for potent cocktails and electro beats. Later on, the bars along shabby rue Verrerie get going, including the eclectic, cave-like *Le Scat,* 11 rue Verrerie (℡04.42.23.00.23), which puts on live music of all sorts. *Hot Brass*, 5km northwest of town on chemin d'Eguilles-Celony (℡04.42.23.13.12, Ⓦwww.hotbrassaix.com), is another dependable venue. Aix's **gay** bar is *Mediterranean Boys*, 6 rue de la Paix.

Festivals

During the annual **music festivals**, the varied contemporary showcase of Aix en Musique (June) and the Festival International d'Art Lyrique (opera and classical concerts; last two weeks of July; ℡04.42.17.34.34), the alternative scene – of street theatre, rock concerts and impromptu gatherings – turns the whole of Vieil Aix into one long party. Tickets and programmes are available from the festival offices in the Palais de l'**Ancien Archevêché** on place des Martyrs-de-la-Résistance (℡04.34.08.02.17, Ⓦwww.festival-aix.com).

Listings

Bike rental Cycles Zammit, 27 rue Mignet
☎04.42.23.19.53.
Books Book in Bar, 1bis rue Cabassol, for English books (closed Mon).
Health Centre Hospitalier, av des Tamaris
☎04.42.33.90.28; SOS Médecins
☎04.42.26.24.00.

Internet The Phone Box, 3 rue Lieutaud; Le Hublot, 17 rue Paul-Bert.
Police 2 cours des Minimes ☎04.42.91.91.11.
Post office 2 rue Lapierre and place de l' Hotel-de-Ville.
Taxis Taxi Radio Aixois ☎04.42.27.71.11 (24hr).

Central Provence

In **central Provence**, it's the landscapes rather than the towns that dominate. The gentle hills and tranquil villages of the Haut-Var make for happy exploration by car or bike, before the foothills of the Alps gradually close in around the citadelle town of **Sisteron** and further east, around **Dignes-les-Bains**. The most exceptional geographical feature is undoubtedly the **Gorges du Verdon** – Europe's answer to the Grand Canyon. So long as you have your own transport, good bases for exploring the majestic peaks, cliffs and lakes of this spectacular area include the small market town of Aups, south of the Gorges, and to the northeast, Castellane, a centre for sports and activities.

Aups

The neat and very pleasant village of **AUPS,** 90km northeast of Aix and 10km north of Salernes, makes an ideal base for drivers touring the Haut-Var or the Grand Canyon du Verdon. While holding all the facilities visitors might need, it remains a vibrant, lived-in community, still earning its living from agriculture, and at its best on Wednesdays and Saturdays, when **market** stalls fill its central squares and the surrounding streets.

Aups centres on three ill-defined and inter-connected squares: place Frédéric-Mistral, the smaller place Duchâtel slightly uphill to the left and the tree-lined gardens of place Martin Bidouré to the right. Beyond these, the tangle of old streets, and the sixteenth-century clock tower with its campanile, make it an enjoyable place to explore. Surprisingly for such a small place, there's a museum of modern art, the **Musée Simon Segal** in the former chapel of a convent on avenue Albert 1er (mid-June to mid-Sept 10am–noon & 4–7pm; €2.50). Its best works are those by the Russian-born painter Simon Segal, but there are interesting local scenes in the other paintings, such as the Roman bridge at Aiguines, now drowned beneath the artificial lake of Sainte-Croix.

Practicalities

The **tourist office** is on place Frédéric-Mistral (April–June & Sept Mon–Sat 8.45am–12.15pm & 2–5.30pm; July & Aug Mon–Sat 9am–12.30pm & 3–6.30pm, plus Sun 9am–12.30pm mid-July to mid-Aug; Oct–May Mon, Tues, Thurs & Fri 8.45am–12.15pm & 1.30–5pm, Wed & Sat 8.45am–12.15pm; ☎04.94.84.00.69, Ⓦwww.aups-tourisme.com). Few villages can boast such a perfect array of good, well-priced hotels: on rue Aloisi, both 🍴 *Auberge de la Tour* (☎04.94.70.00.30, Ⓦwww.aubergedelatour.net; closed Oct–March; ❸) and 🍴 *St-Marc* (☎04.94.70.06.08, Ⓦwww.lesaintmarc.com; closed second half Nov; ❷), have pleasant rooms and appealing restaurants. *Le Gourmet*, 5 rue Voltaire (☎04.94.70.14.97; closed Mon, plus Sun eve Sept–June) is the best stand-alone restaurant, with *menus* from €16.50. The closest **campsite** is the two-star *Camping Les Prés*, to the right off allée Charles Boyer towards Tourtour (☎04.94.70.00.93, Ⓦwww.campinglespres.com; open all year).

Haut-Var villages

The little **villages** in the Haut-Var are among the prettiest in all Provence, and it's essential to have your own wheels to be able to explore them all. Bask in their tranquillity and beauty, wander the maze-like lanes and admire the glorious, verdant landscape – this is rural Provence at its best. The main historical sight in the area is the serene and substantial **Abbaye de Thoronet**, between the villages of Cabasse and Carcès, off the D79.

Around 18km southeast of Aups is lovely **LORGUES**, blessed with a serious gourmet **restaurant**, *Chez Bruno* (☎04.94.85.93.93; closed Mon & Sun eve out of season; ❾), on route de Vidauban, where the truffle reigns supreme on *menus* from €65 to €200, appearing in myriad forms, even in desserts; they also have a few very luxurious rooms. Heading 14km west, **ENTRECASTEAUX** has an ancient stone **laundry** by the river that's still used, and a very beautiful seventeenth-century **château** (Easter–Oct daily except Sat, guided visits 4pm, extra tour 11.30am in Aug; ☎04.94.04.43.95, Ⓦwww.chateau-entrecasteaux.com; €7).

COTIGNAC, 9km west of Entrecasteaux, is the Haut-Var village *par excellence*, with a shaded main square for *pétanque* and passages and stairways bursting with begonias, jasmine and geraniums leading through a cluster of medieval houses. More gardens sprawl at the foot of the bubbly rock cliff that forms the back wall of the village, threaded with troglodyte walkways. **Accommodation** is limited to *chambres d'hôtes*, including the atmospheric *Maison Gonzagues*, in a former tannery at 9 rue Léon Gérard (☎04.94.72.85.40, Ⓦwww.maison-gonzagues-cotignac .com; ❻). If you fancy lunch or a reviving cup of tea, head for the quaint, flower-bedecked 🍴 *Le Temps de Pose* (☎04.94.77.72.07) on 11 place de la Mairie; tasty, fresh sandwiches and quiches cost around €7.

Six kilometres north of Cotignac is **SILLANS-LA-CASCADE**, which has a beautiful walk, signposted off the main road, to an immense waterfall and aquamarine pool (about 20min). **VILLECROZE** (15km) and **TOURTOUR** (21km) further northeast are both suitably picturesque and worth a wander.

Abbaye du Thoronet

East of the **Lac de Carcès** lies the last of the three great Cistercian monasteries of Provence. Even more so than Silvacane and Sénanque, the **Abbaye du Thoronet** (April–Sept Mon–Sat 10am–6.30pm, Sun 10am–noon & 2–6.30pm; Oct–March Mon–Sat 10am–1pm & 2–5pm, Sun 10am–noon & 2–5pm; €7; Ⓦthoronet.monuments-nationaux.fr) has been unscathed by the vicissitudes of time. During the Revolution, it was kept intact as a remarkable monument of history and art; it's now used occasionally for concerts. It was first restored in the 1850s, while a more recent campaign has brought it to clear-cut perfection. As with the other two abbeys, its interior spaces, delineated by walls of pale rose-coloured stone, are inspiring.

Northwest of Aups

Two little towns worth visiting before embarking on the Gorges du Verdon are situated northwest of Aups: **Quinson**, which marks the start of the Basses Gorges du Verdon, and workaday **Riez**, with its smattering of Roman remains.

Quinson

Around 20km west of Aups lies the small village of **QUINSON**. The chief attraction here is the **Musée de Préhistoire des Gorges du Verdon**, route de Montmeyan (May, June & Sept daily except Tues 10am–7pm; July & Aug daily 10am–8pm; Oct to mid-Dec & Feb–April daily except Tues 10am–6pm; Ⓦ www.museeprehistoire.com; €7), designed by the British architect Sir Norman Foster in a clean and sympathetic modern style, so that despite its immense size it does not dominate the village. Europe's largest museum of human prehistory, it charts a million years of human habitation in Provence, with a multimedia presentation of the cave of Baume Bonne and a 15-metre-long reconstruction of the caves of the canyon of Baudinard, with their six-thousand-year-old red sun paintings. A themed path leads from the museum past reconstructed prehistoric homes and through a Neolithic garden to the most important of the sixty or so archeological sites in and around Quinson, the cave of **Baume Bonne** itself, where human occupation has been traced back 400,000 years.

Riez

Fifteen kilometres west of Moustiers, in bustling **RIEZ**, the main business is derived from the lavender fields that cover this corner of Provence. The antiquity of the town soon becomes clear: four stately **Roman columns** stand in a field just off avenue Frédéric Mistral at the bottom of allées Louis Gardiol, while over the river on the left of the road are the disappointing scant remains of a sixth-century **cathedral** (freely visited).

For a **walk** with good views over town, head for the clock tower above Grande-Rue and then go up the steps past the cemetery where a stony, curving path brings you to a cedar-shaded platform on the hilltop where the pre-Roman Riezians lived. The only building now occupying the site is the eighteenth-century Chapelle Ste-Maxime, with a gaudily patterned interior.

The **Maison de l'Abeille**, 1km north of the village (Mon 10am–12.30pm; Tues–Sun 10am–12.30pm & 2.30–7.30pm; closed Jan & Feb; free), is a fascinating research centre where you can buy various **honeys** as well as hydromel, or mead – the honey alcohol of antiquity. Enthusiastic staff share their knowledge of all aspects of a bee's life, from biology to sexuality and physiology; they may even show you the actual bees.

The **tourist office** is on place de la Marie (July & Aug Mon–Sat 9.30am–12.30pm & 3–7pm, Sun 9.30am–12.30pm; Sept–June Mon–Fri 8.30am–noon & 1.30–5pm, Sat 8.30am–noon; ☎ 04.92.77.99.09, Ⓦ www.ville-riez.fr). Given the general lack of accommodation hereabouts, it's best just to stop by during the day. For a long, relaxing lunch, head for *Le Rempart*, 17 rue du Marché (☎ 04.92.77.89.54) where superb Italian and Provençal *plats* cost around €16. If you're pushed for time, *L'Arts des Mets*, 26 allées Louis Gardiol (☎ 04.92.77.82.60), serves great salads and pizzas for €10.

The Gorges du Verdon and around

The **Gorges du Verdon** is also labelled the Grand Canyon du Verdon; while it's on a much smaller scale, the breathtaking drama and beauty of the French landscape isn't far off its American counterpart. Peppered with spectacular viewpoints, plunging crevices up to 700m deep, and glorious azure-blue lakes, the area is absolutely irressible; don't leave Provence without spending at least a day here. The river falls from Rougon at the top of the gorge, disappearing into tunnels, decelerating for shallow, languid moments and finally exiting in full, steady flow at the **Pont du Galetas**, next to the huge artificial **Lac de Sainte-Croix**, which is great for swimming when the water levels are high; otherwise the beach becomes a bit sludgy.

With so many hairpin bends and twisting, narrow roads, it takes a full, rather exhausting day to get right round the Gorges; the entire circuit is 130km long and it's cycling country solely for the preternaturally fit. Beginning at Moustiers-Ste-Marie or Lac-Ste-Croix, it's possible to drive along the **North Rim** (D952) – which runs 31km east to Pont-de-Soleils, passing La Palud-sur-Verdon and Rougon – or the more protracted **South Rim** (D71), which goes through Aiguines and Trigance en route to the junction at Pont-de-Soleils. Both routes hold spectacular lookout points and breathtaking scenery.

Alternatively, you may prefer to detour as you head along the North Rim onto the more dramatic, looping **Routes des Crêtes**. There's nothing to stop you driving straight off into the abyss on its highest stretches, and at some points you look down a sheer 800m drop to the sliver of water below. The mid-section of the Route des Crêtes is one-way (westbound only), so if you want to do it all you'll have to start from the more scenic eastern end. It closes each winter from November 15 to March 15.

West of the gorge

The loveliest village on the fringes of the gorge, **MOUSTIERS-STE-MARIE** occupies a magnificent site near its western end, 15km east of Riez. Set high enough to command fine views down to the Lac de Sainte-Croix, it straddles a plummeting stream that cascades between two golden cliffs. A mighty star slung between them on a chain, originally suspended by a returning Crusader, completes the perfect picture.

Moustiers gets very crowded in summer, when visitors throng its winding lanes and pretty bridges, and fill the stores and galleries that sell the local speciality, glazed pottery. To escape the throngs, puff your way up to the aptly-named chapel of **Notre-Dame de Beauvoir**, high above the village proper.

The **tourist office** is on place de l'Église (March & Oct daily 10am–noon & 2–5.30pm; April–June daily 10am–12.30pm & 2–6pm; July & Aug Mon–Fri 9.30am–7pm, Sat & Sun 9.30am–12.30pm & 2–7pm; Sept daily 10am–12.30pm & 2–6.30pm; Nov daily 10am–noon & 2–5.30pm; Dec–Feb daily 10am–noon & 2–5pm; ☎04.92.74.67.84, ⓦwww.moustiers.fr). The two most central hotels are the *Hotel-Café du Relais,* beside the main bridge (☎04.92.74.66.10, ⓦwww.lerelais-moustiers.com; ❹; closed Nov–March, plus Fri except in July & Aug), which serves good *menus* on a glassed-in terrace overlooking the stream, and the orange *Belvédère* on the east bank (☎04.92.74.66.04; ❷; closed Oct–March), which also has a little garden restaurant (closed Wed). **Chambres d'hôtes** include the *Clerissy,* place du Chevalier du Blacas (☎04.92.74.62.67, ⓦwww.clerissy.fr; ❷; closed mid-Nov to mid-March), which has a good-value pizzeria.

GORGES DU VERDON

Comps-sur-Artuby & Draguignan

Castellane

Moustiers-Ste-Marie & Riez

Aups

Aups

Lac de Ste-Croix

D957

D952

D71

D619

Aiguines

Pont du Galetas

River Verdon

Col d'Illoire

CORNICHE SUBLIME

Mayresste

D952

GR4

D23

La Palud-sur-Verdon

D17

CORNICHE RIVE DROITE

GR4

Chalet de la Maline

Passerelle de l'Estellié (Closed)

Falaise des Cavaliers

Belvédère des Glacières

Belvédère du Tilleul

ROUTE DES CRÊTES

Sentier Martel

River Verdon

Belvédère de l'Escalès

Couloir Samson

Point Sublime

Rougon

GR4

Clue de Carejuan

River Jabron

D955

Pont de Soleils

D955

Trigance

D90

D71

D71

CORNICHE SUBLIME

Balcons de la Mescla

R. Artuby

Pont de l'Artuby

0   2 km

North of the gorge

Along the northern rim, the two most-visited towns are **LA PALUD–SUR-VERDON**, where the Route de Crêtes begins and ends (see p.889) and **ROUGON**, 8km to the east. Peace, tranquillity and breathtaking scenery reign supreme here – whether you're staying for a while or just passing through, take the time to wander around the narrow, rambling streets and enjoy a meal or drink at a traditional restaurant or café.

La Palud is the place to go for information on **sports and activities** in the Gorges: the **Bureau des Guides** (hours erratic; ℡04.92.77.30.50, Ⓦwww .escalade-verdon.fr), where you can find out about guided walks, climbing, canyoning, rafting and other activities, is on Grande Rue. The **Maison des Gorges du Verdon**, in the château in the heart of town (daily except Tues: mid-March to mid-June and mid-Sept to mid-Nov 10am–noon & 4–6pm; mid-June to mid-Sept 10am–1pm & 4–7pm; ℡04.92.77.32.02, Ⓦwww.lapalud surverdon.com; exhibition €4), is a centre for environmental tourism that includes the **tourist office** and an exhibition on the gorge.

Accommodation close to La Palud includes *Le Provence*, in a stunning position on the route de la Maline (℡04.92.77.38.88, Ⓦwww.verdonprovencehotel.com; ❸; closed Nov–March), and the *Auberge des Crêtes*, 1km east towards Castellane (℡04.92.77.38.47, Ⓦwww.provenceweb.fr/04/aubergedescretes; ❹; closed early Nov to late March). Right in the village centre, the *Perroquet Vert* B&B (℡04.92.77.33.39, Ⓦwww.leperroquetvert.com; ❸; two-night minimum stay; closed Nov–March) is a rendezvous for climbers and walkers, and also serves simple meals. The two-star municipal **campsite** is 800m east on the route de Castellane (℡04.92.77.38.13, Ⓦwwwlapaludsurverdon.com; closed Oct–March).

South of the gorge

Extremely popular with climbers who come to enjoy its dramatic, rocky backdrop, **AIGUINES**, perched high above the **Lac de Sainte-Croix** on its eastern side, is known for its turreted Renaissance château (not open to the public) and abundance of craft shops – from woodwork and watercolours to pottery and faïence.

Aiguines has a little tourist office on Allées de Tilleul (July & Aug Mon–Sat 9am–1pm & 2–6pm; Sept–June Mon–Fri 9am–12.30pm & 2–5.30pm; ℡04.94.70.21.64, Ⓦwww.aiguines.com). There are two lovely **hotels** in the heart of the village nearby: *Le Vieux Château* on place de la Fontaine (℡04.94.70.22.95, Ⓦwww.hotelvieuxchateau.fr; ❹; closed Nov–March), which has a nice terrace bar and restaurant that serves a €24 *menu terroir*; and the fancier *Altitudes 823*, at the hairpin bend where the main road reaches the centre (℡04.98.10.22.17, Ⓦwww .altitude823-verdon.com; ❻; closed Nov to mid-March), which has far-reaching views and only accepts guests on *demi-pension*.

The best campsite here is *Le Galetas* (℡04.94.70.20.48; open April to mid-Oct; Ⓦwww.aiguines.com/galetas), almost within diving distance of the lake, a long way down from the village. However, the best place to stay on the south side – as long as you don't suffer from vertigo – is the *Hôtel du Grand Canyon du Verdon* by the dramatic precipice of the Falaise des Cavaliers (℡04.94.76.91.31, Ⓦwww .hotel-canyon-verdon.com; half-board only; ❻; open mid-April to Nov) on the Corniche Sublime, a good 20km from Aiguines, with stunning views. Its restaurant (closed Tues eve & Wed except July & Aug) serves tasty food.

Castellane

Huddled at the foot of a sheer 180m cliff, the grey and rather severe-looking town of **CASTELLANE** is primarily a gateway community for visitors to the Gorges du Verdon, 17km southwest. In summer, thanks to its wide range of restaurants, hotels and cafés, it enjoys an animation rare in these parts.

Houses in Castellane's old quarter, the Vieille Ville, are packed close together; some lanes are barely shoulder-wide. A footpath from behind the parish church winds its way up to the chapel of Notre-Dame du Roc at the top of the cliff. Not as demanding as it might at first appear, it soon passes the machicolated **Tour Pentagonal** on the lower slopes. Twenty to thirty minutes should see you at the top; you won't actually see the gorge, but there's a good view of the river disappearing into it and the mountains circling the town.

The **tourist office** is at the top of rue Nationale (July & Aug Mon–Sat 9am–12.30pm & 1.30–7pm, Sun 10am–1pm; Sept–June Mon–Fri 9am–noon & 2–6pm; ☎04.92.83.61.14, ⓦwww.castellane.org). The finest local **hotel**, the comfortable and very central *Ａ Commerce* on place de l'Église (☎04.92.83.61.00, ⓦhotel-fradet.com; ❺; closed Nov–Feb), serves wonderful **food** in its garden, with dinner *menus* at €25 and €36. Cheaper alternatives include the neighbouring *Roc*, 3 place de l'Église (☎04.92.83.62.65, ⓦwww.hotelduroc04.com; ❷; closed Mon & all Nov). The closest **campsite** to town, a mere hundred metres off place Marcel Sauvaire on boulevard Frédéric-Mistral, is *Le Frédéric Mistral* (☎04.92.83.62.27, ⓦwww.camping-fredericmistral.com; €18; closed mid-Nov to Feb).

Castellane is packed with adventure activity specialists offering everything from **canyoning** and **canoeing** to **mountain biking** and **horseriding** in the Gorges du Verdon: Aboard Rafting (☎04.92.83.76.11, ⓦwww.aboard-rafting.com) and Base Sport et Nature (☎04.93.05.41.18, ⓦbasesportnature.com) both offer water-based activities, while Ferme Équestre du Pesquier (☎04.92.83.63.94, ⓦwww.cheval verdon.com) arranges horseriding, and day-trips that combine rides with rafting.

Alpes de Haute-Provence

North of Castellane, the **Route Napoléon** passes through the barren scrubby rocklands of the **Alpes de Haute-Provence**. The road was built in the 1930s to commemorate the great leader's journey north through Haute-Provence on return from exile on Elba in 1815, in the most audacious and vain recapture of power in French history. Using mule paths still deep with winter snow, Napoleon and his seven hundred soldiers forged ahead towards **Digne-les-Bains** and **Sisteron** on their way to Grenoble – a total of 350km – in just six days. One hundred days later, he lost the battle of Waterloo, and was subsequently dispatched to the island of St Helena for permanent exile.

Digne-les-Bains

The retirement spa of **DIGNE-LES-BAINS** is by far the largest town in northeastern Provence. Despite the almost metropolitan swank of its main street, a

---

The Chemin de Fer de la Provence

To see some of the most breathtaking scenery – glittering rivers, lush dark-green forests, dramatic cliff faces, plunging gorges – in the region, take a trip on the narrow-gauge **Chemin de Fer de la Provence**, also known as the **Train des Pignes** (named after the pine-cones that were originally used as fuel). The line runs between Dignes-les-Bains and Nice, with stops including Annot and St-André-les-Alpes. A single ticket from Dignes to Nice is €17.65 per person, and the journey takes around three hours. For more information, see ⓦwww.trainprovence.com.

handful of interesting museums, and its superb position between the Durance Valley and the start of the real mountains, it's not all that exciting, and is best seen as an overnight base for trips into the surrounding mountains.

Digne enjoys a somewhat unlikely connection with Tibet. The **Musée Alexandra David-Néel**, 27 av du Maréchal Juin (guided visits daily 10am, 2pm & 3.30pm; free; T 04.92.31.32.38, W www.alexandra-david-neel.org), is dedicated to the memory of an extraordinary, tenacious explorer who spent over fourteen years travelling the length and breadth of Tibet. David-Néel lived out the remainder of her life in this house, eventually dying in 1969, aged almost 101. It's stuffed with fascinating photographs tracing her journeys, as well as old Tibetan ornaments, masks and paintings.

Paling in comparison, but still worth a visit for its interesting temporary exhibitions, is the municipal **Musée Gassendi**, 64 bd Gassendi (daily except Tues: April–Sept 11am–7pm; Oct–March 1.30–5.30pm; €4), which holds sixteenth- to nineteenth-century paintings and pays homage to seventeenth-century mathematician and savant Pierre Gassendi.

The largest geological reserve in Europe, the **Réserve Naturelle Géologique de Haute-Provence**, covers over 150,000 hectares north and east of Dignes. To learn more about its 300-million-year-old fossils, head to the ammonite-laden **Musée-Promenade** (April–June, Sept & Oct daily 9am–noon & 2–5pm, closes Fri 4.30pm; July & Aug Mon–Fri 10am–1pm & 2–7pm, Sat & Sun 10.30am–12.30pm & 2–7pm; Nov–March Mon–Thurs 9am–noon & 2–5pm, Fri 9am–noon & 2–4.30pm; €5; W www.resgeol04.org), immediately north of the town to the left of the bridge across the river on the D900A towards Barles.

Practicalities

The **tourist office** is on the *rond point* du 11 Novembre 1918 (June–Sept Mon–Sat 8.45am–12.30pm & 2–6.30pm, Sun 10am–noon; Oct–May Mon–Sat 8.45am–noon & 2–6pm; T 04.92.36.62.62, W www.ot-dignelesbains.fr), with the **gare routière** adjacent. The **gare Chemin de Fer de la Provence** is to the west over the river on avenue Pierre Sémard (see box opposite). **Hotel** options include a spacious, comfortable budget option near the tourist office, the *Central*, 26 bd Gassendi (T 04.92.31.31.91, W www.lhotel-central.com; ❷), and the more luxurious *Grand Paris*, 19 bd Thiers (T 04.92.31.11.15, W www.hotel-grand -paris.com; ❺; open March–Nov), which has a very good restaurant (closed Mon, Tues & Wed lunchtime out of season; *menus* from €32), along with a surprising menagerie in the reception. For cheaper food, go for the modern *Taverne*, 36 bd Gassendi (T 04.92.31.30.82; closed Sun), a brasserie that serves *raclette* (€16) and traditional *menus* from €18.

Sisteron

The Route Napoléon leads eventually to **SISTERON**, 25km northwest of Digne, and the most important mountain gateway to Provence. The site has been fortified since time immemorial; even now, half-destroyed by the Anglo-American bombardment of 1944, its citadelle stands as a fearsome sentinel over the city and the solitary bridge across the River Durance.

Even the quickest of visits should include a trip up to the magnificent **citadelle** (April–Nov daily 9am–dusk; €6); the views from the remparts are breathtaking. A small **historical museum** with a room dedicated to Napoleon lies just inside the walls, while further up the vertiginous late-medieval chapel, **Notre-Dame-du-Château**, has been restored to its Gothic glory and equipped with lovely stained-glass windows. The future king of Poland, Jan Kazimierz, was imprisoned here in 1639; the main tower holds a stuffed model of the unfortunate royal, and a reconstruction of his room. In late July and early August, the Nuits de la Citadelle festival includes open-air performances of music, drama and dance in the citadel grounds.

Back in Sisteron's old town, the three huge **towers** belonged to the citadelle ramparts, built in 1370. Beside them is the **Cathédrale Notre-Dame-des-Pommiers** (daily 3–6pm), a cool and well-proportioned twelfth-century church. From the cathedral, rue Deleuze leads to **place de l'Horloge**, where the Wednesday and Saturday **market** is held and where, on the second Saturday of every month, there's a fair. If you fancy a **swim**, take a dip in the large artificial lake between the allée de Verdun and the river (summer only).

Practicalities

From Sisteron's **gare SNCF**, head right, along avenue de la Libération, to reach place de la République, and the **tourist office** (July–Aug Mon–Sat 9am–7pm, Sun 10am–5pm; Sept–June Mon–Sat 9am–noon & 2–5pm; ☎04.92.61.36.50, ⓦwww.sisteron.fr) plus the **gare routière**. The genteel and old-fashioned *Grand Hôtel du Cours* on allée de Verdun (☎04.92.61.04.51, ⓦwww.hotel-lecours.com; ❹; open March–Dec), is the best **hotel**. For cheap, clean rooms with great views of the imposing landscape, try *La Citadelle*, 126 rue Saunerie (☎04.92.61.13.52, ⓦwww.hotel-lacitadelle.com; ❷). Sisteron's four-star **campsite**, *Les Prés Hauts*, is across the river and 2km along the D951 (☎04.92.61.19.69, ⓦwww.camping-sisteron.com; open March–Oct).

Of Sisteron's **restaurants**, *Le Cours* (see above) serves traditional *plats* for around €20, including the renowned *gigot d'agneau de Sisteron*, while *Les Becs Fins* (☎04.92.61.12.04, ⓦbecsfins.free.fr; out of season, closed Sun eve & Wed), 16 rue Saunerie, is a decent place to sample pricey fish dishes.

Northeast Provence

Depending on the season, the **northeastern corner of Provence** can be two different worlds. In winter, the sheep and shepherds find warmer pastures, leaving the snowy heights to horned mouflons, chamois and the perfectly camouflaged ermine. The villages where shepherds came to summer markets are battened down for the long, cold haul, while modern conglomerations of Swiss-style chalet houses, sports shops and discotheques come to life around the ski lifts. The seasonal dichotomy is particularly evident in towns like **Colmars-les-Alpes** and **Barcelonnette**.

The **Alpes-Maritimes** make up much of northeastern Provence, encompassing a large amount of the magnificent **Parc National du Mercantour** (see box, p.896), which runs south of Barcelonnette to the Italian border villages of Tende, Breil-sur-Roya and Sospel. Base yourself in one of the small Alpes-Maritimes towns, which include **St-Étienne-de-Tinée**, **St-Martin-Vésubie**, **St-Sauveur-sur-Tinée** and from the **upper Roya valley**.

Colmars-les-Alpes

On the western periphery of the Parc National du Mercantour, the charming village of **Colmars-les-Alpes** makes an ideal journey's break, even when it's

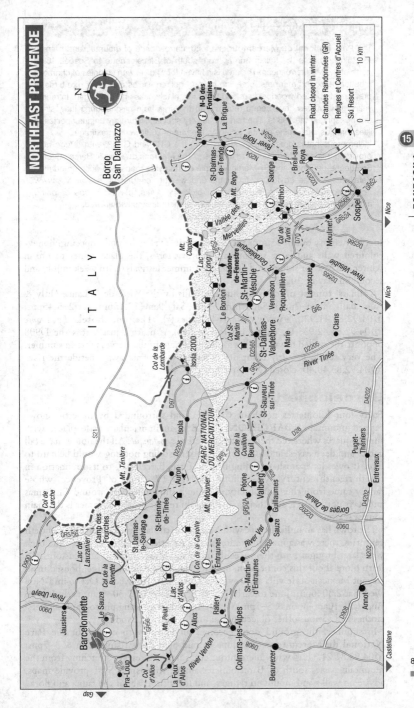

ITALY

Borgo
San Dalmazzo

N-D des
Fontaines

La Brigue

Tende

St-Dalmas-
de-Tende

Mt. Bégo

Saorge

Breil-sur-
Roya

Vallée des
Merveilles

Authion

Mt. Clapier

Lac
Long

Col de Turini

Moulinet

Sospel

Madone-
de-Fenestre

St-Martin-
Vésubie

Bordrésagne

Lantosque

River Vésubie

Venanson

Roquebillière

Le Boréon

Col St-
Martin

St-Dalmas-
Valdeblore

Marie

Clans

Col de la
Lombarde

Isola 2000

St-Sauveur-
sur-Tinée

River Tinée

PARC NATIONAL
DU MERCANTOUR

Mt. Ténibre

Isola

Col de la
Coullole

Beuil

Puget-
Théniers

Entrevaux

Col de
Larche

Auron

Mt. Mounier

Péone

Valberg

Guillaumes

Gorges de Daluis

Camp des
Fourches

St-Etienne-
de-Tinée

Sauze

Lac de
Lauzanier

St-Dalmas-
le-Selvage

Col de la Cayolle

Entraunes

River Var

St-Martin-
d'Entraunes

Annot

Jausiers

River Ubaye

Le Sauze

Col de la
Bonette

Mt. Pelat

Lac
d'Allos

Ratery

Allos

Colmars-
les-Alpes

Beauvezer

Barcelonnette

Pra-Loup

Col -
d'Allos

La Foux
d'Allos

River Verdon

Castellane

895

The Parc National du Mercantour

The **Parc National du Mercantour** is a long, narrow band of mountainland running for 75km close to the Italian border, from south of Barcelonnette to Sospel, 16km north of the Mediterreanean. The area is a haven for wildlife, with colonies of chamois, mouflon, ibex and marmots, breeding pairs of golden eagles and other rare birds of prey, great spotted woodpeckers and hoopoes, blackcocks and ptarmigan. In recent years grey wolves have begun returning to the area from neighbouring Italy, since disappearing in the 1930s. The flora too is very special, with many unique species of lilies, orchids and Alpine plants, including the rare multi-flowering saxifrage.

Numerous paths cross the park, including the GR5 and GR52, with *refuge* huts providing basic food and bedding for hikers. The **Maisons du Parc** in Barcelonnette, St-Étienne-de-Tinée and St-Martin-Vésubie can provide maps and accommodation details as well as advice on footpaths and weather conditions; see also ⓦwww .mercantour.eu. Camping, lighting fires, picking flowers, playing radios or doing anything that might disturb the delicate environment is strictly outlawed.

spookily empty out of season. Secreted away in a valley behind imposing, honey-coloured walls and large seventeenth-century *portes*, the place comes to life in winter as a base for skiiers, and during the summer festivals (third week in July and second Sunday in August).

Colmars' **tourist office** is outside the walls by the Porte de la Lance (July & Aug daily 8am–7pm; Sept–June Tues–Sat 9am–12.15pm & 2–5.45pm; ⓣ04.92.83.41.92, ⓦwww.colmars-les-alpes.fr). The one **hotel**, *Le France* (ⓣ04.92.83.42.93; ❸; closed Jan to late Feb), is nearby, just across the D908 opposite the walled town, and has a garden restaurant that serves pizza in summer. The very scenic *Bois Joly* **campsite** is ten minutes' walk away, beside the river (ⓣ04.92.83.40.40; closed Oct–April).

Barcelonnette

Forty-four kilometres north of Colmars, and surrounded by majestic snow-capped mountains, **BARCELONNETTE** is an immaculate little place, with sunny squares where old men wearing berets play *pétanque*. All the houses have tall gables and deep eaves, and a more ideal spot for doing nothing would be hard to find. It owes its Spanish-sounding name, "Little Barcelona", to its foundation in the thirteenth century by Raimond Béranger IV, count of Provence, whose family came from the Catalan city. Although snow falls here around Christmas and stays until Easter, and there are several ski resorts nearby, summer is the main tourist season.

The town has an unlikely link with Mexico: in the late nineteenth and twentieth centuries, there was a mass migration to the Americas, and those who came back years later brought with them wealth and many Mexican habits and customs. To learn more about this connection, head for the **Musée de la Vallée**, housed in an elegant Mexican-style villa at 10 av de la Libération (Jan–May & Oct to mid-Nov Wed–Sat 2.30–6pm; June to early July & Sept Tues–Sat 2.30–6pm; early July to Aug daily 10am–noon & 3–7pm; €3.50). It holds engrossing photographs, letters, clothes and various other objects pertaining to the mass exodus.

In summer, the ground floor becomes an information centre for the **Parc National du Mercantour** (mid-June to mid-Sept daily 10am–noon & 3–7pm; ⓣ04.92.81.21.31, ⓦwww.mercantour.eu), a national reserve stretching from the mountain passes south of Barçelonnette almost to **Sospel**. Staff provide maps, advise on walks and mountain refuges, and tell visitors about the fauna and flora.

Practicalities

Barcelonnette's **tourist office** is just off place Frédéric Mistral (July & Aug daily 9am–12.30pm & 1.30–7.30pm; Sept–June Mon–Sat 9am–noon & 2–6pm; ℡04.92.81.04.71, ⓦwww.barcelonnette.com). The top **hotel** is the Mexican-style *Azteca* on rue François Arnaud (℡04.92.81.46.36, ⓦwww.azteca-hotel .fr; ❹), while the traditional *Cheval Blanc*, 12 rue Grenette (℡04.92.81.00.19, ⓦwww.chevalblancbarcelonnette.com; closed Nov; ❸), is cheaper. The closest of the three **campsites** is the three-star *Du Plan* at 52 av E.Aubert (℡04.92.81.08.11, ⓦwww.campingduplan.fr; closed Oct to mid-May).

The best **restaurant** in the area is 9km east in **Jausiers**: *Villa Morelia* (℡04.92.84.67.78) serves sophisticated *nouvelle cuisine* in a neo-Mexican folly that also houses a plush spa hotel, with *menu* from €68). In Barcelonnette itself, sample some cheap and cheerful Mexican food at *Adelita* (℡04.92.81.16.12; closed Thurs) on rue Donnadieu, while *La Plancha* (℡04.92.81.12.97) on place Paul Reynaud serves mountain dishes such as *tartiflette*, potato gratin and meat platters from €15. Be sure also to taste the local juniper liqueur, *Genepy*, generally available in the town on market days (Wed & Sat).

The Alpes-Maritimes

With an economy driven mostly by tourism, the towns of the Alpes-Maritimes make great bases for exploring the Parc du Mercantour. From Barcelonnette (the D64) it's a breathtaking journey across the Cime de la Bonette pass, which reaches over 2800m and is is claimed to be the highest in Europe. It's only open for three months of the year, from the end of June until September. The air is cold even in summer and the green and silent spaces of the approach to the summit, circled by barren peaks, are magical.

The Towns

Once over the pass, you descend into the Tinée valley and its highest town, **ST-ÉTIENNE-DE-TINÉE**, which springs awake for its sheep fairs, held twice every summer, and the Fête de la Transhumance at the end of June. On the west side of the town off boulevard d'Auron, a cable car then chair lift climb to the summit of **La Pinatelle**, linking the village to the ski resort of **AURON**. In **summer** a handful of the lifts are open to hikers and mountain bikers (July & Aug; €9 day; ⓦwww .auron.com) while in **winter** skiers come to enjoy the 42 pistes (€29.50 per day).

There are two welcoming **hotel-restaurants** on offer: the *Regalivou*, 8 bd d'Auron (℡04.93.02.49.00, ⓦleregalivou.free.fr; ❸), and *Des Amis*, 1 rue Val-Gélé (℡04.93.02.40.30; ❷). On the edge of the village, you'll find a small **campsite** (open June–Sept; ℡04.93.02.41.57) adjacent to the **Maison du Parc** (July & Aug daily 9.30am–noon & 2–6pm; Oct–May open until 5.30pm; ℡04.93.01.42.27).

The next stretch downstream from St-Étienne has nothing but white quartz and heather, with only the silvery sound of crickets competing with the water's roar before reaching **Isola**, an uneventful village at the bottom of the climb to the purpose-built ski resort of **ISOLA 2000** (ⓦwww.isola2000.com), a jumble of concrete apartment blocks high in the mountain, built to accommodate skiers using the 22 lifts and 120km of piste (Dec–April; €29.50 per day).

After Isola, the road – now the D2205 – and river turn south through the **Gorges de Valabres** to **ST-SAUVEUR-SUR-TINÉE**, a pleasantly sleepy place that's home to a cosy, cheap **hotel**: the *Auberge de la Gare*, 1 av des Blavets (℡04.93.02.00.67; ❶).

Shifting east to the Vésubie valley, you come to the lovely little town of **ST-MARTIN-VÉSUBIE** where a cobbled, narrow street with a channelled stream runs through the old quarter beneath the overhanging roofs and balconies of Gothic houses. The **tourist office** on place Félix-Faure (July & Aug daily 9am–noon & 2–7pm; Sept–June Mon–Sat 9am–noon & 2–6pm, Sun 9am–noon; ☎04.93.03.21.28, ⊛www.saintmartinvesubie.fr) provides details on walks and *gîtes/refuges* in the vicinity. At the *Alpha* **wolf reserve** in Le Boréon, a small, scenic mountain retreat 8km north, you can see newborn wolf puppies in spring (May–Aug daily 10am–6pm, last admission 4.30pm; April, Sept & school hols daily 10am–5pm, last admission 4pm; otherwise hours irregular, closed most of March, Nov & Dec; €12; ⊛www.alpha-loup.com).

Hotels in St-Martin include the *Châtaigneraie* (☎04.93.03.21.22, ⊛www.raiberti.com; ❹; closed Oct–May), set in lovely gardens on the allées de Verdun, which has comfortable rooms that can sleep up to five guests and a good restaurant, and the cute little *Gélas*, 27 rue Cagnoli (☎04.93.03.21.81, ⊛www.hotel-gelas.com; ❹). The closest **campsite** is the *Ferme St-Joseph* (☎06.70.51.90.14, ⊛www.camping-alafermestjoseph.com; open early May to late Sept), on the route de Nice by the lower bridge over La Madone.

The Roya valley

The thickly forested **Roya valley** – divided into **upper** and **lower** sections – runs from Col de Tende on the French–Italian border down to Breil-sur-Roya. The major highlight in the upper valley is the **Vallée des Merveilles**, a jumble of lakes and tumbled rocks on the western flank of Mont Bego; the first person to stumble on the area in the modern era was a fifteenth-century traveller who had lost his way. He described it as "an infernal place with figures of the devil and thousands of demons scratched on the rocks": a pretty accurate description, except that some of the carvings are of animals, tools, people working and mysterious symbols, dated to some time in the second millennium BC. In the lower valley, head for the sleepy Italianate town of **Sospel**.

Getting around is relatively time-consuming; the roads are narrow and steep so driving can be slow, and the once-daily **Train des Merveilles** (departs Nice 9am; €24 return), with an English commentary (May–Oct), trundles along the Nice–Cuneo line at a leisurely pace. There are also normal trains running along the same line, for those who want a later start.

The upper Roya valley

TENDE, the highest town on the Roya, guards the access to the Col de Tende, which connects Provence with Piedmont but is now bypassed by a road tunnel. Though not especially attractive, Tende is fairly busy, with plenty of cheap accommodation, places to eat, bars to lounge around in and shops to browse round.

At the beautifully designed **Musée des Merveilles**, av 16 Septembre 1947 (May to mid-Oct daily 10am–6.30pm; mid-Oct to April daily 10am–5pm; closed 2 weeks in March & 2 weeks in Nov; free, tours €22.85; ⊛www.museedesmerveilles.com), you can check out reproductions of the engravings on the Vallée des Merveilles. The **tourist office** is nearby at 103 av 16 Septembre 1947 (daily 9am–noon & 2–6pm; ☎04.93.04.73.71, ⊛www.tendemerveilles.com). Inexpensive **hotels** include the *Miramonti*, by the station at 5–7 av Vassalo (☎04.93.04.61.82; ❷; closed mid-Nov to mid-Dec).

One stop south from Tende, pretty **LA BRIGUE** makes a good base for the Vallée des Merveilles. While you're here, make the trip 4km east of town to the sanctuary of **Notre-Dame-des-Fontaines** (daily 9.30am–7pm; €2.50). From the exterior this looks like a graceful retreat, but inside it's more like a slasher movie: all its fifteenth-century frescoes, ranging from Christ's torment on the Cross to devils claiming their victims and, ultimate gore, Judas's disembowelment, are full of violent movement and colour. The local **tourist office** is on place St-Martin (daily 9am–12.30pm & 2–5.30pm; ℡04.93.79.09.34, ⓦwww .labrigue.fr). Two hotels on the same square – the *Auberge St-Martin* (℡04.93.04.62.17, ⓦwww.auberge-st-martin.fr; ❸), and the *Fleurs des Alpes* (℡04.93.04.61.05, ⓔhotel.fleurdesalpes@tiscali.fr; ❸; closed Wed, plus Dec–Feb) – have **restaurants** that serve very satisfying meals for less than €20.

The Vallée des Merveilles is best approached from **ST-DALMAS-DE-TENDE** one stop south of La Brigue. The easiest route is the ten-kilometre hike (6–8hr there and back) that starts at *Les Mesches Refuge*, 8km west on the D91. The engravings are beyond the *Refuge des Merveilles*. Note that certain areas are out of bounds unless accompanied by an official guide – and remember that blue skies and sun can quickly turn into violent hailstorms and lightning, so go prepared, properly shod and clothed, and take your own food and water. For details of **guided walks**, contact the Maison du Mercantour in Tende (℡04.93 04.73.71), or local tourist offices.

The lower Roya valley

The best place to spend a relaxed day, or couple of days, in the lower Roya valley is **SOSPEL**, situated 36km south of St-Dalmas-de-Tende. You may find it over-tranquil after the excitements of the high mountains or the flashy speed of the Côte d'Azur, but it can make a pleasant break.

Sospel

Sospel's main street, avenue Jean-Médecin, follows the river on its southern bank; halfway down is the **Vieux Pont**, built originally in the thirteenth century to link the town centre on the south bank with its suburb across the river. The town centre is made up of dark, narrow lanes, with its heart at **place St-Michel**, a riot of colourful Baroque facades and arcaded houses, dominated by the large Cathédrale St-Michel. For something a little more contemporary, head ten minutes out of town, left along boulevard de Verdun to **Fort St-Roch**, part of the ignominious interwar Maginot line, where the **Musée de la Résistance** is housed in an imposing concrete bunker (April–June Sat & Sun 2–6pm; July–Sept Tues–Sun 2–6pm; €5).

The best view of the town is reached via a relatively easy three-hour **hike** up Col d'Agaisen, starting from the Pont de la Libération and walking away from the old town. The tourist office (see below) has a map of the route, and there are plenty of signs to point you in the right direction.

Practicalities
Sospel's friendly **tourist office** is at 19 av Jean-Médecin (Mon–Sat 10am–4pm, Sun 10am–12.30pm; ℡04.93.04.15.80, ⓦwww.sospel-tourisme.com). The **gare SNCF** is southeast of town on avenue A-Borriglione.

The two best-value hotels are side by side on boulevard de Verdun, just across the eastern bridge: the cheaper *France* at no. 9 (℡04.93.04.00.01, ⓦwww.hoteldefrance -sospel.com; ❸; closed mid-Nov to mid-Dec) has comfortable, colourful rooms, while the smarter *Étrangers*, no. 7 (℡04.93.04.00.09, ⓦwww.sospel.net; ❺; closed Dec–Feb), has a pool and a good restaurant (closed Tues & Wed lunch), with *menus* at €25–55. Of the four local **campsites**, the closest is the two-star *Le Mas Fleuri*, 2km upstream along the D2566 in Quartier La Vasta (℡04.93.04.14.94, Ⓦwww.camping-mas-fleuri.com; closed Oct–March), which has a pool.

Restaurants include the *Sout'a Laupia*, 13 rue St-Pierre (℡04.93.04.24.23), which serves delicious traditional local cuisine at good prices; and the *Relais du Sel*, 3 bd de Verdun (℡04.93.04.00.43; closed Fri in low season), where you dine on a terrace above the river, with excellent *menus* starting at €22. *Bar Moderne*, 17 av Jean-Médecin (℡04.97.00.00.42), doubles as an **internet café** and is a pleasant early-evening drinking spot next to the river.

Travel details

Trains

Aix-en-Provence to: Marseille (every 20–30min; 30–45min).

Aix-en-Provence TGV to: Avignon TGV (22 daily; 20min); Marseille (frequent daily; 15min); Paris (8 daily; 3hr); Paris CDG Airport (4 daily; 3hr 30min).

Arles to: Avignon (17 daily; 20min); Avignon TGV (2 daily; 20min); Lyon (7–9 daily; 2hr 30min); Marseille (23 daily; 45min–1hr).

Avignon to: Arles (hourly; 20–45min); Cavaillon (9–14 daily; 35min); Lyon (12 daily; 2hr 30min); Marseille (14 daily; 1hr 5min); Orange (17 daily; 15min); Valence (12 daily; 1hr 20min).

Avignon TGV to: Aix-en-Provence TGV (22 daily; 20min); Lille-Europe (5 daily; 4hr 30min); London St Pancras (summer 1 on Sat only: 5hr 53min; Lyon (14 daily; 1hr 10min); Marseille (half-hourly; 30min); Paris (17 daily; 2hr 40min); Paris CDG Airport (5 daily; 3hr 30min); Valence TGV (9 daily; 30–40min).

Digne to: Nice, via Aix en Provence (4 daily; 6hr).

Orange to: Paris (2 daily; 2hr 30min).

Sospel to: La Brigue (1–3 daily; 50min); Nice (4 daily; 50min); St-Dalmas-de-Tende (3 daily; 45min); Tende (3 daily; 55min).

Buses

Aix-en-Provence to: Apt (2 daily; 1hr 45min); Arles (3 daily; 1hr 25min); Avignon (4 daily; 1hr 30min); Carpentras (3–4 daily; 1hr 30min); Cavaillon (4 daily; 1hr 20min); Marseille (very frequent; 30–50min); Sisteron (3 daily; 2hr).

Arles to: Aix (4 daily; 1hr 30min); Avignon (8 daily; 1hr); Avignon TGV (8 daily; 55min); Stes-Maries-de-la-Mer (4–7 daily; 55min); St-Rémy (4 daily; 25–30min).

Aups to: Aiguines (1 daily; 35min); Cotignac (3 daily; 25min).

Avignon to: Apt (7 daily; 1hr 10min–1hr 30min); Carpentras (frequent; 35–45min); Cavaillon (9 daily; 35min); Digne (3–4 daily; 3hr–3hr 30min); Fontaine-de-Vaucluse (4 daily; 55min); L'Isle-sur-la-Sorgue (10 daily; 40min); Orange (every 30–45min; 50min); St-Rémy (8 daily; 40min); Vaison (3 daily; 1hr 25min).

Barcelonnette to: Digne (2 daily; 1hr 45min); Gap (3 daily; 1hr 20min); Marseille (2 daily; 3hr 50min).

Carpentras to: Cavaillon (2–5 daily; 45min); Gigondas (1–3 daily; 30min); L'Isle-sur-la-Sorgue (5 daily; 20min); Marseille (3 daily; 1hr 15min–2hr 5min); Orange (3 daily; 40–45min); Vaison (4 daily; 45min).

Cavaillon to: Gordes (3–4 daily; 30min).

Digne to: Aix (4 daily; 2hr); Avignon (3 daily; 3hr 30min); Barcelonnette (2 daily; 1hr–1hr 30min); Marseille (4 daily; 2hr–2hr 20min); Nice (2 daily; 3hr–3hr 15min); Riez (3 daily; 1hr 15min); Sisteron (3 daily; 1hr 15min).

Orange to: Châteauneuf-du-Pape (1 Thurs; 30min); Séguret (2 daily; 40min); Sérignan (7 daily; 15min); Vaison (2 daily; 40–50min).

Quinson to: Riez (1 daily; 35min).

St-Rémy to: Les Baux (4 daily; 15–20min).

Riez to: Digne-les-Bains (3 daily; 1hr 15min); Moustiers-Ste-Marie (2 daily; 20min).

The Côte d'Azur

CHAPTER 16 # Highlights

* **Vieux Port, Marseille** The old trading port, with its restaurants, beautiful sunsets and nightlife, attracts the most colourful characters in southern France. See p.908

* **Les Calanques** The limestone cliffs between Marseille and Cassis make for excellent hikes leading to isolated coves in which to go swimming. See p.916

* **Îles de Port-Cros and St-Honorat** Well-preserved island offering a glimpse of what much of the coast must have looked like a hundred years ago. See p.922

* **Massif des Maures** This undeveloped range of hazy coastal hills is a world apart from the glitz and glamour of the Côte. See p.924

* **Fondation Maeght** Modern art, architecture and landscape fuse to create a stunning visual experience. See p.948

* **Nice** The Riviera's capital of street life is laid-back, surprisingly cultured and easy to enjoy, whatever your budget. See p.949

▲ View over the promenade des Anglais, Nice

The Côte d'Azur

The **Côte d'Azur** polarizes opinion like few places in France. To some, it remains the ultimate Mediterranean playground, while for others it has become an overdeveloped victim of its own hype. But in the gaps between the urban sprawl, on the islands, in the remarkable beauty of the hills, the mimosa blossom in February and the impossibly blue water after which the coast is named, the Côte d'Azur remains undeniably captivating. The great city of **Marseille** possesses its own special magnetism, while eastwards along the coast are opportunities for swimming and sailing around the *calanques*. Out of season, the coast between sedate **Hyères**, Roman **Fréjus**, flashy **St-Raphaël** and its backdrop of wooded hills holds its own against the cynicism engendered by tourist brochure overkill. The magic lies in the scented Mediterranean vegetation, silver beaches, secluded islands and medieval **hilltop villages** such as Le Lavandou, Cavalaire-sur-Mer and Ste-Maxime. To add to these are the wonderful **Îles d'Hyères** where you can experience unspoilt landscapes with some of the best fauna and flora in Provence. Back along the coast east of the islands is a chain of seaside resorts – **La Croix-Valmer** is probably the most pleasant, while overhyped **St-Tropez** – where the summer crush really can be unbearable – is a must if only for a day-trip.

The **Riviera**, the seventy-odd kilometres of coast between **Cannes** and **Menton** by the Italian border, was once an inhospitable shore with few natural harbours, its tiny communities preferring to cluster round feudal castles high above the sea. It wasn't until the nineteenth century that the first foreign aristocrats began to winter in the region's mild climate. In the interwar years the aristocrats were gradually supplanted by new elites – film stars, artists and writers. Nowadays, it's an almost uninterrupted promenade, lined by palms and megabuck hotels, with speeding sports cars on the Corniche and yachts like ocean liners moored at each resort. Attractions, however, still remain, most notably in the legacies of the artists who stayed here: Picasso, Léger, Matisse, Renoir and Chagall. **Nice**, too, has real substance as a major city.

Transport can be a problem in the area. There is a regular bus service along the coast, but traffic is extremely slow in high season, and cycling doesn't get you very far unless you're Tour de France material. The months to avoid are July and August, when hotels are booked up, overflowing campsites become health hazards, the locals get short-tempered, and the vegetation is at its most barren, and November, when many museums, hotels and restaurants close and the weather is wet.

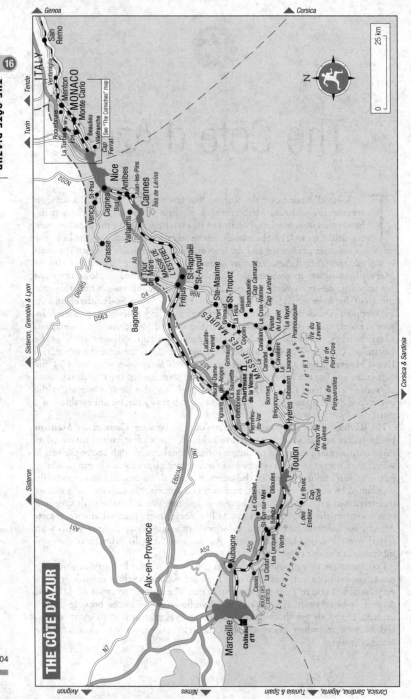

THE CÔTE D'AZUR

25 km

N

Genoa

Corsica

Turin

Tende

San Remo

Ventimiglia

Menton

MONACO

Monte Carlo

Roquebrune

La Turbie

Èze

Beaulieu

Villefranche

Cap Ferrat

See "The Corniches" map

ITALY

N202

Nice

Antibes

St-Paul

Vence

Cagnes

Biot

Juan-les-Pins

Cannes

Îles de Lérins

Vallauris

Grasse

A8

D6085

La Tour de Mare

MASSIF DE L'ESTEREL

St-Raphaël

St-Aygulf

Fréjus

D4

Bagnols

D563

Sisteron, Grenoble & Lyon

Ste-Maxime

D98N

Port Grimaud

St-Tropez

La Foux

Gassin

Ramatuelle

Cap Camarat

Grimaud

Cogolin

Cap Lardier

La Croix-Valmer

Pointe du Layet

LaGarde-Freinet

MASSIF DES MAURES

Cavalaire

Canadel

Pramousquier

Le Rayol

Île du Levant

Notre-Dame-des-Anges

La Sauvette

Chartreuse de la Verne

Cavalière

Île de Port-Cros

Pignans

Collobrières

Bormes

Brégançon

Cabasson

Lavandou

Îles d'Hyères

Corsica & Sardinia

Pierrefeu-du-Var

Hyères

Île de Porquerolles

A57

Presqu'île de Giens

Toulon

DN7

Le Brusc

Cap Sicié

Sisteron

E80/A8

Ollioules

St-Cyr-sur-Mer

Bandol

Î. des Embiez

I. Verte

Aix-en-Provence

A52

A50

Aubagne

Le Castellet

Les Lecques

La Ciotat

Cassis

Les Calanques

ROUTE DES CRÊTES

Marseille

Château d'If

N7

A51

Avignon

Nîmes

Corsica, Sardinia, Algeria, Tunisia & Spain

Food and wine of the Côte d'Azur

The **Côte d'Azur**, as part of Provence, shares its culinary fundamentals of olive oil, garlic and herbs, gorgeous vegetables and fruits (plus Menton's lemons), the goat's cheeses and, of course, the predominance of fish.

The fish soups of **bouillabaisse**, famous in Marseille, and **bourride**, accompanied by a garlic and chilli-flavoured mayonnaise known as *rouille*, are served all along the coast, as are **fish** covered with Provençal herbs and grilled over an open flame. **Seafood** – from spider crabs to clams, sea urchins to crayfish, crabs, lobster, mussels and oysters – are piled onto huge *plateaux de mer*, which don't necessarily represent Mediterranean harvest, more the luxury associated with this coast.

The **Italian influence** is strong, with delicate ravioli stuffed with spinach, prawns, wild mushrooms or *pistou*, pizzas with wafer-thin bases and every sort of pasta as a vehicle for anchovies, olives, garlic and tomatoes. Nice has its own specialities, such as *socca*, a chickpea flour pancake, *pissaladière*, a tart of fried onions with anchovies and black olives, *salade niçoise* and *pan bagnat*, both of which combine egg, olives, salad, tuna and olive oil, and *mesclun*, a salad of bitter leaves including dandelion: consequently, Nice is about as good a spot to enjoy cheap street food as you'll find. *Petites farcies* – stuffed aubergines, peppers or tomatoes – are a standard feature on Côte d'Azur *menus*.

As for **wine**, the rosés of Provence might not have great status in the French viniculture hierarchy, but for baking summer days they are hard to beat. The best of the Côte wines come from Bandol: Cassis too has its own *appellation*, and around Nice the Bellet wines are worth discovering. Fancy cocktails are a Côte speciality, and *pastis* is the preferred thirst quencher at any time of the day.

Marseille

The most renowned and populated city in France after Paris, **MARSEILLE** has both prospered and been ransacked over the centuries. It has lost its privileges to sundry French kings and foreign armies, recovered its fortunes, suffered plagues, religious bigotry, republican and royalist Terror and had its own Commune and Bastille-storming. It was the presence of so many Marseillais revolutionaries marching from the Rhine to Paris in 1792 that gave the *Hymn of the Army of the Rhine* its name of *La Marseillaise*, later to become the national anthem.

In recent years Marseille has undergone a renaissance, shaking off much of its old reputation for sleaze and danger to attract a wider range of visitors taking advantage of the TGV link from the north. The march of progress is not, however, relentless: too often last year's prestige civic project becomes this year's broken, bottle-strewn fountain. But that's Marseille. If you don't like your cities gritty and underground, it may not be for you. See past its occasional squalor, though, and chances are you will warm to this down-to-earth, cosmopolitan, artistic metropolis.

Note that reconstruction work is currently taking place in the city as it gets ready to become European Capital of Culture in 2013; some places of interest may be partially or entirely closed for renovation.

Arrival, information and city transport

The city's **airport**, the Aéroport Marseille-Provence (T 04.42.14.14.14, W www .mrsairport.com), is 20km northwest of the city, linked to the **gare SNCF** by bus (every 20min 5.10am–0.10am; €8.50). The **gare SNCF St-Charles** (T 3635) is on the northern edge of the 1er arrondissement on square Narvik with the **gare routière** alongside at 3 rue Honnorat (T 08.91.02.40.25). From the *gare SNCF*, a

MARSEILLE

◄ Cassis

◄ Toulon

EATING & DRINKING

Aux 3G	2
Chez Fonfon	10
Les Docks des Suds	8
La Gentiane	3
L'Intermédiaire	7
La Maronaise	11
New Cancan	6
Le Poste à Galène	1
Pussy Twisters	5
Bar Le Petit Nice	4
Le Red Lion	9

ACCOMMODATION

Le Corbusier	A
Edmond-Rostand	B
HI Youth Hostel	
Bonneveine	C

MONTAGNE DE MARSEILLEVEYRE ►

LA MADRAGUE

Port de Plaisance de la Pte Rouge

Musée de la Faïence

MAC

Château Borély

Parc Borély

Ballet National de Marseille

Unité d' Habitation

Football Stadium

ROND-POINT DU PRADO

Palais Longchamp

Hôtel du Département

La Friche la Belle de Mai

Gare SNCF

Gare Maritime

Les Docks

Basilique Notre-Dame-de-la-Garde

See "Marseille: Le Vieux Port map"

Avant Port Nord

Anse des Auffes

Rochers de Pendus

Rade de Marseille

Digue du Large

MALMOUSQUE

Rade d'Endoume

Îles d'Endoume

Plage du Prado

Rade de Marseilleveyre

1er · 2e · 3e · 4e · 5e · 6e · 7e · 8e · 10e · 14e · 15e

LE PANIER

LA JOLIETTE

BD. MICHELET · AVENUE DU PRADO · AVENUE DE PRADO · RUE DE ROME · BD. BAILLE · BOULEVARD CHAVE · BD. RABATAU · BD. SCHLOESING · RUE ROMAIN ROLLAND

— Tramway

0   1 km

N

monumental staircase leads down to boulevard d'Athènes and on to La Canebière, Marseille's main street. The **tourist office** is at 4 La Canebière (Mon–Sat 9am–7pm, Sun & public hols 10am–5pm; ℡04.91.13.89.00, Ⓦwww.marseille -tourisme.com), down by the Vieux Port.

Marseille has an efficient **bus, tram** and **métro** network (Ⓦwww.rtm.fr). The métro runs from 5am until 10.30pm on weekdays and until after midnight at weekends; trams run from 5am to after midnight. Night buses run from 9.30pm to around 12.30am. You can get a plan of the transport system from most métro stations' **points d'accueil** office (daily 6.40am–7.40pm) or at the tourist office. **Tickets** are flat-rate for buses, trams and the métro and can be used for journeys combining all three as long as they take less than one hour. You can buy individual tickets (€1.70) from bus and tram drivers, and from métro ticket offices, or **multi-journey Cartes Libertés** (in increments of €6.30 and €12.60), which are valid for five and ten journeys respectively; these can be bought from métro stations, RTM kiosks and shops displaying the RTM sign. Consider the good-value one-day **Carte Journée** (€4.60) or three-day **Carte 3 Jours** (€10.50). Tickets must be punched in the machines on the bus, on tramway platforms or at métro gates.

Accommodation

Since Marseille is not predominately a tourist city, **finding a room** in July or August is less tricky than elsewhere on the coast. Hotels are plentiful, though if you get stuck the tourist office can help and you can also book online via their website.

Hotels

Alizé 35 quai des Belges, 1ᵉʳ ℡04.91.33.66.97, Ⓦwww.alize-hotel.com. Comfortable, freshly renovated and soundproofed rooms, with the more expensive ones looking out onto the Vieux Port. ❹–❺

Le Corbusier Unité d'Habitation, 280 bd Michelet, 8ᵉ ℡04.91.16.78.00, Ⓦwww.hotellecorbusier .com. Landmark hotel on the third floor of this renowned architect's iconic high-rise with fabulous views. ❺–❼

Edmond-Rostand 31 rue Dragon, 8ᵉ ℡04.91.37.74.95, Ⓦwww.hoteledmondrostand .com. Comfortable, smallish rooms with free wi-fi and friendly service. ❹–❺

Etap Hotel Vieux Port 46 rue Sainte, 1ᵉʳ ℡08.92.68.05.82, Ⓦwww.etaphotel.com. Though this is a branch of a budget chain, it is well worth a stay for its location alone, close to the Vieux Port. Situated in a historic building, some of the rooms have timber beams – it's incredibly popular so book ahead. ❸

Hermes 2 rue Bonneterie, 2ᵉ ℡04.96.11.63.63, Ⓦwww.hotelmarseille.com. Apart from the more expensive "Nuptial" room 5 on the wonderful roof terrace overlooking the Vieux Port, the rooms are pretty dull, but the location and views are superb. ❹

Lutétia 38 allée Léon-Gambetta, 1ᵉʳ ℡04.91.50.81.78, Ⓦwww.hotelmarseille.com. Soundproofed and a/c rooms; the cheaper ones with shower only. Group reductions are available. ❹–❺

Newhotel of Marseille 71 bd Charles Livon, 7ᵉ ℡04.91.31.53.15, Ⓦwww .new-hotel.com. Part of an upmarket chain, this four-star design hotel in the Le Pharo area boasts a unique art collection. If you can't afford to stay here, treat yourself to the poolside Sunday champagne brunch at €29. Better room rates are available on their website. ❾

Du Palais 26 rue Breteuil, 6ᵉ ℡04.91.37.78.86, Ⓦwww.hotelmarseille.com. Nicely appointed hotel in a good location a short walk from the Vieux Port. The standard rooms are a little small. ❺–❼

Relax Place de L'Opéra, 1ᵉʳ ℡04.91.33.15.87, Ⓦwww.hotelrelax.fr. Homely and very friendly, right next to the Opéra and close to all the action. ❸

Vertigo 42 rue des Petites Maries, 1ᵉʳ ℡04.91.91.07.11, Ⓦwww.hotelvertigo.fr. Funky backpacker hotel and hostel near the train and bus stations, with simple but stylish decor, youthful staff, guest kitchen and dorm beds from €25. The rooms fill up fast, so book those in advance. ❸

Hostels

HI Youth Hostel Bonneveine Impasse Bonfils, av J.-Vidal, 8ᵉ ℡04.91.17.63.30, Ⓦwww.fuaj.org. Mᵒ Rd-Pt-du-Prado, then bus #44 (direction "Floralia Rimet", stop "Place Bonnefon") or night bus #583 from Vieux Port. Friendly hostel just 200m from the beach, with internet access. Reception 7am–10pm, closed at meal times. Dorm bed €18.60. Closed mid-Dec to mid-Jan.

Vertigo Vieux Port 38 rue Fort Notre-Dame ☏04.91.54.42.95. Close to the Vieux Port, this brand new sister hostel to *Vertigo* (see p.907) above has a similarly cool atmosphere, but with dorm beds only; from €26, breakfast included.

The City

Marseille is divided into fifteen arrondissements which spiral out from the focal point of the city, the **Vieux Port**. Due north lies the old town, **Le Panier**, site of the original Greek settlement of Massalia, and beyond that the rapidly regenerating area of **Les Docks**. The wide boulevard leading from the head of the Vieux Port, La Canebière is the central east–west axis of the town. The **Centre Bourse** and the little streets of **quartier Belsunce** border it to the north, while the main shopping streets lie to the south. The main north–south axis is **rue d'Aix**, becoming cours Belsunce then rue de Rome, avenue du Prado and finally boulevard Michelet. The lively quarter around place Jean-Jaurès and cours Julien lies east of rue de Rome. From the headland west of the Vieux Port, the **corniche** heads south past the city's most favoured residential districts towards the **beaches** and promenade nightlife of the **Plage du Prado**.

The Vieux Port

The cafés around the east end of the **Vieux Port** indulge the sedentary pleasures of observing street life, as well as the glistening fish sold straight off the boats on quai des Belges. A prime afternoon café-lounging spot is the north (Le Panier) side, where the terraces are sunnier and the views better.

Two **fortresses** guard the harbour entrance. **St-Jean**, on the north side, dates from the Middle Ages, when Marseille was an independent republic; the building is currently undergoing conversion to create the new national Musée des Civilisations d'Europe et de la Méditerranée, due to be completed in 2012. The construction of **St-Nicolas** on the south side of the port represents the city's final defeat as a separate entity: Louis XIV ordered the new fort to keep an eye on the city after he had sent in an army, suppressed the city's council, fined it, arrested all opposition and – in an early example of rate-capping – set ludicrously low limits on Marseille's subsequent expenditure and borrowing. The best view of the Vieux Port is from the **Palais du Pharo**, on the headland beyond Fort St-Nicolas, or, for a wider angle, from **Notre-Dame-de-la-Garde** (daily: summer 7am–7.15pm; winter 7am–6.15pm; bus #60 or tourist train from Vieux Port), the city's Second Empire landmark atop the La Garde hill. It is the highest point of the city – and the most distinctive – crowned by a monumental gold Virgin that gleams to ships far out at sea. Inside, model ships hang from the rafters while the paintings and drawings displayed are by turns kitsch, unintentionally comic or deeply moving, as they depict the shipwrecks, house fires and car crashes from which the Virgin has supposedly rescued grateful believers.

A short way inland from the Fort St-Nicolas, above the Bassin de Carénage, is Marseille's oldest church, the **Basilique St-Victor** (daily 9am–7pm; €2 entry to crypt). Originally part of a monastery founded in the fifth century on the burial site of various martyrs, the church was built, enlarged and fortified – a vital requirement given its position outside the city walls – over a period of two hundred years

Marseille City Pass

If you're going to be visiting several of Marseille's museums it may be worth considering the **Marseille City Pass**, which for €22 or €29 for one or two days respectively includes free admission to museums, city guided tours, entry to the Château d'If and free use of the métro and bus system.

from the middle of the tenth century. It looks and feels like a fortress, though the interior has an austere power and the **crypt** is a fascinating, crumbling warren containing several sarcophagi, including one with the remains of St Maurice.

Le Panier and les Docks

To the north of the Vieux Port is the oldest part of Marseille, **Le Panier**, where, up until World War II, tiny streets, steep steps and houses of every era formed a *vieille ville* typical of the Côte. In 1943, however, with Marseille under German occupation, the quarter became an unofficial ghetto for **Untermenschen** of every sort, including Resistance fighters, Communists and Jews. The Nazis gave the twenty thousand inhabitants one day's notice to leave; many were deported to the camps. Dynamite was laid, and everything from the waterside to rue Caisserie was blown sky-high, except for three old buildings that appealed to the fascist aesthetic: the seventeenth-century **Hôtel de Ville**, on the quay; the **Hôtel de Cabre**, on the corner of rue Bonneterie and Grande-Rue; and the **Maison Diamantée**, on rue de la Prison, which houses the interesting, **Musée du Vieux-Marseille**. After the war, archeologists reaped some benefits from this destruction when they discovered the remains of a Roman dockside warehouse, equipped with vast food-storage jars, which can be seen *in situ* at the **Musée des Docks Romains**, on place de Vivaux (Tues–Sun: June–Sept 11am–6pm; Oct–May 10am–5pm; €2).

At the junction of rue de la Prison and rue Caisserie, the steps of montée des Accoules lead up to **place de Lenche**, site of the Greek *agora* and a good café stop. What's left of old Le Panier is above montée des Accoules, though many of the tenements have been demolished. At the top of rue du Réfuge stands the restored **Hospice de la Vieille Charité**, a seventeenth-century workhouse with a gorgeous Baroque chapel surrounded by columned arcades; only the tiny grilled exterior windows recall its original use. It's now a cultural centre, and empty except during its major temporary exhibitions – usually brilliant – and evening concerts. It also houses two museums (both Tues–Sun: June–Sept 11am–6pm; Oct–May 10am–5pm; €2; combined ticket for entire complex €4.50): the **Musée d'Archéologie Méditerranéenne** with some very beautiful pottery and glass and an Egyptian collection with a mummified crocodile; and the dark and spooky **Musée des Arts Africains, Océaniens et Amérindiens**.

The expansion of Marseille's **Joliette docks** started in the first half of the nineteenth century. Like the cathedral, wide boulevards and Marseille's own Arc de Triomphe – the **Porte d'Aix** at the top of cours Belsunce/rue d'Aix – the docks were paid for with the profits of military enterprise, most significantly the conquest of Algeria in 1830. Anyone fascinated by industrial architecture should visit the mammoth old warehouse building, **Les Docks** (follow rue de la République to the end), now restored as part of the ambitious **Euroméditerranée** regeneration scheme. Alongside the docks looms the town's massive late nineteenth-century **Cathédrale de la Nouvelle Major**, architecturally a blend of neo-Romanesque and neo-Byzantine, with a distinctive pattern of alternating bands of stone.

La Canebière

La Canebière, the occasionally tatty boulevard that runs for about a kilometre down to the port, is the city's hub, though it's more a place to move through than to linger. It takes its name from the hemp (*canabé*) that once grew here and was used for the town's rope-making trade. La Canebière neatly divides the moneyed southern *quartiers* and the ramshackle **quartier Belsunce** to the north – an extraordinary, dynamic, mainly Arab area. The **central library**, with its great café, on cours Belsunce is another of the regeneration projects gradually supplanting the dilapidated tenements.

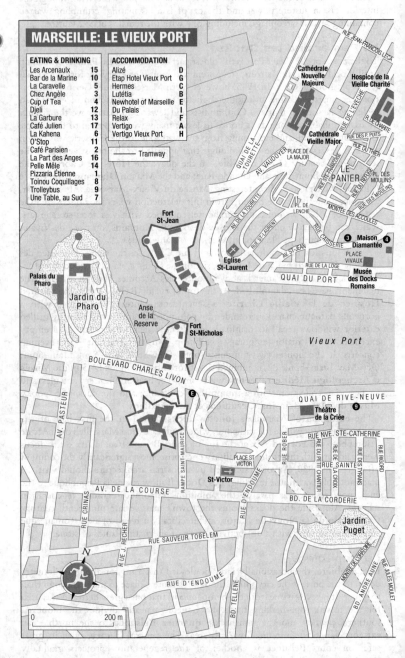

MARSEILLE: LE VIEUX PORT

EATING & DRINKING

Les Arcenaulx	15
Bar de la Marine	10
La Caravelle	5
Chez Angèle	3
Cup of Tea	4
Djeli	12
La Garbure	13
Café Julien	17
La Kahena	6
O'Stop	11
Café Parisien	2
La Part des Anges	16
Pelle Mêle	14
Pizzaria Étienne	1
Toinou Coquillages	8
Trolleybus	9
Une Table, au Sud	7

ACCOMMODATION

Alizé	D
Etap Hotel Vieux Port	G
Hermes	C
Lutétia	B
Newhotel of Marseille	E
Du Palais	I
Relax	F
Vertigo	A
Vertigo Vieux Port	H

--- Tramway

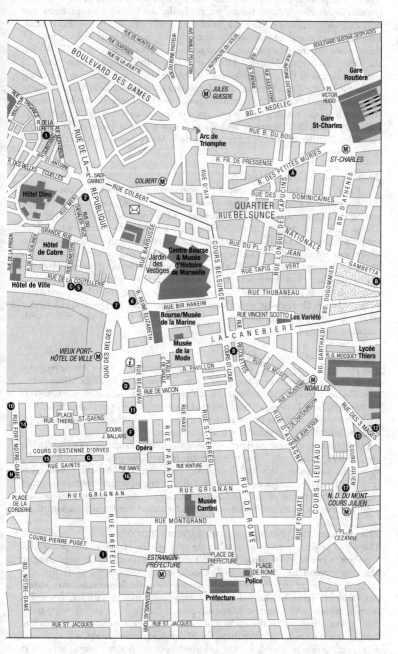

RUE DE MONTOLIEU
RUE DUVERGER
AVE CAMILLE PELLETAN
RUE DE LA JOUETTE
BOULEVARD GUSTAVE DESPLACES
BOULEVARD DES DAMES
RUE DU RENE PASTEUR
L'AUTOROUTE DU SOLEIL
RUE DE TURENNE
RUE ANTOINE ZATTARA
RUE ILES FERRI
Gare
Routière
RUE ST-TRIANCE
R DE LA LOFETTE
RUE MONTBRION
RUE CAMILLE PELLETAN
JULES
GUESDE
PL.
VICTOR
HUGO
BD. C. NEDELEC
R DE LA GUIRANDE
ST-ANTOINE
RUE DE LA-
Arc de
Triomphe
RUE B. DU BOIS
Gare
St-Charles
R. DES BELLES ECUELLES
R. FR. DE PRESSENSE
R. DES PETITES MORIES
ST-CHARLES
PL. SADI-
CARNOT
RUE COLBERT
COLBERT
RUE D'AIX
RUE DES CAPUCINS
DOMINICAINES
BD. D'ATHENES
Hôtel Dieu
RUE MERY
RUE MERY
RÉPUBLIQUE
QUARTIER
BELSUNCE
RUE BELSUNCE
RUE LONGUE DES CAPUCINS
NATIONALE
L. GAMBETTA
GRANDE RUE
RUE DU CHEVALIER ROZE
RUE BARBUSSE
Centre Bourse
& Musée
d'Histoire
de Marseille
COURS BELSUNCE
RUE DU PL. ST-
JEAN
Hôtel
de Cabre
RUE DE LA PRISON
Jardin
des
Vestiges
RUE TAPIS
VERT
BD. DUGOMMIER
Hôtel de Ville
RUE DE LA COUTELLERIE
RUE RENE ELIZABETH
RUE THUBANEAU
Bourse/Musée
de la Marine
RUE BIR HAKEIM
RUE VINCENT SCOTTO
Les Variété
LA CANEBIERE
Musée
de la
Mode
QUAI DES BELGES
VIEUX PORT-
HÔTEL DE VILLE
COURS ST-LOUIS
RECOLLETTES
RUE DU MUSÉE
BD. GARTHALDI
Lycée
Thiers
R.G. MOCQUET
PLACE DU C. DE GAULLE
R. PAVILLON
RUE BEAUVAU
RUE DE VACON
RUE L'ACADÉMIE
NOAILLES
RUE DES 3 MAGES
PLACE
ST-SAENS
RUE THIERS
RUE FORT NOTRE-DAME
COURS
J. BALLARD
Opéra
RUE HAXO
RUE ST-FERREOL
RUE DE CHATEAUREDON
RUE D'AUBAGNE
COURS JULIEN
COURS D'ESTIENNE D'ORVES
RUE SAINTE
RUE SAINTE
RUE PARADIS
RUE VENTURE
RUE JEAN ROQUE
COURS LIEUTAUD
N. D. DU MONT
COURS JULIEN
PLACE
DE LA
CORDERIE
RUE GRIGNAN
RUE GRIGNAN
Musée
Cantini
RUE DE ROME
RUE MONTGRAND
RUE FONGATE
PL. P.
CEZANNE
COURS PIERRE PUGET
BD. NOTRE-DAME
RUE BRETEUIL
ESTRANGIN-
PRÉFECTURE
PLACE DE
PREFECTURE
PLACE
DE ROME
Police
RUE STANISLAS TORR
Préfecture
RUE ST. JACQUES
RUE ST. JACQUES

Immediately west of cours Belsunce, the ugly **Centre Bourse** provides a stark contrast to this dynamic area. Behind it is the **Jardin des Vestiges**, where the ancient port extended, curving northwards from the present quai des Belges. Excavations have revealed a stretch of the Greek port and bits of the **city wall** with the bases of three square towers and a gateway, dated to the second or third century BC. Within the Centre Bourse, the **Musée d'Histoire de Marseille** (Mon–Sat noon–7pm; €2) presents the rest of the finds, including a third-century wreck of a Roman trading vessel. Back at the Vieux Port end of La Canebière is the **Musée de la Marine** (Tues–Sun: June–Sept 11am–6pm; Oct–May 10am–5pm; €2), housed in the Neoclassical stock exchange and with a superb collection of shipbuilders' models, including the legendary 1930s liner *Normandie* and Marseille's own prewar queen of the seas, the *Providence*. Further up at no. 11, the **Musée de la Mode** displays fashion from 1945 to the present day.

The Palais Longchamp

The **Palais Longchamp**, 2km east of the port at the end of boulevard Longchamp (Mº Longchamp–Cinq-Avenues or Tramway 2 same stop), forms the grandiose conclusion of an aqueduct that once brought water from the Durance to the city. The palace's north wing is the city's **Musée des Beaux-Arts** (currently closed for renovation), with a fair share of delights, including works by Rubens, Jordaens, Corot and Signac and a room devoted to the nineteenth-century satirist from Marseille, Honoré Daumier. The other wing is occupied by the **Musée d'Histoire Naturelle** (Tues–Sun: June–Sept 11am–6pm; Oct–May 10am–5pm; €4), and its collection of stuffed animals and fossils. Opposite the palace, at 140 bd Longchamp, is the **Musée Grobet-Labadi** (Tues–Sun: June–Sept 11am–6pm; Oct–May 10am–5pm; €2) an elegant late-nineteenth-century town house filled with exquisite *objets d'art*.

South of La Canebière

The prime shopping district of Marseille is encompassed by three streets running **south from La Canebière**: rue Paradis, rue St-Ferréol and **rue de Rome**. The most elegant boutiques and galleries cluster in the area around the **Musée Cantini**, 19 rue Grignan (Tues–Sun: June–Sept 11am–6pm; Oct–May 10am–5pm; €3), with Fauvists and Surrealists well represented, plus works by Matisse, Léger, Picasso, Ernst, Le Corbusier, Miró and Giacometti.

A few blocks east of rue de Rome is one of the most pleasant places to idle in the city, **cours Julien** (Mº Notre-Dame-du-Mont–Cours-Julien), with pools, fountains, pavement cafés and boutiques, populated by Marseille's bohemian crowd and diverse immigrant community, all of it buried under copious quantities of graffiti. Streets full of bars and music shops lead east to **place Jean-Jaurès**, locally known as "la Pleine", where the market is a treat, particularly on Saturdays.

The corniche, beaches and Parc Borély

The most popular stretch of sand close to the city centre is the **plage des Catalans**, a few blocks south of the Palais du Pharo. This marks the beginning of Marseille's **corniche**, avenue J.F.-Kennedy, which follows the cliffs past the dramatic statue and arch that frames the setting sun of the **Monument aux Morts des Orients**. South of the monument, steps lead down to an inlet, **Anse des Auffes**, which is the nearest Marseille gets to being picturesque, with small fishing boats beached on the rocks and narrow stairways leading nowhere. The corniche then turns inland, bypassing the **Malmousque peninsula**, whose coastal path gives access to tiny bays and beaches – perfect for swimming when the mistral wind is not inciting the waves.

The corniche ends at the **Plage du Prado**, the city's main sand beach. A short way up **avenue du Prado**, avenue du Parc-Borély leads into the city's best green space, the **Parc Borély** (open during daylight hours), with a boating lake, rose gardens, palm trees and a botanical garden (Tues–Fri 10am–5/6pm; Sat & Sun 11am–5/6pm; €3). The quickest way to the park and the beaches is by bus #19 from métro Rd-Pt-du-Prado; for the corniche, take bus #83 from the Vieux Port.

The Château d'If

The **Château d'If** (Tues–Sun: June–Sept 11am–6pm; Oct–May 10am–5pm; €5) on the tiny island of If is best known as the penal setting for Alexandre Dumas' **The Count of Monte Cristo**. Having made his watery escape after fourteen years of incarceration as the innocent victim of treachery, the hero of the piece, Edmond Dantès, describes the island thus: "Blacker than the sea, blacker than the sky, rose like a phantom the giant of granite, whose projecting crags seemed like arms extended to seize their prey". In reality, most prisoners went insane or died before leaving. The sixteenth-century castle and its cells are horribly well preserved, and the views back towards Marseille are fantastic. **Boats** for If leave regularly from the quai des Belges in the Vieux Port (every 30–45min in summer; less frequent in winter; journey time 20min; €10), with the last boat back timed to coincide with the château's closing time.

The Musée de la Faïence, MAC and the Cité Radieuse

From the plage du Prado the promenade continues all the way to the suburb of **Montredon**, where the nineteenth-century Château Pastré, set in a huge park, contains the **Musée de la Faïence** (Tues–Sun: June–Sept 11am–6pm; Oct–May 10am–5pm; €2). The eighteenth- and nineteenth-century ceramics, most produced in Marseille, are of an extremely high quality, and a small collection of novel modern and contemporary pieces is housed on the top floor. The entrance to the park (free) is at 157 av de Montredon (bus #19 from M° Rd-Pt-du-Prado, stop "Montredon-Chancel"). Along the coast from here are easily accessible *calanques* (rocky inlets), ideal for evening swims and supper picnics as the sun sets.

Between Montredon and **boulevard Michelet**, the main road out of the city, is the contemporary art museum, **MAC** (Tues–Sun: June–Sept 11am–6pm; Oct–May 10am–5pm; €3), at 69 av d'Haïfa (bus #23 or #45 from M° Rd-Pt-du-Prado, stop "Haïfa Marie-Louise"). The permanent collection includes works from the 1960s to the present day by Buren, Christo, Klein, Niki de Saint Phalle, Tinguely and Warhol, as well as Marseillais artists César and Ben.

Set back just west of boulevard Michelet stands a building that broke the mould, Le Corbusier's seventeen-storey block of flats, the **Unité d'Habitation**, designed in 1946 and completed in 1952. It's also known as the **Cité Radieuse**, and many architects the world over have tried to imitate it. Up close, its revolutionary example is apparent: at ground level the building is decorated with Le Corbusier's famous human figure, the Modulor; on the third floor there is a hotel (see p.907) and café. Not all of the iconic rooftop recreation area can be visited, though a circuit of the running track is essential. To reach the Unité, take bus #21 from M° Rd-Pt-du-Prado to "Le Corbusier".

Eating and drinking

Fish and **seafood** are the mainstay of Marseille's diet, and the superstar of dishes is Marseille's own *bouillabaisse*, a saffron- and garlic-flavoured soup with bits of fish, croutons and *rouille* thrown in; theories conflict as to which fish should be included, but one essential is the *rascasse* or scorpion fish. The other speciality is *pieds et paquets* – mutton or lamb belly and trotters.

Good **restaurant** hunting grounds include cours Julien or place Jean-Jaurès (international options), the Vieux Port (touristy and fishy), the Corniche and plage du Prado (glitzy and pricey). Rue Sainte is good for smart, fashionable dining close to the opera and Vieux Port.

Cafés and bars

Aux 3G 3 rue St-Pierre, 5ᵉ. Marseille's most popular lesbian bar, regularly packed at weekends. Open Thurs & Sun 7pm–midnight, Fri & Sat until 2am.

Cup of Tea 1 rue Caisserie, 2ᵉ. A gorgeous bookshop serving teas, coffees and cake. Closed Sun.

Bar de la Marine 15 quai de Rive-Neuve, 1ᵉʳ. A favourite bar for Vieux Port lounging, and inspiration for Pagnol's celebrated Marseille trilogy.

🏃 **O'Stop** 16 rue St-Saëns, 1ᵉʳ. Just opposite the Opera House and serving great value, wholesome grub to all walks of life at very reasonable prices, this is also the place to come to people-watch after hours. Daily 9am–6am.

Café Parisien 1 place Sadi-Carnot, 2ᵉ. Decked out in a stylish mix of old elegance and modern chic, this place offers pasta dishes from around €11 and meat mains from €15. Closed Sun.

Bar Le Petit Nice 26 place Jean-Jaurès, 1ᵉʳ. The place to head for on Saturday morning during the market, with a great selection of beers. Open Mon–Sat from 6.30am.

Le Red Lion 231 av Pierre-Mendès-France, 8ᵉ. Large British-style pub close to plage Borély, with twelve beers on draught. Open until 4am Fri & Sat.

Restaurants

Les Arcenaulx 25 cours d'Estienne-d'Orves, 1ᵉʳ ☎04.91.59.80.30. This lovely place has an atmospheric and intellectual vibe, as it's also a bookshop and salon de thé; there's a light €18 *menu*, otherwise €27 and €57. Last orders 11pm. Closed Sun.

Chez Angèle 50 rue Caisserie, 2ᵉ ☎04.91.90.63.35. Packed Le Panier local, dishing up fresh pasta (great ravioli) and pizza, starting at €12. Closed lunchtimes Sat & Sun.

Chez Fonfon 140 Vallon des Auffes, 7ᵉ ☎04.91.52.14.38. There's no debate about the

quality of the *bouillabaisse* here, for this chic restaurant overlooking a small fishing harbour is one of an elite band of restaurants guarding the true recipe of the dish. Expect to pay €46 for it; closed Sun, Mon lunch and all day Mon in winter.

La Garbure 9 cours Julien, 6ᵉ ☎04.91.47.18.01. Rich specialities from southwest France, including duck *cassoulet*. Wonderfully romantic and stylish; it's advised to book. Lunch *menu* €24; dinner *menus* from €35. Closed Sat midday & Sun.

🏃 **La Gentaine** Rue des Trois-Rois, 1ᵉʳ ☎04.91.42.88.80. Resolutely French, the service here is friendly and the food is superb. Great bohemian location, parallel to cours Julien. *Menus* around €20.

La Kahena 2 rue de la République, 2ᵉ ☎04.91.90.61.93. Great Tunisian restaurant near the Vieux Port, with grills and couscous from €10. Open daily.

🏃 **La Part des Anges** 33 rue Sainte, 1ᵉʳ ☎04.91.33.55.70. Wonderful *cave de vins* serving hearty food and cheese platters to mop up the classy wines; *plats* around €14. Open daily.

Pizzaria Étienne 43 rue Lorette, 2ᵉ. A fabulous old-fashioned Le Panier pizzeria; hectic, cramped and crowded. €8 per person/4 people at €19. Also specializes in squid.

Toinou Coquillages 18 cours Saint-Louis, 1ᵉʳ ☎04.91.33.14.94. Popular with locals and visitors alike for the choice of over forty types of shellfish, sold both prepared in the restaurant and fresh from the outdoor counter. Main courses start at €15, platters for two around €40.

Une Table, au Sud 2 quai du Port, 2ᵉ ☎04.91.90.63.53. Stylish gastronomic restaurant overlooking the Vieux Port, where chef Lionel Lévy's creative and contemporary take on Provençal cooking is changed bi-monthly to reflect the season's offerings. *Menus* start at €52. Closed Sun & Mon.

Nightlife and entertainment

Marseille's **nightlife** has something for everyone, with plenty of live music, nightclubs and discos, as well as theatre, opera and classical concerts. The Virgin Megastore at 75 rue St-Ferréol, the book- and record shop FNAC in the Centre Bourse and the tourist office's ticket bureau are the best places to go for **tickets and information**. Virgin also stocks English books and is open Monday to Saturday until 8.30pm and on Sundays 2–8pm. There is a free weekly **listings** mag, *Ventilo*, and a monthly, *César,* which you can pick up from FNAC, Virgin, tourist offices, museums and cultural centres.

Live music and clubs

La Caravelle 34 quai du Port, 2e. Cabaret on the first floor of the *Hôtel Bellevue* with portside views and tapas. Live jazz weekends. Daily till 2am.

Djeli 9 rue des Trois Mages, 1er ☎06.46.73.93.48. Small performance space between cours Julien and place Jean-Jaurès, presenting world music and theatre with a strong focus on Africa and Asia via a big bassy sound system. Daily 9.30pm–2am.

Les Docks des Suds 12 rue Urbain V, 3e ☎04.91.99.00.00. Vast warehouse that serves as the venue for Marseille's annual Fiesta des Suds world-music festival (Oct) and as a regular live venue.

L'Intermédiare 63 place Jean-Jaurès, 6e ☎04.91.47.01.25. Loud and hip bar with live bands and DJs, from rock to electro and world music. Mon–Sat 6pm–2am.

Café Julien 39 cours Julien, 6e ☎04.91.24.34.10. Part of the vibrant Espace Julien arts centre. Regular live music; performances start 8.30–10pm.

La Maronaise Rte de la Maronaise, Les Goudes, 8e. From May–Sept this open-air nightclub, visited by the elite and in a wild setting by the sea, is the most alluring place to dance in Marseille. Tues–Sun 1pm–dawn.

New Cancan 3 rue Sénac, 1er. It's pretty cheesy, but the *New Cancan* is nevertheless Marseille's best-known and longest running gay disco, with regular cabaret nights. Thurs–Sun 11pm–dawn; Fri & Sat entry charges are steep.

Pelle Mêle 8 place aux Huiles, 1er. Intimate, smart and lively jazz bistro and piano bar with weekend DJs. 5pm–2am Tues–Sat.

Le Poste à Galène 103 rue Ferrari, 5e ☎04.91.47.57.99. Live pop, folk, rock and electro plus 1980s DJ nights and a bar. Entry price varies depending on event; opening times also vary.

Pussy Twisters 2 rue Crudère, 6e. In a side street off cours Julien, this small and friendly bar with a curious name plays 1950s, 60s and 70s music. Thurs–Sat 6.30pm–2am.

Trolleybus 24 quai de Rive-Neuve, 7e. Atmospheric bar and club in a series of vaulted rooms; house, pop, electro, hip-hop, reggae and techno. Open Thurs–Sat.

Film, theatre and concerts

Alhambra 2 rue du Cinéma, 16e ☎04.91.03.84.66. Art house cinema occasionally showing undubbed English-language films (v.o.).

Ballet National de Marseille 20 bd Gabès, 8e ☎04.91.32.72.72. The home venue of the famous dance company, founded in 1972 by Roland Petit.

La Friche la Belle de Mai 41 rue Jobin, 3e ☎04.95.04.95.04. Interdisciplinary arts complex occupying a former industrial site in the north of the city, hosting theatre, dance, live music and arts exhibitions.

Opéra 2 rue Moliére, 1er ☎04.91.55.11.10. Symphony concerts and operas in a magnificent setting, part Neoclassical, part Art Deco.

Théâtre National la Criée 30 quai de Rive Neuve, 7e ☎04.91.54.70.54. Home of the Théâtre National de Marseille and Marseille's best theatre.

Les Variétés 37 rue Vincent Scotto, 1er ☎04.96.11.61.61. Downtown cinema offering *v.o.* films.

Listings

Bike rental Blue bicycles belonging to Le Vélo scheme can be rented from 80 self-service rental points throughout the city using a bank card (€1 for first half-hour then €1 for each additional half-hour). Mountain bikes can be rented from Tandem, 16 av du Parc Borély ☎04.91.22.64.80.

Bookstore Virgin, 75 rue St-Ferréol, 1er, has an English books section; Maupetit, 140 La Canebière, 1er, is a good general French bookshop.

Car rental Avis, Gare St-Charles ☎08.20.61.16.36; National Citer, Square Narvik, 1er ☎04.91.05.90.86; Europcar, 59 allées Léon Gambetta, 1er ☎04.91.10.74.90. These and others also have head offices at the airport.

Consulates UK, 24 av du Prado, 6e ☎04.91.15.72.10; USA, place Varian Fry, 6e ☎04.91.54.92.00.

Ferries SNCM (61 bd des Dames ☎32.60, ⊛www.sncm.fr) runs ferries to Corsica, Tunisia and Algeria.

Health Ambulance ☎15; SOS Médecins ☎04.91.52.91.52; 24hr casualty departments at La Conception, 144 rue St-Pierre, 5e ☎04.91.38.00.00; and SOS Voyageurs, Gare St-Charles, 3e ☎04.91.62.12.80.

Internet Cyber Café, 1 rue de la Republique, 2e ☎04.91.90.46.23.

Lost property 41 bd de Briançon, 3e ☎04.91.14.68.97.

Pharmacy Pharmacie du Vieux Port, 4 quai du Port (open daily) ☎04.91.91.63.10.

Police Commissariat Central, 2 rue Antoine-Becker, 2e (24hr; ☎04.91.39.80.00).

Post office 1 place de l'Hôtel-des-Postes, 1er.

Taxis Taxi Radio Marseille ☎04.91.02.20.20; Taxi Radio Tupp ☎04.91.05.80.80; Taxi Plus ☎04.91.03.60.03.

Cassis

Many people rate **CASSIS**, 23km east of Marseille, as the best resort this side of St-Tropez; hemmed in by cliffs, its development has been necessarily modest, making it a pleasant stop-over or a day-trip escape from Marseille's hustle and bustle.

Arrival and information

Buses from Marseille arrive at rond-point de la Gendarmerie from where it's a short walk to the port and beach. The **gare SNCF** is 3.5km from town, connected by bus (Mon–Fri; 15min). The **tourist office** is on the port at quai des Moulins (March–June, Sept & Oct Mon–Fri 9am–12.30pm & 2–6pm, Sat 9.30am–12.30pm & 2–5.30pm, Sun 10am–12.30pm; July & Aug Mon–Fri 9am–7pm, Sat & Sun 9.30am–12.30pm & 3–6pm; Nov–Feb Mon–Fri 9.30am–12.30pm & 2–5.30pm, Sat 10am–12.30pm & 2–5pm, Sun 10am–12.30pm; ☏08.92.25.98.92, ⓦwww .ot-cassis.com).

Accommodation

Cassis is small, so demand for cheaper **rooms** in high season is intense – be sure to book in advance.

Le Clos des Arômes 10 rue Abbé P. Mouton ☏04.42.01.71.84, ⓦwww.le-clos-des-aromes .com. Next to the church, this hotel has its own decent restaurant with seating in a lovely garden. ❹

Le Commerce 12 rue St-Clair ☏04.42.01.09.10, ⓦwww.hotel-lecommerce.fr. A budget option, some rooms with sea view. There is also a cottage, which sleeps up to 19 people. Closed mid-Nov to mid-Jan. ❷–❹

Le Golfe Place du Grand-Carnot ☏04.42.01.00.21, ⓦwww.legolfe-cassis.fr. Most rooms have a lovely view over the port, but the decor is a little dated for the price. Closed Nov–March. ❺

Le Provençal 7 av Victor-Hugo ☏04.42.01.72.13, ⓦwww.cassis-le-provencal.com. Small and cheap hotel close to the port, where breakfast is served to your room. ❸–❹

Hostel and campsite

Les Cigales Just off the D559, inland 2.5km from Cassis. ☏04.42.01.07.34, ⓦwww.campingcassis .com. Closed mid-Nov to mid-March.

La Fontasse In the hills above the *calanques* west of Cassis ☏04.42.01.02.72, ⓦwww.fuaj.org. Basic hostel in a scenic location. €11.20 per night. Reception 8–10.30am & 5–9pm. Mid-March to Dec.

The Town

Portside posing and sunbathing aside, don't miss a boat trip to the **calanques** (from around €13) – fjord-like inlets that cut deep into the limestone cliffs. Several companies operate from the port and you should be prepared for rough seas. If you're feeling energetic, follow the well-marked footpath from the route des Calanques behind the western beach; it's about ninety minutes' walk to the furthest and best *calanque*, **En Vau**, where you can reach the shore. The water is deep blue and swimming between the cliffs is pure heaven. In summer the fire risk is high; smoking and fires are prohibited and you're advised not to head inland off the coastal path if the wind is high. There are no refreshment stops, so take water.

You can hire kayaks or boats in Cassis, sometimes including a skipper, and there are a couple of diving outfits; the tourist office has details. The spectacular clifftop **route des Crêtes** links Cassis with La Ciotat; regular belvederes allow you to stop and take the perfect shot of distant headlands receding into the sunset – vertigo permitting. The route is closed during high winds.

Eating and drinking

Restaurants are abundant in Cassis. They are proud of their *bouillabaisse* at *Chez Gilbert*, 19 quai Baux (☎04.42.01.71.36; *menu* €32; closed Tues eve & Wed out of season) and **El Sol** at no. 23 (☎04.42.01.76.10; closed Mon all day & Tues lunch), with *terroir* cuisine, costs a bit less with mains around €20.

La Ciotat

Cranes still loom over the little port of **LA CIOTAT**, where vast oil tankers were once built. Today, the unpretentious town relies on tourism and yachting and is less a place for sightseeing than relaxing, with good, sandy beaches and a lively waterfront.

Arrival, information and accommodation

The **gare SNCF** is 5km from the town but bus #40 is frequent at peak times and gets you to the Vieux Port in around fifteen minutes. The old town and port look out across the Baie de la Ciotat, whose inner curve provides the beaches and resort lifestyle of La Ciotat's modern extension, **La Ciotat-Plage**. The **gare routière** is at the end of boulevard Anatole-France by the Vieux Port right beside the **tourist office** (June–Sept Mon–Sat 9am–8pm, Sun 10am–1pm; Oct–May Mon–Sat 9am–noon & 2–6pm; ☎04.42.08.61.32, ⓦwww.tourisme-laciotat.com).

For **hotels**, the best cheapies are *La Marine*, 1 av Fernand Gassion (☎&ⓕ04.42.08.35.11; ❶–❷), and *La Rotonde*, 44 bd de la République (☎04.42.08.67.50, ⓦwww.hotel-larotonde.fr; ❷–❸), both on the fringes of the old town. In La Ciotat-Plage, *Miramar*, 3 bd Beaurivage (☎04.42.83.33.79, ⓦwww.miramarlaciotat.com; ❼), is right on the palm-fringed seafront. La Ciotat has five **campsites**, the most central being *Le Soleil*, avenue Emile Bodin (☎04.42.71.55.32, ⓦwww.camping-dusoleil.com; €20 for tent and two people in high season, mobile homes (€45 for two) and bungalows (€55 for up to four) are also available).

The Town

In 1895, **Auguste and Louis Lumière** filmed the first moving pictures in La Ciotat – the town's main claim to fame. The world's oldest movie house, the **Eden Cinéma**, still stands on the corner of boulevard A.-France and boulevard Jean-Jaurès; you can view the interior through glass (closed for renovation until 2012). The town has an annual film festival and the brothers are also commemorated by a monument on plage Lumière.

The streets of the old town, apart from rue des Poilus, are uneventful, though the increasing numbers of boutiques and *immobiliers* reflect the change from shipyard to pleasure port. For a day-trip, Île Verte Navette (☎06.63.59.16.35) makes the crossing to the islet of **Île Verte** daily, while Catamaran Le Citharista (☎06.09.35.25.68) runs trips to the *calanques* of Cassis and Marseille (€14–26) from quai Ganteaume.

Alternatively, take a walk through the **Parc du Mugel** (daily: April–Sept 8am–8pm; Oct–March 9am–6pm; bus #30, stop "Mugel"), with its strange cluster of rock formations on the promontory beyond the shipyards. A path leads up through overgrown vegetation to a narrow terrace overlooking the sea. If you continue on bus #30 to Figuerolles you can reach the **Anse de Figuerolles** *calanque* down the avenue of the same name, and its neighbour, the **Gameau.**

Eating and drinking

There are plenty of **restaurants**, cafés and brasseries around the port. *Coquillages Franquin*, 13 bd Anatole-France (☎04.42.83.59.50), serves well-prepared fish on a €19 *menu*. For a treat, with a *menu* at €34 and a pricey winelist, try *Roche Belle* at Corniche du Liouquet (☎04.42.71.47.60; closed Mon), 8km toward Les Lecques.

Les Lecques and Bandol

Across La Ciotat bay are the fine sand and shingle beaches of the family resort of **LES LECQUES**, an offshoot of the inland town of **St-Cyr-sur-Mer**, to which it is fused by modern suburbs. The **train station** is in St-Cyr, but the tourist office (July & Aug Mon–Sat 9am–7pm, Sun 10am–1pm & 4–7pm; March–June & Sept–Oct Mon–Fri 9am–6pm, Sat 9am–noon & 2–6pm; Nov–Feb Mon–Fri 9am–5pm, Sat 9am–noon & 1–5pm; ☎04.94.26.73.73, ⓦwww.saintcyrsurmer.com) is 2km away, on place de l'Appel du 18 Juin, on the seafront in Les Lecques, serviced by irregular buses. Most **accommodation** is in two-star hotels clustered near the sea in Les Lecques.

A ten-kilometre **coastal path** (signposted) runs from the east end of Les Lecques' beach through a stretch of secluded beaches and *calanques* to the unpretentious resort of **BANDOL**, while inland *dégustation* signs announce the *appellation* Bandol, whose **vineyards** produce some of the best wines on the Côte. The reds are highly reputed; the pale rosé is sublime on a warm summer's evening. In Bandol there are several reasonable **hotels** near the centre, including *Hôtel Florida*, 26 impasse de Nice (☎04.94.29.41.72, ⓦwww.villaflorida.fr; ❺), and *La Cigale Bleue* at 177 av de la Gare (☎04.94.29.41.40; ❷). The pleasant *Hotel Key Largo*, 19 corniche Bonaparte (☎04.94.29.46.93, ⓦwww.hotel-key-largo.com; ❺) is right by the sea with a view of Île de Bendor. The **tourist office**, on allée Vivien by the quayside (late June & early Sept Mon–Sat 9am–noon & 2–6pm; July & Aug daily 9.30am–7pm; Sept–June Mon–Sat 9am–noon & 2–5pm; ☎04.94.29.41.35, ⓦwww.bandol.fr), will help if you're stuck during the high season.

Hyères

HYÈRES is the oldest resort on the Côte, listing Queen Victoria and Tolstoy among its early admirers, but the lack of a central seafront meant it lost out when the foreign rich switched from winter convalescents to quayside strollers, and today it exports cut flowers and exotic plants – the most important being the date palm, which graces every street – and it's a garrison town, the home of the French army's 54th artillery regiment.

Arrival, information and accommodation

The **gare SNCF** is on place de l'Europe, 1.5km south of the centre, with frequent buses (#29, #39 or #67) to the **gare routière** on place Mal-Joffret, two blocks south of the entrance to the old town (☎08.25.00.06.50, ⓦwww.reseaumistral.com). Hyères-Toulon **airport** (☎08.25.01.83.87, ⓦwww.toulon-hyeres.aeroport.fr) is between Hyères and Hyères-Plage, 3km from the centre, to which it's connected by an infrequent bus service (#102). The **tourist office** is at the Forum du Casino, 3 av Ambroise Thomas (July & Aug daily 9am–7pm; Sept–June Mon–Fri 9am–6pm, Sat 10am–4pm; ☎04.94.01.84.50, ⓦwww.hyeres-tourisme.com). **Bikes** and **mopeds** can be hired from Holiday Bikes, 10 rue Jean d'Agrève, near port Saint-Pierre (☎04.94.38.79.45, ⓌWwww.holiday-bikes.com).

Hotels in the old town are sparse, the best one being *Hôtel du Soleil*, on rue du Rempart (☎04.94.65.16.26, Ⓦwww.hoteldusoleil.com; ❺; rates are better if you book via their website), in a renovated house at the foot of the parc St-Bernard. If you are heading for the islands on day-trips, you are better off staying by the port: a basic and friendly option by Port Saint-Pierre is *Le Calypso*, 36 av de la Méditeranée (☎04.94.58.02.09; ❶–❷). There are plenty of **campsites** on the coast. Two smaller ones are *Camping-Bernard*, a two-star in Le Ceinturon (☎04.94.66.30.54; closed Oct–Easter), and *Clair de Lune*, avenue du Clair de Lune (☎04.94.58.20.19, Ⓦwww.campingclairedelune.fr; closed mid-Nov to Feb), which is three-star and on the Presqu'Île de Giens and also has bungalows and mobile homes to rent.

The Town

Walled and medieval **old Hyères** perches on the slopes of Casteou hill, 5km from the sea; below it lies the **modern town**, with avenue Gambetta the main north–south axis. At the coast, the **Presqu'Île de Giens** is leashed to the mainland by an isthmus, known as **La Capte**, and a parallel sand bar enclosing the salt marshes and a lake.

From place Clemenceau, a medieval gatehouse – the **Porte Massillon** – opens into the old town on rue Massillon, lined with tempting shops selling fruit and vegetables, chocolate, soaps, olive oil and wine. It ends at **place Massillon**, a perfect Provençal square with terraced cafés overlooking the twelfth-century **Tour des Templiers**, the remnant of a Knights Templar fort elegantly converted into exhibition space for contemporary art (April–Oct daily except Tues 10am–noon & 4–7pm; Nov–March Wed–Sun 10am–noon & 2–5pm; free). Behind the tower, rue Ste-Catherine leads uphill to place St-Paul, from which you have a panoramic view over the Golfe de Giens.

Wide steps fan out from the Renaissance door of the former collegiate **church of St-Paul** (closed at time of writing; contact tourist office for opening times), whose distinctive belfry is pure Romanesque, as is the choir, though the simplicity of the design is masked by the collection of votive offerings hung inside. To the right of St-Paul, a Renaissance house bridges rue St-Paul, its turret supported by a pillar rising beside the steps. Through this arch you can head up rue Ste-Claire to **Parc Ste-Claire** (daily 8am–5/7pm; free), the exotic gardens around **Castel Ste-Claire**, once home to the American writer Edith Wharton and now the offices of the Parc National de Port-Cros. Cobbled paths lead up the hill towards the **Parc St-Bernard** (daily 8am–5/7pm; free), full of almost every Mediterranean flower known. At the top, above montée des Noailles, is the **Villa Noailles**, a Cubist mansion enclosed within part of the old citadel walls, designed by Mallet-Stevens in the 1920s and a home to all the luminaries of Dada and Surrealism. It now hosts contemporary art and design exhibitions (July–Sept Mon & Wed–Sun 2–7pm, Fri 4–10pm; free). To the west of the park and further up the hill are the immaculate remains of the eleventh-century **castle**, whose keep and ivy-clad towers give stunning views out to the Îles d'Hyères and east to the Massif des Maures.

The switch from medieval to eighteenth- and nineteenth-century Hyères at **avenue des Îles-d'Or** and its continuation, **avenue Général-de-Gaulle**, is abrupt, with wide boulevards, opulent villas and palms creating a spa town atmosphere. If you're keen on the ancient history of this coast, the **Site Archéologique d'Olbia** (☎04.94.65.51.49) in Almanarre (July–Aug daily 9.30am–noon & 3.30pm–7pm; April–June & Sept–Oct Tues–Sat 9.30am–noon & 2–5.30pm; Nov–March on phone reservation; €5) is worth a visit for its Greek, Roman and medieval remains, including those of the abbey of Saint-Pierre de l'Almanarre. An alternative pastime is to wander around the spectacular array of cacti and palms in the **Jardins Olbius-Riquier**, just to the southeast of avenue Gambetta (daily 7.30am–6/7pm; free). It has a small zoo and miniature train to keep kids happy. Hyères' coastal suburbs have plenty of **beaches**, or alternatively, take the **route du Sel** to the **Presqu'Île de Giens** (closed mid-Nov to mid-April) for a glimpse of the saltworks and flamingoes on the adjoining lake.

Eating and drinking

For **eating and drinking**, place Massillon, filled with restaurant tables and with an unmistakably Mediterranean atmosphere in the evening, is the best option. Of its restaurants *Le Bistrot de Marius*, 1 place Massillon (℡04.94.35.88.38; Wed–Sun, plus Tues in Aug), specializes in fish and seafood; *menus* €18–32. In the new town, *Les Jardins de Bacchus*, 32 av Gambetta (℡04.94.65.77.63; *menus* from €29; closed Sat lunch, Sun dinner & Mon), serves gastro fusion as well as Provençal dishes with a good wine list, while *Les Jardins de Saradam*, 35 av de Belgique (℡04.94.65.97.53; closed Sun eve & Mon out of season; eve only July & Aug; book ahead), is a reliable North African restaurant with a pretty garden and filling couscous and tagines on offer from around €13.

The Îles d'Hyères

A haven from tempests in ancient times, then the peaceful home of monks and farmers, the **Îles d'Hyères** became, from the Middle Ages onwards, the target of piracy and coastal attacks. The three main islands, **Porquerolles**, **Port-Cros** and **Levant**, are covered in half-destroyed, rebuilt or abandoned forts, dating from the sixteenth century, when François I started a trend of under-funded fort building, up to the twentieth century, when the German gun positions on Port-Cros and Levant were put out of action by the Americans. Porquerolles and Levant are not yet free of garrisons, thanks to the knack of the French armed forces for securing prime beauty sites for their bases. Their presence has helped prevent development and, in the non-military areas, the islands' fragile environment is protected by the Parc National de Port-Cros and the Conservatoire Botanique de Porquerolles. The fire risk in summer is extreme: at times large sections of the islands are closed off and visitors must stick to marked paths.

The islands' wild, scented greenery and fine sand beaches are a reminder of what much of the mainland was like forty years ago. You can **stay** on Levant – accommodation must be booked months in advance – or on Porquerolles, although accommodation here is limited, sought after and expensive; on Port-Cros it's almost nonexistent. All visitors should observe signs forbidding smoking (away from the ports), flower-picking and littering.

Île de Porquerolles

The most easily accessible of the islands is **Porquerolles**, whose permanent village, also called **PORQUEROLLES**, has a few hotels and restaurants, plenty of cafés, a market and interminable games of *boules*. It dates from a nineteenth-century military settlement, and the village still focuses around the central **place d'Armes**. In summer its population explodes to over ten thousand, but there is some activity all year round. This is the only cultivated island of the three, with a few olive groves and three Côtes de Provence *domaines*, which you can visit.

Ferries to the Îles d'Hyères

Departures from:

Bandol port de Bandol (☎04.94.29.13.13, Ⓦwww.atlantide1.com). Occasional excursions to Porquerolles in summer; the trip includes five hours on the island.

La Tour Fondue Presqu'Île de Giens (☎04.94.58.21.81, Ⓦwww.tlv-tvm.com). The closest port to Porquerolles; all year round to Porquerolles, plus summer two-island trip to Porquerolles and Port-Cros.

Le Lavandou Gare maritime (☎04.94.71.01.02, Ⓦwww.vedettesilesdor.fr). The closest port to Port-Cros and Levant; year-round daily services to Levant and Port-Cros; thrice-weekly service April–Oct to Porquerolles (daily July & Aug). The same line runs less frequent seasonal services from Cavalaire to Port Cros and Porquerolles.

La Londe Port Miramar (☎04.94.05.21.14, Ⓦwww.bateliersdelacotedazur.com) Porquerolles and Port Cros, March–Oct only.

Port d'Hyères Hyères-Plage (☎04.94.57.44.07, Ⓦwww.tlv-tvm.com). Services to Port-Cros and Levant all year.

St-Raphaël Quai Nomy, Vieux Port (☎04.94.95.17.46, Ⓦwww.tmr-saintraphael.com). Services to Port-Cros July & Aug.

Porquerolles is big enough to find yourself alone amid its stunning landscapes. The **lighthouse** (closed to the public), due south of the village, and the *calanques* to its east make good destinations for an hour's walk, though the southern shoreline is all cliffs, with scary paths meandering close to the edge through heather and exuberant maquis scrub. Just off the path to the lighthouse at the southern end of the village is the **Maison du Parc** (daily: July & Aug 9.45am–12.30pm & 2.30–6.45pm; April–June, Sept & Oct 9.30am–12.30pm & 2–6pm) with a garden of palms from around the world, information on the national park's activities and tours of the nearby Mediterranean botanic garden of **Le Hameau**. The longest beach is the **plage Notre-Dame**, 3km northeast of the village just before the *terrain militaire* on the northern tip. The nearest beach to the village is the **plage d'Argent**, 1km away (continue west from the port past the Arche de Noë and take the first, well-signed right). This 500m strip of white sand fringes a curving bay backed by pine forests, and has a pleasant **restaurant**, *La Plage d'Argent* (☎04.94.58.32.48; closed Oct–March; lunchtime *plat du jour* €14–26).

Practicalities

There's a small **information centre** by the harbour (daily: April–Sept 8.30am– 3.30pm; Oct–March 9am–12.30pm; ☎04.94.58.33.76, Ⓦwww.porquerolles .com) where you can get basic maps (€2). You can hire **bikes** from several outlets: La Bécane, rue de la Poste (☎06.74.64.94.26) and L'Indien, place d'Armes (☎04.94.58.30.39).

Expect to pay upwards of €160 a night for **hotel** accommodation in Porquerolles in season; there are no budget hotels. You could try *Les Mèdes*, rue de la Douane (☎04.94.12.41.24, Ⓦwww.hotel-les-medes.fr; ❻; closed early Nov to late Dec), or *Villa Sainte-Anne*, on place d'Armes (☎04.98.04.63.00, Ⓦwww.sainteanne .com; ❻; closed early Nov to mid-March), which has more character. There's no campsite and *camping sauvage* is strictly forbidden, so don't miss the last ferry to the mainland.

Most of the cafés and **restaurants** in the village are pure tourist fodder; if you want gourmet cuisine you'll need to make the trek to the idyllic and Michelin-starred *Le Mas du Langoustier* (☎04.94.58.30.09; closed early October to late April) in the west of the island with *menus* starting from €55. You can buy sandwiches and *pan bagnat* on the place d'Armes for around €5, and there's also a supermarket and fruit and vegetable stall here.

⑯ Île de Port-Cros

The dense vegetation and mini-mountains of **Port-Cros** (ⓦwww.portcros parcnational.fr) make its exploration much tougher than Porquerolles, though it's less than half the size. Aside from ruined forts and the handful of buildings around the port, the only intervention is the classification labels on some of the plants and the extensive network of paths; you're not supposed to stray from these and it would be difficult to do so given the thickness of the undergrowth. The entire island is a protected zone, and has the richest fauna and flora of all the islands. Kestrels, eagles and sparrowhawks nest here; there are shrubs that flower and bear fruit at the same time, and more common species like broom, lavender, rosemary and heather flourish. One kilometre from the port (and a 45min walk) is the nearest beach, **plage de la Palud**; it takes rather longer to reach Mont Vinaigre, the island's highest point, via the **Vallon de la Solitude** – a three-hour round trip. From here there are views over the island's south coast and the islet of Gabinière. Except for those close to the beaches, the island's 30km of paths are all liable to closure during times of high fire risk.

There are two **hotels**: *Le Manoir d'Hélène* (ⓣ04.94.05.90.52, ⓦhotelmanoir portcros.monsite-orange.fr; ❽ per person, half-board; closed Oct to mid-April; *menus* €43) books up fast; there are five half-board rooms at the restaurant, *Hostellerie Provençale* (ⓣ04.94.05.90.43, ⓦwww.hostellerie-provencale.com; ❼ per person, half-board; closed mid-Nov to March). Almost as expensive is dining in the few **restaurants** around the port, though you can get a sandwich or a slice of pizza. Once you leave the village, however, there's nothing; at the very least, walkers should be sure they carry enough water. Camping is forbidden.

Île du Levant

The **Île du Levant** – ninety percent military reserve – is almost always humid and sunny. Cultivated plant life goes wild, with the result that giant geraniums and nasturtiums climb three-metre hedges, overhung by gigantic eucalyptus trees and yuccas. The tiny bit of the island spared by the military is the **nudist colony** of **HELIOPOLIS**, set up in the 1930s. About sixty people live here all year round, joined by thousands who come for the summer, and by tens of thousands of day-trippers, who are treated as voyeurs; if you **stay**, even for one night, you'll receive a friendlier reception. The most reasonable **hotels** are *La Brise Marine* (ⓣ04.94.05.91.15, ⓦwww.labrisemarine.net; ❺; closed Oct–March) and *Gaëtan* (ⓣ04.94.05.91.78, ⓦwww.hotelgaetan.com; ❻; price is for half-board; closed Oct–March). There are two **campsites**: *Le Colombero* (ⓣ04.94.05.90.29; open April–Sept) and *La Pinède* (ⓣ04.94.05.92.81, ⓦcampingdulevant.free.fr; open April–Sept), the latter with a pool and reasonably priced bungalows (❸).

Levant has a better choice of **restaurants** than Port-Cros, though price and quality still don't match; *Le Minimum* and *La Pomme d'Adam* are among the cheaper options.

The Corniche des Maures

The Côte really gets going with the resorts of the **Corniche des Maures**, multi-million-dollar residences lurk in the hills, luxurious yachts bob in the bays, and seafront prices become alarming. American actor Douglas Fairbanks Jr, the late Grand Duke of Luxembourg and sundry other titled names have pushed this coastline into legend.

The Corniche des Maures is spectacular, with its beaches that shine silver (from the mica crystals in the sand), tall dark pines, oaks and eucalyptus to shade them, glittering rocks of purple, green and reddish hue and chestnut-forested hills keeping winds away.

Bormes-les-Mimosas

Seventeen kilometres east of Hyères, chic **BORMES-LES-MIMOSAS** is medieval in flavour, with a ruined but restored **castle** at the summit of its hill, protected by spiralling lines of pantiled houses backing onto immaculately restored flights of steps. The mimosas here, and all along the Côte d'Azur, are no more indigenous than the people passing in their Porsches: the tree was introduced from Mexico in the 1860s, but the town still has some of the most luscious climbing flowers of any Côte town, and in summer, the displays of bougainvillea and oleander are impressive.

Two **hotels** worth trying in old Bormes are the simple but attractive *Bellevue*, on place Gambetta (T04.94.71.15.15, W bellevuebormes.fr.st; ❸; closed mid-Nov to Jan), or the fancier *Hostellerie du Cigalou* opposite (T04.94.41.51.27, W www .hostellerieducigalou.com; ❽). All **campsites** are just below the main road or in La Favière, closer to Le Lavandou than to Bormes. One of the best is *Clau-Mar-Jo* at 895 chemin de Bénat (T04.94.71.53.39, W www.camping-clau-mar-jo.fr; closed mid-Oct to mid-March).

The **tourist office** in Bormes is on place Gambetta (April–Sept daily 9am–12.30pm & 2.30–6.30pm; Oct–March Mon–Sat 9am–12.30pm & 1.30–5.30pm; T04.94.01.38.38, W www.bormeslesmimosas.com). Good **restaurants** include *La Tonnelle* on place Gambetta (T04.94.71.34.84; closed mid-Nov to mid-Dec; lunch *menus* from €27), specializing in local recipes; *La Cassole* at 1 ruelle du Moulin (T04.94.71.14.86; *menus* from €25), which serves Provençal specialities in unpretentious, yet classy, surroundings; and *Pâtes…et Pâtes*, on place du Bazar (T04.94.64.85.75; closed Tues), which serves the best pasta in town from around €11.

Le Lavandou and around

LE LAVANDOU, a few kilometres east of Bormes, is a pleasantly unpretentious seaside town known for its good beaches. Its name derives from *lavoir* or "wash-house" rather than "lavender". From the central promenade of quai Gabriel-Péri the sea is all but invisible thanks to the pleasure boats moored at the three harbours; demand from restaurateurs also keeps a few fishing boats in business. The town beach is quite broad and sandy, but if you're after the fabled silver beaches you need to head out of town and east along the corniche to **Cavalière**, **Pramousquier**, **Le Canadel** and **Le Rayol**. It's hardly countryside, but you can explore the Pointe du Layet headland just east of Cavalière, follow the sinuous D27 up to the Col du Canadel for breathtaking views and beautiful cork-oak woodland, and, in Le Rayol, visit a superb garden, the **Domaine de Rayol** (daily: summer 9.30am–7.30pm; spring & autumn 9.30am–6.30pm; winter 9.30am–5.30pm; €9) which has plants from differing parts of the world that share the Mediterranean climate.

If you want to indulge in watersports or nightlife, Le Lavandou's **tourist office** on quai Gabriel-Péri (July & Aug daily 9am–12.30pm & 2.30–6.30pm; May, June & Sept Mon–Sat 9am–12.30pm & 2.30–6pm, Sun 10am–noon & 4–6pm; Nov–March Mon–Sat 9am–noon & 2.30–6pm; T04.94.00.40.50, W www .ot-lelavandou.fr) will happily advise. For **accommodation**, try the *Hôtel L'Oustaou*, 20 av Général-de-Gaulle (T04.94.71.12.18, W www.lavandou-hotel -oustaou.com; ❷), a clean, family-run place in the town centre.

La Croix-Valmer

Beyond Le Rayol the corniche climbs away from the coast through 3km of open countryside, scarred almost every year by fires. As abruptly as this wilderness commences, it ends with the sprawling family resort of **Cavalaire-sur-Mer**. From here another exceptional stretch of coastline, dressed only in its natural covering of rock and woodlands, is visible across the Baie de Cavalaire. This is the **Domaine de Cap Lardier**, a wonderful coastal conservation area around the southern tip of the St-Tropez peninsula, easily accessible from **LA CROIX-VALMER**. The resort's centre is 2.5km from the sea; some of the land in between is taken up by vineyards producing a very decent Côte de Provence.

La Croix-Valmer's **tourist office** is at Esplanade de la Gare (mid-June to mid-Sept Mon–Sat 9.15am–12.30pm & 2.30–7pm, Sun 9am–1pm; mid-Sept to mid-June Mon–Fri 9.15am–noon & 2–6pm, Sat & Sun 9.15am–noon; ☎04.94.55.12.12, ⓦwww.lacroixvalmer.fr), just up from the junction of the D559 and D93. A good-value **hotel** near the beach, in the Cavalaire bay, is the family-run *Hostellerie La Ricarde*, plage du Débarquement (☎04.94.79.64.07, ⓦwww.hotel-la-ricarde.com; ❸; closed Oct–March), while at the other end of the scale is *Le Château de Valmer,* 7km away on route de Gigaro (☎04.94.55.15.15, ⓦwww.chateauvalmer.com; ❾; closed Nov to early April), a luxurious old mansion within walking distance of the sea. You can **camp** at the four-star *Sélection*, on boulevard de la Mer (☎04.94.55.10.30, ⓦwww.selectioncamping.com; closed mid-Oct to mid-March; booking advisable), 400m from the sea and with excellent facilities. Good pizzas are guaranteed (from €11) at **L'Italien** (☎04.94.79.67.16) on plage de Gigaro, just before the conservation area. Two other good but expensive **restaurants** on this beach are *La Brigantine* and *Souleïas*.

The Massif des Maures

The secret of the Côte d'Azur is that however vulgar the coast, Provence is still just behind – sparsely populated, village-oriented and exploiting the land for produce, not real estate. The most bewitching hinterland is the **Massif des Maures**, stretching from Hyères to Fréjus. The highest point of these hills stops short of 800m, but the quick succession of ridges, the sudden drops and views, and the curling, looping roads, are pervasively mountainous. In spring, the sombre forest is enlivened by millions of wild flowers and the roads are busy with cyclists; in winter, this is the haunt of hunters. Amid the brush crawl the last of the Hermann's tortoises, which once could be found along the whole of the northern Mediterranean coast.

Much of the Massif is inaccessible even to walkers. However, the **GR9 footpath** follows the highest and most northerly ridge from Pignans on the N97 past Notre-Dame-des-Anges, La Sauvette, **La Garde-Freinet** and down to the head of the Golfe de St-Tropez. For **cyclists**, the D14 that runs for 42km through the middle, parallel to the coast, from Pierrefeu-du-Var, north of Hyères, to **Cogolin** near St-Tropez, is manageable and stunning, climbing from 150m to 411m above sea level.

Collobrières

At the heart of the Massif is the ancient village of **COLLOBRIÈRES**, reputed to have been the first place in France to learn from the Spanish that a certain tree bark plugged into bottles allows a wine industry to grow. From the Middle Ages until supplanted by the sweet chestnut, cork production was the major business of the village. The church, the *mairie* and houses don't seem to have been modernized for a century, but the **Confiserie Azurienne** on boulevard Koenig (9.30am–12.30pm

& 1.30–6.30pm) exudes efficiency and modern business skill in the manufacture of all things chestnut: ice cream, jam, nougat, purée and *marrons glacés*. There's also a small outdoor café there where you can enjoy the delicious ice cream.

Collobrières' **tourist office** on boulevard Charles Caminat (April–June & Sept–Oct Tues–Sat 10am–12.30pm & 3–5pm; July–Aug daily 9am–12.30pm & 2–5pm; ☎04.94.48.08.00, ⓦwww.collobrieres-tourisme.com; not always open during its published opening hours) can supply details of walks in the surrounding hills. There are two **hotels**: ⚓ *Notre-Dame*, 15 av de la Libération (☎04.94.48.07.13, ⓦwww.hotelnotredame-provence.com; ❺) has individually decorated rooms with huge bathrooms and a lovely patio restaurant by a stream with excellent wines; and the excellent-value *Hôtel des Maures*, 19 bd Lazare Carnot (☎04.94.48.07.10, ⓦwww.hoteldesmaures.fr; ❶). A municipal **campsite** (bookings only through the tourist office), the *St-Roch*, south of the village near place Charles-de-Gaulle, is open in July and August. **Camping sauvage** is forbidden.

For food other than chestnuts, the **restaurant** *La Petite Fontaine*, 6 place de la République (☎04.94.48.00.12; closed Sun eve & Mon), is congenial and affordable, with *menus* from €26, but books up fast. If you want to buy some local **wines**, visit Les Vignerons de Collobrières close to the *Hôtel Notre-Dame* at the western entrance to the village. **Market** days are Thursday and Sunday.

La Chartreuse de la Verne

Hidden in the forest, 12km from Collobrières off the D14 towards Grimaud, is a huge and now largely restored twelfth-century monastery, **La Chartreuse de la Verne** (daily except Tues: Feb–May & Oct–Dec 11am–5pm; June–Sept 11am–6pm; €6), abandoned at the time of the Revolution. These days it looks a little too pristine, though there's no denying the wonder of its setting. The access road deteriorates into a rutted track for the last 500m.

Grimaud

GRIMAUD, 25km east of Collobrières along the twisting D14 and more easily reached from St-Tropez or La Croix Valmer, is a film set of a **village perché**. The cone of houses enclosing the eleventh-century church and culminating in the ruins of a medieval castle appears as a single, perfectly unified entity, though the effect of timelessness is undermined by the glass lift that whisks visitors up into the village from the main road. The most vaunted street is the arcaded **rue des Templiers**, which leads up to the Romanesque **Église de St-Michel** and a house of the Knights Templar, while the view from the **castle** ruins is superb. Grimaud's celebrated coastal extension, **PORT GRIMAUD**, stands at the head of the Golfe de St-Tropez, just north of La Foux. Created in the 1960s with waterways for roads and yachts everywhere, it's exquisitely tasteful, though the complex is surrounded by car parks rather than fields of lavender and there's an inevitable air of theme-park artificiality. The inhabitants include a certain Joan Collins. The main entrance is well signed off the N98. You don't have to pay to get in, but you can't explore all the islands without hiring a boat (€20 for 30min) or joining a crowded boat tour (€4).

Grimaud's **tourist office** is at 1 bd des Aliziers (Mon–Sat: April–June & Sept 9am–12.30pm & 2.30–6.15pm; July & Aug 9am–12.30pm & 3–7pm; Oct–March Mon–Sat 9am–12.30pm & 2.15–5.30pm; ☎04.94.55.43.83, ⓦwww.grimaud -provence.com), just off the main road which passes by the old village and the little folk museum, the **Musée des Arts et Traditions** (May–Sept Mon–Sat 2.30–6pm; Oct–April Mon–Sat 2–5.30pm; free). Excellent, if pricey, *menus* from €45 are offered at *Le Coteau Fleuri*, place des Pénitents (☎04.94.43.20.17, ⓦwww.coteau fleuri.fr; closed Tues except July & August), which also has fourteen **rooms** (❺).

La Garde-Freinet

The attractive village of **LA GARDE-FREINET**, 10km northwest of Grimaud, was founded in the late twelfth century by people from the nearby villages of Saint-Clément and Miramer. The original fortified settlement sat further up the hillside, and the foundations of the fortress are still visible above the village beside the ruins of a fifteenth-century castle (take the path from La Planette car park at the northwestern end of the village). The medieval charm; easy walks to stunning panoramas; markets twice a week (Wed & Sun); a chestnut cooperative on the northern approach to the village; tempting food shops selling organic produce and good local wines; and very reasonable accommodation are all presumably reasons for the high number of ex-pats buying property in this peaceful village.

The **tourist office** operates from the Chapelle St Jean, on place de l'Hôtel de Ville (April–June & Sept Mon–Sat 9.30am–12.30pm & 3.00–5.30pm; July–Aug Mon–Sat 9.30am–1pm & 4–6.30pm, Sun 10am–12.30pm; Oct–March Mon–Sat 9.30am–12.30pm & 2–5pm; ℡04.94.43.67.41, ⓦwww.lagardefreinet.com), and will provide details for the entire Maures region, including suggesting **walks** and hikes such as the spectacular 21km GR9 route des Crêtes. The danger of forest fires is particularly high here; the current risk level is posted up outside the tourist office in summer. Next door is the **Conservatoire du Patrimoine** (Tues–Sat 10am–12.30pm & 2.30–5.30pm; free), which organizes guided walks on various local topics and has exhibits on local sericulture and a model of the old fortress.

For **rooms**, *La Claire Fontaine* on place Vieille (℡&ⓕ04.94.43.63.76; ❸) is incredibly good value. One kilometre out of town at Quartier Le Défend Nord is the gorgeous *Le Mouron Rouge* (℡04.94.43.66.33, ⓦwww.lemouronrouge.com) with well-equipped apartments (for 2–6 people; €110 per night) and studios (for 2–4 people; €95 per night) and a large pool. There's also a campsite, *La Ferme de Bérard*, 5km along the D558 towards Grimaud (℡04.94.43.21.23; closed Nov–Feb).

The place to be of an evening is **Le Carnotzet** bar, art gallery and **restaurant**, on the exquisite place du Marché (℡04.94.43.62.73; *plats du jour* from €18; occasional live music). *La Colombe Joyeuse*, on place Vieille (℡04.94.43.65.24; closed Tues in winter; *menu* from €20), offers excellent Provençal dishes, while *La Faucado*, on the main road (℡04.94.43.60.41; closed Tues in winter; mains around €35), is overpriced, but serves beautiful dishes from local produce in a pretty garden setting.

St-Tropez

The origins of **ST-TROPEZ** are unremarkable: a fishing village that grew up around a port founded by Marseille's Greeks, destroyed by Saracens in 739 and finally fortified in the late Middle Ages. Its sole distinction was its inaccessibility: stuck on a small peninsula that never warranted proper roads, reached only by boat till the end of the nineteenth century.

Soon after, bad weather forced the painter Paul Signac to moor in St-Tropez. He promptly decided to build a house here, to which he invited his friends. Matisse was one of the first to accept, with Bonnard, Marquet, Dufy, Derain, Vlaminck, Seurat and Van Dongen following suit, and by World War I St-Tropez was an established bohemian hangout. The 1930s saw a new influx, of writers as much as painters: Cocteau, Colette and Anaïs Nin, whose journal records "girls riding bare-breasted in the back of open cars". In 1956, Roger Vadim filmed Brigitte Bardot in **Et Dieu… Créa la Femme**; the international cult of Tropézian sun, sex and celebrities promptly took off and the place has been groaning under the weight of visitors ever since.

As the summer playground of Europe's youthful rich, St-Tropez remains undeniably glamorous, its oversized yachts and infamous champagne "spray" parties creating an air of expensive, hedonistic excess.

Arrival and information

Infrequent buses run between the main coast road at **La Foux** and St-Tropez, 5.5km away, dropping you at the **gare routière** on avenue Général-de-Gaulle. From here it's a short walk along avenue du 8-Mai-1945 to the **Vieux Port**, where you'll find the **tourist office** on quai Jean-Jaurès (daily: April–June & Sept–Oct 9.30am–12.30pm & 2–7pm; July & Aug 9.30am–1.30pm & 3–8pm; Nov–March 9.30am–12.30pm & 2–6pm; ℡04.94.97.45.21, ⓦwww.ot-saint-tropez.com). **Bikes** and **motorbikes** can be rented at Rolling Bikes, 12 av G.-Leclerc (℡04.94.97.09.39, ⓦwww.rolling-bikes.com).

Accommodation

Accommodation is a problem; between April and September you'll be lucky to find a room unless you've booked in advance or are prepared to pay exorbitant prices. The tourist office can help with last-minute reservations (€10), but transport permitting, you might be better off staying elsewhere in the surrounding areas. Many hotels close out of season. **Camping** near St-Tropez can be expensive, with many sites more geared towards chalet lets than providing emplacements for tents. There are a couple of overcrowded and expensive beaches on plage de Pampelonne. Overnighting in vehicles is not permitted.

Hotels

Le 12 Rue Saint-Jean 12 rue Saint-Jean ℡06.16.05.21.76, ⓦwww.aucoeurdesainttropez .com. With only three, beautifully decorated, rooms this stylish *chambre d'hôtes* is great value and centrally located. Book well in advance. ❼
B. Lodge 23 rue de l'Aïoli ℡04.94.97.06.57, ⓦwww.hotel-b-lodge.com. Overlooking the citadelle, this place is quieter than hotels in the centre and has stylish decor and its own bar. ❼
Byblos Av Paul-Signac ℡04.94.56.68.00, ⓦwww .byblos.com. The perennial favourite if money really is no object and you need to be with the in-crowd, with doubles over €600 a night in July & Aug. ❾
Ermitage Av Paul Signac ℡04.94.97.52.33, ⓦwww.ermitagehotel.fr. Newly opened, decadent 1950s Art Decor hotel with a restaurant and fabulous views. ❾

Lou Cagnard 18 av Paul Roussel ℡04.94.97.04.24, ⓦwww.hotel-lou-cagnard.com. The best cheapish option. Chalet type rooms with a garden. ❹–❺
Les Lauriers Rue du Temple ℡04.94.97.04.88, ⓦwww.hotelleslauriers.com. Just behind Place des Lices, this friendly hotel is relaxed and has a pleasant garden. ❺–❻
Le Sube 15 quai Suffren ℡04.94.97.30.04, ⓦwww.hotel-sube.com. Right in the thick of it, with a bar and some – more expensive – rooms offering fantastic views over the port. ❼

Campsites

La Rouillère Quartier la Rouillère ℡04.94.79.28.67, ⓦwww.camping-larouillere.fr. Closed Nov–March.
Les Tournels Rte de Camarat, 3km from Ramatuelle ℡04.94.55.90.90, ⓦwww.tournels.com. Closed Jan to mid-March.

The Town

Beware of St-Tropez in high summer. Even getting to it is an ordeal, unless you waft in by helicopter, yacht or on the ferry from Sainte-Maxime, as the traffic jams can be appalling. It gets crowded around the port and the beaches aren't the cleanest. Save your visit for a spring or autumn day and you'll understand better why this place has had such hype.

The **Vieux Port**, rebuilt after its destruction in World War II, defines the French word *frimer*, which means to stroll ostentatiously in places like St-Tropez. You'll either love it or hate it.

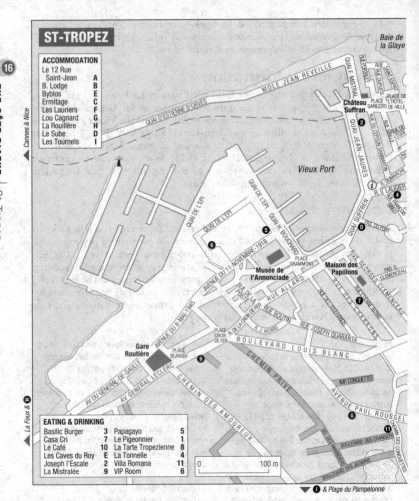

ST-TROPEZ

Baie de la Glaye

ACCOMMODATION
Le 12 Rue	
Saint-Jean	A
B. Lodge	E
Byblos	C
Ermitage	F
Les Lauriers	G
Lou Cagnard	H
La Rouillère	D
Le Sube	
Les Tournels	I

Vieux Port

Château Suffren

Musée de l'Annonciade

Maison des Papillons

Gare Routière

EATING & DRINKING
Basilic Burger	3	Papagayo	5
Casa Cri	7	Le Pigeonnier	1
Le Café	10	La Tarte Tropezienne	8
Les Caves du Roy	E	La Tonnelle	4
Joseph l'Escale	2	Villa Romana	11
La Mistralée	9	VIP Room	6

0   100 m

▼ ● & Plage du Pampelonne

Up from the port, at the end of quai Jean-Jaurès, you enter place de l'Hôtel-de-Ville, with the **Château Suffren**, originally built in 980 by Count Guillaume 1er of Provence, and the very pretty *mairie*. A street to the left leads down to the rocky **baie de la Glaye**, while straight ahead rue de la Ponche passes through an ancient gateway to place du Revelin above the exceptionally pretty **fishing port** and its tiny beach. Turning inland and upwards, you finally reach the open space around the beautiful sixteenth-century **citadelle**, which also houses a **maritime museum** (closed for renovation at time of writing) and glorious views of the gulf and the town – views which haven't changed much since they were painted in the first half of the last century. Some of these paintings you can see at the marvellous **Musée de l'Annonciade** (daily except Tues: July–Aug 10am–noon & 2–6pm; Sept–June 10am–noon & 2–6pm; €5) in the deconsecrated sixteenth-century chapel on place Georges Grammont, right on the port. The Annonciade features works by Signac, Matisse and most of the other artists who worked here: grey, grim, northern views of Paris, Boulogne and Westminster, and then local, brilliantly sunlit scenes by the

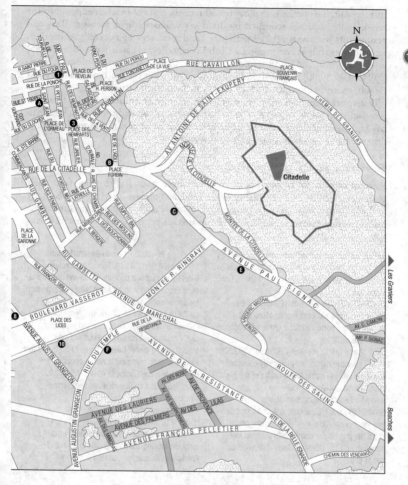

Citadelle

Les Graniers ▶

Beaches ▶

same brush – a real delight and unrivalled outside Paris for the 1890 to 1940 period of French art.

The other pole of St-Tropez's life, south of the Vieux Port, is **place des Lices**, where you can still sit on benches in the shade of decayed but surviving plane trees and watch, or join, the *boules* games.

The beaches

The beach within easiest walking distance is **Les Graniers**, below the citadelle just beyond the port des Pêcheurs along rue Cavaillon. From here, a path follows the coast around the **baie des Canebiers**, with its small beach, to Cap St-Pierre, Cap St-Tropez, the very crowded **Les Salins** beach and right round to Tahiti-Plage, about 11km away.

Tahiti-Plage is the start of the almost straight, 5km north–south **Pampelonne** beach, famous bronzing belt of St-Tropez and world initiator of the topless bathing cult. The water is shallow for 50m or so, and the beach is exposed to the wind, and sometimes scourged by dried sea vegetation and garbage. **Bars** and **restaurants** line the beach, all with patios and sofas, serving cocktails, gluttonous ice creams and full-blown meals. **Le Club 55** on boulevard Patch (℡ 04.94.55.55.55) is the original and most famous; **Maison Ocoa**, also on boulevard Patch (℡ 04.94.79.89.80), is *über*-trendy, almost a nightclub on the beach; and **Nikki Beach**, route de l'Epi (℡ 04.94.79.82.04), is the celebrity hangout.

Transport from St-Tropez is provided by a frequent **minibus** service from the *gare routière* to Salins, or bus #7705 to Ramatuelle. If you're driving, you'll have to pay high parking charges at all the beaches, or to leave your car or motorbike some distance from the sea and easy prey to thieves.

Eating and drinking

Restaurants in St-Tropez obsess as much over how stylish they (and their customers) look as over the quality of the food, and budget offerings are distinctly in the minority. You should reckon on paying quite a bit more than in comparable places in other resorts in the Var, and be aware that price doesn't necessarily correspond to quality.

Basilic Burger Place des Remparts
℡ 04.94.97.29.09. If you need a simple and decent burger, omelette or salad, head straight here. Lunch *menu* €15.

Le Café Place des Lices ℡ 04.94.97.44.69. Old-school, landmark brasserie. *Menu* €30. *Boules* can be borrowed for a game of *pétanque* in the square.

Casa Cri 12 rue Berny ℡ 04.94.97.42.52. Inventive Italian, set in a lovely courtyard down a quiet side street in the centre of the old town. Closed Oct–April.

Joseph l'Escale 9 quai Jean-Jaurès
℡ 04.94.97.00.63. Slick quayside restaurant with two sister restaurants (one cheaper, one pricier) and a bar around the corner, with *plats du jour* from around €19. *Côtes de Boeuf Béarnaise* for two at €80.

La Mistralée 1 av du Général Leclerc
℡ 04.98.12.91.12. This small, exclusive hotel-restaurant has poolside BBQs and gastro à la carte French food with an Asian twist (€35), perfect for a romantic dinner.

La Tarte Tropézienne 36 rue G.-Clemenceau. Patisserie claiming to have invented the rather sickly eponymous sponge and custard cake, though you no longer have to come to St-Tropez to sample it – the company is now a chain.

La Tonelle 6 rue Gambetta ℡ 04.94.54.82.02. Good Italian in a central location, with pizzas starting at €12.

Villa Romana Chemin des Conquettes
℡ 04.94.97.15.50. Pricey Italian and French restaurant with a bar. Don't be fooled by the innocent-looking entrance, inside is a cave of flamboyant debauchery. Closed Oct–April.

Nightlife

In season St-Tropez stays up late. You can spend the evening trying on clothes in the couturier shops; the *boules* games on place des Lices continue well after dusk; and the portside spectacle doesn't falter till the early hours. Places to see and be seen include: *Les Caves du Roy*, in the *Hôtel Byblos* on rue Paul Signac (the most expensive and exclusive); *Papagayo*, on the port, which has a restaurant terrace overlooking the yachts; and the *VIP Room* on the Nouveau Port. There's also a gay club, *Le Pigeonnier*, in rue de la Ponche.

Gassin

In delightful contrast to the overcrowded coast, the interior of the **St-Tropez peninsula** remains undeveloped, thanks to government intervention, complex ownerships and the value of some local wines. The best view of this richly green countryside is from the hilltop village of Gassin, only 8km from St Tropez. **GASSIN** is the shape and size of a ship perched on a summit; once an eighth-century Muslim stronghold, it's an excellent place for a big dinner, sitting outside by the village wall with a spectacular panorama east over the peninsula. Of the handful of **restaurants** *Bello Visto*, 9 place des Barrys (℡04.94.56.17.30; restaurant closed Nov–March), serves good Provençal specialities on a €30 *menu*, plus nine rooms at excellent prices for this glorious setting (❸).

Ste-Maxime

Facing St-Tropez across its gulf, **STE-MAXIME** is the perfect Côte stereotype: palmed corniche and enormous pleasure-boat harbour, beaches crowded with bronzed windsurfers and water-skiers, and estate agents outnumbering any other businesses by something like ten to one. It sprawls a little too much – merging with its northern neighbours to create a continuous suburban strip up to Fréjus. But though hardly as colourful as St-Tropez, it's less pretentious and the beaches are cleaner.

Arrival, information and accommodation

Buses into town stop outside the **tourist office** on the promenade Simon-Lorière (June & Sept Mon–Sat 9am–noon & 2–7pm; July & Aug Mon–Sat 9am–8pm, Sun 10am–noon & 4–7pm; Oct–May Mon–Sat 9am–noon & 2–6pm; ℡04.94.55.75.55, ⓦwww.ste-maxime.com), which can give information on trips and advice on hotel vacancies – once again, rare in summer. If you're heading for St-Tropez from Ste-Maxime, an alternative to the bus is to go by **boat**; the twenty-minute service from Ste-Maxime's *gare maritime* on the port (€12.50 return) runs from February to early November and over Christmas and New Year, with more frequent crossings in July and August. **Bikes** can be rented at ADA/Holiday Bikes, 16 bd Frédéric-Mistral (℡04.94.96.16.25).

Hotels

Auberge Provençale 19 rue Aristide-Briand ℡04.94.55.76.90. Central and very welcoming, this hotel also has its own restaurant. ❸–❹

Castellamar 8 av G.-Pompidou ℡04.94.96.19.97. The best of the cheaper hotels and on the west side of the river, but still close to the town centre and the sea. ❸

Hôtellerie de la Poste 11 bd Frédéric-Mistral ℡04.94.96.18.33, ⓦwww.hotelleriedusoleil.com. Comfortable, plush hotel with a pool. ❼–❽

Campsite

Les Cigalons Quartier de la Nartelle ℡04.94.96.05.51, ⓦwww.campingcigalon.com. By the sea, this place rents out holiday bungalows. Closed mid-Oct to April.

The Town

If your budget denies you the pleasures of watersports, you might find Ste-Maxime a little lacking in diversions. You can, at least, eat at reasonable cost, since there are plenty of crêperies, *glaciers* and snack places along the central avenue Charles-de-Gaulle. For the spenders, the east-facing plage de la Nartelle, 5km east from the centre towards Les Issambres, is the strip of sand to head for. Here, at **Barco Beach** and its seven neighbours, you'll pay for shaded cushioned comfort, watersports, grilled fish and have drinks brought to your mattress and listen to a piano player as dusk falls. A kilometre or so further on, **plage des Éléphants** recalls the town's link to Jean de Brunhoff, creator of Babar the elephant, who had a holiday home in Ste-Maxime.

Ste-Maxime's *vieille ville* has several good **markets**: a covered flower and food market on rue Fernand-Bessy (mid-June to Sept daily 7.30am–1pm & 4–8pm; Oct to mid-June Tues–Sun 8am–1pm); a Thursday morning food market on place du Marché; *prêt-à-porter* every Wednesday morning on place Jean Mermoz; and arts and crafts in the pedestrian streets (mid-June to mid-Sept daily 5–11pm).

High up in the Massif des Maures on the road to Le Muy, some 10km north of Ste-Maxime, the marvellous **Musée du Phonographe et de la Musique Mécanique**, in the parc St-Donat (Easter–Oct Wed–Sun 10am–noon; July & Aug also 4–6.30pm; €3), is the result of one amazing woman's forty-year obsession with collecting audio equipment, amassing a wide selection of automata, musical boxes and pianolas, plus one of Thomas Edison's "talking machines" dating from 1878.

Eating

For non-beach **eating**, the *Hostellerie de la Belle Aurore*, 5 bd Jean-Moulin (℡04.94.96.02.45; closed Wed Sept–June; weekday *menu* from €40), offers gourmet food on a sea-view terrace; less expensive is the classic French cuisine at *La Table des Gémeaux*, 33 rue des Maures (℡04.94.49.16.54; *menus* start at €25, lunch €15).

Fréjus

FRÉJUS – along with its neighbour **St-Raphaël** (see p.935) 3km south – has a history dating back to the Romans. It was established as a naval base under Julius Caesar and Augustus, and its ancient port – known as Forum Julii – consisted of 2km of quays connected by a walled canal to the sea (which was considerably closer then). After the battle of Actium in 31 BC, the ships of Antony and Cleopatra's defeated fleet were brought here.

The area between Fréjus and the sea is now the suburb of **Fréjus-Plage** with a vast 1980s marina, **Port-Fréjus**. Both Fréjus and Fréjus-Plage merge with St-Raphaël, which in turn merges with **Boulouris** to the east. The population of Fréjus's *vieille ville*, which lies within the Roman perimeter, was greater in the first century BC than it is today. Little remains of the Roman walls that once circled the city, and the harbour that made it an important Mediterranean port silted up and was finally filled in after the Revolution.

Arrival, information and accommodation

Regular daily trains stop at Fréjus's **gare SNCF**, just five to eight minutes away from St-Raphaël. Trains to St-Raphaël itself are much more frequent, and it's usually easiest to alight there and then take the #1, #3, #4, #5, #6, #7 or #10 Agglobus, which run frequently between the two towns. The **gare routière** is on the east side of the town centre on place Paul-Vernet (℡04.94.53.78.46), opposite which is the **tourist office**, at 325 rue Jean-Jaurès (June & Sept Mon–Fri 9am–6pm, Sat 9.30am–noon & 2pm–6pm; July & Aug daily 9am–7pm; Oct–May Mon–Fri 9am–noon & 2–6pm; ℡04.94.51.83.83, 🌐www.frejus.fr). If you're planning to visit most of Fréjus's sights it may be worth getting a **Fréjus'Pass** (€6.60), which is valid for seven days and includes access to the amphitheatre, Roman theatre and Musée Archéologique. You can pick up the pass at the sights themselves. The tourist office can also help with bike trails in the **Massif de L'Esterel** mountain range. Cycles Patrick Béraud at 337 rue de Triberg (℡04.94.51.20.20), and Location Loisirs, Base Nature (for the Massif de L'Esterel), boulevard de la Mer (☎06.74.83.86.42), have **bikes** for hire. The main **market days** are Wednesday and Saturday.

Hotels

Aréna 145 rue du Général-de-Gaulle
☎04.94.17.09.40, ⊛www.arena-hotel.com.
Comfortable hotel with a restaurant, serving good fish and seafood. Also has a pool. ❼
Le Bellevue Place Paul-Vernet ☎04.94.17.12.20.
Basic, but close to the bus station – and a large car park. ❶
La Riviera 90 rue Grisolle ☎04.94.51.31.46, or 04.06.17.75.98.59. Basic, but with a decent brasserie – book in advance as owners are not always there. ❶

Hostel and campsite

Les Acacias 370 rue Henri-Giraud
☎04.94.53.21.22, ⊛www.campingacacias.fr.
Moderate-sized and with a pool, 2.5km from the town centre. April–Oct.
HI Hostel 675 chemin du Counillier
☎04.94.53.18.75, ⊛www.fuaj.org.
2km northeast from the centre, take bus #10 from St Raphaël *gare routière*. Reception 8am–noon & 5.30–9.30pm. Dorm bed €14.40; April–Oct.

The Roman town

A tour of the Roman remains will give you a good idea of the extent of Forum Julii, but they are scattered throughout and beyond the town centre and take a full day to get around. Turning right out of the *gare SNCF* and then right down boulevard Severin-Decuers brings you to the **Butte St-Antoine**, against whose east wall the waters of the port would have lapped, and which once was capped by a fort. It was one of the port's defences, and one of the ruined **towers** may have been a lighthouse. A path around the southern wall follows the quayside (some stretches are visible) to the medieval **Lanterne d'Auguste**, built on the Roman foundations of a structure marking the entrance of the canal into the ancient harbour.

In the other direction from the station, past the Roman **Porte des Gaules** and along rue Henri-Vadon, you come to the **amphitheatre** (Tues–Sun: May–Oct 9.30am–12.30pm & 2–6pm; Nov–April 9.30am–12.30pm & 2–5pm; €2), with capacity of around ten thousand, used for concerts today. Its upper tiers have been reconstructed in the same greenish local stone used by the Romans, but the vaulted galleries on the ground floor are largely original. The Roman **theatre** (same hours and prices) is north of the town, along avenue du Théâtre-Romain, its original seats long gone, though it's still used for shows in summer. Northeast of it, in the parc Aurélien at the far end of avenue du XVème-Corps-d'Armée, six arches are visible of the forty-kilometre **aqueduct**, once as high as the ramparts. Closer to the centre, on rue des Moulins, are the arcades of the **Porte d'Orée**, positioned on the former harbour's edge alongside what was probably a **bath complex**.

The medieval town

The **Cité Episcopale**, or cathedral close, takes up two sides of **place Formigé**, the marketplace and heart of both contemporary and medieval Fréjus. It comprises the **cathedral** (Sept–May Tues–Sun 9am–noon & 2–5pm; June–Aug daily 9am–6/6.30pm; €5), flanked by the fourteenth-century bishop's palace (now the Hôtel de Ville), the baptistry, chapterhouse, cloisters and archeological museum. Visits to the cloisters and baptistry are guided with some English language tours.

The oldest part of the complex is the **baptistry**, built in the fourth or fifth century and so contemporary with the decline of the city's Roman founders. Its two doorways are of different heights, signifying the enlarged spiritual stature of the baptized. Bits of the early Gothic **cathedral** may belong to a tenth-century church, but its best features, apart from the bright diamond-shaped tiles on the spire, are Renaissance: the choir stalls, a wooden crucifix on the left of the entrance and the intricately carved doors with scenes of a Saracen massacre, only opened for the guided tours. The most engaging component of the whole ensemble, however, is the **cloisters**. In a small garden of scented bushes around a well, slender twelfth-century marble columns support a fourteenth-century ceiling painted with apocalyptic creatures. The treasures of the **Musée Archéologique** (same hours and prices as amphitheatre) on the upper storey of the cloisters include a complete Roman mosaic of a leopard and a copy of a double-headed bust of Hermes.

Eating, drinking and entertainment

One of the best **restaurants** in the old town is the tiny *Les Potiers*, 135 rue des Potiers (℡04.94.51.33.74; closed Tues), which has *menus* of fresh seasonal ingredients from €25. Cheaper eats are on place Agricola, place de la Liberté and the main shopping streets. *Cadet Rousselle*, at the top of place Agricola (℡04.94.53.36.92), is a crêperie with crêpes starting at €7. Equally good value are the massive salads at the *Brasserie Hermès* (℡04.94.17.26.02) opposite the cathedral at 15 place Formigé. At Fréjus-Plage there's a string of eating options, though *menus* are monotonously alike, with more upmarket *plateau des fruits de mer* outlets at Port-Fréjus.

Around Fréjus

Unlikely remnants of the more recent past come in the shape of a Vietnamese pagoda and an abandoned mosque, both built by French colonial troops. The **Mosquée Missiri de Djenné** (Tues–Sun 9.30am–12.30pm & 2–6pm) is on the left off the D4 to Bagnols, in the middle of an army camp 2km from the RN7 junction. A strange, guava-coloured, fort-like building, it's a replica of a Sudanese mosque in Mali, sadly fenced off, though much of the interior is visible from outside. The **pagoda Hong Hien** (daily: summer 9am–7pm; winter 9am–5pm; €2), still maintained as a Buddhist temple, is on the crossroads of the RN7 to Cannes and the D100, about 2km out of Fréjus. Alongside it is the massive memorial to the dead of the Indo–Chinese wars of the 1940s and 1950s (daily except Tues 10am–5.30pm). It is inscribed with the name of every fallen Frenchman; the sheer length of the lists suggesting the years 1950–54 were the most bloody. Just off the RN7 at La Tour-de-Mare is the last of Jean Cocteau's artistic landmarks, the chapel of **Notre-Dame-de-Jerusalem** (same hours as amphitheatre; free). Conceived as the church for a failed artistic community, the octagonal building was not completed until after Cocteau's death in 1963, and the interior was completed to Cocteau's plans by Édouard Dermit. The Last Supper scene inside includes a self-portrait of Cocteau.

There are a number of **mountain biking** trails that start in the Base Nature, just west of Port-Fréjus along the coast, and head up into the forested hills of the **Massif de l'Esterel** to the northeast of the town. The trails range from a flat, five-kilometre ride around a marsh to more serious 35-kilometre rides in the massif; the tourist office in St Raphaël can give information and sells a **walking guide** to the surrounding district for €8.50.

Appealing to children, there's a **zoo** in Le Capitou, close to exit 38 on the D4 heading north (daily: March–May & Sept–Oct 10am–5pm; June–Aug 10am–6pm; Nov–Feb 10.30am–4.30pm; €14, children under 9 €9.50; bus #1 or #2), and a water amusement park, **Aqualand** (daily from mid-June to mid-Sept: 10am–6pm, 7pm in July & Aug; €25, children under 12 €18.50; bus #9), off the RN98 to St-Aygulf.

St-Raphaël

ST-RAPHAËL became fashionable at the beginning of the twentieth century, but lost many of its seafront *belle-époque* mansions and hotels to World War II bombardment, but you may prefer to stay here rather than in Fréjus for its better restaurants, family friendly atmosphere and access to the beach.

Arrival, information and accommodation

St-Raphaël's **gare SNCF**, in the centre of town, is the main station for the Marseille–Ventimiglia line; the **gare routière** is on square du Dr-Régis, across the rail line behind the **gare SNCF**. Information on the surrounding region is available from the **tourist office**, facing the Vieux Port at quai Albert 1er (July & Aug daily 9.30am–7.30pm; Sept–June Mon–Sat 9am–12.30pm & 2–6.30pm; ℡04.94.19.52.52, ⓦwww.saint-raphael.com). Car hire outlets cluster around the *gare SNCF*. **Bikes** can be rented from Esterel Côte D'Azur at rue Waldeck Rousseau (℡04.94.19.10.60). **Food markets** are held every day except Monday on place Victor-Hugo and place de la République.

Hotels

Ambassador 89 rue Böetman ℡04.98.11.82.00, ⓦwww.ambassador-saint-raphael.com. This charming place has lovely decor; some rooms have their own sitting area and four-poster beds. ❺
Bellevue 840 bd Félix Martin ℡04.94.19.90.10. Basic, but cheap and smells nice, being above a bakery. ❸
🏃 **Cyrnos** 840 bd Alphonse Juin ℡04.94.95.17.13, ⓦwww.hotel-cyrnos.com. A fabulous and super-friendly place to

unwind for a few days. Located 2km from the station, from where the owners can pick you up. ❹
Excelsior Promenade René-Coty ℡04.94.95.02.42, ⓦwww.excelsior-hotel.com. Well-equipped rooms at this elegant seafront hotel. ❽

Campsite

Camping de L'Ile d'Or 98 rue du Nord ℡&ℱ04.94.95.52.13. 2km from the centre, on the N98 in Boulouris, two-star and close to the beach. Late-March to late-Oct.

The Town

The **old town** beyond place Carnot on the other side of the railway line is pleasantly low-key, no longer the commercial focus of the town but a good place to stroll and browse. On rue des Templiers a crumbling fortified Romanesque church has fragments of the Roman aqueduct that brought water from Fréjus in its courtyard, along with a local history and underwater archeology **museum** (Tues–Sat 9am–noon & 2–6pm; entry to church & museum free).

The **beaches** stretch between the Jardin Bonaparte at the entrance to the old port and the modern **Marina Santa Lucia**, with opportunities for every kind of watersport. You can also take boat trips to St-Tropez and the **calanques** of the Esterel coast from the quai Nomy on the south side of the Vieux Port. When you're tired of sea and sand you can lose whatever money you have left at the **casino** (daily 10am–dawn) on Square de Gand overlooking the Vieux Port.

Eating, drinking and nightlife

Key dining areas are on place Victor-Hugo, place de la République, around the Vieux Port, Port Santa Lucia and along the promenades. Of the more expensive establishments on the port, one of the best is **Le Sirocco**, 35 quai Albert 1er (℡04.94.95.39.99), which specializes in fish (*menus* from €19.50); alternatively, try **Le Bishop** at 84 rue Jean Aicard (℡04.94.54.64.06) for traditional Provençal cuisine (*menus* from €19).

For **drinking**, try the selection of lethal cocktails at the **Allbarino** at 105 bd Général-de-Gaulle (open till 3am in summer, closed Monday); **Aux Ambassadeurs**, a brasserie in the Casino complex that attracts a young crowd (till around midnight; or one of the beachfront discos like **La Réserve** on promenade **René Coty** or **L'Odysée** or **La Playa** in Fréjus-Plage. There's also one gay club, *La Gaymence*, on rue Charabois behind the *mairie*.

Cannes

With its immaculate seafront hotels and exclusive beach concessions, glamorous yachts and designer boutiques, **CANNES** is in many ways the definitive Riviera resort of popular fantasy. It's a place where appearances count, especially during the film festival in May, when the orgy of self-promotion reaches its annual peak. The ugly seafront Palais des Festivals is the heart of the film festival but also hosts conferences, tournaments and trade shows throughout the year. Despite its glittery image Cannes works surprisingly well as a big seaside resort, with plenty of free, sandy public beaches away from the famed plage de la Croisette, and if it all gets too much the **Îles de Lérins**, just offshore, offer a sublime contrast. Alternatively, you can escape the glitz of present-day Cannes by exploring the nineteenth-century glitz of La Croix des Gardes and La Californie, the aristocratic suburbs once populated by Russian and British royals.

Arrival, information and transport

The **gare SNCF** is on rue Jean-Jaurès, five blocks north of the concrete Palais des Festivals on the seafront. There are **tourist offices** (all using the same number: ☎04.92.99.84.22, ⓦwww.cannes.com) at the train station (Mon–Sat 9am–1pm & 2pm-6pm; at the Palais des Festivals (daily 9am–7/8pm); and at 1 av Pierre Sémard in Cannes-La Bocca (Tues–Sat 9am–noon & 2.30–6.30pm; ☎04.93.47.04.12). There are two **gares routières**: one on place B.-Cornut-Gentille between the *mairie* and Le Suquet, serving coastal destinations; and the other next to the *gare SNCF* for buses inland to places such as Grasse and Vallauris. Bus Azur runs 24 lines and five night buses, serving all of Cannes and the surrounding area (☎08.25.82.55.99; €1 single ticket). **Bikes** can be hired from Elite Rent a Bike, 32 av du Maréchal Juin (☎04.93.94.30.34) or Holiday Bike, 44 bd Lorraine (☎04.97.06.07.07).

Accommodation

The best concentration of **hotels** – including the limited selection of budget options – is in the centre, between the *gare SNCF* and the sea, around the central axis of rues Antibes and Félix Faure.

Alizé 29 rue Bivouac Napoleon ☎04.97.06.64.64, ⓦwww.hotel-alize-cannes.com. A central hotel with large, newly renovated rooms and a/c – this is great value in the lower end of this price range. ❺

Alnea 20 rue Jean de Riouffe ☎04.93.68.77.77, ⓦwww.hotel-alnea.com. Centrally located with somewhat outdated decor and pleasant service. ❹

Canberra 120 rue d'Antibes ☎04.97.06.95.00, ⓦwww.hotel-cannes-canberra.com. Luxury hotel with large rooms, a pool, sauna, gym, restaurant and cocktail bar with decor inspired by the 50s. ❾

Carlton InterContinental 58 La Croisette ☎04.93.06.40.06, ⓦwww.intercontinental.com. Legendary *belle-époque* palace hotel that starred in Hitchcock's *To Catch a Thief*, along with Cary Grant and Grace Kelly. ❾

Chanteclair 12 rue Forville ☎04.93.39.68.88, ⓦwww.hotel-chanteclair-cannes.cote.azur.fr. Reasonable cheapie, right next to the old town, approached across a private courtyard. ❸–❹

La Villa Tosca 11 rue Hoche ☎04.93.38.34.40, ⓦwww.villa-tosca.com. This place has well

equipped rooms with an airy sitting and breakfast room on the first floor. There is a cheaper (❹) sister hotel a few doors down. ❼
Martinez 73 La Croisette ☎04.92.98.73.00, ⓦwww.hotel-martinez.com. Art Deco palace with a trendy private beach, the best restaurant in Cannes

and a reputation as *the* place to stay during the Festival. ❾
Provence 9 rue Molière ☎04.93.38.44.35, ⓦwww.hotel-de-provence.com. Some rooms have bathtubs in this charmingly decorated and well-appointed place with its own bar. ❻–❼

The Town

The old town, known as **Le Suquet** after the hill on which it stands, provides a great panorama of the 12km beach, and has, on its summit, the remains of the fortified priory lived in by Cannes' eleventh-century monks and the beautiful twelfth-century Chapelle Ste-Anne. These house the **Musée de la Castre** (April–June & Sept Tues–Sun 10am–1pm & 2–6pm; July–Aug daily 10am–7pm; Oct–March Tues–Sun 10am–1pm & 2–5pm; €3.40), which has an extraordinary collection of musical instruments from all over the world, along with pictures and prints of old Cannes and an ethnology and archeology section. Just a few hundred metres to the west of Le Suquet on avenue du Dr-Raymond-Picaud in La Croix des Gardes is the **Château Eléonore**, the villa built by the retired British Chancellor Lord Brougham after his enforced stay in the then-unknown village of Cannes in 1834; he couldn't reach Nice because of a cholera epidemic but, liking what he found in Cannes, he built his villa here and laid the foundations for Cannes' development as an aristocratic resort.

You'll find the non-paying **beaches** to the west of Le Suquet towards the suburb of **La Bocca** along the **plages du Midi**, though there's also a tiny public section of beach on **La Croisette**, just east of the Palais des Festivals. La Croisette is certainly the sight to see, with its palace hotels on one side and private beaches on the other. It's possible to find your way down to the beach without paying, but not easy (you can of course walk along it below the rows of sun beds). The beaches, owned by the deluxe *palais-hôtels* – the *Martinez*, *Carlton* and *Noga Hilton* – are where you're most likely to spot a face familiar in celluloid or a topless hopeful, especially during the film festival, though you'll be lucky to see further than the sweating backs of the paparazzi. Alternative entertainment can be had buying your own food in the **Forville covered market** two blocks behind the *mairie*, or by wandering through the day's flower shipments on the allées de la Liberté, just back from the Vieux Port.

Eating, drinking and nightlife

Cannes has hundreds of **restaurants** catering for every budget, with Rue Meynadier, Le Suquet and quai St-Pierre being the best places to head for. There are tons of trendy, exclusive **bars** and **clubs**, especially in the grid of streets bounded by rue Macé, rue V. Cousin, rue Dr G.-Monod and rue des Frères Pradignac, where most are open till 4am.

Restaurants

Auberge Provençale 10 rue Saint-Antoine ☎04.92.99.27.17. Allegedly the oldest restaurant in Cannes, serving Niçoise specialities.

🏃 **Barbarella** 16 rue Saint-Dizier, Le Suquet ☎04.92.99.17.33. Stylish and fun, with an oriental-influenced fusion *menu* and superb *bellinis*. *Menus* from €40. Tues–Sun eves only, daily during festival.

Aux Bons Enfants 80 rue Meynadier. Small, friendly and rustic, this place serves very reliable

Provençal cuisine with *menus* at €25. Cash only. Closed Sun & Mon.

Chez Vincent & Nicolas 90 rue Meynadier ☎04.93.68.35.39. With a lovely setting in a square just off the main street, the scallops wrapped in bacon are worth a try. Mains start at €18.

La Mère Besson 13 rue des Frères Pradignac ☎04.93.39.59.24. A Cannes favourite with local specialities, such as braised beef in red wine and a great place to try *aioli*. *Menus* at €22 and €35. Closed Sun.

▲ Le Cannet, Mougin & autoroute   ▲ Vallauris

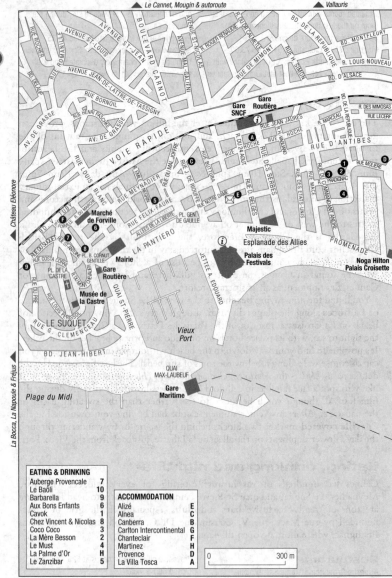

Château Eléonore ▶

◀ La Bocca, La Napoule & Fréjus

EATING & DRINKING	
Auberge Provencale	7
Le Baôli	10
Barbarella	9
Aux Bons Enfants	6
Cavok	1
Chez Vincent & Nicolas	8
Coco Coco	3
La Mère Besson	2
Le Must	4
La Palme d'Or	H
Le Zanzibar	5

ACCOMMODATION	
Alizé	E
Alnea	C
Canberra	B
Carlton Intercontinental	G
Chanteclair	F
Martinez	H
Provence	D
La Villa Tosca	A

0 ———————— 300 m

La Palme d'Or *Hôtel Martinez*, 73 La Croisette
℡04.92.98.74.14. The place to go and celebrate if
you've just won a film festival prize. *Menus* start at
€90. Closed Sun & Mon.

Bars and clubs

Le Baôli Port Pierre Canto. If you want to rub
shoulders with celebrities the place to head is this
exclusive exotic outdoor disco–restaurant with palms
lit up at night – dress the part. Daily from 8pm.

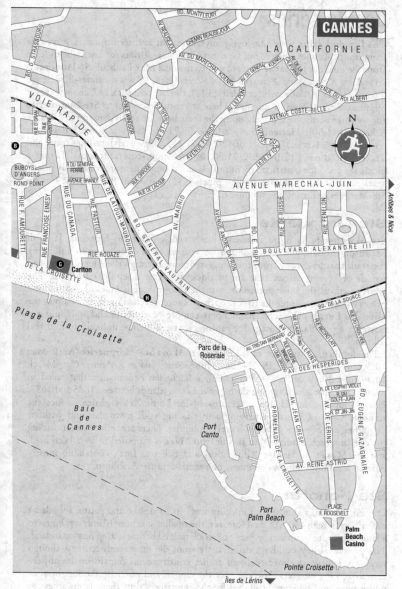

CANNES

Cavok 19 rue des Frères Pradignac. Small and with chilled music, this is a good place to relax from the hustle and bustle of these streets.
Coco Loco 4 Rue des Frères Pradignac. Cocktails with umbrellas, a punchy punch and a Creole vibe.

Le Must 14 rue du Batéguier. Trendy and with live music, there's a restaurant, too, but most come for the shisha pipes. Daily 6pm–2.30am.
Le Zanzibar 85 rue Félix-Faure. The oldest gay bar in Cannes. Daily 6pm–4am.

Îles de Lérins

The **Îles de Lérins** would be lovely anywhere, but at fifteen minutes' ferry ride from frantic Cannes, they're not far short of paradise. **Boats** for both islands leave from the quai des Îles at the seaward end of the quai Max Laubeuf. **St-Honorat** is served by Compagnie Planaria (ⓣ04.92.98.71.38, ⓦwww.cannes-ilesdelerins .com; summer 10 daily, winter 8 daily; €12); the last boat back to Cannes leaves at 5pm in winter & 6pm in summer. There are regular services to **Ste-Marguerite** run by three companies, mostly using the same boat (up to 18 departures 7.30am–5.30pm; €11.50): Horizon Sarl (ⓣ04.92.98.71.36, ⓦwww.horizon-iles-lerins -cannes.com), Riviera Lines (ⓣ04.92.98.71.31, ⓦwww.riviera-lines.com) and Trans Côte d'Azur (ⓣ04.92.98.71.30, ⓦwww.trans-cote-azur.com). Taking a picnic is a good idea, particularly out of season, though there are reasonably priced snack stalls and a restaurant serving pizzas (€15) and *menus* (€28) by the fort on Ste-Marguerite during the summer months.

Ste-Marguerite

Ste-Marguerite is more touristy than its neighbour, St-Honorat. It's still beautiful, though, and large enough for visitors to find seclusion by following the trails that lead away from the congested port, through the Aleppo pines and woods of evergreen oak that are so thick they cast a sepulchral gloom. The western end is the most accessible, but the lagoon here is brackish, so the best places to swim are along the rocky southern shore, reached most easily along the **allée des Eucalyptus**. The channel between Ste-Marguerite and St-Honorat is however a popular anchorage for motor yachts, so you're unlikely to find real solitude.

The dominating structure of the island is the **Fort Ste-Marguerite** (April–May 10.30am–1.30pm & 2.15–5.45pm; June–Sept 10am–5.45pm; Oct–March 10.30am–1.30pm & 2.15–4.45pm; €3), a Richelieu commission that failed to prevent the Spanish occupying both of the Lérins islands between 1635 and 1637. Later, Vauban rounded it off, presumably for Louis XIV's **gloire** – since the strategic value of greatly enlarging a fort facing your own mainland without upgrading the one facing the sea is pretty minimal. There are cells to see, including the one in which Dumas' **Man in the Iron Mask** is supposed to have been held, and the **Musée de la Mer** (same hours and ticket as fort), containing mostly Roman local finds but also remnants of a tenth-century Arab ship.

Ste-Honorat

Owned by monks almost continuously since its namesake and patron founded a monastery here in 410 AD, **St-Honorat**, the smaller southern island, was home to a famous bishops' seminary, where St Patrick trained before setting out for Ireland. The present **abbey** buildings date mostly from the nineteenth century, though some vestiges of the medieval and earlier constructions remain in the austere church and the cloisters. You can visit the church and purchase the sought-after white wine and liqueurs produced by the monastery, but there is no access to the residential part, unless you're staying there on a spiritual retreat. Behind the cloisters on the sea's edge stands the eleventh-century fortified monastery.

There's one tourist restaurant near the landing stage (April–Oct only), but no bars, hotels or cars: just vines, lavender, herbs and olive trees mingled with wild poppies and daisies, and pine and eucalyptus trees shading the paths beside the white rock shore.

Vallauris

Pottery and Picasso are the twin attractions of **VALLAURIS**, an otherwise unremarkable town in the hills above Golfe-Juan, 6km east of Cannes (bus #18 from *gare routière* by *gare SNCF*). It was here that Picasso first began to use clay, thereby reviving one of the traditional crafts of this little town. Today the main street, **avenue Georges Clemenceau**, sells nothing but pottery, much of it garish bowls or figurines that could feature in souvenir shops anywhere. Picasso used to work in the **Madoura workshop** on avenue des Anciens Combattants-d'AFN, to the left as you ascend avenue Georges Clemenceau, but this is now closed.

The bronze statue of **Man with a Sheep**, Picasso's gift to the town, stands in the main square, place Paul Isnard, beside the church and castle. In 1952, he also decorated the deconsecrated early medieval **chapel** in the castle courtyard (daily June–Aug 10am–6pm; Sept–May except Tues 10am–12.15pm & 2–5pm; €3.25), under suggestion of the local authorities; his subject was war and peace. The space is tiny, with the architectural simplicity of an air-raid shelter, and at first it's easy to be unimpressed by the painted panels covering the vault – as many critics still are – since the work looks mucky and slapdash, with paint-runs on the plywood panel surface. But stay a while and the passion of this violently drawn display of pacifism slowly emerges. The ticket for the chapel also gives admission to the **Musée de la Céramique/Musée Magnelli** in the castle (same hours and ticket), which exhibits Picasso's and other ceramics.

Regular buses from Cannes and from Golfe-Juan SNCF arrive at the rear of the château. The **tourist office** is at the bottom of avenue Georges Clemenceau, in the outskirts of town, on square du 8 Mai 1945 (July & Aug daily 9am–7pm; Sept–June Mon–Sat 9am–12.15pm & 1.45–6pm; ☏04.93.63.82.58, ⓦwww .vallauris-golfe-juan.fr), which is where you'll also find the main tourist **car park**.

Grasse

GRASSE, 16km inland from Cannes is the world capital of *parfumiers* and has been for almost three hundred years; it is easy to visit as a day-trip from the coast. These days it promotes a perfumed image of a medieval hill town surrounded by scented flowers, though in truth, the glamour of this friendly place is mostly bottled. Making perfumes is presented as a mysterious process, an alchemy, turning the soul of the flower into a liquid of luxury and desire, and the industry is at pains to keep quiet about modern innovations and techniques.

Arrival, information and accommodation

Grasse's **gare routière** is just north of the old town at place de la Buanderie. Head downhill on avenue Thiers, which becomes boulevard du Jeu-de-Ballon (where there's an annexe of the tourist office) and you'll find the major museums fronting place du Cours, with the main **tourist office** on cours Honoré-Cresp (July–Sept Mon–Sat 9am–7pm, Sun 9am–6pm; Oct–June Mon–Sat 9am–12.30pm & 2–6pm; ☏04.93.36.66.66, ⓦwww.grasse-riviera.com). Should you arrive into the **gare SNCF**, take bus #2, #3 or #4 into town as it's a long walk uphill.

Accommodation options at the budget end of the market are limited and you would be better off basing yourself elsewhere, but if you get stuck, the *Charm Hôtel du Patti*, place du Patti (☏04.93.36.01.00, ⓦwww.hotelpatti.com; ⑤), is just below the bus station and on the edge of the old town.

The Town

Place aux Aires, at the top of **Vieux Grasse**, is the main meeting point of the town. This square is ringed by arcades of different heights and at one time was the exclusive preserve of the tanning industry. At the opposite end of Vieux Grasse lie the **cathedral** – containing various paintings, including one by local boy Jean-Honoré Fragonard, three by Rubens and a wondrous triptych by the sixteenth-century Niçois painter Louis Bréa – and the **bishop's palace**, now the Hôtel de Ville, both built in the twelfth century.

Though the main purpose of going to Grasse is to purchase perfume, it has several worthwhile small museums. The **Musée d'Art et d'Histoire de Provence**, 2 rue Mirabeau (May–Sept Mon–Sat 10am–7pm; Oct–April Mon–Sat 11am–6pm; €3), is housed in a luxurious town house commissioned by Mirabeau's sister as a place to entertain. As well as all the gorgeous fittings and an eighteenth-century kitchen, the collections are highly eclectic and include eighteenth- to nineteenth-century faïence from Apt and Le Castellet, Mirabeau's death mask, a tin bidet and six prehistoric bronze leg bracelets. The fascinating **Musée International de la Parfumerie**, 8 place du Cours (same hours as Musée d'Histoire; free), displays perfume bottles from the ancient Greeks via Marie-Antoinette to the present, and has a reconstruction of a perfume factory.

You can see more works by Jean-Honoré Fragonard in the **Villa-Musée Fragonard** at 23 bd Fragonard (same hours as Musée d'Histoire; free), where the celebrated Rococo painter returned to live after the Revolution. The staircase has impressive wall paintings by his son Alexandre-Evariste, while the salon is graced by copies of **Love's Progress in the Heart of a Young Girl**, which Jean-Honoré painted for Madame du Barry.

The perfume factories

There are thirty-odd **parfumeries** in and around Grasse, most of them making not perfume but essences-plus-formulas which are then sold to Dior, Lancôme, Estée Lauder and the like, who make up their own brand-name perfumes. One litre of pure rose essence can cost as much as €19,000; perfume contains twenty percent essence (eau de toilette and eau de Cologne considerably less). The grand Parisian couturiers, whose clothes, on strictly cost-accounting grounds, serve simply to promote the perfume, go to inordinate lengths to sell their latest fragrance, spending millions of euros a year on advertising alone.

The ingredients that the "nose" – as the creator of the perfume's formula is known – has to play with include resins, roots, moss, beans, bark, civet (extract of deer genitals also known as musk), ambergris (whale vomit), bits of beaver and musk from Tibetan goats. You can visit the various **showrooms**, with overpoweringly fragrant shops and guided tours in English, of the traditional perfume factory set-up (the actual working industrial complexes are strictly out of bounds). These visits are free and usually open daily without interruption in summer. There are three to choose from: **Fragonard**, 20 bd Fragonard (Feb–Oct daily 9am–6pm; Nov–Jan 9am–12.30pm & 2–6pm; ⓦ www.fragonard.com); **Galimard**, 73 route de Cannes (guided visits daily: summer 9am–7.30pm; winter 9am–noon & 2–6pm; ⓦ www.galimard.com); and **Molinard** at 60 bd Victor-Hugo (April–Sept daily Mon–Fri 9am–6.30pm; Oct–March Mon–Fri 9am–noon & 2–6pm, Sat 9am–noon & 2–6pm; ⓦ www.molinard.com).

Eating and drinking

Compared with the coastal towns Grasse isn't terribly well endowed with **restaurants**, though on place aux Aires there are a few along with friendly bars. The best in town is the four-star *La Bastide Saint-Antoine*, 48 rue Henri-Dunant (☏04.93.70.94.94, ⓦwww.jacques-chibois.com; ⓞ), which serves *cuisine gourmande* with a Provençal twist (lunch *menus* €59; otherwise *menus* from €145). Alternatively, *Lou Fassum*, 10km southeast of town at 381 rte de Plascassier (☏04.93.60.14.44; closed Tues in July & Aug; lunch *menu* €39), is a gourmet Provençal restaurant with an excellent lamb stew. At *Maison Venturini*, 1 rue Marcel Journet (☏04.93.36.20.47; closed Sun & Mon), you can buy sweet *fougassettes* – a local brioche, flavoured with the Grasse speciality of orange blossom – to take away.

Antibes and around

Graham Greene, who lived in **Antibes** for more than twenty years, considered it the only place on this stretch of coast to have preserved its soul. And although Antibes and its twin, **Juan-les-Pins**, have not escaped the overdevelopment that

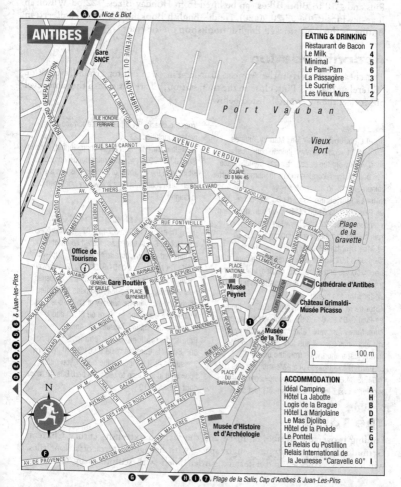

blights much of this region, they have avoided its worst excesses. Antibes itself is a pleasing old town, extremely animated, with one of the finest **markets** on the coast and the best **Picasso collection** in its ancient seafront castle; and the southern end of the Cap d'Antibes still has its woods of pine, in which some of the most exclusive mansions on the Riviera hide.

Arrival and information

Antibes' **gare SNCF** lies north of the old town at the top of avenue Robert Soleau. Turn right out of the station and three minutes' walk along avenue R.Soleau will bring you to place de Gaulle. The **tourist office** is on this square, at no. 11 (July & Aug daily 9am–7pm; Sept–June Mon–Fri 9am–12.30pm & 1.30–6pm, Sat 9am–noon & 2–6pm; plus Sun 10am–noon during April–June & Sept; ☎04.97.23.11.11, ⓦwww.antibesjuanlespins.com) with an annexe in Juan-les-Pins. The **gare routière** is east of here on place Guynemer with frequent buses to and from the **gare SNCF**. Bus #2 goes to Cap d'Antibes, bus #3 to Juan-les-Pins and #10 to Biot. **Bikes** can be hired from Holiday Bikes, 122 bd Wilson in Juan-les-Pins (☎04.93.20.90.20). Heidi's English Bookshop at place Audiberti in Antibes is the most stocked English **bookshop** on the coast.

Accommodation

The cheapest **hotels** in the Antibes-Juan-les-Pins area cluster around avenue de l'Estérel in Juan-les-Pins, close to the train station; all are basic with the same level of service, the nicer hotels listed below.

Hotels

Hôtel La Jabotte 13 av Max Maurey, Antibes ☎04.93.61.45.89, ⓦwww.jabotte.com. Just a short walk from the beach, this gay friendly place has beautifully decorated rooms in vibrant, cheerful colours – book in advance. ⑥–⑦

Hôtel La Marjolaine 15 av du Docteur Fabre, Juan-les-Pins ☎04.93.61.06.60. Romantically decorated rooms in a beautiful villa, between Juan-les-Pins train station and the beach. Parking €5. ④–⑤

Le Mas Djoliba 29 av de Provence, Antibes ☎04.93.34.02.48, ⓦwww.hotel-djoliba.com. With a pool, *boules* and a fabulous garden, this is a great hide away from the bustle of town and not too far from the beach. ⑦–⑧

Hôtel de la Pinède 7 av Georges Gallice, Juan-les-Pins ☎04.93.61.03.95, ⓦwww.hotel-pinede .com. Newly renovated with a friendly owner, this place has a small sun terrace and is in the centre, just a short walk from the beach. ⑤

Le Ponteil 11 impasse Jean-Mensier, Antibes ☎04.93.34.67.92, ⓦwww.leponteil.com. This large villa is set in residential streets just back from the beach. Breakfast on the terrace and parking included. ⑤–⑥

Le Relais du Postillon 8 rue Championnet, Antibes ☎04.93.34.20.77, ⓦwww.relaisdupostillon.com. Situated in the old town of Antibes, this has the feel of an old inn and also has a low-key bar (open till midnight). ④–⑤

Hostel and campsites

Idéal Camping ☎04.93.74.27.07, ⓦwww.ideal camping.fr. Small two-star, located south of the station and also en route to Nice. Closed Oct–April.

Logis de la Brague ☎04.93.33.54.72, ⓦwww .camping-logisbrague.com. As with all campsites near Antibes, this three-star campsite is situated north of the city in the *quartier* of La Brague (bus #10 or one train stop to "Gare de Biot") and is closest to the station. Closed Oct–April.

Relais International de la Jeunesse "Caravelle 60" Bd de la Garoupe ☎04.93.61.34.40, ⓦwww .clajsud.fr. As it is right by the beach, you must book well in advance to secure a bed. Bus #2 stops right outside. €18.

The Town

Lording it over the Antibes ramparts and the sea, the sixteenth-century **Château Grimaldi** is a beautifully cool, light space, with hexagonal terracotta floor tiles, windows over the sea and a terrace garden filled with sculptures by Germaine

Richier, Miró, César and others. In 1946 Picasso was offered the dusty building – by then already a museum – as a studio. Several extremely prolific months followed before he moved to Vallauris (see p.941), leaving all his Antibes output to what is now the **Musée Picasso** (mid-June to mid-Sept Tues–Sun 10am–6pm, Wed & Fri in July & Aug until 8pm; mid-Sept to mid-June Tues–Sun 10am–noon & 2–6pm; €6). Although Picasso donated other works later on, the bulk of the collection belongs to this one period. Picasso himself is the subject of works here by other painters and photographers, including Man Ray, Hans Hartung and Bill Brandt; there are also several anguished canvases by Nicolas de Staël, who stayed in Antibes for a few months from 1954 to 1955. Alongside the castle is the **Cathédrale d'Antibes**, built on the site of an ancient temple. The choir and apse survive from the Romanesque building that served the city in the Middle Ages while the nave and stunning ochre facade are Baroque. Inside, in the south transept, is a sumptuous medieval altarpiece surrounded by immaculate panels of tiny detailed scenes.

One block inland, the morning **covered market** (June–Aug daily 6am–1pm; Sept–May Tues–Sun 6am–1pm) on cours Masséna overflows with Provençal goodies and cut **flowers**, the traditional and still-flourishing Antibes business. In the afternoons (3–4pm), a **craft market** (June–Sept Tues & Thurs–Sun; Oct–May Fri, Sat & Sun only) takes over, and when the stalls pack up, café tables take their place.

Cap d'Antibes

Plage de la Salis, the longest Antibes beach, runs along the eastern neck of Cap d'Antibes, with no big hotels squatting its sands – an amazing rarity on the Riviera. To the south, at the top of chemin du Calvaire, you have superb views from the **Chapelle de la Garoupe** (daily 10am–noon & 2.30–5pm), which contains Russian spoils from the Crimean War and hundreds of **ex votos**. To the west, on boulevard du Cap between chemins du Tamisier and G.Raymond, you can wander around the **Jardin Thuret** (Mon–Fri: summer 8am–6pm, winter 8.30am–5.30pm; closed Sat & Sun; free; guided tours on request to ☎04.97.21.25.02), botanical gardens belonging to a national research institute. Back on the east shore, further south, lies a second public beach, **plage de la Garoupe**. From here a footpath follows the shore to join the chemin des Douaniers. At the southern end of the Cap d'Antibes, on avenue L.D. Beaumont, stands the grandiose **Villa Eilenroc** (gardens Tues & Wed 9am–5pm; villa Wed 9am–noon & 1.30–5pm; closed in July & Aug; free), designed by Charles Garnier, architect of the casino at Monte-Carlo, and surrounded by lush gardens. There are more sandy coves and little harbours along the western shore, where you'll also find the **Musée Napoléonien** (Tues–Sat: mid-June to mid-Sept 10am–6pm; mid-Sept to mid-June 10am–4.30pm; €3), at the end of avenue J.-F.-Kennedy. This documents the great man's return from Elba along with the usual Bonaparte paraphernalia of hats, cockades and signed commands. Much of the southern tip of the **cap** is a warren of private roads, including the area around the fabled **Hotel du Cap Eden Roc** and the so-called "bay of millionaires".

Juan-les-Pins

JUAN-LES-PINS, less than 2km from the centre of Antibes (a 15min walk or bus #1; 6.30am–9pm; €1), had its heyday in the interwar years, when the summer season on the Riviera first took off and the resort was the haunt of film stars like Charlie Chaplin, Maurice Chevalier and Lilian Harvey, the polyglot London-born 1930s musical star who lingered here until 1968, long after her fame had faded. Juan-les-Pins isn't as glamorous as it once was either, though it still has a casino and a certain cachet; the beaches are sand, so it is an attractive tourist destination.

Juan's **international jazz festival** – known simply as Jazz à Juan – takes place in the middle two weeks of July. It's the best in the region and is held in the central pine grove, the **Jardin de La Pinède** (known simply as La Pinède), and **square Gould** above the beach by the casino. A Hollywood-style walk of fame immortalizes various jazz greats at La Pinède, set into the pavement.

Eating, drinking and entertainment

Place Nationale and cours Masséna in Antibes are lined with **cafés**; rue James Close is nothing but **restaurants**, while there's a smattering of big pubs and ethnic places close to the port. Juan-les-Pins is not blessed with particularly memorable restaurants, so take pot luck from the countless *menus* on offer on the boulevards around La Pinède, in particular avenue du Docteur Dautheville. **Juan-les-Pins** still cuts a dash in the nightlife stakes, though. The fads and reputations of the different **discos** may change, but in general opening hours are midnight to dawn, and hefty entrance fees apply. Some of the current hotspots include *Le Milk* on avenue G.-Gallice and *Minimal* on boulevard Wilson. The most popular cocktail bar with frequent **live music** is *Le Pam-Pam*, 137 bd Wilson.

La Passagère Hotel Belles Rives 33 bd Édouard Baudoin, Juan-les-Pins ⊤ 04.93.61.02.79. Serves up modern Mediterranean delights in lovely, restored Art Deco surroundings with wonderful views over the bay; mains between €30 and €60.

Restaurant de Bacon Bd de Bacon, Cap d'Antibes, Antibes ⊤ 04.93.61.50.02. With excellent fish and a view of the sea, *Restaurant de Bacon* is renowned locally and has *menus* from €49. Closed Mon, Tues lunch & Nov–March.

Le Sucrier 6 rue des Bains, Antibes ⊤ 04.93.34.85.40. If you fancy tucking into *escargots sautés au Pernod*, this cosy and stylish restaurant is the place to go. *Menus* start at €26. Closed Mon.

Les Vieux Murs Av de l' Amiral-de-Grasse, Antibes ⊤ 04.93.34.06.73. Serves classy food in a perfect setting on the castle ramparts. Closed Mon all day & Tues lunch out of season. Lunch *menu* from €34, dinner *menu* €60.

Biot

Bus #10 connects Antibes with **BIOT**, 8km to the north, where Fernand Léger lived for a few years at the end of his life. A stunning collection of his intensely life-affirming works, created between 1905 and 1955, is on show at the **Musée Fernand Léger** (daily except Tues: June–Oct 10am–6pm; Nov–May 10am–5pm; €6.50). The museum is just east of the village on the chemin du Val de Pome, stop "Fernand Léger" on the Antibes bus, or a rather unpleasant and dangerous thirty-minute walk from Biot's *gare SNCF*.

The village itself is beautiful and oozes with art in every form – architectural, sculpted, ceramic, jewelled, painted and culinary. The **tourist office**, 46 rue Saint-Sébastien, at the western entrance to the village (June–Aug Mon–Fri 9.30am–6.30pm, Sat & Sun 11am–5pm; April, May & Sept Mon–Fri 9.30am–12.30pm & 1.30–6pm, Sat & Sun 2–6pm; ⊤ 04.93.65.78.00, W www .biot.fr) can provide a map showing the various glassworks – the traditional industry that brought Léger here, and which produces the famous hand-blown **bubble glass**.

If you book well in advance you could stay at the very reasonable *Hôtel des Arcades*, 16 place des Arcades (⊤ 04.93.65.01.04, ⓕ 04.93.65.01.05; ❸–❹), full of old-fashioned charm and with huge rooms in the medieval centre of the village. Its **café-restaurant**, which doubles as an art gallery, serves delicious Provençal food (closed Sun evening & Mon; *plats du jour* around €17).

Above the Baie des Anges

Between Antibes and Nice, the **Baie des Anges** laps at a long stretch of undistinguished built-up twentieth-century resorts and stores. The old towns such as **Cagnes**, lie inland. Cagnes is associated in particular with Renoir – as is **St-Paul-de-Vence**, which houses the wonderful modern art collection of the Fondation Maeght. **Vence** has a small chapel decorated by Matisse, and is a relaxing place to stay with no night life to speak of.

Cagnes

CAGNES is a confusing agglomeration, made up of the seaside district of Cros-de-Cagnes, the immaculate medieval village of Haut-de-Cagnes overlooking the town from the northwest, and Cagnes-sur-Mer, the traffic-choked town centre wedged between the two.

From Cagnes-sur-Mer, chemin des Collettes leads two kilometres off to the left up to **Les Collettes**, the house that Renoir had built in 1908 and where he spent the last twelve years of his life. It's now a **museum** (daily except Tues: May–Sept 10am–noon & 2–6pm; Oct–April 10am–noon & 2–5pm; check with museum for dates of annual winter closure; €4), and you can wander around the house and through the olive and rare orange groves that surround it. One of the two studios in the house is arranged as if Renoir had just popped out. Albert André's painting, *A Renoir Painting*, shows the ageing artist hunched over his canvas, plus there's a bust of him by Aristide Maillol, and a crayon sketch by Richard Guido. Bonnard and Dufy were also visitors to Les Collettes; Dufy's *Hommage à Renoir*, transposing a detail of *Le Moulin de la Galette*, hangs here. Renoir's own work is represented by several sculptures, some beautiful watercolours and ten paintings from his Cagnes period.

Arty **Haut-de-Cagnes** lives up to everything dreamed of in a Riviera *village perché*. The ancient village backs up to a crenellated feudal **château** (daily except Tues: May–Sept 10am–noon & 2–6pm; Oct–April 10am–noon & 2–5pm; free shuttle bus from bus station, or by foot, the steep ascent along rue Général-Bérenger and montée de la Bourgade), with a stunning Renaissance interior, housing museums of local history, olive cultivation, the **donation Solidor** – a diverse collection of paintings of the famous cabaret artist Suzy Solidor – plus an **olive museum** and exhibition space for **contemporary art**.

Practicalities

The **gare SNCF** Cagnes-sur-Mer (one stop from the *gare SNCF* Cros-de-Cagnes) is southwest of the centre alongside the autoroute; turn right on the northern side of the autoroute along avenue de la Gare to head into town. The sixth turning on your right, rue des Palmiers, leads to the **tourist office** at 6 bd Maréchal-Juin (Mon–Fri 9am–noon & 2–6pm, Sat 9am–noon, closed Sun); ☎04.93.20.61.64, ⓦwww.cagnes-tourisme.com). Buses #42, #49, #56 and #200 all make the short run from the *gare SNCF* to the **gare routière** on square Bourdet.

Cros-de-Cagnes has a good choice of **hotels** by the seafront, but also – despite recent traffic calming efforts – plenty of traffic. If you're feeling flush, try *Le Cagnard* on rue Sous-Barri (☎04.93.20.73.21, ⓦwww.le-cagnard.com; ❾), the beautiful guardroom for the castle further inland. **Campsites** are plentiful, and mostly in wooded locations inland; the two-star *Le Val Fleuri*, approximately 4km north (bus #41 during July & Aug) of Cros-de-Cagnes at 139 chemin Vallon des Vaux (☎04.93.31.21.74, ⓦwww.campingvalfleuri.fr; closed Nov–Jan), has a pool, bar and free wi-fi.

The best places to **eat** are in Haut-de-Cagnes, and, for café lounging, place du Château or place Grimaldi, to either side of the castle, are the obvious spots. *Fleur de Sel* at no 85 montée de la Bourgade (T04.92.20.33.33; closed Wed & Thurs lunch) serves octopus salad and *bourride de lotte*, with *menus* starting at €32, or there's *Josy-Jo*, 2 rue du Planastel (T04.93.20.68.76; mains around €30; closed Sat lunch & Sun) with Provençal delicacies dished up in the space that served as Expressionist painter Chaïm Soutine's workshop in the interwar years.

In summer there are free **jazz concerts** on place du Château and, at the end of August, a bizarre **square boules** competition takes place down montée de la Bourgade.

St-Paul-de-Vence: the Fondation Maeght

Further into the hills, the fortified village of **ST-PAUL-DE-VENCE** is home to yet another artistic treat, and one of the best in the whole region: the remarkable **Fondation Maeght** (daily: July–Sept 10am–7pm; Oct–June 10am–6pm; €14), created in the 1950s by Aimé and Marguerite Maeght, art collectors and dealers who knew all the great artists who worked in Provence. The Nice–Vence **bus** has two stops in St-Paul: alighting at the Village-Fondation Maeght stop, the first on the way up from Nice, the Fondation is a left turn up the hill from the round-about; from the village centre, head uphill along the steep street opposite the entrance to the village itself. By **car** or **bike**, follow the signs just before you reach the village, off the D7 from La-Colle-sur-Loup or the D2 from Villeneuve.

Through the gates is a sublime fusion of art, modern architecture and landscape. Alberto Giacometti's *Cat* stalks along the edge of the grass; Miró's *Egg* smiles above a pond; it's hard not to be bewitched by the Calder mobile swinging over watery tiles, by Léger's *Flowers, Birds and a Bench* on a sunlit rough stone wall, or by the clanking tubular fountain by Pol Bury. The building itself is superb: multi-levelled, flooded with daylight and housing a fabulous collection of works by Braque, Miró, Chagall, Léger and Matisse, among others. Not everything is exhibited at any one time, apart from what is permanently featured in the garden. There is also a good shop selling prints and some originals.

The other famous sights are in the extremely busy but beautiful *vieux village*. The hotel-restaurant **La Colombe d'Or** on place du Général-de-Gaulle (T04.93.32.80.02; W www.la-colombe-dor.com; O ; *plats du jour* from around €30 and up; closed Nov to late Dec) is celebrated not just for its food but for the art on its walls, donated in lieu of payment for meals by the then-impoverished Braque, Picasso, Matisse and Bonnard in the lean years following World War I. Rather fewer visitors make the pilgrimage to the simple grave of **Marc Chagall** on the right-hand side of the little **cemetery** (open during daylight hours) at the southern end of the village, running the gauntlet of the boutiques and galleries on rue Grande to get there.

Vence

A few kilometres north, **VENCE** has always been a town of some significance. The old town is blessed with numerous ancient houses, gateways, fountains, chapels and a **cathedral** containing Roman funeral inscriptions and a Chagall mosaic. In the 1920s it became a haven for painters and writers: André Gide, Raoul Dufy, D.H. Lawrence (who died here in 1930 while being treated for tuber-culosis contracted in England) and Marc Chagall were all long-term visitors, along with **Matisse** whose work is the reason most people come here.

Towards the end of World War II, Matisse moved to Vence to escape the Allied bombing of the coast, and his legacy is the town's most famous and exciting building, the **Chapelle du Rosaire**, at 466 av Henri-Matisse (Mon, Wed & Sat and school holidays 2–5.30pm, Tues & Thurs 10–11.30am & 2–5.30pm; closed mid-Nov to mid-Dec; €3.20), off the road to St-Jeannet, which leaves the town from carrefour Jean-Moulin at the top of avenue des Poilus. The chapel was his last work – consciously so – and not, as some have tried to explain, a religious conversion. "My only religion is the love of the work to be created, the love of creation, and great sincerity", he said in 1952 when the five-year project was completed.

The drawings on the chapel walls – black outline figures on white tiles – were executed by Matisse with a paintbrush fixed to a two-metre-long bamboo stick specifically to remove his own stylistic signature from the lines. He succeeded in this to the extent that many people are bitterly disappointed, not finding the "Matisse" they expect. Yet it is a total work – every part of the chapel is Matisse's design – and one that the artist was content with.

Vieux Vence has its share of chic boutiques and arty restaurants, but it also has an everyday feel about it, with ordinary people and run-of-the-mill cafés. On place du Frêne, by the western gateway, the fifteenth-century **Château de Villeneuve Fondation Emile Hugues** (Tues–Sun: 10am–12.30pm & 2–6pm; €5) provides a beautiful temporary exhibition space for the works of artists such as Matisse, Dufy, Dubuffet and Chagall.

Practicalities

Arriving by bus, you'll be dropped close to the **tourist office** on place du Grand-Jardin (July–Aug Mon–Sat 9am–7pm, Sun 10am–6pm; March–June & Sept–Oct Mon–Sat 9am–6pm; Nov–Feb Mon–Sat 9am–5pm; ℡04.93.58.06.38, ⓦwww .ville-vence.fr). You can rent **bikes** at Tendanas Cycles on avenue Henri Giraud.

Vence has some reasonable **places to stay**, such as the welcoming and peaceful *La Closerie des Genêts*, 4 impasse Maurel (℡04.93.58.35.18; ❷), off avenue M.-Maurel to the south of the old town with its own restaurant, and *Le Provence*, 9 av M.-Maurel (℡04.93.58.04.21, ⓦwww.hotelleprovence.com; ❷–❹), with a pleasant garden and a room with a small roof terrace. A little more luxury, including a pool, is on offer at *La Villa Roseraie*, avenue Henri Giraud (℡04.93.58.02.20, ⓦwww.villaroseraie.com; ❻–❼). There's a **campsite**, *La Bergerie*, 3km west off the road to Tourettes-sur-Loup (℡04.93.58.09.36, ⓦwww .camping-domainedelabergerie.com; closed mid-Oct to late March).

For a special **meal** in a beautiful courtyard, try *La Farigoule*, 15 av Henri Isnard (℡04.93.58.01.27; closed Tues; *menus* from €29). For more run-of-the-mill cuisine, try the astounding choice of pizzas from €13 at *Le Pêcheur du Soleil*, 1 place Godeau.

Nice

The capital of the Riviera and fifth largest city in France, **NICE** lives off a glittering reputation, its former glamour now gently faded. First popularized by English aristocrats in the eighteenth century, Nice reached its zenith in the *belle époque* of the late nineteenth century, an era that left the city with several extraordinary architectural flights of fancy. Today, more than a quarter of Nice's residents are over 60, their pensions and investments contributing to the high ratio of per capita income to economic activity.

Far too large to be considered simply a beach resort, Nice has all the advantages and disadvantages of a major city: superb culture, wonderful street life and excellent shopping, eating and drinking, but also a high crime rate, graffiti and horrendous traffic, all set against a backdrop of blue skies, sparkling sea and sub-tropical greenery kept lush by sprinklers.

Nice's charm is at odds with its history of reactionary **politics**. For decades municipal power was the monopoly of a dynasty whose corruption was finally exposed in 1990, when Mayor Jacques Médecin fled to Uruguay, only to be extradited and jailed. From his prison cell, he backed Jacques Peyrat, a former Front National member and frie nd of Jean-Marie Le Pen, in the 1995 local elections. Peyrat won with ease and retained the mayoralty until 2008, when he was defeated

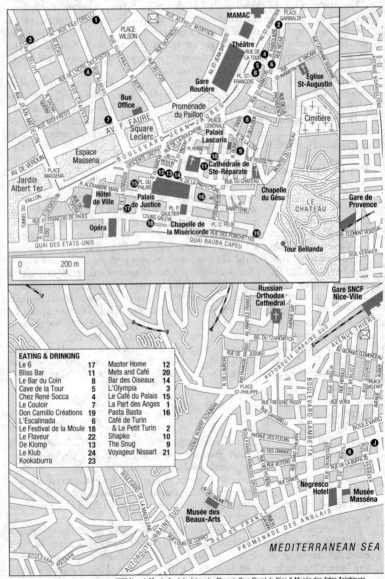

EATING & DRINKING

Le 6	17	Master Home	12
Bliss Bar	11	Mets and Café	20
Le Bar du Coin	8	Bar des Oiseaux	14
Cave de la Tour	5	L'Olympia	3
Chez René Socca	4	Le Café du Palais	15
Le Couloir	7	La Part des Anges	1
Don Camillo Créations	19	Pasta Basta	16
L'Escalinada	6	Café de Turin	
Le Festival de la Moule	18	& Le Petit Turin	2
Le Flaveur	22	Shapko	10
De Klomp	13	The Snug	9
Le Klub	24	Voyageur Nissart	21
Kookaburra	23		

▼ *Airport, Musée Anatole Jakovsky, Phoenix Parc Floral de Nice & Musée des Artes Asiatiques*

by Christian Estrosi, the locally-born son of Italian parents and the candidate of the mainstream centre-right Nice Ensemble.

Nice has retained its historical styles almost intact: the medieval rabbit warren of **Vieux Nice**, the Italianate facades of **modern Nice** and the rich exuberance of **fin-de-siècle residences** dating from when the city was Europe's most fashionable winter retreat. It has also retained mementos from its ancient past, when the

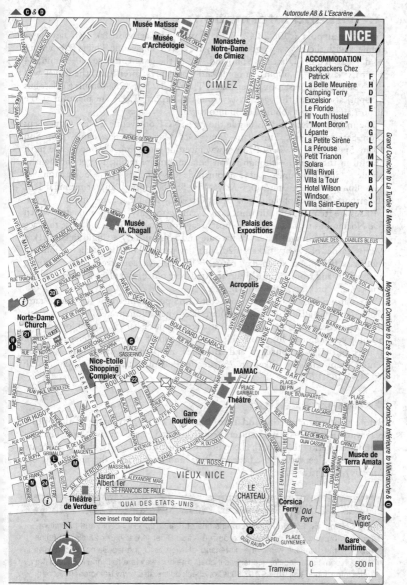

▲ **C** & **D**

Autoroute A8 & L'Escarène ▲

NICE

Musée Matisse

Musée d'Archéologie

Monastère Notre-Dame de Cimiez

CIMIEZ

ACCOMMODATION

Backpackers Chez Patrick	F
La Belle Meunière	H
Camping Terry	D
Excelsior	I
Le Floride	E
HI Youth Hostel "Mont Boron"	O
Lépante	G
La Petite Sirène	L
La Pérouse	P
Petit Trianon	M
Solara	N
Villa Rivoli	K
Villa la Tour	B
Hotel Wilson	A
Windsor	J
Villa Saint-Exupery	C

Grand Corniche to La Turbie & Menton ▶

Moyenne Corniche to Eze & Monaco ▶

Corniche Inférieure to Villefranche & **O** ▶

Musée M. Chagall

Palais des Expositions

AVENUE DES DIABLES BLEUS ▶

TUNNEL MALRAUX

Acropolis

BOULEVARD PIERRE SOLA

Norte-Dame Church

MAMAC

Nice-Etoile Shopping Complex

Théâtre

Gare Routière

VICTOR HUGO

Jardin Albert 1er

VIEUX NICE

LE CHATEAU

Musée de Terra Amata

Théâtre de Verdure

QUAI DES ETATS-UNIS

See inset map for detail

Corsica Ferry

Old Port

Parc Vigier

N

QUAI RAUBA CAPEU

PLACE GUYNEMER

Gare Maritime

Tramway

0   500 m

Romans ruled the region from here, and earlier still, when the Greeks founded the city. Nice's many museums are a treat for art lovers: within France the city is second only to Paris for art.

Of late the city has been smartening up its act with extensive **refurbishment** of its public spaces and the construction of a new **tramway**. Conservative it may be, but Nice does not rest on its laurels.

Arrival and information

From the **airport** (☎08.20.42.33.33, ⓦwww.nice.aeroport.fr), two fast buses connect with the city: #99 goes to the **gare SNCF** on avenue Thiers (25–30min; €4 day pass required, last bus 9pm) and #98 to the **gare routière** (20–35min; €4 day pass; last bus 11.50pm) on boulevard Jean-Jaurès; after 9pm, the driver will take you to the train station when asked. The regular bus #23 (40min; €1; last bus 8.50pm) also serves the *gare SNCF* from the airport. **Taxis** are plentiful at the airport and will cost about €30–35 into town.

The main **tourist office** is beside the *gare SNCF* on avenue Thiers (June–Sept Mon–Sat 8am–8pm, Sun 9am–7pm; Oct–May Mon–Sat 8am–7pm, Sun 10am–5pm; ☎08.92.70.74.07, ⓦwww.nicetourisme.com). It's one of the most helpful in the region – though it can be a nightmare trying to get through by phone – and has annexes at 5 promenade des Anglais (June–Sept Mon–Sat 8am–8pm, Sun 9am–7pm; Oct–May Mon–Sat 9am–6pm), and at terminal 1 of the airport (June–Sept daily 8am–9pm; Oct–May Mon–Sat 8am–9pm).

Buses are frequent and run until early evening (roughly 7.30–9pm), after which five Noctambus night buses serve most areas from Station Bermand close to place Masséna until 1.10am. Fares are flat-rate and you can buy a single ticket (€1), a Multi+ carnet of twenty tickets (€20), or a day pass (€4) on the bus; a ten-journey multipass (€10) and seven-day passes (€15) are available from *tabacs*, kiosks, newsagents and from Ligne d'Azur, the transport office, at 3 place Masséna, where you can also pick up a free route map.

Taxis around town are scarce, and cost €1.68 per kilometre by day; night rates (7pm–7am and all day at weekends) are €2.24 per kilometre. There are various surcharges. Scams are not unknown: if a restaurant or bar calls a cab for you, it's possible you'll enjoy a luxurious ride home in a top-of-the-range Mercedes – with a hefty bill at your journey's end. **Bicycles**, **mopeds** and **motorbikes** can be rented from Holiday Bikes at 23 rue de Belgique just by the *gare SNCF* (☎04.93.16.01.62).

Accommodation

Before hunting for **accommodation**, it's worth taking advantage of the **online reservation service** (ⓦwww.niceres.com) operated by the tourist office. The area around the station teems with cheap hotels, some of them seedy, though there are a few gems. Sleeping on the beach is illegal and impractical: the promenade des Anglais is brightly illuminated.

Chemin de Fer de Provence

The **Chemin de Fer de Provence** runs one of France's most scenic and fun railway routes, from the Gare de Provence on rue Alfred Binet (4 daily; 3hr 25min). The line runs up the Var valley into the hinterland of Nice to Digne-les-Bains, and climbs through some spectacular scenery as it goes. The one-way fare to Digne is €17.65 (for more information call ☎04.97.03.80.80 or check online at ⓦwww.trainprovence.com).

Hotels

Excelsior 19 av Durante ☎04.93.88.18.05, ⓦwww.excelsiornice.com. Nicely appointed rooms, with slightly outdated decor, and a lovely garden where guests can eat breakfast. ❸–❺

Le Floride 52 bd de Cimiez ☎04.93.53.11.02, ⓦwww.hotel-floride.fr. Friendy, small hotel in Cimiez, with some cheap singles. Free private parking. ❸

Lépante 6 rue Lépante ☎04.93.62.20.55, ⓦwww .hotellepante.com. Smart, comfortable and gay-friendly, with a central location, wi-fi, a/c and a first-floor sunny balcony with lots of seating. ❺–❻

La Pérouse 11 quai Rauba-Capeu ☎04.93.62.34.63, ⓦwww.hotel-la-perouse.com. The best-situated hotel in central Nice, at the foot of Le Château with a roof-top pool. This is where to go if you get lucky in Monte-Carlo. ❾

Petit Trianon 11 rue Paradis ☎04.93.87.50.46, ⓔhotel.nice.lepetittrianon@orange.fr. Recently refurbished hotel in a great location; each room has its own laptop providing free wi-fi. ❺

🏃 **La Petite Sirène** 8 rue Maccarani ☎04.97.03.03.40, ⓦwww.sirene-fr.com. Hans Christian Andersen-inspired paintings adorn the walls of these well-equipped rooms, some with huge terraces. There is also a pricey penthouse on the top floor. ❻–❼

Solara 7 rue de France ☎04.93.88.09.96, ⓦwww.hotelsolara.com. With double-glazing, a/c, fridge and balcony, this renovated hotel is great value. There is also a large room sleeping four. ❺

Villa Rivoli 10 rue de Rivoli ☎04.93.88.80.25, ⓦwww.villa-rivoli.com. Sweet hotel with a lovely breakfast room and 3 parking spaces (€15). ❹–❼

Villa la Tour 4 rue de la Tour ☎04.93.80.08.15, ⓦwww.villa-la-tour.com. Lovely place located in Vieux Nice, this has a few rooms with great views over the city. It's next to a nightclub, so avoid Thurs–Sat nights, unless you're a deep sleeper. ❺–❼

🏃 **Hotel Wilson** 39 rue de l'Hôtel-des-Postes ☎04.93.85.47.79, ⓦwww.hotel-wilson -nice.com. A stylish and gay-friendly guesthouse on the third floor in a great location, with a quirky fingerprint entry system. ❷–❸

Windsor 11 rue Dalpozzo ☎04.93.88.59.35, ⓦwww.hotelwindsornice.com. Appealing hotel, close to the casino and with a small pool in a partially shaded garden, overgrown with bamboo. ❼

Hostels

Backpackers Chez Patrick First floor (there is another hostel downstairs), 32 rue Pertinax ☎04.93.80.30.72, ⓦwww.backpackerschez patrick.com. Clean and a/c hostel close to the station, with eating facilities and no curfew. €25.

La Belle Meunière 21 av Durante ☎04.93.88.66.15, ⓦwww.bellemeuniere.com. Efficient and friendly backpacker hotel in a lovely old bourgeois house. Some rooms are shabby, but clean enough and there is a front yard with seating area. Closed Dec and Jan. Dorm €18–24 including breakfast. Rooms sleeping up to three people ❸ are also available.

HI Youth Hostel "Mont Boron" Rte Forestière du Mont-Alban ☎04.93.89.23.64, ⓦwww.fuaj.org. Four kilometres out of town. Take bus #14 from Station J.C. Bermond (direction "place du Mont-Boron", stop "L'Auberge"); the last bus that runs as far as the hostel leaves at 7.35pm. €18.20 per dorm bed. Reception 7–10am & 5–midnight. Open June–Sept.

🏃 **Villa Saint-Exupery** 22 av Gravier ☎04.93.84.42.83, ⓦwww.vsaint.com. Impressively well-equipped family-run hostel in an old nunnery, some way out of central Nice, with bar, internet, kitchen and laundry facilities. Tram from Place Masséna direction Las Planas, stop "Comte de Falicon", where staff will pick you up. €30.

Campsite

Camping Terry 768 rte de Grenoble, St-Isidore ☎04.93.08.11.58. The only campsite anywhere near Nice, 6.5km north of the airport on the D6202; take the #59 bus from the *gare routière* to "Saint-Isidore" stop (or ask the driver to drop you at the site), or the Chemins de Fer de la Provence train to "Bellet".

The City

It doesn't take long to get a feel for the layout of Nice. Shadowed by mountains that curve down to the Mediterranean east of its port, it still breaks up more or less into old and new. **Vieux Nice**, the old town, groups about the hill of **Le Château**, its limits signalled by **boulevard Jean-Jaurès**, built along the course of the River Paillon. Along the seafront, the celebrated **promenade des Anglais** runs a cool 5km until forced to curve inland by the sea-projecting runways of the airport. The central square, **place Masséna**, is at the bottom of the modern city's main street, **avenue Jean-Médecin**, while off to the north is the exclusive hillside suburb of **Cimiez**.

The château and Vieux Nice

For initial orientation, with fantastic sea and city views, fresh air and the scent of Mediterranean vegetation, head for **Le Château park** (daily: April, May & Sept 9am–7pm; June–Aug 9am–8pm; Oct–March 10am–6.30pm). It's where Nice began as the ancient Greek city of Nikaïa, hence the mosaics and stone vases in mock Grecian style. There's no château to see, just wonderful views over the scrambled rooftops and gleaming mosaic tiles of Vieux Nice and along the sweep of the promenade des Anglais. To reach the park, you can take the lift by the Tour Bellanda (€0.90 one way, €1.20 both ways) at the eastern end of quai des États-Unis, or climb the steps from rue de la Providence or montée du Château in the old town.

Vieux Nice has been greatly gentrified in recent years, but the expensive shops, smart restaurants and art galleries still coexist with humbler shops, there's washing strung between the tenements overhead, and away from the showpiece squares a certain shabbiness lingers. Tourism now dominates Vieux Nice: throbbing with life day and night in August, much of it seems deserted in November. It is best explored on foot.

The central square is **place Rossetti**, where the soft-coloured Baroque **Cathédrale de Ste-Réparate** (Mon–Sat 9am–noon & 2–6pm, Sun 3–6pm) just manages to be visible in the concatenation of eight narrow streets. There are cafés to relax in, and a fabulous ice-cream parlour, *Fenocchio*, with an extraordinary choice of flavours. The real magnet of the old town, though, is **cours Saleya** and the adjacent place Pierre-Gautier and place Charles-Félix. These are wide-open, sunlit spaces alongside grandiloquent municipal buildings and Italianate chapels, and are the site of the city's main **market**. Every day except Monday from 6am to 1.30pm there are gorgeous displays of fruit, vegetables, cheeses and sausages, plus cut flowers and potted roses, mimosa and other scented plants displayed till at least 5.30pm (except Sunday afternoons); on Monday the stalls sell bric-a-brac and secondhand clothes (5.30am–6pm). Café and restaurant tables fill the *cours* on summer nights.

To feast your eyes on Baroque splendour, pop into the **chapels** and **churches** of Vieux Nice (opening times vary depending on activity): La Chapelle de la Miséricorde, on cours Saleya; L'Église du Gésu, on rue Droite; or L'Église St-Augustin, on place St-Augustin, which also contains a fine pietà by Louis Bréa.

Also on rue Droite is the **Palais Lascaris** (daily except Tues 10am–6pm; free), a seventeenth-century palace built by the Duke of Savoy's Field-Marshal, Jean-Paul Lascaris, whose family arms, engraved on the ceiling of the entrance hall, bear the motto "Not even lightning strikes us". It's all very sumptuous, with frescoes, tapestries and chandeliers, along with a collection of porcelain vases from an eighteenth-century pharmacy.

For contemporary graphic and photographic art, check out the best **art galleries** (all Tues–Sat 10am–6pm; free) which include: Galerie de la Marine, 59 quai des États-Unis; Galerie des Ponchettes, 77 quai des États-Unis; and Galerie a, 14 rue Sainte-Réparate (closed 1–2pm).

Place Masséna and around

The stately, largely pedestrianized **place Masséna** is the hub of the new town, built in 1835 across the path of the River Paillon. A balustraded terrace and steps on the south of the square lead to Vieux Nice; the new town lies to the north. A short walk to the west lie the **Jardins Albert 1er**, where the Théâtre de Verdure occasionally hosts summer concerts.

The covered course of the Paillon northeast of place Masséna is the site of the city's more recent prestige projects. Most appealing of these is the marble **Musée d'Art Moderne et d'Art Contemporain**, or MAMAC (Tues–Sun 10am–6pm; Ⓦwww.mamac-nice.org; free), with rotating exhibitions of avant-garde French and American movements from the 1960s to the present. New Realism (smashing, burning, squashing and wrapping the detritus or mundane objects of everyday life) and Pop Art feature strongly with works by Warhol, Klein, Lichtenstein, César, Arman and Christo.

Running north from place Masséna, **avenue Jean–Médecin** is the city's nondescript main shopping street, cheered up slightly by the revamped Nice-Étoile **shopping complex** between rue Biscarra and boulevard Dubouchage; there are branches of FNAC and Virgin nearby for books, CDs and concert tickets. **Couturier** shops sit west of place Masséna on rue du Paradis and rue Alphonse Karr. Both these streets intersect with the pedestrianized **rue Masséna** and the end of **rue de France** – true holiday territory, all ice-cream parlours and big brasseries, and always crammed.

Western Nice is chiefly memorable for its flamboyant and exotic flights of architectural fancy, like the **Russian Orthodox Cathedral** (daily except Sun morn: mid-Feb to April & Oct 9.15am–noon & 2.30–5.30pm; May–Sept 9am–noon & 2.30–6pm; Nov to mid-Feb 9.30am–noon & 2.30–5pm; €3), at the end of avenue Nicolas-II, which runs off boulevard du Tsaréwitch, reached by bus #14 or #17 (stop Tzaréwitch).

The promenade des Anglais and the beaches

The point where the Paillon flows into the sea marks the beginning of the **promenade des Anglais**, created by nineteenth-century English residents for their afternoon strolls. Today, along with lots of traffic, it boasts some of the most fanciful turn-of-the-twentieth-century architecture on the Côte d'Azur. At nos. 13–15, the Palais de la Méditerranée is once again a luxurious casino, though the splendid Art Deco facade is all that remains of the 1930s original.

Most celebrated of all is the opulent, vaguely eccentric **Negresco Hotel** at no. 37 built in 1906, and occupying the block between rues de Rivoli and Cronstadt. Provided you're wearing *tenue correcte* you can try wandering in to see the Salon Louis XIV and the Salon Royale. Salon Louis XIV, on the left of the foyer, has a seventeenth-century painted oak ceiling and mammoth fireplace, plus royal portraits, all from various French châteaux. The Salon Royale, in the centre of the hotel, is a vast domed oval room, decorated with 24-carat gold leaf and the biggest carpet ever to have come out of the Savonnerie workshops. The chandelier is one of a pair commissioned from Baccarat by Tsar Nicholas II – the other hangs in the Kremlin.

Just before the *Negresco*, with its entrance at 65 rue de France, stands the **Musée Masséna** (open daily except Tues 10am–6pm), the city's art and history museum, which charts the city's development from Napoleonic times up to the 1930s. A kilometre or so down the promenade and a couple of blocks inland at 33 av des Baumettes lies the **Musée des Beaux-Arts** (Tues–Sun 10am–6pm; free; bus #23, stop "Grosso"), where the chief glory is the collection of 28 works by Raoul Dufy, who is intimately connected with the visual image of Nice. Continuing southwest along the promenade des Anglais towards the airport, you'll find the **Musée International d'Art Naïf Anatole Jakovsky** (daily except Tues 10am–6pm; free), home to a surprisingly good collection of amateur art from around the world.

The **beach** below the promenade des Anglais is all pebbles and mostly public, with showers provided. It's not particularly clean and you need to watch out for broken glass. There are fifteen private beaches, clustering at the more scenic, eastern end of the bay close to Vieux Nice. If you don't mind rocks, you might want to try the string of coves beyond the port that starts with the **plage de la Réserve**, opposite Parc Vigier (bus #20 or #30).

On the far side of the castle sits the **old port**, flanked by gorgeous red and ochre eighteenth-century buildings and headed by the Neoclassical Notre-Dame du Port; it's full of yachts but has little quayside life despite the restaurants along quai Lunel.

Cimiez

Packed with vast *belle-époque* piles, many of them former hotels, the northern suburb of **Cimiez** has always been posh. The heights of Cimiez were the social centre of the local elite some 1700 years ago, when the town was capital of the Roman province of Alpes-Maritimae. Part of a small amphitheatre still stands, and excavations of the **Roman baths** have revealed enough detail to distinguish the sumptuous and elaborate facilities for the top tax official and his cronies, the plainer public baths and a separate complex for women. All the finds, plus an illustration of the town's history up to the Middle Ages, are displayed in the **Musée d'Archéologie**, 160 av des Arènes (daily except Tues 10am–6pm; free; bus #15, #17 or #22, stop "Arènes").

The seventeenth-century villa between the excavations and the arena is the **Musée Matisse** (daily except Tues 10am–6pm; Ⓦ www.musee-matisse-nice.org; free). Matisse spent his winters in Nice from 1916 onwards, staying in hotels on the promenade – from where *A Storm at Nice* was painted – and then from 1921 to 1938 renting an apartment overlooking place Charles Félix. It was here that he painted his most sensual, colour-flooded canvases of odalisques posed against exotic draperies. As well as the Mediterranean light, Matisse loved the cosmopolitan aspect of Nice and the presence of fellow artists Renoir, Bonnard and Picasso in neighbouring towns. He died in Cimiez in November 1954, aged 85.

The Roman remains and the Musée Matisse back onto an old olive grove, one of the best open spaces in Nice and venue for the July **jazz festival**. At its eastern end are the sixteenth-century buildings and exquisite gardens of the **Monastère Notre-Dame de Cimiez** (Mon–Sat 10am–noon & 3–6pm; free); the oratory has brilliant murals illustrating alchemy, while the church houses three masterpieces of medieval painting by Louis and Antoine Bréa.

At the foot of Cimiez hill, just off boulevard Cimiez on avenue du Docteur Menard, **Chagall's Biblical Message** is housed in a **museum** (daily except Tues: May–Oct 10am–6pm; Nov–April 10am–5pm; €7.50, €9.50 during temporary exhibitions; bus #22, stop "Musée Chagall") built specially for the work and opened by the artist in 1972. The rooms are light, white and cool, with windows allowing you to see the greenery of the garden beyond the indescribable shades between pink and red of the *Song of Songs* canvases. The seventeen paintings are all based on the Old Testament and complemented with etchings and engravings.

The Phoenix Parc Floral de Nice

Right out by the airport, the **Phoenix Parc Floral de Nice**, 405 promenade des Anglais (daily: April–Sept 9.30am–7.30pm; Oct–March 9.30am–6pm; €2; exit St-Augustin from the highway from Nice or Promenade des Anglais from Cannes or bus #9, #10 or #23 from Nice), is a cross between a botanical garden, aviary and tacky theme park. The best reason to visit is to see the **Musée Départemental des Arts Asiatiques** (daily except Tues: May to mid-Oct 10am–6pm; mid-Oct to April 10am–5pm; Ⓦ www.arts-asiatiques.com; free), housed in a beautiful building designed by Japanese architect Kenzo Tange. It houses a collection of ethnographic artefacts, including silk goods and pottery, as well as traditional and contemporary art.

Eating, drinking and entertainment

Nice is a great place for **eating**, whether you're picnicking on market fare, snacking on Niçois specialities or dining in the palace hotels. The Italian influence is strong, with pasta on every *menu*; seafood is also a staple. For **snacks**, many of the cafés sell sandwiches with typically Provençal fillings such as fresh basil, olive oil, goat's cheese and *mesclun*, the unique green salad mix of the region. Despite the usual fast-food chains and tourist traps dotted around, most areas of Nice have plenty of reasonable restaurants. Vieux Nice has a dozen on every street catering for a wide variety of budgets; the port quaysides have good, but pricey, fish restaurants. In summer it's wise to book tables or turn up before 8pm, especially in Vieux Nice.

Vieux Nice is also the centre of Nice's lively **pub** and **club** scene, much of it anglophone in character. A good place to set out is along rue Central in the old town, where many pubs have early-evening happy hours. Many Vieux Nice bars boast huge selections of beers and spirits and offer regular live music. As for Niçois nightclubs, bouncers judging your wallet or exclusive membership lists are the rule.

Nice's **lesbian and gay** nightlife scene is surprisingly active given the city's reactionary reputation, and for lesbian and gay visitors the city has a relaxed feel. The annual Pink Parade takes place in early summer.

The **Mardi Gras Carnival** opens the year's events in Nice in February (Ⓦ www .nicecarnaval.com), with the last week of July taken up by the **Nice Jazz Festival** in the Parc de Cimiez (Ⓦ www.nicejazzfestival.fr for info, or contact the main tourist office in May/June).

Cafés

Le Café du Palais Place du Palais. A prime alfresco lounging spot on the handsome square by the Palais de Justice.
Cave de la Tour 3 rue de la Tour Ⓣ 04.93.80.03.31. Local *bar à vins* that serves wine from the bottle or, for the more daring, straight from huge vats. Dishes around €10.
L'Olympia 42 rue Pastorelli. This place serves carpaccio and tartare for around €10 and solid, French food. 6.30am–9pm. Closed Sun.

Restaurants

🏃 **Le Bar du Coin** 2 rue Droite Ⓣ 04.93.62.32.59. Popular with the locals and set in a square in the old town. Pizzas start at €8 and are very tasty indeed.
Chez René Socca 2 rue Miralhéti, off rue Pairolière. The cheapest meal in town: you can buy helpings of *socca*, *pissaladière*, stuffed peppers, pasta or *calamares* at the counter up to 9pm and eat with your fingers; the bar opposite serves the drinks. Closed Mon & Jan.
Don Camillo Créations 5 rue des Ponchettes Ⓣ 04.93.85.67.95. Elegant modern restaurant with contemporary Niçois/Italian cooking on a €42 *menu*. Closed Sun & Mon.
L'Escalinada 22 rue Pairolière Ⓣ 04.93.62.11.71. Good Niçois specialities on a €24 *menu* – *pissaladière* to start, then you help yourself to chickpea salad from a huge pot. The location is pretty, at the foot of a stepped side street.
Le Festival de la Moule 20 cours Saleya Ⓣ 04.93.62.02.12. If you like mussels, come here. There are eleven sauces to choose from and a pot is around €14 with free refills.
Le Flaveur 25 rue Gubernati Ⓣ 04.93.62.53.95. Friendly gastro restaurant with creative dishes, such as salmon with kiwano fruit, that make this a

new local favourite. *Menus* from €15 (lunch) to €55. Closed Sat lunch & Sun and Mon.
Kookaburra 20 quai des Docks Ⓣ 04.89.00.12.65. Charming Aussie-run place with emu on the *menu* and live jazz on Mon. Around €20 for mains.
Mets and Café 28 rue Assalit Ⓣ 04.93.80.30.85. Busy budget brasserie close to many of the backpacker hostels, with a €10.50 *menu*. Closed Sun.
🏃 **La Part des Anges** 17 rue Gubernati Ⓣ 04.93.62.69.80. A wine lover's haven. Classic French food and fabulous wines are served from 10.30am–8pm on weekdays and open till midnight Fri & Sat.
Pasta Basta 18 rue de la Préfecture Ⓣ 04.93.80.03.57. Excellent fresh pasta and sauce from around €10 – the choice is bewildering – and they hand you the block of parmesan to grate yourself. Inexpensive pizza and bruschetta too.
Café de Turin & Le Petit Turin 5 place Garibaldi Ⓣ 04.93.62.29.52. So good, they had to branch out, but thankfully only next door. There's a great emphasis on *fruits de mer*, €20–€40.
🏃 **Voyageur Nissart** 19 rue Alsace-Lorraine Ⓣ 04.93.82.19.60. Excellent, stable French food like your (French) mum made it, along with a great crème brûlée. *Menus* start at €16. Closed Sat lunch & Mon.

Bars, clubs and live entertainment

Le 6 6 rue Raoul Bosio. Popular lesbian and gay music bar, with regular live entertainment and DJs. Tues–Sun from 10pm.
Bar des Oiseaux 5 rue St-Vincent. Named for the birds that once nested in the loft of this bar. There's also an old-fashioned small cabaret stage. Lunch-times Mon–Fri and eves Thurs–Sat.

Bliss Bar 12 rue de L'Abbaya. Funk, groove and disco in this fun and stylish clubbing place with a doorman, who decides if you get in or not. Tues–Sat 8pm–2am.

Le Couloir 1 rue Alberti. Friendly gay place where the bar stretches the length of the tiny room – it's almost impossible not to get chatting.

De Klomp 6 rue Mascoïnat. Dutch-style brown café with big selection of beers and whiskies and regular live music. Mon–Sat 5.30pm–2.30am.

Le Klub 6 rue Halévy. Nice's largest and best gay club attracts a young, stylish crowd including women and some heteros. Open Wed–Sun; entry charge varies according to night.

Master Home 11 rue de la Préfecture. With live music Wed & Sun 7–10 and DJs otherwise playing everything from chill out or clubbing to Top 50, this is the current mainstream place in town; open till 2am. Closed Sun & Mon.

Shapko 5 rue Rossetti. Intimate and friendly place with a relaxed crowd and live music every night except Tuesday, when there's karaoke. Sometimes decent live electronica. Happy hour Tues/Wed all night. Closed Mon.

The Snug 22 rue Droite. Small and low-key Irish bar with a friendly atmosphere and a few tables outside, close to place Rossetti.

Listings

Books The Cat's Whiskers, 30 rue Lamartine, sells English-language books.

Car rental Major firms have offices at the airport and/or at the *gare SNCF* on av Thiers. Try also: Avis, 2 av Phocéens ⑂04.93.80.63.52; Europcar, 3 av Gustave-V ⑂08.25.82.76.74; or Hertz, 9 av Gustav-V ⑂04.93.87.11.87.

Cinema Rialto, 4 rue de Rivoli (⑂08.92.68.00.41) shows subtitled films in the original language (v.o.).

Consulates Canada, 2 place Franklin ⑂04.93.92.93.22; UK, 22 av Notre-Dame ⑂04.93.62.94.95; USA, 7 av Gustave-V, 3rd floor ⑂04.93.88.89.55.

Disabled travellers Transport for people with reduced mobility ⑂04.97.11.40.53.

Ferries SNCM *gare maritime*, quai du Commerce ⑂04.93.13.66.99, ⑽www.sncm.fr; Corsica Ferries, quai Amiral-Infernet ⑂08.25.09.50.95.

Health SOS Médecins ⑂08.10.85.01.01; Riviera Medical Services (English-speaking doctors) ⑂04.93.26.12.70; Hôpital St-Roch, 5 rue Pierre Dévoluy ⑂04.92.03.33.33; SOS Dentaire ⑂04.93.01.14.14.

Internet Internet Café, 30 rue Pertinax; Taxi Phone Internet, 10 rue de Belgique and at 25 rue Paganini.

Lost property 1 rue Raoul Bosio ⑂04.97.13.44.10.

Police Commissariat Central de Police, 1 av Maréchal Foch ⑂04.92.17.22.22.

Post office 21 av Thiers.

Taxis ⑂04.93.13.78.78. 24hr service.

The Corniches

Three **corniche roads** run east from Nice to the independent principality of Monaco and to Menton, the last town of the French Riviera. Napoleon built the **Grande Corniche** on the route of the Romans' Via Julia Augusta, and the **Moyenne Corniche** dates from the first quarter of the twentieth century, when aristocratic tourism on the Riviera was already causing congestion on the lower, coastal road, the **Corniche Inférieure**. The upper two are the classic location for car commercials, and for movie car crashes. Real deaths occur too – most notoriously that of Princess Grace of Monaco – a bitter irony, since the corniches had been the backdrop to one of her greatest film successes, *To Catch a Thief*.

Buses take all three routes; the **train** follows the lower corniche, and all three are superb means of seeing the most mountainous stretch of the Côte d'Azur. **Hotel** rooms between Nice and Menton are relatively scarce and mostly expensive.

The Corniche Inférieure

VILLEFRANCHE-SUR-MER is on the far side of Mont Alban from Nice. The cruise liners attracted by the deep-water anchorage in its beautiful bay can somewhat spoil the ambiance, but as long as your visit doesn't coincide with shore

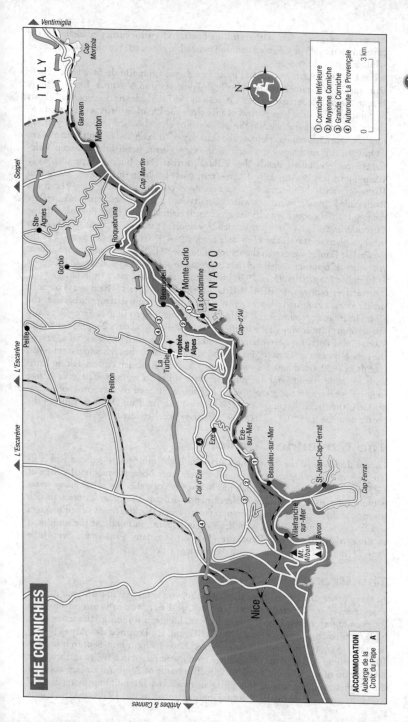

THE CÔTE D'AZUR

16

THE CORNICHES

Ventimiglia

ITALY

Cap Mortola

Sospel

Garavan
Menton

Cap Martin

Ste-Agnes

Roquebrune

Gorbio

Beausoleil

Monte Carlo

MONACO

La Condamine

Peille

Cap-d'Ail

L'Escarène

Trophée des Alpes

La Turbie

L'Escarène

Peillon

Col d'Eze

Eze

Eze-sur-Mer

Beaulieu-sur-Mer

St-Jean-Cap-Ferrat

Cap Ferrat

Villefranche-sur-Mer

Mt. Boron

Mt. Alban

Nice

Antibes & Cannes

① Corniche Inférieure
② Moyenne Corniche
③ Grande Corniche
④ Autoroute La Provençale

N

0   3 km

ACCOMMODATION
Auberge de la
Croix du Pape   A

959

excursions, the old town, with its fishing boats, sixteenth-century citadelle and the covered medieval rue Obscure running beneath the houses, is a charming place to while away an afternoon.

The tiny harbour is overlooked by the medieval **Chapelle de St-Pierre** (Tues– Sun: spring & summer 10am–noon & 3–7pm; autumn & winter 10am–noon & 2–6pm; €2.50), decorated by Jean Cocteau in 1957 in shades he described as "ghosts of colours". The drawings portray scenes from the life of St Peter and homages to the women of Villefranche and the gypsies. The chapel is used just once a year, on June 29, when fishermen celebrate the feast day of St Peter and St Paul with a Mass.

On the main road along the neck of the **Cap Ferrat peninsula**, between Ville- franche and Beaulieu, stands the **Villa Ephrussi** (Feb–June & Sept–Oct daily 10am–6pm; July & Aug daily 10am–7pm; Nov–Jan Mon–Fri 2–6pm, Sat & Sun 10am–6pm; €10, €3 extra to visit first-floor collections). Built in 1912 for a Rothschild heiress, it overflows with decorative art, paintings, sculpture and artefacts ranging from the fourteenth to the nineteenth centuries, and from European to Far Eastern origins. The villa is surrounded by elaborate gardens. Without spending too much, a place to **stay** is the *Hôtel de la Darse* (T04.93.01.72.54; ❹–❺) at 32 av du Général de Gaulle, west from the station and close to the citadelle and the sea. There are plenty of **restaurants** behind the chapel in the old town; a good choice is *Le Serre* at 16 rue de May (T04.93.76.79.91) with *menus* at €17 and pizza from €6.

Attractive, *belle-époque* **BEAULIEU** overlooks the pretty Baie des Fourmis, sheltered by a ring of hills that ensure some of the highest temperatures on the Côte. Its main attraction is the **Villa Kérylos** (mid-Feb to June & Sept–Oct daily 10am–6pm; July & Aug daily 10am–7pm; Nov–Feb weekdays 2–6pm, Sat & Sun 10am–6pm; €8.50), a near-perfect reproduction of an ancient Greek villa, east of the casino on avenue Gustave Eiffel. Théodore Reinach, the archeologist who had it built in 1900, lived here for twenty years, as if an Athenian citizen, taking baths with his male friends and assigning separate suites to women. The villa is five minutes' walk from the **gare SNCF**. For those tempted to **stay**, an economical option is the friendly, family-run *Hôtel Riviera* at 6 rue Paul Doumer, right in the centre near the sea (T04.93.01.04.92; W www.hotel-riviera.fr; ❸–❹).

The Moyenne Corniche

Of the three roads, the **Moyenne Corniche** is the most photogenic, a real cliff- hanging, car-chase highway. Eleven kilometres from Nice, the medieval village of **ÈZE** winds round its conical rock just below the corniche. No other *village perché* is more infested with antique dealers, pseudo-artisans and other caterers to rich tourists, and it requires a major mental feat to recall that the tiny vaulted passages and stairways were designed with defence, not charm, in mind. At the summit, a cactus garden, the **Jardin Exotique** (July & Aug daily 9am–8pm; Sept–June 9am–6/7pm; €5), covers the site of the former castle.

The Grande Corniche

At every other turn on the **Grande Corniche**, you're invited to park your car and enjoy a *belvédère*. At certain points, such as **Col d'Èze**, you can turn off upwards for even higher views; bus #82 goes to here. Eighteen stunning kilometres from Nice, you reach the village of **LA TURBIE** and its **Trophée des Alpes** (Tues– Sun: mid-May to mid-Sept 9.30am–1pm & 2.30–6.30pm; mid-Sept to mid-May 10am–1.30pm & 2.30–5pm; €5), a huge monument raised in 6 BC to celebrate the subjugation of the tribes of Gaul. Originally a statue of Augustus Caesar stood on the 45-metre plinth, which was pillaged, ransacked for building materials and blown up over the centuries. Painstakingly restored in the 1930s, it now stands statueless, 35m high; viewed from a distance, it still looks imperious. Infrequent buses run from here to Nice, from Monday to Saturday.

As the corniche descends towards Cap Martin, it passes the eleventh-century castle of **ROQUEBRUNE**, its village nestling round the base of the rock. The **castle** (daily: Jan, Nov & Dec 10am–12.30pm & 2–5pm; Feb, March & Oct 10am–12.30pm & 2–6pm; April–June & Sept 10am–12.30pm & 2–6.30pm; July & Aug 10am–12.30pm & 3–7.30pm; €3.70) has been kitted out enthusiastically in medieval fashion, while the tiny vaulted passages and stairways of the village are almost too good to be true. One thing that hasn't been restored is the vast millennial **olive tree** that lies just to the east of the village on the chemin de Menton. To get to the *vieux village* from the **gare SNCF**, turn east and then right up avenue de la Côte d'Azur, then first left up escalier Corinthille, across the Grande Corniche and up escalier Chanoine-J.-B.-Grana. The best **hotel** in the old village is *Les Deux Frères*, place des Deux-Frères (℡04.93.28.99.00, Ⓦ www.lesdeuxfreres.com; ❺), which is worth booking in advance to try to get one of the rooms with a sea view. The hotel also has a good restaurant (*menu* €48; closed Mon).

Southeast of the old town is the peninsula of **Cap Martin**, with a **coastal path** giving access to a wonderful shoreline of white rocks, secluded beaches and wind-bent pines. The path is named after **Le Corbusier**, who spent several summers in Roquebrune. He drowned off Cap Martin in 1965 and his grave – designed by himself – is in the **cemetery** (square J near the flagpole), high above the old village on promenade 1ᵉʳ-DFL.

A great **restaurant** to head for is *Auberge de la Croix du Pape* (℡04.93.57.83.03; booking advised in the evening), on the Grande Corniche by the turn-off to the observatory, above Èze. Lunch *menu* at €20.

Monaco

Viewed from a distance, there's no mistaking the cluster of towers that is **MONACO**. Rampant development in the 1960s and 1970s rescued the tiny principality from postwar decline but elbowed aside much of its previous prettiness – not for nothing was **Prince Rainier**, who died in 2005, known as the Prince Bâtisseur ("Prince Builder"). Nevertheless, this tiny state, no bigger than London's Hyde Park, retains its comic opera independence. It has been in the hands of the autocratic Grimaldi family since the thirteenth century, and in theory would become part of France were the royal line to die out. It remains home to six thousand well-heeled British expats – including Roger Moore and Shirley Bassey – out of a total population of 32,000.

The oldest part of the tiny principality is **Monaco-Ville**, around the palace on the rocky promontory, with the **Fontvieille** marina in its western shadow. **La Condamine** is the old port on the other side of the promontory; the ugly bathing resort of **Larvotto** extends to the eastern border; and **Monte-Carlo** is in the middle.

Along with its wealth, Monaco latterly acquired an unwelcome reputation for wheeler-dealer **sleaze**. On his accession in 2005, the US-educated Prince Albert II set about trying to get the principality off an OECD list of uncooperative tax havens, declaring he no longer wished Monaco to be known – in the words of Somerset Maugham – as "a sunny place for shady people". The annual Formula 1 **Monaco Grand Prix** takes place at the end of May. Every space in sight of the circuit is inaccessible without a ticket and prices soar to ridiculous levels.

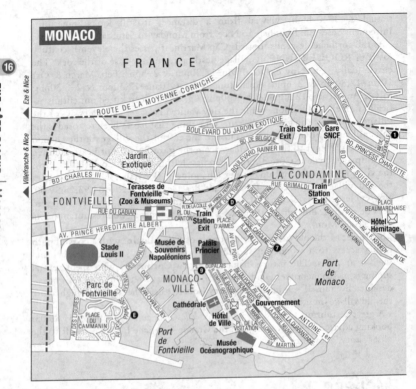

Arrival, information and accommodation

The **gare SNCF** is wedged between boulevard Rainier III and boulevard Princess Charlotte and has several handy exits, signposted clearly. Signs for Monte Carlo/Beausoleil indicate the main exit. Signs for La Condamine/Jardin Exotique/Hôpital will lead to either boulevard Rainier III and the exotic gardens, or by place Sainte-Dévote right by the port; signs for Fontvielle/Monaco-Ville will deposit you by Place d'Armes for the steps up to the old town. Municipal buses ply the length of the principality from 7am to 9pm (€1 single; ten-trip card €6). Buses following the lower corniche stop at place d'Armes; other routes have a variety of stations; most also stop in Monte-Carlo. Local buses #1 & #2 run to the "Casino-Tourisme" stop, close to the **tourist office** at 2a bd des Moulins (Mon–Sat 9am–7pm, Sun 10am–noon; ℡92.16.61.16, @www.visitmonaco.com), with an annexe at the *gare SNCF* (daily 9am–5pm). Clean and efficient **lifts** link the lower and higher streets. **Bicycles** can be hired from Monte-Carlo-Rent, quai des États-Unis (℡99.99.97.79) on the port. The best area for reasonably priced **hotels** is Beausoleil, just across the border in France and a five-minute walk from the action. Monaco has no campsite, and caravans are illegal – as are bathing costumes, bare

Phoning Monaco

Monaco's international code is +377 and numbers have eight digits (omit 0).

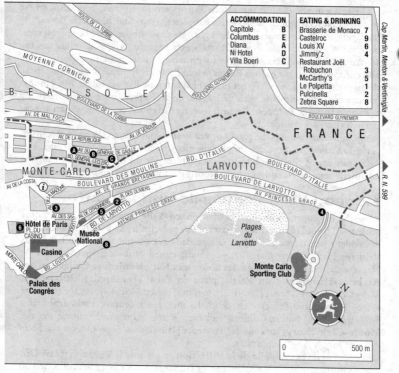

ACCOMMODATION

Capitole	B
Columbus	E
Diana	A
Ni Hotel	D
Villa Boeri	C

EATING & DRINKING

Brasserie de Monaco	7
Castelroc	9
Louis XV	6
Jimmy'z	4
Restaurant Joël Robuchon	3
McCarthy's	5
Le Polpetta	1
Pulcinella	2
Zebra Square	8

feet and chests once you step off the beach. Camper vans have to be parked at the Parking des Écoles, in Fontvieille, and even then not overnight.

Hotels

Capitole 19 bd du Général-Leclerc, Beausoleil ☎ 04.93.28.65.65, ⓦ www.hotelcapitole.fr. Very friendly and newly renovated with well-equipped rooms. ⑥–⑦

Columbus 23 av des Papalins, Fontvieille ☎ 92.05.90.00, ⓦ www.columbushotels.com. A boutique alternative to the steep prices of the palace hotels with sea views. ⑨

Diana 17 bd du Général-Leclerc, Beausoleil ☎ 04.93.78.47.58,

ⓦ www.monte-carlo.mc/hotel-diana-beausoleil. The cheapest option and needs a little repair, but is passable for a night or two. ③–④

Ni Hotel 1 rue Grimaldi, La Condamine ☎ 97.97.51.51, ⓦ www.nihotel.com. Suave, new hotel with a sister bar and restaurant. ⑧–⑨

Villa Boeri 29 bd du Général-Leclerc, Beausoleil ☎ 04.93.78.38.10, ⓦ www.hotelboeri.com. The rooms are bright and clean, but nothing special and there's a nice breakfasting terrace. ④

Monte-Carlo

Monte-Carlo is the area of Monaco where the real money is flung about, and its famous **casino** (ⓦ www.casinomontecarlo.com; bus #1, #2 or #6) demands to be seen. Entrance is restricted to over-18s and you may have to show your passport; dress code is rigid, with shorts and T-shirts frowned upon, though most visitors are scarcely the last word in designer chic. Skirts, jackets and ties are obligatory for the more interesting sections. Bags and large coats are checked at the door.

The first gambling hall is the **Salons Européens** (open from 2pm; €10) where slot machines surround the American roulette, craps and blackjack tables, the managers are Vegas-trained and the lights are low. Above this slice of Nevada, however, the decor is *fin-de-siècle* Rococo extravagance, while the ceilings in the adjoining Pink Salon Bar are adorned with female nudes smoking cigarettes. The heart of the place is the **Salons Privés** (Mon–Fri from 4pm, Sat & Sun from 3pm), through the Salles Touzet. To get in, you have to look like a gambler, not a tourist (no cameras), and dispense with €20 at the door. Rather larger and more richly decorated than the European Rooms, its early afternoon or out-of-season atmosphere is that of a cathedral.

Adjoining the casino is the gaudy **opera house**, and around the palm-tree-lined place du Casino are more casinos plus the city's palace-hotels and *grands cafés*. The American Bar of the **Hôtel de Paris** is *the* place for the elite to meet, while the twentieth-century **Hermitage** has a beautiful Gustave Eiffel iron-and-glass dome.

Monaco-Ville, Fontvieille and Larvotto

After the casino, the amusements of **Monaco-Ville** (bus #1 or #2) are rather quainter. The old town is the one part of the principality to have been spared the developer's worst. You can take a self-guided tour around the Lilliputian **Palais Princier** (daily: April–Oct 10am–6.15pm; closed Nov–March; €8); examine Napoleonic relics at the **Musée des Souvenirs Napoléoniens et Collection des Archives Historiques du Palais**, place du Palais (Jan–April 10.30am–5pm; May–Oct 10am–6.15pm; Dec 10.30am–5pm; closed Nov; €4); see the tombs of Prince Rainier and Princess Grace in the nineteenth-century **cathedral** (daily 8.30am–6.45pm) on rue Colonel; and even watch "Monaco the movie", at the **Monte-Carlo Story**, parking des Pêcheurs (Jan–June & Sept–Oct on the hour 2–5pm; July & Aug 2–6pm; €7).

The **Musée de la Chapelle de la Visitation** on place de la Visitation (May–Dec Tues–Sun 10am–4pm; €3) displays part of Barbara Piasecka Johnson's collection of religious art, a small but exquisite collection including works by Zurbarán, Rubens and Vermeer.

One of Monaco's best sights is the aquarium in the imposing **Musée Océanographique** (April–June & Sept 9.30am–7pm; July & Aug 9.30am–7.30pm; Oct–March 10am–6pm; €13), where the fishy beings outdo the weirdest Kandinsky or Hieronymus Bosch creations. Less exceptional but still peculiar, cactus equivalents can be viewed in the **Jardin Exotique**, on boulevard du Jardin Exotique high above Fontvieille (mid-May to mid-Sept 9am–7pm; mid-Sept to mid-May 9am–6pm or dusk; €7; bus #2).

There are yet more museums in **Fontvieille**, below the rock of Monaco-Ville. They include the **Collection de Voitures Anciennes de SAS le Prince de Monaco** (daily 10am–6pm; €6), an enjoyable miscellany of old and not-so-old cars, with everything from a 1928 Hispano-Suiza worthy of Cruella de Ville to Princess Grace's elegant 1959 Renault Florida Coupé; the **Musée Naval** (daily 10am–6pm; €4), containing 250 model ships; the **zoo** (March–May 10am–noon & 2–6pm; June–Sept 9am–noon & 2–7pm; Oct–Feb 10am–noon & 2–5pm; €4), with exotic birds, a black panther and a white tiger; and the museum of stamps and coins, the **Musée des Timbres et des Monnaies** (daily: July–Aug 9.30am–6pm; Sept–June 9.30am–5pm; €3), which has rare stamps, money and commemorative medals dating back to 1640.

At the other end of the principality near the Larvotto beach, the **Musée National**, 17 av Princesse Grace (daily 10am–6pm; €6), is dedicated to the history of **dolls and automata**, and is better than you would think: some of the dolls' house scenes and the creepy automata are quite surreal and fun.

Eating and drinking

La Condamine and the old town are replete with **restaurants**, but good food and reasonable prices don't exactly match; prices near the casino can be absurd. The best-value cuisine is Italian.

Restaurants

Castelroc Place du Palais ☎93.30.36.68. This place is situated in the old town and specialises in fish and Monégasque dishes. Closed Sat.

Louis XV Hôtel de Paris, place du Casino ☎98.06.88.64. Alain Ducasse's famed restaurant is the most prestigious place in town. Lunch *menu* €140. Closed Tues, Wed & Dec.

Le Polpetta 2 rue Paradis ☎93.50.67.84. Serves good pasta dishes, including *tortellini en brodo* from €12.

Pulcinella 17 rue du Portier in Monte-Carlo ☎93.30.73.61. A reliable Italian offering *menus* for around €30, *plats du jour* from €12.

Restaurant Joël Robuchon *Hôtel Metropole*, 4 av de la Madone ☎98.06.88.64. The cooking is under the aegis of one of France's most respected chefs. *Menus* €75–150.

Bars and clubs

Brasserie de Monaco 36 rte de la Piscine. Situated in the port and with Monaco's only beer brewed on the premises, this smart place is often guested by internationally known DJs.

Jimmy'z Le Sporting Club, av Princess Grace. A local favourite – it's pricey with drinks around €30, but there is no entrance fee. Buy a bottle of spirits if you're a group.

Zebra Square Atop the Grimaldi Forum. Flash nightclub that's open until 3am, with regular celeb DJs.

Menton

Of all the Côte d'Azur resorts, **MENTON**, ringed by protective mountains, is the warmest and most Italianate, being right on the border. In 1861 a British doctor, James Henry Bennet, published a treatise on the benefits of Menton's mild climate to tuberculosis patients, and soon thousands of well-heeled sufferers were flocking here in the vain hope of a cure along this tranquil bay.

Arrival and information

Roquebrune and Cap Martin merge into Menton along the 3km shore of the Baie du Soleil. The old town and old port mark the end of Baie du Soleil and beginning of Baie de Garavan, reached by a ten-minute walk down Promenade du Soleil from the Casino at the end of avenue de Verdun; the main thoroughfare from the **gare SNCF**. Avenue de Verdun and avenue Boyer are divided by the Jardins Biovès – central location for citrus sculptures during February's **Fête du Citron**. The **tourist office** is at 8 av Boyer (Sept–June Mon–Sat 8.30am–12.30pm & 2pm–6pm, Sun 9am–12.30pm; July–Aug daily 8.30am–7pm; ☎04.92.41.76.76, Ⓦ www.menton.fr), in the Palais de l'Europe, a former casino. The **gare routière** is north of the *gare SNCF* on avenue de Sospel, which becomes avenue de Verdun by the railway bridge. Local bus lines (€1) all pass through the *gare routière*.

Accommodation

Menton is no less popular than the other major resorts and there is plenty of **accommodation** on offer. In summer, it's advised to book in advance, which you can do online through the tourist office website.

Hotels

L'Aiglon 7 av de la Madone ☎04.93.57.55.55, Ⓦ www.hotelaiglon.net. Spacious rooms in a nineteenth-century residence with a garden, pool and restaurant just back from the sea on the Roquebrune end of the Menton shore. ⑥–⑧

Beauregard 10 rue Albert 1ᵉʳ ℡04.93.28.61.63, ℮beauregard.menton.wanadoo.fr. A couple of minutes' walk from the train station is this friendly, basic and clean place with a garden. The cheapest beds in town. ❷

Napoléon 29 porte de France, Baie de Garavan ℡04.93.35.89.50, ⓦwww.napoleon-menton.com. Modern and friendly seafront hotel with a private beach across the road (€13 per day) and attached gourmet restaurant. ❼

Hostel and campsite

Camping St-Michel Rte des Ciappes ℡04.93.35.81.23, ⓦwww.menton.fr/camping. Reasonably priced campsite in the hills above the town; follow directions for youth hostel. Closed mid-Oct to March except for Fête du Citron.

HI hostel Plateau St-Michel ℡04.93.35.93.14. Up a gruelling flight of steps (signposted Camping St-Michel) from the northern side of the railway to the east of the station, or take bus #6 from the *gare routière*. Reception open 7–10am & 6–10pm (11pm July & Aug). Curfew. Closed mid-Oct to April. €17.90.

The Town

The **promenade du Soleil** runs along the pebbly beachfront of the Baie du Soleil, stretching from the quai Napoléon III past the casino towards Roquebrune. The most diverting building is a seventeenth-century fort by the quai Napoléon III in front of the old town, now the **Musée Jean Cocteau** (daily except Tues 10am–noon & 2–6pm; €3), set up by the artist himself. It contains pictures of his Mentonnaise lovers in the *Inamorati* series, a collection of delightful *Fantastic Animals* and the tapestry of *Judith and Holofernes* telling the sequence of seduction, assassination and escape. There are also photographs, poems, ceramics and a portrait by his friend Picasso.

As the *quai* bends around the western end of the Baie de Garavan from the Cocteau museum, a long flight of pebbled steps leads up into the **vieille ville** to the **Parvis de la Basilique**, an attractive Italianate square hosting concerts in summer and giving a good view out over the bay. The frontage of the **Église St-Michel** (Mon–Fri 10am–noon & 3–5.15pm, Sat & Sun 3–5.15pm) proclaims its Baroque supremacy in perfect pink-and-yellow proportions; a few more steps up will reward you with the beautiful facade of the **chapel of the Pénitents-Blancs** in apricot and white (not open to the public, except for the classical Festival de Music held first two weeks in August). The crumbly **cemetery**, at the top of the old town on the site once occupied by the town's château, is hauntingly sad – many of the young tuberculosis sufferers who ended their days in Menton are buried here – but also bewitchingly beautiful, with views along the coast into Italy.

On avenue de la Madone, at the other end of the modern town, an impressive collection of paintings from the Middle Ages to the twentieth century are displayed in the **Palais Carnolès** (daily except Tues 10am–noon & 2–6pm; free; bus #7 from Menton) the old summer residence of the princes of Monaco. Of the early works, the *Madonna and Child with St Francis* by Louis Bréa is exceptional. The most recent include canvases by Graham Sutherland, who spent some of his last years in Menton.

If it's cool enough, the gardens of **Garavan**'s villas make a change from shingle beaches. The best is **Les Colombières**, just north of boulevard de Garavan and designed by the artist Ferdinand Bac between 1918 and 1927, but it's privately owned; guided visits (see the tourist office for details or contact Service du Patrimoine ℡04.92.10.97.10) take place during the summer months. Alternatively, try the **Jardin Exotique Val Rameh** (daily except Tues: April–Sept 10am–12.30pm & 2–5pm; Oct–March 10am–12.30pm & 3.30–6pm; €6) below boulevard de Garavan or **Fontana Rosa** (guided visits Friday at 10am; €5) on avenue Blasco-Ibañez, the former home of the Spanish author Vicente Blasco Ibañez and bright with ceramic decoration.

Eating and drinking

Menton's **restaurants** tend towards the informal; the pedestrianized rue St-Michel is promising ground for cheap eats, and in summer there is no shortage of touristy places along the promenade de la Mer. *Le Bruit qui Court* on the port at 31 quai Bonaparte (T 04.93.35.94.64) serves good French cuisine including *foie gras*, while a popular choice with the locals is *Le Petit Port* at 30 rue du Jonquier, facing Musée Jean Cocteau (T 04.93.35.82.62) and for seafood, try *La Coquille d'Or* at quai Bonaparte in the square (T 04.93.35.80.67); all have *menus* around €25.

Travel details

Trains

Cannes to: Antibes (approx. every 20min peak time; 10–15min); Biot (approx. every 20min–1hr; 17min); Cagnes-sur-Mer (every 20min peak time; 20min); Golfe Juan-Vallauris (approx. every 20min–1hr; 7min); Juan-les-Pins (approx. every 20min–1hr; 11min); Marseille (every 15min–1hr; 2hr); Nice (approx. every 20min peak time; 25–59min); St-Raphaël (every 20min–1hr; 32–40min); Villeneuve-Loubet-Plage (approx. every 30min–2hr; 23min).

Marseille to: Arles (up to 20 direct daily; 50min); Avignon (up to 20 daily; 1hr 10min); Bandol (approx. every 30min–1hr 30min; 42min); Cannes (approx. hourly; 2hr); Cassis (approx. every 30min–1hr 30min; 27min); Cavaillon (3 daily; 55min–1hr 20min); Hyères (1–2 daily; 1hr 20min, otherwise change in Toulon); La Ciotat (approx. every 30min–1hr 30min; 34min); Lyon (up to 10 daily; 3hr 40min); Nice (10–18 daily; 2hr 30min); Paris (20 daily; 3hr 15min); St-Cyr/Les Lecques (approx. every 30min–1hr 30min; 35–45min); St-Raphaël (every 30min–1hr 30min; 1hr 30min–1hr 45min); Salon (2–3 daily; 55min); Toulon (every 20min at peak times; 40min–1hr 5min).

Nice to: Beaulieu (every 15–30min; 11min); Cannes (every 20min at peak times; 25–50min); Digne (4 daily; 3hr 25min); Èze-sur-Mer (every 35min–1hr; 15min); Marseille (every 30min–1hr 30min; 2hr 30min–3hr); Menton (hourly; 1hr 25min); Monaco (every 10–35min; 20–25min); Paris (up to 10 daily; 5hr 40min–10hr); St-Raphaël (approx. half hourly at peak times; 55min–1hr 30min); Sospel (5 daily; 45–55min); Tende (1 daily; 1hr 45min); Villefranche (every 15–45min; 8min).

St-Raphaël to: Cannes (every 20–55min; 25–40min); Nice (every 20–55min; 50min–1hr 25min).

Buses

Antibes to: Biot (approx. every hour; 20min); Cannes (every 15–40min; 35min); Juan-les-Pins (every 20–30min; 8min); Nice (every 15–40min; 50–55min); Nice airport (every 30min; 20–47min).

Cannes to: Antibes (every 15–30min; 20–25min); Cagnes (every 30min; 40–45min); Grasse (every 20min; 1hr); Nice (every 15min; 1hr 30min); Nice airport (every 30min; 50min); Vallauris (hourly; 15min).

Grasse to: Cagnes (every 15–50min; 40min); Cannes (every 15–30min; 40–55min); Nice (every 25–50min; 1hr 30min).

Hyères to: Bormes (hourly; 25min); La Croix-Valmer (11 daily; 1hr 10min); Le Lavandou (approx. hourly; 35min); Le Rayol (11 daily; 50min); St-Tropez (11 daily; 1hr 30min–1hr 50min); Toulon (every 25–45min; 35min–1hr 10min).

Le Lavandou to: Bormes (approx. hourly; 10min); Hyères (approx. hourly; 40min); La Croix-Valmer (11 daily; 45min); Le Rayol (11 daily; 20min); St-Tropez (11 daily; 1hr 15min); Toulon (approx. hourly; 1hr 10min).

Marseille to: Aix (every 10min at peak times; 30–50min); Barcelonnette (2–3 daily; 4hr 30min); Carpentras (2–3 daily; 2hr–2hr 20min); Cassis (2–4 daily; 45min); Digne (3–7 daily; 2hr 15min–2hr 40min); Grenoble (1 daily; 4hr 25min); La Ciotat (hourly; 45min); Manosque (3 daily; 1hr 30min); Sisteron (2–4 daily; 2hr 10min–2hr 45min).

Menton to: Monaco (every 20–30min; 30min); Nice (every 20–30min; 1hr 25min).

Monaco to: Èze (every 20–30min; 20min); La Turbie (3–6 daily; 30min); Menton (every 20–30min; 30min); Nice (every 20–30min; 45min).

Nice to: Aix (3–5 daily; 2hr 15min–3hr 30min); Antibes (every 30min; 50min); Beaulieu (every 20–30min; 16min); Cagnes-sur-Mer (every 15–30min; 45min); Cannes (every 15–30min;

1hr 45min); Digne (1 daily; 3hr); Èze-Village (every 20–30min; 20min); Grasse (every 30–45min; 1hr 30min); Marseille (3–5 daily; 2hr 45min–4hr); Menton (every 20–30min; 1hr 15min); Monaco (every 20–30min; 35–40min); Roquebrune (every 20–30min; 45min); St-Paul (every 30–45min; 50min); Sisteron (1 daily; 3hr); Vence (every 30–45min; 1hr 10min); Villefranche (every 20–30min; 13min).

St-Raphaël to: Fréjus (frequent; 20min); Grimaud (every 1hr 30min–2hr; 1hr); La Foux (every 1hr 30min–2hr; 1hr 10min); Ste-Maxime (every 1hr 30min–2hr; 40min); St-Tropez; (every 1hr 30min–2hr; 1hr 20min).

St-Tropez to: Bormes (6–12 daily; 45min–1hr 5min); Gassin (4 daily; 35min); Grimaud (every 1hr 30min; 25min); Hyères (9 daily; 1hr 30min–1hr 50min); Hyères airport (3 daily; 1hr 10min); La Croix-Valmer (6 daily; 15min); La Garde-Freinet (1–3 daily; 40min); Le Lavandou (6 daily; 50min); Ste-Maxime (10 daily; 40min–1hr); St-Raphaël

(10 daily; 1hr 20min–1hr 55min); Toulon (6 daily; 1hr 30min–2hr).

Toulon to: Aix (4 daily; 1hr 15min–1hr 45min); Bandol (7 daily; 50min); Collobrières (2 daily; 1hr 20min–1hr 30min); Hyères (every 30min; 30min–1hr); La Croix-Valmer (8 daily; 1hr 55min); Le Lavandou (hourly; 1hr 15min); St-Tropez (8 daily; 2hr–2hr 30min).

Vence to: Cagnes (every 30–40min; 30min); Nice (every 30–40min; 50min–1hr 10min); St-Paul-de-Vence (every 30–40min; 10min).

Ferries

For Îles d'Hyères and Îles de Lérins services, see p.921 & p.940.

Marseille to: Corsica (1–5 daily; 7hr 45min–12hr).

Nice to: Corsica (summer 4–5 daily, winter reduced service; 5hr 30min–8hr).

Toulon to: Corsica (summer 3–4 daily, winter reduced service; 6hr 15min–9hr 30min).

Corsica

CHAPTER 17 # Highlights

✳ **Plage de Saleccia** Soft white shell sand, turquoise water and barely a building in sight. See p.984

✳ **Calvi** Corsica's hallmark resort, framed by snow peaks and a spectacular blue gulf. See p.987

✳ **The GR20** Gruelling 170km footpath, which takes in spectacular mountain scenery – but is only for the fit. See p.990

✳ **Girolata** The only fishing village on the island still inaccessible by road, set against a backdrop of red cliffs and dense maquis. See p.992

✳ **Les Calanches de Piana** A mass of porphyry, eroded into dogs' heads, witches and devils. See p.994

✳ **Filitosa menhirs** Among the Western Mediterranean's greatest archeological treasures, unique for their carved faces. See p.1004

✳ **Boat trips from Bonifacio** Catch a navette from the harbour visited by Odysseus for imposing views of the famous chalk cliffs and haute ville. See p.1011

✳ **Corte** A nationalist stronghold, with loads of eighteenth-century charm and a rugged mountain setting. See p.1015

▲ Menhirs at Filitosa

Corsica

A round three million people visit **Corsica** each year, drawn by the mild climate and some of the most diverse landscapes in all Europe. Nowhere in the Mediterranean has beaches finer than the island's perfect half-moon bays of white sand and transparent water, or seascapes more dramatic than the red porphyry Calanches of the west coast. Even though the annual visitor influx now exceeds the island's population nine times over, tourism hasn't spoilt the place: there are a few resorts, but overdevelopment is rare and high-rise blocks are confined to the main towns.

Bastia, capital of the north, was the principal Genoese stronghold, and its fifteenth-century citadelle has survived almost intact. It's a purely Corsican city, and commerce rather than tourism is its main concern. Also relatively undisturbed, the northern Cap Corse harbours inviting sandy coves and fishing villages such as **Macinaggio** and **Centuri-Port**. Within a short distance of Bastia, the fertile region of the Nebbio contains a scattering of churches built by Pisan stone-workers, the prime example being the Cathédrale de Santa Maria Assunta at the appealingly chic little port of **St-Florent**.

To the west of here, **L'Île-Rousse** and **Calvi**, the latter graced with an impressive citadelle and fabulous sandy beach, are major targets for holiday-makers. The spectacular **Scandola nature reserve** to the southwest of Calvi is most easily visited by boat from the tiny resort of **Porto**, from where walkers can also strike into the wild **Gorges de Spelunca**. **Corte**, at the heart of Corsica, is the best base for exploring the mountains and gorges of the interior which form part of the **Parc Naturel Régional** that runs almost the entire length of the island.

Sandy beaches and rocky coves punctuate the west coast all the way down to **Ajaccio**, Napoleon's birthplace and the island's capital, where pavement cafés and palm-lined boulevards are thronged with tourists in summer. Slightly fewer make it to nearby **Filitosa**, greatest of the many prehistoric sites scattered across the south. **Propriano**, the town perhaps most transformed by the tourist boom, lies close to stern **Sartène**, former seat of the wild feudal lords who once ruled this region and still the quintessential Corsican town.

More megalithic sites are found south of Sartène on the way to **Bonifacio**, a comb of ancient buildings perched atop furrowed white cliffs at the southern tip of the island. Equally popular, **Porto-Vecchio** provides a springboard for excursions to the amazing beaches of the south. The eastern plain has less to boast of, but the Roman site at **Aléria** is worth a visit for its excellent museum.

Some history

Set on the western Mediterranean trade routes, Corsica has always been of strategic and commercial appeal. Greeks, Carthaginians and Romans came in

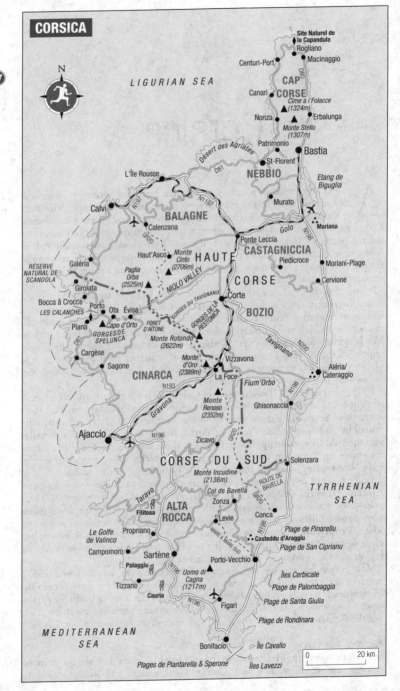

CORSICA

N

LIGURIAN SEA

Site Naturel de
la Capandula
Rogliano
Centuri-Port ● Macinaggio
CAP
CORSE
Canari ● Cime a i Folacce
(1324m) ▲
Nonza ● ● Erbalunga
Monte Stello
(1307m)
Patrimonio ●
St-Florent ● ● Bastia
NEBBIO *Etang de*
Biguglia
L'Île Rousse ● *Désert des Agriates*
D81
Murato ●
Calvi ● N197 BALAGNE ● Mariana
Calenzana
GR20 Golo
Haut'Asco ● Monte CASTAGNICCIA
Cinto HAUTE
RÉSERVE (2706m) ▲ Ponte Leccia
NATURAL DE Galéria ● Piedicroce ● Morlani-Plage
SCANDOLA *Paglia* CORSE
Orba NIOLO VALLEY
Girolata ● *(2525m)* ▲ ● Cervione
Bocca à Crocce Corte ●
Porto ● Ota Évisa ● BOZIO
LES CALANCHES FORÊT
Piana ● *Capo d'Orto* D'AITONE *Tavignano* N200
▲ GORGES DE *Monte Rotondo*
SPELUNCA *(2622m)* ▲ Aléria/
Cargèse ● Monte Cateraggio
Sagone ● *d'Oro* Vizzavona ●
(2389m) ▲
CINARCA La Foce *Fium'Orbo*
N193 ▲
Gravona *Monte* Ghisonaccia ●
Renoso
(2352m)
Ajaccio ● N196 GR20
Zicavo ● ● Solenzara
CORSE DU SUD
Monte Incudine ROUTE DE
(2136m) ▲ BAVELLA *TYRRHENIAN*
Col de Bavella *SEA*
Taravo Zonza ● GR20
Filitosa ALTA
ROCCA
Propriano ● Levie ● Conca ●
Le Golfe *Plage de Pinarellu*
de Valinco Casteddu d'Araggiu ●●
Sartène ● *Plage de San Ciprianu*
Campomoro ●
Palaggiu Porto-Vecchio ●
Uomo di *Îles Cerbicale*
Tizzano ● *Cagna* *Plage de Palombaggia*
Cauria *(1217m)* ▲
N196 *Plage de Santa Giulia*
Figari ●
Plage de Rondinara

MEDITERRANEAN
SEA

0   20 km

Bonifacio ● ● *Île Cavallo*
Plages de Piantarella & Sperone *Îles Lavezzi*

The food of Corsica

It's the herbs – thyme, marjoram, basil, fennel and rosemary – of the maquis (the dense, scented scrub covering lowland Corsica) that lend the island's cuisine its distinctive aromas.

You'll find the best **charcuterie** in the hills of the interior, where pork is smoked and cured in the cold cellars of village houses – it's particularly tasty in Castagniccia, where wild pigs feed on the chestnuts which were once the staple diet of the locals. Here you can also taste chestnut fritters (*fritelli a gaju frescu*) and chestnut porridge (*pulenta*) sprinkled with sugar or *eau de vie*. **Brocciu**, a soft mozzarella-like cheese made with ewe's milk, is found everywhere on the island, forming the basis for many dishes, including omelettes and cannelloni. *Fromage corse* is also very good – a hard **cheese** made in the sheep- and goat-rearing central regions, where *cabrettu à l'istrettu* (kid stew) is a speciality.

Game – mainly stews of hare and wild boar but also roast woodcock, partridge and wood pigeon – features throughout the island's mountain and forested regions. Here blackbirds (*merles*) are made into a fragrant pâté, and eel and trout are fished from the unpolluted rivers. **Sea fish** like red mullet (*rouget*), bream (*loup de mer*) and a great variety of shellfish is eaten along the coast – the best crayfish (*langouste*) comes from around the Golfe de St-Florent, whereas oysters (*huîtres*) and mussels (*moules*) are a speciality of the eastern plain.

Corsica produces some excellent, and still little-known, **wines**, mostly from indigenous vinestocks that yield distinctive, herb-tinged aromas. Names to look out for include: Domaine Torraccia (Porto-Vecchio); Domaine Fiumicicoli (Sartène); Domaine Saparale (Sartène); Domaine Gentille (Patrimonio); Domaine Leccia (Patrimomio); and Venturi-Pieretti (Cap Corse). In addition to the usual whites, reds and rosés, the last also makes the sweet muscat for which Cap Corse was renowned in previous centuries. Another popular aperitif is the drink known as Cap Corse, a fortified wine flavoured with quinine and herbs. Note that **tap water** is particularly good quality in Corsica, coming from the fresh mountain streams.

successive waves, driving native Corsicans into the interior. The Romans were ousted by Vandals, and for the following thirteen centuries the island was attacked, abandoned, settled and sold as a nation-state, with generations of islanders fighting against foreign government. In 1768 France bought Corsica from Genoa, but over two hundred years of French rule have had a limited effect and the island's Baroque churches, Genoese fortresses, fervent Catholic rituals and a Tuscan-influenced indigenous language and cuisine show a more profound affinity with Italy.

Corsica's uneasy relationship with the mainland has worsened in recent decades. Economic neglect and the French government's reluctance to encourage Corsican language and culture spawned a nationalist movement in the early 1970s, whose clandestine armed wing – the FLNC (Fronte di Liberazione Nazionale di a Corsica) – and its various off-shoots have been engaged ever since in a bloody conflict with the central government. The violence seldom affects tourists but signs of the "troubles" are everywhere, from the graffiti-sprayed roadsigns to the bullet holes disfiguring public buildings.

Relations between the island's hard-line nationalists and Paris may be perennially fraught, but there's little support among ordinary islanders for total independence. Bankrolled by Paris and Brussels, Corsica is the most heavily subsidized region of France. Moreover, Corsicans are exempt from social security contributions and the island as a whole enjoys preferential tax status, with one-third of the permanent population an employee of the state. Increasingly, nationalist violence is seen as biting the hand that feeds it.

Getting to Corsica

One French company, SNCM – along with its freight subsidiary CMN – dominates **ferry** services to Corsica. In addition, an Italian operator, Corsica Ferries, has superfast services from **Nice** to Calvi and Bastia. Crossings take between seven and twelve hours on a regular ferry, and from two and a half to three and a half hours on the giant hydrofoil ("NGV", or *navire à grande vitesse*). The cost depends on the season, with the lowest between October and May; during July and August fares quadruple. A one-way crossing for a foot passenger costs anything from €8 to €120 per person, plus €55 to €275 per vehicle, depending on the date of the journey.

Regular ferries run all year round to various ports around the island from **Marseille**, **Toulon** and **Nice**. You can **book** SNCM and CNM tickets via their central reservation desk (☏08.36.67.95.00, ⊛www.sncm.fr). For Corsica Ferries contact ☏04.92.00.42.93, ⊛www.corsicaferries.fr. Note that reservations are essential for journeys in July and August.

Direct **flights** to Corsica depart from most major French cities with charters cheaper than scheduled services. The largest operator is Air France (☏08.20.82.08.20, ⊛www.airfrance.fr), whose fourteen-day advance fares from Paris rise to €450 return in July and August, dropping to €160 out of season. Corse Méditerranée (☏08.02.80.28.02, ⊛www.ccm-airlines.com) offers routes from a range of mainland airports. Their fares from the Côte d'Azur vary little: €125–250 return depending on season.

Getting around

With public transport woefully inadequate, the most convenient way of getting around Corsica is by **rental car**. All the big firms (see Basics, p.39) have offices at airports and towns across the island, allowing you to collect and return vehicles in different places. Even if your budget won't stretch to a week, it's worth renting for a couple of days to explore the back roads of the interior.

Bus services are fairly frequent between Bastia, Corte and Ajaccio, and along the east coast from Bastia to Porto-Vecchio and Bonifacio. Elsewhere in the island, services tend to peter out in the winter months or are relatively infrequent. Getting accurate timetable information for bus services can also be difficult – the best way to check information is at a tourist office or, better still, online at ⊛www.corsicabus.org. See "Travel details" at the end of this chapter for a roundup of routes and frequencies.

Corsica's diminutive **train**, the *Micheline* or *Trinighellu* (little train; ⊛www.ter-sncf.com), rattles through the mountains from Ajaccio to Bastia via Corte, with a branch line running northwest to Calvi. The route had a major upgrade in 2008, and is a notch quicker than the bus – plus it takes you through some stupendous scenery. Again, current timetable information and fares can be viewed online at ⊛www.corsicabus.org.

Opinion, however, remains divided on the best way forward for the island. While the centre-right UMP (Union Pour un Mouvement Populaire) party, which until recently held a majority in the Corsican assembly, pushes for an all-out promotion of tourism as an socio-economic cure-all, local nationalist groups resist large-scale development, claiming it will irrevocably damage the pristine environment visitors come to enjoy. Such opposition achieved resounding popular support in the territorial elections of 2010, in which the nationalists gained an historic 35 percent of the vote thanks largely to their anti-development policies. This, however, was not enough to win them control of L'Assemblée Corse, which went by a narrow margin to Paul Giacobbi's centre-left coalition.

Bastia and around

The dominant tone of Corsica's most successful commercial town, **BASTIA**, is one of charismatic dereliction, as the city's industrial zone is spread onto the lowlands to the south, leaving the centre of town with plenty of aged charm. The old quarter, known as the Terra Vecchia, comprises a tightly packed network of haphazard streets, flamboyant Baroque churches and lofty tenements, their crumbling golden-grey walls set against a backdrop of maquis-covered hills. Terra Nova, the historic district on the opposite side of the old port, is a tidier area that's now Bastia's trendy quarter.

The city dates from Roman times, when a base was set up at Biguglia to the south, beside a freshwater lagoon. Little remains of the former colony, but the site merits a day-trip for the well-preserved pair of Pisan churches at Mariana, rising from the southern fringes of Poretta airport. Bastia began to thrive under the Genoese, when wine was exported to the Italian mainland from Porto Cardo, forerunner of Bastia's Vieux Port, or Terra Vecchia. Despite the fact that in 1811 Napoleon appointed Ajaccio capital of the island, initiating a rivalry between the two towns which exists to this day, Bastia soon established a stronger trading position with mainland France. The Nouveau Port, created in 1862 to cope with the increasing traffic with France and Italy, became the mainstay of the local economy, exporting chiefly agricultural products from Cap Corse, Balagne and the eastern plain.

Arrival and information

Bastia's Poretta **airport** (☎04.95.54.54.54, ⓦwww.bastia.aeroport.fr) is 16km south of town, just off the Route Nationale (N193). **Shuttle buses** into the centre coincide with flights; the stop (marked by a single post with a small timetable on it) is easy to miss – it stands immediately outside the terminal concourse, 20m from the exit. Tickets cost €9. You can be dropped at the north side of Bastia's square, place St-Nicolas, or at the terminus outside the train station. **Taxis** from the airport cost a hefty €50/60 (day/night). **Ferries** arrive at the **Nouveau Port**, just a five-minute walk from the centre of town. Bastia doesn't have a proper bus station, which can cause confusion, with services arriving and departing from different locations around the north side of the main square. A summary of times and departure points is available at the **tourist office**, at the north end of place St-Nicolas (June to mid-Sept daily 8am–8pm; mid-Sept to May Mon–Sat 8am–6pm, Sun 9am–1pm; ☎04.95.54.20.40, ⓦwww.bastia -tourisme.com).

Accommodation

The choice of **hotels** is not great, particularly at the budget end of the scale, and rooms tend to be booked well in advance, especially on weekends.

Hotels

🏃 **Central** 3 rue Miot ☎04.95.31.69.72, ⓦwww.centralhotel.fr. Eighteen pleasantly furnished rooms (plus a handful of larger studios), with textured walls and sparkling bathrooms, just off the southwest corner of place St-Nicolas. By far the most pleasant and best-value place to stay in the centre. Advance reservation essential. ❺

Posta-Vecchia Quai des Martyrs-de-la-Libération ☎04.95.32.32.38, ⓦwww.hotel-postavecchia .com. The only hotel in the Vieux Port, and good value, with views across the sea from the (pricier) rooms at the front. There are smaller, cheaper rooms in the old block across the lane (❹); all have a/c. ❺

Riviera 1bis rue du Nouveau-Port ☎04.95.31.07.16, ⓦwww.corsehotelriviera.com.

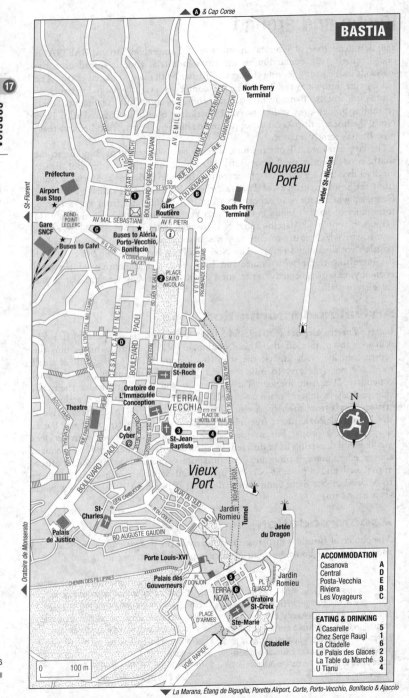

BASTIA

& Cap Corse

North Ferry
Terminal

Nouveau
Port

Jetée St-Nicolas

Préfecture

Airport
Bus Stop

St-Florent

ROND-
POINT
LECLERC

Gare
SNCF

Buses to Calvi

AV MAL SÉBASTIANI

BOULEVARD GÉNÉRAL GRAZIANI

R CÉSAR CAMPINCHI

AV EMILE SARI

RUE DU COMMT LUCE DE CASTABIANCA

RUE CHANOINE LESCHI

SQ
ST-VICTOR

R DU NOUVEAU PORT

Gare
Routière

South Ferry
Terminal

Buses to Aléria,
Porto-Vecchio,
Bonifacio

AV F. PIETRI

R G PÉRI

R CONVENTIONNEL
SALICETI

PLACE
SAINT-
NICOLAS

VOIE RAPIDE

PROMENADE DES QUAIS

BD DE GAULLE

BOULEVARD

PAOLI

RUE CÉSAR CAMPINCHI

RUE MIOT

RUE NAPOLEON

CHEMIN DE L'HÔPITAL MILITAIRE

Oratoire de
St-Roch

Oratoire de
L'Immaculée
Conception

QUAI DES MARTYRS DE LA LIBÉRATION

TERRA
VECCHIA

PLACE DE
L'HÔTEL DE VILLE

Theatre

RUE FAVALELLI

BOULEVARD GÉNÉRAL GIRAUD

BOULEVARD PAOLI

RUE DES TERRASSES

Le
Cyber

St-Jean
Baptiste

Vieux
Port

St-
Charles

R GEN CARBUCCIA

QUAI DU SUD

R DU DOUBLE

Jardin
Romieu

VOIE RAPIDE

Tunnel

Jetée
du Dragon

Oratoire de Monserato

Palais
de Justice

BD AUGUSTE GAUDIN

Porte Louis-XVI

CHEMIN DES FILLIPINES

Palais des
Gouverneurs

PL
DONJON

TERRA
NOVA

PL T
GUASCO

Jardin
Romieu

Oratoire
St-Croix

PLACE
D'ARMES

Ste-Marie

Citadelle

VOIE RAPIDE

N

La Marana, Étang de Biguglia, Poretta Airport, Corte, Porto-Vecchio, Bonifacio & Ajaccio

0   100 m

ACCOMMODATION
Casanova	A
Central	D
Posta-Vecchia	E
Riviera	B
Les Voyageurs	C

EATING & DRINKING
A Casarelle	5
Chez Serge Raugi	1
La Citadelle	6
Le Palais des Glaces	2
La Table du Marché	3
U Tianu	4

Basic and a bit noisy, with modern rooms behind a period facade, but very near the harbour – and all the rooms are en suite, with a/c. ❸

Les Voyageurs 9 av du Maréchal Sébastiani ☎04.95.34.90.80, ⓦ www.hotel-lesvoyageurs .com. Smart three-star near the train station, done out in pale yellow and with three categories of differently themed rooms ("Jules Verne", "Indians" & "Cinema"): the larger, more expensive ones have tubs instead of showers. No views to speak of, but

fine for a night or two. Secure parking and central a/c. ❻

Campsite

Casanova Miomo, 5km north of town ☎04.95.33.24. The most convenient campsite if you're relying on public transport; frequent buses leave from the top of place St-Nicolas opposite the tourist office. Open April–Oct.

The Town

The centre of Bastia is not especially large, and all its sights can easily be seen in a day without the use of a car. The spacious **place St-Nicolas** is the obvious place to get your bearings: open to the sea and lined with shady trees and cafés, it's the main focus of town life. Running parallel to it on the landward side are boulevard Paoli and rue César Campinchi, the two main shopping streets, but all Bastia's historic sights lie within **Terra Vecchia**, the old quarter immediately south of place St-Nicolas, and **Terra Nova**, the area surrounding the Citadelle. Tucked away below the imposing, honey-coloured bastion is the much-photographed **Vieux Port**, with its boat-choked marina and crumbling eighteenth-century tenement buildings.

Terra Vecchia

From place St-Nicolas the main route into Terra Vecchia is **rue Napoléon**, a narrow street with some ancient offbeat shops and a pair of sumptuously decorated chapels on its east side. The first of these, the **Oratoire de St-Roch**, is a Genoese Baroque extravagance built in 1604, with walls of finely carved wooden panelling and a magnificent gilt organ.

A little further along stands the **Oratoire de L'Immaculée Conception**, built in 1611 as the showplace of the Genoese in Corsica, who used it for state occasions. The austere facade belies a flamboyant interior of gilt and velvet, whose centrepiece (behind the High Altar) is one of Bartolomé Esteban Murillo's celebrated depictions of the Immaculate Conception.

Just behind the oratoire, the place de l'Hôtel-de-Ville is commonly known as **place du Marché** after the lively farmers' market that takes place here each morning, from around 7am until 2pm. Dominating the south end of the square is the **church of St-Jean-Baptiste**, an immense ochre edifice that dominates the Vieux Port. Its twin campaniles are iconic of the city, but the interior – a hideous Rococo overkill of multicoloured marble – is less impressive.

Around the church extends the oldest and most photogenic part of Bastia, the **Vieux Port** – a secretive zone of dark alleys, vaulted passageways and seven-storey houses. Site of the original Roman settlement of Porto Cardo, the harbour later bustled with Genoese traders, but since the building of the ferry terminal and commercial docks to the north it has become a backwater.

Terra Nova

The military and administrative core of old Bastia, **Terra Nova** (or the citadelle) is focused on **place du Donjon**, which gets its name from the squat round tower that formed the nucleus of Bastia's fortifications: it was used by the Genoese to incarcerate Corsican patriots, among them the nationalist rebel Sampiero Corso in 1657, who was held in the dungeon for four years.

Facing the *place* is the impressive fourteenth-century **Palais des Gouverneurs**, a building with a distinctly Moorish feel originally built for the Genoese governor and bishop. It became a prison after the French transferred the capital to Ajaccio, and was then destroyed during a British attack of 1794 (in which an ambitious young captain named Horatio Nelson played a decisive part). The subsequent rebuilding was not the last, as parts of it were mistakenly blown up by American B-52s in the bungled attack of 1943 – which devastated the city centre on the day after the island's liberation. Today, the Palais hosts the recently revamped **Musée de Bastia** (Tues–Sun 10am–6pm; €5; Ⓦ www.musee-bastia.com), a state-of-the-art museum charting the city's evolution as a trade and artistic centre. Its collection includes part of Cardinal Fesch's famous hoard of Renaissance art (see p.1001).

Back in place du Donjon, if you cross the square and follow rue Notre-Dame you come out at the **Église Ste-Marie**. Built in 1458 and overhauled in the seventeenth century, it was the cathedral of Bastia until 1801, when the bishopric was transferred to Ajaccio. Inside, the church's principal treasure is a small silver statue of the Virgin (housed in a glass case on the right wall as you face the altar), which is carried through Terra Nova and Terra Vecchia on August 15, the Festival of the Assumption. Immediately behind Ste-Marie in rue de l'Évêché stands the **Oratoire Sainte-Croix**, a sixteenth-century chapel decorated in Louis XV style, with lashings of rich blue paint and gilt scrollwork. It houses another holy item, the *Christ des Miracles*, a blackened oak crucifix much venerated by Bastia's fishermen.

L'Oratoire de Monserato

One of Bastia's most extraordinary monuments, the **Oratoire de Monserato**, lies a pleasant two-kilometre uphill walk from the town centre. The building itself looks unremarkable from the outside, but its interior houses the much revered **Scala Santa**, a replica of the Holy Steps of the Basilica of Saint John of Lateran in Rome. Penitents who ascend it on their knees as far as its high altar may be cleansed, or so it is believed, of all sins, without the intercession of a priest.

Eating and drinking

Lively **place St-Nicolas**, lined with smart café-restaurants, is the place to be during the day, particularly between noon and 3pm, when the rest of town is deserted. Along **boulevard Paoli** and **rue César Campinchi**, chi-chi *salons de thé* offer elaborate patisseries, local chestnut flan and doughnuts (*beignets*).

Drinking is serious business in Bastia. The **Casanis** pastis factory is on the outskirts in Lupino, and this is indisputably the town's drink – order a "*Casa*" and you'll fit in well.

Bars and cafés

Chez Serge Raugi 2bis rue Capanelle, off bd Général Graziani, at the north end of place St-Nicolas. Arguably Corsica's greatest ice-cream maker, from an illustrious line of local *glaciers*. Tables on a cramped pavement terrace or upstairs on an even smaller mezzanine floor. In winter, they also do a legendary chickpea tart to take away.

La Citadelle In front of the Palais des Gouverneurs, Terra Nova. Basically a sandwich and ice-cream bar that would have little to recommend it were it not for the superb location overlooking the Vieux Port.

Restaurants

🏃 **A Casarelle** 6 rue Ste-Croix ☏ 04.95.32.02.32. Innovative Corsican–French cuisine (swordfish steaks in flaky pastry with aubergine and mint, for example) served on a terrace on the edge of the citadelle. The chef's specialities are traditional dishes of the Balagne, such as *casgiate* (nuggets of fresh cheese baked in fragrant chestnut leaves) or the rarely prepared *storzapretti* – balls of *brocciu*, spinach and herbs in tomato sauce. *Menu* at €30 for lunch. Closed Sat lunchtime and all day Sun.

Le Palais des Glaces Place St-Nicolas ☏ 04.95.35.05.01. One of the few dependable lunch

spots on the main square, frequented as much by Bastiais as visitors. Their good-value €27 menu, served under swish awnings beneath the plane trees, often includes the house favourite: fish bruschettas.
La Table du Marché Place du Marché ⊕04.95.31.64.25. Offering far better value than most places on the nearby Vieux Port, this smart terrace restaurant serves a tempting €27.50 menu régional featuring local crayfish, east-coast oysters and filets du St-Pierre. The à la carte menu is dominated by fancier gastro seafood, and is much more expensive. Closed Sun.
U Tianu 4 rue Rigo ⊕04.95.31.36.67. Tiny, family-run restaurant with lots of atmosphere, hidden in a narrow backstreet behind the Vieux Port. Their limited but excellent-value menus (€25–30) feature typical country dishes such as figatellu pâté, blackbird terrine, sardines stuffed with brocciu, and fiadone soaked in home-made eau de vie.

Listings

Bike rental Holiday Bikes, at 35 Rue César Campinchi (⊕04.95.31.48.95, ⓦwww.holiday -bikes.com), rents out bicycles by the day (€22) or for longer periods, as does Velo Corse, based at Borgo to the south of the city (⊕04.95.44.49.67, ⓦwww.velo-corse.com).
Car rental Avis (Ollandini), 40 bd Paoli ⊕04.95.31.95.64, airport ⊕04.95.54.55.46; Europcar, 1 rue du Nouveau-Port ⊕04.95.31.59.29, airport ⊕04.95.30.09.50; Hertz, square St-Victor ⊕04.95.31.14.24, airport ⊕04.95.30.05.00.

Ferry offices Corsica Ferries, 5bis rue du Chanoine-Leschi and sales counter at Nouveau Port, South Terminal ⊕00-33/4.92.00.43.76, ⓦwww.corsicaferries.com; Mobylines, Sarl Colonna D'Istria & Fils, 4 rue Luce de Casablanca, just behind the Nouveau Port ⊕04.95.34.84.94, ⓦwww.mobylines.com; SNCM, Nouveau Port ⊕04.95.54.66.99, ⓦwww.sncm.fr.
Internet access Le Cyber, Rue des Jardins, just behind the Vieux Port (daily 10–2am).
Post office Av du Maréchal Sebastiani, between the train station and place St-Nicolas.

South of Bastia

Fed by the rivers Bevinco and Golo, the **ÉTANG DE BIGUGLIA**, to the south of the city, is the largest lagoon in Corsica, and one of its best sites for rare migrant birds. The Roman town of **MARIANA**, on the southern shore of the étang, can be approached by taking the turning for Poretta airport, 16km along the N193, or the more scenic coastal route through **LA MARANA**. It was founded in 93 BC as a military colony, but today's houses, baths and basilica are too ruined to be of great interest. It's only the square baptistry, with its remarkable mosaic floor decorated with dancing dolphins and fish looped around bearded figures representing the four rivers of paradise, that is worth seeking out.

Adjacent to Mariana stands the **church of Santa Maria Assunta**, known as **La Canonica**. Built in 1119 close to the old capital of Biguglia, it's the finest of around three hundred churches built by the Pisans in their effort to evangelize the island. Modelled on a Roman basilica, the perfectly proportioned edifice is decorated outside with Corinthian capitals plundered from the main Mariana site and with plates of Cap Corse marble. Another ancient church, **San Parteo**, built in the eleventh and twelfth centuries, stands 300m further south.

Cap Corse

Until Napoléon III had a coach road built around **Cap Corse** in the nineteenth century, the promontory was effectively cut off from the rest of the island, relying on Italian maritime traffic for its income – hence its distinctive Tuscan dialect. Many Capicursini later left to seek their fortunes in the colonies of the Caribbean, which explains the distinctly ostentatious mansions, or palazzi, built by the successful émigrés (nicknamed "les Américains") on their return. For all the changes brought by the modern world, Cap Corse still feels like a separate country, with wild flowers in profusion, vineyards and quiet, traditional fishing villages.

Forty kilometres long and only fifteen across, the peninsula is divided by a spine of mountains called the Serra, which peaks at **Cima di e Folicce**, 1324m above sea level. The coast on the east side of this divide is characterized by tiny ports, or *marines*, tucked into gently sloping rivermouths, alongside coves which become sandier as you go further north. The villages of the western coast are sited on rugged cliffs, high above the rough sea and tiny rocky inlets that can be glimpsed from the corniche road.

The main villages on Cap Corse are connected to Bastia's *gare routière* by **bus**. Services are fairly frequent during the summer, but drop off considerably between October and May. Running up the east coast to Pietracorbara, the Bastia municipal bus company, SAB (T 04.95.31.06.65, W www.bastiabus.com), lays on hourly services from Monday to Saturday, the first departing at 6.30am. Transports Micheli (T 04.95.35.14.64) also runs two daily services all the way to Macinaggio. It's advisable to check all timings before departure via the Bastia tourist office or online at W www.corsicabus.org.

Erbalunga

Built along a rocky promontory 10km north of Bastia, the small port of **ERBALUNGA** is the highlight of the east coast, with aged, pale buildings stacked like crooked boxes behind a small harbour and ruined Genoese watchtower. A little colony of French artists lived here in the 1920s, and the village has drawn a steady stream of admirers ever since. Come summer it's transformed into something of a cultural enclave, with concerts and art events adding a spark to local nightlife. The town is most famous, however, for its Good Friday procession, known as the **Cerca** (Search), which evolved from an ancient fertility rite. Hooded penitents, recruited from the ranks of a local religious brotherhood, form a spiral known as a *Granitola*, or snail, which unwinds as the candlelit procession moves into the village square.

The one **hotel**, the gorgeous *Castel Brando* (T 04.95.30.10.30, W www.castel brando.com; mid-March to mid-Nov; ◐), stands at the entrance to the *place*, shaded by a curtain of mature date palms, like the backdrop to a classic Visconti movie. It's an elegant, old, stone-floored *palazzu* with a lovely pool and its own car park. Pick of the harbourside **restaurants** is the renowned ⅄ *Le Pirate* (T 04.95.33.24.20, W www.restaurantlepirate.com; open Easter–Oct), for whose *haute gastronomie* well-heeled Bastiais flock here throughout the year. Local seafood and meat delicacies, such as braised *cabri* (suckling kid) or lobster tagliatelli served with wild asparagus, dominate their *menu* (€35/65/90 for lunch/dinner). A more affordable option is *A Piazzetta* (T 04.95.33.28.69), in the tiny square behind the harbour, which does quality pizzas, veal in Cap Corse liqueur, excellent *moules frites* and possibly Corsica's best sorbets; count on €25–30 for three courses, plus wine.

Macinaggio

A port since Roman times, well-sheltered **MACINAGGIO**, 20km north of Erbalunga, was developed by the Genoese in 1620 for the export of olive oil and wine to the Italian peninsula. The Corsican independence leader, Pascal Paoli, landed here in 1790 after his exile in England, whereupon he kissed the ground and uttered the words "*O ma patrie, je t'ai quitté esclave, je te retrouve libre*" ("Oh my country, I left you as a slave, I rediscover you a free man") – a plaque commemorating the event adorns the wall above the ship chandler's. There's not much of a historic patina to the place nowadays, but with its packed **marina** and line of colourful seafront awnings, Macinaggio has a certain appeal, made all the stronger by its proximity to some of the wildest landscape on the Corsican coast. Daily **boat trips** from the marina on board the *San Paulu* (☎04.95.35.07.09, ⓦwww .sanpaulu.com; €14–22) transport visitors to some of the best of them, as well as the remote islands off the north coast of the cape. Another reason to linger is to sample the superb **Clos Nicrosi** wines, grown in the terraces above the village, which you can taste at the domaine's little shop on the north side of the Rogliano road, opposite the *U Ricordu* hotel.

The only commendable **accommodation** in Macinaggio is the *U Libecciu*, a modern two-star down the lane leading from the marina to the plage de Tamarone (☎04.95.35.43.22, ⓦwww.u-libecciu.com; open mid-March to mid-Nov; ❻). The village **campsite**, *U Stazzu*, lies 1km north of the harbour and is signposted off the Rogliano road (☎04.95.35.43.76; open May to mid-Sept). The ground is like rock, but it's cheap and there's ample shade and easy access to the nearby **beach**; the site's little café serves particularly good breakfasts and pizzas.

Decent places to eat in Macinaggio itself include the *Pizzeria San Columbu*, at the end of the port facing out to sea, which does a tasty seafood pizza for under €15. For more local seafood, you won't do better than *Le Vela d'Oro* (☎04.95.35.42.46; open year round), tucked away down a narrow alleyway running off the little square opposite the marina. Offering *menus* at around €17–22, they serve mainly *capcorsin* seafood specialities – such as local crayfish in home-made spaghetti – in a cosy dining room decorated with old nautical maps. The other place worth a try is *Osteria di u Portu* (☎04.95.35.40.49; open April–Sept), facing the marina, where you can dine on fish straight off local boats, suckling lamb stew and tender free-range veal – at honest prices (*menus* from €23–26).

Site Naturel de la Capandula

North of the town lie some beautiful stretches of sand and clear sea – an area demarcated as the **Site Naturel de la Capandula**. A marked footpath, known as **Le Sentier des Douaniers** because it used to be patrolled by customs officials, threads its way across the hills and coves of the reserve, giving access to an area that cannot by reached by road. The **Baie de Tamarone**, 2km along this path, is a good place for diving and snorkelling. Just behind the beach, the piste forks: follow the left-hand track for twenty minutes and you'll come to a stunning arc of turquoise sea known as the **rade de Santa Maria**, site of the isolated Romanesque **Chapelle Santa-Maria**. The bay's other principal landmark is the huge **Tour Chiapelle**, a ruined three-storeyed watchtower dramatically cleft in half and entirely surrounded by water. The **tourist office** in Macinaggio will furnish you with a free **map** and route description of the path. Otherwise get hold of a copy of IGN #4347 OT, which covers the entire route to Centuri-Port (7–8hr). The *San Paulu* launch (see above) runs a twice-daily shuttle service for walkers between Macinaggio and Centuri-Port (July & Aug; by reservation only; €14).

Centuri-Port

When Dr Johnson's biographer, James Boswell, arrived here from England in 1765, the former Roman settlement of **CENTURI-PORT** was a tiny fishing village, recommended to him for its peaceful detachment from the dangerous turmoil of the rest of Corsica. Not much has changed since Boswell's time: Centuri-Port exudes tranquillity despite a serious influx of summer residents, many of them artists who come to paint the fishing boats in the slightly prettified harbour, where the grey-stone wall is highlighted by the green serpentine roofs of the encircling cottages, restaurants and bars. The only drawback is the beach, which is disappointingly muddy and not ideal for sunbathing.

Centuri-Port has more **hotels** than anywhere else on Cap Corse. *Hôtel-Restaurant du Pêcheur* (☎04.95.35.60.14; Easter to mid-Nov; ❺), the pink building in the harbour, is among the most pleasant and has a popular restaurant. The *Vieux Moulin* (☎04.95.35.60.15, ⓦwww.le-vieux-moulin.net; March–Oct; ❺), at the entrance to the village, is the most stylish option: a converted *maison d'Américain* with a wonderful terrace and attractively furnished en-suite rooms.

Nonza

Set high on a black rocky pinnacle that plunges vertically into the sea, the village of **NONZA**, 18km south of Centuri, is one of the highlights of the Cap Corse shoreline. It was formerly the main stronghold of the da Gentile family, and the remains of their **fortress** are still standing on the overhanging cliff. Reached by a flight of six hundred steps, Nonza's long grey **beach** is discoloured as a result of pollution from the now disused asbestos mine up the coast. This may not inspire confidence, but the locals insist it's safe (they take their own kids there in summer), and from the bottom you get the best view of the tower, which looks as if it's about to topple into the sea.

The village has two **accommodation** options: a stylish little B&B called *Casa Maria* (☎04.95.37.80.95, ⓦwww.casamaria-corse.com; open April–Oct; ❺), in a restored schist house above the square; and the *Casa Lisa* (☎04.95.37.83.52, ⓦcasalisa.free.fr; ❹), further down the hillside at the bottom fringes of the village, which has equally gorgeous rooms with exposed beams, original tiled floors and shuttered windows looking across the gulf to the Désert des Agriates.

The Nebbio (U Nebbiu)

Taking its name from the thick mists that sweep over the region in winter, the **Nebbio** has for centuries been one of the most fertile parts of the island, producing honey, chestnuts and some of the island's finest wine. An amphitheatre of rippled chalk hills, vineyards and cultivated valleys surrounds the area's main town, **St-Florent**, half an hour's drive west over the mountain from Bastia at the base of Cap Corse. Aside from EU subsidies, the major money-earner here is viticulture: the village of **Patrimonio** is the wine-growing hub, with *caves* offering *dégustations* lined up along its main street.

St-Florent is the obvious base for day-trips to the beautifully preserved Pisan church of Santa Maria Assunta, just outside the town, and the **Désert des Agriates**, a wilderness of parched maquis-covered hills across the bay whose rugged coastline harbours one of Corsica's least accessible, but most picturesque, beaches.

The principal **public transport** serving the Nebbio is the twice-daily bus from Bastia to St-Florent, operated by Transports Santini (☎04.95.37.02.98). Timings can be checked at ⓦwww.corsicabus.org, or at the tourist office in St-Florent.

St-Florent

Viewed from across the bay, **ST-FLORENT** (San Fiurenzu) appears as a bright line against the black tidal wave of the Tenda hills, the pale stone houses seeming to rise straight out of the sea, overlooked by a squat circular citadelle. It's a relaxing town, with a decent beach and a good number of restaurants, but the key to its success is the **marina**, which is jammed with expensive boats throughout the summer. Neither the tourists, however, nor indeed St-Florent's proximity to Bastia, entirely eclipse the air of isolation conferred on the town by its brooding backdrop of mountains and scrubby desert.

Arrival and information

St-Florent's compact **tourist office** stands next to the post office at the top of the village (July & Aug Mon–Fri 8.30am–12.30pm & 2–7pm, Sat & Sun 9am–noon & 3–6pm; Sept–June Mon–Fri 9am–noon & 2–5pm, Sat 9am–noon; ℡&℉04.95.37.06.04), 100m north of place des Portes. There's a small **cyber café** just off the square, on the left (north) side of the road leading to Santa Maria Assunta. The photography shop opposite the turning also offers internet access.

Accommodation

St-Florent is a popular resort, and **hotels** fill up quickly, especially at the height of summer when prior booking is essential. A fair number of **campsites** are dotted about the coast, but are packed in August and closed out of season.

Du Centre Rue de Fornellu ℡04.95.37.00.68, ℉04.95.37.41.01. Refreshingly unpretentious, old-fashioned place of a kind that's fast disappearing on the island. The modest rooms, all en suite and with showers, are kept impeccably clean by the feisty Mme Casanova. Ask for "*côté jardin*". **❹**

De l'Europe Place des Portes ℡04.95.37.00. 03, ⓦwww.hotel-europe2.com. Simply refurbished old building in the village centre next to the square, with original flagstone floors and modern comforts. Rooms are on the small side, but all are en suite and well aired, and some overlook the marina. **❻**

Maloni On the Bastia road, 2km northeast of town ℡04.95.37.14.30, ⓦwww.malonihotel.com. An excellent little budget hotel, especially popular with bikers, with simple but pleasant en-suite rooms opening on to a leafy garden. **❺**

Maxime Rte d'Oletta, just off place des Portes ℡04.95.38.39.39, ℉04.95.37.13.07. Bright, modern hotel in the centre. Rooms to the rear of the building have French windows and little balconies overhanging a small water channel. **❺**

U Palazzu Serenu Oletta ℡04.95.37.00.68, ⓦwww.upalazzuserenu.com. Beautiful art-boutique hotel in a restored seventeenth-century mansion on the edge of a pretty hill village 6km inland. Works by Anish Kapoor, Wendy Wischer and others adorn the nine rooms. The pool is heated, and there's small restaurant and spa on site. Peak season rates start at €340 per double. **❾**

Campsite

Camping Kallisté Rte de la Plage ℡04.95.37.03.08. Closest to town and most congenial. Closed Oct–May.

The Village

In Roman times, a settlement called Cersunam – referred to as Nebbium by chroniclers from the ninth century onwards – existed a kilometre east of the present village. Few traces of it remain, and in the fifteenth century it was eclipsed by the port that developed around the new Genoese citadelle. St-Florent prospered as one of Genoa's strongholds, and it was from here that Paoli set off for London in 1796, never to return.

Place des Portes, the centre of village life, has café tables facing the sea in the shade of plane trees, and in the evening fills with strollers and *pétanque* players. The fifteenth-century circular **citadelle** can be reached on foot from place Doria at the seafront in the old quarter. Destroyed by Nelson's bombardment in 1794, it was renovated in the 1990s and affords superb views from its terrace.

Just a kilometre to the east of the town down a small lane running off place des Portes, on the original site of Cersanum, the **church of Santa Maria Assunta** – the so-called "cathedral of the Nebbio" – is a fine example of Pisan Romanesque architecture. Built of warm yellow limestone, the building has gracefully symmetrical blind arcades decorating its western facade, and at the entrance twisting serpents and wild animals adorning the pilasters on each side of the door. In the nave, immediately to the right of the entrance stands a glass case containing the mummified figure of St Flor, a Roman soldier martyred in the third century.

Eating

St-Florent is renowned for the seafood from its gulf and there's no better location to enjoy it than down on the quayside, le Quai d'Honneur, where a handful of swish gourmet places stand alongside standard pizzerias and tourist **restaurants**. With *menus* from €40, *La Rascasse* (T04.95.37.06.09) has become renowned for its imaginative spins on local seafood: lobster cannelloni, mussel and chestnut fritters, and rock fish sautéed in cured ham. In a similar price bracket is the nearby *La Gaffe* (T04.95.37.00.12; closed Tues, except in July & Aug), where you can order sumptuous devilfish stew on a bed of tagliatelle, with *menus* at €33 and €60.

Patrimonio (Patrimoniu)

Leaving St-Florent by the Bastia road, the first village you come to, after 6km, is **PATRIMONIO**, centre of the first Corsican wine region to gain *appellation contrôlée* status. Apart from the renowned local muscat, which can be sampled in the village or at one of the *caves* along the route from St-Florent, Patrimonio's chief asset is the sixteenth-century **church of St-Martin**, occupying its own little hillock and visible for kilometres around. The colour of burnt sienna, it stands out vividly against the rich green vineyards and chalk hills. In a garden 200m south of the church stands a limestone **statue-menhir** known as U Nativu, a late megalithic piece dating from 900–800 BC. A carved T-shape on its front represents a breast-bone, and two eyebrows and a chin can also be made out.

U Nativu takes pride of place next to the stage at Patrimonio's annual open-air **guitar festival** (W www.festival-guitare-patrimonio.com), held in the last week of July next to the church, when performers and music aficionados from all over Europe converge on the village.

The Désert des Agriates

Extending westwards from the Golfe de St-Florent to the mouth of the Ostriconi River, the **Désert des Agriates** is a vast area of uninhabited land, dotted with clumps of cacti and scrub-covered hills. It may appear inhospitable now, but during the time of the Genoese this rocky moonscape was, as its name implies, a veritable breadbasket (*agriates* means "cultivated fields"). In fact, so much wheat was grown here that the Italian overlords levied a special tax on grain to prevent any build-up of funds that might have financed an insurrection. Fires and soil erosion eventually took their toll, however, and by the 1970s the area had become a total wilderness.

Numerous crackpot schemes to redevelop the Désert have been mooted over the years – from atomic weapon test zones to concrete Club-Med-style resorts – but during the past few decades the government has gradually bought up the land from its various owners (among them the Rothschild family) and designated it as a protected nature reserve.

A couple of rough pistes wind into the desert, but without some kind of 4WD vehicle the only feasible way to explore the area and its rugged coastline, which includes two of the island's most beautiful **beaches**, is on foot. From St-Florent, a pathway winds northwest to **plage de Perajola**, just off the main Calvi highway (N1197), in three easy stages. The first takes around 5hr 30min, and leads past the famous **Martello tower** and much-photographed **plage de Loto** to **plage de Saleccia**, a huge sweep of soft white sand and turquoise sea that was used as a location for the invasion sequences in the film *The Longest Day*. There's a seasonal **campsite** here, *U Paradisu* (℡04.95.37.82.51; open mid-June to Sept). From plage de Saleccia, it takes around three hours to reach the second-night halt, **plage de Ghignu**, where a simple *gîte d'étape* (℡04.95.37.09.86) provides basic facilities for €14 per night. The last stretch to Perajola can be covered in under six hours.

Note that the only water sources along the route are at Saleccia and Ghignu, so take plenty with you. It's also worth knowing that between May and October, **excursion boats**, leaving throughout the day from the jetty in St-Florent marina (€17 return), ferry passengers across the gulf to and from plage de Loto. If you time your walk well, you can pick one up for the return leg back to town.

The Balagne (A Balagna)

The **Balagne**, the region stretching west from the Ostriconi valley as far as the red-cliffed wilderness of Scandola, has been renowned since Roman times as "Le Pays de l'Huile et Froment" (Land of Oil and Wheat). Backed by a wall of imposing, pale grey mountains, the characteristic outcrops of orange granite punctuating its spectacular coastline shelter a string of idyllic beaches, many of them sporting ritzy marinas and holiday complexes. These, along with the region's two honeypot towns, **L'Île Rousse** and **Calvi**, get swamped in summer, but the scenery more than compensates. In any case, Calvi, with its cream-coloured citadelle, breathtaking white-sand bay and mountainous backdrop, should not be missed.

L'Île Rousse

Developed by Pascal Paoli in the 1760s as a "gallows to hang Calvi", the port of **L'ÎLE ROUSSE** (Isula Rossa) simply doesn't convince as a Corsican town, its palm trees, smart shops, neat flower gardens and colossal pink seafront hotel creating an atmosphere that has more in common with the French Riviera. Pascal Paoli had great plans for his new town on the Haute-Balagne coast, which was laid out from scratch in 1758 as a port to export the olive oil produced in the region. A large part of it was built on a grid system, quite at odds with the higgledy-piggledy nature of most Corsican villages and towns. Thanks to the busy trading of wine and oil, it soon began to prosper and, two and a half centuries later, still thrives as a successful port. These days, however, the main traffic consists of holiday-makers, lured here by brochure shots of the nearby beaches. This is officially the hottest corner of the island, and the town is deluged by sun-worshippers in July and August. Given the proximity of Calvi, and so much unspoilt countryside, it's hard to see why you should want to stop here for more than a couple of hours.

Arrival and information

The **train station** (℡04.95.60.00.50) is on route du Port, 500m south of where the ferries arrive. The Bastia–Calvi **bus** stops just south of place Paoli in the town's main thoroughfare, avenue Piccioni. The CFC office is on avenue J. Calizi (℡04.95.60.09.56), and the **tourist office** on the south side of place Paoli (April–June & Sept–Oct Mon–Fri 9am–noon & 2–5pm; July & Aug daily 9am–1pm & 2.30–7.30pm; ℡04.95.60.04.35, ⓦwww.ot-ile-rousse.fr). For **internet** access, go to Movie Stores (Mon–Sat 10am–2am), diagonally opposite the supermarket on the crossroads where the Route Nationale cuts through the centre of town.

Accommodation

L'Île Rousse fills up early in the year and it can be difficult to find a **hotel** at any time from mid-June to September.

Hotels

Le Grillon 10 av Paul Doumer ☎04.95.60.00.49, ⓦwww.hotel-grillon.net. The best cheap hotel in town, just 1km from the centre on the St-Florent/Bastia road. Nothing special, but quiet and immaculately clean. April–Oct. ❸

Santa Maria Rte du Port ☎04.95.63.05.05, ⓦwww.hotelsantamaria.com. Next to the ferry port, this is one of the larger and best-value three-star places. Their a/c rooms have small balconies or patios opening onto a garden and pool, and there's exclusive access to a tiny pebble beach. Open year round. ❻

Splendid 4 bd Valéry-François ☎04.95.60.00.24, ⓦwww.le-splendid-hotel.com. Well-maintained, 1930s-style building with a small curvi-form pool and some sea views from upper floors; restrained tariffs, given the central location. Closed Jan–mid-March. ❻

Campsites

Le Bodri 3km west off the main Calvi road ☎04.95.16.19.70, ⓦwww.campinglebodri.com. Slap on a beach, this campsite can be reached direct by rail – ask for "l'arrêt Bodri".

Les Oliviers 1km east of town ☎04.95.60.19.92.

The town and beaches

All roads in L'Île Rousse lead to **place Paoli**, a shady square that's open to the sea and has as its focal point a fountain surmounted by a bust of "U Babbu di u Patria" (Father of the Nation), one of many local tributes to Pascal Paoli. There's a French-ified covered **market** at the entrance to the square, which hosts a popular artisan-cum-antiques sale on Saturday mornings, while on the west side rises the grim facade of the **church of the Immaculate Conception**.

To reach the **Île de la Pietra**, the islet that gives the town its name, continue north, passing the station on your left. Once over the causeway, you can walk through the crumbling mass of red granite as far as the lighthouse at the far end, from where the view of the town is spectacular, especially at sundown, when you get the full effect of the red glow of the rocks.

Immediately in front of the promenade, the **town beach** is a crowded Côte d'Azur-style strand, blocked by ranks of sun loungers and parasols belonging to the row of lookalike café-restaurants behind it. Two much more enticing beaches, Bodri and Giuncheto, lie a couple of kilometres around the headland to the west; you can get there on the four to six daily tramway services shuttling between L'Île Rousse and Calvi.

Eating and drinking

Though there's an abundance of mediocre **eating** places in the narrow alleys of the old town, a few restaurants do stand out, some offering stylish gourmet *menus* and others serving superb fresh seafood. The best cafés are found under the plane trees lining the southern side of place Paoli.

L'Escale Rue Notre-Dame ☎04.95.60.10.53. Giant fresh mussels, prawns and crayfish from the east coast *étangs* are the thing here, served in various *menus* (€18–28) on a spacious terrace looking across the tramway line to the bay. Brisk, courteous service, copious portions and for once the house white (by the glass or *pichet*) is palatable. The *menu pêcheur* (a mixed platter) is especially good value.

L'Ostéria Place Santelli ☎04.95.60.08.39. On a quiet backstreet in the old quarter, this established Corsican speciality restaurant offers a great value

set *menu* (€20), featuring courgette fritters, *soupe de nos villages*, tarragon-scented *gratin d'aubergines*, stuffed sardines and fresh pan-fried prawns. You can sit in a vaulted room adorned with farm implements or on the shaded terrace.

Le Pasquale Paoli 2 place Paoli ☎04.95.46.67.70. One of the few restaurants on the island to have earned a Michelin star. Gastronomic renditions of Corsican standards are its forté: the octopus in olive oil and lemon confit is hard to top, and there are plenty of wonderful vegetarian options. Count on around €70–90 à la carte.

Calvi

Seen from the water, **CALVI** is a beautiful spectacle, with its three immense bastions topped by a crest of ochre buildings, sharply defined against a hazy backdrop of mountains. Twenty kilometres west along the coast from L'Île Rousse, the town began as a fishing port on the site of the present-day *ville basse* below the citadelle, and remained just a cluster of houses and fishing shacks until the Pisans conquered the island in the tenth century. Not until the arrival of the Genoese, however, did the town become a stronghold when, in 1268, Giovaninello de Loreto, a Corsican nobleman, built a huge citadelle on the windswept rock overlooking the port and named it Calvi. A fleet commanded by Nelson launched a brutal two-month attack on the town in 1794; he left saying he hoped never to see the place again, and very nearly didn't see anywhere else again, having sustained the wound that cost him his sight in one eye.

The French concentrated on developing Ajaccio and Bastia during the nineteenth century, and Calvi became primarily a military base. A hangout for European glitterati in the 1950s, the town these days has the ambience of a slightly kitsch Côte d'Azur resort, whose glamorous marina, souvenir shops and fussy boutiques jar with the down-to-earth villages of its rural hinterland. It's also an important base for the French Foreign Legion's parachute regiment, the 2ᵉ REP, and immaculately uniformed legionnaires are a common sight around the bars lining avenue de la République.

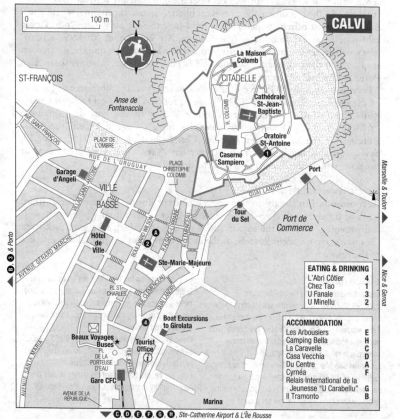

CALVI

0   100 m

N

ST-FRANÇOIS

Anse de Fontanaccia

CITADELLE

La Maison Colomb

Cathédrale St-Jean-Baptiste

R. COLOMB

Oratoire St-Antoine

Caserne Sampiero

PLACE DE L'OMBRE

RUE DE L'URUGUAY

PLACE CHRISTOPHE COLOMB

AVE SAINT-FRANÇOIS

Garage d'Angeli

VILLE BASSE

Port

QUAI LANDRY

Tour du Sel

Port de Commerce

Marseille & Toulon ▶

Nice & Genoa ▶

Hôtel de Ville

BOULEVARD WILSON

R. ALSACE-LORRAINE

R. CLEMENCEAU

Ste-Marie-Majeure

AVENUE GÉRARD MARCHE

◀ B 3 & Porto

PL ST-CHARLES

RUE CLEMENCEAU

QUAI LANDRY

Boat Excursions to Girolata

Beaux Voyages Buses

Tourist Office

PL DE LA PORTEUSE D'EAU

RUE JOFFRE

AVENUE SANTA MARIA

Gare CFC

AVENUE DE LA RÉPUBLIQUE

Marina

▼ C D E F G H, Ste-Catherine Airport & L'Île Rousse

EATING & DRINKING	
L'Abri Côtier	4
Chez Tao	1
U Fanale	3
U Minellu	2

ACCOMMODATION	
Les Arbousiers	E
Camping Bella	H
La Caravelle	C
Casa Vecchia	D
Du Centre	A
Cyrnéa	F
Relais International de la Jeunesse "U Carabellu"	G
Il Tramonto	B

The GR20 Trailhead

Getting to Calenzana from Calvi, trailhead for the **GR20** (see box, p.990), is no easy feat given the sporadic nature of public transport. It's straightforward enough during the summer holidays (July–early Sept), when two daily buses leave from the Porteuse d'Eau roundabout in Calvi (2.30pm & 7.30pm; €7, plus €1 for luggage); but for the rest of the year, this service only operates once daily in term time on Mondays, Tuesdays, Thursdays and Fridays (3.45pm). Timetables may be consulted at ⓦwww .corsicabus.org, or direct via the bus company, Beaux Voyages (3 Rue Joffre; ☎04.95.65.11.35, ⓦwww.corsicar.com).

If you find yourself heading off to the GR20 on a day when the bus isn't running, your only option is to jump in an expensive cab (around €43 from Calvi, Calvi airport or Lumio, the nearest train station to Calenzana). Be warned if you're tempted to cover the stretch on foot that the road makes a seriously unpleasant, and in places downright dangerous, walk – especially at night (when, inevitably, the taxi fare rises to around €50).

Arrival and information

Ste-Catherine airport lies 7km south of Calvi (☎04.95.65.88.88, ⓦwww.calvi .aeroport.fr); the only public transport into town is by **taxi**, which shouldn't cost more than €20 weekdays (or €25 on weekends). The **train station** (Gare CFC; ☎04.95.65.00.61) is on avenue de la République, close to the marina, where you'll find the **tourist office** on quai Landry (mid-June to Sept daily 9am–7pm; Oct to mid-June Mon–Fri 9am–noon & 2–5.30pm, Sat 9am–noon; ☎04.95.65.16.67, ⓦwww.balagne-corsica.com). **Buses** from Bastia and towns along the north coast stop outside the train station on place de la Porteuse d'Eau, whereas those from Porto pull in behind the marina.

Ferries, including NGV hydrofoils, dock at the Port de Commerce at the foot of the citadelle. Tramar (aka "CCR"), agents for **SNCM**, are on the quai Landry (☎04.95.65.00.63); Corsica Ferries' office is over in the Port de Commerce (☎04.95.65.43.21). You can **rent bicycles** from Garage d'Angeli, rue Villa-Antoine, on the left just west of place Christophe-Colomb (☎04.95.65.02.13, ⓦwww.garagedangeli.com) from €13 per day. Take along your credit card or passport, which they'll need to secure the deposit.

Accommodation

Accommodation is easy to find in Calvi except during the jazz festival (third week of June). Hotels range from inexpensive pensions to luxury piles with pools and sweeping views of the bay. If you're on a tight budget, take your pick from the town's two excellent **hostels**, or the dozen **campsites** within walking distance of the centre.

Hotels

Les Arbousiers Rte de Pietra-Maggiore ☎04.95.65.04.47, ⓦwww.arbousiers.com. Large, ochre-painted place set back from the main road, 1km south of town and 150m from the beach, with very well maintained, reasonably priced rooms ranged around a quiet courtyard. ⑤
La Caravelle Marco Plage, 1km south of centre ☎04.95.65.95.50, ⓦwww.hotel-la-caravelle.com. An impeccably clean, modern hotel virtually on the beach, with ground-floor rooms set around a

garden; those on the first floor are more luxurious. Buffet breakfasts are served on a sunny patio, and there's a nice bar-restaurant. Good value in this bracket considering the location, quality of the property and service. ⑧
Casa Vecchia Rte de Santore ☎04.95.65.09.33, ⓦwww.hotel-casa-vecchia.com. Small chalets set in a leafy garden, 500m east of town, and 200m from the beach. Half-board obligatory in July & Aug. Friendly management. Open May–Sept. ⑤

Du Centre 14 rue Alsace-Lorraine ☎04.95.65.02.01. Old-fashioned *pension*, with a hospitable owner, occupying a former police barracks in a narrow, pretty street near Église Ste-Marie-Majeure and harbourside. Its rooms are large for the price, but plain with shared WC. The cheapest option in town – by a long chalk. Open June–Oct. **❷**

Cyrnea Rte de Bastia ☎04.95.65.03.35, ⊛www.hotel-cyrnea.fr. Large budget hotel, a twenty-minute walk south of town, and 300m from the beach. Good-sized rooms for the price, all with bathrooms and balconies (ask for one with "*vue montagne*" to the rear), and there's even a pleasant pool. Outstanding value for money, especially in high season. Open April–Nov. **❹**

Il Tramonto Rte de Porto ☎04.95.65.04.17, ⊛www.hotel-iltramonto.com. Excellent little budget hotel, with clean, comfortable and light rooms on the far north side of town. Definitely worth splashing out on one with "*vue mer*", which have little terraces and a superb panorama over Punta de la Revellata. **❸**

Hostel and campsite

Relais International de la Jeunesse "U Carabellu" 4km from the centre of town on rte Pietra-Maggiore ☎04.95.65.14.16 or 04.93.81.27.63, ⊛www.clajsud.fr. Follow the N197 for 2km, turn right at the sign for Pietra-Maggiore, and the hostel – two little houses with spacious, clean dormitories at €18/29 per bed (B&B/half-board), looking out over the gulf – is in the village another 2km further up the lane. Book in advance. May–Oct.

Camping Bella Vista Rte de Pietra-Maggiore, 1km southeast of the centre (700m inland from the beach) ☎04.95.65.11.76, ⊛www.camping-bellavista.com. The best option for backpackers as it's much closer to the centre of town than the competition – though you pay a couple of euros per night extra for the privilege. Plenty of shade, nice soft ground and clean toilet blocks. Closed Nov–March.

The town and citadelle

Social life in Calvi focuses on the restaurants and cafés of the **quai Landry**, a spacious seafront walkway linking the marina and the port. This is the best place to get the feel of the town, but the majority of Calvi's sights are found within the walls of the **citadelle**.

"Civitas Calvis Semper Fidelis" – always faithful – reads the inscription of the town's motto, carved over the ancient gateway into the fortress. The best way of seeing the citadelle is to follow the ramparts connecting the three immense bastions, the views from which extend out to sea and inland to Monte Cinto. Within the walls the houses are tightly packed along tortuous stairways and narrow passages that converge on the place d'Armes. Dominating the square is the **Cathédrale St-Jean-Baptiste**, set at the highest point of the promontory. This chunky ochre edifice was founded in the thirteenth century, but was partly destroyed during the Turkish siege of 1553 and then suffered extensive damage twelve years later, when the powder magazine in the governor's palace exploded. It was rebuilt in the form of a Greek cross. The church's great treasure is the **Christ des Miracles**, housed in the chapel on the right of the choir; this crucifix was brandished at marauding Turks during the 1553 siege, an act which reputedly saved the day.

To the north of place d'Armes in rue du Fil stands **La Maison Colomb**, the shell of a building which Calvi believes – as the plaque on the wall states – was Christopher Columbus's birthplace, though the claim rests on pretty tenuous circumstantial evidence. The house itself was destroyed by Nelson's troops during the siege of 1794, but as recompense a statue was erected in 1992, the 500th anniversary of Columbus's "discovery" of America; the date of this historic landfall, October 12, is now a public holiday in Calvi.

Calvi's **beach** sweeps round the bay from the end of quai Landry, but most of the first kilometre or so is owned by bars which rent out sun loungers for a hefty price. To avoid these, follow the track behind the sand, which will bring you to the start of a more secluded stretch. The sea might not be as sparklingly clear as at many other Corsican beaches, but it's warm, shallow and free of rocks.

Winding some 170km from Calenzana (12km from Calvi) to Conca (22km from Porto-Vecchio), the **GR20** is Corsica's most demanding long-distance footpath. Only one-third of the 18,000–20,000 hikers who start it each season complete all sixteen stages (*étapes*), which can be covered in ten to twelve days if you're in good physical shape – if you're not, don't even think about attempting this route. Marked with red-and-white splashes of paint, it comprises a series of harsh ascents and descents, sections of which exceed 2000m and become more of a scramble than a walk, with stanchions, cables and ladders driven into the rock as essential aids. The going is made tougher by the necessity of carrying a sleeping bag, all-weather kit and two or three days' food with you. That said, the rewards more than compensate. The GR20 takes in the most spectacular mountain terrain in Corsica and along the way you can spot the elusive mouflon (mountain sheep), glimpse lammergeier (a rare vulture) wheeling around the crags, and swim in ice-cold torrents and waterfalls.

The first thing you need to do before setting off is get hold of the Parc Régional's indispensable **Topo-guide**, published by the Fédération Française de la Randonnée Pédestre, which gives a detailed description of the route, along with relevant sections of IGN contour maps, lists of refuges and other essential information. Most good bookshops in Corsica stock them, or call at the park office in Ajaccio (see p.998).

The route can be undertaken in either **direction**, but most hikers start in the north at Calenzana, tackling the most demanding *étapes* early on. The hardship is alleviated by extraordinary mountainscapes as you round the Cinto massif, skirt the Asco, Niolo, Tavignano and Restonica valleys, and scale the sides of Monte d'Oro and Rotondo. At Vizzavona on the main Bastia–Corte–Ajaccio road, roughly the halfway mark, you can call it a day and catch a bus or train back to the coast, or press on south across two more ranges to the needle peaks of Bavella.

Accommodation along the route is provided by **refuges**, where, for around €12–15, you can take a hot shower, use an equipped kitchen and bunk down on mattresses. Usually converted *bergeries*, these places are staffed by wardens during the peak period (June–Sept). Advance reservations can be made online via the national park (PNRC) website, ⓦwww.parc-corse.org, for an advance payment of €5 per bed; any unbooked places are allocated on a first-come-first-served basis, so be prepared to bivouac if you arrive late. Another reason to be on the trail soon after dawn is that it allows you to break the back of the *étape* before 2pm, when clouds tend to bubble over the mountains and obscure the views.

The **weather** in the high mountains is notoriously fickle. A sunny morning doesn't necessarily mean a sunny day, and during July and August violent storms can envelop the route without warning. It's therefore essential to take good wet-weather gear with you, as well as a hat, sunblock and shades. In addition, make sure you set off on each stage with adequate **food** and **water**. At the height of the season, most *refuges* sell basic supplies (*alimentation* or *ravitaillement*), but you shouldn't rely on this service; ask hikers coming from the opposite direction where their last supply stop was and plan accordingly (basic provisions are always available at the main passes of Col de Vergio, Col de Vizzavona, Col de Bavella and Col de Verde). The refuge wardens (*gardiens*) will be able to advise you on how much water to carry at each stage.

Finally a word of **warning**: each year, injured hikers have to be airlifted to safety off remote sections of the GR20, normally because they strayed from the marked route and got lost. Occasionally, fatal accidents also occur for the same reason, so always keep the paint splashes in sight, especially if the weather closes in – don't rely purely on the many cairns that punctuate the route, as these sometimes mark more hazardous paths to high peaks.

Eating and drinking

Eating is a major pastime in Calvi, and you'll find restaurants and snack bars on almost every street. Fish restaurants predominate in the marina, where – at a price – you can eat excellent seafood fresh from the bay. **Cafés**, fronted with fashionable parasols and teak furniture, line the marina, becoming more expensive the nearer they are to the foot of the citadelle.

Cafés, bars and clubs

Chez Tao Rue St-Antoine, in the citadelle ℡ 04.95.65.00.73. Legendary nightclub, opened in the wake of the Bolshevik Revolution by a Muslim White Russian, and long the haunt of the Riviera's glitterati. Now turned into a pricey piano bar from 11.30pm–2am, after which DJs take over. June–Sept 10am–4am.

Restaurants

L'Abri Côtier On quai Landry, but entrance on rue Joffre ℡ 04.95.65.12.76. Mostly seafood dishes (such as sea bass with fennel) and pizzas (from €13), served on a lovely terrace looking out to sea. Their set *menus* (€25–40) and *suggestions du jour* are invariably the best deals.

 U Fanale Rte de Porto, just outside the centre of town on the way to Punta de la

Revellata ℡ 04.95.65.18.82. Worth the walk out here for their delicious, beautifully presented Corsican specialities – mussels or lamb simmered in ewe's cheese and white wine, a fine *soupe Corse*, and melt-in-the-mouth *fiadone* (traditional flan). *Menus* €18–28 plus a full à la carte choice, and pizzas from €14. You can dine outside in the garden or inside their *salle panoramique*, with views across the bay to Punta de la Revellata.

U Minellu Off bd Wilson, nr Ste-Marie-Majeure ℡ 04.95.65.05.52. Wholesome Corsican specialities served in a narrow stepped alley, or on a shady terrace with pretty mosaic tables. Their menu features baked lamb, *cannelloni al brocciu*, spider crab dressed "*à la Calvaise*", and a cheese platter – good value at €20.

The Réserve Naturelle de Scandola

The extraordinary **Réserve Naturelle de Scandola** takes up the promontory dividing the Balagne from the Golfe de Porto. Composed of striking red porphyry granite, its sheer cliffs and gnarled claw-like outcrops were formed by Monte Cinto's volcanic eruptions 250 million years ago, and subsequent erosion has fashioned shadowy caves, grottoes and gashes in the rock. Scandola's colours are as remarkable as the shapes, the hues varying from the charcoal grey of granite to the incandescent rusty purple.

The headland and its surrounding water were declared a nature reserve in 1975 and now support significant colonies of sea birds, dolphins and seals, as well as 450 types of seaweed and some remarkable fish such as the grouper, a species more commonly found in the Caribbean. In addition, nests belonging to the rare Audouin's gull are visible on the cliffs, and you might see the odd fish eagle (*Balbuzard pêcheur*) – there used to be only a handful of nesting pairs at one time, but careful conservation has increased their numbers considerably over the past two decades.

Scandola is off-limits to hikers and can be viewed only by **boat** (Colombo Lines ℡ 04.95.62.32.10, Ⓦ www.colombo-line.com), which means taking one of the daily excursions from Calvi or Porto. These leave morning and afternoon from Calvi, and from Porto at various intervals throughout the daytime and early evening (April–Oct), the first two stopping for two hours at **Girolata** (see p.992) and returning in the late afternoon. It's a fascinating journey and well worth the steep fare, although it's a good idea to take a picnic if you're on a tight budget, as the restaurants in Girolata are very pricey.

Girolata

Connected by a mere mule track to the rest of the island (1hr 30min on foot from the nearest road), the tiny fishing haven of **GIROLATA**, immediately east of Scandola, has a dreamlike quality that's highlighted by the vivid red of the surrounding rocks. A short stretch of stony beach and a few houses are dominated by a stately watchtower, built by the Genoese later in the seventeenth century in the form of a small castle on a bluff overlooking the cove. For most of the year, this is one of the most idyllic spots on the island, with only the odd yacht and party of hikers to threaten the settlement's tranquillity. From June to September, though, daily boat trips from Porto and Calvi ensure the village is swamped during the middle of the day, so if you want to make the most of the scenery and peace and quiet, walk here and stay a night in one of the *gîtes*.

The head of the Girolata trail is at **Bocca â Crocce** (Col de la Croix), on the Calvi–Porto road, from where a clear path plunges downhill through dense maquis and forest to a flotsam-covered cove known as **Cala di Tuara** (30min). The more rewarding of the two tracks that wind onwards to Girolata is the gentler one running left around the headland, but if you feel like stretching your legs, follow the second, more direct route uphill to a pass.

In Girolata, *La Cabane du Berger* (☎04.95.20.16.98; May–Oct; €40 per person for dorm bed, half-board) offers a choice of **accommodation** in dorms or small wood cabins in the garden behind (these accommodate two people); you can also put your tent up here. Meals are served in their quirky wood-carved bar, but the food isn't up to much. The same is true of the other *gîte*, *Le Cormorant*, among the houses at the north end of the cove (☎04.95.20.15.55; July & Aug; €40; half-board obligatory), which has eighteen dorm spaces and a small restaurant overlooking the boat jetty. Unless you're staying at one of the *gîtes*, you'll be better off paying a little extra to eat at one of the two restaurants just up the steps. With a terrace overlooking the beach, *Le Bel Ombra* is the pricier of the pair, offering local seafood specialities, including fresh Scandola lobster. *Le Bon Espoir*, next door, is marginally cheaper. Note that neither restaurant accepts credit cards.

Porto (Portu) and around

The overwhelming proximity of the mountains, combined with the pervasive eucalyptus and spicy scent of the maquis, give **PORTO**, 30km south of Calvi, a uniquely intense atmosphere that makes it one of the most interesting places to stay on the west coast. Except for a watchtower erected here by the Genoese in the second half of the sixteenth century, the site was only built upon with the onset of tourism since the 1950s; today the village is still so small that it can become claustrophobic in July and August, when overcrowding is no joke. Off-season, the place becomes eerily deserted, so you'd do well to choose your times carefully; the best months are May, June and September.

The crowds and traffic jams tend to be most oppressive passing the famous **Calanches**, a huge mass of weirdly eroded pink rock just southwest of Porto, but you can easily sidestep the tourist deluge in picturesque **Piana**, which overlooks the gulf from its southern shore, or by heading inland from Porto through the **Gorges de Spelunca**. Forming a ravine running from the sea to the watershed of the island, this spectacular gorge gives access to the equally grandiose **Forêt d'Aïtone**, site of Corsica's most ancient Laricio pine trees and a deservedly popular hiking area. Throughout the forest, the river and its tributaries are punctuated by strings of *piscines naturelles* (natural swimming pools) – a refreshing alternative to the beaches hereabouts. If you're travelling between Porto and Ajaccio, a worthwhile place to break the journey is the clifftop village of **Cargèse** where the two main attractions are the Greek church and spectacular beach.

Arrival and information

Buses from Calvi, via Galéria, and from Ajaccio, via Cargèse, pull into the junction at the end of route de la Marine, opposite the Banco supermarket, en route to the marina. Timetables are posted at the stops themselves, and at the **tourist office**, down in the marina (May, June & Sept daily 9am–6pm; July & Aug daily 9am–7pm; Oct–April Mon–Fri 9am–5pm; ℡04.95.26.10.55, Ⓦwww .porto-tourisme.com), where you can buy Topo-guides and brochures for hikes in the area. Timetable information and tickets for the **boat excursions** to Scandola, the Calanches and Girolata are available in advance from the operators at their counters around the marina.

Accommodation

Competition between **hotels** is more cut-throat in Porto than in any other resort on the island. During slack periods towards the beginning and end of the season, most places engage in a full-on price war, pasting up cheaper tariffs than their neighbours – all of which is great for punters. In late July and August, however, the normal high rates prevail. Photos of all the hotels listed below are posted on the local tourist office website (see "Arrival and information", above).

Hotels

Le Belvédère Porto marina ℡04.95.26.12.01, Ⓦwww.hotel-le-belvedere.com. This three-star is the smartest of the hotels overlooking the marina, with great views from its comfortable rooms and terraces of Capo d'Orto. Reasonable rates given the location. ❹

Brise de Mer On the left of rte de la Marine as you approach the tower from the village, opposite the telephone booths ℡04.95.26.10.28, Ⓦwww.brise -de-mer.com. A large, old-fashioned place with very friendly service and a congenial terrace restaurant. Rooms at the back have the best views. April to mid-Oct. ❺

Le Colombo At the top of the village opposite the turning for Ota ℡04.95.26.10, Ⓦwww.hotel -colombo-porto.com. An informal, sixteen-room hotel overlooking the valley, imaginatively decorated in sea-blue colours with driftwood and flotsam sculpture. ❻

Le Golfe At the base of the rock in the marina ℡04.95.26.13.33. Small, cosy and unpretentious;

every room has a balcony with a sea view. Among the cheapest at this end of the village. May–Oct. ❹

🏃 **Le Maquis** At the top of the village just beyond the Ota turning ℡04.95.26.12.19, Ⓦwww.hotel-lemaquis.com. A perennially popular, well-maintained budget hotel; rooms are basic, but comfortable enough, and they give good off-season discounts. Advance booking recommended; rates double in Aug; at other times, tariffs stay under €50 per double. ❺

Campsites

Camping Les Oliviers ℡04.95.26.14.49, Ⓦwww .camping-oliviers-porto.com. Top-notch two-star site, boasting a huge multi-layered pool. April–Nov.

Camping Sole e Vista At the main road junction near the supermarkets ℡04.95.26.15.71, Ⓦwww .camping-sole-e-vista.com. A superb location on shady terraces ascending a steep hillside with a small café at the top. Great views of Capo d'Orto cliffs opposite, and immaculate toilet blocks. April–Nov.

The Town

Eucalyptus-bordered **route de la Marine** links the two parts of the resort. The village proper, known as **Vaïta**, comprises a strip of supermarkets, shops and hotels 1km from the sea, but the main focus of activity is the small **marina**, located at the avenue's end. Overlooking the entrance to the harbour is the much-photographed **Genoese Tower** (May–Sept daily 9am–8.45pm; €2.50), a square chimney-shaped structure that was cracked by an explosion in the seventeenth century, when it was used as an arsenal. An awe-inspiring view of the crashing sea and maquis-shrouded mountains makes it worth the short climb. Occupying a converted powder house down in the square opposite the base of the tower is the **Aquarium de la Poudrière** (June–Aug daily 10am–10pm; Sept–May Mon–Sat 10am–7pm; €5.50), where you can view the various species of sea life that inhabit the gulf, including grouper, moray eels and sea-horses.

The **beach** consists of a pebbly cove south beyond the shoulder of the massive rock supporting the tower. To reach it from the marina, follow the little road that skirts the rock, cross the wooden bridge which spans the River Porto on your left, then walk through the car park under the trees. Although it's rather rocky and exposed, and the sea very deep, the great crags overshadowing the shore give the place a vivid, wild atmosphere.

Eating and drinking

The overall standard of restaurants in Porto is pitiably poor, with overpriced food and indifferent service the norm, particularly during high season. There are, however, a couple of exceptions. At the budget end, *Le Maquis*, in the hotel of the same name (see p.993), serves honest, affordable home cooking in a cosy bar or on a tiny terrace that hangs over the valley. Their good-value €20 *menu* includes delicious scorpion fish in mussel sauce. Down in the port, *La Mer*, opposite the tower (☎04.95.26.11.27), is the posh option, and one of the finest seafood restaurants in the area, with fish fresh from the gulf, imaginatively prepared and served in an ideal setting. *Menus* range from €22–40 and it's best to reserve early for a seat with a view.

The Calanches

The UNESCO-protected site of the **Calanches**, 5km southwest of Porto, takes its name from *calanca*, the Corsican word for creek or inlet, but the outstanding characteristics here are the vivid orange and pink rock masses and pinnacles which crumble into the dark blue sea. Liable to unusual patterns of erosion, these tormented rock formations and porphyry needles, some of which soar 300m above the waves, have long been associated with different animals and figures, of which the most famous is the Tête de Chien (Dog's Head) at the north end of the stretch of cliffs. Other figures and creatures conjured up include a Moor's head, a monocled bishop, a bear and a tortoise.

One way to see the fantastic cliffs of the Calanches is by boat from Porto; excursions leave daily in summer, cost €25/17 (adults/children 5–10) and last about an hour. Alternatively, you could drive along the corniche road that weaves through the granite archways on its way to Piana. Eight kilometres along the road from Porto, the *Roches Bleues* café is a convenient landmark for walkers.

Piana

Picturesque **PIANA** occupies a prime location overlooking the Calanches, but for some reason does not suffer the deluge of tourists that Porto endures. Retaining a sleepy feel, the village comprises a cluster of pink houses ranged around an eighteenth-century church and square, from the edge of which the panoramic views over the Golfe de Porto are sublime.

If you want to **stay**, look no further than *Les Roches Rouges* (☎04.95.27.81.81, ⓦwww.lesrochesrouges.com; April–Oct; ⑧), an elegant old *grand hôtel* rising from the eucalyptus canopy on the outskirts. Having lain empty for two

Calanches walks

The rock formations visible from the road are not a patch on what you can see from the waymarked **trails** winding through the Calanches, which vary from easy ambles to strenuous stepped ascents. An excellent leaflet highlighting the pick of the routes is available free from tourist offices. Whichever one you choose, leave early in the morning or late in the afternoon to avoid the heat in summer, and take plenty of water.

The most popular walk is to the **Château Fort** (1hr), which begins at a sharp hairpin in the D81, 700m north of the *Café Roches Rouges* (look for the car park and signboard at the roadside). Passing the famous **Tête de Chien**, it snakes along a ridge lined by dramatic porphyry forms to a huge square chunk of granite resembling a ruined castle. Just before reaching it there's an open platform from where the views of the gulf and Paglia Orba, Corsica's third highest mountain, are superb – one of the best sunset spots on the island – but bring a torch to help find the path back.

For a more challenging extension to the above walk, begin instead at the **Roches Rouges café**. On the opposite side of the road, two paths strike up the hill: follow the one on your left nearest the stream (as you face away from the café), which zigzags steeply up the rocks, over a pass and down the other side to rejoin the D81 in around 1hr 15min. About 150m west of the spot where you meet the road is the trailhead for the Château Fort walk, with more superb views.

A small oratory niche in the cliff by the roadside, 500m south of *Café Roches Rouges*, contains a Madonna statue, Santa Maria, from where the wonderful **sentier muletier** (1hr) climbs into the rocks above. Before the road was blasted through the Calanches in 1850, this old paved path, an extraordinary feat of workmanship supported in places by dry-stone banks and walls, formed the main artery between the villages of Piana and Ota. After a very steep start, the route contours through the rocks and pine woods above the restored mill at Pont de Gavallaghiu, emerging after one hour back on the D81, roughly 1.5km south of the starting point. Return by the same path.

decades, the building was restored with most of its original fittings and furniture intact, and possesses loads of *fin-de-siècle* style. The rooms are huge and light, with large shuttered windows, but make sure you get one facing the water. Non-residents are welcome to drop in for a sundowner on the magnificent terrace, or for a meal in the fresco-covered restaurant, whose *menus gastronomiques* (€32–70), dominated by local seafood delicacies, are as sophisticated as the ambience.

The Gorges de Spelunca

Spanning the 2km between the villages of Ota and Évisa, a few kilometres inland from Porto, the **Gorges de Spelunca** are a formidable sight, with bare orange granite walls, 1km deep in places, plunging into the foaming green torrent created by the confluence of the rivers Porto, Tavulella, Onca, Campi and Aïtone. The sunlight, ricocheting across the rock walls, creates a sinister effect that's heightened by the dark jagged needles of the encircling peaks. The most dramatic part of the gorge can be seen from the road, which hugs the edge for much of its length.

ÉVISA's bright orange roofs emerge against a lush background of chestnut forests about 10km from Ota, on the eastern edge of the gorge, and the village makes the best base for hiking in the area. Situated 830m above sea level, it caters well for hikers and makes a pleasant stop for a taste of mountain life – the air is invariably crisp and clear, and the food particularly good.

The best **place to stay** is the rambling *La Châtaigneraie*, on the west edge of the village on the Porto road (℡04.95.26.24.47, ⓦwww.hotel-la-chataigneraie.com; mid-April–mid-Oct; ❸). Set amid chestnut trees, this traditional schist and granite building has a dozen smart, cosy rooms (with and without toilets) in an annexe around the back of the main building. On the front side, a pleasant little restaurant serves mountain cooking such as wild boar stew with *pulenta* made from local chestnuts. The *patronne* is American, so English is spoken. If you're just passing through and in search of a decent meal, you won't do better than *A Tràmula*, in the middle of the village (℡04.95.26.24.39; *menu* at €23), where Patricia and Mathieu Ceccaldi serve traditional local cuisine – quality charcuterie, veal, chestnut dishes and other delights – with ingredients sourced in or from the farms in the immediate area. Ask for a table on the tiny balcony overlooking the valley.

For **campers**, the *Camping Acciola* (℡04.95.26.23.01), a small site with a café-bar and great panorama over the mountains, lies roughly 3km out of Evisa: take the D84 for 2km, and turn right at the T-junction towards Cristinacce; the site lies another 400m on your left.

Cargèse (Carghjese)

Sitting high above a deep blue bay on a cliff scattered with olive trees, **CARGÈSE**, 20km southwest of Porto, exudes a lazy charm that attracts hundreds of well-heeled summer residents to its pretty white houses and hotels. The full-time locals, half of whom are descendants of Greek refugees who fled the Turkish occupation of the Peloponnese in the seventeenth century, seem to accept with nonchalance this inundation – and the proximity of a large Club Med complex – but the best times to visit are May and late September, when Cargèse is all but empty.

Two churches stand on separate hummocks at the heart of the village, a reminder of the old antagonism between the two cultures (resentful Corsican patriots ransacked the Greeks' original settlement in 1715 because of the newcomers' refusal to take up arms against their Genoese benefactors). The **Roman Catholic church** was built for the minority Corsican families in 1828 and is one of the latest examples of Baroque with a trompe-l'oeil ceiling. The **Greek church**, however, is the more interesting of the two: a large granite neo-Gothic edifice built in 1852 to replace a building that had become too small for its congregation. Inside, the outstanding feature is an unusual iconostasis, a gift from a monastery in Rome, decorated with uncannily modern-looking portraits. Behind it hang icons brought over from Greece with the original settlers – the graceful Virgin and Child, to the right-hand side of the altar, is thought to date as far back as the twelfth century.

The best beach in the area, **plage de Pero**, is 2km north of the village – head up to the junction with the Piana road and take the left fork down to the sea.

Practicalities

There's a **tourist office** on rue Dr-Dragacci (daily: July–Sept 9am–noon & 4–7pm; Oct–June 3–5pm; ℡04.95.26.41.31, ⓦwww.cargese.net), which can help find accommodation and sells tickets for summer boat trips to the Calanches, costing €46 (ⓦwww.naveva.com). **Buses** for Ajaccio and Porto stop outside the tiny main square in the centre of the village.

There are plenty of hotels to choose from in Cargèse. Overlooking the crossroads at the top of the village, two comfortable mid-scale options are *Le Continental* (℡04.95.26.42.24, ⓦwww.continentalhotel.free.fr; ❹) and *St Jean* (℡04.95.26.46.68, ⓦwww.lesaintjean.com; ❹). Better still, head down the lane dropping from opposite these last two places to the wonderful plage de Pero beach, where you'll find the beautifully situated *Les Lentisques* (℡04.95.26.42.34,

@www.leslentisques.com; ⑤), a congenial, family-run three-star with a large, breezy breakfast hall and ten simple rooms (fully en suite and sea-facing). The nearest **campsite**, *Camping Torraccia* (☎04.95.26.42.39, @www.camping -torraccia.com), is 4km north of Cargèse on the main road.

A fair number of **restaurants** are scattered about the village, as well as the standard crop of basic pizzerias, but the most tempting places to eat are down in the harbour. On a raised deck overlooking the jetty, *Le Cabanon de Charlotte* serves local seafood in a wooden cabin, with *menus* at €15–30, or you can go for their fresh fish of the day.

Ajaccio (Aiacciu)

Edward Lear claimed that on a wet day it would be hard to find so dull a place as **AJACCIO**, a harsh judgement with an element of justice. The town has none of Bastia's sense of purpose and can seem to lack a definitive identity of its own, but it is a relaxed and good-looking place, with an exceptionally mild climate, and a wealth of smart cafés, restaurants and shops.

Although it's an attractive idea that Ajax, hero of the Trojan War, once stopped here, the name of Ajaccio actually derives from the Roman *Adjaccium* (place of rest), a winter stop-off point for shepherds descending from the mountains to stock up on goods and sell their produce. This first settlement was destroyed by the Saracens in the tenth century, and modern Ajaccio grew up around the citadelle founded in 1492. **Napoleon** gave the town international fame, but though the self-designated *Cité Impériale* is littered with statues and street names related to the Bonaparte family, you'll find the Napoleonic cult has a less dedicated following here than you might imagine: the emperor is still considered by many Ajacciens as a self-serving Frenchman rather than as a Corsican.

Since the early 1980s, Ajaccio has gained an unwelcome reputation for nation-alist violence. The most infamous terrorist atrocity of recent decades was the murder, in February 1998, of the French government's most senior official on the island, Claude Erignac, who was gunned down as he left the opera. However, separatist violence rarely (if ever) affects tourists, and for visitors Ajaccio remains memorable for the things that have long made it attractive – its battered old town, relaxing cafés and the encompassing view of its glorious bay.

Arrival and information

Ajaccio's Campo dell'Oro **airport** (☎04.95.23.56.56, @www.2a.cci.fr) is 6km south of town; shuttle buses (three per hour 6.30am–10.45pm; ☎04.95.23.29.41) provide an inexpensive link with the centre, stopping on cours Napoléon, the main street – tickets cost €4.50 one way, and the journey takes around twenty minutes. Heading in the other direction, the best place to pick up buses to the airport is the car park adjacent to the main **bus station** (*terminal routière*), a five-minute walk north of the centre (☎04.95.51.55.45). Ferries also dock nearby, and the SNCM office is directly opposite at quai l'Herminier (☎04.95.29.66.99). The **gare CFC** lies almost a kilometre north along boulevard Sampiero (☎04.95.23.11.03, @www.ter-sncf.com), a continuation of quai l'Herminier.

The **tourist office** on the place du Marché, behind the Hôtel de Ville (April–June & Sept Mon–Sat 8am–7pm, Sun 9am–1pm; July & Aug Mon–Sat 8am–8.30pm, Sun 9am–1pm & 4–7pm; Oct–March Mon–Fri 8.30am–6pm, Sat 8.30am–noon; ☎04.95.51.53.03, @www.ajaccio-tourisme.com), hands out large free glossy maps and posts transport timetables for checking departure times.

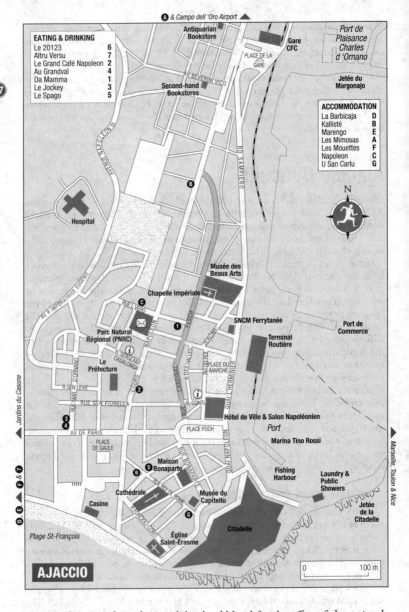

EATING & DRINKING

Le 20123	6
Altru Versu	7
Le Grand Café Napoleon	2
Au Grandval	4
Da Mamma	1
Le Jockey	3
Le Spago	5

ACCOMMODATION

La Barbicaja	D
Kallisté	B
Marengo	E
Les Mimosas	A
Les Mouettes	F
Napoleon	C
U San Carlu	G

AJACCIO

0   100 m

Anyone planning a long-distance hike should head for the office of the national parks association, the **Parc Naturel Régional de Corse**, 2 rue Sergeant-Casalonga, around the corner from the *préfecture* on cours Napoléon (Mon–Fri 8am–noon & 2–6pm; ☎04.95.51.79.00, ⓦwww.parc-corse.org), where you can buy Topo-guides, maps, guidebooks and leaflets. Cars can be rented from Rent-a-Car, at the *Hôtel Kallisté*, 51 cours Napoléon (☎04.95.51.34.45) and the airport (☎04.95.23.56.36); and Avis-Ollandini, 1 rue Colonna d'Istria (☎04.95.23.92.50) and the airport (☎04.95.21.28.01). **Internet access** is free in the lobby of the *Hotel Kallisté* on cours Napoléon.

Accommodation

Ajaccio suffers from a dearth of inexpensive **accommodation**, but there are a fair number of mid- and upscale places. Whatever your budget, it's essential to **book ahead**, especially for weekends between late May and September, when beds are virtually impossible to come by at short notice.

Hotels

Kallisté 51 cours Napoléon ☎04.95.51.34.45, ⓦwww.hotel-kalliste-ajaccio.com. Revamped three-storey hotel right in the centre, with plenty of parking space. Sound-proofed rooms for up to four people, all with cable TVs and bathrooms. Internet facilities in lobby, and the staff speak English. The best choice in this category. ❺

Marengo 12 bd Mme-Mère ☎04.95.21.43.66, ⓦwww.hotel-marengo.com. A ten-minute walk west of the centre, up a quiet side street off bd Mme-Mère. Slightly boxed in by tower blocks, but it's a secluded, quiet and pleasant small hotel (with only 16 rooms) away from the city bustle, offering bargain rates. Open mid-March to mid-Nov. ❸

Les Mouettes 9 cours Lucien-Bonaparte ☎04.95.50.40.40, ⓦwww.hotellesmouettes.fr. Luxuriously renovated nineteenth-century villa off the Routes des Sanguinaires, shaded by mature palms and pines, with direct access to its own private cove. The pricier rooms, facing the pool and sun terrace, enjoy expansive views of the bay and have well shaded balconies. ❼

Napoleon 4 rue Lorenzo-Vero ☎04.95.51.54.00, ⓦwww.hotel-napoleon-ajaccio.fr. Dependable mid-scale hotel slap in the centre of town, up a side road off cours Napoléon, in a recently revamped Second Empire style. Comfortable, very welcoming and good value for the location. ❻

U San Carlu 8 bd Danielle-Casanova ☎04.95.21.13.84, ⓦwww.hotel-sancarlu.com. Sited opposite the citadelle and close to the beach, this three-star hotel is the poshest option in the old town, with sunny, well-furnished rooms, all fully a/c, and a special suite for disabled guests in the basement – but no parking. ❺

Campsites

Le Barbicaja 4.5km west along the rte des Sanguinaires ☎04.95.52.01.17. Crowded and dirty site, but close to the beach and easier to reach by bus (#5 from place de Gaulle) than *Les Mimosas*. Open April–Oct.

Les Mimosas 3km northwest of town ☎04.95.20.99.85, ⓦwww.camping-lesmimosas.com. Much the better option of the two: shady and well-organized, with clean toilet blocks, friendly management and fair rates, though it's a fair old trudge if you're loaded with luggage. Open May–Oct.

The Town

The core of the **old town** – a cluster of ancient streets spreading north and south of **place Foch**, which opens out to the seafront by the port and the marina – holds the most interest in Ajaccio. Nearby, to the west, **place de Gaulle** forms the modern centre and is the source of the main thoroughfare, **cours Napoléon**, which extends parallel to the sea almost 2km to the northeast. West of place de Gaulle stretches the modern part of town fronted by the **beach**, overlooked at its eastern end by the citadelle.

Place Foch

Once the site of the town's medieval gate, **place Foch** lies at the heart of old Ajaccio. A delightfully shady square sloping down to the sea, it gets its local name – place des Palmiers – from the row of palms bordering the central strip. Dominating the top end, a fountain of four marble lions provides a mount for the inevitable statue of Napoleon. A humbler effigy occupies a niche high on the nearest wall – a figurine of Ajaccio's patron saint, **La Madonnuccia**, dating from 1656, the year in which Ajaccio's local council, fearful of infection from

Napoleon and Corsica

Napoleon Bonaparte was born in Ajaccio in 1769, a year after the French took over the island from the Genoese. They made a thorough job of it, crushing the Corsican leader Paoli's troops at Ponte Nuovo and driving him into exile. Napoleon's father Carlo, a close associate of Paoli, fled the scene of the battle with his pregnant wife in order to escape the victorious French army. But Carlo's subsequent behaviour was quite different from that of his former leader – he came to terms with the French, becoming a representative of the newly styled Corsican nobility in the National Assembly, and using his contacts with the French governor to get a free education for his children.

At the age of 9, Napoleon was awarded a scholarship to the **Brienne military academy**, an institution specially founded to teach the sons of the French nobility the responsibilities of their status, and the young son of a Corsican Italian-speaking household used his time well, leaving Brienne to enter the exclusive **École Militaire** in Paris. At the age of 16 he was commissioned into the artillery. When he was 20 the Revolution broke out in Paris and the scene was set for a remarkable career.

Always an ambitious opportunist, he obtained leave from his regiment, returned to Ajaccio, joined the local Jacobin club and – with his eye on a colonelship in the Corsican militia – promoted enthusiastically the interests of the Revolution. However, things did not quite work out as he had planned, for Pascal Paoli had also returned to Corsica.

Carlo Bonaparte had died some years before, and Napoleon was head of a family that had formerly given Paoli strong support. Having spent the last twenty years in London, **Paoli** was pro-English and had developed a profound distaste for revolutionary excesses. Napoleon's French allegiance and his Jacobin views antagonized the older man, and his military conduct didn't enhance his standing at all. Elected second-in-command of the volunteer militia, Napoleon was involved in an unsuccessful attempt to wrest control of the citadelle from royalist sympathizers. He thus took much of the blame when, in reprisal for the killing of one of the militiamen, several people were gunned down in Ajaccio, an incident which engendered eight days of civil war. In June 1793, Napoleon and his family were chased back to the mainland by the Paolists.

Napoleon promptly renounced any special allegiance he had ever felt for Corsica. He Gallicized the spelling of his name, preferring Napoléon to his baptismal Napoleone. And, although he was later to speak with nostalgia about the scents of the Corsican countryside, he put the city of his birth fourth on the list of places where he would like to be buried.

plague-struck Genoa, placed the town under the guardianship of the Madonna in a ceremony conducted on this spot.

At the northern end of place Foch stands the **Hôtel de Ville** of 1826. Its first floor is given over to the **Salon Napoléonien** (mid-June to mid-Sept Mon–Sat 9–11.45am & 2–5.45pm; mid-Sept to mid-June Mon–Fri 9–11.45am & 2–4.45pm; €2.30), which contains a replica of the ex-emperor's death mask, along with a solemn array of Bonaparte family portraits and busts. A smaller medal room has a fragment from Napoleon's coffin and part of his dressing case, plus a model of the ship that brought his body back from St Helena.

South of place Foch

The south side of place Foch, standing on the former dividing line between the poor district around the port and the bourgeoisie's territory, gives access to **rue Bonaparte**, the main route through the latter quarter. Built on the promontory rising to the citadelle, the secluded streets in this part of town –

with their dusty buildings and hole-in-the-wall restaurants lit by flashes of sea or sky at the end of the alleys – retain more of a sense of the old Ajaccio than anywhere else.

Napoleon was born in what's now the colossal **Maison Bonaparte**, on place Letizia (April–Sept Mon daily 9am–noon & 2–6pm; Oct–April Tues–Sun 9am–noon & 2–4.45pm; €7), off the west side of rue Napoléon. The house passed to Napoleon's father in the 1760s and here he lived, with his wife and family, until his death. But in May 1793, the Bonapartes were driven from the house by Paoli's partisans, who stripped the place down to the floorboards. Requisitioned by the English in 1794, Maison Bonaparte became an arsenal and a lodging house for English officers until Napoleon's mother Letizia herself funded its restoration. Owned by the state since 1923, the house now bears few traces of the Bonaparte family's existence. One of the few original pieces of furniture left in the house is the wooden sedan chair in the hallway – the pregnant Letizia was carried back from church in it when her contractions started. The upper floors house an endless display of portraits, miniatures, weapons, letters and documents.

Napoleon was baptized in 1771 in the **cathedral** (Mon–Sat 8am–1.30pm & 2.30–6pm; no tourist visits on Sun), around the corner in rue Forcioli-Conti. Modelled on St Peter's in Rome, it was built in 1587–93 on a much smaller scale than intended, owing to lack of funds – an apology for its diminutive size is inscribed in a plaque inside, on the wall to the left as you enter. Inside, to the right of the door, stands the font where he was dipped at the age of 23 months. Before you go, take a look in the chapel to the left of the altar, which houses a gloomy Delacroix painting of the Virgin.

North of place Foch

The dark narrow streets backing onto the port to the north of place Foch are Ajaccio's traditional trading ground. Each weekday and Saturday morning (and on Sundays during the summer), the square directly behind the Hôtel de Ville hosts a small **fresh produce market** – a rarity in Corsica – where you can browse and buy top-quality fresh produce from around the island, including myrtle liqueur, wild-boar sauces, ewe's cheese from the Niolo valley and a spread of fresh vegetables, fruit and flowers.

Behind here, the principal road leading north is **rue Cardinal-Fesch**, a delightful meandering street lined with boutiques, cafés and restaurants. Halfway along, set back from the road behind iron gates, stands Ajaccio's – indeed Corsica's – finest art gallery, the resplendent **Palais Fesch: Musée des Beaux Arts** (May–Sept Mon, Wed & Sat 10.30am–6pm, Thurs, Fri & Sun noon–6pm; Oct–April Mon, Wed & Sat 11am–5pm, Thurs, Fri & Sat noon–5pm; €8). Cardinal Joseph Fesch was Napoleon's step-uncle and bishop of Lyon, and he used his lucrative position to invest in large numbers of paintings, many of them looted by the French armies in Holland, Italy and Germany. His bequest to the town includes seventeenth-century French and Spanish masters, but it's the Italian paintings that are the chief attraction: Titian, Bellini, Veronese, Botticelli and Michelangelo are all represented in state-of-the-art air-con galleries.

You'll need a separate ticket for the **Chapelle Impériale** (same hours; €1.50), which stands across the courtyard from the museum. With its gloomy monochrome interior the chapel itself is unremarkable, and its interest lies in the crypt, where various members of the Bonaparte family are buried. It was the cardinal's dying wish that all the Bonaparte family be brought together under one roof, so the chapel was built in 1857 and the bodies – all except Napoleon's – subsequently ferried in.

Eating, drinking and nightlife

At mealtimes, the alleyways and little squares of Ajaccio's old town become one large, interconnecting **restaurant** terrace lit by rows of candles. All too often, however, the breezy locations and views of the gulf mask indifferent cooking and inflated prices. With the majority of visitors spending merely a night or two here in transit, only those places catering for a local clientele attempt to provide real value for money. **Bars** and **cafés** jostle for pavement space along cours Napoléon, generally lined with people checking out the promenaders, and on place de Gaulle, where old-fashioned cafés and *salons de thé* offer a still more sedate scene. If you fancy a view of the bay, try one of the flashy cocktail bars that line the seafront on boulevard Lantivy, which, along with the casino, a few cinemas and a handful of overpriced clubs, comprise the sum total of Ajaccio's **nightlife**.

Bars and cafés

Au Grandval 4 rue Maréchal-Ornano. Lively neighbourhood bar that's famous for its collection of antique photos of Ajaccio (mostly evocative portraits). Only a couple of doors down from *Le Jockey* (see below), which stays open later.

Le Jockey 1 rue Maréchal-Ornano. An Ajaccien institution, renowned above all for its extraordinary list of wines, which you can order by the glass or bottle: Saint-Amour, Cantemerle, Morgon, Sancerre, Chasse-Spleen, Châteauneuf du Pâpe and all the local stars. The decor's a quirky but cosy hotch-potch of ephemera and old memorabilia, with a soundtrack to match.

Restaurants

Le 20123 2 rue Roi-de-Rome ☎04.95.21.50.05, ⓦwww.20123.fr. Decked out like a small hill village, complete with *fontaine* and parked Vespa, the decor here's a lot more frivolous than the food: serious Corsican gastronomy featured on a single €34 *menu*. Top-notch cooking, and organic AOC wine. Closed Mon, except in July & Aug.

L'Altru Versu Les Sept Chapelles, Route des Sanguinaires ☎04.95.50.05.22, ⓦwww .laltruversu.com. Classy Corsican speciality place hosted by one of the island's top young chefs. The menu's a mouthwatering array of traditional fare given a gourmet twist: seabass soufflé with *brocciu* and fresh mint, chestnut tagliatelle. *Menus* €34–40; count on €50–75 à la carte.

Da Mamma Passage Guinghetta ☎04.95.21.39.44. Tucked away down a narrow passageway connecting cours Napoléon and rue Cardinal-Fesch. Authentic but affordable Corsican cuisine – such as *cannelloni al brocciu*, roast kid and seafood – on set *menus* from €14 to €29 served in a stone-walled dining room or under a rubber tree in a tiny courtyard.

Le Grand Café Napoléon 10 cours Napoléon ☎04.95.21.42.54. With its studiously Second Empire decor, this is Ajaccio's most genteel meeting place. Drop by for a pastry at the chi-chi *salon de thé*, or dine in Napoleon III splendour in the restaurant. *Menus* €28–45; or around €50 for three courses, plus wine.

Le Spago rue Roi-de-Rome ☎04.95.21.15.71. Thanks largely to its idiosyncratic designer interior, this funky little lounge restaurant has become one of Ajaccio's hippest places to eat. Techno DJs and local bands frequently enliven meals, and the modern Corsican food is reasonably priced. Try their tasty *raclette*, or Bonifacien-style baked aubergine; and leave room for one of the tempting desserts. Most mains around €15–20.

Le Golfe de Valinco

From Ajaccio, the vista of whitewashed villas and sandy beaches lining the opposite side of the gulf may tempt you out of town when you first arrive. On closer inspection, however, **Porticcio** turns out to be a faceless string of leisure settlements for Ajaccio's smart set, complete with tennis courts, malls and flotillas of jet-skis. Better to skip this stretch and press on south along the Route Nationale (RN194) which, after scaling the **Col de Celaccia**, winds down to the stunning **Golfe de Valinco**. A vast blue inlet bounded by rolling, scrub-covered hills, the gulf presents the first dramatic scenery along the coastal highway. It also marks the start of militant and Mafia-ridden south Corsica, more closely associated with vendetta, banditry and separatism than any other part of the island. Many of the mountain villages glimpsed from the roads hereabouts are riven with age-old divisions, exacerbated in recent years by the spread of organized crime and nationalist violence. But the island's seamier side is rarely discernible to the hundreds of thousands of visitors who pass through each summer, most of whom stay around the small port of **Propriano**, at the eastern end of the gulf. In addition to offering most of the area's tourist amenities, this busy resort town lies within easy reach of the menhirs at **Filitosa**, one of the western Mediterranean's most important prehistoric sites.

The Golfe de Valinco region is reasonably well served by public **transport**, with buses running four times per day between Ajaccio and Bonifacio, via Propriano and Sartène. Note, however, that outside July and August there are no services along this route on Sundays.

Propriano (Pruprià)

Tucked into the narrowest part of the Golfe de Valinco, the small port of **PROPRIANO**, 57km southeast of Ajaccio, centres on a fine natural harbour that was exploited by the ancient Greeks, Carthaginians and Romans, but became a prime target for Saracen pirate raids in the sixteenth century, when it was largely destroyed. Redeveloped in the 1900s, it now boasts a thriving marina, and handles ferries to Toulon, Marseille and Sardinia. During the summer, tourists come here in droves for the area's **beaches**. The nearest of these, **plage du Lido**, lies 1km west, just beyond the Port de Commerce, but it's nowhere near as pretty as the coves strung along the northern shore of the gulf around **Olmeto plage**, where an abundance of campsites are on offer (see below). You can reach Olmeto on the three daily buses from Propriano to Porto.

Practicalities

Ferries from the mainland and Sardinia dock in the Port de Commerce, ten minutes' walk from where the **buses** stop at the top of rue du Général-de-Gaulle, the town's main street. The SNCM office is on quai Commandant-L'Herminier (☎04.95.76.04.36), while the **tourist office** is down in the harbourmaster's office in the marina (June & Sept Mon–Sat 9am–noon & 3–7pm; July & Aug daily 8am–8pm; Oct–May Mon–Fri 9am–noon & 2–6pm; ☎04.95.76.01.49, ⓦwww .sartenaisvalinco.com).

There's a reasonable choice of **hotels** in the centre of town, including the high-tech *Loft*, 3 rue Camille Pietri (☎04.95.76.17.48; ❺), directly behind the port; and the *Bellevue* on avenue Napoléon (☎04.95.76.01.86, ⓦwww.hotel -bellevue-propriano.com; ❺), overlooking the marina and with the cheapest central rooms. If you have a car, one other place worth trying is the *Arcu di Sole*, 3km northeast on the route de Baracci (☎04.95.76.05.10, ⓦwww.arcudisole .fr.st; ❻), which has a pool and gourmet restaurant.

Campers are well provided for, although the best sites are well out of town: for the best facilities go to *Camping Colomba* (☎04.95.76.06.42, ⓦwww.camping -colomba.com), 3km north along route de Baracci, which has a swimming pool.

Cafés and **restaurants** are concentrated along the marina's avenue Napoléon. For fresh seafood, you can't beat *Terra Cotta*, at 29 av Napoléon (☎04.95.74.23.80) – the town's swankiest restaurant, with tables in a cool, Moroccan-style bistro, or out on a seafront terrace. *Formules* at lunchtime start at €20; count on €50–60 à la carte. A less pricey option is *U Famale*, a funky little pizzeria on the plage du Phare (☎04.95.76.43.06), which occupies a great spot facing the beach and gulf. They do a reasonably priced €24 *menu* featuring *mussels à la crème*, fish of the day and various *grillades* (or *croustillant d'aubergines* for veggies), and host live Corsican music most evenings.

Filitosa

Set deep in the countryside of the fertile Vallée du Taravo, the extraordinary **Station Préhistorique de Filitosa** (Easter–Oct 8am–sunset, out of season by arrangement only; €7; ☎04.95.74.00.91, ⓦwww.filitosa.fr), 17km north of Propriano, comprises a wonderful array of statue-menhirs and prehistoric structures encapsulating some eight thousand years of history. There's no public transport to the site; vehicles should be parked in the small car park five minutes' walk from the entrance in the village.

Filitosa was settled by Neolithic farming people who lived here in rock shelters until the arrival of navigators from the east in about 3500 BC. These invaders were the creators of the menhirs, the earliest of which were possibly phallic symbols worshipped by an ancient fertility cult. When the seafaring people known as the Torréens (after the towers they built on Corsica) conquered Filitosa around 1300 BC, they destroyed most of the menhirs, incorporating the broken stones into the area of dry-stone walling surrounding the site's two *torri*, or towers, examples of which can be found all over the south of Corsica. The site remained undiscovered until a farmer stumbled across the ruins on his land in the late 1940s.

Filitosa V looms up on the right shortly after the main entrance to the site. The largest statue-menhir on the island, it's an imposing spectacle, with clearly defined facial features and a sword and dagger outlined on the body. Beyond a sharp left turn lies the *oppidum* or central monument, its entrance marked by the **eastern platform**, thought to have been a lookout post. The cave-like structure sculpted out of the rock is the only evidence of Neolithic occupation and is generally agreed to have been a burial mound. Straight ahead, the Torréen **central monument** comprises a scattered group of menhirs on a circular walled mound, surmounted by a dome and entered by a corridor of stone slabs and lintels. Nobody is sure of its exact function.

Nearby **Filitosa XIII** and **Filitosa IX**, implacable lumps of granite with long noses and round chins, are the most impressive of the menhirs. Filitosa XIII is typical of the figures made just before the Torréen invasion, with its vertical dagger carved in relief – **Filitosa VII** also has a clearly sculpted sword and shield. **Filitosa VI**, from the same period, is remarkable for its facial detail. On the eastern side of the central monument stand some vestigial Torréen houses, where fragments of ceramics dating from 5500 BC were discovered; they represent the most ancient finds on the site, and some of them are displayed in the museum.

The **western monument**, a two-roomed structure built underneath another walled mound, is thought to have been some form of Torréen religious building. A flight of steps leads to the foot of this mound, where a footbridge opens onto a meadow that's dominated by five statue-menhirs arranged in a semicircle beneath a thousand-year-old olive tree. A bank separates them from the quarry from which the megalithic sculptors hewed the stone for the menhirs – a granite block is marked ready for cutting.

The **museum** is a downbeat affair, but the artefacts themselves are fascinating. The major item here is the formidable **Scalsa Murta**, a huge menhir dating from around 1400 BC and discovered at Olmeto. Like other statue-menhirs of this period, this one has two indents in the back of its head, which are thought to indicate that these figures would have been adorned with headdresses. Other notable exhibits are **Filitosa XII**, which has a hand and a foot carved into the stone, and **Trappa II**, a strikingly archaic face.

Sartène (Sartè) and around

Prosper Mérimée famously dubbed **SARTÈNE** "*la plus corse des villes corses*" (the most Corsican of Corsican towns), but the nineteenth-century German chronicler Gregorovius put a less complimentary spin on it when he described it as a "town peopled by demons". Sartène hasn't shaken off its hostile image, despite being a smart, better groomed place than many small Corsican towns. The main square, Place Porta, doesn't offer many diversions once you've explored the enclosed *vielle ville*, and the only time of year Sartène teems with tourists is at Easter for **U Catenacciu**, a Good Friday procession that packs the main square with onlookers.

Close to Sartène are some of the island's best-known **prehistoric sites**, most notably Filitosa, the megaliths of **Cauria** and the **Alignement de Palaggiu** – Corsica's largest array of prehistoric standing stones – monuments from which are displayed in the town's excellent museum.

Arrival, information and accommodation

Arriving in Sartène by **bus**, you'll be dropped either at the top of avenue Gabriel Péri or at the end of cours Général-de-Gaulle. The **tourist office** is on cours Soeur Amélie (summer only Mon–Fri 9am–noon & 2.30–6pm; ℡04.95.77.15.40, Ⓦwww.oti-sartenaisvalinco.com). The only **hotel** in Sartène worth consideration is the Swiss-owned *U San Damianu* (℡04.95.70.55.41, Ⓦwww.sandamianu.fr; ❸), just across the bridge from the *vieille ville*, beneath the convent of the same name. A three-star occupying a plum spot with spectacular views over the town and valley, it offers all the comforts and amenities you'd expect for a hotel in this class, although it's a bit bland. With a car, the best **B&B** option in the area is the *Domaine de Croccano*, 3km down the D148 (℡04.95.77.11.37, Ⓦwww.corsenature.com; ❺), a gorgeous eighteenth-century farmhouse hidden in a fold of the Rizzanese Valley, with panoramic views over the Sartenais from its vine-covered terraces. The welcoming hosts also offer horseriding and guided walks. Tariffs hover around €90 per double, although in July–August you have to stay for a minimum of one week (€700). The nearest **campsite**, the very pleasant and friendly *U Farrandu*, lies 1km down the main Propriano road (℡04.95.73.41.69; closed Nov–April).

The Town

Place Porta – its official name, place de la Libération, has never caught on – forms Sartène's nucleus. Once the arena for bloody vendettas, it's now a well-kept square opening onto a wide terrace. Flanking the north side is the **church of Ste-Marie**, built in the 1760s but completely restored to a smooth granitic appearance. Inside the church, the most notable feature is the weighty wooden cross and chair carried through the town by hooded penitents during the Easter **Catenacciu** procession.

A flight of steps to the left of the **Hôtel de Ville**, formerly the governor's palace, leads past the post office to a ruined **lookout tower** (*échauguette*), which is all that remains of the town's twelfth-century ramparts. This apart, the best of the *vieille ville* is to be found behind the Hôtel de Ville in the **Santa Anna** district, a labyrinth of constricted passageways and ancient fortress-like houses. Featuring few windows and often linked to their neighbours by balconies, these houses are entered by first-floor doors which would have been approached by ladders – dilapidated staircases have replaced these necessary measures against unwelcome intruders.

Sartène's other noteworthy attraction is the recently revamped **Musée départemental de préhistoire corse et d'archéologie** (daily 9am–7pm; €5; Ⓦwww.prehistoire-corse.org). Exhibits comprise mostly Neolithic and Torréen pottery fragments, with some bracelets and glass beads from the Iron Age, and painted ceramics from the thirteenth to sixteenth centuries.

Eating

For **restaurants**, a dependable choice is the *Restaurant du Cours ("Chez Jean")* at 20 cours Soeur Amélie (☎04.95.77.19.07), which serves wholesome, honest *cuisine sartenaise* (pork stews, stuffed courgettes and local liver sausage grilled over an open fire), as well as inexpensive pizzas, in a stone-walled inn. The house *menus* are priced at €15–24. For more refined local gastronomy, head down the mountainside to the *Auberge Santa Barbara* (☎04.95.77.09.66), 2km out of town on the Propriano road, where you can enjoy fine, authentic Sartenais dishes from both the coast and interior, served in a lovely garden: langoustine salad, roast pigeon with wild myrtle berries, *courgettes al brocciu*, and divine *milles feuilles aux fruits rouges* – in addition to Mme Lovich''s legendary *flan grandemère*. **Cafés** cluster around place Porta, and are great places for crowd-watching.

The megalithic sites

Sparsely populated today, the rolling hills of the southwestern corner of Corsica are rich in prehistoric sites. The megaliths of **Cauria**, standing in ghostly isolation 10km southwest from Sartène, comprise the Dolmen de Fontaccia, the best-preserved monument of its kind on Corsica, while the nearby alignments of **Stantari** and **Renaggiu** have an impressive congregation of statue-menhirs.

More than 250 menhirs can be seen northwest of Cauria at **Palaggiu**, another rewardingly remote site. Equally wild is the coast hereabouts, with deep clefts and coves providing some excellent spots for diving and secluded swimming.

Cauria

To reach the **Cauria megalithic site**, you need to turn off the N196 about 2km outside Sartène, at the Col de l'Albitrina (291m), taking the D48 towards Tizzano. Four kilometres along this road a left turning brings you onto a winding road through maquis, until eventually the **Dolmen de Fontaccia** comes into view on the horizon, crowning the crest of a low hill amidst a sea of maquis. A blue sign at the parking space indicates the track to the dolmen, a fifteen-minute walk away.

Known to the locals as the **Stazzona del Diavolu** (Devil's Forge), a name that does justice to its enigmatic power, the Dolmen de Fontaccia is in fact a burial chamber from around 2000 BC. This period was marked by a change in burial customs – whereas bodies had previously been buried in stone coffins in the ground, they were now placed above, in a mound of earth enclosed in a stone chamber. What you see today is a great stone table, comprising six huge granite blocks nearly 2m high, topped by a stone slab that remained after the earth eroded away.

The twenty "standing men" of the **Alignement de Stantari**, 200m to the east of the dolmen, date from the same period. All are featureless, except two which have roughly sculpted eyes and noses, with diagonal swords on their fronts and sockets in their heads where horns would probably have been attached.

Across a couple of fields to the south is the **Alignement de Renaggiu**, a gathering of forty menhirs standing in rows amid a small shadowy copse, set against the enormous granite outcrop of Punta di Cauria. Some of the menhirs have fallen, but all face north to south, a fact that seems to rule out any connection with a sun-related cult.

Palaggiu

To reach the **Alignement de Palaggiu**, the largest concentration of menhirs in Corsica, regain the D48 and head southwards past the Domaine la Mosconi vineyard (on your right, 3km after the Cauria turn-off), 1500m beyond which a green metal gate on the right side of the road marks the turning. From here a badly rutted dirt track leads another 1200m to the stones, lost in the maquis, with vineyards spread over the hills in the half-distance. Stretching in straight lines across the countryside like a battleground of soldiers, the 258 menhirs include three statue-menhirs with carved weapons and facial features – they are amid the first line you come to. Dating from around 1800 BC, the statues give few clues as to their function, but it's a reasonable supposition that proximity to the sea was important – the famous Corsican archeologist Roger Grosjean's theory is that the statues were some sort of magical deterrent to invaders.

Bonifacio (Bonifaziu)

BONIFACIO enjoys a superbly isolated location at Corsica's southernmost point, a narrow peninsula of dazzling white limestone creating a town site unlike any other. The much-photographed **haute ville**, a maze of narrow streets flanked by tall Genoese tenements, rises seamlessly out of sheer cliffs that have been hollowed and striated by the wind and waves, while on the landward side the deep cleft between the peninsula and the mainland forms a perfect natural harbour. A haven for boats for centuries, this inlet is nowadays a chic marina that attracts yachts from around the Med. Its geography has long enabled Bonifacio to maintain a certain temperamental detachment from the rest of Corsica, and the town today remains distinctly more Italian than French in atmosphere. It retains Renaissance features found only here, and its inhabitants have their own dialect based on Ligurian, a legacy of the days when this was practically an independent Genoese colony.

Such a place has its inevitable drawbacks: exorbitant prices, overwhelming crowds in August and a commercial cynicism that's atypical of Corsica as a whole. However, the old town forms one of the most arresting spectacles in the Mediterranean, and warrants at least a day-trip. If you plan to come in peak season, try to get here early in the day before the bus parties arrive at around 10am.

Arrival and information

Figari **airport**, 17km north of Bonifacio (℡04.95.71.10.10, ⓦwww.2a.cci.fr), handles flights from mainland France and a few charters from the UK. There's a seasonal **bus** service operated by Transports Rossi (℡04.95.71.00.11) that in theory should meet incoming flights, stopping at Bonifacio en route to Porto-Vecchio; otherwise, your only option is to take a taxi into town – around €50–55. If you're coming by bus from other parts of the island you'll be dropped at the car park by the marina, close to most of the hotels. The **tourist office**, in the *haute ville* at the bottom of rue F. Scamaroni (July–Sept daily 9am–8pm; Oct–June Mon–Fri 9am–12.30pm & 2–5.15pm; ℡04.95.73.11.88, ⓦwww.bonifacio.fr), sells discount passes for the town's attractions (Pass Culturel; €6; see box below), and

---

Pass Culturel

The local tourist office sell a money-saving day pass, the **Pass Culturel**, entitling bearers to enter up to four of Bonifacio's fee-entry attractions for a flat rate of €6.

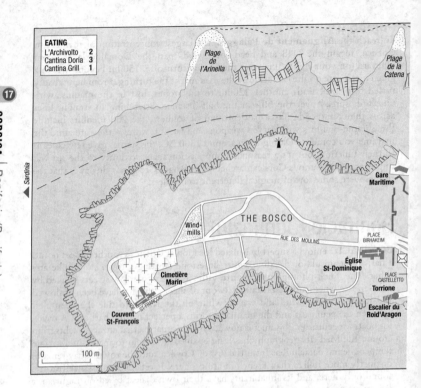

EATING

L'Archivolto	2
Cantina Doria	3
Cantina Grill	1

has audio-guides for hire in English and French (€5 for 1hr 30min tour). **Cars** may be rented from Avis, quai Banda del Ferro (☏04.95.73.01.28); Citer, quai Noel Beretti (☏04.95.73.13.16); Hertz, quai Banda del Ferro (☏04.95.73.06.41). All of the above also have branches at the airport. If you need to change money, note that Bonifacio's only **ATM**, at the Société Générale on quai J. Comparetti, frequently runs out of cash, so get there early in the day or you'll be at the mercy of the rip-off bureaux de change dotted around the town. Bomiboom.com, on quai Comparetti, offers pricey **internet** access.

Accommodation

Finding a **place to stay** can be a chore, as Bonifacio's hotels are quickly booked up in high season; for a room near the centre, reserve well in advance. Better still, save yourself the trouble, and a considerable amount of money, by finding a room somewhere else and travelling here for the day; tariffs in this town are the highest on the island. The same applies to the large campsites dotted along the road to Porto-Vecchio, which can get very crowded.

Hotels

La Caravelle 35 quai J. Comparetti ☏04.95.73.00.03, ⊛www.hotel-caravelle-corse .com. Long-established place in prime location on the quayside, whose standard rooms are on the small side for the price. ❼

Centre Nautique On the marina ☏04.95.73.02.11, ⊛www.centre-nautique.com. Chic but relaxed hotel on the waterfront, fitted out with mellow wood and nautical charts. All rooms are stylishly furnished and consist of two storeys connected with a spiral staircase. ❾

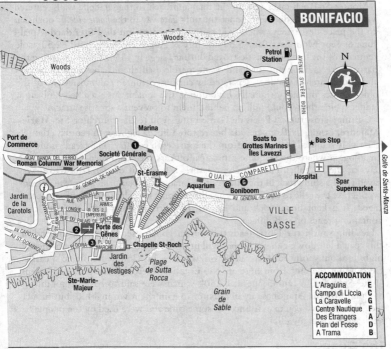

Des Étrangers 4 av Sylvère-Bohn
☎04.95.73.01.09, ⓦhoteldesetrangers.ifrance.com.
Simple rooms (the costlier ones have TV and a/c)
facing the main road, just up the main Porto-Vecchio
road from the port. Nothing special, but good value
for Bonifacio, especially in July & Aug, when rooms
go for under €55. April–Oct. ❷

A Trama 1.5km from Bonifacio along the rte de
Santa Manza ☎04 95 73 17 17, ⓦa-trama.com.
Discreet three-star, hidden behind a screen of
maquis, palms, pines and dry-stone chalk walls. The
rooms, all with private terraces, are grouped around
a garden and pool, and there's a classy restaurant
(*Le Clos Vatel*). Expensive in high summer, but more
affordable off-season. Open all year. ❽

Campsites

L'Araguina Av Sylvère-Bohn ☎04.95.73.02.96.
Closest place to town, but unwelcoming, cramped
in season, and with inadequate washing and toilet
facilities. Avoid unless desperate – though it's
undoubtedly the most convenient if you're
backpacking. April–Sept.

Campo di Liccia 3km north towards Porto-
Vecchio ☎04.95.73.03.09. Well shaded and large,
so you're guaranteed a place. April–Oct.

Pian del Fosse 4km out of town on the rte de
Santa Manza ☎04.95.73.16.34. Big three-star site
that's very peaceful and quiet in June & Sept, and
well placed for the beaches. April to mid-Oct.

The Town

At the end of the café-lined **quai Comparetti**, just before the **port commercial**
where ferries leave for Sardinia, a flight of steps – **Montée Rastello** – leads uphill
to the **haute ville**. The climb is rewarded by a magnificent view of the white
limestone cliffs tapering to Capu Persutau, and the huge lump of fallen rock-face
called the Grain de Sable. The tiny **Chapelle St-Roch**, at the head of the steps,
was built on the spot where the last plague victim died in 1528; another, narrower
stone staircase twists down to the tiny beach of **Sutta Rocca**.

Montée St-Roch takes you up the final approach to the citadelle walls, entered via the great **Porte de Gênes**, once the only gateway to the *haute ville*. It opens on to the place des Armes, where you can visit the **Bastion de l'Étendard** (April–June & Sept Mon–Sat 10am–5.30pm; July & Aug daily 9am–9pm; €2.50), sole remnant of the fortifications destroyed during a siege in 1554. While exploring the narrow streets, look out for flamboyant marble escutcheons above the doorways and double-arched windows separated by curiously stunted columns. Many of the older houses did not originally have doors; the inhabitants used to climb up a ladder which they would pull up behind them to prevent a surprise attack.

Cutting across rue du Palais de Garde brings you to the church of **Ste-Marie-Majeure**, originally Romanesque but restored in the eighteenth century, though the richly sculpted belfry dates from the fourteenth century. The façade is hidden by a loggia where the Genoese municipal officers used to dispense justice in the days of the republic. The church's treasure, a fragment of the True Cross, was saved from a shipwreck in the Straits of Bonifacio; for centuries after, the citizens would take the relic to the edge of the cliff and pray for calm seas whenever storms raged. It is kept under lock and key in the sacristy, along with an ivory cask containing relics of St Boniface.

Heading south, rue Doria leads towards the Bosco (see below); at the end of this road a left down rue des Pachas will bring you to the **Torrione**, a 35-metre-high lookout post built in 1195 on the site of Count Bonifacio's castle. Descending the cliff from here are the **Escalier du Roi d'Aragon**'s 187 steps (June–Sept daily 11am–5.30pm; €2.50), which were said to have been built in one night by the Aragonese in an attempt to gain the town in 1420, but in fact they had already been in existence for some time and were used by the people to fetch water from a well.

The Bosco

To the west of the Torrione lies the **Bosco**, a quarter named after the wood that used to cover the far end of the peninsula in the tenth century. In those days a community of hermits dwelt here, but nowadays the limestone plateau is open and desolate. The entrance to the Bosco is marked by the **Église St-Dominique** (admission €2.50), a rare example of Corsican Gothic architecture – it was built in 1270, most probably by the Templars, and later handed over to the Dominicans.

Beyond the church, rue des Moulins leads on to the ruins of three **mills** dating from 1283, two of them decrepit, the third restored. Behind them stands a memorial to the 750 people who died when a troopship named *Sémillante* ran aground here in 1855, on its way to the Crimea, one of the many disasters wreaked by the notoriously windy straits.

The tip of the plateau is occupied by the **Cimetière Marin**, its white crosses standing out sharply against the deep blue of the sea. Open until sundown, the cemetery is a fascinating place to explore, with its flamboyant mausoleums displaying a jumble of architectural ornamentations. Next to the cemetery stands the **Couvent St-François**, allegedly founded after St Francis sought shelter in a nearby cave – the story goes that the convent was the town's apology to the holy man, over whom a local maid had nearly poured a bucket of slops. Immediately to the south, the **Esplanade St-François** commands fine views across the bay to Sardinia.

Eating, drinking and nightlife

Eating possibilities in Bonifacio might seem unlimited, but it's best to avoid the chintzy restaurants in the marina, few of which merit their exorbitant prices. For a snack, try the boulangerie-patisserie *Faby*, 4 rue St-Jean-Baptiste, in the *haute* *ville*, a tiny local bakery serving Bonifacien treats such as *pain des morts* (sweet buns with walnuts and raisins) and *migliacis* (buns made with fresh ewe's cheese), in addition to the usual range of spinach and *brocciu bastelles*, baked here in the traditional way – on stone. For a scrumptious Bonifacien breakfast you can buy a *pain des morts* warm out of the oven at the *Patisserie Sorba* (follow the smell of baking bread to the bottom of the montée Rastello steps) and take it to *Bar du Quai* a couple of doors down.

The **bars** and **cafés** further along quai Comparetti are the social focus for the town and what little nightlife there is revolves around the terraces here.

Restaurants

L'Archivolto Rue de l'Archivolto ℡ 04.95.73.17.48. With its candlelit, antique- and junk-filled interior, this would be the most commendable place to eat in the *haute ville* were the cooking a little less patchy and the prices fairer. But it still gets packed out – advance reservation is recommended. Lunch *menus* around €17.50–23; evening à la carte only, around €30–35 for three courses. Open Easter–Oct.

Cantina Doria 27 rue Doria ℡ 04.95.73.50.49. Down-to-earth Corsican specialities at down-to-earth prices. Their popular three-course €17 *menu* – which includes the

house speciality, aubergines *à la bonifacienne* – offers unbeatable value for the *haute ville*, though you'll soon bump up your bill if you succumb to the temptations of the excellent wine selection.

Cantina Grill Quai Banda del Ferro ℡ 04.95.70.49.86. Same *patron* as the popular *Cantina Doria* in the citadelle, but down in the marina and with a better choice of seafood (octopus risotto, swordfish steaks, fish soup). They also do succulent *grillades* with a selection of different sauces. The food is dependably fresh, well prepared and presented, and the prices great value.

Around Bonifacio

There are impressive views of the citadelle from the **cliffs** at the head of the montée Rastello (reached via the pathway running left from the top of the steps), but they're not a patch on the spectacular panorama from the sea. Throughout the day, a flotilla of excursion **boats** ferries visitors out to the best vantage points, taking in a string of caves and other landmarks only accessible by water en route, including the **Îles Lavezzi**, the scattering of small islets where the troopship *Sémillante* was shipwrecked in 1855, now designated as a nature reserve. The whole experience of bobbing around to an amplified running commentary is about as touristy as Bonifacio gets, but it's well worth enduring just to round the mouth of the harbour and see the *vieille ville*, perched atop the famous chalk cliffs. The Lavezzi islets themselves are surrounded by wonderfully clear sea water, offering Corsica's best snorkelling. On your way back, you skirt the famous **Île Cavallo**, or "millionaire's island", where the likes of Princess Caroline of Monaco and other French and Italian glitterati have luxury hideaways. The boats leave from the east side of the marina: tickets cost €15–20 for trips to the caves, and around €25–30 for the longer excursions to Lavezzi. Drivers should note that the rival firms offer **free parking** in lots on the town's outskirts to customers.

The **beaches** within walking distance of Bonifacio are generally smaller and less appealing than most in southern Corsica. For a dazzling splash of turquoise, you'll have to follow the narrow, twisting lane east of town in the direction of Pertusatu lighthouse, turning left when you see signs for **Piantarella**, Corsica's kite-surfing hotspot. A twenty-minute walk south around the shore from here takes you past the remains of a superbly situated Roman villa to a pair of divine little coves, Grand Sperone and Petit Sperone – both shallow and perfect for kids.

Another superb beach in the area is **Rondinara**, a perfect shell-shaped cove of turquoise water enclosed by dunes and a pair of twin headlands. Located 10km north (east of N198), it's sufficiently off the beaten track to remain relatively peaceful (outside school holidays). Facilities are minimal, limited to a smart wooden beach restaurant, paying car park and campsite, the *Camping Rondinara* (℡04.95.70.43.15, ⓦwww.rondinara.fr; open mid-May to Sept). Shade is at a premium, so come armed with a parasol.

Porto-Vecchio and around

Set on a hillock overlooking a beautiful deep blue bay, **PORTO-VECCHIO**, 25km north of Bonifacio, was rated by James Boswell as one of "the most distinguished harbours in Europe". It was founded in 1539 as a second Genoese stronghold on the east coast, Bastia being well established in the north. The site was perfect: close to the unexploited and fertile plain, it benefited from secure high land and a sheltered harbour, although the mosquito population spread malaria and wiped out the first Ligurian settlers within months. Things began to take off mainly thanks to the cork industry, which still thrived well into the twentieth century. Today most revenue comes from tourists, the vast majority of them well-heeled Italians who flock here for the fine outlying **beaches**. To the northwest, the little town of **Zonza** makes a good base for exploring the dramatic forest that surrounds one of Corsica's most awesome road trips, the **route de Bavella**.

Around the centre of town there's not much to see, apart from the well-preserved **fortress** and the small grid of **ancient streets** backing onto the main place de la République. East of the square you can't miss the **Porte Génoise**, which frames a delightful expanse of sea and salt pans and through which you'll find the quickest route down to the modern marina, lined with cafés and restaurants.

Practicalities

Porto-Vecchio doesn't have a **bus** station; instead, the various companies who come here stop and depart outside their agents' offices on the edge of the *haute ville*, centred on a picturesque stone square, place de l'Hôtel-de-Ville. This is where you'll find Porto-Vecchio's efficient **tourist office** (May–Sept Mon–Sat 9am–8pm, Sun 9am–1pm; Oct–May Mon–Fri 9am–12.30pm & 2–6pm; ℡04.95.70.09.58, ⓦwww.ot-portovecchio.com).

Accommodation is easy to come by except in high summer. One of the least expensive places is the *Panorama*, 12 rue Jean-Nicoli, just above the old town (℡04.95.70.07.96; ❹), which isn't all that well maintained but offers the cheapest beds in the centre of town. Moving up a couple of brackets, the *San Giovanni* (℡04.95.70.22.55, ⓦwww.hotel-san-giovanni.com; ❼), a couple of kilometres south of Porto-Vecchio on the D659 towards Arca, has thirty comfortable chalet-style rooms set in landscaped gardens, with a pool and tennis courts. It's well run, peaceful and good value.

Of the many **campsites** in the area, *Matonara* (℡04.95.70.37.05, ⓦwww.lamatonara.com), just north of the centre at the Quatre-Chemins intersection, is the most easily accessible. Lying within easy reach of the "Hyper U" supermarket, it's large and shaded by stands of cork trees.

For a pitstop of quality local **food**, try *U Sputinu*'s copious *grande assiette* – a selection of quality charcuterie, cheese, spinach pasties (*chaussons herbes*), savoury fritters (*migliacciu*) and mint omelettes (€17.50) – served on rustic wooden tables in the little square in front of the church. In the nearby rue Borgo, *A Furana* (℡04.95.70.58.03; *formules* from €20–23; or around €35 à la carte) serves fragrant local cuisine in a vaulted Genoese dining hall, or on a romantic terrace boasting panoramic gulf views. Plenty of other places to eat are clustered around the marina and *port de commerce*, but none rustles up pizzas more delectable than those served at *U Corsu* (℡04.95.70.13.91). Reserve early for a sea view on their *pieds dans l'eau* terrace.

Golfe de Porto-Vecchio

Much of the coast of the **Golfe de Porto-Vecchio** and its environs is character-ized by ugly development and hectares of swampland, yet some of the clearest, bluest sea and whitest beaches on Corsica are also found around here. The most frequented of these, Palombaggia and Santa Giulia, can be reached by **bus** from the town in summer, timetables for which are posted in the tourist office (see above) and online at ⓦwww.corsicabus.org; at other times you'll need your own transport. The same applies to the **Casteddu d'Araggiu**, one of the island's best-preserved Bronze Age sites, which stands on a ledge overlooking the gulf to the north of town.

The beaches

Heading south of Porto-Vecchio along the main N198, take the turning signposted for **Palombaggia**, a golden semicircle of sand edged by short twisted umbrella pines that are punctuated by fantastically shaped red rocks. This might be the most beautiful beach on the island were it not for the crowds, which pour on to it in such numbers that a wattle fence has had to be erected to protect the dunes. A few kilometres further along the same road takes you to **Santa Giulia**, a sweeping sandy bay backed by a lagoon. Despite the presence of several sprawling holiday villages, crowds are less of a problem here, and the shallow bay is an extraordinary turquoise colour.

North of Porto-Vecchio, the first beach worth a visit is **San Cipriano**, a half-moon bay of white sand, reached by turning left off the main road at the Elf petrol station. Carry on for another 7km, and you'll come to the even more pictur-esque beach at **Pinarellu**, an uncrowded, long sweep of soft white sand with a Genoese watchtower and, like the less inspiring beaches immediately north of here, benefiting from the spectacular backdrop of the Massif de l'Ospédale.

Casteddu Araggiu

The coast between Porto-Vecchio and Solenzara is also strewn with **prehistoric monuments**. The most impressive of these, Casteddu d'Araggiu, lies 12km north along the D759. From the site's car park (signposted off the main road), it's a twenty-minute stiff climb through maquis and scrubby woodland to the ruins. Built in 2000 BC, the *casteddu* consists of a complex of chambers built into a massive circular wall of pink granite from the top of which the views over the gulf are superb.

The route de Bavella

Starting from the picture-postcard-pretty mountain village of **ZONZA**, 40km northwest of Porto-Vecchio, and running northeast towards the coast, the D268 – known locally as the **route de Bavella** – is perhaps the most dramatic road in all Corsica. Well served by buses, it also affords one of the simplest approaches to the spectacular landscapes of the interior. The road penetrates a dense expanse of old pine and chestnut trees as it rises steadily to the **Col de Bavella** (1218m), where a towering statue of **Notre-Dame-des-Neiges** marks the windswept pass itself. An amazing panorama of peaks and forests spreads out from the col: to the northwest the serrated granite ridge of the Cirque de Gio Agostino is dwarfed by the pink pinnacles of the Aiguilles de Bavella; behind soars Monte Incudine.

Just below the pass, the seasonal hamlet of **BAVELLA** comprises a handful of congenial cafés, corrugated-iron-roofed chalets and hikers' hostels from where you can follow a series of waymarked **trails** to nearby viewpoints. Deservedly the most popular of these is the two-hour walk to the **Trou de la Bombe**, a circular opening that pierces the Paliri crest of peaks. From the car park behind the *Auberge du Col* follow the red-and-white waymarks of GR20 for 800m, then head right when you see orange splashes.

From Bavella, it's a steep descent through what's left of the **Forêt de Bavella**, which was devastated by fire in 1960 but still harbours some huge Laricio pines. The winding road offers numerous breathtaking glimpses of the Aiguilles de Bavella and plenty of places to pull over for a swim in the river.

The best **place to stay** locally is Zonza, which has a cluster of hotels, all with more than decent restaurants, such as *Le Tourisme*, set back on the west side of the Quenza road north of the village (℡04.95.78.67.72, Ⓦwww.hoteldutourisme .fr; ❼; April–Oct), or *L'Aiglon* in the village centre (℡04.95.78.67.72, Ⓦwww .aiglonhotel.com; ❹; April–Dec).

Aléria

Built on the estuary at the mouth of the River Tavignano on the island's east coast, 40km southeast of Corte along the N200, **ALÉRIA** was first settled in 564 BC by a colony of Greek Phoceans as a trading port for copper and lead, as well as wheat, olives and grapes. After an interlude of Carthaginian rule, the Romans arrived in 259 BC, built a naval base and re-established its importance in the Mediterranean. Aléria remained the east coast's principal port right up until the eighteenth century. Little is left of the historic town except Roman ruins and a thirteenth-century Genoese fortress, which stands high against a background of chequered fields and green vineyards. To the south, a strip of modern buildings straddling the main road makes up the modern town, known as **Cateraggio**, but it's the village set on the hilltop just west of here that's the principal focus for visitors. Aléria/Cateraggio can be reached on any of the daily **buses** running between Bastia and the south of the island via the east coast.

To sample the famous Nustale oysters hauled fresh each day from the nearby Étang de Diane lagoon, head 1.2km north and look for a signboard on the right (east) side of the road pointing the way down a surfaced lane to the *Aux Coquillages de Diana* **restaurant** (℡04.95.57.04.55, Ⓦwww.auxcoquillagesdediana.fr). Resting on stilts above the water, it serves a great-value €24 seafood platter, featuring clams, mussels and a terrine made from dried mullet's roe called *poutargue* – the kind of food one imagines the Romans must have feasted on when they farmed the *étang* two millennia ago.

The Site

Before looking around the ruins of the ancient city, set aside an hour for the **Musée Jerôme Carcopino** (mid-May to Sept daily 8am–noon & 2–7pm; Oct to mid-May Mon–Sat 8am–noon & 2–5pm; €2), housed in the Fort Matra. It houses remarkable finds from the **Roman site**, including Hellenic and Punic coins, rings, belt links, elaborate oil lamps decorated with Christian symbols, Attic plates and a second-century marble bust of Jupiter Ammon. Etruscan bronzes fill another room, with jewellery and armour from the fourth to the second century BC.

A dusty track leads from here to the Roman site itself (closes 30min before museum; same ticket), where most of the excavation was done as recently as the 1950s. Most of the site still lies beneath ground and is undergoing continuous digging, but the balneum (bathhouse), the base of Augustus's triumphal arch, the foundations of the forum and traces of shops have already been unearthed.

Corte (Corti)

Stacked up the side of a wedge-shaped crag against a spectacular backdrop of granite mountains, **CORTE** epitomizes *l'âme corse*, or "Corsican soul" – a small town marooned amid a grandiose landscape, where a spirit of dogged patriotism is never far from the surface. Corte has been the home of Corsican nationalism since the first National Constitution was drawn up here in 1731, and was also where **Pascal Paoli**, "U Babbu di u Patria" (Father of the Nation), formed the island's first democratic government later in the eighteenth century. Self-consciously insular and grimly proud, it can seem an inhospitable place at times, although the presence of the island's only university lightens the atmosphere noticeably during term-time, when the bars and cafés lining its long main street fill with students. For the outsider, Corte's charm is concentrated in the tranquil *haute ville*, where the forbidding **citadelle** – site of a modern **museum** – presides over a warren of narrow, cobbled streets. Immediately behind it, the Restonica and Tavignano gorges afford easy access to some of the region's most memorable mountain scenery, best enjoyed from the marked trails that wind through them.

Arrival and information

Buses from Ajaccio and Bastia stop in the centre of town on avenue Xavier-Luciani; the **gare CFC** (T04.95.46.00.97) is at the foot of the hill near the university, a ten-minute walk from the centre and campsites. If you're driving, the best place to **park** is at the top of avenue Jean-Nicoli, the road which leads into town from Ajaccio. Corte's **tourist office** is situated just inside the main gates of the citadelle, near the museum (July–Aug Mon, Wed & Sat 10am–5pm, Tues, Thurs & Fri 9am–7pm; Sept–June Mon–Fri 9am–noon & 2–6pm; T04.95.46.26.70, Wwww .corte-tourisme.com). In the same building is the information office of the **Parc Régional** (same hours and phone number).

Accommodation

Finding a **place to stay** can be a problem from mid-June until early September, when it's advisable to book in advance. With three **campsites** in the town, and a couple a short drive away, tent space is at less of a premium, although the sites across the river get crowded in high season.

Hotels

L'Albadu Ancienne rte d'Ajaccio, 2.5km southwest of town T04.95.46.24.55, Wwww.hebergement-albadu.fr. Simply furnished rooms with showers (shared toilets) on a working farm-cum-equestrian centre. Warm family atmosphere, beautiful horses, fine views and Corsican speciality food (for a bargain €50 half-board). Advance reservation essential. ❺

HR Allée du 9 Septembre T04.95.45.11.11, Wwww.hotel-hr.com. This converted concrete-block *gendarmerie*, 200m southwest of the *gare*

CFC, looks grim from the outside, but its 125 rooms are comfortable enough and its rates rock-bottom; bathroom-less options are the best deal. No credit cards. ❷

Motel La Vigna Chemin de Saint-Pancrace T04.95.46.02.19. Tucked away on the leafy northern edge of town, this small but rather swish students' hall of residence is vacated between early June and the end of September and converted into a motel. The rooms are simple and lacking character by Corte standards, but clean and all en suite, with balconies. Open June–Sept. ❸

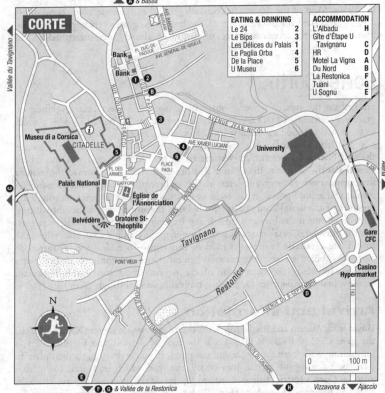

CORTE

EATING & DRINKING	
Le 24	2
Le Bips	3
Les Délices du Palais	1
Le Paglia Orba	4
De la Place	5
U Museu	6

ACCOMMODATION	
L'Albadu	H
Gîte d'Étape U	
Tavignanu	C
HR	D
Motel La Vigna	A
Du Nord	B
La Restonica	F
Tuani	G
U Sognu	E

Du Nord 22 cours Paoli ☏04.95.46.00.33,
ⓦwww.hoteldunord-corte.com. Pleasant, clean
place right in the centre, with oodles of charm. Its
variously priced rooms are large for the tariffs. **⑥**

La Restonica Vallée de la Restonica, 2km
southwest from town ☏04.95.46.09.58,
ⓦwww.aubergerestonica.com. Sumptuous comfort
in a wood-lined riverside hotel set up by a former
French-national footballer, Dominique Colonna.
Hunting trophies, old paintings, salon with open
fireplace and leather-upholstered furniture create
an old-fashioned atmosphere, and there's a large
pool and garden terrace. **⑧**

Hostels and campsites

L'Albadu 2.5km southwest of town
☏04.95.46.24.55, ⓦwww.hebergement
-albadu.fr. Perfect little *camping à la ferme*,
situated on a hillside above Corte. Basic, but
much nicer than any of the town sites, and well
worth the walk.

Gîte d'Étape U Tavignanu ("Chez M. Gambini")
Behind the citadelle ☏04.95.46.16.85.

Run-of-the-mill hikers' hostel with small dorms
and a relaxing garden terrace that looks over the
valley. Peaceful, secluded, and the cheapest place
to stay after the campsites. Follow the signs for the
Tavignano trail (marked with orange spots of paint)
around the back of the citadelle. €17 per bed
(includes breakfast).

Tuani Vallée de la Restonica, 7km
southeast ☏04.95.46.11.62, ⓦwww
.campingtuani.com. Too far up the valley without
your own car, but the wildest and most atmospheric of the campsites around Corte, overlooking
a rushing stream, deep in the woods. Ideally
placed for an early start on Monte Rotondo.
Basic facilities, although they do have a cheerful
little café serving good *bruschettas* and other
hot snacks.

U Sognu Rte de la Restonica ☏04.95.46.09.07.
At the foot of the valley, a 15min walk from the
centre. Has a good view of the citadelle, plenty of
poplar trees for shade, and toilets in a converted
barn. There's also a small bar and restaurant
(in summer).

The Town

Corte is a very small town whose centre effectively consists of one street, **cours Paoli**, which runs from place Paoli at the southern end, a tourist-friendly zone packed with cafés, restaurants and market stalls, to **place du Duc-de-Padoue**, an elegant square of Second Empire buildings.

The old **haute ville**, immediately above cours Paoli, centres on the **Place Gaffori**, dominated by a statue of General Gian-Pietru Gaffori pointing vigorously towards the church. On its base a bas-relief depicts the siege of the Gaffori house by the Genoese, who attacked in 1750 when the general was out of town and his wife Faustina was left holding the fort. Their residence still stands, right behind, and you can clearly make out the bullet marks made by the besiegers.

For the best view of the citadelle, follow the signs uphill to the viewing platform, the **Belvédère**, which faces the medieval tower, perched high above the town on its pinnacle of rock and dwarfed by the immense crags behind. The platform also gives a wonderful view of the converging rivers and encircling forest – a summer bar adds to the attraction.

Just above the place Gaffori, left of the gateway to the citadelle, stands the **Palais National**, a great, solid block of a mansion that's the sole example of Genoese civic architecture in Corte. Having served as the seat of Paoli's government for a while, it became the Università di Corsica in 1765, offering free education to all (Napoleon's father studied here). The university closed in 1769 when the French took over the island after the Treaty of Versailles, not to be resurrected until 1981. Today several modern buildings have been added, among them the Institut Universitaire d'Études Corses, dedicated to the study of Corsican history and culture.

The Museu di a Corsica and citadelle

The monumental gateway just behind the Palais National leads from place du Poilu into Corte's Genoese citadelle, whose lower courtyard is dominated by the modern buildings of **Museu di a Corsica** (April to June 21 & Sept 21 to Oct daily except Tues 10am–6pm; June 22 to Sept 20 daily 10am–8pm; Nov–March Tues–Sat 10am–6pm; €5.30; ⓦ www.musee-corse.com), a state-of-the-art museum housing the collection of ethnographer Révérend Père Louis Doazan, a Catholic priest who spent 27 years amassing a vast array of objects relating to the island's traditional transhumant and peasant past: principally old farm implements, craft tools and peasant dress.

The museum's entrance ticket also admits you to Corte's principal landmark, the **citadelle**. The only such fortress in the interior of the island, the Genoese structure served as a base for the Foreign Legion from 1962 until 1984, but now houses a pretty feeble exhibition of nineteenth-century photographs. It's reached by a huge staircase of Restonica marble, which leads to the medieval tower known as the **Nid d'Aigle** (Eagle's Nest). The fortress, of which the tower is the only original part, was built in 1420, and the barracks were added during the mid-nineteenth century. These were later converted into a prison, in use as recently as World War II, when the Italian occupiers incarcerated Corsican Resistance fighters in tiny cells. Adjacent to the cells is a former **watchtower** which at the time of Paoli's government was inhabited by the hangman.

Eating and drinking

Corte has only four **restaurants** worthy of note, plus the usual handful of pizzerias and crêperies. As a rule of thumb, avoid anywhere fronted by gaudy food photographs and multilingual menus; their dishes may be cheap, but they offer poor value for money – for not much more you'll eat a lot better in one of the places listed below.

Cafés and bars

Les Délices du Palais Cours Paoli. Frilly little crêperie-cum-*salon-de-thé* whose bakery sells a selection of delicious Corsican patisserie: try their *colzone* (spinach pasties) or *brocciu* baked in flaky chestnut-flour pastry.

De la Place Place Paoli. On the shady side of the main square, this is the place to hole up for a spot of crowd-watching over a *barquette de frites* (a pile of chips) and draught Pietra.

Restaurants

Le 24 24 cours Paoli ☎04.95.46.02.90. Served by an enthusiastic young crew against a backdrop of vaulted stone walls and stylish designer furniture, the food in this hip Corsican speciality place is innovative yet full of traditional flavours: pan-fried foie gras with chestnut crumble; salmon rolled in onion seeds with creamy red-onion velouté sauce; sublime chocolate mousse. *Menus* €19–25; or around €35 à la carte.

Le Bips 14 cours Paoli ☎04.95.46.06.26. Hugely popular budget restaurant on the main drag,

serving fragrant, copious pasta dishes, salads, steaks and some local specialities at down-to-earth rates. Hidden away in an eighteenth-century cellar, it's tricky to find: you have to cut down a back alley off the main street to a rear door. And expect to wait for a table unless you arrive early.

Le Paglia Orba 1 av Xavier-Luciani ☎04.95.61.07.89. Quality Corsican cooking at very reasonable prices, served on a raised terrace overlooking the street. Most people come for their succulent pizzas (€9–14), but there is also plenty of choice à la carte, particularly for vegetarians. Pan-fried veal served with *stozapreti* (nuggets of *brocciu* and herbs) is their *plat de résistance*. *Menus* from €17.

U Museu Rampe Ribanelle in the *haute ville* at the foot of the citadelle, 30m down rue Colonel-Feracci ☎04.95.61.08.36. Congenial and well-situated place. Try the €19 *menu corse*, featuring lasagne in wild boar sauce, trout, and *tripettes* (imaginatively translated as "trips"). Great value for money, atmospheric terrace and the house wines are local AOC.

Central Corsica

Central Corsica is a nonstop parade of stupendous scenery, and the best way to immerse yourself in it is to get onto the region's ever-expanding network of trails and forest tracks. The ridge of granite mountains forming the spine of the island is closely followed by the epic **GR20** footpath, which can be picked up from various villages and is scattered with refuge huts, most of them offering no facilities except shelter. For the less active there also are plenty of roads penetrating deep into the **forests** of Vizzavona, La Restonica and Rospa Sorba, crossing lofty passes that provide exceptional views across the island.

The most popular attractions in the centre, though, are the magnificent **gorges** of La Restonica and Tavignano, both within easy reach of Corte.

Gorges du Tavignano

A deep cleft of ruddy granite beginning 5km to the west of Corte, the **Gorges du Tavignano** offers one of central Corsica's great walks, marked in yellow paint flashes alongside the broad cascading River Tavignano. You can pick up the trail from opposite the Chapelle Sainte-Croix in Corte's *haute ville* and follow it as far as the Lac de Nino, 30km west of the town, where it joins the GR20. There's a very well set-up **refuge**, *A Sega* (dorm beds €12, bivouac €5; advance reservation essential: ☎06.10.71.77.26), situated at the halfway point, which serves filling breakfasts and evening meals (half-board €35 to bivouac or €55 in a dorm), and can supply packed lunches (€8.50).

Gorges de la Restonica

The glacier-moulded rocks and deep pools of the **Gorges de la Restonica** make the D936 running southwest from Corte the busiest mountain road in Corsica – if you come in high summer, expect to encounter traffic jams all the way up to the car park at the **Bergeries de Grotelle**, 15km from Corte. **Minibuses** run from Corte to the Bergeries, costing €13; taxis charge around €40. The gorges begin after 6km, just beyond where the route penetrates the **Forêt de la Restonica**, a glorious forest of chestnut, Laricio pine and the tough maritime pine endemic to Corte. Not surprisingly, it's a popular place to walk, picnic and bathe in the many pools fed by the cascading torrent of the River Restonica, easily reached by scrambling down the rocky banks.

From the *bergeries*, a well-worn path winds along the valley floor to a pair of beautiful glacial lakes. The first and larger, **Lac de Melo**, is reached after an easy hour's hike through the rocks. One particularly steep part of the path has been fitted with security chains, but the scramble around the side of the passage is perfectly straightforward, and much quicker. Once past Lac de Melo, press on for another forty minutes along the steeper marked trail over a moraine to the second lake, **Lac de Capitello**, the more spectacular of the pair. Hemmed in by vertical cliffs, the deep turquoise-blue pool affords fine views of the Rotondo massif on the far side of the valley, and in clear weather you can spend an hour or two exploring the surrounding crags.

Travel details

Note that the details apply to June–Sept only; during the winter both train and bus services are considerably scaled down. Current timetables for all public transport services on the island can be viewed online at Ⓦ www.corsicabus.org.

Trains

Ajaccio to: Bastia (4 daily; 3hr 30min); Calvi (2 daily; 4hr 6min); Corte (4 daily; 1hr 30min); L'Île Rousse (2 daily; 3hr 35min).

Bastia to: Ajaccio (2–4 daily; 3hr 34min); Calvi (2 daily; 3hr 10min); Corte (2–4 daily; 1hr 41min); L'Île Rousse (2 daily; 2hr 30min).

Calvi to: Ajaccio (2 daily; 4hr 10min); Bastia (2 daily; 3hr 15min); Corte (2 daily; 2hr 24min); L'Île Rousse (2–10 daily; 30min).

Corte to: Ajaccio (4 daily; 1hr 50min); Bastia (4 daily; 1hr 35min); Calvi (2 daily; 2hr 30min); L'Île Rousse (2 daily; 1hr 40min).

L'Île Rousse to: Ajaccio (2 daily; 4hr 7min); Bastia (2 daily; 2hr 30min); Corte (2 daily; 2hr 9min).

Buses

Ajaccio to: Bastia (2 daily; 3hr); Bonifacio (2–3 daily; 3hr 15min); Cargèse (2–3 daily; 1hr); Corte (2 daily; 1hr 45min); Évisa (1–3 daily; 2hr); Porto (1–2 daily; 2hr); Porto-Vecchio (2–5 daily; 3hr 30min); Propriano (2–6 daily; 1hr 50min); Sartène (2–6 daily; 2hr); Zonza (3 daily; 2hr).

Aléria/Cateraggio to: Bastia (2 daily; 1hr 30min); Corte (3 weekly; 1hr); Porto-Vecchio (2 daily; 1hr 30min).

Bastia to: Ajaccio (2 daily; 3hr); Aléria/Cateraggio (2 daily; 1hr 30min); Calvi (2 daily; 2hr); Centuri (3 weekly; 2hr); Corte (2–3 daily; 1hr 15min); Erbalunga (hourly; 30–50min); L'Île Rousse (2 daily; 1hr 30min); Porto-Vecchio (2 daily; 3hr); St-Florent (2 daily; 45min–1hr).

Bonifacio to: Ajaccio (2 daily; 3hr 30min); Bastia (2–4 daily; 3hr 25min); Porto-Vecchio (1–4 daily; 30–40min); Propriano (2–4 daily; 1hr 40min); Sartène (2 daily; 1hr 25min).

Calvi to: Bastia (1 daily; 1hr 45min–2hr 15min); L'Île Rousse (2 daily; 40min); Porto (1 daily; 2hr 30min).

Cargèse to: Ajaccio (1–2 daily; 1hr 10min); Porto (2–3 daily; 1hr).

Corte to: Ajaccio (2 daily; 1hr 45min–2hr); Bastia (2 daily; 1hr 15min); Évisa (4 daily; 2hr); Porto (1 daily; 2hr 30min).

Évisa to: Ajaccio (1–3 daily; 1hr 45min).

Porto to: Ajaccio (1–2 daily; 2hr 5min); Calvi (1 daily; 2hr 30min); Cargèse (2–3 daily; 1hr).

Porto-Vecchio to: Ajaccio (2–4 daily; 3hr 30min); Bastia (2 daily; 2hr 45min–3hr); Bonifacio (1–4 daily; 30–40min); Propriano (2–4 daily; 1hr 40min); Sartène (2–4 daily; 1hr 35min).

Propriano to: Ajaccio (2–4 daily; 1hr 50min); Bonifacio (2–4 daily; 1hr 35min); Porto-Vecchio (2–4 daily; 1hr 45min); Sartène (2–4 daily; 20min).

Ferries

Marseille to: Ajaccio (4–7 weekly; 11–12hr overnight, or 4hr 30min NGV); Bastia (2–4 weekly; 10hr); L'Île Rousse (1–4 weekly; 11hr 30min overnight); Porto-Vecchio (2–5 weekly; 14hr overnight); Propriano (1 weekly; 12–13hr overnight).

Nice to: Ajaccio (1–5 weekly; 12–13hr overnight); Bastia (1–12 weekly; 6hr, or 2hr 30min NGV); Calvi (2–5 weekly; 2hr 40min NGV); L'Île Rousse (1–3 weekly; 7hr overnight, or 2hr 50min NGV).
Toulon to: Ajaccio (2–4 weekly; 10hr overnight); Bastia (2–4 weekly; 8hr 30min–9hr overnight).

Contexts

Contexts

History

E
ver since Julius Caesar observed that "Gaul" was divided into quite distinct parts, and then conquered and unified the country, France has been perceived as both a nation and a collection of fiercely individualistic pays, or localities. The two Frances have often come into conflict. Few countries' governments have centralized as energetically, or have imposed such radical change from above. Equally, few peoples have been so determined to hold on to their local traditions. Charles de Gaulle famously complained that it was impossible to govern a country with 246 different kinds of cheeses. Yet each of those cheesemaking regions, as de Gaulle was well aware, was proud to belong to the kind of impossibly, quarrelsomely traditional nation that could have so many cheeses.

The themes of nationalism and localism, of central control and popular resistance, of radicalism and conservatism, continue to define France today. What follows is necessarily a brief account of major events in the country's past. For more in-depth coverage see the recommendations given in "Books", p.1068.

Caves to Celts

Traces of human existence are rare in France until about 50,000 BC. Thereafter, beginning with the stone tools of the Neanderthal "Mousterian civilization", they become ever more numerous, with an especially heavy concentration of sites in the Périgord region of the Dordogne, where, near the village of Les Eyzies, remains were discovered in 1868 of a late Stone Age people, subsequently dubbed "Cro-Magnon". Flourishing from around 25,000 BC, these cave-dwelling hunters seem to have developed quite a sophisticated culture, the evidence of which is preserved in the beautiful paintings and engravings on the walls of the region's caves.

By 10,000 BC, human communities had spread out widely across the whole of France, and by about 7000 BC, **farming and pastoral communities** had begun to develop. By 4500 BC, the first **dolmens** (megalithic stone tombs) showed up in Brittany, while dugout canoes dating back to the same epoch have been unearthed in Paris. It seems that a thriving trade followed the rivers, while the land between was heavily forested.

By 1800 BC, the **Bronze Age** had arrived in the east and southeast of the country, and trade links had begun with Spain, central Europe, southern Britain and around the Mediterranean – **Greek colonists** founded Massalia (Marseille) in around 600 BC.

The first Celts made an appearance in around 500 BC. Whether these were the same people known to the Romans as "long-haired" Gauls isn't certain. Either way, the inhabitants of France were far from shaggy-haired barbarians. The Gauls, as they became known, invented the barrel and soap and were skilful manufacturers and prolific traders – as was proved by the "chariot tomb" of **Vix**, where the burial goods included rich gold jewellery, a metal-wheeled cart and elaborate Greek vases.

Roman Gaul

By 100 BC the **Gauls** had established large **hilltop towns with merchant communities**. The area equivalent to modern **Provence** became a Roman colony in 118 BC and when, in 58 BC, **Julius Caesar** arrived to complete the Roman conquest of Gaul, there were perhaps fifteen million people living in the area now occupied by modern France. **Tribal rivalries** made the Romans' job of conquering the north fairly easy, and when the Gauls finally united under **Vercingétorix** in 52 BC, it only made their defeat at the battle of **Alésia** more final.

This **Roman victory** was one of the major turning points in the history of France, fixing the frontier between Gaul and the Germanic peoples at the Rhine, saving Gaul from disintegrating because of internal dissension and making it a Roman province. During the five centuries of peace that followed, the Gauls farmed, manufactured and traded, became urbanized and educated – and learnt Latin. The emperor Augustus founded numerous cities – including Autun, Limoges and Bayeux – built roads and settled Roman colonists on the land. Vespasian secured the frontiers beyond the Rhine, thus ensuring a couple of hundred years of peace and economic expansion.

Serious **disruptions** of the Pax Romana only began in the third century AD. Oppressive aristocratic rule and an economic crisis turned the destitute peasantry into gangs of marauding brigands – precursors of the medieval *jacquerie*. But most devastating of all, there began a series of incursions across the Rhine frontier by various restless **Germanic tribes**, the first of which, the Alemanni, pushed down as far as Spain, ravaging farmland and destroying towns.

In the fourth century the reforms of the emperor **Diocletian** secured some decades of respite from both internal and external pressures. Towns were rebuilt and fortified, foreshadowing feudalism and the independent power of the nobles. By the fifth century, however, the Germanic invaders were back: **Alans**, **Vandals** and **Suevi**, with **Franks** and **Burgundians** in their wake. While the Roman administration assimilated them as far as possible, granting them land in return for military duties, they gradually achieved independence from the empire.

The Franks and Charlemagne

By 500 AD, the **Franks**, who gave their name to modern France, had become the dominant invading power. Their most celebrated king, **Clovis**, consolidated his hold on northern France and drove the Visigoths out of the southwest into Spain. In 507 he made the until-then insignificant little trading town of Paris his capital and became a Christian, which inevitably hastened the **Christianization** of Frankish society.

Under the succeeding **Merovingian** dynasty the kingdom began to disintegrate until, in 732, **Charles Martel** reunited the kingdom and saved western Christendom from the northward expansion of Islam by defeating the Spanish Moors at the **battle of Poitiers**.

In 754 Charles's son, Pepin, had himself crowned king by the pope, thus inaugurating the **Carolingian dynasty** and establishing for the first time the principle of the divine right of kings. His son was **Charlemagne**, who extended Frankish control over the whole of what had been Roman Gaul, and far beyond. On Christmas Day in 800, he was crowned emperor of the **Holy Roman Empire**, though the kingdom again fell apart following his death in squabbles over who was to inherit various parts of his empire. At the Treaty of Verdun in 843, his grandsons agreed on a division of territory that corresponded roughly with the extent of modern France and Germany.

Charlemagne's administrative system had involved the royal appointment of counts and bishops to govern the various provinces of the empire. Under the destabilizing attacks of Norsemen/Vikings (who evolved into the Normans) during the ninth century, Carolingian kings were obliged to delegate more power and autonomy to these **provincial governors**, whose lands, like **Aquitaine** and **Burgundy**, already had separate regional identities as a result of earlier invasions.

Gradually the power of these governors overshadowed that of the king, whose lands were confined to the Île-de-France. When the last Carolingian died in 987, it was only natural that they should elect one of their own number to take his place. This was Hugues Capet, founder of a dynasty that lasted until 1328.

The rise of the French kings

The years 1000 to 1500 saw the gradual extension and consolidation of the power of the **French kings**, accompanied by the growth of a centralized administrative system and bureaucracy. Foreign policy was chiefly concerned with restricting papal interference in French affairs and checking the English kings' continuing involvement in French territory. Conditions for the overwhelming majority of the population, meanwhile, remained remarkably unchanged.

Surrounded by vassals much stronger than themselves, **Hugues Capet** and his successors remained weak throughout the eleventh century, though they made the most of their feudal rights.

At the beginning of the twelfth century, having successfully tamed his own vassals in the Île-de-France, Louis VI had a stroke of luck. **Eleanor**, daughter of the powerful duke of Aquitaine, was left in his care on her father's death, so he promptly married her off to his son, the future Louis VII, though the marriage ended in divorce and in 1152, Eleanor married Henry of Anjou, shortly to become **Henry II** of England. Thus the **English** crown gained control of a huge chunk of French territory, stretching almost from the Channel to the Pyrenees. Though their fortunes fluctuated over the ensuing three hundred years, the English rulers remained a perpetual thorn in the side of the French kings, with a dangerous potential for alliance with any rebellious French vassals.

Philippe Auguste (1179–1223) made considerable headway in undermining English rule by exploiting the bitter relations between Henry II and his three sons, one of whom was Richard the Lionheart. By the end of his reign Philippe had recovered all of Normandy and the English possessions north of the Loire.

For the first time, the royal lands were greater than those of any other French lord. The foundations of a systematic administration and civil service had been established in **Paris**, and Philippe had firmly and quietly marked his independence from the papacy by refusing to take any interest in the **crusade** against the heretic Cathars of Languedoc. When Languedoc and Poitou came under royal control in the reign of his son Louis VIII, France was by far the greatest power in western Europe.

The Hundred Years' War

In 1328 the Capetian monarchy had its first succession crisis, which led directly to the ruinous **Hundred Years' War** with the English. Charles IV, last of the line, had only daughters as heirs, and when it was decided that France could not be ruled by a queen, the English king **Edward III** claimed the throne of France for himself – on the grounds that his mother was Charles's sister.

The French chose **Philippe, Count of Valois**, instead, and Edward acquiesced for a time. But when Philippe began whittling away at his possessions in Aquitaine,

Edward renewed his claim and embarked on war. With its population of about twelve million, France was the far richer and more powerful country, but its army was no match for the superior organization and tactics of the English. Edward won an outright victory at **Crécy** in 1346 and seized the port of Calais as a permanent bridgehead. Ten years later, his son, the Black Prince, actually took the French king, Jean le Bon, prisoner at the **battle of Poitiers**.

Although by 1375 French military fortunes had improved to the point where the English had been forced back to Calais and the Gascon coast, the strains of war and administrative abuses, as well as the madness of Charles VI, caused other kinds of damage. In 1358 there were **insurrections** among the Picardy peasantry (the *jacquerie*) and among the townspeople of Paris under the leadership of Étienne Marcel. Both were brutally repressed, as were subsequent risings in Paris in 1382 and 1412.

When it became clear that the king was mad, two rival camps began to vie for power: the **Burgundians**, led by the king's cousin and Duke of Burgundy, Jean sans Peur, and the **Armagnacs**, who gathered round the Duke of Orléans, Charles's brother. The situation escalated when Jean sans Peur had Orléans assassinated, and when fighting broke out between the two factions, they both called on the English for help. In 1415 Henry V of England inflicted another crushing defeat on the French army at **Agincourt**. The Burgundians seized Paris, took the royal family prisoner and recognized Henry as heir to the French throne. When Charles VI died in 1422, the English and their Burgundian allies assumed control of much of France, leaving the young French heir, the Dauphin Charles, barely clinging on to a rump state around the Loire Valley.

The French state might well have been finally exterminated had it not been for the arrival at court, in 1429, of Joan of Arc, a peasant girl who promised divine support for an aggressive military campaign. The English were driven back from their siege of Orléans, the Dauphin crowned as Charles VII at Reims in July 1429, Paris was retaken in 1436 and the English finally driven from France altogether (except for a toehold at Calais) in 1453. Joan's own end was less triumphant: she fell into the hands of the Burgundians and was burnt at the stake in 1431.

From the 1450s, court life was centred on pleasure-seeking in the Loire valley. Even for the **peasantry** life grew less hard. The threats of war and plague steadily receded, and from 1450 the harvests did not fail for seventy unbroken years. The population began to grow again, and a kind of peasant aristocracy took shape in the form of the smallholder *fermiers*. In the towns, meanwhile, the *aisés*, or well-to-do merchants and artisans, began to form the basis of what would become the bourgeoisie.

By the end of the fifteenth century, **Dauphiné**, **Burgundy**, **Franche-Comté** and **Provence** were under royal control, and an effective standing army had been created. The taxation system had been overhauled, and France had emerged from the Middle Ages a rich, powerful state, firmly under the centralized authority of an absolute monarch.

The Wars of Religion

After half a century of self-confident but inconclusive pursuit of military glory in Italy, brought to an end by the **Treaty of Cateau-Cambrésis** in 1559, France was plunged into another period of devastating internal conflict. The **Protestant** ideas of Luther and Calvin had gained widespread adherence among all classes of society, despite sporadic brutal attempts by François I and Henri II to stamp them out.

Catherine de Médicis, acting as regent for her son, later Henri III, implemented a more tolerant policy, provoking violent reaction from the ultra-Catholic faction led by the **Guise** family. Their massacre of a Protestant congregation coming out of church in March 1562 began a civil **War of Religion** that, interspersed with ineffective truces and accords, lasted for the next thirty years.

Well organized and well led by the Prince de Condé and Admiral Coligny, the **Huguenots** – French Protestants – kept their end up very successfully, until Condé was killed at the battle of Jarnac in 1569. Three years later came one of the blackest events in the memory of French Protestants, even today: the **massacre of St Bartholomew's Day**. Coligny and three thousand Protestants who had gathered in Paris for the wedding of Marguerite, the king's sister, to the Protestant Henri of Navarre were slaughtered at the instigation of the Guises, and the bloodbath was repeated across France, especially in the south and west where the Protestants were strongest.

In 1584 Henri III's son died, leaving his brother-in-law, **Henri of Navarre**, heir to the throne, to the fury of the Guises and their Catholic league, who seized Paris and drove out the king. In retaliation, Henri III murdered the Duc de Guise, and found himself forced into alliance with Henri of Navarre, whom the pope had excommunicated. In 1589 Henri III was himself assassinated, leaving Henri of Navarre to become Henri IV of France. It took another four years of fighting and the abjuration of his faith for the new king to be recognized. "Paris is worth a Mass," he is reputed to have said.

Once on the throne, Henri IV set about reconstructing and reconciling the nation. By the **Edict of Nantes** of 1598, the Huguenots were accorded freedom of conscience, freedom of worship in certain places, the right to attend the same schools and hold the same offices as Catholics, their own courts and the possession of a number of fortresses as a guarantee against renewed attack, the most important being La Rochelle and Montpellier.

Kings and cardinals

In the seventeenth century, France was largely ruled by just two kings, **Louis XIII** (1610–43) and **Louis XIV** (1643–1715). In the *grand siècle*, as the French call it, or "Great Century", the state grew ever stronger, ever more centralized, and ever more embodied in the person of the king. France also expanded significantly, with frontiers secured in the Pyrenees, on the Rhine and in the north; conflict with the neighbouring Habsburg kings of Spain and Austria, however, helped exhaust the state's resources.

Louis XIII had the good fortune to be served by the extraordinarily capable minister **Cardinal Richelieu**, who began his services by crushing a revolt led by Louis XIII's brother Gaston, Duke of Orléans. He then confronted Protestantism. Believing that the Protestants' retention of separate fortresses within the kingdom was a threat to security, and the absolute power of the king, he attacked and took La Rochelle in 1627. Although he was unable to extirpate their religion altogether, Protestants were never again to present a military threat.

Richelieu also actively promoted economic self-sufficiency – **mercantilism** – by encouraging the growth of the luxury craft industries. France was to excel in textile production right up to the Revolution. On the foreign front, he built up the navy and granted privileges to companies involved in establishing **colonies** in North America, Africa and the West Indies. He adroitly kept France out of actual military engagement, meanwhile, by funding the Swedish king and general, Gustavus Adolphus, to make war against the Habsburgs in Germany. When in 1635 the French were finally obliged to commit their own troops, they made significant gains against the Spanish in the Netherlands, Alsace and Lorraine, and won Roussillon for France.

The Sun King

Richelieu died just a few months before Louis XIII in 1642. As Louis XIV was still an infant, his mother, Anne of Austria, acted as regent, served by Richelieu's upstart protégé, **Cardinal Mazarin**, who was hated just as much as his predecessor by the traditional aristocracy and the *parlements*. They were anxious that their privileges, including the collection of taxes, would be curtailed. Spurred by these grievances, which were in any case exacerbated by the ruinous cost of the Spanish wars, various groups in French society combined in a series of revolts, known as the **Frondes**. The first Fronde, in 1648, was led by the *parlement* of Paris, which resented royal oversight of tax collection. It was quickly followed by an aristo-cratic Fronde, supported by various peasant risings round the country. All were suppressed easily enough.

In 1659 Mazarin successfully brought the Spanish wars to an end. Two years later, **Louis XIV** came of age, declaring that he would rule without a first minister. He embarked on a long struggle to modernize the administration. The war ministers, Le Tellier and his son Louvois, provided Louis with a well-equipped and well-trained professional army that could muster some 400,000 men by 1670. But the principal reforms were carried out by **Colbert**, who tackled corruption, set up a free-trade area in northern and central France, established the French East India Company, and built up the navy with a view to challenging the commercial supremacy of the Dutch.

Alongside his promotion of wise governance, Louis XIV certainly liked to gild his own throne, earning himself the title Le Roi Soleil, the "**Sun King**". His grandiosity was expressed in two ruinously expensive forms: his extravagant new royal palace at Versailles and incessant military campaigns. His war against the Dutch, in 1672, ultimately resulted in the acquisition of Franche-Comté and a swathe of Flanders, including the city of Lille. In 1681 he simply grabbed Strasbourg, and got away with it.

In 1685, under the influence of his very Catholic mistress, Madame de Maintenon, the king removed all privileges from the **Huguenots** by revoking the Edict of Nantes. The result was devastating. Many of France's most skilled artisans, its wealthiest merchants and its most experienced soldiers were Protestants, and they fled the country in huge numbers – over 200,000 by some estimates. Protestant countries promptly combined under the auspices of the League of Augsburg to fight the French. Another long and exhausting war followed, ending, most unfavourably for Louis XIV, in the **Peace of Rijswijk** (1697).

No sooner was this concluded than Louis became embroiled in the question of who was to succeed the moribund Charles II of Spain as ruler of the Hapsburg domains in Europe. William of Orange, now king of England as well as ruler of the Dutch United Provinces, organized a Grand Alliance against Louis. The so-called **War of the Spanish Succession** broke out and dragged on until 1713, leaving France totally impoverished. The Sun King, finally, was eclipsed. He died in 1715, after ruling for 72 years over a country that had grown to dominate Europe, and had become unprecedentedly prosperous, largely because of colonial trade. Louis XIV's power and control, however, had masked growing tensions between central government and traditional vested interests.

Louis XV and the parlements

Louis XIV had outlived both his son and grandson. His successor, **Louis XV**, was only 5 when his great-grandfather died. During the **Regency**, the traditional aristocracy and the *parlements* scrambled to recover a lot of their lost power and prestige. An experiment with government by aristocratic councils failed, however, and attempts to absorb the immense national debt by selling shares in an overseas trading company ended in a huge collapse. When the prudent and reasonable **Cardinal Fleury** came to prominence upon the regent's death in 1726, the nation's lot began to improve (though the disparity in wealth between the countryside and the towns continued to increase). The Atlantic seaboard towns grew rich on slavery and trade with the American and Caribbean colonies, though in the middle of the century France lost out to England in the **War of Austrian Succession** and the **Seven Years War** – both in effect contests for control of America and India. The need to finance the wars led to the introduction of a new tax, the Twentieth, which was to be levied on everyone. The *parlement*, which had successfully opposed earlier taxation and fought the Crown over its religious policies, dug its heels in again, leading to renewed conflict over Louis' pro-Jesuit religious policy.

The division between the *parlements* and the king and his ministers only sharpened during the reign of **Louis XVI**, which began in 1774. Strangely enough, the one radical attempt to introduce an effective and equitable tax system led directly to the Revolution. Calonne, finance minister in 1786, tried to get his proposed tax approved by an **Assembly of Notables**, a device that had not been employed for more than a hundred years. His purpose was to bypass the *parlement*, which could be relied on to oppose any radical proposal. The attempt backfired, the *parlement* demanding a meeting of the **Estates-General**, representing the nobles, the clergy and the bourgeoisie – this being the only body competent to discuss such matters. As law and order began to break down, the king gave in and agreed to summon the Estates-General on May 17, 1789.

Revolution and empire

Against a background of deepening economic crisis and general misery, the **Estates-General** proved unusually radical. On June 17, 1789, the Third Estate – the representatives of the bourgeoisie – seized the initiative and declared itself the National Assembly, joined by some of the lower clergy and liberal nobility. Louis XVI appeared to accept the situation, and on July 9 the National Constituent Assembly declared itself. However, the king then called in troops, unleashing the anger of the people of Paris, the *sans-culottes* (literally, "without trousers").

On July 14 the *sans-culottes* stormed the fortress of the **Bastille**, symbol of the oppressive nature of the king's *"ancien régime"*. Throughout the country, peasants attacked landowners' châteaux, destroying records of debt and other symbols of oppression. On the night of August 4, the Assembly abolished the feudal rights and privileges of the nobility – a momentous shift of gear in the Revolutionary process. Later that month they adopted the **Declaration of the Rights of Man**. In December church lands were nationalized.

Bourgeois elements in the Assembly tried to bring about a compromise with the nobility, with a view to establishing a constitutional monarchy, but these overtures were rebuffed. Émigré aristocrats were already working to bring about foreign invasion to overthrow the Revolution. In June 1791 the king was arrested trying to escape from Paris. The Assembly, following an initiative of the wealthier bourgeois **Girondin** faction, decided to go to war to protect the Revolution.

On August 10, 1792, the *sans-culottes* set up a **Revolutionary Commune** in Paris and imprisoned the king, marking a radical turn in the Revolution. A new National Convention was elected and met on the day the ill-prepared Revolutionary armies finally halted the Prussian invasion at Valmy. A major rift swiftly developed between the more moderate **Girondins** and the **Jacobins** and *sans-culottes* over the abolition of the monarchy. The radicals carried the day, and, in January 1793, Louis XVI was executed. By June, the Girondins had been ousted.

Counter-Revolutionary forces were gathering in the provinces and abroad. A Committee of Public Safety was set up as chief organ of the government. Left-wing popular pressure brought laws on general conscription and price controls and a deliberate policy of secularization, and **Robespierre** was pressed onto the Committee as the best hope of containing the pressure from the streets, marking the beginning of the **Terror**.

As well as ordering the death of the hated queen, Marie-Antoinette, Robespierre felt strong enough to guillotine his opponents on both Right and Left. But the effect of so many rolling heads was to cool people's faith in the Revolution; by mid-1794, Robespierre himself was arrested and executed, and his fall marked the end of radicalism. More conservative forces gained control of the government, deregulating the economy, limiting suffrage and establishing a five-man executive Directory, in 1795.

Napoleon

In 1799, **General Napoleon Bonaparte**, who had made a name for himself as commander of the Revolutionary armies in Italy and Egypt, returned to France and took power in a coup d'état. He became First Consul, with power to choose officials and initiate legislation. He redesigned the tax system, created the Bank of France, replaced the power of local institutions by a corps of *préfets* answerable to himself, and made judges into state functionaries – in short, laid the foundations of the modern French administrative system.

Although alarmingly revolutionary in the eyes of the rest of Europe, Napoleon was no Jacobin. He restored unsold property to émigré aristocrats, reintroduced slavery in the colonies, and recognized the Church once more. The authoritarian, militaristic nature of his regime, meanwhile, became more and more apparent. In 1804 he crowned himself **emperor** in the presence of the pope.

The tide began to turn in 1808. Spain, which was then under the rule of Napoleon's brother, rose in revolt, aided by the British, and in 1812, Napoleon threw himself into the disastrous **Russian campaign**. He reached Moscow, but the long retreat in terrible winter conditions annihilated his veteran Grande Armée. The nation was now weary of the burden of unceasing war and in 1814 Napoleon was forced to abdicate by a coalition of European powers. They installed **Louis XVIII**, brother of the decapitated Louis XVI, as monarch. In a last effort to recapture power, Napoleon escaped from exile in Elba and reorganized his armies, only to meet final defeat at **Waterloo** on June 18, 1815. Louis XVIII was restored to power.

Restorations and revolutions

In the **White Terror**, which followed Napoleon's downfall, aristocrats attempted to wipe out all trace of the Revolution and restore the *ancien régime*. **Louis XVIII** resisted these moves, however, at least until the Duc de Berry was assassinated in an attempt to wipe out the Bourbon family. In response to reactionary outrage, the king was forced to dismiss his moderate royalist minister, Decazes. Censorship became more rigid and education was once more subjected to the authority of the Church. Then, in 1824, Louis was succeeded by the thoroughly reactionary **Charles X**, who pushed through a law indemnifying émigré aristocrats for property lost during the Revolution.

When the liberal opposition won a majority in the elections of 1830, the king dissolved the Chamber and restricted the already narrow suffrage. Barricades went up in the streets of Paris. Charles X abdicated and parliament was persuaded to accept **Louis-Philippe**, Duc d'Orléans, as king. On the face of it, divine right had been superseded by popular sovereignty as the basis of political legitimacy. The **1814 Charter**, which upheld Revolutionary and Napoleonic reforms, was reaffirmed, censorship abolished, the tricolour restored as the national flag, and suffrage widened.

However, the **Citizen King**, as he was called, had somewhat more absolutist notions about being a monarch. He began the colonization of Algeria and resisted attempts to enfranchise even the middle ranks of the bourgeoisie. A growing economic crisis brought bankruptcies, unemployment and food shortages, helping to radicalize the growing urban working class, whose hopes of a more just future received a theoretical basis in the **socialist writings** and activities of Blanqui, Fourier, Louis Blanc and Proudhon, among others.

1848 and the Second Republic

In February 1848 workers and students took to the streets, and when the army fired on a demonstration and killed forty people, civil war appeared imminent. The Citizen King fled to England, a provisional government was set up and a **republic** proclaimed. The government quickly extended the vote to all adult males – an unprecedented move for its time. But by the time elections were held in April, a new tax designed to ameliorate the financial crisis had antagonized the countryside, and a massive conservative majority was re-elected. Three days of bloody street fighting at the barricades followed, when General Cavaignac, who had distinguished himself in the suppression of Algerian resistance, turned the artillery on the workers. More than 1500 were killed and 12,000 arrested and exiled.

A reasonably democratic constitution was drawn up and elections called to choose a president. To everyone's surprise, Louis-Napoléon, nephew of the emperor, romped home. In spite of his liberal reputation, he restricted the vote again, censored the press and pandered to the Catholic Church. In 1852, following a coup and further street fighting, he had himself proclaimed Emperor Napoléon III.

Empire and Commune

Napoléon III's authoritarian regime oversaw rapid growth in industrial and economic power. When he came to power, over half the country subsisted on the land (a figure down from three-quarters at the Revolution), two-thirds of road traffic took the form of a mule and France itself remained a semi-continent made up as much of wilderness – forests, mountains, moorlands and grassy wastes – as land under cultivation. The peasant population was overwhelmingly enmired in debt, poverty and hunger: in 1865, life expectancy for those who made it to 5 years old was 51 years.

Industrialization, however, was now under way, and the explosive expansion of the railways began to lift the provinces out of their previous isolation. By 1888, 22,000 miles of track had been laid. Disaster, however, was approaching in the shape of the **Franco–Prussian** war. Involved in a conflict with Bismarck and the rising power of Germany, Napoléon III declared war. The French army was quickly defeated and the emperor himself taken prisoner in 1870. The result at home was a universal demand for the proclamation of a **third republic**. The German armistice agreement insisted on the election of a national assembly to negotiate a proper peace treaty. France lost Alsace and Lorraine and was obliged to pay hefty war reparations.

Outraged by the monarchist majority re-elected to the new Assembly and by the attempt of its chief minister, Thiers, to disarm the National Guard, the people of Paris created their own municipal government known as the **Commune**. However, it had barely existed two months before it was savagely crushed. On May 21, the "*semaine sanglante*" began in which government troops fought with the Communards street by street, massacring around 25,000, the last of them lined up against the wall of Père Lachaise cemetery and shot. It was a brutal episode that left a permanent scar on the country's political and psychological landscape.

The Third Republic

In the wake of the Commune, competing political factions fought it out for control. Legitimists supported the return of a Bourbon to the throne, while Orléanists supported the heir of Louis-Philippe. Republicans, of course, would have none of either. Thanks in part to the intransigence of the Comte de Chambord, the Bourbon claimant who refused to accept a constitutional role, the Third Republic was declared. The Crown Jewels were sold off in 1885, and France never again seriously considered having a monarch.

From 1894, the **Dreyfus Affair** dramatically widened the split between right and left. Captain Dreyfus was a Jewish army officer convicted of spying for the Germans and shipped off to the penal colony of Devil's Island. It soon became clear that he had been framed – by the army itself – yet they refused to reconsider his case. The affair immediately became an issue between the anti-Semitic, Catholic Right and the Republican Left, with Radical statesman Clemenceau, Socialist leader Jean Jaurès and novelist Émile Zola coming out in favour of Dreyfus. Charles Maurras, founder of the fascist Action Française – precursor of Europe's Blackshirts – took the part of the army.

Dreyfus was officially rehabilitated in 1904, but in the wake of the affair the more radical element in the Republican movement began to dominate the administration, bringing the army under closer civilian control and dissolving most of the religious orders. In 1905 the Third Republic affirmed its anti-clerical roots by introducing a law on the **separation of church and state**.

The War years

In the years preceding **World War I**, the country enjoyed a period of renewed prosperity. Yet the conflicts in the political fabric of French society remained unresolved. With the outbreak of war in 1914, France found itself swiftly overrun by Germany and its allies, and defended by its old enemy, Britain. The cost of the war was even greater for France than for the other participants because it was fought largely on French soil. Over a quarter of the eight million men called up were either killed or injured; industrial production fell to sixty percent of the prewar level. This – along with memories of the Franco–Prussian war of 1870 – was the reason that the French were more aggressive than either the British or the Americans in seeking war reparations from the Germans.

In the **postwar struggle for recovery** the interests of the urban working class were again passed over, save for Clemenceau's eight-hour-day legislation in 1919. As the **Depression** deepened in the 1930s, Nazi power across the Rhine became ever more menacing. In 1936, the left-wing **Front Populaire** won the elections with a handsome majority, ushering in **Léon Blum**, France's first socialist and first Jewish Prime Minister. He pushed through progressive reforms, but his government quickly fell – and the Left would remain out of power until 1981. France meanwhile, had more pressing concerns, as it was drawn into war by the German invasion of Poland, in September 1939.

World War II

For eight months, France waited out what it called a *drôle de guerre*, or "funny kind of war". Then, in May 1940, Germany attacked. With terrifying speed. In just six weeks, France was overrun as the government fled south, along with up to ten million refugees, or roughly a quarter of the population. **Maréchal Pétain**, a conservative veteran of World War I, emerged from retirement to sign an armistice with Hitler and head the collaborationist **Vichy government**, which ostensibly governed the southern part of the country, while the Germans occupied the strategic north and the Atlantic coast. Pétain's prime minister, Laval, believed it was his duty to adapt France to the new authoritarian age heralded by the Nazi conquest of Europe.

There has been endless controversy over who collaborated, how much and how far it was necessary. One thing at least is clear: Nazi occupation provided a good opportunity for out-and-out French fascists to track down Communists, Jews, Resistance fighters, freemasons – all those who they considered "alien" bodies in French society. While some Communists were involved in the **Resistance** right from the start, Hitler's attack on the Soviet Union in 1941 brought them into the movement on a large scale. Resistance numbers were further increased by young men taking to the hills to escape conscription as labour in Nazi industry. General de Gaulle's radio appeal from London on June 18, 1940, resulted in the Conseil National de la Résistance, unifying the different Resistance groups in May 1943.

Although British and American governments found him irksome, **de Gaulle** was able to impose himself as the unchallenged spokesman of the Free French. Even the Communists accepted his leadership. Representatives of his provisional government moved quickly into liberated areas of France behind the Allied advance after D-Day, thereby saving the country from localized outbreaks of civil war – and saving France, in de Gaulle's view, from the threat of Communist uprising.

The aftermath of war

France emerged from the war demoralized, bankrupt and bomb-wrecked. Almost half its people were peasants, still living off the land, and its industry was in ruins. Under a new constitution, in which **French women** were granted the vote for the first time, elections resulted in a large and squabblesome left-wing majority. De Gaulle resigned in disgust. The new **Fourth Republic** was weak and fractious, but thanks in part to American aid in the form of the Marshall Plan, France achieved enormous industrial **modernization and expansion** in the 1950s. France opted to remain in the US fold, but at the same time aggressively and independently pursued **nuclear technology**, finally detonating its own atom bomb in early 1960. France also took the lead in promoting closer **European integration**, a process culminating in 1957 with the creation of the European Economic Community.

Colonial wars

On the surrender of Japan to the Allies in 1945, **Vietnam**, the northern half of the French Indochina colony, came under the control of Ho Chi Minh and his Communist organization, Vietminh. An eight-year armed struggle ended with French defeat at Dien Bien Phu and partition of the country at the Geneva Conference in 1954 – at which point the Americans took over in the south, with well-known consequences.

In the same year the **Algerian war of liberation began**. The French government was legally, economically and, it felt, morally committed to maintaining its rule over Algeria. Legally, the country was a *département*, an integral part of France, and the million-odd settlers, or *pieds noirs*, were officially French. And there was oil in the south. By 1958, half a million troops, most of them conscripts, had been committed to a bloody and brutal war that cost some 700,000 lives.

In 1958, it began to seem as if the government would take a more liberal line towards Algeria. In response, hard-line Rightists among the settlers and in the army staged a putsch and threatened to declare war on France. General de Gaulle let it be known that in its hour of need and with certain conditions – ie stronger powers for the president – the country might call upon his help. Thus, on June 1, 1958, the National Assembly voted him full powers for six months and the Fourth Republic came to an end.

De Gaulle and his successors

As prime minister, then newly powerful president of the **Fifth Republic, de Gaulle** wheeled and dealed with the *pieds noirs* and Algerian rebels. Meanwhile the war continued, and violence in France – including a secret massacre of two hundred demonstrating French Algerians in Paris in 1961 – escalated. Eventually, in 1962, a referendum gave an overwhelming yes to **Algerian independence**, and *pieds noirs* refugees flooded into France. At the same time, a French labour shortage led to massive recruitment campaigns for workers in North Africa, Portugal, Spain, Italy and Greece. When the immigrants arrived in France, however, they found themselves underpaid, ill-housed and discriminated against both socially and officially.

De Gaulle's leadership was haughty and autocratic in style, and his quirky strutting on the world stage irritated France's partners. He blocked British entry to the European Economic Community, cultivated the friendship of the Germans, rebuked the US for its imperialist policies in Vietnam, withdrew from NATO, refused to sign a nuclear test ban treaty and called for a "free Québec".

Still, the sudden over-boiling of **May 1968** took everyone by surprise. Beginning with student protests at the University of Nanterre, outside Paris, the movement of revolt rapidly spread to the Sorbonne and out into factories and offices. On the night of May 10, barricades went up in the streets of the Quartier Latin in Paris, and the CRS (riot police) responded by wading in. A **general strike** followed, and within a week more than a million people were out, marching under vaguely radical slogans. De Gaulle appealed to the nation to elect him as the only effective barrier against left-wing dictatorship, and dissolved parliament. The "silent majority", frightened and shocked by *les événements* – "the events", as they were nervously called – voted massively in his favour. When the smoke cleared, little had changed.

Pompidou and Giscard

Having petulantly staked his presidency on the outcome of yet another referendum (on a couple of constitutional amendments) and lost, de Gaulle once more took himself off to his country estate and retirement. He was succeeded as president in 1969 by his business-oriented former prime minister, **Georges Pompidou** and then, in 1974, by **Valéry Giscard d'Estaing**, who announced that his aim was to make France "an advanced liberal society". But, aside from reducing the voting age to 18 and liberalizing divorce laws, little progress was made. Giscard fell foul of various scandals and fell out with his ambitious prime minister, **Jacques Chirac**, who set out to challenge the leadership with his own RPR Gaullist party.

The Left seemed well placed to win the coming 1978 elections, until the fragile union between the Socialists and Communists cracked, the latter fearing their roles as the coalition's junior partners. The result was another right-wing victory, with Giscard able to form a new government, grudgingly supported by the RPR. Law and order and immigrant controls were the dominant features of Giscard's second term.

The Mitterrand and Chirac era

When **François Mitterrand** won the presidential elections over Giscard in 1981, inaugurating the first Socialist government for decades, expectations were sky high. By 1984, however, the flight of capital, inflation and budget deficits had forced a complete turnaround, and the 1986 parliamentary election saw the Right, under Jacques Chirac, winning a clear majority in parliament. Thus began a period marked by what the French call *cohabitation*, in which the head of state (the president) and head of government (the prime minister) belong to opposite sides of the political divide.

As Prime Minister, Chirac embarked on a policy of privatization and monetary control, but the greatest change of the era was instituted by Mitterrand. In 1992, the president staked his reputation on the **Maastricht referendum** on creating closer political union in Europe. The vote was carried by a narrow margin in favour. On the whole, poorer rural areas voted "No" while rich urbanites and political parties voted "Yes". Only the extreme ends of the political spectrum, the Communists and the Front National, remained determinedly anti-Europe.

In the 1990s, emerging scandals over cover-ups, corruption and the dubious war records of senior politicians tainted both the major parties, and Mitterrand tottered on to the end of his presidential term, looking less and less like the nation's favourite uncle. Several mayors ended up in jail, but it seemed as if the Paris establishment was above the law. By the time Mitterrand finally stepped down, he had been the French head of state for fourteen years, during a period when crime rose and increasing numbers of people found themselves excluded from society by racism, poverty and homelessness. Support for extreme Right policies propelled Jean-Marie Le Pen's Front National from a minority faction to a serious electoral force.

Chirac's first presidency

Elected as president in 1995 and winning a second mandate in 2002, Chirac showed himself every bit as astute a politician as Mitterrand, and no less prone to scandal and controversy. An early sign of the rocky road ahead came when his Prime Minister, Alain Juppé, introduced **austerity measures**, designed to prepare France for European monetary union. Reforms to pensions and healthcare spending provoked a series of damaging strikes in 1995 and 1996, and led to growing popular disenchantment with the idea of closer European integration.

The **Front National** played up their image of standing up for the small man against the corrupt political establishment, and at municipal elections in June 1995 gained control of three towns, including the major port of Toulon. The **Algerian bomb attacks** which rocked Paris in the mid-1990s – designed to punish France for supporting Algeria's anti-Islamist military government – further played into the hands of the far Right and diminished public confidence in the government as guardian of law and order.

Feeling increasingly beleaguered and unable to deliver on the economy, Chirac called a snap parliamentary election in May 1997. His gamble failed spectacularly, and he was forced into a weak *cohabitation* with a Socialist parliament headed by **Lionel Jospin**, who promptly introduced the 35-hour working week, a 50:50 gender quota for representatives of political parties and, in 1999, the **Pacs** or Pacte Civile de Solidarité, a contract giving cohabiting couples, particularly gay couples, almost the same rights as married people.

Skeletons in the mayoral cupboard

The most persistent **corruption scandals** focused on the finances of the Paris town hall, dating back to the 1980s. In 1995 it was revealed that Alain Juppé had rented a luxury flat in Paris for his son at below-market rates, and in 1998 the conservative Paris mayor **Jean Tiberi** was implicated in a scam involving subsidized real-estate and fake town-hall jobs – with real salaries – for party activists and relatives. Prosecutors edged ever closer to Chirac himself. In 2001 the president was accused of using some three million francs in cash from illegal sources to pay for luxury holidays, and in 2003 it was revealed that in eight years in office as mayor of Paris he and his wife had run up grocery bills of 2.2 million euros – over half of which had been reimbursed in cash. When investigating magistrates tried to question Chirac he claimed presidential immunity, a position that was upheld by France's highest court. The great escaper is due to come to trial in early 2011.

The election earthquake

In the run-up to the **presidential elections of 2002**, everyone in France assumed that the race was between Chirac and Jospin. Both far left and far right were damagingly split – and Front National leader **Jean-Marie Le Pen** had lost much support for punching a woman Socialist candidate in 1998. Lionel Jospin's hopes had been bolstered by the election of Socialist **Bertrand Delanoë** as Mayor of Paris in March 2001 but in the run-up to the elections, however, the economy began to falter, unemployment was once more on the rise and fears over crime were widespread. Chirac talked up issues of immigration and law and order and when the results of the first round came through, Jospin had been beaten into third place by Le Pen – leaving Chirac and Le Pen to stand against each other in the final run-off in May.

The result was widely referred to as an "earthquake", shaking voters out of their disillusioned apathy. On May 1, 800,000 people packed the boulevards of Paris to protest against Le Pen and Socialists called on their supporters to vote for Chirac. He duly swept the board and, in the **ensuing parliamentary elections**, his new right-wing party, the **Union for a Presidential Majority**, swept convincingly to power. In an attempt to address widespread concerns about lack of representation and government accountability, one of Chirac's first measures was a **devolution** bill, giving more power to 26 regional assemblies and ending centuries of central government steadily accruing power to itself.

Iraq, Muslims and climate change

In March 2003, a reinvigorated Chirac declared that he would wield France's Security Council veto if the US tried to table a resolution that contained an ultimatum leading to war in Iraq. Both nationalists on the right and imperialists on the left lapped it up in an orgy of anti-Americanism, and even some international observers applauded France's principled defence of international law, or perhaps of European power. Others saw Chirac's actions as cynical political posturing.

Either way, the result was an almighty spat that seriously damaged the cherished Franco–American relationship. One thing France's tough stance wasn't based on was any particularly pro-Arab or pro-Islamic bias, despite the presence of 5 million or more **Muslims** in France – the largest community in Europe. During 2003, Chirac presided over a government setting expulsion targets for illegal immigrants and enacting a hugely controversial bill – though it was backed by almost two-thirds of the population and passed in parliament by 494 votes to 36 – banning "ostensibly religious" signs, notably Islamic headscarves, from schools and hospitals. Proposing the measure in December 2003, Chirac avowed that "Secularity is one of the republic's great achievements … We must not allow it to be weakened."

In 2003 **climate change** also bludgeoned its way onto the headlines, due to Parisian temperatures in August regularly topping 40°C (104°F) – more than ten degrees above the average maximum for that time of year. Fifteen thousand people died. No one seemed willing to take responsibility for doing anything about it.

Reforms, resistance and riots

Faced with an ageing population, unemployment flatlining at around ten percent and a budget deficit persistently exceeding the eurozone's three-percent ceiling, the newly confident Right decided it would reform the public sector once and for all. First to go under the knife would be the state's generous pensions and unemployment benefits, then worker-friendly hiring and firing rights, and finally the world-leading health service. Most of France saw the programme less as prudent milk-rationing and more as getting their sacred cows ready to be sent off to slaughter. By mid-May 2003, two million workers were out on strike; and on May 26 half a million protested in the streets of Paris. And this was only in defence of pensions.

In the regional elections of March 2004, the electoral map turned a furious pink. Then, in the referendum of May 2005, 55 percent of French voters rejected the proposed new EU constitution when all the major political parties had urged them to vote "Yes". French voters, it seemed, did not want to join the new, economically liberal, globalized world.

Neither did disaffected French youths. In October 2005, two teenagers in a run-down suburb outside Paris were electrocuted while hiding from police they believed were chasing them. Local anger led speedily to three weeks of nightly, nationwide riots and confrontations. Youths torched cars, buses, schools and even police and power stations – anything connected with the hated state. Almost 9000 vehicles and property worth €200 million went up in smoke, and almost over 2900 people were arrested. The ambitious Interior Minister, Nicolas Sarkozy, demanded the neighbourhoods be cleaned with power-hoses. Young people who actually lived in the "hot" suburbs saw the main cause as anger at **racism** and social and economic exclusion. Many of the worst-affected areas were home to communities of largely African or North-African origin, where youth unemployment runs as high as fifty percent – double the already high average among young people.

Even as the *banlieue* burned, Prime Minister Dominique de Villepin attempted to tackle the problem of youth unemployment and economic stagnation by giving small companies the right to dismiss new employees without having to give cause. This looked suspiciously like neoliberal or "Anglo-Saxon" capitalism. So, in October 2005, a million workers across the country marched against the new labour law. When, in early 2006, the laws were to be extended to all companies employing workers under the age of 26, the young responded with fury. In

March, students in Paris **occupied the Sorbonne**, in conscious imitation of May 1968. And just as in 1968, people protested across France in their millions – only this time in the hope not that France would radically change, but that everything would stay the same. On April 10, Dominique de Villepin withdrew the law.

Sarko

In the wake of the employment rights debacle, Nicolas Sarkozy, by now known popularly (and not affectionately) as "Sarko", was confirmed as the UMP's candidate for the 2007 presidential election. By a narrow margin, he defeated his centrist Socialist rival, **Ségolène Royal**. He had promised ongoing, radical reform, but major surprises followed his victory. First, he appointed a notably conciliatory cabinet. Next, his wife left him, and he took up with the model, singer and Euro-jetsetter Carla Bruni, marrying her in February 2008. Suddenly, the media spotlight was on his Presidency, and it was asking more questions about the lifts in his shoes than his economic policies.

Then came the global financial crisis of 2008–09. Suddenly, the "Anglo-Saxon" form of market-led, laissez-faire capitalism seemed exactly what French socialists had always said it was: a debt-fuelled castle built on sand. In response, Sarkozy performed an astonishing political about-turn, pledging to wield the power of the state to ensure stability. Strong-state *dirigisme* was back. National reform, again, would have to wait. France never teetered on the edge of banking meltdown like its Atlantic rivals, but it was hit by recession nonetheless. In 2009, unemployment in France began racing towards the ten percent figure.

The usual corruption scandals, meanwhile, started to circle over Sarkozy's beleaguered administration. In 2009, his former political associate Dominique de Villepin was tried for his alleged role in the Clearstream affair, a supposed smear campaign in which a fake list of dodgy bank accounts, containing Sarkozy's name, was passed to an investigating judge. Sarkozy was accused of becoming a "French Berlusconi", by putting pressure on his powerful media friends to ensure a compliant press. Members of his party were accused of accepting illegal donations from the L'Oréal heir, Liliane Bettencourt, and in July 2010 Sarkozy himself was forced into making an unprecedented TV address to deny ever receiving money stuffed into an envelope. *Plus ça change*, as they say in France, *plus c'est la même chose.*

Art

Since the Middle Ages, France has held – with occasional gaps – a leading position in the history of European painting, with Paris, above all, attracting artists from the whole continent. The story of French painting is one of richness and complexity, partly due to this influx of foreign painters and partly due to the capital's stability as an artistic centre.

Beginnings

In the late Middle Ages, the itinerant life of the nobles led them to prefer small and transportable works of art; splendidly **illuminated manuscripts** were much praised and the best painters, usually trained in Paris, continued to work on a small scale until the fifteenth century. Many illuminators were also panel painters, and foremost among them was **Jean Fouquet** (c.1420–81). Born in Tours in the Loire valley he became court painter to Charles VIII, drawing from both Flemish and Italian sources and utilizing the new fluid oil technique that had been perfected in Flanders.

Two other fifteenth-century French artists could be said to represent distinctive northern and southern strands. **Enguerrand Quarton** (c.1410–1466) was the most famous Provençal painter of the time. His *Coronation of the Virgin*, which hangs at Villeneuve-lès-Avignon, ranks as one of the first city/landscapes in the history of French painting: Avignon itself is faithfully depicted and the Mont Ste-Victoire, later to be made famous by Cézanne, is recognizable in the distance. The **Master of Moulins**, active in the 1480s and 1490s, was noticeably more northern in temperament, painting both religious altarpieces and portraits commissioned by members of the royal family or the fast-increasing bourgeoisie.

Mannerism and Italian influence

At the end of the fifteenth and the beginning of the sixteenth centuries, the French invasion of Italy brought both artists and patrons into closer contact with the Italian Renaissance.

The most famous of the artists who were lured to France was **Leonardo da Vinci**, spending the last three years of his life (1516–19) at the court of François 1er. From the Loire valley, which until then had been his favourite residence, the French king moved nearer to Paris, where he had several palaces decorated. Italian artists were once again called upon, and two of them, **Rosso** and **Primaticcio**, who arrived in France in 1530 and 1532 respectively, were to shape the artistic scene in France for the rest of the sixteenth century.

Both artists introduced to France the latest Italian style, **Mannerism**, with its emphasis on the fantastic, the luxurious and the large-scale decorative. It was first put to the test in the revamping of the palace at Fontainebleau, and most French artists worked at the château at some point in their career, or were influenced by its homogeneous style, leading to what was subsequently called the **School of Fontainebleau**.

Antoine Caron (c.1520–1600), who often worked for Catherine de Médicis, the widow of Henri II, contrived complicated allegorical paintings in which elongated figures are arranged within wide, theatre-like scenery packed with ancient monuments and Roman statues. Even the Wars of Religion, raging in the 1550s and 1560s, failed to rouse French artists' sense of drama, and representations of the many massacres then going on were detached and fussy in tone.

Portraiture tended to be more inventive, and very French in its general sobriety. The portraits of **Jean Clouet** (c.1485–1541) and his son **François** (c.1510–72), both official painters to François 1er, combined sensitivity in the rendering of the sitter's features with a keen sense of abstract design in the arrangement of the figure, conveying with great clarity social status and giving clues to the sitter's profession.

The seventeenth century

In the **seventeenth century**, Italy continued to be a source of inspiration for French artists, most of whom were drawn to Rome – at that time the most exciting artistic centre in Europe, dominated by Italian painters such as Michelangelo Merisi da Caravaggio and Annibale Carracci.

Some French painters like **Moise Valentin** (c.1594–1632) worked in Rome and were directly influenced by Caravaggio; others, such as the great painter from Lorraine, **Georges de la Tour** (1593–1652), benefited from his innovations at one remove, gaining inspiration from the Utrecht Caravaggisti who were active at the time in Holland. La Tour produced deeply felt religious paintings in which figures appear to be carved out of the surrounding gloom by the magical light of a candle. Sadly, his output was very small – just some forty or so works in all.

Lowlife subjects and attention to naturalistic detail were also important aspects of the work of the **Le Nain brothers**, especially **Louis** (1593–1648), who depicted with great sympathy, but never with sentimentality, the condition of the peasantry. He chose moments of inactivity or repose within the lives of the peasants, and his paintings achieve timelessness and monumentality by their very stillness. The other Italian artist of influence, the Bolognese **Annibale Carracci** (d.1609), impressed French painters not only with his skill as a decorator but, more tellingly, with his ordered, balanced landscapes, which were to prove of prime importance for the development of the classical landscape in general, and in particular for those painted by **Claude Lorrain** (1600–82). Born in Lorraine, he studied and travelled in Italy, which would provide him with subjects of study for the rest of his life. His landscapes are airy compositions in which religious or mythological figures are lost within an idealized, Arcadian nature, bathed in tranquil light.

Landscapes, harsher and even more ordered, but also recalling the Arcadian mood of antiquity, were painted by the other French painter who elected to make Rome his home, **Nicolas Poussin** (1594–1665). Like Claude, Poussin selected his themes from the rich sources of Greek, Roman and Christian myths and stories; unlike Claude, however, his figures are not subdued by nature but rather dominate it, in the tradition of the masters of the High Renaissance, such as Raphael and Titian, whom he greatly admired. Poussin only briefly returned to Paris, called by the king, Louis XIII, to undertake some large decorative works quite unsuited to his style or character.

Many other artists visited Italy, but most returned to France, the luckiest to be employed at the court to boost the royal images of Louis XIII and XIV and their respective ministers, Richelieu and Colbert. **Simon Vouet** (1590–1649), **Charles Le Brun** (1619–90) and **Pierre Mignard** (1612–95) all performed that task with skill, often using ancient history and mythology to suggest flattering comparisons with the reigning monarch.

The official aspect of their works was paralleled by the creation of the new **Academy of Painting and Sculpture** in 1648, an institution that dominated the arts in France for the next few hundred years, if only by the way artists reacted against it. **Philippe de Champaigne** (1602–74), a painter of Flemish origin, alone stands out at the time as remotely different, removed from the intrigues and pleasures of the court and instead strongly influenced by the teaching and moral code of Jansenism, a purist and severe form of the Catholic faith. But it was the more courtly, fun-loving portraits and paintings by such artists as Mignard that were to influence most of the art of the following century.

The early eighteenth century

The semi-official art encouraged by the foundation of the Academy became more frivolous and light-hearted in the **eighteenth century**. The court at Versailles lost its attractions, and many patrons now were to be found among the hedonistic bourgeoisie and aristocracy living in Paris. History painting, as opposed to genre scenes or portraiture, retained its position of prestige, but at the same time many artists tried their hands at landscape, genre, history or decorative works, often merging aspects of one genre with another. **Salons**, at which painters exhibited their works, were held with increasing frequency and bred a new phenomenon in the art world – the art critic.

Possibly the most complex personality of the eighteenth century was **Jean-Antoine Watteau** (1684–1721). Primarily a superb draughtsman, Watteau's use of soft and yet rich, light colours reveals how much he was struck by the great seventeenth-century Flemish painter Rubens. His subtle depictions of dreamy couples, often seen strolling in delicate, mythical landscapes, are known as "*Fêtes Galantes*". They convey a mood of melancholy and poignancy largely lacking in the works of followers such as Nicolas Lancret and J.-B. Pater.

The work of **François Boucher** (1703–70) was probably more representative of the eighteenth century: the pleasure-seeking court of Louis XV found the lightness of morals and colours in his paintings immensely congenial. Boucher's virtuosity is seen at its best in his paintings of women, always rosy, young and fantasy-erotic. **Jean-Honoré Fragonard** (1732–1806) continued this exploration of licentious themes but with an exuberance, a richness of colour and a vitality (*The Swing*) that was a feast for the eyes and raised the subject to a glorification of love. Far more restrained were the paintings of **Jean-Baptiste-Siméon Chardin** (1699–1779), who specialized in homely genre scenes and still lifes, painted with a simplicity that belied his complex use of colours, shapes and space to promote a mood of stillness and tranquillity. **Jean-Baptiste Greuze** (1725–1805) chose stories that anticipated reaction against the laxity of the times; the moral, at times sentimental, character of his paintings was all-pervasive, reinforced by a stage-like composition well suited to cautionary tales.

Neoclassicism

This new seriousness became more severe with the rise of **Neoclassicism**, a movement for which purity and simplicity were essential components of the systematic depiction of edifying stories from the classical authors. Roman history and legends were the most popular subjects. Many of the paintings of **Jacques-Louis David** (1748–1825) are reflections of republican ideals and of contemporary history, from the *Death of Marat* to events from the life of Napoleon, who was his patron. For the emperor and his family, David painted some of his most successful portraits – *Madame Recamier* is not only an exquisite example of David's controlled use of shapes and space and his debt to antique Rome, but can also be seen as a paradigm of Neoclassicism.

Two painters, **Jean-Antoine Gros** (1771–1835) and **Baron Gérard** (1770–1837), followed David closely in style and in themes (portraits, Napoleonic history and legend), but often with a touch of softness and heroic poetry that pointed the way to Romanticism.

Jean-Auguste-Dominique Ingres (1780–1867) was a pupil of David; he also studied in Rome before coming back to Paris to develop the purity of line that was the essential and characteristic element of his art. His effective use of it to build up forms and bind compositions can be admired in conjunction with his recurrent theme of female nudes bathing, or in his magnificent and stately portraits that depict the nuances of social status.

Romanticism

Completely opposed to the stress on drawing advocated by Ingres, two artists created, through their emphasis on colour, form and composition, pictures that look forward to the later part of the nineteenth century and the Impressionists. **Théodore Géricault** (1791–1824), whose short life was still dominated by the heroic vision of the Napoleonic era, explored dramatic themes of human suffering in such paintings as *The Raft of the Medusa*, while his close contemporary, **Eugène Delacroix** (1798–1863), epitomized the **Romantic movement** – its search for emotions and its love of nature, power and change.

Delacroix was deeply aware of tradition, and his art was influenced, visually and conceptually, by the great masters of the Renaissance and the seventeenth and eighteenth centuries. In many ways he may be regarded as the last great religious and decorative French painter, but through his technical virtuosity, freedom of brushwork and richness of colours, he can also be seen as the essential forerunner of the Impressionists.

Other painters working in the Romantic tradition were still haunted by the Napoleonic legends, as well as by North Africa (Algeria) and the Middle East, which had become better known to artists and patrons alike during the Napoleonic wars. These were the subjects of paintings by **Horace Vernet** (1789–1863), **Théodore Chassériau** (1819–56) and the enormously popular but now little-regarded giant of old-fashioned Classicism, **Jean-Louis-Ernest Meissonier** (1815–91).

Among their contemporaries was **Honoré Daumier** (1808–79): very much an isolated figure, influenced by the boldness of approach of caricaturists, he was content to depict everyday subjects such as a laundress or a third-class rail car – caustic commentaries on professions and politics that work as brilliant observations of the times.

Landscape painting and realism

The first part of the **nineteenth century** saw nature, unadorned by artistic conventions, become a subject for study. Running parallel to this was the realization that painting could be the visual externalization of the artist's own emotions and feelings. **Jean-Baptiste-Camille Corot** (1796–1875) started to paint landscapes that were influenced as much by the unpretentious and realistic country scenes of seventeenth-century Holland as by the balanced compositions of Claude. His loving and attentive studies of nature were much admired by later artists, including Monet.

At the same time, a whole group of painters developed similar attitudes to landscape and nature, helped greatly by the practical improvement of being able to buy oil paint in tubes rather than as unmixed pigments. Known as the **Barbizon School** after the village on the outskirts of Paris around which they painted, they soon discovered the joy and excitement of *plein-air* (open-air) painting. **Théodore Rousseau** (1812–67) was their nominal leader, his paintings of forest undergrowth and forest clearings displaying an intimacy that came from the immediacy of the image. **Charles-François Daubigny** (1817–78), like Rousseau, often infused a sense of drama into his landscapes.

Jean-François Millet (1814–75) is perhaps the best-known associate of the Barbizon group, though he was more interested in the human figure than simple nature. Landscapes, however, were essential settings for his figures; indeed, his most famous pictures are those exploring the place of people in nature and their struggle to survive. *The Sower*, for instance, reflected a typical Millet theme, suggesting the heroic working life of the peasant. As is so often the case for painters touching on new themes or on ideas that are uncomfortable to the rich and powerful, Millet enjoyed little success during his lifetime, and his art was only widely appreciated after his death.

The moralistic and romantic undertone in Millet's work was something that **Gustave Courbet** (1819–77) strove to avoid. After an initial resounding success in the Salon exhibition of 1849, he endured constant criticism from the academic world and patrons alike, his scenes of ordinary life regarded as unsavoury and wilfully ugly. Breaking with the Salon tradition, Courbet put on a private exhibition of some forty of his works. Inscribed on the door in large letters was one word: **"Realism"**.

Impressionism

Like Courbet, **Edouard Manet** (1832–83) was strongly influenced by Spanish painters. Unlike Courbet, however, he never saw himself as a rebel or avant-garde painter – yet his technique and his themes were both new and shocking. Manet used bold contrasts of light and very dark colours, giving his paintings a forcefulness that critics often took for a lack of sophistication. And his detractors saw much to decry in his reworking of an old subject originally treated by the sixteenth-century Venetian painter, Giorgione, *Le Déjeuner sur l'Herbe*. Manet's version was shocking because he placed naked and dressed figures together, and because the men were dressed in the costume of the day, implying a pleasure party too specifically contemporary to be "respectable".

Manet's most successful pictures are reflections of ordinary life in bars and public places, where respectability was certainly lacking. To Manet, painting was to be enjoyed for its own sake and not as a tool for moral instruction – in itself an outlook that marked a definite break with the past. From the 1870s, Manet began to adopt the new techniques of painting out-of-doors, and his work became lighter and freer. He began to be seen as a much-admired member of a burgeoning group of mould-breaking young painters, alongside **Claude Monet** (1840–1926). Born in Le Havre, Monet came into contact with **Eugène Boudin** (1824–98), whose colourful beach scenes anticipated the way the Impressionists approached colour. Monet discovered that, for him, light and the way in which it builds up forms and creates an infinity of colours was the element that governed all representations. Under the impact of Manet's bright hues and his unconventional attitude ("art for art's sake"), Monet soon began using pure colours side by side, blended together to create areas of brightness and shade.

In 1874, a group of thirty artists exhibited together for the first time. Among them were some of the best-known names of this period of French art: Degas, Monet, Renoir, Pissarro. One of Monet's paintings was entitled *Impression: Sun Rising*, a title that was singled out by the critics to ridicule the colourful, loose and unacademic style of these young artists. Overnight they became, derisively, the "**Impressionists**".

Camille Pissarro (1830–1903) was slightly older than most of them and seems to have played the part of an encouraging father-figure, always keenly aware of any new development or new talent. Not a great innovator himself, Pissarro was a very gifted artist whose use of Impressionist technique was supplemented by a lyrical feeling for nature and its seasonal changes. But it was really with **Monet** that Impressionist theory ran its full course: he painted and repainted the same motif under different light conditions, at different times of the day, and in different seasons, producing whole series of paintings such as *Grain Stacks*, *Poplars* and, much later, his *Waterlilies*.

Auguste Renoir (1841–1919), who started life as a painter of porcelain, was swept up by Monet's ideas for a while, but soon felt the need to look again at the old masters and to emphasize the importance of drawing to the detriment of colour. Renoir regarded the representation of the female nude as the most taxing and rewarding subject that an artist could tackle. Like Boucher in the eighteenth century, Renoir's nudes are luscious, but rarely, if ever, erotic – although in his later paintings they can become cloyingly, almost overpoweringly, sweet. Better were his portraits of women fully clothed, both for their obvious and innate sympathy and for their keen sense of design.

Edgar Degas (1834–1917) was yet another artist who, although he exhibited with the Impresssionists, did not follow their precepts very closely. The son of a rich banker, he was trained in the tradition of Ingres: design and drawing were an integral part of his art, and, whereas Monet was fascinated mainly by light, Degas wanted to express movement in all its forms. His pictures are vivid expressions of the body in action, usually straining under fairly exacting circumstances – dancers and circus artistes were among his favourite subjects, as well as more mundane depictions of laundresses and other working women.

Like so many artists of the day, Degas had his imagination fired by the discovery of **Japanese prints**, which could for the first time be seen in quantity. These provided him with new ideas of composition, not least in their asymmetry of design and the use of large areas of unbroken colour. **Photography**, too, had an impact, if only because it finally liberated artists from the task of producing accurate, exacting descriptions of the world.

Degas' extraordinary gift as a draughtsman was matched only by that of the Provençal aristocrat **Henri de Toulouse-Lautrec** (1864–1901). Toulouse-Lautrec, who had broken both his legs as a child, was unusually small, a physical deformity that made him particularly sensitive to free and vivacious movements. A great admirer of Degas, he chose similar themes: people in cafés and theatres, working women and variety dancers all figured large in his work. But, unlike Degas, Toulouse-Lautrec looked beyond the body, and his work is scattered with social comment, sometimes sardonic and bitter. In his portrayal of Paris prostitutes, there is sympathy and kindness; to study them better he lived in a brothel, revealing in his paintings the weariness and sometimes gentleness of these women.

Post-Impressionism

Though a rather vague term, as it's difficult to date exactly when the backlash against Impressionism took place, **Post-Impressionism** represents in many ways a return to more formal concepts of painting – in composition, in attitudes to subject and in drawing.

Paul Cézanne (1839–1906), for one, associated only very briefly with the Impressionists and spent most of his working life in relative isolation, obsessed with rendering, as objectively as possible, the essence of form. He saw objects as basic shapes – cylinders, cones, and so on – and tried to give the painting a unity of texture that would force the spectator to view it not so much as a representation of the world but rather as an entity in its own right, as an object as real and dense as the objects surrounding it. It was this striving for pictorial unity that led him to cover the entire surface of the picture with small, equal brush strokes which made no distinction between the textures of a tree, a house or the sky.

The detached, unemotional way in which Cézanne painted was not unlike that of the seventeenth-century artist Poussin, and he found a contemporary parallel in the work of **Georges Seurat** (1859–91). Seurat was fascinated by current theories of light and colour, and he attempted to apply them in a systematic way, creating different shades and tones by placing tiny spots of pure colour side by side, which the eye could in turn fuse together to see the colours mixed out of their various components. This **pointillist** technique also had the effect of giving monumentality to everyday scenes of contemporary life.

While Cézanne, Seurat and, for that matter, the Impressionists sought to represent the outside world objectively, several other artists – the **Symbolists** – were seeking a different kind of truth, through the subjective experience of fantasy and dreams. **Gustave Moreau** (1840–98) represented, in complex paintings, the intricate worlds of the romantic fairy tale, his visions expressed in a wealth of naturalistic details. The style of **Puvis de Chavannes** (1824–98) was more restrained and more obviously concerned with design and the decorative. And a third artist, **Odilon Redon** (1840–1916), produced some weird and visionary graphic work that especially intrigued Symbolist writers; his less frequent works in colour belong to the later part of his life.

The subjectivity of the Symbolists was of great importance to the art of **Paul Gauguin** (1848–1903). He started life as a stockbroker who collected Impressionist paintings, a Sunday artist who gave up his job in 1883 to dedicate himself to painting.

During his stay in Pont-Aven in Brittany, Gauguin worked with a number of artists who called themselves the **Nabis**, among them **Paul Sérusier** and **Émile Bernard**. He began exploring ways of expressing concepts and emotions by means of large areas of colour and powerful forms, and developed a unique style that was heavily indebted to his knowledge of Japanese prints and of the tapestries and stained glass of medieval art. His search for the primitive expression of primitive emotions took him eventually to the Pacific, where, in Tahiti, he found some of his most inspiring subjects.

A similar derivation from Symbolist art and a wish to exteriorize emotions and ideas by means of strong colours, lines and shapes underlies the work of **Vincent Van Gogh** (1853–90), a Dutch painter who came to live in France. Like Gauguin, with whom he had an admiring but stormy friendship, Van Gogh started painting relatively late in life, lightening his palette in Paris under the influence of the Impressionists, and then heading south to Arles where, struck by the harshness of the Mediterranean light, he turned out such frantic expressionistic pieces as

The Reaper and *Wheatfield with Crows*. In all his later pictures the paint is thickly laid on in increasingly abstract patterns that follow the shapes and tortuous paths of his deep inner melancholy.

Édouard Vuillard (1868–1940) and **Pierre Bonnard** (1867–1947) explored the Nabi artists' interest in Japanese art and in the decorative surface of painting. They produced intimate images in which figures and objects blend together in complicated patterns. In the works of Bonnard, in particular, the glowing design of the canvas itself becomes as important as what it's trying to represent.

Fauvism, Cubism, Surrealism

The **twentieth century** kicked off to a colourful start with the **Fauvist** exhibition of 1905, an appropriately anarchic beginning to a century which, in France above all, was to see radical changes in attitudes towards painting. The painters who took part in the exhibition included, most influentially, **Henri Matisse** (1869–1954), **André Derain** (1880–1954), **Georges Rouault** (1871–1958) and **Albert Marquet** (1875–1947), and they were quickly nicknamed the Fauves (Wild Beasts) for their use of bright, wild colours that often bore no relation whatsoever to the reality of the object depicted. Skies were just as likely to be green as blue since, for the Fauves, colour was a way of composing, of structuring a picture, and not necessarily a reflection of real life. Raoul Dufy (1877–1953) used Fauvist colours in combination with theories of abstraction to paint an effervescent industrial age.

Fauvism was just the beginning: the first decades of the twentieth century were times of intense excitement and artistic activity in Paris, and painters and sculptors from all over Europe flocked to the capital to take part in the liberation from conventional art that individuals and groups were gradually instigating. This loose, cosmopolitan grouping of artists gradually became known as the **École de Paris**, though it was never a "school" as such. **Pablo Picasso** (1881–1973) was one of the first to arrive in Paris – from Spain, in 1900. He soon started work on his first Blue Period paintings, which describe the sad and squalid life of itinerant actors in tones of blue. Later, while Matisse was experimenting with colours and their decorative potential, Picasso came under the sway of Cézanne and his organization of forms into geometrical shapes. He also learned from so-called "primitive", and especially African, sculpture, and out of these studies came a painting that heralded a definite new direction, not only for Picasso's own style but for the whole of modern art – *Les Demoiselles d'Avignon*. Executed in 1907, this painting combined Cézanne's analysis of forms with the visual impact of African masks.

It was from this semi-abstract picture that Picasso went on to develop the theory of **Cubism**, inspiring artists such as **Georges Braque** (1882–1963) and **Juan Gris** (1887–1927), another Spaniard, and formulating a whole new movement. The Cubists' aim was to depict objects not so much as they saw them but rather as they knew them to be: a bottle and a guitar were shown from the front, from the side and from the back as if the eye could take in all at once every facet and plane of the object. Braque and Picasso first analysed forms into these facets (analytical Cubism), then gradually reduced them to series of colours and shapes (synthetic Cubism), among which a few recognizable symbols such as letters, fragments of newspaper and numbers appeared. The complexity of different planes overlapping one another made the deciphering of Cubist paintings sometimes difficult, and the very last phase of Cubism tended increasingly towards abstraction.

Spin-offs of Cubism were many: such movements as **Orphism**, headed by **Robert Delaunay** (1885–1941) and **Francis Picabia** (1879–1953), who experimented not with objects but with the colours of the spectrum. **Fernand Léger** (1881–1955), one of the main exponents of the so-called School of Paris, exploited his fascination with its smoothness and power to create geometric and monumental compositions of technical imagery that were indebted to both Cézanne and Cubism.

The war, meanwhile, had affected many artists: in Switzerland, **Dada** was born out of the scorn artists felt for the petty bourgeois and nationalistic values that had led to the bloodshed. It was best exemplified in the work of the Frenchman **Marcel Duchamp** (1887–1968), who selected everyday objects ("ready-mades") and elevated them, without modification, to the rank of works of art simply by putting them on display – his most notorious piece was a urinal which he called *Fontaine* and exhibited in New York in 1917. His conviction that art could be made out of anything would be hugely influential.

Dada was a literary as well as an artistic movement, and through one of its main poets, André Breton, it led to the inception of **Surrealism**. It was the unconscious and its dark unchartered territories that interested the Surrealists: they derived much of their imagery from Freud and even experimented in words and images with free-association techniques. Strangely enough, most of the "French" Surrealists were foreigners, primarily the German **Max Ernst** (1891–1976) and the Spaniard **Salvador Dalí** (1904–89), though Frenchman **Yves Tanguy** (1900–55) also achieved international recognition. Mournful landscapes of weird, often terrifying images evoked the landscape of nightmares in often very precise details and with an anguish that went on to influence artists for years to come. **Picasso**, for instance, shocked by the massacre at the Spanish town of Guernica in 1936, drew greatly from Surrealism to produce the disquieting figures of his painting of the same name.

Towards Nouveau Réalisme

At the outbreak of **World War II** many artists emigrated to the US, where the economic climate was more favourable. France was no longer the artistic melting pot of Europe, though Paris itself remained full of vibrant new work. Sculptors like the Romanian **Brancusi** (1876–1957) and the Swiss **Giacometti** (1886–1966) lived most of their lives in that city. Reacting against the rigours of Cubism, many French artists of the 1940s and 1950s opened themselves instead to the language and methods of American Abstract Expressionism, emanating from a vibrant New York. French painters such as **Pierre Soulages** (b.1919) and **Jean Dubuffet** (1901–85) pursued **Tachisme**, also known as **l'Art informel**. Dubuffet was heavily influenced by **Art Brut** – that is, works created by children, prisoners or the mentally ill. He produced thickly textured, often childlike paintings, pioneering the depreciation of traditional artistic materials and methods, fashioning junk, tar, sand and glass into the shape of human beings. His work (which provoked much outrage) influenced the French-born American, **Arman** (1928–2005), and **César** (1921–98), both of whom made use of scrap metals – their output ranging from presentations of household debris to towers of crushed and compressed cars.

These artists, among others, began to constitute what would be seen as the last coherent French art movement of the century: **Nouveau Réalisme**. A phenom-enon largely of the late 1950s and 1960s, this movement rejected traditional materials and artistic genres, and concentrated instead on the distortion of the objects and signs of contemporary culture. It is often compared to Pop Art. Nouveau Réaliste sculpture is best represented by the works of the Swiss **Jean Tinguely** (1925–91), whose work was concerned mainly with movement and the machine, satirizing technological civilization. His most famous work, executed in collaboration with **Niki de Saint Phalle** (1926–2002), is the exuberant fountain outside the Pompidou Centre, featuring fantastical birds and beasts shooting water in all directions.

Loosely associated with the Nouveaux Réalistes, though resisting all classification, **Yves Klein** (1928–1962) laid the foundations for several currents in contemporary art. He is seen as a precursor of Minimalism thanks to his exhibition "Le Vide" in 1958, in which he redefined the void and the immaterial as having a pure energy. He was fascinated by the colour blue, which he considered to possess a spiritual quality. He even patented his own colour, International Klein Blue, employing it in a series of "body prints" in which he covered female models with paint, thus prefiguring performance art.

Conceptual and contemporary

The chief legacy of Surrealism in 1960s France was the way avant-garde artists regularly banded together – and often quickly disbanded – around ideological or conceptual manifestos. These groups were not art schools as such, more conscious experiments in defining and limiting what art could be, in the search for political or theoretical meaning – in search, some would say, of coherence. One of the first such self-constituted groups of the 1960s, **GRAV** (Groupe de recherche d'art visuel) played with abstraction in the form of mirrors, visual tricks and **kinetic art** – which had a strong heritage in France from Duchamp and Alexander Calder. Among the leading figures were **François Morellet** (b.1926), who focused on geometric works, and the Argentine-born **Julio Le Parc** (b.1928). GRAV's goal, as its 1963 *Manifesto* declared, was to demystify art by tricking the spectator into relaxing in front of the artwork.

Perhaps the most significant group launched itself in January 1967, when Daniel Buren, Olivier Mosset, Michel Parmentier and Niele Toroni removed their own works from the walls of the Salon de la Jeune Peinture, in protest against the reactionary nature of painting itself – and, paradoxically, to reaffirm the relevance of painting as an art form existing in itself, without interpretation. It was an early taste of the politics of 1968. The works of **BMPT** – the name was taken from the four men's surnames – focused on abstract colour, often in regular patterns. The best-known of the four, **Daniel Buren** (b.1938), caused a furore in 1985–6 with his installation in the courtyard of the Palais Royal consisting of numerous black-and-white, vertically striped columns of differing heights. Now, however, this one-time *enfant terrible* has become one of France's most respected living artists.

Following BMPT's lead, the geometrically abstract **Supports-Surfaces** group emerged in Nice in 1969, founded by the likes of **Daniel Dezeuze** (b.1942), **Jean-Pierre Pincemin** (1944–2005) and **Claude Villat** (b.1936). The group stressed the importance of the painting as object – as paint applied to a surface.

The 1977 opening of the Musée National d'Art Moderne, in Paris's Pompidou Centre, was a sign of the increased state support that French contemporary art was beginning to attract – a support that would be hugely boosted in the early 1980s by the active buying policy of the Socialist government. The landmark Pompidou exhibition of 1979, *Tendances de l'art en France*, showed artists in three groupings. The first was broadly abstract, the second, figurative. It was the third, however, which would look most prophetic of future directions; it focused on **conceptual artists**, many of them working with unconventional materials. This third group included the BMPT iconoclasts, along with three artists who would become landmark figures in French contemporary art: **Christian Boltanski** (b.1944) and

Annette Messager (b.1943) – who were then husband and wife – and Bertrand Lavier (b.1949). All three work with found objects: Boltanski's often harrowing work has even employed personal property lost in public places, while Messager has drawn on toys and needlework to create unsettling works, often challenging perceptions of women. Lavier, meanwhile, is best known for playing with art and reality – principally by applying paint to industrial objects.

A quintessentially French reaction to minimalist and conceptual art emerged in 1981 with **Figuration Libre**, a movement which absorbed comic-strip art and graffiti in an explosion of punk creativity. Among the key figures were **Jean-Charles Blais** (b.1956), **Robert Combas** (b.1957), **François Boisrond** (b.1959) and **Herve di Rosa** (b.1959). Despite such breakout movements, the juggernaut of conceptual art continued to roll on through the last two decades. Large-scale installation has become important, particularly in the works of **Jean-Marc Bustamante** (b.1952) and **Jean-Luc Vilmouth** (b.1952), who have been known to co-opt buildings themselves, resulting in a blurring of the aesthetic and the functional. Artists crossing and recrossing generic boundaries is another ongoing theme. Bustamante, for example, also works with photography, and in the early 1980s he collaborated for three years with the sculptor Bernard Bazile (b.1952) under the name **Bazile Bustamante**.

A new generation of artists is using non-traditional media, including video, photography, electronic media and found objects. Recent work could hardly be more diverse, but a common thread seems to be the use of films and installations which explore the relationships between reality and fiction, between interiority and the exterior world – ideas which resonate in the films, puppet shows and "public interventions" of **Pierre Huyghe** (b.1962). Huyghe is often associated with – and has worked with – the Algerian-born **Philippe Parreno** (b.1964), who in 2006 released a feature film which followed the footballer Zinédine Zidane for ninety minutes of relentless close-up. Two other associated artists are **Dominique Gonzalez-Foerster** (b.1965), who works with films, photographs, installations and even métro stations and shop windows to create worlds where fantasy and reality seem to overlap, and **Claude Closky** (b.1963), whose "books" and videos restructure everyday flotsam and jetsam. Closky has declared, "My work bears on all that daily life has made banal, on things that are never called into question." Similarly eclectic in his choice of media is **Fabrice Hybert** (b.1961), who has created the world's largest-ever bar of soap (at 22 tons) and a working television studio. His playful, interactive work taps into what he describes as the "enormous reservoir of the possible". **Sophie Calle** (b.1953) blends texts and photographs; among her most publicized works have been her intimate documentations of the lives of both strangers and – after she asked her mother to hire a private detective for the purpose – Calle herself.

In such a multimedia milieu, some critics have claimed that actual painting is moribund in France. Bucking this trend is the celebrated Lyonnais painter **Marc Desgrandchamps** (b.1960). He may work with traditional oils, but Desgrandchamps is hardly a traditionalist. His figures often appear partially transparent, or are presented as fragments, thus overlaying doubt and disquiet over the perception of reality.

Architecture

Fance's architectural legacy reflects the power and personality of Church and the state, the "great men" vying to outdo their peers with lavish statements in stone. Many of France's architectural trends were born in Italy – Romanesque, Renaissance and Baroque – but they were refined and developed in uniquely French ways. Rococo grew from Baroque, Neoclassicism came from the Renaissance, and Art Nouveau was a brilliant, confused jumble of Baroque features combined with the newly developed cast-iron industry. France's last great architectural flowerings can be seen in the work of the early twentieth-century Modernists, Auguste Perret and Le Corbusier, but the contemporary scene is potentially as exciting, with Jean Nouvel and Christian de Portzamparc as its preeminent stars.

The Romans

The **Romans**, who had colonized the south of France by around 120 BC, were fine town-planners, linking complexes of buildings with straight roads punctuated by decorative fountains, arches and colonnades. They built essentially in the Greek style, and their large, functional buildings were concerned more with strength and solidity than aesthetics. A number of substantial Roman building works survive: in **Nîmes** you can see the Maison Carrée, the best-preserved Roman temple still standing, and the Temple of Diana, one of just four vaulted Roman temples in Europe. Gateways remain at **Autun**, **Orange**, **Saintes** and **Reims**, and largely intact amphitheatres can be seen at Nîmes and **Arles**. The **Pont du Gard** aqueduct outside Nîmes is still a magnificent and ageless monument of civil engineering, built to carry the town's fresh water over the gorge, and Orange has its massive theatre, with Europe's only intact Roman facade. There are excavated archeological sites at **Glanum** near St-Rémy, **Vienne**, **Vaison-la-Romaine** and **Lyon**.

Romanesque

Charlemagne's ninth-century **Carolingian dynasty** attempted to revive the symbols of civilized authority by recourse to Roman models. Of this era, very few buildings remain, though the motifs of arch and vault and the plan of semicircular apse and basilican nave and aisles would be hugely influential.

The style later dubbed "**Romanesque**" (*Roman* in French, as opposed to *Romain* which, confusingly, means Roman/classical) only really developed from the eleventh century onwards. Classical Roman architecture was not so much a direct model as a distant inspiration, filtered partly through the Carolingian heritage and partly through Byzantine models – as imported by returning crusaders and arriving artisans from Italy. The new style was also shaped by the particular needs of monastic communities, which began to burgeon in the period, and the requirements of pilgrims, who began to tour shrines in ever-greater numbers.

The key characteristics of Romanesque are thick walls with small windows, round arches on Roman-style piers and columns, and a proliferation of stone sculpture and wall paintings – these last often being the first victims of wear-and-tear and iconoclasm. Romanesque is as diverse as the various regions of France. In the south, the classical inheritance of Provence is strong, with stone barrel vaults, aisleless naves and domes. **St-Trophime** at Arles (1150) has a porch directly derived from Roman models and, with the church at St-Gilles nearby, exhibits a delight in carved ornament peculiar to the south at this time. The presence of the wealthy and powerful Cluniac order, in Burgundy, made this region a veritable powerhouse of architectural experiment, while the south was the readiest route for the introduction of new cultural developments. The pointed arch and vault are probably owed to Spanish Muslim sources, and appear first in churches such as **Notre-Dame** at Avignon, Notre-Dame-la-Grande at Poitiers, the cathedral at **Autun** and **Ste-Madeleine** at Vézelay (1089–1206).

In Normandy, the nave with aisles is more usual, capped by twin western towers. The emphasis in general is on mass and size, and geometrical design is favoured over figurative sculpture. The **Abbaye aux Hommes** at Caen (1066–77) is typical – and also contains many of the elements later identified as "Gothic", notably ribbed vaults and spires.

Gothic

The reasons behind the development of the **Gothic style** (twelfth to sixteenth centuries) lie in the pursuit of the sublime; to achieve great height without apparent great weight would seem to imitate religious ambition. Its development in the north is partly due to the availability of good building stone and soft stone for carving, but perhaps more to the growth of royal aspiration and power based in the Île de France, which, allied with the papacy, stimulated the building of the great **cathedrals** of Paris, Bourges, Chartres, Laon, Le Mans, Reims and Amiens in the twelfth and thirteenth centuries.

The Gothic phase is said to begin with the building of the choir of the **abbey of St-Denis** near Paris in 1140. In France, the style reigned supreme until the end of the fifteenth century. Architecturally, it encompasses the development of spacious windows of coloured glass and the flying buttress, a rib of external stone that resists the outward push of the vaulting. But, above all, French Gothic is characterized by verticality.

In the south, as at Albi and Angers, the great churches are generally broader and simpler in plan and external appearance, with aisles often almost as high as the nave. Many secular buildings survive – some of the most notable in their present form being the work of Viollet-le-Duc, the pre-eminent nineteenth-century restorer – and even whole towns, for example **Carcassonne** and **Aigues Mortes**; **Avignon** has the bridge and the papal palace.

Even castles began to lend themselves to the disappearing walls of the Gothic style, as windows steadily increased in size in response to more settled times. Fine Gothic stone-carving was applied to doors and windows, and roofscapes came alive with balustrades, sculpted gables and exquisite leadwork finials and ridges. Some of the most elaborate châteaux, as at **Châteaudun** and **Saumur**, in the Loire valley, were veritable palaces. Yet they still incorporated the old defensive feudal tower in their design, perhaps in the form of a elaborately sculpted open staircase. In the Dordogne region, a series of colonial settlements, the **bastides**, or fortified towns, are a refreshing antidote to triumphal French bombast.

Renaissance

French military adventures in Italy in the early sixteenth century hastened the arrival of a new style borrowing heavily from the Italian **Renaissance**. The persistence of Gothic traditions, however, and the necessity of steep roofs and tall chimneys in the more northerly climate, gave the newly luxurious castles, or châteaux, a distinctively French emphasis on the vertical line, with an elaboration of detail on the facade at the expense of the clear modelling of form.

Gradually, these French forms were supplanted by a purely classical style – a development embodied by the **Louvre** palace, which was worked over by all the grand names of French architecture from Lescot in the early sixteenth century, via François Mansart and Claude Perrault in the seventeenth, to the later years of the nineteenth century.

At Blois and **Maisons Lafitte** (1640), Mansart began to experiment with a new suavity and elegance, attitudes that appear again in the eighteenth century in the town houses of the Rococo period. On the other hand, **Claude Perrault** (1613–88), who designed the great colonnaded east front of the Louvre, gives an austere face to the official architecture of despotism, magnificent but far too imperial to be much enjoyed by common mortals. The high-pitched roofs, which had been almost universal until then, are replaced here by the classical balustrade and pediment, the style grand but cold and supremely secular. Art and architecture were at the time organized by boards and academies, including the Académie Royale d'Architecture, and style and employment were strictly controlled by royal direction. With such a limitation of ideas at the source of patronage, it's hardly surprising that there was a certain dullness to the era.

Baroque

In a similar way to the preceding century, the churches of the **seventeenth and eighteenth centuries** have a coldness quite different from the German, Flemish and Italian **Baroque**. When the Renaissance style first appeared in the early sixteenth century, there was no great need for new church building, the country being so well endowed from the Gothic centuries. **St-Étienne-du-Mont** (1517–1620) and **St-Eustache** (1532–89), both in Paris, show how old forms persisted with only an overlay of the new style.

It was with the Jesuits in the seventeenth century that the Church embraced the new style to combat the forces of rational disbelief. In Paris the churches of the **Sorbonne** (1653) and **Val-de-Grâce** (1645) exemplify this, as do a good number of other grandiose churches in the **Baroque** style, through **Les Invalides** at the end of the seventeenth century to the **Panthéon** of the late eighteenth century. Here is the Church triumphant, rather than the state, but no more beguiling.

The architect of Les Invalides was **Jules Hardouin–Mansart**, a product of the Académie Royale d'Architecture, which harked back to the ancient, classical tradition. Mansart also greatly extended the palace of **Versailles** and so created the Cinemascope view of France with that seemingly endless horizon of royalty. As an antidote to this pomposity, the **Petit Trianon** at Versailles is as refreshing now as it was to Louis XV, who had it built in 1762 as a place of escape for his mistress. This is even more true of that other pearl formed of the grit of boredom in the enclosed world of Versailles – **La Petite Ferme**, where Marie-Antoinette played at being a milkmaid, which epitomizes the Arcadian and "picturesque" fantasy of the painters Boucher and Fragonard.

The lightness and charm that was undermining official grandeur with Arcadian fancies and **Rococo** decoration was, however, snuffed out by the Revolution. There's no real Revolutionary architecture, as the necessity of order and authority soon asserted itself and an autocracy every bit as absolute returned with Napoleon, drawing on the old grand manner but with a stronger trace of the stern old Roman.

In Paris it was not the democratic Doric but the imperial Corinthian order that re-emerged triumphant in the church of the **Madeleine** (1806) and, with the **Arc de Triomphe** like some colossal paperweight, reimposed the authority of academic architecture in contrast to the fancy-dress structures of contemporary Regency England.

The nineteenth century

The restoration of legitimate monarchy after the **fall of Napoleon** stimulated a revival of interest in older Gothic and early Renaissance styles, which offered a symbol of dynastic reassurance not only to the state but also to the newly rich. So in the private and commercial architecture of the nineteenth century these earlier styles predominate – in mine-owners' villas and bankers' headquarters.

From 1853, the overgrown and insanitary medieval capital was ruthlessly transformed into an urban utopia. In half a century, half of Paris was rebuilt. Napoléon III's authoritarian government provided the force – land was compulsorily purchased and boulevards bulldozed through old quarters – while banks and private speculators provided the cash. The poor, meanwhile, provided the labour – and were shipped out to the suburban badlands in their tens of thousands to make way for richer tenants. The presiding genius was Napoléon III's architect-in-chief, **Baron Haussmann** (1809–91). In his brave new city, every apartment building was seven storeys high. Every facade was built in golden limestone, often quarried from under the city itself, with unobtrusive Neoclassical details sculpted around the windows. Every second and fifth floor had its wrought-iron balcony and every lead roof sloped back from the streetfront at precisely 45 degrees.

Competing with Haussmann's totalitarian sobriety was a voluptuous, exuberant **neo-Baroque** strain, exemplified by Charles Garnier's Opéra in Paris (1861–74), and a third, engineering-led approach, embodied in the official **School of Roads and Bridges**. The teachings of Viollet-le-Duc, the great restorer who reinterpreted Gothic style as pure structure, led to the development of new techniques out of which "modern" architectural style was born. Iron was the first significant new material, often used in imitation of Gothic forms and destined to be developed as an individual architectural style in America. In the enormously controversial **Eiffel Tower** (1889), France set up a potent symbol of things to come.

Le Corbusier to Art Deco

The sinous, organic **Art Nouveau** style, which was at the height of fashion around the turn of the nineteenth and twentieth centuries, quickly found its winding way onto the facades of many Parisian buildings, including the department stores Printemps and La Samaritaine. The most famous expression of the style, however, is the entrances to the Paris métro, whose twisting metal railings and antennae-like orange lamps were deeply controversial when **Hector Guimard** first designed them in the 1900s. Few of the early entrances now remain, however (**Place des**

Abbesses is one), partly because conservatives fought back under **Charles Garnier**, architect of the Opéra Garnier. He demanded classical marble and bronze porticoes for every station; his line was followed, on a less grandiose scale, wherever the métro steps surfaced by a major monument, putting Guimard out of a job.

Even as Art Nouveau sought lithe and living forms, brutal **Modernism** powered ahead. Towards the end of the nineteenth century, France pioneered the use of reinforced concrete, most notably in buildings by **Auguste Perret**, such as his 1903 apartment house at 25 rue Franklin in Paris. Perret and other **modernists** designed gigantic skyscraper avenues and suburban rings, which now look like totalitarian horror-movie sets.

The greatest proponent of this style was Swiss-born **Le Corbusier**. His stature may now appear diminished by the ascendancy of a blander style in concrete boxing, as well as by the significant technical and social failures of his buildings – not to mention his total disregard for historic streets and monuments – but he remains France's most influential modern architect. Surprisingly few of his works were ever built, but the **Cité Radieuse** in Marseille and plenty of lesser examples in Paris bear witness to the ideas of the man largely responsible for changing the face and form of buildings throughout the world.

The more acceptable face of Modernism, in the 1920s and 30s, was the simple geometry of the modern or International Style, which was allied to the glamorously functional **Art Deco look**; again, you're most likely to come across it in the capital, either on apartment block facades or in mega-projects such as the Palais de Tokyo.

Contemporary

The miserable 1950s and 1960s buildings found all over the country are probably best skipped over. From the 1970s onwards, however, France again established itself as one of the most exciting patrons of international **contemporary architecture**. The **Pompidou Centre**, by **Renzo Piano** and **Richard Rogers**, derided, adored and visited by millions, maximizes space by putting the service elements usually concealed in walls and floors on the outside. It is one of the great contemporary buildings in western Europe – for its originality, popularity and practicality.

In the 1980s, under President Mitterrand's grandiose *grands projets* ("grand projects"), it was decided that the grand axis from the Louvre to the Arc de Triomphe was to be extended westwards towards the **Grande Arche de la Défense**, symbol of the new La Défense business district. Designed by Von Spreckelsen, it isn't really an arch but a huge hollow cube. At the other end of the grand axis stands Ieoh Ming Pei's glass **pyramid** in the Cour Napoléon, the main entrance to the Louvre. Hugely controversial at first, it's now widely accepted and admired.

As part of the wider reorganization of the Louvre, the **Ministry of Finance** decamped to a new building in **Bercy** designed by Paul Chemetov and nicknamed the "steamboat" because of its titanic length and its anchoring in the Seine. Formerly full of wine warehouses, Bercy is now extensively redeveloped. Also in the Parc de Bercy stands Frank Gehry's (architect of Bilbao's Guggenheim Museum) free-form, exuberant **American Centre**. Another mega-project from broadly the same era is the **Parc de la Villette** complex, which was built on the site of an old abattoir. It houses the Cité des Sciences, Bernard Tschumi's 21 *"folies"* of urban life and the **Cité de la Musique** concert hall and conservatoire complex, designed by acclaimed architect Christian de Portzamparc to be like a symphony, its various sections creating a harmonious ensemble.

Perhaps the least successful of Mitterrand's grand projects was the **Bibliothèque Nationale**. Designed by Dominique Perrault, it's made up of four L-shaped tower blocks, resembling four open books, set around an inaccessible sunken garden. The most outstanding, by contrast, is arguably the **Institut du Monde Arabe**. Designed by **Jean Nouvel**, France's most eminent contemporary architect, it ingeniously marries high-tech architecture and motifs from traditional Arabic culture. Jean Nouvel's airy, green-themed buildings in Paris continue to multiply in Paris, from the Fondation Cartier, with its glass wall, to the curving, light-filled **Quai Branly** museum, which traverses on stilts over a lush garden designed by Gilles Clément, who landscaped the Parc André Citroën.

Paris continues to find space for new architecture. The futuristically twisting double-ribbon of the **Passarelle Simone de Beauvoir** now bridges the Seine opposite Perrault's Bibliothèque. Upstream, the University Paris 7 is now installed in the massive **Grands Moulins de Paris** and **Halle aux Farines**, and a new school of architecture – appropriately enough – resides in the handsomely arched, late nineteenth-century **SUDAC** building. Christian de Portzamparc's blade-like **Tour Granite** is now one of the most distinctive silhouettes in the La Défense skyline, a vigorous foil to the incised cylinders of the twin Société Générale towers. Jakob + MacFarlane's **Cité de la Mode et du Design** has a lime-green glass tube apparently pouring through it. And at the time of writing, Frank Gehry's **Fondation Louis Vuitton pour la Création** was slowly taking shape in the Bois de Boulogne; judging by the plans, Gehry's fantasy looks less like the advertised "cloud of glass" than a glazed armadillo which has burst out of its own skin.

In **Marseille** there's Will Alsop's mammoth seat of regional government, while the first cathedral to be built in France since the nineteenth century, the **Cathédrale d'Évry**, masterminded by Swiss Mario Botta and finished in 1995, is a huge cylindrical red-brick tower which, besides being a place of worship, houses an art centre, concert hall and cinema screen. The new **European Parliament** building in **Strasbourg**, designed by the Architecture Studio group, was finished in 1997. A huge, boomerang-shaped structure with a glass dome and metal tower, it sits across the river from the eccentric, high-tech Richard Rogers-designed **European Court of Human Rights**.

Museums across the country continue to attract innovative architects. In **Nîmes**, Norman Foster's **Carré d'Art** modern art museum (1993) is characterized by its simple transparent design, while his **Musée de Préhistoire des Gorges du Verdon** (2001) in **Provence** uses local materials – part of the museum is folded into the landscape and blends on one side into an existing stone wall, while the entrance hall resembles the very caves the museum celebrates.

The country's ever-advancing **transport network** has fuelled some of the most state-of-the-art design and engineering in Europe, as in **Roissy**, around the Charles-de-Gaulle airport, and at **Euralille**, the large complex around Lille's TGV/Eurostar station, masterminded by Dutch architect Rem Koolhaas. Most dramatic of all is the **Millau Viaduct**, a bridge so huge in scale and ambition that its impact could almost be described as geographical. Designed by engineer Michel Virlogeux and Norman Foster's firm, and opened in December 2004, its sleekness belies its size: the largest of its soaring white pylons is actually taller than the Eiffel Tower.

Even as they push towards a high-tech future, the French are particularly good at preserving the past – too good, some would say. A passion for restoring "*la patrimoine*" results in many fine old buildings being practically rebuilt – the dominant restoration theory in France is to restore to perfection rather than halt decay. More often than not, restoration is carried out by the **Maisons de Compagnonnage**, the old craft guilds, which have maintained traditional building skills, handing them down as of old from master to apprentice (and never to women), while also taking on new industrial skills.

Futures

In 2009 the government invited ten leading architectural firms to submit proposals for **Le Grand Pari** – de l'agglomération Parisienne (⊛www.legrandparis.culture .gouv.fr) the Greater, Greener Paris of the future. The architects envisioned new *"Grands Axes"*, avenues as radical as any bulldozed by Haussmann – but in this case linking city and *banlieue*. President Sarkozy favoured high-speed rail links down the Seine towards the port of Le Havre; Richard Rogers called for a green network covering the train lines leading out of the northern stations; Christian de Portzamparc wanted a high-speed elevated train running circles around the ring road. The radical left-wing architect Roland Castro mildly proposed that perhaps the suburbs might have their share of government offices and cultural institutions.

Meanwhile, real works progress apace in **Paris**, and beyond. From 2010, the capital's old, murky underground mall of **Les Halles** is being transformed by architect David Mangin into light-filled spaces under a giant glass roof. Also in 2010, the Louvre has begun work on its annexe of glossy pavilions, sited in the northern town of Lens (it is a modest partner to the equally new Abu Dhabi annexe, designed by – who else – Jean Nouvel), while the Pompidou Centre has opened its own curvaceously geometric satellite in **Metz**, designed by Shigeru Ban and Jean de Gastines to echo of the shape of a Chinese hat. In the Défense business district, the **Tour Phare**, a boldy curvaceous eco-scraper, will rival the height of the Eiffel Tower by 2014. Jean Nouvel's **Tour sans Fins** or "endless tower", has been cancelled, however. It was supposed to dissipate its 425m in the clouds above La Défense; in the end, it was the budget which dissipated, along with the economy. Others may replace it, however: in 2008, ominously, Paris's city council dropped the legal ban on skyscrapers. The capital may yet lose its radical uniformity.

Cinema

The first (satisfied) cinema audience in the world was French. Screened to patrons of the Grand Café, on Paris's boulevard des Capucines, in December 1895, Louis **Lumière**'s single-reelers may have been jerky documentaries, but they were light-years ahead of anything that had come before. Soon after, Georges Méliès's magical-fantastical features were proving a big hit with theatre audiences, and the twin cinematic poles of Realism and Surrealism had been established. France took to cinema with characteristic enthusiasm and seriousness. Ciné-clubs were formed all over the country, journals were published, critics made films and film-makers became critics. The avant-garde wing of French cinema acquired the moniker of **French Impressionism**, a genre characterized by experimental directors such as Louis Delluc, Jean Epstein and Abel Gance, who used experimental, highly visual techniques to express altered states of consciousness. It was only a short step from here to the all-out **Surrealism** of the artist-polymath Jean Cocteau, and the Spanish director Luis Buñuel.

Towards the end of the 1920s, histrionic adaptations of novels, epic historical dramas and broad comedies attracted mass audiences, but the silent heyday ended abruptly with the advent of sound in 1929. Most silent stars faded into obscurity, but a number of directors successfully made the transition, notably Jean Renoir, the son of the painter, René Clair, Julien Duvivier, Jean Gremillon and Abel Gance. Among the newcomers were Jean Vigo, who died young in 1934, and Marcel Carné, who worked with the powerful scripts of the poet Jacques Prévert. The film-makers of the 1930s developed a bold new style, dubbed **Poetic Realism** for its pessimism, powerful visual aesthetic – high-contrast, often nocturnal – and devotion to "realistic", usually working-class, settings.

In 1936 the collector Henri Langlois set up the **Cinémathèque Française**, devoted to the preservation and screening of old and art films – an indication of the speed with which the "*septième art*" had found its niche within the pantheon of French culture. Langlois played an important role in saving thousands of films from destruction during the war, but the Occupation had surprisingly little effect on the industry. Renoir and Clair sought temporary sanctuary in Hollywood, and domestic production dipped, but hundreds of films continued to be made in Vichy France at a time when audiences sought the solace and comfort of the cinema in record numbers.

Postwar and pre-television, the late 1940s and early 1950s was another boom time for French cinema. Poetic Realism morphed into **film noir**, whose emphasis on darkness and corruption gave birth in turn to the thriller, a genre exemplified by the films of Henri-Georges Clouzot and Jean-Pierre Melville. During this period the mainstream cinema industry became highly organized and technically slick, older directors such as Clair, Renoir and Jacques Becker making superbly controlled masterpieces spanning genres as diverse as thrillers, comedies and costume dramas.

The first shot of the coming revolution – a warning shot only – was fired by the acerbic young critic François Truffaut, writing in the legendary film magazine, **Les Cahiers du cinéma**, in the mid-1950s. In opposition to what he and fellow critics dubbed *la tradition de qualité*, Truffaut envisaged a new kind of cinema based on the independent vision of a writer-director, an *auteur* (author), who would make films in a purer and more responsive manner. Directors such as Melville and Louis Malle – who made his first film with the diver Jacques Cousteau – were beginning to make moves in this direction, but Truffaut's vision was only fully realized towards the end of the decade, when the **Nouvelle Vague** ("New Wave") came rolling in. Claude Chabrol's *Les Cousins*, Truffaut's own *Les Quatre-cents* *coups*, Eric Rohmer's *Le Signe du lion*, Alain Resnais' *Hiroshima, mon amour* and Jean-Luc Godard's *À Bout de souffle* were all released in 1959. The trademark freedom of these *auteur*-directors' films – loosely scripted, highly individualistic and typically shot on location – ushered in the modern era.

The 1960s was the heyday of the *auteur*. Truffaut established his pre-eminent status by creating an extraordinary oeuvre encompassing science fiction, thriller, autobiography and *film noir*, all his films characteristically elegant and excitingly shot. But the "new wave" hadn't carried all before it: René Clément, Henri-Georges Clouzot and even Jean Renoir were still working throughout the decade, Jean-Pierre Melville continued shooting his characteristically *noir* **films policiers** (crime-thrillers), and the Catholic director Robert Bresson carried on making films on his favourite theme of salvation. And Jacques Tati, the maverick genius behind the legendary comic character M. Hulot, made two of his greatest and most radical quasi-silent films, *Playtime* and *Trafic*, at either end of the 1960s.

The 1970s is probably the least impressive decade in terms of output, but a shot in the arm was delivered in the 1980s by the **Cinéma du Look**, a genre epitomized in the films of Jean-Jacques Beineix, Luc Besson and Leos Carax. Stylish, image-conscious and postmodern, films such as *Diva* or *Betty Blue* owed much to the look of American pulp cinema and contemporary advertising. Meanwhile, throughout the 1980s and into the 1990s, high-gloss costume dramas – historical or adaptations of novels – were the focus of much attention. Often called **Heritage Cinema**, the best films of this genre are the superbly crafted creations of Claude Berri, though Jean-Pierre Rappeneau's *Cyrano de Bergerac* is probably the internationally recognized standard-bearer. At the other end of the scale lies **cinéma beur**: naturalistic, socially responsible and low-budget films made by French-born film-makers of North African origin – *les beurs* in French slang. The newest trends in contemporary art cinema follow a related path of social realism. In recent years, a number of younger directors, notably Mathieu Kassovitz, have made films set in the deprived suburbs (*la banlieue*), creating a number of sub-genres that have been acclaimed variously as **New Realism**, **cinéma de banlieue** and **le jeune cinéma** ("young cinema").

Today, France remains the second-largest exporter of films in the world. The industry's continued health is largely due to the intransigence of the French state, which continues to protect and promote domestic cinema as part of its policy of **l'exception culturelle** – despite the complaints of the free-marketeers who would have the French market "liberalized". Half of the costs of making a feature film in France are paid for by state subsidies, levied on television stations, box-office receipts and video sales. Currently, American-made films capture around fifty percent of the French market, while home-grown productions make up around forty percent. But the future looks promising: recent years have seen the number of films made in France rise to almost two hundred a year, most of them domestically funded.

Note that the **films reviewed below** are only intended to point out a few landmarks of French cinema; we can't review every Godard film nor cover every significant director. As such, they can all be considered as highly recommended. Alternative English titles are given for those films renamed for the main foreign release.

Cinema pre-1945

L'Atalante Jean Vigo, 1934. Aboard a barge, a newly married couple struggle to reconcile themselves to their new situation. Eventually, the wife, Juliette, tries to flee, but is brought back by the unconventional deck-hand, Père Jules, superbly portrayed by the great Michel Simon. This sensual and naturalistic portrait of a relationship was made just before Vigo died, and is his only feature film.

La Belle équipe/They Were Five
Julien Duvivier, 1936. A group of
unemployed workers wins the lottery
and sets up a cooperative restaurant.
The version with an upbeat conclusion
was a huge hit with contemporary
audiences; Duvivier himself preferred
his darker ending. Jean Gabin stars as
the defeated hero, as in Duvivier's
other greats, *La Bandéra* (1935) and the
cult classic, *Pépé-le-Moko* (1937).

**Un Chien andalou/An Andalusian
Dog** Luis Buñuel, 1929. Made in
collaboration with Salvador Dalí, this
short opens with a woman's eye being
cut into with a razorblade. While it
doesn't get any less weird or shocking
for the rest of its twenty-minute
length, it's surprisingly watchable –
when it came out, it was a big hit at
Paris's Studio des Ursulines cinema.
Buñuel further developed his
Surrealist techniques in the feature-
length talkie *L'Age d'or* (1930).

🏃 **Les Enfants du Paradis** Marcel
Carné, 1945. Probably the
greatest of the collaborations between
Carné and the poet-scriptwriter,
Jacques Prévert, this film is set in the
low-life world of the popular theatre of
1840s Paris. Beautiful and worldly
actress Garance (the great Arletty) is
loved by arch-criminal Lacenaire,
ambitious actor Lemaître, and brilliant,
troubled mime Baptiste – unforgettably
played by the top mime of the 1940s,
Jean-Louis Barrault. The outstanding
character portrayals and romantic,
humane ethos are reminiscent of a great
nineteenth-century novel.

Le Jour se lève/Daybreak Marcel
Carné, 1939. This brooding classic from
the Poetic Realist stable has Jean Gabin,
the greatest star of the era, playing
another of his iconic working-class hero
roles. After shooting his rival, the
villainous old music-hall star Valentin,
François (Gabin) is holed up in a hotel
bedroom. In the course of the night, he
recalls the events that led up to the
murder. Also stars the great female idol
of the 1930s, Arletty, and a superb
script by the poet Jacques Prévert.
Carné's *Hôtel du Nord* (1938) and *Quai
des brumes* (1938) are in a similar vein.

Le Million René Clair, 1931. In 1930
Clair had made the first great French
talkie, *Sous les toits de Paris*, but it
wasn't until *Le Million* that the true
musical film was born. A hunt for a
lost winning lottery ticket provides
plenty of opportunity for madcap
comedy, suspense and romance.

🏃 **La Règle du jeu/The Rules of
the Game** Jean Renoir, 1939.
Now hailed as the foremost masterpiece of the prewar era, this was a
complete commercial failure when it
was released. The Marquis de la
Chesnaye invites his wife, mistress and
a pilot friend to spend a weekend
hunting and partying in the countryside. Matching the four are a group of
four servants with similarly inter-
weaved love lives. Renoir himself
plays Octave, who moves between the
two groups. A complex, almost
farcical plot based around misunder-
standing and accusations of infidelity
moves inexorably towards disaster.

Postwar cinema

**Ascenseur pour l'échafaud/Elevator
to the Gallows/Frantic** Louis Malle,
1957. This thriller is Louis Malle's
remarkable debut. Two lovers (Jeanne
Moreau and Maurice Ronet) murder
the woman's husband but get trapped
by a series of unlucky coincidences.
Beautifully shot – especially when

Jeanne Moreau wanders through the
streets of Paris, accompanied by Miles
Davis' superb original score – and as
breathtaking as any Hitchcock film.

🏃 **La Belle et la bête/Beauty and
the Beast** Jean Cocteau, 1946.
Cocteau's theatrical rendition of the
"Beauty and the Beast" tale teeters on

the edge of the surreal, but the pace is as compelling as any thriller. *Orphée* (1950) is more widely considered to be Cocteau's masterpiece, a surreal retelling of the Orpheus tale in a setting strongly redolent of wartime France.

Casque d'or/Golden Marie Jacques Becker, 1952. Becker's first great film depicts the ultimately tragic romance between a gangster and a beautiful, golden-haired prostitute, portrayed with legendary seductiveness by Simone Signoret. Underneath the love story lurks the moral corruption of a brilliantly recreated turn-of-the-century Paris. Becker went on to make the seminal crime thriller, *Touchez pas au grisbi/Honour Among Thieves* (1953).

Un Condamné à mort s'est échappé/A Man Escaped Robert Bresson, 1956. A prisoner, Fontaine (François Leterrier), calmly plans his escape from prison, working with a painstaking slowness that is brilliantly matched by the intensely absorbed camerawork. Working with real locations and amateur actors, Bresson echoed the work of the Italian Neo-realists, and foreshadowed the work of the Nouvelle Vague directors. Sometimes entitled *Le Vent souffle où il veut*.

Et Dieu ... créa la femme/And God ... Created Woman Roger Vadim, 1956. This film should be called "And Roger Vadim created Brigitte Bardot", as its chief interest is not its harmless plot – love and adultery in St-Tropez – but its scantily clad main actress, who spends most of the time sunbathing and dancing in front of fascinated males. Deemed "obscene" by the moralizing authorities of the time, it helped liberate the way the body was represented in film.

Les Jeux interdits René Clément, 1952. A small Parisian girl loses her parents and her dog in a Stuka attack on a column of refugees, and is rescued and befriended by a peasant boy. Together, they seek solace from the war by building an animal cemetery in an abandoned barn. This moving meditation on childhood and death extracted two remarkable performances from the child actors.

Le Salaire de la peur/The Wages of Fear Henri-Georges Clouzot, 1953. This is the tensest, most suspense-driven of all the films made by the "French Hitchcock", focusing on four men driving an explosive-laden lorry hundreds of miles to a burning, third-world oil field. Tight and shatteringly sustained right up to the magnificent finale.

Les Vacances de Monsieur Hulot/Mr Hulot's Holiday Jacques Tati, 1951. The slapstick comic mime Jacques Tati created his most memorable character in Hulot, the unwitting creator of chaos and nonchalant hero of this gut-wrenchingly funny film. So full of brilliantly conceived and impeccably timed sight gags that you hardly notice the innovative absence of much dialogue or plot. Groundbreaking cinema, and superlative entertainment. The later *Mon oncle* (1958) has an edgier feel, adopting a distinctly critical attitude to modern life.

The Nouvelle Vague

A Bout de souffle/Breathless Jean-Luc Godard, 1959. This is the film that came nearest to defining the Nouvelle Vague: insolent charm, cool music and sexy actors. Jean-Paul Belmondo is a petty criminal, Michel, while Jean Seberg plays Patricia, his American girlfriend. The film's revolutionary style, with its jerky, unconventional narrative, abrupt cuts and rough camerawork, proved one of the most influential of the twentieth century.

Les Cousins/The Cousins Claude Chabrol, 1959. The Balzac-inspired plot centres around Charles (Gérard Blain), an earnest provincial student, who comes to live in Neuilly with his glamorous cousin Paul (Jean-Claude Brialy). A near-caricature of the Nouvelle Vague – idle students in the Quartier Latin, extravagant parties, convertible cars and exciting music.

Hiroshima, mon amour Alain Resnais, 1959. On her last days of shooting a film in Hiroshima, a French actress (Emmanuelle Riva) falls in love with a Japanese architect (Eiji Okada). Gradually, she reveals the story of her affair with a German soldier during the Occupation, and her subsequent disgrace. Based on an original script by Marguerite Duras, Resnais' first film masterfully weaves together past and present in a haunting story of love and memory.

Ma Nuit chez Maude/My Night at Maud's Eric Rohmer, 1969. Rohmer's career-long obsessions with sexuality, conversation, existential choices and the love triangle are given free rein in this moody, lingering portrait of a flirtation. Jean-Louis Trintignant plays a handsome egotist who, during the course of one long night, is drawn into a strange and inconclusive relationship with his friend's friend, the hypnotically attractive Maude (Françoise Fabian).

Les Quatre-cents coups/The 400 Blows François Truffaut, 1959. A young *cinéphile* and critic turned film-maker, François Truffaut triumphed at the 1959 Cannes film festival with this semi-autobiographical film, showing a Parisian adolescent (Jean-Pierre Léaud) trying to escape his lonely, loveless existence, and slowly drifting towards juvenile delinquency. Léaud's poignant performance, and Truffaut's sensitive, sympathetic observation, make this one of the most lovable films of the Nouvelle Vague.

Comedies

Belle de jour Luis Buñuel, 1966. Catherine Deneuve plays Séverine, who lives out her sexual fantasies and obsessions in a brothel. At first sight, this is a far cry from Buñuel's prewar collaborations with Dalí, though the film moves away from the initial acerbic comedy towards surrealism.

La Cage aux folles/Birds of a Feather Edouard Molinaro, 1978. Renato runs a cabaret nightclub at which his boyfriend, Albin, is the headlining drag act. When Renato's son, Laurent, decides to get married, the couple are drawn into an escalating farce as they try to present themselves as a conventional mother-and-son couple to Laurent's conservative in-laws. A supremely camp international hit.

Le Fabuleux destin d'Amélie Poulain/Amélie Jean-Pierre Jeunet, 2001. This sentimental, feel-good portrait of a youthful ingenue wandering around a romanticized Montmartre was a worldwide hit. Amélie (Audrey Tatou) is on a mission to help the world find happiness; her own is harder to fix up.

La Grande vadrouille Gérard Oury, 1966. Head and shoulders the biggest blockbuster in French cinema history, "The Big Jaunt" stars Bourvil and Louis de Funès as a conductor and a decorator. Set in wartime Paris, the comic plot sees three Allied soldiers parachuting down on the hapless pair. In their desperation to be rid of the parachutists, they end up leading them to the free zone.

Playtime Jacques Tati, 1967. Tati once more plays Hulot, cinema's most radical slapstick creation. From a simple premise – he is showing a group of tourists round a futuristic Paris – he creates an intimately observed and perfectly controlled farce. Just as the city has somehow been transformed into a refined and faceless world of glass and steel. Tati's comedy has become infinitely subtle and reflective.

Les Visiteurs/The Visitors Jean-Marie Poiré, 1993. A medieval knight and his squire are transported to present-day France, where they discover their castle has been turned into a country hotel by their descendants. The earthily comic encounters between time-travellers and modern middle-classes make for an extremely funny comedy of manners. French

audiences so loved being sent up that this became the third most successful film in French history.

Zazie dans le métro/Zazie Louis Malle, 1960. In one of his few comedies, Malle successfully rendered novelist Raymond Queneau's verbal experiments by using cartoon-like visual devices. Twelve-year-old Catherine Demongeot is perfect as the delightfully rude little girl driving everybody mad; and the film offers some great shots of Paris, climaxing in a spectacular scene at the top of the Eiffel Tower.

Thrillers/films policiers

L'Armée des ombres/The Army in the Shadows Jean-Pierre Melville, 1969. A small group of Resistance fighters, played by Yves Montand, Simone Signoret and Jean-Pierre Meurisse, are betrayed, questioned and then released. The tight, minimalist style creates a suffocating tension which culminates in an unforgettable conclusion.

Le Boucher/The Butcher Claude Chabrol, 1969. A young schoolteacher in a tiny southwest village lives in an apartment above her school. Her loneliness is eased by a surprising fledgling romance with the local butcher – a kindly yet sinister figure – until a sequence of schoolgirl murders sows doubt in her mind. This would be gripping as a portrayal of village life even without the underlying tension and lurking violence.

Caché/Hidden Michael Haneke, 2005. The smooth bourgeois life of literary TV presenter Georges (Daniel Auteuil) and his wife Anne (Juliette Binoche) is disrupted when they receive a chillingly innocuous videotape of their own home under surveillance. In what has been widely read as a metaphor for France's attitude to its own colonial past, Georges is forced to confront a childhood friend,

Majid (Maurice Bénichou), and his own troubled conscience.

Coup de Torchon/Clean Slate Bertrand Tavernier, 1981. The setting is colonial West Africa, 1938. Ineffective, humiliated police chief Cordier (Philippe Noiret) decides to take murderous revenge on his wife, her lover, his mistress's husband and the locals he views as uniformly corrupt. As much an extremely black comedy as a true thriller.

Irréversible Gaspar Noé, 2002. One of the more disturbing films ever made: not just for the nightmarish rape and murder scenes but for the evisceration of the most terrifying elements of the male sexual psyche. A giddy, swooping camera traces the events of one night backwards in time from a brutal murder to a post-coital couple (Vincent Cassel and Monica Bellucci) getting ready for a party.

Monsieur Hire Patrice Leconte, 1989. A slow-moving, unsettlingly erotic psychological thriller. Michel Blanc plays the spookily impassive Monsieur Hire, a voyeur who witnesses his neighbour's boyfriend commit a murder, and becomes the prime suspect.

Ne le dis à personne/Tell No one Guillaume Canet, 2006. Disturbing psycho-thriller in which a doctor who is slowly rebuilding his life after the murder of his wife, eight years earlier, is suddenly implicated in two fresh murders. To complicate matters further, he is sent evidence that his wife is still alive. As much *Mulholland Drive* as *Frantic*, and more exciting than either.

Pierrot-le-fou Jean-Luc Godard, 1965. Godard's fascination with American pulp fiction is most brilliantly exploited in this highly charged and deeply sophisticated thriller. Accidentally caught up in a murderous gangland killing, Ferdinand (Jean-Paul Belmondo) flees with his babysitter (Godard's then-wife, Anna Karina) to the apparent safety of a Mediterranean island. The bizarre and tragic denouement is one of the great scenes of French cinema.

Films d'amour

L'Ami de mon amie/ Boyfriends and Girlfriends Eric Rohmer, 1987. Two glossy young women in a flashy new town outside Paris – Cergy-Pontoise – become friends. While Blanche is away, Léa falls in love with Blanche's boyfriend Alexandre; when Blanche comes back, she in turn falls in love with Léa's boyfriend, Fabien. Behind the light comedy and seemingly inconsequential dialogue lurks a profound film about love and free will.

Baisers volés/Stolen Kisses François Truffaut, 1968. The third of Truffaut's five-part semi-autobiographical sequence, which began with *Les Quatre-cents coups*, is probably the simplest and most delightful. Returning from military service, idealistic young Antoine Doinel (Jean-Pierre Léaud) mooches about Paris while working variously as a hotel worker, private detective and TV repairman. Through various amorous and bizarre adventures he slowly finds his way back towards the girl he loved and left behind.

La Belle noiseuse Jacques Rivette, 1991. "The beautiful troublemaker" originally stretched to four hours, though the more commonly screened "Divertimento" cut is half that length. A washed-out painter (the splendidly stuttering Michel Piccoli) lives in the deep south with his wife (Jane Birkin). An admiring younger painter offers his beautiful girlfriend (Emmanuelle Béart) as a nude model. Her fraught sittings become the catalyst for all the latent tensions in the two relationships to quietly explode.

Un Coeur en hiver/A Heart in Winter/A Heart of Stone Claude Sautet, 1992. In this thoughtful, fresh *ménage à trois* scenario, violinist Camille (Emmanuelle Béart) is paired first with Maxime (André Dussolier), a violin shop owner, and then with loner Stéphane (Daniel Auteuil), the chief craftsman. As the title "A Heart in Winter" suggests, this is a moody but ultimately sentimental film about love, and the fear of love.

Le Dernier métro/The Last Metro François Truffaut, 1980. This huge commercial success stars Catherine Deneuve and Gérard Depardieu as two actors who fall in love while rehearsing a play during the German Occupation. Wartime Paris is evoked through lavish photography and a growing feeling of imprisonment inside the confined space of the theatre. Swept the Césars that year, for Best Film, Director, Actor and Actress.

Le Mari de la coiffeuse/The Hairdresser's Husband Patrice Leconte, 1990. Leconte's film about a man who grows up obsessed with hairdressers, and ends up marrying one, epitomizes the best in French romantic film-making. A quirky, subtle and engagingly twisted portrait of an obsessive relationship.

Les Parapluies de Cherbourg/The Umbrellas of Cherbourg Jacques Demy, 1964. Demy's most successful film also gave Catherine Deneuve one of her first great roles. It is an extraordinarily stylized musical, shot in bright, artificial-looking colours, and entirely sung rather than spoken. Demy disturbingly twists the traditional cheerfulness of the musical genre to give a dark, bitter ending to this story of love and abandonment, set during the Algerian war.

Trois Couleurs: Rouge/Three Colours: Red Krzysztof Kieslowski, 1994. The final part of Polish-born director's Kieslowski's "tricolore" trilogy is perhaps the most satisfying, though to get the most out of the powerful denouement, in which all the strands are pulled together through a series of chances and accidents, you really need to have watched *Bleu* and *Blanc* as well. A young model, Valentine (Irène Jacob), runs over a dog and traces its owner, a reclusive retired judge (Jean-Louis Trintignant) who assuages his loneliness by tapping his neighbours' phone calls. The film's "colour" is expressed through presiding red-brown tones and the theme of *fraternité*, the third principle of the French Republic.

Heritage cinema

Cyrano de Bergerac Jean-Paul Rappeneau, 1990. It's hard to know what's finest about this extravagantly romantic film: Rostand's original story, set in seventeenth-century France, or Gérard Depardieu's landmark performance as the big-nosed swashbuckler-poet, Cyrano, who hopelessly loves the brilliant and beautiful Roxanne. The film's panache is matched by the verse dialogue – brilliantly rendered into English subtitles by Anthony Burgess. Hilarious, exciting and sublimely weepy.

Jean de Florette Claude Berri, 1986. This masterful adaptation of Marcel Pagnol's novel created the rose-tinted genre, *cinéma du patrimoine*. In the gorgeous setting of inland, prewar Provence, Gérard Depardieu plays a deformed urban refugee struggling to create a rural utopia. He is opposed by the shrewd peasant Papet (Yves Montand) and a simpleton, Ugolin (Daniel Auteuil), who dreams of giant fields of carnations. The excellent sequel, *Manon des Sources* (1987), launched the stellar career of the improbably pouting Emmanuelle Béart.

Au Revoir les enfants/Goodbye, Children Louis Malle, 1987. Malle's autobiographical tale is one of the finest film portraits of the war, and of school life in general. It is minutely observed, and desperately moving without being unduly sentimental. Three Jewish boys are hidden among the pupils at a Catholic boys' boarding school. Eventually, the Gestapo discover the ruse.

Cinéma du look

37°2 le matin/Betty Blue Jean-Jacques Beineix, 1986. Pouty Béatrice Dalle puts on a compellingly erotic performance as Betty, a free-thinking girl who lives in a beach house with struggling writer Zorg. The film opens in romantic mood with a sustained and passionate sex scene but rapidly spirals towards its disturbing ending. The film's intense and sometimes weird stylishness, along with its memorable score, made it an international hit.

Les Amants du Pont-Neuf Léos Carax, 1991. Homeless painter Michèle (Juliette Binoche) is losing her sight. One day, on Paris's Pont-Neuf, she meets an indigent, fire-eating acrobat (Denis Lavant), and they tumble together into a consuming love, madly played out against the background of their life on the streets. An intense and beautiful film.

Delicatessen Jean-Pierre Jeunet/ Marc Caro, 1991. Set in a crumbling apartment block in a dystopian fantasy city – Occupation Paris meets comic book – a grotesque local butcher murders his assistants and sells them as human meat, until his daughter falls in love with the latest butcher boy and the subterranean vegetarian terrorists find out. Hilarious and bizarre in equal measure, with superb cameos from the neighbours.

Subway Luc Besson, 1985. The favoured urban-nocturnal setting of the *cinéma du look* is given its coolest expression in *Subway*. A hock-headed Christophe Lambert is hunted by police and criminals alike for a cache of documents he shouldn't have. He hides out in the Paris métro where he manages to form a rock band – before being found by Isabelle Adjani. Film noir meets MTV.

New realism: beur, banlieue and jeune

Comme une image/Look at Me Agnès Jaoui, 2004. Agnès Jaoui manages to be both sensitive and hard-hitting in this exploration of the dysfunctional relationship between a self-conscious, under-confident daughter (Marilou Berry) and her monstrously egotistical, literary lion of a father – a role played superbly by Jean-Pierre Bacri, who co-wrote the script with Jaoui.

La Haine/Hate Mathieu Kassovitz, 1995. The flagship film of the *cinéma de banlieue*, films of the tough suburbs, centres on three friends: Hubert, of black African origin; Saïd, a *beur* (from North Africa); and Vinz, who has white Jewish roots – and a gun. They spend a troubled night wandering Paris before heading back to the *banlieue* and a violent homecoming. Brilliantly treads the line between gritty realism and street cool – the fact that it's shot in black-and-white helps, as does the soundtrack from French rapper MC Solaar, among others.

Hexagone Malik Chibane, 1991. Shooting in just 24 days, and using amateur actors, Chibane somehow pulled off exactly what he planned: to raise the profile of the new generation of *beurs*. The story is a simple enough rite-of-passage tale focused on five young friends who get in trouble, but the recurring motif of the sacrifice of Abraham gives it a thoughtful twist. The street-slang peppered script and cinematography – strong on handheld shots of the inner city landscape – are superb.

Un prophète Jacques Audiard, 2009. A prison movie that becomes a gangland thriller, this film is lifted beyond the confines of either genre by its bitter political message and by its magnificent anti-hero, the *naïf*-but turned-ruthless young Arab man played brilliantly by Tahir Rahim.

La Ville est tranquille/The Town Is Quiet Robert Guédiguian, 2000. Notwithstanding its title, this harrowing film describes the dysfunctional society of a far-from-quiet city – Marseille – focusing on the hardships of Michèle (Ariane Ascaride), a 40-year-old woman working in a fish factory while fighting to save her heroin-addict daughter. After a series of light, happy tales, Robert Guédiguian magnificently turns here to a more realistic and political tone.

1065

James McConnachie and Eva Lœchner

Listed below is a highly selective recommendation of works – mostly novels – that are rooted in the various French regions, and which would make good holiday reading.

Paris and around
Honoré de Balzac *Old Goriot*
Muriel Barbery *The Elegance of the Hedgehog*
Charles Baudelaire *Baudelaire's Paris*
André Breton *Nadja*
Blaise Cendrars *To the End of the World*
Helen Constantine (ed) *Paris Tales*
Didier Daeninckx *Murder in Memoriam*
Gustave Flaubert *A Sentimental Education*
André Gide *The Counterfeiters*
Faiza Guène *Kif Kif Demain/Just Like Tomorrow*
Victor Hugo *Les Misérables*
Anaïs Nin *Journals 1917–1974*
George Orwell *Down and Out in Paris and London*
Daniel Penac *Monsieur Malaussène*
Georges Perec *Life: A User's Manual*
Marcel Proust *Remembrance of Things Past*
Paul Rambali *French Blues*
Jean Rhys *Quartet, Good Morning Midnight*
Jean-Paul Sartre *Roads to Freedom* trilogy
Georges Simenon Any Maigret thriller
Michel Tournier *The Golden Droplet*
Émile Zola *Nana, L'Assommoir, La Bête Humaine, Le Ventre de Paris*

The north
Sebastian Faulks *Birdsong*
Julien Gracq *A Balcony in the Forest, The Opposing Shore*
Irène Nemirovsky *All Our Worldly Goods*
Émile Zola *Germinal, La Débâcle, La Terre*

Alsace, Franche-Comté and Jura
John Berger *Pig Earth*
Bernard Clavel *The Spaniard*
Colette *My Mother's House*
Pierre Gascar *Women and the Sun*
Stendhal *Scarlet and Black*

Normandy and Brittany
Honoré de Balzac *Les Chouans*, *Modeste Mignon*
Colette *Ripening Seed*
Gustave Flaubert *Madame Bovary*
André Gide *Strait is the Gate*
Pierre Loti *Pêcheur d'Islande*
Guy de Maupassant *Selected Short Stories*
Jean Rouard *Fields of Glory*, *Of Illustrious Men*
Jean-Paul Sartre *La Nausée*

The Loire
Honoré de Balzac *Eugénie Grandet*
Alain Fournier *Le Grand Meaulnes*
George Sand *The Devil's Pool*

Burgundy
Gabriel Chevallier *Clochemerle*, *Atlantic Coast*
François Mauriac *Thérèse*

The Pyrenees
Pierre Loti *Ramuntcho*

Languedoc
Hannah Closs *High Are the Mountains*

Rhône valley and Provence
Lawrence Durrell *The Avignon Quintet*
Jean Giono *The Horseman on the Roof*, *The Man Who Planted Trees*, *Joy of Man's Desiring*
Marcel Pagnol *Jean de Florette*, *Manon des Sources*
Émile Zola *Fortune of the Rougons*

Côte d'Azur
Colette *Collected Stories*
Alexandre Dumas *The Count of Monte Cristo*
F. Scott Fitzgerald *Tender is the Night*
Graham Greene *Loser Takes All*, *May We Borrow Your Husband?*
Katherine Mansfield *Selected Short Stories*
Françoise Sagan *Bonjour Tristesse*

Corsica
Prosper Mérimée *Colomba*

Books

Publishers are detailed below in the form of British publisher/American publisher, where both exist. Where books are published in one country only, UK or US follows the publisher's name. Books marked ✴ are highly recommended. Abbreviations: UP (University Press).

Travel

Marc Augé *In the Metro* (University of Minnesota Press, 2002). A philosophically minded anthropologist descends deep into metro culture and his own memories of life in Paris. Brief and brilliant.

Walter Benjamin *The Arcades Project* (Harvard, 2002). An all-encompassing portrait of Paris from 1830 to 1870, in which the *passages* are used as a lens through which to view Parisian society. Never completed, Benjamin's magnum opus is a kaleidoscopic assemblage of essays, notes and quotations, gathered under such headings as "Baudelaire", "Prostitution", "Mirrors" and "Idleness".

Adam Gopnik *Paris to the Moon* (Vintage/Random House). Intimate and acutely observed essays from the Paris correspondent of the *New Yorker* on society, politics, family life and shopping.

Julien Green *Paris* (Marion Boyars, 2005). A collection of very personal sketches and impressions of the city, by an American who has lived all his life in Paris, writes in French, and is considered one of the great French writers of the century. Bilingual text.

Richard Holmes *Footsteps* (Flamingo, 2004/Vintage, 1996). A marvellous mix of objective history and personal account, such as the tale of the author's own excitement at the events of May 1968 in Paris, which led him to investigate and reconstruct the experiences of the British in Paris during the 1789 Revolution.

Michael de Larrabeiti *French Leave* (Robert Hale, 2003). In the summer of 1949, aged just 15, Michael de Larrabeiti set off on his own by bicycle to Paris from the UK. This book provides a wonderfully evocative testimony to his love of France as he looks back over fifty years of working and travelling throughout the country.

Robert Louis Stevenson *Travels with a Donkey* (Penguin/Echo, 2006). Mile-by-mile account of Stevenson's twelve-day trek in the Haute-Loire and Cévennes uplands with the donkey Modestine. His first book, *Inland Voyage*, took him round the waterways of the north.

History

General

✴ **Eric Hazan** *The Invention of Paris* (Verso). Weighty but utterly compelling "psychogeographical" account of the city, picking over its history *quartier* by *quartier* in a thousand *aperçus* and anecdotes.

Colin Jones *The Cambridge Illustrated History of France* (CUP, 1999). A political and social history of France from prehistoric times to the mid-1990s, concentrating on issues of regionalism, gender, race and class. Good illustrations and a friendly, non-academic writing style.

Colin Jones *Paris: Biography of a City* (Penguin, 2006). Jones focuses tightly on the actual life and growth of the city, from the Neolithic past to the future. Five hundred pages flow by easily, punctuated by thoughtful but accessible "boxes" on characters, streets and buildings whose lives were especially bound up with Paris's, from the Roman *arènes* to Zazie's métro. The best single book on the city's history.

Ross King *The Judgement of Paris* (Pimlico/Walker). High-octane account of the artistic culture wars of the 1860s and 1870s, focusing on the fascinating parallel lives of the well-established painter Meissonier and the radical upstart Manet.

Graham Robb *The Discovery of France* (2007). Captivating, brilliant study of France which makes a superb antidote to the usual narratives of kings and state affairs. With affection and insight, and in fine prose, Robb describes a France of vast wastes inhabited by "faceless millions" speaking mutually unintelligible dialects, and reveals how this France was gradually discovered and, inevitably, "civilized".

Robert Tombs & Isabelle Tombs *That Sweet Enemy: The British and the French from the Sun King to the Present* (Pimlico/Arrow, 2007). A fascinating, original and mammoth study of a strangely intimate relationship. The authors are a French woman and her English husband, and they engage in lively debate between themselves. Covers society, culture and personalities, as well as politics.

The Middle Ages and Renaissance

Natalie Zemon Davis *The Return of Martin Guerre* (Harvard UP, 1984). A vivid account of peasant life in the sixteenth century and a perplexing and titillating hoax in the Pyrenean village of Artigat.

J.H. Huizinga *The Waning of the Middle Ages* (Dover, 1999). Primarily a study of the culture of the Burgundian and French courts – but a masterpiece that goes far beyond this, building up meticulous detail to recreate the whole life and mentality of the fourteenth and fifteenth centuries.

R.J. Knecht *The French Renaissance Court* (Yale, 2008). The definitive work by a genuine authority. Not exactly a racy read, but successfully mixes high politics with sharp detail on life at court life, backed up by plentiful illustrations.

Marina Warner *Joan of Arc* (UCal Press, 2000). Brilliantly places France's patron saint and national heroine within historical, spiritual and intellectual traditions.

Eighteenth and nineteenth centuries

Vincent Cronin *Napoleon* (Harper-Collins, UK, 1990). Enthusiastic and accessible biography.

Christopher Hibbert *The French Revolution* (Penguin, 1982/ Harper, 1999). Well-paced and entertaining narrative treatment by a master historian.

Alistair Horne *The Fall of Paris* (Pan, 2002). A very readable and humane account of the extraordinary period of the Prussian siege of Paris in 1870 and the ensuing struggles of the Commune.

Ross King *The Judgement of Paris: The Revolutionary Decade That Gave the World Impressionism* (Pimlico/Walker, 2006). Lively account of the stormy early years when the Impressionists were refused entry to official exhibitions.

Lucy Moore *Liberty: The Lives and Times of Six Women in Revolutionary France* (HarperCollins, 2006). This engaging and original book follows the lives of six influential – and very different women – through the Revolution, taking in everything from sexual scandal to revolutionary radicalism.

Graham Robb *Parisians* (Picador). This playful but magnificently researched book tells the story of Paris from 1750 to today, looking through the eyes of the people who have played key roles in its turbulent life, from Marie Antoinette fleeing the Tuileries to Hitler's day-trip conqueror's tour.

Ruth Scurr *Fatal Purity: Robespierre and the French Revolution* (Chatto & Windus/Metropolitan, 2006). This myth-busting biography of the "remarkably odd" figure of the man they called The Incorruptible, and who went on to orchestrate the notorious Terror, ends up being one of the best books on the Revolution in general.

Twentieth century

Marc Bloch *Strange Defeat* (Norton, 1999). Moving personal study of the reasons for France's defeat and subsequent caving-in to fascism. Found among the papers of this Sorbonne historian after his death at the hands of the Gestapo in 1942.

Carmen Callil *Bad Faith: A Forgotten History of Family and Fatherland* (Vintage/Knopf, 2006). This quietly angry biography of the loathsome Louis Darquier, the Vichy state's Commissioner for Jewish Affairs, reveals the banality of viciousness in wartime France.

Geoff Dyer *The Missing of the Somme* (Weidenfeld, 2001). Structured round the author's visits to the war graves of northern France, this is a highly moving meditation on the

trauma of World War I and the way its memory has been perpetuated.

Jonathan Fenby *The General: Charles de Gaulle and the France He Saved* (Simon & Schuster 2010). This monumental but utterly readable biography does not always get under the famously private president's skin, but does show how de Gaulle not only shaped but embodied the ideals and ambitions of the postwar nation – or a certain, proudly, idealistically reactionary segment of it, at least.

Ian Ousby *Occupation: The Ordeal of France 1940–1944* (Pimlico, 1999/Cooper Square, 2000). Revisionist 1997 account which shows how relatively late resistance was, how widespread collaboration was, and why.

Society and politics

John Ardagh *France in the New Century: Portrait of a Changing Society* (Penguin, 2000). Long-time writer on France gets to grips with the 1980s and 1990s. Attempts to be a comprehensive

survey, but gets rather too drawn into party politics and statistics.

Julian Barnes *Something to Declare* (Picador/Knopf, 2002). This journalistically highbrow collection of essays on French culture – films, music, the Tour de France, and of course Flaubert – wears its French-style intellectualism on its sleeve, but succeeds in getting under the skin anyway.

Roland Barthes *Mythologies* (Vintage, 1993; Hill & Wang, 1972). *Mythologies* is a brilliant and witty structuralist critique on the socio-historical importance of myth and its signs in France today, based on a series of quirky examples.

Mary Blume *A French Affair: The Paris Beat 1965–1998* (Plume, 2000). Incisive and witty observations on contemporary French life by the *International Herald Tribune* reporter who was stationed there for three decades.

Jonathan Fenby *On the Brink* (Abacus, 2002/Arcade, 2000). While France isn't perhaps quite as endangered as the title suggests, this provocative book takes a long, hard look at the problems facing contemporary France. Somewhat dated, but the issues have changed surprisingly little.

Mark Girouard *Life in the French Country House* (Knopf, 2000). Girouard meticulously recreates the social and domestic life that went on between the walls of French châteaux, starting with the great halls of early castles and ending with the commercial marriage venues of the twentieth century.

Tim Moore *French Revolutions: Cycling the Tour De France* (Vintage, 2002/ St Martin's, 2003). A whimsical bicycle journey along the route of the Tour by a genuinely hilarious writer. Lots of witty asides on Tour history and French culture.

Jim Ring *Riviera: The Rise and Rise of the Cote d'Azur* (John Murray, 2005). A fascinating portrait of France's most anomalous region, taking in its discovery by aristocratic pleasure-seekers in the nineteenth century, the golden years of the 1920s when it was the playground of artists, film stars and millionaires, and the inevitable fall from grace.

Charles Timoney *Pardon My French: Unleash Your Inner Gaul* (Penguin, UK, 2007). Incisive and often very droll dissection of contemporary culture through the words and phrases that the French use all the time. Looks and maybe sounds like a gift book, but it's rather brilliant.

Gillian Tindall *Célestine: Voices from a French Village* (Minerva, UK, 1996). Intrigued by some nineteenth-century love letters left behind in the house she has bought in Chassignolles, Berry, Tindall researches the history of the village back to the 1840s. A brilliant piece of social history.

Lucy Wadham *The Secret Life of France* (Faber UK, 2010). Funny and insightful insider-eye view of the French, written by an expat who married one of them. Particularly good on women and female culture, and generally more intelligent than most in this genre.

Theodore Zeldin *The French* (Harvill UK, 1997). A wise and original book that attempts to describe a country through the prism of the author's intensely personal conversations with a fascinating range of French people. Chapter titles include "How to be chic" and "How to appreciate a grandmother".

Art, architecture and poetry

Philip Ball *Universe of Stone: Chartres Cathedral and the Triumph of the Medieval Mind* (The Bodley Head, UK, 2008). Ball gets hopelessly sidetracked into potted histories of all kinds of aspects of medieval life, but at the core of this book is a fascinating letter of love to an extraordinary building.

André Chastel *French Art* (Flammarion, France, 1995–96). Authoritative, three-volume study by one of France's leading art historians. Discusses individual works of art in some detail in an attempt – from architecture to tapestry, as well as painting – to locate the Frenchness of French art. With glossy photographs and serious-minded but readable text.

David Cairns *Berlioz: The Making of an Artist 1803–1832* (Penguin, 2000). The multiple-award winning first volume of Cairns' two-part biography is more than just a life of the passionate French composer, it's an extraordinary evocation of

post-Napoleonic France and its burgeoning Romantic culture.

John Richardson *The Life of Picasso* (Pimlico/Random House, various dates). No twentieth-century artist has ever been subjected to as much scrutiny as Picasso receives in Richardson's brilliantly illustrated biography. Three of an expected four volumes have been published to date.

Stephen Romer (editor) *20th-Century French Poems* (Faber, 2002). A collection of around 150 French poems spanning the whole of the century. Although there's no French text, many of the translations are works of art in themselves, consummately rendered by the likes of Samuel Beckett, T.S. Eliot and Paul Auster.

Rolf Toman (editor) *Romanesque: Architecture, Sculpture, Painting*. Huge, sumptuously illustrated volume of essays on every aspect of the genre across Europe, with one chapter specifically devoted to France.

Guides

Glynn Christian *Edible France* (Interlink, 1998). A guide to food rather than restaurants: regional produce, local specialities, markets and best shops for buying goodies to bring back home. Dated, but still reliable for the provinces, if not Paris.

Cicerone Walking Guides (Cicerone, UK). Neat, durable guides with detailed route descriptions. Titles include *Tour of Mont Blanc*; *Chamonix-Mont Blanc*; *Tour of the Oisans* (GR54); *French Alps* (GR5); *The Way of Saint James* (GR65); *Tour of the Queyras*; *The Pyrenean Trail* (GR10); *Walks and Climbs in the Pyrenees*; *Walking in the Alps*.

Philippe Dubois *Where to Watch Birds in France* (Helm, 2006). Maps, advice

on when to go, habitat information, species' lists – everything you need.

David Hampshire *Living and Working in France* (Survival Books, 2007). An invaluable guide for anyone considering residence or work in France; packed with ideas and advice on job hunting, bureaucracy, tax, health and so on. Usually updated every two years.

Richard Holmes *Fatal Avenue: A Traveller's History of the Battlefields of France and Flanders 1346–1945* (2008). Excellent combination of guidebook and storytelling from a renowned military historian.

Language

Language

French

F rench can be a deceptively familiar language because of the number of words and structures it shares with English. Despite this, it's far from easy, though the bare essentials are not difficult to master and can make all the difference. Even just saying "Bonjour Madame/Monsieur" and then gesticulating will often get you a smile and helpful service. People working in tourist offices, hotels and so on almost always speak English and tend to use it when you're struggling to speak French.

Pronunciation

One easy rule to remember is that **consonants** at the ends of words are usually silent: the most obvious example is Paris, pronounced "Paree", while the phrase *pas plus tard* (not later) sounds something like "pa-plu-tarr". The exception is when the following word begins with a vowel, in which case you generally run the two together: *pas après* (not after) becomes "pazaprey". Otherwise, consonants are much the same as in English, except that: *ch* is always "sh", *c* is "s", *h* is silent, *th* is the same as "t" , and *r* is growled (or rolled). And to complicate things a little, *ll* after *i* usually sounds like the "y" in yes – though there are exceptions, including common words like *ville* (city), and *mille* (thousand). And *w* is "v", except when it's in a borrowed English word, like *le whisky* or *un weekend*.

Vowels are the hardest sounds to get exactly right, but they rarely differ enough from English to make comprehension a problem. The most obvious differences are that *au* sounds like the "o" in "over"; *aujourd'hui* (today) is thus pronounced

---

Phrasebooks and courses

Breakthrough French (Palgrave Macmillan). One of the best teach-yourself courses, with three levels to choose from. Each comes with a book and CD-ROM.

The Complete Merde! The Real French You Were Never Taught at School (HarperCollins). More than just a collection of swearwords, this book is a passkey into everyday French, and a window into French culture.

Get Into French Course Pack (BBC Worldwide). Comes with an audio CD, book and CD-ROM which allows you to set up your own role-play situations. The BBC offers a whole range of French learning products – see Ⓦ www.bbc.co.uk/languages/french, which also offers a basic "Quick Fix", with free MP3 downloads, and a free, 24-part online audio course: "French Steps".

Oxford Essential French Dictionary (OUP). Very up-to-date French–English and English–French dictionary, with help on pronunciation and verbs, and links to free online products.

Pardon My French (Penguin). See review on p.1071.

Rough Guide French Phrasebook (Rough Guides). Mini dictionary-style phrasebook with both English–French and French–English sections, along with cultural tips, a menu reader and downloadable scenarios read by native speakers.

"oh-jor-dwi". Another one to listen out for is *oi*, which sounds like "wa"; *toi* (to you) thus sounds like "twa". Lastly, adding "m" or "n" to a vowel, as in *en* or *un*, adds a nasal sound, as if you said just the vowel with a cold.

Basic words and phrases

French nouns are divided into masculine and feminine. This causes difficulties with adjectives, whose endings have to change to suit the nouns they qualify – you can talk about *un château blanc* (a white castle), for example, but *une tour blanche* (a white tower). If you're not sure, stick to the simpler masculine form – as used in this glossary.

Essentials

hello (morning or afternoon)	bonjour	big	grand
		small	petit
hello (evening)	bonsoir	more	plus
good night	bonne nuit	less	moins
goodbye	au revoir	a little	un peu
thank you	merci	a lot	beaucoup
please	s'il vous plaît	inexpensive	pas cher/bon marché
sorry	pardon/Je m'excuse	expensive	cher
excuse me	pardon	good	bon
yes	oui	bad	mauvais
no	non	hot	chaud
OK/agreed	d'accord	cold	froid
help!	au secours!	with	avec
here	ici	without	sans
there	là	entrance	entrée
this one	ceci	exit	sortie
that one	celà	man	un homme
open	ouvert	woman	une femme
closed	fermé		(pronounced "fam")

Numbers

1	un	13	treize
2	deux	14	quatorze
3	trois	15	quinze
4	quatre	16	seize
5	cinq	17	dix-sept
6	six	18	dix-huit
7	sept	19	dix-neuf
8	huit	20	vingt
9	neuf	21	vingt-et-un
10	dix	22	vingt-deux
11	onze	30	trente
12	douze	40	quarante

50	cinquante	101	cent-et-un
60	soixante	200	deux cents
70	soixante-dix	300	trois cents
75	soixante-quinze	500	cinq cents
80	quatre-vingts	1000	mille
90	quatre-vingt-dix	2000	deux mille
95	quatre-vingt-quinze	5000	cinq mille
100	cent	1,000,000	un million

Time

today	aujourd'hui	now	maintenant
yesterday	hier	later	plus tard
tomorrow	demain	at one o'clock	à une heure
in the morning	le matin	at three o'clock	à trois heures
in the afternoon	l'après-midi	at ten thirty	à dix heures et demie
in the evening	le soir	at midday	à midi

Days and dates

January	janvier	Sunday	dimanche
February	février	Monday	lundi
March	mars	Tuesday	mardi
April	avril	Wednesday	mercredi
May	mai	Thursday	jeudi
June	juin	Friday	vendredi
July	juillet	Saturday	samedi
August	août	August 1	le premier août
September	septembre	March 2	le deux mars
October	octobre	July 14	le quatorze juillet
November	novembre	November 23	le vingt-trois novembre
December	décembre	2011	deux mille onze

Talking to people

When addressing people a simple *bonjour* is not enough; you should always use *Monsieur* for a man, *Madame* for a woman, *Mademoiselle* for a young woman or girl. This has its uses when you've forgotten someone's name or want to attract someone's attention. "Bonjour" can be used well into the afternoon, and people may start saying "bonsoir" surprisingly early in the evening, or as a way of saying goodbye.

Do you speak English?	Parlez-vous anglais?	I'm ...	Je suis ...
		... English	... anglais[e]
How do you say it in French?	Comment ça se dit en français?	... Irish	... irlandais[e]
		... Scottish	... écossais[e]
What's your name?	Comment vous appelez-vous?	... Welsh	... gallois[e]
		... American	... américain[e]
My name is ...	Je m'appelle ...	... Australian	... australien[ne]

... Canadian	... canadien[ne]	Fine, thanks	Très bien, merci
... a New Zealander	... néo-zélandais[e]	I don't know	Je ne sais pas
... South African	... sud-africain[e]	Let's go	Allons-y
I understand	Je comprends	See you tomorrow	À demain
I don't understand	Je ne comprends pas	See you soon	À bientôt
Could you speak more slowly?	S'il vous plaît, parlez moins vite	Leave me alone (aggressive)	Laissez-moi tranquille
How are you?	Comment allez-vous?/ Ça va?	Please help me	Aidez-moi, s'il vous plaît

Finding the way

bus	autobus/bus/car	I'm going to ...	Je vais à ...
bus station	gare routière	I want to get off at ...	Je voudrais descendre à ...
bus stop	arrêt	the road to ...	la route pour ...
car	voiture	near	près/pas loin
train/taxi/ferry	train/taxi/bac or ferry	far	loin
boat	bâteau	left	à gauche
plane	avion	right	à droite
shuttle	navette	straight on	tout droit
train station	gare (SNCF)	on the other side of	à l'autre côté de
platform	quai	on the corner of	à l'angle de
What time does it leave?	Il part à quelle heure?	next to	à côté de
What time does it arrive?	Il arrive à quelle heure?	behind	derrière
a ticket to ...	un billet pour ...	in front of	devant
single ticket	aller simple	before	avant
return ticket	aller retour	after	après
validate/stamp your ticket	compostez votre billet	under	sous
valid for	valable pour	to cross	traverser
ticket office	vente de billets	bridge	pont
how many kilometres?	combien de kilomètres?	town centre	centre ville
how many hours?	combien d'heures?	all through roads (road sign)	toutes directions
hitchhiking	autostop	other destinations (road sign)	autres directions
on foot	à pied	upper town	ville haute/haute ville
Where are you going?	Vous allez où?	lower town	ville basse/basse ville
		Old Town	vieille ville

Questions and requests

The simplest way of asking a question is to start with *s'il vous plaît* (please), then name the thing you want in an interrogative tone of voice. For example:

Where is there a bakery?	S'il vous plaît, la boulangerie?	Which way is it to the Eiffel Tower?	S'il vous plaît, la route pour la Tour Eiffel?

Can we have a room for two	S'il vous plaît, une chambre pour deux?	
Can I have a kilo of oranges?	S'il vous plaît, un kilo d'oranges?	

Question words

where?	où?
how?	comment?
how many/how much?	combien?
when?	quand?
why?	pourquoi?
at what time?	à quelle heure?
what is/which is?	quel est?

Accommodation

a room for one/two persons	une chambre pour une/deux personne(s)
a double bed	un grand lit/un lit matrimonial
a room with two single beds/twin	une chambre à deux lits
a room with a shower	une chambre avec douche
a room with a bath	une chambre avec salle de bain
for one/two/three nights	pour une/deux/trois nuits
Can I see it?	Je peux la voir?
a room on the courtyard	une chambre sur la cour
a room over the street	une chambre sur la rue
first floor	premier étage
second floor	deuxième étage
with a view	avec vue
key	clé
to iron	repasser
do laundry	faire la lessive
sheets	draps
blankets	couvertures
quiet	calme
noisy	bruyant
hot water	eau chaude
cold water	eau froide
Is breakfast included?	Est-ce que le petit déjeuner est compris?
I would like breakfast	Je voudrais prendre le petit déjeuner
I don't want breakfast	Je ne veux pas de petit déjeuner
bed and breakfast	chambres d'hôte
Can we camp here?	On peut camper ici?
campsite	camping/terrain de camping
tent	tente
tent space	emplacement
hostel	foyer
youth hostel	auberge de jeunesse

Driving

service station	garage
service	service
to park the car	garer la voiture
car park	un parking
no parking	défense de stationner/ stationnement interdit
petrol/gas station	poste d'essence
fuel	essence
unleaded	sans plomb
leaded	super
diesel	gazole
oil	huile
air line	ligne à air
put air in the tyres	gonfler les pneus
battery	batterie
the battery is dead	la batterie est morte
plug (for appliance)	prise
to break down	tomber en panne
petrol can	bidon
insurance	assurance
green card	carte verte
traffic lights	feux rouges

Sign language

Défense de... It is forbidden to...
Fermé closed
Ouvert open
Rez-de-chaussée (RC) ground floor
Sortie exit

Health matters

doctor	médecin	pain	douleur
I don't feel well	Je ne me sens pas bien	it hurts	ça fait mal
medicines	médicaments	chemist/pharmacist	pharmacie
prescription	ordonnance	hospital	hôpital
I feel sick	Je suis malade	condom	préservatif
I have a headache	J'ai mal à la tête	morning-after pill /emergency contraceptive	pilule du lendemain
stomach ache	mal à l'estomac		
period	règles	I'm allergic to …	Je suis allergique à …

Other needs

bakery	boulangerie	tobacconist	tabac
food shop	alimentation	stamps	timbres
delicatessen	charcuterie, traiteur	bank	banque
cake shop	patisserie	money	argent
cheese shop	fromagerie	toilets	toilettes
supermarket	supermarché	police	police
to eat	manger	telephone	téléphone
to drink	boire	cinema	cinéma
tasting, eg wine tasting	dégustation	theatre	théâtre
		to reserve/book	réserver
camping gas	camping gaz		

Restaurant phrases

I'd like to reserve a table	Je voudrais réserver une table	Waiter! (never "garçon")	Monsieur/Madame!/ s'il vous plaît!
for two people, at eight thirty	pour deux personnes, à vingt heures et demie	the bill/check please	l'addition, s'il vous plaît
I'm having the €30 set menu	Je prendrai le menu à trente euros		

Food and dishes

Basic terms

l'addition	bill/check	cru	raw
beurre	butter	cuillère	spoon
bio or biologique	organic	cuit	cooked
bouteille	bottle	emballé	wrapped
carafe d'eau	jug of water	à emporter	takeaway
la carte	the menu	entrée	starter
chauffé	heated	formule	lunchtime set menu
couteau	knife	fourchette	fork

fumé	smoked	plat	main course
gazeuse	fizzy	poivre	pepper
lait	milk	salé	salted/savoury
le menu	set menu	sel	salt
moutarde	mustard	sucre	sugar
oeuf	egg	sucré	sweet
offert	free	table	table
pain	bread	verre	glass
pimenté	spicy	vinaigre	vinegar

Snacks

un sandwich/une	a sandwich	oeufs	eggs
baguette	with ham, no butter	au plat	fried
jambon beurre	with ham and butter	à la coque	boiled
au fromage	with cheese, no butter	durs	hard-boiled
mixte	with ham and cheese	brouillés	scrambled
au pâté (de	with pâté	omelette	omelette
campagne)	(country-style)	nature	plain
croque-monsieur	grilled cheese and ham sandwich	aux fines herbes	with herbs
		au fromage	with cheese
panini	toasted Italian sandwich	salade de tomates	tomato salad
tartine	buttered bread or open sandwich, often with jam	salade verte	green salad

Pasta (pâtes), pancakes (crêpes), tartes and couscous

nouilles	noodles	couscous	steamed semolina grains, usually served with meat or veg, chickpea stew and chilli sauce
pâtes fraîches	fresh pasta		
crêpe au sucre/aux oeufs	pancake with sugar/ eggs		
galette	buckwheat pancake		
pissaladière	tart of fried onions with anchovies and black olives	couscous Royale	couscous with spicy merguez sausage, chicken and beef or lamb kebabs
tarte flambée	thin pizza-like pastry topped with onion, cream and bacon		

Soups (soupes)

bisque	shellfish soup	garbure	potato, cabbage and meat soup
bouillabaisse	soup with five fish		
bouillon	broth or stock	pistou	parmesan, basil and garlic paste added to soup
bourride	thick fish soup		
consommé	clear soup		
		potage	thick vegetable soup

| potée auvergnate | cabbage and meat soup | soupe à l'oignon | onion soup with rich cheese topping |
| rouille | red pepper, garlic and saffron mayonnaise served with fish soup | velouté | thick soup, usually fish or poultry |

Starters (hors d'oeuvres)

| assiette de charcuterie | plate of cold meats | crudités | dressed raw vegetables |
| assiette composée | mixed salad plate, usually cold meat and veg | hors d'oeuvres | combination of the above often with smoked or marinated fish |

Fish (poisson), seafood (fruits de mer) and shellfish (crustaces or coquillages)

anchois	anchovies	homard	lobster
anguilles	eels	huîtres	oysters
barbue	brill	langouste	spiny lobster
baudroie	monkfish or anglerfish	langoustines	saltwater crayfish (scampi)
bigourneau	periwinkle		
brème	bream	limande	lemon sole
cabillaud	cod	lotte de mer	monkfish
calmar	squid	loup de mer	sea bass
carrelet	plaice	maquereau	mackerel
claire	type of oyster	merlan	whiting
colin	hake	moules (marinière)	mussels (with shallots in white wine sauce)
congre	conger eel		
coques	cockles	oursin	sea urchin
coquilles	scallops St-Jacques	palourdes	clams
crabe	crab	poissons de roche	fish from shoreline rocks
crevettes grises	shrimp		
crevettes roses	prawns	praires	small clams
daurade	sea bream	raie	skate
éperlan	smelt or whitebait	rouget	red mullet
escargots	snails	saumon	salmon
flétan	halibut	sole	sole
friture	assorted fried fish, often like whitebait	thon	tuna
		truite	trout
gambas	king prawns	turbot	turbot
hareng	herring	violet	sea squirt

Fish dishes and terms

aïoli	garlic mayonnaise	assiette de pêcheur	assorted fish
anchoïade	anchovy paste or sauce	beignet	fritter
arête	fish bone	darne	fillet or steak

la douzaine	a dozen
frit	fried
friture	deep-fried small fish
fumé	smoked
fumet	fish stock
gigot de mer	large fish baked whole
grillé	grilled

hollandaise	butter and vinegar sauce
à la meunière	in a butter, lemon and parsley sauce
mousse/mousseline	mousse
pané	breaded
poutargue	mullet roe paste
quenelles	light dumplings

Meat (viande) and poultry (volaille)

agneau (de pré-salé)	lamb (grazed on salt marshes)
andouille	cold pork and tripe sausage
andouillette	hot, cooked tripe sausage
bavette	flank-like steak
boeuf	beef
boudin blanc	sausage of white meats
boudin noir	black pudding
caille	quail
canard	duck
caneton	duckling
contrefilet	sirloin roast
coquelet	cockerel
la cuisson?	how would sir/madam like his/her steak done?
dinde/dindon	turkey
entrecôte	rib steak
faux filet	sirloin steak
foie	liver
foie gras	(duck/goose) liver
gibier	game
gigot (d'agneau)	leg (of lamb)
grenouilles (cuisses de)	frogs' (legs)

langue	tongue
lapin/lapereau	rabbit/young rabbit
lard/lardons	bacon/diced bacon
lièvre	hare
merguez	spicy, red sausage
mouton	mutton
museau de veau	calf's muzzle
oie	goose
onglet	tasty, flank-like steak
os	bone
poitrine	breast
porc	pork
poulet	chicken
poussin	baby chicken
rillettes	pork mashed with lard and liver
ris	sweetbreads
rognons	kidneys
rognons blancs	testicles
sanglier	wild boar
steak	steak
tête de veau	calf's head (in jelly)
tournedos	thick slices of fillet
tripes	tripe
tripoux	mutton tripe
veau	veal
venaison	venison

Meat and poultry dishes and terms

| aïado | roast shoulder of lamb stuffed with garlic and other ingredients |
| aile | wing |

| blanquette, daube, estouffade, hochepôt, navarin, ragoût | types of stew |
| blanquette de veau | veal in cream and mushroom sauce |

boeuf bourguignon	beef stew with Burgundy, onions and mushrooms	gésier	gizzard
		grillade	grilled meat
		grillé	grilled
brochette	kebab	hâchis	chopped meat or mince hamburger
carré	best end of neck, chop or cutlet		
		magret de canard	duck breast
cassoulet	casserole of beans, sausages and duck/goose	marmite	casserole
		médaillon	round piece
		mijoté	stewed
choucroute	sauerkraut with peppercorns, sausages, pork and ham	pavé	thick slice
		pieds et paques	mutton or pork tripe and trotters
		poêlé	pan-fried
civet	game stew	poulet de Bresse	chicken from Bresse
confit	meat preserve	râble	saddle
coq au vin	chicken slow-cooked with wine, onions and mushrooms	rôti	roast
		sauté	lightly fried in butter
		steak au poivre (vert/rouge)	steak in a black peppercorn sauce (green/red peppercorn)
côte	chop, cutlet or rib		
cuisse	thigh or leg		
en croûte	in pastry		
épaule	shoulder	steak tartare	raw chopped beef, topped with a raw egg yolk
farci	stuffed		
au feu de bois	cooked over wood fire		
		tagine	North African casserole
au four	baked	viennoise	fried in egg and bread crumbs
garni	with vegetables		

Terms for steaks

bleu	almost raw	bien cuit	well done
saignant	rare	très bien cuit	ruined
à point	medium rare		

Garnishes and sauces

américaine	sauce of white wine, cognac and tomato	bordelaise	in a red wine, shallot and bone-marrow sauce
auvergnat	with cabbage, sausage and bacon	boulangère	baked with potatoes and onions
béarnaise	sauce of egg yolks, white wine, shallots and vinegar	bourgeoise	with carrots, onions, bacon, celery and braised lettuce
beurre blanc	sauce of white wine and shallots, with butter	chasseur	sauce of white wine, mushrooms and shallots
bonne femme	with mushroom, bacon, potato and onions	châtelaine	with artichoke hearts and chestnut purée

diable	strong mustard seasoning	périgourdine	sauce with foie gras and possibly truffles
façon	in the style of ...	piquante	with gherkins or capers, vinegar and shallots
forestière	with bacon and mushroom		
fricassée	rich, creamy sauce	provençale	sauce of tomatoes, garlic, olive oil and herbs
mornay	cheese sauce		
pays d'auge	cream and cider		
		savoyarde	with gruyère cheese

Vegetables (légumes), grains (grains), herbs (herbes) and spices (épices)

ail	garlic	haricots	beans
anis	aniseed	verts	green beans
artichaut	artichoke	rouges	kidney beans
asperge	asparagus	laurier	bay leaf
avocat	avocado	lentilles	lentils
basilic	basil	maïs	maize (corn)
betterave	beetroot	menthe	mint
blette/bette	Swiss chard	moutarde	mustard
cannelle	cinnamon	oignon	onion
capre	caper	panais	parsnip
cardon	cardoon	persil	parsley
carotte	carrot	petits pois	peas
céleri	celery	piment rouge/vert	red/green chilli pepper
champignons, cèpes, ceps, girolles, chanterelles, pleurotes	mushrooms	pois chiche	chickpeas
		pois mange-tout	mange-tout
		pignons	pine nuts
chou (rouge)	(red) cabbage	poireau	leek
choufleur	cauliflower	poivron (vert, rouge)	sweet pepper (green, red)
concombre	cucumber		
cornichon	gherkin	pommes de terre	potatoes
échalotes	shallots	primeurs	spring vegetables
endive	chicory	radis	radish
épinards	spinach	riz	rice
estragon	tarragon	safran	saffron
fenouil	fennel	sarrasin	buckwheat
fèves	broad beans	thym	thyme
flageolets	flageolet beans	tomate	tomato
gingembre	ginger	truffes	truffles

Vegetable dishes and terms

à l'anglaise	boiled	farci	stuffed
beignet	fritter	feuille	leaf
duxelles	fried mushrooms and shallots with cream	fines herbes	mixture of tarragon, parsley and chives

gratiné	browned with cheese or butter	parmentier	with potatoes
à la grecque	cooked in oil and lemon	petits farcis	stuffed tomatoes, aubergines, courgettes and peppers
jardinière	with mixed diced vegetables	râpée	grated or shredded
mousseline	mashed potato with cream and eggs	à la vapeur	steamed
à la parisienne	sautéed potatoes, with white wine and shallot sauce	en verdure	garnished with green vegetables

Fruit (fruit) and nuts (noix)

abricot	apricot	mangue	mango
acajou	cashew nut	marron	chestnut
amande	almond	melon	melon
ananas	pineapple	mirabelle	small yellow plum
banane	banana	myrtille	bilberry
brugnon, nectarine	nectarine	noisette	hazelnut
cacahouète	peanut	noix	walnuts; nuts
cassis	blackcurrant	orange	orange
cérise	cherry	pamplemousse	grapefruit
citron	lemon	pastèque	watermelon
citron vert	lime	pêche	peach
datte	date	pistache	pistachio
figue	fig	poire	pear
fraise (de bois)	strawberry (wild)	pomme	apple
framboise	raspberry	prune	plum
fruit de la passion	passion fruit	pruneau	prune
grenade	pomegranate	raisin	grape
groseille	redcurrant	reine-claude	greengage

Fruit dishes and terms

agrumes	citrus fruits	crème de marrons	chestnut purée
beignet	fritter	flambé	set aflame in alcohol
compôte	stewed fruit	frappé	iced
coulis	sauce of puréed fruit		

Desserts (desserts), pastries (pâtisserie) and cheeses (fromages)

brebis	sheep's milk cheese	charlotte	custard and fruit in lining of almond biscuits or sponge
bombe	moulded ice-cream dessert		
brioche	sweet breakfast roll	chèvre	goat's cheese
		clafoutis	heavy custard and fruit tart

crème Chantilly	vanilla-flavoured and sweetened whipped cream	marrons Mont Blanc	chestnut purée and cream on a rum-soaked sponge cake
crème fraîche	sour cream	palmier	caramelized puff pastry
crème pâtissière	thick, eggy pastry-filling	parfait	frozen mousse, sometimes ice cream
crêpe suzette	thin pancake with orange juice and liqueur	petit-suisse	a smooth mixture of cream and curds
fromage blanc	cream cheese	petits fours	bite-sized cakes/pastries
gaufre	waffle		
glace	ice cream	plâteau de fromages	cheeseboard
Île flottante/oeufs à la neige	whipped egg-white floating on custard	poires belle hélène	pears and ice cream in chocolate sauce
macaron	macaroon	tarte tatin	upside-down apple tart
madeleine	small sponge cake	yaourt/yogourt	yoghurt

Glossary of architectural terms

These are either terms you'll come across in the Guide, or come up against while travelling around.

abbaye abbey

ambulatory passage round the outer edge of the choir of a church

apse semicircular termination at the east end of a church

Baroque mainly seventeenth-century style of art and architecture, distinguished by ornate Classicism

basse ville lower town

bastide walled town

capital carved top of a column

Carolingian dynasty (and art, sculpture etc) named after Charlemagne; mid-eighth to early tenth centuries

château mansion, country house, castle

château fort castle

chevet east end of a church

choir the eastern part of a church between the altar and nave, used by the choir and clergy

Classical architectural style incorporating Greek and Roman elements: pillars, domes, colonnades, etc, at its height in France in the seventeenth century and revived, as Neoclassical, in the nineteenth century

clerestory upper storey of a church, incorporating the windows

Cloître cloister

donjon castle keep

église church

flamboyant florid, late (c.1450–1540) form of Gothic

Gallo-Roman from the Roman era in France

Gothic late-medieval architectural style characterized by pointed arches, verticality and light

hôtel (particulier) mansion or townhouse

Merovingian dynasty (and art etc) ruling France and parts of Germany from sixth to mid-eighth centuries

narthex entrance hall of church

nave main body of a church

porte gateway

Renaissance Classically influenced art/ architectural style imported from Italy to France in the early sixteenth century

retable altarpiece

Roman Romanesque (easily confused with Romain, which means Roman)

Romanesque early medieval architecture distinguished by squat, rounded forms and naive sculpture, called Norman in Britain

stucco plaster used to embellish ceilings etc

tour tower

transepts transverse arms of a church

tympanum sculpted panel above a church door

voussoir sculpted rings in arch over church door

Travel
store

From Paris to Saint-Tropez, explore the best that France has to offer in the comfort and luxury of an Avis car.

With over 500 rental stations located at airports, train stations, and in towns and cites across the country, Avis lets you pack more into your trip.

- Avis GPS available
- Quick and easy rental process
- No hidden costs

Avis – car hire from a name you can trust.

To book visit avis.co.uk
or call 0844 581 0147 for more details.

We try
harder

FAIR FARES from NORTH SOUTH TRAVEL

Our great-value air fares cover the world, from Abuja to Zanzibar and from Zurich to Anchorage. North South Travel is a fund-raising travel agency, owned by the NST Development Trust.

ALL our profits go to development organisations.

Small print and
Index

A Rough Guide to Rough Guides

Published in 1982, the first Rough Guide – to Greece – was a student scheme that became a publishing phenomenon. Mark Ellingham, a recent graduate in English from Bristol University, had been travelling in Greece the previous summer and couldn't find the right guidebook. With a small group of friends he wrote his own guide, combining a highly contemporary, journalistic style with a thoroughly practical approach to travellers' needs.

The immediate success of the book spawned a series that rapidly covered dozens of destinations. And, in addition to impecunious backpackers, Rough Guides soon acquired a much broader and older readership that relished the guides' wit and inquisitiveness as much as their enthusiastic, critical approach and value-for-money ethos.

These days, Rough Guides include recommendations from shoestring to luxury and cover more than 200 destinations around the globe, including almost every country in the Americas and Europe, more than half of Africa and most of Asia and Australasia. Our ever-growing team of authors and photographers is spread all over the world, particularly in Europe, the US and Australia.

In the early 1990s, Rough Guides branched out of travel, with the publication of Rough Guides to World Music, Classical Music and the Internet. All three have become benchmark titles in their fields, spearheading the publication of a wide range of books under the Rough Guide name.

Including the travel series, Rough Guides now number more than 350 titles, covering: phrasebooks, waterproof maps, music guides from Opera to Heavy Metal, reference works as diverse as Conspiracy Theories and Shakespeare, and popular culture books from iPods to Poker. Rough Guides also produce a series of more than 120 World Music CDs in partnership with World Music Network.

Visit www.roughguides.com to see our latest publications.

Rough Guide credits

Text editors: Lucy White, Lara Kavanagh, Andy Turner
Layout: Jessica Subramanian
Cartography: Rajesh Mishra
Picture editor: Jess Carter
Production: Rebecca Short
Proofreader: Stewart Wild
Cover design: Dan May, Nicole Newman, Chlöe Roberts
Photographers: Marc Dubin, Lydia Evans, Michelle Grant, Greg Ward
Editorial: London Keith Drew, Edward Aves, Alice Park, Jo Kirby, James Smart, Natasha Foges, James Rice, Emma Beatson, Emma Gibbs, Kathryn Lane, Monica Woods, Mani Ramaswamy, Harry Wilson, Lucy Cowie, Alison Roberts, Eleanor Aldridge, Ian Blenkinsop, Joe Staines, Matthew Milton, Tracy Hopkins; **Delhi** Madhavi Singh, Jalpreen Kaur Chhatwal, Jubbi Francis

Design & Pictures: London Scott Stickland, Dan May, Diana Jarvis, Mark Thomas, Nicole Newman, Sarah Cummins; **Delhi** Umesh Aggarwal, Ajay Verma, Ankur Guha, Pradeep Thapliyal, Sachin Tanwar, Anita Singh, Nikhil Agarwal, Sachin Gupta
Production: Liz Cherry, Louise Daly, Erika Pepe
Cartography: London Ed Wright, Katie Lloyd-Jones; **Delhi** Rajesh Chhibber, Ashutosh Bharti, Animesh Pathak, Jasbir Sandhu, Swati Handoo, Deshpal Dabas, Lokamata Sahu
Marketing, Publicity & roughguides.com: Liz Statham
Digital Travel Publisher: Peter Buckley
Reference Director: Andrew Lockett
Operations Coordinator: Becky Doyle
Operations Assistant: Johanna Wurm
Publishing Director (Travel): Clare Currie
Commercial Manager: Gino Magnotta
Managing Director: John Duhigg

Publishing information

This twelfth edition published April 2011 by
Rough Guides Ltd,
80 Strand, London WC2R 0RL
11, Community Centre, Panchsheel Park, New Delhi 110017, India

Distributed by the Penguin Group

Penguin Books Ltd,
80 Strand, London WC2R 0RL

Penguin Group (USA)
375 Hudson Street, NY 10014, USA

Penguin Group (Australia)
250 Camberwell Road, Camberwell, Victoria 3124, Australia

Penguin Group (NZ)
67 Apollo Drive, Mairangi Bay, Auckland 1310, New Zealand

Rough Guides is represented in Canada by Tourmaline Editions Inc. 662 King Street West, Suite 304, Toronto, Ontario M5V 1M7

Cover concept by Peter Dyer.

Typeset in Bembo and Helvetica to an original design by Henry Iles.

Printed in Italy by L.E.G.O. S.p.A, Lavis (TN)
© Rough Guides 2011
Maps © Rough Guides
No part of this book may be reproduced in any form without permission from the publisher except for the quotation of brief passages in reviews.
1112pp includes index
A catalogue record for this book is available from the British Library
ISBN: 978-1-84836-723-4
The publishers and authors have done their best to ensure the accuracy and currency of all the information in **The Rough Guide to France**, however, they can accept no responsibility for any loss, injury, or inconvenience sustained by any traveller as a result of information or advice contained in the guide.

1   3   5   7   9   8   6   4   2

MIX
Paper from responsible sources
FSC www.fsc.org   FSC™ C018179

Help us update

We've gone to a lot of effort to ensure that the twelfth edition of **The Rough Guide to France** is accurate and up-to-date. However, things change – places get "discovered", opening hours are notoriously fickle, restaurants and rooms raise prices or lower standards. If you feel we've got it wrong or left something out, we'd like to know, and if you can remember the address, the price, the hours, the phone number, so much the better.

Please send your comments with the subject line "Rough Guide France Update" to ®mail @uk.roughguides.com. We'll credit all contributions and send a copy of the next edition (or any other Rough Guide if you prefer) for the very best emails.

Find more travel information, connect with fellow travellers and book your trip on ⓦwww .roughguides.com

Acknowledgements

Colleen Brousil Special thanks to Joyce Malloy for her diligent research.

Brian Catlos Thanks to Núria Silleras-Fernández and Hélène Aznar.

Anette dal Jensen Merci beaucoup to Bill Sillery, Lucy White, Jo Kirby, Carole Mendy, Christian & Tamsin, Jane-Claire Bulmer, Gemma Riggs, JJ Maurage, Claudia Fitzgerald, Helene at Cyrnos, Kirsty Chestnutt, Mathilde Pineau, Barney Duly, Belinda Rasmussen, Funky Jim, Matt Brooks, Nibs & Wizard, the Festinho crew, beautiful France and particularly amazing Marseille. Love it!

James McConnachie would like to thank Claire Helen Williams.

Charlotte Melville would like to thank M. and Mme. Giboury for their kindness in both Parthenay and on the Île de Ré, and to Bruno Conchin for his help and insight on countless subjects. Also to the Colver family for their hospitality in Lacanau, including their invaluable lessons on Ikea furnishings and windsurfing. Thanks also to Lucy White, the editor, for her continual encouragement and meticulous attention to detail throughout.

Sophie Nellis Thanks to Maureen Waugh and Mike Nellis for their support and encouragement, and Róisín Cameron for her inspiration.

Kate Turner Thank you to Jaime Hall for the Lyon eating and drinking tips.

Greg Ward would like to thank Sam for being there, and being here, and also everyone at Rough Guides for making the book better than ever.

Richard Watkins Thanks to Lydie Galloppe in Briançon, Pierre Kovacic and Eric Belavoire in Gap, Magali Boudières in Grenoble, Isabelle Faure of Rhône-Alpes Tourism, Philippe and Énid Lanthelme-Tournier and Gérard Charpin in Chambéry, Aurélie Nétillard in Belfort and Emilie Meirland-Le Meunier in Montbéliard.

Lucy White would like to thank all those who helped her negotiate a rather rainy Alsace and Lorraine, including Manuela Kaiser and Leslie Collins. Thanks also to Charlie who sorted the car, and to her co-editor and desk buddy, Lara Kavanagh.

Readers' letters

Thanks to all the readers who have taken the time to write in with comments and suggestions (and apologies if we've inadvertently omitted or misspelt anyone's name):

A Betts, J. S Boreham, Malvern Dann, Monica Gilbert, Christopher and Helena Hilton, Nicole Jorge do Marco, David Nixon, D. S Theophilus.

SMALL PRINT

Photo credits

All photos © Rough Guides except the following:

Introduction

Haute-Loire, poppy field © Christian Guy/Getty
Beynac-et-Cazenac © Laurie Noble/Getty
Horse trekking, Belle-Île, Brittany © Slow Images/
Getty
Uttenhoffen, Alsace © Travel Ink/Getty
Cours Saleya Nice © Sandra Raccanello/Getty
View of market produce, Aix-en-Provence
© Grant Faint/Getty
Honfleur, Calvados © Anger O/Getty

Things not to miss

01 Château Azay le Rideau, Loire Valley © Shaun
Egan/Getty
02 Issenheim altarpiece, Unterlinden Museum,
Colmar © Yadid Levy/Photolibrary
03 Perrier-Jouet champagne © Stevens Fremont/
Corbis
05 Gulf of Porto © Riccardo Spila/Getty
07 Jardin du Luxembourg, Paris © D A Barnes/
Alamy
08 Boating in the Gorges du Verdon © Sergio
Pitamitz/Corbis
09 Amiens Cathedral © Pascal Deloche/Godong/
Corbis
10 Menec, Carnac © Joe Cornish/Getty
12 Bastille Day celebrations, Champ de Mars
© Benoit Tessier/Corbis
13 Bouchon, rue Mercière, Lyon © Jean-Pierre
Lescourret/Corbis
15 Cycling, Mont Ventoux © Andrew Bain/Alamy
16 Monpazier, Dordogne © Peet Simard/Corbis
17 Canal du Midi, Languedoc © Travelpix Ltd/
Getty
18 Aix-en-Provence, Provence © Bertrand
Rieger/Getty
19 Calanque d'en Vau © Catherine Karnow/Corbis
20 Annecy © Pierre Jacques/Corbis
22 Cathar ruins, Aude valley © Laurence
Delderfield/Getty
23 Edward the Confessor, Bayeux Tapestry
© Heritage Images/Corbis
24 Paintings, Lascaux caves © Dea/G. Dagli Orti/
Getty
25 Bocca a Reta, GR20, Corsica © Jef Maion/
Alamy
26 Fontenay Cistercian Abbey © Sylvain Sonnet/
Corbis
27 Pont d'Arc, Ardeche © Stockfolio/Alamy
28 Carcassonne © Brian Lawrence/Getty
29 Méribel, Les Trois Vallées © Gavin Hellier/
Robert Harding World Imagery/Getty

French wine colour section

Nuits St-George harvest © Owen Franken/Corbis
Grape harvest, Burgundy © Jean-Marc Charles/
Photolibrary

Champagne cork and grapes, Champagne
© Grant Faint/Getty
Bottle of Ardois Chardonnay © Owen Franken/
Corbis
Taittinger champagne cellar, Reims © Godong/
Getty
Merlot grapevines, Pomerol, Bordeaux © John
Harper/Corbis
White wine on display, Sancerre © David Thorpe/
Alamy
Châteauneuf-du-Pape winery, Rhône © FirstShot/
Alamy
Le Baron Rouge, Paris © Owen Franken/Corbis
Wine being poured, Île-de-Ré © Emilio Suetone/
Corbis

Walking in France colour section

Hiking in Savoie © Photoalto/Photolibrary
Hiking in Les Saisies, Mont Blanc © Pierre
Jacques/Getty
Base camp at Cirque de Gavarnie © Douglas
Pearson/Getty
Emergency Hut at the ascent of Mont Blanc
© imagebroker rf/Photolibrary
Family hiking with a donkey, Cévennes © Look
Die Bilagenur de Fotografen/Alamy
Lac de Melo, Corsica © Juergen Richter/Getty
Sunflower and lavender fields, Provence
© Raimund Linke/Getty
Hiking near Mont Blanc © James Denk/
Photolibrary
Aveyron, Conques © Godong Godong/
Photolibrary

Black and whites

p.168 Givet, Ardennes © Wilmar Photography/
Alamy
p.228 Place Stanislas © Jean-Pierre de Mann/
Corbis
p.384 Villandry © Marc Dozier, Getty
p.444 Beaune © Christophe Boisvieux/Corbis
p.488 La Rochelle © Paul Miles/Axiom/Getty
p.544 *Saucissons* at a traditional French market
© Trevor Peterson/Alamy
p.668 Roman aqueduct, Pont du Gard © David
Stubbs/Getty
p.716 Ardèche gorges © Emmanuel Lattes/
Alamy
p.758 Cable car to Pointe Helbronner © David
Madison/Getty
p.814 Lyon restaurant © Art Kowalsky/Alamy
p.902 Promenade des Anglais, Nice © Roy
Rainford/Robert Harding World Imagery/
Getty
p.970 Filitosa, Corsica © x-drew/istockphoto

SMALL PRINT

Index

Map entries are in colour.

P

I

INDEX

1107

Map symbols

maps are listed in the full index using coloured text

- - -	Chapter division boundary		★	Bus stop
-----·	International boundary		🏮	Fuel station
·-·-·	Regional boundary		◆	Point of interest
▬▬▬	Autoroute		@	Internet café
═══	Major road		ⓘ	Tourist office/information point
───	Minor road		⊠	Post office
▬▬▬	Pedestrianized street		⊞	Hospital
▥▥▥▥	Steps		◉	Accommodation
)········(	Tunnel		⚠	Campsite
═══	Railway		⚒	Concentration Camp
▬■▬	TGV line		🏠	Gîte d'Étape/Mountain refuge
▥▥▥▥▥	Funicular railway		◐	Cave
- - - - -	Footpath		∴	Ruin
───	River		♜	Fort
— - —	Ferry		⚔	Battlefield
───	Wall/fortification		📡	Lighthouse
⊠—⊠	Gate		⊛	Swimming pool
)(	Bridge/mountain pass		⊙	Statue/memorial
▼▼▼▼▼	Cutting		▥	Monastery/abbey
⩟	Mountain range		⛪	Château
▲	Mountain peak		⣿	Race Circuit
ꙮ	Rocks		▭	Market
⩔	Swamp		▬	Building
⩔	Viewpoint		⊞	Church
✈	Airport		◯	Stadium
®	RER station		⊹⊹⊹	Cemetery
Ⓜ	Métro station		░░░	Park
Ⓣ	Tram stop		⠿⠿	Beach

So now we've told you about the things not to miss, the best places to stay, the top restaurants, the liveliest bars and the most spectacular sights, it only seems fair to tell you about the best travel insurance around

WorldNomads.com
keep travelling safely

Recommended by Rough Guides

About the Author

Following his poem *Fireworks Fireworks Bang Bang Bang* at the age of six, Mason eventually took the whole writing thing a little more seriously, graduating in 2009 from London Metropolitan University, having received first class honours in Creative Writing, finishing within the university's top 50 students. In his second year, he won the Sandra Ashman award for his poem *Mother Theresa in the Winner's Enclosure*. He has subsequently had work published in *Succour* magazine and *Brand* magazine. Mason is currently developing his next novel; in addition to this, he writes, co-produces and hosts the award-winning monthly cabaret night The Double R Club (as Benjamin Louche, winner of "Best Host" at the London Cabaret Awards). He also worked as a creature performer on *Star Wars: The Force Awakens* & *The Last Jedi*. He lives in East London with his wife, a cat called Monkey, and a collection of antique medical equipment.

MasonBall.co.uk
Facebook MasonBallnotJasonBell
Twitter @MasonBallauthor

The Thirty Five Timely & Untimely Deaths Of Cumberland County

THE THIRTY FIVE TIMELY & UNTIMELY DEATHS OF CUMBERLAND COUNTY

or The Dutch Wives & How They Went At Their
Fearful Work

Mason Ball

This edition first published in 2018

Unbound

6th Floor Mutual House, 70 Conduit Street, London W1S 2GF

www.unbound.com

ISBN (eBook): 978-1-911586-71-5
ISBN (Paperback): 978-1-911586-70-8

Design by Mecob

Cover image: © Shutterstock.com

Printed and bound in Great Britain by Clays Ltd, Elcograf S.p.A.

For Elisabeth,

beautiful personification of more luck than this man
deserves

and for Kris,

much missed, without whom nothing I write would
be quite what it is

Author's Note

*All facsimiles of medical documents included herein
are reproduced from the originals.*

Is God willing to prevent evil but unable to do so?
Then he is not omnipotent. Is God able to prevent
evil but unwilling to do so? Then he is malevolent
(or at least less than perfectly good). If God is both
willing and able to prevent evil then why is there
evil in the world?

– Epicurus

And nothing is written in the book,
reality is made by you,
And every lie that you pursue,
eventually turns true,
And I was told that your eyes would shine,
a light up into space,
And infinity would then consume
this ordinary place.

– Michael Gira

Dear Reader,

The book you are holding came about in a rather different way to most others. It was funded directly by readers through a new website: Unbound.

Unbound is the creation of three writers. We started the company because we believed there had to be a better deal for both writers and readers. On the Unbound website, authors share the ideas for the books they want to write directly with readers. If enough of you support the book by pledging for it in advance, we produce a beautifully bound special subscribers' edition and distribute a regular edition and e-book wherever books are sold, in shops and online.

This new way of publishing is actually a very old idea (Samuel Johnson funded his dictionary this way). We're just using the internet to build each writer a network of patrons. Here, at the back of this book, you'll find the names of all the people who made it happen.

Publishing in this way means readers are no longer just passive consumers of the books they buy, and authors are free to write the books they really want. They get a much fairer return too – half the profits their books generate, rather than a tiny percentage of the cover price.

If you're not yet a subscriber, we hope that you'll want to join our publishing revolution and have your name listed in one of our books in the future. To get you started, here is a £5 discount on your first pledge. Just visit unbound.com, make your pledge and type MASON18 in the promo code box when you check out.

Thank you for your support,

Dan, Justin and John
Founders, Unbound

I

It can be overstated how most anyplace is built on little more than blood. But that's not to say it idn true. Everyplace people settle that is, everywhere they come to rest, finish up. We spill it, then hunker down. Start to build. Any farmer will tell you bone meal is your crop's best friend.

We were influenza to the Indians. We were smallpox. We swept in, wiped them away. Chalk dust offa slate. The Abenaki have a name for it, call it The Great Dyin. Don't suppose there's much help to be had in wishin it weren't so. One day no doubt our own influenza will march in and make *us* history; maybe it's already here. Our towns, our cities, are wild flowers on a grave, from sea to shining sea.

There's a violence in all things, just as there is a love. Deep seated. In the heart. Nature is blind, alive and burning with the hot coals of it.

People muddle along, step over what they'd rather not look at too closely. People do good, they fall in love, raise kids, they help their neighbor. They do, I've seen em; don't pretend you haven't too. Good *is* everywhere. But the good and the bad in people, in the meat of things, is a specially odious kind of nonsense. What my father used to call, if you'll forgive me, *Solid Gold Bullshit*. Good and bad are whichever eyeglasses you look at them through. Don't you doubt it.

I guess you could say love can only exist if hate follows on its tail but all that's just a mess of words. A chair is called a chair because we named it that. A spade a spade. I guess what I'm saying is that you can just as well grow good as you can bad from blood. Not even sure there's a choice to be made which it is, weeds or crops, and no one to tell you which is which. Don't look at it too closely. Change eyeglasses, hunker down and build.

I say *almost* anyplace because, hell, what do I know? I haven't seen the plains of Africa, nor hobnobbed with the crowned heads of Europe but I figure people are the same all over. Any which color, any which place. But I'm just an old man, some say ornery, what do I know?

It can be overstated then, certainly, but hardly ignored or denied. Let me say it again, almost anyplace is built on blood; Cumberland County, Maine, you can be sure is no different.

I should know. Cumberlander my whole life. Born here, likely die here too. This here whole area sprung from four what they call "grants". You had your Baldwin, your Bridgton, Otisfield and your Raymond. Naples, Casco, Harrison and Sebago was later cut from them four. Like slices acake. This is called Casco, you live here now, you now live in Sebago, you in Harrison; this is a chair, this is a spade. Same thing. And there was my mother always telling us kids you couldn't live on cake.

These "grants" were reward for those Massachusetts folks that stepped forward for King Willy's war. 1690, the Battle of Quebec they called it. Like it was some Clark Gable picture. The English had decided that New France, as it was called then, looked very much like a patch of dirt they wanted so they invaded. The English have a habit athis. Read any history book. They had the money and the inclination, which is all I guess that's needed.

They marched those Bay Staters up there to Canada with promises of plunder and it was all going well by Port Royal, which fell just like that. Spirits musta been high as kites.

These Frenchies drank with their pinkies held out and stank of perfume. Surely. They'd be a feather wall in a high wind. And we're back to our piece of cake. But then the Quebec basin was a horse of a different color altogether.

They was out-soldiered is the truth and the French, led by a fella name of Frontenac, held all the cards every which way. They knew it, the English guy Phips knew it. Still the English sent a man up there to demand the Frenchmen's surrender. A people will do all manner of dumb things when runnin on pure grade arrogance. Frontenac looks at the English guy and says "I have no reply to make to your general other than from the mouths of my cannons and muskets."

Anyhow the thing I'm coming to is, people *died* in this squabble, as they do in all these squabbles, and blood was spilt,

3

on both sides; but the Bay Staters came off worse. Much worse. Those that come home, tails between their legs, were rewarded with a little slice of Maine. And they built on blood.

Naples, Raymond, Bridgton; Maine

July, 1934

The old woman rests on the muddy bank, breathing hard. She blinks wildly, a wide rictus, almost a smile, grasping desperately at each inhalation. For a moment it seems as if she may collapse, pass out, perhaps even suffer a heart attack. She doesn't.

Her head falls forward, rocking with each breath. Through her thinning hair beads of lake water weave and roll forward, collecting, before racing in rivulets over the sharp ridges of her eyebrows and down her face.

She'll be alright in a minute, she'll be alright in a minute.

The knots of her fingers flutter lightly in the air about her knees, wrinkled and aquiver in the warm midday air. Wisps of thin white hair hang down her cheeks in ropes, deep lines criss-cross her taut chin and wrinkled, hanging neck. Rags of wet clothes cling to her rawboned arms and legs, blister with moisture and stick to her shriveled, soft gut, her fallen chest.

She's been old for as long as she can remember.

Even through exhaustion, features poke their way through. A strong jaw line, speaking of past stoicisms, of gristle and strength; rheumy eyes, a sadness hiding in pale blue irises, a hard-heartedness, perhaps even cruelty, hiding behind that. Large putty-colored ears, swollen and doughy with age, a twist to the pitted nose betraying a break, never properly set; a corrugation of forehead, ploughed by lifetimes of concern, of hard and thankless work.

Her breath is returning, as it always does, the feathery weakness in her limbs congealing into something approaching strength enough to stand, to move on.

Nearby on the bank sit her shoes, scuffed and patient; men's shoes. The cool Sebago licks playfully at her gnarled and naked toes as they sink into the mud, something of an echo of the invisible animal of cold and drowning that the old woman knows only too well lies hungry and blind along the lake bed.

Submerged, she's oftentimes heard the lake whisper in its raw bass tones, the torn, empty kettle sound of bubbles, a silt-edged whisper that to crawl up and sleep down there was just about the best idea you ever had. She knows the voice well, intimately, like sweet nothings, a tryst of more years' standing than she cares to recall. Sometimes it sounds like her own voice.

She wonders distantly how many of the folks that lived around those parts had heard it too, how many of them had heard it and made it back to the surface. But then she knows the answer to that question.

Gingerly she maneuvers onto all fours and taking one final deep breath, pushes herself into a crooked standing position. There are places to be, things to get done, and no other way to get there than shanks' mare. Gaining uneasy balance from an obliging tree, she steps first into her shoes and finally back into the woods whence she came.

Doctor John Bischoffberger sat reading in his small back-room office, full of a late if meager lunch and as stilled as he was able. Turning a page, he exhaled the morning.

Oxygen and carbon dioxide be damned. Schooling had taught him the biology of breathing, the mechanics, yet still he held on to a fragment of something he'd thought as a child; that breathing *in* drew things into you, sometimes bad things, whereas breathing *out* was somehow ridding you of these things. A childish but instinctive piece of foolishness. In his young mind inhaling had become of less value than exhaling; he recalled the fear of swallowing bad smells, holding his breath. Exhaling cleansed him. So he exhaled Mrs Abbott's boils and Myron Walker's rattling lungs, the Winant boy's swollen tonsils; a stubbed toe, automobile trouble threatening a return to Higgins Garage, the beggar he passed on Lambs Mill Road, the shoeless child on Quaker Ridge. He read on, emptying himself.

His neglected paperwork glared reproachfully at him; paperless, his Underwood 5 typewriter petulantly bared its teeth.

Organon of the Healing Art by S. Hahnemann seemed to John a book both fascinating and fascinatingly absurd. Published in 1810, Hahnemann's 'law of similars' stated that any effective medicine would produce symptoms in a healthy patient which mirror those it might be used to treat in an ailing one. An idea apparently perverse and backward; a corruption of Shakespeare's *sweets to the sweet* thought John, perhaps *bane to the blighted*. The genesis of homeopathy.

As John read, his hand toyed with the contents of his desk, as if let loose to play on its own, picking up his fountain pen, thumbing through a neat stack of records, shifting his inkwell to and fro across the blotter. Ros called him The Careful Fidget. When in thought his fingers would unconsciously and carefully explore his surroundings, desk, letter opener, medical bag, shirt buttons, as if in search of something. Or perhaps seeking to ensure that all was as it should be, all as he'd left it, before he then left on his ideation, which he did often.

To avoid any serious ill effects, Hahnemann proposed that sub-stances used homeopathically be given only in 'extreme dilutions', a step which made much of the medical profession suggest that while such tiny amounts of substances were unlikely to do any great harm, due to their weakness, it was equally unlikely that they could do any real good either. As such, many dismissed homeopa-thy's claimed successes as mere placebo. John was inclined to agree.

Ros always told him that when they met he "looked like a man chasin somethin", to which he always wryly replied, "And I found that somethin when I found you, my dear." Much as John knew that their courtship had been true and their mar-riage as sound as any and sounder than most, in truth he doubted somehow that this search of his was over, whatever it was for; something about the medical mindset, the eternal unconscious hunt for the magical panacea. A small but peren-nial disquiet.

When prescribing a placebo John knew you had to wrap it up quick in something strong and convincing, lest it spoil; something off the cuff. Dwell too long and the patient might see the lie in it. It was worth remembering that doctors were gods to some but no more than snake oil charlatans to others. Quick and strong was the rule.

But then perhaps all Herr Hahnemann had done was to have found another way. Dressed it up maybe. Ostentation and rig-marole. Slow and fancy. Maybe that's all homeopathy was. The question was, if it worked, did it matter?

Aside from inappropriate use to treat, say, a life-threatening illness, or if it were to preclude *actual* treatment to the detri-ment of the patient; apart from such an eventuality he thought the practice perhaps none too far away from harmless.

The innately 'folksy' nature of so many of homeopathy's remedies might well appeal greatly to many of his patients, he thought, particularly those with a keen skepticism of this Pennsylvanian doctor 'from away' with his pills and his oint-ments, his city tinctures and tonics. Maybe he'd look into it, give it a try. Maybe.

The phone rang.

State of Maine.

Cumberland **ss.**

I certify that I was notified on the _10th_ day _July_ A. D. 19_34_

at _3_ h. and _10_ m. in the _after_ noon by _Camp Kinoni_

of _Naples_ of the finding of the dead body of

David H. Hancock of _Brooklyn N.Y._

supposed to have come to h death by violence or unlawful act; that I forthwith repaired to the place

where said body lies and took charge of the same, and before said body is removed make, or cause to be made,

this written description of the location and position of said body, viz:

    The body was that of a man about five feet eleven inches
tall, weighing 198 pounds, having blond hair, blue eyes and
smooth shaven. He was dressed in blue swimming trunks. The
body was viewed on the shore of Sebago Lake at Naples, near
Stony Ledge cottage.

    There was frothy mucous at the nose and mouth, face, neck
and extremities were cyanosed, rigor mortis was just setting
in.

    The deceased was on his way home with two boys from camp
and another councilor in a canoe. Occupants of canoe stated
that canoe was upset about 150 feet from shore, it being quite
a windy day. He was instructed to hold on to canoe, while the
boys were helped ashore. He was supporting himself in the
water by holding on to canoe. After getting boys ashore they
looked for him but he had gone to the bottom of the lake.
The body was recovered after one hour by Theodore Schrecker
of Camp Kinoni, Naples, Maine.

    Cause of death: Drowning, accidental.

8/20/34

Hen M Bischoffberger M.D.
Medical Examiner

Date   19   *Medical Examiner.*

The room was heavy with warmth, thick with the smell of the thin dinner to come; the overworked remains of last week's ham. Dusk was slowly staining the view from the windows. John pulled the curtains on them. Sitting at the dining table he took up his book, read the same sentence three times.

Rosamond entered with bowls of piping soup and that smile she wore on one side of her mouth. Her hair was up, as were her sleeves. She looked harried but pretty, he thought, and counted himself lucky.

"Bisch, will you stop reading for five minutes and fetch the bread? I believe there's a nubbin in the box yonder."

John put down *Organon of the Healing Art* and fetched the bread. She kissed him gently on the cheek. "And just what book is it you think fit for the dinner table? The Good Book perhaps? William Shakespeare?" He smiled and shifted the book away from his bowl, shook his head.

"An engaging nonsense."

Ros sat and let out a slow breath, before bowing her head and closing her eyes; her fingers laced themselves together in the rising steam of her soup.

"Lord, bless us and these Thy gifts which we are about to receive, we give thanks for Thy bounty through Christ our Lord, amen."

John sat silently and watched her, his hands stilled beside his bowl.

"Amen," he said quietly; she opened her eyes and they ate.

"Ma wrote again concerning Wilson."

"He still suffering with his head?"

"Somethin awful Ma says. Hardly surprising, what with the bank fit to move on him. And him without a bean."

"He's in good company. Is he taking the pills I prescribed?"

"She didn't say. She asks could you go see him."

"*Again?*"

"She asked that I ask."

"Wilson Chaplin is the biggest hypochondriac in all of

Maine, maybe the country. And your mother knows it." Ros smiled. John shook his head ruefully, secretly pleased that Cousin Wilson might be an ideal test for Herr Hahnemann's concoctions. "Ecce Homeopathica," he said to himself. Husband and wife swapped glances that said *I'll go see him* and *Thank you* respectively. The soft clink and drag of spoon on china.

"The newspaper informs me that we are out of Haiti," she said at last.

"So I hear. All good neighbors now," he said, eyebrows raised. He thought of more generals, more soldiers playing further games of checkers who knew where else in the world; something knotted in him, before relaxing.

People were still talking up and down the President's Fireside Chat of two months back, Ros told him, talk of the housing act, of whether it could possibly work; and he thought of foreclosures spreading like an opportunistic infection, or like a slow tumor.

He told her he had patients who still resented Roosevelt's intrusion into their home via the wireless. John had even heard a patient of his compare it to "nothin short of trespass".

"I have faith he is doing all he can," she said.

"I do hope so," he replied. Despite the president's assurances, still the country felt a little like a house built on sand.

"Did you speak with Elmer, dear?" she asked, "he called earlier, I wrote it down."

"Yes, *Deputy Stuart* and I spoke," he replied, "it was nothing important."

"That young man needs a wife, a man shouldn't only be married to his uniform. I shall have a think."

"Matchmaker now? That poor boy. And him all of twenty-five." In lieu of children of their own, Ros' displaced maternal instinct was cause for much gentle ribbing between them, an acknowledgment of, and resignation to, the loss it represented.

"Hey there, Bisch," Elmer had said, "just to let you know I informed the Hussode family down there in Brooklyn that their David had drowned in our lake. Gave em our condolences. Arrangements are being made." John had asked to be told. He'd thanked the deputy and hung up.

The soup was good, peppery and surprisingly hearty, extinguishing a chill he hadn't known he'd been holding on to.

♦

The pale hand grew out of the dark sandy earth like some rarefied tulip, incongruous and impossible, filthy fingers reaching upwards for something, sunlight maybe; fresh air. John rested on his haunches where the lawn met the mud and looked over at it, his own fingers wandering along the seams of his blazer, perhaps counting stitches. A hand. A tulip, he thought, or an orchid stripped of its terrarium.

Some foot or so away from the hand, a pillowcase covered a small rise in the ground, leeching the wet mud into its whiteness, looking for all the world like a dropped handkerchief; a warm breeze tugged at it, briefly describing the face hidden beneath, an eye socket, the bridge of a nose.

The hand had a relaxed quality, a nonchalance that didn't belong. John recalled picture books he'd seen as a child, Adam's hand on the ceiling of the Sistine Chapel: Adam impassive, aloof almost, in contrast to God's hand reaching, almost greedily, at creation. Despite Michelangelo's artistry, young John had always been drawn to the space between them. He'd marveled at the idea that God could create man without even touching him. Abracadabra. *Man touches to create*, his mother had replied, *God don't need to more than think and it's done*. Alakazam. Still the reaching had troubled the boy.

A sudden silhouette threw the hand in shade.

"Sorry you was called, Bisch." Deputy Lewellyn Welch hooked his thumbs into his pants, winced into the sun. "Ol' Deihlan's off with Dean to scare up some shovels. Take them an me a long hour to dig Walter out. You don't mind waitin, sure Cora won't mind you doin so in the house."

The doctor stood on crunching knees, smiling away the inference that he was in the way of things.

Some Mainers still held him at a cordial arm's length, an innate suspicion and dislike of all things *outside*; and him having been there coming on eight and a half years. They were far and away from impolite or unfriendly, there being a genuine warmth just as intrinsic to their collective nature, often spilling over into friendship of the truest kind; yet still a distance existed, though Rosamond would tell him it was all in his head. Perhaps it was. Sometimes townsfolk even used the phrase "from away" within his earshot, a candor which he flattered himself might speak of some kind of progress toward integration, or as near to it as he was ever likely to get.

"She still make that pound cake, Lew?"

"I believe I smell the oven from here. We'll come call you when we get the fella out." They nodded at one another, threw glances at the road, the trees beyond, and back up at the house. John stroked at his mustache, stalling for time so as not to feel like a child doing as he was told; he thought the deputy knew it too. Lewellyn nodded again, as if deciding the doctor needed further persuasion. "We don't get him out of there before noon the sun'll be up higher and bake him like he's in a clay oven, that happens I don't know what."

John had treated Walter last spring but couldn't recall what for. Ulcer maybe. Big eyes, dark rings, turkey's wattle and thinning hair streaked flat to the scalp with pomade. Had a son all grown up, moved over Casco way. He tried to join the hand poking out of the mud with the man but struggled. The hand was its own thing now, its own creation, un-needful of a man to carry it around, to employ it with the business of the doing of human things.

He recoiled a little at the thought of Walter's last moments, of drowning in dirt, the weight and grip of it, the panic. He replaced the feeling with a sadness and duty.

"You'll worry the handle right off that bag ayours, Doc." Perhaps a note of insistence, of patience being lost. John stilled his thumb on the thick leather seam, took a fresh hold.

"You come call me," he said. Flickering a smile, he headed for the house, stealing one last look as he did so: the pillowcase now fringed in brown, the blossoming hand pale and reaching.

Cora Gottam met him at the door, fingers clasped bloodless, graying hair escaping the hastily pinned 'pug' on her head.

"It's terrible, Doctor. Poor Mr Sylvester. His poor wife. They've struggled so. He's gone to his glory now. His father, his baby sister. Did you know the family, Doctor? The earth here is so loose they say. Sandy. Do you think it was the earth, Doctor? I feel so terrible. I only asked that he— He'd done the same for a friend of mine over in Harrison. We needed a well. I knew he and Mr Deihlan needed money. Do you think it was the Raymond earth?" John had no answer that didn't make him feel fraudulent in some way, but spoke nonetheless.

He told her he'd known Walter, he told her he didn't know about Raymond earth, that it was just a terrible accident and that was that. He settled for *The earth does what it wants, Mrs Gottam*, adding, *We all have to drink water.* They sat in the kitchen over coffee and Cora caught her breath. The kitchen felt empty, the house cold; vacant shelves and an unlit stove. No pound cake and no ingredients to make it. Thin times. Cora asked after Ros, said there was a recipe she meant to pass on, her hands calming against the warm cup. She apologized for what she called her hysteria, told him she'd say a prayer for Walter come Sunday in church. He told her he'd see her there and she looked at him with an unreadable sadness, as if perhaps she doubted it.

State of Maine.

Cumberland ss.

I certify that I was notified on the _15th_ day _July_ A. D. 19 3 4

at _10_ h. and _15_ m. in the _fore_ noon by _Deputy Sheriff L. W. Welch_

of _Raymond_ of the finding of the dead body of

Walter R. Sylvester of _Somerville, Mass_

supposed to have come to h death by violence or unlawful act; that I forthwith repaired to the place

where said body lies and took charge of the same, and before said body is removed make, or cause to be made,

this written description of the location and position of said body, viz:

The body was that of a man about five feet eight inches tall, weighing 140 pounds, having white hair, blue eyes, and smooth shaven. He was dressed in dark trousers and grey shirt. He had on a pair of rubber boots. His pockets contained $25.37 in cash and his keys. His mouth and nostrils were filled with sand. Face and extremities were cyanosed. A lower set of false teeth were in the mouth but the upper set could not be found.

The deceased was engaged in digging a well on the property of Cora Cottam at Raymond, Maine, Mr. Harry Deihlan, who was assisting him, states that the deceased was standing in the bottom of the excavation shoveling sand, which he, Deihlan, was removing by bucket attached to a rope. Suddenly a part of the banking caved in covering the deceased completely over. Help was secured and the deceased head was uncovered but he was dead when removed from the well. The body was removered by Dep. Sheriffs Dean Pray of Windham and Lewellyn Welch of South Casco. Cause of death : Suffocation accidental by caving in of well.

9/20/34   Medical Examiner.

Date   19   _Medical Examiner._

The little girl sits on the fallen tree and looks out through the busy crowd of trunk and leaf at the nothing beyond. It's as if she's waiting but has forgotten what for. Her shoes play absentmindedly in the dirt, wrestling one another among desiccating twigs and sun-drunk, wandering fire ants. Her legs are dirty, having walked for days with no particular place to end up. Her hands, thoroughly caked in a dark, granular earth, join almost seamlessly with the bark on which she sits. A small embroidered cloth bag hangs grimy from her right wrist; perhaps a purse, more likely a keepsake.

Her whole body, the shape it cuts in the air, the hunch of its shoulders, the slackened lower lip, her entire aspect, all sing a kind of distant and distracted music, as if she is humming to herself, which she isn't. She's a stilled and silent exclamation among the breeze and indifference of the woods. Like a shout you can see.

For a moment the hundreds of corridors made by the trees, the pathways and arteries of the forest, seem all to lead inwardly towards her, as if she represents some kind of vital focal point; perhaps an answer of some kind.

But then of course if this is true then the opposite could also be true: that she is in fact the origin of something rather than the answer: perhaps she's the seed of the paths which splay out from her, some unspecified genesis.

She is perhaps six years old, no more than eight. Her sallow face has a blunt if appealing quality, the pragmatism and cruelty possessed by children born of a specific kind of poverty play about her mouth; something of the beauty she might grow into, if grow up she will, rests patiently in brown eyes ringed in long, dark lashes.

Some inner vibration beyond the normal electricity of youth makes her inertia on the fallen tree seem a particularly sharp and unnecessary waste of time; almost profane.

She blinks and seems to have returned from a journey somewhere. Lifting her hands she stares at the dark mud in the creases of skin, the merest trace of distaste crinkling her freck-led nose. It's under her fingernails too. Perhaps she's consider-ing washing them clean in the lake.

Just then a large wasp, perhaps drawn confusedly to the evaporating moisture in the dirt on her hand, perhaps to the slow pendulum of the embroidered bag on her wrist, lands in her right palm. Feelers working, legs no doubt no more than the tiniest of tickles. Again the little girl blinks. She bites her lip, perhaps with anxiety, perhaps indecision. She quickly snaps her hand shut on the wasp, making as tight a fist as she can, squeezing and squeezing. If she is stung, her face fails to register it.

She looks out through the busy crowd of trees at the nothing beyond.

His old roadster pitched and yawed along Flint Street, rat-tletrap and wheezing; his mind pitched and yawed along with it. He tried to focus on the matter at hand: Miss Edan Wilby, twenty-one years of age, fever, nausea and vomiting, appendicitis to rule out; this afternoon Rosamond's cousin Wilson. Still he drifted.

Earlier, out on the Portland Road, an old woman had walked quickly out of the trees and into his path. A hot flash in his stomach, he had sounded the horn but been forced to skid to a stop. At this the old woman too had halted.

She was dressed poorly, her sack-like shift dress little more than a rag; dirty green, stained near black under the arms and muddied to the hips. The smell of old sweat reached out to him on a sudden warm gust. Her arms were thin and bore thick veins like scars, speaking of strength, looking to John like little more than bundles of tendon. Not a scrap of fat bulged from under her dress, she appeared all angles and cartilage.

Described in the hard sunlight, her face was an explosion of lines, her nose blunted, her white hair wild in the breeze. She looked impossibly old; he guessed in the neighborhood of seventy. She wore a stern but distant look, as if troubled by something huge and insurmountable. There was something familiar about her, but then perhaps he thought it was merely the recognition of a barrenness, an all-too-common paucity that he saw in her.

Trees nodded as far as the eye could see; an enormous quiet settled on the road, not another soul in sight. They stared at one another.

John wondered when she had last eaten. Where she made her bed at night. What she might do come winter. He called out to her, asked if she needed anything. His words felt ridiculous in the open space, tiny and brittle.

He stopped himself from calling out that he was sorry, unsure as to what he might be sorry for.

Eventually she had dropped her head a little in acknowledgment and carried on her way across the road. Reaching the other side, she had disappeared once more into the woods. At that moment he had been struck with the strangest of impressions, that it had been her very presence on the road that had troubled him, her incongruity.

She had appeared to him suddenly as a kind of feral animal, yet more than that, something more—he had struggled before coming to the word *elemental*. He'd caught her in a limbo between one tree line and another, yet it was in the woods that such a creature belonged, away from the towns, villages, the cities that had doubtless taken her money, perhaps her home, as they had taken so many others' homes since the depression had flooded the country. Trees stood apart from the things of man and now, perhaps, so must she. His hands worried the steering wheel. *The trees will look after her*, he'd thought absurdly.

He'd found himself moved, disconcertingly so, and had sat motionless for some minutes, just him and the Portland Road, before finally going on his way.

He drove into Bridgton confounded by the encounter and somewhat abashed, missing the turning onto Main Street and having to turn the roadster around. At this simple maneuver the automobile complained vehemently, a moan and a rattle singing out from under the hood; John pursed his lips and all but prayed to avoid breakdown.

Automobile trouble meant a trip south to Standish, Standish meant Higgins Garage, Higgins Garage meant Elmer Higgins. But then Elmer Higgins wasn't the problem, *he* was. He willed the car on.

Edan Wilby no more had appendicitis than he did. The woman had a bug, albeit a disagreeable one, a condition that seemed aggravated by the presence of her mother, visiting from Bellows Falls. The daughter sat before the fire, mummified in blankets, greasy-faced and drowsy. The smell of sickness and excrement in the house cut bluntly through attempts to disguise it; rose water and candles.

The mother, Hannah, a pear-shaped woman in her forties, exuded a kind of euphoric distress and seemed intent on talking loudly to John of her new life back in Vermont, the house

21

left to her, her husband dead these three years from a tumor, she said, and was he looking forward to the Naples centenary celebrations? Her eyes were small but bright, reminding John somewhat of dewy mollusks; she seemed hungry for attention, a kind of neurotic agitation throwing sparks just below the surface.

In his current mood the house felt busy and oppressive, the mother standing too close, the smell creeping inside him with every breath. He felt anxious and scrutinized, his bedside manner on trial. Hannah insincerely bemoaned the lot of a mother whose child falls ill, while all the while reveling in her melodrama. John reticently admitted to himself both irritation and jealousy in equal measure.

"Do you have any children, Doctor Bischoffberger?" she asked inevitably. He gave his stock reply.

"My wife and myself have not been so blessed Mrs Wilby, no." Memories of the speckled bedding, of the tiny bundle by candlelight. Pink fingers were duly laid at the crook of his elbow, a slow blink of condolence given. He felt moved to speak, if only to distance himself from further pity. "I saw the strangest old woman on my way over here," he began, without realizing exactly what he had been about to say.

Mother and daughter listened politely as he related the meeting on the Portland Road, mother blinking her mollusks quickly, daughter drifting in and out of consciousness. He told them the woman had vanished back into the woods like some kind of wild animal. There was a silence in the room. He felt himself blush, as if he'd related something too personal, beyond the bounds of the doctor-patient relationship.

The mother smiled tightly, perhaps embarrassed, he thought. For the briefest moment he imagined he saw a flash of fright; the daughter was asleep, or pretending to be so. Eventually the mother spoke.

"There are so many poor and unfortunate people on the road these days." Her words sounded flat, as if she were reciting them. He made his excuses and left.

At first the car refused to fire and he made fists in his lap, clenching his face at the steering wheel; he sat back, exhausted by the effort, allowing himself a forced laugh at his own expense. What a ridiculous sight he must make, a grown man, a doctor no less, making faces at his automobile. He gazed out over the calm stretch of Highland Lake, the yawning blue sky and the deep green of the woods beyond. He let the immensity of the open space push him down into his seat, let it ground him against his sudden anger, anger at the car, at Elmer Higgins, at Hannah Wilby; at the woman on the road. He took a deep breath, held it for a moment, and attempted to exhale them all.

♦

Bloodroot, so a pamphlet informed him, could be found all over Cumberland County. Perennial, herbaceous and flowering, it was known also by the names bloodwort, red puccoon root, and in some regions, tetterwort. Toxic and aggressive, the sap from the root growth, or rhizome, had been known to burn and scar upon contact with the skin; and now a whisper of it lay drowned in a small bottle in his medical bag—*an extreme dilution.*

Wilson Chaplin lived not half an hour from the Bischoffberger's door, through town and then north into the trees, and so to save undue wear on the protesting roadster, John chose to make the house call on foot.

The midday sun had peaked and begun to wane, content at having turned the roads to dust and put wide-brimmed hats on all who chose to venture out. What locals called a *scotcha.* On Village Street John lifted his hat to Mrs Dyer and further on, opposite the white spire of the Union Church, he gave an "afternoon" to Joseph Allen, in his old curling shoes and grimy collar, who threw one of his wry inscrutable smiles back. Joseph was what some called a character, others a scoundrel; John simply thought of him as gloriously improper. Naples born and bred, Joseph Allen wore a full white beard and clothes that Ros had once said looked "like he sleeps in them"; his suits were threadbare and greasy and his hair, when released from under his ragged hat, was long and oftentimes the wrong side of dirty. They said he drank, had skewed manners and smiled too much at the wrong things; his favorite expression, often loudly voiced, was *Solid Gold Bullshit*. No way for a man of his advanced years to present himself. And yet all these things belied the real Joseph, and John thought that perhaps this was the reason some took against him; there was a story about Joseph Allen that all in town knew.

Back in 1911 or so, an evangelist met an unkempt man by the draw bridge. Asked why he had not attended church earlier in the day, the man replied, "I'm afraid I do not look fit to go to church." Seizing on this charitable opportunity to save another's soul, a subscription was immediately started to raise money to buy the poor man a suit of clothes. Doors were knocked on and collection plates rattled; however, the enterprise was quickly halted when it was discovered that the unkempt man in question was one Mr Joseph Allen, arguably the richest man in all of the county.

John wasn't sure if the story was true but had chosen to believe it; the fact of Allen's considerable wealth in contrast to his shabby appearance was certainly a matter of common knowledge. The doctor found himself feeling something of an unspecified kinship with Joseph, an outsider's bond. Their conversation had been sparse over the years and they could not be called friends exactly, but John thought that each one recognized himself to some extent in the other. Conversation between them usually ran the same way, as it did on this particular July afternoon.

"Goodday, Doc. Still hawkin them pills?"

"I'm trying to, Mr Allen."

"Well I'll not keep you then." Each touched his hat and they went on their opposite ways.

Wilson opened the door in his long underwear, a wet rag tied about his head; every inch the bachelor. He winced a pained greeting.

"Uh, hey Bisch, come on in," his voice low and thin. The uncharitable part of John suspected Charlie Pitts' popskull wine, maybe a quart or two of Pickwick Ale, as the culprit of Wilson's headache. He bit down hard on his cynicism. The house was, John thought, about as far from the touch of a woman as it was possible to get; Wilson seemed to have his own way and that way had little to do with housework or conventional order.

"You got folks worried, Wilson."

"I told Aunt Hattie not to call, you don't need botherin with my heads." Even through the obvious pain Wilson's tone was disingenuous: if *he* hadn't asked her then no one had.

"She didn't call, she wrote a letter."

"She *did*? Hell, what that woman has against the telephone I don't know. Sure don't hamper her talkin any." They laughed together politely and Wilson grimaced, buckling for a moment.

John had decided some time ago that Wilson's suffering was real enough, although the likely cause he put down to nothing more than the knots people tied themselves in when they thought themselves ill; it was, to his mind, the closest thing to magic there was. It was as if these people fell under their own hexes. You think it long enough and hard enough and it'll turn up, knocking on your door.

John sat Wilson on an old ladder-back by the kitchen window and examined him, as he had before, checked for paralysis, lack of sensation, looked for clues he knew weren't there in the eyes.

"You taking the pills I prescribed?"

"Took em, taken em, all gone."

"Did they ease the pain?"

"Barely touched it most times. But they did some."

"And have the attacks grown in frequency?"

"Bout the same I'd say, every two months or so. Sometimes longer. Sometimes worse than others."

The bottle hummed from inside the bag at John's feet. He decided to change tack.

"How've you been otherwise? I hear the bank's fit to move on you."

"So they tell me. Same as it ever was, sonsabitches want a stone to bleed."

"I'm sorry to hear that, Wilson, I truly am."

"I appreciate it."

"How bad is it?"

"Not as bad as it might be, worse than I'd want it. There's many worse off. The wolf's not at the door just yet but he sure

25

as shit is in the yard." He gave a sour grin, a resigned lift of his eyebrows. "They say the Devil dances in an empty pocket."

John's hand played about the clasp on his bag. The bottle inside felt like a leap in another direction, like a kind of reliquary, inside an absurd relic of some sort; *bane to the blighted*. For a moment he hesitated, cursing his prevarication. If it was a mistake, it was of a lesser type than feeding more pills to the bottomless pit of Wilson's hypochondria.

"You ever hear of bloodroot, Wilson?"

It was to be found, so the pamphlet told him, growing wild in woodland underbrush or shrubbery, near lakeshores or brooks; bloodroot shunned open spaces, preferring instead to hide in copses or forests.

Parking on Kimball Corner, he'd left the car and headed on foot beyond the dense tree line. Stumbling, tripped by tree roots and kicking up earth, feeling foolish yet strangely boyish and excited, he'd scanned the woods for the irregular palmate leaves with their crenelated lobes he'd noted in diagrams, searching the chaos of green for a particular geometry; on finally finding a specimen he'd laughed out loud. Crouching, he'd carefully pulled at the stalk, gently easing it from the earth, revealing the brownish knuckle of its rhizome.

Once at home, closely following directions, he'd added the suggested quantity of the reddish sap to a small bottle of distilled water and as directed *shaken it vigorously, some thirty times or more*.

This process is known as Succussion and will release and activate the vital energy of the diluted substance. The resulting mixture, the pamphlet informed him, *is known as the First Potency*. He then poured away all but a few drops of the liquid as instructed, *three drops is sufficient*, before refilling the bottle with more distilled water until half full and again shaking the contents. This was the Second Potency. He repeated the process, pouring away, leaving only three drops, refilling, again and again until the dilution, or "Potentization", was known as the Sixth Potency. He held the bottle up to the sunlight; clear, to all intents and purposes simply a bottle of distilled water, not a whisper of the sap's color remaining.

"Ridiculous," he'd said to himself but placed the bottle in his bag nonetheless.

John had first set foot on Naples soil February 11, 1926. The coldest day he'd ever known; he was to know colder days still in the years to come, but for a city dweller the sheer depth of the Naples winter came as if a slap to the face.

The question *Why Maine?* leveled at him by friends and family, chiefly his father, upon his decision to quit the city, was as unanswerable as it was unfair.

His father had begun to stack the bricks of John's future life when he was still in school; a Pennsylvanian doctor, well married, acquaintances in high places, a father of sons. A hand in local affairs, a large house and rich sons to carry forward the Bischoffberger name like some totemic, gauche heirloom. His father disagreed with his going to war, claimed even at the last moment to be able to extricate him from it should he abjure; he had further disagreed with John's "retreating", as he called it, to "some rural backwater to cure the sordid, gynecological minutiae of farmer's wives".

But certain things had borne down on John in the years since his return from the war, and the countryside felt just about right, felt like the ability to take a deep breath again. From Pittsburgh, he'd upped sticks to Westbrook, Maine. Following a certain period of cajoling from Ansel Morton, a County Deputy, poultry farmer and band leader from Edes Falls, John had then moved north from Westbrook to Naples. When Morton had brought the offer John had hesitated, before realizing that perhaps a certain expanse, a wildness, was just what he needed.

It felt like stepping out of a warm house into some fantastic wilderness. Maine in the summer was one thing but Maine in winter he found truly arresting; at once incredibly beautiful and yet somewhat despairing. Cut off, hard edged. It was true they had streets as Pittsburgh had streets, though a little smaller in scale, they had stores and they had houses; these were no country hicks or rural savages, whatever his father may have thought. Naples was picturesque, popular with vacationers, and yet the yawning field of white that Cumberland County became as the nights grew longer made it feel isolated

27

and cruel, as if somehow the cold was a plague visited exclusively on Maine, while perhaps across the state line temperatures soared, outsiders laughing, blithe and balmy, at the poor bucolic Mainers and their biting seasonal arctic. In winter at least Mainers' ire towards those "from away" seemed some way towards understandable.

As the narrow-gauge had plunged deeper into the snow-laden woods, Ansel Morton had grinned at the younger man sat across from him, at his wide eyes.

"Beautiful aint she?" he'd said, laughing quietly to himself. John had agreed wordlessly with a nod. "You'll grow to love her as we do, you'll see." The older man had winked, as if disbelieving the nod. "Naples needs you, Doc, and I'm guessin just by looking at you, maybe you need her too." John had merely smiled, wondered at his withdrawal from the world, its conflicts, its events, its hue and cry; he fought not to think of the word *retreat*, the word *hiding*.

He'd been told that as Medical Examiner cataloguing those deceased that came by that state under unusual or curious circumstance fell under his purview, as well as performing postmortem examinations on the same; "maintaining death records and the like" Morton had said. He was asked if he typed, and he'd replied in the affirmative, adding that he even had his own machine on which to do so, at which Morton had grinned and nodded in a way that seemed to say *but of course you do*.

They'd been met in Bridgton by Ray Crossman and Skipper Bartlett, all hats, scarves, smiles and steaming breath. Children were throwing snowballs in the fading light, their shrieks of hysteria and the soft *crump* of the snowballs as they hit throwing the immense country silence into sharp relief. But then it wasn't silence, not really, it was something else. The cold had gripped him as he'd stepped down from the train and he'd had the queer sensation that the sky was in fact bigger there. The three men had shaken mittened hands and as if to cement John's feeling of otherworldliness, climbed into a large horse-drawn sleigh for the nine-mile journey to Naples. The trees had swallowed the sleigh and soon after, the night had swallowed the trees.

John made sure that Wilson saw him carefully draw the bloodroot dilution into the pipette, made sure he pulled an appropriately somber and clinical expression as he did so, as if the solution was of such vehement potency that too much might well blow the patient's head clean off. He had Wilson tip back his head and curl his tongue to the roof of his mouth, so that he could drip in the ten or so drops, counting each one under his breath as it fell.

Not for the last time that day he imagined himself diluted like the bloodroot, diluted within the sprawl of Cumberland County, a Pennsylvanian needle in a New England haystack, prescribed to the indigenous population one drop at a time; each drop perhaps drawing him further into the community, towards some kind of belonging, or cure. Perhaps Joseph Allen and he both were indeed like the bloodroot, he thought as he dripped: drowned, outnumbered; the germ of something *other*, swimming in a lake of those who belonged. Perhaps this explained John's feelings toward the old man.

By the time John left him, Wilson was already claiming that the pain had eased, loudly extolling the virtues of this new tincture of John's as "nothin short of a miracle".

The old woman sits on a small rise and watches the little girl between a thin stand of pitch pines: walking aimlessly through the woods, staring up at the treetops, swinging her arms, kicking twigs. For a few moments she dances, oblivious and unguarded. The old woman wonders whether she was ever that young, that cut loose from things of weight and worry. She fancies the woods at that moment as some kind of mirror, reaching back to a reflection of herself as she might have been as a child, if she could but recall. But then impossible was called *impossible* for a reason.

The girl stops, and bending down, picks up something small and pale from the earth. She studies it for a moment, spits on her fingers, cleans it off. It catches the sun.

"What you lookin on me for?" she says suddenly, before glancing up at the old woman.

The old woman starts, surprise not being something she's used to. She sets her jaw tight, wondering at the boldness of youngsters these days. For a moment or two she struggles for an answer.

"Not much else but trees to look on," she replies at last. The girl shrugs and looks about her, as if she hadn't until that moment noticed she was in the woods. She opens a small embroidered bag hung on a loop from her wrist and drops the small pale something inside, pulling the drawstring tight. The old woman leans on a pine trunk, walks her hands up it into a standing position, loudly exhales at the effort it takes to do so. It feels strange to talk to another soul, it's been so long. Seeing folks from a way off is one thing, she thinks, them seeing *her* is another; but speaking to them is a whole rarer kettle of fish. It's easy to lose yourself in the woods, should you feel so inclined. "What you got there? You find a shell out here? A pretty stone?"

"You can't have it. Finders and keepers."

"Don't you worry, stones isn't something I want for. What you doin in the woods by yerself? You lost?"

"Lookin."

"What you looking for?"

"They call it parousia."

"Never heard of it."

The little girl grins to herself, pretending to be distracted by the bag on her wrist.

"I like to collect flowers. Sticks, stones, sometimes shells."

"Paroosha aint like no flower I ever heard of. Platanthera leucophaea maybe, but what you say it was called?"

"You know *every* flower there is?" A note of petulance, a toying with backchat.

"Thought I did. What's your name little girl?"

A ripple of fear across the young face.

"Not sposed to say."

"You're not sposed to say?"

The girl shakes her head, kicks her shoe into the dirt, her eyes never leaving the old woman. She looks about ready to run.

"Well why on this here Earth are you not sposed to say?"

"Cause— Cause when they got your name they gotcha."

The old woman nods slowly.

"Is that so?"

"Swhat they say." The sun moves behind a cloud, an expression of the pause that's grown between them.

"Where you from little girl?"

"Not—"

"You're not supposed to say," a roll of the old woman's eyes, "don't know your face. You aint a Cumberlander are you? New Yorker maybe, lookin at your getup. They aint no Cumberlander kid clothes. Where you from?"

"New York," the girl smiles, "maybe." Her smile holds something wrong in it, which makes the old woman frown, draw back a little.

"You don't need be afraid of me."

"I aint," she snaps back, "why would I be afraid of an *old lady*?"

"You'd be surprised those that are." The old woman takes a step toward the girl, a test of sorts. The girl stands her ground. "Your ma an pa not missin you?"

"Got none."

"Well then how you been gettin by? How you been eatin?"

"Maybe I steal, what you think on that?"

The old woman lets out a short sound of indifference.

"I look like a school mistress to you?"

"Stealing is *wrong*." The girl relishes saying it.

"*Wrong*," repeats the old woman under her breath, as if only to feel the ludicrous shape of the word in her mouth; she steps down from the rise and approaches the girl. "Times is hard and *wrong* fades away." When there's only a few feet between them the girl tightens, a cornered cat.

"You try takin my bag an I'll kill you soon as look at you."

The old woman walks by her, dogged and stooped.

"Then I'd best not try to steal your bag," she says from the side of her mouth, pushing on into the woods.

After a brief to and fro inside of herself, the girl catches the old woman up, walks alongside, throwing three steps for every one of the old woman's. The trees hiss above and around them in a breeze, birds streak their shadows across the dirt ground; nature seems on the move, and they on the move inside it.

"I'll show you what's inside the bag if you want," pipes up the girl eventually.

"Better not, I might get me a mind to steal it, then you'd have to kill me."

The little girl scowls, stops in her tracks, only moments from a petulant stamp of the foot.

"You wanna see or don't you?"

There's an expression on the old woman's face that says she's wasted enough time talking to the child, that she's been distracted and foolish, that she needs to be somewhere else; things to be done. She too stops.

"Show me then *get*," she holds out her large knotted hand, "I'm no more a nurse maid than I am a school mistress."

The little girl opens the bag and tips its contents into the wrinkled palm. A few pebbles, one still damp with spittle, brass cogs and the like from a fob watch, a shell, a polished penny, a large bent nail, a pressed flower brown and rotten with age, and a silver charm in the shape of the letter L. She shakes the bag some more and an upper set of dentures fall into the old woman's hand, their crude pink and white horseshoe polished and grinning in the bright air. The old woman's mouth opens, her jaw working silently awhile before speaking.

"Son of a bitch," she says, before looking hard at the little girl, "what in Hell's name did you do?"

The girl leans forward, mischievous, as if imparting a secret.

"I think you know," she whispers.

Church surrounded him, the cool air and the hot stale bodies forcing a kind of blank meditation in lieu of prayer; but then he supposed they might be the same thing.

The heat had done its best to keep sleep at arm's length the night before, and when, covers thrown, he'd finally slipped fitfully away, he'd dreamed of the old woman on the road. She had been standing, impassive and implacable, in his kitchen, his office, his bedroom, the street outside; a series of banal scenes in which other people moved around her as if she were furniture, or as if she weren't there. He woke early, the room yellow and stifling with sun, with the distinct and impossible impression that he'd dreamed of her before.

Church became an exercise in not allowing its calming air to seduce him into sleep. He concentrated on Reverend Grundy's words, on the shuffling noises about him, the intermittent clearing of throats. The acoustics of the church shaved diction and corners from the reverend's voice, smoothing syllables like pebbles in a creek.

"And Jesus sat over against the treasury, and beheld how the people cast money into the treasury: and many that were rich cast in much."

The same voice had sounded John out as they'd arrived that morning, concerning the performance of *The Prodigal Son* for the Naples Centenary Celebrations next month; did he think he might be interested in joining the company? He did not, though he thought he managed to say so politely. The Reverend's smile told him that the suggestion had been little more than a conversational formality; perhaps the very idea of the doctor joining in to that extent with the celebrations was absurd, improper even; perhaps it had been a joke of sorts.

He looked forward to the next hymn for distraction, to Rosamond's clear high voice as she sang beside him, the combination of the standing and the noise a welcome diversion.

"And there came a certain poor widow, and she threw in two mites, which make a farthing. And he called unto him his disciples, and saith unto them, Verily I say unto you, That this poor widow hath cast more in, than all they which have cast into the treasury: For all they did cast in of their abundance; but she of her want did cast in all that she had, even all her living."

In the end he fell back on a common vice of his while in church. The quiet and the cool forced an introspection, forced his mind to meander, toying with his dream, with homeopathy, with Joseph Allen, with the roadster, but in time losing a hold on the mundane and forcing him, as always, back to Europe. His hands held each other still in his lap. He heard the Reverend say the words *Let us pray*.

A young man lain on a cold smear of muddy ground; France, had it been Meuse? Memory had let that go, holding on instead to sordid detail: arms thrown outward, legs absurdly crossed at the ankle, his mousy hair, his shaving rash, the contemplative set of his eyes, their metronomic blinking. His breathing a jagged panting.

In early incarnations of the memory John had held the man's hand, but recently he could no longer be sure of this detail's accuracy, the gesture seeming like too much of a romantic imposition on something as blunt and as vulgar as the war.

Army greens against such pale skin, the missing piece of his head, sheared diagonally, nipping off the top of his right ear, the eyebrow gone altogether; his mouth slack and trying to vocalize. He'd looked directly at John and forced out the word *can't* then vanished before John's eyes, becoming only crude meat, torn open and utterly without animacy.

John had stood in the freezing rain and asked himself where it was that the young man had gone to, where he might possibly exist at that moment. Sinking to his haunches, he'd stared out over the field to the sparse hedgerow and to the road beyond, seeing not another soul; then the trees and the revolver. The Reverend's voice brought him back, its rounded circles in the air, the word *prodigal*, the word *wasteful*.

"And he said unto him, Son, thou art ever with me, and all that I have is thine. It was meet that we should make merry, and be glad: for this thy brother was dead, and is alive again; and was lost, and is found."

John took a long breath, Meuse dissolving. Ros shifted herself on the pew and they exchanged a look.

They'd had the conversation just once but it had lasted all night. He'd told her he envied her certainty, in fact only a half truth. Eyes tearing, she'd asked what it was he believed in. He'd answered that he didn't know, he'd answered medicine, he'd answered Mother Nature, he'd answered Rosamond Bischoff-berger.

Church held him like a gloved hand, cool, gray and heavy; held him lightly but held him nonetheless. He had the queer sensation of having the rules explained to him of a game he'd long been disqualified from playing.

W ilfred York reaches out over the water, flame-haired and straining for the raft, only the thinnest branch anchoring him to the shore. The other boys watch as he stretches himself above his own reflection, both Wilfreds biting their lower lips, no doubt damning their own meager twelve years and the stunted boyish limbs that refuse to do the job. His fingers brush lightly at the wooden planks but serve only to push the raft further out into the brook.

He curses loudly. The other boys giggle, one suggests the climbing of trees, another pooh sticks, a third that they should go throw stones at his sister and her friends. Wilfred throws the three his best glare.

"But we can't reach it," says the tree climber.

"Can't be no moren up to my chest," says Wilfred. The stone thrower whines that he's hungry. While they squabble the raft continues to skate, slow and frictionless, across the brook's surface and away from them.

Upstream a stretch, unseen among the trees, the old woman turns to the little girl, her face as stone, forefinger near jousting with the girl's nose.

"Now you stay right here like we agreed and don't you go messin around on me. *Right here*, you hear?"

The girl smiles puckishly.

"Here hear," she mimics, "herehearhere."

The old woman slaps the girl hard across the face; the girl swallows a yelp, falling against a tree, holding her cheek. The old woman's hand becomes a finger again.

"What did I say? *What* did I say? Don't play your fool games with me. You think I'm afraid of you? I don't care what your name is, you aint nearly too old for a whuppin. *What* did I say?"

The girl's eyes seethe, her swollen mouth all teeth and bitter spittle, all but snarling.

"I'll kill you," she says quietly.

"What do you want, little girl?"

A hardness settles on miniature features.

"*To burn the world down*," she spits. There is a moment before she thaws, adding, "All I want is to watch. Herehear's *fine*."

The old woman holds the girl's gaze a moment longer, as if to fasten her to the spot, then turns and makes for the brook.

Wilfred spits, steels himself, then marches in, shoes and all; the warm water soon swallows his knees, then his waist. The shock of the cold at the bottom, more biting the further in he wades, catches the breath in his throat. It seems impossible that the sun hasn't been able to reach that deep. Water creeps to his shoulders and he's dancing tiptoe across the brook bed, ankles frozen where they leave his shoes. He is gripped with the sudden need to pee.

The stone thrower throws a stone that narrowly misses him, splashing his face. The boys try to hide their laughter. Wilfred pirouettes awkwardly, the brook lapping at his chin, his voice strained through a tight jaw.

"Do— do that again an— an you'll re—" a breath, "gret it." A mouth of brook water makes him choke for a moment, cough.

Lifting up the skirt of her dress the old woman steps, with barely a ripple, into the water. Each considered footstep sees her deeper and deeper until, shoulders submerged, face austere and resolute, she dips her head and is gone, now little more than a gray shape; the sun reflecting off the surface, a trick of the light, perhaps the side of a striped bass. The little girl watches avidly from behind her tree, absentmindedly tonguing her bloodied lip.

The old woman's thin arms propel her along the dimness of the brook bed, hands grasping at rocks, claws in the mud, her white hair alive. That torn, empty kettle sound; the swirl of sediment, the reaching weeds. Above her, two small shoes kicking at the nothing. Anchoring her bare feet among a tangle of roots, the old woman reaches up into the warmer water, takes a firm hold on the boy's trouser cuffs and pulls. Wilfred stiffens, sliding down through the silvered surface, his neck arching to steal a last instant in the world before he goes under.

His young face is screwed into a fist, nostrils spewing bubbles as they fill. His arms are paddling uselessly, hands spread, eyes shut tight. His legs kick out, shoes impacting on her shoulders, her cheek, her chin, and for a moment he breaks free, piercing the surface; she can hear his raw intake of breath, dulled by the weight of the water, his exclamation, his panic. The other boys' voices call out from another world. She takes hold anew and draws him under again. He kicks, but weaker now, robbed of something, diluted. The old woman grabs his waist and pulls him to her, down into the cold, like a mother quelling an unnecessary tantrum. He's making a high, dulled screaming sound from deep inside his body. He tears uselessly at her grip, which only tightens. His fingers feel hers; a second of identification and a kind of understanding. His eyes open and he and the old woman look at one another. The old woman does not smile. His mouth opens, a scream that doesn't quite fulfill its own criteria, rendered almost comical because of this, and the remaining air tumbles out of him towards the surface. She feels his body lose buoyancy as his lungs fill, his features distorting with the pain of it; a warm stream of urine dissipates against her thigh. The old woman embraces him, holding him tightly for as long as is necessary.

John looked down at the freckled boy; the freckled boy for his part seemed to look back, albeit without seeing. The brook whispered at the bank, slow moving, flashing in the sun, faceless, seeming to deny its complicity in the event. He crouched beside the body, making his notes.

Behind a tree stood Will Walker, looking at his shoes, unable to stand still; it was clear that he wanted to be anywhere but where he stood.

"You okay, Will?"

"I'm fine, Bisch, I'm okay." There was a weariness in his answer that John had heard before. Death did strange things, particularly when the young were concerned, bled something out of you that it took time to replace, or to ignore the loss of. It had been a profound disappointment when, years ago, John had learned that far from being unswayed by such things, doctors merely learned how to swallow them, perhaps to mend a little quicker. John didn't recognize the boy, in all likelihood had never treated him, and for that at least he was grateful.

"You say you knew the boy?"

"I did. Known the Yorks some fifteen year. Terrible thing." A breathlessness in him.

"You can wait up with the deputy you know, Will."

"I know it. Just don't seem right. Leavin him."

"He'll be fine with me, Will. Elmer's gonna want to talk to you anyway." Will took a breath, narrowed his eyes. "Honest, Will, you go on. He'll be fine. I promise." Will gave a humorless smile of thanks.

"Well if you think I should, Bisch. I'll be honest I don't feel real good."

Up through the trees by the road, three boys were staring through the deputy as he asked them questions; shivering, distracted and bloodshot, their attention instead focused on the slivers they could still see through the trees of the pale boy on the bank.

Alone again, John finished his notes and stood, kicking out

his stiffened knees. He looked at the boy's body one last time, lips pursed, nodding slowly, though for what purpose he couldn't have said.

He thought back on his words to Cora Gottam: *The earth does what it wants.* He wasted a moment wondering on the truth of this.

Some two hundred or so yards away, through the trees on the opposite bank, a small figure moved and for a brief moment John imagined it to be the boy, Wilfred York, having become somehow separated from his body, now making his way back to tell the doctor he was sorry for the trouble but it was fine, he'd found his way and could be alive again; just slip back into place and everything would go on as before. John blinked.

It was a little girl, skipping, dirty and frayed looking, grimy legs, hair uncombed straw. Another figure. The old woman from the Portland Road, walking beside the girl, both dissolving gradually into the woods. They made a strange family, he thought, perhaps forged merely of a shared poverty, perhaps blood. Did the old woman glance back at him? He couldn't be sure. As the pair finally vanished, he caught a glimpse of the old woman taking the little girl's hand, or perhaps vice versa. It was a gesture that should have been touching but for some reason he saw it as anything but. He wondered if one were leading the other, or whether in fact they were merely holding hands so as not to be alone. Joined in this way, they disappeared between the trunks.

A breeze picked up over the brook, the sun slid behind a cloud, casting shapes onto the earth. Up by the road, one of the boys was crying. At John's feet, Wilfred York was still as dead as anyone had ever been.

3

Cumberland   ss.

I certify that I was notified on the 30 day of July   A. D. 19 34

at 2 h. and 45 m. in the after noon by Sheriffs Department

of Bridgton Me   of the finding of the dead body of

Wilfred Chas York   of Bridgton

supposed to have come to h__ is death by violence or unlawful act; that I forthwith repaired to the place

where said body lies and took charge of the same, and before said body is removed make, or cause to be made,

this written description of the location and position of said body, viz:

    The body was that of a boy about four feet six inches tall, weighing 72 pounds, having light red hair and blue eyes. He was dressed in blue overalls and blue shirt. The body was viewed on the shore of Willet Brook, about a ¼ of a mile below railway station at Bridgton, Maine.

    There was slight cyanosis of ears and extremities, rigor mortis was just setting in.

    Witnesses stated that, not knowing the water was quite deep at this point, he attempted to wade into brook to recover a raft which had drifted out from shore. He sank to bottom, came to surface once, then sank again. Body was recovered by William Walker of Bridgton.

    Cause of death: Drowning, accidental.

8/20/34

               Jhn M Bischoffberger M. D.
                     Medical Examiner

Medical Examiner.

Date   19

II

Any rock will tell you that a hundred years is no time at all. Goddamn blink. Time will make a fool of every one of us. You just wait. Meanwhile we try an paint every era with our version of things, *our* story.

Every people has its own way of telling it. Time. Seems to me nowadays we measure it in men, in presidents. We say Washington this, Jackson that, Lincoln the other. The Indians have their own way of telling it.

The Abenaki cut history into three slices. Durin what they call the Ancient Age, men was as animals, no difference between em. You might often be tempted to think that way today, the way some carry on; but that's hardly fair on the animals now is it?

Next they have the Golden Age. In this Golden Age they tell that men had strayed a little further from the beasts, praps standin on two legs now, praps talkin, I don't rightly know the ins and outs. What I do know is the Abenaki have a god name of Gluskab, who durin this time they say taught them to hunt, to build shelters, use tools, whathaveyou. Gluskab's appearance heralded the Golden Age and his departure ended it, just like that. They say one day he'll return and bring with him a new Golden Age. That sound familiar to you?

The name Gluskab means "man who came from nothin", or, if you wanna get literal about it, "man created outta speech". That sure as shit sounds familiar to me. How many men you know ride on their words alone? How many stories color your view of another person? If I've heard that story of the shabby godless man at the draw bridge one time, I've heard it a million. Story made me infamous in this town. Raised eyebrows, haughty men andcluckin hen women. To this day no one's asked me if it's true and so I spose it don't much matter. Lack of church in a person has got to be seen as tantamount to felony.

Seems like more and more a man is what he says, or what is said about him, and not what he is, not what he does. Everybody's sellin you somethin and I for one aint in the market.

A depression it seems aint no depression for blowhards and hucksters, it's an opportunity. Opportunity to lie to those that are sick of hearin the truth.

In the Abenaki's third age, what they call the Present Age, man is seen as totally different from animal. Ravens and writing desks and never the twain. Sounds like this Present Age kicks in and man gets too big for his britches. Above his station. You ask me this is as good a history lesson as any they teach in school.

You ever see a coyote with a fob watch? You think that beautiful view you love so loves you back? We're less than ants. We're fleas. We're fleas on the *backs* of fleas. I seen men lose their minds in these woods, get swallowed up. It's a matter of realizin that we're outnumbered by the trees, by everythin that crawls or grows and slithers out there. A man thinks too much of hisself, such a realization can hit him pretty hard.

History is the history of universal indifference. The man said those as can't remember the past are doomed to repeat it. Live your life dammit. Take a walk. Work at what pleases you. Read a damn book. Keep yer britches where they fit.

Fleas on fleas.

Naples, Otisfield, Bridgton; Maine

August, October, December, 1934

The thin man stumbles shoeless, his filthy feet a confusion of knots, fabric wrapped around them and around; here and there the burgundy brown of dried blood. His sparrow legs step with difficulty over tree roots, all knees and tendons, wending their way between the trees.

He cuts a strange and fragile figure, at once luminously pale, sooty and emaciated; resembling little more than an arrangement of spent matches. He is perhaps in his thirties, though walks as if worn down by years too numerous to reckon. Each movement has its own particular vibrato, papery and unsound.

He walks seemingly without destination, though tenaciously, as if lost but unwilling to admit the fact. Somewhere to go but not quite sure where that somewhere might be. He tells himself he'll know when he gets there.

His mouth hangs open as he walks, face pinched by exhaustion, pained and breathless. He is all but naked, what look like the rag remains of some kind of long underwear hanging about his waist, his narrow chest bare and greasy, ribs described in shades of dirt.

About his shoulders he holds a blanket stolen from a clothesline, gripped tightly by hands also bandaged, also perhaps once bloodied; his sunken face is bearded unevenly, forehead traced with scratches, perhaps from a fall. Lice pepper his limbs, gambol and hop from follicle to follicle, dipping their mouthparts from time to time into the thin gruel of his bloodstream, hiding in the warmth of a crook, a nest of hairs, or a fold of the blanket; along for the ride. His skin sings with a maddening, falsetto itch.

The thin man's eyes speak of past kindnesses and yet everything else about him shouts of misfortune heaped upon misfortune, of hunger and of destitution, throwing any benevolence that remains in his eyes into sharp relief.

By his count he's been walking for some five or so months, fevered and delirious for much of the time, perhaps from sickness, perhaps hunger. Walking and falling, hiding from the roads, stealing food where he can, slipping in and out of sleep, even as he walks. He drifts in and out of awareness, the forest passing him in snapshots; here, then elsewhere, hungry then dreaming, wanting to lie down but knowing that to do so would be to never get up again.

The trees, while shading him, otherwise seem to serve only as obstacles, forcing a circuitous path where a straight one would have been so much easier, making every two steps four. Zigzagging, the thin man pushes up a small hill and stops, breathing wearily.

Row on row of trees hiss at him, uninterested, malignant even; *a strange kind of company to keep*, he thinks.

Somewhere a songbird calls and is answered some mile or more away. Everywhere photosynthesis, perpetual motion; everywhere tiny bodies running, fighting, feeding. The sun lances down at him through the leafy canopy. He blinks and presses on, nowhere to go, no time to waste in getting there.

All in attendance agreed that the celebrations had been a triumph. An unprecedented tens of thousands visited during the three days, those from near and far, expatriates and tourists alike descending on Naples to mark the passing of its first hundred years. Some claimed that as many as 1700 cars had been counted parked here and there about the town. In the face of the shadow that remained over the country, this "Great Depression" so dubbed by the president, it seemed a triumph peculiarly and undeniably human, and the town was intoxicated with it.

There were boat races, swimming matches, baseball and polo games; lake and field alike rang to the cheers of spectators. The Fifth Infantry Band played and hymns were sung. In cooperation with the Army Air Base of Boston, faux air battles were staged in the early evening sky, much to the delight of upturned faces. There were riding exhibitions, a Century Of Progress parade, fiercely fought bouts of tug-of-war; with great pomp and ceremony the church was rededicated.

The centenary drawing so many together, accident and mishap ran amok and John was kept busy. Old man Treadwell fell among the crowd and was treated for minor cuts and bruises; the youngest of the Leavitt boys was vomiting and fevered, something he ate from a roadside stand his mother said; Miss Louisa Jackson, 71, became unaccountably hysterical on her way to the festivities and required sedation.

To John it felt a little like the town was being squeezed, the sight of so many cars alone startling, the multitudes of wishful sunhats and parasols set aglow by the August light conjuring unwanted feelings of invasion or trespass. Something in the air was taut, excitable; a sense of tenterhooks, the streets overcrowded with smiles.

Just the act of weaving his way along the busy sidewalks John found exhausting and infuriating; Ros laughed that he was finally becoming the spleeny old curmudgeon he'd always accused his father of being. He'd become accustomed to his wilderness, he realized, protective of it even; a recognition of belonging he used to temper his discomfort.

Friday had been an explosion of physicality and of youth, a day of games and pennants, of grass stains and upraised voices; the bleachers rang with it and the Lake House grounds vibrated in the yellow light with a kind of nervous exuberance. There was something of *tomorrow* about the day, of looking forward, and John found himself caught up in it, cheering himself almost hoarse when, at baseball, locals Morton's Pavilion beat Bridgton Pequawket 5 to 4.

Saturday morning saw the Mainers taking to the water, in boats and in bathing suits, plowing up the silvered lake, furrows echoing soundlessly outwards, erasing themselves; bodies dripping wet on the shore, beaming, holding trophies. If John thought at all of Wilfred York pulled from the grip of Willet Brook, then it was briefly, a moment soon swept away in the crowd's enthusiasm, in the day's benign, perhaps even reciprocal, interaction with the waters. Saturday afternoon saw the parade, followed by the first of the recitations and performances.

Postmaster Loton Pitts had given a rousing, if timorous, rendition of his poem written for the celebrations, and it was this that had stayed with John beyond the day's excitements. Broad-faced and balding, Pitts had stood before the crowd, the typewritten sheets shaking in his hand as he read, his breaths often ending before the line, forcing a hurried intake, cutting the poem into anxious snatches.

"New England's blood is in the veins of this New England Town. A stalwart sense of pride runs concourse through her heart. And underneath it all, is a soul of sweet humility." Heads had nodded, people had smiled. Loton had cleared his throat and continued. "God-given gifts of Nature's best make beautiful her being. Her hills and lakes; her woods cathedralled here and there gainst the sky, are frescoes done in prayer."

"That's right," someone sitting behind John had said under their breath, a smile in the way they said it.

"Beautiful," came another.

"Our Native Mother calls us back today. And we pay tribute to her comely years, and braid within her golden hair the laurels that are hers. Some could not come to be with her, understands, and there are some – her sons who shall not come – the ones she gave to war. And though she has a Spartan heart – her soul cries out for peace – she cannot understand the reason why her children had to die. Why war must be, or what it's all about."

Later, as the Boston airplanes wheeled above the town, buoyed on the soft *oohs* and *ahhs* from below, all engine purr and firecracker reports, lest his mind turn to bitter memory, John had made his excuses and returned home early.

On the Sunday, Mary G. Perley, 76, collapsed on the porch of Gus Bove's Spa & Luncheonette, out on the causeway; John received the call just as he and Ros were leaving for the rededication. He told her he'd see her there, and if not then, he'd be sure to make the History and Fellowship service that afternoon. Ros kissed him gently and told him to just make sure he saw to old Mary.

"Who'd be married to a doctor?" she asked.

"Only the lucky few," he replied, and she was gone, out into the bright day.

He found Mary sat on the boards by the Spa entrance, surrounded by a gaggle of concerned expressions, one of which was offering her a glass of ice water which she waved irritably away. Gray, weary but well kept, Mary wore her Sunday Best, hiding frailty and embarrassment behind a thin, lacy costume of dignity. As John stepped onto the porch she fixed him with a vinegar stare.

"Told me they'd called *you*."

"And they told *me* you'd collapsed, Mary."

"Time was doctors called me Miss Perley."

"What happened, *Miss Perley?*"

"Felt kinda feathery is all. Headache. Had to lie down, nothin else for it."

"Did you hit your head?"

"Told you I lay down, Doctor, didn't *fall*."

"Who was with you?"

"Don't need no keeper."

"I saw it," piped a voice in the crowd, Dora Welch, wife

to Raymond's Deputy Welch, pushing herself forward, finger raised as if in school. John threw a nod.

"Dora. Did Miss Perley lose consciousness at all?"

"Don't believe so, Bisch, went down complainin, hasn't stopped since." Good-natured laughter rippled around the concerned expressions. Mary shuffled uncomfortably, smoothed her dress over her knees, no longer the center of things.

"Have you drank much today, Miss Perley?"

"Cup of coffee. You gonna pronounce me deceased Doctor I'd sooner you did it quick, I aim to be at the evening service tonight. I'm not gonna make that, I'd sooner you'd just roll me on into the lake now and have done."

"If it's all the same to you we'll throw you in Brandy Pond another day, Mary— *Miss Perley*. I believe what's wrong with you is a little dehydration is all."

John crouched beside her, measuring the slow drub of her pulse by his wristwatch. She eyed him suspiciously.

"Hear you gave Wilson Chaplin a magic potion."

"I believe you know as well as I do that there isn't any such thing."

"Know nothin of the kind. Says it worked wonders." She pursed her lips. "So, gypsy now is it?" He smiled away the slight.

Wanting to move her out of the sun, he asked her could she stand.

"Since before I was one year old. Don't plan on spending my life on the damn causeway, so I guess I'd better move." More hands than were strictly required helped Mary to her feet and then into a chair in the shade. She grudgingly accepted the ice water.

Sumner Newcombe's ice truck passed by, the peeling legend on the side proclaiming *Come Summer, Come Sumner*. The truck pulled in to the back of the luncheonette and a convoy of four cars chugging eagerly behind were forced to slow. Horns sang out, hand gestures and remonstrations. Folks from *away*. John exhaled, shook his head.

"You ever seen Naples so busy, Mary?"

"No, sir, I have not."

52

"Better visitors than vagrants," said a woman behind them. A general murmur of agreement from the crowd.

"Well. Times is tough," said another voice, this time a man's. Dora said Gus had told her that only the day before he'd caught two itinerants, a woman and child, out back of the luncheonette, eating straight from the garbage cans like a couple of raccoons. A smattering of sighs and shaken heads. Something quickened in John.

"A little *girl?*" he asked.

"Child was all he said."

"An old woman?"

"A woman. Don't know about old. I can ask Gus for you if you like." John waved away the suggestion. "You missin someone, Bisch?"

"No, I—" John had little idea how to finish the sentence, stumbled over himself for a second or two before adding, "a pair of vagrants I saw a while back," and finishing with, "Sad times when a child eats out of a garbage can." The man who'd spoken before shook his head, adjusted his hat.

"Seems we're seein more folks on the roads every week. Beggars on the streets. There's a bunch of fellas they say livin rough in the woods over Convene way. Like the city was picked up and shaken." Another murmur of agreement. The scene had taken on the feel of an ad hoc town meeting.

"Depression's all over. What makes some folks think that the answer is *here?*" Her constitution revived, Mary was indignant.

"New Deal my eye," said another voice.

Dora said it put her in mind of that monkey picture, asked had John seen the King Kong? He said he had. She said it was like these people were fleeing the monster, which gave John the disquieting mental image of a tide of ragged, hungry cityfolk sweeping northwards into the trees; something monstrous clawing through the woods behind them. Conversation bloomed around him, the concerned expressions finally finding their voices, focus shifting about the circle.

"People is turnin to animals."

"Animals."

"Listen to you. *Animals.* A chipmunk ever pick your pocket, Phyllis?"

"Lock your doors is all I'm sayin, Albert. Hungry people will do all kinds."

"The Devil dances in an empty pocket."

"Well they won't stand for it."

"Who won't stand fer what?"

"Gunned that Dillinger down didn they?"

"These folks is just poor, they aint about to rob no banks."

"Bonnie and Clyde too. Won't stand for it."

"That poor girl. Aint right shootin a woman, I don't think they oughta be shootin a woman."

"Poor girl my eye."

"Well, our Lord said it. For ye have the poor with you always, and whensoever ye will, ye may do them good. But me ye have not always."

John let himself drift, his fingers playing about his belt loops, as he gazed out over the road to where the causeway joined once again with the mainland, realizing that the place where he stood, the space under his feet for who knew how far down, had once been only water.

◆

All engaged in Reverend Grundy's staging of *The Prodigal Son* put in a good showing. In particular Philip Cole as the prodigal, it was agreed, proved most arresting in the role. The prodigal's heartfelt contrition had been deftly expressed, it was said, the final scene of forgiveness and redemption between father and son prompting not a few tears from those assembled.

The hall had rung with ovation, some even standing, and John had applauded too, despite his barely confronted misgivings concerning the parable, thoughts of his own father, of whether John himself would ever go home, wherever that might be.

That night Ros seemed preoccupied as she prepared for bed. Something in the over-deliberate way she coiled her special occasion pearls on the dresser, or folded her best green patterned day dress; shoes meticulously parallel by the chair.

He watched her, handsome in her pensiveness, faraway in her thoughts, thought perhaps that he knew what she was thinking.

They talked around the evening's performance as they both undressed, neither one straying into the biblical, instead expressing themselves in vague if heartfelt pleasantries concerning the celebrations, how spectacular the air battles had been, how glorious the parade had looked, what a beautiful three days the town had enjoyed.

John, somewhat relieved at the ending of festivities, could almost feel visitors draining out of the town, the image of a wave retreating across a beach, back out to sea. The ability to take a deep breath once more.

"Thought this town would never shrink back," he joked as he climbed into bed, and Ros couldn't suppress a smile at his only partly feigned sense of umbrage. Still her eyes remained a little sad, an echo of her tears at *The Prodigal Son*. She reached out and held his hand.

"I guess it'll find you if and when it finds you," she said quietly, "I love you, Bisch."

"I love *you*," he whispered, leaning gently on the word, hoping to erase any differences between them. They kissed slowly and he felt her hand on his cheek; separating, they stared at one another for a time.

He placed his hand gently on the small rise of her belly, and they both looked down at it. A moment of realization or understanding came and went. Something about the empty box room. No dollhouse, no baseball in the yard and no child to play with either. As if his hand had acted autonomously, John frowned, gave an almost invisible shake of his head, something towards an apology, and moved the hand slowly down between her legs, catching her breath in her throat, drawing them magnetically back into a kiss.

♦

Oftentimes John's dreams were such that they would dissolve upon waking, stealing back into his thoughts in sudden tableaux throughout the day, pallid, insubstantial things, somehow akin to hearing his name called from faraway. Remembered dreams seemed to inhabit a place outside of the natural span of time, neither long ago nor present, but somehow *other*, recollection wandering from the dream's incidence, leaving him unsure as to when the dream occurred, prompting foolish thoughts of the prophetic. On the last night of the festivities, however, he dreamed sharply and with a depth that fixed itself in time and survived the morning.

Mary Perley lay prone on the bank of Willet Brook, peeled open, chest to groin. Streamers of pale offal were hanging from out of the tear-shaped hole; each bloodless feeler shook as she shook. Mary's hands crawled over her face, obscuring it, her muffled voice repeating the word *no*, over and over, her feet wrangling anxiously with each other. A single shoe was kicked off, legs crossed at the ankle.

A sturdy dining table stood by the body, accompanied by two chairs. Sat at the table were the old woman and the little straw-haired girl, each holding a knife and fork, each gazing hungrily down at what was left of poor Mary, shivering in the dirt.

Joseph Allen was knelt beside her, enthusiastically delving into her body cavity, pulling anemic morsel after anemic morsel from out of her, shirtsleeves rolled, greasy to the elbow, laughing and laughing and laughing.

Though the sky remained as night, the whole impossible scene was lit by a fevered, jaundiced sun, a terrible vibration in the air, something immense, black and pitiless.

The thin man breaks the tree line and stands stock still on the threshold. Reaching out before him is a shorn hayfield, blonde, wide and open, patterned by the teeth of a buck rake, like the nap of a luxurious carpet left to ruin. The clement weather is on the turn, he can smell it. The hay has already been cut. He scratches at his head, then at an armpit, his tiny passengers making merry on him. In the distance a pasture, the wasted shape of a solitary cow. A feeling of being lost comes and goes, of impermanence.

The tree line curves around the hayfield up a slow rise to a narrow lane, where rests a dusty farmhouse, roof tiles missing, one window blinded. On the farmhouse's steps sits a rangy figure in browning denims and a raggedy straw hat. The thin man stares at the figure for a time, wondering what to do next.

Across the way Sydney H. Kemp sits on the step and regards the queer character who has just stepped out of the woods. The man, who appears to be wearing very little at all, begins to make his way across the field. A moment of recognition sparks in Sydney, perhaps merely the similarity in their physiques, their angularity, but perhaps the recognition is of something else.

Sydney's clothes hang on him, heavy bags under his eyes, salt and pepper mustache overgrown; the stranger is similarly disheveled, though more comprehensively so. Sydney's mother, so long dead, would have said that the stranger looked like he'd been *dragged a mile through Hell's own backyard.* Sydney stares. The stranger could be him, an echo, or reflection, though quite some way younger and a few more rungs down the ladder. Taller maybe. But doesn't he look like someone?

Sydney doesn't look too closely at the question. Sydney is a man who falls through holes. More and more of late, the holes through which he falls turn things around on him, steal memories, put this there and that somewheres else, confusing or frustrating him, causing his wife to treat him like a child, causing him to shout that she didn't oughta talk to him like he was a simpleton, causing her to weep and him to skulk off to the hay-field and do likewise.

In time the thin man approaches the house and stops just beyond the yard. Sydney looks him square in the eye.

"*You* again?" He spits in the dirt. To the thin man, Sydney looks old and frayed, cornered and aggressive, then all of a sudden his face blanches, perhaps a little frightened. "Beg your pardon, sir," Sydney says, blinking, confused, "thought you was Francis. You aint Francis." There's a distance in the old man, a disconnectedness that the thin man can't help but pity.

"No, Sydney, I'm not Francis."

"You even a Mainer?"

"No, Sydney."

"We ever meet?"

"No."

The open space hisses and chirrups about them; a breath of wind. Sydney studies the thin man's bandaged feet.

"No shoes," he whispers.

"I wonder... might you spare somethin to eat?" says the thin man, "Been walkin a long time." Sydney frowns at the stranger.

"You oughta get yerself some shoes. What with fall comin." He looks down at his own boots. "But I guess we could spare some bread, maybe a little honey. That do?" The thin man smiles and Sydney stands, wincing a touch, and goes into the house, returning with two tough slices of home baked loaf, a scraping of honey on each. The stranger feeds with great relish and Sydney looks away, thinking it probably rude to watch a starving man eat. When he's finished the stranger thanks him, which he nods away as if nothing.

"You wanna sit awhile?"

"Thank you, I should be getting on."

"Well okay, but you're welcome."

"Who is Francis, Sydney?"

"*Francis?*" It's as if he's never heard the name before, then something coalesces in him. "Francis. Son of mine. Or... brother. Died some ten, twenny year or more ago, I believe."

"Sorry to hear that," says the thin man, but Sydney has fallen through another hole, all at once transfixed by a parade of ants traversing the stranger's sorry looking feet.

The thin man suddenly feels a huge burning compassion for the man sat on the step, almost painful in its size, unwieldy, somehow dangerous; a crushing burden. Sydney glances up at him, all at once a little boy.

"If... you see Francis, tell him to come home. I think he's gotten lost somewheres."

"You loved Francis very much." The past tense of the thin man's *loved* muddies Sydney's head.

"Whole lot." He makes a face. "Didn help any."

"But love is all we have, Sydney."

"Aint much else left." He tries a laugh, doesn't quite make it.

"There never was."

"I guess."

The thin man places his dirty hand on Sydney's shoulder. Sydney stares at the ground, but the ants have moved on. Then the thin man speaks quietly, little more than a breath.

"The next time we meet, I will tell you a secret."

Sydney watches the stranger cross the hayfield back the way he came. Alone on the step once more, tumbling through hole after hole, he sings to himself, little more than a tuneless mumble.

"I got shoes, you got shoes, all God's chillun got shoes, when I get to Heabn I'm gonna put on my shoes, I'm gonna walk all over God's Heabn."

There was nothing else for it, the bullet would have to be bitten, the roadster had to be seen to. He had a good few months before the snows, before the car became nothing but an idea, unemployable on the virtual rink the roads became. Season of the snowmobile and of Old Pinkham, the recalcitrant mare he rented annually from Ed Larsen.

Winter in Maine was a regression into some pre-human age, a period when any and all contrivances of man were rendered arrogant and childish; rocks thrown at the moon. Winter there was beautiful but hard. John couldn't say that he wished its appearance any sooner than it came.

Pushing south down the Sebago Road he enjoyed the mild weather while it lasted, the pitch pines inclining this way and that, to his left Sebago Lake a field of dark swells; he drove past the lonely copse of Spider Island and finally onto Richville Road and into the trees.

All at once, and from no specific source, he had the urge to stop the car, to sit on the road and to wait; without questioning why, he did so.

The engine ticked and cooled, John hoped he hadn't made a mistake in stopping, hoped he'd be able to get it started again; still he sat, nothing but a benign expanse, thin clouds skating overhead, the sound of the trees and the silence that wasn't really silence. Everything felt like a breath taken and held.

Perhaps, he thought, he wished to enjoy the emptiness after the crush of the celebrations. Perhaps. He wondered at what the country might have been like a hundred years ago: wilder certainly, but had it been more peaceful?

They said that Naples had been so named due to the shape and geography of its bay mimicking, by some chance of nature, that of the Italian city. Another stolen name for the jigsaw of America. At its birth, he thought America must have appeared as a set of stage flats, unpainted, a country that any man willing to play the part might sculpt into whatever he wanted it to be, whatever he wanted to pretend it was.

He'd been sitting there for some ten or more minutes and nothing had passed him on the road. He wondered if he were perhaps waiting for the old woman to appear, as she had done on the Portland Road, but he didn't think it was that.

Truth was, a moment was waiting for him at Higgins Garage, perhaps in the shop, perhaps by the counter, a tiny pocket of awkward time and a crippling pain in his gut. Elmer Higgins was a good man, but he was waiting to do that thing he always did, and somewhere John was waiting to feel that same pang of loss, that same sense of falling.

He needed to pee and so climbed from his seat and walked around the car to the edge of the woods, part of him sure that all he was really doing was prevaricating. He stood on the tree line and stared between the trunks but saw nothing. No old women, no little girls, nothing but trees. Nothing but everything. He stood and stared and tried his best not to think of terrible, awful things. He would have to step further into the woods to pee, he thought, to preserve his modesty should anyone pass by. It wouldn't do for a doctor to be seen relieving himself by the road like some hobo. Nevertheless he peed where he stood; luckily no one passed as he did so.

As John pulled the roadster off the Ossipee Trail he noticed down the side of the garage Elmer's broad back bent over the dirty skeleton of a Model T. The driveway bell *ding-dinged* as he parked by the gas pumps. A cool breeze blew curls of dust across the trail; the air was changing color, even as he sat there, graying toward fall. A blonde stocky boy no more than fifteen meandered out to the car.

"Fillerup, mister?" John looked at the boy for a little too long before answering.

"Sure. Elmer busy?"

"When aint he? Go ask him." He nodded to where Elmer was hunched over the Ford. Again John hesitated.

Elmer greeted him with an affable smile, wiping his hands on a rag tucked in his overalls.

"Well hey, Bisch."

Then came the moment he'd been avoiding for some three or more months, the salute, and time did that terrible elastic thing it always did, while John stood, smiling absurdly, willing his right hand not to follow suit, standing there and standing there until finally, inevitably, saluting back, smarting memories ricocheting around inside his chest, clinging to his smile like it were a life buoy.

Elmer had been a sergeant, had been at Cantigny and seemed to be able to carry this fact around with him in a way that John envied, a way he never could. To Elmer it seemed the war was a terrible thing but a matter of pride nonetheless; to John the war felt queerly like the death of a parent, something acknowledged but painful to dwell on, almost impossible to look at directly. For a minute or more John's stomach became a cold, heavy thing in him, excruciating, and he rode it out as best he could.

"She still balky?" Elmer threw a nod to the roadster. Over his smile, John knitted his brows, willing away the weight in him.

"*Something's* not right." His words hung for a while between them; they both nodded at nothing for a time.

Making their way to the car he noticed Elmer favoring his left leg, and asked if there was something he could do. Elmer rubbed at his right knee.

"Just my prayer handle flares up some as it gets cold." John felt an unexpected easing in him.

"I happen to have a rhododendron preparation in my bag, could well sort you out."

"The *flower*? Like a perfume?" Elmer was kidding with him, "You mean to court me, Doc?" John felt his smile melt a little into something more authentic.

"You needn't worry, Elmer, it's odorless, tasteless. It's the *essence* of the plant. A kind of folk medicine."

"I heard it all now but ok," Elmer laughed, "now let's see if we can't fix up yer automobile, fore you fix me up."

John laughed, suddenly finding himself ridiculous. He'd been foolish, had built up the inevitable salute into something it wasn't; perhaps the specter of the war was finally losing strength within him, diluted by distance. He surely hoped so.

Driving back north, where the Fort Hill Road became Richville, he passed a sign: *Jobless Men Turn Back. No Jobs Here.*

The hayfield is lit by the moon in gunpowder blues as the thin man breaks the tree line for the second time. The cold is a solid thing, makes the air sharp, and he hugs the blanket tightly about him, his shivering convulsive. His feet, newly wrapped in rags, feel like crudely carved wood, insensate yet screaming. Breath boils out of him.

He crosses the field, hunched yet purposeful, toward the Kemp house, which seems smaller against the night, its windows black.

The screen door opens with a faint moan, the door behind it is unlocked. In the pitch dark hallway, the stilled interior of the house gradually draws itself upon the air: tired furniture, an old coat hung on a nail, a row of gnarled shoes, a framed embroidery which reads *Come home with me, and refresh thyself, and I will give thee a reward.*

He stands awhile, soaking in the relative heat, before carefully climbing the narrow stairs. He walks deliberately to the third door on the right and gently pushes it open.

Sydney is already awake, sat up in bed, covers clutched to his chest, watching the door as it swings into the room. He can't be sure if he expected the door to move, or even how long he's been awake, staring at it. Perhaps he's been willing it to open, perhaps the very act of doing so has caused it to happen. Mae is asleep beside him, a thousand miles away, the soft rhythms of her breathing almost palpable in the dark bedroom. Sydney holds his breath.

A thin man stands in the doorway, wrapped in a blanket, familiar yet alien; his face is an unreadable smudge of shadow. They look at one another for a time. The dark seems to hold everything in its place, fixtures, fittings, the two men; there's an anesthetic quality to the quiet. The improbability of the scene is at once frightening and absurd. Mae's breathing becomes all there is. A word comes to the surface inside Sydney: *intruder*, forces him into action.

He reaches to the foot of the bed, to his discarded pants,

rifles through the pockets and brings out a straight razor, which he opens, holding it out before him, waving it once in the air, a threat.

"You get away now," he says quietly through his teeth, "you get *away*." The bed moves as his wife stirs, turns over, settles. There is the briefest moment when Sydney wonders whether the thin man is in fact being dreamed by his wife, an impossible escapee. The two men stare at one another. Finally the thin man whispers, a sound so low it's barely a sound at all.

"Francis is in Stone's pasture, Sydney. Follow me." He turns and Sydney is alone, holding his razor out to no one. He hears the stairs creak lightly as the intruder descends.

The thin man waits in the freezing hayfield, thinking with some longing of the old coat in the hall, breathing staccato plumes in the dark. A greater part of him wishes to be anywhere else: he would curl up in the crawlspace under the house, in a woodshed, a barn, in a pile of leaves, anywhere away from the raw air; instead duty fixes him to his purpose, and he waits.

Sydney appears in the doorway, stumbling into a pair of boots, buttoning his shirt, breathless; again they look at one another, the thin man breaking the standoff with a nod, turning and making for the pasture.

Somewhere a voice calls out Sydney's name, and then again.

The cow the thin man had glimpsed all those days ago is nowhere to be seen, only the animal's water trough remains, evidence of its dung here and there; again a feeling of being lost, of being present yet elsewhere. He pulls the blanket about him, walks in place and waits as patiently as the bitter cold will allow.

Eventually Sydney enters the pasture at a hobbling run, a hand axe quivering above his head, breathless and unsteady on his feet. He's angry but close to tears, as if he knows more about what's happening than he cares to admit, to say out loud.

"Whadda you want in my house, you cocksucker? A man doesn enter another man's house. I see you here again I'll kill you I swear it."

"Do you recognize me, Sydney?"

"Plant this between your eyes you ever come back."

"*Do you recognize me, Sydney?*" Something in the old man knots this moment to that and the axe falls to his side.

"Sure," he frowns, unsure, "you're that fella."

"We met before. Do you remember?" Sydney looks at the ground, as if searching for something.

"Is this another day? Have I been asleep since then?"

"Do you remember we talked about Francis?"

"*Francis?*" It's unclear whether Sydney is merely pretending to be confused, stalling.

"How is it that I recall Francis and you don't, Sydney?" This sets the older man's words stumbling.

"I don't— I'm not real sure—" The thin man interrupts him, keeps his voice low, enunciates through his teeth.

"Seems to me, Sydney, that Francis was a son of a bitch." Sydney could not have flinched any more if the thin man had reached out and struck him. He sways, dumbfounded.

"You shut your mouth, mister." His voice cracks.

"So you remember him? Francis?" The thin man remains matter-of-fact. Sydney is in free-fall.

"I don't— at least I thought— You didn oughta be callin him no—"

The thin man's smile cuts a sudden snarl in the dark, animal and frightening on his placid features, incongruous, like a tiger in your yard.

"*A son of a bitch*, Sydney, and you're glad he's gone."

"You shut your mouth." He's raised his voice and both hands, in one the axe, the other a fist, a sad, brittle gesture.

"*A son of a Goddamned bitch.*"

"*You're* a sunovabitch, *you* are." Sydney is shouting now. "Sticks and stones you sunovabitch, you shut your damn mouth." His face blanches in the moonlight, pained, greasy, crooked brown teeth bared; he's crying, but it has yet to reach his face. A silence stretches out and no one and nothing moves.

"I told you that the next time we met I would tell you a secret, do you remember?" The thin man's voice is calm again, soothing. Sydney screws his face into a fist, a plaintive moan snaking out of him.

The thin man steps forward and places a dirty hand on Sydney's shoulder. Leaning in, as if for a kiss, he whispers something in the other man's ear.

Sydney falls, right where he stands, simply falls, arms still upraised, his face smacking into the earth with a wet thud.

The thin man kneels and pulls the axe from Sydney's grip. Standing, he turns the blade in his hand, feeling its weight. He stares out over the dark field to the sparse hedgerow and to the house beyond, a light on in the window, seeing not another soul. The cold bites at him.

"The wind bloweth where it listeth," he says to no one, "and thou hearest the sound thereof, but canst not tell whence it cometh, and whither it goeth: so is every one that is born of the Spirit." He takes a breath and holds on to it. His mouth buckles. He's crying, but it has yet to reach his face.

Of the grieving, for John, the worst were those who remained calm. The uncomfortable truth he carried unspoken within him was that death was catastrophe, the worst of all possible outcomes. It was categorical failure. At best it was a quiet submission to the inevitable, at worst tragedy and violence of the most unimaginable kind. In the face of such disaster, solemn acceptance seemed to him almost profane.

Death was a failure to move forward, a definite *period* stamping down on an indefinite problem. No more do-overs. That some appeared to meet it with little more than a shrug turned John's understanding around, confused and frightened him. He saw the lack of charity, the childishness in this stance of his, and it was a view he had long tried to lose; yet still an iota of it clung on, unattractive and unexpressed, a secret burden.

Mae Kemp sat in her small, spotless kitchen, her husband's hat hanging forever useless in the hall, and tightening her jaw, simply nodded as John spoke.

"What with the trouble Sydney had, it's likely to have been his heart, Mae." She reached out and touched his hand briefly.

"Well, I thank you." Sadness was certainly evident, a weariness, but also resignation. "You can only tell me what happened, Bisch, but not the *why*." John was stymied, nearly said *he was an old man, Mae*, a sentence which felt so obvious and absurd in his mouth; but the widow's mind had turned to practicalities. "I'll make suren bury him in his Sunday duds. Maybe have to sell up, if anyone's buyin. Got a sister lives over in Harrison, if she'll have me." John returned the gesture of touching her hand and stood, nodding a yes to an unasked question.

He found the searching party in the narrow hall, shuffling about awkwardly, silently busying themselves with nothing very much. Gerry Scribner had noticed that the hall table had one leg shorter than the others, and had set about trying to fix it. Wesley Brackett and Almon Hirst were scratching their heads, crouched by him, as if their mere proximity might get the job done. John cleared his throat and they stood.

"Thanks for your help, boys."

"How's she holdin up?" asked Almon. John took a breath.

"She's holdin up." He squeezed a tight smile. "How's Mary's rheumatism, Wesley?"

"O she says fine, thank you, Bisch, but she's not one to harp on."

"And she's taking the preparation I gave her?" Wesley seemed unsure. "The Causticum?"

"I believe she is, yes, Doc." Another tight smile, another silence.

"Okay then."

"She's comin over later. Sit with Mae. Thought it'd be best."

"Good idea. Well, I'll see you gentlemen another day then."

"Not too soon I hope." Almon was smiling, which told John that his comment had been a joke. He smiled back but couldn't quite manage a laugh. "I mean to say, not that we don't wish to see you, Bisch, just that—"

John put him out of his misery.

"That's okay, Al, no one wants to get sick."

"Any you boys want a cup of coffee?" came Mae's voice from the kitchen.

"Sure, Mae, but there's no sense you fussin, let me make it. I'll see you, Doc." Gerry shook John's hand and went to help, the others following suit.

Outside in the cold of the morning, John searched the tree line for the old woman, the little girl; searched a few moments and only then realized what he was doing.

Without destination, he drove south, mind meandering, unable to settle.

Finding himself in the area, and purely on a whim, he stopped at the Two Trails store, where Pequawket Trail branched off from the Ossipee Trail, and bought a roadmap of Standish; held it in his hand, felt a little more anchored because of it.

Climbing back into the car, he ruminated on the old woman, on the little girl, imagined briefly these vagrants, these wretches, as some kind of markers to the deceased, hapless auguries, nature drawing them somehow; he thought of cows lying down before the rain, of dogs barking to herald an earthquake, vultures dogging a starving man.

Driving home, he passed just such a ragged, starving man, bundled in a filthy tarp or blanket by the roadside, no doubt begging, only the man's bearded face and wild hair could be seen atop the folds of dirty cloth, as if severed, lain by the roadside as some kind of warning. He thought again of the sign he'd seen, *Jobless Men Turn Back. No Jobs Here*. The man's hollow eyes followed him as he passed.

4

State of Maine.

Cumberland ss.

I certify that I was notified on the *10 th* day *October* A. D. 19 *34*

at *5* h. and *30* m. in the *fore* noon by *Almon Hirst*

of *East Otisfield* of the finding of the dead body of

Sydney H. Kemp of *East Otisfield*

supposed to have come to h *is* death by violence or unlawful act; that I forthwith repaired to the place

where said body lies and took charge of the same, and before said body is removed make, or cause to be made,

this written description of the location and position of said body, viz:

The body was that of a man about six feet tall, weighing
one hundred forty pounds, having grey hair, blue eyes, and grey
mustache. He was dressed in dark greytrousers, blue shirt, and
rubber boots. His pockets contained a razor and a handkerchief.
His face was covered with mud, there was cyanosis under the nails.
Rigor mortis had not set in.

The body was lying face downward in a small depression in
Pratts field midway between the residences of S H. Kemp and
H. M. Stone on Scribner Hill about 250 Yards from the highway.
At this point there was a mixture of mud and water caused by water
draining from a brook nearby. The mouth and nostrils were submerged
in the mud and water but apparently no water had entered the lungs.
There were slight abrasions on each elbow which were probably
sustained when he fell. There were no other marks of external violence.
His arms were outstretched. There was edema of the scrotum, probably
due to heart disease from which he was suffering at the time of his
death.

His wife states that he had been ill for the past three years
with heart disease. He had been quite unstable mentally for the past
year. At 1 A. M., on the day of his death, he arose from his bed
telling his wife he was going out for a few minutes. She heard him at
the barn door, watched him start toward thepasture, and she started
after him but was unable to catch up with him so she returned to the
house and raised an alarm. A searching party was raised which resulted
in the discovery of the body as stated. The body was discovered by
Gerry Scribner, Almon Hirst, and Wesley Brackett of Otisfield. Cause
of death: Acute dilatation of the heart.

John W. Stroudbysburger
Medical Examiner.

Date *10/11* 19 *34*

70

Winter is a silent flood, choking all, hanging heavy on branches and laying in thick sugary drifts across roof and street alike. Roads are crude glass, dirty onyx waiting for unschooled wheels, to send them into ditches, into trees, down embankments and into the woods.

The air itself seems crystalline, sharp and fragile. Certain things have retreated from the cold and into hibernation; certain other things it seems have advanced, taking this as their time.

A soft crunch of snow and the old woman appears among the trunks. She wears an enormous poncho of caribou hide, weathered by more winters than she cares to recall, smothering her slight, knotted frame, making her misshapen and fantastical in the lambent December light. She makes for a bizarre flaw in the perfect white, as if a narrow face rode atop a shambling mound of earth; she traipses willfully among the trees, leaning on them for support, breath steaming.

The little girl runs on ahead, apple-cheeked in the cold, laughing, excited, kicking through rotting leaves hidden under the snow; out of breath but glowing.

"Almost there!" she calls out.

The old woman has always gone her own way. It's in her bones, on this matter she is implacable; she got where she needed to be, and if that *somewhere* was nowhere, or lost, then so be it. The damn fool girl running ahead no more meant that the old woman was following her, than wearing a big hat made the sun rise. While the wind blows them in the same direction, let the girl hold her foolish daydreams of leading the way, she thinks.

They sleep at night wrapped in the caribou hide, on the frigid cushion of snow banks and in the yawn of hollow trees, in dells and under bushes, if they're lucky in an unlocked barn or woodshed, the girl curled like a hot stone beside her, the wind running amok through the dark woods.

For some months now the girl has been disappearing, sneaking away, often early in the morning or late at night, as the old woman dozed. Each time the old woman wakes alone she wonders if the child might never return, which in turn takes her to wondering just why they've formed this lopsided confederacy of theirs. But the girl always reappears, just as the last hope of her doing so is fading. The old woman castigates herself for waiting on this whelp: what is the whelp to her, or for that matter she to the whelp? There's something maternal in it she supposes, but something else besides, a bond less umbilical and more... pragmatic? Instinctive? Whichever it is, these disappearances trouble the old woman, though for no reason she can get her teeth into.

On her vanishings, the little girl is unforthcoming, throwing black looks at any questions, garbled talk of *work* and of the old woman minding her own damn business; mention again of that nonsense word of hers, *paroosha*.

To the old woman the little girl is a queer one, fearsome yet oddly enchanting, like an explosion or a house fire. Oscillating between incandescent fury and coquettish playfulness, tantrums break out across the girl like a smear of hives, and she screams bloody murder to the indifferent trees; other times she's sugar and spice, won't say boo to goose nor gander. But the false teeth had told a different tale.

The old woman saw her kill a cottontail with a rock, just for fun. A baring of teeth masquerading as a smile, bringing the stone down again and again; red fingered and feral. She'd watched the girl throw its torn, still warm body into the lake, laughing, before it could be explained to her that the rabbit was food, that she'd barely eaten for days. The girl had shrugged and said *I'll do what I damn well please*.

The woods open onto the back of a modest cabin, its roof pitched and frosted, its windows steamed. The old woman stands on the tree line and watches the little girl use all her strength to push over a large chopping stump, rolling it through the snow to the cabin wall, before righting it again and climbing onto it to reach the window. Brushing snow from the sill, she works her tiny fingers into the frame and pulls it open, turning, beaming proudly, holding out a large bent nail which the old woman remembers from the girl's bag of keepsakes.

"Stops the window closin," the girl stage-whispers, brandishing the nail, before jamming it into the window frame. The old woman rolls her eyes, outwardly exasperated, yet inside not liking the look of this one bit. The cabin feels like somewhere neither of them should be.

The girl reaches into her bag and pulls out a small glass jar, containing what appears to be milk. One last grin to the old woman and the girl places the jar on the sill, before hoisting herself up and through the window. Her hand reappears, grips the jar and vanishes once again into the cabin's interior.

Minutes pass with only the cold, quiet air, the old woman thinking of leaving but knowing in truth that she'll stay to find out just what the whelp is up to. Birdsong and the shadows of clouds passing overheard.

The jar, now empty, reappears on the sill. The girl climbs back through the window, places the jar and the nail back into her bag with a tiny clink, closes the window and jumps down. She packs a handful of snow onto the sill, then rolls the stump back to where she found it, rubbing out the path it makes with her feet; a meticulousness that suggests she's done this before, perhaps many times.

The woman and the girl look at one another, the latter's smile meeting with the former's pinched disapproval.

"What in hell's name you up to in there?"

"You'll see."

"Where'd you steal that milk from?"

"Who says I *stole*? Maybe I squeezed it outta my little titties, what you think on that?" The girl enjoys her moment of profanity; the old woman snorts.

"Yaint got no titties, ya little fool."

"Maybe I milked me a wild dog. A jackal."

"Aint no jackals hereabouts." The little girl laughs theatrically.

"Well then who says it was milk?" She shrugs. "We'd best *get*. It'll wake up soon." The old woman takes a step backwards, something heavy inside her.

"What'll wake up?" The girl points at the cabin.

"The thing that lives in there."

They push on through the trees, high steps in deep snow, neither one talking of whatever it was they left back at the cabin.
This time the old woman leads the way, joints singing with the
cold, whether wandering or homing toward some unspecified
destination she couldn't rightly say. The little girl skips some
way behind, pitching snowballs at tree trunks and humming
made-up songs.

A shape that doesn't belong makes the old woman stop;
some kind of foreign geometry. Instinctively, the girl too halts,
her humming falling away.

A thin man in a brown suit stands still not two hundred
yards off in the woods. He's unkempt and wild-looking, with
a dirty beard and long hair. He's carrying in his right hand a
small axe and is looking intently at the girl and the old woman.
The old woman peers back, she doesn't like the look of this fellow one bit. Nobody moves.

"Who in hell's that?" the old woman asks under her breath.

"That," says the little girl gleefully, "is parousia." And sets
off at a run towards the man.

"Wait!" shouts the old woman and to her surprise the little
girl does as she's told.

"You aint *scared*, are you?" The girl herself doesn't seem
scared at all. The old woman is firm.

"Let him come to *us*. If he's a mind." Surely enough the
thin man begins walking towards them. The old woman looks
about her for a rock or a fallen branch as possible weapons.
When no more than ten yards separate them, she throws up a
hand. "Close enough," she barks and the man stops and looks
at the ground, scolded. Up close the suit is pinstriped and double breasted, with the look of having been in a drawer too long,
creased, trouser legs a little too short, showing off his spindly,
sockless ankles and rag-wrapped feet, which have been stuffed
into a pair of wingtips too large for him; under the suit he's
bare-chested. He walks in place a while in the snow, the axe jig-
ging nervously in his hand. "What you all dressed up for out
here?" she asks at last. He looks pained and nervous, frail.

"These are my Sunday duds, ma'am."

"Taint Sunday, *genius*," jeers the little girl from the old woman's side.

"Which way you ladies headed?" he asks, trying a smile. The old woman sets her jaw.

"You move along, mister, we aint lookin for no travelling companions."

"I killed a man," he says quietly. The whelp giggles. The old woman notices a large rock, some four feet away, wonders how quickly her aching joints might allow her to reach it, lift it up.

"That so?" she says. The thin man makes eye contact.

"I believe you know that it is."

"You chop his head off with that?" She gestures to the hand axe, aware that the rock is too far, that it might as well be in the next state.

"No, I— This here is *his* axe. I took it."

"So then how'd you kill this fella?" pipes up the girl.

"I— I spoke to him. Whispered in his ear."

"You bore him to death?" The girl dissolves into mocking laughter. The old woman shushes her.

"You killed a man by speakin to him?"

"I wasn't raised to lie, ma'am."

Again the whelp speaks up:

"By the look of you, you wasn't *raised* at all, your mama ever tell you to how to wash? Comb that hair ayours? You *stink*, mister, *poo-ee!*" Again, laughter.

"Now you speakin to *us*, aint you?" says the old woman, "How come we aint got our legs in the air, your words are so powerful?" The thin man looks down at the axe in his bandaged hand, then out into the woods.

"Don't know. You aint like him, the fella I killed. You ladies aint like him, are you?" The old woman sighs heavily, all at once so terribly tired.

"No. No, sir, we aint."

W alking into the cabin was like walking into a dream. In the dim light nothing seemed tangible, everything a kind of smoky facsimile of itself. John felt a sense of the room being buried under earth, of being far away from the world; sound appeared flat, smothered.

It was true that the windows were small, but it seemed as if the mood in the room were somehow responsible for the dearth of light; something bad had come and gone, leaving its ink in the air, like a startled squid. Everything was merely a shape, the outline of a chair, the outline of a bedpost, a table, a crib. The Faddens were just one more shape against the back wall: he standing, she seated. Their breath steamed about them and was extinguished.

John imagined that to them, he too must appear as a mere shadow sat at their dining table; he imagined that the unwrapped bundle on the table must, to them, have glowed in the dimness.

Philip Fadden was crying a thin, strangled sound and trying his best to swallow it. Ellen Fadden sounded hollowed out, worn away.

"You're entrusted with this beautiful, beautiful thing, this blessing, and then it just slips away."

If the cabin were indeed a dream, John thought that it would be a dream of falling. He blinked and saw Ros' face in the dark, the door to the box room, he saw another bundle, there and then gone; he kept falling.

The child's ribs had pronounced beading, the rosary formation stretching down both sides of the infant's chest and around towards its back. Eyes still open, it lay on the table as if the carcass of yesterday's dinner, wasted to near nothing, bird bones advancing through flesh; a tiny skull atop a bundle of twigs.

"How can it just slip away like that?" came Ellen's voice from somewhere in the dimness.

"*She*," managed Philip. The shape of his wife nodded.

"Two weeks—" She wrestled her voice under control, "Two weeks off a year old," and she fell into painful crying jags. The shape of her husband curled himself tightly around her, adding his own muffled groans.

John supposed that the situation could be argued to the right side of *neglect* but thought it an argument somewhat untenable. This was the first he'd seen of the child since her birth and as far as he knew no other doctor had attended to her either. Lord only knew what they'd been feeding it, but the poor mite's ribs, crooked limbs and emaciated features all spoke of a chronic nutrient deficiency. "Nearly everything I fed her she spit up," Ellen had said, wringing her hands, "wouldn't take the tit neither." Some minor stomach complaint exacerbated by lack of medical attention, he thought. He pondered cruelty for a moment before, surprisingly, pity beat it back. It broke John's heart to look at the child on the table like that, but he looked nonetheless.

Old Pinkham greeted him with her usual inscrutable shake of that immense head, the tiny step forward then back she always did as John swung the reins over her head before mounting, a mark of her irritability at being mastered by so inexperienced a horseman. As they moved on to the frigid Denmark Road, Pinkham choosing the pace as much as he, three figures stepped out of the trees some way off to the west. A man, an old woman and a child. He'd already steered the horse right, toward home, and Pinkham wasn't about to stand for any indecision on his part. He tried turning her but to no avail: she sidestepped once, then a second time, then continued on her way. He twisted about in the saddle to watch the trio cross the road, sure it was the same old woman, now wrapped in something huge against the cold, the same child; he wondered who the slim, bearded, suited man with them might be. John's stomach clenched and burned for a moment, some kind of meaning settling in him; something awful.

All too soon the three were gone, into the woods, and he faced back to the road ahead. The ride home became an exercise in not thinking about the foolish and the impossible, in not dwelling on the dead Fadden child, or imagining King Kong bursting out onto the road, his immense, furry arms clawing up the asphalt, his queerly comical grin. Instead he concentrated on the cold, on the weaving tracks left by Percy Batchelder's snowplow, on improving his horsemanship, concentrating on the image of home.

When he finally got into his small backroom office, away from the bitter wind, Ros kissed hello, divested of coat, gloves, hat and scarf, he fixed himself a rare afternoon whiskey to drink as he typed up his notes.

There was a pleasing order to the task, something that fought against the truth of it; the deceased reduced to date, to place and time, to evidence, to injury and pathology. All suffering, all tragedy, bleached away.

A guilt would often flutter, moth-like, about the simple pleasure he took in the task, yet the process eased his anxiety at the pure and unvarnished fact of their passing. As he typed, the sharp *snap* of the old Underwood 5's typebars striking the page, arrhythmic and satisfying, perversely kept from his mind the loss it described; somewhat akin to the rhythm of a song, he supposed there was something of whistling past the graveyard in it. But typing in a child's age inevitably made the task harder, the climb a little steeper, the song a little strained. Letting out a slow, sour breath, he pasted the entry into the book.

Three whiskies later he found himself staring out of the darkening window at nothing, wondering at his analogy of these itinerants as some kind of natural phenomenon, cows lying down, sentinels to the newly dead. The thought of them as something considerably less benign churned something up in him, muddied his thoughts.

He tried to recall the infant's name but had to refer to his notebook. Virginia.

Reviewing the journal he noticed that he'd dated the entry wrongly, jumping the gun into 1935, but after staring at the error for a time, he left it. What did it matter?

5

State of Maine.

I certify that I was notified on the 5th day December A. D. 19 35

at 9 h. and 20 m. in the noon by E. S. Abbott M. D

of Bridgton of the finding of the dead body of Virginia

Ethel Fadden of Bridgton, Me

supposed to have come to h er death by violence or unlawful act; that I forthwith repaired to the place

where said body lies and took charge of the same, and before said body is removed make, or cause to be made,

this written description of the location and position of said body, viz:

    The body was that of an infant, twenty-one inches tall,
weighing seven pounds, having blond hair and blue eyes. It was
unclothed and wrapped in a cotton blanket.
    The body was viewed at the home of Phillip Fadden, the father
on the Denmark Road, Bridgton, Maine. There was cyanosis of the
extremeties, marked riger mortis. The body was emaciated, abdomen
distended, fontanelles were open, and there was a rachitis resary
on ribs.
    The mother stated that the babies food had not agreed with it
since birth, it had vomited constantly. At one-thirty A.M. on the
day of death she had given the baby its bottle and left it
apparently as well as usual. The baby cried about three A.M. and
at five-thirty A.M. when the mother rose she looked at the baby,
and could not arouse it. She called a physician who pronounced the
child dead.

        Cause of Death-   Malnutrition, Rickets.

Medical Examiner.

Date Dec 5 / -   19 34

80

III

Anyhow, I've drifted some from my point about blood. About building on blood. You don't think there's a violence in all things, I don't know what to tell you.

Don't get me wrong. I don't believe we should moon about it, beat our breasts. I never shot no Indian nor murdered a man in cold blood, guilt for these things wouldn't serve me. Guilt is for what you did, not what you read about, not what you saw and couldn't help. But neither should we forget that which we live upon. The ugliness. Forget this and we're sendin it an invite: "Come back, all is forgotten." Ignore it and it'll bite you in the ass is all I'm sayin.

But build we do and we are industrious sonsabitches. We come together. And I guess that's the message of towns, the comin together, the neighborly aspect. An it's fine. Aint sayin otherwise. Towns, cities, states, countries. We weave ourselves together and we get strong, it's true.

About the queerest, truest thing I ever heard was about British Soldiers.

British Soldiers is the name of a lichen, they call it. Grows hereabouts. Looks like spots of blood on the ground. Really. Tiny red things. Got their name acourse after the redcoats of the British durin the revolutionary war. Sometimes I wonder what the lichen was called before that war, or if it arrived on the boats with the Englishmen. Maybe it sprung up new from the fallen.

See, the interestin part is, lichen isn't one thing. A lichen is a fungus and an algae workin together. Look it up. The fungus gives the algae a place to live, an the algae provides food for the fungus. They're both separate things that can live just fine by themselves, but they do better together. Stronger together. That seems kinda poetic to me. But then the blood red color isn't there if they stay apart, only when they work together. Blood together, bloodless apart. Well that's people, right there.

I say people, but there's persons within that that walk apart.

I hazard, without pride, that I am one of em. Young Doc Bisch, I think, is another.

He's a strange fish as the poet said; caught between. There's a worry in him that I can't get to, can't tree. He's from away but he's been here atime and there's a real warmth toward him; I feel it, even if he don't. Maybe he does. Yet I fancy he counts himself the outsider still.

"You've driven yer stake into the Maine earth an belong here as much as any Mainer I know," I told him, "Oftentimes folks feel they belong somewhere due to little more than geography of birth, over familiarity and abject lack of imagination. Never knowin anyplace else is a paltry foundation for belongin. But you have sought this place out, for whatever reason, and that weighs as strongly as any birthright to my mind. A person no more belongs in a place due to their birth than they own it for the same reason. You've hammered in your stake an here you are."

But still there's this fret in him. He aint a nervous man, I wouldn't want you to think that of him, nor is he a melancholic. It's clear right off that he's capable, damn capable. A good man it's clear and a good doctor. There's somethin in him though, some trouble. But then I guess he sees more of the other side of the coin than the rest of us, so he's entitled.

I have seen the dead. My pa. Men in uniform lain across the plains of Manila. Fella down the way that was beat to death by his brother-in-law. Them funny little vehicles we leave behind, so much useless tissue once whatever loved and raged and hated and laughed has gone on its way. A dead person don't look like a person. It don't. O sure it's a likeness but it ain't nothin more. The man said a pound of feathers won't fly, cause there's no bird in it. There's nothin more sad nor more terrible nor more shop-worn and likely than the dead. Yeah I seen em. Though to do so as a matter of your every day, your trade, must be hard to bear, doctor or no.

He called me Mr Allen and I never insisted on Joseph. I never called him by his name. Chiefly cause my pa's name was John but truth is, never was a man more his job, in action and likeness, than this young doctor, and never was a job more honorable a badge. If a fella says to you "What line are you in?" and you can tell him "The easin of pain, the killin of diseases," well that's a medal of more weight than any gold.

We would happen across one another from time to time, touch our hats, go on our ways. One day though, woulda been an April I think, we found ourselves both milling about the same street corner, or under the same tree or what have you, and so the mere touchin of hats fell a little short of etiquette.

We fell into conversation, talked the weather up and down a while. It was a cool one, the sky big an white. I told him my father had always said "Know enough to come outta the rain and don't fall asleep by the water." We laughed at that.

"Whatever did he suppose would happen if you slept by the water?" asked the doc.

"Who knows ain't tellin. Fathers."

We musta stood there for nigh on an hour chewin the fat and it was suggested, by one or other of us, that we meet upon a future date to do the same. He asked me did I play the game of chess but I told him that I did not. We agreed then that a simple perambulation was all that either of us required from these proposed meetings. Little conversation. And I felt that this tendered friendship of ours went some way towards confirmation of our shared apartness within the scheme of things. And so we began to meet, we met and we walked apart.

After a pause that first day I recall he said, as much to the sky as to myself, "The harvest is past, the summer is ended, and we are not saved."

"What's that?" I asked.

"Something *my* father used to say," he rolled his eyes. It seemed like a queer quotation, what with the month, but it felt like somethin he'd been chewin away at for sometime so I let it pass.

Before we parted he asked me a question. He said "Mr Allen, what do you suppose happens when a person dies?" I said hell if I knew but that I wasn't expectin any gilded staircases. He said "No," he said, such ideas were attributed to us *after* we died. But what did I suppose happened *when* we died.

"The moment of passing itself?" I asked.

"The moment," he said.

"Hell if I know," was the best I could offer.

Bridgton, Windham; Maine.

August, September, 1935

"Are we to keep score?" says the old woman, "we makin sport now?"

The little girl turns her scowl to the woods.

"He aint pullin his share is all I said."

The thin man wears a chastened look, walks in place, mumbles something under his breath.

"What's that?" snaps the girl, "What's that you say you bony sunovabitch?"

"I done my share," he answers quietly, unable to meet her eyes.

"Pay no mind. The whelp aims to be referee." It's only morning and the old woman is already sick of their squabbling. Once she works the age and the sleep out of her limbs, she sets off north. The other two follow. The little girl catches her up.

"How come that shitbird's with *us* now?" she sneers.

"He ain't with no one. He can go as he pleases, leave if he wants. So, for that matter, can you."

"He's an imbecile *I* think," the girl raises her voice so the thin man can hear, "so dumb he'd crawl over a glass wall to see what's on the other side." Pleased with her joke she turns and laughs at him. The thin man for his part merely walks on, tired and pained as ever.

Soon they're picking their way through thinning trees and scrubland and houses appear, washed out in the early sun; a narrow roadway drawn between the trees. The three cross as if tarmac were no more than an idea yet unrealized.

Richard Palmer claws patterns into the lawn, deftly guiding any debris down to the sidewalk with the rake, ignoring the soreness in his back, his wrists; methodical and lost in thought.

He has in the past made much of his being a farmer of many years, reduced to tending the yards of others, and for a pittance at that. "At my age it aint seemly," he has frequently said; but the truth is he finds peace in the endeavor, and as long as his joints hold out he aims to keep at it.

He glances upward. The sky is an untarnished blue. A car

passes and he and the driver exchange raised hands. It'll be a hot one, he'll not need his jacket come noon. He promises himself a sit down in a half hour or so, perhaps some of Em Davis' lemonade, tart though it is, and he works towards it.

The three stand in the shade of an outhouse some two hundred yards away. The little girl is arguing for the drawing of lots. The old woman is having none of it.

"That aint the way an you know it. Now hush yer yap."

"Fuck you, old woman, you aint—" The old woman raises her hand in warning and the whelp cowers and shoots daggers. Still she keeps at it. "I want him. The fucker's pathetic. An old man rakin, and for *beans*."

"Excuse me, duchess, but didn't I yesterday see you eat a maggoty apple and like it?"

"*Hey!*" The thin man has dropped his axe and is already crossing the street in the direction of Richard Palmer. Out in the sun, his awkward asymmetrical walk in his too-big shoes, his disorderly arrangement of hair, his stoop in the brown suit. The little girl tries to run after him but the old woman pulls her back by the scruff; she struggles, hisses and spits like a fire.

They watch him approach Richard Palmer; even at this distance they see the older man's reaction to the disheveled stranger, a small step back, a wariness, the rake held between them.

"He's gonna fuck it up," hisses the girl, still held fast.

"*Hush.*"

The thin man is saying something. Richard Palmer listens for a moment, then his stance thaws a little and he says something back, before pointing off down the street.

"Askin directions. Aint as dumb as he looks." The old woman lets go a begrudging smile. While Richard Palmer points westward, the thin man leans in close to his ear. Almost immediately the old man falls backwards, inanimate before he's hit the ground, emptied of something.

The little girl squirms free and sits on the ground, arms folded, face of thunder. She kicks at the axe.

"He gloats about this I'll cut his throat. Cut off his hands and feet," she says quietly.

The old woman closes her eyes for a long, weary moment.

"Stop acting like a child," she whispers. She opens her eyes and the thin man is already making his way back across the street. As he nears them, it's clear that he's crying, the force of each sob shaking his walk. He's carrying something.

"What in hell's that?"

The thin man blinks away tears, struggles to get his lurching breaths in check, holds it out for them to see. A small leather bag, shiny with wear.

"There is money in here," he says, chancing a smile, "quite a sum."

The old woman's face darkens.

"Take it back. That aint the way."

"But I thought we might buy food, the girl—"

"*Take it back.* It aint yours." She's struggling with her temper. Who was it set these fools on her, or she among these fools?

"But... The girl looks so hungry, I only meant to—"

"*Take it back.* Money aint part of it."

"How much is in there exactly?" asks the girl, craning her neck. The old woman ignores her, places a foot on the axe, fixes the thin man with a cold stare that reads: *last chance.*

"Take it back."

The meat of it was to keep The Notion in check. The three were ever in his thoughts, The Notion a kind of weight, but he kept a tight hold on it as he went about his work and this, he thought, was the best he could make of it; it would pass, he had little doubt.

It had though, with time, ballooned in him, grown distended, tumorous and fantastic; as implausible as it was ill-fitting. It gainsaid all he knew, both as a doctor and as a man, yet it remained, queerly compelling.

He'd seen the little girl near where they found the Renwick boy last month over in Harrison, a tiny shape fleeing into the woods, he was sure; the thin man he was convinced he sighted on the far bank of Island Pond while examining the body of that Berlsheiser fellow who drowned. They were quick and they were clever but he'd seen them.

Joseph Allen had once told him that his father used to say "Joseph, never, *never* fall asleep by the water" and though he'd laughed he'd felt something frightening in it, something old and true; a caveat on complacency in the face of something ageless and without pity for the conceits of men.

His own father would cherry pick from Proverbs: "An ungodly man diggeth up evil: and in his lips there is as a burning fire."

Maybe he was being that ungodly man, he thought, looking for trouble where trouble simply didn't exist. Looking for trouble in a small, impossible pocket of neverwas.

The phone rang, bringing him news of Richard Palmer's passing.

8

State of Maine.

Cumberland ss.

I certify that I was notified on the 1st day august A. D. 1935

at 10 h. and 30 m. in the fore noon by Dr. Friberg

of Bridgton of the finding of the dead body of Richard

Palmer of Bridgton, Me

supposed to have come to h   death by violence or unlawful act; that I forthwith repaired to the place

where said body lies and took charge of the same, and before said body is removed make, or cause to be made,

this written description of the location and position of said body, viz:

The body was that of a man five feet six inches tall, weighing one hundred, fifty-five pounds, having white hair and blue eyes. There was one days growth of beard on the face, he had false teeth. His face and arms were deeply tanned, there was cyanosis under the finger nails, rigor mortis had not set in. There were no marks of external violence.

He was dressed in heather jacket, blue shirt, black striped trousers. brown socks and black oxfords, the pockets of his trousers contained the following articles: One gold watch hunting case, one leather pocket book containing two one dollar bills, thirty-four cents in change. One leather tobacco pouch containing twelve hundred forty dollars in bills of ten, twenty and five dollar denominations, one house key, one pocket knife, one white handkerchief.

The body was viewed in the yard of Sumner Davis at the corner of Green and Main Street, Bridgton, Maine. His body was found lying under a tree by Mrs. Lena O'Brion and Mrs. Leah Sylvester of Bridgton, about nine-forty A.M. He was last seen alive by Mrs. H. H. Bisbee of Bridgton, who saw him walking towards the Davis property about nine-thirty A.M. A rake which he carried was lying across his chest when the body was found.

He had been under medical treatment for some time and was evidently stricken b a fatal heart attack while working about the Davis property.

Cause of Death- Angina Pectoris, Arteriosclerosis.

John W. Bushcoppberger M.D.
Medical Examiner.

Date my 19   1935

91

The boy bit down hard on the wooden spoon as John wrapped the leg. The bit was at the boy's own insistence, and though John knew the setting of a break was far from painless, he thought it oddly theatrical for a thirteen-year-old.

From her armchair Emily Fowler, the boy's mother, explained her little Franklin's fascination with books concerning the civil war:

"In particular those with grisly scenes of battlefield surgery, amputations and the like," she shook her head. "Positively devours such foolishness."

"Charlsh T. Pepper yooshed shpoons they shay," spat the boy with difficulty.

"Is that so?" John couldn't help but smile.

"Grisly and morbid my husband calls it."

"O I suppose I was much the same at his age."

"I find that hard to credit." She seemed to mean it. Did he appear so serious? So staid?

"A childhood without foolishness of one kind or another is no kind of childhood," he said, which made them both laugh. He saw in her face that she wanted to ask after his own children, but then watched her remember, her expression rearranging itself; he was glad not to have to wave away any comment like it was nothing. When she asked could she pay him a week Tuesday and in the meantime handed him two loaves of gray-looking bread, he smiled and told her "That'll be just fine, Mrs Fowler."

On his way to his next appointment he met Wilson Chaplin on Lake House Road. Wilson carried a large sack which he told John contained a number of keepsakes he planned to sell, should a buyer be found; he said his finances were such that he might *cartwheel through the eye of a needle wearin a tall hat, right into heaven.* His clothes looked thin and dusty, his eyes hollowed; he'd lost weight. His face was tight and creased looking. His "heads" had returned, it was clear, yet neither of them mentioned it. John invited Wilson over to dinner later in the week, which Wilson accepted thankfully.

He recalled the first time he'd been sent to Cousin Wilson regarding his heads. Hattie had told Ros, who'd told him. Hattie was "sick of seein him walkin around like a man with stones in his shoes". As Wilson said his goodbyes and went on his way, John could see what she had meant: every step he took was stabbing at his head, holding his gait in a pinch of discomfort. His heads had returned, despite the bloodroot. John wondered for a moment if they had ever left.

Returning home, he'd barely hung his hat when Ros stepped into the hall, face red with crying, fingers knotted, a snatched breath.

"Mother's heart," was all she said.

♦

Northern Cumberland Memorial Hospital always made him think of his college days, the size and scope of the building, something about the color of its brick, the sound of footfalls in tiled corridors and dim stairwells, the smell of disinfectant and agitation; it made him think of examinations and nervous coughs in quiet rooms. Why the building failed also to conjure nostalgia for a time before war and responsibilities, some fabled golden era of youth, seemed unclear; indeed, the work John did at Maine General, at Mercy, or at Maine Eye and Ear, similarly failed to induce fond memory. He'd long since resigned himself to being a doctor perversely at odds with hospitals.

The attack had come upon Hattie whilst she peeled potatoes for the evening meal. She had been found on the floor, surrounded by peelings and pieces of broken bowl, knife still in hand, as if to defend herself against some unseen assailant.

A frantic phone call from Eugene Chaplin had found John out setting Franklin Fowler's leg, another call had found his brother Wilson out doing Lord only knew what, and so Eugene had driven Hattie to Bridgton himself, cursing the roads, his truck, his brother, the damn fool who'd sold her the potatoes, for every mile of the way.

Doctors told Eugene that the attack had been mild but that by no means did this mean that his aunt was out of the woods. Eugene sat and ground his teeth until his cousin and her doctor husband arrived.

All this he related to Ros and John when they found him hunched in the waiting room, the cousins embracing briefly before the details of Hattie's condition were relayed.

He said she'd complained of feeling unusually weary in the week prior, and had experienced a "terrible deep ache" in her chest twice in the preceding days. Eugene cursed himself for believing her hard-headed explanations, putting it down to indigestion.

John watched Ros compose herself as Eugene spoke, drawing in her tears, gathering everything back into place, a deep breath and a hasty mend. He wondered at her composure in the face of the possibility that her mother might cease to be at any moment; the heart spasms, switches off, *poof*, and she's gone forever. He thought of Mae Kemp and her profane resignation, wondered if it were he lying in the hospital, whether Ros would be equally resigned, equally subservient to circumstance. If it were Ros in that bed he thought he might scream, crumble, tear in two, turn inside out.

Eugene implored him to speak to someone at the hospital, as if a simple word from another doctor would unlock some hidden reservoir of healing power, some trick or miracle pill kept secret from mere mortals.

"*Aint out of the woods,* they said. Aint that about the dumbest phrase you ever heard?" John frowned, declined to answer. He told Eugene he'd see about finding someone to speak to. Squeezing Ros' hand, he kissed her on the cheek and told her that he was sure everything was being done; she smiled back, eyes brimming.

He wanted to tell her that everything would be fine, that her mother would live through the attack, that she'd live so long as three malign and magical vagrants didn't somehow gain entrance to the hospital, somehow get into Hattie's ward, somehow find her bed, somehow— but there his imagination dried, faith in his own foolish ideas dissolving. Patients died in hospitals every day, nothing on earth needed less explanation than that.

He strode off purposefully down the hallway, ostensibly to find clarification on Hattie's status, but in reality also to steal five minutes alone to clear his head; to hide. He thought maybe he might climb some stairs, find a window, to see if there was a tree line close enough to view, to keep watch on.

B oth whelp and thin man are gone. The old woman is awake, mustering the impetus to rise and face the new morning. The sun is warm and liquid on her face. She stares at the ground on which her head rests, studies leaves, tiny things moving this way and that; her right ear listens to the grumble of burrowing things below, her left to the tidal susurrations of the trees above.

Steeling herself, she turns over, and groaning, pulls herself up the side of a convenient pine until she stands, albeit stooped; regaining her breath, nodding at nothing, perhaps merely at the victory of standing erect once more. It feels good to be alone again, feels right. She will not look for them, will not act as nursemaid.

She licks a finger, holds it up, and starts out west. Almost immediately she comes across a clearing in which the thin man sits on a tree stump, the little girl on his lap. Her heart sinks a little, alone no longer. They haven't noticed her and so she watches them silently, gladly stealing time without their questions, without their bickering.

But the whelp is on his lap and that doesn't fit, doesn't fit at all. The old woman blinks.

The thin man sits, knees together; his eyes are shut tight. The little girl sits indeed on his lap, one arm about his neck, the other guiding his right hand up under her dress. His mouth is crooked in discomfort, he shakes his head, all but weeping. The girl grabs his hair and pulls hard, pulls his ear closer, her voice hisses, carries across the clearing: *do it you spineless cocksucker*. His hand inches a little higher.

"*You stop that.*" The old woman has closed the gap between her and the pair in remarkable time. She grabs a fist of the girl's hair and yanks her from the thin man's lap and onto the ground. She then squares off and punches the thin man, hard in the eye; he pitches backwards with a yelp, holding his face, and as he falls, as if time has slowed, the old woman notices that his fly is unbuttoned. She quickly turns and places her foot on the girl's neck, pressing down. "You do that again I'll drag you to the lake and drown you." The girl squirms and spits. "You hear me you little bitch?" The thin man is crawling around the stump, whining, apologizing over and over, *I'm sorry, I'm so sorry*, hiding his face in his hands. The old woman snarls at him.

"What kind of a man *are* you? Who's stronger, you or... *that*?" He replies through his fingers:

"I pleaded, I tried to tell her it was wrong. But I am not a violent man. What am I to do? Striking a child would be wrong." The old woman makes a short sound of disgust.

"A *child*. Mister, she's right, you are an imbecile. She's no more a child than you are a man. We all wearin costumes out here." Under her foot, between strangled breaths, the little girl is giggling.

"Heart killed my pa, his brother too. Took four such spells to kill Uncle Ellery though; man was carved outta rock." Joseph glanced at the ground, let out a sigh. "Like the man said, growin up aint for children." Charlotte Norton passed them, touched her hat, smiled at John, raised her brows at Joseph, her disapproval magnified by her eyeglasses.

"Ma'am," said John. Joseph touched his hat, gave a dry laugh. The Sunday went on about them. Finally John spoke, "Hattie might be cast in iron, weak as a kitten but she fights it."

"She's sayin *not today*. Good for old Hattie."

"Ros visits every day. I've been once or twice. It's a scare." Someone John had treated but whose name he couldn't recall passed by, waved, he waved back.

"The Great Fright my ma used to call it. Yknow the Indians called their cemeteries Boskeniganiko, meanin *a forest of coffins*."

"Do you do anything with your days other than read books, Mr Allen?" Joseph smiled.

"I walk and chew the fat with learned fellows such as yourself. Then I go home, *then* I read books."

"Sir, you are a library of information."

"Not all of it useful neither. I reckon if I fully comprehend one solitary thing before I hand in my dinner pail, it'll have been time well spent."

"Ever read anything on homeopathy?" The question felt like a mistake, even as he was asking it.

"A little. It's an interestin turn on herbal remedies, but speakin as a layman can't say I found it all that convincin." John fought not to feel hurt, not to feel stupid. He considered bringing up the placebo effect but decided against it.

"And economics?"

"I've tried. Readin economics feels a little too much like pissin in the ocean. Far as I can gather economics is a joke told by someone who only pretends to understand it, told *to* someone who is the butt of the joke."

"Well I wish someone somewhere understood it. People without roofs, without food."

"Maybe the Abenaki had it right. Live on, off and for the land. Forget pitched roofs, get yerselves a wigwam. Learn to hunt."

"I hear there's some people living in the woods over Convene way."

"Not Indians."

"No, no, white. Road people."

"Vagrants?"

"So they tell me. In the woods off Hogfat Hill. That's if they're still there. However can they survive the winter?"

"The human animal can be remarkably hardy, Doc." Joseph made a sour face. "But it won't be easy."

John took a deep breath, closed his eyes.

"I've been considering going to meet with them." His stomach did a queasy little dance as he said it. Joseph seemed surprised.

"You *have?* To offer medical care, that sorta thing?"

"Well, perhaps, if they required it."

"Then what the hell else?"

John's whole body rebelled against him answering the question truthfully, limbs tightening, throat shrinking, mind conjuring thoughts of him thrown in the booby hatch up in Augusta; the word *insane* rose up in his mind before receding.

"I guess I don't know," was the best he could do. Joseph stopped walking.

"I hope you don't take this wrong, Doc, but poor folk aint no zoo. Many aint too proud to take charity but my guess is none wants to be stared at while they do it."

"O no, nothing like that, I just—" he clenched his teeth for a moment, let a bit of the truth leak out, immediately regretting it. "I guess I'm looking for someone. Three someones."

"Who you lookin for?"

"A woman, a man, a child," John found himself surprised at his ability to improvise a lie. "A young family. I came across them on the Portland Road some time ago. The little girl looked... sickly, unwell. I've since grown concerned that I should have offered treatment then, certain symptoms could suggest—" but his invention was faltering under its own weight, he steadied himself, "I thought these Hogfat Hill people might know of the family's whereabouts."

Joseph narrowed his eyes, ran his tongue around the inside of his mouth.

"You want me to come with you? I could bring my rifle. Poor don't equal bloodthirsty bandit in my book, but, well, out there in the woods you might be easy pickins for anyone desperate enough to raise a stone gainst his brother."

John floundered. Why had he even mentioned it? Merely to have The Notion out there, at least in part, to throw light on it? To see if it became nonsense and fled?

"No, thank you, no, I don't think that will be necessary. I shall be sure to take nothing worth stealing and to carry no money."

"You plan on wearin shoes you'll have somethin worth stealin."

"Please, poor doesn't equal bloodthirsty bandit in my book either. I shall keep my distance and at the first sign of trouble I shall flee. I ran for my school you know." John threw a smile in the hopes of getting one back. Joseph nodded reticently, rasped his fingernails across his whiskers. He clearly feared for this green Pennsylvania doctor out alone in the Maine wilds.

"I don't know. The woods is no place to wander, you don't wanna end up like Frank Mayes, imagined he saw somethin one night that didn't agree with him, knocked him on his ass with a heart attack."

"I recall. It was past midnight when I got the call from Searge. And weren't they both drunk as fiddlers?"

They couldn't help but smile; Joseph's was the first to vanish. He set his jaw, pointed a gnarled finger at John.

"Alright then, how bout this. Make sure you take a bag. I guess you do anyhow bein a doctor so that'll do. If things turn a little... salty, put your hand into that bag and *leave it there*. Look the biggest of em hard in the eye and ask em if they've ever seen a man get shot."

For the first time since the three met, the thin man leads the way. The old woman is next, then the little girl; the old woman has demanded this arrangement, that she stay between them "to prevent any further unnaturalness". The whelp had laughed aloud, the thin man had looked at his feet in shame.

He picks through the underbrush as if hugging himself, as if still clutching the blanket about his shoulders, his gait as yet unable to acknowledge the ill-fitting suit; the blanket itself trails behind him, catches on thorns, snags on branches. The old woman's knees are screaming.

"Where's the scrawny halfwit takin us?" she says under her breath. The girl skips up behind her, whispers:

"Maybe to a quiet dell somewheres, maybe he means to seduce me again."

The old woman makes a fist.

"Shut yer mouth."

After an hour or so he calls a stop and sits, removing his shoes. His feet have been bleeding again and he sets about changing their wrappings. Underneath their bindings the feet are filthy and crusted with flakes of old blood, yet at the center of his injuries there glistens a fresh wetness. The other two watch him.

"Don't you never stop leakin?" asks the girl, sneering; he ignores her. He checks under the wrappings on his hands, and though they're damp, he decides against changing them. The little girl spits. "You got the bleedin sickness aint you? I seen it before. Mister, you get a nick in the wrong place and all of you'll just squirt right out the hole onto the ground." She kicks her feet and laughs. Replacing his shoes he stands, stamps once or twice, wincing, then moves off into the trees. The other two follow.

It's not another ten minutes before he stops again. Placing his axe carefully on the ground, he turns to the old woman. He looks at the earth, then up at the sky, then at her; he holds out his hands.

"Now," he bites his lower lip, "I have met with this gentleman before. We have spoken, at length. If you and the girl would agree to wait here I will go to his residence and return with him."

"What's wrong with *us* goin to his 'residence'?" The girl mimics his voice.

"He is not alone there." He shakes his head, troubled. "We cannot work there."

"How far is it?" asks the old woman.

"Not far, less than a mile."

"Fine, you go get yer friend. We'll wait."

In their fifteen or so minutes of waiting, the old woman and the little girl speak not a word. The old woman seethes to herself and the whelp knows better than to push her.

The thin man leads a stranger into their clearing, the rags of his right hand resting on the man's shoulder. The man looks tired and hollowed, eyes bloodshot, his face and clothing speckled with white flecks. His thin gray hair is swept over to conceal a bald spot, oily with pomade. The thin man gestures between the old woman and the stranger.

"This is Mr Preston L. Mann."

Preston holds out his hand.

"Ma'am. Little girl," he says. The old woman doesn't move, doesn't shake his hand, the girl sticks out her tongue. Preston looks back at the thin man, unsure. The thin man pats his arm, blinks slowly to reassure him.

"These are my—" he throws a worried look, as if about to step beyond his rightful place, "My colleagues, Mr Mann."

Preston smiles weakly.

"Please, call me Preston," he says, his forced bonhomie dissolving. His hands are shaking, his breathing shallow and pained. The old woman rolls her eyes, the little girl stifles a laugh with her hand. The thin man takes Preston by the shoulders and looks him in the eye. It takes Preston some time to meet his gaze.

"You need not be afraid, we are your friends."

"Friends."

"That's right, Preston, that's right." The thin man embraces him, the man's jagged breaths shaking the both of them. Holding him tight, in time the thin man works a bandaged hand down the man's back, untying the length of rope Preston wears coiled at his hip. "That's right, that's right," the thin man keeps saying, now barely a whisper, "*Thaaaat's riiiiight*." He lets the rope fall to the floor and the little girl runs over and picks it up, quickly fashioning a knot.

"Rigmarole," says the old woman to herself, disgusted, though no one hears.

The thin man breaks the embrace, staring once more into Preston's eyes; Preston blinks away tears, tries smiling, doesn't quite make it.

"We love you, Preston."

"Thank you, sir, thank you all."

The little girl jumps up and throws the rope around Preston's neck. Preston's breathing degenerates again to short bursts, his eyes widen. He reaches up, holds on to the rope.

"Preston, *Preston*," the thin man slaps him across the face and he seems to calm. He's shaking his head.

"No, wait. Alright now. Hold on. I need a moment, to think, I need—" whatever else he says is lost as the rope tightens on his throat and he's lifted from the ground. The toes of his shoes scratch at the earth. Behind him the old woman strains as she pulls on the rope, tendons lifting under skin, a swallowed scream at the effort. The rope, thrown over a branch, lifts Preston still higher. The little girl runs to the old woman and she too pulls, the thin man watching in wonder as Preston ascends.

"Bless you," he says, tears in his eyes.

Preston spasms, his fingers working at the rope, reaching behind to the knot, his legs piston wildly, kicking scars into the tree bark. The little girl laughs, her grip on the rope slipping.

"Kick! Kick you sunovabitch!" she screams. The thin man joins the old woman and together the three hold the rope fast. Preston tries to climb the tree, swiping and scratching at it, sending him spinning. Gradually his convulsions fade and his hands drop; his face seems to bulge on its skull, swelling, the whites of his eyes pepper with red spots, as if it were raining blood. His bladder voids and he gives a tiny twitch of his hand, as if in embarrassment. He swings back and forth, urine painting an ever decreasing ellipse on the dirty ground.

The rope is tied off by the old woman, the thin man support-ing the body until it's done. The little girl makes a face, telling him he's gonna smell of dead man's pee. While the old woman walks about in frustration, spits on her burning hands, and the thin man respectfully turns his back, the little girl, unseen, goes through Preston's pockets, stealing a fob watch and a few dollar bills. Hastily stuffing the loot into her bag lest she be discovered, she fails to notice the moment when the polished penny, a keepsake for so long, escapes and falls, unnoticed, in the earth at her feet.

Soon there is nothing more to be done. The thin man watches the body's weakening arc, reaches up, places a hand on Preston's chest to steady him; he fights off weeping. He attempts to lead the group in a prayer but the other two have already vanished into the trees. He dallies for a time but then follows after them.

B y the time John arrived, the body had been hanging for
some two hours. For the most part it remained totally still,
though every so often the wind would set it swaying, perhaps
give it a slow turn; it was a man no longer, nothing remained.
Now it was merely an extension of the tree, an extravagant
bloom pointing down at the earth from which it grew. A group
of four or five men milled about, not looking at it, chatting, as
if it were not the very reason they each found themselves there
and nowhere else.

John was greeted with a wave of nods which he returned. He
studied the body's hands, the face, bent the arm at the elbow,
ran his little finger along the rope where it cut a valley into
the fleshy neck. He marveled at the surety of the step this man
had taken, even as he doubted that the man had acted alone.
Self-murder was among the blackest things, and he puzzled on
whether murder somehow constituted something better. Sheriff Pray wandered over while John was taking notes.

"Bisch."

"Dean." John didn't look up, continued writing.

"Got the wife waitin up by the road. We cut him down?"

"Yes, for Christ's sake cut the man down." John had barked
at him, surprising himself, pushing his pencil too hard into the
paper, tearing a hole. The sheriff looked at him blankly for a
moment before turning to Deputy Welch.

"You heard him, Lew, cut the man down."

John didn't watch them cut the rope, knew they'd handle the
operation thoughtfully, had seen them decant the dead from
this place to that, that vehicle to the other; he'd done all he
needed to, didn't need to see it again. He stood with his back to
them, looking at nothing, working the pencil through his fingers, feeling the differences of texture, paint, wood, the glassy
tip, searching every bite mark, retreating from the scene.

Something winked at him from the ground, a bronzed point
of light. He bent and picked up a penny, wondering at some-

thing so bright, so gleaming, in such a place. *Find a penny, pick it up, and all the day you'll have good luck.*

He had the car and the rarity of an afternoon free. He pocketed the coin, fought to imagine his whereabouts on the map; he turned.

"Sheriff?"

"Doc." They were bringing the wife, he could hear a female voice through the trees, getting closer.

"The best way to get to Convene is Chadbourne then Richville up, am I right?"

"It is."

John held out his hand and the sheriff shook it.

"Thank you, sheriff," *and my apologies,* he meant to say.

State of Maine.

Cumberland ss.

I certify that I was notified on the 9 th day *august* A. D. 1935

at 1 h. and 30 m. in the *after* noon by *the Sheriffs Department*

of *Portland* of the finding of the dead body of *Preston C.*

Mann of *North Windham*

supposed to have come to h *is* death by violence or unlawful act; that I forthwith repaired to the place

where said body lies and took charge of the same, and before said body is removed make, or cause to be made,

this written description of the location and position of said body, viz:

The body was that of a man five feet eight inches tall, weighing one hundred sixty pounds, partially bald, having grey hair, brown eyes and being smooth shaven. He was dressed in blue overalls, blue shirt brown trousers, blue socks and black oxfords, light underwear. There was nothing of value in his pockets.

The body was viewed in the woods at Windham Pines about a quarter of a mile from Pettingill Shores, No. Windham, Maine. The body was hanging from a branch of a small pine tree on a piece of quarter inch hemp rope six feet long, one end of which had been fastened to the branch by a sailors knot, the other end having a slip knot which was fastened just beneath the angle of the jaw.

There were a few marks on the tree evidently made by his shoes when climbing the tree. The face was pale, there was a deep ridge around his neck made by the pressure of the rope. There was pine pitch on both hands, face and extremities were not cyanosed, rigor mortis had not set in.

His wife stated that he had threatened suicide the day before. On the day of his death he and his wife were painting their cottage, working on opposite sides. About eleven A.M. she missed him, when she could not find him she notified Sheriff Dean Pray of No. Windham, who organized a searching party locating the body about twelve forty-five P.M.

Cause of Death- Suicide by Hanging.

Date *Aug 19* 1935

John W. Dischypflarger M. D.
Medical Examiner.

The apple seller grimaced into the late afternoon sun.

"These folks owe you money?"

"No, nothing like that. I'm a doctor from over Naples way, I merely wish to offer them medical care."

"So that then they'll owe you money."

"No sir, gratis, uh, free of—"

"I know what gratis means." The man looked him over, unsure. A young boy, huge in his denim shirt and overalls, sat up on the cart, reading, lips moving under a straw hat. The apple seller turned.

"Walt, you know anythin about folks livin in the woods here?" The boy glanced slowly down at them, shook his head and went back to reading. "Walt says no." John took a breath.

"How about you, sir? I'm told they've been here some time. Somewhere off Hogfat Hill they say."

"Is that what they say?" He looked up and down the road, slapped his hands down onto his knees. "I tell you what, you buy some apples maybe I'll recall what I heard."

"Just like that?"

"Just like that. Call it a miracle."

John pointed to the sign: APPLES 5¢, CANADIAN MONEY NOT ACCEPTED.

"Five cents?"

"Just like it says."

"It a little early for apples?" tried John. The man shrugged. "Little."

"They still good?"

"Five cents apiece, bag for eighteen."

"Four in a bag?"

"Tell you what, you get a maggot I won't charge you extra."

The boy stopped reading and turned a page.

"Two bags," said John.

♦

Two threadbare men sat on their haunches by the remains of a fire, a small boy sat by them, poking at the ashes with a stick, a third man squatted a way off in the trees smoking, trousers at his ankles, calmly defecating; a small dark-haired girl holding a rag bear stared up at John, sooty-faced and thin. Their clothes were torn and dirty, the men wore hats that were ragged and had peeling brims. There were cans, bottles and blankets strewn about the place; makeshift shelters had been tethered to nearby trees like the sails on some craft dry-docked or run aground. It seemed to John as if the girl was the only one who had noticed him.

"We saw your sign," said one of the men suddenly, without looking his way, "if that's what you come to ask. But jobs or no, we aint hurtin no one. You got goods or livestock missin, you best bring the police you plan on accusin anyone."

"No, I— Nothing like that, sir, I'm a doctor from over in Naples, and hearing that there were people living in the woods I thought I might—"

"We're fine," interrupted the man; he spat, before speaking to the boy. "You ailin from somethin, Nate?" The boy shook his head, continued to poke at the ash. "We're *fine*," repeated the man.

"I'm... heartened to hear that, sir. But I wonder—" The other man stood and turned to face him, stopping him short. The man approached, brushing his hands on his trousers. He had a narrow face, tanned, his chin dappled with white and brown whiskers, eyes deep set, wrinkled and kind; his eyebrows arched in apology. He smiled and offered his hand, which John shook, feeling its dirt and rough skin; he thought momentarily of the bark of a tree, wondered how long you lived like this before your skin grew that way. The man led him a little way away from the others.

"Don't you mind Henry," he made a face, "a good man, but he spooks easy."

"I understand. Completely. I apologize. It cannot have been easy for you."

"Well I appreciate it, I surely do."

"However will you cope come winter?"

"You lookin fer cunt, mister?" The sounds of the woods rushed in to fill the silence that followed the question.

"I beg your pardon?" John managed finally.

"I believe you heard me fine," said the man. His eyes now were screwed up in anything but kindness, brows knitted. "Are you lookin for cunt?"

"W-why?" John spoke quietly, struggling with what could possibly be happening. "Why are you asking me this?"

"The girl there may look dirty but her mouth's clean." John ran cold.

"Sir, she must be all of seven years old." He was falling back on formality.

"All of."

"Is she your— daughter?"

"That make a difference?"

"Now listen— I came here—" he steadied himself, swallowed his anger, "I would ask you *not* to say that again."

"Maybe you prefer the boy there? Couple dollars'll get you a shot at that sweet little asshole ahis." The man made a circle of his thumb and forefinger, brought it to his lips, made a kissing sound.

"*Sir.*"

"Cecil," the man's smile returned, albeit fraudulently. John spoke through his teeth.

"Do not ask me that again."

"Well now aint you a slippery customer."

"*You son of a bitch.*" John wasn't sure he'd used that phrase in close to ten years. Cecil smiled two rows of nut-brown teeth.

"You a long way into the woods to be gettin judgmental, mister."

"I came here to—"

"Fer some theater? To get beaten, stripped, murdered maybe?"

"To ask— I came here to find someone, three people, an old woman, a young girl and a man."

"You see em?"

"What?"

"Do you see em here?"

"No but I thought you, or some of your people may—"

"*They aint here, mister.*" Had he stressed the word *they*? Cecil slid his hand into his pocket. "You ever see a man's throat cut?"

"I have a gun," barked John suddenly; it sounded foolish, unconvincing, "I will not hesitate to shoot you, sir." The man laughed hoarsely.

"What you lookin for aint here, mister. I've given you a story to tell, now take off, fore I stick you, send you back to the road with a scar you won't easy forget."

John held his ground for a moment or two, jaw tight, nostrils flaring, flushed and ridiculous, before turning and making his way back to the road. Behind him the man's laughter rang out: "It a terrible world, aint it, mister?"

◆

The whiskey level had crept down the bottle in his office with every week that passed; The Notion had yet to abate. He found himself remarkably calm, unafraid. He slept well and dreamlessly, or at least dreamed in such a way that any image failed to make it past waking. He performed his job, laughed with patients, cajoled others; he made love to his wife. He chose to read this ability to cope as a lack of faith in The Notion itself, perhaps even of the waning of it in his mind.

It was true, however, that moments of tension would fall upon him, the acid burn of his embarrassment in the Convene woods returning, an uncomfortable echo that curled his toes in his shoes and shortened his temper. He had shouted at another driver on Lambs Mill Road that they ought to stick to their own damn side; he'd broken a cup on purpose when the hot coffee had burned his hand. Little things.

Always the quietive was Ros. Cumberland County had been moving under his feet for months unacknowledged, perhaps longer, shifting and impermanent, the landscape redrawing itself, rules changing, truths growing thin; yet Ros was some unspecified hub, a center around which everything span. Home anchored him and he was grateful for it.

When she came home from the hospital that night he'd already started dinner, though in truth all it amounted to was the heating through of the soup Ros had made the previous day, and the boiling of several potatoes; and he had a feeling he'd overdone the latter. She looked tired and when she saw him at the stove, sleeves rolled, she took his head in her hands and kissed him hard on the lips; the kiss dissolved into her laughing wearily, then apologizing.

"I'm sure you've done fine. Did you not want the apron?" They both smiled.

"How's your mother?"

"Remarkable. You know they're talking about her coming home in a day or two?"

"*Really*? They think that's—" he stopped himself, "but of course they do. That's wonderful, truly wonderful."

Ros eased herself into a dining chair.

"Doctor Wolcott says it's okay, she's to go home with Gene, Thursday."

"Then tonight we shall dine on over-boiled potatoes and soup in celebration. I told Mr Allen, I said, that woman is cast iron."

When Ros said grace that night, she added "And thank you for looking over your faithful servant Harriet Chaplin, and for returning her to us, her family, who love her so." John wondered what his wife thought God might possibly have been thinking to allow Hattie's heart to malfunction as it did, to let her suffer so. Still he whispered his token *amen* and they ate.

"And she's fine in herself?"

"She's thin and she's awful weak but she's all there underneath. She can talk only in whispers, which is novel for my mother."

"Does she recall the attack itself?"

"She looked at me and she said *Rosamond, you don't need be afraid but dyin feels kinda like havin Fatty Arbuckle standin on you, dancin a jig.*" John laughed, he could hear Hattie's voice in Ros. "I mean," she went on, "expecting to see angels and what you get is Gene's dopey face looking down at you. It's enough to put the scare on anyone." Again they laughed but it had begun to feel forced and so quickly fell away. The words *expecting to see angels* reverberated in him and sank slowly.

113

"It'll be an uphill struggle but if anyone can do it, it's your mother."

"God willing." They ate for a time, John unable to stop himself wondering what that little boy, that small girl, might be eating out there in the Convene woods. "My concern, excuse me," began Ros, swallowing, "is that Gene has been enquiring about that WPA work down in Portland, which would leave poor Margaret with little Edwin *and* Mother to care for."

"I warned Margaret not to marry into this family."

"As your father warned me not to marry into yours."

John raised his eyebrows, knowing it had not so much been a lighthearted warning from his father as an ill-informed and pompous wish.

"Is the WPA work certain?"

"They're laying road like it was licorice, they say," she sighed, "and Lord knows he and Margaret need the money."

John suddenly saw where the conversation was headed.

"So you're saying..."

"Well. If this Portland work comes good I was thinking that maybe I'd move in with Margaret, for a time, to help with mother's convalescence." John's stomach made a fist. The thought of himself rattling around alone in the house, with only The Notion to keep him company, frightened him, made him want a drink.

"Right," was the best he could manage in answer, "I understand."

◆

If Convene was a dead end then John was at a loss. The noxious Cecil had said that what John was looking for wasn't there; *they aint here, mister.* But *had* he stressed the word 'they'? He played it over and again in his memory but failed to pin down the man's intonation. Perhaps Cecil knew the three and was simply saying that they weren't to be found in Convene. Perhaps he was saying nothing of the kind. He wondered if poverty somehow brought a person closer to the impossible, tolerant of the preternatural. The more he played it the less authentic it became, Cecil growing ever more grotesque, all but slavering, something afraid in his eyes as he indeed stressed the word *they*. But misremembrance wouldn't help John any and could only hurt, so he cut the possibility loose.

The day of Hattie's homecoming approached, Ros busy gathering her things for the move. With every item Ros packed, the house grew around him, the empty space unfolding, swallowing him up.

Through the trees they traipse, to where exactly none of the three can say. The little girl is picking at the thin man as if he were a thread, hoping to unravel him with her jibes and insinuation.

"You know you got things livin on you?" Instinctively the thin man scratches at himself. "You lousy, mister." She watches the specks hop about on the back of his neck, jumps up and tries to pinch one off of him, instead pinching flesh, squeezing too hard. He flinches, claps his hand to the offended area.

"They aint hurtin you, little girl. They mean no harm."

"They're bugs you fool. They spread diseases."

"They just need warmth like the rest of us. I'm just givin em a ride."

"They suck on your blood, you know that?"

"They're welcome to it if it sustains em, I got enough for them *an* me."

"You wake up an they've made off with a whole arm, you'll feel pretty fuckin dumb."

She runs to catch up with the old woman, skipping alongside her for a time. The old woman refuses to look at her, speaks from the corner of her mouth.

"What now?"

"Nothin," smiles the girl, "excited is all."

"You see how excited you are if one day we get there and the subject is *you*."

The girl laughs.

"Never gonna happen an you know it."

"Not if you shut yer mouth an do as yer told."

The girl blows a Bronx cheer. They go on. The whelp wonders aloud.

"I think I liked Mr Mann the best. It was slow, he kicked and kicked. It was funny," she stifles a coquettish giggle. "If only they all had but one neck to stretch."

Still the old woman speaks without looking at her.

"But then what would you do for laughs?"

The girl studies her feet as she walks.

"I guess," she bites her lip, serious, "but I liked Mr Mann the best."

The trees end rudely, the path yawning onto a wide, gray scar in the earth which rises and falls, as if in swelling, before falling away into a large dusty basin. The old woman stops, frowning, kicks the toe of her shoe into the colorless earth. She spits, gives a slow liquid motion to her shoulders as if her dress suddenly doesn't fit.

"Well?" says the girl.

"Are we arrived?" comes the thin man's voice from behind. He shakes his head. "I do not think we are quite there."

The old woman's lips buckle in disgust.

"Place is a fuckin shit stain."

"I like it," chirps the girl contrarily.

"Shut up," says the old woman.

They come to a deep hollow and climbing down into it, stones sliding under their feet, they each find a spot and sit, waiting. The little girl counts pebbles as the light fails.

Expecting to see angels. He wondered what it must be like to expect angels, how such an expectation might possibly produce anything other than alarm, or outrage. Frank Mayes that night had seen something in the woods, maybe angels, maybe blue devils the amount of popskull he'd drank, and his heart had nearly upped and killed him.

John was typing up notes, letting his mind stray, but at this thought his fingers failed on the keys. Joseph's words: *imagined he saw somethin one night that didn't agree with him.*

He stood and crossed to the patient files, slid open the drawer, walked his fingers to the letter M.

A man steps out of the woods, hands in pockets, shoes kicking up dust. He walks with a purpose not just because his stomach yearns for an evening meal, but because he knows full well that in half an hour or so he won't be able to tell his own hand in front of his face; already stars are showing through the waning blue above.

As he nears a hollow in the ground a figure stands up out if it, making him start, and he cries out in surprise.

"Jesus. You scared me," his eyes strain, the figure grows definition, perhaps as the moon rises; if he gives an expression of recognition or of fright, it is swallowed in dusk. "Hello?"

A frayed old woman contemplates him with just about the saddest look he's ever seen, perhaps merely the blankest. A crunch of stones and a little girl's face appears over the edge of the hollow, rising up as if out of the ground itself, then arms, then legs; a little girl crawling up out of the earth on all fours, feral-eyed, teeth bared, more thing than child. The thing breathes spittle; did its eyes glow a dull red? He takes a step away from them; this isn't right, is terrible strange. Something inside him hastens its cold tattoo. Next a man reveals himself, gaunt, kind eyes over a tattered beard, his pencil arms raised in welcome, his suit jacket hanging on him; in the dimness, his hands glisten wetly. He speaks softly as he nods a greeting.

"Hello, Frank."

John stood on the tree line, the fingers of his right hand working overtime on the handle of his bag, and stared over at the shape on the gravel. Deputy Walker suppressed a yawn as he made his way over from the body.

"Mornin, Bisch."

"Harry."

"Friday thirteenth, unlucky fer some alright."

Frank lay on his side, eyes open, as if looking back at them. At any moment he might smile, or throw a wink. John closed his eyes. He found himself unconvinced by the idea of luck, good or bad, or of coincidence; they felt watery and unsound. The polished penny, transferred from pants pocket to pants pocket, something of a charm, felt warm against his thigh. He opened his eyes, the body hadn't moved. It was a telegram, a wagging finger, a *we know who you are*.

Things had the feeling about them of acceleration. This could not be allowed to continue.

State of Maine.

Cumberland **ss.**

I certify that I was notified on the *13 th* day *of September* A. D. 19 *35*

at *7* h. and *15* m. in the *fore* noon by *Deputy Sheriff H. Walker*

of *Naples* of the finding of the dead body of *Frank E.*

Hayes of *Naples*

supposed to have come to h *is* death by violence or unlawful act; that I forthwith repaired to the place

where said body lies and took charge of the same, and before said body is removed make, or cause to be made,

this written description of the location and position of said body, viz:

The body was that of a man five feet six inches tall, weighing
one hundred thirty-five pounds, having grey hair, blue eyes and
blond mustache, teeth false.
He was dressed in black shoes, black striped trousers, heather
sweater, blue shirt and blue tie.
His pockets contained a pipe, can of tobacco, a jackknife,
one key ring on which were seven keys, an open face gold watch
which had not stopped, a small pocket book containing sixteen
cents in change, two ten dollar bills, one ruler.
The body was found under a pine tree on the Dillingham Estate
in Naples near the gravel pit.
There was cyanosis of the extremities, head was retracted ,
there were no marks of external violence, rigor mortis had set in.
He was last seen by E. R. Wiggins, Jr. walking towards his home.
When he did not get home that night his brother in law instituted
a search for him finding his body in the above stated place. He had
been suffering from heart trouble for a year, having had an attack
of coronary thrombosis just about a year before his death.

Cause of Death-   Coronary Thrombosis.

Date *Dec 2.6* 19 *35*

John M Bishopperger
Medical Examiner.

IV

Nobody ever knew everything. I sure don't pretend to and any man who does is a stone cold liar an a fool. Things get mixed up, forgotten, lost in some translation. What the British call Chinese whispers. You may know it as Telephone, or Pass The Message. Words passed along from person to person become elastic, lose their shape.

I have a favorite word. Contrary to what much of Naples would have you credit, it aint a curse word. It aint *solid*, it aint *gold* and it aint *bullshit*, though I freely admit to usin them three more than others I praps oughta concentrate on. No. My favorite word is Obfuscate.

It means to confuse, bewilder or stupefy, to make unclear.

Obfuscate is a word for what politicians do, what I spose they're *for*. Priests, preachers, salesmen of every stripe, bunco artists and carnies, unfaithful spouses and lawyers; obfuscators all.

Things have a habit of bein buried, covered over, smoothed so as you'd never know they had ever been, or how real they ever were.

Like the story about the idols. You believe that? Well, I know some of it's true, I can tell you that for sure, but then it goes off somewhere, gets muddied with nonsense til no one knows what to believe.

The Hill brothers, Charles and Reuben, were either tea mer-chants or railroad men, dependin on who you talk to. They sailed over to China to make their fortune and make it they did, not least by looting a local temple of gold, precious stones what have you, together with three golden idols, a haul that was rumored to top $30,000; back then one hell of a tidy sum and not so mean now either. Some ascribe the looting to that Boxer Rebellion they had over there but I've read a few books and I'm not at all convinced the dates match up; anyway. Some say that inside the idols were jewels, others that they contained written scrolls, stories and prayers offered by acolytes of whatever Celestial faith over hundreds ayears, hidden there for who knows what god to peruse.

There were two smaller idols and one big one, this larger fella standing some eight feet tall, a grand grotesque thing, made of bronze, or brass or somesuch. Wasn't gold like some will tell you. And I know that much because I saw it.

Anyhow, the brothers come home to Naples with their treasure, tore down the family home on Long Lake and threw up a mansion, sixteen rooms an all. Called the place Bellevue Terrace. It was there I saw the big fella. In the front hallway, at the foot of the staircase, standin glaring out the door like some gilded monster. Some kind of party, function, what I was doin there hell only knows. People were being led through the house to the garden. Musta been summer cause the doors were open and the sun came in and seemed to set that thing afire. Looked like a soldier to me. Wearin some kind of armor, tall helmet. Giant hands together in prayer, face calm but terrible. Let me tell you that face left an impression.

A little while later the brothers hit hard times and the money began to dwindle. Despite what some might think, you don't stay rich by drinkin champagne and sittin on your ass. So they decided to return to China and trade tea or lay railroad tracks, whichever it was, and while they're over there they happened upon the temple they stole the idols from and wouldn't you know it, the monks there recognized em, chased em down, caught and killed em. Stories of beheadings and skinnins in the streets are, I think, nothin but ghoulish embroidery. People love that shit.

So now folks back home start to talk of a curse on the idols that lead to Reuben an Charlie's deaths. Curses are always talked up after the fact. The grieving family, spooked by talk of such witchcraft, threw the two smaller idols in the lake, where they sank like stones and for all I know they lay to this day. The big fella in the hallway, well he just disappeared; some said buried on the house grounds.

The house was sold to the White family. John S. White had a son, another Charles, a writer they say. Awhile later Charles was murdered on the Portland Waterfront. White sold up to the Sodens, who renamed the house The Hayloft, traded in antiques and ran a restaurant for tourists; one day Charles Soden hanged himself in one of the upstairs bedrooms. Little more than a year later the widow Soden, seemingly the picture of health, dropped dead on the back porch. If tragedy has likewise struck the current owners, they've kept it pretty quiet.

In the meantime, in 1889, the big fella turns up in the Boston Museum of Fine Arts, a little tarnished but large as life and twice as gruesome; whether he walked all the way to Boston himself isn't recorded.

This whole thing is, I note not without a sense of irony considerin the source of the supposed curse, naught but a game of that Chinese whispers. Telephone. Things get added, taken away, forgotten altogether. Some will tell you that the statue was fifteen feet tall, that its eyes were rubies, that its expression changed when a death occurred, the smile gettin wider. Elements have been woven together, one part to another in a way that doesn't fit, other elements discarded because they don't fit the story as most would like it to be. Most want the curse to be real, maybe because then the story holds a moral: if you transgress, you will be punished. For some there's a comforting order in that, if a somewhat pitiless one. But of course that's nothin but solid gold bullshit, or maybe solid brass.

History is a slow, steady process of wiping away, of muddying, making faint, of obfuscation. You know this when you've lived enough of it. Things are buried all over, we walk on them daily, and every footstep pushes the earth down a little tighter.

So you may not know it, be able to prove it with pen and paper, but you know. You know there aint no curse and never was any such a thing. Nonsense. You may not know you know it, may not wish to know it, but know it you most certainly do.

Naples, Casco; Maine

February, May, July, December, 1936

The three, resting, huddled together against a wide bank of snow, somewhere among the trees. Wrapped in a blanket, the thin man studies his bandages, wincing, the little girl watches him with unconcealed disgust. Atop her caribou hide, the old woman's eyes are closed, lips parted, her breaths a slow, regular issue of steam. A wind whistles through and about them. The girl's distaste spills over into speech.

"I hate you, you know that? I truly do."

"I know," answers the thin man quietly, pulls his blanket about him.

"Wouldn't spit in your face if your head was on fire." At this he merely nods. "An you're gonna sit there and pretend like you don't hate me back, aint that right?" He seems surprised.

"I don't hate you."

"So you're better than me is that it?"

"Better? No."

"Then what? You feel sorry for me? Tell me you feel sorry for me and I'll cut your throat where you sit, you sunovabitch."

He spends a moment in thought before answering.

"You are wicked."

The little girl stifles a laugh with her hand.

"I *am*?" Her eyes widen and she leans toward him, a tremor of excitation in her voice, "I tell you what you gimme some tinder and box a matches an you'll see fuckin wicked."

"It's not your fault. You're wicked because you have not known love. Love begets love. All that is fostered by hatred is yet more hatred. I do not judge."

"An you better not try it neither," she spits, mutters, "better than me my ass."

An automobile passes somewhere nearby, revealing them to be closer to a road than they had thought; the old woman stirs, brows corrugating; she mouths some profanity or other and grows still. The other two watch her sleep, both perhaps a little afraid of her, if truth be told. In that moment a current passes between them, something shared, and despite her enmity, the little girl is moved to lean into him, to whisper.

"Listen, how about the next one we do, you keep the old witch here talkin and I'll pick the person's pocket, we split the winnings?"

"That aint the way," he whispers back.

"That's *her* talkin."

"Stealing is a sin."

"You took that old man's wallet that time."

"It was wrong, I took it back, I—"

"What do the dead want with money? Aint there enough folks on the road hereabouts in need of it? Hungry people?"

"It aint right."

"But think of the good you could do with it."

"Thou shalt not steal."

"Aint you hungry? Aint I?"

"*Thou shalt not steal.*"

"So you'd deny me food so some dead old man can keep his pockets fulla change?"

"Sinful."

"You deny me food, you fuck?" spits the girl. The old woman's voice cuts through them and they both start.

"MONSTERS DON'T EAT," she says loudly, eyes still closed, "cept when they're pretendin to be otherwise." Her eyes open, narrow. "How bout we all stop this fuckin playacting?"

Ros never finished packing her case. It had been returned, empty, to its place in the hall, reminding John every morning of the moment when The Notion had become a proposition. To look at it in any other way than obliquely would be to regret it, to see it as terrible, and so he looked the other way as best he could, ingesting the guilt and going on with it.

The suggestion that Hattie move in with he and Ros, rather than Margaret and Eugene, the selling of this proposition with the shameless mention of the vacant, childless box room, John knew he had made with less authenticity than it appeared. He received his wife's tearful thanks with discomfort, told himself it was his only course of action.

If those proximate to death, whether ailing or merely misadventurous, drew these creatures from the woods, then it stood to reason, if reason might squeeze into such a notion, that the best way to catch them might be with just such bait. Hattie as lure. He thought this most likely the worst thing he'd ever done, yet this realization failed to break his stride. It was here of course that his guilt came into it, an unwelcome pang, and was promptly pushed away.

They brought her home mid-September, thin and gray, maneuvering her through the house on a stretcher, carefully threading her through door after door, before depositing her in the box room. Doctor Wolcott had been firm: Hattie was not to move a muscle for six weeks, she was to become a living statue, John was to administer the prescribed medical treatment and Ros was to care for her.

In addition to prescription, John made homeopathic dilutions of Cactus grandiflorus, as his literature dictated for Hattie's condition, the plants themselves bought mail-order from Mexico, arriving wrapped in wax paper with a hand-written label which read *Reina de la Noche*; he added drops of the dilution to Hattie's morning glass of water.

Wolcott called every week or so to check on her progress, but as the cold gradually fell on Naples, the snow along with it, it became just the three of them in the house, a strange mirror of the family they'd always wanted.

Though repainted, the room still glowed invisibly with the birth that had failed therein, the loss of that imagined life, where Ros had wept as if something had broken open within her, some levee or earthwork; wept as if she might never stop, wept as he held her, held her as he felt stupid and incompetent. The speckled bedding, the tiny bundle by candlelight; that little collection of pale limbs, perfect in all but its lack of breath, of color. Sometimes John imagined the child that never was as some malignancy from wherever people came from, unwilling to be born, uneager and disinclined to enter the world, to become his child.

Hattie indicated that she liked the room just fine. Ros waited patiently for recovery or disaster, John for the impossible.

With an indomitable will, Hattie became as stone for those six weeks, speaking no more than a handful of hoarse words. She slept a great deal and while awake simply stared into nothing until sleep returned. Ros bathed her and dealt with her bedpan, John aided in the changing of bedding. The weeks passed and no one came to kill her.

By early November she was able, with no great speed, to cross the room to use a commode, and the bedpan was put away. A chair and table were brought in so she could eat her meals sitting, as she put it, "like a person". John thought Hattie moved as if she were made of paper and afraid a sudden draft might carry her off.

Thanksgiving arrived, then Christmas, and for both they sat about the kitchen table, Hattie dressed as if for church, and for the first time in his own house, so as not to draw attention to himself, John closed his eyes and pretended to pray as grace was said, smarting with every word.

♦

Sumner Newcombe was doubled over with stomach pains. "FOLDED IN HALF, THINKS HE MIGHT BE DYIN," Maisie Newcombe shouted through a neighbor's telephone. John saddled up Old Pinkham and rode out into the snow, checking the tree line as he went; he thought Hattie over the worst, his plan a failure, but it would do no good at all to miss the three should they make a play whilst he was out.

Sumner lay curled in bed at the back of the small house, winced his *hey, Doc*. A heavy, burnt, not entirely unpleasant smell hung in the room.

"Hello, Sumner. It lessened any?"

Sumner gave a grimacing nod.

"Some."

"You been eating okay?"

"Well as I can. Maisie there could make a feast outta wood chips."

"And no more popskull?"

"No, sir."

John lifted Sumner's nightshirt and felt about his stomach, pushing to feel for any masses hiding inside. The patient endured the examination through a pained attempt at a smile. "Tomorra's harvest, Doc, I be okay fer that?" John looked down his throat, smelt his breath. He sighed, shaking his head. He should have recognized the burnt smell.

"You've been cooking coffee again."

Sumner ran his tongue around the inside of his mouth, gave a half-shrug. "Maisie?" John found her at the stove. A scorched pan holding pitch-black coffee grounds sent off waves of heat. "Maisie, I've told Sumner but he won't listen so I'm telling you. I know times are thin but you can't just keep grounds and keep grounds, add water when you need them. You worry them too much they leak a poison. Two or three times is the limit. When they're done they're done."

Maisie Newcombe reminded John of a prize fighter, harried but stoic; undefeated. She met his statement with an unsmiling nod.

"He be okay?"

"This time he will, Maisie. But no more of this, okay?"

"I appreciate it," she nodded, "what with the harvest an all."

He thought of Sumner and his men out on the frozen lake, tracing out a grid, sawing huge cubes of ice, raising them up onto the cart. Hard, bitter work in a Maine February. The blocks would be packed in sawdust to survive until the warm weather made folks need it and willing to pay for it. John thought it a strange trade, like a magic trick, something out of nothing; frozen water into money. Hide it away in sawdust and it'd survive for months, hold it to the sun and it'd leak through your fingers to nothing; something unsettling resonated in him.

He reached into his bag and brought out a bottle of *Dr. Herring's Ginger Ale*, which he thought was all the doctor Sumner's indigestion required. Maisie took the bottle with thanks and asked what they owed him. Her eyes told him they were up against it, that only a fool would buy ice in winter.

"You buy me a drink in return sometime, throw me some of that white gold come summer and we'll call it quits."

Maisie merely nodded, showing neither gratitude nor surprise, though John felt them nonetheless; as he left she shook his hand.

His ride home was plagued with the certainty that when he arrived he'd find footprints in the snow at the back of the house, a window prised open and Hattie smothered in her bed. He found no such thing.

Cats curl about the old woman's legs, purring like motors as she works the ache out of her fingers. They're done but the thin man has asked that they remain in the room awhile so he can get warm. He hugs the blanket about himself and walks in place. The little girl lays back on the bed alongside the dead man. Hands behind her head, she studies the ceiling.

"This one was too quick," she says, "don't see the point when there's no sport in it."

"Quiet, monster," says the old woman. The girl smiles.

"I'm a monster what's that make you? Or the imbecile there?"

The thin man stamps his feet.

"Just need a little longer," he says quietly. The girl makes a short noise of disdain.

"When that stove burns out the temperature's gonna fall like a stone anyways," she says, yawning. "I coulda killed ten men while you're foolin around."

The old woman sits on a chair in the corner, clenching and unclenching her hands. How has it come to this? She's worked alone for so long but now the very idea seems like a dream, as if she's always been part of the three. The thin man reaches to pick up one of the cats, a large tortoiseshell, perhaps to leech its warmth, but it hisses at him, claws his hand and he cries out. The little girl laughs, then all at once her face darkens; something has occurred to her.

"Wait a second, was this one different? And the last one?"

"Nothins different," says the old woman.

"It aint? This one and that Frank fella on the gravel, they weren't different?"

"Same."

"They weren't different?"

"What did I just say? That aint how it works."

"What's this fella's name?"

"Searge," answers the thin man; he risks a smile at having been a help.

"Where do I know that name?" The little girl strains to recall.

"You don't."

"I don't? They weren't a warning, this one and the last one?"

The thin man stops stamping his feet, stops sucking at his cat scratch, looks at the little girl, then at the old woman.

"I don't understand," he says, "what does she mean *different*? *Warning*?"

The old woman stands.

"Nothins different."

"You standin there and tellin me this one and the last one weren't a message to someone?" The girl is smiling horribly in revelation.

"To who?" asks the thin man, and he begins to blink fretfully.

"Shut up, can't you see she's tryin to aggravate you?"

"A message to who?" he asks again, close to tears.

"Is someone on to us? Are we bein hunted?" asks the girl gleefully "Because that's what I'd call sport." She throws herself back onto the bed in excitement, the dead man bobbing and rocking beside her. The thin man walks in place again, though this time with agitation rather than cold; the old woman forces herself to sit back down. He kneels down by her.

"I don't understand," he says. "What does she mean? Are we in trouble? Did we do wrong?"

The old woman closes her eyes, takes a deep breath. He begins to sob, lays his head on her lap, and she stiffens. She takes a handful of his hair and pulls until they're looking at one another, noses inches apart. She speaks quietly through her teeth:

"I'll not say this again so you listen. *She* is not your friend. She's a liar an she will bullshit you from here to hell an back. She's here to get you all turned around, chasin yer tail. She talks big but she aint nothin but a gnat, like you. Yer both nothin but this mornin's bowel movement. Do not pay her no mind. There's a line and o she dances around it, but make no mistake she crosses moren inch over and I'll drown her in a fuckin sack. If you had a fuckin backbone stead of a wet noodle you'd see that. And I aint here for you to cry on neither, just so

135

you know there's a line fer you too. Next time you talk to me like I'm yer mama I'll give you moren a fuckin scoldin. Are we clear?"

The thin man nods and she lets go of his hair. He gets awkwardly to his feet, sniffing, wrestling his breathing under control. The old woman stands. "So let's move on," she says.

The little girl is on all fours, hunched over the man on the bed. Her head is working sinuously on her neck in slow circles, as if in the act of kissing. Wet sounds can be heard above the dying crackle of the stove.

"Hey," barks the old woman. The girl turns and her face is a nightmare.

John dug at the splinter with a pin. Pushing too hard, he flinched and his finger began to bleed. He thought it felt colder inside than it did out.

It had taken three of them to break through the door, men clumsy in their overcoats and winter boots, puffing out steaming breaths laced with whispered curse words.

Inside, four large cats had eyed the men suspiciously from the windowsill. Jed Harmon was the first to see Searge and covering his mouth with a gloved hand, ran from the house, refusing to return. Every so often when the wind was right, the rest of them caught his voice outside as he paced in the snow, repeating the same phrase over and over: *the cats, o God, the cats, o God.*

Everett Dearborn simply said "Son of a bitch" and fell silent. Frank Pitts fixed his jaw, and went about looking for any liquor that might calm Jed. As he left the room he patted John on the shoulder, muttered "Awful shame."

The mess left of Searge's face had transformed him into a kind of awful clown, a huge meat grin stretching from ear to ear, tiny pinkish teeth pearl-like among the red; his nose and chin were pitted with nibbles as if by buckshot. That there was no blood on the pillow, suggesting the injuries had happened post mortem, did little to ameliorate the abhorrence John felt at the scene. *The cats,* came Jed's voice again, *o God.*

John had known full well that Searge had been with Frank Mayes that night; it had been Searge that called him, drunk as a lord, screaming about chest pains. *Imagined he saw somethin one night that didn't agree with him.* It was well known Searge had been ailing with his blood pressure more or less ever since. If Frank had seen something that night then maybe Searge had too. John had known this and yet he'd willfully disregarded it. He'd been stupid and cowardly. Searge was laughing at him for letting him die, mocking him from his death bed with his chewed-up smile and blank eyes. And all the while John had been playing snipe hunt with his poor mother-in-law. *They* were laughing at him, wherever they were.

State of Maine.

Cumberland ss.

I certify that I was notified on the 22nd day February A. D. 19 36

at 2 h: and 45 m. in the after noon by F. O. Pitts

of Naples of the finding of the dead body of George

Southworth of Naples

supposed to have come to h is death by violence or unlawful act; that I forthwith repaired to the place

where said body lies and took charge of the same, and before said body is removed make, or cause to be made,

this written description of the location and position of said body, viz:

The body was that of a man about six feet tall, weighing about
one-hundred seventy-five pounds, partially bald, having dark hair
streaked with grey and grey beard. The eyes were brown. Both cheeks,
the chin, nostrils and lips had been gnawed away by cats which were
shut in the house with the body. The body was frozen, there were no
marks of external violence.

The body was found on the bed in the home of the deceased, dressed
in grey flannel shirt, grey woolen socks and woolen underwear. His
trousers hung near the foot of the bed.

In one shirt pocket was a leather purse containing four ten dollar
bills, one five dollar bill, one lincoln penny. The other shirt pocket
contained another purse filled with receipted store bills. His trousers
pockets held a leather purse containing eighty cents in change; a key
ring holding four keys, one Elgin open face watch, one tobacco pouch.

He was last seen alive on Tuesday, Feb. 18,1936, by a neighbor
P. K. Spiller of Cooks Mills, who states that at this time he was in
his usual health. He was not seen alive after this. On Saturday,
Feb. 22, having noticed no signs of life about his house, Mrs. Spiller
notified the selectmen of Naples, who in company with myself broke
into the house finding the body as described. The deceased had been
suffering from high blood pressure for several years. About seven
months previously he had been treated for shock, his health having
been poor since then. Death evidently occurred in his sleep from shock.

Cause of Death: Cerebral Hemorrhage.

John M Bishopberger M.D.
Medical Examiner.

Date Mar 1 193 6

Her tiny hands move about under the clear water, over pebbles, letting off a pinkish mist which curls in the current and vanishes. The sun is warm and flashes on the ripples she makes. The thin man comes to the water, pulling at his jacket, peering down, double chinned despite his leanness.

"I got a little on me," he says. The girl ignores him. He reaches down and wets his fingers, wiping at his lapel, scratching a dirty thumbnail over a dark stain. The sound of the lake is bright, crystalline, the air alive with yellow sun, trees vividly green. He pauses a moment to enjoy the day, before going back at his lapel.

"It washin off?" asks the girl without looking. He surveys his handiwork.

"Some. Not really." He sinks a little in disappointment.

The girl cups her hands and splashes him, giggling. After a moment he smiles and, bending down, splashes her back. They play at it for a time, now both wet and breathless. The old woman bellows out from the trees:

"*I'll count to five.*" They stop and the thin man turns, waves his acquiescence, perhaps an implied apology. As he turns back the little girl launches a nugget of sharp rock at him, striking him on the forehead with a loud *knock*. He cries out and claps his hands to the injury. The girl laughs a wide, true laugh and, reaching up, wipes her wet hands on his beard before skipping away. Smarting and hangdog once more, he follows after.

The question hung, rude and ungainly, Joseph chewing soundlessly at it. The shadow of a bird smeared past the open window. Sounds of traffic and a warm breeze. John became aware of the noise of the outside world in contrast to the quiet of the room. He took off his tie and played with it, fingering the seam, coiling and uncoiling it; his eyelids heavy with whiskey.

"I don't have you an answer to that," Joseph said finally.

"No." John refreshed their glasses, his head nodding as Joseph's shook, each the counterpoint to the other. They both looked at their glasses.

"You are sure in your own mind about this?"

"I have tried not to be so."

"And yet you know that—"

"It cannot be."

"Then I don't have you an answer."

John relished the sting of the alcohol in his throat.

"This winter. Searge. You know as well as I do he was there that night with Frank."

"I do, he was." Joseph was unmoved. John floundered again, all attempts at explanation leading him to naught.

"I'm sorry, Joseph."

"What in hell's name are you sorry for?"

"For asking you."

"Hell, don't be sorry for *that*. I've heard bigger damn fool things in my time." Their eyes met. "But not too many," which made them both laugh quietly. The room, stirred with levity, settled again.

"I've fought it every step and haven't stopped yet."

"I'm glad of that. What you're doin is, you're takin a lot of maybes and makin somethin unwarranted, you can't just—"

"Yesterday I viewed the body of Esther Archer."

"I heard."

"There was part of a little hand print. A child's. In blood. On the cheek," he pointed to his own face. Joseph's chin rose.

"Others saw it?"

"It was all but wiped away. There was a sort of clean spot too, on the other side."

"Okay."

"My guess would be that Esther was beaten on the one side, causing the blood, then the girl held Esther's head in her hands and beat it hard against the bedpost, perhaps three or four times. Perhaps the others kicked her."

"She didn't fall. This child killed her."

"Yes."

"Not the bronchitis. Not the..."

"Pneumonia."

"Not the pneumonia. You put that in your notes? Type it up, put it in yer book?"

"I did not."

"What stopped you?"

"I guess the fact that it's impossible. And absurd."

"And yet..."

"And yet."

The older man drank, fidgeted in his seat, ran his hand through his mess of hair. John felt his friend's disappointment as he might a dog bite, took a sharp inward breath. Joseph's hand worked at the air, lips failing to shape the words he needed. Eventually he spoke.

"I am not a believer in things," he waved the hand, "*other.* Things that cannot be measured, touched. I believe such things are childish nonsense that we have yet to outgrow. I believe you, as a man of medicine, believe this too. So you surprise me. I talk about folks. I am ornery, I'll admit. The human animal is of no great weight to me. But truth is, killin someone, when not a rash thing, when not in anger, when not the result of some derangement of mind, cold murder, is a rare thing. Rare thing indeed and we may be grateful to whatever or whoever we please that it's so. Killin folks aint as easy as some would have it. Trust me."

"I am not a Christian man, it's true." Something cold burned all over John as he said it, an admission never before made aloud; embers of a kind of betrayal. "I find such things," he

141

fought himself, "insubstantial. Wishful. Santa Claus too is a fine idea, but—"

Joseph interrupted:

"I killed a fella once, though I don't like to speak of it. Fact, not sure I ever have but if you ask me I'll tell you, because I know you know of war."

John swallowed, gave a tiny nod "Please."

The old man took a breath.

"Filipino come upon me while I was at my rations. Manila. Why there was only him I will never know. Lost maybe. There I was, pants and suspenders, not much else. I just looked up at him, can in hand, doornail dead an dumb. His rifle jammed. I bless that moment of mechanical caprice to this day. My bones would be on the other side of the world now. An so we rolled around some and I managed to force my can opener into him, pushed it in there, held him til his eyes winked out. The earth opened up an I fell through the world. Don't think I spoke moren three words for a month. Don't ask for any more detail as I won't give it." Joseph shook his head, "It aint so easy to go about killin folks."

John thought of the young soldier in France, the word *can't* whispered in cold rain, the feeling of mud forever under his fingernails. He thought of the abstract creature that the war had become within him, the collection of spurious images he kept secret, magnifications, dreams and phantasms; the immense and terrible sound, the shaking of the earth. Something of dirty white rags running on all fours through and above the trenches, dark eyes and a baring of tiny teeth, leaping on men, small hands gripping then twisting their heads with a sharp, wet crack; shovel-handed, blunt, cleaving parts and limbs from their owners, pruning men and gone before they fell, before even blood; a rigid finger quickly poking red holes in faces, bodies, as if made by bullets.

Joseph was studying him intently.

"I guess what I'm asking for is help," said John at last, "because for whatever reason, I find myself a believer." He sank the whiskey, made a face.

"I understand the draw of such thought, I do. No human mind does not. So you knew Frank, you knew Searge. Frank said he saw somethin. But Frank was drunk an this is a small town."

"I feel... targeted."

"They know you know."

"Yes."

"Frank and Searge are dead because of you."

"Yes."

"Why not just come kill *you?*"

"I don't know."

"Just as easy to kill one fella as another."

"They want me to look the other way."

"As they go about killin folk."

"Yes."

"And if you don't?"

"Others will die. Because of me."

"People will die no matter what."

"Maybe people I love."

"And yet Hattie's on the mend."

"They know I know."

"Three characters are roaming around hereabouts, killin people."

"Yes."

"A man, an old woman, an a child."

"Yes. Or at least that's what they appear to be. Outwardly."

"How they appear outwardly."

"Yes."

"An they're killin folk."

"Yes."

"Are they killin anyone outside of Cumberland County?"

"I don't know."

"Is anyone dyin in Cumberland County without these three killin them?"

"I don't know."

"But all those dead that you are called on to deal with are bein killed by them."

"Yes."

"Which is impossible."

"And yet..."

"You drinkin more?"

143

John let go the tiniest hesitation.

"I am."

"Tried not to?"

"Not so far."

After a moment Joseph stood, let out a deep breath.

"Alright," he said. "You are in a tough line of work, my friend. Can't say I'd swap you. Yknow my pa would say, *death always wins, but that don't mean you gotta let it beatcha.*"

"Something's beating these people, Mr Allen."

"Somethin always has, Doc." Joseph looked at him for a long while. "Don't you tell another soul about this. They won't understand."

"You understand?" The question seemed to force the older man's eyes away.

"Don't tell no one else."

12

State of Maine.

Cumberland ss.

I certify that I was notified on the _18_ day _May_ A. D. 19 36

at _4_ h. and _15_ m. in the _after_ noon by _Myron S. Hall_

of _Casco_ of the finding of the dead body of _Esther_

V Archer of _Casco_

supposed to have come to h _er_ death by violence or unlawful act; that I forthwith repaired to the place

where said body lies and took charge of the same, and before said body is removed make, or cause to be made,

this written description of the location and position of said body, viz:

 The body was that of a female, five feet, three inches tall, weighing about ninety-eight pounds, having grey hair and blue eyes. There was a discoloration of the left eye caused by laceration and contusion of same, a small bruise on the forehead and several bruises on the abdomen.
 The body was viewed in the undertaking parlor of Myron J. Hall, of Casco, Maine.
 Her daughter-in-law, Jesse R. Archer, with whom she resided states that she had been under the care of a Christian science practitioner for one month prior to her death.
 On May 14th 1936 she was confined to her bed by an acute cold she became delirious and while trying to get out of bed, while her attendant was out of the room she fell striking the end of the bed and sustaining the injuries found on the body. She became rapidly worse and passed away at four fifteen P.M. May 18th 1936.

Cause of Death; Acute Bronchitis
       Terminal Broncho-Pneumonia
       Accidental Fall

John W. Bischoffberger M.D.
Medical Examiner.

Date _May 26_ 193 6

July fourth they drowned little Oscar Bough, then later that month they struck down old Louis Rufus as he mowed the tennis courts over at Camp Wenonah. On the 25th, *something* caused Herbert B. Nelson to swerve his car suddenly, causing an automobile driven by Franklin C. Meade to collide with it, spinning it about and throwing from the car Nelson's passenger, one Mr Henry Small of Berlin, New Hampshire. Not killed instantly, Small was removed to the Central Maine Hospital at Lewiston. He vomited frothy blood several times on the way and died shortly after reaching the hospital.

In all cases John duly arrived after the fact, scooping up the dead with his notebook, feeling not unlike a man with a shovel that walks behind a horse.

A mound of dark hide shivers in a narrow hallway. Three breaths curl out into the bitter gloom, three heads sprouting from the hide, as if of one beast.

Somewhere in the house a yellow light shifts, perhaps being carried about an upper room, but does little to reach them. The light picks out colored paper chains hung about the doors, a child's drawing of a Christmas tree; beyond the light, the house is a clutter of shapes, untidy and chaotic. The hide's feet shuffle, walk in place.

In the dark, whispering voices, though it is near impossible to hear what is being said, or indeed from which head the whispers originate. Footsteps above. They fall quiet.

"This is mine," says the girl.

"Be quiet, monster."

"I'm tellin you, this one is mine, I claim it."

"And I'm tellin you to be fuckin quiet. He'll hear us."

"Isn't he—" says the thin man, before lowering his voice. "I'm sorry, but isn't he supposed to hear us?"

"In time." The old woman nods, takes a slow breath, but the girl cannot wait.

"In time hell. *Now*."

Again footsteps above, a muffled questioning word; the meager light shifts again before pouring down the staircase and through the doorway.

"Who's there?" A man's voice. "Gene?" A pair of black galoshes and a ragged fawn overcoat descend with heavy steps. Wilson has one eye closed below his fur hat and carries his head as if afraid it might suddenly disengage, fall to the floor and shatter. Once he's reached the bottom step he surveys the three, who stand wincing at his lamp. A cold moment passes. He is framed in the doorway, a golden figure in the black.

"Who're you?" he asks simply, a weariness overpowering any concern.

"We come to deliver a message," says the girl.

"*Shut up.*" The old woman grabs her by the scruff and she twists in the grip.

"You didn't oughta just walk into a man's house, aint you heard of knockin on a door?" He addresses the thin man, who bites at his lower lip and looks at the floor. Wilson closes his eyes for a time; forces them open. The three look to him to be little more than tatters and he shivers at the idea of the wind outside. "Aint got much by way of food but I'll see—"

"We aint hungry." The girl spits it, excited.

"You cold?"

"You reckon that's about the dumbest question that's ever come outta your mouth?" She brings to mind a dog straining on a leash.

"Wasn a question." Wilson looks to the old woman. "Your grandchild there needs a coat. An some manners."

"I aint no grandchild and you buttoned your last coat, you sunovabitch. You won't see mornin." Wilson is taken aback by the child. There is an instant of nothing. He lifts the lamp, leans forward. "What you fuckin starin at?" she asks.

"I'd be lyin if I said I knew. Tryin to figure out if you're real I guess."

"You in the habit of seein things?"

"Nope, but my head hurts fierce tonight and I guess there's always a first time."

"A last one too."

"Your head hurts?" The thin man steps away from the three. Wilson regards him suspiciously.

"Like I said."

"May I see?" He takes another step and Wilson rises a stair; the silhouettes of everything angle downwards.

"Thanks, I got a doctor." The thin man lifts his hand, reaches out, whether to shield his eyes from the lamp or for some other purpose seems unclear. Wilson reiterates, "Don't need no healer." The thin man stays in his queer pose, eyes tightly shut, arm extended, and they all watch him; his lips move without sound. Wilson fidgets, "Hey, I said—"

"Everythin is possible for those that believe," says the thin man quietly. Wilson looks at him, then at the old woman, then the girl; he is shaking his head, his mouth creases, the tip of his tongue plays about his teeth.

"No. You aint here. No, you get out. All of you, get out, get outta my house." The three fail to move. "*Get outta my goddamn house.*" The lamp sways and everything else sways with it, jaundiced and dizzying; still the three fail to move. Wilson pulls the door shut and is heard hurriedly stamping his way upstairs. The three are lightless again. The girl hisses a laugh, perhaps into her hand; the old woman sighs, the thin man is silent, perhaps praying. They wait.

Clattering and the slamming of doors thunders overhead, the shattering of something glass, perhaps china. The rectangle of the closed door is described in weak yellow light.

Footfalls descend and the light flares bright. The door flies open and Wilson brandishes a rifle, the barrel fed through the lamp handle, the lamp swinging back and forth, clacking against the trigger guard as he levels the gun at each of them in turn. The world pendulates. He's breathless and his hat has fallen somewhere in the rush.

"Real or not you get out of my house." The girl steps forward and the old woman lets her. Bathed in light, she looks up at him, calm, smiling sweetly.

"How do you want it?" she asks. Wilson keeps the rifle trained on the other two.

"I want not to have to shoot your friends here but I will."

"It's going to hurt and you're going to want to scream," says the girl brightly. Wilson lowers the gun to her face and the lamp slides away from him. The girl catches it by the handle as it falls from the barrel. "Oops," she says. They look at one another.

"Don't," is all he can manage. She swings the lamp playfully on her finger and everything goes head over heels.

149

The indoors was now outdoors, had escaped screaming into the woods on the back of the fire. All seemed to be its own opposite, all a contradiction.

John stood looking out of what had been the kitchen window. The trees and the trees and the trees. An old ladder-back had been reduced to sticks at his feet, everything was black. The smell was thick, acrid, and he recalled the burnt smell at the Newcombe place; he wasted moments wondering on the notion of prophecy and premonition before letting it drop. A biting wind blew through what remained of the house, lifting drifts of ash; here and there embers still died, still let smoke. Deputy Walker's gloved hand on his shoulder.

"Bisch? I can get Dandridge up here in a quick hour, you can go home, be with Ros and Hattie."

"No, thank you. You're a doctor long enough you will bury your own." The aphorism, taught him at college, had surfaced without thought. John tried a reassuring smile but it felt coarse on his face. "Thank you, Myron."

He imagined the scene hours before: the house alive, fire in the snow in the night, a ravenous orange light in the dark; all was its own opposite. He turned and opened his notebook.

Three Edes Falls men, who had begrudgingly stopped fighting the flames and solemnly watched the fire until dawn, lingered in the ruin, kicking through the debris. One, Robert Meserve, a close friend of Wilson's, could only make gloved fists and shake his head.

Among pieces of the fallen bedroom floor, now littering the kitchen, a kind of long blackened cushion, crudely sewn, lay among the timbers. Meserve picked it up and brushed it off.

"What's that? Pillow?" asked one of the Edes Falls men. Meserve said nothing. They stood there and looked at it; John felt moved to answer.

"It's a Dutch Wife, I think. Aids sleep in hot weather, or for some who suffer from joint pain. Knees or hips. The back." He felt as if he were giving a lecture or reading from a textbook, his voice strange in the cold and the quiet. "It aids sleep. Gives comfort." John had seen them used in the war, embraced in trenches, wept into, used to smother cries. One of the men, sooty and scrawny, let a short *well I'll be* laugh.

"Company too I'll bet," he said. "Robert, check that ol' bachelor Wilson didn cut no little hole in there." Robert struck the man solidly in the jaw, sending him down into the ashes, and the two had to be separated by Deputy Walker. Curse words were thrown, charcoal kicked up, and the man who had been struck was told to go the hell home before folks formed a queue to knock him down some more.

John scratched at his pencil with a thumbnail, lost in a thought that refused to make itself clear, staring at the blanket thrown over what remained of Wilson. He closed his eyes and held them that way for some time. The scorched walls clicked and popped lightly, the trees whispered in reply. It began to snow.

♦

Church, again. It seemed months since he'd been inside: patients, urgent call-outs in poor weather, illicit meetings with Joseph; work, white lies and avoidance. It seemed larger, the ceiling higher; it was cold, hats were held but none removed their coats. A low murmur of voices, he and Ros drawing looks from those who didn't know what to say, or didn't care to search for the words, their own troubles weighing enough thank you very much. A simple pine coffin, Wilson inside; what they could find of him.

As they made their way through the thin crowd of mourners, Charlotte Norton had touched Ros' arm, her mouth pursing dimly behind a fraying veil; Ros had nodded in appreciation of the sentiment but Charlotte had held on, eventually forcing out a low "Wilson always spoke the truth and shamed the Devil." John smiled tightly in thanks as he led Ros away, when in fact what he wanted was to tell the woman that she was a fool and that she had better grow up before certain things came knocking at her door, as they had at Wilson's.

They sat beside Eugene, who'd already maneuvered a frail

Hattie to her seat; any looks between the family remained strangely open and without focus, nothing to impart, no meaning or comfort to be had from so sudden a death, so early a passing.

John stared at nothing and thought of William Bray's insomnia, Caleb Burnham's gout, Winifred Cole's diarrhea; made lists and timetables in his head.

The Notion, this lie of his, had become the only way he knew to live, the only way not to send things tumbling. Time and again he'd wanted to tell Ros all but had not.

Reverend Grundy began to speak and John retreated, drifted, not back to Meuse, to Europe and the dying soldier, but to a blissful nowhere, void of thought or consequence. A single sob from Ros at his side and his retreat was spoiled. He gripped her hand, as if to keep from falling.

The lamp is out and Wilson is burning; John can see it. The church is gone, as is all its ceremony and consolation. Wilson is burning. He doesn't scream but merely moans an insistent muted tone, as if impatient, or gagged. He boils with fire, his clothes curl up on him and vanish, cinders rising up like lightning bugs; flames slither upwards, fingers forcing their way into his mouth and down to his lungs as he tries to snatch a last breath. The house burns around him and everything is afire, curling with orange, crawling with smoke.

Everyone rose to sing and John was forced back into the church. Standing, the organ blew its plaintive note and the hymn began. John opened his mouth but no words came; he fancied he felt a black plume coughed up between his teeth. The world swayed a little.

As they sat, he heard the Reverend say the words *Let us pray*.

Aconite Napellus for William Bray's insomnia, Colchicum for Caleb Burnham's gout, Arsenicum Album for Winifred Cole's diarrhea; Actaea Racemosa for Carroll Leavitt's rheumatism, Rhus Toxicodendron for Lydia Ann Perley's menstrual cramps, Podophyllum for Harry Paul's gallstones.

State of Maine.

I certify that I was notified on the _23rd_ day _December_   A. D. 19_36_

at _7_ h. and _30_ m. in the _fore_ noon by _Deputy Myron Walker_

of _Naples_   of the finding of the dead body of _Wilson Chaplin_

of _Naples_

supposed to have come to h _is_ death by violence or unlawful act; that I forthwith repaired to the place

where said body lies and took charge of the same, and before said body is removed make, or cause to be made,

this written description of the location and position of said body, viz:

The body was that of a man about five feet, seven inches tall, burned beyond recognition.

The limbs were missing except for small portions of the bones of the extremities.

The pelvis bones were intact and covered with portions of charred flesh to which adhered small pieces of charred clothing. A few fragments of the arms, hands, legs and feet were recovered. The skull was cremated with the exceptions of a few small pieces.

The remains were found in one corner of a room near a door leading upstairs to the bed room. A twenty two calibre single shot rifle lay across the left arm. Portions of a lamp bracket and lamp chimney were scattered about near the body.

He was last seen alive by his brother, Eugene Chaplin of Cooks Mills, who in company with Louville Edwards, also of Cooks Mills, called on him the afternoon of December twenty-second, leaving him about three-thirty P. M. His brother states that he had been in ill health for several days and complained that he was having severe pains in his head.

About twelve o'clock on the night of December twenty-second, Ellis Stone of Otisfield noticed the reflection of the flames. He drove about for several hours before he located the fire. He then aroused inhabitants of the village of Edes Falls, but when they arrived the buildings had been completely burned to the ground.

It is surmised that when preparing to retire the deceased picked up his kerosene lamp which he usually kept on a table in his living room and started for his chamber. Before reaching the stairs he was evidently overcome by a fainting spell or cerebral hemorrage falling to the floor, dropping the lamp and setting the building afire. As he was evidently unconscious he remained on the floor and was consumed in the fire which followed.

Cause of Death: Accidently Burned to death in burning buildings.

Medical Examiner.

Date   19

V

B ut then everythin is both ways, all the time. Simultaneous. If blood was all there was then we'd have all gone up in fire long since. Maybe we will yet. I guess it's just a case of which stays with you longest, which makes the biggest splash in you, which leaves the biggest stain; this I guess dictates how you see the world.

Like that, whattheycallit, The McIntosh Homicide.

George Peirce Jr., the first ever settler around here, rolled up at Crooked River around 1775, what now they call Edes Falls. And this first white man of Naples was quite the man. Businessman, lawyer, physician, surgeon, millwright, could, by all accounts, "write as plain as print" and never was there a stronger back nor so hardy a human. How much of this is hyperbole is anyone's guess but that's all by the by and gone to the obfuscation of history; believe half of it and he still comes out pretty damn well.

Now George had a neighbor, a Scotsman name of John McIntosh. McIntosh had taken a likin to George's youngest, Molly, and petitioned her father for her hand in marriage. For whatever reason George was not moved to agree and refused the match.

Some days later, in October of 1789, McIntosh, drunk, accosts Peirce at his home, finds him in the construction of a new harrow and words are exchanged, no doubt his suit put forth anew and summarily rejected anew. McIntosh attacks Peirce in anger, some say with an axe but I don't know about that, and Peirce defends himself with the tool he happens to be holdin, a large mallet, strikin the Scotsman across the skull, after which McIntosh flees and Peirce, fearin a return of the Scotsman with reinforcements or fresh weaponry, barricades hisself in his home.

In fact the wounded McIntosh made his way to the home of Eleazer Bartlett, some half mile or more away, who he begged to examine his wounds and tell him if he thought them mortal. Bartlett told him he thought they were not and McIntosh then asked him to go fetch a quantity of rum from his home while he rested at Bartlett's. Bartlett did so but on his journey back met McIntosh on the road, all fired up and suggestin that they both return to McIntosh's home, which they did, and where the Scotsman took up a broadsword he kept about the place and full of bad blood and fevered anger, instructed Bartlett to go and bring back "Percy" as he called Peirce, and swearin that he would see to the "whoreson" "if I have to tear the boards off his house to do so".

Bartlett no doubt hesitated, knowin full well the murder in McIntosh's eyes. But McIntosh then seemed to weaken and said that he wished Peirce called merely to tend his wounds, somethin which Peirce was known for thereabouts, possessin as he did equipment to bleed folks and to pull teeth, whathaveyou.

Bartlett indeed went to Peirce but only to warn him *not* to come for fear of further violence. Upon his return to the Scotsman, McIntosh's injuries had indeed worsened and Bartlett set forth again, this time returning with Peirce, who attempted unsuccessfully to bleed McIntosh and who then remained with him until he eventually succumbed to his injuries.

The death reported, Peirce immediately surrendered himself to the authorities and was tried and found guilty of manslaughter. Served eight months up in Portland Gaol and paid the sum of two hundred pounds, as was then the legal tender. Quite the Renaissance man, George Peirce Jr. even wrote a book while under lock and key.

Now here's a man, who when attacked, *provoked*, in his own home, defended himself, some might say defended his daughter, his family, from the murderous McIntosh. An this was an attack that can have been nothin but ferocious to set a man like Peirce barricading himself in his home. And yet when asked a second time he goes to this man, this drunken, sword-wieldin man, and attempts to save him from his wounds. This is astonishin to me. Can't say it'd take so few requests for mercy to get me to that bedside. Would it you? Beyond the mere sensationalism of the tale itself, this is the meat of The McIntosh Homicide for me.

This man saw the blood he'd spilled in defense of his family, the reality and truth of that, and he saw a man, that same man who'd come at him, askin for help and the bigger of the two for him was the latter.

And I'm not sayin he's wrong. I'm sayin he's rare, real rare, and perhaps the unappetizing thing I'm sayin is maybe he should be rare. His is the Christian reaction as I understand it, it truly is, but should it be the human one? I'm not talkin revenge or retribution, I'm not. I guess what I'm sayin is, is this a way to continue? As a species. Is this rational? Is this right?

It's not a question of should violence beget violence, it already did, Peirce defended himself; it's a question of whether violence should beget compassion, directly, or whether compassion has more deserving recipients, better places to be.

If McIntosh had an axe or not doesn't matter, the fact is had Peirce not had the mallet things may have gone the other way for him.

I don't hold with these fellas who parade their collections of guns around like some badge of foolishness, point it at the little man who aint got one, think it means somethin. I'm not pushin my chest out, there's no swagger in me.

All I know is that when I killed that Filipino that time it was because he was plannin on doing likewise to me and I never once felt it was wrong. I felt it was awful, dumb, regrettable even, but what else was I to do?

It *was* awful. Worst thing I can think of, but then maybe that speaks of a lack of imagination. That same day I told a sergeant to go fuck himself, then just stopped talkin. Got kicked around some, lost this here tooth and spent who knows how long in the stockade. Slept mostly. I didn't count the days, was grateful for the solitude. But I never thought it was a mistake. Had I merely injured him should I have nursed him? Maybe I'm glad I never had to decide. You don't set a broken leg on a rabid dog. And maybe I'm wrong but I'm just askin. Askin myself as much as askin you.

And in the end the answer is I don't know. Peirce saw beyond the blood and I'm not sure I could, not sure I'd want to. All I know is that it'd take more requests than most men have breath in em to get me to that Scotsman's bedside.

Harrison, Bridgton, Naples; Maine

May, June, July, 1937

An observer would be forgiven for thinking that the little girl and the thin man are dancing, perhaps a stilted or mannered waltz, but of course they are not. Her left hand is between his legs, making a fist of something soft there, tendons raised across her knuckles. His hands rest lightly on her shoulders, bandaged fingers every so often flutter, as if toying with the idea of closing themselves around her throat. His mouth is a crescent grimace, breathing hard.

A Mr Harold S. Caswell is crawling about at their feet, as if having dropped something; one red spattered hand is held at his neck, he is hissing between his teeth. Between his fingers blood seeps, discharging enthusiastically whenever he stumbles, whenever his hand lessens its pressure; his mustache is thick with it. He leaves a trail on the floorboards. He moans constantly, unintelligible sounds that rise every so often to high whines, terminating in wet glottal stops, a hurried intake of breath, before beginning again.

The old woman sits by a cooling fire grate and looks at and through this lunatic scene, lost somewhere else altogether. She appears bored, or spent, or both.

Harold has discovered the shotgun under the girl's right foot and using all the strength he can gather he tugs at it, whether to defend himself or finish the job half done is uncertain; the girl holds it fast under her, kicks at him with her free foot. Her eyes never leave those of the thin man.

"I told you to hold him you dumb halfwit." Her hand tightens, he squirms on the end of her arm, a puppet. Harold wetly mumbles what sounds like the word *Lord*.

"I— Sorry, he— Moved, he moved, I'm sorry he moved, please—" The thin man has turned his end of the waltz into a jig.

"Someone puts a shotgun under *your* chin, you'd fuckin move, wouldn't you?" says the girl.

"I'm sorry, please—"

"Are we gonna act *right*? Do we have a job of work to do? You gonna be a man? Or dyou like it when I do this?" A tightening.

From Harold, perhaps the word *Jesus*.

"No, I— Please—"

She moves in closer to the thin man, as if unable to hear him; she stands on tiptoes.

"You do, dontcha? You like this. You want I should crush em? Wait, is some— Is somethin gettin bigger down there? You growin in my hand, little man?" She laughs.

Harold suddenly bucks and bays a gargling howl of frustration at the ceiling; perhaps it's a kind of torn speech, perhaps the words *I can't*. Holding his breath, he rises, slow and excruciating, face fit to burst, to his feet. Interrupted, the dancing couple watch him.

"Well, look at you," says the little girl.

Wild-eyed, choked syllables are all that Harold can manage following his exertion. Another treacly discharge between his fingers. A light black rash of powder burn, like a handprint in coal dust, runs up his left cheek. He looks from the girl to the thin man, then to the old woman behind them, then again: girl, man, old woman, then again.

"Aint we a picture?" says the girl. Harold sways on his feet, looks at them incredulously, breathes with difficulty. The girl lets the thin man go and he falls into a pained stoop. "Go get more shells, halfwit. We'll keep doin this til we get it right." The thin man shuffles away. Harold and the girl watch one another. "Don't you worry, sir, we'll see you done," she smiles. He looks at her with what can only be described as a total lack of understanding. "We'll put you right," she says, and cannot help but laugh. Harold begins a kind of choked panting, pacing to and fro about the room. The girl studies him. "Why don't he run?" she asks the old woman. "You'd think he'd at least *try* to run." The woman doesn't answer. "I asked you—"

"Heard you."

Moments pass with only Harold's stumbling footfalls, wet breaths and frantic, bloodshot stare. The thin man returns with a handful of shells, the other hand cupped between his legs.

"I gottem, here they are, I gottem."

"Why don't he run?" the girl asks him. They both look at Harold.

"Maybe he knows," the thin man replies, then repeats, "I gottem." The girl picks up the shotgun. On end, it's taller than she is. She breaks it, and snatching a shell, loads it. Harold flinches as she snaps it shut.

"Well alright."

Perhaps the word *Hurts*. Perhaps *Help*.

"You want I should hold him again?" asks the thin man.

The girl throws him a disdainful glance, a gesture to the old woman.

"Well she aint gonna do it for you."

The old woman doesn't move. He leans in to the girl.

"She okay?"

"O she's thinkin about that fella."

"She *is*?" He ponders awhile. "Fella?"

"That doctor fella."

The old woman addresses the room through tight lips, speaking to no one in particular:

"Is that what he is? Doctor?" She gives out a short breath of disgust. "Seems to me the man's an accountant. At best."

State of Maine.

I certify that I was notified on the _2nd_ day _May_ A. D. 19_37_

at _9_ o'h. and _5_ m. in the _fore_ noon by _Deputy, Earl Davis_

of _Harrison_ of the finding of the dead body of _Harold G._

Caswell of _Harrison_

supposed to have come to h _is_ death by violence or unlawful act; that I forthwith repaired to the place

where said body lies and took charge of the same, and before said body is removed make, or cause to be made,

this written description of the location and position of said body, viz:

The body was that of a man five feet ten inches tall, weighing about one-hundred seventy-five pounds, having iron grey hair, blue eyes and black mustache. He was clothed in grey shirt and black trousers, brown socks and no shoes on the feet. The body lay face downward in a pool of blood, head toward the door and almost touching door jamb. A twelve gauge shot gun with empty shell lay over his right leg just below the knees.

The left half of the face was completely blown off, including the left eye, part of forehead, left half of nose and left half of chin, the left side and front of the mandible were missing, the palate and most of tongue were gone, the teeth had all been blown out of mouth, some being imbedded in the brain and others scattered over walls and ceiling of camp. The frontal bone was fractured. There were powder burns on under side of chin.

The body was discovered by Frank Stokes of Harrison on Sunday morning, May second, who had come to consult him about some work. He found the doors unlocked and on opening them discovered the body.

The deceased was last seen by Theodore Koten of Harrison, who talked with him on the previous Friday at four-thirty P.M. He states that he was acting strangely at this time. Several neighbors saw him going back and forth between his camp and barn on the day of his death, but saw him only from a distance.

No money was found on the body, his pockets containing a pen knife and open face watch.

A safe which stood in one corner was locked, this was opened by the sheriff and was found to contain his pocket book, which held fifty-seven dollars in cash. There was also a ten dollar gold piece, two silver dollars, several old coins, a watch and various papers and stock certificates. There was one dollar and eighty-two cents in small change in the house.

It is surmised that the deceased shot himself twice, the first time either because of holding the gun at an incorrect angle or jerking his head involuntarily to one side on pulling the trigger he merely grazed his neck, puncturing a vein in the neck causing severe bleeding but not disabling him. He then wandered about the camp as shown by blood stains on the floor, secured another shell for his gun and this time made a successful attempt at suicide.

Neighbors state that he had been acting strangely for some time. He was subject to fits of despondency.

Cause of Death; Suicide by shooting self in head with shot gun.

The day is warm, the trees brilliant above them, the three grimy and tattered in the breezy shade below. At four paces they are an indecorous, visual eccentricity in the woods, at forty paces they are invisible.

The subject of the doctor has refused to abate, despite the old woman's flat out ignoring the other two's questions.

"Perhaps he's next. Is he next?" whispers the thin man to the little girl. She spits at him, mimics his voice in falsetto.

"*Is he next?*"

The old woman turns on them. They both halt.

"Of course he's next," she says, "everyone's next. It's just there's an order is all. Now shut your mouths and come on." She walks on, batting branch and bush aside easily, leaving them to whip back into the little girl's face; the girl barely blinks. The thin man is agitated, insistent.

"But is he huntin us?"

"Maybe we're huntin him," answers the girl slyly.

"Which is it?" He's confused. The old woman's voice barks back at them:

"I guess we'll know when it's over. The one wins is the hunter. The other fella just thought he was."

♦

The thin man is gnawing noisily around the wormy patches on a small red apple, the little girl is sucking the last morsels off a collection of cold chicken bones. She tongues the gristle with something more than hunger. The old woman faces away into the trees, refuses to watch them at it, to entertain any longer such foolishness.

She believes that the time of these cretins will soon be done, that they'll both fall away eventually, vanish, and that in time she'll forget they ever were. Still she flirts with the notion of leaving them somehow, of escape back to a time when there was no one but herself, the trees, and the job at hand.

She sets about the slow and painful act of standing, a matter of balance, of popping sockets and sandy joints, of inhalation held. When upright, she takes a moment to gather fresh breath and sets off again, without so much as a backward glance. The little girl drops her bones, wipes her hands on the thin man's beard, which he receives without protest, and follows; he runs to catch up.

It's late morning and the sun is falling upwards to its peak, honeyed and oily in the blue. In time a small house makes itself known among the trees and they each stop and peer over at it. A woman is cutting kindling while a small girl watches on; a man's voice calls out from somewhere and the woman answers. Behind the house some way is a field, the man working away at it, to what purpose it is unclear at such distance.

"Come on," says the old woman, and makes to leave. The girl tugs at her dress.

"Wait a second, how bout we do these? Do the whole lot of em in one go? Paint the house red."

The old woman bats the girl's hand away.

"Be quiet. We got somewhere to be."

"Bull*shit*, what difference does it make?" The girl is working towards petulant, a favorite tone of hers. The old woman simply repeats herself.

"We got somewhere to be."

"Where?"

"Wherever we end up is where, come on."

The thin man is still peering over at the house. He takes a step towards it.

"These are honest people," he says.

"Shut up. Honest people." The old woman spits. "You tell that by lookin?"

"No. Look. This man here he works with his hands, he makes things. Farms the land. A hard workin man, like my daddy. These are good people, honest people doin the best they can with what little the Lord has provided. Times are tough all over, you seen it, we see it all over."

"Your daddy was a farmer?" asks the girl with feigned interest, relishing any reason to postpone following the old woman's orders to move on.

"Sure. Somethin with his hands... Sure, he was a farmer, why not? Like this here fella. A good man."

Teasing, she prods him with a finger.

"You don't seem half sure."

His face creases.

"I'm sure. I recall it."

"You don't seem sure."

"I'm sure."

"You don't remember any such fuckin thing," says the old woman.

"I do so." She purses her lips, her look says O *really?*

"What he think of what you're doin with us then, this farmer pappy ayours?" she says. The thin man is abashed, as if some fraud of his has been rumbled.

"Couldn't say. We doin what we must," he too purses his lips, "but it's an awful burden is all."

"O boo-hoo," pipes up the girl, tears up a handful of grass and throws it in his direction.

"Takes its toll is what I'm gettin at," he tries.

"Maybe you should think of retirement then, kick back, live off your fortune. Like these good, honest folks," sneers the old woman.

"I don't mean to sound ungrateful. This is wonderful. A good thing we're doin here. A fine brotherhood—" The girl interrupts him, aggressive, her prods turning to play punches:

"*Brotherhood?* You see many brothers here? You're the only brother here, *brother*, as close to a man as we got, or would be if you had anythin moren a peanut to pee out of down there." He flinches and retreats a step. The old woman leans against a tree and turns away, impatient but unwilling to be drawn further into their squabbling.

"Sorry," tries the thin man, "no, brotherhood is the wrong—" but the girl is on him in a flash, apology a chink she can exploit for sport.

"We a gang? A party?" she goads.

"No, I—"

"Hey, how about we're a trinity? I like the sounda that."

"No, I don't, I couldn't say— but I know, what I meant to say is, we do good, we are a good— I'm not tryin to say otherwise, nor—" He fidgets with his bandages. "Good work it's true. But it's a burden is all. I've been havin dreams. Bad dreams. This big, dark thing crawlin on me, puttin its fingers in my mouth, filthy, and I wake up not breathin. Dreams. About things I can't— I don't rightly understand." He takes a breath, fixes her with a plaintive stare. "I don't remember much of anything before this, do you?"

"Before what, imbecile?"

"Before this, before us, this enterprise of ours."

"Next time you wake up not breathin, give serious thought to stayin that way," she says. He sits down, right where he is, perturbed, fingers working at the air as if they might find there an answer to his troubles. The old woman turns to face him, irritated at his sitting, at his having anchored them to the spot by doing so. He looks to them both, eyes pleading.

"But I don't understand how I can't remember," he whines. The girl's tease has lost none of its momentum.

"Besides yer daddy, you remember *him*, so you say."

"Sure. I think so. But how can it be I don't recall much of anything else? Do you?" he asks the girl. "Do *you*?" he asks the old woman.

"*SHUT YOUR MOUTHS*," she bellows and they all start, the girl takes a step back and the thin man stands as if commanded to do so. The old woman goes on: "I don't remember nothin. I'm just a foolish old woman. Old as the hills. But despite aches, despite people bein ugly," thrown at the girl, "and dumb," at the thin man, "despite you two sons of bitches I will push on. You two are foolish and you're playin at it but I have work to do dammit. I'll still be walkin hereabouts when you two are smoke, are a memory, and I won't recall you at all. You'll be gone so absolutely. I don't remember nothin cus I don't need to. There aint nothin that changes so memory aint no use. You wanna remember what was? Look ahead, cus here it comes again."

♦

Inside the wardrobe the three twist and fidget, limbs of uncertain ownership push and dig at ribs and at rumps. The old woman's knees scream at her, but persuaded into the wardrobe she will not be the first out, she will see it through. Only a narrow blade of light illuminates this nest of arms and legs, perhaps a mouth twisted in discomfort, perhaps the pained closing of an eye.

"Nonsense," hisses the old woman.

"Ssshhh," hisses back the little girl.

"Shut your fuckin mouth." Somewhere in the dark, giggling. Somewhere in the dark, the thin man is breathing long and low. "Is that fool asleep?" says the old woman. "Give that son of a bitch a jab." A snort and a start, a syllable of enquiry as to his whereabouts; an apology. "Fool."

Having climbed in through the window, the old woman had labeled the proposed climbing into the wardrobe as *needless malarkey and folderol* and she had stuck by that, even as she climbed inside.

"I been workin on this fella," the little girl had said, "this is the way this one has to be, I told him already."

"What you mean, workin on him?"

"You know, workin on him, told him a thinga two, showed him a thinga two. Put the spook on him."

"So now why the hell the goddamn cabinet?"

"That's where I appeared to him the first time so I kept it up."

"Why in hell's name you do that?"

"I dunno. Little somethin they call theatrics."

"We a fuckin circus act now?"

"It worked. Shoulda seen his face."

"Folderol."

"You can wait outside if you like, behind a tree, til we're done." But the old woman didn't trust the girl to do things right on her own, and the girl knew it too, knew she'd get them all in the wardrobe and took great pleasure in her machinations. For his part the thin man never raised so much as a word in protest.

The thin man is still apologizing for falling asleep, blaming the pains in his hands and feet. Both the girl and the old woman tell him to shut the hell up. Somewhere in the house there are voices, a woman and a boy, the clattering of cutlery, the hard ceramic sound of crockery. There is a smell of cheese and old bread, the smell sour somehow and lacking substance; no doubt whatever ingredients there are have been stretched too far and for too long. The three wait in darkness as these people's lives go on beside them. After a time, the thin man whispers, barely a breath.

"Can I ask a question?"

"Can you do so while keepin yer mouth shut?" snaps the old woman.

"I— I'm sorry but it seems we needs must speak about this doctor fella."

"O we needs must, must we?"

"Gettin airs now, this bony sacka shit," laughs the girl. He goes on:

"It seems that our enterprise is threatened."

"By this doctor fella," says the old woman.

"Yes."

"Bullshit."

"He knows of us, yes?"

"I believe what he knows *entire* you could write on the head of a pin, and what he knows of us wouldn't amount to less than half of what we know of him."

"And yet he troubles you."

"O you think so?"

"Forgive me but I do, yes."

"Fuck him and fuck you."

"You said there's an order. I propose we make to move him up it somewhat." Suddenly the girl's voice:

"Hell yeah, let's do that, let's move him up the list."

"We'll do no such thing," hisses the old woman, "not until I say so. And that's an end to it." A pause, before he starts up again:

"But please, I only mean to say—"

"You think because I can't see you I can't reach out and black your eye? Trust me *I can see you* and I'll knock you clean through the side athis thing."

Somewhere in the house the young boy is singing quietly to himself, bouncing a rubber ball on floor and wall.

"Listen," starts the old woman, "maybe we keep an eye on this doctor, go see him maybe."

"Hell yeah," whispers the girl, "let's go see the fucker. Put the spook on him."

The old woman makes a face that can't be seen in the dark.

"Maybe."

"His confidence shall be rooted out of his tabernacle, and it shall bring him to the king of terrors," says the thin man from somewhere.

A crash from outside and another voice in the house, male, shouted words, diction slowed and rounded by alcohol. The woman's voice. The breaking of a plate. The woman's voice is cut short and the boy cries out.

"Do you have the knife?" asks the thin man.

"You better believe it," replies the girl, "an the gun's in the hall."

"You best be quick you wanna pull that trigger."

"O, I'll be quick."

"Wait for it," says the old woman quietly, "wait for it..."

State of Maine.

Cumberland ss.

I certify that I was notified on the 30th day May A. D. 19 3 7

at 1 P. m. and 15 m. in the after noon by E. S. Abbott M. D.

of Bridgton, Me of the finding of the dead body of Norris E

Allen of Bridgton

supposed to have come to h is death by violence or unlawful act; that I forthwith repaired to the place

where said body lies and took charge of the same, and before said body is removed make, or cause to be made,

this written description of the location and position of said body, viz:

    The body was that of a man five feet seven inches tall,
weighing about one-hundred ninety pounds, having brown hair and
brown eyes. The deceased was dressed in black pants, black belt,
shoes and stockings, he wore no shirt.
    The deceased lay on his back on the dining room floor in
a pool of blood, a small paring knife with blood on blade and
handle lay at his feet. A twelve gauge shot gun containing one
exploded shelllay at his right side.
    There was a knife wound about two inches long in the right
side of neck exposing posterior portion of trachea and a gunshot
wound surrounded by powder burns in epigastric region of stomach.
A gold seal ring was the only thing of value found on the body.
    The deceased returned home at about twelve fifteen P. M.
on the day of his death evidently under the influence of liquor.
Upon entering the house he assaulted his wife and foster son.
Harold Fogg his half brother states that he went into the house
during the assault and took the wife and boy to a neighbors. Upon
his return he states his brother stood in the room with a gun
and said he was going to kill himself. Fogg immediately turned
and ran from the house and as he reached the piazza steps heard a
shot.
    William Foster, constable of Bridgton, was called by a
neighbor, he arrived about one fifteen P. M. and states that
Allen was breathing but unable to speak. Death occured shortly after.

Cause of Death: Self inflicted laceration of neck
                 Self inflicted gunshot wound of abdomen.

Date June 22 19 3 7

John M Bumbszinger
Medical Examiner.

They come fresh from a muted undertaking, an early morning engagement, an easy job; for the little girl a disappointment. She walks in disgruntled silence awhile until moved to speak.

"All I'm sayin is, when we jus do em in their sleep like that, there's no point in it."

"The point is they get done," growls the old woman.

"Ours is not to reason why," chirrups the thin man.

"What you so fuckin pleased with yerself about?" The girl gives him a push, he stumbles. His mood remains undiminished.

"He was so peaceful is all. It was quite beautiful."

"Fuck you. Beautiful." She turns back to the old woman. "An if it's reaction you want why not add some," she searches for the word, throws a hand in the air, "flair to it?"

"What I *want* is to get it done without your pissin and moanin but I guess that's too much to hope for."

"Gauge the fella's reaction you said."

"And gauge it we shall, where you think we're goin?"

"You wanna gauge reaction like you said then spill blood is all I'm sayin, spill some fuckin blood, at *least*."

"Shut up."

"Fer Chrisakes. Some blood."

"Shut up, we're almost there."

"Coulda taken maybe an eye. Finger at least. Hell, if I had my way, we'da cut his damn pecker off an—"

The old woman wheels about and strikes the girl with a closed fist. The thin man gasps, the girl flies backwards, blonde hair trailing after her. The thin man claps his hands to his face, perhaps in alarm, perhaps to stifle a smile.

"*Told you to shut up.*"

The girl writhes, back arched painfully over tree roots; she's winded and cannot speak, making do instead with a kind of anguished inhalation, a hissing. A red mark on her cheek is already blooming towards a bruise. The thin man turns away, indeed laughing quietly between his fingers. The old woman speaks with tightened jaw and both hands fists. "Now you and he is here under sufferance and I will not just take your shit and take your shit. You pickin away and pickin away at what you *know* is the way things is done. You and he both got the cradle marks still and I'm tellin you to stop your goddamn nonsense and to do it now."

The girl turns herself over and crouches on all fours, still hissing, hair dirty and hung in matted ropes hiding her face; she rocks with each snatched breath.

"I—" she tries, swallows, "*I will kill you.*"

"Stop it now." The old woman looks tired; then, to the thin man: "You, help her up, we got somewhere to be." The girl springs at her, propelled by some feral, extended and unintelligible syllable of rage. The old woman backhands her and the girl yet again blunders, ending on the ground. "*Stop it now dammit.*"

The trees stand around them yet fail to pass comment, impassive witnesses. The girl spits breathy blood. She nods. After a time, with difficulty, she stands, shoulders rising and falling with exhaustion. She opens her hands at her sides, stretches out her fingers, shaking. Her face cannot be seen behind dirty hair but her nodding has not ceased. There is a time of waiting, of embarrassments and a sour resignation masquerading as calm. Still the trees hold their tongues. The old woman turns and they push on.

♦

Some time is taken to wait for the street to clear, so they may cross unnoticed and circumnavigate to the rear of the Bischoff-berger house. The little girl hasn't said a word since the beating but she follows behind nonetheless, her lower lip fat and her eye swelling towards shut.

They find a window, open just a crack, but it holds no sign of the doctor. It shows a rich brown room of books and of heavy furniture. A cluttered desk supports a precarious mound of books, scattered papers and what looks like a collection of small clear flasks of water. Under the window itself a short leather couch and a small table which holds an all but empty whiskey bottle and two glasses, one broken into several pieces.

In the next window, a small dimly lit room, an elderly woman lain upon a bed in dirty blue light, eyes open as if considering some feature on the ceiling. She might be dead but for her intermittent blinking and the up and down of the coverlet at her shallow respirations. No doctor.

Moving around to the far side of the house they find him. The kitchen window shows the doctor sat at a dining table, disconsolate at his breakfast. The old woman and thin man stare in at him, the girl too short to see; neither offers to lift her. The doctor's spoon plays about his bowl of oatmeal, gaze unfocused, free hand toying with his mustache. The old woman thinks how much older he looks than when they met on the road some three years ago; troubled, hollow now somehow.

A woman enters the kitchen, and the two flinch, as if another figure would break some kind of trance, would make them obvious in their spying. At the woman's appearance the doctor lifts, sits straighter, adapts his tautness into a smile. The woman bends and kisses him; the old woman looks away, noticing for the first time that the little girl is no longer beside them. She nudges the thin man away from his watching, whispers:

"Go get the whelp. She didn't oughta be wanderin." He creeps around back and quickly returns.

"She aint there." A glance back at the kitchen and the kissing-woman runs her hand over the doctor's shoulders and leaves the room. The old woman leaves the window and peers around the corner of the house. No girl.

"You stay with yer eye on the doctor," she tells the thin man. "Come get me if he moves."

The dirty blue room with the elderly woman in the bed now also holds the kissing-woman, settling by the bedside, opening a book.

The brown room of books reveals the window open, the little girl inside. She stands stock still in the very center of the room, a statuette, back to the window, pale dress aglow in the dimness. The embroidered bag swings lightly at her hip, the only sign of movement there is.

The old woman drums a fingernail on the sill.

"*Hey,*" she rasps low. The girl turns, bloody lip darker in the house, black eye a shadow, face illegible. "Get the hell outta there, what you thinkin? Get the hell outta there." The girl does not move. "Come on now," tries the old woman. The thin man is at her shoulder, close to hysteria, dancing about like a man with a full bladder and nowhere to relieve it:

"He's finished. He aint in the kitchen no more. *He aint there no more.*" The old woman all but screams, throat stiffening and stretching, teeth bared and parted, everything but the sound itself. Still the girl stands. The old woman runs to the dirty blue window. The kissing-woman is reading to the woman in the bed, snatched words: *There were giants in the earth in those days, and also after that.* Back at the brown room the girl hasn't moved and behind her the door handle is turning. The old woman grips the thin man's lapels and drags him down below the sill and they wait in silence.

Sounds of the doctor in the room separated by interminable silences, creak of leather, the dropping of something, the purr of a book's leaves, clack of a typewriter. As to sounds of surprise or alarm at the discovery of a small intruder, there are none. Finally, a distant telephone ring and the doctor's footsteps leaving the room.

A pale leg hooks over the window frame above the crouching two, then another, then the little girl slides down and out of the house. Hunkered down, she and the old woman trade blank stare and dagger look while the thin man blinks away fretful tears. From inside, and for the first time, they hear the doctor's voice, an accent *from away*, a measured timbre:

"I believe I do, yes. Indeed. I shall be there presently." In time, the sound of the front door and of his automobile and they up and leave, across the street and back among the trees. Eventually the old woman can hold her tongue no more.

"What the hell were you thinkin?"

The girl shrugs.

"Thought maybe I'd go inside is all."

"O you thought maybe you'd go inside?"

"I did. And so I did."

"You stupid little bitch, you realize—"

"He didn't see me."

"What does it matter? He sure coulda seen you."

"He didn't see me."

The thin man's eyes widen; he stoops to look at her.

"Like you was invisible?"

The girl rolls her eyes.

"Like maybe I hid, genius." They walk on, the old woman detailing punishments should the girl ever do the same thing again, the girl paying little mind, remaining remote and impassive. She lags behind the two, all the while hugging to herself her keepsake bag, fingering the shape inside of the doctor's stolen letter opener, buoyed along by thoughts of where she might plant it, how she might twist it in the wound, and the look on the old woman's face as she did so.

State of Maine.

Cumberland ss.

I certify that I was notified on the *19* day *June* A. D. 19 *3 7*

at *9* h. and *15* m. in the *fore* noon by *Geo Bowley*

of *Bridgton* of the finding of the dead body of *Edward F*

Flaggett of *Bridgton*

supposed to have come to h *is* death by violence or unlawful act; that I forthwith repaired to the place

where said body lies and took charge of the same, and before said body is removed make, or cause to be made,

this written description of the location and position of said body, viz:

The body was that of a man about six feet tall weighing one-hundred ninety pounds, having black hair and brown eyes. He was lying in bed dressed in his night clothes. There was cyanosis of the face and extremities, rigor mortis had set in.

The deceased was last seen returning home from his work about ten P. M. the night before his death. He appeared to be in his usual health and did not complain of feeling ill. When he did not appear at his work the next morning his employer, H. E. Burnham of Bridgton tried to arouse him by ringing his door bell. Being unable to arouse him he entered the house in company with a neighbor, Geo. Bowley, who entered the house by means of a pass key. They looked into his bed room and saw that he was dead.

His Physician, I. E. Mabry of Bridgton, states that he has been in good health as far as he knew, but that various times he spoke of vague pains in the upper abdomen, though these were not severe enough for him to seek medical attention.

Cause of Death;   Angina Pectoris
                  Chronic Myocarditis.

Date *June 22* 193 *7*

John M Buckmauofburgen M.D.
Medical Examiner.

A black interruption in the trees, the road is darker than the woods somehow. There is no light save that filtered down from a bearded moon, egg-like and waxing gibbous. Above the three as they wait on the tree line the sky is powdered with stars, streaked with thin cloud. The night is warm, yet still the thin man shivers intermittently, walking in place.

The old woman stands, austere and arms folded. Every so often she casts a look down the road northwest. The little girl is stilled and quiet, has been for some weeks. The keepsake bag is tied at her waist, her left hand hangs inside it, as if it were a pocket, the hand holding on to something within; perhaps for luck, perhaps something else.

"Hey, I been thinkin," says the thin man, "maybe we make nice with this doctor fella. Talk to him. Maybe he'd see." The old woman's face creases in disgust.

"Shut up. There aint no nice. You want we should wash his fuckin windows too?"

"I only thought..." but he trails off, something in his meaning dissolving under her glare. The night pushes down on them, on the road. Little creatures call out from the trees, calling the old woman back, she who has no place on such a thing as flat and as even as a road; the other two seem oblivious to the call.

"How we know we're all waitin for the same thing?" says the little girl quietly. The other two turn to face her.

"*What?*" says the old woman. "You decided to start talkin again? Wonderful."

"What dyou mean?" asks the thin man.

"What *do* you mean? Or are you just stirrin the pot like always?"

The girl takes her time to answer, fingers working themselves in her bag.

"What I mean is, what if what *you're* waitin for idn what he's waitin for? What *I'm* waitin for?" She stares malevolently up at the old woman, the old woman's face hardens and her arms tighten, ready to deliver another beating.

"Can't we jus once wait without flappin our fuckin gums?"

"What if?" asks the girl simply, almost a whisper. The old woman spits, turns her back on them, looks down the road.

Nothing happens, and it seems clear that nothing will, yet the old woman reminds herself that the gap between the two, between nothing and something, is no more than a hair and gone in a breath just as easy.

"What's to happen?" asks the thin man.

"We'll see. But it's comin from up yonder." Again a look down the road.

A white point of light blinks into life in the distance. She looks the other way and there is nothing, then back at the light. The three stare at it.

In time the light splits, two lights throwing a diffuse triangle onto the road, an automobile's throaty grumble reaching out in the dark. The little girl takes a step forward to stand beside the old woman, takes something out of her bag. The bright metallic glint of a radiator grille is drawn in the black, a visual echo of something held in the little girl's hand.

The thin man adopts the aspect of an athlete about to run a race: knees bent, head forward; but he takes only a single step, and in so doing gives a mighty push, all his meager weight behind it, sending the little girl flailing headlong into the road.

What it is the driver sees no one will ever know, perhaps he thinks it an animal of some kind, perhaps he sees a child. He slams on the brakes and the automobile glides, screaming, across the road towards the little girl.

Her face in the blaze of the headlamps is one of utter, almost comical surprise, bleached, her hair burning white, hands thrown back in a vain attempt at balance, keepsake bag swinging, before the car hits her. With a muted report like far-off artillery, she buckles, lifeless, and is thrown.

Its slide uninterrupted, the car comes about, moving sideways like a skiff in a strong current, then capsizes. Its bodywork crunches and gives, glass explodes, throws sparks, the roof ruches and crumples, flips up like a toupee as the car turns over again, bodies flung out, lit in their flight by the surviving headlamp as it spins. One-eyed, the automobile ends on its back and in a fog of golden dust, comes to rest.

State of Maine.

Cumberland ss.

I certify that I was notified on the *17th* day *July* A. D. 19 *37*

at *10* h. and *45* m. in the *after* noon by *F. O. Pitts*

of *Naples* of the finding of the dead body of *Cora*

Dyer of *Bridgton, Me.*

supposed to have come to h *er* death by violence or unlawful act; that I forthwith repaired to the place

where said body lies and took charge of the same, and before said body is removed make, or cause to be made,

this written description of the location and position of said body, viz:

    The body was that of a female five feet six inches tall, weighing one hundred seventy-five pounds, having red hair and blue eyes. She was clothed in blue slacks, white sweat shirt and white shoes. A Waltham wrist watch was on the right wrist.

    There was a depressed fracture of the skull over the right parietal bone, the right arm was fractured at the shoulder joint and a large bruise extended the length of the right arm. There were three small abrasions on left side of face, and a bruise on the right ankle. Rigor mortis had not set in.

    The body was lying in the middle of the highway about one quarter mile north of residence of F. O. Pitts, Naples, Maine.

    She had been thrown from a car in which she was riding from Harrison, Me., accompanied by Annie Burnham of Naples, and driven by Jeremiah Potts of Casco who was also killed when the car skidded and overturned.

Cause of Death; Fracture of skull sustained in automobile accident.

Date *July 27* 193*7*   *John M. Bishopberger M. D.*
                                             Medical Examiner.

VI

People won't step back, and that's the problem. You believe whatever you want. Knew a man once thought that wood could think; a chair, a table. Thought his woodshed was haunted by the spirits a murdered trees. Knew another thought that colored folks could have three babies a year. But if you can't back up, look at it with another fella's eye, objectively, then you are no kinda person, and your belief is no kinda belief if it can't hold water.

Because for better or worse, no church is a conversation. It's like a river, only flows in one direction and many folks feel empty that way an that's their business. But if you can't step back, walk around somethin then I don't know what.

But then I guess you have the other kind. Rare it's true but some folks can walk around it, see the charade, see the foot-lights and the flats, and yet still can't let it go. These things are in there like a tick, like a mite, they're burrowed in there deep and cannot be shaken. Maybe these beliefs are more powerful because of it but as to truer I couldn't rightly say.

Richard Lee was somewhere near a friend of mine. Business acquaintance might be closer to it. Knew him more years than I care to count and there was many more years fore I even met the man, when he moved himself all the way up from Providence and telegrams and the like ceased to be our only way of talkin. Richard was a shrewd man and a good man. He died August of '37 and he did so in a way many aspire to. O he'd been havin attacks for some time before it where he'd fall down, go blue, and though I never witnessed one of these seizures I can't say they sound like a whole lotta fun. But then he still appears to have wrestled the brass ring from the situation in that he died in his sleep. How many people you heard say they wanna go that way? Lay back, close your eyes and *boom*, out like a candle, never knowin hide nor hair of it. O it's the brass ring alright.

As to how false that notion is we have, that idea of blissful, instant, unknowin death, who knows? Maybe it was just like that, maybe. Maybe he suffered terribly, woke up, couldn't scream, could barely breathe, could only look out into the dark room, the back of his wife's head, maybe for hours, before he died. But hell, we'll give him the brass ring, he deserved it. Fact is, he went to bed, never got up. His heart upped and quit. It'd complained for months prior, throwin little tantrums but finally it had coughed and failed. This is what happened, this is how Richard Lee left the game. We all go some way an this was Richard's. Those that knew him might shed a tear, those that didn't might take off their hats.

But then you got young Doc Bisch, also a friend of mine, and he sees Richard havin gone in his sleep like that, knows the truth of it moren you or I, he walks around it some but can't let go of a belief that this isn't at all the way it happened. And this is a fella smarter than you and me. He sticks with this idea ahis, the idea of the three, goin about the place killin folks.

He is one of this other kind I mentioned. He sees the flats and footlights. He knows horseshit when he smells it, like you do, like I do. He can look at it from every angle and yet he cannot help but believe what it is he finds himself believin.

Richard didn die in his sleep. No. Richard went to bed and was visited by a man in the night. Man in a raggedy brown suit. This scrawny fella sneaks into Richard's house, leavin no signs mind you of entry. This fella waits fer Richard's wife Alma to fall asleep, then creeps into the bedroom, wakes Richard with a hand on his chest and whispers words into his ear, some kinda magic words that cause him to up and die right there, just like that.

An that's nonsense but still preferable to my scenario of lyin, unable to scream, the darkness and the backa Alma's head. But it aint the truth because it can't be. And it aint what the doctor wrote up in his book either. Showed it to me. Big old thing, looked more like a ledger to me, which I guess it is, asorts. Marbled burgundy spine and corners, cover rough like a sharkskin, made by Merril & Webber over in Auburn. *Medical Examiner's Record Vol 103* it says on the cover. I flicked the pages and people fell to this and to that as I did so, old and young alike, some I'd known, some not, all written up, typed up, documented and sent off to posterity. On Richard's page, page 22, it reads *Cause*

of Death: Acute Coronary Thrombosis, Chronic Coronary Sclerosis.
And yet I knew Bisch knew how to spell *Strange man in brown*
suit spoke magic words. He hadn't typed that cus it's impossible
but I could tell he'd wanted to. We drank moren we should and
joked with little mirth about keepin two books; "One true, one
more than true," he said.

More than true is a phrase I can't get outta my head. People
will do all kindsa acrobatics to explain things, they are ingenious. Belief is a funny thing but it aint no laughin matter. A
belief is a shrill edict is what it is. A shoutin voice in your ear.
And maybe it's true, this belief, but if you can't ask it a question, walk around it, I'd say look away, I'd say run a fuckin mile.

Harrison, Naples, Casco, Raymond; Maine

June, August, 1938

They work their way up a slow hill between the trunks, in and out of shade, she leading the way, he following ten or so paces back. Every mile or so she throws a look behind her but still he's there. Neither has spoken for nigh on five hours, though he at times seems to be mumbling to himself, something more than a breath, something less than words.

The boards of a house make themselves known, porch and door, a pitched roof planted in a gap among the trees. They stop and the old woman sits, waves a hand at the house.

"This one's mine," says the thin man in a low voice, unsure. She nods.

"This one's yours."

"Cus awhat I done. Like we said."

"That's right."

"Reward."

"Call it what you damn please."

"Fer what I done, in pushin the girl."

The old woman answers only by spitting and glancing away, before looking back at him. He looks somewhat shamefaced at the ground. The old woman doesn't like to call it a reward, doesn't like to speak of it at all if she can help it, though not from any wish that it had not taken place, but because the incident went beyond what she knew to be possible. It rewrote rules, dislodged what she'd taken for granted as The Way Of Things, threw the equilibrium. She'd found the letter opener on the road and held no illusions as to its intended use or destination; instead the girl's passing made her wonder at the fragility of any one of them, of him, of herself. Unsettled deeply, she'd wondered long and hard and gotten nowhere at all. So on they had walked.

"This one's yours," she repeats. He fumbles with his bandages, nods nervously.

"This one's mine cus there won't be no pain, it'll be peaceful, like I like."

"Far as I know." This back and forth, this call and answer

liturgy, has become something he likes to enact before an appointment, and something she barely tolerates. "I lain the ground work on this one," she says, "that there window stands open. Do as I told you."

"Peaceful," he says; her patience falters.

"And do it *now*."

A winter has come and gone since the girl's passing, with no more meaning gleaned from that night for all the months they'd chewed on it. They'd dragged her little body into the woods, each holding a foot, until her bloody dress had ridden up, exposing her hairless sex, and the old woman had insisted they turn her about, pull at her hands instead.

A hole was dug with the thin man's axe and the old woman's fingers, clawing a hollow deep enough so as to leave the broken remains undisturbed by any passing animal. When the old woman had suggested the burying of the keepsake bag with the body, the thin man had looked afraid, had clutched it to his breast, insisted that it must be buried elsewhere.

"Therefore their goods shall become a booty, and their houses a desolation," he'd whispered. He'd said a prayer over the grave while the old woman had paced and made fists. In time they'd left the heap of tilled earth and gone on into the night.

♦

He sits on haunches, back in a corner, all knees and elbows in the narrow triangular space behind the armchair. He traces the ribbed floral pattern across the blanched red-brown upholstery, absentmindedly fingering frayed tears, the horsehair escaping from within. He waits and fights sleep. He listens to voices in other rooms. He feels invisible and magical, apart from, yet among the voices, and it warms him. Eventually those voices drift closer, unsure steps and hoarseness, emphatic steps and concern; two men. The chair gives, shifts back a little, and the thin man retracts, fearing discovery. The chair back bulges, swelling, as if from infection.

"Throat's awful dry," says the hoarse voice.

"Set tight, I'll bring you a glassa water," says the other.

"You feel free to wash out the glass with whiskey."

"I'll feel free to do no such thing."

The thin man is so close to the voices, yet they are utterly incognizant of his presence. He feels like a ghost, feels these people's lives spinning forward on their spastic and unknown trajectories, feels their awkward ignorance and loves them silently for it. Again, a warmth. He holds up a hand, presses it lightly to the back of the chair. He mouths the word *peaceful*. He closes his eyes.

State of Maine.

Cumberland ss.

I certify that I was notified on the 2nd day Jan A. D. 19 38

at 2 h. and 30 m. in the after noon by Dr. W. D. Smith

of Bridgton of the finding of the dead body of Wm Fleury

Austin of Harrison

supposed to have come to h is death by violence or unlawful act; that I forthwith repaired to the place

where said body lies and took charge of the same, and before said body is removed make, or cause to be made,

this written description of the location and position of said body, viz:

    The body was that of a man, five feet ten inches tall, weighing
about two hundred pounds. Having grey hair and beard and blue eyes.
He was dressed in a brown sweater, brown trousers, white woolen socks
and rubber overshoes. There was oedema of the legs. He was found
sitting in a chair in the living room of his sons home.
    The deceased had suffered from heart trouble for several years.
He had been unable to lie down for two days previous to his death
on account of difficulty in breathing and had remained in his chair.
His condition was apparently about the same on the day of his death.
He had requested a drink of water and while trying to swallow it he
passed away.

Cause of death; Chronic Myocarditis
              Congestive heart failure.

Date March 31   1938   Jno Bischopsberger M. D.
                                    Medical Examiner.

John left the Austin place as if he'd never been there at all, thinking that he may as well not have been for all the matter it made. He had of late become equal parts disconsolate and fanciful, toying with ideas of daydreaming himself into being, of never having come to Naples, of never having left childhood, dreaming his adult self from his boyhood bedroom; then in time he would be torn from reverie and thrown headlong into the real, or indeed the real as he found it. It was a madness, he knew, something above mere fancy, but it was a madness he kept a tight hold on, lest it get away from him.

Left sitting in the midday glare, the car was hot, the steering wheel fevered, almost alive in his hands; the engine panted, sickly and emphysemic, as if with every mile it died a little more under him.

He was buoyed somewhat when Sumner Newcombe's truck drove by where the Naples Road met Rocky Point; they waved and John felt a little warmth from his advice concerning Sumner's coffee intake, advice it seemed being adhered to still. By all appearances business was good, Newcombe's ice much in demand and Sumner himself in rude health. Such little victories John counted as the bread and butter of doctoring.

The image of his stake driven into the Maine earth sprang to mind, Joseph's metaphor from years back, his relocation, his belonging. There was a time when he'd pictured this claim of his, his placeholder, the stake itself, as dry, gray wood, the earth hard and unyielding; now though he felt the stake had perhaps taken root, was now a tree, anchored, healthier certainly, a little green, though perhaps in certain lights or certain seasons indistinguishable from those around it.

Yet still his stomach burned nervously as his mind swung from small victories to terrible losses; and he craved the sanctuary of his office, the reconstituting properties of a small whiskey, perhaps a chip or two of Newcombe's ice.

Edan Wilby waved him down on the Lake House Road, smiling from under her hat in the afternoon sun, asking after Ros, after Hattie, telling him her mother was visiting again, asking if he recalled her mother, asking if he thought it had been a glorious day. He said it had indeed been glorious and of course he recalled her mother and asked was she well. A memory of the mother's small mollusk eyes came and went.

"She has been out of sorts of late, truth be told," she said wearily, "been under a Doctor Ogilvie up there in Brattlebora, do you know Doctor Ogilvie at all?" He admitted that he did not. "She has a nervous condition, he says that explains her bouts of despondency, thought a toucha Naples sunshine might be just the ticket."

"That it might," he offered, "you wish her well from me."

"Wonderin if you might not come see her." He sank a little in his seat; seeing another physician's patient seldom served any good purpose.

"Has she asked for me, Miss Wilby?"

"Not as such but— Well, it'd sure put my mind to rest if you could see your way clear to a visit. If you have the time, I know you're a busy man Doctor Bischoffberger." His title and full surname did it. He slipped a gear into bedside manner and heard himself say he would indeed go see her, felt a smile on his face, an affirmative nod of his head.

♦

Sat curled in his office, the bright square of outside reaching uninvited through the window, he felt the qualities of *inside* as the polar opposite of the *out* with a greater strength than ever before. The inside was dimly lit, was safe, while also somehow unfriendly, somehow lessening him as a man with every moment he spent hiding in it. The out was bright, was burning, was hope, but was chaos. The house felt an unwelcoming, alien thing. He'd typed up his notes and pasted in the entry before realizing he had accidentally skipped a page in the record, page 23, had pasted this new entry on page 24, and this little mistake disheartened him somehow; he left it, sipped at his whiskey, stared, distant and misgiven, at nothing.

He took out the penny he'd found at the scene of Preston Mann's hanging, some three years ago now, incredible though it seemed; turned it over in his hands, wondered at his still not having spent it. He'd stood and stared at it while they'd carried out the body of Harold Caswell, another gone by his own hand, feeling no luck resonate within it, keeping it nonetheless. In a way he failed to understand, the penny anchored him to something in the passing of these men and he could not help but imagine himself in their place; trying the idea on for fit and for comfort.

Ros breezed into the room and they both gave a start, he pocketed the coin and put down his glass; they smiled and kissed briefly. She seemed out of place in his mood, having punctured it somehow as she always managed.

"You look beat," she said, "tough day?"

"O nothing so unusual."

She looked him over.

"Think your hair needs cutting."

"I have no doubt."

"After dinner then."

"As you say."

"I shall try not to relieve you of an ear," she winked and made to leave. Something in him rose up.

"Ros, I've been meaning to talk."

"You have?"

"Your mother," words shrank back momentarily, "seems— *Is* much better, and Gene is long back from Portland, Edwin almost five. I wondered if she might not be happier with more— If it might not be time to— That she might like to live with Gene and Margaret again." The look on Ros' face hurt him a little. He was trying to take her mother away, he was being small and selfish.

"She's no trouble now is she?"

A twist in him.

"No, Ros, all I— I only mean to say—"

"I enjoy looking after her. Reading to her."

"I understand and I apologize—" He noticed her hands had begun to flutter, her breath to shorten. She gripped his hand.

"I know it cannot have been easy to adjust but she was so ill, and gave us all such a scare. And after Wilson's passing." She grimaced as she said it. He knew she still bore her cousin's death like a bruise that wouldn't shift, supposed that this was what people did with terrible things that could not be helped.

"I'm sorry," he said, "forgive me," and sat heavily in his chair, the movement tearing their hands apart. He looked at the contents of his desk and she at the blankness of his face. A desperate, undeniable moment passed. "I'm sorry," he repeated at last. She took a broken breath.

"You're unhappy."

"No it's fine, Hattie can stay, she *should* stay, of course."

"But you're so unhappy. I see it in you. Every day. I smell it on your breath."

"O, that's just whiskey," he tried, smiling up at her in a way that failed to reach his eyes and fell away.

"No, John, it is unhappiness."

"I'm sorry," he tried again. Her eyes brimmed.

"What *is it*, John?" She knelt, took his hands again. *I should not have to make a pantomime of prayer in my own home*, he thought of saying, felt the sting of its pettiness.

"I am being foolish. But sometimes I feel that I cannot be myself about her. At mealtimes. Grace." The very words embarrassed him, pained him in the saying. Ros' eyes lowered. "I believe I am a good man, endeavor to be so at least. That I cannot believe as she does, as you do, should not be held in punishment over me. In my own home. I care for your mother, truly, but her disapproving stare—"

"She does not disapprove of you, John, she never has. All this is in your mind."

"She sees me wince at prayer, knows I go to church only when nothing else can be substituted to prevent me. You see it too, I know. I may be unworthy of you, I admit—"

"Are we talking of my mother, or of me?"

"Rosamond, a man should not be made to pretend." She stood, and he found himself unable to look at her.

"However did you marry such a petty, sanctimonious woman, John?" Her voice was thick with tears; he felt wretched.

"I apologize. You are no such thing." He forced himself to meet her stare. "But I am incapable of this belief of yours."

She rallied.

"There is no such thing as a man incapable, John."

"I'm afraid that there is, and you are married to one."

"This is Mr Allen talking."

"No, Ros, it is your husband. I know my mind and I know my truth." He took a breath, and in a tone he hoped would end the matter, said deliberately, "There are terrible things."

M ona Bell pushes out into the cool water, legs kicking, grimacing at the droplets of river that leap up to spatter against her eyelids, that bead her lashes. She darts forward, turns effortlessly, regards her sister still crouched in the shallows. Mary is luxuriating in the feel of the mud seeping between her toes. Mona thinks that while only thirteen months separate them, eleven is a whole world away from twelve. She dunks herself under, pushing off the bottom and breaking the surface, smoothes back her red hair, tucks it behind her ears.

Tommy Leavitt is splashing Fatty Maggie Morgan, the Maxfield brothers are racing between rowboats moored for the purpose; balls are batted about, laughter. Play is still being had, but there's a strained nature to it, knowledge of a day nearly done. Tommy's splashes reach Mary and this pushes her further into the river to join her sister.

Dry, the girls look not unlike twins viewed at different distances, the older of the two a slight magnification, the younger sister shorter, perhaps a little stockier; the only stark variance being their difference in hair color. They swim together a little away from the others, talk about nothing so much.

"One day poor Maggie'll bloody his nose, then he'll see."

"If he ever seen her pitch a rock he wouldn't be so keen to rile her." The river corrugates with a slow breeze as they swim.

"Who's that?" asks Mary, pointing to the far shore. Mona turns and they both tread water, blinking at the distance. Some hundred or so feet away, a man sits on the tree line in the weakening afternoon light. His face is a bush of dark beard, his head a mass of hair, almost shoulder length. His grimy trousers hang off his pointed knees like pennants, the shoulders of his jacket poke out, empty, no real shoulders to fill them. He looks like what their mom calls an Oakie, what their father calls a Road Man. The man appears to be making some motion with his hand; has he just waved, blown them a kiss? Mona squints at the figure.

"Jus some hobo fella."

"Guess. Looks awful hungry." Mary returns the supposed wave. The man seems to cover his face with both hands, perhaps the preamble to a game of peek-a-boo.

A large shape glides under them and Mona, without urgency, says, "That weren't no brook trout."

H is simply stating that there were "terrible things" had of course not been sufficient to end the discussion. He'd tried his best to choose his words carefully but a few reckless ones had crept through; tears had been shed, voices raised. He'd stewed over it for some months, the coolness in their conversations thawing, yet still he held on to it, worked it over and over.

Mary Bell lay under a blanket at his feet, abstract patterns of water soaking through the rough wool, leaking in a narrow rivulet back down the sloping bank to rejoin the river.

Deputy Walker was up by the road, quietly decanting blank-faced children into the care of their parents. It was growing dark and the trees were filling in the spaces of light with their blooming shadows; already stars were pinpricking the sky. The temperature was falling, Mary Bell's body temperature falling in tandem with it. Strands of dark hair that had escaped the blanket were drying blonde.

"Suffering has no currency with me," he'd told Ros, "it is dumb and ugly. It is cruel and it is everywhere, *still*."

"Why must you always gravitate toward pain, toward suffering? Why not toward compassion, John, toward love?"

"You think me without love?"

"I think you without enough of it." And he had felt the dearth of something he did not possess, or something that, through neglect, he had allowed to wither.

With the sound of shearing twigs a woman came crashing through the trees, breathing hard, the deputy on her heels. A man in overalls stood up by the road, jaundiced in the headlights of the sheriff's car, mouth buckling, head shaking in an attempt at indignation, refuting absolutely something huge and terrible told him. John stepped back as the woman tore aside the blanket and scooped up the girl, kneeling, holding the thin white body to her breast, whispering *my girl my girl my girl my girl*, convulsions transmitting through her body to that of her daughter's, limp hands quivering at the child's side as if uninterested in this gauche public display of affection; and all John could do was look on, and all John could do was finish his notes and go home.

"You tell me that He," here he had edited himself from adding *this mascot of yours*, "loves us all, that He loves me. Well I do not love him, though nor do I hate him, because I have looked and Ros, He is not there. One might as well love a gust of wind, or a creak on the stair." She had been appalled, he had appalled her. He knew himself to be a hypocrite; what was one set of impossibilities over another? One superstition for another. He recalled, as a child, the very real dread upon stepping on a crack in the sidewalk, a dread that might stop his heart like a rock inside him, as real as anything a boy knew, real as breath, real as Jesus. He'd looked away from Ros' face, had felt the penny glow in the dark of his pocket. *Find a penny, pick it up, and all the day you'll have good luck.*

Deputy Walker led the father down to the shore to comfort his wife but all the man seemed capable of doing was shaking John's hand, to thank him, for what John had no idea. John had nodded an uncomfortable acknowledgment; the father's head still shaking *no*. They all waited for some unspecific moment or finale to the scene and it grew dark. The deputy stood, hands on hips, and looked at the earth, then out over the water. John buttoned his jacket, raised the collar against the cold.

He wasn't at all sure that he hadn't lied when he'd told Ros he didn't hate *Him*; often he thought he did indeed hate this idea, this autocrat, this player of games and snuffer of candles, this mean-spirited, despotic patrician. But not much sense was to be had in the hating of someone whose existence you failed to believe in.

More than a minute of silence had passed before any of them noticed. The river lapped and the wind blew the trees into voice but the mother had ceased her crying. She looked up at the deputy, then at John, red-faced and staring.

"But where is Mona?" she whispered.

State of Maine.

Cumberland ss.

I certify that I was notified on the *1st* day *of august* A. D. 19*38*

at *7* h. and *30* m. in the *after* noon by *Myron Walker*

of *Naples*   of the finding of the dead body of *Mary Bell*

of *Edes Falls, Naples, Me*

supposed to have come to h~~er~~ death by violence or unlawful act; that I forthwith repaired to the place

where said body lies and took charge of the same, and before said body is removed make, or cause to be made,

this written description of the location and position of said body, viz:

    The body was that of a girl four feet four inches tall weighing about eighty pounds having flaxen hair and hazel eyes. She was dressed in a red one piece bathing suit.

    There were post mortem bruises on right cheek and right side of neck. A bruise at the base of each lung from artificial respiration.

    There was cyanosis of face and bloody mucous from mouth and nose. Rigor mortis had not set in.

    While swimming with a group of children in Crooked River above Edes Falls, she went beyond her depth and sank. The body was recovered in about one hour.

                        Cause Of Death: Accidental Drowning

John M. Bird M. D.
Medical Examiner.

Date *Aug 1*   19*38*

She is to be a keepsake, thinks the old woman, that word bringing painfully to mind the one she is replacing; a pain born not of sadness or loss, but of a fear the old woman still cannot get a grip on. Fear of change, fear of the usurping of one set of rules by another; fear of a kind of death, of a wiping away of her own presence from these woods. A fear that has the feel of falling to it.

It is full night and has been for some hours. Mona sits under the thin man's filthy jacket, hugs her knees and shivers terribly, legs milk-white, teeth chattering, eyes wide. The old woman looks on. This was a good idea, the only idea; this was a foolish idea, desperate and ill thought out. But then the balance had been thrown, the vacuum had to be filled, did it not? This was a good idea; and so on.

The thin man was all in favor, said a prayer over the new arrival and now sits beside her, smiling, trying to tie some kind of doll from reeds plucked nearby.

"She is older than the other," he addresses the old woman as he works, "seems of quieter disposition. Think she'll be a fine addition." Whatever oscillates inside of Mona, causing her to shake so, works to some kind of crescendo and with a caught breath she seems to wake from her trance. She looks at the two of them.

"Where's Mary?" she says quietly. The thin man places a hand on her shoulder.

"Gone to her glory. You're with us now."

Mona doesn't seem to have understood; she looks about her.

"When can I go get her? We should be home, mom will be ever so mad, what time is it? Do you have my clothes? I'm cold."

"We are your home." She looks at him, smells him and her face creases.

"You that Oakie we saw."

He smiles.

"I was on the bank when you were swimming, you remember?"

All at once the girl looks frightened.

"Where's Mary?"

"Mary is gone."

"Gone where?"

The thin man looks to the old woman for help.

"Gone to the bottom of the river," is all the help she gives. Mona wells with tears, looks between the two of them, breath shortening.

"No, no but— but where is she? An— an— where's my shoes, my daddy bought me them shoes an he'll be awful mad if they're lost." She stands, gives her bare foot an ineffectual stamp, her tantrum diluted by cold and confusion. She wipes her nose with the back of her hand. "You gimme back my shoes an my sister now or so help me my daddy'll call the sheriff, send you to jail."

The clearing seems to get a little smaller, little darker. Mona, shivering again, skinny and ridiculous in her bathing suit, red hair in ropes, looks at the old woman. The thin man reaches up for the girl's slender hand and she flinches away. Her shoulders raise up and she stares down at nothing, begins to sob.

"No, it's fine, you'll be fine," tries the thin man; the girl says something lost to her tears, a word stretched out to a wail then swallowed, choked on. "You're with us now, you'll be fine, you'll see."

"No," says the old woman sharply. She spits. She's been a fool. "It aint right. Aint the way." The thin man stands, arms outstretched in a gesture of desperate placation. He's seen the turn in her.

"No, wait, she'll be fine, she's just new, and cold, we get her some duds, teach her the job, she'll be fine. She's a good girl aint ya? Itta be peachy."

The old woman's mouth sets somewhere between disgust and resolution; an anger flickers about the corners.

"No. She is not like the other. She is only what the other masqueraded as. This is stupid. Can't believe I thought it anythin but."

"She's not like the other, no, she's better don't you see? She is pure. This puts somethin back but makes it better."

"Equilibrium so called wasn thrown by the girl's passin, any-moren it is restored by this newun." What threw it, the old woman knows in that moment, was the whelp's arrival, was *his* arrival, and what will get it back is not this hasty surrogate, but the removal of the last of its causes.

She had thought these two anchors on her time indelible, irremovable. Her bitter lot. But the girl's passing seemed to gainsay this. A new course of action: she will have back her autonomy, by hook or by crook. The old woman resolves to remove the thin man at the earliest possible opportunity, fair means or foul, resolves to merely wait for a favorable circumstance to present itself; but first, the new girl. The thin man steps in front of the shivering Mona.

"*Wait*," he tries, his tone betraying his infirmity of purpose, "please, this can work, it'll be the three of us again, please, like before but—"

"No. Aint right. Things aint been right since you an the whelp. Well now she's gone an anytime you wanna take that axe ayours an go home is alright with me."

He stands to his full height, makes bandaged fists.

"*You will not harm this child*," he says, eyes unable to match the boldness of his words.

"Step aside."

"Please."

"Won't tell you again."

"But if we—"

The old woman's fist strikes him in the mouth and he feels a tooth wrenched free, others shaken loose; a popping sound and the iron taste of blood. The world slides out of focus and then another fist explodes in his belly, he closes up like a pocket knife and the floor leaps up at him.

He wakes with his missing tooth laying on his tongue like a piece of candy. He spits it into his hand, looks at it, wondering how long he's been unconscious. He turns his head and the silhouette of the old woman's legs crosses his field of vision. He blinks. A blur of her walking away. She stoops to pick something up and he blinks again; a metallic glimmer. The axe.

"Time you left our merry little band too, I reckon. You done her, now maybe I'll do you," she hisses, walking back to where he lays. He tries to speak but words won't come, he feels tired and adrift on something; perhaps a rowboat, maybe a raft. And yet he is still in the clearing, among the trees. He can't remember ever learning to swim and feels suddenly afraid. He raises his hand, the one holding the tooth, almost tries to say *candy?*

The old woman steps on the hand, grinds it into the dirt and he feels his own tooth bite into his palm; in lieu of crying out, his mouth opens soundlessly, neck arching in pain.

"Good riddance," she says through her teeth and raises the axe, and then, addressing Mona, "You might not wanna see this." Still no words come to him and he resolves to die silently.

The tiniest of sounds, a movement of earth or rustle of flora perhaps and the axe falls onto his chest, dropped; the old woman vanishes.

In time he raises himself up onto elbows, looks at his bleeding hand, perhaps a finger broken, the bandage soaked through again, looks about him. He is quite alone, the old woman and the little girl Mona are gone. He looks up, as if he might blearily glimpse them rocketing skyward into some heaven or other above.

♦

In woods, in the dark, silent escape is an impossibility. Mona rips through branches, stumbles and dirties her knees, cries out, runs almost blind until the trees fall away and she slides to a halt, all at once ankle deep in cold river water. The open space after the trees is bewildering, everything picked out in a pale, distant blue, the reach of the water, the trees on the opposite bank; the sky speckled with stars. She stands in wonder for a moment at somewhere so familiar rendered so strange. Something silent pushes at her back, prickling the skin, and she spins about. The old woman is right there, hands on knees and breathless, eyes burning, her ancient face varnished with sweat. They breathe at one another for a time in the moonlight. There's no sign of the skinny Oakie. Finally, through a grimace, the old woman speaks:

"You gonna run again?" Mona shakes her head. "Cause I am old and I am slow but I will catch you and it'll still go the same way."

"Where's my sister?"

"I told you already."

The girl begins to cry.

"You gonna hurt me?"

"That is not my intention but maybe, a little."

"A little?"

"Maybe a lot."

"Can't you jus let me go?"

"No I can't."

"You *can't*?"

"No, I cannot."

"I won't tell. I promise I won't tell."

"I know you won't."

"But—" Mona takes a backwards step, deeper into the river, "But— But what if I swim? Over there," she casts a glance behind her, wrestles her crying under control, "across the way, climb up, run home."

"You'll never see the opposite shore."

"I'm a pretty good swimmer. I can make it."

"You'll make it harder is all you'll make it." The old woman shakes her head, peevish. "What is it with you people?"

The girl's voice dips, low and reedy.

"I won't tell no one."

"I know it." The old woman steps out of her shoes. Mona mouths the word *please*, searches that old face for anything in the way of sympathy. Finds nothing; tears return, syllables elongate.

"But I— I don't understand."

Unmoved, the old woman steps forward into the river to take a hold on her.

"Nor will you neither," she says.

State of Maine.

Cumberland ss.

I certify that I was notified on the *2nd* day *of august* A. D. 19*38*

at *6* h. and *15* m. in the *fore* noon by *Deputy Bryant*

of *Windham* of the finding of the dead body of *Mona Bell*

of *Edes Falls, Naples, ME*

supposed to have come to h *er* death by violence or unlawful act; that I forthwith repaired to the place

where said body lies and took charge of the same, and before said body is removed make, or cause to be made,

this written description of the location and position of said body, viz:

The body was that of a girl four feet eleven inches tall having red hair, hazel eyes weighing about 95 pounds. She was dressed in a blue one piece bathing suit.

The body was recovered from Crooked River above Edes Falls. There was cyanosis of the lips and fingers, a bloody froth was coming from the mouth and nose. Rigor mortis had set in.

The deceased, in company with her sister and several other children, was swimming in Crooked River. Her younger sister, Mary, slipped beyond her depth and sank. Mona went to her aid and sank.

Cause Of Death: Accidental Drowning

John M Bischoffbugos M.D.
Medical Examiner.

Date *8/3* 19*38*

Two days after the finding of the second Bell girl, the heavens opened. With scant warning a mighty cloudburst descended on Cumberland County, rain so thick and heavy anyone brave or foolish enough to venture out had to part the deluge like a curtain. The air was a sketched gauze, as if fashioned by hasty pencil strokes, roads ran muddy and impassable, roofs were battered into leaking, the causeway flooded and Gus Bove began joking he'd soon need to receive customers by skiff.

Up in North Sebago, the bridge over Bachelder Brook was washed out in two places by the flooding, so too were other bridges in the area and even stretches of road. Three people perished when the bridge over Breakneck Brook in West Baldwin was overcome by the tide and swept away.

Reverend Grundy's sermon the following Sunday, for those who could make it in, concerned the plagues of Egypt, in truth to remind parishioners that a mere downpour did not compare, as of course some had begun to facetiously suggest.

John sat, chagrined in his pew, nonetheless feeling sympathy with this dismissed idea of plague, of immense things breaking down, bleeding onto the earth; a punishment or some perverse godly incontinence.

"Such wrath should *not* be blithely thought equal to mere precipitation," warned the pulpit. Still the allusion persisted, Elva Babb claiming that not even Pharaoh himself would have stood up under such a deluge; George MacVane, who rescued the Goulds from their waterlogged homestead out at Sokokis Point, was known for all of a week as *Our Noah MacVane*.

On the day the bridges in Baldwin were lost, John was east on Bonny Eagle Road, Standish, leaving the Dillingham place, breathless and wet after a dash to the car, its interior feeling small, dark and under siege. While the roadster started with ease, the bodywork felt like it was taking gunfire as he drove and after a scant hundred or so yards, visibility reaching no further than the steaming hood, he surrendered to the fusillade.

He pulled to the side of the road, resigned to wait it out, hoping for the roof to hold. He sat in the dimness while a million fingers drummed over his head, deafening and aggressive; sat and thought of controlled madnesses, of how little anyone truly knew of what went on in a man's head, wondered where the thin man and the old woman might be taking shelter, what folks thought God could possibly be thinking with such weather, or with such a world.

◆

Hands in pockets, the two men wandered along Ward's Cove, gazing out over the swollen lake, jackets buttoned, hunched a little under a pale gray ceiling of sky. The air was cool but felt cleansed by the rainfall, fresh and clear. They talked of the deluge, of Reverend Grundy, of this and that.

John had detailed his conversation with Ros some months ago, the strictest confidence of their friendship unnecessary to reaffirm.

"I handled it badly, of course."

"Of course," said Joseph with a smile.

"Found myself telling her there were terrible things."

"Well you didn't lie any."

"But this grace business. What next, I begin to avoid meals? In my own house?"

"And you feel ol' Hattie unresponsive to your point of view."

"I do. Most certainly." It was John's turn to smile. "Women are a mysterious breed."

Joseph halted.

"I'll just stop you there. Any sentence that starts with 'women are' will only get you into trouble. 'Men are' too. Knew a fella once would juggle live eels. Sold em at market. An he had a hat and cane routine that'd killya. Does he stand for all men? Can you do that? I know I cannot. Knew a gal called Irene once, would give it away like she thought it'd spoil. My Louise was not like that, an I know your wife aint neither."

John held up his hands in surrender.

All seemed prematurely hunkered down for the onset of fall, pregnant with the promise of longer nights and the fanfare of blazing leaves, preparation for the war of attrition that was the Maine winter; month upon month of dusk. As they walked, soiled clouds slid overhead, huge and indifferent. Joseph had brought a flask along and they both shared what the older man called *a nip*, leaned on a fence and considered the expanse.

"I meant to say," said John, "I believe the three now to be two." Joseph stood upright in consideration of the statement.

"One has gone," he replied.

"Gone. Yes."

"I'd say that's a step in the right direction."

"It is. Yet I feel a kind of anticipation. Something akin to a quickening."

"That might just be The Notion itself fightin its own wanin in your mind."

"It might be so."

"Anticipation. Of what?"

At this, John also stood, turning his back on the lake, looking into the trees.

"Of—" He shrugged. "Doing something about it, playing a part. Maybe putting a stop to it." His tone was matter-of-fact; perhaps, he realized, out of place when talking of murders, of magic, yet to commit emotionally felt like one madness too many. "Though if I'm honest, I have no idea," he said. They walked on.

"Still I'd say two better than three. Soon maybe two will become one, then none."

"At which point I shall be welcomed back into the fold of the sane." They both enjoyed the joke, though it left discomfort and a strange taste.

"Open arms."

"It's a nice thought."

"Certainly moving in the right direction."

John stopped.

"Still, I never found my letter opener."

"Forgetful in your old age. Misplaced it perhaps. Threw it away by accident."

"Perhaps."

♦

Joseph held forth concerning stories gleaned from the newspapers, of uprisings and disaster, of invention and artistic endeavor; the world in print, disseminated in an endless sea of names, places and incident.

"Sometimes I look at it and think I'll be damned if things don't never stop happenin."

"It's tempting to think that it wasn't always like this."

"It is." Time had gotten away from them and they'd let it, gladly. John had no appointments and it seemed a pleasing indulgence to drift along, but evening was well on the way so they turned back toward the car. "Sometimes I think the war cracked the world, let somethin out," said Joseph.

"I told Ros the war was like waking up. Wanted to ask her, if she had seen what I have seen, would she still believe so?"

"Well many people did and many people still do. They held onto it, though it seems to me at times their knuckles sure as hell are white with it." They wandered on, draining the flask between them. Joseph's gaze became unfocused, transported elsewhere; he shook his head. "The war cracked the world," he said quietly. John thought maybe the whiskey had touched a little deeper than his friend had meant it to. "We'd run forward an the bullets would fizz by like hornets," Joseph went on. "Men would die right by you. Right there. I'd sing. *Walk jawbone, Jenny come along*, you know it? Sing as I ran, under my breath. If I got to the end of the song then I wasn't dead and that's about all there was. Hornets and song and maybe one day home." He screwed the cap on the flask and put it in his pocket. A light squall of rain blew across the waters and they upped their pace.

They reached the roadster just as the rain began again in earnest. Joseph opened the passenger door but didn't climb in.

"The Lakota Sioux," he said across the roof of the car, "had a war-cry, *Hoka Hey!* which means *Today is a good day to die!*" He gave a practiced squint. "Yknow what our war-cry is, the white man? *Death to the other fella.* Over an over. Forever. And now Europe is callin again, you read this? I wonder, will we answer? I tell you, Doc, sometimes it's good to be too old."

♦

As John drove, Joseph sang quietly, his hand clapping on his knee:

"Walk jawbone, Jenny come along, in come Sally with the booties on..."

People held on to all kinds. Don Rogers once told John he'd been taught that a crane fly, if caught and asked where the cattle was, would point the way with its antenna. Frank Brooks had told him that he may well laugh, but hens that roost in the morning were plain bad luck, foretold a death, and that was all there was to it. If John were mad, and he knew some would certainly think him so, believing as he did, then who was not?

The Sebago Road swept by, a smear of trees and houses, and Joseph's voice lifted in volume.

"They made me a scarecrow in the field, and a buzzard come to get his meal, but in his face I blowed my breath, and he was a case for ol' Jim Death. Walk jawbone, Jenny come along..."

By the time they made Naples, the rain had stopped and they sat awhile, sated with something and a little weary. Joseph seemed to fight with a thought for a time before speaking.

"I am not a believer, as you know." He flung a gesture with both hands that seemed to say *so what?* "But it would be a more arrogant man than I who would be so sure that it wasn't *built in* to a man to believe. Somewhere in the meat of us maybe. Our rightful position and purpose. Like we're supposed to be afraid afire, of the dark, maybe we're supposed to construct these totems to cushion the blow of things. Give solace. Comfort. Help us sleep easier at nights. I been thinkin, might not this notion ayours be a window into that? A way toward the faithful? Albeit in a way as yet unclear?" Joseph was still trying to solve him, John realized. He mirrored his friend's *so what?* gesture, yet in a way which seemed to say *who knows?* But it didn't sit well with him.

"If it is a way of seeing God, it is a way of seeing him indulging in the grossest cruelty imaginable, the most wanton and needless violence. This is a window to nothing good."

"They are no emissaries from heaven."

"They hardly seem it."

"Well wait a second, they seem, as you tell it, not a whole hell of a lot different from some things I heard of in Sunday school."

Joseph's logic tensed something in John.

"The Portland Road runs nowhere near Damascus."

"No it don't."

"Are these two monsters to be worshipped?" he asked, a little irked; Joseph shrugged.

"The Lord our God, so called, if you listen to the Reverend, brought the floods, did he not? Killed the firstborn of every man and woman in Egypt, and yet folks seem to have no trouble worshippin him."

John was frowning, no longer wishing to discuss it.

"I, however, do have such trouble."

"We both do. But to hear it told it's a blissful surrender: 'all this must be for a purpose beyond our ken', you know the idea."

"I do. But there is no peace for me in that."

Joseph sighed.

"Nor for me." Something in the atmosphere of the car had waned, John's irritation curdling the air a little. Joseph took out the flask, then recalling its emptiness, put it back, smiling ruefully. "Hell," he said, "this notion ayours hasn't harmed you so much. Least not that I can see. You've not started to talk to the moon or nothin. You've gotten along with it. But this grace business as you call it. Ol' Hattie's disapprovin stare. Can it hurt to say the words? What can it last, a minute? Less? You think maybe you're worried you start joining in it'll take?" John did his best for his face to read *I don't know*. "But I aint tellin you what to do in yer home." They traded nods and Joseph patted his jacket where the flask lay. "Well I'll see you again, Doc. You take care." They shook hands.

"Mr Allen," said John.

♦

He dreams painful things. He opens the door to the house and calls out Ros' name. It's day but the house is dark and something within it that does not move, nor make a sound, scares him more than it should. He knows, in the way one knows things while asleep, *knows* she's in there but she does not answer. He steps into the hall but doesn't close the door, using the daylight to illuminate his way further into the house. Still no answer. Nothing. He climbs the stairs to an upper floor barely touched by the warmth or light of the sun.

In the bedroom, Ros lies naked in the arms of the thin man. He is filthy, even unclothed, limbs knucklesome and wasted; in contrast her skin is pristine, obscene and crawling with his bandaged hands. Long fingers leave smudges on her arms, her breasts. She looks at John in the doorway but makes no attempt to speak, to cover herself. John slams the door, runs past windows black as if painted, runs up another flight of stairs, stairs which have no place in his real house, which do not exist.

In another bedroom the old woman is bent over a chest of drawers, her dress hiked up, Joseph hunched over her, trousers around his ankles, fucking her. Even in his dream, that word makes John balk, but it is the only word for what Joseph is doing; his face, that repulsive, animal grin. They ignore him and he stumbles away.

In the living room, dark, stripped of rug, furniture and ornament, Wilson stands alone in his overalls. He looks happy to see John, and that's the worst of it. They look at one another and John tells him: "I called but she didn't answer." Wilson lets an awkward smile, as if his presence might be some imposition, points at the fireplace. The fireplace is boarded up, old and blackened. As Wilson points at the boards, there comes an awful scratching sound from the other side, like something is trapped beyond. Wilson speaks quiet and thin, catarrhal, uncomfortable to hear:

"Crow come down your chimney, John." The scratching sound. Wilson is Wilson and he's not Wilson at all. John can't move, is terrified and sick. "Crow come down your chimney."

♦

He rose early from a threadbare sleep, the bedroom ceiling or the washstand appearing through patches worn thin with the anxiety of his dream; seesawing between this world and another.

Dressed while Ros still dozed, he spent an hour or more in his office, typing up notes and making dilutions for that day's patients, his tiredness showing itself as an intense fastidiousness.

Harriet Lawrence had called the previous day and told him that her neighbor, Widow Scribner, was suffering a terrible attack of what she referred to as *the arthritis*, and was having trouble looking after herself.

"In pain somethin awful," she told him, "barely hold a cup of coffee, can't make no fire, an time will soon be when she'll surely need one. Taint proper for an ol' woman to suffer so. Martyr as she is, she denies the existence of it even, won't ask fer help."

So it was with a certain measure of excitement that he read in his homeopathy literature, a collection of books and pamphlets which had steadily grown into something approaching a library, of Arnica Montana; a plant he'd ordered some time ago and that now rested somewhere in a drawer with other prospective ingredients. Commonly known as leopard's bane, or mountain tobacco, it was a flowering plant from Europe which was used in treatment for arthritis, but also in cases where the sufferer was unwilling to accept their ailment: *Should the patient refuse to admit that they are ill, if they are highly strung, suffer from rheumatoid arthritis, specifically cases in which the pain is made worse by the damp or cold.*

As he diluted, his credulity was hindered a little by the idea that treatment for physical symptoms might also treat those of a mental nature, namely the widow's denial, yet he completed the procedure, intent on giving her the choice of a more usual treatment for her condition, as well as the arnica solution.

The day was dry, yet threatened rain with every cloud that blew over. His eyes felt parched and a little too large for their sockets, lack of sleep creeping in on him as he drove; he blinked it away.

"My hands hurt when there's storms is all," said the widow, screwing her face up in irritated dismissal. "Never was any such thing as arthritis, not in my daddy's day. Made-up word from doctors on the make. O I don't blame you, we all gotta eat, but we don't say that word in this house," and then she did just that, over enunciating it as if it were the most ridiculous thing in the world: "*Arthritis.*"

Her hands were tree-like, knuckles enormous, fingers splayed at dreadful angles; he examined them as delicately as he could; she for her part, he could tell, tried her best not to wince too much as he did so.

"It's just the storms, Doctor," she said, "nothin more to it. And I'll be damned if we haven't had some rain of late." He played along, telling himself that at least she'd agreed to accept treatment, even as she rejected diagnosis.

"Weatherman says the worst is by us," he said. She snorted dismissively.

"I don't pay mind to what the weatherman says. My Henry would say you get paid to be wrong so much of the time, it sure must beat workin."

Leaving the Scribner house he drove north on Edes Falls Road, perhaps holding the wheel a little too tightly, turning south west onto Pike Hill and into the trees. Leaving the car, hands clenched at his sides, he walked, stiffly and with purpose, into the woods. Very quickly the road had vanished behind him. At first there were thin paths worn into the earth but he eschewed these in favor of ground uneven with tree roots, a circuitous route which took him, with every step, further from town and from any human being. The ground was soft after the rains and spattered his shoes and trousers. He walked, rudderless, until he felt himself far enough away from anything manmade, anything practical or straight of edge, right of angle, and then stopped. Nothing but trees, and in between those trees, more trees, and more and more, in all directions; yet still he fancied them watching, scrutinizing this fool adrift in *their* playground, *their* province, this queer haunting a shadow on all he did, giving the lie to much he said.

Birds called overhead and branches inclined this way and that, their leaves hissing like one huge exhalation all about him.

Are these two monsters to be worshipped? he'd asked Joseph, and he'd been angry at the thought; but overnight conviction had deserted him and driven him into the trees.

"Hey," he shouted, his voice fell away and was swallowed, then again, louder, "*Hey!*" But there was no answer and search as he might, no human shapes could he see among the trunks, no movement of anything beyond that blown by the wind, or scurrying to its burrow or home. What had Joseph called them? *Emissaries from heaven.* He felt foolish yet it failed to embarrass or stop him. In his mind he told himself that a man who believes the impossible is only ever moments away from embracing any number of irrationalities.

He took from his pocket the polished penny, turned it over in his hand. Lincoln, stony-faced, *In God We Trust, E Pluribus Unum*; no answers to be had in it, nor luck it appeared. He crouched and clawed a small hole in the mud with his fingers, before dropping the penny into it. He paused awhile, looked about him once, then filled in the hole, patted down the mud with his palm, leaving the hand there a moment, as if feeling for some warmth forcing its way up through the earth from the coin; the gesture felt like a prayer, the earth some way towards a shrine.

"Not I, nor mine," he said quietly. "All I ask. Not I, nor mine," and heading back in the direction he thought the car to be, left this betrayal of himself with the trees.

S carcely more than an hour later the old woman reaches into the cool earth and draws out the coin, spitting into her hand, wiping away the dirt with her thumb. She stares at the inscription yet gains no meaning from it. The penny winks coppery in the shadow of the trees like a tiny circle of fire.

♦

A steady distance is maintained between them, out of reach of blows or projectiles, yet near enough to see, to hear; it's as if a tow rope separates them, and he quick to brake lest they grow too near and risk collision. The old woman walks with one fist, something held within.

"What's that you got there?" he asks. She does not look back at him, hesitates to answer.

"You don't talk to me," she says at last. As they walk he plays with his broken finger, wonders will it ever heal.

All at once she stops, turns back and holds out her free hand.

"Gimme the axe."

He takes a backward step, shakes his head.

"Gimme the axe."

"You aim to do murder on me."

"I aint aimin to do any such thing, now give it to me damnit."

"Chop me up like firewood. Leave me for the birds to peck at."

"Don't make me take it from you. *The damn axe.*" They look at one another for a long time, her arm still outstretched, hand still open. They are both fragile, and both believe so, both vulnerable to a bad end like the girl before them. After a time he throws the axe to the ground between them and backs off a ways into the woods. She picks it up and begins chipping lightly at the side of a tree with it, stopping every so often to pick something out of the bark with her fingers, placing whatever it is in her mouth.

"You gone crazy?" he shouts, "You eatin woodchips now?"

"Gum," she says, mouth full, dropping the axe, walking away. She moves the wad of gum about in her mouth as she walks, still one fist closed. In time he takes up the axe and follows.

♦

Frank Selbo brings the splitting maul down in an arc over his head, right hand sliding down the handle, gripping it anew at the right moment, upper body tensing as he drives the blade down into the fat log with all the force he can gather. The way his daddy taught him, one cut in each "corner", then work the split through on both sides and cut the rest as you would any smaller piece. The broad log bristles with amputated branches and proves damp, knotty and unyielding. He told Watkins they should have been kept better, what with the rains. He swings again.

Ben Libby is stacking wood already split. He halts for a moment and watches Frank swing.

"You got a rock there, Frank, can't be no tree is that hard."

"She'll give, just gotta work her."

"Knew a girl like that once," says Ben and they both laugh, Frank's laugh robbing his swing of force. He stops and takes off his hat, wipes his forehead.

"You think Henry's still got some athat ginger beer he's always talkin up?"

"If not I'll bet he's got summa the non ginger kind," tries Ben. Frank nods, looks up at the graying sky, makes a face that reads as *why not?* He hangs his hat on the upturned maul handle and both men head off toward the house.

Their backs turned, the old woman breaks the tree line and is at the chopping block in seconds. She bites off a piece of the spruce gum and spits it into her hand. Opening her fist, she takes the penny plucked from the Maine earth, places it on the cushion of gum, and sticks it to the inside of Frank's hat; her hands are shaking.

And the hat is back hanging on the axe handle, the old woman back among the trees, the whole process having taken less than a minute.

Hidden once more, though no calmer for it, she paces like a tethered hound, carrying two fists now, her face alternating between a kind of blank, desperate anger and a fury of frustration, head nodding then shaking as if in answer to a volley of stupid questions, or accusations.

The thin man whispers from somewhere off in the woods, a phantom, still keeping his distance.

"What's happenin? What you do there?"

"You don't talk to me," she says, pacing still.

"What's wrong? What's wrong? You scarin me."

"You *don't talk to me*."

"Didn't it go right? Won't the right one pass? Shouldn't we fix it? Can we fix it?" Panic leaks into his whisper. "You scarin me."

She halts, addresses him as if he is the trees, has been absorbed somehow into their trunks and leaves, a swallowed spirit.

"Hate these is all. Seen this before, nothin good comes from these, this is a warnin is what it is, never leads nowhere good, when you get one of these somethin bad is always around the corner, this is a message, says there's a sea change on the way, somethin you don't never wanna see is comin an there's less than nothin you can do about it."

"One athese? One of what? Message?" The voice from the trees is close to tears. "Sayin what?" The old woman turns her back on him, wherever he is; he is not the trees, he's nothing but a hiding fool. He goes on: "From who? Aint *you* in charge?" Her voice lowers, forced through her teeth:

"Aint no one in charge."

"What?" asks the phantom. She looks out over the open space, at the hat hung on the axe handle.

"Sea change on the way so you poor sunsabitches better get yer affairs in order."

In time the men return to their work and the two in the trees watch them, she opening and closing her hands, he crouched and crooked with anticipation.

It begins to rain and the men cover the wood, work for a time in it, Frank donning his hat, shoulders giving off a thin steam, but as the downpour increases, they retreat under a nearby

tree, shaking themselves off and joking. Ben Libby lights a cigarette and they watch the rain.

"Good thing we got most of it done afore this, wood left
won't chop for shit for months," says Frank, enjoying his
moment of idleness.

Half an hour passes and the rain appears to lose its enthusiasm for the ruining of logs, for the soaking of men, and begins
to peter; the smear of charcoal across the sky turns chalky. Ben
steps out to test the air, turns and shrugs at Frank leaning on
his maul.

"We're back on," he says.

There is an enormous tearing sound and the air solidifies
with light, Frank swallowed in the white-blue center of it.
Ben's ears feel like he's underwater, perhaps drowning in phos-
phorescence. Time snags on something and is unable to move
on. Only sound and light. Ben is pushed back on his heels by
an immense momentary heat, he feels the hairs on his arms
stand out from the skin, the whole front side of his body hums
with it, a white-hot image of a jagged strip or ladder of something reaching up glows across his retinas long after the sound
has gone, the light winked out.

♦

The thin man is curled on his knees, head in hands, hands on
the earth, wet sibilant murmurs leaking through his fingers in
between sobs.

"What in hell you doin?" she asks. She steps toward him but
he doesn't rise, doesn't run, his voice merely rises in volume.

"Hallowed be your name. Your— thy kingdom come, your
will— it be done, here on the earth—"

She kicks him lightly in the ribs but he does not stop. Disgusted, she spits on him, saliva frothy amongst his matted hair.

"Girl was right about you, you aint got brains enough to
grease a griddle. You know no more about the state athings
than a hole in the ground."

At this he falls quiet, looks up at her, tear tracks worn into
the grime on his face, eyes bloodshot and frightened.

"You know— about the state athings?" he asks, perhaps in

hope of greater answers. She looks at him for a time before leaning down, her face pinched and ferocious, blood pooling under the wrinkled skin, old yellow teeth bared; her words are more a convulsion, a vomiting, than they are mere words:

"I *am* the state athings."

Europe is calling again, Joseph had said, and so it was. The *Portland Press Herald* made everything sound distant, queerly exotic and mannered; these people with their strange customs and names, so very far away. This German fellow, jostling for position and entitlement like some belligerent drunk in search of a bar tab. Weaker nations cowering, calling for support; salvos of diplomatic words lobbed this way and that.

John wondered if war was inevitable, knowing immediately that of course it was, that of course it always was, and that while his war had been a muddy, lumpen and awkward affair, that the next would be larger, would be a ravenous, automated nightmare of a thing; such had been man's wondrous advancements. He wondered if young men would one day die again in Meuse, perhaps on the very spot where he'd watched the young soldier disappear before his eyes.

John had an image of thousands of identical bearded men in greatcoats, dark-eyed, indeterminate of race or allegiance, moving across the French countryside, slowly, almost ceremoniously, deliberate and quietly pompous; unstoppable. Something was mustering its forces, a current in the air.

He had searched the ground around the blackened tree on the Watkins place but had not found the coin; nor had he found Frank's hat. Still an uncomfortable feeling of culpability sat heavy in him; when he'd talked to Joseph of *playing a part*, this was not at all what he'd had in mind.

The top of Frank's head was still smoking when he arrived, letting off the merest scent of cooked meat. Liquid in the tree had boiled and its trunk burst, showering the grass in splinters, baring the pale flesh within; it smelled of old soot and hot, pungent sap, a smell that crept in and clung to the back of John's throat, washed away only when Henry gave him a glass of his wife's celebrated ginger beer. He'd almost asked for something stronger.

Ben Libby sat up on the Watkins' porch cradling his own

glass, face pallid and waxy, voice a guarded stutter. John had checked him over, laid what felt like an ineffectual hand on his shoulder and told him to go home, get some rest.

John was calm, attentive, took his notes, drank his ginger beer, while his insides were pitching and yawing, tying themselves in knots. He felt punchy and off balance, a little numb, bringing to mind past instances of a blow to the head, a darkening, a loss of focus, the sensation of reeling. Thoughts of Germany's posturing, of war, of The Notion, of Ros and of Joseph became mixed up in him and he dizzied himself trying to separate them, to find their ends.

The walk back to the roadster brought an unwelcome thought: that the two had perhaps become three once more, and following the offering of the penny, that he now played the part of the third.

State of Maine.

Cumberland ss.

I certify that I was notified on the *16th* day *August* A. D. 19 *38*

at 3 *—* h. and *15* m. in the *after* noon by *Mrs.*

of *Casco* of the finding of the dead body of *Frank Gilbo*

of *Casco, me*

supposed to have come to h *is* death by violence or unlawful act; that I forthwith repaired to the place

where said body lies and took charge of the same, and before said body is removed make, or cause to be made,

this written description of the location and position of said body, viz:

    The body was that of a man six feet tall having gray hair and brown eyes and smooth shaven, he was dressed in blue denims, wool socks, rubber overshoes. There was a laceration on back of head near vertex. There was cyanosis of face and neck.

    The deceased had been cutting wood on the Henry Watkins place in company with Benjamin Libby of Casco.

    A thundershower came up and he took refuge under a large pine tree. A bolt of lightning struck the tree followed down the trunk striking his head and passing thru his body causing his death.

           Cause Of Death: Electrocution By Lightning

Jhn M Bisslopper M.D.
Medical Examiner.

Date *8/16* 19 *38*

Seldom did he talk to Ros of his patients, or mention the dead he'd attended to, and yet he told her about Frank Selbo. It was an attack of sorts, he knew, a finger pointed, and childish though he accepted it was, he told himself that he had little choice but to speak of it. The scene had resonated with something in him, had stayed with him like a weight, birthing an imperative.

"Dear Lord that's awful," she said. "His poor wife."

"Two boys," replied John, "seven and nine."

"Would it at least have been quick?"

"I think so. Hope so." *Your man allowed this*, part of him wanted to say, *yours*.

"It struck the tree?"

"Travelled down it, struck him. In the head."

"The poor man." *The poor man*, repeated John in his head, the real weight bringing itself to bear, *the poor man that I killed with a penny*.

He looked up at her and thought that she looked older, before realizing that this was what concern, pity, pain by proxy did to the human face, tightening the skin year on year into a mask of collected woes; what the Bible called tribulation. He wondered did people who cared only for themselves never grow old, before thinking that maybe age was as much a mask of love as it was distress. And he loved her, with a scope and fullness that made him cold for a moment. He wanted to stand and kiss her but the memory of the scent of Frank Selbo's charred scalp kept him in his seat, insinuated the pull of whiskey as a pale substitute.

◆

On his way back from the lightning strike, his journey taking him across the Causeway, he had called in at Gus Bove's and bought road maps of Bridgton and of Raymond to add to his collection. The collection, housed in a drawer in his office, barely glanced at, puzzled him, worried him. Perhaps, he thought, it gave him some sense of belonging, of ownership, over the county; some kind of documentary proof of what the land truly was, where hills sat, where woods grew, where roads lay, and where they lead.

It's not yet six and the sun is crawling up out of the trees, cutting them as a string of black paper dolls against the coppered sky.

The old woman stands, shoeless, by the water, arms folded, watches the thin man leading a large woman in a white nightgown through the trees to the shore. The large woman holds his bandaged hand daintily, like a debutante, though barefoot, hair tangled from her bed. The nightgown moves about her ample frame, tugged by the breeze off the lake, diaphanous in the dawn light.

The old woman had hoped to hurry the job along, still nervous of possible echoes of yesterday's lightning, repercussions, or whatever that blinding flare augured. But still she had had to wait while the thin man crept tiptoe about the exterior of the house, tapping on windows, hiding in bushes while first one woman left the house, then another. Eventually he had coaxed the subject from the building and the old woman had kicked off her shoes in preparation.

"This is Mrs Hannah Wilby," he says as they near the shore. The old woman spits.

"Miss," Hannah corrects him lightly, "my Percy left us some years gone."

"Miss," repeats the thin man.

"Of a tumor," says Hannah, smiling.

"Gone to his glory," says the thin man.

"Pleased to meet you," says Hannah politely, holding out a hand to be shaken. The scene has taken on an aspect of absurd formality. The woman's body is that of a corpulent adult but her round, taut face she holds open like a child's; small, bright eyes, yet containing something bitter and doleful.

"Alright now giver here," says the old woman.

"And you are?" tries Hannah as she is taken by the wrist and elbow.

"We're here to take you onward," says the thin man from behind her.

"Are we to go on a trip?" she asks, craning her neck to see the unkempt stranger as she is led into the lake; she starts. "Oh but the water's awful cool!"

"Cool but cleansing, Miss Wilby, cool but cleansing." The thin man has his hands clasped together, brows knitted with concern. The old woman leads Hannah a little further in before turning her. Hannah smiles at the unkempt man on the bank, chances a wave which he does not return.

"Are you not coming with us, sir?" The thin man only smiles a tight smile, tears welling. The old woman hooks a leg behind Hannah and, placing a hand on her chest, pushes her off balance and over. Hannah's arms fly up in surprise and before she goes under she says, "But what of E—"

The old woman holds Hannah on the bottom, the lake licking at her own shoulders, Hannah's fingers batting wildly at the surface, splashing, grasping at the old woman's dress. Her face is clearly visible beneath the water, eyes wide, magnified and frightened, mouth open, trying to speak perhaps, or cry out; her hair reaching, sinuous on the undertow. The old woman fancies she can see the path of the lake as it floods into the Wilby woman's mouth; lines in the water.

Curious, the thin man wades in a little to watch, to pray under his breath, nodding his unspoken *yes*. When Hannah's hands fall still and the white of her nightgown blooms amber with urine, he wrinkles his nose and turns away, disgusted, perhaps disappointed, striding back to the shore, shaking his head in an unspoken *no*.

H is shoes were filling with mud, the water cold, and still he waded farther out. When the lake was at his knees, he heard Elmer's call from the shore. When the lake was at his hips, he heard splashes behind, felt the sheriff's hand on his shoulder.

"What you doin there, Bisch?" John turned and looked at Elmer like that was just about the dumbest question. Behind the deputy John could see people standing on the shore watching the two of them, stood there, ridiculous in the water. John saw Mary Putney, hands to her mouth, beside her Ben Libby's father, Norman; perhaps, John thought, wondering on just what the hell was going on, that one day his son should witness something like Frank Selbo's immolation, and then the next he himself should see this. Beside those on the shore lay Hannah Wilby, white and incongruous on the muddy shore, pristine under a bruised morning sky. John looked from the body to Elmer, blinked. He felt distant and knew that when he spoke he would sound it.

"Thought I saw— Just looking for something, thought perhaps—" He turned to the far shore, to Knowles Point some half a mile or so across the way, where he'd seen the shape, then down into the water, waved his hand as if looking for something, some evidence perhaps, doctorly and arcane, before nodding. "But no, there's nothing, it— just a trick of the light perhaps." Elmer looked worried.

"You okay, Bisch?"

"I guess we must look pretty foolish. Stood here in the lake." John gave a weak smile.

"I guess we must." The disquiet remained on Elmer's face.

"I thought I had seen something. In the water." His mind grasped at excuses. "A belonging of Miss Wilby's. Or a garment, floating," he applied greater strength in fashioning a smile, "but there is nothing." Elmer nodded.

"Nothin out here but us fish," said the deputy.

He shook everyone's hand as he left the scene, by way of some kind of explanation, or excuse, perhaps a reaffirmation that he was a doctor dammit, a professional, and should he act in a way that appeared irrational, then there was most certainly an explanation that, just because he didn't trouble them with it, was no less weighty or legitimate.

He half ran back to the car, all eyes following him, pant legs sopping and shoes spitting tiny bubbles from their seams with every sodden step. He'd seen the old woman across the water, knew it, and had decided to drive over there as quickly as he could, maybe catch the two making their escape, maybe catch them drying off, maybe dozing, luxuriating in their easy murder; for what possible reason did they have to flee? Who was he to interfere in their business? And just what damn fool would even try?

The roadster strummed and murmured irritably at its top speed, adding a falsetto hiss to its choir of complaint as he willed it up Chadbourne Hill and on to Upper Ridge Road. He pulled at the steering wheel, rocking in his seat; cursed the machinery under him. He'd find them and he'd tell them it was over, that he knew all about it, and that they could just damn well stop their filthy business, that if three could be two then why couldn't two be none. His thin wish that their mere anonymity was all that allowed them to operate with impunity, unchallenged by the people whose families they were decimating, failed to catch any real conviction in him, yet still he raced on; the doubting part of him telling himself he'd know what to do when he caught them.

A hasty left onto Big Sandy Road led him to a dead end at the northernmost point of the lake, tantalizingly close to Knowles Point but inaccessible by road, forcing a retreat back to Upper Ridge, around to Summit Drive and down Commons, a five or so mile detour, every inch of which gave the two extra opportunities for flight.

When he reached the point, it was deserted, the road weaving through the thinning trees, bearing no sign of murderers, the vista opening out towards the tip of the peninsula, the road terminating in a turning point, beyond which lay only the shore and the reach of the lake.

Either he was too late, had tarried too long on Big Sandy, or the two had never been there; had never *been*. Perhaps they possessed the power of flight, perhaps of dematerialization.

He stood on the patch of ground on which he'd seen the old woman stand and looked over the water at the tiny figures of the sheriff, of Mary Putney and of the white dot of Hannah Wilby's body; he spent a moment looking for his own shape among them. He closed his eyes and swallowed the word *fuck*.

Edan Wilby had asked him to visit her mother, when had that been, back in June? He'd sat in his car and said that he would, and then put it out of his mind. Hannah Wilby, he knew, was a marker in all of this. He had first met Hannah the day he'd seen the old woman on the Portland Road; the beginning of it all. They'd spoken of the sighting, he recalled, whilst the daughter sat drowsy in her blankets. He remembered the stench of shit in the house, which somehow now felt oddly meaningful, portentous. It seemed strange that the mother now lay dead opposite him, impossible that it could be unconnected to that day, to him.

Not I, nor mine he'd asked the woods, ridiculously, neglecting to understand that in his professional capacity there were precious few, if any, that did not fall in some way under that umbrella.

In this way it struck him with some pain that every part of him was a target, as if he were a body made up of many bodies, an amalgam or the fulcrum of many beings, one who held them in his care, one who might save them, yet in all likelihood would not; ineffectual nursemaid, murderer of the world.

28

State of Maine.

Cumberland ss.

I certify that I was notified on the *17* day *of august* A. D. 19 *38*
at *7* h. and *30* m. in the *fore* noon by *Deputy Elmer O Stewart*
of *Bridgton* of the finding of the dead body of *Hannah Wilby*
of *Lebanon, N. H.*

supposed to have come to h *er* death by violence or unlawful act; that I forthwith repaired to the place

where said body lies and took charge of the same, and before said body is removed make, or cause to be made,

this written description of the location and position of said body, viz:

The body was that of a woman five feet six inches tall, having grey
hair and blue eyes, dressed in white night gown. There was cyanosis of
lips and face.
The body was found floating in Highland Lake, Bridgton, Maine.,
about eighty feet from shore in Front of cottage occupied by deceased and
her daughter.
Mrs Mary Putney who was employed as housekeeper stated that Mrs.
Wilby's daughter left for Portland, Me., early in the morning leaving
her mother in bed and as she supposed asleep.
Mrs Putney started to prepare breakfast leaving the house for a
short time to secure a bucket of water from a nearby cottage. When she
returned she could not find Mrs. Wilby and after searching for her for
a time called a neighbor, Mr. Norman Libby to help in the search. He
noticed the body floating in the lake. He then called Deputy Elmer Stuart
of Bridgton who removed the body.
The deceased had been despondent for three years and had attempted
suicide at previous times. She had been released from State Sanitoriun
at Brattlebora, Vermont under the care of her daughter Miss Edan Wilby
just beforecoming to Bridgton.

Cause of Death   Suicide by Drowning.

John M Bischoffberger
Medical Examiner.

Date *8/17* 19 *38*

S he feels the heart throb within him, flutter like a thing trapped, beat once further, then fall still. His arms and legs work at her for a time but to no avail, his breath leaves him in a series of ascending silver bubbles; he contracts in her hands, muscles bunching, then he simply seems to relax into his leaving.

She leaves go on him and glides away into the lake, hair streaming, sand curling up from the lake bed in her wake; she hears dulled cries of consternation through the water before she's even reached the shore, before she's even surfaced. And this one is done.

◆

He watches the old woman, knowing too well not to speak until she's fought her breath back, lest her only reply be to strike him. She is so old, he thinks, so frail; her bones might be carnival glass, her skin no thicker than a Bible page. Oftentimes he wonders that she does not simply fall to pieces, tear open and spill, a machine hastily built, a construction of old lady parts that cannot possibly fulfill their function, let alone what use she puts them to.

Though she has cautioned him many times for doing so, in moments like these he thinks of her as his mother, his existence impossible without her; other times he feels he may have sprung from an egg, so little do they have in common. He loves her, yet does not understand her, is afraid of her.

At first he thought with the girl gone, he and the old woman might grow closer; then he began to think that she had designs on killing him, perhaps in his sleep, perhaps in broad daylight, brutal and ugly. He knows too well she has ugliness within her. Now though he thinks this time of murder passed, the demarcation of types of job rendering the two of them pieces which fit together, each having his or her own purpose within the business; he: the peaceful ones, she: everything else.

Head clearing, she glances over at the thin man, imagines a log brought down upon that vacant look, a rock driven into that cheek, those eyes widened and panicked under three feet of lake. He is a fool, aberrant in the woods somehow, out of place most anywhere, like an imitation of something she can't place, weak and cockamamie. And with whatever is coming following the lightning strike, this event, this arrival, felt like some pressure in her ears, some weight in her belly, she can do without playing wet-nurse to an imbecile. He will not leave of his own accord, she knows that, she will look for the moment and send him on his way and out of hers. And *then* the matter of the doctor fella.

"You're not wearin the hat I gotcha," she says.

He's surprised, pats his jacket.

"I— have it in my pocket, for colder weather. Thank you."

She turns to face him.

"Put it on," she says.

"Thank you but—"

"Put it on." She even manages a smile as she says it. He pulls out the ruined hat and smoothing his wild hair as best he can, forces it onto his head. A large hole has been torn into its very top, blackened at the shredded edges; the wind teases strands of his hair through it, like some comically decrepit headdress.

"Pretty as a picture," she says with barely a touch of disgust, standing, gesturing at the trees, almost a bow. "Shall we?"

J ohn marveled at his own performance, his evenness of
   voice, his methodical approach to the body, handwriting
reined in and neatened, his professional camaraderie, even
bonhomie, with Joe Bodge; he was Doctor Bischoffberger to a
tee.

Doctor Joe had grown somewhat fatter since last John had
seen him, a little grayer, walked a little worse perhaps, but had
surrendered none of his good humor, nor indeed his seriousness when it came to his job. He'd practiced thereabouts for
more years than John had been in the state and showed as
much resignation as regret when telling of the boy's drowning.

"They fished him out pretty damn quick but he wouldn't
take the breath. Did all I know how to do. Thirteen."

"They say the boy had heart trouble."

"So they told me."

"Pinkham." John busied himself with wondering if he knew
the family.

"Eugene."

John felt scrutinized, that Joe would surely see through his
playacting as the good Doc Bisch, see the cracks opening up
under him.

Several boys were sat some way off, their backs to the dead
boy, somber as a counselor addressed them. Elsewhere in the
camp other boys, unaware, laughed and shouted through some
game or other. John closed his notebook, fought off the need to
flee.

"How's Julia, is she well?" he tried.

"She is, thank you. Touch of the rheumatism for which she
blames the Maine winter; I just nod, better blame that than
blame forty or more years married to me." John's laugh surprised him. Joe went on, "And Rosamond is just as cunnin as
she always was?"

"She is that."

"Handsome woman. Good eyes, smart eyes."

"Picked me, not sure how smart that makes her."

"Constant effort and frequent mistakes are the stepping stones of genius." Joe winked at him, held out his hand to be shaken; the performance could end, John was free to go.

♦

Somewhere on Plains Road, the roadster drifted right and he let it go. His thoughts were everywhere at once, everywhere but behind the wheel, and it took the gravel on the shoulder to shudder him back into the here and now, braking just in time to shear off a sapling, splintered twigs clawing at the car's underbelly, just before he ran into a ditch proper and ran the risk of likewise shearing an axle.

He was out of the car and running before he knew it, almost as if the car had spat him. Heart racing, he ran on by the side of the road, past Rocky Point and on, open mouthed, arms wheeling, shoes smacking the tarmac, shirt dampening with sweat. He ran as he hadn't run since he was a boy, ran with no idea where he might be running to, or what he thought might be chasing him.

State of Maine.

Cumberland **ss.**

I certify that I was notified on the *19th* day *of August* A. D. 19 *38*

at *1* h. and *10* m. in the *after* noon by *Camp Hinds*

of *Raymond, Me* of the finding of the dead body of *Eugene*

Pinkham of *Portland, Maine*

supposed to have come to h *is* death by violence or unlawful act; that I forthwith repaired to the place

where said body lies and took charge of the same, and before said body is removed make, or cause to be made,

this written description of the location and position of said body, viz:

The body was that of a boy five feet tall, weighing about one hundred pounds, having brown hair and brown eyes and wearing brown swimming trunks There was cyanosis of ears and neck.

The deceased was swimming near dock at Camp Hinds, Raymong, Maine. He had climbed on dock from row boat and then jumped from dock into Lake. After swimming about for a few minutes he started for dock ladder. One of his companions looked back and saw him floating face downward in the water.

A counsilor, E. A. F. Anderson states that the deceased was taken from water within two minutes and artificial respiration applied a nd adrenalin administered by Dr. Bodge who happened to be in camp at the time.

Camp health records showed that he had come to camp with a statement from his physician that he had a weak heart.

Cause of Death Valvular heart dewease
                Myocarditis
                Heart Failure while swimming.

Date *Aug 19* 19 *38*

Medical Examiner.

235

VII

Oftentimes I think we are bound for this whether we know it or not, whether we like it or not, strapped in there and on our way. O some of us may jimmy loose, jump the train, but the ticket is there, I think, from birth. Godbound, whether he's there when we arrive or not.

Our compulsion toward the fantastical, the absurd, the intangible, toward God, toward Solid Gold Bullshit, has its germ, I believe, in love.

Ask someone why they hate someone and they'll tell you, make you a list you give em paper an a pencil. Give you specifics. Ask someone why they love someone and they'll flounder, fall down on cliché, they'll talk poetry and song; they'll compare thee to a summer's day.

They say love is the opposite ahate but I'm not so sure. Maybe the opposite alove is indifference. Hate is tangible, has blood in it, has bone, viscera, love has nothin to hold on to, but it's there. Hate is like makin a chair, choppin the wood, workin it, planin it down. Love is like wishin you had somewhere nice to sit, trustin that you do have somewhere nice to sit, then sittin down without lookin behind you to see if it's there. Hate is like there's no gravity an you're holdin on to the world, love is openin your hand and floatin up and up.

For near two thousand years we've argued against hate, pointed at the obviousness of its costs, but who argues against love? O the cuckolded will rail and gnash their teeth at it but you sit em down an all argument will fall apart. Who stands up and makes the case against love?

O I'm not sayin love is a fraud, that those who love are fooled into doin so by some collective hysteria. I'm jus sayin, you've felt it, I've felt it, and neither of us can explain it. Love is the most attractive of intangibles. It is the reason so often given for us bein so called "spiritual beings", but is it?

I don't know.

What if next week some fella, scientist, was to prove what love is? He says, see there's these sixteen switches in your brain, why sixteen I don't know but however many. Maybe it's a hundred, maybe two. But this fella says these sixteen switches you're born with, every one of us born with different versions of these sixteen. Maybe one's hair color. One maybe the way they laugh, another some kinda geometry in em, their face, way they think; an all the time these switches are gettin flicked: brown eyes, flick, and a bell rings, make you laugh, ding, another bell.

An while you're flickin switches, they are too, and likely more than one ayours is dependent on how ever many atheirs you throw and so on until, dingdingding, jackpot, all or most of the sixteen are flicked on both sides and there you are. Love.

If that were *proven* tomorrow, would it matter to you? That it was only a successful score card that made love rather than a meetin of souls? An equation or jigsaw puzzle, not fate, not some grand romantic epiphany? See, love lies in the shadows a little don't it? We can't quite make it out but we feel we know it's there because every so often we reach in an it bites us somethin fierce.

An what then if this scientist fella told you he could make a pill that'd take it away? A pill to reset the machine, the switches. Heart broke? Take this and in the mornin you won't care about her no more, him no more; you can go lookin for another to flick your switches, if you'll pardon. Would you take that pill? Many would I'm sure, those bites do sting some. But would it make love less somehow? Kill the magic? Explainin it wouldn't stop it happenin any more than explainin why heated water turns to steam stopped a train workin.

But if that same scientist could explain God to you in the same way, I think it'd be a horse of another color; think maybe the need for it might just dissolve. Maybe. But I'm not sure explanation for either will ever come.

Some say you're lookin for your daddy, your mommy in the one you love, others say *soul mate*, they say *fated* and when there is no proof, well then magic tends to take the lead I think. And then what's one irrationality over another? Why do I cleave to one unexplainable and reject another?

There's plenty awhat they call anecdotal evidence for love. We all have our stories don't we? But then so is there for God.

Folks feel it, they do, they aint lyin. I guess it comes down to what you see worth in. What you think we need as a people, what pushes us on, what holds us down. We tried many things over thousands ayears and some just don't work no more. Don't help. You ask an I'll tell you, to me, God is a millstone, love an aeroplane.

No, not many talk against love. Like I said the cuckold will curse it, make vows against it foolin him a second time but he remains a believer; he just wishes he weren't.

Bridgton, Naples; Maine

September, 1938

There is no light in the room and no window. There is only the petrified air and the quiet. Heavy, timbered walls stand sentinel, one bulwark within another, the space between packed with sawdust, strangling any outside warmth before it can finger its way inside.

In the dark, something.

If a person were stood in this room, they would be forgiven for thinking that it has no smell to it, just a certain cleanness of air, a kind of frigid purity; but it has a smell.

Nothing else smells like an ice house. Something clean yet always on the edge of rotten, wet wood held just the right side of putrefaction; a suspension of deterioration. That cleanness lays over everything, cloaked in a biting cold; the smell of the lake itself is there, albeit stilled, nature rendered unnatural.

If a person were stood within, shivering, the air would steam with breath, were there light with which to see it, but there is neither. No person is here.

If the door were opened and the warm August light let in, the ice would glow a vivid blue, stacked in huge bricks, a monument to winter, defiant, surviving out of its time. As it is, these slabs, sawn from the lake in February, sit in utter darkness and hold tight to their form, resist the slow drip of the incremental melt, defy the inevitable.

Outside, voices, blanketed into unintelligibility by the walls; a man and a woman. He seems to be standing still, she moving off. Words are impossible to discern but the tone is familiar, warm. The man's voice rises, perhaps in farewell, as the distance between them grows greater and all sound falls away; perhaps a heavy footfall on a porch step, the closing of the door to the house.

It is August 27th, nine days before Labor Day and what will likely be the last call for ice this year.

The light in the room was paltry; nonetheless it threw shadow on his face, shading the hollow cheeks, his sallow complexion, dry cracked lips and the dirty smear of a three-day beard. William Clifford had always been a somewhat narrow man, but now he looked positively gaunt and disarranged; he stank and his bloodshot gaze looked sore.

"Can't see no reason in it," he said, voice pained, as if pulled through a wet gauze. "No reason, at all. In nothin." John laid a practiced hand on his shoulder.

"Things really that bad?" he said, brows knitted, a slight squeeze of the hand. William's lower lip fluttered around his reply, hands made fists.

"I know things have got better for some, but I can't seem to get a foot up. House in tatters, can't afford lumber to fix her. Kids hungry, nother on the way, poor Janey's worn to a bastin thread. Brother Earl was sendin dollars home when he could but we aint heard from Earl in close to six months. We're right out straight tryin to keep our heads above it but we're drownin is the truth of it."

"How is Janey faring?"

"O she's strong as a horse, you know."

"That she is." John measured his words, let them out in small parcels, thought out his movements, where he'd sit on the chair, the angle of his head, what his hands should do; he thought of it like a dance.

"Have you been sleeping?"

"I have not. I jus feel so low an fear doin somethin awful. I don't hold with suicide, Doc, believe it's a sin bad as any there is, but I'm real low and sinkin further feels like. I wasn brought up to complain nor make a fuss—"

"Asking a doctor for help is not making a fuss, William, people stopped doing that I'd be out of a job."

"Don't want the electric cure neither, scares me stupid. Gave that to Arthur Wiley's sister. I jus thought, if there was somethin you could give me. Pep me up, yknow?"

"Electric cure scares me a little too, you want the truth." John leaned in, let go a smile. "I've got a few things we could try before we let General Electric have a go at you." A short tap on his bag let forth the satisfying tinkle of bottles. "You know what a cuttlefish is, William?"

He held up the dilution and explained that it contained a tiny amount of something called sepia, and that sepia is derived from the ink of the cuttlefish. He told him that the dilution was utterly without toxicity, yet was used to treat, and here he quoted the literature verbatim: *those of a fractious or fretful disposition, particularly in cases where they have become overwhelmed by family duties and obligations.*

"Do you think this something you'd like to try?" he asked. William stared at the clear liquid.

"And that's got squid ink in it?"

"In a sense. It's got something in it that is found in squid ink."

William was transfixed.

"You can't see a thing."

"Amazing, isn't it?"

"Well I'll be."

"Do you think this something you'd like to try?"

William seemed unsure, looked at John, then back at the flask.

"Hell, I'll try anythin fore I let em wire me up like a damn lightbulb."

◆

"Bless, O Lord, this food for thy use, and make us ever mindful of the wants and needs of others. Amen." The words fell out of him with an ease that flattered his performance; though it was not his wife's indifferent custodian he thought of as he spoke, nor her murdered carpenter's son, but of the filthy pair in the woods, no doubt as he spoke on their way to steal away yet another man, another woman or child.

Ros had been visibly startled when he'd suggested that it was he that say grace, and he thought he'd seen the tiniest smile from Hattie, a rare enough thing in of itself since her attack, a smile which he'd struggled to define as either happiness or victory.

They ate and he retreated to the authentic John inside, replaying The Notion's spoils lain on riverbanks and in woods, on spattered floorboards and beside quiet roads; bodies naked and clothed, broken and seemingly untouched, bloody and brimful with lake water. In none of these tableaux did Ros' God feature.

Upon the clearing of plates, Ros had looked him in the eye and asked if everything was okay. He'd replied that it was, had kissed her on the forehead, adding, "It is, now."

His depiction of what he'd come to call The Goodly Doctor remained flawless, though exhausting, more than once forcing an afternoon nap, patients permitting, on the couch in his office. If ever he struggled to sleep, whiskey was always there to sing him off. Sometimes when Ros came to speak to him, he'd merely pretend to be asleep.

He'd begun, over the past month or two, quite unconsciously at first, to fill his pockets with tiny things. Odds and ends picked up here and there: a triangle of glass broken who knew when or from what, worn smooth by the elements; a paperclip, a bottle cap, a horseshoe nail, a watch cog, a thimble. Often his pockets rattled and jingled as he walked.

Sometimes as he drove to or from a patient, he would pick out something from this collection and throw it into the trees, or try to skip a button over the water, or while walking he'd drop it by the shoulder of the road and press it into the earth with his shoe. Tiny, votive things gathered only to discard, as if to artificially lighten his load, or invested with some phantom worry then dropped; perhaps offerings.

There is blood in his eye and as he runs, he presses his bandaged hand against it. The angry split in his forehead feels hot, and he imagines it to be incandescent, letting forth a fierce white light between his fingers. His ribs burn and there is a tear in his jacket. He stumbles into trees and trips over roots, yet does not stop. Somewhere behind him the old woman gives chase and he daren't halt to glance back, nor indeed look back while fleeing, half-blind as he is.

It's a dirty trick to sneak up on a man as he takes a leak, he thinks; he puts his axe down to piss, that's a dirty trick. Were it not for the rainfall and so the wet footfall, he'd never have heard her, would have been put asunder, hacked to scraps on the forest floor. But he'd heard and he'd turned and the blade had swung short, had travelled down his forehead, then down his side, ruined a perfectly good jacket and made his vision swim pinkish with blood.

Behind him some way, the old woman runs long-legged and strangely, like a series of collapses which impossibly end in still more, each convulsive stride, each chaotic swing of her arms giving impetus somehow to the next then the next.

Even if he were faster she could follow him by his breathlessness she thinks, by his whimpers, his intermittent, choked cries of *You leave me be* and *My God, my God*. So on they run.

♦

Sumner hasn't prayed since he was a boy, and then with more obligation than enthusiasm. He has never heard God's voice, nor seen him, yet he knows He's there, like he knows that the sun rises and that water freezes. Prayer always seemed to him like so much applesauce; unnecessary, a nonsense. He is not a man of fanciful sensibilities. He has never seen anything that couldn't be explained one way or another, never seen the wendigos nor white phantoms that some folks spoke of; so it is queer that in the hush of night, sometime toward three, he finds himself in conversation with someone who he cannot see.

"*What?*" His voice is strange in the dark, hoarse and too loud. "Sure." He draws a hand down his face, blinks to pull himself further up from sleep; his other hand rests on Maisie's side of the bed, empty. "Sure. But—" He is interrupted. The room slowly sketches itself; no one is there. "I am. Who—" Interrupted again. "I guess." Sumner swings his legs from the bedclothes and pushes fingers through his wiry hair. "My wife, Mae." He stands with a groan. "No. Took the bus. Sister's. Down there in Poughkeepsie. *Long* way. Brother-in-law's gotten himself—" Again, he's cut off, he waves his hands in weary acquiescence. "Okay, okay, don't get so aerated." He pulls on his pants, shuffles into his shoes. "I will, I will." He halts, cocks his head like a hound. "Wh— You're *where?*" A pause. "What in hell's name you doin in there?"

Outside on the porch he halts, still full of sleep, frowns, does a troubled little to and fro. This isn't right, is strange and dumb; yet he knows he won't return to the house until he's taken a look.

The night sky is clear and a rich dark blue, the moon a pale curl of rind. He lights the lamp hanging by the porch steps, shaking his head. He goes to the barn, pulls out the ice pick from the beam by the door and holds it behind his back as he approaches the icehouse. Putting the lamp on the ground and one-handed, he works with difficulty at the heavy door catch. Open, a faint gray moonlight is thrown from the warm night into the cold. Even in the dark, the blue of the ice. Sumner stands in the doorway, breath tumbling out along the moonlight.

Some way in the back, a number of blocks are untidily stacked together, forming a largish, disordered cube. Inside, a smear, a shadow or shape; maybe driftwood, maybe leaves. He lifts the lamp, cranes his neck, peers in; shadows slide all over, black like oil.

A large gouge in the cube reveals what appears to be part of a face, nostrils, a mouth. Pale lips beaded with moisture. The head must be angled back, as if caught in pain or exaltation; the eyes, the forehead, still buried. The jaw works on its hinge, as if in an attempt to fidget the rest of the head free; a muted cartilaginous sound in the quiet. The appearance is of a person trapped inside a box or a solid block of stone, perhaps gnawing themselves free. The sight is at once frightening and compelling. Cold reaches out to Sumner and he lets a shiver. Can there really be a person folded up, sealed up, in there? His fingers tighten and blanch around the ice pick nestled in the small of his back. As he steps inside, the mandible falls still, before speaking aloud.

"Sumner." It's a greeting but also a statement of acknowledgment, and perhaps of intent: his name is known. He nods in return, a purse of his lips. "Hey, Sumner." The voice is quiet but strangely weighty, strangled sounding. He takes a while to answer.

"Hey yourself."

"Do you recognize me?" *Recognize what?* he thinks.

"Can't say as I do. Aint much moren a fraction I can see."

"Are you surprised to see me?"

"Surprised to see anyone in there. Aint you cold?"

"Do you have a notion why I might be here?"

"In the ice?"

"No. The ice is just the where, not the why." The voice carries a cruel, mannered exactness, clinging to affect and pomposity. "I mean do you know why I might be here, with you."

"I do not."

He knows he should be worrying about the door standing ajar but he isn't, knows the longer the door is open the closer the blocks edge toward slickness, toward melt. He knows this scene should seem to him stranger than it does but still he stands and converses with a mouth in his ice. That this might be some terrible phantasm, some malignant spirit has crossed his mind and so he keeps his distance, keeps that one hand hidden. If he were to wake up this instant he'd sure have a story to tell, though in truth he's unsure as to whether he'd tell a soul.

"It's awful close in here, think you might like to chip me out a little with that pick?"

His grip lessens on it and he feels scolded, a little stupid, thinks: *It don't have eyes worth a damn, but it can see the pick.*

"You can't get out?"

"I can do whatever I want. I'm wondering if you might like to help me."

"Help you."

"Help me out."

Sumner has no inclination to do any such thing, so he stalls.

"You... get trapped when the lake froze?"

The lips crinkle in dissatisfaction.

"Is that something you really think likely?"

"I guess not."

"I guess not too. You haven't asked me what I'm doing here."

"What brings you here?"

"That's a different question."

"What— What are you doin here?"

"What am I doing here? What am I currently doing? What action am I engaged in? I'm being angry, that's what I'm doing."

"Angry."

"*Furious.*" This is spoken through teeth. Sumner nods, unsure how to reply.

"Okay."

"Are you an angry man, Sumner?" A smile in the way it's said. He waves a hand.

"O, once maybe. Anger's a young man's game."

The lips straighten.

"No, Sumner, it isn't."

John woke with a breath snatched as if he'd been underwater. It was dark and he was standing. An anemic moon pushed through the window in a blue wash that lit the living room. Ros' ornaments, the rug his father had given them. The mantel clock read a quarter after two. For an instant he had the sense that the world had moved under him, that he hadn't wandered down there an unconscious blank, but that the earth had repositioned itself like a tumbler in a safe, while he had remained fixed. He stood facing the fireplace and was reminded of his dream, of Wilson and the sounds of something trapped; but there were no boards covering the hearth and the room was just as he'd left it upon retiring earlier that evening.

Crow come down your chimney, John.

He stared for a time at the blackness of the hearth, trying not to see faces there, phantoms or questions, before turning and retracing his steps back up to bed.

♦

For the rest of that night he dreamt of flying.

He is all at once terribly tired and closes his eyes for a long time. Opening them, he hunts about for something on which to sit, finds an old scrap of sacking, bends his aching legs and sits, the pick by his side. Behind him, through the open door, the night makes scurrying, creaking sounds; before him the icehouse is unbearably quiet. The night feels deep, entrenched, dawn an impossibility, a week or more away. He looks over at the fragment of face in the lamplight and considers what he might say next, whether he shouldn't ask just why the hell it's woken him, asked him there.

"How's business, Sumner?"

"Been better. Worse."

"The ice business. Not much better than selling fresh air, is it?" A certain taunt in the tone.

"If you say so."

"Maybe it's not just I who says so."

"Folks find it queer, or disagreeable, they don't have to buy it." The mouth smiles and he feels like running. Instead he tries to move things along. "How'd you get in there?"

"How do you think?"

"Well I don't reckon you just walked in."

"You don't think I could just walk into a block of ice?"

"If you could I imagine you'd just as easy walk on out."

"Very good, Sumner. But as I said, I was hoping you might help me out."

"An you weren't in there when we cut those blocks in February."

"No."

"So maybe someone put you in there."

"I would applaud if it were possible. You see, *my arms*. Thought anymore about using that ice pick?"

The cry of bedsprings, a Mr Harold Bisbee bucking and arching, face a mixture of restlessness and embarrassed discomfort. Working men didn't get sick, they moved on and through, past such trivialities. No more than six years older than John and already he was suffering from something that, barring any catastrophic mishap, would likely see him out. Inside him, Mr Bisbee's heart spluttered, nervous and tired.

The rest of the ward lay around, did nothing very much, read, waited on visitors, looked for sleep or made their way to and fro on papery legs; men-marionettes stripped to bare fibers and bloodshot eyes.

Bisbee insisted John call him Harold, complained he thought he was sharing his bed with a dozen or more goddamn rocks. John asked his questions, made comforting noises where appropriate.

His times at Northern Cumberland, at the other hospitals, were spent wading through a disgruntled hubbub, a murmurous ambient ache, trying not to feel held down by the sheer weight of so many of the unwell collected into such an enormous building. He'd move about the corridors feeling a little incongruous: something improper in the imposition of white tile, of disinfectant, among the Maine woods. *A hundred years ago what had stood on this spot?*

That morning he'd stopped as if to tie a shoelace and had pressed a bottle cap into the earth of the potted Parlor Maple in the lobby; closed his eyes, a little wordless moment, another idiot, impotent prayer.

He allowed himself a glance at his watch. Lunchtime, yet hope of lunch forever at arm's length, John halted in a stairwell and stared out of the window, took a moment to regroup, to watch the calm sway of the trees in the bright day, the intermittent cars buzzing along the road and into the distance.

Joseph Allen descended the steps from the main entrance and set off towards town. The suit he wore might not have been new but it was pressed, his hat clean and straight of brim. John watched him as if he were a stranger. No more than sixty feet separated them yet he'd never felt so distant from the old man, from their friendship. Would he tell Joseph he'd seen him? Perhaps. Would he ever tell Joseph of his little offerings, the buttons, the pennies, of his impromptu dip in Highland Lake? Perhaps. Did The Notion itself have an end, a resolution? Perhaps. Perhaps not.

He is a voice in the advancing dusk. The bright day is clawing its way reticently down the sky as he squats in shade, wringing bandaged hands, fending off tears, hoping that dark will be his escape. The old woman holds the axe in both hands, stands still and waits.

"You leave me be. I aint never hurt you." His voice comes from all over.

"O sure. You're just a sweetheart, you never hurt a fly."

"The girl was wicked, you wanted it done as much as me, she was low-down as a person can get."

"She was wicked. An you're weak an you're dumb an that's as good as in my book."

"She was low-down. I am dumb. Well you are... stern and unfeelin. You— You are cruel whether you mean to be or not, you don't care about nothin."

"Care about the rules, care about the way things are meant to be done."

"Even if they're wrong? Even if they're cold-blooded an— an bestial?"

"I done this long before you, before the whelp, an I'll be doin it long after you. You aint needed, mister."

"Then let me leave, I'll go away, won't bother you, I swear."

"Is that right?"

"I will, go far away."

"An where will you go? An just how will you keep your mouth shut? I don't believe you can. It aint in you, mister." There passes a silent moment in which his fear, his panic, his frustration, are as loud as if they were in fact shouted.

A gray shape flashes into life, describes a low arc in the dimness; she sidesteps before the rock can hit her and it impacts quietly against tree. She makes a face, spits. Another rock flies at her from out of the gloom and she ducks; another clangs against the axe blade, another *tocks* loudly against her right knee and she draws a hissing breath.

"Child," she snarls and bolts in the direction from which the rocks came. Something in the shadows skids and scuttles away from her and the chase begins again.

♦

The ice has turned glassy and small rivulets are pooling on the boards, describing dark lines in the grain of the wood like blood in the palm of a hand. The mandible works itself, chewing at the air; Sumner watches and yearns for sunrise.

A corner of ice cracks and shears off to the floor. An eye. Sumner grasps the ice pick. The teeth grit and growl and the top third of the cube breaks into pieces which slide away. Wet, matted hair, a smallish head, features surprising and discomfiting. It is breathless and works its head in circles on its neck.

"I fuckin *told you* I could get out of here," it spits with an animalism that belies its appearance, "An with no help from *you*, Sumner." The mannered pomposity falters, a colloquial ire forcing its way through here and there. Sumner stands, walks in place, churned up inside. He barks:

"What you want here? What you want in my icehouse? You didn't oughta be here. This time anight. Playin games like this."

"I'm here to do the worst things, Sumner, just the worst things." The eyes widen and Sumner halts.

"What things? Who to?"

"To you, Sumner, ya dumb halfwit, to you."

Sumner runs his tongue around the inside of his mouth, narrows his eyes.

"You don't look so big," he says, though in truth, beneath the bravado, his mind is once again turning to flight.

"You lookin pretty small yerself right about now, Sumner."

His face falls a little; it sees him, just as it saw the pick when there was no way it could have done so. He armors himself in counterfeit offense. This thing treating him so, on his own property?

"How about I bring this here pick over there, make you a few holes in that head?"

A wet, glutinous laugh.

"Bring it over, do. I'll be needing it in a moment."

"Fuck you." He is pleased with the delivery of the words, yet afraid of how little fortitude lies behind them.

The thing's evident incapacity vies with his fright. He's never really killed anything, never was much of a hunter; his brother claimed to have killed a black bear once but Owen was full of shit mostly and this is quite another thing. His mind is flailing. Dawn seems to be hiding, as if waiting for some resolution before it will show its face.

Sumner has the sense that if he runs, perhaps hides in the woods, it will be there waiting for him; if he counts the whole scene a dream and goes back to bed, he will find it curled up on his pillow; if he climbs the roof it will be sat astride the weathercock and nothing will be changed. And so he changes nothing, he stands still and the ice grows wetter, the night he'll never see the other side of fossilizing at his back.

"What do you know of dreams?" he had asked. Joseph had frowned.

"Interpretation or physiology?"

"Interpretation. Meaning."

"I know that anyone who tells you they can interpret them for you without knowin a great deal about the dreamer is a stone cold liar. *Dreamin of teeth is a dream about money* they say. Solid gold bullshit. For a dentist, maybe."

"And dreams of flying?"

"Ah, a stalwart dream of man, ever since he had mind enough to raise his eyes. As to meaning, well, like I say, depends on the dreamer, what birds, what flight, means to the dreamer. Escape? Freedom? The ability to see everything at once, from a distance, at a glance?" John nodded, pictured his dreams of flight, a carpet of trees sliding under him, without uniformity, despite their number; things seen scurrying between. "The Indians talk of a giant bird of prey, name of Culloo. Bird that would eat people. So big it could carry off children in its mighty talons." John imagined Culloo carrying off the two Bell girls, tiny limbs squirming, borne up into the clouds. "Nother called Wuchowsen," said Joseph, "a bird spirit. Bird of such size that its wings are what makes the wind." John's mind reached to conceive of such scale but fell short, even in daydream.

◆

Drunk and alone, sliding about in his thoughts, John grimaced clumsily, grasping around for the idea that had flitted so quickly across his mind, something that felt important; a sensation akin to hunting for a silver dollar in sand.

Would they come out then? Show themselves then?

Because they'd be drawn, surely, pulled through the trees to that place, to where it had happened. Was going to happen. They were there at all the others, why not then? But he'd have to mean it, mean to see it through or they would sense his infirmity of purpose, stay away, giggle at him from the branches and know him a fool and a pretender.

He clenched his teeth, held the thought fast until he could see it clearly.

For the sake of argument alone, if he took someone somewhere, meant to do them harm, hell, call a spade a spade, made to kill them, maybe took a rock, maybe a gun—

For the sake of argument if he did this, then they'd show, the two would turn up to finish the deed; and he could turn the gun on them. But if this was his plan, this deception, then they'd know and stay away. It couldn't possibly work unless he was willing to trust that in attempting to kill, in being willing to follow through, he would be stopped; all but full commitment to the task would be useless. He was Abraham, he realized, his proposed victim, this someone, his Isaac.

He put his head in his hands, laughed once, fought off tears. Faith was what was required, absolute faith. The plan became stupid and ugly and fell away.

The night doesn't move a muscle, while in the icehouse time goes wild, races, the melt showing the lamp's reflection in silvers and golds. Sumner shuffles his feet.

"You're not makin sense."

"You're thinking of running again."

"Because you're not makin *sense*."

"If that were reason enough to flee, however would anyone ever stop running their whole lives?"

"It aint real."

"It aint?"

"None of it."

"You asked and I told you. Now how about you come on over here and hand me that pick?"

"But my wife—"

"Better off without you. Give it a week, folks'll have to struggle to bring to mind your name, let alone your face."

"Aint real."

"Your record's broke, Sumner."

"Please—"

"Business is in the toilet, you're past your usefulness and the ice is melting."

"Aint so bad."

"Is too."

"I don't wanna go."

"Well that's good cause you aint goin nowheres."

"Don't say that. You didn't oughta say *that*."

A dull crack from the cube and a molasses-thick laugh.

"Tell you what, you see any pearly gates, meet any angels, you be sure to write me. But I aint about to hold my breath for it."

Sumner flounders, tries to recall the last words he spoke to Mae. The lamp's flame gutters and dims, the room do-si-dos around them.

"What's it like?"

"It's like nothin at all."

"Should I be afraid?"

"Of course."

♦

In the real thick of it, he can't see his hand before his face, so dense are the branches; but should one or more bow, or bend just so, the moon spears him in blue and his path appears then vanishes, his feet then having to recall the ups and downs of the earth to save him from a spill. But the moon is falling behind him and the darkest hour could all too easily see him fall with it, be caught and cut into pieces.

She seems to have no such trouble, her tread uninterrupted behind him, the occasional ringing sound of the axe glancing off trunks as she comes. Were the trees sidestepping to let her pass?

They tear along, through bushes and bracken, blind and breathing hard. He tries to double back but she follows, he tries hiding but loses his nerve the closer she gets and he bolts.

As the moon falls behind them, so he feels the earth tipping, as some immense disc, with the weight of its descent, he running uphill in an attempt to level it out, to tip it forwards and reveal the sun, as if some salvation lay in it. As exhaustion tightens its grip, he imagines the planet whirling under him, like a treadwheel, he merely moving his legs so as not to be thrown backwards into the old woman and to his certain dismemberment.

How long or how far they travel he can't tell; miles flow under him and his lungs scream and his head swims.

Finally, as dawn breaks and a bruised mauve light rises, he comes ripping through leaves and into an open space, where he stops, wheezing and hoarse. In the half light, a house, two large outbuildings; a recumbent truck slouching on its suspension. As good a place to die as any. He collapses onto all fours and dry heaves, each spasm stealing still more breath he can ill-afford to lose. Even through his pain, something registers and he raises his head, looks about. This place is a strange one, has a resonance that he cannot place nor understand.

The old woman strides into the clearing and immediately

feels it too. She stands still, as if listening for a quiet voice, or trying to remember an old song. The thin man looks up at her from the ground.

"Have we been here before?" he says at last.

"No." She looks thrown and confused.

"I think I— recognize it, or somethin."

"We've never been here before."

He stands uneasily and keeping a small distance between them they approach the first outbuilding, its doors wide open. On the floor a lamp burns low, almost out; large pieces of ice are scattered about the room, pools of water stain the floorboards.

They walk on. The second outbuilding, a barn, holds nothing so much: few tools, few crates. They circle around the house, perhaps afraid to go inside. At the back, a door stands open, inside a man hangs from his neck by a rope. In the dimness of the house, his face is a darker smudge, swollen and vague, as if wiped away by a sooty hand.

"Dear God, the poor fella," whispers the thin man, peering in, "we know him?"

"We do not," she replies. The hanging man pendulates an inch or so back and forth and they stand together and watch him in silence.

The thin man cries out, sharp and loud, and they spring apart; the old woman raises the axe. Between them stands the little girl, wet through, both hands on the handle of the letter opener, the blade of which is now buried in the thin man's side. For the longest time nothing happens.

He arches, strained and pinched, buckles slowly, face an awful mask.

"I'm sorry," he manages.

"I'm not," spits back the little girl and turns the handle in him; he cries out again. He mouths what she thinks might be the word *forgive* and she laughs, letting go of the letter opener, which he takes with him to the ground.

He wriggles in his blood for a good half hour before dying, cries out and weeps loudly, and they both watch; the old woman tired and cheated, the little girl beside herself, giggling through her fingers.

When it's done, they drag him a short way into the woods and cover him with fallen branches. The old woman toys with the axe for a time before throwing it off into the trees. The little girl lifts up her dirty dress, squats near the body and urinates, smiling; steam rises up from her in the cool morning air.

"You know it aint done," says the old woman. The girl shrugs, standing.

"Was worth it," she says.

He finished his notes standing on the porch, keeping the Newcombe house between himself and what remained of the ice man, tried to recall the scorched coffee scent of the interior while the corrupt smell he'd fled the body to escape bled through the house like an intruder, tainted its familiarity, embraced him, clung to the roof of his mouth.

He descended the steps, drawing a shallow breath from fresher air.

He swerved thought to the matter at hand, dismissed as best he could all speculation, all imagination. Whether or not a patch of ground off to the right had a strange dark brown tinge to it, or was merely in shadow, he refused to investigate; he glanced into the trees for a moment, then quickly away, not wishing to see what might or might not be hidden within.

He thought of Meuse, of the trees and of the revolver. The lieutenant finding him, snatching away the gun and ordering him back to the men. As he'd walked back through the rain, he'd thought to himself that it had been the young soldier's terrible inanimacy that had forced him into the trees with the revolver, and yet the threat of that same inanimacy that had kept him from using it. Still from time to time the same strange pull he'd felt that day reared up in him.

The peeling legend on the side of the ice truck alluded to Summer, even as a fierce winter was gathering forces, even as the truck's owner had vanished from any future season, clement or inclement. He thought of Maisie receiving the telegram down there at her sister's, wondered what grief would look like on that hard face, whether it would show at all or simply be ingested, swallowed and held down like a bad olive. John made his notes and held himself in check. Behind him, familiar hushed voices, workmanlike yet respectful. Elmer and the boys were in the back room cutting Sumner down, wrapping him like a prize ham, faces covered with bandanas and kerchiefs, like cowboy bandits in the movies, wincing at their task, eyes watering in the miasma rising up from the man they had known.

John plucked a grimy brass washer from his pocket, dropped it and trod it into the ground. What he might possibly be doing with the accumulation, the dispersal of these little things, these tiny offerings, he had only barely addressed within himself, and never with any detail or justification. There he was, a man, a *doctor*, dropping bric-a-brac, curios, hiding these souvenirs to nothing so very much, peppering the county with them. Fleeting answers as to why these things had occurred, though none of any help or satisfactory fit: an animal marking its territory, breadcrumbs in a forest, scratches marking time on a cell wall. Burying the penny had felt like a prayer, but this motive had since curdled and no longer sat right with him.

Though answers were unforthcoming, still he carried on, still some compulsion that spoke in ungrasped vagaries compelled him; this had importance, he told himself, there was meaning here, all this led somewhere, to some as yet hidden conclusion or completion.

He felt the approach of something and for a moment grew afraid, before recognizing the feeling as something approximate to his perpetual state; this was what it was to live as Doctor John M. Bischoffberger: something else always advancing. He did his best to wrestle a sliver of comfort from the realization.

State of Maine.

Cumberland **ss.**

I certify that I was notified on the *1st* day *of September* A. D. 19 *38*

at *5* h. and *5* m. in the *after* noon by *Elmer O. Stewart Deputy*

of *Bridgton, Me* of the finding of the dead body of *Sumner*

O. Newcombe of *Bridgton, Me*

supposed to have come to h *is* death by violence or unlawful act; that I forthwith repaired to the place

where said body lies and took charge of the same, and before said body is removed make, or cause to be made,

this written description of the location and position of said body, viz:

```
     The body was that of a man five feet nine inches tall, having gray
hair, blue eyes, dressed in brown slacks, brown striped jersey,tan shoes
and stockings. His pockets contained at empty wallet and $35.30 in cash.
     The body was badly decomposed, there was cyanosis of face, congestion
of neck muscles and protrusion of eyes, mucous extented from mouth,
rigor mortis had set in.
     He was found hanging from a rope in a storeroom in the back part
of house. The rope had been fastened to an ice pick driven into the
timbers of a small storage space above. A slip knot had been fastened
about the neck. A stool upon which the deceased had stood,while placing
noose, stood to one side of the body.
     The deceased was last seen alive on August 27th 1938. On Sept 1st.
Judge Pike and Judge Corless of Bridgton requested Deputy Elmer Stewart's
help in locating him. Unable to get into the house they broke in and
found body as described.

     Cause of Death.  Suicide by Hanging.
```

Date *Sept 1* 19 *3 8* *John M. Bischoffberger*

Medical Examiner.

The missing page. Page 23 had only the gaps left in the printed text, gaps into which he was meant to have slotted a body. Only a date was scrawled, in his hand, at the bottom: March 31st, 1938. He checked the rest of the journal; no other entries bore that date. The date meant nothing to him. He kept no diary, and threw away his notes once transcribed, so if something had occurred on that day and he had forgotten it, he had no way of remembering. Still it felt like a day stolen, or lost to something unknown and unknowable. It felt clumsy and undoctorly; a slip. A blank page in the course of events known and recorded felt uncomfortably metaphoric.

He drained his glass, refilled it.

He pictured again Joseph's figurative stake that John had supposedly driven into the Maine earth on his arrival, and somehow the image doubled and intermingled with an image from his youth, a stake in the ground, a rope tied to that stake, a dog tied to that rope; memories of the Hudsons' dog on Vine Street.

Dwight Hudson's barber's shop on Vine Street, just down from the Post Office and Schlachter's Market. Dwight kept the dog out back tied to a length of steel pipe hammered into the ground. The dog was a gray and matted thing, like something that might've been pulled from a drain. It barked incessantly, seemingly without effort or fatigue, straining at the rope that bound it to the pipe. As a boy John had spent many a moment watching, agape, fascinated at this strange and futile display. Then one day the dog simply wasn't there, the pipe uprooted, the ground smoothed over. Harold Willis at school said the dog had escaped, killed a cat two towns over. John's father had said that Hudson the barber had "put the beast out of its and everyone else's misery". When young John had asked how, his father had replied cryptically "with the tool of his trade, son" and when little John had asked why, his father had told him not to ask such damn fool questions.

He drained his glass, refilled it.

The rain beat hard against the window, the morning's storm mustering belligerence hour on hour. A fresh deluge had begun some four days before and had refused to let up. Floods were rife and rivers were rising; winds were tearing at the trees.

The day before, Tuesday, sheltering in Thompsons Beer Parlor, John had heard Clifford Whitney use the word *hurricane* and be laughed off of his stool and out of the door. He'd watched the drunk and disgruntled Whitney leave, had tried not to think of the weather as some reaction to the two becoming three again, if indeed they had; some upsetting of the natural scheme of things, albeit within this little pocket of unnaturalness.

He had dreamed again that night of flying above the trees and of glimpsing those hidden within; had woken disquieted.

Because the hiding was the thing, he told himself, his finger tap-tapping on the desk, as if trying to make a point to an uninterested room; they were *hiding*. He wondered disjointedly how wide a road had to be. If they couldn't hide then they couldn't operate. The trees were the thing.

They operated in secret, hid themselves until it was time for them to act, sprung from the woods, did the deed, then vanished once again. The trees were the thing.

Take away the trees and they would be exposed. He tried to picture a map of Cumberland County, the masses of trees dissected by roads, and wondered how wide a road had to be to effectively halt a forest fire.

Eight? Nine fires set round about and who knew how far it would spread, how much ground would be cleared? The ash would fall, the embers settle and there they'd be, between blackened trunks, perhaps hugging one another, perhaps weeping, vulnerable. And then everyone would see them.

But he was reaching, and drunk. He would never set any fires, it was preposterous. And besides, no fire would catch after such a downpour.

As they walk, trees moan flatly about them like a deaf choir; clawed at, branches tear off and fall, leaves are ripped to tatters. The rain strikes their faces like a handful of pebbles thrown, and they grimace and hunch over as they make their way, wet to the skin. In the storm, a raised voice is the only means of communication.

"THIS ONE IS *MINE*," shouts the girl.

"O YOU THINK SO?" bellows the old woman. "IT AINT THERE TO GIVE YOU JOLLIES."

"DON'T THINK SO, I *KNOW* SO. THIS ONE IS MINE AN YOU'LL JUST WATCH. *YOU* BECAUSE YOU COULDN'T BEAR TO HAVE ANYTHIN HAPPEN LESS IT'S UNDER YOUR BEADY EYE, AN *HIM* BECAUSE HE'LL DO AS HE'S FUCKIN TOLD."

"*THIS AINT FOR YOUR JOLLIES.*"

"DON'T MATTER WHAT IT'S HERE FOR, IT'S HERE AINT IT?"

"PERHAPS JOLLIES IS THE WRONG WAY OF SAYIN IT," shouts the thin man. "A PERSON SHOULD FEEL PEACE, IS THAT PERHAPS WHAT YOU MEANT?"

The girl shoots him a look through the rain.

"YOU SEE ANY 'PEOPLE' HERE, DUMB FUCK?" she growls. He lowers his eyes, wipes his sopping hair from his face.

"WHAT I MEAN TO SAY IS—"

"*SHUT YER MOUTH*. THIS ONE IS *MINE*. THINGS ARE DIFFERENT NOW. JUST HOLD YER TONGUE OR I'LL KILL YOU ALL OVER AGAIN." She walks on and, despite themselves, they follow.

The hurricane made landfall on Long Island and tore up Westhampton Beach's Dune Road, killing twenty nine. A nearby movie house was picked up, patrons, projectionist and all, and thrown two miles out to sea, where all twenty souls drowned. In New York City, the Empire State Building swayed drunkenly.

A further one hundred people died as the winds hit Westerly, Rhode Island, the storm following the Connecticut River north into Massachusetts and killing another ninety-nine. In New Hampshire another thirteen lost their lives; Vermont escaped with a death toll of only five.

Later, John would imagine the storm to be the result of air churned up in the wake of something massive tearing north across the country, trailing a widening V of destruction behind it; perhaps drawn towards something, inhaled like a sharp breath before screaming. He put it all together in his mind in a way that fitted, conspiring to see the chain of events culminating in their arrival in Naples. He daydreamed of the immense Indian bird spirit Joseph had talked of, its wings like the sky, their beating pushing air that threw down trees, that likewise destroyed the white man's vain and petty additions to the surface of the land.

When the hurricane did indeed reach Maine, roofs were torn off and tossed, as if some delinquent child were searching doll's houses for someone hiding within. Trees fell like tenpins, squashing cars and caving in roofs; barns were blown away, debris thrown into Thompson Lake. There were widespread power outages, shop frontages were denuded, signage hurled and windows put in; cellars in Bangor were flooded.

A man in Lewiston was hit by a falling branch, and another man likewise struck in Waterville; in Farmington a woman crashed her motorcycle into a fallen tree, breaking her arm. Of the six states affected, Maine was the only one to escape without fatalities.

♦

Something akin to a waking dream: again, the stake in the ground. A tree no longer, reduced, demoted once again to that gray length of timber. A dog tied to it, the animal walking around and around, on and on, its tread describing a perfect circle in the dirt; perhaps the Hudsons' dog of his childhood. But no, not the Hudsons' dog but a soot-black, hairless thing, somehow a sight both pitiful and frightening. Silent, it walked around and around and went nowhere.

They stand and watch from under the open window, each of them dripping silently onto the rug, as the girl carefully lifts the infant, holding him to her flat chest, rocking him a little in a pantomime of heavyhearted endearment, making eye contact first with the old woman, then with the thin man, her mouth turned comically down at the corners.

The house is rattled about them as the storm howls and beats at its outside. And they stand and watch, the old woman seething with inaction, with a lack of plays to be made; the thin man cowed and resigned, perhaps still reeling from his return and the echo of the act that sent him away.

"Things are different now," says the girl.

"Nothins ever different," says the old woman quietly, though with little conviction.

"I'm just warmin up," says the girl.

"Warmin up," repeats the old woman.

"To somethin more. Somethin bigger."

"*Bigger?*" The old woman injects all the scorn she can muster into that one word.

"Whole street maybe, whole *town.*"

"Whole town. Listen to you."

"Listen to *you.* You of all of us shouldn't doubt the possibility."

"Possibility of *what?*"

"Plague, or fire, or earthquake, or madness. Told you once I wanted to burn the world, maybe we start with a town and see how we go on."

"You're a whelp an you're stupid and you'll ruin things with your foolishness."

"What you gonna do, kill me?"

"This aint the way."

"O boo hoo."

The girl pushes out her bottom lip, lays her head on its side, before shifting the baby gingerly in her arms and placing him face down on the quilt, laying a hand on the back of his small head and pressing gently down, her pantomimic sad expression creasing under the weight of just how funny she finds the whole business.

I t took forty some minutes to reach the Knight place, despite it being only on the other side of Naples. Almost every road was littered with downed trees and impassable; a series of indistinct barricades lying in the dark like fallen animals, forcing a meager speed and many a backtrack and re-route. Everywhere the thunderous clamor of the storm, like the sound of some catastrophic collapse that never came to rest. The car felt fragile and awkward, a clumsy machine unwilling to be steered through the chaos and around the haphazard obstacles; yet walking felt perilous at best.

With every intersection he reached, the wind tore at the roadster, trying its best to tip it over, the air roaring and full of small pieces of the world picked up and scattered about. Every so often something large fell heavily nearby.

He was met at the door by Annie Proctor, a neighbor, who offered him the brief sketch of a smile before ushering him inside out of the winds.

Even with the door closed the sound in the house was incredible, and it seemed no less appropriate an accompaniment to the scene waiting for him in the small back bedroom than the parents' sobbing that crept through the walls whenever the storm paused for breath.

State of Maine.

Cumberland ss.

I certify that I was notified on the 21st day September A. D. 19 37

at 7 h. and 30 m. in the after noon by Mrs. Annie Proctor

of Naples of the finding of the dead body of Donald

Walter Knight Jr. of Naple

supposed to have come to h is death by violence or unlawful act; that I forthwith repaired to the place

where said body lies and took charge of the same, and before said body is removed make, or cause to be made,

this written description of the location and position of said body, viz:

The body was that of a male infant, twenty-six inches tall
having blue eyes, blond hair and weighing about eighteen pounds.
He was dressed in a white dress, white shoes and white stockings
a white bonnet was held on his head by a tie beneath the chin.
There was cyanosis of the lips and congestion of the neck and face.
There were no marks of external violence. Rigor mortis was just
setting in.
The mother stated the baby was apparently alive at five P. M.
while she was preparing the evening meal. The father came home at
seven P. M. and found the baby lying on its face, on turning it
over he saw it was dead.
Post mortem signs indicated that the baby must have died
about three P. M.

Cause of Death; Accidental Suffocation.

Date March 31 1938

John M Bradley Myers M. D.
Medical Examiner.

On the walk back to the car, things flashed and flew in the dark woods, catching what light there was as they span, smears in his peripheral vision; he fancied them the shapes of people, yet he kept walking, hunched and dogged. Through the screaming air, the impact of something to his left, the splintering of something to his right. Wuchowsen roared and careened about, spread its wings and took full flight.

The rain stung, hitting him in waves, darting capriciously on the whim of the winds, one moment at his back, then slap in his face; it was hard to take a full breath. Standing still was impossible.

John stopped as he reached the car, hand on the door handle, performing a strange little jig as he was pushed this way and that. He wondered if any of his little offerings, his bottle caps and coins, his cogs and paperclips, had been disinterred by the storm and thrown about, whether they might race around the streets at terrific speeds, dangerous as bullets.

Stood in that rain, buffeted and beaten by the storm, alone at night on that road, he felt oddly surrounded, inundated by the detritus of some mighty discharge put forth from the world, swimming about him, careening through the air like shrapnel in a self-perpetuating fusillade. Everything crowded in on him and it all felt bad and unending, and he thought that maybe he'd spent so much of his time in the eye of it, untouched and oblivious, that now he was *in it*, deep in the flow and bite, he felt the terrible weight as never before.

He turned his back on the car and walked falteringly into the trees.

VIII

How do we spend our time is the question, I think. This short spool that unravels while we hold on too tightly like some boy fisherman.

Maybe we spend it gatherin things together, money, maybe turnin out children, maybe buildin things, bein kind, crushin those that oppose us; maybe we just stand still and gape at the enormity of life until it's too late to do anythin with it.

I've thought about this a lot, whole lot; how should we spend our time? I have come to the conclusion that we should spend it askin questions.

I am not a believer, as you know, but if God himself turned up on my doorstep tomorrow, it's true I'd feel pretty foolish, but then I'd certainly have quite a few questions to ask the son of a bitch.

"Alas, how terrible is wisdom when it brings no profit to the man that's wise!" so says Sophocles and he's right, he is. You dig around too much you may not like all you find, but if you don't dig you won't find nothin; gold weren't never found with a garden rake, only a pick, a shovel.

Why does this fella over here believe what he believes? And what about this other fella? Is there somethin in *that*?

Why do these folks have everythin, while those folks over there have nothin at all?

Are fear and violence inescapable? Are they what man truly yearns for?

Does good always triumph? And if so, whose good?

Why does this fella turn the other cheek and that fella put a bullet between yer eyes? And who's more human for it? And what does that word even mean?

Is there reason to be had in searchin for an answer that will never be found? An how do you know it'll never be found less you look?

A fool I once knew would tell me "a man lookin for answers is chasin his tail," he would say, endin with the idiot flourish of "The tail you understand isn't the object of his chase, but the asshole hangin beneath it." This imbecile and blowhard would talk loudly to anyone who'd listen, an he bothered many who wouldn't. He'd be dead now, or nigh on a hundred and four. Wherever he finished up. Whatever became of him I do not know but I can tell you with certainty that he did not end well. An ignorant man never dies happy, for he never lives.

Me? I'll go on askin. This particular boy fisherman is tryin to land the unlandable, the one that, no matter what, *will* get away; but it won't get away without a tussle.

Harrison; Maine

June, July, 1939

The car rockets and growls, its passage headlong and frantic, trees smearing by on either side. Perched on a fruit crate, the little girl glares through the steering wheel, daring the world before them not to step aside, to risk impact and glorious catastrophe.

Beside the girl the body of Joseph Walker lolls and slouches, his head little more than a tethered balloon; the old woman and the thin man are tossed around on the back seat.

The girl throws the Sunbeam Coupe onto Edes Falls Road, and all inside lurch to the right. Her eyes huge and wild, she whispers under her breath:

"*Fasterfasterfasterfasterfaster*—" They swerve around other cars in a blink, leaving behind angry horns and hasty braking.

"Fuck you!" she cries out, laughing, and rocks in the driver's seat, willing the three of them on to who knows what. Joseph Walker slides limply down into the footwell and the old woman reaches forward, pulling him back up by his shirt collar; there is an oily sheen of sweat on her face and neck.

"We done here?" she snaps at the girl. "This is stupid and ugly. I hate these fuckin things."

"*You're* stupid an ugly, how about that?"

"Listen—"

"I— don't feel so good," says the thin man from the back.

"See?" says the girl, "You've made the fool all nauseated."

"Stop this thing," snarls the old woman.

"Think I'm gonna puke," moans a tiny voice behind them.

"I'm tellin you to stop this fuckin contraption."

"Or what? What'll you do? This is the new way now, we're movin forward, I'm warmin up." They streak past a couple out walking, causing them to leap into a ditch by the roadside; an angry *Hey!* falls away as they speed on.

"Stop it."

"What if I don't?" The girl is giggling.

"*Stop it.*"

"New way," says the girl, "forward."

"Please—" moans the thin man.

"This is foolish and reckless, folks'll see."

"You're not gonna have another tantrum are you?"

"They'll *see*."

"Let em see. Who cares?"

"I hate these things," says the old woman again, quietly to herself, then: "*Stop this fuckin car now!*"

The little girl howls madly, a long and loud *hoooooo* sound, and veers across the road; all inside fall and rattle about, the old woman screaming something lost to the shrill outcry of the tires, reaching for the door handle, the thin man holding his bandaged hands to his mouth, eyes tightly shut as the car tips onto its side and then onto its back. The detritus of Joseph Walker's life takes to the air in a thousand little pieces: loose change dropped, pebbles brought in on the soles of shoes, a matchbook, weightless now, motes of dust sparkle, catch the light. Glass breaks, a door flies open, then another, and light streams in, bleaching the interior as first the old woman, then the rest, are flung from the car as if it were alive and shaking itself free of irksome parasites.

The old woman falls horizontally through the air and into the woods, turning, landing among nettles; the thin man hits tarmac and rolls and rolls, skinning his face, his knees and elbows, letting forth a pale crescent of vomit from his grimace as he spins. The little girl simply *flies*, knees bent, arms outstretched, a wide grin across her face which breaks into a laugh as Joseph Walker sails past her, slack-limbed and oddly graceful, already broken before he hits the ground.

M aine felt pitted and corrupted somehow. The ground had broken up under him, roads sinking and cracking, 'frost heave' having lifted the earth in large plates, as subterranean ice had thawed and frozen and thawed again, winter throwing its final punches before going down for another year. Even in the early days of June, the spring mud that had clawed at shoes and boots long having abated, many of these potholes and miniature peaks had yet to be flattened or filled.

John parked the roadster where Lewis Road met Harrison and took a moment to compose himself.

"Nothing new and nothing to worry about," he said, forcing himself to nod and smile once in a kind of rehearsal. Before leaving the car he took a sip from his pewter flask and left it on the passenger seat, concealed beneath a newspaper.

Deputy Elmer Stuart was talking baseball with Patrolman Ralph Price, something about *them Tigers eatin them Yankees alive*. They greeted John with a wave and a wincing look into the sun.

"Bisch."

"Now, Ralph, I thought you'd be over there in Niagara Falls today meeting King George," tried John, smiling, forcing a cordiality in place of the distance he felt.

"Invite never arrived can you believe it?"

"How are you, Bisch?" asked Elmer.

"O I'm fine, and you? And Mary?"

"O you know, married life suits me but not my waistline. I'll take you over to poor Mr Walker over here."

John was aware that his pockets jangled with collected bits and pieces as he walked, and he tried to measure his steps to lessen the sound. If anyone at the scene noticed the jangle, or any scent of whiskey, or indeed that he had neglected to shave that morning, no one said a word, nor treated him any differently than they ever had; for this he was grateful.

In addition, no one spoke of his time off following the hurricane, though they all knew that Doctor Joe Bodge and Doctor Wendel Smith had picked up the slack of his caseload, as he recovered from whatever it was he'd taken ill with. Some said pneumonia, others speculated in wilder directions; talk of a nervous exhaustion, of heart trouble, of straight-out madness. John never confirmed nor denied any of these speculations.

The night had raged about him as he walked, whipping at his face and casting branches in his path, strange pressure changes fingering his eardrums painfully, his medical bag becoming an almost intolerable weight that he longed to put down. He'd walked and walked, one arm outstretched, so absolute was the dark, moving between the trees like a blind man in a busy railway station. When the clouds were momentarily torn from the moon, a full barn door came wheeling between the trees, miraculously missing them all, spinning on its way into the night; half seen things, some animal blown and caught in the high branches, perhaps a large dog, breathing hoarsely, tugged at by the storm.

He'd returned home in the early hours, cold and in disarray, the knees to his trousers muddy, as if he'd fallen, or been kneeling. Ros met him in the hall, embraced him too tightly, her face pale and harried. Her late-night calls around had met with no sign of him, the consensus being that he more than likely had been forced by the storm into seeking refuge in a nearby household. A search party during the hurricane was impossible, she was told, yet Elmer had assured her that come morning one would be mounted.

John had spent a little over two weeks in bed, in a strange and what he felt to be an indulgent and malingering echo of Hattie's convalescence; a further two weeks had been spent wandering about the house, getting under Ros' feet and staring through windows at the outside world, feeling discomposed and vaguely adversarial toward all that lay out there. Ros never spoke a word about that night, nor raised an objection when he said that he was not going to return to work until he felt able, despite the financial implications. She fed and shaved him, when he was up and about gave him little jobs to do to occupy his time. He read a little, fixed up the table in Hattie's room, stripped and re-stained the hall chair, caught up on paperwork, but mostly his time was taken up with a quiet and exhausting attempt to avoid thought; still his mind wandered in circles, loose and ungoverned in its ideation.

In his mind he saw the stake again, the dog, sometimes the

Hudsons' mutt, sometimes the black thing; other times a drawing a child might make of a dog, ungainly and shambling in its
proportions, all teeth and fierce, irregular eyes. In whichever
incarnation, the dog went around and around on its rope, but
now the rope had caught somehow, the knot refusing to turn,
and so the dog, with every circle, drew closer and closer to the
center, to the stake.

It walked a spiral toward that center, drawing ever closer to
the stake, to him, to John. He had, perhaps vainly, driven himself into the Maine earth, planted his flag, and something was
circling in on him.

Such were the thoughts that chewed at him.

Much of the night spent in the storm remained a blank to
him, a series of shapes in the black, the smell of something
unearthed, damp and rotten; the terrible bawling of the wind.

State of Maine.

Cumberland ss.

I certify that I was notified on the   day   A. D. 19 *39*

at *3* h. and *45* m. in the *after* noon by *Patrolman Ralph Prince*

of *Bridgton*   of the finding of the dead body of *Joseph*

Walker   of *Harrison Maine*

supposed to have come to h ~~is~~ death by violence or unlawful act; that I forthwith repaired to the place

where said body lies and took charge of the same, and before said body is removed make, or cause to be made,

this written description of the location and position of said body, viz:

The body was that of a man five feet eight inches tall, weighing about one hundred eighty pounds, having grey hair and brown eyes, brown mustacke. He was dressed in blue shirt, with cord trousers and high leather boots.

There was Fracture of neck at base of skull, abrasion of forehead, lacerations above and below left eye. Post mortem abrasions on chest.

The body was found on the highway two miles North of Naples village in an overturned coupe was nearby. He had evidently been driving toward Naples at an excessive rate of speed and upset when failing to make curve at this point in road throwing him from car and causing injuries as stated.

Cause of Death   Fracture of Neck in Automobile accident.

John M Bachop Reyes
Medical Examiner.

Date   19

Dust kicked up by the Sunbeam Coupe still hangs in the air as the old woman sits up in the woods, dazed, leaves in her hair. Over at the junction, capsized, the coupe's wheels still turn on nothing, sounds of the accident having left a queer resonant trace, absent yet ever sharp, ever loud and grating.

The thin man and the little girl stand on the sunbaked road, staring across the tree line at the old woman sat in the shade. The thin man's suit pants are shredded, his knees bloody within; he is picking splinters of the fruit crate out of his forehead with raw fingers. The little girl appears unscathed, her hands playing about the hem of her dress, smiling at the old woman as if to say *wasn't that just about the most fun you ever had?*

Slowly the dust settles and the sound recedes to mere memory. The old woman stands falteringly, reins her balance in, winces at the bite of nettles on her hands, blinks, stamps her feet on the earth, takes inventory of any injuries; the little girl mimics her, stamping on the hard, dark ribbon of the roadway. Confused, the thin man does likewise.

The old woman looks at the two out in the sunlight and a strange epiphany hits, forcing her back a step. She looks at them in the light, they at her among the shade. A surprise as much to herself as to the others, she begins to laugh, quietly at first but soon with volume and a doubling over at the waist, muscles she'd misplaced or forgotten aching like warm stones.

"What in hell's name's with you?" asks the girl. The old woman struggles to find breath for a reply.

"She lost her wits maybe?" asks the thin man, peering, wiping a bead of blood from his forehead. "Bump on the head?"

"You go on," the old woman manages at last, "you two go on. You're ridiculous, the both ayou."

"Go on where?" asks the thin man, face folded up and worried looking.

"Jus go."

"An you aint comin?"

"I aint." A long moment sails by.

"But it's us three, you, me an her. It's the way it is," he says at last.

"No it aint. Just the way I thought it had to be. But it's ludicrous, you're ludicrous. I'm done with you. Both ayou."

"Fuck you then," shouts the little girl, then aside to the thin man, "We don't need her." The old woman has already turned, stepping away into the woods, wiping tears and calming her laughter. "We aint about to stop workin!" the girl shouts after her.

"I'd wish you luck but I wouldn't mean it," replies the old woman over her shoulder and is gone.

"We aint about to stop fuckin workin," says the girl again.

The same newspaper that had told John of the royal visit in Niagara, with which he'd weakly teased Patrolman Price, had also told him of the MS *St. Louis*, an ocean liner packed with almost a thousand Jews fleeing the savagery mustering in Germany. The liner, having been turned away from sanctuary in Cuba, after much waiting, had been denied permission to land in Florida and was on its way back to whatever awaited it in Europe. He imagined the passengers as his bearded men in trench coats, homogeneous, eyes downcast. Sometimes he saw them as identical copies of the dying soldier in Meuse; it was difficult not to imagine them sailing back into some vast and hungry mouth.

On the afternoon of reading this, driving back from the scene of the automobile accident, he'd thrown three separate offerings from the moving car; a button, a small key, and the propeller broken from a toy airplane.

Perhaps it was the wildness, the untamed nature about him that he feared, he thought, perhaps what he was doing was sowing these tiny pieces of the manmade, the detritus of human industry and society, to reclaim that which frightened him so; perhaps what he was saying was: *man treads here, we makers of things, wild nature no longer holds sway*. Perhaps. The idea withered.

He'd stopped at Gibson's General Store, where he'd bought another map, left the store with Baldwin tucked under his arm, fought to feel marginally better for it.

◆

The usual manner of their meetings was this: they'd drive somewhere, park up, walk arbitrarily for half hour or so on one side of the road, then about turn and walk back on the other. Sometimes they would veer off onto tributaries they knew to hook back around, other times they would cut through the woods, or stand awhile at the water's edge.

The day was bright and warm, the men leaving their jackets in the car, pulling down their brims to shield their eyes. It had been two months or more since their last meeting, and Joseph seemed happy to see John, clapping him on the back and telling him he looked well and that hurricanes were obviously good for a man's constitution. Joseph's bonhomie jarred with John's mood but he did his best to match it, to perform The Goodly Doctor as well as he could. He had decided ahead of their meeting not to bring up The Notion, that no use was to be had from its further discussion; one might as well discuss how to halt the seasons, or bleed a stone. He hoped that Joseph could be steered away from any questioning, and that his own mind might be saved from wandering.

They passed houses, bright white and freckled with shadow under lazy, dipping branches; they exchanged raised hands with George Mann, shouted their good-days.

Joseph mentioned a book he was reading, *Three Guineas* by a Virginia Woolf, which used as its opening gambit the question of how all war might be prevented.

"And does Mrs Woolf come to an answer?"

"Teach the young to hate war. Educate women."

"So simple?"

"*Scarcely a human being in the course of history has fallen to a woman's rifle*, she says."

"She has a point," admitted John. Joseph stopped.

"Does she? I used to think of women in that way, until I was married. Now don't get me wrong, the point about a woman's rifle is well-made and surely true, but if you've ever seen a woman in full anger..." He paused for a moment, half-smiling, "I guess I just think it'll get awful crowded up on that pedestal. Sayin a woman aint capable of war given the right circumstances is like sayin she aint nearly human." They walked on, Joseph shrugged, "But it's true Woolf makes a powerful case."

"You think Europe a foregone conclusion?" asked John.

"O I think we both do, don't we?" They crossed the road, hung a left.

"Think America will sign up?"

"Not if she can help it." Joseph cleared his throat, seemed uncomfortable with the topic. "You're well though?"

"I am."

"After the hurricane I mean. That was one sunovabitch of a wind. Fella I know Lewiston way says he saw a tin roof ripped off, folded like it was paper."

"It was—" John reached for a description and failed, "quite a wind." They walked on, John snatching at memories of that night, only to have them bleed away; his hands crept to his pockets and worked their fingers at the tiny offerings, turning a coin, scratching at a button.

"I ask you a question, an you'll be honest with me?"

"Of course." John sank a little within himself, feeling sure that talk was now to turn to the three in the woods.

"If we do sign up, send boys over there to get blown to pieces, will it matter? To you, I mean. You'll be here, knowin better, will it matter to you? Really?"

John was wrong-footed. He shook himself, brought the question into focus.

"Yes," he replied, "yes, of course."

Joseph looked him in the eye for a moment, then nodded sadly.

"To me too. It'd matter but there's not a damn thing I could do about it. This, I think, is an old man's burden." Joseph looked tired and before he'd decided to do so, John was moved to speak of something he'd decided not to mention.

"I saw you at the hospital. Last August, September it must have been."

The older man looked surprised.

"You said nothin about it."

"Didn't like to. Can I ask why you didn't come to me?"

"Well I guess I didn't like to. A friend is a friend and a doctor is another creature entirely."

"Is it serious?" asked John, to which Joseph laughed.

"O at my age there's nothin but." John's bedside manner stumbled in the face of friendship.

"But it's... in hand?"

"I guess you could say it is, one way or another."

♦

Someone sits on the end of his bed, a shape somehow managing the properties of a silhouette without the catalyst of light to draw it on the dark air. Something there that cannot be seen. He stares at it for some time before realizing just what it is, what it means. He should be afraid, he reasons, but isn't; Ros' steady breathing beside him an antidote to anxiety.

"What do you want?" he whispers, realizing that he might just as easily have replaced the *what* with *who*. He feels a grim smile thrown back at him.

"Thought I'd come see you, up close, see what the great doctor looks like," says the old woman.

"Well now you've seen me," he says.

"Now I've seen you," she replies.

"You're alone?"

"You're here aint you?"

"The other two. You know what I mean."

"You are a fool."

"Am I?"

"If you're not I aint never seen one."

"You're a murderer," he says. The voice seems to ignore the accusation.

"You an me aint friends. We each act in the opposite of one another."

"Where are the others?"

"They are..." he thinks he detects a tilt of the head, perhaps a dismissive gesture, "abroad. Workin. *You* know."

"Murdering."

Another invisible smile.

"Aint no such thing."

"Does this have an end?" he asks, feeling something slip away, perhaps the old woman leaving him, dissolving into the dark.

"Too many to count." Was her voice more distant? By the door, the window?

"Is Joseph Allen dying?"

"Of course."

"Are there to be more killings?"

291

"Too many to count."

"I'll find you."

"You won't have to."

♦

John slides sideways out of sleep and into a black wakefulness. A jolt of cool air, a moment of wondering whether his eyes were open or closed. Trees sketched silvery in the dark, the spaces between them fading to gray, to black, to a bottomless nothing whatsoever.

He was standing in the woods, barefoot on earth. He turned and behind him some hundred feet or so, framed in an oval of branches, lay the road and beyond that, his house. He should have been afraid but he wasn't, failed to find the energy to be so. He sat on the ground in his pajamas and hid his face in his hands, waited for the impetus to return home and climb back into bed.

The day is blazing, the air soupy and vibrating with heat and insects; the sky is immense and bright, yet pushes down on any who venture out under it like the basement ceiling of a house on fire. The water flashes, blinding and inviting.

The thin man has sweated through his ruined jacket, a triangular streak up the back and dark rings under the arms, turning the brown serge to black; his hair is a stringy mass, like something pulled from a drain, sticking to his greasy face and neck.

How much longer?

The shade he'd clung to that morning has gradually been pulled out from under him as midday advanced and he's been left with his face hanging in the shadow of his knees, stones making a numbness of his backside, the back of his neck slowly reddening and growing sore. He eases giddily to his feet and stands. The water beckons and flares. He shakes off the jacket, undoes his button flies, stepping jaybird naked down the gravel bank on filthy, bandaged feet. His face and a stripe down his chest are a nutty brown, the rest of him pale and gray with dirt. The pink scars on his knees tighten his gait, the red weal under his ribs is still angry and itches, and for a moment he feels the letter opener again; the hatband of scabs on his forehead from the fruit crate splinters looks infected. Arms lifted, he walks slowly into the water. He is not yet to his waist when there is a splash across the way and he starts.

A young man surfaces and steals a breath, smoothing down his hair and treading water. The thin man can just make out the redness of the young man's face, the broadness of his shoulders breaking the surface. In time the young man turns in the water and sees him.

"Hey!" he shouts, waving.

"Hey," replies the thin man.

"Real scotcha aint it?" shouts the young man.

"Somethin fierce," replies the thin man. They observe each other for a time, the young man swimming a stroke or two back and forth, the thin man standing shoulders raised and thigh deep, the short thumb of his penis dipping and floating absurdly, as if thirsty.

"That's some scratch you got on you there," says the young man, and the thin man looks down at the weal, unsure as to a suitable reply. "You a vagrant fella, huh?" says the man, then "Why doncha come in?" Something under the water moves and the thin man makes to turn away, nodding.

"I'm sorry," he says but is too late in his turning to avoid seeing the young man pulled under.

He dresses to the sound of splashes and torn breaths, stealing shameful thrills with every arm that breaks the surface, every glimpse of wide eye or gaping mouth, letting go tiny prayers, like belches, with every one. He waits patiently back among the trees for the young man to die and the little girl to return. The little girl, it appears, is in no hurry to bring the matter to a conclusion.

State of Maine.

Cumberland **ss.**

I certify that I was notified on the   day   A. D. 19

at   h. and   m. in the   noon by *W. D. Smith M.D*

of *Harrison Me*   of the finding of the dead body of *Thisdow*

      Kobey   of *Harrison Me*

supposed to have come to h *is* death by violence or unlawful act; that I forthwith repaired to the place

where said body lies and took charge of the same, and before said body is removed make, or cause to be made,

this written description of the location and position of said body, viz:

     The body was that of a boy five feet tall, weighing about one hundred thirty pounds, having brown hair and blueeyes and smooth shaven. There was a gold ring on little finger, the body was unclothed.
     The body was viewed in the undertaking parlor of David H. Green of Harrison, Maine.
     The deceased had been working in hay field on Whitney Place in Otisfield, Maine.
     While overheated he dove into an unused gravel pit nearby, was siezed by cramps and drowned.

     Cause of Death   Accidental Drowning.

M Barker Burgess M.D
Medical Examiner.

Date   19

H e dreamt of something terrible, and woke with an idea.

◆

Folds and creases in the paper gave Maine a whole new topography, redrew all he'd learned in his years there; here a valley that didn't exist, there a poker-straight ridge cutting blithely through lake, road and river alike. Houses he knew to stand were uprooted, hills and hollows changed places and land was parceled into a neat grid system of rectangles. Same street names, different world.

One by one he opened the maps and spread them across the thinning carpet; here Bridgton, there Naples, Harrison. With every fresh unfolding, Cumberland County bloomed under him, flooding the floor of his office. He slid them into sequence, an overlapping montage of towns, of neighborhoods and waterways, smoothing them with his hands, then holding them in place with a series of thumbtacks pushed clean through the carpet and into the boards of the house. He stood in the doorway and surveyed his Maine, as if from a cloud. He thought momentarily of his dreams of flight.

Next he took the Medical Examiner's Record and turned to the first page. 1934. *David H. Hussode, accidental death by drowning. Near Stony Ledge Cottage*, it read. He fought to recall the scene, the young man's face; but there was nothing. Shoeless now, and on hands and knees, he found the place on the map of Naples where the cottage stood, ran his finger toward Sebago Lake and with a red pencil drew a small circle, marked it #1 – Hussode.

For the next hour he annotated the collage of maps with his pencil, tiny red circles and names peppering the roadways and fields, the hills and woods, like the symptom of some cartographic ringworm. Finished, he sat in his chair and poured a drink, watched the rings intently, half hoping they'd move about the pages like bugs, or vanish; imaginary from the first.

He span the chair and feeding a sheet into his typewriter, began to make a list of all the places, starting with the polished penny, he could remember leaving one of his little offerings. When he had an, admittedly only partial, list, he tore it from the typewriter and attacked it with the red pencil, correcting any chronological mis-ordering, scoring out some, writing them in later or earlier, crossing out numbers, drawing lines, arrows.

Two hours later, near three in the morning, he was drunk and had transcribed the list in red onto the maps, each offering marked with a number and an 'x'. He had counted 37 little objects which he had secreted beneath the dermis of Maine, numbered them roughly in the order he thought they had been left. His eye darted about the maps; #9 – *bottle cap, Parlor Maple, Northern Cumberland Hosp*... #11 – *brass washer, Newcombe place, near Dearborn Hill, Bridgton*... #22 – *shirt button, Roosevelt Trail, tossed from car, South Casco?*

Next, using the edge of his copy of *Organon of the Healing Art*, he drew straight lines between the deaths, in the order they occurred, charting a general route the three had taken between murders; even in his inebriation, it felt some way toward an achievement, some undefined progress. He was recording, he was documenting, dragging himself toward a bleary understanding; a doctor giant crawling drunkenly over his kingdom, head swimming, the soft crump of paper under knees, pencil quivering like a dowser's wand.

He fell asleep sprawled across the county, his head cradled in West Bridgton, spots of saliva staining Moose Pond, hands fidgeting over Steep Falls, Standish; his stocking feet lay in the shadow of no man's land under the desk. He dreamt of flight. He dreamt of standing on a red x while all around him the world burned.

The weather is turning, albeit by increments, night clawing back its share for the season to come, holding on just that little while longer with every day that passes. Something else is turning, the air is off-color, stained with it; something is bruised and yellowing.

The thin man and the little girl sit among a dense stand of pitch pines, he staring at the ground, lips working on his thoughts, she toying with her collection of keepsakes, laying them out neatly in rows, meticulously rearranging their order.

"Yknow," starts the thin man, and the girl tenses, drawing a quick scowl, "I believe I feel more at peace now the old woman has gone."

"O you *do*? I'm so very glad, halfwit. Tell me a fuckin nother, do."

He goes on as if she hasn't spoken.

"We will go on well together, working, doing what must be done."

"O *I'll* go on, *you'll* bitch and moan like a stupid child. But you'll be *my* stupid child, an I'll drag you on. An you'll do as yer fuckin told. Things are different now. Folks will beg, beg even as I put their fuckin lights out. I'll piss on em and light fires. I'm just warmin up."

The thin man is confused but blinks it away.

"We are more kindred than I had first thought. You an I. O sure you are wicked, as I once told you, but she, I think, she was somethin worse. Much worse. I used to think she was cruel but she aint cruel."

"She *aint*?" the girl snorts.

"No, she don't care enough to be cruel. An that's the sin of it. I'm glad she aint here no more."

The girl looks at him with utter contempt, shakes her head.

"You think she aint here?"

"She aint here," he says, then seems unnerved, looks about him, seeing only trees, "is she?" Deciding that the girl is only pulling his leg, he says again, "She aint here."

"I know," says the girl seriously, attention back at her keep-sakes, "but she's here."

John beat flat-handed on the door, knuckles already skinned, the other hand feeling at his unshaven face, as if some answer might be found there to gain entry. His heart leaped about in him like something caught in a snare.

It was midday and he felt eyes on him, the doctor on the doorstep, perhaps flailing and mad. He took a moment to steady himself; all passersby saw was the doctor they knew knocking, albeit vigorously, on a door; he fought the image of him as this whirling lunatic or dervish, some imaginary projection of his inner state. He took a breath, knocked again, though his knuckles smarted.

Joseph opened the door, bloodshot and old, long underwear hung on him, swagged between his legs like a sail. He ran his hand through wild hair and leaned on the doorjamb for support, whiskered and wan, tired, widening his eyes as if just woken.

"What is it, Doc, what's the matter?" his voice cracked.

"They are at war," said John. "Europe." Joseph cleared his throat, closed his eyes for a time.

"Then I guess you'd better come on in."

IX

Deep down, I think, what we really crave is for the prospect of our passing to be met with a terrible outpourin of rage, for folks to rear up, fingers clawed, tear at the skies; issue forth cries of "Not *him*, surely, any of us but *him*!" Voices raised in protest, in horror, some crusade mounted, some petition to whatever imagined administrative power, to end all this damn death business. But you can't end it. For one thing, where in hell's name would everybody live?

Shakespeare died, Mozart, da Vinci too, and with perhaps more fanfare but with no more opposition to the act of dyin as an undeniable constant at the heart of all things. "A damn shame, I liked much of his plays, his music, his paintings, made me laugh, made me cry, made life better, enriched the very act of breathin, and now he's gone. Now what's for fuckin dinner?"

No one will protest that you happen to be subject to the same conclusion, the same eternal interruption, as them; no matter who you are. Those that love you will bemoan the timin. "Just a little longer," they'll say, bemoan maybe the circumstances of your dyin, for certain the fact that you will no longer be around; but the specific fact of you dyin?

No protest will be made, no banner flown, no complaint filed, no voice upraised. Many of us I think, if my father is anythin to go by, spend our final days indignant at this fact. Who the holy fuck are you, am I, that we should be singled out? Well, we're *us*, aint we? We're *me*, every last one of us, we're the person we've shared every single second of our lives with; surely we deserve some special dispensation? Some loophole? But no.

You too shall vanish. The minutiae of you, things you never told a soul but which are the real inner you, will be gone forever and never known nor lamented; books half-read, choices never taken nor discussed, loves swallowed, that time you cheated in school, gone. And when those who loved you are gone too, only traces of you will stick around, mark the way to where you once stood.

We're all The Hinkey Dink, y'know? Gone. Gone yet still here.

There might be a photograph floatin around somewheres an they'll say *who's that old guy?* Or some hazy shard of memory, *didn't there used to be that fella...?*

Maybe a house this guy built stands after him, maybe a name carved into a tree somewhere; coat of paint on a fence. We leave a tiny mark, most of us, scratches at the world, minor damage; whether those scratches can be used to accurately reconstruct us, in thought, in memory, when we are no more, seems unlikely. Our scratches will be for those still drawin breath to interpret, those barely interested archeologists of the mundane spoor we leave behind. And that's okay, that time is theirs to rewrite, just as our time was ours.

The Hinkey Dink, excuse me, was a, *is* a canal boat up on the Songo. Been moored up there beyond Scribners Mills, half sank, wastin away for who knows how many years now. Don't know who owned it, why they left it there, don't know a soul who does. It's just there. Rotten and sorry for itself. Someone owned it, worked it up and down the river to Portland who knows how many years, carryin freight, carryin passengers, it was a workin boat, sixty footer. But now that boat, that little scratch at the world, is all that's left.

I know some young folks now say the old boat is haunted, tales of drowned sailors and the like; you know. That's what they've made of it and I guess that's okay, guess that's their job.

One day maybe I'll be a hat in a yard sale, an folks will maybe wonder at whose head fit up in there, or I'll be that path I laid through to Lambs Mill Road that summer damn near broke my back, or I'll be a story of when an evangelist met an unkempt man by the draw bridge and I guess that's okay, that'll just be me, the me that's left. Believe it or don't, hold on to it or let it go.

Bridgton; Maine

January, 1940

The air is bitter, cutting sharply through the thin man's ragged blanket as he hugs it to himself, arms wrapped tightly about his ribs, as if to stop the last kernel of warmth within him from escaping. He wishes he still had the lightning fella's hat given him by the old woman, but it was lost. The night before, the bandages on his hands had frozen stiff, and upon waking he had felt them crack as he made his morning fists.

They have walked for months and the landscape has swollen white and unkind around them with the onset of winter. They have found no persons to kill in all that time and felt no particular impetus to govern their journey. They have not seen hide nor hair of the old woman, though the little girl has often spoken of her as if she hid behind every tree.

They cross a dirt track, and stepping over a shallow snow bank, stomp back down into the woods; the girl swings her keepsake bag, fatter now, heavy now.

"When you suppose we get back to it?" he asks.

"We'll get back to it when we get where we're goin, an we'll get where we're goin when we get there," she answers without breaking her stride, without even a turn of her head. They walk on.

"I was jus thinkin. It's pretty funny how I used to cry when I done one," he gives a short exclamation, as if an example of laughter were required. "I'd cry because I didn realize that it was jus the way, it's what needs to be done. Pretty funny idn it? How I used to cry?" The girl walks on without answering. The thin man presses her. "But I'm thinkin, if this is what they call a vocation, a callin, an so forth, hadn we better get back to it? Important work is all."

"You'll do as yer damn well told like I said."

"You did. I will. I'm jus thinkin—"

"No yer not. What you're doin is a pantomime athinkin. You haven't the balls nor the brains to carry off the real thing."

"But didn we oughta—"

She's down to her haunches, back up and a rock has glanced painfully off of his cheekbone before he knows it. He staggers, slides and lands hard on his back in the snow. She's on him in a blink, worms the fingers of one hand into his knotted hair while the other tears at his beard and she knocks his head three times hard on the frozen ground, breathing heavily, no longer a little girl, snapping at the air with her teeth as if perhaps she means to bite him. *Haaah-haaah-haaah!* she screams, inches from his face, all spittle and bad breath steaming, *Haaaaaah!* slapping at his chest, digging her fingernails into his face, yanking painfully on his ears, looking up from her frenzy every so often as if an animal jealously guarding its meal, or fearful that another might be watching, might intervene. She howls and scratches and beats at him with tiny fists and he, in turn, plays his part and cowers wretchedly, waits for the onslaught to end.

She collapses onto him after a full five minutes of this mania and they lie for a time, like lovers in the snow, both breathing heavily. Finally she sits up, brushes back her hair and smiling, hands on his chest, raises herself up a little and urinates. He feels heat run across his belly, soak into his pants; crouched over him, wide-eyed, she is shrouded in steam.

Weeping now, black-eyed, he opens his mouth to cry out, but daren't let go his voice.

◆

That afternoon they come upon a small horse, tied to a fence in the northern corner of a large field. Its coat is a light brown and shaggy with neglect, hairless in patches; its ribs show through, there are old scars about its face and flanks. Dung is scattered round about, hard and dusted with snow. Hay too is strewn about its hooves and a tin pail of water stands nearby, a hole broken through the inch-thick ice, which even now is growing a fresh skin, like a cataract. The sorry creature blinks and steps back and forth, eyes them blankly. The girl looks about them, nervous at being out in the open like this, looks down at the pail.

"Someone's been here, not so long ago," she says.

"Poor girl," says the thin man, reaching out to stroke the horse. It flinches, then steps closer. "Poor girl," he says again.

"Poor wittle wamb," mocks the girl. "What a shabby sacka shit."

"Someone oughta be lookin after you didn they, girl?"

"Give her a bucket didn they?" The girl moves to get a closer look at the animal and the horse pulls away, tugging at the rope holding it to the fence. She smiles, takes hold of the rope and pulls hard on it; the knot is fast and the rope strong. She looks off across the field, then back at the thin man as he strokes its muzzle.

"How about we do the horse?" she says. There is a cold moment. He looks at the girl like she just fell out of the sky.

"But," he says, lost, "but that aint the job."

She rolls her eyes.

"O bull*shit*. The job that finds you is the job that is."

A reply fails him for a moment.

"We don't do... animals. We do folks, persons. I—"

"Aint it the same?"

"No, I— No, I don't think that it is. Is it? I don't *think* it is."

She enjoys his confusion, affects a girlishness that is gauche on her wind-bitten face.

"Why not be the adder in the path, uh? Bite at the horse's heels?"

"You jokin?"

She climbs the fence and drops into the snow on the other side; the horse pulls again at the rope.

"Maybe," she says. He shakes his head, unable to make her out at all. She toes the pail absentmindedly, lifts her foot to push at the ice. Pushing through it, she yelps playfully as her shoe goes under a little, eliciting the trace of a smile from the thin man.

She finds the pail's handle and, with difficulty, lifts it, walking a circle around the fretting horse, making tiny shushing sounds as she heaves the bucket, first to her hip, then onto her shoulder. The horse's eyes show their whites as it strains to keep watch on her, moving itself back against the fence. When close enough, with a small hop, she pours the ice water over the horse's back. It bucks and makes a raw inhaling sound; the rope holds. The girl laughs, covers her mouth with her hand. The horse stamps and paces within the space allowed by its tether.

"*What you do that for?*" asks the thin man, appalled, but she fails to answer, moving about the anxious, fidgeting horse, her eyes wide, swinging the bucket. Finally, she tilts her head, eyes him from behind a veil of dirty blonde hair.

"Like you said, we been away from it for so long. Maybe look on this as a run-up. A breath. An apprentice piece."

"A breath?" He's trying again to stroke the horse but the animal is now too wary. The girl's disgust is striking.

"Look at *you*. I think you've grown weak. Weak*er*. For all your talk of vocation. I aint even sure you're up to it anymore." A short hesitation and she swings the pail high, bringing it down hard on the beast's backbone; her feet leave the ground a moment before impact. The pail hits with a report like a cracked drum. The animal whinnies and bucks some more, tries to turn to face her. The thin man stifles a cry with his hands.

"Please," he says, at last. The girl sneers.

"There's some difficult work ahead. However will you manage when we expand our operations?" She swings the pail again, the horse grunts and kicks at the fence, nostrils steaming. The thin man moans behind bandaged hands. "Things I got in mind? Mommy's boy like you?"

"You're teasin me and I get it an let's have that be an end to it."

"Teasin? I told you, we got a world to *burn*."

"An burn it we shall, I promise, but this—"

"An we'll visit that doctor fella again."

"The doctor fella?"

"He thinks us animals," says the girl contemptuously, "no bettern dogs. Well dogs bite you sunovabitch, you fuckin clerk."

"Dog bit me once," says the thin man glancing down at his bandaged hands, "least, I think so. Once. This look like a dog bite to you? I don't know." The girl ignores him.

"We'll set his house afire, cut the hands off his wife, put out her eyes, pull him to pieces. You can't do a fuckin horse, how you gonna do what's required when the chips are down, when there's that arrogant fuck beggin you not to cut off that nose he's so fuckin keen to push into *our fuckin business?*" As she grows ever more incensed, she punctuates her speech by swinging the pail against the beast's head as hard as she is able. The horse, blood now beading its long eyelashes, jerks at the rope, whinnies and raises its head in an attempt to draw it out of the girl's reach; its eyes, black as polished stones, roll, show their whites, seem to grasp something beyond its mere beating.

The thin man adopts a look of pained seriousness, grinds his teeth and peers at the ground; it is some time before he realizes she has stopped speaking. When he looks up, she is holding the empty pail out to him.

"*Imagine the horse is the doctor*," she hisses. The thin man stares at her. "Well?"

"No," he says, quietly.

"No? Fuckin *no*? Choose your words careful, fore I pitch this fuckin pail at *your* head. Tell me again, no?"

"No." As she raises her arm, he holds up a hand. "Don't need the pail. I still got this." He is holding the letter opener, still smeared black-burgundy with his own dried blood, something wildly ungoverned in his stare. "I got this."

As he works, as his jaw distends, his tongue plays about his teeth, breath shallow, something accelerating behind his eyes, flinching at the horse's cries yet pushing on regardless, climbing over it as it kicks, struggles and having been brought to the ground, is opened up; the girl sits on the fence and watches, nodding.

"You aint cryin now," she says quietly, "no you aint."

The dog went around, ever smaller circles, closer, closer. It shambled and wandered on its circumnavigations, drew nearer, and the nearer it drew, the more it spent time as the child's drawing of teeth and malevolence.

Things were going along as always, yet there seemed an inevitability in some kind of finish or culmination; some event of uncertain form or outcome felt imminent.

◆

His thinking ran thus: no one could have found the polished penny by chance; no one. If the three had been somehow drawn to it, then perhaps they had also been drawn to his other "offerings". Perhaps he had, unwittingly, been directing the three across Cumberland County, object by object, offering by offering, perhaps even directing them toward their next subject. Perhaps ever since Frank Selbo was struck by lightning John had in fact been in charge of the whole shooting match. Maybe this was what the objects meant, this their role, *his* role. The penny had felt like a prayer, but then what was a prayer but a child's tugging at its mother's apron? A demand for attention. Had he been calling for their attention? Had they answered?

He stared intently at the maps spread across his office floor, traced the lines between the deaths, noted each "x" in relation to them. The lines were asymmetrical, haphazard and ungainly, like some occult star collapsed under the weight of its own implausibility, points splaying out into the countryside.

His records told him that he planted the polished penny a week or so after the finding of the second Bell girl and the coming of the rains. If he traced the line from Mona Bell to Frank Selbo, it took him almost directly through where he estimated that he had left the penny. He imagined these magical itinerant creatures pulled toward it, then allowing the momentum to carry them on down to Casco and the site of the lightning strike. At finding this his breath shortened.

Next had come Hannah Wilby up there at Highland Lake. The line drawn from Selbo to Wilby, if extended less than half inch onwards, intersected with an "x" which stood for the horseshoe nail he'd tossed into someone's front yard off the Dugway Road, Bridgton; house call, sprained ankle, concussion, he couldn't recall.

Whichever it was, he thought it had been roughly a day or so after planting the penny. He sat down for some time, set his jaw, snarled at the idea of a whiskey that fluttered about the back of his mind before retreating.

He imagined the offerings, these thoughts of his buried all over: a button, a bead, a tiny brass cog trodden into the earth and invisible; these objects had called out to them somehow, flashed on the periphery of whatever understanding these creatures had, like a series of beacons, each one drawing them toward its gravity, the strange mass of these wishful things exerting some impossible pull. He thought of migratory birds, of flocks, of swarms, the unthinking wisdom of animals; something magnetic and mysterious.

Had he, through some indirect action, killed these people? What business would these creatures have had in Bridgton that day without the presence, the pull, of his horseshoe nail?

But they had, of course, he told himself, been killing before the advent of his offerings, and while he took some solace from this fact, the idea that he may have gone on to blindly point them in the direction of their prey tightened his stomach painfully, made his head swim.

He quickly checked the next name. Eugene Pinkham, all the way down there in Raymond; then the next. Sumner Newcombe. They didn't fit. Neither of the connecting lines ran through or near the next offering on the list, but ran instead through or near previously left offerings. The three did seem drawn to objects he'd left, but in no chronological order. From this he deduced that the offerings were not stepping stones so much as they were magical fragments, scraps of minutiae exerting an influence, and some it appeared exerted more than others. He thought of the orbits of planets, of comets flaring through the dark of space. He ran through them one by one. Metal seemed to have a stronger pull that stone, and coins were among the strongest metal objects, it appeared. Plastic was stronger than wood, he noted, before realizing that in some cases it might even be stronger than metal, the brass washer left on the Newcombe place failing to pull the three from the influence of a small plastic wheel from a toy truck, left on the line between Newcombe and the home of the next victim, Joseph Walker.

He felt like he'd stumbled onto something huge yet oddly pedestrian, some order in the world of tiny things and of death that seemed perverse yet improbable enough to be true; and that whiskey edged a little closer.

◆

After his impromptu visit and their talk in September, war had not been mentioned between the friends. They had exhausted it that day, or at least lanced momentarily whatever carbuncle had been expanding within them. That day Joseph had coughed hoarsely, pulled himself up from whatever sleep John had interrupted, and they'd talked it up and down, hypothesized and estimated, toyed with the wishful thought that Germany might flinch at the weight of international consternation tilted against it, just slink back to within its borders by the end of the year. They'd shaken their heads and swapped their own stories, stories held on to like secret and favorite sores; John had spoken of the young soldier at Meuse. When they parted both men had been run ragged by talk; the handshake had been a little warmer, held on to a little longer.

As the month had crept by, he had read of the Soviets flooding into Poland to meet the Germans, a race across that country like brutish homesteaders hungry for land; yet no crops would be planted, and any harvests would be of quite another kind.

Elsewhere ships were sinking in boiling seas, men were dying, torn and already forgotten it seemed. He struggled to keep up to date with the blossoming war's progress.

Men were being pulled out of the world thousands of miles away, yet still he was drawn to his maps, to the confusion of lines drawn across them, some grand graffito scratched into the surface of the county, some talisman heralding something immense and indifferent.

From time to time, all they have to pinpoint the man on the dark road is the plume of his breath, struck white in the moonlight. The size and bulk of his coat makes him shambling and ungainly, his narrow legs revealing the deliberate gait of the inebriated, head lolling yet every booted step placed with calculated precision in the snow.

"This sacka shit," says the girl; the thin man merely nods and shivers. "Can't hold his damn liquor."

"Where you suppose he's goin?"

"Where dya think?"

"Is it him?"

"Him who?"

"Him. The next one."

"It's him. It's all of em."

"They are corrupt."

"They're fuckin weak. Look at this sacka shit."

"Who's to do him? You or me?"

"What we need is a gun. Big one. Line em up down the street, single file. All of em. *Boom*. One shot. *Boom*, straight down the line. Hundreds maybe. Thousands. Like dominos. Blood in the gutters. Leave em by the roadside for the fuckin crows. Town after town."

Lights seep through the trees as they round a bend and soon the man is a silhouette. The two hang back and watch him enter the beer parlor, the rise of hubbub and thrum from inside, the warm glow, and with the slamming of the door, quiet again and dark, cold.

"He have a gun on him, that fella?" asks the thin man.

"No he don't have a fuckin gun, imbecile."

"But you s—"

"Shut your fuckin mouth what I said," the girl spits words through grinding teeth.

"You alright?" he asks.

"I'm *fine*."

"So, it weren't him."

"It's him."

"It's him?"

"Him. Them. All of em. *Fuck.*" This last word comes out like an involuntary retch, or cough, accompanied with a pronounced contraction of her body.

"So we wait?" he tries, but the girl isn't listening, she's contorting her features into alarming knots.

"I wanna do em all, every fuckin, tear em, fuckin, haah, I fuck— fuckin, *haah*, haa-uckin scream an burn the fuckin—" she devolves into growling and barking sounds, doubled over, as if about to collapse to all fours, doglike, body all a-spasm with her raging, feet walking in place, hands alternately claws and fists, head darting about as if troubled by the buzz and flitter of unseen insects. "Fucking, fuck-fuck, fuck-fuck, fuck-*burning-fuck.*" The thin man steps away from her and hugs himself, waits for the fit to subside. This is as bad as he's ever seen her mania; he's afraid, yet he waits.

She has been worsening of late, he thinks, screwed up inside, paler, yet enlivened somehow.

"Funny aint it," he'd tried a day or so before, "you hate em so much, yet I love them. But we do the same job." It had been an attempt at amelioration, to gently steer her to his way of thinking.

"You find that funny?"

"Amusing. Peculiar. Interesting, yes. Don't you?"

"I think it's pathetic," she'd replied, her eyes telling him that of the two attitudes, love and hate, his, of course, was the weaker.

This time her raging is interrupted by the beer parlor door. It's the man again, now holding his coat, tripping backwards out into the night; in the doorway a large man in an apron. Arms worming back into his coat sleeves, the drunken man gesticulates, shouting.

"You still sell beer dontcha? Sell me a damn beer. One lousy—"

"Go home ya bum," says the man in the apron, and closes the door on him. Still the ejected drunk shouts:

"I'm meetin my wife. She's in there. *She's right in there.*" He turns around twice, throwing his arms about him, exasperated.

"Dammit." He turns to leave, putting on a fur hat then taking it off, striding back to the door. "Treat a— a man like that, goddamn— sunovabitch." He throws it open and marches in. Moments later he's pushed out again, this time stumbling, falling back, twisted and lying still in the snow. The large man in the apron rolls his eyes, gives a weary *goddammit*, before dragging the drunkard up against the building in a seated position; he slaps his face once, then twice, but there is no reaction. The door, now ajar, breathes an orange glow into the dark.

"*Martha!*" shouts the man in the apron and disappears inside; raised voices from within the glow.

A woman appears, drunk and hair like rags, skids some in the snow, turns several times and looks down at the man, out cold against the wall. She stares at him for some five minutes or more, swaying in the night, hand working at her chin, forcing her way into as deep a thought as she can muster. Finally, she gives a *fuck you Clifford*, quietly under her breath, spits and goes back inside, closing the door behind her.

The thin man looks back to the little girl, whose raging is fading, allowing her to stand more or less erect once again.

"You okay?" he tries.

"Shut up."

"Should we do him now?" He gestures at the man, a shape hunched against the beer parlor.

"Shut up." They stand and they wait and nothing happens. The thin man again feels moved to speak.

"I've been thinkin about what you said the other day. About love and hate? About it not mattering which you— in which one's name you do— we do the things we do."

"Don't you go puttin words in my mouth."

"But didn—"

"I didn't say that."

"You didn't?"

"I recall what I said was that you was pathetic and should shut yer hole."

"Do you think it matters though? Whether love or hate?"

"I don't think *you* matter is what I think. Love or hate. No difference is what I think."

"Then— Then when you say that you hate me, as you have said many times, does that mean in fact that you—"

"It means shut the hell up is what it means. You talk an you talk an you aint never said a word worth hearin."

In time the man in the apron comes out again, sees the drunkard unmoving, throws up his arms and goes back inside.

"Now? We do him now?" The thin man is getting nervous, they've been waiting around on the roadside for too long, someone might come, might see them. "I could put his head in with a rock, maybe strangle him?"

"Look at the pathetic sunovabitch. Slave to liquor," she says. The thin man nods sagely.

"The demon drink."

"It's wretched. I've half a mind not to do him. Let the fuck suffer. Let him pickle in it."

"Truly? Just... let him go?" The idea had never occurred to him.

"All I'm sayin is, sometimes what we do is a kindness and quite frankly, fuck kindness."

"But what would happen if we just let him go?"

"Kindness don't make the fuckin world go round."

"Would he jus go on, forever?"

"We could watch him eaten from the inside out, and never a respite, never relief."

"He'd jus go on and on and never die?"

"Best fuckin curse there is."

The thin man is unnerved by this suggestion, the reversal of all he knows.

"I think maybe I oughta kill him jus the same." A sudden idea raises his eyebrows. "We could make it hurt. You'd like that. Put out an eye maybe."

They're still debating when the patrol car rounds the bend and pulls up outside the beer parlor.

"Time to go," says the girl quickly, "it aint far," and darts into the trees. The thin man dawdles for a moment.

"So, we aint—?" But she's gone. He runs after her.

♦

Forcing the sticky door, they tiptoe into the dark house and find the drunken man, Clifford Whitney, still unconscious, on a couch in a small living room; a vibrato to his breathing betrays a shiver. Down the hall, his wife's snoring resonates, buzzes the grimy picture frames on the wall; she can be spied through the doorway, akimbo under the covers, head open-mouthed on the pillow.

The air in the living room is petrified and still, the grate having been cold for hours, maybe all day; cruel winter has crept in and occupied the space.

The girl quickly tears off the plaid blanket that's been thrown across Whitney and straddles his lap, pinches his cheek.

"He's freezin," she says lightly. "Bring me over the rock."

"You gonna put his head in?"

"In? No. But I'll give him a knocka two, rattle that peanut in there."

"With the rock?"

"Less you wanna."

"I do."

"You do, do you?" She turns, surprised. The thin man is standing in the cold dark, weighing the rock in his hand, eyes wide in the dimness.

"I do, yes."

"You grow a pair since the horse?"

"Love and hate," he mumbles.

"What's that?"

"This one is mine. I feel it."

"O so you feel it?"

"I do." He is rocking from side to side now, anxious. She climbs off of Whitney, approaches him.

"An you aint gonna cry like a baby after?"

"I aint gonna cry."

"Tell me this," she narrows her eyes, "you love this man?"

"What?"

"You love this man? This dipsomaniac?"

He frowns, shrugs.

"You said there weren't no difference."

"You don't believe that though."

He takes a difficult breath.

"I'm tryin."

"You gonna put the rock to this man's head?"

After a time, he nods.

"This our son is stubborn and rebellious," he says quietly, "he will not obey our voice; he is a glutton, and a drunkard."

This amuses the girl greatly.

"That he is! You go on then," she laughs, motioning theatrically towards Whitney. The thin man stands over him for a second or two before swinging the rock, knocking the unconscious man over; Whitney lets out a wet *foooh* sound as he falls sideways onto the couch. The girl props him back up, giggling, steps aside.

"You hit like a girl. *AGAIN*."

State of Maine.

Cumberland ss.

I certify that I was notified on the _19_ day of _January_ A. D. 19 _40_
at _8_ h. and _15_ m. in the _afte_ noon by _Deputy Elmer O Stewart_
of _Bridgton, Me_ of the finding of the dead body of _Clifford Whitney_ of _Bridgton, Me_
supposed to have come to h _is_ death by violence or unlawful act; that I forthwith repaired to the place

where said body lies and took charge of the same, and before said body is removed make, or cause to be made,

this written description of the location and position of said body, viz:

Body was that of a man five feet ten inches tall, weighing about
one hundred sixty pounds, having black hair and gray eyes. Body was
viewed in Potter Mortuary, Bridgton, Maine, having been removed from
place of death.
     There was cyanosis of lips and finger nails. There were abrasions
of ring finger left hand, left forehead and over left eye.
     The deceased had appeared at Thompsons beer parlor on Flint Street
Bridgton the previous night in an intoxicated condition. On being refused
beer by the clerk he created a disturbance and was asked to leave, after
leaving he attempted to reenter beer parlor and when pushed away from
door fell in an unconscious condition. He was placed against building
and his wife was asked to take him home, this was aboutten-thirty P. M.
     His wife returned stating he had left and she could not find him.
About eleven P. M. the owner of the beer parlor decided to search for
him and found him lying outdoors where he had been placed at ten-thirty.
He then called the Bridgton police, who removed him to his home and
placed him on a couch. Mrs. Whitney stated she would take care of him,
but went to sleep leaving him in a cold room overnight.
     The next morning at eight-thirty being unable to arouse him she
called Dr. Irtin Mabry of Bridgton, who found him unconscious and in
a dying condition, death occured at about eight P. M. on the same day.

     Cause of Death; Brain Injury ?
                      Acute Alcoholism
                      Exposure

Medical Examiner.

Date _Jan 19_ 19 _40_

He typed up Whitney, scored and tore the paper as neatly as he could, pasted it into the book, before realizing that he'd skipped two pages. Pages 33 and 34 had been left featureless, as if two days had never happened, or two deaths, lives, had been rendered imaginary, or wiped away. It was sloppy, and the glue already drying. When had he become so careless in his work? Suddenly tired, he leafed through the record.

The one before had been the Koley fellow, over at Green's; the coolness and the coffins stacked like lunchboxes, he remembered. He flicked back a page, then forward. July? He had failed to note down the month. Again, sloppy.

♦

"I was wondering when your—" here she paused to find the right word, put her book down on the coverlet, smiled, "*project* might be over so I can get into your office to clean it. Dust must be an inch thick."

"Soon," he smiled back, pretending to read, even then charting in his mind strange connections on the maps pinned to the floor downstairs, unable to prevent an inaudible *never* leaking out under his breath. Ros went on telling him about the pipes that had burst over on Bird Hill, how Tom Jeffries over there got himself all cut up in the cold trying to fix it himself, how his wife Phyllis near had a conniption.

John nodded and gave out appropriate *hmmm*s, saw the little girl pulling at Whitney's wedding ring, gnawing at it, unable to wrench it free; he imagined the hemorrhage flowering across the jelly of Whitney's brain from the thin man's blows. She was saying his name.

"Mmm?"

"Are you to shave this week? You're beginning to look a little... wild."

He had a brief image of himself being ingested by the countryside, spat out changed, made one of its own. He thought of his stake driven into the Maine earth; the rope flaccid, the dog loosed.

"I thought I might try a beard, what do you think?"

She ran a hand over his cheek, seemed unconvinced by the idea.

"I swear you become more like that old goat Joseph by the day," she answered, and kissed him to show the jest in it.

John thought of object sixteen: *razorblade (blunt)* – *Bell Hill, Otisfield, near Pond View Dr.*, and resolved to shave the following day. He fought to recall the objects either side of the razorblade on the list, his methodology for memorizing them all:

> #17 – *what looked like the broken mouthpiece to a pipe, tortoiseshell?* – *Lewis Road, Harrison*
> #15 – *.22 shell casing (spent)* – *Wildwood Road, Bridgton*

He thought of Joseph's Winder musket, offered as protection for John's ill-advised jaunt into the Convene woods all of five years ago. He thought of Wilson's rifle, tinted an unearthly blue by the fire, as if borne through hell yet left undischarged. Wilson's Winchester Low Wall, which still lay downstairs, wrapped in burlap, secreted behind the leather couch in his office; yet undischarged.

X

The first fella that ever believed in God, how long did he keep it to himself for fear that others would think him mad?

I think about this sometimes. Wouldn't *you* keep it a secret?

Think about it. We know there was a time before Jesus, people lived, they died, went about their business; we know there was a time before the Hebrew Bible, people had jobs, fell in love, stubbed their toes and lost money on games achance. Then along comes a new idea, or a new setta clothes for an old idea; maybe the oldest idea. Strikes me every god has a first fella.

He's sittin there one day an he realizes that everyone's got it wrong, hits him like a thunderbolt *boom* that this idea he's just had, revelation whathaveyou, this new god is the real McCoy, the genuine article, and I mean he *knows* this, knows it to be the truth.

Why is it all the stories we have of these first fellas are always stories of men who can't wait to tell everyone about it?

Not sure I'd be so forthright, would you?

I mean what the first fella is sayin is this: Hey, did you know up is down? *Up is what?* Up is down. *Is that right?* That's right alright. *Well how come you know that up is down?* An this fella, this first fella, smiles wide and says: The sky told me. An eyes get rolled, brows knit, witch doctors are sent for, scaffolds built, fires lit. How come they don't keep it to themselves I don't know.

Asked this question once of a man I knew, good man, outta Kansas City, a believer, I asked *How come they don't keep it to themselves?* An he thought for a time an he said:

"If you knew the building was on fire and you were the only one that knew where the fire escape was, wouldn't you tell everyone?" Which makes a certain kinda sense I guess. But, I said, that makes you a man shoutin *fire* in a crowded theater, a crowded theater where there is no visible nor olfactory evidence of smoke whatsoever and nary a flame to be seen.

Bridgton; Maine

April, 1940

U p on the screen, Stan Laurel, in doughboy helmet and bat-tledress, sits and eats beans in the trenches, oblivious to peacetime, throws the can onto a mountain of twenty years of empties; the darkness breaks into laughter. Heads, outlined in dim sketches, rock on shoulders.

The girl spots him three seats from the aisle, eight rows back. Mustached, narrow-headed, haloed in the fingers of light reaching out from the projection booth, motes swimming about the penumbra and shine off his pomade. She stands to the left of the screen, its glow painting the corner all the blacker, making her all but invisible. She stands and she waits.

The doctor's eye is drawn from the light and movement, nagged into wandering by the faintest imprint of a shape that has no place being where it is. He blinks but it remains, a small figure, perhaps a child, out of its seat and stood in the corner; whether it faces into the corner, as if scolded, or out into the theater he cannot tell. A glance at his wife beside him makes it plain she has seen nothing; she laughs, still mesmerized by the screen. When he looks again, the child is gone.

He refocuses on Laurel peppering an innocent German air-plane with bullets, and then she's at his ear, a hot current of air from the row behind; words described less in voice than in the wet meeting and parting of lips, the rigid curl of a tiny tongue in a bitter mouth: *Do you remember me?* and then: *Make your excuses.*

Without a thought, he leans into his wife, whispers the words "I gotta step out," to which she nods, still watching the movie. As he stands, the dark ripples again with laughter.

The girl is waiting for him outside in the parking lot; the doctor keeps his distance, buttons then unbuttons his jacket; he takes out his eyeglasses, puts them away. He struggles to stand still, lights a cigarette, lets it burn in his hand. The night is cool, the last glow of the blue day looms over the trees as it retreats.

"Hi, Wendel," says the girl.

"What do you want, callin me out here?"

"I asked you a question."

"I heard you. Now what do you want?"

"*Let's be polite.*" These three words of hers are all teeth, he imagines a heat haze in the chilly dark.

"What do you want?"

"For starters, an answer to my question."

He closes his eyes for a time.

"Sure, I remember you." Speaking to this child feels to him somehow like speaking to a painting, or a statue, absurd and worrisome.

"Where you know me from, Wendel?"

"All over. Know you and I know your buddy over there behind the tree." A short way off, the thin man steps out onto the road, chagrined, like a child found out at hide and go seek; he raises his chin in weak acknowledgment. "I'm a doctor. I know who you are. What you are."

"I'm a wittle girl." She plucks at her hem, sways coquettishly. Wendel is unmoved.

"If you are then so am I."

"You look scared, Wendel."

He thinks for a moment of denying it, but knows it would be less than convincing.

"Then you must feel right at home," he replies. She steps forward and Wendel stands his ground, grips perhaps too tightly at the idea that this is his decision and not her wish. She reaches out, strokes his thigh, her touch painful, scalding. He sets his jaw and stands his ground.

"Can't we be friends?" she says.

"You aint gonna kill me."

"I aint?"

"No you aint."

"Why ever not, Wendel?"

"Because, you sunovabitch, I don't buy it."

"You don't?"

"I do not."

The girl laughs, throws her arms in an unconvincing pretense of exasperated defeat.

"Well I guess you got us beat then, Wendel. You don't buy it, we can't touch you, isn't that it?"

"That's it."

"Well okay," she turns to the thin man, "we're beat. We'd best leave Doctor Smith alone then, he's too smart for us." They all stare at one another for a time, the doctor tremulous, the girl simmering and amused, the thin man unsure. "Go on home, Wendel," she barks at last, "we'll talk again." She turns and heads back toward the thin man and the woods; Wendel feels a sudden heat between his fingers and drops the cigarette on the road. "Physician heal thyself!" shouts the girl behind her and laughs her way into the trees.

♦

"What now?" The two are weaving their way between the trunks, in and out of moonlight.

"His house, that's what. Up here aways."

"Do him there, ymean? Like before, with the drunkard and the rock? You want I should find a rock?"

"Not this time."

"Why did we have to meet him outside the picture house?"

"To talk."

"You wanted to talk to him?"

"Not particularly, no."

"Then, I don't underst—"

She lets loose a strangled and angry sound that stops him, her body contracts, twitches, and her arms shoot out momentarily, broken looking, bringing to mind some kind of injured bird or insect. She rights herself and goes on walking, goes on speaking, as if nothing whatever has occurred.

"Fella knows whats comin fears it all the more, that's all, stretches it out, makes it delicious. Couldn't you taste it on him?"

♦

The handgun, he thinks, weighs almost as much as the rock he'd swung at the drunkard that time before. It shines dully in his palm, cold and dumb.

"Beauty aint it?" says the girl, wide-eyed.

"It's very," he ponders, "impressive," he says at last, quickly handing it back. The girl holds the grip tight, worms her finger around the inside of the trigger guard. In her tiny hand it looks monstrous.

"It's a beauty."

"Will it be loud?"

"Loud as hell."

"Why do you suppose he keeps it in the kitchen drawer?"

"Hides it. It frightens him."

"Is— Is this the gun you talked about? The one you said we oughta get?"

"They're *all* the one we oughta get."

"But—"

Footsteps, voices, and the kitchen is empty in seconds.

♦

The girl climbs out of the kitchen cabinet already speaking, as if hours had not passed since last they spoke.

"I meant to ask you, Wendel." The doctor visibly jumps, backs up against the sink, spills a little liquor from the coffee cup in his hand.

"Jesus fucking Christ," he hisses, then throws a look into the next room. When he looks back, the thin man's face smiles, well-meaning, from the dim recesses of the cupboard. Wendel covers his face with his hand. "Get out of my house."

"I meant to ask: you know us, seen us around."

"I *told* you."

"Never up close though, eh, Wendel? Tell me, do I look, up close, how you imagined? You look *precisely* how I imagined."

"You people are like a fucking virus."

"People? You forget yourself, Wendel."

"Get out. *My brother's in the next room for Christ's sake.*"

"You seen us. All over, you said. And you never told a soul. Not a word."

"Get out."

"You got a lot of secrets dontcha, Wendel? The time you set fire to the Petersons' barn when you was a boy. That woman in Chicago your wife don't know about. That little boy patient you thought you coulda saved. Your unhappiness. Your terrible unhappiness, Wendel. You don't talk much, do you?"

"Not to you I won't."

"So many secrets."

Wendel drains his cup, tightens his lips, anemically resolute.

"I'm done talking to you."

"Secretive Wendel."

"My business." There is quiet, while the girl wanders about the kitchen, opening drawers, running her finger over surfaces to check for dust, wrinkling her face disapprovingly.

"But we aint gonna kill you because you don't buy it," she says at last.

"I do not!" As he says this, the doctor points furiously at the girl. She feigns an almost parental disappointment.

"I thought you people believed your eyes. And here I am. Here we are."

"Hallucination," he mumbles unconvincingly. She laughs.

"*An undigested bit of beef, a blot of mustard, a crumb of cheese, a fragment of underdone potato, that it?*"

Wendel merely sighs wearily, draws his hand over his face, rubs his eyes.

"Asked you to leave."

"Well then I guess it just aint your time."

"So then get out."

"Well then you won't care if we play a little game." She holds out her hand and the thin man climbs awkwardly from the cupboard, all elbows and knees. He hands her the revolver gingerly, like it was something live and feral. The girl deftly pops out the cylinder, empties out the rounds, replaces a single cartridge and spins the cylinder before clicking it back into place with a practiced flick of her wrist. She holds it out to Wendel, with a smile. "Point this at your head and pull the trigger."

The doctor puts down his cup, sets his jaw defiantly. She holds out the gun a little higher, her eyebrows raised in question.

"Look on it as a test of faith."

"How dumb do you think I am?"

"It aint your time, right? Said so yourself."

"Just put it down and *leave*, bothayou."

"If it aint your time, like you said, you don't buy it, we can't kill you, then you won't get the lead bye-bye, right?"

"I aint doin it."

"Don't tell me you aint thought about it, puttin a slug in the ol' melon. What with your terrible unhappiness an all."

"Never thought about doin it because someone told me to."

"Just put it to your head. Pull the trigger. Click. I look like a fool and you'll never see us again."

"No."

"I think maybe you *do* buy it, maybe you think we *can* kill you."

"I aint doin it."

"You *do* buy it, you mendacious sunovabitch."

"My brother is in the next fucking room for Christ's sake."

"Charlie boy? O he drifted off readin. He's dreamin of swimmin with bow-legged women."

"My wife's asleep in bed."

"O she's dreamin about—" here the girl narrows her eyes, frowns, as if straining to hear a distant voice. "Well, what do you know, *she's* dreamin about brother Charlie."

Wendel turns away from her but cannot force himself to remain so and turns back.

"Please leave now," he says quietly. The girl tries another tack, gestures at the thin man.

"My skinny friend here's got all kindsa diseases, lice too. He'd just love to run them dirty hands all over your wife, Wendel. Put his thing in her, I half bet she'd like it too." The thin man blanches, considers his shoes.

"You are a coward," spits the doctor. The girl rolls her eyes.

"No such thing. That word exists so folks like you can imagine that everyone thinks like you think, wants what you want." She fixes the doctor with a stare. "*And they don't, yknow.*" Changing tone, she adopts one of playful flippancy, "So should I let my friend have a ride of your wife, or will you play our little game and we can leave?"

"You— You'd wake Charlie, then what would you do?"

"Take his fuckin head off," she replies, monotone. She holds out the revolver again, cocks her head a little.

"I won't do it," he says.

"I'm gonna count to three."

"Count. I won't do it."

"One."

The doctor snatches the revolver, points it in the girl's face and pulls the trigger. There is a sharp click and he drops it as if bitten.

"*Fuck!*" He bends double, closes his eyes. Laughing, the girl picks up the gun, pops the chamber, spins it and closes it again.

"Well what do you know, not my time either. I'm gonna count to three again."

"Please leave." Still bent over, he looks the girl in the eye, "Get out."

"One."

"*Stop playing games,*" he hisses, "I won't do this."

"One and one half."

"I don't want to do this. You can't make me."

"Two."

The thin man snatches the revolver from the girl, lurches forward and with a low growl forces the barrel into Wendel's mouth, knocking through teeth with a porcelain clink, clapping his hand to the back of the doctor's neck, pulling the trigger. There is a loud crack and Wendel's head erupts in red mist; in the muted flash, the image of Wendel wearing some elaborate headdress of crimson feathers. There is the dull crunch of a ricochet somewhere in the room and the coffee cup explodes; the doctor's nostrils and mouth stream with blood, gush and spatter, and he collapses backwards, soaking the thin man, who instinctively embraces the body and is pulled to the floor. He leaps away, disgusted and smeared in oily blood, appalled; Wendel quivers once on the ground and is still. The thin man holds his red hand to his mouth, when he takes it away it has left an imprint, like a bloody star across his beard.

The girl and the thin man look down at Wendel, then at each other, then down at Wendel; the air rings with a clear, crystalline sound.

They leave quickly by the window they came in, scuttle into the trees just as someone in the house starts to yell, then to scream.

State of Maine.

Cumberland   ss.

I certify that I was notified on the *6 th* day *of april* A.D. 19 *40*

at *2* h. and *20* m. in the *fore* noon by *David H Green*

of *Harrison, Me* of the finding of the dead body of *Wendel D.*

Smith M. D. of *Bridgton, Me*

supposed to have come to h *is* death by violence or unlawful act; that I forthwith repaired to the place

where said body lies and took charge of the same, and before said body is removed make, or cause to be made,

this written description of the location and position of said body, viz:

     The body was that of a man about six feet tall, weighing one-hundred seventy-five pounds. He had black hair and brown eyes, black mustach. The deceased was fully clothed with exception of his shirt.

     On entering kitchen from living room, body lay in opposite corner from door, at an angle to stand which stood against right hand wall, the head was near kitchen sink and lay in a pool of blood. Pieces of broken coffee cup were scattered under and about the head. A revolver was found under the body which a friend, Richard Whitney of Harrison, stated "was a 38 or 44 magnus revolver". The deceased lay on his back with left hand resting on left knee and right hand outflung to right.

     There were two holes in ceiling above and to left of body. The head lay in a pool of blood which had formed from a wound in back of head apparently caused by exit of bullet, both parietal bones were fractured and comminuted.

     The mouth and nostrils were filled with clotted blood. The two upper incisor teeth to left of midline were missing and the maxilla was fractured to left of midline. On removing clotted blood from mouth, the point of entrance of the bullet, was found in roof of mouth surrounded by a blackened area, also a blackened area on back of tongue. There was an alcoholic odor from the mouth. There were abrasions about both knees and a burn sustained some time before on left thigh.

     The deceased went to a moving picture show with his wife the night of his death. Shortly after arriving at the show, about eight-thirty, the deceased left but did not state where he was going.

     At eleven P. M. a call came to the theatre for the deceased, his wife left at this time to locate him, on arriving home she found that he had gone to make a call on which his brother, Charles B. Smith, accompanied him.

     She retired and some time after the clock had struck one she heard a shot, shortly after this the brother of the deceased informed her that the doctor had shot himself.

     The brother of the deceased states that he went on a call with the Doctor about eleven P. M. April 5th. They returned about one A. M. After having some coffee, Charles Smith sat in the front room reading while the Doctor remained in the kitchen. He heard a shot and on going into the kitchen found his brother as described.

     Cause of Death: Suicide by bullet wound from revolver.

Date *april 6*   19 *40*   *Jhn M Bischoffsberger*
                                     Medical Examiner.

H e stood beside the roadster on The Mattocks Road, bag in hand, and his thoughts splayed, loitered on this and on that. He thought of Joseph, recalled Ros' tease that he was becoming *more like that old goat by the day*. He saw the older man as something of a reflection of himself, a mirror image reaching forward to a man he might become; Joseph his analogue, another him. He felt something closing in on him as it was closing in on Joseph, perhaps illness, perhaps misfortune.

The sky over Baldwin remained aloof and impervious to question; time hid in plain sight and kept its wicked secrets.

◆

They talked the morning out, yet not one undisguised word was spoken of either man's burden. John was reminded of something his mother would say: *If it can't be helped, talking of it can only hurt*, and he wondered on the truth of this. They walked less and less of late it seemed, Joseph a little more tired a little more quickly, and so they sat and they talked. Village Street sprang to slow life about them. As conversation came and went, John's mind span wildly on some separate gyroscope of thought known only to him.

He told Joseph how he'd worked with Doctor Smith at Cumberland Memorial, how Wendel and Joe Bodge had picked up the slack of his caseload following the hurricane.

"He a good doctor?"

"Always seemed so to me. I mean, we weren't close, but we'd spoken, toasted his daughter's birth; and he helped me out when I needed it. Ros knows his wife Molly a little, I think."

The older man shook his head.

"Suicide's a horror." Joseph noticed that John refused to meet his eye, he thought the doctor looked a little bilious, like he'd lost weight, fatigued and wrung out. "Knew a few fellas tried it, couple succeeded. It don't leave behind a whole hell of a lot worth much."

"Had an uncle," said John, "Uncle Paul. Caught him crying once when I was a kid. Walked in on him, crying. Someone said he went crazy and then suddenly he didn't live with Aunt Catherine any more. Then they said he'd gone to live in Canada but I don't know." John fought a little with his words. "Well. It was quick at least."

"Wendel?"

"Wendel." The name felt strange in his mouth, had yet to become the name of a dead man.

"How is his wife? If it aint too stupid a question."

"Utterly at a loss. Like a sleepwalker."

"She had no idea? Had seen nothin comin?"

"Apparently not."

"That is a horror."

A few moments passed and John took to listing in his mind the first five and the last five objects on his list of offerings.

"You know who was there?" he said finally. "At the Smith place? Richard Whitney."

Joseph thought for a moment.

"Whitney, Whitney. The lawyer?"

"That's him."

"He related?"

"Family friend I think. Helping out." They had both heard chatter of impropriety following Wendel's passing.

"You think the lawyer really has inclinations toward the widow?"

"O I know some have said so, but I think it was more a case of the mourning being drawn to the mourning."

"Misery loving company."

"What with Richard having lost his brother not two months since."

"Clifford liked a drink," said Joseph, taking out his flask; a tiny smile. John's mind drifted, he thought of his maps, of the line that ran between a doll's eye and an old house key he'd planted, that ran almost directly between, or at the very least little more than a stone's throw from the Smith place and the picture house; his words ran ahead of his thoughts:

"Sometimes it seems almost like it travels by connections. The path of least resistance. Brothers. Friends. Connections.

He dies, then his wife's brother, then some guy he knew, and on like that. Some guy he worked with once. Some logic at work." A look was exchanged between the two men.

"O seems don't make it so. Small towns. Most everyone knows most everyone else." Joseph threw a nod to a passing car, as if to underline his point. The moment stretched out between them, John fixated on the words *small towns*, on the color and shade of blood in Wendel's kitchen struck by the dawn light, the doctor dead and ridiculous among it. He had the sensation of everything slowing down and speeding up simultaneously; something pedestrian yet dizzying.

"You have any plans?" asked Joseph at last. "To do—" he waved a hand, "something, anything, I mean." John fought not to see something accusatory or judgmental in the vagaries of the question. He tried to imagine the moment before the gun-shot, before Wendel had winked out like a light bulb, tried to live that moment himself, to wear it like a costume; wondered if in that terrible second there might not have been a scintilla of relief hidden there.

"Plans? Like what?"

Joseph exhaled tiredly, shrugged.

"I don't know. Tell me somethin." People passed them by, cars, folks in Sunday Best were coming out of the Union Church.

"I'm not sure I know yet," replied John at last, "But something. Soon."

"Be careful," said Joseph, almost a whisper. He took another chug of bourbon. The day felt done, though barely afternoon, and John knew his friend needed to go home, to rest up.

Joseph stood with difficulty, stood awhile and turning, smiled, gestured with his flask.

"The first fella that ever believed in God, how long dya suppose did he keep it to himself for fear—"

"Joseph Allen! Drinking, in the street, on a Sunday. Opposite a church!" Charlotte Norton stood before them, gloved hands fists at her hips, wrinkles pursed and furious under an impressive hat. Joseph blinked.

"Miss Norton," he smiled, putting away the flask. "What a beautiful day—"

"Does your disrespect know no bounds, sir?"

"I apologize, ma'am, it was not my intention to offend you." Joseph tried his best smile, though John could see it was somewhat strained.

"Not your intention? Pray, sir, what *was* your intention gulping down whiskey on a Sunday morning?"

Joseph let go a sigh and his pretense at apology began to fail him.

"My intention? I don't know, to feel a little better, to oil the wheels of conversation between my friend and I," here his patience grew threadbare, "or perhaps merely to mind my own business and trust others to do likewise."

Charlotte screwed up her face.

"Well you should be ashamed."

"Well I aint." His reply came a little too quickly on the heels of hers to pass as cordial. Charlotte, in her anger, was momentarily at a loss for words. Had Joseph chosen that time to take out the flask and steal a sip, John thought she might have reached up and struck him.

"*Opposite a church*," she said with all the disgust and disbelief she could muster. John stood, to cool the situation, perhaps to move Joseph away; Charlotte failed even to notice his presence. Joseph regained his smile.

"Like the Sawyer boy said: church ain't shucks to a circus," he said.

"Why of all the irreligious, impious—" Her face was growing pinker, shaking with anger, eyes immense behind her eyeglasses. John thought it wise to curb the situation before things ran out of hand.

"Now, I think perhaps—" he tried but was interrupted.

"The lord of that servant will come in a day when he looketh not for him, and at an hour when he is not aware, and will cut him in sunder, and will appoint him his portion with the unbelievers," she barked. Joseph was taken aback.

"I'm impressed, Miss Norton," he said, thinking for a moment, then added playfully, "The way to see by faith is to shut the eye of reason. Ben Franklin."

The old woman narrowed her eyes.

"He answered and said, I will not: but afterward he repented, and went," she said, proudly. Joseph raised his eyebrows, stole a glance at John. All at once he exhibited none of the weariness that had marked his disposition that morning. He took out his flask and stole a quick, and John thought purely theatrical, sip. Charlotte gave a snort of repulsion. Joseph gave another look at John and a wink; he took a breath.

"Shake off all the fears of servile prejudices, under which weak minds are servilely crouched. Fix reason firmly in her seat, and call on her tribunal for every fact, every opinion." He faltered, closed his eyes, searching for the words. "Question with boldness even the existence of a god; because, if there be one, he must more approve of the homage of reason than that of blindfolded fear. Thomas Jefferson."

Charlotte came back at him, her viciousness all the more ludicrous in her Sunday Best.

"Repent ye therefore, and be converted, that your sins may be blotted out, when the times of refreshing shall come from the presence of the Lord."

"Times of refreshing? I like that. I'll drink to that," said Joseph and raised the flask.

"Don't you *dare!*"

He lifted his hands in appeasement, put the flask away.

"Let me see," he said, "Religion is all bunk. Thomas Edison. Faith means not wanting to know what is true. Nietzsche. Our remedies oft in ourselves do lie, which we ascribe to Heaven. Shakespeare. Things that you're liable to read in the Bible—"

"You are vain and craven, you use the words of others to elevate yourself, sir."

Joseph feigned puzzlement.

"I do. For this is how we learn. And so do you, madam. But my gentlemen are asking questions, yours are transcribing, playin Telephone, interpreting, obfuscating."

"You speak of things that you cannot know."

"I do. But then nor can I know if every night you climb on a broomstick and haunt the skies over Muddy Bog, but I doubt that you do, madam."

She was breathless for a short moment, at a loss.

"I've never been so insulted."

"That I find hard to believe, ma'am."

Pitch and temper had risen on both sides. John's attempts at placation had been all but ignored by both parties. Passersby had begun to gawp and to linger.

"There is but one book I need," Charlotte was getting shrill and ever pinker.

"Then I feel sorry for you, ma'am."

"Don't you dare feel sorry for me, the word of God, Mr Allen—"

"Who wrote the book of Matthew?"

"Why, you should know full well that—"

"Chances are a fella never even set foot in the Holy Land, that's who."

Charlotte was dumbfounded.

"You have lost your mind."

"A scrapbook. At best. Shabby anthology. Rumor and embroidery. Written by countless men hundreds ayears after the fact, men who weren't even there, likely had never even visited the places written of, editors, theological politicians with agendas too convoluted and rich in perverse unreason, illogic and irrationality to be granted even the least morsel of credence."

"You—" she almost choked on her words, "old— stubborn drunkard, you are a blight on this town! On this state! They oughta run you out on a rail, mister, if I had my way—" Here Joseph quickly leaned in to her, close enough to shake her into silence.

"*This aint Scopes*," he said low, and with more belligerence that John had thought it possible for him to possess. The old woman made a few exasperated sounds, kept Joseph's gaze for as long as she could before marching off down Village Street, waving her hands and talking to herself, no doubt to suggest that she would not be spoken to like this and was on her way to put things right; all at once Joseph looked tired again and sat back down on the bench. The thin crowd dissipated and after a time John laid his hand on his friend's shoulder.

"Come on, let's get you home."

♦

In an attempt to make light, he'd suggested to Joseph that he was a firebrand; Joseph countered that he was no such thing but instead, a fool. John had tried another tack:

"She's been hectoring folks for years, we might have sold tickets to see her put in her place."

"Is that what I did?" The reply was melancholic, disappointed.

After dropping Joseph at his house, offering to see him inside, to see him comfortable (an offer politely refused) John bid his friend farewell, told him to lay off the liquor, and took his own quiet madness for a drive.

He drove in a wide, elongated arc up the Roosevelt Trail, left onto Perley, away from the yawn and expanse of Long Lake and onward to Grist Mill Road. Heading south east on Kings Hill, the road pushed through the trees which bowed gently to one another in the breeze, like debutantes or courtiers, mute creatures held down by some natural etiquette; their roots both feeding them and keeping them in place at the same time. He felt a little nauseous, his stomach queer and ill-shaped within him, tumorous. He let his mind splay out in all directions.

Some half mile or so above the turn to Two Pond Road, a bright shape of daylight between the trees caught his eye. It set loose in him so strange a feeling that he pulled the roadster over and held his breath, watched the space for it to happen again. He thought of fire, of miraculous conflagrations, of spontaneous materializations of impossible persons and flashes of holy light; he thought of someone or something signaling to him with a piece of broken mirror. But the trees remained in shadow.

After some minutes of walking up and down the roadway, staring intently into the woods, the shape turned out to be a clearing, what looked like some thirty or so feet beyond the tree line, the rows of trunks conspiring by chance to form a kind of crooked alleyway between their number, revealing the space to any passerby stood, or happening to glance left, while at a specific point on the road. It was like a secret pocket of light and space among so much of nature's confusion. John left the car and walked into the trees, making his way toward the clearing.

Roughly oval in shape and spanning something like fifteen feet of treeless earth, it appeared as if perhaps the ground had been salted centuries ago, or that some mighty hand had reached down and uprooted all that stood there; while the forest around was hardly thick, still the clearing felt anomalous, uncanny.

John stood there for close to an hour while something approaching a design or scheme crept up on him, drifted by on the breeze, doubled back and gathered about him like the scent of smoke bringing news of a burning building many miles away.

The thin man throws a worried look behind him, then, after no more than four or five further steps throws another. The girl stops.

"What the hell you lookin for?"

"Nothin." And they press on; still he snatches glances.

They come to a lake, wide and dim in the oncoming night, and navigate lazily along its shore, the little girl kicking pebbles into the shallows.

"Sorry I left the gun," he says at last, sighs, as if by saying this, some great weight has been lifted from him; the girl merely shrugs.

"There's others."

"But after you said we needed a gun and me havin one right in my hand like that, but it fell, under him an then we didn have no time to go back and get it, an I really shoulda—"

The girls turns and claps her hands to silence him.

"*Hey!*" she snaps, "quit your whinin. There's other guns. Hundreds, *thousands*. They're like secrets. Like peccadilloes. Like weakness. Like ways in, apertures, fears. They're everywhere."

"Good," he says. The blood star is flaking and peeling from his beard.

"That won't be the last trigger you pull, alright?"

He nods.

"I know. Good. I— I enjoyed it," he says quietly, instinctively holds a bandaged hand momentarily between his legs as he says it. They set off again and the sun ducks, aloof, behind the serrated stage-flat of the distant horizon.

XI

So there is good and there is bad and much that is in between. So what? Them answers still elude me as they elude you, if you are honest.

We go on, you and I. Long as we're allowed.

There is blood, spilled for all manner astupid reasons, some good, many not so. Men and women fall and timber is cut, bricks are laid, countries spring up. Millions afolks now dead will never be remembered, yet this world would not be here, how it is, in all its wonder and horror were it not for their lives. It would be a different world and who knows if better or worse.

Good and bad. But such words can have you turnin summersaults. Is there such a thing as a bad man? Known many I considered so and many a bad action I have witnessed but sometimes, often early in the mornin, or when stood by water on a calm day, or when the sun strikes a stand atrees in that way it does, I think perhaps there is no good nor bad. These bad fellas I've known are merely of faulty construction and while their actions are terrible, or brutal, their origin is from malfunction, some kinda illness caught by bein alive maybe or defect from birth.

But then if bad is nothin but a balky machine and a defect, then why not good? And if good, then who are we, and what would we be without life's ravages upon us? We can never know because to be a person without life's influence is to be dead and to be dead is to be no kinda person at all. These are the summersaults I spoke of.

We are a hapless montage. We are wonderful, foolish, beautiful, weak, inventive, cruel, selfless and frightened; chiefly I think this last one.

Chiefly.

Now I think on it, probly every wantonly violent man I ever knew was afraid. Like Aristotle says Men are swayed more by fear than by reverence. But scared awhat? I guess the big one. Guess we're all a little scared of the Great Fright. Difficult to dislodge that one, but the more you indeed do think on it, the more foolish it feels, I think.

Bein scared adyin is natural, scared adeath though is just foolishness. Life is fulla dangers. I recall somethin a man once told me, he said, looked me in the eye and he said "Life is dangerous, dying is dangerous but death, well there aint nothin safer than death."

An *No one knows whether death, which people fear to be the greatest evil, may not be the greatest good.* Plato said that.

I don't know.

A fat man of vulgar habits and intemperance reels an says *hell, aint nobody ever died healthy,* an he's right and he's wrong in about equal measure.

Yknow?

They are eradicating smallpox in America, which is a good, nay great thing; this is how ingenious we are. But like my Ma used to say: "We all gotta die of somethin."

I mean—

Blood is everywhere.

So what, you say? I guess the *what* is down to you.

Otisfield; Maine

June, 1941

Muscles curl and harden, tendons stand out, taut, like some internal rigging suffering a terrible storm. Arms and legs make a cripple's geometry, stiff, sharp, painful looking. Only disjointed syllables make it past the gritted teeth, the spittle and whistling breath: *Yn, Nh, Fh, Fuh, FUH*— Legs shake and when knees bend to allow it, heels plough up and chop at the earth; hands are claws and fists. At this moment she appears less a girl than an engine, loosely bolted, doing its damnedest to shake itself into its constituent parts.

There appears, he thinks, to be something huge within her, some rage or similar animal, something larger than any avenue it has to be expressed, or to escape from. It is therefore vented in bursts, this thing, vomited out in little parcels that her tiny throat, her thin body can accommodate. As used to it as he has become, still it frightens him.

The thin man decided some months ago that his path is one of pilgrimage, though to what end he could not hope to fathom. Since the old woman left them, he has become closer and closer to the girl, has begun to, even gladly, accept her verbal attacks, her beatings, as some kind of protracted penance. He has even acquiesced to touching her where and when she demands it, and as such, and to his buried relief, she appears to have lost interest in doing so.

He sits on the warm ground and watches her spasm and convulse, enjoying the early sun on his face, wondering at what the day holds for him, what the girl might decide is to be done.

The study carpet had been free of paper and pushpins for months now, winter having seen Ros' temper thin a little at the accumulation of inaccessible dust and clutter in the room, leading to John's grudging acquiescence. Her questioning of his 'project' had gone no further than his vague admission to some local historical interest.

All that remained of the conglomeration of maps now was a single abstract section, pieces Scotch-taped together, three or so feet long, cut roughly from the whole with a pair of scissors and folded up in John's jacket pocket. The cutting itself had felt to him like decisive action, like the narrowing down of his area of concentration, like the inauguration of a plan; and so it had been.

For her part, Ros had charted her husband's increasing eccentricity across the years with concern, his devolution from The Careful Fidget into something quite other, a worried man adrift in his own sea of doubt. There was a tremor in him, but then, she supposed, there was in so many, times being what they were, what the president called "the philosophy of force" amok in the world.

Violet Porter, a friend, herself married for some fifty years, had once commented that men are only ever boys until they are old men, the process one of the gradual dismantling of fanciful and childish ideas on the world, and the acceptance of the world as it truly is; and all *just about the time it's too damn late to help*. Ros refused such blanket judgment on the other sex, yet could not help but feel the pull of Violet's rationale.

So it was that John's behavior was filtered through this idea that it was merely his reaction to some process beyond his control; still her worry lurked on the periphery.

♦

In May of that year, as Roosevelt leaned toward war, just as much of America strained to distance itself from the call of

Europe, John wrote two letters. Eschewing the clatter and smudge of his typewriter, he wrote by hand, carefully, each word considered, each phrase invested with as much of himself as he felt he could spare. His hand cramped and he shook it to loosen the words.

The isolationist rhetoric, though somewhat shrill, attracted John greatly, in a sense told him what he wanted to hear, that America need not be brought to blows with Germany and its allies in a fight which, it could be argued, was not her own; yet a certain terrible inevitability in the newsreels, in the death tolls and photographs from the front lent an ever more hysterical air to calls to let the old world battle, while the new world blithely prospered.

He mentioned the war in both letters. To Joseph he wrote *As I write, we stumble to this dreadful and inescapable conflagration in Europe,* to Ros he wrote *this awful slaughter of young men*; both letters moved on from the subject with the line *yet closer to home I have, as you know, been suffering from an accumulated disquiet.* Hours fell past as he wrote.

When finished, he sealed the letters in envelopes, addressed one to *My good friend, Joseph Allen,* the other simply to *My darling Rosamond.* He locked them in his desk drawer and dropped the key into the breast pocket of his jacket, before retrieving it and placing it instead in his left jacket pocket, unable to recall how often he had checked the breast pocket of a body he'd dealt with.

The girl lies exhausted, gathering herself together to stand, arms plagued with bruises, back with knots, neck with pangs.

"It's gettin worse, aint it?" he says. She makes a face.

"It's a fever. It'll break." She widens her eyes, gives her head a shake.

"Then you'll be all better?"

She sits up, brushes dirt from her dress.

"An a whole lotta folks will be worse." She stands and her right leg buckles like some supporting string has been cut, and she lets forth a great cry of pain. "Dammitfuck!" The thin man jumps to his feet, wringing his hands. On all fours now, the girl bares her teeth while she works out the offending leg, the knee bending fine but the ankle causing yet another explosion, "*Fuck!*"

"You okay?" he asks.

"I'd say that question is a mite fuckin redundant wouldn you?" she spits.

"What is it?"

"My damn ankle."

"You want me to bind it up? You wanna bandage?" He makes to untie those about his hands.

"Get those dirty rags away from me, moron."

"You want I should help you up?"

"Help me up shit, this fucker's broke." She winces, waves him closer, impatient. "I want you should fuckin carry me is what I want." There is the tiniest hesitation in him before he reaches down and takes her under the arms, until she's balancing on one foot, then sweeps an arm under her and lifts her. She is heavier than he'd thought and he staggers a little.

"To the lake maybe?" he manages through a tightened throat. "Give the offendin leg a dip?"

"What am I, a sacka fuckin potatoes? Up higher, you fuck."

He struggles and almost falls a number of times before she's sat on his shoulders.

"Now the lake?"

"I'll let you know. Onward, fool!" she cries out, kicking her good heel at his ribs, pointing the way.

The queer creature stumbles into the trees, a chimera eight-limbed and two-headed, the head atop grinning from ear to ear.

Despite everything that was, and indeed anything that might be, circumstance and eventuality, life was normal, he reasoned, it went on, and while this thought was certainly true, its inanity was troubling; yet it held within it a kernel of strange comfort.

♦

In candlelight, years were wiped away, both of them appearing to the other as the selves they had been upon their first meeting; perhaps, thought John, this was the origin of the tradition. Anything not lit fell in shadow and anything in shadow felt insubstantial to him, of less import or weight.

She thought he looked calmer and more relaxed than she had seen him in months; his laugh truer, his words less guarded. Their plates glistened greasily between them, cleaned; wineglasses bled.

"Rosamond," he said. She waited for him to continue but he did not.

"Mother only ever used my full Christian name when I was in hot water," she said. He smiled, looked a little embarrassed.

"I use it because I like the sound of it, all three syllables."

She watched him take a breath and let it go, pretending, upon seeing her watching, that it was nothing but an expression of having eaten too much. His guarded nature could infuriate her, yet it was, in its way, endearing.

"What do you suppose would have become of us had we not married?" she asked.

"And lived in infamy and sin, you mean?"

Ros laughed.

"Charlotte Norton needs no more ammunition for her outrage. No," she said, "had we not met at all, I meant. Ships passing." There was the tiniest moment while they both considered this.

"I know very well what would have become of me," said

John, seriously, "a ruin." Ros smiled, picked up her glass, and seeing it empty, placed it back down.

"I'm the power behind the throne?" she said, playfully.

"Throne? Hardly. But, sure. Behind, around, within, under," even in the dimness, he saw her blush, "through, between. I mean it." He looked at her, amazing to him. "You are the best thing I ever had anything to do with." She slid the candlestick to one side and the shadows coasted over the walls and over her face; she leant across the table and kissed him, warm, the scent of wine, the scent of dinner, of her; yet she felt distant to him and his heart broke a little at the feeling. He gathered her in as best he could.

◆

He saw a road laid out before him and felt that he could do little but walk along it. He thought for a moment of Gene and his WPA work in Portland, *laying road like it was licorice.* All was uncertain and frightening; but, he reasoned, when all was such, what other choice existed, where else did he have to go?

◆

Franklin Fowler was now nineteen and a far cry from the child who'd bitten down on a wooden spoon while John had set his leg. He was tall and gruff sounding, affected a light mustache, stood in a way that suggested an enthusiasm for his sudden maleness that had little to do with any understanding or acceptance of the real thing. He was engaged to be married to a Mary Harmon from Harrison, he said, showed John a picture of a plain, doe-eyed girl with a startled expression.

He'd fallen from his horse, Budd, *tryin some foolishness,* and had fractured his wrist. No spoons were employed this time; instead he bore the pain with the fierce arrogance of youth, perhaps, thought John, to impress him, the older man.

"Your mother once thought you'd become a surgeon I seem to recall," said John as he worked.

"Ma has her head in the clouds. So says Pa. Fowler boy becomin a surgeon," he scoffed.

"You liked to read," said John.

"I did." He leaned gently on the past tense.

"The civil war," said John. Franklin seemed surprised, a little embarrassed.

"You got a good memory, Doc."

"You still read?"

"Don't got time, farm keeps me pretty busy."

"But now, with your wrist, you need to be resting. Maybe you can catch up on a book or two?"

Franklin pulled the face a young man pulls when he feels he's being treated like a child.

"Maybe."

On his way back to the roadster, John thought to himself that, with Washington in two minds, nineteen was just about the worst age a boy could be.

♦

Something unsaid spoke of friendship, of the times they had remaining in each other's company, a portion that had always been finite and unfair. John thought that Joseph had always felt this limitation, perhaps as the older and wiser of the two of them; it hung between them, at once sad and somehow urgent and gladdening.

Joseph lay on a couch by the window, blanket thrown, motes floating on the sunlight streaming through the open window. Books were piled about the couch, open, closed, bristling with bookmarks; whiskey glowed amber in bottle and glass, the remains of a sandwich dried and curled on a plate on the floor. A cane rested by his shoulder, though John had yet to see him use it to walk.

"Abe wakes up next to his wife, Maud," said Joseph. "Abe is eighty years of age, Maud is seventy-eight. He turns over, gives Maud a kiss. 'You leave me alone!' screams Maud. Abe says 'Leave you alone? Why?' Maud says 'Cos I'm dead, you fool!' Abe says 'Dead? How can you be dead? I'm talkin, you can hear me, you're talkin back.' 'I'm dead!' insists Maud. 'How do you know you're dead?' asks Abe, an she comes right back: 'Cos I woke up this mornin an nothin hurts!'"

They laughed and they talked. There was a lull and Joseph

clawed a hand at his beard, John surveyed the paintings on the walls, the chaos of papers on the desk by the window. Joseph watched him keenly. The doctor seemed less perturbed than he had seen him in some time, the trouble in him having abated, or at least lessened.

"You'll be alright," said Joseph, seemingly apropos of nothing. John smiled but failed to reply, felt a little like he'd let go a lie by doing so.

◆

If a dog will not come when called, it must be coaxed, it must be fooled. He reckoned one object every six feet or so would suffice, though further spaced on the roads. He emptied his leather bag of bottles, of instruments, medicines, and decanted all the offerings he had remaining, adding his latest additions: a snarled knot of picture wire, three loose buttons, the lid from an old bottle of metal polish, the thumbtacks he'd used to secure the maps; these little scraps and corners broken from doohickeys and whachamacallits, pinched and snapped from things pedestrian and seldom noted, let alone valued. Half full, the bag rattled and hissed when tipped, recalling pebbles clawed at by the tide; a miscellany of useless pieces carried forth to end death or to die in so doing.

A giant of a man sits on the bed in the dark, sits on it as if it were a miniature thing of novelty, as if perspective or scale in that room were somehow skewed. His giant face lays in his giant hands and he weeps. His nightshirt billows and shakes with every smothered sob. From the warm night, they watch him through the open window, the girl still atop the thin man's shoulders.

"He's a big fella aint he?" whispers the thin man.

"Big? Like this we're biggern he is."

"Look at the size of his hands, his arms, legs." The thin man is all agog, like a rube on the midway.

"Fucker must hafta duck to go through doors."

"What's this fella's name?" he asks.

"Name don't matter. Look at him. He's all men." On the bed, the man cries and cries, his sniffs and whimpers such that they mask the thin man and the girl's balancing act entrance through the window and into the house.

They stand before him for some time, monstrous and absurd in their doubleness, before he notices them; perhaps a subtle change in the room's atmosphere, the stifled giggles of the little girl, perhaps the stench of the thin man.

When the giant looks up at them he is bloodshot and hollow of eye but seems unsurprised. He wipes his nose on the back of his hand, perhaps a little embarrassed, clears his throat.

"What?" he asks, hoarse, face gray and drawn. At the tiniest impetus from his rider, the thin man holds onto her shins and leans forward, like they practiced; the girl widens her eyes and through her teeth says:

"Buck up, Hancock you sorry fuck, we come to kill you."

"What?" says the man again, wiping his face. He looks up at them, at each face in turn, then gives a short exhalation of a laugh. "You two? You're going to kill me?"

"We are," sneers the girl. At this, the man laughs again.

"You can't kill me, I'm already dyin, you fools."

"Dyin aint dead and dead's what you'll be afore we leave here."

"That right? An what do you suppose this is for?" He lifts a rifle, until then stood by the bedside. "What you suppose this is for, bedbugs?" He stands slowly, towers in his bare feet, the merest trace of a wince betraying the enormous pain and effort of remaining upright. He raises his shoulders in question, "Hmm?" The girl just blinks, thrown and wordless.

"Listen here you— you damn— cryin fool," spits the thin man, fury ungainly on him. "We are here to kill you dead, that's what we do. We are killers of men, of women and of children, an you will scream before you breathe your last tonight."

Hancock makes a pantomime of confusion, still a little dizzy with tears.

"Scream you say? You don't think I've screamed? I'm dyin, mister, I've cried an I've screamed and can't sleep most nights with the pain, my insides so eaten up and rotten. Every hour I'm awake I'm on fire. I'm dyin, you understand? You can't threaten a man who aint got nothin left to lose, don't you know that?"

The little girl has pulled herself together. She squirms down from the thin man and limps, grimacing, toward the giant.

"Maybe we kill your wife first, eh? You got that to lose aint you? My pal here put his thing in her, cut her throat an fuck her in the ass."

Hancock all at once looks tired.

"You won't do a goddamn thing to my wife you stupid little bitch an you know it. She aint sick, *I'm* sick, she aint sat here cryin with a gun by her side, *I* am. You're nothin but a little girl—"

"I aint no damn little girl."

Hancock holds up a giant hand, almost an apology.

"No you aint. You're a dogsbody. Paltry messenger, the both ayou."

"We are killers."

"Yes you are but so what?" Both girl and thin man are stymied, she boiling with rage unspent, he close to tears. "I'm here dyin. So what, right? So what. But then you two foolish imps or some such swagger in here like a poor man's circus acrobats. You are a joke is what you are, spirits or no."

The girl is red-faced and raging inside, veins worming fat across her forehead, body beginning to convulse; her words, when they come, are barely words at all.

"*I will burn the world,*" she hisses. Hancock makes a face.

"That sunovabitch will burn regardless. Now you can watch or you can get outta my fuckin house." He sits on the bed and it is rendered Lilliputian again. His long arms maneuver the rifle into position.

"You son of a damn whore I'll fuck— fucking kill you," barks the thin man, himself now weeping, school-boyish and at a loss. "I'll fucking kill you!"

"O quiet, you. You never did nothin," replies Hancock. He pauses for a moment, a shake of his head, "You know what? I always knew death would be strange, but this? This is outright comical."

"*I'm a killer, we're fuckin killers, mister, an you better—*"

"You're a punchline, both ayou," Hancock says, tiredly, "I pity you. Go on, get out, go home. I'm tired. I'm leavin." And with this, he aligns the barrel of the rifle, pulls back the lever, pushes it home, closes his eyes, takes a breath and squeezes the trigger.

S pare sheets had been put down in the hall and had blos-
somed in little red spots, recalling the algae of British Soldiers. There were red flecks on the doorjamb and on the
wallpaper.

John fancied he could still feel the echo of the explosion in
the stunned air around him, still reverberating with it, its nap
rubbed the wrong way, ruched up and feathered.

He sat on the end of the bed and took the deceased's mighty
hand in his, felt its meat coldness, wanted to say out loud to
those who milled respectfully about the house "If only he'd
held off a day, who knows what would have become of him?"
but somehow the act of touching earthed the sentiment and it
fell away, became something counterfeit. This was to be John's
last moment of doubt on the subject, soon swept away.

Edna Hancock, blankly adrift in her new widowhood, spoke
her part calmly, answered his questions, while something huge
and awful butted up against the backs of her eyes waiting to
pour forth and she, oblivious, even smiled at John and thanked
him as he left.

He allowed himself a moment of stillness on the Hancock
stoop, smelled the dawn air, felt his own body, its flesh and
bone, its solidity and participation in the world, before moving
on to do what had to be done.

State of Maine.

Cumberland   **ss.**

I certify that I was notified on the _13_ **day** _June_   A. D. 19 _41_

at   h. and   m. in the   noon by

of   of the finding of the dead body of _John Hancock_

of _Balster Mills Me._

supposed to have come to h _is_ death by violence or unlawful act; that I forthwith repaired to the place

where said body lies and took charge of the same, and before said body is removed make, or cause to be made,

this written description of the location and position of said body, viz:

The body was that of a man six feet, four inches tall, having brown hair and blue eyes. He wore a white night shirt. Rigor Mortis had not set in.

The body was found in deceased bed room lying on floor beside bed on south side of room. He head was towards the head of the bed and feet at foot of bed. He lay on right side with right arm under him and left arm slightly bent. A 32 special Winchester rifle lay between his legs with muzzle towards his head. Hte rifle contained one exploded shell and four unexploded shells, fifteen shells remained in package of shells on bed.

The skull was blown out from just above a line extending from about the level of the eyes to the anterior portion of occipital bone. The brains had been lown from the head and flesh was scattered about the room and into the next room, four holes made by splinters of bullet were noticed in the ceiling above center of bed. There were no sighs of any struggle in room.

The deceased evidently sat on edge of bed, stuck muzzle of gun in mouth and pulled trigger.

Mrs. Hancock states that he had appeared quite normal all day, altho he had been having frequent crying spells since his return from the hospital on the preceding Thesday, where he had been for observation, and been told that he had an incurable desease. They both retired about ten-thirty P. M. on the night of the 13th. Mrs. Hancock to her room upstairs. Mr. Hancock to his bed room on the first floor. Mrs. Hancock awoke about twelve-fifteen A. M. and thought she smelled smoke. She went down to the cellar first where she had some incubators going, finding everything all right in cellar she returned to her husbands room, turned on light and found him as described.

His physician, Dr. Bean of Norway, states he has been treating him for the past two years, that he has been despondent, and on several occasions stated it would be better if he finished things.

Cause of Death: Self inflicted gun shot wound in mouth.

Date _June 14_   19 _41_   _Medical Examiner._

Taking Haskell Hill, the bag open beside him, he went tossing his tiny objects from the car; a button, a flattened thimble, a woodscrew, counting to ten, sometimes twenty, between each throw.

Turning right onto Maple Ridge Road he threw an empty cotton reel, a small rusted key and a wine cork, and on and on; instinctively he threw more objects where there were more trees and fewer where there were fewer. Driving through Main Street, Harrison, he threw nothing at all.

Norway Road saw a pencil eraser, the handle to a fruit knife broken loose from its blade, a doll's shoe. Hooking around the top of Long Lake he bore left onto Bridgton Road and south toward Naples.

By Grist Mill Road the count between throws went as low as five, as bottle tops and pen nibs span out into the trees, two, three at a time; by Kings Hill, handfuls. A Mahjong piece described with what appeared to be the hilt of a sword scratched in red, a mahogany knight from a chess set, the buckle from a lady's bag. Leaning against his shoulder, as if a drunken passenger wrapped in burlap, Wilson's Winchester Low Wall nudged at him with every bump and turn.

He could not recall a time when he felt a greater calm or surety of purpose.

◆

Once parked, it took him a half hour or so to find the clearing again.

He seeded the perimeter of the bare oval of ground with his buttons, nails, a bent curtain ring, a paperclip, thumbtacks. The thumbtacks indeed gave the scene a strange ceremonial feel, a sense that in sewing these objects, he was in fact holding something down to the ground, as he had held the maps in his office, securing it, fixing it in place, keeping something from wandering further; the offerings both lure and snare. The offerings formed a rough ring around the clearing, glinted here and there, shone dully.

Unwrapping the Winchester, he walked into the woods, cradling it. Some fifteen feet away lay a fallen tree; he spread the burlap on it and sat down, both hands around the rifle's forestock, barrel pointing to the sky. He sat and he waited.

S he walks quickly and in anger, her limp throwing her limbs into strange angles and counterbalances. She tears off branches that block her way, ripping up their leaves, her fingers green and wet; despite the pain she leans in to the walk like it were an unseasonal downpour.

The thin man follows, as if someone robbed of something precious and thrown to the mercies of the wilderness. He has cried and been beaten by the girl. He blinks too much and tries on various pained expressions, searching for an appropriate mask or response. The girl has already warned him against repeating the phrases *But I don't understand*, and *But didn you say*; his worldview, such as it is, is all aflame. He settles with the here and now.

"Nother gun we left behind."

"Shut up."

"Coulda used it, killed hundreds. Like you said."

"Aint gonna tell you again."

Denied conversation, he is alone again as they walk and he wrestles with his need to weep, makes bandaged fists, throws worried looks behind him.

The girl stops.

"Wait," she says, eyes scanning the trees, disquieted, "wait," then: "*shit.*" The thin man feels it too, frowns, closes his eyes.

"I don't feel so good," he says quietly.

There is the sensation of all coming to a halt, of a dreadful stillness, and they both reel for a moment; she has the mental image of flotsam circling a drain, of being drawn down, of coming to rest somewhere deep and inescapable. The thin man bends double, dry heaves, feels like he's being bled, like something is being pulled out of him, stitches on a wound maybe, tugging at the flesh, queasy, smarting and strange feeling.

"Where are we?" he asks her, pinched-sounding and pained.

"Nowhere," she hisses, then: "The doctor fella."

The doctor walks carefully through the trees toward them,

circumspect and deliberate, head cocked toward the rifle he holds, muzzle dancing between the two of them.

"*The doctor fella*," echoes the thin man. The doctor's breathing is slow and even but his eyes are wild.

They stand and they stare, the Winchester's muzzle snaking between them. The girl is hunched, jaw set and hackles up, the thin man stooped, wretched, flinching whenever the rifle points his way.

The air vibrates queerly, in a way that suggests that they stand not in a forest clearing but underwater, sound is oddly muted, light filters through clouds as if down through waves; a chaos of dust and leaves, insects, drift and are buffeted on invisible currents.

"You think you can just shoot us and go on your way?" says the girl, dropped now to all fours. "Just how fuckin dumb are you?" The doctor says nothing, and they each stand, and they stare, and do nothing.

"Why you been huntin us?" whimpers the thin man, "what we ever do to you?" and he begins to weep. "You must hate the world so," he says at last.

"What you waitin for?" snarls the girl. "Shoot us, you wanna see what good it does you. I'll pop back up, tear you to fuckin ribbons, mister. Think you're so fuckin clever." The doctor shifts his feet, readjusts his grip on the rifle; purposeful, businesslike. "What if this aint a trap?" tries the girl. "What if it's a door? What if you just set me loose? Where you think I'll go next? You know very well where, dontcha?"

There is a shift in the disposition of the atmosphere; perhaps the clearing growing a little smaller, perhaps the light a little brighter. The old woman does not step into the clearing; she is not there, and then she is there. The same sack-like shift dress little more than a rag, the same hardwood features, weathered and implacable, impossibly old, the same tendon and mettle.

"O God," whines the thin man, "o *God*," and sinks to his knees. He's holding his bandaged hands together, talking into them, fervent and unintelligible, as if they are some primitive telephone to who knows what friend or savior.

The old woman simply stands, surveys them all, blankly furious, radiating an anger of ambiguous origin or target.

"Hail, hail, the gang's all here," says the little girl.

Time goes slowly. Out in the woods, the indifferent trees perform their moan and whisper; within the clearing however, for the longest time, nothing stirs.

The doctor lowers the rifle and after a brief hesitation, lets it fall to the ground; the little girl eyes it jealously where it rests.

The thin man is shuffling on his knees toward the old woman.

"We tried to do right, we did, you went off an we tried. An she, the girl, she made me do terrible things an I let her make me I admit it, but you was gone an never no one but her to tell me how things should be." The old woman ignores him, looks instead at the doctor, fury replaced with something approaching disappointment; the doctor looks back at her tiredly, hanging on to some last vestige of fight.

On hands and feet the girl crawls along the earth toward the rifle, jackal-like, edges along slowly, eyes never leaving her two compatriots; under her breath she sings the mantra:

"Hail, hail, the gang's all here, what the heck do we care? What the heck do we care? Hail, hail, the gang's all here, what the heck do we care now?"

The thin man is tearing at his bandages, scratching and beating at his face, crying, begging, saying that he's sorry, if only she hadn't left them.

The doctor gives a short sigh.

The old woman crouches, and summoning up something from deep inside her, opens her mouth and bellows a vast syllable of force, of determination, of will, standing as she does so, as if to propel the sound from her, raising her arms to the sky, bellowing, howling. The light in the clearing shifts and is stained by something of indeterminate nature, color or opacity. A wind picks up, throwing leaves, throwing dirt. The doctor reels.

Hand on the stock of the rifle, hair rampant on the wind, the little girl writhes and twists in the throes of a fit, muscles pulling her this way and that, fingers unable to fasten, to grip, to lift, to aim, or to fire.

The old woman's arms stretch out impossibly, her ribs distend and twist, her legs lengthen, her wrinkles crack and darken; fingers sprout fingers sprout fingers, snake upwards. Her clothes tear and are carried away as rags on the wind; she rises and she rises and she rises.

Something of the old woman remains in the black oak she has become.

Tremors relenting, the girl stands, breathless, and stumbles about the clearing. Before she has taken a step she is afire, some spark or other from within catching and flowering into thick orange flames that curl and blacken her dress, that pucker and blister her flesh. Her hair is gone in seconds, her dress rises off of her in red embers. She roars, runs at the black oak, throwing her flaming arms about its trunk, raging and raging as she burns; she kicks and she wrestles, as if trying to fell the tree, all the time screeching a terrible torn sound. The air is alive with the smell of her as she cooks, with the sound of her immense acrimony and savagery.

Soon the sound trails off to nothing and she slides down the tree and lays still, still burning, a girl-shaped pyre at the foot of the tree; though the oak's bark is charred, it fails to catch or to burn.

The thin man is standing, tear-stained and abject, staring at the doctor. He looks cored, like little more than a skin, cured and held up by some invisible contrivance, perhaps for exhibition, perhaps for sale. When it comes, his voice is tiny:

"I have loved you. All of you. Yet it did no good." He turns and approaches the black oak. After a few awkward slips and losses of footing, he begins to climb the tree, grunting with the exertion, bleating and mewling, higher and higher; he loses a shoe, which tocks hollow off branches as it falls, landing among the smoldering remains of the girl, there blackening and curling. The doctor watches him climb, up and up, until he is lost in the blinding white of the summer sky.

The letters burned eagerly and he felt like a part of him had remained sore, held too tightly, until they were gone. The memory of his certainty as he had written them still frightened him. He returned the key to its drawer.

He checked his disbelief and found it still present and correct; he thought of night in the clearing, the pure dark of it, and knew he would never return there.

Sounds of Ros somewhere upstairs warmed him, shamed him a little at her extraordinary legitimacy in the world, compared to what he felt was his relative insubstantiality.

He sat for a time, stared through the open window at the bright day, evened out his breathing, listened to Ros upstairs singing to herself; he didn't catch the words, perhaps all she sang was melody, but her voice filled the house with something intangible, quieting. He closed his eyes.

In the hall, the phone rang.

Out in the woods, the old woman walked.

Afterword

I first came into contact with the Medical Journal of Doctor John M. Bischoffberger by way of my thirtieth birthday. My then girlfriend (now wife) decided that at such a grand age I should collect something; grudges, kidney stones and CDs apparently did not count.

Knowing me as well as she did, she chose antique medical instruments, and to this day I have a beautiful array of strange, hinged, sharpened, dusty, rusty metal implements to dazzle and disgust in equal measure.

While hunting online for another addition to my collection, she came across the medical journal and her fascination overpowering her lack of funds, she bought it.

On reading through the journal, an old idea from many years ago was rekindled and this book began to make itself known.

Beyond the deaths themselves, several other incidents included herein also took place: details of the centenary celebrations, the path and wreckage of the hurricane, the tale of the Chinese idols, etc. are all true; though I'm sure I don't need to specify certain incidents which, of course, are fabrications.

On top of this, I will state for the record that I have no knowledge of the real Dr. Bischoffberger's religious beliefs or any concrete details of whether he had children; though research did provide me with the fact that he utilized homeopathic treatments as well as conventional medicine, which played neatly into my story.

In fact, many of the real events included (co-opted) into my narrative were pilfered purely because they aided my ends, which is after all a methodology at the heart of all "magical thinking", a subject which is itself woven into the book's DNA.

I am indebted to *Now I Will Tell You... The Story of Naples, Maine, Its History and Legends* compiled by Robert Jordan Dingley for the Naples Historical Society, a curious volume of snippets and stories which gave me more than enough to work with and to pilfer from, including fascinating details, actual incidents and common local names with which to construct fictional townsfolk when they were required; one very real detail is the centenary poem in chapter two, which was written by the very real Mr Loton Pitts, postmaster.

Another book that proved incredibly useful was *Images of America: Sebago Lake, West Shore, Standish, Baldwin, Sebago, And Naples*, compiled by Diane and Jack Barnes, and which includes a wealth of wonderful old photographs of the area. It was in this book that I discovered, not only the "Hinkey Dink", the causeway and the store at Two Trails, but also, to my great surprise, a picture of Dr. Bischoffberger himself, with his wife Rosamond, taken in 1970; a strange and unexpected discovery that quickened the pulse I can tell you.

These photographs enabled me to visualize the streets that Bisch walked and, while precise or exhaustive description was never my interest, I think gave me a mental image within which my fictional events could take place, a fitting home for my characters, living, dead and otherwise.

I'd like to take this opportunity to heap oodles of thanks to all who made this book firstly a possibility and finally a reality: firstly to my university tutor Carolyn Hart who oversaw and encouraged the first chapter (which served as my dissertation), my wife who read early drafts without complaint, to my editor Scott Pack who was the recipient of my first ever "book pitch", and indeed to all the Unbound editing team; to Jodee DeBeau, who did such sterling work scanning the pages from the fragile medical record, and to Dom Strickland and Matthew Ball, who used their skills to sharpen those images, to Kathy Burke whose Tweet first inspired me to pitch to Unbound, to Michael Gira who very graciously, after a paltry Facebook message, agreed to allow the inclusion of his lyric at the start of the book; and of course to all of my Unbound pledgers for flinging their hard-earned money at a strange man with a strange book.

Any mistakes, omissions or anachronisms are my fault alone; this is not an historical novel so much as a strange tale hung on the bare bones of historical fact. In my defense, if defense is needed, I echo the words of Joseph Allen to Charlotte Norton:

> *A scrapbook. At best. Shabby anthology. Rumor and embroidery. Written by... men who weren't even there, likely had never even visited the places written of, editors... with agendas too convoluted and rich in perverse unreason, illogic and irrationality to be granted even the least morsel of credence.*

Mason Ball, London, 2018

Patrons

Ian Bowden
Richard Boyce
Sinan Bozkurt
Anthony Bradnum
Lyn Breakwell
Marnie Brederoo
Christine Brown
Simon Brown
Ian Bruce
Jools Bryan
Philip Burns
Jodie Butler
Rob Cage
Peter Canty
Victoria Carlin
Alex Carnegie
Tom Carradine
Abbi De Carteret-Feazey
Catia Ciarico
Christian Clavadetscher
Toby Coe
Fiona Coffey
Aaron Cohen
Graham Cooke
Porl Cooper
Johan Coveliers
Shaun Crook
Ian Crouch
Susan Dean
Oliver Deans
Jodee Debeau
Susan Debelle
Shaun Dellenty
Anil Desai
Torie Dieppe
Jenny Doughty
Caroline Doyle
David Duchin
Veronica Dyreng

Gabriel Edvy
Jon Ellis
Vicky Falconer-Pritchard
Stuart Faulkner
Charlotte Featherstone
Snake Fervor
Rob Fletcher
Tomas Ford
Lain Freefall
Victoria Futterweit
Kate Gamble
Jatinder Ghataora
Shane Gilliver
Izaskun Gonzalez
David Green
Kevin Gude
Venetia & Andy Hadley
Laurence Vander Haeghen
America Hart
Fred Hartman
Jimmy Havoc
Michael Hekimian
Brian Herring
Claire Hibbins
Jon Hicks
Nancy Hitzig
Louise Holland
Yvonne Holland
Clive Holland
Yvette Hughes
Kelly Humphreys
Nadia Hussein
Malik Ibheis
Al J Jacob
Alisa James
Rebecca Johnson
Lesley Jones
Amelia Kallman
Nada Karsakov

Neil 'Nez' Kendall
Dan Kieran
Shona Kinsella
Tessa Kuragi
Claire Laffar
Sumitra Lahiri
Teresa Larkin
Johanna Lee
Jess Lee-Short
Francis Liming
Shell Lock
Simone Longley
Mark Lycett
Nange Magro
Damian Marais
Edward Marlowe
Ruby Martin
Michelle Maskell
Em Mason
Kye Matheson
Belinda May
Henry Maynard
David McGavin
Hannah McGavin
Mark McInnes
Wendy McQueen
Kimberley Michelle
Philip Middleton
Laura Miller
Helana Miller
John Mitchinson
Sean Mooney
Jonathan Moore
Adam Moriarty
Mhairi-Gael Morrison
Deborah Muir
Catherine Muller
Roxanne Murray
Irene Newell

Sandy Nicholson
Bronagh O'Neill
Mike Oakley
Guilherme Oconnor
B. Orbax
Laurence Owen
Scott Pack
Louise Parker-Jones
John Pash
Jim Paterson
Deano Peppers
Dave Pickens
Lynda Dearborn Pietroforte
Steve Pledger
Justin Pollard
Lisa Pouncer
Patricia Price
Stagecoach Principal
Michael Prior
Paul Pryke
Graeme Puttock
Polly Rae
Michael Rae
Xandi Rae
Shorn Rah
Shehzad Raj
Juliet Reeves
Laura Riach
Anna Richards
Moe Rocksmoore
Michael Roulston
Mario Ruiz
Jacob Sabotig
Amanda Saint
Ian Rob Salmon
Red Sarah
Kim Scopes
Doug Segal
Juliet Shalam

Neil Shaylor
Antony Simpson
Arcane Sin
Lang Skrimshire
Martin Small
Helen Smedley
Fred Snow
Emma Stafford
Tallulah Starr
Alston Stephanus
Niki Stevens
Emma Streeb-Greebling
Matt Stuttle
Rebecca Super-Tedd
Jennifer Sweet
Anna Swiczeniuk
Dee Tails
Christian Talbot
Shema Tariq
Dylan Tate
Brigid Taylor-Beeson
Sarah Taylor-Harman
Rasp Thorne
Lesley Thurston-Brown
Rachel Upson
Mark Vent
Tricity Vogue
Amy Walker
Dave White
Toby Whithouse
The Widow Stanton
Nathan Williams
Damian Williams
Noah Wise
Andrew Wood
Ruth Young
Sarah-Louise Young